The Middle Ages • SIMPSON / ORLEMANSKI

The Sixteenth Century • GREENBLATT / STERN

The Early Seventeenth Century
MAUS / CRAWFORD

The Restoration and the Eighteenth Century
NOGGLE / SMITH

The Romantic Period • LYNCH / EISNER

The Victorian Age • ROBSON / ABLOW

The Twentieth and Twenty-First Centuries
RAMAZANI / VADDE

THE NORTON ANTHOLOGY OF
ENGLISH LITERATURE

ELEVENTH EDITION

VOLUME B

THE SIXTEENTH CENTURY
AND
THE EARLY SEVENTEENTH CENTURY

Rachel Ablow
PROFESSOR OF ENGLISH, UNIVERSITY AT BUFFALO, SUNY

Julie Crawford
MARK VAN DOREN PROFESSOR OF HUMANITIES, COLUMBIA UNIVERSITY

Eric Eisner
ASSOCIATE PROFESSOR OF ENGLISH, GEORGE MASON UNIVERSITY

Deidre Shauna Lynch
ERNEST BERNBAUM PROFESSOR OF LITERATURE AND PROFESSOR OF ENGLISH,
HARVARD UNIVERSITY

Katharine Eisaman Maus
JAMES BRANCH CABELL PROFESSOR OF ENGLISH, UNIVERSITY OF VIRGINIA

James Noggle
PROFESSOR OF ENGLISH, WELLESLEY COLLEGE

Julie Orlemanski
ASSOCIATE PROFESSOR OF ENGLISH, UNIVERSITY OF CHICAGO

Jahan Ramazani
UNIVERSITY PROFESSOR AND EDGAR F. SHANNON PROFESSOR OF ENGLISH,
UNIVERSITY OF VIRGINIA

Catherine Robson
PROFESSOR OF ENGLISH, NEW YORK UNIVERSITY

James Simpson
DOUGLAS P. AND KATHERINE B. LOKER RESEARCH PROFESSOR OF ENGLISH, HARVARD UNIVERSITY

Courtney Weiss Smith
ASSOCIATE PROFESSOR OF ENGLISH, WESLEYAN UNIVERSITY

Tiffany Stern
PROFESSOR OF SHAKESPEARE AND EARLY MODERN DRAMA, THE SHAKESPEARE INSTITUTE,
UNIVERSITY OF BIRMINGHAM

Aarthi Vadde
ASSOCIATE PROFESSOR OF ENGLISH, DUKE UNIVERSITY

M. H. Abrams, *Founding Editor*
LATE OF CORNELL UNIVERSITY

THE NORTON ANTHOLOGY OF
ENGLISH LITERATURE

ELEVENTH EDITION

Stephen Greenblatt, *General Editor*
COGAN UNIVERSITY PROFESSOR OF THE HUMANITIES
HARVARD UNIVERSITY

VOLUME B

THE SIXTEENTH CENTURY AND
THE EARLY SEVENTEENTH CENTURY

Stephen Greenblatt   Katharine Eisaman Maus
Tiffany Stern   Julie Crawford

W. W. Norton & Company
Celebrating a Century of Independent Publishing

W. W. Norton & Company has been independent since its founding in 1923, when William Warder Norton and Mary D. Herter Norton first published lectures delivered at the People's Institute, the adult education division of New York City's Cooper Union. The firm soon expanded its program beyond the Institute, publishing books by celebrated academics from America and abroad. By midcentury, the two major pillars of Norton's publishing program—trade books and college texts—were firmly established. In the 1950s, the Norton family transferred control of the company to its employees, and today—with a staff of five hundred and hundreds of trade, college, and professional titles published each year—W. W. Norton & Company stands as the largest and oldest publishing house owned wholly by its employees.

Copyright © 2024, 2018, 2012, 2006, 2000, 1993, 1986, 1979, 1974, 1968, 1962 by W. W. Norton & Company, Inc.
All rights reserved

Editor: Marian Johnson
Assistant Editor: Serin Lee
Manuscript Editors: Katharine Ings, Alice Falk, Harry Haskell
Media Editor: Sarah Rose Aquilina
Associate Media Editor: Jessica Awad
Assistant Media Editor: Emma Daugherty
Marketing Manager, Literature: Megan DeBono Zwilling
Managing Editor: Kim Yi
Project Editor: Diane Cipollone
Production Manager: Benjamin Reynolds
Director of College Permissions: Megan Schindel
Permissions Clearing: Nancy J. Rodwan
Photo Editors: Amla Sanghvi and Ted Szczepanski
Cartographer: Adrian Kitzinger
Composition: Westchester Book Company
Manufacturing: Marquis Book Printing

Since this page cannot legibly accommodate all the copyright notices, the Permissions Acknowledgments constitute an extension of the copyright page.

ISBN: 978-0-393-54329-2

W. W. Norton & Company, Inc., 500 Fifth Avenue, New York, NY 10110
wwnorton.com

W. W. Norton & Company Ltd., 15 Carlisle Street, London W1D 3BS

1 2 3 4 5 6 7 8 9 0

Printed in Canada

Contents

PREFACE xxiii

ACKNOWLEDGMENTS xxxv

The Sixteenth Century (1485–1603)

INTRODUCTION 3

TIMELINE 36

JOHN SKELTON (ca. 1460–1529)   38
Mannerly Margery Milk and Ale 39
With Lullay, Lullay, Like a Child 40
The Tunning of Elinour Rumming 41
    Secundus Passus 41

SIR THOMAS MORE (1478–1535)   43
Utopia 46

SIR THOMAS WYATT THE ELDER (1503–1542)   120
The Long Love That in My Thought Doth Harbor 122
    Petrarch, Rima 140 123
Whoso List to Hunt 123
    Petrarch, Rima 190 124
I Find No Peace 124
    Petrarch, Rima 134 124
My Galley 125
    Petrarch, Rima 189 125
What Vaileth Truth? 126
Madam, Withouten Many Words 126
They Flee from Me 127
The Lover Showeth How He Is Forsaken of Such as He
    Sometime Enjoyed 127
My Lute, Awake! 128
Forget Not Yet 129

Stand Whoso List 130
Who List His Wealth and Ease Retain 130
Mine Own John Poins 131

HENRY HOWARD, EARL OF SURREY (1517–1547) 134
The Soote Season 135
    Petrarch, Rima 310 135
Love, That Doth Reign and Live Within My Thought 136
Alas! So All Things Now Do Hold Their Peace 136
    Petrarch, Rima 164 136
So Cruel Prison How Could Betide 137
Wyatt Resteth Here, That Quick Could Never Rest 138
O Happy Dames, That May Embrace 139

FAITH IN CONFLICT 141

THE ENGLISH BIBLE: 1 Corinthians 13 143
  From Tyndale's Translation 144
  From The Geneva Bible 144
  From The Douay-Rheims Version 146
  From The Authorized (King James) Version 146
WILLIAM TYNDALE: The Obedience of a Christian Man 147
  [The Forgiveness of Sins] 147
  [Scriptural Interpretation] 148
THOMAS MORE: A Dialogue Concerning Heresies 149
  From Book 1, Chapter 28 149
JOHN CALVIN: The Institution of Christian Religion 151
  From Book 3, Chapter 21 151
ANNE ASKEW: *From* The First Examination of Anne Askew 154
JOHN FOXE: Acts and Monuments 157
  [The Death of Anne Askew] 159
ANNE COOKE BACON: *From* John Jewel's *Apology* 159
BOOK OF COMMON PRAYER: *From* The Form of Solemnization of Matrimony 161
BOOK OF HOMILIES: *From* An Homily Against Disobedience and Willful Rebellion 164
ANNE VAUGHAN LOCKE: A Meditation of a Penitent Sinner 166
  4 ("Have mercy, Lord, have mercy") 167
RICHARD HOOKER: Of the Laws of Ecclesiastical Polity 167
  Book 1, Chapter 3 168
    [On the Several Kinds of Law, and on the Natural Law] 168
ROBERT SOUTHWELL: The Burning Babe 170

Roger Ascham (1515–1568) — 171
The Schoolmaster 172
    The First Book for the Youth 172
        [Teaching Latin] 172
        [The Italianate Englishman] 174

Sir Thomas Hoby (1530–1566) — 176
Castiglione's *The Courtier* 176
    Book 1, Sections 25–26 176
        [Grace]
    Book 4, Sections 49–73 178
        [The Ladder of Love]

Isabella Whitney (fl. 1566–1573) — 193
Will and Testament 193

Women and Power — 201

Mary I (Mary Tudor) — 203
Letter to Henry VIII 204
From An Ambassadorial Dispatch to the Holy Roman Emperor, Charles V: The Coronation of Mary I 205
The Oration of Queen Mary in the Guildhall, on the First of February 1554 207

Lady Jane Grey — 209
Roger Ascham's *Schoolmaster* 210
    [A Talk with Lady Jane] 210
From A Letter of the Lady Jane to M. H., Late Chaplain to the Duke of Suffolk, Her Father 211
A Letter of the Lady Jane, Sent unto Her Father 213
A Prayer of the Lady Jane 214
A Second Letter to Her Father 215
Foxe's *Acts and Monuments* 215
    The Words and Behavior of the Lady Jane upon the Scaffold 215

Mary, Queen of Scots — 217
From Casket Letter Number 2 219
A Letter to Elizabeth I, May 17, 1568 222
From Narrative of the Execution of the Queen of Scots 224

Elizabeth I — 230
Verses Written with a Diamond 232
From The Passage of Our Most Dread Sovereign Lady Queen Elizabeth through the City of London to Westminster on the Day before Her Coronation 233
Speech to the House of Commons, January 28, 1563 235

From A Speech to a Joint Delegation of Lords and Commons,
    November 5, 1566 236
From A Letter to Mary, Queen of Scots, February 24, 1567 239
The Doubt of Future Foes 240
On Monsieur's Departure 240
A Letter to Robert Dudley, Earl of Leicester, February 10, 1586 241
A Letter to Sir Amyas Paulet, August 1586 241
A Letter to King James VI of Scotland, February 14, 1587 242
Verse Exchange between Elizabeth and Sir Walter Ralegh 243
Speech to the Troops at Tilbury 244
The "Golden Speech" 245

ANNE COOKE BACON   248
   To the Right Worshipful and Worthily Beloved Mother 248
MARGARET TYLER   249
   To the Reader 249
ANNE DOWRICHE   252
   To the Right Worshipful Her Loving Brother 252
JANE ANGER   253
   To All Women in General 253
   Eiusdem ad Lectorem 254

EDMUND SPENSER (1552?–1599)   254
   The Shepheardes Calender 257
       To His Booke 257
       October 258
   The Faerie Queene 263
       A Letter of the Authors 265
       Book 1 269
       Mutabilitie Cantos 422
   Amoretti *and* Epithalamion
       Amoretti
           1 ("Happy ye leaves when as those lilly hands")   452
           34 ("Lyke as a ship that through the Ocean wyde")   452
           37 ("What guyle is this, that those her golden tresses") 453
           54 ("Of this worlds Theatre in which we stay")   453
           64 ("Coming to kisse her lyps [such grace I found]")   453
           67 ("Lyke as a huntsman after weary chace")   454
           75 ("One day I wrote her name upon the strand")   454
           79 ("Men call you fayre, and you doe credit it")   455
       Epithalamion 455

Commonplace Book 466

AGING 467
George Gascoigne: The Lullaby of a Lover 467
Michael Drayton: There's Nothing Grieves Me, But That Age Should Haste 468
Samuel Daniel: When Men Shall Find Thy Flower, Thy Glory, Pass 469
Anonymous: The Queen's Champion Retires 470

BAWDY 470
Anonymous: Will Ye Buy a Fine Dog? 471
Anonymous: On a Maidenhead 471

CARPE DIEM 472
Thomas Lodge: Pluck the Fruit and Taste the Pleasure 472

DEATH 473
Fulke Greville: You That Seek What Life Is in Death 473
Emma Foxe: To You That Life Possess 473
Sir Walter Ralegh: *From* The History of the World 474

DRINK 475
William Stevenson/John Still: Jolly Good Ale and Old 475
Thomas Dekker: Troll the Bowl, the Jolly Nut-Brown Bowl 477

EXECUTION 478
Chidiock Tichborne: Tichborne's Elegy 478
Sir Walter Ralegh: To His Son 478
Sir Walter Ralegh: The Author's Epitaph, Made by Himself 479

FOREIGNERS 480
Anonymous: The Dutch Libel 480
William Shakespeare: *From* Sir Thomas More 482

IMAGINATION 483
Fulke Greville: In Night When Colors All to Black Are Cast 483
Michael Drayton: How Many Paltry, Foolish, Painted Things 484

LYING 484
Sir Walter Ralegh: The Lie 484

LOVE: HAPPY 487
John Davies of Hereford: If There Were (Oh!) an Hellespont of Cream 487
Thomas Campion: My Sweetest Lesbia 488
Thomas Campion: I Care Not for These Ladies 489
Thomas Campion: Now Winter Nights Enlarge 490
Richard Barnfield: Cynthia, Sonnets 9 and 11 490

LOVE: UNHAPPY 491
Michael Drayton: Nothing but "No" and "I" and "I" and "No"? 491
George Gascoigne: And If I Did, What Then? 492
Michael Drayton: As in Some Countries Far Remote from Hence 493
Sir Walter Ralegh: Farewell, False Love 493

PASTORAL LOVE 495
  Christopher Marlowe: The Passionate Shepherd to His Love 495
  Sir Walter Ralegh: The Nymph's Reply to the Shepherd 496
PLAGUE 496
  Thomas Nashe: A Litany in Time of Plague 496
  John Davies of Hereford: *From* The Triumph of Death 498
SIMPLE LIFE 499
  Thomas Campion: Jack and Joan, They Think No Ill 499
TIME 500
  Robert Greene: Doralicia's Ditty 500
  John Dowland: It Was a Time When Silly Bees Could Speak 501
  Sir Walter Ralegh: Nature, That Washed Her Hands in Milk 502
  William Shakespeare: *From* The Rape of Lucrece 503
TOBACCO 503
  Robert Wisdome: A Religious Use of Taking Tobacco 503
  Tobias Hume: Tobacco 504
TRADE 505
  Robert Wilson: New Brooms 505
  Robert Wilson: Hunting for Hire 506
  Anonymous: Cries of London 506
  Anonymous: Soldiers' Song 508
  Anonymous: Mariners' Song 508
WOMEN 509
  Sir John Harington: A Certain Man 509
  Lady Mary Cheke: The Reply 510
  Lady Anne Southwell: All Married Men Desire to Have Good Wives 510

JOHN LYLY (1554–1606) 511
  Euphues: The Anatomy of Wit 511
    [Euphues Introduced] 511

SIR PHILIP SIDNEY (1554–1586) 514
  The Countess of Pembroke's Arcadia 515
    From Book 1 516
    From Book 2 519
  From The Defense of Poesy 525
  Astrophil and Stella 540
      1 ("Loving in truth, and fain in verse my love to show") 541
      2 ("Not at first sight, nor with a dribbèd shot") 541
      15 ("You that do search for every purling spring") 542
      18 ("With what sharp checks I in myself am shent") 542
      20 ("Fly, fly, my friends, I have my death-wound, fly") 542
      27 ("Because I oft, in dark abstracted guise") 543

28 ("You that with allegory's curious frame") 543
31 ("With how sad steps, O Moon, thou climb'st the skies") 544
34 ("Come, let me write. 'And to what end?'") 544
41 ("Having this day my horse, my hand, my lance") 544
45 ("Stella oft sees the very face of woe") 545
47 ("What, have I thus betrayed my liberty?") 545
49 ("I on my horse, and Love on me doth try") 545
54 ("Because I breathe not love to every one") 546
56 ("Fie, school of Patience, fie, your lesson is") 546
69 ("O joy, too high for my low style to show") 547
71 ("Who will in fairest book of Nature know") 547
72 ("Desire, though thou my old companion art") 547
74 ("I never drank of Aganippe well") 548
81 ("O kiss, which dost those ruddy gems impart") 548
Fourth Song ("Only joy, now here you are") 548
87 ("When I was forced from Stella ever dear") 550
89 ("Now that of absence the most irksome night") 550
91 ("Stella, while now by Honor's cruel might") 550
106 ("O absent presence, Stella is not here") 551
108 ("When Sorrow [using mine own fire's might]") 551

MARY (SIDNEY) HERBERT, COUNTESS OF PEMBROKE (1562–1621)   552
To the Thrice-Sacred Queen Elizabeth 553
Psalm 52 556
Psalm 119: O 557
Psalm 139 557
From Robert Garnier's *Marc Antoine* 560

CHRISTOPHER MARLOWE (1564–1593)   561
Hero and Leander 563
Doctor Faustus 581
    The Tragical History of Doctor Faustus 582
    The Two Texts of *Doctor Faustus* 618

WILLIAM SHAKESPEARE (1564–1616)   620
Sonnets 624
    1 ("From fairest creatures we desire increase") 625
    3 ("Look in thy glass and tell the face thou viewest") 625
    12 ("When I do count the clock that tells the time") 626
    15 ("When I consider every thing that grows") 626
    18 ("Shall I compare thee to a summer's day?") 626
    19 ("Devouring Time, blunt thou the lion's paws") 627
    20 ("A woman's face with Nature's own hand painted") 627
    23 ("As an unperfect actor on the stage") 628
    29 ("When, in disgrace with Fortune and men's eyes") 628
    30 ("When to the sessions of sweet silent thought") 628

33 ("Full many a glorious morning have I seen") 629
35 ("No more be grieved at that which thou hast done") 629
55 ("Not marble nor the gilded monuments") 629
60 ("Like as the waves make towards the pebbled shore") 630
62 ("Sin of self-love possesseth all mine eye") 630
65 ("Since brass, nor stone, nor earth, nor boundless sea") 630
71 ("No longer mourn for me when I am dead") 631
73 ("That time of year thou may'st in me behold") 631
74 ("But be contented; when that fell arrest") 631
80 ("O, how I faint when I of you do write") 632
87 ("Farewell: thou art too dear for my possessing") 632
94 ("They that have power to hurt and will do none") 633
97 ("How like a winter hath my absence been") 633
98 ("From you have I been absent in the spring") 633
105 ("Let not my love be called idolatry") 634
106 ("When in the chronicle of wasted time") 634
107 ("Not mine own fears, nor the prophetic soul") 634
110 ("Alas, 'tis true I have gone here and there") 635
116 ("Let me not to the marriage of true minds") 635
126 ("O thou, my lovely boy, who in thy power") 636
127 ("In the old age black was not counted fair") 636
128 ("How oft when thou, my music, music play'st") 636
129 ("Th' expense of spirit in a waste of shame") 637
130 ("My mistress' eyes are nothing like the sun") 637
135 ("Whoever hath her wish, thou hast thy *Will*") 637
138 ("When my love swears that she is made of truth") 638
144 ("Two loves I have of comfort and despair") 638
146 ("Poor soul, the center of my sinful earth") 638
147 ("My love is as a fever, longing still") 639
152 ("In loving thee thou know'st I am forsworn") 639

Othello 640
The Tempest 726

ENGLAND AND THE WORLD 787

SIR WALTER RALEGH: *From* The Discovery of the . . . Empire of Guiana 790
THOMAS HARIOT: *From* A Brief and True Report of the New-found Land of Virginia 802
WILLIAM STRACHEY: *From* A True Reportory of the Wreck . . . upon . . . the Islands of the Bermudas 809
JOHN SMITH: *From* The General History of Virginia, New England, and the Summer Isles 822
RICHARD LIGON: *From* A True and Exact History of the Island of Barbados 830

The Early Seventeenth Century (1603–1660)

INTRODUCTION 849

TIMELINE 880

JOHN DONNE (1572–1631) 882
    Songs and Sonnets 886
        The Flea 886
        The Good-Morrow 887
        Song ("Go and catch a falling star") 887
        The Sun Rising 888
        The Indifferent 889
        The Canonization 889
        Song ("Sweetest love, I do not go") 891
        Air and Angels 892
        Break of Day 892
        A Valediction: Of Weeping 893
        A Nocturnal upon Saint Lucy's Day, Being the Shortest Day 894
        The Bait 895
        The Apparition 896
        A Valediction: Forbidding Mourning 897
        The Ecstasy 898
        The Funeral 900
        The Relic 901
        A Lecture upon the Shadow 902
    Elegy 16. On His Mistress 903
    Elegy 19. To His Mistress Going to Bed 904
    Satire 3 905
    To Sir Henry Wotton 908
    Holy Sonnets 910
        1 ("Thou hast made me, and shall thy work decay?") 910
        5 ("I am a little world made cunningly") 911
        7 ("At the round earth's imagined corners, blow") 911
        9 ("If poisonous minerals, and if that tree") 912
        10 ("Death, be not proud, though some have callèd thee") 912
        11 ("Spit in my face ye Jews, and pierce my side") 912
        13 ("What if this present were the world's last night?") 913
        14 ("Batter my heart, three-personed God; for you") 913
        17 ("Since she whom I loved hath paid her last debt") 914
        18 ("Show me, dear Christ, thy spouse so bright and clear") 914
        19 ("Oh, to vex me, contraries meet in one") 915
    Good Friday, 1613. Riding Westward 915
    Hymn to God My God, in My Sickness 916
    A Hymn to God the Father 917

Devotions upon Emergent Occasions 918
    Meditation 4 918
    Meditation 17 919
    From Expostulation 19 920
From Death's Duel 922

AEMILIA LANYER (1569–1645)   924

Salve Deus Rex Judaeorum 925
    From To the Queen's Most Excellent Majesty 925
    From To the Lady Anne, Countess of Dorset 927
    From Salve Deus Rex Judaeorum 928
    The Description of Cookham 936

BEN JONSON (1572–1637)   941

Volpone, or The Fox 944
The Masque of Blackness 1039
Epigrams 1049
    To My Book 1049
    On Something, That Walks Somewhere 1049
    To Fine Lady Would-Be 1049
    On My First Daughter 1050
    On My First Son 1050
    To Lucy, Countess of Bedford, with Mr. Donne's Satires 1051
    To Sir Thomas Roe 1051
    Inviting a Friend to Supper 1052
    On Gut 1053
The Forest 1053
    To Penshurst 1053
    Song: To Celia 1055
    To Heaven 1056
Underwood 1057
    A Sonnet, to the Noble Lady, the Lady Mary Wroth 1057
    My Picture Left in Scotland 1057
    To the Immortal Memory and Friendship of That Noble Pair, Sir Lucius Cary and Sir H. Morison 1059
Queen and Huntress 1062
To the Memory of My Beloved, The Author, Mr. William Shakespeare 1063
Ode to Himself 1065

MARY WROTH (1587–1651?)   1067

The Countess of Montgomery's Urania 1069
    From The First Book 1069
    Song ("Love what art thou? A vain thought") 1073
Pamphilia to Amphilanthus 1074
    1 ("When night's black mantle could most darkness prove") 1074
    16 ("Am I thus conquered? Have I lost the powers") 1075
    25 ("Like to the Indians scorched with the sun") 1075

26 ("When everyone to pleasing pastime hies") 1075
28 Song ("Sweetest love, return again") 1076
39 ("Take heed mine eyes, how you your looks do cast") 1076
40 ("False hope which feeds but to destroy and spill") 1077
64 ("Love like a juggler comes to play his prize") 1077
68 ("My pain still smothered in my grievèd breast") 1077
74 Song ("Love a child is ever crying") 1078
From A Crown of Sonnets Dedicated to Love 1078
   77 ("In this strange labyrinth how shall I turn?") 1078
103 ("My muse now happy lay thyself to rest") 1079

JOHN WEBSTER (1580?–1625?)   1079
The Duchess of Malfi 1080

SIR FRANCIS BACON (1561–1626)   1156
Essays 1157
   Of Truth 1157
   Of Marriage and Single Life 1158
   Of Great Place 1160
   Of Superstition 1162
   Of Plantations 1163
   Of Negotiating 1165
   Of Masques and Triumphs 1166
   Of Studies [1597 version] 1167
   Of Studies [1625 version] 1168
The Advancement of Learning 1169
   [The Abuses of Language] 1169
From Novum Organum 1171
The New Atlantis 1175
   [Solomon's House] 1175

GEORGE HERBERT (1593–1633)   1180
The Temple 1182
   The Altar 1182
   Redemption 1182
   Easter 1183
   Easter Wings 1184
   Affliction (1) 1184
   Prayer (1) 1186
   Jordan (1) 1186
   Church Monuments 1187
   The Windows 1188
   Denial 1188
   Virtue 1189
   Man 1189
   Jordan (2) 1191
   Affliction (4) 1191

The Bunch of Grapes 1192
The Holdfast 1193
The Collar 1194
The Pulley 1195
The Flower 1195
The Forerunners 1196
Discipline 1197
Death 1198
Love (3) 1199

Henry Vaughan (1621–1695) — 1200

Silex Scintillans 1201
    Regeneration 1201
    The Retreat 1203
    Silence, and Stealth of Days! 1204
    Corruption 1205
    Unprofitableness 1206
    The World 1206
    Cock-Crowing 1208
    The Waterfall 1209
    Quickness 1210

Richard Crashaw (ca. 1613–1649) — 1211

Steps to the Temple 1212
    Acts 8. On the Baptized Aethiopian 1212
    To the Infant Martyrs 1212
    I Am the Door 1213
    Luke 11.[27] 1213
    On the Wounds of Our Crucified Lord 1214
    On Our Crucified Lord Naked and Bloody 1214
Carmen Deo Nostro 1215
    The Flaming Heart 1215

Robert Herrick (1591–1674) — 1219

Hesperides 1220
    The Argument of His Book 1220
    Upon the Loss of His Mistresses 1220
    The Vine 1221
    Dreams 1221
    Delight in Disorder 1221
    Corinna's Going A-Maying 1222
    To the Virgins, to Make Much of Time 1224
    The Hock Cart, or Harvest Home 1224
    Upon the Nipples of Julia's Breast 1226
    Upon His Verses 1226
    Upon Julia's Clothes 1226
    Upon Prue, His Maid 1226
    To His Book's End 1227

      Noble Numbers 1227
          To His Conscience 1227
          Another Grace for a Child 1227

HESTER PULTER (1605–1678)   1228
   Upon the Death of My Dear and Lovely Daughter, Jane Pulter 1228
   View But This Tulip 1230
   Dear God, from Thy High Throne Look Down 1231

RICHARD LOVELACE (1617–1657)   1232
   Lucasta 1232
      To Lucasta, Going to the Wars 1232
      The Grasshopper 1233
      To Althea, from Prison 1233
      La Bella Bona Roba 1235
   A Black Patch on Lucasta's Face 1236
   Love Made in the First Age. To Chloris 1237

LUCY HUTCHINSON (1620–1681)   1239
   From Translation of Lucretius's *De rerum natura* 1240
   To the Garden at Owthorpe 1242
   Order and Disorder 1243
      Canto 5 1243

KATHERINE PHILIPS (1632–1664)   1258
   A Married State 1259
   An Answer to Another Persuading a Lady to Marriage 1260
   Upon the Double Murder of King Charles 1261
   Friendship's Mystery, To My Dearest *Lucasia* 1262
   To Mrs. M. A. at Parting 1263
   Epitaph: On Her Son H. P. at St. Syth's Church, Where Her Body Also Was
      Interred 1264

ANDREW MARVELL (1621–1678)   1265
   The Coronet 1267
   Bermudas 1267
   A Dialogue Between the Soul and Body 1268
   The Nymph Complaining for the Death of Her Fawn 1270
   To His Coy Mistress 1272
   The Definition of Love 1274
   The Picture of Little T. C. in a Prospect of Flowers 1275
   The Mower Against Gardens 1276
   Damon the Mower 1277
   The Mower to the Glowworms 1279
   The Mower's Song 1279
   The Garden 1280
   An Horatian Ode 1282
   Upon Appleton House 1287

Crisis of Authority 1310

PETITIONING
  A True Copy of the Petition of Gentlewomen and Tradesmen's Wives 1310
REPORTING THE NEWS 1316
  The Moderate, No. 28 1317
    [The Trial of King Charles I, the First Day] 1317
  A Perfect Diurnal of Some Passages in Parliament, No. 288 1320
    [The Execution of Charles I] 1320
POLITICAL WRITING 1324
  ROBERT FILMER: *From* Patriarcha 1325
  JOHN MILTON: *From* The Tenure of Kings and Magistrates 1328
  GERRARD WINSTANLEY: *From* A New Year's Gift Sent to the Parliament and Army 1331
  THOMAS HOBBES: *From* Leviathan 1337
HISTORY AND LIFE-WRITING 1350
  EDWARD HYDE, EARL OF CLARENDON: The History of the Rebellion 1350
    [The Character of Oliver Cromwell] 1350
  DOROTHY WAUGH: A Relation Concerning Dorothy Waugh's Cruel Usage by the Mayor of Carlisle 1354

MARGARET CAVENDISH (1623–1673) 1356
  Poems and Fancies 1357
    The Poetess's Hasty Resolution 1357
    A World Made by Atoms 1358
    Of Many Worlds in This World 1358
    The Hunting of the Hare 1359
  Of Sense and Reason Exercised in Their Different Shapes 1361
  From The Description of a New World, Called The Blazing World 1364

JOHN MILTON (1608–1674) 1381
  Poems 1385
    On the Morning of Christ's Nativity 1385
    On Shakespeare 1393
    L'Allegro 1393
    Il Penseroso 1397
    Lycidas 1401
  The Reason of Church Government Urged Against Prelaty 1408
    [Plans and Projects] 1408
  From Areopagitica 1413
  Sonnets 1423
    How Soon Hath Time 1423
    On the New Forcers of Conscience under the Long Parliament 1424
    To the Lord General Cromwell, May 1652 1425

    When I Consider How My Light Is Spent 1426
    On the Late Massacre in Piedmont 1426
    Methought I Saw My Late Espousèd Saint 1427
Paradise Lost 1427

Appendices   A1

General Bibliography A3
Literary Terminology A13
Geographic Nomenclature A35
British Money A37
The British Baronage A43
    The Royal Lines of England and Great Britain A45
Religions in Great Britain A49
Illustration: The Universe According to Ptolemy A55
Illustration: A London Playhouse of Shakespeare's Time A57

PERMISSIONS ACKNOWLEDGMENTS   A59

INDEX   A61

Preface

The Norton Anthology of English Literature is a massive cultural space. In it the selections are in conversation, echoing and imitating, and also expanding, contracting, observing, playing, arguing, and dissenting, among a host of other responses. To enter this space as a reader is to recognize that works of literature, even the greatest of them, are never strictly solitary. They belong to larger communities, and within these communities they participate in ongoing dialogues. *The Norton Anthology of English Literature* represents one such community, formed by a shared relation to the English language as it emerged in the British Isles and has evolved, changed shape, and spread over the centuries. Literary relations often cross boundaries from one language to another, but their interactions tend to be most concentrated and intense within a shared linguistic community—a community that can be both massive and intimate, both cohesive and fractured, but always part of a wider world.

With this Eleventh Edition of *The Norton Anthology of English Literature*, a new generation of editors has assumed the principal responsibility for revising each of the periods of this community. The result is the most thoroughgoing rethinking in the anthology's long and storied life. Though the great landmarks remain, familiar and beloved works of literature find themselves in unfamiliar and sometimes surprising company. It is our hope that fresh perceptions and new conversations will arise out of these changes in the overall anthology environment.

M. H. Abrams, the distinguished literary critic who brought together the original team of editors more than sixty years ago and, with characteristic insight, diplomacy, and humor, oversaw the first seven editions of the anthology, understood that scholarly discoveries and the shifting interests of readers constantly alter the landscape of literary history. As he said, "A vital literary culture is always on the move." Thus, for example, the First Edition included just 6 women writers. But the sustained work of scholars over the decades has recovered dozens of significant authors who had been marginalized or neglected by a male-dominated literary tradition and has deepened our understanding of those women writers who managed, against considerable odds, to claim a place in that tradition. The Eleventh Edition includes 119 women writers. So too the First Edition included no writers of color and 8 writers whose origins lay outside the British Isles. This edition features 49 writers of color and 78 writers from beyond Britain. Significant change is apparent as well in the expansion of selections from writers already present in earlier editions, including Anne Finch, Margaret Cavendish,

Lucy Hutchinson, Olaudah Equiano, Mary Prince, Charles Darwin, Alfred, Lord Tennyson, Elizabeth Barrett Browning, Christina Rossetti, Philip Larkin, and Seamus Heaney. And it is strikingly manifested in the host of writers who appear in these volumes for the first time, among them Clemence of Barking, Meir of Norwich, "John Mandeville," the anonymous author of the Welsh *Lady of the Fountain*, Hester Pulter, the anonymous authors of *The Arabian Nights Entertainments*, Henry Louis Vivian Derozio, Mary Seacole, Rabindranath Tagore, Mohandas Gandhi, Mulk Raj Anand, Elizabeth Bowen, Arundhati Roy, Ali Smith, and Rachel Cusk.

Such rethinking extends, of course, beyond individual writers to the larger community of the anthology. The geographical space occupied by that community has continued to expand. For centuries now English literature has not been confined to the British Isles; it is a global phenomenon. Though on pragmatic grounds, we have followed the lead of most college courses in distinguishing between English and American literature, we have, in keeping with the multinational, multicultural, and hugely expansive character of the language, incorporated a substantial number of texts by authors from other countries, among them Phillis Wheatley, Samson Occom, Dean Mahomet, Mary Seacole, Rabindranath Tagore, Toru Dutt, and Bessie Head.

This border-crossing is not a phenomenon of modernity only. It is fitting that among the first works here is *Beowulf*, a powerful epic written in the Germanic language known as Old English about a singularly restless Scandinavian hero. *Beowulf*'s translator in *The Norton Anthology of English Literature*, Seamus Heaney, is one of the great contemporary masters of English literature—he was awarded the Nobel Prize for Literature in 1995—but it would be misleading to call him an "English poet" for he was born in Northern Ireland and was not in fact English. It would be still more misleading to call him a "British poet," as if the British Empire were the most salient fact about the language he spoke and wrote in or the culture by which he was shaped. What matters is that the language in which Heaney wrote is English, and this fact links him powerfully with the authors assembled in these volumes, a linguistic community that stubbornly refuses to fit comfortably within any firm geographical or ethnic or national boundaries.

So too do other authors and texts in the anthology lie outside familiar boundaries: in the twelfth century, the noblewoman Marie de France wrote her short stories in an Anglo Norman dialect at home on both sides of the channel; in the sixteenth century William Tyndale, in exile in the Low Countries and inspired by German religious reformers, translated the New Testament from Greek and thereby changed the course of the English language; in the seventeenth century Aphra Behn touched readers with a story that moves from Africa, where its hero is born, to South America, where Behn herself may have witnessed some of the tragic events she describes; and early in the twentieth century Joseph Conrad, born in Ukraine of Polish parents, wrote in eloquent English a novella whose brooding vision of European colonialism in Africa is trenchantly challenged in our pages by Caryl Phillips, born in St. Kitts, and Chimamanda Ngozi Adichie, born in Nigeria.

These contemporary responses to *Heart of Darkness* point to a further, quite crucial feature of this edition of *The Norton Anthology of English Literature*. Within the cultural space defined by English literature, the nature and the parameters of the conversation are constantly changing.

Eloquent voices call into question the stance of works that had once been viewed as morally impeccable. Authors whose literary style or identity had condemned them to marginality are reappraised and celebrated as centrally important. Historical events that had been overlooked or dismissed as irrelevant come to seem essential to a full understanding of a period and its writing. Topics that few or none had explicitly raised emerge as vital not only to contemporary readers but also to writers of the past who turn out to have engaged with them in significant ways.

Alert to these changes in the cultural conversation, the editors of the Eleventh Edition have not only included many new works but have also taken full advantage of a key feature introduced at the anthology's origin and developed and expanded over the years: the topical cluster. These groupings of short texts, on a wide range of subjects keyed to each period, enable readers to explore the boundaries between writing that was clearly understood at the time it was created as "literary" and writing that, for various reasons, fell outside this category. The boundaries are explored outside of the clusters as well, in the presence of Ottobah Cugoano alongside Samuel Johnson, for example, or of Mohandas Gandhi alongside Rudyard Kipling. The question of what constitutes literature is an open one, and, as the *Norton Anthology* makes clear, the answers are constantly being revised.

The topical clusters serve many additional purposes. They allow a sharp focus on issues that captured the imagination and focused the energy of a community of writers, such as "God's Body" in the Middle Ages, "Crisis of Authority" in the Early Seventeenth Century, or "Science, Speculation, and Experiment" in the Romantic Period. They introduce key writing practices, forms, and artistic movements—such as the commonplace book in the Sixteenth Century, the novel in the Restoration and the Eighteenth Century, and digital literature in the Twentieth and Twenty-First Centuries—that help define a period. They assemble a range of voices that speak out on such crucial subjects as "Britain and Transatlantic Slavery" in the Restoration and the Eighteenth Century, "Settler Colonialism" in the Victorian Age, and "Nation, Race, and Language" in the Twentieth and Twenty-First Centuries. Here as elsewhere in the *Norton Anthology* the conversation not only illuminates adjacent works but extends across the periods. The texts in "England and the World," the topic forming a bridge between the Sixteenth and Seventeenth centuries, illuminate the two Shakespeare plays, *Othello* and *The Tempest,* and at the same time open up into the major topics on empire in the Restoration and the Eighteenth Century and the Victorian Age. So too in the Victorian Age "The Promise and Price of Industrialization," with its section on environmental degradation, leads into "Environmental Literature and Climate Change" in the Twentieth and Twenty-First Centuries.

The presence in this latter topic of powerful contemporary voices—Ben Okri, Arundhati Roy, Amitav Ghosh, Patience Agbabi, and others—reminds us that literature can be a call to action as well as a mode of reflection and representation. The way we live our lives, including the actions we take or fail to take, depends upon our understanding of the world and of ourselves, and that understanding is and has always been shaped by the stories we tell, the pictures we draw, the songs we sing. Art making in its myriad forms is one of the essential attributes of humanity; it helps to define us as a species. The astonishingly evocative paintings on the walls of caves from 35,000 years ago, together with even older sculptured figures and bone flutes, bear witness to the foundational nature of our impulse to represent the world and to make sense of our experience through art. This is what the world looks and feels like to us, the pictures say; this is what we love and what we fear; this is how we register our sense of beauty and tell our stories; this is how we make or hope to make things happen; this is who we are. The artists who created the images sometimes pressed their hands to the wall and blew pigment around them, leaving their prints on the walls like signatures: remember us, the handprints tell us; we were here once.

Verbal art making almost certainly reaches at least as far back in our collective past as these archaic images, but it could leave no material trace for future generations until writing was invented, some five thousand years ago in Mesopotamia. From this moment onward, works of literature have helped at once to define and to explore what it means to be human. The Mesopotamian tablets in which words were first inscribed were devised at a time when cities were developing and their inhabitants turned to storytellers to reflect on the human condition. At every point since then our species has looked to its writers for the special guidance that comes from artistic representation. For a host of reasons—from alarming fissures in our social and political order, to the astonishing advances in artificial intelligence, to the critical state of our planet—there has never been a moment in which the written outpouring of the human imagination has been more important than it is now. There is much talk at the moment about a crisis of the humanities, but the more important issue we face is a crisis of the human. In order to confront this crisis—to orient ourselves, to know more fully who we are, and, above all, to respond creatively to the challenges we face—we need literature.

PERIOD-BY-PERIOD REVISIONS

Volume A: The Middle Ages

Edited by Julie Orlemanski and James Simpson, this period, huge in its eight-century scope and immensely varied in its voices, offers exciting surprises, many new to this edition. The heart of the Old English portion is the great elegiac epic *Beowulf,* in the acclaimed translation by Seamus Heaney. Many texts in the anthology resonate with *Beowulf* in various ways. And while *Beowulf* is set in Scandinavia, two new texts offer contrasting responses to the Scandinavian invasions of England from the eighth to the early eleventh centuries: King Alfred's call to resuscitate learning ("Preface to *Pastoral Care*"); and the "Sermon to the English" by Wulfstan of York, which is addressed to Christian listeners under attack by polytheistic invaders. Literature of the Twelfth and Thirteenth Centuries—a key sub-period between the Old and Middle English sections—offers an illuminating cluster on the genre of romance, with four subtle narratives (one new) by Marie de France; a rich new text translated from Welsh, *The Lady of the Fountain*; three texts about *Tristan and Ysolt*; and *Sir Orfeo*, a comedic version of the Orpheus and Eurydice story. Also new is a selection from the life of the learned, feisty Saint Catherine of Alexandria, by a female author, Clemence of Barking. As always, the Middle English section offers a generous selection from *The Canterbury Tales*. The *Tales* are presented from the new edition by David Lawton, with additional modifications for ease of reading. Among other notable additions is a cluster focused on religious exclusions: fierce expressions of Christian/Jewish relations by the persecuted and persecutors (respectively Meir of Norwich and the *Croxton Play of the Sacrament*) and a text that defines and deepens the divisions between Christian and Muslim (*The King of Tars*). "What the Animals Say" includes, alongside brilliant bird poems by Chaucer and Henryson, a selection from the vivacious debate poem *The Owl and the Nightingale*, in a new translation by Simon Armitage, and a text about a wolf-man by Marie de France. At every point we strive to render these texts, written in a variety of languages, accessible to readers of Modern English. All the relevant Middle English texts (notably all works by Chaucer) are presented in modernized spelling wherever such modernization does not injure meter or rhyme. Plentiful, discreet glosses offer consistent aid.

Volume B: The Sixteenth Century

New to this period, edited by Tiffany Stern and Stephen Greenblatt, are Isabella Whitney, Anne Cooke Bacon, Margaret Tyler, Anne Dowriche, Mary Cheke, and Anne Southell, who add their voices to those of Mary Tudor, Lady Jane Grey, Mary, Queen of Scots, and Elizabeth I. New as well is a cluster that reproduces an influential practice widespread in this period: the "commonplace book." Texts, often surprising, striking, and always memorable, are grouped according to miscellaneous topics, ranging from "Aging," "Death," and "Drink" to "Tobacco," "Trade," and "Women." Not only will readers enjoy this diverse array, but we hope they will be encouraged to assemble their own commonplace books. Included for the first time too is Shakespeare's remarkable late romance *The Tempest*, with its haunting blend of shipwreck, magic, enslavement, and forgiveness. This play, together with *Othello*, offers readers insight into the period's fascination with encountering those it regarded as "other." "England and the World," a topical cluster that serves as a bridge to the Early Seventeenth Century, suggests that this fascination was only beginning. In addition to texts by Thomas Hariot and Walter Ralegh, it includes, new to the anthology, portions of a letter by William Strachey about a momentous wreck of English ships on the Bermudas; a generous selection from Richard Ligon's *A True and Exact History of the Island of Barbados*, the first account of the English colonization of Barbados and the rise of the sugar industry that would change the global economy forever; and a selection from John Smith's *The General History of Virginia, New England, and the Summer Isles*.

Volume B: The Early Seventeenth Century

At the heart of this period, edited by Julie Crawford and Katharine Maus, is John Milton's *Paradise Lost*, presented complete. New to the Eleventh Edition is Canto 5 of Lucy Hutchinson's contemporaneous epic poem *Order and Disorder*, which offers a different account of Adam and Eve's fall and its aftermath. The Eleventh Edition also offers other selections from Hutchinson's work, including from her translation of Lucretius and her elegies; three poems by the (relatively) newly discovered Hester Pulter; a wholly revised entry on Margaret Cavendish, including a much more substantive and representative selection from her mind-bending utopia *The Blazing World*; and a fully revised entry on Aemilia Lanyer, which offers a new selection from her most ambitious poem, "Salve Deus Rex Judaeorum." Ben Jonson's *The Masque of Blackness* appears in its entirety, offering a rich intertext for the two Shakespeare plays and Richard Ligon's and John Smith's colonial fantasies. The revised cluster "Crisis of Authority" includes the full text of a petition women presented to the House of Commons in February 1641, arguing for their rights as citizens. The period also offers new poems by Donne, Jonson, Herbert, Wroth, Crashaw, Lovelace, and Philips.

Volume C: The Restoration and the Eighteenth Century
This volume, edited by Courtney Weiss Smith and James Noggle, situates eighteenth-century British literature in a global context. New to the period are the stories of Scheherazade and Ali Baba from the *Arabian Nights Entertainments*, a work of complex global provenance, as well as writing by Phillis Wheatley, Ignatius Sancho, Samson Occom, Dean Mahomet, and "Ossian" (a medieval Gaelic bard ventriloquized by an eighteenth-century Scotsman). Five new topical clusters address themes and issues whose legacies shape our world today. "Global Commerce and Empire" and "Britain and Transatlantic Slavery" explore the violent histories of this period and literature's role in helping people grapple with them. This edition also offers more work by women writers, including Anne Finch, Mary Wortley Montagu, Mary Collier, Charlotte Lennox, and Frances Burney; and a new cluster featuring explorations of gender and sexuality, with works such as Hannah Snell's *The Female Soldier* and Henry Fielding's *The Female Husband*. Also new are clusters on the histories of science and of sentimental emotion. The Eleventh Edition shows that classic works long in the anthology—such as Behn's *Oroonoko*, Congreve's *The Way of the World*, Swift's *Gulliver's Travels*, Gay's *The Beggar's Opera*, Johnson's *Rasselas*, and influential poetry by Dryden, Pope, and Gray—become even more interesting when read alongside a wider and more diverse array of voices.

Volume D: The Romantic Period
Edited by Eric Eisner and Deidre Lynch, this volume contains new texts that demonstrate just how conscious Romantic-period authors were of living in an expanded, interconnected world. The "Revolution Controversy" cluster has been retitled "An Age of Revolutions," registering its inclusion of material on the conflict that led to Haiti's independence and its development as the first Black republic. Also new is William Blake's *America: A Prophecy*, which approaches revolution through a transatlantic frame. Additions to the cluster "Slavery and the Literature of Abolition" deepen coverage of the painful interval between the British Parliament's abolition of the slave trade in 1807 and its abolition of slavery in Britain's Caribbean colonies in 1833: significantly expanding the excerpt from Mary Prince's 1831 *History*, the volume now includes an excerpt from a periodical dedicated to antislavery and working-class resistance written and published in 1817 by Robert Wedderburn, the son of a Scottish Jamaican planter and an African-born enslaved woman. A new cluster, "Science, Speculation, and Experiment," showcases the striking forms science writing could take in this period of tre-

mendous scientific advances and controversy. It gathers texts by scientist-poet Erasmus Darwin, natural history writer Gilbert White, astronomer Caroline Herschel, and others. The representation of writing by women continues to increase, with new texts by Charlotte Smith, Dorothy Wordsworth, Felicia Hemans, and Letitia Elizabeth Landon. A substantial new excerpt from the "London cantos" of Byron's *Don Juan* enlivens the presentation of Romantic writers' fascination with modern urban experience. The volume now concludes with poems by Henry Louis Vivian Derozio, author of the first books of English-language poetry published in India, whose work reinvents popular Romantic models in assembling an idiom for an Indian national identity.

Volume E: The Victorian Age
Edited by Rachel Ablow and Catherine Robson, this volume has been substantially revised, as signaled by "Great Britain's Imperial Mission," a major topic that includes the following sections: "Slavery, Abolition, and the Plantation System"; "India: The 'Jewel in the Crown'"; "Settler Colonialism: Canada, Australia, New Zealand, South Africa"; and "The British Isles: Ireland, Scotland, Wales." One of the first new entries is a sizable excerpt from *The Wonderful Adventures of Mrs. Seacole*, the memoir of a Jamaican nurse and businesswoman who ministered to British soldiers during the Crimean War. Seacole's text anchors a host of additions that highlight the extent and literary consequences of British imperial aggression. The much-expanded opening cluster provides important historical context for both Seacole's text and the writings that follow, among them work by Toru Dutt, Rabindranath Tagore, and Mohandas Gandhi from India; Tekahionwake/E. Pauline Johnson and Susanna Moodie from Canada; and Olive Schreiner from South Africa. Another major addition is the novella *The Lifted Veil*, by George Eliot, which introduces the central concerns of nineteenth-century realism. Also new are texts focused on the environmental and human consequences of industrialization—by Friedrich Engels, Henry Mayhew, Elizabeth Gaskell, Adelaide Procter, and Thomas Hardy. And we offer longer excerpts from Charles Darwin's major works, as well as a wider range of perspectives on gender and sexuality in the period. Newly added are poems by major authors that address issues of empire (Elizabeth Barrett Browning, Tennyson, Christina Rossetti), as well as texts for two women writers whose work was central to the period: Amy Levy and Augusta Webster.

Volume F: The Twentieth and Twenty-First Centuries
This volume, edited by Aarthi Vadde and Jahan Ramazani, has undergone substantial revision. Major highlights include two new clusters. The first, "Environmental Literature and Climate Change," addresses the impact of environmental crises on how writers, including J. G. Ballard, Bessie Head, Ben Okri, Arundhati Roy, and Robert Macfarlane, have depicted the convergence of nature and culture. A special subsection of poetry captures the richness of verse responding to human-caused climate change; it includes anthology favorites such as Seamus Heaney and Simon Armitage alongside newcomers such as Pascale Petit and Vahni Capildeo. The second cluster, "Born-Digital Literature," features works composed on and for the computer screen by writers who have used digital media to push the boundaries of poetic and narrative form. Poets bpNichol and Caroline Bergvall make

their anthology debut here as do novelists Ali Smith, Teju Cole, and David Mitchell. Joseph Conrad's *Heart of Darkness* and Virginia Woolf's *Mrs. Dalloway* continue to serve as exemplars of the modernist novel, with Conrad's novella now framed by responses from Caryl Phillips and Chimamanda Ngozi Adichie. New to the Eleventh Edition are Wole Soyinka's *Death and the King's Horseman* and Caryl Churchill's *Top Girls*, which join Samuel Beckett's *Waiting for Godot* to provide a varied look at modern drama. We have increased the selections for Claude McKay and contemporary poet Patience Agbabi as well as added a new poem by Philip Larkin. In response to reader requests, the short story "The Demon Lover" by Elizabeth Bowen now appears in "Voices from World War II" while Una Marson and Samuel Selvon join the celebrated cluster "Nation, Race, and Language." Indian novelist Mulk Raj Anand and British novelist Rachel Cusk appear here for the first time, and Zadie Smith is now represented by "The Embassy of Cambodia."

COMPLETE LONGER TEXTS

As in past editions, *The Norton Anthology of English Literature*, Eleventh Edition, includes a generous selection of complete longer texts:

Beowulf (Heaney translation)
The Lady of the Fountain
The York Play of the Crucifixion
The Wakefield Second Shepherds' Play
The King of Tars
The Croxton Play of the Sacrament
Sir Orfeo
Sir Gawain and the Green Knight (Armitage translation)
Everyman
Thomas More, *Utopia*
Christopher Marlowe, *Doctor Faustus* and *Hero and Leander*
William Shakespeare, *Othello* and *The Tempest*
Ben Jonson, *Volpone*
John Webster, *The Duchess of Malfi*
John Milton, *Paradise Lost*
Aphra Behn, *Oroonoko*
William Congreve, *The Way of the World*
John Gay, *The Beggar's Opera*
Eliza Haywood, *Fantomina*
Samuel Johnson, *Rasselas*
William Blake, *Vision of the Daughters of Albion*, *The Marriage of Heaven and Hell*, and *America: A Prophecy*
Jane Austen, *Love and Friendship*
Byron, *Manfred*
Charles Dickens, *A Christmas Carol*
George Eliot, *The Lifted Veil*
Robert Louis Stevenson, *The Strange Case of Dr. Jekyll and Mr. Hyde*
Oscar Wilde, *The Importance of Being Earnest*

Arthur Conan Doyle, *The Speckled Band*
Rudyard Kipling, *The Man Who Would Be King*
Joseph Conrad, *Heart of Darkness*
Virginia Woolf, *Mrs. Dalloway*
James Joyce, *The Dead*
T. S. Eliot, *The Waste Land*
Samuel Beckett, *Waiting for Godot*
Wole Soyinka, *Death and the King's Horseman*
Caryl Churchill, *Top Girls*

The presence of so many complete longer works highlights the anthology's extraordinary value when compared to the cost of purchasing each of these works individually. And through the inclusion of hundreds of brilliant poems and prose pieces, these works are integrated into a much larger vision of the literary achievements of their periods. Indeed, the six volumes by themselves constitute a small but surprisingly comprehensive library.

VISUAL IMAGES

Now, as in the past, cultures define themselves through language. But the central importance of visual media in contemporary culture has heightened our awareness of the ways in which songs and stories have always been closely linked to the images that societies have produced and viewed. The Eleventh Edition of *The Norton Anthology of English Literature* features fifty-six pages of color plates (in seven color inserts) and more than 120 black-and-white illustrations throughout the volumes, including six maps. In selecting visual material—from the Sutton Hoo treasure of the seventh century to Yinka Shonibare's *Nelson's Ship in a Bottle* in the twenty-first century—the editors sought to provide images that illuminate the culture of a particular literary period; that conjure up, whether directly or indirectly, the literature of the section; and that relate specifically to works in the anthology.

EDITORIAL PROCEDURES AND FORMAT

The Eleventh Edition adheres to the principles that have always characterized *The Norton Anthology of English Literature*. Period introductions, headnotes, and annotations are designed to enhance students' reading and, without imposing an interpretation, to give students the information they need to understand each text. The aim of these editorial materials is to make the anthology self-sufficient, so that it can be read anywhere—in a coffeeshop, on a bus, under a tree. The availability of the ebook makes this aim even easier to realize.

The Norton Anthology of English Literature prides itself on both the scholarly accuracy and the readability of its texts. To ease students' encounter with some works, we have normalized spelling and capitalization in texts up to and including the Romantic period—for the most part they now follow the conventions of modern English. We leave unaltered, however, texts in which such modernizing would change semantic or metrical qualities. From the Victorian period onward, we have used the original spelling and punctuation. We continue other editorial procedures that have proved useful in the past. After each work, we cite the date of first publication on the right; in some instances, this date is followed by the date of a revised edition for which the author was responsible. Dates of composition, when they differ from those of publication and when they are known, are provided on the left. We use square brackets to indicate titles supplied by the editors for the convenience of readers. Whenever a portion of a text is omitted, we indicate that omission with three asterisks. If the omitted portion is important for following the plot or argument, we provide a brief summary within the text or in a footnote. Finally, we have reconsidered annotations throughout and increased the number of marginal glosses for archaic, dialect, or unfamiliar words.

The Eleventh Edition includes the useful Literary Terminology appendix, an alphabetical glossary with examples from works in the anthology. We have also updated the General Bibliography, as well as the period and author bibliographies, which appear online.

New and Expanded Resources for Students and Instructors

For the Eleventh Edition, we have added exciting new resources and improved and updated existing resources to make them more useful and easy to find online.

THE NORTON EBOOK READER

Dynamic new features exclusive to the Norton Ebook Reader platform offer students a supportive, accessible environment for thoughtful reading—all at a great price. Readers of the ebook will find it easy to highlight, take notes, search, read offline, and more. In addition to audio recorded by the anthology editors, the anthology's period introductions feature embedded videos that help situate the literature of a particular time and place and highlight overarching themes.

Annotation tools encourage close reading, and instructors can even embed their own content for students directly on the page. An introduction to annotation—available in the Norton Ebook Reader and enriched with videos—walks students through the general *whats*, *whys*, and *hows* of annotation before they delve into the anthology.

Along with these interactive features, the Norton Ebook Reader includes page numbers and selections that match those of the Full Edition print books. The Full Edition includes all selections in the Shorter Edition (and more). Page references corresponding to the Shorter Edition also appear in the margins of relevant selections, making the digital edition more versatile than ever. Many of the black-and-white images in the print anthology *appear in color in the ebook*.

To access and learn more about the Norton Ebook Reader for *The Norton Anthology of English Literature*, reach out to your Norton representative or contact us at literature@wwnorton.com.

STUDENT SITE

The Student Site for *The Norton Anthology of English Literature* features the videos from the Norton Ebook Reader, a curated selection of links to Spotify recordings, and more. Access to this site is available with all new copies of the book or as an affordable standalone purchase option for students with used copies.

TEACHING RESOURCES

Extensive materials are available to adopters to help with course preparation. These include:

- ***Teaching with* The Norton Anthology of English Literature: *A Guide for Instructors*.** In addition to new thematic tables of contents, this downloadable file features "Quick Read" summaries, teaching notes, and writing suggestions for authors, works, and clusters.
- **Reading Comprehension Quizzes.** Norton Testmaker brings high-quality testing and quizzing materials online. Quizzes feature multiple-choice questions on often-taught works and can be easily exported to Microsoft Word or as Common Cartridge files for your LMS.
- **Image Files.** All the images from the anthology are available in PowerPoint with alt text and in JPEG format.

PACKAGE OPTIONS WITH THE NORTON LIBRARY

Select a paperback from our new series of classics to bundle for free with *The Norton Anthology of English Literature*. Edited and produced with the same care that Norton devotes to its anthologies, volumes in the Norton Library include enticing introductions and helpful but unobtrusive annotations by leading scholars. Visit wwnorton.com/norton-library for a complete list of titles and to request examination copies.

The editors would like to express appreciation for their assistance to Sukanya Banerjee (University of California, Berkeley), Ayelet Ben-Yishai (University of Haifa), Liza Blake (University of Toronto), Gabriel Bloomfield (United States Naval Academy), Shamma Boyarin (University of Victoria), Jacqueline

Burek (George Mason University), Jordan Burke (University of Virginia), Evan Reed Butler (Columbia University), Allison Cardon (College of Wooster), Al Coppola (John Jay College, CUNY), Rachel Eisendrath (Barnard College), Kevis Goodman (University of California, Berkeley), Spencer Grayson (University of Virginia), Daniel Grimley (University of Oxford), Andrew Hadfield (University of Sussex), Daniel Hack (University of Michigan), Stephanie Insley Hershinow (Baruch College, CUNY), Lorna Hutson (University of Oxford), Ian Jayne (University of Virginia), Hannah Jorgensen (Duke University), Mary Ellen Lamb (Southern Illinois University at Carbondale), Stephen Leonard, Thomas Leonard-Roy (Harvard University), Tricia Lootens (University of Georgia), Kathleen Lubey (St. John's University), Christina Luckyj (Dalhousie University), Ruth Mack (University at Buffalo, SUNY), Nathaniel Mackey (Duke University), Nicholas Mason (Brigham Young University), Margaret Maurer (Colgate University), Richard McCabe (University of Oxford), Harry McCarthy (University of Cambridge), Claire McManus (University of Roehampton), James Mulholland (North Carolina State University), Lucy Munro (King's College London), Molly Murray (Columbia University), Vivek Narayanan (George Mason University), David Norbrook (University of Oxford), Juan Christian Pellicer (University of Oslo), Manushag Powell (Purdue University), Lisa Rodensky (Wellesley College), Benjamin A. Saltzman (University of Chicago), Elaine Savory (The New School), Wolfram Schmidgen (Washington University in St. Louis), Ana Schwartz (University of Texas at Austin), Daniel Shore (Georgetown University), Yasmin Solomonescu (University of Notre Dame), Samantha Stephens (University of Virginia), Dustin Stewart (Columbia University), Ramie Targoff (Brandeis University), Anna Tjeltveit (Wesleyan University), Teresa Trout (Academy at Penguin Hall), Wendy Wall (Northwestern University), Paul Westover (Brigham Young University), Alexander Wragge-Morley (Lancaster University), Carlisle Yingst (Harvard University), Saskia Ziolkowski (Duke University), and Eugenia Zuroski (McMaster University).

    We also thank the many people at Norton, an employee-owned publishing house with a commitment to excellence, who contributed to the Eleventh Edition. In planning this edition and overseeing its innumerable changes, Marian Johnson served not only as the inhouse supervisor but also as our unfailingly wise and effective collaborator. Her colleague Serin Lee, assistant editor, guided us through the permissions and production processes and contributed deeply to our work on the image program, including the color inserts. Sarah Rose Aquilina, electronic media and course guide editor, oversaw creation of the ebook, fashioned the new video modules, and brought together the web resources and other pedagogical aids. In addition we thank Katharine Ings, Harry Haskell, and Alice Falk, manuscript editors; Megan DeBono Zwilling, marketing manager; Benjamin Reynolds, production manager; Nancy Rodwan, permissions clearance; Amla Sanghvi and Ted Szczepanski, photo editors; Diane Cipollone, ebook project editor; and Jessica Awad and Emma Daugherty, associate media editor and assistant media editor, respectively. All these friends provided the editors with indispensable help in meeting the challenge of representing the unparalleled range and *variety of* English literature.

STEPHEN GREENBLATT

Acknowledgments

We express appreciation and thanks to the close to two hundred teachers who completed surveys and provided reviews. Their participation has been crucial as we look to strengthen the selection of more traditional works while adding texts that reflect the expansion and continued transformation of the field of English studies.

Elizabeth Acosta (El Paso Community College), Rachel Adcock (Keele University), Diann Ainsworth (Weatherford College), Laura Alexander (High Point University), Nadia Alexis (University of Mississippi), Carla Anderson (Temple University), Jessica Assink (Baylor University), Alison Baker (Cal Poly Pomona), Michael Baker (Florida Gateway College), Samuel Baker (University of Texas at Austin), Leah Benedict (Kennesaw State University), Brian Blackley (North Carolina State University), Lindy Brady (University of Mississippi), Paul Bowers (Northern Oklahoma College), Julie Brannon (Jacksonville University), Nathan Branson (Carteret Community College), Jim Brisson (Robeson Community College), Katherine Calloway (Baylor University), Sarah Canfield (Shenandoah University), William Carroll (Abilene Christian University), Amanda L. Chapman (Glenville State College), David Chapman (Samford University), King-Kok Cheung (University of California, Los Angeles), Ashley L. Cohen (University of Southern California), Michael C. Cohen (University of California, Los Angeles), Rita Colanzi (Immaculata University), Daniel Compton (Midlands Technical College–Beltline), Charles Conaway (University of Southern Indiana), Lisa Cooper (University of Wisconsin-Madison), Alison Cope (Lone Star College), Jenny Crisp (Dalton State College), Thomas H. Crofts (East Tennessee State University), Noel Currie (Langara College), Linda J. Daigle (Houston Community College), Catherine England (Francis Marion University), Kasey Evans (Northwestern University), Rhonda Fabrizi Cuyahoga Community College), Anne Fertig (University of North Carolina at Chapel Hill), Douglas Field (University of Manchester), John Flood (University of Groningen), Elizabeth Fowler (University of Virginia), Peter Francev (Victor Valley College), Alan Friedman (University of Texas), Emily C. Friedman (Auburn University), Noelle Gallagher (University of Manchester), Royce Clifton Garner (North Central Texas College), Jennifer Garrison (St. Mary's University), Kim Allen Gleed (Harrisburg Area Community College), Kevis Goodman (University of California, Berkeley),

Jill Gos (Lee College), Andrea Green (Motlow State Community College), Darragh Greene (University College Dublin), Meg Gregory (Webster University), Joel Grossman (Queen Mary University of London), Gary R. Grund (Rhode Island College), Adam Hadley (Kansas City Kansas Community College), John Halbrooks (University of South Alabama), Gabriel Haley (Concordia University Nebraska), Marjory Hall (Florence-Darlington Technical College), Robin Hammerman (Stevens Institute of Technology), Ginger Hanchey (Baylor University), Matthew Hart (Columbia University), Richard Hartnett (Trident Technical College), Brandon W. Hawk (Rhode Island College), Nathan K. Hensley (Georgetown University), Natalie Hewitt (Hope International University), Douglas Higbee (University of South Carolina Aiken), Linda Holland-Toll (University of Mount Olive), Sylvia Hunt (Laurentian University), Zach Hyde (Valencia College), Robin Inboden (Wittenberg University), Christopher Ivic (Bath Spa University), Sujata Iyengar (University of Georgia), David James (University of Birmingham), Jill Johnson (Tyler Junior College), Harold Johnson (Northwest Mississippi Community College), Betty Joseph (Rice University), George Justice (Arizona State University), Wei-Hung Kao (National Taiwan University), Christopher Keirstead (Auburn University), Jim Knowles (North Carolina State University), Julie Kratt (Cowley College), Christopher Krejci (Temple College), Laura S. Krohn (Oral Roberts University), James M. Lang (Assumption College), Douglas Lanier (University of New Hampshire), Alex Lawrie (University of Edinburgh), Miles Leeson (University of Chichester), Eric Lindstrom (University of Vermont), Jeremy Lopez (University of Toronto), Derek Lowe (University of South Alabama), Sara Luttfring (Penn State Behrend), Ruth Mack (University at Buffalo, SUNY), Joseph Mansky (University of Oklahoma), Kelly Mayhew (San Diego City College), Comanchette McBee (Iowa Western Community College), Heidi M. McConnell (El Paso Community College), Cameron McFarlane (Nipissing University), Jenny McHenry (Tallahassee Community College), Raj Mehta (Camosun College), David Merrell (Abilene Christian University), Christine Mihelich (Marywood University), Lindsay Milam (Cuyahoga Community College), Carey Millsap-Spears (Moraine Valley Community College), Feisal G. Mohamed (Yale University), James Morey (Emory University), Elizabeth Napier (Middlebury College), Jim Neilson (Wake Technical Community College), Leila Neti (Occidental College), Ralph Norris (Sam Houston State University), Niamh Pattwell (University College Dublin), Michelle Paulsen (Victoria College), Heidi L. Pennington (James Madison University), Michael Piero (Cuyahoga Community College), Albert Pionke (University of Alabama), Christine Pristash (Jefferson Community College, SUNY), Katherine Quinsey (University of Windsor), David Ragsdale (Lone Star College–Kingwood), Dominic Rainsford (Aarhus University), Neil Ramsey (University of New South Wales), Erin Ranft (Lone Star College–North Harris), Mark Rankin (James Madison University), Joshua Reid (East Tennessee State University), Jennifer Richardson (Lone Star College–Tomball), Jim Richey (Tyler Junior College), Jessica Riddell (Bishop's University), Robert Rogan (Brunswick Community College), Cordelia Ross (University of Alabama), Kelly Ross (Rider University), Cheryl Saba (Cape Fear Community College), Nicholas Sabo (University of Mississippi), Allen J. Salerno (Auburn University), Elizabeth Scala (University of Texas), Terry Scarborough (Okanagan College), Chester N. Scoville (University of Toronto), Michael Schwartz (Moreno Valley College), Edel Semple (University College Cork), Daniel Shore (Georgetown University), Debora Shuger (University of California, Los Angeles), Cassander Smith (University of Alabama), Helen Smith (Kentucky State University), Sara Smith (Pensacola State College), William H. Smith (Weatherford College), Sebastian Sobecki (University of Groningen), Yasmin Solomonescu (University of Notre Dame), Vivasvan Soni (Northwestern University), Janet Sorensen (University of California, Berkeley), Julie M. Sorge Way (James Madison University), Lauren Springer (Mt. San Jacinto College), Tyesha Stafford-McGilbrey (Tarrant County College), Erin Stephens (Somerset Community College), Timothy L. Stinson (North Carolina State University), Ellen Stockstill (Penn State Harrisburg), Ashley Streeter (San Jacinto College), Cara Swafford (Lincoln Land Community College), Steve Tedeschi (University of Alabama), Dennis Yi Tenen (Columbia University), Kristin Teston (University of Mississippi), Arvind Thomas (University of California, Los Angeles), Mary Ives Thompson (Sussex County Community College), Heidi Thomson (Victoria University of Wellington), Christopher W. Thurley (Gaston College), Margaret Torrell (SUNY Old Westbury), Ryan Trimm (University of Rhode Island), Roy Turner (Lone Star College–Montgomery), William A. Ulmer (University of Alabama), Kees de Vries (University of Groningen), Vallie Watson (University of North Carolina Wilmington), Rachel Webster (Baylor University), Kristen Weinzapfel (North Central Texas College), Deborah Weiss (University of Alabama), Clifford Werier (Mount Royal University), Paul Westover (Brigham Young University), Cathy L. Whaley (East Tennessee State University), Gwen Whitehead (Lamar State College Orange), Helen Williams (Northumbria University), Jocelyn Williams (St. Mary's University), Jessica Wolfe (University of North Carolina at Chapel Hill), Mou-Lan Wong (National Taiwan University), Jennifer Young (Cape Fear Community College), Kim Zarins (California State University at Sacramento), and Jay Zysk (University of Massachusetts Dartmouth).

THE NORTON ANTHOLOGY OF
ENGLISH LITERATURE

ELEVENTH EDITION

VOLUME B

THE SIXTEENTH CENTURY
AND
THE EARLY SEVENTEENTH CENTURY

The Sixteenth Century 1485–1603

1485: Accession of Henry VII inaugurates the Tudor dynasty
1509: Accession of Henry VIII
1517: Martin Luther's Wittenberg Theses; beginning of the Reformation
1534: Henry VIII declares himself head of the English Church
1557: Publication of Tottel's *Songs and Sonnets*, containing poems by Sir Thomas Wyatt; Henry Howard, Earl of Surrey; and others
1558: Accession of Elizabeth I
1576: Building of The Theatre, the first round permanent structure in England for the presentation of plays
1588: Defeat of the Spanish Armada
1603: Death of Elizabeth I and accession of James I, the first of the Stuart kings

England came late to the Renaissance. It was in the fourteenth century that Italy had begun its "Renaissance," the word meaning "rebirth." What was reborn in Italy was a fascination with its own classical past, including its Latin literature, philosophy, and art. England, however, reached its Renaissance only a century later, and in fact this was a new birth rather than a rebirth. An island, England was slow to adopt Italy's focus on the classics.

As the Renaissance swept across Europe, Latin became the international language: all significant schooling was in Latin, and Latin was the language for international

The Life and Death of Sir Henry Unton (detail), anonymous, ca. 1597. A masque of musicians and dancers performs for a dinner party of Unton's friends. Theatrical life in this period, which often included music and dancing, was not restricted to the playhouse; it extended into other social settings, such as this one.

trade. The English language, by contrast, was not very useful. There were those at home who thought it too primitive ever to serve as a suitable medium for serious, elevated, or elegant discourse—or, consequently, writing. One of the first works in this anthology's selection of English Renaissance literature, Thomas More's *Utopia*, for instance, was not first written in English: More, who began his great book in 1515 when he was on a diplomatic mission in the Netherlands, was intending his work for an international intellectual community, and so his language of choice was the European one, Latin. His work, though it became famous throughout Europe, was not even translated into English until the 1550s. Yet by the end of that same century, English had developed and grown beyond recognition: it had been fashioned into the powerful expressive medium whose cadences in the works of Marlowe, Shakespeare, and the translators of the Bible continue to thrill readers after more than four centuries.

How did it come about that so many remarkable poems, plays, and prose works were written in English by the end of the sixteenth century? The answer lies in part in the spectacular creativity of a succession of brilliant writers, the best of whom are represented in these pages. Still, a vital literary culture is the product of complex processes, involving thousands of more modest, half-hidden creative acts sparked by a wide range of motives, some of which will briefly be explored over the following pages.

THE COURT AND THE CITY

The development of the English language in the sixteenth century is linked at least indirectly to the consolidation and strengthening of the English state. Through most of the previous century, the English had been preoccupied by violent clashes between the militarized servants of rival barons and had had limited time and inclination to cultivate rhetorical skills. The social and economic health of the nation had been further damaged by the so-called Wars of the Roses, a vicious, decades-long struggle for royal power between the noble houses of York, whose symbol was a white rose, and Lancaster, whose symbol was a red rose. The struggle was resolved by the establishment of what was called the Tudor dynasty, named for Owen Tudor, an ambitious Welshman who himself had no claim to the throne but who married Catherine of Valois, widow of the Lancastrian king Henry V. Their grandson, the Earl of Richmond, became the first Tudor monarch: he won the crown by leading the army that defeated and killed the reigning Yorkist king, Richard III, at the battle of Bosworth Field. When the victorious Richmond, descendent of the house of Lancaster, was crowned King Henry VII in 1485, he married Elizabeth of the house of York. The result was a Tudor dynasty that united the two rival factions of York and Lancaster. Their union was symbolized in a floral device, the "Tudor rose," which consists of a red rose of Lancaster enclosing a white rose of York.

Because they had been impoverished and divided by their own wars, England's barons could not effectively oppose the new power of the Tudor Crown. Moreover, the leaders of the Church also supported royal power. So Henry VII was able to counter the multiple and competing power structures characteristic of feudal society and impose a much stronger central authority and order on the nation. By the reign of the last Tudor—Henry's granddaughter, Elizabeth I—even though the ruler still needed the consent of Parliament on crucial matters (including the all-important one of levying taxes), the royal court had concentrated in itself much of the nation's power.

The court was a center of culture as well as power: court entertainments such as theater and masque (a sumptuous, elaborately costumed performance of dance, song, and poetry); court fashions in dress and speech; court tastes in painting, music, and poetry—all shaped the taste and the imagination of the country as a whole. Culture and power were not, in any case, easily separable in Tudor England. In a society with little freedom of speech (as we understand it) and with mass communication limited to word of mouth and the announcing and hanging up of official proclamations (newspapers, called "corantoes," were not to be published until the 1620s), important public issues were often aired indirectly, through what we might now regard as entertainment.

Whereas in the Middle Ages noblemen had guarded their power by keeping their distance from London and the king, in the Tudor era the route to power lay in proximity to royalty. (One of the coveted positions in the court of Henry VIII was Groom of the Stool, "close stool" being the Tudor term for toilet.) The monarch's chief ministers and favorites dispensed favors to courtiers who competed for offices in the court, the government bureaucracies, the royal household, the army, the Church, and the universities or who sought titles or grants or leases of land. But proximity to royalty had dangers of its own. Festive evenings with the likes of the ruthless Henry VIII were not occasions for relaxation. The court was a place of competition, even paranoia, with an accompanying obsession with secrecy, spying, duplicity, and betrayal.

Tudor courtiers were torn between the needs to protect and to display themselves. For lessons in the art of intrigue, many turned to the Italian Machiavelli's notorious *Il Principe* (The Prince), with its cool guidance on how power may be gained and kept. For advice on the cultivation and display of the self, they could resort to the still more influential Italian book *Il Cortegiano* (The Courtier) by Count Baldassare Castiglione. It was particularly important, Castiglione wrote, to conceal the effort that lay behind elegant accomplishments, so that they would seem natural. (*Sprezzatura* was the name for this invaluable skill.) In this anxious atmosphere, courtiers became highly practiced at implementing what these Italian writers recommended and at crafting and coining new and graceful words with double or triple meanings. The English language expanded as a result, not least because a habit of Anglifying Latin quickly doubled the number of words available in English ("sweat" *and* "perspiration," "drink" *and* "beverage"—the frank Anglo-Saxon vying with the ponderous Latin). And, hardly surprisingly, several of the best poets in the period—Sir Thomas Wyatt, Sir Philip Sidney, Sir Walter Ralegh, and others—were courtiers.

Other forces in Tudor England pulled toward a more public sphere. Markets expanded significantly, international trade flourished, and cities throughout the realm experienced a rapid surge in size and importance. London's population soared, from 60,000 in 1520, to 120,000 in 1550, to 375,000 a century later, making it the largest and fastest-growing city not only in England but in all of Europe. Every year in the first half of the seventeenth century about 10,000 people migrated to London from other parts of England—wages in London tended to be around 50 percent higher than in the rest of the country—and it is estimated that one in eight English people lived in London at some point in their lives. Elderly Londoners in the 1590s could barely recognize the city of their childhood; London's boom was one factor among many contributing to the sense of a culture moving with increasing swiftness away from its historical roots. That expansion, too, found its voice in literature, in songs celebrating markets and trade, and fueled the import of merchandise from overseas like tobacco and spices.

About a decade before Henry VII won his throne, the art of printing, a German invention, had been introduced into England by William Caxton (ca. 1422–1491). Caxton, who was an author and a translator as well as a printer, attempted to cater to courtly tastes by producing works whose tone was more medieval than modern. As often in an age of alarming novelty, many people looked back to an idealized past. Indeed the great innovations of the Tudor era—intellectual, governmental, and religious—were all presented, at the time, as attempts to restore ancient traditions. Printing made books cheaper and more plentiful, providing more opportunity to read and more incentive to learn. Though reliable statistics are impossible to come by, literacy seems to have increased during the fifteenth century and still more during the sixteenth as printed texts became more widely accessible. The greater availability of books may also have reinforced the trend toward silent reading, a practice that gradually transformed what had been a communal experience into a more intimate encounter with a text, though communal singing ensured that certain varieties of lyric remained shared—some of which are included in this volume.

Social class often determined writers' attitude to print. As Sir Thomas Smith explained in 1583, "We in England divide our men commonly into four sorts, gentlemen, citizens or burgesses, yeomen artificers, and laborers." But while citizens, artificers, and laborers bought and increasingly wrote texts, leading to a flourishing trade in plays, ballads, romances, sermons, jests, and a rich range of other books and pamphlets, court poets were wary of the "stigma of print" that might mark their verse as less exclusive. Among "gentlemen"—the elite—manuscripts retained considerable prestige, and court texts often circulated in notebooks and commonplace books without ever reaching print.

RENAISSANCE HUMANISM

To Renaissance intellectuals and artists, the achievements of the pagan philosophers of ancient Greece and Rome came to seem compelling, and the medieval submission of the human spirit to penitential discipline gave way to unleashed curiosity, individual self-assertion, and a powerful conviction that man was the measure of all things. In Italy, in the brilliant, intensely competitive, and vital world of the artists Leonardo da Vinci and Michelangelo, the human figure was placed at the center of the Renaissance worldview. "We have made thee neither of heaven nor of earth, neither mortal nor immortal," God tells Adam, in the Florentine Pico della Mirandola's *Oration on the Dignity of Man* (1486), "so that with freedom of choice and with honor, as though the maker and molder of thyself, thou mayest fashion thyself in whatever shape thou shalt prefer." "As though the maker and molder of thyself": this vision of self-fashioning may be glimpsed too in the works of other artists—the poetry of Petrarch, the sculpture of Donatello, and the statecraft of Lorenzo de' Medici.

But in England it was not until the accession of Henry VIII that the Renaissance began to flower—and not, as in Italy, in painting, sculpture, and architecture. It came rather in the intellectual program and literary vision known as humanism (from the Italian name for an educator of classical literature, *umanista*). In England, Renaissance humanism was bound up with struggles over the purposes of education and curriculum reform. English humanists, including John Colet (who, as dean of St. Paul's Cathedral, recast its grammar school on humanist principles), Roger Ascham (tutor to Princess Elizabeth), and Sir Thomas Elyot, wrote treatises on education to promote the kind of learning they regarded as the most suitable preparation for public service. That education shifted from training for the Church to the general acquisition of "literature," in the sense both of literacy and of cultural knowledge. For some of the more intellectually ambitious humanists, that knowledge extended to ancient Greek (largely lost in

Tudor Schoolroom. In this woodcut from the sixteenth century, the pupils sit on "forms," or benches, with few if any desks. As an early school statute explains, "When they have to write, let them use their knees for a table." All the lessons, for the different age groups, are taught in the same room: the younger boys (left) are learning their letters, while the students at the upper right are studying music. The schoolmaster, seated, holds a birch, while the usher, or assistant master, is beating a student. The windows of the schoolroom are set high in the walls, to cut down on distractions. Next to the far pillar is an hourglass used in marking time for various lessons. The school's valuable books are kept in a locked chest, behind the schoolmaster.

the West between the fourth and thirteenth centuries), whose enthusiastic followers began to challenge the preeminence of Latin.

Still, at the core of the curriculum remained the study of Latin. The purpose was to train the sons (and, very occasionally, daughters) of the nobility and gentry to speak and write good Latin, the language of diplomacy, of the professions, and of all higher learning. Women were primarily educated at home or in other noble houses, where they chiefly learned modern languages, religion, music, and needlework. While women seldom received the thorough training in the ancient languages and classical literature so central to the dominant culture, some, including Elizabeth I and Mary Sidney Herbert—and the daughters of Sir Thomas More—were able to play central roles in the translation and production of literary texts. Through Latin-based training, Elizabethan schoolmasters sought to impart rhetorical elegance, but the books their students laboriously pored over—from the *Sententiae Pueriles* (Maxims for Children) for beginners to the dramatists Terence, Plautus, and Seneca; the poets Virgil and Horace; and the orator Cicero—also offered moral, political, and philosophical wisdom and cultural capital. Though originating in pagan times, ancient truths could, in the opinion of many humanists, be reconciled to the moral vision of Christianity. The result, perplexing for some modern readers, is that pagan gods and goddesses flourish on the pages of even such a devoutly Christian poem as Edmund Spenser's *Faerie Queene*.

Humanists committed to classical learning were faced with the question of whether to write in Latin or in English. To many learned men, influenced both by the humanist elevation of the classical languages and by a Renaissance desire for eternal fame, national languages seemed unstable and impermanent in a way that Latin did not. Works by English scientists such as William Gilbert, William Harvey, and Francis Bacon easily joined those by such Continental writers as Nicolaus Copernicus, Johannes Kepler, and Andreas Vesalius in the common linguistic medium of Latin. But throughout Europe, nationalism and the expansion of the reading public were steadily strengthening the power and allure of native languages. The famous English schoolmaster Richard Mulcaster (ca. 1530–1611), teacher of the poet Spenser, captured this emergent sense of national identity when he compared Latin to his native tongue:

> Is it not . . . a marvelous bondage, to become servants to one tongue for learning's sake the most of our time, with loss of most time, whereas we may have the very same treasure in our own tongue, with the gain of more time? our own bearing the joyful title of our liberty and freedom, the Latin tongue remembering us of our thralldom and bondage? I love Rome, but London better; I favor Italy, but England more; I honor the Latin, but I worship the English.

These two impulses within learned writers—humanist reverence for the classics and English pride in their native language—gave rise to many distinguished translations throughout the century: Homer's *Iliad* and *Odyssey* by George Chapman, Plutarch's *Lives of the Noble Grecians and Romans* by Sir Thomas North, and Ovid's *Metamorphoses* by Arthur Golding. Translators also sought to make available in English the most notable literary works in the modern languages: Castiglione's *Il Cortegiano* by Sir Thomas

"How You Ought to Hold Your Pen." Humanist concern with literacy led to a proliferation of writing books. These books typically explained how to cut and shape a goose quill to make a pen, how to hold that pen (and how not to), and how to write in both "secretary" and "Italian" (italic) hand.

Hoby, Ariosto's *Orlando furioso* (Orlando Mad) by Sir John Harington, and Montaigne's *Essais* by John Florio. The London book trade of the sixteenth century was a thoroughly international affair.

THE REFORMATION

Officially, England in the early sixteenth century had a single religion, Catholicism. Because its acknowledged head was the pope in Rome, England was bound to Italy in terms of religion as well as language and culture. The most sacred Catholic ritual was Mass, a ceremony performed in Latin during which the congregation could regularly witness a miracle: the priest held up bread and wine, which his words transformed into the body and blood of God. This act gave the male priests great power, at once spiritual and material, over their largely illiterate flocks—power conveyed through systems of confession, pardons, penance, absolution, indulgences, sacred relics, and ceremonies. The Bible, the church services, and most of the theological discussions were in Latin, which few laypeople could understand. However, religious doctrine and spirituality were mediated to them by the priests, by beautiful church art and music, and by the liturgical ceremonies of daily life: festivals, holy days, baptisms, marriages, exorcisms, and funerals.

In the past, heretical movements had occasionally emerged and were suppressed, but a more serious threat arose in the sixteenth century. In November 1517, an Augustinian monk and a professor of theology at the University of Wittenberg, named Martin Luther, began to question several of the key doctrines and practices of the Catholic Church. What began in November 1517 as an academic disputation grew with amazing speed into a bitter, far-reaching, and bloody revolt that forever ruptured the unity of Western Christendom.

A person of formidable intellectual energy, eloquence, and rhetorical violence, Luther rose up against the ancient Catholic Church, in the name of private conscience enlightened by a personal reading of the scriptures. He maintained that the Church had degenerated and was a corrupt, worldly conspiracy; that it exploited its credulous believers and subverted nonreligious authority; and that the pope and his hierarchy were the servants of Satan. Luther argued that all people should have direct access to the word of God and be able to make their own analyses of the Bible: he therefore also thought the Bible should be translated out of Latin and into native languages. The movement Luther sparked, the Reformation as it came to be known (because it aimed to *reform* the Catholic Church), was governed by the terms *sola scriptura* and *sola fide*, according to which only the scriptures (not the Church or tradition or the clerical hierarchy) have authority in matters of religion and should determine what an individual must believe and practice; and only the faith of the individual (not good works or the scrupulous observance of religious rituals) can effect a Christian's salvation.

These tenets, heretical in the eyes of the Catholic Church, spread and gathered force, especially in northern Europe, where major leaders like the Swiss pastor Ulrich Zwingli in Zurich and the French theologian John Calvin in Geneva, elaborating various and sometimes conflicting doctrinal principles, organized the populace to overturn the existing church and established new institutional structures. In England, in contrast, the Reformation began less with popular discontent and theological disputation than with politics and royal greed. Henry VIII, who had received from Pope Leo X the title Defender of the Faith for writing a diatribe against Luther, craved a legitimate son to succeed to the throne, and his queen, Catherine of Aragon, failed to give him one. (Catherine had borne six children, but only a daughter, Mary, survived infancy.) After lengthy negotiations, the pope, under pressure from Catherine's powerful Spanish family, refused to grant the king the divorce he sought in order to marry Anne Boleyn, who, he hoped, might finally bear him a son.

A series of momentous events followed, as England lurched away from the Church of Rome. In 1531 Henry forced the entire clergy of England to beg pardon for having administered canon law (which governed such matters as divorce), which, he claimed, should be understood as a royal prerogative, not controlled by Rome. Two years later Henry's marriage to Catherine was officially declared null and void and Anne Boleyn was crowned queen. The king was promptly excommunicated by the pope, Clement VII. In the following year, all adult male subjects were required by a parliamentary "Act of Succession" to accept as "undoubted, true, sincere and perfect" the king's marriage to Anne. Thomas More and John Fisher, the bishop of Rochester, were among the small number who stuck to their Catholic beliefs and refused. The Act of Supremacy, passed later in the year, formally declared the king to be "Supreme Head of the Church in England" and again required an oath to this effect. In 1535 and 1536 further acts made it treasonous to refuse the oath of royal supremacy or, as More had tried to do, to remain silent. Three monks of the Catholic Carthusian order who rejected the oath—"How could the king, a layman," said one of them, "be Head of the Church of England?"—in May 1535 were hanged, drawn (tied to a horse and dragged), and quartered (torn apart by four horses pulling in different directions). A few weeks later Fisher and More were con-

The Pope as Antichrist. In this satirical woodcut, the pope, riding the seven-headed Beast of the Apocalypse, holds in his hand a banner on which he urges his followers to be traitors and kill their princes. His message, carried by three froglike devils, flies into the gaping mouths of a knight, a bishop, and a monk. The devils are a reference to Revelation 16:13: "And I saw three unclean spirits like frogs come out of the mouth of the dragon, and out of the mouth of the beast, and out of the mouth of the false prophet." From *Fierie Tryall of God's Saints* (1611; author unknown).

victed and beheaded. Between 1536 and 1539, under the direction of Henry's powerful secretary of state, Thomas Cromwell, England's Catholic monasteries were suppressed. Their vast wealth was seized by the Crown and transferred, by either gift or sale, to the king's followers.

Royal defiance of the authority of Rome was a key element in the English Reformation. But in the same year that Fisher and More were martyred for their adherence to Roman Catholicism, twenty-five Protestants (a label applied to adherents of any form of Christianity that "protested" or rejected Catholicism), members of a sect known as Anabaptists, were also burned for heresy on a single day. Through most of his reign, Henry remained an equal-opportunity persecutor, pitiless to Catholics loyal to Rome and hostile to many of those who espoused Reformation ideas, though these ideas, aided greatly by the printing press, gradually established themselves on English soil.

Having produced only a daughter, Elizabeth, the marriage between Henry and Anne Boleyn ended in disaster: the king had his wife beheaded on charges of treason and adultery. Henry's third wife, Jane Seymour, finally gave birth to the son he craved, and this son, Edward, succeeded to the throne upon the king's death in 1547. Both the ten-year-old Edward and his successive Protectors, the dukes of Somerset and Northumberland, were Protestants. Reformers hastened to transform the English Church accordingly. During Edward's brief reign, Thomas Cranmer, the archbishop of Canterbury, formulated the forty-two articles of religion that became the core of English Protestantism and wrote the first *Book of Common Prayer*, which was officially adopted in 1549 as the basis of English worship services.

The sickly Edward VI died in 1553, only six years after his accession to the throne. He was succeeded by his half-sister Mary (Henry VIII's daughter by his first wife, Catherine), who immediately took steps to return her kingdom to Roman Catholicism. Though she was unable to get Parliament to agree to return Church lands seized under Henry VIII, she restored the Catholic Mass, once again affirmed the authority of the pope, and subdued a rebellion that sought to depose her. With her ardently Catholic husband, Philip II, king of Spain, she initiated a series of bloodthirsty religious persecutions—she had almost three hundred Protestants burned "at the stake" (that is, tied to posts and burned)—that earned her (from her enemies) the name "Bloody Mary." Hundreds of Protestants, including John Jewel and Anne Vaughan Locke, took refuge abroad in cities like Calvin's Geneva. Yet for thousands of English men and women, Mary's reign came as a liberation; the return of old Catholic ornaments to parish churches all over England indicates that they had not been confiscated or destroyed as ordered, but hidden away, in hopes of a return to the true faith.

Mary died childless in 1558, and her younger half-sister, Elizabeth, became queen. Elizabeth's succession had been by no means assured. For if Protestants regarded as invalid Henry VIII's Catholic marriage to Catherine and hence deemed Mary illegitimate, so Catholics regarded as invalid his Protestant marriage to Anne Boleyn and hence deemed *her* daughter illegitimate. Moreover, though Elizabeth outwardly complied with the official Catholic religious observances throughout her sister's reign, Mary and her advisers rightly suspected her of Protestant leanings and set traps for her: her life was often in danger. When Elizabeth ascended the throne, the country's future religious course was once again in question. During her coronation procession, when a girl in an allegorical pageant presented her with a Bible in English translation—banned under Mary's reign—Elizabeth kissed the book, held it up reverently, and laid it to her breast. By this simple yet profound (and carefully choreographed) gesture, Elizabeth signaled England's return to Protestantism, as well as the central role the Book, and books in general, would play in her court.

Many English men and women, of all classes, remained loyal to the old Catholic faith, but English authorities under Elizabeth demanded at least the appearance of conformity to Protestantism. Recusants (those who refused to attend regular Sunday services in their parish churches) were heavily fined. Anyone who wished to receive a university degree, to be ordained as a priest in the Church of England, or to be named as an officer of the state had to swear an oath to the ruler's supremacy as head of the church. Bishops were directed to investigate whether parish clergy had, as commanded, "removed, abolished, and destroyed" all images that were thought superstitious. Commissioners were sent throughout the land to confirm that religious services were following the officially approved liturgy and to investigate any reported backsliding into Catholic practice. At the other extreme were the Protestant exiles who returned to England eager to carry the Reformation much further than it had gone. A minority, whom their enemies called Puritans—for their attempts to "purify" the Church from any vestige of Catholicism—sought to purge the church service of ritual practices deemed to have no basis in scripture, to dress *the* clergy in simple garb, and to smash "idolatrous" statues, crucifixes, and altarpieces. They also objected to the calendar of "pagan" folk customs, including dancing around the maypole to mark the start of summer, and "mumming"—dressing up in disguise and performing plays and antics at friends' houses—to mark the Christmas period. Throughout her long reign, however, Elizabeth remained cautiously conservative and determined to hold Puritanism as well as Catholicism in check.

In the space of a single lifetime, England's official religion had changed from Roman Catholicism, to Catholicism under the supreme headship of the English king, to a guarded Protestantism, to a more radical Protestantism, to a renewed and aggressive Roman Catholicism, and finally to Protestantism again. Each of these shifts was accompanied by danger, persecution, and death. It was enough to make people wary. Or skeptical. Or extremely agile.

QUEEN ELIZABETH I

In the last year of Mary's reign, the Scottish minister John Knox, who was a Calvinist—a follower of the extreme French Protestant reformer Calvin—thundered against what he called "the monstrous regiment of women." After the Protestant Elizabeth came to the throne the following year, Knox and his religious brethren were less inclined to denounce all female rulers; but in England, as elsewhere in Europe, there remained a widespread conviction that women were unsuited to wield power over men. Many men seem to have regarded rational thought as exclusively male; women, they assumed, were led only by their passions. While gentlemen mastered the arts of rhetoric and warfare, gentlewomen were expected to display the virtues of silence and good housekeeping. Among upper-class males, the will to dominate others was acceptable and indeed admired; the same will in women was condemned as a grotesque and dangerous aberration.

Admirers of Queen Elizabeth countered these prejudices by pointing out that history offered inspiring examples of just female rulers—notably Deborah, the biblical prophetess who had judged Israel. In the legal sphere, Crown lawyers advanced the theory of "the king's [or, in this instance, queen's] two bodies." As England's crowned head, Elizabeth had a mortal "body natural" and an immortal "body politic." While the queen's natural body was subject to decay and death, the office of monarch was eternal. In political terms, therefore, Elizabeth's sex was a matter of no consequence.

Elizabeth, who had received a fine humanist education and an extended, dangerous lesson in the art of survival, made it immediately clear that she intended to rule in more than name only. Though she assembled a group of trustworthy advisers, foremost among them William Cecil (later created Lord Burghley), she insisted on making many of the crucial decisions herself. Like many Renaissance monarchs, Elizabeth was drawn to the theory that ultimate power was quite properly concentrated in her person and indeed that God had appointed her to be his deputy in the kingdom. Opposition to her rule, in this view, was against the will of God and therefore blasphemous. Supporters of "absolutism" maintained that God commands that the people obey even wicked rulers (whom he has sent to punish the sinfulness of humankind). Such arguments were routinely made in speeches and political tracts and from the pulpits of churches, where they were incorporated into the *Book of Homilies* that clergymen were required to read out to their congregations.

In reality, Elizabeth's power was not absolute. The government had a network of spies, informers, and agents provocateurs, but it lacked a standing army, a national police force, an efficient system of communication, and an extensive bureaucracy. Above all, the queen had limited financial resources and needed to turn periodically to an independent Parliament, which had the sole right to levy taxes and to grant subsidies. Members of the House of Commons were elected from their towns (known as "boroughs"), not appointed by the monarch, and the queen could not dictate their policies. Under these constraints, Elizabeth ruled through a combination of political maneuvering and imperious command, while establishing an extraordinary, and largely literary, cult of love with her at the center.

"We all loved her," Elizabeth's godson Sir John Harington wrote, with just a touch of irony, a few years after the queen's death, "for she said she loved us." Ambassadors, courtiers, and parliamentarians all submitted to Elizabeth's cult of love, in which the queen's sex was cunningly transformed from a potential liability into a significant asset. Those who approached her generally did so on their knees and were expected to address her with the most extravagant compliments; she in turn spoke, when it suited her to do so, in a comparable language of love. The court favored an atmosphere of romance, with music, dancing, plays, and the elaborate fancy dress entertainments called masques. The queen adorned herself in dazzling clothes and rich jewels. When she went on one of her summer "progresses," ceremonial journeys through her land, she looked like an exotic, sacred image in a religious cult of love, and her noble hosts virtually bankrupted themselves to lavish upon her the costliest pleasures. England's leading artists, such as the poet Edmund Spenser and the painter Nicholas Hilliard, celebrated Elizabeth's mystery by likening her to the goddesses of mythology and the heroines of the Bible: Diana, Astraea, Cynthia, Deborah. The cultural sources of the cult of Elizabeth were both secular (her courtiers could pine for her as the cruelly chaste mistress celebrated in love poetry) and sacred (the veneration that under Catholicism had been due to the Virgin Mary could now be directed toward England's semidivine queen).

There was a sober, even grim aspect to these poetical fantasies: Elizabeth was brilliant at playing off one dangerous faction against another, now turning her gracious smiles on one favorite, now honoring his hated rival, now suddenly looking elsewhere and raising an obscure upstart to royal favor. And when she was disobeyed or when she felt that her prerogatives had been challenged, she was capable of an anger that, as Harington put it, with a reference to Henry VIII, "left no doubtings whose daughter she was." Thus when Sir Walter Ralegh, one of the queen's glittering favorites, married without her knowledge and consent, he found himself imprisoned in the Tower of London. Or when the controversial Protestant writer John Stubbes published a pamphlet denouncing the queen's proposed marriage to the French Catholic Duke of Anjou, he and his publisher were arrested and had their right hands chopped off. (After receiving the blow, the now prudent Stubbes lifted his hat with his remaining hand just before he fainted and cried, "God save the Queen!")

THE KINGDOM IN DANGER

Beset by Catholic and Protestant extremists, Elizabeth's careful compromises enabled her realm to avert the massacres and civil wars that poisoned France and other countries on the Continent. But menace was never far off, and there were continual fears of conspiracy, rebellion, and assassination. Suspicion swirled around Elizabeth's second cousin the Catholic Mary, Queen of Scots, who had been driven from Scotland in 1568 and had taken refuge in England. The presence, under a kind of house arrest, of a Catholic queen with a plausible claim to the English throne was the source of widespread anxiety. There were recurrent rumors that Mary was plotting to seize the English throne. Some of these were real enough, others imaginary, still others fabricated by the secret agents of the government's intelligence service under the direction of Elizabeth's spymaster, Sir Francis Walsingham. Fears of Catholic conspiracies intensified greatly after imperial armies of Catholic Spain invaded the Netherlands to stamp out Protestant rebels (1567), after the St. Bartholomew's Day Massacre of Huguenots (French Protestant followers of Calvin) in France (1572), and after the assassination of Europe's other major Protestant leader, William of Orange (1584).

Elizabeth's life seemed to be in even greater danger after Pope Gregory XIII's proclamation in 1580 that, as she was a great heretic (she had been excommunicated a decade before), her assassination would not constitute a mortal sin. The immediate effect of the proclamation was to make life more difficult for English Catholics, most of whom were loyal to the queen but who fell under grave suspicion. Suspicion was heightened by the presence of English Jesuits, a militant religious order of the Catholic Church, who had been trained abroad and smuggled back into England to serve the Roman Catholic cause. When, after several botched conspiracies had been disclosed, Walsingham unearthed another plot to assassinate Elizabeth in the letters between the Queen of Scots and the Catholic Anthony Babington, the wretched Mary's fate was sealed. After a public display of indecision and perhaps with genuine regret, Elizabeth signed the death warrant, and her cousin was beheaded.

The long-anticipated military confrontation with Catholic Spain was now unavoidable. Elizabeth learned that Philip II of Spain, her former brother-in-law and onetime suitor, was preparing to send an enormous fleet against her island realm. The Spanish Armada was to sail first to the Netherlands, where a Spanish army would be waiting to embark and invade England. Barring its way was England's small fleet of well-armed and highly maneuverable fighting vessels, backed up by ships from the merchant navy. The Armada reached English waters in July 1588, but, in one of the most famous and decisive naval battles in European history, it was defeated. Then, in what many viewed as an act of God on behalf of Protestant England, the Spanish fleet was dispersed and all but destroyed by violent storms.

As England braced for an invasion that, as it turned out, never materialized, Elizabeth appeared in person to review some of her soldiers who had assembled at Tilbury, on the Thames estuary. Dressed in a white gown and a silver breastplate, she declared that though some among her councillors had urged her not to appear before a large crowd of armed men, she would

Armada Portrait. This portrait of Queen Elizabeth, painted ca. 1588–89, is attributed to George Gower. Through the windows to the left and right can be glimpsed the arrival and then the defeat of the Spanish Armada, wrecked in violent storms. The queen, glowing with the pearls that symbolized her chastity, rests her hand on a globe, her fingers in effect claiming the Americas for her empire.

never fail to trust the loyalty of her faithful and loving subjects. Nor did she fear the Spanish armies. "I know I have the body but of a weak and feeble woman," Elizabeth declared, "but I have the heart and stomach [that is, valor] of a king, and of a king of England too." In this celebrated, widely publicized speech, Elizabeth displayed many of her most memorable qualities: her great personal courage, her subtle blending of magniloquent rhetoric and the language of love, her strategic appropriation of traditionally masculine qualities, and her self-consciously theatrical command of grand public occasions. "We princes," she once remarked, "are set on stages in the sight and view of all the world."

ENGLAND AND THE WORLD

In 1485 most English people would have devoted little thought to their national identity. If asked to describe their sense of belonging, they would probably have spoken of the international community of Christendom and *of their local* region, such as Kent or Cornwall. The extraordinary events of the Tudor era, from the encounter with the New World to the break with Rome, made many people more aware and proud of their Englishness. At the same time, they began to perceive those who lay outside the national community in new (and often negative) ways. Like most national communities, the English defined themselves largely in terms of what or who they were not. In the wake of the Reformation, the most prominent "others" were those who had until recently been more or less the same—that is, the Catholics of Western Christendom. But other groups were also instrumental in the project of English self-definition.

Elizabethan London had a large population of foreign residents, mainly artisans and merchants and their families, from Portugal, Italy, Spain, Germany, and, above all, France and the Netherlands. Many of these people were Protestant refugees, and they were accorded some legal and economic protection by the government. But they were not always welcomed by the local populace. Throughout the sixteenth century, London was the site of repeated demonstrations and, on occasion, bloody riots against the communities of foreign artisans, who were accused of taking jobs away from Englishmen. There was widespread hostility as well toward other people occupying the same island as England, the Welsh and Scots, and the island opposite, the Irish, whom the English had for centuries been unsuccessfully struggling to subdue. The kings of England claimed to be rulers of Ireland, but in reality they effectively controlled only a small area known as the Pale, extending north from Dublin. The great majority of the Irish population remained stubbornly Catholic and, despite English burning of villages, destruction of crops, seizure of land, and massacres, fiercely independent.

Medieval England's Jewish population, the recurrent object of persecution, extortion, and massacre, had been officially expelled by King Edward I in 1290—the earliest such mass expulsion in Europe—but Elizabethan England harbored a small number of Jews or Jewish converts to Christianity. They were the objects of suspicion and hostility. Elizabethans appear to have been fascinated by Jews and Judaism but quite uncertain whether the terms referred to a people, a foreign nation, a set of strange practices, a living faith, a defunct religion, a villainous conspiracy, or a messianic inheritance. Protestant Reformers brooded deeply on the Hebraic origins of Christianity; government officials ordered the arrest of those "suspected to be Jews"; villagers paid pennies to traveling fortune-tellers who claimed to be descended from Abraham or masters of kabbalistic mysteries; and London playgoers enjoyed the spectacle of the downfall of the wicked Barabas in Christopher Marlowe's *The Jew of Malta* and the forced conversion of Shylock in Shakespeare's *The Merchant of Venice*. Jews were not officially permitted to resettle in England until the middle of the seventeenth century, and even then their legal status was ambiguous.

Of equal fascination was "the Turk": Muslims from the Ottoman Empire. The phrase "to turn Turk" originates from this period and signified Christians who converted to Islam, sometimes through enforced slavery, but sometimes by choice. Eager for trade, Queen Elizabeth would not vilify the Ottoman Empire entirely, though she worried about its expansionist aggression (so similar to her own) and was fearful of the compelling nature of its religion. Plays about Muslims stage this conflicted approach. Characters such as Marlowe's Tamberlaine in the play of that name are magnificent, eloquent, and sensual—as well as displaying overweening pride and cruelty.

Sixteenth-century England also had a small African population, brought into the country by mariners and merchants, who worked as servants, entertainers, and craftspeople. Their skin color was the subject of pseudo-

Etching of a Black Woman, 1645, by Wenceslaus Hollar. The Bohemian-born Hollar lived and worked for most of his career in Antwerp and in London. He drew portraits of many men and women, including this depiction of a Black woman, probably a servant.

scientific speculation and theological debate. Some Elizabethans believed that Africans' blackness resulted from the climate of the regions where they lived, where, as one traveler put it, they were "so scorched and vexed with the heat of the sun, that in many places they curse it when it riseth." Others held that blackness was a curse inherited from their forefather Cush, the son of Ham (who had, according to the first book of the Bible, Genesis, wickedly exposed the nakedness of his drunken father, Noah). George Best, a proponent of this theory of inherited skin color, reported that "I myself have seen an Ethiopian as black as coal brought into England, who taking a fair English woman to wife, begat a son in all respects as black as the father was, although England were his native country, and an English woman his mother: whereby it seemeth this blackness proceedeth rather of some natural infection of that man."

As the word *infection* suggests, Elizabethans frequently regarded blackness as a physical defect; though some of the Black people who lived in England and Scotland throughout the sixteenth century were accepted, others were treated as exotic curiosities. At his marriage to Anne of Denmark, James VI of Scotland (the son of Mary, Queen of Scots; as James I of England, he succeeded Elizabeth, in 1603) entertained his bride and her family by commanding four naked Black youths to dance before him in the snow. (The youths died of pneumonia shortly afterward.) In 1594, in the festivities celebrating the baptism of James's son, a "Black-Moor" entered pulling an elaborately decorated chariot that was, in the original plan, supposed to be pulled by a lion. In England there was a Black trumpeter in the courts of Henry VII and Henry VIII, while Elizabeth, who drafted a proclamation saying that Black people should be deported (though she may never have promulgated it), had at least one male Black servant, and a female servant, perhaps a midget, called Ipolyta the Tartarian (Tartary being the name for much of central and north Asia).

The legal status of slavery in England was ambiguous. In 1569 a man called Cartwright claimed that he should be allowed to beat an enslaved person he had brought over from Russia, but the court ruled "that England was too Pure an Air for Slaves to breathe in." Nevertheless, by the mid-sixteenth century the English had become involved in the profitable trade that carried African slaves to the New World. In 1562 John Hawkins embarked on his first slaving voyage, transporting some three hundred Africans from the Guinea coast to Hispaniola, where they were sold for ten thousand pounds. Elizabeth is reported to have said that this venture was "detestable and would call down the vengeance of Heaven upon the undertakers." She did, however, invest profitably in Hawkins's subsequent voyages and loaned him ships.

Elizabeth also invested in other enterprises that combined aggressive nationalism and the pursuit of profit in enslaved people. In 1493 the pope had divided the New World between the Spanish and the Portuguese by drawing a line from pole to pole (hence Brazil is a Portuguese-speaking country today and the rest of Latin America is Spanish-speaking): the English were not in the picture. But by the end of Edward VI's reign, the Company of Merchant Adventurers had been founded, and Englishmen had begun to explore Asia and North America. Some were looking for new lands in which to live, or new sources of gold, or simply new commodities to be sold. These people were fascinated, worried, and sometimes—they hinted—impressed by their encounters with other nations and cultures that seemed to function so well and without Christianity. Several of these adventurers turned to piracy, preying on Spanish ships that were returning laden with wealth extracted by enslaved natives from Spain's New World possessions. (The pope had ruled that the native peoples were human beings—and hence could be converted to Christianity—but the ruling did nothing to prevent their enslavement and brutal exploitation.) English acts of piracy soon became a private undeclared war, with the queen and her courtiers covertly investing in the raids but accepting no responsibility for them. The greatest of many astounding exploits was the voyage of Francis Drake (1577–80): he sailed through the Strait of Magellan, pillaged Spanish towns on the Pacific, reached as far north as San Francisco, crossed to the Philippines, and returned around the Cape of Good Hope; he came back with a million pounds in treasure, and his investors earned a dividend of 5,000 percent. Queen Elizabeth knighted him on the deck of his ship, *The Golden Hind*. His was the first English voyage to pass through the Magellan Straits from the Atlantic Ocean to the Pacific Ocean, and only the second circumnavigation in history. Yet, during the circumnavigation, Drake executed his sometime friend and fellow commander Thomas Doughty in dubious circumstances, and abandoned a pregnant Black woman, Maria, on an island in Indonesia.

WRITERS, PRINTERS, AND PATRONS

Printers, who owned printing presses, and publishers, who had the right to print texts, were all known by one name, "stationer." A "stationer" might be a man or, sometimes, his widow—for women had the right to take over their dead husband's business. When in 1557 the Worshipful Company of Stationers, formed in 1403, received a royal charter, the tasks of printers and publishers were defined. Printers were only to print those texts formally licensed by the stationers: for which the publisher would have to pay. In 1559 the process of licensing was further formalized: books had to be approved by either six privy councilors or the archbishop of Canterbury and the bishop of London. There was, then, no notion of the freedom of the press.

Despite the strict regulations of the Stationers' Company, "scandalous, malicious, schismatical, and heretical" works were never effectively suppressed. Though there were occasional show trials and horrendous punishments—the printer William Carter was hanged for treason in 1584 because he had published a Catholic pamphlet; the Protestant separatists John Penry, Henry Barrow, and John Greenwood were executed in 1593 under a statute that made it a capital offense to "devise and write, print or set forth, any manner of book . . . letter, or writing containing false, seditious, and slanderous matter to the defamation of the Queen's Majesty"—active censorship was not as frequent or thorough as we might expect.

The censors largely focused their attention on works of history, which often had political implications for the present, and on religious treatises. In this, they shared the public's taste. Plays and secular poetry occasionally sold well (Shakespeare's *Henry IV, Part 1*, was printed seven times in twenty-five years), but they could not compete with publishing blockbusters such as *The Plain Man's Pathway* (sixteen editions in twenty-five years), let alone *The Psalms in English Meter* (published 124 times between 1583 and 1608). Publishers were largely interested in profit margins, and the predominance of devotional texts among the surviving books from the period attests to their greater marketability. The format in which works of literature were usually published is also telling. We normally find plays and poetry in quartos (or octavos), small volumes that had four (or eight) pages printed on each side of a sheet that was then folded twice (or three times) and stitched together with other such folded sheets to form the book. The more imposing folio format (in which the paper was folded only once, at two pages per side of a sheet) tended to be reserved not just for longer works but for those regarded as needing especially respectful treatment. In 1577 Raphael Holinshed's massive history *The Chronicles of England, Scotlande, and Irelande* appeared in a woodcut-illustrated folio; ten years later, a second edition was published, again in the large format. In contrast, Edmund Spenser's huge poem *The Faerie Queene* was printed as a quarto both in 1590 and in 1596. A decade after his death, though, as the poet's reputation grew, his epic appeared again (1609), this time as a folio.

Printed books were mainly to be purchased from the bookshops that filled the churchyard of St. Paul's Cathedral. Dissolved chapels—chantries—were taken over by bookshops in the 1540s; church officials leased out their residences near the church's north door to members of the Stationers' Company; and eventually bookstores two stories high and more filled the bays between the cathedral's buttresses. St. Paul's was also the main center of business in the capital. The church itself served as a meeting place and its columns as bulletin boards; publishers would post there, and elsewhere in the city, the title pages of new books as advertisements. Those title pages listed the wholesaler for the work, but customers could have bought popular books too at most of the shops in St. Paul's Yard. The location ensured the trade's connection with the heart of English Protestantism and its values.

It is a mistake, however, to imagine that most texts were printed or that most writers dreamed of print permanence. Poetry in particular frequently circulated in manuscript, copied by reader after reader, often into commonplace books where individual works were categorized by subject rather than author. The texts that have come down to us in printed form often bear an uncertain relation to authorial manuscripts and were frequently published only after their actual authors were dead. That is because the career of professional writer in sixteenth-century England was almost impossible: there was no such thing as author's copyright, no royalties paid to an author when books were sold, and virtually no notion that anyone could make a decent living through the creation of works of literature. Writers sold their manuscripts to the publisher outright, for what now seem like ridiculously low prices, or kept them for private circulation in manuscript, without ever sending them to the press at all.

Elizabethan writers of exalted social standing, like the Earl of Surrey or Sir Philip Sidney, who thought of themselves as courtiers, statesmen, and landowners, did not view writing as a profession but a social (and political) grace—a deeply pleasurable, exalted form of game. Only people of lower rank, such as Samuel Daniel and Michael Drayton, sought careers as writers—or, rather, as civil servants, secretaries, tutors, and clerics; they might take up more or less permanent residence in a noble household or, more casually, offer their literary work to actual or prospective patrons, in the hope of protection, career advancement, or financial reward. Ambitious authors eager to rise from penniless obscurity often looked to the court for notice and encouragement, and sometimes hoped for jobs there too: but their great expectations were not generally met. "A thousand hopes, but all nothing," wailed John Lyly, alluding to his long wait to be given the exalted office of Master of the Revels, the organizer of royal entertainments, "a hundred promises but yet nothing."

Financial rewards for writing prose or poetry came mostly in the form of support or gifts from wealthy patrons, who sought to enhance their status and gratify their vanity through the achievements and lavish praises of their clients. Some Elizabethan patrons, though, were well-educated humanists motivated by aesthetic interests, and with them patronage extended beyond financial support to the creation of lively literary and intellectual circles. Poems by Samuel Daniel, as well as prose by Thomas Nashe, bear witness to the sustaining intelligence and sophistication, as well as the generosity, of their benefactors. But the experience of Robert Greene is equally revealing: he had sixteen different patrons for seventeen books, suggesting that he did not find much favor or support from any one of them. Indeed, a practice grew up, among those who printed texts, of writing different dedications to be inserted into particular copies of a book so that an author in need of money could deceive several patrons into thinking that they in particular had been honored by the volume.

In addition to patronage from the court and great families, the city of London and the only universities at the time, Oxford and Cambridge, also had a substantial impact on the period's literature. London was the center of the book trade, and the home of the public theaters. Before Elizabeth's time, the universities were mainly devoted to educating the clergy, and that remained an important part of their function. But in the second half of the century, the sons of the gentry and the aristocracy began going in increasing numbers to the universities and the Inns of Court (law schools), not to take religious orders or to practice law but to prepare for public service or the management of their estates. Other,

Margaret Roper, Thomas More's eldest child, was educated at home by William Gonnell, who found her so impressive that he suggested she publish a book. More, however, warned that for a woman to publish would be "vain and low." Despite her father's disapproval, Roper did eventually become the first non-royal woman to have one of her translations printed.

less affluent students, such as Marlowe and Spenser, attended Oxford or Cambridge on scholarship. A group of graduates, including Thomas Nashe, Robert Greene, and George Peele, enlivened the literary scene in London in the 1590s, but the precarious lives of these so-called university wits testify to the difficulties they encountered in their attempt to survive by their writing skill. The diary of Philip Henslowe, a leading theatrical manager, has entry after entry showing university graduates who were playwrights for his company in prison or in debt or eking out a meagre existence by adding new passages into old plays.

Women had no access to grammar schools, the universities, or the Inns of Court, and tended not to have the education, patronage, or income to write or publish work. Occasionally, however, women in great houses were privately educated following a model adopted by Sir Thomas More. He had tried having his daughters schooled in Latin alongside his son as an experiment: the result was that his eldest daughter, Margaret, became not only one of the most learned women in the land, but also one of the first to publish a book (a translation of a Latin work by Erasmus, *Precatio Dominica*). Female literacy improved in the sixteenth century more generally, aided by Protestantism with its emphasis on reading scripture, and women translators ultimately made a crucial print contribution to the humanist movement—though they had to show their skills obliquely through the way in which they rendered into English texts by men. Often adopting what was called a "modesty topos," in which they asked to be forgiven for a lack of rhetorical skill (while actually displaying it, of course), women also still seem to have felt obliged, like Anne Dowriche, to apologize for their sex itself: "if anything . . . fits not your liking, remember, I pray, that it is a woman's doing."

TUDOR STYLE: ORNAMENT, PLAINNESS, AND WONDER

Renaissance literature is the product of a rhetorical culture whose members were steeped in the arts of persuasion and trained to process complex verbal signals. (The contemporary equivalent would be the ease with which we deal in movies with complex visual signals, effortlessly processing such devices as fade-out, montage, crosscutting, and morphing.) In 1512, Erasmus published a work called *De copia* that taught its readers how to cultivate "copiousness," verbal richness, in discourse. The work obligingly provides, as an example, a list of 144 different ways of saying "Thank you for your letter."

In Renaissance England certain forms or patterns of words known as "figures" (also called "schemes") were shaped and repeated to confer verbal beauty or heighten expressive power. Figures were usually known by their Greek and Latin names, though in an Elizabethan rhetorical manual, *The Arte of English Poesie*, George Puttenham made a valiant attempt to give them English equivalents, such as "Hyperbole, or the Overreacher" and "Ironia, or the Dry Mock." Those who received a grammar school education throughout Europe at almost any point between the Roman Empire and the eighteenth century probably knew by heart the names of up to one hundred such figures, just as they knew by heart their multiplication tables. According to one scholar's count, William Shakespeare knew and made use of about two hundred.

Lessons from *De copia* and similar rhetorical guides could make for very wordy texts. Elizabethans had a taste for elaborate ornament in language as in clothing, jewelry, and furniture; and if we are to appreciate their accomplishments, it helps to set aside the modern preference, particularly in prose, for simplicity and directness. When, in one of the age's most fashionable works of prose fiction, John Lyly wishes to explain that the virtues of his young hero, Euphues, are being offset by his vices, he offers a series of synonymous images: "The freshest colors soonest fade, the teenest [keenest] razor soonest turneth his edge, the finest cloth is soonest eaten with moths." Lyly's multiplication of balanced rhetorical figures sparked a small literary craze known as "Euphuism," which was soon ridiculed by Shakespeare and others for its excesses. Yet such devices were a source of deep-rooted pleasure in rhetorical culture, and most of the greatest Renaissance writers used them to extraordinary effect. Consider, for example, the succession of images in Shakespeare's sonnet 73:

> That time of year thou may'st in me behold
> When yellow leaves, or none, or few, do hang
> Upon those boughs which shake against the cold,
> Bare ruined choirs, where late the sweet birds sang.
> In me thou seest the twilight of such day
> As after sunset fadeth in the west;
> Which by and by black night doth take away,
> Death's second self that seals up all in rest.
> In me thou seest the glowing of such fire
> That on the ashes of his youth doth lie,
> As the deathbed whereon it must expire,
> Consumed with that which it was nourished by.
>   This thou perceiv'st, which makes thy love more strong,
>   To love that well, which thou must leave ere long.

Here, the perception of decay is carried through a succession of images from winter (or late fall) to twilight to the last glow of a dying fire. Each of these images is sensitively explored, so that, for example, the season is figured by bare boughs that shiver, as if they were human, and then these anthropomorphized tree branches in turn are refigured as the ruined choirs of a church where services were once sung. No sooner is the image of singers in a church choir evoked than these singers are instantaneously transmuted back into the songbirds who, in an earlier season, had sat upon the boughs, while these sweet birds in turn conjure up the poet's own vanished youth. And this nostalgic gaze extends, at least glancingly, to the chancels of the Catholic abbeys reduced to ruins by Protestant iconoclasm and the dissolution of the monasteries. All of this within the first four lines: here and elsewhere Shakespeare, along with other poets of his time, contrives to give the small compass and tight formal constraints of the sonnet—fourteen lines of rhymed iambic pentameter, with a "volta," or turn, before the final couplet—remarkable emotional intensity, psychological nuance, and imagistic complexity.

Elizabethans were certainly capable of admiring plainness of speech—in *King Lear* Shakespeare contrasts the severe directness of the virtuous Cordelia to the "glib and oily art" of her wicked sisters—and such poets as George Gascoigne, Thomas Nashe, and, in the early seventeenth century, Ben Jonson, wrote restrained, aphoristic, moralizing lyrics in a plain style whose power depends precisely on the avoidance of figurative verbal games. This power is readily apparent in the wintry spareness of Nashe's "A Litany in Time of Plague," with its grim refrain of "Lord, have mercy on us," the warning words written on the nailed-shut front doors of those who were dying of the plague:

> Wit with his wantonness
> Tasteth death's bitterness;
> Hell's executioner
> Hath no ears for to hear
> What vain art can reply.
> I am sick, I must die.
> Lord, have mercy on us!

Here linguistic playfulness—the "wit" beloved by Elizabethan culture—is scorned as an ineffectual "vain art" to which the executioner, death, is utterly indifferent.

Even plain poetry referred to or negotiated with more complex poetry, and all poetry was, writes Puttenham, "more delicate to the ear than prose is, because it is more current and slipper upon the tongue [that is, more flowing and easily pronounced], and withal tunable and melodious, as a kind of Music, and therefore may be termed a musical speech or utterance." The sixteenth century was an age of superb vocal music. The renowned composers William Byrd, Thomas Morley, and John Dowland, as well as others scarcely less distinguished, wrote a rich profusion of madrigals (part songs for two to eight voices, unaccompanied) and airs (songs for solo voice, generally accompanied by the lute). These works, along with hymns, catches, and other forms of song, enjoyed immense popularity, not only in the royal court, where musical skill was regarded as an important accomplishment, and in aristocratic households, where professional musicians were employed as entertainers, but also in less exalted social circles. Fairgrounds, marketplaces, ale houses, milking sheds—all encouraged group singing of known songs, often with a rousing chorus. Widespread genteel

Notation Knives. These knives have a pre-meal blessing inscribed on one side and a post-meal grace on the other. As each represents a part for a singer, perfect harmony will only occur when a set of knives is "performed" at the same time. Presumably such knives were sung from at banquets, fusing music and feasting with prayer.

musical literacy is reflected in a splendid array of music for the lute, viol, recorder, harp, and virginal as well as vocal music; popular music is reflected in ballad texts, airs, catches, glees, and rounds—though intriguingly the same music often doubles for both art and popular forms.

Many sixteenth-century poems were written to be set to music; others were written to already-known tunes. The division between musical lyric and poem was not always clear. In poetry and music, as in gardens, architecture, and dance, Elizabethans had a taste for elaborate, intricate, but perfectly regular designs. They admired form, valued the artist's manifest control of the medium, and took pleasure in the highly patterned surfaces of things. Modern responses to art often show a suspicion of surfaces, impatience with order, the desire to rip away the mask to discover a hidden core: these responses are far less evident in Renaissance aesthetics than is a delight in pattern. Indeed, many writers of the time expressed the faith that the universe itself had in its basic construction the beauty, concord, and harmonious order of a poem or a piece of music. "The world is made by Symmetry and proportion," wrote Thomas Campion, who was both a poet and a composer, "and is in that respect compared to Music, and Music to Poetry." The design of an exquisite work of art is deeply linked in this view to the design of the cosmos.

Such an emphasis on conspicuous pattern might seem to encourage an art as stiff as the starched ruffs that, on special occasions, ladies and gentlemen wore around their necks, but the period's fascination with order came with a profound interest in the movements of the mind and heart. Syntax in the sixteenth century was looser, more flexible than our own, and punctuation less systematic. If the effect is sometimes confusing, it also enabled writers to follow the twists and turns of thought or perception. Consider, for example, Roger Ascham's account, in his book on archery, of a day when he saw the wind blowing the new-fallen snow:

> That morning the sun shone bright and clear, the wind was whistling aloft, and sharp according to the time of the year. The snow in the highway lay loose and trodden with horse feet: so as the wind blew, it took the loose snow with it, and made it so slide upon the snow in the

> field which was hard and crusted by reason of the frost overnight, that thereby I might see very well, the whole nature of the wind as it blew that day. And I had a great delight and pleasure to mark it, which maketh me now far better to remember it. Sometime the wind would be not past two yards broad, and so it would carry the snow as far as I could see. Another time the snow would blow over half the field at once. Sometime the snow would tumble softly, by and by it would fly wonderful fast. And this I perceived also, that the wind goeth by streams and not whole together. . . . And that which was the most marvel of all, at one time two drifts of snow flew, the one of the West into the East, the other out of the North into the East: And I saw two winds by reason of the snow the one cross over the other, as it had been two highways. . . . The more uncertain and deceivable the wind is, the more heed must a wise Archer give to know the guiles [cunning] of it.

What is delightful here is not only the author's happy moment of sharpened perception but his confidence that this moment—a glimpse of baffling complexity and uncertainty—can be captured in the restless succession of sentences and then neatly summed up in the pithy conclusion. (This effect parallels that of the couplet that sums up the complexities of a Shakespearean sonnet.) A similar confidence emanates from Sir Walter Ralegh's deeply melancholy, deeply ironic address to Death at the close of *The History of the World*, written when he was a prisoner in the Tower of London:

> O eloquent, just, and mighty Death! Whom none could advise, thou hast persuaded; what none hath dared, thou hast done; and whom all the world hath flattered, thou only hast cast out of the world and despised; thou hast drawn together all the far-stretched greatness, all the pride, cruelty, and ambition of man, and covered it all over with these two narrow words: *Hic jacet!* [Here lies!]

Death is triumphant here, but so is Ralegh's eloquent, just, and mighty language.

The sense of *wonder* in both of these prose passages—as if the world were being seen clearly and distinctly for the first time—characterizes much of the period's poetry as well. The mood need not always be solemn. For example, one can sense laughter rippling just below the surface of Marlowe's admiring description of the beautiful maiden Hero's boots:

> Buskins of shells all silvered usèd she,
> And branched with blushing coral to the knee,
> Where sparrows perched, of hollow pearl and gold,
> Such as the world would wonder to behold;
> Those with sweet water oft her handmaid fills;
> Which, as she went, would chirrup through the bills.

Seashells were beloved by Renaissance collectors because their intricate designs, functionally inexplicable, seemed the work of an ingenious, infinitely playful craftsman. Typically, the shells did not simply stand by themselves in cabinets but were gilded or silvered and then turned into other *objects*: cups, miniature ships, or, in Marlowe's fantasy, boots further decorated with coral and mechanical sparrows made of precious materials and designed, as he puts it deliciously, to "chirrup." The poet knows perfectly well that the boots would be implausible footwear in the real world, but he invites us into an imaginary world in which the heroine's costume includes a skirt "whereon was many a stain, / Made with the blood of wretched lovers slain" and a veil of "artificial flowers and leaves, / Whose workmanship both man and beast deceives." The veil reflects an admiration for an art of successful imitation—bees are said to look in vain for honey amid the artificial flowers—but it is cunning illusion rather than realism that excites Marlowe's wonder. Renaissance poetry is interested not in reality or accuracy but in the magical power of exquisite workmanship to draw its readers into fabricated worlds.

In his *Defense of Poesy*, the most important work of literary criticism in sixteenth-century England, Sidney claims that this magical power is also a moral power. All other arts, he argues, are constrained by fallen, imperfect nature, but the poet alone is free to range "within the zodiac of his own wit" and create a second nature, superior to the one we are condemned to inhabit: nature's "world is brazen, the poets only deliver a golden." The poet's golden world in this account is not an escapist fantasy: it is a model to be emulated in actual life. It is difficult to say, of course, how seriously this project of realization was taken—though Sidney's own battlefield death (he is said, when mortally wounded, to have given his water to a fellow soldier, saying, "Thy necessity is yet greater than mine")—suggest that he was maintaining to the end the golden ideal of Protestant chivalry. His sister Mary Sidney Herbert advised Queen Elizabeth to model herself on poetry; if the queen could "sing what God doth"—in particular, the psalms that the Sidneys had translated—she would be enabled to "do what men may sing," that is, perform the triumphant acts that people write poetry about. Other Elizabethan poets too believed that poetry could mark the way to a more virtuous and fulfilled existence. And not only mark the way: poetry, Sidney, his sister, and others argue, has a unique persuasive force that impels readers toward the good they glimpse in its ravishing lines.

This force, attributed to the energy and vividness of figurative language, made poetry a fitting instrument for such high-minded enterprises as moral exhortation, prayer, and praise; for such uplifting narratives as the legends of religious and national heroes and also for such verbal actions as cursing, lamenting, flattering, and seducing. Conventions in the period defined the major literary modes (or "kinds," as Sidney terms them): pastoral, heroic, lyric, satiric, elegiac, tragic, and comic. They helped shape subject matter, attitude, tone, and values, and in some cases—sonnet, verse epistle, epigram, funeral elegy, and masque, to name a few—they also governed formal structure, meter, style, length, and occasion. We can glimpse some of the ways in which these literary codes worked by looking briefly at two that are, for modern readers, among the least familiar: pastoral and heroic.

In the pastoral mode, the idyllic fictional world is inhabited by shepherds and shepherdesses, often with Greek names, who tend their flocks, fall in love, and engage in friendly singing contests. The mode celebrated leisure, humility, and contentment, exalting the country life over the city and its business, the military camp and its violence, the court and its burdens of rule. Pastoral songs commonly expressed the joys of the shepherd's life or his disappointment in love. Pastoral dialogues between shepherds might conceal serious, satiric comment on abuses in the great world under the guise of homely, local concerns. There were pastoral funeral elegies, pastoral dramas, pastoral prose fictions called "romances," and even pastoral episodes within epics. The most famous pastoral poem of the period is a song (it was even published as a broadsheet ballad), Marlowe's "The Passionate Shepherd to His Love," but the shepherd who woos his potential love with promises of gold buckles, coral clasps, and amber studs serves to remind us that the mode is only superficially of the country and is really sophisticated and urban.

With its rustic characters, simple concerns, and modest scope, the pastoral mode was regarded as situated at the opposite extreme from the heroic, with its values of honor, martial courage, loyalty, leadership, and endurance, as well as its glorification of a nation or people. The chief genre that employed the heroic was the epic: typically a long, ambitious poem in the high style, based on a story from the nation's distant past and imitating Homer and Virgil in structure and motifs. Renaissance poets throughout Europe undertook to honor their nations and their vernacular languages by writing this most prestigious kind of poetry. In sixteenth-century England the major success in heroic poetry is Spenser's *Faerie Queene*. Yet the success of *The Faerie Queene* owes much to the fact that the poem is a generic hybrid, in which the conventions of classical epic mingle with those of romance, medieval allegory, pastoral, satire, mythological narrative, comedy, philosophical meditation, and many others in a strange, wonderful blend. The spectacular mixing of genres in Spenser's poem is only an extreme instance of a general Elizabethan indifference to the generic purity admired by writers on the Continent. English poets tended to approach the different genres in the spirit of Sidney's inclusivism: "if severed they be good, the conjunction cannot be hurtful."

THE ELIZABETHAN THEATER

While Sidney welcomed the experimental intertwining of genres in his own *Arcadia*, there was one place where he found it absurd: the theater. He condemned the conjunction of high and low characters in "mongrel" tragicomedies that mingled "kings and clowns." Moreover, he had the belief, whose origin was attributed to Aristotle, that plays should keep to what were called the three "dramatic unities" of action (plays should have one principal action), time (the events in plays should happen within a day), and place (plays should be set in one location). For Sidney, then, the action on the bare stage "where you shall have Asia of the one side and Afric of the other" violated the laws of time and place. "Now you shall have three ladies walk to gather flowers," he writes in *The Defense of Poesy*, "and then we must believe the stage to be a garden. By and by we hear news of shipwreck in the same place: and then we are to blame if we accept it not for a rock." The irony is that this mocking account, written probably in 1579, anticipates by a few years the stupendous achievements of Marlowe and Shakespeare, whose plays joyously break every rule that Sidney thought it essential to observe.

A permanent, freestanding public theater in England dates only from Shakespeare's own lifetime. A London playhouse, the Red Lion, is first mentioned in 1567, and James Burbage's round playhouse, The Theatre, was built in 1576. Before the construction of these theaters, people in late medieval England had mounted elaborate cycles of plays (sometimes called "mystery plays") in the towns and villages of the land, depicting the great biblical stories, from the creation of the world to Christ's Passion and its miraculous aftermath. Many of these plays have been lost, but among those that survive are several magnificent and complex works of art. At once civic and religious festivals, the cycles were performed into the reign of Elizabeth, but their close links to popular Catholic piety led Protestant authorities in the later sixteenth century to suppress them.

Early English theater was not restricted to these annual festivals. Performers acted in town halls and the halls of guilds and aristocratic households, on scaffolds erected in town squares and marketplaces, on pageant wagons in the streets, and in innyards. By the fifteenth century, and probably earlier, there were organized companies of players traveling under noble patronage. Such companies earned a precarious living providing amusement, while enhancing the prestige of the patron whose livery they wore and whose protection they enjoyed. (Actors without a patron or another, ordinary trade risked being classified as vagabonds and whipped or branded.) When theatre was professionalized in the latter half of the sixteenth century, the acting companies still attached themselves to a nobleman and remained technically servants. The company for which Christopher Marlowe wrote was the Lord Admiral's Men; Shakespeare wrote for the Lord Chamberlain's Men, and so on. The only exception was children's companies, which arose from boy choirs and consisted almost entirely of pre-adolescent boys; they were typically named after their place of performance, like the Children of Paul's and the Blackfriars' Children.

Before the construction of the public theaters, the playing companies often performed short plays called "interludes" that were, in effect, staged dialogues on religious, moral, and political themes. Henry Medwall's *Fulgens and Lucrece* (ca. 1490–1501), for example, pits a wealthy but dissolute nobleman against a virtuous public servant of humble origins, while John Heywood's *The Play of the Weather* (ca. 1525–33) stages a debate among social rivals, including a gentleman, a merchant, a forest ranger, and two millers. The structure of such plays reflects the training in argumentation that students received in Tudor schools and, in particular, the sustained practice in examining both sides of a difficult question. Some of Shakespeare's amazing ability to look at critical issues from multiple perspectives may be traced back to this practice and the dramatic interludes it helped inspire.

Another major form of theater that flourished in England in the fifteenth century and continued into the sixteenth was the morality play, a dramatization of the spiritual struggle of the Christian soul. As *Everyman* (included in Volume A, "The Middle Ages") demonstrates, these dramas derived their power from the poignancy and terror of an individual's encounter with death. Often this somber power was supplemented by the extraordinary comic vitality of the evil character, or Vice.

If such plays sound more than a bit like sermons, it is because they were. The Church was a profoundly different institution from the theater, but its professionals shared some of the same rhetorical skills. It would be grossly misleading to regard churchgoing and playgoing as comparable entertainments, but clerical attacks on the theater sometimes make it sound as if ministers thought themselves to be in direct competition with professional players. The players, for their part, were generally too discreet to present themselves in a similar light, yet they almost certainly understood their

The "Long View" of London, 1647, by Wenceslaus Hollar. In this detail from Hollar's engraving of London, one can glimpse, on the south bank of the Thames, the Globe Theater and an arena for bearbaiting. The labels were accidentally transposed in the original: the Globe is the round structure on the left.

craft as relating to sermons, with an uneasy blend of emulation and rivalry. When, in 1610, the theater manager Philip Rosseter was reported to have declared that plays were as good as sermons, he was summoned before the bishop of London to recant; but Rosseter had said no more than what many players must have privately thought.

By the later sixteenth century, many churchmen, particularly those with Puritan leanings, were steadfastly opposed to the theater, but some early Protestant Reformers, such as John Bale, tried their hand at writing plays. Thomas Norton, who with a fellow lawyer, Thomas Sackville, wrote the first English tragedy in blank verse, *Gorboduc, or Ferrex and Porrex* (1561), was also a translator of the great Reformer John Calvin. There is no evidence that Norton felt a tension between his religious convictions and his theatrical interests, nor was his play a private exercise. The five-act tragedy, a grim vision of faction-driven Britain descending into civil war, was performed at the Inner Temple (one of London's law schools) and subsequently acted before the queen.

Gorboduc was closely modeled on the works of the Roman playwright Seneca, and Senecan influence—including violent plots, resounding rhetorical speeches, and ghosts thirsting for blood—remained pervasive in the Elizabethan theater, giving rise to the subgenre we now call revenge tragedy (the term itself is modern), in which a wronged protagonist plots and executes revenge, destroying himself or herself in the process. An early, highly influential example is Thomas Kyd's *Spanish Tragedy* (1592); and, despite its unprecedented psychological complexity, Shakespeare's *Hamlet* is another instance. A related but distinct kind is the villain tragedy, in which the protagonist is blatantly evil: in his *Poetics,* Aristotle had advised against attempting to use a wicked person as the hero of a tragedy, but Shakespeare's *Richard III* and *Macbeth* amply justify the general English indifference to classical rules. Some Elizabethan tragedies, such as *Arden of Feversham* (whose author is unknown), are concerned not with the fall of great men but with domestic violence; others, such as Christopher Marlowe's *Tamburlaine,* are concerned with "overreachers," larger-than-life heroes who challenge the limits of human possibility. Certain tragedies in the period, such as *Richard III*, intersect with another Elizabethan genre, the history play, in which dramatists staged the great events, most often conspiracies, rebellions, and wars, of the nation. Not all of the events commemorated in history plays were tragic, but they tend to circle around the act that epitomized what for this period was the ultimate challenge to authority: the killing of a king. When the English cut off the head of their king in 1649, they were performing a deed that they had been rehearsing, literally, for most of a century.

English schoolboys would read and occasionally perform comedies by the great Roman playwrights Plautus and Terence. Shortly before midcentury, a schoolmaster, Nicholas Udall, used these as a model for a comedy in English, *Ralph Roister Doister.* At about the same time, another comedy, *Gammar Gurton's Needle,* which put vivid, native English material into classical form, was amusing the students at Cambridge; a song from that play is included in this volume. From the classical models English playwrights derived some elements of structure and content: plots based on intrigue, division into scenes, and type characters such as the rascally servant and the *miles gloriosus* (cowardly braggart soldier). The latter type appears in *Ralph Roister Doister* and is a remote ancestor of Shakespeare's Sir John Falstaff in the two parts of *Henry IV* and *The Merry Wives of Windsor.* But early plays such as *Gorboduc* and *Ralph Roister Doister* are, in terms of both dramatic structure and style, comparatively crude.

Around 1590, when most commercial theater had come to be concentrated in London, an extraordinary change overcame the English drama, transforming it almost overnight into a vehicle for unparalleled poetic and dramatic expression. Many factors contributed to this transformation, but probably the chief was the eruption onto the scene of Christopher Marlowe. Here are the lines in Marlowe's *Doctor Faustus* (ca. 1592–93) with which Faustus greets the conjured figure of the most beautiful woman who has ever lived, Helen of Troy:

> Was this the face that launched a thousand ships,
> And burnt the topless towers of Ilium?
> Sweet Helen, make me immortal with a kiss:
> Her lips sucks forth my soul, see where it flies!
> Come Helen, come, give me my soul again.
> Here will I dwell, for heaven be in these lips,
> And all is dross that is not Helena! (scene 12, lines 81–87)

Marlowe had mastered a new theatrical language—a superb unrhymed iambic pentameter, or blank verse.

Playacting, whether of tragedies, comedies, or any of the other Elizabethan genres, took its place alongside other forms of public expression and entertainment as well. Perhaps the most important, from the perspective of the theater, were music and dance, because these surrounded the theaters—ballad singers/sellers were situated directly outside—and were repeatedly incorporated into plays. Moreover, virtually all plays in the period, including Shakespeare's, apparently ended with a jig—a ballad in the form of a dance and song, often comic.

Plays, music, and dancing were by no means the only shows in town. There were jousts, tournaments, royal entries, religious processions, pageants in honor of newly installed civic officials or ambassadors arriving from abroad; wedding masques, court masques, and costumed entertainments known as disguisings or mummings; exhibitions of swordsmanship, mountebanks, folk healers, storytellers, magic shows; bearbaiting, bullbaiting, cockfighting, and other blood sports. For several years, Elizabethan Londoners were delighted by a trained animal—Banks's Horse—that could, it was thought, do arithmetic, answer questions, and dance a brisk galliard. And there was always the grim but compelling spectacle of public shaming, mutilation, and execution.

Most English towns had stocks and whipping posts. Drunks, fraudulent merchants, adulterers, and quarrelers could be placed in carts or mounted backward on asses and paraded through the streets for crowds to jeer and throw refuse at. Women accused of being scolds could be publicly muzzled by an iron device called a branks or tied to a "cucking stool" and dunked in the river. Convicted criminals could have their ears cut off, their noses slit, their bodies branded. Ben Jonson the playwright, for instance, was branded with a "T" on his left thumb, for "Tyburn": the place where he might otherwise have been executed for killing an actor in a duel. Public beheadings and hangings were common. In the worst cases, felons were sentenced to be "hanged by the neck, and being alive cut down, and your privy members to be cut off, and your bowels to be taken out of your belly and there burned, you being alive." In the B text of *Doctor Faustus*, Faustus's limbs are, after his death, "torn asunder" and scattered over the stage, so the audience witnessed the theatrical equivalent of the execution of criminals and traitors that they could have also watched in the flesh, as it were, nearby.

Doctor Faustus was performed by the Lord Admiral's Men at the Rose Playhouse, one of four major public playhouses that by the mid-1590s were feverishly competing for crowds of spectators. These playhouses (including Shakespeare's famous Globe, owned by Shakespeare's company, which opened in 1599) each accommodated some two thousand spectators and generally followed the same design: they were round in shape, with an unroofed yard in the center around which stood the people who paid least, the "groundlings" (apprentices, servants, and others of the lower classes) and three rising tiers around the yard for men and women who chose to pay a higher price for places to sit with a roof over their heads. A large platform stage thrust out into the yard, surrounded on three sides by spectators (see the conjectural drawing of an Elizabethan playhouse in the appendixes to this volume). These financially risky ventures relied on admission charges—it was an innovation of this

Scold's Bridle, or Branks. First recorded in Scotland, the scold's bridle was a device to humiliate and torture women who were regarded as "riotous" or "troublesome" in speech. The metal gag was designed to inflict maximum pain if the victim attempted to speak. In England, unruly women were also humiliated by being dragged through the streets in chairs known as "cucking stools," to be dunked.

period to have money advanced in the expectation of pleasure rather than offered afterward as a reward—and counted on habitual playgoing.

The public playhouses were all located in "liberties": generally areas outside the city walls or opposite the city on the other side of the Thames; they were thus outside the legal jurisdiction of the city of London, which was generally hostile to dramatic spectacles. Eventually, expensive indoor theaters, lit by candles and patronized by a more select audience, were built; they too were in "liberties," though often inside the city itself. The Blackfriars Playhouse, for instance—occupied by a boy company and later, when rebuilt nearby, by the King's Men, Shakespeare's company—was constructed inside a former monastery and retained its exemption from London's puritanical rules.

About forty plays might be put on in a season, and typically a different play was performed every day (there were no play runs); thus although popular plays were regularly repeated, a steady supply of new plays was also essential. The fact that many plays had to be learned in a short period of time affected rehearsal, performance, and the way plays were written in the first place. Actors learned their roles not from full copies of plays but from what were called "parts" (they were just part of the play), consisting of the lines that they would speak and a cue of, generally, the one to three words preceding their speeches. Given the time constraints under which they performed, actors focused on learning their parts by heart, but did not always have a full grasp of the whole of the play. Playwrights who were actors, like Shakespeare, wrote with "parts" in mind, and parts were often an aspect of their creative writing and thinking too.

The response to what we now regard as one of the undisputed glories of the age was often hostility. But why? One answer, curiously enough, is traffic: plays drew large audiences, and nearby residents objected to the crowds, the noise, and the crush of carriages. Other, more serious concerns were public health and crime. It was thought that many diseases, including the dreaded bubonic plague, were spread by noxious odors, and the packed playhouses were obvious breeding grounds for infection. (Patrons often tried to protect themselves by sniffing nosegays or stuffing cloves in their nostrils.) And the large crowds drew pickpockets, cutpurses, and other scoundrels. On one memorable afternoon, recalls Shakespeare's clown William Kemp, a cutpurse was caught in the act and tied for the duration of the play to one of the posts that held up the canopy above the stage. The theater was, moreover, a well-known haunt of prostitutes and, it was alleged, a place where innocent maids were seduced and respectable matrons corrupted or lured to the taverns, disreputable inns, and brothels that were close at hand.

There were other charges as well. Plays were performed in the afternoon and therefore drew people, especially the young, away from their work. They were schools of idleness, luring apprentices from their trades, law students from their studies, housewives from their kitchens, and potentially pious souls from the sober meditations to which they might otherwise devote themselves. Moralists warned that the theaters were nests of sedition, and religious polemicists, especially Puritans, obsessively focusing on the use of boy actors to play the female parts, charged that theatrical transvestism was ungodly—the Bible held that dressing to deceive as to one's sex was an "abomination"—and that, additionally, it excited illicit sexual desires, both heterosexual and homosexual.

But the playing companies had powerful allies. Queen Elizabeth kept many companies alive by agreeing to the notion that public performance was a necessary "rehearsal" for private performance in front of her at court; a surprisingly large number of women as well as men with money became playhouse investors and shareholders; and people of all classes attended theaters. One theater historian has estimated that between the late 1560s and 1642, when the playhouses were shut down by the English Civil War, well over fifty million visits were paid to the London theater, an astonishing figure for a city that had, by our standards, a very modest population of 220,000 (it is now over 8 million). Plays were performed without the act breaks and intermissions to which we are accustomed; there was little scenery—handheld props often had to substitute (jingling keys for a jailor and hence a jail; a spade for a gravedigger and hence a churchyard)—but costumes were usually costly and elaborate, often hand-me-downs from the nobility or court. The players formed what would now be called repertory companies—that is, they filled the roles of each play from members of their own group, not employing outsiders beyond "hirelings" who were paid by the day to take on tiny roles. Sometimes principal actors were, like Shakespeare, shareholders in the profits of the company. An actor who was a freeman of the city—a status acquired by completing an apprenticeship in one of the guilds—could take on apprentices, so boys were effectively apprenticed to actors. As a result, boys apprenticed to a livery company like the haberdashers or the goldsmiths might actually be taught acting. They took the women's parts in plays, at least until their voices changed and sometimes afterwards.

The plays performed might be bought for the company from freelance writers; or, as in Shakespeare's company, the group might include an actor-playwright who could supply it with some (though by no means all) of its plays. The script remained the property of the company, but a popular play was eagerly sought by readers; and the companies, which sometimes tried to keep their plays from appearing in print, at other times seem to have released them to the press, particularly if a corrupt version had come out already. A market developed for playbooks in print, though major libraries remained wary of accepting them: Thomas Bodley, planning which books should be accepted for Oxford's new great library, warned against such "riff-raffs" and "baggage books" as almanacs and plays. The status of plays and playwrights started to rise, however, as a result of the fact that people could read and analyze the texts they had seen performed. As an unsigned note to Ben Jonson's *Every Men Out of His Humour* put it in 1600, publishing a play gave readers "leave and leisure to judge with distinction." We have been doing so ever since.

SURPRISED BY TIME

All of the ways we cut up time into units are inevitably distortions. The dividing line between centuries was not, as far as we can tell, a highly significant one for people in the Renaissance, and many of the most important literary careers cross into the seventeenth century without a self-conscious moment of reflection. But virtually everyone must have been aware, by the end of the 1590s, that the long reign of Queen Elizabeth was nearing its end, and this impending closure occasioned considerable anxiety. Childless, the last of her line, Elizabeth had steadfastly refused to name a successor. She continued to make brilliant speeches, to receive the extravagant compliments of her flatterers, and to exercise her authority—in 1601, she had her favorite, the headstrong Earl of Essex, executed for attempting to raise an insurrection. But, as her seventieth birthday approached, she was clearly, as Ralegh put it, "a lady surprised by time." She suffered from bouts of ill health and melancholy; her godson Sir John Harington was dismayed to see her pacing through the rooms of her palace, striking at the tapestries with a sword. Her more astute advisers—among them Lord Burghley's son, Sir Robert Cecil, who had succeeded his father as her principal councillor—secretly entered into correspondence with the likeliest claimant to the throne, James VI of Scotland. Though the English queen had executed his Catholic mother, Mary, Queen of Scots, the Protestant James had continued to exchange polite letters with Elizabeth. It was at least plausible, as officially claimed, that in her dying breath, on March 24, 1603, Elizabeth designated James as her successor. A jittery nation that had feared a possible civil war at her death lit bonfires to welcome its new king. But in just a very few years, the English began to express nostalgia for the rule of "Good Queen Bess" and to look back on her reign as a magnificent high point in the history and culture of their nation.

THE SIXTEENTH CENTURY

TEXTS	CONTEXTS
	1485 Accession of Henry VII inaugurates Tudor dynasty
	ca. 1504 Leonardo da Vinci paints the *Mona Lisa*
ca. 1505–07 Amerigo Vespucci, *New World* and *Four Voyages*	1508–12 Michelangelo paints Sistine Chapel ceiling
	1509 Death of Henry VII; accession of Henry VIII
1511 Desiderius Erasmus, *Praise of Folly*	
	1513 James IV of Scotland killed at Battle of Flodden; succeeded by James V
1516 Thomas More, *Utopia*; Ludovico Ariosto, *Orlando furioso*	
ca. 1517 John Skelton, "The Tunning of Elinour Rumming"	1517 Martin Luther's Ninety-Five Theses; beginning of the Reformation in Germany
	1519 Cortés invades Mexico; Magellan begins his voyage around the world
1520s–30s Thomas Wyatt's poems circulating in manuscript	1521 Pope Leo X names Henry VIII "Defender of the Faith"
1525 William Tyndale's English translation of the New Testament	
1528 Baldassare Castiglione, *The Courtier*	
	1529–32 More is Lord Chancellor
1532 Niccolò Machiavelli, *The Prince* (written 1513)	1532–34 Henry VIII divorces Catherine of Aragon to marry Anne Boleyn; Elizabeth I born; Henry declares himself head of the Church of England
	1535 More beheaded
1537 John Calvin, *The Institution of Christian Religion*	1537 Establishment of Calvin's theocracy at Geneva
	1542 Roman Inquisition; James V of Scotland dies, succeeded by infant daughter, Mary
1543 Copernicus, *On the Revolution of the Spheres*	
1547 *Book of Homilies*	1547 Death of Henry VIII; accession of Protestant Edward VI
1549 *Book of Common Prayer*	
	1553 Death of Edward VI; failed attempt to put Protestant Lady Jane Grey on throne; accession of Catholic Queen Mary, daughter of Catherine of Aragon
	1554 Execution of seventeen-year-old Lady Jane Grey, along with her husband and father-in-law
	1555–56 Archbishop Cranmer and former bishops Latimer and Ridley burned at the stake
1557 Tottel's *Songs and Sonnets* (printing poems by Wyatt, Surrey, and others)	

TEXTS	CONTEXTS
	1558 Mary dies; succeeded by Protestant Elizabeth I
1563 John Foxe, *Acts and Monuments*	
1565 Thomas Norton and Thomas Sackville, *Gorboduc*, first English blank-verse tragedy (acted in 1561)	
1567 Arthur Golding, translation of Ovid's *Metamorphoses*	**1567–68** Mary, Queen of Scots, forced to abdicate; succeeded by her son James VI; Mary imprisoned in England
	1570 Elizabeth I excommunicated by Pope Pius V
	1572 St. Bartholomew's Day Massacre of French Protestants
	1576 James Burbage's playhouse, The Theatre, built in London
	1577–80 Drake's circumnavigation of the globe
1578 John Lyly, *Euphues*	
1579 Edmund Spenser, *The Shepheardes Calender*	
1580 Montaigne, *Essais*	
	1583 Irish rebellion crushed
	1584–87 Sir Walter Ralegh's earliest attempts to colonize Virginia
	1586–87 Mary, Queen of Scots, tried for treason and executed
ca. 1587–90 Marlowe's *Tamburlaine* acted; Shakespeare begins career as actor and playwright	
1588 Thomas Hariot, *A Brief and True Report of . . . Virginia*	**1588** Failed invasion by the Spanish Armada
1589 Richard Hakluyt, *The Principal Navigations . . . of the English Nation*	
1590 Sir Philip Sidney, *Arcadia* (posthumously published); Spenser, *The Faerie Queene*, Books 1–3	
1591 Sidney, *Astrophil and Stella* published	
ca. 1592 John Donne's earliest poems circulating in manuscript	
1595 Sidney, *The Defense of Poesy* published	**1595** Ralegh's voyage to Guiana
1596 Spenser, *The Faerie Queene*, Books 4–6 (with Books 1–3)	
1598 Ben Jonson, *Every Man in His Humor*	
	1599 Globe Theatre opens
	1603 Elizabeth I dies; succeeded by James VI of Scotland (as James I), inaugurating the Stuart dynasty

JOHN SKELTON
ca. 1460–1529

John Skelton was not a tame poet. There was something wild about him that continues to provoke, baffle, and fascinate readers. It is difficult to fit the varied pieces of his life together: gifted rhetorician, translator, Latin tutor to the young prince who became Henry VIII, disgruntled courtier, political pamphleteer, visionary, biting satirist, and ordained priest. He was also the major English poet of the first quarter of the sixteenth century, with the title of poet laureate from both Oxford and Cambridge. His poetic achievement, remarkable though it is, is equally difficult to place; as C. S. Lewis observes, Skelton had "no real predecessors and no important disciples" in the history of English verse. His poetry draws, to be sure, on a long tradition of medieval anticlerical satire and carnivalesque parody, but Skelton brings to his mature works a fresh, often extremely eccentric voice.

His early works were more routinely conventional—ornate compliments, dutiful elegies, occasional verses, and the like—but in a satire written at the end of the fifteenth century, *The Bowge of Court*, Skelton gave unusually powerful expression to the anxiety of living in the dangerous, viciously competitive precincts of royal power. (The poem's main character is called "Dread.") A few years later, whether self-exiled or sent away by his enemies, Skelton was living far from the court: about 1503 he became the rector of the parish church at Diss, in Norfolk, where he remained for some eight years. By 1512 he had returned to court, having been appointed *orator regius*, or "the king's orator." He moved to a house in the sanctuary of Westminster Abbey in 1518 and shortly thereafter, in a series of satires including *Speak, Parrot*; *Colin Clout*; and *Why Come Ye Not to Court?* (1521–22), began vituperative attacks on Cardinal Wolsey, the great prelate-statesman. Wolsey had Skelton briefly imprisoned but released him and promptly hired his services for himself.

Skelton's poems gain their most startling effects by mixing high and low styles and by playing bawdy and scatological verbal games with some of his culture's most respected and authoritative texts: the ancient classics, the poetry of Chaucer, the canonical works of logic and rhetoric taught at Oxford and Cambridge, and even the Catholic liturgy. The latter games were not necessarily sacrilegious—the Catholic Church, before the challenge of the Reformation, was capable of tolerating a wide range of expression—but they seem deliberately risk-taking, provocative, and obstreperous, an impression heightened by the way they are written. In the satires, Skelton rejects the ornate rhetorical devices and grandiloquent language that characterized his period's most ambitious poetry; he writes in short rhymed lines, having from two to five beats, and the lines can keep on rhyming helter-skelter until the resources of the language give out. To many of his poems, with their aggressive and restless energies, this strange verse form is singularly appropriate. "The Tunning of Elinour Rumming," for example, is a wonderfully clattering, apparently disordered portrait of an alewife, and the "skeltonics," as this way of writing has come to be called, contribute to the effect of disorder. The voice of the narrator of the satires has a breathless urgency that was much admired by twentieth-century poets, while to contemporary ears its attention to detail, madcap rhymes, and brash tone are strikingly reminiscent of rap.

The English Reformation, which was set in motion shortly after Skelton's death, would drastically alter the context in which his work was received. English Protestants later in the century had trouble knowing what to make of the "rude railing rhymer," as the Elizabethan critic George Puttenham called Skelton. On the one hand, his satires of Cardinal Wolsey made him ripe for inclusion (with William Langland and others) in the honor roll of supposedly proto-Protestant poets. Yet on the other hand, as a foul-mouthed and frivolous priest, Skelton could serve equally well as an emblem of the alleged corruption of the Catholic clergy. He also became associated with various tales and jests that seemed nostalgically to recall the innocence and "merriment" of pre-Reformation England. (In one of these, Skelton proudly ascends the pulpit to show off his naked illegitimate baby to his astonished parishioners.) For English society, as for English poetry, Skelton quickly came to represent the path not taken.

Mannerly Margery Milk and Ale[1]

  Aye, beshrew° you, by my fay,°   *curse / faith*
  These wanton clerks[2] be nice° alway,   *foolish*
  Avaunt, avaunt, my popagay![3]
  "What, will ye do nothing but play?"
5 Tilly vally straw,[4] let be I say!
  Gup,[5] Christian Clout, gup, Jack of the Vale!
  With Mannerly Margery milk and ale.

  "By God, ye be a pretty pode,°   *toad*
  And I love you an whole cartload."
10 Straw, James Foder, ye play the fode,°   *deceiver, flatterer*
  I am no hackney° for your rod:°   *horse / riding*
  Go watch a bull, your back is broad!
  Gup, Christian Clout, gup, Jack of the Vale!
  With Mannerly Margery milk and ale.

15 Ywis° ye deal uncourteously;   *truly*
  What, would ye frumple° me? now fie!   *rumple, tumble*
  "What, and ye shall not be my pigsny?"[6]
  By Christ, ye shall not, no hardily:
  I will not be japed° bodily!   *tricked, deceived*
20 Gup, Christian Clout, gup, Jack of the Vale!
  With Mannerly Margery milk and ale.

  "Walk forth your way, ye cost me naught;
  Now have I found that° I have sought: *that which*
  The best cheap flesh that ever I bought."
25 Yet, for his love that hath all wrought,
  Wed me, or else I die for thought.°   *of distress*
  Gup, Christian Clout, your breath is stale!
  With Mannerly Margery milk and ale!

---

1. The poem is a song for three voices. The seducer's lines are in quotation marks; Margery sings the rest, except the chorus, which is sung by a bass.
2. Educated men: students, scholars, clergymen.
3. Popinjay, parrot—that is, vain fellow.
4. An exclamation of impatience: Nonsense!
5. "Go on!" (usually addressed to horses).
6. Pig's eye. Here used as a (rough) term of endearment.

Gup, Christian Clout, gup, Jack of the Vale!
30 With Mannerly Margery milk and ale.

ca. 1495   1523

With Lullay, Lullay, Like a Child

With lullay, lullay, like a child,
Thou sleepest too long, thou art beguiled.°   *deceived*
"My darling dear, my daisy flower,
Let me," quod° he, "lie in your lap."   *quoth, said*
5   "Lie still," quod she, "my paramour,°   *lover*
Lie still, hardily,° and take a nap."   *confidently*
His head was heavy, such was his hap,°   *fortune, lot*
All drowsy dreaming, drowned in sleep,
That of his love he took no keep.°   *care*
10 With hey lullay, lullay, like a child,
Thou sleepest too long, thou art beguiled.

With ba, ba, ba! and bas,[1] bas, bas!
She cherished him, both cheek and chin,
That he wist° never where he was;   *knew*
15 He had forgotten all deadly sin.
He wanted wit[2] her love to win,
He trusted her payment and lost all his prey;
She left him sleeping and stale° away,   *stole*
With hey lullay, lullay, like a child,
20 Thou sleepest too long, thou art beguiled.

The rivers rowth,° the waters wan,   *rough*
She sparèd not to wet her feet;
She waded over, she found a man
That halsèd° her heartily and kissed her sweet—   *embraced*
25 Thus after her cold she caught a heat.
"My lief,"° she said, "routeth° in his bed;   *lover / snores*
Ywis° he hath an heavy head."   *truly*
With hey lullay, lullay, like a child,
Thou sleepest too long, thou art beguiled.

30 What dreamest thou, drunkard, drowsy pate?°   *head*
Thy lust and liking[3] is from thee gone.
Thou blinkard blowboll,[4] thou wakest too late:
Behold thou liest, luggard,° alone!   *sluggard*
Well may thou sigh, well may thou groan,
35 To deal with her so cowardly.
Ywis, pole-hatchet, she bleared thine eye.[5]

1495–1500   1527

1. Kiss. "Ba": the "by" of *lullaby*.
2. Lacked sufficient intelligence.
3. Your pleasure and enjoyment.
4. Blink-eyed drunkard.
5. Deceived you. "Pole-hatchet": a soldier who carried a poleax.

From The Tunning of Elinour Rumming[1]
Secundus Passus[2]

    Some have no money
    That thither comey,
    For their ale to pay;
    That is a shrewd array!°   *sorry state of affairs*
5   Elinour sweared, "Nay,
    Ye shall not bear away
    My ale for nought,
    By Him that me bought."°   *redeemed*
    With, "Hey, dog, hey,
10   Have these hogs away!"
    With, "Get me a staff,
    The swine eat my draff!°   *refuse, dregs*
    Strike the hogs with a club,
    They have drunk up my swilling-tub!"°   *tub for stirring*
15   For, be there never so much prese,°   *crowd*
    These swine go to the high dese;[3]
    The sow with her pigs;
    The boar his tail wrigs,°   *wriggles*
    His rump also he frigs°   *rubs*
20   Against the high bench!
    With, "Fo, there is a stench!
    Gather up, thou wench;
    Seest thou not what is fall?°   *has fallen*
    Take up dirt° and all,   *dung*
25   And bear out of the hall:
    God give it ill preving°   *ill success*
    Cleanly as evil cheving!"°   *bad luck*
      But let us turn plain
    There° we left° again.   *where / left off*
30   For as ill a patch° as that   *poor piece of ground*
    The hens run in the mash-fat;°   *mixing vat*
    For they go to roost
    Straight over the ale-joust,°   *ale pot*
    And dung, when it comes,
35   In the ale tuns.°   *barrels*
    Then Elinour taketh
    The mash-bowl, and shaketh
    The hens' dung away,
    And skommeth° it in a tray   *skims*
40   Whereas the yeast is,
    With her mangy fistis,°   *fists*
    And sometime she blens
    The dung of her hens
    And the ale together;

---

1. This rowdy poem—whose heroine really did keep an alehouse in Surrey—recounts Elinour's brewing practices ("tunning") and the social life in her establishment.
2. *Second Section* (Latin).
3. Go to the dais; that is, take the best place.

45	And saith, "Gossip,° come hither,	*friend*
	This ale shall be thicker,	
	And flower° the more quicker;	*froth*
	For I may tell you,	
	I learned it of a Jew,	
50	When I began to brew,	
	And I have found it true;	
	Drink now while it is new;	
	And ye may it brook,[4]	
	It shall make you look	
55	Younger than ye be,	
	Years two or three,	
	For ye may prove it by me.	
	Behold," she said, "and see	
	How bright I am of ble!°	*complexion*
60	Ich° am not cast away,	*I*
	That can my husband say,	
	When we kiss and play	
	In lust and in liking;	
	He calleth me his whiting,[5]	
65	His mulling and his miting,	
	His nobs° and his cony,°	*dear / bunny*
	His sweeting and his honey,	
	With, 'Bas,° my pretty bonny,	*kiss*
	Thou art worth good° and money!'	*goods*
70	Thus make I my falyre fonny,°	*make my fellow foolish*
	Till that he dream and dronny,°	*laze*
	For after all our sport,	
	Then will he rout° and snort;	*snore*
	Then sweetly together we lie	
75	As two pigs in a sty."	
	To cease meseemeth best,	
	And of this tale to rest,	
	And for to leave this letter,°	*text, subject*
	Because it is no better,	
80	And because it is no sweeter;	
	We will no farther rhyme	
	Of it at this time,	
	But we will turn plain	
	Where we left again.[6]	

1517?   ca. 1545

---

4. If you can tolerate it.
5. A small white fish—here a term of endearment, like "mulling" (meaning unclear) and "miting" (mite) in line 65.
6. That is, go back to where we left off.

SIR THOMAS MORE
1478–1535

Sir Thomas More, a brilliant, compelling, and disturbing figure, has been the hero of people who hated each other: the Catholic Church, Communists, and liberals. Each of these groups has also been deeply troubled by aspects of More's life and writings: the Catholic bishops of sixteenth-century Spain and Portugal placed *Utopia* on their list of banned prohibited books; Karl Marx reserved his most bitter scorn for impractical socialists he branded "utopian"; and liberals have noticed uneasily that More embraced the idea of the forced labor camp. Robert Bolt's play (and film) *A Man for All Seasons* celebrates More for his integrity and humanity, while Hilary Mantel's novels *Wolf Hall* and *Bring Up the Bodies* depict him as a dangerous, wily fanatic.

Born in London, More was the son of a prominent lawyer. As a youth he served as a page in the grand household of the archbishop of Canterbury, John Morton, who was also King Henry VII's lord chancellor. At Christmastime, when plays were performed at the archbishop's palace, the boy would join in and improvise a part for himself. This early talent for improvisation characterized More throughout his life, as did a lingering sense that he was never quite at home in any of the parts he played. (In the famous portrait of More by Hans Holbein the Younger—included in the color insert in this volume—More may well have been wearing a hair shirt, designed to lacerate his skin, under his rich robe of office.)

After studying at Oxford, More was trained in the law, but he was torn between law as a career, with its promise of wealth and access to power, and a life of religious devotion. He lived, for a while, as a layman among the ascetic monks in London's Charterhouse; but deciding that he wanted to marry and have a family, he turned toward a career in public affairs. Still, amid his busy engagements in law, diplomacy, and government, More constantly reserved some part of himself for other realms. One of those realms was his growing family, to whom he was a devoted and loving father, though he complained to a friend that it took him away from the life of the mind. Shortly after the completion of his law studies, he gave a series of public lectures on Saint Augustine's monumental work *The City of God*, whose religious vision continued to fascinate him until his death. He also had a passion for ancient literature, the Greek and Latin classics that lay at the heart of the cultural movement known as Renaissance humanism. He shared this passion with his close friend Desiderius Erasmus of Rotterdam (ca. 1466–1536), the greatest humanist scholar of the Northern Renaissance.

Erasmus and More also shared an ardent Christian piety, a suspicion of the philosophical distinctions drawn by generations of scholastic theologians, a delight in rhetoric, and a lively interest in experimental, unsettling wit. For Erasmus this interest bore fruit in his most enduring work, *Moriae Encomium*—whose punning title meant both *In Praise of More* and *In Praise of Folly* (1511)—which he completed as a guest in More's London house and dedicated to him. More's love of playful, subversive wit culminated in his book *Utopia*, which he began in 1515 while in the Netherlands on a diplomatic mission for Henry VIII and finished the next year. Both works, written in Latin and quickly circulated among humanists throughout Europe, daringly question the period's most cherished assumptions.

Utopia follows Plato's *Republic* in proposing a radically communal society, but it also reflects more contemporary influences: communities of monks, which forbade private property and required everyone to labor; emerging market societies, with their emphasis on education and social mobility and their dislike of inherited privilege and the old warrior aristocracy; the outcries of peasant rebels demanding a more just distribution of wealth; and, explicitly, Amerigo Vespucci's published accounts of his voyages to the newly encountered lands across the Atlantic Ocean. Those voyages revealed countries organized on principles utterly unlike those that governed European societies, and seemingly free of the inequality, economic exploitation, dynastic squabbles, and legal trickery that More observed everywhere around him.

The lands that the Europeans called "America," in honor of Vespucci, had entirely changed the view of the world. Vespucci's letters, part factual, part wild fantasy, helped More imagine an alternative to the familiar social and political order. Book II of *Utopia* (the part of the work More composed first) describes in detail the laws and customs of an imagined country that bears some striking physical resemblances to England. But, in other ways, how unlike England it is! The abolition of money and private property has prevented any attachment to goods and status, and the hated ruling classes—nobles, lawyers, idle priests, rapacious soldiers—have been eliminated. In Utopia, a well-ordered political democracy, education is free and universal. Instead of the misery of oppressed peasants, there are prosperous collective farms. Instead of stench and suffering in crowded, crooked streets, there are gleaming, rational cities, with free hospitals and child care. Since everyone works, no one is overburdened; and there is ample time for all citizens to pursue the arts of peace and the pleasures of the mind and the body.

The picture of England in Book I of *Utopia*—beggars in the streets, convicted small-time thieves hanging from the gallows, hungry farmers displaced from lands fenced off for more profitable sheep rearing, cynical flatterers encouraging the king to embark on imperialistic wars—makes the sharpest contrast imaginable with the ordered and peaceable state described in Book II. Yet Book I is not directly a call for revolutionary social reform. It is a dialogue on the question of whether intellectuals should involve themselves in politics. The speakers are a traveler named Raphael Hythloday and someone named Thomas More, who closely resembles (but perhaps should not be identified precisely with) the real More. More argues that Hythloday should offer his services as a councillor to one of the great monarchs of Europe. Hythloday replies that kings, who want only flattery from their councillors, would never dream of adopting the policies that might lead to a good society, such as the abandonment of warfare and the abolition of private property. In the dialogue, Hythloday is the detatched idealist, unwilling to dirty his hands in a pointless cause; More is the practical one, prepared to compromise with the system and seek to change it from within rather than give up on any possibility of action.

Hythloday's account of his visit to Utopia, which takes place in Book II, is also in some sense a dialogue, a complex meditation on the nature of the ideal commonwealth. The dialogue structure employed throughout *Utopia* not only allows the author some cover for critiques of the social policy of his own country but also encourages the reader to notice the disturbing underside of the imaginary society: Utopia employs slavery, including enslavement for social deviance. There is no variety in dress or housing or cityscape, and no privacy. Citizens are encouraged to value pleasure, but they are constantly monitored, to make sure their pursuit of pleasure doesn't pass the strict bounds set by "nature" or "reason." There are the state guarantees of freedom of thought and toleration of religious diversity, but people who fail to believe in divine providence and the afterlife are regarded as subhuman and, accordingly, not treated as citizens.

The Utopians officially despise war, but they nevertheless appear to fight a good many of them. It is very difficult to gauge More's attitude toward his imaginary commonwealth; perhaps he himself could not have said with any absolute certainty what it was.

If there is deep ambivalence in More's attitude toward Utopia, there is no similar ambivalence in the writings on theology, moral philosophy, and religious controversy that occupied much of his life. (A representative excerpt is included in the section "Faith in Conflict.") Though his characteristic wit and irony are visible everywhere in these writings, they are part of an increasingly desperate struggle. The struggle was against Lutheranism, which began to make inroads into England precisely during the period of More's rise to great power. More, an ardent Catholic, hated the main beliefs of the Protestant Reformation and fought their advocates with every means at his disposal, including book burnings, imprisonment, torture, and execution. As Henry VIII's trusted friend and, finally, lord chancellor (1529–32), he played for a time a significant role in the war on heresy. He resigned his high office when the king, seeking a divorce in order to marry Anne Boleyn, broke away from the Roman Catholic Church. When More was required to take the oath for the Act of Succession, acknowledging that the claim to the throne would lie with Henry's children by his new wife Anne, and to state his approval of the Act of Supremacy, affirming that the king rather than the pope was the supreme head of the Church in England, he declined. He attempted to remain silent on the matter, but the king treated silence as refusal and refusal as treason. More maintained his silence, choosing, as he put it, "to die the king's good servant, but God's first." In 1535 he was beheaded. Four hundred years later he was made Saint Thomas More by the Catholic Church.

Utopia[1]

CONCERNING THE BEST STATE OF A COMMONWEALTH AND THE NEW ISLAND OF UTOPIA

A Truly Golden Handbook
No Less Beneficial Than Entertaining
by the Most Distinguished and Eloquent Author
THOMAS MORE
Citizen and Undersheriff[2] of the Famous City
of London

Thomas More to Peter Giles,[3] Greetings

My very dear Peter Giles, I am almost ashamed to be sending you after nearly a year this little book about the Utopian commonwealth, which I'm sure you expected in less than six weeks. For, as you were well aware, I faced no problem in finding my materials, and had no reason to ponder the arrangement of them. All I had to do was repeat what you and I together heard Raphael[4] describe. There was no occasion, either, for labor over the style, since what he said, being extempore and informal, couldn't be couched in fancy terms. And besides, as you know, he's a man not so well versed in Latin as in Greek; so that my language would be nearer the truth, the closer it approached to his casual simplicity. Truth in fact is the only quality at which I should have aimed, or did aim, in writing this book.

I confess, friend Peter, that having all these materials ready to hand left hardly anything at all for me to do. Otherwise, thinking through a topic like this from scratch and disposing it in proper order might have demanded no little time and work even if a man were not entirely deficient in talent and learning. And then if the matter had to be set forth with eloquence, not just factually, there's no way I could have done that, however hard I worked, for however long a time. But now when I was relieved of all these problems, over which I could have sweated forever, there was nothing for me to do but simply write down what I had heard. Well, little as it was, that task was rendered almost impossible by my many other obligations. Most of my day is given to the law—pleading some cases, hearing others, compromising

---

1. More coined the word "Utopia" from Greek *ou* (not)+*topos* (place): "Noplace"; perhaps with a pun on *eu*+*topos*, "Happy" or "Fortunate" Place. The book was written in Latin and published—elaborately titled, as shown—on the European continent under the supervision of More's friend the great Dutch humanist Desiderius Erasmus (ca. 1466–1536). This translation is by Robert M. Adams, as published in the Norton Critical Edition of *Utopia* (3rd ed., 2011), with revisions by George M. Logan.
2. As an undersheriff, More's principal duty was to serve as a judge in the Sheriff's Court, a city court that heard a wide variety of cases.
3. Giles (ca. 1486–1533) was both a humanistic scholar and a practical man of affairs, city clerk of Antwerp. Erasmus had recommended him and More to each other, and they met in Antwerp in the summer of 1515; *Utopia* seems to have originated in conversations between them. In the first edition of the book, this letter is called its preface.
4. That is, the fictitious character Raphael Hythloday. His given name associates him with the archangel Raphael, traditionally a guide and healer.

others, and deciding still others. I have to visit this man because of his official position and that man because of his business; and so almost the whole day is devoted to other people's business and the rest to my own; and then for myself—that is, my studies—there's nothing left.

For when I get home, I have to talk with my wife, chatter with my children, and consult with the servants. All these matters I consider part of my business, since they have to be done, unless a man wants to be a stranger in his own house. Besides, you are bound to bear yourself as agreeably as you can toward those whom nature or chance or your own choice has made the companions of your life. But of course you mustn't spoil them with your familiarity, or by overindulgence turn the servants into your masters. And so, amid these concerns, the day, the month, and the year slip away.

What time do I find to write, then? especially since I still have taken no account of sleeping or even of eating, to which many people devote as much time as to sleep itself, which consumes almost half of our lives.[5] My own time is only what I steal from sleeping and eating. It isn't very much, but it's something, and so I've finally been able to finish *Utopia*, even though belatedly, and I'm sending it to you now. I hope, my dear Peter, that you'll read it over and let me know if you find anything that I've overlooked. Though I'm not really afraid of having forgotten anything important—I wish my judgment and learning were up to my memory, which isn't half bad—still, I don't feel so sure of it that I would swear I've missed nothing.

For my servant John Clement[6] has raised a great doubt in my mind. As you know, he was there with us, for I always want him to be present at conversations where there's profit to be gained. (And one of these days I expect we'll get a fine crop of learning from this young sprout, who's already made excellent progress in Greek as well as Latin.) Anyhow, as I recall matters, Hythloday said the bridge over the Anyder at Amaurot[7] was five hundred yards long; but my John says that is two hundred yards too much—that in fact the river is not more than three hundred yards wide there. So I beg you, consult your memory. If your recollection agrees with his, I'll yield to the two of you, and confess myself mistaken. But if you don't recall the point, I'll follow my own memory and keep my present figure. For, as I've taken particular pains to avoid having anything false in the book, so, if anything is in doubt, I'd rather say something untrue than tell a lie. In short, I'd rather be honest than clever.

But the whole matter can easily be cleared up if you'll ask Raphael about it—either face to face or else by letter. And I'm afraid you must do this anyway, because of another problem that has cropped up—whether through my fault, or yours, or Raphael's, I'm not sure. For it didn't occur to us to ask, nor to him to say, in what area of the New World Utopia is to be found. I wouldn't have missed hearing about this for a sizable sum of money, for I'm quite ashamed not to know even the name of the ocean where this island

---

5. More's 16th-century biographer Thomas Stapleton says he slept four or five hours a night, rising at 2 A.M.

6. Clement (d. 1572) had entered More's household by 1514, as servant and pupil. He later became a respected physician.

7. From Greek: "made dark or dim." "Hythloday": its first root is surely Greek *hythlos*, "nonsense"; the second part is probably from *daiein*, "to distribute"—hence, together, "nonsense-peddler." "Anyder": waterless (also from Greek).

lies about which I've written so much. Besides, there are various people here, and one in particular, a devout man and a professor of theology, who very much wants to go to Utopia. His motive is not by any means idle curiosity, a hankering after new sights, but rather a desire to foster and further the growth of our religion, which has made such a happy start there. To do this properly, he has decided to arrange to be sent there by the pope, and even to be named bishop to the Utopians. He feels no particular scruples about applying for this post, for he considers it a holy ambition, arising not from motives of glory or gain, but simply from religious zeal.[8]

Therefore I beg you, my dear Peter, to get in touch with Hythloday—in person if you can, or by letters if he's gone—and make sure that my work contains nothing false and omits nothing true. It would probably be just as well to show him the book itself. If I've made a mistake, there's nobody better qualified to correct me; but even he cannot do it, unless he reads over my book. Besides, you will be able to discover in this way whether he's pleased or annoyed that I have written the book. If he has decided to write out his own story himself, he may not want me to do so; and I should be sorry, too, if, in publicizing the Utopian commonwealth, I had robbed him and his story of the flower of novelty.

But to tell the truth, I'm still of two minds as to whether I should publish the book at all. For the tastes of mortals are so various, the tempers of some are so severe, their minds so ungrateful, their judgments so foolish, that there seems no point in publishing something, even if it's intended for their advantage, that they will receive only with contempt and ingratitude. Better simply to follow one's own natural inclinations, lead a merry life, and ignore the vexing problems of publication. Most people know nothing of learning; many despise it. The clod rejects as too difficult whatever isn't cloddish. The pedant dismisses as mere trifling anything that isn't stuffed with obsolete words. Some readers approve only of ancient authors; many men like only their own writing. Here's a man so solemn he won't allow a shadow of levity, and there's one so insipid of taste that he can't endure the salt of a little wit. Some dullards dread satire as a man bitten by a rabid dog dreads water;[9] some are so changeable that they like one thing when they're seated and another when they're standing.

These people lounge around the taverns, and as they swill their ale pass judgment on the intelligence of writers. With complete assurance they condemn every author by his writings, just as they think best, plucking each one, as it were, by the beard. But they themselves remain safe and, as the proverb has it, out of harm's way. No use trying to lay hold of them; they're shaved so close, there's not so much as a hair of their heads to catch them by.

Finally, some people are so ungrateful that even though they're delighted with a work, they don't like the author any better because of it. They are like rude guests who, after they have stuffed themselves with a splendid dinner, go off, carrying their full bellies homeward without a word of thanks to the host who invited them. A fine task, providing at your own

---

8. Tradition has it that this zealous theologian was Rowland Phillips, warden of Merton College, Oxford. But there is no real support for the identification, and the passage may be wholly fabricated.
9. A late-stage symptom of rabies, which gives the disease its other name, hydrophobia.

expense a banquet for men of such finicky palates and such various tastes, who will remember and reward you with such thanks!

At any rate, my dear Peter, will you take up with Hythloday the points I spoke of? After I've heard from him, I'll take a fresh look at the whole matter. But since I've already taken the pains to write up the subject, it's too late to be wise. In the matter of publication, I hope we can have Hythloday's approval; after that, I'll follow the advice of my friends—and especially yours. Farewell, my dear Peter Giles. My regards to your excellent wife. Love me as you have always done; I am more fond of you than ever.

THE BEST STATE OF A COMMONWEALTH
A DISCOURSE BY THE EXTRAORDINARY
RAPHAEL HYTHLODAY
AS RECORDED BY THE NOTED THOMAS MORE
CITIZEN AND UNDERSHERIFF OF LONDON
THE FAMOUS CITY OF GREAT BRITAIN

Book I

The most invincible king of England, Henry, the eighth of that name, a prince adorned with the royal virtues beyond any other, had recently some differences of no slight import with Charles, the most serene prince of Castille,[1] and sent me into Flanders as his spokesman to discuss and settle them. I was companion and associate to that incomparable man Cuthbert Tunstall,[2] whom the king has recently created master of the rolls, to everyone's great satisfaction. I will say nothing in praise of this man, not because I fear the judgment of a friend might be questioned, but because his integrity and learning are greater than I can describe and too well known everywhere to need my commendation—unless I would, according to the proverb, "light up the sun with a lantern."

Those appointed by the prince to deal with us, all excellent men, met us at Bruges by prearrangement. Their head and leader was the mayor of Bruges, a most distinguished person. But their main speaker and guiding spirit was Georgius de Theimseke, the provost of Cassel, a man eloquent by nature as well as by training, very learned in the law, and most skillful in diplomatic affairs through his ability and long practice. After we had met several times, certain points remained on which we could not come to agreement; so they adjourned the meetings and went to Brussels for some days to learn their prince's pleasure.

Meanwhile, since my business required it, I went to Antwerp.[3] Of those who visited me while I was there, no one was more welcome than Peter Giles.

---

1. Later (1519), as Charles V, he became the Holy Roman Emperor. By 1515 he had already (at age fifteen) inherited the Low Countries, and he was soon to become king of Spain. The matters in dispute between him and Henry VIII concerned especially the trade in English wool.
2. An admired scholar and influential cleric, Tunstall (1474–1559) was appointed ambassador to Brussels in May 1515 and a year later became master of the rolls (principal clerk of the Chancery Court).
3. Antwerp and Brussels are about equidistant (sixty miles) from Bruges.

He was a native of Antwerp, a man of high reputation, already appointed to a good position and worthy of the very best: I hardly know whether the young man is more distinguished in learning or in character. Apart from being cultured, virtuous, and courteous to all, with his intimates he is so open-hearted, affectionate, loyal, and sincere that you would be hard-pressed to find anywhere a man comparable to him in all the points of friendship. No one is more modest or more frank; none better combines simplicity with wisdom. His conversation is so pleasant, and so witty without malice, that the ardent desire I felt to see again my native country, my wife, and my children (from whom I had been separated more than four months) was much eased by his agreeable company and delightful talk.

One day after I had heard mass at Nôtre Dame, the most beautiful and most popular church in Antwerp, I was about to return to my quarters when I happened to see him talking with a stranger, a man of quite advanced years. The stranger had a sunburned face, a long beard, and a cloak hanging loosely from his shoulders; from his appearance and dress, I took him to be a ship's captain. When Peter saw me, he approached and greeted me. As I was about to return his greeting, he drew me aside, and, indicating the stranger, said, "Do you see that fellow? I was just on the point of bringing him to you."

"He would have been very welcome on your behalf," I answered.

"And on his own too, if you knew him," said Peter, "for there is no mortal alive today can tell you so much about unknown peoples and lands; and I know that you're always greedy for such information."

"In that case," said I, "my guess wasn't a bad one, for at first glance I supposed he was a skipper."

"Then you're far off the mark," he replied, "for his sailing has not been like that of Palinurus, but more that of Ulysses, or rather of Plato.[4] This man, who is named Raphael—his family name is Hythloday—knows a good deal of Latin, and is particularly learned in Greek. He studied Greek more than Latin because his main interest is philosophy, and in that field he found that the Romans have left us nothing very valuable except certain works of Seneca and Cicero.[5] Being eager to see the world, he left to his brothers the patrimony to which he was entitled at home (he is a native of Portugal) and took service with Amerigo Vespucci.[6] He was Vespucci's constant companion on the last three of his four voyages, accounts of which are now common reading everywhere; but on the last voyage, he did not return home with the commander. After much persuasion and expostulation he got Amerigo's permission to be one of the twenty-four men who were left in a fort at the farthest point of the last voyage.[7] Being marooned in this way was altogether agreeable to him, as he was more anxious to pursue his travels than afraid of death. He would often say, 'The man who has no grave is covered by the sky,'

---

4. Palinurus—Aeneas's pilot, who dozed over his steering oar and fell overboard (*Aeneid* 5.833–71)—is an exemplar of the careless traveler; Ulysses, of the person who learns from traveling; and Plato (who made trips to Sicily and Egypt), of the person who travels to learn.

5. The great orator Cicero (106–43 B.C.E.), though *not a philosopher*, in his writings rehearsed at length the views of the various philosophical schools. Seneca (ca. 4 B.C.E.–65 C.E.) was the foremost Roman Stoic philosopher.

6. The Florentine explorer was sponsored first by the king of Spain and later by the king of Portugal and was reputed to have made four trips to the New World, starting in 1497. Accounts of his voyages published in the opening years of the 16th century were widely circulated and made his exploits more famous than the more substantial explorations of Columbus and Cabot.

7. Reputedly at Cape Frio, east of present-day Rio de Janeiro.

and 'The road to heaven is the same length from all places.'[8] Yet this frame of mind would have cost him dear, if God had not been gracious to him. After Vespucci's departure, he traveled through many countries with five companions from the garrison. At last, by strange good fortune, he got, via Ceylon, to Calicut, where he opportunely found some Portuguese ships; and so, beyond anyone's expectation, he returned to his own country."[9]

When Peter had told me this, I thanked him for his great kindness in wishing to introduce me to a man whose conversation he hoped I would enjoy, and then I turned to Raphael. After we had greeted each other and exchanged the usual civilities of strangers upon their first meeting, we all went off to my house. There in the garden we sat down on a bench covered with turf, to talk together.

He told us that when Vespucci sailed away, he and his companions who had stayed behind in the fort often met with the people of the countryside, and by ingratiating speeches gradually won their friendship. Before long they came to dwell with them safely and even affectionately. The prince (I have forgotten his name and that of his country) also gave them his favor, furnishing Raphael and his five companions not only with ample provisions but with means for traveling—rafts when they went by water, wagons when they went by land. In addition, he sent with them a most trusty guide, who was to conduct them to other princes to whom he heartily recommended them. After many days' journey, he said, they came to towns and cities, and to commonwealths that were both very populous and not badly governed.

To be sure, under the equator and as far on both sides of the line as the sun moves, there lie vast empty deserts, scorched with perpetual heat. The whole region is desolate and squalid, grim and uncultivated, inhabited by wild beasts, serpents, and also by men no less wild and dangerous than the beasts themselves. But as you go on, conditions gradually grow milder. The sun is less fierce, the earth greener, the creatures less savage. At last you reach people, cities, and towns which not only trade among themselves and with their neighbors but even carry on commerce by sea and land with remote countries. After that, he said, they were able to visit different lands in every direction, for he and his companions were welcome as passengers aboard any ship about to make a journey.

The first vessels they saw were flat-bottomed, he said, with sails made of stitched papyrus-reeds or wicker, or elsewhere of leather. Farther on, they found ships with pointed keels and canvas sails, in every respect like our own.[1] The seamen were not unskilled in managing wind and water; but they were most grateful to him, Raphael said, for showing them the use of the compass, of which they had been ignorant. For that reason, they had formerly sailed with great timidity, and only in summer. Now they have such trust in the compass that they no longer fear winter at all, and tend to be overconfident rather than cautious. There is some danger that through their imprudence this device, which they thought would be so advantageous to them, may become the cause of much mischief.

---

8. Both these dicta have classical sources: the epic poet Lucan (Seneca's nephew), *Pharsalia* 7.819; and Cicero, *Tusculan Disputations* 1.43.104.
9. Thus becoming the first circumnavigator of the globe. (Magellan's men completed the trip in 1522.) Calicut is a seaport on the west coast of India.
1. As a matter of fact, the indigenous peoples of South America, when they traveled by water, used canoes made from hollowed logs. In general, More's depiction is fanciful.

It would take too long to repeat all that Raphael told us he had observed in each place, nor would it make altogether for our present purpose. Perhaps on another occasion we shall tell more about the things that are most profitable, especially the wise and sensible institutions that he observed among the civilized nations. We asked him many eager questions about such things, and he answered us willingly enough. We made no inquiries, however, about monsters, for nothing is less new or strange than they are. Scyllas, ravenous Celaenos, man-eating Lestrygonians,[2] and that sort of monstrosity you can hardly avoid, but well and wisely trained citizens you will hardly find anywhere. While he told us of many ill-considered usages in these new-found nations, he also described quite a few other customs from which our own cities, nations, races, and kingdoms might take example in order to correct their errors. These I shall discuss in another place, as I said. Now I intend to relate only what he told us about the customs and institutions of the Utopians,[3] first recounting the conversation that led him to speak of that commonwealth. Raphael had been talking very sagely about the faulty arrangements and also the wise institutions found in that hemisphere and this (many of both sorts in each), speaking as shrewdly about the manners and governments of each place he had visited as though he had lived there all his life. Peter was amazed.

"My dear Raphael," he said, "I'm surprised that you don't enter some king's service; for I don't know of a single prince who wouldn't be eager to employ you. Your learning and your knowledge of various countries and peoples would entertain him, while your advice and your supply of examples would be very helpful in the council chamber. Thus you might advance your own interests and be useful at the same time to all your relatives and friends."

"I am not much concerned about my relatives and friends," he replied, "because I consider that I have already done my duty by them. While still young and healthy, I distributed among my relatives and friends the possessions that most men do not part with till they are old and sick (and then only reluctantly, because they can no longer keep them). I think they should be content with this gift of mine, and not expect that for their sake I should enslave myself to any king whatever."

"Well said," Peter replied; "but I do not mean that you should be in servitude to any king, only in his service."

"The difference is only a matter of one syllable," said Raphael.

"All right," said Peter, "but whatever you call it, I do not see any other way in which you can be so useful to your friends or to the general public, in addition to making yourself happier."

"Happier indeed!" exclaimed Raphael. "Would a way of life so absolutely repellent to my spirit make my life happier? As it is now, I live as I please, and I fancy very few courtiers, however splendid, can say that. As a matter of fact, there are so many men soliciting favors from the powerful that it will be no great loss if they have to do without me and a couple of others like me."

---

2. Scylla and the Lestrygonians were Homeric bogeys: the former, a six-headed sea monster (*Odyssey* 12.85–101); the latter, giant cannibals (*Odyssey* 10.80–132). Celaeno, one of the Harpies (birds with women's faces), appears in the *Aeneid* (3.209–18).
3. As J. H. Hexter argues (*More's "Utopia": The Biography of an Idea* [1952], pp. 18–21), it is almost certain that at this point More opened a seam in the original version of *Utopia*—which evidently included only the account of the Utopian commonwealth (now Book II) and the opening pages of what is now Book I—to insert the additions that constitute the remainder of Book I.

Then I said, "It is clear, my dear Raphael, that you seek neither wealth nor power, and indeed I value and revere a man of such a disposition as much as I do the mightiest persons in the world. Yet I think if you would devote your time and energy to public affairs, you would do a thing worthy of a generous and philosophical nature, even if you did not much like it. You could best perform such a service by joining the council of some great prince and inciting him to just and noble actions (as I'm sure you would): for a people's welfare or misery flows in a stream from their prince, as from a never-failing spring. Your learning is so full, even if it weren't combined with experience, and your experience is so great, even apart from your learning, that you would be an extraordinary counselor to any king in the world."

"You are twice mistaken, my dear More," he replied, "first in me and then in the situation itself. I don't have the capacity you ascribe to me, and if I had it in the highest degree, the public would still not be any better off if I exchanged my contemplative leisure for this kind of action. In the first place, most princes apply themselves to the arts of war, in which I have neither ability nor interest, instead of to the good arts of peace. They are generally more set on acquiring new kingdoms by hook or by crook than on governing well those they already have. Moreover, the counselors of kings are all so wise already that they need no advice from anyone else (or at least that's the way they see it). At the same time, they approve and even flatter the most absurd statements of favorites through whose influence they seek to stand well with the prince. It is only natural, of course, that each man should think his own opinions best: the crow loves his fledgling, and the ape his cub.

"Now in a court composed of people who envy everyone else and admire only themselves, if a man should suggest something he had read of in other ages or seen in practice elsewhere, the other counselors would think their reputation for wisdom was endangered and they would look like simpletons, unless they could find fault with his proposal. If all else failed, they would take refuge in some remark like this: 'The way we're doing it was good enough for our ancestors, and I only hope we're as wise as they were.' And with this deep thought they would take their seats, as though they had said the last word on the subject—implying, of course, that it would be a very dangerous matter if anyone were found to be wiser in any point than his ancestors were. As a matter of fact, we have no misgivings about neglecting the best examples they have left us; but if something better is proposed, we eagerly seize upon the excuse of reverence for times past and cling to it desperately. Such proud, obstinate, ridiculous judgments I have encountered many times, and once even in England."

"What!" I said. "Were you ever in my country?"

"Yes," he answered, "I spent several months there. It was not long after the revolt of the Cornishmen against the king had been put down, with the miserable slaughter of the rebels.[4] During my stay I was deeply beholden to the reverend father John Cardinal Morton,[5] archbishop of Canterbury, and in

---

4. Angered by the greedy taxation of Henry VII, an army of Cornishmen marched on London in 1497 but were defeated at the Battle of Blackheath.

5. Morton (1420–1500) was a distinguished prelate, statesman, and administrator. More's father, following a custom of the age, sent his son to serve as a page for two years (1490–92) in the cardinal's household; the seventy-year-old Morton is said to have been so impressed with the twelve-year-old More that he arranged for his education at Oxford.

addition at that time lord chancellor of England. He was a man, my dear Peter (for More knows about him, and can tell what I'm going to say), as much respected for his wisdom and virtue as for his authority. He was of medium height, not bent over despite his years; his looks inspired respect rather than fear. In conversation, he was not forbidding, though serious and grave. When suitors came to him on business, he liked to test their spirit and presence of mind by speaking to them sharply, though not rudely. He liked to uncover these qualities, which were those of his own nature, as long as they were not carried to the point of effrontery; and he thought such men were best qualified to carry on business. His speech was polished and pointed; his knowledge of the law was great; he had an incomparable understanding and a prodigious memory, for he had improved extraordinary natural abilities by study and practice. At the time when I was in England, the king relied heavily on his advice, and he seemed the chief support of the nation as a whole. He had been taken from school to court when scarcely more than a boy, had devoted all his life to important business, and had acquired from weathering violent changes of fortune and many great perils a supply of practical wisdom, which is not soon lost when so purchased.

"One day when I was dining with him, there was present a layman, learned in the laws of your country, who for some reason took occasion to praise the rigid execution of justice then being practiced upon thieves. They were being executed everywhere, he said, with as many as twenty at a time being hanged on a single gallows. And then he declared that he could not understand how so many thieves sprang up everywhere, when so few of them escaped hanging. I ventured to speak freely before the cardinal, and said, 'There is no need to wonder: this way of punishing thieves goes beyond the call of justice, and is not, in any case, for the public good. The penalty is too harsh in itself, yet it isn't an effective deterrent. Simple theft[6] is not so great a crime that it ought to cost a man his life, yet no punishment however severe can withhold those from robbery who have no other way to eat. In this matter not only you in England but a good part of the world seem to imitate bad schoolmasters, who would rather whip their pupils than teach them. Severe and terrible punishments are enacted against theft, when it would be much better to enable every man to earn his own living, instead of being driven to the awful necessity of stealing and then dying for it.'

"'Oh, we've taken care of that,' said the fellow. 'There are the trades and there is farming, by which men may make a living unless they choose deliberately to be rogues.'

"'Oh no you don't,' I said, 'you won't get out of it that way. We may disregard for the moment the cripples who come home from foreign and civil wars, as lately from the Cornish battle and before that from your wars with France. These men, who have lost limbs in the service of king and country, are too badly crippled to follow their old trades, and too old to learn new ones. But since wars occur only from time to time, let us, I say, disregard these men, and consider what happens every day. There are a great many noblemen who live idly like drones off the labor of others, their tenants whom they bleed white by constantly raising their rents. (This is the only

---

6. Theft is "simple" when not accompanied by violence or intimidation.

instance of their tightfistedness, because they are prodigal in everything else, ready to spend their way to the poorhouse.) These noblemen drag around with them a great train of idle servants,[7] who have never learned any trade by which they could earn a living. As soon as their master dies, or they themselves fall ill, they are promptly turned out of doors, for lords would rather support idlers than invalids, and the son is often unable to maintain as big a household as his father had, at least at first. Those who are turned off soon set about starving, unless they set about stealing. What else can they do? Then when a wandering life has left their health impaired and their clothes threadbare, when their faces look pinched and their garments tattered, men of rank will not care to engage them. And country people dare not do so, for they don't have to be told that one who has been raised softly to idle pleasures, who has been used to swaggering about with sword and buckler, is likely to look down on the whole neighborhood and despise everybody else as beneath him. Such a man can't be put to work with spade and mattock; he will not serve a poor man faithfully for scant wages and sparse diet.'

"'But we ought to encourage these men in particular,' said the lawyer. 'In case of war the strength and power of our army depend on them, because they have a bolder and nobler spirit than workmen and farmers have.'

"'You may as well say that thieves should be encouraged for the sake of wars,' I answered, 'since you will never lack for thieves as long as you have men like these. In fact thieves don't make bad soldiers, and soldiers turn out to be pretty good robbers—so nearly are these two ways of life related. But the custom of keeping too many retainers is not peculiar to this nation; it is common to almost all of them. France suffers from an even more grievous plague. Even in peacetime—if you can call it peace—the whole country is crowded with foreign mercenaries, imported on the same principle that you've given for your noblemen keeping idle servants.[8] Wise fools think that the public safety depends on having ready a strong army, preferably of veteran soldiers. They think inexperienced men are not reliable, and they sometimes hunt out pretexts for war, just so they may have trained soldiers and experienced cutthroats—or, as Sallust neatly puts it, that "hand and spirit may not grow dull through lack of practice."[9] But France has learned to her cost how pernicious it is to feed such beasts. The examples of the Romans, the Carthaginians, the Syrians,[1] and many other peoples show the same thing; for not only their governments but their fields and even their cities were ruined more than once by their own standing armies. Besides, this preparedness is unnecessary: not even the French soldiers, practiced in arms from their cradles, can boast of having often got the best of your raw recruits.[2] I shall say no more on this point, lest I seem to flatter present

---

7. Some of these were household servants; others were the last vestiges of the private armies by which, under feudalism, every lord was followed.
8. Charles VII of France (reigned 1422–61) had tried to establish a national army, but his successors reverted to mercenaries, mostly Swiss infantrymen.
9. Paraphrasing the *Catiline* (16.3) of the Roman historian Sallust (86–35 B.C.E.).
1. The Romans and Carthaginians both had to fight wars against enslaved gladiators and mercenaries. The victimizers of the Syrians that Hythloday has in mind are probably the Mamelukes, a military caste of foreign extraction that ruled, from the 13th century to the early 16th, a state that included much of the Middle East.
2. Past English victories over the French included Crécy (1346), Poitiers (1356), and Henry V's triumph at Agincourt (1415).

company. At any rate, neither your town workmen nor your rough farm laborers—except for those whose physiques aren't suited for strength or boldness, or whose spirits have been cowed by inability to feed their families—seem to be much afraid of fighting the idle attendants of noblemen. So you need not fear that retainers, once strong and vigorous (for that's the only sort noblemen deign to corrupt), but now soft and flabby because of their idle, effeminate life, would be weakened if they were taught practical crafts to earn their living, and trained to manly labor. Anyway, I cannot think it's in the public interest to maintain for the emergency of war such a vast multitude of people who trouble and disturb the peace. You never have war unless you choose it, and peace is always more to be considered than war. Yet this is not the only circumstance that makes thieving necessary. There is another one, which, I believe, applies more especially to you Englishmen.'

"'What is that?' asked the cardinal.

"'Your sheep,' I replied, 'that used to be so meek and eat so little. Now they have become so greedy and fierce that they devour human beings themselves, as I hear.[3] They devastate and depopulate fields, houses, and towns. For in whatever parts of the land the sheep yield the softest and most expensive wool, there the nobility and gentry, yes, and even some abbots—holy men—are not content with the old rents that the land yielded to their predecessors. Living in idleness and luxury, without doing any good to society, no longer satisfies them; they have to do positive harm. For they leave no land free for the plow: they enclose every acre for pasture; they destroy houses and abolish towns, keeping only the churches, and those for sheep-barns. And as if enough of your land were not already wasted on woods and game-preserves, these worthy men turn all human habitations and cultivated fields back to wilderness. Thus one greedy, insatiable glutton, a frightful plague to his native country, may enclose many thousand acres of land within a single hedge. The tenants are dismissed; some are stripped of their belongings by trickery or brute force, or, wearied by constant harassment, are driven to sell them. By hook or by crook these miserable people—men, women, husbands, wives, orphans, widows, parents with little children, whole families (poor but numerous, since farming requires many hands)—are forced to move out. They leave the only homes familiar to them, and they can find no place to go. Since they cannot afford to wait for a buyer, they sell for a pittance all their household goods, which would not bring much in any case. When that little money is gone (and it's soon spent in wandering from place to place), what remains for them but to steal, and so be hanged—justly, you'd say!—or to wander and beg? And yet if they go tramping, they are jailed as idle vagrants. They would be glad to work, but they can find no one who will hire them. There is no need for farm labor, in which they have been trained, when there is no land left to be planted. One herdsman or shepherd can look after a flock of beasts large enough to stock an area that would require many hands if it were plowed and harvested.

---

3. This vivid image introduces Hythloday's treatment of the social dislocation brought about by "enclosure"—the gradual amalgamation and fencing, over a period extending from the 12th century to the 19th, of the open fields of the feudal system: one incentive to the practice was the increasing profitability of the wool trade.

"'This enclosing has had the effect of raising the price of food in many places. In addition, the price of raw wool has risen so much that poor people who used to make cloth are no longer able to buy it, and so great numbers are forced from work to idleness. One reason is that after the enlarging of the pasture-land, a murrain killed a great number of sheep—as though God were punishing greed by sending a plague upon the animals, which in justice should have fallen on the owners! But even if the number of sheep should increase greatly, their price will not fall a penny. The reason is that the wool trade, though it can't be called a monopoly, because it isn't in the hands of one single person, is concentrated in few hands (an oligopoly, you might say), and these so rich that the owners are never pressed to sell until they have a mind to, and that is only when they can get their price.

"'For the same reason other kinds of livestock also are priced exorbitantly, the more so because with so many farmhouses being pulled down, and farming in a state of decay, there are not enough people to look after the breeding of animals. These rich men will not breed other animals as they do lambs, but buy them lean and cheap, fatten them in their own pastures, and then sell them at a high price. I don't think the full impact of this bad system has yet been felt. We know these dealers raise prices where the fattened animals are sold. But when, over a period of time, they keep buying beasts from other localities faster than they can be bred, then as the supply gradually diminishes where they are purchased, a severe shortage is bound to ensue. So your island, which seemed especially fortunate in this matter, will be ruined by the crass avarice of a few. For the high food prices cause everyone to dismiss as many retainers as he can from his household; and what, I ask, can these men do, but rob or beg? And a man of courage is more likely to steal than to cringe.

"'To make this hideous poverty and scarcity worse, they exist side by side with wanton luxury.[4] Not only the servants of noblemen, but tradespeople, even some farmers, and people of every social rank are given to ostentatious dress and gluttonous greed. Look at the eating houses, the bawdy houses, and those other places just as bad, the wine bars and alehouses. Look at all the crooked games of chance, dice, cards, backgammon, tennis, bowling, and quoits, in which money slips away so fast. Don't all these lead their habitués straight to robbery? Banish these blights, make those who have ruined farmhouses and villages restore them, or hand them over to someone who will rebuild. Restrict the right of the rich to buy up anything and everything, and then to exercise a kind of monopoly. Let fewer people be brought up in idleness. Let agriculture be restored and the wool manufacture revived as an honest trade, so there will be useful work for the whole crowd of those now idle—whether those whom poverty has already made into thieves, or those whom vagabondage and habits of lazy service are converting, just as surely, into the robbers of the future.

"'If you do not find a cure for these evils, it is futile to boast of your justice in punishing theft. Your policy may look superficially like justice, but in

---

4. Luxurious living was not, in fact, characteristic of the reign of the parsimonious Henry VII (when Hythloday is supposed to be addressing Cardinal Morton). More is projecting onto the earlier period, perhaps unconsciously, a kind of extravagant display that began in 1509 with the accession of Henry VIII.

reality it is neither just nor practical. If you allow young folk to be abominably brought up and their characters corrupted, little by little, from childhood; and if then you punish them as grownups for committing crimes to which their early training has inclined them, what else is this, I ask, but first making them thieves and then punishing them for it?'

"As I was speaking thus, the lawyer had made ready his answer, choosing the usual style of disputants who are better at summing up than at replying, and who like to show off their memory. So he said to me, 'You have talked very well for a stranger, but you have heard about more things than you have been able to understand correctly. I will make the matter clear to you in a few words. First, I will summarize what you have said; then I will show how you have been misled by ignorance of our customs; finally, I will demolish all your arguments and reduce them to rubble. And so to begin where I promised, on four points you seemed to me—'

"'Hold your tongue,' said the cardinal, 'for you won't be finished in a few words, if this is the way you start. We will spare you the trouble of answering now, and reserve the pleasure of your reply till our next meeting, which will be tomorrow, if your affairs and Raphael's permit it. Meanwhile, my dear Raphael, I am eager to hear why you think theft should not be punished with death, or what other punishment you think would be more in the public interest. For I'm sure even you don't think it should go unpunished entirely. Even as it is, the fear of death does not restrain evildoers; once they were sure of their lives, as you propose, what force or fear could restrain them? They would look on a lighter penalty as an open invitation to commit more crimes—it would be like offering them a reward.'

"'It seems to me, most kind and reverend father,' I said, 'that it's altogether unjust to take someone's life for taking money. Nothing in the world that fortune can bestow is equal in value to a human life. If they say the thief suffers not for the money, but for violation of justice and transgression of laws, then this extreme justice should really be called extreme injury.[5] We ought not to approve of these fierce Manlian edicts[6] that invoke the sword for the smallest violations. Neither should we accept the Stoic view that considers all crimes equal,[7] as if there were no difference between killing a man and taking a coin from him. If equity means anything, there is no proportion or relation at all between these two crimes. God has said, "Thou shalt not kill"; shall we kill so readily for the theft of a bit of small change? Perhaps it will be argued that God's commandment against killing does not apply where human law allows it. But then what prevents men from making other laws in the same way—perhaps even laws legalizing rape, adultery, and perjury? God has taken from each person the right not only to kill another, but even to kill himself. If mutual consent to human laws on manslaughter entitles men freely to exempt their agents from divine law and allows them to kill those condemned by human decrees where God has given no precedent, what is this but preferring the law of man to the law of God? The result will be that in every situation men will decide for themselves how far it suits

---

5. Echoing the classical adage *summum ius, summa iniuria*, long cited in discussions of equity.
6. Proverbially strict, like those imposed by the Roman consul Titus Manlius in the 4th century B.C.E. Manlius executed his own son for disobeying one of them.
7. This view was actually maintained by some of the ancient Stoic philosophers.

them to observe the laws of God. The law of Moses was harsh and severe, as for an enslaved and stubborn people, but it punished theft with a fine, not death.[8] Let us not think that in his new law of mercy, where he rules us with the tenderness of a father, God has given us greater license to be cruel to one another.

"'These are the reasons why I think it is wrong to put thieves to death. But surely everybody knows how absurd and even harmful to the public welfare it is to punish theft and murder alike. If theft carries the same penalty as murder, the thief will be encouraged to kill the victim whom otherwise he would only have robbed. When the punishment is the same, murder is safer, since one conceals both crimes by killing the witness. Thus while we try to terrify thieves with extreme cruelty, we really invite them to kill the innocent.

"'As for the usual question of what more suitable punishment can be found, in my judgment it would be much easier to find a better one than a worse. Why should we question the value of the punishments long used by the Romans, who were most expert in the arts of government? They condemned those convicted of heinous crimes to work, shackled, for life, in stone quarries and mines. But of all the alternatives, I prefer the method which I observed in my Persian travels, among the people commonly called the Polylerites.[9] They are a sizable nation, not badly governed, free and subject only to their own laws, except that they pay annual tribute to the Persian king. Living far from the sea, they are nearly surrounded by mountains. Being contented with the products of their own land, which is by no means unfruitful, they do not visit other nations, nor are they much visited. According to their ancient customs, they do not try to enlarge their boundaries, and easily protect themselves behind their mountains by paying tribute to their overlord. Thus they have no wars and live in a comfortable rather than a showy manner, more contented than renowned or glorious. Indeed, I think they are hardly known by name to anyone but their next-door neighbors.

"'In their land, whoever is found guilty of theft must make restitution to the owner, not (as elsewhere) to the prince; they think the prince has no more right to the stolen goods than the thief. If the stolen property has disappeared, its value is repaid from the thief's possessions. Whatever remains of those is handed over to his wife and children, while the thief himself is sentenced to hard labor.

"'Unless their crimes were compounded with atrocities, thieves are neither imprisoned nor shackled, but go freely and unconstrained about their work on public projects. If they shirk and do their jobs slackly, they are not chained, but they are whipped. If they work hard, they are treated without any indignities, except that at night after roll call they are locked up in their dormitories. Apart from constant work, they undergo no discomfort in living. As they work for the public good, they are decently fed out of the public stores, though arrangements vary from place to place. In some districts they are supported by alms. Unreliable as this support may seem, the Polylerites are so compassionate that no way is found more rewarding. In other places, public revenues are set aside for their support, or a special tax is levied on

---

8. The Mosaic law is that spelled out in the first verses of Exodus 22. It provides various penalties for theft, but nowhere death. This is contrasted with the "new law" of Christ, under which England is supposed to be operating.
9. From Greek: "the People of Much Nonsense."

every individual for their use; and sometimes they do not do public work, but anyone in need of workmen can go to the market and hire some of them by the day at a set rate, a little less than that for free men. If they are lazy, it is lawful to whip them. Thus they never lack for work, and each one of them brings a little profit into the public treasury beyond the cost of his keep.

"'They are all dressed in clothes of the same distinctive color. Their hair is not shaved but trimmed close about the ears,[1] and the tip of one ear is cut off. Their friends are allowed to give them food, drink, or clothing, as long as it is of the proper color; but to give them money is death, both to the giver and to the taker. It is just as serious a crime for any free man to take money from them for any reason whatever; and it is also a capital crime for any of these slaves (as the condemned are called) to carry weapons. In each district of the country they are required to wear a special badge. It is a capital crime to throw away the badge, to go beyond one's own district, or to talk with a slave of another district. Plotting escape is no more secure than escape itself: it is death for any other slave to know of a plot to escape, and slavery for a free man. On the other hand, there are rewards for informers—money for a free man, freedom for a slave, and for both of them pardon and amnesty. Thus it can never be safer for them to persist in an illicit scheme than to renounce it.

"'Such are their laws and policies in this matter. It is clear how mild and practical they are, for the aim of the punishment is to destroy vices and save men. The criminals are treated so that they become good of necessity, and for the rest of their lives they atone for the wrong they have done before. There is so little danger of relapse that travelers going from one part of the country to another think slaves the most reliable guides, changing them at the boundary of each district. The slaves have no means of committing robbery, since they are unarmed, and any money in their possession is evidence of a crime. If caught, they would be punished, and there is no hope of escape anywhere. Since every bit of a slave's clothing is unlike the usual clothing of the country, how could a slave escape, unless he fled naked? Even then his cropped ear would give him away. Might not the slaves form a conspiracy against the government? Perhaps. But the slaves of one district could hardly expect to succeed unless they first involved in their plot the slave-gangs of many other districts. And that is impossible, since they are not allowed to meet or talk together or even to greet one another. No one would risk a plot when they all know joining is so dangerous to the participant and betrayal so profitable to the informer. Besides, no one is quite without hope of gaining his freedom eventually if he accepts his punishment in the spirit of obedience and patience, and gives promise of future good conduct. Indeed, every year some are pardoned as a reward for their submissive behavior.'

"When I had finished this account, I added that I saw no reason why this system could not be adopted even in England, and with much greater advan-

---

1. At this point in the text, the early editions have a marginal gloss—in translation, "Yet nowadays the servants of noblemen think such a haircut *quite* handsome." This is one of a series of some two hundred glosses, which were supplied by Peter Giles after Erasmus shared More's manuscript with him. The glosses range in length from a single word to a full sentence and provide a valuable record of the response to *Utopia* (especially to Book II, where they are heavily concentrated) by a particularly well-positioned member of the humanist audience for it. The present edition includes a selection of the more pungent glosses, as footnotes.

tage than the 'justice' which my legal antagonist had praised so highly. But the lawyer replied that such a system could never be established in England without putting the commonwealth in serious peril. And so saying, he shook his head, made a wry face, and fell silent. And all the company sided with him.

"Then the cardinal remarked, 'It is not easy to guess whether this scheme would work well or not, since nobody has yet tried it out. But perhaps when the death sentence has been passed on a thief, the king might reprieve him for a time without right of sanctuary,[2] and thus see how the plan worked. If it turned out well, then he might establish it by law; if not, he could execute immediate punishment on the man formerly condemned. This would be neither less nor more unjust than if the condemned man had been put to death at once, and the experiment would involve no risk. I think vagabonds too might be treated this way, for though we have passed many laws against them, they have had no real effect as yet.'

"When the cardinal had concluded, they all began praising enthusiastically ideas which they had received with contempt when I suggested them; and they particularly liked the idea about vagabonds, because it was the cardinal's addition.

"I don't know whether it is worthwhile telling what followed, because it was silly, but I'll tell it anyhow, for there's no harm in it, and it bears on our subject. There was a hanger-on standing around, who was so good at playing the fool that you could hardly tell him from the real thing. He was constantly making jokes, but so awkwardly that we laughed more at him than at them; yet sometimes a rather clever thing came out, confirming the old proverb that a man who throws the dice often will sooner or later make a lucky cast. One of the company happened to say that in my speech I had taken care of the thieves, and the cardinal had taken care of the vagabonds, so now all that was left to do was to take care of the poor whom sickness or old age had reduced to poverty and kept from earning a living.

"'Leave that to me,' said the fool, 'and I'll set it right at once. These are people I'm eager to get out of my sight, having been so often vexed with them and their woeful complaints. No matter how pitifully they beg for money, they've never whined a single penny out of my pocket. They can't win with me: either I don't want to give them anything, or I haven't anything to give them. Now they're getting wise; they know me so well, they don't waste their breath, but let me pass without a word or a hope—no more, by heaven, than if I were a priest. But I would make a law sending all these beggars to Benedictine monasteries, where the men could become lay brothers,[3] as they're called, and the women could be nuns.'

"The cardinal smiled and passed it off as a joke; the rest took it seriously. But a certain friar, a theologian, took such pleasure in this jest at the expense of priests and monks that he too began to make merry, though generally he was grave to the point of sourness. 'Even so, you will not get rid of the beggars,' he began, 'unless you take care of us friars[4] too.'

---

2. In earlier days almost any criminal could take sanctuary in any church and be safe from the law. By More's time the privilege had been considerably abridged.
3. Men who lived and worked in monasteries (mostly performing menial tasks) but who were not admitted to clerical orders.
4. Members of a mendicant (begging) order, as opposed to monks, who live, and labor, in a cloister.

"'You have been taken care of already,' retorted the fool. 'The cardinal provided for you splendidly when he said vagabonds should be arrested and put to work, for you friars are the greatest vagabonds of all.'

"When the company, watching the cardinal closely, saw that he admitted this jest like the other, they all took it up with vigor—except for the friar. He, as you can easily imagine, was stung by the vinegar,[5] and flew into such a rage that he could not keep from abusing the fool. He called him a knave, a slanderer, a sneak, and a 'son of perdition,'[6] quoting the meanwhile terrible denunciations from Holy Scripture. Now the joker began to jest in earnest, for he was clearly on his own ground.

"'Don't get angry, good friar,' he said, 'for it is written, "In your patience possess ye your souls."'[7]

"In reply, the friar said, and I quote his very words, 'I am not angry, you gallows-bird, or at least I do not sin, for the psalmist says, "Be ye angry, and sin not."'[8]

"At this point the cardinal gently cautioned the friar to calm down, but he answered: 'No, my lord, I speak only from righteous zeal, as I ought to. For holy men have had great zeal. That is why Scripture says, "the zeal of thine house hath eaten me up,"[9] and we sing in church, "those who mocked Elisha as he went up to the house of God, felt the zeal of the baldhead,"[1] just as this mocker, this rascal, this guttersnipe may very well feel it.'

"'Perhaps you mean well,' said the cardinal, 'but you would act in a holier, and certainly in a wiser way, if you didn't set your wit against a fool's wit and try to spar with a buffoon.'

"'No, my lord,' he replied, 'I would not act more wisely. For Solomon himself, the wisest of men, said, "Answer a fool according to his folly,"[2] and that's what I'm doing now. I am showing him the pit into which he will fall if he does not take care. For if the many mockers of Elisha, who was only one bald man, felt the effects of his zeal, how much more effect shall be felt by a single mocker of many friars, who include a great many baldheads! And besides, we have a papal bull,[3] by which all who mock us are excommunicated.'

"When the cardinal saw there was no end to the matter, he nodded to the fool to leave, and turned the conversation to another subject. Soon after, he rose from table, and, going to hear petitioners, dismissed us.

"Look, my dear More, what a long story I have inflicted on you. I would be quite ashamed, if you had not yourself asked for it, and seemed to listen as if you did not want any part to be left out. Though I ought to have related this conversation more concisely, I did feel bound to recount it, so you might see how those who rejected what I said at first approved of it immediately afterward, when they saw the cardinal did not disapprove. In fact they went so far in their flattery that they indulged and almost took seriously ideas

---

5. Alluding to a phrase in Horace's *Satires* 1.7.32: *italo perfusus aceto*, "soaked in Italian vinegar."
6. John 17:12; 2 Thessalonians 2:3.
7. Luke 21:19.
8. Psalms 4:4. The Vulgate Bible translates as *Irascimini* (Be angry) the Hebrew word that is rendered as "Stand in awe" in the King James Version.
9. Psalms 69:9.
1. Some children mocked Elisha, son of Elijah the prophet, for his baldness; but he called two bears out of the woods, and they tore the bad children to pieces (2 Kings 23–24). The friar quotes a hymn that was based on this cautionary tale.
2. Proverbs 26:5. But compare the previous verse: "Answer not a fool according to his folly, lest thou also be like unto him."
3. A formal papal document, named after the seal (Latin *bulla*) that authenticated it.

that he tolerated only as the jesting of a fool. From this episode you can see how little courtiers would value me or my advice."

To this I answered, "You have given me great pleasure, my dear Raphael, for everything you've said has been both wise and witty. As you spoke, I seemed to be a child and in my own native land once more, through the pleasant recollection of that cardinal in whose court I was brought up as a lad. Dear as you are to me on other accounts, you cannot imagine how much dearer you are because you honor his memory so highly. Still, my friend Raphael, I don't give up my former opinion: I think if you could overcome your aversion to court life, your advice to a prince would be of the greatest advantage to the public welfare. This, after all, is the chief duty of every good man, including you. Your friend Plato thinks that commonwealths will become happy only when philosophers become kings or kings become philosophers.[4] No wonder we are so far from happiness, when philosophers do not condescend even to assist kings with their counsels."

"They are not so ungracious," Raphael replied, "but that they would gladly do it; in fact, they have already done it in a great many published books, if the rulers would only read their good advice. But doubtless Plato was right in foreseeing that unless kings became philosophical themselves, they would never take the advice of real philosophers, drenched as they are and infected with false values from boyhood on. Plato certainly had this experience with Dionysius of Syracuse.[5] If I proposed wise laws to some king, and tried to root out of his soul the seeds of evil and corruption, don't you suppose I would be either banished forthwith, or treated with scorn?

"Imagine, if you will, that I am at the court of the king of France.[6] Suppose I were sitting in his royal council, meeting in secret session with the king himself presiding, and all the cleverest councillors were hard at work devising a set of crafty machinations by which the king might keep hold of Milan, recover Naples, which has proved so slippery;[7] then overthrow the Venetians and subdue all Italy; next add Flanders, Brabant, and the whole of Burgundy to his realm, besides some other nations he has in mind to invade. One man urges him to make an alliance with the Venetians for just as long as the king finds it convenient—perhaps to develop a common strategy with them, and even allow them some of the loot, which can be recovered later when things work out according to plan. While one recommends hiring German mercenaries, his neighbor proposes paying the Swiss to stay neutral.[8] A fourth voice suggests soothing the offended divinity of the emperor with an offering of gold.[9] Still another, who is of a different mind, thinks a settlement should be made with the king of Aragon, and that, to cement the

---

4. Plato, *Republic* 5.473.
5. Plato is reported to have made three visits to Syracuse (in Sicily), where his attempts to reform the tyrant Dionysius the Elder, and later his son Dionysius the Younger, were notoriously unsuccessful.
6. At the time of writing, Francis I; at the time of Hythloday's supposed visit to England, either Charles VIII (d. 1498) or Louis XII (d. 1515). All three were would-be imperialists with hereditary claims to Milan and Naples, and all three bogged down in the intricacies of Italian political intrigue.
7. A marginal gloss at this point says, "Indirectly he discourages the French from seizing Italy." France gained Milan in 1499, lost it in 1512, and regained it at the Battle of Marignano in September 1515. Naples was won in 1495, lost in 1496, won again in 1501, and lost again in 1504. But, as Hythloday goes on to suggest, French territorial ambitions in the period extended almost limitlessly.
8. Among foot soldiers for hire, the Swiss ranked first, the Germans second.
9. Maximilian of Austria, Holy Roman Emperor, had grandiose schemes (he even dreamed of being pope) but little money. He was always accessible to a bribe.

peace, he should be allowed to take Navarre[1] from its proper ruler. Meanwhile, someone suggests snaring the prince of Castille into a marriage alliance—a first step would be to buy up some nobles of his court with secret pensions.[2]

"The hardest problem of all is what to do about England. They all agree that peace should be made, and that the alliance, which is weak at best, should be strengthened as much as possible; but while the English are being treated as friends, they should also be suspected as enemies. And so the Scots must be kept in constant readiness, poised to attack the English in case they stir ever so little.[3] Also a banished nobleman with some pretensions to the English throne must be secretly encouraged (there are treaties against doing it openly), and in this way pressure can be brought to bear on the English king, and a ruler kept in check who can't really be trusted.[4]

"Now in a meeting like this one, where so much is at stake, where so many brilliant men are competing to think up intricate strategies of war, what if an insignificant fellow like me were to get up and advise going on another tack entirely? Suppose I said the king should leave Italy alone and stay at home, because the single kingdom of France all by itself is almost too much for one man to govern well, and the king should not dream of adding others to it? Then imagine I told about the decrees of the Achorians,[5] who live off the island of Utopia toward the southeast. Long ago, these people went to war to gain another realm for their king, who had inherited an ancient claim to it through marriage. When they had conquered it, they soon saw that keeping it was going to be as hard as getting it had been. The seeds of war were constantly sprouting, their new subjects were continually rebelling or being attacked by foreign invaders, the Achorians had to be constantly at war for them or against them, and they saw no hope of ever being able to disband their army. In the meantime, they were being heavily taxed, money flowed out of their kingdom, their blood was being shed for the advantage of others, and peace was no closer than it had ever been. The war corrupted their own citizens by encouraging lust for robbery and murder; and the laws fell into contempt because their king, distracted with the cares of two kingdoms, could give neither one his proper attention.

"When they saw that the list of these evils was endless, the Achorians took counsel together and very courteously offered their king his choice of keeping whichever of the two kingdoms he preferred, because he couldn't rule them both. They were too numerous a people, they said, to be ruled by half a king; and they added that a man would not even hire a muledriver, if he had to divide his services with somebody else. The worthy king was thus obliged to be content with his own realm and give his new one to a friend, who before long was driven out.

---

1. A small independent enclave astride the Pyrenees, long disputed between Spain and France.
2. The future emperor Charles V was a great matrimonial and diplomatic catch. (Before he was twenty, he had been engaged ten times.) The question of a French marriage that would unite the two greatest Continental and Catholic powers was continually in the air.
3. The Scots, as traditional enemies of England, were traditional allies of France.
4. The French had in fact supported various pretenders to the English throne—most recently, Richard de la Pole, the inheritor of the Yorkist claim.
5. The name arises from Greek *a* (without) and *chora* (place): "the People without a Country."

"Finally, suppose I told the French king's council that all this warmongering, by which so many different nations were kept in turmoil as a result of one man's connivings, would exhaust his treasury and demoralize his people, and yet in the end come to nothing, through some mishap or other.[6] And therefore he should look after his ancestral kingdom, improve it as much as he could, cultivate it in every conceivable way. He should love his people and be loved by them; he should live among them, govern them kindly, and let other kingdoms alone, since his own is big enough, if not too big, for him. How do you think, my dear More, the other councillors would take this speech of mine?"

"Not very well, I'm sure," said I.

"Well, let's go on," he said. "Suppose the councillors of some other king are discussing various schemes for raising money to fill his treasury. One man recommends increasing the value of money when the king pays his debts and devaluing it when he collects his revenues.[7] Thus he can discharge a huge debt with a small payment, and collect a large sum when only a small one is due him. Another suggests a make-believe war, so that money can be raised under pretext of carrying it on; then, when the money is in, he can conclude a ceremonious peace treaty—which the deluded common people will attribute to the piety of their prince and his careful compassion for the lives of his subjects.[8] Another councillor calls to mind some old motheaten laws, antiquated by long disuse, which no one remembers being made and consequently everyone has transgressed. By imposing fines for breaking these laws, the king will get great sums of money, as well as credit for upholding law and order, since the whole procedure can be made to look like justice.[9] Another recommendation is that he forbid under particularly heavy fines a lot of practices that are contrary to the public interest; afterward, he can dispense with his own rules for large sums of money. Thus he pleases the people and makes a double profit, one from the heavy fines imposed on lawbreakers, and the other from selling dispensations. Meanwhile he seems careful of his people's welfare, since it is plain he will not allow private citizens to do anything contrary to the public interest, except for a huge price.

"Another councillor proposes that he work on the judges so that they will decide every case in favor of the king. They should be summoned to court often, and invited to debate his affairs in the royal presence. However unjust his claims, one or another of the judges, whether from love of contradiction, or desire to seem original, or simply to serve his own interest, will be bound to find some way of twisting the law in the king's favor. If the judges can be brought to differ, then the clearest matter in the world will be obscured, and the truth itself brought into question. The king is given leverage to interpret the law as he will, and everyone else will acquiesce from shame or fear. The judges will have no hesitation about supporting the

---

6. Francis I lost Milan in 1520 (that is, four years after More wrote this passage) and, in a catastrophic effort to regain it in 1525, was defeated and taken prisoner by Charles V.
7. Both Henry VII and (after *Utopia* was written) Henry VIII fiddled with the English currency in ways like those suggested here.
8. Something like this happened in 1492, when Henry VII not only pretended war with France on behalf of Brittany and levied taxes for the war (which was hardly fought) but collected a bribe from Charles VIII for not fighting it.
9. This had been common practice under Henry VII, whose ministers Empson and Dudley enforced many forgotten laws for strictly mercenary purposes.

royal interest, for there are always plenty of pretexts for giving judgment in favor of the king. Either equity is on his side, or the letter of the law happens to make for him, or the words of the law can be twisted into obscurity—or, if all else fails, he can appeal above the law to the royal prerogative, which is a never-failing argument with judges who know their 'duty.'

"Then all the councillors agree with the famous maxim of Crassus: a king can never have too much gold, because he must maintain an army.[1] Further, that a king, even if he wants to, can do no wrong, for all property belongs to the king, and so do his subjects themselves; a man owns nothing but what the king, in his goodness, sees fit to leave him. The king should in fact leave his subjects as little as possible, because his own safety depends on keeping them from growing insolent with wealth and freedom. For riches and liberty make people less patient to endure harsh and unjust commands, whereas meager poverty blunts their spirits, makes them docile, and grinds out of the oppressed the lofty spirit of rebellion.

"Now at this point, suppose I were to get up again and declare that all these counsels are both dishonorable and ruinous to the king? Suppose I said his honor and his safety alike rest on the people's resources rather than his own? Suppose I said that the people choose a king for their own sake, not for his, so that by his efforts and troubles they may live in comfort and safety? This is why, I would say, it is the king's duty to take more care of his people's welfare than of his own, just as it is the duty of a shepherd who cares about his job to feed his sheep rather than himself.[2]

"They are absolutely wrong when they say that the people's poverty safeguards public peace—experience shows the contrary. Where will you find more squabbling than among beggars? Who is more eager for revolution than the man who is most discontented with his present position? Who is more reckless about creating disorder than the man who knows he has nothing to lose and thinks he may have something to gain? If a king is so hated or despised by his subjects that he can rule them only by mistreatment, plundering, confiscation, and pauperization of his people, then he'd do much better to abdicate his throne—for under these circumstances, though he keeps the name of authority, he loses all the majesty of a king. A king has no dignity when he exercises authority over beggars, only when he rules over prosperous and happy subjects. This was certainly what that noble and lofty spirit Fabricius[3] meant when he said he would rather be a ruler of rich men than be rich himself.

"A solitary ruler who enjoys a life of pleasure and self-indulgence while all about him are grieving and groaning is acting like a jailer, not a king. Just as an incompetent doctor can cure his patient of one disease only by throwing him into another, so it's an incompetent king who can rule his

---

1. Adapted from Cicero, *On Moral Obligation* 1.8.25. Crassus was a rich Roman who joined with Pompey and Caesar to form the First Triumvirate, which dominated Rome from 60 B.C.E. to Crassus's death seven years later. Legend has it that he died when a Parthian general, after defeating and capturing Crassus at the Battle of Carrhae, disproved his maxim by pouring molten gold down his throat.

2. This metaphor is one of the great commonplaces. Ezekiel 34:2 reads: "Woe be to the shepherds of Israel that do feed themselves! should not the shepherds feed the flocks?"

3. Gaius Fabricius Luscinus, who took part in the wars against Pyrrhus, king of Epirus (280–275 B.C.E.). The saying attributed to him here was actually coined by his colleague Manius Curius Dentatus, but it is quite in his spirit.

people only by depriving them of all life's pleasures. Such a king openly confesses that he does not know how to rule free men.

"A king of this stamp should correct his own sloth or arrogance, because these are the vices that cause people to hate or despise him. Let him live on his own income without wronging others, and limit his spending to his income. Let him curb crime, and by wise training of his subjects keep them from misbehavior, instead of letting it breed and then punishing it. Let him not suddenly revive antiquated laws, especially if they have been long forgotten and never missed. And let him never take money as a fine when a judge would regard an ordinary subject as a low fraud for claiming it.

"Suppose I should then describe for them the law of the Macarians,[4] a people who also live not far from Utopia? On the day that their king first assumes office, he must take an oath confirmed by solemn ceremonies that he will never have in his treasury at any one time more than a thousand pounds in gold, or its equivalent in silver. They say this law was made by an excellent king, who cared more for his country's prosperity than for his own wealth; he established it as a barrier against any king heaping up so much money as to impoverish his people.[5] He thought this sum would enable the king to put down rebellions or repel hostile invasions, but would not tempt him into aggressive adventures. His law was aimed chiefly at keeping the king in check, but he also wanted to ensure an ample supply of money for the daily business transactions of the citizens. Besides, a king who has to distribute all his excess money to the people will not be much disposed to seek out opportunities for extortion. Such a king will be both a terror to evildoers and beloved by the good.—Now, don't you suppose if I set such ideas before men strongly inclined to the contrary, they would turn deaf ears to me?"

"Stone deaf, indeed, there's no doubt about it," I said, "and no wonder! To tell you the truth, I don't think you should offer advice or thrust on people ideas of this sort, that you know will not be listened to. What good can it do? When your listeners are already prepossessed against you and firmly convinced of opposite opinions, how can you win over their minds with such out-of-the-way speeches? This academic philosophy is quite agreeable in the private conversation of close friends, but in the councils of kings, where grave matters are being authoritatively decided, there is no place for it."

"That is just what I was saying," Raphael replied. "There is no place for philosophy in the councils of kings."

"Yes, there is," I said, "but not for this school philosophy which supposes that every topic is suitable for every occasion. There is another philosophy that is better suited for political action, that takes its cue, adapts itself to the drama in hand, and acts its part neatly and appropriately. This is the philosophy for you to use. Otherwise, when a comedy of Plautus is being played,[6] and the household slaves are cracking trivial jokes together, you propose to come on stage in the garb of a philosopher and repeat Seneca's speech to Nero from the *Octavia*.[7] Wouldn't it be better to take a silent role than to say

---

4. From Greek *makarios*, "blessed," "happy."

5. Once again More glances at the previous English monarch, Henry VII, who died the richest prince in Christendom and probably the most hated. He combined unscrupulous greed with skinflint stinginess.

6. Most of the plays of the Roman comic dramatist Plautus (ca. 250–184 B.C.E.) involve low intrigue: needy young men, expensive prostitutes, senile moneybags, and clever slaves, in predictable combinations.

7. The Latin tragedy *Octavia* involves Seneca

something wholly inappropriate, and thus turn the play into a tragicomedy? You pervert and ruin a play when you add irrelevant speeches, even if they are better than the original. So go through with the drama in hand as best you can, and don't spoil it all simply because you happen to think of a play by someone else that would be better.

"That's how things go in the commonwealth, and in the councils of princes. If you cannot pluck up bad ideas by the root, if you cannot cure long-standing evils as completely as you would like, you must not therefore abandon the commonwealth. Don't give up the ship in a storm because you cannot hold back the winds. And don't force strange ideas on people who you know have set their minds on a different course from yours. You must strive to influence policy indirectly, handle the situation tactfully, and thus what you cannot turn to good, you may at least make as little bad as possible. For it is impossible to make everything good unless you make all men good, and that I don't expect to see for a long time to come."

"The only result of this," he answered, "will be that while I try to cure others of madness, I'll be raving along with them myself. If I am to speak the truth, I will simply have to talk in the way I have described. For all I know, it may be the business of a philosopher to tell lies, but it certainly isn't mine. Though my advice may be repugnant and irksome to the king's councillors, I don't see why they should consider it eccentric to the point of folly. What if I told them the kind of thing that Plato advocates in his republic, or that the Utopians actually practice in theirs? However superior those institutions might be (and as a matter of fact they are), yet here they would seem inappropriate, because private property is the rule here, and there all things are held in common.

"People who have made up their minds to rush headlong down the opposite road are never pleased with someone who calls them back and tells them they are on the wrong course. But, apart from that, what did I say that could not and should not be said anywhere and everywhere? If we dismiss as out of the question and absurd everything which the perverse customs of men have made to seem alien to us, we shall have to set aside most of the commandments of Christ, even in a community of Christians. Yet he forbade us to dissemble them, and even ordered that what he had whispered to his disciples should be preached openly from the housetops.[8] Most of his teachings differ more radically from the common customs of mankind than my discourse did. But preachers, like the crafty fellows they are, have found that people would rather not change their lives to conform to Christ's rule, and so, just as you suggest, they have accommodated his teaching to the way people live, as if it were a leaden yardstick.[9] At least in that manner they can get the two things to correspond in some way or other. The only real thing they accomplish that I can see is to make people feel more secure about doing evil.

"And this is all that I could accomplish in the councils of princes. For either I would have different ideas from the others, and that would come to

---

as a character and was long thought to have been written by him. In the speech More refers to (lines 440–592), Seneca lectures Nero on the *abuses of power*. Interestingly, Seneca in fact committed suicide on the orders of Nero (whom he actually had tutored).

8. Matthew 10:27; Luke 12:3.

9. A flexible measuring rod of lead was particularly helpful in constructing the many curved moldings used in a kind of building associated, in antiquity, with the Greek isle of Lesbos. This "Lesbian rule" became proverbial as a metaphor for adaptable moral standards.

the same thing as having no ideas at all, or else I would agree with them, and that, as Mitio says in Terence, would merely confirm them in their madness.[1] When you say I should 'influence policy indirectly,' I simply don't know what you mean; remember, you said I should try hard to handle the situation tactfully, and what can't be made good I should try to make as little bad as possible. In a council, there is no way to dissemble, no way to shut your eyes to things. You must openly approve the worst proposals, and consent to the most vicious policies. A man who went along only halfheartedly even with the worst decisions would immediately get himself a name as a spy and perhaps a traitor. How can one individual do any good when he is surrounded by colleagues who would more readily corrupt the best of men than do any reforming of themselves? Either they will seduce you by their evil ways or, if you keep yourself honest and innocent, you will be made a screen for the knavery and folly of others. Influencing policy indirectly! You wouldn't have a chance.

"This is why Plato in a very fine comparison declares that wise men are right in keeping clear of public business.[2] They see the people swarming through the streets and getting soaked with rain, and they cannot persuade them to go indoors and get out of the wet. They know if they go out themselves, they can do no good but only get drenched with the rest. So they stay indoors and are content to keep at least themselves dry, since they cannot remedy the folly of others.

"But as a matter of fact, my dear More, to tell you what I really think, as long as you have private property, and as long as money is the measure of all things, it is scarcely ever possible for a commonwealth to be just or happy. For justice cannot exist where all the best things in life are held by the worst people; nor can anyone be happy where property is limited to a few, since even those few are always uneasy, and the many are utterly wretched.

"So I reflect on the wonderfully wise and sacred institutions of the Utopians, who are so well governed with so few laws. Among them virtue has its reward, yet everything is shared equally, and everyone lives in plenty. I contrast them with the many other nations, which are constantly passing new ordinances and yet can never order their affairs satisfactorily. In these other nations, whatever a man can get he calls his own private property; but all the mass of laws old and new don't enable him to secure his own, or defend it, or even distinguish it from someone else's property—as is shown by innumerable and interminable lawsuits, fresh ones every day. When I consider all these things, I become more sympathetic to Plato and do not wonder that he declined to make laws for any people who refused to share their goods equally.[3] Wisest of men, he saw easily that the one and only road to the welfare of all lies through the absolute equality of goods. I doubt whether such equality can ever be achieved where property belongs to individuals. However abundant goods may be, when everyone tries to get as much as he can for his own exclusive use, a handful of men end up sharing the whole pile,

---

1. The allusion is to a comedy—*The Brothers* (lines 145–47)—by the Roman playwright Terence (ca. 190–159 B.C.E.).
2. *Republic* 6.496.
3. Diogenes Laertius (3rd century C.E.) reports that the Arcadians and Thebans united to build a great city and asked Plato to be its legislator. He made communism a condition of his going there, and when the inhabitants would not consent, he declined their offer (*Lives of Eminent Philosophers* 3.23).

and the rest are left in poverty. The result generally is two sorts of people whose fortunes ought to be interchanged: the rich are rapacious, wicked, and useless, while the poor are unassuming, modest men who work hard, more for the benefit of the public than of themselves.

"Thus I am wholly convinced that unless private property is entirely done away with, there can be no fair or just distribution of goods, nor can the business of mortals be happily conducted. As long as private property remains, by far the largest and the best part of the human race will be oppressed by a heavy and inescapable burden of cares and anxieties. This load, I admit, may be lightened to some extent, but I maintain it cannot be entirely removed. Laws might be made that no one should own more than a certain amount of land or receive more than a certain income. Or laws might be passed to prevent the prince from becoming too powerful and the populace too unruly. It might be made unlawful for public offices to be solicited, or put up for sale, or made burdensome for the officeholder by great expense. Otherwise, officials are tempted to get their money back by fraud or extortion, and only rich men can afford to accept positions which ought to be held by the wise. Laws of this sort, I agree, may have as much effect as poultices continually applied to sick bodies that are past cure. The social evils I mentioned may be alleviated and their effects mitigated for a while, but so long as private property remains, there is no hope at all of effecting a cure and restoring society to good health. While you try to cure one part, you aggravate the disease in other parts. Suppressing one symptom causes another to break out, since you cannot give something to one person without taking it away from someone else."[4]

"But I don't see it that way," I replied. "It seems to me that people cannot possibly live well where all things are in common. How can there be plenty of commodities where every man stops working? The hope of gain will not spur him on; he will rely on others, and become lazy. If men are driven by need, and yet cannot legally protect what they have gained, what can follow but continual bloodshed and turmoil, especially when respect for magistrates and their authority has been lost? I for one cannot conceive of authority existing among men who are equal to one another in every respect."[5]

"I'm not surprised," said Raphael, "that you think of it this way, since you have no idea, or only a false idea, of such a commonwealth. But you should have been with me in Utopia, and seen with your own eyes their manners and customs as I did—for I lived there more than five years, and would never have left, if it had not been to make that new world known to others. If you had seen them, you would frankly confess that you had never seen a people well governed anywhere but there."

"You will have a hard time persuading me," said Peter Giles, "that people in that new land are better governed than in the world we know. Our minds are not inferior to theirs, and our governments, I believe, are older. Long experience has helped us develop many conveniences of life, and by good luck we have discovered many other things which human ingenuity could never have hit upon."

---

4. Plato also employs the metaphor of societal disease, and of the statesman as physician (*Republic* 4.425E–426A; *Statesman* 297E–298E; Epistle 7, 330C–331A).

5. These objections to communism derive from the critique of the *Republic* in Aristotle's *Politics* 2.1–5.

"As for the relative ages of the governments," Raphael replied, "you might judge more accurately if you had read their histories. If we believe these records, they had cities before there were even people here. What ingenuity has discovered or chance hit upon could have turned up just as well in one place as the other. For the rest, I believe that even if we surpass them in natural intelligence, they leave us far behind in their diligence and zeal to learn.

"According to their chronicles, they had heard nothing of ultra-equatorials (that's their name for us) until we arrived, except that once, some twelve hundred years ago, a ship which a storm had blown toward Utopia was wrecked on their island. Some Romans and Egyptians were cast ashore, and never departed. Now note how the Utopians profited, through their diligence, from this one chance event. They learned every single useful art of the Roman empire either directly from their guests or indirectly from hints and surmises on which they based their own investigations. What benefits from the mere fact that on a single occasion some Europeans landed there! If a similar accident has hitherto brought anyone here from their land, the incident has been completely forgotten, as it will perhaps be forgotten in time to come that I was ever in their country. From one such accident they made themselves masters of all our useful inventions, but I suspect it will be a long time before we accept any of their institutions which are better than ours. This willingness to learn is, I think, the really important reason for their being better governed and living more happily than we do, though we are not inferior to them in brains or resources."

"Then let me implore you, my dear Raphael," said I, "to describe that island to us. Do not try to be brief, but explain in order everything relating to their land, their rivers, towns, people, manners, institutions, laws—everything, in short, that you think we would like to know. And you can take it for granted that we want to know everything that we don't know yet."

"There's nothing I'd rather do," he replied, "for these things are fresh in my mind. But it will take quite some time."

"In that case," I said, "let's first go to lunch. Afterward, we shall have all the time we want."

"Agreed," he said. So we went in and had lunch. Then we came back to the same spot, and sat down on the bench. I ordered my servants to take care that no one should interrupt us. Peter Giles and I urged Raphael to keep his promise. When he saw that we were attentive and eager to hear him, he sat silent and thoughtful a moment, and then began as follows.

Book II

[THE GEOGRAPHY OF UTOPIA][1]

The island of the Utopians is two hundred miles across in the middle part, where it is widest, and is nowhere much narrower than this except toward the two ends, where it gradually tapers. These ends, drawn toward one

---

1. The early editions of *Utopia* include, in Book II, eight section headings. These help in locating the treatment of particular topics in Hythloday's rather sprawling discourse, but since in several instances the headings identify only the *initial* topic of a section, they can also be misleading. In the present edition, they are supplemented by additional headings, enclosed in brackets to identify them as editorial insertions.

Woodcut map of Utopia, by Ambrosius Holbein (brother of the more famous Hans Holbein the Younger). This map appeared in the two 1518 editions.

another as if in a five-hundred-mile circle, make the island crescent-shaped, like a new moon.[2] Between the horns of the crescent, which are about eleven miles apart, the sea enters and spreads into a broad bay. Being sheltered from the wind by the surrounding land, the bay is never rough, but quiet and smooth instead, like a big lake. Thus nearly the whole inner coast is one great harbor, across which ships pass in every direction, to the great advantage of the people. What with shallows on one side and rocks on the

---

2. The island is similar to England in size, though not at all in shape.

other, the entrance into the bay is perilous. Near the middle of the channel, there is one rock that rises above the water, and so presents no danger in itself; on top of it a tower has been built, and there a garrison is kept. Since the other rocks lie underwater, they are very dangerous to navigation. The channels are known only to the Utopians, so hardly any strangers enter the bay without one of their pilots; and even they themselves could not enter safely if they did not direct their course by some landmarks on the coast. If these landmarks were shifted about, the Utopians could easily lure to destruction an enemy fleet coming against them, however big it was.

On the outer side of the island there are likewise occasional harbors; but the coast is rugged by nature, and so well fortified that a few defenders could beat off the attack of a strong force. They say (and the appearance of the place confirms this) that their land was not always an island. But Utopus, who conquered the country and gave it his name (it had previously been called Abraxa),[3] and who brought its rude and uncouth inhabitants to such a high level of culture and humanity that they now excel in that regard almost every other people, also changed its geography. After winning the victory at his first landing, he cut a channel fifteen miles wide where their land joined the continent, and caused the sea to flow around the country. He put not only the natives to work at this task, but all his own soldiers too, so that the vanquished would not think the labor a disgrace. With the work divided among so many hands, the project was finished quickly, and the neighboring peoples, who at first had laughed at his folly, were struck with wonder and terror at his success.

There are fifty-four cities on the island, all spacious and magnificent, identical in language, customs, institutions, and laws. So far as the location permits, all of them are built on the same plan and have the same appearance. The nearest are twenty-four miles apart, and the farthest are not so remote that a person cannot go on foot from one to the other in a day.

Once a year each city sends three of its old and experienced citizens to Amaurot to consider affairs of common interest to the island. Amaurot lies at the navel of the land, so to speak, and is convenient to every other district, so it acts as a capital. Every city has enough ground assigned to it so that at least twelve miles of farm land are available in every direction, though where the cities are farther apart, they have much more land.[4] No city wants to enlarge its boundaries,[5] for the inhabitants consider themselves good tenants rather than landlords. At proper intervals all over the countryside they have built houses and furnished them with farm equipment. These houses are inhabited by citizens who come to the country by turns. No rural household has fewer than forty men and women in it, besides two slaves bound to the land. A master and mistress, serious and mature persons, are in charge of each household. Over every thirty households is placed a single phylarch.[6] Each year twenty persons from each household move back to the city, after

---

3. The Greek Gnostic Basilides (2nd century C.E.) postulated 365 heavens and called the highest of them Abraxas. The Greek letters that constitute the word have numerical equivalents summing to 365, but what it actually *means* is unknown.
4. Each consisting of a central metropolis and the surrounding countryside, the Utopian cities recall the ancient Greek city-states.
5. Marginal gloss: "But today this is the curse of all countries." Although Utopia exists in the present, the glosses repeatedly refer to it as if it belonged to the distant past, like classical Greece and Rome.
6. From Greek *phylarchos*, "ruler of a tribe."

completing a two-year stint in the country. In their place, twenty others are sent out from town, to learn farm work from those who have already been in the country for a year and are therefore better skilled in farming. They, in turn, will teach those who come the following year. If all were equally unskilled in farm work, and new to it, they might harm the crops out of ignorance. This custom of alternating farm workers is the usual procedure, so that no one will have to do such hard work unwillingly for more than two years; but many of them, who take a natural pleasure in farm life, are allowed to stay longer.

The farm workers till the soil, feed the animals, hew wood, and take it to the city by land or by water, as is more convenient. They breed an enormous number of chickens by a marvelous method. The farmers, not hens, hatch the eggs, by keeping them in a warm place at an even temperature. As soon as they come out of the shell, the chicks recognize the humans, follow them around, and are devoted to them instead of to their mothers.

They raise very few horses, and those full of mettle, which they keep only to exercise the young people in the art of horsemanship.[7] For all the work of plowing and hauling they use oxen, which they agree are inferior to horses over the short haul, but which can hold out longer under heavy burdens, are less subject to disease (as they suppose), and can be kept with less cost and trouble. Moreover, when oxen are too old for work, they can be used for meat.

Grain they use only to make bread.[8] They drink wine, apple or pear cider, or simple water, which they sometimes boil with honey or licorice, of which they have an abundance. Although they know very well, down to the last detail, how much food each city and its surrounding district will consume, they produce much more grain and cattle than they need for themselves, and share the surplus with their neighbors. Whatever goods the folk in the country need which cannot be produced there, they request of the town magistrates, and since there is nothing to be paid or exchanged, they get what they want without any trouble. They generally go to town once a month in any case, for the feast day. When harvest time approaches, the phylarchs in the country notify the town magistrates how many hands will be needed. Crews of harvesters come just when they're wanted, and in one day of good weather they can usually get in the whole crop.

THEIR CITIES, ESPECIALLY AMAUROT

If you know one of their cities, you know them all, for they're exactly alike, except where geography itself makes a difference. So I'll describe one of them, and no matter which. But what one rather than Amaurot, the most worthy of all?—since its eminence is acknowledged by the other cities, which send representatives to the annual meeting there; besides which, I know it best, because I lived there for five full years.

Well, then, Amaurot lies up against a gently sloping hill; the town is almost square in shape. From a little below the crest of the hill, it runs down about two miles to the river Anyder, and then spreads out along the river bank for a

---

7. In fact, horses had long been extinct in the Western Hemisphere, before Europeans imported them.

8. That is, they don't, like the English, use it to make beer and ale.

somewhat greater distance. The Anyder rises from a small spring about eighty miles above Amaurot, but other streams flow into it, two of them being pretty big, so that, as it runs past Amaurot, the river has grown to a width of five hundred yards. It continues to grow even larger until at last, sixty miles farther along, it is lost in the ocean. In all this stretch between the sea and the city, and also for some miles above the city, the river is tidal, ebbing and flowing every six hours with a swift current.[9] When the tide comes in, it fills the whole Anyder with salt water for about thirty miles, driving the fresh water back. Even above that, for several miles farther, the water is brackish; but a little higher up, as it runs past the city, the water is always fresh, and when the tide ebbs, the river runs clean and sweet all the way to the sea.

The two banks of the river at Amaurot are linked by a bridge, built not on wooden piles but on remarkable stone arches. It is placed at the upper end of the city, farthest removed from the sea, so that ships can sail along the entire length of the city quays without obstruction. There is also another stream, not particularly large, but very gentle and pleasant, which gushes from the hill on which the city is situated, flows down through the center of town, and into the Anyder. The inhabitants have walled around the source of this river, which takes its rise a little outside the town, and joined it to the town proper so that if they should be attacked, the enemy would not be able to cut off the stream or divert or poison it. Water from the stream is carried by tile piping into various sections of the lower town. Where the terrain makes this impractical, they collect rain water in cisterns, which serve just as well.

The town is surrounded by a thick, high wall, with many towers and bastions. On three sides it is also surrounded by a dry ditch, broad and deep and filled with thorn hedges; on its fourth side the river itself serves as a moat. The streets are conveniently laid out for use by vehicles and for protection from the wind. Their buildings are by no means shabby; unbroken rows of houses face each other across the streets along the whole block. The streets are twenty feet wide.[1] Behind each row of houses—at the center of every block and extending the full length of the street—there are large gardens.

Every house has a door to the street and another to the garden. The doors, which are made with two leaves, open easily and swing shut automatically, letting anyone enter who wants to—so there is nothing private anywhere. Every ten years, they change houses by lot. The Utopians are very fond of these gardens of theirs. They raise vines, fruits, herbs, and flowers, so well cared for and flourishing that I have never seen any gardens more productive or elegant than theirs. They keep interested in gardening, partly because they delight in it, and also because of the competition between different blocks, which challenge one another to produce the best gardens. Certainly you will not easily find anything else in the whole city more useful or more pleasant to the citizens. And this gives reason to think that the founder of the city paid particular attention to the siting of these gardens.

They say that in the beginning the whole city was planned by Utopus himself, but that he left to posterity matters of adornment and improvement

---

9. Many of the details of Amaurot—its situation on a tidal river, its stone bridge (next paragraph), though not the location of that bridge—are reminiscent of London.
1. Lavish, by 16th-century standards.

such as could not be perfected in one man's lifetime. Their records began 1,760 years ago with the conquest of the island, have been diligently compiled, and are carefully preserved. From these it appears that the first houses were low, like cabins or peasant huts, built out of any sort of timber, with mud-plastered walls and pointed roofs thatched with straw. But now their houses are all three stories high and handsomely constructed; the fronts are faced with fieldstone, quarried rock, or brick, over rubble construction. The roofs are flat, and are covered with a kind of plaster that is cheap but fireproof, and more weather-resistant even than lead.[2] Glass (which is plentiful there) is used in windows to keep out the weather;[3] and they also use thin linen cloth treated with oil or gum so that it lets in more light and keeps out more wind.

THEIR OFFICIALS

Once a year, every group of thirty households elects an official, formerly called the syphogrant,[4] but now called the phylarch. Over every group of ten syphogrants with their households there is another official, once called the tranibor but now known as the head phylarch. All the syphogrants, two hundred in number, elect the governor. They take an oath to choose the man they think best qualified; and then by secret ballot they elect the governor from among four men nominated by the people of the four sections of the city. The governor holds office for life, unless he is suspected of aiming at a tyranny. Though the tranibors are elected annually, they are not changed for light or casual reasons. All their other officials hold office for a single year only.

The tranibors meet to consult with the governor every other day, and more often if necessary: they discuss affairs of state, and settle any disputes between private parties (there are very few), acting as quickly as possible.[5] The tranibors always invite two syphogrants to the senate chamber, different ones every day. There is a rule that no decision can be made on a matter of public business unless it has been discussed in the senate on three separate days. It is a capital offense to make plans about public business outside of the senate or the popular assembly. The purpose of these rules, they say, is to prevent the governor and the tranibors from conspiring together to alter the government and enslave the people. Therefore all matters which are considered important are first laid before the assembly of the syphogrants. They talk the matter over with the households they represent, debate it with one another, then report their recommendation to the senate. Sometimes a question is brought before the general council of the whole island.

The senate also has a standing rule never to discuss a matter on the day when it is first introduced; all new business is deferred to the next meeting.[6] They do this so that a man will not blurt out the first thought that occurs to

2. Used in More's time to roof important buildings.
3. During More's day in England window glass was not common; oiled cloth and lattices of wicker or wood were more frequent.
4. The word appears to be constructed from Greek *sophos* (wise)—or perhaps *sypheos* (of the sty)—plus *gerontes* (old men). The etymology for "tranibor" (below) seems to be *traneis* or *tranos* (clear, plain, distinct) plus *boros* (devouring, gluttonous). There is no explanation of why Hythloday consistently uses the "older" form of the titles.
5. Marginal gloss: "A quick ending to disputes, which now are endlessly and deliberately prolonged."
6. Marginal gloss: "Would that the same rule prevailed in our modern councils."

him, and then devote all his energies to defending those foolish impulses, instead of considering impartially the public good. They know that some men would rather jeopardize the general welfare than admit to having been heedless and shortsighted—so perverse and preposterous is their sense of pride. They should have had enough foresight at the beginning to speak with prudence rather than haste.

THEIR OCCUPATIONS

Agriculture is the one occupation at which everyone works, men and women alike, with no exceptions. They are trained in it from childhood, partly in the schools, where they learn theory, and partly through field trips to nearby farms, which make something like a game of practical instruction. On these trips they not only watch the work being done, but frequently pitch in and get a workout by doing the jobs themselves.

Besides farm work (which, as I said, everybody performs), each person is taught a particular trade of his own, such as wool-working, linen-making, masonry, metal-work, or carpentry. There is no other craft that is practiced by any considerable number of them.[7] Throughout the island people wear, and throughout their lives always wear, the same style of clothing, except for the distinction between the sexes, and between married and unmarried persons. Their clothing is attractive, does not hamper bodily movement, and serves for warm as well as cold weather; what is more, each household makes its own.

Every person (and this includes women as well as men) learns a second trade, besides agriculture. As the weaker sex, women practice the lighter crafts, such as working in wool or linen; the heavier jobs are assigned to the men. As a rule, the son is trained to his father's craft, for which most feel a natural inclination. But if anyone is attracted to another occupation, he is transferred by adoption into a family practicing the trade he prefers. Both his father and the authorities make sure that he is assigned to a grave and responsible householder. After someone has learned one trade, if he wants to learn another he gets the same permission. When he has learned both, he pursues whichever he likes better, unless the city needs one more than the other.

The chief and almost the only business of the syphogrants is to manage matters so that no one sits around in idleness, and assure that everyone works hard at his trade. But no one has to exhaust himself with endless toil from early morning to late at night, as if he were a beast of burden. Such wretchedness, really worse than slavery, is the common lot of workmen almost everywhere except Utopia.[8] Of the day's twenty-four hours, the Utopians devote only six to work. They work three hours before noon, when they go to lunch. After lunch they rest for a couple of hours, then go to work for another three hours. Then they have supper, and at eight o'clock (counting the first hour after noon as one) they go to bed, and sleep eight hours.

---

7. Would not considerable numbers also be employed making such things as pottery, harnesses, bread, and books, as well as in mining and the merchant marine? Presumably all the professionals—doctors, for example—are drawn from the class of scholars.

8. For example, in England a law of 1514–15 required workmen to be present at the workplace from daybreak to nightfall in fall and winter and from 5 A.M. to between 7 and 8 P.M. in spring and summer. (There were breaks for meals and, in summer, for a brief afternoon nap.)

The other hours of the day, when they are not working, eating, or sleeping, are left to each person's individual discretion, provided that free time is not wasted in roistering or sloth but used properly in some chosen occupation. Generally these periods are devoted to intellectual activity. For they have an established custom of giving daily public lectures before dawn;[9] attendance at these lectures is required only of those who have been specially chosen to devote themselves to learning, but a great many other people, both men and women, choose voluntarily to attend. Depending on their interests, some go to one lecture, some to another. But if anyone would rather devote his spare time to his trade, as many do who don't care for the intellectual life, this is not discouraged; in fact, such persons are commended as especially useful to the commonwealth.

After supper, they devote an hour to recreation, in their gardens in summer, or during winter in the common halls where they have their meals. There they either play music or amuse themselves with conversation. They know nothing about gambling with dice, or other such foolish and ruinous games.[1] They do play two games not unlike chess. One is a battle of numbers, in which one number captures another. The other is a game in which the vices fight a battle against the virtues. The game is ingeniously set up to show how the vices oppose one another, yet combine against the virtues; then, what vices oppose what virtues, how they try to assault them openly or undermine them insidiously; how the defenses of the virtues can break the strength of the vices or skillfully elude their plots; and finally, by what means one side or the other gains the victory.[2]

But in all this, you may get a wrong impression, if we don't go back and consider one point more carefully. Because they allot only six hours to work, you might think the necessities of life would be in scant supply. This is far from the case. Their working hours are ample to provide not only enough but more than enough of the necessities and even the conveniences of life. You will easily appreciate this if you consider how large a part of the population in other countries exists without doing any work at all. In the first place, hardly any of the women, who are a full half of the population, work;[3] or, if they do, then as a rule their husbands lie snoring in bed. Then there is a great lazy gang of priests and so-called religious.[4] Add to them all the rich, especially the landlords, who are commonly called gentlemen and nobles. Include with them their retainers, that mob of swaggering bullies. Finally, reckon in with these the sturdy and lusty beggars who go about feigning some disease as an excuse for their idleness. You will certainly find that the things which satisfy our needs are produced by far fewer hands than you had supposed.

And now consider how few of those who do work are doing really essential things. For where money is the standard of everything, many vain, superfluous trades are bound to be carried on simply to satisfy luxury and

---

9. Renaissance universities got under way early: first lecture was between 5 and 7 A.M.
1. Marginal gloss: "But now dicing is the sport of princes."
2. *Moral games* of this general character were popular with Renaissance educators.
3. A strange statement, since in More's time most women selected, prepared, and cooked the family food; did the family laundry; performed a thousand other routine tasks of domestic drudgery; and were responsible for taking care of the children. In Utopia too they are responsible for at least some of these duties—cooking, child care—in addition to practicing a craft and taking their turn at farmwork.
4. That is, members of the various religious orders.

licentiousness. Suppose the multitude of those who now work were limited to a few trades, and set to producing just those commodities that nature really requires. They would be bound to produce so much that prices would drop and the workmen would be unable to gain a living. But suppose again that all the workers in useless trades were put to useful ones, and that all the idlers (who now guzzle twice as much as the workingmen who make what they consume) were assigned to productive tasks—well, you can easily see how little time would be enough and more than enough to produce all the goods that human needs and conveniences require—yes, and human pleasure too, as long as it's true and natural pleasure.

The experience of Utopia makes this perfectly apparent. In each city and its surrounding countryside barely five hundred of those men and women whose age and strength make them fit for work are exempted from it.[5] Among these are the syphogrants, who by law are free not to work; yet they don't take advantage of the privilege, preferring to set a good example to their fellow citizens. Some others are permanently exempted from work so that they may devote themselves to study, but only on the recommendation of the priests[6] and through a secret vote of the syphogrants. If any of these scholars disappoints their hopes, he becomes a workman again. On the other hand, it happens from time to time that a craftsman devotes his leisure so earnestly to study, and makes such progress as a result, that he is relieved of manual labor and promoted to the class of learned men. From this class of scholars are chosen ambassadors, priests, tranibors, and the governor himself, who used to be called Barzanes, but in their modern tongue is known as Ademus.[7] Since almost all the rest of the population is neither idle nor occupied in useless trades, it is easy to see why they produce so much in so short a working day.

Apart from all this, in several of the necessary crafts their way of life requires less total labor than does that of people elsewhere. In other countries, building and repairing houses requires the constant work of many men, because what a father has built, his thriftless heir lets fall into ruin; and then his successor has to repair, at great expense, what could easily have been maintained at a very small charge. Further, when a man has built a splendid house at vast cost, someone else may think he has finer taste, let the first house fall to ruin, and then build another one somewhere else for just as much money. But among the Utopians, where everything has been well ordered and the commonwealth properly established, building a brand-new home on a new site is a rare event. They are not only quick to repair damage, but foresighted in preventing it. The result is that their buildings last for a very long time with minimal repairs; and the carpenters and masons sometimes have so little to do that they are set to hewing timber and cutting stone in case some future need for it should arise.

---

5. That is, are exempted from manual labor. As Hythloday proceeds to explain, in each city those exempted include the 200 syphogrants and the class of scholars, from which is chosen the other exempted individuals: the twenty tranibors, the governor, ambassadors, and the thirteen priests.

6. Who are in charge of the education of children.

7. Marginal gloss: "Only the learned hold public office." "Ademus": from Greek for "Without People." "Barzanes": "Son of Zeus" (Hebrew—*bar*—plus Greek).

Consider, too, how little labor their clothing requires. Their work clothes are unpretentious garments made of leather, which last seven years. When they go out in public, they cover these rough working-clothes with a cloak. Throughout the entire island, these cloaks are of the same color, which is that of natural wool.[8] As a result, they not only need less wool than people in other countries, but what they do need is less expensive. Even so, they use linen cloth most, because it requires least labor. They like linen cloth to be white and wool cloth to be clean; but they put no price on fineness of texture. Elsewhere a man may not be satisfied with four or five woolen cloaks of different colors and as many silk shirts; or if he's a clotheshorse, even ten are not enough. But there everyone is content with a single cloak, and generally wears it for two years. There is no reason at all why he should want any others, for if he had them, he would not be better protected against the cold, nor would he appear in any way better dressed.

Since there is an abundance of everything, as a result of everyone working at useful trades and the trades requiring less work, they sometimes assemble great numbers of people to work on the roads, if any of them need repairing. And when there is no need even for this sort of work, then the officials very often proclaim a shorter workday, since they never force their citizens to perform useless labor. The chief aim of their constitution is that, whenever public needs permit, all citizens should be free to withdraw as much time as possible from the service of the body and devote themselves to the freedom and culture of the mind. For in that, they think, is the real happiness of life.

SOCIAL RELATIONS

Now I must explain how the citizens behave toward one another, the nature of their social relations, and how they distribute their goods within the society.

Each city, then, consists of households, the households consisting generally of blood-relations. When the women grow up and are married, they move into their husbands' households. On the other hand, male children and after them grandchildren remain in the family, and are subject to the oldest member, unless his mind has started to fail, in which case the next oldest takes his place. To keep the cities from becoming too large or too small, they take care that there should be no more than six thousand households in each (exclusive of the surrounding countryside), each family containing between ten and sixteen adults.[9] They do not, of course, try to regulate the number of minor children in a family. The limit on adults is easily observed by transferring individuals from a household with too many into a household with not enough. Likewise if a city has too many people, the extra persons serve to make up a shortage of population in other cities. And if the population throughout the entire island exceeds the quota, they enroll citizens out of

---

8. In a letter to Erasmus of ca. December 4, 1516, More identifies this garment as the habit of a Franciscan friar.

9. If an average household includes thirteen adults, and there are 6,000 households per city (not counting those on the surrounding farms), then there are about 78,000 adults per city; allowing for children and slaves, the total population must be well in excess of 100,000, making every Utopian city larger than all but the greatest European cities of the time. Whether More actually made these calculations (or whether there is really much point in making them) is another matter.

every city and plant a colony under their own laws on the mainland near them, wherever the natives have plenty of unoccupied and uncultivated land. Those natives who want to live with the Utopian settlers are taken in. When such a merger occurs, the two peoples gradually and easily blend together, sharing the same way of life and customs, much to the advantage of both. For by their policies the Utopians make the land yield an abundance for all, though previously it had seemed too poor and barren even to support the natives. But if the natives will not join in living under their laws, the Utopians drive them out of the land they claim for themselves, and if they resist make war on them. They think it is perfectly justifiable to make war on people who leave their land idle and waste, yet forbid the use of it to others who, by the law of nature, ought to be supported from it.

If for any reason one of their cities shrinks so sharply in population that it cannot be made up from other cities without bringing them too under proper strength, the numbers are restored by bringing people back from the colonies. This has happened only twice, they say, in their whole history, both times as a result of a frightful plague. They would rather that their colonies disappeared than that any of the cities on their island should get too small.

But to return to their manner of living. The oldest of every household, as I said, is the ruler. Wives are subject to their husbands, children to their parents, and generally the younger to their elders.[1] Every city is divided into four equal districts, and in the middle of each district is a market for all kinds of commodities. Whatever each household produces is brought here and stored in warehouses, each kind of goods in its own place. Here the head of each household looks for what he or his family needs, and carries off what he wants without any sort of payment or compensation. Why should anything be refused him? There is plenty of everything, and no reason to fear that anyone will claim more than he needs. Why would anyone be suspected of asking for more than is needed, when everyone knows there will never be any shortage? Fear of want, no doubt, makes every living creature greedy and rapacious—and, in addition, man develops these qualities out of sheer pride, pride which glories in getting ahead of others by a superfluous display of possessions. But this kind of vice has no place whatever in the Utopian way of life.

Next to the marketplace of which I just spoke are the food markets, where people bring all sorts of vegetables, fruit, and bread. Fish, meat, and poultry are also brought there from designated places outside the city, where running water can carry away all the blood and refuse. Bondsmen do the slaughtering and cleaning in these places: citizens are not allowed to do such work. The Utopians feel that slaughtering our fellow creatures gradually destroys the sense of compassion, which is the finest sentiment of which our human nature is capable. Besides, they don't allow anything dirty or filthy to be brought into the city, lest the air become tainted by putrefaction and thus infectious.

---

1. Utopian women enjoy considerably more equality with men than did their 16th-century European counterparts, but Utopian social relations as a whole exhibit the same patriarchal structure that had always been prevalent in Europe and was sanctioned in classical and biblical texts (for example, Aristotle, Politics 1.12.1–2; Ephesians 5:22–6:4) as well as in many later ones.

Each block has its own spacious halls, equally distant from one another, and each known by a special name. In these halls live the syphogrants. Thirty families are assigned to each hall, to take their meals in common[2]—fifteen live on one side of the hall, fifteen on the other. The stewards of all the halls meet at a fixed time in the market and get food according to the number of persons for whom each is responsible.

But first consideration goes to the sick, who are cared for in public hospitals. Every city has four of these, built at the city limits, slightly outside the walls, and spacious enough to appear like little towns. The hospitals are large for two reasons: so that the sick, however numerous they may be, will not be packed closely and uncomfortably together, and also so that those who have a contagious disease, such as might pass from one to the other, may be isolated. The hospitals are well ordered and supplied with everything needed to cure the patients, who are nursed with tender and watchful care. Highly skilled physicians are in constant attendance. Consequently, though nobody is sent there against his will, there is hardly anyone in the city who would not rather be treated for an illness at the hospital than at home.

When the hospital steward has received the food prescribed for the sick by their doctors, the best of the remainder is fairly divided among the halls according to the number in each, except that special regard is paid to the governor, the high priest, and the tranibors, as well as to ambassadors and foreigners, if there are any. In fact, foreigners are very few; but when they do come, they have certain furnished houses assigned to them.

At the hours of lunch and supper, a brazen trumpet summons the entire syphogranty to assemble in their hall, except for those who are bedridden in the hospitals or at home. After the halls have been served with their quotas of food, nothing prevents an individual from taking food home from the marketplace. They realize that no one would do this without good reason. For while it is not forbidden to eat at home, no one does it willingly, because it is not thought proper; and besides, it would be stupid to take the trouble of preparing a worse meal at home when there is an elegant and sumptuous one near at hand in the hall.

In this hall, slaves do all the particularly dirty and heavy work. But planning the meal, as well as preparing and cooking the food, is carried out by the women alone, with each family taking its turn. Depending on their number, they sit down at three or more tables. The men sit with their backs to the wall, the women on the outside, so that if a woman has a sudden qualm or pain, such as occasionally happens during pregnancy, she may get up without disturbing the others and go off to the nurses.

A separate dining room is assigned to the nurses and infants, with a plentiful supply of cradles, clean water, and a warm fire. Thus the nurses may lay the infants down, or remove their swaddling clothes and let them refresh themselves by playing freely before the fire. Each child is nursed by its own mother, unless death or illness prevents. When that happens, the wives of the syphogrants quickly find a nurse. The problem is not difficult. Any

---

2. The institution of the common messes has precedents in ancient Sparta and in the designs for an ideal commonwealth by Plato (*Republic* 3.416E) and Aristotle (*Politics* 7.10.10). It has also been a feature of other communities with a utopian bent—for example, the Israeli kibbutzim.

woman who can, gladly volunteers for the job, since everyone applauds her kindness and the child itself regards its nurse as its natural mother.

Children under the age of five sit together in the nursery. All other minors, both boys and girls up to the age of marriage, either wait on table or, if not old and strong enough for that, stand by in absolute silence. Both groups eat whatever is handed to them by those sitting at the table, and have no other set time for their meals.

The syphogrant with his wife sits at the middle of the first table, in the highest part of the dining hall. This is the place of greatest honor, and from this table, which is placed crosswise to the others, the whole gathering can be seen. Two of the eldest sit with them, for they always sit in groups of four; if there is a church in the district, the priest and his wife sit with the syphogrant, so as to preside.[3] On both sides of them sit younger people, next to them older people again, and so through the hall: those of about the same age sit together, yet are mingled with others of a different age. The reason for this, as they explain it, is that the dignity of the aged, and the respect due them, may restrain the younger people from improper freedom of words and gestures, since nothing said or done at table can pass unnoticed by the old, who are present on every side.

Dishes of food are not served down the tables in order from top to bottom, but all the old persons, who are seated in conspicuous places, are served with the best food; and then equal shares are given to the rest. The old people, as they feel inclined, give their neighbors a share of those delicacies which are not plentiful enough to be served to everyone. Thus due respect is paid to seniority, yet everyone enjoys some of the benefits.

They begin every lunch and supper with some reading on a moral topic,[4] but keep it brief lest it become a bore. Taking that as an occasion, the elders introduce proper topics of conversation, which they try not to make gloomy or dull. They never monopolize the conversation with long monologues, but are eager to hear what the young people say. In fact, they deliberately draw them out, in order to discover the natural temper and quality of each one's mind, as revealed in the freedom of mealtime talk.

Their lunches are light, their suppers rather more elaborate, because lunch is followed by work, supper by rest and a night's sleep, which they think particularly helpful to good digestion. No evening meal passes without music, and the dessert course is never scanted; during the meal, they burn incense and scatter perfume, omitting nothing which will make the occasion festive. For they are somewhat inclined to think that no kind of pleasure is forbidden, provided harm does not come of it.

This is the pattern of life in the city; but in the country, where they are farther removed from neighbors, they all eat in their own homes. No family lacks for food, since, after all, whatever the city-dwellers eat comes originally from those in the country.

---

3. Marginal gloss: "Priest before prince. But now even bishops act as servants to royalty."
4. Humanists were fond of this social custom, the origins of which were part monastic, part classical.

THE TRAVELS [AND TRADE] OF THE UTOPIANS

Anyone who wants to visit friends in another city, or simply to see the place itself, can easily obtain permission from his syphogrant and tranibor, unless for some special reason he is needed at home. They travel together in groups, taking a letter from the governor granting leave to travel and fixing a day of return. They are given a wagon and a public slave to drive the oxen and look after them, but unless women are in the company they dispense with the wagon as an unnecessary bother. Wherever they go, though they take nothing with them, they never lack for anything, because they are at home everywhere. If they stay more than a day in one place, each one practices his trade there, and is kindly received by his fellow artisans.

Anyone who takes upon himself to leave his district without permission, and is caught without the governor's letter, is treated with contempt, brought back as a runaway, and severely punished. If he is bold enough to try it a second time, he is made a slave. Anyone who wants to stroll about and explore the extent of his own district is not prevented, provided he first obtains his father's permission and his wife's consent. But wherever he goes in the countryside, he gets no food until he has completed either a morning's or an afternoon's stint of work. On these terms, he may go where he pleases within his own district, yet be just as useful to the city as if he were at home.

So you see there is no chance to loaf or any pretext for evading work; there are no wine bars or alehouses or brothels, no chances for corruption, no hiding places, no spots for secret meetings. Because they live in the full view of all, they are bound to be either working at their usual trades or enjoying their leisure in a respectable way. Such customs must necessarily result in plenty of life's good things, and since they share everything equally, it follows that no one can ever be reduced to poverty or forced to beg.

In the senate at Amaurot (to which, as I said before, three representatives come every year from each city), they survey the island to find out where there are shortages and surpluses, and promptly satisfy one district's shortage with another's surplus. These are outright gifts; those who give receive nothing in return from those to whom they give. Though they give freely to one city, asking nothing in return, they get freely from another to which they gave nothing; and thus the whole island is like a single family.

After they have accumulated enough for themselves—and this they consider to be a full two-years' store, because next year's crop is always uncertain—then they export their surpluses to other countries: great quantities of grain, honey, wool, flax, timber, scarlet and purple dyestuffs, hides, wax, tallow, and leather, as well as livestock. One-seventh of their cargo they give freely to the poor of the importing country, and the rest they sell at moderate prices. In exchange they receive not only such goods as they lack at home (in fact, about the only important thing they lack is iron) but immense quantities of silver and gold. They have been carrying on trade for a long time now, and have accumulated a greater supply of the precious metals than you would believe possible. As a result, they now care very little whether they sell for cash or on credit, and most payments to them actually take the *form of promissory notes*. However, in all such transactions, they never trust individuals but insist that the foreign city become officially responsible. When the day of payment comes, the city collects the money due from private debtors, puts it into the treasury, and enjoys the use of it till the Utopians claim payment. Most of it, in fact, is never claimed. The Utopians think it hardly right to take what they don't need away from people who do need it. But if they need to lend some part of the money to another nation, then they call it in—as they do also when they must wage war. This is the only reason that they keep such an immense treasure at home, as a protection against extreme peril or sudden emergency. They use it above all to hire, at extravagant rates of pay, foreign mercenaries, whom they would much rather risk in battle than their own citizens. They know very well that for large enough sums of money many of the enemy's soldiers can themselves be bought off or set at odds with one another, either secretly or openly.[5]

[THEIR ATTITUDE TO GOLD AND SILVER]

For this reason, therefore, they have accumulated a vast treasure; but they do not keep it like a treasure. I'm really quite ashamed to tell you how they do keep it, because you probably won't believe me. I would not have believed it myself if someone had just told me about it; but I was there, and saw it with my own eyes. It is a general rule that the more different anything is from what people are used to, the harder it is to accept. But, considering that all their other customs are so unlike ours, a sensible judge will perhaps not be surprised that they treat gold and silver quite differently from the way we do. After all, they never do use money among themselves, but keep it only for a contingency which may or may not actually arise. So in the meanwhile they take care that no one shall overvalue gold and silver, of which money is made, beyond what the metals themselves deserve. Anyone can see, for example, that iron is far superior to either; men could not live without iron, by heaven, any more than without fire or water. But Nature granted to gold and silver no function with which we cannot easily dispense. Human folly has made them precious because they are rare. In contrast, Nature, like a most indulgent mother, has placed the best things out in the open, like air, water, and the earth itself; but vain and unprofitable things she has hidden away in remote places.

If in Utopia gold and silver were kept locked up in some tower, foolish heads among the common people might concoct a story that the governor and senate were out to cheat ordinary folk and get some advantage for themselves. They might indeed put the gold and silver into plate-ware and such handiwork, but then in case of necessity the people would not want to give up such articles, on which they had begun to fix their hearts, only to melt them down for soldiers' pay. To avoid all these inconveniences, they thought of a plan which conforms with their institutions as clearly as it contrasts with our own. Unless one has actually seen it working, their plan may seem incredible, because we prize gold so highly and are so careful about protecting it. While they eat from pottery dishes and drink from glass cups, well made but inexpensive, their chamber pots and all their humblest vessels, for use in the common halls and even in private homes, are made of gold and silver.[6] The chains and heavy fetters of slaves are also made of these metals.

---

5. Marginal gloss: "Better to avoid war by bribery or guile than to wage it with great loss of human blood."

6. Marginal gloss: "O magnificent scorn for gold!" Vespucci had reported Native Americans' indifference to gold and gems.

Finally, criminals who are to bear the mark of some disgraceful act are forced to wear golden rings in their ears and on their fingers, golden chains around their necks, and even golden headbands. Thus they hold gold and silver up to scorn in every conceivable way. As a result, if they had to part with their entire supply of these metals, which other nations give up with as much agony as if they were being disemboweled, the Utopians would feel it no more than the loss of a penny.

They pick up pearls by the seashore, and diamonds and garnets from certain cliffs, but never go out of set purpose to look for them. If they happen to find some, they polish them and give them to the children, who, when they are small, feel proud and pleased with such gaudy decorations. But after, when they grow a bit older, and notice that only babies like such toys, they lay them aside. Their parents don't have to say anything; the children simply put these trifles away out of shame, just as our children when they grow up put away their marbles, baubles, and dolls.

These customs so different from those of other people produce quite different attitudes: this never became clearer to me than it did in the case of the Anemolian[7] ambassadors, who came to Amaurot while I was there. Because they came to discuss important business, the national council had assembled ahead of time, three citizens from each city. The ambassadors from nearby nations, who had visited Utopia before and knew something of their customs, understood that fine clothing was not respected in that land, silk was despised, and gold a badge of contempt; therefore they always came in the very plainest of their clothes. But the Anemolians, who lived farther off and had had fewer dealings with the Utopians, had heard only that they all dressed alike and very simply; so they took for granted that their hosts had nothing to wear that they didn't put on. Being themselves rather more proud than wise, they decided to dress as resplendently as the very gods, and dazzle the eyes of the poor Utopians by the glitter of their garb.

Consequently the three ambassadors made a grand entry with a suite of a hundred attendants, all in clothing of many colors, and most in silk. Being noblemen at home, the ambassadors were arrayed in cloth of gold, with heavy gold chains on their necks, gold earrings, gold rings on their fingers, and sparkling strings of pearls and gems on their caps. In fact, they were decked out in all the articles which in Utopia are used to punish slaves, shame wrongdoers, or entertain infants. It was a sight to see how they strutted when they compared their finery with the dress of the Utopians, who had poured out into the streets to see them pass. But it was just as funny to see how wide they fell of the mark, and how far they were from getting the consideration they wanted and expected. Except for a very few Utopians who for some special reason had visited foreign countries, all the onlookers considered this pomp and splendor a mark of disgrace. They therefore bowed to the humblest of the party as lords, and took the ambassadors, because of their golden chains, to be slaves, passing them by without any reverence at all. You might have seen children, who had themselves thrown away their

---

7. From Greek *anemolios*, "windy." The story of the Anemolian ambassadors owes much to "Nigrinus," a dialogue by the Syrian satirist Lucian (2nd century C.E.) in which a rich Roman makes a fool of himself by stalking around Athens in a purple robe. More and Erasmus had published a volume of Latin translations of Lucian (who wrote in Greek) in 1506.

pearls and gems, nudge their mothers when they saw the ambassadors' jeweled caps, and say:

"Look at that big lummox, mother, who's still wearing pearls and jewels as if he were a little boy!"

But the mother, in all seriousness, would answer:

"Hush, son, I think he is one of the ambassadors' fools."

Others found fault with the golden chains as useless, because they were so flimsy any slave could break them, and so loose that he could easily shake them off and run away whenever he wanted, footloose and fancy-free. But after the ambassadors had spent a couple of days among the Utopians, they saw the immense amounts of gold which were as thoroughly despised there as they were prized at home. They saw too that more gold and silver went into making the chains and fetters of a single runaway slave than into costuming all three of them. Somewhat ashamed and crestfallen, they put away all the finery in which they had strutted so arrogantly, especially after they had talked with the Utopians enough to learn their customs and opinions.

[THEIR PHILOSOPHY]

The Utopians marvel that any mortal can take pleasure in the dubious sparkle of a little jewel or bright gemstone, when he has a star, or the sun itself, to look at. They are amazed at the foolishness of any man who considers himself a nobler fellow because he wears clothing of specially fine wool. No matter how delicate the thread, they say, a sheep wore it once, and still was nothing but a sheep.[8] They are surprised that gold, a useless commodity in itself, is everywhere valued so highly that man himself, who for his own purposes conferred this value on it, is considered far less valuable than the gold. They do not understand why a dunderhead with no more brains than a post, and who is as depraved as he is foolish, should command a great many wise and good men simply because he happens to have a great pile of gold. Yet if this master should lose his money to the lowest rascal in his household (as can happen by chance, or through some legal trick—for the law can produce reversals as violent as Fortune herself), he would promptly become the servant of his servant, as if he were personally attached to the coins, and a mere appendage to them.[9] Even more than this, the Utopians are appalled at those people who practically worship a rich man, though they neither owe him anything nor are obligated to him in any way. What impresses them is simply that the man is rich. Yet all the while they know he is so mean and grasping that as long as he lives not a single penny out of that great mound of money will ever come their way.

These and the like attitudes the Utopians have picked up partly from their upbringing, since the institutions of their commonwealth are completely opposed to such folly, and partly from instruction and their reading of good books. For though not many people in each city are excused from labor and assigned to scholarship full-time (these are persons who from childhood have given evidence of excellent character, unusual intelligence, and devotion to learning), every child gets an introduction to good literature, and throughout

---

8. Echoing Lucian's "Demonax" (sec. 41).
9. Alongside this passage and obviously applying to several sentences in it, a marginal gloss proclaims, "How much wiser are the Utopians than the ruck of Christians!"

their lives a large part of the people, men and women alike, spend their leisure time in reading.

They study all the branches of learning in their native tongue, which is not deficient in terminology or unpleasant in sound, and adapts itself as well as any to the expression of thought. Just about the same language is spoken throughout that entire area of the world, though elsewhere it is corrupted to various degrees.

Before we came there, the Utopians had never so much as heard about a single one of those philosophers[1] whose names are so celebrated in our part of the world. Yet in music, dialectic, arithmetic, and geometry they have found out just about the same things as our great men of the past. But while they equal the ancients in almost all subjects, they are far from matching the inventions of our modern logicians.[2] In fact they have not discovered even one of those elaborate rules about restrictions, amplifications, and suppositions which our own young men study in the *Little Logicbook*.[3] They are so far from being able to speculate on "second intentions" that not one of them was able to see "man-in-general,"[4] though I pointed straight at him with my finger, and he is, as you well know, bigger than any giant, maybe even a colossus. On the other hand, they have learned to plot expertly the courses of the stars and the movements of the heavenly bodies. They have devised a number of different instruments by which they compute with the greatest exactness the course and position of the sun, the moon, and the other stars that are visible in their area of the sky. As for the conjunctions and oppositions of the planets, and that whole deceitful business of divination by the stars, they have never so much as dreamed of it.[5] From long experience in observation, they are able to forecast rains, winds, and other changes in the weather. But as to the causes of the weather, of the tides in the sea and its saltiness, and the origins and nature of the heavens and the earth, they have various opinions. They agree with our ancient philosophers on some matters, but on others, just as the ancients disagreed with one another, so the Utopians differ from all the ancients and yet reach no consensus among themselves.

In matters of moral philosophy, they carry on the same arguments as we do. They inquire into the nature of the good, distinguishing goods of the body from goods of the mind and external goods.[6] They ask whether the name of "good" may be applied to all three, or applies only to goods of the mind. They discuss virtue and pleasure, but their chief concern is what to think of human happiness, and whether it consists of one thing or of more. On this point, they seem overly inclined to the view of those who think that all or most human happiness consists of pleasure.[7] And what is more surpris-

---

1. As the next sentence indicates, the idea of "philosophy" here is the old, broad one that encompasses learning in general (the sense that survives in the title doctor of philosophy).
2. The Scholastic philosophers, constantly deprecated by humanists.
3. Probably the *Parva logicalia*, a textbook of logic by Peter of Spain, later Pope John XXI (d. 1277).
4. *Man conceived of as a "universal."* "Second intentions": in Scholastic discourse, purely abstract conceptions, derived from "first intentions" (the direct apprehensions of things). The sentence is typical of the way humanists liked to ridicule, in the name of common sense, the Scholastics' abstractions.
5. Marginal gloss: "Yet these astrologers are revered by Christians to this day."
6. This threefold classification of goods is associated especially with Aristotle (*Nicomachean Ethics* 1.8.2, *Politics* 7.1.3–4).
7. That is, the Utopians' primary affinity in moral philosophy is with the hedonistic school founded by Epicurus (341–271 B.C.E.). Compare Vespucci on the Native Americans: "I deem their manner of

ing, they seek support for this comfortable opinion from their religion, which is serious and strict, indeed almost stern and forbidding. For they never discuss happiness without joining to their philosophic rationalism certain principles drawn from religion. Without these religious principles, they think that reason by itself is weak and defective in its efforts to investigate true happiness.

Their religious principles are of this nature: that the soul of man is immortal, and by God's goodness born for happiness; that after this life, rewards are appointed for our virtues and good deeds, punishments for our sins. Though these are indeed religious beliefs, they think that reason leads us to believe and accept them. And they add unhesitatingly that if these beliefs were rejected, no one would be so stupid as not to feel that he should seek pleasure, regardless of right and wrong. His only care would be to keep a lesser pleasure from standing in the way of a greater one, and to avoid pleasures that are inevitably followed by pain.[8] They think you would have to be actually crazy to pursue harsh and painful virtue, give up the pleasures of life, and suffer pain from which you can expect no advantage. For if there is no reward after death, you have no compensation for having passed your entire existence without pleasure, that is, miserably.

To be sure, they believe happiness is found, not in every kind of pleasure, but only in good and honest pleasure. Virtue itself, they say, draws our nature to this kind of pleasure, as to the supreme good. There is an opposed school which declares that virtue is itself happiness.[9]

They define virtue as living according to nature;[1] and God, they say, created us to that end. When an individual obeys the dictates of reason in choosing one thing and avoiding another, he is following nature. Now the first rule of reason is to love and venerate the Divine Majesty to whom we owe our existence and our capacity for happiness. The second rule of nature is to lead a life as free of anxiety and as full of joy as possible, and to help all one's fellow men toward that end. The most hard-faced eulogist of virtue and the grimmest enemy of pleasure, while they invite us to toil and sleepless nights and self-laceration, still admonish us to relieve the poverty and misfortune of others as best we can. It is especially praiseworthy, they tell us, when we provide for our fellow creatures' comfort and welfare. Nothing is more humane (and humanity is the virtue most proper to human beings) than to relieve the misery of others and, by removing all sadness from their lives, restore them to enjoyment, that is, pleasure. Well, if this is the case, why doesn't nature equally invite us to do the same thing for ourselves? Either a joyful life (that is, one of pleasure) is a good thing, or it isn't. If it isn't, then you should not help anyone to it—indeed, you ought to take it away from everyone you can, as being harmful and deadly to them. But if such a life is good, and if we are supposed, indeed obliged, to help others to it, why shouldn't we first of all seek it for ourselves, to whom we owe no less charity

---

life to be Epicurean." Contrary to popular opinion, however, Epicurus himself did not mean, by the pursuit of pleasure, mere undiscriminating sensual indulgence: like the Utopians, he placed primary emphasis on the pleasures of a virtuous, rational life.

8. These rules for choosing among pleasures are attributed to Epicurus (Diogenes Laertius, *Lives of Eminent Philosophers* 10.129).

9. This is the position of the Stoics, who asserted that virtue constitutes happiness whether or not it leads to pleasure.

1. Another Stoic precept.

than to anyone else? When nature prompts you to be kind to your neighbors, she does not mean that you should be cruel and merciless to yourself.[2] Thus they say that nature herself prescribes for us a joyous life, in other words, pleasure, as the goal of our actions; and living according to her prescriptions is to be defined as virtue. But as nature bids mortals to make one another's lives merrier, to the extent that they can, so she warns us constantly not to seek our own advantage in ways that cause misfortune to our fellows. And the reason for this is an excellent one; for no one is placed so far above the rest that he is nature's sole concern: she cherishes alike all those living beings to whom she has granted the same form.

Consequently, the Utopians maintain that one should not only abide by private agreements but also obey all those public laws which control the distribution of vital goods, such as are the very substance of pleasure. Any such laws, provided they have been properly promulgated by a good king, or ratified by a people free of force and fraud, should be observed; and as long as they are observed, to pursue your own interests is prudent; to pursue the public interest as well is pious; but to pursue your own pleasure by depriving others of theirs is unjust. On the other hand, deliberately to decrease one's own pleasure in order to augment that of others is a work of humanity and benevolence which never fails to reward the doer over and above his sacrifice. You may be repaid for your kindness; and in any case you are conscious of having done a good deed. Your mind draws more joy from recalling the affection and good will of those whom you have benefited than your body would have drawn pleasure from the things you gave up. Finally, they believe (as religion easily persuades a well-disposed mind to believe) that God will recompense us, for surrendering a brief and transitory pleasure here, with immense and neverending joy in heaven. And so they conclude, after carefully considering and weighing the matter, that all our actions and the virtues exercised within them look toward pleasure and happiness as their ultimate end.

By pleasure they understand every state or movement of body or mind in which we find delight in accordance with the behests of nature. They are right in adding that the desire must accord with nature. By simply following our senses and right reason[3] we may discover what is pleasant by nature: it is a delight that does not injure others, that does not preclude a greater pleasure, and that is not followed by pain. But a pleasure which is against nature, and which men call "delightful" only by the emptiest of fictions (as if one could change the real nature of things just by changing their names), does not, they hold, really make for happiness; in fact, they say it often precludes happiness. And the reason is that men whose minds are filled with false ideas of pleasure have no room left for true and genuine delight. As a matter of fact, there are a great many things which have no genuine sweetness in them but are for the most part actually bitter, yet which, through the perverse enticements of evil desires, are considered very great pleasures, and even included among the supreme goals of life.

---

2. *Marginal gloss:* "But now some people cultivate pain as if it were the essence of religion, rather than incidental to performance of a pious duty or the result of natural necessity—and thus to be borne, not pursued."

3. The power, thought to have been implanted by God in all humankind, to apprehend truth and moral law; conscience.

Among the devotees of this false pleasure, they include those whom I mentioned before, the people who think themselves finer fellows because they wear finer clothes. These people are twice mistaken: first in thinking their clothes better than anyone else's, and then in thinking themselves better because of their clothes. As far as a garment's usefulness goes, what does it matter if it was woven of fine thread or coarse? Yet they act as if they were set apart by Nature herself, rather than their own fantasies; they strut about, and put on airs. Because they have a fancy suit, they think themselves entitled to honors they would never have expected if they were dressed in homespun, and they grow indignant if someone passes them by without showing special respect.

It is the same kind of absurdity to be pleased by empty, ceremonial honors. What true and natural pleasure can you get from someone's bent knee or bared head? Will the creaks in your own knees be eased thereby, or the madness in your head? The phantom of false pleasure is illustrated by others who run mad with delight over their own blue blood, plume themselves on their nobility, and applaud themselves for all their rich ancestors (the only ancestors that count nowadays), and especially for all their ancient family estates. Even if they don't have the shred of an estate themselves, or if they've squandered every penny of their inheritance, they don't consider themselves a bit less noble.

In the same class the Utopians put those people I described before who are mad for jewelry and gems, and think themselves divinely happy if they find a good specimen, especially of the sort that happens to be fashionable in their country at the time—for stones vary in value from one market to another. The collector will not make an offer for a stone till it's taken out of its gold setting, and even then he will not buy unless the dealer guarantees and gives security that it is a true and genuine stone. What he fears is that his eyes will be deceived by a counterfeit. But if you consider the matter, why should a counterfeit give any less pleasure, when your eyes cannot distinguish it from a real gem? Both should be of equal value to you—as they would be, in fact, to a blind man.[4]

What about those who pile up money not because they want to do anything with the heap, but so they can sit and look at it? Is that true pleasure they experience, or aren't they simply cheated by a show of pleasure? Or what of those with the opposite vice, who hide away gold they will never use and perhaps never even see again? In their anxiety to hold onto it, they actually lose it. For what else happens when you deprive yourself, and perhaps other people too, of a chance to use your gold, by burying it in the ground? And yet when you've hidden your treasure away, you exult over it as if your mind were now free to rejoice. Suppose someone stole it, and you died ten years later, knowing nothing of the theft. During all those ten years, what did it matter whether the money was stolen or not? In either case, it was equally useless to you.

To these false and foolish pleasures they add gambling, which they have heard about, though they've never tried it, as well as hunting and hawking. What pleasure can there be, they wonder, in throwing dice on a table? If

---

4. In *The Praise of Folly*, Erasmus tells a story about More giving his young wife some false gems, which he passed off as being real and highly valuable.

there were any pleasure in the action, wouldn't doing it over and over again quickly make one tired of it? What pleasure can there be in listening to the barking and yelping of dogs—isn't that rather a disgusting noise? Is there any more pleasure felt when a dog chases a hare than when a dog chases a dog? If what you like is fast running, there's plenty of that in both cases; they're just about the same. But if what you really want is slaughter, if you want to see a living creature torn apart under your eyes—you ought to feel nothing but pity when you see the little hare fleeing from the hound, the weak creature tormented by the stronger, the fearful and timid beast brutalized by the savage one, the harmless hare killed by the cruel dog. The Utopians, who regard this whole activity of hunting as unworthy of free men, have assigned it accordingly, to their butchers, who, as I said before, are all slaves.[5] In their eyes, hunting is the lowest thing even butchers can do. In the slaughterhouse, their work is more useful and honest, since there they kill animals only from necessity; but the hunter seeks merely his own pleasure from the killing and mutilating of some poor little creature. Even in beasts, taking such relish in the sight of death reveals, in the Utopians' opinion, a cruel disposition, or else one that has become so through the constant practice of such brutal pleasures.

Common opinion considers these activities, and countless others like them, to be pleasures; but the Utopians say flatly they have nothing at all to do with real pleasure, since there's nothing naturally pleasant about them. They often please the senses, and in this they are like pleasure, but that does not alter their basic nature. The enjoyment doesn't arise from the experience itself, but only from the perverse habits of the mob, as a result of which they mistake the bitter for the sweet, just as pregnant women, whose taste has been turned awry, sometimes think pitch and tallow taste sweeter than honey. A person's taste may be similarly depraved by disease or by custom, but that does not change the nature of pleasure, or of anything else.

They distinguish several different classes of true pleasure, some being pleasures of the mind and others pleasures of the body. Those of the mind are knowledge and the delight which rises from contemplating the truth, also the gratification of looking back on a well-spent life and the unquestioning hope of happiness to come.

Pleasures of the body they also divide into two classes. The first is that which fills the senses with immediate delight. Sometimes this happens when bodily organs that have been weakened by natural heat are restored with food and drink; sometimes it happens when we eliminate some excess in the body, as when we move our bowels, generate children, or relieve an itch somewhere by rubbing or scratching it. Now and then pleasure arises, not from restoring a deficiency or discharging an excess, but from something that excites our senses with a hidden but unmistakable force, and attracts them to itself. Such is the power of music.

The second kind of bodily pleasure they describe as nothing but the calm and harmonious state of the body, its state of health when undisturbed by any disorder. Health itself, when not oppressed by pain, gives pleasure, without any external excitement at all. Even though it appeals less directly to the

---

5. Marginal gloss: "Yet today this is the chosen art of our court-divinities."

senses than the gross gratifications of eating and drinking, many consider this to be the greatest pleasure of all. Most of the Utopians regard it as the foundation and basis of all the pleasures, since by itself alone it can make life peaceful and desirable, whereas without it there is no possibility of any other pleasure. Mere absence of pain, without positive health, they regard as insensibility, not pleasure.

Some have maintained that a stable and tranquil state of health is not really a pleasure, on the grounds that the presence of health cannot be felt except through some external stimulus.[6] The Utopians (who have considered the matter thoroughly) long ago rejected this opinion. On the contrary, they nearly all agree that health is crucial to pleasure. Since pain is inherent in disease, they argue, and pain is the bitter enemy of pleasure, just as disease is the enemy of health, then pleasure must be inherent in quiet good health. You may say pain is not the disease itself, simply an accompanying effect; but they argue that that makes no difference, since the effect is the same either way. For whether health is itself a pleasure or is merely the cause of pleasure (as fire is the cause of heat), the fact remains that those who have stable health must also have pleasure.

When we eat, they say, what happens is that health, which was starting to fade, takes food as its ally in the fight against hunger. While our health gains strength, the simple process of returning vigor gives us pleasure and refreshment. If our health feels delight in the struggle, will it not rejoice when the victory has been won? When at last it is restored to its original strength, which was its aim all through the conflict, will it at once become insensible, and fail to recognize and embrace its own good? The idea that health cannot be felt they consider completely wrong. Every man who's awake, they say, feels that he's in good health—unless he isn't. Is anyone so torpid and dull that he won't admit health is delightfully agreeable to him? And what is delight except pleasure under another name?

Of all the different pleasures, they seek primarily those of the mind, and prize them most highly. The foremost mental pleasure, they believe, arises from the practice of the virtues and the consciousness of a good life. Among the pleasures of the body, they give the first place to health. As for eating and drinking and other delights of that sort, they consider them desirable, but only for the sake of health. They are not pleasant in themselves, but only as ways to withstand the insidious attacks of sickness. A wise man would rather escape sickness altogether than have a good cure for it; he would rather prevent pain than find a palliative for it. And so it would be better not to need this kind of pleasure at all than to be assuaged by it.

Anyone who thinks happiness consists of this sort of pleasure must confess that his ideal life would be one spent in an endless round of hunger, thirst, and itching, followed by eating, drinking, scratching, and rubbing. Who can fail to see that such an existence is not only disgusting but miserable? These pleasures are certainly the lowest of all, as they are the most adulterate— for they never occur except in connection with the pains that are their contraries. Hunger, for example, is linked to the pleasure of eating, and far from equally, since the pain is sharper and lasts longer; it precedes the pleasure,

---

6. This is, especially, the position of Plato: for example, *Republic* 9.583C–585A.

and ends only when the pleasure ends with it. So the Utopians think pleasures of this sort should not be much valued, except insofar as they are necessary to life. Yet they enjoy these pleasures too, and acknowledge gratefully the kindness of Mother Nature, who coaxes her children with allurements and cajolery to do what in any case they must do from necessity. How wretched life would be if the daily diseases of hunger and thirst had to be overcome by bitter potions and drugs, like some other diseases that afflict us less often!

Beauty, strength, and agility, as special and pleasant gifts of nature, they joyfully accept. The pleasures of sound, sight, and smell they also pursue as the special seasonings of life, recognizing that nature intended these delights to be the particular province of man. No other kind of animal admires the shape and loveliness of the universe, or enjoys odors, except in the way of searching for food, or distinguishes harmonious from dissonant sounds. But in all their pleasures, the Utopians observe this rule, that the lesser pleasure must not interfere with the greater, and that no pleasure shall carry pain with it as a consequence. If a pleasure is dishonorable, they think it will inevitably lead to pain.

Moreover, they think it is crazy for a man to despise beauty of form, to impair his own strength, to grind his energy down to lethargy, to exhaust his body with fasts, to ruin his health, and to scorn all other natural delights, unless by so doing he can better serve the welfare of others or the public good. Then indeed he may expect a greater reward from God. But otherwise for a man to inflict pain on himself does no one any good. He gains, perhaps, the empty and shadowy reputation of virtue; and no doubt he hardens himself against fantastic adversities which may never occur. But such a person the Utopians consider absolutely crazy—cruel to himself, as well as most ungrateful to Nature—as if, to avoid being in her debt, he rejects all her gifts.

This is the way they think about virtue and pleasure. Human reason, they believe, can attain to no surer conclusions than these, unless a revelation from heaven should inspire men with holier notions. In all this, I have no time now to consider whether they are right or wrong, and don't feel obliged to do so. I have undertaken only to describe their principles, not to defend them. But of this I am sure, that whatever you think of their ideas, there is not a more excellent people or a happier commonwealth anywhere in the whole world.

In body they are nimble and lively, and stronger than you would expect from their stature, though they're by no means tiny. Their soil is not very fertile, nor their climate of the best, but they protect themselves against the weather by temperate living, and improve their soil by industry, so that nowhere do grain and cattle flourish more plentifully, nowhere are people more vigorous, and liable to fewer diseases. There you can see not only that they do all the things farmers usually do to improve poor soil by hard work and technical knowledge, but you can see a forest which they uprooted with their own hands and moved to another site. They did this not so much for the sake of better growth but to make transport easier, by having wood closer to *the sea, the rivers, or the* cities themselves. For grain is easier than wood to carry by land over a long distance.

[THEIR DELIGHT IN LEARNING]

The people in general are easygoing, cheerful, clever, and like their leisure. When they must, they can stand heavy labor, but otherwise they are not very fond of it. In intellectual pursuits, they are tireless. When they heard from us about the literature and learning of the Greeks (for we thought there was nothing in Latin, except the historians and poets, that they would value), it was wonderful to behold how eagerly they sought to be instructed in Greek. We therefore began to study a little of it with them, at first more to avoid seeming lazy than out of any expectation that they would profit by it. But after a short trial, their diligence convinced us that our efforts would not be wasted. They picked up the forms of the letters so easily, pronounced the language so aptly, memorized it so quickly, and began to recite so accurately that it seemed like a miracle. Most of our pupils were established scholars, of course, picked for their unusual ability and mature minds; and they studied with us, not just of their own free will, but at the command of the senate.[7] Thus in less than three years they had perfect control of the language and could read the best authors fluently, unless the text was corrupt. I have a feeling they picked up Greek more easily because it was somewhat related to their own tongue. Though their language resembles Persian in most respects, I suspect their race descends from the Greeks, because their language retains some vestiges of Greek in the names of cities and in official titles.

Before leaving on the fourth voyage, I placed on board, instead of merchandise, a good-sized packet of books; for I had resolved not to return at all rather than come home soon. Thus they received from me most of Plato's works and more of Aristotle's, as well as Theophrastus's book *On Plants*, though the latter, I'm sorry to say, was somewhat mutilated.[8] During the voyage I carelessly left it lying around, a monkey got hold of it, and from sheer mischief ripped out a few pages here and there and tore them up. Of the grammarians they have only Lascaris, for I did not take Theodorus with me, nor any dictionary except that of Hesychius; and they have Dioscorides.[9] They are very fond of Plutarch's writings, and delighted with the witty persiflage of Lucian.[1] Among the poets they have Aristophanes, Homer, and Euripides, together with Sophocles in the small typeface of the Aldine edition.[2] Of the historians they possess Thucydides and Herodotus, as well as Herodian.[3]

As for medical books, a comrade of mine named Tricius Apinatus brought with him some small treatises by Hippocrates, and the *Microtechne* of

7. Marginal gloss: "But now clods and blockheads are assigned to learning, while the best minds are corrupted by pleasures."
8. Theophrastus, Aristotle's pupil, was studied in the Renaissance not as a quaint curiosity but because his views were still current in botany.
9. Dioscorides (1st century C.E.) wrote a treatise on drugs and herbs that was printed in 1499. The Renaissance scholars Constantine Lascaris and Theodore of Gaza wrote grammars of Greek. The Greek dictionary of Hesychius of Alexandria (5th century C.E.) was published in 1514.
1. The Syrian-born ironist who was admired, translated, and imitated by both More and Erasmus (see p. 86, n. 7). The writings of Plutarch (ca. 46–ca. 120 C.E.) referred to presumably include his *Moral Essays* as well as his *Parallel Lives* of eminent Greeks and Romans.
2. The first printed edition of Sophocles was that of Aldus Manutius in 1502. The house of Aldus, established in Venice toward the end of the 15th century, not only was the first establishment to print Greek texts in Greek type but was responsible for some of the best-designed books in the history of the art.
3. Thucydides and Herodotus (both 5th century B.C.E.) are the preeminent Greek historians. Herodian (ca. 175–250 C.E.) wrote a history of the Roman emperors of the 2nd and 3rd centuries.

VTOPIENSIVM ALPHABETVM. 13

a b c d e f g h i k l m n o p q r s t u x y

TETRASTICHON VERNACVLA VTO-
PIENSIVM LINGVA.

Vtopos ha Boccas peula chama.

polta chamaan.

Bargol he maglomi baccan

soma gymnosophaon.

Agrama gymnosophon labarem

bacha bodamilomin.

Voluala barchin heman la

lauoluola dramme pagloni.

HORVM VERSVVM AD VERBVM HAEC
EST SENTENTIA.

Vtopus me dux ex non insula fecit insulam.
Vna ego terrarum omnium absq; philosophia.
Ciuitatem philosophicam expressi mortalibus.
Libenter impartio mea, non grauatim accipio meliora.

b 3

This sample of the Utopian language, which first appeared in the earliest edition of More's book (1516), reveals affinities with Greek and Latin and has enough internal consistency to suggest that it was worked out with care (evidently by Peter Giles). The stilted Latin quatrain at the end, which purports to be a literal translation, can itself be translated as follows: "Me, once a peninsula, Utopus the king made an island. / Alone among all nations, and without complex abstractions, / I set before men's eyes the philosophical city. / What I give is free; what is better I am not slow to take from others."

Galen.[4] They were delighted to have these books. Even though there's hardly a country in the world that needs doctors less, medicine is nowhere held in greater honor: they consider it one of the finest and most useful parts of philosophy. They think that when, with the help of philosophy, they explore the secrets of nature they are gratifying not only themselves but the author and maker of nature. They suppose that, like other artists, he created this beautiful mechanism of the world to be admired—and by whom, if not by man, who is alone in being able to appreciate so great a thing? Therefore he is bound to prefer a careful observer and sensitive admirer of his work before one who, like a brute beast, looks on the grand spectacle with a stupid and blockish mind.

Once stimulated by learning, the minds of the Utopians are wonderfully quick to seek out those various arts which make life more agreeable. Two inventions, to be sure, they owe to us: the art of printing and the manufacture of paper. At least they owe these arts partly to us, though partly to their own ingenuity. While we were showing them the Aldine editions of various works, we talked about papermaking and how letters are printed, though without going into detail, for none of us had had any practical experience of either skill. But with great sharpness of mind they immediately grasped the basic principles. While previously they had written only on vellum, bark, and papyrus, they now undertook to make paper and to print with type. Their first attempts were not altogether successful, but with practice they soon mastered both arts. They became so proficient that, if they had texts of the Greek authors, they would soon have no lack of volumes; but as they have no more than those I mentioned, they have contented themselves with reprinting each in thousands of copies.

Any sightseer coming to their land who has some special intellectual gift, or who has traveled widely and seen many countries, is sure of a warm welcome, for they love to hear what is happening throughout the world. This is why we were received so kindly. Few merchants, however, go there to trade. What could they import except iron—or else gold and silver, which everyone would rather bring home than send abroad? As for the export trade, the Utopians prefer to do their own transportation, rather than invite strangers to do it. By carrying their own cargos they are able to learn more about foreign countries on all sides, and keep up their skill in navigation.

SLAVES[5]

The only prisoners of war the Utopians enslave are those captured in wars they fight themselves. The children of slaves are not automatically enslaved,[6]

---

4. Hippocrates (5th century B.C.E.) and Galen (2nd century C.E.) were the most influential Greek medical writers. The *Microtechne* is a medieval summary of Galen's ideas. The name Tricius Apinatus (like Hythloday) is a learned joke: in classical Italy, Trica and Apina were extinct towns whose names, taken together, were proverbial for trifling, worthless things.

5. The institution of slavery—with prisoners of war (civilians as well as combatants) as a major source of the people to be enslaved—was ubiquitous in the ancient world, including the Greek and Roman civilizations that Utopia resembles in various ways. In Europe, slavery declined in the Middle Ages, being replaced as a source of labor by feudal serfdom, in which individuals were bound to the land rather than to a particular owner. Chattel slavery, however, revived strongly in the European colonies in the New World: the enslavement of Native Americans began with the earliest settlements, in the 1490s, and enslaved people from Africa were imported from Spain to Hispaniola in the Caribbean in 1502.

6. This fact sharply distinguishes Utopian slavery from both classical and early modern slavery and medieval serfdom.

nor are slaves obtained from foreign countries. Their slaves are either their own citizens, enslaved for some heinous offense, or else foreigners who were condemned to death in their own land. Most are of the latter sort. Sometimes the Utopians buy them at a very modest rate, more often they ask for them, get them for nothing, and bring them home in considerable numbers. Both kinds of slaves are kept constantly at work, and are always fettered. But the Utopians deal with their own people more harshly than with the others, feeling that their crimes are worse and deserve stricter punishment because they had an excellent education and the best of moral training, yet still couldn't be restrained from wrongdoing. A third class of slaves consists of hardworking penniless drudges from other nations who voluntarily choose to become slaves in Utopia. Such people are treated well, almost as well as citizens, except that they are given a little extra work, on the score that they're used to it. If one of them wants to leave, which seldom happens, no obstacles are put in his way, nor is he sent off emptyhanded.

[SUICIDE AND EUTHANASIA]

As I said before, the sick are carefully tended, and nothing is neglected in the way of medicine or diet which might cure them. Everything possible is done to mitigate the pain of those who are suffering from incurable diseases; and visitors do their best to console them by sitting and talking with them. But if the disease is not only incurable but excruciatingly and constantly painful, then the priests and public officials come and urge the invalid not to endure such agony any longer. They remind him that he is now unfit for any of life's duties, a burden to himself and to others; he has really outlived his own death. They tell him he should not let the disease prey on him any longer, but now that life is simply torture, he should not hesitate to die but should rely on hope for something better. Since life has become a mere prison cell, where he is bitterly tormented, he should free himself, or let others free him, from the rack of living. This would be a wise act, they say, since for him death would put an end not to pleasure but to agony. In addition, he would be obeying the advice of the priests, who are the interpreters of God's will; which ensures that it would be a holy and pious act.[7]

Those who have been persuaded by these arguments either starve themselves to death or, having been put to sleep, are freed from life without any sensation of dying. But they never force this step on a man against his will; nor, if he decides against it, do they lessen their care of him. Under these circumstances, when death is advised by the authorities, they consider self-destruction honorable. But the suicide, who takes his own life without the approval of priests and senate, they consider unworthy either of earth or fire, and throw his body, unburied and disgraced, into a bog.

[MARRIAGE AND DIVORCE]

Women do not marry till they are eighteen, nor men till they are twenty-two. Premarital intercourse, if discovered and proved, brings severe punishment

---

7. In ancient Rome, suicide was regarded as an honorable way out of deep personal or political difficulties, but neither suicide nor euthanasia has ever been acceptable in Catholic Christianity. See Hythloday's earlier reference to God's prohibition of suicide.

on both man and woman, and the guilty parties are forbidden to marry during their whole lives, unless the governor by his pardon remits the sentence. In addition both the father and mother of the household where the offense occurred suffer public disgrace for having been remiss in their duty. The reason they punish this offense so severely is that they suppose few people would join in married love—with confinement to a single partner, and all the petty annoyances that married life involves—unless they were strictly restrained from a life of promiscuity.

In choosing marriage partners, they solemnly and seriously follow a custom which seemed to us foolish and absurd in the extreme. Whether she is a widow or a virgin, the woman is shown naked to the suitor by a responsible and respectable matron; and similarly, some respectable man presents the suitor naked to the woman.[8] We laughed at this custom and called it absurd; but they were just as amazed at the folly of all other peoples. When men go to buy a colt, where they are risking only a little money, they are so suspicious that, though the beast is almost bare, they won't close the deal until the saddle and blanket have been taken off, lest there be a hidden sore underneath. Yet in the choice of a mate, which may cause either delight or disgust for the rest of their lives, people are completely careless. They leave all the rest of her body covered up with clothes and estimate the attractiveness of a woman from a mere handsbreadth of her person, the face, which is all they can see. And so they marry, running great risk of bitter discord, if something in either's person should offend the other. Not all people are so wise as to concern themselves solely with character; and even the wise appreciate physical beauty, as a supplement to the virtues of the mind. There's no question but that deformity may lurk under clothing, serious enough to make a man hate his wife when it's too late to be separated from her. If some disfiguring accident occurs after marriage, each person must bear his own fate; but beforehand everyone should be legally protected from deception.

There is extra reason for them to be careful, because in that part of the world they are the only people who practice monogamy. Their marriages are seldom terminated except by death, though they do allow divorce for adultery or for intolerably offensive behavior. A husband or wife who is the aggrieved party in such a divorce is granted permission by the senate to remarry, but the guilty party is considered disreputable and is permanently forbidden to take another mate.[9] They absolutely forbid a husband to put away his wife against her will and without any fault on her part, just because of some bodily misfortune; they think it cruel that a person should be abandoned when most in need of comfort; and they add that old age, since it not only entails disease but is actually a disease itself, needs more than a precarious fidelity.

It happens occasionally that a married couple cannot get along, and have both found other persons with whom they hope to live more harmoniously. After getting the approval of the senate, they may then separate by mutual consent and contract new marriages. But such divorces are allowed only after the senators and their wives have carefully investigated the case. They allow divorce only very reluctantly, because they know that husbands and

---

8. Marginal gloss: "Not very modest, but not so imprudent, either."
9. In Europe, the Catholic Church allowed separation in cases of adultery but did not allow even the aggrieved party to remarry.

wives will find it hard to settle down together if each has in mind that a new marriage is easily available.

They punish adulterers with the strictest form of slavery. If both parties were married, they are both divorced, and the injured parties may marry one another, if they want, or someone else. But if one of the injured parties continues to love such an undeserving spouse, the marriage may go on, providing the innocent person chooses to share in the labor to which the slave is condemned. And sometimes it happens that the repentance of the guilty and the devotion of the innocent party move the governor to pity, so that he restores both to freedom. But a second conviction of adultery is punished by death.

[PUNISHMENTS AND REWARDS; CUSTOMS AND LAWS]

No other crimes carry fixed penalties; the senate sets specific penalties for each particular misdeed, as it is considered atrocious or venial. Husbands chastise their wives, and parents their children, unless the offense is so serious that public punishment is called for. Generally, the gravest crimes are punished by slavery, for they think this deters offenders just as much as getting rid of them by immediate capital punishment, and is more beneficial to the commonwealth. In addition, slaves contribute more by their labor than by their death, and they are permanent and visible reminders that crime does not pay. If the slaves rebel against their condition, then, like savage beasts which neither bars nor chains can tame, they are finally put to death. But if they are patient, they are not left altogether without hope. When subdued by long hardships, if they show by their behavior that they regret the crime more than the punishment, their slavery is lightened or remitted altogether, sometimes by the governor's pardon, sometimes by popular vote.

Attempted seduction is subject to the same penalty as seduction itself. They think that a crime clearly and deliberately attempted is as bad as one committed, and that failure should not confer advantages on a criminal who did all he could to succeed.

They are very fond of fools, and think it contemptible to insult them.[1] There is no prohibition against enjoying their foolishness, and they even regard this as beneficial to the fools. If anyone is so serious and solemn that the foolish behavior and comic patter of a clown do not amuse him, they don't entrust him with the care of such a person, for fear that a man who gets not only no use from a fool but not even any amusement—a fool's only gift—will not treat him kindly.

To mock a person for being deformed or crippled is considered ugly and disfiguring, not to the victim but to the mocker, who stupidly reproaches the cripple for something he cannot help.

They think it a sign of a weak and sluggish character to neglect one's natural beauty, but they consider cosmetics a detestable affectation. From experience they have learned that no physical beauty recommends a wife to her husband so effectually as goodness and respect. Though some men are captured by beauty alone, none are held except by virtue and compliance.

---

1. More's household included a fool, Henry Patenson.

As they deter people from crime by penalties, so they incite them to virtue by public honors. They set up in the marketplace statues of distinguished men who have served their country well, thinking thereby to preserve the memory of their good deeds and to spur on the citizens to emulate the glory of their ancestors.

Any man who campaigns for a public office is disqualified for all of them. They live together harmoniously, and the public officials are never arrogant or unapproachable. Instead, they are called "fathers," and that is the way they behave. Because the officials never extort respect from the people against their will, the people respect them spontaneously, as they should. Not even the governor is distinguished from his fellow citizens by a robe or crown; he is known only by a sheaf of grain he carries, just as the high priest is distinguished by a wax candle borne before him.[2]

They have very few laws, and their training is such that they need no more. The chief fault they find with other nations is that, even with infinite volumes of laws and interpretations, they cannot manage their affairs properly. They think it completely unjust to bind people by a set of laws that are too many to be read and too obscure for anyone to understand. As for lawyers, a class of men whose trade it is to manipulate cases and multiply quibbles, they exclude them entirely.[3] They think it is better for each man to plead his own case, and say the same thing to the judge that he would tell his lawyer. This makes for less ambiguity, and readier access to the truth. A man speaks his mind without tricky instructions from a lawyer, and the judge examines each point carefully, taking pains to protect simple folk against the false accusations of the crafty. It is hard to find this kind of plain dealing in other countries, where they have such a multitude of incomprehensibly intricate laws. But in Utopia everyone is a legal expert. For the laws are very few, as I said, and they consider the most obvious interpretation of any law to be the fairest. As they see things, all laws are promulgated for the single purpose of teaching every man his duty. Subtle interpretations teach very few, since hardly anybody is able to understand them, whereas the more simple and apparent sense of the law is open to everyone. If laws are not clear, they are useless; for simpleminded men (and most men are of this sort, and need to be told where their duty lies), there might as well be no laws at all as laws which can be interpreted only by devious minds after endless disputes. The dull common man cannot understand this legal chicanery, and couldn't even if he studied it his whole life, since he has to earn a living in the meantime.

[FOREIGN RELATIONS]

Some of the Utopians' free and independent neighbors (many of whom were previously liberated by them from tyranny), having learned to admire Utopian virtues, have made a practice of asking the Utopians to supply magistrates for them. Some of these magistrates serve one year, others five. When their service is over, they bring them home with honor and praise, and take back new ones to their country. These peoples seem to have settled on an

---

2. Grain and candle evidently symbolize the special function of each ruler: to ensure prosperity and to provide spiritual vision.

3. Marginal gloss: "The useless crowd of lawyers." More was, of course, one himself.

excellent scheme to safeguard the commonwealth. Since the welfare or ruin of a commonwealth depends on the character of its officials, where could they make a more prudent choice than among Utopians, who cannot be tempted by money? For money is useless to them when they go home, as they soon must, and they can have no partisan or factional feelings, since they are strangers in the city over which they rule. Wherever they take root in men's minds, these two evils, greed and faction, are the destruction of all justice—and justice is the strongest bond of any society. The Utopians call these people who have borrowed magistrates from them their *allies*; others whom they have benefited they call simply *friends*.

While other nations are constantly making treaties, breaking them, and renewing them, the Utopians never make any treaties at all. If nature, they say, doesn't bind man adequately to his fellow man, will an alliance do so? If a man scorns nature herself, is there any reason to think he will care about mere words? They are confirmed in this view by the fact that in that part of the world, treaties and alliances between kings are not generally observed with much good faith.

In Europe, of course, the dignity of treaties is everywhere kept sacred and inviolable, especially in those regions where the Christian religion prevails. This is partly because the kings are all so just and virtuous, partly also because of the reverence and fear that everyone feels toward the popes.[4] Just as the popes themselves never promise anything which they do not most conscientiously perform, so they command all other princes to abide by their promises in every way. If someone declines to do so, they compel him to obey by means of pastoral censure and sharp reproof. The popes rightly declare that it would be particularly disgraceful if people who are specifically called "the faithful" acted in bad faith.

But in that new world, which is as distant from ours in customs and way of life as in the distance the equator puts between us, nobody trusts treaties. The greater the formalities, the more numerous and solemn the oaths, the sooner the treaty will be broken. The rulers will easily find some defect in the wording of it, which often enough they deliberately inserted themselves. No treaty can be made so strong and explicit that a government will not be able to worm out of it, breaking in the process both the treaty and its own word. If such craft, deceit, and fraud were practiced in private contracts, the politicians would raise a great outcry against both parties, calling them sacrilegious and worthy of the gallows. Yet the very same politicians think themselves clever fellows when they give this sort of advice to kings. As a consequence, people are apt to think that justice is a humble, plebeian virtue, far beneath the majesty of kings. Or else they conclude that there are two kinds of justice, one which is only for the common herd, a lowly justice that creeps along the ground, hedged in everywhere and encumbered with chains; and the other, which is the justice of princes, much more free and majestic, so that it can do anything it wants and nothing it doesn't want.

This royal practice of keeping treaties badly there is, I suppose, the reason the Utopians don't make any; doubtless if they lived here in Europe they would change their minds. However, they think it a bad idea to make trea-

---

4. In fact the crowned heads of Europe and the popes alike were ruthless and casual violators of treaties.

ties at all, even if they are faithfully observed. A treaty implies that people who are separated by some natural obstacle as slight as a hill or a brook are joined by no bond of nature; it assumes that they are born rivals and enemies, and are right in aiming to destroy one another except insofar as a treaty restrains them. Moreover, they see that treaties do not really promote friendship; for both parties still retain the right to prey upon one another to whatever extent incautious drafting has left the treaty without sufficient provisions against it. The Utopians think, on the other hand, that no one should be considered an enemy who has done you no harm, that the fellowship of nature is as good as a treaty, and that men are united more firmly by good will than by pacts, by their hearts than by their words.

MILITARY PRACTICES

They despise war as an activity fit only for beasts, yet practiced more by man than by any other creature. Unlike almost every other people in the world, they think nothing so inglorious as the glory won in battle. Yet on certain fixed days, men and women alike carry on vigorous military training, so they will be fit to fight should the need arise. But they go to war only for good reasons: to protect their own land, to protect their friends from an invading army, or to liberate an oppressed people from tyranny and servitude. Out of human sympathy, they not only protect their friends from present danger but sometimes avenge previous injuries; they do this, however, only if they themselves have previously been consulted, have approved the cause, and have demanded restitution in vain. Then and only then they think themselves free to declare war. They take this final step not only when their friends have been plundered but also, and even more fiercely, when their friends' merchants have been subjected to extortion in another country, either on the pretext of laws unjust in themselves or through the perversion of good laws.

This and no other was the cause of the war which the Utopians waged a little before our time on behalf of the Nephelogetes against the Alaopolitans.[5] Under pretext of right, a wrong (as they saw it) had been inflicted on some Nephelogete traders residing among the Alaopolitans. Whatever the rights and wrongs of the quarrel, it developed into a fierce war, into which, apart from the hostile forces of the two parties themselves, the neighboring nations poured their efforts and resources. Some prosperous nations were ruined completely, others badly shaken. One trouble led to another, and in the end the Alaopolitans were crushed and reduced to slavery (since the Utopians weren't involved on their own account) by the Nephelogetes—a people who, before the war, had not been remotely comparable in power to their rivals.

So severely do the Utopians punish wrong done to their friends, even in matters of mere money; but they are not so strict in enforcing their own rights. When they are cheated out of their goods, so long as no bodily harm is done, their anger goes no further than cutting off trade relations with that nation till restitution is made. The reason is not that they care more for their allies' citizens than for their own, but simply this: when the merchants

---

5. "People Born from the Clouds" versus "Citizens of a Country without People."

of their friends are cheated, it is their own property that is lost, but when the Utopians lose something, it comes from the common stock, and is bound to be in plentiful supply at home; otherwise they wouldn't have been exporting it. Hence no one individual even notices the loss. So small an injury, which affects neither the life nor the livelihood of any of their own people, they consider it cruel to avenge by the deaths of many soldiers. On the other hand, if one of their own is maimed or killed anywhere, whether by a government or by a private citizen, they first send envoys to look into the circumstances; then they demand that the guilty persons be surrendered; and if that demand is refused, they are not to be put off, but at once declare war. If the guilty persons are surrendered, their punishment is death or slavery.

The Utopians are not only troubled but ashamed when their forces gain a bloody victory, thinking it folly to pay too high a price even for the best goods. But if they overcome the enemy by skill and cunning, they exult mightily, celebrate a public triumph, and raise a monument as for a hard-won victory. They think they have really acted with manly virtue when they have won a victory such as no animal except man could have won—a victory achieved by strength of understanding. Bears, lions, boars, wolves, dogs, and other wild beasts fight with their bodies, they say; and most of them are superior to us in strength and ferocity; but we outdo them all in shrewdness and rationality.

The only thing they aim at, in going to war, is to secure what would have prevented the declaration of war, if the enemy had conceded it beforehand. Or if they cannot get that, they try to take such bitter revenge on those who have provoked them that they will be afraid ever to do it again. These are their chief aims, which they try to achieve quickly, yet in such a way as to avoid danger rather than to win fame and glory.

As soon as war is declared, therefore, they have their secret agents simultaneously post many placards, each marked with their official seal, in the most conspicuous places throughout the enemy territory. In these proclamations they promise immense rewards to anyone who will kill the enemy's king. They offer smaller but still very substantial sums for killing any of a list of other individuals whom they name. These are the persons whom they regard as most responsible, after the king, for plotting aggression against them. The reward for an assassin is doubled for anyone who succeeds in bringing in one of the proscribed men alive. The same reward, plus a guarantee of personal safety, is offered to any one of the proscribed men who turns against his comrades. As a result, the enemies of the Utopians quickly come to suspect everyone, particularly one another; and the many perils of their situation lead to panic. They know perfectly well that many of them, including their princes, have been betrayed by those in whom they placed complete trust—so effective are bribes as an incitement to crime. Knowing this, the Utopians are lavish in their promises of bounty. Being well aware of the risks their agents must run, they make sure that the payments are in proportion to the peril; thus they not only offer, but actually deliver, enormous sums of gold, as well as large landed estates in very secure locations on the territory of their friends.

Everywhere else in the world, this process of bidding for and buying the *life of* an enemy is condemned as the cruel villainy of a degenerate mind; but the Utopians consider it good policy, both wise and merciful. In the first place, it enables them to win tremendous wars without fighting any actual battles; and in the second place it enables them, by the sacrifice of a few guilty men, to spare the lives of many innocent persons who would have died in battle, some on their side, some on the enemy's. They pity the mass of the enemy's soldiers almost as much as their own citizens, for they know common people do not go to war of their own accord, but are driven to it by the madness of princes.

If assassination does not work, they sow the seeds of dissension in enemy ranks by inciting the prince's brother or some other member of the nobility to scheme for the crown. If internal discord dies down, they try to rouse up neighboring peoples against the enemy by reviving forgotten claims to dominion, of which kings always have an ample supply.

When they promise their resources to help in a war, they send money very freely, but commit their own citizens only sparingly. They hold their own people dear, and value them so highly that they would not willingly exchange one of their citizens for an enemy's prince. Since they keep their gold and silver for the purpose of war alone, they spend it without hesitation; after all, they will continue to live just as well even if they expend the whole sum. Besides the wealth they have at home, they have a vast treasure abroad, since, as I said before, many nations owe them money. So they hire mercenary soldiers from all sides, especially the Zapoletes.[6]

These people live five hundred miles to the east of Utopia, and are rude, rough, and fierce. The forests and mountains where they are bred are the kind of country they like: tough and rugged. They are a hard race, capable of standing heat, cold, and drudgery, unacquainted with any luxuries, careless of what houses they live in or what they wear; they don't till the fields but raise cattle instead. Most of them survive by hunting and stealing. These people are born for battle and are always eager for a fight; they seek one out at every opportunity. Leaving their own country in great numbers, they offer themselves for cheap hire to anyone in need of warriors. The only art they know for earning a living is the art of taking life.

They fight with great courage and incorruptible loyalty for the people who pay them, but they will not bind themselves to serve for any fixed period of time. If someone, even the enemy, offers them more money tomorrow, they will take his side; and day after tomorrow, if a trifle more is offered to bring them back, they'll return to their first employers. Hardly a war is fought in which a good number of them are not engaged on both sides. It happens every day that men who are united by ties of blood and have served together in friendship, but who are now separated into opposing armies, meet in battle. Forgetful of kinship and comradeship alike, they furiously run one another through, driven to mutual destruction for no other reason than that they were hired for paltry pay by opposing princes. They care so much about money that they can easily be induced to change sides for an increase of only a penny a day. They have picked up the habit of avarice, but none of the profit; for what they earn by shedding blood, they quickly squander on debauchery of the most squalid sort.

Because the Utopians give higher pay than anyone else, these people are ready to serve them against any enemy whatever. And the Utopians, who seek

---

6. "Busy sellers." The Zapoletes resemble the Swiss, who produced the best and most feared mercenaries of Europe (a remnant still survives as the Swiss Guard in the Vatican).

out the best possible men for proper uses, hire these, the worst possible men, for improper uses. When the situation requires, they thrust the Zapoletes into the positions of greatest danger by offering them immense rewards. Most of them never come back to collect their pay, but the Utopians faithfully pay off those who do survive, to encourage them to try it again. As for how many Zapoletes get killed, the Utopians never worry about that, for they think they would deserve very well of all mankind if they could exterminate from the face of the earth that entire disgusting and vicious race.

Besides the Zapoletes, they employ as auxiliaries the soldiers of the people for whom they have taken up arms, and then squadrons of their other friends. Last, they add their own citizens, including some man of known bravery to command the entire army. In addition, they appoint two substitutes for him, who hold no rank as long as he is safe. But if the commander is captured or killed, the first of these two substitutes becomes his successor, and in case of a mishap to him, the other. Thus, though the accidents of war cannot be foreseen, they make sure that the whole army will not be disorganized through the loss of their leader.

In each city, soldiers are chosen from those who have volunteered. No one is forced to fight abroad against his will, because they think a man who is naturally fearful will act weakly at best, and may even spread panic among his comrades. But if their own country is invaded, they call everyone to arms, posting the fearful (as long as they are physically fit) on shipboard among braver men, or here and there along fortifications, where there is no place to run away. Thus shame at failing their countrymen, desperation at the immediate presence of the enemy, and the impossibility of flight often combine to overcome their fear, and they make a virtue out of sheer necessity.

Just as no man is forced into a foreign war against his will, so women are allowed to accompany their men on military service if they want to—not only not forbidden, but encouraged and praised for doing so. Each goes with her husband to the front, and stands shoulder to shoulder with him in the line of battle; in addition, they place around a man his children and blood- or marriage-relations, so that those who by nature have most reason to help one another may be closest at hand for mutual aid. It is a matter of great reproach for either partner to come home without the other, or for a son to return after losing a parent. The result is that if the enemy stands his ground, the hand-to-hand fighting is apt to be long and bitter, ending only when everyone is dead.

As I observed, they take every precaution to avoid having to fight in person, so long as they can bring the war to an end with mercenaries. But when they are forced to take part in battle, they are as bold in the struggle as they were prudent in avoiding it while they could. In the first charge they are not fierce, but gradually as the fighting goes on they grow more determined, putting up a steady, stubborn resistance. Their spirit is so strong that they will die rather than yield ground. They are certain that everyone at home will be provided for, and they have no worries about the future of their families (and that sort of worry often daunts the boldest courage); so their spirit is exalted and unconquerable. Their skill in the arts of war gives them extra confidence; also from childhood they have been trained in sound principles of conduct (which their education and the good institutions of their commonwealth reinforce); and that too adds to their courage. They don't hold life so cheap that they throw it away recklessly, nor so dear as to grasp it avidly at the price of shame, when duty bids them give it up.

At the height of the battle, a band of the bravest young men, who have taken a special oath, devote themselves to seeking out the opposing general. They attack him directly, they lay secret traps for him, they hit at him from near and far. A long and continuous supply of fresh men keep up the assault as the exhausted drop out. In the end, they rarely fail to kill or capture him, unless he takes to flight.

When they win a battle, it never ends in a massacre, for they would much rather take prisoners than cut throats. They never pursue fugitives without keeping one line of their army drawn up under the colors. They are so careful of this that if they win the victory, with this last reserve force (supposing the rest of their army has been beaten), they would rather let the enemy army escape than pursue fugitives with their own ranks in disorder. They remember what has happened more than once to themselves: that when the enemy seemed to have the best of the day, had routed the main Utopian force and, exulting in their victory, had scattered to pursue the fugitives, a few Utopians held in reserve and watching their opportunity have suddenly attacked the dispersed and scattered enemy at the very moment when he felt safe and had lowered his guard. Thereby they changed the fortune of the day, snatched certain victory out of the enemy's hands, and, though conquered themselves, conquered their conquerors.

It is not easy to say whether they are more crafty in laying ambushes or more cautious in avoiding those laid for them. Sometimes they seem to be on the point of breaking and running when that is the last thing they have in mind; but when they really are ready to retreat, you would never guess it. If they are outnumbered, or if the terrain is unsuitable, they shift their ground silently by night or slip away from the enemy by some stratagem. Or if they have to withdraw by day, they do so gradually, and in such good order that they are as dangerous to attack then as if they were advancing. They fortify their camps very carefully with a deep, broad ditch all around them, the earth being thrown inward to make a wall; the work is done not by workmen but by the soldiers themselves with their own hands. The whole army pitches in, except for an armed guard posted around the rampart to prevent a surprise attack. With so many hands at work, they complete great fortifications, enclosing wide areas with unbelievable speed.

The armor they wear is strong enough to protect them from blows, but does not prevent easy movement of the body; in fact, it doesn't interfere even with their swimming, and part of their military training consists of swimming in armor. For long-range fighting they use arrows, which they fire with great force and accuracy, and from horseback as well as on foot. At close quarters they use not swords but battle-axes, which because of their sharp edge and great weight are lethal weapons, whether used in slashing or thrusting. They are very skillful in inventing machines of war, but conceal them with the greatest care, since if they were made known before they were needed, they might be more ridiculous than useful. Their first consideration in designing them is to make them easy to move and aim.[7]

---

7. The military devices of the Utopians represent a patchwork of notions from the common knowledge of the day. Their camps are fortified like Roman ones. Their reliance on archery links them with the

When the Utopians make a truce with the enemy, they observe it religiously, and will not break it even if provoked. They do not ravage the enemy's territory or burn his crops; indeed, so far as possible, they avoid any trampling of the fields by men or horses, thinking they may need the grain themselves later on. Unless he is a spy, they injure no unarmed man. When cities are surrendered to them, they keep them intact; even when they have stormed a place, they do not plunder it, but put to death the men who prevented surrender, enslave the other defenders, and do no harm to the civilians. If they find any inhabitants who recommended surrender, they give them a share in the property of the condemned, and present their auxiliaries with the rest; for the Utopians themselves never take any booty.

After a war is ended, they collect the cost of it, not from the allies for whose sake they undertook it, but from the conquered. They take as indemnity not only money, which they set aside to finance future wars, but also landed estates, from which they may enjoy forever a substantial annual income. They now have revenues of this sort in many different countries, acquired little by little in various ways, till it now amounts to over seven hundred thousand ducats a year.[8] As managers of these estates, they send abroad some of their own citizens to serve as collectors of revenue. Though they live on the properties in grand style and conduct themselves like great lords, plenty of income is still left over to be put in the public treasury, unless they choose to give the conquered nation credit. They often do the latter, until they happen to need the money, and even then it's rare for them to call in the entire debt. Some of the estates are given, as I've already described, to those who have risked great dangers on their behalf.

If any prince takes up arms and prepares to invade their land, they immediately attack him in full force outside their own borders. They are most reluctant to wage war on their own soil, and no necessity could ever compel them to admit foreign auxiliaries onto their island.

THE RELIGIONS OF THE UTOPIANS

There are different forms of religion throughout the island, and even in individual cities. Some worship as a god the sun, others the moon, and still others one of the planets. There are some who worship a man of past ages who was conspicuous either for virtue or glory; they consider him not only a god but the supreme god. The vast majority, however, and these by far the wisest, believe nothing of the sort: they believe in a single power, unknown, eternal, infinite, inexplicable, beyond the grasp of the human mind, and diffused throughout the universe, not physically, but in influence. Him they call their parent, and to him alone they attribute the origin, increase, progress, changes, and ends of all things; they do not offer divine honors to any other.

English, whose archers had played key roles in the famous victories over the French at Crécy and Agincourt—though the Utopians' skill in shooting arrows from horseback recalls the ancient Parthians and Scythians. Their "machines" are presumably like Roman dart hurlers, battering rams, and stone throwers, but the emphasis on their portability probably reflects contemporary experience with cannon, which were extremely hard to drag over the muddy roads of the time.

8. Gold coins of this name were minted by several European states. Four ducats of Venice, Burgundy, or Hungary were roughly equivalent to an English pound, and the pound itself was worth several hundred times its value today. The point is that the Utopians' annual income from the estates is huge.

Though the other sects of the Utopians differ from this main group in various particular doctrines, they agree with them in this single head, that there is one supreme power, the maker and ruler of the universe, whom they all call in their native language Mithra.[9] Different people define him differently, and each supposes the object of his worship is that one and only nature to whose divine majesty, by the consensus of all nations, the creation of all things is attributed. But gradually they are coming to forsake this mixture of superstitions, and to unite in that one religion which seems more reasonable than any of the others. And there is no doubt that the other religions would have disappeared long ago, had not various unlucky accidents that befell certain Utopians who were thinking about changing their religion been interpreted, out of fear, as signs of divine anger, not chance, as if the deity who was being abandoned were avenging an insult against himself.

But after they had heard from us the name of Christ, and learned of his teachings, his life, his miracles, and the no less marvelous constancy of the many martyrs whose blood, freely shed, has drawn many nations far and near into the Christian fellowship, you would not believe how eagerly they assented to it, either through the mysterious inspiration of God, or because Christianity seemed very like the religion already prevailing among them. But I think they were also much influenced by the fact that Christ approved a communal way of life for his disciples, and that among the truest communities of Christians the practice still prevails.[1] Whatever the reason, no small number of them chose to join our communion, and received the holy water of baptism. By that time, two of our group had died, and among us four survivors there was, I am sorry to say, no priest; so, though they received the other sacraments, they still lack those which in our religion can be administered only by priests.[2] They do, however, understand what these are, and earnestly desire them. In fact, they dispute vigorously whether a man chosen from among themselves could legitimately assume the functions of a priest without the dispatch of a Christian bishop. Though they seemed on the point of selecting such a person, they had not yet done so when I left.

Those who have not accepted Christianity make no effort to restrain others from it, nor do they criticize new converts to it. While I was there, only one of the Christians was interfered with. As soon as he was baptized, he took upon himself to preach the Christian religion publicly, with more zeal than discretion. We warned him not to do so, but he soon worked himself up to a pitch where he not only set our religion above the rest but condemned all others as profane in themselves, leading their impious and sacrilegious followers to the hell-flames they richly deserved. After he had been going on in this style for a long time, they arrested him. He was tried on a charge, not of despising their religion, but of creating a public disorder, convicted, and sentenced to exile. For it is one of their oldest rules that no man's religion, as such, shall be held against him.

---

9. In ancient Persian religion, Mithra (or Mithras) was the spirit of light.
1. The communist practice of the early Christians is described in Acts 2:44–45 and 4:32–35. Many monastic and ascetic orders still made a practice of abolishing private property for their members.
2. Of the seven Catholic sacraments, only baptism and matrimony can be conferred by laymen. Priests are created by ordination by a bishop (the Utopian priests are elected; see below).

Utopus had heard that before his arrival the inhabitants were continually quarreling over religious matters. In fact, he found it was easy to conquer the country because the different sects were too busy fighting one another to oppose him. As soon as he had gained the victory, therefore, he decreed that everyone could cultivate the religion of his choice, and strenuously proselytize for it too, provided he did so quietly, modestly, rationally, and without bitterness toward others. If persuasion failed, no one was allowed to resort to abuse or violence. Anyone who fights wantonly about religion is punished by exile or enslavement.

Utopus laid down these rules not simply for the sake of peace, which he saw was in danger of being destroyed by constant quarrels and implacable hatreds, but also for the sake of religion itself. In matters of religion, he was not at all quick to dogmatize, because he suspected that God perhaps likes diverse and manifold forms of worship and has therefore deliberately inspired different people with different views. On the other hand, he was quite sure that it was arrogant folly for anyone to enforce conformity with his own beliefs on everyone else by means of threats or violence.[3] He supposed that if one religion is really true and the rest false, the true one will sooner or later emerge and prevail by its own natural strength, provided only that men consider the matter reasonably and moderately. But if they try to decide these matters by fighting and rioting, since the worst men are always the most headstrong, the best and holiest religion in the world will be crowded out by blind superstitions, like grain choked out of a field by thorns and briars. So he left the whole matter open, allowing each individual to choose what he would believe. The only exception he made was a solemn and strict law against any person who should sink so far below the dignity of human nature as to think that the soul perishes with the body, or that the universe is ruled by mere chance rather than divine providence.

Thus the Utopians all believe that after this life vices are to be punished and virtue rewarded; and they consider that anyone who denies this proposition is not even one of the human race, since he has degraded the sublimity of his own soul to the base level of a beast's wretched body. Still less will they count him as one of their citizens, since he would openly despise all the laws and customs of society, if not prevented by fear. Who can doubt that a man who has nothing to fear but the law, and no hope of life beyond the grave, will do anything he can to evade his country's laws by craft or break them by violence, in order to gratify his own private greed? Therefore a person who holds such views is offered no honors, entrusted with no offices, and given no public responsibility; he is universally regarded as low and torpid. Yet they do not afflict him with punishments, because they are persuaded that no one can choose to believe by a mere act of the will. They do not compel him by threats to dissemble his views, nor do they tolerate in the matter any deceit or lying, which they detest as next door to deliberate

---

3. This was not the attitude More took a decade after *Utopia*, when, the Reformation schism having begun, he was involved in the prosecution of Protestant heretics, sometimes to the death. In the *Dialogue Concerning Heresies* (1529), he wrote that "if it were now doubtful and ambiguous whether the church of Christ were in the right rule of doctrine or not, then were it very necessary to give them all good audience that could and would anything dispute on either party for it or against it, to the end that if we were now in a wrong way, we might leave it and walk in some better." Utopia was in this hypothetical situation; England, in More's view, was not.

malice. The man may not argue with the common people in behalf of his opinion; but in the presence of the priests and other important persons, in private, they not only permit but encourage it. For they are confident that in the end his madness will yield to reason.

There are some others, in fact no small number of them, who err in the opposite direction, in supposing that animals too have immortal souls,[4] though not comparable to ours in excellence, nor destined to equal felicity. These people are not thought to be evil, their opinion is not thought to be wholly unreasonable, and so they are not interfered with.

Almost all the Utopians are absolutely convinced that human bliss after death will be enormous; thus they lament every individual's sickness, but mourn over a death only if the person was torn from life anxiously and unwillingly. Such behavior they take to be a very bad sign, as if the soul, despairing and conscious of guilt, dreaded death through a secret premonition of punishments to come. Besides, they suppose God can hardly be well pleased with the coming of one who, when he is summoned, does not come gladly but is dragged off reluctantly and against his will. Such a death fills the onlookers with horror, and they carry the corpse out to burial in melancholy silence. There, after begging God to have mercy on his spirit and to pardon his infirmities, they commit his body to the earth. But when someone dies blithely and full of good hope, they do not mourn for him but carry the body cheerfully away, singing and commending the dead man's soul to God. They cremate him in a spirit more of reverence than of grief, and erect a column on which the dead man's honors are inscribed. After they have returned home, they talk of his character and deeds, and no part of his life is mentioned more frequently or more gladly than his joyful death.

They think that recollecting the dead person's goodness helps the living to behave virtuously and is also the most acceptable form of honor to the dead. For they think that dead people are actually present among us, and hear what we say about them, though through the dullness of human sight they are invisible to our eyes. Given their state of bliss, the dead must be able to travel freely where they please, and it would be unkind of them to cast off every desire of revisiting their friends, to whom they had been bound by mutual affection and charity during their lives. Like all other good things, they think that after death charity is increased rather than decreased in good men; and thus they believe the dead come frequently among the living, to observe their words and actions. Hence they go about their business the more confidently because of their trust in such protectors; and the belief that their forefathers are physically present keeps them from any secret dishonorable deed.

Fortune-telling and other vain forms of superstitious divination, such as other peoples take very seriously, they have no part of and consider ridiculous. But they venerate miracles which occur without the help of nature, considering them direct and visible manifestations of the divine power. Indeed, they report that miracles have frequently occurred in their country. Sometimes in great and dangerous crises they pray publicly for a miracle, which they then anticipate with great confidence, and obtain.

---

4. These Utopians resemble the ancient Pythagoreans, who, as a facet of their doctrine of the transmigration of souls, conceded them to animals.

They think that the contemplation of nature, and the sense of reverence arising from it, are acts of worship to God. There are some people, however, and not just a few of them, who from religious motives reject learning and pursue no studies; but none of them is the least bit idle. Constant dedication to the offices of charity, these people think, will increase their chances of happiness after death; and so they are always busy in the service of others. Some tend the sick; others repair roads, clean ditches, rebuild bridges, dig turf, sand, or stones; still others fell trees and cut them up, and transport wood, grain, or other commodities into the cities by wagon. They work for private citizens as well as for the public, and work even harder than slaves. They undertake with cheery good will any task that is so rough, hard, and dirty that most people refuse to tackle it because of the toil, boredom, and frustration involved. While constantly engaged in heavy labor themselves, they secure leisure for others, and yet they claim no credit for it. They do not criticize the way other people live, nor do they boast of their own doings. The more they put themselves in the position of slaves, the more highly they are honored by everyone.

These people are of two sects. The first are celibates who abstain not only from sex but also from eating meat, and some of them from any sort of animal food whatever. They reject all the pleasures of this life as harmful, and look forward only to the joys of the life to come, which they hope to deserve by hard labor and all-night vigils. As they hope to attain it soon, they are cheerful and active in the here and now. The other kind are just as fond of hard work, but prefer to marry. They don't despise the comforts of marriage, but think that, as their duty to nature requires work, so their duty to their country requires them to beget children. They avoid no pleasure unless it interferes with their labor, and gladly eat meat, precisely because they think it makes them stronger for any sort of heavy work. The Utopians regard the second sort as more sensible, but the first sort as holier. If they claimed to prefer celibacy to marriage, and a hard life to a comfortable one, on grounds of reason alone, the Utopians would think them absurd. But since these men claim to be motivated by religion, the Utopians respect and revere them. There is no subject on which they are warier of jumping to conclusions than in this matter of religion. These then are the men whom in their own language they call Buthrescas, a term which may be translated as "the especially religious."

Their priests are of great holiness, and therefore very few. In each city, there are no more than thirteen, one for each church. In case of war, seven of them go out with the army, and seven substitutes are appointed to fill their places for the time being. When the regular priests come back, the substitutes return to their former posts—that is, they serve as assistants to the high priest, until one of the regular thirteen dies, and then one of them succeeds to his position. The high priest is, of course, in authority over all the others. Priests are elected, just like all other officials, by secret popular vote, in order to avoid partisan feeling. After election they are ordained by the college of priests.

They preside over divine worship, attend to religious matters, and act as *censors of public* morality. For a man to be summoned before them and scolded for not living an honorable life is considered a great disgrace. As the duty of the priests is simply to counsel and advise, so correcting and punishing offenders is the duty of the governor and the other officials, though the priests do exclude from divine service persons whom they find to be extraordinarily wicked. Hardly any punishment is more dreaded than this; the excommunicate incurs great disgrace, and is tortured by the fear of damnation. Not even his body is safe for long, for unless he quickly convinces the priests of his repentance he will be seized and punished by the senate for impiety.

The priests are entrusted with teaching the children and young people.[5] Instruction in morality and virtue is considered just as important as the accumulation of learning. From the very first they try to instill in the pupils' minds, while they are still young and tender, principles which will be useful to preserve the commonwealth. What is planted in the minds of children lives on in the minds of adults, and is of great value in strengthening the commonwealth: the decline of society can always be traced to vices which arise from wrong attitudes.

Women are not debarred from the priesthood, but only a widow of advanced years is ever chosen, and it doesn't happen often. The wives of the male priests are the very finest women in the whole country.

No official in Utopia is more honored than the priest. Even if one of them commits a crime, he is not brought into a court of law, but left to God and his own conscience. They think it is wrong to lay human hands on a man, however guilty, who has been specially consecrated to God as a holy offering, so to speak. This custom is the easier for them to observe because their priests are very few and very carefully chosen. Besides, it rarely happens that a man selected for his goodness and raised to high dignities wholly because of his moral character will fall into corruption and vice. And even if such a thing should happen, human nature being as changeable as it is, no great harm is to be feared, because the priests are so few and have no power beyond that which derives from their good reputation. In fact, the reason for having so few priests is to prevent the order, which the Utopians now esteem so highly, from being cheapened by numbers.[6] Besides, they think it would be hard to find many men qualified for a dignity for which merely ordinary virtues are not sufficient.

Their priests are esteemed no less highly abroad than at home, which can be seen from the following fact: Whenever their armies join in battle, the Utopian priests are to be found, a little removed from the fray but not far, wearing their sacred vestments and down on their knees. With hands raised to heaven, they pray first of all for peace, and then for victory to their own side, but without much bloodshed on either hand.[7] Should their side be victorious, they rush among the combatants and restrain the rage of their own men against the enemy. If any of the enemy see these priests and call to them, it is enough to save their lives; to touch the flowing robes of a priest will save all their property from confiscation. This custom has brought them such veneration among all peoples, and given them such genuine authority, that they have saved the Utopians from the rage of the enemy as often as

---

5. Presumably the priests only *supervise* the teaching: there are only thirteen of them per city, whereas each city is home to thousands of children.

6. Marginal gloss: "But what a crowd of them we have!"

7. Marginal gloss: "O priests far holier than our own!"

they have protected the enemy from Utopians. Instances of this are well known. Sometimes when the Utopian line has buckled, when the field was lost, and the enemy was rushing in to kill and plunder, the priests have intervened to stop the carnage and separate the armies, and an equitable peace has been concluded. There was never anywhere a tribe so fierce, cruel, and barbarous as not to hold their persons sacrosanct and inviolable.

The Utopians celebrate the first and last days of every month, and likewise of each year, as feast days. They divide the year into months which they measure by the orbit of the moon, just as they measure the year itself by the course of the sun. In their language, the first days are known as the Cynemerns and the last days as the Trapemerns, which is to say "First-feasts" and "Last-feasts."[8] Their churches are beautifully constructed, finely adorned, and large enough to hold a great many people. This is a necessity, since churches are so few. Their interiors are all rather dark, not from architectural ignorance but from deliberate policy; for the priests think that in bright light the congregation's thoughts will go wandering, whereas a dim light tends to concentrate the mind and encourage devotion.

Though there are various religions in Utopia, all of them, even the most diverse, agree in the main point, which is worship of the divine nature; they are like travelers going to one destination by different roads. So nothing is seen or heard in the churches that does not square with all the creeds. If any sect has a special rite of its own, that is celebrated in a private house; the public service is ordered by a ritual which in no way derogates from any of the private services. Therefore in the churches no image of the gods is to be seen, so that each person may be free to form his own image of God according to his own religion, in any shape he pleases. They do not invoke God by any name except Mithra. Whatever the nature of the divine majesty may be, they all agree to refer to it by that single word, and their prayers are so phrased as to accommodate the beliefs of all the different sects.

On the evening of the "Last-feast" they meet in their churches, and while still fasting they thank God for their prosperity during that month or year which is just ending. Next day, which is "First-feast," they all flock to the churches in the morning, to pray for prosperity and happiness in the month or year which is just beginning. On the day of "Last-feast," in the home before they go to church, wives kneel before their husbands and children before their parents, to confess their various sins of commission or of negligence and beg forgiveness for their offenses. Thus if any cloud of anger or resentment has arisen in the family, it is dispersed, and they can attend divine services with clear and untroubled minds—for they consider it sacrilege to worship with a rankling conscience. If they are conscious of hatred or anger toward anyone, they do not take part in divine services till they have been reconciled and have cleansed their hearts, for fear of some swift and terrible punishment.

As they enter the church, they separate, men going to the right side and women to the left.[9] Then they take their seats so that the males of each household are placed in front of the head of that household, while the women-

---

8. The Greek coinage *Trapemerns* actually means "turning-days"; *Cynemerns* means "dog-days" (or perhaps "starting-days").

9. Separation of the sexes in church had been customary since the early Christian centuries.

folk are directly in front of the mother of the family. In this way they ensure that everyone's behavior in public is supervised by the same person whose authority and discipline direct him at home. They take great care that the young are everywhere placed in the company of their elders. For if children were trusted to the care of other children, they might spend in childish foolery the time they should devote to developing a religious fear of the gods, which is the greatest and almost the only incitement to virtue.

They do not slaughter animals in their sacrifices, and do not think that a merciful God, who gave life to all creatures precisely so that they might live, will be gratified with the shedding of blood. They burn incense, scatter perfumes, and display a great number of candles—not that they think these practices profit the divine nature in any way, any more than human prayers do; but they like this harmless kind of worship. They feel that sweet smells, lights, and other such rituals elevate the mind and lift it with a livelier devotion toward the adoration of God.

When they go to church, the people all wear white. The priest wears robes of various colors, wonderful for their workmanship and decoration, though not of materials as costly as one would suppose. The robes have no gold embroidery nor any precious stones, but are decorated with the feathers of different birds so skillfully woven together that the value of the handiwork far exceeds the cost of the most precious materials.[1] Also, certain symbolic mysteries are hidden in the patterning of the feathers on the robes, the meaning of which is carefully handed down among the priests. These messages serve to remind them of God's benefits toward them, and consequently of the devotion they owe to God, as well as of their duty to one another.

As the priest in his robes appears from the vestibule, the people all fall to the ground in reverence. The stillness is so complete that the scene strikes one with awe, as if a divinity were actually present. After remaining in this posture for some time, they rise at a signal from the priest. Then they sing hymns to the accompaniment of musical instruments, most of them quite different in shape from those in our part of the world. Many of them produce sweeter tones than ours, but others are not even comparable. In one respect, however, they are beyond doubt far ahead of us, because all their music, both vocal and instrumental, renders and expresses natural feelings and perfectly matches the sound to the subject. Whether the words of the hymn are supplicatory, cheerful, troubled, mournful, or angry, the music represents the meaning through the contour of the melody so admirably that it penetrates and inspires the minds of the ardent hearers. Finally, the priest and the people together recite certain fixed forms of prayer, so composed that what they all repeat in unison each individual can apply to himself.

In these prayers, the worshipers acknowledge God to be the creator and ruler of the universe and the author of all good things. They thank God for benefits received, and particularly for the divine favor which placed them in the happiest of commonwealths and inspired them with religious ideas which they hope are the truest. If they are wrong in this, and if there is some sort of society or religion more acceptable to God, they pray that he will, in his goodness, reveal it to them, for they are ready to follow wherever he

---

1. Perhaps related to Vespucci's observation that the Native Americans' wealth "consists of feathers of many-hued birds . . . and of many other things to which we attach no value."

leads. But if their form of society is the best and their religion the truest, then they pray that God will keep them steadfast, and bring other mortals to the same way of life and the same religious faith—unless, indeed, there is something in this variety of religions which delights his inscrutable will.

Then they pray that after an easy death God will receive each of them to himself, how soon or how late it is not for them to say. But if God's divine majesty so please, they ask to be brought to him soon, even by the hardest possible death, rather than be kept away from him longer, even by the most fortunate of earthly lives. When this prayer has been said, they prostrate themselves on the ground again; then after a little while they rise and go to lunch. The rest of the day they pass in games and military training.

Now I have described to you as accurately as I could the structure of that commonwealth which I consider not only the best but indeed the only one that can rightfully claim that name. In other places men talk very liberally of the commonwealth, but what they mean is simply their own wealth; in Utopia, where there is no private business, everyone zealously pursues the public business. And in both places people are right to act as they do. For among us, even though the commonwealth may flourish, there are very few who do not know that unless they make separate provision for themselves, they may perfectly well die of hunger. Bitter necessity, then, forces them to think that they must look out for themselves rather than for others, that is, for the people. But in Utopia, where everything belongs to everybody, no one need fear that, so long as the public warehouses are filled, anyone will ever lack for anything he needs. For the distribution of goods is not niggardly; in Utopia no one is poor, there are no beggars, and though no one owns anything, everyone is rich.

For what can be greater riches than to live joyfully and peacefully, free from all anxieties, and without worries about making a living? No man is bothered by his wife's querulous entreaties about money, no man fears poverty for his son, or struggles to scrape up a dowry for his daughter. Everyone can feel secure of his own livelihood and happiness, and of his whole family's as well: wife, sons, grandsons, great-grandsons, great-great-grandsons, and that whole long line of descendants that gentlefolk are so fond of contemplating. Indeed, even those who once worked but can no longer do so are cared for just as well as those who are still working.

Now here I'd like to see anyone try to compare this equity of the Utopians with the so-called justice that prevails among other peoples—among whom let me perish if I can discover the slightest scrap of justice or fairness. What kind of justice is it when a nobleman or a goldsmith or a moneylender, or someone else who makes his living by doing either nothing at all or something completely useless to the commonwealth, gets to live a life of luxury and grandeur, while in the meantime a laborer, a carter, a carpenter, or a farmer works so hard and so constantly that even a beast of burden could scarcely endure it? Although this work of theirs is so necessary that no commonwealth could survive a year without it, they earn so meager a living and lead such miserable lives that beasts of burden would really seem to be better off. Beasts do not have to work every minute, and their food is not much worse; in fact they like it better. And besides, they do not have to worry about their future. But workingmen not only have to sweat and suffer without present reward, but agonize over the prospect of a penniless old age. Their daily wage is inadequate even for their present needs, so there is no possible chance of their saving toward the future.

Now isn't this an unjust and ungrateful commonwealth? It lavishes rich rewards on so-called gentry, goldsmiths, and the rest of that crew, who don't work at all or are mere parasites, purveyors of empty pleasures. And yet it makes no provision whatever for the welfare of farmers and colliers, laborers, carters, and carpenters, without whom the commonwealth would simply cease to exist. After society has taken the labor of their best years, when they are worn out by age and sickness and utter destitution, then the thankless commonwealth, forgetting all their sleepless nights and great services, throws them out to die a miserable death. What is worse, the rich constantly try to grind out of the poor part of their meager wages, not only by private swindling but by public laws. Before, it appeared to be unjust that people who deserve most from the commonwealth should receive least; but now, by promulgating law, they have palmed injustice off as "legal." When I run over in my mind the various commonwealths flourishing today, so help me God, I can see in them nothing but a conspiracy of the rich, who are fattening up their own interests under the name and title of the commonwealth.[2] They invent ways and means to hang onto whatever they have acquired by sharp practice, and then they scheme to oppress the poor by buying up their toil and labor as cheaply as possible. These devices become law as soon as the rich, speaking for the commonwealth—which, of course, includes the poor as well—say they must be observed.

And yet, when these insatiably greedy and evil men have divided among themselves all the goods which would have sufficed for the entire people, how far they remain from the happiness of the Utopian republic, which has abolished not only money but with it greed! What a mass of trouble was cut away by that one step! What a multitude of crimes was pulled up by the roots! Everyone knows that if money were abolished, fraud, theft, robbery, quarrels, brawls, altercations, seditions, murders, treasons, poisonings, and a whole set of crimes which are avenged but not prevented by the hangman would at once die out. If money disappeared, so would fear, anxiety, worry, toil, and sleepless nights. Even poverty, the one condition which seems more than anything else to need money for its relief, would die away if money were entirely abolished.

Consider, if you will, this example. Take a barren year of failed harvests, when many thousands of people have been carried off by famine. If at the end of the scarcity the barns of the rich were searched, I dare say positively that enough grain would be found in them to have kept all those who died of starvation and disease from even realizing that a shortage ever existed—if only it had been divided among them. So easily might people get the necessities of life if that cursed money, that marvelous invention which is supposed to provide access to them, were not in fact the only barrier to our getting what we need to live. Even the rich, I'm sure, understand this. They must

---

2. Marginal gloss: "Reader, note well!" In the text at this point, More may be alluding to the judgment of Saint Augustine in *The City of God* 4.4: "Take away justice, and what are kingdoms but great robber bands?" As a young man, More had given a series of public lectures on Augustine's book.

know that it's better to have enough of what we really need than an abundance of superfluities, much better to escape from our many present troubles than to be burdened with great masses of wealth. And in fact I have no doubt that every man's perception of where his true interest lies, along with the authority of Christ our Savior (whose wisdom could not fail to recognize the best, and whose goodness would not fail to counsel it), would long ago have brought the whole world to adopt Utopian laws, if it were not for one single monster, the prime plague and begetter of all others—I mean Pride.

Pride measures her advantages not by what she has but by what others lack. Pride would not condescend even to be made a goddess, if there were no wretches for her to sneer at and domineer over. Her good fortune is dazzling only by contrast with the miseries of others, her riches are valuable only as they torment and tantalize the poverty of others. Pride is a serpent from hell that twines itself around the hearts of men; and it acts like a suckfish[3] in holding them back from choosing a better way of life.

Pride is too deeply fixed in human nature to be easily plucked out. So I am glad that the Utopians at least have been lucky enough to achieve this commonwealth, which I wish all mankind would imitate. The institutions they have adopted have made their community most happy, and, as far as anyone can tell, capable of lasting forever. Now that they have rooted up the seeds of ambition and faction at home, along with most other vices, they are in no danger from internal strife, which alone has been the ruin of many cities that seemed secure. As long as they preserve harmony at home, and keep their institutions healthy, the Utopians can never be overcome or even shaken by all the envious princes of neighboring countries, who have often attempted their ruin, but always in vain.

When Raphael had finished his story, I was left thinking that not a few of the customs and laws he had described as existing among the Utopians were quite absurd. These included their methods of waging war, their religious practices, as well as other customs of theirs, but my chief objection was to the basis of their whole system, that is, their communal living and their moneyless economy. This one thing alone takes away all the nobility, magnificence, splendor, and majesty which (in the popular view) are the true ornaments and glory of any commonwealth. But I saw Raphael was tired with talking, and I was not sure he could take contradiction in these matters, particularly when I remembered what he had said about certain people who were afraid they might not appear wise unless they found out something to criticize in the ideas of others. So with praise for the Utopian way of life and his account of it, I took him by the hand and led him in to supper. But first I said that we would find some other time for thinking of these matters more deeply, and for talking them over in more detail. And I still hope such an opportunity will present itself someday.

Meanwhile, though he is a man of unquestionable learning, and highly experienced in the ways of the world, I cannot agree with everything he

---

3. A fish (the remora) with a suction plate atop its head, by which it attaches itself to the underbelly of larger fishes or the hulls of ships. Impressed by the tenacity of its grip, the ancients fabled that it could stop ships in their courses.

said. Yet I freely confess there are very many things in the Utopian commonwealth that in our own societies I would wish rather than expect to see.

1515–16   1516

Thomas More to His Friend Peter Giles, Warmest Greetings[1]

My dear Peter, I was absolutely delighted with the judgment of that very sharp fellow you recall, who posed this dilemma about my *Utopia*: if the story is put forward as fact, he said, then I see a number of absurdities in it; but if it's fiction, then it seems to me that in various respects More's usual good judgment is at fault. I suspect this fellow of being learned, and I see that he's a friend; but whoever he is, I'm much obliged to him. By this frank opinion of his, he has pleased me more than anyone else since the book was published.

For in the first place, either out of fondness for me or for the work itself, he seems to have borne up under the burden of reading the book all the way through—and that not perfunctorily or hastily, the way priests read the divine office—those, at least, who read it at all.[2] No, he read slowly and attentively, noting all the particular points. Then, having singled out certain matters for criticism, and not very many, as a matter of fact, he gives careful and considered approval to the rest. And finally, in the very expressions he uses to criticize me, he implies higher praises than some of those who have put all their energies into compliment. It's easy to see what a high opinion he has of me, when he expresses disappointment over reading something imperfect or inexact—whereas I don't expect, in treating so many different matters, to be able to say more than a few things which aren't totally ridiculous.

Still, I'd like to be just as frank with him as he was with me; and, in fact, I don't see why he should think himself so acute (so "sharp-sighted," as the Greeks would say) just because he's discovered some absurdities in the institutions of Utopia, or caught me putting forth some half-baked ideas about the constitution of a republic. Aren't there any absurdities elsewhere in the world? And did any one of the philosophers who've offered a pattern of a society, a ruler, or even a private household set down everything so well that nothing ought to be changed? Actually, if it weren't for the great respect I retain for certain highly distinguished names, I could easily produce from each of them a number of notions which I can hardly doubt would be universally condemned as absurd.

But when he wonders whether *Utopia* is fact or fiction, then I find *his* judgment, in turn, sorely at fault. I do not deny that if I'd decided to write about a commonwealth, and a tale of this sort had occurred to me, I might have spread a little fiction, like so much honey, over the truth, to make it more acceptable. But I would certainly have tempered the fiction a little, so that, while it deceived the common folk, I gave hints to the more learned

---

1. This second letter of More to Giles appeared only in the second edition of *Utopia* (Paris, 1517), where it immediately follows Book II. The letter praises a supposedly perspicacious critique of *Utopia* by a "very sharp fellow," whose identity is unknown—if indeed More didn't simply invent him.

2. Priests read the "divine office"—the daily round of prescribed prayers to be recited at set hours—with varying degrees of enthusiasm, according to More.

which would enable them to see what I was about. So, if I'd done nothing but give special names to the governor, the river, the city, and the island, which hinted to the learned that the island was nowhere, the city a phantom, the river waterless, and that the governor had no people,[3] that would not have been hard to do, and would have been far more clever than what I actually did. Unless I had a historian's devotion to fact, I am not so stupid as to have used those barbarous and senseless names of Utopia, Anyder, Amaurot, and Ademus.

Still, my dear Giles, I see some people are so suspicious that what we simple-minded and credulous fellows have written down of Hythloday's account can hardly find any credence at all with these circumspect and sagacious persons. I'm afraid my personal reputation, as well as my authority as a historian, may be threatened by their skepticism; so it's a good thing that I can defend myself by saying, as Terence's Mysis says about Glycerium's boy, to confirm his legitimacy, "Praise be to God there were some free women present at his birth."[4] And so it was a good thing for me that Raphael told his story not just to you and me, but to a great many perfectly respectable and serious-minded men. Whether he told them more things, and more important things, I don't know; but I'm sure he told them no fewer and no less important things than he told us.

Well, if these doubters won't believe such witnesses, let them consult Hythloday himself, for he is still alive. I heard only recently from some travelers coming out of Portugal that on the first of last March he was as healthy and vigorous a man as he ever was. Let them get the truth from him—dig it out of him with questions, if they want. I only want them to understand that I'm responsible for my own work, and my own work alone, not for anyone else's credibility.

Farewell, my dearest Peter, to you, your charming wife, and your clever little girl—to all, my wife sends her very best wishes.

1517

3. This is of course precisely what the names do mean.
4. *The Lady of Andros*, lines 770–71.

SIR THOMAS WYATT THE ELDER
1503–1542

Thomas Wyatt made his career in the shifting, dangerous currents of Renaissance courts, whose power struggles, sexual intrigues, and sophisticated tastes shaped his remarkable achievements as a poet. Educated at St. John's College, Cambridge, Wyatt entered the service of Henry VIII, becoming clerk of the king's jewels, a member of diplomatic missions to France and the Low Countries, and, in 1537–39, ambassador to Spain at the court of the Holy Roman Emperor, Charles V.

The years he spent abroad as a diplomat had a significant impact on his writing, imbuing it with the spirit of Continental Renaissance poetry. Diplomacy, with its veiled threats, rhetorical manipulation, and cynical role-playing, may have had a more indirect impact as well, reinforcing the lessons in self-presentation and self-concealment that Wyatt would have received at the English court.

Life in the orbit of the ruthless, unpredictable Henry VIII was competitive and risky. When, in the late 1530s, Wyatt wrote to his son of the "thousand dangers and hazards, enmities, hatreds, prisonments, despites [insults], and indignations" he had faced, he was not exaggerating. He probably came closest to the executioner's ax when in 1536 he was imprisoned in the Tower of London along with several others accused of having committed adultery with the queen, Anne Boleyn. As his poem "Who List His Wealth and Ease Retain" suggests, Wyatt may have watched from his cell the execution of the queen and her alleged lovers; but he himself was spared, as he was spared a few years later, when he was again imprisoned in the Tower, on charges of high treason brought by his enemies at court. His death, at the age of thirty-nine, came from a fever.

It is not surprising, given his career, that many of Wyatt's poems, including his satires and his psalm translations, express an intense longing for "steadfastness" and an escape from the corruption, anxiety, and duplicity of the court. The praise, in his verse epistle to John Poins, of a quiet retired life in the country and the harsh condemnation of courtly hypocrisy derive from his own experience. But the eloquent celebration of simplicity and truthfulness can itself be a cunning strategy. Wyatt was a master of the game of poetic self-display. Again and again he represents himself as a plain-speaking and steadfast man, betrayed by the "doubleness" of a fickle mistress or the instability of fortune. At this distance it is impossible to know how much this account corresponds to reality, but we can admire, as Wyatt's contemporaries did, the rhetorical deftness of the performance.

In a move with momentous consequences for English poetry, Wyatt introduced into English the sonnet, a fourteen-line poem in iambic pentameter with a complex, intertwining rhyme scheme and the development of one or more sustained metaphors or "conceits." For the most part, he took his subject matter from the sonnets of Francesco Petrarca (anglicized as "Petrarch"; 1304–1374), an Italian poet who, over twenty years, wrote obsessive poems about his love for the unattainable "Laura." But while Petrarch's sonnets consist of an "octave," rhyming *abba abba*, followed, after a turn (*volta*) in the sense, by a "sestet" with various rhyme schemes (such as *cd cd cd* and *cde cde*), Wyatt's most common sestet scheme is *cddc ee*. He began the process of changing the Petrarchan sonnet into what was to become the characteristic "English" structure for the sonnet: three quatrains and a closing couplet.

In his freest translations of Petrarchan sonnets, such as "Whoso List to Hunt," Wyatt tends to turn the idealizing of the woman into disillusionment and complaint. For the lover in Petrarch's poems, love is an ongoing, transcendent experience, extending beyond the boundaries of life itself; for the lover in Wyatt's poems, it is all too transient and embittering. The tone of bitterness carries over to many poems less closely linked to Italian and French models, poems with short stanzas and refrains that associate them with the native English song tradition. Some of Wyatt's songs, to be sure, strike a note of jaunty independence, often tinged with misogyny; but melancholy complaint is rarely very distant. Perhaps the poem that most brilliantly captures his blend of passion, anger, cynicism, longing, and pain is "They Flee from Me."

Wyatt never published a collection of his own poems, and very few of them appeared in print during his lifetime. Carefully crafted pieces in an elaborate and sometimes risky erotic chess game, many of them may have been designed for specific social occasions, to be recited or sometimes set to music and sung to the accompaniment of a lute. In addition to such oral performances, the poems were written out, exchanged, and circulated in manuscript, both within a small, exclusive circle of friends and among those beyond the court who were eager to enjoy the latest poetic fashions.

Contemporaries clearly took pleasure in staging and savoring the drama of sexual relations: the Devonshire Manuscript, one of the chief sources for Wyatt's verse, collects a variety of poetic perspectives on courtship. The miscellany contains not only several male-authored poems in a female voice but also a number of poems probably written by women, along with many more transcribed by female hands. Wyatt was writing within a larger game of social competition and exchange.

In 1557 (fifteen years after Wyatt's death), 97 poems attributed to him were included by the printer Richard Tottel among the 271 poems in his miscellany, *Songs and Sonnets*. By the time this collection was published, Wyatt's deliberately rough, vigorous, and expressive metrical practice was felt to be crude, and Tottel (or perhaps some intermediary) smoothed out the versification. We reprint "They Flee from Me" both in Tottel's "improved" version and in the version found in the Egerton Manuscript, which contains poems in Wyatt's own hand and corrections he made to scribal copies of his poems.

In the following selections we have divided the poems into three generic groups: sonnets, other lyrics, and finally a satire. Within each of the first two groups, the poems are printed in the order in which they appear in the manuscripts. There is no reason to think that this is a chronological ordering.

The Long Love That in My Thought Doth Harbor[1]

    The long love that in my thought doth harbor,
    And in mine heart doth keep his residence,
    Into my face presseth with bold pretense
    And therein campeth, spreading his banner.[2]
5   She that me learneth° to love and suffer   *teaches me*
    And will that my trust and lust's negligence[3]
    Be reined by reason, shame, and reverence,
    With his hardiness taketh displeasure.
    Wherewithal° unto the heart's forest he fleeth,   *because of which*
10 Leaving his enterprise with pain and cry,
    And there him hideth, and not appeareth.
    What may I do, when my master feareth,
    But in the field with him to live and die?
    For good is the life ending faithfully.

                                                                       E. MS.

---

1. Wyatt's version of poem 140 of Petrarch's *Rime sparse* (Scattered Rhymes); his younger friend the Earl of Surrey also translated it (p. 136).
2. *That is, the speaker's blush.* The first four lines of this sonnet introduce the "conceit" (elaborately sustained metaphor) of Love as a warrior who, "with bold pretense" (that is, making bold claim), flaunts his presence by means of the "banner." Elaborate metaphors of this kind are common in Petrarchan (and Elizabethan) love poetry, and often, as in this instance, an entire sonnet will turn on a single conceit.
3. That is, my open and careless revelation of my love.

Petrarch, Rima 140
A MODERN PROSE TRANSLATION[4]

Love, who lives and reigns in my thought and keeps his principal seat in my heart, sometimes comes forth all in armor into my forehead, there camps, and there sets up his banner.

She who teaches us to love and to be patient, and wishes my great desire, my kindled hope, to be reined in by reason, shame, and reverence, at our boldness is angry within herself.

Wherefore Love flees terrified to my heart, abandoning his every enterprise, and weeps and trembles; there he hides and no more appears outside.

What can I do, when my lord is afraid, except stay with him until the last hour? For he makes a good end who dies loving well.

Whoso List to Hunt[1]

Whoso list° to hunt, I know where is an hind,°   *cares / female deer*
But as for me, alas, I may no more.
The vain travail° hath wearied me so sore,°   *labor / sorely, seriously*
I am of them that farthest cometh behind.
5   Yet may I, by no means, my wearied mind
Draw from the deer, but as she fleeth afore,
Fainting I follow. I leave off, therefore,
Since in a net I seek to hold the wind.
Who list her hunt, I put him out of doubt,°   *assure him*
10   As well as I, may spend his time in vain.
And graven with diamonds in letters plain
There is written, her fair neck round about,
"*Noli me tangere,* for Caesar's I am,
And wild for to hold, though I seem tame."

E. MS.

---

4. This and the prose translations of Rime 190, 134, and 189 are by Robert K. Durling.
1. An adaptation of Petrarch's Rima 190, perhaps influenced by commentators on Petrarch, who said that *Noli me tangere quia Caesaris sum* (Touch me not, for I am Caesar's) was inscribed on the collars of Caesar's hinds, which were then set free and were presumably safe from hunters. Wyatt's sonnet is usually supposed to refer to Anne Boleyn, in whom Henry VIII became interested in 1526.

Petrarch, Rima 190

A MODERN PROSE TRANSLATION

A white doe on the green grass appeared to me, with two golden horns, between two rivers, in the shade of a laurel, when the sun was rising in the unripe season.

Her look was so sweet and proud that to follow her I left every task, like the miser who as he seeks treasure sweetens his trouble with delight.

"Let no one touch me," she bore written with diamonds and topazes around her lovely neck. "It has pleased my Caesar to make me free."

And the sun had already turned at midday; my eyes were tired by looking but not sated, when I fell into the water, and she disappeared.

I Find No Peace[1]

I find no peace, and all my war is done,
I fear and hope, I burn and freeze like ice,
I fly above the wind, yet can I not arise,
And naught I have, and all the world I seize on.
5   That° looseth nor locketh holdeth me in prison,   *that which*
And holdeth me not, yet can I 'scape nowise;
Nor letteth me live nor die at my devise,°   *my own will*
And yet of death it giveth me occasion.
Without eyen° I see, and without tongue I plain;°   *eyes / complain*
10 I desire to perish, and yet I ask health;
I love another, and thus I hate myself;
I feed me in sorrow, and laugh in all my pain.
Likewise displeaseth me both death and life,
And my delight is causer of this strife.

E. MS.

Petrarch, Rima 134

A MODERN PROSE TRANSLATION

Peace I do not find, and I have no wish to make war; and I fear and hope, and burn and am of ice; and I fly above the heavens and lie on the ground; and I grasp nothing and embrace all the world.

One has me in prison who neither opens nor locks, neither keeps me for his own nor unties the bonds; and Love does not

---

1. Translated from Petrarch's Rima 134.

kill and does not unchain me, he neither wishes me alive nor frees me from the tangle.

I see without eyes, and I have no tongue and yet cry out; and I wish to perish and I ask for help; and I hate myself and love another.

I feed on pain, weeping I laugh; equally displeasing to me are death and life. In this state am I, Lady, on account of you.

My Galley[1]

My galley charged° with forgetfulness[2]   *freighted*
Thorough° sharp seas, in winter nights doth pass   *through*
'Tween rock and rock; and eke° mine enemy, alas,   *also*
That is my lord, steereth with cruelness;
5   And every oar a thought in readiness,
As though that death were light in such a case.[3]
An endless wind doth tear the sail apace°   *swiftly*
Of forced sighs and trusty fearfulness.°   *fear to trust*
A rain of tears, a cloud of dark disdain,
10   Hath done the wearied cords great hinderance;
Wreathed° with error and eke with ignorance.   *twisted*
The stars be hid that led me to this pain.
Drowned is reason that should me consort,°   *accompany*
And I remain despairing of the port.

                                                              E. MS.

Petrarch, Rima 189

A MODERN PROSE TRANSLATION

My ship laden with forgetfulness passes through a harsh sea, at midnight, in winter, between Scylla and Charybdis,[4] and at the tiller sits my lord, rather my enemy;

each oar is manned by a ready, cruel thought that seems to scorn the tempest and the end; a wet, changeless wind of sighs, hopes, and desires breaks the sail;

a rain of weeping, a mist of disdain wet and loosen the already weary ropes, made of error twisted up with ignorance.

My two usual sweet stars are hidden; dead among the waves are reason and skill; so that I begin to despair of the port.

---

1. Translated from Petrarch's Rima 189. For Edmund Spenser's adaptation of the same poem, see p. 452.
2. That is, obliviousness of everything except love.
3. As though my destruction would not matter much.
4. The monster and the whirlpool that threaten Odysseus's ship on either side of the Strait of Messina, in *Odyssey* 12.

What Vaileth Truth?[1]

What vaileth° truth? or by it to take pain, — *avails*
To strive by steadfastness for to attain.
To be just and true and flee from doubleness;
Sithens all° alike, where ruleth craftiness, — *since exactly*
5 Rewarded is both false and plain?
Soonest he speedeth° that most can feign; — *succeeds*
True-meaning heart is had in disdain.
Against deceit and doubleness,
    What vaileth truth?

10 Deceived is he by crafty train° — *treachery*
That meaneth no guile and doth remain
Within the trap without redress.° — *remedy*
But for° to love, lo, such a mistress, — *except*
Whose cruelty nothing can refrain,° — *restrain*
15   What vaileth truth?

                                   E. MS.

Madam, Withouten Many Words

Madam, withouten many words,
Once,° I am sure, ye will or no. — *sometime*
And if ye will, then leave your bordes,° — *jests*
And use your wit° and show it so. — *mind*

5 And with a beck ye shall me call.
And if of one that burneth alway
Ye have any pity at all,
Answer him fair with yea or nay.

If it be yea, I shall be fain.° — *glad*
10 If it be nay, friends as before.
Ye shall another man obtain,
And I mine own and yours no more.

                                   E. MS.

---

1. A rondeau: a difficult French verse form in which the unrhymed refrain "rounds" back to the opening words, and the rest of the poem uses only two rhyme sounds.

They Flee from Me

They flee from me, that sometime did me seek
With naked foot stalking° in my chamber.　　　　　*walking softly*
I have seen them gentle, tame, and meek
That now are wild and do not remember
5　That sometime they put themself in danger
To take bread at my hand; and now they range,
Busily seeking with a continual change.

Thanked be fortune it hath been otherwise
Twenty times better; but once in special,
10　In thin array, after a pleasant guise,
When her loose gown from her shoulders did fall,
And she me caught in her arms long and small,°　　　*slender*
Therewithal° sweetly did me kiss　　　　　　　　　*with that*
And softly said, "Dear heart, how like you this?"

15　It was no dream, I lay broad waking.
But all is turned, thorough° my gentleness,　　　　*through*
Into a strange fashion of forsaking;
And I have leave to go, of her goodness,
And she also to use newfangleness.°　　　　　　　*fickleness*
20　But since that I so kindly[1] am served,
I fain would° know what she hath deserved.　　　　*would like to*

　　　　　　　　　　　E. MS.

The Lover Showeth How He Is Forsaken of Such as He Sometime Enjoyed

They flee from me, that sometime did me seek
With naked foot stalking within my chamber.
Once have I seen them gentle, tame, and meek
That now are wild and do not once remember
5　That sometime they have put themselves in danger
To take bread at my hand; and now they range,
Busily seeking in continual change.

Thankèd be fortune, it hath been otherwise
Twenty times better; but once especial,
10　In thin array, after a pleasant guise,
When her loose gown did from her shoulders fall,

---

1. Naturally (from *kind*: "nature," but with an ironic suggestion of the modern meaning of "kindly"). In Wyatt's spelling, the word should presumably be pronounced as three syllables.

       And she me caught in her arms long and small,
       And therewithal so sweetly did me kiss
       And softly said, "Dear heart, how like you this?"

15 It was no dream, for I lay broad awaking.
       But all is turned now, through my gentleness,
       Into a bitter fashion of forsaking;
       And I have leave to go, of her goodness,
       And she also to use newfangleness.
20 But since that I unkindly so am served,
       How like you this? What hath she now deserved?

TOTTEL, 1557

My Lute, Awake!

       My lute, awake! Perform the last
       Labor that thou and I shall waste,
       And end that I have now begun:
       For when this song is sung and past,
5   My lute be still, for I have done.

       As to be heard where ear is none,
       As lead to grave in marble stone,[1]
       My song may pierce her heart as soon.
       Should we then sigh or sing or moan?
10 No, no, my lute, for I have done.

       The rocks do not so cruelly
       Repulse the waves continually
       As she my suit and affectiön.
       So that I am past remedy,
15 Whereby my lute and I have done.

       Proud of the spoil that thou hast got
       Of simple hearts, thorough° Love's shot,   *through*
       By whom, unkind, thou hast them won,
       Think not he hath his bow forgot,
20 Although my lute and I have done.

       Vengeance shall fall on thy disdain
       That makest but game on earnest pain.
       Think not alone under the sun
       Unquit° to cause thy lovers plain,°   *unrevenged / to complain*
25 Although my lute and I have done.

---

1. That is, when sound may be heard with no ear to hear it or when soft lead is able to carve ("grave") hard marble.

　　　　Perchance thee lie[2] withered and old
　　　　The winter nights that are so cold,
　　　　Plaining in vain unto the moon.
　　　　Thy wishes then dare not be told.
30　　　Care then who list,° for I have done.　　　　　　　　　likes

　　　　And then may chance thee to repent
　　　　The time that thou hast lost and spent
　　　　To cause thy lovers sigh and swoon.
　　　　Then shalt thou know beauty but lent,
35　　　And wish and want as I have done.

　　　　Now cease, my lute. This is the last
　　　　Labor that thou and I shall waste,
　　　　And ended is that we begun.
　　　　Now is this song both sung and past;
40　　　My lute be still, for I have done.

　　　　　　　　　　　　　　　　　　　　　　　　　　　E. MS.

Forget Not Yet

　　　　Forget not yet the tried intent
　　　　Of such a truth° as I have meant,　　　　　　　　　fidelity
　　　　My great travail so gladly spent,
　　　　　　Forget not yet.

5　　　Forget not yet when first began
　　　　The weary life ye know since when,
　　　　The suit,° the service[1] none tell can,　　　　　　pursuit, wooing
　　　　　　Forget not yet.

　　　　Forget not yet the great essays,°　　　　　　　　　trials
10　　　The cruel wrong, the scornful ways,
　　　　The painful patience in denays,°　　　　　　　　　denials, refusals
　　　　　　Forget not yet.

　　　　Forget not yet, forget not this,
　　　　How long ago hath been and is
15　　　The mind that never meant amiss,
　　　　　　Forget not yet.

　　　　Forget not then thine own approved,
　　　　The which so long hath thee so loved,
　　　　Whose steadfast faith yet never moved,
20　　　　Forget not this.

　　　　　　　　　　　　　　　　　　　　　　　　　　　D. MS.

2. Perhaps it may befall you to lie.
1. Actions of a lover, often called the lady's "servant."

Stand Whoso List[1]

Stand whoso list° upon the slipper° top   *cares to / slippery*
Of court's estates,° and let me here rejoice   *high positions*
And use me quiet without let or stop,[2]
Unknown in court, that hath such brackish[3] joys.
5   In hidden place so let my days forth pass
That when my years be done withouten noise,
I may die aged after the common trace.°   *way*
For him death grippeth right hard by the crop°   *throat*
That is much known of other, and of himself, alas,
10   Doth die unknown, dazed, with dreadful° face.   *fearful*

A. MS.

Who List His Wealth and Ease Retain[1]

Who list° his wealth° and ease retain,   *desires / well-being*
Himself let him unknown contain.[2]
Press not too fast in at that gate
Where the return stands by disdain:
5   For sure, *circa regna tonat*.[3]

The high mountains are blasted oft
When the low valley is mild and soft.
Fortune with Health stands at debate.[4]
The fall is grievous from aloft.
10   And sure, *circa regna tonat*.

These bloody days have broken my heart.
My lust,° my youth did then depart,   *pleasure*
And blind desire of estate.°   *status*
Who hastes to climb seeks to revert.°   *fall back*
15   Of truth, *circa regna tonat*.

The Bell Tower showed me such sight
That in my head sticks day and night.
There did I learn out of a grate,°   *barred window*
For all favor, glory, or might,[5]
20   That yet *circa regna tonat*.

---

1. A translation of Seneca, *Thyestes*, lines 391–403.
2. Comport myself quietly without hindrance or impediment.
3. Spoiled by mixture, as of seawater with fresh.
1. This poem was almost certainly written at the time of Wyatt's imprisonment in 1536, during which he witnessed from the Bell Tower the execution of Anne Boleyn.
2. That is, let him keep himself unknown.
3. "He [that is, Jupiter] thunders around thrones" (Seneca, *Phaedra*, line 1140). The first two stanzas of Wyatt's poem paraphrase lines from that play. "The return stands by disdain": that is, "you will be disdained as you make your (forced) exit."
4. That is, fortune and well-being are always at odds.
5. That is, whatever one's favor, glory, or might.

> By proof,° I say, there did I learn: *experience*
> Wit helpeth not defense to yerne,
> Of innocence to plead or prate.[6]
> Bear low°, therefore, give God the stern,[7] *be humble*
> 25 For sure, *circa regna tonat*.

B. MS.

Mine Own John Poins[1]

> Mine own John Poins, since ye delight to know
> The cause why that homeward I me draw
> (And flee the press of courts, whereso they go,
> Rather than to live thrall under the awe
> 5 Of lordly looks) wrapped within my cloak,
> To will and lust° learning to set a law; *desire*
> It is not for because I scorn or mock
> The power of them to whom Fortune hath lent
> Charge over us, of right to strike the stroke.[2]
> 10 But true it is that I have always meant
> Less to esteem them than the common sort,
> Of outward things that judge in their intent,
> Without regard what doth inward resort.
> I grant sometime that of glory the fire
> 15 Doth touch my heart; me list not to report
> Blame by honor, and honor to desire.[3]
> But how may I this honor now attain,
> That cannot dye the color black a liar?[4]
> My Poins, I cannot frame my tune to feign,
> 20 To cloak the truth for praise, without desert,
> Of them that list° all vice for to retain. *desire*
> I cannot honor them that sets their part
> With Venus and Bacchus all their life long,[5]
> Nor hold my peace of° them although I smart. *concerning*
> 25 I cannot crouch nor kneel nor do so great a wrong
> To worship them like God on earth alone
> That are as wolves these sely° lambs among. *innocent*
> I cannot with my words complain and moan
> And suffer naught,° nor smart without complaint, *wickedness*

---

6. That is, intelligence does not help one earn ("yerne") a defense, [nor does it help] to plead or prattle about one's innocence.
7. Let God do the steering.
1. Poins was a friend of Wyatt's. This verse epistle of informal satire is based on the tenth satire of the Italian Luigi Alamanni but is personalized and Anglicized in detail by Wyatt. It was apparently written during his banishment from court, in 1536. Lines 1–52 of the poem are missing from the authoritative Egerton Manuscript and are here supplied from the Devonshire Manuscript.

2. That is, my retirement from court is not because I scorn the powerful, or their prerogatives of rule and punishment. But I esteem them less than do the "common sort" of people, who judge by externals only (lines 10–13).
3. That is, I do not wish to attack honor or to call dishonorable desire honorable.
4. That is, cannot pretend that black is not black.
5. That is, I cannot honor those who devote their lives to Venus (goddess of love) and Bacchus (god of drinking).

30 Nor turn the word that from my mouth is gone;
    I cannot speak and look like a saint,
    Use wiles for wit° and make deceit a pleasure,   *wisdom*
    And call craft° counsel, for profit still to paint;°   *craftiness / deceive*
    I cannot wrest the law to fill the coffer,
35 With innocent blood to feed myself fat,
    And do most hurt where most help I offer.
    I am not he that can allow° the state°   *approve / exaltation*
    Of high Caesar and damn Cato[6] to die,
    That with his death did 'scape out of the gate
40 From Caesar's hands, if Livy[7] do not lie,
    And would not live where liberty was lost,
    So did his heart the common weal apply.[8]
    I am not he such eloquence to boast
    To make the crow singing as the swan,
45 Nor call the lion of coward beasts the most,
    That cannot take a mouse as the cat can;
    And he that dieth for hunger of the gold,
    Call him Alexander,[9] and say that Pan
    Passeth° Apollo in music many fold;[1]   *surpasses*
50 Praise Sir Thopas for a noble tale,
    And scorn the story that the Knight told;[2]
    Praise him for counsel that is drunk of ale;
    Grin when he laugheth that beareth all the sway,°   *power*
    Frown when he frowneth, and groan when he is pale;
55 On other's lust° to hang both night and day—   *wishes*
    None of these points would ever frame in me;°   *appeal to me*
    My wit° is naught:° I cannot learn the way;   *intellect / worthless*
    And much the less of things that greater be,
    That asken help of colors of device°   *tricks of rhetoric*
60 To join the mean with each extremity:
    With the nearest virtue to cloak alway the vice,
    And, as to purpose likewise it shall fall,[3]
    To press the virtue that it may not rise;
    As drunkenness, good fellowship to call;
65 The friendly foe, with his double face,
    Say he is gentle and courteous therewithal;°   *besides*
    And say that favel° hath a goodly grace   *flattery*
    In eloquence; and cruelty to name
    Zeal of justice, and change in time and place;[4]
70 And he that suffereth offense° without blame,   *allows offenses*
    Call him pitiful,° and him true and plain   *compassionate*
    That raileth reckless° to every man's shame;   *recklessly*

---

6. Cato the Younger, the famous Roman patriot who committed suicide rather than submit to Caesar.
7. Titus Livius (59 B.C.E.–17 C.E.), the great Roman historian.
8. So much did he devote himself to the common good.
9. Compare him to Alexander the Great with his towering ambition.
1. According to classical mythology, the music of the nature god Pan was far inferior to that of Apollo, patron of music and art.
2. The silly tale of Sir Thopas, in *The Canterbury Tales*, is told by Chaucer himself, until the Host forces him to stop. *The Knight's Tale* is the most courtly and dignified of the tales.
3. That is, as will also be opportune.
4. That is, to miscall cruelty zeal for justice, and to rationalize it by appeals to altered circumstances.

Say he is rude° that cannot lie and feign, *uneducated*
The lecher a lover, and tyranny
75 To be the right of a prince's reign.
I cannot, I: no, no, it will not be.
This is the cause that I could never yet
Hang on their sleeves that weigh, as thou mayst see,
A chip of chance more than a pound of wit.
80 This maketh me at home to hunt and hawk
And in foul weather at my book to sit;
In frost and snow then with my bow to stalk.
No man doth mark° whereso I ride or go. *note*
In lusty leas° at liberty I walk, *pleasant fields*
85 And of these news I feel nor weal nor woe,
Save that a clog doth hang yet at my heel.[5]
No force° for that, for it is ordered so *no matter*
That I may leap both hedge and dike full well.
I am not now in France, to judge the wine,
90 With sav'ry sauce the delicates° to feel; *delicacies*
Nor yet in Spain, where one must him incline,
Rather than to be, outwardly to seem.
I meddle not with wits that be so fine;
Nor Flanders' cheer[6] letteth° not my sight to deem *hinders*
95 Of black and white, nor taketh my wit away
With beastliness they, beasts, do so esteem.
Nor am I not where Christ is given in prey
For money, poison, and treason—at Rome[7]
A common practice, used night and day.
100 But here I am in Kent and Christendom,
Among the Muses, where I read and rhyme;
Where if thou list, my Poins, for to come,
Thou shalt be judge how I do spend my time.

D. MS., E. MS.

---

5. That is, I feel neither happiness nor unhappiness about current political affairs, except that a "clog" (that is, his confinement on parole to his estate) keeps me from traveling far. Note that *news* is a plural in Elizabethan English.
6. That is, the drinking for which, in the 16th century, Flemings were notorious.
7. In *Tottel's Miscellany*, published in the reign of the Catholic Queen Mary, these lines were altered as follows: "where *truth* is given in prey / For money, poison, and treason—*of some*."

HENRY HOWARD, EARL OF SURREY
1517–1547

The ax that decapitated Surrey at the age of thirty had been hanging over his head for much of his life. In the court of Henry VIII, it was dangerous to be a potential claimant to the throne, and Surrey was descended from kings on both sides of his family. He was brought up at Windsor Castle as the close companion of Henry VIII's illegitimate son, the Duke of Richmond, who married Surrey's sister. As the eldest son of the Duke of Norfolk, the chief bulwark of the old Catholic aristocracy against the rising tide of "new men" and the reformed religion, Surrey was the heir not only to the Howard family's great wealth but also to the family's immense pride, its sense at once of noble privilege and of obligation. Like his father and grandfather, he was a brave and able soldier, serving in Henry VIII's French wars as "Lieutenant General of the King on Sea and Land." He was also repeatedly imprisoned for rash behavior, on one occasion for striking a courtier, on another for wandering through the streets of London breaking the windows of sleeping townspeople. In 1541 Surrey used his family connections—his first cousin, Catherine Howard, was queen—to secure the release from the Tower of his close friend the poet Thomas Wyatt, who had been accused of treason. But a year later, Catherine Howard was executed for adultery, like Anne Boleyn before her. Power returned to the rival family of the former queen Jane Seymour, who had died in childbirth giving a son and heir to the aging Henry VIII. Surrey's situation was already precarious, and his vocal opposition to the Seymours, with their strong Protestant leanings, sealed his fate. Convicted of treason, he had the grim distinction of being Henry's last victim.

Poets and critics of the later sixteenth century, fascinated by Surrey's noble rank and his tragic fate, routinely praised him as one of the very greatest English poets. The full title of Tottel's influential miscellany, published in 1557 (ten years after Surrey's death), is *Songs and Sonnets Written by the Right Honorable Lord Henry Howard Late Earl of Surrey and Other.* The principal "other" here is his older friend Wyatt, with whose poetry Surrey's is closely linked. Poets who circulated their verse in manuscript in a courtly milieu, the two shared a passion for French and Italian poetry, especially for Petrarch's sonnets. Surrey established a form for these that was used by Shakespeare and that has become known as the English sonnet: three quatrains and a couplet, all in iambic pentameter and rhyming *abab cdcd efef gg.* Even more significant, he was the first English poet to publish in blank verse—unrhymed iambic pentameter—a verse form so popular in the succeeding centuries that it has come to seem almost native to the language. The work in which he used his "strange meter," as the publisher called it, was a translation of part of Virgil's *Aeneid,* a Latin epic poem telling the legendary story of Aeneas of Troy and written between 29 and 19 B.C.E. Managing the five-stress line with exceptional skill, Surrey initiated the rhythmic fluency that distinguishes so many Elizabethan lyrics. It is striking that his two great literary innovations, the English sonnet and blank verse, should emerge in the same period that saw radical upheavals in traditional religious and social life. It is possible that he was drawn to Virgil's epic because it offered a model of continuity in the face of disaster. Aeneas cannot prevent the fall of Troy, but, carrying his household gods with him, he leads his followers to a new land, Italy, where his descendants will found a city, the future Rome.

As a conventional love poet Surrey is not very convincing: in 1593 Thomas Nashe wrote sardonically that Surrey "was more in love with his own curious forming fancy" than with this mistress's face. His verse comes alive when he writes about his deep male friendships ("So Cruel Prison" and the moving epitaph he published on Wyatt), or imagines himself as a woman longing for her absent man ("O Happy Dames").

Our selections from Surrey are divided into two groups: sonnets are followed by lyric and reflective poems.

The Soote Season[1]

    The soote° season, that bud and bloom forth brings,   *sweet, fragrant*
    With green hath clad the hill and eke° the vale.   *also*
    The nightingale with feathers new she sings;
    The turtle to her make° hath told her tale.   *turtledove to her mate*
5   Summer is come, for every spray now springs.
    The hart hath hung his old head on the pale;°   *fence, paling*
    The buck in brake° his winter coat he flings;   *thicket*
    The fishes float with new repairèd scale;
    The adder all her slough° away she slings;   *cast-off skin*
10 The swift swallow pursueth the fliès small;
    The busy bee her honey now she mings.°   *mingles*
    Winter is worn, that was the flowers' bale.°   *harm*
    And thus I see among these pleasant things,
    Each care decays, and yet my sorrow springs.

1557

Petrarch, Rima 310

A MODERN PROSE TRANSLATION[2]

Zephyrus returns and leads back the fine weather and the flowers and the grass, his sweet family, and chattering Procne and weeping Philomena,[3] and Spring, all white and vermilion;

the meadows laugh and the sky becomes clear again, Jupiter is gladdened looking at his daughter,[4] the air and the waters and the earth are full of love, every animal takes counsel again to love.

But to me, alas, come back heavier sighs, which she draws from my deepest heart, she who carried off to Heaven the keys to it;

and the singing of little birds, and the flowering of meadows, and virtuous gentle gestures in beautiful ladies are a wilderness and cruel, savage beasts.

---

1. This poem is a free adaptation of Petrarch's Rima 310, one of the sonnets written after the death of the poet's beloved.
2. This and the prose translation of Rima 164 are by Robert K. Durling.
3. The swallow and the nightingale, respectively. Zephyrus is the west wind.
4. Jupiter and his daughter Venus are here the planets, in favorable astrological relation.

Love, That Doth Reign and Live Within My Thought[1]

    Love, that doth reign and live within my thought,
    And built his seat within my captive breast,
    Clad in the arms wherein with me he fought,
    Oft in my face he doth his banner rest.
5 But she that taught me love and suffer pain,
    My doubtful hope and eke° my hot desire   *also*
    With shamefast° look to shadow and refrain,°   *modest / restrain*
    Her smiling grace converteth straight to ire.
    And coward Love then to the heart apace°   *at once*
10 Taketh his flight, where he doth lurk and plain,°   *complain*
    His purpose lost, and dare not show his face.
    For my lord's guilt thus faultless bide° I pain,   *endure*
    Yet from my lord shall not my foot remove:
    Sweet is the death that taketh end by love.

                                              1557

Alas! So All Things Now Do Hold Their Peace[1]

    Alas! so all things now do hold their peace,
    Heaven and earth disturbèd in no thing.
    The beasts, the air, the birds their song do cease;
    The nightès chare[2] the stars about doth bring;
5 Calm is the sea, the waves work less and less.
    So am not I, whom love, alas, doth wring,
    Bringing before my face the great increase
    Of my desires, whereat I weep and sing,
    In joy and woe, as in a doubtful ease:
10 For my sweet thoughts sometime do pleasure bring,
    But by and by° the cause of my disease[3]   *immediately*
    Gives me a pang that inwardly doth sting,
    When that I think what grief it is, again,
    To live, and lack the thing should rid my pain.

                                              1557

Petrarch, Rima 164

A MODERN PROSE TRANSLATION

Now that the heavens and the earth and the wind are silent, and sleep reins in the beasts and the birds, Night drives her starry car about, and in its bed the sea lies without a wave,

I am awake, I think, I burn, I weep; and she who destroys me is always before me, to my sweet pain: war is my state, full of sorrow and suffering, and only thinking of her do I have any peace.

---

1. Compare Surrey's version of Petrarch's Rima 140 with Wyatt's translation of the same original (pp. 122–23; with a modern prose translation).

1. Adapted from Petrarch's Rima 164.
2. From Italian *carro* (the Great Bear).
3. Dis-ease; that is, discomfort.

Thus from one clear living fountain alone spring the sweet and the bitter on which I feed; one hand alone heals me and pierces me.

And that my suffering may not reach an end, a thousand times a day I die and a thousand am born, so distant am I from health.

So Cruel Prison How Could Betide[1]

So cruel prison how could betide,[2] alas,
As proud Windsor, where I in lust° and joy   *pleasure*
With a king's son my childish° years did pass   *youthful*
In greater feast than Priam's sons of Troy?[3]

5 Where each sweet place returns a taste full sour:
The large green courts, where we were wont to hove,°   *linger*
With eyes cast up unto the Maidens' Tower,
And easy sighs, such as folk draw in love.

The stately sales,° the ladies bright of hue,   *halls*
10 The dances short, long tales of great delight,
With words and looks that tigers could but rue,[4]
Where each of us did plead the other's right.

The palm play° where, dispoilèd° for the game,   *handball / stripped*
With dazed eyes oft we by gleams of love
15 Have missed the ball and got sight of our dame,
To bait° her eyes, which kept the leads[5] above.   *attract, as in fishing*

The graveled ground, with sleeves° tied on the helm,   *ladies' favors*
On foaming horse, with swords and friendly hearts,
With cheer° as though the one should overwhelm,   *countenance*
20 Where we have fought and chasèd oft with darts.°   *spears*

With silver drops the meads yet spread[6] for ruth,°   *pity*
In active games of nimbleness and strength,
Where we did strain, trailèd by swarms of youth,
Our tender limbs that yet shot up in length.

25 The secret groves which oft we made resound
Of pleasant plaint and of our ladies' praise,
Recording soft what grace° each one had found,   *favor*
What hope of speed,° what dread of long delays.   *success*

---

1. In the summer of 1537 Surrey was imprisoned at Windsor Castle for striking another courtier. The poem recalls his boyhood stay there (1530–32) with Henry Fitzroy, illegitimate son of Henry VIII.
2. That is, how could there happen to be.
3. Priam, king of Troy in the *Iliad*, had fifty sons.
4. Take pity on, despite tigers' legendary fierceness.
5. Who was on the lead-covered roof.
6. That is, when the dew, like tears, was still on the meadows.

The wild forest, the clothèd holts° with green,   *wooded hills*
30 With reins availed° and swift ybreathèd horse,   *slackened*
With cry of hounds and merry blasts° between,   *of the horn*
Where we did chase the fearful hart a force.[7]

The void° walls eke° that harbored us each night,   *empty / also*
Wherewith, alas, revive within my breast
35 The sweet accord, such sleeps as yet delight,
The pleasant dreams, the quiet bed of rest,

The secret thoughts imparted with such trust,
The wanton° talk, the divers change of play,   *playful*
The friendship sworn, each promise kept so just,
40 Wherewith we passed the winter nights away.

And with this thought, the blood forsakes my face,
The tears berain my cheeks of deadly hue,
The which as soon as sobbing sighs, alas,
Upsuppèd have, thus I my plaint renew:

45 "O place of bliss, renewer of my woes,
Give me accompt,° where is my noble fere,[8]   *account*
Whom in thy walls thou didst each night enclose,
To other lief,° but unto me most dear."   *dear*

Each stone, alas, that doth my sorrow rue,°   *pity*
50 Returns thereto a hollow sound of plaint.
Thus I alone, where all my freedom grew,
In prison pine with bondage and restraint.

And with remembrance of the greater grief
To banish the less, I find my chief relief.

1537   1557

Wyatt Resteth Here, That Quick Could Never Rest

Wyatt resteth here, that quick° could never rest,   *alive*
Whose heavenly gifts, increasèd by disdain[1]
And virtue, sank the deeper in his breast:
Such profit he by envy could obtain.

5 A head where wisdom mysteries° did frame,   *subtle meanings*
Whose hammers beat still in that lively brain
As on a stith,° where that some work of fame   *anvil*
Was daily wrought to turn to Britain's gain.

---

7. That is, to run it down.
8. Companion. Henry Fitzroy had died the year before, at age seventeen.

1. Hostility (equivalent to "envy" in line 4). That is, he could turn hostility toward him to his advantage.

A visage stern and mild, where both did grow
10　Vice to contemn,° in virtue to rejoice;　　　　　　　　　　　　*despise*
　　　Amid great storms whom grace assurèd so
　　　To live upright and smile at fortune's choice.

　　　A hand that taught what might be said in rhyme,
　　　That reft° Chaucer the glory of his wit[2]—　　　　　　　　　*bereft*
15　A mark the which, unperfited° for time,　　　　　　　　　　　*unperfected*
　　　Some may approach, but never none shall hit.

　　　A tongue that served in foreign realms his king;
　　　Whose courteous talk to virtue did inflame
　　　Each noble heart: a worthy guide to bring
20　Our English youth by travail° unto fame.　　　　　　　　　　*labor*

　　　An eye whose judgment none affect° could blind,　　　　　*no partiality*
　　　Friends to allure and foes to reconcile,
　　　Whose piercing look did represent a mind
　　　With virtue fraught, reposèd, void of guile.

25　A heart where dread yet never so impressed
　　　To hide the thought that might the truth advance;
　　　In neither fortune loft nor yet repressed[3]
　　　To swell in wealth° or yield unto mischance.　　　　　　　*well-being*

　　　A valiant corpse[4] where force and beauty met,
30　Happy°—alas, too happy, but° for foes;　　　　　　　　　　*fortunate / if not*
　　　Lived and ran the race that Nature set,
　　　Of manhood's shape, where she the mold did lose.[5]

　　　But to the heavens that simple° soul is fled,　　　　　　　　*innocent*
　　　Which left, with such as covet Christ to know,
35　Witness of faith[6] that never shall be dead,
　　　Sent for our health,° but not receivèd so.　　　　　　　　　*welfare*

　　　Thus for our guilt, this jewel have we lost;
　　　The earth his bones, the heavens possess his ghost.°　　*spirit*

1542

O Happy Dames, That May Embrace[1]

　　　O happy dames,° that may embrace　　　　　　　　　　　　*wives*
　　　The fruit of your delight,
　　　Help to bewail the woeful case

---

2. Genius. That is, Wyatt (supposedly) replaced Chaucer as England's greatest poet.
3. That is, neither overly elated by good fortune nor downcast by bad.
4. Body (not, as now, a dead one).
5. A conventional praise—that Nature, in creating someone, made a masterpiece and then lost the pattern.
6. That is, which left with Christians ("such as covet Christ to know") a testimony of faith.
1. The speaker is a woman. The poem was probably written for Surrey's wife, from whom he was separated while on military duty in France in the 1540s.

And eke° the heavy plight   *also*
5   Of me, that wonted° to rejoice   *was accustomed*
The fortune of my pleasant choice:
Good ladies, help to fill my mourning voice.

In ship, freight° with rememberance   *loaded*
Of thoughts and pleasures past,
10   He sails that hath in governance
My life while it will last;
With scalding sighs, for lack of gale,
Futhering his hope, that is his sail,
Toward me, the sweet port of his avail.°   *destination*

15   Alas, how oft in dreams I see
Those eyes that were my food,
Which sometime so delighted me,
That yet they do me good;
Wherewith I wake with his return,
20   Whose absent flame did make me burn:
But when I find the lack, Lord how I mourn!

When other lovers in arms across°   *embracing*
Rejoice their chief delight,
Drowned in tears to mourn my loss
25   I stand the bitter night
In my window, where I may see
Before the winds how the clouds flee.
Lo, what a mariner love hath made me!

And in green waves when the salt flood
30   Doth rise by rage of wind,
A thousand fancies in that mood
Assail my restless mind.
Alas, now drencheth° my sweet foe,[2]   *drowns*
That with the spoil° of my heart did go   *plunder, booty*
35   And left me; but, alas, why did he so?

And when the seas wax calm again,
To chase from me annoy,°   *distress*
My doubtful hope doth cause me plain,°   *to complain*
So dread cuts off my joy.
40   Thus is my wealth° mingled with woe,   *happiness*
And of each thought a doubt doth grow:
Now he comes! Will he come? Alas, no, no!

1557

---

2. A conventional expression for a loved one, going back to medieval love poetry.

Faith in Conflict

When, in the late 1520s, the Catholic authorities of England tried to burn all copies of William Tyndale's English translation of the New Testament, they were attempting to stop the spread of what they viewed as a dangerous new plague of heresies. The plague was the Protestant Reformation, a movement opposed to crucial aspects of both the belief system and the institutional structure of Roman Catholicism.

The movement had been launched by the German theologian Martin Luther, who in 1517 challenged the authority of the pope and attacked several key doctrines of the Catholic Church. According to Luther, the Church, with its elaborate hierarchical structure centered in Rome, its rich monasteries and convents, and its enormous political influence, had become a hopelessly corrupt conspiracy of cynical priests who manipulated popular superstitions to enrich themselves and amass worldly power. Luther began by vehemently attacking the sale of indulgences—certificates promising the remission of punishments to be suffered in the afterlife by souls sent to "Purgatory" (a place or state where souls could be punished to make amends for their earthly sins before being allowed into heaven). Purgatory, he argued, had no foundation in scripture, which in his view was the only legitimate source of religious truth (*sola scriptura*). Christians would be saved not by scrupulously following the ritual practices fostered by the Catholic Church—observing fast days, reciting the ancient Latin prayers, endowing chantries to say prayers for the dead, invoking the protection of individual saints, and so on—and not even by the performance of good deeds, but by faith and faith alone (*sola fide*).

This challenge spread and gathered force, especially in northern Europe, where major Protestant leaders like the French theologian Jean Calvin (who, after his break with Catholicism, established a theocracy in Geneva) transformed religious institutions and elaborated various and sometimes conflicting doctrinal principles. Calvin, whose thought came to be particularly influential in England and Scotland, emphasized the obligation of governments to implement God's will in the world. He advanced too the doctrine of predestination, by which, as he put it, "God adopts some to hope of life and sentences others to eternal death." God's "secret election" of the saved troubled Calvin, but his study of the scriptures had led him to conclude that "only a small number, out of an incalculable multitude, should obtain salvation." Some Christians found this idea horrifying. How, they asked, could a loving creator condemn the great majority of his creatures to an eternity of torment? And was it not possible for humans to avert the severe decree through virtuous actions? But for Calvin predestination was a mystery bound up with faith, confidence, and an active engagement in the fashioning of a Christian community.

The Reformation had a direct and powerful impact on those realms where it gained control. Monasteries were sacked, their possessions seized by princes or sold off to the highest bidder; monks and nuns, expelled from their cloisters, were encouraged to break their vows of chastity and find spouses, as Luther and his wife, a former nun, had done. In the great cathedrals and in hundreds of smaller churches and chapels, the elaborate altarpieces, bejeweled crucifixes, crystal reliquaries holding the bones of saints, venerated statues, and paintings were attacked as "idols." Condemned for their Catholic doctrinal content and accused of violating the biblical prohibition on the making of "graven images," they were often defaced or destroyed. Protestant congregations continued, for the most part, to celebrate the most sacred Christian ritual—the Eucharist, or Lord's Supper—but they did so in a profoundly different spirit from the Catholic Church. For them it was a commemoration (in which the bread and wine symbolized Christ) rather than a miracle (in which the bread and wine turned into Christ), and the service was conducted not in the old liturgical Latin but in the local language.

The Reformation was at first vigorously resisted in England. Protestant writings were seized by officials of the Church and the state and burned. Protestants who made their views known were persecuted—driven to flee the country or arrested, put on trial, and burned at the stake. But the situation changed drastically after Henry VIII decided to seek a divorce from his first wife, Catherine of Aragon, to marry Anne Boleyn. When the Roman Catholic Church, under pressure from Catherine's powerful family, refused to grant the divorce, Henry defied papal authority, declared himself head of the Church in England, seized the wealth of the monasteries, and unleashed Protestant energies, including fierce bursts of iconoclasm in which many religious images in churches were painted over, broken, or otherwise destroyed. On most doctrinal questions, however, Henry remained an orthodox Catholic, and in the latter part of his reign his clerical authorities renewed the persecution of Protestants.

The turn toward the Reformation was more decisive in the reign (1547–53) of Henry's heir, Edward VI; and the attempt by Edward's successor, Mary (daughter of Henry VIII's first wife, the Catholic Catherine of Aragon), to reimpose Roman Catholicism as the national religion came to an end with her death, in 1558. The long reign (1558–1603) of Henry's daughter by Anne Boleyn, Elizabeth I, firmly established Protestantism as the faith of the Church of England. Reformation doctrine shaped the English liturgy eloquently formulated in the officially sanctioned *Book of Common Prayer* and was reinforced in the series of homilies, or sermons, that ministers were commanded to deliver to their parishioners.

The Reformation did not spread quickly or easily in England. Like Henry VIII himself, most English people in the decades after the break with Rome were far from being full-fledged Protestants. Emotional attachment to the traditional religion ran deep, as did resentment of an aggressively intolerant Protestant officialdom. From the 1530s to the end of the century, a significant number of individuals, including Thomas More and the Jesuit Robert Southwell, were prepared to die for the old faith. Many more, though still a small minority, stubbornly rejected the new orthodoxy, absenting themselves from obligatory Protestant worship; these recusants, as they were known, were subjected to fines and sometimes worse punishments. A much greater number conformed in public but remained largely untouched by Protestant doctrine.

Though Protestantism and Catholicism were exposed, under different regimes, to brutal persecution, both faiths proved impossible to eradicate. In large part this tenacity arose from the passionate, often suicidal heroism of men and women who felt that their soul's salvation depended on the precise character of their Christianity and who consequently embraced martyrdom rather than repudiate their beliefs. It arose too from a mid-fifteenth-century technological innovation that made it extremely difficult to suppress unwelcome ideas: the printing press. Early Protestants quickly grasped that with a few clandestine presses they could defy the Catholic authorities and flood the country with their texts. "How many printing presses there be in the world," wrote the Protestant polemicist and martyrologist John Foxe, "so many blockhouses there be against the high castle" of the pope in Rome, "so that either the pope must abolish knowledge and printing or printing at length will root him out." By the century's end, it was the outlawed Catholics, as well as the more radical Protestant dissenters known as Puritans, who were using the clandestine press to propagate their beliefs in the face of official persecution.

THE ENGLISH BIBLE

Protestant insistence that true belief must be based on the Holy Scriptures alone made the translation and dissemination of the Bible in English and other vernacular languages a matter of utmost urgency. Before the Reformation, the Roman Catholic Church had not always and everywhere opposed vernacular translations of the Bible, but it generally preferred that the populace encounter the scriptures through the interpretations of its priests, trained to read the Latin translation known as the Vulgate. In times of great conflict this preference hardened into outright prohibition of vernacular translation and into persecution and book burning. The late fourteenth-century English translation associated with John Wycliffe was vehemently attacked as heretical, and its suppression led to an edict banning any unauthorized attempt to translate the Bible into English. Throughout the fifteenth century no authorization was granted.

It was in the face of such fierce opposition that zealous Protestants all over Europe set out to put the Bible into the hands of the general populace, rather than the clergy. A remarkable translation of the New Testament by an English follower of Luther named William Tyndale was printed on the Continent and smuggled into England in 1526; Tyndale's translation of the Pentateuch, the first five books of the Hebrew Bible, followed in 1530. Many copies of these translations were seized and destroyed, as was the translator himself, but the printing press made it extremely difficult for authorities to eradicate books for which there was a passionate demand.

Tyndale's translation of the Bible was completed by an associate, Miles Coverdale, whose rendering of the Psalms proved to be particularly influential. Their joint labor was the basis for the Great Bible (1539), a copy of which was ordered to be placed in every church in the kingdom. Four years later, as Henry VIII sought to halt the tide of reform, a law was passed forbidding women, craftsmen, servants, and laborers from reading the Bible either in public or in private. Yet at this stage it was already too late to get the scriptures out of the hands of the populace. Though there would be further opposition in years to come—innumerable Bible translations were printed under Edward VI, only to be burned during the reign of his half-sister Mary—the English Bible was a force that could not be suppressed, and it became, in its various forms, the single most important book of the sixteenth century.

The persecution of Protestants under the Queen Mary was indirectly responsible for what would become the most scholarly Protestant English Bible, known as the Geneva Bible. This translation was prepared, with extensive, learned, and often fiercely polemical marginal notes, by English exiles in Calvin's Geneva and widely diffused in England after Elizabeth came to the throne. In addition, Elizabethan church authorities ordered a careful revision of the Great Bible, and this version, known as the Bishops' Bible, was the one read in the churches. The success of the Geneva Bible in particular finally prompted those Elizabethan Catholics who now in turn found themselves in exile to bring out a vernacular translation of their own, the Douay-Rheims version, to counter the Protestant readings and glosses.

After Elizabeth's death, in 1603, King James I and his bishops ordered that a revised translation of the entire Bible be undertaken by a group of forty-seven scholars. The result, published in 1611, was the Authorized Version, more popularly known as the King James Bible. This translation, whose diction and rhythms have had an immense influence on English literature, continues to be read and treasured.

In the passage selected here, 1 Corinthians 13, Tyndale's use of the word *love*, echoed by the Geneva Bible, is set against the Catholic *charity*. The latter term gestures toward the religious doctrine of salvation through actions, against the Protestant insistence on salvation by faith alone. It is a sign of the conservative, moderate Protestantism of the King James Version that it too opts for *charity*.

1 Corinthians 13

From *Tyndale's Translation*

Though I spake with the tongues of men and angels, and yet had no love, I were even as sounding brass: or as a tinkling cymbal. And though I could prophesy, and understood all secrets, and all knowledge: yea, if I had all faith, so that I could move mountains out of their places, and yet had no love, I were nothing. And though I bestowed all my goods to feed the poor, and though I gave my body even that I burned, and yet had no love, it profiteth me nothing.

Love suffereth long, and is courteous. Love envieth not. Love doth not forwardly,[1] swelleth not, dealeth not dishonestly, seeketh not her own, is not provoked to anger, thinketh not evil, rejoiceth not in iniquity: but rejoiceth in the truth, suffereth all things, believeth all things, hopeth all things, endureth in all things. Though that prophesying fail, other[2] tongues shall cease, or knowledge vanish away, yet love falleth never away.

For our knowledge is unperfect and our prophesying is unperfect. But when that which is perfect is come, then that which is unperfect shall be done away. When I was a child, I spake as a child, I understood as a child, I imagined as a child. But as soon as I was a man, I put away childishness. Now we see in a glass, even in a dark[3] speaking: but then shall we see face to face. Now I know unperfectly: but then shall I know even as I am known. Now abideth faith, hope, and love, even these three: but the chief of these is love.

1525, 1535

From *The Geneva Bible*

Though I speak with the tongues of men and Angels, and have not love, I am as sounding brass, or a tinkling cymbal. And though I had the gift of prophecy, and knew all secrets and all knowledge, yea, if I had all faith, so that I could remove mountains, and had not love, I were nothing. And though I feed the poor with all my goods, and though I give my body, that I be burned, and have not love, it profiteth me nothing. Love suffereth long: it is bountiful: love envieth not: love doth not boast itself: it is not puffed up: It disdaineth not: it seeketh not her own things: it is not provoked to anger: it thinketh not evil: It rejoiceth not in iniquity, but rejoiceth in the truth: It suffereth all things: it believeth all things: it hopeth all things: it endureth all things. Love doth never fall away, though that prophesyings be abolished, or the tongues cease, or knowledge vanish away. For we know in part, and we prophesy in part. But when that which is perfect is come, then that which is in part shall be abolished. When I was a child, I spake as a child, I understood as a child, I thought as a child: but when I became a man, I put away childish things. For now we see through a glass darkly:[4] but then shall we see face to face. Now I know in part: but then shall I know even as I am known. And now abideth faith, hope, and love, even these three: but the chiefest of these is love.

1560, 1602

---

1. Perversely, evilly.
2. Or.
3. Obscure, unclear. "Glass": mirror. The metaphor of indirect, imperfect sight seems to derive from Plato's Allegory of the Cave (*Republic* 7).
4. By means of a mirror, obscurely.

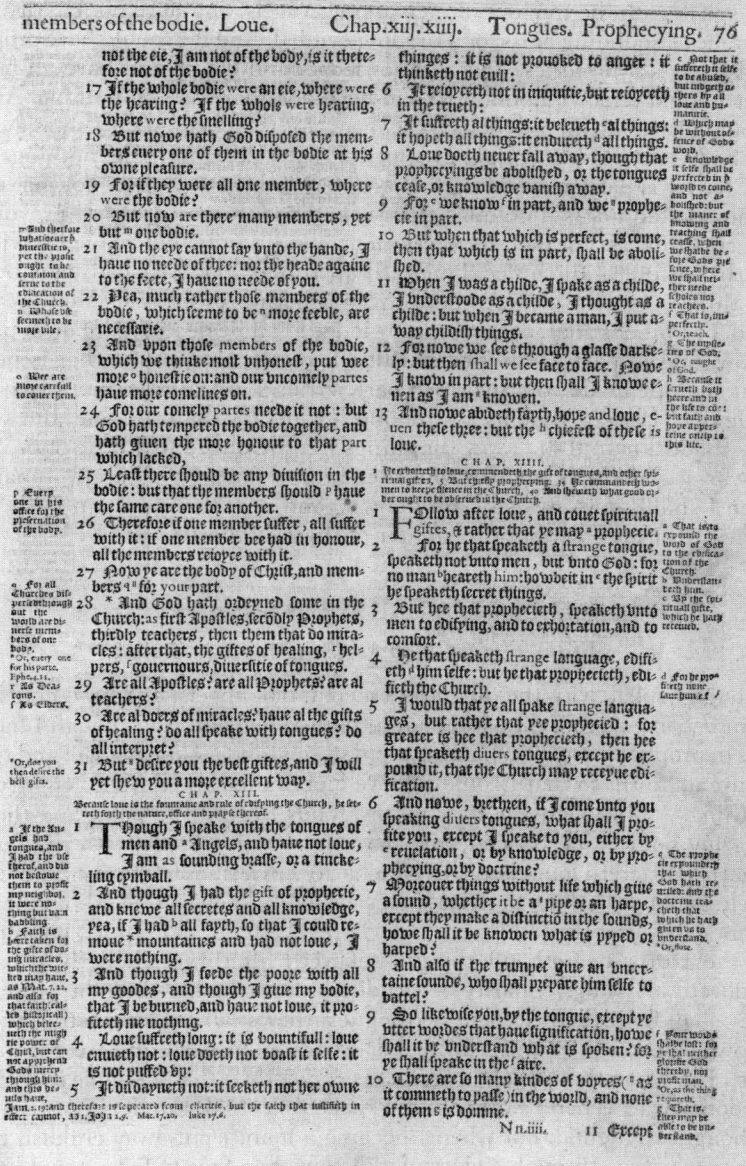

A Page from the Geneva Bible, with Commentary; 1583 Edition. The Geneva Bible includes elaborate marginal notes, often with a sharply Protestant inflection. Some Elizabethan Catholics may have detected such a perspective in one note's anticipation of a redeemed state "where we shal neither nede scholes nor teachers."

From *The Douay-Rheims Version*

If I speak with the tongues of men and of Angels, and have not charity,[5] I am become as sounding brass, or a tinkling cymbal. And if I should have prophecy, and knew all mysteries, and all knowledge, and if I should have all faith so that I could remove mountains, and have not charity, I am nothing. And if I should distribute all my goods to be meat[6] for the poor, and if I should deliver my body so that I burn, and have not charity, it doth profit me nothing.

Charity is patient, is benign: charity envieth not, dealeth not perversely: is not puffed up, is not ambitious, seeketh not her own, is not provoked to anger, thinketh not evil: rejoiceth not upon iniquity, but rejoiceth with the truth: suffereth all things, believeth all things, hopeth all things, beareth all things. Charity never falleth away: whether prophecies shall be made void, or tongues shall cease, or knowledge shall be destroyed. For in part we know, and in part we prophesy. But when that shall come that is perfect, that shall be made void that is in part. When I was a little one, I spake as a little one, I understood as a little one, I thought as a little one. But when I was made a man, I did away the things that belonged to a little one. We see now by a glass in a dark sort: but then face to face. Now I know in part: but then I shall know as also I am known. And now there remain faith, hope, charity, these three, but the greater of these is charity.

1582

From *The Authorized (King James) Version*

Though I speak with the tongues of men and of angels, and have not charity, I am become as sounding brass, or a tinkling cymbal. And though I have the gift of prophecy, and understand all mysteries, and all knowledge; and though I have all faith, so that I could remove mountains, and have no charity, I am nothing. And though I bestow all my goods to feed the poor, and though I give my body to be burned, and have not charity, it profiteth me nothing. Charity suffereth long, and is kind; charity envieth not; charity vaunteth not itself, is not puffed up, doth not behave itself unseemly, seeketh not her own, is not easily provoked, thinketh no evil; rejoiceth not in iniquity, but rejoiceth in the truth; beareth all things, believeth all things, hopeth all things, endureth all things. Charity never faileth: but whether there be prophecies, they shall fail; whether there be tongues, they shall cease; whether there be knowledge, it shall vanish away. For we know in part, and we prophesy in part. But when that which is perfect is come, then that which is in part shall be done away. When I was a child, I spake as a child, I understood as a child, I thought as a child: but when I became a man, I put away childish things. For now we see through a glass, darkly; but then face to face: now I know in part; but then shall I know even as also I am known. And now abideth faith, hope, charity, these three; but the greatest of these is charity.

1611

---

5. From Latin *caritas*, "love"; but also carrying the modern sense.

6. Food (in general).

WILLIAM TYNDALE

Educated at Oxford, William Tyndale (ca. 1490–1536) became a lecturer at Cambridge, where he was associated with a group of humanist scholars who met regularly at the White Horse Inn. Having become convinced that salvation depended on direct access to the word of God, he sought official support to undertake a translation of the Bible into English; but English church authorities, concerned about the spread of heresies, blocked this project. In 1524 Tyndale went to Germany, where, with the financial assistance of wealthy London merchants, he completed a translation of the New Testament the following year. Deeply influenced by the writings of Martin Luther and other reformers, he also wrote a series of doctrinal and polemical works, such as *The Obedience of a Christian Man* (1528), that eloquently express the Protestant hope of salvation through faith alone and reject the principles and practices of Roman Catholicism. Because of their bitter assaults on the Catholic Church, Protestants like Tyndale were often accused of fomenting rebellion. *The Obedience of a Christian Man* attempts to answer the charge by insisting on the subject's absolute secular obligation to obey the king. At Anne Boleyn's urging, Henry VIII read it and is reported to have remarked that "this is a book for me and for all kings to read." Notwithstanding this supposed endorsement, English Catholic authorities during Henry's reign managed to lure Tyndale into a trap and had him strangled and burned in Vilvorde, Flanders.

From The Obedience of a Christian Man

[THE FORGIVENESS OF SINS]

* * * For sin we through fragility never so oft, yet as soon as we repent and come into the right way again, and unto the testament[1] which God hath made in Christ's blood, our sins vanish away as smoke in the wind, and as darkness at the coming of light; or as thou castest a little blood, or milk, into the main sea: insomuch that whosoever goeth about to make satisfaction for his sins to God-ward,[2] saying in his heart, This much have I sinned, this much will I do again; or this-wise will I live to make amends withal; or this will I do, to get heaven withal; the same is an infidel, faithless, and damned in his deed-doing, and hath lost his part in Christ's blood; because he is disobedient unto God's testament, and setteth up another of his own imagination, unto which he will compel God to obey. If we love God, we have a commandment to love our neighbor also, as saith John in his epistle;[3] and if we have offended him, to make him amends; or if we have not wherewith, to ask him forgiveness, and to do and suffer all things for his sake, to win him

---

1. Covenant. "Fragility": frailty, moral weakness.
2. That is, in his relationship to God.
3. "If a man say, I love God, and hateth his brother, he is a liar: for he that loveth not his brother whom he hath seen, how can he love God whom he hath not seen? And this commandment have we from him, That he who loveth God love his brother also" (1 John 4:20–21).

to God, and to nourish peace and unity. But to God-ward Christ is an everlasting satisfaction, and ever sufficient.[4]

[SCRIPTURAL INTERPRETATION]

Thou shalt understand, therefore, that the Scripture hath but one sense, which is the literal sense. And that literal sense is the root and ground of all, and the anchor that never faileth, whereunto if thou cleave, thou canst never err or go out of the way. And if thou leave the literal sense, thou canst not but go out of the way. Neverthelater,[5] the Scripture useth proverbs, similitudes, riddles, or allegories, as all other speeches do; but that which the proverb, similitude, riddle, or allegory signifieth, is ever the literal sense, which thou must seek out diligently: as in the English we borrow words and sentences of one thing, and apply them unto another, and give them new significations. We say, "Let the sea swell and rise as high as he will, yet hath God appointed how far he shall go": meaning that the tyrants shall not do what they would, but that only which God hath appointed them to do. "Look ere thou leap": whose literal sense is, "Do nothing suddenly, or without advisement." "Cut not the bough that thou standest upon": whose literal sense is, "Oppress not the commons"; and is borrowed of hewers. When a thing speedeth[6] not well, we borrow speech, and say, "The bishop hath blessed it"; because that nothing speedeth well that they meddle withal. If the porridge be burned too, or the meat over-roasted, we say, "The bishop hath put his foot in the pot," or "The bishop hath played the cook"; because the bishops burn whom they lust,[7] and whosoever displeaseth them. "He is a pontifical fellow"; that is, proud and stately. "He is popish"; that is, superstitious and faithless.

* * *

Beyond all this, when we have found out the literal sense of the Scripture by the process of the text, or by a like text of another place, then go we, and as the Scripture borroweth similitudes of worldly things, even so we again borrow similitudes or allegories of the Scripture, and apply them to our purposes; which allegories are no sense of the Scripture, but free things besides the Scripture, and altogether in the liberty of the Spirit. * * * This allegory proveth nothing, neither can do. For it is not the Scripture, but an ensample[8] or a similitude borrowed of the Scripture, to declare a text or a conclusion of the Scripture more expressly, and to root it and grave[9] it in the heart. For a similitude, or an ensample, doth print a thing much deeper in the wits of a man than doth a plain speaking, and leaveth behind him as it were a sting to prick him forward, and to awake him withal. Moreover, if I could not prove with an open[1] text that which the allegory doth express, then were the allegory a thing to be jested at, and of no greater value than a tale of Robin Hood.

1527, 1528

---

4. To the ecclesiastical commissioners who examined Tyndale's works in 1530, this passage was clearly heretical. One of the commissioners, Sir Thomas More, lambasted it as constituting an encouragement to sin because it made obtaining forgiveness seem such an easy matter.

5. Nevertheless.
6. Succeeds, prospers.
7. Whomever they please.
8. Example.
9. Engrave.
1. Plain, clear.

THOMAS MORE

As early as 1521, when he became Henry VIII's "theological councillor," Thomas More had played an important role in the official campaign against Luther. Initially writing doctrinal attacks on Protestantism under the king's name, by 1529, when he became lord chancellor of England, More was immersed in the anti-Protestant campaign in his own right. His extremely energetic contributions included written attacks, in English, on Tyndale's Bible translations and other prohibited books and extended to active persecution of those defined as heretics. A few years earlier, in *Utopia*, More had imagined a state that would tolerate a diversity of religious convictions, but that view had vanished in the face of actual dissent. "I find that breed of men absolutely loathsome," More wrote to his friend Erasmus; "I want to be as hateful to them as anyone can possibly be." During his tenure as lord chancellor, several Protestants were imprisoned in More's own house while he tried to persuade them to renounce views unacceptable to Roman Catholic orthodoxy, and six people were burned at the stake for heresy. If More was willing to kill in defense of the doctrines in which he passionately believed, he also proved willing in the end to die for his beliefs.

More had two principal quarrels with Lutheranism: (1) he objected to Luther's denial that Christians could contribute to their own salvation through their good works, and (2) he objected to Luther's view of biblical interpretation. For Luther, scripture preceded and ideally determined the form of the Church; for More, the Church preceded and determined the interpretation of scripture.

In *A Dialogue Concerning Heresies* (1529), More raises both issues. Departing from the head-on, bitter attacks of his Latin works, More here adopts a different approach: one of the speakers in his *Dialogue* is a young man on friendly terms with More but infatuated with Protestant ideas; the other speaker is a version of More himself. More's aim seems to be less to attack Luther directly than, by using wit, to dissuade English men and women from embracing Protestantism.

The selection printed here tackles the fundamental issues of biblical interpretation. Who decides on the meaning of scripture: the Church or individual readers? More's interlocutor is in no doubt: scripture is for the most part entirely plain; individual readers have no trouble interpreting it. More strongly counters such simple faith in the plain and literal sense. Everything, he argues (in a passage playing with the consonance of "goose" and "gloss"), requires a commentary. Even to compare one text with another is to gloss it, and any translation of the Bible is itself inevitably a gloss. If commentary is always necessary, then some stable ground for establishing authority over that commentary also becomes necessary. For More that ground is the Catholic Church, whose authority is established by the many centuries of its continued existence and by the consensus of the Church's councils. More casts the young Lutheran's position as that of a single opinionated reader perversely resisting the "common faith" of Christendom.

From A Dialogue Concerning Heresies

From *Book 1, Chapter 28:* * * * *proving the authority of the old interpreters and the infallible authority of the Church* * * *

"* * * in somewhat, ye say, ye will believe the Church, but not in all. In anything beside Scripture ye will not, nor in the interpretation of Scripture ye will not; and so, where ye said that ye believe the Church in somewhat, in very deed ye believe the Church in right nought. For wherein will ye believe it, if ye believe it not in the interpretation of Scripture? For as touching the text, ye believe the Scripture self, and not the Church."

"Methinketh," quod[1] he, "the text is good enough and plain enough, needing no gloss[2] if it be well considered, and every part compared with other."

"Hard it were," quod I, "to find anything so plain that it should need no gloss at all."

"In faith," quod he, "they make a gloss to some texts that be as plain as it is that twice two make four."

"Why," quod I, "needeth that no gloss at all?"

"I trow[3] so," quod he. "Or else the devil is on it."

"Iwis,"[4] quod I, "and yet though ye would believe one that would tell you that twice two ganders made always four geese, yet ye would be advised[5] ere ye believed him that would tell you that twice two geese made always four ganders. For therein might ye be deceived. And him would ye not believe at all, that would tell you that twice two geese would always make four horse."

"Tut," quod he, "this is a merry[6] matter. They must be all the twice twain always of one kind. But geese and horse be of diverse."

"Well," quod I, "then every man that is neither goose nor horse seeth that there is one gloss yet.[7] But now," quod I, "the geese and the ganders be both of one kind, and yet twice two geese make not always four ganders."

"A sweet matter," quod he. "Ye wot[8] what I mean well enough."

"I think I do," quod I. "But I think if ye bring it forth it will make another gloss to your text, as plain as your text is; and[9] ye will in all Holy Scripture have no gloss at all. And yet will ye have collation made of one text with another, and show how they may be agreed together[1]—as though all that were no gloss."

"Yea," quod he, "but would you that we should believe the Church if it set a gloss that will in no wise[2] agree with the text, but that it appeareth plainly that the text, well considered, saith clean the contrary?"

"To whom doth that appear," quod I, "so plainly, when it appeareth one to you, and to the whole Church another?"

"Yet if I see it so," quod he, "though holy doctors and all the whole Church would tell me the contrary, methinketh I were no more bounden to believe them all, that the Scripture meaneth as they take it, than if they would all tell me that a thing were white which I see myself is black."

"Of late," quod I, "ye would believe the Church in something. And now not only ye would believe it in nothing, but also whereas God would the Church should be your judge, ye would now be judge over the Church. And ye will by your wit[3] be judge whether the Church, in the understanding of Holy Scripture that God hath written to His Church, do judge aright or err. As for your white and black, never shall it be that ye shall see the thing black that all other shall see white. But ye may be sure that if all other see it white, and ye take it for black, your eyen[4] be sore deceived. For the

---

1. Quoth, said.
2. Interpretation, commentary.
3. Believe.
4. Certainly.
5. Warned.
6. Frivolous.
7. Still.
8. Know.
9. Whereas.
1. Reconciled.
2. Way.
3. Intellect.
4. Eyes.

Church will not, I think, agree to call it other than it seemeth to them. And much marvel were it, if ye should in Holy Scripture see better than the old holy doctors and Christ's whole Church."

* * *

1528–29   1529

JOHN CALVIN

Born to middle-class parents in Picardy, France, and trained as a lawyer, Calvin (1509–1564) was steeped in the Greek and Latin learning associated with Renaissance humanism. He acquired as well a knowledge of Hebrew, so that he was powerfully equipped to respond to the call, from Erasmus and others, for a study of the Bible in its original languages. Drawn increasingly toward Protestantism, Calvin left Catholic France for Switzerland, where he eventually established a stern theocratic rule in Geneva. Through his many writings, he also became the principal theologian of the Protestant Reformation, exercising immense influence in England and Scotland as well as on the Continent. His major work, revised in successive Latin and French editions and widely translated, is *The Institution of Christian Religion*. The passage printed here is from Calvin's famous, troubling account of the doctrine of predestination, according to which God has determined before the foundation of the world whom he will save and whom he will damn, regardless of the merits or defects of these individuals. The good deeds that a virtuous person does in life are a sign of having divine "election" (to be saved), not a means to secure salvation. The translation, closely adhering to the Latin original, is by Thomas Norton (1532–1584), a lawyer and member of Parliament and, with Thomas Sackville, the author of the earliest English tragedy in blank verse, *Gorboduc*—first performed in the same year (1561) that Norton's translation of Calvin appeared.

From The Institution of Christian Religion, written in Latin by Master John Calvin, and translated into English according to the author's last edition

From *Book 3, Chapter 21*
Of the eternal election, whereby God hath predestinate some to salvation, and other some to destruction

But now whereas the covenant of life[1] is not equally preached to all men, and with them to whom it is preached it doth not either equally or continually find like place,[2] in this diversity the wondrous depth of the judgment of God appeareth. For neither is it any doubt but that this diversity also serveth the free choice of God's eternal election.[3] If it be evident that it is wrought by the will of God that salvation is freely offered to some, and other some are

---

1. Promise of salvation.
2. Consideration.
3. Choice; that is, of whom to save.

debarred from coming to it, here by and by[4] arise great and hard questions which cannot otherwise be discussed than if the godly minds have that certainly stablished which they ought to hold[5] concerning election and predestination. This is (as many think) a cumbersome[6] question: because they think nothing to be less reasonable than of the common multitude of men some to be foreordained to salvation, other some to destruction. But how they wrongfully encumber themselves shall afterward be evident by the framing of the matter together.[7] Beside that in the very same darkness which maketh men afraid, not only the profitableness of this doctrine but also the most sweet fruit showeth forth itself. We shall never be clearly persuaded, as we ought to be, that our salvation floweth out of the fountain of the free mercy of God, till his eternal election be known to us, which by this comparison brightly setteth forth the grace of God, that he doth not without difference adopt all into the hope of salvation,[8] but giveth to some that which he denieth to other. How much the ignorance of this principle diminisheth of the glory of God, how much it withdraweth from true humility, it is plain to see.

* * *

They which shut the gates, that none may be bold to come to the tasting of this doctrine, do no less wrong to men than to God: because neither shall any other thing suffice to humble us as we ought to be, neither shall we otherwise feel from our heart how much we are bound[9] to God. Neither yet is there any otherwhere the upholding stay of sound affiance,[1] as Christ himself teacheth, which to deliver us from all fear, and to make us unvanquishable among so many dangers, ambushes, and deadly battles, promiseth that whatsoever he hath received of[2] his Father to keep shall be safe.[3] Whereof we gather that they shall with continual trembling be miserable, whosoever they be that know not themselves to be the proper possession of God; and therefore that they do very ill provide both for themselves and for all the faithful, which, in being blind at these three profits which we have touched,[4] would wish the whole foundation of our salvation to be quite taken from among us. Moreover, hereby the Church appeareth unto us, which otherwise (as Bernard rightly teacheth)[5] were not possible to be found nor to be known among creatures, because both ways in marvelous wise[6] it lieth hidden: within the bosom of blessed predestination, and within the mass of miserable damnation.

But ere I enter into the matter itself, I must beforehand in two sorts speak to two sorts of men.[7] That the entreating[8] of predestination, whereas of itself it is somewhat cumbersome, is made very doubtful, yea, and dangerous, the curiousness of men is the cause: which can by no stops be refrained from wandering into forbidden compasses,[9] and climbing up on high; which,

4. Immediately.
5. Believe. "Stablished": established.
6. Troublesome.
7. That is, from the following discussion.
8. He does not extend the hope of salvation equally to all.
9. Obliged.
1. Trust, faith. "Stay": support.
2. From.
3. "My sheep hear my voice, and I know them, and they follow me: And I give unto them eternal life; and they shall never perish, neither shall any man pluck them out of my hand. My Father, which gave them me, is greater than all; and no man is able to pluck them out of my Father's hand" (John 10:27–29).
4. That is, God's free mercy, God's glory, and our true humility.
5. Saint Bernard of Clairvaux (1090–1153), in his *Sermons on the Song of Songs*.
6. In a marvelous fashion.
7. I must first speak in two different ways about two sorts of men.
8. Treating, discussing.
9. Places.

if it may, will leave to God no secret which it will not search and turn over. Into this boldness and importunacy[1] forasmuch as we commonly see many to run headlong, and among those some that are otherwise not evil men, here is fit occasion to warn them what is in this behalf[2] the due measure of their duty. First, therefore, let them remember that when they inquire upon predestination, they pierce into the secret closets[3] of the wisdom of God: whereinto if any man too carelessly and boldly break in, he shall both not attain wherewith to satisfy his curiousness, and he shall enter into a maze whereof he shall find no way to get out again. For neither is it meet[4] that man should freely search those things which God hath willed to be hidden in himself, and to turn over from very eternity the height of wisdom,[5] which he willed to be honored and not to be conceived, that by it also he mought[6] be marvelous unto us. Those secrets of his will which he hath determined to be opened unto us, he hath disclosed in his Word: and he hath determined, so far as he foresaw to pertain to us and to be profitable for us.[7]

* * *

There be other which, when they have a will to remedy this evil,[8] do command all mention of predestination to be in a manner buried: at the least they teach men to flee from every manner of questioning thereof as from a rock. Although the moderation of these men be herein worthily to be praised, that they judge that mysteries should be tasted of with such sobriety, yet because they descend too much beneath the mean,[9] they little prevail with the wit of man, which doth not lightly suffer[1] itself to be restrained. Therefore, that in this behalf also we may keep a right end,[2] we must return to the Word of the Lord, in which we have a sure rule of understanding. For the Scripture is the school of the Holy Ghost, in which as nothing is left out which is both necessary and profitable to be known, so nothing is taught but that which is behoveful[3] to learn. Whatsoever therefore is uttered in the Scripture concerning predestination, we must beware that we debar not the faithful from it, lest we should seem either enviously[4] to defraud them of the benefit of their God or to blame and accuse the Holy Ghost, who hath published those things which it is in any wise[5] profitable to be suppressed.

* * *

That, therefore, which the Scripture clearly showeth, we say that God by eternal and unchangeable counsel hath once appointed whom in time to come he would take to salvation, and on the other side whom he would condemn to destruction. This counsel as touching the elect,[6] we say to be grounded upon his free mercy, without any respect of[7] the worthiness of man: but whom he appointeth to damnation, to them by his judgment (which

---

1. Pertinacity, stubborn persistence.
2. In this regard.
3. Inner chambers.
4. Fitting.
5. And to search out from eternity itself the sublimest wisdom.
6. Might. "Conceived": understood.
7. That is, God has let us know, in the scriptures, as much about these matters as he foresaw would be useful for us to know.
8. That is, the audacious attempt to learn more about predestination than scripture teaches.
9. That is, fall short of the appropriate middle ground ("mean").
1. Permit. "Wit": intellect.
2. Keep within proper bounds.
3. Useful, advantageous.
4. Out of jealousy; maliciously.
5. In any way.
6. Those predestined to salvation.
7. Regard toward.

is indeed just and irreprehensible but also incomprehensible) the entry of life is foreclosed. Now in the elect we set vocation to be the testimony[8] of election; and then justification[9] to be another sign of the manifest showing of it, till they come to glory, wherein is the fulfilling of it. But as by vocation and election God marketh his elect, so by shutting out the reprobate[1] either from the knowledge of his name or from the sanctification of his spirit, he doth as it were by these marks open what judgment abideth[2] for them. * * *

1561

8. Evidence. "Vocation": a calling; a predisposition to the religious life.
9. The state of being justified; that is, freed from the penalty of sin and accounted righteous by God. The underlying scriptural text for this passage is Romans 8:30: "whom he did predestinate, them he also called: and whom he called, them he also justified: and whom he justified, them he also glorified."
1. Those predestined to damnation.
2. Waits. "Open": reveal.

ANNE ASKEW

In the 1540s, Henry VIII sought to return the English Church to a basically Catholic doctrinal position, and Protestants were subjected to persecution. The outspoken Protestant Anne Askew (1521–1546) was called in for questioning in 1545; the next year, she was tortured on the rack and burned at the stake. Askew's accounts of her two examinations were smuggled out of England by the reformer John Bale, who published them in Germany (1546–47). The texts were later incorporated into John Foxe's *Acts and Monuments* (1563).

Vivid first-person accounts like Askew's were intended to bear witness to the astonishing courage and determination of a small group of ardent Protestants, men and women alike, who were willing to die for their convictions. (When the political tides shifted, there were comparable Catholic figures who endured similar trials for their faith.) Though obedience to authority was instilled in Tudor England and though women in particular were expected to be submissive, social norms could be upended by religious conviction. By the time of the examinations Askew describes, she had already repeatedly defied her Catholic husband, who denounced her publicly and had her arrested. Even when showed the instruments of torture, she refused to name any of her associates or to take back any of her beliefs.

The theological controversies over the meaning of the bread and wine taken in church, the "Eucharist," for which Askew and her companions along with many other Protestants and Catholics were willing to lay down their lives, require some explanation. Catholic doctrine held that if the formula of consecration of the bread and wine was correctly spoken by a properly ordained priest, a miraculous "transubstantiation"—in which the bread or Host became the body of Christ and the wine his blood—would occur, whether or not the priest or the communicant was in a state of grace. Indeed, some Catholic theologians argued that because the bread had objectively been transformed into the body of God, even a mouse nibbling on a consecrated host would be receiving Christ's flesh. In contrast, Protestants argued that an evil priest would not only be damning himself (as Catholics also believed) but would also be turning the Lord's Supper itself into the Devil's Supper.

From The First Examination of Anne Askew

To satisfy your expectation, good people (sayeth she), this was my first examination in the year of our Lord 1545, and in the month of March. First, Christopher Dare examined me at Saddlers' Hall, being one of the quest,[1] and asked if I did not believe that the sacrament hanging over the altar[2] was the very body of Christ really. Then I demanded[3] this question of him: wherefore Saint Stephen was stoned to death.[4] And he said he could not tell. Then I answered that no more would I assoil[5] his vain question.

Secondly, he said that there was a woman which did testify that I should read[6] how God was not in temples made with hands. Then I showed him the seventh and the seventeenth chapters of the Acts of the Apostles, what Stephen and Paul had said therein.[7] Whereupon he asked me how I took those sentences.[8] I answered that I would not throw pearls among swine,[9] for acorns were good enough.

Thirdly, he asked me wherefore I said that I had rather to read five lines in the Bible than to hear five masses in the temple. I confessed that I said no less. Not for the dispraise of either the Epistle or Gospel, but because the one did greatly edify me and the other[1] nothing at all. As Saint Paul doth witness in the fourteenth chapter of his first Epistle to the Corinthians, whereas he doth say: "If the trumpet giveth an uncertain sound, who will prepare himself to the battle?"

Fourthly, he laid unto my charge that I should say: "If an ill[2] priest ministered, it was the Devil and not God." My answer was that I never spake such thing. But this was my saying: "That whatsoever he were which ministered unto me, his ill conditions could not hurt my faith, but in spirit I received nevertheless the body and blood of Christ." He asked me what I said concerning confession. I answered him my meaning, which was as Saint James sayeth, that every man ought to knowledge[3] his faults to other, and the one to pray for the other.

Sixthly, he asked me what I said to the king's book.[4] And I answered him that I could say nothing to it, because I never saw it.

Seventhly, he asked me if I had the spirit of God in me. I answered if I had not, I was but reprobate or cast away. Then he said he had sent for a priest to examine me, which was there at hand. The priest asked me what I said to the sacrament of the altar.[5] And required much to know therein my meaning. But I desired him again to hold me excused concerning that matter. None other answer would I make him, because I perceived him a papist.[6]

---

1. Inquest. "Saddlers' Hall": belonging to the guild of saddle makers.
2. The holy wafers were sometimes held in a hanging vessel in the shape of a dove, symbolizing the Holy Ghost.
3. Asked.
4. Stephen was martyred in Jerusalem after proclaiming that God "dwelleth not in temples made with hands" and accusing the priests of the temple of resisting the Holy Ghost and persecuting the prophets (Acts 7:48–60). "Wherefore": why.
5. Resolve.
6. Would teach.
7. Acts 17:24 repeats the assertion of Acts 7 that God does not dwell in temples built by human hands.
8. Interpreted those pronouncements.
9. Matthew 7:6.
1. "The one . . . the other": that is, the Bible . . . the mass.
2. Wicked.
3. Acknowledge. See James 5:16.
4. *A Necessary Doctrine and Erudition for Any Christian Man* (1543), with a preface by the king, sought to put a brake on reformers' "sinister understanding of Scripture, presumption, arrogancy, carnal liberty, and contention," by affirming a number of basically Catholic positions.
5. The Eucharist.
6. Follower of the pope; that is, Roman Catholic.

Eighthly, he asked me if I did not think that private masses did help souls departed.[7] And [I] said it was great idolatry to believe more in them than in the death which Christ died for us. Then they had me thence unto my lord mayor and he examined me, as they had before, and I answered him directly in all things as I answered the quest afore. Besides this, my lord mayor laid one thing unto my charge which was never spoken of[8] me but of them. And that was whether a mouse eating the host received God or no. This question did I never ask, but indeed they asked it of me, whereunto I made them no answer, but smiled. Then the bishop's chancellor rebuked me and said that I was much to blame for uttering the Scriptures. For Saint Paul (he said) forbade women to speak or to talk of the word of God. I answered him that I knew Paul's meaning as well as he, which is, 1 Corinthians 14, that a woman ought not to speak in the congregation by the way of teaching. And then I asked him how many women he had seen go into the pulpit and preach? He said he never saw none. Then I said he ought to find no fault in poor women, except[9] they had offended the law. Then my lord mayor commanded me to ward.[1] I asked him if sureties[2] would not serve me, and he made me short answer, that he would take none.

Then was I had to the Counter,[3] and there remained eleven days, no friend admitted to speak with me. But in the meantime there was a priest sent to me which said that he was commanded of the bishop to examine me and to give me good counsel, which he did not. But first he asked me for what cause I was put in the Counter. And I told him I could not tell. Then he said it was great pity that I should be there without cause, and concluded that he was very sorry for me.

Secondly, he said it was told him that I should deny the sacrament of the altar. And I answered him again that, that[4] I had said, I had said. Thirdly, he asked me if I were shriven.[5] I told him, so that I might have one of these three, that is to say, Doctor Crome, Sir William, or Huntingdon,[6] I was contented, because I knew them to be men of wisdom. "As for you or any other I will not dispraise, because I know ye not."

Then he said, "I would not have you think but that I or another that shall be brought you shall be as honest as they. For if we were not, ye may be sure, the king would not suffer us to preach."

Then I answered by the saying of Solomon, "By communing with the wise, I may learn wisdom: But by talking with a fool, I shall take scathe"[7] (Proverbs 1).

Fourthly, he asked me, if the host should fall and a beast did eat it, whether the beast did receive God or no. I answered, "Seeing ye have taken the pains to ask this question, I desire you also to assoil[8] it yourself. For I will not do it, because I perceive ye come to tempt me." And he said it was against the order of schools that he which asked the question should answer it. I told him I was but a woman and knew not the course of schools.[9] Fifthly, he asked me if I

---

7. By shortening their time in Purgatory.
8. By.
9. Unless.
1. Imprisonment.
2. Guarantors of good behavior.
3. A London prison.
4. What.
5. Absolved after confessing to a priest.
6. Reformist preachers. "So": if.
7. Injury.
8. Answer.
9. Rules governing Catholic theological debates; scholastic procedures.

intended to receive the sacrament at Easter or no. I answered that else I were no Christian woman, and that I did rejoice that the time was so near at hand. And then he departed thence with many fair words.

* * *

In the meanwhile he commanded his archdeacon to common[1] with me, who said unto me, "Mistress, wherefore are ye accused and thus troubled here before the bishop?"

To whom I answered again and said, "Sir, ask, I pray you, my accusers, for I know not as yet."

Then took he my book out of my hand and said, "Such books as this hath brought you to the trouble you are in. Beware," sayeth he, "beware, for he that made this book and was the author thereof was an heretic, I warrant you, and burnt in Smithfield."[2]

Then I asked him if he were certain and sure that it was true that[3] he had spoken. And he said he knew well the book was of John Frith's making.[4] Then I asked him if he were not ashamed for to judge of the book before he saw it within, or yet knew the truth thereof. I said also that such unadvised and hasty judgment is token apparent of a very slender wit.[5] Then I opened the book and showed it to him. He said he thought it had been another, for he could find no fault therein. Then I desired him no more to be so unadvisedly rash and swift in judgment, till he thoroughly knew the truth; and so he departed from me. * * *

1546–47, 1563

1. Converse.
2. Smithfield Market, just outside the London city walls, was a site of public executions until the 17th century.
3. What.
4. The reformer John Frith was executed in 1533. *A Book Made by John Frith, Prisoner in the Tower of London, Answering unto Master More's Letter . . . Concerning the Sacrament of the Body and Blood of Christ*, published in that year, was reissued in revised form in 1546, a few weeks before Askew was executed.
5. Shallow mind.

JOHN FOXE

When the Catholic Mary Tudor became queen, in 1553, and began to persecute Protestants, John Foxe (1516–1587), who had been a fellow at Oxford University and had served as a tutor to the children of noble families, fled to the Continent. The book for which he became famous was already under way: the first version (Strasbourg, 1554) was in Latin and dealt with the persecutions suffered by the early reformers, particularly John Wycliffe and John Hus. But his book grew and grew as Foxe received from England and Scotland accounts of the persecutions, including hideous tortures, being inflicted on the Protestants there. When Elizabeth came to the throne, in 1558, Foxe returned at once to England, and there he translated his Latin volume, adding to it hundreds of stories of those martyred under Queen Mary (many based on eyewitness testimony, some on hearsay and rumor). The English edition was first published in 1563; often called "Foxe's Book of Martyrs," the work was titled *Acts and Monuments of these latter and perilous*

The Burning of Thomas Cranmer, from Foxe's *Acts and Monuments*. Cranmer, archbishop of Canterbury, was arrested, tried for treason, and burned at the stake in front of Balliol College, Oxford, on March 21, 1556. Here he stretches his right hand into the fire, since that hand had been responsible for writing (or at least signing) a recantation of his Protestant faith, an apostasy that he repudiated just before his execution. The image also shows Cranmer crying out, "Lord, receive my spirit," traditionally said to be part of the dying words of the first Christian martyr, Saint Stephen.

days, touching matters of the church, wherein are comprehended and described the great persecution and horrible troubles that have been wrought and practiced by the Romish prelates from the year of Our Lord a thousand to the time now present.

Foxe saw life as an apocalyptic struggle between good and evil, Christ and Antichrist. Immediately and enormously popular, his book is a compendium of memoirs, stories, personal letters, court records, and the like, rendering the words, acts, and sufferings of some hundreds of martyrs in graphic—if often fictionalized—detail. The final version of the book (1583) is massive—more than six thousand folio pages, containing four million words. Though vehemently criticized by Catholics for its distortions and errors, it helped shape for generations of men and women across the broad social spectrum a sense of collective identity and destiny. Apart from fanning the flames of anti-Catholic feeling, Foxe had an immense influence on English nationalism. His stories—from the medieval crypto-Protestants burned for heresy to the Protestant martyrs who passed through the fiery trials of the Marian persecutions—portrayed England as the land of a new chosen people, destined to lead the way toward the kingdom of God on earth. Foxe's second edition (1570) was placed, by government order, in churches throughout England.

From Acts and Monuments

[THE DEATH OF ANNE ASKEW]

Hitherto we have entreated of[1] this good woman; now it remaineth that we touch somewhat as touching her end and martyrdom. She being born of such stock and kindred that she might have lived in great wealth and prosperity, if she would rather have followed the world than Christ, but now she was so tormented, that she could neither live long in so great distress, neither yet by the adversaries be suffered[2] to die in secret. Wherefore the day of her execution was appointed, and she brought into Smithfield[3] in a chair, because she could not go on her feet, by means[4] of her great torments. When she was brought unto the stake she was tied by the middle with a chain that held up her body. When all things were thus prepared to the fire, the king's letters of pardon were brought, whereby to offer her safeguard of her life if she would recant, which she would neither receive neither[5] yet vouchsafe once to look upon. Shaxton[6] also was there present, who, openly that day recanting his opinions, went about with a long oration to cause her also to turn, against whom she stoutly resisted. Thus she being troubled so many manner of ways, and having passed through so many torments, having now ended the long course of her agonies, being compassed in with flames of fire, as a blessed sacrifice unto God, she slept in the Lord, in anno[7] 1546, leaving behind her a singular example of Christian constancy for all men to follow.

1563

1. Treated, discussed.
2. Allowed.
3. See p. 157, n. 2.
4. Because.
5. Nor.
6. Nicholas Shaxton, formerly bishop of Salisbury.
7. The year.

ANNE COOKE BACON

It was while he was a student at Oxford University that John Jewel (1522–1571) became devoted to the Protestant cause. But when, later, he advanced to the position of public orator of Oxford, he had to compose a Latin epistle in honor of the Catholic Mary I, who had just ascended to the throne. Because he retained his allegiance to Protestantism, for his own safety he fled to Frankfurt, returning to England only after the Protestant Elizabeth I was crowned.

An Apology is a book Jewel wrote, as bishop of Salisbury, against Catholicism and in defense of the establishment of the English Protestant Church. The section provided here, from the end of the book, maintains that English Protestant Reformers are simply bringing back the values of a historic "old" church, in the face of a viciously corrupt Catholicism. In 1609 Archbishop Richard Bancroft ordered that Jewel's *Apology* be placed in all churches in the land.

Anne Cooke Bacon (ca. 1527–1610), one of the five daughters of Sir Anthony Cooke, was said to be the most learned women in England. Married to Nicholas Bacon, privy councillor and lord keeper of the great seal under Queen Elizabeth,

Bacon had two children; her younger son was the philosopher Francis Bacon. Bacon knew Jewel and shared his Protestant beliefs. She translated his Latin work as *An Apology or Answer in Defence of the Church of England* in 1564, rendering his Latin text into spare, accessible, and punchy prose.

From John Jewel's *An Apology or Answer in Defence of the Church of England*

We have said that we abandon and detest, as plagues and poisons, all those old heresies which either the sacred scriptures, or the ancient councils, have utterly condemned. That we call home again, as much as ever we can, the right[1] discipline of the Church, which our adversaries have quite brought into a poor and weak case.[2] That we punish all licentiousness of life, and unruliness of manners, by the old and long-continued laws, and with as much sharpness[3] as is convenient, and lieth in our power. That we maintain still the state of kingdoms in the same condition and plight wherein we have found them, without any diminishing or alteration, reserving unto our princes their majesties and worldly pre-eminence, safe and without impairing, to our possible power. That we have so gotten ourselves away from that Church—which they had made a den of thieves,[4] and wherein nothing was in good frame,[5] or once like to the Church of God, and which, themselves confessed, had erred many ways, even as Lot in times past gat him[6] out of Sodom, or Abraham out of Chaldea—not upon a desire of contention, but by the warning of God Himself.[7] And that we have searched out of[8] the Holy Bible, which we are sure cannot deceive, one sure form of religion, and have returned again unto the primitive Church of the ancient fathers and Apostles—that is to say, to the first ground[9] and beginning of things, as unto the very foundations and headsprings of Christ's Church. And in very truth we have not tarried[1]—for, in this matter, the authority or consent of the Tridentine council,[2] wherein we saw nothing done uprightly, nor by good order; where also everybody was sworn to the maintenance of one man;[3] where our prince's ambassadors were contemned;[4] where not one of our divines could be heard, and where partstaking and ambition was openly and earnestly procured and wrought—but, as the holy fathers in former time, and as our predecessors have commonly done, we have restored our churches by a provincial convocation,[5] and have clean shaken off, as our duty was, the yoke and tyranny of the bishop of Rome,[6] to whom we were not bound; who also had no manner of thing like,

---

1. Correct. "Call home": call to a virtuous life.
2. Condition.
3. Keenness.
4. "That church" is the Catholic Church, here compared to the money changers in the temple, to whom Jesus said: "It is written, My house shall be called the house of prayer; but ye have made it a den of thieves" (Matthew 21:13).
5. Order.
6. Got himself away.
7. Not because we desired strife, but because God himself gave the order for it (just as Lot got out of Sodom, Genesis 19:1–16, and Abraham out of Canaan, Genesis 12).
8. Made diligent efforts to find in.
9. Original foundation.
1. Delayed our beginning.
2. The Council of Trent (1545–63), held in Trento (Latin name, "Tridentum") in northern Italy. Called to respond to the Protestant Reformation, it helped launch the Counter-Reformation.
3. The pope.
4. Despised.
5. An assembly of the clergy, called together to deliberate on church matters.
6. The pope.

neither to Christ, nor to Peter,[7] nor to an Apostle, nor yet like to any bishop at all. Finally, we say, that we agree amongst ourselves touching[8] the whole judgment and chief substance of Christian religion, and with one mouth, and with one spirit, do worship God, and the Father of our Lord Jesus Christ.

1564

7. Saint Peter was the first bishop of Rome and thus, according to Catholic tradition, the first pope.
8. Concerning.

BOOK OF COMMON PRAYER

The Protestant attack on Catholic rituals and the demand for worship in the vernacular led during the reign of Edward VI to the preparation of an English liturgical book, authorized to be the official and only text for public worship in England. The work was initiated by the Act of Uniformity in 1549, and its principal architect was Thomas Cranmer (1489–1556). Cranmer, the archbishop of Canterbury, was at first careful to translate and shape the old Latin liturgy into a moderate, occasionally ambiguous compromise between Catholic and Protestant positions. His thorough revision in 1552, however, put the *Book of Common Prayer* much more decisively into the Protestant camp. Banned by the Catholic Mary Tudor, during whose reign Cranmer was executed, the *Book of Common Prayer* was restored, with small revisions, by Elizabeth and has remained the basis of Anglican worship ever since. Cranmer was, among his other accomplishments, a brilliant prose stylist, and the cadences of his book have had a profound influence on the English language. The selection, part of the marriage service, is from the version used during the reign of Elizabeth.

From The Book of Common Prayer and Administration of the Sacraments and Other Rites and Ceremonies in the Church of England

From *The Form of Solemnization of Matrimony*

* * * At the day appointed for solemnization of matrimony, the persons to be married shall come into the body of the church with their friends and neighbors. And there the priest shall thus say:

Dearly beloved friends, we are gathered together here in the sight of God, and in the face of his congregation, to join together this man and this woman in holy matrimony, which is an honorable estate,[1] instituted of God in paradise, in the time of man's innocency, signifying unto us the mystical union that is betwixt Christ and his church:[2] which holy estate Christ adorned and beautified with his presence and first miracle that he wrought in Cana of Galilee,[3] and is commended of Saint Paul to be honorable among

1. State, condition.
2. Compare Ephesians 5:31–32: "For this cause shall a man leave his father and mother, and shall be joined unto his wife, and they two shall be one flesh. This is a great mystery: but I speak concerning Christ and the church."
3. He changed water into wine at a wedding (John 2:1–11).

all men,[4] and therefore is not to be enterprised[5] nor taken in hand unadvisedly, lightly, or wantonly, to satisfy men's carnal lusts and appetites, like brute beasts that have no understanding; but reverently, discreetly, advisedly, soberly, and in the fear of God, duly considering the causes for the which matrimony was ordained. One was, the procreation of children, to be brought up in the fear and nurture of the Lord, and praise of God. Secondly, it was ordained for a remedy against sin, and to avoid fornication, that such persons as have not the gift of continency might marry, and keep themselves undefiled members of Christ's body.[6] Thirdly, for the mutual society, help, and comfort that the one ought to have of the other, both in prosperity and adversity: into the which holy estate these two persons present come now to be joined. Therefore if any man can show any just cause why they may not lawfully be joined together, let him now speak, or else hereafter forever hold his peace.

And also speaking to the persons that shall be married, he shall say:

I require and charge you (as you will answer at the dreadful day of judgment, when the secrets of all hearts shall be disclosed) that if either of you do know any impediment why ye may not be lawfully joined together in matrimony, that ye confess it. For be ye well assured, that so many as be coupled together otherwise than God's word doth allow are not joined together by God, neither is their matrimony lawful.

At which day of marriage, if any man do allege and declare any impediment why they may not be coupled together in matrimony by God's law or the laws of this realm; and will be bound, and sufficient sureties with him, to the parties, or else put in a caution,[7] to the full value of such charges as the persons to be married doth sustain, to prove his allegation: then the solemnization must be deferred unto such time as the truth be tried. If no impediment be alleged, then shall the curate[8] say unto the man,

N.[9] Wilt thou have this woman to thy wedded wife, to live together after God's ordinance in the holy estate of matrimony? Wilt thou love her, comfort her, honor and keep her, in sickness and in health? And forsaking all other, keep thee only to her, so long as you both shall live?

The man shall answer,
I will.
Then shall the priest say to the woman,

N. Wilt thou have this man to thy wedded husband, to live together after God's ordinance in the holy estate of matrimony? Wilt thou obey him and serve him, love, honor, and keep him, in sickness and in health, and forsaking all other, keep thee only unto him, so long as you both shall live?

---

4. "Marriage is honorable in all, and the bed *undefiled*: but whoremongers and adulterers God will judge" (Hebrews 13:4).
5. Undertaken.
6. The church.
7. Surety.
8. A clergyman who has charge of a parish.
9. Name; that is, the minister inserts the man's given name here.

The woman shall answer,
I will.
Then shall the minister say,

Who giveth this woman to be married unto this man?

And the minister receiving the woman at her father or friend's hands, shall cause the man to take the woman by the right hand, and so either to give their troth[1] to other. The man first saying:

I N. take thee N. to my wedded wife, to have and to hold from this day forward, for better, for worse, for richer, for poorer, in sickness and in health, to love and to cherish, till death us depart,[2] according to God's holy ordinance: and thereto I plight thee my troth.

Then shall they loose their hands, and the woman taking again the man by the right hand shall say:

I N. take thee N. to my wedded husband, to have and to hold from this day forward, for better, for worse, for richer, for poorer, in sickness and in health, to love, cherish, and to obey, till death us depart, according to God's holy ordinance: and thereto I give thee my troth.

Then shall they again loose their hands, and the man shall give unto the woman a ring, laying the same upon the book with the accustomed duty[3] to the priest and clerk. And the priest taking the ring, shall deliver it unto the man, to put it upon the fourth finger of the woman's left hand. And the man taught by the priest shall say:

With this ring I thee wed: with my body I thee worship: and with all my worldly goods I thee endow. In the name of the Father, and of the Son, and of the Holy Ghost. Amen.

Then the man leaving the ring upon the fourth finger of the woman's left hand, the minister shall say:

O eternal God, creator and preserver of all mankind, giver of all spiritual grace, the author of everlasting life: send thy blessing upon these thy servants, this man and this woman, whom we bless in thy name; that as Isaac and Rebecca lived faithfully together,[4] so these persons may surely perform and keep the vow and covenant betwixt them made, whereof this ring given and received is a token and pledge, and may ever remain in perfect love and peace together, and live according unto thy laws: through Jesus Christ our Lord. Amen.

Then shall the priest join their right hands together, and say:

Those whom God hath joined together, let no man put asunder.[5]

Then shall the minister speak unto the people:

---

1. Truth; that is, pledge.
2. Part.
3. Payment. "Book": Bible.
4. In Genesis 24–27.
5. From Mark 10:9.

Forasmuch as N. and N. have consented together in holy wedlock, and have witnessed the same before God and this company, and thereto have given and pledged their troth, either to other, and have declared the same by giving and receiving of a ring, and by joining of hands: I pronounce that they be man and wife together. In the name of the Father, and of the Son, and of the Holy Ghost. Amen.

And the minister shall add this blessing:

God the Father, God the Son, God the Holy Ghost, bless, preserve, and keep you: the Lord mercifully with his favor look upon you, and so fill you with all spiritual benediction and grace that you may so live together in this life that in the world to come you may have life everlasting. Amen.

1559

BOOK OF HOMILIES

The first Protestant archbishop of Canterbury, Thomas Cranmer, was responsible in 1547 for the publication of the *Book of Homilies*. Hoping to curb the influence of "ignorant preachers" and fearing the spread of unauthorized beliefs, Cranmer brought together twelve sermons that were, by royal and ecclesiastical decree, to be read over and over, in the order in which they were set forth, in parish churches throughout the realm. The *Homilies*, revised and reissued during the reign of Elizabeth, are political as well as religious documents. As the "Homily Against Disobedience" (added in 1570 in the aftermath of a Catholic uprising the preceding year) amply demonstrates, the intention was to teach the English people "to honor God and to serve their king with all humility and subjection, and godly and honestly to behave themselves toward all men." Artfully crafted and tirelessly reiterated, these sermons would have been familiar to almost everyone in the latter half of the sixteenth century.

From An Homily Against Disobedience and Willful Rebellion

* * * How horrible a sin against God and man rebellion is cannot possibly be expressed according unto the greatness thereof. For he that nameth rebellion nameth not a singular, or one only sin, as is theft, robbery, murder, and suchlike, but he nameth the whole puddle and sink[1] of all sins against God and man, against his prince, his country, his countrymen, his parents, his children, his kinfolks, his friends, and against all men universally: all sins, I say, against God and all men heaped together nameth he that nameth rebellion. For concerning the offense of God's majesty, who seeth not that rebellion riseth first by *contempt of God* and of his holy ordinances and laws, wherein he so straitly[2]

---

1. Cesspool.   2. Strictly.

commandeth obedience, forbiddeth disobedience and rebellion?[3] And besides the dishonor done by rebels unto God's holy name by their breaking of the oath made to their prince with the attestation of God's name and calling of his majesty to witness, who heareth not the horrible oaths and blasphemies of God's holy name that are used daily amongst rebels, that is either amongst them or heareth the truth of their behavior? Who knoweth not that rebels do not only themselves leave all works necessary to be done upon workdays undone, whiles they accomplish their abominable work of rebellion, and do compel others that would gladly be well occupied to do the same, but also how rebels do not only leave the sabbath day of the Lord unsanctified, the temple and church of the Lord unresorted unto, but also do by their works of wickedness most horribly profane and pollute the sabbath day, serving Satan, and by doing of his work making it the devil's day instead of the Lord's day? Besides that they compel good men that would gladly serve the Lord assembling in his temple and church upon his day, as becometh the Lord's servants, to assemble and meet armed in the field to resist the fury[4] of such rebels. Yea, and many rebels, lest they should leave any part of God's commandments in the first table of his law[5] unbroken or any sin against God undone, do make rebellion for the maintenance of their images and idols, and of their idolatry committed or to be committed by them, and, in despite of God, cut and tear in sunder his Holy Word, and tread it under their feet, as of late ye know was done.[6]

As concerning the second table of God's law, and all sins that may be committed against man, who seeth not that they be all contained in rebellion? For first, the rebels do not only dishonor their prince, the parent of their country, but also do dishonor and shame their natural parents, if they have any, do shame their kindred and friends, disherit[7] and undo forever their children and heirs. Thefts, robberies, and murders, which of all sins are most loathed of most men, are in no men so much, nor so perniciously and mischievously, as in rebels. For the most arrant thieves and cruelest murderers that ever were, so long as they refrain from rebellion, as they are not many in number, so spreadeth their wickedness and damnation unto a few: they spoil[8] but a few, they shed the blood but of few in comparison. But rebels are the cause of infinite robberies and murders of great multitudes, and of those also whom they should defend from the spoil and violence of other; and, as rebels are many in number, so doth their wickedness and damnation spread itself unto many. And if whoredom and adultery amongst such persons as are agreeable to such wickedness are (as they indeed be) most damnable, what are the forcible oppressions[9] of matrons and men's wives, and the violating and deflowering of virgins and maids, which are most rife with rebels; how horrible and damnable, think you, are they? Now, besides that rebels, by breach of their faith given and oath made to their prince, be guilty of most damnable perjury, it is wondrous to see what false

---

3. Romans 13:1–2: "Let every soul be subject unto the higher powers. For there is no power but of God: the powers that be are ordained of God. Whosoever therefore resisteth the power, resisteth the ordinance of God: and they that resist shall receive to themselves damnation."
4. Violence.
5. The first of the two "tables" (tablets) of stone on which God wrote the Ten Commandments (Deuteronomy 5:22): those on the first table specify our obligations to God, those on the second (see the following paragraph) our obligations to one another.
6. These wicked deeds were purportedly perpetrated by the Catholic rebels who, in the winter of 1569, rose in the north of England against Queen Elizabeth and in support of her Catholic cousin, Mary, Queen of Scots (who had been imprisoned in England since May 1568).
7. Disinherit.
8. Despoil, plunder.
9. Rapes.

colors and feigned causes, by slanderous lies made upon their prince and the counselers, rebels will devise to cloak their rebellion withal, which is the worst and most damnable of all false-witness-bearing that may be possible. For what should I speak of coveting or desiring of other men's wives, houses, lands, goods, and servants in rebels, who by their wills would leave unto no man anything of his own?

Thus you see that all God's laws are by rebels violated and broken, and that all sins possible to be committed against God or man be contained in rebellion: which sins, if a man list[1] to name by the accustomed names of the seven capital or deadly sins, as pride, envy, wrath, covetousness, sloth, gluttony, and lechery, he shall find them all in rebellion, and amongst rebels. For first, as ambition and desire to be aloft, which is the property of pride, stirreth up many men's minds to rebellion, so cometh it of a luciferian pride and presumption that a few rebellious subjects should set themselves up against the majesty of their prince, against the wisdom of the counselors, against the power and force of all nobility, and the faithful subjects and people of the whole realm. As for envy, wrath, murder, and desire of blood, and covetousness of other men's goods, lands, and livings, they are the inseparable accidents of all rebels, and peculiar properties[2] that do usually stir up wicked men unto rebellion. Now such as by riotousness, gluttony, drunkenness, excess of apparel, and unthrifty[3] games have wasted their own goods unthriftily, the same are most apt unto and most desirous of rebellion, whereby they trust to come by other men's goods unlawfully and violently. And where other gluttons and drunkards take too much of such meats and drinks as are served to tables, rebels waste and consume in short space all corn in barns, fields, or elsewhere, whole graners,[4] whole storehouses, whole cellars, devour whole flocks of sheep, whole droves of oxen and kine.[5] And as rebels that are married, leaving their own wives at home, do most ungraciously, so much more do unmarried men than any stallions or horses, being now by rebellion set at liberty from correction of laws which bridled them before, which abuse by force other men's wives and daughters, and ravish virgins and maidens most shamefully, abominably, and damnably. Thus all sins, by all names that sins may be named, and by all means that all sins may be committed and wrought, do all wholly upon heaps follow rebellion, and are to be found all together amongst rebels.

1570

1. Wants.
2. Distinctive characteristics. "Inseparable accidents": unavoidable accompaniments.
3. Dissolute.
4. Granaries. "Corn": grain.
5. Cattle.

ANNE VAUGHAN LOCKE

Born to parents who served in the court of Henry VIII, Anne Vaughan Locke (ca. 1530–ca. 1590) received a privileged education in languages and became deeply involved in the Protestant Reformation, living among English exiles in Calvinist Geneva during the reign of Mary I and later exerting her influence in England, in part by translating religious works and writing her own. Her verse paraphrase of Psalm 51 is arguably the first English sonnet sequence as well as an early example of the Protestant devotional lyric that led to the religious poetry of John Donne and George Herbert.

From A Meditation of a Penitent Sinner

Sonnet 4

Have mercy, Lord, have mercy: for I know
How much I need thy mercy in this case.
The horror of my guilt doth daily grow,
And, growing, wears[1] my feeble hope of grace.
5 I feel and suffer in my thrallèd[2] breast
Secret remorse and gnawing of my heart.
I feel my sin, my sin that hath oppressed
My soul with sorrow and surmounting smart.[3]
Draw me to mercy: for so oft as I
10 Presume to mercy to direct my sight,
My Chaos[4] and my heap of sin doth lie
Between me and thy mercy's shining light.
Whatever way I gaze about for grace,
My filth and fault are ever in my face.°   *sight*

1560

1. That is, wears down, weakens.
2. Enthralled, enslaved (to sin).
3. Exceeding pain.
4. Alluding to the "great gulf" (in Latin, *chaos*) stretching between heaven and hell; see Luke 16:26. In classical mythology, Chaos is vaguely personified as a primordial deity.

RICHARD HOOKER

Out of the long and bitter controversy over the government of the church in sixteenth-century England emerged one literary masterpiece. It is a work in eight books called *Of the Laws of Ecclesiastical Polity* (that is, the governmental system of the church). The author was the Oxford-educated Richard Hooker (1554–1600), a scholar and minister. In 1585 Hooker was master of the Temple, a royal church in London; one of his subordinates was a Puritan intellectual named Walter Travers (1548–1635). Between them a contentious debate developed on the question of how the Church should be governed. The Puritan view was that no organization or authority in the church was valid unless it was based clearly and specifically on the Bible; the whole hierarchical system of the English Church, with its deacons, priests, bishops, and archbishops, was accordingly wrong, along with its liturgy and most of its rituals. The position Hooker undertook to defend was that the scriptures, or divine revelation, are not the only guide given to Christians for organizing and administering the Church. Another guide is the law of nature, also divinely given, but able to be discerned by the use of human reason unassisted by revelation.

In the book that grew out of his controversy with Travers, Hooker explained how the law of nature affords principles that justify the existing organization and practices of the English Church. Book 1 of *Ecclesiastical Polity* deals with law in general and the several kinds of law; it pictures the entire universe, and also human society, as founded on reason and operating under various natural and divine laws. Book 2 deals with the nature, authority, and adequacy of scripture. Books 3 to 5 explain and defend the rites, ceremonies, worship, and government of the English Church. Books 6, 7, and 8 deal with various embodiments of authority, legitimate and illegitimate—elders, bishops, kings, and popes.

Hooker was a close and effective reasoner; avoiding the fiery invective or impassioned rhetoric that characterized most disputants of his time, he wrote in a calm, reasonable, and judicious manner. His defense of existing ecclesiastical practices went back to fundamental principles, to a philosophy of nature and our place in it, to the subordination of the individual to a larger community and to God. It is this worldview, set forth in what is perhaps the period's most sonorous and quietly elegant prose, that makes *Ecclesiastical Polity* of enduring interest.

From Of the Laws of Ecclesiastical Polity
From *Book 1, Chapter 3*

[ON THE SEVERAL KINDS OF LAW, AND ON THE NATURAL LAW]

I am not ignorant that by law eternal the learned for the most part do understand the order, not which God hath eternally purposed himself in all his works to observe, but rather that which with himself he hath set down as expedient to be kept by all his creatures, according to the several[1] conditions wherewith he hath indued them. They who thus are accustomed to speak apply the name of *Law* unto that only rule of working which superior authority imposeth; whereas we, somewhat more enlarging the sense thereof, term any kind of rule or canon whereby actions are framed[2] a law. Now that law, which as it is laid up in the bosom of God they call *eternal*, receiveth according unto the different kinds of things which are subject unto it different and sundry kinds of names. That part of it which ordereth natural agents,[3] we call usually *nature's* law; that which angels do clearly behold, and without any swerving observe, is a law *celestial* and heavenly; the law of *reason* that which bindeth creatures reasonable in this world, and with which by reason they may most plainly perceive themselves bound; that which bindeth them, and is not known but by special revelation from God, *divine* law; *human* law, that which, out of the law either of reason or of God, men probably[4] gathering to be expedient, they make it a law. All things, therefore, which are as they ought to be, are conformed unto *this second law eternal*, and even those things which to this *eternal* law are not conformable are notwithstanding in some sort ordered by *the first eternal law*. For what good or evil is there under the sun, what action correspondent to or repugnant unto the law which God hath imposed upon his creatures, but in or upon it God doth work according to the law which himself hath eternally purposed to keep, that is to say, the *first law eternal?* So that a twofold law eternal being thus made, it is not hard to conceive how they both take place in all things. Wherefore to come to the law of nature, albeit thereby we sometimes mean that manner of working which God hath set for each created thing to keep, yet forasmuch as those things are termed

1. Different.
2. Directed.
3. Referring to the mineral, vegetable, and animal agents, traditionally distinguished from human agents by their lack of rationality.
4. Plausibly.

most properly natural agents, which keep the law of their kind[5] unwittingly, as the heavens and elements of the world, which can do no otherwise than they do, and forasmuch as we give unto intellectual natures the name of voluntary agents, that so we may distinguish them from the other, expedient it will be that we sever[6] the law of nature observed by the one from that which the other is tied unto. Touching the former, their strict keeping of one tenure statute[7] and law is spoken of by all, but hath in it more than men have as yet attained to know, or perhaps ever shall attain, seeing the travail of wading herein is given of God to the sons of men, that perceiving how much the least thing in the world hath in it more than the wisest are able to reach unto, they may by this means learn humility. Moses in describing the work of creation attributeth speech unto God: "God said, Let there be light, Let there be a firmament; Let the waters under the heaven be gathered together into one place; Let the earth bring forth; Let there be lights in the firmament of heaven."[8] Was this only the intent of Moses, to signify the greatness of God's power by the easiness of his accomplishing such effects without travail, pain, or labor? Surely it seemeth that Moses had herein besides this a further purpose: namely, first to teach that God did not work as a necessary, but a voluntary, agent, intending beforehand and decreeing with himself that which did outwardly proceed from him; secondly, to show that God did then institute a law natural to be observed by creatures, and therefore according to the manner of laws, the institution thereof is described as being established by solemn injunction. His commanding those things to be which are, and to be in such sort as they are, to keep that tenure and course which they do, importeth[9] the establishment of nature's law. This world's first creation, and the preservation since of things created, what is it but only so far forth a manifestation by execution, what the eternal law of God is concerning things natural? And as it cometh to pass in a kingdom rightly ordered, that after a law is once published, it presently[1] takes effect far and wide, all states[2] framing themselves thereunto; even so let us think it fareth[3] in the natural course of the world: since the time that God did first proclaim the edicts of his law upon it, heaven and earth have hearkened unto his voice, and their labor hath been to do his will. He made a law for the rain. He gave his decree unto the sea, that the waters should not pass his commandment.[4]

Now if Nature should intermit[5] her course and leave altogether, though it were but for a while, the observation of her own laws; if those principal and mother elements of the world, whereof all things in this lower world are made, should lose the qualities which now they have; if the frame of that heavenly arch erected over our heads should loosen and dissolve itself; if celestial spheres should forget their wonted[6] motions and by irregular volubility[7] turn themselves any way as it might happen; if the prince of the lights of heaven, which now as a giant doth run his unwearied course, should as it

---

5. Species, nature.
6. Distinguish.
7. Decree establishing the domains of the various creatures and the conditions of service by which they hold these domains.
8. Genesis 1:3, 6, 9, 11, 14. In this period, Moses was generally assumed to be the author of the book of Genesis.
9. Signifies, implies.
1. Immediately.
2. Classes.
3. Happens.
4. Proverbs 8:29. "Pass": overstep.
5. Interrupt.
6. Accustomed.
7. Revolution, rotation.

were through a languishing faintness begin to stand[8] and to rest himself; if the moon should wander from her beaten way, the times and seasons of the year blend themselves by disordered and confused mixture, the winds breathe out their last gasp, the clouds yield no rain, the earth be defeated[9] of heavenly influence, the fruits of the earth pine away as children at the withered breasts of their mother no longer able to yield them relief, what would become of man himself, whom these things now do all serve? See we not plainly that obedience of creatures unto the law of nature is the stay[1] of the whole world? Notwithstanding with nature it cometh sometimes to pass as with art. Let Phidias[2] have rude[3] and obstinate stuff to carve, though his art do that[4] it should, his work will lack that beauty which otherwise in fitter matter it might have had. He that striketh an instrument with skill may cause notwithstanding a very unpleasant sound, if the string whereon he striketh chance to be uncapable of harmony. In the matter whereof natural things consist, that of Theophrastus taketh place:[5] "much of it is oftentimes such as will by no means yield to receive that impression which were best and most perfect." Which defect in the matter of things natural, they who gave themselves unto the contemplation of nature among the heathen observed often; but the true original cause thereof divine malediction,[6] laid for the sin of man upon those creatures which God had made for the use of man. This, being an article of that saving truth which God hath revealed unto his church, was above the reach of their[7] merely natural[8] capacity and understanding. But howsoever these swervings[9] are now and then incident into[1] the course of nature, nevertheless so constantly the laws of nature are by natural agents observed, that no man denieth but those things which nature worketh are wrought either always or for the most part after one and the same manner. * * *

1593

8. Stand still.
9. Deprived.
1. Mainstay, support.
2. The greatest of ancient Greek sculptors (5th century B.C.E.).
3. Rough, undressed (that is, unprepared).
4. What.
5. That is, "that remark of Theophrastus carries weight." The Greek philosopher Theophrastus (ca. 370–ca. 285 B.C.E.), Aristotle's pupil and successor, became best-known among postclassical readers for his *characters*, thirty sketches of different moral types; the quotation is from his *Metaphysics*.
6. God's curse in Eden, which fell not only on sinful humankind but on the earth as well.
7. That is, the ancient pagans'.
8. That is, unaided by revelation.
9. Deviations.
1. Likely to happen in.

ROBERT SOUTHWELL

Robert Southwell (1561–1595), the younger son of a prominent Roman Catholic family, went to the English seminary for Catholics at Douai, France, in his youth, and then to Rome, where he entered the Society of Jesus (the Jesuits). In 1586 he returned to England to minister to English Catholics. His mission was dangerous because of laws that proscribed Roman Catholic worship and banished priests; in 1592 he was apprehended, imprisoned, tortured, and, three years later, executed as a traitor in the usual grisly manner—by being hanged, disemboweled, and then beheaded. Southwell wrote a good deal of religious prose and verse; the most famous of his lyrics is "The Burning Babe." Ben Jonson told his friend William Drummond of Hawthornden that if he had written "The Burning Babe" he would have been content to destroy many of his own poems.

The Burning Babe

As I in hoary winter's night stood shivering in the snow,
Surprised I was with sudden heat which made my heart to glow;
And lifting up a fearful eye to view what fire was near,
A pretty babe all burning bright did in the air appear;
5   Who, scorchèd with excessive heat, such floods of tears did shed
As though his floods should quench his flames which with his tears
    were fed.
"Alas," quoth he, "but newly born in fiery heats I fry,°   *burn*
Yet none approach to warm their hearts or feel my fire but I!
My faultless breast the furnace is, the fuel wounding thorns,
10 Love is the fire, and sighs the smoke, the ashes shame and scorns;
The fuel justice layeth on, and mercy blows the coals,
The metal in this furnace wrought are men's defilèd souls,
For which, as now on fire I am to work them to their good,
So will I melt into a bath to wash them in my blood."
15 With this he vanished out of sight and swiftly shrunk away,
And straight¹ I callèd unto mind that it was Christmas day.

1602

1. Straightaway, immediately.

ROGER ASCHAM
1515–1568

When she heard of the death of her former tutor and Latin secretary, Queen Elizabeth is said to have exclaimed, "I would rather have cast ten thousand pounds in the sea than parted from my Ascham." Educated at St. John's College, Cambridge, one of the great centers of humanism in England, Roger Ascham passionately believed in the study of the Greek and Latin classics, not merely for erudition and aesthetic pleasure but for guidance in moral values and in political activity. He both corresponded widely in Latin with learned men on the Continent and was eager to influence his countrymen, whether they read Latin or not. His important books written in English include *Toxophilus*, a dialogue in praise of archery with the traditional English longbow, and *A Report and Discourse of the State of Germany*, based on his experience as secretary to the English ambassador there in 1550–53. His most famous work in English was *The Schoolmaster*, published two years after his death.

The Schoolmaster eloquently opposes the widespread use of corporal punishment in schools. Instilling a love of learning, rather than a fear of physical pain, inspires young children to excel in their studies. Ascham advocates "double translation" as the most effective way of acquiring a sound Latin style: students would translate a passage from Latin to English and then, without consulting the Latin original, translate the English back into Latin; they would then compare their version with the author's. The approach thus downplays rote learning of the rules of grammar and emphasizes instead a sense of style.

Misused, Ascham's method (which included discouraging students from speaking Latin, for fear that engagement with everyday life would corrupt the linguistic purity of classical antiquity) could, like so many other educational reforms, become torturous. But his ultimate goal was not to make students into gifted imitators but to fashion them ethically and aesthetically. Deeply fearing what he called the "divorce between the tongue and the heart," he believed that education should teach a person to join language and values in a way that achieved what *The Schoolmaster* calls "decorum." Ascham's most despairing vision of a society without this moral decorum comes in his account of a brief trip to Italy, which he viewed as an evil seductress, luring unwitting Englishmen away from their ethical and religious values.

From The Schoolmaster[*]

From *The First Book for the Youth*

[TEACHING LATIN]

There is a way, touched in the first book of Cicero *De oratore*,[1] which, wisely brought into schools, truly taught, and constantly used, would not only take wholly away this butcherly fear in making of Latins[2] but would also, with ease and pleasure and in short time, as I know by good experience, work a true choice and placing of words, a right ordering of sentences, an easy understanding of the tongue, a readiness to speak, a facility to write, a true judgment both of his own and other men's doings, what tongue soever he doth use.

The way is this. After the three concordances[3] learned, as I touched before, let the master read unto him the epistles of Cicero gathered together and chosen out by Sturmius[4] for the capacity of children.

First, let him teach the child, cheerfully and plainly, the cause and matter[5] of the letter; then, let him construe[6] it into English so oft as the child may easily carry away the understanding of it; lastly, parse[7] it over perfectly. This done thus, let the child, by and by,[8] both construe and parse it over again so that it may appear that the child doubteth in nothing that his master taught him before. After this, the child must take a paper book and, sitting in some place where no man shall prompt him, by himself, let him translate into

---

[*] Another excerpt from *The Schoolmaster*—on Ascham's last conversation with Lady Jane Grey—is found on pp. 210–11.
[1] Cicero's *On the Orator* (55 B.C.E.) consists of three parts, or books.
[2] That is, in Latin composition.
[3] Agreement of noun and adjective, verb and noun, relative with antecedent.
[4] Johannes Sturm (1507–1589), German scholar and educator.
[5] Occasion and content.
[6] Translate.
[7] Give a grammatical analysis.
[8] Immediately.

English his former lesson. Then, showing it to his master, let the master take from him his Latin book, and, pausing an hour at the least, then let the child translate his own English into Latin again in another paper book. When the child bringeth it turned into Latin, the master must compare it with Tully's[9] book and lay them both together, and where the child doth well, either in choosing or true placing of Tully's words, let the master praise him and say, "Here ye do well." For I assure you, there is no such whetstone to sharpen a good wit and encourage a will to learning as is praise.

But if the child miss, either in forgetting a word, or in changing a good with a worse, or misordering the sentence, I would not have the master either frown or chide with him, if the child have done his diligence and used no truantship therein. For I know by good experience that a child shall take more profit of two faults gently warned of than of four things rightly hit. For then the master shall have good occasion to say unto him:

> N[omen],[1] Tully would have used such a word, not this; Tully would have placed this word here, not there; would have used this case, this number, this person, this degree,[2] this gender; he would have used this mood, this tense, this simple rather than this compound; this adverb here, not there; he would have ended the sentence with this verb, not with that noun or participle, etc.

In these few lines I have wrapped up the most tedious part of grammar and also the ground of almost all the rules that are so busily taught by the master, and so hardly[3] learned by the scholar, in all common schools, which after this sort[4] the master shall teach without all error, and the scholar shall learn without great pain, the master being led by so sure a guide, and the scholar being brought into so plain and easy a way. And therefore we do not contemn[5] rules, but we gladly teach rules, and teach them more plainly, sensibly, and orderly than they be commonly taught in common schools. For when the master shall compare Tully's book with his scholar's translation, let the master, at the first, lead and teach his scholar to join the rules of his grammar book with the examples of his present lesson, until the scholar by himself be able to fetch out of his grammar every rule for every example, so as the grammar book be ever in the scholar's hand and also used of him, as a dictionary, for every present use. This is a lively and perfect way of teaching of rules, where the common way, used in common schools, to read the grammar alone by itself, is tedious for the master, hard for the scholar, cold and uncomfortable to them both.

Let your scholar be never afraid to ask you any doubt,[6] but use discreetly the best allurements ye can to encourage him to the same, lest his overmuch fearing of you drive him to seek some misorderly shift,[7] as to seek to be helped by some other book, or to be prompted by some other scholar, and so go about to beguile you much, and himself more.

---

9. Common English name for Marcus Tullius Cicero.
1. Name (Latin). The teacher will substitute the child's name.
2. The level of intensity of an adjective or adverb.
3. With such difficulty.
4. Method.
5. Disdain.
6. Question.
7. Subterfuge.

[THE ITALIANATE ENGLISHMAN]

* * * But I am afraid that overmany of our travelers into Italy do not eschew the way to Circe's court but go[8] and ride and run and fly thither; they make great haste to come to her; they make great suit[9] to serve her; yea, I could point out some with my finger that never had[1] gone out of England but only to serve Circe in Italy. Vanity and vice and any license to ill-living in England was counted stale and rude[2] unto them. And so, being mules and horses before they went, returned very[3] swine and asses home again; yet everywhere very foxes with subtle and busy heads and, where they may, very wolves with cruel malicious hearts. A marvelous monster which for filthiness of living, for dullness to learning himself, for wiliness in dealing with others, for malice in hurting without cause, should carry at once in one body the belly of a swine, the head of an ass, the brain of a fox, the womb of a wolf. If you think we judge amiss and write too sore against you, hear what the Italian saith of the Englishman, what the master reporteth of the scholar, who uttereth plainly what is taught by him and what is learned by you, saying, *Inglese italianato è un diavolo incarnato*; that is to say, "You remain men in shape and fashion but become devils in life and condition." This is not the opinion of one, for some private spite, but the judgment of all in a common proverb which riseth of that learning and those manners which you gather in Italy—a good schoolhouse of wholesome doctrine, and worthy masters of commendable scholars, where the master had rather defame himself for his teaching than not shame his scholar for his learning: a good nature of the master, and fair conditions of the scholars. And now choose you, you Italian Englishmen, whether you will be angry with us for calling you monsters, or with the Italians for calling you devils, or else with your own selves, that take so much pains and go so far to make yourselves both. If some yet do not well understand what is an Englishman Italianated, I will plainly tell him: he that by living and traveling in Italy bringeth home into England out of Italy the religion, the learning, the policy,[4] the experience, the manners[5] of Italy. That is to say, for religion, papistry[6] or worse; for learning, less, commonly, than they carried out with them; for policy, a factious heart, a discoursing head, a mind to meddle in all men's matters; for experience, plenty of new mischiefs never known in England before; for manners, variety of vanities and change of filthy living. These be the enchantments of Circe brought out of Italy to mar men's manners in England: much by example of ill life but more by precepts of fond[7] books, of late translated out of Italian into English, sold in every shop in London, commended by honest titles the sooner to corrupt honest manners, dedicated overboldly to virtuous and honorable personages, the easier to beguile simple and innocent wits. It is pity that those which have authority and charge to allow and disallow books to be printed be no more circumspect herein than they are. Ten sermons at Paul's Cross[8] do not so much good for moving men to true

---

8. Walk. Circe was an enchantress in Homer's *Odyssey* who changed men into swine and other animals.
9. Petition.
1. Would never have.
2. Unrefined.
3. True.
4. Politics.
5. Morals.
6. Catholicism.
7. Foolish.
8. An outdoor pulpit near St. Paul's Cathedral where important ministers preached.

doctrine as one of those books do harm with enticing men to ill-living. Yea, I say farther, those books tend not so much to corrupt honest living as they do to subvert true religion. More papists be made by your merry books of Italy than by your earnest books of Louvain.[9] And because our great physicians do wink at the matter and make no count[1] of this sore, I, though not admitted one of their fellowship, yet having been many years a prentice to God's true religion, and trust to continue a poor journeyman therein all days of my life, for the duty I owe and love I bear both to true doctrine and honest living, though I have no authority to amend the sore myself, yet I will declare my good will to discover[2] the sore to others.

St. Paul saith that sects and ill opinions be the works of the flesh and fruits of sin.[3] This is spoken no more truly for the doctrine than sensibly for the reason. And why? For ill-doings breed ill-thinkings, and of corrupted manners spring perverted judgments. And how? There be in man two special[4] things: man's will, man's mind. Where will inclineth to goodness the mind is bent to truth; where will is carried from goodness to vanity the mind is soon drawn from truth to false opinion. And so the readiest way to entangle the mind with false doctrine is first to entice the will to wanton living. Therefore, when the busy and open[5] papists abroad could not by their contentious books turn men in England fast enough from truth and right judgment in doctrine, then the subtle[6] and secret papists at home procured bawdy books to be translated out of the Italian tongue, whereby overmany young wills and wits, allured to wantonness, do now boldly contemn all severe books that sound to[7] honesty and godliness. In our forefathers' time, when papistry as a standing pool covered and overflowed all England, few books were read in our tongue, saving certain books of chivalry, as they said, for pastime and pleasure, which, as some say, were made in monasteries by idle monks or wanton canons; as one for example, *Morte Darthur*,[8] the whole pleasure of which book standeth in two special points—in open manslaughter and bold bawdry; in which book those be counted the noblest knights that do kill most men without any quarrel and commit foulest adulteries by subtlest shifts:[9] as Sir Lancelot with the wife of King Arthur his master, Sir Tristram with the wife of King Mark his uncle, Sir Lamorak with the wife of King Lot that was his own aunt. This is good stuff for wise men to laugh at or honest men to take pleasure at. Yet I know when God's Bible was banished the court and *Morte Darthur* received into the prince's chamber.[1] * * *

1570

---

9. Town in Belgium noted in the 16th century for its Catholic university, especially the theological faculty.
1. Account. "Wink at": shut their eyes to, connive at.
2. Reveal.
3. Galatians 5:19–21.
4. That is, specific to the human species.
5. Meddlesome and openly declared.
6. Deceitful.
7. Treat of. "Severe": serious.
8. Sir Thomas Malory's collection of Arthurian romances.
9. Stratagems.
1. Referring to the prohibition of the Protestant translations of the Bible during the reign of the Catholic Queen Mary I (1553–58).

SIR THOMAS HOBY
1530–1566

One of the most influential books of the Renaissance was *Il Cortegiano* (The Courtier), published in 1528 in Italian by Count Baldassare Castiglione (1478–1529) and soon translated into all the major European languages. The English translation, by the humanist and diplomat Sir Thomas Hoby, was not published until 1561 but had been written earlier, probably during the reign of Queen Mary (1553–58), when Hoby was living abroad as a Protestant exile.

Castiglione's book describes, by means of four fictitious dialogues—on successive evenings, among actual men and women living at the court of the duke of Urbino in 1504–08—the qualities of the ideal courtier. Supreme among these qualities is grace, the mysterious attribute that renders a person's speech and actions not merely impressive or accomplished but persuasive, touching, and beautiful. Though few people are born with grace, it is possible to acquire it by the mastery of certain techniques. In a famous passage, one of *The Courtier*'s speakers, Count Lodovico Canossa, defines the most important of these techniques as *sprezzatura*, or, as Hoby translates it, "recklessness." *Sprezzatura* is in fact close to the opposite of recklessness, as we ordinarily understand the term; it is a device for manipulating appearances and masking all the tedious memorizing of lines and secret rehearsals that underlie successful social performances. The paradox here is still evident in many social settings: success requires the painstaking mastery of complex codes of behavior, yet there is no surer recipe for failure than to be seen to be trying too hard.

The most famous passage in *The Courtier* presents an elegant version of an ideal of love that ultimately derives from Plato's *Symposium*. In the ancient Greek original, dating from the late fourth century B.C.E., that ideal is principally focused on the love of men for beautiful boys; in Castiglione's dialogue, the poet and scholar Peter Bembo recasts it as both heterosexual and Christian. Bembo declares that love is not the mere gratification of the senses but is the yearning of the soul after beauty, which is finally identical with the eternal good, as perceived by such holy visionaries as Saint Francis and Saint Paul. Love properly understood is, therefore, a kind of ladder by which the soul progresses from lower to higher things. As he pursues his theme, Bembo becomes more and more enraptured and ends with a vision of the soul ravished by heavenly beauty, purged of the flesh, and admitted to the feast of the angels. One of the spirited ladies in the court, Emilia Pia, plucks his garment and gently reminds him that he also has a body.

From Castiglione's *The Courtier*
From *Book 1, Sections 25–26*
[GRACE]

"* * * Perhaps I am able to tell you what a perfect Courtier ought to be, but *not to teach you how ye should do to be one*. Notwithstanding, to fulfill your request in what I am able, although it be (in manner) in a proverb that

Grace[1] *is not to be learned,* I say unto you, whoso mindeth to be gracious or to have a good grace in the exercises of the body (presupposing first that he be not of nature unapt) ought to begin betimes, and to learn his principles of cunning[2] men. The which thing how necessary a matter Philip, king of Macedonia,[3] thought it, a man may gather in that his will was that Aristotle, so famous a philosopher, and perhaps the greatest that ever hath been in the world, should be the man that should instruct Alexander, his son, in the first principles of letters. And of men whom we know nowadays, mark how well and with what a good grace Sir Galeazzo Sanseverino, master of the horse to the French king, doth all exercises of the body; and that because, besides the natural disposition of person that is in him, he hath applied all his study to learn of cunning men, and to have continually excellent men about him, and, of every one, to choose the best of that they have skill in. For as in wrestling, in vaulting, and in learning to handle sundry kind of weapons he hath taken for his guide our Master Peter Mount, who (as you know) is the true and only master of all artificial[4] force and sleight, so in riding, in jousting, and in every other feat, he hath always had before his eyes the most perfectest that hath been known to be in those professions.

"He therefore that will be a good scholar, beside the practicing of good things, must evermore set all his diligence to be like his master, and, if it were possible, change himself into him. And when he hath had some entry,[5] it profiteth him much to behold sundry men of that profession; and, governing himself with that good judgment that must always be his guide, go about to pick out, sometime of one and sometime of another, sundry matters. And even as the bee in the green meadows flieth always about the grass choosing out flowers, so shall our Courtier steal this grace from them that to his seeming have it, and from each one that parcel[6] that shall be most worthy praise. And not do as a friend of ours whom you all know, that thought he resembled much King Ferdinand the Younger, of Aragon, and regarded not to resemble him in any other point but in the often lifting up his head, wrying, therewithal,[7] a part of his mouth, the which custom the king had gotten by infirmity. And many such there are that think they do much, so they resemble a great man in somewhat, and take many times the thing in him that worst becometh him.

"But I, imagining with myself often times how this grace cometh, leaving apart such as have it from above, find one rule that is most general which in this part (methink) taketh place[8] in all things belonging to a man, in word or deed, above all other. And that is to eschew as much as a man may, and as a sharp and dangerous rock, *Affectation* or curiosity,[9] and, to speak a new word, to use in everything a certain Recklessness, to cover art[1] withal, and seem whatsoever he doth and sayeth to do it without pain, and, as it were, not

---

1. *Grace* had a wide range of meanings for Elizabethans, and many puns were made on the word. It refers especially to a natural, easy manner, and also to that favor of God that can be neither earned nor deserved. "In manner": in the manner of; almost.
2. Knowing. "Betimes": early.
3. Philip II (ca. 382–336 B.C.E.), the father of Alexander the Great.
4. Artful, skillful.
5. Introduction.
6. Aspect. "To his seeming": in his opinion.
7. Twisting awry, moreover.
8. Precedence.
9. Overfastidiousness.
1. Artifice. "Recklessness": care-lessness; that is, nonchalance. The Italian word, whose sense Hoby's translation does not clearly convey, is *sprezzatura*: a natural, easy grace.

minding[2] it. And of this do I believe grace is much derived, for in rare matters and well brought to pass every man knoweth the hardness of them, so that a readiness therein maketh great wonder. And contrariwise to use force and, as they say, to hale by the hair, giveth a great disgrace and maketh everything, how great soever it be, to be little esteemed. Therefore that may be said to be a very[3] art that appeareth not to be art; neither ought a man to put more diligence in anything than in covering it, for in case it be open, it loseth credit clean, and maketh a man little set by.[4] And I remember that I have read in my days that there were some most excellent orators which among other their cares enforced themselves to make every man believe that they had no sight[5] in letters, and dissembling their cunning, made semblant[6] their orations to be made very simply, and rather as nature and truth made them than study and art, the which if it had been openly known would have put a doubt in the people's mind, for fear lest he beguiled them. You may see then how to show art and such bent[7] study taketh away the grace of everything. * * *"

From *Book 4, Sections 49–73*

[THE LADDER OF LOVE]

Then the Lord Gaspar:[8] "I remember," quoth he, "that these lords yesternight, reasoning of the Courtier's qualities, did allow him to be a lover; and in making rehearsal[9] of as much as hitherto hath been spoken, a man may pick out a conclusion that the Courtier which with his worthiness and credit must incline his prince to virtue[1] must in manner of necessity be aged, for knowledge cometh very seldom-time before years, and specially in matters that be learned with experience. I cannot see, when he is well drawn[2] in years, how it will stand well with him to be a lover, considering, as it hath been said the other night, love frameth not with[3] old men, and the tricks that in young men be gallantness, courtesy, and preciseness[4] so acceptable to women, in them are mere follies and fondness[5] to be laughed at, and purchase him that useth them hatred of women and mocks of others. Therefore, in case this your Aristotle, an old Courtier, were a lover and practiced the feats that young lovers do, as some that we have seen in our days, I fear me he would forget to teach his prince; and peradventure boys would mock him behind his back, and women would have none other delight in him but to make him a jesting-stock."

Then said the Lord Octavian:[6] "Since all the other qualities appointed to the Courtier are meet[7] for him, although he be old, methink we should not then bar him from this happiness to love."

---

2. Noticing.
3. True.
4. Lightly regarded. "Clean": entirely.
5. Skill, insight.
6. Pretended.
7. Assiduous.
8. Gaspar Pallavicino, *a young man whose attitude in the dialogue is usually that of the misogynist.*
9. Reviewing.

1. The courtier's role in counseling his prince had been discussed in the preceding part of Book 4.
2. Advanced.
3. Is not suitable to.
4. Excessive neatness.
5. Foolishness. "In them": that is, in old men.
6. Ottaviano Fregoso, a soldier, later doge of Genoa.
7. Suitable.

"Nay rather," quoth the Lord Gaspar, "to take this love from him is a perfection over and above, and a making him to live happily out of misery and wretchedness."

* * *

Then M. Peter[8] after a while's silence, somewhat settling himself as though he should entreat upon a weighty matter, said thus: "My lords, to show that old men may love not only without slander, but otherwhile[9] more happily than young men, I must be enforced to make a little discourse to declare what love is, and wherein consisteth the happiness that lovers may have. Therefore I beseech you give the hearing with needfulness, for I hope to make you understand that it were not unfitting for any man here to be a lover, in case he were fifteen or twenty years elder than M. Morello."[1]

And here, after they had laughed awhile, M. Peter proceeded: "I say, therefore, that according as it is defined of the wise men of old time, love is nothing else but a certain coveting to enjoy beauty;[2] and forsomuch as coveting longeth for nothing but for things known, it is requisite that knowledge go evermore before coveting, which of his own nature willeth the good, but of himself is blind and knoweth it not. Therefore hath nature so ordained that to every virtue[3] of knowledge there is annexed a virtue of longing. And because in our soul there be three manner ways to know, namely, by sense, reason, and understanding:[4] of sense ariseth appetite or longing, which is common to us with brute beasts; of reason ariseth election or choice, which is proper[5] to man; of understanding, by the which man may be partner with angels, ariseth will. Even as therefore the sense knoweth not but sensible matters and that which may be felt, so the appetite or coveting only desireth the same; and even as the understanding is bent but to behold things that may be understood, so is that will only fed with spiritual goods. Man of nature endowed with reason, placed, as it were, in the middle between these two extremities, may, through his choice inclining to sense or reaching to understanding, come nigh to the coveting sometime of the one, sometime of the other part. In these sorts therefore may beauty be coveted; the general name whereof may be applied to all things, either natural or artificial, that are framed in good proportion and due temper,[6] as their nature beareth. But speaking of the beauty that we mean, which is only it that appeareth in bodies, and especially in the face of man, and moveth this fervent coveting which we call love, we will term it an influence of the heavenly bountifulness, the which for all it stretcheth over all things that be created (like the light of the sun), yet when it findeth out a face well proportioned, and framed with a certain lively agreement of several colors, and set forth with lights and shadows, and with an orderly distance and limits of lines, thereinto it distilleth itself and appeareth most well favored, and decketh out and lighteneth the subject where it shineth with a marvelous grace and

---

8. Pietro Bembo (1470–1547), poet, Platonist, grammarian, and historian, later a cardinal. He undertakes to prove that it is suitable for an older courtier to be (in a special sense) a lover.
9. Sometimes.
1. Morello da Ortona, an elderly courtier and musician. "In case": even if.
2. The definition derives from Plato's Symposium.
3. Power.
4. Direct intellectual apprehension, without need of reasoning. "Manner": kinds of.
5. Distinctive.
6. The right mixture or combination of elements. Bembo's definition of beauty, as of love, derives from Plato.

glistering,[7] like the sunbeams that strike against beautiful plate of fine gold wrought and set with precious jewels, so that it draweth unto it men's eyes with pleasure, and piercing through them imprinteth himself in the soul, and with an unwonted sweetness all to-stirreth[8] her and delighteth, and setting her on fire maketh her to covet him.

* * *

"Do you believe, M. Morello," quoth then Count Lewis,[9] that beauty is always so good a thing as M. Peter Bembo speaketh of?"

"Not I, in good sooth," answered M. Morello. "But I remember rather that I have seen many beautiful women of a most ill inclination, cruel and spiteful, and it seemeth that, in a manner, it happeneth always so, for beauty maketh them proud, and pride, cruel."

Count Lewis said, smiling: "To you perhaps they seem cruel, because they content you not with it that you would have. But cause M. Peter Bembo to teach you in what sort old men ought to covet beauty, and what to seek at their ladies' hands, and what to content themselves withal; and in not passing out of these bounds ye shall see that they shall be neither proud nor cruel, and will satisfy you with what you shall require."

M. Morello seemed then somewhat out of patience, and said: "I will not know the thing that toucheth[1] me not. But cause you to be taught how the young men ought to covet this beauty that are not so fresh and lusty as old men be."

Here Sir Frederick,[2] to pacify M. Morello and to break their talk, would not suffer Count Lewis to make answer, but interrupting him said: "Perhaps M. Morello is not altogether out of the way in saying that beauty is not always good, for the beauty of women is many times cause of infinite evils in the world—hatred, war, mortality, and destruction, whereof the razing of Troy[3] can be a good witness; and beautiful women for the most part be either proud and cruel, as is said, or unchaste; but M. Morello would find no fault with that. There be also many wicked men that have the comeliness of a beautiful countenance, and it seemeth that nature hath so shaped them because they may be the readier to deceive, and that this amiable look were like a bait that covereth the hook."

Then M. Peter Bembo: "Believe not," quoth he, "but[4] beauty is always good."

Here Count Lewis, because he would return again to his former purpose, interrupted him and said: "Since M. Morello passeth[5] not to understand that which is so necessary for him, teach it me, and show me how old men may come by this happiness of love, for I will not care to be counted old, so it may profit me."

M. Peter Bembo laughed, and said: "First will I take the error out of these gentlemen's mind, and afterward will I satisfy you also." So beginning

---

7. Glittering, sparkling.
8. Moves violently. In this passage, "it" and "him" refer to beauty, "her" to the soul.
9. *Lodovico Canossa*, who had earlier discoursed on grace.
1. Concerns.
2. Federico Fregoso, later archbishop of Salerno.

3. The destruction of Troy by the Greeks, celebrated in Homer's *Iliad*, was caused by the Trojan Paris's abduction of Helen, the most beautiful woman in the world.
4. That is, anything but that.
5. Cares.

afresh: "My Lords," quoth he, "I would not that with speaking ill of beauty, which is a holy thing, any of us as profane and wicked should purchase him the wrath of God. Therefore, to give M. Morello and Sir Frederick warning, that they lose not their sight, as Stesichorus did—a pain most meet[6] for whoso dispraiseth beauty—I say that beauty cometh of God and is like a circle, the goodness whereof is the center. And therefore, as there can be no circle without a center, no more can beauty be without goodness. Whereupon doth very seldom an ill[7] soul dwell in a beautiful body. And therefore is the outward beauty a true sign of the inward goodness, and in bodies this comeliness is imprinted, more and less, as it were, for a mark of the soul, whereby she is outwardly known; as in trees, in which the beauty of the buds giveth a testimony of the goodness of the fruit. And the very same happeneth in bodies, as it is seen that palmisters[8] by the visage know many times the conditions and otherwhile the thoughts of men. And, which is more, in beasts also a man may discern by the face the quality of the courage,[9] which in the body declareth itself as much as it can. Judge you how plainly in the face of a lion, a horse, and an eagle, a man shall discern anger, fierceness, and stoutness; in lambs and doves, simpleness and very innocency; the crafty subtlety in foxes and wolves; and the like, in a manner, in all other living creatures. The foul,[1] therefore, for the most part be also evil, and the beautiful good. Therefore it may be said that beauty is a face pleasant, merry, comely, and to be desired for goodness; and foulness a face dark, uglesome,[2] unpleasant, and to be shunned for ill. And in case you will consider all things, you shall find that whatsoever is good and profitable hath also evermore the comeliness of beauty. Behold the state of this great engine of the world,[3] which God created for the health and preservation of everything that was made: the heaven round beset with so many heavenly lights; and in the middle the earth environed with the elements and upheld with the very weight of itself; the sun, that compassing about[4] giveth light to the whole, and in winter season draweth to the lowermost sign,[5] afterward by little and little climbeth again to the other part; the moon, that of him taketh her light, according as she draweth nigh or goeth farther from him; and the other five stars[6] that diversely keep the very same course. These things among themselves have such force by the knitting together of an order so necessarily framed that, with altering them any one jot, they should all be loosed and the world would decay. They have also such beauty and comeliness that all the wits men have cannot imagine a more beautiful matter.

"Think now of the shape of man, which may be called a little world, in whom every parcel of his body is seen to be necessarily framed by art and not by hap,[7] and then the form altogether most beautiful, so that it were a hard matter to judge whether the members (as the eyes, the nose, the mouth, the ears, the arms, the breast, and in like manner the other parts) give either more profit to the countenance and the rest of the body, or comeliness. The

---

6. Fitting. Stesichorus: "a notable [ancient Greek] poet which lost his sight for writing against Helena, and recanting, had his sight restored him again" [Hoby's note].
7. Evil.
8. Fortune-tellers.
9. Heart.
1. Ugly.

2. Horribly ugly (apparently first used by Hoby).
3. Mechanism of the universe.
4. Revolving.
5. Of the zodiac.
6. That is, the five other planets then known: Mercury, Venus, Mars, Jupiter, and Saturn.
7. By skill rather than by chance.

like may be said of all other living creatures. Behold the feathers of fowls, the leaves and boughs of trees, which be given them of nature to keep them in their being, and yet have they withal a very great sightliness. Leave nature, and come to art. What thing is so necessary in sailing vessels as the forepart, the sides, the main yards, the mast, the sails, the stern, oars, anchors, and tacklings? All these things notwithstanding are so well-favored in the eye that unto whoso beholdeth them they seem to have been found out as well for pleasure as for profit. Pillars and great beams uphold high buildings and palaces, and yet are they no less pleasureful unto the eyes of the beholders than profitable to the buildings. When men began first to build, in the middle of temples and houses they reared the ridge of the roof, not to make the works to have a better show, but because the water might the more commodiously avoid[8] on both sides; yet unto profit there was forthwith adjoined a fair sightliness, so that if, under the sky where there falleth neither hail nor rain, a man should build a temple without a reared ridge, it is to be thought that it could have neither a sightly show nor any beauty. Besides other things, therefore, it giveth a great praise to the world in saying that it is beautiful. It is praised in saying the beautiful heaven, beautiful earth, beautiful sea, beautiful rivers, beautiful woods, trees, gardens, beautiful cities, beautiful churches, houses, armies. In conclusion, this comely and holy beauty is a wondrous setting out of everything. And it may be said that good and beautiful be after a sort one self[9] thing, especially in the bodies of men; of the beauty whereof the nighest cause, I suppose, is the beauty of the soul; the which, as a partner of the right and heavenly beauty, maketh sightly and beautiful whatever she toucheth, and most of all if the body where she dwelleth be not of so vile a matter that she cannot imprint in it her property.[1] Therefore beauty is the true monument and spoil[2] of the victory of the soul, when she with heavenly influence beareth rule over material and gross nature, and with her light overcometh the darkness of the body. It is not, then, to be spoken that beauty maketh women proud or cruel, although it seem so to M. Morello. Neither yet ought beautiful women to bear the blame of that hatred, mortality, and destruction which the unbridled appetites of men are the cause of. I will not now deny but it is possible also to find in the world beautiful women unchaste; yet not because beauty inclineth them to unchaste living, for it rather plucketh them from it, and leadeth them into the way of virtuous conditions, through the affinity that beauty hath with goodness; but otherwhile[3] ill bringing-up, the continual provocations of lovers' tokens,[4] poverty, hope, deceits, fear, and a thousand other matters overcome the steadfastness, yea, of beautiful and good women; and for these and like causes may also beautiful men become wicked."

Then said the Lord Cesar:[5] "In case the Lord Gaspar's saying be true of yesternight, there is no doubt but the fair women be more chaste than the foul."

"And what was my saying?" quoth the Lord Gaspar.

The Lord Cesar answered: "If I do well bear in mind, your saying was that the women that are sued to always refuse to satisfy him that sueth to them,

---

8. *Escape.*
9. *Same.*
1. Attribute, quality.
2. Reward, trophy.

3. Sometimes.
4. Gifts.
5. Cesar Gonzaga, cousin of Castiglione.

but those that are not sued to, sue to others. There is no doubt but the beautiful women have always more suitors, and be more instantly laid at[6] in love, than the foul. Therefore the beautiful always deny, and consequently be more chaste than the foul, which, not being sued to, sue unto others."

M. Peter Bembo laughed, and said: "This argument cannot be answered to."

Afterward he proceeded: "It chanceth also, oftentimes, that as the other senses, so the sight is deceived and judgeth a face beautiful which indeed is not beautiful. And because in the eyes and in the whole countenance of some woman a man beholdeth otherwhile a certain lavish wantonness painted, with dishonest flickerings,[7] many, whom that manner delighteth because it promiseth them an easiness to come by the thing that they covet, call it beauty; but indeed it is a cloaked un-shamefastness,[8] unworthy of so honorable and holy a name."

M. Peter Bembo held his peace, but those lords still were earnest upon him to speak somewhat more of this love and of the way to enjoy beauty aright, and at the last, "Methink," quoth he, "I have showed plainly enough that old men may love more happily than young, which was my drift;[9] therefore it belongeth not to me to enter any farther."

Count Lewis answered: "You have better declared the unluckiness of young men than the happiness of old men, whom you have not as yet taught what way they must follow in this love of theirs; only you have said that they must suffer themselves to be guided by reason, and the opinion of many is that it is unpossible for love to stand with reason."

Bembo notwithstanding sought to make an end of reasoning, but the duchess[1] desired him to say on, and he began thus afresh: "Too unlucky were the nature of man, if our soul, in which this so fervent coveting may lightly[2] arise, should be driven to nourish it with that only which is common to her with beasts, and could not turn it to the other noble part,[3] which is proper to her. Therefore, since it is so your pleasure, I will not refuse to reason upon this noble matter. And because I know myself unworthy to talk of the most holy mysteries of Love, I beseech him to lead my thought and my tongue so that I may show this excellent Courtier how to love contrary to the wonted[4] manner of the common ignorant sort; and even as from my childhood I have dedicated all my whole life unto him, so also now that my words may be answerable to the same intent, and to the praise of him. I say, therefore, that since the nature of man in youthful age is so much inclined to sense, it may be granted the Courtier, while he is young, to love sensually; but in case afterward also, in his riper years, he chance to be set on fire with this coveting of love, he ought to be good and circumspect, and heedful that he beguile not himself to be led willfully into the wretchedness that in young men deserveth more to be pitied than blamed, and contrariwise in old men more to be blamed than pitied. Therefore when an amiable counte-

---

6. Persistently urged.
7. Hints of lewdness.
8. Immodesty.
9. Purpose. In a passage omitted above, Bembo had argued that old men, whose senses have cooled, find it easier than young men to be guided in love by reason and can therefore more easily avoid the miseries that, he argues, inevitably follow from sensual love.
1. Elisabetta Gonzaga, Duchess of Urbino, the presiding figure in the life of the court and in these dialogues.
2. Easily, readily.
3. That is, reason.
4. Accustomed.

nance of a beautiful woman cometh in his sight, that is accompanied with noble conditions and honest[5] behaviors, so that, as one practiced in love, he wotteth well that his hue[6] hath an agreement with hers, as soon as he is aware that his eyes snatch that image and carry it to the heart, and that the soul beginneth to behold it with pleasure, and feeleth within herself the influence that stirreth her and by little and little setteth her in heat, and that those lively spirits[7] that twinkle out through the eyes put continually fresh nourishment to the fire, he ought in this beginning to seek a speedy remedy and to raise up reason, and with her to fence the fortress of his heart, and to shut in such wise[8] the passages against sense and appetites that they may enter neither with force nor subtle practice.[9] Thus, if the flame be quenched, the jeopardy is also quenched. But in case it continue or increase, then must the Courtier determine, when he perceiveth he is taken, to shun throughly[1] all filthiness of common love, and so enter into the holy way of love with the guide of reason, and first consider that the body where that beauty shineth is not the fountain from whence beauty springeth, but rather because beauty is bodiless and, as we have said, an heavenly shining beam, she loseth much of her honor when she is coupled with that vile subject[2] and full of corruption: because the less she is partner thereof, the more perfect she is, and, clean sundered from it, is most perfect. And as a man heareth not with his mouth, nor smelleth with his ears, no more can he also in any manner wise enjoy beauty, nor satisfy the desire that she stirreth up in our minds, with feeling, but with the sense unto whom beauty is the very butt to level at,[3] namely, the virtue[4] of seeing. Let him lay aside, therefore, the blind judgment of the sense, and enjoy with his eyes the brightness, the comeliness, the loving sparkles, laughters, gestures, and all the other pleasant furnitures[5] of beauty, especially with hearing the sweetness of her voice, the tunableness[6] of her words, the melody of her singing and playing on instruments (in case the woman beloved be a musician); and so shall he with most dainty food feed the soul through the means of these two senses which have little bodily substance in them and be the ministers of reason, without entering farther toward the body with coveting unto any longing otherwise than honest. Afterward, let him obey, please, and honor with all reverence his woman, and reckon her more dear to him than his own life, and prefer all her commodities[7] and pleasures before his own, and love no less in her the beauty of the mind than of the body. Therefore let him have a care not to suffer her to run into any error, but with lessons and good exhortations seek always to frame her to modesty, to temperance, to true honesty, and so to work that there may never take place in her other than pure thoughts and far wide from all filthiness of vices. And thus in sowing of virtue in the garden of that mind, he shall also gather the fruits of most beautiful conditions, and savor them with a marvelous good relish. And this shall be the right engendering and imprinting of beauty in beauty, the which some hold opinion to be the end[8] of love. In this manner shall our Courtier

5. Virtuous (as also several times in the following pages). "Conditions": personal qualities.
6. Aspect. "Wotteth": knows.
7. *Vital, animating powers.* See p. 186, n. 2.
8. In such a way.
9. Treachery.
1. Thoroughly.

2. That is, the body.
3. Target to aim at.
4. Power.
5. Ornaments.
6. Musical quality.
7. Conveniences.
8. Goal.

be most acceptable to his lady, and she will always show herself toward him tractable, lowly,[9] and sweet in language, and as willing to please him as to be beloved of him; and the wills of them both shall be most honest and agreeable, and they consequently shall be most happy."

Here M. Morello: "The engendering," quoth he, "of beauty in beauty aright were the engendering of a beautiful child in a beautiful woman; and I would think it a more manifest token a great deal that she loved her lover, if she pleased him with this than with the sweetness of language that you speak of."

M. Peter Bembo laughed, and said: "You must not, M. Morello, pass your bounds. I may tell you it is not a small token that a woman loveth when she giveth unto her lover her beauty, which is so precious a matter; and by the ways that be a passage to the soul (that is to say, the sight and the hearing) sendeth the looks of her eyes, the image of her countenance, and the voice of her words, that pierce into the lover's heart and give a witness of her love."

M. Morello said: "Looks and words may be, and oftentimes are, false witnesses. Therefore whoso hath not a better pledge of love, in my judgment he is in an ill assurance. And surely I looked[1] still that you would have made this woman of yours somewhat more courteous and free toward the Courtier than my Lord Julian[2] hath made his; but meseemeth ye be both of the property[3] of those judges that, to appear wise, give sentence against their own."

Bembo said: "I am well pleased to have this woman much more courteous toward my Courtier not young than the Lord Julian's is to the young; and that with good reason, because mine coveteth but honest matters, and therefore may the woman grant him them all without blame. But my Lord Julian's woman, that is not so assured of the modesty of the young man, ought to grant him the honest matters only, and deny him the dishonest. Therefore more happy is mine, that hath granted him whatsoever he requireth, than the other, that hath part granted and part denied. And because[4] you may moreover the better understand that reasonable love is more happy than sensual, I say unto you that selfsame things in sensual ought to be denied otherwhile, and in reasonable granted; because in the one they be honest, and in the other dishonest. Therefore the woman, to please her good lover, besides the granting him merry countenances, familiar and secret talk, jesting, dallying, hand-in-hand, may also lawfully and without blame come to kissing, which in sensual love, according to the Lord Julian's rules, is not lawful. For since a kiss is a knitting together both of body and soul, it is to be feared lest the sensual lover will be more inclined to the part of the body than of the soul; but the reasonable lover wotteth well that although the mouth be a parcel[5] of the body, yet is it an issue for the words that be the interpreters of the soul, and for the inward breath, which is also called the soul; and therefore hath a delight to join his mouth with the woman's beloved with a kiss, not to stir him to any unhonest desire, but because he feeleth that that bond is the opening of an entry to the souls, which, drawn with a coveting the one of the other, pour themselves by turn the one into the other's body,

---

9. Modest.
1. Expected.
2. Giuliano de' Medici, younger son of Lorenzo the Magnificent. In Book 3, discussing the ideal courtier's female counterpart, he expresses the opinions alluded to here.
3. Nature.
4. So that.
5. Part.

and be so mingled together that each of them hath two souls, and one alone, so framed of them both, ruleth, in a manner, two bodies. Whereupon a kiss may be said to be rather a coupling together of the soul than of the body, because it hath such force in her that it draweth her unto it, and, as it were, separateth her from the body. For this do all chaste lovers covet a kiss as a coupling of souls together. And therefore Plato,[6] the divine lover, saith that in kissing his soul came as far as his lips to depart out of the body. And because the separating of the soul from the matters of the sense, and the thorough coupling of her with matters of understanding, may be betokened by a kiss, Solomon saith[7] in his heavenly book of ballads, 'Oh that he would kiss me with a kiss of his mouth,' to express the desire he had that his soul might be ravished through heavenly love to the beholding of heavenly beauty in such manner that, coupling herself inwardly with it, she might forsake the body."

They stood all hearkening heedfully to Bembo's reasoning, and after he had stayed[8] a while and saw that none spake, he said: "Since you have made me to begin to show our not-young Courtier this happy love, I will lead him yet somewhat farther forwards; because to stand still at this stay were somewhat perilous for him, considering, as we have oftentimes said, the soul is most inclined to the senses, and for all[9] reason with discourse chooseth well, and knoweth that beauty not to spring of the body, and therefore setteth a bridle to the unhonest desires, yet to behold it always in that body doth oftentimes corrupt the right judgment. And where no other inconvenience ensueth upon it, one's absence from the wight[1] beloved carrieth a great passion with it; because the influence of that beauty when it is present giveth a wondrous delight to the lover and, setting his heart on fire, quickeneth and melteth certain virtues in a trance and congealed in the soul, the which, nourished with the heat of love, flow about and go bubbling nigh the heart, and thrust out through the eyes those spirits which be most fine vapors made of the purest and clearest part of the blood, which receive the image of beauty[2] and deck it with a thousand sundry furnitures. Whereupon the soul taketh a delight, and with a certain wonder is aghast, and yet enjoyeth she it, and, as it were, astonied[3] together with the pleasure, feeleth the fear and reverence that men accustomably have toward holy matters, and thinketh herself to be in paradise. The lover, therefore, that considereth only the beauty in the body loseth this treasure and happiness as soon as the woman beloved with her departure leaveth the eyes without their brightness, and consequently the soul as a widow without her joy. For since beauty is far off, that influence of love setteth not the heart on fire, as it did in presence. Whereupon the pores be dried up and withered, and yet doth the remembrance of beauty somewhat stir those virtues of the soul in such wise that they seek to scatter abroad the spirits, and they, finding the ways closed up, have no issue, and still they seek to get out, and so with those shootings enclosed prick the soul and torment her bitterly, as young children when in

---

6. Plato's discussion of love in *The Symposium*.
7. Song of Solomon 1:2. "Betokened": symbolized.
8. Paused.
9. And although.
1. Person.

2. Love "melts" certain elements ("virtues") that were before "congealed," releasing the vital blood "spirits" that take in the image of beauty through the eyes.
3. Stunned.

their tender gums they begin to breed teeth. And hence come the tears, sighs, vexations, and torments of lovers; because the soul is always in affliction and travail and, in a manner, waxeth wood,[4] until the beloved beauty cometh before her once again, and then she is immediately pacified and taketh breath, and, throughly bent to it, is nourished with most dainty food, and by her will would never depart from so sweet a sight. To avoid, therefore, the torment of this absence, and to enjoy beauty without passion, the Courtier by the help of reason must full and wholly call back again the coveting of the body to beauty alone, and, in what he can, behold it in itself simple and pure, and frame it within his imagination sundered from all matter, and so make it friendly and loving to his soul, and there enjoy it, and have it with him day and night, in every time and place, without mistrust ever to lose it; keeping always fast in mind that the body is a most diverse[5] thing from beauty, and not only not increaseth but diminisheth the perfection of it. In this wise shall our not-young Courtier be out of all bitterness and wretchedness that young men feel, in a manner continually, as jealousies, suspicions, disdains, angers, desperations, and certain rages full of madness, whereby many times they be led into so great error that some do not only beat the women whom they love, but rid themselves out of their life. He shall do no wrong to the husband, father, brethren, or kinsfolk of the woman beloved. He shall not bring her in slander. He shall not be in case with[6] much ado otherwhile to refrain his eyes and tongue from discovering his desires to others. He shall not take thought[7] at departure or in absence, because he shall evermore carry his precious treasure about with him shut fast within his heart. And besides, through the virtue of imagination, he shall fashion within himself that beauty much more fair than it is indeed. But among these commodities the lover shall find another yet far greater, in case he will take this love for a stair, as it were, to climb up to another far higher than it. The which he shall bring to pass, if he will go and consider with himself what a strait bond it is to be always in the trouble to behold the beauty of one body alone. And therefore, to come out of this so narrow a room,[8] he shall gather in his thought by little and little so many ornaments that, meddling[9] all beauties together, he shall make a universal concept, and bring the multitude of them to the unity of one alone, that is generally spread over all the nature of man. And thus shall he behold no more the particular beauty of one woman, but an universal, that decketh out all bodies. Whereupon, being made dim with this greater light, he shall not pass upon[1] the lesser, and, burning in a more excellent flame, he shall little esteem it that[2] he set great store by at the first. This stair of love, though it be very noble and such as few arrive at it, yet is it not in this sort to be called perfect, forsomuch as where the imagination is of force to make conveyance, and hath no knowledge but through those beginnings that the senses help her withal, she is not clean purged from gross darkness; and therefore, though she do consider that universal beauty in sunder and in itself alone, yet doth she not well and clearly discern it, nor without some doubtfulness, by reason of the

---

4. Becomes mad, crazy.
5. Very different.
6. In the situation of having.
7. Be distressed.
8. Space.
9. Mingling.
1. Concern himself with.
2. That is, the thing that.

agreement that the fancies have with the body. Wherefore such as come to this love are like young birds almost flush,[3] which for all they flutter a little their tender wings, yet dare they not stray far from the nest, nor commit themselves to the wind and open weather. When our Courtier, therefore, shall be come to this point, although he may be called a good and happy lover, in respect of them that be drowned in the misery of sensual love, yet will I not have him to set his heart at rest, but boldly proceed farther, following the highway, after his guide[4] that leadeth him to the point of true happiness. And thus, instead of going out of his wit[5] with thought, as he must do that will consider the bodily beauty, he may come into his wit to behold the beauty that is seen with the eyes of the mind, which then begin to be sharp and through-seeing when the eyes of the body lose the flower of their sightliness.

"Therefore the soul, rid of vices, purged with the studies of true philosophy, occupied in spiritual, and exercised in matters of understanding, turning her to the beholding of her own substance, as it were raised out of a most deep sleep, openeth the eyes that all men have and few occupy,[6] and seeth in herself a shining beam of that light which is the true image of the angel-like beauty partened[7] with her, whereof she also partneth with the body a feeble shadow; therefore, waxed blind about earthly matters, is made most quick of sight about heavenly. And otherwhile,[8] when the stirring virtues of the body are withdrawn alone through earnest beholding, either[9] fast bound through sleep, when she is not hindered by them, she feeleth a certain privy[1] smell of the right angel-like beauty, and, ravished with the shining of that light, beginneth to be inflamed, and so greedily followeth after, that in a manner she waxeth drunken and beside herself, for coveting to couple herself with it, having found, to her weening,[2] the footsteps of God, in the beholding of whom, as in her happy end, she seeketh to settle herself. And therefore, burning in this most happy flame, she ariseth to the noblest part of her, which is the understanding, and there, no more shadowed with the dark night of earthly matters, seeth the heavenly beauty; but yet doth she not for all that enjoy it altogether perfectly, because she beholdeth it only in her particular[3] understanding, which cannot conceive the passing[4] great universal beauty; whereupon, not throughly satisfied with this benefit, love giveth unto the soul a greater happiness. For like as through the particular beauty of one body he guideth her to the universal beauty of all bodies, even so in the last degree of perfection through particular understanding he guideth her to the universal understanding. Thus the soul kindled in the most holy fire of heavenly love fleeth to couple herself with the nature of angels, and not only clean forsaketh sense, but hath no more need of the discourse of reason, for, being changed into an angel, she understandeth all things that may be understood; and without any veil or cloud she seeth the main sea of the pure heavenly beauty, and receiveth it into her, and enjoyeth that sovereign happiness that cannot be comprehended of the senses. Since, therefore, the beauties which we daily see with these our dim eyes in bodies

---

3. Fledged, fit to fly.
4. That is, reason.
5. *Mind, intellect.*
6. Use.
7. Shared.
8. Sometimes.
9. Or.
1. Intimate.
2. Thinking, opinion.
3. Individual.
4. Surpassing.

subject to corruption, that nevertheless be nothing else but dreams and most thin shadows of beauty, seem unto us so well favored and comely that oftentimes they kindle in us a most burning fire, and with such delight that we reckon no happiness may be compared to it that we feel otherwhile through the only look[5] which the beloved countenance of a woman casteth at us; what happy wonder, what blessed abashment, may we reckon that to be that taketh the souls which come to have a sight of the heavenly beauty? What sweet flame, what sweet incense, may a man believe that to be which ariseth of the fountain of the sovereign and right beauty? Which is the origin of all other beauty, which never increaseth nor diminisheth, always beautiful, and of itself, as well on the one part as on the other, most simple, only like itself, and partner of none other, but in such wise beautiful that all other beautiful things be beautiful because they be partners of the beauty of it.

"This is the beauty unseparable from the high bounty which with her voice calleth and draweth to her all things; and not only to the endowed with understanding giveth understanding, to the reasonable reason, to the sensual sense and appetite to live, but also partaketh with plants and stones, as a print of herself, stirring, and the natural provocation of their properties.[6] So much, therefore, is this love greater and happier than others, as the cause that stirreth it is more excellent. And therefore, as common fire trieth gold and maketh it fine, so this most holy fire in souls destroyeth and consumeth whatsoever is mortal in them, and relieveth and maketh beautiful the heavenly part, which at the first by reason of the sense was dead and buried in them. This is the great fire in the which, the poets write, that Hercules was burned on the top of the mountain Oeta,[7] and, through that consuming with fire, after his death was holy and immortal. This is the fiery bush of Moses;[8] the divided tongues of fire;[9] the inflamed chariot of Elias;[1] which doubleth grace and happiness in their souls that be worthy to see it, when they forsake this earthly baseness and flee up into heaven. Let us, therefore, bend all our force and thoughts of soul to this most holy light, which showeth us the way which leadeth to heaven; and after it, putting off the affections we were clad withal at our coming down, let us climb up the stairs which at the lowermost step have the shadow of sensual beauty, to the high mansion place where the heavenly, amiable, and right beauty dwelleth, which lieth hid in the innermost secrets of God, lest unhallowed eyes should come to the sight of it; and there shall we find a most happy end for our desires, true rest for our travails, certain remedy for miseries, a most healthful medicine for sickness, a most sure haven in the troublesome storms of the tempestuous sea of this life.

"What tongue mortal is there then, Oh most holy Love, that can sufficiently praise thy worthiness? Thou most beautiful, most good, most wise,

---

5. Through the look alone.
6. That is, motion ("stirring") and, as we would say, their natural instincts.
7. "A mountain between Thessalia and Macedonia where is the sepulcher of Hercules" [*Hoby's note*].
8. "And the angel of the Lord appeared unto . . . [Moses] in a flame of fire out of the midst of a bush: and he looked, and, behold, the bush burned with fire, and the bush was not consumed" (Exodus 3:2).
9. "And there appeared unto them [that is, the Apostles] cloven tongues like as to fire, and it sat upon each of them. And they were all filled with the Holy Ghost, and began to speak with other tongues, as the Spirit gave them utterance" (Acts 2:3–4).
1. The prophet Elijah. "And it came to pass, as they still went on, and talked, that, behold, there appeared a chariot of fire, and horses of fire, and parted them both asunder; and Elijah went up by a whirlwind into heaven" (2 Kings 2:11).

art derived of the unity of heavenly beauty, goodness, and wisdom, and therein dost thou abide, and unto it through it, as in a circle, turnest about. Thou the most sweet bond of the world, a mean betwixt heavenly and earthly things, with a bountiful temper bendest the high virtues[2] to the government of the lower, and turning back the minds of mortal men to their beginning, couplest them with it. Thou with agreement bringest the elements in one, and stirrest nature to bring forth that which ariseth and is born for the succession of the life.[3] Thou bringest severed matters into one, to the unperfect givest perfection, to the unlike likeness, to enmity amity, to the earth fruits, to the sea calmness, to the heaven lively light. Thou art the father of true pleasures, of grace, peace, lowliness, and goodwill, enemy to rude wildness and sluggishness—to be short, the beginning and end of all goodness. And forsomuch as thou delightest to dwell in the flower of beautiful bodies and beautiful souls, I suppose that thy abiding-place is now here among us, and from above otherwhile showest thyself a little to the eyes and minds of them that be worthy to see thee. Therefore vouchsafe, Lord, to hearken to our prayers, pour thyself into our hearts, and with the brightness of thy most holy fire lighten our darkness, and, like a trusty guide in this blind maze, show us the right way; reform the falsehood of the senses, and after long wandering in vanity give us the right and sound joy. Make us to smell those spiritual savors that relieve the virtues of the understanding, and to hear the heavenly harmony so tunable that no discord of passion take place any more in us. Make us drunken with the bottomless fountain of contentation that always doth delight and never giveth fill, and that giveth a smack[4] of the right bliss unto whoso drinketh of the running and clear water thereof. Purge with the shining beams of thy light our eyes from misty ignorance, that they may no more set by[5] mortal beauty, and well perceive that the things which at the first they thought themselves to see be not indeed, and those that they saw not, to be in effect. Accept our souls that be offered unto thee for a sacrifice. Burn them in the lively flame that wasteth[6] all gross filthiness, that after they be clean sundered from the body they may be coupled with an everlasting and most sweet bond to the heavenly beauty. And we, severed from ourselves, may be changed like right lovers into the beloved, and, after we be drawn from the earth, admitted to the feast of the angels, where, fed with immortal ambrosia and nectar,[7] in the end we may die a most happy and lively death, as in times past died the fathers of old time, whose souls with most fervent zeal of beholding, thou didst hale from the body and coupledst them with God."

When Bembo had hitherto spoken with such vehemency that a man would have thought him, as it were, ravished and beside himself, he stood still without once moving, holding his eyes toward heaven as astonied; when the Lady Emilia,[8] which together with the rest gave most diligent ear to this talk, took him by the plait of his garment and plucking him a little, said: "Take heed, M. Peter, that these thoughts make not your soul also to forsake the body."

2. Powers.
3. That is, for the perpetuation of life.
4. Taste.
5. Set store by.
6. Consumes.
7. The food and drink of the gods in classical mythology.
8. Emilia Pia, a widow living at court, the faithful companion of the duchess Elisabetta and the mistress of ceremonies of the discussions.

"Madam," answered M. Peter, "it should not be the first miracle that love hath wrought in me."

Then the Duchess and all the rest began afresh to be instant[9] upon M. Bembo that he would proceed once more in his talk, and everyone thought he felt in his mind, as it were, a certain sparkle of that godly love that pricked him, and they all coveted to hear farther; but M. Bembo: "My Lords," quoth he, "I have spoken what the holy fury of love hath, unsought for, indited[1] to me; now that, it seemeth, he inspireth me no more, I wot not what to say. And I think verily that Love will not have his secrets discovered any farther, nor that the Courtier should pass the degree that his pleasure is I should show him, and therefore it is not perhaps lawful to speak any more in this matter."

"Surely," quoth the Duchess, "if the not-young Courtier be such a one that he can follow this way which you have showed him, of right he ought to be satisfied with so great a happiness, and not to envy the younger."

Then the Lord Cesar Gonzaga: "The way," quoth he, "that leadeth to this happiness is so steep, in my mind, that I believe it will be much ado to get to it."

The Lord Gaspar said: "I believe it be hard to get up for men, but unpossible for women."

The Lady Emilia laughed, and said: "If you fall so often to offend us, I promise you you shall be no more forgiven."

The Lord Gaspar answered: "It is no offense to you in saying that women's souls be not so purged from passions as men's be, nor accustomed in beholdings,[2] as M. Peter hath said is necessary for them to be that will taste of the heavenly love. Therefore it is not read that ever woman hath had this grace; but many men have had it, as Plato, Socrates, Plotinus,[3] and many other, and a number of our holy fathers, as Saint Francis, in whom a fervent spirit of love imprinted the most holy seal of the five wounds.[4] And nothing but the virtue[5] of love could hale up Saint Paul the Apostle to the sight of those secrets which is not lawful for man to speak of; nor show Saint Stephen the heavens open."[6]

Here answered the Lord Julian: "In this point men shall nothing pass women, for Socrates himself doth confess that all the mysteries of love which he knew were oped unto him by a woman, which was Diotima.[7] And the angel that with the fire of love imprinted the five wounds in Saint Francis hath also made some women worthy of the same print in our age. You must remember, moreover, that Saint Mary Magdalen[8] had many faults forgiven her, because she loved much; and perhaps with no less grace than Saint Paul was she many times through angelic love haled up to the third heaven. And

---

9. Insistent.
1. Dictated. "Fury": frenzy; enthusiasm of one possessed as by a god.
2. Contemplations.
3. Plotinus (205–270 C.E.) was the founder of the Neoplatonic philosophical school of late antiquity—the tradition revived by Bembo and, especially, his predecessor the great Florentine philosopher Marsilio Ficino (1433–1499).
4. Saint Francis of Assisi (1182–1226) is supposed to have received the stigmata, marking on his body the five wounds of Jesus on the Cross.
5. Power.
6. Before being stoned to death, Saint Stephen, the first Christian martyr, said, "Behold, I see the heavens opened, and the Son of man standing on the right hand of God" (Acts 7:56). Saint Paul's vision of the "third heaven" is in 2 Corinthians 12:2–4.
7. In Plato's *Symposium*, Socrates claims that a wise woman, Diotima, taught him his philosophy of love. "Oped": opened, disclosed.
8. Traditionally though baselessly regarded as a converted prostitute, she became one of Jesus's most faithful followers.

many other, as I showed you yesterday more at large, that for love of the name of Christ have not passed upon[9] life, nor feared torments, nor any other kind of death how terrible and cruel ever it were. And they were not, as M. Peter will have his Courtier to be, aged, but soft and tender maidens, and in the age when he saith that sensual love ought to be borne withal[1] in men."

The Lord Gaspar began to prepare himself to speak, but the Duchess: "Of this," quoth she, "let M. Peter be judge, and the matter shall stand to his verdict, whether women be not as meet[2] for heavenly love as men. But because the plead[3] between you may happen be too long, it shall not be amiss to defer it until tomorrow."

"Nay, tonight," quoth the Lord Cesar Gonzaga.

"And how can it be tonight?" quoth the Duchess.

The Lord Cesar answered: "Because it is day already," and showed her the light that began to enter in at the clefts of the windows. Then every man arose upon his feet with much wonder, because they had not thought that the reasonings had lasted longer than the accustomed wont, saving only that they were begun much later, and with their pleasantness had deceived so the lords' minds that they wist[4] not of the going away of the hours. And not one of them felt any heaviness of sleep in his eyes, the which often happeneth when a man is up after his accustomed hour to go to bed. When the windows then were opened on the side of the palace that hath his prospect toward the high top of Mount Catri, they saw already risen in the east a fair morning like unto the color of roses, and all stars voided,[5] saving only the sweet governess of the heaven, Venus, which keepeth the bounds of the night and the day, from which appeared to blow a sweet blast that, filling the air with a biting cold, began to quicken the tunable notes of the pretty birds among the hushing woods of the hills at hand. Whereupon they all, taking their leave with reverence of the Duchess, departed toward their lodgings without torch, the light of the day sufficing.

And as they were now passing out at the great chamber door, the Lord General[6] turned him to the Duchess and said: "Madam, to take up the variance between the Lord Gaspar and the Lord Julian, we will assemble this night with the judge sooner than we did yesterday."

The Lady Emilia answered: "Upon condition that in case my Lord Gaspar will accuse women, and give them, as his wont is, some false report, he will also put us in surety to stand to trial:[7] for I reckon him a wavering starter."[8]

1561

9. Cared for.
1. Put up with.
2. Fitted.
3. *Controversy.*
4. Knew.
5. Vanished.
6. Francesco Maria della Rovere, nephew and adopted heir of the duke.
7. That is, he must give us some pawn ("surety") to guarantee that he will answer the charge of falsely accusing women. "Wont": habit.
8. That is, one who is likely to "start"—suddenly desert his post.

ISABELLA WHITNEY
fl. 1566–1573

The poet Isabella Whitney was one of the small number of women in early modern England able to break through the social barriers that inhibited female appearance in print. Making her achievement even more impressive was that she, unlike most of the other women in this volume, apparently started her career not at court but as a maidservant—and, because of slander, she had even been dismissed from that position. That she was the sister of a well-known writer of emblems, Geoffrey Whitney, may have given her entrée to the up-and-coming London printer Richard Jones, who printed a set of her verse epistles on love and inconstancy (*The Copy of a Letter*, 1567), perhaps to help her with her family finances. In 1573 she followed this initial effort with *A Sweet Nosegay or Pleasant Posy: Containing a Hundred and Ten Philosophical Flowers*. This work begins with a series of moral adages adapted from Sir Hugh Plat's *Flowers of Philosophy* (1572). A second section returns to the genre of the epistle, with a collection of letters between family and friends that provide her an opportunity to comment on social and economic problems. The work's third and concluding section is the author's satirical "Will and Testament," included here.

Will and Testament

The author (though loath to leave the city) upon her friend's procurement is constrained to depart, wherefore she feigneth as she would die and maketh her will and testament, as followeth, with large legacies of such goods and riches which she most abundantly hath left behind her, and thereof maketh London sole executor to see her legacies performed.

A communication which the author had to
London, before she made her will

    The time is come I must depart
      from thee, ah famous city.
    I never yet, to rue my smart,°   *pain*
      did find that thou hadst pity.
5   Wherefore small cause there is that I
      should grieve from thee [to] go.
    But many women foolishly,
      like me, and other mo'e,°   *more*
    Do such a fixèd fancy set
10   on those which least deserve,
    That long it is ere° wit we get,   *before*
      away from them to swerve.°   *turn*
    But time with pity oft will tell
      to those that will her try,
15 Whether it best be more to mell,°   *associate with*
      or utterly defy.
    And now hath time me put in mind

        of thy great cruelness,
    That never once a help would find
20   to ease me in distress.
    Thou never yet wouldst credit give
        to board me for a year,
    Nor with apparel me relieve
        except thou payèd were.
25   No, no, thou never didst me good,
        nor ever wilt, I know;
    Yet I am in no angry mood,
        but will, or ere I go,
    In perfect love and charity
30   my testament here write,
    And leave to thee such treasury
        as I in it recite.
    Now stand aside and give me leave
        to write my latest will:
35   And see that none you do deceive
        of that I leave them till.°   *to them*

The manner of her will, and what she left to London and to all those in it at her departing

    I whole in body and in mind,
        but very weak in purse,
    Do make and write my testament
40   for fear it will be worse.
    And first I wholly do commend
        my soul and body eke°   *also*
    To God the Father and the Son,
        so long as I can speak.
45   And after speech, my soul to him,
        and body to the grave,
    Till time that all shall rise again,
        their judgment for to have.
    And then I hope they both shall meet
50   to dwell for aye° in joy   *ever*
    Whereas° I trust to see my friends   *where*
        released from all annoy.
    Thus have you heard touching my soul
        and body what I mean;
55   I trust you all will witness bear,
        I have a steadfast brain.
    And now let me dispose such things
        as I shall leave behind,
    That those which shall receive the same
60   may know my willing mind.
    I first of all to London leave,
        because I there was bred,
    Brave° buildings rare, of churches store,°   *splendid / abundance*
        and Paul's to the head.[1]

---

1. "And St. Paul's Cathedral foremost among them."

> 65 Between the same, fair streets there be
>   and people goodly store;
>   Because their keeping craveth° cost, — *requires*
>   I yet will leave hem° more. — *them*
>   First for their food, I butchers leave,
> 70   that every day shall kill;
>   By Thames you shall have brewers store,
>   and bakers at your will.
>   And such as orders do observe,
>   and eat fish thrice a week,[2]
> 75 I leave two streets full fraught therewith;
>   they need not far to seek.
>   Watling Street and Canwick Street
>   I full of woolen leave,
>   And linen store in Friday Street,
> 80   if they me not deceive.
>   And those which are of calling such
>   that costlier they require,
>   I mercers[3] leave, with silk so rich
>   as any would desire.
> 85 In Cheap,[4] of them they store shall find,
>   and likewise in that street
>   I goldsmiths leave, with jewels such
>   as are for ladies meet.° — *suitable*
>   And plate° to furnish cupboards with — *silver-plated dishes*
> 90   full brave there shall you find,
>   With purl° of silver and of gold — *thread or cord*
>   to satisfy your mind.
>   With hoods, bongraces,° hats, or caps, — *sunshades*
>   such store are in that street,
> 95 As if on tone side you should miss,
>   the tother[5] serves you feat.° — *nicely*
>   For nets° of every kind of sort, — *hairnets*
>   I leave within the pawn,[6]
>   French ruffs, high purls,° gorgets,° and sleeves — *ruff pleats / wimples*
> 100   of any kind of lawn.° — *fine linen*
>   For purse or knives, for comb or glass,
>   or any needful knack,
>   I by the Stocks[7] have left a boy
>   will ask you what you lack.
> 105 I hose do leave in Birchin Lane,
>   of any kind of size,
>   For women stitched, for men both trunks
>   and those of Gascon guise,[8]
>   Boots, shoes, or pantables° good store, — *overshoes*
> 110   Saint Martin's hath for you;
>   In Cornwall,[9] there I leave you beds,
>   and all that 'longs° thereto. — *belongs*

2. To encourage the fishing industry, an Act of 1563 ordered that fish was to be eaten three days a week.
3. Dealers in silk and other costly materials.
4. Cheapside Market, near St. Paul's.
5. "Tone . . . tother": the one . . . the other.
6. The upper walk or gallery of the Royal Exchange.
7. A market in the center of London.
8. Two kinds of breeches: trunk-hose (full and baglike) and gaskins (wide breeches).
9. "Cornwallish ground" in Vintry Ward.

> For women, shall you tailors have:
> by Bow,[1] the chiefest dwell;
> In every lane you some shall find
> can do indifferent well.
> And for the men, few streets or lanes,
> but body-makers° be,   *tailors*
> And such as make the sweeping cloaks
> with guards° beneath the knee.   *ornamental borders*
> Artillery° at Temple Bar   *weapons*
> and dagges° at Tower Hill;   *pistols*
> Swords and bucklers of the best
> are nigh the Fleet until.°   *near to Fleet Street*
> Now when thy folk are fed and clad
> with such as I have named,
> For dainty mouths and stomachs weak
> some junkets° must be framed.   *milk puddings*
> Wherefore I 'pothecaries[2] leave,
> with banquets in their shop;
> Physicians also for the sick,
> diseases for to stop.
> Some roisters° still must bide in thee   *roisterers, bullies*
> and such as cut it out,°   *make a show*
> That with the guiltless quarrel will,
> to let their blood about.
> For them I cunning surgeons leave,
> some plasters° to apply,   *poultices*
> That ruffians may not still be hanged,
> nor quiet persons die.
> For salt, oatmeal, candles, soap,
> or what you else do want,
> In many places shops are full,
> I left you nothing scant.°   *scarce*
> If they that keep what I you leave
> ask money, when they sell it,
> At Mint there is such store it is
> unpossible to tell it.
> At Steelyard[3] store of wines there be,
> your dullèd minds to glad,
> And handsome men that must not wed
> except they leave their trade.[4]
> They oft shall seek for proper girls,
> and some perhaps shall find
> That need compels or lucre lures
> to satisfy their mind.
> And near the same I houses leave
> for people to repair,°   *resort*
> To bathe themselves, so to prevent
> infection of the air.
> On Saturdays I wish that those

---

1. The Church of St. Mary Bow.
2. Apothecaries sold various dainty dishes ("banquets").
3. The place of business of the Hanseatic merchants, known for their Rhenish wines.
4. That is, the men are apprentices, who were not allowed to marry.

which all the week do drug°   *drudge*
Shall thither trudge to trim them up
    on Sundays to look smug.°   *neat, trim*
165 If any other thing be lacked
    in thee, I wish them look;
For there it is: I little brought,
    but nothing from thee took.
Now for the people in thee left,
170   I have done as I may,
And that the poor, when I am gone,
    have cause for me to pray,
I will to prisons portions leave,
    what though but very small,
175 Yet that they may remember me
    occasion be it shall.
And first the Counter° they shall have,   *a debtors' prison*
    lest they should go to wrack,°   *ruin*
Some coggers° and some honest men   *cheats*
180   that sergeants° draw aback.   *police officers*
And such as friends will not them bail,
    whose coin is very thin,
For them I leave a certain hole,
    and little ease within.
185 The Newgate° once a month shall have   *a prison for felons*
    a sessions° for his share,   *court*
Lest being heaped,° infection might   *overcrowded*
    procure a further care.
And at those sessions some shall 'scape
190   with burning near the thumb,°   *branding*
And afterward to beg their fees[5]
    till they have got the sum.
And such whose deeds deserveth death,
    and twelve° have found the same,   *a jury*
195 They shall be drawn up Holborn Hill
    to come to further shame.[6]
Well, yet to such I leave a nag
    shall soon their sorrows cease,
For he shall either break their necks
200   or gallop from the preace.°   *press, crowd*
The Fleet° not in their circuit is,   *another prison*
    yet if I give him nought,
It might procure his curse, ere I
    unto the ground be brought.
205 Wherefore I leave some papist old
    to underprop his roof,
And to the poor within the same,
    a box° for their behoof.°   *money box / benefit*
What makes you standers-by to smile,
210   and laugh so in your sleeve,
I think it is because that I
    to Ludgate° nothing give.   *debtors' prison*

---

5. That is, the discharge fees that prisoners were required to pay.

6. The road to Tyburn—the place of execution—ran by Holborn Hill.

I am not now in case to° lie,   *in a position to*
   here is no place of jest:
215 I did reserve that for myself,
   if I my health possessed°   *retained*
And ever came in credit so
   a debtor for to be,
When days of payment did approach,
220   I thither meant to flee,
To shroud myself amongst the rest
   that choose to die in debt
Rather than any creditor
   should money from them get.
225 Yet 'cause I feel myself so weak
   that none me credit dare,
I here revoke, and do it leave
   some bankrupts to his share.°   *to Ludgate's share*
To all the bookbinders by Paul's,°   *St. Paul's*
230   because I like their art,
They every week shall money have
   when they from books depart.°   *sell their books*
Amongst them all my printer must
   have somewhat to his share;
235 I will my friends these books to buy
   of him, with other ware.
For maidens poor, I widowers rich
   do leave, that oft shall dote
And by that means shall marry them,
240   to set the girls afloat.
And wealthy widows will I leave
   to help young gentlemen,
Which when you° have, in any case   *the young gentlemen*
   be courteous to them then.
245 And see their plate and jewels eke
   may not be marred with rust,
Nor let their bags too long be full,
   for fear that they do burst.
To every gate under the walls
250   that compass thee about,
I fruitwives° leave to entertain   *fruit sellers*
   such as come in and out.
To Smithfield[7] I must something leave,
   my parents there did dwell:
255 So careless for to be of it,
   none would accompt° it well.   *account*
Wherefore it thrice a week shall have
   of horse and neat° good store;   *oxen*
And in his spittle° blind and lame   *hospital*
260   to dwell for evermore.
And Bedlam° must not be forgot,   *the lunatic asylum*
   for that was oft my walk:
I people there too many leave
   that out of tune do talk.

---

7. West Smithfield, known for its horse market.

265	At Bridewell° there shall beadles be,	*a workhouse for the poor*
	and matrons that shall still	
	See chalk well-chopped and spinning plied,	
	and turning of the mill.	
	For such as cannot quiet be,	
270	but strive for house or land,	
	At th'Inns of Court[8] I lawyers leave	
	to take their cause in hand.	
	And also leave I at each Inn	
	of Court or Chancery,	
275	Of gentlemen a youthful rout°	*crowd*
	full of activity:	
	For whom I store of books have left	
	at each bookbinder's stall,	
	And part of all that London hath	
280	to furnish them withal.°	*with*
	And when they are with study cloyed,	
	to recreate their mind,	
	Of tennis courts, of dancing schools,	
	and fence° they store shall find.	*fencing*
285	And every Sunday at the least	
	I leave, to make them sport,	
	In divers places players° that	*actors*
	of wonders shall report.	
	Now, London, have I (for thy sake),	
290	within thee and without,	
	As comes into my memory	
	dispersèd round about	
	Such needful things as they should have	
	here left now unto thee:	
295	When I am gone, with conscience	
	let them dispersèd be.	
	And though I nothing namèd have	
	to bury me withal,	
	Consider that above the ground	
300	annoyance be I shall°	*I shall be*
	And let me have a shrouding sheet	
	to cover me from shame,	
	And in oblivion bury me	
	and never more me name.	
305	Ringings° nor other ceremonies	*of church bells*
	use you not for cost,°	*because of the expense*
	Nor at my burial make no feast,	
	your money were but lost.	
	Rejoice in God that I am gone	
310	out of this vale so vile,	
	And that of each thing left such store	
	as may your wants exile.[9]	
	I make thee sole executor, because	
	I loved thee best.	
315	And thee I put in trust to give	

---

8. The Inns of Court and Inns of Chancery trained and housed lawyers.

9. That is, rejoice that I've left you such abundance of everything that you will have no further needs.

     the goods unto the rest.
Because thou shalt a helper need
     in this so great a charge,°   *task*
I wish Good Fortune be thy guide, lest
320   thou shouldst run at large.
The happy days and quiet times
     they both her servants be,
Which well will serve to fetch and bring
     such things as need° to thee.   *are needed*
325 Wherefore (good London) not refuse
     for helper her to take:
Thus being weak and weary both,
     an end here will I make.
To all that ask what end I made,
330   and how I went away,
Thou answer mayst: "like those which here
     no longer tarry may."
And unto all that wish me well
     or rue that I am gone,
335 Do me commend, and bid them cease
     my absence for to moan.
And tell them further, if they would
     my presence still have had,
They should have sought to mend my luck,
340   which ever was too bad.
So fare thou well a thousand times,
     God shield thee from thy foe,
And still make thee victorious
     of those that seek thy woe.
345 And though I am persuade that I
     shall never more thee see,
Yet to the last I shall not cease
     to wish much good to thee.
This twenty of October, I,
350   in Anno Domini[1]
A thousand five hundred seventy-three,
     as almanacs descry,°   *declare*
Did write this will with mine own hand
     and it to London gave,
355 In witness of the standers-by,
     whose names if you will have,
Paper, Pen, and Standish° were   *inkstand*
     at that same present by,
With Time, who promised to reveal,
360   so fast as she could hie,
The same, lest of my nearer kin
     for any thing should vary:[2]
So finally I make an end,
     no longer can I tarry.

1573

---

1. In the year of the Lord (Latin).
2. Time will hasten ("hie") to reveal the will, lest kinsfolk begin to quarrel over her property.

Women and Power

An act of Parliament in 1544 reaffirmed the long-standing legal prohibition upon the writing of wills by certain groups or classes of people, including persons under the age of twenty-one, idiots, madmen—and wives. Thus for a woman to write her own will, let alone to publish it, was to lay claim to a certain legal, social, and economic independence. Isabella Whitney adopts this stance in order to survey the institutions, occupations, and commodities of London and, in leaving her mock bequests, to articulate a series of sharp criticisms. She writes in the voice of an impoverished gentlewoman who is compelled by her circumstances to leave the city and does so in a mood that mingles regret, complaint, irony, and aggression.

Though Tudor England was a patriarchal society, from 1553 to 1603 it experienced five uninterrupted decades of female rule. What effect did this have on the society's discourse of gender relations? On one level, precious little. Women governed the realm, but Tudor men, with very few exceptions, clung to and reiterated their misogynistic views. None of the royal women introduced in this section showed either an interest in improving the lot of less privileged women in their society or a sense of solidarity with their powerful female peers. Two of them, Mary Tudor and Elizabeth, signed the death warrants of the two others, Jane Grey and Mary Stuart (Queen of Scots). In addition, Mary Tudor probably came close to having her half-sister, Elizabeth, executed, and Mary Stuart plotted her cousin Elizabeth's assassination. These women are fascinating because they found themselves thrust into positions of almost unbelievable complexity, challenge, and danger. That one of them—Elizabeth I—not only flourished but also managed to use to her advantage the fact that she was a woman is one of the age's great stories.

Though public affirmations of male superiority continued, condemnations of the female sex could not, under Elizabeth, be quite so sweeping or absolute as in previous times. When the prominent humanist Sir Thomas Smith thought of how he should describe his country's social order, he declared that "we do reject women, as those whom nature hath made to keep home and to nourish their family and children, and not to meddle with matters abroad, nor to bear office in a city or commonwealth." Then, with a kind of nervous glance over his shoulder, he made an exception of those few in whom "the blood is respected, not the age nor the sex"—for example, the queen.

But even at the top, women could not easily escape being defined by their marital status, sexual behavior, and reproductive potential. Such was the case for Jane Grey, matched to Guildford Dudley as a move in a dangerous political game; for Mary Tudor, with her marriage to a foreign king and her phantom pregnancies; and for Mary Stuart, with her string of disastrous marriages and reputed sexual liaisons. Imagining how the careers of these contemporary women appeared in the eyes of Elizabeth helps explain her choice not to marry.

Before the Reformation, learned and ambitious women had been able, in convents, to gain a modicum of education that offered them scope for both literary expression and the exercise of authority. With the dissolution of the monasteries under Henry VIII, however, that option was closed; and as Protestantism gathered strength, the emphasis on marriage further narrowed for women the possibilities of an independent life. Nonetheless, many Tudor women ran households and businesses; others played prominent roles in city life and were influential in regional politics and church appointments. Though in practice many women had more influence and authority than official doctrine acknowledged, that doctrine affirmed

Women in Charge. This engraving is from a 1597 cookbook by Switzerland's first culinary author, Anna Wecker. Intended for a popular, rather than aristocratic readership, the book provides simple, accessible recipes. Of the two women in this picture, the one on the left, proudly supervising her kitchen, is probably Wecker herself.

the subordination of women in public, private, economic, and spiritual life. Sermon writers and moralists cited alleged scriptural, medical, moral, historical, and philosophical "proofs" of male superiority and urged women to be chaste, silent, and obedient. At the same time, Protestant insistence on scripture as the crucial guide to faith also placed a sharply increased emphasis on literacy, which contributed, over the course of the sixteenth century, to a gradual increase in the number of women writers. Translation was a field that educated women could enter, as it allowed them to claim to be the mouthpieces of men while giving them a medium for displaying their linguistic and technical skills. The dedicatory matter provided here, in which the translators Anne Cooke Bacon and Mary Tyler address their own "authorship" as well as that of the people they are translating, shows the extent to which women were able to exploit male voices to express their own concerns.

Two further dedications join Bacon's and Tyler's as early examples of *querelles de femme*. This French term, meaning "the woman question," was used of a range of European books written from 1500 onward that discussed women's nature, abilities, and status in society—issues particularly pressing in England with Mary I and then Elizabeth I on the throne. Women who defend their right to authorship are participating in the *querelles de femme* debate; here two authors of original texts, Anne Dowriche and Jane Anger, explain why they feel they have the ability and right to write for themselves. Anne Dowriche tells her brother that she can pen an epic poem about the French wars because, though she is a woman, her subject justifies the Protestant Reformation; Jane Anger maintains that she can write as she does because she needs to confront the arrogant men who seduce and subjugate women. Anger's furious text is, however, further contradictory, as it is unclear whether it is genuinely by a woman or is by a man adopting an angry woman's voice and stance. In one way or another, the male voice regularly intrudes into the woman's—but, as these examples show, the reverse is also true.

MARY I (MARY TUDOR)

Mary Tudor (1516–1558) was the only surviving child of Henry VIII's first wife, Catherine of Aragon. The king saw his daughter as a useful bargaining chip in international diplomacy—at the age of six she was engaged to be married to her cousin Charles V, the Holy Roman Emperor and England's chief ally against France—but balked at the thought of leaving his kingdom to a female heir. Blaming Catherine for failing to produce a son, he determined to seek a divorce. The pope's refusal to grant it precipitated the Protestant Reformation in England.

In the years immediately following the royal divorce and the break with Rome, Mary had good reason to believe that her life was in danger. When she refused to take the Oaths of Succession and Supremacy (affirming, respectively, the invalidity of her parents' marriage and her father's supreme authority over the English Church), Henry came close to having her arrested for treason. At length, her own Catholic councillors prevailed on her to sign the oaths rather than lose her life. Sparing her no humiliation, the Privy Council insisted that she add a postscript acknowledging that Henry VIII's marriage to her mother had been "incestuous and unlawful," thus effectively declaring herself a bastard. In his will, however, Henry VIII made Mary second in line for the throne, after her younger half-brother, Edward.

Harassed for harboring priests and attending Mass during Edward's reign, Mary very nearly did not survive the attempt, at its end, to establish as successor the Protestant Jane Grey. But when, somewhat surprisingly, Protestants as well as Catholics rallied firmly to Mary's cause, she ascended the throne, and Jane Grey and her supporters went to the scaffold. The early eagerness of Protestants to accept Henry VIII's legitimate heir as their queen, regardless of her religion, diminished sharply when it became clear that Mary intended to marry a foreign ruler, Philip II of Spain. (Eleven years her junior, Philip was the son of her childhood fiancé, Charles V.) Sir Thomas Wyatt, son of the poet of the same name, led an uprising in January 1554 to prevent the match. Urged to flee, Mary instead went to the Guildhall in London and made a forceful speech that garnered popular support.

Wyatt's rebellion was subdued a week later, but there would never thereafter be real peace between Mary and her subjects. Her determination to restore the Catholic religion was probably welcomed by the majority, but there was no hope of avoiding confrontation with committed Protestants, and Mary did not attempt to avoid it. Between the beginning of 1555 and the end of her reign in 1558, she had 283 Protestants, from famous bishops to village zealots, executed for heresy. The immediate popular response of horror and resentment, which would soon solidify into the lurid historical legend of "Bloody Mary," had less to do with the number of executions than with the nature of the charge and with the grisly method employed. In reality both Henry VIII and Elizabeth executed many more people in the course of their reigns than did Mary. But Henry and Elizabeth, who were disposed to treat religious dissent as treason, typically had their victims executed as traitors—that is, hanged or beheaded. The pious Mary attempted to stamp out heresy and had *her* victims burned at the stake.

Impelled to marry for political reasons, Mary seemed to fall genuinely in love with her husband, who, however, did not reciprocate her feelings. On two occasions in her reign, she believed and announced herself to be pregnant, but both were phantom pregnancies. The melancholy from which she had always suffered intensified in the later years of her reign, when she grappled with bitter disappointments: many of her subjects incorrigibly heretical, her husband aloof and usually absent, her body apparently incapable of childbearing. In 1558 Mary died, leaving the throne to her Protestant half-sister. The two royal half-sisters are buried in a single tomb in Westminster Abbey.

Letter to Henry VIII

To the King's Most Gracious Highness, my father:[1]

Most humbly prostrate before the feet of Your Most Excellent Majesty, your most humble, faithful, and obedient subject, which hath so extremely offended Your Most Gracious Highness that my heavy and fearful heart dare not presume to call you father, ne[2] Your Majesty hath any cause by my deserts, saving the benignity of your most blessed nature doth surmount all evils, offenses, and trespasses, and is ever merciful and ready to accept the penitent calling for grace in any convenient time. Having received this Thursday at night certain letters from Mr. Secretary,[3] as well advising me to make my humble submission immediately to yourself, which because I durst not without your gracious license presume to do before, I lately sent unto him, as signifying that your most merciful heart and fatherly pity had granted me your blessing, with condition that I should persevere in that I had commenced and begun, and that I should not eftsoons[4] offend Your Majesty by the denial or refusal of any such articles and commandments as it may please Your Highness to address unto me for the perfect trial of mine heart and inward affection. For the perfect declaration of the bottom of my heart and stomach,[5] first, I knowledge[6] myself to have most unkindly and unnaturally offended Your Most Excellent Highness, in that I have not submitted myself to your most just and virtuous laws, and for mine offense therein, which I must confess were in me a thousandfold more grievous than they could be in any other living creature, I put myself wholly and entirely to your gracious mercy; at whose hands I cannot receive that punishment for the same[7] that I have deserved. Secondly, to open my heart to Your Grace in these things which I have hitherto refused to condescend[8] unto, and have now written with mine own hand, sending the same to Your Highness herewith; I shall never beseech Your Grace to have pity and compassion of me, if ever you shall perceive that I shall privily or apertly[9] vary or alter from one

---

1. After the execution of Anne Boleyn on May 19, 1536, Mary thought that she would quickly be restored to her father's favor. Henry, though, persisted in the demand that he had been making of her for several years: that she acknowledge in writing his supremacy over the English Church, as well as the invalidity of his marriage to her mother. In the weeks after Anne's beheading, Mary's continuing refusal to comply with this demand infuriated Henry to the point that he threatened her (not for the first time) with death. *Finally*, lambasted by Henry's secretary and principal adviser Thomas Cromwell, who had supported her until the king's rage made him fear for his own safety, and urged to submit even by her Spanish allies, Mary yielded, signing the prescribed articles on a Thursday night in June (either the 15th or the 22nd) and writing her father this supplicatory letter (which may have been drafted by Cromwell).
2. Nor.
3. Cromwell.
4. Again.
5. The stomach, like the heart, was often designated the inward seat of thought and feeling.
6. Acknowledge.
7. That is, for my offense.
8. Consent.
9. Secretly or openly.

piece of that I have written and subscribed, or refuse to confirm, ratify, or declare the same where Your Majesty shall appoint me. Thirdly, as I have and shall, knowing your excellent learning, virtue, wisdom, and knowledge, put my soul into your direction, and, by the same, hath and will, in all things, from henceforth direct my conscience, so my body I do wholly commit to your mercy and fatherly pity; desiring no state, no condition, nor no manner degree of living, but such as Your Grace shall appoint unto me; knowledging and confessing that my state cannot be so vile as either the extremity of justice would appoint unto me, or as mine offenses have required and deserved. And whatsoever Your Grace shall command me to do, touching any of these points, either for things past, present, or to come, I shall as gladly do the same, as Your Majesty can command me. Most humbly therefore, beseeching your mercy, most gracious sovereign lord and benign father, to have pity and compassion of your miserable and sorrowful child, and with the abundance of your inestimable goodness so to overcome my iniquity towards God, Your Grace, and your whole realm, as I may feel some sensible[1] token of reconciliation, which, God is my judge, I only desire, without other respect.[2] To Whom I shall daily pray for the preservation of Your Highness, with the Queen's Grace,[3] and that it may please Him to send you issue. From Hunsdon, this Thursday, at 11 of the clock at night.

Your Grace's most humble and
obedient daughter and handmaid,
Mary

1536   1830

From An Ambassadorial Dispatch to the Holy Roman Emperor, Charles V: The Coronation of Mary I[1]

Your Highness's own cousin,[2] Queen Mary, now wears the crown of this kingdom. She was crowned on the first day of this month,[3] with the pomp and ceremonies customary here, which are far grander than elsewhere, as I shall briefly show; and according to the rites of the old religion.[4] On the eve of her coronation-day, the queen was removed from the Tower and castle of London to Westminster Palace, where the sovereigns of England are by custom wont to reside in London. She was accompanied by the earls, lords, gentlemen, ambassadors, and officers, all dressed in rich garments. The queen was carried in an open litter covered with brocade. Two coaches followed her: the Lady Elizabeth and the Lady of Cleves[5] rode in one; some of the ladies of the court in the other. The streets were hung with tapestries

---

1. Evident. "As": so that.
2. Regard.
3. Jane Seymour, whom Henry had married on May 30 (eleven days after the execution of Anne Boleyn).
1. Translated from Spanish, in *Calendar of State Papers, Spanish*, vol. 5, pt. 1.
2. Mary and Charles were first cousins.

3. October 1553.
4. That is, Catholicism.
5. Anne of Cleves, the German noblewoman who had been Henry VIII's fourth wife, was the only one of the six still alive in 1553. Henry had had the marriage annulled after seven months, but Anne had remained in England. "Lady Elizabeth" is Mary's half-sister, the future Elizabeth I.

and strewn with grass and flowers; and many triumphal arches were erected along her way. The next day, coronation-day, the queen went from the Hall of Parliament and Justice to the church,[6] in procession with the bishops and priests in full canonical dress, the streets being again covered with flowers and decked with stuffs.[7] She mounted a scaffolding that was erected at the church for this purpose, and showed herself to the people. The queen's coronation was proclaimed to them and the question asked of them if they were willing to accept her as their queen. All answered: Yes; and the ordinary ceremonies were then gone through, the queen making an offering of silver and silken stuffs. The bishop of Winchester, who officiated, gave her the scepter and the orb, fastened on the spurs, and girt her with the sword; he received the oath, and she was twice anointed and crowned with three crowns. The ceremonies lasted from ten in the morning till five o'clock in the afternoon. She was carried from the church to the Parliament Hall, where a banquet was prepared. The queen sat on a stone chair[8] covered with brocade, which they say was carried off from Scotland in sign of a victory, and was once used by the kings of Scotland at their crowning; she rested her feet upon two of her ladies, which is also a part of the prescribed ceremonial, and ate thus. She was served by the earls and lords, Knights of the Order[9] and officers, each one performing his own special office. The meats[1] were carried by the Knights of the Bath. These knights are made by the kings on the eve of their coronation and at no other time; and their rank is inferior to the other order. The queen instituted twenty fresh ones. They are called Knights of the Bath because they plunge naked into a bath with the king and kiss his shoulder. The queen being a woman, the ceremony was performed for her by the earl of Arundel, her great master of the household. The earl marshal and the lord steward[2] directed the ceremonies mounted on horseback in the great hall. When the banquet was over, an armed knight rode in upon a Spanish horse and flung down his glove,[3] while one of the kings-of-arms[4] challenged anyone who opposed the queen's rights to pick up the glove and fight the champion in single combat. The queen gave him a gold cup, as it is usual to do. Meanwhile the earls, vassals, and councillors paid homage to her, kissing her on the shoulder; and the ceremonies came to an end without any of the interruptions or troubles that were feared on the part of the Lutherans, who would rejoice in upsetting the queen's reign. They were feared especially because of the Lady Elizabeth, who does not feel sincerely the oath she took at the coronation; she has had intelligence with the king of France, which has been discovered.[5] A remedy is to be sought at the convocation of the estates,[6] which is to take place on the

---

6. That is, from Westminster Hall to Westminster Abbey.
7. Pieces of cloth.
8. The coronation throne—not itself stone, but having the Stone of Scone (taken from Scotland by Edward I in 1292) encased in its seat.
9. The Order of the Garter.
1. Food in general (not just animal flesh).
2. The Earl of Arundel was both the lord steward and the lord great master of the household. The earl marshal was the Duke of Norfolk.
3. That is, threw down the gauntlet. The challenge by the "king's champion" (a hereditary office) was a part of the coronation ritual until 1821.
4. The title of the three chief heralds of the College of Arms.
5. There is, at least now, no evidence of Elizabeth's conniving with the French king. "Intelligence": communication.
6. That is, Parliament. Statutes declaring both Mary and Elizabeth illegitimate were already in place; Parliament nullified those pertaining to Mary, but left unrepealed the ones concerning Elizabeth.

fifth of this month: Elizabeth is to be declared a bastard, having been born during the lifetime of Queen Catherine, mother of the queen. The affairs of the kingdom are unsettled because the vassals and people are prone to scandal, and seekers after novelties; they are strange and troublesome folk.

* * *

1553   1916

The Oration of Queen Mary in the Guildhall, on the First of February, 1554[1]

I am come unto you in mine own person, to tell you that which already you see and know; that is, how traitorously and rebelliously a number of Kentishmen have assembled themselves against both us and you. Their pretense (as they said at the first) was for a marriage determined for us: to the which, and to all the articles thereof, ye have been made privy. But since,[2] we have caused certain of our Privy Council to go again unto them, and to demand the cause of this their rebellion: and it appeared then unto our said council that the matter of the marriage seemed to be but a Spanish cloak to cover their pretended purpose against our religion; for that[3] they arrogantly and traitorously demanded to have the governance of our person, the keeping of the Tower,[4] and the placing of our councillors.

Now, loving subjects, what I am, ye right well know. I am your queen, to whom at my coronation, when I was wedded to the realm and laws of the same (the spousal ring whereof I have on my finger, which never hitherto was, nor hereafter shall be, left off), you promised your allegiance and obedience unto me. And that I am the right and true inheritor of the crown of this realm of England, I take all Christendom to witness. My father, as ye all know, possessed the same regal state, which now rightly is descended unto me: and to him always ye showed yourselves most faithful and loving subjects; and therefore I doubt not, but ye will show yourselves likewise to me, and that ye will not suffer a vile traitor to have the order and governance of our person, and to occupy our estate,[5] especially being so vile a traitor as Wyatt is; who most certainly, as he hath abused mine ignorant subjects which be on his side, so doth he intend and purpose the destruction of you,

---

1. When, in the early months of Mary's reign, it became clear that she intended to marry the heir to the Spanish throne (the future Philip II, son of her cousin Charles V), discontent broke into insurrection. In late January 1554, a sizable army led by the Kentishman Sir Thomas Wyatt II began an advance on London. In the crisis, Mary went to the Guildhall and made this rousing speech to the assembled Londoners. They rallied to her side, and when Wyatt reached the city he found an unreceptive populace. The uprising collapsed, and he and other rebel leaders were executed. The version of Mary's speech given here was printed, with grudging admiration, by the Protestant martyrologist John Foxe, in his *Acts and Monuments*.
2. Subsequently.
3. Because.
4. That is, the Tower of London.
5. Position.

and spoil[6] of your goods. And this I say to you, on the word of a prince: I cannot tell how naturally the mother loveth the child, for I was never the mother of any; but certainly, if a prince and governor may as naturally and earnestly love her subjects, as the mother doth the child, then assure yourselves that I, being your lady and mistress, do as earnestly and as tenderly love and favor you. And I, thus loving you, cannot but think that ye as heartily and faithfully love me; and then I doubt not but we shall give these rebels a short and speedy overthrow.

As concerning the marriage, ye shall understand that I enterprised not the doing thereof without advice, and that by the advice of all our Privy Council, who so considered and weighed the great commodities[7] that might ensue thereof, that they not only thought it very honorable, but also expedient, both for the wealth[8] of our realm and also of all you our subjects. And as touching myself, I assure you, I am not so bent to my will, neither so precise nor affectionate,[9] that either for mine own pleasure I would choose where I lust,[1] or that I am so desirous as needs[2] I would have one. For God, I thank him, to whom be the praise therefore, I have hitherto lived a virgin, and doubt nothing[3] but with God's grace am able so to live still. But if, as my progenitors have done before, it might please God that I might leave some fruit of my body behind me to be your governor, I trust ye would not only rejoice thereat, but also I know it would be to your great comfort. And certainly, if I either did think or know that this marriage were to the hurt of any of you my commons, or to the impeachment[4] of any part or parcel of the royal state of this realm of England, I would never consent thereunto, neither would I ever marry while I lived. And on the word of a queen I promise you that if it shall not probably[5] appear to all the nobility and commons in the high court of Parliament that this marriage shall be for the high benefit and commodity of the whole realm, then I will abstain from marriage while I live.

And now, good subjects, pluck up your hearts, and like true men stand fast against these rebels, both our enemies and yours, and fear them not; for I assure you, I fear them nothing at all. And I will leave with you my Lord Howard and my lord treasurer,[6] who shall be assistants with the mayor for your defense.

1554   1563

6. Despoliation, pillage.
7. Benefits.
8. *Well-being.*
9. Nor so fastidious nor willful.
1. Where I please.
2. So full of desire that it is necessary.

3. Not at all.
4. Injury; discrediting.
5. Plausibly.
6. Sir William Paulet, Marquis of Winchester. "My Lord Howard": William Howard, Earl of Warwick.

LADY JANE GREY

Jane Grey (1537–1554) was unlucky in her parents, the Duke and Duchess of Suffolk. They were, by her own account, impossible to please, subjecting her to taunts, threats, and physical abuse whenever she made a minor error in performance or deportment. Much worse for Jane, her mother was a granddaughter of Henry VII with a distant but plausible claim to the English throne. This fact, more than any action of her own, determined the course of Jane's life and death.

In 1553 England was ruled in name by the boy-king Edward VI, but in reality by John Dudley, Duke of Northumberland (1504–1553), who as head of state (Lord Protector) stood atop an aggressively Protestant regime. With Edward's health in decline and his Catholic half-sister Mary next in line to the throne, Protestant nobles feared for their future and for England's. For Northumberland, Jane Grey's Protestantism and bloodline offered an elegant solution. At age fifteen, Lady Jane was married to Northumberland's son, Guildford Dudley. Within six weeks of the marriage, Edward VI was dead, having named Jane Grey as his successor. The Privy Council, pressured by Northumberland, denounced Mary Tudor as a bastard and declared Jane queen of England.

Jane's reign lasted a mere nine days, July 9–18. For the first seventy-two hours, there seemed some hope of success; even the hostile ambassadors of Catholic powers were ready to hail Jane as queen. But the nobility and the common people, Protestant as well as Catholic, soon began to shift their allegiance to Mary, who at the time downplayed her religion. Personal connections to Mary's household and local grievances, along with Catholic sympathies, motivated much of the gentry to rally around her. Within weeks Northumberland was defeated, arrested, and executed. Jane, who had briefly reigned from the Tower of London, was now made prisoner there. The victorious Mary initially had no intention of executing Jane or her young husband, who, she recognized, had been no more than pawns in their parents' political games. But in January 1554 the Duke of Suffolk, Jane's father, joined in an ill-fated rebellion intended to reinstate his daughter on the throne. Mary's councillors convinced her that Jane would pose a danger as long as she remained alive. On the morning of February 12, 1554, Jane watched from a Tower window as her husband, Guildford, went to his public execution; within an hour she too had been beheaded, privately, on Tower Green.

Jane Grey was never really a woman in power. Her ability to command her own destiny, let alone that of others, was hardly greater when she was queen of England than when she was prisoner in the Tower. Yet it is clear from her writings and the testimony of others that Jane possessed a firm, even fiery will. In her brief stint as queen, she shocked her controllers by refusing to allow Guildford to take the title of king and rule jointly with her, and again by insisting that Northumberland, rather than her father, Suffolk, should lead her forces against Mary. Her will was harnessed to a militant and unshakable Protestantism; from an early age she mocked Catholic beliefs. In the Tower, where a politic conversion to Catholicism might well have saved her life, she instead wrote a violent and soon public letter to her onetime tutor Thomas Harding, who had converted, lambasting him as a "seed of Satan." Yet far from being an ignorant bigot, Jane was, though dead at sixteen, among the most learned women of her century; she had mastered Latin and Greek and was a student of Hebrew. She rivaled Elizabeth in intellectual brilliance and—to her fatal cost—exceeded her greatly in religious fervor.

From Roger Ascham's *Schoolmaster*[1]

[A TALK WITH LADY JANE]

* * * One example whether love or fear doth work more in a child for virtue and learning I will gladly report; which may be heard with some pleasure and followed with more profit. Before I went into Germany,[2] I came to Broadgate in Leicestershire to take my leave of that noble Lady Jane Grey, to whom I was exceeding much beholding. Her parents, the duke and the duchess, with all the household, gentlemen and gentlewomen, were hunting in the park. I found her in her chamber reading *Phaedon Platonis*[3] in Greek, and that with as much delight as some gentleman would read a merry tale in Boccaccio.[4] After salutation and duty done, with some other talk, I asked her why she would lose[5] such pastime in the park. Smiling she answered me, "Iwis,[6] all their sport in the park is but a shadow to that pleasure that I find in Plato. Alas, good folk, they never felt what true pleasure meant." "And how came you, madam," quoth I, "to this deep knowledge of pleasure, and what did chiefly allure you unto it, seeing not many women, but very few men, have attained thereunto?" "I will tell you," quoth she, "and tell you a truth which perchance ye will marvel at. One of the greatest benefits that ever God gave me is that he sent me so sharp and severe parents and so gentle a schoolmaster. For when I am in presence either of father or mother, whether I speak, keep silence, sit, stand, or go,[7] eat, drink, be merry or sad, be sewing, playing, dancing, or doing anything else, I must do it, as it were, in such weight, measure, and number even so perfectly as God made the world, or else I am so sharply taunted, so cruelly threatened, yea, presently sometimes, with pinches, nips, and bobs,[8] and other ways which I will not name for the honor I bear them,[9] so without measure misordered, that I think myself in hell till time come that I must go to Master Aylmer,[1] who teacheth me so gently, so pleasantly, with such fair allurements to learning, that I think all the time nothing whilst I am with him. And when I am called from him, I fall on weeping, because whatsoever I do else but learning is full of grief, trouble, fear, and whole misliking unto me. And thus my book hath been so much my pleasure, and bringeth daily to me more pleasure and more, that in respect of it all other pleasures in very deed be but trifles and troubles unto me." I remember this talk gladly, both because it is so worthy of memory and because also it was the last talk that ever I had, and the last time that ever I saw, that noble and worthy lady.

1570

---

1. On Ascham—the preeminent humanist educational theorist of mid-16th-century England—see p. 171.
2. In 1550, as secretary of the English ambassador to the emperor Charles V. So Lady Jane was thirteen at the time of the conversation Ascham recounts.
3. Plato's dialogue *Phaedo*, which recounts the last hours of Socrates and affirms the immortality of the soul.
4. Boccaccio's *Decameron* (1348–53), a collection of one hundred "merry," sometimes licentious, tales, not translated into English in Ascham's time.
5. Miss, forgo.
6. Truly.
7. Walk.
8. Raps, blows. "Presently": on the spot.
9. Her parents.
1. John Aylmer (1521–1594). As a schoolboy he attracted the notice of Jane's father, who provided for his education at Cambridge and appointed him tutor to his daughters. In 1577 Queen Elizabeth made him bishop of London.

From A Letter of the Lady Jane to M. H., Late Chaplain to the Duke of Suffolk, Her Father, and Then Fallen from the Truth of God's Most Holy Word[1]

So oft as I call to mind the dreadful and fearful saying of God, "That he which layeth hold upon the plough, and looketh back, is not meet for the kingdom of heaven,"[2] and, on the other side, the comfortable[3] words of our Savior Christ to all those that, forsaking themselves, do follow him, I cannot but marvel at thee, and lament thy case, which seemed sometime to be the lively member of Christ, but now the deformed imp[4] of the devil; sometime the beautiful temple of God, but now the stinking and filthy kennel of Satan; sometime the unspotted spouse of Christ, but now the unshamefaced paramour of Antichrist; sometime my faithful brother, but now a stranger and apostate; sometime a stout Christian soldier, but now a cowardly runaway. Yea, when I consider these things, I cannot but speak to thee, and cry out upon thee, thou seed of Satan, and not of Judah,[5] whom the devil hath deceived, the world hath beguiled, and the desire of life subverted, and made thee of a Christian an infidel. Wherefore hast thou taken the testament of the Lord in thy mouth? Wherefore hast thou preached the law and the will of God to others? Wherefore hast thou instructed others to be strong in Christ, when thou thyself dost now so shamefully shrink, and so horribly abuse the testament and law of the Lord? when thou thyself preachest not to steal, yet most abominably stealest, not from men but from God, and, committing most heinous sacrilege, robbest Christ thy Lord of his right members, thy body and thy soul, and choosest rather to live miserably with shame to the world, than to die and gloriously with honor to reign with Christ, in whom even in death is life? Why dost thou now show thyself most weak, when indeed thou oughtest to be most strong? The strength of a fort is unknown before the assault: but thou yieldest thy hold before any battery be made.

O wretched and unhappy man, what art thou, but dust and ashes? and wilt thou resist thy maker that fashioned thee and framed thee? Wilt thou now forsake Him that called thee from the custom gathering among the Romish Antichristians,[6] to be an ambassador and messenger of his eternal word? He that first framed thee, and since thy first creation and birth preserved thee, nourished, and kept thee, yea, and inspired thee with the spirit of knowledge (I cannot say of grace), shall he not now possess thee? Darest thou deliver up thyself to another, being not thine own, but his? How canst thou, having knowledge, or how darest thou neglect the law of the Lord and follow the vain traditions of men, and whereas thou hast been a public professor of his name, become now a defacer of his glory? Wilt thou refuse the true God, and worship the invention of man, the golden calf, the whore of

---

1. Taken from the 2nd edition (1570) of John Foxe's *Acts and Monuments*. In a subsequent edition, "M. H." is identified as "Master Harding"—the eminent theologian Thomas Harding, who was one of Lady Jane's tutors. Like many other English clergymen, Harding had renounced his Protestantism after Mary I made clear her determination to restore Catholicism. Jane wrote to him from her prison in the Tower.
2. Luke 9:62. "Meet": fit.
3. Comforting.
4. Offshoot.
5. Patriarch of the biblical kingdom of the Hebrews.
6. In the late 1540s, Harding had studied in Catholic Italy.

Babylon,[7] the Romish religion, the abominable idol, the most wicked Mass? Wilt thou torment again, rend and tear the most precious body of our Savior Christ, with thy bodily and fleshly teeth?[8] Wilt thou take upon thee to offer up any sacrifice unto God for our sins, considering that Christ offered up himself, as Paul saith, upon the cross, a lively sacrifice once for all? Can neither the punishment of the Israelites (which, for their idolatry, they so oft received), nor the terrible threatenings of the prophets, nor the curses of God's own mouth, fear thee to honor any other god than him? Dost thou so regard Him that spared not his dear and only son for thee, so diminishing, yea, utterly extinguishing his glory, that thou wilt attribute the praise and honor due unto him to the idols, "which have mouths and speak not, eyes and see not, ears and hear not";[9] which shall perish with them that made them?

* * *

Return, return again into Christ's war, and, as becometh a faithful warrior, put on that armor that St. Paul teacheth to be most necessary for a Christian man.[1] And above all things take to you the shield of faith, and be you provoked by Christ's own example to withstand the devil, to forsake the world, and to become a true and faithful member of his mystical body, who spared not his own body for our sins.

Throw down yourself with the fear of his threatened vengeance for this so great and heinous an offense of apostasy; and comfort yourself, on the other part, with the mercy, blood, and promise of him that is ready to turn unto you whensoever you turn unto him. Disdain not to come again with the lost son,[2] seeing you have so wandered with him. Be not ashamed to turn again with him from the swill of strangers[3] to the delicates of your most benign and loving Father, acknowledging that you have sinned against heaven and earth: against heaven, by staining the glorious name of God and causing his most sincere and pure word to be evil-spoken-of through you; against earth, by offending so many of your weak brethren, to whom you have been a stumbling-block through your sudden sliding. Be not abashed to come home again with Mary,[4] and weep bitterly with Peter,[5] not only with shedding the tears of your bodily eyes, but also pouring out the streams of your heart—to wash away, out of the sight of God, the filth and mire of your offensive fall. Be not abashed to say with the publican,[6] "Lord be merciful unto me a sinner."

Last of all, let the lively remembrance of the last day[7] be always before your eyes, remembering the terror that such shall be in at that time, with the runagates[8] and fugitives from Christ, which, setting more by the world than

---

7. Revelation 17–19. Protestants often identified her with the Church of Rome. "The golden calf": the idol fashioned by the Israelites while Moses was on Mount Sinai receiving the Ten Commandments (Exodus 32).
8. Alluding to the bitter controversy over transubstantiation: Catholic doctrine holds that although the bread and wine of the Eucharist retain their normal appearance, they are miraculously transformed into the actual body and blood of Christ; Protestants believe that the identification is symbolic rather than substantive.
9. Psalm 115.
1. Ephesians 6:11–18.
2. The Prodigal Son (Luke 15:10–32).

3. The Prodigal journeyed into a "far country," where, having "wasted his substance with riotous living," he "would fain have filled his belly with the husks that the swine did eat."
4. Christ's follower Mary Magdalene, long regarded (though without substantive basis in the Gospels) as a repentant sinner.
5. After thrice denying Christ, Peter wept bitterly for his apostasy (Matthew 26:75; Luke 22:62).
6. Luke 18:13. "Publican": in Christ's parable of the Pharisee and the publican (tax collector—agent of the hated Roman occupiers), the latter humbles himself before God and is forgiven.
7. Judgment Day.
8. Runaways; that is, apostates.

by heaven, more by their life than by him that gave them life, did shrink, yea did clean fall away, from him that forsook not them; and, contrariwise, the inestimable joys prepared for them that, fearing no peril nor dreading death, have manfully fought and victoriously triumphed over all power of darkness, over hell, death, and damnation, through their most redoubted[9] captain, Christ, who now stretcheth out his arms to receive you, ready to fall upon your neck and kiss you, and, last of all, to feast you with the dainties and delicates of his own precious blood: which undoubtedly, if it might stand with his determinate purpose, he would not let[1] to shed again, rather than you should be lost. To whom, with the Father and the Holy Ghost, be all honor, praise, and glory everlasting. Amen.

> Be constant, be constant; fear not for pain:
> Christ hath redeemed thee, and heaven is thy gain.

1553–54   1563, 1570

A Letter of the Lady Jane, Sent unto her Father[1]

Father, although it hath pleased God to hasten my death by you, by whom my life should rather have been lengthened; yet can I so patiently take it, as I yield God more hearty thanks for shortening my woeful days than if all the world had been given into my possession, with life lengthened at my own will. And albeit I am well assured of your impatient dolors, redoubled manifold ways, both in bewailing your own woe and especially, as I hear, my unfortunate state, yet, my dear father (if I may without offense rejoice in my own mishaps), meseems in this I may account myself blessed, that washing my hands with the innocency of my fact,[2] my guiltless blood may cry before the Lord, Mercy, mercy to the innocent! And yet, though I must needs acknowledge that, being constrained and, as you wot well enough, continually assayed,[3] in taking upon me I seemed to consent,[4] and therein grievously offended the queen and her laws: yet do I assuredly trust that this mine offense towards God is so much the less in that, being in so royal estate as I was, mine enforced honor never agreed with mine innocent heart. And thus, good father, I have opened unto you the state wherein I presently stand; whose death at hand, although to you perhaps it may seen right woeful, to me there is nothing that can be more welcome than from this vale of misery to aspire to that heavenly throne of all joy and pleasure with Christ our savior. In whose steadfast faith (if it may be lawful for the daughter so to write

---

9. Reverenced; dreaded.
1. Hesitate.

1. Written shortly before her execution and later published in Foxe's *Acts and Monuments*. Lady Jane's father, the Duke of Suffolk, had been pardoned by Mary I for his involvement in the attempt to put Jane on the throne following the death of Edward VI; Jane herself, though remaining in custody, also had good hopes of being pardoned. But when Suffolk joined in the insurrection of January 1554 against Mary, the queen decided that both must die. Suffolk was executed eleven days after his daughter, on February 23.
2. Actions. Jane had had to be coerced to accept the crown in July 1553 and was in no way involved in the later uprising.
3. Assailed; that is, browbeaten. "Wot": know.
4. That is, though I accepted the crown only under intense pressure, nonetheless, by accepting it at all I apparently consented to Mary's displacement.

to the father) the Lord that hitherto hath strengthened you so continue you that at the last we may meet in heaven with the Father, the Son, and the Holy Ghost.[5]

1554   1570

A Prayer of the Lady Jane[1]

O Lord, thou God and Father of my life, hear me, poor and desolate woman, which flieth unto thee only, in all troubles and miseries. Thou, O Lord, art the only defender and deliverer of those that put their trust in thee: and therefore I, being defiled with sin, encumbered with affliction, unquieted with troubles, wrapped in cares, overwhelmed with miseries, vexed with temptations, and grievously tormented with the long imprisonment of this vile mass of clay, my sinful body, do come unto thee, O merciful Savior, craving thy mercy and help, without the which so little hope of deliverance is left that I may utterly despair of any liberty.

Albeit it is expedient, that, seeing our life standeth upon trying,[2] we should be visited sometime with some adversity, whereby we might both be tried whether we be of thy flock or no, and also know thee and ourselves the better, yet thou, that saidst thou wouldst not suffer us to be tempted above our power,[3] be merciful unto me now, a miserable wretch, I beseech thee; which with Solomon[4] do cry unto thee, humbly desiring thee that I may neither be too much puffed up with prosperity, neither too much pressed down with adversity, lest I, being too full, should deny thee, my God, or being too low brought, should despair and blaspheme thee, my Lord and Savior.

O merciful God, consider my misery, best known unto thee; and be thou now unto me a strong tower of defense, I humbly require[5] thee. Suffer me not to be tempted above my power, but either be thou a deliverer unto me out of this great misery, either[6] else give me grace patiently to bear thy heavy hand and sharp correction. It was thy right hand that delivered the people of Israel out of the hands of Pharaoh, which for the space of four hundred years did oppress them and keep them in bondage. Let it, therefore, likewise seem good to thy fatherly goodness to deliver me, sorrowful wretch (for whom thy son Christ shed his precious blood on the cross), out of this miserable captivity and bondage wherein I am now.

How long wilt thou be absent? forever? O Lord, hast thou forgotten to be gracious, and hast thou shut up thy loving-kindness in displeasure? Wilt thou be no more entreated? Is thy mercy clean gone forever, and thy promise come utterly to an end for evermore?[7] Why dost thou make so long tarrying? Shall I despair of thy mercy, O God? Far be that from me. I am thy

---

5. As Foxe noted, this final sentence amounts to *an admonition* that Suffolk not renounce his Protestantism.
1. Also written shortly before her death.
2. Trial.
3. 1 Corinthians 10:13.
4. Proverbs 30:7–9.
5. Ask.
6. Or.
7. Psalm 77:8.

workmanship, created in Christ Jesu: give me grace, therefore, to tarry thy leisure, and patiently to bear thy works; assuredly knowing that as thou canst, so thou wilt deliver me when it shall please thee, nothing doubting or mistrusting thy goodness towards me; for thou knowest better what is good for me than I do: therefore do with me in all things what thou wilt, and plague me what way thou wilt. Only in the meantime, arm me, I beseech thee, with thy armor,[8] that I may stand fast, my loins being girded about with verity, having on the breastplate of righteousness and shod with the shoes prepared by the gospel of peace; above all things, taking to me the shield of faith, wherewith I may be able to quench all the fiery darts of the wicked, and taking the helmet of salvation and the sword of the spirit, which is thy most holy Word: praying always with all manner of prayer and supplication, that I may refer myself wholly to thy will, abiding thy pleasure and comforting myself in those troubles that it shall please thee to send me; seeing such troubles be profitable for me, and seeing I am assuredly persuaded that it cannot be but well, all that thou doest.

Hear me, O merciful Father, for His sake whom thou wouldst should be a sacrifice for my sins: to whom with thee and the Holy Ghost, be all honor and glory. Amen.

1554   1563

A Second Letter to Her Father[1]

The Lord comfort your grace, and that in his Word, wherein all creatures only are to be comforted. And though it hath pleased God to take away two of your children,[2] yet think not, I most humbly beseech your grace, that you have lost them, but trust that we, by losing this mortal life, have won an immortal life. And I for my part, as I have honored your grace in this life, will pray for you in another life. Your grace's humble daughter,

Jane Dudley

1554   1850

From Foxe's *Acts and Monuments*[1]

The Words and Behavior of the Lady Jane upon the Scaffold

These are the words that the Lady Jane spake upon the scaffold, at the hour of her death. First, when she mounted upon the scaffold, she said to the people standing thereabout, "Good people, I am come hither to die, and by a law I am condemned to the same. The fact[2] against the queen's highness

---

8. The allegorical armor of Ephesians 6:11–18. The ensuing passage closely echoes these verses.
1. Lady Jane inscribed this farewell message in a prayer book, now in the British Library.

2. That is, his daughter and son-in-law.
1. On the Protestant martyrologist John Foxe (1516–1587), see p. 157.
2. Act.

was unlawful, and the consenting thereunto by me; but, touching the procurement and desire thereof by me, or on my behalf, I do wash my hands thereof in innocency before God and the face of you, good Christian people, this day." And therewith she wrung her hands, wherein she had her book.[3] Then said she, "I pray you all, good Christian people, to bear me witness that I die a true Christian woman, and that I do look to be saved by no other mean but only by the mercy of God,[4] in the blood of his only Son Jesus Christ; and I confess that when I did know the word of God I neglected the same, loved myself and the world; and therefore this plague and punishment is happily and worthily happened unto me for my sins; and yet I thank God of his goodness that he hath thus given me a time and respite to repent. And now, good people, while I am alive, I pray you assist me with your prayers."[5] And then, kneeling down, she turned her to Feckenham,[6] saying, "Shall I say this psalm?" And he said, "Yea." Then said she the psalm of *Miserere mei Deus*[7] in English, in most devout manner, throughout to the end; and then she stood up, and gave her maiden, Mistress Ellen, her gloves and handkerchief, and her book to Master Brydges.[8] And then she untied her gown, and the hangman pressed upon her to help her off with it;[9] but she, desiring him to let her alone, turned towards her two gentlewomen, who helped her off therewith, and also with her frau's paste[1] and neckerchief, giving her a fair handkerchief to knit about her eyes.

Then the hangman kneeled down and asked her forgiveness, whom she forgave most willingly. Then he willed her to stand upon the straw;[2] which doing, she saw the block. Then she said, "I pray you, dispatch me quickly." Then she kneeled down, saying, "Will you take it off before I lay me down?" And the hangman said, "No, madam." Then tied she the kerchief about her eyes, and feeling for the block she said, "What shall I do? Where is it? Where is it?" One of the standers-by guiding her thereunto, she laid her head down upon the block, and then stretched forth her body and said, "Lord, into thy hands I commend my spirit";[3] and so finished her life, in the year of our Lord God 1554, the twelfth day of February.

1563

---

3. Prayer book.
4. Asserting the Protestant doctrine of salvation by faith alone.
5. Implicitly challenging the Catholic doctrine of the efficacy of prayers for the *dead*.
6. John de Feckenham, Queen Mary's confessor, who at her behest had tried unsuccessfully, in *Lady Jane's* last days, to convert her to Catholicism. A gifted and tolerant man, Feckenham was later put in charge of Mary's project of restoring the Benedictine monastery of Westminster Abbey, where he thus became the last abbot.
7. Psalm 51, which opens "Have mercy upon me, O God."
8. Sir John Brydges, lieutenant of the Tower.
9. The victim's adornments were part of the executioner's fee.
1. A type of elaborate headdress worn by married women.
2. Strewn about the execution block to soak up some of the blood.
3. Echoing Christ's dying words, Luke 23:46.

MARY, QUEEN OF SCOTS

Mary Stuart (1542–1587) was born on December 8, and within a week, following the death of her father, King James V, she had inherited the throne of Scotland. Remembered as the "Queen of Scots," she spent very few years in Scotland, never spoke its language as easily as French, and was forced to abdicate at the age of twenty-four.

Determined to foil the ambitions of Henry VIII, who sought to force a union between England and Scotland by having Mary married to his son, Edward, Mary's guardians sent her at the age of five to the court of France, where she would be brought up. At age fifteen she married Francis, the French dauphin, who became king in 1559. A year later, Francis II died, and at eighteen Mary returned to her own kingdom, Scotland, a land she could barely remember. As a Catholic woman coming to rule over a patriarchal society in which militant Protestantism was gathering force, Mary could hardly hope for a unanimously warm welcome. Her subsequent decisions destroyed whatever chance she may have had of enjoying a peaceful reign. In 1565 she married her vain and erratic cousin, Henry Stewart, Lord Darnley (1546–1567), with whom she was soon deeply unhappy. In 1566 Darnley was implicated in the murder of Mary's secretary, David Rizzio, who was rumored to be her lover. In 1567 Darnley was murdered in turn, certainly with the connivance of the powerful James Hepburn, Earl of Bothwell. Soon Mary was married to Bothwell, though her own will in the matter remains unclear. The scandal of this marriage alienated many of her supporters and helped provoke an uprising of the Scottish nobility. Mary was imprisoned at Lochleven Castle and forced to abdicate in favor of her one-year-old son, James. Though she escaped, she failed to rally the Scottish people to her side, and in 1568 she fled across the border into England, where she appealed for help from her cousin Elizabeth.

The arrival on English soil of the twenty-five-year-old Queen of Scots was not welcome news to the Protestant queen Elizabeth I and her wary advisers. As a descendant of Henry VII with a good claim to the English throne, Mary was seen to be a dangerous and destabilizing presence. She was immediately taken prisoner and remained so until her execution at the age of forty-four. She was tried in England in 1568–69 on the charge of murdering her second husband. At this point her Scottish accuser produced the notorious Casket Letters, which had supposedly been discovered in a silver casket seized from an associate of Bothwell's. The casket, it was said, contained eight letters and twelve sonnets, all in French, testifying (if they are authentic) to an adulterous relationship with Bothwell and, more ambiguously, to Mary's involvement in the murder of Darnley. Mary herself was not permitted to inspect the letters, which were withdrawn shortly after being displayed in court and subsequently disappeared, though not before translations of them had been made into English and Scots. The result of the trial was inconclusive; Elizabeth declared that nothing had been proven that would make her "conceive an evil opinion of her good sister"; yet she kept Mary prisoner, moving her from one place of confinement to another for the next nineteen years.

Mary quickly became the focus for the aspirations of discontented Catholics at home and abroad. She conspired with these adherents by means of secret messages, written in ciphers or in invisible ink on white taffeta, smuggled in and out of her prison hidden in such things as beer barrels. The conspiracies were monitored, and to some extent even engineered, by Elizabeth's spymaster, Francis Walsingham, who was setting a trap for the Queen of Scots and English Catholics generally. In 1586 Mary was found to be communicating with a young Englishman named

Mary, Queen of Scots, is shown here in a mourning costume with a prayer book in her left hand and a crucifix in her right. An inset picture under the crucifix depicts her execution. This full-length portrait is dated ca. 1610–40; the artist is unknown.

Anthony Babington, who was plotting to assassinate Elizabeth and place Mary on the throne. Babington and his co-conspirators were drawn and quartered, their heads displayed on Tower Bridge. Though she insisted that, as the sovereign queen of another country, she could not be charged with treason against England's queen, Mary was convicted as a traitor and sentenced to death. Elizabeth vacillated for some time over carrying out the sentence, worrying about the reaction abroad and the precedent involved in executing a monarch. Eventually she was prevailed upon *to sign the death warrant,* and Mary was beheaded on February 8, 1587. A week later, Elizabeth wrote to the orphaned James VI of Scotland, lamenting the "miserable accident, which far contrary to my meaning hath befallen."

Many of the words that seem to speak to us most eloquently of Mary's self and circumstances are not in fact her own. Throughout her life, Mary encountered no shortage of people—some who were admirers and others deadly foes—who were eager to seize control of her voice. The controversy over the Casket Letters thus crystallizes the more general problem of locating the "real" Mary Stuart. It will probably never be possible to prove whether the letters are products of Mary's own hand or cunning forgeries designed to incriminate her, and indeed it is this impossibility that lends them much of their fascination, opening them up for the endless play of interpretation. Yet if the interpretation of the Casket Letters has become a kind of intellectual game, it began as a matter of life or death. If Mary was in one respect a text with many authors, she was also a singular woman inhabiting a body that, on the orders of another woman, was at last cut in two.

From Casket Letter Number 2[1]

* * * This day I have wrought[2] till two of the clock upon this bracelet, to put the key in the cleft[3] of it, which is tied with two laces. I have had so little time that it is very ill,[4] but I will make a fairer; and in the meantime take heed that none of those that be here do see it: for all the world would know it, for I have made it in haste in their presence. I go to my tedious talk.[5] You make me dissemble so much that I am afraid thereof with horror; and you make me almost to play the part of a traitor. Remember that if it were not for obeying you, I had rather be dead;[6] my heart bleedeth for it. To be short, he will not come[7] but with condition that I shall promise to be with him as heretofore at bed and board,[8] and that I shall forsake him no more; and upon my word[9] he will do whatsoever I will, and will come, but he hath prayed me to tarry till after tomorrow. * * * But now, to make him trust me, I must feign something unto him; and therefore when he desired me to promise that when he should be whole[1] we should make but one bed, I told him (feigning to believe his fair promises) [that if he][2] did not change his mind between this time and that, I was contented, so as[3] he would say nothing thereof: for (to tell it between us two) the lords wished no ill to him,[4] but did fear lest (considering the threatenings which he made in case we did agree together) he would make them feel the small account[5] they have made of him, and that he would persuade me to pursue some of them; and for this respect should be in jealousy if at one instant,[6] without their knowledge, I did break a game made to the contrary in their presence.[7] And he said unto

---

1. The English translation was made shortly after the French originals of the Casket Letters were produced at Mary's first trial in England (1568–69).
2. Worked.
3. That is, lock.
4. Badly made.
5. That is, with Darnley. He was lying ill (probably from syphilis, though smallpox was given out as the cause) at Glasgow; Mary had joined him there.
6. That is, than play the traitor.
7. That is, to Craigmillar Castle, outside Edinburgh. "To be short": in short.
8. That is, to live again with him as husband and wife.
9. That is, if I give my word to do this.
1. Well.
2. The manuscript of the English translation has a tear at this point; the missing words have been inferred from the contemporary Scottish translation.
3. Provided that.
4. Darnley—weak, arrogant, and vicious—had many bitter enemies among the other Scottish lords.
5. Make them suffer for the low estimate.
6. Suddenly. "Respect": reason.
7. At their urging, Mary had authorized a confederacy of nobles to find a way for her to divorce Darnley. "Game": undertaking.

Coded Letter. Mary, Queen of Scots, was such a threat to the throne that she was imprisoned by Queen Elizabeth I for the last nineteen years of her life. During that time, she was involved in several plots to dethrone her cousin. In the secret, coded letter above, she writes about the poor conditions of her captivity and her hopes for release.

me, very pleasant and merry, "Think you that they do the more esteem you therefore? But I am glad that you talk to me of the lords. I hear[8] that you desire now that we shall live a happy life—for if it were otherwise, it could not be but greater inconvenience should happen to us both than you think. But I will do now whatsoever you will have me do, and will love all those that you shall love, so as you make them to love me also. For, so as they seek not my life, I love them all equally."

Thereupon I have willed this bearer to tell you many pretty[9] things; for I have too much to write, and it is late, and I trust him, upon your word. To be short, he[1] will go anywhere upon my word. Alas! and I never deceived anybody; but I remit[2] myself wholly to your will. And send me word what I shall do, and whatever happen to me, I will obey you. Think also if you will not find some invention more secret, by physic,[3] for he is to take physic at Craigmillar, and the baths also, and shall not come forth of[4] long time. To be short, for that that[5] I can learn, he hath great suspicion, and yet nevertheless trusteth upon my word, but not to tell me as yet anything. Howbeit, if you will that I shall *avow*[6] him, I will know all of him; but I shall never be willing[7] to beguile one who putteth his trust in me. Nevertheless, you may do all.[8] And do not esteem me the less therefore, for you are the cause thereof; for, for my own revenge, I would not do it.

He giveth me certain charges[9] (and those strong) of that that I fear: even to say that his faults be published, but there be that commit some secret faults and fear not to have them spoken of so loudly, and that there is speech of great and small. And even touching the Lady Reres,[1] he said, "God grant

8. That is, I am convinced.
9. Small(er). "This bearer": the bearer of the letter.
1. That is, Darnley.
2. Submit.
3. Medicine (that is, a poisoned drink). "Invention": contrivance. If Mary wrote this sentence, it shows her complicit in the plot to murder Darnley, who was in fact strangled—and the house he was occupying at Kirk O'Field, just outside Edinburgh, *blown up*—on the night of February 9–10, 1567.
4. For a.
5. As far as.
6. Assure him by taking a vow. "Howbeit": however.
7. That is, without reluctance.
8. That is, you may command me in all things.
9. Admonitions. The idea seems to be that Darnley hinted that he might reveal Mary's secrets.
1. She was acting as wet nurse to Mary's son, James (later James VI of Scotland and, in 1603, James I of England).

that she serve you to your honor," and that men may not think, nor he neither, that mine own power was not in myself,[2] seeing I did refuse his offers. To conclude, for a surety he mistrusteth us of that that you know,[3] and for his life. But in the end, after I had spoken two or three good words to him, he was very merry and glad. I have not seen him this night, for ending[4] your bracelet; but I can find no clasps for it. It is ready thereunto,[5] and yet I fear lest it should bring you ill hap, or that it should be known if you were hurt.[6] Send me word whether you will have it, and more money,[7] and when I shall return, and how far I may speak. * * *

He hath sent to me, and prayeth me to see him rise tomorrow in the morning early. To be short, this bearer shall declare unto you the rest; and if I shall learn anything, I will make every night a memorial[8] thereof. He shall tell you the cause of my stay.[9] Burn this letter, for it is too dangerous; neither is there anything well said in it, for I think upon nothing but upon grief if you be at Edinburgh.[1]

Now if to please you, my dear life, I spare neither honor, conscience, nor hazard, nor greatness, take it in good part, and not according to the interpretation of your false brother-in-law,[2] to whom I pray you give no credit against the most faithful lover that ever you had, or shall have.

See not also her whose feigned tears you ought not more to regard than the true travails which I endure to deserve her place, for obtaining of which, against my own nature I do betray those that could let[3] me. God forgive me, and give you, my only friend,[4] the good luck and prosperity that your humble and faithful lover doth wish unto you: who hopeth shortly to be another thing unto you, for the reward of my pains. I have not made[5] one word, and it is very late, although I should never be weary in writing to you, yet will I end, after kissing of your hands. Excuse my evil[6] writing, and read it over twice. Excuse also that [I scribbled,[7] for I had yesternight no paper, when I took the paper of a memorial.[8] . . . Remember your friend, and write unto her, and often. Love me al[ways, as I shall do you].[9]

1567   1571

2. That is, that I was not acting of my own will.
3. The thing that you know about. "For a surety": for certain.
4. Because I was finishing.
5. Apart from that.
6. Recognized if you were wounded (and thus powerless to conceal the bracelet). "Ill hap": misfortune.
7. That is, whether you want more money.
8. Memorandum.
9. Delay.
1. The Scottish translation makes this clause the beginning of a new sentence, which says, in effect, "If you are in Edinburgh when you receive this, send me word soon."
2. Presumably the brother of Bothwell's wife, Jean Gordon, who in turn is presumably the person referred to in the following sentence.

3. Prevent.
4. Lover.
5. Possibly "reade"—in which case the meaning is "I have not read over a word."
6. Poor.
7. Words torn off the English manuscript here; reading inferred from the Scottish translation.
8. She apologizes for having had to use paper already used for memoranda.
9. Again words torn from the English manuscript are inferred from the Scottish translation. The latter continues with what seem to be the memoranda—to herself or perhaps to the bearer of the letter—mentioned earlier: "Remember zow [you] of the purpois of the Lady Reres. Of the Inglismen. Of his mother. Of the Erle of Argyle. Of the Erle Bothwell. Of the ludgeing [lodging] in Edinburgh."

A Letter to Elizabeth I, May 17, 1568[1]

Madam my good sister,[2] I believe you are not ignorant how long certain of my subjects, whom from the least of my kingdom I have raised to be the first, have taken upon themselves to involve me in trouble, and to do what it appears they had in view from the first. You know how they purposed to seize me and the late king my husband, from which attempt it pleased God to protect us, and to permit us to expel them from the country, where, at your request, I again afterwards received them; though, on their return, they committed another crime, that of holding me a prisoner, and killing in my presence a servant of mine, I being at the time in a state of pregnancy.[3] It again pleased God that I should save myself from their hands; and, as above said, I not only pardoned them, but even received them into favor. They, however, not yet satisfied with so many acts of kindness, have, on the contrary, in spite of their promises, devised, favored, subscribed to, and aided in a crime[4] for the purpose of charging it falsely upon me, as I hope fully to make you understand. They have, under this pretence, arrayed themselves against me, accusing me of being ill-advised, and pretending a desire of seeing me delivered from bad counsels, in order to point out to me the things that required reformation. I, feeling myself innocent, and desirous to avoid the shedding of blood, placed myself in their hands, wishing to reform what was amiss.[5] They immediately seized and imprisoned me. When I upbraided them with a breach of their promise, and requested to be informed why I was thus treated, they all absented themselves. I demanded to be heard in council, which was refused me. In short, they have kept me without any servants, except two women, a cook, and a surgeon; and they have threatened to kill me, if I did not sign an abdication of my crown, which the fear of immediate death caused me to do,[6] as I have since proved before the whole of the nobility, of which I hope to afford you evidence.

After this, they again laid hold of me in parliament, without saying why, and without hearing me; forbidding, at the same time, every advocate to plead for me; and, compelling the rest to acquiesce in their unjust usurpation of my rights, they have robbed me of everything I had in the world, not permitting me either to write or to speak, in order that I might not contradict their false inventions.

At last, it pleased God to deliver me,[7] when they thought of putting me to death, that they might make more sure of their power, though I repeatedly

---

1. This letter (translated from the French by Agnes Strickland) was written just after Mary, in flight from her Scottish enemies, made her fateful crossing into England. Its account of her troubles is, though not exaggerated, inevitably one-sided. In 1565, Mary's ill-advised marriage to her cousin Lord Darnley had upset the power structure of the nation's factious and violent nobility. A group of nobles rebelled against her, led by Mary's illegitimate half-brother James Stewart, Earl of Moray, who had previously been her key supporter and adviser.
2. *Fellow queen.*
3. The servant was David Rizzio, Mary's secretary and confidant. At the time of his murder, Mary was six months pregnant with her only child, the future King James VI. She omits the fact that Darnley was involved in the murder.
4. The murder of Darnley.
5. Unhappy about the elevation of Bothwell to the position of Mary's consort (she had married him three months after Darnley's murder, in which he was well known to have been the principal conspirator), the nobles brought an army against the royal couple in June 1567. With their own forces melting away, Bothwell escaped, and Mary surrendered herself to the nobles.
6. In late July. Her infant son was then crowned king on July 29, in a Protestant church. Moray became regent.
7. Mary escaped from captivity on May 2, 1568.

offered to answer any thing they had to say to me, and to join them in the punishment of those who should be guilty of any crime. In short, it pleased God to deliver me, to the great content of all my subjects, except Moray, Morton, the Humes, Glencairn, Mar, and Sempill, to whom, after that my whole nobility was come from all parts, I sent to say that, notwithstanding their ingratitude and unjust cruelty employed against me, I was willing to invite them to return to their duty, and to offer them security of their lives and estates, and to hold a parliament for the purpose of reforming every thing. I sent twice. They seized and imprisoned my messengers, and made proclamation, declaring traitors all those who should assist me, and guilty of that odious crime. I demanded that they should name one of them, and I would give him up, and begged them, at the same time, to deliver to me such as should be named to them. They seized upon my officer and my proclamation. I sent to demand a safe-conduct for my Lord Boyd, in order to treat of an accommodation, not wishing, as far as I might be concerned, for any effusion of blood. They refused, saying that those who had not been true to their regent and to my son, whom they denominate king, should leave me and put themselves at their disposal, a thing at which the whole nobility were greatly offended.

Seeing, therefore, that they were only a few individuals, and that my nobility were more attached to me than ever, I was in hope that, in course of time, and under your favor, they would be gradually reduced; and, seeing that they said they would either retake me or all die, I proceeded toward Dumbarton,[8] passing at the distance of two miles from them, my nobility accompanying me, marching in order of battle between them and me; which they seeing, sallied forth, and came to cut off my way and take me. My people seeing this, and moved by that extreme malice of my enemies, with a view to check their progress, encountered them without order, so that, though they were twice their number, their sudden advance caused them so great a disadvantage that God permitted them to be discomfited, and several killed and taken; some of them were cruelly put to death when taken on their retreat. The pursuit was immediately interrupted, in order to take me on my way to Dumbarton; they stationed people in every direction, either to kill or take me. But God through his infinite goodness has preserved me, and I escaped to my Lord Herries's,[9] who, as well as other gentlemen, have come with me into your country,[1] being assured that, hearing the cruelty of my enemies, and how they have treated me, you will, conformably to your kind disposition and the confidence I have in you, not only receive me for the safety of my life but also aid and assist me in my just quarrel; and I shall solicit other princes to do the same. I entreat you to send to fetch me as soon as you possibly can,[2] for I am in a pitiable condition, not only for a queen, but for a gentlewoman; for I have nothing in the world but what I had on my person when I made my escape, traveling across the country the first day, and not having since ever ventured to proceed except in the night, as I hope to declare before you, if it pleases you to have pity, as I trust you will, upon my extreme misfortune; of

---

8. In the west of Scotland. The royal army passed near Glasgow, in a deliberate attempt to draw Moray's army, which was smaller, into battle.
9. Herries was a magnate of southwestern Scotland, which remained strongly Catholic.
1. Crossing the Solway Firth in a fishing boat, Mary and twenty supporters landed in the Cumberland port of Workington on May 16, 1568.
2. Elizabeth never granted Mary an audience; two days after arriving in England, she was conducted to Carlisle Castle, where her nineteen years of English captivity began.

which I will forbear complaining, in order not to importune you, and pray to God that he may give to you a happy state of health and long life, and to me patience, and that consolation which I expect to receive from you, to whom I present my humble commendations. From Workington, the 17th of May.

> Your most faithful and affectionate good
> sister, and cousin, and escaped prisoner,
> Mary R.[3]

1568   1844

From Narrative of the Execution of the Queen of Scots. In a Letter to the Right Honorable Sir William Cecil[1]

It may please your lordship to be advertised[2] that, according as your honor gave me in command, I have here set down in writing the true order and manner of the execution of the Lady Mary, late queen of Scots, the 8th of February last, in the great hall within the castle of Fotheringhay,[3] together with relation of all such speeches and actions spoken and done by the said queen or any others, and all other circumstances and proceedings concerning the same, from and after the delivery of the said Scottish queen to Thomas Andrews, Esquire, high sheriff for Her Majesty's county of Northampton, unto the end of the said execution: as followeth.

It being certified the 6th of February last to the said queen, by the right honorable the earl of Kent, the earl of Shrewsbury, and also by Sir Amyas Paulet and Sir Drue Drury, her governors,[4] that she was to prepare herself to die the 8th of February next, she seemed not [to] be in any terror, for aught that appeared by any her outward gesture or behavior (other than marveling she should die), but rather with smiling cheer and pleasing countenance digested and accepted the said admonition of preparation to her (as she said) unexpected execution, saying that her death should be welcome unto her, seeing Her Majesty was so resolved, and that that soul were too too far unworthy the fruition of joys of heaven forever, whose body would not in this world be content to endure the stroke of the executioner for a moment. And that spoken, she wept bitterly and became silent.

The said 8th day of February being come, and time and place appointed for the execution, the said queen, being of stature tall, of body corpulent, round-shouldered, her face fat and broad, double-chinned, and hazel-eyed, her borrowed hair auburn, her attire was this. On her head she had a dressing of lawn edged with bone lace,[5] a pomander chain[6] and an *Angus Dei* about her

---

3. A royal signature: "R." = "Regina" (Latin for "Queen").
1. Elizabeth's lord high treasurer and principal minister. The author of the letter (of which there are various versions extant) was Robert Wingfield, Cecil's nephew, sent by him to report on the execution.
2. Informed.
3. In Northamptonshire. Mary had been moved to Fotheringhay in September 1586 and was there tried and convicted of treason against Elizabeth (though she was not Elizabeth's subject).
4. Keepers. The earls of Kent and Shrewsbury were sent by the royal council to oversee the execution. Paulet had been Mary's principal custodian since January 1585; Drury joined him in his charge in November 1586.
5. Lace that is woven with bobbins made of bone. "Lawn": fine linen.
6. Pomander is a mixture of aromatic substances; a small bag of it was sometimes suspended from a necklace.

neck,[7] a crucifix in her hand, a pair of beads at her girdle,[8] with a silver cross at the end of them. A veil of lawn fastened to her caul,[9] bowed out with wire and edged round about with bone lace. Her gown was of black satin painted, with a train and long sleeves to the ground, set with acorn buttons of jet trimmed with pearl, and short sleeves of satin black cut,[1] with a pair of sleeves of purple velvet whole under them. Her kirtle[2] whole, of figured black satin, and her petticoat skirts of crimson velvet, her shoes of Spanish leather with the rough side outward, a pair of green silk garters, her nether stockings[3] worsted colored watchet,[4] clocked[5] with silver, and edged on the tops with silver, and next her leg a pair of jersey[6] hose, white, etc. Thus apparelled, she departed her chamber, and willingly bended her steps towards the place of execution.

As the commissioners and divers other knights were meeting the queen coming forth, one of her servants, called Melvin,[7] kneeling on his knees to his queen and mistress, wringing his hands and shedding tears, used these words unto her: "Ah, Madam, unhappy me: what man on earth was ever before the messenger of so important sorrow and heaviness as I shall be, when I report that my good and gracious queen and mistress is beheaded in England?" This said, tears prevented him of further speaking. Whereupon the said queen, pouring forth her dying tears, thus answered him: "My good servant, cease to lament, for thou hast cause rather to joy than to mourn. For now shalt thou see Mary Stuart's troubles receive their long-expected end and determination. For know (said she), good servant, all the world is but vanity, and subject still to more sorrow than a whole ocean of tears can bewail. But I pray thee (said she), carry this message from me, that I die a true woman to my religion, and like a true queen of Scotland and France. But God forgive them (said she) that have long desired my end and thirsted for my blood, as the hart doth for the water brooks. Oh God (said she), thou that art the author of truth, and truth itself, knowest the inward chamber of my thought, how that I was ever willing that England and Scotland should be united together. Well (said she), commend me to my son, and tell him that I have not done anything prejudicial to the state and kingdom of Scotland"; and so resolving[8] herself again into tears, said, "Good Melvin, farewell"; and with weeping eyes and her cheeks all besprinkled with tears as they were, kissed him, saying once again, "Farewell, good Melvin, and pray for thy mistress and queen."

And then she turned herself unto the lords, and told them she had certain requests to make unto them. One was, for certain money to be paid to Curle, her servant. Sir Amyas Paulet, knowing of that money, answered to this effect, "it should." Next, that her poor servants might have that with quietness[9] which she had given them by her will, and that they might be favorably entreated,[1] and to send them safely into their countries. "To this (said she) I

---

7. A medallion bearing the figure of a lamb: an emblem of Christ. From "Agnus Dei" ("Lamb of God"; Latin), a part of the Mass beginning with those words.
8. Belt. "Beads": rosary beads.
9. Close-fitting cap.
1. Slashed, to reveal the contrasting-colored sleeves beneath.
2. Outer petticoat.

3. "Nether stockings" means simply "stockings." ("Nether" = "of the legs.")
4. Light blue.
5. Embroidered.
6. Worsted.
7. Sir Andrew Melville.
8. Dissolving.
9. Without contestation.
1. Treated.

conjure[2] you." Last, that it would please the lords to permit her poor distressed servants to be present about her at her death, that their eyes and hearts may see and witness how patiently their queen and mistress would endure her execution, and so make relation, when they came into their country, that she died a true constant Catholic to her religion. Then the earl of Kent did answer thus: "Madam, that which you have desired cannot conveniently be granted. For if it should, it were to be feared lest some of them, with speeches or other behavior, would both be grievous to Your Grace and troublesome and unpleasing to us and our company, whereof we have had some experience. For if such an access might be allowed, they would not stick to put some superstitious trumpery in practice, and if it were but dipping their handkerchiefs in Your Grace's blood, whereof it were very unmeet[3] for us to give allowance."

"My lord," said the queen of Scots, "I will give my word, although it be but dead, that they shall not deserve any blame in any the actions you have named. But alas, poor souls, it would do them good to bid their mistress farewell; and I hope your mistress" (meaning the queen), "being a maiden queen, will vouchsafe in regard of[4] womanhood that I shall have some of my own people about me at my death: and I know Her Majesty hath not given you any such strait[5] charge or commission but that you might grant me a request of far greater courtesy than this is, if I were a woman of far meaner calling[6] than the queen of Scots." And then, perceiving that she could not obtain her request without some difficulty, burst out into tears, saying, "I am cousin to your queen, and descended from the blood royal of Henry the Seventh, and a married queen of France, and an anointed queen of Scotland." Then, upon great consultation had betwixt the two earls and the others in commission, it was granted to her what she instantly[7] before earnestly entreated, and desired her to make choice of six of her best-beloved men and women. Then of her men she chose Melvin, her apothecary, her surgeon, and one old man more;[8] and of her women, those two which did lie in her chamber. Then, with an unappalled countenance, without any terror of the place, the persons, or the preparations, she came out of the entry into the hall, stepped up to the scaffold, being two foot high and twelve foot broad, with rails round about, hanged and covered with black, with a low stool, long fair cushion, and a block covered also with black. The stool brought her, she sat down. The earl of Kent stood on the right hand, the earl of Shrewsbury on the other, other knights and gentlemen stood about the rails. The commission for her execution was read (after silence made) by Mr. Beale, clerk of the council;[9] which done, the people with a loud voice said, "God save the Queen!" During the reading of this commission, the said queen was very silent, listening unto it with so careless a regard as if it had not concerned her at all, nay, rather with so merry and cheerful a countenance as if it had been a pardon from Her Majesty for her life; and withal[1] used such a strangeness in her words as if she had not known any of the assembly, nor had been anything seen[2] in the English tongue.

2. Earnestly entreat.
3. Unfitting.
4. For the sake of.
5. Strict.
6. Far lower station.
7. Importunely.
8. Her aged porter, Didier.
9. That is, the royal council.
1. As well.
2. At all fluent.

Then Mr. Doctor Fletcher, dean of Peterborough,[3] standing directly before her without[4] the rails, bending his body with great reverence, uttered the exhortation following:

"Madam, the Queen's Most Excellent Majesty (whom God preserve long to reign over us), having (notwithstanding this preparation for the execution of justice justly to be done upon you for your many trespasses against her sacred person, state, and government) a tender care over your soul, which presently departing out of your body must either be separated in the true faith in Christ or perish forever, doth for Jesus Christ offer unto you the comfortable[5] promises of God, wherein I beseech Your Grace, even in the bowels of Jesus Christ,[6] to consider these three things:

"First, your state past, and transitory glory;

"Secondly, your condition present, of death;

"Thirdly, your estate to come, either in everlasting happiness or perpetual infelicity.

"For the first, let me speak to Your Grace with David the King: Forget, Madam, yourself, and your own people, and your father's house; forget your natural birth, your regal and princely dignity: so shall the King of Kings have pleasure in your spiritual beauty, etc.[7]

"Madam, even now, Madam, doth God Almighty open you a door into a heavenly kingdom; shut not therefore this passage by the hardening of your heart, and grieve not the Spirit of God, which may seal your hope to a day of redemption."

The queen three or four times said unto him, "Mr. Dean, trouble not yourself nor me: for know that I am settled in the ancient Catholic and Roman religion, and in defense thereof, by God's grace, I mind to spend my blood."

Then said Mr. Dean, "Madam, change your opinion, and repent you of your former wickedness. Settle your faith only upon this ground, that in Christ Jesus you hope to be saved." She answered again and again, with great earnestness, "Good Mr. Dean, trouble yourself not anymore about this matter, for I was born in this religion, have lived in this religion, and am resolved to die in this religion."

Then the earls, when they saw how far uncomfortable[8] she was to hear Mr. Dean's good exhortation, said, "Madam, we will pray for Your Grace with Mr. Dean, that you may have your mind lightened with the true knowledge of God and his word."

"My lords," answered the queen, "if you will pray with me, I will even from my heart thank you, and think myself greatly favored by you; but to join in prayer with you in your manner, who are not of one[9] religion with me, it were a sin, and I will not."

Then the lords called Mr. Dean again, and bade him say on, or what he thought good else. The dean kneeled and prayed. * * *[1]

---

3. That is, of the Anglican cathedral there.
4. Outside.
5. Comforting, reassuring.
6. "In the bowels of Jesus Christ": in the name of Christ's pity. The bowels were regarded as the seat of pity and compassion.
7. The dean paraphrases Psalm 45:10–11, a passage addressed to the bride of a king: "forget also thine own people, and thy father's house; So shall the king greatly desire thy beauty."
8. Unwilling.
9. The same.
1. The dean prays at considerable length, beseeching God to wash away Mary's "blindness and ignorance of heavenly things."

All the assembly, save the queen and her servants, said the prayer after Mr. Dean as he spake it, during which prayer the queen sat upon her stool, having her *Agnus Dei*, crucifix, beads, and an office[2] in Latin. Thus furnished with superstitious trumpery, not regarding what Mr. Dean said, she began very fastly[3] with tears and a loud voice to pray in Latin, and in the midst of her prayers, with overmuch weeping and mourning, slipped off her stool, and kneeling presently said diverse other Latin prayers. Then she rose, and kneeled down again, praying in English for Christ's afflicted church, an end of her troubles, for her son, and for the Queen's Majesty, to God for forgiveness of the sins of them in this island: she forgave her enemies with all her heart, that had long sought her blood. This done, she desired all saints to make intercession for her to the Savior of the World, Jesus Christ. Then she began to kiss her crucifix and to cross herself, saying these words: "Even as thy arms, oh Jesu Christ, were spread here upon the cross, so receive me into the arms of mercy." Then the two executioners kneeled down unto her, desiring her to forgive them her death. She answered, "I forgive you with all my heart. For I hope this death shall give an end to all my troubles." They, with her two women helping, began to disrobe her, and then she laid the crucifix upon the stool. One of the executioners took from her neck the *Agnus Dei*, and she laid hold of it, saying she would give it to one of her women, and, withal, told the executioner that he should have money for it.[4] Then they took off her chain. She made herself unready[5] with a kind of gladness, and, smiling, putting on a pair of sleeves with her own hands, which the two executioners before had rudely[6] put off, and with such speed as if she had longed to be gone out of the world.

During the disrobing of this queen, she never altered her countenance, but smiling said she never had such grooms before to make her unready, nor ever did put off her clothes before such a company. At length, unattired and unapparelled to her petticoat and kirtle, the two women burst out into a great and pitiful shrieking, crying, and lamentation, crossed themselves, and prayed in Latin. The queen turned towards them: "Ne criez vous; j'ai promis pour vous";[7] and so crossed and kissed them, and bade them pray for her.

Then with a smiling countenance she turned to her menservants, Melvin and the rest, crossed them, bade them fare well, and pray for her to the last.

One of the women having a Corpus Christi cloth,[8] lapped[9] it up three-corner-wise and kissed it, and put it over the face of her queen, and pinned it fast upon the caul of her head. Then the two women departed. The queen kneeled down upon the cushion resolutely, and without any token of fear of death, said aloud in Latin the Psalm *"In te, Domine, confido."*[1] Then, groping for the block, she laid down her head, putting her chain over her back with both her hands, which, holding there still,[2] had been cut off, had they not been espied.

---

2. Prayer book.
3. Steadfastly.
4. A condemned person's adornments were normally perquisites of the executioner.
5. *Undressed.*
6. Roughly.
7. "Don't make an outcry; I promised you wouldn't."
8. The veil (also known as the "pyx cloth") that covered the vessel holding the consecrated Host the Communion. "Corpus Christi": the body of Christ (Latin).
9. Folded.
1. Psalm 10 (Vulgate), 11 (King James): "In the Lord put I my trust."
2. That is, if her hands had remained there.

The Execution of Mary, Queen of Scots. Though this watercolor image was not painted until some years after Mary's execution, it reflects eyewitness accounts. The minister depicted is likely Dr. Richard Fletcher, dean of Peterborough, who was so nervous that he stammered and never actually delivered his sermon because he was interrupted by Mary herself. Mary wears a Corpus Christi cloth around her head as a blindfold. On the stool beside her is a prayer book, and in her hands a crucifix. Her gentlewomen stand weeping to the left of the scaffold, which is covered in black cloth. On the far left of the image is a bonfire, for burning any cloth or other items with Mary's blood on them so that they could not serve as Catholic relics after her death.

    Then she laid herself upon the block most quietly, and stretching out her arms and legs cried out: *"In manus tuas, Domine, commendo spiritum meum,"*[3] three or four times.

    At last, while one of the executioners held her straitly[4] with one of his hands, the other gave two strokes with an axe before he did cut off her head, and yet left a little gristle behind.

    She made very small noise, no part stirred from the place where she lay. The executioners lifted up the head, and bade God save the Queen. Then her dressing of lawn fell from her head,[5] which appeared as gray as if she had been threescore and ten years old,[6] polled[7] very short. Her face much altered, her lips stirred up and down almost a quarter of an hour after her head was cut off. Then said Mr. Dean: "So perish all the Queen's enemies!" The earl of Kent came to the dead body, and with a loud voice said, "Such end happen to all the Queen's and Gospel's enemies." One of the executioners, plucking off her garters, espied her little dog, which was crept under her clothes, which would not be gotten forth but with force, and afterwards would not depart from the dead corpse, but came and laid between her head and shoulders: a thing much noted. The dog, imbrued in her blood, was carried away and

---

3. Luke 13:46: "Father, into thy hands I commend my spirit": the words of Christ on the Cross.
4. Tightly.
5. That is, her headcovering and auburn wig came off in the executioner's hand.
6. She was actually forty-four.
7. Cut.

washed, as all things else were that had any blood, save those things which were burned. The executioners were sent away with money for their fees, not having any one thing that belonged unto her. Afterwards everyone was commanded forth of the hall, saving[8] the sheriff and his men, who carried her up into a great chamber made ready for the surgeons to embalm her; and there she was embalmed.

And thus I hope (my very good lord) I have certifieth Your Honor of all actions, matters, and circumstances as did proceed from her or any other at her death: wherein I dare promise unto your good lordship (if not in some better or worse words than were spoken I am somewhat mistaken), in matter I have not in any whit offended.[9] Howbeit,[1] I will not so justify my duty herein but that[2] many things might well have been omitted, as not worthy noting. Yet because it is your lordship's fault to desire to know all, and so I have certified all, it is an offense pardonable. So, resting at Your Honor's further commandment, I take my leave this 11th of February, 1587.

Your Honor's in all humble service to command,
R. W.

1587   1843

---

8. Except. "Forth of": out of.
9. That is, though I may not have gotten the speeches word-for-word, I promise that my account is completely accurate in substance.
1. However.
2. That is, I will concede that.

ELIZABETH I

Elizabeth I (1533–1603), queen of England from 1558 to her death, set her mark indelibly on the age that has come to bear her name. Endowed with intelligence, courage, eloquence, and a talent for self-display, she managed to survive and flourish in a world that would easily have crushed a weaker person. Her birth was a disappointment to her father, Henry VIII, who had hoped for a male heir to the throne, and her prospects were further dimmed when her mother, Anne Boleyn, was executed a few years later on charges of adultery and treason. By an act of Parliament she was ruled illegitimate. At six years old, observers noted, Elizabeth had as much gravity as if she had been forty.

Under distinguished tutors, including the Protestant humanist Roger Ascham, the young princess received a rigorous education, with training in classical and modern languages, history, rhetoric, theology, and moral philosophy. Her own religious orientation was also Protestant, which put her in great danger during the reign of her Catholic older half-sister, Mary. Imprisoned in the Tower of London, interrogated and constantly spied upon, Elizabeth steadfastly professed innocence, loyalty, and a pious abhorrence of heresy. Upon Mary's death, she ascended the throne and quickly made clear that the official religion of the land would be Protestantism.

When she came to the throne, at twenty-five, speculation about a suitable match, already widespread, intensified. It remained for decades at a fever pitch, for the stakes were high. If Elizabeth died childless, the Tudor line would come to an end. The nearest heir was her cousin Mary, Queen of Scots, a Catholic whose claim was

Princess Elizabeth. This picture depicts Elizabeth at the age of thirteen, standing by the Old Testament, and holding the New. Designed to show her modesty and piety, it equally broadcasts the fact that she is a woman of learning. The portrait dates from ca. 1546 and may be by Guillim Scrots, an artist from the Netherlands.

supported by France and by the papacy, and whose penchant for sexual and political intrigue soon confirmed the worst fears of English Protestants. The obvious way to avert the nightmare was for Elizabeth to marry and produce an heir, and the pressure on her to do so was intense.

More than the royal succession hinged on the question of the queen's marriage; Elizabeth's perceived eligibility was a vital factor in the complex machinations of international diplomacy. A dynastic marriage between the queen of England and a foreign ruler could forge an alliance sufficient to alter the balance of power in Europe. The English court hosted a steady stream of ambassadors from kings and princelings eager to win the hand of the royal maiden, and Elizabeth played her romantic part with exemplary skill, sighing and spinning the negotiations out for months and even years. Most probably, she never meant to marry any of her numerous foreign (and domestic) suitors. "She is determined," a shrewd Spanish observer wrote to his king, at the moment that Elizabeth ascended to the throne, "to be governed by no one." Marriage would have meant the end of her independence as well as the end of the complex diplomatic game by which she played off one power against another. One day she would seem to be on the verge of accepting a proposal; the next, she would vow never to forsake her virginity. "She is a princess," the French ambassador remarked, "who can act any part she pleases." Ultimately she refused all offers and declared repeatedly that she was wedded to her country.

In the face of deep skepticism about the ability of any woman to rule, Elizabeth strategically blended imperiousness with an elaborate cult of love. Quickly making it clear that she would not be a figurehead, she gathered around her an able group of advisers, but she held firmly to the reins of power, subtly manipulating factional disputes, conducting diplomacy, and negotiating with an often contentious Parliament. Her courtiers and advisers, on their knees, approached the queen, glittering in jewels and gorgeous gowns, and addressed her in extravagant terms that conjoined romantic passion and religious veneration. Artists and poets celebrated her in mythological guise—as Diana, the chaste goddess of the moon; Astraea, the goddess of justice; Gloriana, the queen of the fairies. Though she could suddenly veer, whenever she chose, toward bluntness and anger, Elizabeth often contrived to transform the language of politics into the language of love. "We all loved her," her godson John Harington wrote, "for she said she loved us."

Throughout her life, Elizabeth took pride in her command of languages (she spoke fluent French and Italian and read Latin and Greek) and in her felicity of expression. Her own writing includes carefully crafted letters and speeches on several state occasions; a number of prayers; prose and verse translations, including works of Horace, Seneca, Plutarch, Boethius, Calvin, and the French Protestant Queen Margaret of Navarre; and a few original poems. The original poems known to be hers deal with actual events in her life. They show her to have been an exceptionally agile, poised, and self-conscious writer, a gifted role-player fully in control of the rhetorical as well as political situation in which she found herself. The texts printed here, occasionally altered in light of variant versions, are from *Elizabeth I: Collected Works*, ed. Leah Marcus, Janel Mueller, and Mary Beth Rose (2000).

Verses Written with a Diamond

In her imprisonment at Woodstock, these verses she wrote with her diamond in a glass window:[1]

    Much suspected by[2] me,
    Nothing proved can be.
        Quod[3] Elizabeth the prisoner

1554–55   1563

---

1. This is the heading given to the verses in John Foxe's *Acts and Monuments*. After the insurrection of January 1554 against Mary I, Elizabeth was imprisoned in the Tower of London. Extensive interrogation and investigation yielded against her no firm evidence of treason, but she was transferred to the royal manor at Woodstock in Oxfordshire and held there in close custody for a year.
2. About.
3. Quoth, said.

From The Passage of Our Most Dread Sovereign Lady Queen Elizabeth through the City of London to Westminster on the Day before Her Coronation[1]

* * * Her grace, by holding up her hands and merry countenance to such as stood far off, and most tender and gentle language to those that stood nigh to her grace, did declare herself no less thankfully to receive her people's goodwill than they lovingly offered it unto her. To all that wished her grace well she gave hearty thanks, and to such as bade God save her grace she said again,[2] God save them all, and thanked them with all her heart. So that on either side there was nothing but gladness, nothing but prayer, nothing but comfort. The queen's majesty rejoiced marvelously to see it so exceedingly showed toward her grace which all good princes have ever desired: I mean, so earnest love of subjects, so evidently declared even to her grace's own person being carried in the midst of them. The people, again, were wonderfully ravished with welcoming answers and gestures of their princess, like to the which they had before tried at her first coming to the Tower from Hatfield.[3] This her grace's loving behavior, preconceived in the people's heads, upon these considerations was thoroughly confirmed, and indeed implanted a wonderful hope in them touching her worthy government in the rest of her reign. For in all her passage she did not only show her most gracious love toward the people in general, but also privately. If the baser personages had either offered her grace any flowers or such like as a signification of their goodwill, or moved to her any suit, she most gently, to the common rejoicing of all the lookers-on and private comfort of the party, stayed her chariot[4] and heard their requests. So that if a man should say well, he could not better term the City of London that time than a stage wherein was showed the wonderful spectacle of a noble-hearted princess toward her most loving people and the people's exceeding comfort in beholding so worthy a sovereign and hearing so princelike a voice. * * *

Out at the windows and penthouses of every house did hang a number of rich and costly banners and streamers, till her grace came to the upper end of Cheap.[5] And there, by appointment, the right worshipful Master Ranulph Cholmley, recorder[6] of the City, presented to the queen's majesty a purse of crimson satin richly wrought with gold, wherein the City gave unto the queen's majesty a thousand marks[7] in gold, as Master Recorder did declare briefly unto the queen's majesty, whose words tended to this end: that the lord mayor, his brethren, and commonality of the City, to declare their

---

1. By Richard Mulcaster (ca. 1530–1611), who became an authority on the education of children. Elizabeth had succeeded to the throne upon the death of Mary I on November 17, 1558, but her coronation did not take place until January 15, 1559. By custom, the ceremonies began the day before the coronation itself, with the ruler being conducted across the city in procession from the Tower of London to Westminster. See the account of Mary's coronation procession on p. 205.
2. That is, said in reply.
3. Elizabeth had set out from the royal manor at Hatfield (in Hertfordshire) to London on November 23.
4. Wearing a robe made of gold and silver cloth, trimmed with ermine, and overlaid with gold lace, Elizabeth rode in a litter trimmed to the ground with gold damask.
5. Also known as Cheapside or Westcheap: the chief market street in London. (The name derives from the Old English word for "market.")
6. Senior law officer.
7. The mark was valued at two-thirds of a pound sterling, and the pound was worth far more than at present—so this was a very large gift.

gladness and goodwill towards the queen's majesty, did present her grace with that gold, desiring her grace to continue their good and gracious queen and not to esteem the value of the gift, but the mind of the givers. The queen's majesty with both her hands took the purse and answered to him again marvelous pithily, and so pithily that the standers-by, as they embraced entirely her gracious answer, so they marveled at the couching thereof, which was in words, truly reported these:

> I thank my lord mayor, his brethren, and you all. And whereas your request is that I should continue your good lady and queen, be ye ensured that I will be as good unto you as ever queen was to her people. No will in me can lack, neither do I trust shall there lack any power. And persuade yourselves that for the safety and quietness of you all I will not spare, if need be, to spend my blood. God thank you all.

Which answer of so noble an hearted princess, if it moved a marvelous shout and rejoicing, it is nothing to be marveled at, since both the heartiness thereof was so wonderful, and the words so jointly[8] knit.

But because princes be set in their seat by God's appointing and therefore they must first and chiefly tender[9] the glory of Him from whom their glory issueth, it is to be noted in her grace that forsomuch as God hath so wonderfully placed her in the seat of government over this realm, she in all doings doth show herself most mindful of His goodness and mercy showed unto her. And amongst all other, two principal signs thereof were noted in this passage. First in the Tower, where her grace, before she entered her chariot, lifted up her eyes to heaven and said:

> O Lord, almighty and everlasting God, I give Thee most hearty thanks that Thou hast been so merciful unto me as to spare me to behold this joyful day. And I acknowledge that Thou hast dealt as wonderfully and as mercifully with me as Thou didst with Thy true and faithful servant Daniel, Thy prophet, whom Thou deliveredst out of the den from the cruelty of the greedy and raging lions.[1] Even so was I overwhelmed and only by Thee delivered. To Thee (therefore) only be thanks, honor, and praise forever, amen.

The second was the receiving of the Bible at the Little Conduit[2] in Cheap. For when her grace had learned that the Bible in English[3] should there be offered, she thanked the City therefor, promised the reading thereof most diligently, and incontinent[4] commanded that it should be brought. At the receipt whereof, how reverently did she with both her hands take it, kiss it, and lay it upon her breast, to the great comfort of the lookers-on! God will undoubtedly preserve so worthy a prince, which at His honor so reverently taketh her beginning. For this saying is true and written in the book of truth: he that first seeketh the kingdom of God shall have all other things cast unto him.[5]

---

8. Concordantly.
9. *Have regard to.*
1. Daniel 6:16–23.
2. The smaller of two lead pipe water conduits situated at the west end of Cheap Street.
3. In contrast to the Latin Bibles of the restored Catholicism of Mary's reign.
4. Immediately.
5. Matthew 6:33.

Now, therefore, all English hearts and her natural people must needs praise God's mercy, which hath sent them so worthy a prince, and pray for her grace's long continuance amongst us.

1559

Speech to the House of Commons, January 28, 1563[1]

Williams,[2] I have heard by you the common request of my Commons, which I may well term (methinketh) the whole realm, because they give, as I have heard, in all these matters of Parliament their common consent to such as be here assembled. The weight and greatness of this matter might cause in me, being a woman wanting both wit[3] and memory, some fear to speak and bashfulness besides, a thing appropriate to my sex. But yet the princely seat and kingly throne wherein God (though unworthy) hath constituted me, maketh these two causes to seem little in mine eyes, though grievous perhaps to your ears, and boldeneth me to say somewhat in this matter, which I mean only to touch but not presently to answer. For this so great a demand[4] needeth both great and grave advice. I read of a philosopher whose deeds upon this occasion I remember better than his name[5] who always when he was required to give answer in any hard question of school points would rehearse over his alphabet before he would proceed to any further answer therein, not for that he could not presently have answered, but have his wit the riper and better sharpened to answer the matter withal.[6] If he, a common man, but[7] in matters of school took such delay the better to show his eloquent tale, great cause may justly move me in this, so great a matter touching the benefits of this realm and the safety of you all, to defer mine answer till some other time, wherein I assure you the consideration of my own safety (although I thank you for the great care that you seem to have thereof) shall be little in comparison of that great regard that I mean to have of the safety and surety of you all. And although God of late seemed to touch me rather like one that He chastised than one that He punished, and though death possessed almost every joint of me,[8] so as I wished then that the feeble thread of life, which lasted (methought) all too long, might by Clotho's hand[9] have quietly been cut off, yet desired I not then life (as I have some witnesses here) so much for mine own safety, as for yours. For I know that in exchanging of this reign I should have enjoyed a better reign where residence is perpetual.

---

1. Because a secure royal succession depended on Elizabeth's marrying and producing an heir, Parliament had been concerned about her single state from the beginning of her reign. The Commons raised the matter with her (not for the first time) in January 1563; the speech printed here is a later, written version of her extemporaneous response.
2. Thomas Williams, speaker of the Parliament.
3. Intellect.
4. Question.
5. According to the *Moral Essays* of Plutarch (ca. 46–ca. 120 C.E.), the philosopher was Athenodorus.
6. By that means.
7. Merely.
8. Elizabeth had nearly died of smallpox the past October.
9. Clotho is one of the three Fates of classical mythology, who spin and eventually cut the thread of each individual life.

There needs no boding of my bane.[1] I know now as well as I did before that I am mortal. I know also that I must seek to discharge myself of that great burden that God hath laid upon me; for of them to whom much is committed, much is required.[2] Think not that I, that in other matters have had convenient[3] care of you all, will in this matter touching the safety of myself and you all be careless. For I know that this matter toucheth me much nearer than it doth you all, who if the worst happen can lose but your bodies. But if I take not that convenient care that it behoveth me to have therein, I hazard to lose both body and soul. And though I am determined in this so great and weighty a matter to defer mine answer till some other time because I will not in so deep a matter wade with so shallow a wit, yet have I thought good to use these few words, as well to show you that I am neither careless nor unmindful of your safety in this case, as I trust you likewise do not forget that by me you were delivered whilst you were hanging on the bough ready to fall into the mud—yea, to be drowned in the dung; neither[4] yet the promise which you have here made concerning your duties and due obedience, wherewith, I assure you, I mean to charge[5] you, as, further, to let you understand that I neither mislike any of your requests herein, nor the great care that you seem to have of the surety and safety of yourselves in this matter.

Lastly, because I will discharge[6] some restless heads in whose brains the needless hammers beat with vain judgment that I should mislike this their petition, I say that of the matter and sum thereof I like and allow very well. As to the circumstances, if any be, I mean upon further advice further to answer. And so I assure you all that though after my death you may have many stepdames, yet shall you never have any a more mother than I mean to be unto you all.

1563   1921

From A Speech to a Joint Delegation of Lords and Commons, November 5, 1566[1]

* * * Was I not born in the realm? Were my parents born in any foreign country? Is there any cause I should alienate myself from being careful over this country? Is not my kingdom here? Whom have I oppressed? Whom have I enriched to others' harm? What turmoil have I made in this commonwealth, that I should be suspected to have no regard to the same? How have

---

1. Prognosticating of my death.
2. Luke 12:48.
3. Befitting.
4. Nor. "Mud . . . dung": harsh characterizations of the Roman Catholicism that Mary I had been restoring to England.
5. Exhort.
6. Disabuse.

1. The birth on June 19, 1566, of a son—James—to Mary, Queen of Scots, imparted new urgency to the concern about Elizabeth's unmarried state. Mary was Elizabeth's second cousin and, in the absence of any child of Elizabeth's own, had a strong claim to be her heir; Mary's male child would have an even stronger one. On November 5, a delegation of sixty members of the Lords and Commons met with Elizabeth, to urge her to marry and also to establish formally the line of succession. After the meeting, a member of the delegation wrote down Elizabeth's impromptu response.

I governed since my reign? I will be tried by envy itself.[2] I need not to use many words, for my deeds do try me.

Well, the matter whereof they[3] would have made their petition, as I am informed, consisteth in two points: in my marriage and in the limitation of the succession of the crown, wherein my marriage was first placed as for manner[4] sake. I did send them answer by my Council I would marry, although of mine own disposition I was not inclined thereunto. But that was not accepted nor credited, although spoken by their prince. And yet I used so many words that I could say no more. And were it not now I had spoken those words, I would never speak them again. I will never break the word of a prince spoken in public place, for my honor[5] sake. And therefore I say again I will marry as soon as I can conveniently, if God take not him away with whom I mind to marry, or myself, or else some other great let[6] happen. I can say no more except[7] the party were present. And I hope to have children; otherwise I would never marry. A strange order of petitioners, that will make a request and cannot be otherwise ascertained[8] but by the prince's word, and yet will not believe it when it is spoken! But they, I think, that moveth the same will be as ready to mislike him with whom I shall marry as they are now to move it, and then it will appear they nothing meant it. I thought they would have been rather ready to have given me thanks than to have made any new request for the same. There hath been some that have, ere this, said unto me they never required more than that they might once hear me say I would marry. Well, there was never so great a treason but might be covered under as fair a pretense.

The second point was the limitation of the succession of the crown, wherein was nothing said for my safety, but only for themselves. A strange thing that the foot should direct the head in so weighty a cause, which cause hath been so diligently weighed by us for that[9] it toucheth us more than them. I am sure there was not one of them that ever was a second person,[1] as I have been, and have tasted of the practices against my sister, who I would to God were alive again. I had great occasions to hearken to their motions,[2] of whom some of them are of the Common House. But when friends fall out truth doth appear, according to the old proverb, and were it not for my honor, their knavery should be known. There were occasions in me at that time: I stood in danger of my life, my sister was so incensed against me. I did differ from her in religion and I was sought for divers ways; and so shall never be my successor.

I have conferred before this time with those that are well learned and have asked their opinions touching the limitation of succession, who have been silent—not that by their silence after lawlike manner[3] they have seemed to assent to it, but that indeed they could not tell what to say, considering the great peril to the realm and most danger to myself. But now the matter

---

2. That is, envy itself could not fault my governance.
3. Parliament, which had planned to submit a written petition to the queen.
4. Manners'.
5. Honor's.
6. Hindrance. At the time, there were negotiations for a possible match with Archduke Charles of Austria.
7. Unless.
8. Assured.
9. Because.
1. Next in line to the throne, as Elizabeth had been under her half-sister, Mary I.
2. To pay heed to their doings.
3. In accordance with the legal maxim (that silence implies consent).

must needs go trimly and pleasantly, when the bowl runneth all on the one side.[4] And alas, not one amongst them all would answer for us, but all their speeches was for the surety[5] of their country. They would have twelve or fourteen limited in succession, and the mo[6] the better. And those shall be of such uprightness and so divine as in them shall be divinity itself. Kings were wont to honor philosophers, but if I had such[7] I would honor them as angels, that should have such piety in them that they would not seek where they are the second to be the first, and where the third to be the second, and so forth.

It is said I am no divine.[8] Indeed, I studied nothing else but divinity till I came to the crown, and then I gave myself to the study of that which was meet[9] for government, and am not ignorant of stories wherein appeareth what hath fallen out for[1] ambition of kingdoms, as in Spain, Naples, Portingal,[2] and at home. And what cocking[3] hath been between the father and the son for the same! You would have a limitation of succession. Truly if reason did not subdue will in me, I would cause you to deal in it, so pleasant a thing it should be unto me. But I stay[4] it for your benefit; for if you should have liberty to treat of it, there be so many competitors—some kinsfolk, some servants, and some tenants; some would speak for their master, and some for their mistress, and every man for his friend—that it would be an occasion of a greater charge than a subsidy.[5] And if my will did not yield to reason, it should be that thing I would gladly desire, to see you deal in it.

Well, there hath been error—I say not errors, for there were too many in the proceeding in this matter. But we will not judge that these attempts were done of any hatred to our person, but even for lack of good foresight. I do not marvel though *Domini Doctores*[6] with you, my lords, did so use themselves therein, since after my brother's[7] death they openly preached and set forth that my sister and I were bastards.[8] Well, I wish not the death of any man, but only this I desire: that they which have been the practitioners herein may before their deaths repent the same and show some open confession of their faults, whereby the scabbed[9] sheep may be known from the whole. As for my own part, I care not for death, for all men are mortal; and though I be a woman, yet I have as good a courage answerable to my place as ever my father had. I am your anointed queen. I will never be by violence constrained to do anything. I thank God I am indeed endued with such qualities that if I were turned out of the realm in my petticoat, I were able to live in any place of Christendom.

* * *

1566   1949

4. A metaphorical extension of the preceding clause: in the game of bowls, the ball has a flat place: rolled unskillfully, it wobbles, bounces, and prematurely stops; rolled well ("all on the one side"), it runs smoothly.
5. Security.
6. More.
7. That is, such virtuous potential successors.
8. Theologian.
9. Relevant to. Elizabeth's claim that before ascending the throne she studied nothing but the*ology is an exaggeration, but it is true that she had devoted much effort to the subject, as evidenced by her translations of several religious works.
1. Happened as a result of.

2. Portugal.
3. Cockfighting: strife, contention.
4. Stop.
5. That is, it would cost more than a tax. Subsidies were tax levies granted to the sovereign to meet special expenses.
6. The Doctors of the Lord: her derisive Latin term for the bishops who had supported the petition in the House of Lords.
7. Edward VI's.
8. Presumably in support of the claim of Lady Jane Grey to the throne.
9. Infected with scab (the skin disease also known as scabies).

From A Letter to Mary, Queen of Scots, February 24, 1567[1]

Madame:

My ears have been so deafened and my understanding so grieved and my heart so affrighted to hear the dreadful news of the abominable murder of your mad husband and my killed cousin[2] that I scarcely yet have the wits to write about it. And inasmuch as my nature compels me to take his death in the extreme, he being so close in blood, so it is that I will boldly tell you what I think of it. I cannot dissemble that I am more sorrowful for you than for him. O madame, I would not do the office of faithful cousin or affectionate friend if I studied rather to please your ears than employed myself in preserving your honor. However, I will not at all dissemble what most people are talking about: which is that you will look through your fingers at[3] the revenging of this deed, and that you do not take measures that touch those who have done as you wished, as if the thing had been entrusted in a way that the murderers felt assurance in doing it.[4] Among the thoughts in my heart I beseech you to want no such thought to stick at this point. Through all the dealings of the world I never was in such miserable haste to lodge and have in my heart such a miserable opinion of any prince as this would cause me do. Much less will I have such of her to whom I wish as much good as my heart is able to imagine or as you were able a short while ago to wish. However, I exhort you, I counsel you, and I beseech you to take this thing so much to heart that you will not fear to touch even him whom you have nearest to you[5] if the thing touches him, and that no persuasion will prevent you from making an example out of this to the world: that you are both a noble princess and a loyal wife. I do not write so vehemently out of doubt that I have, but out of the affection that I bear you in particular. For I am not ignorant that you have no wiser counselors than myself. Thus it is that, when I remember that our Lord had one Judas out of twelve, and I assure myself that there could be no one more loyal than myself, I offer you my affection in place of this prudence.

* * *

1567   1900

---

1. Written after news reached Elizabeth of the murder of Henry Stuart, Lord Darnley, the arrogant and erratic Scottish nobleman whom Mary had ill-advisedly married in 1565.
2. Darnley, like Mary, was Elizabeth's second cousin and a potential claimant to the throne of England.
3. Wink at.
4. Because Mary and Darnley had been estranged, there were immediately rumors that she had been complicit in his murder.
5. Evidently an allusion to James Hepburn, Earl of Bothwell, whom Mary married (under much-disputed circumstances) three months after Darnley's death, although Bothwell was known to have been one of the chief conspirators in the murder.

The Doubt of Future Foes[1]

The doubt° of future foes exiles my present joy, — *fear*
And wit° me warns to shun such snares as threatens mine — *intelligence*
   annoy.[2]
For falsehood now doth flow, and subjects' faith doth ebb,[3]
Which should not be, if reason ruled or wisdom weaved the web.
5 But clouds of toys° untried do cloak aspiring minds, — *tricks*
Which turns to rain of late repent, by course of changèd winds.[4]
The top of hope supposed, the root of rue° shall be, — *regret*
And fruitless all their grafted guile,[5] as shortly you shall see.
Their dazzled eyes with pride, which great ambition blinds,
10 Shall be unsealed° by worthy wights° whose foresight — *opened / men*
   falsehood finds.
The daughter of debate,[6] that discord aye° doth sow, — *continually*
Shall reap no gain where former rule[7] still° peace hath taught — *stable*
   to grow.
No foreign banished wight shall anchor in this port:
Our realm brooks no seditious sects—let them elsewhere resort.
15 My rusty sword through rest[8] shall first his edge employ
To poll their tops[9] who seek such change or gape for future joy.
            Vivat Regina[1]

ca. 1571   1589

On Monsieur's Departure[1]

I grieve and dare not show my discontent,
I love and yet am forced to seem to hate,
I do, yet dare not say I ever meant,
I seem stark mute but inwardly do prate.° — *chatter*
5   I am and not, I freeze and yet am burned,
   Since from myself another self I turned.

My care is like my shadow in the sun,
Follows me flying, flies when I pursue it,
Stands and lies by me, doth what I have done.[2]
10 His too familiar care[3] doth make me rue° it. — *regret*
   No means I find to rid him from my breast,
   Till by the end of things it be suppressed.

---

1. The poem concerns Mary, Queen of Scots, who in 1568 sought refuge in England from her rebellious subjects.
2. That is, threaten to do me harm ("annoy").
3. That is, the tide of faith (loyalty) is ebbing, yielding to the rising tide of falsehood.
4. Clouds of tricks not yet tested or detected hide the "aspiring minds" of ambitious foes, but those clouds will turn at last into rains of repentance.
5. The deception ("guile") grafted into them will not bear fruit.
6. Strife. Mary Stuart also was sometimes called "Mother of Debate," because she was constantly the focus of conspiracies and plots.
7. Either the reign of Henry VIII or that of Edward VI, which established the Reformation in England.
8. Sword rusty from disuse.
9. Strike off their heads.
1. Long live the queen (Latin).
1. The heading, present in a 17th-century manuscript, identifies the occasion of this poem as the breaking off of marriage negotiations between Elizabeth and the French Duke of Anjou, in 1582.
2. Does everything I do.
3. That is, my own care, which he caused.

    Some gentler passion slide into my mind,
    For I am soft and made of melting snow;
15 Or be more cruel, love, and so be kind.
    Let me or° float or sink, be high or low.   either
    Or let me live with some more sweet content,
    Or die and so forget what love e'er° meant.   ever

ca. 1582   1823

A Letter to Robert Dudley, Earl of Leicester, February 10, 1586[1]

How contemptuously we conceive ourselves to have been used by you, you shall by this bearer[2] understand: whom we have expressly sent unto you to charge you withal. We could never have imagined (had we not seen it fall out[3] in experience) that a man raised up by ourself and extraordinarily favored by us, above any other subject of this land, would have in so contemptible a sort broken our commandment in a cause that so greatly toucheth us in honor. Whereof although you have showed yourself to make but little account in so most undutiful a sort, you may not therefore think that we have so little care of the reparation thereof as we mind to pass so great a wrong in silence unredressed. And therefore our express pleasure and commandment is that, all delays and excuses laid apart, you do presently upon the duty of your allegiance obey and fulfill whatsoever the bearer hereof shall direct you to do in our name.[4] Whereof fail you not, as you will answer the contrary at your uttermost peril.

1586   1935

A Letter to Sir Amyas Paulet, August 1586[1]

Amyas, my most careful and faithful servant,

    God reward thee treblefold in the double for thy most troublesome charge[2] so well discharged. If you knew, my Amyas, how kindly, besides dutifully, my careful[3] heart accepts your double labors and faithful actions, your wise orders and safe regards performed in so dangerous and crafty[4] a charge, it

---

1. Leicester (ca. 1532–1588) had been the queen's greatest favorite from the beginning of her reign and was for a time her suitor and possibly lover. Sent to the Netherlands to assist the revolt of the Dutch Protestants against Spanish rule, however, he incurred her rage by accepting, without her permission, the offer of the Dutch to make him their absolute governor. They had been without a leader since the assassination of William of Orange, in 1584, and had offered Elizabeth herself the sovereignty of the United Provinces (which she declined) the preceding summer.
2. Sir Thomas Heneage, one of Elizabeth's most trusted courtiers.
3. Happen.
4. Heneage was instructed to direct Leicester to resign the governorship immediately. Though it was several months before Leicester did so, Elizabeth was by April already addressing him fondly again.

1. Paulet was the keeper of Mary, Queen of Scots. In 1586 a number of her supporters, led by Anthony Babington, plotted to murder Elizabeth and place Mary on the throne. The plot was discovered, and the plotters were executed in September. Mary, who had been complicit with them, was placed under stricter confinement, and then tried for treason.
    Elizabeth's letter to Paulet circulated widely in manuscript: to her contemporaries, it was evidently the single best-known of the queen's letters.
2. Duty, responsibility.
3. Full of care.
4. Requiring skill.

would ease your troubles' travail and rejoice your heart. In which I charge you to carry this most nighest thought: that I cannot balance in any weight of my judgment the value that I prize you at. And suppose no treasure to countervail[5] such a faith, and condemn me in that behalf which I never committed if I reward not such deserts. Yea, let me lack when I have most need if I acknowledge not such a merit with a reward *non omnibus datum*.[6]

But let your wicked mistress know how, with hearty sorrow, her vile deserts compels these orders; and bid her, from me, ask God forgiveness for her treacherous dealing towards the saver of her life many years, to the intolerable peril of her own.[7] And yet not content with so many forgivenesses, must fall again so horribly, far passing a woman's thought, much more a princess', instead of excusing, whereof not one can serve, it being so plainly confessed by the actors[8] of my guiltless death. Let repentance take place; and let not the fiend possess her so as her best part be lost, which I pray with hands lifted up to Him that may both save and spill,[9] with my loving adieu and prayer for thy long life.

Your most assured and loving sovereign in heart,
by good desert induced, *Elizabeth Regina*.

1586   1854

A Letter to King James VI of Scotland, February 14, 1587

My dear brother,[1]

I would you knew though not felt the extreme dolor that overwhelms my mind for that miserable accident,[2] which far contrary to my meaning hath befallen. I have now sent this kinsman of mine,[3] whom ere now it hath pleased you to favor, to instruct you truly of that which is too irksome for my pen to tell you. I beseech you that—as God and many more know—how innocent I am in this case, so you will believe me that if I had bid aught I would have bid by it.[4] I am not so base minded that fear of any living creature or prince should make me afraid to do that[5] were just or, done, to deny the same. I am not of so base a lineage nor carry so vile a mind; but as not to disguise fits most a king, so will I never dissemble my actions but cause them show even as I meant them. Thus assuring yourself of me that, as I know this was deserved, yet if I had meant it I would never lay it on others' shoulders, no more will I not damnify[6] myself that thought it not. The circumstance it may please you to have of this bearer. And for your part, think you have not in the world a more loving kinswoman nor a more dear friend than myself, nor any that will watch more carefully to preserve you and your

---

5. To be equal in value to.
6. Not given to all (Latin).
7. That is, Elizabeth's own life.
8. That is, the conspirators.
9. Destroy.
1. Fellow ruler.
2. That is, the execution, six days before, of James's mother, Mary, Queen of Scots. In the aftermath of the Babington plot, Elizabeth decided to have Mary tried and convicted of treason—legally an outrageous charge, since she was not a subject of England. Mary was sentenced to death, and Elizabeth, after much vacillation, signed the warrant for her execution. Once the sentence had been carried out, however, the queen went to great lengths to exculpate herself, even in her own mind, from responsibility for her cousin's death.
3. Sir Robert Carey, related to Elizabeth on her mother's side.
4. That is, if I had commanded her death, I would have abided by my decision. ("Bid" is a form of the past participle of both *bid* and *bide*.)
5. That is, the thing that.
6. Wrong.

estate.[7] And who shall otherwise persuade you, judge them more partial to others than you. And thus in haste, I leave to trouble you, beseeching God to send you a long reign. The 14 of February, 1587.

> Your most assured, loving sister and cousin,
> Elizabeth R.[8]

1587   1834

Verse Exchange between Elizabeth and Sir Walter Ralegh[1]

[RALEGH TO ELIZABETH]

Fortune hath taken away my love,
My life's joy and my soul's heaven above.
Fortune hath taken thee away, my princess,
My world's joy and my true fantasy's mistress.

5   Fortune hath taken thee away from me;
Fortune hath taken all by taking thee.
Dead to all joys, I only live to woe:
So is Fortune become my fantasy's foe.

In vain, my eyes, in vain ye waste your tears;
10   In vain, my sights,° the smoke of my despairs,   sighs (?)
In vain you search the earth and heaven above.
In vain you search, for Fortune keeps my love.

Then will I leave my love in Fortune's hand;
Then will I leave my love in worldlings' band,°   bond
15   And only love the sorrows due to me—
Sorrow, henceforth, that shall my princess be—

And only joy that Fortune conquers kings.
Fortune, that rules the earth and earthly things,
Hath taken my love in spite of virtue's might:
20   So blind a goddess did never virtue right.

With wisdom's eyes had but blind Fortune seen,
Then had my love, my love forever been.
But love, farewell—though Fortune conquer thee,
No fortune base nor frail shall alter me.

[ELIZABETH TO RALEGH]

Ah, silly Pug,[2] wert thou so sore afraid?
Mourn not, my Wat,[3] nor be thou so dismayed.
It passeth fickle Fortune's power and skill

---

7. Position.
8. *Regina* (Queen; Latin).
1. This exchange, which exemplifies the poetic banter that sometimes passed between the queen and her favorites, took place about 1587, when Ralegh believed that the rapid rise of the Earl of Essex in Elizabeth's favor entailed a diminution of his own standing with her.
2. An endearment, which Elizabeth used as her pet name for Ralegh.
3. Short for Walter.

                To force my heart to think thee any ill.
 5   No Fortune base, thou sayest, shall alter thee?
                And may so blind a witch so conquer me?
                No, no, my Pug, though Fortune were not blind,
                Assure thyself she could not rule my mind.
                Fortune, I know, sometimes doth conquer kings,
 10   And rules and reigns on earth and earthly things,
                But never think Fortune can bear the sway
                If virtue watch, and will her not obey.
                Ne° chose I thee by fickle Fortune's rede,°   nor / decision
                Ne she shall force me alter with such speed
 15   But if[4] to try this mistress' jest with thee.[5]
                Pull up thy heart, suppress thy brackish tears,
                Torment thee not, but put away thy fears.
                Dead to all joys and living unto woe,
                Slain quite by her that ne'er gave wise men blow,
 20   Revive again and live without all dread,
                The less afraid, the better thou shalt speed.°   succeed

ca. 1587   ca. 1600?

Speech to the Troops at Tilbury[1]

My loving people, I have been persuaded by some that are careful of[2] my safety, to take heed how I committed myself to armed multitudes, for fear of treachery. But I tell you that I would not desire to live to distrust my faithful and loving people. Let tyrants fear! I have so behaved myself that, under God, I have placed my chiefest strength and safeguard in the loyal hearts and goodwill of my subjects. Wherefore I am come among you at this time but for my recreation and pleasure, being resolved in the midst and heat of the battle to live and die amongst you all,[3] to lay down for my God and for my kingdom and for my people mine honor and my blood even in the dust. I know I have the body but of a weak and feeble woman; but I have the heart and stomach of a king, and of a king of England too[4]—and take foul scorn that Parma[5] or any prince of Europe should dare to invade the borders of my realm. To the which, rather than any dishonor shall grow by me, I myself will venter[6] my royal blood; I myself will be your general, judge, and rewarder of your virtue in the field. I know that already for your forwardness you have

---

4. Unless I do it.
5. Since "thee" has nothing to rhyme with, and since the line is hard to construe, it seems likely that there is a line missing before or after this one.
1. Delivered by Elizabeth on August 9, 1588, to the land forces assembled at Tilbury (in Essex) to repel the anticipated invasion of the Spanish Armada, a fleet of warships sent by Philip II. The Armada was defeated at sea and never reached England, a miraculous deliverance and sign of God's special favor to Elizabeth and to England, in the general view.
2. Anxious about.
3. In another version of the speech (based, like this one, on an auditor's memory), the sentence up to this point reads: "And therefore I am come amongst you, as you see at this time, not for my recreation and disport, but being resolved in the midst and heat of the battle to live or die amongst you all."
4. An allusion to the concept of the king's (or queen's) two bodies, the one natural and mortal, the other an ideal and enduring political construct. "Stomach": valor.
5. Alessandro Farnese, Duke of Parma, allied with the king of Spain and expected to join with him in the invasion of England.
6. Venture, risk.

deserved rewards and crowns,[7] and I assure you in the word of a prince you shall not fail of them. In the meantime, my lieutenant general[8] shall be in my stead, than whom never prince commanded a more noble or worthy subject; not doubting but by your concord in the camp and valor in the field, and your obedience to myself and my general, we shall shortly have a famous victory over these enemies of my God and of my kingdom.

1588   1654

The "Golden Speech"

A speech to Elizabeth's last Parliament, delivered November 30, 1601, and here given as recorded by one of the members. The designation "Golden Speech" stems from the headnote to a version of the speech printed near the end of the Puritan interregnum (1659?): "This speech ought to be set in letters of gold, that as well the majesty, prudence, and virtue of this royal queen might in general most exquisitely appear, as also that her religious love and tender respect which she particularly and constantly did bear to her Parliament in unfeigned sincerity might (to the shame and perpetual disgrace and infamy of some of her successors) be nobly and truly vindicated."

The royal prerogatives included the right to grant or sell "letters patent," which gave the recipient monopoly control of some branch of commerce. (Sir Walter Ralegh, for example, was given the exclusive right, for a period of thirty years, to license all taverns.) Discontent with the monopolies—which had resulted in higher prices for a wide range of commodities, including such basic ones as salt and starch— came to a head in the Parliament of 1601. Under parliamentary pressure (and in return for a subsidy granted to her treasury), Elizabeth agreed to revoke some of the most obnoxious patents and to allow the courts to rule freely on charges brought against the holders of others. She invited members of Parliament who wished to offer thanks for this largesse to come to her in a body, and on November 30 received about 150 of them at Whitehall Palace. After effusive remarks by the speaker of the House of Commons (Sir John Croke), the queen responded more or less as recorded here. (Elizabeth revised the speech for publication; and none of the surviving versions of it—which differ considerably—was printed earlier than about 1628.)

The "Golden Speech"[1]

Mr. Speaker, we have heard your declaration and perceive your care of our estate,[2] by falling into the consideration of a grateful acknowledgment of such benefits as you have received; and that your coming is to present thanks unto us, which I accept with no less joy than your loves can have desire to offer such a present.

I do assure you that there is no prince that loveth his subjects better, or whose love can countervail[3] our loves. There is no jewel, be it of never so rich a price, which I set before this jewel—I mean your loves. For I do more esteem it than any treasure or riches: for that we know how to prize, but love and thanks I count unvaluable.[4] And though God hath raised me high, yet

---

7. The crown was an English coin. "Forwardness": eagerness.
8. The Earl of Leicester led the English troops. Elizabeth's great and powerful favorite, he died just a month later.
1. We print only the words of the queen, omitting various interpolations as well as the opening remarks by the speaker of the Parliament.
2. Rank, position.
3. Match.
4. Invaluable.

this I count the glory of my crown, that I have reigned with your loves. This makes me that I do not so much rejoice that God hath made me to be a queen, as to be a queen over so thankful a people. Therefore I have cause to wish nothing more than to content the subjects, and that is a duty which I owe. Neither do I desire to live longer days than that I may see your prosperity, and that is my only desire. And as I am that person that still,[5] yet under God, hath delivered you, so I trust, by the almighty power of God, that I shall be His instrument to preserve you from envy, peril, dishonor, shame, tyranny, and oppression, partly by means of your intended helps, which we take very acceptable because it manifesteth the largeness of your loves and loyalties unto your sovereign.

Of myself I must say this: I never was any greedy, scraping grasper, nor a strait, fast-holding prince, nor yet a waster. My heart was never set on worldly goods, but only for my subjects' good. What you bestow on me, I will not hoard it up, but receive it to bestow on you again. Yea, my own properties I account yours to be expended for your good, and your eyes shall see the bestowing of all for your good. Therefore render unto them from me, I beseech you, Mr. Speaker, such thanks as you imagine my heart yieldeth but my tongue cannot express.

Mr. Speaker, I would wish you and the rest to stand up, for I shall yet trouble you with longer speech.[6]

Mr. Speaker, you give me thanks, but I doubt[7] me that I have more cause to thank you all than you me; and I charge you to thank them of the Lower House[8] from me. For had I not received a knowledge from you, I might have fallen into the lapse of an error only for lack of true information.

Since I was queen yet did I never put my pen to any grant but that upon pretext and semblance made unto me, it was both good and beneficial to the subject in general, though a private profit to some of my ancient servants who had deserved well. But the contrary being found by experience, I am exceedingly beholding to such subjects as would move the same at the first.[9] And I am not so simple to suppose but that there be some of the Lower House whom these grievances never touched; and for them I think they speak out of zeal to their countries[1] and not out of spleen or malevolent affection, as being parties grieved. And I take it exceedingly gratefully from them, because it gives us to know that no respects or interests had moved them other than the minds they bear to suffer[2] no diminution of our honor and our subjects' love unto us, the zeal of which affection, tending to ease my people and knit their hearts unto me, I embrace with a princely care.

For above all earthly treasures I esteem my people's love, more than which I desire not to merit. That my grants should be grievous to my people and oppressions to be privileged under color[3] of our patents, our kingly dignity shall not suffer it. Yea, when I heard it I could give no rest unto my thoughts until I had reformed it.[4] Shall they (think you) escape unpunished that have thus oppressed you and have been respectless of their duty and regardless of our honor? No, no, Mr. Speaker, I assure you were it not more for conscience'

---

5. Continually.
6. Up to this point, the assemblage had been *kneeling*.
7. Fear.
8. The House of Commons.
9. That is, those members of the House of Commons who had raised the issue of monopolies in previous sessions. "Beholding": beholden.

1. Their constituents.
2. Permit. "Minds": intentions.
3. Pretext.
4. In fact Elizabeth was extremely slow to respond to the grievances, which had, for example, previously been raised in the Parliament of 1597.

sake than for any glory or increase of love that I desire, these errors, troubles, vexations, and oppressions done by these varlets and low persons (not worthy the name of subjects) should not escape without condign punishment. But I perceive they dealt with me like physicians who, ministering a drug, make it more acceptable by giving it a good aromatical savor; or when they give pills, do gild them all over.

I have ever used[5] to set the Last Judgment Day before my eyes and so to rule as I shall be judged, to answer before a higher Judge. To whose judgment seat I do appeal that never thought was cherished in my heart that tended not unto my people's good. And now if my kingly bounties have been abused and my grants turned to the hurts of my people, contrary to my will and meaning, or if any in authority under me have neglected or perverted what I have committed to them, I hope God will not lay their culps[6] and offenses to my charge. Who, though there were danger in repealing our grants, yet what danger would I not rather incur for your good than I would suffer them still to continue?

I know the title of a king is a glorious title, but assure yourself that the shining glory of princely authority hath not so dazzled the eyes of our understanding but that we well know and remember that we also are to yield an account of our actions before the great Judge. To be a king and wear a crown is more glorious to them that see it than it is pleasant to them that bear it. For myself, I was never so much enticed with the glorious name of a king or royal authority of a queen as delighted that God hath made me His instrument to maintain His truth and glory, and to defend this kingdom (as I said) from peril, dishonor, tyranny, and oppression.

There will never queen sit in my seat with more zeal to my country, care to my subjects, and that will sooner with willingness venture her life for your good and safety, than myself. For it is not my desire to live nor reign longer than my life and reign shall be for your good. And though you have had and may have many princes more mighty and wise sitting in this seat, yet you never had or shall have any that will be more careful and loving.

Shall I ascribe anything to myself and my sexly[7] weakness? I were not worthy to live then, and of all most unworthy of the mercies I have had from God, who hath ever yet given me a heart which yet never feared any foreign or home enemy. I speak it to give God the praise as a testimony before you, and not to attribute anything unto myself. For I, O Lord, what am I, whom practices and perils past should not fear?[8] O, what can I do, that I should speak for any glory? God forbid!

This, Mr. Speaker, I pray you deliver unto the House, to whom heartily recommend me. And so I commit you all to your best fortunes and further counsels. And I pray you, Mr. Comptroller, Mr. Secretary,[9] and you of my council, that before these gentlemen depart into their countries,[1] you bring them all to kiss my hand.

1601   1601 (in a summary version)

---

5. Been accustomed.
6. Sins.
7. Characteristic of my sex. "Ascribe": attribute.
8. Frighten. "Practices": treacherous schemes.
9. William Knollys, Earl of Banbury, and Robert Cecil, Earl of Salisbury.
1. Districts.

ANNE COOKE BACON

Anne Cooke Bacon (ca. 1527–1610) here introduces her translation of the sermons of Bernadino Ochino from Italian to English. In this pointed dedication to her mother, who had clearly argued that learning Italian would not help God's cause, she notes that learning the language has enabled her to translate these holy texts. Thus this short epistle shows defiance in its reverence. Ochino (1487–1564) was a Catholic turned Protestant reformer and Calvinist; through his works Bacon, here at the age of twenty-two, first broadcast her own as well as his powerful Protestant beliefs. This translation paved the way for her later translation of Jewel's *Apology*, included earlier in this volume.

To the Right Worshipful and Worthily Beloved Mother, the Lady F., Her Humble Daughter Wisheth Increase of Spiritual Knowledge, with Full Fruition of the Fruits Thereof

Since the original of whatsoever is or may be converted to any good use in me hath freely proceeded—though as the minister of God—of your ladyship's mere careful and motherly goodness, as well in procuring[1] all things thereunto belonging, as in your many and most Godly exhortations (wherein among the rest it hath pleased you, often, to reprove my vain study in the Italian tongue, accounting the seed thereof to have been sown in baren, unfruitful ground, since God thereby is no whit magnified), I have at the last perceived it my duty to prove how much the understanding of your will could work in me towards the accomplishing of the same. And—for that I have well known your chief delight to rest in the destroying of man his glory, and exalting wholly the glory of God, which may not be unless we acknowledge that He doth foresee and determine, from without beginning, all things, and cannot alter or reward after our deserved works, but remain steadfast, according to his immutable will—I have taken in hand to dedicate unto your Ladyship this small number of sermons for the excellent fruit sake in them contained, proceeding from the happy spirit of the sanctified Barnardine, which treat of the election and predestination of God, with the rest (although not of the self-title) appertaining to the same effect, to the end it might appear that your so many worthy sentences touching the same have not utterly been without some note in my weak memory. And albeit they be not done[2] in such perfection as the dignity of the matter doth require, yet I trust and know ye will accept the humble will of the presenter, not weighing so much the excellency of the translation—although of right it ought to be such as should not by the grossness[3] thereof deprive the author of his worthiness. But not meaning to take upon me the reach to his high style of theology, and fearing also, lest in enterprising[4] to set forth the brightness of his eloquence I should manifest myself unapt to attain unto the lowest degree thereof, I descend therefore, to the understanding of mine own debility, only requiring that it may please your ladyship to vouchsafe[5] that this

---

1. Acquiring. "Mere": pure.
2. That is, translated.
3. Coarseness.
4. Attempting.
5. Grant. "Debility": weakness.

my small labor may be allowed at your hands, under whose protection only it is committed, with humble reverence, as yielding some part of the fruit of your motherly admonitions in this my willing service.

Your ladyship's daughter most boundenly[6] obedient. A.C.

6. According to bounden duty.

MARGARET TYLER

The background of Margaret Tyler (ca. 1540–ca. 1590), translator of Spanish, is unknown. As she dedicates this, her only known printed work, to Lord Thomas Howard, it is assumed she was a servant to his aristocratic family. Her *Mirror of Princely Deeds* is a translation of book 1 of Diego Ortúñez de Calahorra, *Espejo de Príncipes y Cavalleros* (1555), a racy romance featuring sorcerers, magic, courageous deeds, and hopeless love; it was regularly reprinted and became a source and model for subsequent English romances. Tyler seems, from the confident dedication supplied here, to have been of mature age when her text, the first romance from a woman's pen in English, came out. She offers here an impassioned defense of women's right to translate stories in addition to pious works, stating that if a woman is allowed to read a story, and be its dedicatee, she should be allowed to translate one too.

To the Reader

Thou hast here, gentle Reader, the history of Trebatio, an Emperor in Greece, whether a true history of him indeed, or a feigned fable, I wot not,[1] neither did I greatly seek after it in the translation, but by me it is done into English for thy profit and delight. The chief matter therein contained is of exploits of wars, and the parties therein named are especially renowned for their magnanimity and courage. The author's purpose appeareth to be this: to animate thereby, and to set on fire, the lusty[2] courages of young gentlemen to the advancement of their line by ensuing[3] suchlike steps. The first tongue wherein it was penned was the Spanish (in which nation, by common report, the inheritance of all worldly commendation hath to this day rested); the whole discourse in respect of the end not unnecessary, for the variety and continual shift of fresh matter very delightful, in the speeches short and sweet, wise in sentence, and wary in the provision of contrary accidents.[4] For I take the grace thereof to be rather in the reporter's device than in the truth of this report, as I would that I could so well impart with thee that delight which myself findeth in reading the Spanish: but seldom is the tale carried clean[5] from another's mouth.

Such delivery[6] as I have made, I hope thou wilt friendly accept, the rather for that it is a woman's work, though[7] in a story profane and a matter more manlike than becometh my sex. But as for the manliness of the matter, thou

1. I do not know.
2. Vigorous. "Animate": inspire.
3. Imitating.
4. Occurrences.
5. Absolutely correctly.
6. Translation.
7. Even if.

knowest that it is not necessary for every trumpeter or drumsler[8] in the war to be a good fighter. They take wage only to incite others, though themselves have privy maims and are thereby recureless.[9] So, gentle reader, if my travail in Englishing this author may bring thee to a liking of the virtues herein commended, and by example thereof in thy princes and country's quarrel to hazard thy person and purchase good name, as for[1] hope of well deserving myself that way, I neither bend myself thereto, nor yet fear the speech of people if I be found backward.[2] I trust every man holds not the plough which would[3] the ground were tilled, and it is no sin to talk of Robin Hood, though you never shot in[4] his bow. * * * The invention, disposition, trimming, and what else[5] in this story, is wholly another man's, my part none therein but the translation, as it were only in giving entertainment to a stranger before this time unacquainted with our country guise.[6] Marry, the worst perhaps is this: that among so many strangers[7] as daily come over, some more ancient, and some but new set forth, some penning matters of great weight and sadness in divinity or other studies (the profession whereof more nearly beseemeth[8] my years), other some discoursing of matters more easy and ordinary in common talk wherein a gentlewoman may honestly employ her travail, I have notwithstanding made countenance only to[9] this gentleman, whom neither his personage might sufficiently commend itself unto my sex, nor his behavior (being light and soldierlike) might in good order acquaint itself[1] with my years.

So the question now ariseth of my choice, not of my labor, wherefore[2] I preferred this story before matter of more importance. For answer whereto, gentle reader, the truth is that as the first motion to[3] this kind of labor came not from myself, so was this piece of work put upon me by others, and they which first counselled me to fall to work took upon them also to be my taskmasters and overseers lest I should be idle. And yet because the refusal was in my power, I must stand[4] to answer for my easy yielding, and may not be unprovided of excuse, wherein if I should allege for myself that matters of less worthiness by as aged years have been taken in hand, and that daily new devices[5] are published, in songs, sonnets, interludes, and other discourses, and yet are borne out[6] without reproach only to please the humor of some men, I think I should make no good plea therein; for besides that I should find thereby so many known enemies as known men have been authors of such idle conceits, yet would my other adversaries be never the rather quieted. For they would say that as well the one as the other were all naught, and though peradventure[7] I might passe unknown amongst a multitude, and not be the only gaze or odd party in my ill[8] doing, yet because there is less merit of pardon if the fault be excused as common, I will not make that my defense which cannot help me, and doth hinder other men. But my defense is by example of the best, amongst which many have dedicated their labors, some

8. Drummer.
9. Incurable. "Privy maims": secret wounds.
1. As regards. "Hazard": risk or stake.
2. Reluctant. "Bend": incline.
3. Who wishes.
4. With. The legendary outlaw hero Robin Hood, the subject of a series of English ballads, was famed for his skill in archery.
5. *What else should be the case.* "Disposition": organization. "Trimming": adornment.
6. Native appearance. "Stranger": foreigner.
7. Here, foreign books. "Marry": indeed.

8. Becomes, befits.
9. Favored only.
1. Familiarize itself. "Light": frivolous. "In good order": decently.
2. Why.
3. Suggestion about.
4. Agree.
5. Ingenious writings.
6. Tolerated.
7. Perhaps. "Naught": nothing.
8. Wrong. "Gaze": object of gaze. "Party": participant.

stories, some of war, some physic, some law, some as concerning government, some divine matters, unto diverse[9] ladies and gentlewomen. And if men may and do bestow such of their travails upon gentlewomen, then may we women read such of their works as they dedicate unto us, and if we may read them, why not farther wade in them to the search of a truth? And then, much more, why not deal by translation in such arguments, especially this kind of exercise, being a matter of more heed than of deep invention or exquisite[1] learning? And they must needs leave this as confessed: that in their dedications they mind[2] not only to borrow names of worthy personages, but the testimonies also for their further credit, which neither the one may demand without ambition, nor the other grant without over-lightness. If women be excluded from the view of such works as appear in their name, or if glory only be sought in our common inscriptions, it mattereth not whether the parties be men or women, whether alive or dead. But to return, whatsomever[3] the truth is, whether that women may not at all discourse in learning (for men lay in[4] their claim to be sole possessioners of knowledge), or whether they may in some manner, that is by limitation or appointment in some kind of learning, my persuasion hath been thus, that it is all one[5] for a woman to pen a story, as for a man to address his story to a woman. But amongst all my ill-willers, some I hope are not so straight[6] that they would enforce me necessarily either not to write or to write of divinity. Whereas neither durst I trust mine own judgment sufficiently, if matter of controversy were handled, nor yet could I find any book in the tongue which would not breed offence to some, but I perceive some may be rather angry to see their Spanish delight turned to an English pastime:[7] they could well allow the story in Spanish, but they may not afford it so cheap, or they would have it proper[8] to themselves. What natures such men be of, I list[9] not greatly dispute, but my meaning hath been to make other partners of my liking, as I doubt not, gentle reader, but if it shall please thee—after serious matters—to sport thyself[1] with this Spaniard, that thou shalt find in him the just reward of malice and cowardice, with the good speed[2] of honesty and courage, being able to furnish thee with sufficient store[3] of foreign example to both purposes. And as in such matters which have been rather devised to beguile time than to breed matter of sad[4] learning, he hath ever borne away the prize which could season such delights with some profitable reading, so shalt thou have this stranger an honest man when need serveth, and at other times either a good companion to drive out a weary night or a merry jest at thy board.[5]

And thus much concerning this present story: that it is neither unseemly for a woman to deal in, neither greatly requiring a less staid age then mine is. But of these two points gentle reader, I thought to give thee warning, lest perhaps understanding of my name and years, thou mightest be carried into a wrong suspect of my boldness and rashness, from which I would gladly free myself by this plain excuse; and if I may deserve thy good favor

9. Different.
1. Careful.
2. Pay attention to, remember. "Leave this as confessed": take it that this is manifest.
3. Whatsoever.
4. Exert themselves in.
5. It is equal.
6. Proper.

7. Diversion.
8. Exclusively.
9. Desire.
1. Divert yourself.
2. Good success.
3. Supply. "Furnish": supply.
4. Serious. "Beguile": wile away.
5. Table.

by like labor, when the choice is mine own, I will have a special regard[6] of thy liking. So I wish thee well.

Thine to use, M[argaret]. T[yler].

6. Esteem.

ANNE DOWRICHE

Anne Dowriche (1560–after 1613) was a Puritan poet and historian who was married to a minister, Hugh Dowriche, a rector in Honiton, Devon. Her long narrative poem, *The French Historie*, published in 1589, told in gruesome detail the story of the recent French wars of religion—her attempt to justify the Protestant Reformation and vilify Catholicism. The dedication, addressed to her much older brother, Sir Pearse Edgecombe (1536–1607/8), details her joy in writing the poem and expresses the hope that its content will make her work acceptable to him. While she seemingly dismisses her own style and writing ability, the length (2,400 lines) and gore of the text point to her boldness.

To the Right Worshipful Her Loving Brother, Master Pearse Edgecombe of Mount Edgecombe in Devon Esquire, Mercy and Peace from Jesus Christ

Right worshipful and my loving brother, I have heard it often and truly reported that laws may be broken but nature cannot be forgotten. I find the force of this in myself: if I find not the like in you, I blame not your nature, but the contrary crossings of those politic affections that hinder the working of it. When I had ended this present pamphlet, I saw that the simplicity[1] of it required a patron, and the often remembrance of your former courtesies enforced me to make bold[2] with you. Consider not therefore the worthiness of the work, but rather the will of the worker: for though the one may justly be condemned, yet the other deserves to be accepted. This book which proceeds under your protection, if you consider the matter, I assure you it is most excellent and well worth the reading; but if you weigh the manner, I confess it is base and scarce worth the seeing. This is therefore my desire: that the simple attire of this outward form may not discourage you from seeking the comfortable[3] taste of the inward substance. You shall find here many things for comfort worthy the considering, and for policy the observing. This hath been my ordinary exercise for recreation at times of leisure for a long space[4] together. If I were sure that you would but take half so much pleasure in reading it as I have in collecting and disposing[5] it, I should not need any farther to commend it. If you find anything that fits not your liking, remember, I pray, that it is a woman's doing. The thing itself will

1. Unembellished appearance.
2. Become bold.
3. Comforting.
4. Duration of time. "Exercise": occupation.
5. Ordering

sufficiently prove this to be true. Thus, committing the patronage of this my recreation unto your protection, and you with my good sister-in-law your wife, and all your children to the Lord's tuition,[6] I cease to trouble you.

Honiton, the 25 day of July 1589
Your loving sister Anne Dowriche

6. Protection.

JANE ANGER

Jane Anger her Protection for women. To defend them against the scandalous reports of a late surfeiting lover, and all other like Venerians that complain so to be overcloyed with women's kindness (1589) announces its content in its title. It was written as a response to a contemporary pamphlet now lost, Thomas Orwin's *Surfeit in Love, with a farwel to the folies of his own fantasy* (1588)—an attack on women. How we assess Anger's work depends on whether it is taken to be a defense of women by an actual woman or an experiment in arguing the women's cause written by a man. In the period, the nature of women (known as the *querelle des femmes*, the "woman question") was often discussed as an intellectual debate, with arguments put forward in favor of or against women, their natures, and their rights. This contribution to the *querelle* may be a powerful offering by a genuine woman—there were women named Jane Anger in early modern England—or by a woman writing under a pseudonym, or by a man taking on an outraged woman's voice. In this dedication, Anger wishes ruin on men who take advantage of women sexually and then complain about them. In her final poem she considers how she has planted her seed of anger in and for women readers.

To All Women in General, and Gentle Reader[s] Whatsoever

Fie on the falsehood of men, whose minds go oft a-madding,[1] and whose tongues cannot so soon be wagging but straight they fall a-railing. Was there ever any so abused, so slandered, so railed upon, or so wickedly handled undeservedly, as are we women? Will the gods permit it, the goddesses stay[2] their punishing judgments, and we ourselves not pursue their undoings[3] for such devilish practices? O Paul's steeple and Charing Cross![4] A halter[5] hold all such persons! Let the streams of the channels in London streets[6] run so swiftly as they may be able alone to carry them from that sanctuary. Let the stones be as ice, the soles of their shoes as glass, the ways steep like Etna,[7] and every blast a *whirlwind puffed out of Boreas*[8] his long throat, that these may hasten their passage to the devils' haven. Shall surfeiters rail on our kindness,[9] you stand still and say nought, and shall not Anger stretch the veins of her brains, the

1. In a furious or mad way.
2. Cease.
3. Ruin.
4. London landmarks that were in ruins: St. Paul's Cathedral lost its steeple to fire in 1561; Charing Cross had had its lower statues pulled out and its cross damaged in the 1580s.
5. Noose.
6. That is, the gutters, used for carrying away refuse and sewage.
7. An active volcano in Sicily.
8. The north wind.
9. Willingness to be loving. "Surfeiters": liberines.

strings of her fingers, and the lists[1] of her modesty, to answer their surfeitings? Yes truly. And herein I conjure[2] all you to aide and assist me in defense of my willingness, which shall make me rest at your commands. Fare you well.

Your friend. Ja. A.

Eiusdem ad Lectorem, de Authore[1]

Though sharp the seed by Anger sown
We all, almost, confess,
And hard his hap° we aye account   *luck*
Who Anger doth possess;
5 Yet hapless° shalt thou, reader, reap   *without (his hard) luck*
Such fruit from ANGER'S soil
As may thee please, and ANGER ease
From long and weary toil—
Whose pains were took,° for thy behoof,°   *efforts were made / benefit*
10 To till that cloddy ground
Where scarce no place free from disgrace
Of female sex was found.
If ought offend, which she doth send,
Impute° it to her mood,   *attribute*
15 For ANGER'S rage must that assuage,
As well is understood.
If to delight aught° come in sight   *anything*
Then deem it for the best.
So you your will may well fulfil,
20 And she have her request.

1589

1. Limits.
2. Entreat.

1. To the reader of the same, from the author (Latin).

EDMUND SPENSER
1552?–1599

Edmund Spenser set out, consciously and deliberately, to become the great English poet of his age. In a culture in which most accomplished poetry was written by those who were, or at least professed to be, principally interested in something else— advancement at court, diplomacy, statecraft, or the Church—Spenser's ambition was altogether remarkable, and it is still more remarkable that he succeeded in reaching his goal. Unlike such poets as Wyatt, Surrey, and Sidney, born to privilege and social distinction, Spenser was born—in London, probably in 1552—to parents of modest social class and limited means. He nonetheless received an impressive education, first at the Merchant Taylors' School—under its demanding, humanist headmaster, Richard Mulcaster—and then at Pembroke College, Cambridge, where he was enrolled as a "sizar," a student who received financial aid in exchange for waiting on tables and other menial tasks. In the Puritan environment of Cambridge, where the popular preacher Thomas Cartwright was beginning to make the authorities uneasy, Spenser began as a poet by translating some poems for a volume of anti-Catholic propaganda. He also began his friendship with Gabriel Harvey, an eccentric Cambridge don, humanist, and pamphleteer. Their correspondence shows they shared a passionate interest in heightening the power and prestige of poetry written in English.

After receiving the B.A. degree in 1573 and the M.A. in 1576, Spenser served as personal secretary and aide to several prominent men, including both Dr. John Young, bishop of Rochester, and Robert Dudley, Earl of Leicester and the queen's principal favorite. During his employment in Leicester's household, Spenser came to know Sir Philip Sidney and his friend Sir Edward Dyer, courtiers who sought to promote a new English poetry. Spenser's contribution to the movement was *The Shepheardes Calender*, published in 1579 and dedicated to Sidney.

In *The Shepheardes Calender* Spenser used a deliberately archaic language—partly in homage to Chaucer, whose work he praised as a "well of English undefiled," and partly to achieve a rustic effect, in keeping with the feigned simplicity of pastoral poetry's shepherd singers. Sidney did not entirely approve, and another contemporary, Ben Jonson, growled that Spenser "writ no language." In the eighteenth century Samuel Johnson described the language of *The Shepheardes Calender* as "studied barbarity." Johnson's characterization is, in a way, quite accurate, for Spenser was attempting to conjure up a native English style to which he could wed the classical mode of the pastoral. Moreover, because pastoral was traditionally viewed as the prelude in a great poet's career, Spenser was also in effect announcing his extravagant ambition to become England's national poet.

Spenser was a prolific and daring experimenter: the poems of *The Shepheardes Calender* use no fewer than thirteen different metrical schemes. In his later poems, he went on to make further innovations: the best known are the special rhyme scheme of the Spenserian sonnet, the remarkably beautiful adaptation of the Italian *canzone* forms for the *Epithalamion* and *Prothalamion*, and the great Spenserian stanza of *The Faerie Queene* (eight iambic pentameters followed by a six-foot line, rhymed *ababbcbcc*). Spenser is sometimes called "the poet's poet," because so many later English poets learned the art of versification from him. In the nineteenth century alone his influence may be seen in Shelley's *Revolt of Islam*, Byron's *Childe Harold's Pilgrimage*, Keats's "Eve of St. Agnes," and Tennyson's "The Lotus-Eaters."

The year after the publication of *The Shepheardes Calender*, Spenser went to Ireland as secretary and aide to Lord Grey of Wilton, lord deputy of Ireland. Although the poet tried continually to obtain appointments in England (which he revisited on several occasions) and to secure the patronage of the queen, he lived in Ireland nearly to the end of his life, holding various minor government posts and hence participating actively in the English struggle against those who resisted colonial occupation. The grim realities of that struggle—massacres, the burning of miserable hovels and of crops with the deliberate intention of starving the inhabitants, the forced relocation of whole communities, the manipulation of treason charges to facilitate the seizure of lands, the endless repetition of acts of military "justice" calculated to intimidate and break the spirit—may be glimpsed in distorted and on occasion direct form throughout Spenser's writings, along with dreamlike depictions of the beauty of the Irish landscape. Those writings include an anonymously published political tract, *A View of the Present State of Ireland*, which was unusual in its time both for its genuine fascination with Irish culture and for the ruthlessness of the policies it prescribed.

Spenser's attitudes toward Ireland and his conduct there raise difficult questions concerning the relationship between literature and colonialism. Are the harsh policies of the *View* echoed, allegorically, in *The Faerie Queene*? What does it mean to admire a poet who might, by modern standards, be judged a war criminal (as his master, Lord Grey, was judged to be, even by notoriously brutal Elizabethan standards)? Does Spenser use his Irish vantage point to launch daring criticisms of Queen Elizabeth and the English form of government? In addition to sharpening racial chauvinism, the experience of Ireland seems to have given English settlers a new perspective on events back home. As one of Spenser's contemporaries remarked, words that would be considered treasonous in England were common table talk among the Irish settlers.

Spenser was rewarded for his efforts in Ireland with a castle and 3,028 acres of expropriated land at Kilcolman, in the province of Munster. There he was visited by another colonist and poet, the powerful and well-connected Sir Walter Ralegh, to whom Spenser showed the great chivalric epic on which he was at work. With Ralegh's influential backing, Spenser traveled to England and published, in 1590, the first three books of *The Faerie Queene*, which made a strong bid for the queen's favor and patronage. He was rewarded with a handsome pension of £50 a year for life, though the queen's principal councillor, Lord Burghley, is said to have grumbled that it was a lot for a song. Soon after, Spenser published a volume of poems called *Complaints*; a pastoral called *Colin Clouts Come Home Againe* (1595), commenting wryly on the court life he had observed during his 1590 visit; his sonnet cycle, *Amoretti*; and two wedding poems: "Prothalamion," celebrating the double marriage of aristocratic sisters, and "Epithalamion," celebrating the poet's own marriage to Elizabeth Boyle. The six-book *Faerie Queene* was published in 1596, with some revisions in the first part and a changed ending to Book 3 to provide a bridge to the added books; the two so-called Mutabilitie Cantos and two stanzas of a third canto—perhaps part of an intended seventh book—appeared posthumously, in the 1609 edition.

In 1598 there was an uprising in Munster, and rebels burned down the house in which Spenser lived. The poet fled with his wife; their newborn baby is said to have died in the flames. Spenser was sent to England with messages from the besieged English garrison. He died in Westminster on January 13, 1599, and was buried near his beloved Chaucer in what is now called the Poets' Corner of Westminster Abbey.

Spenser cannot be put into neatly labeled categories. His work is steeped in classical learning and arcane mysticism, but it is also earthy and practical. A staunch Protestant, influenced by Puritanism, he portrayed the Roman Catholic Church as a demonic villain in *The Faerie Queene*, and yet his understanding of faith and of sin owes much to Catholic thinkers. He is a poet of sensuous images yet also something of an iconoclast, deeply suspicious of the way powerful images (material and verbal) can turn into idols. He is an idealist, drawn to courtesy, gentleness, and exquisite moral refinement, yet also a celebrant of English nationalism, empire, and martial power. He is the author of the most memorable literary idealization of Elizabeth I, yet he fills his poem with coded criticisms of the queen and her court. He is in some ways a backward-looking poet who paid homage to Chaucer, used archaic language, and compared his own age unfavorably with the feudal past. Yet as British epic poet and poet-prophet, he points forward to the poetry of the Romantics and especially to Milton, who himself paid homage to the "sage and serious" Spenser as "a better teacher than Scotus or Aquinas."

Because it was a deliberate choice on Spenser's part that his language should seem antique, his poetry is always printed in the original spelling and punctuation; but a few of the most confusing punctuation marks have been altered in the present text, and we have sometimes added diacritical marks to indicate pronunciation. Spenser also spells words variably, in such a way as to suggest rhymes to the eye or to suggest etymologies (often incorrect ones). This inconsistency in his spellings is typical of his time; in the sixteenth century, people varied the spelling even of their own names.

The Shepheardes Calender

Pastoral poetry—with its idea of shepherds among their flocks piping on their flutes and singing beautiful songs of love, sadness, and complaint—was an influential classical form whose most famous practitioners were the Alexandrian poet Theocritus (third century B.C.E.) and the Roman poet Virgil (first century B.C.E.). The singers of the pastoral, or eclogue, were depicted as simple rustics who inhabited a world in which human beings and nature lived in harmony, but the form was always essentially urban and elite: in his series of twelve eclogues, Spenser, a Londoner, was self-consciously assuming a highly conventional literary role. That role enabled him at once to lay claim to the prestige of classical poetry and to insist on his native Englishness, insistently signaled by the deliberately archaic, pseudo-Chaucerian language. The rustic mask also enabled Spenser, in certain of the eclogues, to make sharply satirical comments on religious and political issues of his day, such as Elizabeth's suppression of Puritan clergy in the Church of England, and to reflect on his own marginal social position.

The eclogues of *The Shepheardes Calender* are titled for the months of the year. Each is prefaced by an illustrative woodcut representing the characters and theme of the poem and picturing in the clouds the dominant sign of the zodiac for that month, and each is accompanied by a commentary ascribed to "E. K.," who also wrote an introductory epistle to the work as a whole. E. K., who has not been identified but must have been someone close to Spenser (or, in the opinion of some, Spenser himself), trumpets the arrival of a "new poet" whose skills are conspicuously displayed in the sequence of poems. "October" deals with the place of poetry and the responsibility of the poet in the world, an important theme throughout the *Calender* and in much of Spenser's work.

From The Shepheardes Calender

To His Booke

Goe little booke:[1] thy selfe present,
As child whose parent is unkent:°   *unknown*
To him that is the president°   *pattern*
Of noblesse and of chevalree,
5 And if that Envie barke at thee,
As sure it will, for succoure° flee   *aid*
Under the shadow of his wing,[2]
And askèd, who thee forth did bring,
A shepheards swaine° saye did thee sing,   *boy*
10 All as his straying flocke he fedde:
And when his honor has thee redde,°   *seen*
Crave pardon for my hardyhedde.°   *boldness*
But if that any aske thy name,
Say thou wert base° begot with blame: *lowly*
15 For thy° thereof thou takest shame.   *therefore*
And when thou art past jeopardee,
Come tell me, what was sayd of mee:
And I will send more after thee.
        IMMERITO.°   *unworthy*

---

1. A deliberate echo of Chaucer's line "Go litel bok, go litel myn tragedye" (*Troilus and Criseyde* 5.1786).

2. That is, the protective sponsorship of Sir Philip Sidney, to whom this poem dedicates the book.

October[3]

Aegloga decima[4]
ARGUMENT

In Cuddie[5] is set out the perfecte paterne of a Poete, which finding no maintenaunce of his state and studies, complayneth of the comtempte of Poetrie, and the causes thereof: Specially having bene in all ages, and even amongst the most barbarous always of singular accounpt[6] and honor, and being indede so worthy and commendable an arte: or rather no arte, but a divine gift and heavenly instinct not to bee gotten by laboure and learning, but adorned with both: and poured into the witte by a certaine *enthousiasmos* and celestiall inspiration, as the Author hereof els where at large discourseth, in his booke called the English Poete,[7] which booke being lately come to my hands, I mynde[8] also by Gods grace upon further advisement to publish.

PIERS   CUDDIE

Cuddie, for shame hold up thy heavye head,
And let us cast with what delight to chace,

---

3. When *The Shepheardes Calender* was published, in 1579, each of the twelve eclogues was followed by a commentary (called a "Glosse") by the mysterious E. K., which contained explications of difficult or archaic words, together with learned discussions of—and disagreements with—Spenser's ideas, imagery, and poetics. Designed to appear authoritative, the commentaries in fact often serve to complicate the process of interpretation. To give the reader some sense of them, we have included several of the individual notes from the "October" Glosse.
4. Tenth Eclogue (Latin). An eclogue ("aeglogue") is a short pastoral poem in the form of a dialogue or *soliloquy*. Spenser's spelling is based on a false etymology (*aix*, "goat" + *logos*, "speech"), signifying, according to E. K., "Goteheards tales." For this eclogue, E. K. identifies as sources Theocritus's *Idyl* 16, which reproves the tyrant Hiero of Syracuse for his neglect of poets, and also Baptista Spagnuoli (1448–1516), called Mantuan (the fifth eclogue). The illustration portrays Cuddie (left) holding a pipe and crowned with a laurel wreath (emblems of a poet). He talks with his fellow shepherd, Piers, in a pastoral landscape, with the court in the background. The astrological sign for October, Scorpio, is at the top of the picture.
5. E. K. queries "whether by Cuddie be specified the authour selfe, or some other," noting that in "August" he was introduced as singing a song "of Colins making. So that some doubt, that the persons be different." It may be that Cuddie and Piers, along with Colin, present different aspects of Spenser the poet.
6. Esteem.
7. *The English Poete* is evidently a lost work by Spenser. "*Enthousiasmos*": inspiration. The Greek word originally meant "possessed by a god."
8. Intend.

And weary thys long lingring Phoebus race.⁹
Whilome thou wont¹ the shepheards laddes to leade,
⁵ In rymes, in ridles, and in bydding base:²
Now they in thee, and thou in sleepe art dead.

CUDDIE

Piers, I have pypèd erst° so long with payne,°   *up to now / care*
That all mine Oten reedes³ bene rent° and wore: *torn*
And my poore Muse hath spent her sparèd° store,   *saved up*
¹⁰ Yet little good hath got, and much lesse gayne.
Such pleasaunce makes the Grashopper so poore,
And ligge so layd,⁴ when Winter doth her straine.°   *constrain*

The dapper° ditties, that I wont⁵ devise,   *pretty*
To feede youthes fancie, and the flocking fry,⁶
¹⁵ Delighten much: what I the bett for thy?⁷
They han° the pleasure, I a sclender prise.°   *have / meager reward*
I beate the bush, the byrds to them doe flye:
What good thereof to Cuddie can arise?

PIERS

Cuddie, the prayse is better, then° the price,   *than*
²⁰ The glory eke° much greater then the gayne: *also*
O what an honor is it, to restraine
The lust° of lawlesse youth with good advice:⁸   *desires*
Or pricke° them forth with pleasaunce of thy vaine°   *spur / talent*
Whereto thou list° their traynèd° willes entice.   *desire / ensnared*

²⁵ Soone as thou gynst° to sette thy notes in frame,   *begin*
O how the rurall routes° to thee doe cleave: *crowds*
Seemeth thou dost their soule of sence bereave,⁹
All as the shepheard, that did fetch his dame
From Plutoes balefull bowre withouten leave:
³⁰ His musicks might the hellish hound did tame.¹

CUDDIE

So praysen babes the Peacoks spotted traine,
And wondren at bright Argus blazing eye:²

---

9. That is, let us see how we may pass this long day pleasantly. In classical mythology, Phoebus was god of the sun.
1. Formerly you were accustomed.
2. A popular game; here, perhaps a poetry contest.
3. The shepherd's pipe, symbol of pastoral poetry.
4. That is, lie so subdued. The reference is to the fable of the industrious ant who laid up supplies for winter, and the carefree grasshopper who did not.
5. Am accustomed to.
6. "A bold Metaphore, forced from the spawning fishes. For the multitude of young fish be called the frye" [E. K.].
7. That is, how am I the better for that?
8. E. K. compares these lines with *The Laws* 1, in which Plato declares "that the first invention of Poetry was of very vertuous intent."

9. That is, hypnotize them. E. K. cites Plato and Pythagoras for the theory that the mind is made of "a certaine harmonie and musicall nombers," and gives several examples of music's irresistible power over the emotions.
1. In classical mythology, the three-headed dog Cerberus guards the entrance to Hades. But he let pass Orpheus, "of whom is sayd, that by his excellent skil in Musick and Poetry, he recovered his wife Eurydice from hell" [E. K.]—that is, from "Plutoes balefull bowre."
2. E. K. alludes to the myth of Argus of the hundred eyes, who, set by Juno to guard Io, Jupiter's current paramour, was lulled asleep by Mercury's music and then killed. Juno placed his eyes in the tail of her bird, the peacock, whose splendor elicits the praises even of "babes."

    But who rewards him ere° the more for thy?°   *at all / therefore*
    Or feedes him once the fuller by a graine?
35 Sike° prayse is smoke, that sheddeth° in the skye,   *such / is dispersed*
    Sike words bene wynd, and wasten soone in vayne.

PIERS

    Abandon then the base and viler clowne,°   *rustic*
    Lyft up thy selfe out of the lowly dust:
    And sing of bloody Mars,[3] of wars, of giusts.°   *jousts*
40 Turne thee to those, that weld° the awful° crowne,   *bear / awesome*
    To doubted° Knights, whose woundlesse[4] armour rusts,   *dreaded*
    And helmes unbruzèd waxen° dayly browne.   *grow*

    There may thy Muse display her fluttryng wing,
    And stretch her selfe at large from East to West:[5]
45 Whither thou list° in fayre Elisa rest,   *choose*
    Or if thee please in bigger notes to sing,
    Advaunce° the worthy whome shee loveth best,   *extol*
    That first the white beare to the stake did bring.[6]

    And when the stubborne stroke of stronger stounds,°   *efforts*
50 Has somewhat slackt[7] the tenor of thy string:
    Of love and lustihead tho° mayst thou sing,   *pleasure then*
    And carrol lowde, and leade the Myllers rownde,[8]
    All° were Elisa one of thilke same ring.[9]   *although*
    So mought our Cuddies name to Heaven sownde.

CUDDIE

55 Indeede the Romish Tityrus,[1] I heare,
    Through his Mecaenas left his Oaten reede,
    Whereon he earst° had taught his flocks to feede,   *formerly*
    And laboured lands to yield the timely eare,
    And eft° did sing of warres and deadly drede,°   *afterward / danger*
60 So as the Heavens did quake his verse to here.[2]

    But ah Mecaenas is yclad in claye,
    And great Augustus long ygoe is dead:
    And all the worthies liggen° wrapt in leade,   *lie*

---

3. Roman god of war.
4. "Unwounded in warre, doe rust through long peace" [E. K.].
5. E. K. explains this "poeticall metaphore" as indicating the heroic subjects available to Cuddie if he wishes to "showe his skill in matter of more dignitie, then [that is, than] is the homely Aeglogue." These include "our most gratious soveraign, whom (as before) he calleth Elisa," and also the "noble and valiaunt men" who deserve his praise and have been his patrons.
6. "He meaneth (as I guesse) the most honorable and renowmed the Erle of Leycester" [E. K.]. Leicester's device was the bear and ragged staff.
7. "That is when thou chaungest thy verse from stately discourse, to matter of more pleasaunce and delight" [E. K.].
8. "A kind of daunce" [E. K.].
9. A "company of dauncers" [E. K.].
1. "Wel knowen to be Virgile, who by Mecaenas means was brought into the favour of the Emperor Augustus, and by him moved to write in loftier kinde, then he erst had doen" [E. K.]. Maecenas ("Mecaenas") was Virgil's patron and counselor to Augustus, and Tityrus was the shepherd-poet in virgil's *Eclogue* 1.
2. "In these three verses are the three severall workes of Virgile intended. For in teaching his flocks to feede, is meant his Aeglogues. In labouring of lands, is hys Georgiques. In singing of wars and deadly dreade, is his divine Aeneis figured" [E. K.]. The *Georgics* ("Georgiques") is Virgil's idealizing poem about farm life.

That matter made for Poets on to play:
65 For ever, who in derring doe³ were dreade,°   *held in awe*
The loftie verse of hem° was lovèd aye.⁴   *them*

But after vertue gan for age to stoupe,
And mighty manhode brought a bedde of° ease:⁵   *to bed by*
The vaunting Poets found nought worth a pease,°   *pea*
70 To put in preace° among the learned troupe.   *present for competition*
Tho° gan the streames of flowing wittes to cease,   *then*
And sonnebright honour pend in shamefull coupe.⁶

And if that any buddes of Poesie,
Yet of the old stocke gan to shoote agayne:
75 Or° it mens follies mote° be forst to fayne,°   *either / must / feign*
And rolle with rest in rymes of rybaudrye:°   *ribaldry*
Or as it sprong, it wither must agayne:
Tom Piper makes us better melodie.⁷

PIERS

O pierlesse Poesye, where is then thy place?
80 If nor in Princes pallace thou doe sitt:
(And yet is Princes pallace the most fitt)
Ne brest of baser birth⁸ doth thee embrace.
Then make thee winges of thine aspyring wit,°   *mind*
And, whence thou camst, flye backe to heaven apace.

CUDDIE

85 Ah Percy it is all to° weake and wanne,   *too*
So high to sore,° and make so large a flight: *soar*
Her peecèd pyneons bene not so in plight,
For Colin fittes such famous flight to scanne:⁹
He, were he not with love so ill bedight,°   *afflicted*
90 Would mount as high, and sing as soote° as Swanne.¹   *sweet*

PIERS

Ah fon,° for love does teach him climbe so hie,   *fool*
And lyftes him up out of the loathsome myre:
Such immortall mirrhor,² as he doth admire,
Would rayse ones mynd above the starry skie.

---

3. "In manhoode and chevalrie" [E. K.].
4. "He sheweth the cause, why Poetes were wont be had in such honor of noble men; that is, that by them their worthines and valor shold through theyr famous Posies be commended to al posterities" [E. K.].
5. "He sheweth the cause of contempt of Poetry to be idlenesse and basenesse of mynd" [E. K.].
6. Coop, cage. That is, poets found nothing worthy to write of, and the spirit of heroic achievement (sun-bright honor) found expression neither in deeds nor in song.
7. "An Ironicall Sarcasmus, spoken in derision of these rude wits, whych make more account of a ryming rybaud, then of skill grounded upon learning and judgment" [E. K.].
8. "The meaner sort of men" [E. K.].
9. Cuddie explains that the imperfect, patched wings ("peecèd pyneons") of his own poetic powers are not in condition, but that it is proper for ("fittes") Colin to attempt ("scanne") such a high poetic flight.
1. "It is sayd of the learned that the swan a little before hir death, singeth most pleasantly" [E. K.].
2. "Beauty, which is an excellent object of Poeticall spirites" [E. K.].

95 And cause a caytive corage³ to aspire,
For lofty love doth loath a lowly eye.

CUDDIE

All otherwise the state of Poet stands,
For lordly love is such a Tyranne fell:°   *fierce*
That where he rules, all power he doth expell.
100 The vaunted verse a vacant head demaundes,
Ne wont with crabbèd care the Muses dwell:
Unwisely weaves, that takes two webbes in hand.⁴

Who ever casts° to compasse° weightye prise,   *tries / attain*
And thinks to throwe out thondring words of threate:
105 Let powre in lavish cups and thriftie bitts of meate,
For Bacchus fruite is frend to Phoebus wise.⁵
And when with Wine the braine begins to sweate,
The nombers° flowe as fast as spring doth ryse.   *verses*

Thou kenst° not Percie howe the ryme should rage.   *knowest*
110 O if my temples were distaind° with wine,   *stained*
And girt in girlonds of wild Yvie⁶ twine,
How I could reare the Muse on stately stage,
And teache her tread aloft in buskin⁷ fine,
With queint Bellona⁸ in her equipage.°   *equipment; retinue*

115 But ah my corage cooles ere it be warme,
For thy,° content us in thys humble shade: *therefore*
Where no such troublous tydes° han us assayde,°   *times / assaulted*
Here we our slender pipes may safely charme.⁹

PIERS

And when my Gates shall han their bellies layd:¹
120 *Cuddie* shall have a Kidde to store his farme.

Cuddies Embleme

*Agitante calescimus illo &c.*²

1579

---

3. "A base and abject minde" [E. K.].
4. That is, the Muses are not accustomed ("wont") to dwell with those afflicted by love ("crabbèd care"); he is an unwise weaver who takes two pieces of cloth ("webbes") in hand at once.
5. That is, let him pour lavish drink but take only a little food, for wine ("Bacchus fruite") promotes poetry ("Phoebus"—Apollo—is the god of poetry).
6. Worn by followers of Bacchus. "He seemeth here to be ravished with a Poetical furie. For (if one rightly mark) the numbers rise so ful, and the verse groweth so big, that it seemeth he hath forgot the meanenesse of shepheards state and stile" [E. K.].
7. Buskins are boots worn by actors in classical tragedies—hence a symbol for tragedy.
8. "Strange Bellona; the goddesse of battaile, that is Pallas" [E. K.]. Pallas Athena, the Greek goddess of wisdom, is not normally identified with Bell, the Roman goddess of war, though she was often portrayed in armor.
9. "Temper and order" [E.K.].
1. That is, when my goats bear their young.
2. The Latin line, of which Spenser gives the first three words, is from Ovid's *Fasti* 6.5: "There is a god within us; it is from his stirring that we feel warm." E. K. comments, "Hereby is meant, as also in the whole course of this Aeglogue, that Poetry is a divine instinct and unnatural rage passing the reache of comen reason."

The Faerie Queene   In a letter to Sir Walter Ralegh, appended to the first, 1590 edition of *The Faerie Queene*, Spenser describes his exuberant, multifaceted poem as an allegory—an extended metaphor or "dark conceit"—and invites us to interpret the characters and adventures in its several books in terms of the particular virtues and vices they enact or come to embody. Thus the Redcrosse Knight in Book 1 is the knight of Holiness (and also Saint George, the patron saint of England); Sir Guyon in Book 2 is the knight of Temperance; the female knight Britomart in Book 3 is the knight of Chastity ("chastity" here meaning chaste love leading to marriage). The heroes of Books 4, 5, and 6 represent Friendship, Justice, and Courtesy. The poem's general end, Spenser writes, is "to fashion a gentleman or noble person in vertuous and gentle discipline," and the individual moral qualities, taken together, constitute the ideal human being.

However, Spenser's allegory is not as straightforward as the letter to Ralegh might suggest, and the fashioning of identity proves to be anything but simple. Far from being the static embodiments of abstract moral precepts, the knights have a surprisingly complex, altogether human relation to their allegorical identities, identities into which they grow only through painful trial and error in the course of their adventures. These adventures repeatedly take the form of mortal combat with sworn enemies—hence the Christian Redcrosse Knight smites the "Saracen" (that is, Muslim) Sansfoy (literally, "Without faith")—but the enemies are revealed more often than not to be weirdly dissociated aspects of the knights themselves: when he encounters Sansfoy, Redcrosse has just been faithless to his lady, Una, and his most dangerous enemy ultimately proves to be his own despair. Accordingly, the meaning of the various characters, episodes, and places is richly complex, revealed to us (and to the characters themselves) only by degrees.

The complexity is heightened by the inclusion, in addition to the moral allegory, of a historical allegory to which Spenser calls attention in the letter to Ralegh; there he observes that both the Faerie Queene and another character, Belphoebe, are representations of Queen Elizabeth. (In fact, they are only two among many oblique representations of Elizabeth.) Throughout the poem there is a dense network of allusions to events, issues, and particular persons in England and the rest of the British Isles—for example, the queen's rival Mary, Queen of Scots, the Spanish Armada, the English Reformation, the controversies over religious images, and the bitter colonial struggles against Irish rebellion. Some of Spenser's characters are identified by conventional symbols and attributes that would have been obvious to readers of his time. For example, they would know immediately that a woman who wears a miter and scarlet clothes and who dwells near the river Tiber represents (in one sense at least) the Roman Catholic Church, which had often been identified by Protestant preachers with the Whore of Babylon in the book of Revelation. Marginal notes jotted in early copies of *The Faerie Queene* suggest, however, that there was no consensus among Spenser's contemporaries about the precise historical referents of other of the poem's myriad figures. (Sir Walter Ralegh's wife, Bess, for example, seems to have identified many of the virtuous female characters as allegorical representations of herself.) Spenser's poem may be enjoyed as a fascinating story with multiple meanings, a story that works on several levels at once and continually eludes the full and definitive allegorical explanation it constantly promises to deliver.

The poem is also an epic. In moving from *The Shepheardes Calender* to *The Faerie Queene*, Spenser deliberately fashioned himself after the great Roman poet Virgil, who began his poetic career with pastoral poetry and moved on to his epic poem, the *Aeneid*. Spenser was acutely conscious that poets elsewhere in Europe, such as Ariosto and Tasso in Italy and Camões in Portugal, had already produced works modeled on Virgil's, in celebration of their respective nations. In drawing on the British legends of Saint George and King Arthur, weaving together classical and medieval sources, and adapting whole episodes from Ariosto and Tasso, Spenser was providing his country with the epic it had lacked.

Like Virgil, Spenser is deeply concerned with the dangerous struggles and painful renunciations required to attain the highest goals. The heroic deeds of his brave knights are the achievements of individual aristocratic men and women, not the triumphs of armies or communities united in serving a common purpose—not even the triumph of the virtually invisible royal court of Gloriana, the Faerie Queene. Yet, taken together, the disjointed adventures of these solitary warriors constitute in Spenser's fervent vision the glory of Britain, the collective memory of its heroic past, and the promise of a still more glorious future. And if the Faerie Queene herself is consigned to the margins of the poem that bears her name, she nonetheless is the symbolic embodiment of a shared national destiny, a destiny that reaches beyond mere political success to participate in the ultimate, millennial triumph of good over evil.

If *The Faerie Queene* is thus an epic celebration of Queen Elizabeth, the Protestant faith, and the English nation, it is also a chivalric romance, full of jousting knights and damsels in distress, dragons, witches, enchanted trees, wicked magicians, giants, dark caves, shining castles, and non-Christian "paynims" or heathens (with French names). A clear, pleasant stream may be dangerous, weakening those who drink its water. A pious hermit may prove to be a cunningly disguised villain. Houses, castles, and gardens are often places of education and challenge or of especially dense allegorical significance, as if they possessed special, half-hidden keys to the meaning of the books in which they appear. As a romance, Spenser's poem is designed to produce wonder, to enthrall its readers with sprawling plots, marvelous adventures, heroic characters, ravishing descriptions, and esoteric mysteries.

In addition to enthralling its readers, the poem habitually entraps, misleads, and deludes them. Like Spenser's protagonists, readers are constantly in danger of mistaking hypocritical evil for good, or cunningly disguised foulness for true beauty. *The Faerie Queene* demands vigilance from its readers, and many passages must be reread in light of what follows after. In some sections, such as the dialogue between Redcrosse and Despaire (Book 1, canto 9), the repeated use of pronouns instead of proper names can lead to confusion as to who is speaking; the effect is intentional, for the promptings of evil are not always easy to disentangle from the voice of conscience.

The whole of *The Faerie Queene* is written in a remarkable nine-line stanza of closely interlocking rhymes (*ababbcbcc*), the first eight lines each with five stresses (iambic pentameter) and the final line with six stresses (iambic hexameter or alexandrine). The stanza gives the work a certain formal regularity, but the various books are composed on quite different structural principles. Book 1 is almost entirely self-contained; it has been called a miniature epic in itself, centering on the adventures of one principal hero, Redcrosse, who at length achieves the quest he undertakes at Una's behest: killing the dragon who has imprisoned her parents and thereby winning her as his bride. The spiritual allegory is similarly self-contained; it presents the Christian struggling heroically against many evils and temptations—doctrinal error, hypocrisy, the Seven Deadly Sins, and despair—to some of which he succumbs before finally emerging triumphant. It shows him separated from the one true faith and, aided by interventions of divine grace, at length reunited with it.

Spenser had outlined a plan for an immense poem twelve or even twenty-four books in length, but he died before he could bring this project anywhere near completion. To some degree a lack of closure characterizes all of *The Faerie Queene*, including the more self-contained of the six finished books, and it is fitting that there survives the fragment of another book, the cantos of Mutabilitie (see below), in which Spenser broods on the tension in nature between systematic order and ceaseless change. The poem as a whole is built around principles that pull tautly against one another: a commitment to a life of constant struggle and a profound longing for rest; a celebration of human heroism and a perception of ineradicable human sinfulness; a vision of evil as a terrifyingly potent force and a vision of evil as mere emptiness and filth; a faith in the supreme value of visionary art and a recurrent suspicion that art is dangerously allied to graven images and deception. That Spenser's knights never quite reach the havens they seek reflects the irresolvable tensions to which we owe much of the power and beauty of this great, unfinished work.

From The Faerie Queene

A Letter of the Authors[1]

EXPOUNDING HIS WHOLE INTENTION IN THE COURSE OF THIS WORKE: WHICH FOR THAT IT GIVETH GREAT LIGHT TO THE READER, FOR THE BETTER UNDERSTANDING IS HEREUNTO ANNEXED

To the Right noble, and Valorous, Sir Walter Raleigh knight, Lo. Wardein of the Stanneryes,[2] and her Majesties liefetenaunt of the County of Cornewayll

Sir knowing how doubtfully all Allegories may be construed, and this booke of mine, which I have entituled the *Faery Queene*, being a continued Allegory, or darke conceit,[3] I have thought good as well for avoyding of gealous opinions and misconstructions, as also for your better light in reading thereof, (being so by you commanded,) to discover unto you the general intention and meaning, which in the whole course thereof I have fashioned, without expressing of any particular purposes or by-accidents[4] therein occasioned. The generall end therefore of all the booke is to fashion a gentleman or noble person in vertuous and gentle[5] discipline: Which for that I conceived shoulde be most plausible and pleasing, being coloured with an historicall fiction, the which the most part of men delight to read, rather for variety of matter, then for profite of the ensample:[6] I chose the historye of King Arthure, as most fitte for the excellency of his person, being made famous by many mens former workes, and also furthest from the daunger of envy, and suspition of present time.[7] In which I have followed all the antique Poets historicall,[8] first

---

1. The Letter was appended—not prefixed—to the 1590 edition of the poem. (It was omitted from the 1596 edition.) We follow the common practice of printing it as a "preface" to the work.
2. That is, the mining districts of Cornwall and Devon. "Lo.": Lord.
3. Obscure or difficult poetic figure.
4. Secondary matters.
5. Pertaining to a gentleman. "Fashion": (1) to represent; (2) to educate.
6. Example. "Then": than.
7. That is, free from current political controversy.
8. That is, epic.

Homere, who in the Persons of Agamemnon and Ulysses hath ensampled a good governour and a vertuous man, the one in his *Ilias*, the other in his *Odysseis:* then Virgil, whose like intention was to doe in the person of Aeneas: after him Ariosto comprised them both in his Orlando: and lately Tasso dissevered them againe, and formed both parts in two persons, namely that part which they in Philosophy call Ethice, or vertues of a private man, coloured in his Rinaldo: The other named Politice in his Godfredo.[9] By ensample of which excellente Poets, I labour to pourtraict in Arthure, before he was king, the image of a brave knight, perfected in the twelve private morall vertues, as Aristotle hath devised,[1] the which is the purpose of these first twelve bookes: which if I finde to be well accepted, I may be perhaps encouraged, to frame the other part of polliticke vertues in his person, after that hee came to be king. To some I know this Methode will seeme displeasaunt, which had rather have good discipline[2] delivered plainly in way of precepts, or sermoned at large, as they use, then thus clowdily enwrapped in Allegoricall devises. But such, me seeme, should be satisfide with the use of these dayes, seeing all things accounted by their showes,[3] and nothing esteemed of, that is not delightfull and pleasing to commune sence.[4] For this cause is Xenophon preferred before Plato, for that the one in the exquisite depth of his judgment, formed a Commune welth such as it should be, but the other in the person of Cyrus and the Persians fashioned a governement such as might best be:[5] So much more profitable and gratious is doctrine by ensample, then by rule. So have I laboured to doe in the person of Arthure: whome I conceive after his long education by Timon, to whom he was by Merlin delivered to be brought up, so soone as he was borne of the Lady Igrayne, to have seene in a dream or vision the Faery Queen, with whose excellent beauty ravished, he awaking resolved to seeke her out, and so being by Merlin armed, and by Timon throughly[6] instructed, he went to seeke her forth in Faerye land. In that Faery Queene I meane glory in my generall intention, but in my particular I conceive the most excellent and glorious person of our soveraine the Queene, and her kingdome in Faery land. And yet in some places els, I doe otherwise shadow[7] her. For considering she beareth two persons, the one of a most royall Queene or Empresse, the other of a most vertuous and beautifull Lady, this latter part in some places I doe express in Belphoebe, fashioning her name according to your owne excellent conceipt of Cynthia,[8] (Phoebe and Cynthia being both names of Diana.[9]) So in the person of Prince Arthure I sette forth magnificence in particular, which vertue for that (according to Aristotle and the rest) it is the perfection of all

---

9. Torquato Tasso (1544–1595) published his chivalric romance *Rinaldo* in 1562 and completed the epic *Gerusalemme liberata* (centered on the heroic figure of Count Godfredo) in 1575. Lodovico Ariosto (1474–1533) was author of the epic romance *Orlando furioso*, first published in 1516.
1. Though Aristotle distinguished between private and public virtues, he did not devise lists of twelve of each. Spenser was in fact relying on more modern philosophers—his friend Lodowick Bryskett and the Italian Alessandro Piccolomini. That Spenser contemplated (as he proceeds to indicate) a poem four times as long as the six books we now have rather staggers the imagination.
2. Teaching.
3. That is, judged according to their appearances.
4. The notions of the many.
5. The allusion is to Plato's *Republic* and Xenophon's *Cyropaedia*.
6. Thoroughly.
7. Picture, portray.
8. Ralegh's poem "The Ocean to Cynthia" praised Queen Elizabeth.
9. In classical mythology, goddess of the moon.

the rest,[1] and conteineth in it them all, therefore in the whole course I mention the deedes of Arthure applyable to that vertue, which I write of in that booke. But of the xii. other vertues, I make xii. other knights the patrones, for the more variety of the history. Of which these three bookes contayn three, The first of the knight of the Redcrosse, in whome I expresse Holynes: The seconde of Sir Guyon, in whome I sette forth Temperaunce: The third of Britomartis a Lady knight, in whome I picture Chastity. But because the beginning of the whole worke seemeth abrupte and as depending upon other antecedents,[2] it needs that ye know the occasion of these three knights severall adventures. For the Methode of a Poet historical is not such, as of an Historiographer.[3] For an Historiographer discourseth of affayres orderly as they were donne, accounting as well the times as the actions, but a Poet thrusteth into the middest,[4] even where it most concerneth him, and there recoursing to the thinges forepaste,[5] and divining of things to come, maketh a pleasing Analysis of all. The beginning therefore of my history, if it were to be told by an Historiographer, should be the twelfth booke, which is the last, where I devise that the Faery Queene kept her Annuall feaste xii. dayes, uppon which xii. severall dayes, the occasions of the xii. severall adventures hapned, which being undertaken by xii. severall knights, are in these xii books severally handled and discoursed. The first was this. In the beginning of the feaste, there presented him selfe a tall clownishe[6] younge man, who falling before the Queen of Faeries desired a boone (as the manner then was) which during that feast she might not refuse: which was that hee might have the atchievement of any adventure, which during that feaste should happen: that being graunted, he rested him on the floore, unfitte through his rusticity for a better place. Soone after entred a faire Ladye in mourning weedes, riding on a white Asse, with a dwarfe behind her leading a warlike steed, that bore the Armes of a knight, and his speare in the dwarfes hand. Shee falling before the Queene of Faeries, complayned that her father and mother an ancient King and Queene, had bene by an huge dragon many years shut up in a brasen Castle, who thence suffred them not to yssew:[7] and therefore besought the Faery Queene to assygne her some one of her knights to take on him that exployt. Presently[8] that clownish person upstarting, desired that adventure: whereat the Queene much wondering, and the Lady much gainesaying, yet he earnestly importuned his desire. In the end the Lady told him that unlesse that armour which she brought, would serve him (that is the armour of a Christian man specified by Saint Paul v. Ephes.[9]) that he could not succeed in that enterprise, which being forthwith put upon him with dewe furnitures[1] thereunto, he seemed the goodliest man in

---

1. For Aristotle, magnanimity ("magnificence" in Spenser)—greatness of soul—is the ultimate virtue.
2. Earlier events.
3. Historian.
4. Referring to the critical dictum that epic should begin, as the Roman poet Horace said, *in medias res*—"in the middle of things" (*Art of Poetry*, lines 147–48).
5. Past.
6. Rustic-looking.
7. Come forth.
8. Immediately.
9. Ephesians 6:11, "Put on the whole armor of God, that ye may be able to stand against the wiles of the devil." The parts (verses 14 to 17) are loins girt about with truth, breastplate of righteousness, feet shod with the gospel of peace, shield of faith "wherewith ye shall be able to quench all the fiery darts of the wicked," helmet of salvation, and "sword of the Spirit, which is the word of God."
1. Suitable equipment.

al that company, and was well liked of the Lady. And eftesoones[2] taking on him knighthood, and mounting on that straunge Courser, he went forth with her on that adventure: where beginneth the first booke, vz.

   A gentle knight was pricking on the playne. &c.

 The second day ther came in a Palmer[3] bearing an Infant with bloody hands, whose Parents he complained to have bene slayn by an Enchaunteresse called Acrasia: and therfore craved of the Faery Queene, to appoint him some knight, to performe that adventure, which being assigned to Sir Guyon, he presently went forth with that same Palmer: which is the beginning of the second booke and the whole subject thereof. The third day there came in, a Groome who complained before the Faery Queene, that a vile Enchaunter called Busirane had in hand a most faire Lady called Amoretta, whom he kept in most grievous torment, because she would not yield him the pleasure of her body. Whereupon Sir Scudamour the lover of that Lady presently tooke on him that adventure. But being unable to performe it by reason of the hard Enchauntments, after long sorrow, in the end met with Britomartis, who succoured him, and reskewed his love.

 But by occasion hereof, many other adventures are intermedled, but rather as Accidents, then intendments.[4] As the love of Britomart, the overthrow of Marinell, the misery of Florimell, the vertuousnes of Belphoebe, the lasciviousnes of Hellenora, and many the like.

 Thus much Sir, I have briefly overronne[5] to direct your understanding to the wel-head of the History, that from thence gathering the whole intention of the conceit,[6] ye may as in a handfull gripe al the discourse, which otherwise may happily[7] seeme tedious and confused. So humbly craving the continuaunce of your honorable favour towards me, and th' eternall establishment of your happines, I humbly take leave.

                  23. January, 1589[8]
                Yours most humbly affectionate.
                       ED. SPENSER.

---

2. Forthwith.
3. *Pilgrim.*
4. That is, there are episodes that are not part of these principal stories.
5. Run through, summarized.
6. Conception.
7. Perhaps.
8. The date is actually 1590, because until England adopted the Gregorian calendar in 1752, the new year began on March 25.

The First Booke of The Faerie Queene

*Contayning
The Legende of the
Knight of the Red Crosse, or
Of Holinesse*

1

Lo I the man, whose Muse whilome did maske,
   As time her taught, in lowly Shepheards weeds,[1]
Am now enforst a far unfitter taske,
For trumpets sterne to chaunge mine Oaten reeds,[2]
And sing of Knights and Ladies gentle° deeds;   *noble*
Whose prayses having slept in silence long,[3]
Me, all too meane,° the sacred Muse areeds°   *low / counsels*
To blazon° broad emongst her learned throng: *proclaim*
Fierce warres and faithfull loves shall moralize[4] my song.

2

Helpe then, O holy Virgin chiefe of nine,[5]
   Thy weaker° Novice to performe thy will,   *too weak*
Lay forth out of thine everlasting scryne°   *a chest for papers*
The antique rolles, which there lye hidden still,
Of Faerie knights and fairest Tanaquill,°   *Gloriana*
Whom that most noble Briton Prince[6] so long
Sought through the world, and suffered so much ill,
That I must rue° his undeserved wrong: *pity*
O helpe thou my weake wit, and sharpen my dull tong.

3

And thou most dreaded impe° of highest Jove,   *offspring*
   Faire Venus sonne,° that with thy cruell dart   *Cupid*
At that good knight so cunningly didst rove,°   *shoot*
That glorious fire it kindled in his hart,
Lay now thy deadly Heben° bow apart,   *ebony*
And with thy mother milde come to mine ayde:
Come both, and with you bring triumphant Mart,[7]
In loves and gentle jollities arrayd,
After his murdrous spoiles and bloudy rage allayd.

4

And with them eke,° O Goddesse heavenly bright,   *also*
   Mirrour of grace and Majestie divine,

---

1. Garb. The poet appeared before ("whilome") as a writer of humble pastoral (that is, *The Shepheardes Calender*). These lines are imitated from the verses prefixed to Renaissance editions of Virgil's *Aeneid*.
2. To write heroic poetry, of which the trumpet is a symbol, instead of pastoral poetry symbolized by the humble shepherd's pipe ("Oaten reeds").
3. This and the preceding line are imitated from the opening of Ariosto's *Orlando furioso*.
4. Provide subjects for moralizing.
5. Scholars have debated whether the reference is to Clio, the Muse of history, or to Calliope, the Muse of epic.
6. That is, Arthur, named in canto 9, stanza 6.
7. Mars, god of war and lover of Venus.

Great Lady of the greatest Isle, whose light
Like Phoebus lampe throughout the world doth shine,
Shed thy faire beames into my feeble eyne,°   *eyes*
And raise my thoughts too humble and too vile,°   *lowly*
To thinke of that true glorious type[8] of thine,
The argument° of mine afflicted stile:°   *subject / humble work*
The which to heare, vouchsafe, O dearest dred° a-while.   *object of awe*

Canto 1

The Patron of true Holinesse,
Foule Errour doth defeate:
Hypocrisie him to entrappe,
Doth to his home entreate.

1

A Gentle Knight was pricking° on the plaine,   *spurring*
  Ycladd[9] in mightie armes and silver shielde,
Wherein old dints of deepe wounds did remaine,
  The cruell markes of many a bloudy fielde;
  Yet armes till that time did he never wield:
His angry steede did chide his foming bitt,
  As much disdayning to the curbe to yield:
Full jolly° knight he seemd, and faire did sitt,   *gallant*
As one for knightly giusts° and fierce encounters fitt.   *jousts, tourneys*

2

But on his brest a bloudie Crosse he bore,
  The deare remembrance of his dying Lord,
For whose sweete sake that glorious badge he wore,
  And dead as living ever him adored:[1]
  Upon his shield the like was also scored,°   *incised*
For soveraine[2] hope, which in his helpe he had:
  Right faithfull true[3] he was in deede and word,
But of his cheere[4] did seeme too solemne sad;°   *grave*
Yet nothing did he dread, but ever was ydrad.°   *dreaded, feared*

3

Upon a great adventure he was bond,
  That greatest Gloriana to him gave,
That greatest Glorious Queene of Faerie Lond,
  To winne him worship,° and her grace to have,   *honor*

---

8. That is, Gloriana is the "type" (prefiguration) of Queen Elizabeth.
9. Imitating Chaucerian English, Spenser sometimes uses the prefix *y* as the sign of a past participle.
1. A compressed reference to Revelation 1:18: "I am he that liveth, and was dead; and, behold, I am alive for evermore."
2. Having greatest power (often applied to medical remedies).
3. Compare Revelation 19:11: "And I saw heaven opened, and behold a white horse; and he that sat upon him was called Faithful and True."
4. Facial expression; mood.

Which of all earthly things he most did crave;
    And ever as he rode, his hart did earne°   *yearn*
    To prove his puissance° in battell brave   *might*
    Upon his foe, and his new force to learne;
Upon his foe, a Dragon horrible and stearne.

4

A lovely Ladie rode him faire beside,
    Upon a lowly Asse more white then° snow,   *than*
    Yet she much whiter, but the same did hide
    Under a vele, that wimpled° was full low,   *lying in folds*
    And over all a blacke stole° she did throw,   *long robe*
    As one that inly° mournd: so was she sad,   *inwardly*
    And heavie sat upon her palfrey slow:
    Seemèd in heart some hidden care she had,
And by her in a line° a milke white lambe she lad.   *on a leash*

5

So pure an innocent, as that same lambe,
    She was in life and every vertuous lore,
    And by descent from Royall lynage came
    Of ancient Kings and Queenes, that had of yore
    Their scepters stretcht from East to Westerne shore,
    And all the world in their subjection held;
    Till that infernall feend with foule uprore
    Forwasted° all their land, and them expeld: *laid waste*
Whom to avenge, she had this Knight from far compeld.°   *summoned*

6

Behind her farre away a Dwarfe did lag,
    That lasie seemd in being ever last,
    Or wearièd with bearing of her bag
    Of needments at his backe. Thus as they past,
    The day with cloudes was suddeine overcast,
    And angry Jove an hideous storme of raine
    Did poure into his Lemans[5] lap so fast,
    That every wight° to shrowd° it did constrain,   *creature / take shelter*
And this faire couple eke° to shroud themselves were fain.°   *also / eager*

7

Enforst to seeke some covert° nigh at hand,   *cover, shelter*
    A shadie grove not far away they spide,
    That promist ayde the tempest to withstand:
    Whose loftie trees yclad with sommers pride,
    Did spred so broad, that heavens light did hide,
    Not perceable° with power of any starre: *penetrable*

---

5. His lover's (that is, the earth's).

And all within were pathes and alleies wide,
  With footing worne, and leading inward farre:
Faire harbour that them seemes; so in they entred arre.

8

And foorth they passe, with pleasure forward led,
  Joying to heare the birdes sweete harmony,
  Which therein shrouded from the tempest dred,°   *fearful*
  Seemd in their song to scorne the cruell sky.
  Much can° they prayse the trees, so straight and hy,   *did*
  The sayling[6] Pine, the Cedar proud and tall,
  The vine-prop Elme, the Poplar never dry,
  The builder Oake, sole king of forrests all,
The Aspine good for staves, the Cypresse funerall.°   *funereal*

9

The Laurell, meed° of mightie Conquerours   *reward*
  And Poets sage, the Firre that weepeth still,[7]
  The Willow worne of forlorne Paramours,
  The Eugh° obedient to the benders will,   *yew*
  The Birch for shaftes, the Sallow° for the mill,   *willow*
  The Mirrhe sweete bleeding in the bitter wound,
  The warlike Beech, the Ash for nothing ill,
  The fruitfull Olive, and the Platane° round,   *plane tree*
The carver Holme,[8] the Maple seeldom inward sound.

10

Led with delight, they thus beguile the way,
  Untill the blustring storme is overblowne;
  When weening° to returne, whence they did stray,   *thinking*
  They cannot finde that path, which first was showne,
  But wander too and fro in wayes unknowne,
  Furthest from end then, when they neerest weene,
  That makes them doubt, their wits be not their owne:
  So many pathes, so many turnings seene,
That which of them to take, in diverse doubt they been.

11

At last resolving forward still to fare,
  Till that some end they finde or° in or out,   *either*
  That path they take, that beaten seemed most bare,
  And like to lead the labyrinth about°   *out of*
  Which when by tract° they hunted had throughout,   *track; tracing*
  At length it brought them to a hollow cave,
  Amid the thickest woods. The Champion stout

---

6. Either because pine was used for ships or because of the tree's soaring height.
7. That is, exudes resin continuously. Spenser in these stanzas imitates Chaucer's catalog of trees in the *Parliament of Fowls*; the convention goes back to Ovid.
8. Holly or holm oak, both suitable for carving.

Eftsoones° dismounted from his courser brave,   *at once*
And to the Dwarfe a while his needlesse spere[9] he gave.

12

"Be well aware,"° quoth then that Ladie milde,   *watchful*
  "Least suddaine mischiefe° ye too rash provoke: *misfortune*
  The danger hid, the place unknowne and wilde,
  Breedes dreadfull doubts: Oft fire is without smoke,
  And perill without show: therefore your stroke
  Sir knight with-hold, till further triall made."
  "Ah Ladie," said he, "shame were to revoke°   *draw back*
  The forward footing for° an hidden shade: *because of*
Vertue gives her selfe light, through darkenesse for to wade."

13

"Yea but," quoth she, "the perill of this place
  I better wot then° you, though now too late   *know than*
  To wish you backe returne with foule disgrace,
  Yet wisedome warnes, whilest foot is in the gate,
  To stay the stepe, ere forcèd to retrate.
  This is the wandring wood, this Errours den,
  A monster vile, whom God and man does hate:
  Therefore I read° beware." "Fly fly," quoth then   *advise*
The fearefull Dwarfe: "this is no place for living men."

14

But full of fire and greedy hardiment,°   *boldness*
  The youthfull knight could not for ought° be staide,   *anything*
  But forth unto the darksome hole he went,
  And lookèd in: his glistring° armor made   *shining*
  A litle glooming light, much like a shade,
  By which he saw the ugly monster plaine,
  Halfe like a serpent horribly displaide,
  But th' other halfe did womans shape retaine,
Most lothsom, filthie, foule, and full of vile disdaine.[1]

15

And as she lay upon the durtie ground,
  Her huge long taile her den all overspred,
  Yet was in knots and many boughtes° upwound,   *coils*
  Pointed with mortall sting. Of her there bred
  A thousand yong ones, which she dayly fed,
  Sucking upon her poisonous dugs, eachone
  Of sundry shapes, yet all ill favorèd:
  Soone as that uncouth° light upon them shone,   *unfamiliar*
Into her mouth they crept, and suddain all were gone.

---

9. Needless because the spear is used only on horseback.
1. Loathsomeness. The description echoes both classical and biblical monsters (see Revelation 9:7–10).

16

Their dam upstart, out of her den efrraide,°   *alarmed*
  And rushèd forth, hurling her hideous taile
  About her cursèd head, whose folds displaid°   *extended*
Were stretcht now forth at length without entraile.°   *coiling*
  She lookt about, and seeing one in mayle
  Armèd to point,° sought backe to turne againe;   *completely*
  For light she hated as the deadly bale,°   *injury*
  Ay wont° in desert darknesse to remain,   *ever accustomed*
Where plaine none might her see, nor she see any plaine.

17

Which when the valiant Elfe[2] perceived, he lept
  As Lyon fierce upon the flying pray,
  And with his trenchand° blade her boldly kept   *cutting*
From turning backe, and forcèd her to stay:
  Therewith enraged she loudly gan to bray,
  And turning fierce, her speckled taile advaunst;
  Threatning her angry sting, him to dismay:°   *defeat*
  Who nought aghast, his mightie hand enhaunst:°   *lifted up*
The stroke down from her head unto her shoulder glaunst.

18

Much daunted with that dint,° her sence was dazd,   *blow*
  Yet kindling rage, her selfe she gathered round,
  And all attonce her beastly body raizd
With doubled forces high above the ground:
  Tho° wrapping up her wrethèd sterne° arownd,   *then / tail*
  Lept fierce upon his shield, and her huge traine°   *tail*
  All suddenly about his body wound,
  That hand or foot to stirre he strove in vaine:
God helpe the man so wrapt in Errours endlesse traine.

19

His Lady sad to see his sore constraint,
  Cride out, "Now now Sir knight, shew what ye bee,
  Add faith unto your force, and be not faint:
Strangle her, else she sure will strangle thee."
  That when he heard, in great perplexitie,[3]
  His gall did grate[4] for griefe° and high disdaine,   *wrath*
  And knitting all his force got one hand free,
  Wherewith he grypt her gorge° with so great paine,   *throat*
That soone to loose her wicked bands did her constraine.

---

2. That is, knight of Faerie Land.
3. In both the usual sense and the sense of "entangled condition."
4. That is, his gallbladder (considered the seat of anger) was violently disturbed.

20

Therewith she spewd out of her filthy maw
  A floud of poyson horrible and blacke,
  Full of great lumpes of flesh and gobbets raw,
  Which stunck so vildly, that it forst him slacke
  His grasping hold, and from her turne him backe:
  Her vomit full of bookes and papers was,[5]
  With loathly frogs and toades, which eyes did lacke,
  And creeping sought way in the weedy gras:
Her filthy parbreake° all the place defilèd has.[6]   *vomit*

21

As when old father Nilus° gins to swell   *the Nile River*
  With timely° pride above the Aegyptian vale,   *in season*
  His fattie° waves do fertile slime outwell,°   *rich / pour forth*
  And overflow each plaine and lowly dale:
  But when his later spring gins to avale,°   *subside*
  Huge heapes of mudd he leaves, wherein there breed
  Ten thousand kindes of creatures, partly male
  And partly female of his fruitfull seed;
Such ugly monstrous shapes elswhere may no man reed.°   *see*

22

The same so sore annoyed° has the knight,   *injuriously affected*
  That welnigh chokèd with the deadly stinke,
  His forces faile, ne° can no longer fight.   *nor*
  Whose corage when the feend perceived to shrinke,
  She pourèd forth out of her hellish sinke[7]
  Her fruitfull cursèd spawne of serpents small,
  Deformèd monsters, fowle, and blacke as inke,
  Which swarming all about his legs did crall,
And him encombred sore, but could not hurt at all.

23

As gentle Shepheard in sweete even-tide,
  When ruddy Phoebus° gins to welke° in west,   *the sun / sink*
  High on an hill, his flocke to vewen wide,
  Markes° which do byte their hasty supper best;   *observes*
  A cloud of combrous° gnattes do him molest,   *encumbering*
  All striving to infixe their feeble stings,
  That from their noyance he no where can rest,
  But with his clownish° hands their tender wings   *rustic*
He brusheth oft, and oft doth mar their murmurings.

---

5. Alluding (at one level) to books and pamphlets of Catholic propaganda, notably attacks on Queen Elizabeth.
6. Revelation 16:13: "And I saw three unclean spirits like frogs come out of the mouth of the dragon, and out of the mouth of the beast, and out of the mouth of the false prophet."
7. Cesspool (that is, her womb or organ of excretion).

24

Thus ill bestedd,° and fearful more of shame,   *situated*
  Then of the certaine perill he stood in,
  Halfe furious unto his foe he came,
  Resolved in minde all suddenly to win,
  Or soone to lose, before he once would lin;°   *cease*
  And strooke at her with more then manly force,
  That from her body full of filthie sin
  He raft° her hatefull head without remorse;   *cut away*
A streame of cole black bloud forth gushèd from her corse.°   *corpse*

25

Her scattred brood, soone as their Parent deare
  They saw so rudely° falling to the ground,   *with great force*
  Groning full deadly, all with troublous feare,
  Gathred themselves about her body round,
  Weening° their wonted entrance to have found   *thinking*
  At her wide mouth: but being there withstood
  They flockèd all about her bleeding wound,
  And suckèd up their dying mothers blood,
Making her death their life, and eke° her hurt their good.   *also*

26

That detestable sight him much amazde,°   *stunned*
  To see th'unkindly Impes° of heaven accurst,   *unnatural offspring*
  Devoure their dam; on whom while so he gazd,
  Having all satisfide their bloudy thurst,
  Their bellies swolne he saw with fulnesse burst,
  And bowels gushing forth: well worthy end
  Of such as drunke her life, the which them nurst;
  Now needeth him no lenger° labour spend,   *longer*
His foes have slaine themselves, with whom he should contend.

27

His Ladie seeing all, that chaunst, from farre
  Approcht in hast to greet° his victorie,   *congratulate*
  And said, "Faire knight, borne under happy starre,
  Who see your vanquisht foes before you lye;
  Well worthy be you of that Armorie,°   *armor*
  Wherein ye have great glory wonne this day,
  And prooved your strength on a strong enimie,
  Your first adventure: many such I pray,
And henceforth ever wish, that like succeed it may."

28

Then mounted he upon his Steede againe,
  And with the Lady backward sought to wend;°   *go*
  That path he kept, which beaten was most plaine,

  Ne ever would to any by-way bend,
   But still did follow one unto the end,
   The which at last out of the wood them brought.
   So forward on his way (with God to frend)°   *with God as friend*
   He passèd forth, and new adventure sought;
  Long way he travelèd, before he heard of ought.°   *aught, anything*

29

  At length they chaunst to meet upon the way
   An agèd Sire, in long blacke weedes yclad,[8]
   His feete all bare, his beard all hoarie° gray,   *silvery*
   And by his belt his booke he hanging had;
   Sober he seemde, and very sagely sad,°   *grave*
   And to the ground his eyes were lowly bent,
   Simple in shew,° and voyde of malice bad,   *show*
   And all the way he prayèd, as he went,
  And often knockt his brest, as one that did repent.

30

  He faire the knight saluted, louting° low,   *bowing*
   Who faire him quited,° as that courteous was: *responded*
   And after askèd him, if he did know
   Of straunge adventures, which abroad did pas.
   "Ah my deare Sonne," quoth he, "how should, alas,
   Silly° old man, that lives in hidden cell,   *simple*
   Bidding his beades° all day for his trespas,   *saying his prayers*
   Tydings of warre and worldly trouble tell?
  With holy father sits not with such things to mell.[9]

31

  "But if of daunger which hereby doth dwell,
   And homebred evill ye desire to heare,
   Of a straunge man I can you tidings tell,
   That wasteth° all this countrey farre and neare."   *lays waste to*
   "Of such," said he, "I chiefly do inquere,
   And shall you well reward to shew the place,
   In which that wicked wight his dayes doth weare.°   *spend*
   For to all knighthood it is foule disgrace,
  That such a cursèd creature lives so long a space."

32

  "Far hence," quoth he, "in wastfull° wildernesse   *desolate*
   His dwelling is, by which no living wight°   *creature*
   May ever passe, but thorough° great distresse."   *through*
   "Now," sayd the Lady, "draweth toward night,
   And well I wote, that of your later° fight   *recent*

---

8. Dressed in long black garments.
9. That is, it is not fitting for a holy hermit to meddle ("mell") with such things.

    Ye all forwearied be: for what so strong,
        But wanting° rest will also want of might?   *lacking*
    The Sunne that measures heaven all day long,
At night doth baite° his steedes the Ocean waves emong.   *feed; refresh*

33

"Then with the Sunne take Sir, your timely rest,
    And with new day new worke at once begin:
    Untroubled night they say gives counsell best."
    "Right well Sir knight ye have advisèd bin,"
    Quoth then that agèd man; "the way to win
    Is wisely to advise:° now day is spent;   *take thought*
    Therefore with me ye may take up your In°   *lodging*
    For this same night." The knight was well content.
So with that godly father to his home they went.

34

A little lowly Hermitage it was,
    Downe in a dale, hard by° a forests side,   *close to*
    Far from resort° of people, that did pas   *access*
    In travell to and froe: a little wyde°   *apart*
    There was an holy Chappell edifyde,°   *built*
    Wherein the Hermite dewly wont° to say   *was accustomed*
    His holy things° each morne and eventyde: *prayers*
    Thereby a Christall streame did gently play,
Which from a sacred fountaine wellèd forth alway.

35

Arrivèd there, the little house they fill,
    Ne looke for entertainement,° where none was: *elegant provision*
    Rest is their feast, and all things at their will;
    The noblest mind the best contentment has.
    With faire discourse the evening so they pas:
    For that old man of pleasing wordes had store,
    And well could file° his tongue as smooth as glas;   *polish*
    He told of Saintes and Popes, and evermore
He strowd an *Ave-Mary*[1] after and before.

36

The drouping Night thus creepeth on them fast,
    And the sad humour° loading their eye liddes,   *heavy moisture*
    As messenger of Morpheus[2] on them cast
    Sweet slombring deaw, the which to sleepe them biddes.
    Unto their lodgings then his guestes he riddes:°   *leads*
    Where when all drownd in deadly sleepe° he findes,   *sleep like death*
    He to his study goes, and there amiddes

---

1. Hail Mary (Latin); that is, a Catholic prayer.
2. Here (as often) Morpheus, the classical god of dreams, is conflated with his father, Somnus, god of sleep.

His Magick bookes and artes of sundry kindes,
He seekes out mighty charmes, to trouble sleepy mindes.

37

Then choosing out few wordes most horrible
(Let none them read), thereof did verses frame,°   *make*
With which and other spelles like terrible,
He bade awake blacke Plutoes griesly Dame,³
And cursèd heaven, and spake reprochfull shame
Of highest God, the Lord of life and light;
A bold bad man, that dared to call by name
Great Gorgon,⁴ Prince of darknesse and dead night,
At which Cocytus quakes, and Styx is put to flight.

38

And forth he cald out of deepe darknesse dred
Legions of Sprights,° the which like little flyes⁵   *spirits*
Fluttring about his ever damnèd hed,
A-waite whereto their service he applyes,
To aide his friends, or fray° his enimies: *frighten*
Of those he chose out two, the falsest twoo,
And fittest for to forge true-seeming lyes;
The one of them he gave a message too,
The other by him selfe staide other worke to doo.

39

He making speedy way through spersèd° ayre,   *dispersed*
And through the world of waters wide and deepe,
To Morpheus house doth hastily repaire.
Amid the bowels of the earth full steepe,
And low, where dawning day doth never peepe,
His dwelling is; there Tethys° his wet bed   *the wife of Ocean*
Doth ever wash, and Cynthia⁶ still° doth steepe   *continually*
In silver deaw his ever-drouping hed,
Whiles sad° Night over him her mantle black doth spred.   *sober*

40

Whose double gates he findeth lockèd fast,
The one faire framed of burnisht Yvory,
The other all with silver overcast;
And wakefull dogges before them farre do lye,
Watching to banish Care their enimy,
Who oft is wont° to trouble gentle Sleepe.   *accustomed*
By them the Sprite doth passe in quietly,

---

3. Proserpine, as patron of witchcraft and wife of Pluto, god of the underworld.
4. Demogorgon, in some myths the progenitor of all the gods, so powerful that the mention of his name causes hell's rivers (Styx and Cocytus) to tremble.
5. The simile associates him with Beelzebub (Lord of Flies), the name given to "the prince of the devils."
6. Diana, as goddess of the moon.

And unto Morpheus comes, whom drownèd deepe
In drowsie fit he findes: of nothing he takes keepe.°   *notice*

41

And more, to lulle him in his slumber soft,
  A trickling streame from high rocke tumbling downe
  And ever-drizling raine upon the loft,°   *aloft, above*
  Mixt with a murmuring winde, much like the sowne°   *sound*
  Of swarming Bees, did cast him in a swowne:°   *swoon*
  No other noyse, nor peoples troublous cryes,
  As still° are wont t'annoy the wallèd towne,   *always*
  Might there be heard: but carelesse° Quiet lyes,   *free from care*
Wrapt in eternall silence farre from enemyes.[7]

42

The messenger approching to him spake,
  But his wast° wordes returnd to him in vaine: *wasted*
  So sound he slept, that nought mought° him awake.   *might*
  Then rudely he him thrust, and pusht with paine,°   *effort*
  Whereat he gan to stretch: but he againe
  Shooke him so hard, that forcèd him to speake.
  As one then in a dreame, whose dryer braine[8]
  Is tost with troubled sights and fancies° weake,   *fantasies*
He mumbled soft, but would not all his silence breake.

43

The Sprite then gan more boldly him to wake,
  And threatned unto him the dreaded name
  Of Hecate:° whereat he gan to quake,   *queen of Hades*
  And lifting up his lumpish° head, with blame   *heavy*
  Halfe angry askèd him, for what° he came.   *why*
  "Hither," quoth he, "me Archimago[9] sent,
  He that the stubborne Sprites can wisely tame,
  He bids thee to him send for his intent
A fit false dreame, that can delude the sleepers sent."°   *senses*

44

The God obayde, and calling forth straight way
  A diverse° dreame out of his prison darke,   *diverting, distracting*
  Delivered it to him, and downe did lay
  His heavie head, devoide of carefull carke,°   *anxious concerns*
  Whose sences all were straight benumbd and starke.[1]
  He backe returning by the Yvorie dore,[2]

---

7. Spenser is imitating descriptions of the caves of Morpheus in Chaucer (*Book of the Duchess*, lines 153–77) and of Somnus in Ovid (*Metamorphoses* 11.592–632).
8. According to the old physiology, elderly people and other light sleepers had too little moisture in the brain.
9. The name can be construed as meaning both "archmagician" and "architect of images."
1. Immediately ("straight") benumbed and paralyzed.
2. According to Homer (*Odyssey* 19.562–67) and Virgil (*Aeneid* 6.893–96), false dreams come through Sleep's ivory gate, true dreams through his gate of horn.

    Remounted up as light as chearefull Larke,
      And on his litle winges the dreame he bore
  In hast unto his Lord, where he him left afore.

45

Who all this while with charmes and hidden artes,
    Had made a Lady of that other Spright,
    And framed of liquid ayre her tender partes
    So lively,° and so like in all mens sight,   *lifelike*
    That weaker° sence it could have ravisht° quight: *too weak / entranced*
    The maker selfe for all his wondrous witt,
    Was nigh beguilèd° with so goodly sight: *deceived*
    Her all in white he clad, and over it
Cast a blacke stole, most like to seeme for Una[3] fit.°   *fitting*

46

Now when that ydle dreame was to him brought
    Unto that Elfin knight he bad him fly,
    Where he slept soundly void of evill thought
    And with false shewes abuse his fantasy,°   *imagination*
    In sort as° he him schoolèd privily: *in the way that*
    And that new creature borne without her dew,°   *unnaturally*
    Full of the makers guile, with usage sly
    He taught to imitate that Lady trew,
Whose semblance she did carrie under feignèd hew.°   *form*

47

Thus well instructed, to their worke they hast
    And comming where the knight in slomber lay
    The one upon his hardy head him plast,°   *placed*
    And made him dreame of loves and lustfull play,
    That nigh his manly hart did melt away,
    Bathèd in wanton blis and wicked joy:
    Then seemèd him his Lady by him lay,
    And to him playnd,° how that false wingèd boy°   *complained / Cupid*
Her chast hart had subdewd, to learne Dame pleasures toy.°   *lustful play*

48

And she her selfe of beautie soveraigne Queene,
    Faire Venus seemde unto his bed to bring
    Her, whom he waking evermore did weene°   *think*
    To be the chastest flowre, that ay° did spring   *ever*
    On earthly braunch, the daughter of a king,
    Now a loose Leman° to vile service bound: *paramour*
    And eke° the Graces seemèd all to sing,   *also*

---

3. Her name means "one, unity." Elizabethan readers would know the Latin phrase *Una Vera Fides* (One True Faith) and also the proverb "Truth is one."

> *Hymen iô Hymen*, dauncing all around,
> Whilst freshest Flora her with Yvie girlond crownd.[4]

49

> In this great passion of unwonted° lust, — *unaccustomed*
>   Or wonted feare of doing ought amis,
> He started up, as seeming to mistrust° — *suspect*
>   Some secret ill, or hidden foe of his:
> Lo there before his face his Lady is,
>   Under blake stole hyding her bayted hooke,
>   And as halfe blushing offred him to kis,
> With gentle blandishment and lovely° looke, — *loving*
> Most like that virgin true, which for her knight him took.

50

> All cleane dismayd to see so uncouth° sight, — *strange; unseemly*
>   And halfe enragèd at her shamelesse guise,
> He thought have slaine her in his fierce despight:° — *indignation*
>   But hasty heat tempring with sufferance° wise, — *patience*
> He stayde his hand, and gan himselfe advise
>   To prove his sense, and tempt° her faignèd truth. — *test*
>   Wringing her hands in wemens pitteous wise,
> Tho can° she weepe, to stirre up gentle ruth,° — *then did / pity*
> Both for her noble bloud, and for her tender youth.

51

> And said, "Ah Sir, my liege Lord and my love,
>   Shall I accuse the hidden cruell fate,
>   And mightie causes wrought in heaven above,
> Or the blind God, that doth me thus amate,° — *dismay*
> For° hopèd love to winne me certaine hate? — *instead of*
> Yet thus perforce° he bids me do, or die. — *forcibly*
> Die is my dew:[5] yet rew° my wretched state — *pity*
>   You, whom my hard avenging destinie
> Hath made judge of my life or death indifferently.° — *impartially*

52

> "Your owne deare sake forst me at first to leave
>   My Fathers kingdome," There she stopt with teares;
> Her swollen hart her speach seemd to bereave,° — *deprive her of*
>   And then againe begun, "My weaker yeares
>   Captived to fortune and frayle worldly feares,
> Fly to your faith for succour and sure ayde:
>   Let me not dye in languor° and long teares." — *sorrow*

---

4. The Three Graces of classical mythology were personifications of grace and beauty; here they sing a call to the pleasures of the marriage bed (Hymen was god of marriage). In the March eclogue of *The Shepheardes Calender*, E. K. glossed Flora as "the Goddesse of flowres, but indede (as saith Tacitus) a famous harlot."
5. That is, I deserve to die.

"Why Dame," quoth he, "what hath ye thus dismayd?
What frayes° ye, that were wont to comfort me affrayd?" — *frightens*

53

"Love of your selfe," she said, "and deare° constraint — *dire*
    Lets me not sleepe, but wast the wearie night
    In secret anguish and unpittied plaint,
    Whiles you in carelesse sleepe are drownèd quight."
    Her doubtfull words made that redoubted[6] knight
    Suspect her truth: yet since no'untruth he knew,
    Her fawning love with foule disdainefull spight
    He would not shend,° but said, "Deare dame I rew, — *reject*
That for my sake unknowne such griefe unto you grew.

54

"Assure your selfe, it fell not all to ground;
    For all so deare as life is to my hart,
    I deeme your love, and hold me to you bound;
    Ne let vaine feares procure your needlesse smart,° — *pain*
    Where cause is none, but to your rest depart."
    Not all content, yet seemd she to appease° — *cease*
    Her mournefull plaintes, beguilèd of her art,° — *foiled in her cunning*
    And fed with words, that could not chuse° but please, — *choose*
So slyding softly forth, she turnd° as to her ease. — *returned*

55

Long after lay he musing at her mood,
    Much grieved to thinke that gentle Dame so light,° — *frivolous; wanton*
    For whose defence he was to shed his blood.
    At last dull wearinesse of former fight
    Having yrockt a sleepe his irkesome[7] spright,
    That troublous dreame gan freshly tosse his braine,
    With bowres and beds, and Ladies deare delight:
    But when he saw his labour all was vaine,
With that misformèd spright[8] he backe returnd againe.

Canto 2

The guilefull great Enchaunter parts
    The Redcrosse Knight from Truth:
    Into whose stead faire falshood steps,
    And workes him wofull ruth.° — *mischief*

1

By this the Northerne wagoner[9] had set
    His seven fold teame behind the stedfast starre,[1]

---

6. Dreaded, but also "doubting again." "Doubtfull": fearful; also questionable, arousing doubt.
7. Tired, but also troublesome.
8. That is, with the spirit impersonating Una.
9. The constellation Boötes, the plowman, who drives a wagon composed of the seven bright stars of Ursa Major (the Big Dipper).
1. The North Star.

That was in Ocean waves yet never wet,
But firme is fixt, and sendeth light from farre
To all, that in the wide deepe wandring arre:
And chearefull Chaunticlere[2] with his note shrill
Had warnèd once, that Phoebus fiery carre[3]
In hast was climbing up the Easterne hill,
Full envious that night so long his roome° did fill.   *place*

2

When those accursèd messengers of hell,
  That feigning dreame, and that faire-forgèd Spright
Came to their wicked maister, and gan tell
  Their bootelesse° paines, and ill succeeding night: *useless*
Who all in rage to see his skilfull might
  Deluded° so, gan threaten hellish paine   *foiled*
  And sad Proserpines wrath, them to affright.
But when he saw his threatning was but vaine,
He cast about, and searcht his balefull° bookes againe.   *deadly*

3

Eftsoones° he tooke that miscreated faire,   *immediately*
  And that false other Spright, on whom he spred
A seeming body of the subtile° aire,   *rarefied*
  Like a young Squire, in loves and lusty-hed
His wanton dayes that ever loosely led,
  Without regard of armes and dreaded fight:
Those two he tooke, and in a secret bed,
  Covered with darknesse and misdeeming° night,   *misleading*
Them both together laid, to joy in vaine delight.

4

Forthwith he runnes with feignèd faithfull hast
  Unto his guest, who after troublous sights
And dreames, gan now to take more sound repast,°   *rest*
  Whom suddenly he wakes with fearefull frights,
As one aghast with feends or damnèd sprights,
  And to him cals, "Rise rise unhappy Swaine,°   *youth; rustic*
That here wex° old in sleepe, whiles wicked wights   *grow*
  Have knit themselves in Venus shamefull chaine;
Come see, where your false Lady doth her honour staine."

5

All in amaze he suddenly up start
  With sword in hand, and with the old man went;
Who soone him brought into a secret part,
  Where that false couple were full closely ment°   *mingled*
In wanton lust and lewd embracèment:

---

2. That is, Chanticleer; generic name for a rooster.   3. Chariot of the sun god, Phoebus Apollo.

Which when he saw, he burnt with gealous fire,
    The eye of reason was with rage yblent,°   *blinded*
    And would have slaine them in his furious ire,
But hardly° was restreinèd of° that agèd sire.   *with difficulty / by*

6

Returning to his bed in torment great,
    And bitter anguish of his guiltie sight,[4]
    He could not rest, but did his stout heart eat,[5]
    And wast his inward gall with deepe despight,°   *malice*
    Yrkesome° of life, and too long lingring night.   *tired*
    At last faire Hesperus[6] in highest skie
    Had spent his lampe, and brought forth dawning light,
    Then up he rose, and clad him hastily;
The Dwarfe him brought his steed: so both away do fly.

7

Now when the rosy-fingred Morning faire,
    Weary of agèd Tithones[7] saffron bed,
    Had spred her purple robe through deawy aire,
    And the high hils Titan° discoverèd,°   *the sun / revealed*
    The royall virgin shooke off drowsy-hed,
    And rising forth out of her baser° bowre,   *too lowly*
    Lookt for her knight, who far away was fled,
    And for her Dwarfe, that wont° to wait each houre: *was accustomed*
Then gan she waile and weepe, to see that woefull stowre.° *affliction*

8

And after him she rode with so much speede
    As her slow beast could make; but all in vaine:
    For him so far had borne his light-foot steede,
    Prickèd with wrath and fiery fierce disdaine,°   *indignation*
    That him to follow was but fruitlesse paine;
    Yet she her weary limbes would never rest,
    But every hill and dale, each wood and plaine
    Did search, sore grievèd in her gentle brest,
He so ungently left her, whom she lovèd best.

9

But subtill° Archimago, when his guests   *cunning*
    He saw divided into double parts,
    And Una wandring in woods and forrests,
    Th' end of his drift,° he praisd his divelish arts   *plot*
    That had such might over true meaning harts;
    Yet rests not so, but other meanes doth make,
    How he may worke unto her further smarts:°   *pains*

---

4. Suggesting guilt in both the sight and the seer.
5. Proverbially, jealousy is a monster that eats the heart.
6. The morning star.
7. Tithonus is the husband of Aurora, goddess of the dawn.

For her he hated as the hissing snake,
And in her many troubles did most pleasure take.

10

He then devisde himselfe how to disguise;
  For by his mightie science° he could take   *knowledge*
  As many formes and shapes in seeming wise,°   *in appearance*
  As ever Proteus[8] to himselfe could make:
  Sometime a fowle, sometime a fish in lake,
  Now like a foxe, now like a dragon fell,°   *fierce*
  That of himselfe he oft for feare would quake,
  And oft would flie away. O who can tell
The hidden power of herbes, and might of Magicke spell?

11

But now seemde best, the person to put on
  Of that good knight, his late beguilèd guest:
  In mighty armes he was yclad anon,
  And silver shield: upon his coward brest
  A bloudy crosse, and on his craven crest
  A bounch of haires discolourd diversly:°   *variously colored*
  Full jolly° knight he seemde, and well addrest,°   *gallant / armed*
  And when he sate upon his courser free,°   *high-spirited*
Saint George himself ye would have deemèd him to be.

12

But he the knight, whose semblaunt° he did beare,   *likeness*
  The true Saint George was wandred far away,
  Still flying from° his thoughts and gealous feare;   *because of*
  Will was his guide, and griefe led him astray.
  At last him chaunst to meete upon the way
  A faithlesse Sarazin[9] all armed to point,°   *completely*
  In whose great shield was writ with letters gay
  Sans foy:[1] full large of limbe and every joint
He was, and carèd not for God or man a point.°   *at all*

13

He had a faire companion of his way,
  A goodly Lady clad in scarlot red,
  Purfled° with gold and pearle of rich assay,[2]   *decorated*
  And like a Persian mitre on her hed
  She wore, with crownes and owches° garnishèd,   *brooches*
  The which her lavish lovers to her gave;[3]

---

8. A sea god who could change his shape at will (*Odyssey* 4.398–424).
9. Saracen; that is, a Muslim, especially the foes of the Christian knights in the Crusades to the Holy Land; sometimes used generically of any non-Christian.
1. Without faith, faithless (French).
2. Proven of rich value.
3. The lady's garb associates her with the biblical Whore of Babylon (Revelation 17:3–4): "And I saw a woman sit upon a scarlet coloured beast, full of names of blasphemy, having seven heads and ten horns. And the woman was arrayed in purple and scarlet colour, and decked with gold and precious stones and pearls, having a golden cup in her hand full of abominations and filthiness of her fornication."

Her wanton° palfrey[4] all was overspred   *unruly, frisky*
  With tinsell trappings, woven like a wave,
Whose bridle rung with golden bels and bosses brave.°   *handsome studs*

14

With faire disport° and courting dalliaunce   *diversion*
  She intertainde her lover all the way:
  But when she saw the knight his speare advaunce,
  She soone left off her mirth and wanton play,
  And bad her knight addresse him to the fray:
  His foe was nigh at hand. He prickt with pride
  And hope to winne his Ladies heart that day,
  Forth spurrèd fast: adowne his coursers side
The red bloud trickling staind the way, as he did ride.

15

The knight of the Redcrosse when him he spide,
  Spurring so hote with rage dispiteous,°   *cruel*
  Gan fairely couch° his speare, and towards ride: *lower*
  Soone meete they both, both fell° and furious,   *fierce*
  That daunted° with their forces hideous,   *dazed*
  Their steeds do stagger, and amazèd° stand,   *stunned*
  And eke° themselves too rudely rigorous,°   *also / violent*
  Astonied° with the stroke of their owne hand,   *stunned*
Do backe rebut,° and each to other yeeldeth land.   *recoil*

16

As when two rams stird with ambitious pride,
  Fight for the rule of the rich fleecèd flocke,
  Their hornèd fronts so fierce on either side
  Do meete, that with the terrour of the shocke
  Astonied both, stand sencelesse as a blocke,
  Forgetfull of the hanging° victory: *in the balance*
  So stood these twaine, unmovèd as a rocke,
  Both staring fierce, and holding idely
The broken reliques of their former cruelty.

17

The Sarazin sore daunted with the buffe
  Snatcheth his sword, and fiercely to him flies;
  Who well it wards,° and quyteth° cuff with cuff: *fends off / requites, repays*
  Each others equall puissaunce envies,°   *power seeks to rival*
  And through their iron sides with cruell spies°   *looks*
  Does seeke to perce: repining courage yields
  No foote to foe. The flashing fier flies
  As from a forge out of their burning shields,
And streames of purple bloud new dies the verdant fields.

---

4. Riding horse (as distinguished from a warhorse); often, as here, a small saddle horse for a woman.

18

"Curse on that Crosse," quoth then the Sarazin,
   "That keepes thy body from the bitter fit;°   *death pangs*
   Dead long ygoe I wote° thou haddest bin,   *know*
   Had not that charme from thee forwarnèd° it: *prevented*
   But yet I warne thee now assurèd° sitt,   *securely*
   And hide thy head." Therewith upon his crest°   *helmet*
   With rigour° so outrageöus he smitt,   *violence*
   That a large share it hewd out of the rest,
And glauncing downe his shield, from blame him fairely blest.[5]

19

Who thereat wondrous wroth, the sleeping spark
   Of native vertue° gan eftsoones° revive,   *strength / again*
   And at his haughtie helmet making mark,°   *taking aim*
   So hugely° stroke, that it the steele did rive,   *mightily*
   And cleft his head. He tumbling downe alive,
   With bloudy mouth his mother earth did kis,
   Greeting his grave: his grudging° ghost did strive   *complaining*
   With the fraile flesh; at last it flitted is,
Whither the soules do fly of men, that live amis.

20

The Lady when she saw her champion fall,
   Like the old ruines of a broken towre,
   Staid not to waile his woefull funerall,°   *death*
   But from him fled away with all her powre;
   Who after her as hastily gan scowre,°   *scurry*
   Bidding the Dwarfe with him to bring away
   The Sarazins shield, signe of the conqueroure.
   Her soone he overtooke, and bad to stay,
For present cause was none of dread her to dismay.[6]

21

She turning backe with ruefull° countenaunce,   *pitiable*
   Cride, "Mercy mercy Sir vouchsafe to show
   On silly° Dame, subject to hard mischaunce,   *helpless*
   And to your mighty will." Her humblesse low
   In so ritch weedes° and seeming glorious show,   *clothes*
   Did much emmove his stout heroicke heart,
   And said, "Deare dame, your suddein overthrow
   Much rueth° me; but now put feare apart,   *grieves*
And tell, both who ye be, and who that tooke your part."

22

Melting in teares, then gan she thus lament;
   "The wretched woman, whom unhappy howre

---

5. Preserved him from harm.   6. That is, there was no reason for her to be afraid.

Hath now made thrall° to your commandèment, — *slave*
Before that angry heavens list to lowre,° — *chose to frown*
And fortune false betraide me to your powre,
Was (O what now availeth that I was!)
Borne the sole daughter of an Emperour,
He that the wide West under his rule has,
And high hath set his throne, where Tiberis doth pas.[7]

23

"He in the first flowre of my freshest age,
Betrothèd me unto the onely haire° — *heir*
Of a most mighty king, most rich and sage;[8]
Was never Prince so faithfull and so faire,
Was never Prince so meeke and debonaire;° — *gracious*
But ere my hopèd day of spousall shone,
My dearest Lord fell from high honours staire,
Into the hands of his accursèd fone,° — *foes*
And cruelly was slaine, that shall I ever mone.

24

"His blessèd body spoild of lively breath,
Was afterward, I know not how, convaid° — *carried away*
And fro° me hid: of whose most innocent death — *from*
When tidings came to me unhappy maid,
O how great sorrow my sad soule assaid.° — *afflicted*
Then forth I went his woefull corse to find,
And many yeares throughout the world I straid,
A virgin widow, whose deepe wounded mind
With love, long time did languish as the striken hind.° — *deer*

25

"At last it chauncèd this proud Sarazin
To meete me wandring, who perforce° me led — *by violence*
With him away, but yet could never win
The fort, that Ladies hold in soveraigne dread.° — *utmost reverence*
There lies he now with foule dishonour dead,
Who whiles he livde, was callèd proud Sans foy,
The eldest of three brethren, all three bred
Of one bad sire, whose youngest is Sans joy,
And twixt them both was borne the bloudy bold Sans loy.[9]

26

"In this sad plight, friendlesse, unfortunate,
Now miserable I Fidessa° dwell, — *Faithful*

---

7. The Tiber River runs through Rome. The lady is hence associated with the Catholic Church. Her father, she says, is ruler of the west—but Una's father had the rule of both east *and* west (canto 1, stanza 5); historically, the true church once embraced east and west.
8. The lady claims to have been betrothed to Christ, bridegroom of the Church (Matthew 9:15).
9. Without law; lawless.

Craving of you in pitty of my state,
    To do none° ill, if please ye not do well."   *no*
He in great passion all this while did dwell,°   *continue*
    More busying his quicke eyes, her face to view,
    Then his dull eares, to heare what she did tell;
    And said, "Faire Lady hart of flint would rew
The undeservèd woes and sorrowes, which ye shew.

27

"Henceforth in safe assuraunce may ye rest,
    Having both found a new friend you to aid,
    And lost an old foe, that did you molest:
    Better new friend than an old foe is° said."   *it is*
    With chaunge of cheare° the seeming simple maid   *countenance*
    Let fall her eyen, as shamefast° to the earth,   *as if modestly*
    And yeelding soft, in that she nought gain-said,°   *objected*
    So forth they rode, he feining° seemely merth,   *simulating*
And she coy lookes: so dainty they say maketh derth.[1]

28

Long time they thus together traveilèd,
    Till weary of their way, they came at last,
    Where grew two goodly trees, that faire did spred
    Their armes abroad, with gray mosse overcast,
    And their greene leaves trembling with every blast,°   *breeze*
    Made a calme shadow far in compasse round:
    The fearefull Shepheard often there aghast
    Under them never sat, ne wont° there sound   *nor was accustomed to*
His mery oaten pipe, but shund th'unlucky ground.

29

But this good knight soone as he them can° spie,   *did*
    For the coole shade him thither hastly got:
    For golden Phoebus now ymounted hie,
    From fiery wheeles of his faire chariot
    Hurlèd his beame so scorching cruell hot,
    That living creature mote° it not abide;   *might*
    And his new Lady it endurèd not.
    There they alight, in hope themselves to hide
From the fierce heat, and rest their weary limbs a tide.°   *time*

30

Faire seemely pleasaunce° each to other makes,   *courtesy*
    With goodly purposes° there as they sit: *courteous conversation*
    And in his falsèd° fancy he her takes   *deceived*
    To be the fairest wight° that livèd yit;   *creature*
    Which to expresse, he bends° his gentle wit,°   *applies / mind*

---

1. A proverb meaning that disdainfulness makes one more to be coveted; here, that coyness creates unsatisfied desire.

And thinking of those braunches greene to frame
   A girlond for her dainty forehead fit,
   He pluckt a bough; out of whose rift there came
Small drops of gory bloud, that trickled downe the same.

31

Therewith a piteous yelling voyce was heard,
   Crying, "O spare with guilty hands to teare
   My tender sides in this rough rynd° embard,°   *bark / imprisoned*
   But fly, ah fly far hence away, for feare
Least° to you hap, that happened to me heare,   *lest*
   And to this wretched Lady, my deare love,
   O too deare love, love bought with death too deare."
   Astond° he stood, and up his haire did hove,°   *stunned / rise*
And with that suddein horror could no member move.

32

At last whenas the dreadfull passiön
   Was overpast, and manhood well awake,
   Yet musing at the straunge occasiön,
   And doubting much his sence, he thus bespake;
"What voyce of damnèd Ghost from Limbo[2] lake,
   Or guilefull spright wandring in empty aire,
   Both which fraile men do oftentimes mistake,°   *mislead*
   Sends to my doubtfull eares these speaches rare,°   *strange*
And ruefull plaints, me bidding guiltlesse bloud to spare?"

33

Then groning deepe, "Nor° damnèd Ghost," quoth he,   *neither*
   "Nor guilefull sprite to thee these wordes doth speake,
   But once a man Fradubio,[3] now a tree,
   Wretched man, wretched tree; whose nature weake,
A cruell witch her cursèd will to wreake,
   Hath thus transformed, and plast in open plaines,
   Where Boreas° doth blow full bitter bleake,   *the north wind*
   And scorching Sunne does dry my secret vaines:
For though a tree I seeme, yet cold and heat me paines."

34

"Say on Fradubio then, or° man, or tree,"   *whether*
   Quoth then the knight, "by whose mischievous arts
   Art thou misshapèd thus, as now I see?
   He oft finds med'cine, who his griefe imparts;°   *expresses*
But double griefs afflict concealing harts,
   As raging flames who striveth to suppresse."
   "The author then," said he, "of all my smarts,

---

2. A region of hell, traditionally the abode of the unbaptized.
3. *Fra* (Italian "in" or "brother") + *dubbio* ("doubt").

The motif of a man imprisoned in a tree derives from Virgil (*Aeneid* 3.27–42) and is used by Ariosto (*Orlando furioso* 6.26–53).

Is one Duessa[4] a false sorceresse,
That many errant° knights hath brought to wretchednesse.   *wandering*

35

"In prime of youthly yeares, when corage hot
　The fire of love and joy of chevalree
　First kindled in my brest, it was my lot
　To love this gentle Lady, whom ye see,
　Now not a Lady, but a seeming tree;
　With whom as once I rode accompanyde,
　Me chauncèd of a knight encountred bee,
　That had a like faire Lady by his syde,
Like a faire Lady, but did fowle Duessa hyde.

36

"Whose forgèd beauty he did take in hand,°   *he maintained*
　All other Dames to have exceeded farre,
　I in defence of mine did likewise stand,
　Mine, that did then shine as the Morning starre:
　So both to battell fierce arraungèd arre,
　In which his harder fortune was to fall
　Under my speare: such is the dye° of warre: *hazard*
　His Lady left as a prise martiäll,°   *spoil of battle*
Did yield her comely person, to be at my call.

37

"So doubly loved of Ladies unlike° faire,   *diversely*
　Th'one seeming such, the other such indeede,
　One day in doubt I cast° for to compare,   *determined*
　Whether° in beauties glorie did exceede;   *which one (of two)*
　A Rosy girlond was the victors meede:°   *reward*
　Both seemde to win, and both seemde won to bee,
　So hard the discord was to be agreede.
　Fraelissa[5] was as faire, as faire mote bee,
And ever false Duessa seemde as faire as shee.

38

"The wicked witch now seeing all this while
　The doubtfull ballaunce equally to sway,
　What not by right, she cast to win by guile,
　And by her hellish science° raisd streight way   *magic*
　A foggy mist, that overcast the day,
　And a dull blast, that breathing on her face,
　Dimmed her former beauties shining ray,
　And with foule ugly forme did her disgrace:
Then was she° faire alone, when none was faire in place.[6]   *Duessa*

---

4. Double Being. *Due* (Italian "two") + *esse* (Latin "being").
5. Frailty (Italian *Fralezza*).
6. When nobody else was fair.

39

"Then cride she out, 'Fye, fye, deformèd wight,
  Whose borrowed beautie now appeareth plaine
  To have before bewitchèd all mens sight;
  O leave her soone, or let her soone be slaine.'
  Her lothly visage viewing with disdaine,
  Eftsoones° I thought her such, as she me told, — *presently*
  And would have kild her; but with faignèd paine,
  The false witch did my wrathfull hand withhold;
So left her, where she now is turnd to treën mould.° — *the form of a tree*

40

"Thens forth I tooke Duessa for my Dame,
  And in the witch unweeting° joyd long time, — *unknowingly*
  Ne ever wist,° but that she was the same, — *knew*
  Till on a day (that day is every Prime,[7]
  When Witches wont° do penance for their crime) — *are accustomed to*
  I chaunst to see her in her proper hew,° — *in her own shape*
  Bathing her selfe in origane and thyme:[8]
  A filthy foule old woman I did vew,
That ever to have toucht her, I did deadly rew.° — *regret*

41

"Her neather partes misshapen, monstruous,
  Were hidd in water, that I could not see,
  But they did seeme more foule and hideous,
  Then° womans shape man would beleeve to bee. — *than*
  Thens forth from her most beastly companie
  I gan refraine, in minde to slip away,
  Soone as appeard safe opportunitie:
  For danger great, if not assured decay° — *destruction*
I saw before mine eyes, if I were knowne to stray.

42

"The divelish hag by chaunges of my cheare° — *demeanor*
  Perceived my thought, and drownd in sleepie night,
  With wicked herbes and ointments did besmeare
  My bodie all, through charmes and magicke might,
  That all my senses were bereavèd quight:° — *quite*
  Then brought she me into this desert waste,
  And by my wretched lovers side me pight,° — *planted*
  Where now enclosd in wooden wals full faste,[9]
Banisht from living wights, our wearie dayes we waste."

---

7. Spring; or the first appearance of the new moon.
8. Oregano and thyme were used to cure scabs and itching.
9. That is, imprisoned within the trees.

43

"But how long time," said then the Elfin knight,
  "Are you in this misformèd house to dwell?"
"We may not chaunge," quoth he, "this evil plight,
  Till we be bathèd in a living well;[1]
  That is the terme prescribèd by the spell."
"O how," said he, "mote° I that well out find,   *might*
  That may restore you to your wonted well?"°   *well-being*
  "Time and suffisèd fates to former kynd
Shall us restore,[2] none else from hence may us unbynd."

44

The false Duessa, now Fidessa hight,°   *called*
  Heard how in vaine Fradubio did lament,
  And knew well all was true. But the good knight
  Full of sad feare and ghastly dreriment,°   *gloom*
  When all this speech the living tree had spent,
The bleeding bough did thrust into the ground,
  That from the bloud he might be innocent,
  And with fresh clay did close the wooden wound:
Then turning to his Lady, dead with feare her found.

45

Her seeming dead he found with feignèd feare,
  As all unweeting of that well she knew,[3]
  And paynd himselfe with busie care to reare
  Her out of carelesse° swowne. Her eylids blew   *unconscious*
  And dimmèd sight with pale and deadly hew°   *deathlike appearance*
  At last she up gan lift: with trembling cheare
  Her up he tooke, too simple and too trew,
  And oft her kist. At length all passèd feare,[4]
He set her on her steede, and forward forth did beare.

Canto 3

Forsaken Truth long seekes her love,
  And makes the Lyon mylde,
Marres° blind Devotions mart,° and fals   *spoils / trade*
  In hand of leachour° vylde.   *lecher*

1

Nought is there under heav'ns wide hollownesse,°   *concavity*
  That moves more deare compassiön of mind,
  Then beautie brought t'unworthy° wretchednesse   *undeserved*

---

1. With allusion to John 4:14, the "well of water springing up into everlasting life."
2. That is, time and the satisfaction of the fates alone can restore us to our former human nature.
3. That is, pretending ignorance of what she knew well.
4. That is, having overcome all fear.

Through envies snares or fortunes freakes° unkind: *sudden changes*
    I, whether lately through her brightnesse blind,
    Or through alleageance and fast fealtie,
    Which I do owe unto all woman kind,
    Feele my heart perst° with so great agonie, *pierced*
When such I see, that all for pittie I could die.

2

And now it is empassionèd° so deepe, *moved*
    For fairest Unas sake, of whom I sing,
    That my fraile eyes these lines with teares do steepe,
    To thinke how she through guilefull handeling,° *treatment*
    Though true as touch,° though daughter of a king, *touchstone*
    Though faire as ever living wight was faire,
    Though nor in word nor deede ill meriting,
    Is from her knight divorcèd° in despaire *separated*
And her due loves derived° to that vile witches share. *diverted*

3

Yet she most faithfull Ladie all this while
    Forsaken, wofull, solitarie mayd
    Farre from all peoples prease,° as in exile, *press, crowd*
    In wildernesse and wastfull° deserts strayd, *desolate*
    To seeke her knight; who subtilly betrayd
    Through that late vision, which th'Enchaunter wrought,
    Had her abandond. She of nought affrayd,
    Through woods and wastnesse° wide him daily sought; *wilderness*
Yet wishèd tydings none° of him unto her brought. *no one*

4

One day nigh wearie of the yrkesome way,
    From her unhastie° beast she did alight, *slow*
    And on the grasse her daintie limbes did lay
    In secret shadow,° farre from all mens sight: *shade*
    From her faire head her fillet she undight,[5]
    And laid her stole aside. Her angels face
    As the great eye of heaven shynèd bright,
    And made a sunshine in the shadie place;
Did never mortall eye behold such heavenly grace.

5

It fortunèd° out of the thickest wood *chanced*
    A ramping° Lyon rushèd suddainly, *raging*
    Hunting full greedie after salvage blood;° *wild game*
    Soone as the royall virgin he did spy,
    With gaping mouth at her ran greedily,
    To have attonce° devoured her tender corse;° *at once / body*

---

5. She took off her headband.

But to the pray when as he drew more ny,
　His bloudie rage asswagèd with remorse,
And with the sight amazd, forgat his furious forse.

6

In stead thereof he kist her wearie feet,
　And lickt her lilly hands with fawning tong,
　As° he her wrongèd innocence did weet.° *as if / understand*
　O how can beautie maister the most strong,
　And simple truth subdue avenging wrong?
　Whose yeelded pride and proud submissiön,
　Still dreading death, when she had markèd long,
　Her hart gan melt in great compassiön,
And drizling teares did shed for pure affectiön.

7

"The Lyon Lord of everie beast in field,"
　Quoth she, "his princely puissance° doth abate, *power*
　And mightie proud to humble weake does yield,
　Forgetfull of the hungry rage, which late
　Him prickt, in pittie of my sad estate:° *condition*
　But he my Lyon, and my noble Lord,
　How does he find in cruell hart to hate
　Her that him loved, and ever most adord,
As the God of my life? why hath he me abhord?"

8

Redounding° teares did choke th'end of her plaint, *overflowing*
　Which softly ecchoed from the neighbour wood;
　And sad to see her sorrowfull constraint° *affliction*
　The kingly beast upon her gazing stood;
　With pittie calmd, downe fell his angry mood.
　At last in close hart shutting up her paine,
　Arose the virgin borne of heavenly brood,° *parentage*
　And to her snowy Palfrey got againe,
To seeke her strayèd Champion, if she might attaine.° *overtake*

9

The Lyon would not leave her desolate,
　But with her went along, as a strong gard
　Of her chast person, and a faithfull mate
　Of her sad troubles and misfortunes hard:
　Still° when she slept, he kept both watch and ward,° *always / guard*
　And when she wakt, he waited diligent,
　With humble service to her will prepard:
　From her faire eyes he tooke commaundèment,
And ever by her lookes conceivèd her intent.

10

Long she thus traveilèd through deserts wyde,
  By which she thought her wandring knight shold pas,
  Yet never shew° of living wight espyde; — *show*
  Till that at length she found the troden gras,
  In which the tract° of peoples footing was, — *track*
  Under the steepe foot of a mountaine hore;° — *gray*
  The same she followes, till at last she has
  A damzell spyde slow footing her before,[6]
That on her shoulders sad° a pot of water bore. — *heavy*

11

To whom approching she to her gan call,
  To weet,° if dwelling place were nigh at hand; — *know*
  But the rude° wench her answered nought at all, — *impolite; ignorant*
  She could not heare, nor speake, nor understand;[7]
  Till seeing by her side the Lyon stand,
  With suddaine feare her pitcher downe she threw,
  And fled away: for never in that land
  Face of faire Ladie she before did vew,
And that dread Lyons looke her cast in deadly° hew. — *deathlike*

12

Full fast she fled, ne ever lookt behynd,
  As if her life upon the wager lay,° — *were at stake*
  And home she came, whereas her mother blynd
  Sate in eternall night: nought could she say,
  But suddaine catching hold, did her dismay
  With quaking hands, and other signes of feare:
  Who full of ghastly fright and cold affray,° — *terror*
  Gan shut the dore. By this arrivèd there
Dame Una, wearie Dame, and entrance did requere.° — *request*

13

Which when none yeelded, her unruly Page
  With his rude° clawes the wicket° open rent, — *rough / door*
  And let her in; where of his cruell rage
  Nigh dead with feare, and faint astonishment,[8]
  She found them both in darkesome corner pent;° — *huddled*
  Where that old woman day and night did pray
  Upon her beades° devoutly penitent; — *rosary*
  Nine hundred *Pater nosters* every day,
And thrise nine hundred *Aves* she was wont to say.[9]

---

6. That is, walking slowly ahead of her.
7. Compare Mark 4:11–12: "unto them that are without, all these things are done in parables: That seeing they may see, and not perceive; and hearing they may hear, and not understand."
8. That is, fainting with amazement.
9. Her prayers are the Lord's Prayer ("Our Father") and the Hail Mary.

14

And to augment her painefull pennance more,
   Thrise every weeke in ashes she did sit,
   And next her wrinkled skin rough sackcloth wore,[1]
   And thrise three times did fast from any bit:°   *food*
But now for feare her beads she did forget.
Whose needlesse dread for to remove away,
   Faire Una framèd words and count'nance fit:
   Which hardly° doen, at length she gan them pray,   *with difficulty*
That in their cotage small, that night she rest her may.[2]

15

The day is spent, and commeth drowsie night,
   When every creature shrowded is in sleepe;
   Sad Una downe her laies in wearie plight,
   And at her feet the Lyon watch doth keepe:
In stead of rest, she does lament, and weepe
For the late° losse of her deare lovèd knight,   *recent*
   And sighes, and grones, and evermore does steepe
   Her tender brest in bitter teares all night,
All night she thinks too long, and often lookes for light.

16

Now when Aldeboran was mounted hie
   Above the shynie Cassiopeias chaire,[3]
   And all in deadly sleepe did drownèd lie,
   One knockèd at the dore, and in would fare;°   *come*
He knockèd fast,° and often curst, and sware,   *insistently*
That readie entrance was not at his call:
   For on his backe a heavy load he bare
   Of nightly stelths and pillage severall,[4]
Which he had got abroad by purchase° criminall.   *acquisition*

17

He was to weete° a stout and sturdie thiefe,   *in fact*
   Wont to robbe Churches of their ornaments,
   And poore mens boxes[5] of their due reliefe,
   Which given was to them for good intents;
The holy Saints of their rich vestiments
He did disrobe, when all men carelesse slept,
   And spoild the Priests of their habiliments,°   *vestments*
   Whiles none the holy things in safety kept;
Then he by cunning sleights in at the window crept.

---

1. Sackcloth and ashes are symbols of penitence and, like the rosary beads and prayers in stanza 13, are associated with Catholicism.
2. That is, that she might rest herself.
3. The star Aldebaran, in the constellation Taurus, mounts over the constellation Cassiopeia.
4. That is, he carried the booty gained from nightly thefts and various kinds of pillage.
5. A box for alms for the poor.

18

And all that he by right or wrong could find,
   Unto this house he brought, and did bestow
   Upon the daughter of this woman blind,
   Abessa daughter of Corceca[6] slow,
   With whom he whoredome usd, that few did know,
   And fed her fat with feast of offerings,
   And plentie, which in all the land did grow;
   Ne sparèd he to give her gold and rings:
And now he to her brought part of his stolen things.

19

Thus long the dore with rage and threats he bet,°   *beat*
   Yet of those fearefull women none durst rize,
   The Lyon frayèd them, him in to let:[7]
   He would no longer stay him to advize,°   *consider*
   But open breakes the dore in furious wize,°   *manner*
   And entring is; when that disdainfull° beast   *indignant*
   Encountring fierce, him suddaine doth surprize,
   And seizing° cruell clawes on trembling brest,   *fastening*
Under his Lordly foot him proudly hath supprest.

20

Him booteth not resist,[8] nor succour° call,   *help*
   His bleeding hart is in the vengers hand,
   Who streight° him rent in thousand peeces small,   *immediately*
   And quite dismembred hath: the thirstie land
   Drunke up his life; his corse left on the strand.°   *ground*
   His fearefull friends weare out the wofull night,
   Ne dare to weepe, nor seeme to understand
   The heavie hap,° which on them is alight,°   *lot / fallen*
Affraid, least to themselves the like mishappen might.[9]

21

Now when broad day the world discovered° has,   *revealed*
   Up Una rose, up rose the Lyon eke,°   *also*
   And on their former journey forward pas,
   In wayes unknowne, her wandring knight to seeke,
   With paines farre passing that long wandring Greeke,
   That for his love refusèd deitie;[1]
   Such were the labours of this Lady meeke,
   Still seeking him, that from her still did flie,
Then furthest from her hope, when most she weenèd nie.°   *believed near*

---

6. Blind heart. Abessa's name comes from "abbess," also *ab+esse* (Latin): "from being"; that is, without substance.
7. That is, neither of the women dared rise to let him in because the lion terrified ("frayed") them.
8. It does him no good to resist.
9. That is, lest the same thing might happen amiss ("mishappen") to them.
1. Odysseus, who rejected immortality and the love of the nymph Calypso for his wife, Penelope.

22

Soone as she parted thence, the fearefull twaine,
  That blind old woman and her daughter deare
  Came forth, and finding Kirkrapine° there slaine,   *church robber*
  For anguish great they gan to rend their heare,
  And beat their brests, and naked flesh to teare.
  And when they both had wept and wayld their fill,
  Then forth they ranne like two amazèd deare,
  Halfe mad through malice, and revenging will,°   *desire of revenge*
To follow her, that was the causer of their ill.

23

Whom overtaking, they gan loudly bray,
  With hollow howling, and lamenting cry,
  Shamefully at her rayling all the way,
  And her accusing of dishonesty,°   *unchastity*
  That was the flowre of faith and chastity;
  And still amidst her rayling, she[2] did pray,
  That plagues, and mischiefs, and long misery
  Might fall on her, and follow all the way,
And that in endlesse error° she might ever stray.   *wandering*

24

But when she saw her prayers nought prevaile,
  She backe returnèd with some labour lost;
  And in the way as she did weepe and waile
  A knight her met in mighty armes embost,°   *encased*
  Yet knight was not for all his bragging bost,°   *boast*
  But subtill Archimag, that Una sought
  By traynes° into new troubles to have tost: *tricks*
  Of that old woman tydings he besought,
If that of such a Ladie she could tellen ought.[3]

25

Therewith she gan her passion to renew,
  And cry, and curse, and raile, and rend her heare,°   *hair*
  Saying, that harlot she too lately knew,
  That causd her shed so many a bitter teare,
  And so forth told the story of her feare:
  Much seemèd he to mone her haplesse chaunce,
  And after for that Ladie did inquere;
  Which being taught, he forward gan advaunce
His fair enchaunted steed, and eke his charmèd launce.

---

2. Corceca. (Abessa cannot speak.)
3. Anything. That is, if she could tell anything about such a lady.

26

Ere long he came, where Una traveild slow,
  And that wilde Champion wayting° her besyde: *attending*
  Whom seeing such, for dread he durst not show
  Himselfe too nigh at hand, but turnèd wyde
  Unto an hill; from whence when she him spyde,
  By his like seeming shield, her knight by name
  She weend it was, and towards him gan ryde:
  Approching nigh, she wist° it was the same,   *believed*
And with faire fearefull humblesse° towards him shee came.   *humility*

27

And weeping said, "Ah my long lackèd Lord,
  Where have ye bene thus long out of my sight?
  Much fearèd I to have bene quite abhord,
  Or ought° have done, that ye displeasen might,   *aught*
  That should as death unto my deare hart light:[4]
  For since mine eye your joyous sight did mis,
  My chearefull day is turnd to chearelesse night,
  And eke my night of death the shadow is;
But welcome now my light, and shining lampe of blis."

28

He thereto meeting[5] said, "My dearest Dame,
  Farre be it from your thought, and fro my will,
  To thinke that knighthood I so much should shame,
  As you to leave, that have me lovèd still,
  And chose in Faery court of meere° goodwill,   *pure*
  Where noblest knights were to be found on earth:
  The earth shall sooner leave her kindly° skill   *natural*
  To bring forth fruit, and make eternall derth,°   *desert*
Then I leave you, my liefe,° yborne of heavenly berth.   *beloved*

29

"And sooth to say, why I left you so long,
  Was for to seeke adventure in strange place,
  Where Archimago said a felon strong
  To many knights did daily worke disgrace;
  But knight he now shall never more deface:°   *discredit*
  Good cause of mine excuse; that mote° ye please   *may*
  Well to accept, and evermore embrace
  My faithfull service, that by land and seas
Have vowd you to defend, now then your plaint appease."°   *cease*

---

4. That is, be as a deathblow to my loving heart. ("Deare" can also mean heavy or sore.)
5. Answering in like manner.

30

His lovely° words her seemd due recompence   *loving*
   Of all her passèd paines: one loving howre
   For many yeares of sorrow can dispence:°   *make amends*
   A dram of sweet is worth a pound of sowre:
   She has forgot, how many a wofull stowre°   *trouble*
   For him she late endured; she speakes no more
   Of past: true is, that true love hath no powre
   To looken backe; his eyes be fixt before.
Before her stands her knight, for whom she toyld so sore.

31

Much like, as when the beaten marinere,
   That long hath wandred in the Ocean wide,
   Oft soust° in swelling Tethys[6] saltish teare,   *soaked*
   And long time having tand his tawney hide
   With blustring breath of heaven, that none can bide,
   And scorching flames of fierce Orions hound,[7]
   Soone as the port from farre he has espide,
   His chearefull whistle merrily doth sound,
And Nereus crownes with cups;[8] his mates him pledg° around.   *toast*

32

Such joy made Una, when her knight she found;
   And eke° th'enchaunter joyous seemd no lesse,   *also*
   Then the glad marchant, that does vew from ground
   His ship farre come from watrie wildernesse,
   He hurles out vowes, and Neptune oft doth blesse:
   So forth they past, and all the way they spent
   Discoursing of her dreadfull late distresse,
   In which he askt her, what the Lyon ment:
Who told her all that fell in journey as she went.[9]

33

They had not ridden farre, when they might see
   One pricking° towards them with hastie heat,   *spurring*
   Full strongly armd, and on a courser free,°   *eager to charge*
   That through his fiercenesse fomèd all with sweat,
   And the sharpe yron° did for anger eat,   *bit*
   When his hot ryder spurd his chauffèd° side;   *chafed; heated*
   His looke was sterne, and seemèd still to threat
   Cruell revenge, which he in hart did hyde,
And on his shield Sans loy in bloudie lines was dyde.

---

6. The wife of Ocean; here, the ocean itself.
7. Sirius, the dog star, symbolizing hot weather (the dog days).
8. Nereus, a benevolent sea god, to whom the mariner in gratitude makes libations.
9. That is, she told all that had befallen her on her journey.

34

When nigh he drew unto this gentle payre
   And saw the Red-crosse, which the knight did beare,
   He burnt in fire, and gan eftsoones° prepare   *immediately*
   Himselfe to battell with his couchèd° speare.   *leveled*
   Loth was that other, and did faint° through feare,   *lose heart*
   To taste th'untryed dint° of deadly steele;   *blow*
   But yet his Lady did so well him cheare,
   That hope of new good hap° he gan to feele;   *fortune*
So bent° his speare, and spurnd[1] his horse with yron heele.   *lowered*

35

But that proud Paynim° forward came so fierce,   *pagan*
   And full of wrath, that with his sharp-head speare
   Through vainely crossèd shield[2] he quite did pierce,
   And had his staggering steede not shrunke for feare,
   Through shield and bodie eke he should him beare:°   *thrust*
   Yet so great was the puissance° of his push,   *force*
   That from his saddle quite he did him beare:
   He tombling rudely° downe to ground did rush,   *violently*
And from his gorèd wound a well of bloud did gush.

36

Dismounting lightly from his loftie steed,
   He to him lept, in mind to reave° his life,   *take*
   And proudly said, "Lo there the worthie meed°   *recompense*
   Of him, that slew Sansfoy with bloudie knife;
   Henceforth his ghost freed from repining strife,
   In peace may passen over Lethe[3] lake,
   When mourning altars purgd° with enemies life,   *cleansed*
   The blacke infernall Furies[4] doen aslake:°   *appease*
Life from Sansfoy thou tookst, Sansloy shall from thee take."

37

Therewith in haste his helmet gan unlace,
   Till Una cride, "O hold that heavie hand,
   Deare Sir, what ever that thou be in place:°   *whoever you are*
   Enough is, that thy foe doth vanquisht stand
   Now at thy mercy: Mercie not withstand:
   For he is one the truest knight alive,[5]
   Though conquered now he lie on lowly land,°   *low on the ground*
   And whilest him fortune favourd, faire did thrive
In bloudie field: therefore of life him not deprive."

---

1. Spurred.
2. The cross on Archimago's shield was false and did not give him the protection the Redcrosse knight received in his fight with Sansfoy (see canto 2, stanza 18).
3. The river of forgetfulness in Hades (but Styx, the river at hell's entrance, would seem more appropriate here; see canto 5, stanza 10).
4. Spirits of discord and revenge.
5. That is, do not withhold mercy, for he is the one truest knight.

38

Her piteous words might° not abate his rage,   *could*
  But rudely rending up his helmet, would
  Have slaine him straight: but when he sees his age,
  And hoarie head of Archimago old,
  His hastie hand he doth amazèd hold,
  And halfe ashamèd, wondred at the sight:
  For the old man well knew he, though untold,[6]
  In charmes and magicke to have wondrous might,
Ne ever wont° in field, ne in round lists[7] to fight.   *accustomed*

39

And said, "Why Archimago, lucklesse syre,
  What doe I see? what hard mishap is this,
  That hath thee hither brought to taste mine yre?
  Or thine the fault, or mine the error is,
  In stead of foe to wound my friend amis?"
  He answered nought, but in a traunce still lay,
  And on those guilefull dazèd eyes of his
  The cloud of death did sit. Which doen away,°   *when the swoon passed*
He left him lying so, ne would no lenger stay.

40

But to the virgin comes, who all this while
  Amasèd stands, her selfe so mockt° to see   *deceived*
  By him, who has the guerdon° of his guile,   *reward*
  For so misfeigning her true knight to bee:
  Yet is she now in more perplexitie,°   *trouble*
  Left in the hand of that same Paynim bold,
  From whom her booteth not° at all to flie;   *is of no use*
  Who by her cleanly° garment catching hold,   *pure*
Her from her Palfrey pluckt, her visage to behold.

41

But her fierce servant full of kingly awe°   *awesomeness*
  And high disdaine,° whenas his soveraine Dame   *indignation*
  So rudely handled by her foe he sawe,
  With gaping jawes full greedy at him came,
  And ramping° on his shield, did weene° the same   *rearing / intend*
  Have reft away with his sharpe rending clawes:
  But he was stout, and lust did now inflame
  His corage more, that from his griping pawes
He hath his shield redeemed,° and foorth his swerd he drawes.   *recovered*

---

6. That is, without needing to be told.   7. Enclosures for fighting tournaments.

42

O then too weake and feeble was the forse
   Of salvage beast, his puissance to withstand:
   For he was strong, and of so mightie corse,°   *body*
   As ever wielded speare in warlike hand,
   And feates of armes did wisely° understand.   *skillfully*
   Eftsoones he percèd through his chaufèd° chest   *angry*
   With thrilling° point of deadly yron brand,°   *penetrating / blade*
   And launcht° his Lordly hart: with death opprest   *pierced*
He roared aloud, whiles life forsooke his stubborne brest.

43

Who now is left to keepe the forlorne maid
   From raging spoile° of lawlesse victors will?   *plunder*
   Her faithfull gard removed, her hope dismaid,
   Her selfe a yeelded pray to save or spill.°   *destroy*
   He now Lord of the field, his pride to fill,
   With foule reproches, and disdainfull spight
   Her vildly° entertaines, and will or nill,   *basely*
   Beares her away upon his courser light:[8]
Her prayers nought prevaile; his rage is more of might.

44

And all the way, with great lamenting paine,
   And piteous plaints she filleth his dull° eares,   *deaf*
   That stony hart could riven have in twaine,
   And all the way she wets with flowing teares:
   But he enraged with rancor, nothing heares.
   Her servile beast° yet would not leave her so,   *the palfrey*
   But followes her farre off, ne ought° he feares, *aught; anything*
   To be partaker of her wandring woe,
More mild in beastly kind,° then that her beastly foe. *nature*

Canto 4

To sinfull house of Pride, Duessa
   guides the faithfull knight,
Where brothers death to wreak° Sansjoy   *avenge*
   doth chalenge him to fight.

1

Young knight, what ever that dost armes professe,
   And through long labours huntest after fame,
   Beware of fraud, beware of ficklenesse,
   In choice, and change of thy deare lovèd Dame,

---

8. Quickly. That is, he treats her basely and quickly bears her away, willing or not, on his horse.

  Least thou of her beleeve too lightly blame,[9]
   And rash misweening° doe thy hart remove: *misjudgment*
   For unto knight there is no greater shame,
   Then lightnesse and inconstancie in love;
  That doth this Redcrosse knights ensample° plainly prove.   *example*

2

  Who after that he had faire Una lorne,°   *forsaken*
   Through light misdeeming° of her loialtie,   *misjudging*
   And false Duessa in her sted had borne,°   *taken as companion*
   Called Fidess', and so suppos'd to bee;
   Long with her traveild, till at last they see
   A goodly building, bravely garnishèd,°   *adorned*
   The house of mightie Prince it seemd to bee:
   And towards it a broad high way[1] that led,
  All bare through peoples feet, which thither traveilèd.

3

  Great troupes of people traveild thitherward
   Both day and night, of each degree and place,°   *rank*
   But few returnèd, having scapèd hard,°   *with difficulty*
   With balefull° beggerie, or foule disgrace,   *wretched*
   Which ever after in most wretched case,
   Like loathsome lazars,° by the hedges lay.   *lepers*
   Thither Duessa bad him bend his pace:°   *direct his steps*
   For she is wearie of the toilesome way,
  And also nigh consumèd is the lingring day.

4

  A stately Pallace built of squarèd bricke,
   Which cunningly was without morter laid,
   Whose wals were high, but nothing strong, nor thick,
   And golden foile° all over them displaid,   *thin layer of gold*
   That purest skye with brightnesse they dismaid:°   *outdid*
   High lifted up were many loftie towres,
   And goodly galleries farre over laid,°   *placed above*
   Full of faire windowes, and delightfull bowres;
  And on the top a Diall told the timely howres.[2]

5

  It was a goodly heape° for to behould,   *building*
   And spake the praises of the workmans wit;°   *skill*
   But full great pittie, that so faire a mould°   *structure*
   Did on so weake foundation ever sit:
   For on a sandie hill,[3] that still did flit,°   *shift*

---

9. Lest you too readily believe accusations about her.
1. "Broad is the way, that leadeth to destruction" (Matthew 7:13).

2. A sundial measured the hours of the day.
3. Matthew 7:26–27: "A foolish man . . . built his house upon the sand: And the rain descended, and the floods came, and the winds blew, and

And fall away, it mounted was full hie,
That every breath of heaven shakèd it:
And all the hinder parts, that few could spie,
Were ruinous and old, but painted cunningly.

6

Arrivèd there they passèd in forth right;
  For still° to all the gates stood open wide,   *always*
  Yet charge of them was to a Porter hight°   *committed*
  Cald Malvenù,[4] who entrance none denide:
  Thence to the hall, which was on every side
  With rich array and costly arras dight:[5]
  Infinite sorts of people did abide
  There waiting long, to win the wishèd sight
Of her, that was the Lady of that Pallace bright.

7

By them they passe, all gazing on them round,
  And to the Presence[6] mount; whose glorious vew
  Their frayle amazèd senses did confound:
  In living Princes court none ever knew
  Such endlesse richesse, and so sumptuous shew;°   *show*
  Ne° Persia selfe, the nourse° of pompous pride   *nor / breeding ground*
  Like ever saw. And there a noble crew
  Of Lordes and Ladies stood on every side,
Which with their presence faire, the place much beautifide.

8

High above all a cloth of State° was spred,   *canopy*
  And a rich throne, as bright as sunny day,
  On which there sate most brave embellishèd°   *handsomely clad*
  With royall robes and gorgeous array,
  A mayden Queene, that shone as Titans° ray,   *the sun's*
  In glistring gold, and peerelesse pretious stone:
  Yet her bright blazing beautie did assay°   *attempt*
  To dim the brightnesse of her glorious throne,
As envying her selfe, that too exceeding shone.

9

Exceeding shone, like Phoebus fairest childe,
  That did presume° his fathers firie wayne,°   *usurp / chariot*
  And flaming mouthes of steedes unwonted° wilde   *unusually*
  Through highest heaven with weaker° hand to rayne;   *too weak*
  Proud of such glory and advancement vaine,
  While flashing beames do daze his feeble eyen,°   *eyes*

---

beat upon that house; and it fell: and great was the fall of it."
4. Unwelcome. In courtly love allegories, the porter is often called Bienvenu or Bel-accueil (Welcome).
5. Decorated with costly wall hangings.
6. Presence chamber, where a sovereign receives guests.

He leaves the welkin° way most beaten plaine, — *heavenly*
And rapt° with whirling wheeles, inflames the skyen, — *carried away*
With fire not made to burne, but fairely for to shyne.⁷

10

So proud she shynèd in her Princely state,
　Looking to heaven; for earth she did disdayne,
　And sitting high; for lowly° she did hate: — *lowliness*
　Lo underneath her scornefull feete, was layne
　A dreadfull Dragon with an hideous trayne,° — *tail*
　And in her hand she held a mirrhour bright,⁸
　Wherein her face she often vewèd fayne,° — *with pleasure*
　And in her selfe-loved semblance tooke delight;
For she was wondrous faire, as any living wight.

11

Of griesly° Pluto she the daughter was, — *horrid*
　And sad Proserpina the Queene of hell;
　Yet did she thinke her pearelesse worth to pas° — *surpass*
　That parentage, with pride so did she swell,
　And thundring Jove, that high in heaven doth dwell,
　And wield° the world, she claymèd for her syre, — *govern*
　Or if that any else did Jove excell:
　For to the highest she did still aspyre,
Or if ought° higher were then that, did it desyre. — *anything*

12

And proud Lucifera men did her call,
　That made her selfe a Queene, and crownd to be,
　Yet rightfull kingdome she had none at all,
　Ne heritage of native soveraintie,
　But did usurpe with wrong and tyrannie
　Upon the scepter, which she now did hold:
　Ne ruld her Realmes with lawes, but pollicie,° — *political cunning*
　And strong advizement of six wisards old,
That with their counsels bad her kingdome did uphold.

13

Soone as the Elfin knight in presence came,
　And false Duessa seeming Lady faire,
　A gentle Husher,° Vanitie by name — *usher*
　Made rowme, and passage for them did prepare:
　So goodly° brought them to the lowest staire — *graciously*
　Of her high throne, where they on humble knee
　Making obeyssance,° did the cause declare, — *submission*

---

7. Phaëthon tried to drive the chariot of his father, Phoebus, the sun god, but set the skies on fire and fell.

8. Pride and figures associated with her in Renaissance literature and art often hold a mirror, emblematic of self-love.

Why they were come, her royall state to see,
To prove° the wide report of her great Majestee. — *verify*

14

With loftie eyes, halfe loth to looke so low,
　　She thankèd them in her disdainefull wise,° — *manner*
　　Ne other grace vouchsafèd them to show
　　Of Princesse worthy, scarse them bad° arise. — *bade*
　　Her Lordes and Ladies all this while devise° — *make ready*
　　Themselves to setten forth to straungers sight:
　　Some frounce° their curlèd haire in courtly guise, — *frizzle*
　　Some prancke° their ruffes, and others trimly dight° — *pleat / arrange*
Their gay attire: each others greater pride does spight.[9]

15

Goodly they all that knight do entertaine,
　　Right glad with him to have increast their crew:
　　But to Duess' each one himselfe did paine
　　All kindnesse and faire courtesie to shew;
　　For in that court whylome° her well they knew: — *formerly*
　　Yet the stout Faerie mongst the middest° crowd — *thickest*
　　Thought all their glorie vaine in knightly vew,
　　And that great Princesse too exceeding prowd,
That to strange° knight no better countenance° allowd. — *stranger / favor*

16

Suddein upriseth from her stately place
　　The royall Dame, and for her coche doth call:
　　All hurtlen° forth and she with Princely pace, — *rush*
　　As faire Aurora in her purple pall,[1]
　　Out of the East the dawning day doth call:
　　So forth she comes: her brightnesse brode° doth blaze; — *abroad*
　　The heapes of people thronging in the hall,
　　Do ride° each other, upon her to gaze: — *climb up on*
Her glorious glitterand° light doth all mens eyes amaze. — *glittering*

17

So forth she comes, and to her coche does clyme,
　　Adornèd all with gold, and girlonds gay,
　　That seemd as fresh as Flora° in her prime, — *the goddess of flowers*
　　And strove to match, in royall rich array,
　　Great Junos golden chaire,° the which they say — *chariot*
　　The Gods stand gazing on, when she does ride
　　To Joves high house through heavens bras-pavèd way
　　Drawne of faire Pecocks, that excell in pride,
And full of Argus eyes their tailes dispredden wide.[2]

---

9. Each despises the others' greater pride.
1. Goddess of dawn, in her crimson robe ("purple pall").
2. Peacocks, with their tails outspread ("dispredden wide"), are a symbol of pride. The hundred-eyed monster Argus was set by Juno to watch Io,

18

But this was drawne of six unequall beasts,
  On which her six sage Counsellours did ryde,
  Taught to obay their bestiall beheasts,°   *bidding*
  With like conditions to their kinds applyde:³
  Of which the first, that all the rest did guyde,
  Was sluggish Idlenesse the nourse of sin;
  Upon a slouthfull Asse he chose to ryde,
  Arayd in habit blacke, and amis thin,⁴
Like to an holy Monck, the service to begin.

19

And in his hand his Portesse° still he bare,   *breviary, prayer book*
  That much was worne, but therein little red,
  For of devotion he had little care,
  Still drownd in sleepe, and most of his dayes ded;
  Scarse could he once uphold his heavie hed,
  To looken, whether it were night or day:
  May seeme the wayne° was very evill led,   *chariot*
  When such an one had guiding of the way,
That knew not, whether right he went, or else astray.

20

From worldly cares himselfe he did esloyne,°   *withdraw*
  And greatly shunnèd manly exercise,
  From every worke he chalengèd essoyne,°   *claimed exemption*
  For contemplation sake: yet otherwise,
  His life he led in lawlesse riotise;°   *riotous conduct*
  By which he grew to grievous malady;
  For in his lustlesse° limbs through evill guise°   *feeble / living*
  A shaking fever raignd continually:
Such one was Idlenesse, first of this company.

21

And by his side rode loathsome Gluttony,
  Deformèd creature, on a filthie swyne,
  His belly was up-blowne with luxury,°   *indulgence*
  And eke° with fatnesse swollen were his eyne,°   *also / eyes*
  And like a Crane his necke was long and fyne,⁵
  With which he swallowd up excessive feast,
  For want whereof poore people oft did pyne;°   *starve*

---

one of Jupiter's loves. When Mercury killed Argus, his eyes were put in the peacock's tail feathers.

3. That is, each bestial rider gave commands to his beast appropriate to its particular nature: the *beasts and riders are suited to each other*. This procession of the Seven Deadly Sins—of which Pride is queen—had a long tradition in medieval art and literature (see also Marlowe, *Dr. Faustus,* scene 5, lines 272–328).

4. Idleness wears the gown ("habit") and hood or amice ("amis") of a monk. Traditionally, Idleness led the procession of the deadly sins.

5. Thin. The crane is a common symbol of gluttony because its long, thin neck allows extended pleasure in swallowing.

And all the way, most like a brutish beast,
He spuèd up his gorge,⁶ that° all did him deteast. *so that*

22

In greene vine leaves he was right fitly clad;
   For other clothes he could not weare for heat,
   And on his head an yvie girland had,⁷
   From under which fast trickled downe the sweat:
   Still as he rode, he somewhat° still did eat, *something*
   And in his hand did beare a bouzing° can, *drinking*
   Of which he supt so oft, that on his seat
   His dronken corse° he scarse upholden can, *body*
In shape and life more like a monster, then° a man. *than*

23

Unfit he was for any worldly thing,
   And eke unhable once° to stirre or go,° *at all / walk*
   Not meet° to be of counsell to a king, *fit*
   Whose mind in meat and drinke was drownèd so,
   That from his friend he seldome knew his fo:
   Full of diseases was his carcas blew,
   And a dry dropsie through his flesh did flow,
   Which by misdiet daily greater grew:
Such one was Gluttony, the second of that crew.

24

And next° to him rode lustfull Lechery, *just after*
   Upon a bearded Goat,⁸ whose rugged° haire, *shaggy*
   And whally° eyes (the signe of gelosy,°) *glaring / jealousy*
   Was like the person selfe, whom he did beare:
   Who rough, and blacke, and filthy did appeare,
   Unseemely man to please faire Ladies eye;
   Yet he of Ladies oft was lovèd deare,
   When fairer faces were bid standen by:° *away*
O who does know the bent of womens fantasy?° *caprice, whim*

25

In a greene gowne he clothèd was full faire,
   Which underneath did hide his filthinesse,
   And in his hand a burning hart he bare,
   Full of vaine follies, and new fangleness:° *fickleness*
   For he was false, and fraught with ficklenesse,
   And learnèd had to love with secret lookes,
   And well could daunce, and sing with ruefulnesse,° *pathos*
   And fortunes tell, and read in loving bookes,⁹
And thousand other wayes, to bait his fleshly hookes.

---

6. Vomited up what he had swallowed.
7. He resembles the drunken satyr Silenus, foster father of Bacchus, god of wine. Ivy is sacred to Bacchus.
8. Traditional symbol of lust.
9. Either manuals on the art of love (for example, Ovid's *Ars Amatoria*) or more ordinary erotica.

26

Inconstant man, that lovèd all he saw,
   And lusted after all, that he did love,
   Ne would his looser° life be tide to law,   *lustful*
   But joyd weake wemens hearts to tempt and prove°   *try*
   If from their loyall loves he might them move;
   Which lewdnesse fild him with reprochfull paine
   Of that fowle evill, which all men reprove,°   *syphilis*
   That rots the marrow, and consumes the braine:
Such one was Lecherie, the third of all this traine.

27

And greedy Avarice by him did ride,
   Upon a Camell loaden all with gold;[1]
   Two iron coffers hong on either side,
   With precious mettall full, as they might hold,
   And in his lap an heape of coine he told;°   *counted*
   For of his wicked pelfe° his God he made,   *money*
   And unto hell him selfe for money sold;
   Accursèd usurie was all his trade,
And right and wrong ylike in equall ballaunce waide.[2]

28

His life was nigh unto deaths doore yplast,[3]
   And thread-bare cote, and cobled° shoes he ware,   *roughly mended*
   Ne scarse good morsell all his life did tast,
   But both from backe and belly still did spare,
   To fill his bags, and richesse to compare;°   *acquire*
   Yet chylde ne° kinsman living had he none   *nor*
   To leave them to; but thorough° daily care   *through*
   To get, and nightly feare to lose his owne,
He led a wretched life unto him selfe unknowne.

29

Most wretched wight, whom nothing might suffise,
   Whose greedy lust° did lacke in greatest store,°   *desire / plenty*
   Whose need had end, but no end covetise,
   Whose wealth was want, whose plenty made him pore,
   Who had enough, yet wishèd ever more;
   A vile disease, and eke in foote and hand
   A grievous gout tormented him full sore,
   That well he could not touch, nor go,° nor stand: *walk*
Such one was Avarice, the fourth of this faire band.

---

1. The camel as a symbol of avarice is based on Matthew 19:24: "It is easier for a camel to go through the eye of a needle, than for a rich man to enter into the kingdom of God."
2. That is, he made no distinction between right and wrong.
3. Avarice was proverbially associated with old age.

30

And next to him malicious Envie rode,
    Upon a ravenous wolfe, and still° did chaw   *continually*
    Betweene his cankred° teeth a venemous tode,   *infected*
    That all the poison ran about his chaw;°   *jaw*
    But inwardly he chawèd his owne maw°   *entrails*
    At neighbours wealth, that made him ever sad;
    For death it was, when any good he saw,
    And wept, that cause of weeping none he had,
But when he heard of harme, he wexèd° wondrous glad.   *waxed, grew*

31

All in a kirtle of discolourd say[4]
    He clothèd was, ypainted full of eyes;
    And in his bosome secretly there lay
    An hatefull Snake,[5] the which his taile uptyes
    In many folds, and mortall sting implyes.°   *enfolds*
    Still as he rode, he gnasht his teeth, to see
    Those heapes of gold with griple Covetyse,°   *grasping Avarice*
    And grudgèd at the great felicitie
Of proud Lucifera, and his owne companie.

32

He hated all good workes and vertuous deeds,
    And him no lesse, that any like did use,°   *perform*
    And who with gracious bread the hungry feeds,
    His almes for want of faith he doth accuse;[6]
    So every good to bad he doth abuse:°   *twist*
    And eke the verse of famous Poets witt
    He does backebite, and spightfull poison spues
    From leprous mouth on all, that ever writt:
Such one vile Envie was, that fifte in row did sitt.

33

And him beside rides fierce revenging Wrath,
    Upon a Lion, loth for to be led;
    And in his hand a burning brond° he hath,   *sword*
    The which he brandisheth about his hed;
    His eyes did hurle forth sparkles fiery red,
    And starèd sterne on all, that him beheld,
    As ashes pale of hew and seeming ded;
    And on his dagger still° his hand he held,   *always*
Trembling through hasty rage, when choler° in him sweld.   *anger*

---

4. Robe or gown of many-colored cloth.
5. Traditional attribute of envy.
6. Envy perversely discounts others' good works by attributing them to a selfish motive: the desire to compensate (in God's eyes) for lack of faith.

34

His ruffin° raiment all was staind with blood,   *disorderly*
  Which he had spilt, and all to rags yrent,°   *torn*
  Through unadvisèd rashnesse woxen wood,°   *grown insane*
  For of his hands he had no governement,°   *control*
  Ne cared for° bloud in his avengement:°   *minded / vengeance*
  But when the furious fit was overpast,
  His cruell facts° he often would repent;   *actions*
  Yet wilfull man he never would forecast,
How many mischieves should ensue his heedlesse hast.[7]

35

Full many mischiefes follow cruell Wrath;
  Abhorrèd bloudshed, and tumultuous strife,
  Unmanly murder, and unthrifty scath,[8]
  Bitter despight,° with rancours rusty knife,   *malice*
  And fretting griefe the enemy of life;
  All these, and many evils moe° haunt ire,°   *more / anger*
  The swelling Splene,[9] and Frenzy raging rife,
  The shaking Palsey, and Saint Fraunces fire:[1]
Such one was Wrath, the last of this ungoldly tire.°   *train*

36

And after all, upon the wagon beame
  Rode Sathan,° with a smarting whip in hand,   *Satan*
  With which he forward lasht the laesie teme,
  So oft as Slowth° still in the mire did stand.   *Idleness*
  Huge routs° of people did about them band,   *crowds*
  Showting for joy, and still before their way
  A foggy mist had covered all the land;
  And underneath their feet, all scattered lay
Dead sculs and bones of men, whose life had gone astray.

37

So forth they marchen in this goodly sort,°   *company*
  To take the solace° of the open aire,   *pleasure*
  And in fresh flowring fields themselves to sport;
  Emongst the rest rode that false Lady faire,
  The fowle Duessa, next unto the chaire
  Of proud Lucifera, as one of the traine:
  But that good knight would not so nigh repaire,°   *approach*
  Him selfe estraunging from their joyaunce° vaine,   *festivity*
Whose fellowship seemd far unfit for warlike swaine.°   *young man*

---

7. That is, he never would foresee ("forecast") the calamities his careless haste caused.
8. That is, inhuman murder and destructive harm.
9. In Renaissance physiology, the spleen was regarded as the seat of ill-humor.
1. Presumably Saint Anthony's fire: erysipelas, or the flaming itch; appropriate to Wrath.

38

So having solacèd themselves a space
    With pleasaunce of the breathing° fields yfed,   *emitting fragrance*
    They backe returnèd to the Princely Place;
    Whereas an errant knight in armes ycled,°   *clad*
    And heathnish shield, wherein with letters red
    Was writ Sans joy, they new arrivèd find:
    Enflamed with fury and fiers hardy-hed,°   *hardihood*
    He seemd in hart to harbour thoughts unkind,
And nourish bloudy vengeaunce in his bitter mind.

39

Who when the shamèd shield[2] of slaine Sans foy
    He spied with that same Faery champions page,°   *the dwarf*
    Bewraying° him, that did of late destroy   *revealing*
    His eldest brother, burning all with rage
    He to him leapt, and that same envious gage°   *envied prize*
    Of victors glory from him snatcht away:
    But th'Elfin knight, which ought that warlike wage,[3]
    Disdaind to loose the meed° he wonne in fray,°   *reward / battle*
And him rencountring° fierce, reskewd the noble pray.   *encountering*

40

Therewith they gan to hurtlen° greedily,   *rush together*
    Redoubted battaile ready to darrayne,°   *contest*
    And clash their shields, and shake their swords on hy,
    That with their sturre° they troubled all the traine;   *tumult*
    Till that great Queene upon eternall paine
    Of high displeasure, that ensewen° might,   *ensue*
    Commaunded them their fury to refraine,
    And if that either to that shield had right,
In equall lists[4] they should the morrow next it fight.

41

"Ah dearest Dame," quoth then the Paynim° bold,   *pagan*
    "Pardon the errour of enragèd wight,°   *creature; man*
    Whom great griefe made forget the raines to hold
    Of reasons rule, to see this recreant° knight,   *cowardly*
    No knight, but treachour° full of false despight°   *traitor / disdain*
    And shamefull treason, who through guile° hath slayn   *deceit*
    The prowest° knight, that ever field did fight,   *bravest*
    Even stout Sans foy (O who can then refrayn?)
Whose shield he beares renverst, the more to heape disdayn.

---

2. Carrying a shield upside down, with the heraldic arms reversed, was a great insult (see stanza 41, line 9).

3. The knight (Redcrosse) who owned ("ought") that spoil of war ("warlike wage").

4. That is, in impartial formal combat.

42

"And to augment the glorie of his guile,
  His° dearest love the faire Fidessa loe   *Sansfoy's*
Is there possessèd of⁵ the traytour vile,
Who reapes the harvest sowen by his foe,
Sowen in bloudy field, and bought with woe:
That° brothers hand shall dearely well requight   *that act*
So be, O Queene, you equall favour showe."⁶
  Him litle answerd th'angry Elfin knight:
He never meant with words, but swords to plead his right.

43

But threw his gauntlet as a sacred pledge,
  His cause in combat the next day to try:
So been they parted both, with harts on edge,
To be avenged each on his enimy.
That night they pas in joy and jollity,
Feasting and courting both in bowre and hall;⁷
  For Steward was excessive Gluttonie,
That of his plenty pourèd forth to all;
Which doen,° the Chamberlain⁸ Slowth did to rest them call.   *done*

44

Now whenas darkesome night had all displayd
  Her coleblacke curtein over brightest skye,
The warlike youthes on dayntie° couches layd,   *fine*
Did chace away sweet sleepe from sluggish eye,
To muse on meanes of hopèd victory.
But whenas Morpheus⁹ had with leaden mace
  Arrested all that courtly company,
Up-rose Duessa from her resting place,
And to the Paynims lodging comes with silent pace.

45

Whom broad awake she finds, in troublous fit,°   *troubled mood*
  Forecasting, how his foe he might annoy,°   *injure*
And him amoves° with speaches seeming fit: *arouses*
"Ah deare Sans joy, next dearest to Sans foy,
Cause of my new griefe, cause of my new joy,
Joyous, to see his ymage in mine eye,
  And greeved, to thinke how foe did him destroy,
That was the flowre of grace and chevalrye;
Lo his Fidessa to thy secret faith I flye."

---

5. Possessed by (that is, sexually).
6. That is, if, O Queen, you show impartiality ("equall favour").
7. That is, feasting in hall, courting in bowers (inner apartments, bedrooms).
8. The court attendant in charge of the bed-chambers.
9. Here, the god of sleep (see canto 1, stanza 36, n. 2).

46

With gentle wordes he can° her fairely° greet,   *did / courteously*
   And bad say on the secret of her hart.
   Then sighing soft, "I learne that litle sweet
Oft tempred is," quoth she, "with muchell° smart: *much*
For since my brest was launcht with lovely dart[1]
Of deare Sansfoy, I never joyèd howre,°   *for an hour*
   But in eternall woes my weaker° hart   *too weak*
   Have wasted, loving him with all my powre,
And for his sake have felt full many an heavie stowre.°   *grief*

47

"At last when perils all I weenèd past,
   And hoped to reape the crop of all my care,
   Into new woes unweeting° I was cast,   *unknowing*
By this false faytor,° who unworthy ware°   *imposter / wore*
His worthy shield, whom he with guilefull snare
Entrappèd slew, and brought to shamefull grave.
   Me silly° maid away with him he bare,   *helpless*
   And ever since hath kept in darksome cave,
For that I would not yeeld, that° to Sans foy I gave.   *what*

48

"But since faire Sunne hath sperst° that lowring clowd,   *dispersed*
   And to my loathèd life now shewes some light,
   Under your beames I will me safely shrowd,°   *take shelter*
From dreaded storme of his disdainfull spight:
To you th'inheritance belongs by right
Of brothers prayse, to you eke longs° his love.   *belongs*
   Let not his love, let not his restlesse spright°   *ghost*
   Be unrevenged, that calles to you above
From wandring Stygian[2] shores, where it doth endlesse move."

49

Thereto said he, "Faire Dame be nought dismaid
   For sorrowes past; their griefe is with them gone:
   Ne yet of present perill be affraid;
For needlesse feare did never vantage° none,   *aid*
And helplesse hap it booteth not to mone.[3]
Dead is Sans-foy, his vitall° paines are past,   *living*
   Though greevèd ghost for vengeance deepe do grone:
   He lives, that shall him pay his dewties° last,   *rites*
And guiltie Elfin bloud shall sacrifice in hast."

---

1. That is, since my breast was pierced with the arrow of love.
2. That is, from wandering on the banks of the river Styx, in Hades.
3. That is, it does not help to moan over that which is beyond help ("helplesse hap").

50

"O but I feare the fickle freakes,"° quoth shee, *unpredictable tricks*
 "Of fortune false, and oddes of armes[4] in field."
"Why dame," quoth he, "what oddes can ever bee,
 Where both do fight alike, to win or yield?"
"Yea but," quoth she, "he beares a charmèd shield,
 And eke enchaunted armes, that none can perce,
 Ne none can wound the man, that does them wield."
"Charmd or enchaunted," answerd he then ferce,° *fiercely*
"I no whit reck,[5] ne you the like need to reherce."° *recount*

51

"But faire Fidessa, sithens° fortunes guile, *since*
 Or enimies powre hath now captivèd you,
 Returne from whence ye came, and rest a while
 Till morrow next, that I the Elfe subdew,
 And with Sans-foyes dead dowry you endew."[6]
"Ay me, that is a double death," she said,
 "With proud foes sight my sorrow to renew:
 Where ever yet I be, my secrete aid
Shall follow you." So passing forth she him obaid.

Canto 5

*The faithfull knight in equall field
subdewes his faithlesse foe,
Whom false Duessa saves, and for
his cure to hell does goe.*

1

The noble hart, that harbours vertuous thought,
 And is with child of° glorious great intent, *pregnant with*
 Can never rest, untill it forth have brought
 Th'eternall brood of glorie excellent:[7]
 Such restlesse passion did all night torment
 The flaming corage° of that Faery knight, *heart; mind*
 Devizing, how that doughtie° turnament *worthy*
 With greatest honour he atchieven might;
Still did he wake, and still did watch for dawning light.

2

At last the golden Orientall gate
 Of greatest heaven gan to open faire,
 And Phoebus[8] fresh, as bridegrome to his mate,

---

4. Advantage of superior arms.
5. *I do not care at all.*
6. That is, endow you with the legacy of the dead Sansfoy.
7. That good must be manifested in action, not in mere intent, is an important Renaissance commonplace.
8. That is, the sun. See Psalm 19:4–5: "In them hath he set a Tabernacle for the sun, Which is as a bridegroom coming out of his chamber."

  Came dauncing forth, shaking his deawie haire:
  And hurld his glistring beames through gloomy aire.
  Which when the wakeful Elfe perceived, streight way
   He started up, and did him selfe prepare,
   In sun-bright armes, and battailous° array: *warlike*
  For with that Pagan proud he combat will that day.

3

  And forth he comes into the commune hall,
   Where earely waite him many a gazing eye,
  To weet° what end to straunger knights may fall.° *learn / befall*
  There many Minstrales maken melody,
  To drive away the dull melancholy,
  And many Bardes, that to the trembling chord
   Can tune their timely° voyces cunningly,   *measured*
  And many Chroniclers, that can record
Old loves, and warres for ladies doen° by many a Lord.[9] *done*

4

Soone after comes the cruell Sarazin,°   *Saracen*
  In woven maile all armèd warily,
  And sternly lookes at him, who not a pin
  Does care for looke of living creatures eye.
  They bring them wines of Greece and Araby,
  And daintie spices fetcht from furthest Ynd,°   *India*
   To kindle heat of courage privily:°   *within*
  And in the wine a solemne oth they bynd
T'observe the sacred lawes of armes, that are assynd.

5

At last forth comes that far renowmèd Queene,
  With royall pomp and Princely majestie;
  She is ybrought unto a palèd° greene,   *fenced*
  And placèd under stately canapee,°   *canopy*
  The warlike feates of both those knights to see.
  On th'other side in all mens open vew
  Duessa placèd is, and on a tree
  Sans-foy his shield is hangd with bloudy hew:
Both those the lawrell girlonds[1] to the victor dew.

6

A shrilling trompet sownded from on hye,
  And unto battaill bad° them selves addresse: *bade*
  Their shining shieldes about their wrestes° they tye, *wrists*
  And burning blades about their heads do blesse,° *brandish*
  The instruments of wrath and heavinesse:°   *rage*

---

9. Minstrels play the music on their instruments; bards sing the words; chroniclers—historians, epic poets—write of love and war.

1. Laurel wreaths were awarded to the victor of a joust.

   With greedy force each other doth assayle,
    And strike so fiercely, that they do impresse
    Deepe dinted furrowes in the battred mayle;
  The yron walles to ward their blowes are weake and fraile.[2]

7

The Sarazin was stout,° and wondrous strong,	*bold*
And heapèd blowes like yron hammers great:	
For after bloud and vengeance he did long.	
The knight was fiers,° and full of youthly heat:	*high-spirited*
And doubled strokes, like dreaded thunders threat:	
For all for prayse and honour he did fight.	
Both stricken strike, and beaten both do beat,	
That from their shields forth flyeth firie light,	
And helmets hewen deepe, shew marks of eithers might.	

8

So th'one for wrong, the other strives for right:	
As when a Gryfon[3] seizèd° of his pray,	*in possession*
A Dragon fiers encountreth in his flight,	
Through widest ayre making his ydle° way,	*casual*
That would his rightfull ravine° rend away:	*plunder*
With hideous horrour both together smight,	
And souce° so sore, that they the heavens affray:°	*strike / startle*
The wise Southsayer° seeing so sad sight,	*soothsayer*
Th'amazèd vulgar tels of warres and mortall fight.	

9

So th'one for wrong, the other strives for right,	
And each to deadly shame would drive his foe:	
The cruell steele so greedily doth bight	
In tender flesh, that streames of bloud down flow,	
With which the armes, that earst° so bright did show,	*at first*
Into a pure vermillion now are dyde:	
Great ruth° in all the gazers harts did grow,	*pity*
Seeing the gorèd woundes to gape so wyde,	
That victory they dare not wish to either side.	

10

At last the Paynim chaunst to cast his eye,	
His suddein° eye, flaming with wrathfull fyre,	*darting*
Upon his brothers shield, which hong thereby:	
Therewith redoubled was his raging yre,°	*anger*
And said, "Ah wretched sonne of wofull syre,	
Doest thou sit wayling by black Stygian lake°	*the river Styx*
Whilest here thy shield is hangd for victors hyre,°	*reward*

---

2. That is, their armor is too frail to withstand such blows.
3. A legendary monster, half-eagle, half-lion.

And sluggish german[4] doest thy forces slake,°   *slacken*
  To after-send his foe, that him may overtake?

11

"Goe caytive° Elfe, him quickly overtake,   *servile*
  And soone redeeme from his long wandring woe;
  Goe guiltie ghost, to him my message make,
  That I his shield have quit° from dying foe."   *rescued*
  Therewith upon his crest he stroke him so,
  That twise he reelèd, readie twise to fall;
  End of the doubtfull battell deemèd tho°   *then*
  The lookers on,[5] and lowd to him gan call
The false Duessa, "Thine the shield, and I, and all."

12

Soone as the Faerie heard his Ladie speake,
  Out of his swowning dreame he gan awake,
  And quickning° faith, that earst was woxen° weake,   *life-restoring / grown*
  The creeping deadly cold away did shake:
  Tho moved with wrath, and shame, and Ladies sake,°   *regard*
  Of all attonce he cast° avengd to bee,   *determined*
  And with so'exceeding furie at him strake,
  That forcèd him to stoupe upon his knee;
Had he not stoupèd so, he should have cloven bee.

13

And to him said, "Goe now proud Miscreant,°   *misbeliever*
  Thy selfe thy message doe° to german deare,   *give*
  Alone he wandring thee too long doth want:
  Goe say, his foe thy shield with his doth beare."
  Therewith his heavie hand he high gan reare,
  Him to have slaine; when loe a darkesome clowd
  Upon him fell: he no where doth appeare,
  But vanisht is. The Elfe him cals alowd,
But answer none receives: the darknes him does shrowd.[6]

14

In haste Duessa from her place arose,
  And to him running said, "O prowest° knight,   *bravest*
  That ever Ladie to her love did chose,
  Let now abate the terror of your might,
  And quench the flame of furious despight,°   *anger*
  And bloudie vengeance; lo th'infernall powres
  Covering your foe with cloud of deadly night,

---

4. Kinsman; here, brother.
5. That is, the onlookers then thought this would end the battle, heretofore in doubt.
6. The device of a god rescuing a hero in danger by hiding him in a cloud has parallels in *Iliad* 3.380, *Aeneid* 5.810–12, and *Gerusalemme liberata* 7.44–45.

Have borne him hence to Plutoes balefull bowres.° — *Hades*
The conquest yours, I yours, the shield, and glory yours."

15

Not all so satisfide, with greedie eye
   He sought all round about, his thirstie blade
   To bath in bloud of faithlesse enemy;
   Who all that while lay hid in secret shade:
   He standes amazèd, how he thence should fade.
   At last the trumpets Triumph sound on hie,
   And running Heralds humble homage made,
   Greeting him goodly° with new victorie, — *respectfully*
And to him brought the shield, the cause of enmitie.

16

Wherewith he goeth to that soveraine Queene,
   And falling her before on lowly knee,
   To her makes present of his service seene;° — *proved*
   Which she accepts, with thankes, and goodly gree,° — *favor*
   Greatly advauncing° his gay chevalree. — *extolling*
   So marcheth home, and by her takes the knight,
   Whom all the people follow with great glee,
   Shouting, and clapping all their hands on hight,° — *aloud*
That all the aire it fils, and flyes to heaven bright.

17

Home is he brought, and laid in sumptuous bed:
   Where many skilfull leaches° him abide,° — *doctors / attend*
   To salve° his hurts, that yet still freshly bled. — *anoint*
   In wine and oyle they wash his woundès wide,
   And softly can embalme° on every side. — *carefully did anoint*
   And all the while, most heavenly melody
   About the bed sweet musicke did divide,° — *descanted*
   Him to beguile of° griefe and agony: — *divert from*
And all the while Duessa wept full bitterly.

18

As when a wearie traveller that strayes
   By muddy shore of broad seven-mouthèd Nile,
   Unweeting° of the perillous wandring wayes, — *unaware*
   Doth meet a cruell craftie Crocodile,
   Which in false griefe hyding his harmefull guile,
   Doth weepe full sore, and shedeth tender teares:[7]
   The foolish man, that pitties all this while
   His mournefull plight, is swallowed up unwares,° — *unexpectedly*
Forgetfull of his owne, that mindes anothers cares.

---

7. Medieval bestiaries popularized the legend of the hypocritical crocodile's tears.

19

So wept Duessa untill eventide,
    That shyning lampes in Joves high house were light:[8]
    Then forth she rose, ne lenger° would abide,   *longer*
    But comes unto the place, where th'Hethen knight
    In slombring swownd nigh voyd of vitall spright,[9]
    Lay covered with inchaunted cloud all day:
    Whom when she found, as she him left in plight,[1]
    To wayle his woefull case she would not stay,
But to the easterne coast of heaven makes speedy way.

20

Where griesly° Night, with visage deadly sad,   *grim, horrible*
    That Phoebus chearefull face durst never vew,
    And in a foule blacke pitchie mantle clad,
    She findes forth comming from her darkesome mew,°   *den*
    Where she all day did hide her hated hew.°   *shape; color*
    Before the dore her yron charet° stood,   *chariot*
    Alreadie harnessèd for journey new;
    And cole blacke steedes yborne of hellish brood,
That on their rustie bits did champ, as° they were wood.°   *as if / mad*

21

Who when she saw Duessa sunny bright,
    Adorned with gold and jewels shining cleare,°   *brightly*
    She greatly grew amazèd at the sight,
    And th'unacquainted° light began to feare: *unfamiliar*
    For never did such brightnesse there appeare,
    And would have backe retyred to her cave,
    Untill the witches speech she gan to heare,
    Saying, "Yet O thou dreaded Dame, I crave
Abide,° till I have told the message, which I have."   *stay*

22

She stayd, and foorth Duessa gan proceede,
    "O thou most auncient Grandmother of all,[2]
    More old then Jove, whom thou at first didst breede,
    Or that great house of Gods caelestiall,
    Which wast begot in Daemogorgons hall,
    And sawst the secrets of the world unmade,°   *before it was made*
    Why suffredst thou thy Nephewes° deare to fall   *grandsons*
    With Elfin sword, most shamefully betrade?
Lo where the stout Sansjoy doth sleepe in deadly shade.

---

8. That is, when ("that") the stars came out.
9. Nearly ("nigh") devoid of life.
1. That is, in the same desperate state in which she had left him.

2. By tradition, Night was eldest of the gods, existing before the world was formed and the Olympian gods were begotten in the hall of Demogorgon (Chaos).

23

"And him before, I saw with bitter eyes
    The bold Sansfoy shrinke underneath his speare;
    And now the pray of fowles in field he lyes,
    Nor wayld of° friends, nor laid on groning beare,[3]   *lamented by*
    That whylome° was to me too dearely deare.   *formerly*
    O what of Gods then boots it° to be borne,   *is it worth*
    If old Aveugles sonnes so evill heare?[4]
    Or who shall not great Nightès children scorne,
When two of three her Nephews are so fowle forlorne?°   *wretchedly lost*

24

"Up then, up dreary Dame, of darknesse Queene,
    Go gather up the reliques° of thy race,   *remnants*
    Or else goe them avenge, and let be seene,
    That dreaded Night in brightest day hath place,
    And can the children of faire light deface."°   *destroy*
    Her feeling speeches some compassion moved
    In hart, and chaunge in that great mothers face:
    Yet pittie in her hart was never proved°   *known*
Till then: for evermore she hated, never loved.

25

And said, "Deare daughter rightly may I rew
    The fall of famous children borne of mee,
    And good successes, which their foes ensew:°   *attend*
    But who can turne the streame of destinee,
    Or breake the chayne of strong necessitee,
    Which fast is tyde to Joves eternall seat?[5]
    The sonnes of Day he favoureth, I see,
    And by my ruines thinkes to make them great:
To make one great by others losse, is bad excheat.°   *exchange*

26

"Yet shall they not escape so freely all;
    For some shall pay the price of others guilt:
    And he the man that made Sansfoy to fall,
    Shall with his owne bloud price° that he hath spilt.   *pay for*
    But what art thou, that telst of Nephews kilt?"
    "I that do seeme not I, Duessa am,"
    Quoth she, "how ever now in garments gilt,
    And gorgeous gold arayd I to thee came:
Duessa I, the daughter of Deceipt and Shame."

---

3. Bier attended by mourners (thus "groning").
4. That is, are so badly thought of. Aveugle (Blind) is the son of Night and father of Sansfoy, Sansjoy, and Sansloy.
5. The golden chain that binds the entire universe. The image goes back as far as Homer (*Iliad* 8.18–27).

27

Then bowing downe her agèd backe, she kist
　The wicked witch, saying; "In that faire face
　The false resemblance of Deceipt, I wist° — *knew*
　Did closely° lurke; yet so true-seeming grace — *secretly*
　It carried, that I scarse in darkesome place
　Could it discerne, though I the mother bee
　Of falshood, and root of Duessaes race.
　O welcome child, whom I have longd to see,
And now have seene unwares.° Lo now I go with thee." — *unexpectedly*

28

Then to her yron wagon she betakes,
　And with her beares the fowle welfavour'd witch:
　Through mirkesome° aire her readie way she makes. — *murky; dense*
　Her twyfold Teme,[6] of which two blacke as pitch,
　And two were browne, yet each to each unlich,° — *unlike*
　Did softly swim away, ne ever stampe,
　Unlesse she chaunst their stubborne mouths to twitch;
　Then foming tarre,° their bridles they would champe, — *black froth*
And trampling the fine element,° would fiercely rampe.° — *the air / rear up*

29

So well they sped, that they be come at length
　Unto the place, whereas the Paynim lay,
　Devoid of outward sense, and native strength,
　Coverd with charmèd cloud from vew of day,
　And sight of men, since his late° luckelesse fray. — *recent*
　His cruell wounds with cruddy° bloud congealed, — *clotted*
　They binden up so wisely,° as they may, — *skillfully*
　And handle softly, till they can be healed:
So lay him in her charet, close in night concealed.

30

And all the while she stood upon the ground,
　The wakefull dogs did never cease to bay,
　As giving warning of th'unwonted° sound, — *unusual*
　With which her yron wheeles did them affray,
　And her darke griesly° looke them much dismay; — *horrid*
　The messenger of death, the ghastly Owle
　With drearie shriekes did also her bewray;° — *reveal*
　And hungry Wolves continually did howle,
At her abhorrèd face, so filthy and so fowle.

31

Thence turning backe in silence soft they stole,
　And brought the heavie corse° with easie pace — *body*

---

6. Twofold team of horses.

    To yawning gulfe of deepe Avernus hole.⁷
       By that same hole an entrance darke and bace°   *low*
       With smoake and sulphure hiding all the place,
       Descends to hell: there creature never past,
       That backe returnèd without heavenly grace;
       But dreadfull Furies, which their chaines have brast,°   *burst*
    And damnèd sprights sent forth to make ill° men aghast.   *evil*

32

    By that same way the direfull dames doe drive
       Their mournefull charet, fild° with rusty blood,   *defiled*
       And downe to Plutoes house are come bilive:°   *quickly; alive*
       Which passing through, on every side them stood
       The trembling ghosts with sad amazèd mood,
       Chattring their yron teeth, and staring wide
       With stonie eyes; and all the hellish brood
       Of feends infernall flockt on every side,
    To gaze on earthly wight, that with the Night durst ride.

33

    They pas the bitter waves of Acheron,
       Where many soules sit wailing woefully,
       And come to fiery flood of Phlegeton,⁸
       Whereas the damnèd ghosts in torments fry,
       And with sharpe shrilling shriekes doe bootlesse° cry,   *without avail*
       Cursing high Jove, the which them thither sent.
       The house of endlesse paine is built thereby,
       In which ten thousand sorts of punishment
    The cursèd creatures doe eternally torment.

34

    Before the threshold dreadfull Cerberus⁹
       His three deformèd heads did lay along,°   *at full length*
       Curlèd with thousand adders venemous,
       And lillèd° forth his bloudie flaming tong: *lolled*
       At them he gan to reare his bristles strong,
       And felly gnarre,° untill dayes enemy   *savagely snarl*
       Did him appease; then downe his taile he hong
       And suffered them to passen quietly:
    For she in hell and heaven had power equally.

35

    There was Ixion turnèd on a wheele,
       For daring tempt the Queene of heaven to sin;
       And Sisyphus an huge round stone did reele°   *roll*
       Against an hill, ne° might from labour lin;°   *nor / cease*

---

7. In classical mythology Avernus is hell, where Pluto (stanza 32) reigns.
8. Acheron and Phlegeton are rivers in hell.
9. The three-headed dog that guards hell. Stanzas 31–35 recall Aeneas's descent into hell (Virgil, *Aeneid* 6.200, 239–40).

There thirstie Tantalus hong by the chin;
And Tityus fed a vulture on his maw;° *liver*
Typhoeus joynts were stretchèd on a gin,° *rack*
Theseus condemned to endlesse slouth° by law, *sloth*
And fifty sisters water in leake vessels draw.[1]

36

They all beholding worldly° wights in place,° *mortal / there*
   Leave off their worke, unmindfull of their smart,° *pain*
   To gaze on them; who forth by them doe pace,
   Till they be come unto the furthest part:
   Where was a Cave ywrought by wondrous art,
   Deepe, darke, uneasie,° dolefull, comfortlesse, *lacking ease*
   In which sad Aesculapius° farre a part *god of medicine*
   Emprisond was in chaines remedilesse,° *beyond any remedy*
For that Hippolytus rent corse° he did redresse.° *body / cure*

37

Hippolytus a jolly° huntsman was, *gallant*
   That wont° in charet chace the foming Bore; *used to*
   He all his Peeres in beautie did surpas,
   But Ladies love as losse of time forbore:
   His wanton stepdame[2] lovèd him the more,
   But when she saw her offred sweets refused
   Her love she turnd to hate, and him before
   His father fierce of treason false accused,
And with her gealous° termes his open eares abused. *arousing jealousy*

38

Who all in rage his Sea-god syre° besought, *Poseidon (Neptune)*
   Some cursèd vengeance on his sonne to cast:
   From surging gulf two monsters straight° were brought, *immediately*
   With dread whereof his chasing steedes aghast,
   Both charet swift and huntsman overcast.
   His goodly corps on ragged cliffs yrent,° *torn*
   Was quite dismembred, and his members chast
   Scattered on every mountaine, as he went,
That of Hippolytus was left no moniment.[3]

39

His cruell stepdame seeing what was donne,
   Her wicked dayes with wretched knife did end,
   In death avowing th'innocence of her sonne.

---

1. Ixion was being punished for attempting to seduce Juno; Sisyphus, for refusing to pray to the gods; Tantalus, for stealing the gods' nectar; Tityus, for his attempted assault on Apollo's mother, Leto; the monster Typhoeus, for creating destructive winds; Theseus, for stealing Persephone from Hades; and forty-nine of the fifty daughters of King Danaus, for having killed their husbands on their wedding night. Tantalus stood chin-deep in water that receded whenever he tried to drink—hence he is "thirstie." Ovid, Virgil, and Homer are Spenser's sources here.
2. Phaedra, the wife of his father, Theseus.
3. That is, no trace of identity.

    Which hearing his rash Syre, began to rend
        His haire, and hastie tongue, that did offend:
        Tho° gathering up the relicks of his smart[4]   *then*
        By Dianes meanes, who was Hippolyts frend,
        Them brought to Aesculape, that by his art
Did heale them all againe, and joynèd every part.

40

    Such wondrous science in mans wit to raine
        When Jove avizd,° that could the dead revive,   *discovered*
        And fates expirèd[5] could renew againe,
        Of endlesse life he might him not deprive,
        But unto hell did thrust him downe alive,
        With flashing thunderbolt ywounded sore:
        Where long remaining, he did alwaies strive
        Himselfe with salves to health for to restore,
And slake the heavenly fire, that raged evermore.

41

    There auncient Night arriving, did alight
        From her nigh wearie waine,[6] and in her armes
        To Aesculapius brought the wounded knight:
        Whom having softly disarayd of armes,
        Tho gan to him discover° all his harmes,   *reveal*
        Beseeching him with prayer, and with praise,
        If either salves, or oyles, or herbes, or charmes
        A fordonne° wight from dore of death mote raise,   *undone*
He would at her request prolong her nephews daies.

42

    "Ah Dame," quoth he, "thou temptest me in vaine,
        To dare the thing, which daily yet I rew,
        And the old cause of my continued paine
        With like attempt to like end to renew.
        Is not enough, that thrust from heaven dew[7]
        Here endlesse penance for one fault I pay,
        But that redoubled crime with vengeance new
        Thou biddest me to eeke?° Can Night defray°   *increase / appease*
The wrath of thundring Jove, that rules both night and day?"

43

    "Not so," quoth she; "but sith° that heavens king   *since*
        From hope of heaven hath thee excluded quight,
        Why fearest thou, that canst not hope for thing,°   *anything*
        And fearest not, that more thee hurten might,
        Now in the powre of everlasting Night?

---

4. That is, his son's remains, which caused his grief.
5. The completed term of life as fixed by the Fates.
6. That is, the horses of Night's chariot ("waine") are nearly exhausted.
7. The proper ("dew") place for a god.

Goe to then, O thou farre renowmèd sonne
Of great Apollo, shew thy famous might
In medicine, that else° hath to thee wonne *already*
Great paines, and greater praise, both never to be donne."° *ended*

44

Her words prevaild: And then the learnèd leach° *doctor*
His cunning hand gan to his wounds to lay,
And all things else, the which his art did teach:
Which having seene, from thence arose away
The mother of dread darknesse, and let stay
Aveugles sonne there in the leaches cure,° *care*
And backe returning tooke her wonted° way, *accustomed*
To runne her timely race,° whilst Phoebus pure *her nightly journey*
In westerne waves his wearie wagon did recure.° *refresh*

45

The false Duessa leaving noyous° Night, *harmful*
Returnd to stately pallace of dame Pride;
Where when she came, she found the Faery knight
Departed thence, albe° his woundès wide *although*
Not throughly heald, unreadie were to ride.
Good cause he had to hasten thence away;
For on a day his wary Dwarfe had spide,
Where in a dongeon deepe huge numbers lay
Of caytive° wretched thrals,° that waylèd night and day. *captive / slaves*

46

A ruefull sight, as could be seene with eie;
Of whom he learnèd had in secret wise
The hidden cause of their captivitie,
How mortgaging their lives to Covetise,
Through wastfull° Pride, and wanton Riotise, *causing desolation*
They were by law of that proud Tyrannesse[8]
Provokt with Wrath, and Envies false surmise,
Condemnèd to that Dongeon mercilesse,
Where they should live in woe, and die in wretchednesse.

47

There was that great proud king of Babylon[9]
That would compell all nations to adore,
And him as onely God to call upon,
Till through celestiall doome° throwne out of dore, *judgment*
Into an Oxe he was transformed of yore:
There also was king Croesus,[1] that enhaunst° *exalted*
His heart too high through his great riches store;

---

8. Lucifera. The noble sinners named in stanzas 47–50 exemplify a theme common in Renaissance morality, the fall of princes.
9. Nebuchadnezzar (Daniel 3–4).
1. King of Lydia, famous for his riches.

And proud Antiochus,[2] the which advaunst
His cursèd hand gainst God, and on his altars daunst.°   *danced*

48

And them long time before, great Nimrod was,
  That first the world with sword and fire warrayd;°   *ravaged*
  And after him old Ninus[3] farre did pas°   *surpass*
  In princely pompe, of° all the world obayd;   *by*
  There also was that mightie Monarch layd
  Low under all, yet above all in pride,
  That name of native° syre did fowle upbrayd,   *natural*
  And would as Ammons sonne be magnifide,
Till scornd of God and man a shamefull death he dide.[4]

49

All these together in one heape were throwne,
  Like carkases of beasts in butchers stall.
  And in another corner wide° were strowne   *lying apart*
  The antique ruines of the Romaines fall:
  Great Romulus the Grandsyre of them all,
  Proud Tarquin, and too lordly Lentulus,
  Stout Scipio, and stubborne Hanniball,
  Ambitious Sylla, and sterne Marius,
High Caesar, great Pompey, and fierce Antonius.[5]

50

Amongst these mighty men were wemen mixt,
  Proud wemen, vaine, forgetfull of their yoke:°   *duty*
  The bold Semiramis,° whose sides transfixt   *wife of Ninus*
  With sonnes owne blade, her fowle reproches spoke;
  Faire Sthenoboea,[6] that her selfe did choke
  With wilfull cord, for wanting° of her will;   *lacking*
  High minded Cleopatra, that with stroke
  Of Aspes sting her selfe did stoutly° kill: *bravely*
And thousands moe the like, that did that dongeon fill.

51

Besides the endlesse routs° of wretched thralles,   *crowds*
  Which thither were assembled day by day,
  From all the world after their wofull falles,

---

2. King of Syria, who desecrated the Jewish temple of Jerusalem (1 Maccabees 1:20–24).
3. In classical mythology, Ninus was founder of Nineveh, archetype of the wicked city (see the book of Jonah). Nimrod, identified as the first tyrant, caused the Tower of Babel to be built in defiance of God (Genesis 10:9–10, 11:1–9).
4. The reference is to Alexander the Great, whose "shamefull death" came ten days after he fell ill at a drinking party. The son of Philip II of Macedon, Alexander was occasionally worshipped as the son of Jupiter Ammon.
5. Romulus was the founder of Rome; Tarquin, a Roman tyrant; Lentulus, a conspirator with Catiline to overthrow the Republic; Scipio, a Roman general, conqueror of Carthage; Hannibal, a Carthaginian general; Sulla, a Roman civil war general; Marius, Sulla's rival. The figures in the final line are Julius Caesar, Pompey the Great, and Mark Antony.
6. Queen of King Proteus of Argos; she lusted after her brother-in-law Bellerophon.

Through wicked pride, and wasted wealthes decay.
But most of all, which in that Dongeon lay
Fell from high Princes courts, or Ladies bowres,
Where they in idle pompe, or wanton play,
Consumèd had their goods, and thriftlesse howres,
And lastly throwne themselves into these heavy stowres.°   *disasters*

52

Whose case wheneas the carefull° Dwarfe had tould,   *wary*
   And made ensample of their mournefull sight
Unto his maister, he no lenger would
There dwell in perill of like painefull plight,
But early rose, and ere that dawning light
Discovered had the world to heaven wyde,
He by a privie Posterne° tooke his flight,   *secret back door*
That of no envious eyes he mote be spyde:
For doubtlesse death ensewd, if any him descryde.°   *descried, observed*

53

Scarse could he footing find in that fowle way,
   For many corses, like a great Lay-stall°   *burial place; rubbish heap*
Of murdred men which therein strowèd lay,
Without remorse, or decent funerall:
Which all through that great Princesse pride did fall
And came to shamefull end. And them beside
Forth ryding underneath the castell wall,
A donghill of dead carkases he spide,
The dreadfull spectacle of that sad house of Pride.[7]

Canto 6

From lawlesse lust by wondrous grace
   fayre Una is releast:
Whom salvage° nation does adore,   *wild; of the woods*
   and learnes her wise beheast.°   *bidding*

1

As when a ship, that flyes faire under saile,
   An hidden rocke escapèd hath unwares,°   *unexpectedly*
That lay in waite her wrack for to bewaile,[8]
The Marriner yet halfe amazèd stares
At perill past, and yet in doubt ne dares
To joy at his foole-happie oversight:°   *lucky ignorance*
So doubly is distrest twixt joy and cares
The dreadlesse° courage of this Elfin knight,   *fearless*
Having escapt so sad ensamples in his sight.

---

7. Named in the argument of canto 4, but in the poem itself, only now, after we have been shown what the name means.

8. That is, cause the shipwreck and thereby cause it to be bewailed.

2

Yet sad he was that his too hastie speed
  The faire Duess' had forst him leave behind;
And yet more sad, that Una his deare dreed°   *object of reverence*
  Her truth had staind with treason so unkind;°   *unnatural*
Yet crime in her could never creature find,
But for his love, and for her owne selfe sake,
She wandred had from one to other Ynd,[9]
Him for to seeke, ne ever would forsake,
Till her unwares the fierce Sansloy did overtake.

3

Who after Archimagoes fowle defeat,
  Led her away into a forrest wilde,
And turning wrathfull fire to lustfull heat,
  With beastly sin thought her to have defilde,
And made the vassall of his pleasures vilde.°   *vile*
Yet first he cast by treatie,° and by traynes,°   *persuasion / tricks*
Her to perswade, that stubborne fort to yilde:
For greater conquest of hard love he gaynes,
That workes it to his will, then° he that it constraines.°   *than / forces*

4

With fawning wordes he courted her a while,
  And looking lovely,° and oft sighing sore,   *lovingly*
Her constant hart did tempt with diverse guile:
  But wordes, and lookes, and sighes she did abhore,
As rocke of Diamond stedfast evermore.[1]
Yet for to feed his fyrie lustfull eye,
He snatcht the vele, that hong her face before;
Then gan her beautie shine, as brightest skye,
And burnt his beastly hart t'efforce° her chastitye.   *violate*

5

So when he saw his flatt'ring arts to fayle,
  And subtile engines bet from batteree,[2]
With greedy force he gan the fort assayle,
  Whereof he weend° possessèd soone to bee,   *thought*
And win rich spoile of ransackt chastetee.
Ah heavens, that do this hideous act behold,
And heavenly virgin thus outragèd see,
How can ye vengeance just so long withhold,
And hurle not flashing flames upon that Paynim bold?

---

9. That is, she would have wandered from the East to the West Indies.
1. The diamond, because of its hardness, was an emblem of fidelity.
2. That is, beaten ("bet") from their fruitless assault ("batteree") on her unmovable virtue.

6

The pitteous maiden carefull° comfortlesse, — *full of cares*
    Does throw out thrilling° shriekes, and shrieking cryes, — *piercing*
    The last vaine helpe of womens great distresse,
    And with loud plaints importuneth the skyes,
    That molten starres do drop like weeping eyes;
    And Phoebus flying so most shamefull sight,
    His blushing face in foggy cloud implyes,° — *buries*
    And hides for shame. What wit of mortall wight
Can now devise to quit a thrall° from such a plight? — *release a captive*

7

Eternall providence exceeding° thought, — *transcending*
    Where none appeares can make her selfe a way:
    A wondrous way it for this Lady wrought,
    From Lyons clawes to pluck the gripèd° pray. — *grasped*
    Her shrill outcryes and shriekes so loud did bray,
    That all the woodes and forestes did resownd;
    A troupe of Faunes and Satyres[3] far away
    Within the wood were dauncing in a rownd,
Whiles old Sylvanus[4] slept in shady arber sownd.

8

Who when they heard that pitteous strainèd voice,
    In hast forsooke their rurall meriment,
    And ran towards the far rebownded° noyce, — *re-echoed*
    To weet,° what wight so loudly did lament. — *learn*
    Unto the place they come incontinent:° — *immediately*
    Whom when the raging Sarazin espide,
    A rude, misshapen, monstrous rablement,
    Whose like he never saw, he durst not bide,
But got his ready steed, and fast away gan ride.

9

The wyld woodgods arrivèd in the place,
    There find the virgin dolefull desolate,
    With ruffled rayments, and faire blubbred° face, — *flooded with tears*
    As her outrageous foe had left her late,° — *shortly before*
    And trembling yet through feare of former hate;
    All stand amazèd at so uncouth° sight, — *strange*
    And gin to pittie her unhappie state,
    All stand astonied° at her beautie bright, — *stupified*
In their rude° eyes unworthie° of so wofull plight. — *rustic / undeserving*

---

3. Woodland deities with men's bodies above the waist and goats' bodies below, noted for their sensuality.

4. Roman god of the woods, who is traditionally associated with fauns.

10

She more amazed, in double dread doth dwell;
  And every tender part for feare does shake:
  As when a greedie Wolfe through hunger fell° — *fierce*
  A seely° Lambe farre from the flocke does take, — *innocent*
  Of whom he meanes his bloudie feast to make,
  A Lyon spyes fast running towards him,
  The innocent pray in hast he does forsake,
  Which quit° from death yet quakes in every lim — *rescued*
With chaunge of feare, to see the Lyon looke so grim.° — *savage*

11

Such fearefull fit assaid° her trembling hart, — *assailed*
  Ne word to speake, ne joynt to move she had:
  The salvage° nation feele her secret smart, — *wild; uncivilized*
  And read her sorrow in her count'nance sad;
  Their frowning forheads with rough hornes yclad,
  And rusticke horror° all a side doe lay, — *rough, rugged looks*
  And gently grenning,° shew a semblance° glad — *grinning / an appearance*
  To comfort her, and feare to put away,
Their backward bent knees teach her humbly to obay.[5]

12

The doubtfull Damzell dare not yet commit
  Her single person to their barbarous truth,[6]
  But still twixt feare and hope amazd does sit,
  Late learnd° what harme to hastie trust ensu'th: — *recently taught*
  They in compassion of her tender youth,
  And wonder of her beautie soveraine,° — *supreme*
  Are wonne with pitty and unwonted ruth,° — *unaccustomed pity*
  And all prostrate upon the lowly plaine,
Do kisse her feete, and fawne on her with count'nance faine.° — *glad*

13

Their harts she ghesseth by their humble guise,° — *appearance*
  And yieldes her to extremitie of time;[7]
  So from the ground she fearelesse doth arise,
  And walketh forth without suspect° of crime: — *suspicion*
  They all as glad, as birdes of joyous Prime,° — *springtime*
  Thence lead her forth, about her dauncing round,
  Shouting, and singing all a shepheards ryme,
  And with greene braunches strowing all the ground,
Do worship her, as Queene, with olive girlond cround.

---

5. That is, teach their knees, bent backward like a goat's, to obey her.
6. That is, her solitary self to their wild allegiance ("barbarous truth").
7. That is, necessity of the time.

14

And all the way their merry pipes they sound,
   That all the woods with doubled Eccho ring,
   And with their hornèd feet do weare the ground,
   Leaping like wanton kids in pleasant Spring.
   So towards old Sylvanus they her bring;
   Who with the noyse awakèd, commeth out,
   To weet° the cause, his weake steps governing,   *learn*
   And agèd limbs on Cypresse stadle° stout,   *staff*
And with an yvie twyne his wast is girt about.

15

Far off he wonders, what them makes so glad,
   Or Bacchus merry fruit they did invent,[8]
   Or Cybeles franticke rites[9] have made them mad;
   They drawing nigh, unto their God present
   That flowre of faith and beautie excellent.
   The God himselfe vewing that mirrhour rare,[1]
   Stood long amazd, and burnt in his intent;[2]
   His owne faire Dryope now he thinkes not faire,
And Pholoe fowle, when her to this he doth compaire.[3]

16

The woodborne people fall before her flat,
   And worship her as Goddesse of the wood;
   And old Sylvanus selfe bethinkès not,° what   *cannot decide*
   To thinke of wight so faire, but gazing stood,
   In doubt to deeme her borne of earthly brood;
   Sometimes Dame Venus selfe he seemes to see,
   But Venus never had so sober mood;
   Sometimes Diana he her takes to bee,
But misseth bow, and shaftes, and buskins° to her knee.   *soft boots*

17

By vew of her he ginneth to revive
   His ancient love, and dearest Cyparisse,[4]
   And calles to mind his pourtraiture alive,[5]
   How faire he was, and yet not faire to° this,   *compared to*
   And how he slew with glauncing dart amisse
   A gentle Hynd, the which the lovely boy
   Did love as life, above all worldly blisse;
   For griefe whereof the lad n'ould° after joy,   *would not*
But pynd away in anguish and selfe-wild annoy.°   *self-willed suffering*

---

8. That is, whether ("or") they did find ("invent") wine grapes.
9. Orgiastic dances in worship of Cybele, goddess of the powers of nature.
1. That is, Una, in the sense that she is a paragon, a perfect reflection of heavenly faith and beauty.
2. Glowed with intense concentration.
3. Dryope and Pholoe were nymphs loved by Faunus and Pan. For Spenser, the names *Faunus*, *Pan*, and *Sylvanus* were apparently interchangeable.
4. A fair youth, beloved of Sylvanus, turned into a cypress tree.
5. That is, his appearance when alive.

18

The wooddy Nymphes, faire Hamadryades[6]
    Her to behold do thither runne apace,
    And all the troupe of light-foot Naiades,°   *water nymphs*
    Flocke all about to see her lovely face:
    But when they vewèd have her heavenly grace,
    They envie her in their malitious mind,
    And fly away for feare of fowle disgrace:
    But all the Satyres scorne their woody kind,°   *woodborn race*
And henceforth nothing faire, but her on earth they find.

19

Glad of such lucke, the luckelesse lucky maid,
    Did her content to please their feeble eyes,
    And long time with that salvage people staid,
    To gather breath in many miseries.
    During which time her gentle wit she plyes,
    To teach them truth, which worshipt her in vaine,
    And made her th'Image of Idolatryes;[7]
    But when their bootlesse° zeale she did restraine   *useless*
From her own worship, they her Asse would worship fayn.°   *willingly*

20

It fortunèd a noble warlike knight
    By just occasion to that forrest came,
    To seeke his kindred, and the lignage right,°   *true*
    From whence he took his well deservèd name:
    He had in armes abroad wonne muchell° fame,   *great*
    And fild far landes with glorie of his might,
    Plaine, faithfull, true, and enimy of shame,
    And ever loved to fight for Ladies right,
But in vaine glorious frayes° he litle did delight.   *frays, fights*

21

A Satyres sonne yborne in forrest wyld,
    By straunge adventure as it did betyde,°   *happen*
    And there begotten of a Lady myld,
    Faire Thyamis the daughter of Labryde,[8]
    That was in sacred bands of wedlocke tyde
    To Therion,[9] a loose unruly swayne;
    Who had more joy to raunge the forrest wyde,
    And chase the salvage beast with busie payne,°   *painstaking care*
Then serve his Ladies love, and wast° in pleasures vayne.   *live idly*

---

6. Spirits of trees, whose lives ended when the tree they inhabited died.
7. The idol of their idolatries.
8. The name means "turbulence." Thyamis means "passion."
9. The name means "wild beast."

22

    The forlorne mayd did with loves longing burne,
        And could not lacke° her lovers company,   *be without*
        But to the wood she goes, to serve her turne,
        And seeke her spouse, that from her still° does fly,   *always*
        And followes other game and venery:[1]
        A Satyre chaunst her wandring for to find,
        And kindling coles of lust in brutish eye,
        The loyall links of wedlocke did unbind,
    And made her person thrall unto his beastly kind.

23

    So long in secret cabin there he held
        Her captive to his sensuall desire,
        Till that with timely° fruit her belly sweld,   *ripening*
        And bore a boy unto that salvage sire:
        Then home he suffred her for to retire,°   *return*
        For ransome leaving him the late borne childe;
        Whom till to ryper yeares he gan aspire,°   *grow up*
        He noursled° up in life and manners wilde,   *reared*
    Emongst wild beasts and woods, from lawes of men exilde.

24

    For all he taught the tender ymp,° was but   *child*
        To banish cowardize and bastard° feare;   *base*
        His trembling hand he would him force to put
        Upon the Lyon and the rugged Beare,
        And from the she Beares teats her whelps to teare;
        And eke° wyld roring Buls he would him make   *also*
        To tame, and ryde their backes not made to beare;
        And the Robuckes[2] in flight to overtake,
    That every beast for feare of him did fly and quake.

25

    Thereby so fearelesse, and so fell° he grew,   *fierce*
        That his owne sire and maister of his guise°   *teacher of his behavior*
        Did often tremble at his horrid vew,°   *rough appearance*
        And oft for dread of hurt would him advise,
        The angry beasts not rashly to despise,
        Nor too much to provoke; for he would learne°   *teach*
        The Lyon stoup to him in lowly wise,
        (A lesson hard) and make the Libbard° sterne   *leopard*
    Leave roaring, when in rage he for revenge did earne.°   *yearn*

26

    And for to make his powre approvèd° more,   *demonstrated*
        Wyld beasts in yron yokes he would compell;

---

1. Hunting; also sexual play.   2. A species of deer noted for its speed.

The spotted Panther, and the tuskèd Bore,
The Pardale° swift, and the Tigre cruell;   *female leopard*
The Antelope, and Wolfe both fierce and fell;°   *savage*
And them constraine in equall teme³ to draw.
Such joy he had, their stubborne harts to quell,
And sturdie courage tame with dreadfull aw,
That his beheast they fearèd, as a tyrans law.

27

His loving mother came upon a day
Unto the woods, to see her little sonne;
And chaunst unwares° to meet him in the way,   *unexpectedly*
After his sportes, and cruell pastime donne,
When after him a Lyonesse did runne,
That roaring all with rage, did lowd requere°   *demand*
Her children deare, whom he away had wonne:°   *seized*
The Lyon whelpes she saw how he did beare,
And lull in rugged armes, withouten childish feare.

28

The fearefull Dame all quakèd at the sight,
And turning backe, gan fast to fly away,
Untill with love revokt° from vaine affright,   *recalled*
She hardly° yet perswaded was to stay,   *with difficulty*
And then to him these womanish words gan say;
"Ah Satyrane,⁴ my dearling, and my joy,
For love of me leave off this dreadfull play;
To dally thus with death, is no fit toy,
Go find some other play-fellowes, mine own sweet boy."

29

In these and like delights of bloudy game
He traynèd was, till ryper yeares he raught,°   *reached*
And there abode, whilst any beast of name
Walkt in that forest, whom he had not taught
To feare his force: and then his courage haught°   *high*
Desird of forreine foemen to be knowne;
And far abroad for straunge adventures sought:
In which his might was never overthrowne,
But through all Faery lond his famous worth was blown.°   *spread*

30

Yet evermore it was his manner faire,
After long labours and adventures spent,
Unto those native woods for to repaire,°   *return*
To see his sire and ofspring° aunccient.   *origin*
And now he thither came for like intent;

---

3. Side by side, yoked together in a team.   4. That is, like a satyr.

Where he unwares the fairest Una found,
  Straunge Lady, in so straunge habiliment,°   *attire*
  Teaching the Satyres, which her sat around,
Trew sacred lore, which from her sweet lips did redound.°   *flow*

31

He wondred at her wisedome heavenly rare,
  Whose like in womens wit he never knew;
  And when her curteous deeds he did compare,
  Gan her admire, and her sad sorrowes rew,°   *pity*
  Blaming of Fortune, which such troubles threw,
  And joyd to make proofe of her crueltie
  On gentle Dame, so hurtlesse,° and so trew: *harmless*
  Thenceforth he kept her goodly company,
And learnd her discipline° of faith and veritie.   *teachings*

32

But she all vowd° unto the Redcrosse knight,   *entirely promised*
  His wandring perill closely° did lament,   *secretly*
  Ne in this new acquaintaunce could delight,
  But her deare° heart with anguish did torment,   *loving*
  And all her wit in secret counsels spent,
  How to escape. At last in privie wise°   *privately*
  To Satyrane she shewèd her intent;
  Who glad to gain such favour, gan devise,
How with that pensive Maid he best might thence arise.° *depart*

33

So on a day when Satyres all were gone,
  To do their service to Sylvanus old,
  The gentle virgin left behind alone
  He led away with courage stout and bold.
  Too late it was, to Satyres to be told,
  Or ever hope recover her againe:
  In vaine he seekes that having cannot hold.
  So fast he carried her with carefull paine,°   *painstaking care*
That they the woods are past, and come now to the plaine.

34

The better part now of the lingring day,
  They traveild had, when as they farre espide
  A wearie wight forwandring° by the way,   *wandering far and wide*
  And towards him they gan in hast to ride,
  To weet of newes, that did abroad betide,
  Or tydings of her knight of the Redcrosse.
  But he them spying, gan to turne aside,
  For feare as seemd, or for some feignèd losse;°   *pretended harm*
More greedy they of newes, fast towards him do crosse.

35

A silly° man, in simple weedes forworne,°   *simple / worn out*
  And soild with dust of the long drièd way;
  His sandales were with toilesome travell torne,
  And face all tand with scorching sunny ray,
  As° he had traveild many a sommers day,   *as if*
  Through boyling sands of Arabie and Ynde;°   *India*
  And in his hand a Jacobs staffe,° to stay   *pilgrim's staff*
    His wearie limbes upon: and eke behind,
His scrip° did hang, in which his needments he did bind.   *bag*

36

The knight approching nigh, of him inquerd
  Tydings of warre, and of adventures new;
  But warres, nor new adventures none he herd.
  Then Una gan to aske, if ought° he knew,   *aught, anything*
  Or heard abroad of that her champion trew,
  That in his armour bare a croslet° red.   *small cross*
  "Aye me, Deare dame," quoth he, "well may I rew
    To tell the sad sight, which mine eies have red:°   *beheld*
These eyes did see that knight both living and eke ded."

37

That cruell word her tender hart so thrild,°   *pierced*
  That suddein cold did runne through every vaine,
  And stony horrour all her sences fild
  With dying fit,° that downe she fell for paine.   *deathlike swoon*
  The knight her lightly° rearèd up againe,   *quickly*
  And comforted with curteous kind reliefe:
  Then wonne from death, she bad him tellen plaine
    The further processe° of her hidden griefe;   *account*
The lesser pangs can beare, who hath endured the chiefe.

38

Then gan the Pilgrim thus, "I chaunst this day,
  This fatall day, that shall I ever rew,°   *rue, regret*
  To see two knights in travell on my way
  (A sory° sight) arraungèd° in battell new,   *grievous / drawn up*
  Both breathing vengeaunce, both of wrathfull hew:
  My fearefull flesh did tremble at their strife,
  To see their blades so greedily imbrew,[5]
    That drunke with bloud, yet thristed after life:
What more? the Redcrosse knight was slaine with Paynim knife."

39

"Ah dearest Lord," quoth she, "how might that bee,
  And he the stoutest° knight, that ever wonne?"°   *bravest; strongest / fought*

---

5. Soak themselves in blood.

"Ah dearest dame," quoth he, "how might I see
The thing, that might not be, and yet was donne?"
"Where is," said Satyrane, "that Paynims sonne,
That him of life, and us of joy hath reft?"
"Not far away," quoth he, "he hence doth wonne°   *stay*
Foreby° a fountaine, where I late him left   *close by*
Washing his bloudy wounds, that through° the steele were cleft."   *by*

40

Therewith the knight thence marchèd forth in hast,
    Whiles Una with huge heavinesse° opprest,   *grief*
    Could not for sorrow follow him so fast;
    And soone he came, as he the place had ghest,
    Whereas that Pagan proud him selfe did rest,
    In secret shadow by a fountaine side:
    Even he it was, that earst° would have supprest°   *before / violated*
    Faire Una: whom when Satyrane espide,
With fowle reprochfull words he boldly him defide.

41

And said, "Arise thou cursèd Miscreaunt,°   *infidel*
    That hast with knightlesse guile and trecherous train[6]
    Faire knighthood fowly shamed, and doest vaunt°   *boast*
    That good knight of the Redcrosse to have slain:
    Arise, and with like treason now maintain°   *defend*
    Thy guilty wrong, or else thee guilty yield."
    The Sarazin this hearing, rose amain,°   *at once*
    And catching up in hast his three square° shield,   *triangular*
And shining helmet, soone him buckled to the field.

42

And drawing nigh him said, "Ah misborne Elfe,[7]
    In evill houre thy foes thee hither sent,
    Anothers wrongs to wreake upon thy selfe:
    Yet ill thou blamest me, for having blent°   *stained*
    My name with guile and traiterous intent;
    That Redcrosse knight, perdie,° I never slew,   *by God (pardieu)*
    But had he beene, where earst his armes were lent,
    Th'enchaunter vaine his errour should not rew:
But thou his errour shalt, I hope now proven trew."[8]

43

Therewith they gan, both furious and fell,°   *fierce*
    To thunder blowes, and fiersly to assaile
    Each other bent° his enimy to quell,°   *determined / kill*

---

6. Deceit. "Knightlesse": unknightly.
7. Base-born knight of Faerie Land ("Elfe").
8. That is, had Redcrosse been wearing his arms, the enchanter Archimago would not have to regret his error in fighting me. But you will now repeat that error and that regret.

That with their force they perst° both plate and maile, *pierced*
And made wide furrowes in their fleshes fraile,
That it would pitty° any living eie. *bring pity to*
Large floods of bloud adowne their sides did raile:° *flow*
But floods of bloud could not them satisfie:
Both hungred after death: both chose to win, or die.

44

So long they fight, and fell revenge pursue,
That fainting° each, themselves to breathen let, *weakening*
And oft refreshèd, battell oft renue:
As when two Bores with rancling malice met,
Their gory sides fresh bleeding fiercely fret,° *tear*
Til breathlesse both them selves aside retire,
Where foming wrath, their cruell tuskes they whet,
And trample th'earth, the whiles they may respire;
Then backe to fight againe, new breathèd and entire.° *fresh*

45

So fiersly, when these knights had breathèd once,
They gan to fight returne, increasing more
Their puissant° force, and cruell rage attonce, *mighty*
With heapèd strokes more hugely, then before,
That with their drerie° wounds and bloudy gore *gory*
They both deformèd,° scarsely could be known. *disfigured*
By this sad Una fraught° with anguish sore, *burdened*
Led with their noise, which through the aire was thrown,
Arrived, where they in erth their fruitles bloud had sown.

46

Whom all so soone as that proud Sarazin
Espide, he gan revive the memory
Of his lewd lusts, and late attempted sin,
And left the doubtfull° battell hastily, *undecided*
To catch her, newly offred to his eie:
But Satyrane with strokes him turning, staid,
And sternely bad him other businesse plie,° *take on*
Then° hunt the steps of pure unspotted Maid: *than*
Wherewith he all enraged, these bitter speaches said.

47

"O foolish faeries sonne, what furie mad
Hath thee incenst, to hast thy dolefull fate?
Were it not better, I that Lady had,
Then that thou hadst repented it too late?
Most sencelesse man he, that himselfe doth hate,
To love another. Lo then for thine ayd
Here take thy lovers token on thy pate."
So they to fight; the whiles the royall Mayd
Fled farre away, of that proud Paynim sore afrayd.

48

But that false Pilgrim, which that leasing° told,   *lie*
  Being in deed old Archimage, did stay
  In secret shadow, all this to behold,
  And much rejoycèd in their bloudy fray:
  But when he saw the Damsell passe away
  He left his stond,° and her pursewd apace,   *place*
  In hope to bring her to her last decay.°   *her death*
  But for to tell her lamentable cace,
And eke° this battels end, will need another place.[9]   *also*

Canto 7

The Redcrosse knight is captive made
  By Gyaunt proud opprest,°   *overwhelmed*
Prince Arthur meets with Una great-
  ly with those newes distrest.

1

What man so wise, what earthly wit so ware,°   *wary*
  As to descry° the crafty cunning traine,°   *perceive / guile*
  By which deceipt doth maske in visour° faire,   *a mask*
  And cast her colours dyèd deepe in graine,[1]
  To seeme like Truth, whose shape she well can faine,°   *feign, imitate*
  And fitting gestures to her purpose frame,
  The guiltlesse man with guile to entertaine?°   *engage*
  Great maistresse of her art was that false Dame,
The false Duessa, clokèd with Fidessaes name.

2

Who when returning from the drery Night,
  She fownd not in that perilous house of Pryde,
  Where she had left, the noble Redcrosse knight,
  Her hopèd pray, she would no lenger bide,
  But forth she went, to seeke him far and wide.
  Ere long she fownd, whereas° he wearie sate,   *where*
  To rest him selfe, foreby° a fountaine side,   *beside*
  Disarmèd all of yron-coted Plate,
And by his side his steed the grassy forage ate.

3

He feedes upon the cooling shade, and bayes°   *bathes*
  His sweatie forehead in the breathing wind,
  Which through the trembling leaves full gently playes
  Wherein the cherefull birds of sundry kind
  Do chaunt sweet musick, to delight his mind:

---

9. In fact Spenser never tells how the battle ended. But Satyrane reappears in Book 3.

1. That is, Deceit disposes her colors, thoroughly dyed, so as to seem like Truth.

The Witch approaching gan him fairely° greet,   *courteously*
  And with reproch of carelesnesse° unkind   *indifference*
  Upbrayd, for leaving her in place unmeet,°   *unfitting*
With fowle words tempring° faire, soure gall with hony sweet.   *mingling*

4

Unkindnesse past, they gan of solace treat,°   *pleasure speak*
  And bathe in pleasaunce of the joyous shade,
  Which shielded them against the boyling heat,
  And with greene boughes decking a gloomy glade,
  About the fountaine like a girlond made;
  Whose bubbling wave did ever freshly well,
  Ne ever would through fervent° sommer fade:°   *hot / dry up*
  The sacred Nymph, which therein wont° to dwell,   *was accustomed*
Was out of Dianes favour, as it then befell.

5

The cause was this: one day when Phoebe[2] fayre
  With all her band was following the chace,°   *hunt*
  This Nymph, quite tyred with heat of scorching ayre
  Sat downe to rest in middest of the race:
  The goddesse wroth° gan fowly her disgrace,   *angered*
  And bad the waters, which from her did flow,
  Be such as she her selfe was then in place.°   *there*
  Thenceforth her waters waxèd dull and slow,
And all that drunke thereof, did faint and feeble grow.

6

Hereof this gentle knight unweeting° was,   *ignorant*
  And lying downe upon the sandie graile,°   *gravel*
  Drunke of the streame, as cleare as cristall glas;
  Eftsoones° his manly forces gan to faile,   *immediately*
  And mightie strong was turnd to feeble fraile.
  His chaunged powres at first themselves not felt,
  Till crudled° cold his corage° gan assaile,   *congealing / vigor*
  And chearefull° bloud in faintnesse chill did melt,   *lively*
Which like a fever fit through all his body swelt.°   *raged*

7

Yet goodly court he made still to his Dame,
  Pourd out in loosnesse[3] on the grassy grownd,
  Both carelesse of his health, and of his fame:°   *reputation*
  Till at the last he heard a dreadfull sownd,
  Which through the wood loud bellowing, did rebownd,
  That all the earth for terrour seemed to shake,
  And trees did tremble. Th'Elfe therewith astownd,°   *amazed*

---

2. That is, Diana, goddess of the moon and of chastity.

3. Spread out in lewdness ("loosnesse"); sexually expended.

Upstarted lightly° from his looser make,[4]   *quickly*
And his unready weapons gan in hand to take.

8

But ere he could his armour on him dight,°   *put on*
  Or get his shield, his monstrous enimy
  With sturdie steps came stalking in his sight,
  An hideous Geant horrible and hye,
  That with his talnesse seemd to threat the skye,
  The ground eke° gronèd under him for dreed;°   *also / dread*
  His living like saw never living eye,
  Ne durst behold: his stature did exceed
The hight of three the tallest sonnes of mortall seed.

9

The greatest Earth his uncouth° mother was,   *vile; strange*
  And blustring Aeolus his boasted sire,[5]
  Who with his breath, which through the world doth pas,
  Her hollow womb did secretly inspire,°   *breathe into*
  And fild her hidden caves with stormie yre,°   *ire, anger*
  That she conceived; and trebling the dew time,
  In which the wombes of women do expire,°   *bring forth*
  Brought forth this monstrous masse of earthly slime,
Puft up with emptie wind, and fild with sinfull crime.

10

So growen great through arrogant delight
  Of th'high descent, whereof he was yborne,
  And through presumption of his matchlesse might,
  All other powres and knighthood he did scorne.
  Such now he marcheth to this man forlorne,°   *abandoned*
  And left to losse:° his stalking steps are stayde°   *destruction / supported*
  Upon a snaggy Oke,[6] which he had torne
  Out of his mothers bowelles, and it made
His mortall° mace, wherewith his foemen he dismayde.[7]   *death-dealing*

11

That when the knight he spide, he gan advance
  With huge force and insupportable mayne,°   *irresistible power*
  And towardes him with dreadfull fury praunce;°   *strut*
  Who haplesse,° and eke hopelesse, all in vaine   *unlucky*
  Did to him pace, sad battaile to darrayne,°   *engage*
  Disarmd, disgrast, and inwardly dismayde,
  And eke so faint in every joynt and vaine,
  Through that fraile° fountaine, which him feeble made,   *enfeebling*
That scarsely could he weeld his bootlesse° single blade.   *useless*

---

4. Too licentious ("looser") companion.
5. Aeolus was keeper of the winds. The giant's descent from Earth and Wind links him to earthquakes.
6. That is, he uses as walking stick a knotty ("snaggy") oak tree.
7. In its usual sense, but also "dis-made, dissolved."

12

The Geaunt strooke so maynly° mercilesse, — *mightily*
  That could have overthrowne a stony towre,
  And were not heavenly grace, that him did blesse,
  He had beene pouldred° all, as thin as flowre: — *powdered*
  But he was wary of that deadly stowre,° — *peril*
  And lightly° lept from underneath the blow: — *quickly*
  Yet so exceeding was the villeins powre,
  That with the wind it did him overthrow,
And all his sences stound,° that still he lay full low. — *stunned*

13

As when that divelish yron Engin° wrought — *cannon*
  In deepest Hell, and framd by Furies skill,
  With windy Nitre and quick Sulphur fraught,[8]
  And ramd with bullet round, ordaind to kill,
  Conceiveth fire, the heavens it doth fill
  With thundring noyse, and all the ayre doth choke,
  That none can breath, nor see, nor heare at will,
  Through smouldry cloud of duskish stincking smoke,
That th'onely breath him daunts,[9] who hath escapt the stroke.

14

So daunted when the Geaunt saw the knight,
  His heavie hand he heavèd up on hye,
  And him to dust thought to have battred quight,
  Untill Duessa loud to him gan crye;
  "O great Orgoglio,[1] greatest under skye,
  O hold thy mortall hand for Ladies sake,
  Hold for my sake, and do him not to dye,° — *do not cause him to die*
  But vanquisht thine eternall bondslave make,
And me thy worthy meed unto thy Leman take."[2]

15

He hearkned, and did stay° from further harmes, — *refrain*
  To gayne so goodly guerdon,° as she spake: — *reward*
  So willingly she came into his armes,
  Who her as willingly to grace° did take, — *favor*
  And was possessèd of his new found make.° — *mate*
  Then up he tooke the slombred° sencelesse corse, — *unconscious*
  And ere he could out of his swowne awake,
  Him to his castle brought with hastie forse,
And in a Dongeon deepe him threw without remorse.

---

8. *Filled* ("fraught") with gunpowder ("Nitre" and "Sulphur").
9. That is, so that the blast or smell alone ("onely") overcomes him.
1. Pride, haughtiness, disdain (Italian).
2. That is, take me, your worthy reward, as your mistress.

16

From that day forth Duessa was his deare,
    And highly honourd in his haughtie eye,
    He gave her gold and purple pall° to weare,   *crimson robe of royalty*
    And triple crowne set on her head full hye,[3]
    And her endowd with royall majestye:
    Then for to make her dreaded more of men,
    And peoples harts with awfull terrour tye,°   *bind*
    A monstrous beast ybred in filthy fen°   *marsh*
He chose, which he had kept long time in darksome den.

17

Such one it was, as that renowmèd Snake
    Which great Alcides in Stremona slew,
    Long fostred in the filth of Lerna lake,[4]
    Whose many heads out budding ever new,
    Did breed° him endlesse labour to subdew: *cause*
    But this same Monster much more ugly was;
    For seven great heads out of his body grew,
    An yron brest, and backe of scaly bras,
And all embrewd° in bloud, his eyes did shine as glas.   *stained*

18

His tayle was stretchèd out in wondrous length,
    That to the house of heavenly gods it raught,°   *reached*
    And with extorted powre, and borrowed strength,
    The ever-burning lamps° from thence it brought,   *stars*
    And prowdly threw to ground, as things of nought;
    And underneath his filthy feet did tread
    The sacred things, and holy heasts foretaught.[5]
    Upon this dreadfull Beast with sevenfold head
He set the false Duessa, for more aw and dread.

19

The wofull Dwarfe, which saw his maisters fall,
    Whiles he had keeping of his grasing steed,
    And valiant knight become a caytive° thrall,   *captive*
    When all was past, tooke up his forlorne weed,°   *abandoned garment*
    His mightie armour, missing most at need;
    His silver shield, now idle maisterlesse;
    His poynant° speare, that many made to bleed,   *sharp*
    The ruefull moniments° of heavinesse,°   *memorials / grief*
And with them all departes, to tell his great distresse.

---

3. Duessa is attired like the Whore of Babylon in Revelation 17:3–4. The triple crown is that of the papacy (see canto 2, stanzas 13 and 22).
4. The nine-headed Lernean hydra slain by Hercules (Alcides). Orgoglio's seven-headed monster recalls the red dragon of Revelation 12:3–9: "behold a great red dragon, having seven heads and ten horns, and seven crowns upon his heads. And his tail drew the third part of the stars of heaven, and did cast them to the earth . . . [he is] that old serpent, called the Devil, and Satan, which deceiveth the whole world." Many Protestants associated the Beast with the Roman Church.
5. Doctrines ("holy heasts") previously taught.

20

He had not travaild long, when on the way
    He wofull Ladie, wofull Una met,
    Fast flying from the Paynims greedy pray,°   *clutch*
    Whilest Satyrane him from pursuit did let:°   *prevent*
    Who when her eyes she on the Dwarfe had set,
    And saw the signes, that deadly tydings spake,
    She fell to ground for sorrowfull regret,°   *grief*
    And lively breath her sad brest did forsake,
Yet might her pitteous hart be seene to pant and quake.

21

The messenger of so unhappie newes
    Would faine° have dyde: dead was his hart within,   *gladly*
    Yet outwardly some little comfort shewes:
    At last recovering hart, he does begin
    To rub her temples, and to chaufe° her chin,   *chafe, rub*
    And every tender part does tosse and turne:
    So hardly he the flitted life does win,
    Unto her native prison to retourne:[6]
Then gins her grievèd ghost° thus to lament and mourne.   *spirit*

22

"Ye dreary instruments of dolefull sight,
    That doe this deadly spectacle behold,
    Why do ye lenger° feed on loathèd light,   *longer*
    Or liking find to gaze on earthly mould,[7]
    Sith° cruell fates the carefull° threeds unfould,   *since / intricate*
    The which my life and love together tyde?
    Now let the stony dart of senselesse cold°   *death*
    Perce to my hart, and pas through every side,
And let eternall night so sad sight fro me hide.

23

"O lightsome day, the lampe of highest Jove,
    First made by him,[8] mens wandring wayes to guyde,
    When darknesse he in deepest dongeon drove,
    Henceforth thy hated face for ever hyde,
    And shut up heavens windowes shyning wyde:
    For earthly sight can nought but sorrow breed,
    And late° repentance, which shall long abyde.   *too late*
    Mine eyes no more on vanitie shall feed,
But seelèd up with death, shall have their deadly meed."°   *reward of death*

---

6. That is, with such difficulty ("so hardly") he persuades ("does win") the life back to her body ("native prison").
7. That is, or find it pleasure to gaze on earthly form ("mould").
8. An allusion to Genesis 1:3: "And God said, Let there be light: and there was light."

24

Then downe againe she fell unto the ground;
  But he her quickly rearèd up againe:
  Thrise did she sinke adowne in deadly swownd,
  And thrise he her revived with busie paine:° — *care*
  At last when life recovered had the raine,° — *rule*
  And over-wrestled his strong enemie,
  With foltring° tong, and trembling every vaine, — *faltering*
  "Tell on," quoth she, "the wofull Tragedie,
The which these reliques° sad present unto mine eie. — *remains*

25

"Tempestuous fortune hath spent all her spight,
  And thrilling° sorrow throwne his utmost dart; — *piercing*
  Thy sad tongue cannot tell more heavy plight,
  Then that I feele, and harbour in mine hart:
  Who hath endured the whole, can beare each part.
  If death it be, it is not the first wound,
  That launchèd° hath my brest with bleeding smart. — *pierced*
  Begin, and end the bitter balefull stound;° — *time (of sorrow)*
If lesse, then that° I feare, more favour I have found." — *than what*

26

Then gan the Dwarfe the whole discourse° declare, — *story*
  The subtill traines° of Archimago old; — *wiles*
  The wanton loves of false Fidessa faire,
  Bought with the bloud of vanquisht Paynim bold:
  The wretched payre transformed to treen mould;° — *shape of a tree*
  The house of Pride, and perils round about;
  The combat, which he with Sansjoy did hould;
  The lucklesse conflict with the Gyant stout,
Wherein captived, of life or death he stood in doubt.

27

She heard with patience all unto the end,
  And strove to maister sorrowfull assay,° — *affliction*
  Which greater grew, the more she did contend,
  And almost rent her tender hart in tway;° — *two*
  And love fresh coles unto her fire did lay:
  For greater love, the greater is the losse.
  Was never Ladie lovèd dearer day,[9]
  Then she did love the knight of the Redcrosse;
For whose deare sake so many troubles her did tosse.

28

At last when fervent sorrow slakèd was,
  She up arose, resolving him to find

---

9. That is, there was never a lady who loved life ("day") more dearly than she loved Redcrosse.

  Alive or dead: and forward forth doth pas,
   All° as the Dwarfe the way to her assynd:°   *just / showed*
   And evermore in constant carefull° mind   *full of care; sorrowful*
   She fed her wound with fresh renewèd bale;°   *anguish*
   Long tost with stormes, and bet° with bitter wind,   *beaten*
   High over hils, and low adowne the dale,
  She wandred many a wood, and measurd many a vale.

29

  At last she chauncèd by good hap to meet
   A goodly knight, faire marching by the way
   Together with his Squire, arayèd meet:°   *properly*
   His glitterand° armour shinèd farre away,   *glittering*
   Like glauncing° light of Phoebus brightest ray;   *flashing*
   From top to toe no place appearèd bare,
   That deadly dint° of steele endanger may: *stroke*
   Athwart his brest a bauldrick[1] brave° he ware,   *splendid*
  That shynd, like twinkling stars, with stons most pretious rare.

30

  And in the midst thereof one pretious stone
   Of wondrous worth, and eke of wondrous mights,°   *powers*
   Shapt like a Ladies head, exceeding shone,
   Like Hesperus° emongst the lesser lights,°   *evening star / stars*
   And strove for to amaze the weaker sights;
   Thereby his mortall blade full comely hong
   In yvory sheath, ycarved with curious slights;°   *designs*
   Whose hilts were burnisht gold, and handle strong
  Of mother pearle, and buckled with a golden tong.°   *pin*

31

  His haughtie helmet, horrid° all with gold,   *bristling*
   Both glorious brightnesse, and great terrour bred;
   For all the crest a Dragon did enfold
   With greedie pawes, and over all did spred
   His golden wings: his dreadfull hideous hed
   Close couchèd on the bever,° seemed to throw   *visor*
   From flaming mouth bright sparkles fierie red,
   That suddeine horror to faint harts did show;
  And scaly tayle was stretcht adowne his backe full low.

32

  Upon the top of all his loftie crest,°   *top of helmet*
   A bunch of haires discolourd° diversly,   *dyed*
   With sprincled pearle, and gold full richly drest,
   Did shake, and seemed to daunce for jollity,
   Like to an Almond tree ymounted hye

---

1. Sash worn over the shoulder to support the sword.

> On top of greene Selinis[2] all alone,
> With blossomes brave bedeckèd daintily;
> Whose tender locks do tremble every one
> At every little breath, that under heaven is blowne.

33

> His warlike shield all closely covered was,
>   Ne might of mortall eye be ever seene;
>   Not made of steele, nor of enduring bras,
>   Such earthly mettals soone consumèd bene:° *been: be, are*
>   But all of Diamond perfect pure and cleene° *clear*
>   It framèd was, one massie entire mould,[3]
>   Hewen out of Adamant rocke with engines° keene, *tools*
>   That point of speare it never percen could,
> Ne dint° of direfull sword divide the substance would. *blow*

34

> The same to wight° he never wont disclose, *creature*
>   But° when as monsters huge he would dismay, *except*
>   Or daunt unequall armies of his foes,
>   Or when the flying heavens he would affray;[4]
>   For so exceeding shone his glistring ray,
>   That Phoebus golden face it did attaint,° *make dim*
>   As when a cloud his beames doth over-lay;
>   And silver Cynthia° wexèd pale and faint, *the moon*
> As when her face is staynd with magicke arts constraint.[5]

35

> No magicke arts hereof had any might,
>   Nor bloudie wordes of bold Enchaunters call,
>   But all that was not such, as seemd in sight,
>   Before that shield did fade, and suddeine fall:
>   And when him list° the raskall routes° appall, *wanted to / unruly mobs*
>   Men into stones therewith he could transmew,° *change*
>   And stones to dust, and dust to nought at all;
>   And when him list the prouder lookes subdew,
> He would them gazing blind, or turne to other hew.° *form*

36

> Ne let it seeme, that credence this exceedes,
>   For he that made the same, was knowne right well
>   To have done much more admirable° deedes. *marvelous*
>   It Merlin was, which whylome° did excell *formerly*
>   All living wightes in might of magicke spell:
>   Both shield, and sword, and armour all he wrought

---

2. Town associated with the palm awarded to victors (Virgil, *Aeneid* 3.705).
3. The shield was made of one solid piece of diamond, unflawed, unpierceable, translucent.
4. That is, when he would frighten ("affray") the revolving constellations.
5. Magicians were said to be able to cause an eclipse of the moon.

For this young Prince,[6] when first to armes he fell;°   *came*
  But when he dyde, the Faerie Queene it brought
To Faerie lond, where yet it may be seene, if sought.

37

A gentle° youth, his dearely lovèd Squire   *noble*
  His speare of heben° wood behind him bare,   *ebony*
  Whose harmefull head, thrice heated in the fire,
Had riven many a brest with pikehead° square;°   *spearhead / stout*
  A goodly person, and could menage° faire   *control*
  His stubborne steed with curbèd canon bit,[7]
  Who under him did trample as the aire,
  And chauft,° that any on his backe should sit;   *fretted*
The yron rowels° into frothy fome he bit.   *ends of the bit*

38

When as this knight nigh to the Ladie drew,
  With lovely court° he gan her entertaine;   *kind courtesy*
  But when he heard her answers loth, he knew
Some secret sorrow did her heart distraine:°   *afflict*
  Which to allay, and calme her storming paine,
  Faire feeling words he wisely gan display,°   *pour forth*
  And for her humour fitting purpose faine,[8]
To tempt° the cause it selfe for to bewray;°   *invite / reveal*
Wherewith emmoved, these bleeding words she gan to say.

39

"What worlds delight, or joy of living speach
  Can heart, so plunged in sea of sorrowes deepe,
  And heapèd with so huge misfortunes, reach?
The carefull° cold beginneth for to creepe,   *afflicting*
  And in my heart his yron arrow steepe,
  Soone as I thinke upon my bitter bale:°   *grief*
  Such helplesse harmes yts better hidden keepe,
Then rip up° griefe, where it may not availe,   *than lay open*
My last left comfort is, my woes to weepe and waile."

40

"Ah Ladie deare," quoth then the gentle knight,
  "Well may I weene,° your griefe is wondrous great;   *suppose*
  For wondrous great griefe groneth in my spright,°   *spirit*
  Whiles thus I heare you of your sorrowes treat.
  But wofull Ladie let me you intrete,
  For to unfold the anguish of your hart:
  Mishaps are maistred by advice discrete,

---

6. The reference to Merlin indicates that the prince is Arthur (who had been mentioned in the canto's prefatory quatrain). In the *Letter to Ralegh*, he is identified with "magnificence," understood as the perfection of all the virtues and containing them all.
7. A smooth, round bit.
8. That is, suited his manner to her mood.

And counsell mittigates the greatest smart;
Found never helpe, who never would his hurts impart."[9]

41

"O but," quoth she, "great griefe will not be tould,
   And can more easily be thought, then said."
"Right so"; quoth he, "but he, that never would,
   Could never: will to might gives greatest aid."[1]
"But grief," quoth she, "does greater grow displaid,°   *when revealed*
   If then it find not helpe, and breedes despaire."
"Despaire breedes not," quoth he, "where faith is staid."°   *firm*
"No faith so fast," quoth she, "but flesh does paire."°   *impair*
"Flesh may empaire," quoth he, "but reason can repaire."

42

His goodly reason, and well guided speach
   So deepe did settle in her gratious thought,
That her perswaded to disclose the breach,°   *wound*
   Which love and fortune in her heart had wrought,
And said; "Faire Sir, I hope good hap° hath brought   *fortune*
   You to inquire the secrets of my griefe,
Or° that your wisedome will direct my thought,   *either*
   Or that your prowesse can me yield reliefe:
Then heare the storie sad, which I shall tell you briefe.

43

"The forlorne° Maiden, whom your eyes have seene   *forsaken*
   The laughing stocke of fortunes mockeries,
Am th'only daughter of a King and Queene,
   Whose parents deare, whilest equall destinies
   Did runne about,[2] and their felicities
The favourable heavens did not envy,
   Did spread their rule through all the territories,
   Which Phison and Euphrates floweth by,
And Gehons golden waves doe wash continually.[3]

44

"Till that their cruell cursèd enemy,
   An huge great Dragon horrible in sight,
Bred in the loathly lakes of Tartary,°   *Tartarus (hell)*
   With murdrous ravine,° and devouring might   *destruction*
   Their kingdome spoild,° and countrey wasted quight: *plundered*
Themselves, for feare into his jawes to fall,
   He forst to castle strong to take their flight,

---

9. That is, he never found help who would not tell his sorrows.
1. That is, he that fails to will something cannot do it: willing gives the greatest help to one's power ("might").
2. That is, while the impartial fates ran their course.
3. Phison, Euphrates, and Gehon, along with the Tigris, were the rivers of the Garden of Eden (Genesis 2:11–14).

Where fast embard° in mightie brasen wall, — *imprisoned*
He has them now foure yeres besiegd to make them thrall.

45

"Full many knights adventurous and stout
    Have enterprizd that Monster to subdew;
    From every coast° that heaven walks about, — *land*
    Have thither come the noble Martiall crew,
    That famous hard atchievements still pursew,
    Yet never any could that girlond win,
    But all still shronke,° and still he greater grew: — *quailed*
    All they for want of faith, or guilt of sin,
The pitteous pray of his fierce crueltie have bin.

46

"At last yledd° with farre reported praise, — *led*
    Which flying fame throughout the world had spread,
    Of doughtie° knights, whom Faery land did raise, — *brave*
    That noble order hight° of Maidenhed,[4] — *called*
    Forthwith to court of Gloriane I sped,
    Of Gloriane great Queene of glory bright,
    Whose kingdomes seat Cleopolis[5] is red,° — *named*
    There to obtaine some such redoubted knight,
That Parents deare from tyrants powre deliver might.

47

"It was my chance (my chance was faire and good)
    There for to find a fresh unprovèd° knight, — *untried*
    Whose manly hands imbrewed in guiltie blood
    Had never bene,[6] ne ever by his might
    Had throwne to ground the unregarded° right: — *unrespected*
    Yet of his prowesse proofe he since hath made
    (I witnesse am) in many a cruell fight;
    The groning ghosts of many one dismaide° — *defeated*
Have felt the bitter dint° of his avenging blade. — *blow*

48

"And ye the forlorne reliques of his powre,
    His byting sword, and his devouring speare,
    Which have endurèd many a dreadfull stowre,° — *conflict*
    Can speake his prowesse, that did earst° you beare, — *before*
    And well could rule: now he hath left you heare,
    To be the record of his ruefull losse,
    And of my dolefull disaventurous deare:° — *sad unfortunate dear one*
    O heavie record of the good Redcrosse,
Where have you left your Lord, that could so well you tosse?° — *handle*

---

4. The type or analogue of the Order of the Garter. Its emblem shows Saint George killing the dragon, and its star is the Red Cross.
5. The name means "famous city."
6. That is, his strong hands had never been guiltily stained ("imbrewed") with blood.

49

"Well hopèd I, and faire beginnings had,
   That he my captive langour should redeeme,[7]
   Till all unweeting,° an Enchaunter bad   *unknowing*
   His sence abusd, and made him to misdeeme°   *misjudge*
   My loyalty, not such as it did seeme;
   That rather death desire, then such despight.[8]
   Be judge ye heavens, that all things right esteeme,°   *judge rightly*
   How I him loved, and love with all my might,
So thought I eke of him, and thinke I thought aright.

50

"Thenceforth me desolate he quite forsooke,
   To wander, where wilde fortune would me lead,
   And other bywaies he himselfe betooke,
   Where never foot of living wight did tread,
   That brought not backe the balefull body dead;°   *who was not killed*
   In which him chauncèd false Duessa meete,
   Mine onely foe, mine onely deadly dread,[9]
   Who with her witchcraft and misseeming° sweete,   *false appearance*
Inveigled him to follow her desires unmeete.°   *improper*

51

"At last by subtill sleights she him betraid
   Unto his foe, a Gyant huge and tall,
   Who him disarmèd, dissolute,° dismaid,   *enfeebled*
   Unwares surprisèd and with mightie mall°   *club*
   The monster mercilesse him made to fall,
   Whose fall did never foe before behold;
   And now in darkesome dungeon, wretched thrall,
   Remedilesse, for aie[1] he doth him hold;
This is my cause of griefe, more great, then may be told."

52

Ere she had ended all, she gan to faint:°   *grow weak; lose heart*
   But he her comforted and faire bespake,
   "Certès,° Madame, ye have great cause of plaint,   *certainly*
   That stoutest heart, I weene, could cause to quake.
   But be of cheare, and comfort to you take:
   For till I have acquit° your captive knight,   *freed*
   Assure your selfe, I will you not forsake."
   His chearefull words revived her chearelesse spright,
So forth they went, the Dwarfe them guiding ever right.

---

7. That is, relieve my state, captive to sadness.
8. That is, I, who prefer death to such treachery ("despight").
9. That is, the only object of my mortal fear.
1. That is, forever ("for aie") without hope of rescue ("remedilesse").

Canto 8

Faire virgin to redeeme her deare
brings Arthur to the fight:
Who slayes the Gyant, wounds the beast,
and strips Duessa quight.

1

Ay me, how many perils doe enfold
   The righteous man, to make him daily fall?
   Were not, that heavenly grace doth him uphold,
   And stedfast truth acquite° him out of all.   *deliver*
   Her love is firme, her care continuall,
   So oft as he through his owne foolish pride,
   Or weaknesse is to sinfull bands° made thrall: *bonds*
   Else should this Redcrosse knight in bands have dyde,
For whose deliverance she this Prince doth thither guide.

2

They sadly traveild thus, untill they came
   Nigh to a castle builded strong and hie:
   Then cryde the Dwarfe, "lo yonder is the same,
   In which my Lord my liege doth lucklesse lie,
   Thrall to that Gyants hatefull tyrannie:
   Therefore, deare Sir, your mightie powres assay."°   *put to trial*
   The noble knight alighted by and by°   *immediately*
   From loftie steede, and bad the Ladie stay,
To see what end of fight should him befall that day.

3

So with the Squire, th'admirer of his might,
   He marchèd forth towards that castle wall;
   Whose gates he found fast shut, ne living wight
   To ward° the same, nor answere commers call.   *guard*
   Then tooke that Squire an horne of bugle° small,   *wild ox*
   Which hong adowne his side in twisted gold,
   And tassels gay. Wyde wonders over all°   *everywhere*
   Of that same hornes great vertues° weren told,[2]   *powers*
Which had approvèd° bene in uses manifold.   *demonstrated*

4

Was never wight, that heard that shrilling sound,
   But trembling feare did feele in every vaine;
   Three miles it might be easie heard around,
   And Ecchoes three answered it selfe againe:
   No false enchauntment, nor deceiptfull traine°   *snare*
   Might once abide the terror of that blast,

---

2. Marvelous tales ("Wyde wonders") told of the horn connect it with the horn of the legendary French hero Roland and the ram's horn of Joshua, with which he razed the walls of Jericho (Joshua 6:5).

But presently° was voide and wholly vaine: *at once*
  No gate so strong, no locke so firme and fast,
But with that percing noise flew open quite, or brast.°   *burst*

5

The same before the Geants gate he blew,
  That all the castle quakèd from the ground,
  And every dore of freewill open flew.
  The Gyant selfe dismaièd with that sownd,
  Where he with his Duessa dalliance° fownd,   *amorous play*
  In hast came rushing forth from inner bowre,
  With staring° countenance sterne, as one astownd,   *glaring*
  And staggering steps, to weet, what suddein stowre°   *disturbance*
Had wrought that horror strange, and dared his dreaded powre.

6

And after him the proud Duessa came,
  High mounted on her manyheaded beast,
  And every head with fyrie tongue did flame,
  And every head was crownèd on his creast,
  And bloudie mouthèd with late cruell feast.
  That when the knight beheld, his mightie shild
  Upon his manly arme he soone addrest,°   *made ready*
  And at him fiercely flew, with courage fild,
And eger greedinesse° through every member thrild. *eagerness for battle*

7

Therewith the Gyant buckled him to fight,
  Inflamed with scornefull wrath and high disdaine,°   *indignation*
  And lifting up his dreadfull club on hight,
  All armed with ragged snubbes° and knottie graine,   *snags*
  Him thought at first encounter to have slaine.
  But wise and warie was that noble Pere,°   *peer*
  And lightly leaping from so monstrous maine,°   *force*
  Did faire° avoide the violence him nere;   *quite*
It booted nought, to thinke, such thunderbolts to beare.[3]

8

Ne shame he thought to shunne so hideous might:
  The idle° stroke, enforcing furious way,   *useless*
  Missing the marke of his misaymèd sight
  Did fall to ground, and with his° heavie sway°   *its / force*
  So deepely dinted in the driven clay,
  That three yardes deepe a furrow up did throw:
  The sad earth wounded with so sore assay,°   *assault*
  Did grone full grievous underneath the blow,
And trembling with strange feare, did like an earthquake show.

---

3. That is, it was useless to think of withstanding such blows.

9

As when almightie Jove in wrathfull mood,
  To wreake° the guilt of mortall sins is bent,°   *punish / disposed*
  Hurles forth his thundring dart with deadly food,°   *hatred (feud)*
  Enrold in flames, and smouldring dreriment,°   *smothering darkness*
  Through riven cloudes and molten firmament;
  The fierce threeforkèd engin° making way,   *weapon*
  Both loftie towres and highest trees hath rent,
  And all that might his angrie passage stay,
And shooting in the earth, casts up a mount of clay.

10

His boystrous° club, so buried in the ground,   *massive*
  He could not rearen up againe so light,°   *easily*
  But that the knight him at avantage found,
  And whiles he strove his combred clubbe to quight[4]
  Out of the earth, with blade all burning bright
  He smote off his left arme, which like a blocke
  Did fall to ground, deprived of native might;
  Large streames of bloud out of the trunckèd stocke°   *truncated stump*
Forth gushèd, like fresh water streame from riven rocke.[5]

11

Dismaièd with so desperate deadly wound,
  And eke° impatient of unwonted paine,[6]   *also*
  He loudly brayd with beastly yelling sound,
  That all the fields rebellowèd againe;
  As great a noyse, as when in Cymbrian[7] plaine
  An heard of Bulles, whom kindly° rage doth sting,   *natural*
  Do for the milkie mothers want complaine,[8]
  And fill the fields with troublous bellowing,
The neighbour woods around with hollow murmur ring.

12

That when his deare Duessa heard, and saw
  The evill stownd, that daungerd her estate,[9]
  Unto his aide she hastily did draw
  Her dreadfull beast, who swolne with bloud of late
  Came ramping° forth with proud presumpteous gate,°   *rearing / gait*
  And threatned all his heads like flaming brands.°   *torches*
  But him the Squire made quickly to retrate,
  Encountring fierce with single° sword in hand,   *only*
And twixt him and his Lord did like a bulwarke stand.

---

4. Strove to release his encumbered club.
5. Compare Exodus 17:6, where Moses smites the rock and water flows forth.
6. That is, unable to bear ("impatient of") this unfamiliar ("unwonted") pain.
7. Jutland, once called the Cimbric peninsula.
8. That is, mourn the cows' absence.
9. That is, the peril ("stownd") that endangered her state.

13

The proud Duessa full of wrathfull spight,
    And fierce disdaine, to be affronted so,
    Enforst her purple° beast with all her might   *scarlet*
    That stop° out of the way to overthroe,   *obstacle*
    Scorning the let° of so unequall foe: *hindrance*
    But nathemore° would that courageous swayne   *never the more*
    To her yeeld passage, gainst his Lord to goe,
    But with outrageous° strokes did him restraine,   *exceedingly fierce*
And with his bodie bard the way atwixt them twaine.

14

Then tooke the angrie witch her golden cup,
    Which still° she bore, replete with magick artes;[1]   *always*
    Death and despeyre did many thereof sup,
    And secret poyson through their inner parts,
    Th'eternall bale° of heavie wounded harts;   *woe*
    Which after charmes and some enchauntments said,
    She lightly sprinkled on his weaker° parts;   *too weak*
    Therewith his sturdie courage soone was quayd,°   *quelled*
And all his senses were with suddeine dread dismayd.

15

So downe he fell before the cruell beast,
    Who on his necke his bloudie clawes did seize,
    That life nigh crusht out of his panting brest:
    No powre he had to stirre, nor will to rize.
    That when the carefull° knight gan well avise,°   *watchful / observe*
    He lightly° left the foe, with whom he fought,   *quickly*
    And to the beast gan turne his enterprise;
    For wondrous anguish in his hart it wrought,
To see his lovèd Squire into such thraldome° brought.   *slavery*

16

And high advauncing° his bloud-thirstie blade,   *lifting up*
    Stroke one of those deformèd heads so sore,[2]
    That of his puissance° proud ensample made;   *strength*
    His monstrous scalpe° downe to his teeth it tore   *skull*
    And that misformèd shape mis-shapèd more:
    A sea of bloud gusht from the gaping wound,
    That her gay garments staynd with filthy gore,
    And overflowèd all the field around;
That over shoes[3] in bloud he waded on the ground.

---

1. An allusion to the golden cup of the woman in Revelation 17:4, which is "full of abominations and filthiness of her fornication"; the chalice of the Roman Church; and the cup of Circe, the sorceress who turned men into beasts (in *Odyssey* 10).
2. "I saw one of his [that is, the beast's] heads as it were wounded to death" (Revelation 13:3).
3. That is, deeply immersed.

17

Thereat he roarèd for exceeding paine,
   That to have heard, great horror would have bred,°   *produced*
   And scourging th'emptie ayre with his long traine,°   *tail*
   Through great impatience of his grievèd hed[4]
   His gorgeous ryder from her loftie sted°   *place*
   Would have cast downe, and trod in durtie myre,
   Had not the Gyant soone her succourèd;°   *aided*
   Who all enraged with smart° and franticke yre,°   *pain / anger*
Came hurtling in full fierce, and forst the knight retyre.

18

The force, which wont° in two to be disperst,   *used*
   In one alone left hand[5] he now unites,
   Which is through rage more strong then both were erst;°   *before*
   With which his hideous club aloft he dites,°   *raises*
   And at his foe with furious rigour° smites,   *violence*
   That strongest Oake might seeme to overthrow:
   The stroke upon his shield so heavie lites,
   That to the ground it doubleth him full low:
What mortall wight could ever beare so monstrous blow?

19

And in his fall his shield, that covered was,
   Did loose his vele° by chaunce, and open flew: *its covering*
   The light whereof, that heavens light did pas,°   *surpass*
   Such blazing brightnesse through the aier threw,
   That eye mote not the same endure to vew.
   Which when the Gyaunt spyde with staring eye,
   He downe let fall his arme, and soft withdrew
   His weapon huge, that heavèd was on hye
For to have slaine the man, that on the ground did lye.

20

And eke the fruitfull-headed° beast, amazed   *many-headed*
   At flashing beames of that sunshiny shield,
   Became starke blind, and all his senses dazed,
   That downe he tumbled on the durtie field,
   And seemed himselfe as conquerèd to yield.
   Whom when his maistresse proud perceived to fall,
   Whiles yet his feeble feet for faintnesse reeld,
   Unto the Gyant loudly she gan call,
"O helpe Orgoglio, helpe, or else we perish all."

---

4. That is, through inability to endure ("impatience") his afflicted ("grievèd") head.

5. That is, in the one hand left to him.

21

At her so pitteous cry was much amooved
    Her champion stout, and for to ayde his frend,°   *lover*
    Againe his wonted° angry weapon prooved:°   *usual / tried*
    But all in vaine: for he has read his end
    In that bright shield, and all their forces spend
    Themselves in vaine: for since that glauncing° sight,   *flashing*
    He hath no powre to hurt, nor to defend;
    As where th'Almighties lightning brond° does light,   *firebrand*
It dimmes the dazèd eyen, and daunts the senses quight.

22

Whom when the Prince, to battell new addrest,
    And threatning high his dreadfull stroke did see,
    His sparkling blade about his head he blest,°   *brandished*
    And smote off quite his right leg by the knee,
    That downe he tombled; as an agèd tree,
    High growing on the top of rocky clift,
    Whose hartstrings with keene steele nigh hewen be,
    The mightie trunck halfe rent, with ragged rift°   *split*
Doth roll adowne the rocks, and fall with fearefull drift.°   *impact*

23

Or as a Castle rearèd high and round,
    By subtile engins and malitious slight[6]
    Is underminèd from the lowest ground,
    And her foundation forst,° and feebled quight,   *shattered*
    At last downe falles, and with her heapèd hight
    Her hastie ruine does more heavie make,
    And yields it selfe unto the victours might;
    Such was this Gyaunts fall, that seemed to shake
The stedfast globe of earth, as° it for feare did quake.   *as if*

24

The knight then lightly° leaping to the pray,   *quickly*
    With mortall steele him smot againe so sore,
    That headlesse his unweldy bodie lay,
    All wallowd in his owne fowle bloudy gore,
    Which flowèd from his wounds in wondrous store.°   *abundance*
    But soone as breath out of his breast did pas,
    That huge great body, which the Gyaunt bore,
    Was vanisht quite, and of that monstrous mas
Was nothing left, but like an emptie bladder was.

---

6. Clever machines of war ("engins") and evil strategy.

25

Whose grievous fall, when false Duessa spide,
  Her golden cup she cast unto the ground,
  And crownèd mitre[7] rudely° threw aside;   *violently*
  Such percing griefe her stubborne hart did wound,
  That she could not endure that dolefull stound,°   *sorrow*
  But leaving all behind her, fled away:
  The light-foot Squire her quickly turned around,
  And by hard meanes enforcing her to stay,
So brought unto his Lord, as his deservèd pray.

26

The royall Virgin, which beheld from farre,
  In pensive° plight, and sad perplexitie,   *anxious*
  The whole achievement of this doubtfull warre,[8]
  Came running fast to greet his victorie,
  With sober gladnesse, and myld modestie,
  And with sweet joyous cheare° him thus bespake;   *countenance*
  "Faire braunch of noblesse, flowre of chevalrie,
  That with your worth the world amazèd make,
How shall I quite° the paines, ye suffer for my sake?   *requite*

27

"And you° fresh bud of vertue springing fast,   *the Squire*
  Whom these sad eyes saw nigh unto deaths dore,
  What hath poore Virgin for such perill past,
  Wherewith you to reward? Accept therefore
  My simple selfe, and service evermore;
  And he that high does sit, and all things see
  With equall° eyes, their merites to restore,°   *impartial / reward*
  Behold what ye this day have done for mee,
And what I cannot quite,° requite with usuree.°   *repay / interest*

28

"But sith° the heavens, and your faire handeling°   *since / conduct*
  Have made you maister of the field this day,
  Your fortune maister eke with governing,[9]
  And well begun end all so well, I pray,
  Ne let that wicked woman scape away;
  For she it is, that did my Lord bethrall,
  My dearest Lord, and deepe in dongeon lay,
  Where he his better dayes hath wasted all.[1]
O heare, how piteous he to you for ayd does call."

---

7. *An allusion to the pope's triple tiara.*
8. That is, the final outcome, which had been in doubt, of this battle.
9. Secure your good fortune also by prudent management.
1. That is, he has consumed ("wasted") there his best days.

29

Forthwith he gave in charge unto his Squire,
    That scarlot whore to keepen carefully;
    Whiles he himselfe with greedie° great desire   *eager*
    Into the Castle entred forcibly,
    Where living creature none he did espye;
    Then gan he lowdly through the house to call:
    But no man cared to answere to his crye.
    There raignd a solemne silence over all,
Nor voice was heard, nor wight was seene in bowre or hall.

30

At last with creeping crooked pace forth came
    An old old man, with beard as white as snow,
    That on a staffe his feeble steps did frame,°   *support*
    And guide his wearie gate° both too and fro: *gait*
    For his eye sight him failèd long ygo,
    And on his arme a bounch of keyes[2] he bore,
    The which unusèd, rust did overgrow:
    Those were the keyes of every inner dore,
But he could not them use, but kept them still in store.

31

But very uncouth° sight was to behold,   *strange*
    How he did fashion his untoward° pace,   *awkward*
    For as he forward mooved his footing old,
    So backward still was turned his wrinclèd face,
    Unlike to men, who ever as they trace,°   *walk*
    Both feet and face one way are wont to lead.
    This was the aunctient keeper of that place,
    And foster father of the Gyant dead;
His name Ignaro° did his nature right aread.°   *Ignorance / declare*

32

His reverend haires and holy gravitie
    The knight much honord, as beseemèd well,°   *seemed proper*
    And gently° askt, where all the people bee,   *courteously*
    Which in that stately building wont to dwell.
    Who answerd him full soft, he could not tell.
    Againe he askt, where that same knight was layd,
    Whom great Orgoglio with his puissaunce fell°   *fierce power*
    Had made his caytive° thrall; againe he sayde,   *captive*
He could not tell: ne ever other answere made.

33

Then askèd he, which way he in might pas:
    He could not tell, againe he answerèd.

---

2. An allusion to "the keys of the kingdom of heaven" (Matthew 16:19). See also Matthew 23:13 and Luke 11:52.

Thereat the curteous knight displeasèd was,
And said, "Old sire, it seemes thou hast not red°   *recognized*
How ill it sits with° that same silver hed   *suits*
In vaine to mocke, or mockt in vaine to bee:
But if thou be, as thou art pourtrahèd
With natures pen, in ages grave degree,
Aread° in graver wise, what I demaund° of thee."   *answer / ask*

34

His answere likewise was, he could not tell.
   Whose sencelesse speach, and doted° ignorance   *foolish*
   When as the noble Prince had markèd well,
   He ghest his nature by his countenance,
   And calmd his wrath with goodly temperance.
   Then to him stepping, from his arme did reach
   Those keyes, and made himselfe free enterance.
   Each dore he opened without any breach;°   *forcing*
There was no barre to stop, nor foe him to empeach.°   *hinder*

35

There all within full rich arayd he found,
   With royal arras° and resplendent gold,   *tapestry*
   And did with store of every thing abound,
   That greatest Princes presence° might behold.   *person*
   But all the floore (too filthy to be told)
   With bloud of guiltlesse babes, and innocents trew,[3]
   Which there were slaine, as sheepe out of the fold,
   Defilèd was, that dreadfull was to vew,
And sacred ashes over it was strowèd° new.   *strewn*

36

And there beside of marble stone was built
   An Altare, carved with cunning imagery,[4]
   On which true Christians bloud was often spilt,
   And holy Martyrs often doen to dye,°   *put to death*
   With cruell malice and strong tyranny:
   Whose blessed sprites from underneath the stone
   To God for vengeance cryde continually,[5]
   And with great griefe were often heard to grone,
That hardest heart would bleede, to heare their piteous mone.

37

Through every rowme he sought, and every bowr,
   But no where could he find that wofull thrall:
   At last he came unto an yron doore,

---

3. Probably alluding to Herod's massacre of the Innocents (Matthew 2:16), who were traditionally viewed as the first martyrs for Christ.
4. Skillfully wrought images.
5. "And when he had opened the fifth seal, I saw under the altar the souls of them that were slain for the word of God, and for the testimony which they held: And they cried with a loud voice, saying, How long, O Lord, holy and true, dost thou not judge and avenge our blood on them that dwell on the earth?" (Revelation 6:9–10).

That fast was lockt, but key found not at all
　Emongst that bounch, to open it withall;
　But in the same a little grate was pight,°　　　　　　　*placed*
Through which he sent his voyce, and lowd did call
With all his powre, to weet,° if living wight　　　　　　*learn*
Were housèd therewithin, whom he enlargen° might.　　*set free*

38

Therewith an hollow, dreary, murmuring voyce
　These piteous plaints and dolours° did resound;　　*laments*
　"O who is that, which brings me happy choyce
Of death,⁶ that here lye dying every stound,°　　　　　*moment*
Yet live perforce in balefull° darkenesse bound?　　　*evil*
For now three Moones have changèd thrice their hew,°　*shape*
　And have beene thrice hid underneath the ground,
　Since I the heavens chearefull face did vew,
O welcome thou, that doest of death bring tydings trew."

39

Which when that Champion heard, with percing point
　Of pitty deare° his hart was thrillèd° sore,　　　*extreme / pierced*
　And trembling horrour ran through every joynt,
For ruth° of gentle knight so fowle forlore:°　　　*pity / grievously lost*
Which shaking off, he rent° that yron dore,　　　　*burst open*
With furious force, and indignation fell;°　　　　*fierce*
　Where entred in, his foot could find no flore,
　But all a deepe descent, as darke as hell,
That breathèd ever forth a filthie banefull smell.

40

But neither darkenesse fowle, nor filthy bands,°　　　*bonds*
　Nor noyous° smell his purpose could withhold,　　　*noxious*
　(Entire° affection hateth nicer° hands)　　*perfect / too fastidious*
But that with constant zeale, and courage bold,
After long paines and labours manifold,
　He found the meanes that Prisoner up to reare;
　Whose feeble thighes, unhable to uphold
His pinèd° corse, him scarse to light could beare,　　*wasted*
A ruefull spectacle of deathe and ghastly drere.°　*sorrow, wretchedness*

41

His sad dull eyes deepe sunck in hollow pits,
　Could not endure th'unwonted° sunne to view;　　*unaccustomed*
　His bare thin cheekes for want of better bits,°　*food*
And empty sides deceivèd° of their dew,　　　　　*cheated*
Could make a stony hart his hap to rew;°　　*to pity his lot*
His rawbone armes, whose mighty brawnèd bowrs°　*brawny muscles*

---

6. That is, the chance or right to choose death.

Were wont to rive steele plates, and helmets hew,
Were cleane consumed, and all his vitall powres
Decayd, and all his flesh shronk up like withered flowres.

42

Whom when his Lady saw, to him she ran
With hasty joy: to see him made her glad,
And sad to view his visage pale and wan,
Who earst° in flowres of freshest youth was clad. *formerly*
Tho° when her well of teares she wasted° had, *then / expended*
She said, "Ah dearest Lord, what evill starre
On you hath frownd, and pourd his influence bad,
That of your selfe ye thus berobbèd arre,
And this misseeming hew° your manly looks doth marre? *unseemly appearance*

43

"But welcome now my Lord, in wele° or woe, *weal, well-being*
Whose presence I have lackt to long a day;
And fie on Fortune mine avowèd foe,
Whose wrathfull wreakes° them selves do now alay. *punishments*
And for these wrongs shall treble penaunce pay
Of treble good: good growes of evils priefe."[7]
The chearelesse man, whom sorrow did dismay,° *unnerve*
Had no delight to treaten° of his griefe; *speak*
His long endurèd famine needed more reliefe.

44

"Faire Lady," then said that victorious knight,° *Arthur*
"The things, that grievous were to do, or beare,
Them to renew,° I wote,° breeds no delight; *recall / know*
Best musicke breeds delight in loathing eare:
But th'onely good, that growes of passèd feare,
Is to be wise, and ware° of like agein. *wary*
This dayes ensample hath this lesson deare
Deepe written in my heart with yron pen,
That blisse may not abide in state of mortall men.

45

"Henceforth sir knight, take to you wonted strength,
And maister these mishaps with patient might;
Loe° where your foe lyes stretcht in monstrous length, *look*
And loe that wicked woman in your sight,
The roote of all your care, and wretched plight,
Now in your powre, to let her live, or dye."
"To do her dye," quoth Una, "were despight,[8]

---

7. That is, Fortune will now make amends for his wrongs with triple benefits, as good comes from evils endured ("priefe").
8. That is, to cause her to die would be spiteful.

And shame t'avenge so weake an enimy;
But spoile° her of her scarlot robe, and let her fly."   *despoil, strip*

46

So as she bad, that witch they disaraid,
    And robd of royall robes, and purple pall,°   *scarlet cloak*
    And ornaments that richly were displaid;
    Ne sparèd they to strip her naked all.
    Then when they had despoild her tire° and call,°   *robe / caul, headdress*
    Such as she was, their eyes might her behold,
    That her misshapèd parts did them appall,
    A loathly, wrinckled hag, ill favoured, old,
Whose secret filth good manners biddeth not be told.

47

Her craftie head was altogether bald,
    And as in hate of honorable eld,°   *age*
    Was overgrowne with scurfe° and filthy scald;[9]   *scabs*
    Her teeth out of her rotten gummes were feld,°   *fallen*
    And her sowre breath abhominably smeld;
    Her drièd dugs,° like bladders lacking wind,   *breasts*
    Hong downe, and filthy matter from them weld;°   *welled*
    Her wrizled° skin as rough, as maple rind,   *wrinkled*
So scabby was, that would have loathd° all womankind.   *revolted*

48

Her neather parts, the shame of all her kind,°   *womankind*
    My chaster° Muse for shame doth blush to write;   *too chaste*
    But at her rompe she growing had behind
    A foxes taile, with dong all fowly dight;°   *covered*
    And eke her feete most monstrous were in sight;
    For one of them was like an Eagles claw,
    With griping talaunts armd to greedy fight,
    The other like a Beares uneven° paw: *rough*
More ugly shape yet never living creature saw.[1]

49

Which when the knights beheld, amazd they were,
    And wondred at so fowle deformèd wight.
    "Such then," said Una, "as she seemeth here,
    Such is the face of falshood, such the sight
    Of fowle Duessa, when her borrowed light
    Is laid away, and counterfesaunce° knowne."   *deceit*
    Thus when they had the witch disrobèd quight,
    And all her filthy feature° open showne,   *form*
They let her goe at will, and wander wayes unknowne.

---

9. A scabby disease of the scalp.
1. The passage alludes to Revelation 17:16: "these shall hate the whore, and shall make her desolate and naked." The animals associated with Duessa were emblematic: foxes of cunning, eagles and bears of rapacity, cruelty, and brutality.

50

She flying fast from heavens hated face,
    And from the world that her discovered° wide,   *exposed to view*
    Fled to the wastfull° wildernesse apace,   *desolate*
    From living eyes her open shame to hide,
    And lurkt in rocks and caves long unespide.
    But that faire crew° of knights, and Una faire   *company*
    Did in that castle afterwards abide,
    To rest them selves, and weary powres repaire,
Where store they found of all, that dainty° was and rare.   *precious*

Canto 9

His loves and lignage° Arthur tells: *lineage*
*   The knights knit friendly bands:°*   *bonds*
*   Sir Trevisan flies from Despayre,*
*   Whom Redcrosse knight withstands.*

1

O goodly golden chaine,[2] wherewith yfere°   *together*
    The vertues linkèd are in lovely wize:°   *manner*
    And noble minds of yore allyèd were,
    In brave poursuit of chevalrous emprize,°   *adventure*
    That none did others safety despize,°   *disregard*
    Nor aid envy° to him, in need that stands,   *begrudge*
    But friendly each did others prayse devize
    How to advaunce with favourable hands,
As this good Prince redeemd the Redcrosse knight from bands.

2

Who when their powres, empaird through labour long,
    With dew repast° they had recurèd° well,   *rest / restored*
    And that weake captive wight now wexèd° strong,   *waxed, grown*
    Them list° no lenger there at leasure dwell,   *they cared*
    But forward fare, as their adventures fell,
    But ere they parted, Una faire besought
    That straunger knight his name and nation tell;
    Least° so great good, as he for her had wrought,   *lest*
Should die unknown, and buried be in thanklesse thought.

3

"Faire virgin," said the Prince, "ye me require
    A thing without the compas of° my wit: *beyond the reach of*
    For both the lignage and the certain Sire,
    From which I sprong, from me are hidden yit.°   *still*
    For all so soone as life did me admit

---

2. The golden chain of love or concord that binds the world and the human race together (compare canto 5, stanza 25, n. 5).

Into this world, and shewèd heavens light,
From mothers pap I taken was unfit:°   *not yet weaned*
And streight delivered to a Faery knight,
To be upbrought in gentle thewes° and martiall might.   *manners*

4

"Unto old Timon[3] he me brought bylive,°   *immediately*
Old Timon, who in youthly yeares hath beene
In warlike feates th'expertest man alive,
And is the wisest now on earth I weene;
His dwelling is low in a valley greene,
Under the foot of Rauran mossy hore,°   *gray*
From whence the river Dee as silver cleene°   *pure*
His tombling billowes rolls with gentle rore:[4]
There all my dayes he traind me up in vertuous lore.

5

"Thither the great Magicien Merlin came,
As was his use,° ofttimes to visit me: *custom*
For he had charge my discipline° to frame,°   *education / direct*
And Tutours nouriture° to oversee.   *tutor's upbringing*
Him oft and oft I askt in privitie,
Of what loines and what lignage I did spring:
Whose aunswere bad me still assurèd bee,
That I was sonne and heire unto a king,
As time in her just terme° the truth to light should bring."   *due course*

6

"Well worthy impe,"° said then the Lady gent,°   *offspring / gentle*
"And Pupill fit for such a Tutours hand.
But what adventure, or what high intent
Hath brought you hither into Faery land,
Aread° Prince Arthur,[5] crowne of Martiall band?"   *declare*
"Full hard it is," quoth he, "to read° aright   *discern*
The course of heavenly cause, or understand
The secret meaning of th'eternall might,
That rules mens wayes, and rules the thoughts of living wight.

7

"For whither he through fatall deepe foresight,[6]
Me hither sent, for cause to me unghest,°   *unknown*
Or that fresh bleeding wound, which day and night
Whilome° doth rancle in my riven° brest,   *all the while / torn*
With forcèd fury following his behest,°   *its command*

---

3. The name means "honor."
4. The hill Rauran is in Wales. The river Dee flows in, and forms part of the boundary of, Wales. The Tudors (Queen Elizabeth's family) were originally Welsh, and the legends of Arthur had their beginnings in the Celtic mythology of early Wales.

5. Arthur had been named in the quatrains that precede cantos 7 and 8, but not previously in the body of the text.
6. That is, whether God ("th'eternall might") sent me here through foresight ordained by fate ("fatall").

Me hither brought by wayes yet never found,
You to have helpt I hold my selfe yet blest."
"Ah curteous knight," quoth she, "what secret wound
Could ever find,° to grieve the gentlest hart on ground?"   *succeed*

8

"Deare Dame," quoth he, "you sleeping sparkes awake,
Which troubled once, into huge flames will grow,
Ne ever will their fervent fury slake
Till living moysture into smoke do flow,
And wasted° life do lye in ashes low.   *consumed*
Yet sithens° silence lesseneth not my fire,   *since*
But told it flames, and hidden it does glow,
I will revele, what ye so much desire:
Ah Love, lay downe thy bow, the whiles I may respire.°   *take breath*

9

"It was in freshest flowre of youthly yeares,
When courage first does creepe in manly chest,
Then first the coale of kindly° heat appeares   *natural*
To kindle love in every living brest;
But me had warnd old Timons wise behest,
Those creeping flames by reason to subdew,
Before their rage grew to so great unrest,
As miserable lovers use° to rew,   *are accustomed*
Which still wex° old in woe, whiles woe still wexeth new.   *grow*

10

"That idle name of love, and lovers life,
As° losse of time, and vertues enimy   *as being*
I ever scornd, and joyd to stirre up strife,
In middest of their mournfull Tragedy,
Ay° wont to laugh, when them I heard to cry,   *always*
And blow the fire, which them to ashes brent:°   *burned*
Their God himselfe, grieved at my libertie,
Shot many a dart at me with fiers intent,
But I them warded all with wary government.[7]

11

"But all in vaine: no fort can be so strong,
Ne fleshly brest can armèd be so sound,
But will at last be wonne with battrie° long,   *siege*
Or unawares at disavantage found;
Nothing is sure, that growes on earthly ground:
And who most trustes in arme of fleshly might,
And boasts, in beauties chaine not to be bound,

---

7. That is, self-control. The descriptions here of Cupid's archery and of the siege of the castle of chastity (in the next stanza) have many echoes from the medieval courtly love tradition.

Doth soonest fall in disaventrous° fight, *disastrous*
And yeeldes his caytive° neck to victours most° despight. *captive / greatest*

12

"Ensample make of him your haplesse joy,° *Redcrosse*
   And of my selfe now mated,° as ye see; *overcome*
   Whose prouder° vaunt that proud avenging boy *too proud*
   Did soone pluck downe, and curbd my libertie.
   For on a day prickt° forth with jollitie *spurred*
   Of looser° life, and heat of hardiment,° *too loose / boldness*
   Raunging the forest wide on courser° free, *warhorse*
   The fields, the floods, the heavens with one consent
Did seeme to laugh on me, and favour mine intent.

13

"For-wearied° with my sports, I did alight *utterly wearied*
   From loftie steed, and downe to sleepe me layd;
   The verdant° gras my couch did goodly dight,° *green / make*
   And pillow was my helmet faire displayd:
   Whiles every sence the humour sweet embayd,[8]
   And slombring soft my hart did steale away,
   Me seemèd, by my side a royall Mayd
   Her daintie limbes full softly down did lay:
So faire a creature yet saw never sunny day.

14

"Most goodly glee° and lovely blandishment° *entertainment / compliment*
   She to me made, and bad me love her deare,
   For dearely sure her love was to me bent,° *given*
   As when just time expirèd[9] should appeare.
   But whether dreames delude, or true it were,
   Was never hart so ravisht with delight,
   Ne living man like words did ever heare,
   As she to me delivered all that night;
And at her parting said, She Queene of Faeries hight.[1]

15

"When I awoke, and found her place devoyd,° *empty*
   And nought but pressèd gras, where she had lyen,
   I sorrowed all so much, as earst° I joyd, *previously*
   And washèd all her place with watry eyen.
   From that day forth I loved that face divine;
   From that day forth I cast° in carefull° mind, *resolved / care-filled*
   To seeke her out with labour, and long tyne,° *hardship*

---

8. That is, while the dew ("humour") of sleep pervaded ("embayd") every sense.
9. A fitting length of time having passed.
1. Was called. In the background are many folk-tales and ballads of a hero bewitched by a fairy. Spenser's letter to Ralegh identifies Gloriana allegorically with glory and with Queen Elizabeth.

    And never vowd° to rest, till her I find,   *vowed never*
    Nine monethes I seeke in vaine yet ni'll° that vow unbind." *will not*

16

Thus as he spake, his visage wexèd pale,
    And chaunge of hew great passion did bewray;°   *reveal*
    Yet still he strove to cloke his inward bale,°   *grief*
    And hide the smoke, that did his fire display,
    Till gentle Una thus to him gan say;
    "O happy Queene of Faeries, that hast found
    Mongst many, one that with his prowesse may
    Defend thine honour, and thy foes confound:
True Loves are often sown, but seldom grow on ground."

17

"Thine, O then," said the gentle Redcrosse knight,
    "Next to that Ladies love shalbe the place,
    O fairest virgin, full of heavenly light,
    Whose wondrous faith, exceeding earthly race,
    Was firmest fixt in mine extremest case.°   *plight*
    And you, my Lord, the Patrone° of my life,   *protector*
    Of that great Queene may well gaine worthy grace:
    For onely worthy you through prowes priefe° *demonstration of prowess*
Yf living man mote° worthy be, to be her liefe."°   *may / love*

18

So diversly discoursing of their loves,
    The golden Sunne his glistring° head gan shew,   *glittering*
    And sad remembraunce now the Prince amoves,
    With fresh desire his voyage to pursew:
    Als° Una earnd° her traveill to renew.   *also / yearned*
    Then those two knights, fast friendship for to bynd,
    And love establish each to other trew,
    Gave goodly gifts, the signes of gratefull mynd,
And eke as pledges firme, right hands together joynd.

19

Prince Arthur gave a boxe of Diamond sure,°   *true*
    Embowd° with gold and gorgeous ornament,   *bound*
    Wherein were closd few drops of liquor pure,
    Of wondrous worth, and vertue° excellent,   *power*
    That any wound could heale incontinent:°   *immediately*
    Which to requite, the Redcrosse knight him gave
    A booke, wherein his Saveours testament
    Was writ with golden letters rich and brave;°   *splendid*
A worke of wondrous grace, and able soules to save.

20

Thus beene they parted, Arthur on his way
  To seeke his love, and th'other for to fight
  With Unas foe, that all her realme did pray:°   *prey on*
  But she now weighing the decayèd plight,
  And shrunken synewes of her chosen knight,
  Would not a while her forward course pursew,
  Ne bring him forth in face of dreadfull fight,
  Till he recovered had his former hew:°   *appearance*
For him to be yet weake and wearie well she knew.

21

So as they traveild, lo they gan espy
  An armèd knight towards them gallop fast,
  That seemèd from some fearèd foe to fly,
  Or other griesly thing, that him agast.°   *terrified*
  Still° as he fled, his eye was backward cast,   *continually*
  As if his feare still followed him behind;
  Als flew his steed, as he his bands had brast,°   *broken*
  And with his wingèd heeles did tread the wind,
As he had beene a fole of Pegasus his kind.[2]

22

Nigh as he drew, they might° perceive his head   *could*
  To be unarmd, and curld uncombèd heares
  Upstaring° stiffe, dismayd with uncouth° dread;   *bristling / strange*
  Nor drop of bloud in all his face appeares
  Nor life in limbe: and to increase his feares,
  In fowle reproch° of knighthoods faire degree,°   *disgrace / condition*
  About his neck an hempen rope he weares,
  That with his glistring armes does ill agree;
But he of rope or armes has now no memoree.

23

The Redcrosse knight toward him crossèd fast,
  To weet,° what mister° wight was so dismayd: *learn / kind of*
  There him he finds all sencelesse and aghast,
  That of him selfe he seemd to be afrayd;
  Whom hardly° he from flying forward stayd,   *with difficulty*
  Till he these wordes to him deliver might;
  "Sir knight, aread° who hath ye thus arayd,   *declare*
  And eke from whom make ye this hasty flight:
For never knight I saw in such misseeming° plight."   *unseemly*

---

2. That is, as if he had been a foal of a horse like Pegasus, the flying horse of classical mythology.

24

He answerd nought at all, but adding new
   Feare to his first amazment, staring wide
   With stony eyes, and hartlesse hollow hew,³
   Astonisht stood, as one that had aspide
   Infernall furies, with their chaines untide.
   Him yet againe, and yet againe bespake
   The gentle knight; who nought to him replide,
   But trembling every joynt did inly quake,
And foltring tongue at last these words seemd forth to shake.

25

"For Gods deare love, Sir knight, do me not stay;
   For loe he comes, he comes fast after mee."
   Eft° looking backe would faine have runne away;   *again*
   But he him forst to stay, and tellen free
   The secret cause of his perplexitie:°   *distress*
   Yet nathemore° by his bold hartie speach,   *not at all*
   Could his bloud-frosen hart emboldned bee,
   But through his boldnesse rather feare did reach,
Yet forst, at last he made through silence suddein breach.

26

"And am I now in safetie sure," quoth he,
   "From him, that would have forcèd me to dye?
   And is the point of death now turnd fro mee,
   That I may tell this haplesse history?"°   *story of misfortune*
   "Feare nought:" quoth he, "no daunger now is nye."
   "Then shall I you recount a ruefull cace,"°   *pitiable event*
   Said he, "the which with this unlucky eye
   I late beheld, and had not greater grace
Me reft° from it, had bene partaker of the place.⁴   *carried*

27

"I lately chaunst (Would I had never chaunst)
   With a faire knight to keepen companee,
   Sir Terwin⁵ hight,° that well himselfe advaunst   *named*
   In all affaires, and was both bold and free,
   But not so happie as mote happie bee:
   He loved, as was his lot, a Ladie gent,°   *gentle*
   That him againe° loved in the least degree: *in return*
   For she was proud, and of too high intent,°   *mind*
And joyd to see her lover languish and lament.

---

3. That is, with blanched, bloodless countenance.
4. That is, shared the same fate.
5. His name may connote weariness or fatigue ("terwyn").

28

"From whom returning sad and comfortlesse,°   *desolate*
  As on the way together we did fare,
  We met that villen (God from him me blesse°)   *defend*
  That cursèd wight, from whom I scapt whyleare,°   *a while before*
  A man of hell, that cals himselfe Despaire;[6]
  Who first us greets, and after faire areedes°   *tells*
  Of tydings strange, and of adventures rare:
  So creeping close, as Snake in hidden weedes,
Inquireth of our states, and of our knightly deedes.

29

"Which when he knew, and felt our feeble harts
  Embost° with bale,° and bitter byting griefe,   *exhausted / sorrow*
  Which love had launchèd° with his deadly darts,   *pierced*
  With wounding words and termes of foule repriefe,°   *insult, scorn*
  He pluckt from us all hope of due reliefe,
  That earst° us held in love of lingring life;   *formerly*
  Then hopelesse hartlesse, gan the cunning thiefe
  Perswade us die, to stint° all further strife: *end*
To me he lent this rope, to him a rustie° knife.   *bloodstained*

30

"With which sad instrument of hastie death,
  That wofull lover, loathing lenger° light,   *longer*
  A wide way made to let forth living breath.
  But I more fearefull, or more luckie wight,
  Dismayd with that deformèd dismall sight,
  Fled fast away, halfe dead with dying feare:°   *fear of death*
  Ne yet assur'd of life by you, Sir knight,
  Whose like infirmitie like chaunce may beare:
But God you never let his charmèd speeches heare."[7]

31

"How may a man," said he, "with idle speach
  Be wonne, to spoyle° the Castle of his health?"   *destroy*
  "I wote,"° quoth he, "whom triall° late did teach,   *know / experience*
  That like would not[8] for all this worldes wealth:
  His subtill tongue, like dropping honny, mealt'th°   *melts*
  Into the hart, and searcheth every vaine,
  That ere one be aware, by secret stealth
  His powre is reft,° and weaknesse doth remaine.   *taken by force*
O never Sir desire to try° his guilefull traine."°   *test / treachery*

---

6. Despair is the ultimate Christian sin, denying the possibility of divine mercy and grace.
7. That is, may God never let you hear his mesmerizing ("charmèd") speeches.
8. That is, would not do the like again.

32

"Certès,"° said he, "hence shall I never rest,   *surely*
   Till I that treachours art have heard and tride;
And you Sir knight, whose name mote° I request,   *might*
   Of grace° do me unto his cabin° guide."   *favor / cave*
"I that hight° Trevisan,"⁹ quoth he, "will ride   *am called*
   Against my liking backe, to doe you grace:°   *a favor*
But nor for gold nor glee¹ will I abide
   By you, when ye arrive in that same place;
For lever° had I die, then° see his deadly face."   *rather / than*

33

Ere long they come, where that same wicked wight
   His dwelling has, low in an hollow cave,
Farre underneath a craggie clift ypight,°   *placed*
   Darke, dolefull, drearie, like a greedie grave,
That still° for carrion carcases doth crave: *continually*
   On top whereof aye° dwelt the ghastly Owle,²   *ever*
Shrieking his balefull note, which ever drave
   Farre from that haunt all other chearefull fowle;
And all about it wandring ghostes did waile and howle.

34

And all about old stockes° and stubs of trees,   *stumps*
   Whereon nor fruit, nor leafe was ever seene,
Did hang upon the ragged rocky knees;°   *crags*
   On which had many wretches hangèd beene,
Whose carcases were scattered on the greene,
   And throwne about the cliffs. Arrivèd there,
That bare-head knight for dread and dolefull teene,°   *grief*
   Would faine° have fled, ne durst approachen neare,   *gladly*
But th' other forst him stay, and comforted in feare.

35

That darkesome cave they enter, where they find
   That cursèd man, low sitting on the ground,
Musing full sadly in his sullein° mind;   *morose*
   His griesie° lockes, long growen, and unbound,   *gray*
Disordred hong about his shoulders round,
   And hid his face; through which his hollow eyne
Lookt deadly dull, and starèd as astound;°   *as if stunned*
   His raw-bone cheekes through penurie and pine,°   *starvation*
Were shronke into his jawes, as° he did never dine.   *as if*

---

9. The meaning is uncertain, but may be "flight" or "dread."

1. Beauty. That is, not for anything in the world.
2. Traditionally a messenger of death.

36

His garment nought but many ragged clouts,°   *scraps*
  With thornes together pind and patchèd was,
  The which his naked sides he wrapt abouts;
  And him beside there lay upon the gras
  A drearie corse,° whose life away did pas,   *bloody corpse*
  All wallowd in his owne yet luke-warme blood,
  That from his wound yet wellèd fresh alas;
  In which a rustie knife fast fixèd stood,
And made an open passage for the gushing flood.

37

Which piteous spectacle, approving° trew   *confirming*
  The wofull tale that Trevisan had told,
  When as the gentle Redcrosse knight did vew,
  With firie zeale he burnt in courage bold,
  Him to avenge, before his bloud were cold,
  And to the villein said, "Thou agèd damnèd wight,
  The author of this fact,° we here behold,   *deed*
  What justice can but judge against thee right,
With thine owne bloud to price° his bloud, here shed in sight?" *pay for*

38

"What franticke fit," quoth he, "hath thus distraught
  Thee, foolish man, so rash a doome° to give?   *judgment*
  What justice ever other judgement taught,
  But he should die, who merites not to live?
  None else to death this man despayring drive,°   *drove*
  But his owne guiltie mind deserving death.
  Is then unjust to each his due to give?
  Or let him die, that loatheth living breath?
Or let him die at ease, that liveth here uneath?°   *in hardship*

39

"Who travels by the wearie wandring way,
  To come unto his wishèd home in haste,
  And meetes a flood, that doth his passage stay,
  Is not great grace to helpe him over past,
  Or free his feet, that in the myre sticke fast?
  Most envious man, that grieves at neighbours good,
  And fond,° that joyest in the woe thou hast,   *foolish*
  Why wilt not let him passe, that long hath stood
Upon the banke, yet wilt thy selfe not passe the flood?

40

"He there does now enjoy eternall rest
  And happie ease, which thou doest want and crave,
  And further from it daily wanderest:
  What if some little paine the passage have,

That makes fraile flesh to feare the bitter wave?
Is not short paine well borne, that brings long ease,
And layes the soule to sleepe in quiet grave?
Sleepe after toyle, port after stormie seas,
Ease after warre, death after life does greatly please."³

41

The knight much wondred at his suddeine wit,°   *quick intelligence*
   And said, "The terme of life is limited,
   Ne may a man prolong, nor shorten it;
   The souldier may not move from watchfull sted,⁴
   Nor leave his stand, untill his Captaine bed."°   *commands*
"Who life did limit by almightie doome,"
   Quoth he, "knowes best the termes establishèd;
   And he, that points the Centonell his roome,°   *station*
Doth license him depart at sound of morning droome.⁵

42

"Is not his deed, what ever thing is donne,
   In heaven and earth? did not he all create
   To die againe? all ends that was begonne.
   Their times in his eternall booke of fate
   Are written sure, and have their certaine° date.   *fixed*
Who then can strive with strong necessitie,
   That holds the world in his still chaunging state,
   Or shunne the death ordaynd by destinie?
When houre of death is come, let none aske whence, nor why.

43

"The lenger° life, I wote° the greater sin,   *longer / know*
   The greater sin, the greater punishment:
   All those great battels, which thou boasts to win,
   Through strife, and bloud-shed, and avengement,
   Now praysd, hereafter deare° thou shalt repent: *bitterly*
For life must life, and bloud must bloud repay.⁶
   Is not enough thy evill life forespent?°   *already spent*
   For he, that once hath missèd the right way,
The further he doth goe, the further he doth stray.

44

"Then do no further goe, no further stray,
   But here lie downe, and to thy rest betake,
   Th'ill to prevent, that life ensewen may.⁷
   For what hath life, that may it lovèd make,

---

3. Despaire's arguments on behalf of suicide as against a painful life are derived, like those of *Hamlet* in his third soliloquy (*Hamlet* 3.1.58–90), principally from Seneca, Marcus Aurelius, other ancient Stoics, and Old Testament statements on divine justice.

4. The sentry post assigned him.
5. Drum, with a pun on *doom*.
6. An echo of Genesis 9:6: "Whoso sheddeth man's blood, by man shall his blood be shed."
7. That is, to prevent the evil that will ensue in the rest of your life.

And gives not rather cause it to forsake?
Feare, sicknesse, age, losse, labour, sorrow, strife,
Paine, hunger, cold, that makes the hart to quake;
And ever fickle fortune rageth rife,° *widely*
All which, and thousands mo° do make a loathsome life. *more*

45

"Thou wretched man, of death hast greatest need,
If in true ballance thou wilt weigh thy state:
For never knight, that darèd warlike deede,
More lucklesse disaventures° did amate:° *mishaps / daunt*
Witnesse the dongeon deepe, wherein of late
Thy life shut up, for death so oft did call;
And though good lucke prolongèd hath thy date,° *span of life*
Yet death then, would the like mishaps forestall,
Into the which hereafter thou maiest happen fall.° *happen to fall*

46

"Why then doest thou, O man of sin, desire
To draw thy dayes forth to their last degree?
Is not the measure of thy sinfull hire° *service to sin*
High heapèd up with huge iniquitie,
Against the day of wrath,° to burden thee? *Judgment Day*
Is not enough that to this Ladie milde
Thou falsèd° hast thy faith with perjurie,° *betrayed / oath-breaking*
And sold thy selfe to serve Duessa vilde,° *vile*
With whom in all abuse thou hast thy selfe defilde?

47

"Is not he just, that all this doth behold
From highest heaven, and beares an equall° eye? *impartial*
Shall he thy sins up in his knowledge fold,° *cover up*
And guiltie be of thine impietie?
Is not his law, Let every sinner die:[8]
Die shall all flesh? what then must needs be donne,
Is it not better to doe willinglie,
Then° linger, till the glasse° be all out ronne? *than / hourglass*
Death is the end of woes: die soone, O faeries sonne."

48

The knight was much enmovèd with his speach,
That as a swords point through his hart did perse,
And in his conscience made a secret breach,° *wound*
Well knowing true all, that he did reherse,° *recount*
And to his fresh remembrance did reverse° *bring back*
The ugly vew of his deformèd crimes,

---

8. Despaire cites only half of the scripture verse: "The wages of sin is death; but the gift of God is eternal life through Jesus Christ our Lord" (Romans 6:23).

That all his manly powres it did disperse,
    As he were charmèd with inchaunted rimes,
That oftentimes he quakt, and fainted° oftentimes. — *lost heart*

49

In which amazement, when the Miscreant° — *misbeliever*
    Perceivèd him to waver weake and fraile,
    Whiles trembling horror did his conscience dant,° — *daunt*
    And hellish anguish° did his soule assaile, — *fear of hell*
    To drive him to despaire, and quite to quaile,° — *be dismayed*
    He shewed him painted in a table° plaine, — *picture*
    The damnèd ghosts, that doe in torments waile,
    And thousand feends that doe them endlesse paine
With fire and brimstone, which for ever shall remaine.

50

The sight whereof so throughly him dismaid,
    That nought but death before his eyes he saw,
    And ever burning wrath before him laid,
    By righteous sentence of th'Almighties law:
    Then gan the villein him to overcraw,° — *exult over*
    And brought unto him swords, ropes, poison, fire,
    And all that might him to perdition draw;
    And bad him choose, what death he would desire:
For death was due to him, that had provokt Gods ire.

51

But when as none of them he saw him take,
    He to him raught° a dagger sharpe and keene, — *reached*
    And gave it him in hand: his hand did quake,
    And tremble like a leafe of Aspin greene,
    And troubled bloud through his pale face was seene
    To come, and goe with tydings from the hart,
    As it a running messenger had beene.
    At last resolved to worke his finall smart,° — *pain*
He lifted up his hand, that backe againe did start.

52

Which when as Una saw, through every vaine
    The crudled° cold ran to her well of life,° — *congealing / heart*
    As in a swowne: but soone relived° againe, — *revived*
    Out of his hand she snatcht the cursèd knife,
    And threw it to the ground, enragèd rife,° — *deeply*
    And to him said, "Fie, fie, faint harted knight,
    What meanest thou by this reprochfull° strife? — *deserving reproach*
    Is this the battell, which thou vauntst to fight
With the fire-mouthèd Dragon, horrible and bright?

53

"Come, come away, fraile, feeble, fleshly wight,
   Ne let vaine words bewitch thy manly hart,
   Ne divelish thoughts dismay thy constant spright.°   *spirit*
   In heavenly mercies hast thou not a part?
   Why shouldst thou then despeire, that chosen[9] art?
   Where justice growes, there grows eke° greater grace,   *also*
   The which doth quench the brond° of hellish smart,   *firebrand*
   And that accurst hand-writing[1] doth deface.°   *blot out*
Arise, Sir knight arise, and leave this cursèd place."

54

So up he rose, and thence amounted° streight.   *mounted his horse*
   Which when the carle° beheld, and saw his guest   *churl*
   Would safe depart, for° all his subtill sleight,   *in spite of*
   He chose an halter° from among the rest,   *noose*
   And with it hung himselfe, unbid° unblest.   *unprayed for*
   But death he could not worke himselfe thereby;
   For thousand times he so himselfe had drest,°   *made ready*
   Yet nathelesse it could not doe° him die,   *make*
Till he should die his last, that is eternally.

Canto 10

Her faithfull knight faire Una brings
to house of Holinesse,
Where he is taught repentance, and
the way to heavenly blesse.°   *bliss*

1

What man is he, that boasts of fleshly might,
   And vaine assurance of mortality,°   *mortal life*
   Which all so soone, as it doth come to fight,
   Against spirituall foes, yeelds by and by,°   *immediately*
   Or from the field most cowardly doth fly?
   Ne let the man ascribe it to his skill,
   That thorough° grace hath gainèd victory.   *through*
   If any strength we have, it is to ill,
But all the good is Gods, both power and eke° will.[2]   *also*

---

9. Compare 2 Thessalonians 2:13: "God hath from the beginning chosen you to salvation through sanctification of the Spirit and belief of the truth." This is one of several similar passages in the epistles of Saint Paul that form the basis of the theological doctrine of predestination.
1. An echo of Colossians 2:14: "Blotting out the handwriting of ordinances [that is, the Old Testament law] that was against us, which was contrary to us, and took it out of the way, nailing it to his cross."
2. "For by grace are ye saved through faith; and that not of yourselves: it is the gift of God: Not of works, lest any man should boast" (Ephesians 2:8–9); "it is God which worketh in you both to will and to do of his good pleasure" (Philippians 2:13).

2

By that, which lately hapned, Una saw,
  That this her knight was feeble, and too faint;
  And all his sinews woxen weake and raw,°   *unready*
  Through long enprisonment, and hard constraint,°   *affliction*
  Which he endurèd in his late restraint,
  That yet he was unfit for bloudie fight:
  Therefore to cherish° him with diets daint,°   *foster / choice*
  She cast° to bring him, where he chearen° might,   *resolved / be cheered*
Till he recovered had his° late decayèd plight.   *from his*

3

There was an auntient house not farre away,
  Renowmd throughout the world for sacred lore,
  And pure unspotted life: so well they say
  It governd was, and guided evermore,
  Through wisedome of a matrone grave and hore;°   *hoar, venerable*
  Whose onely joy was to relieve the needes
  Of wretched soules, and helpe the helpelesse pore:
  All night she spent in bidding of her bedes,°   *saying prayers*
And all the day in doing good and godly deedes.

4

Dame Caelia° men did her call, as thought   *Heavenly*
  From heaven to come, or thither to arise,
  The mother of three daughters, well upbrought
  In goodly thewes,° and godly exercise:°   *habits / deeds*
  The eldest two most sober, chast, and wise,
  Fidelia and Speranza virgins were,
  Though spousd,° yet wanting° wedlocks solemnize;[3]   *betrothed / lacking*
  But faire Charissa to a lovely fere°   *loving mate*
Was linckèd, and by him had many pledges dere.[4]

5

Arrivèd there, the dore they find fast lockt;
  For it was warely watchèd night and day,
  For feare of many foes: but when they knockt,
  The Porter opened unto them streight way:
  He was an agèd syre, all hory gray,
  With lookes full lowly cast, and gate° full slow,   *gait*
  Wont° on a staffe his feeble steps to stay,   *accustomed*
  Hight Humilta.° They passe in stouping low;   *called Humility*
For streight and narrow was the way, which he did show.[5]

---

3. Solemnization.
4. That is, many children. The daughters' names mean Faith, Hope, and Charity; compare the three Saracens: Sansfoy, Sansjoy, and Sansloy. This canto draws heavily on scriptural references, especially 1 Corinthians 13:13: "And now abideth faith, hope, charity, these three; but the greatest of these is charity." Many aspects of the House of Holiness oppose their counterparts in the House of Pride (canto 4).
5. Alluding to Matthew 7:13–14: see stanza 10, n. 9.

6

Each goodly thing is hardest to begin,
  But entred in a spacious court they see,
  Both plaine, and pleasant to be walkèd in,
  Where them does meete a francklin[6] faire and free,
  And entertaines with comely courteous glee,
  His name was Zele,° that him right well became,   *Zeal*
  For in his speeches and behaviour hee
  Did labour lively to expresse the same,
And gladly did them guide, till to the Hall they came.

7

There fairely them receives a gentle Squire,
  Of milde demeanure, and rare courtesie,
  Right cleanly clad in comely sad° attire;   *sober*
  In word and deede that shewed great modestie,
  And knew his good° to all of each degree,   *proper respect*
  Hight Reverence. He them with speeches meet°   *fitting*
  Does faire entreat; no courting nicetie,[7]
  But simple true, and eke unfainèd sweet,
As might become a Squire so great persons to greet.

8

And afterwards them to his Dame he leades,
  That agèd Dame, the Ladie of the place:
  Who all this while was busie at her beades:
  Which doen, she up arose with seemely grace,
  And toward them full matronely[8] did pace.
  Where when that fairest Una she beheld,
  Whom well she knew to spring from heavenly race,
  Her hart with joy unwonted° inly sweld,°   *unaccustomed / swelled*
As feeling wondrous comfort in her weaker eld.°   *too weak age*

9

And her embracing said, "O happie earth,
  Whereon thy innocent feet doe ever tread,
  Most vertuous virgin borne of heavenly berth,
  That to redeeme thy woefull parents head,
  From tyrans rage, and ever-dying dread,°   *constant fear of death*
  Hast wandred through the world now long a day°   *many a long day*
  Yet ceasest not thy wearie soles to lead,
  What grace hath thee now hither brought this way?
Or doen° thy feeble feet unweeting° hither stray?   *do / unwittingly*

---

6. Freeholder, landowner.
7. He treats them courteously ("faire"); no courtly affectation ("nicetie").
8. Like a matron, that is, a woman in charge of an establishment.

10

"Strange thing it is an errant° knight to see   *wandering*
  Here in this place, or any other wight,
  That hither turnes his steps. So few there bee,
  That chose the narrow path, or seeke the right:
  All keepe the broad high way, and take delight
  With many rather for to go astray,
  And be partakers of their evill plight,
  Then with a few to walke the Tightest way;[9]
O foolish men, why haste ye to your owne decay?"

11

"Thy selfe to see, and tyred limbs to rest,
  O matrone sage," quoth she, "I hither came,
  And this good knight his way with me addrest,°   *directed*
  Led with thy prayses and broad-blazèd fame,
  That up to heaven is blowne."[1] The auncient Dame
  Him goodly greeted in her modest guise,
  And entertaynd them both, as best became,
  With all the court'sies,° that she could devise,   *courtesies*
Ne wanted ought,° to shew her bounteous or wise.   *nor lacked anything*

12

Thus as they gan of sundry things devise,°   *talk*
  Loe two most goodly virgins came in place,
  Ylinkèd arme in arme in lovely wise,°   *loving fashion*
  With countenance demure, and modest grace,
  They numbred even steps and equall pace:
  Of which the eldest, that Fidelia hight,
  Like sunny beames threw from her Christall face,
  That could have dazd° the rash beholders sight,   *dazzled*
And round about her head did shine like heavens light.

13

She was araièd° all in lilly white,   *arrayed*
  And in her right hand bore a cup of gold,
  With wine and water[2] fild up to the hight,
  In which a Serpent[3] did himselfe enfold,
  That horrour made to all, that did behold;
  But she no whit did chaunge her constant mood:°   *expression*
  And in her other hand she fast did hold

---

9. An echo of Matthew 7:13–14: "Broad is the way, that leadeth to destruction, and many there be which go in thereat: . . . strait is the gate, and narrow is the way, which leadeth unto life, and few there be that find it."
1. That is, your praises and fame are widely celebrated ("blazèd"), reaching ("blowne") up to heaven.
2. Signifying the sacrament of Communion.
3. A symbol of the crucified Christ (of whom the serpent lifted up by Moses, Numbers 21:9, is a recognized "type" or prefiguration).

A booke,⁴ that was both signd and seald with blood,
Wherein darke° things were writ, hard to be understood.⁵   *obscure*

14

Her younger sister, that Speranza hight,
    Was clad in blew, that her beseemèd° well;   *suited*
    Not all so chearefull seemèd she of sight,°   *in appearance*
    As was her sister; whether dread° did dwell,   *fear*
    Or anguish in her hart, is hard to tell:
    Upon her arme a silver anchor⁶ lay,
    Whereon she leanèd ever, as befell:°   *as was fitting*
    And ever up to heaven, as she did pray,
Her stedfast eyes were bent, ne swarvèd other way.

15

They seeing Una, towards her gan wend,°   *walk*
    Who them encounters° with like courtesie;   *meets*
    Many kind speeches they betwene them spend,
    And greatly joy each other well to see:
    Then to the knight with shamefast° modestie   *humble*
    They turne themselves, at Unas meeke request,
    And him salute with well beseeming glee;°   *appropriate joy*
    Who faire them quites,° as him beseemèd best,   *requites*
And goodly gan discourse of many a noble gest.°   *deed*

16

Then Una thus; "But she your sister deare,
    The deare Charissa where is she become?°   *gone to*
    Or wants° she health, or busie is elsewhere?"   *is lacking*
    "Ah no," said they, "but forth she may not come:
    For she of late is lightned of her wombe,
    And hath encreast the world with one sonne more,⁷
    That her to see should be but troublesome."
    "Indeede," quoth she, "that should her trouble sore,
But thankt be God, that her encrease so evermore."⁸

17

Then said the agèd Caelia, "Deare dame,
    And you good Sir, I wote° that of your toyle,   *know*
    And labours long, through which ye hither came,
    Ye both forwearied° be: therefore a whyle   *utterly weary*
    I read° you rest, and to your bowres recoyle."⁹   *counsel*
    Then callèd she a Groome, that forth him led
    Into a goodly lodge, and gan despoile°   *disrobe*

---

4. That is, the New Testament.
5. See 2 Peter 3:16, which notes that in the epistles of the apostle Paul "are some things hard to be understood."
6. The iconographic symbol of hope.
7. Charity, the fruitful virtue, is often depicted as a mother with many children.
8. That is, God be thanked, who continually increases her thus.
9. Retire to your rooms.

Of puissant armes, and laid in easie° bed; — *comfortable*
His name was meeke Obedience rightfully arèd.° — *understood*

18

Now when their wearie limbes with kindly° rest, — *natural*
   And bodies were refresht with due repast,° — *repose*
   Faire Una gan Fidelia faire request,
   To have her knight into her schoolehouse plaste,° — *placed*
   That of her heavenly learning he might taste,
   And heare the wisedome of her words divine.
   She graunted, and that knight so much agraste,° — *favored*
   That she him taught celestiall discipline,° — *instruction*
And opened his dull eyes, that light mote in them shine.

19

And that her sacred Booke, with bloud° ywrit, — *the blood of Christ*
   That none could read, except she did them teach,
   She unto him disclosèd every whit,° — *bit*
   And heavenly documents° thereout did preach, — *doctrines*
   That weaker wit° of man could never reach, — *too weak mind*
   Of God, of grace, of justice, of free will,
   That wonder was to heare her goodly speach:
   For she was able, with her words to kill,
And raise againe to life the hart, that she did thrill.° — *pierce*

20

And when she list° poure out her larger spright,° — *chose to / greater power*
   She would commaund the hastie Sunne to stay,
   Or backward turne his course from heavens hight;
   Sometimes great hostes of men she could dismay,
   Dry-shod to passe, she parts the flouds in tway;° — *two*
   And eke huge mountaines from their native seat
   She would commaund, themselves to beare away,
   And throw in raging sea with roaring threat.
Almightie God her gave such powre, and puissance great.[1]

21

The faithfull knight now grew in litle space,° — *time*
   By hearing her, and by her sisters lore,
   To such perfection of all heavenly grace,
   That wretched world he gan for to abhore,[2]
   And mortall life gan loath, as thing forelore,° — *doomed*
   Greeved with remembrance of his wicked wayes,
   And prickt with anguish of his sinnes so sore,

---

1. Joshua made the sun stand still (Joshua 10:12); *Hezekiah* made it turn backward (2 Kings 20:10). With 300 men Gideon was victorious over the Midianite hosts (Judges 7:7). Moses led the Israelites through the parted waters of the Red Sea (Exodus 14:21–31). Faith, said Christ, can move mountains (Matthew 21:21). All these are miracles of faith.
2. That is, he began to abhor the world.

That he desirde to end his wretched dayes:
So much the dart of sinfull guilt the soule dismayes.

22

But wise Speranza gave him comfort sweet,
    And taught him how to take assurèd hold
    Upon her silver anchor, as was meet;
    Else had his sinnes so great, and manifold
    Made him forget all that Fidelia told.
    In this distressèd doubtfull° agonie,   *fearful*
    When him his dearest Una did behold,
    Disdeining life, desiring leave to die,
She found her selfe assayld with great perplexitie.°   *distress*

23

And came to Caelia to declare her smart,°   *pain*
    Who well acquainted with that commune° plight,   *common*
    Which sinfull horror° workes in wounded hart,   *horror of sin*
    Her wisely comforted all that she might,
    With goodly counsell and advisement right;
    And streightway sent with carefull diligence,
    To fetch a Leach,° the which had great insight   *doctor*
    In that disease of grievèd° consciënce,   *distressed*
And well could cure the same; His name was Patiënce.

24

Who comming to that soule-diseasèd knight,
    Could hardly° him intreat, to tell his griefe: *with difficulty*
    Which knowne, and all that noyd° his heavie spright   *troubled*
    Well searcht,° eftsoones° he gan apply reliefe   *probed / immediately*
    Of salves and med'cines, which had passing priefe,[3]
    And thereto added words of wondrous might:
    By which to ease he him recurèd briefe,°   *restored quickly*
    And much asswaged the passion° of his plight,   *suffering*
That he his paine endured, as seeming now more light.

25

But yet the cause and root of all his ill,
    Inward corruption, and infected sin,[4]
    Not purged nor heald, behind remainèd still,
    And festring sore did rankle yet within,
    Close° creeping twixt the marrow and the skin.   *secretly*
    Which to extirpe,° he laid him privily   *extirpate*
    Downe in a darkesome lowly place farre in,
    Whereas° he meant his corrosives to apply,   *where*
And with streight° diet tame his stubborne malady.   *strict*

---

3. Which had extraordinary power.   4. Apparently, the effects of original sin.

26

In ashes and sackcloth⁵ he did array
    His daintie corse,° proud humors⁶ to abate,   *handsome body*
    And dieted with fasting every day,
    The swelling of his wounds to mitigate,
    And made him pray both earely and eke late:
    And ever as superfluous flesh did rot
    Amendment readie still at hand did wayt,
    To pluck it out with pincers firie whot,°   *hot*
That soone in him was left no one corrupted jot.

27

And bitter Penance with an yron whip,
    Was wont him once to disple° every day: *discipline*
    And sharpe Remorse his hart did pricke and nip,
    That drops of bloud thence like a well did play;
    And sad Repentance usèd to embay°   *bathe*
    His bodie in salt water smarting sore,
    The filthy blots of sinne to wash away.⁷
    So in short space they did to health restore
The man that would not live, but earst° lay at deathes dore.   *formerly*

28

In which his torment often was so great,
    That like a Lyon he would cry and rore,
    And rend his flesh, and his owne synewes eat.
    His own deare Una hearing evermore
    His ruefull shriekes and gronings, often tore
    Her guiltlesse garments, and her golden heare,
    For pitty of his paine and anguish sore;
    Yet all with patience wisely she did beare;
For well she wist, his crime could else be never cleare.°   *cleansed*

29

Whom thus recovered by wise Patiënce,
    And trew Repentance they to Una brought:
    Who joyous of his curèd consciënce,
    Him dearely kist, and fairely° eke besought   *courteously*
    Himselfe to chearish,° and consuming thought   *cheer; cherish*
    To put away out of his carefull° brest.   *care-full*
    By this° Charissa, late° in child-bed brought,   *by this time / recently*
    Was woxen° strong, and left her fruitfull nest;   *grown*
To her faire Una brought this unacquainted guest.

---

5. Symbols of penitence.
6. That is, the bodily fluids that conduce to pride. In Renaissance physiology, the proportions of the various fluids ("humors") determine one's temperament.
7. "Wash me throughly from mine iniquity, and cleanse me from my sin" (Psalm 51:2).

30

She was a woman in her freshest age,
   Of wondrous beauty, and of bountie° rare,   *goodness*
   With goodly grace and comely personage,°   *appearance*
   That was on earth not easie to compare;°   *rival*
   Full of great love, but Cupids wanton snare
   As hell she hated, chast in worke and will;
   Her necke and breasts were ever open bare,
   That ay° thereof her babes might sucke their fill;   *ever*
The rest was all in yellow robes arayèd still.[8]

31

A multitude of babes about her hong,
   Playing their sports, that joyd her to behold,
   Whom still she fed, whiles they were weake and young,
   But thrust them forth° still, as they wexèd old: *weaned them*
   And on her head she wore a tyre° of gold,   *headdress*
   Adornd with gemmes and owches° wondrous faire,   *jewels*
   Whose passing° price uneath° was to be told;   *surpassing / scarcely*
   And by her side there sate a gentle paire
Of turtle doves,[9] she sitting in an yvorie chaire.

32

The knight and Una entring, faire her greet,
   And bid her joy of that her happie brood;
   Who them requites with court'sies seeming meet,°   *appropriate*
   And entertaines with friendly chearefull mood.
   Then Una her besought, to be so good,
   As in her vertuous rules to schoole her knight,
   Now after all his torment well withstood,
   In that sad° house of Penaunce, where his spright   *solemn*
Had past° the paines of hell, and long enduring night. *passed through*

33

She was right joyous of her just request,
   And taking by the hand that Faeries sonne,
   Gan him instruct in every good behest,°   *command*
   Of love, and righteousness, and well to donne,°   *right action*
   And wrath, and hatred warely° to shonne,   *warily*
   That drew on men Gods hatred, and his wrath,
   And many soules in dolours° had fordonne:° *misery / destroyed*
   In which when him she well instructed hath,
From thence to heaven she teacheth him the ready° path. *direct*

---

8. Always. Her yellow (saffron) robe is the color of marriage, fertility, and maternity. Her chaste, fruitful love (Christian *agapē*) is opposed to "Cupid's wanton snare" (*erōs*).

9. Emblem of true love and faithful marriage.

34

Wherein his weaker° wandring steps to guide,   *too weak*
  An aunciet matrone she to her does call,
  Whose sober lookes her wisedome well descride:°   *made known*
  Her name was Mercie, well knowne over all,
  To be both gratious, and eke liberall:
  To whom the carefull charge of him she gave,
  To lead aright, that he should never fall
  In all his wayes through this wide worldès wave,°   *expanse*
That Mercy in the end his righteous soule might save.

35

The godly Matrone by the hand him beares°   *leads*
  Forth from her° presence, by a narrow way,   *Charissa's*
  Scattred with bushy thornes, and ragged breares,°   *briers*
  Which still before him she removed away,
  That nothing might his ready passage stay:°   *hinder*
  And ever when his feet encombred were,
  Or gan to shrinke, or from the right to stray,
  She held him fast, and firmely did upbeare,
As carefull Nourse her child from falling oft does reare.

36

Eftsoones unto an holy Hospitall,°   *hospice*
  That was fore° by the way, she did him bring,   *close*
  In which seven Bead-men° that had vowèd all   *men of prayer*
  Their life to service of high heavens king
  Did spend their dayes in doing godly thing:
  Their gates to all were open evermore,
  That by the wearie way were travelling,
  And one sate wayting ever them before,
To call in commers-by, that needy were and pore.[1]

37

The first of them that eldest was, and best,°   *chiefest*
  Of all the house had charge and governement,
  As Guardian and Steward of the rest:
  His office° was to give entertainement   *duty*
  And lodging, unto all that came, and went:
  Not unto such, as could him feast againe,°   *host in return*
  And double quite,° for that he on them spent,   *repay*
  But such, as want of harbour° did constraine:°   *shelter / afflict*
Those for Gods sake his dewty was to entertaine.

---

1. That is, one beadsman sat in front of the gates, to call in needy wayfarers.

38

The second was as Almner[2] of the place,
    His office was, the hungry for to feed,
    And thristy give to drinke, a worke of grace:
    He feard not once him selfe to be in need,
    Ne cared to hoord for those, whom he did breede:°   *his children*
    The grace of God he layd up still in store,
    Which as a stocke° he left unto his seede;°   *resource / children*
    He had enough, what need him care for more?
And had he lesse, yet some he would give to the pore.

39

The third had of their wardrobe custodie,
    In which were not rich tyres,° nor garments gay,   *attire*
    The plumes of pride, and wings of vanitie,
    But clothes meet to keepe keene could° away,   *cold*
    And naked nature seemely° to aray;   *decently*
    With which bare wretched wights he dayly clad,
    The images of God in earthly clay;
    And if that no spare clothes to give he had,
His owne coate he would cut, and it distribute glad.

40

The fourth appointed by his office was,
    Poore prisoners to relieve with gratious ayd,
    And captives to redeeme with price of bras,°   *payment of money*
    From Turkes and Sarazins, which them had stayd;°   *held captive*
    And though they faultie were, yet well he wayd,°   *considered*
    That God to us forgiveth every howre
    Much more then that, why° they in bands° were layd,   *for which / bonds*
    And he that harrowd hell[3] with heavie stowre,°   *assault*
The faultie° soules from thence brought to his heavenly bowre.   *sinful*

41

The fift had charge sicke persons to attend,
    And comfort those, in point of death which lay;
    For them most needeth comfort in the end,
    When sin, and hell, and death do most dismay
    The feeble soule departing hence away.
    All is but lost, that living we bestow,°   *store up*
    If not well ended at our dying day.
    O man have mind of that last bitter throw;°   *throes of death*
For as the tree does fall, so lyes it ever low.[4]

---

2. An almoner distributed charity (*alms*) to the poor.
3. Christ, who journeyed to hell to deliver those good people who lived before his time, according to a story popular in the Middle Ages. It originated in the apocryphal gospel of Nicodemus (compare *Piers Plowman*, Passus 18).
4. "In the place where the tree falleth, there it shall be" (Ecclesiastes 11:3).

42

The sixt had charge of them now being dead,
    In seemely sort their corses to engrave,°   *bodies to bury*
    And deck with dainty flowres their bridall bed,
    That to their heavenly spouse° both sweet and brave°   *Christ / fair*
    They might appeare, when he their soules shall save.
    The wondrous workemanship of Gods owne mould,[5]
    Whose face he made, all beasts to feare,° and gave   *frighten*
    All in his hand,[6] even dead we honour should.
Ah dearest God me graunt, I dead be not defould.°   *defiled*

43

The seventh now after death and buriall done,
    Had charge the tender Orphans of the dead
    And widowes ayd, least° they should be undone: *lest*
    In face of judgement° he their right would plead,   *in court*
    Ne ought° the powre of mighty men did dread   *nor at all*
    In their defence, nor would for gold or fee°   *bribe*
    Be wonne their rightfull causes downe to tread:
    And when they stood in most necessitee,
He did supply their want, and gave them ever free.[7]

44

There when the Elfin knight arrivèd was,
    The first and chiefest of the seven, whose care
    Was guests to welcome, towardes him did pas:
    Where seeing Mercie, that his steps up bare,°   *supported*
    And alwayes led, to her with reverence rare°   *uncommon*
    He humbly louted° in meeke lowlinesse,   *bowed*
    And seemely welcome for her did prepare:
    For of their order she was Patronesse,
Albe° Charissa were their chiefest founderesse.   *although*

45

There she awhile him stayes, him selfe to rest,
    That to the rest more able he might bee:
    During which time, in every good behest°   *command*
    And godly worke of Almes and charitee
    She him instructed with great industree;
    Shortly therein so perfect he became,
    That from the first unto the last degree,
    His mortall life he learnèd had to frame
In holy righteousnesse, without rebuke or blame.

---

5. The human body is God's own image ("mould") *and a "mould"* of God's making (see Genesis 1:26–30, 2:7).

6. "And the fear of you and the dread of you shall be upon every beast of the earth, and upon every fowl of the air, upon all that moveth upon the earth, and upon all the fishes of the sea; into your hand are they delivered" (Genesis 9:2).

7. Always freely. The seven beadsmen here correspond to, and perform, the seven works of charity, or corporal mercy: lodging the homeless, feeding the hungry, clothing the naked, redeeming the captive, comforting the sick, burying the dead, and succoring the orphan.

46

Thence forward by that painfull way they pas,
  Forth to an hill, that was both steepe and hy;
  On top whereof a sacred chappell was,
  And eke a litle Hermitage thereby,
  Wherein an agèd holy man did lye,°   *live*
  That day and night said his devotiön,
  Ne other worldly busines did apply;[8]
  His name was heavenly Contemplatiön;
Of God and goodnesse was his meditatiön.

47

Great grace that old man to him given had;
  For God he often saw from heavens hight,
  All° were his earthly eyen both blunt° and bad,   *although / dim*
  And through great age had lost their kindly° sight,   *natural*
  Yet wondrous quick and persant° was his spright,°   *piercing / spirit*
  As Eagles eye, that can behold the Sunne:[9]
  That hill they scale with all their powre and might,
  That his frayle thighes nigh° wearie and fordonne°   *almost / exhausted*
Gan faile, but by her helpe the top at last he wonne.

48

There they do finde that godly agèd Sire,
  With snowy lockes adowne his shoulders shed,
  As hoarie frost with spangles doth attire
  The mossy braunches of an Oke halfe ded.
  Each bone might through his body well be red,°   *seen*
  And every sinew seene through° his long fast: *because of*
  For nought he cared his carcas long unfed;
  His mind was full of spirituall repast,
And pyned° his flesh, to keepe his body low° and chast.   *starved / weak*

49

Who when these two approching he aspide,
  At their first presence grew agrievèd sore,[1]
  That forst him lay his heavenly thoughts aside;
  And had he not that Dame respected more,°   *greatly*
  Whom highly he did reverence and adore,
  He would not once have movèd for the knight.
  They him saluted standing far afore;°   *away*
  Who well them greeting, humbly did requight,°   *respond*
And askèd, to what end they clomb° that tedious height.   *had climbed*

50

"What end," quoth she, "should cause us take such paine,
  But that same end, which every living wight

---

8. That is, he did not attend to any worldly activities.
9. The eagle able to gaze directly at the sun is the symbol of Saint John the Divine, whose visions are recorded in Revelation.
1. That is, he was at first sorely grieved at their arrival.

    Should make his marke,° high heaven to attaine? — *goal*
    Is not from hence the way, that leadeth right
    To that most glorious house, that glistreth° bright — *glistens*
    With burning starres, and everliving fire,
    Whereof the keyes are to thy hand behight° — *entrusted*
    By wise Fidelia? she doth thee require,
  To shew it to this knight, according° his desire." — *granting*

51

"Thrise happy man," said then the father grave,
    "Whose staggering steps thy° steady hand doth lead, — *Mercy's*
    And shewes the way, his sinfull soule to save.
    Who better can the way to heaven aread° — *direct*
    Then thou thy selfe, that was both borne and bred
    In heavenly throne, where thousand Angels shine?
    Thou doest the prayers of the righteous sead° — *seed*
    Present before the majestie divine,
  And his avenging wrath to clemencie incline.

52

"Yet since thou bidst, thy pleasure shalbe donne.
    Then come thou man of earth,[2] and see the way,
    That never yet was seene of Faeries sonne,
    That never leads the traveiler astray,
    But after labours long, and sad delay,
    Brings them to joyous rest and endlesse blis.
    But first thou must a season fast and pray,
    Till from her bands the spright assoilèd° is, — *spirit released*
  And have her strength recured° from fraile infirmitis." — *recovered*

53

That done, he leads him to the highest Mount;
    Such one, as that same mighty man° of God, — *Moses*
    That bloud-red billowes like a wallèd front
    On either side disparted° with his rod, — *parted asunder*
    Till that his army dry-foot through them yod,° — *went*
    Dwelt fortie dayes upon; where writ in stone
    With bloudy letters by the hand of God,
    The bitter doome of death and balefull mone[3]
  He did receive, whiles flashing fire about him shone.

54

Or like that sacred hill, whose head full hie,
    Adornd with fruitfull Olives all arownd,

---

2. An allusion to humankind's formation from the dust of the earth (Genesis 2:7) and also to the knight's name (see stanza 66 and n. 6).
3. That is, the Ten Commandments ("bloudy letters") carried with them the judgment ("doome") of death and pain, causing sorrowful moans ("balefull mone").

Is, as it were for endlesse memory
Of that deare Lord, who oft thereon was fownd,
For ever with a flowring girlond crownd:
Or like that pleasaunt Mount, that is for ay°   *forever*
Through famous Poets verse each where° renownd,   *everywhere*
On which the thrise three learned Ladies play
Their heavenly notes, and make full many a lovely lay.[4]

55

From thence, far off he unto him did shew
A litle path, that was both steepe and long,
Which to a goodly Citie led his vew;
Whose wals and towres were builded high and strong
Of perle and precious stone,[5] that earthly tong
Cannot describe, nor wit of man can tell;
Too high a ditty° for my simple song;   *subject*
The Citie of the great king hight° it well,   *is called*
Wherein eternall peace and happinesse doth dwell.

56

As he thereon stood gazing, he might° see   *could*
The blessed Angels to and fro descend
From highest heaven, in gladsome companee,
And with great joy into that Citie wend,°   *proceed*
As commonly° as friend does with his frend.[6]   *familiarly*
Whereat he wondred much, and gan enquere,
What stately building durst so high extend
Her loftie towres unto the starry sphere,
And what unknowen nation there empeopled were.°   *dwelt*

57

"Faire knight," quoth he, "Hierusalem that is,
The new Hierusalem, that God has built
For those to dwell in, that are chosen his,
His chosen people purged from sinfull guilt,
With pretious bloud, which cruelly was spilt
On cursèd tree, of that unspotted lam,[7]
That for the sinnes of all the world was kilt:
Now are they Saints all in that Citie sam,°   *together*
More deare unto their God, then younglings to their dam."[8]

---

4. Song. The mountain is successively compared to Mount Sinai, where Moses, after parting the "bloud-red billowes" (stanza 53) of the Red Sea, received the tablets of the Ten Commandments; to the Mount of Olives, associated with Christ; and to Mount Parnassus, where the Nine Muses of the arts and learning dwelt.
5. Compare Revelation 21:10–21.
6. Compare Jacob's ladder, which "reached to heaven; and behold the angels of God ascending and descending on it" (Genesis 28:12).
7. Christ (the lamb of God), whose death on the Cross ("cursèd tree") purged the guilt of sin from "His chosen people."
8. Than offspring to their mother. The New Jerusalem is described in Revelation 21–22; compare "the nations of them which are saved shall walk in the light of it" (21:24).

58

"Till now," said then the knight, "I weenèd° well,   *supposed*
 That great Cleopolis,[9] where I have beene,
 In which that fairest Faerie Queene doth dwell,
 The fairest Citie was, that might be seene;
 And that bright towre all built of christall cleene,°   *clear*
 Panthea,[1] seemd the brightest thing, that was:
 But now by proofe° all otherwise I weene;   *experience*
 For this great Citie that[2] does far surpas,
And this bright Angels towre quite dims that towre of glas."

59

"Most trew," then said the holy agèd man;
 "Yet is Cleopolis for earthly frame,°   *structure*
 The fairest peece,° that eye beholden can: *masterpiece*
 And well beseemes° all knights of noble name,   *becomes*
 That covet in th'immortall booke of fame
 To be eternizèd, that same to haunt,°   *frequent*
 And doen their service to that soveraigne Dame,
 That glorie does to them for guerdon° graunt: *reward*
For she is heavenly borne, and heaven may justly vaunt.[3]

60

"And thou faire ymp,° sprong out from English race,   *youth*
 How ever now accompted° Elfins sonne,   *accounted*
 Well worthy doest thy service for her grace,°   *favor*
 To aide a virgin desolate foredonne.°   *undone*
 But when thou famous victorie hast wonne,
 And high emongst all knights hast hong thy shield,
 Thenceforth the suit° of earthly conquest shonne,°   *pursuit / shun*
 And wash thy hands from guilt of bloudy field:
For bloud can nought but sin, and wars but sorrowes yield.

61

"Then seeke this path, that I to thee presage,°   *show prophetically*
 Which after all to heaven shall thee send;
 Then peaceably thy painefull° pilgrimage   *laborious*
 To yonder same Hierusalem do bend,
 Where is for thee ordaind a blessèd end:
 For thou emongst those Saints, whom thou doest see,
 Shalt be a Saint, and thine owne nations frend
 And Patrone: thou Saint George shalt callèd bee,
Saint George of mery England, the signe of victoree."[4]

---

9. City of Fame; in the historical allegory, London or Westminster.
1. Reminiscent of the temple of glass in Chaucer's *House of Fame*; perhaps intended to allude to Westminster Abbey as pantheon of the English great.
2. That is, the New Jerusalem far surpasses Cleopolis ("that").
3. That is, may justly boast ("vaunt") that heaven is her home.
4. Spenser's conception of Saint George, patron saint of England, draws on the *Legenda Aurea*

62

"Unworthy wretch," quoth he, "of so great grace,
   How dare I thinke such glory to attaine?"
"These that have it attaind, were in like cace,"
   Quoth he, "as wretched, and lived in like paine."
"But deeds of armes must I at last be faine,°   *content (to leave)*
   And Ladies love to leave so dearely bought?"
"What need of armes, where peace doth ay° remaine,"   *ever*
   Said he, "and battailes none are to be fought?
As for loose° loves are° vaine, and vanish into nought."   *wanton / they are*

63

"O let me not," quoth he, "then turne againe
   Backe to the world, whose joyes so fruitlesse are;
But let me here for aye in peace remaine,
   Or streight way on that last long voyage fare,°   *travel*
That nothing may my present hope empare."°   *impair*
   "That may not be," said he, "ne maist thou yit
Forgo that royall maides bequeathèd care,°   *charge*
   Who did her cause into thy hand commit,
Till from her cursèd foe thou have her freely quit."°   *released*

64

"Then shall I soone," quoth he, "so God me grace,
   Abet° that virgins cause disconsolate,   *maintain*
And shortly backe returne unto this place
   To walke this way in Pilgrims poore estate.
But now aread,° old father, why of late   *declare*
   Didst thou behight° me borne of English blood,   *call*
Whom all a Faeries sonne doen nominate?"°   *name*
   "That word shall I," said he, "avouchen° good,   *prove*
Sith° to thee is unknowne the cradle of thy brood.[5]   *since*

65

"For well I wote,° thou springst from ancient race   *know*
   Of Saxon kings, that have with mightie hand
And many bloudie battailes fought in place°   *there*
   High reard their royall throne in Britane land,
And vanquisht them,° unable to withstand: *the ancient Britons*
   From thence a Faerie thee unweeting reft,°   *secretly stole*
There as thou slepst in tender swadling band,
   And her base Elfin brood° there for thee left.   *offspring*
Such men do Chaungelings call, so chaungd by Faeries theft.

(*The Golden Legend*, a medieval manual of ecclesiastical lore, translated into English by William Caxton in 1487) and on pictures, tapestries, pageants, and folklore.

5. The place from which your race derives.

66

"Thence she thee brought into this Faerie lond,
   And in an heapèd furrow did thee hyde,
   Where thee a Ploughman all unweeting fond,°   *inadvertently found*
   As he his toylesome teme° that way did guyde,   *team of oxen*
   And brought thee up in ploughmans state to byde,
   Whereof Georgos he thee gave to name;[6]
   Till prickt° with courage, and thy forces pryde,   *spurred*
   To Faery court thou cam'st to seeke for fame,
And prove thy puissaunt° armes, as seemes thee best became."[7]   *powerful*

67

"O holy Sire," quoth he, "how shall I quight°   *repay*
   The many favours I with thee have found,
   That hast my name and nation red° aright,   *declared*
   And taught the way that does to heaven bound?"°   *go*
   This said, adowne he lookèd to the ground,
   To have returnd, but dazèd° were his eyne,   *dazzled*
   Through passing° brightnesse, which did quite confound   *surpassing*
   His feeble sence, and too exceeding shyne.
So darke are earthly things compard to things divine.

68

At last whenas° himselfe he gan to find,°   *when / recover*
   To Una back he cast him to retire;°   *resolved to return*
   Who him awaited still with pensive° mind.   *anxious*
   Great thankes and goodly meed° to that good syre,   *gift*
   He thence departing gave for his paines hyre.°   *reward*
   So came to Una, who him joyd to see,
   And after litle rest, gan him desire,
   Of her adventure mindfull for to bee.
So leave they take of Caelia, and her daughters three.

Canto 11

The knight with that old Dragon fights
two dayes incessantly:
The third him overthrowes, and gayns
most glorious victory.

1

High time now gan it wex° for Una faire,   *grow*
   To thinke of those her captive Parents deare,
   And their forwasted kingdome to repaire:[8]
   Whereto whenas they now approachèd neare,
   With hartie° words her knight she gan to cheare,   *bold*

---

6. That is, as a name. "Georgos": farmer (Greek); compare Virgil's *Georgics*, on farming.
7. As best suited you.
8. That is, to restore their kingdom, laid waste (by the dragon).

And in her modest manner thus bespake;
"Deare knight, as deare, as ever knight was deare,
That all these sorrowes suffer for my sake,
High heaven behold the tedious toyle, ye for me take.

2

"Now are we come unto my native soyle,
And to the place, where all our perils dwell;
Here haunts that feend,° and does his dayly spoyle,   *fiend*
Therefore henceforth be at your keeping well,°   *be well on your guard*
And ever ready for your foeman fell.°   *fierce*
The sparke of noble courage now awake,
And strive your excellent selfe to excell;
That shall ye evermore renowmèd make,
Above all knights on earth, that batteill undertake."

3

And pointing forth, "lo yonder is," said she,
"The brasen towre in which my parents deare
For dread of that huge feend emprisond be,
Whom I from far see on the walles appeare,
Whose sight my feeble soule doth greatly cheare:
And on the top of all I do espye
The watchman wayting tydings glad to heare,
That O my parents might I happily
Unto you bring, to ease you of your misery."

4

With that they heard a roaring hideous sound,
That all the ayre with terrour fillèd wide,
And seemd uneath° to shake the stedfast ground.   *almost*
Eftsoones° that dreadfull Dragon they espide,   *immediately*
Where stretcht he lay upon the sunny side
Of a great hill, himselfe like a great hill.
But all so soone, as he from far descride
Those glistring armes, that heaven with light did fill,
He rousd himselfe full blith,° and hastned them untill.°   *joyfully / toward*

5

Then bad° the knight his Lady yede° aloofe,   *bade / go*
And to an hill her selfe withdraw aside,
From whence she might behold that battailles proof°   *outcome*
And eke° be safe from daunger far descryde:°   *also / observed from afar*
She him obayd, and turnd a little wyde.°   *aside*
Now O thou sacred Muse, most learnèd Dame,
Faire ympe° of Phoebus, and his agèd bride,[9]   *child*
The Nourse of time, and everlasting fame,
That warlike hands ennoblest with immortall name;

---

9. That is, Mnemosyne (memory), mother of the Muses.

6

 O gently come into my feeble brest,
  Come gently, but not with that mighty rage,
  Wherewith the martiall troupes thou doest infest,°   *arouse*
  And harts of great Heroes doest enrage,
  That nought their kindled courage may aswage,°   *allay*
  Soone as thy dreadfull trompe° begins to sownd;   *trumpet*
  The God of warre with his fiers equipage°   *military equipment*
  Thou doest awake, sleepe never he so sownd,
 And scarèd nations doest with horrour sterne astown.°   *appall*

7

 Faire Goddesse lay that furious fit° aside,   *strain*
  Till I of warres and bloudy Mars do sing,[1]
  And Briton fields with Sarazin° bloud bedyde,°   *Saracen / dyed*
  Twixt that great faery Queene and Paynim° king,   *pagan*
  That with their horrour heaven and earth did ring,
  A worke of labour long, and endlesse prayse:
  But now a while let downe that haughtie string,
  And to my tunes thy second tenor rayse,[2]
 That I this man of God his godly armes may blaze.°   *proclaim*

8

 By this the dreadfull Beast drew nigh to hand,
  Halfe flying, and halfe footing° in his hast,   *walking*
  That with his largenesse measurèd much land,
  And made wide shadow under his huge wast;°   *girth*
  As mountaine doth the valley overcast.
  Approching nigh, he rearèd high afore
  His body monstrous, horrible, and vast,
  Which to increase his wondrous greatnesse more,
 Was swolne with wrath, and poyson, and with bloudy gore.

9

 And over, all with brasen scales was armd,
  Like plated coate of steele, so couchèd neare,°   *placed so closely*
  That nought mote perce,[3] ne might his corse° be harmd   *body*
  With dint of sword, nor push of pointed speare;
  Which as an Eagle, seeing pray appeare,
  His aery Plumes doth rouze,° full rudely dight,°   *shake / ruggedly arrayed*
  So shakèd he, that horrour was to heare,
  For as the clashing of an Armour bright,
 Such noyse his rouzèd scales did send unto the knight.

---

1. Perhaps a reference to a projected but unwritten book of *The Faerie Queene*.
2. The high-pitched ("haughtie") mode would be appropriate to a large-scale epic war; a lower pitch ("second tenor") suits this present battle.
3. Nothing might pierce.

10

His flaggy° wings when forth he did display, — *drooping*
    Were like two sayles, in which the hollow wynd
    Is gathered full, and worketh speedy way:
    And eke the pennes, that did his pineons bynd,
    Were like mayne-yards, with flying canvas lynd,[4]
    With which whenas him list° the ayre to beat, — *he chose*
    And there by force unwonted° passage find, — *unaccustomed*
    The cloudes before him fled for terrour great,
And all the heavens stood still amazèd with his threat.

11

His huge long tayle wound up in hundred foldes,
    Does overspred his long bras-scaly backe,
    Whose wreathèd boughts° when ever he unfoldes, — *coils*
    And thicke entangled knots adown does slacke,
    Bespotted as with shields° of red and blacke, — *scales*
    It sweepeth all the land behind him farre,
    And of three furlongs[5] does but litle lacke;
    And at the point two stings in-fixèd arre,
Both deadly sharpe, that sharpest steele exceeden farre.

12

But stings and sharpest steele did far exceed° — *were far exceeded by*
    The sharpnesse of his cruell rending clawes;
    Dead was it sure, as sure as death in deed,° — *in its effect*
    What ever thing does touch his ravenous pawes,
    Or what within his reach he ever drawes.
    But his most hideous head my toung to tell
    Does tremble: for his deepe devouring jawes
    Wide gapèd, like the griesly° mouth of hell, — *horrid*
Through which into his darke abisse all ravin° fell. — *prey; booty*

13

And that° more wondrous was, in either jaw — *what*
    Three ranckes of yron teeth enraungèd° were, — *arranged*
    In which yet trickling bloud and gobbets raw° — *chunks of unswallowed food*
    Of late° devourèd bodies did appeare, — *recently*
    That sight thereof bred cold congealèd feare:
    Which to increase, and all at once to kill,
    A cloud of smoothering smoke and sulphur seare° — *burning*
    Out of his stinking gorge° forth steemèd still, — *maw*
That all the ayre about with smoke and stench did fill.

---

4. That is, the ribs of his wings were like the massive spars (main yards) to which a ship's mainsail is affixed.

5. That is, three-eighths of a mile.

14

His blazing eyes, like two bright shining shields,
   Did burne with wrath, and sparkled living fyre;
   As two broad Beacons, set in open fields,
   Send forth their flames farre off to every shyre,°   *shire*
And warning give, that enemies conspyre,
   With fire and sword the region to invade;
   So flamed his eyne° with rage and rancorous yre:°   *eyes / ire, anger*
   But farre within, as in a hollow glade,
Those glaring lampes were set, that made a dreadfull shade.

15

So dreadfully he towards him did pas,
   Forelifting up aloft his speckled brest,
   And often bounding on the brusèd gras,
   As for great joyance of his newcome guest.
Eftsoones he gan advance his haughtie crest,
   As chauffèd° Bore his bristles doth upreare,   *angry*
   And shoke his scales to battell readie drest;°   *prepared*
   That made the Redcrosse knight nigh quake for feare,
As bidding bold defiance to his foeman neare.

16

The knight gan fairely couch° his steadie speare,   *level*
   And fiercely ran at him with rigorous° might: *violent*
   The pointed steele arriving rudely° theare,   *roughly*
   His harder hide would neither perce, nor bight,
But glauncing by forth passèd forward right;
   Yet sore amovèd with so puissant push,
   The wrathfull beast about him turnèd light,°   *quickly*
   And him so rudely passing by, did brush
With his long tayle, that horse and man to ground did rush.

17

Both horse and man up lightly rose againe,
   And fresh encounter towards him addrest:
   But th'idle° stroke yet backe recoyld in vaine,   *useless*
   And found no place his° deadly point to rest.   *its*
Exceeding rage enflamed the furious beast,
   To be avengèd of so great despight;°   *outrage*
   For never felt his imperceable brest
   So wondrous force, from hand of living wight;
Yet had he proved° the powre of many a puissant knight.   *tested*

18

Then with his waving wings displayèd wyde,
   Himselfe up high he lifted from the ground,
   And with strong flight did forcibly divide
   The yielding aire, which nigh° too feeble found   *nearly*

Her flitting° partes, and element unsound,°   *moving / weak*
    To beare so great a weight: he cutting way
    With his broad sayles, about him soarèd round:
    At last low stouping with unweldie sway,°   *ponderous force*
Snatcht up both horse and man, to beare them quite away.

19

Long he them bore above the subject plaine,°   *the ground below*
    So farre as Ewghen° bow a shaft may send,   *yewen, of yew*
    Till struggling strong did him at last constraine,
    To let them downe before his flightès end:
    As hagard° hauke presuming to contend   *untamed*
    With hardie fowle, above his hable might,°   *able power*
    His wearie pounces° all in vaine doth spend,   *claws*
    To trusse° the pray too heavie for his flight;   *seize*
Which comming downe to ground, does free it selfe by fight.

20

He so disseizèd of his gryping grosse,[6]
    The knight his thrilant° speare againe assayd   *piercing*
    In his bras-plated body to embosse,°   *plunge*
    And three mens strength unto the stroke he layd;
    Wherewith the stiffe beame quakèd, as affrayd,
    And glauncing from his scaly necke, did glyde
    Close under his left wing, then broad displayd.
    The percing steele there wrought a wound full wyde,
That with the uncouth° smart the Monster lowdly cryde.   *unfamiliar*

21

He cryde, as raging seas are wont° to rore,   *accustomed*
    When wintry storme his wrathfull wreck° does threat,   *ruin*
    The rolling billowes beat the ragged shore,
    As° they the earth would shoulder° from her seat,   *as if / push*
    And greedie gulfe° does gape, as he would eat   *the sea*
    His neighbour element° in his revenge: *earth*
    Then gin the blustring brethren° boldly threat,   *the winds*
    To move the world from off his stedfast henge,°   *axis*
And boystrous battell make, each other to avenge.°   *take vengeance on*

22

The steely head stucke fast still in his flesh,
    Till with his cruell clawes he snatcht the wood,
    And quite a sunder broke. Forth flowèd fresh
    A gushing river of blacke goarie° blood,   *clotted*
    That drownèd all the land, whereon he stood;
    The stream thereof would drive a water-mill.
    Trebly augmented was his furious mood

---

6. Freed from his formidable grip.

With bitter sense of his deepe rooted ill,° — injury
That flames of fire he threw forth from his large nosethrill.° — nostril

23

His hideous tayle then hurlèd he about,
    And therewith all enwrapt the nimble thyes° — thighs
    Of his froth-fomy steed, whose courage stout
    Striving to loose the knot, that fast him tyes,
    Himselfe in streighter° bandes too rash implyes,[7] — tighter
    That to the ground he is perforce° constraynd — of necessity
    To throw his rider: who can° quickly ryse — did
    From off the earth, with durty bloud distaynd,° — defiled
For that reprochfull fall right fowly he disdaynd.° — resented

24

And fiercely tooke his trenchand° blade in hand, — sharp
    With which he stroke so furious and so fell,° — fiercely
    That nothing seemd the puissance could withstand:
    Upon his crest the hardned yron fell,
    But his more hardned crest was armd so well,
    That deeper dint therein it would not make;[8]
    Yet so extremely did the buffe° him quell,° — blow / dismay
    That from thenceforth he shund the like to take,
But when he saw them come, he did them still forsake.° — avoid

25

The knight was wrath to see his stroke beguyld,° — foiled
    And smote againe with more outrageous might;
    But backe againe the sparckling steele recoyld,
    And left not any marke, where it did light;
    As if in Adamant rocke it had bene pight.° — struck against
    The beast impatient of his smarting wound,
    And of so fierce and forcible despight,° — powerful injury
    Thought with his wings to stye° above the ground; — mount
But his late wounded wing unserviceable found.

26

Then full of griefe and anguish vehement,
    He lowdly brayd, that like was never heard,
    And from his wide devouring oven sent
    A flake of fire, that flashing in his beard,
    Him all amazd, and almost made affeard;
    The scorching flame sore swingèd° all his face, — singed
    And through his armour all his bodie seard,
    That he could not endure so cruell cace,° — plight; suit of armor
But thought his armes to leave, and helmet to unlace.

---

7. That is, too quickly entangles.   8. That is, it could not make a deep gash there.

27

Not that great Champion of the antique world,°   *Hercules*
  Whom famous Poetes verse so much doth vaunt,
  And hath for twelve huge labours high extold,
  So many furies and sharpe fits did haunt,
  When him the poysoned garment did enchaunt
  With Centaures bloud, and bloudie verses charmed,
  As did this knight twelve thousand dolours° daunt,   *pains*
  Whom fyrie steele now burnt, that earst° him armed,   *formerly*
That erst him goodly armed, now most of all him harmed.[9]

28

Faint, wearie, sore, emboylèd,° grievèd, brent°   *boiled; enraged / burned*
  With heat, toyle, wounds, armes, smart, and inward fire
  That never man such mischiefes° did torment;   *misfortunes*
  Death better were, death did he oft desire,
  But death will never come, when needes require.
  Whom so dismayd when that his foe beheld,
  He cast to suffer° him no more respire,°   *allow / live*
  But gan his sturdie sterne° about to weld,°   *tail / lash*
And him so strongly stroke, that to the ground him feld.

29

It fortunèd (as faire it then befell)
  Behind his backe unweeting,° where he stood,   *unnoticed*
  Of auncient time there was a springing well,
  From which fast trickled forth a silver flood,
  Full of great vertues,° and for med'cine good.   *powers*
  Whylome,° before that cursèd Dragon got   *formerly*
  That happie land, and all with innocent blood
  Defyld those sacred waves, it rightly hot°   *was called*
The Well of Life,[1] ne yet his vertues had forgot.

30

For unto life the dead it could restore,
  And guilt of sinfull crimes cleane wash away,
  Those that with sicknesse were infected sore,
  It could recure, and agèd long decay
  Renew, as one were borne that very day.
  Both Silo this, and Jordan did excell,
  And th'English Bath, and eke the german Spau,

---

9. Redcrosse's fire baptism is compared with the burning shirt of Nessus, which killed Hercules. His "twelve huge labours" are paralleled to the knight's "twelve thousand dolours."
1. An allusion to Revelation 22:1–2: "And he showed me a pure river of water of life, clear as crystal, proceeding out of the throne of God and of the Lamb. In the midst of the street of it, and on either side of the river, was the tree of life, which bare twelve manner of fruits, and yielded her fruit every month: and the leaves of the tree were for the healing of the nations."

Ne can Cephise, nor Hebrus match this well:
Into the same the knight backe overthrowen, fell.[2]

31

Now gan the golden Phoebus for to steepe
  His fierie face in billowes of the west,
  And his faint steedes watred in Ocean deepe,
  Whiles from their journall° labours they did rest,   *daily*
  When that infernall Monster, having kest°   *cast*
  His wearie foe into that living well,
  Can° high advaunce his broad discoloured brest,   *did*
  Above his wonted pitch,° with countenance fell,°   *height / sinister*
And clapt his yron wings, as victor he did dwell.°   *remain*

32

Which when his pensive° Ladie saw from farre,   *anxious*
  Great woe and sorrow did her soule assay,°   *assail*
  As weening° that the sad end of the warre,   *thinking*
  And gan to highest God entirely° pray,   *earnestly*
  That feared chaunce° from her to turne away;   *fate*
  With folded hands and knees full lowly bent
  All night she watcht, ne once adowne would lay
  Her daintie limbs in her sad dreriment,°   *dismal condition*
But praying still did wake, and waking did lament.

33

The morrow next gan early to appeare,
  That° Titan° rose to runne his daily race;   *when / the sun god*
  But early ere the morrow next gan reare
  Out of the sea faire Titans deawy face,
  Up rose the gentle virgin from her place,
  And lookèd all about, if she might spy
  Her lovèd knight to move° his manly pace: *moving*
  For she had great doubt of his safety,
Since late she saw him fall before his enemy.

34

At last she saw, where he upstarted brave
  Out of the well, wherein he drenchèd lay;
  As Eagle fresh out of the Ocean wave,
  Where he hath left his plumes all hoary gray,
  And deckt himselfe with feathers youthly gay,
  Like Eyas hauke° up mounts unto the skies,   *unfledged hawk*
  His newly budded pineons to assay,°   *test*

---

2. The Well of Life, with its powers of renewal, is successively compared with waters of the *Bible,* of England and Europe, and of classical antiquity. In the pool of Siloam ("Silo"), a blind man was cured by Christ (John 9:7). Water of the river Jordan cured Naaman of leprosy (2 Kings 5:14) and Christ was baptized therein (Matthew 3:16). The towns of Bath and Spa ("Spau") were famed for their medicinal waters. Cephise and Hebrus, in Greece, were rivers noted for purifying and healing powers.

And marveiles at himselfe, still as he flies:
So new this new-borne knight to battell new did rise.

35

Whom when the damnèd feend so fresh did spy,
   No wonder if he wondred at the sight,
   And doubted, whether his late enemy
   It were, or other new supplièd knight.
   He, now to prove° his late renewèd might,   *try*
   High brandishing his bright deaw-burning blade,
   Upon his crested scalpe so sore did smite,
   That to the scull a yawning wound it made:
The deadly dint° his dullèd senses all dismaid.   *blow*

36

I wote° not, whether the revenging steele   *know*
   Were hardnèd with that holy water dew,
   Wherein he fell, or sharper edge did feele,
   Or his baptizèd hands now greater° grew;   *stronger*
   Or other secret vertue° did ensew;   *power*
   Else never could the force of fleshly arme,
   Ne molten mettall in his bloud embrew:°   *plunge*
   For till that stownd° could never wight him harme,   *moment*
By subtilty, nor slight,° nor might, nor mighty charme.   *trickery*

37

The cruell wound enragèd him so sore,
   That loud he yellèd for exceeding paine;
   As hundred ramping° Lyons seemed to rore,   *rearing*
   Whom ravenous hunger did thereto constraine:
   Then gan he tosse aloft his stretchèd traine,°   *tail*
   And therewith scourge the buxome° aire so sore,   *yielding*
   That to his force to yeelden it was faine;°   *obliged*
   Ne ought his sturdie strokes might stand afore,[3]
That high trees overthrew, and rocks in peeces tore.

38

The same advauncing high above his head,
   With sharpe intended° sting so rude° him smot,   *extended / roughly*
   That to the earth him drove, as stricken dead,
   Ne living wight would have him life behot:[4]
   The mortall sting his angry needle shot
   Quite through his shield, and in his shoulder seasd,
   Where fast it stucke, ne would there out be got:
   The griefe° thereof him wondrous sore diseasd,°   *pain / afflicted*
Ne might his ranckling paine with patience be appeasd.

---

3. That is, neither could anything ("ought") stand before his violent ("sturdie") strokes.

4. Promised. That is, no one would have thought he could survive the blow.

39

But yet more mindfull of his honour deare,
    Then° of the grievous smart, which him did wring,°   *than / torment*
    From loathèd soile he can° him lightly reare,   *did*
    And strove to loose the farre infixèd sting:
    Which when in vaine he tryde with struggeling,
    Inflamed with wrath, his raging blade he heft,°   *heaved*
    And strooke so strongly, that the knotty string
    Of his huge taile he quite a sunder cleft,
Five joynts thereof he hewd, and but the stump him left.

40

Hart cannot thinke, what outrage,° and what cryes,   *violent clamor*
    With foule enfouldred[5] smoake and flashing fire,
    The hell-bred beast threw forth unto the skyes,
    That all was coverèd with darknesse dire:
    Then fraught° with rancour, and engorgèd° ire,   *filled / swollen*
    He cast at once him to avenge for all,
    And gathering up himselfe out of the mire,
    With his uneven wings did fiercely fall
Upon his sunne-bright shield, and gript it fast withall.

41

Much was the man encombred with his hold,
    In feare to lose his weapon in his paw,
    Ne wist° yet, how his talents° to unfold;   *knew / talons*
    Nor harder was from Cerberus[6] greedie jaw
    To plucke a bone, then from his cruell claw
    To reave° by strength the gripèd gage° away: *seize / prize*
    Thrise he assayd° it from his foot to draw,   *tried*
    And thrise in vaine to draw it did assay,
It booted nought to thinke, to robbe him of his pray.

42

Tho° when he saw no power might prevaile,   *then*
    His trustie sword he cald to his last aid,
    Wherewith he fiercely did his foe assaile,
    And double blowes about him stoutly laid,
    That glauncing fire out of the yron plaid;
    As sparckles from the Andvile° use to fly,   *anvil*
    When heavie hammers on the wedge are swaid;°   *struck*
    Therewith at last he forst him to unty°   *loosen*
One of his grasping feete, him to defend thereby.

43

The other foot, fast fixèd on his shield,
    Whenas no strength, nor stroks mote° him constraine   *might*

---

5. Black as a thundercloud.   6. The dog that guards the mouth of Hades.

To loose, ne yet the warlike pledge to yield,
He smot thereat with all his might and maine,° — strength
That nought so wondrous puissance might sustaine;
Upon the joynt the lucky steele did light,
And made such way, that hewd it quite in twaine;
The paw yet missèd not his minisht° might, — lessened
But hong still on the shield, as it at first was pight.° — placed

44

For griefe° thereof, and divelish despight, — pain
From his infernall fournace forth he threw
Huge flames, that dimmèd all the heavens light,
Enrold in duskish smoke and brimstone blew;
As burning Aetna[7] from his boyling stew° — cauldron
Doth belch out flames, and rockes in peeces broke,
And ragged ribs of mountaines molten new
Enwrapt in coleblacke clouds and filthy smoke,
That all the land with stench, and heaven with horror choke.

45

The heate whereof, and harmefull pestilence
So sore him noyd,° that forst him to retire — troubled
A little backward for his best defence,
To save his bodie from the scorching fire,
Which he from hellish entrailes did expire.° — breathe out
It chaunst (eternall God that chaunce did guide)
As he recoylèd backward, in the mire
His nigh forwearied° feeble feet did slide, — exhausted
And downe he fell, with dread of shame sore terrifide.

46

There grew a goodly tree him faire beside,
Loaden with fruit and apples rosie red,
As they in pure vermilion had beene dide,
Whereof great vertues over all were red:° — everywhere were told
For happie life to all, which thereon fed,
And life eke everlasting did befall:
Great God it planted in that blessed sted° — place
With his almightie hand, and did it call
The Tree of Life, the crime of our first fathers fall.[8]

47

In all the world like was not to be found,
Save in that soile, where all good things did grow,

---

7. Mount Etna, an active volcano in Sicily.
8. Genesis 2:9 describes the Tree of Life and also the Tree of Knowledge of Good and Evil, both of which God planted in the Garden of Eden. The "crime of our first fathers fall" is that Adam, in eating of the second and being banished from Eden, separated himself—and (according to Christian doctrine) his descendants—from the first. The Tree of Life appears again in the New Jerusalem (Revelation 22:2).

    And freely sprong out of the fruitfull ground,
        As incorrupted Nature did them sow,
        Till that dread Dragon all did overthrow.
        Another like faire tree eke grew thereby,
        Whereof who so did eat, eftsoones° did know   *soon after*
        Both good and ill: O mornefull memory:
    That tree through one mans fault hath doen us all to dy.°   *killed us*

48

    From that first tree forth flowd, as from a well,
        A trickling streame of Balme, most soveraine°   *powerful for cures*
        And daintie deare,° which on the ground still fell,   *precious*
        And overflowèd all the fertill plaine,
        As it had deawèd bene with timely° raine: *seasonable*
        Life and long health that gratious° ointment gave,   *full of grace*
        And deadly woundes could heale, and reare° againe   *raise*
        The senselesse corse appointed° for the grave.   *made ready*
    Into that same he fell: which did from death him save.[9]

49

    For nigh thereto the ever damnèd beast
        Durst not approch, for he was deadly made,°   *a child of death*
        And all that life preservèd, did detest:
        Yet he it oft adventured° to invade.   *attempted*
        By this the drouping day-light gan to fade,
        And yeeld his roome° to sad succeeding° night,   *its place / following after*
        Who with her sable mantle gan to shade
        The face of earth, and wayes of living wight,
    And high her burning torch set up in heaven bright.

50

    When gentle Una saw the second fall
        Of her deare knight, who wearie of long fight,
        And faint through losse of bloud, moved not at all,
        But lay as in a dreame of deepe delight,
        Besmeard with pretious Balme, whose vertuous might
        Did heale his wounds, and scorching heat alay,[1]
        Againe she stricken was with sore affright,
        And for his safetie gan devoutly pray;
    And watch the noyous° night, and wait for joyous day.   *noxious*

51

    The joyous day gan early to appeare,
        And faire Aurora from the deawy bed
        Of agèd Tithone gan her selfe to reare,[2]

---

9. The healing balm flowing from the Tree of *Life is understood to be* Christ's blood, shed to redeem humankind from eternal damnation.
1. Compare Revelation 2:7: "To him that overcometh will I give to eat of the tree of life" and 2:11: "He that overcometh shall not be hurt of the second death" (that is, the eternal death, of the soul).
2. Aurora is goddess of the dawn. Tithonus is her husband ("agèd" because he was granted everlasting life without everlasting youth).

With rosie cheekes, for shame as blushing red;
　Her golden lockes for haste were loosely shed
　About her eares, when Una her did marke
　Clymbe to her charet,° all with flowers spred,　　*chariot*
　From heaven high to chase the chearelesse darke;
With merry note her loud salutes the mounting larke.

52

Then freshly up arose the doughtie° knight,　　*valiant*
　All healèd of his hurts and woundès wide,
　And did himselfe to battell readie dight;°　　*prepare*
　Whose early foe awaiting him beside
　To have devourd, so soone as day he spyde,
　When now he saw himselfe so freshly reare,
　As if late fight had nought him damnifyde,°　　*injured*
　He woxe° dismayd, and gan his fate to feare;　　*grew*
Nathlesse° with wonted° rage he him advauncèd neare.　　*nevertheless / usual*

53

And in his first encounter, gaping wide,
　He thought attonce him to have swallowed quight,
　And rusht upon him with outragious pride;
　Who him r'encountring fierce, as hauke in flight,
　Perforce rebutted° backe. The weapon bright　　*drove*
　Taking advantage of his open jaw,
　Ran through his mouth with so importune° might,　　*violent*
　That deepe emperst his darksome hollow maw,°　　*throat*
And back retyrd,³ his life bloud forth with all did draw.

54

So downe he fell, and forth his life did breath,
　That vanisht into smoke and cloudès swift;
　So downe he fell, that th'earth him underneath
　Did grone, as feeble so great load to lift;
　So downe he fell, as an huge rockie clift,
　Whose false° foundation waves have washt away,　　*insecure*
　With dreadfull poyse° is from the mayneland rift,°　　*falling weight / split*
　And rolling downe, great Neptune doth dismay;
So downe he fell, and like an heapèd mountaine lay.

55

The knight himselfe even trembled at his fall,
　So huge and horrible a masse it seemed;
　And his deare Ladie, that beheld it all,
　Durst not approch for dread, which she misdeemed,°　　*misjudged*
　But yet at last, when as the direfull feend
　She saw not stirre, off-shaking vaine affright,
　She nigher drew, and saw that joyous end:

---

3. That is, on being drawn back.

Then God she praysd, and thankt her faithfull knight,
That had atchiev'd so great a conquest by his might.

Canto 12

Faire Una to the Redcrosse knight
betrouthèd is with joy:
Though false Duessa it to barre
her false sleights doe imploy.

1

Behold I see the haven nigh at hand,
    To which I meane my wearie course to bend;
    Vere the maine shete, and beare up with the land,[4]
    The which afore is fairely to be kend,°   *recognized*
    And seemeth safe from stormes, that may offend;
    There this faire virgin wearie of her way
    Must landed be, now at her journeyes end:
    There eke° my feeble barke° a while may stay,   *also / ship*
Till merry° wind and weather call her thence away.   *favorable*

2

Scarsely had Phoebus in the glooming East°   *dawn*
    Yet harnessèd his firie-footed teeme,
    Ne reard above the earth his flaming creast,°   *crest*
    When the last deadly smoke aloft did steeme,
    That signe of last outbreathèd life did seeme
    Unto the watchman on the castle wall;
    Who thereby dead that balefull° Beast did deeme,   *evil*
    And to his Lord and Ladie lowd gan call,
To tell, how he had seene the Dragons fatall fall.

3

Uprose with hastie joy, and feeble speed
    That agèd Sire, the Lord of all that land,
    And lookèd forth, to weet,° if true indeede   *know*
    Those tydings were, as he did understand,
    Which whenas true by tryall he out fond,
    He bad° to open wyde his brazen gate,   *bade*
    Which long time had bene shut, and out of hond°   *straightaway*
    Proclaymèd joy and peace through all his state;
For dead now was their foe, which them forrayèd late.[5]

4

Then gan triumphant Trompets sound on hie,
    That sent to heaven the ecchoed report

---

4. Release the mainsail line and sail toward the land. The nautical metaphor echoes many classical authors and Chaucer's *Troilus and Criseyde* (2.1–7).
5. Had recently ravaged.

Of their new joy, and happie victorie
Gainst him, that had them long opprest with tort,° *wrong*
And fast imprisonèd in siegèd fort.
Then all the people, as in solemne feast,
To him assembled with one full consort,° *all together*
Rejoycing at the fall of that great beast,
From whose eternall bondage now they were releast.

5

Forth came that auncient Lord and agèd Queene,
Arayd in antique robes downe to the ground,
And sad habiliments right well beseene;[6]
A noble crew about them waited round
Of sage and sober Peres,° all gravely gownd; *peers*
Whom farre before did march a goodly band
Of tall young men, all hable armes to sownd,[7]
But now they laurell braunches bore in hand;
Glad signe of victorie and peace in all their land.

6

Unto that doughtie Conquerour they came,
And him before themselves prostrating low,
Their Lord and Patrone° loud did him proclame, *defender*
And at his feet their laurell boughes did throw.
Soone after them all dauncing on a row
The comely virgins came, with girlands dight,° *adorned*
As fresh as flowres in medow greene do grow,
When morning deaw upon their leaves doth light:
And in their hands sweet Timbrels° all upheld on hight. *tambourines*

7

And them before, the fry° of children young *crowd*
Their wanton° sports and childish mirth did play, *playful*
And to the Maydens sounding tymbrels sung
In well attunèd notes, a joyous lay,° *song*
And made delightfull musicke all the way,
Untill they came, where that faire virgin stood;
As faire Diana° in fresh sommers day *goddess of the hunt*
Beholds her Nymphes, enraunged° in shadie wood, *ranged*
Some wrestle, some do run, some bathe in christall flood.

8

So she beheld those maydens meriment
With chearefull vew; who when to her they came,
Themselves to ground with gratious humblesse° bent, *humility*
And her adored by honorable name,° *with titles of honor*
Lifting to heaven her everlasting fame:

---

6. That is, sober, appropriate ("right well beseene") attire. 7. Able to fight with weapons.

Then on her head they set a girland greene,
    And crownèd her twixt earnest and twixt game:°   *half in fun*
    Who in her selfe-resemblance well beseene,[8]
Did seeme such, as she was, a goodly maiden Queene.

9

And after all, the raskall many° ran,   *rabble throng*
    Heapèd together in rude rablement,°   *confusion*
    To see the face of that victorious man:
    Whom all admirèd,° as from heaven sent,   *wondered at*
And gazd upon with gaping wonderment.
    But when they came, where that dead Dragon lay,
    Stretcht on the ground in monstrous large extent,
    The sight with idle° feare did them dismay,   *baseless*
Ne durst approch him nigh, to touch, or once assay.°   *venture to*

10

Some feard, and fled; some feard and well it faynd;°   *concealed*
    One that would wiser seeme, then all the rest,
    Warnd him not touch, for yet perhaps remaynd
    Some lingring life within his hollow brest,
Or in his wombe might lurke some hidden nest
    Of many Dragonets,° his fruitfull seed;   *young dragons*
    Another said, that in his eyes did rest
    Yet sparckling fire, and bad thereof take heed;
Another said, he saw him move his eyes indeed.

11

One mother, when as her foolehardie chyld
    Did come too neare, and with his talants° play,   *talons*
    Halfe dead through feare, her litle babe revyld,°   *scolded*
    And to her gossips° gan in counsell° say;   *women friends / private*
"How can I tell, but that his talants may
    Yet scratch my sonne, or rend his tender hand?"
    So diversly themselves in vaine they fray;°   *frighten*
    Whiles some more bold, to measure him nigh stand,
To prove° how many acres he did spread of land.   *determine*

12

Thus flockèd all the folke him round about,
    The whiles that hoarie° king, with all his traine,   *gray-haired*
    Being arrivèd, where that champion stout
    After his foes defeasance° did remaine,   *defeat*
Him goodly greetes, and faire does entertaine,
    With princely gifts of yvorie and gold,
    And thousand thankes him yeelds for all his paine.
    Then when his daughter deare he does behold,
Her dearely doth imbrace, and kisseth manifold.°   *many times*

---

8. That is, looking appropriately like herself.

13

And after to his Pallace he them brings,
  With shaumes, and trompets, and with Clarions[9] sweet;
  And all the way the joyous people sings,
  And with their garments strowes the pavèd street:
  Whence mounting up, they find purveyance° meet — *provisions*
  Of all, that royall Princes court became,° — *suited*
  And all the floore was underneath their feet
  Bespred with costly scarlot of great name,° — *famous scarlet cloth*
On which they lowly sit, and fitting purpose frame.[1]

14

What needs me tell their feast and goodly guize,° — *behavior*
  In which was nothing riotous nor vaine?
  What needs of daintie dishes to devize,° — *talk*
  Of comely° services, or courtly trayne?° — *becoming / assembly*
  My narrow leaves cannot in them containe
  The large discourse° of royall Princes state. — *full description*
  Yet was their manner then but bare and plaine:
  For th'antique world excesse and pride did hate;
Such proud luxurious pompe is swollen up but late.° — *just recently*

15

Then when with meates and drinkes of every kinde
  Their fervent appetites they quenchèd had,
  That aunciant Lord gan fit occasion finde,
  Of straunge adventures, and of perils sad,° — *grave*
  Which in his travell him befallen had,
  For to demaund° of his renowmèd guest: — *inquire*
  Who then with utt'rance grave, and count'nance sad,
  From point to point,° as is before exprest, — *from first to last*
Discourst his voyage long, according° his request. — *granting*

16

Great pleasure mixt with pittifull° regard, — *sympathetic*
  That godly King and Queene did passionate,° — *feel and express*
  Whiles they his pittifull° adventures heard, — *deserving pity*
  That oft they did lament his lucklesse state,
  And often blame the too importune° fate, — *severe*
  That heapd on him so many wrathfull wreakes:° — *vengeful injuries*
  For never gentle knight, as he of late,
  So tossèd was in fortunes cruell freakes;° — *whims*
And all the while salt teares bedeawd the hearers cheaks.

---

9. Trumpet calls. "Shaumes": the shawm was the medieval and Renaissance predecessor of the oboe.
1. Make seemly conversation.

17

Then said that royall Pere in sober wise:
  "Deare Sonne, great beene the evils, which ye bore
  From first to last in your late enterprise,
  That I note,° whether prayse, or pitty more: *know not*
  For never living man, I weene,° so sore   *think*
  In sea of deadly daungers was distrest;
  But since now safe ye seisèd° have the shore,   *reached*
  And well arrivèd are (high God be blest),
Let us devize° of ease and everlasting rest."   *think*

18

"Ah dearest Lord," said then that doughty knight,
  "Of ease or rest I may not yet devize;
  For by the faith, which I to armes have plight,°   *pledged*
  I bounden am streight° after this emprize,°   *immediately / enterprise*
  As that your daughter can ye well advize,
  Backe to returne to that great Faerie Queene,
  And her to serve six yeares in warlike wize,°   *manner*
  Gainst that proud Paynim king, that workes her teene:°   *sorrow*
Therefore I ought° crave pardon, till I there have beene."[2]   *must*

19

"Unhappie falles that hard necessitie,"
  Quoth he, "the troubler of my happie peace,
  And vowèd foe of my felicitie;
  Ne° I against the same can justly preace:°   *nor / press, contend*
  But since that band° ye cannot now release,   *obligation*
  Nor doen undo (for vowes may not be vaine),[3]
  Soone as the terme of those six yeares shall cease,
  Ye then shall hither backe returne againe,
The marriage to accomplish vowd betwixt you twain.

20

"Which for my part I covet to performe,
  In sort as° through the world I did proclame,   *even as*
  That who so kild that monster most deforme,°   *hideous*
  And him in hardy battaile overcame,
  Should have mine onely daughter to his Dame,°   *wife*
  And of my kingdome heire apparaunt bee:
  Therefore since now to thee perteines° the same,   *belongs*
  By dew desert of noble chevalree,
Both daughter and eke kingdome, lo I yield to thee."

---

2. The final Christian triumph, the marriage of Christ and the true Church, will be achieved only at the end of time. Meanwhile, the struggle against evil (and the Roman Church) continues.

3. That is, you cannot undo what is done ("doen"), for vows may not be (made) vain.

21

Then forth he callèd that his daughter faire,
   The fairest Un' his onely daughter deare,
   His onely daughter, and his onely heyre;
   Who forth proceeding with sad° sober cheare,°   *grave / countenance*
   As bright as doth the morning starre appeare
   Out of the East, with flaming lockes bedight,°   *bedecked*
   To tell that dawning day is drawing neare,
   And to the world does bring long wishèd light;
So faire and fresh that Lady shewd her selfe in sight.

22

So faire and fresh, as freshest flowre in May;
   For she had layd her mournefull stole[4] aside,
   And widow-like sad wimple° throwne away,   *veil*
   Wherewith her heavenly beautie she did hide,
   Whiles on her wearie journey she did ride;
   And on her now a garment she did weare,
   All lilly white, withoutten spot, or pride,°   *ornament*
   That seemed like silke and silver woven neare,°   *tightly*
But neither silke nor silver therein did appeare.[5]

23

The blazing brightnesse of her beauties beame,
   And glorious light of her sunshyny face[6]
   To tell, were as to strive against the streame.
   My ragged rimes are all too rude and bace,
   Her heavenly lineaments for to enchace.°   *adorn*
   Ne wonder; for her owne deare lovèd knight,
   All° were she dayly with himselfe in place,   *although*
   Did wonder much at her celestiall sight:
Oft had he seene her faire, but never so faire dight.°   *arrayed*

24

So fairely dight, when she in presence came,
   She to her Sire made humble reverence,
   And bowèd low, that her right well became,
   And added grace unto her excellence:
   Who with great wisdome, and grave eloquence
   Thus gan to say. But eare° he thus had said,   *ere*
   With flying speede, and seeming great pretence,°   *purpose*
   Came running in, much like a man dismaid,
A Messenger with letters, which his message said.

---

4. Her black robe (canto 1, stanza 4).
5. "The marriage of the Lamb is come, and his wife hath made herself ready. And to her was granted that she should be arrayed in fine linen, clean and white: for the fine linen is the righteousness of saints" (Revelation 19:7–8).
6. Revelation 21:9, 11 describes the New Jerusalem as "the bride, the Lamb's wife . . . her light was like unto a stone most precious."

25

All in the open hall amazèd stood,
   At suddeinnesse of that unwarie° sight,   *unexpected*
   And wondred at his breathlesse hastie mood.
   But he for nought would stay his passage right°   *direct*
   Till fast° before the king he did alight;   *close*
   Where falling flat, great humblesse he did make,
   And kist the ground, whereon his foot was pight;°   *placed*
   Then to his hands that writ° he did betake,°   *document / deliver*
Which he disclosing, red thus, as the paper spake.

26

"To thee, most mighty king of Eden faire,
   Her greeting sends in these sad lines addrest,
   The wofull daughter, and forsaken heire
   Of that great Emperour of all the West;
   And bids thee be advizèd for the best,
   Ere thou thy daughter linck in holy band
   Of wedlocke to that new unknowen guest:
   For he already plighted his right hand
Unto another love, and to another land.

27

"To me sad mayd, or rather widow sad,
   He was affiauncèd long time before,
   And sacred pledges he both gave, and had,
   False erraunt knight, infamous, and forswore:
   Witnesse the burning Altars, which° he swore,   *by which*
   And guiltie heavens of° his bold perjury,   *and heavens polluted by*
   Which though he hath polluted oft of yore,
   Yet I to them for judgement just do fly,
And them conjure° t'avenge this shamefull injury.   *implore*

28

"Therefore since mine he is, or° free or bond,°   *whether / bound*
   Or false or trew, or living or else dead,
   Withhold, O soveraine Prince, your hasty hond°   *hand*
   From knitting league with him, I you aread;°   *advise*
   Ne wene° my right with strength adowne to tread,   *think*
   Through weakenesse of my widowhed, or woe:
   For truth is strong, her rightfull cause to plead,
   And shall find friends, if need requireth soe,
So bids thee well to fare, Thy neither friend, nor foe, Fidessa."

29

When he these bitter byting words had red,
   The tydings straunge did him abashèd make,

That still he sate long time astonishèd
   As in great muse,° ne word to creature spake.   *amazement*
   At last his solemne silence thus he brake,
   With doubtfull eyes fast fixèd on his guest:
   "Redoubted° knight, that for mine onely sake[7]   *honored*
   Thy life and honour late adventurest,
Let nought be hid from me, that ought to be exprest.

30

"What meane these bloudy vowes, and idle threats,
   Throwne out from womanish impatient mind?
   What heavens? what altars? what enragèd heates
   Here heapèd up with termes of love unkind,°   *unnatural*
   My conscience cleare with guilty bands° would bind?   *bonds of guilt*
   High God be witnesse, that I guiltlesse ame.
   But if your selfe, Sir knight, ye faultie° find,   *guilty*
   Or wrappèd be in loves of former Dame,
With crime do not it cover, but disclose the same."

31

To whom the Redcrosse knight this answere sent,
   "My Lord, my King, be nought hereat dismayd,
   Till well ye wote by grave intendiment,°   *serious investigation*
   What woman, and wherefore doth me upbrayd
   With breach of love, and loyalty betrayd.
   It was in my mishaps, as hitherward
   I lately traveild, that unwares I strayd
   Out of my way, through perils straunge and hard;
That day should faile me, ere I had them all declard.

32

"There did I find, or rather I was found
   Of this false woman, that Fidessa hight,°   *is called*
   Fidessa hight the falsest Dame on ground,
   Most false Duessa, royall richly dight,
   That easie was t'invegle weaker° sight: *deceive too weak*
   Who by her wicked arts, and wylie skill,
   Too false and strong for earthly skill or might,
   Unwares me wrought unto her wicked will,
And to my foe betrayd, when least I fearèd ill."

33

Then steppèd forth the goodly royall Mayd,
   And on the ground her selfe prostrating low,
   With sober countenaunce thus to him sayd:
   "O pardon me, my soveraigne Lord, to show

---

7. For my sake alone.

The secret treasons, which of late I know
  To have bene wroght by that false sorceresse.
  She onely she it is, that earst° did throw   *formerly*
  This gentle knight into so great distresse,
That death him did awaite in dayly wretchednesse.

34

"And now it seemes, that she subornèd hath
  This craftie messenger with letters vaine,
  To worke new woe and improvided scath,°   *unexpected harm*
  By breaking of the band° betwixt us twaine;   *bond*
  Wherein she usèd hath the practicke paine°   *treacherous skill*
  Of this false footman, clokt with simplenesse,
  Whom if ye please for to discover plaine,
  Ye shall him Archimago find, I ghesse,
The falsest man alive; who tries° shall find no lesse."   *investigates*

35

The king was greatly movèd at her speach,
  And all with suddein indignation fraight,°   *filled*
  Bad° on that Messenger rude° hands to reach.   *bade / harsh*
  Eftsoones° the Gard, which on his state did wait,   *immediately*
  Attacht° that faitor° false, and bound him strait: *arrested / impostor*
  Who seeming sorely chauffèd° at his band,   *angered*
  As chainèd Beare, whom cruell dogs do bait,
  With idle force did faine° them to withstand,   *feign*
And often semblaunce made to scape out of their hand.

36

But they him layd full low in dungeon deepe,
  And bound him hand and foote with yron chaines.
  And with continuall watch did warely° keepe;   *vigilantly*
  Who then would thinke, that by his subtile trains°   *tricks*
  He could escape fowle death or deadly paines?[8]
  Thus when that Princes wrath was pacifide,
  He gan renew the late forbidden banes,[9]
  And to the knight his daughter deare he tyde,
With sacred rites and vowes for ever to abyde.

37

His owne two hands the holy knots did knit,
  That none but death for ever can devide;

---

[8]. "And he laid hold on the dragon, that old serpent, which is the Devil, and Satan, and bound him a thousand years, And cast him into the bottomless pit, and shut him up, and set a seal upon him, that he should deceive the nations no more, till the thousand years should be fulfilled: and after that he must be loosed a little season" (Revelation 20:2–3).

[9]. Banns; that is, proclamation or public notice of an intended marriage. Una and Redcrosse are now betrothed; the consummation of their marriage is postponed.

His owne two hands, for such a turne° most fit, — *act*
The housling° fire did kindle and provide, — *sacramental*
And holy water thereon sprinckled wide;[1]
At which the bushy Teade° a groome did light, — *nuptial torch*
And sacred lampe in secret chamber hide,
Where it should not be quenchèd day nor night,
For feare of evill fates, but burnen ever bright.

38

Then gan they sprinckle all the posts with wine,
   And made great feast to solemnize that day;
   They all perfumde with frankencense divine,
   And precious odours fetcht from far away,
   That all the house did sweat with great aray:
   And all the while sweete Musicke did apply
   Her curious° skill, the warbling notes to play, — *intricate*
   To drive away the dull Melancholy;
The whiles one sung a song of love and jollity.

39

During the which there was an heavenly noise
   Heard sound through all the Pallace pleasantly,
   Like as it had bene many an Angels voice,
   Singing before th'eternall majesty,
   In their trinall triplicities[2] on hye;
   Yet wist° no creature, whence that heavenly sweet° — *knew / delight*
   Proceeded, yet each one felt secretly° — *inwardly*
   Himselfe thereby reft of his sences meet,° — *proper*
And ravishèd with rare impression in his sprite.[3]

40

Great joy was made that day of young and old,
   And solemne feast proclaimd throughout the land,
   That their exceeding merth may not be told:
   Suffice it heare by signes to understand
   The usuall joyes at knitting of loves band.
   Thrise happy man the knight himselfe did hold,
   Possessèd of his Ladies hart and hand,
   And ever, when his eye did her behold,
His heart did seeme to melt in pleasures manifold.

---

1. Marriages in ancient times were solemnized with sacramental fire and water.
2. The nine angelic orders, divided into three groups of three, the whole hierarchy corresponding to the nine spheres of the universe. The music heard in this stanza is the music of the spheres, not audible on earth since the Fall.
3. Spirit. "Let us be glad and rejoice, and give honour to him: for the marriage of the Lamb is come" (Revelation 19.7). In Revelation, the marriage of Christ and the New Jerusalem signals the general redemption.

41

Her joyous presence and sweet company
  In full content he there did long enjoy,
    Ne wicked envie, ne vile gealosy
    His deare delights were able to annoy:
  Yet swimming in that sea of blisfull joy,
  He nought forgot, how he whilome° had sworne,   *formerly*
    In case he could that monstrous beast destroy,
    Unto his Faerie Queene backe to returne:
The which he shortly did, and Una left to mourne.

42

Now strike your sailes ye jolly Mariners,
  For we be come unto a quiet rode,°   *harbor*
    Where we must land some of our passengers,
    And light this wearie vessell of her lode.
  Here she a while may make her safe abode,
  Till she repairèd have her tackles spent,°   *worn out*
    And wants supplide. And then againe abroad
    On the long voyage whereto she is bent:
Well may she speede and fairely finish her intent.

                                              1590, 1596

Mutabilitie Cantos   In 1609, in an edition of *The Faerie Queene* published ten years after Spenser's death, two cantos and a two-stanza fragment of a third one appeared for the first time. If they actually are, as their editor's note suggests, part of an uncompleted book of the poem, centered on the virtue of constancy, they constitute a longer digression from the main story than any in the other books. The cantos give Spenser's reflections on change and permanence in the world—a subject that fascinated and disturbed him and his contemporaries. How is it possible to secure any stable meaning in a world that is forever in flux? Where can beauty and truth be found in the midst of relentless strife? In a great trial scene, the Goddess of Nature rules against Mutabilitie in favor of Jove's principle of underlying order. But in the moving two-stanza fragment, the poet discloses his longing for eternal rest in the changeless realm of heaven.

Two Cantos of *Mutabilitie*:

Which, both for Forme and Matter, appeare to be parcell of some following Booke of the Faerie Queene

(∴)

Under the Legend of Constancie.

Canto 6

Proud Change (not pleasd, in mortall things,
beneath the Moone, to raigne)[1]
Pretends,° as well of Gods, as Men   claims
to be the Soveraine.

1

What man that sees the ever-whirling wheele
   Of Change, the which all mortall things doth sway,°   rule
   But that therby doth find, and plainly feele,
   How Mutability in them doth play
Her cruell sports, to many mens decay?°   destruction
Which that to all may better yet appeare,
I will rehearse° that whylome° I heard say,   relate / formerly
How she at first her selfe began to reare,
Gainst all the Gods, and th'empire sought from them to beare.

2

But first, here falleth fittest to unfold
   Her antique race and linage ancient,
   As I have found it registred of old,
   In Faery Land mongst records permanent:
She was, to weet,° a daughter by descent   to wit, in fact
Of those old Titans,[2] that did whylome strive
With Saturnes sonne for heavens regiment.°   rule
Whom, though high Jove of kingdome did deprive,
Yet many of their stemme° long after did survive.   race

3

And many of them, afterwards obtained
   Great power of Jove, and high authority;

---

1. The old cosmology held that change occurred only in the sublunary realm.
2. The Titans were the sons and daughters of sky and earth; their king was Cronus (Time). Jove, Cronus's son, dethroned him and established the rule of the gods. But some descendants of the original Titans, such as Prometheus and Hecate, survived. Spenser invents another, a Titaness called Mutabilitie.

As Hecate,[3] in whose almighty hand,
He plac't all rule and principality,
To be by her disposèd diversly,
To Gods, and men, as she them list° divide: *chose to*
And drad° Bellona,[4] that doth sound on hie *dreaded*
Warres and allarums unto Nations wide,
That makes both heaven and earth to tremble at her pride.

4

So likewise did this Titanesse aspire,
Rule and dominion to her selfe to gaine;
That as a Goddesse, men might her admire,° *wonder at*
And heavenly honours yield, as to them twaine.[5]
And first, on earth she sought it to obtaine;
Where she such proofe and sad° examples shewed *grievous*
Of her great power, to many ones great paine,
That not men onely (whom she soone subdewed)
But eke° all other creatures, her bad dooings rewed.° *also / rued*

5

For, she the face of earthly things so changed,
That all which Nature had establisht first
In good estate,° and in meet° order ranged, *condition / fitting*
She did pervert,° and all their statutes burst: *overturn*
And all the worlds faire frame (which none yet durst
Of Gods or men to alter or misguide)
She altered quite, and made them all accurst
That God had blest; and did at first provide
In that still° happy state for ever to abide. *continually*

6

Ne° shee the lawes of Nature onely brake, *nor*
But eke of Justice, and of Policie;° *government*
And wrong of right, and bad of good did make,
And death for life exchangèd foolishlie:
Since which, all living wights° have learned to die, *creatures*
And all this world is woxen° daily worse. *grown*
O pittious worke of Mutabilitie!
By which, we all are subject to that curse,
And death in stead of life have suckèd from our Nurse.° *Nature*

7

And now, when all the earth she thus had brought
To her behest,° and thrallèd to her might, *bidding*
She gan to cast° in her ambitious thought, *resolve*

---

3. A goddess of Hades but also often associated with the powerful and generally benevolent goddess Artemis (in Rome, Diana). Her name is pronounced *HEK-a-tee*.
4. Roman goddess of war.
5. Those two; that is, Hecate and Bellona.

    T'attempt° the empire of the heavens hight,   *attack*
    And Jove himselfe to shoulder from his right.
    And first, she past the region of the ayre,
    And of the fire,[6] whose substance thin and slight,
    Made no resistance, ne could her contraire,°   *withstand*
But ready passage to her pleasure did prepare.

8

Thence, to the Circle of the Moone[7] she clambe,
    Where Cynthia[8] raignes in everlasting glory,
    To whose bright shining palace straight she came,
    All fairely deckt with heavens goodly story;[9]
    Whose silver gates (by which there sate an hory
    Old aged Sire, with hower-glasse in hand,
    Hight° Tyme) she entred, were he liefe or sory:[1]   *called*
    Ne staide till she the highest stage° had scand,°   *level / mounted to*
Where Cynthia did sit, that never still did stand.°   *remain*

9

Her sitting on an Ivory throne shee found,
    Drawne of two steeds, th'one black, the other white,
    Environd with tenne thousand starres around,
    That duly her attended day and night;
    And by her side, there ran her Page, that hight
    Vesper, whom we the Evening-starre intend:°   *call*
    That with his Torche, still twinkling like twylight,
    Her lightened all the way where she should wend,°   *journey*
And joy to weary wandring travailers did lend:

10

That when the hardy Titanesse beheld
    The goodly building of her Palace bright,
    Made of the heavens substance, and up-held
    With thousand Crystall pillors of huge hight,
    Shee gan to burne in her ambitious spright,°   *spirit*
    And t'evnie her that in such glorie raigned.
    Eftsoones she cast[2] by force and tortious° might,   *wrongful*
    Her to displace; and to her selfe to have gained
The kingdome of the Night, and waters by her wained.°   *drawn*

11

Boldly she bid the Goddesse downe descend,
    And let her selfe into that Ivory throne;

---

6. The highest sublunary region.
7. The transparent sphere that, in the Ptolemaic cosmology, revolved around the earth, carrying the moon along. (The sun, the other known planets, and, collectively, the fixed stars were similarly carried by *their* spheres.)
8. Cynthia, Diana, or Phoebe, the moon goddess, often associated with Queen Elizabeth.
9. That is, the constellations.
1. That is, whether he liked it or not.
2. Soon, she resolved.

> For, shee her selfe more worthy thereof wend,°   *weened, thought*
> And better able it to guide alone:
> Whether to men, whose fall she did bemone,
> Or unto Gods, whose state she did maligne,°   *envy*
> Or to th'infernall Powers, her need give lone
> Of her faire light, and bounty most benigne,
> Her selfe of all that rule shee deemèd most condigne.°   *worthy*

12

> But shee that had to her that soveraigne seat
> By highest Jove assigned, therein to beare
> Nights burning lamp, regarded not her threat,
> Ne yielded ought for favour or for feare;
> But with sterne countenaunce and disdainfull cheare,°   *aspect*
> Bending her hornèd browes,[3] did put her back:
> And boldly blaming her for comming there,
> Bade her attonce from heavens coast to pack,°   *depart*
> Or at her perill bide the wrathfull Thunders wrack.°   *destruction*

13

> Yet nathemore° the Giantesse forbare: *not at all*
> But boldly preacing-on,° raught forth her hand   *advancing*
> To pluck her downe perforce° from off her chaire;   *by force*
> And there-with lifting up her golden wand,
> Threatned to strike her if she did with-stand.
> Where-at the starres, which round about her blazed,
> And eke the Moones bright wagon,° still did stand,   *chariot*
> All beeing with so bold attempt amazed,
> And on her uncouth habit[4] and sterne looke still gazed.

14

> Meane-while, the lower World, which nothing knew
> Of all that chauncèd here, was darkned quite;
> And eke the heavens, and all the heavenly crew
> Of happy wights, now unpurvaide° of light,   *deprived*
> Were much afraid, and wondred at that sight;
> Fearing least° Chaos broken had his chaine,   *lest*
> And brought againe on them eternall night:
> But chiefely Mercury, that next doth raigne,[5]
> Ran forth in haste, unto the king of Gods to plaine.°   *complain*

---

3. Cynthia's bent brows are the horns of the crescent moon.
4. Strange behavior.
5. In the Ptolemaic system the sphere of Mercury was next beyond that of the moon. In mythology Mercury was the messenger of the gods. In stanza 19, his Greek name, Hermes, is used. "Chaos": in Greek mythology, the first created being—the scarcely personified, profoundly unordered primordial soup.

15

All ran together with a great out-cry,
  To Joves faire Palace, fixt in heavens hight;
  And beating at his gates full earnestly,
  Gan call to him aloud with all their might,
  To know what meant that suddaine lack of light.
  The father of the Gods when this he heard,
  Was troubled much at their so strange affright,
  Doubting least° Typhon[6] were againe upreared,   *fearing that*
Or other his old foes, that once him sorely feared.°   *frightened*

16

Eftsoones the sonne of Maia° forth he sent   *Mercury*
  Downe to the Circle of the Moone, to knowe
  The cause of this so strange astonishment,
  And why shee did her wonted° course forslowe;°   *accustomed / delay*
  And if that any were on earth belowe
  That did with charmes or Magick her molest,
  Him to attache,° and downe to hell to throwe: *seize*
  But, if from heaven it were, then to arrest
The Author, and him bring before his presence prest.°   *immediately*

17

The wingd-foot God, so fast his plumes did beat,
  That soone he came where-as the Titanesse
  Was striving with faire Cynthia for her seat:
  At whose strange sight, and haughty hardinesse,°   *boldness*
  He wondred much, and fearèd her no lesse.
  Yet laying feare aside to doe his charge,°   *assigned task*
  At last, he bade her (with bold stedfastnesse)
  Ceasse to molest the Moone to walke at large,[7]
Or come before high Jove, her dooings to discharge.°   *account for*

18

And there-with-all, he on her shoulder laid
  His snaky-wreathèd Mace,[8] whose awfull power
  Doth make both Gods and hellish fiends affraid:
  Where-at the Titanesse did sternely lower,°   *scowl*
  And stoutly answered, that in evill hower
  He from his Jove such message to her brought,
  To bid her leave faire Cynthias silver bower;
  Sith° shee his Jove and him esteemèd nought,   *since*
No more then° Cynthia's selfe; but all their kingdoms sought.   *than*

---

6. A giant who had rebelled against Jove.
7. That is, stop interfering with the moon's free movement.
8. That is, the caduceus, Mercury's rod, which could bring spirits from the underworld.

19

    The Heavens Herald staid not to reply,
        But past away, his doings to relate
    Unto his Lord; who now in th'highest sky,
    Was placed in his principall Estate,°   *position of state*
        With all the Gods about him congregate:
    To whom when Hermes had his message told,
        It did them all exceedingly amate,°   *dismay*
        Save Jove; who, changing nought his count'nance bold,
Did unto them at length these speeches wise unfold;

20

"Harken to mee awhile yee heavenly Powers;
        Ye may remember since th'Earths cursèd seed
    Sought to assaile the heavens eternall towers,
    And to us all exceeding feare did breed:
    But how we then defeated all their deed,
        Yee all doe knowe, and them destroied quite;
        Yet not so quite, but that there did succeed
        An off-spring of their bloud, which did alite
Upon the fruitfull earth, which doth us yet despite.°   *disdain*

21

"Of that bad seed is this bold woman bred,
        That now with bold presumption doth aspire
    To thrust faire Phoebe[9] from her silver bed,
    And eke our selves from heavens high Empire,
    If that her might were match to her desire:
        Wherefore, it now behoves us to advise°   *consider*
        What way is best to drive her to retire;
        Whether by open force, or counsell wise,
Areed° ye sonnes of God, as best ye can devise."   *advise*

22

So having said, he ceast; and with his brow
        (His black eye-brow, whose doomefull dreaded beck[1]
    Is wont to wield° the world unto his vow,°   *sway / will*
    And even the highest Powers of heaven to check)
    Made signe to them in their degrees to speake:
        Who straight gan cast[2] their counsell grave and wise.
        Mean-while, th'Earths daughter, thogh she nought did reck[3]
        Of Hermes message; yet gan now advise,
What course were best to take in this hot bold emprize.°   *enterprise*

---

9. The moon as the twin sister of Phoebus Apollo, the sun god.
1. That is, his awesome nod of judgment.
2. Deliver. "Straight": straightaway.
3. Care. "Earths daughter": that is, Mutabilitie.

23

Eftsoones she thus resolved; that whil'st the Gods
  (After returne of Hermes Embassie)
  Were troubled, and amongst themselves at ods,
  Before they could new counsels re-allie,°   *form again*
  To set upon them in that extasie;°   *astonishment*
  And take what fortune time and place would lend:
  So, forth she rose, and through the purest sky
  To Joves high Palace straight cast° to ascend,   *resolved*
To prosecute her plot: Good on-set boads good end.

24

Shee there arriving, boldly in did pass;
  Where all the Gods she found in counsell close,°   *secret*
  All quite unarmed, as then their manner was.
  At sight of her they suddaine all arose,
  In great amaze,° ne wist° what way to chose.   *bewilderment / knew*
  But Jove, all fearelesse, forc't them to aby;°   *remain*
  And in his soveraine throne, gan straight dispose°   *arrange*
  Himselfe more full of grace and Majestie,
That mote encheare° his friends, and foes mote terrifie.   *cheer*

25

That, when the haughty Titanesse beheld,
  All° were she fraught with pride and impudence,   *although*
  Yet with the sight thereof was almost queld;
  And inly quaking, seemed as° reft of sense,   *as if*
  And voyd of speech in that drad° audience;   *dread*
  Until that Jove himself, her selfe bespake:
  "Speake thou fraile woman, speake with confidence,
  Whence art thou, and what doost thou here now make?° *intend*
What idle errand hast thou, earths mansion to forsake?"

26

Shee, halfe confusèd with his great commaund,
  Yet gathering spirit of her natures pride,
  Him boldly answered thus to his demaund:
  "I am a daughter, by the mothers side,
  Of her that is Grand-mother magnifide°   *glorified*
  Of all the Gods, great Earth, great Chaos child:[4]
  But by the fathers (be it not envide°)   *begrudged*
  I greater am in bloud (whereon I build°)   *base my claim*
Then all the Gods, though wrongfully from heaven exiled.

27

"For, Titan (as ye all acknowledge must)
  Was Saturnes elder brother by birth-right;

---

4. Earth is the offspring of Chaos, in Hesiod and later mythologies.

  Both, sonnes of Uranus: but by unjust
  And guilefull meanes, through Corybantes slight,°   *trickery*
  The younger thrust the elder from his right:[5]
  Since which, thou Jove, injuriously° hast held   *wrongfully*
  The Heavens rule from Titans sonnes by might;
  And them to hellish dungeons downe hast feld:
Witnesse ye Heavens the truth of all that I have teld."

28

  Whil'st she thus spake, the Gods that gave good eare
   To her bold words, and markèd well her grace,
   Beeing of stature tall as any there
   Of all the Gods, and beautifull of face,
  As any of the Goddesses in place,°   *present*
  Stood all astonied, like a sort° of Steeres;   *herd*
  Mongst whom, some beast of strange and forraine race,
  Unwares° is chaunc't, far straying from his peeres: *unexpectedly*
So did their ghastly gaze bewray° their hidden feares.   *reveal*

29

Till having pauzed awhile, Jove thus bespake;
  "Will never mortall thoughts ceasse to aspire,
  In this bold sort, to Heaven claime to make,
  And touch celestiall seates with earthly mire?
  I would have thought, that bold Procrustes[6] hire,°   *reward*
  Or Typhons fall, or proud Ixions paine,
  Or great Prometheus, tasting of our ire,
  Would have suffized, the rest for to restraine;
And warned all men by their example to refraine:

30

  "But now, this off-scum of that cursèd fry,°   *brood*
   Dare to renew the like bold enterprize,
   And chalenge° th'heritage of this our skie;   *lay claim to*
   Whom what should hinder, but that we likewise
  Should handle as the rest of her allies,
  And thunder-drive to hell?" With that, he shooke
  His Nectar-deawèd locks,[7] with which the skyes
  And all the world beneath for terror quooke,°   *quaked*
And eft° his burning levin-brond[8] in hand he tooke.   *then*

---

5. In this variant myth, Titan, eldest son of Uranus, abdicated in favor of his younger brother Saturn on condition that Saturn would eat all his own male children, thus assuring the succession would eventually revert to Titan's line. When Jove was born to Rhea, Saturn's wife, she gave Saturn a stone to swallow instead of the baby, and her attendants, the Corybantes, beat on their shields to drown out the baby's cries. Eventually Jove deposed his father.
6. Procrustes was a robber who waylaid strangers and made them fit his bed by cutting or stretching them. (Spenser includes him among those punished by Jove, though the standard version of the myth has Theseus in that role.) Typhon was a hundred-headed monster overthrown by Jove. Ixion tried to seduce Jove's wife and was punished by being bound to a wheel of fire in hell. Prometheus stole fire from heaven and gave it to humankind, for which Jove punished him by chaining him to a cliff where an eagle fed on his liver, which grew back every night.
7. That is, his locks were sprinkled with a fragrant balm. "Nectar" more often referred to the drink of the gods.
8. Lightning bolt.

31

But, when he lookèd on her lovely face,
  In which, faire beames of beauty did appeare,
  That could the greatest wrath soone turne to grace
  (Such sway° doth beauty even in Heaven beare) — *power*
  He staide his hand: and having changed his cheare,° — *mood*
  He thus againe in milder wise began;
  "But ah! if Gods should strive with flesh yfere,° — *together*
  Then shortly should the progeny of Man
Be rooted out, if Jove should doe still° what he can: — *always*

32

"But thee faire Titans child, I rather weene,° — *suppose*
  Through some vaine errour or inducement light,° — *slight*
  To see that° mortall eyes have never seene; — *that which*
  Or through ensample° of thy sisters might, — *example*
  Bellona; whose great glory thou doost spight,° — *envy*
  Since thou hast seene her dreadfull power belowe,
  Mongst wretched men (dismaide with her affright)[9]
  To bandie Crownes, and Kingdomes to bestowe:
And sure thy worth, no lesse then hers doth seem to showe.

33

"But wote° thou this, thou hardy Titanesse, — *know*
  That not the worth of any living wight
  May challenge ought in Heavens interesse,[1]
  Much lesse the Title of old Titans Right:
  For, we by Conquest of our soveraine might,
  And by eternall doome of Fates decree,
  Have wonne the Empire of the Heavens bright;
  Which to our selves we hold, and to whom wee
Shall worthy deeme partakers of our blisse to bee.

34

"Then ceasse thy idle claime thou foolish gerle,
  And seeke by grace and goodnesse to obtaine
  That place from which by folly Titan fell;
  There-to thou maist perhaps, if so thou faine° — *desire*
  Have Jove thy gratious Lord and Soveraigne."
  So, having said, she thus to him replide;
  "Ceasse Saturnes sonne, to seeke by proffers vaine
  Of idle hopes t'allure mee to thy side,
For to betray my Right, before I have it tride.

---

9. Through fear of her.
1. That is, no living person, however worthy, can claim any title to power or authority in heaven.

35

"But thee, O Jove, no equall° Judge I deeme *impartial*
    Of my desert, or of my dewfull° Right; *due*
That in thine owne behalfe maist partiall seeme:
But to the highest him, that is behight° *called*
    Father of Gods and men by equall might;[2]
    To weet, the God of Nature, I appeale."
There-at Jove wexèd° wroth, and in his spright° *waxed, grew / spirit*
    Did inly grudge, yet did it well conceale;
And bade Dan Phoebus Scribe[3] her Appellation° seale. *appeal*

36

Eftsoones the time and place appointed were,
    Where all, both heavenly Powers, and earthly wights,
    Before great Natures presence should appeare,
    For triall of their Titles and best Rights:
    That was, to weet, upon the highest hights
    Of Arlo-hill[4] (Who knowes not Arlo-hill?)
    That is the highest head (in all mens sights)
    Of my old father Mole, whom Shepheards quill
Renownèd hath with hymnes fit for a rurall skill.

37

And, were it not ill fitting for this file,[5]
    To sing of hilles and woods, mongst warres and Knights,
    I would abate the sternenesse of my stile,
    Mongst these sterne stounds° to mingle soft delights; *clashes*
    And tell how Arlo through Dianaes spights
    (Beeing of old the best and fairest Hill
    That was in all this holy-Islands[6] hights)
    Was made the most unpleasant, and most ill.° *evil*
Meane while, O Clio, lend Calliope[7] thy quill.

38

Whylome,° when Ireland florishèd in fame *formerly*
    Of wealths and goodnesse, far above the rest
    Of all that beare the British Islands name,
    The Gods then used[8] (for pleasure and for rest)
    Oft to resort there-to, when seemed them best:
    But none of all there-in more pleasure found,
    Then Cynthia;[9] that is soveraine Queene profest° *acknowledged*

---

2. That is, who is called father of gods and humans, with equal authority over both. Androgynous Nature is here male, but in the following canto female.
3. Evidently Spenser makes Phoebus Apollo the secretary ("Scribe") of the gods because he is the god of poetry.
4. That is, Galtymore, a peak of the mountain range Spenser calls "my old father Mole," near Kilcolman Castle, where he lived in Ireland. The last two lines of the stanza refer to Spenser's praise of Mole in his pastoral eclogue *Colin Clouts Come Home Againe*.
5. Thread (of the story).
6. Ireland is called the "holy-Island" because, according to legend, Christianity first found a foothold there and thence spread to the rest of the British Isles.
7. Calliope is the Muse of epic poetry. Clio is the Muse of history.
8. Were accustomed to.
9. That is, as Diana, goddess of forests, fond of hunting.

Of woods and forrests, which therein abound,
Sprinkled with wholsom waters, more then most on ground.

39

But mongst them all, as fittest for her game,°   *recreation*
  Either for chace of beasts with hound or boawe,
  Or for to shroude in shade from Phoebus flame,
  Or bathe in fountaines that doe freshly flowe,
  Or° from high hilles, or from the dales belowe,   *either*
  She chose this Arlo; where shee did resort
  With all her Nymphes enrangèd on° a rowe,   *arranged in*
  With whom the woody Gods did oft consort:°   *sexually*
For, with the Nymphes, the Satyres love to play and sport.[1]

40

Amongst the which, there was a Nymph that hight
  Molanna; daughter of old father Mole,
  And sister unto Mulla,[2] faire and bright:
  Unto whose bed false Bregog whylome stole,
  That Shepheard Colin dearely did condole,°   *keenly bewailed*
  And made her lucklesse loves well knowne to be.
  But this Molanna, were she not so shole,°   *shallow*
  Were no lesse faire and beautifull then shee:
Yet as she is, a fairer flood may no man see.

41

For, first, she springs out of two marble Rocks,
  On which, a grove of Oakes high mounted growes,
  That as a girlond seemes to deck the locks
  Of som faire Bride, brought forth with pompous[3] showes
  Out of her bowre,° that many flowers strowes: *chamber*
  So, through the flowry Dales she tumbling downe,
  Through many woods, and shady coverts° flowes   *thickets*
  (That on each side her silver channell crowne)
Till to the Plaine she come, whose Valleyes shee doth drowne.

42

In her sweet streames, Diana usèd oft
  (After her sweatie chace and toilesome play)
  To bathe her selfe; and after, on the soft
  And downy grasse, her dainty limbes to lay
  In covert° shade, where none behold her may: *secret*
  For, much she hated sight of living eye.
  Foolish God Faunus, though full many a day

---

1. Nymphs in Greek mythology were minor female deities of streams, springs, trees, and other parts of nature. Satyrs were minor male gods of the woods, given to drinking and sensual pleasure. The Romans identified them with their goat-footed fauns; hence "Faunus" (stanza 42) and "Faune" (stanza 46).
2. The river Awbeg, whose joining with the river Bregog is told in *Colin Clouts Come Home Againe*. The Molanna is the shallow, rocky river Behanna.
3. Magnificent.

He saw her clad, yet longèd foolishly
To see her naked mongst her Nymphes in privity.[4]

43

No way he found to compasse° his desire, — *accomplish*
   But to corrupt Molanna, this her maid,
   Her to discover° for some secret hire:° — *reveal / reward*
So, her with flattering words he first assaid;
And after, pleasing gifts for her purvaid,° — *provided*
   Queene-apples,[5] and red Cherries from the tree,
   With which he her allurèd and betraid,
   To tell what time he might her Lady see
When she her selfe did bathe, that he might secret° bee. — *hidden*

44

There-to hee promist, if she would him pleasure
   With this small boone, to quit° her with a better; — *requite*
   To weet, that where-as she had out of measure
Long loved the Fanchin, who by nought did set her,[6]
That he would undertake, for this to get her
   To be his Love, and of him likèd well:
   Besides all which, he vowed to be her debter
   For many moe° good turnes then he would tell; — *more*
The least of which, this little pleasure should excell.

45

The simple maid did yield to him anone;° — *at once*
   And eft him placèd where he close[7] might view
   That° never any saw, save onely one; — *that which*
Who, for his hire to so foole-hardy dew,° — *due*
Was of his hounds devoured in Hunters hew.[8]
   Tho,° as her manner was on sunny day, — *then*
   Diana, with her Nymphes about her, drew
   To this sweet spring; where, doffing her array,
She bathed her lovely limbes, for Jove a likely pray.° — *proper prey*

46

There Faunus saw that pleasèd much his eye,
   And made his hart to tickle° in his brest, — *be thrilled*
   That for great joy of some-what he did spy,
He could him not containe in silent rest;
But breaking forth in laughter, loud profest
   His foolish thought. A foolish Faune indeed,
   That couldst not hold thy selfe so° hidden blest, — *thus*

---

4. Privacy. Spenser here adapts the classical story of Actaeon with local Irish geographical references. Actaeon while hunting happened to see Diana bathing; he was turned into a stag and pursued and killed by his own hounds.
5. Noted for their redness and early ripening.
6. That is, who cared nothing for her. Fanchin is the river Funsheon.
7. Secretly; close up.
8. That is, as a due reward to one so foolhardy, he was devoured by his hunting dogs in the slaughter ("hew") that follows a hunt.

But wouldest needs thine owne conceit[9] areed.°   *make known*
Babblers unworthy been of so divine a meed.°   *reward*

47

The Goddesse, all abashèd with that noise,
   In haste forth started from the guilty brooke;
   And running straight where-as she heard his voice,
   Enclosed the bush about, and there him tooke,
   Like darrèd[1] Larke; not daring up to looke
   On her whose sight before so much he sought.
   Thence, forth they drew him by the hornes, and shooke
   Nigh all to peeces, that they left him nought;°   *good for nothing*
And then into the open light they forth him brought.

48

Like as an huswife, that with busie care
   Thinks of her Dairie to make wondrous gaine,
   Finding where-as some wicked beast unware°   *unexpected*
   That breakes into her Dayr'house, there doth draine
   Her creaming pannes, and frustrate all her paine;°   *effort*
   Hath in some snare or gin° set close behind,   *trap*
   Entrappèd him, and caught into her traine,°   *snare*
   Then thinkes what punishment were best assigned,
And thousand deathes deviseth in her vengefull mind:

49

So did Diana and her maydens all
   Use silly Faunus, now within their baile:°   *power, custody*
   They mocke and scorne him, and him foule miscall;°   *revile*
   Some by the nose him pluckt, some by the taile,
   And by his goatish beard some did him haile:°   *pull*
   Yet he (poore soule) with patience all did beare;
   For, nought against their wils might countervaile:°   *avail*
   Ne ought he said what ever he did heare;
But hanging downe his head, did like a Mome° appeare.   *fool*

50

At length, when they had flouted him their fill,
   They gan to cast° what penaunce him to give.   *consider*
   Some would have gelt° him, but that same would spill[2]   *castrated*
   The Wood-gods breed, which must for ever live:
   Others would through the river him have drive,°   *forced to go*
   And duckèd deepe: but that seemed penaunce light;
   But most agreed and did this sentence give,
   Him in Deares skin to clad; and in that plight,°   *condition*
To hunt him with their hounds, him selfe save how hee might.

---

9. Thought; vanity or pride.   2. Destroy.
1. Paralyzed with fear.

51

But Cynthia's selfe, more angry then the rest,
   Thought not enough, to punish him in sport,
   And of her shame to make a gamesome° jest;   *sportive*
   But gan examine him in straighter° sort,   *stricter*
   Which of her Nymphes, or other close consort,°   *secret confederate*
   Him thither brought, and her to him betraid?
   He, much affeard, to her confessèd short,°   *soon*
   That 'twas Molanna which her so bewraid.°   *betrayed*
Then all attonce their hands upon Molanna laid.

52

But him (according as they had decreed)
   With a Deeres-skin they covered, and then chast
   With all their hounds that after him did speed;
   But he more speedy, from them fled more fast
   Then any Deere: so sore him dread aghast.°   *terrified*
   They after followed all with shrill out-cry,
   Shouting as they the heavens would have brast:°   *burst*
   That all the woods and dales where he did flie,
Did ring againe, and loud reeccho to the skie.

53

So they him followed till they weary were;
   When, back returning to Molann' againe,
   They, by commaund'ment of Diana, there
   Her whelmed with stones.[3] Yet Faunus (for her paine)°   *trouble*
   Of her belovèd Fanchin did obtaine,
   That her he would receive unto his bed.
   So now her waves passe through a pleasant Plaine,
   Till with the Fanchin she her selfe doe wed,
And (both combined) themselves in one faire river spred.

54

Nath'lesse,° Diana, full of indignatiön,   *nonetheless*
   Thence-forth abandond her delicious brooke;
   In whose sweet streame, before that bad occasiön,
   So much delight to bathe her limbes she tooke:
   Ne onely her,° but also quite forsooke   *the brook*
   All those faire forrests about Arlo hid,
   And all that Mountaine, which doth over-looke
   The richest champian that may else be rid,[4]
And the faire Shure,[5] in which are thousand Salmons bred.

---

3. This overwhelming with stones accounts for the shallowness of the river, mentioned in stanza 40.
4. The richest plain to be seen anywhere.
5. The river Suir.

55

Them all, and all that she so deare did way,°   *esteem*
    Thence-forth she left; and parting from the place,
    There-on an heavy haplesse curse did lay,
    To weet, that Wolves, where she was wont to space,°   *roam*
    Should harboured be, and all those Woods deface,
    And Thieves should rob and spoile[6] that Coast° around.   *region*
    Since which, those Woods, and all that goodly Chase,[7]
    Doth to this day with Wolves and Thieves abound:
Which too-too true that lands in-dwellers since have found.

Canto 7

Pealing,° from Jove, to Natur's Bar,   *appealing*
    bold Alteration° pleades   *Mutabilitie*
Large° Evidence: but Nature soone   *copious*
    her righteous Doome areads.[8]

1

Ah! whither doost thou now thou greater° Muse[9]   *very great*
    Me from these woods and pleasing forrests bring?
    And my fraile spirit (that dooth oft refuse
    This too high flight, unfit for her weake wing)
    Lift up aloft, to tell of heavens King
    (Thy soveraine Sire)[1] his fortunate successe,
    And victory, in bigger° noates to sing,   *louder*
    Which he obtained against that Titanesse,
That him of heavens Empire sought to dispossesse.

2

Yet sith° I needs must follow thy behest,   *since*
    Doe thou my weaker° wit with skill inspire,   *too weak*
    Fit for this turne;° and in my feeble brest   *task*
    Kindle fresh sparks of that immortall fire,
    Which learnèd minds inflameth with desire
    Of heavenly things: for, who but thou alone,
    That art yborne of heaven and heavenly Sire,
    Can tell things doen in heaven so long ygone;
So farre past memory of man that may be knowne.

3

Now, at the time that was before agreed,
    The Gods assembled all on Arlo hill;
    As well those that are sprung of heavenly seed,
    As those that all the other world° doe fill,   *the earth*

---

6. Despoil.
7. Hunting ground.
8. Proclaims her righteous judgment.
9. Calliope, though possibly Clio. See canto 6, stanza 37 and n. 7.
1. Jove fathered the Muses on the Titaness Mnemosyne (Memory).

And rule both sea and land unto their will:
   Onely th'infernall Powers might not appeare;
   Aswell for horror of their count'naunce ill,
   As for th'unruly fiends which they did feare;[2]
Yet Pluto and Proserpina were present there.[3]

4

And thither also came all other creatures,
   What-ever life or motion doe retaine,
   According to their sundry kinds of features;
   That Arlo scarsly could them all containe;
   So full they fillèd every hill and Plaine:
   And had not Natures Sergeant (that is Order)
   Them well disposèd by his busie paine,°   *care*
   And raungèd° farre abroad in every border,   *arranged*
They would have causèd much confusion and disorder.

5

Then forth issewed (great goddesse) great dame Nature,
   With goodly port° and gracious Majesty;   *bearing*
   Being far greater and more tall of stature
   Then any of the gods or Powers on hie:
   Yet certes° by her face and physnomy,°   *certainly / countenance*
   Whether she man or woman inly were,
   That could not any creature well descry:
   For, with a veile that wimpled° every where,   *covered in folds*
Her head and face was hid, that mote to none appeare.

6

That some doe say was so by skill devized,
   To hide the terror of her uncouth hew,°   *strange appearance*
   From mortall eyes that should be sore agrized;°   *terrified*
   For that her face did like a Lion shew,
   That eye of wight could not indure to view:
   But others tell that it so beautious was,
   And round about such beames of splendor threw,
   That it the Sunne a thousand times did pass,°   *surpass*
Ne° could be seene, but° like an image in a glass.   *nor / except*

7

That well may seemen true: for, well I weene
   That this same day, when she on Arlo sat,°   *in judgment*
   Her garment was so bright and wondrous sheene,°   *shining*
   That my fraile wit cannot devize to what
   It to compare, nor finde like stuffe° to that,   *fabric*
   As those three sacred Saints, though else most wise,
   Yet on mount Thabor quite their wits forgat,

---

2. Meaning either that the infernal powers controlled the fiends by fear or that the heavenly and earthly powers feared *them*.

3. King and queen of the Underworld.

When they their glorious Lord in strange disguise
Transfigured sawe; his garments so did daze° their eyes.[4]   *dazzle*

8

In a fayre Plaine upon an equall° Hill,   *level-topped*
   She placèd was in a paviliön;
   Not such as Craftes-men by their idle° skill   *vain*
   Are wont for Princes states° to fashiön: *canopied thrones*
   But th'earth her self of her owne motiön,
   Out of her fruitfull bosome made to growe
   Most dainty trees; that, shooting up anon,°   *at once*
   Did seeme to bow their bloosming° heads full lowe,   *blossoming*
For homage unto her, and like a throne did shew.°   *appear*

9

So hard it is for any living wight,
   All her array and vestiments to tell,
   That old Dan° Geffrey (in whose gentle spright   *Master, Sir*
   The pure well head of Poesie did dwell)
   In his *Foules parley* durst not with it mel,°   *meddle*
   But it transferd° to Alane, who he thought   *referred*
   Had in his *Plaint of kindes* described it well:[5]
   Which who will read set forth so as it ought,
Go seek he out that Alane where he may be sought.

10

And all the earth far underneath her feete
   Was dight° with flowres, that voluntary grew   *decked*
   Out of the ground, and sent forth odours sweet,
   Tenne thousand mores° of sundry sent and hew,   *plants*
   That might delight the smell, or please the view:
   The which, the Nymphes, from all the brooks thereby
   Had gathered, which they at her foot-stoole threw;
   That richer seemed then any tapestry,
That Princes bowres adorne with painted imagery.

11

And Mole[6] himself, to honour her the more,
   Did deck himself in freshest faire attire,
   And his high head, that seemeth alwaies hore°   *hoary*
   With hardned frosts of former winters ire,
   He with an Oaken girlond now did tire,°   *attire*
   As if the love of some new Nymph late seene,
   Had in him kindled youthfull fresh desire,
   And made him change his gray attire to greene;
Ah gentle Mole! such joyance hath thee well beseene.[7]

---

4. Peter, James, and John saw Jesus transfigured on a mountain (traditionally Mount Tabor, in Galilee). See Matthew 17:1–8.
5. Chaucer, in his *Parliament of Fowls*, lines 316–18, refers to Alain de Lille's *De Planctu Naturae* as Aleyn's *Pleynt of Kynde* (Complaint of Nature).
6. See canto 6, stanza 36 and n. 4.
7. Well becomes you.

12

Was never so great joyance since the day,
   That all the gods whylome assembled were,
   On Haemus hill in their divine array,
   To celebrate the solemne° bridall cheare,   *sacred*
   Twixt Peleus, and dame Thetis[8] pointed° there;   *appointed*
   Where Phoebus self, that god of Poets hight,
   They say did sing the spousall hymne full cleere,
   That all the gods were ravisht with delight
Of his celestiall song, and Musicks wondrous might.

13

This great Grandmother of all creatures bred
   Great Nature, ever young yet full of eld,°   *age*
   Still° mooving, yet unmovèd from her sted;°   *always / place*
   Unseene of any, yet of all beheld;
   Thus sitting in her throne as I have teld,
   Before her came dame Mutabilite;
   And being lowe before her presence feld,°   *prostrated*
   With meek obaysance and humilitie,
Thus gan her plaintif Plea, with words to amplifie;

14

"To thee O greatest goddesse, onely° great,   *uniquely*
   An humble suppliant loe, I lowely fly
   Seeking for Right, which I of thee entreat;
   Who Right to all dost deale indifferently,°   *impartially*
   Damning all Wrong and tortious° Injurie,   *wrongful*
   Which any of thy creatures doe to other
   (Oppressing them with power, unequally)°   *unjustly*
   Sith of them all thou are the equall° mother,   *impartial*
And knittest each to each, as brother unto brother.

15

"To thee therefore of this same Jove I plaine,
   And of his fellow gods that faine° to be,   *feign*
   That challenge° to themselves the whole worlds raign;   *claim*
   Of which, the greatest part is due to me,
   And heaven it selfe by heritage in Fee:°   *absolute possession*
   For, heaven and earth I both alike do deeme,°   *adjudge*
   Sith heaven and earth are both alike to thee;
   And, gods no more then men thou doest esteeme:
For, even the gods to thee, as men to gods do seeme.

16

"Then weigh, O soveraigne goddesse, by what right
   These gods do claime the worlds whole soverainty;

---

8. Mortal king and sea goddess, the parents of Achilles. Haemus is a mountain in Thrace. (But in the standard accounts the wedding is said to have taken place on Mount Pelion, in Greece.)

And that° is onely dew unto thy might   *that which*
   Arrogate to themselves ambitiously:
   As for the gods owne principality,°   *sovereignty*
   Which Jove usurpes unjustly; that to be
   My heritage, Jove's self cannot deny,
   From my great Grandsire Titan, unto mee,
Derived by dew descent; as is well knowen to thee.

17

"Yet mauger° Jove, and all his gods beside,   *despite*
   I doe possesse the worlds most regiment;°   *rule*
   As, if ye please it into parts divide,
   And every parts inholders° to convent,°   *inhabitants / convene*
   Shall to your eyes appeare incontinent.°   *at once*
   And first,[9] the Earth (great mother of us all)
   That only° seems unmoved and permanent,   *alone*
   And unto Mutability not thrall;
Yet is she changed in part, and eeke° in generall.   *also*

18

"For, all that from her springs, and is ybredde,
   How-ever fayre it flourish for a time,
   Yet see we soone decay; and, being dead,
   To turne again unto their earthly slime:
   Yet, out of their decay and mortall crime,[1]
   We daily see new creatures to arize;
   And of their Winter spring another Prime,°   *spring*
   Unlike in forme, and changed by strange disguise:
So turne they still about, and change in restlesse wise.

19

"As for her tenants; that is, man and beasts,
   The beasts we daily see massacred dy,
   As thralls and vassalls unto mens beheasts:
   And men themselves doe change continually,
   From youth to eld, from wealth to poverty,
   From good to bad, from bad to worst of all.
   Ne doe their bodies only flit and fly:
   But eeke their minds (which they immortal call)
Still change and vary thoughts, as new occasions fall.

20

"Ne is the water in more constant case;
   Whether those same on high, or these belowe.[2]
   For, th'Ocean moveth stil, from place to place;

---

9. In what follows, Mutabilitie argues the ubiquity of change in each of the traditional four elements (see stanza 25): earth, water, air, and fire. The most notable sources are Ovid, *Metamorphoses* 15, and Lucretius, *De rerum natura* 5.

1. That is, death and disintegration.

2. As in Genesis 1:7, where God divides "the waters which were under the firmament from the waters which were above the firmament."

And every River still doth ebbe and flowe:
   Ne any Lake, that seems most still and slowe,
   Ne Poole so small, that can his smoothnesse holde,
   When any winde doth under heaven blowe;
   With which, the clouds are also tost and rolled;
Now like great Hills; and, streight, like sluces, them unfold.[3]

21

"So likewise are all watry living wights
   Still tost, and turnèd, with continuall change,
   Never abyding in their stedfast plights.°   *conditions*
   The fish, still floting,° doe at randon° range,   *swimming / random*
   And never rest; but evermore exchange
   Their dwelling places, as the streames them carrie:
   Ne have the watry foules a certaine grange,°   *abode*
   Wherein to rest, ne in one stead° do tarry;   *place*
But flitting still doe flie, and still their places vary.

22

"Next is the Ayre: which who feels not by sense
   (For, of all sense it is the middle meane[4])
   To flit still? and, with subtill influence°   *flowing*
   Of his thin spirit, all creatures to maintaine,
   In state of life? O weake life! that does leane
   On thing so tickle° as th'unsteady ayre;   *uncertain; changeable*
   Which every howre is changed, and altred cleane°   *altogether*
   With every blast that bloweth fowle or faire:
The faire doth it prolong; the fowle doth it impaire.

23

"Therein the changes infinite beholde,
   Which to her creatures every minute chaunce;
   Now, boyling hot: streight, friezing deadly cold:
   Now, faire sun-shine, that makes all skip and daunce:
   Streight, bitter storms and balefull countenance,
   That makes them all to shiver and to shake:
   Rayne, hayle, and snowe do pay them sad penance,
   And dreadfull thunder-claps (that make them quake)
With flames and flashing lights that thousand changes make.

24

"Last is the fire: which, though it live for ever,
   Ne can be quenchèd quite;° yet, every day,   *entirely*
   We see his parts, so soone as they do sever,
   To lose their heat, and shortly to decay;
   So, makes himself his owne consuming pray.
   Ne any living creatures doth he breed:
   But all, that are of others bredd, doth slay;

---

3. Open. "Streight": immediately.   4. The conductor or medium.

And, with their death, his cruell life dooth feed;
Nought leaving, but their barren ashes, without seede.

25

"Thus, all these fower° (the which the ground-work bee   *four*
    Of all the world, and of all living wights)
    To thousand sorts of Change we subject see:
    Yet are they changed (by other wondrous slights°)   *devices*
    Into themselves,° and lose their native mights;   *into one another*
    The Fire to Aire, and th'Ayre to Water sheere,°   *clear*
    And Water into Earth: yet Water fights
    With Fire, and Aire with Earth approaching neere:
Yet all are in one body, and as one appeare.

26

"So, in them all raignes Mutabilitie;
    How-ever these, that Gods themselves do call,
    Of them doe claime the rule and soverainty:
    As, Vesta, of the fire aethereall;
    Vulcan, of this, with us so usuall;
    Ops,⁵ of the earth; and Juno of the Ayre;
    Neptune, of Seas; and Nymphes, of Rivers all.
    For, all those Rivers to me subject are:
And all the rest, which they usurp, be all my share.

27

"Which to approven° true, as I have told,   *prove*
    Vouchsafe, O goddesse, to thy presence call
    The rest which doe the world in being hold:
    As, times and seasons of the yeare that fall:
    Of all the which, demand° in generall,   *ask*
    Or judge thy selfe, by verdit° of thine eye,   *verdict*
    Whether to me they are not subject all."
    Nature did yeeld thereto; and by-and-by,°   *immediately*
Bade Order call them all, before her Majesty.

28

So, forth issewed the Seasons of the yeare;
    First, lusty° Spring, all dight in leaves of flowres   *vigorous*
    That freshly budded and new bloosmes° did beare   *blossoms*
    (In which a thousand birds had built their bowres
    That sweetly sung, to call forth Paramours°):   *lovers*
    And in his hand a javelin he did beare,
    And on his head (as fit for warlike stoures°)   *encounters*
    A guilt° engraven morion° he did weare;   *gilded / helmet*
That as some did him love, so others did him feare.

---

5. Roman goddess of plenty and fertility, who rules over earth. Vesta, goddess of the hearth, is assigned by Spenser to rule over the fire that is above the air. Vulcan, the blacksmith god, rules over earthly fire ("this, with us so usuall").

29

Then came the jolly Sommer, being dight
   In a thin silken cassock° coloured greene,   *cloak*
   That was unlynèd all, to be more light:
   And on his head a girlond well beseene[6]
   He wore, from which as he had chauffèd° been   *heated*
   The sweat did drop; and in his hand he bore
   A boawe and shaftes, as he in forrest greene
   Had hunted late the Libbard° or the Bore,   *leopard*
And now would bathe his limbes, with labor heated sore.°   *severely*

30

Then came the Autumne all in yellow clad,
   As though he joyèd in his plentious store,
   Laden with fruits that made him laugh, full glad
   That he had banisht hunger, which to-fore°   *formerly*
   Had by the belly oft him pinchèd sore.
   Upon his head a wreath that was enrold°   *enfolded*
   With eares of corne,° of every sort he bore: *grain*
   And in his hand a sickle he did holde,
To reape the ripened fruits the which the earth had yold.°   *yielded*

31

Lastly, came Winter cloathèd all in frize.[7]
   Chattering his teeth for cold that did him chill,
   Whil'st on his hoary beard his breath did freese;
   And the dull drops that from his purpled bill°   *nose*
   As from a limbeck° did adown distill.   *alembic*
   In his right hand a tippèd° staffe he held,   *with metal*
   With which his feeble steps he stayèd still:°   *continually*
   For, he was faint with cold, and weak with eld;
That scarse his loosèd limbes he hable was to weld.°   *wield; move*

32

These, marching softly,° thus in order went,   *slowly*
   And after them, the Monthes all riding came;
   First, sturdy° March[8] with brows full sternly bent,   *stern; surly*
   And armèd strongly, rode upon a Ram,
   The same which over Hellespontus swam:[9]
   Yet in his hand a spade he also hent,°   *grasped*
   And in a bag all sorts of seeds ysame,°   *together*
   Which on the earth he strowèd as he went,
And fild her womb with fruitfull hope of nourishment.

---

6. Seen to look well; attractive.
7. A coarse woolen cloth.
8. In the Julian calendar (used in England until 1752), the year began on March 25.
9. A ram, sometimes identified as Jove in one of the many forms he took for purposes of ravishment or seduction, carried Helle through the air. But she fell off into a body of water that has since borne her name: the Hellespont.

33

Next came fresh Aprill full of lustyhed,° — *vigor*
  And wanton as a Kid whose home new buds:
  Upon a Bull he rode, the same which led
  Europa floting through th'Argolick fluds:¹
  His homes were gilden all with golden studs,
  And garnishèd with garlonds goodly dight
  Of all the fairest flowres and freshest buds
  Which th'earth brings forth, and wet he seemed in sight.
With waves, through which he waded for his loves delight.

34

Then came faire May, the fayrest mayd on ground,
  Deckt all with dainties of her seasons pryde,
  And throwing flowres out of her lap around:
  Upon two brethrens shoulders she did ride,
  The twinnes of Leda;² which on eyther side
  Supported her like to their soveraine Queene.
  Lord! how all creatures laught, when her they spide,
  And leapt and daunc't as they had ravisht° beene! — *enraptured*
And Cupid selfe about her fluttred all in greene.

35

And after her, came jolly June, arrayd
  All in greene leaves, as he a Player³ were;
  Yet in his time, he wrought° as well as playd, — *worked*
  That by his plough-yrons° mote right well appeare: — *ploughshares*
  Upon a Crab he rode, that him did beare
  With crooked crawling steps an uncouth pase,
  And backward yode,° as Bargemen° wont to fare — *went / rowers*
  Bending their force contrary to their face,
Like that ungracious crew which faines demurest grace.⁴

36

Then came hot July boyling like to fire,
  That all his garments he had cast away:
  Upon a Lyon raging yet with ire
  He boldly rode and made him to obay:
  It was the beast that whylome did forray° — *ravage*
  The Nemaean forrest, till th'Amphytrionide⁵
  Him slew, and with his hide did him array;
  Behinde his back a sithe,° and by his side — *scythe*
Under his belt he bore a sickle⁶ circling wide.

---

1. The Argolic Gulf of the Aegean Sea. The bull was Jupiter in disguise. He swam with Europa from the ancient Middle Eastern city of Tyre to Crete, off the southern coast of the continent that was supposedly named after her.
2. Castor and Pollux (the zodiacal sign of Gemini). Each month brings its zodiacal sign to the conference.
3. Actor. Actors appearing as wild or savage men were attired in leafy costumes.
4. Like those who, in excessive and false politeness, walk backward as they leave a room.
5. That is, Hercules, whose mother was the wife of King Amphitryon (though his father was Jupiter). Strangling the supernaturally powerful lion that had terrorized the region of Nemea in Greece was the first of Hercules' Twelve Labors.
6. July both mows (with his scythe) and reaps.

37

    The sixth was August, being rich arrayd
      In garment all of gold downe to the ground:
      Yet rode he not, but led a lovely Mayd
      Forth by the lilly hand, the which was cround
      With eares of corne, and full her hand was found;
      That was the righteous Virgin,[7] which of old
      Lived here on earth, and plenty made abound;
      But, after Wrong was loved and Justice solde,
    She left th'unrighteous world and was to heaven extold.°   *raised*

38

    Next him, September marchèd eeke on foote;
      Yet was he heavy laden with the spoyle
      Of harvests riches, which he made his boot,°   *booty*
      And him enrich with bounty of the soyle:
      In his one hand, as fit for harvests toyle,
      He held a knife-hook; and in th'other hand
      A paire of waights, with which he did assoyle°   *determine*
      Both more and lesse, where it in doubt did stand,
    And equall° gave to each as Justice duly scanned.°   *equitably / judged*

39

    Then came October full of merry glee:
      For, yet his noule was totty of the must,[8]
      Which he was treading in the wine-fats see,[9]
      And of the joyous oyle, whose gentle gust°   *taste*
      Made him so frollick and so full of lust:°   *lustiness*
      Upon a dreadful Scorpion he did ride,
      The same which by Dianaes doom° unjust   *judgment*
      Slew great Orion:[1] and eeke by his side
    He had his ploughing share, and coulter[2] ready tyde.

40

    Next was November, he full grosse and fat,
      As fed with lard, and that right well might seeme;
      For, he had been a fatting° hogs of late,   *fattening*
      That yet his browes with sweat, did reek and steem,
      And yet the season was full sharp° and breem;°   *rough / cold*
      In planting eeke he took no small delight:
      Whereon he rode, not easie was to deeme;°   *determine*
      For it a dreadfull Centaure was in sight,
    The seed of Saturne, and faire Naïs, Chiron[3] hight.

---

7. Astraea, the goddess of justice. After leaving earth—in despair—she became the constellation Virgo.
8. That is, his head was unsteady from the new wine.
9. Wine vats' sea.
1. According to one myth Orion boasted that he could kill anything that came from the earth. Indignant at his arrogance Diana sent a scorpion that stung and killed him.
2. The iron blade of a plow, which makes a vertical cut in the soil ahead of the plowshare, which cuts the furrow.
3. He was stellified as the zodiacal sign Sagittarius.

41

And after him, came next the chill December:
   Yet he through merry feasting which he made,
   And great bonfires, did not the cold remember;
   His Saviours birth his mind so much did glad:
   Upon a shaggy-bearded Goat he rade,°   *rode*
   The same wherewith Dan Jove in tender yeares,
   They say, was nourisht by th'Idaean mayd;[4]
   And in his hand a broad deepe boawle he beares;
Of which, he freely drinks an health to all his peeres.

42

Then came old January, wrappèd well
   In many weeds° to keep the cold away;   *clothes*
   Yet did he quake and quiver like to quell,°   *perish*
   And blowe his nayles to warme them if he may:
   For, they were numbd with holding all the day
   An hatchet keene, with which he fellèd wood,
   And from the trees did lop the needlesse spray:°   *twigs*
   Upon an huge great Earth-pot steane[5] he stood;
From whose wide mouth, there flowèd forth the Romane floud.[6]

43

And lastly, came cold February, sitting
   In an old wagon, for he could not ride;
   Drawne of two fishes° for the season fitting,   *Pisces*
   Which through the flood before[7] did softly slyde
   And swim away: yet had he by his side
   His plough and harnesse fit to till the ground,
   And tooles to prune the trees, before the pride°   *splendor*
   Of hasting Prime° did make them burgein° round: *spring / bud*
So past the twelve Months forth, and their dew places found.

44

And after these, there came the Day, and Night,
   Riding together both with equall pase,
   Th'one on a Palfrey° blacke, the other white;   *saddle horse*
   But Night had covered her uncomely face
   With a blacke veile, and held in hand a mace,
   On top whereof the moon and stars were pight,°   *placed*
   And sleep and darknesse round about did trace:°   *go*
   But Day did beare, upon his scepters hight,
The goodly Sun, encompast all with beamès bright.

---

4. The nymph Amalthea, of Mount Ida in Crete. Jove was saved by his mother, Rhea, from being eaten by Cronus, his father. He was brought up in Crete and suckled by a goat identified with the zodiacal sign Capricorn.

5. Urn; here standing for the constellation Aquarius.

6. That is, the Tiber River.

7. That is, the water flowing from Aquarius's urn.

45

Then came the Howres, faire daughters of high Jove,
    And timely[8] Night, the which were all endewed
    With wondrous beauty fit to kindle love;
    But they were Virgins all, and love eschewed,
    That might forslack[9] the charge to them fore-shewed
    By mighty Jove; who did them Porters make
    Of heavens gate (whence all the gods issued)
    Which they did dayly watch, and nightly wake°   *guard*
By even turnes, ne ever did their charge forsake.

46

And after all came Life, and lastly Death;
    Death with most grim and griesly visage seene,
    Yet is he nought but parting of the breath;
    Ne ought to see, but like a shade to weene,°   *conceive*
    Unbodièd, unsouled, unheard, unseene.
    But Life was like a faire young lusty boy,
    Such as they faine Dan Cupid to have beene,
    Full of delightfull health and lively joy,
Deckt all with flowres, and wings of gold fit to employ.

47

When these were past, thus gan the Titanesse:
    "Lo, mighty mother, now be judge and say,
    Whether in all thy creatures more or lesse
    Change doth not raign and beare the greatest sway:
    For, who sees not, that Time on all doth pray?°   *prey*
    But Times do change and move continually.
    So nothing here long standeth in one stay:
    Wherefore, this lower world who can deny
But to be subject still° to Mutabilitie?"   *always*

48

Then thus gan Jove: "Right true it is, that these
    And all things else that under heaven dwell
    Are chaunged of Time, who doth them all disseise°   *deprive*
    Of being: But, who is it (to me tell)
    That Time himselfe doth move and still compell
    To keepe his course? Is not that namely wee
    Which poure that vertue° from our heavenly cell,   *power*
    That moves them all, and makes them changèd be?
So them we gods doe rule, and in them also thee."

---

8. Temporal, belonging to time; in contrast to "high Jove," who is immortal.
9. Cause (them) to neglect.

49

To whom, thus Mutability: "The things
   Which we see not how they are moved and swayd,
   Ye may attribute to your selves as Kings,
   And say they by your secret powre are made:
   But what we see not, who shall us perswade?
   But were they so, as ye them faine to be,
   Moved by your might, and ordred by your ayde;
   Yet what if I can prove, that even yee
Your selves are likewise changed, and subject unto mee?

50

"And first, concerning her that is the first,[1]
   Even you faire Cynthia, whom so much ye make
   Joves dearest darling, she was bred and nurst
   On Cynthus hill,[2] whence she her name did take:
   Then is she mortall borne, how-so° ye crake;°   *howsoever / brag*
   Besides, her face and countenance every day
   We changèd see, and sundry forms partake,
   Now hornd, now round, now bright, now brown° and gray: *dark*
So that 'as changefull as the Moone' men use° to say.   *are accustomed*

51

"Next, Mercury, who though he lesse appeare
   To change his hew, and alwayes seeme as one;
   Yet, he his course doth altar every yeare,
   And is of late far out of order gone:[3]
   So Venus eeke, that goodly Paragone,°   *model of excellence*
   Though faire all night, yet is she darke all day;
   And Phoebus self, who lightsome is alone,°   *alone is radiant*
   Yet is he oft eclipsed by the way,°   *in his course*
And fills the darkned world with terror and dismay.

52

"Now Mars that valiant man is changèd most:
   For, he some times so far runs out of square,
   That he his way doth seem quite to have lost,
   And cleane without° his usuall sphere to fare;   *outside*
   That even these Star-gazers stonisht are
   At sight thereof, and damne their lying bookes:
   So likewise, grim Sir Saturne oft doth spare°   *restrain*
   His sterne aspect,[4] and calme his crabbèd° lookes: *harsh*
So many turning cranks° these have, so many crookes.   *twists*

---

1. The moon is first because its orbit is closest to the earth.
2. Mount Cynthus, on the Greek isle Delos.
3. The actual orbits of Mercury and the other planets were not accurately predictable by the Ptolemaic (earth-centric) astronomical model.
4. Punning on the astrological sense of "aspect" as the relative position of planets, which supposedly affects their influence. Saturn often runs so far out of his course that his generally baleful influence is lessened.

53

"But you Dan Jove, that only constant are,
    And King of all the rest, as ye do clame,
    Are you not subject eeke to this misfare?°   *going astray*
    Then let me aske you this withouten blame,
    Where were ye borne? some say in Crete by name,
    Others in Thebes, and others other-where;
    But wheresoever they comment° the same,   *devise*
    They all consent that ye begotten were,
And borne here in this world, ne other[5] can appeare.

54

"Then are ye mortall borne, and thrall to me,
    Unless the kingdome of the sky yee make°   *claim to be*
    Immortall, and unchangeable to bee;
    Besides, that power and vertue[6] which ye spake,
    That ye here worke, doth many changes take,
    And your owne natures change: for, each of you
    That vertue have, or° this, or that to make,   *either*
    Is checkt and changèd from his nature trew,
By others opposition or obliquid view.[7]

55

"Besides, the sundry motions of your Spheares,[8]
    So sundry waies and fashions as clerkes° faine,   *learned men*
    Some in short space, and some in longer yeares;
    What is the same but alteration plaine?
    Onely the starrie skie[9] doth still remaine:°   *remains constant*
    Yet do the Starres and Signes therein still move,
    And even it self is moved, as wizards saine.°   *wise men say*
    But all that moveth, doth mutation love:
Therefore both you and them to me I subject prove.

56

"Then since within this wide great Universe
    Nothing doth firme and permanent appeare,
    But all things tost and turned by transverse:°   *turned away*
    What then should let,° but I aloft should reare   *hinder*
    My Trophee, and from all, the triumph beare?
    Now judge then (O thou greatest goddesse trew!)
    According as thy selfe doest see and heare,
    And unto me addoom that° is my dew;   *judge that which*
That is the rule of all, all being ruled by you."

---

5. Nor anything else.
6. Power; that is, the paired words are synonymous.
7. Referring to the fundamental idea of astrology: that each planet has a "vertue" (power) that it sheds on earth, but that the effect depends on its position and the position of other planets. "Opposition" and "obliquity" are technical terms for the relative position of celestial bodies. "Obliquid" (found only here) is a coinage from *oblique*, presumably for the sake of the meter.
8. See canto 6, stanza 8, n. 7.
9. The crystalline sphere that bore all the fixed stars, beyond the spheres of the moon, sun, and planets.

57

So having ended, silence long ensewed,
  Ne° Nature to or fro¹ spake for a space,   *nor*
  But with firme eyes affixt, the ground still viewed.
  Meane while, all creatures, looking in her face,
  Expecting° th'end of this so doubtfull case,   *awaiting*
  Did hang in long suspence what would ensew,
  To whether° side should fall the soveraigne place: *which*
  At length, she looking up with chearefull view,
The silence brake, and gave her doome in speeches° few.   *phrases*

58

"I well consider all that ye have sayd,
  And find that all things steadfastnes doe hate
  And changèd be: yet being rightly wayd°   *weighed*
  They are not changèd from their first estate;°   *state, condition*
  But by their change their being doe dilate:²
  And turning to themselves at length againe,
  Doe worke their owne perfection so by fate:
  Then over them Change doth not rule and raigne;
But they raigne over change, and doe their states maintaine.

59

"Cease therefore daughter further to aspire,
  And thee content thus to be ruled by me:
  For thy decay° thou seekst by thy desire;   *downfall*
  But time shall come that all shall changèd bee,
  And from thenceforth, none no more change shall see."³
  So was the Titaness put downe and whist,°   *silenced*
  And Jove confirmed in his imperiall see.°   *throne*
  Then was that whole assembly quite dismist,
And Natur's selfe did vanish, whither no man wist.°   *knew*

The 8 Canto, unperfite.°   *unfinished*

1

When I bethinke me on that speech whyleare,°   *earlier*
  Of Mutability, and well it way:°   *weigh, consider*
  Me seemes, that though she all unworthy were
  Of the Heav'ns Rule; yet very sooth to say,
  In all things else she beares the greatest sway.
  Which makes me loath this state of life so tickle,°   *uncertain; changeable*
  And love of things so vaine to cast away;
  Whose flowring pride, so fading and so fickle,
Short Time shall soon cut down with his consuming sickle.

---

1. For or against.
2. Expand, as they fulfill their natures.
3. Compare 1 Corinthians 15:51, 54: "we shall all be changed. . . . when this corruptible shall have put on incorruption, and this mortal shall have put on immortality, then shall be brought to pass the saying that is written, Death is swallowed up in victory."

2

Then gin° I thinke on that which Nature sayd, — *begin*
  Of that same time when no more Change shall be,
  But stedfast rest of all things firmely stayd
  Upon the pillours of Eternity,
That is contrayr to° Mutabilitie: — *the opposite of*
  For, all that moveth, doth in Change delight:
  But thence-forth all shall rest eternally
  With Him that is the God of Sabbaoth hight:
O that great Sabbaoth God, graunt me that Sabaoths sight.[4]

1609

From Amoretti

1

Happy ye leaves[1] when as those lilly hands,
  Which hold my life in their dead doing° might, — *killing*
  Shall handle you and hold in loves soft bands,° — *bonds*
  Lyke captives trembling at the victors sight.
5 And happy lines, on which with starry light,
  Those lamping° eyes will deigne sometimes to look — *flashing*
  And reade the sorrowes of my dying spright,° — *spirit*
  Written with teares in harts close° bleeding book. — *secret*
And happy rymes bath'd in the sacred brooke
10 Of Helicon[2] whence she derivèd is,
  When ye behold that Angels blessèd looke,
  My soules long lackèd foode, my heavens blis.
Leaves, lines, and rymes, seeke her to please alone,
  Whom if ye please, I care for other none.

34[3]

Lyke as a ship that through the Ocean wyde,
  By conduct of some star doth make her way,
  Whenas a storme hath dimd her trusty guyde,
  Out of her course doth wander far astray:
5 So I whose star, that wont° with her bright ray — *was accustomed*
  Me to direct, with cloudes is overcast,
  Doe wander now in darknesse and dismay,
  Through hidden perils round about me plast.° — *placed*
Yet hope I well, that when this storme is past

---

4. Spenser here confuses, perhaps intentionally, the Hebrew word for "armies, hosts" (*Sabaoth*) with that for "rest" (*Sabbath*).
1. That is, of the book: pages.
2. The "sacred brooke" is Hippocrene, which flows from Mount Helicon, the mountain sacred to the Muses.
3. An adaptation of Petrarch's Rima 189. See p. 125 for Sir Thomas Wyatt's verse translation of the sonnet, as well as a modern prose translation of it.

     My Helice[4] the lodestar° of my lyfe   *guiding star*
        Will shine again, and looke on me at last,
        With lovely light to cleare my cloudy grief.
     Till then I wander carefull° comfortlesse,   *full of cares*
        In secret sorow and sad pensivenesse.

37

     What guyle is this, that those her golden tresses,
        She doth attyre under a net of gold:
     And with sly° skill so cunningly them dresses,   *clever*
        That which is gold or heare,° may scarse be told?   *hair*
5   Is it that mens frayle eyes, which gaze too bold,
        She may entangle in that golden snare:
        And being caught may craftily enfold
        Theyr weaker harts, which are not wel aware?°   *wary*
     Take heed therefore, myne eyes, how ye doe stare
10   Henceforth too rashly on that guilefull net,
        In which if ever ye entrappèd are,
        Out of her bands ye by no means shall get.
     Fondnesse° it were for any being free,   *foolishness*
        To covet fetters, though they golden bee.

54

     Of this worlds Theatre in which we stay,
        My love like the Spectator ydly sits
     Beholding me that all the pageants° play,   *dramatic scenes*
        Disguysing diversly my troubled wits.
5   Sometimes I joy when glad occasion fits,
        And mask in myrth lyke to a Comedy:
        Soone after when my joy to sorrow flits,
        I waile and make my woes a Tragedy.
     Yet she beholding me with constant° eye,   *unmoved*
10   Delights not in my merth nor rues my smart:°   *pities my hurt*
        But when I laugh she mocks, and when I cry
        She laughes and hardens evermore her hart.
     What then can move her? if nor merth nor mone,°   *moan*
        She is no woman, but a sencelesse stone.

64[5]

     Comming to kisse her lyps (such grace I found)
        Me seemd I smelt a gardin of sweet flowres
     That dainty odours from them threw around,
        For damzels fit to decke their lovers bowres.
5   Her lips did smell lyke unto Gillyflowers,°   *carnations*
        Her ruddy cheeks lyke unto Roses red;

---

4. A name for the Big Dipper (after the nymph who, in classical mythology, was transformed into it).

5. Much of the imagery of this sonnet is imitated from the Song of Solomon 4:10–16.

      Her snowy browes lyke budded Bellamoures,[6]
        Her lovely eyes like Pincks but newly spred,
  Her goodly bosome lyke a Strawberry bed,
10   Her neck lyke to a bounch of Cullambynes;
        Her brest lyke lillyes, ere theyr leaves be shed,
      Her nipples lyke yong blossomd Jessemynes.°   *jasmines*
Such fragrant flowres doe give most odorous smell,
  But her sweet odour did them all excell.

67[7]

Lyke as a huntsman after weary chace,
  Seeing the game from him escapt away,
  Sits downe to rest him in some shady place,
  With panting hounds beguilèd° of their pray: *deluded*
5 So after long pursuit and vaine assay,°   *attempt*
  When I all weary had the chace forsooke,
  The gentle deare returnd the selfe-same way,
  Thinking to quench her thirst at the next° brooke.   *nearby*
There she beholding me with mylder looke,
10 Sought not to fly, but fearelesse still did bide:
  Till I in hand her yet halfe trembling tooke,
  And with her owne goodwill hir fyrmely tyde.
Strange thing me seemd to see a beast so wyld,
  So goodly wonne with her owne will beguyld.[8]

75

One day I wrote her name upon the strand,°   *shore*
  But came the waves and washèd it away:
  Agayne I wrote it with a second hand,
  But came the tyde, and made my paynes his pray.°   *prey*
5 "Vayne man," sayd she, "that doest in vaine assay,°   *attempt*
  A mortall thing so to immortalize,
  For I my selve shall lyke to this decay,
  And eek° my name bee wypèd out lykewize."   *also*
"Not so," quod° I, "let baser things devize°   *said / contrive*
10 To dy in dust, but you shall live by fame:
  My verse your vertues rare shall eternize,
  And in the heavens wryte your glorious name.
Where whenas death shall all the world subdew,
  Our love shall live, and later life renew."

---

6. Unidentified flower, evidently white.
7. An imitation of Petrarch's Rima 190, but with a very different ending. Compare Sir Thomas Wyatt's adaptation ("Whoso List to Hunt") of the same sonnet, and the prose translation of the Petrarchan original appended to it, on p. 123.
8. Entrapped; won over.

79

    Men call you fayre, and you doe credit° it,   *believe*
      For that your selfe ye dayly such doe see:
        But the trew fayre,° that is the gentle wit,°   *beauty / intelligence*
        And vertuous mind, is much more praysd of° me.   *by*
5   For all the rest, how ever fayre it be,
      Shall turne to nought and loose that glorious hew:°   *form*
      But onely that is permanent and free
        From frayle corruption, that doth flesh ensew.°   *outlast*
    That is true beautie: that doth argue° you   *prove*
10   To be divine and borne of heavenly seed:
      Deriv'd from that fayre Spirit,° from whom al true   *God*
      And perfect beauty did at first proceed.
    He onely fayre, and what he fayre hath made:
    All other fayre, lyke flowres, untymely fade.

                                                                     1595

Epithalamion

    Ye learnèd sisters° which have oftentimes   *the Muses*
    Beene to me ayding, others to adorne:[1]
    Whom ye thought worthy of your gracefull rymes,
    That even the greatest did not greatly scorne
5   To heare theyr names sung in your simple layes,°   *songs*
    But joyèd in theyr prayse.
    And when ye list° your owne mishaps to mourne,   *chose*
    Which death, or love, or fortunes wreck did rayse,
    Your string could soone to sadder tenor° turne,   *mood*
10   And teach the woods and waters to lament
    Your dolefull dreriment.°   *sorrow*
    Now lay those sorrowfull complaints aside,
    And having all your heads with girland crownd,
    Helpe me mine owne loves prayses to resound,
15   Ne° let the same of° any be envide: *nor / by*
    So Orpheus did for his owne bride,[2]
    So I unto my selfe alone will sing,
    The woods shall to me answer and my eccho ring.

    Early before the worlds light giving lampe,
20   His golden beame upon the hils doth spred,
    Having disperst the nights unchearefull dampe,
    Doe ye awake, and with fresh lustyhed°   *vigor*
    Go to the bowre° of my belovèd love,   *bedchamber*
    My truest turtle dove,

---

1. To write poems in praise of others.
2. Orpheus, archetype of the poet in classical antiquity, was famous for his love for his wife, Eurydice.

25	Bid her awake; for Hymen³ is awake,	
	And long since ready forth his maske to move,	
	With his bright Tead⁴ that flames with many a flake,°	spark
	And many a bachelor to waite on him,	
	In theyr fresh garments trim.	
30	Bid her awake therefore and soone her dight,°	dress
	For lo the wishèd day is come at last,	
	That shall for al the paynes and sorrowes past,	
	Pay to her usury° of long delight:	interest
	And whylest she doth her dight,	
35	Doe ye to her of joy and solace° sing,	pleasure
	That all the woods may answer and your Eccho ring.	

Bring with you all the Nymphes that you can heare°   *can hear you*
Both of the rivers and the forrests greene:
And of the sea that neighbours to her neare,
40 Al with gay girlands goodly wel beseene.°   *beautified*
And let them also with them bring in hand,
Another gay girland
For my fayre love of lillyes and of roses,
Bound truelove wize° with a blew silke riband.   *in a love knot*
45 And let them make great store° of bridale poses,°   *abundance / posies*
And let them eeke° bring store of other flowers   *also*
To deck the bridale bowers.
And let the ground whereas° her foot shall tread,   *where*
For feare the stones her tender foot should wrong
50 Be strewed with fragrant flowers all along,
And diapred lyke the discolorèd mead.⁵
Which done, doe at her chamber dore awayt,
For she will waken strayt,°   *straightaway*
The whiles doe ye this song unto her sing,
55 The woods shall to you answer and your Eccho ring.

Ye Nymphes of Mulla⁶ which with careful heed,
The silver scaly trouts doe tend full well,
And greedy pikes which use° therein to feed,   *are accustomed*
(Those trouts and pikes all others doo excell)
60 And ye likewise which keepe the rushy lake,°   *bordered by rushes*
Where none doo fishes take,
Bynd up the locks the which hang scatterd light,
And in his waters which your mirror make,
Behold your faces as the christall bright,
65 That when you come whereas° my love doth lie,   *where*
No blemish she may spie.
And eke ye lightfoot mayds which keepe the deere,⁷
That on the hoary° mountayne use to towre,⁸   *gray; venerable*

---

3. The god of marriage, who leads a "maske" or procession at weddings.
4. A ceremonial torch, associated with marriages since classical times.
5. Ornamented like the many-colored meadow.
6. A river near Spenser's home in Ireland.
7. All wild animals, kept by the woodland nymphs.
8. A falconry term meaning to occupy heights.

And the wylde wolves which seeke them to devoure,
70 With your steele darts° doo chace from comming neer,   *spears*
Be also present heere,
To helpe to decke her and to help to sing,
That all the woods may answer and your eccho ring.

Wake now my love, awake; for it is time,
75 The Rosy Morne long since left Tithones bed,[9]
All ready to her silver coche° to clyme,   *coach*
And Phoebus° gins° to shew his glorious hed.   *the sun god / begins*
Hark how the cheerefull birds do chaunt theyr laies
And carroll of loves praise.
80 The merry Larke hir mattins° sings aloft,   *morning prayers*
The thrush replyes, the Mavis descant[1] playes,
The Ouzell shrills, the Ruddock[2] warbles soft,
So goodly all agree with sweet consent,°   *harmony*
To this dayes merriment.
85 Ah my deere love why doe ye sleepe thus long,
When meeter° were that ye should now awake,   *more fitting*
T'awayt the comming of your joyous make,°   *mate*
And hearken to the birds lovelearnèd song,
The deawy leaves among.
90 For they of joy and pleasance to you sing,
That all the woods them answer and theyr eccho ring.

My love is now awake out of her dreame,
And her fayre eyes like stars that dimmèd were
With darksome cloud, now shew° theyr goodly beams   *show*
95 More bright then° Hesperus° his head doth rere.   *than / evening star*
Come now ye damzels, daughters of delight,
Helpe quickly her to dight,°   *attire*
But first come ye fayre houres[3] which were begot
In Joves sweet paradice, of Day and Night,
100 Which doe the seasons of the yeare allot,
And al that ever in this world is fayre
Doe make and still° repayre.   *continuously*
And ye three handmayds of the Cyprian Queene,[4]
The which doe still adorne her beauties pride,
105 Helpe to addorne my beautifullest bride:
And as ye her array, still throw betweene°   *at intervals*
Some graces to be seene,
And as ye use° to Venus, to her sing,   *are accustomed*
The whiles the woods shal answer and your eccho ring.

---

9. See Song of Solomon 2:10–13: "Rise up, my love, my fair one, and come away. For, lo, the winter is past, the rain is over and gone; The flowers appear on the earth; the time of the singing of birds is come." In classical myth, Tithonus is the aged husband of Aurora, the dawn.
1. A melody or counterpoint written above a musical theme—a soprano obbligato. "Mavis": the song thrush.
2. The European robin. "Ouzell": the blackbird (which sings in England). The birds' concert is a convention of medieval love poetry.
3. The Hours, or Horae, are Olympian deities who attend to natural growth and to social order. They were traditionally the daughters of Jove and the Titaness Themis, but in the Mutabilitie Cantos of *The Faerie Queene* (above), Spenser says Jove fathered them on Night.
4. Venus. "Three handmayds": the Graces, representing brightness, joy, and abundance.

  Now is my love all ready forth to come,   110
  Let all the virgins therefore well awayt,
  And ye fresh boyes that tend upon her groome
  Prepare your selves; for he is comming strayt.°   *straightaway*
  Set all your things in seemely good aray°   *order*
  Fit for so joyfull day,   115
  The joyfulst day that ever sunne did see.
  Faire Sun, shew forth thy favourable ray,
  And let thy lifull° heat not fervent° be   *life-giving / hot*
  For feare of burning her sunshyny face,
  Her beauty to disgrace.°   120   *mar*
  O fayrest Phoebus, father of the Muse,[5]
  If ever I did honour thee aright,
  Or sing the thing, that mote° thy mind delight,   *might*
  Doe not thy servants simple boone° refuse,   *request*
  But let this day let this one day be myne,   125
  Let all the rest be thine.
  Then I thy soverayne prayses loud wil sing,
  That all the woods shal answer and theyr eccho ring.

  Harke how the Minstrels gin to shrill aloud
  Their merry Musick that resounds from far,   130
  The pipe, the tabor,° and the trembling Croud,[6]   *small drum*
  That well agree withouten breach or jar.°   *discord*
  But most of all the Damzels doe delite,
  When they their tymbrels° smyte,   *tambourines*
  And thereunto doe daunce and carrol sweet,   135
  That all the sences they doe ravish quite,
  The whyles the boyes run up and downe the street,
  Crying aloud with strong confusèd noyce,
  As if it were one voyce.
  Hymen[7] *iô Hymen, Hymen* they do shout,   140
  That even to the heavens theyr shouting shrill
  Doth reach, and all the firmament doth fill,
  To which the people standing all about,
  As in approvance doe thereto applaud
  And loud advaunce her laud,°   145   *praise*
  And evermore they *Hymen Hymen* sing,
  That all the woods them answer and theyr eccho ring.

  Loe where she comes along with portly° pace,   *stately*
  Lyke Phoebe from her chamber of the East,
  Arysing forth to run her mighty race,[8]   150
  Clad all in white, that seemes° a virgin best.   *beseems, suits*
  So well it her beseems that ye would weene°   *think*
  Some angell she had beene.

---

5. Phoebus Apollo, god of the sun, was also god of music and poetry, but he was not normally regarded as the father of the Nine Muses (Zeus was).
6. Primitive fiddle. Spenser here designates Irish, not classical, instruments and music for the classical masque or ballet.
7. The name of the classical god of marriage, used as a conventional exclamation at weddings in ancient Greece.
8. Phoebe is the moon, a virgin like the bride; the reference to her anticipates the night.

>   Her long loose yellow locks lyke golden wyre,
> 155 Sprinckled with perle, and perling flowres a tweene,⁹
>   Doe lyke a golden mantle her attyre,
>   And being crownèd with a girland greene,
>   Seeme lyke some mayden Queene.
>   Her modest eyes abashèd to behold
> 160 So many gazers, as on her do stare,
>   Upon the lowly ground affixèd are.
>   Ne dare lift up her countenance too bold,
>   But blush to heare her prayses sung so loud,
>   So farre from being proud.
> 165 Nathlesse doe ye still loud her prayses sing,
>   That all the woods may answer and your eccho ring.
>
>   Tell me ye merchants daughters did ye see
>   So fayre a creature in your towne before,
>   So sweet, so lovely, and so mild as she,
> 170 Adornd with beautyes grace and vertues store,°   *abundance*
>   Her goodly eyes lyke Saphyres shining bright,
>   Her forehead yvory white,
>   Her cheekes lyke apples which the sun hath rudded,°   *made red*
>   Her lips lyke cherryes charming men to byte,
> 175 Her brest like to a bowle of creame uncrudded,°   *uncurdled*
>   Her paps° lyke lyllies budded,   *breasts*
>   Her snowie necke lyke to a marble towre,
>   And all her body like a pallace fayre,
>   Ascending uppe with many a stately stayre,
> 180 To honors seat and chastities sweet bowre.¹
>   Why stand ye still ye virgins in amaze,
>   Upon her so to gaze,
>   Whiles ye forget your former lay to sing,
>   To which the woods did answer and your eccho ring.
>
> 185 But if ye saw that which no eyes can see,
>   The inward beauty of her lively spright,°   *living spirit, soul*
>   Garnisht with heavenly guifts of high degree,
>   Much more then would ye wonder at that sight,
>   And stand astonisht lyke to those which red°   *saw*
> 190 Medusaes mazeful hed.²
>   There dwels sweet love and constant chastity,
>   Unspotted fayth° and comely womanhood,   *fidelity*
>   Regard of honour and mild modesty,
>   There vertue raynes as Queene in royal throne,
> 195 And giveth lawes alone.
>   The which the base° affections doe obay,   *lower*
>   And yeeld theyr services unto her will,
>   Ne thought of thing uncomely ever may

---

9. Between. "Perling": winding.
1. The head, where the higher faculties are. The catalog of qualities is a convention in love poetry (compare Song of Solomon 4–8).
2. Medusa, one of the Gorgons, had serpents instead of hair (hence a "mazeful hed"): to stone.

Thereto approch to tempt her mind to ill.
200 Had ye once seene these her celestial threasures,
And unrevealèd pleasures,
Then would ye wonder and her prayses sing,
That all the woods should answer and your Echo ring.

Open the temple gates unto my love,
205 Open them wide that she may enter in,[3]
And all the postes adorne as doth behove,[4]
And all the pillours deck with girlands trim,
For to recyve this Saynt with honour dew,
That commeth in to you.
210 With trembling steps and humble reverence,
She commeth in, before th'almighties vew,
Of her ye virgins learne obedience,
When so ye come into those holy places,
To humble your proud faces:
215 Bring her up to th'high altar, that she may
The sacred ceremonies there partake,
The which do endless matrimony make,
And let the roring° Organs loudly play   *resounding*
The praises of the Lord in lively notes,
220 The whiles with hollow° throates   *fully open*
The Choristers the joyous Antheme sing,
That all the woods may answere and theyr eccho ring.

Behold whiles she before the altar stands
Hearing the holy priest that to her speakes
225 And blesseth her with his two happy hands,
How the red roses flush up in her cheekes,
And the pure snow with goodly vermill° stayne,   *vermilion*
Like crimsin dyde in grayne,°   *fast color*
That even th'Angels which continually,
230 About the sacred Altare doe remaine,
Forget their service and about her fly,
Ofte peeping in her face that seemes more fayre,
The more they on it stare.
But her sad° eyes still° fastened on the ground,   *serious / ever*
235 Are governèd with goodly modesty,
That suffers° not one looke to glaunce awry,   *permits*
Which may let in a little thought unsownd.°   *flawed*
Why blush ye love to give to me your hand,
The pledge of all our band?°   *bond, tie*
240 Sing ye sweet Angels, Alleluya sing,
That all the woods may answere and your eccho ring.

Now al is done; bring home the bride againe,
Bring home the triumph of our victory,

---

3. See Psalms 24:7: "Lift up your heads, O ye gates; and be ye lift up, ye everlasting doors; and the King of glory shall come in."

4. As is proper. The doorposts were trimmed for weddings in classical times, and the custom was often referred to in classical and later love poetry.

   Bring home with you the glory of her gaine,[5]
245 With joyance bring her and with jollity.
   Never had man more joyfull day then this,
   Whom heaven would heape with blis.
   Make feast therefore now all this live long day,
   This day for ever to me holy is,
250 Poure out the wine without restraint or stay,°   *limit*
   Poure not by cups, but by the belly° full,   *wineskin*
   Poure out to all that wull,°   *want it*
   And sprinkle all the postes and wals with wine,
   That they may sweat, and drunken be withall.
255 Crowne ye God Bacchus° with a coronall,°   *god of wine / garland*
   And Hymen also crowne with wreathes of vine,
   And let the Graces daunce unto the rest;
   For they can doo it best:
   The whiles the maydens doe theyr carroll sing,
260 To which the woods shall answer and theyr eccho ring.

   Ring ye the bels, ye young men of the towne,
   And leave your wonted° labors for this day: *usual*
   This day is holy; doe ye write it downe,
   That ye for ever it remember may.
265 This day the sunne is in his chiefest hight,
   With Barnaby the bright,[6]
   From whence declining daily by degrees,
   He somewhat loseth of his heat and light,
   When once the Crab[7] behind his back he sees.
270 But for this time it ill ordainèd was,
   To chose the longest day in all the yeare,
   And shortest night, when longest fitter weare:
   Yet never day so long, but late° would passe.   *at last*
   Ring ye the bels, to make it weare away,
275 And bonefiers° make all day,   *bonfires*
   And daunce about them, and about them sing:
   That all the woods may answer, and your eccho ring.

   Ah when will this long weary day have end,
   And lende me leave to come unto my love?
280 How slowly do the houres theyr numbers[8] spend?
   How slowly does sad Time his feathers move?[9]
   Hast° thee O fayrest Planet to thy home   *haste*
   Within the Westerne fome:
   Thy tyred steedes long since have need of rest.[1]
285 Long though it be, at last I see it gloome,°   *begin to darken*
   And the bright evening star with golden creast°   *crest*
   Appeare out of the East.

---

5. That is, the glory of gaining her.
6. Saint Barnabas's Day, at the time of the summer solstice.
7. The constellation Cancer between Gemini and Leo. The sun, passing through the zodiac, leaves the Crab behind toward the end of July.
8. That is, the number of minutes or the numbers depicted on a clock.
9. In traditional iconography, Time is winged.
1. The sun's chariot completes its daily course in the western sea ("fome").

> Fayre childe of beauty, glorious lampe of love
> That all the host of heaven in rankes doost lead,
> And guydest lovers through the nightès dread,   [290]
> How chearefully thou lookest from above,
> And seemst to laugh atweene thy twinkling light
> As joying in the sight
> Of these glad many which for joy doe sing,
> That all the woods them answer and theyr echo ring.   [295]
>
> Now ceasse ye damsels your delights forepast;°   *previous*
> Enough is it, that all the day was youres:
> Now day is doen, and night is nighing° fast: *approaching*
> Now bring the Bryde into the brydall boures.
> Now night is come, now soone her disaray,°   *undress*   [300]
> And in her bed her lay;
> Lay her in lillies and in violets,
> And silken courteins over her display,°   *spread*
> And odourd° sheetes, and Arras° coverlets.   *perfumed / tapestry*
> Behold how goodly my faire love does ly   [305]
> In proud humility;
> Like unto Maia,[2] when as Jove her tooke,
> In Tempe,[3] lying on the flowry gras,
> Twixt sleepe and wake, after she weary was,
> With bathing in the Acidalian brooke.[4]   [310]
> Now it is night, ye damsels may be gon,
> And leave my love alone,
> And leave° likewise your former lay to sing: *cease*
> The woods no more shall answere, nor your echo ring.
>
> Now welcome night, thou night so long expected,   [315]
> That long daies labour doest at last defray,°   *pay for*
> And all my cares, which cruell love collected,
> Hast sumd° in one, and cancellèd[5] for aye:°   *combined / forever*
> Spread thy broad wing over my love and me,
> That no man may us see,   [320]
> And in thy sable° mantle us enwrap,   *black*
> From feare of perrill and foule horror free.
> Let no false treason seeke us to entrap,
> Nor any dread disquiet once annoy°   *interfere with*
> The safety of our joy: [325]
> But let the night be calme and quietsome,
> Without tempestuous storms or sad afray:°   *fear*
> Lyke as when Jove with fayre Alcmena[6] lay,
> When he begot the great Tirynthian groome:
> Or lyke as when he with thy selfe[7] did lie,   [330]

---

2. The eldest and most beautiful of the seven daughters of Atlas. (They were stellified as the Pleiades.) Jove fathered Mercury on her.
3. *The Vale of Tempe* in Thessaly (not, however, traditionally the site of Jove's encounter with Maia).
4. Associated with Venus.
5. Annulled or rendered void (as with a debt); compensated for.
6. The mother of Hercules ("the great Tirynthian groome"). Jove made that first night last as long as three.
7. Night. This is Spenser's own myth.

And begot Majesty.
And let the mayds and yongmen cease to sing:
Ne let the woods them answer, nor theyr Eccho ring.

Let no lamenting cryes, nor dolefull teares,
335 Be heard all night within nor yet without:
Ne let false whispers, breeding hidden feares,
Breake gentle sleepe with misconceivèd dout.°   *groundless fear*
Let no deluding dreames, nor dreadful sights
Make sudden sad affrights;
340 Ne let housefyres, nor lightnings helpelesse° harmes,   *without remedy*
Ne let the Pouke,[8] nor other evill sprights,
Ne let mischivous witches with theyr charmes,
Ne let hob Goblins, names whose sence we see not,
Fray° us with things that be not.   *terrify*
345 Let not the shriech Oule, nor the Storke be heard:
Nor the night Raven that still° deadly yels,[9]   *always*
Nor damnèd ghosts cald up with mighty spels,
Nor griesly° vultures make us once affeard: *horrid*
Ne let th'unpleasant Quyre of Frogs still croking
350 Make us to wish theyr choking.
Let none of these theyr drery accents sing;
Ne let the woods them answer, nor theyr eccho ring.

But let stil Silence trew night watches keepe,
That sacred peace may in assurance rayne,
355 And tymely Sleep, when it is tyme to sleepe,
May poure his limbs forth on your pleasant playne,
The whiles an hundred little wingèd loves,°   *cupids (or amoretti)*
Like divers fethered doves,
Shall fly and flutter round about your bed,
360 And in the secret darke, that none reproves,
Their prety stealthes shal worke, and snares shal spread
To filch away sweet snatches of delight,
Conceald through covert night.
Ye sonnes of Venus, play your sports at will,
365 For greedy pleasure, carelesse of your toyes,°   *amorous dallying*
Thinks more upon her paradise of joyes,
Then° what ye do, albe it° good or ill.   *than / albeit, although*
All night therefore attend your merry play,
For it will soone be day:
370 Now none doth hinder you, that say or sing,
Ne will the woods now answer, nor your Eccho ring.

Who is the same, which at my window peepes?
Or whose is that faire face, that shines so bright,
Is it not Cinthia,[1] she that never sleepes,

---

8. Puck, Robin Goodfellow—here more powerful and evil than Shakespeare made him in *A Midsummer Night's Dream*.
9. The owl and the night raven were birds of ill omen. The stork, in Chaucer's *Parliament of Fowls*, is called an avenger of adultery.
1. Cynthia (or Diana) is goddess of the moon.

But walkes about high heaven al the night? 375
O fayrest goddesse, do thou not envy
My love with me to spy:
For thou likewise didst love, though now unthought,°   *not thought of*
And for a fleece of woll,° which privily,   *wool*
The Latmian shepherd[2] once unto thee brought, 380
His pleasures with thee wrought.
Therefore to us be favorable now;
And sith° of wemens labours thou hast charge,[3]   *since*
And generation goodly dost enlarge,
Encline thy will t'effect our wishfull vow, 385
And the chast wombe informe° with timely seed,   *give life to*
That may our comfort breed:
Till which we cease our hopefull hap° to sing,   *fortune we hope for*
Ne let the woods us answer, nor our Eccho ring.

And thou great Juno, which with awful° might 390   *awesome*
The lawes of wedlock still dost patronize,°   *watch over*
And the religion° of the faith first plight°   *sanctity / pledged*
With sacred rites hast taught to solemnize:
And eeke° for comfort often callèd art   *also*
Of women in their smart,° 395   *(labor) pains*
Eternally bind thou this lovely band,°   *bond*
And all thy blessings unto us impart.
And thou glad Genius,[4] in whose gentle hand,
The bridale bowre and geniall bed remaine,
Without blemish or staine, 400
And the sweet pleasures of theyr loves delight
With secret ayde doest succour° and supply,   *help*
Till they bring forth the fruitfull progeny,
Send us the timely fruit of this same night.
And thou fayre Hebe,[5] and thou Hymen free, 405
Grant that it may so be.
Til which we cease your further prayse to sing,
Ne any woods shall answer, nor your Eccho ring.

And ye high heavens, the temple of the gods,
In which a thousand torches flaming bright 410
Doe burne, that to us wretched earthly clods,
In dreadful darknesse lend desirèd light;
And all ye powers which in the same remayne,
More then we men can fayne,°   *imagine*
Poure out your blessing on us plentiously, 415
And happy influence upon us raine,
That we may raise a large posterity,

---

2. Endymion, beloved of the moon. The "fleece of woll," however, comes from another story—that of Pan's enticement of the moon.
3. Diana is, as Lucina, patroness of births. The "labours" are, of course, those of childbirth.
4. God of generation and birth. "Geniall": a puns on his name having both the usual sense and the sense of *generative*.
5. Goddess of youth and freedom.

                Which from the earth, which they may long possesse,
                With lasting happinesse,
420   Up to your haughty° pallaces may mount,   lofty
                And for the guerdon° of theyr glorious merit   reward
                May heavenly tabernacles there inherit,
                Of blessèd Saints for to increase the count.
                So let us rest, sweet love, in hope of this,
425   And cease till then our tymely joyes to sing,
                The woods no more us answer, nor our eccho ring.

                Song made in lieu of many ornaments,
                With which my love should duly have bene dect,°   adorned
                Which cutting off through hasty accidents,
430   Ye would not stay your dew time to expect,°   await
                But promist both to recompens,
                Be unto her a goodly ornament,
                And for short time an endlesse moniment.[6]

                                                                           1595

---

6. The envoy (brief final stanza addressed to the poem itself) is traditionally apologetic in tone: the poem is offered as a substitute for presents ("ornaments") that did not arrive in time for the wedding. But this elaborate poem is itself a "goodly ornament," for it stands as a timeless monument of art to the passing day that it celebrates.

Commonplace Book

Many of the authors in this volume—including, famously, Elizabeth I—recorded their writings, and those of other people, in "commonplace books." These were personal anthologies, written out and organized by their compilers under subject headings (or "places," in the sense of the Greek *topoi*, or "topics"). Essentially handwritten scrapbooks, commonplace books combined favorite passages, revered bits of text, and observations needing further thought; they at once provided an account and a summary of their owners' reading, a handy guide for conversation, and a template for imitation. As commonplace books were generally written in one hand, they gave a sameness and unity to vastly different material, which might have its source in printed texts, manuscripts, and sometimes oral exchanges. And compilers often further personalized the snippets they had chosen to record by adding their own words to them or making other changes. That is why the "same" texts preserved in more than one commonplace book often differ. Thus several selections in the commonplace book here—including Sir John Harington's "A Certain Man," Marlowe's "The Passionate Shepherd to His Love," and Robert Wisdome's "A Religious Use of Taking Tobacco"—exist in variant forms, which may be explained by authorial revision or by the commonplace book culture. Commonplace books make it hard to know what the "real author" or the "real text" is and, indeed, whether those are the correct questions to ask.

Though Erasmus had set down rules for possessing and organizing commonplace books, which he thought essential to the education of the humanist, surviving commonplace books seldom have educational improvement as their (only) goal. Some are funny, some bawdy, some practical, and some mixtures of all of these. What follows, a commonplace book compiled by the Norton anthology editors from a range of early modern sources, reflects the mingled seriousness and humor typical of many commonplace books: it shows writers of the period being frank, annoyed, and humorous as well as decorous and pastoral. The headings chosen, too, are editorial, and are arranged in alphabetical order, and it will be clear that several poems could easily have been slotted into other "places" and put into dialogue with other texts.

Of the poems and prose in this section, some are sourced from commonplace books of the time; others are taken from print or manuscript texts regularly quoted in commonplace books; and still others have been commonplaced by the Norton editors. As sixteenth-century commonplace books ranged over oral, sung, and written texts, so this commonplace book includes all three types, setting the voices of the literate by those of the illiterate (who often recorded their thoughts in popular song), working men and women by courtiers, the young by the old, the ill by the well, and the successful by the unsuccessful. As often happens in commonplace books, some of the texts here are anonymous, meaning that the sex, race, and age of their writers cannot always be determined. As with any commonplace book, this one contains texts that are not easily datable, so some may not fit exactly into the period of this volume.

Commonplace books reveal as well as dictate the active way in which individuals read in the period: they show how some readers were "collectors," searching texts for discrete passages to add to their compilations. Some of the extraordinary literary exuberance included in this volume—the rhymes, the puns, the conceits, the sententiae, the proverbial wisdom, the euphuisms—may have been written to be excerpted: written, that is to say, with commonplace books and their construction in mind.

AGING

George Gascoigne   The son of a respectable country gentleman, Gascoigne (1534/5–1577) lived a turbulent life. Having squandered his inheritance in an attempt to establish himself at court, he failed both as a lawyer and as a soldier and was constantly in search of occupation and patronage. As part of this search, his writing, which included courtly entertainments, plays, literary criticism, moral tracts, a hunting treatise, military reportage, and a brilliant work of prose fiction as well as many poems, won him considerable esteem. But the esteem was not unmixed—some of his work was criticized as obscene—and Gascoigne seems to have died, as he lived, in financial straits. In this grown-up lullaby, the aging Gascoigne sings farewell to his youth and sexual energy—or does he?

The Lullaby of a Lover

    Sing lullaby, as women do,
    Wherewith they bring their babes to rest,
    And lullaby can I sing too,
    As womanly as can the best.
 5 With lullaby they still the child,
    And if I be not much beguiled,°   deceived
    Full many wanton° babes have I,   unruly (but with sexual overtones)
    Which must be stilled with lullaby.

    First, lullaby my youthful years,
10 It is now time to go to bed,
    For crooked age and hoary hairs
    Have won the haven° within my head.   come to harbor
    With lullaby then, youth, be still,
    With lullaby content thy will,¹
15 Since courage quails and comes behind,
    Go sleep, and so beguile thy mind.

    Next, lullaby my gazing eyes,
    Which wonted were° to glance apace:° were accustomed / unhesitatingly
    For every glass° may now suffice   mirror
20 To show the furrows in my face.
    With lullaby then wink° awhile,   close your eyes
    With lullaby your looks beguile.
    Let no fair face nor beauty bright
    Entice you eft° with vain delight.   again

25 And lullaby my wanton will,
    Let reason's rule now rein thy thought,

---

1. With an overtone from the common 16th-century sense of "will" as "sexual desire." "Courage" (line 15): vigor, but also sexual desire.

Since all too late I find by skill°   experience
How dear I have thy fancies bought.
With lullaby now take thine ease,
30 With lullaby thy doubts appease.
For trust to this, if thou be still,
My body shall obey thy will.

Eke° lullaby my loving boy,   also
My little Robin,° take thy rest.   his penis
35 Since age is cold and nothing coy,°   not at all lascivious
Keep close thy coin, for so is best.
With lullaby be thou content,
With lullaby thy lusts relent.°   relinquish
Let others pay which hath mo° pence;   more
40 Thou art too poor for such expense.[2]

Thus lullaby, my youth, mine eyes,
My will, my ware,° and all that was.   genitals
I can no mo delays devise,
But welcome pain, let pleasure pass.
45 With lullaby now take your leave,
With lullaby your dreams deceive,
And when you[3] rise with waking eye,
Remember then this lullaby.

Ever or never.

1573, 1575

Michael Drayton

The son of a Warwickshire butcher or tanner, Drayton (1563–1631) had a long and productive career as a professional writer. He collaborated on plays and wrote scriptural paraphrases, pastorals, satires, odes, poetic epistles, verse legends, and a historical epic. His masterpiece is *Poly-Olbion*, a 15,000-line historical-geographical poem celebrating all the counties of England and Wales. He contributed as well to the period's vogue for sonnets, publishing a sequence of fifty-one sonnets called *Idea's Mirror* (1594), which, following substantial revision, he republished as *Idea*. In this poem he takes malicious delight in what time will do to the woman who has rejected him.

There's Nothing Grieves Me, But That Age Should Haste

There's nothing grieves me, but that° age should haste,   *the possibility that*
That° in my days I may not see thee old;   *with the result that*
That where those two clear, sparkling eyes are placed,
Only two loopholes then I might behold;

---

2. Punning on "expense" as ejaculation; compare Shakespeare, sonnet 129, line 1 (p. 637, below). Each ejaculation was thought to shorten life by a day—a cost that, Gascoigne suggests, old age cannot afford.
3. That is, youth, eyes, will, and ware in the first lines of the stanza: despite the lullaby, they won't sleep long.

5   That lovely archèd, ivory, polished brow
    Defaced with wrinkles that I might but see;
    Thy dainty hair, so curled and crispèd now,
    Like grizzled moss upon some agèd tree;
    Thy cheek, now flush with roses, sunk and lean;
10 Thy lips, with age as any wafer thin;
    Thy pearly teeth out of thy head so clean,°   *entirely*
    That when thou feed'st, thy nose shall touch thy chin.
       These lines that now thou scorn'st, which should delight thee,
       Then would I make thee read, but to despite° thee.   *spite*

1594   1619

Samuel Daniel

A poet, playwright, historian, and translator, Daniel (1562/3–1619) was a member of the circle of Mary Sidney, Countess of Pembroke, and he later held various offices in the household of Anne of Denmark, James I's queen. He wrote tragedies, court masques, a historical epic, a prose history of England, a defense of rhyme, several fine verse epistles, a verse dialogue on the purpose of writing poetry, a popular "complaint" poem in which the ghost of a king's mistress laments her fate, and one of the best Elizabethan sonnet sequences, *Delia*. This poem imagines the aging of the woman who has rejected him. Will she feel pity then?

When Men Shall Find Thy Flower, Thy Glory, Pass

       When men shall find thy flower, thy glory, pass,
       And thou, with careful° brow sitting alone,   *full of care; sorrowful*
       Receivèd hast this message from thy glass,°   *mirror*
       That tells thee truth, and says that all is gone,
5   Fresh shalt thou see in me the wounds thou madest,
       Though spent thy flame, in me the heat remaining:
       I that have loved thee thus before thou fadest,
       My faith shall wax,° when thou art in thy waning. *fidelity shall increase*
          The world shall find this miracle in me,
10   That fire can burn when all the matter's spent;
       Then, what my faith hath been thyself shall see,
       And that thou wast unkind thou may'st repent.
          Thou may'st repent that thou hast scorned my tears,
          When winter snows upon thy golden hairs.

                                                              1592

Anonymous   Sir Henry Lee (1533–1611), Master of the Armory, served as the Queen's Champion, defending her honor against all comers, at annual tournaments or jousts, from 1559 to 1590. He retired, at the age of fifty-seven, in favor of the Earl of Cumberland. On that occasion this lyric was sung by Robert Hales, the queen's lutenist, on behalf of Lee. The authorship, sometimes ascribed to George Peele because the poem was first printed at the end of his *Polyhymnia*, is uncertain. It may be by Lee himself.

The Queen's Champion Retires

His golden locks time hath to silver turned;
O time too swift, O swiftness never ceasing!
His youth 'gainst time and age hath ever spurned,
But spurned in vain; youth waneth by increasing:[1]
5 Beauty, strength, youth are flowers but fading seen;
Duty, faith, love are roots, and ever green.

His helmet now shall make a hive for bees;
And lovers' sonnets turned to holy psalms;
A man-at-arms must now serve on his knees
10 And feed on prayers, which are age's alms:[2]
But though from court to cottage he depart,
His saint[3] is sure of his unspotted heart.

And when he saddest[4] sits in homely cell,°   *humble dwelling*
He'll teach his swains this carol for a song:
15 "Blessed be the hearts that wish my sovereign well;
Cursed be the souls that think her any wrong."
Goddess,[5] allow this agèd man his right
To be your beadsman[6] now, that was your knight.

1590

1. That is, paradoxically, as one's growth increases, one's youth decreases.
2. That is, prayers are the only alms a retired, aged man can give.
3. Ladylove.
4. In a serious mood (not "melancholy").
5. Queen Elizabeth, often honored as the moon goddess Diana (Cynthia).
6. One who offers prayers on behalf of someone.

BAWDY

Anonymous   These lyrics are sometimes said to be by Thomas Morley (1557–1642), who published them in *Airs* (1600), along with a musical setting. They purportedly give the "cry" of a peddler selling goods for the female market—in particular, a "dog" with "a hole in his head": a fillable dildo with an opening at its top.

Will Ye Buy a Fine Dog?

Will ye buy a fine dog, with a hole in his head[1]
With a dildo, dildo, dildo;
Muffs, cuffs, rebatoes,° and fine sister's thread,[2] *wired lace collars*
With a dildo, with a dildo, with a dildo?

5 I stand not on points,[3] pins, periwigs,
   Combs, glasses,
   Gloves, garters; girdles,
   Busks° for the brisk° lasses, *headdresses / lively*

But I have other dainty tricks,
10 Sleekstones[4] and potting sticks,° *stirrers*
With a dildo, with a dildo, diddle dildo.

And for a need my pretty pods,° *bags*
Amber,[5] civet, and musk cods,° *(scent) glands*
With a dildo, with a dildo, diddle, diddle dildo!

1600

Anonymous   This poem, in riddle form, is from a commonplace book in the Houghton Library, Harvard, which contains verses from the 1590s through the 1630s. Authorship and date are unknown.

On a Maidenhead

Yes, that a maidenhead we call:
A thing° by standing makes it fall. *that is, a penis*
At fifteen rare, at eighteen strange,
Which both do lose[1] when they it change;° *replace it*
5 A thing oft smothered in a bed,
Which few have now, which all have had;
A thing which lasses bears about
Till putting in doth put it out.

---

1. A dildo that could be filled with warm liquid, which could be shot out at the appropriate moment.
2. Bleached thread.
3. I do not view as important. "Points": tagged cords used for fastening garments The whole phrase is also a pun on "to stand upon points" (that is, to be scrupulous about punctuation).

4. Smooth stones used for polishing.
5. Ambergris, a waxy substance originating in the intestines of sperm whales; it was used in manufacturing perfumes, as were the secretions of African civets and male musk deers.
1. They lose the status both of being maidens and of having a hymen.

CARPE DIEM

Thomas Lodge   The London-born Lodge (1558–1625) was educated at Oxford, studied law, and eventually became a physician. He sailed in 1591 on a disastrous voyage to the New World, which he was fortunate to survive. In a career complicated by his lifelong Catholicism in a time of persecution, he tried his hand at writing poems, literary tracts, plays, translations, and prose fictions (one of which became the source of Shakespeare's *As You Like It*). This is one of several poems interspersed in Lodge's romance *The Famous, True, and Historical Life of Robert, Second Duke of Normandy* (1591).

Pluck the Fruit and Taste the Pleasure

Pluck the fruit and taste the pleasure,
   Youthful lordings,° of delight,   *gentlemen*
Whilst occasion gives you seizure,[1]
   Feed your fancies and your sight:
      After death when you are gone,   5
      Joy and pleasure is there none.

Here on earth no thing is stable,
   Fortune's changes well are known,
Whilst as youth doth then enable,
   Let your seeds of joy be sown: 10
      After death when you are gone,
      Joy and pleasure is there none.

Feast it freely with your lovers,
   Blithe and wanton sweets do fade,
Whilst that lovely Cupid hovers   15
   Round about this lovely shade:
      Sport it freely one to one,
      After death is pleasure none.

Now the pleasant spring allureth,
   And both place and time invites: 20
Out alas,[2] what heart endureth
   To disclaim° his sweet delights?   *renounce; relinquish*
      After death when we are gone,
      Joy and pleasure is there none.

1591

---

1. While you have the opportunity to seize it.
2. "Out" simply intensifies "alas."

DEATH

Fulke Greville The wealthy Fulke Greville, Lord Brooke (1554–1628), was educated at Cambridge, traveled widely on the Continent, served in Parliament, and was a successful courtier under Elizabeth I, James I, and Charles I. Never married, he wrote some conventional love poetry addressed to a woman he called Caelica, but his most passionate expressions of love were for his friend Sir Philip Sidney, whose death, in 1586, he never ceased to mourn. In addition to a number of powerful, brooding short poems, Greville wrote long philosophical verse treatises, several politically charged closet dramas, and a moving biography of Sidney. The end of Greville's life was grimly in keeping with his general pessimism: he was fatally stabbed by a longtime servant who then killed himself.

You That Seek What Life Is in Death

You that seek what life is in death,
Now find it air that once was breath.
New names unknown, old names gone:
Till time end bodies, but souls none.
₅   Reader! then make time while you be
But° steps to your eternity.   *only*

ca. 1586   1633

Emma Foxe This epitaph is on a brass grave monument in St. Peter and St. Paul's Church, Aldeburgh, Suffolk, dated 1570. Written in the voice of Emma Foxe, it may have been penned by her before death, or by a family member afterward, imagining what she might say from the grave. The verse is accompanied by images, also in brass, showing Emma Foxe, her seven sons and seven daughters.

To You That Life Possess

To you that life possess
   Great troubles do befall,°   *belong*
Where we that sleep by death
   Do feel no harm at all.
₅   An honest life doth bring
   A joyful death at last,
And life again begins
   When death is overpassed.°   *overcome, ended*

My loving Foxe farewell:
₁₀   God guide thee with his grace;
Prepare thyself to come
   And I will give thee place.°   *make room for you*

>   My children all adieu,
>   And be right° sure of this: *totally*
> 15 You shall be brought to dust
>   As Emma Foxe your mother is.
>
>   1570

Sir Walter Ralegh

Ralegh wrote *The History of the World* (1614) during his long years in the Tower awaiting execution. He began it with the Creation and ended it, here, with death. The work emphasized the providential punishment of evil princes and projected a treatment of English history—although not of recent events, because, he declared, he who follows truth too closely at the heels might get kicked in the teeth. The work was to have been dedicated to Henry, Prince of Wales, Ralegh's most powerful friend and supporter, who declared, "Only my father would keep such a bird in a cage." But Henry died in 1612, and the dispirited Ralegh broke off his narrative at 168 B.C.E. In this conclusion, Ralegh considers the tremendous leveling power of death.

From The History of the World

[CONCLUSION: ON DEATH]

It is * * * Death alone that can suddenly make man to know himself. He tells the proud and insolent that they are but abjects,[1] and humbles them at the instant; makes them cry, complain, and repent; yea, even to hate their forepassed[2] happiness. He takes the account[3] of the rich, and proves him a beggar, a naked beggar, which hath interest in nothing but in the gravel that fills his mouth. He holds a glass[4] before the eyes of the most beautiful, and makes them see therein their deformity and rottenness, and they acknowledge it.

O eloquent, just, and mighty Death! Whom none could advise, thou hast persuaded; what none hath dared, thou hast done; and whom all the world hath flattered, thou only hast cast out of the world and despised; thou hast drawn together all the far-stretched greatness, all the pride, cruelty, and ambition of man, and covered it all over with these two narrow words: *Hic jacet!*[5]

                                                                1614

---

1. Castoffs.
2. Bygone.
3. Estimate, measure.
4. Mirror.
5. Here lies (Latin); often carved on tombstones.

The Dance and Song of Death. This engraving, which shows skeletons dancing people of all ranks to their death, depicts a wide range of society: the king and the beggar; the old man and the child; the wise man and the fool. In the middle, Sickness sits over a grave on a chair of bones and plays the music. At the corners are (left) a miser and a prisoner and (right) a judge and a pair of lovers; they too are summoned to join the dance by prancing skeletons.

DRINK

William Stevenson/John Still

This drinking song appears in the play *Gammer Gurtons Needle*, published in 1575 and first performed sometime between 1553 and 1562. It was put on at Cambridge and may have been written by William Stevenson (1530–1575), a clergyman, or John Still (1543–1608), master of St. John's and Trinity College, Cambridge, and bishop of Bath and Wells. The text is assumed to be about poverty, which is relieved and cheered by drink, but the song's topic also naturally fits its student environment.

Jolly Good Ale and Old

    Back and side go bare, go bare,
    Both foot and hand go cold.
    But, belly, God send thee good ale enough,
    Whether it be new or old.

5   I cannot eat but little meat,
    My stomach is not good;
    But sure I think that I can drink

      With him that wears a hood.[1]
      Though I go bare, take ye no care,°   *don't you worry*
10 I am nothing a-cold:
      I stuffed my skin, so full within
      Of jolly good ale and old.

      Back and side go bare, go bare,
      Both foot and hand go cold.
15 But, belly, God send thee good ale enough,
      Whether it be new or old.

      I love no roast, but a nut-brown toast
      And a crab laid in the fire,[2]
      A little bread shall do me stead,°   *suffice me*
20 Much bread I not desire.
      No frost nor snow, no wind I trow°   *believe*
      Can hurt me if I would,°   *even if I wished it*
      I am so wrapped, and thoroughly lapped
      Of jolly good ale and old.

25 Back and side go bare, go bare,
      Both foot and hand go cold.
      But, belly, God send thee good ale enough,
      Whether it be new or old.

      And Tib, my wife, that as her life
30 Loveth well good ale to seek,
      Full oft drinks she, till ye may see
      The tears run down her cheeks.
      Then doth she troll° to me the bowl   *pass*
      Even as a malt-worm[3] should,
35 And saith "sweetheart, I took my part
      Of this jolly good ale and old."

      Back and side go bare; go bare,
      Both foot and hand go cold.
      But, belly, God send thee good ale enough,
40 Whether it be new or old.

      Now let them drink till they nod and wink,°   *close their eyes (fall asleep)*
      Even as good fellows° should do.   *drinking companions*
      They shall not miss,° to have the bliss,   *fail*
      Good ale doth bring men to.
45 And all poor souls that have scoured° bowls   *cleared out*
      Or have them lustily° trolled,   *gladly*
      God save the lives of them and their wives
      Whether they be young or old.

---

1. Hoods were worn by authority figures: civic officials, clergymen, and university graduates.
2. Toasted bread and (crab) apples were usual additions to ale, particularly when it was served hot.
3. A heavy drinker (literally, a weevil that infests malt).

Back and side go bare, go bare,
50 Both foot and hand go cold.
But, belly, God send thee good ale enough,
Whether it be new or old.

ca. 1553   1575

Thomas Dekker   This verse is printed at the end of *The Shoemaker's Holiday* (1600), a play by Dekker (1572–1632), a man-about-town who apparently supported himself through writing. The "toast" drunk in the second and fourth stanza, which is to be repeated "as often as there are men to drink," and the fact that the final stanza is preceded by the stage direction "when all have drunk, this verse" show this to be an action poem in which ale is consumed throughout the performance.

Troll the Bowl, the Jolly Nut-Brown Bowl

Cold's the wind and wet's the rain,
    Saint Hugh[1] be our good speed.°   *success, luck*
Ill is the weather that bringeth no gain,
    Nor helps good hearts in need.

5 Troll° the bowl, the jolly nut-brown bowl,[2]   *pass round*
    And here, kind mate, to thee.[3]
Let's sing a dirge° for Saint Hugh's soul,   *lament*
    And down it merrily!

Down-a-down, hey down-a-down,
10   Hey derry derry down-a-down,[4]
Ho well done, to me let come,
    Ring compass,[5] gentle joy.°   *sweetheart*

Troll the bowl, the jolly nut-brown bowl,
    And here, kind[6] mate, to thee.
15 Let's sing a dirge for Saint Hugh's soul,
    And down it merrily!

Cold's the wind and wet's the rain,[7]
    Saint Hugh be our good speed.
Ill is the weather that bringeth no gain,
20   Nor helps good hearts in need.

ca. 1600

1. Patron saint of shoemakers (also sick people and swans), the subjects of the play in which this is sung.
2. Wide-mouthed drinking vessel.
3. A drinking toast meaning "here's to you, kind friend."
4. Nonsense to be sung while the drink is being consumed or "downed." This line is followed by a stage direction "close with the tenor boy," indicating that the largest bell is to be rung.
5. This has been glossed as meaning "ring the full range—compass—of notes"; it seems rather to mean something along the lines of "keep circulating."
6. In the text, this verse is not completed. It stops here with "etc" followed by the stage direction "as often as there be men to drink," indicating that this verse should be repeated until the bowl is empty.
7. This verse is preceded by the stage direction "at last, when all have drunk, this verse."

EXECUTION

Chidiock Tichborne   Tichborne (1562–1586) was part of the Babington conspiracy to assassinate Queen Elizabeth and her chief ministers; release Mary, Queen of Scots, from her long captivity; and promote an uprising of English Catholics to coincide with a Spanish invasion. The detection of this plot by Walsingham, and the proof of Mary's complicity in it, finally cost the Scottish queen her life. Tichborne, one of six conspirators assigned to kill Elizabeth, pled guilty at his trial and was executed. His "Elegy" was published in a volume called *Verses of Praise and Joy Written upon Her Majesty's Preservation*; it was later set to music by three different composers.

Tichborne's Elegy

Written with His Own Hand in the Tower Before His Execution

My prime of youth is but a frost of cares,
My feast of joy is but a dish of pain,
My crop of corn° is but a field of tares,°   *grain / weeds*
And all my good is but vain hope of gain;
5   The day is past, and yet I saw no sun,
And now I live, and now my life is done.

My tale was heard and yet it was not told,
My fruit is fallen and yet my leaves are green,
My youth is spent and yet I am not old,
10   I saw the world and yet I was not seen;
My thread is cut and yet it is not spun,
And now I live, and now my life is done.

I sought my death and found it in my womb,
I looked for life and saw it was a shade,°   *ghost*
15   I trod the earth and knew it was my tomb,
And now I die, and now I was but made;
My glass° is full, and now my glass is run,   *hourglass*
And now I live, and now my life is done.

                                                                1586

Sir Walter Ralegh   Ralegh (1552–1618) called his son by his own name, Walter; writing to him was by extension writing about himself. Here he cautions the younger Walter (1593–1618), a wild "wag," to avoid the gallows—a genuine concern, given that the poem's author was himself executed. Ralegh embraced the manuscript circulation of his poems at court but actively opposed appearing as a poet in print—in one case he forced a printer to recall a volume and paste a slip of paper over his initials. That makes it difficult to put the copies that circulated in manuscript, often in commonplace books, in any reliably chronological order or to date them. This poem may date to around 1600, in which case it is addressed to a naughty child; it may date from later, in which case the "wag" is engaging in adult bad behavior.

Sir Walter Ralegh to His Son[1]

Three things there be that prosper up apace
And flourish, whilst they grow asunder far,
But on a day, they meet all in one place,
And when they meet, they one another mar;
5 And they be these: the wood, the weed,° the wag.   *hemp*
The wood is that which makes the gallow tree;
The weed is that which strings the hangman's bag;[2]
The wag, my pretty knave, betokeneth° thee.   *signifies*
Mark well, dear boy, whilst these assemble not,
10 Green springs the tree, hemp grows, the wag is wild,
But when they meet, it makes the timber rot,
It frets the halter,° and it chokes the child.   *tightens the noose*
    Then bless thee, and beware, and let us pray
    We part not with thee at this meeting day.

ca. 1600

Sir Walter Ralegh   Against orders, men under Ralegh's command in Guiana had attacked a Spanish outpost. His son Walter was killed in the attack, which proved fatal to Ralegh as well, since King James I was determined to repair the breach with Spain. Ralegh, who had had an earlier sentence of execution stayed, was resentenced. The seventeenth-century story, which may be true, was that Ralegh inscribed this poem in his Bible the night before he was beheaded. The epitaph, a version of the last stanza of his "Nature, That Washed Her Hands in Milk" (p. 501 in this volume), completes its brave acknowledgment of death with the trust—or hope—that Ralegh will be resurrected on Judgment Day.

The Author's Epitaph, Made by Himself

Even such is time, which takes in trust
Our youth, our joys, and all we have,
And pays us but with age and dust;
Who in the dark and silent grave,
5 When we have wandered all our ways,
Shuts up the story of our days:
And from which earth, and grave, and dust
The Lord shall raise me up, I trust.

1628

---

1. The sonnet has this title in one of the manuscripts in which it appears.
2. That is, when woven into rope, the hemp secures the hangman's hood ("bag") to the condemned person's neck.

FOREIGNERS

Anonymous The content of this "libel" (a defamatory writing put up in public) is recorded in a manuscript book (ca. 1599–1601) of letters, orations, and various other texts transcribed by John Mansell (1580–1631), a churchman, theologian, philosopher, and later president of Queens' College, Cambridge. The libel itself is apparently about Protestant asylum seekers fleeing religious persecution in the Netherlands; records of the Privy Council attest that it was first hung up, in manuscript, in the churchyard of the so-called Dutch church where the refugees prayed. But Mansell mistitles the work "A libel fixed upon the French Church Wall in London," showing how easy it was to confuse one despised people with another. Said to be in the hand of "Tamberlaine," the name of the title character of two plays by Christopher Marlowe, the poem got Marlowe in trouble with the authorities, who saw him as one of the instigators of anti-alien riots in Southwark in 1593, of which this libel was a part. He is unlikely, though, to have "hidden" his authorship under so obvious a name. "Tamberlaine" probably indicates instead the character as depicted in Marlowe's plays, who cruelly annihilated his enemies. Foreigners ("strangers"), often economic migrants from elsewhere in Europe, were crucial to English commercial expansion, but could be feared and hated. Here they are accused of buying goods and selling them at a higher price, producing better merchandise, being spies, causing rents to increase, having more than one trade, and pretending to be Protestants.

The Dutch Libel

Ye strangers° that do inhabit in this land, *foreigners*
Note this same writing; do it understand.
Conceit° it well—for safeguard° of your lives, *understand / protection*
Your goods, your children and your dearest wives.
5   Your Machiavellian merchant spoils° the state,[1] *despoils, strips*
Your usury doth leave us all for dead,
Your artifex° and craftsman works our fate *artificers, artisans*
And, like the Jews, you eat us up as bread.[2]
The merchant doth ingross° all kind of wares; *buys up wholesale*
10   Forestalls the markets wheresoe'er he goes;[3]
Sends forth his wares by peddlers to the fairs;
Retails at home; and with his horrible shows
Undoeth thousands.

In baskets your wares trot up and down
15   Carried the streets by the country nation.[4]

---

1. "Machiavellian" may suggest being unscrupulous or cunning, as Niccolò Machiavelli, the Italian diplomat and author of *The Prince*, was popularly thought to have been. It is also a shorthand way of insulting Italians.
2. This may allude to accusations that Jews ate Christian babies and desecrated the Church's consecrated host—the Communion bread—or may simply refer to "Jewish bread" (matzoh).
3. *Forestalling* was to buy up goods privately, before they reached the markets; the claim is that the merchants are getting the goods through underhanded means and selling them at profit.
4. Either "your wares are carried by countrymen" or, if the word is in fact *contrary*, "you, of a different nation, carry your wares around."

You are intelligencers° to the state and crown *spies*
And in your hearts do wish an alteration.⁵
You transport goods, and bring us gauds° good store, *playthings, showy ornaments*
Our lead, our vittle, our ordinance and what not,⁶
20 That Egypt's plagues vexed not th'Egyptians more
Than you do us;⁷ then death shall be your lot.
No prize° comes in but you make claim thereto, *payment, duty*
And every merchant hath three trades at least,
And cutthroat-like in selling, you undo
25 Us all, and with our store continually you feast.
We cannot suffer long.

Our poor artificers° do starve and die *artisans*
For that they cannot now be set on work.° *put to work*
And for° your work, more curious° to the eye, *as for / skillful, elaborate*
30 In chambers twenty in one house will lurk—
Raising of rents was never known before—
Living far better than at native home;
And our poor souls are clean thrust out of door
And to the wars are sent abroad to roam
35 To fight it out for France and Belgia
And die like dogs as sacrifice for you.⁸
Expect you therefore such a fatal day
Shortly on you and yours for to ensue
As never was seen.

40 Since words nor threats nor any other thing
Can make you to avoid this certain ill,
We'll cut your throats in your temples praying:
Not Paris massacre⁹ so much blood did spill
As we will do just vengeance on you all
45 In counterfeiting religion for your flight,
When 'tis well known you are loath for to be thrall.°¹ *to be in bondage*
Your coin and you as countries cause to flight.²
With Spanish gold you all are infected³
And with that gold our nobles wink at feats.⁴

---

5. The implication is that the foreigners spy for the state, while in fact desiring a change of government.
6. Lead, food, and furniture and "what not" are the goods that are transported and replaced with (or perhaps made into, or sold as) "gawds" from abroad that are then retailed back in England.
7. See Exodus 7–10, which describes ten natural disasters visited by God on Pharoah to convince him to let the enslaved Israelites leave Egypt.
8. English soldiers often went to the Continent to fight and die on behalf of foreign Protestants—a reference to the queen's engagement in the struggle against the Spanish, or to the Dutch wars, which extended into France and Belgium. See "Soldiers Song," below.
9. The massacre of French Huguenots in Paris on Saint Bartholomew's Day, 1572.

1. The claim is that the foreigners have falsely pretended a passion for Protestantism in order to be welcomed into England.
2. An obscure sentence. "Flight" here rhymes with itself, suggesting eye-skip: other transcription errors are possible. As it stands, the point seems to be that you and your coins set flight to the country's cause. But the line may in fact be something like "as [or 'our'] countries/country's cause to fight"; "as [or 'our'] countries/country's cause to [or 'do'] slight."
3. Spanish coins were in circulation everywhere.
4. Close their eyes at your deeds; that is, turn a blind eye to what you do. The Spanish treasure fleet had brought large quantities of gold and silver from the New World to Europe, causing inflation throughout western Europe.

50 Nobles said I? Nay, men to be rejected:
Upstarts that enjoy the noblest seats,
That wound their country's breast for lucre's° sake, *money's*
And wrong our gracious queen and subjects good
By letting strangers make our hearts to ache,[5]
55 For which our swords are whet to shed their blood.
And, for a truth, let it be understood:
Fly,° fly and never return. *run away hurriedly*

Per.° Tamberlaine *by the hand of*
1593

William Shakespeare   This is a speech from the manuscript play of *Sir Thomas More* (ca. 1591–93), which is written in five anonymous hands: A, B, C, D, and E. Hand D, and the author of this speech, is thought to be Shakespeare. This section of the play depicts a riot against foreigners that occurred in London on May 1, 1517, a day that came to be called "Evil May Day." As it is clearly also a reference to the more recent anti-immigrant unrest in the 1590s (see headnote to "The Dutch Libel"), the text was thought incendiary and was censored; the Master of the Revels, Sir Edmund Tilney, declared that the play should be altered to "leave out the insurrection wholly and the cause thereof." There is no proof that the play ever made it to the stage. In this speech, More pleads with the rioters for tolerance and asks them to consider how they would feel if they themselves were immigrants.

From Sir Thomas More

Grant them[1] removed, and grant that this your noise
Hath chid down° all the majesty of England. *silenced*
Imagine that you see the wretched strangers,
Their babies at their backs and their poor luggage,
5 Plodding to th'ports and coasts for transportation,
And that you sit as kings in your desires,
Authority quite silenced by your brawl,
And you in ruff of your opinions clothed;[2]
What had you got? I'll tell you. You had taught
10 How insolence and strong hand should prevail;
How order should be quelled; and by this pattern
Not one of you should live an agèd man,
For other ruffians, as their fancies wrought,
With selfsame hand, self-reasons, and self-right,
15 Would shark° on you, and men like ravenous fishes *prey*
Would feed on one another.

---

5. *That is,* English noblemen are protecting immigrants and profiting by so doing.
1. Let us suppose that the strangers (that is, foreigners).
2. Wearing the ruffled collar (that is, pride) of your notions.

      You'll put down° strangers,   *subdue*
Kill them, cut their throats, possess their houses,
And lead the majesty of law in lyam,°   *a leash for hounds*
20 To slip him like a hound.[3] Say now the king
(As he is clement° if th'offender mourn)   *merciful*
Should so much come too short of your great trespass
As but to banish you,[4] whither would you go?
What country, by the nature of your error,
25 Should give you harbor? Go you to France or Flanders,
To any German province, to Spain or Portugal,
Nay, anywhere that not adheres to England,
Why, you must needs be strangers. Would you be pleased
To find a nation of such barbarous temper
30 That, breaking out in hideous violence,
Would not afford you an abode on earth;
Whet their detested knives against your throats;
Spurn you like dogs and, like as if that God
Owed° not nor made not you, nor that the claimants°   *owned / benefits claimed*
35 Were not all appropriate to your comforts
But chartered unto° them? What would you think   *reserved to*
To be thus used? This is the strangers' case,°   *situation*
And this your mountainish inhumanity.

                                                                    ca. 1590

3. That is, as if the law were a dog, you'll lead it and then release it.
4. If the king should, through kindness, fail to punish your great wrong as it deserves, and merely banish you.

IMAGINATION

Fulke Greville   The hundredth sonnet from *Caelica* (1633), this poem considers the frightening visions that the "inward" eye reveals in the dark.

In Night When Colors All to Black Are Cast

In night when colors all to black are cast,
Distinction lost, or gone down with the light,
The eye a watch to inward senses placed,
Not seeing, yet still having power of sight,
5 Gives vain alarums to the inward sense,
Where fear stirred up with witty tyranny°   *of imaginings*
Confounds all powers and thorough self-offense° *through self-injury*
Doth forge and raise impossibility:
Such as in thick depriving darknesses
10 Proper reflections of the error be,

>   And images of self-confusednesses,
>   Which hurt imaginations only see;
>   And from this nothing seen tells news of devils,
>   Which but expressions be of inward evils.

ca. 1580–1600   1633

Michael Drayton   From the sonnet cycle *Ideas Mirror* (1594), this poem compares the "things" (women) who will be forgotten with one who will survive—because Drayton has preserved her in verse.

How Many Paltry, Foolish, Painted Things

>   How many paltry, foolish, painted things,
>   That now in coaches trouble every street,
>   Shall be forgotten, whom no poet sings,
>   Ere they be well wrapped in their winding sheet?°   *shroud*
> 5 Where° I to thee eternity shall give,   *whereas*
>   When nothing else remaineth of these days;
>   And queens hereafter shall be glad to live
>   Upon the alms of thy superfluous praise.
>   Virgins and matrons, reading these my rhymes,
> 10 Shall be so much delighted with thy story
>   That they shall grieve they lived not in these times,
>   To have seen thee, their sex's only glory:
>   So shalt thou fly above the vulgar° throng,   *common*
>   Still to survive in my immortal song.

                                                                            1619

LYING

Sir Walter Ralegh   This poem circulated anonymously and in manuscript—but a series of "answer poems," often angry about it, reveal that the text was popularly understood to be by Ralegh. In this relentless, frantic poem, the author "gives the lie to" (accuses of lying—a phrase typically used when challenging someone to a duel) institutions such as the church and the court, types of people held in high esteem, and a manic list of intangibles, from wit to aging.

The Lie

Go, soul, the body's guest,
    Upon a thankless errand;
Fear not to touch° the best;   *speak of; censure*
    The truth shall be thy warrant.
5 Go, since I needs must die,
    And give the world the lie.[1]

Say to the court, it glows
    And shines like rotten wood;°   *with phosphorescence*
Say to the church, it shows
10   What's good, and doth no good.
If church and court reply,
    Then give them both the lie.

Tell potentates they live
    Acting by others' action;
15 Not loved unless they give,
    Not strong but by a faction.
If potentates reply,
    Give potentates the lie.

Tell men of high condition,
20   That manage the estate,°   *state*
Their purpose is ambition,
    Their practice only hate.
And if they once reply,
    Then give them all the lie.
25 Tell them that brave it° most,   *live ostentatiously*
    They beg for more by spending,
Who, in their greatest cost,
    Seek nothing but commending.°   *others' approval*
And if they make reply,
30   Then give them all the lie.

Tell zeal it wants° devotion;   *lacks*
    Tell love it is but lust;
Tell time it is but motion;
    Tell flesh it is but dust.
35 And wish them not reply,
    For thou must give the lie.

Tell age it daily wasteth;°   *decays*
    Tell honor how it alters;
Tell beauty how she blasteth;°   *withers away*
40   Tell favor how it falters.

---

1. "give . . . the lie": accuse of lying.

    And as they shall reply,
        Give every one the lie.

    Tell wit° how much it wrangles   *intellect*
        In tickle points of niceness;°   *in trivial distinctions*
45   Tell wisdom she entangles
        Herself in overwiseness.
    And when they do reply,
        Straight give them both the lie.

    Tell physic° of her boldness;°   *medicine / presumption*
50   Tell skill it is pretension;
    Tell charity of coldness;
        Tell law it is contention.
    And as they do reply,
        So give them still the lie.

55   Tell fortune of her blindness;
        Tell nature of decay;
    Tell friendship of unkindness;
        Tell justice of delay.
    And if they will reply,
60   Then give them all the lie.

    Tell arts[2] they have no soundness,
        But vary by esteeming;[3]
    Tell schools[4] they want profoundness,
        And stand too much on seeming.
65   If arts and schools reply,
        Give arts and schools the lie.

    Tell faith° it's fled the city;   *faithfulness, fidelity*
        Tell how the country erreth;
    Tell manhood shakes off pity;
70   Tell virtue least preferreth.°   *advances*
    And if they do reply,
        Spare not to give the lie.

    So when thou hast, as I
        Commanded thee, done blabbing,°   *revealing secrets*
75   Although to give the lie
        Deserves no less than stabbing,
    Stab at thee he that will,
        No stab thy soul can kill.

ca. 1592   1608

---

2. The seven liberal arts, the basis of the academic curriculum.
3. That is, seem good or bad according to different tastes or judgments.
4. The various philosophical traditions.

LOVE: HAPPY

John Davies of Hereford   Always associated in print with his birthplace in the historic Welsh Marches, an area on the border between England and Wales, in order to avoid confusion with a contemporary poet of the same name, John Davies of Hereford (1564/5–1618) moved to London to work as a writing master, tutoring members of the nobility in penmanship. At the same time, he produced scores of poems, including religious and moral treatises, love sonnets, satires, eclogues, and his best-known work, a collection of epigrams (short, pointed poems), many of them addressed to the era's most prominent writers.

If There Were (Oh!) an Hellespont of Cream

The author loving these homely meats specially, viz., cream, pancakes, buttered pippin pies[1] (laugh, good people), and tobacco, writ to that worthy and virtuous gentlewoman whom he calleth mistress, as followeth:

If there were (oh!) an Hellespont[2] of cream
Between us, milk-white mistress, I would swim
To you, to show to both my love's extreme,
Leander-like[3]—yea, dive from brim to brim.
5   But met I with a buttered pippin pie
Floating upon't, that would I make my boat,
To waft me to you without jeopardy,
Though seasick I might be while it did float.
Yet if a storm should rise, by night or day,
10   Of sugar snows and hail of caraways,[4]
Then, if I found a pancake in my way,[5]
It, like a plank, should bring me to your quays:[6]
   Which having found, if they tobacco kept,
   The smoke should dry me well, before I slept.

1611

---

1. Apple pies. "Meats": foods (not just flesh).
2. The ancient name for the Dardanelles, the strait linking the Aegean Sea and the Sea of Marmara. One to five miles wide, it divides Europe from Asia.
3. According to a late classical legend, Leander swam the Hellespont to reach his ladylove, Hero. See Marlowe's "Hero and Leander" (p. 563).
4. Caraway seeds; here, in sweets.
5. On my route.
6. Or "keys": banks or landing stages strengthened for loading or unloading ships. Here, alluding to the breasts of his "milk-white mistress."

Thomas Campion   After three years at Cambridge, Campion (1567–1620) studied law before finally settling on medicine. A composer, a writer of court masques, and a poet, he wrote his first poetic compositions in Latin, and he remained interested in the possibility of applying the classical principles of quantitative versification to English. His most memorable achievements arose from the fact that he was both poet and composer: his aim, he wrote, was "to couple my words and notes lovingly together." This poem and the two lyrics that follow appeared, with musical settings, in *A Book of Airs*, which contains Campion's first work as a composer. This piece is imitated and partly translated from a poem by Catullus (87–ca. 54 B.C.E.), the Latin lyric poet who often celebrated the charms of an unidentified married woman he called Lesbia.

My Sweetest Lesbia

My sweetest Lesbia, let us live and love,
And though the sager sort our deeds reprove,
Let us not weigh° them: heav'n's great lamps do dive   *heed*
Into their west, and straight° again revive,   *at once*
But soon as once set is our little light,
Then must we sleep one ever-during° night.   *everlasting*

If all would lead their lives in love like me,
Then bloody swords and armor should not be;
No drum nor trumpet peaceful sleeps should move,°   *disturb*
Unless alarm° came from the camp of love.   *the call to arms*
But fools do live, and waste their little light,
And seek with pain their ever-during night.

When timely death my life and fortune ends,
Let not my hearse° be vexed with mourning friends,   *bier*
But let all lovers, rich in triumph, come
And with sweet pastimes grace my happy tomb;
And Lesbia, close up thou my little light,
And crown with love my ever-during night.

1601

Thomas Campion Published in *A Book of Airs* (1601), Campion's song about women and class compares the demands of court "ladies" with the availability of the country maid Amaryllis.

I Care Not for These Ladies

I care not for these ladies
That must be wooed and prayed;
Give me kind Amaryllis,[1]
The wanton country[2] maid.
5   Nature art° disdaineth;   *artifice*
Her beauty is her own.
    Her when we court and kiss,
    She cries "Forsooth,° let go!"   *truly!*
    But when we come where comfort is,
10   She never will say no.

If I love Amaryllis,
She gives me fruit and flowers;
But if we love these ladies,
We must give golden showers.
15   Give them gold that sell love,
Give me the nut-brown° lass   *sun-tanned*
    Who when we court and kiss,
    She cries "Forsooth, let go!"
    But when we come where comfort is,
20   She never will say no.

These ladies must have pillows,
And beds by strangers wrought.°   *imported*
Give me a bower of willows,
Of moss and leaves unbought,
25   And fresh Amaryllis,
With milk and honey fed,
    Who when we court and kiss,
    She cries "Forsooth, let go!"
    But when we come where comfort is,
30   She never will say no.

1601

---

1. In classical and later pastoral poetry, a conventional name for a shepherdess.
2. Probably with an obscene pun.

Thomas Campion Love, in this song from Campion's *Third and Fourth Book of Airs* (1617), is presented as a way of passing the long winter nights.

Now Winter Nights Enlarge

Now winter nights enlarge
  The number of their hours,
And clouds their storms discharge
  Upon the airy towers.
5 Let now the chimneys blaze
  And cups o'erflow with wine,
Let well-tuned words amaze
  With harmony divine.
Now yellow waxen lights
10 Shall wait on honey Love,
While youthful revels, masques,° and courtly sights   *masked balls*
  Sleep's leaden spells remove.

This time doth well dispense
  With[1] lovers' long discourse;
15 Much speech hath some defense,
  Though beauty no remorse.
All do not all things well:
  Some measures[2] comely° tread,   *pleasing*
Some knotted riddles tell,
20 Some poems smoothly read.
The Summer hath his joys,
  And Winter his delights;
Though Love and all his pleasures are but toys,°   *trifles*
  They shorten tedious nights.

1617

Richard Barnfield Barnfield (1574–1620) was sometimes thought to have been the "rival poet" of Shakespeare's sonnets. His first work, *The Affectionate Shepherd* (1594), a pastoral account of "the love of a shepherd to a boy," was criticized for its homoeroticism. As these later sonnets show, gay love remained a focus of much of his writing.

From *Cynthia*[1]

Sonnet 9

Diana (on a time) walking the wood
  To sport herself, of her fair train forlorn,[2]
  Chanced for to prick her foot against a thorn,

---

1. "Dispense / With": permit, allow.
2. Dances; also poetic rhythms. "Some": that is, some people.

1. Cynthia, or Diana, was the chaste huntress goddess, and moon goddess, of classical mythology.
2. Left without her fair retinue (of wood nymphs).

And from thence issued out a stream of blood.
5 No sooner she was vanished out of sight,
    But love's fair queen° came there away by chance,   *Venus*
    And having of this hap° a glimm'ring glance,   *accident, happenstance*
She put the blood into a crystal° bright.   *vessel of crystal*
When being now come unto Mount Rhodope,[3]
10   With her fair hands she forms a shape of snow,
    And blends it with this blood; from whence doth grow
A lovely creature, brighter than the day.
    And being christened in fair Paphos'[4] shrine,
    She called him Ganymede,[5] as all divine.

Sonnet 11

Sighing, and sadly sitting by my love,
    He asked the cause of my heart's sorrowing,
    Conjuring me by heaven's eternal king
To tell the cause which me so much did move.
5 Compelled (quoth I), to thee will I confess
    Love is the cause, and only love it is
    That doth deprive me of my heavenly bliss;
Love is the pain that doth my heart oppress.
And what is she (quoth he) whom thou dost love?
10   Look in this glass° (quoth I), there shalt thou see   *mirror*
    The perfect form of my felicity.
When, thinking that it would strange magic prove,°   *show*
    He opened it: and taking off the cover,
    He straight perceived himself to be my lover.

1595

3. In frigid Thrace, and associated with Diana.
4. A city in Cyprus, sacred to Venus.
5. A Trojan boy, said to be the most beautiful of mortals. Enamored of him, Zeus brought Ganymede away to Olympus, where he was deified and became cupbearer to the gods.

LOVE: UNHAPPY

Michael Drayton   From *Ideas Mirror*, a sequence that Drayton began writing in 1594, this poem puns throughout on the homonyms *aye* (yes) and *I*. Especially in the sonnet's final couplet, a nearly limitless number of interpretations can be produced by varying the punctuation—including the quotation marks, all of which are editorial—and letting the mind play freely with the homonyms.

Nothing but "No" and "I" and "I" and "No"?

Nothing but "No" and "I" and "I" and "No"?
How falls it out° so strangely you reply?   *how does it happen*
I tell ye (fair), I'll not be answered so,

With this affirming "No," denying "I."
5 I say, "I love"; you slightly° answer, "I." *indifferently; carelessly*
I say, "You love"; you pule me out[1] a "No."
I say, "I die"; you echo me with "I."
"Save me," I cry; you sigh me out a "No."
Must Woe and I have nought but "No" and "I"?
10 No I am I, if I no more can have.
Answer no more: with silence make reply,
And let me take myself what I do crave.
   Let "No" and "I" with I and you be so,
   Then answer "No" and "I" and "I" and "No."

1599, 1619

George Gascoigne   This poem appears at the end of Gascoigne's evidently autobiographical novella, *The Adventures of Master F. J.* (1573), which mixes prose and verse; it is occasioned by a conversation between F. J. and his mistress, the wife of his host in Italy. F. J. accuses her of betraying him with her male secretary, "and she . . . denied it, until at last being still urged with such evident tokens [that is, clear proofs] as he alleged, she gave him this bone to gnaw upon: And if I did so (quoth she), what then? Whereunto F. J. made none answer, but departed. . . . And when he was in place solitary, he compiled these following [verses], for a final end of the matter."

And If I Did, What Then?

"And if I did, what then?
Are you aggrieved therefore?
The sea hath fish for every man,
And what would you have more?"

5 Thus did my mistress once
  Amaze° my mind with doubt, *stupefy; perplex*
  And popped a question, for the nonce,° *on purpose; expressly*
  To beat my brains about.

  Whereto I thus replied,
10 "Each fisherman can wish
  That all the sea at every tide
  Were his alone to fish.

  "And so did I (in vain);
  But since it may not be,
15 Let such° fish there as find the gain, *such men*
  And leave the loss for me.

---

1. Peevishly answer me with.

>   "And with such luck and loss,
>   I will content myself,
>   Till tides of turning time may toss
>   20   Such fishers on the shelf.°   *to one side*
>
>   "And when they stick on sands,
>   That every man may see,
>   Then will I laugh and clap my hands,
>   As they do now at me."
>
>   1573

Michael Drayton   The conceit of this sonnet is to draw a parallel between being actually ill and being "lovesick."

As in Some Countries Far Remote from Hence

> As in some countries far remote from hence,
> The wretched creature destinèd to die,
> Having the judgment due to his offense,
> By surgeons begg'd their art° on him to try,   *skill*
> 5 Which° on the living work without remorse,   *who*
> First make incision on each mast'ring vein,°   *major blood vessel*
> Then stanch the bleeding, then transpierce the corse,° *pierce the body*
> And with their balms recure° the wounds again,   *heal*
> Then poison, and with physic° him restore,   *medical treatment*
> 10 Not that they fear the hopeless man to kill,
> But their experience to increase the more:
> Ev'n so my mistress works upon my ill,°   *illness (love's pangs)*
>   By curing me and killing me each hour
>   Only to show her beauty's sov'reign power.
>
>   1605

Sir Walter Ralegh   A series of "vicious bitter" descriptions of "false" love, this poem was set to music by William Byrd in *Psalms, Sonnets and Songs* (1588): as ever, what is a poem and what a song, who is author and who is composer, is hard to disentangle.

Farewell, False Love

>   Farewell, false love, the oracle° of lies,   *authoritative source*
>   A mortal foe and enemy to rest;
>   An envious boy, from whom all cares arise,
>   A bastard vile, a beast with rage possessed;
>   5 A way of error, a temple full of treason,
>   In all effects contrary unto reason.

A poisoned serpent covered all with flowers,
Mother of sighs and murtherer° of repose, — *murderer*
A sea of sorrows from whence are drawn such showers
10 As moisture lends to every grief that grows;
A school of guile, a net of deep deceit,
A gilded hook that holds a poisoned bait.

A fortress foiled° which reason did defend, — *overthrown*
A siren song, a fever of the mind,
15 A maze wherein affection finds no end,
A raging cloud that runs before the wind,
A substance like the shadow of the sun,
A goal of grief for which the wisest run.

A quenchless fire, a nurse of trembling fear,
20 A path that leads to peril and mishap;
A true retreat of sorrow and despair,
An idle boy that sleeps in pleasure's lap,
A deep distrust of that which certain seems,
A hope of that which reason doubtful deems.

25 Sith° then thy trains° my younger years betrayed, — *since / tricks*
And for my faith° ingratitude I find, — *faithfulness*
And sith repentance hath my wrongs bewrayed° — *revealed*
Whose course was ever contrary to kind°— — *nature*
False love, desire, and beauty frail, adieu!
30 Dead is the root whence all these fancies grew.

1588

The Marriage Balance. Love or worth? Cupid and a man are set on one side of the balance; money and a woman, probably a widow—she wears black—are set on the other. They are not equally balanced, and money appears to win out over love. Marriages were often strategic in the period, hence the many texts about unattainable love.

PASTORAL LOVE

Christopher Marlowe   This pastoral lyric of invitation is one of the most famous Elizabethan songs. First published in *The Passionate Pilgrim* (1599), a book of poems attributed to Shakespeare, its author has long been recognized as Marlowe. The poem exists in several different manuscript and print forms and media (including as a single-sheet ballad text). Many poets have written replies to it; the best known of them, by Sir Walter Ralegh, follows.

The Passionate Shepherd to His Love

Come live with me and be my love,
And we will all the pleasures prove°   *test, experience*
That valleys, groves, hills, and fields,
Woods, or steepy mountain yields.

5 And we will sit upon the rocks,
Seeing the shepherds feed their flocks,
By shallow rivers to whose falls
Melodious birds sing madrigals.

And I will make thee beds of roses
10 And a thousand fragrant posies,°   *bouquets (also of poems)*
A cap of flowers, and a kirtle°   *dress*
Embroidered all with leaves of myrtle;

A gown made of the finest wool
Which from our pretty lambs we pull;
15 Fair linèd slippers for the cold,
With buckles of the purest gold;

A belt of straw and ivy buds,
With coral clasps and amber studs:
And if these pleasures may thee move,
20 Come live with me, and be my love.

The shepherd swains shall dance and sing
For thy delight each May morning:
If these delights thy mind may move,
Then live with me and be my love.

1599, 1600

Sir Walter Ralegh

The "nymph's reply" is an answer to the preceding poem.

The Nymph's Reply to the Shepherd

If all the world and love were young,
And truth in every shepherd's tongue,
These pretty pleasures might me move
To live with thee and be thy love.

5 Time drives the flocks from field to fold
When rivers rage and rocks grow cold,
And Philomel° becometh dumb;   *the nightingale*
The rest complains of cares to come.

The flowers do fade, and wanton fields
10 To wayward winter reckoning yields;°   *renders an account*
A honey tongue, a heart of gall,
Is fancy's spring, but sorrow's fall.

Thy gowns, thy shoes, thy beds of roses,
Thy cap, thy kirtle,° and thy posies°   *dress / bouquets*
15 Soon break, soon wither, soon forgotten—
In folly ripe, in reason rotten.

Thy belt of straw and ivy buds,
Thy coral clasps and amber studs,
All these in me no means can move
20 To come to thee and be thy love.

But could youth last and love still breed,
Had joys no date° nor age no need,   *ending*
Then these delights my mind might move
To live with thee and be thy love.

                                                1600

PLAGUE

Thomas Nashe   This poem is from the play *A Pleasant Comedy Called Summer's Last Will and Testament*, acted before the archbishop of Canterbury in his palace at Croydon in 1592 and published in 1600. Composed during an outbreak of the bubonic plague, "A Litany" is a contemplation about death from the perspective of a plague sufferer ("Lord have mercy on us" was written on the door of plague-ridden households). Literally, a litany is a form of public prayer in which each of a series of supplications by the clergy is followed by a response from the congregation, with the same formula of response being repeated several times.

A Litany in Time of Plague

    Adieu, farewell, earth's bliss,
    This world uncertain is;
    Fond° are life's lustful° joys,   *foolish / lusty*
    Death proves them all but toys,°   *trifles*
5   None from his darts° can fly;   *arrows*
    I am sick, I must die.
        Lord, have mercy on us!

    Rich men, trust not in wealth,
    Gold cannot buy you health;
10 Physic himself° must fade,   *medicine itself*
    All things to end are made.
    The plague full swift goes by;
    I am sick, I must die.
        Lord, have mercy on us!

15 Beauty is but a flower
    Which wrinkles will devour;
    Brightness falls from the air,
    Queens have died young and fair,
    Dust hath closed Helen's° eye.   *Helen of Troy*
20 I am sick, I must die.
        Lord, have mercy on us!

    Strength stoops unto the grave,
    Worms feed on Hector[1] brave;
    Swords may not fight with fate,
25 Earth still holds ope her gate.
    "Come, come!" the bells[2] do cry.
    I am sick, I must die.
        Lord, have mercy on us!

    Wit with his wantonness
30 Tasteth death's bitterness;
    Hell's executioner
    Hath no ears for to hear
    What vain art° can reply.   *skill*
    I am sick, I must die.
35   Lord, have mercy on us!

    Haste, therefore, each degree,°   *social rank*
    To welcome destiny;
    Heaven is our heritage,
    Earth but a player's stage;
40 Mount we unto the sky.
    I am sick, I must die.
        Lord, have mercy on us!

1592   1600

1. The greatest of the Trojan warriors—killed, nevertheless, by Achilles.
2. The "passing bell" that was tolled in the parish church to solicit prayers for the dying.

John Davies of Hereford   The following extract is from Davies' long poem *The Triumph of Death*, published in 1609. It is about the 1603 outbreak of plague, which killed one in five Londoners.

From The Triumph of Death

* * *

At London, sink of sin, as at the fount,°   *source*
This all-confounding pestilence began,
According to that plague's most woeful wont,°   *habit*
From whence it, flowing, all the realm o'erran.

5 Which to prevent, at first, they pesterèd
Pesthouses[1] with their murrain-tainted° sick,   *death-contaminated*
But though from them, and thence,° the healthy fled,   *from there*
They, ere suspected, mortified° the quick.°   *killed / living*

Those so infected, being ignorant
10 That so they are, converse with whomsoe'er
Whose open shops and houses all do haunt,[2]
And find most danger where they least do fear.

And so not knowing sick folk from the sound
(For such ill air's not subject to the sense)
15 They one with other do themselves confound,[3]
And so confound all with a pestilence.

* * *

The king himself—O wretched times the while!—
From place to place to save himself did fly;[4]
Which from himself himself did seek t'exile,
20 Who (as amaz'd) not safe knew where to lie.[5]

It's hard with subjects when the sovereign
Hath no place free from plagues his head to hide;
And hardly can we say the King doth reign
That nowhere for just fear can well abide.

25 For nowhere comes he but death follows him
Hard at the heels, and reacheth at his head;
So sinks all sports° that would like triumphs swim,   *recreations*
For what life have we when we all are dead:

Dead in our spirits, to see our neighbors die;
30 To see our king so shift his life to save;
And with his council all conclusions try[6]
To keep themselves from th'insatiate° grave.   *never satisfied*

---

1. Special hospitals for people with infectious diseases.
2. *Are frequented* by everyone.
3. They confuse sick and well (sound) together.
4. King James came to the throne in 1603 as London was overcome with plague, delaying his coronation for some months—and "the Coronation being happily over," notes his proclamation of the time, "the King hereby commands all persons not detained at Court to depart at once." He took his own advice and fled once more.
5. As he, panicked, did not know where he could safely rest, he attempted to exile himself from himself.
6. Experiment with all kinds of solutions.

For hardly could one man another meet,
That in his bosom brought not odious death;
35 It was confusion but a friend to greet,°   *simply to greet a friend*
For, like a fiend, he banèd° with his breath.   *poisoned*

The wildest wastes, and places most remote
From man's repair° are now the most secure;   *abode, haunt*
Happy is he that there doth find a cote°   *shed, stall*
40 To shroud his head from this plague's smoking shower.

A beggar's home, though dwelling in a ditch,
If far from London it were situate,
He might rent out, if pleased him, to the rich,
That now as Hell their London homes do hate.

* * *

1609

SIMPLE LIFE

Thomas Campion   This piece praises, in idealized form, the realities of English rustic life—a contrast to the pastoral poetry of so much of this volume. It appears, with its music, in Campion's *Two Books of Airs* (1613).

Jack and Joan, They Think No Ill

Jack and Joan, they think no ill,
But loving live, and merry still;°   *always*
Do their weekdays' work, and pray
Devotely° on the holyday;   *devoutly*
5 Skip and trip it° on the green,   *caper; dance*
And help to choose the summer queen;
Lash out,° at a country feast,   *squander*
Their silver penny with the best.

Well can they judge of nappy° ale,   *heady, strong*
10 And tell at large a winter tale;[1]
Climb up to the apple loft,
And turn the crabs° till they be soft.   *crab apples (roasting)*
Tib[2] is all the father's joy,
And little Tom the mother's boy.
15 All their pleasure is content;
And care, to pay their yearly rent.[3]

Joan can call by name her cows,
And deck her windows with green boughs;

---

1. An idle tale, old wives' tale (as in Shakespeare's *The Winter's Tale*).
2. Used as a typical name for a woman or girl of lower social status.
3. That is, their only care is to pay their rent.

>   She can wreaths and tutties° make,   *nosegays*
> 20   And trim with plums a bridal cake.
>   Jack knows what brings gain or loss,
>   And his long flail[4] can stoutly toss;
>   Makes the hedge, which others[5] break,
>   And ever thinks what he doth speak.[6]
>
> 25   Now you courtly dames and knights,
>   That study only strange[7] delights,
>   Though you scorn the homespun gray,
>   And revel in your rich array;
>   Though your tongues dissemble deep,
> 30   And can your heads from danger keep;
>   Yet, for all your pomp and train,[8]
>   Securer lives the silly° swain.   *simple; lowly*
>
>   1613

4. A long-handled wooden tool for thrashing grain.
5. Aristocrats, while hunting on horseback.
6. That is, always says what he truly thinks.
7. With the connotation of "foreign," "from elsewhere." "Study": devote (yourselves) to.
8. (1) Attendants; (2) guile.

TIME

Robert Greene   Greene (1558–1592) was a popular writer of prose and romantic comedies for the stage. Probably the first professional author, he was known for his vicious critiques of colleagues, including Shakespeare. The many stories told of and by him—that he abandoned his wife and son; had another son by a mistress who was sister to a famous criminal, whom he called "Infortunatus"; and died of a "surfeit of pickle herring and Rhenish wine"—have led to speculation that he might have been the model for Shakespeare's Falstaff. This verse is sung to a lute by a woman, Doralicia, in one of his prose works, *Arbasto: The Anatomy of Fortune* (1584). It argues that everything can change in time, including one's affections.

Doralicia's Ditty

>   In time we see that silver drops
>   The craggy stones make soft;
>   The slowest snail in time we see,
>   Doth creep and clime aloft.
>
> 5   With feeble puffs the tallest pine
>   In tract of time doth fall;
>   The hardest heart in time doth yield
>   To Venus' luring call.
>
>   Where chilling frost a-late did nip
> 10   There flasheth now a fire;

Where deep disdain bred noisome° hate   *offensive*
There kindleth now desire.

Time causeth hope to have his hap;°   *(good) outcome*
What care in time not eased?
15   In time I loathed that now I love,
In both content and pleased.

1584

John Dowland   Set to music by Dowland (1563–1626) in his *Book of Songs or Airs* (1603), this lyric is likely to be by its composer. Musicians are interested in time from a practical perspective—but this poem, about working hard but being rejected at court, seems particularly personal. An "obstinate Papist," as Queen Elizabeth called him, Dowland was, throughout his life, ill-treated for reasons of his faith. He left England to seek employment in a more forgiving country, becoming court lutenist, singer, and composer for Christian IV of Denmark; when he returned, he was taken into the court of James I. Yet Dowland never seems to have stopped feeling like an outsider, and his melancholy verses and music apparently mirror his frustration.

It Was a Time When Silly Bees Could Speak

It was a time when silly° bees could speak,   *foolish; lowly*
And in that time I was a silly bee
Who fed on time until my heart gan° break,   *began to*
Yet never found the time would favor me.
5   Of all the swarm I only did not thrive,
Yet brought I wax and honey to the hive.

Then thus I buzzed when time no sap would give,
"Why should this blessèd time to me be dry,
Sith by this time the lazy drone° doth live,   *male bee*
10   The wasp, the worm, the gnat, the butterfly?"
Mated° with grief, I kneelèd on my knees,   *overcome*
And thus complained unto the king of bees:

"My liege, gods grant thy time may never end,
And yet vouchsafe° to hear my plaint° of time,   *grant / complaint*
15   Which fruitless flies have found to have a friend,°   *to be a friend*
And I cast down when atomies° do clime."   *motes in the sun*
The king replied but thus, "peace, peevish° bee,   *foolish*
Th'art bound to serve the time, the time not thee."

1603

Sir Walter Ralegh   This poem is divided into halves: three stanzas are on Nature's creation of the visually perfect (but hard-hearted) woman; three stanzas are on Time and how it destroys her. Ralegh adapted the final stanza when writing his own epitaph on the night before his execution (see p. 479).

Nature, That Washed Her Hands in Milk

    Nature, that washed her hands in milk,
        And had forgot to dry them,
    Instead of earth took snow and silk,
        At Love's request to try them,
5   If she a mistress could compose
        To please Love's fancy out of those.

    Her eyes he would should be of light,
        A violet breath, and lips of jelly;
    Her hair not black, nor overbright,
10   And of the softest down her belly;
    As for her inside he'd have it
        Only of wantonness° and wit.   *playfulness*

    At Love's entreaty such a one
        Nature made, but with her beauty
15   She hath framed a heart of stone;
        So as Love, by ill destiny,
    Must die for her whom Nature gave him,
    Because her darling would not save him.

    But Time (which Nature doth despise,
20   And rudely gives her love the lie,
    Makes Hope a fool, and Sorrow wise)
        His hands do neither wash nor dry;
    But being made of steel and rust,
    Turns snow and silk and milk to dust.

25   The light, the belly, lips, and breath,
        He dims, discolors, and destroys;
    With those he feeds but fills not death,
        Which sometimes were the food of joys.
    Yea, Time doth dull each lively wit,
30   And dries all wantonness with it.

    Oh, cruel Time! which takes in trust
        Our youth, our joys, and all we have,
    And pays us but with age and dust;
        Who in the dark and silent grave
35   When we have wandered all our ways
    Shuts up the story of our days.

1902

William Shakespeare   The narrative poem *The Rape of Lucrece* (1594) is about an aristocratic Roman woman who was raped by the heir to the throne, Tarquin, and subsequently committed suicide. The revolt against the Tarquin family, led by Lucrece's husband and family, led to the founding of the Roman Republic (traditionally dated to 509 B.C.E.). In this excerpt, the violated Lucrece considers how our destinies are shaped by time. Time solves problems, but often by obliterating them entirely.

From The Rape of Lucrece

* * *

    Time's glory is to calm contending kings,
940 To unmask falsehood and bring truth to light,
    To stamp the seal of time in agèd things,
    To wake the morn and sentinel° the night,   *guard*
    To wrong the wronger till he render right,
        To ruinate proud buildings with thy hours,
945   And smear with dust their glittering golden towers;

    To fill with wormholes stately monuments,
    To feed oblivion with decay of things,
    To blot old books and alter their contents,
    To pluck the quills from ancient ravens' wings,
950 To dry the old oak's sap and cherish springs,
        To spoil antiquities of hammered steel,
        And turn the giddy round of Fortune's wheel;

    To show the beldam° daughters of her daughter,   *old woman*
    To make the child a man, the man a child,
955 To slay the tiger that doth live by slaughter,
    To tame the unicorn and lion wild,
    To mock the subtle in themselves beguiled,[1]
        To cheer the ploughman with increaseful crops,
        And waste° huge stones with little water drops.   *wear away*

* * *

1594

---

1. The cunning who have been taken in by their own schemes.

TOBACCO

Robert Wisdome   Wisdome (d. 1568) was a Protestant preacher, exiled under Mary Tudor but, under Elizabeth I, made archdeacon of Ely. His published verse is religious, but this poem, preserved in manuscript and not possible to date, shows his interest in worldly pleasures. A reworked version, "Tobacco's but an Indian weed," sometimes attributed to George Wither, was sung as a ballad and made its way to Virginia with the early settlers.

A Religious Use of Taking Tobacco

The Indian° weed witherèd quite—   *Native American*
Green at morn, cut down at night—
Shows thy decay; all flesh is hay:
Thus think, then drink° tobacco.[1]   *smoke*

5 And when the smoke ascends on high,
Think thou behold'st the vanity
Of worldly stuff, gone with a puff:
Thus think, then drink tobacco.

The ashes that are left behind
10 May serve to put thee still in mind
That unto dust return thou must:
Thus think, then drink tobacco.

before 1568   1896

Tobias Hume   This poem appears in *The First Part of Airs, French, Polish, and Others* (1605), by Hume (ca. 1579–1645), a Scottish composer and mercenary who served as officer with both the Swedish and the Russian armies. He was known for his lighthearted rhymes and musical pranks: here, for example, he argues that tobacco and love are alike.

Tobacco

Tobacco, tobacco,
Sing sweetly for tobacco,
Tobacco is like love,
   O love it,
5 For you see I will prove it.

Love maketh lean the fat men's tumor,°   *swollen condition*
  So doth tobacco;
Love still dries up the wanton° humor,   *unruly; promiscuous*
  So doth tobacco;
10 Love makes men sail from shore to shore,
  So doth tobacco;
'Tis fond° love often makes men poor.   *foolish*
  So doth tobacco;
Love makes men scorn all coward fears,
15 So doth tobacco;
Love often sets men by the ears,°   *causes men to quarrel*
  So doth tobacco.

Tobacco, tobacco,
Sing sweetly for tobacco.
20 Tobacco is like love,
   O love it,
For you see I have proved it.

                                                            1605

---

1. Smoke was inhaled and swallowed rather than puffed out.

This commonplace book held in the Beinecke Rare Books Library, Yale University, shows a text that descends from Wisdome's poem about tobacco. In this new form, it is often attributed to George Wither.

TRADE

Robert Wilson   The song of the broom seller is found in *The Three Ladies of London* (1584), a play by the clown and playwright Wilson (active 1572–1600). It may be by him or may originate in a lost ballad entered into the Stationer's Register in 1563–64 called "Buy, Brooms, Buy." Because the text is directed to "maidens" with money or goods to barter, and is sung in the play by a woman, Conscience, it offers a glimpse into female trade and social relationships of the period.

New Brooms

New brooms, green brooms, will you buy any?
Come maidens, come quickly, let me take a penny.

My brooms are not steeped,°   *soft*
    but very well bound;
5 My brooms be not crooked,
    but smooth cut and round.
I wish it should please you
    to buy of my broom;
Then would it well ease me

          if market were done.[1]
10   Have you any old boots,
          or any old shoon,°   shoes
      Pouch-rings,° or buskins,   rings for fastening purses
          to cope° for new broom?   barter
15   If so you have, maidens,
          I pray you bring hither,
      That you and I friendly
          may bargain together.

      New brooms, green brooms, will you buy any:
20   Come maidens, come quickly, let me take a penny.

                                                                               1584

Robert Wilson   This dialogue song, in which potential male servants beg for hire—and are firmly rejected by the distrustful woman called Conscience—is from Wilson's play *The Three Ladies of London* (1584). The characters in this play are depicted by their names: the men in this scene are called Fraud, Dissimulation, Usury, Simony, and Simplicity; the women are called Lucre, Love, and Conscience.

Hunting for Hire

Good ladies, take pity and grant our desire.
    Speak boldly and tell me what is't you require.
Your service,° good ladies, is that we do crave.   to serve you
    We like not nor list° not such servants to have.   desire

5   *If you entertain us, we trusty will be—*
        But if you refrain us, then most unhappy—
    We will come, we will run, we will bend at your beck.°   when you beckon
    We will ply,[1] we will hie,° for fear of a check.°   hurry / reprimand

    You do feign,° you do flatter, you do lie, you do prate;°   pretend / chatter
10   You will steal, you will rob, you will kill in your hate.
    I deny you, I defy you, then cease of your talking,
        I refrain you,° I disdain you, therefore get you walking.   shun you

                                                                               1584

Anonymous   The three poems that follow are all from *Deuteromelia* (1609), a song collection by the composer Thomas Ravenscroft (1588–1635). Ravenscroft was a boy chorister at St. Paul's Cathedral who went on to become a composer in his own right. He also published song collections, which seem to have mingled popular oral music—street cries, songs of trade—with songs of his own. This song, which gathers the street cries of a variety of London vendors, may be by Ravenscroft or may be traditional. In it, we see female and male traders who are made happy or unhappy by their jobs. The poorest people are here said to be the happiest.

1. When the market is finished.
1. Apply ourselves.

Cries of London

Who liveth so merry in all this land
As doth the poor widow that selleth the sand?
    And ever she singeth, as I can guess,
    "Will you buy any sand, any sand, mistress?"

5 The broom-man° maketh his living most sweet   *street sweeper*
With carrying of brooms from street to street.
    Who would desire a pleasanter thing
    Than all the day long to do nothing but sing?

The chimney-sweeper all the long day
10 He singeth and sweepeth the soot away.
    Yet when he comes home, although he be weary,
    With his sweet wife he maketh full merry.

15 The cobbler he sits cobbling till noon,
And cobbleth his shoes till they be done.
    Yet doth he not fear, and so doth say,
    For he knows his work will soon decay.

The merchantman doth sail on the seas,
20 And lie on the shipboard with little ease,
    Always in doubt° the rock is near—   *suspecting*
    How can he be merry and make good cheer?

The husbandman° all day goeth to plow,   *farmer*
And when he comes home he serveth° his sow.   *tends to*
25   He moileth° and toileth all the long year,   *works hard*
    How can he be merry and make good cheer?

The serving-man waiteth° from street to street,   *attends*
With blowing his nails and beating his feet,[1]
    And serveth for forty shillings a year,
30   That 'tis impossible to make good cheer.

Who liveth so merry and maketh such sport
As those that be of thy poorest sort?
    The poorest sort, wheresoever they be,
    They gather together by one, two, and three,
35   And every man will spend his penny:
    What makes such a shot° among a great many?[2]   *payment*

ca. 1609

---

1. Typical actions of someone who is cold.
2. In this final stanza the poorest are gathered in the alehouse spending their hard-earned money.

"Soldier's Song" was probably gathered by Ravenscroft, as it concerns mercenaries returning from the Dutch Revolt (1566/8–1648) against the Spaniards. The French imprecation suggests the soldiers have been fighting alongside the French and have learned some of their phrases. The text combines bravado and desperation: these penniless fighters have returned home desperate for money and drink; the song contains a threat that they may do mischief to those who will not help them.

Soldiers' Song

We be soldiers three,
    Pardonnez-moi je vous en prie,[1]
Lately come forth of the low country,
    With never a penny of money.

5 Here, goodfellow,° I drink to thee,   *drinking companion*
    Pardonnez-moi je vous en prie,
To all goodfellows wherever they be,
    With never a penny of money.

And he that will not pledge me[2] this,
10   *Pardonnez-moi je vous en prie,*
Pays for the shot,[3] whatever it is,
    With never a penny of money.

Charge it° again, boy, charge it again,   *refill it*
    Pardonnez-moi je vous en prie,
15 As long as there is any ink in thy pen[4]
    With never a penny of money.

ca. 1609

"Mariners' Song" may be a companion piece by Ravenscroft to match "Soldiers' Song," though it may be traditional.

Mariners' Song

We be three poor mariners
Newly come from the seas;
We spend our lives in jeopardy
Whiles others live at ease.
5 Shall we go dance the round
And shall we go dance the round?
And he that is a bully boy,° come pledge me on the   *good young man*
    ground.[1]

---

1. Excuse me if you please (French).
2. Drink with me as a sign of friendship.
3. Pays the bill, or, alternatively, pays for the drink—though there is a threat, too, of actual shooting.
4. Presumably to record the debt.
1. Drink a toast to me. The term "ground" mingles a physical place and music: the ground was the plainsong or melody.

We care not for those martial men
That do our states disdain;
10 But we care for those merchantmen
Which do our states maintain.²
To them we dance this round
Around; to them we dance this round.
And he that is a bully boy, come pledge me on the ground.

ca. 1609

2. Because the merchants trade in ships, they maintain mariners.

WOMEN

Sir John Harington, Lady Mary Cheke   This poetic exchange is recorded in a commonplace book of about 1630, kept by Robert Bishop (dates unknown). It consists of a poem by Harington (1561–1612)—published, but in a different form, in 1618—that claims that there once was a "certain" man but has never been a certain woman, not even in the Bible (the joke conflates several senses of *certain*: "particular," "clear," "able to be relied on," and "knowing one's own mind"). The reply, by Cheke (ca. 1532–1616), lady of the privy chamber to Elizabeth I, takes the form of an answer poem: it turns the table on the first poem and corrects it (in a literal but also figurative sense, as, Cheke points out, the phrase "certain woman" *is* in the Bible). By making Harington's statement into the first part of a dialogue, Cheke upstages him to "win" what she has ingeniously rendered a dispute.

Sir John Harington: A Certain Man

It was not certain when a certain preacher—
That having never learned would be° a teacher—   *wanted to be*
And having thus in Latin read his text
Of "Erat quidam homo", much perplexed,
5 He seemed the same with diligence to scan°   *interpret*
In English thus, "'There was *a certain* man'.¹
And now", said he, "good people mark you this,
He saith *there was*, he doth not say *there is*,
For in this age of ours, it is most certain,
10 Of promise, word, deed, oath, there's no man certain,
Yet by my text it's clearly brought to pass°   *brought about*
That surely once a certain man there was.
But this I think, in all the bible no man
Can find *this* text: 'there was a certain woman.'"

before 1612

1. That no such line appears in the Vulgate (Latin) Bible undercuts Harington's story. The preacher is probably looking at "Homo quidam erat dives" (There was a certain rich man; Luke 16:19).

Lady Mary Cheke: The Reply

    That no man yet could in the Bible find
    A certain woman argues men all blind:
    Blind as the preacher who had little learning,
    The certain cause of his so ill° discerning.   *poorly*
5 A certain woman of the multitude
    Said "blessed be the paps° that gave our savior food".[2]   *breasts*
    A certain woman, too, a millstone[3] threw
    And from the wall Abimelech she slew.[4]
    Nay more. By men though it be oversaid,°   *mentioned previously*
10 The text records there was a certain maid,
    Which proves directly certain women then,
    And certain too, more certain far then men.[5]
    Your preacher, then, may well stand much perplexed
    To see how grossly he belied° the text,   *gave a false impression of*
15 And blush that's sermon was no better suited
    Than by a woman thus to be confuted.°   *proved wrong*
    Yet, for his comfort, one true note he made
    When "there is now no certain man" he said.

before 1612

Lady Anne Southwell

Southwell (1574–1636) recorded this poem in a commonplace book dated 1636. The book contained verse that she wrote throughout her life.

All Married Men Desire to Have Good Wives

    All married men desire to have good wives,
    But few give good example by their lives.
    They are our head; they would have us their heels.[1]
    This makes the good wife kick; the goodman° reels.°   *husband / recoils*
5 When God brought Eve to Adam for a bride,
    The text says she was ta'en from out man's side,
    A symbol of that side whose sacred blood
    Flowed for his spouse: the church's saving good.[2]
    This is a mystery° perhaps too deep   *religious truth*
10 For blockish° Adam that was fallen asleep.   *stupid*

before 1637

---

2. See Luke 11:27. Cheke's poem corrects Harington's by pointing out that in the Bible the phrase "a certain woman/girl" can in fact be found, and once again plays on "certain."
3. Large flat stone used for grinding grain.
4. See Judges 9:53.
5. That is, the Bible says "certain women" even more often than it says "certain men."
1. See 1 Corinthians 11:3: "the head of every man is Christ; and the head of the woman is the man."
2. For this creation story, see Genesis 2:21–22. John 19:34 describes the blood and water that flowed from the pierced side of Christ on the Cross; here, as often, his spouse is the church. The notion of a "saving good"—that a good act might indicate status as one of the "elect" destined for heaven—is associated with Protestantism.

JOHN LYLY
1554–1606

John Lyly was the grandson of William Lily, the author of the standard Latin grammar that every English schoolboy studied. After receiving an M.A. degree at Oxford, Lyly went to London, where his prose romance *Euphues* (1578) enjoyed an instant success. He later wrote several elegant, sophisticated plays acted at court by the children's companies and served several terms as a member of Parliament, though his hopes of obtaining a lucrative court appointment were disappointed.

The title *Euphues*, taken from the name of that book's hero, is Greek for "of good natural parts, graceful, witty"; the subtitle, *Anatomy of Wit*, means something like "analysis of the mental faculties." The plot of the work involves a young man who leaves university for the temptations of the city, falls in love, betrays his best friend, is in turn betrayed, repents, and thereafter ladles out great quantities of moral wisdom. But the story is secondary to the prose style, which has come to be known as "euphuism" and which greatly influenced a generation of writers eager to follow the fashion the book established. The style has two distinctive features: a sentence structure based on comparison and antithesis; and a wealth of verbal embellishments, including proverbs, incidents from history and poetry, and fanciful similes drawn from contemporary science, classical texts, or the author's own imagination. Euphuism became a rage for a while, especially at court. The style may have been particularly popular among court women: in 1632 the publisher of Lyly's *Six Court Comedies* informed his readers that "all our ladies were then his [Euphues's or Lyly's] scholars, and the beauty in court who could not parley Euphuism was as little regarded as she which now there speaks not French." When it started to fall out of fashion, euphuism was criticized by Sidney, parodied by Shakespeare, and mocked by Thomas Nashe and Ben Jonson. Although it did not last, Lyly's highly self-conscious, overwrought style is an example of the Elizabethan fascination with ornate language and artifice.

From Euphues: The Anatomy of Wit

[EUPHUES INTRODUCED]

There dwelt in Athens a young gentleman of great patrimony, and of so comely a personage, that it was doubted[1] whether he were more bound to Nature for the lineaments of his person, or to Fortune for the increase of his possessions. But Nature impatient of comparisons, and as it were disdaining a companion or copartner in her working, added to this comeliness of his body such a sharp capacity of mind, that not only she proved Fortune counterfeit, but was half of that opinion that she herself was only current.[2] This young gallant, of more wit[3] than wealth, and yet of more wealth than wisdom, seeing himself inferior to none in pleasant conceits,[4] thought himself superior to all in honest conditions, insomuch that he deemed himself so apt to all things, that he gave himself almost to nothing, but practicing of

1. Doubtful, uncertain.
2. Genuine.
3. Intellect.
4. Witty expressions.

those things commonly which are incident to these sharp wits, fine phrases, smooth quipping, merry taunting, using jesting without mean,[5] and abusing mirth without measure. As therefore the sweetest rose hath his prickle, the finest velvet his brack,[6] the fairest flower his bran,[7] so the sharpest wit hath his wanton will, and the holiest head his wicked way. And true it is that some men write and most men believe, that in all perfect shapes, a blemish bringeth rather a liking every way to the eyes, than a loathing any way to the mind. Venus had her mole in her cheek which made her more amiable: Helen[8] her scar on her chin which Paris called *cos amoris*, the whetsone of love. Aristippus his wart, Lycurgus[9] his wen: So likewise in the disposition of the mind, either virtue is over-shadowed with some vice, or vice overcast with some virtue. Alexander valiant in war, yet given to wine. Tully eloquent in his glozes, yet vainglorious: Solomon wise, yet too too wanton: David holy but yet an homicide:[1] none more witty than Euphues, yet at the first none more wicked. The freshest colors soonest fade, the teenest[2] razor soonest turneth his edge, the finest cloth is soonest eaten with moths, and the cambric sooner stained than the coarse canvas: which appeared well in this Euphues, whose wit being like wax apt to receive any impression, and having the bridle in his own hands, either to use the rein or the spur, disdaining counsel, leaving his country, loathing his old acquaintance, thought either by wit to obtain some conquest, or by shame to abide[3] some conflict, and leaving the rule of reason, rashly ran unto destruction. Who preferring fancy before friends, and his present humor[4] before honor to come, laid reason in water being too salt for his taste, and followed unbridled affection, most pleasant for his tooth.[5] When parents have more care how to leave their children wealthy than wise, and are more desirous to have them maintain the name than the nature of a gentleman; when they put gold into the hands of youth, where they should put a rod under their girdle,[6] when instead of awe they make them past grace, and leave them rich executors of goods, and poor executors of godliness, then is it no marvel that the son, being left rich by his father's will, become retchless by his own will.[7]

It hath been an old-said saw,[8] and not of less truth than antiquity, that wit is the better if it be the dearer bought: as in the sequel of this history[9] shall most manifestly appear. It happened this young imp[1] to arrive at Naples (a place of more pleasure than profit, and yet of more profit than piety), the very walls and windows whereof shewed it rather to be the Tabernacle of Venus than the Temple of Vesta.[2]

There was all things necessary and in readiness that might either allure the mind to lust or entice the heart to folly, a court more meet[3] for an atheist than

---

5. Moderation.
6. Break, flaw.
7. Husk.
8. The Greek queen whom Paris abducted to Troy: the most beautiful woman in the world.
9. The legendary lawgiver of Sparta. Aristippus was a disciple of Socrates and traditionally the founder of the Cyrenaic school of philosophy, which taught that life's goal is pleasure.
1. The biblical King David loved Bathsheba and had her husband, Uriah, killed so he could marry her. Alexander the Great killed his friend Clitus in a drunken brawl. Tully (Marcus Tullius Cicero) was the great Roman orator, famous for his "glozes" (flattering speeches). Solomon, David's son, was famous both for his wisdom and for his many wives.
2. Keenest.
3. Stand firm in.
4. Whimsy.
5. Taste. "Affection": passion.
6. That is, whip them. "Girdle": belt.
7. Appetite, the opposite of reason. "Retchless": reckless.
8. Saying, proverb.
9. Rest of this story.
1. Novice.
2. Symbolizing chastity, in contrast to Venus.
3. Fitting.

for one of Athens, for Ovid than for Aristotle, for a graceless lover than for a godly liver: more fitter for Paris than Hector, and meeter for Flora than Diana.[4]

Here my youth (whether for weariness he could not, or for wantonness would not, go any further) determined to make his abode: whereby it is evidently seen that the fleetest fish swalloweth the delicatest bait, that the highest soaring hawk traineth[5] to the lure, and that the wittiest sconce[6] is inveigled with the sudden view or alluring vanities.

Here he wanted[7] no companions which courted him continually with sundry kinds of devices, whereby they might either soak[8] his purse to reap commodity, or soothe his person to win credit, for he had guests and companions of all sorts.

There frequented to this lodging and mansion house as well the spider to suck poison of his fine wit as the bee to gather honey, as well the drone as the dove, the fox as the lamb, as well Damocles[9] to betray him as Damon[1] to be true to him: yet he behaved himself so warily, that he singled his game[2] wisely. He could easily discern Apollo's music from Pan his pipe,[3] and Venus's beauty from Juno's bravery,[4] and the faith of Laelius[5] from the flattery of Aristippus, he welcomed all but trusted none, he was merry but yet so wary that neither the flatterer could take advantage to entrap him in his talk nor the wisest any assurance of his friendship: who being demanded of[6] one what countryman he was, he answered, "What countryman am I not? If I be in Crete, I can lie, if in Greece I can shift, if in Italy I can court it:[7] if thou ask whose son I am also, I ask thee whose son I am not. I can carouse with Alexander, abstain with Romulus, eat with the Epicure, fast with the Stoic, sleep with Endymion, watch with Chrysippus,"[8] using these speeches and other like. An old gentleman in Naples seeing his pregnant wit,[9] his eloquent tongue somewhat taunting, yet with delight, his mirth without measure yet not without wit, his sayings vainglorious yet pithy, began to bewail his nurture and to muse at his nature, being incensed against the one as most pernicious, and enflamed with the other as most precious: for he well knew that so rare a wit would in time either breed an intolerable trouble or bring an incomparable treasure to the common weal:[1] at the one he greatly pitied, at the other he rejoiced.

1578

4. Diana was the goddess of chastity. Ovid was famous for his love poems, Aristotle for his profound philosophical works. Paris was the lover of Helen, in contrast to his brother Hector, the greatest Trojan warrior. Flora was a fertility goddess whose annual celebrations were noted for lasciviousness.
5. Is attracted to.
6. Head, brain.
7. Lacked.
8. Drain.
9. Famous as a flatterer of Dionysius, who gave him a gorgeous banquet but made him sit with a sword suspended over his head by a single hair, to show how dangerous eminence is.
1. Famous in classical legend as the friend of Pythias, so loyal to him that he offered to be executed in his place.
2. Separated his target animal from the herd—that is, made distinctions.
3. In classical myth, Apollo's music was much superior to that which Pan, god of the wild spaces, produced on his pipes.
4. Splendid attire.
5. Laelius was famous as the faithful friend of Scipio Africanus the Younger.
6. Asked by.
7. Inhabitants of the island of Crete early had a reputation as liars. Lyly is elaborating or inventing when he says that the Greeks "shift" (practice or live by deceit) and that the Italians "court it" (behave in a courtly manner).
8. Chrysippus was a celebrated Stoic philosopher, so devoted to study that he would "watch" (stay up all night) with his books. Romulus was the legendary founder and first king of Rome. Exposed as an infant with his twin brother, Remus, he was rescued and suckled by a she-wolf and became a symbol of abstinence. The followers of Epicurus (Epicureans) were thought to care for nothing but pleasure. The austere Stoics venerated duty. Endymion was a youth in Greek legend renowned for his beauty and his eternal sleep on Mount Latmus, where the moon goddess fell in love with him.
9. Fertile mind.
1. Commonwealth.

SIR PHILIP SIDNEY
1554–1586

Sir Philip Sidney's face was "spoiled with pimples," Ben Jonson remarked in 1619, distancing himself from the virtual cult that had arisen in the years after Sidney's death. Knight, soldier, poet, friend, and patron, Sidney seemed to most Elizabethans to embody all the traits of character and personality they admired: he was Castiglione's perfect courtier come to life. When he was killed in battle in the Low Countries at the age of thirty-two, fighting for the Protestant cause against the hated Spanish, all England mourned. Stories, not all necessarily true, immediately began to circulate about his gallantry on the battlefield—grievously wounded, he gave his water to a dying foot soldier with the words "Thy necessity is yet greater than mine"—and about his astonishing self-composure as he himself lay dying: suffering from his putrifying, gangrenous wound, Sidney composed a song and had it sung by his deathbed. When his corpse was brought back to England for burial, the spectacular funeral procession, one of the most elaborate ever staged, almost bankrupted his father-in-law, Francis Walsingham, the wealthy head of Queen Elizabeth's secret service.

Philip Sidney's father was Sir Henry Sidney, thrice lord deputy (governor) of Ireland, and his mother was a sister of Robert Dudley, Earl of Leicester, the most spectacular and powerful of all the queen's favorites. He entered Shrewsbury School in 1564, at the age of ten, on the same day as Fulke Greville, who became his lifelong friend and his biographer. Greville wrote of Sidney, "Though I lived with him and knew him from a child, yet I never knew him other than a man—with such staidness of mind, lovely and familiar gravity, as carried grace and reverence above greater years." He attended Oxford but left without taking a degree; he completed his education by extended travels on the Continent. There he met many of the most important people of the time, from kings and queens to philosophers, theologians, and poets. In France he witnessed the St. Bartholomew's Day Massacre, which began in Paris on August 24, 1572, and raged through France for more than a month, as Catholic mobs incited by Queen Catherine de Médicis slaughtered perhaps fifty thousand Huguenots (French Protestants). This experience undoubtedly strengthened Sidney's ardent Protestantism. In an intense correspondence with his mentor, the humanist reformer Hubert Languet of Burgundy, France, he brooded on how he could help save Europe from what he viewed as the Roman Catholic menace.

Languet and his associates clearly hoped that this brilliant and wonderfully well-connected young Englishman would be able to steer English royal policy toward active intervention in Europe's wars of religion. Yet when he returned to England, Sidney found the direct path to heroic action blocked by the caution and hard-nosed realism of Queen Elizabeth and her principal advisers. Though she sent him on some modest diplomatic missions, the queen clearly regarded the zealous young man with considerable skepticism. As a prominent courtier with literary interests, Sidney actively encouraged authors such as Edward Dyer, Greville, and, most important, Edmund Spenser, who dedicated *The Shepheardes Calender* to him as "the president [chief exemplar] of noblesse and of chevalree." But he clearly longed to be something more than an influential patron of letters. In 1580 his Protestant *convictions* led him publicly to oppose Queen Elizabeth's projected marriage to the Catholic Duke of Anjou. The queen, who hated interference with her diplomatic maneuvers, angrily dismissed Sidney from the court.

He retired to Wilton, the estate of his beloved and learned sister, Mary Herbert, Countess of Pembroke, and there he wrote a long, elaborate epic romance in prose, called *Arcadia*. Sidney's claim, made with studied nonchalance, that the work was written on the spur of the moment for his sister's private entertainment is belied by its considerable literary, political, and moral ambitions, qualities that were reinforced and intensified in the extensive revisions he began to make to it in 1582. Our selection is from this revised version, which scholars call the *New Arcadia*.

In addition to *Arcadia*, which inspired many imitations, including the *Urania* of Sidney's niece, Lady Mary Wroth, two other influential works by Sidney have had still more lasting importance. One of these, *The Defense of Poesy*, is the major work of literary criticism produced in the English Renaissance. In this long essay Sidney eloquently defends poetry (his term for all imaginative literature) against its attackers and, in the process, greatly exalts the role of the poet, the freedom of the imagination, and the moral value of fiction. Perhaps Sidney's finest literary achievement is *Astrophil and Stella* (Starlover and Star), the first of the great Elizabethan sonnet cycles. The principal focus of these sonnets is not a sequence of events or an unfolding relationship. Rather, they explore the lover's state of mind and soul—the contradictory impulses, intense desires, and frustrations that haunt him.

In his guise as a lovelorn sonneteer, Sidney repeatedly insists that the thought of his beloved drives all more mundane matters from his mind. Yet a number of the sonnets betray a continuing preoccupation with matters of politics and foreign policy. Neither love nor literature could distract Sidney for long from what he took to be his destined role. In 1585 he tried to join Sir Francis Drake's West Indian expedition but was prevented by the queen; instead, she appointed him governor of Flushing in the Netherlands, where as a volunteer and knight-errant he engaged in several vicious skirmishes in the war against Spain. At Zutphen on September 13, 1586, leading a charge against great odds, Sidney was wounded in the thigh, shortly after he had thrown away his thigh armor in an ill-fated chivalric gesture. He died twenty-six days later.

In keeping with the norms of his class, Sidney did not publish any of his major literary works himself. His ambition, continually thwarted, was to be a man of action whose deeds would affect his country's destiny. Yet he was the author of the most ambitious work of prose fiction, the most important piece of literary criticism, and the most influential sonnet cycle of the Elizabethan Age.

The Countess of Pembroke's Arcadia

Sidney wrote his epic romance in two forms, which scholars have dubbed the *Old Arcadia* and the *New Arcadia*. Shortly after the *Old Arcadia* was completed, in five "books," Sidney began to recast and greatly expand it, but he broke off in midsentence and left the revision unfinished. This revised fragment, almost three books, is known as the *New Arcadia*; it was published after his death, in 1590. In 1593 Sidney's sister, the Countess of Pembroke, herself a gifted writer, made some small changes to the *New Arcadia* and the last two books of the *Old*, stitched them together, and published them as a single text. (The complete *Old Arcadia*, as Sidney had left it in manuscript, was not rediscovered and published until the twentieth century.) Both Sidney's original version and his revision are full of oracles, princes in disguise, mistaken identity, melodramatic incidents, and tangled love situations, but the *New Arcadia* has a much more labyrinthine, interwoven plot, as well as a more consistently elevated tone of moral and heroic high seriousness. Some episodes are of political interest, and Sidney clearly put into the work more of his serious thought on statecraft (the responsibilities of a king or queen, the evils of rebellion, and the duties of ministers, judges, and advisers of state) than his claim that the *Arcadia* was mere entertainment suggests. Many poems—pastoral eclogues and songs—are interspersed throughout the narrative; they represent Sidney's experiments with diverse lyric kinds and verse forms.

From The Countess of Pembroke's Arcadia[1]

From *The First Book*

[THE ABSENT URANIA]

It was in the time that the earth begins to put on her new apparel against the approach of her lover, and that the sun, running a most even course, becomes an indifferent arbiter between the night and the day, when the hopeless shepherd Strephon was come to the sands which lie against the island of Cithera; where viewing the place with a heavy kind of delight, and sometimes casting his eyes to the isleward, he called his friendly rival, the pastor[2] Klaius, unto him; and setting first down in his darkened countenance a doleful copy of what he would speak,

"O my Klaius," said he, "hither we are now come to pay the rent for which we are so called unto by over-busy remembrance—remembrance, restless remembrance, which claims not only this duty of us but for it will have us forget ourselves. I pray you, when we were amid our flock, and that of other shepherds some were running after their sheep strayed beyond their bounds, some delighting their eyes with seeing them nibble upon the short and sweet grass, some medicining their sick ewes, some setting a bell for an ensign of a sheepish squadron,[3] some with more leisure inventing new games of exercising their bodies and sporting their wits; did remembrance grant us any holiday either for pastime or devotion—nay either for necessary food or natural rest—but that still it forced our thoughts to work upon this place where we last (alas, that the word *last* should so long last) did graze our eyes upon her ever-flourishing beauty? Did it not still cry within us 'Ah, you base-minded wretches, are your thoughts so deeply bemired in the trade or ordinary worldeings, as for respect of gain some paltry wool may yield you, to let so much time pass without knowing perfectly her estate, especially in so troublesome a season; to leave that shore unsaluted from whence you may see to the island where she dwelleth; to leave those steps unkissed wherein Urania printed the farewell of all beauty?'

"Well, then, remembrance commanded; we obeyed, and here we find that as our remembrance came ever clothed unto us in the form of this place, so this place gives new heat to the fever of our languishing remembrance. . . ." * * *

[*Klaius*] ". . . Hath not the only love[4] of her made us, being silly ignorant shepherds, raise up our thoughts above the ordinary level of the world, so as great clerks[5] do not disdain our conference? Hath not the desire to seem worthy in her eyes made us, when others were sleeping, to sit viewing the course of the heavens; when others were running at base,[6] to run over learned writings; when others mark[7] their sheep, we mark ourselves? Hath not she thrown

---

1. These sections are from chapters 1, 2, and 3 of the *New Arcadia*. The opening section presents Strephon and Klaius, two Arcadian shepherds, lamenting the loss of Urania, a shepherdess whom both love and a figure of Neoplatonic beauty. The next section portrays one of the two young heroes of the work, the shipwrecked Musidorus, being led into the land of Arcadia by the shepherds (who are also the singers of the song "Ye Goat-herd Gods"). They bring him to the house of the wise and noble Kalander, who introduces the central plot of Sidney's romance in the curious situation of King Basilius and his family.
2. Shepherd.
3. That is, tying a bell on the leader of the flock. "Ensign": standard-bearer.
4. Love alone.
5. Scholars.
6. The country game of Prisoner's Base.
7. Consider.

reason upon our desires and, as it were, given eyes unto Cupid?[8] Hath in any but in her, love-fellowship maintained friendship between rivals, and beauty taught the beholders chastity?"

[THE COUNTRY OF ARCADIA]

* * * The third day after, in the time that the morning did strew roses and violets in the heavenly floor against the coming of the sun, the nightingales (striving one with the other which could in most dainty variety recount their wrong-caused sorrow)[9] made them put off their sleep, and rising from under a tree (which that night had been their pavilion) they went on their journey, which by and by welcomed Musidorus' eyes, wearied with the wasted soil of Laconia,[1] with delightful prospects.

There were hills which garnished their proud heights with stately trees; humble valleys whose base estate seemed comforted with refreshing of silver rivers; meadows enameled[2] with all sorts of eye-pleasing flowers; thickets, which, being lined with most pleasant shade, were witnessed so to by the cheerful deposition[3] of many well-tuned birds; each pasture stored with sheep feeding with sober security, while the pretty lambs with bleating oratory craved the dams' comfort; here a shepherd's boy piping as though he should never be old; there a young shepherdess knitting and withal singing, and it seemed that her voice comforted her hands to work and her hands kept time to her voice's music. As for the houses of the country—for many houses came under their eye—they were all scattered, no two being one by the other, and yet not so far off as that it barred mutual succour: a show, as it were, of an accompanable solitariness and of a civil wildness.[4]

"I pray you," said Musidorus, then first unsealing his long silent lips, "what countries be these we pass through which are so divers in show, the one wanting no store,[5] the other having no store but of want?"

"The country," answered Klaius, "where you were cast ashore and now are passed through is Laconia, not so poor by the barrenness of the soil (though in itself not passing fertile) as by a civil war, which being these two years within the bowels of that estate between the gentlemen and the peasants (by them named Helots)[6] hath in this sort as it were disfigured the face of nature, and made it so unhospital[7] as now you have found it: the towns neither of the one side nor the other willingly opening their gates to strangers, nor strangers willingly entering for fear of being mistaken.

"But this country where now you set your foot is Arcadia;[8] and even hard by is the house of Kalander whither we lead you: this country being thus decked with peace and (the child of peace) good husbandry. These houses you see so scattered are of men as we two are that live upon the commodity of their sheep, and therefore in the division of the Arcadian estate are termed shepherds: a happy people, wanting little because they desire not much."

---

8. The god of Love is traditionally blind.
9. Sorrows caused by wrongs.
1. The ancient name of the southeastern district of the Greek Peloponnese, which includes Sparta; much of it is hilly, rugged, and barren.
2. Adorned with varied colors, like enamelwork.
3. Testimony.
4. "Accompanable [that is, sociable] solitariness" and "civil [that is, civilized] wildness" are oxymorons, figures of flat contradiction.
5. Abundance.
6. State-owned serfs in Sparta, probably the original inhabitants of Laconia.
7. Inhospitable.
8. A country in the middle of the Peloponnese, surrounded by mountains and very fertile; beginning with classical Greek and Latin bucolic poetry, it was represented as a paradise.

"What cause then," said Musidorus, "made you venture to leave this sweet life and put yourself in yonder unpleasant and dangerous realm?"

"Guarded with poverty," answered Strephon, "and guided with love."

[KALANDER TELLS ABOUT BASILIUS]

Which Kalander perceiving, "Well," said he, "my dear guest, I know your mind and I will satisfy it. Neither will I do it like a niggardly answerer, going no further than the bounds of the question; but I will discover[9] unto you as well that wherein my knowledge is common with others as that which by extraordinary means is delivered unto me, knowing so much in you (though not long acquainted) that I shall find your ears faithful treasurers." So then sitting down in two chairs and sometimes casting his eye to the picture,[1] he thus spake:

"This country Arcadia among all the provinces of Greece hath ever been had in singular reputation; partly for the sweetness of the air and other natural benefits, but principally for the well-tempered minds of the people who (finding that the shining title of glory, so much affected by other nations, doth indeed help little to the happiness of life) are the only people which, as by their justice and providence give neither cause nor hope to their neighbors to annoy them, so are they not stirred with false praise to trouble others' quiet, thinking it a small reward for the wasting of their own lives in ravening[2] that their posterity should long after say they had done so. Even the Muses[1] seem to approve their good determination by choosing this country for their chief repairing[3] place, and by bestowing their perfections so largely here that the very shepherds have their fancies lifted to so high conceits[4] that the learned of other nations are content both to borrow their names and imitate their cunning.

"Here dwelleth and reigneth this prince (whose picture you see) by name Basilius;[5] a prince of sufficient skill to govern so quiet a country, where the good minds of the former princes had set down good laws, and the well-bringing up of the people did serve as a most sure bond to hold them. But to be plain with you, he excels in nothing so much as in the zealous love of his people, wherein he doth not only pass all his own foregoers but, as I think, all the princes living. Whereof the cause is that though he exceed not in the virtues which get admiration, as depth of wisdom, height of courage, and largeness of magnificence, yet is he notable in those which stir affection, as truth of word, meekness, courtesy, mercifulness, and liberality.

"He, being already well stricken in years, married a young princess named Gynecia,[6] daughter to the king of Cyprus, of notable beauty as by her picture you see: a woman of great wit, and in truth of more princely virtues than her husband; of most unspotted chastity, but of so working a mind and so vehement spirits as a man may say it was happy[7] she took a good course, for otherwise it would have been terrible.

"Of these two are brought into the world two daughters, so beyond measure excellent in all the gifts allotted to reasonable creatures that we may think they were born to show that nature is no stepmother to that sex, how much

---

9. Disclose, reveal.
1. The picture of Basilius, as we learn below.
2. Plundering.
1. The nine goddesses who preside over the different kinds of poetry and the several arts and sciences.
3. Revivifying.
4. Conceptions.
5. The Greek word for "king."
6. The Greek word for "woman."
7. Fortunate.

soever some men, sharp-witted only in evil speaking, have sought to disgrace them. The elder is named Pamela, by many men not deemed inferior to her sister. For my part, when I marked them both, methought there was (if at least such perfections may receive the word of more) more sweetness in Philoclea but more majesty in Pamela: methought love played in Philoclea's eyes and threatened in Pamela's; methought Philoclea's beauty only persuaded, but so persuaded as all hearts must yield; Pamela's beauty used violence, and such violence as no heart could resist. And it seems that such proportion is between their minds: Philoclea so bashful, as though her excellencies had stolen into her before she was aware; so humble, that she will put all pride out of countenance; in sum, such proceeding as will stir hope but teach hope good manners. Pamela of high thoughts, who avoids not pride with not knowing her excellencies, but by making that one of her excellencies, to be void of pride; her mother's wisdom, greatness, nobility, but—if I can guess aright—knit with a more constant temper. Now then, our Basilius—being so publicly happy as to be a prince, and so happy in that happiness as to be a beloved prince, and so in his private blessed as to have so excellent a wife and so over-excellent children—hath of late taken a course which yet makes him more spoken of than all these blessings. For, having made a journey to Delphos[8] and safely returned, within short space he brake up his court and retired himself, his wife and children, into a certain forest hereby which he calleth his desert; wherein, besides a house appointed for stables and lodgings for certain persons of mean calling who do all household services, he hath built two fine lodges. In the one of them himself remains with his younger daughter Philoclea—which was the cause they three were matched together in this picture—without having any other creature living in that lodge with him.

"Which though it be strange, yet not strange as the course he hath taken with the princess Pamela whom he hath placed in the other lodge; but how think you accompanied? Truly with none other but one Dametas, the most arrant doltish clown that I think ever was without the privilege of a bauble,[9] with his wife Miso and daughter Mopsa, in whom no wit can devise anything wherein they may pleasure her but to exercise her patience and to serve for a foil of her perfections."

From *Book Two*

CHAPTER 1[1]

In these pastoral pastimes[2] a great number of days were sent to follow their flying predecessors, while the cup of poison[3] (which was deeply tasted of this noble company) had left no sinew of theirs without mortally searching into it; yet never manifesting his venomous work, till once that the night (parting away angry that she could distill no more sleep into the eyes of lovers) had no sooner given place to the breaking out of the morning light and

---

8. To consult the famous oracle of Apollo there.
9. Jester's baton (which would explain and excuse his folly).
1. Before this chapter, Pyrocles, prince of Macedon, has fallen in love with Philoclea, daughter of Basilius and Gynecia, the king and queen of Arcadia. To gain entrance to the royal household, he has disguised himself as a woman, the Amazon Zelmane. To his dismay, though, both Basilius and Gynecia (who sees through his disguise) have fallen in love with him.
2. The reference is to the elaborate entertainment, featuring a series of pastoral songs, that had concluded Book One.
3. That is, love.

the sun bestowed his beams upon the tops of the mountains, but that the woeful Gynecia (to whom rest was no ease) had left her loathed lodging and gotten herself into the solitary places those deserts[4] were full of, going up and down with such unquiet motions as a grieved and hopeless mind is wont to bring forth. There appeared unto the eyes of her judgment the evils she was like to run into, with ugly infamy waiting upon them: she felt the terrors of her own conscience; she was guilty of a long exercised virtue which made this vice the fuller of deformity. The uttermost of the good she could aspire unto was a mortal wound to her vexed spirits; and lastly, no small part of her evils was that she was wise to see her evils. Insomuch that, having a great while thrown her countenance ghastly about her[5] (as if she had called all the powers of the world to be witness of her wretched estate), at length casting up her watery eyes to heaven:

"O sun," said she, "whose unspotted light directs the steps of mortal mankind, art thou not ashamed to impart the clearness of thy presence to such a dust-creeping worm as I am? O you heavens, which continually keep the course allotted unto you, can none of your influences prevail so much upon the miserable Gynecia as to make her preserve a course so long embraced by her? O deserts, deserts, how fit a guest am I for you, since my heart can people you with wild ravenous beasts, which in you are wanting! O virtue, where dost thou hide thyself? What hideous thing is this which doth eclipse thee? Or is it true that thou wert never but a vain name and no essential thing, which hast thus left thy professed servant when she had most need of thy lovely presence? O imperfect proportion of reason, which can too much foresee and too little prevent! Alas, alas," said she, "if there were but one hope for all my pains or but one excuse for all my faultiness! But wretch that I am, my torment is beyond all succor, and my evil-deserving doth exceed my evil fortune. For nothing else did my husband take this strange resolution to live so solitarily, for nothing else have the winds delivered this strange guest to my country, for nothing else have the destinies reserved my life to this time, but that only I, most wretched I, should become a plague to myself and a shame to womankind. Yet if my desire, how unjust soever it be, might take effect, though a thousand deaths followed it and every death were followed with a thousand shames, yet should not my sepulcher receive me without some contentment. But alas, though sure I am that Zelmane is such as can answer my love, yet as sure I am that this disguising must needs come for some foretaken conceit.[6] And then, wretched Gynecia, where canst thou find any small ground-plot for hope to dwell upon? No, no, it is Philoclea his heart is set upon; it is my daughter I have borne to supplant me. But if it be so, the life I have given thee, ungrateful Philoclea, I will sooner with these hands bereave thee of than my birth[7] shall glory she hath bereaved me of my desires. In shame there is no comfort but to be beyond all bounds of shame."

Having spoken thus, she began to make a piteous war with her fair hair, when she might hear not far from her an extremely doleful voice, but so suppressed with a kind of whispering note that she could not conceive the words distinctly. But as a lamentable tune is the sweetest music to a woeful mind,

---

4. Uninhabited regions. In consequence of an oracle, Basilius has taken the royal family to live in "a certain forest which he calleth his desert."
5. Looked about her in a frightful manner.
6. With some prior purpose.
7. Offspring.

she drew thither near-away[8] in hope to find some companion of her misery; and as she paced on she was stopped with a number of trees so thickly placed together that she was afraid she should, with rushing through, stop the speech of the lamentable party which she was so desirous to understand. And therefore sitting her down as softly as she could (for she was now in distance to hear) she might first perceive a lute excellently well played upon, and then the same doleful voice accompanying it with these verses:

> In vain, mine eyes, you labor to amend
>   With flowing tears your fault of hasty sight;
> Since to my heart her shape you so did send,
>   That her I see, though you did lose your light.
>
> In vain, my heart, now you with sight are burned,
>   With sighs you seek to cool your hot desire;
> Since sighs, into mine inward furnace turned,
>   For bellows serve to kindle more the fire.
>
> Reason in vain, now you have lost my heart,
>   My head you seek, as to your strongest fort;
> Since there mine eyes have played so false a part,
>   That to your strength your foes have sure resort.
>   Then since in vain I find were all my strife,
>   To this strange death I vainly yield my life.

  The ending of the song served but for a beginning of new plaints, as if the mind, oppressed with too heavy a burden of cares, was fain to discharge itself of all sides and, as it were, paint out the hideousness of the pain in all sorts of colors. For the woeful person (as if the lute had evil[9] joined with the voice) threw it to the ground with suchlike words:

  "Alas, poor lute, how much art thou deceived to think that in my miseries thou could'st ease my woes, as in my careless[1] times thou wast wont to please my fancies! The time is changed, my lute, the time is changed; and no more did my joyful mind then receive everything to a joyful consideration than my careful[2] mind now makes each thing taste like the bitter juice of care. The evil is inward, my lute, the evil is inward; which all thou dost doth serve but to make me think more freely of, and the more I think, the more cause I find of thinking, but less of hoping. And alas, what is then thy harmony but the sweetmeats of sorrow? The discord of my thoughts, my lute, doth ill agree to the concord of thy strings; therefore be not ashamed to leave thy master, since he is not afraid to forsake himself."

  And thus much spoken, instead of a conclusion was closed up with so hearty a groaning that Gynecia could not refrain to show herself, thinking such griefs could serve fitly for nothing but her own fortune. But as she came into the little arbor of this sorrowful music, her eyes met with the eyes of Zelmane, which was the party that thus had indicted herself of misery, so that either of them remained confused with a sudden astonishment, Zelmane fearing lest she had heard some part of those complaints which she had risen up that morning early of purpose to breathe out in secret to

---

8. Near to it.
9. Badly.

1. Carefree.
2. Full of care.

herself. But Gynecia a great while stood still with a kind of dull amazement, looking steadfastly upon her. At length returning to some use of herself, she began to ask Zelmane what cause carried her so early abroad. But, as if the opening of her mouth to Zelmane had opened some great floodgate of sorrow whereof her heart could not abide the violent issue, she sank to the ground with her hands over her face, crying vehemently, "Zelmane, help me, O Zelmane have pity on me!"

Zelmane ran to her, marveling what sudden sickness had thus possessed her; and beginning to ask her the cause of her pain and offering her service to be employed by her, Gynecia opening her eyes wildly upon her, pricked with the flames of love and the torments of her own conscience, "O Zelmane, Zelmane," said she, "dost thou offer me physic,[3] which art my only poison? Or wilt thou do me service, which hast already brought me into eternal slavery?"

Zelmane then knowing well at what mark she shot, yet loth to enter into it, "Most excellent lady," said she, "you were best retire yourself into your lodging, that you the better may pass this sudden fit."

"Retire myself?" said Gynecia, "If I had retired myself into myself when thou (to me unfortunate guest) camest to draw me from myself, blessed had I been, and no need had I had of this counsel. But now, alas, I am forced to fly to thee for succor whom I accuse of all my hurt, and make thee judge of my cause, who art the only author of my mischief."

Zelmane the more astonished, the more she understood her, "Madam," said she, "whereof do you accuse me that I will not clear myself? Or wherein may I stead[4] you that you may not command me?"

"Alas!" answered Gynecia, "What shall I say more? Take pity of me, O Zelmane, but not as Zelmane, and disguise not with me in words, as I know thou dost in apparel."

Zelmane was much troubled with that word, finding herself brought to this strait. But as she was thinking what to answer her, they might see old Basilius pass hard by them without ever seeing them, complaining likewise of love very freshly, and ending his complaint with this song, love having renewed both his invention and voice:

> Let not old age disgrace my high desire,
>   O heavenly soul in human shape contained:
> Old wood inflamed doth yield the bravest[5] fire,
>   When younger doth in smoke his virtue[6] spend.
>
> Ne let white hairs which on my face do grow
>   Seem to your eyes of a disgraceful hue,
> Since whiteness doth present the sweetest show,[7]
>   Which makes all eyes do homage unto you.
>
> Old age is wise and full of constant truth;
>   Old age well stayed from ranging humor[8] lives;
> Old age hath known whatever was in youth;

---

3. Medicine.
4. Be of use to.
5. Most splendid.
6. Power.
7. Appearance.
8. Caprice. "Stayed": settled.

> Old age o'ercome, the greater honor gives.
> And to old age since you yourself aspire,
> Let not old age disgrace my high desire.

Which being done, he looked very curiously[9] upon himself, sometimes fetching a little skip as if he had said his strength had not yet forsaken him.

But Zelmane, having in this time gotten some leisure to think for an answer, looking upon Gynecia as if she thought she did her some wrong, "Madam," said she, "I am not acquainted with those words of disguising; neither is it the profession of an Amazon; neither are you a party with whom it is to be used. If my service may please you, employ it, so long as you do me no wrong in misjudging of me."

"Alas, Zelmane," said Gynecia, "I perceive you know full little how piercing the eyes are of a true lover. There is no one beam of those thoughts you have planted in me but is able to discern a greater cloud than you do go in. Seek not to conceal yourself further from me, nor force not the passion of love into violent extremities."

Now was Zelmane brought to an exigent,[1] when the king, turning his eyes that way through the trees, perceived his wife and mistress[2] together; so that framing the most lovely[3] countenance he could, he came straightway towards them, and at the first word, thanking his wife for having entertained Zelmane, desired her she would now return into the lodge, because he had certain matters of estate[4] to impart to the Lady Zelmane. The queen, being nothing troubled with jealousy in that point, obeyed the king's commandment, full of raging agonies, and determinately bent[5] that as she would seek all loving means to win Zelmane, so she would stir up terrible tragedies rather than fail of her intent. And so went she from them to the lodge-ward;[6] with such a battle in her thoughts and so deadly an overthrow given to her best resolutions that even her body (where the field was fought) was oppressed withal, making a languishing sickness wait upon the triumph of passion,[7] which the more it prevailed in her, the more it made her jealousy watchful both over her daughter and Zelmane, having ever one of them entrusted to her own eyes.[8]

But as soon as Basilius was rid of his wife's presence, falling down on his knees, "O lady," said he, "which hast only had the power to stir up again those flames which had so long lain dead in me, see in me the power of your beauty, which can make old age come to ask counsel of youth, and a prince unconquered to become a slave to a stranger. And when you see that power of yours, love that at least in me, since it is yours, although of me you see nothing to be loved."

"Worthy prince," answered Zelmane, taking him up from his kneeling, "both your manner and your speech are so strange unto me as I know not how to answer it better than with silence."

"If silence please you," said the king, "it shall never displease me, since my heart is wholly pledged to obey you. Otherwise, if you would vouchsafe mine ears such happiness as to hear you, they shall convey your words to such a mind which is with the humblest degree of reverence to receive them."

9. Carefully, attentively.
1. Crisis.
2. That is, the woman who rules his heart.
3. Loving.
4. State.
5. Resolutely determined.
6. Toward the lodge.
7. Attend upon passion's victory procession.
8. Always having one of them in her sight.

"I disdain not to speak to you, mighty prince," said Zelmane, "but I disdain to speak to any matter which may bring my honor into question."

And therewith, with a brave counterfeited scorn she departed from the king, leaving him not so sorry for his short answer as proud in himself that he had broken[9] the matter. And thus did the king, feeding his mind with those thoughts, pass great time in writing verses and making more of himself than he was wont to do, that, with a little help, he would have grown into a pretty kind of dotage.

But Zelmane, being rid of this loving but little loved company, "Alas," said she, "poor Pyrocles, was there ever one but I that had received wrong and could blame nobody, that having more than I desire, am still in want of that I would?[1] Truly, love, I must needs say thus much on thy behalf: thou hast employed my love there where all love is deserved, and for recompense hast sent me more love than ever I desired. But what wilt thou do, Pyrocles? Which way canst thou find to rid thee of thy intricate troubles? To her whom I would be known to, I live in darkness; and to her am revealed from whom I would be most secret. What shift[2] shall I find against the diligent love of Basilius? What shield against the violent passions of Gynecia? And if that be done, yet how am I the nearer to quench the fire that consumes me? Well, well, sweet Philoclea, my whole confidence must be builded in thy divine spirit, which cannot be ignorant of the cruel wound I have received by you."

1578–83   1593

The Defense of Poesy

In 1579 Sidney found himself the unwilling dedicatee of a small book titled *The School of Abuse*. Its author, the playwright-turned-moralist Stephen Gosson, attacked poets and actors from a rigidly pious perspective that called into question the morality of any fiction making. Sidney may have shared in the author's militant Protestantism, but he took a very different view of the poet's art, both more sympathetic and more complex. He did not specifically answer Gosson's polemic, but he must have had it in mind when he composed, perhaps in the same year, a major piece of critical prose that was published after his death under two titles, *The Defense of Poesy* and *An Apology for Poetry*. Probably written in 1579 though not published until 1595, *The Defense of Poesy* is an eloquent argument for the dignity, social efficacy, and moral value of imaginative literature in verse or prose.

Sidney gives this argument the underlying form of a classical oration, as if he were a lawyer in ancient Rome defending his client against defamatory accusations. The great masters of Roman rhetoric, Cicero and Quintilian, prescribed a set structure for such orations, and as our footnotes indicate in detail, Sidney adapts his defense to this structure.

Sidney responds to old charges against poetic fictions—charges of irresponsibility and unreality—that had been revived in his own time most strenuously by Puritan moralists. The *Defense* argues both that the poet, liberated from the world, is free to range "within the zodiac of his own wit" and that poetry actively intervenes in the world and transforms it for the better. After slyly putting himself down in the introduction, Sidney points out the antiquity of poetry, its high standing in the biblical and classical worlds, and its universality; also, he cites the names given to poets—*vates* (prophet) by the Romans, and *poiētēs* (maker) by the Greeks—as evidence of their ancient dignity. But he bases his defense essentially on the special

---

9. Broached.
1. Of the thing I desire.
2. Evasion, stratagem.

status of the poetic imagination. While all arts, from astronomy to music to medicine, depend ultimately on nature as their object, poetry, he claims, is uniquely free: "Only the poet, disdaining to be tied to any such subjection, lifted up with the vigor of his own invention, doth grow in effect another nature."

This freedom, Sidney argues, enables the poet to present virtues and vices in a livelier and more affecting way than nature does, as it teaches, delights, and moves the reader at the same time. The poet is superior to both the philosopher and the historian, because he is more concrete than the one and more universal than the other. The *Defense* also refutes the claim of the Greek philosopher Plato that poets are liars, by arguing that the poet "nothing affirms, and therefore never lieth," and it denies as well the Platonic charge that poetry arouses base desires. Tragedy, for example, "openeth the greatest wounds," in Sidney's account, "and showeth forth the ulcers that are covered with tissue," thereby making "kings fear to be tyrants." Surveying the English literary scene of his own century, Sidney finds little to praise except for Surrey's lyrics, the moralizing verse narratives of the popular midcentury collection *A Mirror for Magistrates*, and Spenser's *Shepheardes Calender*; the drama he faults for "mingling kings and clowns" and for unrealistic distortions of time and space. (The great, sprawling plays of Marlowe and Shakespeare, which triumphantly violated many of Sidney's cherished principles, lay just ahead.) The *Defense* ends with a mock conjuration and a playful curse, reminders of the magical power of poetry, a power that lurks beneath both Sidney's idealism and his precepts.

From The Defense of Poesy
[THE POET AS PROPHET AND CREATOR]

Among the Romans a poet was called *vates*, which is as much as a diviner, foreseer, or prophet, as by his conjoined words *vaticinium* and *vaticinari*[1] is manifest: so heavenly a title did that excellent people bestow upon this heart-ravishing knowledge. And so far were they carried into the admiration thereof, that they thought in the chanceable hitting upon any such verses great foretokens of their following fortunes were placed. Whereupon grew the word of *Sortes Virgilianae*,[2] when by sudden opening Virgil's book they lighted upon any verse of his making, whereof the histories of the emperors' lives are full: as of Albinus,[3] the governor of our island, who in his childhood met with this verse

> Arma amens capio nec sat rationis in armis[4]

and in his age performed it. Which, although it were a very vain and godless superstition, as also it was to think spirits were commanded by such verses—whereupon this word charms, derived of *carmina*,[5] cometh—so yet serveth it to show the great reverence those wits[6] were held in; and altogether not without ground, since both the oracles of Delphos and Sibylla's prophecies[7] were wholly delivered in verses. For that same exquisite observing of number and measure in the words, and that high flying liberty of conceit[8] proper to the poet, did seem to have some divine force in it.

---

1. "Prophecy" and "to prophesy."
2. Virgilian lots; that is, accepting as prophecy a line of Virgil chosen by a random ("chanceable") opening of the *Aeneid*.
3. Roman governor of Britain, declared emperor by his troops in 193 C.E. but defeated and killed four years later.
4. Frantic, I take up arms, yet there is little purpose in arms (*Aeneid* 2.314).
5. Songs, poems.
6. Talented people (that is, the poets).
7. The Pythia (priestess) at Delphi in Greece proclaimed Apollo's oracles. Sibylla (Sibyl) was a general name given to various prophetesses in Greek and Roman culture.
8. Imaginative conception.

And may not I presume a little further, to show the reasonableness of this word *vates*, and say that the holy David's[9] Psalms are a divine poem? If I do, I shall not do it without the testimony of great learned men, both ancient and modern. But even the name of Psalms will speak for me, which being interpreted, is nothing but songs; then that it is fully written in meter, as all learned Hebricians agree, although the rules be not yet fully found;[1] lastly and principally, his handling his prophecy, which is merely[2] poetical: for what else is the awaking his musical instruments, the often and free changing of persons, his notable *prosopopoeias*,[3] when he maketh you, as it were, see God coming in His majesty, his telling of the beasts' joyfulness and hills leaping, but a heavenly poesy, wherein almost[4] he showeth himself a passionate lover of that unspeakable and everlasting beauty to be seen by the eyes of the mind, only cleared by faith? But truly now having named him, I fear me I seem to profane that holy name, applying it to poetry, which is among us thrown down to so ridiculous an estimation. But they that with quiet judgments will look a little deeper into it, shall find the end and working of it such as, being rightly applied, deserveth not to be scourged out of the Church of God.

But now let us see how the Greeks named it, and how they deemed of it. The Greeks called him a "poet," which name hath, as the most excellent, gone through other languages. It cometh of this word *poiein*, which is, to make: wherein, I know not whether by luck or wisdom, we Englishmen have met with the Greeks in calling him a maker:[5] which name, how high and incomparable a title it is, I had rather were known by marking the scope of other sciences than by any partial[6] allegation.

There is no art delivered to mankind that hath not the works of nature for his principal object, without which they[7] could not consist, and on which they so depend, as they become actors and players, as it were, of what nature will have set forth. So doth the astronomer look upon the stars, and, by that he seeth, set down what order nature hath taken therein. So doth the geometrician and arithmetician in their diverse sorts of quantities. So doth the musician in times tell you which by nature agree,[8] which not. The natural philosopher thereon[9] hath his name, and the moral philosopher standeth upon[1] the natural virtues, vices, or passions of man; and follow nature (saith he) therein, and thou shalt not err. The lawyer saith what men have determined; the historian what men have done. The grammarian speaketh only of the rules of speech; and the rhetorician and logician, considering what in nature will soonest prove and persuade, thereon give artificial rules, which still are compassed within the circle of a question according to the proposed matter.[2] The physician weigheth[3] the nature of man's body, and the nature of

---

9. The biblical King David, commonly identified in the Renaissance as author of the book of Psalms in its entirety.
1. Many Renaissance scholars who knew some Hebrew ("Hebricians") thought the Psalms were written in verse forms approximating classical Greek and Latin meters.
2. Entirely.
3. Personifications. "Changing of persons": shifts *in narrative perspective*, between first- and third-person expressions.
4. Indeed. "Poesy": art of making poetry.
5. A common word for *poet* in 16th-century England. "Met with": agreed with.
6. Biased. "Marking": noting.
7. The several arts. The following argument owes much to the *Poetics* (1561) of the Renaissance Italian theorist Julius Caesar Scaliger.
8. Which rhythms are naturally consonant.
9. That is, from nature. "Natural philosopher": scientist.
1. Takes as subject matter.
2. The rules of those arts ("artificial rules") are always limited in their application to questions pertaining to the subject at hand.
3. Considers.

things helpful or hurtful unto it. And the metaphysic, though it be in the second and abstract notions, and therefore be counted supernatural,[4] yet doth he indeed build upon the depth of nature. Only the poet, disdaining to be tied to any such subjection, lifted up with the vigor of his own invention, doth grow in effect another nature, in making things either better than nature bringeth forth, or, quite anew, forms such as never were in nature, as the Heroes, Demigods, Cyclops, Chimeras, Furies,[5] and suchlike: so as he goeth hand in hand with nature, not enclosed within the narrow warrant of her gifts, but freely ranging only within the zodiac of his own wit.[6] Nature never set forth the earth in so rich tapestry as divers poets have done; neither with so pleasant rivers, fruitful trees, sweet-smelling flowers, nor whatsoever else may make the too much loved earth more lovely. Her world is brazen, the poets only deliver a golden.[7]

But let those things alone, and go to man—for whom as the other things are, so it seemeth in him her uttermost cunning is employed—and know whether she have brought forth so true a lover as Theagenes, so constant a friend as Pylades, so valiant a man as Orlando, so right a prince as Xenophon's Cyrus,[8] so excellent a man every way as Virgil's Aeneas. Neither let this be jestingly conceived, because the works of the one be essential, the other in imitation or fiction;[9] for any understanding knoweth the skill of each artificer standeth in that *idea* or fore-conceit[1] of the work, and not in the work itself. And that the poet hath that *idea* is manifest, by delivering them forth in such excellency as he had imagined them. Which delivering forth also is not wholly imaginative, as we are wont[2] to say by them that build castles in the air; but so far substantially it worketh, not only to make a Cyrus, which had been but a particular excellency as nature might have done, but to bestow a Cyrus upon the world to make many Cyruses, if they will learn aright why and how that maker made him.

Neither let it be deemed too saucy a comparison to balance the highest point of man's wit with the efficacy of nature; but rather give right honor to the heavenly Maker of that maker, who having made man to His own likeness, set him beyond and over all the works of that second nature:[3] which in nothing he showeth so much as in poetry, when with the force of a divine breath he bringeth things forth surpassing her doings—with no small arguments to the incredulous[4] of that first accursed fall of Adam, since our erected wit maketh us know what perfection is, and yet our infected will[5] keepeth us from reaching unto it. But these arguments will by few be understood, and by fewer granted. This much (I hope) will be given me, that the Greeks with some probability of reason gave him[6] the name above all names of learning.

---

4. Outside the physical world—entirely mental. "Metaphysic": metaphysician.
5. Avenging deities who punish crimes both in this world and after death. "Heroes": in the Greek sense, part human, part divine. "Cyclops": one-eyed giants (the correct plural is "Cyclopes") in Homer's *Odyssey*. "Chimeras": fire-breathing monsters with lion's head, goat's body, and serpent's tail.
6. Intellect.
7. A reference to the classical tradition of "The Four Ages of Man"—the idea that the world has declined from the first and perfect Golden Age, through the Silver, Brass (or Bronze), and Iron ages. "Her": Nature's.
8. Cyrus the Great of Persia, exemplary hero of Xenophon's prose romance, the *Cyropaedia* (4th century B.C.E.). Theagenes, hero of Heliodorus's Greek prose romance, *Aethiopica* (3rd or 4th century C.E.). Pylades, friend of the Greek hero Orestes. Orlando, hero especially of Ariosto's *Orlando furioso* (1516).
9. The works of nature are real ("essential"); those of the poet are fiction.
1. Imaginative plan; conception.
2. Accustomed. "Imaginative": fanciful.
3. Physical nature.
4. That is, skeptics.
5. Will corrupted in the Fall by original sin.
6. That is, poesy.

Now let us go to a more ordinary opening[7] of him, that the truth may be the more palpable: and so I hope, though we get not so unmatched a praise as the etymology of his names will grant, yet his very description, which no man will deny, shall not justly be barred from a principal commendation.

[DEFINITION AND CLASSIFICATION OF POETRY]

Poesy therefore is an art of imitation, for so Aristotle termeth it in the word *mimesis*[8]—that is to say, a representing, counterfeiting, or figuring forth— to speak metaphorically, a speaking picture—with this end, to teach and delight.[9]

Of this have been three general kinds. The chief, both in antiquity and excellency, were they that did imitate the unconceivable excellencies of God. Such were David in his Psalms; Solomon in his Song of Songs, in his Ecclesiastes, and Proverbs; Moses and Deborah in their Hymns;[1] and the writer of Job: which, beside other, the learned Emanuel Tremellius and Franciscus Junius[2] do entitle the poetical part of the Scripture. Against these none will speak that hath the Holy Ghost in due holy reverence. (In this kind, though in a full wrong divinity, were Orpheus, Amphion, Homer in his Hymns,[3] and many other, both Greeks and Romans.) And this poesy must be used by whosoever will follow St. James's counsel in singing psalms when they are merry;[4] and I know is used with the fruit of comfort by some, when, in sorrowful pangs of their death-bringing sins, they find the consolation of the never-leaving goodness.

The second kind is of them that deal with matters philosophical, either moral, as Tyrtaeus, Phocylides, Cato;[5] or natural, as Lucretius and Virgil's *Georgics*; or astronomical, as Manilius and Pontanus; or historical, as Lucan:[6] which who mislike, the fault is in their judgment quite out of taste, and not in the sweet food of sweetly uttered knowledge.

But because this second sort is wrapped within the fold of the proposed subject, and takes not the course of his own invention, whether they properly be poets or no let grammarians dispute, and go to the third, indeed right[7] poets, of whom chiefly this question ariseth: betwixt whom and these second

---

7. Analysis or explanation.
8. *Poetics* 1.2. This begins what Sidney labels the *propositio*—the third part of a judicial oration as Thomas Elyot explains it in *The Art of Rhetoric* (1553), "a pithy sentence, comprehending in a small room the sum of the whole matter." It is followed by the *divisio*, in which the subject is divided into its parts and the orator clarifies which of these are in dispute.
9. The primary authorities for the commonplace notions that a poem is a "speaking picture" and that the end of poetry is "to teach and delight" are, respectively, Plutarch (ca. 46–ca. 120 C.E.), especially in *How to Study Poetry* 17–18, and Horace (65–8 B.C.E.), *Art of Poetry* 343–44. The compounded definition, as well as the threefold classification of poets that follows, stems from Scaliger.
1. See Exodus 15:1–18; Deuteronomy 32:1–44; Judges 5.
2. Two scholars who published a Protestant Latin translation of the Bible, in 1579.
3. The Homeric Hymns are a collection of ancient Greek poems addressed to various gods and formerly attributed to Homer. Similarly, Orpheus (the archetypal poet of Greek mythology) was thought to be the author of a group of poems that expound the beliefs of a Greek mystery-religion. The lyre playing of Amphion (a son of Zeus) moved stones to form themselves into the walls of Thebes.
4. "Is any merry? let him sing psalms" (James 5:13).
5. The Roman Marcus Cato was the author of *Disticha de moribus*, an immensely popular collection, in verse and prose, of moral maxims. Tyrtaeus and Phocylides are among the Greek poets Sidney has previously mentioned.
6. Lucan wrote *De bello civili* (On the Civil War; also known as the *Pharsalia*), an epic poem on the struggle between Caesar and Pompey. Lucretius wrote a philosophical poem, *De rerum natura* (On the Nature of Things). Virgil's *Georgics* exalts the life and work of the farmer. Manilius wrote a long poem titled *Astronomica*. The 15th-century Italian writer Pontanus—the only postclassical poet in this list—was the author of another celebrated astronomical poem, *Urania*.
7. Justly entitled to the name.

is such a kind of difference as betwixt the meaner[8] sort of painters, who counterfeit only such faces as are set before them, and the more excellent, who having no law but wit,[9] bestow that in colors upon you which is fittest for the eye to see: as the constant though lamenting look of Lucretia, when she punished in herself another's fault,[1] wherein he painteth not Lucretia, whom he never saw, but painteth the outward beauty of such a virtue. For these third[2] be they which most properly do imitate to teach and delight, and to imitate borrow nothing of what is, hath been, or shall be; but range, only reined with learned discretion, into the divine consideration of what may be and should be. These be they that, as the first and most noble sort may justly be termed *vates,* so these are waited on in the excellentest languages and best understandings with[3] the fore-described name of poets. For these indeed do merely[4] make to imitate, and imitate both to delight and teach; and delight, to move men to take that goodness in hand, which without delight they would fly as from a stranger; and teach, to make them know that goodness whereunto they are moved—which being the noblest scope to which ever any learning was directed, yet want[5] there not idle tongues to bark at them.

These be subdivided into sundry more special denominations. The most notable be the heroic,[6] lyric, tragic, comic, satiric, iambic, elegiac,[7] pastoral, and certain others, some of these being termed according to the matter they deal with, some by the sorts of verses they liked best to write in; for indeed the greatest part of poets have appareled their poetical inventions in that numbrous[8] kind of writing which is called verse—indeed but appareled, verse being but an ornament and no cause to poetry, since there have been many most excellent poets that never versified, and now swarm many versifiers that need never answer to the name of poets. For Xenophon, who did imitate so excellently as to give us *effigiem iusti imperii,* the portraiture of a just empire, under the name of Cyrus (as Cicero saith of him), made therein an absolute heroical poem. So did Heliodorus in his sugared invention of that picture of love in Theagenes and Chariclea;[9] and yet both these wrote in prose: which I speak to show that it is not rhyming and versing that maketh a poet—no more than a long gown maketh an advocate,[1] who though he pleaded in armor should be an advocate and no soldier. But it is that feigning notable images of virtues, vices, or what else, with that delightful teaching, which must be the right describing note[2] to know a poet by; although indeed the senate of poets hath chosen verse as their fittest raiment, meaning, as in matter they passed all in all,[3] so in manner to go beyond them: not speaking (table-talk fashion or like men in a dream) words as they chanceably fall from the mouth, but peising[4] each syllable of each word by just proportion according to the dignity of the subject.

---

8. Lower.
9. Creative imagination.
1. A notable exemplar of chastity and honor, the Roman matron Lucretia committed suicide after being raped by the son of King Tarquinius Superbus.
2. That is, the right poets.
3. "Waited on . . . with": distinguished by.
4. Only.
5. Lack. "Scope": aim.
6. Epic.
7. Two genres are named after their Greek and Latin verse forms. "Iambic": associated with directly vituperative poetry (as distinguished from the irony of satire). "Elegiac": poetry written in the "elegiac couplet," which was used especially for reflective, lamenting, or erotic poetry.
8. That is, in numbers, poetic meters.
9. The heroine of Heliodorus's *Aethiopica.*
1. Lawyer.
2. The true distinguishing characteristics.
3. All others, in all respects.
4. Weighing.

[POETRY VERSUS PHILOSOPHY AND HISTORY]

Now therefore it shall not be amiss first to weigh this latter sort of poetry by his works, and then by his parts; and if in neither of these anatomies he be condemnable, I hope we shall obtain a more favorable sentence.[5]

This purifying of wit—this enriching of memory, enabling of judgment, and enlarging of conceit[6]—which commonly we call learning, under what name soever it come forth, or to what immediate end soever it be directed, the final end is to lead and draw us to as high a perfection as our degenerate souls, made worse by their clayey lodgings, can be capable of.

This, according to the inclination of the man, bred many-formed[7] impressions. For some that thought this felicity principally to be gotten by knowledge, and no knowledge to be so high or heavenly as acquaintance with the stars, gave themselves to astronomy; others, persuading themselves to be demigods if they knew the causes of things, became natural and supernatural philosophers; some an admirable delight drew to music; and some the certainty of demonstration to the mathematics. But all, one and other, having this scope: to know, and by knowledge to lift up the mind from the dungeon of the body to the enjoying his own divine essence.

But when by the balance of experience it was found that the astronomer, looking to the stars, might fall in a ditch,[8] that the inquiring philosopher might be blind in himself, and the mathematician might draw forth a straight line with a crooked heart, then lo, did proof, the overruler of opinions, make manifest that all these are but serving sciences, which, as they have each a private[9] end in themselves, so yet are they all directed to the highest end of the mistress-knowledge, by the Greeks called *architectonike*,[1] which stands (as I think) in the knowledge of a man's self, in the ethic and politic consideration, with the end of well-doing and not of well-knowing only—even as the saddler's next[2] end is to make a good saddle, but his further end to serve a nobler faculty, which is horsemanship, so the horseman's to soldiery, and the soldier not only to have the skill, but to perform the practice of a soldier. So that, the ending end of all earthly learning being virtuous action, those skills that most serve to bring forth that have a most just title to be princes over all the rest.

Wherein, if we can, show we the poet's nobleness, by setting him before his other competitors. Among whom as principal challengers step forth the moral philosophers, whom, methinketh, I see coming towards me with a sullen gravity, as though they could not abide vice by daylight, rudely clothed for to witness outwardly their contempt of outward things, with books in their hands against glory, whereto they set their names, sophistically[3] speaking against subtlety, and angry with any man in whom they see the foul fault of anger. These men casting largess as they go, of definitions, divisions, and distinctions,[4] with a scornful interrogative do soberly ask whether it be

---

5. Judgment. "Works": effects. "Anatomies": analyses. Here Sidney moves to the central and longest part of the judicial oration, the *confirmatio* or *examinatio*, in which the speaker develops the arguments in support of his (or her) position.
6. Conceptual power. "Wit": intellect; understanding. "Enabling": strengthening.
7. Manifold. "Inclination": natural disposition.
8. As Plato (*Theaetetus* 174) reported of the philosopher and astronomer Thales.
9. Particular.
1. The "chief art," to which all others are subordinate. The term is Aristotle's (*Nicomachean Ethics* 1.1).
2. Nearest.
3. Subtly.
4. That is, bountiful gifts of scholastic terms and arguments.

possible to find any path so ready to lead a man to virtue as that which teacheth what virtue is; and teach it not only by delivering forth his very being, his causes and effects, but also by making known his enemy, vice, which must be destroyed, and his cumbersome[5] servant, passion, which must be mastered; by showing the generalities that containeth it, and the specialities that are derived from it; lastly, by plain setting down how it extendeth itself out of the limits of a man's own little world to the government of families and maintaining of public societies.

The historian scarcely giveth leisure to the moralist to say so much, but that he, laden with old mouse-eaten records, authorizing himself[6] (for the most part) upon other histories, whose greatest authorities are built upon the notable foundation of hearsay; having much ado to accord differing writers and to pick truth out of their partiality;[7] better acquainted with a thousand years ago than with the present age, and yet better knowing how this world goeth than how his own wit runneth; curious for antiquities and inquisitive of novelties; a wonder to young folks and a tyrant in table talk, denieth, in a great chafe,[8] that any man for teaching of virtue and virtuous actions is comparable to him. "I am *testis temporum, lux veritatis, vita memoriae, magistra vitae, nuntia vetustatis.*"[9] "The philosopher," saith he, "teacheth a disputative virtue, but I do an active. His virtue is excellent in the dangerless Academy of Plato, but mine showeth forth her honorable face in the battles of Marathon, Pharsalia, Poitiers, and Agincourt.[1] He teacheth virtue by certain abstract considerations, but I only bid you follow the footing of them that have gone before you. Old-aged experience goeth beyond the fine-witted philosopher, but I give the experience of many ages. Lastly, if he make the songbook, I put the learner's hand to the lute; and if he be the guide, I am the light." Then would he allege you innumerable examples, confirming story by stories, how much the wisest senators and princes have been directed by the credit of history, as Brutus, Alphonsus of Aragon,[2] and who not, if need be? At length the long line of their disputation maketh a point[3] in this, that the one giveth the precept, and the other[4] the example.

Now whom shall we find (since the question standeth for the highest form in the school of learning) to be moderator?[5] Truly, as me seemeth, the poet; and if not a moderator, even the man that ought to carry the title from them both, and much more from all other serving sciences. Therefore compare we the poet with the historian and with the moral philosopher; and if he go beyond them both, no other human skill can match him. For as for the divine,[6] with all reverence it is ever to be excepted, not only for having his scope as far beyond any of these as eternity exceedeth a moment, but even for passing[7]

---

5. Obstructive; troublesome.
6. Basing his authority.
7. Bias. "Accord": reconcile.
8. Temper.
9. "I am the witness of times, the light of truth, the life of memory, the teacher of life, the messenger of antiquity" (Cicero, *De oratore* 2.9.36).
1. At Poitiers (1356) and Agincourt (1415), the English defeated the French. At Marathon, the Greeks defeated the Persians (490 B.C.E.). At Pharsalia, Caesar defeated Pompey (48 B.C.E.).
2. Alfonso V of Aragon (1396–1458) carried the histories of Livy and Caesar into battle with him.

Marcus Brutus was inspired to rise up against Caesar by the history of his great republican ancestor, Junius Brutus, who expelled the Tarquin kings.
3. Comes to a full stop.
4. The historian. "The one": the philosopher.
5. Judge, arbitrator. Sidney images the rival claims of philosophy and history as a formal academic disputation—a standard exercise at the time—engaging the top class ("highest form") in the "school of learning."
6. The theologian.
7. Surpassing.

each of these in themselves. And for the lawyer, though *Ius*[8] be the daughter of Justice, and justice the chief of virtues, yet because he seeketh to make men good rather *formidine poenae* than *virtutis amore*;[9] or, to say righter, doth not endeavor to make men good, but that their evil hurt not others; having no care, so he be a good citizen, how bad a man he be: therefore as our wickedness maketh him[1] necessary, and necessity maketh him honorable, so is he not in the deepest truth to stand in rank with these[2] who all endeavor to take naughtiness away and plant goodness even in the secretest cabinet[3] of our souls. And these four are all that any way deal in that consideration of men's manners,[4] which being the supreme knowledge, they that best breed it deserve the best commendation.

The philosopher, therefore, and the historian are they which would win the goal, the one by precept, the other by example. But both, not having both, do both halt.[5] For the philosopher, setting down with thorny arguments the bare rule, is so hard of utterance and so misty to be conceived, that one that hath no other guide but him shall wade in him till he be old before he shall find sufficient cause to be honest.[6] For his knowledge standeth so upon the abstract and general, that happy[7] is that man who may understand him, and more happy that can apply what he doth understand. On the other side, the historian, wanting[8] the precept, is so tied, not to what should be but to what is, to the particular truth of things and not to the general reason of things, that his example draweth no necessary consequence, and therefore a less fruitful doctrine.

Now doth the peerless poet perform both: for whatsoever the philosopher saith should be done, he giveth a perfect picture of it in someone by whom he presupposeth it was done, so as he coupleth the general notion with the particular example. A perfect picture I say, for he yieldeth to the powers of the mind an image of that whereof the philosopher bestoweth but a wordish description, which doth neither strike, pierce, nor possess the sight of the soul so much as that other doth. For as in outward things, to a man that had never seen an elephant or a rhinoceros, who should tell him most exquisitely[9] all their shapes, color, bigness, and particular marks, or of a gorgeous palace the architecture, with declaring the full beauties, might well make the hearer able to repeat, as it were by rote, all he had heard, yet should never satisfy his inward conceit[1] with being witness to itself of a true lively knowledge; but the same man, as soon as he might see those beasts well painted, or that house well in model, should straightways grow, without need of any description, to a judicial[2] comprehending of them: so no doubt the philosopher with his learned definitions—be it of virtue, vices, matters of public policy or private government[3]—replenisheth the memory with many infallible grounds of wisdom, which, notwithstanding, lie dark before the imaginative and judging power, if they be not illuminated or figured forth[4] by the speaking picture of poesy.

---

8. The system of law (Latin).
9. Through fear of punishment than love of virtue. The distinction is from Horace, *Epistles* 1.16.52–53.
1. That is, the lawyer.
2. The moral philosopher, historian, and poet.
3. Most private chamber. "Naughtiness": wickedness.
4. Moral conduct.

5. Limp (having, after all, only one leg each).
6. Virtuous.
7. Fortunate.
8. Not having.
9. Discriminatingly.
1. Conception.
2. Judicious.
3. Individual conduct (as opposed to "public policy").
4. Given form or shape.

Tully[5] taketh much pains, and many times not without poetical helps, to make us know the force love of our country hath in us. Let us but hear old Anchises speaking in the midst of Troy's flames, or see Ulysses in the fullness of all Calypso's delights bewail his absence from barren and beggarly Ithaca.[6] Anger, the Stoics said, was a short madness:[7] let but Sophocles bring you Ajax on a stage, killing or whipping sheep and oxen, thinking them the army of Greeks,[8] with their chieftains Agamemnon and Menelaus, and tell me if you have not a more familiar insight into anger than finding in the schoolmen his *genus* and difference.[9] See whether wisdom and temperance in Ulysses and Diomedes, valor in Achilles, friendship in Nisus and Euryalus,[1] even to an ignorant man carry not an apparent shining;[2] and, contrarily, the remorse of conscience in Oedipus, the soon repenting pride in Agamemnon, the self-devouring cruelty in his father Atreus, the violence of ambition in the two Theban brothers, the sour-sweetness of revenge in Medea;[3] and, to fall lower, the Terentian Gnatho and our Chaucer's Pandar[4] so expressed that we now use their names to signify their trades: and finally, all virtues, vices, and passions so in their own natural seats laid to the view, that we seem not to hear of them, but clearly to see through them.

But even in the most excellent determination of goodness, what philosopher's counsel can so readily direct a prince, as the feigned Cyrus in Xenophon; or a virtuous man in all fortunes, as Aeneas in Virgil; or a whole commonwealth, as the way of Sir Thomas More's *Utopia*? I say the way, because where Sir Thomas More erred, it was the fault of the man and not of the poet, for that way of patterning a commonwealth was most absolute,[5] though he perchance hath not so absolutely performed it. For the question is, whether the feigned image of poetry or the regular instruction of philosophy hath the more force in teaching: wherein if the philosophers have more rightly showed themselves philosophers than the poets have attained to the high top of their profession, as in truth

>Mediocribus esse poetis,
>Non dii, non homines, non concessere columnae;[6]

it is, I say again, not the fault of the art, but that by few men that art can be accomplished.

Certainly, even our Savior Christ could as well have given the moral commonplaces of uncharitableness and humbleness as the divine narration of

---

5. A common English name for Cicero (Marcus Tullius Cicero).
6. All the charms of the lovely nymph Calypso, and the promise of immortality with her, could not make Odysseus forget his home on the Greek isle of Ithaca (*Odyssey* 5.149–224). Anchises, the father of Aeneas, laments his destroyed homeland in *Aeneid* 2.638–49.
7. The formulation is Horace's (*Epistles* 1.2.62).
8. In fact, Sophocles's *Ajax* does not portray its protagonist's mad actions on the stage but has them reported by Menelaus (lines 1052–61).
9. In the logic of the Scholastic philosophers ("schoolmen"), "differences" are the attributes that distinguish among the species in a genus.
1. All are figures in the story of the Trojan War, as recounted in the *Iliad* and, for the faithful friends Nisus and Euryalus, the *Aeneid* (9.176–449).
2. An evident splendor.

3. All are figures from Greek and Roman tragedy. "The two Theban brothers": Eteocles and Polynices, twin sons of Oedipus, who killed each other in battle. (For Atreus—the father of Agamemnon, leader of the Greeks against Troy—see p. 535, n. 8).
4. The common noun *pander* derives from Pandarus, the go-between in Chaucer's *Troilus and Criseyde*. Similarly, Gnatho—a figure in the *Eunuch* of the Roman comic dramatist Terence—became a type-name for a fawning parasite.
5. Perfect. Sidney approves of More's casting a work of political philosophy as an account of a voyage to a fictional country, but he does not want to be thought of as endorsing all features of the Utopian commonwealth (especially, one surmises, its communism).
6. "That poets be middling, neither gods, nor men, nor booksellers ever allowed" (Horace, *Art of Poetry* 372–73).

Dives and Lazarus; or of disobedience and mercy, as that heavenly discourse of the lost child and the gracious father;[7] but that His through-searching wisdom knew the estate[8] of Dives burning in hell, and of Lazarus in Abraham's bosom, would more constantly (as it were) inhabit both the memory and judgment. Truly, for myself, meseems I see before mine eyes the lost child's disdainful prodigality, turned to envy a swine's dinner: which by the learned divines are thought not historical acts,[9] but instructing parables.

For conclusion, I say the philosopher teacheth, but he teacheth obscurely, so as the learned only can understand him, that is to say, he teacheth them that are already taught; but the poet is the food for the tenderest stomachs, the poet is indeed the right popular philosopher, whereof Aesop's tales give good proof: whose pretty allegories, stealing under the formal[1] tales of beasts, make many, more beastly than beasts, begin to hear the sound of virtue from these dumb speakers.

But now may it be alleged that if this imagining of matters be so fit for the imagination, then must the historian needs surpass, who bringeth you images of true matters; such as indeed were done, and not such as fantastically or falsely may be suggested to have been done. Truly, Aristotle himself, in his discourse of poesy, plainly determineth this question, saying that poetry is *philosophoteron* and *spoudaioteron*, that is to say, it is more philosophical and more studiously serious than history.[2] His reason is, because poesy dealeth with *katholou*, that is to say, with the universal consideration, and the history with *kathekaston*, the particular: now, saith he, the universal weighs what is fit to be said or done, either in likelihood or necessity (which the poesy considereth in his imposed names), and the particular only marks whether Alcibiades did, or suffered, this or that.[3] Thus far Aristotle: which reason of his (as all his) is most full of reason. For indeed, if the question were whether it were better to have a particular act truly or falsely set down, there is no doubt which is to be chosen, no more than whether you had rather have Vespasian's[4] picture right as he was, or, at the painter's pleasure, nothing resembling. But if the question be for your own use and learning, whether it be better to have it set down as it should be, or as it was, then certainly is more doctrinable[5] the feigned Cyrus in Xenophon than the true Cyrus in Justin, and the feigned Aeneas in Virgil than the right Aeneas in Dares Phrygius:[6] as to a lady that desired to fashion her countenance to the best grace, a painter should more benefit her to portrait a most sweet face, writing Canidia upon it, than to paint Canidia as she was, who, Horace sweareth, was full ill-favored.[7]

---

7. The Prodigal Son (Luke 15:11–32); for the parable of the rich Dives and the beggar Lazarus, see Luke 16:19–31.
8. Condition.
9. Records.
1. That is, in the form of.
2. *Poetics* 9.
3. Alcibiades, an Athenian politician and disciple of Socrates, died in 404 B.C.E.—twenty years before Aristotle's birth. Sidney's summary of Aristotle's passage is accurate, with the important exception that he imposes the notion that Aristotelian universals have a morally prescriptive force, weighing "what is *fit* to be said or done." Aristotle says only that "by a universal statement I mean one as to what such or such a kind of man will probably or necessarily say or do."
4. Vespasian was emperor of Rome 69–79 C.E.
5. Instructive.
6. Mentioned in the *Iliad*, Dares Phrygius was the supposed author of an eyewitness account of the Trojan War. Justin was a Roman historian of the 2nd or 3rd century C.E. who wrote an abridgment of a now-lost universal history by one Trogus.
7. For the lost looks of the witch Canidia, see Horace, *Epodes* 5.

If the poet do his part aright, he will show you in Tantalus, Atreus,[8] and suchlike, nothing that is not to be shunned; in Cyrus, Aeneas, Ulysses, each thing to be followed; where the historian, bound to tell things as things were, cannot be liberal (without he will be poetical) of a perfect pattern, but, as in Alexander or Scipio himself,[9] show doings, some to be liked, some to be misliked. And then how will you discern what to follow but by your own discretion, which you had without reading Quintus Curtius? And whereas a man may say, though in universal consideration of doctrine the poet prevaileth, yet that the history,[1] in his saying such a thing was done, doth warrant a man more in that he shall follow[2]—the answer is manifest: that, if he stand upon that was (as if he should argue, because it rained yesterday, therefore it should rain today), then indeed hath it some advantage to a gross conceit;[3] but if he know an example only informs a conjectured likelihood, and so go by reason,[4] the poet doth so far exceed him[5] as he is to frame his example to that which is most reasonable (be it in warlike, politic, or private matters), where the historian in his bare "was" hath many times that which we call fortune to overrule the best wisdom. Many times he must tell events whereof he can yield no cause; or, if he do, it must be poetically.

For that a feigned example hath as much force to teach as a true example (for as for to move, it is clear, since the feigned may be tuned to the highest key of passion), let us take one example wherein an historian and a poet did concur. Herodotus and Justin do both testify that Zopyrus, King Darius' faithful servant, seeing his master long resisted by the rebellious Babylonians, feigned himself in extreme disgrace of his king: for verifying of which, he caused his own nose and ears to be cut off, and so flying to the Babylonians was received, and for his known valor so sure credited, that he did find means to deliver them over to Darius.[6] Much like matter doth Livy record of Tarquinius and his son. Xenophon excellently feigneth such another stratagem performed by Abradatas in Cyrus' behalf. Now would I fain know, if occasion be presented unto you to serve your prince by such an honest dissimulation, why you do not as well learn it of Xenophon's fiction as of the other's verity; and truly so much the better, as you shall save your nose by the bargain: for Abradatas did not counterfeit so far. So then the best of the historian is subject to the poet; for whatsoever action, or faction, whatsoever counsel, policy, or war stratagem the historian is bound to recite, that may the poet (if he list)[7] with his imitation make his own, beautifying it both for further teaching and more delighting, as it please him: having all, from Dante's heaven to his hell, under the authority of his pen.

---

8. Figures from Greek mythology. In one version of his story, Tantalus served up his son at a banquet for the gods; similarly, his grandson Atreus served his brother's children to him.
9. Alexander the Great was often represented—for example, by the Roman historian Quintus Curtius—as having been corrupted by power; and even Scipio Africanus—the conqueror of Hannibal and one of the most unreservedly admired Romans—was, in his later years, accused of political misconduct. "Cannot be liberal . . . of": is not at liberty to give.
1. The historian. "Doctrine": instruction.
2. That is, provides more reliable assurance as to what course one should follow.
3. That is, to a person of undiscriminating intelligence.
4. That is, if a person is sufficiently sophisticated to understand that reason is a better guide than example.
5. That is, the historian.
6. Darius I was king of Persia 521–486 B.C.E. The story of his faithful servant Zopyrus was told in Herodotus's *Histories* 3.153–60 and repeated in Justin's *Histories* 1.10. Somewhat similar stories (see the two following sentences) are recounted by the Roman historian Livy (concerning the last of the Tarquin kings and his son) in *From the Foundation of the City* 1.53–54 and in Xenophon's *Cyropaedia* 6.1.38–44, 6.3.14–20 (though about Cyrus and one Araspas—not, as Sidney has it, Abradatas).
7. Likes.

Which if I be asked what poets have done so, as I might well name some, so yet say I, and say again, I speak of the art, and not of the artificer.

Now, to that which commonly is attributed to the praise of history, in respect of the notable learning is got by marking the success,[8] as though therein a man should see virtue exalted and vice punished—truly that commendation is particular to poetry, and far off from history. For indeed poetry ever sets virtue so out in her best colors, making Fortune her well-waiting handmaid, that one must needs be enamored of her. Well may you see Ulysses in a storm,[9] and in other hard plights; but they are but exercises of patience and magnanimity, to make them shine the more in the near-following prosperity. And of the contrary part, if evil men come to the stage, they ever go out (as the tragedy writer[1] answered to one that misliked the show of such persons) so manacled as they little animate folks to follow them. But the history, being captived to the truth of a foolish world, is many times a terror[2] from well-doing, and an encouragement to unbridled wickedness. For see we not valiant Miltiades[3] rot in his fetters? The just Phocion[4] and the accomplished Socrates put to death like traitors? The cruel Severus[5] live prosperously? The excellent Severus[6] miserably murdered? Sulla and Marius[7] dying in their beds? Pompey and Cicero[8] slain then when they would have thought exile a happiness? See we not virtuous Cato driven to kill himself,[9] and rebel Caesar so advanced that his name yet, after 1600 years, lasteth in the highest honor? And mark but even Caesar's own words of the aforenamed Sulla (who in that only did honestly, to put down his dishonest tyranny), *literas nescivit*, as if want of learning caused him to do well.[1] He meant it not by[2] poetry, which, not content with earthly plagues, deviseth new punishments in hell for tyrants, nor yet by philosophy, which teacheth *occidendos esse*;[3] but no doubt by skill in history, for that indeed can afford you Cypselus, Periander, Phalaris, Dionysius,[4] and I know not how many more of the same kennel, that speed[5] well enough in their abominable injustice of usurpation.

I conclude, therefore, that he[6] excelleth history, not only in furnishing the mind with knowledge, but in setting it forward to that which deserveth to be called and accounted good: which setting forward, and moving to well-doing, indeed setteth the laurel crown upon the poets as victorious, not only of the historian, but over the philosopher, howsoever in teaching it may be questionable.[7]

For suppose it be granted (that which I suppose with great reason may be denied) that the philosopher, in respect of his methodical proceeding, doth

---

8. Outcome.
9. In *Odyssey* 5.291–387.
1. Euripides (as reported by Plutarch, *How to Study Poetry* 4).
2. That is, a deterrent.
3. Athenian general and architect of victory at Marathon over the Persians, later imprisoned by the Athenians.
4. Athenian general and statesman executed for treason because he opposed ill-advised opposition to Athens' Macedonian conquerors.
5. Emperor Lucius Septimius Severus, noted for ruthlessness.
6. Emperor Alexander Severus, a reformer slain by his troops.
7. Political rivals who brought unrest and destruction to Rome for two decades.

8. The great orator, killed at Mark Antony's command. Pompey the Great, defeated by Caesar at Pharsalia and slain in Egypt.
9. Cato the Younger committed suicide after his party failed to defeat Caesar.
1. When Sulla resigned ("put down") his dictatorship, Caesar joked that he was illiterate (*literas nescivit*), since he left the *dictatura* (which means both "dictatorship" and "dictation") to others.
2. With reference to.
3. They [tyrants] must be killed.
4. Four famous tyrants of the classical world: the first two were from Corinth, Phalaris was from Agrigentum, and Dionysus the Elder was from Syracuse.
5. Succeed.
6. That is, poetry.
7. Arguable.

teach more perfectly than the poet, yet do I think that no man is so much *philophilosophos*[8] as to compare the philosopher in moving with the poet. And that moving is of a higher degree than teaching, it may by this appear, that it is well nigh both the cause and effect of teaching. For who will be taught, if he be not moved with desire to be taught? And what so much good doth that teaching bring forth (I speak still of moral doctrine) as that it moveth one to do that which it doth teach? For, as Aristotle saith, it is not *gnosis* but *praxis*[9] must be the fruit. And how *praxis* cannot be, without being moved to practice, it is no hard matter to consider.

The philosopher showeth you the way, he informeth you of the particularities, as well of the tediousness of the way, as of the pleasant lodging you shall have when your journey is ended, as of the many by-turnings that may divert you from your way. But this is to no man but to him that will read him, and read him with attentive studious painfulness;[1] which constant desire whosoever hath in him, hath already passed half the hardness of the way, and therefore is beholding to the philosopher but for the other half. Nay truly, learned men have learnedly thought that where once reason hath so much overmastered passion as that the mind hath a free desire to do well, the inward light each mind hath in itself is as good as a philosopher's book; since in nature[2] we know it is well to do well, and what is well, and what is evil, although not in the words of art which philosophers bestow upon us; for out of natural conceit[3] the philosophers drew it. But to be moved to do that which we know, or to be moved with desire to know, *hoc opus, hic labor est.*[4]

Now therein of all sciences (I speak still of human,[5] and according to the human conceit) is our poet the monarch. For he doth not only show the way, but giveth so sweet a prospect into the way, as will entice any man to enter into it. Nay, he doth, as if your journey should lie through a fair vineyard, at the first give you a cluster of grapes, that full of that taste, you may long to pass further. He beginneth not with obscure definitions, which must blur the margin with interpretations and load the memory with doubtfulness; but he cometh to you with words set in delightful proportion, either accompanied with, or prepared for, the well enchanting skill of music; and with a tale forsooth he cometh unto you, with a tale which holdeth children from play, and old men from the chimney corner. And, pretending no more, doth intend the winning of the mind from wickedness to virtue—even as the child is often brought to take most wholesome things by hiding them in such other as have a pleasant taste, which, if one should begin to tell them the nature of *aloes* or *rhabarbarum*[6] they should receive, would sooner take their physic at their ears than at their mouth.[7] So is it in men (most of which are childish in the best things, till they be cradled in their graves): glad will they be to hear the tales of Hercules, Achilles, Cyrus, Aeneas; and, hearing them, must needs hear the right description of wisdom, valor, and justice; which, if they had been barely, that is to say philosophically, set out, they would swear they be brought to school again.

---

8. A lover of philosophers.
9. Not knowing but doing (*Nicomachean Ethics* 1.3).
1. Painstaking effort.
2. Considering that by nature.
3. Natural understanding, as opposed to the philosophers' special vocabulary ("words of art").
4. This is the task, this is the work to be done (Virgil, *Aeneid* 6.129).
5. As opposed to divine. "Sciences": branches of learning.
6. Two bitter purgatives: aloe and rhubarb.
7. That is, would rather have their ears boxed than take the medicine.

That imitation whereof poetry is hath the most conveniency[8] to nature of all other, insomuch that, as Aristotle saith, those things which in themselves are horrible, as cruel battles, unnatural monsters, are made in poetical imitation delightful.[9] Truly, I have known men that even with reading *Amadis de Gaule*[1] (which God knoweth wanteth much of a perfect poesy) have found their hearts moved to the exercise of courtesy, liberality, and especially courage. Who readeth Aeneas carrying old Anchises on his back, that wisheth not it were his fortune to perform so excellent an act? Whom doth not these words of Turnus move, the tale of Turnus having planted his image in the imagination,

> Fugientem haec terra videbit?
> Usque adeone mori miserum est?[2]

Where the philosophers, as they scorn to delight, so much they be content little to move—saving wrangling whether *virtus*[3] be the chief or the only good, whether the contemplative or the active life do excell—which Plato and Boethius well knew, and therefore made Mistress Philosophy very often borrow the masking raiment of poesy.[4] For even those hard-hearted evil men who think virtue a school name, and know no other good but *indulgere genio*,[5] and therefore despise the austere admonitions of the philosopher, and feel not the inward reason they stand upon, yet will be content to be delighted—which is all the good-fellow poet seemeth to promise—and so steal[6] to see the form of goodness (which seen they cannot but love) ere themselves be aware, as if they took a medicine of cherries.

Infinite proofs of the strange effects of this poetical invention might be alleged; only two shall serve, which are so often remembered as I think all men know them. The one of Menenius Agrippa,[7] who, when the whole people of Rome had resolutely divided themselves from the senate, with apparent show of utter ruin, though he were (for that time) an excellent orator, came not among them upon trust of figurative speeches or cunning insinuations, and much less with far-fet[8] maxims of philosophy, which (especially if they were Platonic) they must have learned geometry before they could well have conceived;[9] but forsooth he behaves himself like a homely and familiar poet. He telleth them a tale, that there was a time when all the parts of the body made a mutinous conspiracy against the belly, which they thought devoured the fruits of each other's labor; they concluded they would let so unprofitable a spender starve. In the end, to be short (for the tale is notorious, and as notorious that it was a tale), with punishing the belly they plagued themselves. This applied by him wrought such effect in the people,

---

8. Congruity; suitability.
9. *Poetics* 4.
1. A chivalric romance of Spanish origin, which became extremely popular in a French translation.
2. *Aeneid* 12.645–46: "Shall this land see Turnus in flight? Is it so bad a thing to die?" The Italian king Turnus is Aeneas's worthy rival, killed by the epic hero in the poem's closing lines. Aeneas carries his father, Anchises, away from burning Troy in 2.705–44.
3. Virtue. "Saving": except. The (satiric) point is that wrangling over standard philosophical questions is unlikely to move anyone other than the wrangling philosophers themselves.
4. In an earlier passage not included here, Sidney argued that the beauty of Plato's work depended on "poetry" (that is, fiction). The *Consolation of Philosophy* of Boethius (476–524 C.E.) is cast as a dialogue between himself and Lady Philosophy, and alternates prose and verse.
5. To follow one's natural inclination.
6. That is, come accidentally.
7. Roman consul in 503 B.C.E. The story of his parable was first related by Livy, *From the Foundation of the City* 2.32.
8. Far-fetched.
9. A medieval tradition held that over the door of Plato's Academy was written: "No man untaught in geometry should enter."

as I never read that only words brought forth but then[1] so sudden and so good an alteration; for upon reasonable conditions a perfect reconcilement ensued. The other is of Nathan the prophet, who, when the holy David had so far forsaken God as to confirm adultery with murder,[2] when he was to do the tenderest office of a friend in laying his own shame before his eyes, sent by God to call again so chosen a servant, how doth he it but by telling of a man whose beloved lamb was ungratefully[3] taken from his bosom? The application most divinely true, but the discourse itself feigned; which made David (I speak of the second and instrumental cause[4]) as in a glass see his own filthiness, as that heavenly psalm of mercy[5] well testifieth.

By these, therefore, examples and reasons, I think it may be manifest that the poet, with that same hand of delight, doth draw the mind more effectually than any other art doth. And so a conclusion[6] not unfitly ensue: that, as virtue is the most excellent resting place for all worldly learning to make his end of, so poetry, being the most familiar[7] to teach it, and most princely to move towards it, in the most excellent work is the most excellent workman.

[CONCLUSION]

So that since the ever-praiseworthy Poesy is full of virtue-breeding delightfulness, and void of no gift that ought to be in the noble name of learning;[8] since the blames laid against it are either false or feeble; since the cause why it is not esteemed in England is the fault of poet-apes,[9] not poets; since, lastly, our tongue is most fit to honor poesy, and to be honored by poesy; I conjure you all that have had the evil luck to read this ink-wasting toy of mine, even in the name of the nine Muses, no more to scorn the sacred mysteries of poesy; no more to laugh at the name of poets, as though they were next inheritors to fools; no more to jest at the reverent title of a rhymer; but to believe, with Aristotle, that they were the ancient treasurers of the Grecians' divinity; to believe, with Bembus, that they were first bringers-in of all civility; to believe, with Scaliger, that no philosopher's precepts can sooner make you an honest man than the reading of Virgil; to believe, with Clauserus, the translator of Cornutus, that it pleased the heavenly Deity, by Hesiod[1] and Homer, under the veil of fables, to give us all knowledge, logic, rhetoric, philosophy natural and moral, and *quid non?*;[2] to believe, with me, that there are many mysteries contained in poetry, which of purpose were written darkly, lest by profane wits it should be abused; to believe, with Landino,[3] that they are so beloved of the gods that whatsoever they write proceeds of a

---

1. Except on that occasion. "Only words": words alone.
2. By killing the husband of his mistress, Bathsheba. For the deed, and Nathan's rebuke, see 2 Samuel 11–12.
3. Cruelly.
4. The *first* cause was God's intention to bring David to repentance.
5. Psalm 51, in which David pleads for God's mercy. "Glass": mirror.
6. That is, to the argument weighing poetry by its "works."
7. Congenial, suitable. "End": aim, objective.
8. This final paragraph constitutes the *peroratio* of Sidney's judicial oration: though it includes a brief recapitulation of arguments, the main function of the peroration is, like that of the exordium, to work on the audience's feelings, leaving it well-disposed toward the speaker and the speaker's client.
9. False poets, who mimic ("ape") the real ones.

1. Early Greek poet whose *Theogony* recounts myths of the birth and warfare of the gods and the origin of the world. For Aristotle, compare *Metaphysics* 3.4.12. Bembus (Pietro Bembo) was an Italian cardinal and grammarian. For Scaliger, see p. 526, n. 7. Conrad Clauser was a German scholar who translated a Greek treatise by Cornutus, a Stoic pedagogue of Nero's time.
2. What not?
3. Christoforo Landino, Florentine humanist who developed this argument in his edition of Dante's *Divine Comedy* (1481).

divine fury;[4] lastly, to believe themselves, when they tell you they will make you immortal by their verses. Thus doing, your name shall flourish in the printers' shops; thus doing, you shall be of kin to many a poetical preface; thus doing, you shall be most fair, most rich, most wise, most all, you shall dwell upon superlatives; thus doing, though you be *libertino patre natus*,[5] you shall suddenly grow *Herculea proles*,[6]

Si quid mea carmina possunt;[7]

thus doing, your soul shall be placed with Dante's Beatrice, or Virgil's Anchises.[8] But if (fie of such a but) you be born so near the dull-making cataract of Nilus that you cannot hear the planet-like[9] music of poetry; if you have so earth-creeping a mind that it cannot lift itself up to look to the sky of poetry, or rather, by a certain rustical disdain, will become such a mome as to be a Momus[1] of poetry; then, though I will not wish unto you the ass's ears of Midas,[2] nor to be driven by a poet's verses, as Bubonax[3] was, to hang himself, nor to be rhymed to death, as is said to be done in Ireland;[4] yet thus much curse I must send you, in the behalf of all poets, that while you live, you live in love, and never get favor for lacking skill of a sonnet;[5] and, when you die, your memory die from the earth for want of an epitaph.

ca. 1579   1595

Astrophil and Stella

Sidney was a jealous protector of his privacy. "I assure you before God," he had written once in an angry letter to his father's private secretary, Molyneux, "that if ever I know you do so much as read any letter I write to my father, without his commandment or my consent, I will thrust my dagger into you. And trust to it, for I speak it in earnest." Yet in *Astrophil and Stella* he seems to hold up a mirror to every nuance of his emotional being. For its original coterie audience, Sidney's sonnet sequence must have been an elaborate game of literary masks, psychological risk-taking, and open secrets. The loosely linked succession of 108 sonnets and eleven songs, with its dazzling display of technical virtuosity, provides tantalizing glimpses of identifiable characters and, still more, a sustained and remarkably intimate portrait of the poet's inner life.

Much biographical speculation has centered on Sidney's ambiguous relationship with Penelope Devereux, the supposed original of Stella. A marriage between the two had been proposed in 1576 and was talked about for some years, but in 1581 she married Lord Robert Rich, and two years later Sidney also married. (At their high social rank, marriages were negotiated in the interests of the powerful families involved, not of the individuals.) Some of the sonnets contain sly puns on the name *Rich*, and it seems likely that there are autobiographical elements in the shadowy narrative sketched by the work. At the same time, however, the "plot" of

---

4. Divinely inspired frenzy.
5. Born of a freed-slave father (Horace, *Satires* 1.6.6).
6. Offspring of Hercules.
7. If my songs are of any avail (*Aeneid* 9.446).
8. That is, in Paradise with Dante's beloved or in the Elysian Fields with Aeneas's honored father.
9. Resembling the music of the spheres, most beautiful of all music. According to Cicero (*Dream of Scipio* 5), the noise of the waterfalls in the upper Nile deafened those who lived nearby.
1. God of ridicule, son of Night; hence, a critic.

"Mome": dunce.
2. He was given ass's ears because he preferred Pan's music to Apollo's (Ovid, *Metamorphoses* 11.146–79).
3. Bupalus, an ancient Greek sculptor who, according to an apocryphal story, hanged himself when his works were satirized by the poet Hipponax. Sidney fuses the two names.
4. Irish bards were thought to be able to cause death with their rhymed charms.
5. Because you are unable to write a sonnet.

the sequence—full of trials, setbacks, much suffering on the part of the lover, and occasional encouragement on the part of the lady—is highly conventional, derived from Petrarch and his many Italian, French, and Spanish imitators.

Poets in this tradition undertook to produce an anatomy of love, displaying its shifting and often contradictory states: hope and despair, tenderness and bitterness, exultation and modesty, bodily desire and spiritual transcendence. Sidney, in the role of Astrophil, protests that he uses no standard conventional phrases, that his verse is original and comes from his heart. This protest is itself conventional, and yet Sidney manages to infuse his sonnets with an extraordinary vigor and freshness. Certain of the sonnets have, within their narrow fourteen-line bounds, the force of the drama: "Fly, fly, my friends, I have my death-wound, fly" or "What, have I thus betrayed my liberty?" Others, in their grappling with insistent desire, have the probing, psychological resonance of private confession: "With what sharp checks I in myself am shent" or "Who will in fairest book of Nature know." Still others ask crucial questions about the whole project of self-representation: "Stella oft sees the very face of woe." Virtually all of them manifest the exceptional *energia*—forcibleness—that Sidney, in *The Defense of Poesy*, says is the key ingredient of good love poetry.

From Astrophil and Stella

1[1]

Loving in truth, and fain° in verse my love to show,   *desirous*
That the dear She might take some pleasure of my pain,
Pleasure might cause her read, reading might make her know,
Knowledge might pity win, and pity grace obtain,
5   I sought fit words to paint the blackest face of woe,
Studying inventions fine, her wits to entertain,
Oft turning others' leaves, to see if thence would flow
Some fresh and fruitful showers upon my sunburned brain.
    But words came halting forth, wanting Invention's stay;[2]
10 Invention, Nature's child, fled step-dame Study's blows,
And others' feet still° seemed but strangers in my way.   *continually*
Thus great with child to speak, and helpless in my throes,
    Biting my truant pen, beating myself for spite,
"Fool," said my Muse to me, "look in thy heart and write."

2

Not at first sight, nor with a dribbèd[3] shot
    Love gave the wound, which while I breathe will bleed,
    But known worth did in mine[4] of time proceed,
Till by degrees it had full conquest got.
5 I saw and liked, I liked but lovèd not,
    I loved, but straight did not[5] what Love decreed;
    At length to Love's decrees, I, forced, agreed,

---

1. One of six sonnets in the sequence written in hexameters.
2. That is, lacking the support of Invention, his words moved haltingly.
3. Ineffectual or at random.
4. Tunnel dug to undermine a besieged fortress.
5. Did not immediately do.

Yet with repining° at so partial° lot.   *complaining / unfair*
  Now even that footstep of lost liberty
10 Is gone, and now like slave-born Muscovite,[6]
I call it praise to suffer tyranny;
And now employ the remnant of my wit°   *mind*
  To make myself believe that all is well,
  While with a feeling skill I paint my hell.

15

You that do search for every purling° spring   *murmuring*
  Which from the ribs of old Parnassus[7] flows,
  And every flower,[8] not sweet perhaps, which grows
Near therabout, into your poesy[9] wring;
5 You that do dictionary's method bring
  Into your rhymes, running in rattling rows;
  You that poor Petrarch's long-deceasèd woes
With new-born sighs and denizened wit° do sing: *naturalized ingenuity*
You take wrong ways, those far-fet° helps be such   *far-fetched*
10 As do bewray a want of inward touch,[1]
And sure at length stolen goods do come to light.
  But if (both for your love and skill) your name
  You seek to nurse at fullest breasts of Fame,
Stella behold, and then begin to indite.°   *compose, write*

18

With what sharp checks° I in myself am shent,°   *rebukes / shamed*
  When into Reason's audit I do go,
  And by just counts myself a bankrout° know   *bankrupt*
Of all those goods, which heaven to me hath lent:
5 Unable quite to pay even Nature's rent,
  Which unto it by birthright I do owe;
  And which is worse, no good excuse can show,
But that my wealth I have most idly spent.
My youth doth waste, my knowledge brings forth toys,[2]
10 My wit° doth strive those passions to defend,   *intellect*
Which for reward spoil it with vain annoys.°   *troubles*
I see my course to lose myself doth bend:°   *turn*
  I see and yet no greater sorrow take,
  Than that I lose no more for Stella's sake.

20

Fly, fly, my friends, I have my death-wound, fly;
  See there that boy, that murth'ring° boy, I say,   *murdering*

---

6. Inhabitant of Muscovy, Russian principality ruled from Moscow; 16th-century travel books describe Muscovites as contented slaves.
7. Mountain near Delphi in Greece, sacred to the Muses.
8. Also, poetic figures ("flowers of rhetoric").
9. Also, a nosegay (posy).
1. Reveal a lack of innate talent.
2. Trifles; that is, these poems.

    Who like a thief hid in dark bush doth lie
    Till bloody bullet get him wrongful prey.
5   So tyran° he no fitter place could spy, —*tyrant*
    Nor so fair level° in so secret stay,° —*aim / stopping place*
    As that sweet black° which veils the heav'nly eye; —*pupil*
    There himself with his shot he close° doth lay. —*secretly*
      Poor passenger,° pass now thereby I did, —*passerby*
10 And stayed, pleased with the prospect of the place,
    While that black hue from me the bad guest hid:
    But straight I saw motions of lightning grace,
      And then descried° the glist'ring° of his dart;° —*saw / glittering / arrow*
    But ere I could fly thence, it pierced my heart.

27

    Because I oft, in dark abstracted guise,
      Seem most alone in greatest company,
      With dearth of words, or answers quite awry,
    To them that would make speech of speech arise,
5   They deem, and of their doom° the rumor flies, —*judgment*
      That poison foul of bubbling pride doth lie
      So in my swelling breast that only I° —*that I do nothing but*
    Fawn on myself, and others do despise.
      Yet pride, I think, doth not my soul possess,
10 Which looks too oft in his unflatt'ring glass;° —*mirror*
    But one worse fault, ambition, I confess,
    That makes me oft my best friends overpass,° —*pass by, ignore*
      Unseen, unheard, while thought to highest place
    Bends all his powers, even unto Stella's grace.° —*beauty, elegance; favor*

28

    You that with allegory's curious frame° —*intricate contrivance*
      Of others' children changelings use° to make, —*are accustomed*
      With me those pains for God's sake do not take:
    I list not° dig so deep for brazen fame. —*I don't care to*
5   When I say Stella, I do mean the same
      Princess of beauty for whose only sake
      The reins of love I love, though never slake,° —*slack*
    And joy therein, though nations count it shame.
      I beg no subject to use eloquence,[3]
10 Nor in hid ways to guide philosophy;
    Look at my hands for no such quintessence,[4]
    But know that I in pure simplicity
      Breathe out the flames which burn within my heart,
    Love only reading unto me this art.

---

3. That is, I don't ask for a topic simply as an excuse to display my rhetorical skills.
4. The mysterious "fifth element" of matter (supplementary to earth, air, fire, and water), which alchemists labored to extract.

31

With how sad steps, O Moon, thou climb'st the skies,
   How silently, and with how wan a face!
   What, may it be that even in heavenly place
That busy archer° his sharp arrows tries?   *Cupid*
5 Sure, if that long-with-love-acquainted eyes
   Can judge of love, thou feel'st a lover's case;
   I read it in thy looks: thy languished grace,
To me that feel the like, thy state descries.°   *reveals*
   Then even of fellowship, O Moon, tell me,
10 Is constant love deemed there but want of wit?°   *lack of intelligence*
Are beauties there as proud as here they be?
Do they above love to be loved, and yet
   Those lovers scorn whom that love doth possess?
   Do they call virtue there ungratefulness?[5]

34

Come, let me write. "And to what end?" To ease
   A burdened heart. "How can words ease, which are
   The glasses° of thy daily vexing care?"   *mirrors*
Oft cruel fights well pictured forth do please.
5 "Art° not ashamed to publish thy disease?"   *are you*
   Nay, that may breed my fame, it is so rare.
   "But will not wise men think thy words fond ware?"° *foolish trinkets*
Then be they close,[6] and so none shall displease.
   "What idler thing, than speak and not be hard?"°   *heard*
10 What harder thing than smart,° and not to speak?   *feel pain*
Peace, foolish wit;° with wit my wit is marred.   *reason; intellect*
Thus while I write I doubt° to write, and wreak° *hesitate; fear / avenge*
   My harms on Ink's poor loss: perhaps some find
   Stella's great powers, that so confuse my mind.

41

Having this day my horse, my hand, my lance
   Guided so well that I obtained the prize,
   Both by the judgment of the English eyes
And of some sent from that sweet enemy France;[7]
5 Horsemen my skill in horsemanship advance;[8]
   Townfolks my strength; a daintier° judge applies   *more discerning*
   His praise to sleight,[9] which from good use° doth rise; *experience*
Some lucky wits impute it but to chance;
   Others, because of both sides I do take

---

5. That is, is the lady's ingratitude considered virtue in heaven (as here)? Also, is the lover's virtue (fidelity) considered distasteful in heaven (as here)?
6. Let them (my words) be kept private.
7. Sidney took part in several jousting tournaments between 1579 and 1585 with French spectators present, but the one in May 1581 was devised specifically to entertain French commissioners.
8. That is, put forward as the reason for my triumph.
9. Skill, dexterity.

10 My blood from them who did excel in this,[1]
    Think Nature me a man of arms did make.
    How far they shoot awry! The true cause is,
        Stella looked on, and from her heavenly face
        Sent forth the beams which made so fair my race.[2]

45

Stella oft sees the very face of woe
    Painted in my beclouded stormy face,
    But cannot skill to° pity my disgrace,°   is unable to / misfortune
Not though thereof the cause herself she know.[3]
5 Yet hearing late a fable which did show,
    Of lovers never known, a grievous case,
    Pity thereof gate° in her breast such place   got
That, from that sea derived, tears' spring did flow.
    Alas, if fancy,° drawn by imaged things,   fantasy
10 Though false, yet with free scope more grace° doth breed   favor
Than servant's wrack, where new doubts honor brings,[4]
    Then think, my dear, that you in me do read
    Of lover's ruin some sad tragedy:
    I am not I; pity the tale of me.

47

What, have I thus betrayed my liberty?
    Can those black beams such burning marks° engrave   brands of slavery
    In my free side? or am I born a slave,
Whose neck becomes° such yoke of tyranny?   is suited to
5 Or want° I sense to feel my misery?   lack
    Or sprite,° disdain of such disdain to have?   spirit
    Who for long faith, though daily help I crave,
May get no alms but scorn of beggary.[5]
    Virtue awake! Beauty but beauty is;
10 I may, I must, I can, I will, I do
Leave following that which it is gain to miss.
    Let her go. Soft, but here she comes. Go to,[6]
    Unkind, I love you not. O me, that eye
    Doth make my heart give to my tongue the lie.°   contradict my tongue

49

I on my horse, and Love on me doth try
    Our horsemanships, while by strange work I prove
    A horseman to my horse, a horse to Love;

---

1. Sidney's father and grandfather and his maternal uncles, the earls of Leicester and Warwick, were frequent participants in tournaments.
2. Course in a tournament.
3. That is, even though she knows she herself is the cause of it.
4. That is, than the ruin of her lover ("servant"), caused by the new scruples ("doubts") her honor brings up.
5. That is, scorn for [my] begging.
6. An emphatic expression, like "I tell you."

And now man's wrongs in me, poor beast, descry.°   *discover*
5   The reins wherewith my rider doth me tie
    Are humbled thoughts, which bit of reverence move,
    Curbed in with fear, but with gilt boss° above   *gold stud*
Of hope, which makes it seem fair to the eye.
    The wand° is will; thou, Fancy, saddle art,[7]   *whip*
10   Girt fast by Memory; and while I spur
My horse, he spurs with sharp desire my heart;
    He sits me fast,° however I do stir,   *tightly*
    And now hath made me to his hand so right
That in the manage[8] myself takes delight.

54

Because I breathe not love to every one,
    Nor do not use set colors for to wear,[9]
    Nor nourish special locks of vowèd hair,[1]
Nor give each speech a full point[2] of a groan,
5   The courtly nymphs, acquainted with the moan
    Of them who in their lips Love's standard° bear,   *ensign*
    "What, he?" say they of me, "now I dare swear
He cannot love; no, no, let him alone!"
    And think so still, so[3] Stella know my mind.
10 Profess indeed I do not Cupid's art;
But you, fair maids, at length this true shall find,
    That his right badge[4] is but worn in the heart:
    Dumb swans, not chatt'ring pies,° do lovers prove;[5]   *magpies*
They love indeed, who quake to say they love.

56

Fie, school of Patience, fie, your lesson is
    Far far too long to learn it without book:°   *by memory*
    What, a whole week without one piece of look,[6]
And think I should not your large precepts miss?°   *forget*
5   When I might read those letters fair of bliss,
    Which in her face teach virtue, I could brook°   *bear*
    Somewhat thy leaden counsels, which I took
As of a friend that meant not much amiss.
    But now that I, alas, do want° her sight,   *lack*
10 What, dost thou think that I can ever take
    In thy cold stuff a phlegmatic° delight?   *sluggish*
    No, Patience, if thou wilt my good, then make
Her come and hear with patience my desire,
And then with patience bid me bear my fire.

---

7. That is, you, Fancy (imagination), are the saddle.
8. *Training or handling of a horse.*
9. Am not accustomed to wear colors associated with a particular woman.
1. That is, lovelocks: long, flowing locks characteristic of amorous courtiers.
2. Final punctuation, period.
3. Go on thinking so, provided only that.
4. True badge, livery.
5. Prove to be (true) lovers.
6. Without the briefest glimpse of her.

69

O joy, too high for my low style to show,
   O bliss, fit for a nobler state than me!
   Envy, put out thine eyes, least° thou do see   *lest*
What oceans of delight in me do flow.
My friend, that oft saw through all masks my woe,
   Come, come, and let me pour myself on thee:
   Gone is the winter of my misery;
My spring appears; O see what here doth grow.
For Stella hath, with words where faith doth shine,
Of her high heart given me the monarchy:
I, I, O I may say that she is mine.
And though she give but thus conditionly
   This realm of bliss, while virtuous course I take,
   No kings be crowned but° they some covenants⁷ make.   *unless*

71

Who will in fairest book of Nature know
   How Virtue may best lodged in beauty be,
   Let him but learn of Love to read in thee,
Stella, those fair lines, which true goodness show.
There shall he find all vices' overthrow,
   Not by rude force, but sweetest sovereignty
   Of reason, from whose light those night-birds⁸ fly;
That inward sun in thine eyes shineth so.
And not content to be Perfection's heir
Thyself, dost strive all minds that way to move,
Who mark° in thee what is in thee most fair.⁹   *perceive*
So while thy beauty draws the heart to love,
   As fast° thy Virtue bends that love to good;   *at the same rate*
   "But, ah," Desire still cries, "give me some food."

72

Desire, though thou my old companion art,
   And oft so clings to my pure Love that I
   One from the other scarcely can descry,°   *distinguish*
While each doth blow the fire of my heart,
Now from thy fellowship I needs must part:
   Venus is taught with Dian's¹ wings to fly;
   I must no more in thy sweet passions lie;
Virtue's gold now must head my Cupid's dart.
   Service and honor, wonder with delight,
Fear to offend, will worthy to appear,²

---

7. Solemn coronation oaths taken by English monarchs, promising to protect the laws and the people.
8. The owl, for example, was an emblem of various vices.
9. That is, her virtue, which is fairer even than her beauty.
1. Diana, goddess of the moon and patron of chastity. Venus, goddess of beauty and love, mother of Cupid.
2. The phrase can mean either "the wish to appear worthy" or "desire that is worthy to appear [that is, not shameful]."

Care shining in mine eyes, faith in my sprite:° *spirit*
These things are left me by my only dear.
   But thou, Desire, because thou wouldst have all,
   Now banished art. But yet alas how shall?

74

I never drank of Aganippe well,[3]
Nor ever did in shade of Tempe[4] sit;
And Muses scorn with vulgar° brains to dwell; *common*
Poor layman I, for sacred rites unfit.
   Some do I hear of poets' fury° tell, *inspiration*
But God wot,° wot not what they mean by it; *knows*
And this I swear by blackest brook of hell,[5]
I am no pick-purse of another's wit.
   How falls it then that with so smooth an ease
My thoughts I speak, and what I speak doth flow
In verse, and that my verse best wits doth please?
   Guess we the cause. "What, is it thus?" Fie no.
   "Or so?" Much less. "How then?" Sure thus it is:
My lips are sweet, inspired with Stella's kiss.[6]

81

O kiss, which dost those ruddy gems impart,
Or° gems, or fruits of new-found Paradise, *either*
Breathing all bliss and sweet'ning to the heart,
Teaching dumb lips a nobler exercise!
   O kiss, which souls, even souls, together ties
By links of Love, and only Nature's art,
How fain° would I paint thee to all men's eyes, *gladly*
Or of thy gifts at least shade out° some part. *sketch*
   But she forbids, with blushing words she says
She builds her fame on higher-seated praise.
But my heart burns, I cannot silent be.
   Then since (dear life) you fain would have me peace,[7]
   And I, mad with delight, want wit[8] to cease,
Stop you my mouth with still still kissing me.

Fourth Song[9]

   Only joy, now here you are,
   Fit to hear and ease my care;
   Let my whispering voice obtain
   Sweet reward for sharpest pain:

---

3. The fountain at the foot of Mount Helicon in Greece, sacred to the Muses.
4. Valley beside Mount Olympus, sacred to Apollo, the god of poetry.
5. The most binding of all oaths were those sworn by the river Styx.
6. A kiss he stole from Stella when he caught her napping (Second Song).
7. You want me to be silent.
8. Lack the mental faculties.
9. Like Petrarch, Sidney intersperses songs (eleven of them, in various verse forms) in his sequence. Some of them incorporate Stella's voice. This song appears between sonnets 85 and 86.

     Take me to thee, and thee to me.
     "No, no, no, no, my dear, let be."

Night hath closed all in her cloak,
Twinkling stars love-thoughts provoke,
Danger hence good care doth keep,
Jealousy itself doth sleep:
     Take me to thee, and thee to me.
     "No, no, no, no, my dear, let be."

Better place no wit can find,
Cupid's yoke to loose or bind;
These sweet flowers on fine bed, too,
Us in their best language woo:
     Take me to thee, and thee to me.
     "No, no, no, no, my dear, let be."

This small light the moon bestows
Serves thy beams but to disclose,
So to raise my hap° more high;   *good fortune*
Fear not else, none can us spy:
     Take me to thee, and thee to me.
     "No, no, no, no, my dear, let be."

That you heard was but a mouse,
Dumb sleep holdeth all the house;
Yet asleep methinks they say,
"Young folks, take time while you may."
     Take me to thee, and thee to me.
     "No, no, no, no, my dear, let be."

Niggard° Time threats, if we miss   *stingy*
This large offer of our bliss,
Long stay° ere he grant the same;   *wait*
Sweet, then, while each thing doth frame,°   *serve*
     Take me to thee, and thee to me.
     "No, no, no, no, my dear, let be."

Your fair mother is abed,
Candles out, and curtains spread;
She thinks you do letters write:
Write, but first let me indite:°   *dictate*
     Take me to thee, and thee to me.
     "No, no, no, no, my dear, let be."

Sweet, alas, why strive you thus?
Concord better fitteth us.
Leave to Mars the force of hands;
Your power in your beauty stands:
     Take me to thee, and thee to me.
     "No, no, no, no, my dear, let be."

                    Woe to me, and do you swear
50   Me to hate? But I forbear.°   *desist*
                    Cursèd be my destines° all,   *fates*
                    That brought me so high to fall:
                    Soon with my death I will please thee.
                    "No, no, no, no, my dear, let be."

87

When I was forced from Stella ever dear,
Stella, food of my thoughts, heart of my heart,
Stella, whose eyes make all my tempests clear,
By iron laws of duty to depart,
   Alas, I found that she with me did smart:°   *suffer*
I saw that tears did in her eyes appear;
I saw that sighs her sweetest lips did part,
And her sad words my sadded sense did hear.
   For me, I wept to see pearls scattered so,
   I sighed her sighs, and wailèd for her woe,
Yet swam in joy, such love in her was seen.
   Thus while th' effect most bitter was to me,
   And nothing than the cause more sweet could be,
I had been° vexed, if vexed I had not been.   *would have been*

89[1]

Now that of absence the most irksome night
   With darkest shade doth overcome my day,
   Since Stella's eyes, wont° to give me my day,   *accustomed*
Leaving my hemisphere, leave me in night,
   Each day seems long, and longs for long-stayed° night,   *long-delayed*
   The night, as tedious, woos th' approach of day;
Tired with the dusty toils of busy day,
Languished with horrors of the silent night,
   Suffering the evils both of the day and night,
   While no night is more dark than is my day,
Nor no day hath less quiet than my night,
   With such bad mixture of my night and day
That, living thus in blackest winter night,
I feel the flames of hottest summer day.

91

Stella, while now by Honor's cruel might
   I am from° you, light of my life, mis-led,   *away from*
   And that fair you, my sun, thus overspread
With absence' veil, I live in Sorrow's night,
   If this dark place yet shew,° like candlelight,   *show*
   Some beauty's piece,[2] as amber-colored head,

---

1. A sonnet with only two rhyme words, *night* and *day*.   2. Some beauties in other women.

      Milk hands, rose cheeks, or lips more sweet, more red,
        Or seeing jets,[3] black, but in blackness bright,
        They please I do confess, they please mine eyes;
10   But why? because of you they models be;
      Models such be wood-globes of glist'ring° skies.[4]   *glittering*
      Dear, therefore be not jealous over me,
        If you hear that they seem my heart to move:
        Not them, O no, but you in them I love.

106

      O absent presence, Stella is not here;
        False flattering Hope, that with so fair a face
        Bare me in hand,° that in this orphan place   *deceived me*
      Stella, I say my Stella, should appear.
5   What say'st thou now? Where is that dainty cheer°   *countenance; food*
        Thou told'st mine eyes should help their famished case?
        But thou art gone, now that self-felt disgrace
      Dost make me most to wish thy comfort near.
        But here I do store° of fair ladies meet,   *abundance*
10   Who may with charm of conversation sweet
      Make in my heavy mold° new thoughts to grow: *earth*
        Sure they prevail as much with me, as he
        That bade his friend, but then new-maimed, to be
      Merry with him, and not think of his woe.

108[5]

      When Sorrow (using mine own fire's might)
        Melts down his lead into my boiling breast,
        Through that dark furnace to my heart oppressed
      There shines a joy from thee, my only light;
5   But soon as thought of thee breeds my delight,
        And my young soul flutters to thee, his nest,
        Most rude Despair, my daily unbidden guest,
      Clips straight° my wings, straight wraps me in his night,   *immediately*
        And makes me then bow down my head and say,
10   "Ah, what doth Phoebus'° gold that wretch avail,   *god of the sun*
      Whom iron doors do keep from use of day?"
        So strangely (alas) thy works in me prevail,
        That in my woes for thee thou art my joy,
      And in my joys for thee my only annoy.°   *trouble, pain*

1582?   1591, 1598

---

3. That is, jet-black eyes.
4. Wooden globes of the heavens, with painted constellations and planets.

5. In many sonnet sequences, as here, the final poem brings no resolution.

MARY (SIDNEY) HERBERT, COUNTESS OF PEMBROKE
1562–1621

When her brother, the celebrated courtier and author Philip Sidney, died in 1586, Mary Sidney, the Countess of Pembroke, became the custodian not only of his writings but also of his last name. Though her marriage in 1577 to Henry Herbert, the second Earl of Pembroke, represented a great social advance for her family—her offspring would be among the nation's tiny hereditary nobility—throughout her life the Countess of Pembroke held on to her identity as a Sidney.

She had good reason to do so. The Sidneys were celebrated for their generous support of poets, clergymen, alchemists, naturalists, scientists, and musicians. The Pembroke country estate, Wilton, quickly became a gathering place for thinkers who enjoyed the countess's patronage and shared her staunch Protestant convictions and her literary interests. Books, pamphlets, and scores of poems in the 1590s and thereafter were dedicated to her, as well as to her brother Robert (whose country house, Penshurst, is praised in a well-known poem by Ben Jonson). Nicholas Breton and Samuel Daniel in particular benefited from her support, as did her niece, goddaughter, and frequent companion, Mary Wroth.

In one of the dedicatory poems to *Salve Deus Rex Judaeorum*, Aemilia Lanyer praises Mary Sidney not only for her generosity toward poets but also for those "works that are more deep and more profound." These include her translations: she joins Anne Bacon, Margaret Tyler, and Anne Locke as a notable female translator of the era. Part of her translation of Robert Garnier's neoclassical French tragedy *Marc Antoine* is provided below; she also translated the religious tract *A Discourse of Life and Death* by the French Protestant Philippe de Mornay. She knew Italian too: her translation of Petrarch's *Triumph of Death* was the first in English to maintain the original *terza rima* (a particularly challenging rhyme scheme for an English versifier). She also dared to write in her own voice. Two of her main themes are her love for her brother Philip Sidney and for Queen Elizabeth—among her original poems was a powerful elegy for Philip and a short pastoral entertainment for the queen; both themes come together in the text provided below, "To the Thrice-Sacred Queen Elizabeth," in which the psalms she co-wrote with her now dead brother are dedicated to the queen.

Mary Sidney was best known for having prepared a composite edition of Philip Sidney's *Arcadia* and for contributing the larger number (107) of the verse translations of the 150 biblical psalms that her brother had begun. Her very free renderings re-create the psalms as English poems, using an amazing variety of stanzaic and metrical patterns and some strikingly effective images. Widely circulated in manuscript, this influential collection was an important bridge between the many metrical paraphrases of psalms in this period and the works of the great religious lyric poets of the seventeenth century, especially George Herbert. Donne's poem "Upon the Translation of the Psalms by Sir Philip Sidney and the Countess of Pembroke His Sister" testifies to that importance: "They tell us *why*, and teach us *how* to sing."

To the Thrice-Sacred Queen Elizabeth   In this complex poem, preserved in two manuscripts, Mary Sidney dedicates her completed translation of the psalms, begun by her brother Philip Sidney, to Queen Elizabeth. She mourns her brother while also maintaining that he and she together have, through their translations, made the psalms and their writer, King David, English. She praises Queen Elizabeth and King David both as artists and as rulers and celebrates the queen's—and England's—political and international successes.

To the Thrice-Sacred Queen Elizabeth

Even now, that care which on thy crown attends[1]—
And with thy happy greatness daily grows—
Tells me, thrice-sacred queen, my muse offends,
And of respect to thee the line outgoes.[2]
5 One instant will (or willing) can she° lose   *that is, the queen*
I say not reading, but receiving rhymes,[3]
On whom in chief dependeth to dispose°   *control*
What Europe acts° in these most active times?   *does*

Yet dare I so: as humbleness may dare
10 Cherish some hope° they° shall acceptance find;   *nurse the hope / the poems*
Not weighing less thy state, lighter thy care,
But knowing more thy grace, abler thy mind.
What heavenly powers thee highest throne assigned,[4]
Assigned thee goodness suiting that degree,°   *station, rank*
15 And by thy strength thy burthen so defined,
To others toil, is exercise to thee.[5]

Cares, though still great, cannot be greatest still,
Business must ebb, though leisure never flow.
Then these the posts of duty and goodwill
20 Shall press° to offer what their senders owe;[6]   *push forward*
Which once in two, now in one subject go,[7]
The poorer left, the richer reft away:°   *plucked away*
Who better might (oh "might"! ah word of woe)[8]
Have given for me what I for him defray.°   *pay for*

25 How can I name whom sighing sighs extend,°   *belong*
And not unstop my tears' eternal spring?
But he did warp, I weaved,[9] this web to end;

---

1. Trouble that accompanies having a crown.
2. The poetic line exceeds its bounds (that is, meter is broken).
3. Can she, or will she, lose a single instant receiving (I won't say reading) rhymes.
4. The heavenly powers that appointed you to the highest throne.
5. What is drudgery to others is customary to you.
6. These poems will offer you what we, the senders of these poems, owe you: duty and goodwill.
7. Because Philip Sidney, her brother and co-translator, is dead.
8. A reference to Philip Sidney's *Astrophil and Stella* 33: "I might! Unhappy word: O me, I might . . ."
9. He laid the lengthwise and I the crosswise yarns.

          The stuff° not ours,[1] our work no curious° thing;   *material / ingenious*
          Wherein yet well we thought the Psalmist King—[2]
30   Now English denizened,° though Hebrew born—   *naturalized*
          Would to thy music undispleasèd° sing,   *pleasingly*
          Oft having worse, without repining,° worn.   *complaining*

          And I the cloth in both our names present,
          A livery robe[3] to be bestowed by thee:
35   Small parcel of° that undischargèd° rent,   *part of / not paid*
          From which nor pains, nor payments can us free.
          And yet enough to cause our neighbours see
          We will our best, though scanted° in our will: *diminished*
          And those nigh° fields where sown thy favors be   *near*
40   Unwealthy do, not else unworthy, till.°   *cultivate*

          For in our work what bring we but thine own?
          What English is, by many names, is thine.
          There humble laurels,° in thy shadows grown   *the crown given to victors*
          To garland others, would themselves repine.°   *complain*
45   Thy breast the cabinet, thy seat the shrine
          Where Muses hang their vowèd memories:
          Where wit, where art, where all that is divine
          Conceivèd best, and best defended lies.

          Which if men did not (as they do) confess,
50   And wronging worlds would otherwise consent:
          Yet here who minds° so meet° a patroness   *recalls / suitable*
          For authors' state or writing's argument?
          A king should only to a queen be sent.
          God's lovèd choice unto his chosen love:
55   Devotion to devotion's president:
          What all applaud, to her whom none reprove.[4]

          And who sees ought, but sees how justly square°   *harmonize; fit*
          His haughty ditties° to thy glorious days?   *lofty songs*
          How well beseeming thee his triumphs are?
60   His hope, his zeal, his prayer, plaint,° and praise,   *lament*
          Needless thy person to their height to raise;
          Less need to bend them down to thy degree;
          These holy garments each good soul assays,°   *tries on*
          Some sorting° all, all sort to none but thee.   *fitting*

65   For even thy rule is painted° in his reign: *represented; prefigured*
          Both clear in right; both nigh° by wrong oppressed;   *closely*
          And each at length (man crossing° God in vain)   *opposing*

---

1. Because the original biblical text is by David.
2. David, original author of the psalms.
3. Uniform worn by household retainers.
4. The king here is King David (God's loved choice, devotion, and the one whom all applaud); it is appropriate to send his psalms to a queen (God's chosen, the patron of devotion, the one whom none reprove).

Possessed of place, and each in peace possessed.
Proud Philistines did interrupt his rest;
70 The foes of Heaven no less have been thy foes.[5]
He with great conquest; thou with greater blessed;
Thou sure to win; and he secure to lose.

Thus hand in hand with him thy glories walk.
But who can trace them where alone they go?
75 Of thee two hemispheres on honor talk,[6]
And lands and seas thy trophies jointly show.
The very winds did on thy party blow,
And rocks in arms thy foemen eft° defy.[7]   *again*
But soft my muse: thy pitch is earthly low;
80 Forbear this heaven where only eagles fly.

Kings on a queen enforced their states to lay;
Mainlands for empire waiting on an isle;
Men drawn by worth a woman to obey;
One moving all, herself unmoved the while:
85 Truth's restitution,° vanity exile,   *restoration*
Wealth sprung of want, war held without annoy,°   *harm*
Let subject be of some inspirèd style,
Till then the object of her subjects' joy.

Thy[8] utmost° can but offer to her sight   *greatest skill*
Her handmaid's task,[9] which most her will endears;
90 And pray unto thy pains life from that light[1]
Which lively lightsome° court and kingdom cheers,   *happy*
What wish she may (far past her living peers
And rival still to Judah's faithful king°)   *David*
In more than he and more triumphant years,
95 Sing what God doth, and do what men may sing.

1599

---

5. Just as the Philistines (the enemies of the Israelites in the Bible) warred against David, so the enemies of heaven (that is, the Spanish) have opposed you.
6. Land and sea, but also the Old and New worlds
7. A reference to the defeat in 1588 of the Spanish Armada, which was damaged when the wind changed and drove the ships against the rocks.
8. Sidney is still addressing her muse.
9. Herbert's task as a servant (translating the psalms).
1. That is, Queen Elizabeth.

Psalm 52

Tyrant, why swell'st thou thus,
    Of mischief vaunting?
Since help from God to us
    Is never wanting.

5 Lewd° lies thy tongue contrives,   *vile*
    Loud lies it soundeth;
Sharper than sharpest knives
    With lies it woundeth.

Falsehood thy wit° approves,   *mind*
10   All truth rejected:
Thy will all vices loves,
    Virtue neglected.

Not words from cursèd thee,
    But gulfs° are pourèd;   *abysses, yawning chasms*
15 Gulfs wherein daily be
    Good men devourèd.

Think'st thou to bear it° so?   *bear it off, triumph*
    God shall displace thee;
God shall thee overthrow,
20   Crush thee, deface° thee.   *destroy*

The just shall fearing see
    These fearful chances,
And laughing shoot at thee
    With scornful glances.

25 Lo, lo, the wretched wight,°   *creature*
    Who, God disdaining,
His mischief made his might,
    His guard his gaining.°   *riches*

I as an olive tree
30   Still green shall flourish:
God's house the soil shall be
    My roots to nourish.

My trust on his true love
    Truly attending,
35 Shall never thence remove,
    Never see ending.

Thee will I honor still,
    Lord, for this justice;
There fix my hopes I will
40   Where thy saints' trust is.

Thy saints trust in thy name,
   Therein they joy them:
Protected by the same,
   Nought° can annoy° them. — *nothing / harm*

Psalm 119: O[1]

Oh, what a lantern, what a lamp of light
   Is thy pure Word to me
To clear my paths and guide my goings right!
   I sware,° and swear again, — *swore*
5   I of the statutes will observer be,
   Thou° justly dost ordain. — *which you*

The heavy weights of grief oppress me sore:° — *sorely, severely*
   Lord, raise me by thy Word,
As thou to me didst promise heretofore.
10   And this unforcèd praise
   I for an off'ring bring, accept, O Lord,
   And show to me thy ways.

What if my life lie naked[2] in my hand,
   To every chance exposed?
15 Should I forget what thou dost me command?
   No, no, I will not stray
From thy edicts, though round about enclosed
   With snares the wicked lay.

Thy testimonies, as mine heritage,
205   I have retainèd still,
And unto them my heart's delight engage—
   My heart which still doth bend,
And only bend to do what thou dost will,
   And do it to the end.

Psalm 139

O Lord, in me there lieth nought
   But to thy search revealèd lies:
      For when I sit
      Thou markest it;° — *you note it*
5 No less thou notest when I rise;

---

1. The 176 lines of Psalm 119 are divided into twenty-two sections of eight verses each, with the sections headed by, and their initial verses beginning with, successive letters of the Hebrew alphabet. Mary Sidney adopts the analogous procedure in English and also uses a different stanzaic form for each of the twenty-two sections.
2. That is, exposed to danger.

Yea, closest closet° of my thought   *most secret private chamber*
　　Hath open windows to thine eyes.

Thou walkest with me when I walk;
　　When to my bed for rest I go,
10　　　　I find thee there,
　　　　And everywhere:
　　Not youngest thought in me doth grow,
No, not one word I cast° to talk   *resolve*
　　But yet unuttered thou dost know.

15 If forth I march, thou goest before,
　　If back I turn, thou com'st behind:
　　　　So forth nor back
　　　　Thy guard I lack,
　　Nay, on me too thy hand I find.
20 Well I thy wisdom may adore,
　　But never reach with earthy mind.

To shun thy notice, leave thine eye,
　　O whither might I take my way?
　　　　To starry sphere?
25　　　　Thy throne is there.
　　To dead men's undelightsome stay?°   *place*
There is thy walk, and there to lie
　　Unknown° in vain I should assay.°   *(to thee) / attempt*

O sun, whom light nor flight can match,
30　　Suppose thy lightful flightful wings
　　　　Thou lend to me,
　　　　And I could flee
　　As far as thee the ev'ning brings:
Even led to west he would me catch,
35　　Nor should I lurk° with western things.   *hide*

Do thou thy best, O secret night,
　　In sable veil to cover me:
　　　　Thy sable veil
　　　　Shall vainly fail;
40　　With day unmasked my night shall be,
　　For night is day and darkness light,
　　　　O father of all lights, to thee.

Each inmost piece in me is thine:
　　While yet I in my mother dwelt,
45　　　　All that me clad
　　　　From thee I had.
　　Thou in my frame° hast strangely dealt: *form*
Needs in my praise thy works must shine,
　　So inly them my thoughts have felt.

50   Thou, how my back was beam-wise laid,
            And raft'ring of my ribs, dost know;
                Know'st every point
                Of bone and joint,
            How to this whole these parts did grow,
55   In brave° embroid'ry fair arrayed,   *splendid*
            Though wrought in shop both dark and low.

        Nay, fashionless, ere form I took,
            Thy all and more beholding eye
                My shapeless shape
60   Could not escape:
            All these, with times appointed by,¹
        Ere one had being, in the book
            Of thy foresight enrolled did lie.

        My God, how I these studies prize,
65   That do thy hidden workings show!
                Whose sum is such
                No sum so much:
            Nay, summed as° sand they sumless grow.   *like*
        I lie to sleep, from sleep I rise,
70   Yet still° in thought with thee I go.   *always*

        My God, if thou but one² wouldst kill,
            Then straight would leave my further chase³
                This cursèd brood
                Inured to blood,
75   Whose graceless taunts at thy disgrace
        Have aimèd oft, and hating still
            Would with proud lies thy truth outface.°   *defy*

        Hate not I them, who thee do hate?
            Thine, Lord, I will the censure be.⁴
80   Detest I not
                The cankered knot
            Whom I against thee banded see?
        O Lord, thou know'st in highest rate
            I hate them all as foes to me.

85   Search me, my God, and prove my heart,
            Examine me, and try° my thought;   *test*
                And mark in me
                If ought° there be   *aught, anything*
            That hath with cause their anger wrought.
90   If not (as not) my life's each part,
            Lord, safely guide from danger brought.

ca. 1595   1823

1. With appropriate times indicated (for each step of the work of creation).
2. Only one (wicked man).
3. Then immediately [the wicked] would stop pursuing me.
4. That is, I leave it to you to censure them.

Robert Garnier's *Marc Antoine* (Mary Sidney's *Tragedie of Antonie*) Mary Sidney's decision to translate a French play into English is a testament to her own approach and beliefs—in the face of those of her brother, Philip Sidney, whose *Defense of Poesy* is ambivalent about the theater. She picked a drama, Robert Garnier's *Marc Antoine* (1578), that had a strong female heroine and translated it into the homely iambic pentameter of conventional staged English dramas (the French text, by contrast, is in twelve-syllable lines called "alexandrines"). Though her play was unperformed, it was made to be in dialogue with other printed dramas of the time. A popular text (printed in 1592 as *Antonius, a tragedie*; reprinted in 1595 as *The Tragedie of Antonie*), this was the first play to be published under a woman's name. It directly influenced Samuel Daniel, whose *Cleopatra* (1594) was written as a sequel to it—and probably also Shakespeare, whose emotional characterization of Antony and Cleopatra in the play of that name echoes Mary Sidney's own.

From Robert Garnier's *Marc Antoine*

ERAS All things do yield to force of lovely face.
CLEOPATRA My face, too lovely, caused my wretched case.°   *situation*
    My face hath so entrapped, so cast us down,
    That for his conquest Caesar[1] may it thank,
5   Causing that Antony one army lost;
    The other° wholly did to Caesar yield.   *that is, army*
    For not enduring (so his amorous sprite°   *spirit*
    Was with my beauty fired) my shameful flight,
    Soon as he saw—from rank° wherein he stood   *battalion*
10 In hottest fight—my gallies° making sail,   *warships*
    Forgetful of his charge° (as if his soul   *responsibility*
    Unto his lady's soul had been enchained)
    He left his men, who so courageously
    Did leave their lives to gain him victory,
15 And careless both of fame and army's loss,
    My oarèd gallies followed with his ships,
    Companion of my flight, by this base part
    Blasting° his former flourishing renown.   *destroying*
ERAS Are you therefore cause of his overthrow?
20 CLEOPATRA I am sole cause: I did it, only I.

                                                                   1592, 1595

---

1. Octavius Caesar, grandnephew and adopted son of Julius Caesar, was brother to Octavia, wife of Antony. Octavius Caesar instigated the battles that are the subject of this play partly because Antony continued his love affair with Cleopatra, despire being married to Octavia.

CHRISTOPHER MARLOWE
1564-1593

The son of a Canterbury shoemaker, Christopher Marlowe was born two months before William Shakespeare. In 1580 he went to Corpus Christi College, Cambridge, on a scholarship that was ordinarily awarded to students preparing for the ministry. He held the scholarship for the maximum time, six years, but did not take holy orders. Instead, he began to write plays. When he applied for his master of arts degree in 1587, the university was about to deny it to him on the grounds that he intended to go abroad to join the dissident English Catholics at Rheims. But the Privy Council intervened and requested that because Marlowe had done the queen "good service" he be granted his degree at the next commencement. "It is not Her Majesty's pleasure," the government officials added, "that anyone employed as he had been in matters touching the benefit of his country should be defamed by those that are ignorant in the affairs he went about." Although much sensational information about Marlowe has been discovered in modern times, we are still largely "ignorant in the affairs he went about." The likeliest possibility is that he served as a spy or an agent provocateur against English Catholics who were conspiring to overthrow the Protestant regime.

Before he left Cambridge, Marlowe had probably already drafted his tremendously successful play *Tamburlaine*. *Tamburlaine* dramatizes the exploits of a fourteenth-century Mongol warrior who rose from humble origins to conquer a huge territory that extended from the Black Sea to Delhi. Marlowe's hero is the vehicle for the expression of boundless energy and ambition, the impulse to strive ceaselessly for absolute dominance. Tamburlaine's conquests are achieved not only by force of arms but also by his extraordinary mastery of language, his "high astounding terms." The English theater audience had never before heard such resonant, immensely energetic blank verse. The great period of Elizabethan drama was launched by what Ben Jonson called "Marlowe's mighty line."

From the time of his first theatrical success, when he was twenty-three, Marlowe had only six years to live. It is remarkable how much he managed to accomplish in so brief and turbulent a time. (Had Shakespeare died in the same year, we would scarcely remember him.) In a raw new entertainment industry, with no strong English models to imitate, Marlowe produced a succession of brilliant plays. In a culture devoted to recovering the ancient classics, he was the first English translator of Ovid's erotic poems, the *Amores*, poems deemed so scandalous that the authorities ordered all copies of his translation burned. In a literary environment that produced many fine lyrics, he was the author of the lyric poem most widely celebrated by his contemporaries, "Come Live with Me and Be My Love." And in an age of wonderful long love poems, he was the author of one of the most wonderful of them all, *Hero and Leander*.

In 1591 Marlowe lived in London with the playwright Thomas Kyd, who later, under torture, gave information to the Privy Council accusing his former roommate of atheism and treason. On May 30, 1593, an informer named Richard Baines submitted a note to the council that, on the evidence of Marlowe's own alleged utterances, branded him with atheism, sedition, and homosexuality. Four days later, at an inn in the London suburb of Deptford, Marlowe was killed by a dagger thrust, purportedly in an argument over the bill. Modern scholars have discovered that the murderer and the others present in the room at the inn had connections to the world of spies, double agents, and swindlers to which Marlowe himself was in some way linked. Those who were arrested in connection with the murder were briefly held and then quietly released.

Hero and Leander   Marlowe's mythological poem is a free and original treatment of a classic tale about two ill-fated lovers. The story derives from a version by the Alexandrian poet Musaeus (ca. fifth century C.E.), but in its blend of poignancy and irony *Hero and Leander* is closer to that of the Roman poet Ovid, who briefly recounts the story in two epistles of his *Heroides*.

Hero and Leander is a rich and elusive poem: it is comic, decorative, cruel; now swiftly narrative, now digressive; playful and yet, in a light way, philosophical. Filled with free-floating erotic energy, both heterosexual and homosexual, it at once celebrates the power of language and calls attention to its irresponsibility and deceptiveness. The characters are evidently not intended to be consistent or psychologically credible; they inhabit a world of fancy, of strange contrasts between innocence and the wild riot of amorous intrigues among the gods that is Ovid's subject matter. Hero is paradoxically a nun vowed to chastity and a devotee of Venus, the love goddess; Leander is both a sharp, sophisticated seducer and a sexual innocent. The deadpan asides, with their irony, hyperbole, and cynicism mingling with exuberant delight in the body's instinctual freedom, heighten the poem's elusiveness, its cunning evasion of all fixed categories.

Hero and Leander cannot be precisely dated. Marlowe's translations of Ovid, to which the poem is closely related in spirit, are generally thought to be from the later 1580s. But, alternatively, Marlowe may have been participating in a vogue for brief erotic epics (epyllia, as they are sometimes called) that dates from the early 1590s, when Shakespeare composed his contribution to the genre, *Venus and Adonis*. Most striking, in either case, is the capacity for innovation. Just as Marlowe's plays displayed an unprecedented dramatic power in their blank verse, *Hero and Leander* manifested for the first time the sophisticated eloquence and tonal range of the heroic couplet.

Marlowe left his poem unfinished; George Chapman, the playwright and translator of Homer, undertook to complete it. Chapman's moralizing, weightily philosophical continuation was published in 1598, shortly after Marlowe's fragment. The work is printed here without Chapman's additions.

Hero and Leander

On Hellespont,[1] guilty of true-loves'° blood, — *sweethearts'*
In view and opposite, two cities stood,
Sea-borderers, disjoined by Neptune's might;
The one Abydos, the other Sestos hight.° — *called*
5 At Sestos Hero dwelt; Hero the fair,
Whom young Apollo courted for her hair,
And offered as a dower his burning throne,
Where she should sit for men to gaze upon.
The outside of her garments were of lawn,[2]
10 The lining purple silk, with gilt stars drawn;
Her wide sleeves green, and bordered with a grove
Where Venus in her naked glory strove
To please the careless and disdainful eyes
Of proud Adonis, that before her lies;[3]
15 Her kirtle° blue, whereon was many a stain, — *long dress*
Made with the blood of wretched lovers slain.[4]
Upon her head she ware a myrtle wreath,
From whence her veil reached to the ground beneath.
Her veil was artificial flowers and leaves,
20 Whose workmanship both man and beast deceives;
Many would praise the sweet smell as she passed,
When 'twas the odor which her breath forth cast;
And there for honey, bees have sought in vain,
And, beat from thence, have lighted there again.
25 About her neck hung chains of pebble-stone,
Which, lightened° by her neck, like diamonds shone. — *illuminated*
She ware no gloves, for neither sun nor wind
Would burn or parch her hands, but to her mind° — *as she wished*
Or° warm or cool them, for they took delight — *either*
30 To play upon those hands, they were so white.
Buskins° of shells all silvered usèd she, — *boots*
And branched with blushing coral to the knee,
Where sparrows perched, of hollow pearl and gold,
Such as the world would wonder to behold;
35 Those with sweet water oft her handmaid fills,
Which, as she went,° would chirrup through the bills. — *walked*
Some say, for her the fairest Cupid pined,
And looking in her face, was strooken blind.
But this is true: so like was one the other,
40 As he imagined Hero was his mother;° — *Venus*
And oftentimes into her bosom flew,
About her naked neck his bare arms threw,
And laid his childish head upon her breast,

---

1. The Dardanelles, in Turkey, a strait that forms part of the boundary between Europe and Asia.
2. A kind of fine linen or thin cambric.
3. Venus's love for the young hunter Adonis and his death in a boar hunt are recounted by Ovid, and by Shakespeare in *Venus and Adonis*.
4. The extravagant claim is made that many "wretched lovers" had committed suicide at her feet because Hero would not have them.

        And with still° panting rocked, there took his rest.   *continual*
45   So lovely fair was Hero, Venus' nun,[5]
        As Nature wept, thinking she was undone,
        Because she took more from her than she left
        And of such wondrous beauty her bereft;
        Therefore, in sign her° treasure suffered wrack,°   *Nature's / destruction*
50   Since Hero's time hath half the world been black.
        Amorous Leander, beautiful and young
        (Whose tragedy divine Musaeus[6] sung),
        Dwelt at Abydos; since him dwelt there none
        For whom succeeding times make greater moan.
55   His dangling tresses that were never shorn,
        Had they been cut and unto Colchos[7] borne,
        Would have allured the vent'rous youth of Greece
        To hazard more than for the Golden Fleece.
        Fair Cynthia° wished his arms might be her sphere;°   *the moon / orbit*
60   Grief makes her pale, because she moves not there.
        His body was as straight as Circe's wand;[8]
        Jove might have sipped out nectar from his hand.
        Even as delicious meat is to the taste,
        So was his neck in touching, and surpassed
65   The white of Pelops' shoulder.[9] I could tell ye
        How smooth his breast was, and how white his belly,
        And whose immortal fingers did imprint
        That heavenly path, with many a curious dint,°   *exquisite indentation*
        That runs along his back; but my rude° pen   *crude*
70   Can hardly blazon forth the loves of men,
        Much less of powerful gods; let it suffice
        That my slack° muse sings of Leander's eyes,   *dull*
        Those orient° cheeks and lips, exceeding his   *shining*
        That leapt into the water for a kiss
75   Of his own shadow,° and despising many,   *reflection*
        Died ere he could enjoy the love of any.[1]
        Had wild Hippolytus[2] Leander seen,
        Enamored of his beauty had he been;
        His presence made the rudest peasant melt,
80   That in the vast uplandish country dwelt;
        The barbarous Thracian soldier, moved with nought,
        Was moved with him, and for his favor sought.
        Some swore he was a maid in man's attire,
        For in his looks were all that men desire:
85   A pleasant smiling cheek, a speaking° eye,   *expressive*
        A brow for love to banquet royally;

---

5. The connotations of these two words are contradictory. Hero is a maiden in attendance at the temple of Venus, who is, of course, the goddess of physical love.

6. The author of the Greek poem on which *Hero and Leander* is remotely based. Though he lived in late antiquity (ca. 5th century C.E.), he was sometimes confused with a legendary early Musaeus, supposed son of Orpheus; hence Marlowe calls him "divine."

7. The country in Asia where the Argonauts ("the vent'rous youth of Greece"; line 57) found the Golden Fleece.

8. The wand with which Circe, in the *Odyssey*, turned men into beasts.

9. Pelops, according to Ovid, had a shoulder of ivory.

1. An allusion to Narcissus.

2. Like Adonis, he preferred hunting to love.

And such as knew he was a man, would say,
"Leander, thou art made for amorous play;
Why art thou not in love, and loved of° all?   *by*
90 Though thou be fair, yet be not thine own thrall."°   *captive*
   The men of wealthy Sestos every year,
For his sake whom their goddess held so dear,
Rose-cheeked Adonis, kept a solemn feast.
Thither resorted many a wandering guest
95 To meet their loves; such as had none at all
Came lovers home from this great festival;
For every street, like to a firmament,
Glistered° with breathing stars, who, where they went,   *glittered*
Frighted the melancholy earth, which deemed
100 Eternal heaven to burn, for so it seemed
As if another Phaëton[3] had got
The guidance of the sun's rich chariot.
But far above the loveliest, Hero shined,
And stole away th' enchanted gazer's mind;
105 For like sea nymphs' inveigling harmony,
So was her beauty to the standers by.
Nor that night-wandering pale and watery star°   *the moon*
(When yawning dragons draw her thirling[4] car°   *chariot*
From Latmos' mount[5] up to the gloomy sky,
110 Where, crowned with blazing light and majesty,
She proudly sits) more over-rules° the flood°   *rules over / tide*
Than she the hearts of those that near her stood.
Even as when gaudy nymphs pursue the chase,°   *hunt*
Wretched Ixion's shaggy-footed race,[6]
115 Incensed with savage heat, gallop amain
From steep pine-bearing mountains to the plain,
So ran the people forth to gaze upon her,
And all that viewed her were enamored on her.
And as in fury of a dreadful fight,
120 Their fellows being slain or put to flight,
Poor soldiers stand with fear of death dead-strooken,
So at her presence all, surprised and tooken,
Await the sentence of her scornful eyes;
He whom she favors lives, the other dies.
125 There might you see one sigh, another rage,
And some, their violent passions to assuage,
Compile sharp satires; but alas, too late,
For faithful love will never turn to hate.
And many, seeing great princes were denied,
130 Pined as they went, and thinking on her, died.
On this feast day, oh, cursèd day and hour!
Went Hero thorough° Sestos, from her tower   *through*

---

3. A son of the sun god, he drove his father's chariot erratically across the sky and almost burned up the world.
4. Flying like a spear.
5. The mountain where the moon visited her lover, Endymion.
6. The centaurs, fathered by Ixion on a cloud. For his presumption in loving Juno, Ixion was chained to a wheel, hence "wretched."

To Venus' temple, where unhappily,
As after chanced, they did each other spy.
135 So fair a church as this had Venus none;
The walls were of discolored° jasper stone,   *many-colored*
Wherein was Proteus[7] carved, and o'erhead
A lively° vine of green sea-agate spread,   *lifelike*
Where, by one hand, light-headed Bacchus[8] hung,
140 And with the other, wine from grapes out-wrung.
Of crystal shining fair the pavement was;
The town of Sestos called it Venus' glass;°   *looking glass*
There might° you see the gods in sundry shapes,   *could*
Committing heady° riots, incest, rapes: *passionate; violent*
145 For know that underneath this radiant floor
Was Danaë's[9] statue in a brazen tower,
Jove slyly stealing from his sister's[1] bed
To dally with Idalian Ganymed,[2]
And for his love Europa bellowing loud,[3]
150 And tumbling with the rainbow in a cloud;[4]
Blood-quaffing Mars heaving the iron net
Which limping Vulcan and his Cyclops set;[5]
Love kindling fire to burn such towns as Troy;
Sylvanus weeping for the lovely boy[6]
155 That now is turned into a cypress tree,
Under whose shade the wood-gods love to be.
And in the midst a silver altar stood;
There Hero sacrificing turtles'[7] blood,
Vailed° to the ground, veiling her eyelids close,   *bowed down*
160 And modestly they opened as she rose;
Thence flew love's arrow with the golden head,[8]
And thus Leander was enamorèd.
Stone still he stood, and evermore he gazed,
Till with the fire that from his countenance blazed,
165 Relenting Hero's gentle heart was strook;
Such force and virtue° hath an amorous look.   *power*
  It lies not in our power to love or hate,
For will in us is overruled by fate.
When two are stripped, long ere the course° begin   *race*
170 We wish that one should lose, the other win;
And one especially do we affect°   *fancy*
Of two gold ingots, like in each respect.
The reason no man knows, let it suffice,
What we behold is censured° by our eyes.   *judged*
175 Where both deliberate, the love is slight;

---

7. A sea god, who could change his shape at will.
8. God of wine and revelry.
9. Imprisoned in a tower, Danaë was visited by Jove in the form of a shower of gold.
1. That is, Juno's. She was Jove's wife.
2. Ganymede was a beautiful youth whom Jove kidnapped from Mount Ida, hence "Idalian."
3. To abduct Europa, Jove took the form of a bull.
4. Jove as Jupiter Pluvius, god of rain, frolicking with Iris, goddess of the rainbow. But no such tryst is found in classical mythology.
5. Vulcan used a net to trap Venus (his wife) and Mars, "blood-quaffing" god of war, in the act of love. "Cyclops": probably plural; members of this one-eyed race worked as Vulcan's assistants.
6. Cyparissus, beloved of the wood god Sylvanus.
7. Turtledoves, symbolic of constancy in love.
8. The "golden head" of some of Cupid's arrows produced love; he had others, of lead, that produced dislike.

Who ever loved, that loved not at first sight?[9]
   He kneeled, but unto her devoutly prayed.
Chaste Hero to herself thus softly said,
"Were I the saint he worships, I would hear him,"
180 And as she spake those words, came somewhat near him.
He started up; she blushed as one ashamed,
Wherewith Leander much more was inflamed.
He touched her hand; in touching it she trembled:
Love deeply grounded hardly° is dissembled.   *with difficulty*
185 These lovers parlèd° by the touch of hands;   *spoke*
True love is mute, and oft amazèd stands.
Thus while dumb signs their yielding hearts entangled,
The air with sparks of living fire was spangled,
And Night, deep drenched in misty Acheron,[1]
190 Heaved up her head, and half the world upon
Breathed darkness forth. (Dark night is Cupid's day.)
And now begins Leander to display
Love's holy fire, with words, with sighs and tears,
Which like sweet music entered Hero's ears,
195 And yet at every word she turned aside
And always cut him off as he replied.
At last, like to a bold sharp sophister,[2]
With cheerful hope thus he accosted° her: *addressed*
"Fair creature, let me speak without offense;
200 I would my rude° words had the influence   *rough*
To lead thy thoughts as thy fair looks do mine;
Then shouldst thou be his prisoner, who is thine.
Be not unkind and fair—misshapen stuff°   *persons*
Are of behavior boisterous and rough.
205 O shun me not, but hear me ere you go;
God knows I cannot force° love, as you do.   *compel*
My words shall be as spotless as my youth,
Full of simplicity and naked truth.
This sacrifice, whose sweet perfume descending
210 From Venus' altar to your footsteps bending,°   *turning*
Doth testify that you exceed her far
To whom you offer and whose nun you are.
Why should you worship her? Her you surpass
As much as sparkling diamonds flaring° glass.   *glaring*
215 A diamond set in lead his worth retains;
A heavenly nymph, beloved of human swains,°   *youths*
Receives no blemish but ofttimes more grace;
Which makes me hope, although I am but base—
Base in respect of° thee, divine and pure—   *in comparison with*
220 Dutiful service may thy love procure;
And I in duty will excel all other,
As thou in beauty dost exceed Love's mother.°   *Venus*

---

9. Shakespeare quotes this famous line in *As You Like It* (3.5.83).
1. One of the rivers of Hades.

2. A sophist is a person skilled in arguments, especially specious ones.

       Nor heaven, nor thou, were made to gaze upon;
       As heaven preserves all things, so save thou one.
225   A stately builded ship, well rigged and tall,
       The ocean maketh more majestical:
       Why vowest thou then to live in Sestos here,
       Who on Love's seas more glorious wouldst appear?
       Like untuned golden strings all women are,
230   Which, long time lie untouched, will harshly jar.³
       Vessels of brass, oft handled, brightly shine;
       What difference betwixt the richest mine°   *ore*
       And basest mold,° but use? for both not used   *earth*
       Are of like worth. Then treasure is abused
235   When misers keep it; being put to loan,
       In time it will return us two for one.
       Rich robes themselves and others do adorn;
       Neither themselves nor others, if not worn.
       Who builds a palace and rams up the gate
240   Shall see it ruinous and desolate.
       Ah, simple Hero, learn thyself to cherish;
       Lone women, like to empty houses, perish.
       Less sins the poor rich man that starves himself
       In heaping up a mass of drossy pelf,°   *wealth*
245   Than such as you: his golden earth remains,
       Which after his decease some other gains.
       But this fair gem, sweet in the loss alone,
       When you fleet hence can be bequeathed to none.
       Or if it could, down from th' enameled° sky   *many-colored*
250   All heaven would come to claim this legacy,
       And with intestine° broils the world destroy   *internal, civil*
       And quite confound Nature's sweet harmony.
       Well therefore by the gods decreed it is,
       We human creatures should enjoy that bliss.
255   One is no number;⁴ maids are nothing then
       Without the sweet society of men.
       Wilt thou live single still? One shalt thou be,
       Though never-singling Hymen⁵ couple thee.
       Wild savages, that drink of running springs,
260   Think water far excels all earthly things;
       But they that daily taste neat° wine despise it.   *undiluted*
       Virginity, albeit° some highly prize it,   *although*
       Compared with marriage, had you tried them both,
       Differs as much as wine and water doth.
265   Base bullion for the stamp's sake⁶ we allow:°   *approve*
       Even so for men's impression do we you;
       By which alone, our reverend fathers⁷ say,
       Women receive perfection every way.

---

3. That is, instruments not played will be out of tune and harsh.
4. A traditional concept, going back to Aristotle.
5. God of marriage. "Never-singling": that is, one who never separates, but always joins.
6. For the impression that makes metal ("bullion") into a coin.
7. Ancient philosophers, like Aristotle.

>   This idol which you term Virginity,
> 270   Is neither essence,° subject to the eye,   *something real*
>   No, nor to any one exterior sense,
>   Nor hath it any place of residence,
>   Nor is 't of earth or mold° celestial,   *form*
>   Or capable of any form at all.
> 275   Of that which hath no being do not boast:
>   Things that are not at all are never lost.
>   Men foolishly do call it virtuous:
>   What virtue is it that is born with us?⁸
>   Much less can honor be ascribed thereto:
> 280   Honor is purchased by the deeds we do.
>   Believe me, Hero, honor is not won
>   Until some honorable deed be done.
>   Seek you for chastity, immortal fame,
>   And know that some have wronged Diana's name?⁹
> 285   Whose name is it, if she be false or not,
>   So she be fair, but some vile tongues will blot?
>   But you are fair, aye me! so wondrous fair,
>   So young, so gentle, and so debonair,°   *gracious*
>   As Greece will think, if thus you live alone,
> 290   Some one or other keeps you as his own.
>   Then, Hero, hate me not, nor from me fly
>   To follow swiftly-blasting° infamy.   *-blighting*
>   Perhaps thy sacred priesthood makes thee loath.
>   Tell me, to whom madest thou that heedless oath?"
> 295   "To Venus," answered she, and as she spake,
>   Forth from those two tralucent cisterns° brake   *translucent eyes*
>   A stream of liquid pearl, which down her face
>   Made milk-white paths whereon the gods might trace°   *go*
>   To Jove's high court. He thus replied: "The rites
> 300   In which Love's beauteous empress most delights
>   Are banquets, Doric music,¹ midnight revel,
>   Plays, masques, and all that stern age counteth evil.
>   Thee as a holy idiot doth she scorn;
>   For thou, in vowing chastity, hast sworn
> 305   To rob her name and honor, and thereby
>   Commit'st a sin far worse than perjury—
>   Even sacrilege against her Deity,
>   Through regular and formal purity.
>   To expiate which sin, kiss and shake hands;
> 310   Such sacrifice as this Venus demands."
>   Thereat she smiled and did deny him so
>   As, put° thereby, yet might he hope for mo.°   *put off / more*
>   Which makes him quickly reinforce his speech
>   And her in humble manner thus beseech:

---

8. That is, a virtue is not a virtue unless it is acquired.
9. That is, no fame for chastity is secure. Even Diana, goddess of chastity, has been slandered.

1. A solemn, military mode. Leander would more appropriately have said "Lydian" (as in Milton's "L'Allegro," line 136); Lydian music was soft and sensual.

315   "Though neither gods nor men may thee deserve,
       Yet for her sake whom you have vowed to serve,
       Abandon fruitless, cold Virginity,
       The gentle Queen of Love's sole enemy.
       Then shall you most resemble Venus' nun,
320   When Venus' sweet rites are performed and done.
       Flint-breasted Pallas[2] joys in single life,
       But Pallas and your mistress are at strife.
       Love, Hero, then, and be not tyrannous,
       But heal the heart that thou hast wounded thus,
325   Nor stain thy youthful years with avarice;[3]
       Fair fools delight to be accounted nice.°   *shy, reluctant*
       The richest corn° dies, if it be not reaped;   *grain*
       Beauty alone is lost, too warily kept."
         These arguments he used, and many more,
330   Wherewith she yielded, that was won before.
       Hero's looks yielded, but her words made war:
       Women are won when they begin to jar.°   *dispute*
       Thus, having swallowed Cupid's golden hook,
       The more she strived, the deeper was she strook.
335   Yet, evilly° feigning anger, strove she still   *badly*
       And would be thought to grant against her will.
       So having paused a while, at last she said:
       "Who taught thee rhetoric to deceive a maid?
       Aye me, such words as these should I abhor,
340   And yet I like them for the orator."
         With that, Leander stooped to have embraced her,
       But from his spreading arms away she cast her,
       And thus bespake him: "Gentle youth, forbear
       To touch the sacred garments which I wear.
345   "Upon a rock, and underneath a hill,
       Far from the town, where all is whist° and still,   *silent*
       Save that the sea, playing on yellow sand,
       Sends forth a rattling murmur to the land,
       Whose sound allures the golden Morpheus[4]
350   In silence of the night to visit us,
       My turret stands, and there, God knows, I play
       With Venus' swans and sparrows[5] all the day.
       A dwarfish beldame° bears me company,   *old hag*
       That hops about the chamber where I lie
355   And spends the night, that might be better spent,
       In vain discourse and apish° merriment.   *silly*
       Come thither." As she spake this, her tongue tripped,
       For unawares "Come thither" from her slipped;
       And suddenly her former color changed
360   And here and there her eyes through anger ranged.

---

2. Athena, a rival goddess of war and wisdom, usually portrayed in armor.
3. That is, by hoarding the treasure of her beauty.
4. God of sleep. "Golden slumbers" was a common expression.
5. Venus was often portrayed in a chariot drawn by swans, and sparrows were associated with her because of their traditionally reputed lechery.

And like a planet, moving several° ways,⁶ — *different*
At one self° instant, she, poor soul, assays,° — *one and the same / tries*
Loving, not to love at all, and every part
Strove to resist the motions of her heart;
365 And hands so pure, so innocent, nay, such
As might have made heaven stoop to have a touch,
Did she uphold to Venus, and again
Vowed spotless chastity, but all in vain.
Cupid beat down her prayers with his wings;
370 Her vows above the empty air he flings.
All deep enraged, his sinewy° bow he bent, — *strong*
And shot a shaft that burning from him went,
Wherewith she, strooken, looked so dolefully
As made Love sigh to see his tyranny.
375 And as she wept, her tears to pearl he turned,
And wound them on his arm, and for her mourned.
Then towards the palace of the Destinies,° — *the Fates*
Laden with languishment and grief, he flies,
And to those stern nymphs humbly made request
380 Both might enjoy each other and be blessed.
But with a ghastly dreadful countenance,
Threatening a thousand deaths at every glance,
They answered Love, nor would vouchsafe° so much — *grant*
As one poor word, their hate to him was such.
385 Harken a while, and I will tell you why:
Heaven's wingèd herald, Jove-born Mercury,
The selfsame day that he asleep had laid
Enchanted Argus,⁷ spied a country maid
Whose careless hair, instead of pearl t' adorn it,
390 Glistered with dew, as one that seemed to scorn it;⁸
Her breath as fragrant as the morning rose,
Her mind pure, and her tongue untaught to glose.° — *deceive*
Yet proud she was, for lofty pride that dwells
In towered courts is oft in shepherds' cells,° — *huts*
395 And too-too well the fair vermilion knew,
And silver tincture of her cheeks, that drew
The love of every swain.° On her, this god — *rustic*
Enamored was, and with his snaky rod⁹
Did charm her nimble feet and made her stay;
400 The while upon a hillock down he lay,
And sweetly on his pipe began to play,
And with smooth speech, her fancy to assay,° — *test*
Till in his twining arms he locked her fast,
And then he wooed with kisses, and at last,
405 As shepherds do, her on the ground he laid,
And tumbling in the grass, he often strayed
Beyond the bounds of shame, in being bold

---

6. In Ptolemaic astronomy each planet moved in its own orbit or sphere but was also carried along in the motion of the surrounding spheres.
7. Mercury (or Hermes), the messenger god with wingèd feet, put to sleep Argus, the hundred-eyed monster whom Juno had placed as a guard over Io, with whom her husband, Jupiter, was in love. The myth that follows is Marlowe's invention.
8. That is, pearl or other jewelry.
9. The caduceus (now the symbol of medicine).

To eye those parts which no eye should behold;
And, like an insolent commanding lover,
410 Boasting his parentage, would needs discover
The way to new Elysium;¹ but she,
Whose only dower was her chastity,
Having striven in vain, was now about to cry
And crave the help of shepherds that were nigh.
415 Herewith he stayed his fury,° and began   *passion*
To give her leave to rise. Away she ran;
After went Mercury, who used such cunning
As she, to hear his tale, left off her running.
Maids are not won by brutish force and might,
420 But speeches full of pleasure and delight.
And knowing Hermes² courted her, was glad
That she such loveliness and beauty had
As could provoke his liking, yet was mute,
And neither would deny nor grant his suit.
425 Still vowed he love; she, wanting° no excuse   *lacking*
To feed him with delays, as women use,°   *as women usually do*
Or thirsting after immortality
(All women are ambitious naturally),
Imposed upon her lover such a task
430 As he ought not perform, nor yet she ask.
A draft of flowing nectar she requested,
Wherewith the king of gods and men is feasted.
He, ready to accomplish what she willed,
Stole some from Hebe (Hebe Jove's cup filled)
435 And gave it to his simple rustic love,
Which being known (as what is hid from Jove?)
He inly stormed and waxed more furious
Than for the fire filched by Prometheus,
And thrusts him down from heaven. He, wandering here,
440 In mournful terms,° with sad and heavy cheer,°   *condition / countenance*
Complained to Cupid. Cupid, for his sake,
To be revenged on Jove did undertake;
And those on whom heaven, earth, and hell relies
(I mean the adamantine³ Destinies)
445 He wounds with love and forced them equally
To dote upon deceitful Mercury.
They offered him the deadly fatal knife
That shears the slender threads of human life;⁴
At his fair feathered feet the engines° laid   *contrivances*
450 Which th' earth from ugly Chaos' den upweighed.⁵
These he regarded not, but did entreat

---

1. In classical mythology, the paradisal home of the favored dead; also known as the Islands of the Blessed.
2. Marlowe uses the names Mercury and Hermes interchangeably, according to the requirements of meter.
3. Of extreme hardness (so called because the Destinies'—or Fates'—decrees were irrevocable).
4. According to classical mythology, the Fates spun and cut the thread that measures each life.
5. The Fates also controlled the supports that had held up ("upweighed") the earth since it arose out of Chaos, the yawning abyss from which all things came.

> That Jove, usurper of his father's seat,
> Might presently° be banished into hell   *immediately*
> And agèd Saturn in Olympus dwell.
> 455 They granted what he craved,° and once again   *requested*
> Saturn and Ops began their golden reign.
> Murder, rape, war, lust, and treachery
> Were with Jove closed in Stygian empery.°   *realm*
> But long this blessèd time continued not;
> 460 As soon as he his wishèd purpose got,
> He, reckless of his promise, did despise
> The love of th' everlasting Destinies.
> They seeing it, both Love and him abhorred,
> And Jupiter unto his place restored.[6]
> 465 And but that Learning, in despite of Fate,
> Will mount aloft and enter heaven gate,
> And to the seat of Jove itself advance,
> Hermes had slept in hell with Ignorance.
> Yet as a punishment they added this,
> 470 That he and Poverty should always kiss.[7]
> And to this day is every scholar poor;
> Gross gold from them runs headlong to the boor.°   *ignorant clod*
> Likewise the angry sisters, thus deluded,
> To venge themselves on Hermes, have concluded
> 475 That Midas' brood[8] shall sit in Honor's chair,
> To which the Muses' sons are only heir.
> And fruitful wits° that inaspiring[9] are   *minds*
> Shall discontent run into regions far;
> And few great lords in virtuous deeds shall joy,
> 480 But be surprised with° every garish toy,°   *captivated by / trifle*
> And still° enrich the lofty servile clown,°   *ever / ignorant person*
> Who, with encroaching guile, keeps learning down.
> Then muse not° Cupid's suit no better sped,   *don't be surprised*
> Seeing in their loves the Fates were injurèd.
> 485   By this, sad Hero, with love unacquainted,
> Viewing Leander's face, fell down and fainted.
> He kissed her and breathed life into her lips,
> Wherewith, as one displeased, away she trips.
> Yet as she went, full often looked behind,
> 490 And many poor excuses did she find
> To linger by the way, and once she stayed

---

6. The story in lines 451–64 may be summarized as follows: Mercury scorns the gifts offered by the Fates but asks instead that Jove be dethroned (Jove had overthrown his father, Saturn, who ruled heaven during the Golden Age). Mercury persuades the Fates to reverse this revolution, so Saturn and his wife, Ops, return to Olympus and Jove is thrust down into "Stygian empery" (line 458), or Hades. During the Golden Age there was no murder, rape, war, lust, or treachery; these came in with Jove, so when he is sent to Hades they go with him. But this second Golden Age did not last long, because once he got what he wanted, Mercury forgot the Destinies and they restored Jove.
7. Mercury, the god of learning, would have slept in hell with Ignorance were it not that Learning is so divine that it always mounts up, even to heaven, the "seat of Jove." But it was not beyond the Fates' power to make Learning and Poverty go together, which they decreed in revenge for Mercury's neglect.
8. The rich, because everything Midas touched turned to gold; also the stupid, because Midas, judging a musical contest between Apollo and Pan, preferred the latter, against all sensible opinion.
9. Not ambitious for riches or power.

      And would have turned again, but was afraid
      In offering parley to be counted light.°   *immodest*
      So on she goes, and in her idle flight
495 Her painted fan of curlèd plumes let fall,
      Thinking to train° Leander therewithal.   *entice*
      He, being a novice, knew not what she meant,
      But stayed, and after her a letter sent,
      Which joyful Hero answered in such sort
500 As he had hope to scale the beauteous fort
      Wherein the liberal Graces¹ locked their wealth,
      And therefore to her tower he got by stealth.
      Wide open stood the door; he need not climb,
      And she herself before the pointed° time   *appointed*
505 Had spread the board,° with roses strewed the room,   *set the table*
      And oft looked out, and mused° he did not come.   *wondered*
      At last he came; O who can tell the greeting
      These greedy lovers had at their first meeting?
      He asked, she gave, and nothing was denied;
510 Both to each other quickly were affied.°   *engaged*
      Look how° their hands, so were their hearts united,   *just as*
      And what he did, she willingly requited.
      (Sweet are the kisses, the embracements sweet,
      When like desires and affections meet,
515 For from the earth to heaven is Cupid raised,
      Where fancy is in equal balance peised.°)   *weighed*
      Yet she this rashness suddenly repented
      And turned aside and to herself lamented,
      As if her name and honor had been wronged
520 By being possessed of him for whom she longed.
      Ay, and she wished, albeit not from her heart,
      That he would leave her turret and depart.
      The mirthful god of amorous pleasure smiled
      To see how he this captive nymph beguiled,°   *deceived*
525 For hitherto he did but fan the fire
      And kept it down that it might mount the higher.
      Now waxed she jealous° lest his love abated,   *possessively fearful*
      Fearing her own thoughts made her to be hated.
      Therefore unto him hastily she goes
530 And, like light Salmacis,² her body throws
      Upon his bosom where, with yielding eyes,
      She offers up herself a sacrifice
      To slake his anger, if he were displeased.
      O what god would not therewith be appeased?
535 Like Aesop's cock,³ this jewel he enjoyed,
      And as a brother with his sister toyed,
      Supposing nothing else was to be done,
      Now he her favor and good will had won.
      But know you not that creatures wanting sense° *lacking intelligence*

---

1. Three goddesses, embodying aspects of beauty.
2. An amorous nymph in Ovid's *Metamorphoses*.
3. In Aesop's fable, a cock, scratching in the barnyard, uncovers a jewel but prefers a barley corn.

540 By nature have a mutual appetence,[4]
And wanting organs to advance a step,
Moved by love's force, unto each other leap?
Much more in subjects having intellect
Some hidden influence breeds like effect.
545 Albeit Leander, rude° in love and raw,   *untutored*
Long dallying with Hero, nothing saw
That might delight him more, yet he suspected
Some amorous rites or other were neglected.
Therefore unto his body, hers he clung;
550 She, fearing on the rushes[5] to be flung,
Strived with redoubled strength; the more she strived,
The more a gentle, pleasing heat revived,
Which taught him all that elder lovers know.
And now the same gan so to scorch and glow,
555 As, in plain terms, yet cunningly,° he craved° it.   *skillfully / asked for*
(Love always makes those eloquent that have it.)
She, with a kind of granting, put him by it,
And, ever as he thought himself most nigh it,
Like to the tree of Tantalus,[6] she fled,
560 And, seeming lavish, saved her maidenhead.
Ne'er king more sought to keep his diadem
Than Hero this inestimable gem.
Above our life we love a steadfast friend;
Yet, when a token of great worth we send,
565 We often kiss it, often look thereon,
And stay the messenger that would be gone.
No marvel then, though Hero would not yield
So soon to part from that she dearly held.
Jewels being lost are found again, this never;
570 'Tis lost but once, and once lost, lost forever.
    Now had the Morn espied her lover's steeds,[7]
Whereat she starts, puts on her purple weeds,°   *clothes*
And, red for anger that he stayed so long,
All headlong throws herself the clouds among.
575 And now Leander, fearing to be missed,
Embraced her suddenly, took leave, and kissed;
Long was he taking leave, and loath to go,
And kissed again, as lovers use° to do.   *are accustomed*
Sad Hero wrung him by the hand and wept,
580 Saying, "Let your vows and promises be kept."
Then, standing at the door, she turned about,
As loath to see Leander going out.
And now the sun that through th' horizon peeps,
As pitying these lovers, downward creeps,
585 So that in silence of the cloudy night,
Though it was morning, did he take his flight.
But what the secret trusty night concealed,

---

4. Attraction, as iron to a magnet.
5. Reeds used as carpeting in Elizabethan homes.
6. Punished in Hades by constantly reaching for fruit from a tree that eluded him and by trying to drink water that also escaped him.
7. The horses that pull the chariot of the sun.

>   Leander's amorous habit° soon revealed.   *dress*
>   With Cupid's myrtle⁸ was his bonnet° crowned;   *hat*
> 590 About his arms the purple riband° wound   *ribbon*
>   Wherewith she wreathed her largely spreading hair;
>   Nor could the youth abstain but he must wear
>   The sacred ring wherewith she was endowed
>   When first religious chastity she vowed;
> 595 Which made his love through Sestos to be known,
>   And thence unto Abydos sooner blown
>   Than he could sail, for incorporeal Fame,
>   Whose weight consists in nothing but her name,
>   Is swifter than the wind, whose tardy plumes
> 600 Are reeking water and dull earthly fumes.⁹
>   Home when he came, he seemed not to be there,
>   But like exilèd air thrust from his sphere,
>   Set in a foreign place, and straight from thence,
>   Alcides-like,¹ by mighty violence
> 605 He would have chased away the swelling main°   *sea*
>   That him from her unjustly did detain.
>   Like as the sun in a diameter²
>   Fires and inflames objects removèd far,
>   And heateth kindly, shining lat'rally,³
> 610 So beauty sweetly quickens° when 'tis nigh,   *gives life*
>   But being separated and removed,
>   Burns where it cherished, murders where it loved.
>   Therefore, even as an index to a book,
>   So to his mind was young Leander's look.
> 615 O none but gods have power their love to hide:
>   Affection by the count'nance is descried.°   *revealed*
>   The light of hidden fire itself discovers,
>   And love that is concealed betrays° poor lovers.   *gives away*
>   His secret flame apparently° was seen;   *openly*
> 620 Leander's father knew where he had been,
>   And for the same mildly rebuked his son,
>   Thinking to quench the sparkles new begun.
>   But love, resisted once, grows passionate,
>   And nothing more than counsel lovers hate.
> 625 For as a hot, proud horse highly disdains
>   To have his head controlled, but breaks the reins,
>   Spits forth the ringled° bit, and with his hooves   *with rings at the ends*
>   Checks° the submissive ground; so he that loves,   *stamps*
>   The more he is restrained, the worse he fares.
> 630 What is it now but mad Leander dares?⁴
>   "O Hero, Hero!" thus he cried full oft,
>   And then he got him to a rock aloft,

---

8. A plant sacred to Venus or Cupid, symbolic of love.
9. That is, are mist and smoke.
1. Like Hercules, with brute force. ("Alcides" is a patronymic of Hercules, derived from the name of his step-grandfather, Alcaeus.)
2. That is, shining straight down at noon.
3. That is, when it is lower in the sky. The idea is that the sun, paradoxically, causes harm only when it appears to be farthest away (at the zenith). Beauty, Marlowe goes on to claim, works the same way.
4. That is, what is there now Leander dares not do?

       Where, having spied her tower, long stared he on 't
       And prayed the narrow toiling Hellespont
635   To part in twain, that he might come and go;
       But still the rising billows answered "No!"
       With that he stripped him to the ivory skin,
       And crying, "Love, I come!" leapt lively in.
       Whereat the sapphire-visaged god° grew proud,[5]   Neptune, god of the sea
640   And made his capering Triton[6] sound aloud;
       Imagining that Ganimed,[7] displeased,
       Had left the heavens, therefore on him seized.
       Leander strived; the waves about him wound
       And pulled him to the bottom, where the ground
645   Was strewed with pearl, and in low coral groves
       Sweet singing mermaids sported with their loves
       On heaps of heavy gold and took great pleasure
       To spurn in careless sort° the shipwreck treasure;   manner
       For here the stately azure palace stood
650   Where kingly Neptune and his train° abode.   attendants
       The lusty god embraced him, called him love,
       And swore he never should return to Jove.
       But when he knew it was not Ganimed,
       For under water he was almost dead,
655   He heaved him up, and looking on his face,
       Beat down the bold waves with his triple mace,[8]
       Which mounted up, intending to have kissed him,
       And fell in drops like tears because they missed him.
       Leander being up, began to swim,
660   And, looking back, saw Neptune follow him;
       Whereat aghast, the poor soul gan to cry,
       "O let me visit Hero ere I die!"
       The god put Helle's bracelet[9] on his arm,
       And swore the sea should never do him harm.
665   He clapped his plump cheeks, with his tresses played,
       And, smiling wantonly, his love bewrayed.°   revealed
       He watched his arms, and as they opened wide,
       At every stroke betwixt them he would slide
       And steal a kiss, and then run out and dance
670   And, as he turned, cast many a lustful glance
       And throw him gaudy toys to please his eye,
       And dive into the water and there pry
       Upon his breast, his thighs, and every limb,
       And up again and close beside him swim,
675   And talk of love. Leander made reply,
       "You are deceived; I am no woman, I."
       Thereat smiled Neptune, and then told a tale
       How that a shepherd, sitting in a vale,

5. The primary sense is probably "became sexually aroused."
6. A subordinate sea god who blew on a conch shell.
7. See p. 566, n. 2.
8. The three-pronged fork carried by Neptune.

9. Helle was the daughter of King Athamas of Thebes. To escape a cruel stepmother, she fled on a winged, golden-fleeced ram but fell off into the Hellespont, which was named for her. Marlowe apparently invented the detail of the bracelet.

> Played with a boy so lovely fair and kind,
> As for his love both earth and heaven pined;
> That of the cooling river durst not drink,
> Lest water nymphs should pull him from the brink;
> And when he sported in the fragrant lawns,
> Goat-footed satyrs and up-staring fawns[1]
> Would steal him thence. Ere half this tale was done
> "Ay me!" Leander cried, "th' enamored sun
> That now should shine on Thetis' glassy bower[2]
> Descends upon my radiant Hero's tower.
> O that these tardy arms of mine were wings!"
> And as he spake, upon the waves he springs.
> Neptune was angry that he gave no ear,
> And in his heart revenging malice bare.
> He flung at him his mace, but as it went
> He called it in, for love made him repent.
> The mace returning back, his own hand hit,
> As meaning to be venged for darting it.
> When this fresh bleeding wound Leander viewed,
> His color went and came, as if he rued°   regretted
> The grief° which Neptune felt. In gentle breasts   pain
> Relenting thoughts, remorse, and pity rests;
> And who have hard hearts and obdurate minds
> But vicious, harebrained, and illit'rate hinds?°   rustics
> The god, seeing him with pity to be moved,
> Thereon concluded that he was beloved.
> (Love is too full of faith, too credulous,
> With folly and false hope deluding us.)
> Wherefore Leander's fancy to surprise,°   to capture his love
> To the rich ocean for gifts he flies.
> 'Tis wisdom to give much; a gift prevails
> When deep persuading oratory fails.
> By this° Leander, being near the land,   by this time
> Cast down his weary feet and felt the sand.
> Breathless albeit he were, he rested not
> Till to the solitary tower he got,
> And knocked and called; at which celestial noise
> The longing heart of Hero much more joys
> Than nymphs and shepherds when the timbrel° rings,   tambourine
> Or crooked[3] dolphin when the sailor sings.
> She stayed not for her robes, but straight arose
> And, drunk with gladness, to the door she goes;
> Where, seeing a naked man, she screeched for fear
> (Such sights as this to tender maids are rare)
> And ran into the dark herself to hide.
> Rich jewels in the dark are soonest spied.
> Unto her was he led, or rather drawn

---

1. Woodland spirits, who prophesied by looking up to the heavens.
2. That is, the sea. Thetis was a sea nymph, mother of the hero Achilles.
3. "Crooked" because of the undulating path of the dolphin in the water. The musician Arion was saved from drowning by a dolphin charmed by his music.

By those white limbs which sparkled through the lawn.° *fine linen*
The nearer that he came, the more she fled,
And, seeking refuge, slipped into her bed.
Whereon Leander sitting, thus began,
730 Through numbing cold, all feeble, faint, and wan:
"If not for love, yet, love, for pity's sake
Me in thy bed and maiden bosom take;
At least vouchsafe° these arms some little room, *grant*
Who, hoping to embrace thee, cheerly° swum. *gladly*
735 This head was beat with many a churlish billow,
And therefore let it rest upon thy pillow."
Herewith affrighted Hero shrunk away
And in her lukewarm place Leander lay;
Whose lively heat, like fire from heaven fet,° *fetched*
740 Would animate gross clay, and higher set
The drooping thoughts of base declining souls
Than dreary° Mars° carousing nectar bowls. *bloody / god of war*
His hands he cast upon her like a snare;
She, overcome with shame and sallow fear,
745 Like chaste Diana when Actaeon[4] spied her,
Being suddenly betrayed, dived down to hide her,
And as her silver body downward went,
With both her hands she made the bed a tent,
And in her own mind thought herself secure,
750 O'ercast with dim and darksome coverture.
And now she lets him whisper in her ear,
Flatter, entreat, promise, protest, and swear;
Yet ever as he greedily assayed° *tried*
To touch those dainties, she the Harpy[5] played,
755 And every limb did, as a soldier stout,
Defend the fort and keep the foeman out.
For though the rising ivory mount he scaled,
Which is with azure circling lines empaled,° *surrounded*
Much like a globe (a globe may I term this,
760 By which love sails to regions full of bliss),
Yet there with Sisyphus[6] he toiled in vain,
Till gentle parley did the truce obtain.[7]
Wherein Leander on her quivering breast,
Breathless spoke something, and sighed out the rest;
765 Which so prevailed, as he, with small ado,
Enclosed her in his arms and kissed her, too.
And every kiss to her was as a charm,
And to Leander as a fresh alarm,° *call to battle*

---

4. A hunter who happened on Diana bathing. She turned him into a stag, and he was killed by his own hounds.
5. A monster, half-bird, half-woman, who snatches away banquets in Virgil's *Aeneid* and Shakespeare's *Tempest*.
6. Condemned in Hades endlessly to roll a stone uphill.
7. In both the authoritative early printings of the poem (1598), the lines here numbered 775–84 follow at this point (that is, they precede the lines here numbered 763–74). Like almost all modern editors, though, we have adopted the rearrangement first made in 1910 by Tucker Brooke, in his edition of Marlowe's *Works*. The original order, Brooke thought, did not make good sense; he hypothesized that two sheets of Marlowe's manuscript had been accidentally reversed by the time (five years after his death) the poem was printed. Students may, though, want to read the passage both ways and make up their own minds as to which order is preferable.

>   So that the truce was broke, and she, alas,
> 770 Poor silly° maiden, at his mercy was.   *innocent*
>   Love is not full of pity, as men say,
>   But deaf and cruel, where he means to prey.
>   Even as a bird which in our hands we wring
>   Forth plungeth and oft flutters with her wing,
> 775 She trembling strove; this strife of hers, like that
>   Which made the world,[8] another world begat
>   Of unknown joy. Treason was in her thought,
>   And cunningly to yield herself she sought.
>   Seeming not won, yet won she was, at length.
> 780 (In such wars women use but half their strength.)
>   Leander now, like Theban Hercules,
>   Entered the orchard of th' Hesperides,
>   Whose fruit none rightly can describe but he
>   That pulls or shakes it from the golden tree.[9]
> 785 And now she wished this night were never done,
>   And sighed to think upon th' approaching sun,
>   For much it grieved her that the bright daylight
>   Should know the pleasure of this blessèd night,
>   And them like Mars and Erycine[1] displayed,
> 790 Both in each other's arms chained as they laid.
>   Again she knew not how to frame her look
>   Or speak to him who in a moment took
>   That which so long so charily° she kept;   *carefully*
>   And fain° by stealth away she would have crept   *gladly*
> 795 And to some corner secretly have gone,
>   Leaving Leander in the bed alone.
>   But as her naked feet were whipping out,
>   He on the sudden clinged her so about
>   That mermaid-like unto the floor she slid:
> 800 One half appeared, the other half was hid.
>   Thus near the bed she blushing stood upright;
>   And from her countenance behold ye might
>   A kind of twilight break, which through the hair,
>   As from an orient° cloud, glims° here and there,   *bright / gleams*
> 805 And round about the chamber this false morn
>   Brought forth the day before the day was born.
>   So Hero's ruddy cheek Hero betrayed,
>   And her all naked to his sight displayed,
>   Whence his admiring eyes more pleasure took
> 810 Than Dis[2] on heaps of gold fixing his look.
>   By this Apollo's golden harp began
>   To sound forth music to the Ocean,
>   Which watchful Hesperus[3] no sooner heard

---

8. The Greek philosopher Empedocles held that creation was the result of love and strife acting in opposition to each other and alternately ruling the universe.
9. One of Hercules' labors was to get the golden apples of the Hesperides, guarded by a dragon. Hercules was born in Thebes.
1. A name for Venus, who was caught in bed with Mars by her husband, Vulcan, who enmeshed them in a fine chain net.
2. Pluto, god of the underworld and of wealth.
3. The evening star; one would expect Lucifer, the morning star.

But he the day's bright-bearing car prepared,
And ran before, as harbinger of light,
And with his flaring beams mocked ugly Night
Till she, o'ercome with anguish, shame, and rage,
Danged° down to hell her loathsome carriage.   *hurled*
        Desunt nonnulla.°   *something is lacking*

                                                            1598

Doctor Faustus

Each of Marlowe's tragic heroes, like the playwright himself, is an overreacher, striving to get beyond conventional boundaries. Marlowe's Faustus seeks the mastery and voluptuous pleasure that come from forbidden knowledge. To achieve his goal Faustus must make—or chooses to make—a bargain with Lucifer. This is an old folklore motif, but it would have been taken seriously in a time when belief in the reality of devils was almost universal. The story's power over its original audience is vividly suggested by the numerous accounts of uncanny events at performances of the play: strange cracking noises in the theater or the extra devil who suddenly appeared when the actors were counted, causing hysteria.

In the opening soliloquy, Doctor Faustus bids farewell to each of his studies—logic, medicine, law, and divinity—as things he has mastered and found unfulfilling. He turns instead to black magic, but the devil exacts a fearful price in exchange: the eternal damnation of Faustus's soul. Whether Faustus freely chooses to pay this price, in order to acquire hidden knowledge, or he is predestined to do so, is unclear. Renaissance theologians fiercely debated the question of fate versus free will, and their arguments are reflected in the play. Faustus's fall is caused by the same pride and ambition that caused the fall of the angels in heaven and of humankind in the garden of Eden. But it is characteristic of Marlowe that he makes this catastrophic aspiration nonetheless a magnificent human venture.

The immediate source of the play is a German narrative called, in its English translation, *The History of the Damnable Life and Deserved Death of Doctor John Faustus*. That source supplies Marlowe's drama with the scenes of horseplay and low practical joking that contrast so markedly with the passages of huge ambition. It is quite possible that these comic scenes are the work of a collaborator; but no other Elizabethan could have written the first scene (with its brilliant representation of the insatiable aspiring mind of the hero), the ecstatic address to Helen of Troy, or the searing scene of Faustus's last hour. And though compared with these celebrated passages the comic scenes often seem crude, they too contribute to the overarching vision of Faustus's fate: the half-trivial, half-daring exploits, the alternating states of bliss and despair, the questions that are not answered and the answers that bring no real satisfaction, the heroic wanderings that lead nowhere.

Marlowe's play exists in two very different forms: the A text (1604) and the much longer B text (1616). Even the earlier version dates from some fifteen years after the play was actually written and contains later interpolations. The B text almost certainly incorporates additions by other hands and was also revised to conform to the severe censorship statutes of 1606. We use Roma Gill's edition, based on the A text. Following the play are parallel versions of a key scene that will enable the reader to compare the two texts.

The Tragical History of Doctor Faustus

Dramatis Personae[1]

CHORUS
DR. JOHN FAUSTUS
WAGNER, *his servant, a student*
VALDES ⎫
CORNELIUS ⎭ *his friends, magicians*
BELZEBUB
OLD MAN
CLOWN
ROBIN ⎫
RAFE ⎭ *ostlers at an inn*
VINTNER
HORSE-COURSER
THE POPE
THE CARDINAL OF LORRAINE
CHARLES V, EMPEROR OF GERMANY
A KNIGHT *at the* EMPEROR'*s court*
DUKE OF VANHOLT
DUCHESS OF VANHOLT
THREE SCHOLARS
GOOD ANGEL
EVIL ANGEL
MEPHASTOPHILIS
LUCIFER
Spirits presenting
THE SEVEN DEADLY SINS
PRIDE
COVETOUSNESS
WRATH
ENVY
GLUTTONY
SLOTH
LECHERY
ALEXANDER THE GREAT *and his* PARAMOUR
HELEN OF TROY
ATTENDANTS, FRIARS, *and* DEVILS

Prologue

[*Enter* CHORUS.][2]

CHORUS Not marching now in fields of Thrasimene,
Where Mars[3] did mate° the Carthaginians,   *join with*
Nor sporting in the dalliance of love,
In courts of kings where state° is overturned,   *political power*
5   Nor in the pomp of proud audacious deeds,
Intends our Muse to vaunt his heavenly verse:
Only this (Gentlemen) we must perform,
The form of Faustus' fortunes good or bad.
To patient judgments we appeal our plaud,°   *applause*
10 And speak for Faustus in his infancy:
Now is he born, his parents base of stock,
In Germany, within a town called Rhodes;[4]
Of riper years to Wittenberg[5] he went,
Whereas° his kinsmen chiefly brought him up.   *where*
15 So soon he profits in divinity,°   *theology*
The fruitful plot of scholarism graced,
That shortly he was graced with doctor's name,[6]

---

1. There is no list of characters in the A text. The one here is an editorial construction.
2. A single actor who recited a prologue to an act or a whole play, and occasionally delivered an epilogue.
3. God of war. The battle of Lake Trasimene (217 B.C.E.) was one of the Carthaginian leader Hannibal's great victories.
4. Roda, or Stadtroda, in Germany.
5. The famous university where Martin Luther studied, as did Shakespeare's Hamlet and Horatio.
6. The lines play on two senses of *graced*: he so (1) adorned the place ("plot") of scholarship—that is, the university—that shortly he was (2) honored with a doctor's degree.

Excelling all whose sweet delight disputes[7]
In heavenly matters of theology.
20   Till, swollen with cunning,° of a self-conceit,   *knowledge*
His waxen wings did mount above his reach,
And melting heavens conspired his overthrow.[8]
For falling to a devilish exercise,
And glutted more with learning's golden gifts,
25   He surfeits upon cursed necromancy:°   *black magic*
Nothing so sweet as magic is to him,
Which he prefers before his chiefest bliss.[9]
And this the man[1] that in his study sits.   [*Exit.*]

SCENE 1

[*Enter* FAUSTUS *in his study.*]

FAUSTUS   Settle thy studies, Faustus, and begin
To sound the depth of that thou wilt profess:
Having commenced, be a divine in show,[2]
Yet level° at the end of every art,   *aim*
5   And live and die in Aristotle's works.
Sweet *Analytics*,[3] 'tis thou hast ravished me.
Bene disserere est finis logices.[4]
Is to dispute well logic's chiefest end?
Affords this art no greater miracle?
10   Then read no more, thou hast attained the end;
A greater subject fitteth Faustus' wit.°   *intellect*
Bid *on kai me on*[5] farewell; Galen[6] come:
Seeing, *ubi desinit philosophus, ibi incipit medicus.*[7]
Be a physician, Faustus, heap up gold,
15   And be eternized for some wondrous cure.
Summum bonum medicinae sanitas:[8]
The end of physic° is our body's health.   *medicine*
Why Faustus, hast thou not attained that end?
Is not thy common talk found aphorisms?[9]
20   Are not thy bills° hung up as monuments,   *prescriptions*
Whereby whole cities have escaped the plague,
And thousand desperate maladies been eased?
Yet art thou still but Faustus, and a man.
Couldst thou make men to live eternally,
25   Or, being dead, raise them to life again,

---

7. Referring to formal disputations, academic exercises that occupied the place now held by examinations.
8. In Greek myth, Icarus flew too near the sun on wings of feathers and wax made by his father, Daedalus; the wax melted, and he fell into the sea and drowned.
9. The salvation of his soul.
1. Apparently a cue for the Chorus to draw aside the curtain to the enclosed space at the rear of the stage.
2. In external appearance. "Commenced": grad-uated, that is, received the doctor's degree.
3. The title of two treatises on logic by Aristotle.
4. To carry on a disputation well is the end [or purpose] of logic (Latin).
5. Being and not being (Greek); here standing for philosophical studies in general.
6. The supreme ancient authority on medicine (2nd century c.e.).
7. Where the philosopher leaves off the physician begins (Latin).
8. The Latin is translated in the following line.
9. That is, generally accepted wisdom.

Then this profession were to be esteemed.
Physic farewell! Where is Justinian?[1]
Si una eademque res legatur duobus,
Alter rem alter valorem rei, etc.[2]
A pretty case of paltry legacies.
Exhereditare filium non potest pater nisi . . .[3]
Such is the subject of the Institute
And universal Body of the Law:
This study fits a mercenary drudge
Who aims at nothing but external trash!
Too servile and illiberal for me.
When all is done, divinity is best.
Jerome's Bible,[4] Faustus, view it well:
Stipendium peccati mors est:[5] ha! *Stipendium, etc.*
The reward of sin is death? That's hard.
Si pecasse negamus, fallimur, et nulla est in nobis veritas:[6]
If we say that we have no sin,
We deceive ourselves, and there's no truth in us.
Why then belike° we must sin,   *in all likelihood*
And so consequently die.
Ay, we must die an everlasting death.
What doctrine call you this? *Che sarà, sarà*:
What will be, shall be? Divinity, adieu!
These metaphysics° of magicians   *occult lore*
And necromantic books are heavenly!
Lines, circles, schemes, letters, and characters!
Ay, these are those that Faustus most desires.
O what a world of profit and delight,
Of power, of honor, of omnipotence
Is promised to the studious artisan![7]
All things that move between the quiet° poles   *unmoving*
Shall be at my command: emperors and kings
Are but obeyed in their several° provinces,   *separate*
Nor can they raise the wind, or rend the clouds;
But his dominion that exceeds in this
Stretcheth as far as doth the mind of man:
A sound magician is a mighty god.
Here, Faustus, try thy brains to gain a deity.
  [*Enter* WAGNER.]
Wagner, commend me to my dearest friends,
The German Valdes and Cornelius,

---

1. Roman emperor and authority on law (483–565 C.E.). The Latin passages that follow paraphrase Justinian's *Institutiones*, a manual included in his *Corpus Iuris* (Body of the Law); see lines 32–33.
2. If something is bequeathed to two persons, one shall have the thing itself, the other something of equal value.
3. A father cannot disinherit his son unless . . .
4. The Latin translation, or Vulgate, of Saint Jerome (ca. 340–420 C.E.).
5. Romans 6:23. But Faustus reads only part of the scripture verse: "For the wages of sin is death; but the gift of God is eternal life through Jesus Christ our Lord."
6. I John 1:8 (translated in the following two lines).
7. A practitioner of an art; here, necromancy.

Request them earnestly to visit me.
WAGNER   I will, sir.   [Exit.]
FAUSTUS   Their conference will be a greater help to me
   Than all my labors, plod I ne'er so fast.
      [Enter the GOOD ANGEL and the EVIL ANGEL.]
70 GOOD ANGEL   O Faustus, lay that damnèd book aside,
   And gaze not on it, lest it tempt thy soul
   And heap God's heavy wrath upon thy head:
   Read, read the Scriptures; that is blasphemy.
   EVIL ANGEL   Go forward, Faustus, in that famous art,
75   Wherein all nature's treasury is contained:
   Be thou on earth as Jove[8] is in the sky,
   Lord and commander of these elements.   [Exeunt.]
FAUSTUS   How am I glutted with conceit° of this!   filled with the idea
   Shall I make spirits fetch me what I please,
80   Resolve me of all ambiguities,
   Perform what desperate° enterprise I will?   reckless
   I'll have them fly to India for gold,
   Ransack the ocean for orient pearl,[9]
   And search all corners of the new-found world
85   For pleasant fruits and princely delicates.
   I'll have them read me strange philosophy,
   And tell the secrets of all foreign kings;
   I'll have them wall all Germany with brass,
   And make swift Rhine circle fair Wittenberg;[1]
90   I'll have them fill the public schools[2] with silk,
   Wherewith the students shall be bravely° clad.   splendidly
   I'll levy soldiers with the coin they bring,
   And chase the Prince of Parma[3] from our land,
   And reign sole king of all our provinces.
95   Yea, stranger engines for the brunt of war
   Than was the fiery keel at Antwerp's bridge,[4]
   I'll make my servile spirits to invent.
   Come German Valdes and Cornelius,
   And make me blest with your sage conference.
      [Enter VALDES and CORNELIUS.]
100   Valdes, sweet Valdes, and Cornelius,
   Know that your words have won me at the last
   To practise magic and concealèd° arts;   occult
   Yet not your words only, but mine own fantasy,°   imagination
   That will receive no object[5] for my head,
105   But ruminates on necromantic skill.

---

8. God—a common substitution in Elizabethan drama.
9. Pearl of Orient—the especially lustrous pearl from the seas around India.
1. Wittenberg is in fact on the Elbe River.
2. The university lecture rooms.
3. The Duke of Parma, the Spanish governor-general of the Low Countries from 1579 to 1592. In 1588 he commanded the Spanish Armada in its failed attempt to invade England.
4. A reference to the burning ship sent by the Protestant Netherlanders in 1585 against the barrier on the river Scheldt that Parma had built as a part of the blockade of Antwerp.
5. That will pay no attention to physical reality.

Philosophy is odious and obscure,
Both law and physic are for petty wits;
Divinity is basest of the three,
Unpleasant, harsh, contemptible, and vile.
'Tis magic, magic that hath ravished me.
Then, gentle friends, aid me in this attempt,
And I, that have with concise syllogisms
Graveled° the pastors of the German church   *confounded*
And made the flowering pride of Wittenberg
Swarm to my problems[6] as the infernal spirits
On sweet Musaeus when he came to hell,[7]
Will be as cunning as Agrippa was,
Whose shadows made all Europe honor him.[8]

VALDES   Faustus, these books, thy wit,° and our experience   *intellect*
Shall make all nations to canonize us.
As Indian Moors[9] obey their Spanish lords,
So shall the spirits of every element
Be always serviceable to us three.
Like lions shall they guard us when we please,
Like Almaine rutters° with their horsemen's staves,   *German horsemen*
Or Lapland giants trotting by our sides;
Sometimes like women, or unwedded maids,
Shadowing° more beauty in their airy brows   *harboring*
Than in the white breasts of the Queen of Love.
From Venice shall they drag huge argosies,°   *merchant ships*
And from America the golden fleece
That yearly stuffs old Philip's treasury,[1]
If learnèd Faustus will be resolute.

FAUSTUS   Valdes, as resolute am I in this
As thou to live, therefore object it not.[2]

CORNELIUS   The miracles that magic will perform
Will make thee vow to study nothing else.
He that is grounded in astrology,
Enriched with tongues,° well seen° in minerals,   *languages / expert*
Hath all the principles magic doth require:
Then doubt not, Faustus, but to be renowned
And more frequented° for this mystery°   *visited / craft*
Than heretofore the Delphian oracle.[3]
The spirits tell me they can dry the sea,
And fetch the treasure of all foreign wrecks,
Ay, all the wealth that our forefathers hid

---

6. Questions posed for public academic disputation.
7. Musaeus was a legendary singer, supposed son of Orpheus; it was, however, Orpheus who charmed the denizens of hell with his music.
8. Cornelius Agrippa, German author of *The Vanity and Uncertainty of Arts and Sciences* (1530), was popularly believed to have had the power of calling up the "shadows" or shades of the dead.
9. Dark-skinned Native Americans. ("India" in the period could refer to either the East Indies or the West Indies.)
1. Comparing the treasures Philip II of Spain received from the Americas to the Golden Fleece taken, in Greek mythology, from Colchis by Jason and the Argonauts. (Evidently the Venetian argosies put Marlowe in mind of Jason's ship, the *Argo*.)
2. That is, do not make an issue of my resolve.
3. The oracle of Apollo at Delphi in Greece.

        Within the massy° entrails of the earth.   *massive*
        Then tell me, Faustus, what shall we three want?°   *lack*
FAUSTUS   Nothing, Cornelius. O this cheers my soul!
150   Come, show me some demonstrations magical,
        That I may conjure in some lusty° grove,   *pleasant*
        And have these joys in full possessiön.
VALDES   Then haste thee to some solitary grove,
        And bear wise Bacon's and Abanus'[4] works,
155   The Hebrew Psalter, and New Testament;
        And whatsoever else is requisite
        We will inform thee ere our conference cease.
CORNELIUS   Valdes, first let him know the words of art,[5]
        And then, all other ceremonies learned,
160   Faustus may try his cunning by himself.
VALDES   First I'll instruct thee in the rudiments,
        And then wilt thou be perfecter° than I.   *more accomplished*
FAUSTUS   Then come and dine with me, and after meat
        We'll canvass every quiddity° thereof: *essential feature*
165   For ere I sleep, I'll try what I can do.
        This night I'll conjure,° though° I die therefore.   *call up spirits / even if*
                                                                                      [*Exeunt.*]

SCENE 2

        [*Enter two* SCHOLARS.]
1 SCHOLAR   I wonder what's become of Faustus, that was wont to make our schools ring with *sic probo*.[6]
2 SCHOLAR   That shall we know; for see, here comes his boy.[7]
        [*Enter* WAGNER.]
1 SCHOLAR   How now, sirra,[8] where's thy master?
5 WAGNER   God in heaven knows.
2 SCHOLAR   Why, dost not thou know?
WAGNER   Yes I know, but that follows not.
1 SCHOLAR   Go to,[9] sirra, leave your jesting, and tell us where he is.
WAGNER   That follows not necessary by force of argument, that you,
10   being licentiates,[1] should stand upon't; therefore acknowledge your error, and be attentive.
2 SCHOLAR   Why, didst thou not say thou knew'st?
WAGNER   Have you any witness on't?
1 SCHOLAR   Yes, sirra, I heard you.
15 WAGNER   Ask my fellow if I be a thief.[2]
2 SCHOLAR   Well, you will not tell us.
WAGNER   Yes sir, I will tell you; yet if you were not dunces you would never ask me such a question. For is not he *corpus naturale*? And is

---

4. Roger Bacon, the 13th-century friar and scientist popularly thought to be a magician, and Pietro d'Abano, 13th-century alchemist.
5. That is, the technical terms.
6. Thus I prove; a phrase in scholastic disputation.
7. In this case, a poor student acting as a servant to earn his living.
8. A variant of "sir," used condescendingly.
9. Come on!
1. Graduate students.
2. That is, the testimony of your companion ("fellow") is worth no more than one thief's testimony for another.

not that *mobile*?³ Then wherefore should you ask me such a question? But that I am by nature phlegmatic,⁴ slow to wrath and prone to lechery—to love I would say—it were not for you to come within forty foot of the place of execution,⁵ although I do not doubt to see you both hanged the next sessions.⁶ Thus having triumphed over you, I will set my countenance like a precisian,⁷ and begin to speak thus: Truly, my dear brethren, my master is within at dinner with Valdes and Cornelius, as this wine, if it could speak, it would inform your worships. And so the Lord bless you, preserve you, and keep you, my dear brethren, my dear brethren.   [*Exit.*]

1 SCHOLAR   Nay then, I fear he is fallen into that damned art, for which they two are infamous through the world.

2 SCHOLAR   Were he a stranger, and not allied to me, yet should I grieve for him. But come, let us go and inform the rector,⁸ and see if he by his grave counsel can reclaim him.

1 SCHOLAR   O but I fear me nothing can reclaim him.

2 SCHOLAR   Yet let us try what we can do.   [*Exeunt.*]

SCENE 3

[*Enter* FAUSTUS *to conjure.*]

FAUSTUS   Now that the gloomy shadow of the earth,
Longing to view Orion's drizzling look,⁹
Leaps from th'antarctic world unto the sky,
And dims the welkin° with her pitchy breath,   *sky*
Faustus, begin thine incantations,
And try if devils will obey thy hest,°   *command*
Seeing thou hast prayed and sacrificed to them.
Within this circle¹ is Jehovah's name,
Forward and backward anagrammatized;
Th'bbreviated names of holy saints,
Figures of every adjunct² to the heavens,
And characters of signs and erring stars,³
By which the spirits are enforced to rise.
Then fear not Faustus, but be resolute,
And try the uttermost magic can perform.
Sint mihi dei Acherontis propitii! Valeat numen triplex Jehovae! Ignei, aerii, aquatici, terreni spiritus salvete! Orientis princeps, Belzebub⁴ inferni ardentis monarcha, et Demogorgon,⁵ propitiamus vos

---

3. *Corpus naturale et mobile* (matter natural and movable) was a scholastic definition of the subject matter of physics. Wagner is here parodying the language of learning at the university.
4. Dominated by the phlegm, one of the four humors (bodily fluids) whose relative proportions were thought to determine a person's physical and psychological qualities.
5. That is, if I were not slow to anger, it would be fatally dangerous for you to come near me.
6. Sittings of a court.
7. Puritan. The rest of his speech is in the style of the Puritans.
8. The head of a German university.
9. The constellation Orion appears at the beginning of winter. The phrase is a reminiscence of Virgil.
1. The magic circle drawn on the ground, within which the magician would be safe from the spirits he conjured.
2. Heavenly body thought to be joined to the solid firmament of the sky.
3. The moving planets. "Characters of signs": signs of the zodiac and the planets.
4. Lord of the Flies; an ancient Phoenician deity. In Matthew 12:24 he is called "the prince of the devils."
5. In Renaissance versions of classical mythology, a mysterious primeval god.

ut appareat et surgat Mephastophilis. Quid tu moraris? Per Jehovam,
Gehennam, et consecratam aquam quam nunc spargo, signumque
crucis quod nunc facio, et per vota nostra, ipse nunc surgat nobis
dicatus Mephastophilis.[6]
[*Enter a* DEVIL.]
I charge thee to return and change thy shape,
Thou art too ugly to attend on me;
Go and return an old Franciscan friar,
That holy shape becomes a devil best. [*Exit* DEVIL.]
I see there's virtue° in my heavenly words!   power
Who would not be proficient in this art?
How pliant is this Mephastophilis,
Full of obedience and humility,
Such is the force of magic and my spells.
Now Faustus, thou art conjurer laureate°   preeminent
That canst command great Mephastophilis.
Quin redis, Mephastophilis, fratris imagine![7]
[*Enter* MEPHASTOPHILIS.]

MEPHASTOPHILIS   Now Faustus, what would'st thou have me do?
FAUSTUS   I charge thee wait upon me whilst I live,
To do whatever Faustus shall command,
Be it to make the moon drop from her sphere,
Or the ocean to overwhelm the world.
MEPHASTOPHILIS   I am a servant to great Lucifer,
And may not follow thee without his leave;
No more than he commands must we perform.
FAUSTUS   Did not he charge thee to appear to me?
MEPHASTOPHILIS   No, I came now hither of mine own accord.
FAUSTUS   Did not my conjuring speeches raise thee? Speak!
MEPHASTOPHILIS   That was the cause, but yet *per accidens*,[8]
For when we hear one rack[9] the name of God,
Abjure° the Scriptures, and his savior Christ,   repudiate
We fly in hope to get his glorious soul;
Nor will we come unless he use such means
Whereby he is in danger to be damned:
Therefore the shortest cut for conjuring
Is stoutly to abjure the Trinity,
And pray devoutly to the prince of hell.
FAUSTUS   So Faustus hath already done, and holds this principle:
There is no chief but only Belzebub,
To whom Faustus doth dedicate himself.
This word damnation terrifies not him,

---

6. Faustus's Latin conjures the devils: "May the gods of the lower regions favor me! Farewell to the Trinity! Hail, spirits of fire, air, water, and earth! Prince of the East, Belzebub, monarch of burning hell, and Demogorgon, we pray to you that Mephastophilis may appear and rise. What are you waiting for? By Jehovah, Gehenna, and the holy water that I now sprinkle, and the sign of the cross that I now make, and by our vows, may Mephastophilis himself now rise to serve us."
7. Return, Mephastophilis, in the shape of a friar.
8. The immediate, not ultimate, cause.
9. Torture; here, by anagrammatizing.

>   For he confounds hell in Elysium:
> 60   His ghost be with the old philosophers.[1]
>   But leaving these vain trifles of men's souls,
>   Tell me, what is that Lucifer thy lord?
> MEPHASTOPHILIS   Arch-regent and commander of all spirits.
> FAUSTUS   Was not that Lucifer an angel once?
> 65 MEPHASTOPHILIS   Yes Faustus, and most dearly loved of God.
> FAUSTUS   How comes it then that he is prince of devils?
> MEPHASTOPHILIS   O, by aspiring pride and insolence,
>   For which God threw him from the face of heaven.
> FAUSTUS   And what are you that live with Lucifer?
> 70 MEPHASTOPHILIS   Unhappy spirits that fell with Lucifer,
>   Conspired against our God with Lucifer,
>   And are forever damned with Lucifer.
> FAUSTUS   Where are you damned?
> MEPHASTOPHILIS   In hell.
> 75 FAUSTUS   How comes it then that thou art out of hell?
> MEPHASTOPHILIS   Why this is hell, nor am I out of it.
>   Think'st thou that I, who saw the face of God,
>   And tasted the eternal joys of heaven,
>   Am not tormented with ten thousand hells
> 80   In being deprived of everlasting bliss?[2]
>   O Faustus, leave these frivolous demands,°   *questions*
>   Which strike a terror to my fainting soul.
> FAUSTUS   What, is great Mephastophilis so passionate
>   For being deprivèd of the joys of heaven?
> 85   Learn thou of Faustus manly fortitude,
>   And scorn those joys thou never shalt possess.
>   Go bear these tidings to great Lucifer:
>   Seeing Faustus hath incurred eternal death
>   By desp'rate thoughts against Jove's deity,
> 90   Say he surrenders up to him his soul,
>   So° he will spare him four and twenty years,   *on condition that*
>   Letting him live in all voluptuousness,
>   Having thee ever to attend on me,
>   To give me whatsoever I shall ask,
> 95   To tell me whatsoever I demand,
>   To slay mine enemies and aid my friends,
>   And always be obedient to my will.
>   Go, and return to mighty Lucifer,
>   And meet me in my study at midnight
> 100   And then resolve me of thy master's mind.[3]
> MEPHASTOPHILIS   I will, Faustus.   [*Exit.*]
> FAUSTUS   Had I as many souls as there be stars,
>   I'd give them all for Mephastophilis.

---

1. Faustus considers hell to be the Elysium of the classical philosophers, not the Christian hell of torment.
2. This is the punishment of loss of God's presence, which is supposed to be the greatest torment of hell.
3. That is, give me his decision.

By him I'll be great emperor of the world,
And make a bridge through the moving air
To pass the ocean with a band of men;
I'll join the hills that bind the Afric shore,
And make that land continent to° Spain,   *connected to*
And both contributory to my crown.
The emperor° shall not live but by my leave,   *Holy Roman Emperor*
Nor any potentate of Germany.
Now that I have obtained what I desire,
I'll live in speculation° of this art   *contemplation*
Till Mephastophilis return again.   [*Exit.*]

SCENE 4

[*Enter* WAGNER *and the* CLOWN.[4]]

WAGNER   Sirra boy, come hither.

CLOWN   How, boy? Zounds,[5] boy! I hope you have seen many boys with such pickadevants as I have. Boy, quotha![6]

WAGNER   Tell me, sirra, hast thou any comings in?[7]

CLOWN   Ay, and goings out too; you may see else.[8]

WAGNER   Alas poor slave, see how poverty jesteth in his nakedness! The villain is bare, and out of service,[9] and so hungry that I know he would give his soul to the devil for a shoulder of mutton, though it were blood raw.

CLOWN   How, my soul to the devil for a shoulder of mutton though 'twere blood raw? Not so good, friend; by'rlady,[1] I had need have it well roasted, and good sauce to it, if I pay so dear.

WAGNER   Well, wilt thou serve me, and I'll make thee go like *qui mihi discipulus*?[2]

CLOWN   How, in verse?

WAGNER   No, sirra; in beaten silk and stavesacre.[3]

CLOWN   How, how, knavesacre?[4] Ay, I thought that was all the land his father left him! Do ye hear, I would be sorry to rob you of your living.

WAGNER   Sirra, I say in stavesacre.

CLOWN   Oho, oho, stavesacre! Why then belike, if I were your man, I should be full of vermin.

WAGNER   So thou shalt, whether thou be'st with me or no. But sirra, leave your jesting, and bind yourself presently unto me for seven years, or I'll turn all the lice about thee into familiars,[5] and they shall tear thee in pieces.

---

4. Not a court jester (as in some of Shakespeare's plays) but an older stock character, a rustic buffoon.
5. God's wounds; an oath.
6. Says he. The point of the clown's retort is that he is a man and wears a beard. "Pickadevants": small, pointed beards.
7. Income, but the clown then puns on the literal meaning.
8. That is, if you don't believe me.
9. Out of a job.

1. By Our Lady; an oath.
2. You who are my pupil (the opening phrase of a poem on how students should behave, from Lily's *Latin Grammar*, ca. 1509). Wagner means "like a proper servant of a learned man."
3. A preparation from delphinium seeds, used for killing vermin.
4. Wordplay, here and in the following lines.
5. Familiar spirits, demons. "Bind yourself": that is, as apprentice. "Presently": immediately.

CLOWN Do you hear, sir? You may save that labor: they are too familiar with me already—zounds, they are as bold with my flesh as if they had paid for my meat and drink.
WAGNER Well, do you hear, sirra? Hold, take these guilders.[6]
CLOWN Gridirons; what be they?
WAGNER Why, French crowns.[7]
CLOWN 'Mass, but for the name of French crowns a man were as good have as many English counters![8] And what should I do with these?
WAGNER Why, now, sirra, thou art at an hour's warning whensoever or wheresoever the devil shall fetch thee.
CLOWN No, no, here take your gridirons again.
WAGNER Truly I'll none of them.
CLOWN Truly but you shall.
WAGNER Bear witness I gave them him.
CLOWN Bear witness I give them you again.
WAGNER Well, I will cause two devils presently to fetch thee away. Baliol[9] and Belcher!
CLOWN Let your Baliol and your Belcher come here, and I'll knock[1] them, they were never so knocked since they were devils! Say I should kill one of them, what would folks say? "Do ye see yonder tall fellow in the round slop?[2] He has killed the devil!" So I should be called "Killdevil" all the parish over.
[*Enter two* DEVILS, *and the* CLOWN *runs up and down crying.*]
WAGNER Baliol and Belcher, spirits, away! [*Exeunt* DEVILS.]
CLOWN What, are they gone? A vengeance on them! They have vile long nails. There was a he devil and a she devil. I'll tell you how you shall know them: all he devils has horns,[3] and all she devils has clefts and cloven feet.
WAGNER Well, sirra, follow me.
CLOWN But do you hear? If I should serve you, would you teach me to raise up Banios and Belcheos?
WAGNER I will teach thee to turn thyself to anything, to a dog, or a cat, or a mouse, or a rat, or anything.
CLOWN How! A Christian fellow to a dog or a cat, a mouse or a rat? No, no, sir, if you turn me into anything, let it be in the likeness of a little pretty frisking flea, that I may be here, and there, and everywhere. O I'll tickle the pretty wenches' plackets![4] I'll be amongst them, i'faith.[5]
WAGNER Well, sirra, come.
CLOWN But do you hear, Wagner . . . ?
WAGNER How? Baliol and Belcher!
CLOWN O Lord I pray, sir, let Banio and Belcher go sleep.

---

6. Coins. "Hold": here.
7. The coins, legal tender in England at this period, were easily counterfeited.
8. Worthless tokens. "'Mass": by the Mass.
9. Probably a corruption of Belial.
1. Beat.
2. Baggy pants. "Tall": fine.
3. Traditional mark both of devils and of cuckolded husbands.
4. Slits in garments—but with an obvious sexual allusion.
5. In faith; an oath.

WAGNER Villain, call me Master Wagner; and let thy left eye be diametarily fixed upon my right heel, with *quasi vestigias nostras insistere.*⁶ [*Exit.*]
CLOWN God forgive me, he speaks Dutch fustian!⁷ Well, I'll follow him, I'll serve him; that's flat. [*Exit.*]

SCENE 5

[*Enter* FAUSTUS *in his study.*]

FAUSTUS Now Faustus, must thou needs be damned,
And canst thou not be saved.
What boots° it then to think of God or heaven? *avails*
Away with such vain fancies, and despair,
Despair in God, and trust in Belzebub.
Now go not backward: no, Faustus, be resolute;
Why waverest thou? O, something soundeth in mine ears:
"Abjure this magic, turn to God again."
Ay, and Faustus will turn to God again.
To God? He loves thee not:
The god thou servest is thine own appetite,
Wherein is fixed the love of Belzebub.
To him I'll build an altar and a church,
And offer lukewarm blood of newborn babes.
  [*Enter* GOOD ANGEL *and* EVIL.]
GOOD ANGEL Sweet Faustus, leave that execrable° art. *accursed*
FAUSTUS Contrition, prayer, repentance: what of them?
GOOD ANGEL O they are means to bring thee unto heaven.
EVIL ANGEL Rather illusions, fruits of lunacy,
That makes men foolish that do trust them most.
GOOD ANGEL Sweet Faustus, think of heaven, and heavenly things.
EVIL ANGEL No, Faustus, think of honor and of wealth. [*Exeunt.*]
FAUSTUS Of wealth!
Why, the signory° of Emden⁸ shall be mine, *lordship*
When Mephastophilis shall stand by me.
What god can hurt thee, Faustus? Thou art safe,
Cast no more doubts. Come, Mephastophilis,
And bring glad tidings from great Lucifer.
Is't not midnight? Come, Mephastophilis:
*Veni, veni, Mephastophile!*⁹
  [*Enter* MEPHASTOPHILIS.]
Now tell, what says Lucifer thy lord?
MEPHASTOPHILIS That I shall wait on Faustus whilst he lives,
So° he will buy my service with his soul. *provided that*
FAUSTUS Already Faustus hath hazarded that for thee.
MEPHASTOPHILIS But Faustus, thou must bequeath it solemnly,
And write a deed of gift with thine own blood,

---

6. A pedantic way of saying "Follow my footsteps." "Diametarily": diametrically.
7. Gibberish.
8. A wealthy German trade center.
9. Come, come, Mephastophilis!

        For that security° craves great Lucifer.   *guarantee*
        If thou deny it, I will back to hell.
FAUSTUS   Stay, Mephastophilis, and tell me,
        What good will my soul do thy lord?
40 MEPHASTOPHILIS   Enlarge his kingdom.
FAUSTUS   Is that the reason he tempts us thus?
MEPHASTOPHILIS   *Solamen miseris socios habuisse doloris.*[1]
FAUSTUS   Have you any pain that tortures others?
MEPHASTOPHILIS   As great as have the human souls of men.
45   But tell me Faustus, shall I have thy soul?
        And I will be thy slave and wait on thee,
        And give thee more than thou hast wit to ask.
FAUSTUS   Ay Mephastophilis, I give it thee.
MEPHASTOPHILIS   Then stab thine arm courageously,
50   And bind thy soul, that at some certain day
        Great Lucifer may claim it as his own,
        And then be thou as great as Lucifer.
FAUSTUS   Lo Mephastophilis, for love of thee,
        I cut my arm, and with my proper° blood   *own*
55   Assure my soul to be great Lucifer's,
        Chief lord and regent of perpetual night.
        View here the blood that trickles from mine arm,
        And let it be propitious for my wish.
MEPHASTOPHILIS   But Faustus, thou must write it
60   In manner of a deed of gift.
FAUSTUS   Ay, so I will; but, Mephastophilis,
        My blood congeals and I can write no more.
MEPHASTOPHILIS   I'll fetch thee fire to dissolve it straight.   [*Exit.*]
FAUSTUS   What might the staying of my blood portend?
65   Is it unwilling I should write this bill?°   *contract*
        Why streams it not, that I may write afresh:
        "Faustus gives to thee his soul"? Ah, there it stayed!
        Why should'st thou not? Is not thy soul thine own?
        Then write again: "Faustus gives to thee his soul."
        [*Enter* MEPHASTOPHILIS *with a chafer° of coals.*]   *a portable grate*
70 MEPHASTOPHILIS   Here's fire, come Faustus, set it on.
FAUSTUS   So, now the blood begins to clear again.
        Now will I make an end immediately.
MEPHASTOPHILIS   O what will not I do to obtain his soul!
FAUSTUS   *Consummatum est,*[2] this bill is ended,
75   And Faustus hath bequeathed his soul to Lucifer.
        But what is this inscription on mine arm?
        Homo fuge.° Whither should I fly?   *O man, fly*
        If unto God, he'll throw me down to hell.
        My senses are deceived, here's nothing writ;
80   I see it plain, here in this place is writ,
        Homo fuge! Yet shall not Faustus fly.

---

1. Misery loves company.
2. It is finished. A blasphemy, because these are the words of Christ on the Cross (John 19:30).

MEPHASTOPHILIS   I'll fetch him somewhat to delight his mind. [*Exit.*]
[*Enter with* DEVILS, *giving crowns and rich apparel to* FAUSTUS, *and dance, and then depart.*]
FAUSTUS   Speak, Mephastophilis, what means this show?
MEPHASTOPHILIS   Nothing, Faustus, but to delight thy mind withal,
And to show thee what magic can perform.
FAUSTUS   But may I raise up spirits when I please?
MEPHASTOPHILIS   Ay, Faustus, and do greater things than these.
FAUSTUS   Then there's enough for a thousand souls!
Here, Mephastophilis, receive this scroll,
A deed of gift of body and of soul:
But yet conditionally, that thou perform
All articles prescribed between us both.
MEPHASTOPHILIS   Faustus, I swear by hell and Lucifer
To effect all promises between us made.
FAUSTUS   Then hear me read them. On these conditions following:
First, that Faustus may be a spirit[3] in form and substance.
Secondly, that Mephastophilis shall be his servant, and at his command.
Thirdly, that Mephastophilis shall do for him, and bring him whatsoever.
Fourthly, that he shall be in his chamber or house invisible.
Lastly, that he shall appear to the said John Faustus at all times, in what form or shape soever he please.
I, John Faustus of Wittenberg, doctor, by these presents,[4] do give both body and soul to Lucifer, Prince of the East, and his minister Mephastophilis; and furthermore grant unto them that, four and twenty years being expired, the articles above-written inviolate, full power to fetch or carry the said John Faustus, body and soul, flesh, blood, or goods, into their habitation wheresoever.
                                              By me John Faustus.
MEPHASTOPHILIS   Speak, Faustus: do you deliver this as your deed?
FAUSTUS   Ay, take it; and the devil give thee good on't.
MEPHASTOPHILIS   Now, Faustus, ask what thou wilt.
FAUSTUS   First will I question with thee about hell:
Tell me, where is the place that men call hell?
MEPHASTOPHILIS   Under the heavens.
FAUSTUS   Ay, but whereabouts?
MEPHASTOPHILIS   Within the bowels of these elements,
Where we are tortured and remain for ever.
Hell hath no limits, nor is circumscribed
In one self place; for where we are is hell,
And where hell is, there must we ever be.
And to conclude, when all the world dissolves,
And every creature shall be purified,
All places shall be hell that is not heaven.
FAUSTUS   Come, I think hell's a fable.

---

3. That is, have the supernatural powers of a spirit.   4. Legal articles.

MEPHASTOPHILIS   Ay, think so still, till experience change thy mind.
FAUSTUS   Why? think'st thou then that Faustus shall be damned?
MEPHASTOPHILIS   Ay, of necessity, for here's the scroll
   Wherein thou hast given thy soul to Lucifer.
FAUSTUS   Ay, and body too; but what of that?
   Think'st thou that Faustus is so fond° to imagine   *foolish*
   That after this life there is any pain?
   Tush, these are trifles and mere old wives' tales.
MEPHASTOPHILIS   But Faustus, I am an instance to prove the
   contrary:
   For I am damned, and am now in hell.
FAUSTUS   How, now in hell? Nay, and this be hell, I'll willingly be
   damned here! What? walking, disputing, etc. . . . But leaving off
   this, let me have a wife, the fairest maid in Germany, for I am
   wanton and lascivious, and cannot live without a wife.
MEPHASTOPHILIS   How, a wife? I prithee Faustus, talk not of a wife.[5]
FAUSTUS   Nay sweet Mephastophilis, fetch me one, for I will have
   one.
MEPHASTOPHILIS   Well, thou wilt have one; sit there till I come.
   I'll fetch thee a wife in the devil's name.   [*Exit.*]
   [*Enter with a* DEVIL *dressed like a woman, with fireworks.*]
MEPHASTOPHILIS   Tell, Faustus, how dost thou like thy wife?
FAUSTUS   A plague on her for a hot whore!
MEPHASTOPHILIS   Tut, Faustus, marriage is but a ceremonial toy;
   If thou lovest me, think no more of it.
   I'll cull thee out the fairest courtesans
   And bring them every morning to thy bed:
   She whom thine eye shall like, thy heart shall have,
   Be she as chaste as was Penelope,[6]
   As wise as Saba,[7] or as beautiful
   As was bright Lucifer before his fall.
   Hold, take this book, peruse it thoroughly:
   The iterating° of these lines brings gold;   *repeating*
   The framing° of this circle on the ground   *drawing*
   Brings whirlwinds, tempests, thunder and lightning.
   Pronounce this thrice devoutly to thyself,
   And men in armor shall appear to thee,
   Ready to execute what thou desirest.
FAUSTUS   Thanks, Mephastophilis, yet fain would I have a book
   wherein I might behold all spells and incantations, that I might
   raise up spirits when I please.
MEPHASTOPHILIS   Here they are in this book.   [*There turn to them.*]
FAUSTUS   Now would I have a book where I might see all characters
   and planets of the heavens, that I might know their motions and
   dispositions.[8]

---

5. Mephastophilis cannot produce a wife for Faustus because marriage is a sacrament.
6. The wife of Ulysses, famed for chastity and fidelity.
7. The queen of Sheba, who tested Solomon's wisdom with "hard questions" (1 Kings 10).
8. Relationships to other planets. "Characters": occult symbols.

	MEPHASTOPHILIS	Here they are too.	[*Turn to them.*]
170			

FAUSTUS   Nay, let me have one book more, and then I have done,
   wherein I might see all plants, herbs, and trees that grow upon the
   earth.
MEPHASTOPHILIS   Here they be.
175 FAUSTUS   O thou art deceived!
MEPHASTOPHILIS   Tut, I warrant⁹ thee.   [*Turn to them.*]
FAUSTUS   When I behold the heavens, then I repent,
   And curse thee, wicked Mephastophilis,
   Because thou hast deprived me of those joys.
180 MEPHASTOPHILIS   Why Faustus,
   Think'st thou that heaven is such a glorious thing?
   I tell thee 'tis not half so fair as thou,
   Or any man that breathes on earth.
FAUSTUS   How prov'st thou that?
185 MEPHASTOPHILIS   It was made for man, therefore is man more excellent.
FAUSTUS   If it were made for man, 'twas made for me:
   I will renounce this magic, and repent.
      [*Enter* GOOD ANGEL *and* EVIL ANGEL.]
GOOD ANGEL   Faustus, repent, yet° God will pity thee.   *still*
EVIL ANGEL   Thou art a spirit,° God cannot pity thee.   *evil spirit, devil*
190 FAUSTUS   Who buzzeth in mine ears I am a spirit?
   Be I a devil, yet God may pity me.
   Ay, God will pity me if I repent.
EVIL ANGEL   Ay, but Faustus never shall repent.   [*Exeunt.*]
FAUSTUS   My heart's so hardened I cannot repent!
195   Scarce can I name salvation, faith, or heaven,
   But fearful echoes thunders in mine ears,
   "Faustus, thou are damned"; then swords and knives,
   Poison, guns, halters,° and envenomed steel   *hangman's nooses*
   Are laid before me to dispatch myself:
200   And long ere this I should have slain myself,
   Had not sweet pleasure conquered deep despair.
   Have I not made blind Homer sing to me
   Of Alexander's¹ love, and Oenon's death?
   And hath not he that built the walls of Thebes
205   With ravishing sound of his melodious harp,²
   Made music with my Mephastophilis?
   Why should I die then, or basely despair?
   I am resolved! Faustus shall ne'er repent.
   Come, Mephastophilis, let us dispute again,
210   And argue of divine astrology.
   Tell me, are there many heavens above the moon?
   Are all celestial bodies but one globe,

---

9. Assure.
1. Alexander is another name for Paris, the lover of Oenone; later he deserted her and abducted Helen, causing the Trojan War. Oenone refused to heal the wounds Paris received in battle, and when he died of them, she killed herself in remorse.
2. The legendary musician Amphion, whose harp caused stones, of themselves, to form the walls of Thebes.

As is the substance of this centric earth?[3]
MEPHASTOPHILIS   As are the elements, such are the spheres,
Mutually folded in each other's orb.
And, Faustus, all jointly move upon one axletree
Whose terminè° is termed the world's wide pole,   *end*
Nor are the names of Saturn, Mars, or Jupiter
Feigned, but are erring stars.[4]
FAUSTUS   But tell me, have they all one motion, both *situ et tempore*?[5]
MEPHASTOPHILIS   All jointly move from east to west in four-and-twenty hours upon the poles of the world, but differ in their motion upon the poles of the zodiac.[6]
FAUSTUS   Tush, these slender trifles Wagner can decide! Hath Mephastophilis no greater skill? Who knows not the double motion of the planets? The first is finished in a natural day, the second thus: as Saturn in thirty years; Jupiter in twelve; Mars in four; the Sun, Venus, and Mercury in a year; the Moon in twenty-eight days. Tush, these are freshmen's suppositions. But tell me, hath every sphere a dominion or *intelligentia*?[7]
MEPHASTOPHILIS   Ay.
FAUSTUS   How many heavens or spheres are there?
MEPHASTOPHILIS   Nine: the seven planets, the firmament, and the empyreal heaven.[8]
FAUSTUS   Well, resolve me then in this question: why have we not conjunctions, oppositions,[9] aspects, eclipses, all at one time, but in some years we have more, in some less?
MEPHASTOPHILIS   *Per inaequalem motum respectu totius.*[1]
FAUSTUS   Well, I am answered. Tell me who made the world?
MEPHASTOPHILIS   I will not.
FAUSTUS   Sweet Mephastophilis, tell me.
MEPHASTOPHILIS   Move° me not, for I will not tell thee.   *urge*
FAUSTUS   Villain, have I not bound thee to tell me anything?
MEPHASTOPHILIS   Ay, that is not against our kingdom; but this is. Think thou on hell, Faustus, for thou art damned.
FAUSTUS   Think, Faustus, upon God, that made the world.
MEPHASTOPHILIS   Remember this.   [*Exit.*]
FAUSTUS   Ay, go accursèd spirit, to ugly hell,
'Tis thou hast damned distressèd Faustus' soul:
Is't not too late?

---

3. Faustus asks whether all the apparently different heavenly bodies really form "one globe" like the earth. Mephastophilis answers that like the elements, which are separate but combined, the heavenly bodies are separate but their spheres are enfolded, and they move (according to the ancient Ptolemaic cosmology) on a single axle.
4. It is appropriate to give individual names to Saturn, Mars, Jupiter, and the other planets—which are called wandering, or "erring" stars. The fixed stars were in the eighth sphere (the firmament, or crystalline sphere).
5. In position and in time.
6. The common axle on which all the spheres revolve.
7. An angel, or intelligence, thought to be the source of motion in each sphere.
8. The ninth sphere was the immovable empyrean.
9. When two planets are most remote from each other. "Conjunctions": the apparent joinings of two planets. These are two of the planetary "aspects" (relative positions) that figure in astrology.
1. Because of their unequal movements in respect of the whole.

[Enter GOOD ANGEL and EVIL.]
EVIL ANGEL   Too late.
GOOD ANGEL   Never too late, if Faustus will repent.
EVIL ANGEL   If thou repent, devils shall tear thee in pieces.
GOOD ANGEL   Repent, and they shall never raze° thy skin.   graze
[Exeunt.]
FAUSTUS   Ah Christ my Savior! seek to save
Distressèd Faustus' soul!
[Enter LUCIFER, BELZEBUB, and MEPHASTOPHILIS.]
LUCIFER   Christ cannot save thy soul, for he is just.
There's none but I have interest in the same.
FAUSTUS   O who art thou that look'st so terrible?
LUCIFER   I am Lucifer, and this is my companion prince in hell.
FAUSTUS   O Faustus, they are come to fetch away thy soul!
LUCIFER   We come to tell thee thou dost injure us.
Thou talk'st of Christ, contrary to thy promise.
Thou should'st not think of God; think of the devil,
And his dam[2] too.
FAUSTUS   Nor will I henceforth: pardon me in this,
And Faustus vows never to look to heaven,
Never to name God, or to pray to him,
To burn his Scriptures, slay his ministers,
And make my spirits pull his churches down.
LUCIFER   Do so, and we will highly gratify thee. Faustus, we are come from hell to show thee some pastime; sit down, and thou shalt see all the Seven Deadly Sins[3] appear in their proper shapes.
FAUSTUS   That sight will be as pleasing unto me as Paradise was to Adam, the first day of his creation.
LUCIFER   Talk not of Paradise, nor creation, but mark this show; talk of the devil and nothing else. Come away.
[Enter the SEVEN DEADLY SINS.]
Now Faustus, examine them of their several names and dispositions.
FAUSTUS   What art thou, the first?
PRIDE   I am Pride: I disdain to have any parents. I am like to Ovid's flea, I can creep into every corner of a wench: sometimes like a periwig,[4] I sit upon her brow; or like a fan of feathers, I kiss her lips. Indeed I do—what do I not! But fie, what a scent[5] is here? I'll not speak another word, except the ground were perfumed and covered with cloth of arras.[6]
FAUSTUS   What art thou, the second?
COVETOUSNESS   I am Covetousness, begotten of an old churl[7] in an old leathern bag; and might I have my wish, I would desire that this

2. Mother. "The devil and his dam" was a common colloquial expression.
3. Pride, avarice, lust, anger, gluttony, envy, and sloth, called deadly because they lead to spirtual death. All other sins are said to grow out of them (compare the procession of the Seven Deadly Sins in Spenser's The Faerie Queene, Book 1, canto 4, stanzas 16–37).
4. Wig. "Ovid's flea": a salacious medieval poem "Carmen de pulice" (Song of the Flea) was attributed to Ovid.
5. Stink.
6. Arras in Flanders exported fine cloth used for tapestry hangings. "Except": unless.
7. Miser.

house, and all the people in it, were turned to gold, that I might lock you up in my good chest. O my sweet gold!

FAUSTUS What art thou, the third?

WRATH I am Wrath. I had neither father nor mother: I leaped out of a lion's mouth when I was scarce half an hour old, and ever since I have run up and down the world with this case[8] of rapiers, wounding myself when I had nobody to fight withal. I was born in hell—and look to it, for some of you[9] shall be my father.

FAUSTUS What art thou, the fourth?

ENVY I am Envy, begotten of a chimney-sweeper and an oyster-wife. I cannot read, and therefore wish all books were burnt; I am lean with seeing others eat—O that there would come a famine through all the world, that all might die, and I live alone; then thou should'st see how fat I would be! But must thou sit and I stand? Come down, with a vengeance!

FAUSTUS Away, envious rascal! What art thou, the fifth?

GLUTTONY Who, I sir? I am Gluttony. My parents are all dead, and the devil a penny they have left me but a bare pension, and that is thirty meals a day and ten bevers[1]—a small trifle to suffice nature. O, I come of a royal parentage: my grandfather was a gammon[2] of bacon, my grandmother a hogshead of claret wine; my godfathers were these: Peter Pickled-Herring, and Martin Martlemas-Beef.[3] O but my godmother! She was a jolly gentlewoman, and well-beloved in every good town and city; her name was Mistress Margery March-Beer.[4] Now, Faustus, thou hast heard all my progeny;[5] wilt thou bid me to supper?

FAUSTUS No, I'll see thee hanged; thou wilt eat up all my victuals.

GLUTTONY Then the devil choke thee!

FAUSTUS Choke thyself, Glutton. What art thou, the sixth?

SLOTH I am Sloth; I was begotten on a sunny bank, where I have lain ever since—and you have done me great injury to bring me from thence. Let me be carried thither again by Gluttony and Lechery. I'll not speak another word for a king's ransom.

FAUSTUS What are you, Mistress Minx, the seventh and last?

LECHERY Who, I sir? I am one that loves an inch of raw mutton better than an ell of fried stockfish;[6] and the first letter of my name begins with Lechery.

LUCIFER Away! To hell, to hell!   [*Exeunt the* SINS.]
Now Faustus, how dost thou like this?

FAUSTUS O this feeds my soul!

LUCIFER Tut, Faustus, in hell is all manner of delight.

FAUSTUS O might I see hell, and return again, how happy were I then!

---

8. Pair.
9. That is, some in the audience.
1. Snacks.
2. The lower side of pork, including the leg.
3. Meat, salted to preserve it during the winter, was prepared around Martinmas (November 11).
4. A rich ale, made in March.
5. Lineage.
6. Dried cod, associated with sexual coldness and impotence. "Mutton": frequently a bawdy term in Elizabethan English; here, the penis. "Ell": forty-five inches.

LUCIFER Thou shalt; I will send for thee at midnight. In meantime, take this book, peruse it thoroughly, and thou shalt turn thyself into what shape thou wilt.
FAUSTUS Great thanks, mighty Lucifer; this will I keep as chary[7] as my life.
LUCIFER Farewell, Faustus; and think on the devil.
FAUSTUS Farewell, great Lucifer; come, Mephastophilis.

[*Exeunt* OMNES.]

SCENE 6

[*Enter* ROBIN *the ostler*[8] *with a book in his hand.*]

ROBIN O this is admirable! here I ha' stolen one of Doctor Faustus' conjuring books, and i'faith I mean to search some circles[9] for my own use: now will I make all the maidens in our parish dance at my pleasure stark naked before me, and so by that means I shall see more than ere I felt or saw yet.

[*Enter* RAFE *calling* ROBIN.]

RAFE Robin, prithee come away, there's a gentleman tarries[1] to have his horse, and he would have his things rubbed and made clean. He keeps such a chafing[2] with my mistress about it, and she has sent me to look thee out. Prithee, come away.

ROBIN Keep out, keep out; or else you are blown up, you are dismembered, Rafe. Keep out, for I am about a roaring[3] piece of work.

RAFE Come, what dost thou with that same book? Thou canst not read!

ROBIN Yes, my master and mistress shall find that I can read—he for his forehead,[4] she for her private study. She's born to bear with me,[5] or else my art fails.

RAFE Why Robin, what book is that?

ROBIN What book? Why the most intolerable[6] book for conjuring that ere was invented by any brimstone devil.

RAFE Canst thou conjure with it?

ROBIN I can do all these things easily with it: first, I can make thee drunk with 'ipocrase[7] at any tavern in Europe for nothing, that's one of my conjuring works.

RAFE Our master parson says that's nothing.

ROBIN True, Rafe! And more, Rafe, if thou hast any mind to Nan Spit, our kitchen maid, then turn her and wind her to thy own use, as often as thou wilt, and at midnight.

RAFE O brave Robin! Shall I have Nan Spit, and to mine own use? On that condition I'll feed thy devil with horsebread as long as he lives, of free cost.[8]

7. Carefully.
8. Hostler, stablehand.
9. Magicians' circles, but with a sexual innuendo.
1. Is waiting.
2. Scolding.
3. Dangerous.
4. That is, Robin intends to give his master horns—cuckold him.
5. That is, bear his weight, or bear him a child.
6. Irresistible.
7. Robin's pronunciation of "hippocras," a spiced wine.
8. Free of charge. "Horsebread": fodder.

ROBIN   No more, sweet Rafe; let's go and make clean our boots which lie foul upon our hands, and then to our conjuring in the devil's name.   [*Exeunt.*]

CHORUS 2

[*Enter* WAGNER *solus.*]
WAGNER   Learned Faustus,
To know the secrets of astronomy
Graven in the book of Jove's high firmament,
Did mount himself to scale Olympus'[9] top.
5   Being seated in a chariot burning bright,
Drawn by the strength of yokèd dragons' necks.
He now is gone to prove cosmography,[1]
And, as I guess, will first arrive at Rome
To see the pope, and manner of his court,
10 And take some part of holy Peter's feast,[2]
That to this day is highly solemnized.   [*Exit* WAGNER.]

SCENE 7

[*Enter* FAUSTUS *and* MEPHASTOPHILIS.]
FAUSTUS   Having now, my good Mephastophilis,
Passed with delight the stately town of Trier,[3]
Environed round with airy mountain tops,
With walls of flint, and deep entrenchèd lakes,°   *moats*
5   Not to be won by any conquering prince;
From Paris next, coasting° the realm of France,   *traversing*
We saw the river Main fall into Rhine,
Whose banks are set with groves of fruitful vines;
Then up to Naples, rich Campania,
10 With buildings fair and gorgeous to the eye,
The streets straight forth, and paved with finest brick,
Quarters the town in four equivalents;
There saw we learned Maro's[4] golden tomb,
The way° he cut, an English mile in length,   *tunnel*
15 Thorough° a rock of stone in one night's space.   *through*
From thence to Venice, Padua, and the rest,
In midst of which a sumptuous temple° stands   *St. Mark's in Venice*
That threats the stars with her aspiring top.
Thus hitherto hath Faustus spent his time.
20 But tell me now, what resting place is this?
Hast thou, as erst° I did command,   *earlier*
Conducted me within the walls of Rome?
MEPHASTOPHILIS   Faustus, I have; and because we will not be unprovided, I have taken up his holiness' privy chamber[5] for our use.

9. The home of the gods in Greek mythology.
1. To test the accuracy of maps.
2. Saint Peter's feast is June 29.
3. Treves (in Prussia).
4. Virgil's. In medieval legend the Roman poet Virgil was considered a magician whose powers produced a tunnel on the promontory of Posilippo at Naples, near his tomb.
5. Private quarters.

25   FAUSTUS   I hope his holiness will bid us welcome.
      MEPHASTOPHILIS   Tut, 'tis no matter, man, we'll be bold with his good cheer.[6]
      And now, my Faustus, that thou may'st perceive
      What Rome containeth to delight thee with,
30   Know that this city stands upon seven hills
      That underprop the groundwork of the same;
      Just through the midst runs flowing Tiber's stream,
      With winding banks, that cut it in two parts;
      Over the which four stately bridges lean,
35   That makes safe passage to each part of Rome.
      Upon the bridge called Ponte Angelo
      Erected is a castle passing[7] strong,
      Within whose walls such store of ordnance are
      And double cannons, framed of carvèd brass,
40   As match the days within one complete year—
      Besides the gates and high pyramides°   *obelisks*
      Which Julius Caesar brought from Africa.
      FAUSTUS   Now by the kingdoms of infernal rule,
      Of Styx, Acheron, and the fiery lake
45   Of ever-burning Phlegethon,[8] I swear
      That I do long to see the monuments
      And situation of bright-splendent Rome.
      Come therefore, let's away.
      MEPHASTOPHILIS   Nay, Faustus, stay. I know you'd fain see the pope,
50   And take some part of holy Peter's feast,
      Where thou shalt see a troop of bald-pate friars,
      Whose *summum bonum*[9] is in belly-cheer.
      FAUSTUS   Well, I am content to compass[1] then some sport,
      And by their folly make us merriment.
55   Then charm me that I may be invisible, to do what I please
      unseen of any whilst I stay in Rome.
      MEPHASTOPHILIS   [*casts a spell on him*]   So Faustus, now do what thou wilt, thou shalt not be discerned.
          [*Sound a sennet;*[2] *enter the* POPE *and the* CARDINAL OF LOR-
          RAINE *to the banquet, with* FRIARS *attending.*]
      POPE   My lord of Lorraine, will't please you draw near?
60   FAUSTUS   Fall to; and the devil choke you and[3] you spare.
      POPE   How now, who's that which spake? Friars, look about.
      1 FRIAR   Here's nobody, if it like[4] your holiness.
      POPE   My lord, here is a dainty dish was sent to me from the bishop of Milan.
65   FAUSTUS   I thank you, sir.   [*Snatch it.*]

---

6. Entertainment.
7. Surpassingly. Actually the castle is on the bank, not the bridge.
8. Classical names for rivers of the underworld.
9. The greatest good; often refers to God.

1. Take part in.
2. A set of notes on the trumpet or cornet.
3. If. "Fall to": start eating.
4. Please.

POPE How now, who's that which snatched the meat from me? Will no man look? My lord, this dish was sent me from the cardinal of Florence.
FAUSTUS You say true? I'll have't. [*Snatch it.*]
POPE What, again! My lord, I'll drink to your grace.
FAUSTUS I'll pledge[5] your grace. [*Snatch the cup.*]
LORRAINE My lord, it may be some ghost newly crept out of purgatory come to beg a pardon of your holiness.
POPE It may be so; friars, prepare a dirge[6] to lay the fury of this ghost. Once again my lord, fall to. [*The* POPE *crosseth himself.*]
FAUSTUS What, are you crossing of your self? Well, use that trick no more, I would advise you.
    [*Cross again.*]
FAUSTUS Well, there's the second time; aware[7] the third! I give you fair warning.
    [*Cross again, and* FAUSTUS *hits him a box of the ear, and they all run away.*]
Come on, Mephastophilis, what shall we do?
MEPHASTOPHILIS Nay, I know not; we shall be cursed with bell, book, and candle.[8]
FAUSTUS How! Bell, book, and candle; candle, book, and bell, Forward and backward, to curse Faustus to hell.
Anon you shall hear a hog grunt, a calf bleat, and an ass bray, Because it is St. Peter's holy day.
    [*Enter all the* FRIARS *to sing the Dirge.*]
1 FRIAR Come brethren, let's about our business with good devotion.
    [*Sing this.*]
    Cursed be he that stole away His Holiness' meat from the table.
        Maledicat Dominus.[9]
    Cursed be he that struck His Holiness a blow on the face.
        Maledicat Dominus.
    Cursed be he that took Friar Sandelo a blow on the pate.
        Maledicat Dominus.
    Cursed be he that disturbeth our holy dirge.
        Maledicat Dominus.
    Cursed be he that took away His Holiness' wine.
        Maledicat dominus.
            Et omnes sancti.[1] Amen.
    [*Beat the* FRIARS, *and fling fireworks among them, and so Exeunt.*]

SCENE 8

[*Enter* ROBIN *and* RAFE *with a silver goblet.*]
ROBIN Come, Rafe, did not I tell thee we were forever made by this Doctor Faustus' book? *Ecce signum!*[2] Here's a simple purchase for horsekeepers: our horses shall eat no hay as long as this lasts.

---

5. Toast.
6. A requiem mass. But what actually follows is a litany of curses.
7. Beware.
8. The traditional paraphernalia for cursing and excommunication.
9. May the Lord curse him.
1. And all the saints (also curse him).
2. Behold the proof.

[*Enter the* VINTNER.]

RAFE But Robin, here comes the vintner.
ROBIN Hush, I'll gull[3] him supernaturally! Drawer,[4] I hope all is paid; God be with you. Come, Rafe.
VINTNER Soft, sir, a word with you. I must yet have a goblet paid from you ere you go.
ROBIN I, a goblet, Rafe? I, a goblet? I scorn you: and you are but a etc.[5] . . . I, a goblet? Search me.
VINTNER I mean so, sir, with your favor. [*Searches* ROBIN.]
ROBIN How say you now?
VINTNER I must say somewhat to your fellow; you, sir!
RAFE Me, sir? Me, sir? Search your fill. Now sir, you may be ashamed to burden honest men with a matter of truth.
VINTNER [*searches* RAFE] Well, t'one of you hath this goblet about you.
ROBIN You lie, drawer; 'tis afore me. Sirra you, I'll teach ye to impeach[6] honest men: [*to* RAFE] stand by. [*to the* VINTNER] I'll scour you for a goblet—stand aside, you were best—I charge you in the name of Belzebub—look to the goblet, Rafe!
VINTNER What mean you, sirra?
ROBIN I'll tell you what I mean: [*he reads*] *Sanctobulorum Periphrasticon*—nay, I'll tickle you, vintner—look to the goblet, Rafe—*Polypragmos Belseborams framanto pacostiphos tostis Mephastophilis, etc.*[7] . . .
   [*Enter* MEPHASTOPHILIS: *sets squibs*[8] *at their backs: they run about.*]
VINTNER *O nomine Domine!*[9] What mean'st thou, Robin? Thou hast no goblet.
RAFE *Peccatum peccatorum!*[1] Here's thy goblet, good vintner.
ROBIN *Misericordia pro nobis!*[2] What shall I do? Good devil, forgive me now, and I'll never rob thy library more.
   [*Enter to them* MEPHASTOPHILIS.]
MEPHASTOPHILIS Vanish, villains, th'one like an ape, another like a bear, the third an ass, for doing this enterprise. [*Exit* VINTNER.]
   Monarch of hell, under whose black survey
   Great potentates do kneel with awful fear;
   Upon whose altars thousand souls do lie;
   How am I vexèd with these villains' charms!
   From Constantinople am I hither come,
   Only for pleasure of these damnèd slaves.
ROBIN How, from Constantinople? You have had a great journey! Will you take sixpence in your purse to pay for your supper, and be gone?

---

3. Trick.
4. Wine drawer.
5. The actor might ad lib abuse at this point.
6. Accuse.
7. Dog-Latin, as Robin attempts to conjure from Faustus's book.
8. Firecrackers. Evidently Mephastophilis is onstage only long enough to set off the firecrackers and is not seen by Robin, Rafe, or the vintner. He then reenters at line 32.
9. In the name of the Lord. The Latin invocations are used in swearing.
1. Sin of sins!
2. Have mercy on us!

MEPHASTOPHILIS Well, villains, for your presumption, I transform
   thee into an ape, and thee into a dog; and so begone!   [*Exit.*]
ROBIN How, into an ape? That's brave:[3] I'll have fine sport with the
   boys; I'll get nuts and apples enow.[4]
RAFE And I must be a dog.
ROBIN I'faith, thy head will never be out of the potage[5] pot.
                                                          [*Exeunt.*]

CHORUS 3

[*Enter* CHORUS.[6]]
CHORUS When Faustus had with pleasure ta'en the view
   Of rarest things, and royal courts of kings,
   He stayed his course, and so returnèd home;
   Where such as bare his absence but with grief—
   I mean his friends and nearest companions—
   Did gratulate his safety with kind words.
   And in their conference of what befell,
   Touching his journey through the world and air,
   They put forth questions of astrology,
   Which Faustus answered with such learnèd skill
   As they admired and wondered at his wit.
   Now is his fame spread forth in every land:
   Amongst the rest the emperor is one,
   Carolus the Fifth,[7] at whose palace now
   Faustus is feasted 'mongst his noblemen.
   What there he did in trial° of his art   *demonstration*
   I leave untold: your eyes shall see performed.   [*Exit.*]

SCENE 9

[*Enter* EMPEROR, FAUSTUS, *and a* KNIGHT, *with Attendants.*]
EMPEROR Master Doctor Faustus, I have heard strange report of thy
   knowledge in the black art, how that none in my empire, nor in the
   whole world, can compare with thee for the rare effects of magic.
   They say thou hast a familiar spirit, by whom thou canst accomplish what thou list! This therefore is my request: that thou let me
   see some proof of thy skill, that mine eyes may be witnesses to confirm what mine ears have heard reported. And here I swear to thee,
   by the honor of mine imperial crown, that whatever thou dost, thou
   shalt be in no ways prejudiced or endamaged.
KNIGHT [*aside*] I'faith, he looks much like a conjuror.
FAUSTUS My gracious sovereign, though I must confess myself far
   inferior to the report men have published, and nothing answerable
   to[8] the honor of your imperial majesty, yet for that love and duty
   binds me thereunto, I am content to do whatsoever your majesty
   shall command me.

---

3. Splendid.
4. Enough.
5. Porridge.
6. That is, Wagner.
7. The Holy Roman Emperor Charles V (reigned 1519–56).
8. Not at all deserving of.

EMPEROR Then Doctor Faustus, mark what I shall say. As I was sometime solitary set within my closet,⁹ sundry thoughts arose about the honor of mine ancestors—how they had won by prowess such exploits, got such riches, subdued so many kingdoms, as we that do succeed, or they that shall hereafter possess our throne, shall (I fear me) never attain to that degree of high renown and great authority. Amongst which kings is Alexander the Great,¹ chief spectacle of the world's pre-eminence:
The bright shining of whose glorious acts
Lightens the world with his reflecting beams;
As when I hear but motion° made of him,   *mention*
It grieves my soul I never saw the man.
If therefore thou, by cunning of thine art,
Canst raise this man from hollow vaults below,
Where lies entombed this famous conqueror,
And bring with him his beauteous paramour,²
Both in their right shapes, gesture, and attire
They used to wear during their time of life,
Thou shalt both satisfy my just desire
And give me cause to praise thee whilst I live.

FAUSTUS My gracious lord, I am ready to accomplish your request, so far forth as by art and power of my spirit I am able to perform.

KNIGHT [*aside*] I'faith, that's just nothing at all.

FAUSTUS But, if it like your grace, it is not in my ability to present before your eyes the true substantial bodies of those two deceased princes, which long since are consumed to dust.

KNIGHT [*aside*] Ay, marry,³ master doctor, now there's a sign of grace in you, when you will confess the truth.

FAUSTUS But such spirits as can lively resemble Alexander and his paramour shall appear before your grace, in that manner that they best lived in, in their most flourishing estate:⁴ which I doubt not shall sufficiently content your imperial majesty.

EMPEROR Go to, master doctor, let me see them presently.⁵

KNIGHT Do you hear, master doctor? You bring Alexander and his paramour before the emperor!

FAUSTUS How then, sir?

KNIGHT I'faith, that's as true as Diana turned me to a stag.

FAUSTUS No sir; but when Actaeon died, he left the horns⁶ for you! Mephastophilis, begone.   [*Exit* MEPHASTOPHILIS.]

KNIGHT Nay, and⁷ you go to conjuring I'll be gone.   [*Exit* KNIGHT.]

FAUSTUS I'll meet with you anon⁸ for interrupting me so. Here they are, my gracious lord.

---

9. Private chamber.
1. The emperor traces his ancestry to the world conqueror (356–323 B.C.E.).
2. Probably Roxana, Alexander's wife.
3. To be sure.
4. Condition.
5. Immediately.
6. Horns were traditionally a sign of the cuckolded husband (see scene 6, lines 14–15). "Actaeon": the hunter of classical legend who happened to see the goddess Diana bathing. For punishment he was changed into a stag; he was then chased and killed by his own hounds.
7. If.
8. Shortly. "Meet with": be revenged on.

[*Enter* MEPHASTOPHILIS *with* ALEXANDER *and his* PARAMOUR.]

EMPEROR Master doctor, I heard this lady, while she lived, had a wart or mole in her neck; how shall I know whether it be so or no?

FAUSTUS Your highness may boldly go and see.

[*The* EMPEROR *examines the lady's neck.*]

EMPEROR Sure, these are no spirits, but the true substantial bodies of those two deceased princes.

[*Exit* ALEXANDER (*and his* PARAMOUR).]

FAUSTUS Will't please your highness now to send for the knight that was so pleasant with me here of late?

EMPEROR One of you call him forth.

[*Enter the* KNIGHT *with a pair of horns on his head.*]

How now, sir knight? Why, I had thought thou hadst been a bachelor, but now I see thou hast a wife that not only gives thee horns but makes thee wear them! Feel on thy head.

KNIGHT Thou damnèd wretch and execrable° dog,   *detestable*
Bred in the concave of some monstrous rock,
How dar'st thou thus abuse a gentleman?
Villain, I say, undo what thou hast done.

FAUSTUS O not so fast, sir, there's no haste but good.⁹ Are you remembered¹ how you crossed me in my conference with the emperor? I think I have met with you for it.

EMPEROR Good master doctor, at my entreaty release him; he hath done penance sufficient.

FAUSTUS My gracious lord, not so much for the injury he offered me here in your presence, as to delight you with some mirth, hath Faustus worthily requited this injurious knight; which being all I desire, I am content to release him of his horns. And, sir knight, hereafter speak well of scholars: Mephastophilis, transform him straight.² Now, my good lord, having done my duty, I humbly take my leave.

EMPEROR Farewell, master doctor; yet ere you go, expect from me a bounteous reward.

[*Exit* EMPEROR (*and his* ATTENDANTS).]

FAUSTUS Now, Mephastophilis, the restless course
That time doth run with calm and silent foot,
Shortening my days and thread of vital life,
Calls for the payment of my latest years;
Therefore, sweet Mephastophilis, let us make haste to Wittenberg.

MEPHASTOPHILIS What, will you go on horseback or on foot?

FAUSTUS Nay, till I am past this fair and pleasant green, I'll walk on foot.

SCENE 10

[*Enter a* HORSE-COURSER.³]

HORSE-COURSER I have been all this day seeking one Master Fustian: 'Mass,⁴ see where he is! God save you, master doctor.

---

9. A proverb: no point hurrying, unless it's to good effect.
1. Have you forgotten.
2. Immediately.

3. Horse trader, traditionally a sharp bargainer or cheat.
4. By the Mass. "Fustian": the horse-courser's comic mistake for Faustus's name.

FAUSTUS What, horse-courser: you are well met.
HORSE-COURSER Do you hear, sir; I have brought you forty dollars[5] for your horse.
FAUSTUS I cannot sell him so: if thou lik'st him for fifty, take him.
HORSE-COURSER Alas sir, I have no more. I pray you speak for me.
MEPHASTOPHILIS I pray you let him have him; he is an honest fellow, and he has a great charge[6]—neither wife nor child.
FAUSTUS Well, come, give me your money; my boy will deliver him to you. But I must tell you one thing before you have him: ride him not into the water at any hand.[7]
HORSE-COURSER Why sir, will he not drink of all waters?
FAUSTUS O yes, he will drink of all waters, but ride him not into the water. Ride him over hedge or ditch, or where thou wilt, but not into the water.
HORSE-COURSER Well sir. Now am I made man forever: I'll not leave my horse for forty! If he had but the quality of hey ding ding, hey ding ding,[8] I'd make a brave living on him! He has a buttock as slick as an eel. Well, God b'y,[9] sir; your boy will deliver him me. But hark ye sir, if my horse be sick, or ill at ease, if I bring his water[1] to you, you'll tell me what it is?

[*Exit* HORSE-COURSER.]

FAUSTUS Away, you villain! What, dost think I am a horse-doctor? What art thou, Faustus, but a man condemned to die?
Thy fatal time° doth draw to final end.   *time allotted by fate*
Despair doth drive distrust unto my thoughts.
Confound these passions with a quiet sleep:
Tush, Christ did call the thief upon the cross.[2]
Then rest thee, Faustus, quiet in conceit.°   *in mind*
[*Sleep in his chair.*]
[*Enter* HORSE-COURSER *all wet, crying.*]

HORSE-COURSER Alas, alas, Doctor Fustian, quotha?[3] 'Mass, Doctor Lopus[4] was never such a doctor! H'as given me a purgation, h'as purged me of forty dollars! I shall never see them more. But yet, like an ass as I was, I would not be ruled by him; for he bade me I should ride him into no water. Now I, thinking my horse had had some rare quality that he would not have had me known of, I, like a vent'rous[5] youth, rid him into the deep pond at the town's end. I was no sooner in the middle of the pond, but my horse vanished away, and I sat upon a bottle[6] of hay, never so near drowning in my life! But I'll seek out my doctor, and have my forty dollars again, or I'll make it the dearest[7] horse. O, yonder is his snipper-snapper![8] Do you hear, you hey-pass,[9] where's your master?

5 Common German coins.
6 Burden.
7 On any account.
8 That is, he wishes his horse were a stallion, not a gelding, so he could put him to stud.
9 Good-bye (contracted from "God be with you").
1 Urine.
2 In Luke 23:39–43 one of the two thieves crucified with Jesus is promised paradise. "Tush": a scoffing exclamation.
3 He said.
4 In February 1594 Roderigo Lopez, the queen's personal physician, was executed for plotting to poison her. Obviously Marlowe, who died in 1593, did not write the line.
5 Adventurous.
6 Bundle.
7 Most expensive.
8 Insignificant youth; a whipper-snapper.
9 A conjurer's phrase.

MEPHASTOPHILIS   Why, sir, what would you? You cannot speak with him.
HORSE-COURSER   But I will speak with him.
MEPHASTOPHILIS   Why, he's fast asleep; come some other time.
HORSE-COURSER   I'll speak with him now, or I'll break his glasswindows[1] about his ears.
MEPHASTOPHILIS   I tell thee, he has not slept this eight nights.
HORSE-COURSER   And he have not slept this eight weeks I'll speak with him.
MEPHASTOPHILIS   See where he is, fast asleep.
HORSE-COURSER   Ay, this is he; God save ye, master doctor, master doctor, master Doctor Fustian, forty dollars, forty dollars for a bottle of hay!
MEPHASTOPHILIS   Why, thou seest he hears thee not.
HORSE-COURSER   So ho ho; so ho ho.[2] [*Halloo in his ear.*] No, will you not wake? I'll make you wake ere I go. [*Pull him by the leg, and pull it away.*] Alas, I am undone! What shall I do?
FAUSTUS   O my leg, my leg! Help, Mephastophilis! Call the officers! My leg, my leg!
MEPHASTOPHILIS   Come villain, to the constable.
HORSE-COURSER   O Lord, sir! Let me go, and I'll give you forty dollars more.
MEPHASTOPHILIS   Where be they?
HORSE-COURSER   I have none about me: come to my ostry[3] and I'll give them you.
MEPHASTOPHILIS   Begone quickly!
[HORSE-COURSER *runs away.*]
FAUSTUS   What, is he gone? Farewell he: Faustus has his leg again, and the horse-courser—I take it—a bottle of hay for his labor! Well, this trick shall cost him forty dollars more.
[*Enter* WAGNER.]
How now, Wagner, what's the news with thee?
WAGNER   Sir, the duke of Vanholt[4] doth earnestly entreat your company.
FAUSTUS   The duke of Vanholt! An honorable gentleman, to whom I must be no niggard of my cunning.[5] Come, Mephastophilis, let's away to him.   [*Exeunt.*]

SCENE 11

[FAUSTUS *and* MEPHASTOPHILIS *return to the stage. Enter to them the* DUKE *and the* DUCHESS; *the* DUKE *speaks.*]

DUKE   Believe me, master doctor, this merriment hath much pleased me.
FAUSTUS   My gracious lord, I am glad it contents you so well: but it may be, madam, you take no delight in this; I have heard that

---

1. Spectacles.
2. The huntsman's cry, when he sights the quarry.
3. Hostelry, inn.
4. The duchy of Anhalt, in central Germany.
5. That is, must generously display my skill.

great-bellied[6] women do long for some dainties or other—what is it, madam? Tell me, and you shall have it.

DUCHESS Thanks, good master doctor; and for I see your courteous intent to pleasure me, I will not hide from you the thing my heart desires. And were it now summer, as it is January and the dead of winter, I would desire no better meat than a dish of ripe grapes.

FAUSTUS Alas madam, that's nothing! Mephastophilis, begone! [*Exit* MEPHASTOPHILIS.] Were it a greater thing than this, so it would content you, you should have it. [*Enter* MEPHASTOPHILIS *with the grapes.*] Here they be, madam; will't please you taste on them?

DUKE Believe me, master doctor, this makes me wonder above the rest: that being in the dead time of winter, and in the month of January, how you should come by these grapes?

FAUSTUS If it like[7] your grace, the year is divided into two circles over the whole world, that when it is here winter with us, in the contrary circle it is summer with them, as in India, Saba,[8] and farther countries in the east; and by means of a swift spirit that I have, I had them brought hither, as ye see. How do you like them, madam; be they good?

DUCHESS Believe me, master doctor, they be the best grapes that ere I tasted in my life before.

FAUSTUS I am glad they content you so, madam.

DUKE Come, madam, let us in, where you must well reward this learned man for the great kindness he hath showed to you.

DUCHESS And so I will, my lord; and whilst I live, rest beholding for this courtesy.

FAUSTUS I humbly thank your grace.

DUKE Come, master doctor, follow us, and receive your reward.

[*Exeunt.*]

CHORUS 4

[*Enter* WAGNER *solus.*]

WAGNER I think my master means to die shortly,
For he hath given to me all his goods.
And yet methinks, if that death were near,
He would not banquet, and carouse, and swill
Amongst the students, as even now he doth,
Who are at supper with such belly-cheer°   *gluttony*
As Wagner ne'er beheld in all his life.
See where they come: belike the feast is ended.   [*Exit.*]

SCENE 12

[*Enter* FAUSTUS (*and* MEPHASTOPHILIS), *with two or three* SCHOLARS.]

1 SCHOLAR Master Doctor Faustus, since our conference about fair ladies, which was the beautifulest in all the world, we have

---

6. Pregnant.
7. Please.

8. The biblical kingdom of Sheba, in southwestern Arabia.

determined with ourselves that Helen of Greece was the admira-
blest lady that ever lived. Therefore, master doctor, if you will do
us that favor as to let us see that peerless dame of Greece, whom
all the world admires for majesty, we should think ourselves much
beholding unto you.

FAUSTUS Gentlemen, for that I know your friendship is unfeigned,
And Faustus' custom is not to deny
The just requests of those that wish him well,
You shall behold that peerless dame of Greece,
No otherways for pomp and majesty
Than when Sir Paris crossed the seas with her
And brought the spoils to rich Dardania.°   *Troy*
Be silent then, for danger is in words.

[*Music sounds, and* HELEN *passeth over the stage.*]

2 SCHOLAR Too simple is my wit to tell her praise,
Whom all the world admires for majesty.

3 SCHOLAR No marvel though the angry Greeks pursued
With ten years' war the rape° of such a queen,   *abduction*
Whose heavenly beauty passeth all compare.

1 SCHOLAR Since we have seen the pride of Nature's works
And only paragon of excellence,
Let us depart; and for this glorious deed
Happy and blest be Faustus evermore.

FAUSTUS Gentlemen, farewell; the same I wish to you.

[*Exeunt* SCHOLARS.]

[*Enter an* OLD MAN.]

OLD MAN Ah Doctor Faustus, that I might prevail
To guide thy steps unto the way of life,
By which sweet path thou may'st attain the goal
That shall conduct thee to celestial rest.
Break heart, drop blood, and mingle it with tears,
Tears falling from repentant heaviness°   *grief*
Of thy most vile and loathsome filthiness,
The stench whereof corrupts the inward soul
With such flagitious° crimes of heinous sins,   *villainous*
As no commiseration may expel
But mercy, Faustus, of thy savior sweet,
Whose blood alone must wash away thy guilt.

FAUSTUS Where art thou, Faustus? Wretch, what hast thou done!
Damned art thou, Faustus, damned; despair and die!
Hell calls for right, and with a roaring voice
Says, "Faustus, come: thine hour is come!"

[MEPHASTOPHILIS *gives him a dagger.*]

And Faustus will come to do thee right.

OLD MAN Ah stay, good Faustus, stay thy desperate steps!
I see an angel hovers o'er thy head
And with a vial full of precious grace
Offers to pour the same into thy soul!
Then call for mercy, and avoid despair.

FAUSTUS Ah my sweet friend, I feel thy words

    To comfort my distressèd soul;
50   Leave me awhile to ponder on my sins.
  OLD MAN I go, sweet Faustus; but with heavy cheer,°   *heavy heart*
    Fearing the ruin of thy hopeless soul.   [*Exit.*]
  FAUSTUS Accursèd Faustus, where is mercy now?
    I do repent, and yet I do despair:
55   Hell strives with grace for conquest in my breast!
    What shall I do to shun the snares of death?
  MEPHASTOPHILIS Thou traitor, Faustus: I arrest thy soul
    For disobedience to my sovereign lord.
    Revolt,[9] or I'll in piecemeal tear thy flesh.
60   FAUSTUS Sweet Mephastophilis, entreat thy lord
    To pardon my unjust presumptiön;
    And with my blood again I will confirm
    My former vow I made to Lucifer.
  MEPHASTOPHILIS Do it then quickly, with unfeignèd heart,
65   Lest greater danger do attend thy drift.°   *intent*
  FAUSTUS Torment, sweet friend, that base and crooked age°   *aged man*
    That durst° dissuade me from thy Lucifer,   *dared to*
    With greatest torments that our hell affords.
  MEPHASTOPHILIS His faith is great, I cannot touch his soul,
70   But what I may afflict his body with
    I will attempt—which is but little worth.
  FAUSTUS One thing, good servant, let me crave of thee,
    To glut the longing of my heart's desire:
    That I might have unto° my paramour   *for*
75   That heavenly Helen which I saw of late,
    Whose sweet embracings may extinguish clean
    These thoughts that do dissuade me from my vow,
    And keep mine oath I made to Lucifer.
  MEPHASTOPHILIS Faustus, this, or what else thou shalt desire,
80   Shall be performed in twinkling of an eye.
     [*Enter* HELEN.]
  FAUSTUS Was this the face that launched a thousand ships,
    And burnt the topless[1] towers of Ilium?°   *Troy*
    Sweet Helen, make me immortal with a kiss:
    Her lips sucks forth my soul, see where it flies!
85   Come Helen, come, give me my soul again.
    Here will I dwell, for heaven be in these lips,
    And all is dross that is not Helena!
     [*Enter* OLD MAN.]
    I will be Paris, and for love of thee,
    Instead of Troy shall Wittenberg be sacked;
90   And I will combat with weak Menelaus,°   *Helen's husband*
    And wear thy colors on my plumèd crest;
    Yea, I will wound Achilles in the heel,[2]

---

9. Turn back (to your allegiance to Lucifer).
1. Immeasurably high; matchless.

2. Achilles could be wounded only in his heel—where he was shot by Paris.

        And then return to Helen for a kiss.
        O thou art fairer than the evening air
95   Clad in the beauty of a thousand stars,
        Brighter art thou than flaming Jupiter
        When he appeared to hapless Semele;[3]
        More lovely than the monarch of the sky
        In wanton Arethusa's azured arms;[4]
100   And none but thou shalt be my paramour.
                    [*Exeunt* (FAUSTUS *and* HELEN).]
  OLD MAN   Accursèd Faustus, miserable man,
        That from thy soul exclud'st the grace of heaven
        And fliest the throne of His tribunal seat!
          [*Enter the* DEVILS.]
        Satan begins to sift me with his pride,[5]
105   As in this furnace God shall try my faith.
        My faith, vile hell, shall triumph over thee!
        Ambitious fiends, see how the heavens smiles
        At your repulse, and laughs your state° to scorn.   *royal power*
        Hence hell, for hence I fly unto my God.
                    [*Exeunt.*]

SCENE 13

[*Enter* FAUSTUS *with the* SCHOLARS.]

FAUSTUS   Ah gentlemen!

1 SCHOLAR   What ails Faustus?

FAUSTUS   Ah my sweet chamber-fellow, had I lived with thee, then had I lived still;[6] but now I die eternally. Look, comes he not, comes he not?

2 SCHOLAR   What means Faustus?

3 SCHOLAR   Belike he is grown into some sickness by being over-solitary.

1 SCHOLAR   If it be so, we'll have physicians to cure him; 'tis but a surfeit:[7] never fear, man.

FAUSTUS   A surfeit of deadly sin, that hath damned both body and soul.

2 SCHOLAR   Yet Faustus, look up to heaven; remember God's mercies are infinite.

FAUSTUS   But Faustus' offense can ne'er be pardoned! The serpent that tempted Eve may be saved, but not Faustus. Ah gentlemen, hear me with patience, and tremble not at my speeches, though my heart pants and quivers to remember that I have been a student here these thirty years—O would I had never seen Wittenberg, never read book—and what wonders I have done, all Wittenberg can witness—yea, all the world; for which Faustus

---

3. A Theban girl, loved by Jupiter and destroyed by the fire of his lightning when he appeared to her in his full splendor.
4. Arethusa was the nymph of a fountain, as well as the fountain itself; she excited the passion of the river god Alpheus, who was by some accounts related to the sun.
5. To test me with his strength.
6. Always.
7. Indigestion caused by overeating.

hath lost both Germany and the world—yea, heaven itself—
heaven, the seat of God, the throne of the blessed, the kingdom of
joy; and must remain in hell forever—hell, ah, hell forever! Sweet
friends, what shall become of Faustus, being in hell forever?
3 SCHOLAR   Yet Faustus, call on God.
FAUSTUS   On God, whom Faustus hath abjured? On God, whom
Faustus hath blasphemed? Ah, my God—I would weep, but the
devil draws in my tears! Gush forth blood, instead of tears—yea,
life and soul! O, he stays my tongue! I would lift up my hands, but
see, they hold them, they hold them!
ALL   Who, Faustus?
FAUSTUS   Lucifer and Mephastophilis! Ah gentlemen, I gave them
my soul for my cunning.
ALL   God forbid!
FAUSTUS   God forbade it indeed, but Faustus hath done it: for the
vain pleasure of four-and-twenty years hath Faustus lost eternal
joy and felicity. I writ them a bill[8] with mine own blood, the date
is expired, the time will come, and he will fetch me.
1 SCHOLAR   Why did not Faustus tell us of this before, that divines
might have prayed for thee?
FAUSTUS   Oft have I thought to have done so, but the devil threatened to tear me in pieces if I named God, to fetch both body and
soul if I once gave ear to divinity; and now 'tis too late. Gentlemen,
away, lest you perish with me!
2 SCHOLAR   O what shall we do to save Faustus?
3 SCHOLAR   God will strengthen me. I will stay with Faustus.
1 SCHOLAR   Tempt not God, sweet friend, but let us into the next
room, and there pray for him.
FAUSTUS   Ay, pray for me, pray for me; and what noise soever ye
hear, come not unto me, for nothing can rescue me.
2 SCHOLAR   Pray thou, and we will pray, that God may have mercy
upon thee.
FAUSTUS   Gentlemen, farewell. If I live till morning, I'll visit you; if
not, Faustus is gone to hell.
ALL   Faustus, farewell.   [*Exeunt* SCHOLARS.]
       [*The clock strikes eleven.*]
FAUSTUS   Ah Faustus,
Now hast thou but one bare hour to live,
And then thou must be damned perpetually.
Stand still, you ever-moving spheres of heaven,
That time may cease, and midnight never come.
Fair Nature's eye, rise, rise again, and make
Perpetual day, or let this hour be but
A year, a month, a week, a natural day,
That Faustus may repent and save his soul.
O lente, lente currite noctis equi![9]

---

8. Document.
9. Slowly, slowly run, O horses of the night (adapted from a line in Ovid's *Amores*).

The stars move still, time runs, the clock will strike,
The devil will come, and Faustus must be damned.
O I'll leap up to my God! Who pulls me down?
See, see where Christ's blood streams in the firmament!°   *sky*
One drop would save my soul, half a drop: ah my Christ—
Ah, rend not my heart for naming of my Christ;
Yet will I call on him—O spare me, Lucifer!
Where is it now? 'Tis gone: and see where God
Stretcheth out his arm, and bends his ireful brows!
Mountains and hills, come, come and fall on me,
And hide me from the heavy wrath of God.
No, no?
Then will I headlong run into the earth:
Earth, gape! O no, it will not harbor me.
You stars that reigned at my nativity,
Whose influence hath allotted death and hell,
Now draw up Faustus like a foggy mist
Into the entrails of yon laboring cloud,
That when you vomit forth into the air
My limbs may issue from your smoky mouths,
So that my soul may but ascend to heaven.[1]
   [*The watch strikes.*]
Ah, half the hour is past: 'twill all be past anon.°   *shortly*
O God, if thou wilt not have mercy on my soul,
Yet for Christ's sake, whose blood hath ransomed me,
Impose some end to my incessant pain:
Let Faustus live in hell a thousand years,
A hundred thousand, and at last be saved.
O no end is limited to damnèd souls!
Why wert thou not a creature wanting° soul?   *lacking*
Or why is this immortal that thou hast?
Ah, Pythagoras' *metempsychosis*[2]—were that true,
This soul should fly from me, and I be changed
Unto some brutish beast:
All beasts are happy, for when they die,
Their souls are soon dissolved in elements;
But mine must live still° to be plagued in hell.   *always*
Cursed be the parents that engendered me!
No, Faustus, curse thy self, curse Lucifer,
That hath deprived thee of the joys of heaven.
   [*The clock striketh twelve.*]
O it strikes, it strikes! Now body, turn to air,
Or Lucifer will bear thee quick° to hell.   *alive*
   [*Thunder and lightning.*]
O soul, be changed into little water drops
And fall into the ocean, ne'er be found.

---

1. Faustus wants to be drawn up into a cloud, which would compact his body into a thunderbolt so that his soul, thus purified, might ascend to heaven.
2. Pythagoras's doctrine of the transmigration of souls.

110 My God, my God, look not so fierce on me!
    [*Enter* DEVILS.]
    Adders and serpents, let me breathe awhile!
    Ugly hell gape not! Come not, Lucifer!
    I'll burn my books—ah, Mephastophilis!
                                [*Exeunt with him.*]

Epilogue

[*Enter* CHORUS.]
Cut is the branch that might have grown full straight,
And burnèd is Apollo's laurel bough,³
That sometime grew within this learnèd man.
Faustus is gone! Regard his hellish fall,
5 Whose fiendful fortune° may exhort the wise   *devilish fate*
Only to wonder at⁴ unlawful things:
Whose deepness doth entice such forward wits°   *aspiring minds*
To practice more than heavenly power permits.
                                          [*Exit.*]

*Terminat hora diem, terminat author opus.*⁵

                                          1604, 1616

---

3. The laurel crown of Apollo symbolizes (among other things) learning and wisdom.
4. Be content simply to observe with awe.
5. The hour ends the day, the author ends his work. This motto was probably added by the printer.

The Two Texts of *Doctor Faustus* The following excerpts enable readers to compare a sample passage (from Scene 12) of the A text (1604) with the corresponding passage of the B text (1616). (On the two texts, see p. 581.) Here the differences in tone and content in the two versions of the Old Man's speech may signal different attitudes toward the finality of Faustus's damnation.

Doctor Faustus, A Text

[*Enter an* OLD MAN.]
OLD MAN Ah Doctor Faustus, that I might prevail
  To guide thy steps unto the way of life,
  By which sweet path thou may'st attain the goal
  That shall conduct thee to celestial rest.
5 Break heart, drop blood, and mingle it with tears,
  Tears falling from repentant heaviness°   *grief*
  Of thy most vile and loathsome filthiness,
  The stench whereof corrupts the inward soul
  With such flagitious° crimes of heinous sins   *villainous*
10 As no commiseration may expel
  But mercy, Faustus, of thy savior sweet,
  Whose blood alone must wash away thy guilt.
FAUSTUS Where art thou, Faustus? Wretch, what hast thou done!
  Damned art thou, Faustus, damned; despair and die!
15 Hell calls for right, and with a roaring voice
  Says, "Faustus, come: thine hour is come!"
    [MEPHASTOPHILIS *gives him a dagger.*]
  And Faustus will come to do thee right.
OLD MAN Ah stay, good Faustus, stay thy desperate steps!
  I see an angel hovers o'er thy head
20 And with a vial full of precious grace
  Offers to pour the same into thy soul!
  Then call for mercy, and avoid despair.
FAUSTUS Ah my sweet friend, I feel thy words
  To comfort my distressèd soul;
25 Leave me awhile to ponder on my sins.
OLD MAN I go, sweet Faustus; but with heavy cheer,°   *heavy heart*
  Fearing the ruin of thy hopeless soul.   [*Exit.*]
FAUSTUS Accursèd Faustus, where is mercy now?
  I do repent, and yet I do despair:
30 Hell strives with grace for conquest in my breast!
  What shall I do to shun the snares of death?
MEPHASTOPHILIS Thou traitor, Faustus: I arrest thy soul
  For disobedience to my sovereign lord.
  Revolt,[1] or I'll in piecemeal tear thy flesh.

---

1. Turn back (to your allegiance to Lucifer).

Doctor Faustus, B Text

[*Enter an* OLD MAN.]

OLD MAN   O gentle Faustus, leave this damnèd art,
This magic that will charm thy soul to hell
And quite bereave thee of salvatiön.
Though thou hast now offended like a man,
5   Do not persèver° in it like a devil.   *persevere*
Yet, yet, thou hast an amiable° soul,   *worthy of (divine) love*
If sin by custom grow not into nature.
Then, Faustus, will repentance come too late;
Then thou art banished from the sight of heaven.
10   No mortal can express the pains of hell.
It may be this my exhortatiön
Seems harsh and all unpleasant; let it not,
For, gentle son, I speak it not in wrath
Or envy of° thee, but in tender love   *ill will toward*
15   And pity of thy future misery.
And so have hope that this my kind rebuke,
Checking° thy body, may amend thy soul.   *rebuking*
FAUSTUS   Where art thou, Faustus? Wretch, what hast thou done?
Hell claims his right, and with a roaring voice
20   Says, "Faustus, come; thine hour is almost come";
And Faustus now will come to do thee right.
[MEPHOSTOPHILIS *gives him a dagger.*]
OLD MAN   O stay, good Faustus, stay thy desperate steps.
I see an angel hover o'er thy head,
And with a vial full of precious grace
25   Offers to pour the same into thy soul.
Then call for mercy and avoid despair.
FAUSTUS   O friend, I feel thy words
To comfort my distressèd soul.
Leave me a while to ponder on my sins.
30   OLD MAN   Faustus, I leave thee, but with grief of heart,
Fearing the enemy of thy hapless soul.   [*Exit.*]
FAUSTUS   Accursèd Faustus, wretch, what hast thou done?
I do repent, and yet I do despair.
Hell strives with grace for conquest in my breast.
35   What shall I do to shun the snares of death?
MEPHOSTOPHILIS   Thou traitor, Faustus, I arrest thy soul
For disobedience to my sovereign lord.
Revolt,[1] or I'll in piecemeal tear thy flesh.

---

1. Turn back (to your allegiance to Lucifer).

WILLIAM SHAKESPEARE
1564–1616

William Shakespeare was born in the small market town of Stratford-upon-Avon in April (probably April 23) 1564. His father, a successful glovemaker, landowner, moneylender, and dealer in agricultural commodities, was elected to several important posts in local government but later suffered financial and social reverses, possibly as a result of adherence to the Catholic faith. Shakespeare, between the ages of seven and fourteen, almost certainly attended the free Stratford grammar school, where he would have acquired a reasonably impressive education, including a respectable knowledge of Latin, but he did not proceed to Oxford or Cambridge. There are legends about Shakespeare's youth but no documented facts. The first unambiguous record we have of his life after his christening is that of his marriage, in 1582, at age eighteen, to Anne Hathaway, eight years his senior. A daughter, Susanna, was born six months later, in 1583, and twins, Hamnet and Judith, in 1585. We possess no information about his activities for the next seven years, but by 1592 he was in London as an actor and apparently already well known as a playwright, for a rival dramatist, Robert Greene, refers to him resentfully in *A Groatsworth of Wit* as "an upstart crow, beautified with our feathers."

At this time, there were several companies of professional actors in London and in the provinces. What links Shakespeare had with one or more of them before 1592 are conjectural, but we do know of his long and fruitful connection, established by 1594, with the most successful troupe, the Lord Chamberlain's Men; later, when James I came to the throne, they became the King's Men. Shakespeare not only acted with this company but eventually became a leading shareholder (he had shares in the company), householder (he had shares in the theatrical buildings), and the principal playwright. Then as now, making a living in the professional theater was not easy: competition among the repertory companies was stiff; civic officials and religious moralists regarded playacting as a sinful, time-wasting nuisance and tried to ban it altogether; government officials exercised censorship over the contents of the plays; and periodic outbreaks of bubonic plague led to temporary closing of the London theaters. But Shakespeare's company, which included some of the most famous actors of the day, nonetheless thrived and in 1599 began to perform in the Globe, a fine, round open-air theater that the company built for itself on the south bank of the Thames. The company also performed frequently at court and, after 1608, at Blackfriars, an oblong private indoor London theater. Already by 1597 Shakespeare had so prospered that he was able to purchase New Place, a handsome house in Stratford-upon-Avon; he could now call himself a gentleman, as his father had (probably with the financial assistance of his successful playwright son) been granted a coat of arms the previous year. Shakespeare's wife and daughters (his son, Hamnet, having died in 1596) resided in Stratford-upon-Avon, while the playwright, living in rented rooms in London, pursued his career. Shortly after writing *The Tempest* (ca. 1611), he retired from direct involvement in the theater and returned to Stratford, buying one of the largest houses there. In March 1616, he signed his will; he died a month later, leaving the bulk of his estate to his daughter Susanna.

Shakespeare began his career as a playwright, probably in the early 1590s, by writing comedies and history plays. The earliest of these histories (in which he may have had one or more collaborators), generally based on accounts of English kings written by Raphael Holinshed and other sixteenth-century chroniclers, seem theatrically vital but crude, as does an early attempt at tragedy, *Titus Andronicus*. But by the later 1590s Shakespeare had created a sequence of profoundly searching and ambitious history plays—*Richard II*, the first and second parts of *Henry IV*, and *Henry V*—which together explore the death throes of feudal England and the birth of the modern nation-state ruled by a charismatic monarch. In the same years he wrote a succession of romantic comedies (*The Merchant of Venice, The Merry Wives of Windsor, Much Ado About Nothing, As You Like It, Twelfth Night*) whose poetic richness and emotional complexity remain unmatched.

Twelfth Night may originally have been written in the same year as *Hamlet* (ca. 1601), which initiated an outpouring of great tragic dramas: *Othello, King Lear, Macbeth, Antony and Cleopatra,* and *Coriolanus*. These plays, written from 1601 to 1607, seem to mark a major shift in sensibility, an existential and metaphysical darkening that many readers think originated in personal anguish. Whatever the truth of this speculation—and we have no direct, personal testimony either to support or to undermine it—there appears to have occurred in the same period a shift as well in Shakespeare's comic sensibility. The comedies written between 1601 and 1604, *Troilus and Cressida, All's Well That Ends Well,* and *Measure for Measure*, are sufficiently different from the earlier comedies—more biting in tone, more uneasy with comic conventions, more ruthlessly questioning of the values of the characters and the resolutions of the plots—that some modern scholars have classified them as "problem plays" or "dark comedies." Another group of plays, among the last that Shakespeare wrote, seem similarly to define a distinct category. *Pericles, Cymbeline, The Winter's Tale,* and *The Tempest*, written between 1608 and 1611, when Shakespeare had developed a remarkably fluid, dreamlike sense of plot and a poetic style that could veer, apparently effortlessly, from the tortured to the ineffably sweet, are now commonly known as the "romances." These plays share an interest in the moral and emotional life less of the adolescents who dominate the earlier comedies than of their parents. The romances are deeply concerned with patterns of loss and recovery, suffering and redemption, despair and renewal. They have seemed to many critics to constitute a self-conscious conclusion to a career that opened with histories and comedies and passed through the dark and tormented tragedies. They are, though, also written after the company's acquisition of the new, Blackfriars playhouse—which was more exclusive and expensive than the Globe—and reflect, too, the tastes of the elevated courtly audience the company was now expecting. In a few of the late plays, Shakespeare worked, as he apparently had at the beginning of his professional life, with collaborators. Perhaps he thought of himself as handing over his vocation to a new generation.

Shakespeare evinced no interest in preserving for posterity the sum of his writings, let alone in clarifying the chronology of his works or in specifying which plays he wrote alone and which with collaborators. He wrote plays for performance by his company, and his scripts existed in his own handwritten manuscripts or in scribal copies, in actors' separate part scripts, in playhouse promptbooks, and probably in pirated texts based on shorthand reports of a performance or, possibly, on reconstructions from memory by a spectator. None of these manuscript versions has survived, with the exception, perhaps, of some of the *Thomas More* passages, one of which is included in this volume (p. 482). Eighteen of his plays were published during his lifetime in the small-format, inexpensive books called quartos; to these were added eighteen other plays, never before printed, in the large, expensive folio volume of *Mr. William Shakespeares Comedies, Histories, & Tragedies* (1623), published seven years after his death. This First Folio, compiled by two of his friends and fellow actors, John Heminges and Henry Condell, is prefaced by a Ben Jonson poem, in which Shakespeare is hailed as "not of an age, but for all time."

That Shakespeare is "for all time" does not mean that he did not also belong to his own age. It is possible to see where Shakespeare adapted the techniques of his contemporaries and where, crucially, he differed from them. Shakespeare rarely invented the plots of his dramas, preferring to work, often quite closely, with stories

Sketch of the Swan Theater. This drawing by Arend van Buchell (ca. 1596), based on the observations of Johannes De Witt, shows features of a public playhouse in Shakespeare's time. Resembling the courtyard of an Elizabethan inn, the Swan had three galleries for the audience, and probably additional room for audience members in the gallery at the back of the stage, above the tiring-house (dressing room). The stage itself had two doors for players' entrances and exits, and the roof over the stage was supported by pillars. The flag flying from the roof signals that a play is to be performed that day, and a trumpeter announces the beginning of the performance (though the sketch shows a performance already under way). De Witt labeled parts of the sketch using Latin names derived from the Roman theater.

he found ready-made in histories, novellas, narrative poems, or other plays. The religious mystery plays and the allegorical morality plays still popular during his childhood taught him that dramas worth seeing must get at something central to the human condition, that they should embody as well as narrate the crucial actions, and that they could reach not only a coterie of the educated elite but also the great mass of ordinary people. From these and other theatrical models, Shakespeare learned how to construct plays around the struggle for the soul of a protagonist, how to create theatrically compelling and subversive figures of wickedness, and how to focus attention on his characters' psychological, moral, and spiritual lives as well as on their outward behavior.

The authors of the morality plays thought they could enhance the broad impact they sought to achieve by stripping their characters of all incidental distinguishing traits and getting to their essences. They believed that their audiences would thereby not be distracted by the irrelevant details of individual identities. Shakespeare grasped that the spectacle of human destiny was in fact vastly more compelling when it was attached not to generalized abstractions but to particular people, people whom he realized with an unprecedented intensity of individuation: not Youth but Viola, not Everyman but Lear. No other writer of his time was able to create and enter into the interior worlds of so many characters, conveying again and again a sense of unique and irreducible selfhood. In the plays of Shakespeare's brilliant contemporary Marlowe, the protagonist overwhelms virtually all the other characters; in Shakespeare, by contrast, even relatively minor characters—Gonzalo in *The Tempest*, for example, or Emilia in *Othello*—make astonishingly powerful claims on the audience's attention. The Romantic critic William Hazlitt observed that Shakespeare had the power to multiply himself marvelously. His plays convey the sense of an inexhaustible imaginative generosity.

Shakespeare was singularly alert to the fantastic vitality of the English language. His immense vocabulary bears witness to an uncanny ability to absorb terms from a wide range of pursuits and to transform them into intimate registers of thought and feeling. He had a seemingly boundless capacity to generate metaphors, and he was virtually addicted to wordplay. Double meanings, verbal echoes, and submerged associations ripple through every passage, deepening the reader's enjoyment and understanding, though sometimes at the expense of a single clear sense. The eighteenth-century critic Samuel Johnson complained with some justice that the quibble, the pun, was "the fatal Cleopatra for which Shakespeare lost the world and was content to lose it." For the power that continually discharges itself throughout his plays and poems, at once constituting and unsettling everything it touches, is the power of language.

Historical accuracy is rarely a concern for Shakespeare. His ancient Romans wear doublets, throw caps into the air and use Christian oaths: to this extent he pulled everything he touched into his contemporary existence. But at the same time he was not a social realist; other writers in this period are better at conveying the precise details of the daily lives of shoemakers, alchemists, and judges. The settings of his plays are rarely realistic representations of particular historical times and places; instead, they function as imaginative displacements into alternative worlds that remain strangely familiar.

Though on occasion he depicts ghosts, demons, and other supernatural figures, the universe Shakespeare conjures up seems resolutely human-centered and secular: the torments and joys that most deeply matter are found in this world, not in the next. Attempts to claim him for one or another religious system have proven unconvincing, as have attempts to assign him a specific political label. Activists and ideologues of all political stripes have viewed him as an ally: he has been admiringly quoted by kings and by revolutionaries, by fascists, liberal democrats, socialists, republicans, and communists. At once an agent of civility and an agent of subversion, Shakespeare seems to have been able to view society simultaneously as an insider and as an outsider. His plays can be interpreted and performed—with deep conviction and compelling power—in utterly contradictory ways. The centuries-long accumulation of these interpretations and performances, far from exhausting Shakespeare's aesthetic appeal, seems only to have enhanced its enduring freshness.

Sonnets

In Elizabethan England aristocratic patronage, with the money, protection, and prestige it alone could provide, was probably a professional writer's most important asset. This patronage, or at least Shakespeare's quest for it, is most visible in his dedication, in 1593 and 1594, of his narrative poems, *Venus and Adonis* and *The Rape of Lucrece*, to the wealthy young nobleman Henry Wriothesley, earl of Southampton. What return the poet got for his exquisite offerings is unknown. We do know that among wits and gallants the poems won Shakespeare a reputation as an immensely stylish and accomplished poet. This reputation was enhanced by manuscript circulation of his sonnets, which were mentioned admiringly in print more than ten years before they were published, in 1609 (apparently without his personal supervision and perhaps without his consent).

Shakespeare's sonnets are quite unlike the other sonnet sequences of his day, notably in his almost unprecedented choice of a beautiful young man (rather than a lady) as the principal object of praise, love, and idealizing devotion and in his portrait of a dark, sensuous, and sexually promiscuous mistress (rather than the usual chaste and aloof blond beauty). Nor are the moods confined to what the Renaissance thought were those of the despairing Petrarchan lover: they include delight, pride, melancholy, shame, disgust, and fear. Shakespeare's sequence suggests a story, although the details are vague, and there is even doubt whether the sonnets as published are in an order established by the poet himself. Certain motifs are evident: an introductory series (1 to 17) celebrates the beauty of a young man and urges him to marry and beget children who will bear his image. The subsequent long sequence (18 to 126), passionately focused on the beloved young man, develops as a dominant motif the transience and destructive power of time, countered only by the force of love and the permanence of poetry. The remaining sonnets focus chiefly on the so-called Dark Lady as an alluring but degrading object of desire. Some sonnets (like 144) intimate a love triangle involving the speaker, the male friend, and the woman; others take note of a rival poet (sometimes identified as George Chapman or Christopher Marlowe). The biographical background of the sonnets has inspired a mountain of speculation, but very little of it has any factual support.

Though there are many variations, Shakespeare's most frequent rhyme scheme in the sonnets is *abab cdcd efef gg*. This so-called Shakespearean pattern often (though not always) calls attention to three distinct quatrains (each of which may develop a separate metaphor), followed by a closing couplet that may either confirm or pull sharply against what has gone before. Startling shifts in direction may occur in lines other than the closing ones; consider, for example, the twists and turns in the opening lines of sonnet 138: "When my love swears that she is made of truth, / I do believe her, though I know she lies." Shakespeare's sonnets as a whole are strikingly intense, conveying a sense of high psychological and moral stakes. They are also remarkably dense, written with a daunting energy, concentration, and compression. Often the main idea of the poem may be grasped quickly, but the precise movement of thought and feeling, the links between the shifting images, and the syntax, tone, and rhetorical structure prove immensely challenging. These are poems that famously reward rereading.

Sonnets

To the Only Begetter of
These Ensuing Sonnets
Mr. W. H. All Happiness
and That Eternity
Promised
By
Our Ever-Living Poet
Wisheth
The Well-Wishing
Adventurer in
Setting Forth
T. T.[1]

1

From fairest creatures we desire increase,
That thereby beauty's rose might never die,
But as the riper should by time decease,
His tender heir might bear his memory;
5 But thou, contracted[2] to thine own bright eyes,
Feed'st thy light's flame with self-substantial[3] fuel,
Making a famine where abundance lies,
Thyself thy foe, to thy sweet self too cruel.
Thou that art now the world's fresh ornament
10 And only[4] herald to the gaudy spring,
Within thine own bud buriest thy content[5]
And, tender churl,[6] mak'st waste in niggarding.°   *hoarding*
   Pity the world, or else this glutton be,
   To eat the world's due, by the grave and thee.[7]

3

Look in thy glass° and tell the face thou viewest   *mirror*
Now is the time that face should form another,
Whose fresh repair° if now thou not renewest,   *state*
Thou dost beguile° the world, unbless some mother.   *cheat*
5 For where is she so fair whose uneared° womb   *unplowed*
Disdains the tillage of thy husbandry?
Or who is he so fond° will be the tomb   *foolish*

---

1. This odd dedication bears the initials of the publisher, Thomas Thorpe. The W. H. addressed here may or may not be the male friend addressed in sonnets 1 to 126. Leading candidates for that role are Henry Wriothesley, Earl of Southampton, the dedicatee of *Venus and Adonis* (1593) and *The Rape of Lucrece* (1594), and William Herbert, earl of Pembroke, a dedicatee of the First Folio. But there is no hard evidence to support these or other suggested identifications of the male friend or of the so-called Dark Lady; these sonnet personages may or may not have had real-life counterparts.
   Since all the sonnets save two were first published in 1609, we do not repeat the date after each one. Numbers 138 and 144 were first published in 1599, in a verse miscellany called *The Passionate Pilgrim*.
2. Betrothed; also, withdrawn into.
3. Of your own substance.
4. Principal, with overtones of single, solitary.
5. What you contain (potential for fatherhood), also what would content you (marriage and fatherhood).
6. Gentle boor (an oxymoron).
7. "This . . . thee": be a glutton by causing what is owed to the world (your posterity) to be consumed by the grave and within yourself.

Of his self-love, to stop posterity?
Thou art thy mother's glass, and she in thee
10 Calls back the lovely April of her prime;
So thou through windows of thine age shalt see,
Despite of wrinkles, this thy golden time.
   But if thou live rememb'red not to be,[8]
   Die single, and thine image dies with thee.

12

When I do count the clock that tells the time
And see the brave° day sunk in hideous night,   *splendid*
When I behold the violet past prime
And sable curls all silvered o'er with white,
5 When lofty trees I see barren of leaves,
Which erst° from heat did canopy the herd,   *formerly*
And summer's green all girded up in sheaves
Borne on the bier with white and bristly beard:
Then of thy beauty do I question make°   *speculate*
10 That thou among the wastes of time must go,
Since sweets and beauties do themselves forsake,
And die as fast as they see others grow,
   And nothing 'gainst Time's scythe can make defense
   Save breed,° to brave° him when he takes thee hence.   *offspring / defy*

15

When I consider every thing that grows
Holds° in perfection but a little moment;   *remains*
That this huge stage presenteth nought but shows[9]
Whereon the stars in secret influence comment;[1]
5 When I perceive that men as plants increase,
Cheered and checked[2] even by the selfsame sky,
Vaunt[3] in their youthful sap, at height decrease,
And wear their brave state out of memory;[4]
Then the conceit° of this inconstant stay   *conception*
10 Sets you most rich in youth before my sight,
Where wasteful Time debateth[5] with Decay
To change your day of youth to sullied° night,   *soiled, blackened*
   And all in war with Time for love of you,
   As he takes from you, I ingraft[6] you new.

18

Shall I compare thee to a summer's day?
Thou art more lovely and more temperate:
Rough winds do shake the darling buds of May,
And summer's lease hath all too short a date;
5 Sometime too hot the eye of heaven shines,

---

8. But if you live to be forgotten.
9. (1) Appearances, (2) performances.
1. That is, the stars secretly affect human actions.
2. Encouraged and reproached or stopped.
3. Exult, display themselves.
4. Wear their showy splendor out and are forgotten.
5. (1) Fights, (2) joins forces.
6. Renew by grafting; implant beauty again (by my verse).

And often is his gold complexion dimmed;
And every fair from fair sometime declines,
By chance or nature's changing course untrimmed.⁷
But thy eternal summer shall not fade,
Nor lose possession of that fair thou ow'st;°   *ownest*
Nor shall death brag thou wander'st in his shade,
When in eternal lines to time thou grow'st:°   *are grafted*
  So long as men can breathe or eyes can see,
  So long lives this,⁸ and this gives life to thee.

19

Devouring Time, blunt thou the lion's paws,
And make the earth devour her own sweet brood;
Pluck the keen teeth from the fierce tiger's jaws,
And burn the long-lived phoenix in her blood;⁹
Make glad and sorry seasons as thou fleet'st,
And do whate'er thou wilt, swift-footed Time,
To the wide world and all her fading sweets,
But I forbid thee one most heinous crime:
O carve not with thy hours my love's fair brow,
Nor draw no lines there with thine antique¹ pen;
Him in thy course untainted² do allow,
For beauty's pattern to succeeding men.
  Yet do thy worst, old Time: despite thy wrong,
  My love shall in my verse ever live young.

20

A woman's face with Nature's own hand painted³
Hast thou, the master mistress of my passion;⁴
A woman's gentle heart but not acquainted
With shifting change as is false women's fashion;
An eye more bright than theirs, less false in rolling,°   *roving*
Gilding the object whereupon it gazeth;
A man in hue all hues⁵ in his controlling,
Which steals men's eyes and women's souls amazeth.
And for a woman wert thou first created,
Till Nature as she wrought thee fell a-doting,⁶
And by addition me of thee defeated,
By adding one thing to my purpose nothing.
  But since she pricked⁷ thee out for women's pleasure,
  Mine be thy love, and thy love's use⁸ their treasure.

---

7. Stripped of gay apparel.
8. That is, the poem. The boast of immortality for one's verse was a convention going back to the Greek and Roman classics.
9. In full vigor of life (a hunting term). The phoenix was a mythical bird that lived five hundred years, then died in flames to rise again from its ashes.
1. (1) Old, (2) fantastic (antic).
2. (1) Undefiled, (2) untouched by a weapon (a term from jousting).
3. That is, not made up with cosmetics.
4. (1) Strong feeling, (2) poem.
5. "Hue" probably means appearance or form. In the first edition, "hues" is spelled *"Hews,"* which some have taken as indicating a pun on a proper name. It has also been suggested that "man in" is a copyist's or compositor's misreading of "maiden."
6. (1) Crazy, (2) infatuated.
7. Marked, with obvious sexual pun.
8. (1) Sexual enjoyment, (2) interest (as in usury).

23

As an unperfect actor on the stage
Who with his fear is put besides° his part, — *forgets*
Or some fierce thing replete with too much rage
Whose strength's abundance weakens his own heart,
5 So I, for fear of trust,° forget to say — *lack of confidence*
The perfect ceremony of love's rite,[9]
And in mine own love's strength seem to decay,
O'er-charged° with burden of mine own love's might. — *overweighed*
O let my books be then the eloquence
10 And dumb presagers° of my speaking breast, — *mute presenters*
Who plead for love, and look for recompense
More than that tongue that more hath more expressed.[1]
   O learn to read what silent love hath writ;
   To hear with eyes belongs to love's fine wit.° — *intelligence*

29

When, in disgrace° with Fortune and men's eyes, — *disfavor*
I all alone beweep my outcast state,
And trouble deaf heaven with my bootless° cries, — *futile*
And look upon myself and curse my fate,
5 Wishing me like to one more rich in hope,
Featured like him, like him with friends possessed,[2]
Desiring this man's art° and that man's scope,° — *skill / ability*
With what I most enjoy contented least;
Yet in these thoughts myself almost despising,
10 Haply I think on thee, and then my state[3]
(Like to the lark at break of day arising
From sullen earth) sings hymns at heaven's gate;
   For thy sweet love remembered such wealth brings
   That then I scorn to change my state with kings.

30

When to the sessions[4] of sweet silent thought
I summon up remembrance of things past,
I sigh the lack of many a thing I sought,
And with old woes new wail° my dear time's waste: — *bewail anew*
5 Then can I drown an eye (unused to flow)
For precious friends hid in death's dateless° night, — *endless*
And weep afresh love's long since canceled woe,
And moan th' expense° of many a vanished sight: — *loss*
Then can I grieve at grievances foregone,° — *former*
10 And heavily from woe to woe tell° o'er — *count*
The sad account of fore-bemoanèd moan,
Which I new pay as if not paid before.

---

9. The first edition has "right," suggesting love's due as well as love's ritual ("rite").
1. More than that (rival) speaker who has more often said more.
2. That is, I wish I had one man's looks, another man's friends.
3. Condition, state of mind; but in line 14 there is a pun on *state* meaning chair of state, throne.
4. Sittings of court. "Summon up" (next line) continues the metaphor.

But if the while I think on thee, dear friend,
All losses are restored and sorrows end.

33

Full many a glorious morning have I seen
Flatter the mountain tops with sovereign eye,°   *sunlight*
Kissing with golden face the meadows green,
Gilding pale streams with heavenly alchemy;
5   Anon° permit the basest° clouds to ride   *(but) soon / darkest*
With ugly rack° on his celestial face,   *cloudy mask*
And from the forlorn world his visage hide,
Stealing unseen to west with this disgrace.
Even so my sun one early morn did shine
10   With all triumphant splendor on my brow;
But out, alack,° he was but one hour mine;   *alas*
The region° cloud hath masked him from me now.   *high*
    Yet him for this my love no whit disdaineth:
    Suns of the world may stain° when heaven's sun staineth.   *darken*

35

No more be grieved at that which thou hast done:
Roses have thorns, and silver fountains mud.
Clouds and eclipses stain° both moon and sun,   *dim*
And loathsome canker° lives in sweetest bud.   *rose worm*
5   All men make faults, and even I in this,
Authorizing thy trespass with compare,°   *comparisons*
Myself corrupting, salving thy amiss,°   *palliating your offense*
Excusing thy sins more than thy sins are;
For to thy sensual fault I bring in sense°—   *reason*
10   Thy adverse party is thy advocate—
And 'gainst myself a lawful plea commence.
Such civil war is in my love and hate
    That I an accessory needs must be
    To that sweet thief which sourly robs from me.

55

Not marble nor the gilded monuments
Of princes shall outlive this powerful rhyme;
But you shall shine more bright in these contents
Than unswept stone, besmeared with sluttish time.[5]
5   When wasteful war shall statues overturn,
And broils° root out the work of masonry,   *battles*
Nor Mars his° sword nor war's quick fire shall burn   *neither Mars's*
The living record of your memory.
'Gainst death and all-oblivious enmity[6]
10   Shall you pace forth; your praise shall still find room
Even in the eyes of all posterity

---

5. That is, than in a stone tomb or effigy that slovenly time wears away and covers with dust.

6. The enmity of oblivion, of being forgotten.

That wear this world out to the ending doom.° *Judgment Day*
  So, till the judgment that yourself arise,[7]
  You live in this, and dwell in lovers' eyes.

60

Like as the waves make towards the pebbled shore,
So do our minutes hasten to their end;
Each changing place with that which goes before,
In sequent toil all forwards do contend.[8]
5 Nativity, once in the main° of light, *broad expanse*
Crawls to maturity, wherewith being crowned,
Crooked° eclipses 'gainst his glory fight, *pernicious*
And Time that gave doth now his gift confound.
Time doth transfix the flourish[9] set on youth,
10 And delves the parallels[1] in beauty's brow,
Feeds on the rarities of nature's truth,
And nothing stands but for his scythe to mow.
  And yet to times in hope° my verse shall stand, *future times*
  Praising thy worth, despite his cruel hand.

62

Sin of self-love possesseth all mine eye,
And all my soul, and all my every part;
And for this sin there is no remedy,
It is so grounded inward in my heart.
5 Methinks no face so gracious° is as mine, *pleasing*
No shape so true,° no truth of such account, *perfect*
And for myself mine own worth do define
As° I all other° in all worths surmount. *as if / others*
But when my glass° shows me myself indeed, *mirror*
10 Beated and chapped with tanned antiquity,
Mine own self-love quite contrary° I read; *differently*
Self so self-loving were iniquity.
  'Tis thee, my self,° that for° myself I praise, *you, my other self / as*
  Painting my age with beauty of thy days.

65

Since[2] brass, nor stone, nor earth, nor boundless sea,
But sad mortality o'ersways their power,
How with this rage° shall beauty hold a plea, *destructive power*
Whose action is no stronger than a flower?
5 O how shall summer's honey breath hold out
Against the wrackful° siege of batt'ring days, *destructive*
When rocks impregnable are not so stout,
Nor gates of steel so strong, but Time decays?
O fearful meditation! Where, alack,

---

7. Until you rise from the dead on Judgment Day.
8. Toiling and following each other, all struggle to move forward.
9. Destroy the embellishment. To "flourish" is also to blossom.
1. Digs the parallel furrows (wrinkles).
2. That is, since there is neither.

10   Shall Time's best jewel from Time's chest[3] he hid?
      Or what strong hand can hold his swift foot back?
      Or who his spoil° of beauty can forbid?   *ravaging*
        O none, unless this miracle have might,
        That in black ink my love may still shine bright.

71

    No longer mourn for me when I am dead
    Than you shall hear the surly sullen bell[4]
    Give warning to the world that I am fled
    From this vile world, with vilest worms to dwell.
5   Nay, if you read this line, remember not
    The hand that writ it; for I love you so,
    That I in your sweet thoughts would be forgot,
    If thinking on me then should make you woe.
    O, if, I say, you look upon this verse
10 When I perhaps compounded am with clay,
    Do not so much as my poor name rehearse,°   *repeat*
    But let your love even with my life decay;
      Lest the wise world should look into your moan,
      And mock you with me after I am gone.

73

    That time of year thou may'st in me behold
    When yellow leaves, or none, or few, do hang
    Upon those boughs which shake against the cold,
    Bare ruined choirs,[5] where late° the sweet birds sang.   *lately*
5   In me thou seest the twilight of such day
    As after sunset fadeth in the west;
    Which by and by black night doth take away,
    Death's second self that seals up all in rest.
    In me thou seest the glowing of such fire
10 That on the ashes of his youth doth lie,
    As the deathbed whereon it must expire,
    Consumed with that which it was nourished by.[6]
      This thou perceiv'st, which makes thy love more strong,
      To love that well, which thou must leave ere long.

74

    But be contented; when that fell[7] arrest
    Without all bail shall carry me away,
    My life hath in this line some interest,[8]
    Which for memorial still° with thee shall stay.   *always*
5   When thou reviewest this, thou dost review

---

3. That is, from being coffered up by Time.
4. The bell was tolled to announce the death of a member of the parish—one stroke for each year of his or her life.
5. The part of a church where divine service was sung.
6. Choked by the ashes of that which once nourished its flame.
7. Cruel. Hamlet says, "this fell sergeant / Death is strict in his arrest" (5.2.278–79).
8. Share, participation. "In this line": that is, in this poetry.

The very part was° consecrate to thee. *which was*
The earth can have but earth, which is his due;
My spirit is thine, the better part of me.
So then thou hast but lost the dregs of life,
10 The prey of worms, my body being dead,
The coward conquest of a wretch's knife,[9]
Too base of° thee to be rememberèd. *by*
    The worth of that is that which it contains,[1]
    And that is this, and this with thee remains.

80

O, how I faint° when I of you do write, *get discouraged*
Knowing a better spirit[2] doth use your name,
And in the praise thereof spends all his might,
To make me tongue-tied, speaking of your fame!
5 But since your worth, wide as the ocean is,
The humble as° the proudest sail doth bear, *as well as*
My saucy bark,° inferior far to his, *impudent boat*
On your broad main° doth willfully° appear. *waters / boldly*
Your shallowest help will hold me up afloat
10 Whilst he upon your soundless° deep doth ride; *bottomless*
Or, being wrecked, I am a worthless boat,
He of tall building[3] and of goodly pride.° *magnificence*
    Then if he thrive and I be cast away,
    The worst was this: my love was my decay.

87

Farewell: thou art too dear[4] for my possessing,
And like enough thou know'st thy estimate.° *value*
The charter° of thy worth gives thee releasing;[5] *deed; contract for property*
My bonds in thee are all determinate.° *expired*
5 For how do I hold thee but by thy granting,
And for that riches where is my deserving?
The cause of this fair gift in me is wanting,° *absent*
And so my patent° back again is swerving.[6] *title*
Thy self thou gav'st, thy own worth then not knowing,
10 Or me, to whom thou gav'st it, else mistaking;° *overestimating*
So thy great gift, upon misprision growing,° *based on error*
Comes home again, on better judgment making.[7]
    Thus have I had thee as a dream doth flatter:
    In sleep a king, but waking no such matter.

---

9. Death's weapon (like Time's scythe).
1. That is, the only value of the body is that it contains the spirit.
2. A rival poet. See the headnote, p. 624.
3. Tall, strong build.
4. (1) Expensive, (2) beloved.
5. Releases you (from love's bonds).
6. That is, reverting to you.
7. That is, when you realize your error.

94

They that have power to hurt and will do none,
That do not do the thing they most do show,[8]
Who, moving others, are themselves as stone,
Unmovèd, cold, and to temptation slow;
5 They rightly do inherit heaven's graces
And husband nature's riches from expense;[9]
They are the lords and owners of their faces,
Others but stewards of their excellence.
The summer's flower is to the summer sweet,
10 Though to itself it only live and die,[1]
But if that flower with base infection meet,
The basest weed outbraves° his dignity: *surpasses*
    For sweetest things turn sourest by their deeds;
    Lilies that fester smell far worse than weeds.

97

How like a winter hath my absence been
From thee, the pleasure of the fleeting year!
What freezings have I felt, what dark days seen!
What old December's bareness everywhere!
5 And yet this time removed[2] was summer's time,
The teeming autumn, big with rich increase,
Bearing the wanton burthen of the prime,[3]
Like widowed wombs after their lords' decease.
Yet this abundant issue° seemed to me *outgrowth*
10 But hope of orphans and unfathered fruit;
For summer and his pleasures wait° on thee, *attend*
And, thou away, the very birds are mute;
    Or, if they sing, 'tis with so dull a cheer° *such a dismal mood*
    That leaves look pale, dreading the winter's near.

98

From you have I been absent in the spring,
When proud-pied[4] April, dressed in all his trim,
Hath put a spirit of youth in everything,
5 That heavy Saturn° laughed and leapt with him. *god of melancholy*
Yet nor° the lays° of birds, nor the sweet smell *neither / songs*
Of different flowers in odor and in hue
Could make me any summer's story tell,
Or from their proud lap pluck them where they grew;
Nor did I wonder at° the lily's white, *admire*
10 Nor praise the deep vermilion in the rose;
They were but sweet, but figures° of delight, *merely emblems*
Drawn after you, you pattern of all those.

---

8. Seem to do, or seem capable of doing.
9. That is, they do not squander nature's gifts.
1. Even if it lives and dies in apparent isolation (unpollinated).
2. That is, when I was absent.
3. Spring, which has engendered the lavish crop ("wanton burthen") that autumn is now left to bear.
4. Magnificent in many colors.

Yet seemed it winter still, and, you away,
As with your shadow I with these did play.

105

Let not my love be called idolatry,
Nor my belovèd as an idol show,
Since all alike my songs and praises be
To one, of one, still° such, and ever so.   *continually*
5 Kind is my love today, tomorrow kind,
Still constant in a wondrous excellence.
Therefore my verse, to constancy confined,
One thing expressing, leaves out difference.°   *variety*
"Fair, kind, and true" is all my argument,°   *theme*
10 "Fair, kind, and true" varying to other words,
And in this change is my invention spent,[5]
Three themes in one, which wonderous scope affords.
   Fair, kind, and true have often lived alone,°   *separately*
   Which three till now never kept seat° in one.   *dwelt permanently*

106

When in the chronicle of wasted° time   *past*
I see descriptions of the fairest wights,°   *persons*
And beauty making beautiful old rhyme
In praise of ladies dead and lovely knights,
5 Then, in the blazon[6] of sweet beauty's best,
Of hand, of foot, of lip, of eye, of brow,
I see their antique pen would have expressed
Even such a beauty as you master now.
So all their praises are but prophecies
10 Of this our time, all you prefiguring;
And, for they looked but with divining eyes,[7]
They had not skill enough your worth to sing:
   For we, which now behold these present days,
   Have eyes to wonder, but lack tongues to praise.

107

Not mine own fears, nor the prophetic soul
Of the wide world dreaming on things to come,[8]
Can yet the lease of my true love control,
Supposed as forfeit to a confined doom.[9]
5 The mortal moon hath her eclipse endured,
And the sad augurs mock their own presage;[1]

---

5. And in varying the words alone my inventiveness is expended.
6. Catalog of excellencies.
7. Because ("for") they were able only ("but") to foresee prophetically.
8. This sonnet refers to contemporary events and the prophecies, common in Elizabethan almanacs, of disaster.
9. That is, can yet put an end to my love, which I thought doomed to early forfeiture.

1. The "mortal moon" is probably Queen Elizabeth; her "eclipse" could be either her death (March 1603) or, perhaps, her "climacteric" year, her sixty-third (thought meaningful because the product of two "significant" numbers, 7 and 9), which ended in September 1596. The sober astrologers ("sad augurs") now ridicule their own predictions ("presage") of catastrophe, because they turned out to be false.

Incertainties now crown themselves assured,
And peace² proclaims olives of endless age.
Now with the drops of this most balmy time
10 My love looks fresh, and death to me subscribes,°   *submits*
Since, spite of him, I'll live in this poor rhyme,
While he insults o'er dull and speechless tribes:
    And thou in this shalt find thy monument,
    When tyrants' crests and tombs of brass are spent.°   *wasted away*

110

Alas, 'tis true I have gone here and there
And made myself a motley° to the view,   *fool, jester*
Gored³ mine own thoughts, sold cheap what is most dear,
Made old offenses of affections° new.   *passions*
5 Most true it is that I have looked on truth°   *fidelity*
Askance and strangely;⁴ but, by all above,
These blenches° gave my heart another youth,   *turnings aside*
And worse essays⁵ proved thee my best of love.
Now all is done, have what shall have no end:
10 Mine appetite I never more will grind°   *whet*
On newer proof,° to try° an older friend,   *experiences / test*
A god in love, to whom I am confined.
    Then give me welcome, next my heaven the best,⁶
    Even to thy pure and most most loving breast.

116

Let me not to the marriage of true minds
Admit impediments;⁷ love is not love
Which alters when it alteration finds,
Or bends with the remover to remove:
5 O, no, it is an ever-fixèd mark,⁸
That looks on tempests and is never shaken;
It is the star to every wand'ring bark,
Whose worth's unknown, although his height⁹ be taken.
Love's not Time's fool,° though rosy lips and cheeks   *plaything*
10 Within his¹ bending sickle's compass come;
Love alters not with his brief hours and weeks,
But bears it out even to the edge of doom.°   *brink of Judgment Day*
    If this be error and upon me proved,
    I never writ, nor no man ever loved.

---

2. Perhaps referring to the peace treaty signed with Spain by Elizabeth's successor, James I, or, if the sonnet refers to the time of Elizabeth's climacteric, to an earlier treaty between England and France.
3. Wounded, pierced.
4. Obliquely or asquint, and coldly (like a stranger).
5. Trials of worse relationships.
6. That is, the next best thing to the Christian heaven.
7. From the Anglican marriage service: "If either of you do know any impediment why ye may not be lawfully joined together . . ."
8. Seamark, such as a lighthouse or a beacon.
9. The star's value is incalculable, although its altitude may be known and used for navigation.
1. Time's (as also in line 11).

126[2]

O thou, my lovely boy, who in thy power
Dost hold Time's fickle glass,[3] his sickle, hour;°   *hourglass*
Who hast by waning grown and therein show'st°   *in contrast*
Thy lovers withering as thy sweet self grow'st;
5 If Nature (sovereign mistress over wrack°)   *destruction*
As thou goest onwards still will pluck thee back,
She keeps thee to this purpose, that her skill
May Time disgrace and wretched minutes kill.
Yet fear her, O thou minion° of her pleasure,   *darling*
10 She may detain, but not still° keep, her treasure!   *always*
   Her audit° (though delayed) answered must be,   *accounting*
   And her quietus° is to render° thee.   *settlement / surrender*

127

In the old age black was not counted fair,[4]
Or, if it were, it bore not beauty's name;
But now is black beauty's successive heir,[5]
And beauty slandered with a bastard shame:°   *declared illegitimate*
5 For since each hand hath put on nature's power,
Fairing the foul with art's false borrowed face,°   *with cosmetics*
Sweet beauty hath no name, no holy bower,[6]
But is profaned, if not lives in disgrace.
Therefore my mistress' brows are raven black,
10 Her eyes so suited,° and they mourners seem   *also black*
At° such who, not born fair, no beauty lack,[7]   *for*
Sland'ring creation with a false esteem:
   Yet so they mourn, becoming of° their woe,   *gracing*
   That every tongue says beauty should look so.

128

How oft when thou, my music, music play'st
Upon that blessèd wood[8] whose motion sounds
With thy sweet fingers when thou gently sway'st°   *govern*
The wiry concord that mine ear confounds,[9]
5 Do I envý those jacks[1] that nimble leap
To kiss the tender inward of thy hand,
Whilst my poor lips, which should that harvest reap,
At the wood's boldness by thee blushing stand.
To be so tickled they would change their state[2]
10 And situation[3] with those dancing chips,
O'er whom thy fingers walk with gentle gait,

---

2. This poem—not a sonnet but six couplets—is an envoy (a closing summary or commentary) marking the end of the sequence addressed to a beloved young man (see the headnote) and formally signaling a change in tone and subject matter in the remaining sonnets.
3. Mirror, fickle because as the subject ages, the mirror reflects a changed image.
4. Beautiful, equated with blond hair and coloring. "Old": former. "Black": dark hair and coloring, equated with ugliness.
5. Heir in line of succession.
6. Shrine. The next line suggests that natural (unpainted) beauty is now discredited.
7. That is, nevertheless possess the appearance of beauty.
8. Keys of the spinet or virginal.
9. The harmony from the strings that overcomes my ear with delight.
1. The keys (actually, "jacks" are the plectra that pluck the strings when activated by the keys).
2. Their place in the order of things.
3. Physical location.

Making dead wood more blessed than living lips.
  Since saucy jacks[4] so happy are in this,
  Give them thy fingers, me thy lips to kiss.

129

Th' expense of spirit in a waste of shame
Is lust in action;[5] and till action, lust
Is perjured, murd'rous, bloody, full of blame,
Savage, extreme, rude,° cruel, not to trust;   *brutal*
5 Enjoyed no sooner but despisèd straight;°   *immediately*
Past reason hunted, and no sooner had,
Past reason hated as a swallowed bait
On purpose laid to make the taker mad:
Mad in pursuit, and in possession so;
10 Had, having, and in quest to have, extreme;
A bliss in proof,[6] and proved, a very° woe;   *true*
Before, a joy proposed; behind, a dream.
  All this the world well knows; yet none knows well
  To shun the heaven that leads men to this hell.

130

My mistress' eyes are nothing like the sun;[7]
Coral is far more red than her lips' red;
If snow be white, why then her breasts are dun;
If hairs be wires, black wires grow on her head.
5 I have seen roses damasked,° red and white,   *dappled*
But no such roses see I in her cheeks;
And in some perfumes is there more delight
Than in the breath that from my mistress reeks.[8]
I love to hear her speak, yet well I know
10 That music hath a far more pleasing sound;
I grant I never saw a goddess go;°   *walk*
My mistress, when she walks, treads on the ground.
  And yet, by heaven, I think my love as rare°   *admirable; extraordinary*
  As any she belied° with false compare.   *misrepresented*

135

Whoever hath her wish, thou hast thy *Will*,[9]
And *Will* to boot, and *Will* in overplus;
More than enough am I that vex thee still,°   *always*
To thy sweet will making addition thus.
5 Wilt thou, whose will is large and spacious,
Not once vouchsafe° to hide my will in thine?   *consent*
Shall will in others seem right gracious,
And in° my will no fair acceptance shine?   *in the case of*

---

4. With a quibble on the sense "impertinent fellows."
5. The word order here is inverted and slightly obscures the meaning. Lust, when put into action, expends "spirit" (life, vitality; also semen) in a "waste" (desert; also with a pun on *waist*) of shame.
6. A bliss during the experience.
7. An anti-Petrarchan sonnet. All of the details commonly attributed by other Elizabethan sonneteers to their ladies (for example, in Spenser's *Amoretti* 64; see p. 453) are here denied to the poet's mistress.
8. Not with our pejorative sense, but simply "emanates."
9. (1) Wishes, (2) carnal desire, (3) the male and female sexual organs, (4) one or more lovers—evidently including Shakespeare—named Will. This is one of several sonnets punning on the word.

The sea, all water, yet receives rain still,
And in abundance addeth to his store,°   *plenty*
So thou being rich in *Will* add to thy *Will*
One will of mine to make thy large *Will* more.
    Let no unkind, no fair beseechers kill;[1]
    Think all but one, and me in that one *Will*.

138

When my love swears that she is made of truth,[2]
I do believe her, though I know she lies,[3]
That she might think me some untutored youth,
Unlearnèd in the world's false subtleties.
Thus vainly thinking that she thinks me young,
Although she knows my days are past the best,[4]
Simply° I credit her false-speaking tongue: *like a simpleton*
On both sides thus is simple truth suppressed.
But wherefore says she not she is unjust?°   *unfaithful*
And wherefore say not I that I am old?
Oh, love's best habit° is in seeming trust,   *clothing, guise*
And age in love loves not to have years told.°   *counted*
    Therefore I lie with her and she with me,
    And in our faults by lies we flattered be.

144

Two loves I have of comfort and despair,[5]
Which like two spirits do suggest me still:°   *tempt me constantly*
The better angel is a man right fair,
The worser spirit a woman colored ill.°   *dark*
To win me soon to hell, my female evil
Tempteth my better angel from my side,
And would corrupt my saint to be a devil,
Wooing his purity with her foul pride.[6]
And whether that my angel be turned fiend
Suspect I may, yet not directly tell;
But being both from° me, both to each° friend,   *away from / each other*
I guess one angel in another's hell.
    Yet this shall I ne'er know, but live in doubt,
    Till my bad angel fire my good one out.[7]

146

Poor soul, the center of my sinful earth,
Lord of[8] these rebel powers that thee array,[9]
Why dost thou pine within and suffer dearth,

---

1. That is, do not kill with unkindness any of your wooers.
2. (1) Is utterly honest, (2) is faithful.
3. With the obvious sexual pun (as also in lines 13–14).
4. Shakespeare was thirty-five or younger when he wrote this sonnet (it first appeared in *The Passionate Pilgrim*, 1599).
5. I have two beloveds, one bringing me comfort and the other despair.
6. (1) Vanity, (2) sexuality.
7. That is, until she infects him with venereal disease.
8. "Lord of" is an emendation. The 1609 edition repeats the last three words of line 1. Other suggestions are "Thrall to," "Starved by," "Pressed by," and leaving the repetition but dropping "that thee" in line 2.
9. The rebellious body that clothes you.

    Painting thy outward walls so costly gay?
5 Why so large cost, having so short a lease,
    Dost thou upon thy fading mansion spend?
    Shall worms, inheritors of this excess,
    Eat up thy charge?[1] Is this thy body's end?°   *destiny; purpose*
    Then, soul, live thou upon thy servant's loss,
10 And let that pine to aggravate thy store;[2]
    Buy terms° divine in selling hours of dross;°   *long periods / rubbish*
    Within be fed, without be rich no more.
       So shalt thou feed on death, that feeds on men,
       And death once dead, there's no more dying then.

147

    My love is as a fever, longing still°   *continually*
    For that which longer nurseth[3] the disease,
    Feeding on that which doth preserve the ill,°   *maintain the illness*
    Th' uncertain sickly appetite[4] to please.
5 My reason, the physician to my love,
    Angry that his prescriptions are not kept,
    Hath left me, and I desperate now approve
    Desire is death, which physic did except.[5]
    Past cure I am, now reason is past care,[6]
10 And frantic mad with evermore unrest;
    My thoughts and my discourse as madmen's are,
    At random from the truth, vainly expressed:[7]
       For I have sworn thee fair, and thought thee bright,
       Who art as black as hell, as dark as night.

152

    In loving thee thou know'st I am forsworn,[8]
    But thou art twice forsworn to me love swearing:
    In act thy bed-vow° broke, and new faith torn   *to husband (or lover)*
    In vowing new hate after new love bearing.[9]
5 But why of two oaths' breach do I accuse thee
    When I break twenty? I am perjured most,
    For all my vows are oaths but to misuse° thee,   *deceive; misrepresent*
    And all my honest faith in thee is lost.
    For I have sworn deep oaths of thy deep kindness,
10 Oaths of thy love, thy truth, thy constancy,
    And to enlighten thee gave eyes to blindness,[1]
    Or made them swear against the thing they see.
       For I have sworn thee fair—more perjured eye°   *(punning on "I")*
       To swear against the truth so foul a lie.

1609

---

1. (1) Your expense, (2) the thing you were responsible for (that is, the body).
2. Let "that" (that is, the body) deteriorate to increase ("aggravate") the soul's riches ("thy store").
3. (1) Nourishes, (2) takes care of.
4. (1) Desire for food, (2) lust.
5. That is, I learn by experience that desire, which rejected reason's medicine, is death.
6. That is, medical care (of me). The line is a version of the proverb "past cure, past care."
7. Wide of the mark and senselessly uttered.
8. That is, am breaking loving vows to another.
9. The object of the "new faith" followed by "new hate" could be either the speaker's young friend or the speaker himself.
1. And to make you fair (or give you insight), I looked blindly on your failings (or pretended to see what I couldn't).

Othello

Othello *Othello* (1603–04), one of a succession of tragic masterpieces that Shakespeare wrote in the early years of the seventeenth century, is unrivaled in its excruciating intensity. With its almost clinical account of a malevolent assault on love and beauty, the play has for centuries aroused in audiences the paradoxical blend of pleasure and acute discomfort characteristic of great tragedy. The performance history of *Othello* includes anecdotes of spectators attempting to intervene by angrily denouncing the villain, shouting advice to the deceived hero, or even rushing onstage to save the doomed heroine. If such stories reveal a fundamental misunderstanding of the nature of theater, they also disclose Shakespeare's brilliant exploitation of the gap between the performers and the audience. We see what is happening; we understand where it is leading; we urgently want to prevent the catastrophe—but, as in a nightmare, we are powerless to do so. *Othello* is a prime instance of what a twentieth-century writer, Antonin Artaud, called "the theater of cruelty."

This cruelty is intensified by the fact that the plot of Shakespeare's tragedy is woven from some of the elements of the joyous comedies in which he had already distinguished himself. *Othello* begins with a miniature version of the traditional comedy of sexual fulfillment. Refusing to allow his daughter to elope with the man of her choosing, an angry father, wellborn, wealthy, and powerful, lodges a formal complaint before the authorities. His daughter, he alleges, has been seduced by means of witchcraft; otherwise, she would never have been attracted to someone so far below her in social class and culture. At first the authorities—the senators of the Venetian Republic—seem inclined to agree, but after hearing testimony from the couple in question, Othello and Desdemona, they dismiss the father's complaint. The rigid hold of the older generation over the desires of the next is broken, paternal possessiveness is defeated, and romantic love triumphs over familial bonds. And lest this triumph should seem to threaten the social order, the romantic couple is legitimated by marriage, the newlywed husband makes clear his devotion to serving the state in its war against the Ottoman Turks, and the spouse who at first seemed socially unsuitable turns out to be the equal of his amorous conquest. "I fetch my life and being," Othello declares, "From men of royal siege" (1.2.21–22). All's well that ends well.

But, of course, it does not end well. Disturbing elements, also with roots in comedy, have already begun to surface in the first scenes. One of these is the familiar farce of January and May: the old man married to the much younger wife who is courted by handsome, unscrupulous suitors. Another is what we might call the comedy of fantastical passion: the person who awakens from the trance of love to find that the object of desire is in fact ridiculous. Still another is the braggart soldier, the preening, self-promoting hero who is revealed to be an empty shell. And yet another is the mocking of the alien, the collective ridiculing of an outsider who hopes to be accepted but whom the natives despise as outlandish, gullible, and grotesque.

There is one person who is particularly sensitive to all of these cruel comic undertones: Othello's devious, resentful third-in-command, Iago. Unable to derail Othello's elopement, Iago seizes on potentially destructive versions of Othello and Desdemona's story. Desdemona fell in love with Othello merely for his bragging, he tells the lovesick Roderigo, but she will soon realize her mistake and long for someone younger, more handsome, more appropriate. When Roderigo doubts that Desdemona can be so easily seduced—"I cannot believe that in her; she's full of most blessed condition"—Iago replies with the cynic's tough, deflating realism: "Blessed fig's-end! The wine she drinks is made of grapes" (2.1.246–49).

The problem for Iago, though, is that none of these conventional comic scenarios seems very promising. Desdemona shows no sign of restlessness with her choice, nor does she register any discomfort with the age difference between herself and her husband. Othello's martial heroism is the real thing, attested to by everyone and elegantly manifested in the serene self-confidence with which he greets the armed followers of his irate father-in-law: "Keep up your bright swords, for the dew will rust them" (1.2.59). It is true that he initially allured Desdemona with exotic tales from

"Men whose heads / Do grow beneath their shoulders" (*Othello* 1.3.143–44), in an engraving by Jodocus Hondius from a 1599 edition of Ralegh's *Discovery of Guiana*. These creatures, known as Blemmyes or Ewaipanoma, are reported as well in *Mandeville's Travels*.

what he calls "the story of my life" (1.3.128), but the bond between them is anything but superficial: consecrating her "soul and fortunes" to her husband, she declares that her "heart's subdued / Even to the very quality of my lord" (1.3.252, 248–49).

The strongest weapon in Iago's arsenal is racism, the contempt and revulsion with which many Europeans in the Middle Ages and the Renaissance routinely stigmatized dark skin and African features. This attitude is also reflected in a document issued by Queen Elizabeth in 1601, complaining about the "great numbers of . . . Blackamoors" who "are crept into this realm." Denouncing these unwelcome people as "infidels, having no understanding of Christ or his Gospel," the queen authorized their deportation (though it is not clear that any such expulsion was carried out). In the tragedy Shakespeare wrote only a few years after this order, his hero is a Moor, whether that refers to an origin in North Africa or in sub-Saharan Africa, and this identity is enough to trigger the vile abuse Iago and Roderigo shout in the darkness in the first moments of the play. Othello is an "old black ram," "a Barbary horse" (1.1.85, 108).

But even this weapon seems blunted. Othello is not a religious outsider, but a Christian. He is the valiant commander to whom the state of Venice turns when it needs to defend its strategic outpost Cyprus against the great Muslim enemy, the Turks. Racial slurs in this play are the hallmarks of viciousness, not the collective judgment of the community. As for Desdemona, her declaration that she "saw Othello's visage in her mind" (1.3.250) suggests, among other things, that her husband's skin is not relevant to the great love that unites them.

How then does Iago do it? How does he succeed in undermining Othello's absolute faith in his wife and in shattering what seems an unshakable bond? Shakespeare depicts the destruction in one of the greatest scenes he ever wrote, a quiet conversation between the two men. The Turkish threat has vanished, blown away by a storm; Othello and Desdemona have been safely reunited in Cyprus; and though a drunken brawl in the night (cunningly instigated by Iago) has temporarily disgraced Othello's lieutenant Cassio, all the significant obstacles to harmony both public and private have been resolved. At this moment of almost perfect security, Iago injects the fatal poison of jealousy into Othello by little more than the intonation of the simple word "indeed" (3.3.101). Without leveling any direct accusation or offering a shred of evidence, with only a succession of apparently naive questions and broken phrases, Iago manages to insert himself into and remake—indeed, destroy—Othello's whole world.

Othello is not naive. He grasps that the verbal feints and dodges Iago is performing could "in a false disloyal knave" (3.3.124) be tricks designed to take in the gullible. But he knows Iago well, he thinks, and has confidence in his honesty. Tormented by the unbearable pain of aroused jealousy, Othello demands "ocular proof" (3.3.361) of Desdemona's adultery with Cassio. Iago, who has been promoted to lieutenant in Cassio's place, then embarks on a devious set of deceptions, centered on an embroidered handkerchief, a gift from Othello, that Desdemona has inadvertently mislaid. "Trifles light as air," Iago gleefully observes, "Are to the jealous confirmations strong / As proofs of holy writ" (3.3.323–25).

What is Iago's motive? Why should he want to destroy Othello, on whom his livelihood depends, and Desdemona, whom his own wife, Emilia, serves as lady's maid? Early in the play Iago presents himself as someone with an eye only for his own interests: "not I for love and duty, / But seeming so, for my peculiar end" (1.1.56–57). But it is difficult to make out how ruining his commander could help Iago. What is his peculiar—that is, personal—end?

As was his usual practice, Shakespeare did not make up the plot of his play from scratch but instead adapted it—in this case, from a short story by the sixteenth-century Italian writer Giraldi Cinthio. In Cinthio's account the villain's pathology is reasonably clear. Having fallen ardently in love with Desdemona, he tried to seduce her. When he did not succeed, the love he felt for the general's wife turned into violent loathing, and he set about to destroy her. Shakespeare discards this motivation. His villain does not dream of possessing Othello's wife, nor is she the particular object of his hatred. To be sure, there is a moment in which Iago seems to be heading in this direction—"Now I do love her too" (2.1.287), he declares in one of his sinister soliloquies—yet he immediately veers away from it toward a farrago of other explanations. Iago's repeated attempts to account for his obsessive, unappeasable hatred of Othello are famously unconvincing. Coleridge called them "the motive-hunting of motiveless malignity." Near the play's end, when he has come to understand that he has been duped into murdering his innocent, loving wife and that his life has been destroyed in the cruelest imaginable way, Othello asks why Iago "hath thus ensnared my soul and body?" Iago's spare, monosyllabic reply—his last utterance in the play—is a refusal to apologize or explain: "What you know, you know. / From this time forth I never will speak word" (5.2.307–9).

But why does Othello succumb? Why should a passion on which he has staked his whole being—"when I love thee not, / Chaos is come again" (3.3.91–92)—prove so fragile? Why should he doubt the faith of a woman so obviously single-minded in her devotion to him and so absolute in her love? The answer in part seems to lie in the terrible vulnerability of trust. As Iago coolly observes, Othello "[i]s of a constant, loving, noble nature" (2.1.285). That nature is bound up with his capacity to cherish his friends, rely on his subordinates, and, above all, open his whole soul to his wife: "My life upon her faith!" (1.3.293). But such openness makes it possible for Iago to penetrate Othello's psychic defenses and refashion his perceptions.

Though Iago has a coarse and reductive account of human nature, he is a brilliant improviser, able to employ whatever comes to hand to shape illusions and to manipulate those around him like puppets in a theatrical performance of his making. He bustles about using people without a trace of moral restraint, shame, or decency, and he has the peculiar liberty of complete fraudulence: "I am not what I am" (1.1.62). In the end, he is exposed—by the wife whom he despises, abuses, and finally murders—but not before he has ruined whatever seemed most beautiful and precious in his world. Such is the power of cunning lies and twisted hatred over someone "that loved not wisely but too well" (5.2.349).

But perhaps this characterization of himself, offered by Othello just before his suicide, is not quite right, or at least not complete. Perhaps there is something disturbing in his love—some strain of anxiety about the future, about sexual pleasure, about his capacity for happiness—that Iago senses he can exploit. "If it were now to die," Othello has declared at the height of his joy,

> 'Twere now to be most happy; for I fear
> My soul hath her content so absolute
> That not another comfort like to this
> Succeeds in unknown fate. (2.1.187–91)

Desdemona attempts to offer reassurance—"The heavens forbid / But that our loves and comforts should increase / Even as our days do grow" (2.1.191–93)—but the malevolent worm of Iago's doubt is more powerful than her generous embrace. Or is it? Desdemona struggles in her last breath to commend herself to her "kind lord" (5.2.128), and Othello, desperately attempting to reestablish a moral order by executing himself, dies kissing the wife whose innocence he knows he has fatally wronged. Readers and audiences have, for more than four centuries, pondered how much these final gestures offer a glimpse of redemption through boundless love.

The Tragedy of Othello, the Moor of Venice*

The Names of the Actors[1]

OTHELLO, the Moor [and General of the Venetian forces]
BRABANTIO, father to Desdemona [and a Venetian Senator]
CASSIO, an honorable lieutenant [to Othello]
IAGO, a villain [and Othello's standard-bearer or ensign]
RODERIGO, a gulled° gentleman   *deceived*
DUKE of Venice
SENATORS
MONTANO, Governor of Cyprus
GENTLEMEN of Cyprus
LODOVICO and GRATIANO, two Noble Venetians [and kinsmen to Brabantio]
SAILORS
OFFICERS
CLOWN
DESDEMONA, wife to Othello
EMILIA, wife to Iago
BIANCA, a courtesan
MESSENGERS
MUSICIANS

---

*Othello exists in two early texts, both of which have a claim to authority: a version published in the small, inexpensive quarto format in 1622 (Q) and a version published in the great First Folio of 1623 (F). There are many small and some substantial differences between them, including 160 lines that are found only in F. The text printed here is adapted from the Norton Critical Edition of *Othello*, edited by Edward Pechter. Like most modern editors of the play, Pechter bases his text on F, corrected by some readings from Q. Significant departures from Pechter's text have been footnoted.

1. The list of characters (with its misleading title) is reproduced from the First Folio, with some bracketed additions.

1.1

Enter RODERIGO *and* IAGO.[1]

RODERIGO Tush, never tell me![2] I take it much unkindly
That thou, Iago, who hast had my purse
As if the strings were thine, shouldst know of this.

IAGO 'Sblood,° but you'll not hear me! If ever I did dream   *by Christ's blood*
Of such a matter, abhor me.

RODERIGO   Thou told'st me
Thou didst hold him in thy hate.

IAGO   Despise me
If I do not. Three great ones of the city,
In personal suit to make me his lieutenant,
Off-capped° to him; and by the faith of man   *took off their caps*
I know my price; I am worth no worse a place.
But he, as loving his own pride and purposes,
Evades them with a bombast circumstance,[3]
Horribly stuffed with epithets of war,°   *military jargon*
Non-suits° my mediators. For "Certes,"° says he,   *denies / certainly*
"I have already chose my officer." And what was he?
Forsooth, a great arithmetician,[4]
One Michael Cassio, a Florentine,
A fellow almost damned in a fair wife,[5]
That° never set a squadron in the field,   *who*
Nor the division° of a battle° knows   *ordering / battalion*
More than a spinster°—unless the bookish theoric,°   *housewife / learning*
Wherein the tonguèd consuls can propose[6]
As masterly as he. Mere prattle without practice
Is all his soldiership. But he, sir, had th'election
And I—of whom his eyes had seen the proof
At Rhodes, at Cyprus, and on other grounds,
Christened and heathen—must be beleed° and calmed[7]   *without wind*
By debitor and creditor. This counter-caster,[8]
He in good time° must his lieutenant be,   *indeed (scornful)*
And I—God bless the mark!°—his Moorship's ancient.[9]   *God help us*

RODERIGO By heaven, I rather would have been his
   hangman.

IAGO Why, there's no remedy. 'Tis the curse of service;
Preferment goes by letter and affection,[1]

1.1 Location: A street in Venice.
1. Iago's name may be related to that of Santiago Matamoros (Saint James the Moor-Slayer), the patron saint of Spain.
2. Expressive of annoyance, disbelief.
3. With an inflated circumlocution. "Bombast": cotton padding in clothes, a metaphor picked up by "stuffed" (line 13) and perhaps "Non-suits" (line 14).
4. Implying that Cassio's knowledge of war is purely theoretical.
5. Obscure. Cassio has not yet met Bianca and is *unmarried* (although in Shakespeare's source he is married). Perhaps Shakespeare's error, a reference to Cassio as a ladies' man, or an oblique anticipation of the main plot.
6. In which the glib senators can debate. In Q the senators are not "tonguèd" but "togaed," that is, toga-wearing.
7. Becalmed.
8. Pejorative term for an accountant (Cassio), as is "debitor and creditor."
9. A variant form of ensign. Iago is something like a standard-bearer or third-in-command. He clearly ranks below "lieutenant" Cassio, the second-in-command. This reference to "his Moorship" is also the first indication of the person about whom Iago has been complaining.
1. Promotion comes through connections and favoritism.

And not by old gradation,° where each second — *traditional seniority*
Stood heir to th'first. Now, sir, be judge yourself
Whether I in any just term am affined° — *am bound in any just way*
To love the Moor.²

RODERIGO   I would not follow him then.

IAGO   O, sir, content you.° — *be content*
I follow him to serve my turn upon him.
We cannot all be masters, nor all masters
Cannot be truly followed. You shall mark
Many a duteous and knee-crooking knave
That, doting on his own obsequious bondage,
Wears out his time much like his master's ass,
For naught but provender;° and when he's old— — *animal feed*
    cashiered.° — *fired*
Whip me° such honest knaves! Others there are — *the hell with*
Who, trimmed° in forms and visages of duty, — *outwardly decorated*
Keep yet their hearts attending on themselves
And, throwing but shows of service on their lords,
Do well thrive by them; and when they have lined their
    coats,
Do themselves homage. These fellows have some soul,
And such a one do I profess myself. For, sir,
It is as sure as you are Roderigo,
Were I the Moor, I would not be Iago.
In following him, I follow but myself.
Heaven is my judge, not I for° love and duty, — *I am not driven by*
But seeming so, for my peculiar° end. — *personal*
For when my outward action doth demonstrate
The native act and figure³ of my heart
In complement extern,° 'tis not long after — *outward appearance*
But I will wear my heart upon my sleeve
For daws° to peck at. I am not what I am. — *crowlike birds*

RODERIGO   What a full fortune does the thick-lips owe° — *own*
If he can carry't thus!

IAGO   Call up her father,
Rouse him, make after him, poison his delight.
Proclaim him in the streets, incense her kinsmen,
And though he in a fertile climate dwell,
Plague him with flies. Though that his joy be joy,
Yet throw such chances of vexation on't,
As it may lose some color.

RODERIGO   Here is her father's house. I'll call aloud.

IAGO   Do, with like timorous accent° and dire yell — *frightening tone*

---

2. A Muslim of the mixed Berber and Arab people inhabiting northwest Africa. This term, like the comparison of Othello to a "Barbary horse" (an Arab, line 108), formerly led to the denial of Othello's blackness. But the passages describing Othello's appearance—"thick-lips," "black ram," "sooty bosom," "black Othello," "I am black," "black / As mine own face" (1.1.63, 85; 1.2.70; 2.3.29; 3.3.265, 388–89)—seem to have greater weight. In the Renaissance, "Moor" often meant sub-Saharan African.
3. The innate operation (or motivation) and shape (or nature).

          As when, by night and negligence, the fire
          Is spied in populous cities.
75   RODERIGO   What ho, Brabantio! Signor Brabantio, ho!
      IAGO   Awake! What ho, Brabantio! Thieves, thieves!
          Look to your house, your daughter, and your bags!
          Thieves, thieves!
                    [*Enter*] BRABANTIO *above at a window.*
      BRABANTIO   What is the reason of this terrible summons?
80   What is the matter there?
      RODERIGO   Signor, is all your family within?
      IAGO   Are your doors locked?
      BRABANTIO   Why? Wherefore ask you this?
      IAGO   'Swounds,° sir, you're robbed! For shame, put on   *by Christ's wounds*
          your gown!
          Your heart is burst, you have lost half your soul.
85   Even now, now, very now, an old black ram
          Is tupping° your white ewe. Arise, arise!   *copulating with*
          Awake the snorting° citizens with the bell,   *snoring*
          Or else the devil will make a grandsire of you.
          Arise, I say!
      BRABANTIO   What, have you lost your wits?
90   RODERIGO   Most reverend signor, do you know my voice?
      BRABANTIO   Not I; what are you?
      RODERIGO   My name is Roderigo.
      BRABANTIO   The worser welcome!
          I have charged thee not to haunt about my doors;
          In honest plainness thou hast heard me say
95   My daughter is not for thee. And now in madness,
          Being full of supper and distemp'ring° draughts,   *destabilizing*
          Upon malicious bravery,° dost thou come   *defiance*
          To start° my quiet.   *upset*
      RODERIGO   Sir, sir, sir—
      BRABANTIO   But thou must needs be sure,
100   My spirits and my place° have in their power   *rank*
          To make this bitter to thee.
      RODERIGO   Patience, good sir.
      BRABANTIO   What tell'st thou me of robbing? This is
          Venice;
          My house is not a grange.°   *country house*
      RODERIGO   Most grave Brabantio,
          In simple and pure soul, I come to you.
105   IAGO   'Swounds, sir, you are one of those that will not
          serve God if the devil bid you. Because we come to do you
          service and you think we are ruffians, you'll have your
          daughter covered with a Barbary horse;[4] you'll have
          your nephews° neigh to you; you'll have coursers for   *grandsons*
110   cousins and jennets for germans.[5]

---

4. Horse from northwest coastal Africa.
5. Close relatives. "Coursers": strong horses. "Cousins": kinsmen. "Jennets": small Spanish horses.

BRABANTIO   What profane wretch art thou?
IAGO   I am one, sir, that comes to tell you your daughter
and the Moor are making the beast with two backs.°   *copulating*
BRABANTIO   Thou art a villain.
IAGO   You are a senator.
BRABANTIO   This thou shalt answer.° I know thee,   *account for*
    Roderigo.
RODERIGO   Sir, I will answer anything. But I beseech you,
    If't be your pleasure, and most wise consent—⁶
    As partly I find it is—that your fair daughter,
    At this odd-even° and dull watch o'th' night,   *late (around midnight)*
    Transported with no worse nor better guard
    But with a knave of common° hire, a gondolier,   *public*
    To the gross clasps of a lascivious Moor—
    If this be known to you, and your allowance,°   *allowed by you*
    We then have done you bold and saucy wrongs.
    But if you know not this, my manners tell me
    We have your wrong rebuke. Do not believe
    That from° the sense of all civility   *in opposition to*
    I thus would play and trifle with your reverence.
    Your daughter, if you have not given her leave,
    I say again, hath made a gross revolt,
    Tying her duty, beauty, wit, and fortunes
    In an extravagant and wheeling stranger⁷
    Of here and everywhere. Straight° satisfy yourself.   *immediately*
    If she be in her chamber or your house,
    Let loose on me the justice of the state
    For thus deluding you.
BRABANTIO   Strike on the tinder,° ho!   *a light*
    Give me a taper,° call up all my people!   *candle*
    This accident° is not unlike my dream;   *event*
    Belief of it oppresses me already.
    Light, I say, light!   *Exit [above].*
IAGO   Farewell, for I must leave you.
    It seems not meet° nor wholesome to my place   *proper*
    To be produced°—as, if I stay, I shall—   *presented as witness*
    Against the Moor. For I do know the state,
    However this may gall him with some check,°   *reprimand*
    Cannot with safety cast° him; for he's embarked°   *dismiss / committed*
    With such loud° reason to the Cyprus wars,   *urgent*
    Which even now stands in act,° that, for their souls,   *are taking place*
    Another of his fathom° they have none   *caliber*
    To lead their business. In which regard,
    Though I do hate him as I do hell pains,
    Yet for necessity of present life
    I must show out a flag and sign of love,

---

6. Lines 118–34 do not appear in Q.
7. In a vagrant and vagabond foreigner.

  Which is indeed but sign. That you shall surely find
   him,
155 Lead to the Sagittary⁸ the raisèd search,°   *awakened searchers*
  And there will I be with him. So farewell.   *Exit.*
    Enter [below] BRABANTIO *in his nightgown, with*
     servants and torches
  BRABANTIO It is too true an evil. Gone she is,
  And what's to come of my despisèd time°   *lifetime*
  Is naught but bitterness. Now, Roderigo,
160 Where didst thou see her?—O unhappy girl!—
  With the Moor, say'st thou?—Who would be a father?—
  How didst thou know 'twas she?—O, she deceives me
  Past thought!—What said she to you?— *[to servants]* Get
   more tapers,
  Raise all my kindred!   *[Exit one or more.]*
  [to RODERIGO*]*   Are they married, think you?
165 RODERIGO Truly, I think they are.
  BRABANTIO O heaven! How got she out? O treason of
   the blood!
  Fathers, from hence trust not your daughters' minds
  By what you see them act. Is there not charms°   *magic*
  By which the property° of youth and maidhood°   *attribute / virginity*
170 May be abused? Have you not read, Roderigo,
  Of some such thing?
  RODERIGO   Yes, sir, I have indeed.
  BRABANTIO *[to servants]* Call up my brother.
  [to RODERIGO*]*   O, would you had had her!
  [to servants] Some one way, some another.
          [Exit one or more.]
  [to RODERIGO*]*   Do you know
  Where we may apprehend her and the Moor?
175 RODERIGO I think I can discover him, if you please
  To get good guard and go along with me.
  BRABANTIO Pray you lead on. At every house I'll call;
  I may command° at most.—Get weapons, ho!   *demand help*
  And raise some special officers of night.—
180 On, good Roderigo; I will deserve° your pains.   *reward*
         Exeunt.

1.2

   Enter OTHELLO, IAGO, *[and] attendants with torches.*
  IAGO Though in the trade of war I have slain men,
  Yet do I hold it very stuff° o'th' conscience   *essence*
  To do no contrived° murder. I lack iniquity,   *premeditated*

---

8. Perhaps indicating an inn named for the astrological sign *Sagittarius*, where Othello and Desdemona are staying. It may also suggest Othello himself, because Sagittarius is depicted as a centaur (a mythological being part man, part horse), and Iago has already likened Othello to a "Barbary horse."
1.2 Location: Another street in Venice, before Othello's lodgings.

Sometime, to do me service. Nine or ten times
I had thought t'have yerked him° here, under the ribs. — stabbed (Roderigo)
OTHELLO 'Tis better as it is.
IAGO   Nay, but he prated
And spoke such scurvy and provoking terms
Against your honor
That, with the little godliness I have,
I did full hard forbear him.[1] But I pray you, sir,
Are you fast° married? Be assured of this, — legitimately
That the magnifico° is much beloved, — (Brabantio)
And hath in his effect a voice potential° — powerful
As double as the duke's. He will divorce you,
Or put upon you what restraint or grievance
The law, with all his might to enforce it on,
Will give him cable.° — scope
OTHELLO   Let him do his spite.
My services, which I have done the signory,° — Venetian government
Shall out-tongue his complaints. 'Tis yet to know°— — not publicly known
Which, when I know that boasting is an honor,
I shall promulgate—I fetch my life and being
From men of royal siege;° and my demerits° — rank / deserts
May speak unbonneted[2] to as proud a fortune
As this that I have reached. For know, Iago,
But that I love the gentle Desdemona,
I would not my unhousèd° free condition — unconfined
Put into circumscription and confine
For the seas' worth. But look, what lights come yond?
    Enter CASSIO, *with officers and torches.*
IAGO Those are the raisèd father and his friends.
You were best go in.
OTHELLO   Not I; I must be found.
My parts,° my title, and my perfect soul[3] — qualities
Shall manifest me rightly. Is it they?
IAGO By Janus,° I think no. — two-faced Roman god
OTHELLO The servants of the duke? And my lieutenant?
The goodness of the night upon you, friends.
What is the news?
CASSIO   The duke does greet you, general,
And he requires your haste-post-haste appearance
Even on the instant.
OTHELLO   What is the matter, think you?
CASSIO Something from Cyprus, as I may divine.
It is a business of some heat.° The galleys — urgency
Have sent a dozen sequent° messengers — successive
This very night at one another's heels,
And many of the consuls, raised and met,
Are at the duke's already. You have been hotly called for;

1. I barely restrained myself from attacking him.   3. My clear conscience.
2. Without deference; modestly.

	When, being not at your lodging to be found,	
45	The senate hath sent about° three several quests	*out*
	To search you out.	

OTHELLO   'Tis well I am found by you.
　　I will but spend a word here in the house
　　And go with you.   [*Exit.*]
CASSIO   Ancient, what makes he here?
50　IAGO   Faith, he tonight hath boarded a land-carrack.[4]
　　If it prove lawful prize, he's made forever.
CASSIO   I do not understand.
IAGO   He's married.
CASSIO   To who?

IAGO Marry,° to— [*Enter* OTHELLO.]	*by Mary (a mild oath)*
Come, captain, will you go?	
OTHELLO Have with you.°	*let's go*

CASSIO   Here comes another troop to seek for you.
　　　Enter BRABANTIO [*and*] RODERIGO, *with officers and
　　　torches.*
55　IAGO   It is Brabantio; general, be advised,
　　He comes to bad intent.
OTHELLO   Holla, stand there!
RODERIGO   Signor, it is the Moor.
BRABANTIO   Down with him, thief!
　　[*They draw on both sides.*]
IAGO   You, Roderigo? Come, sir, I am for you.

OTHELLO Keep up° your bright swords, for the dew will	*put away*
rust them.	

60　Good signor, you shall more command with years
　　Than with your weapons.
BRABANTIO   O thou foul thief, where hast thou stowed
　　my daughter?
　　Damned as thou art, thou hast enchanted her;
　　For I'll refer me to all things of sense,[5]
65　If she in chains of magic were not bound,
　　Whether a maid, so tender, fair, and happy,
　　So opposite to marriage that she shunned
　　The wealthy curlèd darlings of our nation,
　　Would ever have, t'incur a general mock,
70　Run from her guardage to the sooty bosom
　　Of such a thing as thou—to fear, not to delight.
　　Judge me the world if 'tis not gross in sense[6]
　　That thou hast practiced on her with foul charms,
　　Abused her delicate youth with drugs or minerals

That weakens motion.° I'll have't disputed on;[7]	*natural inclination*
'Tis probable and palpable to thinking.	
I therefore apprehend and do attach° thee	*arrest*

　　For an abuser of the world, a practicer

---

4. A carrack is a large merchant ship.
5. For I'll ask, relying on common sense.
6. If it is not patently obvious. Lines 72–77 do not appear in Q.
7. Argued by experts.

Of arts inhibited and out of warrant.° *prohibited and illegal*
80 Lay hold upon him; if he do resist,
Subdue him at his peril!
OTHELLO   Hold your hands,
Both you of my inclining° and the rest. *following*
Were it my cue to fight, I should have known it
Without a prompter. Where will you that I go
To answer this your charge?
85 BRABANTIO   To prison, till fit time
Of law and course of direct session
Call thee to answer.
OTHELLO   What if I do obey?
How may the duke be therewith satisfied,
Whose messengers are here about my side
90 Upon some present business of the state
To bring me to him?
OFFICER   'Tis true, most worthy signor.
The duke's in council, and your noble self
I am sure is sent for.
BRABANTIO   How? The duke in council?
In this time of the night? Bring him away.° *along*
95 Mine's not an idle cause. The duke himself,
Or any of my brothers of the state,
Cannot but feel this wrong as 'twere their own;
For if such actions may have passage free,
Bondslaves and pagans shall our statesmen be.
Exeunt.

1.3

Enter DUKE *and* SENATORS *set at a table, with lights and* OFFICERS.

DUKE   There's no composition in this news
That gives them credit.[1]
FIRST SENATOR   Indeed, they are disproportioned;° *inconsistent*
My letters say a hundred and seven galleys.
DUKE   And mine a hundred forty.
SECOND SENATOR   And mine two hundred.
5 But though they jump not on a just account°— *don't exactly agree*
As in these cases where the aim reports
'Tis oft with difference[2]—yet do they all confirm
A Turkish fleet, and bearing up to Cyprus.
DUKE   Nay, it is possible enough to judgment;
10 I do not so secure me in the error
But the main article I do approve
In fearful sense.[3]

1.3 Location: A Venetian council room.
1. The reports lack the consistency that would make them believable.
2. "Where . . . difference": where the reports are estimates, there are often discrepancies among them.
3. "I do not . . . sense": I am not so reassured by the discrepancies as to dismiss the main concern—the approach of a Turkish fleet.

SAILOR [*within*]　　　　　What ho! what ho! what ho!
　　　Enter SAILOR.
OFFICER　A messenger from the galleys.
DUKE　　　　　　　　　　　　　Now, what's the business?
SAILOR　The Turkish preparation° makes for Rhodes.　　*battle-ready fleet*
15　So was I bid report here to the state
　　By Signor Angelo.[4]
DUKE　How say you by this change?
FIRST SENATOR　　　　　　　　This cannot be
　　By no assay° of reason. 'Tis a pageant　　　　　　　*test*
　　To keep us in false gaze. When we consider
20　Th' importancy of Cyprus to the Turk,
　　And let ourselves again but understand
　　That, as it more concerns the Turk than Rhodes,
　　So may he with more facile question bear it,[5]
　　For that it stands not in such warlike brace,
25　But altogether lacks th'abilities
　　That Rhodes is dressed in—if we make thought of this,
　　We must not think the Turk is so unskillful
　　To leave that latest° which concerns him first,　　*last*
　　Neglecting an attempt of ease and gain
30　To wake and wage° a danger profitless.　　　　　　*risk*
DUKE　Nay, in all confidence, he's not for Rhodes.
OFFICER　Here is more news.
　　　Enter a MESSENGER.
MESSENGER　The Ottomites,° reverend and gracious,[6]　　*Ottoman Turks*
　　Steering with due course toward the isle of Rhodes,
35　Have there injointed them with an after° fleet.　　*joined with another*
FIRST SENATOR　Ay, so I thought. How many, as you guess?
MESSENGER　Of thirty sail; and now they do re-stem°　　*retrace*
　　Their backward course, bearing with frank appearance
　　Their purposes toward Cyprus. Signor Montano,
40　Your trusty and most valiant servitor,
　　With his free duty recommends you thus,[7]
　　And prays you to believe him.
DUKE　'Tis certain then for Cyprus.
　　Marcus Luccicos[8]—is not he in town?
45　FIRST SENATOR　He's now in Florence.
DUKE　Write from us to him post-post-haste. Dispatch!
FIRST SENATOR　Here comes Brabantio and the valiant
　　Moor.
　　　Enter BRABANTIO, OTHELLO, CASSIO, IAGO, RODERIGO,
　　　and OFFICERS.
DUKE　Valiant Othello, we must straight° employ you　　*immediately*

---

4. Not mentioned elsewhere in the play, Angelus Sorianus was a Venetian sea captain who received the Venetian ambassador bearing from Constantinople the Turkish ultimatum to surrender Cyprus, shortly before its capture by the Turks in 1571.

5. So also can the Turkish fleet more easily win it.
6. Addressed to the senators.
7. With his freely given loyalty reports to you thus.
8. Not mentioned elsewhere in the play.

Against the general enemy° Ottoman.   (*of all Christendom*) — general enemy° *noble*

50 [*to* BRABANTIO] I did not see you; welcome, gentle°   *noble*
signor.
We lacked your counsel and your help tonight.
BRABANTIO   So did I yours. Good your grace, pardon me.
Neither my place° nor aught I heard of business   *official duty*
Hath raised me from my bed; nor doth the general care
55 Take hold on me. For my particular grief
Is of so floodgate and o'erbearing nature
That it englutts and swallows other sorrows,
And it is still itself.⁹
DUKE   Why, what's the matter?
BRABANTIO   My daughter, O my daughter!
SENATOR   Dead?
BRABANTIO   Ay, to me.
60 She is abused,° stol'n from me and corrupted   *deluded*
By spells and medicines bought of mountebanks;°   *quacks*
For nature so preposterously to err,
Being not deficient, blind, or lame of sense,
Sans° witchcraft could not.   *without*
65 DUKE Whoe'er he be that in this foul proceeding
Hath thus beguiled your daughter of herself
And you of her, the bloody book of law
You shall yourself read in the bitter letter
After your own sense; yea, though our proper son
Stood in your action.¹
70 BRABANTIO   Humbly I thank your grace.
Here is the man, this Moor, whom now it seems
Your special mandate for the state affairs
Hath hither brought.
ALL   We are very sorry for't.
DUKE [*to* OTHELLO]   What in your own part can you say
to this?
75 BRABANTIO   Nothing, but this is so.
OTHELLO   Most potent, grave, and reverend signors,
My very noble and approved good masters:
That I have ta'en away this old man's daughter
It is most true; true I have married her.
80 The very head and front° of my offending   *height and breadth*
Hath this extent, no more. Rude° am I in my speech,   *unpolished*
And little blessed with the soft phrase of peace;
For since these arms of mine had seven years' pith°   *strength*
Till now some nine moons wasted,° they have used   *nine months ago*
85 Their dearest° action in the tented field;   *most valued*
And little of this great world can I speak
More than pertains to feats of broils° and battle,   *combats*
And therefore little shall I grace my cause

---

9. That it (my grief) can incorporate other sorrows without being affected.
1. That is, you yourself shall interpret the law as you see fit, even if my own son was the one you accuse.

In speaking for myself. Yet, by your gracious patience,
I will a round° unvarnished tale deliver,   *plain*
Of my whole course of love: what drugs, what charms,
What conjuration and what mighty magic—
For such proceeding I am charged withal°—   *with*
I won his daughter.

BRABANTIO   A maiden never bold;
Of spirit so still and quiet that her motion
Blushed at herself[2] and she—in spite of nature,
Of years, of country, credit,° everything—   *reputation*
To fall in love with what she feared to look on?
It is a judgment maimed and most imperfect
That will confess perfection so could err
Against all rules of nature, and must° be driven   *(we therefore) must*
To find out practices of cunning hell
Why this should be. I therefore vouch again
That with some mixtures powerful o'er the blood,°   *passions*
Or with some dram conjured° to this effect,   *enchanted dose*
He wrought upon her.

DUKE   To vouch this is no proof,
Without more wider and more overt test
Than these thin habits and poor likelihoods
Of modern seeming do prefer against him.[3]

SENATOR   But, Othello, speak;
Did you by indirect and forced courses°   *means*
Subdue and poison this young maid's affections?
Or came it by request and such fair question°   *conversation*
As soul to soul affordeth?

OTHELLO   I do beseech you
Send for the lady to the Sagittary,
And let her speak of me before her father.
If you do find me foul in her report,
The trust, the office I do hold of you,
Not only take away, but let your sentence
Even fall upon my life.

DUKE [to OFFICERS]   Fetch Desdemona hither.

OTHELLO   Ancient, conduct them; you best know the
    place.

                    Exit [IAGO and] two or three [attendants].
And till she come, as truly as to heaven
I do confess the vices of my blood,°   *sins of passion*
So justly to your grave ears I'll present
How I did thrive in this fair lady's love
And she in mine.

DUKE   Say it, Othello.

OTHELLO   Her father loved me, oft invited me,

---

2. "Her . . . herself": she blushed at herself at the slightest provocation.

3. "Without . . . him": without fuller and more direct testimony than mere appearances and conjecture based on currently popular beliefs against him.

                Still° questioned me the story of my life   *constantly*
                From year to year, the battles, sieges, fortunes
130   That I have past.
                I ran it through, even from my boyish days
                To th'very moment that he bade me tell it;
                Wherein I spoke of most disastrous chances,°   *events*
                Of moving accidents° by flood and field,   *events*
135   Of hair-breadth scapes i'th' imminent-deadly breach,[4]
                Of being taken by the insolent foe
                And sold to slavery, of my redemption thence
                And portance° in my traveler's history;   *conduct*
                Wherein of antars° vast and deserts idle,   *caves*
140   Rough quarries, rocks, and hills whose heads touch
                    heaven,
                It was my hint° to speak—such was my process° —   *occasion / story*
                And of the cannibals that each other eat,
                The anthropophagi,[5] and men whose heads
                Do grow beneath their shoulders. These things to hear
145   Would Desdemona seriously incline,
                But still the house affairs would draw her thence,
                Which ever as° she could with haste dispatch   *whenever*
                She'd come again and with a greedy ear
                Devour up my discourse; which I, observing,
150   Took once a pliant° hour and found good means   *convenient*
                To draw from her a prayer of earnest heart
                That I would all my pilgrimage dilate,°   *relate*
                Whereof by parcels she had something heard,
                But not intentively.° I did consent   *continuously*
155   And often did beguile her of her tears
                When I did speak of some distressful stroke
                That my youth suffered. My story being done,
                She gave me for my pains a world of kisses;[6]
                She swore in faith 'twas strange, 'twas passing° strange,   *exceptionally*
160   'Twas pitiful, 'twas wondrous pitiful.
                She wished she had not heard it, yet she wished
                That heaven had made her such a man.[7] She thanked me
                And bade me, if I had a friend that loved her,
                I should but teach him how to tell my story,
165   And that would woo her. Upon this hint I spake.
                She loved me for the dangers I had past,
                And I loved her that she did pity them.
                This only is the witchcraft I have used.
                Here comes the lady; let her witness it.
                    Enter DESDEMONA, IAGO, [*and*] *attendants.*

---

4. In the immediately life-threatening gaps in a fortification.
5. Man-eaters. The term is from the ancient Roman writer Pliny the Elder. Shakespeare was also indebted to the travel literature of the Middle Ages (*The Travels of Sir John Mandeville*) and the Renaissance (Hakluyt's *Principal Navigations*, among others).
6. F reads "kisses," Q "sighs." It is hard to explain "kisses" as a textual error.
7. Made such a man for her; made her into such a man.

DUKE I think this tale would win my daughter too.
    Good Brabantio, take up this mangled matter at the
      best.°   *make the best of this*
    Men do their broken weapons rather use,
    Than their bare hands.
BRABANTIO   I pray you hear her speak.
    If she confess that she was half the wooer,
    Destruction on my head if my bad blame
    Light on the man. Come hither, gentle mistress.
    Do you perceive in all this noble company
    Where most you owe obedience?
DESDEMONA   My noble father,
    I do perceive here a divided duty.
    To you I am bound for life and education;
    My life and education both do learn° me   *teach*
    How to respect you; you are the lord of duty;
    I am hitherto your daughter. But here's my husband;
    And so much duty as my mother showed
    To you, preferring you before her father,
    So much I challenge° that I may profess   *assert*
    Due to the Moor my lord.
BRABANTIO   God be with you; I have done.
    Please it° your grace, on to the state affairs;   *if it pleases*
    I had rather to adopt a child than get° it.   *beget*
    Come hither, Moor.
    I here do give thee that° with all my heart   *that which*
    Which, but° thou hast already, with all my heart   *except that*
    I would keep from thee. [*to* DESDEMONA] For your sake,
      jewel,
    I am glad at soul I have no other child,
    For thy escape would teach me tyranny
    To hang clogs[8] on them. I have done, my lord.
DUKE Let me speak like yourself and lay a sentence°   *draw a moral*
    Which, as a grise° or step, may help these lovers   *step*
    Into your favor.
    When remedies are past, the griefs are ended
    By seeing the worst, which late on hopes depended.[9]
    To mourn a mischief that is past and gone
    Is the next way to draw new mischief on.
    What cannot be preserved, when fortune takes,
    Patience her injury a mockery makes.[1]
    The robbed that smiles steals something from the thief;
    He robs himself that spends a bootless° grief.   *pointless*
BRABANTIO So let the Turk of Cyprus us beguile:
    We lose it not, so long as we can smile.

---

8. Blocks of wood tied to criminals' legs to keep them from escaping.
9. By seeing those things come to pass that caused grief in anticipation. The duke paints the moral in rhyming couplets, to which Brabantio replies in kind.
1. Patience laughs at what cannot be helped (and thus reduces the "injury").

210 He bears the sentence° well that nothing bears	*saying; judgment*
But the free comfort which from thence he hears.	
But he bears both the sentence and the sorrow	
That, to pay grief, must of poor patience borrow.	
These sentences, to sugar or to gall,°	*both sweet and bitter*
215 Being strong on both sides, are equivocal.	
But words are words; I never yet did hear	
That the bruised heart was piercèd[2] through the ear.	
I humbly beseech you proceed to th'affairs of state.	

DUKE The Turk with a most mighty preparation makes for
220   Cyprus. Othello, the fortitude of the place is best known
  to you; and though we have there a substitute of most
  allowed sufficiency,° yet opinion, a more sovereign mis- *known ability*
  tress of effects, throws a more safer voice on you.[3] You
  must therefore be content to slubber° the gloss of your *soil*
225   new fortunes with this more stubborn° and boisterous *rougher*
  expedition.

OTHELLO The tyrant custom, most grave senators,
  Hath made the flinty and steel couch of war
  My thrice-driven° bed of down. I do agnize° *sifted / acknowledge*
230 A natural and prompt alacrity
  I find in hardness,° and do undertake *hardship*
  This present wars against the Ottomites.
  Most humbly, therefore, bending to your state,° *authority*
  I crave fit disposition for my wife,
235 Due reference of place, and exhibition,[4]
  With such accommodation and besort° *suitable attendance*
  As levels with her breeding.

DUKE Why, at her father's.
BRABANTIO I will not have it so.
OTHELLO Nor I.
DESDEMONA Nor would I there reside,
240 To put my father in impatient thoughts
  By being in his eye. Most gracious duke,
  To my unfolding° lend your prosperous° ear, *proposal / receptive*
  And let me find a charter° in your voice *an authorization*
  T'assist my simpleness.

245 DUKE What would you, Desdemona?
DESDEMONA That I love the Moor to live with him,
  My downright violence and storm of fortunes[5]
  May trumpet to the world. My heart's subdued
  Even to the very quality[6] of my lord.
250 I saw Othello's visage in his mind,
  And to his honors and his valiant parts° *qualities*
  Did I my soul and fortunes consecrate;

---

2. Surgically lanced (and presumably cured).
3. "Opinion . . . you": public opinion, which determines what gets done, finds greater security with you.
4. Proper accommodation and maintenance.
5. My outright defiance of custom.
6. Essential nature. In the Quarto, Desdemona says that her heart is subdued to Othello's "utmost pleasure."

So that, dear lords, if I be left behind,
A moth of peace, and he go to the war,
The rites° for why I love him are bereft me,   *(of love); (of war?)*
And I a heavy interim shall support
By his dear absence. Let me go with him.
OTHELLO [*to the* DUKE]   Let her have your voice.
Vouch with me, heaven, I therefor beg it not
To please the palate of my appetite,
Nor to comply with heat° (the young affects[7]   *sexual passion*
In me defunct) and proper° satisfaction,   *personal; fitting*
But to be free° and bounteous to her mind;   *liberal*
And heaven defend your good souls that you think
I will your serious and great business scant
When she is with me. No, when light-winged toys°   *diversions*
Of feathered Cupid seel° with wanton dullness   *blind*
My speculative and officed instruments,[8]
That my disports° corrupt and taint my business,   *sexual pleasures*
Let housewives make a skillet of my helm,
And all indign° and base adversities   *undignified*
Make head against my estimation.[9]
DUKE   Be it as you shall privately determine,
Either for her stay or going. Th'affair cries haste,
And speed must answer it.
SENATOR   You must away tonight.
DESDEMONA   Tonight, my lord?
DUKE   This night.[1]
OTHELLO   With all my heart.
DUKE   At nine i'th' morning here we'll meet again.
Othello, leave some officer behind,
And he shall our commission bring to you,
And such things else of quality and respect°   *weight and importance*
As doth import° you.   *concern*
OTHELLO   So please your grace, my ancient;
A man he is of honesty[2] and trust.
To his conveyance I assign my wife,
With what else needful your good grace shall think
To be sent after me.
DUKE   Let it be so.
Good night to every one. [*to* BRABANTIO] And, noble signor,
If virtue no delighted° beauty lack,   *delightful*
Your son-in-law is far more fair than black.
                                      [*Exit* DUKE.]
SENATOR   Adieu, brave Moor; use Desdemona well.
BRABANTIO   Look to her,° Moor, if thou hast eyes to see: *watch her carefully*
She has deceived her father, and may thee.

---

7. The youthful desires.
8. My duty-bound faculties of sense.
9. Raise an army against my good reputation.
1. This exchange between Desdemona and the Duke is only in Q.
2. The first of many references to Iago's "honesty."

Exeunt [BRABANTIO, CASSIO, SENATORS, *and* OFFICERS.]
OTHELLO My life upon her faith!—Honest Iago,
My Desdemona must I leave to thee.
I prithee let thy wife attend on her,
And bring them after in the best advantage.[3]
Come, Desdemona; I have but an hour
Of love, of worldly matter and direction
To spend with thee. We must obey the time.
Exeunt [OTHELLO *the*] *Moor and* DESDEMONA.
RODERIGO Iago?
IAGO What say'st thou, noble heart?
RODERIGO What will I do, think'st thou?
IAGO Why, go to bed and sleep.
RODERIGO I will incontinently° drown myself. — *immediately*
IAGO If thou dost, I shall never love thee after. Why, thou silly gentleman?
RODERIGO It is silliness to live when to live is torment; and then have we a prescription[4] to die when death is our physician.
IAGO O villainous!° I have looked upon the world for four — *absurd* times seven years, and since I could distinguish betwixt a benefit and an injury, I never found man that knew how to love himself. Ere I would say I would drown myself for the love of a guinea-hen,° I would change my humanity — *woman* with a baboon.
RODERIGO What should I do? I confess it is my shame to be so fond, but it is not in my virtue° to amend it. — *native ability*
IAGO Virtue? A fig!° 'Tis in ourselves that we are thus or — *(an obscenity)* thus. Our bodies are our gardens, to the which our wills are gardeners. So that if we will plant nettles or sow lettuce, set hyssop° and weed up thyme, supply it with one — *mint herb* gender° of herbs or distract it with many, either to have it — *kind* sterile with idleness° or manured with industry, why, the — *noncultivation* power and corrigible authority° of this lies in our wills. If — *ability to decide* the balance of our lives had not one scale of reason to poise° another of sensuality, the blood and baseness of — *counterweigh* our natures would conduct us to most preposterous conclusions. But we have reason to cool our raging motions,° — *appetites* our carnal stings or unbitted° lusts; whereof I take this — *unrestrained* that you call love to be a sect or scion.° — *offshoot*
RODERIGO It cannot be.
IAGO It is merely a lust of the blood and a permission of the will. Come, be a man! Drown thyself? Drown cats and blind puppies. I have professed me thy friend, and I confess me knit to thy deserving with cables of perdurable° — *durable* toughness. I could never better stead° thee than now. — *help* Put money in thy purse. Follow thou the wars; defeat thy

---

3. And bring them along at the most favorable moment.
4. Right; doctor's order.

favor with an usurped beard.[5] I say, put money in thy
purse. It cannot be long that Desdemona should continue her love to the Moor—put money in thy purse—
nor he his to her. It was a violent commencement[6] in
her, and thou shalt see an answerable sequestration[7]—
put but money in thy purse. These Moors are changeable in their wills—fill thy purse with money. The food
that to him now is as luscious as locusts[8] shall be to him
shortly as bitter as coloquintida.[9] She must change for
youth: when she is sated with his body, she will find
the error of her choice. Therefore, put money in thy
purse. If thou wilt needs° damn thyself, do it a more °*if you must*
delicate way than drowning—make all the money thou
canst. If sanctimony° and a frail vow betwixt an erring[1] °*holy rite*
barbarian and a super-subtle° Venetian be not too hard °*highly sensitive*
for my wits and all the tribe of hell, thou shalt enjoy
her. Therefore make money. A pox of drowning thyself;
it is clean out of the way.° Seek thou rather to be hanged °*of no use*
in compassing° thy joy than to be drowned and go with- °*encompassing*
out her.

RODERIGO Wilt thou be fast° to my hopes, if I depend on °*duty-bound*
the issue?° °*outcome*

IAGO Thou art sure of me—go make money. I have told
thee often, and I retell thee again and again, I hate the
Moor. My cause is hearted;° thine hath no less reason. °*heartfelt*
Let us be conjunctive° in our revenge against him. If thou °*joined*
canst cuckold him, thou dost thyself a pleasure, me a
sport. There are many events in the womb of time which
will be delivered. Traverse,° go, provide thy money. We °*go (to arms)*
will have more of this tomorrow. Adieu.

RODERIGO Where shall we meet i'th' morning?

IAGO At my lodging.

RODERIGO I'll be with thee betimes.° °*early*

IAGO Go to, farewell. Do you hear, Roderigo?

RODERIGO I'll sell all my land.   *Exit.*

IAGO Thus do I ever make my fool my purse;
For I mine own gained knowledge should profane
If I would time expend with such a snipe° °*fool*
But for my sport and profit. I hate the Moor,
And it is thought abroad° that 'twixt my sheets °*rumored*
H'as done my office. I know not if't be true,
But I for mere suspicion in that kind
Will do° as if for surety. He holds° me well; °*act / esteems*
The better shall my purpose work on him.
Cassio's a proper° man. Let me see now . . . °*handsome*

---

5. Disguise your appearance with a fake beard.
6. An abruptly begun affair.
7. A correspondingly abrupt separation.
8. A sweet, exotic fruit, perhaps carob or honey-suckle.
9. Colocynth, a purgative—one of Iago's many references to the digestive tract.
1. A wandering.

To get his place and to plume up° my will *gratify*
In double knavery—how? how? Let's see . . .
385 After some time, to abuse Othello's ears
That he is too familiar with his wife.[2]
He hath a person and a smooth dispose° *manner*
To be suspected, framed° to make women false. *formed*
The Moor is of a free° and open nature *liberal*
390 That thinks men honest that but seem to be so,
And will as tenderly° be led by th'nose *easily*
As asses are. . . .
I have't! It is engendered! Hell and night
Must bring this monstrous birth to the world's light. *Exit.*

2.1

Enter MONTANO *and two* GENTLEMEN *[one above].*

MONTANO What from the cape can you discern at sea?
FIRST GENTLEMAN Nothing at all; it is a high-wrought
  flood.[1] *very rough sea*
  I cannot 'twixt the heaven and the main° *sea*
  Descry° a sail. *discern*
5 MONTANO Methinks the wind hath spoke aloud at land;
  A fuller blast ne'er shook our battlements
  If it hath ruffianed° so upon the sea, *raged*
  What ribs of oak, when mountains melt on them,
  Can hold the mortise?[1] What shall we hear of this?
10 SECOND GENTLEMAN A segregation° of the Turkish fleet: *separation*
  For do but stand upon the foaming shore,
  The chidden billow[2] seems to pelt the clouds;
  The wind-shaked surge, with high and monstrous mane,
  Seems to cast water on the burning Bear
15 And quench the guards of th'ever-fixèd pole.[3]
  I never did like molestation view° *see such a tumult*
  On the enchafed° flood. *raging*
MONTANO   If that the Turkish fleet
  Be not ensheltered and embayed, they are drowned;
  It is impossible to bear it out.

  Enter a THIRD GENTLEMAN.

20 THIRD GENTLEMAN News, lads! Our wars are done.
  The desperate tempest hath so banged the Turks
  That their designment° halts. A noble ship of Venice *plan*
  Hath seen a grievous wrack and sufferance° *damage*
  On most part of their fleet.
MONTANO How? Is this true?

---

2. "He" is Cassio (as in line 387), but "his" refers to Othello.
2.1 Location: A seaport in Cyprus; outdoors near the harbor.
1. "What . . . mortise": what ship (with "ribs of oak") can hold its joints ("mortise") together when "mountains" of water pour on it?

2. The surging ocean, rebuked ("chidden") by the wind (or repulsed by the land).
3. The "burning Bear" is the constellation Ursa Minor; the "guards" are probably two stars in the constellation that point in a line to the polestar, also in Ursa Minor.

THIRD GENTLEMAN   The ship is here put in,
   A Veronnesa.[4] Michael Cassio,
   Lieutenant to the warlike Moor, Othello,
   Is come on shore; the Moor himself at sea,
   And is in full commission here for Cyprus.
MONTANO   I am glad on't—'tis a worthy governor.
THIRD GENTLEMAN   But this same Cassio, though he speak
      of comfort
   Touching the Turkish loss, yet he looks sadly°   *seriously*
   And prays the Moor be safe; for they were parted
   With foul and violent tempest.
MONTANO   Pray heavens he be,
   For I have served him, and the man commands
   Like a full soldier. Let's to the seaside—ho!—
   As well to see the vessel that's come in
   As to throw out our eyes for brave Othello,
   Even till we make the main and th'aerial blue
   An indistinct regard.[5]
THIRD GENTLEMAN   Come, let's do so;
   For every minute is expectancy
   Of more arrivance.
         Enter CASSIO.
CASSIO   Thanks, you the valiant of the warlike isle,
   That so approve the Moor! O, let the heavens
   Give him defense against the elements,
   For I have lost him on a dangerous sea.
MONTANO   Is he well shipped?
CASSIO   His bark is stoutly timbered, and his pilot
   Of very expert and approved allowance;°   *known ability*
   Therefore my hopes, not surfeited to death,°   *not excessive*
   Stand in bold cure.°   *likely to be rewarded*
VOICES [*within*]   A sail! a sail! a sail!
CASSIO   What noise?
GENTLEMAN   The town is empty; on the brow o'th' sea
   Stand ranks of people, and they cry "A sail!"
CASSIO   My hopes do shape him for° the governor.   *make it out to be*
      [*A shot.*]
SECOND GENTLEMAN   They do discharge their shot of
      courtesy—
   Our friends, at least.
CASSIO   I pray you, sir, go forth
   And give us truth who 'tis that is arrived.
SECOND GENTLEMAN   I shall.   *Exit.*
MONTANO   But, good lieutenant, is your general wived?
CASSIO   Most fortunately: he hath achieved a maid
   That paragons° description and wild fame,   *stands above*

---

4. Meaning unclear: either a ship originally from Verona, though now used by the Venetians; or perhaps a particular *kind* of ship.

5. "Even . . . regard": until we can't distinguish sea from sky.

One that excels the quirks of blazoning° pens,   *praise-giving*
And in th'essential vesture of creation
Does tire the engineer.[6]
   Enter SECOND GENTLEMAN.

How now? Who has put in?
SECOND GENTLEMAN   'Tis one Iago, ancient to the general.
CASSIO   He's had most favorable and happy speed:
Tempests themselves, high seas, and howling winds,
The guttered° rocks and congregated° sands,   *jagged / accumulated*
Traitors ensteeped° to enclog the guiltless keel,   *underwater*
As having sense of beauty, do omit°   *forgo*
Their mortal° natures, letting go safely by   *deadly*
The divine Desdemona.
MONTANO   What is she?
CASSIO   She that I spake of, our great captain's captain,
Left in the conduct of the bold Iago,
Whose footing here anticipates our thoughts
A se'night's speed.[7] Great Jove, Othello guard,
And swell his sail with thine own powerful breath,
That he may bless this bay with his tall ship,
Make love's quick pants in Desdemona's arms,
Give renewed fire to our extinct spirits,
And bring all Cyprus comfort!
   Enter DESDEMONA, IAGO, RODERIGO, *and* EMILIA.
                       O, behold!
The riches of the ship is come on shore.
You men of Cyprus, let her have your knees.
Hail to thee, lady, and the grace of heaven
Before, behind thee, and on every hand
Enwheel thee round.
DESDEMONA   I thank you, valiant Cassio.
What tidings can you tell me of my lord?
CASSIO   He is not yet arrived, nor know I aught
But that he's well and will be shortly here.
DESDEMONA   O, but I fear!—How lost you company?
CASSIO   The great contention of sea and skies
Parted our fellowship.
VOICES *within*   A sail! a sail!
   [*A shot.*]
CASSIO   But hark—a sail.
GENTLEMAN   They give their greeting to the citadel;
This likewise is a friend.
CASSIO   See for the news.
   [*Exit* GENTLEMAN.]
Good ancient, you are welcome. Welcome, mistress.
   [*Kisses* EMILIA.]

---

6. "In . . . engineer": whose natural beauty exhausts the poet's capacity to invent praise.

7. Whose arrival predates our expectations by a week.

    Let it not gall your patience, good Iago,
    That I extend my manners. 'Tis my breeding
    That gives me this bold show of courtesy.
100 IAGO   Sir, would she give you so much of her lips
    As of her tongue she oft bestows on me,
    You would have enough.
  DESDEMONA   Alas, she has no speech.[8]
  IAGO   In faith, too much:
    I find it still° when I have leave to sleep.   *always*
105 Marry, before your ladyship, I grant,
    She puts her tongue a little in her heart[9]
    And chides with thinking.
  EMILIA   You have little cause to say so.
  IAGO   Come on! come on! You are pictures[1] out of door,
110 Bells° in your parlors, wildcats in your kitchens,   *noisy*
    Saints° in your injuries, devils being offended,   *martyrs*
    Players in your huswifery, and huswives[2] in your beds.
  DESDEMONA   O, fie upon thee, slanderer!
  IAGO   Nay, it is true, or else I am a Turk:
115 You rise to play and go to bed to work.
  EMILIA   You shall not write my praise.
  IAGO   No, let me not.
  DESDEMONA   What wouldst write of me, if thou shouldst
    praise me?
  IAGO   O, gentle lady, do not put me to't,
    For I am nothing if not critical.
120 DESDEMONA   Come on, assay.° There's one gone to the   *essay, try*
    harbor?
  IAGO   Ay, madam.
  DESDEMONA   I am not merry, but I do beguile°   *disguise*
    The thing I am° by seeming otherwise.—   *(worried for Othello)*
    Come, how wouldst thou praise me?
125 IAGO   I am about it, but indeed my invention
    Comes from my pate as birdlime[3] does from frieze.° *coarse wool cloth*
    It plucks out brains and all. But my muse labors,°   *(in childbirth)*
    And thus she is delivered:
    "If she be fair and wise, fairness and wit,
130 The one's for use, the other useth it."[4]
  DESDEMONA   Well praised! How if she be black and witty?
  IAGO   "If she be black,[5] and thereto have a wit,
    She'll find a white that shall her blackness fit."[6]
  DESDEMONA   Worse and worse!

---

8. Perhaps both a defense of Emilia and a prod for her to speak.
9. She keeps her (critical) thoughts to herself.
1. Models of silent propriety. In this speech Iago shifts from Emilia to women generally.
2. Pronounced *hussies* and thus carrying opposed suggestions: wanton; businesslike, charily husbanding sexual favors (compare line 115). "Players in your huswifery": deceptive in managing household expenses.
3. Sticky substance used to trap small birds.
4. That is, intelligence makes use of beauty.
5. Dark-haired or dark-complexioned.
6. With sexual double entendre. "White": fair-skinned person (with a pun on *wight*, "person").

EMILIA How if fair and foolish?
IAGO "She never yet was foolish that was fair,
　For even her folly° helped her to an heir."　　　　　*foolishness; lechery*
DESDEMONA These are old fond° paradoxes, to make fools　　*foolish*
laugh i'th' alehouse. What miserable praise hast thou for
her that's foul° and foolish?　　　　　　　　　　　　　*ugly*
IAGO "There's none so foul and foolish thereunto,°　　　*to boot*
But does foul° pranks which fair and wise ones do."　　*lascivious*
DESDEMONA O, heavy ignorance! Thou praisest the worst
best. But what praise couldst thou bestow on a deserv-
ing woman indeed? One that in the authority of her
merit did justly put on the vouch[7] of very malice itself.
IAGO "She that was ever fair, and never proud,
Had tongue at will, and yet was never loud,
Never lacked gold, and yet went never gay,°　　　　　*lavishly clothed*
Fled from her wish, and yet said "now I may";[8]
She that, being angered, her revenge being nigh,
Bade her wrong stay° and her displeasure fly;　　　　*sense of injury end*
She that in wisdom never was so frail
To change the cod's head for the salmon's tail;[9]
She that could think, and ne'er disclose her mind,
See suitors following, and not look behind:
She was a wight (if ever such wights were) . . ."
DESDEMONA To do what?
IAGO "To suckle fools and chronicle small beer."[1]
DESDEMONA O, most lame and impotent conclusion! Do
not learn of him, Emilia, though he be thy husband.
How say you, Cassio? Is he not a most profane and lib-
eral° counselor?　　　　　　　　　　　　　　　　　*outspoken*
CASSIO He speaks home, madam. You may relish him
more in° the soldier than in the scholar.　　　　　　　*as*
IAGO [*aside*] He takes her by the palm. Ay, well said,°　　*well done*
whisper! With as little a web as this will I ensnare as
great a fly as Cassio. Ay, smile upon her, do! I will gyve°　*shackle*
thee in thine own courtship.°—You say true, 'tis so　　　*courtliness*
indeed.—If such tricks as these strip you out of your
lieutenantry, it had been better you had not kissed your
three fingers so oft,[2] which now again you are most apt
to play the sir° in. Very good! well kissed and excellent　*gentleman*
courtesy!—'Tis so indeed.—Yet again, your fingers to
your lips? Would they were clyster pipes° for your sake!　*enema tubes*
　Trumpets within
The Moor! I know his trumpet.
CASSIO 'Tis truly so.
DESDEMONA Let's meet him and receive him.

---

7. Compel the approval.
8. Voluntarily withstood temptation even when given the choice.
9. To make an unworthy exchange.
1. That is, to breastfeed babies and keep track of trivial domestic goods.
2. It would have been better for you not to have blown her so many kisses.

CASSIO Lo, where he comes.
          Enter OTHELLO *and attendants.*
OTHELLO O, my fair warrior!
DESDEMONA   My dear Othello!
OTHELLO It gives me wonder great as my content
  To see you here before me. O! my soul's joy,
  If after every tempest come such calms,
  May the winds blow till they have wakened death,
  And let the laboring bark° climb hills of seas   *small ship*
  Olympus-high,³ and duck again as low
  As hell's from heaven! If it were now to die,⁴
  'Twere now to be most happy; for I fear
  My soul hath her content so absolute
  That not another comfort like to this
  Succeeds° in unknown fate.°   *will follow / future*
DESDEMONA   The heavens forbid
  But that our loves and comforts should increase
  Even as our days do grow.
OTHELLO   Amen to that, sweet powers!
  I cannot speak enough of this content;
  It stops me here; it is too much of joy.
  And this, and this—   *They kiss.*
                      the greatest discords be
  That e'er our hearts shall make!
IAGO [*aside*]   O, you are well tuned now;
  But I'll set down the pegs that make this music,⁵
  As honest as I am.
OTHELLO   Come, let us to the castle.
  News, friends; our wars are done. The Turks are drowned.
  How does my old acquaintance of this isle?—
  Honey, you shall be well desired° in Cyprus;   *welcomed*
  I have found great love amongst them. O, my sweet,
  I prattle out of fashion, and I dote
  In mine own comforts. I prithee, good Iago,
  Go to the bay and disembark my coffers.°   *trunks*
  Bring thou the master° to the citadel;   *captain*
  He is a good one, and his worthiness
  Does challenge° much respect. Come, Desdemona;   *deserve*
  Once more well met at Cyprus.
          Exit OTHELLO *and* DESDEMONA [*and all but* IAGO *and*
          RODERIGO].
IAGO [*to a departing attendant*]   Do thou meet me pres-
  ently at the harbor. [*to* RODERIGO] Come hither. If thou
  be'st valiant—as they say base° men, being in love, have   *lowly born*
  then a nobility in their natures more than is native to
  them—list° me. The lieutenant tonight watches on the   *listen to*

---

3. Mount Olympus, home of the Greek gods and hence too high for mortals.
4. To perish, but also evoking the very common sense "to have an orgasm."
5. I'll untune (by loosening) the "pegs" that hold the strings of the musical instrument taut.

court of guard.⁶ First I must tell thee this: Desdemona is directly in love with him.

RODERIGO With him? Why, 'tis not possible.

IAGO Lay thy finger thus,° and let thy soul be instructed. Mark me with what violence she first loved the Moor, but° for bragging and telling her fantastical lies. To love him still for prating, let not thy discreet heart think it. Her eye must be fed. And what delight shall she have to look on the devil? When the blood is made dull with the act of sport, there should be—again to enflame it, and to give satiety a fresh appetite—loveliness in favor,° sympathy in years, manners, and beauties, all which the Moor is defective in. Now for want of these required conveniences,° her delicate tenderness will find itself abused,° begin to heave the gorge,⁷ disrelish and abhor the Moor. Very nature will instruct her in it and compel her to some second choice. Now, sir, this granted—as it is a most pregnant° and unforced position—who stands so eminent in the degree of⁸ this fortune as Cassio does?—a knave very voluble,° no further conscionable⁹ than in putting on the mere form of civil and humane seeming for the better compass° of his salt¹ and most hidden loose affection. Why none! why none! A slipper° and subtle knave, a finder of occasion, that has an eye can stamp and counterfeit advantages,² though true advantage never present itself. A devilish knave! Besides, the knave is handsome, young, and hath all those requisites in him that folly° and green minds look after. A pestilent° complete knave! And the woman hath found him already.

be silent

only

looks

compatibilities
revolted

obvious; (sexual)

facile

achievement
slippery

wantonness
damnably

RODERIGO I cannot believe that in her; she's full of most blessed condition.

IAGO Blessed fig's-end!° The wine she drinks is made of grapes. If she had been blessed, she would never have loved the Moor. Blessed pudding!° Didst thou not see her paddle with the palm of his hand? Didst not mark that?

(obscene)

sausage

RODERIGO Yes, that I did, but that was but courtesy.

IAGO Lechery, by this hand! an index and obscure° prologue to the history° of lust and foul thoughts.³ They met so near with their lips that their breaths embraced together. Villainous thoughts, Roderigo: when these mutualities so marshal the way, hard at hand comes the master and main exercise,⁴ th'incorporate° conclusion.

encoded
story

in the flesh

---

6. That is, Cassio is in charge of the watch at the guardhouse.
7. Feel nausea.
8. As next in line for.
9. No more ethical.
1. Lewd.
2. Who can (like a counterfeiter) create his own opportunities.
3. The analogy is to a dirty book. "Index": table of contents.
4. When these intimacies have cleared the way, the main event follows close behind. Here, the analogy is to an official procession.

260 Pish! But, sir, be you ruled by me. I have brought you from Venice. Watch you tonight. For the command, I'll lay't upon you.⁵ Cassio knows you not. I'll not be far from you. Do you find some occasion to anger Cassio, either by speaking too loud or tainting° his discipline, or from what °insulting
265 other course you please, which the time shall more favorably minister.° °provide

RODERIGO Well.

IAGO Sir, he's rash and very sudden in choler, and haply° °perhaps may strike at you. Provoke him that he may; for even out
270 of that will I cause these of Cyprus to mutiny; whose qualification shall come into no true taste again⁶ but by the displanting of Cassio. So shall you have a shorter journey to your desires by the means I shall then have to prefer° them, and the impediment most profitably °promote
275 removed without the which there were no expectation of our prosperity.

RODERIGO I will do this if you can bring it to any opportunity.

IAGO I warrant thee. Meet me by and by at the citadel. I
280 must fetch his necessaries⁷ ashore. Farewell.

RODERIGO Adieu.   [*Exit.*]

IAGO That Cassio loves her, I do well believ't;
That she loves him, 'tis apt and of great credit.°   °likely and believable
The Moor, howbeit that I endure him not,
285 Is of a constant, loving, noble nature,
And I dare think he'll prove to Desdemona
A most dear° husband. Now I do love her too,   °affectionate; costly
Not out of absolute lust (though peradventure
I stand accountant° for as great a sin),   °accountable
290 But partly led to diet° my revenge,   °feed
For that I do suspect the lusty Moor
Hath leaped into my seat°—the thought whereof   °slept with my wife
Doth, like a poisonous mineral, gnaw my inwards,°   °innards
And nothing can or shall content my soul
295 Till I am evened with him, wife for wife;
Or failing so, yet that I put the Moor
At least into a jealousy so strong
That judgment cannot cure; which thing to do,
If this poor trash of Venice, whom I trace
300 For his quick hunting, stand the putting on,⁸
I'll have our Michael Cassio on the hip,°   °at my mercy
Abuse° him to the Moor in the rank garb°   °slander / gross manner
(For I fear Cassio with my nightcap° too),   °(as sexual rival)
Make the Moor thank me, love me, and reward me
305 For making him egregiously an ass

---

5. *Stand watch tonight. I'll see that you receive orders.*
6. Who will not be adequately appeased.
7. Othello's possessions.

8. "If . . . on": if Roderigo, whom I follow (?), harness (?), is successfully set on the hunt when incited.

And practicing upon° his peace and quiet — *undermining*
Even to madness. 'Tis here,° but yet confused; — *my plan is here*
Knavery's plain face is never seen till used. *Exit.*

2.2

Enter OTHELLO'S HERALD *with a proclamation.*
HERALD [*reads*] "It is Othello's pleasure, our noble and valiant general, that upon certain tidings now arrived importing the mere perdition° of the Turkish fleet, every — *entire loss*
man put himself into triumph—some to dance, some to make bonfires, each man to what sport and revels his addition° leads him. For besides these beneficial news, it — *inclination*
is the celebration of his nuptial." So much was his pleasure should be proclaimed. All offices° are open, and — *storehouses*
there is full liberty of feasting from this present hour of five till the bell have told eleven. Heaven bless the isle of Cyprus and our noble general Othello! *Exit.*

2.3

Enter OTHELLO, DESDEMONA, CASSIO, *and attendants.*
OTHELLO Good Michael, look you to the guard tonight.
Let's teach ourselves that honorable stop,° — *self-restraint*
Not to outsport° discretion. — *pass the limits of*
CASSIO Iago hath direction what to do;
But notwithstanding, with my personal eye
Will I look to't.
OTHELLO   Iago is most honest.
Michael, goodnight. Tomorrow with your earliest
Let me have speech with you.—Come, my dear love.
The purchase made, the fruits are to ensue,
That profit's yet to come 'tween me and you.[1]
Goodnight.
        Exit [OTHELLO, DESDEMONA, *and attendants*].
    Enter IAGO.
CASSIO Welcome, Iago; we must to the watch.
IAGO Not this hour, lieutenant; 'tis not yet ten o'th' clock.
Our general cast° us thus early for the love of his Desde- — *dismissed*
mona, who let us not therefore blame: he hath not yet made wanton the night with her, and she is sport for Jove.
CASSIO She's a most exquisite lady.
IAGO And, I'll warrant her, full of game.
CASSIO Indeed, she's a most fresh and delicate creature.
IAGO What an eye she has! Methinks it sounds a parley° — *(military) call*
to provocation.
CASSIO An inviting eye; and yet, methinks, right modest.

2.2 Location: A street in Cyprus.
2.3 Location: The citadel at Cyprus.

1. That is, we haven't yet consummated our marriage.

IAGO   And when she speaks, is it not an alarum° to love?   *a call (to arms)*
CASSIO   She is indeed perfection.
IAGO   Well, happiness to their sheets! Come, lieutenant, I have a stoup° of wine, and here without are a brace° of   *two quarts / pair*
Cyprus gallants that would fain have a measure² to the health of black Othello.
CASSIO   Not tonight, good Iago. I have very poor and unhappy brains for drinking. I could well wish courtesy would invent some other custom of entertainment.
IAGO   O, they are our friends; but one cup; I'll drink for you.
CASSIO   I have drunk but one cup tonight, and that was craftily qualified° too; and behold what innovation³ it   *well diluted*
makes here. I am unfortunate in the infirmity and dare not task my weakness with any more.
IAGO   What, man! 'Tis a night of revels—the gallants desire it.
CASSIO   Where are they?
IAGO   Here at the door; I pray you call them in.
CASSIO   I'll do't, but it dislikes me.°   *Exit.*   *I don't like it*
IAGO   If I can fasten but one cup upon him
With that which he hath drunk tonight already,
He'll be as full of quarrel and offense
As my young mistress' dog. Now my sick fool, Roderigo,
Whom love hath turned almost the wrong side out,
To Desdemona hath tonight caroused
Potations pottle-deep; and he's to watch.⁴
Three else of Cyprus (noble swelling° spirits,   *proud*
That hold their honors in a wary distance,⁵
The very elements° of this warlike isle)   *typical residents*
Have I tonight flustered with flowing cups,
And they watch too. Now, 'mongst this flock of drunkards
Am I to put our Cassio in some action
That may offend the isle. But here they come.
   Enter CASSIO, MONTANO, *and* GENTLEMEN [*with wine*].
If consequence do but approve my dream,⁶
My boat sails freely, both with wind and stream.°   *current*
CASSIO   'Fore God, they have given me a rouse° already.   *full draft*
MONTANO   Good faith, a little one; not past a pint, as I am a soldier.
IAGO   Some wine, ho!
   [*Sings*]
         And let me the cannikin° clink, clink,   *drinking vessel*
         And let me the cannikin clink.
         A soldier's a man,
         O man's life's but a span,

2. Would like *to drink.*
3. *Disorder.*
4. "Caroused . . . watch": consumed drink to the bottom of the tankard; and he's assigned guard duty.
5. Who are touchy about their honor.
6. If events turn out as I hope.

                Why then, let a soldier drink.
            Some wine, boys!
70 CASSIO   'Fore God, an excellent song!
    IAGO   I learned it in England, where indeed they are most
        potent in potting.⁷ Your Dane, your German, and your
        swag°-bellied Hollander—drink, ho!—are nothing to   *hanging*
        your English.
75 CASSIO   Is your Englishman so exquisite in his drinking?
    IAGO   Why, he drinks you with facility your Dane dead
        drunk. He sweats not to overthrow your Almaine.° He   *German*
        gives your Hollander a vomit ere the next pottle° can be   *tankard*
        filled.
80 CASSIO   To the health of our general!
    MONTANO   I am for it, lieutenant, and I'll do you justice.⁸
    IAGO   O sweet England!
            [*Sings*]
                King Stephen was and-a worthy peer,
                    His breeches cost him but a crown;⁹
85   He held them sixpence all too dear,
                    With that he called the tailor lown.°   *lout*
                He was a wight of high renown,
                    And thou art but of low degree;
                'Tis pride° that pulls the country down,   *ostentatious clothing*
90   And take thy auld cloak about thee.
            Some wine, ho!
    CASSIO   'Fore God, this is a more exquisite song than the
        other.
    IAGO   Will you hear't again?
95 CASSIO   No, for I hold him to be unworthy of his place
        that does those things. Well, God's above all, and there
        be souls must be saved, and there be souls must not be
        saved.¹
    IAGO   It's true, good lieutenant.
100 CASSIO   For mine own part—no offense to the general,
        nor any man of quality°—I hope to be saved.   *rank*
    IAGO   And so do I too, lieutenant.
    CASSIO   Ay; but by your leave, not before me. The lieuten-
        ant is to be saved before the ancient. Let's have no more
105   of this. Let's to our affairs. God forgive us our sins. Gen-
        tlemen, let's look to our business. Do not think, gentle-
        men, I am drunk. This is my ancient, this is my right
        hand, and this is my left. I am not drunk now. I can
        stand well enough, and I speak well enough.
110 GENTLEMAN   Excellent well.

---

7. Most adept at drinking.
8. Match your drinking.
9. A coin (worth 60 pence).
1. Referring to the doctrine of predestination, the belief held by Calvinist Protestants that some souls are destined from all eternity to be saved and others to be damned.

CASSIO Why, very well then. You must not think, then, that I am drunk. *Exit.*

MONTANO To th'platform, masters; come, let's set the watch. [*Exeunt some* GENTLEMEN.]

IAGO [*to* MONTANO] You see this fellow that is gone before:
He's a soldier fit to stand by Caesar
And give direction. And do but see his vice:
'Tis to his virtue a just equinox,°   *of equal size*
The one as long as th'other. 'Tis pity of him;
I fear the trust Othello puts him in
On some odd time of his infirmity
Will shake this island.

MONTANO   But is he often thus?

IAGO 'Tis evermore his prologue to his sleep.
He'll watch the horologe a double set[2]
If drink rock not his cradle.

MONTANO   It were well
The general were put in mind of it.
Perhaps he sees it not, or his good nature
Prizes the virtue that appears in Cassio
And looks not on his evils. Is not this true?

Enter RODERIGO.

IAGO [*aside*] How now, Roderigo?
I pray you after the lieutenant—go! *Exit* RODERIGO.

MONTANO And 'tis great pity that the noble Moor
Should hazard such a place as his own second
With one of an ingraft° infirmity.   *ingrained*
It were an honest action to say so
To the Moor.

IAGO   Not I, for this fair island.
I do love Cassio well and would do much
To cure him of this evil.

VOICES [*within*] Help, help![3]
                    But hark, what noise?

Enter CASSIO, *pursuing* RODERIGO.

CASSIO 'Swounds, you rogue! you rascal!

MONTANO What's the matter, lieutenant?

CASSIO A knave teach me my duty? I'll beat the knave into a twiggen° bottle.   *wicker-cased*

RODERIGO Beat me?

CASSIO Dost thou prate, rogue? [*Attacks* RODERIGO.]

MONTANO Nay, good lieutenant! I pray you, sir, hold your hand.

CASSIO Let me go, sir, or I'll knock you o'er the mazzard.°   *head*

MONTANO Come, come; you're drunk!

CASSIO Drunk? [CASSIO *and* MONTANO *fight.*]

---

2. He'll stay up twice around the clock.

3. The offstage shouts for help are only in Q.

IAGO [*aside to* RODERIGO]   Away, I say! Go out and cry a
  mutiny.
                              [*Exit* RODERIGO.]
  Nay, good lieutenant! God's will, gentlemen!
  Help ho! Lieutenant! Sir—Montano—Sir!
155 Help, masters! Here's a goodly watch indeed!
      A bell rung.
  Who's that which rings the bell? Diablo,° ho!   *the devil*
  The town will rise. God's will, lieutenant, hold!
  You'll be ashamed forever.
      Enter OTHELLO *and attendants.*
OTHELLO   What is the matter here?
160 MONTANO   'Swounds, I bleed still; I am hurt to th'death.
    [*Attacks* CASSIO] He dies.
OTHELLO   Hold, for your lives!
IAGO   Hold, ho! Lieutenant—Sir—Montano—gentlemen!
  Have you forgot all place of sense and duty?
165 Hold! The general speaks to you. Hold, for shame!
OTHELLO   Why, how now, ho? From whence ariseth this?
  Are we turned Turks? and to ourselves do that
  Which heaven hath forbid the Ottomites?°   (*by raising a storm*)
  For Christian shame, put by this barbarous brawl!
170 He that stirs next, to carve for his own rage,°   *draw a sword in anger*
  Holds his soul light; he dies upon his motion.
  Silence that dreadful bell—it frights the isle
  From her propriety. What is the matter, masters?
  Honest Iago, that looks dead with grieving,
175 Speak. Who began this? On thy love, I charge thee.
IAGO   I do not know. Friends all, but now, even now,
  In quarter° and in terms like bride and groom   *under control*
  Divesting them° for bed; and then, but now,   *getting undressed*
  As if some planet° had unwitted men,   *astrological influence*
180 Swords out and tilting one at other's breasts
  In opposition bloody. I cannot speak
  Any beginning to this peevish odds,°   *silly quarrel*
  And would in action glorious I had lost
  Those legs that brought me to a part of it.
185 OTHELLO   How comes it, Michael, you are thus forgot?
CASSIO   I pray you pardon me; I cannot speak.
OTHELLO   Worthy Montano, you were wont° to be civil;   *were accustomed*
  The gravity and stillness of your youth
  The world hath noted, and your name is great
190 In mouths of wisest censure.° What's the matter,   *judgment*
  That you unlace your reputation thus
  And spend your rich opinion° for the name   *reputation*
  Of a night brawler? Give me answer to it.
MONTANO   Worthy Othello, I am hurt to danger.
195 Your officer, Iago, can inform you—
  While I spare speech, which something now offends me[4]—

---

4. Somewhat now pains me.

Of all that I do know; nor know I aught
By me that's said or done amiss this night,
Unless self-charity° be sometimes a vice, — *care of oneself*
And to defend ourselves it be a sin
When violence assails us.

OTHELLO　　　　　　　　Now, by heaven,
My blood begins my safer guides to rule,
And passion, having my best judgment collied,° — *darkened*
Assays° to lead the way. 'Swounds, if I stir — *tries*
Or do but lift this arm, the best of you
Shall sink in my rebuke. Give me to know
How this foul rout began, who set it on;
And he that is approved° in this offense, — *proven guilty*
Though he had twinned with me, both at a birth,
Shall lose me. What! in a town of war,
Yet° wild, the people's hearts brimful of fear, — *still*
To manage° private and domestic quarrel? — *carry on*
In night, and on the court and guard of safety?[5]
'Tis monstrous. Iago, who began't?

MONTANO　　If partially affined,° or leagued in office, — *biased (for Cassio)*
Thou dost deliver more or less than truth,
Thou art no soldier.

IAGO　　　　　　　　Touch me not so near.
I had rather have this tongue cut from my mouth
Than it should do offense to Michael Cassio;
Yet I persuade myself to speak the truth
Shall nothing wrong him. This it is, general:
Montano and myself being in speech,
There comes a fellow crying out for help,
And Cassio following him with determined sword
To execute upon° him. Sir, this gentleman — *to attack*
Steps in to Cassio and entreats his pause;
Myself the crying fellow did pursue,
Lest by his clamor—as it so fell out—
The town might fall in fright. He, swift of foot,
Outran my purpose; and I returned, the rather
For that I heard the clink and fall of swords
And Cassio high in oath, which till tonight
I ne'er might say before. When I came back—
For this was brief—I found them close together
At blow and thrust, even as again they were
When yourself did part them.
More of this matter cannot I report.
But men are men: the best sometimes forget.
Though Cassio did some little wrong to him,
As men in rage strike those that wish them best,
Yet surely Cassio, I believe, received
From him that fled some strange indignity

---

5. And at the place where safety and security are at stake (on the night watch).

Which patience could not pass.°   *let pass*
OTHELLO   I know, Iago,
Thy honesty and love doth mince° this matter,   *minimize*
245 Making it light to Cassio. Cassio, I love thee,
But never more be officer of mine.—
     Enter DESDEMONA, *attended.*
Look if my gentle love be not raised up!—
I'll make thee an example.
DESDEMONA   What is the matter, dear?
OTHELLO   All's well, sweeting;
250 Come away to bed. [*To* MONTANO] Sir, for your hurts
Myself will be your surgeon. Lead him off.
                 [*Exeunt attendants with* MONTANO.]
Iago, look with care about the town,
And silence those whom this vile brawl distracted.
Come, Desdemona; 'tis the soldier's life
255 To have their balmy slumbers waked with strife.
     Exeunt [OTHELLO *the*] *Moor,* DESDEMONA, *and attendants.*
IAGO   What, are you hurt, lieutenant?
CASSIO   Ay, past all surgery.
IAGO   Marry, God forbid!
CASSIO   Reputation, reputation, reputation! O, I have lost
260 my reputation! I have lost the immortal part of myself, and
what remains is bestial. My reputation, Iago, my reputation!
IAGO   As I am an honest man, I had thought you had
received some bodily wound; there is more sense in that
than in reputation. Reputation is an idle and most false
265 imposition,° oft got without merit and lost without   *artificial notion*
deserving. You have lost no reputation at all, unless you
repute yourself such a loser. What, man! there are more
ways to recover the general again. You are but now cast in
his mood, a punishment more in policy⁶ than in malice,
270 even so as one would beat his offenseless dog to affright
an imperious lion. Sue to° him again, and he's yours.   *petition*
CASSIO   I will rather sue to be despised than to deceive
so good a commander with so slight, so drunken, and so
indiscreet an officer. Drunk? And speak parrot?° And   *rant on*
275 squabble? Swagger? Swear? And discourse fustian° with   *nonsense*
one's own shadow? O, thou invisible spirit of wine! if
thou hast no name to be known by, let us call thee devil.
IAGO   What was he that you followed with your sword?
What had he done to you?
280 CASSIO   I know not.
IAGO   Is't possible?
CASSIO   I remember a mass of things, but nothing distinctly; a quarrel, but nothing wherefore.° O God! that   *but not why*
men should put an enemy in their mouths to steal away

---

6. "Cast . . . policy": dismissed in anger—a matter of policy (of public example).

their brains! that we should with joy, pleasance, revel, and applause transform ourselves into beasts!

IAGO Why, but you are now well enough. How came you thus recovered?

CASSIO It hath pleased the devil drunkenness to give place to the devil wrath; one unperfectness shows me another, to make me frankly despise myself.

IAGO Come, you are too severe a moraler. As the time, the place, and the condition of this country stands, I could heartily wish this had not befallen; but since it is as it is, mend it for your own good.

CASSIO I will ask him for my place again. He shall tell me I am a drunkard. Had I as many mouths as Hydra,[7] such an answer would stop them all. To be now a sensible man, by and by a fool, and presently a beast!—O, strange! Every inordinate cup is unblessed, and the ingredient is a devil.

IAGO Come, come; good wine is a good familiar creature if it be well used. Exclaim no more against it. And, good lieutenant, I think you think I love you.

CASSIO I have well approved° it, sir—I drunk?   *tested*

IAGO You or any man living may be drunk at a time, man. I tell you what you shall do. Our general's wife is now the general. I may say so in this respect, for that he hath devoted and given up himself to the contemplation, mark, and devotement° of her parts[8] and graces. Confess   *observation*
yourself freely to her; importune her help to put you in your place again. She is of so free,° so kind, so apt, so   *generous*
blessed a disposition, she holds it a vice in her goodness not to do more than she is requested. This broken joint between you and her husband entreat her to splinter,[9] and my fortunes against any lay° worth naming, this   *wager*
crack of your love shall grow stronger than it was before.

CASSIO You advise me well.

IAGO I protest,° in the sincerity of love and honest   *insist*
kindness.

CASSIO I think it freely; and betimes° in the morning I   *early*
will beseech the virtuous Desdemona to undertake for me. I am desperate of my fortunes if they check° me.   *stop*

IAGO You are in the right. Good night, lieutenant; I must to the watch.

CASSIO Good night, honest Iago.   *Exit* CASSIO.

IAGO And what's he then that says I play the villain,
When this advice is free I give and honest,
Probal° to thinking, and indeed the course   *wise*
To win the Moor again? For 'tis most easy
Th'inclining° Desdemona to subdue   *well-disposed*

---

7. A mythical serpent with many heads, who grew two more when one was cut off.
8. Qualities.
9. Heal with a splint.

In any honest suit: she's framed as fruitful°   *generous*
As the free elements; and then for her
To win the Moor, were't to renounce his baptism,
335 All seals and symbols of redeemèd sin,
His soul is so enfettered to her love
That she may make, unmake, do what she list,
Even as her appetite° shall play the god   *wishes*
With his weak function.° How am I then a villain   *faculties*
340 To counsel Cassio to this parallel° course   *suitable*
Directly to his good? Divinity° of hell!   *theology*
When devils will the blackest sins put on,
They do suggest at first with heavenly shows,
As I do now. For whiles this honest fool
345 Plies Desdemona to repair his fortune,
And she for him pleads strongly to the Moor,
I'll pour this pestilence into his ear:
That she repeals him° for her body's lust,   *appeals for him*
And by how much she strives to do him good
350 She shall undo her credit with the Moor.
So will I turn her virtue into pitch,[1]
And out of her own goodness make the net
That shall enmesh them all.
    Enter RODERIGO.
How now, Roderigo?
355 RODERIGO   I do follow here in the chase, not like a hound
that hunts, but one that fills up the cry.° My money is   *a pack follower*
almost spent; I have been tonight exceedingly well cud-
geled; and I think the issue will be I shall have so
much° experience for my pains, and so, with no money   *only this much*
360 at all and a little more wit, return again to Venice.
IAGO   How poor are they that have not patience!
What wound did ever heal but by degrees?
Thou know'st we work by wit and not by witchcraft,
And wit depends on dilatory° time.   *gradually unfolding*
365 Does't not go well? Cassio hath beaten thee,
And thou by that small hurt hath cashiered° Cassio.   *dismissed*
Though other things grow fair against the sun,
Yet fruits that blossom first will first be ripe.[2]
Content thyself awhile. By the Mass,° 'tis morning!   *(a mild oath)*
370 Pleasure and action make the hours seem short.
Retire thee; go where thou art billeted.
Away! I say; thou shalt know more hereafter.
Nay, get thee gone!   *Exit* RODERIGO.
    Two things are to be done:
My wife must move for Cassio to her mistress—
375 I'll set her on—
Myself a while to draw the Moor apart

---

1. Black, sticky substance used as a snare.
2. That is, although others may appear to be prospering, your plan will be successful soonest because it was set in motion first.

And bring him jump° when he may Cassio find — *exactly*
Soliciting his wife. Ay, that's the way!
Dull not device by coldness and delay.³   *Exit.*

3.1

Enter CASSIO, MUSICIANS, *and* CLOWN.

CASSIO   Masters, play here—I will content° your pains— — *reward*
Something that's brief; and bid "Good morrow, general."
CLOWN   Why, masters, have your instruments been in
Naples, that they speak i'th' nose thus?¹
5 MUSICIAN   How, sir? how?
CLOWN   Are these, I pray you, wind instruments?²
MUSICIAN   Ay, marry, are they, sir.
CLOWN   O, thereby hangs a tail!
MUSICIAN   Whereby hangs a tale, sir?
10 CLOWN   Marry, sir, by many a wind instrument that I know.
But, masters, here's money for you; and the general so
likes your music that he desires you for love's sake to
make no more noise with it.
MUSICIAN   Well, sir, we will not.
15 CLOWN   If you have any music that may not° be heard, to't — *cannot*
again. But, as they say, to hear music the general does
not greatly care.
MUSICIAN   We have none such, sir.
CLOWN   Then put up your pipes in your bag, for I'll away.
20   Go! Vanish into air, away!   *Exeunt* MUSICIANS.
CASSIO   Dost thou hear, mine honest friend?
CLOWN   No, I hear not your honest friend: I hear you.
CASSIO   Prithee keep up thy quillets.³ There's a poor piece
of gold for thee. If the gentlewoman that attends the
25   general be stirring, tell her there's one Cassio entreats
her a little favor of speech. Wilt thou do this?
CLOWN   She is stirring, sir. If she will stir hither, I shall
seem° to notify unto her. — *arrange*
CASSIO   Do, good my friend.   *Exit* CLOWN.
Enter IAGO   In happy time,° Iago. — *well met*
30 IAGO   You have not been abed then?
CASSIO   Why, no; the day had broke before we parted.
I have made bold, Iago, to send in to your wife.
My suit to her is that she will to virtuous Desdemona
Procure me some access.
IAGO   I'll send her to you presently;° — *immediately*
35   And I'll devise a mean to draw the Moor
Out of the way, that your converse and business

---

3. Don't let sluggishness and slowness to act weaken the plot.
3.1 *Location:* Outside Othello and Desdemona's room.
1. That they sound so nasal; perhaps a reference to venereal disease, often associated with Naples, or a phallic or anal joke.
2. The exchange that follows depends on the connections among wind instruments, flatulence, and "tale/tail."
3. Pack up your puns.

May be more free.
CASSIO   I humbly thank you for't.   *Exit* [IAGO].
                         I never knew
A Florentine more kind and honest.
    Enter EMILIA
EMILIA   Good morrow, good lieutenant. I am sorry
For your displeasure, but all will sure° be well.   surely
The general and his wife are talking of it,
And she speaks for you stoutly. The Moor replies
That he you hurt is of great fame in Cyprus
And great affinity,° and that in wholesome wisdom   well connected
He might not but refuse you; but he protests he loves you
And needs no other suitor but his likings
To bring you in again.
CASSIO   Yet I beseech you,
If you think fit, or that it may be done,
Give me advantage of some brief discourse
With Desdemon alone.
EMILIA   Pray you come in.
I will bestow you where you shall have time
To speak your bosom° freely.   heart
CASSIO   I am much bound to you.
                                        Exeunt.

3.2

Enter OTHELLO, IAGO, *and* GENTLEMEN
OTHELLO   These letters give, Iago, to the pilot,
And by him do my duties° to the senate.   send my respects
That done, I will be walking on the works;°   fortifications
Repair° there to me.   come
IAGO   Well, my good lord; I'll do't.
OTHELLO   This fortification, gentlemen, shall we see't?
GENTLEMAN   We'll wait upon your lordship.   *Exeunt.*

3.3

Enter DESDEMONA, CASSIO, *and* EMILIA.
DESDEMONA   Be thou assured, good Cassio, I will do
All my abilities in thy behalf.
EMILIA   Good madam, do. I warrant it grieves my husband
As if the cause were his.
DESDEMONA   O, that's an honest fellow. Do not doubt, Cassio,
But I will have my lord and you again
As friendly as you were.
CASSIO   Bounteous madam,
Whatever shall become of Michael Cassio,
He's never anything but your true servant.

3.2 Location: The citadel.
3.3 Location: The citadel's garden.

DESDEMONA I know't; I thank you. You do love my lord;
You have known him long; and be you well assured
He shall in strangeness stand no farther off
Than in a politic distance.¹
CASSIO   Ay, but, lady,
That policy may either last so long,
Or feed upon such nice and wat'rish diet,
Or breed itself so out of circumstances,²
That—I being absent, and my place supplied°—   filled
My general will forget my love and service.
DESDEMONA Do not doubt° that. Before Emilia here,   fear
I give thee warrant° of thy place. Assure thee,   assurance
If I do vow a friendship, I'll perform it
To the last article. My lord shall never rest:
I'll watch him tame and talk him out of patience;³
His bed shall seem a school, his board a shrift;°   confessional
I'll intermingle everything he does
With Cassio's suit. Therefore be merry, Cassio,
For thy solicitor° shall rather die   advocate
Than give thy cause away.°   up
      Enter OTHELLO *and* IAGO.
EMILIA Madam, here comes my lord.
CASSIO Madam, I'll take my leave.
DESDEMONA Why, stay and hear me speak.
CASSIO Madam, not now: I am very ill at ease,
Unfit for mine own purposes.
DESDEMONA Well, do your discretion.   *Exit* CASSIO.
IAGO Ha! I like not that.
OTHELLO   What dost thou say?
IAGO Nothing, my lord; or if . . . I know not what.
OTHELLO Was not that Cassio parted from my wife?
IAGO Cassio, my lord? No, sure, I cannot think it
That he would steal away so guilty-like,
Seeing your coming.
OTHELLO   I do believe 'twas he.
DESDEMONA How now, my lord?
I have been talking with a suitor here,
A man that languishes in your displeasure.
OTHELLO Who is't you mean?
DESDEMONA Why, your lieutenant, Cassio. Good my lord,
If I have any grace or power to move you,
His present reconciliation take;°   accept him now
For if he be not one that truly loves you,
That errs in ignorance and not in cunning,°   not knowingly
I have no judgment in an honest face.

---

1. *He will distance himself from you only as much as good diplomacy requires.*
2. "Or feed . . . circumstances": or persist based on such unimportant and poor justifications, or continue by chance.
3. I'll keep him awake until he obeys me, and talk to him beyond his endurance.

I prithee call him back.
OTHELLO Went he hence now?
DESDEMONA Yes, faith; so humbled
That he hath left part of his grief with me
To suffer with him. Good love, call him back.
OTHELLO Not now, sweet Desdemon; some other time.
DESDEMONA But shall't be shortly?
OTHELLO The sooner, sweet, for you.
DESDEMONA Shall't be tonight, at supper?
OTHELLO No, not tonight.
DESDEMONA Tomorrow dinner° then? *midday meal*
OTHELLO I shall not dine at home;
I meet the captains at the citadel.
DESDEMONA Why then, tomorrow night, on Tuesday morn,
On Tuesday noon or night, on Wednesday morn.
I prithee name the time, but let it not
Exceed three days. In faith, he's penitent;
And yet his trespass, in our common reason°— *normal judgment*
Save that, they say, the wars must make example
Out of her° best—is not almost a fault *(war's)*
T'incur a private check.[4] When shall he come?
Tell me, Othello. I wonder in my soul
What you would ask me that I should deny,
Or stand so mamm'ring° on? What? Michael Cassio, *hesitating*
That came a-wooing with you? and so many a time,
When I have spoke of you dispraisingly,
Hath ta'en your part—to have so much to do
To bring him in?° By'r Lady, I could do much[5]— *into favor*
OTHELLO Prithee, no more. Let him come when he will:
I will deny thee nothing.
DESDEMONA Why, this is not a boon;
'Tis as I should entreat you wear your gloves,
Or feed on nourishing dishes, or keep you warm,
Or sue to you to do a peculiar° profit *particular*
To your own person. Nay, when I have a suit
Wherein I mean to touch your love indeed,
It shall be full of poise° and difficult weight, *balanced judgment*
And fearful to be granted.
OTHELLO I will deny thee nothing.
Whereon I do beseech thee grant me this,
To leave me but a little to myself.
DESDEMONA Shall I deny you? No. Farewell, my lord.
OTHELLO Farewell, my Desdemona; I'll come to thee
straight.° *immediately*
DESDEMONA Emilia, come. [*to* OTHELLO] Be as your
fancies teach° you. *as your whims lead*

---

4. Is barely worth even private criticism.
5. Do much to make you regret your reluctance (?).

Whate'er you be, I am obedient.
Exeunt DESDEMONA *and* EMILIA.

OTHELLO Excellent wretch!° Perdition catch my soul   (*affectionate*)
But I do love thee! and when I love thee not,
Chaos is come again.
IAGO My noble lord . . .
OTHELLO   What dost thou say, Iago?
IAGO Did Michael Cassio, when you wooed my lady,
Know of your love?
OTHELLO   He did, from first to last.
Why dost thou ask?
IAGO But for a satisfaction of my thought,
No further harm.
OTHELLO   Why of thy thought, Iago?
IAGO I did not think he had been acquainted with her.
OTHELLO O yes, and went between us very oft.
IAGO Indeed?
OTHELLO Indeed? Ay, indeed. Discern'st thou aught in that?
Is he not honest?
IAGO Honest, my lord?
OTHELLO Honest? Ay, honest.
IAGO My lord, for aught I know.
OTHELLO What dost thou think?
IAGO Think, my lord?
OTHELLO "Think, my lord?" By heaven, thou echo'st me
As if there were some monster in thy thought
Too hideous to be shown. Thou dost mean something:
I heard thee say even now thou lik'st not that,
When Cassio left my wife. What didst not like?
And when I told thee he was of my counsel,°   *in my confidence*
Of my whole course of wooing, thou cried'st "Indeed?"
And didst contract and purse thy brow together
As if thou then hadst shut up in thy brain
Some horrible conceit.° If thou dost love me,   *thought*
Show me thy thought.
IAGO My lord, you know I love you.
OTHELLO   I think thou dost;
And for° I know thou'rt full of love and honesty,   *since*
And weigh'st thy words before thou giv'st them breath,
Therefore these stops° of thine fright me the more: *reluctances*
For such things in a false disloyal knave
Are tricks of custom;° but in a man that's just,   *habitual*
They're close dilations,[6] working from the heart
That passion cannot rule.°   *control*
IAGO   For Michael Cassio,
I dare be sworn I think that he is honest.
OTHELLO I think so too.

---

6. That is, involuntary revelations of interior, close-kept secrets.

IAGO   Men should be what they seem,
130 Or those that be not, would they might seem none.⁷
     OTHELLO   Certain, men should be what they seem.
     IAGO   Why then, I think Cassio's an honest man.
     OTHELLO   Nay, yet there's more in this.
       I prithee speak to me as to thy thinkings,
135   As thou dost ruminate, and give thy worst of thoughts
       The worst of words.
     IAGO   Good my lord, pardon me.
       Though I am bound to every act of duty,
       I am not bound to that all slaves are free to:⁸
       Utter my thoughts? Why, say they are vile and false—
140   As where's that palace whereinto foul things
       Sometimes intrude not? Who has that breast so pure
       But some uncleanly apprehensions
       Keep leets and law-days, and in sessions sit
       With meditations lawful?⁹
145 OTHELLO   Thou dost conspire against thy friend,° Iago,   (Othello)
       If thou but think'st him wronged and mak'st his ear
       A stranger to thy thoughts.
     IAGO   I do beseech you,
       Though I perchance am vicious° in my guess   mistaken
       (As I confess it is my nature's plague
150   To spy into abuses, and oft my jealousy
       Shapes faults that are not), that your wisdom
       From one that so imperfectly conceits°   imagines
       Would take no notice, nor build yourself a trouble
       Out of his scattering° and unsure observance.   incoherent
155   It were not for your quiet, nor your good,
       Nor for my manhood, honesty, and wisdom,
       To let you know my thoughts.
     OTHELLO   What dost thou mean?
     IAGO   Good name in man and woman, dear my lord,
       Is the immediate jewel of their souls;
160   Who steals my purse steals trash: 'tis something, nothing;
       'Twas mine, 'tis his, and has been slave to thousands.
       But he that filches from me my good name
       Robs me of that which not enriches him
       And makes me poor indeed.
     OTHELLO   By heaven, I'll know thy thoughts!
165 IAGO   You cannot, if my heart were in your hand,
       Nor shall not, whilst 'tis in my custody.
     OTHELLO   Ha?
     IAGO   O, beware, my lord, of jealousy!

---

7. "Or . . . none": if only those who are not what they seem didn't seem to be what they are not.
8. That is, I am not obligated to reveal my inner thoughts, something about which even slaves have a choice.

9. "Uncleanly . . . lawful": illegitimate thoughts meet in court ("leets") from time to time (on "law-days") and debate (in court "sessions") with legitimate ones.

                    It is the green-eyed monster, which doth mock
                    The meat it feeds on.¹ That cuckold lives in bliss
170   Who, certain of his fate, loves not his wronger;²
                    But O, what damnèd minutes tells he o'er
                    Who dotes yet doubts, suspects yet strongly loves!
     OTHELLO   O misery!
     IAGO   Poor and content is rich, and rich enough,
175   But riches fineless° is as poor as winter   *boundless*
                    To him that ever fears he shall be poor.
                    Good God, the souls of all my tribe defend
                    From jealousy!
     OTHELLO   Why, why is this?
                    Think'st thou I'd make a life of jealousy,
180   To follow still the changes of the moon°   *to renew endlessly*
                    With fresh suspicions? No! To be once in doubt
                    Is once to be resolved.° Exchange me for a goat   *to be finally settled*
                    When I shall turn the business of my soul
                    To such exsufflicate and blowed° surmises,   *inflated and blown up*
185   Matching thy inference. 'Tis not to make me jealous
                    To say my wife is fair, feeds well, loves company,
                    Is free of speech, sings, plays, and dances:
                    Where virtue is, these are more virtuous.
                    Nor from mine own weak merits will I draw
190   The smallest fear or doubt of her revolt,°   *or fear of her betrayal*
                    For she had eyes and chose me. No, Iago,
                    I'll see before I doubt; when I doubt, prove;
                    And on the proof there is no more but this:
                    Away at once with love or jealousy!
195 IAGO   I am glad of this; for now I shall have reason
                    To show the love and duty that I bear you
                    With franker spirit. Therefore, as I am bound,
                    Receive it from me. I speak not yet of proof.
                    Look to your wife; observe her well with Cassio;
200   Wear your eyes thus: not jealous, nor secure.
                    I would not have your free and noble nature
                    Out of self-bounty be abused.³ Look to't.
                    I know our country disposition well:
                    In Venice they do let God see the pranks
205   They dare not show their husbands; their best conscience
                    Is not to leave't undone, but keep't unknown.
     OTHELLO   Dost thou say so?
     IAGO   She did deceive her father, marrying you,
                    And when she seemed to shake, and fear your looks,
                    She loved them most.
     OTHELLO   And so she did.

---

1. That is, tortures, as it consumes, the heart of the jealous person.
2. Who, knowing it is his fate to be cuckolded, doesn't love his wife.
3. Be deceived on account of your own goodness.

210 IAGO   Why, go to° then.   *that's it*
     She that, so young, could give out such a seeming
     To seel her father's eyes up close as oak,⁴
     He thought 'twas witchcraft . . . ; but I am much to blame.
     I humbly do beseech you of your pardon
     For too much loving you.
215 OTHELLO   I am bound to thee forever.
    IAGO   I see this hath a little dashed your spirits.
    OTHELLO   Not a jot, not a jot.
    IAGO   I'faith, I fear it has.
     I hope you will consider what is spoke
     Comes from my love. But I do see you're moved.
220 I am to pray you not to strain my speech
     To grosser issues° nor to larger reach   *greater conclusions*
     Than to suspicion.
    OTHELLO   I will not.
    IAGO   Should you do so, my lord,
     My speech should fall into such vile success
225 Which my thoughts aimed not. Cassio's my worthy
       friend—
     My lord, I see you're moved.
    OTHELLO   No, not much moved;
     I do not think but Desdemona's honest.
    IAGO   Long live she so! and long live you to think so!
    OTHELLO   And yet how nature, erring from itself—
230 IAGO   Ay, there's the point! as to be bold with you,
     Not to affect° many proposed matches   *desire*
     Of her own clime, complexion, and degree,
     Whereto we see in all things nature tends—
     Foh! one may smell in such a will most rank,
235 Foul disproportions, thoughts unnatural.
     But, pardon me, I do not in position°   *argument*
     Distinctly speak of her, though I may fear
     Her will,° recoiling° to her better judgment,   *desire / submitting*
     May fall to match you with her country forms,⁵
     And happily° repent.   *perhaps*
240 OTHELLO   Farewell, farewell.
     If more thou dost perceive, let me know more.
     Set on thy wife to observe. Leave me, Iago.
    IAGO [*going*]   My lord, I take my leave.
    OTHELLO   Why did I marry? This honest creature,
       doubtless,
245 Sees and knows more, much more, than he unfolds.
    IAGO [*returning*]   My lord, I would I might entreat your
       honor

---

4. Perhaps: to cover ("seel" means "to blind") her father's eyes as tightly as oak (a fine-grained wood).

5. May happen to compare you with Venetian standards.

To scan this thing no farther; leave it to time.
Although 'tis fit that Cassio have his place
(For sure he fills it up with great ability),
Yet if you please to hold him off awhile,
You shall by that perceive him and his means.[6]
Note if your lady strain his entertainment°   *urge his reception*
With any strong or vehement importunity;
Much will be seen in that. In the meantime
Let me be thought too busy° in my fears   *meddlesome*
(As worthy cause I have to fear I am),
And hold her free,° I do beseech your honor.   *believe her innocent*

OTHELLO   Fear not my government.°   *self-conduct*

IAGO   I once more take my leave.   *Exit.*

OTHELLO   This fellow's of exceeding honesty,
And knows all qualities° with a learned spirit   *(human) types*
Of human dealings. If I do prove her haggard,°   *wild (from falconry)*
Though that her jesses were my dear heartstrings,
I'd whistle her off and let her down the wind
To prey at fortune.[7] Haply for° I am black,   *perhaps because*
And have not those soft parts of conversation°   *easy manners*
That chamberers° have, or for I am declined   *gallants*
Into the vale of years—yet that's not much—
She's gone, I am abused,° and my relief   *deceived*
Must be to loathe her. O curse of marriage!
That we can call these delicate creatures ours
And not their appetites! I had rather be a toad
And live upon the vapor of a dungeon
Than keep a corner in the thing I love
For others' uses. Yet 'tis the plague of great ones:
Prerogatived° are they less than the base;°   *privileged / lowborn*
'Tis destiny unshunnable, like death;
Even then this forkèd plague is fated to us
When we do quicken.[8]

    Enter DESDEMONA *and* EMILIA.

              Look where she comes!
If she be false, O then heaven mocks itself;
I'll not believe't.

DESDEMONA   How now, my dear Othello?
Your dinner, and the generous° islanders   *noble*
By you invited, do attend° your presence.   *wait for*

OTHELLO   I am to blame.

DESDEMONA   Why do you speak so faintly?
Are you not well?

OTHELLO   I have a pain upon my forehead, here.°   *(from cuckold's horns)*

---

6. Method (for restoring himself to favor).
7. "Though . . . fortune": even if what tied her ("jesses" are leg straps put on a hawk) were my own heartstrings, I'd set her loose downwind forever to hunt on her own.
8. "Even . . . quicken": the "plague" of horns (imagined to grow from the forehead of a cuckold) is our fate as soon as we live.

DESDEMONA Faith, that's with watching;° 'twill away *from lack of sleep*
  again.
  Let me but bind it hard, within this hour
  It will be well.
OTHELLO   Your napkin° is too little; *handkerchief*
      [*The handkerchief is dropped.*]
290 Let it alone. Come, I'll go in with you.
DESDEMONA I am very sorry that you are not well.
      Exeunt OTHELLO *and* DESDEMONA.
EMILIA I am glad I have found this napkin;
  This was her first remembrance° from the Moor. *keepsake*
  My wayward husband hath a hundred times
295 Wooed me to steal it. But she so loves the token
  (For he conjured her° she should ever keep it) *made her swear*
  That she reserves it evermore about her
  To kiss and talk to. I'll have the work ta'en out,° *embroidery copied*
  And giv't Iago; what he will do with it
300 Heaven knows, not I:
  I nothing° but to please his fantasy. *intend nothing*
      Enter IAGO.
IAGO How now? What do you here alone?
EMILIA Do not you chide; I have a thing for you.
IAGO You have a thing for me? It is a common thing⁹—
305 EMILIA Ha?
IAGO To have a foolish wife.
EMILIA O, is that all? What will you give me now
  For that same handkerchief?
IAGO   What handkerchief?
EMILIA What handkerchief?
310 Why, that the Moor first gave to Desdemona,
  That which so often you did bid me steal.
IAGO Hast stolen it from her?
EMILIA No, faith; she let it drop by negligence,
  And to th'advantage° I, being here, took't up. *taking the occasion*
  Look, here 'tis.
315 IAGO   A good wench! Give it me.
EMILIA What will you do with't, that you have been so
    earnest
  To have me filch it?
IAGO [*taking it*]   Why, what is that to you?
EMILIA If it be not for some purpose of import,
  Giv't me again. Poor lady, she'll run mad
  When she shall lack it.
320 IAGO   Be not acknown on't;° *don't let it be known*
  I have use for it. Go—leave me! *Exit* EMILIA.
  I will in Cassio's lodging lose this napkin
  And let him find it. Trifles light as air

---

9. It is a vagina ("thing") available to all.

>   Are to the jealous confirmations strong
> 325   As proofs of holy writ. This may do something.
>   The Moor already changes with my poison:
>   Dangerous conceits° are in their natures poisons,   *ideas*
>   Which at the first are scarce found to distaste,
>   But with a little act° upon the blood   *effect*
>   Burn like the mines of sulphur.¹
> 330   *Enter* OTHELLO.   I did say so—
>   Look where he comes! Not poppy nor mandragora²
>   Nor all the drowsy syrups of the world
>   Shall ever medicine thee to that sweet sleep
>   Which thou owedst° yesterday.   *owned*
>   OTHELLO   Ha! ha! false to me?
> 335 IAGO   Why, how now, general? No more of that!
>   OTHELLO   Avaunt! be gone! Thou hast set me on the rack.
>   I swear 'tis better to be much abused°   *mistreated; deceived*
>   Than but to know't a little.
>   IAGO   How now, my lord?
>   OTHELLO   What sense had I of her stol'n hours of lust?
> 340   I saw't not, thought it not; it harmed not me;
>   I slept the next night well, fed well, was free and merry;
>   I found not Cassio's kisses on her lips.
>   He that is robbed, not wanting° what is stol'n,   *missing*
>   Let him not know't, and he's not robbed at all.
> 345 IAGO   I am sorry to hear this.
>   OTHELLO   I had been happy if the general camp,
>   Pioneers° and all, had tasted her sweet body,   *manual laborers*
>   So° I had nothing known. O, now forever   *if*
>   Farewell the tranquil mind! farewell content!
> 350   Farewell the plumèd troops and the big wars
>   That makes ambition virtue! O, farewell!
>   Farewell the neighing steed and the shrill trump,°   *trumpet*
>   The spirit-stirring drum, th'ear-piercing fife,
>   The royal banner and all quality,°   *aspects*
> 355   Pride,° pomp, and circumstance° of glorious war!   *magnificence / ceremony*
>   And O you mortal engines° whose rude throats   *deadly cannons*
>   Th'immortal Jove's dread clamors° counterfeit,   *thunderclaps*
>   Farewell! Othello's occupation's gone!
>   IAGO   Is't possible, my lord?
> 360 OTHELLO   [*grabs* IAGO *by the throat*]   Villain, be sure
>   thou prove my love a whore!
>   Be sure of it, give me the ocular proof,
>   Or by the worth of mine eternal soul,
>   Thou hadst been better have been born a dog
>   Than answer my waked wrath.
>   IAGO   Is't come to this?

---

1. Pliny the Elder (23/24–79 C.E.) describes two islands of sulfur between mainland Italy and Sicily that were rumored to be always on fire.
2. A sleep-inducing substance made from the mandrake root.

OTHELLO Make me to see't, or at the least so prove it
That the probation° bear no hinge nor loop — *proof*
To hang a doubt on, or woe upon thy life!
IAGO My noble lord—
OTHELLO If thou dost slander her and torture me,
Never pray more; abandon all remorse;
On horror's head horrors accumulate;
Do deeds to make heaven weep, all earth amazed;
For nothing canst thou to damnation add
Greater than that.
IAGO   O grace! O heaven forgive me!
Are you a man? Have you a soul? or sense?
God buy you; take mine office.[3] O wretched fool,° — *(to himself)*
That lov'st to make thine honesty a vice!° — *fault*
O monstrous world! Take note, take note, O world:
To be direct and honest is not safe.
I thank you for this profit,° and from hence — *profitable lesson*
I'll love no friend, sith° love breeds such offense. — *since*
OTHELLO Nay, stay; thou shouldst be honest.
IAGO I should be wise; for honesty's a fool
And loses that° it works for. — *what*
OTHELLO   By the world,[4]
I think my wife be honest, and think she is not;
I think that thou art just, and think thou art not.
I'll have some proof. My name, that was as fresh
As Dian's[5] visage, is now begrimed and black
As mine own face. If there be cords or knives,
Poison, or fire, or suffocating streams,
I'll not endure it. Would I were satisfied!
IAGO I see you are eaten up with passion;
I do repent me that I put it to you.
You would be satisfied?
OTHELLO   Would? Nay, and I will.
IAGO And may . . . but how? how satisfied, my lord?
Would you, the supervisor,° grossly gape on? — *observer*
Behold her topped?
OTHELLO   Death and damnation! O!
IAGO It were a tedious° difficulty, I think, — *painful*
To bring them to that prospect. Damn them then,
If ever mortal eyes do see them bolster° — *share a pillow*
More° than their own.° What then? How then? — *other / own eyes*
What shall I say? Where's satisfaction?
It is impossible you should see this,
Were they as prime° as goats, as hot as monkeys, — *lustful*
As salt as wolves in pride,[6] and fools as gross

---

3. Good-bye, I resign my official position (ensign).
4. Othello's speech (lines 384–91) does not appear in Q.
5. Diana, goddess of chastity and of the (pale) moon. The Second Quarto (1630) replaces "My" (line 387) with "Her," a plausible but arguably less powerful reading that lacks textual authority.
6. As lecherous as wolves in heat.

As ignorance made drunk. But yet, I say,
If imputation and strong circumstances⁷
Which lead directly to the door of truth
Will give you satisfaction, you might have't.

410 OTHELLO Give me a living° reason she's disloyal.   *sustainable; valid*
IAGO I do not like the office.°   *task*
But sith I am entered in this cause so far,
Pricked to't° by foolish honesty and love,   *prodded on*
I will go on. I lay with Cassio lately,
415 And being troubled with a raging tooth,
I could not sleep. There are a kind of men
So loose of soul that in their sleeps will mutter
Their affairs; one of this kind is Cassio.
In sleep I heard him say "Sweet Desdemona,
420 Let us be wary, let us hide our loves!"
And then, sir, would he gripe° and wring my hand,   *grip*
Cry "O sweet creature!" then kiss me hard,
As if he plucked up kisses by the roots
That grew upon my lips, lay his leg o'er my thigh,
425 And sigh, and kiss, and then cry "Cursèd fate
That gave thee to the Moor!"
OTHELLO O monstrous! monstrous!
IAGO   Nay, this was but his
   dream.
OTHELLO But this denoted a foregone conclusion;°   *an earlier event*
'Tis a shrewd doubt,° though it be but a dream.⁸   *reasonable fear*
430 IAGO And this may help to thicken other proofs
That do demonstrate thinly.
OTHELLO   I'll tear her all to pieces!
IAGO Nay, yet be wise; yet we see nothing done;
She may be honest yet. Tell me but this:
Have you not sometimes seen a handkerchief
435 Spotted with strawberries in your wife's hand?
OTHELLO I gave her such a one; 'twas my first gift.
IAGO I know not that; but such a handkerchief—
I am sure it was your wife's—did I today
See Cassio wipe his beard with.
OTHELLO   If it be that—
440 IAGO If it be that, or any that was hers,
It speaks against her with the other proofs.
OTHELLO O that the slave° had forty thousand lives!   *(Cassio)*
One is too poor, too weak for my revenge.
Now do I see 'tis true. Look here, Iago:
445 All my fond love thus do I blow to heaven.
'Tis gone.
Arise, black vengeance, from the hollow hell!

---

7. If inference and strong circumstantial evidence.
8. Q gives this line to Iago.

	Yield up, O love, thy crown and hearted throne°	*rule of the heart*
	To tyrannous hate! Swell, bosom, with thy fraught,°	*burden*
	For 'tis of aspics'° tongues!	*poisonous snakes'*
450	IAGO Yet be content.	

OTHELLO   O, blood! blood! blood!
IAGO   Patience, I say; your mind may change.
OTHELLO   Never, Iago. Like to the Pontic Sea,°   *Black Sea*
  Whose icy current and compulsive course
455 Ne'er keeps retiring ebb but keeps due on
  To the Propontic and the Hellespont,[9]
  Even so my bloody thoughts with violent pace
  Shall ne'er look back, ne'er ebb to humble love,
  Till that a capable° and wide revenge   *capacious*
  Swallow them up.   OTHELLO *kneels.*
460   Now, by yond marble heaven,
  In the due reverence of a sacred vow,
  I here engage my words.
IAGO   Do not rise yet.   IAGO *kneels.*
  Witness, you ever-burning lights above,
  You elements that clip° us round about,   *embrace*
465 Witness that here Iago doth give up
  The execution° of his wit, hands, heart,   *command*
  To wronged Othello's service. Let him command,
  And to obey shall be in me remorse,°   *pity (for Othello)*
  What bloody business ever.°   [*They rise.*]   *soever*
OTHELLO   I greet thy love,
470 Not with vain thanks but with acceptance bounteous,
  And will upon the instant put thee to't.°   *immediately test it*
  Within these three days let me hear thee say
  That Cassio's not alive.
IAGO   My friend is dead;
  'Tis done at your request. But let her live.
475 OTHELLO   Damn her, lewd minx!° O, damn her! damn   *wanton*
  her!
  Come, go with me apart; I will withdraw
  To furnish me with some swift means of death
  For the fair devil. Now art thou my lieutenant.
IAGO   I am your own forever.   *Exeunt.*

3.4

Enter DESDEMONA, EMILIA, *and* CLOWN.

DESDEMONA   Do you know, sirrah,[1] where Lieutenant
  Cassio lies?
CLOWN   I dare not say he lies anywhere.
DESDEMONA   Why, man?

---

9. The Propontic was the body of water bounded by the straits of Bosphorus and the Dardanelles (Hellespont), the latter strait leading to the Aegean.
3.4 Location: Before the citadel.
1. A form of address to an inferior.

CLOWN He's a soldier, and for me to say a soldier lies, 'tis
stabbing.
DESDEMONA Go to; where lodges he?
CLOWN To tell you where he lodges is to tell you where
I lie.
DESDEMONA Can anything be made of this?
CLOWN I know not where he lodges, and for me to devise
a lodging and say he lies here or he lies there were to lie in
mine own throat.°   *lie outrageously*
DESDEMONA Can you inquire him out and be edified by
report?
CLOWN I will catechize the world for him—that is, make
questions and by them answer.
DESDEMONA Seek him, bid him come hither. Tell him I
have moved° my lord on his behalf and hope all will be   *petitioned*
well.
CLOWN To do this is within the compass° of man's wit,   *scope*
and therefore I will attempt the doing it.   *Exit* CLOWN.
DESDEMONA Where should° I lose the handkerchief,   *did*
Emilia?
EMILIA I know not, madam.
DESDEMONA Believe me, I had rather have lost my purse
Full of crusadoes,° and but° my noble Moor   *gold coins / except that*
Is true of mind and made of no such baseness
As jealous creatures are, it were enough
To put him to ill-thinking.
EMILIA   Is he not jealous?
DESDEMONA Who, he? I think the sun where he was born
Drew all such humors from him.²
        Enter OTHELLO.
EMILIA   Look where he comes.
DESDEMONA [*aside*] I will not leave him now till Cassio be
Called to him.—How is't with you, my lord?
OTHELLO Well, my good lady. [*Aside*] O, hardness to dissemble!—
How do you, Desdemona?
DESDEMONA   Well, my good lord.
OTHELLO Give me your hand. This hand is moist, my lady.
DESDEMONA It hath felt no age nor known no sorrow.
OTHELLO This argues fruitfulness and liberal heart.³
Hot, hot and moist. This hand of yours requires
A sequester from liberty: fasting and prayer,
Much castigation, exercise devout;
For here's a young and sweating devil here
That commonly rebels. 'Tis a good hand,
A frank° one.   *(sexually) open*
DESDEMONA   You may indeed say so,

---

2. As if the African sun dried up the bodily fluids ("humors") that produce jealousy.
3. This demonstrates fertility (perhaps, by implication, lust) and a generous (hinting at "loose") heart. A moist hand was thought to be a sign of active desire.

For 'twas that hand that gave away my heart.
OTHELLO A liberal hand. The hearts of old gave hands,
But our new heraldry is hands, not hearts.[4]
DESDEMONA I cannot speak of this. Come now, your promise.
OTHELLO What promise, chuck?°   *woodchuck (affectionate)*
DESDEMONA I have sent to bid Cassio come speak with you.
OTHELLO I have a salt and sorry rheum° offends me;   *badly watering eyes*
Lend me thy handkerchief.
DESDEMONA   Here, my lord.
OTHELLO That which I gave you.
DESDEMONA   I have it not about me.
OTHELLO Not?
DESDEMONA No, faith, my lord.
OTHELLO   That's a fault. That handkerchief
Did an Egyptian to my mother give.
She was a charmer° and could almost read   *sorceress*
The thoughts of people. She told her, while she kept it,
'Twould make her amiable° and subdue my father   *desirable*
Entirely to her love; but if she lost it
Or made a gift of it, my father's eye
Should hold her loathèd, and his spirits should hunt
After new fancies. She, dying, gave it me,
And bid me, when my fate would have me wived,
To give it her.° I did so; and—take heed on't!—   *to my wife*
Make it a darling like your precious eye.
To lose't or give't away were such perdition°   *loss; damnation*
As nothing else could match.
DESDEMONA   Is't possible?
OTHELLO 'Tis true. There's magic in the web of it:
A sibyl° that had numbered in the world   *female prophet*
The sun to course two hundred compasses,[5]
In her prophetic fury° sewed the work;   *rapture*
The worms were hallowed that did breed the silk,
And it was dyed in mummy,[6] which the skillful
Conserved of° maidens' hearts.   *preserved out of*
DESDEMONA   I'faith? Is't true?
OTHELLO Most veritable; therefore look to't well.
DESDEMONA Then would to God that I had never seen't!
OTHELLO Ha? wherefore?
DESDEMONA Why do you speak so startingly and rash?°   *fitfully and urgently*
OTHELLO Is't lost? Is't gone? Speak, is't out o'th'way?
DESDEMONA Heaven bless us!
OTHELLO Say you?
DESDEMONA It is not lost; but what an if° it were?   *an if = if*
OTHELLO How?

---

4. That is, these days the joining of hands doesn't signify the joining of hearts.
5. "That . . . compasses": who was two hundred years old.
6. Fluid drained from mummified bodies, supposedly magical.

DESDEMONA I say it is not lost.
OTHELLO Fetch't, let me see't!
DESDEMONA Why, so I can; but I will not now.
  This is a trick to put me from my suit.
  Pray you let Cassio be received again.
OTHELLO Fetch me the handkerchief, my mind misgives—
DESDEMONA Come, come!
  You'll never meet a more sufficient° man—   *complete*
OTHELLO The handkerchief!
DESDEMONA   I pray, talk me of Cassio.
OTHELLO The handkerchief!⁷
DESDEMONA   A man that all his time
  Hath founded his good fortunes on your love,
  Shared dangers with you—
OTHELLO   The handkerchief!
DESDEMONA I'faith, you are to blame.
OTHELLO 'Swounds!   *Exit* OTHELLO.
EMILIA Is not this man jealous?
DESDEMONA I ne'er saw this before.
  Sure, there's some wonder in this handkerchief;
  I am most unhappy in the loss of it.
EMILIA 'Tis not a year or two shows us a man.⁸
  They are all but° stomachs, and we all but food;   *nothing but*
  They eat us hungrily, and when they are full
  They belch us.
            Enter IAGO *and* CASSIO.
                      Look you, Cassio and my husband.
IAGO There is no other way; 'tis she must do't;
  And lo the happiness!⁹ go and importune her.
DESDEMONA How now, good Cassio, what's the news
  with you?
CASSIO Madam, my former suit. I do beseech you
  That by your virtuous means I may again
  Exist and be a member of his love
  Whom I, with all the office° of my heart,   *duty; loyal service*
  Entirely honor. I would not be delayed.
  If my offense be of such mortal° kind   *deadly*
  That nor° my service past nor present sorrows   *neither*
  Nor purposed merit in futurity
  Can ransom me into his love again,
  But to know so° must be my benefit;   *even to know this*
  So° shall I clothe me in a forced content   *if so*
  And shut° myself up in some other course   *give*
  To fortune's alms.
DESDEMONA   Alas, thrice-gentle Cassio,
  My advocation is not now in tune.¹

---

7. Desdemona's "I pray, talk me of Cassio" and Othello's "The handkerchief!" are only in Q.
8. That is, it doesn't take long to see what a man is.
9. What a happy coincidence (seeing Desdemona).
1. My advocacy isn't working properly.

                My lord is not my lord, nor should I know him,
                Were he in favor° as in humor° altered. *appearance / mood*
                So help me every spirit sanctified
                As I have spoken for you all my best
                And stood within the blank² of his displeasure
                For my free speech. You must awhile be patient.
                What I can do I will, and more I will
                Than for myself I dare. Let that suffice you.
IAGO   Is my lord angry?
EMILIA   He went hence but now,
                And certainly in strange unquietness.
IAGO   Can he be angry? I have seen the cannon
                When it hath blown his ranks into the air
                And, like the devil, from his very arm
                Puffed his own brother³—and is he angry?
                Something of moment then. I will go meet him;
                There's matter in't indeed if he be angry.
DESDEMONA   I prithee do so.   *Exit* [IAGO].
                                     Something sure of state⁴—
                Either from Venice, or some unhatched practice°   *unfinished plot*
                Made demonstrable here in Cyprus to him—
                Hath puddled his clear spirit; and in such cases
                Men's natures wrangle with inferior things,
                Though great ones are their object. 'Tis even so.
                For let our finger ache, and it endues°   *induces*
                Our other, healthful members even to a sense
                Of pain. Nay, we must think men are not gods,
                Nor of them look for such observancy°   *careful attention*
                As fits the bridal.°—Beshrew me° much, Emilia.   *wedding / (mild curse)*
                I was, unhandsome° warrior as I am,   *unskilled*
                Arraigning his unkindness with my soul;
                But now I find I had suborned the witness,
                And he's indicted falsely.⁵
EMILIA   Pray heaven it be
                State matters, as you think, and no conception
                Nor no jealous toy° concerning you.   *whim*
DESDEMONA   Alas the day! I never gave him cause.
EMILIA   But jealous souls will not be answered so;
                They are not ever jealous for the cause,
                But jealous for they're jealous. It is a monster
                Begot upon itself, born on itself.
DESDEMONA   Heaven keep the monster from Othello's mind!
EMILIA   Lady, amen!
DESDEMONA   I will go seek him; Cassio, walk here about.
                If I do find him fit, I'll move your suit
                And seek to effect it to my uttermost.

---

2. The "blank" was the white spot at the center of a target.
3. Blew up his own brother (and Othello wasn't angry even then).
4. Surely some official business.
5. Made the witness lie and so accused Othello falsely.

CASSIO   I humbly thank your ladyship.

Exeunt DESDEMONA *and* EMILIA.

Enter BIANCA.[6]

BIANCA   Save you,° friend Cassio!   *God save you*
CASSIO   What make° you from home?   *brings*
How is't with you, my most fair Bianca?
I'faith, sweet love, I was coming to your house.
BIANCA   And I was going to your lodging, Cassio.
What? keep a week away? seven days and nights?
Eightscore-eight hours? And lovers' absent hours
More tedious than the dial eightscore times![7]
O weary reckoning!°   *calculating*
CASSIO   Pardon me, Bianca;
I have this while with leaden thoughts been pressed,
But I shall in a more continuate° time   *opportune*
Strike off° this score of absence. Sweet Bianca,   *make up*
        [*Gives her* DESDEMONA's *handkerchief.*]
Take me this work out.°   *copy this embroidery*
BIANCA   O, Cassio! whence came this?
This is some token from a newer friend;
To the felt absence now I feel a cause.
Is't come to this? Well, well.
CASSIO   Go to,° woman!   *stop it*
Throw your vile guesses in the devil's teeth,
From whence you have them. You are jealous now
That this is from some mistress some remembrance;
No, by my faith, Bianca.
BIANCA   Why, whose is it?
CASSIO   I know not neither; I found it in my chamber.
I like the work well; ere it be demanded,°   *sought out*
As like° enough it will, I would have it copied.   *likely*
Take it and do't, and leave me for this time.
BIANCA   Leave you? Wherefore?
CASSIO   I do attend here on the general,
And think it no addition,° nor my wish,   *(to my cause)*
To have him see me womaned.
BIANCA   Why, I pray you?
CASSIO   Not that I love you not.
BIANCA   But that you do not love me.
I pray you bring me on the way a little,
And say if I shall see you soon at night.
CASSIO   'Tis but a little way that I can bring you,
For I attend here; but I'll see you soon.
BIANCA   'Tis very good—I must be circumstanced.[8]

Exeunt.

---

6. "Bianca" means "white" in Italian—an ironic reversal of conventional color imagery, given that Bianca is a "customer" (courtesan, 4.1.119).
7. "Lovers'... times": each hour lovers are parted is eightscore (160) times more tedious than normal clock time.
8. Content with what circumstances offer.

4.1

Enter OTHELLO *and* IAGO.

IAGO Will you think so?
OTHELLO   Think so, Iago?
IAGO   What,
  To kiss in private?
OTHELLO   An unauthorized kiss!
IAGO Or to be naked with her friend in bed
  An hour or more, not meaning any harm?
5 OTHELLO Naked in bed, Iago, and not mean harm?
  It is hypocrisy against the devil.[1]
  They that mean virtuously, and yet do so,
  The devil their virtue tempts, and they tempt heaven.[2]
IAGO If they do nothing, 'tis a venial slip;°   *an excusable sin*
10 But if I give my wife a handkerchief—
OTHELLO What then?
IAGO Why then, 'tis hers, my lord; and being hers,
  She may, I think, bestow't on any man.
OTHELLO She is protectress of her honor too;
15 May she give that?
IAGO Her honor is an essence that's not seen;
  They° have it very oft that have it not.   *they are reputed to*
  But for the handkerchief—
OTHELLO By heaven, I would most gladly have forgot it!
20 Thou said'st—O, it comes o'er my memory
  As doth the raven o'er the infectious° house,[3]   *plague-infested*
  Boding to all!—he had my handkerchief.
IAGO Ay, what of that?
OTHELLO   That's not so good now.
IAGO What if I had said I had seen him do you wrong?
25 Or heard him say—as knaves be such abroad[4]
  Who (having by their own importunate suit
  Or voluntary dotage° of some mistress   *doting*
  Convincèd or supplied° them) cannot choose   *seduced or satisfied*
  But they must blab—
OTHELLO   Hath he said anything?
30 IAGO He hath, my lord, but be you well assured,
  No more than he'll unswear.
OTHELLO   What hath he said?
IAGO Faith, that he did . . . I know not what he did.
OTHELLO What? What?
IAGO Lie . . .
OTHELLO   With her?

4.1 Location: Before the citadel.
1. That is, by appearing to act sinfully while actually being good.
2. Those who mean well ("virtuously") but act in this lascivious fashion ("so") open themselves to temptation by the devil, and they tempt heaven (to give them over). "Thou shalt not tempt the Lord thy God" (Matthew 4:7).
3. The raven was thought to be an ill omen and a carrier of plague.
4. As such knaves do exist in the world.

IAGO   With her, on her; what you will.

OTHELLO Lie with her? lie on her? We say lie on her when
they belie° her. Lie with her? 'Swounds, that's ful-   *slander*
some.°— Handkerchief! confessions! handkerchief!—To[5]   *nauseating*
confess, and be hanged for his labor. First to be hanged,
and then to confess: I tremble at it. Nature would not
invest herself in such shadowing passion without some
instruction.[6] It is not words that shakes me thus. Pish!
Noses, ears, and lips! Is't possible? Confess? Handkerchief? O devil!   *Falls in a trance.*

IAGO Work on;
My medicine works! Thus credulous fools are caught,
And many worthy and chaste dames even thus,
All guiltless, meet reproach.—What ho! my lord!
My lord, I say! Othello!
       Enter CASSIO.
                     How now, Cassio?

CASSIO What's the matter?

IAGO My lord is fallen into an epilepsy.
This is his second fit; he had one yesterday.

CASSIO Rub him about the temples.

IAGO   No, forbear.
The lethargy° must have his° quiet course;   *trance / its*
If not, he foams at mouth and by and by
Breaks out to savage madness. Look, he stirs.
Do you withdraw yourself a little while;
He will recover straight.° When he is gone,   *immediately*
I would on great occasion° speak with you.   *important matters*
                              [*Exit* CASSIO.]
How is it, general? Have you not hurt your head?[7]

OTHELLO Dost thou mock me?

IAGO   I mock you not, by heaven.
Would you would bear your fortune like a man!

OTHELLO A hornèd man's a monster and a beast.

IAGO There's many a beast then in a populous city,
And many a civil° monster.   *city-dwelling*

OTHELLO Did he confess it?

IAGO   Good sir, be a man:
Think every bearded fellow that's but yoked
May draw with you.[8] There's millions now alive
That nightly lie in those unproper beds
Which they dare swear peculiar.[9] Your case is better.
O, 'tis the spite of hell, the fiend's arch-mock,°   *devil's greatest mock*
To lip° a wanton in a secure° couch   *kiss / an unsuspected*

---

5. The rest of the speech does not appear in Q.
6. "Nature . . . instruction": it isn't natural that I would feel such overwhelming ("shadowing") emotion (*jealousy*) unless there were some cause for it.
7. Othello takes this as suggesting that he has grown cuckold's horns.
8. Every married man ("yoked," like an ox, to his wife and hence to cuckoldry) labors ("draws") under the same fate.
9. Who lie in beds that don't belong entirely to them but that they would swear are exclusively their own.

And to suppose her chaste. No, let me know;
And knowing what I am,° I know what she shall be. *(a cuckold)*

OTHELLO O, thou art wise, 'tis certain.

IAGO   Stand you a while apart,
75 Confine yourself but in a patient list.° *boundary*
Whilst you were here, o'er-whelmèd with your grief—
A passion most unsuiting such a man—
Cassio came hither. I shifted him away
And laid good 'scuses upon your ecstasy,° *for your fit*
80 Bade him anon return and here speak with me,
The which he promised. Do but encave° yourself, *hide*
And mark the fleers,° the gibes, and notable scorns *sneers*
That dwell in every region of his face;
For I will make him tell the tale anew:
85 Where, how, how oft, how long ago, and when
He hath and is again to cope° your wife. *copulate with*
I say, but mark his gesture. Marry, patience!
Or I shall say you're all in all in spleen,° *completely impulsive*
And nothing of a man.

OTHELLO   Dost thou hear, Iago?
90 I will be found most cunning in my patience;
But—dost thou hear?—most bloody.

IAGO   That's not amiss,
But yet keep time° in all. Will you withdraw? *maintain control*
    [OTHELLO *withdraws*.]
Now will I question Cassio of Bianca,
A huswife° that by selling her desires *hussy*
95 Buys herself bread and cloth. It is a creature
That dotes on Cassio—as 'tis the strumpet's plague
To beguile many and be beguiled by one.
He, when he hears of her, cannot restrain
From the excess of laughter. Here he comes.
    Enter CASSIO.
100 As he shall smile, Othello shall go mad;
And his unbookish° jealousy must conster° *ignorant / construe*
Poor Cassio's smiles, gestures, and light behaviors
Quite in the wrong. How do you, lieutenant?

CASSIO The worser that you give me the addition° *title*
105 Whose want even kills me.

IAGO Ply Desdemona well, and you are sure on't.
Now if this suit lay in Bianca's power,
How quickly should you speed!

CASSIO   Alas, poor caitiff!° *wretch*

OTHELLO Look how he laughs already!

110 IAGO I never knew woman love man so.

CASSIO Alas, poor rogue! I think, i'faith, she loves me.

OTHELLO Now he denies it faintly and laughs it out.

IAGO Do you hear, Cassio?

OTHELLO   Now he importunes him

To tell it o'er. Go to! well said, well said!
IAGO She gives it out that you shall marry her.
Do you intend it?
CASSIO Ha, ha, ha!
OTHELLO Do ye triumph, Roman?[1] do you triumph?
CASSIO I marry? What! a customer?° Prithee bear some *courtesan*
charity to my wit;° do not think it so unwholesome. Ha, ha, *sense*
ha!
OTHELLO So, so, so, so! they laugh that wins.
IAGO Faith, the cry goes that you marry her.
CASSIO Prithee say true.
IAGO I am a very villain else.° *if it's not true*
OTHELLO Have you scored° me? Well. *scored off*
CASSIO This is the monkey's own giving out.[2] She is persuaded I will marry her out of her own love and flattery, not out of my promise.
OTHELLO Iago beckons me; now he begins the story.
[OTHELLO *draws closer.*]
CASSIO She was here even now; she haunts me in every place. I was the other day talking on the sea-bank with certain Venetians, and thither comes the bauble° and *toy*
falls me thus about my neck—
OTHELLO Crying "O dear Cassio!" as it were: his gesture imports° it. *indicates*
CASSIO So hangs and lolls and weeps upon me, so shakes and pulls me. Ha, ha, ha!
OTHELLO Now he tells how she plucked him to my chamber. O, I see that nose of yours, but not that dog I shall throw it to.[3]
CASSIO Well, I must leave her company.
IAGO Before me! look where she comes!
Enter BIANCA.
CASSIO 'Tis such another fitchew![4] marry, a perfumed one! What do you mean by this haunting of me?
BIANCA Let the devil and his dam° haunt you! What did *mother*
you mean by that same handkerchief you gave me even now? I was a fine fool to take it. I must take out° the *copy*
work? A likely piece of work,[5] that you should find it in your chamber and know not who left it there! This is some minx's token, and I must take out the work? There, give it your hobby-horse!° Wheresoever you had it, I'll *mountable woman*
take out no work on't.
CASSIO How now, my sweet Bianca?
How now? how now?

---

1. Othello draws on associations either with Rome's imperial successes (and subsequent collapse) or with the Roman practice of holding celebratory *processions* (called *triumphs*) for military victors.
2. That is, this is Bianca's own story.
3. That is, I'm envisioning my revenge, but the time is not yet quite right.
4. Polecat, associated with prostitutes because of its bad smell and supposed lecherousness.
5. An implausible story.

OTHELLO By heaven, that should° be my handkerchief! — *must*
BIANCA If you'll come to supper tonight, you may; if you will not, come when you are next prepared for.[6] *Exit.*
IAGO After her, after her!
160 CASSIO Faith, I must; she'll rail in the streets else.
IAGO Will you sup there?
CASSIO Faith, I intend so.
IAGO Well, I may chance to see you, for I would very fain speak with you.
165 CASSIO Prithee come, will you?
IAGO Go to; say no more. *Exit CASSIO.*
OTHELLO [*comes forward*] How shall I murder him, Iago?
IAGO Did you perceive how he laughed at his vice?
OTHELLO O Iago!
170 IAGO And did you see the handkerchief?
OTHELLO Was that mine?
IAGO Yours, by this hand! and to see how he prizes the foolish woman, your wife! She gave it him, and he hath given it his whore.
175 OTHELLO I would have him nine years a-killing![7]—A fine woman, a fair woman, a sweet woman!
IAGO Nay, you must forget that.
OTHELLO Ay, let her rot and perish and be damned tonight, for she shall not live! No, my heart is turned to
180 stone; I strike it, and it hurts my hand.—O, the world hath not a sweeter creature! She might lie by an emperor's side and command him tasks.
IAGO Nay, that's not your way.° — *(the way to think)*
OTHELLO Hang her!—I do but say what she is: so delicate
185 with her needle; an admirable musician (O, she will sing the savageness out of a bear!); of so high and plenteous wit and invention!° — *imagination*
IAGO She's the worse for all this.
OTHELLO O, a thousand, a thousand times!—And then of
190 so gentle° a condition! — *highly born*
IAGO Ay, too gentle.° — *generous (sexually)*
OTHELLO Nay, that's certain.—But yet the pity of it, Iago! O Iago, the pity of it, Iago!
IAGO If you are so fond° over her iniquity, give her patent° — *foolish / license*
195 to offend; for if it touch not you, it comes near nobody.
OTHELLO I will chop her into messes!° Cuckold me! — *pieces of food*
IAGO O, 'tis foul in her.
OTHELLO With mine officer!
IAGO That's fouler.
200 OTHELLO Get me some poison, Iago, this night. I'll not expostulate with her, lest her body and beauty unprovide my mind° again. This night, Iago. — *weaken my resolve*

6. Come next time I prepare for you (never).   7. I would like to spend nine years killing him.

IAGO Do it not with poison. Strangle her in her bed, even
the bed she hath contaminated.
OTHELLO Good, good! The justice of it pleases. Very
good!
IAGO And for Cassio, let me be his undertaker.°   *murderer*
hear more by midnight.
OTHELLO Excellent good!
    A trumpet [within].
What trumpet is that same?
IAGO I warrant something from Venice.
    Enter LODOVICO, DESDEMONA, *and attendants.*
'Tis Lodovico; this comes from the duke.
See, your wife's with him.
LODOVICO God save you, worthy general.
OTHELLO With all my heart,° sir.   *thank you*
LODOVICO The duke and the senators of Venice greet you.
    [*Gives him a letter.*]
OTHELLO I kiss the instrument° of their pleasures.°   *bearer / commands*
    [*Opens the letter and reads.*]
DESDEMONA And what's the news, good cousin Lodovico?
IAGO I am very glad to see you, signor.
Welcome to Cyprus.
LODOVICO I thank you. How does Lieutenant Cassio?
IAGO Lives, sir.
DESDEMONA Cousin, there's fallen between him and my lord
An unkind° breach; but you shall make all well.   *unnatural*
OTHELLO Are you sure of that?
DESDEMONA My lord?
OTHELLO [*reads*] "This fail you not to do, as you will . . ."
LODOVICO He did not call: he's busy in the paper.
Is there division 'twixt my lord and Cassio?
DESDEMONA A most unhappy one; I would do much
T'atone° them, for the love I bear to Cassio.   *to reconcile*
OTHELLO Fire and brimstone!
DESDEMONA   My lord?
OTHELLO   Are you wise?
DESDEMONA What, is he angry?
LODOVICO   May be the letter moved him;
For, as I think, they do command him home,
Deputing Cassio in his government.°   *official position*
DESDEMONA By my troth, I am glad on't.
OTHELLO   Indeed!
DESDEMONA   My lord?
OTHELLO I am glad to see you mad.⁸
DESDEMONA   Why, sweet Othello?
OTHELLO Devil! [*Strikes her.*]

---

8. Othello is pleased that Desdemona is rejoicing in Cassio's promotion and thus revealing their adulterous affair, which she would be "mad" to do in public and in front of him.

DESDEMONA I have not deserved this.
LODOVICO My lord, this would not be believed in Venice,
   Though I should swear I saw't. 'Tis very much;°   *going too far*
   Make her amends—she weeps.
OTHELLO   O devil, devil!
   If that the earth could teem with° woman's tears,   *become pregnant by*
   Each drop she falls would prove a crocodile.[9]
   Out of my sight!
DESDEMONA   I will not stay to offend you.
LODOVICO Truly obedient lady!
   I do beseech your lordship call her back.
OTHELLO Mistress!
DESDEMONA My lord?
OTHELLO What would you° with her, sir?   *do you wish*
LODOVICO   Who, I, my lord?
OTHELLO Ay, you did wish that I would make her turn.°   *return*
   Sir, she can turn, and turn,° and yet go on   *(sexually)*
   And turn again. And she can weep, sir, weep.
   And she's obedient; as you say, obedient,
   Very obedient.—Proceed you in your tears.—
   Concerning this, sir—O well-painted passion!—
   I am commanded home.—Get you away!
   I'll send for you anon.—Sir, I obey the mandate
   And will return to Venice.—Hence, avaunt!°   *begone*
         [*Exit* DESDEMONA.]
   Cassio shall have my place. And, sir, tonight
   I do entreat that we may sup together.
   You are welcome, sir, to Cyprus.—Goats and monkeys![1]
                                                Exit.
LODOVICO Is this the noble Moor whom our full senate
   Call all-in-all sufficient? Is this the nature
   Whom passion could not shake? whose solid virtue
   The shot of accident nor dart of chance
   Could neither graze nor pierce?
IAGO   He is much changed.
LODOVICO Are his wits safe? Is he not light of brain?
IAGO He's that he is; I may not breathe my censure.
   What he might be—if what he might he is not—
   I would to heaven he were.
LODOVICO   What! Strike his wife?
IAGO 'Faith, that was not so well; yet would I knew
   That stroke would prove the worst.
LODOVICO   Is it his use?°   *custom*
   Or did the letters work upon his blood°   *passions*
   And new create his fault?
IAGO   Alas, alas!

---

9. Each drop would cause the earth to conceive a crocodile (crocodiles proverbially wept false tears for their victims).
1. Symbols of lust.

>   It is not honesty in me to speak
>   What I have seen and known. You shall observe him,
>   And his own courses° will denote him so   *actions*
>   That I may save my speech. Do but go after
> 280   And mark how he continues.
>   LODOVICO   I am sorry that I am deceived in him.
>   *Exeunt.*

4.2

Enter OTHELLO *and* EMILIA.

OTHELLO   You have seen nothing then?
EMILIA   Nor ever heard, nor ever did suspect.
OTHELLO   Yes, you have seen Cassio and she together.
EMILIA   But then I saw no harm, and then I heard
5   Each syllable that breath made up between them.
OTHELLO   What, did they never whisper?
EMILIA   Never, my lord.
OTHELLO   Nor send you out o'th' way?
EMILIA   Never.
OTHELLO   To fetch her fan, her gloves, her mask, nor nothing?
10   EMILIA   Never, my lord.
OTHELLO   That's strange.
EMILIA   I durst, my lord, to wager she is honest,
    Lay down my soul at stake. If you think other,
    Remove your thought; it doth abuse your bosom.
15   If any wretch have put this in your head,
    Let heaven requite it with the serpent's curse,[1]
    For if she be not honest, chaste, and true,
    There's no man happy. The purest of their wives
    Is foul as slander.
OTHELLO   Bid her come hither—go.   *Exit* EMILIA.
20   She says enough; yet she's a simple bawd
    That cannot say as much.[2] This is a subtle whore:
    A closet lock and key° of villainous secrets;   *a hider*
    And yet she'll kneel and pray; I have seen her do't.
            Enter DESDEMONA *and* EMILIA.
DESDEMONA   My lord, what is your will?
OTHELLO   Pray you, chuck,
    come hither.
DESDEMONA   What is your pleasure?
25   OTHELLO   Let me see your eyes.
    Look in my face.
DESDEMONA   What horrible fancy's this?
OTHELLO [*to* EMILIA]   Some of your function,[3] mistress:
    Leave procreants° alone and shut the door;   *copulators*

4.2 Location: The citadel.
1. In Genesis, the curse that God laid on the serpent who deceived Eve.
2. Yet it would be a simpleminded go-between who couldn't say as much as she did.
3. Fulfill your bawd's function by guarding the door.

Cough or cry "hem" if anybody come.
Your mystery, your mystery!° Nay, dispatch! *Exit* EMILIA.   *profession*
DESDEMONA   Upon my knees, what doth your speech import?
I understand a fury in your words,
But not the words.
OTHELLO   Why? What art thou?
DESDEMONA   Your wife, my lord, your true and loyal wife.
OTHELLO   Come, swear it! damn thyself!
Lest, being° like one of heaven, the devils themselves   *appearing*
Should fear to seize thee. Therefore be double-damned:
Swear thou art honest!
DESDEMONA   Heaven doth truly know it.
OTHELLO   Heaven truly knows that thou art false as hell.
DESDEMONA   To whom, my lord? With whom? How am I false?
OTHELLO   Ah, Desdemon! away, away, away!
DESDEMONA   Alas the heavy day! Why do you weep?
Am I the motive of these tears, my lord?
If haply° you my father do suspect   *perhaps*
An instrument of this your calling back,
Lay not your blame on me. If you have lost him,
I have lost him too.
OTHELLO   Had it pleased heaven
To try me with affliction, had they rained
All kind of sores and shames on my bare head,
Steeped me in poverty to the very lips,
Given to captivity me and my utmost hopes,
I should have found in some place of my soul
A drop of patience. But, alas, to make me
The fixèd figure for the time of scorn
To point his slow and moving finger at!⁴
Yet could I bear that too—well, very well;
But there where I have garnered° up my heart,   *stored*
Where either I must live or bear no life,
The fountain from the which my current runs
Or else dries up; to be discarded thence,
Or keep it as a cistern for foul toads
To knot and gender⁵ in!—Turn thy complexion there,
Patience,⁶ thou young and rose-lipped cherubin;
Ay, here look grim as hell!
DESDEMONA   I hope my noble lord esteems me honest.
OTHELLO   O, ay, as summer flies are in the shambles,°   *slaughterhouse*
That quicken even with blowing.⁷ O thou weed,
Who art so lovely fair and smell'st so sweet

---

4. The designated object of scorn for this scornful time to point (as on a clock face) its slowly moving hand at.
5. To couple and engender.
6. Change color at the thought of that, Patience.
7. Who come to life (or bring their offspring to life and hence make the meat foul) as soon as the eggs are deposited. The point seems to be the speed of breeding, inferred from Desdemona's supposed infidelity.

    That the sense aches at thee,
70   Would thou hadst never been born!
DESDEMONA Alas, what ignorant sin have I committed?
OTHELLO Was this fair paper, this most goodly book,
    Made to write "whore" upon? What committed?
    Committed?[8] O, thou public commoner!°   *prostitute*
75   I should make very forges of my cheeks
    That would to cinders burn up modesty
    Did I but speak thy deeds. What committed?
    Heaven stops the nose at it, and the moon winks;°   *closes its eyes*
    The bawdy° wind that kisses all it meets   *promiscuous*
80   Is hushed within the hollow mine of earth°   *within a cave*
    And will not hear't. What committed?
DESDEMONA By heaven, you do me wrong!
OTHELLO Are not you a strumpet?
DESDEMONA   No, as I am a Christian!
    If to preserve this vessel for my lord
85   From any other foul unlawful touch
    Be not to be a strumpet, I am none.
OTHELLO What, not a whore?
DESDEMONA   No, as I shall be saved!
OTHELLO Is't possible?
DESDEMONA   O, heaven forgive us!
OTHELLO   I cry you mercy° then. *I beg your pardon*
90   I took you for that cunning whore of Venice
    That married with Othello.—You! Mistress!
    That have the office opposite to Saint Peter
    And keeps the gate of hell. You, you!
      Enter EMILIA.
             Ay, you.
    We have done our course;° [*giving her money*] there's *business*
     money for your pains;
95   I pray you turn the key and keep our counsel.   *Exit.*
EMILIA Alas, what does this gentleman conceive?°   *believe*
    How do you, madam? how do you, my good lady?
DESDEMONA Faith, half asleep.
EMILIA Good madam, what's the matter with my lord?
DESDEMONA With who?
100 EMILIA   Why, with my lord, madam.
DESDEMONA Who is thy lord?
EMILIA   He that is yours, sweet lady.
DESDEMONA I have none. Do not talk to me, Emilia;
    I cannot weep, nor answers have I none
    But what should go by water.° Prithee tonight *appear in tears*
105   Lay on my bed my wedding sheets, remember;
    And call thy husband hither.
EMILIA   Here's a change indeed!
                Exit.

---

8. Lines 74–77 do not appear in Q.

DESDEMONA 'Tis meet° I should be used so, very meet. — *fitting*
How have I been behaved that he might stick
The small'st opinion on my least misuse?[9]
Enter IAGO *and* EMILIA.
IAGO What is your pleasure, madam? How is't with you?
DESDEMONA I cannot tell. Those that do teach young babes
Do it with gentle means and easy tasks.
He might have chid me so; for in good faith
I am a child to chiding.
IAGO   What is the matter, lady?
EMILIA Alas, Iago, my lord hath so bewhored her,° — *called her a whore*
Thrown such despite° and heavy terms upon her, — *spite*
That true hearts cannot bear it.
DESDEMONA Am I that name, Iago?
IAGO   What name, fair lady?
DESDEMONA Such as she said my lord did say I was.
EMILIA He called her whore. A beggar in his drink
Could not have laid such terms upon his callet.° — *whore*
IAGO Why did he so?
DESDEMONA I do not know; I am sure I am none such.
IAGO Do not weep, do not weep. Alas the day!
EMILIA Hath she forsook so many noble matches,
Her father and her country and her friends,
To be called whore? Would it not make one weep?
DESDEMONA It is my wretched fortune.
IAGO   Beshrew° him for't! — *curse*
How comes this trick° upon him? — *behavior*
DESDEMONA   Nay, heaven doth know.
EMILIA I will be hanged if some eternal villain,
Some busy° and insinuating rogue, — *meddling*
Some cogging,° cozening° slave, to get some office, — *deceiving / cheating*
Have not devised this slander. I will be hanged else.
IAGO Fie! there is no such man; it is impossible.
DESDEMONA If any such there be, heaven pardon him.
EMILIA A halter° pardon him, and hell gnaw his bones! — *hangman's noose*
Why should he call her whore? Who keeps her company?
What place? what time? what form? what likelihood?
The Moor's abused by some most villainous knave,
Some base notorious knave, some scurvy fellow.
O heaven, that such companions thou'dst unfold,° — *reveal*
And put in every honest hand a whip
To lash the rascals naked through the world
Even from the east to th' west!
IAGO   Speak within door.° — *more softly*
EMILIA O, fie upon them! Some such squire° he was — *fellow*
That turned your wit the seamy side without° — *wrong side out*
And made you to suspect me with the Moor.

---

9. "That . . . misuse": that would cause him to suspect even slightly the least fault (?).

IAGO You are a fool; go to.
DESDEMONA   O God,[1] Iago,
    What shall I do to win my lord again?
    Good friend, go to him; for by this light of heaven,
    I know not how I lost him. Here I kneel:[2]
    If e'er my will did trespass 'gainst his love,
    Either in discourse of thought or actual deed,
    Or that mine eyes, mine ears, or any sense
    Delighted them in any other form,[3]
    Or that I do not yet,° and ever did,   *still*
    And ever will (though he do shake me off
    To beggarly divorcement) love him dearly—
    Comfort forswear me!° Unkindness may do much,   *deny me divine solace*
    And his unkindness may defeat my life,
    But never taint my love.   [*She rises.*]
                                I cannot say "whore."
    It does abhor[4] me now I speak the word.
    To do the act that might the addition° earn,   *label*
    Not the world's mass of vanity° could make me.   *all worldly splendor*
IAGO I pray you be content; 'tis but his humor;°   *mood*
    The business of the state does him offense.
DESDEMONA If 'twere no other—
IAGO   It is but so, I warrant.
    [*Trumpets within.*]
    Hark how these instruments summon to supper.
    The messengers of Venice stays the meat;°   *are waiting to eat*
    Go in, and weep not; all things shall be well.
                                Exeunt DESDEMONA *and* EMILIA.
        Enter RODERIGO.
    How now, Roderigo?
RODERIGO I do not find that thou deal'st justly with me.
IAGO What in the contrary?
RODERIGO Every day thou doff'st me with some device,[5]
    Iago, and rather, as it seems to me now, keep'st from me
    all conveniency° than suppliest me with the least advan-   *opportunity*
    tage of hope. I will indeed no longer endure it. Nor am I
    yet persuaded to put up in peace what already I have
    foolishly suffered.
IAGO Will you hear me, Roderigo?
RODERIGO Faith, I have heard too much; and your words
    and performances are no kin together.
IAGO You charge me most unjustly.
RODERIGO With naught but truth. I have wasted myself
    out of my means. The jewels you have had from me to
    deliver Desdemona would half have corrupted a votarist.°   *nun*

---

1. The folio reads "Alas," in keeping with the censorship of oaths that led to many changes from the quarto text. Q's reading here, "O Good," is probably a misprint for "O God."
2. Lines 151–64 (beginning with "Here") do not appear in Q.
3. Took pleasure in anyone but him.
4. Fill me with abhorrence; make me abhorrent, with a pun on "ab-whore."
5. You put me off with some trick.

You have told me she hath received them, and returned me expectations and comforts of sudden respect and acquaintance, but I find none.

190 IAGO Well, go to, very well.

RODERIGO "Very well"! "go to"! I cannot go to,° man, nor 'tis not very well. Nay, I think it is scurvy, and begin to find myself fopped° in it.

succeed sexually

made a fool

IAGO Very well.

195 RODERIGO I tell you 'tis not very well. I will make myself known to Desdemona. If she will return me my jewels, I will give over my suit and repent my unlawful solicitation. If not, assure yourself I will seek satisfaction of you.

200 IAGO You have said° now.

finished

RODERIGO Ay, and said nothing but what I protest intendment of doing.

IAGO Why, now I see there's mettle in thee, and even from this instant do build on thee a better opinion than
205 ever before. Give me thy hand, Roderigo. Thou hast taken against me a most just exception, but yet I protest I have dealt most directly in thy affair.

RODERIGO It hath not appeared.

IAGO I grant indeed it hath not appeared, and your suspi-
210 cion is not without wit and judgment. But, Roderigo, if thou hast that in thee indeed which I have greater reason to believe now than ever—I mean purpose, courage, and valor—this night show it. If thou the next night following enjoy not Desdemona, take me from this world
215 with treachery and devise engines for° my life.

plots against

RODERIGO Well, what is it? Is it within reason and compass?°

possibility

IAGO Sir, there is especial commission come from Venice to depute Cassio in Othello's place.

220 RODERIGO Is that true? Why, then Othello and Desdemona return again to Venice.

IAGO O no; he goes into Mauritania[6] and taketh away with him the fair Desdemona, unless his abode be lingered here by some accident; wherein none can be so
225 determinate° as the removing of Cassio.

effectual

RODERIGO How do you mean "removing" him?

IAGO Why, by making him uncapable of Othello's place—knocking out his brains.

RODERIGO And that you would have me to do.

230 IAGO Ay, if you dare do yourself a profit and a right. He sups tonight with a harlotry, and thither will I go to him. He knows not yet of his honorable fortune.° If you will watch his going thence, which I will fashion° to fall out

his promotion

arrange

---

6. Country in the western Sahara.

between twelve and one, you may take him at your pleasure. I will be near to second your attempt, and he shall fall between us. Come, stand not amazed at it, but go along with me. I will show you such a necessity in his death that you shall think yourself bound to put it on him. It is now high suppertime, and the night grows to waste. About it!

RODERIGO   I will hear further reason for this.
IAGO   And you shall be satisfied.   *Exeunt.*

4.3

Enter OTHELLO, LODOVICO, DESDEMONA, EMILIA, *and attendants.*

LODOVICO   I do beseech you, sir, trouble yourself no further.
OTHELLO   O, pardon me; 'twill do me good to walk.
LODOVICO [*to* DESDEMONA]   Madam, good night. I humbly thank your ladyship.
DESDEMONA   Your honor is most welcome.
OTHELLO   Will you walk, sir?
O, Desdemona—
DESDEMONA   My lord?
OTHELLO   Get you to bed on th'instant. I will be returned forthwith. Dismiss your attendant there. Look't be done.
DESDEMONA   I will, my lord.
            Exeunt [OTHELLO *with* LODOVICO *and attendants*].
EMILIA   How goes it now? He looks gentler than he did.
DESDEMONA   He says he will return incontinent,°   *immediately*
And hath commanded me to go to bed,
And bid me to dismiss you.
EMILIA   Dismiss me?
DESDEMONA   It was his bidding; therefore, good Emilia,
Give me my nightly wearing, and adieu.
We must not now displease him.
EMILIA   I would you had never seen him.
DESDEMONA   So would not I: my love doth so approve him
That even his stubbornness, his checks, his frowns—
Prithee unpin¹ me—have grace and favor in them.
            [EMILIA *helps* DESDEMONA *undress*.]
EMILIA   I have laid those sheets you bade me on the bed.
DESDEMONA   All's one.° Good faith, how foolish are our   *it doesn't matter*
minds!
If I do die before thee, prithee shroud me
In one of these same sheets.
EMILIA   Come, come—you talk.
DESDEMONA   My mother had a maid called Barbary;

4.3 Location: Scene continues.
1. To "unpin" a woman was to undo her dress, by the removal of pins.

She was in love, and he she loved proved mad
And did forsake her. She had a Song of "Willow"—
An old thing 'twas, but it expressed her fortune—
And she died singing it. That song tonight
30 Will not go from my mind; I² have much to do
But to³ go hang my head all at one side
And sing it, like poor Barbary. Prithee dispatch.°   *make haste*
EMILIA   Shall I go fetch your nightgown?
DESDEMONA   No. Unpin me here.
This Lodovico is a proper man.
35 EMILIA   A very handsome man.
DESDEMONA   He speaks well.
EMILIA   I know a lady in Venice would have walked barefoot
to Palestine for a touch of his nether° lip.   *lower*
DESDEMONA [*sings*]
    The poor soul sat sighing by a sycamore tree,
40   Sing all a green willow;⁴
    Her hand on her bosom, her head on her knee,
        Sing willow, willow, willow.
    The fresh streams ran by her and murmured her moans,
        Sing willow, willow, willow;
45   Her salt tears fell from her and softened the stones,
        Sing willow—
[*to* EMILIA] Lay by these.°   *put these things aside*
[*sings*]
        willow, willow.
[*to* EMILIA] Prithee hie° thee—he'll come anon.°   *hurry / straightaway*
[*sings*]
50   Sing all a green willow must be my garland.
        Let nobody blame him, his scorn I approve.
Nay, that's not next. Hark, who is't that knocks?
EMILIA   It's the wind.
DESDEMONA [*sings*]
    I called my love false love, but what said he then?⁵
55   Sing willow, willow, willow;
    If I court more women, you'll couch with more men.
[*to* EMILIA] So, get thee gone, good night. Mine eyes do
    itch—
Doth that bode° weeping?   *foretell*
EMILIA   'Tis neither here nor there.
DESDEMONA   I have heard it said so. O, these men, these men!⁶
60 Dost thou in conscience think—tell me, Emilia—
That there be women do abuse their husbands
In such gross kind?°   *fashion*
EMILIA   There be some such, no question.
DESDEMONA   Wouldst thou do such a deed for all the world?

---

2. Lines 30–52 ("I . . . next") do not appear in Q.   5. Lines 54–56 do not appear in Q.
3. I can barely bring myself not to.   6. Lines 59–62 do not appear in Q.
4. A conventional symbol of disappointed love.

EMILIA   Why, would not you?
DESDEMONA   No, by this heavenly light!
EMILIA   Nor I neither, by this heavenly light:
I might do't as well i'th' dark.
DESDEMONA   Wouldst thou do such a deed for all the world?
EMILIA   The world's a huge thing: it is a great price for a
small vice.
DESDEMONA   In troth, I think thou wouldst not.
EMILIA   In troth, I think I should—and undo't when I had
done. Marry, I would not do such a thing for a joint
ring,[7] nor for measures of lawn,° nor for gowns, petti-   *linen*
coats, nor caps, nor any petty exhibition.° But for all the   *gift*
whole world—'Uds° pity! who would not make her hus-   *God's*
band a cuckold to make him a monarch? I should venture
purgatory for't.
DESDEMONA   Beshrew me if I would do such a wrong for
the whole world!
EMILIA   Why, the wrong is but a wrong i'th' world; and
having the world for your labor, 'tis a wrong in your own
world, and you might quickly make it right.
DESDEMONA   I do not think there is any such woman.
EMILIA   Yes, a dozen; and as many to'th' vantage as
would store the world they played for.[8]
But I do think it is their husbands' faults[9]
If wives do fall. Say that they slack their duties°   *marital duties*
And pour our treasures into foreign laps;[1]
Or else break out in peevish jealousies,
Throwing restraint upon us; or say they strike us,
Or scant our former having in despite.[2]
Why, we have galls;° and though we have some grace,[3]   *tempers*
Yet have we some revenge. Let husbands know
Their wives have sense like them. They see, and smell,
And have their palates both for sweet and sour,
As husbands have. What is it that they do
When they change us for others? Is it sport?
I think it is. And doth affection° breed it?   *lust*
I think it doth. Is't frailty that thus errs?
It is so too. And have not we affections,
Desires for sport, and frailty, as men have?
Then let them use us well; else let them know,
The ills we do, their ills instruct us so.
DESDEMONA   Good night, good night. God me such uses°   *habits*
send,
Not to pick bad from bad, but by bad, mend![4]   *Exeunt.*

---

7. A cheap ring in separable halves.
8. And as many more as it would take to populate the world they gained by doing it.
9. Lines 86–103 do not appear in Q.
1. And give the semen that belongs to us to other women.
2. Or reduce our allowances out of spite.
3. Capacity for goodness, forgiveness.
4. Not to take bad behavior as an example to be followed, but to learn from it what to avoid.

5.1

Enter IAGO *and* RODERIGO.

IAGO Here, stand behind this bulk,° straight¹ will he come. — *shop stall*
   Wear thy good rapier bare, and put it home.° — *drive it into him*
   Quick, quick, fear nothing! I'll be at thy elbow.
   It makes us or it mars us; think on that
5 And fix most firm thy resolution.
RODERIGO Be near at hand; I may miscarry in't.
IAGO Here, at thy hand. Be bold, and take thy stand.
   [*Stands aside.*]
RODERIGO I have no great devotion to the deed,
   And yet he hath given me satisfying reasons;
10 'Tis but a man gone. Forth my sword: he dies!
IAGO I have rubbed this young quat° almost to the sense,² — *pimple*
   And he grows angry. Now, whether he kill Cassio
   Or Cassio him, or each do kill the other,
   Every way makes my gain. Live Roderigo,° — *if Roderigo lives*
15 He calls me to a restitution large
   Of gold and jewels that I bobbed from him° — *defrauded him of*
   As gifts to Desdemona.
   It must not be. If Cassio do remain,
   He hath a daily beauty in his life
20 That makes me ugly; and besides, the Moor
   May unfold° me to him; there stand I in much peril. — *reveal*
   No, he must die. But so—I hear him coming.
   Enter CASSIO
RODERIGO I know his gait; 'tis he. Villain, thou diest!
   [*Thrusts at* CASSIO.]
CASSIO That thrust had been mine enemy indeed,
25 But that my coat is better° than thou know'st. — *thicker; more armored*
   I will make proof of° thine. [*Wounds* RODERIGO.] — *test*
RODERIGO   O, I am slain!
   [IAGO *wounds* CASSIO *in the leg and exits.*]
CASSIO I am maimed forever! Help, ho! murder! murder!
   Enter OTHELLO.
OTHELLO The voice of Cassio. Iago keeps his word.
RODERIGO O, villain that I am!
OTHELLO   It is even so.
30 CASSIO O, help ho! light! a surgeon!
OTHELLO 'Tis he. O brave Iago, honest and just,
   That hast such noble sense of thy friend's wrong!
   Thou teachest me. Minion,° your dear lies dead, — *hussy (Desdemona)*
   And your unblest fate hies.° Strumpet, I come. — *damnation hurries on*
35 Forth of° my heart those charms, thine eyes, are blotted. — *out of*

5.1 Location: A street in Cyprus.   2. To the quick.
1. Right away.

Thy bed, lust-stained, shall with lust's blood be spotted.
              Exit OTHELLO.
    Enter LODOVICO *and* GRATIANO.
CASSIO What ho! no watch? no passage?° Murder, murder! *passerby*
GRATIANO 'Tis some mischance; the voice is very direful.
CASSIO O help!
40 LODOVICO Hark!
RODERIGO O wretched villain!
LODOVICO Two or three groan. 'Tis heavy° night; *dark*
 These may be counterfeits; let's think't unsafe
 To come into° the cry without more help. *go near*
45 RODERIGO Nobody come? Then shall I bleed to death.
    Enter IAGO *with a light*.
LODOVICO Hark.
GRATIANO Here's one comes in his shirt, with light and
 weapons.
IAGO Who's there? Whose noise is this that cries on murder?
LODOVICO We do not know.
IAGO   Do not you hear a cry?
CASSIO Here, here! for heaven's sake, help me!
50 IAGO   What's the matter?
GRATIANO This is Othello's ancient, as I take it.
LODOVICO The same indeed, a very valiant fellow.
IAGO What are you here that cry so grievously?
CASSIO Iago? O, I am spoiled, undone by villains!
55 Give me some help.
IAGO O me, lieutenant! What villains have done this?
CASSIO I think that one of them is hereabout
 And cannot make away.
IAGO   O treacherous villains!
 [*to* LODOVICO *and* GRATIANO] What are you there? Come
 in, and give some help.
60 RODERIGO O, help me there!
CASSIO That's one of them.
IAGO   O murd'rous slave! O villain!
 [*Stabs* RODERIGO.]
RODERIGO O damned Iago! O inhuman dog!
IAGO Kill men i'th' dark?—Where be these bloody thieves?—
 How silent is this town!—Ho, murder, murder!—
65 [*to* LODOVICO *and* GRATIANO] What may you be? Are you
 of good or evil?
LODOVICO As you shall prove us, praise us.
IAGO Signor Lodovico?
LODOVICO He, sir.
IAGO I cry you mercy. Here's Cassio hurt by villains.
70 GRATIANO Cassio?
IAGO How is't, brother?
CASSIO My leg is cut in two.
IAGO   Marry, heaven forbid!
 Light, gentlemen. I'll bind it with my shirt.

Enter BIANCA.

BIANCA What is the matter, ho? Who is't that cried?
IAGO Who is't that cried?
BIANCA   O, my dear Cassio!
  My sweet Cassio! O Cassio, Cassio, Cassio!
IAGO O notable strumpet! Cassio, may you suspect
  Who they should be that have thus mangled you?
CASSIO No.
GRATIANO I am sorry to find you thus; I have been to seek
  you.
IAGO Lend me a garter.³ So ... O for a chair°   litter
  To bear him easily hence!
BIANCA Alas, he faints! O Cassio, Cassio, Cassio!
IAGO Gentlemen all, I do suspect this trash
  To be a party in this injury.—
  Patience awhile, good Cassio.—Come, come!
  Lend me a light. Know we this face or no?
  Alas! my friend and my dear countryman,
  Roderigo! No—yes, sure! O heaven, Roderigo!
GRATIANO What, of Venice?
IAGO   Even he, sir. Did you know him?
GRATIANO Know him? Ay.
IAGO Signor Gratiano? I cry your gentle pardon.
  These bloody accidents must excuse my manners
  That so neglected you.
GRATIANO   I am glad to see you.
IAGO How do you, Cassio? O, a chair, a chair!
GRATIANO Roderigo?
IAGO He, he, 'tis he. [*Enter attendants with a litter.*]
              O, that's well said, the chair.
  Some good man bear him carefully from hence;
  I'll fetch the general's surgeon.—For you, mistress,
  Save you your labor.—He that lies slain here, Cassio,
  Was my dear friend. What malice was between you?
CASSIO None in the world, nor do I know the man.
IAGO [*to* BIANCA] What, look you pale? [*To attendants*] O,
  bear him out o'th'air.⁴
              [*Exeunt attendants with* CASSIO *in the
              litter and with* RODERIGO'*s body.*]
  Stay you, good gentlemen.—Look you pale, mistress?—
  Do you perceive the gastness° of her eye?—   terror
  Nay, if you stare, we shall hear more anon.—
  Behold her well; I pray you look upon her.
  Do you see, gentlemen? Nay, guiltiness will speak
  Though tongues were out of use.
        Enter EMILIA.

---

3. A band worn as a sash or belt. Iago wants to use one as a tourniquet.

4. Out of the open air (thought to be bad for wounds).

EMILIA Alas, what is the matter? what is the matter, husband?
IAGO Cassio hath here been set on in the dark
  By Roderigo and fellows that are scaped.
  He's almost slain, and Roderigo quite dead.
EMILIA Alas, good gentleman! alas, good Cassio!
IAGO This is the fruits of whoring. Prithee, Emilia,
  Go know of Cassio where he supped tonight.—
  What, do you shake at that?
BIANCA He supped at my house, but I therefore shake not.
IAGO O did he so? I charge you go with me.
EMILIA O fie upon thee, strumpet!
BIANCA   I am no strumpet, but of life as honest
  As you that thus abuse me.
EMILIA   As I? Fie upon thee!
IAGO Kind gentlemen, let's go see poor Cassio dressed.⁵—
  Come, mistress, you must tell's another tale.
  Emilia, run you to the citadel
  And tell my lord and lady what hath happed.
                                      [*Exit* EMILIA.]
  Will you go on afore?   *Exeunt* [*all but* IAGO].
       This is the night
  That either makes me or fordoes° me quite.   [*Exit.*]   undoes

5.2

Enter OTHELLO *with a light,* DESDEMONA *in her bed* [*asleep*].

OTHELLO It is the cause,¹ it is the cause, my soul.
  Let me not name it to you, you chaste stars.
  It is the cause. Yet I'll not shed her blood,
  Nor scar that whiter skin of hers than snow,
  And smooth as monumental alabaster.°   stone used in tombs
  Yet she must die, else she'll betray more men.
  Put out the light, and then put out the light.²
  If I quench thee, thou flaming minister,°   light that serves me
  I can again thy former light restore,
  Should I repent me. But once put out thy light,
  Thou cunning'st pattern of excelling nature,³
  I know not where is that Promethean heat⁴
  That can thy light relume.° When I have plucked thy rose   relight
  I cannot give it vital growth again;
  It needs must wither. I'll smell thee on the tree.
    [*He smells, then kisses her.*]
  O balmy breath, that dost almost persuade

---

5. That is, see his wound dressed.
5.2 Location: Desdemona and Othello's bedroom.
1. That is, Desdemona's infidelity is the "cause" of—the *thing that demands*—justice, which Othello sees himself as being required to execute.
2. This and the following lines compare the light of Othello's lamp or torch to Desdemona's "light" of life.
3. You most cleverly wrought example of nature's surpassing work.
4. Life-giving fire. In Greek mythology, Prometheus stole fire from heaven to give it to humankind; in a different tradition, he is credited with animating humankind from clay.

Justice to break her sword! One more; one more.
   [*He kisses her.*]
Be thus when thou art dead, and I will kill thee
And love thee after. One more, and that's the last.
   He kisses her.
So sweet was ne'er so fatal. I must weep,
But they are cruel tears. This sorrow's heavenly:
It strikes where it doth love.[5] She wakes.

DESDEMONA   Who's there? Othello?
OTHELLO   Ay, Desdemona.
DESDEMONA   Will you come to bed, my lord?
OTHELLO   Have you prayed tonight, Desdemon?
DESDEMONA   Ay, my lord.
OTHELLO   If you bethink yourself of any crime
Unreconciled as yet to heaven and grace,
Solicit° for it straight.   °*ask forgiveness*
DESDEMONA   Alack, my lord, what may you mean by that?
OTHELLO   Well, do it, and be brief; I will walk by.
I would not kill thy unprepared spirit.
No, heavens forfend! I would not kill thy soul.
DESDEMONA   Talk you of killing?
OTHELLO   Ay, I do.
DESDEMONA   Then heaven
Have mercy on me!
OTHELLO   Amen, with all my heart!
DESDEMONA   If you say so, I hope you will not kill me.
OTHELLO   Humh.
DESDEMONA   And yet I fear you, for you're fatal then
When your eyes roll so. Why I should fear, I know not,
Since guiltiness I know not; but yet I feel I fear.
OTHELLO   Think on thy sins.
DESDEMONA   They are loves I bear to you.
OTHELLO   Ay, and for that thou diest.
DESDEMONA   That death's unnatural that kills for loving.
Alas, why gnaw you so your nether lip?
Some bloody passion shakes your very frame.
These are portents; but yet I hope, I hope,
They do not point on me.
OTHELLO   Peace, and be still.
DESDEMONA   I will so. What's the matter?
OTHELLO   That handkerchief,
Which I so loved and gave thee, thou gav'st to Cassio.
DESDEMONA   No, by my life and soul! Send for the man
And ask him.
OTHELLO   Sweet soul, take heed; take heed of perjury;
Thou art on thy deathbed.
DESDEMONA   Ay, but not yet to die.

---

5. See Hebrews 12:6: "For whom the Lord loveth, he chasteneth."

OTHELLO   Presently.°   *immediately*
   Therefore confess thee freely of thy sin;
   For to deny each article with oath
   Cannot remove nor choke the strong conception
   That I do groan withal.⁶ Thou art to die.
DESDEMONA   Then Lord have mercy on me!
OTHELLO   I say amen.
DESDEMONA   And have you mercy too! I never did
   Offend you in my life, never loved Cassio
   But with such general warranty of heaven
   As I might love. I never gave him token.
OTHELLO   By heaven, I saw my handkerchief in's hand!
   O perjured woman! thou dost stone° my heart,   *harden*
   And makes me call what I intend to do
   A murder, which I thought a sacrifice.
   I saw the handkerchief.
DESDEMONA   He found it then.
   I never gave it him. Send for him hither.
   Let him confess a truth.
OTHELLO   He hath confessed.
DESDEMONA   What, my lord?
OTHELLO   That he hath used thee.
DESDEMONA   How? unlawfully?
OTHELLO   Ay.
DESDEMONA   He will not say so.
OTHELLO   No, his mouth is stopped.
   Honest Iago hath ta'en order for't.
DESDEMONA   O, my fear interprets! What, is he dead?
OTHELLO   Had all his hairs been lives, my great revenge
   Had stomach for them all.
DESDEMONA [*weeping*]   Alas, he is betrayed and I undone!
OTHELLO   Out, strumpet! Weep'st thou for him to my face?
DESDEMONA   O banish me, my lord, but kill me not!
OTHELLO [*attacking her*]   Down, strumpet!
DESDEMONA   Kill me tomorrow, let me live tonight!
OTHELLO   Nay, if you strive—
DESDEMONA   But half an hour!
OTHELLO   Being done, there is no pause.⁷
DESDEMONA   But while I say one prayer!
OTHELLO   It is too late.
   Smothers her.
DESDEMONA   O Lord, Lord, Lord!
EMILIA *calls within*   My lord, my lord! What ho! My lord,
   my lord!

---

6. Cannot change the strong conviction I have of your guilt (or the firm plan to kill you), which makes me groan so. The metaphor is from childbirth.
7. Now that I've started, there's no stopping.

OTHELLO   What noise is this? Not dead? not yet quite dead?
   I that am cruel am yet merciful;
   I would not have thee linger in thy pain.
   So, so.
EMILIA *within*   What ho? my lord, my lord!
OTHELLO   Who's there?
EMILIA [*within*]   O good my lord, I would speak a word with
   you.
OTHELLO [*calling*]   Yes.—'Tis Emilia.—[*calling*] By and
   by.°—She's dead.   *in a moment*
   'Tis like she comes to speak of Cassio's death.
   The noise was high.° Ha, no more moving?   *commotion was loud*
   Still as the grave. Shall she come in? Were't good?
   I think she stirs again. No. What's best to do?
   If she come in, she'll sure speak to my wife.
   My wife, my wife! What wife? I have no wife.
   O insupportable! O heavy hour!
   Methinks it should be now a huge eclipse
   Of sun and moon, and that th'affrighted globe
   Should yawn at alteration.⁸
EMILIA [*within*]   I do beseech you
   That I may speak with you. O good my lord!
OTHELLO   I had forgot thee. O, come in, Emilia.
   Soft,° by and by; let me the curtains draw.   *quiet*
   [*He closes the bed curtains.*]
   Where art thou? What's the matter with thee now?
   [*He unlocks the door.*] *Enter* EMILIA.
EMILIA   O my good lord, yonder's foul murders done!
OTHELLO   What? now?
EMILIA   But° now, my lord.   *just*
OTHELLO   It is the very error° of the moon;   *deviation*
   She comes more nearer earth than she was wont
   And makes men mad.
EMILIA   Cassio, my lord, hath killed
   A young Venetian called Roderigo.
OTHELLO   Roderigo killed? and Cassio killed?
EMILIA   No, Cassio is not killed.
OTHELLO   Not Cassio killed? Then murder's out of tune,
   And sweet revenge grows harsh.
DESDEMONA   O falsely, falsely murdered!
EMILIA   O Lord! what cry is that?
OTHELLO   That? What?
EMILIA   Out and alas! that was my lady's voice.
   [*She opens the bed curtains.*]
   Help, help ho, help! O, lady, speak again!
   Sweet Desdemona, O sweet mistress, speak!
DESDEMONA   A guiltless death I die.
EMILIA   O, who hath done this deed?

8. Should gape at the change. Earthquakes were associated with eclipses.

DESDEMONA Nobody. I myself. Farewell.
   Commend me to my kind lord. O, farewell!
      She dies.
OTHELLO Why, how should she be murdered?
EMILIA   Alas, who knows?
OTHELLO You heard her say herself it was not I.
EMILIA She said so; I must needs report the truth.
OTHELLO She's like a liar gone to burning hell!
   'Twas I that killed her!
EMILIA   O, the more angel she,
   And you the blacker devil!
OTHELLO She turned to folly,° and she was a whore. °*wantonness*
EMILIA Thou dost belie her, and thou art a devil.
OTHELLO She was false as water.
EMILIA   Thou art rash as fire to say
   That she was false. O, she was heavenly true!
OTHELLO Cassio did top her. Ask thy husband else.° °*if you doubt it*
   O, I were damned beneath all depth in hell
   But that I did proceed upon just grounds
   To this extremity! Thy husband knew it all.
EMILIA My husband?
OTHELLO Thy husband.
EMILIA That she was false to wedlock?
OTHELLO Ay, with Cassio. Had she been true,
   If heaven would make me such another world
   Of one entire and perfect chrysolite,° °*topaz*
   I'd not have sold her for it.
EMILIA   My husband?
OTHELLO Ay, 'twas he that told me on her first.
   An honest man he is, and hates the slime
   That sticks on filthy deeds.
EMILIA   My husband?
OTHELLO What needs this iterance,° woman? °*repetition*
   I say, thy husband.
EMILIA O mistress, villainy hath made mocks with° love![9] °*at*
   My husband say she was false?
OTHELLO   He, woman;
   I say, thy husband; dost understand the word?
   My friend, thy husband; honest, honest Iago.
EMILIA If he say so, may his pernicious soul
   Rot half a grain a day! He lies to th'heart.
   She was too fond of her most filthy bargain.[1]
OTHELLO Ha?
EMILIA Do thy worst.
   This deed of thine is no more worthy heaven
   Than thou wast worthy her.
OTHELLO   Peace, you were best!° °*it would be best for you*
EMILIA Thou hast not half that power to do me harm

---

9. Lines 155–58 do not appear in Q.
1. That is, her marriage, or her husband.

As I have to be hurt. O gull,° O dolt!   *fool*
As ignorant as dirt! Thou hast done a deed—
   [*He draws his sword.*]
I care not for thy sword; I'll make thee known,
170 Though I lost twenty lives. Help, help, ho, help!
The Moor hath killed my mistress! Murder, murder!
    Enter MONTANO, GRATIANO, IAGO, *and others.*
MONTANO   What is the matter? How now, general?
EMILIA   O, are you come, Iago? You have done well,
That men must lay their murders on your neck.
175 GRATIANO   What is the matter?
EMILIA [*to* IAGO]   Disprove this villain, if thou be'st a man.
He says thou told'st him that his wife was false.
I know thou didst not; thou'rt not such a villain.
Speak, for my heart is full.
180 IAGO   I told him what I thought, and told no more
Than what he found himself was apt and true.
EMILIA   But did you ever tell him she was false?
IAGO   I did.
EMILIA   You told a lie, an odious damnèd lie!
185 Upon my soul, a lie! a wicked lie!
She false with Cassio? Did you say with Cassio?
IAGO   With Cassio, mistress! Go to, charm° your tongue!   *silence*
EMILIA   I will not charm my tongue; I am bound to speak:
My mistress here lies murdered in her bed—[2]
190 ALL   O heavens forfend!—
EMILIA [*to* IAGO]   And your reports have set the murder on.
OTHELLO   Nay, stare not, masters; it is true indeed.
GRATIANO   'Tis a strange truth.
MONTANO   O monstrous act!
195 EMILIA   Villainy, villainy, villainy!
I think upon't, I think I smell't. O villainy!
I thought so then.—I'll kill myself for grief!
O villainy! villainy!
IAGO   What, are you mad? I charge you get you home!
200 EMILIA   Good gentlemen, let me have leave to speak.
'Tis proper I obey him, but not now.
Perchance, Iago, I will ne'er go home.
OTHELLO   O! O! O!
   Falls on the bed.
EMILIA   Nay, lay thee down and roar,
205 For thou hast killed the sweetest innocent
That e'er did lift up eye.°   *(to heaven)*
OTHELLO [*rising*]   O, she was foul!
[*to* GRATIANO] I scarce did know you, uncle. There lies
   your niece,
Whose breath, indeed, these hands have newly stopped.
I know this act shows° horrible and grim.   *appears*

---

2. Lines 189–98 do not appear in Q.

210	GRATIANO Poor Desdemon, I am glad thy father's dead;	
	Thy match° was mortal to him, and pure grief	*marriage*
	Shore his old thread in twain.³ Did he live now,	
	This sight would make him do a desperate turn;°	*act*
	Yea, curse his better angel from his side	
215	And fall to reprobance.⁴	
	OTHELLO 'Tis pitiful; but yet Iago knows	
	That she with Cassio hath the act of shame	
	A thousand times committed. Cassio confessed it,	
	And she did gratify his amorous works	
220	With that recognizance° and pledge of love	*token*
	Which I first gave her. I saw it in his hand;	
	It was a handkerchief, an antique token	
	My father gave my mother.	
	EMILIA O God! O heavenly God!	
	IAGO 'Swounds, hold your peace!	
225	EMILIA 'Twill out, 'twill out! I peace?	
	No, I will speak as liberal as the north;⁵	
	Let heaven and men and devils, let them all,	
	All, all cry shame against me, yet I'll speak!	
	IAGO Be wise, and get you home.	
	[IAGO *threatens* EMILIA *with his sword.*]	
	EMILIA I will not!	
230	GRATIANO Fie! Your sword upon a woman?	
	EMILIA O thou dull Moor, that handkerchief thou speak'st of	
	I found by fortune and did give my husband;	
	For often with a solemn earnestness—	
	More than indeed belonged to such a trifle—	
	He begged of me to steal't.	
235	IAGO Villainous whore!	
	EMILIA She give it Cassio? No, alas, I found it,	
	And I did giv't my husband.	
	IAGO Filth, thou liest!	
	EMILIA By heaven, I do not! I do not, gentlemen.—	
	O murderous coxcomb!° What should such a fool	*fool*
	Do with so good a wife?	
240	OTHELLO Are there no stones° in heaven	*thunderbolts*
	But what serves for the thunder? Precious° villain!	*absolute*
	The Moor runs at IAGO. [MONTANO *disarms* OTHELLO.]	
	IAGO [*stabs*] *his wife.*	
	GRATIANO The woman falls; sure he hath killed his wife.	
	EMILIA Ay, ay. O lay me by my mistress' side. *Exit* IAGO.	
	GRATIANO He's gone, but his wife's killed.	
245	MONTANO 'Tis a notorious villain. Take you this weapon,	
	Which I have here recovered from the Moor.	
	Come, guard the door without; let him not pass,	
	But kill him rather. I'll after that same villain,	

---

3. Cut the thread of his life.
4. Suicide, the unforgivably sinful act of despair.
5. As freely as the north wind.

For 'tis a damnèd slave.
    Exeunt MONTANO, GRATIANO *[and all but* OTHELLO *and*
    EMILIA*].*
OTHELLO   I am not valiant neither,
But every puny whipster° gets my sword.   *insignificant person*
But why should honor outlive honesty?[6]
Let it go all.
EMILIA   What did thy song bode, lady?[7]
Hark, canst thou hear me? I will play the swan,
And die in music. [*Sings*] "Willow, willow, willow."
Moor, she was chaste. She loved thee, cruel Moor.
So come my soul to bliss as I speak true!
So speaking as I think, alas, I die.   *She dies.*
OTHELLO   I have another weapon in this chamber;
It was a sword of Spain, the ice-brook's temper.°   *tempered in icy water*
O, here it is.—Uncle, I must come forth.
GRATIANO [*within*]   If thou attempt it, it will cost thee dear;
Thou hast no weapon and perforce must suffer.
OTHELLO   Look in upon me then and speak with me,
Or, naked° as I am, I will assault thee.   *unarmed*
    [*Enter* GRATIANO.]
GRATIANO   What is the matter?
OTHELLO   Behold, I have a weapon;
A better never did itself sustain
Upon a soldier's thigh. I have seen the day
That with this little arm and this good sword
I have made my way through more impediments
Than twenty times your stop.° But O, vain boast!   *power to stop*
Who can control his fate? 'Tis not so now.
Be not afraid, though you do see me weaponed.[8]
Here is my journey's end, here is my butt°   *destination*
And very seamark° of my utmost sail.   *beacon*
Do you go back dismayed? 'Tis a lost° fear.   *an unnecessary*
Man but a rush° against Othello's breast   *aim even a reed*
And he retires.° Where should Othello go?   *falls back*
[*to* DESDEMONA] Now, how dost thou look now? O
    ill-starred wench,
Pale as thy smock. When we shall meet at count,°   *Judgment Day*
This look of thine will hurl my soul from heaven,
And fiends will snatch at it.
    [*He touches her.*]
                Cold, cold, my girl?
Even like thy chastity. O cursèd, cursèd slave!
Whip me, ye devils,
From the possession of this heavenly sight!

---

6. Why should military reputation outlive integrity?
7. Lines 252–54 ("What . . . willow.'") do not appear in Q.
8. Lines 272–78 do not appear in Q.

285		Blow me about in winds, roast me in sulfur,	
		Wash me in steep-down gulfs of liquid fire!	
		O Desdemon! dead Desdemon; dead. O, O!	
		Enter LODOVICO, CASSIO *in a chair,* MONTANO, *and* IAGO, *with* OFFICERS.	
	LODOVICO	Where is this rash and most unfortunate man?	
	OTHELLO	That's he that was Othello; here I am.	
290	LODOVICO	Where is that viper? Bring the villain forth.	
	OTHELLO	I look down towards his feet,[9] but that's a fable;	
		If that thou be'st a devil, I cannot kill thee.	
		[*Wounds* IAGO.]	
	LODOVICO	Wrench his sword from him.	
	IAGO	I bleed, sir, but not killed.	
	OTHELLO	I am not sorry, neither; I'd have thee live,	
295		For in my sense° 'tis happiness to die.	state of feeling
	LODOVICO	O thou Othello, that was once so good,	
		Fallen in the practice° of a cursèd slave,	plot
		What shall be said to thee?	
	OTHELLO	Why, anything:	
		An honorable murderer, if you will;	
300		For naught I did in hate, but all in honor.	
	LODOVICO	This wretch hath part confessed his villainy.	
		Did you and he consent in Cassio's death?	
	OTHELLO	Ay.	
	CASSIO	Dear general, I never gave you cause.	
305	OTHELLO	I do believe it, and I ask your pardon.	
		Will you, I pray, demand° that demi-devil	ask
		Why he hath thus ensnared my soul and body?	
	IAGO	Demand me nothing. What you know, you know.	
		From this time forth I never will speak word.	
	LODOVICO	What, not to pray?	
310	GRATIANO	Torments° will ope your lips.	tortures
	OTHELLO	Well, thou dost best.	
	LODOVICO	Sir, you shall understand what hath befall'n,	
		Which, as I think, you know not. Here is a letter	
		Found in the pocket of the slain Roderigo,	
315		And here another. The one of them imports	
		The death of Cassio, to be undertook	
		By Roderigo.	
	OTHELLO	O villain!	
	CASSIO	Most heathenish and most gross!°	monstrous
	LODOVICO	Now here's another discontented paper	
320		Found in his pocket too; and this, it seems,	
		Roderigo meant t'have sent this damnèd villain,	
		But that, belike,° Iago in the interim	most likely
		Came in and satisfied him.	

---

9. To look for the devil's cloven feet.

OTHELLO O thou pernicious caitiff!°— — *wretch*
How came you, Cassio, by that handkerchief
That was my wife's?
CASSIO I found it in my chamber;
And he himself confessed it, but even now,
That there he dropped it for a special purpose
Which wrought to his desire.
OTHELLO O fool, fool, fool!
CASSIO There is besides in Roderigo's letter
How he upbraids Iago that he made him
Brave° me upon the watch, whereon it came — *defy*
That I was cast;° and even but now he spake, — *dismissed*
After long seeming dead, Iago hurt him,
Iago set him on.
LODOVICO [*to* OTHELLO] You must forsake this room and
go with us.
Your power and your command is taken off,
And Cassio rules in Cyprus. For this slave,
If there be any cunning cruelty
That can torment him much and hold him° long, — *(alive)*
It shall be his. You shall close° prisoner rest — *tightly confined*
Till that the nature of your fault be known
To the Venetian state. [*to officers*] Come, bring away.
OTHELLO Soft you;° a word or two before you go. — *wait*
I have done the state some service, and they know't;
No more of that. I pray you, in your letters,
When you shall these unlucky deeds relate,
Speak of me as I am. Nothing extenuate,
Nor set down aught in malice. Then must you speak
Of one that loved not wisely but too well;
Of one not easily jealous but, being wrought,
Perplexed in the extreme; of one whose hand,
Like the base Judean,[1] threw a pearl away
Richer than all his tribe, of one whose subdued° eyes, — *(by grief)*
Albeit unusèd to the melting mood,
Drops tears as fast as the Arabian trees
Their medicinable gum.° Set you down this; — *myrrh*
And say besides that in Aleppo once,
Where a malignant and a turbaned Turk
Beat a Venetian and traduced the state,
I took by th'throat the circumcisèd dog
And smote him—thus!
He stabs himself.
LODOVICO O bloody period!° — *conclusion*
GRATIANO All that is spoke is marred.

---

1. Probably alludes to Judas Iscariot, betrayer of Jesus. "Base Indian," in the quarto, suggests naive gullibility rather than malice.

OTHELLO [*to* DESDEMONA]   I kissed thee ere I killed thee.
  No way but this,
Killing myself, to die upon a kiss.
  He [*kisses* DESDEMONA *and*] *dies.*
CASSIO   This did I fear, but thought he had no weapon;
  For he was great of heart.
LODOVICO [*to* IAGO]   O Spartan dog,[2]
  More fell° than anguish, hunger, or the sea,   *cruel*
  Look on the tragic loading of this bed:
  This is thy work. The object poisons sight;
  Let it be hid. Gratiano, keep the house
  And seize upon the fortunes of the Moor,
  For they succeed on you. [*to* CASSIO] To you, lord
    governor,
  Remains the censure° of this hellish villain;   *sentence*
  The time, the place, the torture—O, enforce it!
  Myself will straight aboard, and to the state
  This heavy act with heavy heart relate.   *Exeunt.*

1603–04   1623

2. A bloodhound; hence a relentless, bloodthirsty man. Also, the people of ancient Sparta were reputed to be inhumane and unfeeling.

The Tempest

The title of this play, *The Tempest*, has its roots in the Latin *tempestas*, meaning "storm," as well as *tempus*, or "time"—it is a storm/time drama. The storm is present in the opening stage direction, its sounds preceding any of the words of the play: "A tempestuous noise of thunder and lightning heard." In the fiction, it is this storm that brings a shipload of dignitaries, on their way back from a wedding in Tunis in Africa, crashing onto a magical island. But the plot and relationships that form the rest of the drama are in their own way also tempestuous: Prospero meets again the brother who stole his dukedom and banished him, and survives an attempt on his life. His daughter, Miranda, sees a man for the first time, falls in love, and becomes engaged. Ferdinand, mourning the death of his father at sea, falls for Miranda before learning that his father miraculously lives. Ariel yearns for freedom from servitude and receives it. In private theaters like Blackfriars—the expensive indoor theater owned by Shakespeare's company, for which this play was written—play titles were suspended on "title boards." The word "tempest" would have hung throughout the performance, its meaning changing from literal to figurative as the play progressed.

That the play is equally about time is demonstrated by its conformity—unusual for a Shakespearean drama—to the "unities" of time, place, and action suggested in Aristotle's *Poetics*: it happens in real time (between 2 and 6 P.M. in a single afternoon), is staged in one place (a magical island), and concerns—if not analyzed too closely—one action (the tempest and its aftermath). But Shakespeare is usually playful with rules, and this work is no exception. Ferdinand, falling in love with Miranda, says that "'tis fresh morning with me / When you are by at night" (3.1.33–34), though, given the play's time constraints, he has never seen her in the morning or the evening. The story of the drama is beyond time, as is to be expected in a *world in* which shattered ships can be made instantly whole, wet clothes instantly dry, and swords freeze midstroke. Yet when Prospero, at the end of the play, declares that he will "retire me to my Milan, where / Every third thought shall be my grave" (5.1.312–13), he acknowledges that, magician though he may be, time has aged him, and he must prepare for death. This play, then, simultaneously explores stage, magic, and biological time.

Published for the first time in Shakespeare's 1623 folio, seven years after the playwright's death, *The Tempest* is somewhat easy to date. For a start, we know it to have been performed at court in 1611, and again in 1612–13, when it was one of the fourteen plays put on by Shakespeare's company for the betrothal of King James's daughter Elizabeth to Frederick, Elector Palatine of Germany. Indeed, the single version of *The Tempest* that has come down to us contains details that may have been added specifically for that royal wedding: its "betrothal masque," featuring Juno, goddess of marriage and childbirth, as well as Iris and Ceres, goddesses of fruitfulness, is particularly suited to a noble marriage, which depended on fertility to ensure the continuance of bloodlines. But the play itself was probably first written around 1609/10; its plot, with its fearful storm and its wrecked seafarers finding themselves on a fertile but troubling island, closely resembles tales of the shipwreck of the *Sea Venture* onto the Bermudas in 1609, told vividly in this volume by William Strachey. Sometimes Strachey's own account is said to be behind *The Tempest*, though it is just as likely that Shakespeare learned the story from returning mariners. The play's pointed reference to the "still-vexed Bermudas" (1.2.229) ensures that those islands, and their storms, are at the forefront of the audience's mind, even if—given that the wedding guests are sailing from Africa to Italy—Prospero's actual island must itself be in the Mediterranean.

The play also touches on different narratives of colonialist expansion. We learn that when Prospero had originally arrived on the island he had been helped by Caliban, who had shown him where the fresh water was, and what berries he could eat. Later, however, Prospero had enslaved Caliban; indeed, he generally calls him "slave" instead of using his name. And while he is kinder to Ariel, Prospero has also enslaved that native island spirit; Ariel does his "master" Prospero's magical bidding in order to win his longed-for freedom. In these respects, Prospero is a prototypical colonial enslaver. But Shakespeare confuses the narrative by his depiction of Caliban as a victimizer as well as a victim: he is a would-be rapist and killer (he falls victim to the drunken clowns, Stephano and Trinculo, because he thinks they can help him murder Prospero); and his very name seems intended to hint at the word "cannibal." Moreover, though Caliban maintains that "this island's mine" (1.2.331), his own right to it is dependent on an earlier act of colonization: his mother, the witch Sycorax, had claimed the island on her arrival and had herself made Ariel a slave, imprisoning him in a cloven pine when he refused to do her bidding. The strange parallels between Prospero and Sycorax may recall English and Spanish competing claims and bad behavior—as in Ralegh's account of his "discovery" of Guiana in this volume. The play portrays the problems of contentions over ownership for other people's land and people. At the end of the play, Ariel is finally freed by Prospero: but what will, or should, happen to Caliban?

The Tempest shares with Shakespeare's other late plays—or "romances," as they are often called—a set of themes: *The Winter's Tale, Cymbeline, Pericles,* and *The Tempest* are all tragicomedies, meaning that they explore tragic issues but have happy endings; they all feature redemption and forgiveness, and all end with long-separated families coming together; they are all about fathers with daughters of marriageable age; they all contain fantastical plots, lengthy passages of narration, and extraordinarily lyrical poetry. They are also all highly musical. This was partly for practical reasons. Blackfriars, which Shakespeare's company was able to use from 1608 on, was an enclosed, wooden indoor space, with fine acoustics. And Shakespeare's company, which became the King's Men in 1603—technically, servants to King James—now also had access to the court's leading composers. Robert Johnson (1583–1633), lutenist to Prince Henry, King James's son, wrote the music for *The Tempest*. The result is a play in which, like the other late plays, some of the most evocative passages had musical settings and were intended to be sung rather than spoken. Ferdinand is not told that his father has drowned, but instead hears a song about how a drowned man is metamorphosed into something rich and strange: "Those are pearls that were his eyes" (1.2.397). The song's refrain is the sound of a death knell—the bell rung for a funeral—rung under the water by sea nymphs.

But the play also picks up on ideas and themes from the period's earlier drama. Prospero recalls Doctor Faustus. His magic, which comes from books, gives him a sense that he has godlike powers: "I have bedimmed / The noontide sun"; "Graves at my command / Have waked their sleepers" (5.1.41–42, 48–49). When, at the play's close, he determines to burn his books and drown his magic staff, he rejects not just magic but also the claims of earlier drama, and perhaps the theater itself. This play, which some see as the last written solely by Shakespeare, has often been described as Shakespeare's own farewell to the stage. Certainly *The Tempest*, with its interest in the limitations of knowledge, in the abuse—but also the abusing nature—of power, and in the nature and purpose of art, gathers together many of the preoccupations of Shakespeare's writing career and brings them to a haunting conclusion. At the end of *The Tempest*, Prospero tells the spectators that he will remain trapped on the island unless released by their applause: "As you from crimes would pardoned be, / Let your indulgence set me free" (Epilogue 19–20). The epilogue may suggest that we, the audience, have found Prospero, a noble magician and magus, imprisoned on an island, and can now decide whether to continue his confinement or, in light of his good deeds, free him. Alternatively, the epilogue suggests that we are enslavers and, at that same shocking moment of discovery, that we can right our wrongs by forgiving and applauding Prospero, the play, and, by extension, Shakespeare.

The Tempest

THE PERSONS OF THE PLAY

PROSPERO, the right Duke of Milan
MIRANDA, daughter to Prospero
ANTONIO, his brother, the usurping Duke of Milan

ALONSO, King of Naples
SEBASTIAN, his brother
FERDINAND, son to Alonso

GONZALO, an honest old councillor
ADRIAN and FRANCISCO, lords

ARIEL, an airy spirit
CALIBAN, a savage and deformed slave

TRINCULO, a jester
STEFANO, a drunken butler

MASTER of a ship
BOATSWAIN
MARINERS

SPIRITS *appearing as*
IRIS
CERES
JUNO
Nymphs
Reapers

THE SCENE: *An uninhabited island.*

1.1

A tempestuous noise of thunder and lightning heard.
Enter a ship['s] MASTER *and a* BOATSWAIN.[1]

MASTER Boatswain!
BOATSWAIN Here, Master. What cheer?
MASTER Good,[2] speak to th' mariners. Fall to't yarely,° or   *promptly*
  we run ourselves aground. Bestir, bestir!   *Exit.*
  Enter MARINERS.

1.1 Location: A ship at sea.
1. The Boatswain probably enters after the shipmaster calls him; the latter is perhaps on the upper stage.
2. Acknowledging the Boatswain's presence; or perhaps short for "good man."

BOATSWAIN Heigh, my hearts!° Cheerly, cheerly, my hearts! —*hearties*
Yare, yare! Take in the topsail.³ Tend° to th' Master's whistle. —*attend*
[*to the storm*] Blow till thou burst thy wind, if room
enough!⁴

Enter ALONSO, SEBASTIAN, ANTONIO, FERDINAND,
GONZALO, *and others.*

ALONSO Good Boatswain, have care. Where's the Master?
[*to the* MARINERS] Play the men!° —*act like men*
BOATSWAIN I pray now, keep below.
ANTONIO Where is the Master, Boatswain?
BOATSWAIN Do you not hear him? You mar our labor. Keep
your cabins: you do assist the storm!
GONZALO Nay, good,° be patient. —*good man*
BOATSWAIN When the sea is. Hence! What cares these
roarers for the name of king?⁵ To cabin! Silence! Trouble
us not.
GONZALO Good, yet remember whom thou hast aboard.
BOATSWAIN None that I more love than myself. You are a
councillor:⁶ if you can command these elements to silence
and work the peace of the present,⁷ we will not hand° a rope —*handle*
more. Use your authority! If you cannot, give thanks you
have lived so long, and make yourself ready in your cabin
for the mischance of the hour, if it so hap.° [*to the* MARINERS] —*happen*
Cheerly, good hearts! [*to* GONZALO] Out of our way, I say!
Exit [BOATSWAIN *with* MARINERS].
GONZALO I have great comfort from this fellow. Methinks
he hath no drowning mark⁸ upon him; his complexion is
perfect gallows.⁹ Stand fast, good Fate, to his hanging;
make the rope of his destiny our cable,¹ for our own doth
little advantage.° If he be not born to be hanged, our —*good*
case is miserable.

Exeunt [GONZALO, ALONSO, SEBASTIAN,
ANTONIO, *and* FERDINAND].

Enter BOATSWAIN.

BOATSWAIN Down with the topmast!² Yare! Lower, lower!
Bring her to try with main-course.³ (*A cry within.*) A plague
upon this howling! They are louder than the weather or
our office.⁴

Enter SEBASTIAN, ANTONIO, *and* GONZALO.

---

3. To reduce the surface area of the sail and thereby lessen the force of the wind pushing the ship toward the island.
4. Blow as hard as you like, as long as we have room between the ship and the rocks.
5. "Roarers," referring to the waves, was also a term for riotous people.
6. Member of the king's council; also an adviser or persuader.
7. Of the present circumstances.
8. Birthmark whose position was held to portend death by drowning. "He that was born to be hanged will never be drowned" was proverbial.
9. His physiognomy, or appearance, shows that he will certainly be hanged.
1. Anchor cable (an anchor is actually useless in a storm).
2. To reduce the top weight of the ship and make it more stable.
3. Bring the ship close to the wind, sailing only with the mainsail.
4. Duties (in shouting orders).

Yet again? What do you here? Shall we give o'er° and   *up*
drown? Have you a mind to sink?
SEBASTIAN A pox o' your throat, you bawling, blasphe-
40 mous, incharitable dog!
BOATSWAIN Work you, then.
ANTONIO Hang, cur! Hang, you whoreson insolent noise-
maker! We are less afraid to be drowned than thou art.
GONZALO I'll warrant him from drowning,[5] though° the   *even if*
45 ship were no stronger than a nutshell and as leaky as an
unstanched° wench.   *freely menstruating*
BOATSWAIN Lay her a-hold, a-hold! Set her two courses![6]
Off to sea again! Lay her off!
    Enter MARINERS, *wet*.
MARINERS All lost! To prayers, to prayers! All lost!
    [*Exeunt* MARINERS.]
50 BOATSWAIN What, must our mouths be cold?[7]
GONZALO The King and Prince at prayers! Let's assist
them, for our case is as theirs.
SEBASTIAN I'm out of patience.
ANTONIO We are merely° cheated of our lives by drunk-   *utterly*
55 ards. This wide-chopped° rascal—would thou mightst   *large-mouthed*
lie drowning the washing of ten tides![8]
GONZALO He'll be hanged yet, though every drop of water
swear against it and gape at widest to glut° him.   *its widest to swallow*
    A confused noise within.
MARINERS [*within*] Mercy on us! We split, we split! Fare-
60 well, my wife and children! Farewell, brother! We split,
we split, we split!
    [*Exit* BOATSWAIN.]
ANTONIO Let's all sink wi'th' King.
SEBASTIAN Let's take leave of him.   *Exit* [*with* ANTONIO].
GONZALO Now would I give a thousand furlongs of sea for
65 an acre of barren ground: long heath, brown furze,[9] anything. The wills above be done, but I would fain die a dry
death.   *Exit.*

1.2

    Enter PROSPERO *and* MIRANDA.
MIRANDA[1] If by your art,[2] my dearest father, you have
Put the wild waters in this roar, allay them.
The sky, it seems, would pour down stinking pitch

---

5. I'll guarantee him against drowning.
6. Set the foresail in addition to the mainsail.
7. To be cold in the mouth—to be dead—was proverbial; may also suggest that the mariners warm their mouths with liquor.
8. Pirates were hanged on the shore at low-water mark and left there for the ebbing and flowing of three tides.
9. Heather and gorse—both shrubs that grow in poor soil.
1.2 Location: The rest of the play is set in various parts of Prospero's island.
1. "Miranda" in Latin means "admirable" or "wondering." Miranda uses the formal "you," contrasting with Prospero's more familiar "thou."
2. Skill; magic; learning; science.

　　　　　But that the sea, mounting to th' welkin's° cheek,　　　　　*sky's*
5　　　　Dashes the fire out. Oh, I have suffered
　　　　　With those that I saw suffer: a brave° vessel—　　　　　　*splendid*
　　　　　Who had, no doubt, some noble creature in her—
　　　　　Dashed all to pieces! Oh, the cry did knock
　　　　　Against my very heart! Poor souls, they perished.
10　　　Had I been any god of power, I would
　　　　　Have sunk the sea within the earth or ere°　　　　　　　　*before*
　　　　　It should the good ship so have swallowed and
　　　　　The fraughting souls³ within her.
　　　PROSPERO⁴　　　　　　　　　　Be collected.
　　　　　No more amazement.° Tell your piteous° heart　　　*consternation / pitying*
　　　　　There's no harm done.
　　　MIRANDA　　　　　　　　Oh, woe the day!
15　　PROSPERO　　　　　　　　　　　　　　No harm.
　　　　　I have done nothing but in care of thee—
　　　　　Of thee, my dear one, thee, my daughter—who
　　　　　Art ignorant of what thou art, naught knowing
　　　　　Of whence I am, nor that I am more better°　　　　　　*higher in rank*
20　　　Than Prospero, master of a full poor cell⁵
　　　　　And thy no greater father.
　　　MIRANDA　　　　　　　　　　More to know
　　　　　Did never meddle with° my thoughts.　　　　　　　　*intrude upon*
　　　PROSPERO　　　　　　　　　　　　　　'Tis time
　　　　　I should inform thee farther. Lend thy hand
　　　　　And pluck my magic garment from me.—
　　　　　[*She helps him remove the cloak, and he puts it aside.*]
　　　　　　　　　　　　　　　　　　　　—So,
25　　　Lie there, my art. —Wipe thou thine eyes; have comfort.
　　　　　The direful spectacle of the wreck, which touched
　　　　　The very virtue of compassion in thee,
　　　　　I have with such provision° in mine art　　　　　　　　*foresight*
　　　　　So safely ordered that there is no soul—
30　　　No, not so much perdition° as an hair　　　　　　　　　*loss*
　　　　　Betid° to any creature in the vessel　　　　　　　　　　*happened*
　　　　　Which° thou heard'st cry, which thou saw'st sink. Sit down,　*whom*
　　　　　For thou must now know farther.
　　　MIRANDA　　　　　　　　　　　　　　You have often
　　　　　Begun to tell me what I am, but stopped
35　　　And left me to a bootless inquisition,°　　　　　　　　*profitless inquiry*
　　　　　Concluding, "Stay: not yet."
　　　PROSPERO　　　　　　　　　　The hour's now come;
　　　　　The very minute bids thee ope° thine ear.　　　　　　*open*
　　　　　Obey, and be attentive. Canst thou remember
　　　　　A time before we came unto this cell?

---

3. *Souls* constituting the freight; perhaps also suggesting "burdened."
4. "Prospero" in Italian and Spanish means "fortunate" or "prosperous."
5. Suggesting a hermit's or a poor man's dwelling. "Full": very.

40 I do not think thou canst, for then thou wast not
Out° three years old. — *fully*
MIRANDA   Certainly, sir, I can.
PROSPERO   By what? By any other house or person?
Of anything the image tell me that
Hath kept with thy remembrance.
MIRANDA   'Tis far off,
45 And rather like a dream than an assurance° — *a certainty*
That my remembrance warrants.° Had I not — *guarantees is true*
Four or five women once that tended me?
PROSPERO   Thou hadst, and more, Miranda. But how is it
That this lives in thy mind? What seest thou else
50 In the dark backward° and abysm of time? — *past*
If thou rememb'rest aught° ere thou cam'st here, — *anything*
How thou cam'st here thou mayst.
MIRANDA   But that I do not.
PROSPERO   Twelve year since, Miranda, twelve year since,
Thy father was the Duke of Milan[6] and
A prince of power.
55 MIRANDA   Sir, are not you my father?
PROSPERO   Thy mother was a piece° of virtue,° and — *perfect example / chastity*
She said thou wast my daughter, and thy father
Was Duke of Milan, and his only heir
And princess no worse issued.° — *no less nobly born*
MIRANDA   O the heavens!
60 What foul play had we that we came from thence?
Or blessèd° was't we did? — *providential*
PROSPERO   Both, both, my girl.
By foul play, as thou say'st, were we heaved thence,
But blessedly holp° hither. — *helped*
MIRANDA   Oh, my heart bleeds
To think o'th' teen° that I have turned you to, — *sorrow; trouble*
65 Which is from° my remembrance! Please you, farther. — *out of*
PROSPERO   My brother and thy uncle, called Antonio—
I pray thee mark me, that a brother should
Be so perfidious!—he whom next° thyself — *after*
Of all the world I loved, and to him put
70 The manage° of my state, as at that time — *control*
Through all the signories° it was the first — *lordships*
And Prospero the prime° duke, being so reputed — *foremost*
In dignity, and for the liberal arts[7]
Without a parallel. Those being all my study,
75 The government I cast upon my brother
And to my state grew stranger, being transported[8]

---

6. Pronounced with stress on the first syllable.
7. As opposed to the "mechanical arts," the "liberal arts" encompassed the trivium (grammar, logic, and rhetoric) and the quadrivium (arithmetic, geometry, music, and astronomy).
8. Enraptured, with suggestions of "conveyed to another place." "Grew stranger": grew alienated from; became a foreigner to.

　　　　　And rapt in secret studies. Thy false uncle—
　　　　　Dost thou attend me?
MIRANDA　　　　　　　Sir, most heedfully.
PROSPERO　Being once perfected how to grant suits,⁹
80　　　　How to deny them, who t'advance, and who
　　　　　To trash for overtopping,¹ new created
　　　　　The creatures° that were mine, I say, or changed 'em,　　　　*dependents*
　　　　　Or else new formed 'em;² having both the key°　　　　*control*
　　　　　Of officer and office, set all hearts i'th' state
85　　　　To what tune pleased his ear, that° now he was　　　　*so that*
　　　　　The ivy which had hid my princely trunk
　　　　　And sucked my verdure° out on't. Thou attend'st not.　　　　*vitality; power*
MIRANDA　　O good sir, I do.
PROSPERO　　　　　　　I pray thee, mark me.
　　　　　I, thus neglecting worldly ends, all dedicated
90　　　　To closeness° and the bettering of my mind　　　　*seclusion*
　　　　　With that which, but° by being so retired,　　　　*merely*
　　　　　O'er-prized all popular rate,³ in my false brother
　　　　　Awaked an evil nature; and my trust,
　　　　　Like a good parent,⁴ did beget of him
95　　　　A falsehood in its contrary° as great　　　　*inverse qualities*
　　　　　As my trust was, which had indeed no limit,
　　　　　A confidence sans° bound. He being thus lorded　　　　*without*
　　　　　Not only with what my revenue yielded,
　　　　　But what my power might else exact, like one
100　　　Who, having into truth by telling of it,
　　　　　Made such a sinner of his memory
　　　　　To credit his own lie,⁵ he did believe
　　　　　He was indeed the duke, out o'th'° substitution　　　　*as a consequence of the*
　　　　　And executing° th'outward face° of royalty　　　　*portraying / image*
105　　　With all prerogative. Hence his ambition growing—
　　　　　Dost thou hear?
MIRANDA　　　　　　Your tale, sir, would cure deafness.
PROSPERO　To have no screen between this part he played
　　　　　And him he played it for, he needs will be
　　　　　Absolute Milan.⁶ Me,° poor man, my library　　　　*as for me*
110　　　Was dukedom large enough. Of temporal royalties°　　　　*rule*
　　　　　He thinks me now incapable; confederates,°　　　　*(he) plots*
　　　　　So dry° he was for sway,° wi'th' King of Naples　　　　*thirsty / power*
　　　　　To give him annual tribute, do him homage,
　　　　　Subject his coronet to his crown,⁷ and bend

---

9. Having mastered the handling of formal requests.
1. For rising too high. "Trash": restrain, hold back (as by a leash).
2. "Changed . . . formed 'em": changed the duties and allegiance of existing officials, or created new ones.
3. Became too precious for the people to value or understand.
4. From the colloquial "Good parents breed bad children."
5. "Like one . . . lie": like someone who comes to believe his own repeatedly stated lie. "To": So as to.
6. "To have . . . Milan": He wanted to be the Duke of Milan in actual fact, rather than merely exercising power as the Duke's proxy. "Screen": partition, barrier.
7. Subject Antonio's coronet to Alonso's crown. "Coronet": a lesser crown indicating the wearer's inferiority to the sovereign.

  The dukedom yet unbowed—alas, poor Milan!—
  To most ignoble stooping.[8]
MIRANDA   O the heavens!
PROSPERO Mark his condition° and th'event;° then tell me *treaty / outcome*
  If this might be a brother.
MIRANDA   I should sin
  To think but° nobly of my grandmother.   *anything but*
  Good wombs have borne bad sons.[9]
PROSPERO   Now the condition.
  This King of Naples, being an enemy
  To me inveterate, hearkens my brother's suit;
  Which was that he, in lieu o'th' premises[1]
  Of homage and I know not how much tribute,
  Should presently extirpate me and mine
  Out of the dukedom and confer fair Milan,
  With all the honors, on my brother. Whereon,
  A treacherous army levied, one midnight
  Fated to th' purpose did Antonio open
  The gates of Milan, and i'th' dead of darkness,
  The ministers° for th' purpose hurried thence   *agents*
  Me and thy crying self.
MIRANDA   Alack, for pity!
  I, not remembering how I cried out then,
  Will cry it o'er again; it is a hint°   *an occasion*
  That wrings mine eyes to't.
PROSPERO   Hear a little further,
  And then I'll bring thee to the present business
  Which now's upon's, without the which this story
  Were most impertinent.°   *irrelevant*
MIRANDA   Wherefore did they not
  That hour destroy us?
PROSPERO   Well demanded, wench:[2]
  My tale provokes that question. Dear, they durst not,
  So dear the love my people bore me, nor set
  A mark so bloody on the business, but
  With colors fairer painted their foul ends.
  In few,° they hurried us aboard a bark,°   *short / ship*
  Bore us some leagues to sea, where they prepared
  A rotten carcass of a butt,[3] not rigged,
  Nor tackle, sail, nor mast—the very rats
  Instinctively have quit it. There they hoist us
  To cry to th' sea that roared to us; to sigh
  To th' winds, whose pity, sighing back again,
  Did us but loving wrong.[4]

---

8. "And bend . . . stooping": by making Milan, previously free, a tributary subject of Naples.
9. Antonio's character need not imply that his mother was a bad parent (see line 94).
1. In return for the conditions agreed upon.
2. A young woman; also, term of endearment to wife, daughter, or sweetheart.
3. Cask or tub: here, deprecatory for "boat."
4. The winds, responding sympathetically to our sighs, only blew us farther out to sea.

MIRANDA   Alack, what trouble
  Was I then to you!
PROSPERO   Oh, a cherubin
  Thou wast that did preserve me. Thou didst smile,
  Infusèd with a fortitude from heaven,
  When I have decked° the sea with drops° full salt,   *covered; adorned / tears*
  Under my burden groaned,⁵ which° raised in me   *(Miranda's smile)*
  An undergoing stomach° to bear up   *a courage*
  Against what should ensue.
MIRANDA   How came we ashore?
PROSPERO   By Providence divine.
  Some food we had and some fresh water that
  A noble Neapolitan, Gonzalo,
  Out of his charity—who being then appointed
  Master of this design—did give us, with
  Rich garments, linens, stuffs, and necessaries,
  Which since have steaded° much. So, of his gentleness,⁶   *been useful*
  Knowing I loved my books, he furnished me
  From mine own library with volumes that
  I prize above my dukedom.
MIRANDA   Would I might
  But ever see that man.
PROSPERO   Now I arise.⁷
  Sit still,° and hear the last of our sea-sorrow.   *continue to sit*
  Here in this island we arrived, and here
  Have I, thy schoolmaster, made thee more profit°   *profit more*
  Than other princes⁸ can, that have more time
  For vainer hours, and tutors not so careful.°   *caring*
MIRANDA   Heavens thank you for't. And now I pray you, sir,
  For still 'tis beating in my mind, your reason
  For raising this sea-storm?
PROSPERO   Know thus far forth:
  By accident most strange, bountiful Fortune,
  Now my dear lady,⁹ hath mine enemies
  Brought to this shore; and by my prescience
  I find my zenith¹ doth depend upon
  A most auspicious star,² whose influence
  If now I court not but omit,° my fortunes   *disregard*
  Will ever after droop. Here cease more questions.
  Thou art inclined to sleep. 'Tis a good dullness,°   *drowsiness*
  And give it way. I know thou canst not choose.
    [MIRANDA *sleeps.*]

5. The secondary sense provides an image of giving birth.
6. Nobility; kindness.
7. Referring to the action of standing; or to Prospero's rising fortunes (as in lines 179–84). The former might visually reinforce the latter, especially if Prospero also resumes his magical powers by putting on his cloak.
8. A generic plural for "princes and princesses."
9. Traditional characterization of Fortune as a woman changeable in her affections.
1. Highest point, as of a star in the sky.
2. Referring to the belief that celestial bodies had astrological influence on people and events.

[*to* ARIEL] Come away,° servant, come! I am ready now.   *come here*
Approach, my Ariel.³ Come!
    Enter ARIEL.
ARIEL   All hail, great master; grave sir, hail! I come
To answer thy best pleasure, be't to fly,
To swim, to dive into the fire, to ride
On the curled clouds. To thy strong bidding task
Ariel and all his quality.°   *cohorts; faculties*
PROSPERO   Hast thou, spirit,
Performed to point° the tempest that I bade thee?   *in detail*
ARIEL   To every article.
I boarded the King's ship. Now on the beak,°   *prow*
Now in the waist,° the deck,° in every cabin,   *midship / poop*
I flamed amazement.⁴ Sometimes I'd divide
And burn in many places;⁵ on the topmast,
The yards, and bowsprit would I flame distinctly,
Then meet and join. Jove's lightning, the precursors
O'th' dreadful thunderclaps, more momentary
And sight-outrunning° were not. The fire and cracks   *quicker than the eye*
Of sulfurous⁶ roaring the most mighty Neptune
Seem to besiege and make his bold waves tremble,
Yea, his dread trident shake.
PROSPERO   My brave spirit!
Who was so firm, so constant, that this coil°   *turmoil*
Would not infect his reason?
ARIEL   Not a soul
But felt a fever of the mad° and played   *such as madmen feel*
Some tricks of desperation. All but mariners
Plunged in the foaming brine and quit the vessel,
Then all afire with me; the King's son Ferdinand,
With hair upstaring°—then like reeds, not hair—   *standing on end*
Was the first man that leapt, cried, "Hell is empty,
And all the devils are here!"
PROSPERO   Why, that's my spirit.
But was not this nigh shore?
ARIEL   Close by, my master.
PROSPERO   But are they, Ariel, safe?
ARIEL   Not a hair perished.
On their sustaining⁷ garments not a blemish,
But fresher than before; and, as thou bad'st° me,   *commanded*
In troops° I have dispersed them 'bout the isle.   *groups*
The King's son have I landed by himself,
Whom I left cooling of° the air with sighs   *cooling*
In an odd angle° of the isle, and sitting,   *corner*

---

3. Ariel's name, along with sounding like "airy," also means in Hebrew "lion of God." The name appears as that of a magical spirit in various occult texts.
4. I appeared as flames, causing terror.
5. The phosphorescent effect of St. Elmo's fire, caused in a thunderstorm by the charge of static electricity that builds up particularly around metal projections.
6. Sulfur was popularly associated with thunder and lightning.
7. Buoying up, and thus suggesting "life-giving."

His arms in this sad knot.[8]
PROSPERO   Of the King's ship,
The mariners, say how thou hast disposed,
And all the rest o'th' fleet.
ARIEL   Safely in harbor
Is the King's ship; in the deep nook where once
Thou called'st me up at midnight to fetch dew
From the still-vexed° Bermudas, there she's hid; *ever-stormy*
The mariners all under hatches stowed,
Who, with° a charm joined to° their suffered labor, *by virtue of / with*
I have left asleep; and for the rest o'th' fleet,
Which I dispersed, they all have met again
And are upon the Mediterranean float,° *billow; sea*
Bound sadly home for Naples,
Supposing that they saw the King's ship wrecked
And his great person perish.
PROSPERO   Ariel, thy charge
Exactly is performed; but there's more work.
What is the time o'th' day?
ARIEL   Past the mid-season.° *noon*
PROSPERO At least two glasses.° The time twixt six and now *hourglasses*
Must by us both be spent most preciously.
ARIEL Is there more toil? Since thou dost give me pains,° *tasks*
Let me remember° thee what thou hast promised, *remind*
Which is not yet performed me.
PROSPERO   How now? Moody?
What is't thou canst demand?
ARIEL   My liberty.
PROSPERO Before the time be out? No more.
ARIEL   I prithee,
Remember I have done thee worthy service,
Told thee no lies, made no mistakings, served
Without or° grudge or grumblings. Thou did promise *either*
To bate° me a full year. *remit; excuse*
PROSPERO   Dost thou forget
From what a torment I did free thee?
ARIEL   No.
PROSPERO Thou dost, and think'st it much to tread the ooze
Of the salt deep,
To run upon the sharp wind of the north,
To do me business in the veins[9] o'th' earth
When it is baked° with frost. *dried and hardened*
ARIEL   I do not, sir.
PROSPERO Thou liest, malignant thing! Hast thou forgot
The foul witch Sycorax, who with age and envy
Was grown into a hoop?° Hast thou forgot her? *bent over with age*

8. Folded sadly, like this (folded arms implied sorrow).
9. Mineral veins or subterranean rivers.

ARIEL No, sir.
PROSPERO   Thou hast. Where was she born? Speak. Tell me.
ARIEL Sir, in Algiers.
PROSPERO   Oh, was she so? I must
 Once in a month recount what thou hast been,
 Which thou forgett'st. This damned witch Sycorax,
 For mischiefs manifold and sorceries terrible
 To enter human hearing, from Algiers,
 Thou know'st, was banished. For one thing she did
 They would not take her life.[1] Is not this true?
ARIEL Ay, sir.
PROSPERO This blue-eyed[2] hag was hither brought with child
 And here was left by th' sailors. Thou, my slave,
 As thou report'st thyself, was then her servant;
 And for° thou wast a spirit too delicate   because
 To act her earthy[3] and abhorred commands,
 Refusing her grand hests,° she did confine thee,   commands
 By help of her more potent ministers,°   agents; slaves
 And in her most unmitigable rage,
 Into a cloven pine; within which rift
 Imprisoned thou didst painfully remain
 A dozen years, within which space she died
 And left thee there, where thou didst vent thy groans
 As fast as millwheels strike.° Then was this island—   hit the water
 Save for the son that she did litter° here,   give birth to
 A freckled whelp, hag-born—not honored with
 A human shape.
ARIEL   Yes, Caliban her son.
PROSPERO Dull thing, I say so:[4] he, that Caliban
 Whom now I keep in service. Thou best know'st
 What torment I did find thee in: thy groans
 Did make wolves howl, and penetrate° the breasts   arouse sympathy in
 Of ever-angry bears. It was a torment
 To lay upon the damned, which Sycorax
 Could not again undo. It was mine art,
 When I arrived and heard thee, that made gape
 The pine and let thee out.
ARIEL   I thank thee, master.
PROSPERO If thou more murmur'st, I will rend an oak
 And peg thee in his° knotty entrails till   its
 Thou hast howled away twelve winters.
ARIEL   Pardon, master.
 I will be correspondent° to command   compliant
 And do my spriting gently.°   graciously

---

1. "For . . . life": Only because she got pregnant. Capital sentences were commuted for pregnant women; ordinarily, condemned witches were either hanged or burned at the stake.
2. The description of Sycorax as "blue-eyed" has puzzled many readers, and editors have proposed a variety of emendations and interpretations.
3. Difficult for Ariel, whose element is air; also, grossly material, coarse.
4. You dullard, that's just what I said.

PROSPERO   Do so, and after two days
            I will discharge thee.⁵
         ARIEL   That's my noble master!
300   What shall I do? Say what, what shall I do?
         PROSPERO   Go make thyself like a nymph o'th' sea. Be subject
            To no sight but thine and mine, invisible
            To every eyeball else.⁶ Go, take this shape°   *appearance; disguise*
            And hither come in't. Go! Hence with diligence.
                                                    Exit [ARIEL].
305   [*to* MIRANDA] Awake, dear heart, awake! Thou hast slept well.
            Awake.
         MIRANDA   The strangeness of your story put
            Heaviness° in me.   *sleepiness*
         PROSPERO   Shake it off. Come on;
            We'll visit Caliban, my slave, who never
            Yields us kind answer.
         MIRANDA   'Tis a villain, sir,
            I do not love to look on.
310   PROSPERO   But, as 'tis,
            We cannot miss° him. He does make our fire,   *avoid; do without*
            Fetch in our wood, and serves in offices°   *capacities; duties*
            That profit us. What ho! Slave! Caliban!
            Thou earth, thou: speak!
         CALIBAN (*within*)   There's wood enough within.
315   PROSPERO   Come forth, I say! There's other business for thee.
            Come, thou tortoise! When?
                  Enter ARIEL *like a water nymph.*
            —Fine apparition! My quaint⁷ Ariel,
            Hark in thine ear.
                  [*He whispers.*]
         ARIEL   My lord, it shall be done.   *Exit.*
         PROSPERO   Thou poisonous slave, got° by the devil⁸ himself   *begot*
320   Upon thy wicked dam,° come forth!   *harmful, foul mother*
                  Enter CALIBAN.
         CALIBAN   As wicked dew as e'er my mother brushed⁹
            With raven's feather from unwholesome fen°   *bog*
            Drop on you both! A southwest¹ blow on ye
            And blister you all o'er!
325   PROSPERO   For this, be sure, tonight thou shalt have cramps,
            Side-stitches that shall pen thy breath up; urchins²

---

5. Prospero reduces this to within two days at lines 419–20 and actually releases Ariel in about four hours' time.
6. "Be . . . else": Ariel may wear a conventional costume, indicating his invisibility to other characters onstage.
7. The term could simultaneously mean "ingenious," "curious in appearance," and "elegant."
8. Not merely an insult, but also an allusion to Caliban's birth from the devil (incubus) and witch.
9. Brushed up, collected. Dew was a common ingredient of magical potions.
1. A southerly wind was considered plague-bearing.
2. Hedgehogs; but here spirits disguised as hedgehogs.

                Shall forth at vast of° night that they may work   *during the boundless*
                All exercise on thee;³ thou shalt be pinched
                As thick as honeycomb,⁴ each pinch more stinging
                Than bees that made 'em.°   *(honeycomb cells)*
330 CALIBAN   I must eat my dinner.
                This island's mine by Sycorax my mother,
                Which thou tak'st from me. When thou cam'st first
                Thou strok'st me and made much of me; wouldst give me
                Water with berries in't, and teach me how
335   To name the bigger light and how the less⁵
                That burn by day and night. And then I loved thee
                And showed thee all the qualities o'th' isle:
                The fresh springs, brine-pits, barren place and fertile.
                Cursèd be I that did so! All the charms°   *spells*
340   Of Sycorax—toads, beetles, bats—light on you!
                For I am all the subjects that you have,
                Which first was mine own king; and here you sty me°   *pen me up*
                In this hard rock whiles you do keep from me
                The rest o'th' island.
     PROSPERO   Thou most lying slave,
345   Whom stripes° may move, not kindness. I have used° thee,   *lashes / treated*
                Filth as thou art, with humane care, and lodged thee
                In mine own cell till thou didst seek to violate
                The honor of my child.
     CALIBAN   Oh ho, oh ho! Would't had been done!
                Thou didst prevent me; I had peopled else
                This isle with Calibans.
350 MIRANDA⁶   Abhorrèd slave,
                Which any print° of goodness wilt not take,   *impression*
                Being capable of° all ill. I pitied thee,   *susceptible to*
                Took pains to make thee speak, taught thee each hour
                One thing or other. When thou didst not, savage,
355   Know thine own meaning but wouldst gabble like
                A thing most brutish, I endowed thy purposes
                With words that made them known. But thy vile race,°   *hereditary nature*
                Though thou didst learn, had that in't which good natures
                Could not abide to be with; therefore wast thou
360   Deservedly confined into this rock,
                Who hadst deserved more than a prison.
     CALIBAN You taught me language, and my profit on't
                Is I know how to curse. The red plague rid you⁷
                For learning me your language!
     PROSPERO   Hag-seed,° hence!   *offspring of a hag*

---

3. In order that they may perform their habitual activity.
4. The pinch marks will be as closely packed as, and of similar texture to, the cells of a honeycomb.
5. See Genesis 1:16: "God then made two great lights: the greater light to rule the day, and the less light to rule the night."
6. For roughly two and a half centuries, editors reassigned this speech to Prospero, finding it inappropriate for Miranda.
7. The plague that gives red sores destroy, kill you.

365		Fetch us in fuel; and be quick, thou'rt best,	
		To answer other business.° Shrugg'st thou, malice?	*perform other tasks*

                Fetch us in fuel; and be quick, thou'rt best,
                To answer other business.° Shrugg'st thou, malice?   *perform other tasks*
                If thou neglect'st or dost unwillingly
                What I command, I'll rack thee with old[8] cramps,
                Fill all thy bones with aches,[9] make thee roar,
                That beasts shall tremble at thy din.
370 CALIBAN   No, pray thee.
                [*aside*] I must obey. His art is of such power
                It would control my dam's god Setebos[1]
                And make a vassal of him.
     PROSPERO   So, slave, hence.
                                                  Exit CALIBAN.
                Enter FERDINAND, *and* ARIEL, *invisible,
                playing and singing.*[2]
     ARIEL [*sings*] Come unto these yellow sands,
375   And then take hands.
                       Curtsied when you have, and kissed,
                       The wild waves whist.[3]
                       Foot it featly° here and there,   *dance nimbly*
                       And sweet sprites bear°   *spirits sing*
380   The burden.[4]
     SPIRITS [*within, sing the*] (*burden dispersedly*)
                       Hark, hark! Bow-wow!
                       The watch-dogs bark: bow-wow!
     ARIEL   Hark, hark. I hear
                       The strain of strutting Chanticleer°   *a rooster*
385   Cry cock-a-diddle-dow.
     FERDINAND Where should this music be? I'th' air or th'earth?
                It sounds no more; and sure it waits° upon   *attends*
                Some god o'th' island. Sitting on a bank,
                Weeping again the King my father's wreck,
390   This music crept by me upon the waters,
                Allaying both their fury and my passion°   *grief*
                With its sweet air.° Thence I have followed it,   *melody*
                Or it hath drawn me rather; but 'tis gone.
                No, it begins again.
395 ARIEL [*sings*] Full fathom five thy father lies;
                       Of his bones are coral made;
                       Those are pearls that were his eyes;
                       Nothing of him that doth fade,
                       But doth suffer a sea-change
400   Into something rich and strange.
                       Sea-nymphs hourly ring his knell.

---

8. As of aged people; long-accustomed.
9. As a noun, this was probably pronounced "aitches."
1. A name found in travel narratives as a god of the *Patagonians*.
2. This probably does not imply that Ferdinand enters first, even though such a staging is possible if Ferdinand is bewildered as to where this music is coming from. Ariel is invisible to all but Prospero and the audience. He is probably still dressed as a water nymph.
3. Become hushed and attentive.
4. "Burden" is a technical term from Renaissance music meaning "refrain" or "undersong," but its other associations may lend extra significance to Ariel's use of the word in this song.

SPIRITS [*within, sing the*] (*burden*)   Ding dong.
ARIEL   Hark, now I hear them.
SPIRITS [*within*]   Ding dong, bell.
FERDINAND   The ditty does remember⁵ my drowned father.
This is no mortal° business, nor no sound   *human*
That the earth owes.° I hear it now above me.   *owns*
PROSPERO [*to* MIRANDA]   The fringèd curtains of thine
   eye advance°   *raise*
And say what thou seest yond.
MIRANDA   What is't? A spirit?
Lord, how it looks about. Believe me, sir,
It carries a brave° form. But 'tis a spirit.   *splendid; gallant*
PROSPERO   No, wench, it eats and sleeps and hath such
   senses
As we have—such. This gallant° which thou seest   *fine gentleman*
Was in the wreck; and but° he's something° stained   *except that / somewhat*
With grief—that's beauty's canker⁶—thou mightst call him
A goodly person. He hath lost his fellows
And strays about to find 'em.
MIRANDA   I might call him
A thing divine, for nothing natural
I ever saw so noble.
PROSPERO [*aside*]⁷   It° goes on, I see,   (*my plan*)
As my soul prompts it. [*to* ARIEL] Spirit, fine spirit, I'll free
   thee
Within two days for this.
FERDINAND   Most sure, the goddess
On whom these airs attend!⁸ Vouchsafe° my prayer   *grant*
May know if you remain° upon this island,   *dwell*
And that you will some good instruction give
How I may bear me° here. My prime request,   *conduct myself*
Which I do last pronounce, is—O you wonder!⁹—
If you be maid¹ or no?
MIRANDA   No wonder, sir,
But certainly a maid.
FERDINAND   My language? Heavens!
I am the best² of them that speak this speech,
Were I but where 'tis spoken.
PROSPERO   How? The best?
What wert thou if the King of Naples heard thee?
FERDINAND   A single³ thing, as I am now, that wonders

---

5. Commemorate. "Ditty": the words of the song.
6. Cankerworm; caterpillar ("beauty" being seen as a flower); spreading sore.
7. Prospero's asides here and at lines 437, 449, and 492 may be either private utterances or addressed to Ariel. If the former, Ariel may nevertheless hear them; Prospero speaks to Ariel after all these instances. Their import may well be purposefully enigmatic.
8. Probably spoken aside, but possibly an invocation. "Most sure, the goddess": an echo of Aeneas's reaction to seeing Venus after his shipwreck, "o dea certe" (*Aeneid* 1.328). "Airs": Ariel's melodies.
9. Miracle, punning on the meaning of Miranda's name.
1. Unmarried virgin; made (human).
2. Highest in rank, assuming he has succeeded his father.
3. Weak and helpless; solitary; one and the same.

                To hear thee speak of Naples. He does hear me,[4]
                And that he does I weep. Myself am Naples,°   King of Naples
                Who with mine eyes, never since at ebb,° beheld   ceasing to flow
                The King my father wrecked.
435   MIRANDA   Alack, for mercy!
        FERDINAND   Yes, faith, and all his lords, the Duke of Milan
                And his brave son[5] being twain.
        PROSPERO [aside]   The Duke of Milan
                And his more braver daughter could control[6] thee
                If now 'twere fit to do't. At the first sight
440   They have changed eyes.[7] [to ARIEL] Delicate° Ariel,   graceful; artful
                I'll set thee free for this! [to FERDINAND] A word, good sir.
                I fear you have done yourself some wrong.[8] A word.
        MIRANDA   Why speaks my father so ungently?° This   discourteously
                Is the third man that e'er I saw, the first
445   That e'er I sighed for. Pity move my father
                To be inclined my way.
        FERDINAND   Oh, if a virgin,
                And your affection not gone forth,[9] I'll make you
                The Queen of Naples.
        PROSPERO   Soft, sir! One word more.
                [aside] They are both in either's powers. But this swift
                    business
450   I must uneasy° make, lest too light[1] winning   difficult
                Make the prize light. [to FERDINAND] One word more! I
                    charge thee
                That thou attend me. Thou dost here usurp
                The name thou ow'st° not, and hast put thyself   own
                Upon this island as a spy to win it
                From me, the lord on't.°   of it
455   FERDINAND   No, as I am a man.
        MIRANDA   There's nothing ill can dwell in such a temple.[2]
                If the ill spirit have so fair a house,
                Good things will strive to dwell with't.
        PROSPERO [to FERDINAND]   Follow me.
                [to MIRANDA] Speak not you for him: he's a traitor.
                    [to FERDINAND] Come!
460   I'll manacle thy neck and feet together.
                Sea-water shalt thou drink; thy food shall be
                The fresh-brook mussels,[3] withered roots, and husks
                Wherein the acorn cradled. Follow!
        FERDINAND   No.

---

4. "He" and "me" both refer to Ferdinand. Presuming his father to be dead, Ferdinand takes himself to be the new king of Naples (and as such, he hears himself speaking). Alternatively, Ferdinand thinks his father's spirit hears him.
5. The *only* instance in which Antonio is mentioned as having a son.
6. Challenge; take to task; exercise power over.
7. Exchanged loving glances; fallen in love at first sight.
8. Euphemistic for "told a lie about yourself."
9. Given over to someone else.
1. Easy; playing on the meanings of "little valued" and also "promiscuous" in line 451.
2. A common metaphor for the body; also, a conventional Renaissance notion that moral qualities were physically manifest.
3. Freshwater mussels are inedible.

> I will resist such entertainment° till   *treatment*
> Mine enemy has more power.
>   *He draws [his sword], and is charmed from moving.*
465 MIRANDA   O dear father,
> Make not too rash a trial of him, for
> He's gentle and not fearful.[4]
> PROSPERO   What, I say,
> My foot° my tutor? *[to* FERDINAND*]* Put thy sword up,   *inferior*
>   traitor,
> Who mak'st a show but dar'st not strike, thy conscience
470 Is so possessed with guilt. Come from thy ward,°   *defensive stance*
> For I can here disarm thee with this stick°   *magician's wand*
> And make thy weapon drop.
> MIRANDA   Beseech you, father—
> PROSPERO   Hence! Hang not on my garments.
> MIRANDA   Sir, have pity.
> I'll be his surety.
> PROSPERO   Silence! One word more
475 Shall make me chide thee, if not hate thee. What,
> An advocate for an imposter? Hush!
> Thou think'st there is no more such shapes° as he,   *forms; men*
> Having seen but him and Caliban. Foolish wench,
> To° th' most of men this is a Caliban,   *compared to*
> And they to him are angels.
480 MIRANDA   My affections
> Are then most humble. I have no ambition
> To see a goodlier man.
> PROSPERO *[to* FERDINAND*]*   Come on, obey.
> Thy nerves° are in their infancy again,   *sinews*
> And have no vigor in them.
> FERDINAND   So they are.
485 My spirits,° as in a dream, are all bound up.   *mental powers*
> My father's loss, the weakness which I feel,
> The wreck of all my friends, nor this man's threats
> To whom I am subdued, are but light to me,
> Might I but through my prison once a day
490 Behold this maid. All corners else o'th' earth
> Let liberty make use of; space enough
> Have I in such a prison.
> PROSPERO *[aside]*   It works. *[to* FERDINAND*]* Come on!
>   *[to* ARIEL*]* Thou hast done well, fine Ariel. *[to* FERDINAND*]*
>   Follow me.
>   *[to* ARIEL*]* Hark what thou else shalt do me.
> MIRANDA *[to* FERDINAND*]*   Be of comfort;
495 My father's of a better nature, sir,
> Than he appears by speech. This is unwonted°   *unusual*
> Which now came from him.

---

4. He's noble and, therefore, not cowardly. Alternatively, not fearsome.

746 | WILLIAM SHAKESPEARE

PROSPERO [*to* ARIEL]   Thou shalt be as free
  As mountain winds; but then° exactly do   *until then*
  All points of my command.
ARIEL   To th' syllable.
500 PROSPERO [*to* FERDINAND]   Come, follow. [*to* MIRANDA]
  Speak not for him.   *Exeunt.*

2.1

Enter ALONSO, SEBASTIAN, ANTONIO, GONZALO, ADRIAN, *and*
  FRANCISCO.

GONZALO   Beseech you, sir, be merry. You have cause—
  So have we all—of joy; for our escape
  Is much beyond our loss. Our hint° of woe   *occasion*
  Is common: every day some sailor's wife,
5 The masters of some merchant, and the merchant[1]
  Have just° our theme of woe. But for the miracle—   *exactly*
  I mean our preservation—few in millions
  Can speak like us. Then wisely, good sir, weigh
  Our sorrow with° our comfort.   *against*
ALONSO   Prithee, peace.[2]
10 SEBASTIAN [*to* ANTONIO]   He receives comfort like cold
  porridge.°   *broth*
ANTONIO [*to* SEBASTIAN]   The visitor[3] will not give him o'er
  so.°   *leave him alone*
SEBASTIAN   Look, he's winding up the watch of his wit; by
15 and by it will strike.
GONZALO [*to* ALONSO]   Sir—
SEBASTIAN   One. Tell.°   *keep count*
GONZALO   When every grief is entertained° that's offered,   *harbored*
  comes to th'entertainer[4]—
20 SEBASTIAN   A dollar.[5]
GONZALO   Dolor° comes to him, indeed. You have spoken   *sorrow*
  truer than you purposed.
SEBASTIAN   You have taken it wiselier than I meant you
  should.
25 GONZALO [*to* ALONSO]   Therefore, my lord—
ANTONIO   Fie, what a spendthrift is he of his tongue!
ALONSO   I prithee, spare.°   *spare your words*
GONZALO   Well, I have done. But yet—
SEBASTIAN   He will be talking.
30 ANTONIO   Which of he or Adrian, for a good wager, first
  begins to crow?[6]
SEBASTIAN   The old cock.

2.1
1. The chief officers of some merchant ship and its owner.
2. Sebastian takes this as "pease," as in "pease porridge."
3. Antonio compares Gonzalo with one who visits and comforts the sick and distressed.
4. There comes to the person who accepts that grief.
5. English name for the German thaler.
6. Which of the two will first begin to speak ("crow")?

ANTONIO The cockerel.[7]
SEBASTIAN Done. The wager?
ANTONIO A laughter.[8]
SEBASTIAN A match.
ADRIAN Though this island seem to be desert°—   *uninhabited*
ANTONIO Ha, ha, ha!
SEBASTIAN So, you're paid.[9]
ADRIAN Uninhabitable and almost inaccessible—
SEBASTIAN Yet—
ADRIAN Yet—
ANTONIO He could not miss't.
ADRIAN It must needs be of subtle, tender, and delicate[1] temperance.°   *climate*
ANTONIO Temperance was a delicate wench.[2]
SEBASTIAN Ay, and a subtle, as he most learnedly delivered.[3]
ADRIAN The air breathes upon us here most sweetly.
SEBASTIAN As if it had lungs, and rotten ones.
ANTONIO Or as 'twere perfumed by a fen.°   *bog*
GONZALO Here is everything advantageous to life.
ANTONIO True, save° means to live.   *except*
SEBASTIAN Of that there's none, or little.
GONZALO How lush and lusty° the grass looks! How green!   *tender and luxuriant*
ANTONIO The ground indeed is tawny.
SEBASTIAN With an eye[4] of green in't.
ANTONIO He misses not much.
SEBASTIAN No, he doth but mistake the truth totally.
GONZALO But the rarity[5] of it is, which is indeed almost beyond credit—
SEBASTIAN As many vouched° rarities are.   *alleged; accepted*
GONZALO That our garments being, as they were, drenched in the sea, hold notwithstanding their freshness and gloss, being rather new-dyed than stained with salt water.
ANTONIO If but one of his pockets[6] could speak, would it not say he lies?
SEBASTIAN Ay, or very falsely pocket up his report.[7]
GONZALO Methinks our garments are now as fresh as when we put them on first in Africa, at the marriage of the King's fair daughter Claribel to the King of Tunis.

---

7. "The young cock crows as the old hears" was proverbial. "Old cock" refers to Gonzalo and "cockerel" to Adrian.
8. From the proverb "He laughs that wins."
9. Antonio's laugh is his prize.
1. Exquisite, but in Antonio's usage (line 46), "given to pleasure." "Subtle": fine, but in Sebastian's usage (line 47), "sexually expert" or "crafty."
2. Antonio takes "Temperance" to be the name of a girl.
3. "Learnedly delivered" was a popular phrase among Puritans who wanted to appear pious.
4. A tinge. In Antonio's reply, an "eye of green" refers to Gonzalo's optimistic capacity to see green.
5. Exceptional quality; but in Sebastian's usage (line 62), "uncommon thing."
6. Seen as the garments' "mouth"; also implying that Gonzalo's pockets are stained.
7. The evidence of stained pockets would confute Gonzalo's words and reputation for honesty. "Pocket up": suppress, or keep silent; also, receive unprotestingly.

SEBASTIAN 'Twas a sweet marriage, and we prosper well in our return.
ADRIAN Tunis was never graced before with such a paragon to° their queen. —for
GONZALO Not since widow Dido's[8] time.
ANTONIO Widow?[9] A pox o' that! How came that "widow" in? Widow Dido!
SEBASTIAN What if he had said "widower Aeneas" too? Good Lord, how you take° it! —fuss about
ADRIAN "Widow Dido," said you? You make me study of° that: she was of Carthage, not of Tunis. —examine
GONZALO This Tunis, sir, was Carthage.[1]
ADRIAN Carthage?
GONZALO I assure you, Carthage.
ANTONIO His word is more than the miraculous harp.[2]
SEBASTIAN He hath raised the wall, and houses too.
ANTONIO What impossible matter will he make easy next?
SEBASTIAN I think he will carry this island home in his pocket and give it his son for an apple.
ANTONIO And sowing the kernels° of it in the sea, bring forth more islands. —seeds
GONZALO Ay.[3]
ANTONIO Why, in good time.
GONZALO [to ALONSO] Sir, we were talking, that our garments seem now as fresh as when we were at Tunis at the marriage of your daughter, who is now queen.
ANTONIO And the rarest that e'er came there.
SEBASTIAN Bate,[4] I beseech you, widow Dido.
ANTONIO Oh, widow Dido? Ay, widow Dido.
GONZALO Is not, sir, my doublet as fresh as the first day I wore it? I mean, in a sort.[5]
ANTONIO That "sort" was well fished for.
GONZALO When I wore it at your daughter's marriage.
ALONSO You cram these words into mine ears against
The stomach of my sense.[6] Would I had never
Married my daughter there; for coming thence
My son is lost, and, in my rate,° she too, —consideration
Who is so far from Italy removed
I ne'er again shall see her. O thou mine heir
Of Naples and of Milan, what strange fish
Hath made his meal on thee?

---

8. Queen of ancient Carthage, whose tragic love affair with Aeneas is related in Virgil's *Aeneid*.
9. Antonio picks on this designation for a woman abandoned by her lover as being either irrelevant or conspicuously prudish. Dido, however, was in fact a *widow* when she met Aeneas.
1. The city of Tunis was actually built ten miles from the site of Carthage.
2. A reference to Amphion's harp; at its music the walls (but not the houses) of Thebes arose.
3. Affirming his belief that Tunis was Carthage; Antonio mocks the length of time this took.
4. Except (as a verb); don't mention.
5. Comparatively speaking; Antonio plays on "drawing lots."
6. The image is of one being force-fed words against the appetite ("stomach") for hearing them.

FRANCISCO　　　　　　　　　Sir, he may live.
　　I saw him beat the surges under him
　　And ride upon their backs. He trod the water
115　Whose enmity he flung aside, and breasted
　　The surge, most swol'n, that met him. His bold head
　　'Bove the contentious waves he kept, and oared
　　Himself with his good arms in lusty° stroke　　　　　　　　　*vigorous*
　　To th' shore, that o'er his wave-worn basis bowed,[7]
120　As° stooping to relieve him. I not° doubt　　　　　　　*as if / do not*
　　He came alive to land.
ALONSO　　　　　　　　　No, no, he's gone.
SEBASTIAN　Sir, you may thank yourself for this great loss,
　　That would not bless our Europe with your daughter,
　　But rather loose° her to an African,　　　　　　　　　　*lose; release*
125　Where she, at least, is banished from your eye,
　　Who° hath cause to set the grief on't.　　　　　　　　　　*(Claribel)*
ALONSO　　　　　　　　　Prithee, peace.
SEBASTIAN　You were kneeled to and importuned otherwise[8]
　　By all of us; and the fair soul herself
　　Weighed, between loathness and obedience, at
130　Which end o'th' beam should bow.[9] We have lost your son,
　　I fear, forever. Milan and Naples have
　　More widows in them of this business' making
　　Than we bring men to comfort them. The fault's
　　Your own.
ALONSO　　　　　So is the dearest o'th' loss.[1]
135　GONZALO　My lord Sebastian,
　　The truth you speak doth lack some gentleness,
　　And time° to speak it in. You rub the sore[2]　　　　　*(appropriate time)*
　　When you should bring the plaster.[3]
SEBASTIAN　　　　　　　　　Very well.
ANTONIO　And most chirurgeonly.°　　　　　　　　　　　　　*surgeonlike*
140　GONZALO　[*to* ALONSO]　It is foul weather in us all, good sir,
　　When you are cloudy.
SEBASTIAN　　　　　　　Foul weather?
ANTONIO　　　　　　　　　　　　　Very foul.
GONZALO　Had I plantation[4] of this isle, my lord—
ANTONIO　He'd sow't with nettle-seed.
SEBASTIAN　　　　　　　　　　Or docks, or mallows.[5]
GONZALO　And were the king on't, what would I do?
145　SEBASTIAN　Scape being drunk for want of wine.

---

7. That extended out and drooped over the foot of the cliff, which had been eroded by waves.
8. To act differently.
9. Weighed loathness to marry against obedience to her father to find out which end of the scales' beam would sink.
1. That is, the most grievous, or costliest, part of the loss is also my own.
2. "To rub the sore" was proverbial.
3. A soothing remedy.
4. Had I responsibility for colonization of the island; but also interpreted as "planting" by Antonio and Sebastian.
5. Cited as wild plants prone to grow on uncultivated land; but dock is a traditional soother of nettle stings, and mallow roots were used to make soothing ointment.

GONZALO   I' th' commonwealth I would by contraries
Execute all things.⁶ For no kind of traffic° —commerce
Would I admit; no name of magistrate;
Letters° should not be known; riches, poverty, —writing; erudition
And use of service,° none; contract, succession,⁷ —servants
Bourn,° bound of land, tilth,° vineyard, none; —boundary / tillage
No use of metal, corn,° or wine, or oil; —grain
No occupation, all men idle, all;
And women too, but innocent and pure;⁸
No sovereignty—
SEBASTIAN   Yet he would be king on't.
ANTONIO   The latter end of his commonwealth forgets the
beginning.
GONZALO   —All things in common° nature should produce —for communal use
Without sweat or endeavor. Treason, felony,
Sword, pike, knife, gun, or need of any engine° —weapon
Would I not have; but nature should bring forth
Of it own kind, all foison,° all abundance, —plenty
To feed my innocent people.
SEBASTIAN   No marrying⁹ 'mong his subjects?
ANTONIO   None, man, all idle: whores and knaves.
GONZALO   I would with such perfection govern, sir,
T'excel the golden age.¹
SEBASTIAN   Save° his majesty! —God save
ANTONIO   Long live Gonzalo!
GONZALO   And do you mark me, sir?
ALONSO   Prithee, no more. Thou dost talk nothing to me.
GONZALO   I do well believe your highness, and did it to
minister occasion² to these gentlemen, who are of such
sensible° and nimble lungs that they always use° to laugh —sensitive / are
at nothing.   accustomed
ANTONIO   'Twas you we laughed at.
GONZALO   Who in this kind of merry fooling am nothing
to you. So you may continue, and laugh at nothing still.
ANTONIO   What a blow was there given!
SEBASTIAN   An it had not fallen flatlong.³
GONZALO   You are gentlemen of brave mettle;⁴ you would
lift the moon out of her sphere if she would continue in
it five weeks without changing.⁵
        Enter ARIEL [*invisible,*] *playing solemn music.*
SEBASTIAN   We would so, and then go a-bat-fowling.⁶

---

6. I would advance the opposite to what would be usual. This speech is based on a passage in John Florio's translation of Montaigne's essay "Of Cannibals."
7. Inheritance of property.
8. Idleness proverbially begets lust.
9. Seen as irrelevant to sexually innocent people; also *a* form of contract.
1. In classical mythology, the earliest of the ages—a time without strife, labor, or injustice, when abundant food grew without cultivation.
2. Afford opportunity.
3. If it had not fallen on the flat, harmless side of the sword.
4. Courage; punning on "metal," as of a sword blade.
5. You would even steal the moon, if she were to stand still in her orbit ("sphere").
6. Trapping birds by using light to attract them and bats to strike them down; may also mean swindling and victimizing the simple.

ANTONIO Nay, good my lord, be not angry.
GONZALO No, I warrant you, I will not adventure my discretion so weakly.[7] Will you laugh me asleep, for I am very heavy?°   *tired; serious*
ANTONIO Go sleep, and hear us.
    [*All sleep, except* ALONSO, SEBASTIAN, *and* ANTONIO.]
ALONSO What, all so soon asleep? I wish mine eyes
Would, with themselves, shut up my thoughts. I find
They are inclined to do so.
SEBASTIAN   Please you, sir,
Do not omit° the heavy offer° of it.   *neglect / opportunity*
It seldom visits sorrow; when it doth,
It is a comforter.
ANTONIO   We two, my lord,
Will guard your person while you take your rest,
And watch your safety.
ALONSO   Thank you. Wondrous heavy.
    [ALONSO *sleeps. Exit* ARIEL.]
SEBASTIAN What a strange drowsiness possesses them!
ANTONIO It is the quality o'th' climate.
SEBASTIAN   Why
Doth it not then our eyelids sink? I find
Not myself disposed to sleep.
ANTONIO Nor I: my spirits are nimble.
They fell together all as by consent;°   *consensus*
They dropped, as by a thunderstroke. What might,
Worthy Sebastian, oh, what might—? No more.
And yet methinks I see it in thy face
What thou shouldst be. Th'occasion speaks° thee, and   *opportunity speaks to*
My strong imagination sees a crown
Dropping upon thy head.
SEBASTIAN   What? Art thou waking?°   *awake*
ANTONIO Do you not hear me speak?
SEBASTIAN   I do, and surely
It is a sleepy language, and thou speak'st
Out of thy sleep. What is it thou didst say?
This is a strange repose, to be asleep
With eyes wide open; standing, speaking, moving,
And yet so fast asleep.
ANTONIO   Noble Sebastian,
Thou lett'st thy fortune sleep—die rather; wink'st°   *shut your eyes*
Whiles thou art waking.
SEBASTIAN   Thou dost snore distinctly;°   *meaningfully*
There's meaning in thy snores.
ANTONIO I am more serious than my custom. You
Must be so too, if heed° me; which to do   *if you heed*
Trebles thee o'er.[8]

---

7. I will not put my sound judgment at risk so foolishly.
8. Makes you three times as great.

220	SEBASTIAN	Well, I am standing water.[9]	
	ANTONIO	I'll teach you how to flow.	
	SEBASTIAN	Do so. To ebb	
		Hereditary sloth[1] instructs me.	
	ANTONIO	Oh!	
		If you but knew how you the purpose cherish	
		Whiles thus you mock it;[2] how in stripping it	
225		You more invest° it. Ebbing° men, indeed,	clothe / declining
		Most often do so near the bottom run	
		By their own fear or sloth.	
	SEBASTIAN	Prithee, say on.	
		The setting° of thine eye and cheek proclaim	fixed look
		A matter° from thee; and a birth, indeed,	something important
230		Which throes[3] thee much to yield.	
	ANTONIO	Thus, sir:	
		[indicating GONZALO] Although this lord of weak	
		remembrance,° this,	memory
		Who shall be of as little memory°	as little remembered
		When he is earthed,° hath here almost persuaded—	buried
		For he's a spirit of persuasion, only	
235		Professes[4] to persuade—the King his son's alive,	
		'Tis as impossible that he's undrowned	
		As he that sleeps here swims.	
	SEBASTIAN	I have no hope	
		That he's undrowned.	
	ANTONIO	Oh, out of that no hope	
		What great hope have you! No hope that way° is	(that he's not drowned)
240		Another way so high a hope that even	
		Ambition cannot pierce a wink° beyond,	catch a glimpse
		But doubt discovery there.[5] Will you grant with me	
		That Ferdinand is drowned?	
	SEBASTIAN	He's gone.	
	ANTONIO	Then tell me,	
		Who's the next heir of Naples?	
	SEBASTIAN	Claribel.	
245	ANTONIO	She that is Queen of Tunis; she that dwells	
		Ten leagues beyond man's life;° she that from Naples	lifetime journey
		Can have no note,° unless the sun were post°—	information / messenger
		The man i'th' moon's too slow—till newborn chins	
		Be rough and razorable; she that from° whom	returning from
250		We all were sea-swallowed, though some cast again,[6]	
		And by that destiny to perform an act	

9. Between tides, and thus open to suggestion; also, associated with being slothful.
1. Inherited laziness, or the slowness to attain prosperity arising from being born a younger brother.
2. If you only understood that your mockery reveals how great your aspirations really are; also, the hereditary position you mock is actu-ally to your advantage. "Cherish": hold dear; cultivate.
3. Which puts in agony, as in childbirth.
4. "Only / Professes": his sole vocation is.
5. Doubt that there is anything to achieve beyond the high hope of the crown.
6. Regurgitated, cast ashore; also, possibly, theatrical role-playing.

Whereof what's past is prologue, what to come
In yours and my discharge.° — *performance*
SEBASTIAN   What stuff is this? How say you?
'Tis true my brother's daughter's Queen of Tunis;
So is she heir of Naples, twixt which regions
There is some space.
ANTONIO   A space whose ev'ry cubit° — *about 18 to 22 inches*
Seems to cry out, "How shall that Claribel
Measure us° back to Naples? Keep° in Tunis, — *(the cubits) / stay*
And let Sebastian wake."° Say this were death — *(to his opportunity)*
That now hath seized them: why, they were no worse
Than now they are. There be that° can rule Naples — *those that*
As well as he that sleeps; lords that can prate
As amply and unnecessarily
As this Gonzalo; I myself could make
A chough of as deep chat.[7] Oh, that you bore
The mind that I do! What a sleep were this
For your advancement! Do you understand me?
SEBASTIAN   Methinks I do.
ANTONIO   And how does your content
Tender° your own good fortune? — *regard; care for*
SEBASTIAN   I remember
You did supplant your brother Prospero.
ANTONIO   True:
And look how well my garments sit upon me,
Much feater° than before. My brother's servants — *more trimly*
Were then my fellows; now they are my men.
SEBASTIAN   But for your conscience?
ANTONIO   Ay, sir, where lies that? If 'twere a kibe,[8]
'Twould put me to° my slipper; but I feel not — *make me wear*
This deity in my bosom. Twenty consciences
That stand twixt me and Milan, candied[9] be they,
And melt ere they molest. Here lies your brother,
No better than the earth he lies upon
If he were that which now he's like—that's dead—
Whom I with this obedient steel,° three inches of it, — *sword*
Can lay to bed forever; whiles you, doing thus,
To the perpetual wink for aye° might put — *sleep forever*
This ancient morsel, this Sir Prudence, who
Should not upbraid our course. For all the rest,
They'll take suggestion° as a cat laps milk; — *prompting to evil*
They'll tell the clock° to any business that — *chime; agree*
We say befits the hour.
SEBASTIAN   Thy case, dear friend,
Shall be my precedent. As thou gott'st Milan,

---

7. I could train a jackdaw (known for imitating speech) to speak as profoundly.
8. Chilblain; sore on the heel.
9. Turned to sugar; crystallized in sugar.

I'll come by Naples. Draw thy sword: one stroke
Shall free thee from the tribute which thou payest,
And I the King shall love thee.

ANTONIO   Draw together;
And when I rear my hand, do you the like
To fall it on Gonzalo.

295 SEBASTIAN   Oh, but one word.

Enter ARIEL, [*invisible,*] *with music and song.*

ARIEL   My master through his art foresees the danger
That you his friend are in, and sends me forth—
For else° his project dies—to keep them[1] living.   *otherwise*

[*He*] *sings in Gonzalo's ear.*

While you here do snoring lie,
300   Open-eyed conspiracy
His time° doth take.   *opportunity*
If of life you keep a care,
Shake off slumber and beware.
Awake, awake!

305 ANTONIO   Then let us both be sudden.

[ANTONIO *and* SEBASTIAN *draw their swords.*]

GONZALO [*waking*]   Now, good angels preserve the King.

[*He wakes* ALONSO.]

ALONSO   Why, how now? Ho! Awake! Why are you° drawn?   *your weapons*
Wherefore this ghastly° looking?   *fearful*

GONZALO   What's the matter?

SEBASTIAN   Whiles we stood here securing° your repose,   *guarding*
310   Even now we heard a hollow burst of bellowing,
Like bulls, or rather lions. Did't not wake you?
It struck mine ear most terribly.

ALONSO   I heard nothing.

ANTONIO   Oh, 'twas a din to fright a monster's ear,
To make an earthquake: sure it was the roar
Of a whole herd of lions.

315 ALONSO   Heard you this, Gonzalo?

GONZALO   Upon mine honor, sir, I heard a humming,
And that a strange one too, which did awake me.
I shaked you, sir, and cried.° As mine eyes opened,   *called out*
I saw their weapons drawn. There was a noise,
320   That's verily.° 'Tis best we stand upon our guard,   *the truth*
Or that we quit this place. Let's draw our weapons.

ALONSO   Lead off this ground, and let's make further search
For my poor son.

GONZALO   Heavens keep him from these beasts,
For he is sure i'th' island.

ALONSO   Lead away.

325 ARIEL[2]   Prospero my lord shall know what I have done.
So, King, go safely on to seek thy son.   *Exeunt.*

---

1. Gonzalo and Alonso.
2. Ariel's following lines are spoken as the other characters depart; he probably exits in another direction.

2.2

Enter CALIBAN *with a burden of wood.*

CALIBAN   All the infections that the sun sucks up
From bogs, fens, flats,° on Prosper fall, and make him   *marshes*
By inchmeal° a disease!   *inch by inch*
   A noise of thunder heard.[1]
             His spirits hear me,
And yet I needs must curse. But they'll nor pinch,
5   Fright me with urchin-shows,[2] pitch me i'th' mire,
Nor lead me like a firebrand in the dark
Out of my way, unless he bid 'em. But
For every trifle are they set upon me;
Sometime like apes that mow° and chatter at me   *grimace*
10 And after bite me; then like hedgehogs, which
Lie tumbling in my barefoot way and mount
Their pricks at my footfall; sometime am I
All wound with° adders, who with cloven tongues   *entwined by*
Do hiss me into madness.
   Enter TRINCULO.[3]
             Lo, now, lo!
15 Here comes a spirit of his, and to torment me
For bringing wood in slowly. I'll fall flat.
Perchance he will not mind° me.   *notice*

TRINCULO   Here's neither bush nor scrub to bear off° any   *ward off*
20 weather at all, and another storm brewing: I hear it sing
i'th' wind. Yond same black cloud, yond huge one, looks
like a foul bombard[4] that would shed his liquor. If it
should thunder as it did before, I know not where to hide
my head. Yond same cloud cannot choose but fall by pail-
fuls. [*He sees* CALIBAN.] What have we here? A man or a
25 fish? Dead or alive? A fish: he smells like a fish; a very
ancient and fishlike smell; a kind of not-of-the-newest
poor-john.[5] A strange fish. Were I in England now, as once
I was, and had but this fish painted,[6] not a holiday fool
there but would give a piece of silver. There would this
30 monster make a man;[7] any strange beast there makes a
man. When they will not give a doit° to relieve a lame   *small coin*
beggar, they will lay out ten to see a dead Indian.[8] Legged
like a man, and his fins like arms. Warm, o'my troth! I do
now let loose my opinion, hold it no longer: this is no fish,
35 but an islander that hath lately suffered by a thunderbolt.
[*Thunder.*] Alas, the storm is come again. My best way is
to creep under his gaberdine; there is no other shelter
hereabout. Misery acquaints a man with strange bedfel-

2.2
1. Caliban takes this as a response to his curse.
2. With the sight of hedgehog-like spirits.
3. Trinculo is probably dressed in traditional fool's motley (many-colored garment).
4. Large leather drinking vessel; stone-throwing military engine.
5. Dried hake, a poor person's staple.
6. On a sign to attract spectators.
7. Make a fortune for a man; become a man.
8. An allusion to exhibitions of Native Americans in London.

lows. I will here shroud° till the dregs⁹ of the storm   *take cover*
be past.
    [*He crawls under Caliban's cloak.*]
    Enter STEFANO *singing.*
STEFANO   I shall no more to sea, to sea,
        Here shall I die ashore.
This is a very scurvy tune to sing at a man's funeral.
Well, here's my comfort.
    [*He*] *drinks* [*and*] *sings.*
        The master, the swabber, the boatswain and I,
        The gunner and his mate,
        Loved Moll, Meg, and Marian, and Margery,
        But none of us cared for Kate.
        For she had a tongue with a tang,°   *sting*
        Would cry to a sailor, "Go hang!"
        She loved not the savor of tar nor of pitch,
        Yet a tailor might scratch her where'er she did itch.¹
        Then to sea, boys, and let her go hang!
This is a scurvy tune, too; but here's my comfort.
    [*He*] *drinks.*
CALIBAN   Do not torment me! Oh!
STEFANO   What's the matter?° Have we devils here? Do   *what's going on?*
you put tricks upon 's with savages and men of Ind?°   *India*
Ha? I have not scaped drowning to be afeared now of
your four legs; for it hath been said, "As proper a man as
ever went on four legs² cannot make him give ground";
and it shall be said so again, while Stefano breathes at'°   *at the*
nostrils.
CALIBAN   The spirit torments me! Oh!
STEFANO   This is some monster of the isle with four legs
who hath got, as I take it, an ague.° Where the devil   *a fit of fever*
should he learn our language? I will give him some relief
if it be but for that. If I can recover° him and keep him   *cure*
tame and get to Naples with him, he's a present for any
emperor that ever trod on neat's leather.°   *cowhide; shoes*
CALIBAN   Do not torment me, prithee! I'll bring my wood
home faster.
STEFANO   He's in his fit now, and does not talk after° the   *in the manner of*
wisest. He shall taste of my bottle. If he have never drunk
wine afore, it will go near to° remove his fit. If I can recover   *almost*
him and keep him tame, I will not take too much for him.³
He shall pay for him that hath° him, and that soundly.   *gets*
CALIBAN   Thou dost me yet but little hurt; thou wilt anon,
I know it by thy trembling. Now Prosper works upon thee.

---

9. *Last drinks,* as from the bottom of a "bombard" of wine.
1. Implying sexual desire and gratification. Tailors were often mocked for supposed lack of virility.
2. Comically varying "on two legs" (upright); also suggesting "on crutches."
3. No sum can be too high for him.

STEFANO Come on your ways.° Open your mouth: here is   come on
   that which will give language to you, cat.[4] Open your
   mouth: this will shake° your shaking, I can tell you, and   dislodge
   that soundly. [CALIBAN *drinks*.] You cannot tell who's
   your friend. Open your chaps again.
TRINCULO I should know that voice. It should be—but he
   is drowned, and these are devils. Oh, defend me!
STEFANO Four legs and two voices: a most delicate° mon-   exquisitely made
   ster! His forward voice now is to speak well of his friend;
   his backward voice is to utter foul speeches and to detract.
   If all the wine in my bottle will recover him,[5] I will help
   his ague. Come. [CALIBAN *drinks*.] Amen.° I will pour some   enough
   in thy other mouth.
TRINCULO Stefano!
STEFANO Doth thy other mouth call me? Mercy, mercy!
   This is a devil and no monster. I will leave him; I have
   no long spoon.[6]
TRINCULO Stefano? If thou beest Stefano, touch me and
   speak to me, for I am Trinculo—be not afeard—thy
   good friend Trinculo.
STEFANO If thou beest Trinculo, come forth: I'll pull thee by
   the lesser legs. If any be Trinculo's legs, these are they. [*He
   pulls him out.*] Thou art very° Trinculo indeed! How   actual
   cam'st thou to be the siege° of this mooncalf?[7] Can he   excrement
   vent° Trinculos?   defecate
TRINCULO I took him to be killed with a thunderstroke.
   But art thou not drowned, Stefano? I hope now thou
   art not drowned. Is the storm overblown? I hid me under
   the dead mooncalf's gaberdine, for fear of the storm.
   And art thou living, Stefano? O Stefano, two Neapolitans
   scaped!
STEFANO Prithee, do not turn me about, my stomach is
   not constant.
CALIBAN [*aside*] These be fine things, an if° they be not   an if = if
   sprites. That's a brave° god, and bears celestial liquor. I   excellent; fine
   will kneel to him.
STEFANO How didst thou scape? How cam'st thou hither?
   Swear by this bottle how thou cam'st hither. I escaped
   upon a butt of sack[8] which the sailors heaved o'erboard,
   by this bottle, which I made of the bark of a tree, with
   mine own hands, since I was cast ashore.
CALIBAN I'll swear upon that bottle to be thy true subject, for the liquor is not earthly.
STEFANO Here. Swear then how thou escaped'st.

---

4. "Ale will make a cat speak" was proverbial.
5. If it takes all the wine in my bottle to cure him.
6. From the proverbial "He should have a long spoon that sups with the devil."
7. Deformed creature; miscarriage, owing to the supposed detrimental influence of the moon.
8. Cask of Spanish or Canary wine.

TRINCULO Swum ashore, man, like a duck. I can swim like a duck, I'll be sworn.
STEFANO [*giving* TRINCULO *the bottle*] Here, kiss the Book.⁹ Though thou canst swim like a duck, thou art made like a goose.¹
TRINCULO O Stefano, hast any more of this?
STEFANO The whole butt, man. My cellar is in a rock by the seaside, where my wine is hid. [*to* CALIBAN] How now, mooncalf, how does thine ague?
CALIBAN Hast thou not dropped from heaven?
STEFANO Out o'th' moon I do assure thee. I was the man i'th' moon, when time was.°   *once upon a time*
CALIBAN I have seen thee in her, and I do adore thee. My mistress° showed me thee, and thy dog, and thy bush.²   *(Miranda)*
STEFANO [*giving the bottle to* CALIBAN] Come, swear to that: kiss the Book. I will furnish it anon with new contents. Swear.
TRINCULO By this good light,° this is a very shallow monster. I afeared of him? A very weak monster. The man i'th' moon? A most poor credulous monster. Well drawn,° monster, in good sooth.   *sun*   *drunk*
CALIBAN I'll show thee every fertile inch o'th' island, and I will kiss thy foot. I prithee, be my god.
TRINCULO By this light, a most perfidious and drunken monster! When 's god's asleep he'll rob his bottle.
CALIBAN I'll kiss thy foot. I'll swear myself thy subject.
STEFANO Come on, then: down and swear.
TRINCULO I shall laugh myself to death at this puppy-headed monster. A most scurvy monster. I could find in my heart to beat him—
STEFANO [*to* CALIBAN] Come, kiss.
TRINCULO —but that the poor monster's in drink.° An abominable monster.   *drunk*
CALIBAN I'll show thee the best springs; I'll pluck thee berries; I'll fish for thee, and get thee wood enough. A plague upon the tyrant that I serve! I'll bear him no more sticks but follow thee, Thou wondrous man.
TRINCULO A most ridiculous monster, to make a wonder of a poor drunkard.
CALIBAN I prithee, let me bring thee where crabs° grow;   *crab apples*
And I with my long nails will dig thee pig-nuts,°   *edible tubers*
Show thee a jay's nest, and instruct thee how

---

9. Confirming an oath by kissing the Bible; or the proverbial "Kiss the cup" ("Drink").
1. *Probably* alluding to Trinculo's outstretched neck with the bottle as a beak; also, a byword for giddiness and unsteadiness on the feet.
2. A dog and a thornbush were traditional attributes of the man in the moon.

To snare the nimble marmoset. I'll bring thee
To clust'ring filberts, and sometimes I'll get thee
Young scamels³ from the rock. Wilt thou go with me?

STEFANO   I prithee now lead the way without any more talking. Trinculo, the King and all our company else being drowned, we will inherit here. [*to* CALIBAN] Here, bear my bottle. —Fellow Trinculo, we'll fill him° by and by again.   °*it*

CALIBAN (*sings drunkenly*)⁴   Farewell, master; farewell, farewell.

TRINCULO   A howling monster, a drunken monster.

CALIBAN [*continuing to sing*]   No more dams I'll make for° fish,   °*to trap*

    Nor fetch in firing°   °*firewood*
    At requiring,
    Nor scrape trencher, nor wash dish,
    'Ban, 'Ban, Ca-Caliban
    Has a new master: get a new man.⁵

Freedom, high-day;° high-day, freedom; freedom, high-day, freedom!   °*holiday*

STEFANO   O brave° monster, lead the way!   *Exeunt.*   °*excellent; fine*

3.1

Enter FERDINAND, *bearing a log.*

FERDINAND   There be some sports are painful, and their labor
Delight in them sets off.¹ Some kinds of baseness
Are nobly undergone, and most poor matters
Point to rich ends. This my mean° task   °*lowly*
Would be as heavy to me as odious, but°   °*except that*
The mistress which I serve quickens° what's dead   °*enlivens*
And makes my labors pleasures. Oh, she is
Ten times more gentle than her father's crabbed,
And he's composed of harshness. I must remove
Some thousands of these logs and pile them up,
Upon a sore° injunction. My sweet mistress   °*harsh*
Weeps when she sees me work and says such baseness
Had never like executor. I forget;
But these sweet thoughts do even refresh my labors,
Most busil'est,² when I do it.°   °(*labor*)

Enter MIRANDA, *and* PROSPERO [*unseen*].

---

3. Shakespeare may have invented this exotic word, which appears nowhere else in the English language, but it seems more likely that "scamel" was the result of an error in transmission.
4. This stage direction may be misplaced and may actually refer to the following song, "No more dams."
5. Addressed to the old master, Prospero.

3.1
1. The greater effort invested amounts to more pleasure; the labor of painful activities ("sports") is offset by whatever delight we take in them.
2. Most busily (giving a double superlative).

MIRANDA   Alas now, pray you,
   Work not so hard. I would the lightning had
   Burnt up those logs that you are enjoined to pile.
   Pray set it down and rest you. When this burns
   'Twill weep³ for having wearied you. My father
   Is hard at study. Pray now, rest yourself.
   He's safe° for these three hours.   *we are safe from him*
FERDINAND   O most dear mistress,
   The sun will set before I shall discharge
   What I must strive to do.
MIRANDA   If you'll sit down
   I'll bear your logs the while. Pray give me that:
   I'll carry it to the pile.
FERDINAND   No, precious creature,
   I had rather crack my sinews, break my back,
   Than you should such dishonor undergo
   While I sit lazy by.
MIRANDA   It would become me
   As well as it does you; and I should do it
   With much more ease, for my goodwill is to it,
   And yours it is against.
PROSPERO [*aside*]   Poor worm, thou art infected:⁴
   This visitation⁵ shows it.
MIRANDA   You look wearily.
FERDINAND   No, noble mistress, 'tis fresh morning with me
   When you are by at night. I do beseech you,
   Chiefly that I may set it in my prayers,
   What is your name?
MIRANDA   Miranda. —O my father,
   I have broke your hest° to say so!   *disobeyed your command*
FERDINAND   Admired⁶ Miranda!
   Indeed the top of admiration, worth
   What's dearest to the world. Full many a lady
   I have eyed with best regard, and many a time
   Th' harmony of their tongues hath into bondage
   Brought my too diligent° ear. For several virtues   *attentive*
   Have I liked several° women; never any   *various*
   With so full soul but some defect in her
   Did quarrel with the noblest grace she owed°   *owned*
   And put it to the foil.⁷ But you, O you,
   So perfect and so peerless, are created
   Of every creature's best.
MIRANDA   I do not know
   One of my sex; no woman's face remember

---

3. By exuding drops of resin.
4. *Afflicted with lovesickness.* "Worm": an expression of tenderness; but a worm was often thought to carry disease.
5. Suggesting a pastoral or charitable visit to the sick; or perhaps indicating a visit by the plague—here, lovesickness.
6. Playing on the meaning of Miranda's name.
7. Foiled it, or made it ineffectual; challenged it, as in a fencing match (see "quarrel" in line 45).

50	Save, from my glass,° mine own. Nor have I seen	*mirror*
	More that I may call men than you, good friend,	
	And my dear father. How features are abroad[8]	
	I am skilless° of; but by my modesty,°	*ignorant / virginity*
	The jewel in my dower,° I would not wish	*dowry*
55	Any companion in the world but you,	
	Nor can imagination form a shape	
	Besides° yourself to like of. But I prattle	*other than*
	Something° too wildly, and my father's precepts	*somewhat*
	I therein do forget.	
	FERDINAND I am in my condition°	*rank*
60	A prince, Miranda; I do think a king—	
	I would° not so!—and would no more endure	*wish it were*
	This wooden slavery[9] than to suffer	
	The flesh fly[1] blow my mouth. Hear my soul speak:	
	The very instant that I saw you did	
65	My heart fly to your service, there resides	
	To make me slave to it, and for your sake	
	Am I this patient log-man.	
	MIRANDA Do you love me?	
	FERDINAND O heaven, O earth, bear witness to this sound,	
	And crown what I profess with kind event°	*favorable outcome*
70	If I speak true! If hollowly,° invert	*falsely*
	What best is boded° me to mischief!° I,	*foretold to / misfortune*
	Beyond all limit of what° else i'th' world,	*whatsoever*
	Do love, prize, honor you.	
	MIRANDA I am a fool	
	To weep at what I am glad of.	
	PROSPERO [*aside*] Fair encounter	
75	Of two most rare affections. Heavens rain grace	
	On that which breeds between 'em.	
	FERDINAND Wherefore weep you?	
	MIRANDA At mine unworthiness, that dare not offer	
	What I desire to give, and much less take	
	What I shall die to want.[2] But this is trifling,	
80	And all the more it seeks to hide itself	
	The bigger bulk it shows.[3] Hence, bashful cunning,°	*artful shyness*
	And prompt me, plain and holy innocence!	
	I am your wife if you'll marry me;	
	If not, I'll die your maid.° To be your fellow°	*virgin; servant / equal*
85	You may deny me, but I'll be your servant	
	Whether you will or no.	
	FERDINAND My mistress,° dearest,	*sweetheart*
	And I thus humble ever.	
	MIRANDA My husband, then?	

8. What people look like elsewhere.
9. The log as a symbol of Prospero's oppression.
1. Species of fly that deposits its eggs ("blows") in dead flesh.

2. Miranda is not at liberty to bestow her virginity or to obtain the consummation that she desires and lacks.
3. An image of secret pregnancy.

FERDINAND   Ay, with a heart as willing°   *desirous*
As bondage e'er of freedom. Here's my hand.[4]
MIRANDA   And mine, with my heart in't. And now farewell
Till half an hour hence.
FERDINAND   A thousand thousand!°   *(farewells)*
    Exeunt [FERDINAND *and* MIRANDA, *separately*].
PROSPERO   So glad of this as they I cannot be,
Who are surprised withal;° but my rejoicing   *overwhelmed by all*
At nothing can be more. I'll to my book,°   *book of magic*
For yet ere suppertime must I perform
Much business appertaining.   *Exit.*

3.2

Enter CALIBAN, STEFANO, *and* TRINCULO.

STEFANO   Tell not me. When the butt is out we will drink water, not a drop before. Therefore bear up and board 'em.[1] —Servant monster, drink to me!
TRINCULO   "Servant monster"? The folly° of this island!   *absurdity*
They say there's but five upon this isle. We are three of them; if th'other two be brained° like us, the state totters.   *have brains*
STEFANO   Drink, servant monster, when I bid thee. Thy eyes are almost set° in thy head.   *fixed by drunkenness*
TRINCULO   Where should they be set° else? He were a   *placed*
brave monster indeed if they were set in his tail.
STEFANO   My man-monster hath drowned his tongue in sack. For my part, the sea cannot drown me. I swam, ere I could recover the shore, five and thirty leagues,° off and   *about 100 miles*
on.[2] By this light, thou shalt be my lieutenant, monster, or my standard.[3]
TRINCULO   Your lieutenant, if you list;° he's no standard.   *wish*
STEFANO   We'll not run, Monsieur Monster.
TRINCULO   Nor go° neither, but you'll lie[4] like dogs and   *walk*
yet say nothing neither.
STEFANO   Mooncalf, speak once in thy life, if thou beest a good mooncalf.
CALIBAN   How does thy honor? Let me lick thy shoe.
I'll not serve him; he is not valiant.
TRINCULO   Thou liest, most ignorant monster; I am in case°   *prepared*
to jostle a constable. Why, thou debauched fish thou, was there ever man a coward that hath drunk so much sack as I do today? Wilt thou tell a monstrous lie, being but half a fish and half a monster?

---

4. "I am your wife . . . hand" (lines 83–89): such an exchange could actually have constituted a marriage ceremony. In Shakespeare's time, weddings did not need to be witnessed and performed in a church to be valid (compare 4.1.14–19).
3.2
1. Force a way aboard, continuing the terminology of naval warfare; take onboard (drink). "Bear up": sail to the attack.
2. Tacking away from and toward the shore.
3. Standard-bearer; but in Trinculo's reply, "one who can stand up."
4. Lie (down); tell lies; excrete.

CALIBAN Lo, how he mocks me. Wilt thou let him, my lord?
TRINCULO "Lord," quoth he? That a monster should be
such a natural!⁵
CALIBAN Lo, lo again! Bite him to death, I prithee.
STEFANO Trinculo, keep a good tongue in your head. If
you prove a mutineer, the next tree!° The poor monster's   *(for a gallows)*
my subject, and he shall not suffer indignity.
CALIBAN I thank my noble lord. Wilt thou be pleased
To hearken once again to the suit I made to thee?
STEFANO Marry, will I. Kneel and repeat it. I will stand,
and so shall Trinculo.
   Enter ARIEL *invisible.*
CALIBAN As I told thee before, I am subject to a tyrant,
A sorcerer, that by his cunning hath
Cheated me of the island.
ARIEL   Thou liest.
CALIBAN [*to* TRINCULO] Thou liest, thou jesting monkey, thou!
I would my valiant master would destroy thee.
I do not lie.
STEFANO Trinculo, if you trouble him any more in 's tale,
by this hand, I will supplant° some of your teeth.   *uproot*
TRINCULO Why, I said nothing.
STEFANO Mum, then, and no more. —Proceed.
CALIBAN I say by sorcery he got this isle;
From me he got it. If thy greatness will
Revenge it on him—for I know thou dar'st,
But this thing⁶ dare not—
STEFANO That's most certain.
CALIBAN Thou shalt be lord of it, and I'll serve thee.
STEFANO How now shall this be compassed?° Canst thou   *accomplished*
bring me to the party?°   *person concerned*
CALIBAN Yea, yea, my lord. I'll yield him thee asleep,
Where thou mayst knock a nail into his head.⁷
ARIEL Thou liest; thou canst not.
CALIBAN What a pied ninny's° this! Thou scurvy   *fool in motley*
patch!°   *jester; idiot*
I do beseech thy greatness give him blows
And take his bottle from him. When that's gone,
He shall drink naught but brine, for I'll not show him
Where the quick freshes° are.   *fast-flowing springs*
STEFANO Trinculo, run into no further danger. Interrupt
the monster one word further and, by this hand, I'll turn
my mercy out o' doors and make a stockfish of thee.⁸
TRINCULO Why, what did I? I did nothing. I'll go farther off.

---

5. An idiot, punning on the idea that monsters were unnatural.
6. Trinculo; or perhaps Caliban himself.
7. As Jael murdered the sleeping the Sisera in Judges 4:21 and 5:26.
8. Proverbial allusion to the beating of dried fish before cooking it.

STEFANO   Didst thou not say he lied?
ARIEL   Thou liest.
STEFANO   Do I so?
     [*He beats* TRINCULO.]
   Take thou that! As you like this, give me the lie° another   *call me a liar*
   time.
TRINCULO   I did not give the lie! Out o'your wits, and
   hearing too? A pox o'your bottle. This can sack and
   drinking do. A murrain° on your monster, and the devil   *plague*
   take your fingers!
CALIBAN   Ha, ha, ha!
STEFANO   Now forward with your tale. —Prithee stand
   further off.
CALIBAN   Beat him enough. After a little time I'll beat him
   too.
STEFANO   Stand farther. —Come, proceed.
CALIBAN   Why, as I told thee, 'tis a custom with him
   I'th' afternoon to sleep. There° thou mayst brain him,   *then*
   Having first seized his books; or with a log
   Batter his skull, or paunch° him with a stake,   *disembowel*
   Or cut his weasand° with thy knife. Remember   *windpipe*
   First to possess his books, for without them
   He's but a sot° as I am, nor hath not   *stupid fool*
   One spirit to command—they all do hate him
   As rootedly as I. Burn but his books.
   He has brave utensils,⁹ for so he calls them,
   Which, when he has a house, he'll deck withal.
   And that most deeply to consider is
   The beauty of his daughter. He himself
   Calls her a nonpareil.° I never saw a woman   *one without equal*
   But only Sycorax my dam and she;
   But she as far surpasseth Sycorax
   As great'st does least.
STEFANO   Is it so brave° a lass?   *excellent; fine*
CALIBAN   Ay, lord. She will become thy bed, I warrant,
   And bring thee forth brave brood.
STEFANO   Monster, I will kill this man. His daughter and I
   will be king and queen—save° our graces—and Trinculo   *God save*
   and thyself shall be viceroys. Dost thou like the plot,
   Trinculo?
TRINCULO   Excellent.
STEFANO   Give me thy hand. I am sorry I beat thee. But
   while thou liv'st, keep a good tongue in thy head.
CALIBAN   Within this half hour will he be asleep.
   Wilt thou destroy him then?
STEFANO   Ay, on mine honor.
ARIEL [*aside*]   This will I tell my master.

---

9. Perhaps confusing implements for magic and household goods.

CALIBAN Thou mak'st me merry. I am full of pleasure;
Let us be jocund. Will you troll° the catch° *sing / round; song*
You taught me but whilere?° *a short time ago*
STEFANO At thy request, monster, I will do reason, any
reason.° Come on, Trinculo, let us sing. *anything reasonable*
(*Sings.*)¹   Flout 'em, and scout 'em
                And scout° 'em, and flout 'em. *mock*
                Thought is free.
CALIBAN That's not the tune.
   ARIEL *plays the tune on a tabor and pipe.*²
STEFANO What is this same?
TRINCULO This is the tune of our catch, played by the
picture of Nobody.³
STEFANO If thou beest a man, show thyself in thy likeness. If thou beest a devil, take't as thou list.° *wish*
TRINCULO Oh, forgive me my sins!
STEFANO He that dies pays all debts.⁴ I defy thee! Mercy
upon us!⁵
CALIBAN Art thou afeard?
STEFANO No, monster, not I.
CALIBAN Be not afeard: the isle is full of noises,
Sounds and sweet airs° that give delight and hurt not. *tunes*
Sometimes a thousand twangling instruments
Will hum about mine ears; and sometimes voices,
That, if I then had waked after long sleep,
Will make me sleep again; and then, in dreaming,
The clouds methought would open and show riches
Ready to drop upon me, that when I waked
I cried to dream again.
STEFANO This will prove a brave kingdom to me, where I
shall have my music for nothing.⁶
CALIBAN When Prospero is destroyed.
STEFANO That shall be by and by:° I remember the story. *very soon*
        [*Exit* ARIEL *playing music.*]
TRINCULO The sound is going away; let's follow it, and
after do our work.
STEFANO Lead, monster, we'll follow. I would I could see
this taborer: he lays it on.⁷
TRINCULO [*to* CALIBAN] Wilt come? I'll follow Stefano.
                                    Exeunt.

1. The stage direction suggests that the others cannot manage the catch and remain in bewildered silence. But Trinculo, and perhaps Caliban, may attempt to join in.
2. The tabor was a small drum slung on the left-hand side of the body; the tabor pipe was a long narrow pipe played with the left hand. The combination was associated with rustic dances and merrymaking.
3. "Nobody" was a character in a comedy who was depicted on the title page of the printed text. Large breeches up to his neck made him appear to have no trunk.
4. Varying the proverbial "Death pays all debts."
5. Stefano's defiance comically collapses.
6. James I spent large sums on court music, but not typically of the popular kind Ariel now plays.
7. He sets himself to his music vigorously. Stefano deserts Caliban in order to follow the music. Trinculo and Caliban in turn follow Stefano.

3.3

Enter ALONSO, SEBASTIAN, ANTONIO, GONZALO, ADRIAN, *and* FRANCISCO.

GONZALO By'r lakin,[1] I can go no further, sir.
My old bones aches. Here's a maze trod indeed
Through forthrights and meanders.° By your   *direct and winding paths*
    patience,
I needs must rest me.
ALONSO   Old lord, I cannot blame thee,
5 Who am myself attached° with weariness   *seized*
To th' dulling of my spirits. Sit down and rest.
Even° here I will put off my hope, and keep it   *exactly*
No longer for° my flatterer: he is drowned   *as*
Whom thus we stray to find, and the sea mocks
10 Our frustrate° search on land. Well, let him go.   *vain*
ANTONIO [*aside to* SEBASTIAN] I am right glad that he's so
    out of hope.
Do not, for° one repulse, forgo the purpose   *on account of*
That you resolved t'effect.
SEBASTIAN [*aside to* ANTONIO] The next advantage
Will we take throughly.°   *thoroughly*
ANTONIO [*aside to* SEBASTIAN] Let it be tonight;
15 For now they are oppressed with travail,° they   *journey; effort*
Will not nor cannot use such vigilance
As when they are fresh.
SEBASTIAN [*aside to* ANTONIO] I say tonight: no more.
    Solemn and strange music. [Enter] PROSPERO *on the
    top,[2] invisible.*
ALONSO What harmony is this? My good friends, hark!
GONZALO Marvelous sweet music.
    *Enter several strange shapes, bringing a banquet; and
    dance about it with gentle actions of salutations, and
    inviting the King etc. to eat, they depart.*
20 ALONSO Give us kind keepers,° heavens! What were these?   *guardian angels*
SEBASTIAN A living drollery.[3] Now I will believe
That there are unicorns; that in Arabia
There is one tree, the phoenix' throne, one phoenix[4]
At this hour reigning there.
ANTONIO   I'll believe both;
25 And what does else want credit,° come to me,   *lack belief*
And I'll be sworn 'tis true. Travelers ne'er did lie,[5]
Though fools at home condemn 'em.
GONZALO   If in Naples
I should report this now, would they believe me?

3.3
1. Ladykin: a colloquial form of reference to the Virgin Mary.
2. A small acting area above the upper stage.
3. A puppet show with live actors.
4. The unicorn and phoenix, a bird, were two mythological creatures that sometimes figured in travelers' tales. Only one phoenix was said to exist in the world at any one time.
5. Proverbially, "A traveler may lie with authority."

If I should say I saw such islanders—
For certes° these are people of the island—   *certainly*
Who, though they are of monstrous shape, yet note
Their manners are more gentle, kind, than of
Our human generation you shall find
Many, nay, almost any.
PROSPERO [*aside*]   Honest lord,
Thou hast said well; for some of you there present
Are worse than devils.
ALONSO   I cannot too much muse°   *marvel at*
Such shapes, such gesture, and such sound, expressing—
Although they want the use of tongue°—a kind   *language*
Of excellent dumb discourse.
PROSPERO [*aside*]   Praise in departing.[6]
FRANCISCO   They vanished strangely.
SEBASTIAN   No matter, since
They have left their viands° behind; for we have   *food*
  stomachs.°   *good appetites*
Wilt please you taste of what is here?
ALONSO   Not I.
GONZALO   Faith, sir, you need not fear. When we were boys,
Who would believe that there were mountaineers,°   *mountain dwellers*
Dewlapped like bulls, whose throats had hanging at 'em
Wallets° of flesh? Or that there were such men   *pouches*
Whose heads stood in their breasts?[7] Which now we find
Each putter-out of five for one[8] will bring us
Good warrant of.
ALONSO   I will stand to and feed;°   *begin eating*
Although my last, no matter, since I feel
The best is past. Brother, my lord the duke,
Stand to and do as we.
    [ALONSO, SEBASTIAN, *and* ANTONIO *approach the table.*]
    Thunder and lightning.
    Enter ARIEL, *like a harpy;*[9] *claps his wings upon*
    the table, and with a quaint device° *the*   *an ingenious mechanism*
    banquet vanishes.[1]
ARIEL   You are three men of sin, whom destiny—
That hath to° instrument this lower world   *as its*
And what is in't—the never-surfeited sea
Hath caused to belch up you, and on this island,

---

6. Reserve your praise until the end of the event.
7. Such headless people were described by classical writers, including Pliny the Elder (*Natural History* 5.8), as located in North Africa.
8. A traveler could profit from a voyage by laying down a sum with a broker before departing and undertaking to bring back evidence of having reached his destination; if successful, he was repaid fivefold.
9. A mythological monster with a vulture's wings and claws and a woman's face. Aeneas and his companions encountered these harpies, who stole their meals and threatened to punish them with slow starvation. "Thunder and lightning": both spectacular and functional for disguising the mechanics of the "quaint device."
1. The simplest effective staging is by means of a rotating tabletop with the vessels of the banquet fixed to its surface. Leg-to-leg planks supporting the tabletop or a hanging cloth would conceal the vanished banquet. The harpy's wings would hide the mechanics from the audience, and clapping them would provide a visual distraction.

Where man doth not inhabit—you 'mongst men
Being most unfit to live. I have made you mad;
And even with suchlike valor[2] men hang and drown
Their proper selves.° — *themselves*
    [ALONSO, SEBASTIAN, *and* ANTONIO *draw their
    swords.*][3]

60 You fools, I and my fellows
Are ministers of fate. The elements
Of whom your swords are tempered[4] may as well
Wound the loud winds, or with bemocked-at stabs
Kill the still-closing[5] waters, as diminish
65 One dowl° that's in my plume.° My fellow ministers — *featherlet / plumage*
Are like° invulnerable. If you could hurt, — *similarly*
Your swords are now too massy° for your strengths — *heavy*
And will not be uplifted. But remember—
For that's my business to you—that you three
70 From Milan did supplant good Prospero;
Exposed unto the sea, which hath requit it,
Him and his innocent child; for which foul deed
The powers, delaying not forgetting,[6] have
Incensed the seas and shores—yea, all the creatures[7]—
75 Against your peace. Thee of thy son, Alonso,
They have bereft; and do pronounce by me
Ling'ring perdition[8]—worse than any death
Can be at once—shall step by step attend
You and your ways; whose[9] wraths to guard you from,
80 Which here in this most desolate[1] isle else falls
Upon your heads, is nothing° but heart's sorrow — *there is no alternative*
And a clear life° ensuing. — *a life innocent of sin*
    He vanishes[2] *in thunder; then, to soft music, enter
    the shapes again, and dance with mocks and mows,*° — *grimaces*
    and [then exeunt], carrying out the table.
PROSPERO [*aside*] Bravely the figure of this harpy hast thou
Performed, my Ariel; a grace it had, devouring.[3]
85 Of my instruction hast thou nothing bated° — *omitted*
In what thou hadst to say. So with good life[4]
And observation strange[5] my meaner ministers° — *lesser spirits*
Their several kinds° have done.° My high charms — *various roles / performed*
    work,
And these mine enemies are all knit up

---

2. Fearlessness that comes from madness.
3. Ariel perhaps ascends beyond their reach here. Aeneas's companions, like Alonso here, similarly attempted to kill the harpies with swords.
4. Compounded and hardened. Metal was sometimes thought of as being compounded of earth and fire, here contrasted with winds and waters.
5. Self-healing, since they close immediately once parted.
6. Related to the proverb "God stays long but strikes at last."
7. Compare Genesis 1:21: "Then God created . . . everything living and moving."

8. Slow starvation; hell on earth of spiritual suffering. The phrase is first the object of "pronounce" and then the subject of "shall . . . attend."
9. That is, "the powers" in line 73.
1. Joyless, wretched; barren, deserted.
2. Ariel is raised out of sight into the canopy.
3. In clapping his wings, Ariel has created the illusion of having devoured the banquet.
4. Convincingly; with vitality. "So": in the same way.
5. Remarkable attention to the requirements of their parts, or instructions.

In their distractions. They now are in my power;
And in these fits I leave them, while I visit
Young Ferdinand, whom they suppose is drowned,
And his and mine loved darling. [*Exit.*]
GONZALO I'th' name of something holy, sir, why stand you
In this strange stare?
ALONSO   Oh, it is monstrous, monstrous!
Methought the billows spoke and told me of it,
The winds did sing it to me, and the thunder,
That deep and dreadful organ pipe, pronounced
The name of Prosper. It did bass my trespass.⁶
Therefore° my son i'th' ooze is bedded, and   *for that*
I'll seek him deeper than e'er plummet sounded,
And with him there lie mudded. [*Exit.*]
SEBASTIAN   But one fiend at a time,
I'll fight their legions o'er!°   *from beginning to end*
ANTONIO   I'll be thy second.
              Exeunt [SEBASTIAN *and* ANTONIO].
GONZALO All three of them are desperate:° their great   *in despair; reckless*
  guilt,
Like poison given to work° a great time after,   *take effect*
Now gins to bite the spirits. I do beseech you
That are of suppler joints, follow them swiftly,
And hinder them from what this ecstasy°   *madness*
May now provoke them to.
ADRIAN   Follow, I pray you.   *Exeunt.*

4.1

Enter PROSPERO, FERDINAND, *and* MIRANDA.

PROSPERO [*to* FERDINAND] If I have too austerely punished
  you,
Your compensation makes amends, for I
Have given you here a third¹ of mine own life—
Or that for which I live—who° once again   *whom*
I tender° to thy hand. All thy vexations   *offer*
Were but my trials of thy love, and thou
Hast strangely° stood the test. Here, afore heaven,   *wonderfully*
I ratify this my rich gift. O Ferdinand,
Do not smile at me that I boast her off,°   *sing her praises*
For thou shalt find she will outstrip all praise
And make it halt° behind her.   *limp*
FERDINAND   I do believe it against an oracle.²
PROSPERO   Then, as my guest, and thine own acquisition

---

6. The thunder proclaimed my sin ("trespass") in a bass voice, or with a bass background; perhaps, wordplay on the "utter baseness" of trespass.

4.1
1. Miranda. The usual poetic conceit was a half; commentators variously conjecture the other third to be his dukedom, his books, or his late wife.
2. I would believe it even if an oracle said otherwise.

Worthily purchased,° take my daughter. But   *gained by effort*
If thou dost break her virgin-knot° before   *hymen*
All sanctimonious° ceremonies may   *holy*
With full and holy rite be ministered,
No sweet aspersion° shall the heavens let fall   *shower of grace*
To make this contract grow; but barren hate,
Sour-eyed disdain, and discord shall bestrew
The union of your bed with weeds[3] so loathly
That you shall hate it both. Therefore take heed,
As Hymen's[4] lamps shall light you.

FERDINAND   As I hope
For quiet days, fair issue,° and long life,   *children*
With such love as 'tis now, the murkiest den,°   *cave*
The most opportune place, the strong'st suggestion°   *temptation*
Our worser genius can,[5] shall never melt
Mine honor into lust, to take away
The edge° of that day's celebration   *unblunted desire*
When I shall think or° Phoebus' steeds are foundered,[6]   *either*
Or night kept chained below.

PROSPERO   Fairly spoke.
Sit then and talk with her: she is thine own.
—What,° Ariel! My industrious servant, Ariel!   *now then*
    Enter ARIEL.
ARIEL   What would my potent master? Here I am.
PROSPERO   Thou and thy meaner° fellows your last service   *lesser*
Did worthily perform, and I must use you
In such another trick. Go bring the rabble[7]
O'er whom I give thee pow'r here to this place.
Incite them to quick motion, for I must
Bestow upon the eyes of this young couple
Some vanity[8] of mine art. It is my promise,
And they expect it from me.
ARIEL   Presently?°   *at once*
PROSPERO   Ay, with a twink.[9]
ARIEL   Before you can say "come" and "go,"
And breathe twice and cry "so, so,"
Each one tripping on his toe,
Will be here with mop and mow.[1]
Do you love me, master? No?
PROSPERO   Dearly, my delicate Ariel. Do not approach
Till thou dost hear me call.
ARIEL   Well; I conceive.°   *Exit.*   *understand*

---

3. Weeds in place of the flowers traditionally strewn on the marriage bed; wordplay on both "marriage bed" and "seedbed."
4. Classical god of marriage.
5. Is *capable of*. "Worser genius": evil spirit corresponding to a guardian angel.
6. Collapsed and made lame. "Phoebus' steeds": the mythological horses that drew the chariot of the sun. Ferdinand anticipates that on his wedding day he will, in his impatience, think that the night will never come.
7. Troupe of lesser spirits. "Trick": theatrical device, or clever artifice.
8. Trifle; conceit; illusion; display.
9. In the twinkling of an eye.
1. With derisive and grimacing gestures.

PROSPERO [*to* FERDINAND]   Look thou be true;[2] do not
        give dalliance
    Too much the rein.[3] The strongest oaths are straw
    To th' fire i'th' blood. Be more abstemious,
    Or else good night your vow.
FERDINAND   I warrant you, sir,
55 The white cold virgin snow upon my heart
    Abates the ardor of my liver.[4]
PROSPERO   Well.
    —Now come, my Ariel: bring a corollary°   *surplus*
    Rather than want° a spirit. Appear, and pertly.°   *lack / briskly*
        Soft music.
    No tongue, all eyes! Be silent!
        Enter IRIS.[5]
60 IRIS   Ceres, most bounteous lady, thy rich leas[6]
    Of wheat, rye, barley, vetches,[7] oats, and peas;
    Thy turfy mountains where live nibbling sheep,
    And flat meads° thatched with stover,[8] them to keep;   *meadows*
    Thy banks with pionèd and twillèd[9] brims,
65 Which spongy° April at thy hest betrims[1]   *wet*
    To make cold nymphs chaste crowns; and thy
        broom-groves,[2]
    Whose shadow the dismissèd bachelor° loves,   *rejected suitor*
    Being lass-lorn; thy poll-clipped vineyard,[3]
    And thy sea-marge,° sterile and rocky-hard,   *seashore*
70 Where thou thyself dost air°—the queen o'th' sky,[4] *take fresh air*
    Whose wat'ry arch° and messenger am I,   *rainbow*
    Bids thee leave these, and with her sovereign grace,
    Here on this grass-plot,[5] in this very place
    To come and sport. Her peacocks fly amain.[6]
75 Approach, rich Ceres, her to entertain.
        Enter CERES.[7]
CERES   Hail, many-colored messenger, that ne'er
    Dost disobey the wife of Jupiter;°   (*Juno*)
    Who with thy saffron wings upon my flowers
    Diffusest honey-drops, refreshing showers,

---

2. Take care that you remain faithful to your promise. Prospero may have caught the lovers just indulging in dalliance.
3. To "give the rein" is to make a horse gallop.
4. Virgin snow lies on his heart because he has remained chaste, never having given in to his ardent liver. The liver was held to be the seat of passion.
5. Goddess of the rainbow and messenger of Juno; her apparel is in the colors of the rainbow, and she wears "saffron wings" (line 78).
6. Arable land. Ceres was the Roman goddess of agriculture and generative nature.
7. Pealike plants grown for fodder.
8. Hay for winter fodder.
9. Reinforced with channels ("pioned") and with entwined branches ("twilled") to prevent riverbank erosion.
1. Adorns with flowers; this recalls the colloquial "April showers bring forth May flowers."
2. Thickets of gorse, yellow-flowered shrubs. "Cold": chaste.
3. Vineyard with vines embracing, twined around, their supporting poles; pruned vineyard. "Vineyard" was pronounced as three syllables. "Lass-lorn": abandoned by the girl he wooed. "Poll-clipped": pruned short.
4. Juno, queen of the heavens and goddess of women, held to protect marriages and preside over childbirth.
5. Compare "this short-grassed green" (line 83) and "this green land" (line 130): a green carpet on the acting area is indicated.
6. In haste. Peacocks, sacred to Juno, drew her chariot.
7. Her part is probably played by Ariel (see line 167).

	And with each end of thy blue bow dost crown	
80	My bosky⁸ acres and my unshrubbed down,	
	Rich scarf⁹ to my proud earth. Why hath thy queen	
	Summoned me hither to this short-grassed green?	

IRIS   A contract of true love to celebrate
85   And some donation freely to estate°   *bestow*
     On the blessed lovers.
     CERES   Tell me, heavenly bow,°   *rainbow*
     If Venus or her son,¹ as° thou dost know,   *as far as*
     Do now attend the Queen? Since they did plot
     The means that dusky Dis² my daughter got,
90   Her and her blind boy's scandaled° company   *scandalous; notorious*
     I have forsworn.
     IRIS   Of her society
     Be not afraid. I met her deity
     Cutting the clouds towards Paphos,³ and her son
     Dove-drawn⁴ with her. Here thought they to have done
95   Some wanton charm upon⁵ this man and maid,
     Whose vows are that no bed-right⁶ shall be paid
     Till Hymen's torch be lighted;⁷ but in vain.
     Mars's hot minion° is returned again;   *lover; Venus*
     Her waspish-headed⁸ son has broke his arrows,
100 Swears he will shoot no more but play with sparrows,⁹
     And be a boy right out.°   *an ordinary boy*
        JUNO *descends*.¹
     CERES   Highest queen of state,
     Great Juno comes; I know her by her gait.°   *majestic bearing*
     JUNO   How does my bounteous sister? Go with me
     To bless this twain that they may prosperous be
105 And honored in their issue.
                [JUNO *and* CERES] *sing*.²
                    Honor, riches, marriage-blessing,
                    Long continuance and increasing,
                    Hourly joys be still° upon you,   *always*
                    Juno sings her blessings on you.
110 CERES   Earth's increase and foison° plenty,   *abundance*
                    Barns and garners° never empty,   *granaries*
                    Vines with clust'ring bunches growing,
                    Plants with goodly burden bowing;

---

8. Covered with bushes and thickets.
9. Ornamental and hung across the body rather than around the neck.
1. Cupid, proverbially blind.
2. King of the underworld in classical mythology. Venus and her son Cupid made him fall in love with Ceres' daughter Proserpine, whom he abducted (Ovid, *Metamorphoses* 5.385–571).
3. City in Cyprus associated with Venus.
4. Doves were sacred to Venus and drew her chariot.
5. "Done . . . upon": cast a lustful spell upon.
6. Right to consummate the marriage; also, suggesting a rite, as in line 17.
7. Until the wedding ceremony is performed.
8. Peevish, irritable, and with arrows like the wasp's sting.
9. Sparrows were associated with Venus because they were proverbially lustful.
1. Although most editors place "JUNO *descends*" at the point where Juno enters and speaks, in the Folio (1623) this stage direction appears around line 74.
2. Ceres and Juno might be raised together in the flight apparatus and sing suspended above the stage. They would then vanish (line 138 stage direction) by being raised into the heavens.

                    Spring come to you at the farthest,
                    In the very end of harvest.³
                    Scarcity and want shall shun you,
                    Ceres' blessing so is on you.
FERDINAND   This is a most majestic vision, and
    Harmonious charmingly.⁴ May I be bold°   would I be right
    To think these spirits?
PROSPERO   Spirits, which by mine art
    I have from their confines⁵ called to enact
    My present fancies.
FERDINAND   Let me live here ever!
    So rare a wondered° father and a wise⁶   endowed with wonders
    Makes this place paradise.
         JUNO and CERES whisper, and send IRIS on employment.
PROSPERO   Sweet° now, silence.   softly
    Juno and Ceres whisper seriously.
    There's something else to do. Hush and be mute,
    Or else our spell is marred.
IRIS You nymphs called naiads of the wind'ring⁷ brooks,
    With your sedged crowns° and ever-harmless looks,   garlands of reeds
    Leave your crisp channels, and on this green land
    Answer your summons; Juno does command.
    Come, temperate nymphs, and help to celebrate
    A contract of true love. Be not too late.
         Enter certain Nymphs.
    —You sunburned sicklemen° of August weary,   harvesters
    Come hither from the furrow and be merry;
    Make holiday; your rye-straw hats put on,
    And these fresh nymphs encounter every one
    In country footing.
         *Enter certain Reapers, properly habited.⁸ They
         join with the Nymphs in a graceful dance, towards
         the end whereof PROSPERO starts suddenly and speaks, after
         which, to a strange, hollow, and confused noise, they heavily vanish.⁹*
PROSPERO   I had forgot that foul conspiracy
    Of the beast Caliban and his confederates
    Against my life. The minute of their plot
    Is almost come. [*to the Spirits*] Well done. Avoid;° no more!   begone
FERDINAND   This is strange: your father's in some passion
    That works° him strongly.   agitates
MIRANDA   Never till this day
    Saw I him touched with anger so distempered.°   troubled; distracted
PROSPERO   You do look, my son, in a movèd sort,°   disturbed manner

---

3. Let spring return immediately after harvest, without any intervening winter. (In Greek mythology, winter was originally caused by Ceres abandoning the earth in search of Proserpine.)
4. Delightfully; magically; harmoniously.
5. Regions of dwelling. The word is accented on the second syllable.
6. Since the eighteenth century, some editors have changed "wise" to "wife," an emendation backed by disputed typographical evidence but with implications for the play's representation of women.
7. Perhaps a conflation of "wandering" and "winding." The naiads were mythical river nymphs.
8. Either appropriately or finely dressed.
9. Sorrowfully depart (probably not implying a trick of staging).

              As if you were dismayed. Be cheerful, sir.
              Our revels¹ now are ended. These our actors,
              As I foretold you,° were all spirits and   told you before
150   Are melted into air, into thin air;
              And like the baseless fabric² of this vision,
              The cloud-capped towers, the gorgeous palaces,
              The solemn temples, the great globe³ itself,
              Yea, all which it inherit,⁴ shall dissolve,
155   And, like this insubstantial pageant faded,
              Leave not a rack° behind. We are such stuff   wisp of cloud
              As dreams are made on,° and our little life   of
              Is rounded⁵ with a sleep. Sir, I am vexed.
              Bear with my weakness: my old brain is troubled.
160   Be not disturbed with my infirmity.
              If you be pleased, retire into my cell
              And there repose. A turn or two I'll walk
              To still my beating mind.
     FERDINAND *and* MIRANDA   We wish your peace.   *Exeunt.*
     PROSPERO   Come with a thought.⁶ I thank thee, Ariel. Come.
                 Enter ARIEL.
     ARIEL   Thy thoughts I cleave to. What's thy pleasure?
165 PROSPERO   Spirit,
              We must prepare to meet with Caliban.
     ARIEL   Ay, my commander. When I presented⁷ Ceres
              I thought to have told thee of it, but I feared
              Lest I might anger thee.
170 PROSPERO   Say again, where didst thou leave these varlets?°   ruffians
     ARIEL   I told you, sir, they were red hot with drinking;
              So full of valor that they smote the air
              For breathing in their faces, beat the ground
              For kissing of their feet; yet always bending°   aiming
175   Towards their project. Then I beat my tabor,°   side drum
              At which like unbacked° colts they pricked their ears,   never-ridden
              Advanced° their eyelids, lifted up their noses   opened
              As° they smelt music. So I charmed their ears   as if
              That calf-like they my lowing° followed through   mooing
180   Toothed briars, sharp furzes, pricking gorse,° and thorns, prickly shrubs
              Which entered their frail shins. At last I left them
              I' th' filthy-mantled⁸ pool beyond your cell,
              There dancing up to th' chins, that° the foul lake   so that
              O'erstunk⁹ their feet.

---

1. Entertainment, in both festive and theatrical senses.
2. An edifice or substance without foundations; insubstantial, alluding to buildings in masque scenery.
3. World; also a passing allusion to the Globe theater.
4. All who come into possession of it.
5. Rounded off; surrounded; or, possibly, crowned.
6. Come as fast as thought, a colloquial simile.
7. Acted; produced the masque of; introduced while playing Iris.
8. Covered with filthy scum.
9. Made smelly; smelled worse than.

PROSPERO   This was well done, my bird.° — *chick; dear*
Thy shape invisible retain thou still.
The trumpery° in my house, go bring it hither — *cheap goods*
For stale° to catch these thieves. — *decoy; bait*
ARIEL   I go, I go.   *Exit.*
PROSPERO   A devil, a born devil, on whose nature
Nurture can never stick; on whom my pains,
Humanely taken, all, all lost, quite lost;
And, as with age his body uglier grows,
So his mind cankers.° I will plague them all, — *festers*
Even to roaring.
   Enter ARIEL, *laden with glistering apparel, etc.*
   —Come, hang them on this line.¹
   Enter CALIBAN, STEFANO, *and* TRINCULO, *all wet.*
CALIBAN   Pray you tread softly, that the blind mole may not
Hear a foot fall. We now are near his cell.
STEFANO   Monster, your fairy, which you say is a
harmless fairy, has done little better than played the
jack° with us. — *knave; will-o'-the-wisp*
TRINCULO   Monster, I do smell° all horse-piss, at which my — *smell of*
nose is in great indignation.
STEFANO   So is mine. Do you hear, monster? If I should
take a displeasure against you, look you—
TRINCULO   Thou wert but a lost monster.
CALIBAN   Good my lord, give me thy favor still.
Be patient, for the prize I'll bring thee to
Shall hoodwink² this mischance. Therefore speak softly;
All's hushed as midnight yet.
TRINCULO   Ay, but to lose our bottles in the pool!
STEFANO   There is not only disgrace and dishonor in that,
monster, but an infinite loss.
TRINCULO   That's more to me than my wetting. Yet this is
your harmless fairy, monster.
STEFANO   I will fetch off³ my bottle, though I be o'er ears° — *drowned*
for my labor.
CALIBAN   Prithee, my king, be quiet. Seest thou here:
This is the mouth o'th' cell. No noise, and enter.
Do that good mischief which may make this island
Thine own forever, and I, thy Caliban,
For aye° thy foot-licker. — *ever*
STEFANO   Give me thy hand. I do begin to have bloody
thoughts.
TRINCULO   O King Stefano, O peer! O worthy Stefano,
look what a wardrobe here is for thee.⁴
CALIBAN   Let it alone, thou fool. It is but trash.

---

1. Variant of lind, the lime tree or linden, probably indicating a stage property tree.
2. Blind with a hood, as was done to pacify a hawk—hence, make harmless; also, put out of sight.
3. Recover; rescue; drink off.
4. Recalling "King Stephen was and a worthy peer, / His breeches cost him but a crown," a popular ballad about King Stephen, sung in part in *Othello* 2.3.

225 TRINCULO Oh ho, monster! We know what belongs to a
frippery.° O King Stefano! *old-clothes shop*
STEFANO Put off that gown, Trinculo: by this hand, I'll
have that gown.
TRINCULO Thy grace shall have it.
230 CALIBAN The dropsy[5] drown this fool! What do you mean
To dote thus on such luggage?° Let't alone *encumbrances*
And do the murder first. If he awake,
From toe to crown he'll fill our skins with pinches,
Make us° strange stuff. *turn us into*
235 STEFANO Be you quiet, monster. Mistress line, is not this
my jerkin?° Now is the jerkin under the line.[6] Now, jer- *leather jacket*
kin, you are like to lose your hair and prove a bald jerkin.[7]
TRINCULO Do, do! We steal by line and level,[8] an't like° *if it please*
your grace.
240 STEFANO I thank thee for that jest. Here's a garment for't.
Wit shall not go unrewarded while I am king of this
country. "Steal by line and level" is an excellent pass of
pate.[9] There's another garment for't.
TRINCULO Monster, come, put some lime upon your fin-
245 gers[1] and away with the rest.
CALIBAN I will have none on't. We shall lose our time
And all be turned to barnacles,[2] or to apes
With foreheads villainous° low. *wretchedly*
STEFANO Monster, lay to° your fingers. Help to bear this *apply*
250 away, where my hogshead of wine is, or I'll turn you out
of my kingdom. Go to, carry this.
TRINCULO And this.
STEFANO Ay, and this.

A noise of hunters heard. Enter diverse° SPIRITS in shape *various*
of dogs and hounds, hunting them about, PROSPERO and
ARIEL setting them on.

PROSPERO Hey, Mountain, hey!
255 ARIEL Silver! There it goes, Silver!
PROSPERO Fury, Fury! There, Tyrant, there! Hark, hark!
[CALIBAN, STEFANO, *and* TRINCULO *are chased off by* SPIRITS.]
[*to* ARIEL] Go, charge my goblins that they grind their joints
With dry convulsions, shorten up their sinews
With agèd cramps, and more pinch-spotted[3] make them

---

5. A disease characterized by the accumulation of fluid in connective tissue.
6. Below the lime tree; south of the equator; below the waist. Also, a possible allusion to the proverb "Thou hast stricken the ball under the line," meaning "You have cheated." Stefano has taken the jerkin from the lime tree.
7. Baldness caused either through tropical disease or by sailors who customarily shaved the heads of passengers when they crossed the line of the equator for the first time. "Under the [waist]line" could also be an allusion to baldness from syphilis.
8. An idiomatic expression for "properly, by the rules"—literally, "by plumb line and carpenter's level"; also, punning on "lime." "Do, do": an expression of approval.
9. Thrust of wit (fencing term).
1. Be "lime-fingered," sticky-fingered (alluding to birdlime, a gluey substance used to catch birds).
2. Barnacle geese, also known as "tree geese" and supposed to begin life as barnacle shells.
3. Spotted with bruises from pinches. "Agèd cramps": the convulsions of old age.

Than pard or cat o'mountain.[4]
ARIEL   Hark, they roar!
PROSPERO   Let them be hunted soundly.° At this hour   *thoroughly*
Lies at my mercy all mine enemies.
Shortly shall all my labors end, and thou
Shalt have the air at freedom. For a little,
Follow and do me service.   *Exeunt.*

5.1

Enter PROSPERO *in his magic robes, and* ARIEL.

PROSPERO   Now does my project gather to a head:[1]
My charms crack not, my spirits obey, and time
Goes upright with his carriage.[2] How's the day?
ARIEL   On the sixth hour; at which time, my lord,
You said our work should cease.
PROSPERO   I did say so
When first I raised the tempest. Say, my spirit,
How fares the King and 's° followers?   *and his*
ARIEL   Confined together
In the same fashion as you gave in charge,
Just as you left them; all prisoners, sir,
In the line-grove which weather-fends[3] your cell:
They cannot budge till your release.° The King,   *you release them*
His brother, and yours abide all three distracted,° *out of their wits*
And the remainder mourning over them,
Brimful of sorrow and dismay; but chiefly
Him that you termed, sir, the good old Lord Gonzalo:
His tears runs down his beard like winter's drops
From eaves of reeds.° Your charm so strongly works 'em   *thatched roofs*
That if you now beheld them, your affections°   *feelings*
Would become tender.
PROSPERO   Dost thou think so, spirit?
ARIEL   Mine would, sir, were I human.
PROSPERO   And mine shall.
Hast thou, which art but air, a touch,° a feeling   *sense*
Of their afflictions, and shall not myself—
One of their kind, that relish all as sharply
Passion as they[4]—be kindlier[5] moved than thou art?
Though with their high° wrongs I am struck to th' quick,   *great*
Yet with my nobler reason 'gainst my fury
Do I take part.° The rarer action is   *side*
In virtue than in vengeance. They being penitent,

---

4. Both terms are synonymous with "leopard"; the second is from Jeremiah 13:23: "May a man of Ind change his skin, and the cat of the mountain her spots?" (Bishops' Bible).
5.1
1. Draw to its fulfillment. "Project" suggests an alchemical projection or experiment.
2. Because his carriage, or burden, is now light.
3. Which protects from the weather.
4. Who feel as much strong emotion as they do.
5. More tenderly; more naturally.

The sole drift of my purpose doth extend
Not a frown further. Go, release them, Ariel.
My charms I'll break, their senses I'll restore,
And they shall be themselves.

ARIEL   I'll fetch them, sir.   *Exit.*
     [PROSPERO makes a circle on the stage.][6]
PROSPERO[7] Ye elves of hills, brooks, standing lakes, and groves,
And ye that on the sands with printless foot
Do chase the ebbing Neptune, and do fly him
When he comes back; you demi-puppets[8] that
By moonshine do the green sour ringlets[9] make,
Whereof the ewe not bites; and you, whose pastime
Is to make midnight°-mushrooms, that rejoice   *springing up overnight*
To hear the solemn curfew;[1] by whose aid—
Weak masters[2] though ye be—I have bedimmed
The noontide sun, called forth the mutinous winds,
And twixt the green sea and the azured vault°   *the sky*
Set roaring war; to the dread rattling thunder
Have I given fire, and rifted° Jove's stout oak   *split*
With his own bolt;° the strong-based promontory   *lightning bolt*
Have I made shake, and by the spurs° plucked up   *roots*
The pine and cedar. Graves at my command
Have waked their sleepers, oped, and let 'em forth
By my so potent art. But this rough[3] magic
I here abjure; and when I have required°   *summoned*
Some heavenly music—which even now I do—
To work mine end upon their senses that°   *the senses of whom*
This airy[4] charm is for, I'll break my staff,
Bury it certain° fathoms in the earth,   *several*
And deeper than did ever plummet sound
I'll drown my book.
     Solemn music.
     Here enters ARIEL *before; then* ALONSO *with a frantic gesture,*
     attended by GONZALO; SEBASTIAN *and* ANTONIO *in like manner,*
     attended by ADRIAN *and* FRANCISCO. *They all enter the circle*
     which PROSPERO *had made, and there stand charmed; which*
     PROSPERO *observing, speaks.*[5]
A solemn air° and° the best comforter   *song / which is*
To an unsettled fancy° cure thy brains,   *imagination*
Now useless, boiled within thy skull. There stand,
For you are spell-stopped.

---

6. The original text does not indicate when the circle is drawn. Other possibilities are at the beginning of the scene or before the entry at line 57.
7. Prospero's speech closely follows Ovid's *Metamorphoses* 7.265–77, in Arthur Golding's translation (1567); the speaker in Ovid is the sorceress Medea, who uses her witchcraft to vengeful ends.
8. Puppets; elves; quasi-puppets.
9. Fairy rings: distinctive circles of grass supposed to be caused by dancing fairies but actually caused by mushrooms.
1. The bell rung at nightfall, indicating the time when spirits are abroad.
2. Ineffectual when acting independently; without supernatural power; subordinate spirits.
3. Violent; discordant; crudely approximate.
4. Wrought by spirits of the air.
5. Prospero remains invisible and inaudible to Alonso and his party until he greets Alonso at line 106.

Holy Gonzalo, honorable man,
Mine eyes, e'en sociable° to the show° of thine,   *sympathetic / appearance*
Fall fellowly drops. [*aside*] The charm dissolves apace
65 And, as the morning steals upon the night,
Melting the darkness, so their rising senses
Begin to chase the ignorant fumes[6] that mantle°   *envelop*
Their clearer° reason. —O good Gonzalo,   *growing clearer*
My true preserver and a loyal sir°   *gentleman*
70 To him thou follow'st, I will pay° thy graces   *requite*
Home° both in word and deed. Most cruelly   *fully*
Didst thou, Alonso, use me and my daughter.
Thy brother was a furtherer° in the act: *an accomplice*
Thou art pinched° for't now, Sebastian. Flesh and blood,   *tortured; afflicted*
75 You, brother mine, that entertained ambition,
Expelled remorse and nature,[7] whom° with Sebastian—   *who*
Whose inward pinches therefore are most strong—
Would here have killed your king, I do forgive thee,
Unnatural though thou art. [*aside*] Their understanding
80 Begins to swell,° and the approaching tide   *(as does a tide)*
Will shortly fill the reasonable shore
That now lies foul and muddy. Not° one of them   *there is not*
That yet looks on me or would know me. —Ariel,
Fetch me the hat and rapier[8] in my cell.
            [ARIEL *exits and returns.*]
85 I will discase° me and myself present   *undress*
As I was sometime Milan.[9] Quickly, spirit!
Thou shalt ere long be free.
        ARIEL *sings and helps to attire him.*
ARIEL   Where the bee sucks, there suck I;
          In a cowslip's bell I lie;
90   There I couch when owls do cry;
          On the bat's back I do fly
          After summer merrily.
        Merrily, merrily shall I live now,
        Under the blossom that hangs on the bough.
95 PROSPERO   Why, that's my dainty Ariel! I shall miss
Thee, but yet thou shalt have freedom.—So, so, so.[1]
To the King's ship, invisible as thou art;
There shalt thou find the mariners asleep
Under the hatches. The Master and the Boatswain
100 Being awake, enforce them to this place,
And presently,° I prithee.   *immediately*
ARIEL   I drink the air before me and return
Or ere° your pulse twice beat.   *Exit.*   *before*
GONZALO   All torment, trouble, wonder, and amazement°   *bewilderment*

---

6. Fogs of ignorance; the image is of the sun ("rising senses") dissipating morning mist.
7. Pity and brotherly affection.
8. Elements of normal aristocratic dress.
9. Formerly, when duke of Milan.
1. Prospero arranges his attire approvingly.

Inhabits here. Some heavenly power guide us
Out of this fearful° country!   *fearsome*
PROSPERO   Behold, sir King,
The wrongèd Duke of Milan, Prospero.
For more assurance that a living prince
Does now speak to thee, I embrace thy body
And to thee and thy company I bid
A hearty welcome.
ALONSO   Whe'er° thou beest he or no,   *whether*
Or some enchanted trifle[2] to abuse° me—   *delude; maltreat*
As late I have been—I not know. Thy pulse
Beats as of flesh and blood; and since I saw thee,
Th'affliction of my mind amends, with which,
I fear, a madness held me. This must crave°—   *requires, as explanation*
An if this be at all[3]—a most strange story.
Thy dukedom[4] I resign and do entreat
Thou pardon me my wrongs. But how should Prospero
Be living, and be here?
PROSPERO [*to* GONZALO]   First, noble friend,
Let me embrace thine age,° whose honor cannot   *old body*
Be measured or confined.
GONZALO   Whether this be
Or be not, I'll not swear.
PROSPERO   You do yet taste
Some subtleties[5] o'th' isle, that will not let you
Believe things certain. Welcome, my friends all.
[*aside to* SEBASTIAN *and* ANTONIO] But you, my brace° of   *pair*
    lords, were I so minded
I here could pluck his highness' frown upon you
And justify° you traitors. At this time   *prove*
I will tell no tales.
SEBASTIAN [*to* ANTONIO]   The devil speaks in him!
PROSPERO   No.
[*to* ANTONIO] For you, most wicked sir, whom to call brother
Would even infect my mouth, I do forgive
Thy rankest fault—all of them—and require
My dukedom of thee, which perforce° I know   *necessarily*
Thou must restore.
ALONSO   If thou beest Prospero,
Give us particulars of thy preservation;
How thou hast met us here, whom three hours since
Were wrecked upon this shore, where I have lost—
How sharp the point of this remembrance is—
My dear son Ferdinand.
PROSPERO   I am woe° for't, sir.   *I grieve*
ALONSO   Irreparable is the loss, and patience

---

2. With a suggestion of the old sense of "trifle" as "deception."
3. If this is really happening.
4. Alonso's rights of homage and tribute from it.

5. You still experience some of the illusions. "Subtleties" were also sweet confections shaped like castles, temples, beasts, allegorical figures, and the like, and arranged like a pageant.

Says it is past her cure.
PROSPERO   I rather think
You have not sought her help, of° whose soft grace° *by / mercy*
For the like loss I have her sovereign aid
And rest myself content.
ALONSO   You the like loss?
PROSPERO   As great to me as late;° and supportable   *recent*
To make the dear loss[6] have I means much weaker
Than you may call to comfort you, for I
Have lost my daughter.[7]
ALONSO   A daughter?
O heavens, that they were living both in Naples,
The King and Queen there! That they were, I wish
Myself were mudded in that oozy bed
Where my son lies. When did you lose your daughter?
PROSPERO   In this last tempest. I perceive these lords
At this encounter do so much admire°   *wonder*
That they devour their reason[8] and scarce think
Their eyes do offices of truth,° their words   *function accurately*
Are natural breath. But, howsoe'er you have
Been jostled from your senses, know for certain
That I am Prospero, and that very duke
Which was thrust forth of Milan, who most strangely
Upon this shore where you were wrecked, was landed
To be the lord on't. No more yet of this,
For 'tis a chronicle of day by day,
Not a relation for a breakfast, nor
Befitting this first meeting. Welcome, sir;
This cell's my court. Here have I few attendants
And subjects none abroad.[9] Pray you look in.
My dukedom since you have given me again,
I will requite you with as good a thing;
At least bring forth a wonder to content ye
As much as me my dukedom.

Here PROSPERO *discovers*[1] FERDINAND *and* MIRANDA
playing at chess.

MIRANDA   Sweet lord, you play me false.°   *trick me*
FERDINAND   No, my dearest love,
I would not for the world.
MIRANDA   Yes, for a score of kingdoms you should wrangle,
And I would call it fair play.[2]
ALONSO   If this prove
A vision of the island, one dear son
Shall I twice lose.

---

6. "Supportable . . . loss": in order to make the heartfelt loss bearable.
7. Prospero apparently means that Alonso still has a child, his daughter Claribel, to comfort him.
8. "Reason" has the additional sense of "discourse"; hence, the phrase is an extension of "swallow their words."
9. Elsewhere about the island; beyond the cell.
1. Reveals by drawing back a curtain hanging in front of the discovery space.
2. You could quarrel for twenty kingdoms, and I would still call it fair play.

SEBASTIAN   A most high miracle!
FERDINAND   Though the seas threaten, they are merciful:
     I have cursed them without cause.
          [FERDINAND *kneels*.]
ALONSO   Now all the blessings
     Of a glad father compass thee about!°   *surround you*
     Arise, and say how thou cam'st here.
MIRANDA   Oh, wonder!
     How many goodly creatures are there here!
     How beauteous mankind is! Oh, brave new world
     That has such people in't!
PROSPERO   'Tis new to thee.
ALONSO [*to* FERDINAND]   What is this maid with whom
          thou wast at play?
     Your eld'st° acquaintance cannot be three hours.   *longest*
     Is she the goddess that hath severed us
     And brought us thus together?
FERDINAND   Sir, she is mortal;
     But by immortal Providence she's mine.
     I chose her when I could not ask my father
     For his advice, nor thought I had one. She
     Is daughter to this famous Duke of Milan—
     Of whom so often I have heard renown
     But never saw before—of whom I have
     Received a second life; and second father
     This lady makes him to me.
ALONSO   I am hers.[3]
     But oh, how oddly will it sound that I
     Must ask my child° forgiveness!   (*Miranda*)
PROSPERO   There, sir, stop.
     Let us not burden our remembrances with
     A heaviness° that's gone.   *sorrow*
GONZALO   I have inly wept,
     Or should have spoke ere this. Look down, you gods,
     And on this couple drop a blessèd crown.
     For it is you that have chalked forth° the way   *marked out*
     Which brought us hither.
ALONSO   I say "Amen," Gonzalo.
GONZALO   Was Milan° thrust from Milan that his issue   *the Duke of Milan*
     Should become kings of Naples? Oh, rejoice
     Beyond a common joy and set it down
     With gold on lasting pillars:[4] in one voyage
     Did Claribel her husband find at Tunis,
     And Ferdinand her brother found a wife
     Where he himself was lost; Prospero his dukedom
     In a poor isle; and all of us ourselves
     When no man was his own.[5]

---

3. I will be her second father: Alonso's assent to the betrothal.
4. Suggesting, perhaps, the triumphal arches commissioned to celebrate notable occasions.
5. When we all had lost our senses.

ALONSO [to FERDINAND and MIRANDA]   Give me your hands.
　　Let grief and sorrow still° embrace his heart　　　　　　*always*
　　That° doth not wish you joy.　　　　　　　　　　　　　*who*
215 GONZALO　　　　　　　　Be it so. Amen.
　　　Enter ARIEL, *with the* MASTER *and* BOATSWAIN
　　　　amazedly following.
　　Oh, look, sir, look, sir: here is more of us.
　　I prophesied if a gallows were on land
　　This fellow could not drown. [*to* BOATSWAIN] Now,
　　　　blasphemy,°　　　　　　　　　　　　　　　　　　*blasphemer*
　　That swear'st grace o'erboard, not an oath on shore?
220 　Hast thou no mouth by land? What is the news?
　BOATSWAIN   The best news is that we have safely found
　　Our king and company; the next, our ship,
　　Which but three glasses° since we gave out° split,　　*hourglasses / declared*
　　Is tight and yare⁶ and bravely rigged as when
225 　We first put out to sea.
　ARIEL [*to* PROSPERO]   Sir, all this service
　　Have I done since I went.
　PROSPERO [*to* ARIEL]   My tricksy° spirit!　　　　　　*capricious; neat*
　ALONSO   These are not natural events; they strengthen°　*increase*
230 　From strange to stranger. Say, how came you hither?
　BOATSWAIN   If I did think, sir, I were well awake,
　　I'd strive to tell you. We were dead of° sleep　　　　　*with*
　　And—how we know not—all clapped° under hatches,　　*shut up*
　　Where but even now with strange and several° noises　　*various*
235 　Of roaring, shrieking, howling, jingling chains,
　　And more diversity of sounds, all horrible,
　　We were awaked; straightway at liberty,
　　Where we, in all our trim, freshly beheld
　　Our royal, good, and gallant ship, our Master
240 　Cap'ring to eye° her. On° a trice, so please you,　　*dancing to see / in*
　　Even in a dream were we divided from them
　　And were brought moping° hither.　　　　　　　　　　*dazed*
　ARIEL [*to* PROSPERO]　　　　　　　Was't well done?
　PROSPERO [*to* ARIEL]   Bravely, my diligence. Thou shalt be free.
　ALONSO   This is as strange a maze as e'er men trod,
245 　And there is in this business more than nature
　　Was ever conduct° of. Some oracle　　　　　　　　　　*conductor*
　　Must rectify our knowledge.
　PROSPERO　　　　　　　Sir, my liege,
　　Do not infest° your mind with beating on⁷　　　　　　*trouble*
　　The strangeness of this business. At picked leisure,
250 　Which shall be shortly, single° I'll resolve you—　　　*in private*
　　Which to you shall seem probable°—of every　　　　　*plausible*
　　These happened accidents.° Till when, be cheerful　　*occurrences*

---

6. Is sound and ready to sail.　　　7. With repeatedly worrying about.

And think of each thing well. [*to* ARIEL] Come hither, spirit.
Set Caliban and his companions free:
Untie the spell. [*Exit* ARIEL.]
[*to* ALONSO]   How fares my gracious sir?
There are yet missing of your company
Some few odd lads that you remember not.
      Enter ARIEL, *driving in* CALIBAN, STEFANO, *and*
      TRINCULO *in their stolen apparel.*

STEFANO   Every man shift for all the rest, and let no man
take care for himself;[8] for all is but fortune. *Coraggio*,
bully monster,[9] *coraggio!*

TRINCULO   If these° be true spies which I wear in my head,   *these eyes*
here's a goodly sight!

CALIBAN   O Setebos, these be brave spirits indeed!
How fine° my master is! I am afraid   *splendidly dressed*
He will chastise me.

SEBASTIAN   Ha, ha! What things are these, my lord Antonio?
Will money buy 'em?

ANTONIO   Very like.° One of them   *likely*
Is a plain° fish, and no doubt marketable.   *mere*

PROSPERO   Mark but the badges[1] of these men, my lords;
Then say if they° be true. This misshapen knave,   *(the men); (the badges)*
His mother was a witch, and one so strong
That could control the moon, make flows and ebbs,
And deal in her command without her power.[2]
These three have robbed me, and this demi-devil[3]—
For he's a bastard one—had plotted with them
To take my life. Two of these fellows you
Must know and own;[4] this thing of darkness I
Acknowledge mine.

CALIBAN   I shall be pinched to death.

ALONSO   Is not this Stefano, my drunken butler?

SEBASTIAN   He is drunk now. Where had he wine?

ALONSO   And Trinculo is reeling-ripe.° Where should they   *drunk*
Find this grand liquor that hath gilded[5] 'em?
How cam'st thou in this pickle?[6]

TRINCULO   I have been in such a pickle since I saw you last
that I fear me will never out of my bones: I shall not fear
flyblowing.[7]

SEBASTIAN   Why, how now, Stefano?

---

8. Stefano drunkenly confuses the saying "Every man for himself."
9. Gallant monster. "*Coraggio*": take courage (Italian).
1. Livery. Servants often wore their master's emblem, but Prospero probably refers to the stolen apparel.
2. And wield her (the moon's) power without her authority, or beyond the reach of her might.
3. Being the offspring of Sycorax and the devil.
4. And acknowledge to be yours.
5. Probably alluding to the alchemical elixir ("liquor") known as *aurum potabile* (drinkable gold); hence, "gilded" (flushed).
6. Sorry plight; Trinculo takes up the literal sense of "preserving liquid," recalling both his drunkenness and his drenching in the lake.
7. Not fear being infested with flies, since he has been "pickled" (preserved).

STEFANO Oh, touch me not! I am not Stefano, but a cramp.
PROSPERO You'd be king o'the isle, sirrah?
STEFANO I should have been a sore° one then.   *an inept; severe; pained*
ALONSO [*indicating* CALIBAN] This is a strange thing as
    e'er I looked on.
PROSPERO He is as disproportioned in his manners[8]
    As in his shape. Go, sirrah, to my cell;
    Take with you your companions. As you look
    To have my pardon, trim° it handsomely.   *tidy; decorate*
CALIBAN Ay, that I will; and I'll be wise hereafter
    And seek for grace. What a thrice-double ass
    Was I to take this drunkard for a god
    And worship this dull fool!
PROSPERO   Go to, away.
ALONSO Hence, and bestow your luggage where you found it.
SEBASTIAN Or stole it rather.
        [*Exeunt* CALIBAN, STEFANO, *and* TRINCULO.]
PROSPERO Sir, I invite your highness and your train
    To my poor cell, where you shall take your rest
    For this one night; which—part of it°—I'll waste°   *part of which / spend*
    With such discourse as, I not doubt, shall make it
    Go quick away: the story of my life
    And the particular accidents° gone by   *events*
    Since I came to this isle. And in the morn
    I'll bring you to your ship, and so to Naples,
    Where I have hope to see the nuptial
    Of these our dear-belovèd solemnized,
    And thence retire me to my Milan, where
    Every third thought shall be my grave.
ALONSO   I long
    To hear the story of your life, which must
    Take° the ear strangely.   *captivate*
PROSPERO   I'll deliver° all,   *relate*
    And promise you calm seas, auspicious gales,
    And sail so expeditious that shall° catch   *it will*
    Your royal fleet far off. —My Ariel, chick,
    That is thy charge. Then to the elements
    Be free, and fare thou well. —Please you draw near.
        Exeunt all [*except* PROSPERO].[9]

---

8. Behavior; moral character.
9. The general exeunt is through Prospero's cell; Ariel departs in another direction.

Epilogue

Spoken by PROSPERO.

Now my charms are all o'erthrown,
And what strength I have's mine own,
Which is most faint. Now 'tis true
I must be here confined by you,
5 Or sent to Naples. Let me not,
Since I have my dukedom got
And pardoned the deceiver, dwell
In this bare island° by your spell,   *(the stage)*
But release me from my bands°   *fetters*
10 With the help of your good hands.°   *(applause)*
Gentle breath° of yours my sails   *favorable comment*
Must fill or else my project fails,
Which was to please. Now I want°   *lack*
Spirits to enforce, art to enchant;
15 And my ending[1] is despair,
Unless I be relieved by prayer,
Which pierces so that it assaults
Mercy itself and frees all faults.
As you from crimes would pardoned be,
20 Let your indulgence[2] set me free.   [*Exit.*]

Epilogue
1. Punning on the sense "death."   2. Approval; appeasement; remission for sin.

England and the World

Othello first captured Desdemona's attention, he recalls, by telling her his "traveler's history,"

> Wherein of antars [caves] vast and deserts idle,
> Rough quarries, rocks, and hills whose heads touch heaven,
> It was my hint to speak—such was my process—
> And of the cannibals that each other eat,
> The anthropophagi, and men whose heads
> Do grow beneath their shoulders. (1.3.139–44)

The Venetian heiress was not the only person who found such stories thrilling. In the sixteenth century, narratives of adventure, exploration, trade, and reconnaissance proliferated throughout western Europe, circulating widely in both manuscript and print. Public interest in them was not entirely new. Shakespeare probably found some of the details in Othello's stories in *Mandeville's Travels*, an immensely popular fourteenth-century text still widely read in the Renaissance. Columbus took a copy with him on his first voyage, and even a century later, despite growing skepticism about the book's wilder claims, Sir Walter Ralegh continued to be on the lookout for "men whose heads / Do grow beneath their shoulders" in what is now Venezuela.

But in the wake of Columbus's encounter with the Americas and the voyages and colonial projects that followed, there came a flood of new reports about places and peoples whose existence had been unknown to Europeans. Readers' interest was about far more than idle curiosity. With Muslim powers in control of the key eastern Mediterranean ports and trade routes, Europeans had long been searching for an alternative route to the spices and silks of the East. Columbus believed that he had discovered such a route—he initially thought he had reached islands off the coast of India or China when he arrived at the Americas—but the enormous quantities of gold, silver, and pearls that treasure fleets began to carry back to Spain after the brutal conquests of the Mexica-Aztec and Inca empires heralded a new world orientation in trade, colonization, and enslavement. The major European states strengthened their fleets, supplied them with weapons, recruited armies and navies, and fiercely competed with one another to reach, and claim ownership of, potentially lucrative overseas territories.

The New World was not the only site of contest. Islands in the Mediterranean, including Sicily, Cyprus, Malta, and Rhodes were particularly vulnerable to attempted invasion by one or another European power and by the Muslim states of Turkey and North Africa. Competition existed as well along the coast of Africa, where access to trade in gold, ivory, and, increasingly, human beings, aroused the greed of privateers and merchants and their royal protectors. Wherever there was the promise of gain—in Russia, Scandinavia, Poland, and elsewhere—there were diplomatic maneuverings and trade agreements. In such a constantly shifting scene, traditional allies could suddenly become dangerous rivals; conversely, bitter enemies could forge convenient alliances. From a position of relative isolation—a Protestant island-nation at the geographical margins of Europe—England proved itself a remarkably energetic and brutal participant in this increasingly global, and increasingly genocidal, competition.

Though the English failed to equal the astonishing Spanish and Portuguese enterprises of exploration and conquest, they nonetheless undertook many naval,

John Hawkins's coat of arms, granted in 1568, features an enslaved person, with arms bound, representing the trade that Hawkins himself introduced to the English. The text, expanded and modernized, reads: "Sir John Hawkins Knight: The canton [that is, emblem for a shield] given by Robert Cook, clarenceux [that is, officer of arms]: 1568."

overland, and colonial ventures in the sixteenth century. While several other Englishmen had already taken and enslaved people from Africa by the mid-fifteenth century, John Hawkins effectively set the pattern for English triangular trade between England, Africa, and the Americas. In 1562, Hawkins led an expedition in which he captured 300 Africans in Sierra Leone (and from other slavers) and transported them to Spanish plantations in the Americas, where he traded them for pearls, animal hides, and sugar. His mission was so lucrative that Queen Elizabeth I sponsored his subsequent journeys, providing ships, supplies, and guns. She also gave him coat of arms, reproduced above, which featured an enslaved African man. In four voyages to Sierra Leone between 1564 and 1569, Hawkins took a total of 1,200 Africans across the Atlantic to sell to Spanish colonists in the Caribbean. Several West Africans returned to England from these voyages as well, assimilating into English life. In a three-year voyage from 1577 to 1580, Hawkins's protégé Sir Francis Drake circumnavigated the globe on his ship *The Golden Hind*, laying claim to California on behalf of the queen and bringing home untold riches. (His crew of wage-earning sailors included Diego, a Cimarron—an African fleeing slavery—who had joined him in Panama in 1572.) At one point in his journey, Drake, who was said to be critical of the trade in human beings, left two Black men and "a proper Negro wench" taken from a Spanish ship during an earlier raid on a deserted island off the Celebes in what is now Indonesia. In addition to the queen (who retained the right to "disavow" responsibility for any actions taken by the men), Drake's investors in his raids on the Spanish West Indies included Robert Dudley, Earl of Leicester, and Sir Walter Ralegh. Sometime before 1591, Elizabeth gave

Drake a jewel, reproduced in the color insert in this volume, which features profile heads of a Black male figure in front of a White female head. The jewel was enclosed in a case featuring a Nicholas Hilliard miniature of the queen. A few years later, Thomas Cavendish followed Drake in circumnavigating the globe. His 120-ton, eighteen-cannon ship was called the *Desire*.

The English desire for territory and colonies in the Americas led Philip Amadas and Arthur Barlowe to make an expedition, financed by Sir Walter Ralegh, to Virginia in the mid-1580s. The failure of the short-lived colony at Roanoke would haunt all subsequent colonial efforts in North America. Included below are accounts in which Ralegh himself ventures up the Orinoco delta in what is now Venezuela in search of the golden city of "El Dorado"; Thomas Hariot visits Virginia to see how many of its commodities might support a settlement there and/or be imported back to England; and Thomas Strachey, landing unexpectedly in the Bermudas, realizes that the island is, as he carefully puts it, "habitable"; it was to be officially added to England's territories in 1612. Also included below are Captain John Smith's later account of Virginia, which shows the progress, and fantasies, of English colonial efforts in America, and Richard Ligon's account of the colonization of Barbados in the 1650s, which reveals how the work of enslaved Indians from Guiana, enslaved Africans, and indentured and enslaved Europeans made the West Indian sugar colony "one of the richest spots of earth" in the world.

Many accounts of England's early exploratory and colonial efforts were collected by the clergyman, geographer, and tireless promoter of empire Richard Hakluyt (1552?–1616), and published as *The principal navigations, voyages, traffiques, and discoveries of the English Nation* (1589; three-volume edition 1598–1600). Bartolemé de las Casas' *Brevísima relación de la destrucción de las Indias* (1552), which described Spanish atrocities against the Indigenous peoples of the Americas, was printed in English for the first time in 1583, and Spain's Protestant Northern European rivals used this account to demonize the Spanish Empire and counter its influence and power. English commentators and writers, including Hakluyt, amplified Catholic mistreatment of Indigenous Americans in order to suggest an apparent contrast with "reformed" English behavior. Hakluyt also understood that his nation's success in the competitive, often violent struggle to explore, chart, and exploit the natural and human resources of the globe depended on assembling as much reliable information as possible, preferably from European eyewitnesses. To be of full use, both for England's practical endeavors and for the general goal of understanding the world, that information would have to reach beyond physical geography to the social practices and beliefs of the Indigenous inhabitants of the territories being explored and colonized. Hence, for example, Sir Walter Ralegh sent the mathematician and natural scientist Thomas Hariot to observe the Algonquin natives of Virginia and to describe in detail their technology, society, and conceptions of the world. Hariot's ethnographic observations were supplemented by beautiful watercolors by the artist and cartographer John White, one of which is included in the color insert in this volume. Expeditions brought back native plants and their products (including tomatoes, potatoes, pineapples, chocolate, and tobacco), animals, cultural artifacts, and, on occasion, native people themselves, most often seized against their will. There were exhibitions in London of a kidnapped Inuit with his kayak and of Algonquins with their canoes. Most of these captives, violently uprooted and vulnerable to European diseases, quickly perished, but even in death they were evidently valuable property: while the English will not give one small coin "to relieve a lame beggar," one of the characters in *The Tempest* remarks, "they will lay out ten to see a dead Indian" (2.2.30–31). As we see in the selections from John Smith below, the Powhatan "Princess" Pocahontas died during a much-publicized embassy to England, right before she was set to sail for home.

The Algonquin were new to the English and therefore aroused particular curiosity, but a comparable attention extended to parts of the world that were at least partially known and to peoples traditionally regarded as mortal enemies. In 1600 a protégé of Hakluyt, John Pory, translated and published the *Geographical History of Africa* (completed in 1526) by "John Leo Africanus," a Muslim-born traveler whose vivid descriptions were widely regarded as a crucial resource for understanding that entire continent. Also around the turn of the seventeenth century, Thomas Dallam and Richard Knolles wrote accounts of the Ottoman Empire that displayed often nuanced and ambivalent attitudes to the great and fearsome Islamic power. During the sixteenth century around 35,000 Europeans, including captured English sailors, were enslaved on the Barbary Coast. ("Barbary" was the name given to the coastal regions of North Africa, or Maghreb, specifically the Ottoman borderlands consisting of the regencies in Algiers and Tripoli, as well as the Beylik of Tunis and the Sultanate of Morocco.) Popular plays on the Elizabethan stage featured parodic versions of the Muslim enemy—and the occasional "Christian turned Turk"—but Queen Elizabeth's foreign policy contemplated the possibility of an alliance with rulers in Turkey and Morocco against the Spanish. For the first time in this period English readers begin to find reasonably detailed accounts not only of the Ottoman Sultan's court and the organization of his state, but also of Islam. Elizabeth I's negotiations with the Moroccan ruler Mulay Ahmed al-Mansur for a proposed military alliance against Spain is commemorated by the remarkable portrait of his ambassador, Abd al-Wahid bin Masoud bin Muhammad-al-Annuri, which is included in the color insert in this volume.

The principal way in which English men and women encountered the wider world was through eyewitness accounts, some in print, many others in manuscript or in casual conversation—Strachey's narration below, for instance, is still in letter form. Travelers' tales had an ancient and well-deserved reputation for self-inflation, exaggeration, and lying, and Elizabethan and Jacobean writers strove for the effect of factual directness, simplicity, and trustworthiness rather than for rhetorical brilliance, from title onward: Hariot's account is called a "true report," Strachey's a "true repertory," and Ligon's "a true and exact history." Their content, however, was nonetheless often fantastical.

SIR WALTER RALEGH

The brilliant and versatile Sir Walter Ralegh (1552–1618) was a soldier, courtier, philosopher, explorer and colonist, student of science, historian, and poet. Born to West Country gentry of modest means, Ralegh amassed great wealth thanks to his position at court, leading him to be denounced by some as a social upstart and hated by others as a greedy monopolist. He fought ruthlessly in Ireland and the Spanish city of Cádiz, directed the colonization of Virginia, made the smoking of tobacco fashionable in England, brought Edmund Spenser from Ireland to the English court, conducted scientific experiments, led a 1595 expedition to Guiana (now part of Venezuela) in an unsuccessful effort to find gold, and urged England to challenge Spanish dominance in the New World. A selection from his account of the 1595 expedition to Guiana is included here. His goal was to find and take possession of the fabled "El Dorado," or golden city, before the Spanish did: his failure to find such a city is downplayed in his exaggerated account of the golden promise of the area. The alliances he made with the native peoples of Guiana laid the groundwork for future colonization.

Ralegh was known for his violent temper, his dramatic sense of life, his extravagant dress, his skepticism in religious matters, his bitter hatred of Spain, and his great favor with Queen Elizabeth, who knighted him in 1585. (A portrait of Ralegh is included in the color insert to this volume.) In 1592, after Ralegh seduced and married one of her ladies-in-waiting, Elizabeth Throckmorton, Elizabeth suspended her favor and briefly imprisoned him in the Tower of London. His long, remorseful poem to the queen, "The Ocean to Cynthia," survived in manuscript fragments, one of more than five hundred lines. Released from the tower in 1593, Ralegh was elected to Parliament, traveled, and built what is now Sherborne New Castle in Dorset.

After Elizabeth's death Ralegh was again imprisoned, this time for his supposed role in a plot to remove James I from the throne and put Lady Arbella Stuart in his place. He remained in the Tower for the rest of his life, save for an ill-fated second expedition to Guiana in 1618, which again failed to discover gold but succeeded in infuriating the Spanish. To appease the Spanish, with whom James I hoped to be on better terms, Ralegh was beheaded on the old treason charge in October 1618.

From The Discovery of the Large, Rich, and Beautiful Empire of Guiana, with a Relation of the Great and Golden City of Manoa (Which the Spaniards Call El Dorado)

* * *

The next day we arrived at the port of Morequito, and anchored there, sending away one of our pilots[1] to seek the king of Aromaia, uncle to Morequito, slain by Berreo[2] as aforesaid. The next day following, before noon, he came to us on foot from his house, which was fourteen English miles, himself being a hundred and ten years old, and returned on foot the same day; and with him many of the borderers,[3] with many women and children, that came to wonder at our nation and to bring us down victual,° *food* which they did in great plenty, as venison, pork, hens, chickens, fowl, fish, with divers sorts of excellent fruits and roots, and great abundance of pinas,° the princess of *pineapples* fruits that grow under the sun, especially those of Guiana. They brought us, also, store of bread and of their wine, and a sort of paraquitos° no bigger than wrens, and *parrots* of all other sorts both small and great. One of them gave me a beast called by the Spaniards armadillo, which they call cassacam, which seemeth to be all barred over with small plates somewhat like to a rhinoceros, with a white horn growing in his hinder parts as big as a great huntinghorn, which they use to wind° instead of a trumpet. *to blow wind into* Monardus writeth that a little of the powder of that horn put into the ear cureth deafness.[4]

---

1. Those who steer ships.
2. Antonio de Berrío (1527–1597), Spanish soldier, governor, and explorer; one of Ralegh's informants.
3. People dwelling close by.
4. Nicolás Monardes, trader between Seville and the New World, wrote the *Historia Medicinal* (in three parts, 1565, 1571, and 1574). It detailed treatments that he learned from indigenous people and medicines that he made using products from the New World.

After this old king had rested awhile in a little tent that I caused to be set up, I began by my interpreter to discourse with him of the death of Morequito his predecessor, and afterward of the Spaniards; and ere I went any farther, I made him know the cause of my coming thither, whose servant I was, and that the Queen's pleasure was I should undertake the voyage for their defense, and to deliver them from the tyranny of the Spaniards, dilating° at large, as I had done before to those of Trinidad, her Majesty's greatness, her justice, her charity to all oppressed nations, with as many of the rest of her beauties and virtues as either I could express or they conceive.° All which being with great admiration attentively heard and marvelously° admired, I began to sound° the old man as touching Guiana and the state thereof, what sort of commonwealth it was, how governed, of what strength and policy, how far it extended, and what nations were friends or enemies adjoining, and finally of the distance and way to enter the same. He told me that himself and his people, with all those down the river towards the sea as far as Emeria, the province of Carapana, were of Guiana, but that they called themselves Orenoqueponi,[5] and that all the nations between the river and those mountains in sight, called Wacarima, were of the same cast° and appellation;° and that on the other side of those mountains of Wacarima there was a large plain (which after I discovered in my return) called the valley of Amariocapana. In all that valley the people were also of the ancient Guianians.

    I asked what nations those were which inhabited on the further side of those mountains, beyond the valley of Amariocapana. He answered with a great sigh (as a man which had inward feeling of the loss of his country and liberty, especially for that° his eldest son was slain in a battle on that side of the mountains, whom he most entirely loved) that he remembered in his father's lifetime, when he was very old and himself a young man, that there came down into that large valley of Guiana a nation from so far off as the sun slept (for such were his own words), with so great a multitude as they could not be numbered nor resisted, and that they wore large coats and hats of crimson color, which color he expressed by shewing a piece of red wood wherewith my tent was supported, and that they were called Orejones and Epuremei;[6] that those had slain and rooted out° so many of the ancient people as there were leaves in the wood upon all

describing

understand
greatly
examine

type / designation

because

eradicated

---

5. That is, people who live on the boarders of the Orenoque River.
6. Orejones: a Spanish term meaning 'having big ears,' used to describe native noble Guianians who wore plugs in their pierced earlobes; Epuremei: supposedly elite native Guianians, but possibly, given their Spanish characteristics, an invention of Ralegh's.

the trees, and had now made themselves lords of all, even to that mountain foot called Curaa, saving only of two nations, the one called Iwarawaqueri and the other Cassipagotos; and that in the last battle fought between the Epuremei and the Iwarawaqueri his eldest son was chosen to carry to the aid of the Iwarawaqueri a great troop of the Orenoqueponi, and was there slain with all his people and friends, and that he had now remaining but one son; and farther told me that those Epuremei had built a great town called Macureguarai at the said mountain foot, at the beginning of the great plains of Guiana, which have no end; and that their houses have many rooms, one over the other, and that therein the great king of the Orejones and Epuremei kept three thousand men to defend the borders against them, and withal° daily to invade and slay them; but that of late years, since the Christians offered to° invade his territories and those frontiers, they were all at peace, and traded one with another, saving only the Iwarawaqueri and those other nations upon the head of the river of Caroli called Cassipagotos, which we afterwards discovered, each one holding the Spaniard for a common enemy.

After he had answered thus far, he desired leave to depart, saying that he had far to go, that he was old and weak, and was every day called for by death (which was also his own phrase). I desired him to rest with us that night, but I could not entreat him; but he told me that at my return from the country above he would again come to us, and in the meantime provide for us the best he could of all that his country yielded. The same night he returned to Orocotona, his own town; so as° he went that day eight-and-twenty miles, the weather being very hot, the country being situate between four and five degrees of the equinoctial.° This Topiawari is held for the proudest and wisest of all the Orenoqueponi, and so he behaved himself towards me in all his answers at my return, as I marveled to find a man of that gravity and judgment and of so good discourse that had no help of learning nor breed.° The next morning we also left the port and sailed westward up to the river to view the famous river called Caroli, as well because° it was marvelous of itself, as also for that I understood it led to the strongest nations of all the frontiers, that were enemies to the Epuremei, which are subjects to Inga, emperor of Guiana and Manoa.[7] And that night we anchored at another island called Caiama, of some five or six miles in length; and the next day arrived at the mouth of Caroli.

likewise
proposed

in such a way that

equator

racial origin

not only because

---

7. The Inga, or Inca; the supposed ruler of Guiana and its chief city, Manoa.

When we were short of it° as low or further down as the port of Morequito, we heard the great roar and fall of the river. But when we came to enter with our barge and wherries,° thinking to have gone up some forty miles to the nations of the Cassipagotos, we were not able with a barge of eight oars to row one stone's cast° in an hour; and yet the river is as broad as the Thames at Woolwich, and we tried both sides, and the middle, and every part of the river. So as° we encamped upon the banks adjoining, and sent off our Orenoquepone, which came with us from Morequito, to give knowledge to the nations upon the river of our being there, and that we desired to see the lords of Canuria which dwelt within the province upon that river, making them know that we were enemies to the Spaniards; for it was on this river side that Morequito slew the friar, and those nine Spaniards which came from Manoa, the city of Inga, and took from them 14,000 pesos of gold. So as the next day there came down a lord or cacique,[8] called Wanuretona, with many people with him, and brought all store of provisions to entertain us as the rest had done. And as I had before made my coming known to Topiawari, so did I acquaint this cacique therewith, and how I was sent by her Majesty for the purpose aforesaid and gathered also what I could of him touching° the estate of Guiana. And I found that those also of Caroli were not only enemies to the Spaniards, but most of all to the Epuremei, which abound in gold. And by this Wanuretona I had knowledge that on the head of this river were three mighty nations, which were seated on a great lake from whence this river descended, and were called Cassipagotos, Eparegotos, and Arawagotos, and that all those either against the Spaniards or the Epuremei would join with us, and that if we entered the land over the mountains of Curaa we should satisfy ourselves with gold and all other good things. He told us farther of a nation called Iwarawaqueri, before spoken of, that held daily war with the Epuremei that inhabited Macureguarai, and first civil town of Guiana, of the subjects of Inga, the emperor.

Upon this river one Captain George, that I took with Berreo, told me that there was a great silver mine, and that it was near the banks of the said river. But by this time as well Orenoque, Caroli, as all the rest of the rivers were risen four or five feet in height, so as it was not possible by the strength of any men, or with any boat whatsoever, to row into the river against the stream. I therefore

not quite at it

light rowing boats

throw

for that reason

concerning

---

8. Indigenous chief. The term is a Spanish transliteration of a word from a Central American Indian language.

sent Captain Thynn, Captain Greenville, my nephew John Gilbert, my cousin Butshead[9] Gorges, Captain Clarke, and some thirty shot° more to coast° the river by land, and to go to a town some twenty miles over the valley called Amnatapoi; and they found guides there to go farther towards the mountain foot to another great town called Capurepana, belonging to a cacique called Haharacoa, that was a nephew to old Topiawari, king of Aromaia, our chiefest friend, because this town and province of Capurepana adjoined to Macureguarai, which was a frontier town of the empire. And the meanwhile myself with Captain Gifford, Captain Caulfield, Edward Hancock, and some half-a-dozen shot marched overland to view the strange overfalls° of the river of Caroli, which roared so far off; and also to see the plains adjoining, and the rest of the province of Canuri. I sent also Captain Whiddon, William Connock, and some eight shot with them to see if they could find any mineral stone alongst the river's side. When we were come to the tops of the first hills of the plains adjoining to the river, we beheld that wonderful breach of waters° which ran down Caroli; and might from that mountain see the river how it ran in three parts, above° twenty miles off, and there appeared some ten or twelve overfalls in sight, every one as high over the other as a church tower, which fell with that fury that the rebound of water made it seem as if it had been all covered over with a great shower of rain; and in some places we took it at the first for a smoke that had risen over some great town. For mine own part I was well persuaded from thence to have returned, being a very ill footman;° but the rest were all so desirous to go near the said strange thunder of waters as° they drew me on by little and little till we came into the next valley where we might better discern the same. I never saw a more beautiful country nor more lively prospects;° hills so raised here and there over the valleys; the river winding into divers branches;° the plains adjoining without bush or stubble, all fair green grass; the ground of hard sand, easy to march on, either for horse or foot; the deer crossing in every path; the birds towards the evening singing on every tree with a thousand several° tunes; cranes and herons of white, crimson, and carnation, perching in the river's side; the air fresh with a gentle easterly wind; and every stone that we stooped to take up promised either gold or silver by his complexion.[1] Your Lordship shall see of° many sorts, and I hope some of them cannot be bet-

soldiers / skirt

waterfalls

breaking of waves

over

poor pedestrian that

vistas

streams

separate

have sight of

---

9. Name for a historic estate in the parish of St. Budeaux in Devon, now known as Budockshed; it was lived in by the Gorges family.

1. Seemed by its texture and appearance to give promise of containing gold or silver.

tered under the sun; and yet we had no means but with our daggers and fingers to tear them out here and there, the rocks being most hard of that mineral spar° afore- said, which is like a flint, and is altogether as hard or harder, and, besides, the veins lie a fathom or two deep in the rocks. But we wanted° all things requisite° save only° our desires and good will to have performed more if it had pleased God. To be short, when both our compa- nies returned, each of them brought also several sorts of stones that appeared very fair but were such as they found loose on the ground, and were for the most part but colored, and had not any gold fixed in them. Yet such as had no judgment or experience kept all that glistered and would not be persuaded but[2] it was rich because of the luster;° and brought of those, and of marcasite[3] withal, from Trinidad, and have delivered of° those stones to be tried in many places and have thereby bred an opinion that all the rest is of the same. Yet some of these stones I shewed afterward to a Spaniard of the Caracas who told me that it was "el madre del oro" that is, the mother of gold, and that the mine was farther in the ground.

    But it shall be found a weak policy in me either to betray myself or my country with imaginations; neither am I so far in love with that lodging, watching,° care, peril, dis- eases, ill savors,° bad fare,° and many other mischiefs that accompany these voyages as to woo myself again into any of them, were I not assured that the sun covereth not so much riches in any part of the earth. Captain Whid- don, and our chirurgeon,° Nicholas Millechamp, brought me a kind of stones like sapphires; what they may prove° I know not. I shewed them to some of the Orenoqueponi, and they promised to bring me to a mountain that had of them very large pieces growing diamond-wise; whether it be crystal of the mountain, Bristol diamond,[4] or sapphire, I do not yet know, but I hope the best; sure I am that the place is as likely as° those from whence all the rich stones are brought and in the same height or very near. On the left hand of this river Caroli are seated those nations which I called Iwarawaqueri before remembered,° which are enemies to the Epuremei; and on the head of it, adjoining to the great lake Cassipa, are situated those other nations which also resist Inga, and the Epuremei, called Cassipagotos, Eparegotos, and Arawagotos. I far- ther understood that this lake of Cassipa is so large as° it is above° one day's journey for one of their canoas to cross, which may be some forty miles; and that thereinto fall

---

2. Could not be dissuaded from the idea that.
3. White iron pyrite; sometimes known as "fool's gold."
4. Quartz crystals found in the Avon Gorge in Bristol, England.

Gloss (right margin, in order): crystalline minerals; lacked / appropriate; except; sheen; presented; wakefulness; bad smells / bad food; surgeon; turn out to be; similar to; reflected on; that; over divers rivers, and that great store° of grains of gold are found in the summer time when the lake falleth by the banks in those branches. *abundant supply*

There is also another goodly river beyond Caroli, which is called Arui, which also runneth through the lake Cassipa, and falleth into Orenoque farther west, making all that land between Caroli and Arui an island; which is likewise a most beautiful country. Next unto Arui there are two rivers, Atoica and Caura, and on that branch which is called Caura are a nation of people whose heads appear not above their shoulders,[5] which though it may be thought a mere fable, yet for mine own part I am resolved it is true, because every child in the provinces of Aromaia and Canuri affirm the same. They are called Ewaipanoma; they are reported to have their eyes in their shoulders and their mouths in the middle of their breasts, and that a long train of hair groweth backward between their shoulders.

* * *

For the rest, which myself have seen, I will promise these things that follow which I know to be true. Those that are desirous to discover and to see many nations may be satisfied within this river which bringeth forth so many arms and branches leading to several countries and provinces, above 2,000 miles east and west and 800 miles south and north, and of these the most either rich in gold or in other merchandises. The common soldier shall here fight for gold, and pay himself, instead of pence, with plates of half-a-foot broad, whereas he breaketh his bones in other wars for provant° and penury. Those commanders and chieftains that shoot at° honor and abundance shall find there more rich and beautiful cities, more temples adorned with golden images, more sepulchers filled with treasure than either Cortes found in Mexico or Pizarro in Peru.[6] And the shining glory of this conquest will eclipse all those so far-extended beams of the Spanish nation. There is no country which yieldeth more pleasure to the inhabitants, either for those common delights of hunting, hawking, fishing, fowling and the rest, than Guiana doth; it hath so many plains, clear rivers, and abundance of pheasants, partridges, quails, rails, cranes, herons, and all other fowl; deer of all sorts, porks, hares, lions, tigers, leopards, and divers other sorts of beasts, either for chase or food. It hath a kind of beast called cama or anta, as big as an English beef, and in great *an allowance of food* *aspire to*

---

5. See *Othello* 1.3.143–44 and the image on p. 641 for reference to this notion.
6. Hernán Cortés (1485–1547), leader of a Spanish expedition that conquered the Aztec empire in Mexico; Francisco Pizzaro (ca. 1476–1541), leader of a Spanish expedition that conquered the Inca empire in Peru.

plenty. To speak of the several sorts of every kind I fear would be troublesome to the reader, and therefore I will omit them, and conclude that both for health, good air, pleasure, and riches, I am resolved it cannot be equaled by any region either in the east or west. Moreover, the country is so healthful as, of an hundred persons and more, which lay without shift° most sluttishly,° and were every day almost melted with heat in rowing and marching, and suddenly wet again with great showers, and did eat of all sorts of corrupt fruits, and made meals of fresh fish without seasoning, of tortugas,° of lagartos or crocodiles, and of all sorts good and bad, without either order or measure, and besides lodged in the open air every night, we lost not any one, nor had one ill-disposed to my knowledge; nor found any calenture⁷ or other of those pestilent diseases which dwell in all hot regions and so near the equinoctial line. *[underclothing / repulsively]* *[tortoises]*

Where there is store of gold it is in effect needless to remember other commodities for trade. But it hath, towards the south part of the river, great quantities of Brazil-wood and divers berries that dye a most perfect crimson and carnation; and for painting,° all France, Italy, or the East Indies yield none such. For the more the skin is washed, the fairer the color appeareth, and with which even those brown and tawny women spot themselves and color their cheeks. All places yield abundance of cotton, of silk, of balsamum⁸ and of those kinds most excellent and never known in Europe, of all sorts of gums, of Indian pepper,° and what else the countries may afford within the land we know not, neither had we time to abide the trial and search. The soil besides is so excellent and so full of rivers as it will carry sugar, ginger, and all those other commodities which the West Indies have. *[cosmetics]* *[probably chili pepper]*

The navigation is short, for it may be sailed with an ordinary wind in six weeks and in the like time back again; and, by the way,° neither lee shore,⁹ enemies' coast, rocks, nor sands. All which in the voyages to the West Indies and all other places we are subject unto; as the channel of Bahama, coming from the West Indies, cannot well be passed in the winter, and when it is at the best it is a perilous and a fearful place; the rest of the Indies for calms° and diseases very troublesome, and the sea about the Bermudas a hellish sea for thunder, lightning, and storms. *[along the way]* *[absences of wind]*

This very year° there were seventeen sail¹ of Spanish ships lost in the channel of Bahama, and the great Philip,² like to have sunk at the Bermudas, was put back *[1595]*

---

7. A tropical sailors' disease, characterized by delirium in which the patient, it is said, believes the sea to be green fields and wants to leap into it.
8. An aromatic resinous vegetable juice.
9. The shore that the wind blows on.
1. A collective singular for sailing vessels.
2. The *Saint Philip* was the largest ship in the navy of Spain.

to St. Juan de Puerto Rico; and so it falleth out in that navigation every year for the most part. Which in this voyage are not to be feared; for the time of year to leave England is best in July, and the summer in Guiana is in October, November, December, January, February and March, and then the ships may depart thence in April and so return again into England in June. So as they shall never be subject to winter weather, either coming, going, or staying there: which, for my part, I take to be one of the greatest comforts and encouragements that can be thought on, having, as I have done, tasted in this voyage by the West Indies so many calms, so much heat, such outrageous gusts, such weather and contrary winds.

To conclude, Guiana is a country that hath yet her maidenhead, never sacked, turned, nor wrought; the face of the earth hath not been torn, nor the virtue and salt of the soil spent by manurance.[3] The graves have not been opened for gold, the mines not broken with sledges,° nor their images pulled down out of their temples. It hath never been entered by any army of strength, and never conquered or possessed by any Christian prince. It is, besides, so defensible° that if two forts be builded in one of the provinces which I have seen, the flood° setteth in so near the bank—where the channel also lieth—that no ship can pass up but within a pike's length of the artillery, first of the one, and afterwards of the other. Which two forts will be a sufficient guard both to the empire of Inga, and to an hundred other several kingdoms lying within the said river, even to the city of Quito in Peru.

There is therefore great difference between the easiness of the conquest of Guiana, and the defense of it being conquered,[4] and the West or East Indies. Guiana hath but one entrance by the sea, if it hath that, for any vessels of burden.[5] So as whosoever shall first possess it, it shall be found unaccessible for any enemy, except° he come in wherries, barges, or canoas, or else in flat-bottomed boats; and if he do offer° to enter it in that manner, the woods are so thick two hundred miles together upon the rivers of such entrance, as a mouse cannot sit in a boat unhit from the bank. By land it is more impossible to approach, for it hath the strongest situation of any region under the sun, and it is so environed° with impassable mountains on every side as it is impossible to victual any company in the passage. Which hath been well proved by the Spanish nation, who since the conquest of Peru have never left five years free from attempting° this empire or discovering some way into it; and yet of

° sledgehammers

° easy to defend
° tide

° unless

° attempt

° surrounded

° attacking

---

3. Guiana is here described as a virgin country that has not been raped, plundered, or exhausted through labor. "Manurance": manuring; that is, (over)cultivating the land—so, here, an occupation.
4. Once it has been conquered.
5. Ships capable of carrying a significant load.

three-and-twenty several gentlemen, knights, and noblemen, there was never any that knew which way to lead an army by land, or to conduct ships by sea, anything near the said country. Orellana, of whom the river of Amazons taketh name, was the first, and Don Antonio de Berreo, whom we displanted,° the last: and I doubt much whether he himself—or any of his—yet know the best way into the said empire. It can therefore hardly be regained, if any strength° be formerly set down, but in one or two places, and but two or three crumsters[6] or galleys built and furnished° upon the river within. The West Indies have many ports, watering places,[7] and landings; and nearer than three hundred miles to Guiana, no man can harbor a ship, except he know one only place, which is not learned in haste, and which I will undertake° there is not any one of my companies that knoweth, whosoever hearkened° most after it.

uprooted

fortress

fitted with appliances

affirm
eavesdropped

Besides, by keeping one good fort, or building one town of strength, the whole empire is guarded; and whatsoever companies shall be afterwards planted within the land, although in twenty several provinces, those shall be able all to reunite themselves upon any occasion either by the way of one river or be able to march by land without either wood, bog, or mountain. Whereas in the West Indies there are few towns or provinces that can succor or relieve one the other by land or sea. By land the countries are either desert, mountainous, or strong enemies. By sea, if any man invade to the eastward, those to the west cannot in many months turn against the breeze and eastern wind. Besides, the Spaniards are therein so dispersed as they are nowhere strong but in Ñueva Espana[8] only; the sharp mountains, the thorns, and poisoned prickles, the sandy and deep ways in the valleys, the smothering heat and air, and want of water in other places are their only and best defense; which, because those nations that invade them are not victualled or provided to stay, neither have any place to friend° adjoining, do serve them instead of good arms and great multitudes.

on intimate terms

The West Indies were first offered her Majesty's grandfather by Columbus,[9] a stranger,° in whom there might be doubt° of deceit; and besides it was then thought incredible that there were such and so many lands and regions never written of before. This Empire is made known to her Majesty by her own vassal,° and by him that oweth to

foreigner
fear

subordinate

---

6. Kromsteven or Kromster (Dutch), a vessel with a bent prow.
7. *Places* where fresh water can be obtained.
8. Literally, "New Spain"—the territorial land claimed by Spain extended over large parts of the Americas and had its capital in Mexico City.
9. In 1488 Bartholomew Columbus petitioned Henry VII to sponsor his brother Christopher in an attempt to find a new route to the (East) Indies by sailing west. The king declined, so Christopher sought the sponsorship of Queen Isabella of Spain.

her more duty than an ordinary subject; so that it shall ill sort° with the many graces and benefits which I have received to abuse her Highness, either with fables or imaginations. The country is already discovered, many nations won to her Majesty's love and obedience, and those Spaniards which have latest and longest labored about the conquest, beaten out, discouraged and disgraced, which among these nations were thought invincible. Her Majesty may in this enterprise employ all those soldiers and gentlemen that are younger brethren,[1] and all captains and chieftains that want° employment, and the charge° will be only the first setting out in victualling and arming them; for after the first or second year I doubt not but to see in London a contractation-house of more receipt° for Guiana than there is now in Seville for the West Indies.[2]

°badly fit

°lack
°cost

°money

And I am resolved° that if there were but a small army afoot in Guiana, marching towards Manoa, the chief city of Inga, he would yield to her Majesty by composition° so many hundred thousand pounds yearly as should both defend all enemies abroad, and defray all expenses at home; and that he would besides pay a garrison of three or four thousand soldiers very royally to defend him against other nations. For he cannot but know how his predecessors, yea, how his own great uncles, Guascar and Atabalipa, sons to Guiana-Capac, emperor of Peru, were, while they contended for the empire, beaten out by the Spaniards, and that both of late years and ever since the said conquest, the Spaniards have sought the passages and entry of his country; and of their cruelties used to the borderers he cannot be ignorant. In which respects no doubt but he will be brought to tribute with great gladness; if not, he hath neither shot nor iron weapon in all his empire and therefore may easily be conquered.

°certain

°treaty

And I further remember that Berreo confessed to me and others, which I protest° before the Majesty of God to be true, that there was found among the prophecies in Peru, at such time as the empire was reduced to the Spanish obedience, in their chiefest temples, amongst divers others which foreshadowed the loss of the said empire, that from Inglatierra° those Ingas should be again in time to come restored, and delivered from the servitude of the said conquerors. And I hope, as we with these few hands have displanted the first garrison and driven them out of the said country, so her Majesty will give order for the rest, and either defend it, and hold it as tributary,[3] or conquer and keep it as empress of the same. For

°affirm

°England

---

1. Younger brothers were seen as likely recruits because they were without patrimony.
2. An exchange or treasury in Seville, the Casa de Contratación, where contracts were made in connection with West Indian trade.
3. Nation that pays tribute to the sovereign nation.

whatsoever prince shall possess it shall be greatest; and if the king of Spain enjoy it, he will become unresistible. Her Majesty hereby shall confirm and strengthen the opinions of all nations as touching° her great and princely actions. And where the south border of Guiana reacheth to the dominion and empire of the Amazons, those women shall hereby hear the name of a virgin, which is not only able to defend her own territories and her neighbors, but also to invade and conquer so great empires and so far removed.

 To speak more at this time I fear would be but troublesome: I trust in God, this being true, will suffice, and that he which is King of all Kings, and Lord of Lords, will put it into her heart which is Lady of Ladies to possess it. If not, I will judge those men worthy to be kings thereof, that by her grace and leave will undertake it of themselves.

concerning

1596, 1599

THOMAS HARIOT

Thomas Hariot (1560–1621), mathematician, astronomer, linguist, and surveyor in the service of Sir Walter Ralegh, was observing sunspots and using a telescope at about the same time as Galileo; he also made important discoveries in algebra, navigational techniques, and optics.

 Hariot matriculated at Oxford University in 1577, where he met Richard Hakluyt, who may have interested him in the subject of travel and colonization. After Hariot graduated in 1580, Ralegh hired him to keep accounts, design ships, and improve navigational methods with a view to traveling to the New World. Over that period, Hariot also became friendly with two Native Americans, the Algonquins Manteo and Wanchese, who had been brought to England, and who taught him their language. Hariot accompanied Sir Richard Grenville's expedition to the Roanoke Colony in 1585, and his account of it, extracted here, was intended to describe the virtues of the place and people and to promote colonization. To this end, he supplies information about the geography and climate, details the vegetation and wildlife that can be eaten, and offers an account of the inhabitants, about whom the English were intensely curious. Reports had begun to circulate in England about tensions with the Algonquin Indians, on whom the colonists were almost completely dependent for food, and Hariot's brief ethnographic observations are meant to reassure readers that the Indigenous people "are not to be feared." First published in 1588, his account was printed by Theodor de Bry in 1590, with maps and engravings of Native American life based on the watercolors by John White.

 After he returned to England in 1586, Hariot worked for Henry Percy, ninth Earl of Northumberland, and continued to do so when his patron was imprisoned for his close connections with the 1605 Gunpowder Plot. Hariot was among the first people to use a telescope; in 1611, he produced the first map of the moon. Hariot died in 1621, apparently from cancer of the nose—possibly caused by the habit of taking tobacco that he had acquired in the New World.

From A Brief and True Report of the New-Found land of Virginia

A brief and true report of the new-found land of Virginia; of the commodities there found and to be raised—as well merchantable,° as others for victual, building and other necessary uses—for those that are and shall be the planters there, and of the nature and manners of the natural inhabitants. Discovered by the English Colony there seated° by *Sir Richard Grenville Knight*[1] in the year 1585, which remained under the government of Ralph Lane Esquire,[2] one of her Majesty's Esquires, during the space of twelve months, at the special charge and direction of the Honorable SIR WALTER RALEGH, Knight, lord Warden of the Stannaries,[3] who therein hath been favored and authorized by her MAJESTY and her letters patents.

    salable

    placed

Directed to the adventurers, favorers and well-willers of the action for the inhabiting and planting there. By Thomas Hariot, servant to the above-named Sir WALTER, a member of the colony, and there employed in discovering. 1588

The first part: of merchantable commodities.

* * *

The second part: of such commodities as Virginia is known to yield for victual and sustenance of man's life, usually fed upon by the natural inhabitants, as also by us during the time of our abode. And first of such as are sowed and husbanded.°

    cultivated

* * *

The third and last part: of such other things as is behoveful° for those which shall plant and inhabit to know of, with a description of the nature and manners of the people of the country.

    necessary

Of commodities for building and other necessary uses.

Those other things which I am more to make rehearsal of° are such as concern building and other mechanical necessary uses—as diverse sorts of trees for house and ship timber and other uses else; also lime, stone, and brick, lest that being not mentioned some might have been doubted of, or by some that are malicious reported the contrary.

    further to relate

Oaks there are as fair, straight, tall, and as good timber as any can be, and also great store,° and in some places very great.

    in abundance

---

1. Richard Grenville (1542–1591), English privateer and explorer.
2. Ralph Lane (ca. 1532–1603), English explorer and colonizer.
3. Tin mines in Cornwall and Devon.

Walnut trees, as I have said before, very many. Some have been seen excellent fair timber of four and five fathom[4] and above fourscore° foot straight without bough. °eighty

Fir trees fit for masts of ships, some very tall and great.

Rakiock,[5] a kind of trees so called that are sweet wood of which the inhabitants that were near unto us do commonly make their boats or canoes of the form of trows,[6] only with the help of fire, hatchets of stones, and shells; we have known some so great being made in that sort° of one tree that they have carried well twenty men at once besides much baggage; the timber being great, tall, straight, soft, light, and yet tough enough I think (besides other uses) to be fit also for masts of ships. °in that manner

Cedar, a sweet wood good for ceilings, chests, boxes, bedsteads, lutes, virginals[7] and many things else, as I have also said before. Some of our company, which have wandered in some places where I have not been, have made certain affirmation of *Cyprus* which for such and other excellent uses is also a wood of price and no small estimation.° °in great number

Maple, and also *Witch-hazel,* whereof the inhabitants use to make their bows.

Holly, a necessary thing for the making of birdlime.[8]

Willows, good for the making of weirs and weels[9] to take fish after the English manner, although the inhabitants use only reeds which, because they are so strong as also° flexible, do serve for that turn° very well and sufficiently. °as well as / °fulfil the purpose

Beech and *Ash,* good for cask, hoops,[1] and if need require,° plough work, as also for many things else. °necessary

Elm.

Sassafras trees.

Ascopo° a kind of tree very like unto laurel. The bark is hot in taste and spicy; it is very like to that tree which Monardus[2] describeth to be *Cassia Lignea* of the West Indies.[3] °sweet bay tree

There are many other strange trees whose names I know not but in the Virginian language, of which I am not now able, neither is it so convenient for the present, to trouble you with particular relation,° seeing that for timber and other necessary uses I have named sufficient. °tell you

---

4. Six feet (the length covered by the outstretched arms).
5. What tree this is has not been determined. A tulip tree, perhaps.
6. A type of boat used for fishing in early modern England.
7. Instruments consisting of keyboards in a box.
8. A sticky substance spread on trees to catch birds.
9. Weirs were fences in rivers that would channel fish toward a trap; weels were wicker traps for catching fish.
1. That is, the staves of barrels and the hoops that bind them
2. Nicolás Monardes (1493–1588) wrote an account of the plants of the New World and their medical uses in 1574; it was translated into English 1580.
3. A variety of cinnamon.

And of many of the rest, but that they may be applied to good use, I know no cause to doubt.

Now for stone, brick, and lime, thus it is. Near unto the seacoast where we dwelt, there are no kind of stones to be found (except a few small pebbles about four miles off) but such as have been brought from farther out of the main.° In some of our voyages, we have seen diverse hard, raggy° stones, great pebbles, and a kind of grey stone like unto marble, of which the inhabitants make their hatchets to cleave wood. Upon enquiry we heard that a little further up into the country were of all sorts very many, although of quarries they are ignorant, neither have they use of any store whereupon they should have occasion to seek any. For if every household have one or two to crack nuts, grind shells, whet copper, and sometimes other stones for hatchets, they have enough. Neither use they any digging, but only for graves about three foot deep, and therefore no marvel that they know neither quarries nor limestones, which both may be in places nearer than they wot° of. *sea*
 ragged

know

In the meantime, until there be discovery of sufficient store in some place or other convenient, the want° of you which are and shall be the planters therein may be as well supplied by brick, for the making whereof in diverse places of the country there is clay both excellent good and plenty, and also by lime° made of oyster shells, and of others burnt, after the manner as they use in the isles of Thanet and Sheppey,[4] and also in diverse other places of England, which kind of lime is well known to be as good as any other. And of oyster shells there is plenty enough. For besides diverse other particular places where are abundance, there is one shallow sound along the coast where, for the space of many miles together in length and two or three miles in breadth, the ground is nothing else being but half a foot or a foot under water for the most part. *lack*

mortar

This much can I say furthermore of stones: that about one hundred twenty miles from our fort near the water in the side of a hill was found by a gentleman of our company a great vein of hard raggy stones, which I thought good to remember° unto you. *mention*

OF THE NATURE AND MANNERS OF THE PEOPLE

It resteth° I speak a word or two of the natural inhabitants, their natures and manners * * * *remains that*

---

4. A peninsula and island respectively off the coast of Kent in southern England. Oyster shells can be burned to create lime, then mixed with water, sand, ash, and other shells to create a kind of concrete (to be known, later, as tabby).

They are a people clothed with loose mantles° made of   *sleeveless cloaks*
deerskins, and aprons of the same round about their
middles, all else naked; of such a difference of statures
only as we in England; having no edge tools[5] or weapons
of iron or steel to offend us withal, neither know they
how to make any. Those weapons that they have are only
bows made of witch hazel and arrows of reeds, flat-edged
truncheons also of wood about a yard long, neither have
they anything to defend themselves but targets° made of   *shields*
barks, and some armors made of sticks wickered° together   *enclosed with wicker*
with thread.

Their towns are but small and near the seacoast but
few, some containing but ten or twelve houses, some
twenty. The greatest that we have seen hath been but of
thirty houses. If they be walled, it is only done with barks
of trees made fast° to stakes, or else with poles only fixed   *fastened*
upright and close one by another.

Their houses are made of small poles made fast at the
tops in round form after the manner as is used in many
arbories° in our gardens of England, in most towns covered   *arbors*
with barks, and in some with artificial° mats, made of long   *manufactured (woven)*
rushes, from the tops of the houses down to the ground.
The length of them is commonly double to the breadth. In
some places they are but twelve and sixteen yards long,
and in other some we have seen of four-and-twenty.

In some places of the country only one town belongs to
the government, of a *werowance* or chief lord;[6] in other some
two or three, on some six, eight, and more. The greatest
werowance that yet we had dealing with had but eighteen
towns in his government, and able to make° not above seven   *muster*
or eight hundred fighting men at the most. The language
of every government is different from any other, and the
farther they are distant, the greater is the difference.

Their manner of wars amongst themselves is either by
sudden surprising one another, most commonly about the
dawning of the day or moonlight, or else by ambushes, or
some subtle devices. Set battles are very rare, except it fall
out° where there are many trees, where either part may have   *happen*
some hope of defense, after the delivery of every arrow, in
leaping behind some or other.

If there fall out any wars between us and them, what
their fight is likely to be, we having advantages against
them for many manner of ways—as by our discipline, our
strange° weapons and devices else,° especially ordnance°   *unfamiliar / in addition /*
great and small—it may be easily imagined, by the experi-   *artillery*
ence we have had in some places, the turning up of their
heels against us in running away was their best defense.

---

5. Tools with sharp, cutting edges.
6. Name for a chief among the Native Americans of what is now Virginia, Maryland, and North Carolina.

In respect of° us they are a people poor, and for want of skill and judgement in the knowledge and use of our things, do esteem° our trifles before things of greater value. Notwithstanding in their proper° manner, considering the want of such means as we have, they seem very ingenious. For although they have no such tools nor any such crafts, sciences, and arts as we, yet in those things they do, they show excellency of wit.° And by how much they upon due consideration shall find our manner of knowledges and crafts to exceed theirs in perfection, and speed for doing or execution,° by so much the more is it probable that they should desire our friendship and love and have the greater respect for pleasing and obeying us. Whereby may be hoped if means of good government be used that they may in short time be brought to civility and the embracing of true religion.

° *in comparison with*
° *regard, value*
° *own*
° *intelligence*
° *carrying into effect*

Some religion they have already which although it be far from the truth, yet being as it is, there is hope it may be the easier and sooner reformed.

They believe that there are many gods, which they call *Mantoac*, but of different sorts and degrees, one only chief and great god, which hath been from all eternity. Who, as they affirm, when he purposed to make the world, made, first, other gods of a principal order to be as means and instruments to be used in the creation and government to follow; and, after, the sun, moon, and stars as petty gods and the instruments of the other order more principal. First, they say, were made waters, out of which by the gods was made all diversity of creatures that are visible or invisible.

For mankind, they say, a woman was made first, which by the working of one of the gods conceived and brought forth children. And in such sort, they say, they had their beginning.

But how many years have passed since, they say, they can make no relation,° having no letters° nor other such means as we do to keep records of the particularities of times past, but only tradition from father to son.

° *cannot tell / writing*

They think that all the gods are of human shape, and therefore they represent them by images in the forms of men, which they call *Kewasowok*. One alone is called *Kewas*. Them they place in houses appropriate, or temples which they call *Machicomuck*, where they worship, pray, sing, and make many times offering unto them. In some *Machicomuck* we have seen but one *Kewas*, in some two, and in other some three. The common sort think them to be also gods.

They believe also the immortality of the soul: that after this life, as soon as the soul is departed from the body according to the works it hath done, it is either carried to

heaven, the habitacle° of gods, there to enjoy perpetual   *habitation*
bliss and happiness, or else to a great pit or hole, which they think to be in the furthest parts of their part of the world toward the sunset, there to burn continually. The place they call *Popogusso*.

For the confirmation of this opinion, they told me two stories of two men that had been lately dead and renewed°   *spiritually reborn*
again. The one happened but few years before our coming, in the country of a wicked man which, having been dead and buried, the next day the earth of the grave being seen to move, was taken up again, who made declaration where his soul had been—that is to say very near entering into *Popogusso*—had not one of the gods saved him and gave him leave to return again, and teach his friends what they should do to avoid that terrible place of torment.

The other happened in the same year we were there, but in a town that was threescore° miles from us, and it   *sixty*
was told me for strange news: that one being dead, buried, and taken up again as the first, showed that although his body had lien dead in the grave, yet his soul was alive, and had traveled far in a long broad way, on both sides whereof grew most delicate and pleasant trees, bearing more rare and excellent fruits than ever he had seen before or was able to express;° and at length came to most   *put into words*
brave° and fair houses, near which he met his father that   *splendid*
had been dead before, who gave him great charge[7] to go back again and show his friends what good they were to do to enjoy the pleasures of that place, which, when he had done he should after come again.

What subtlety° soever be in the *Wiroances* and priests,   *craftiness*
this opinion° worketh so much in many of the common   *belief*
and simple sort of people that it maketh them have a great respect to their governors and also great care what they do to avoid torment after death and to enjoy bliss. Although, notwithstanding, there is punishment ordained for malefactors, as° stealers, whoremongers,[8] and other sorts of   *such as*
wicked-doers: some punished with death, some with forfeitures,° some with beating, according to the greatness of   *fines*
the facts.°   *deeds*

And this is the sum of their religion, which I learned by having special familiarity with some of their priests. Wherein they were not so sure grounded, nor gave such credit to their traditions and stories, but through conversing with us they were brought into great doubts of their own,[9] and no small admiration of ours, with earnest desire

---

7. Commanded him powerfully.
8. People who use/procure prostitutes.

9. That is, of their own religion.

in many to learn more than we had means—for want of perfect utterance in their language—to express.

Most things they saw with us, as mathematical instruments, sea compasses, the virtue° of the lodestone° in drawing iron, a perspective glass° whereby was showed many strange sights, burning glasses,[1] wildfire works,° guns, books, writing and reading, spring-clocks that seem to go of themselves, and many other things that we had were so strange unto them and so far exceeded their capacities to comprehend the reason and means how they should be made and done, that they thought they were rather the works of gods than of men, or at the leastwise they had been given and taught us of the gods. Which made many of them to have such opinion of us as, that if they knew not the truth of God and religion already, it was rather to be had from us, whom God so especially loved, than from a people that were so simple (as they found themselves to be in comparison of us). Whereupon greater credit was given unto that we spake of concerning such matters.

power / magnet
magnifying glass
fireworks

Many times, and in every town where I came according as° I was able, I made declaration of the contents of the bible: that therein was set forth the true and only God and his mighty works; that therein was contained the true doctrine of salvation through Christ; with many particularities of miracles and chief points of religion as I was able then to utter and thought fit° for the time. And although I told them the book materially and of itself was not of any such virtue, as I thought they did conceive, but only the doctrine therein contained, yet would many be glad to touch it, to embrace it, to kiss it, to hold it to their breasts, and heads, and stroke over all their body with it to show their hungry desire of that knowledge which was spoken of.

as far as

proper

The *Wiroans* with whom we dwelt [was] called *Wingina*, and many of his people would be glad many times to be with us at our prayers and many times call upon us, both in his own town, as also in others (whither he sometimes accompanied us to pray and sing psalms) hoping thereby to be partaker of the same effects which we by that means also expected.

Twice this *Wiroance* was so grievously sick that he was like to die, and as he lay languishing, doubting of any help by his own priests—and thinking he was in such danger for offending us and thereby our God—sent for some of us to pray and be a means to our God that it would please Him either that he might live or after death dwell with Him in bliss, so likewise were the requests of many others in the like case.

---

1. Concave mirrors used to concentrate the sun's rays.

On a time also when their corn began to wither by reason of a drought which happened extraordinarily,° fearing that it had come to pass by reason that in something they had displeased us, many would come to us and desire us to pray to our God of England that he would preserve their corn, promising that, when it was ripe, we also should be partakers of the fruit.

very unusually

There could at no time happen any strange sickness, losses, hurts, or any other cross° unto them, but that they would impute° to us the cause or means thereof for offending or not pleasing us.

affliction
attribute

One other rare and strange accident,° leaving others, will I mention before I end, which moved the whole country that either knew or heard of us to have us in wonderful admiration.° There was no town where we had any subtle device° practiced against us we leaving it unpunished or not revenged (because we sought by all means possible to win them by gentleness) but that within a few days after our departure, from every such town, the people began to die very fast, and many in short space; in some towns about twenty, in some forty, in some sixty, and in one sixscore,° which in truth was very many in respect of° their numbers. This happened in no place that we could learn but where we had been, where they used some practice against us, and after such time. The disease also was so strange that they neither knew what it was nor how to cure it; the like by report of the oldest men in the country never happened before, time out of mind, a thing specially observed by us as also by the natural inhabitants themselves.

occurrence

high regard
contrivance, plot

one hundred and
twenty
in proportion to

Insomuch that when some of the inhabitants which were our friends and especially the *Wiroance Wingina* had observed such effects in four of five towns to follow their[2] wicked practices, they were persuaded that it was the work of our God through our means, and that we by Him might kill and slay whom we would° without weapons and not come near them.

wanted to

And thereupon when it had happened that they had understanding that any of their enemies had abused us in our journeys, hearing that we had wrought no revenge with our weapons, and fearing upon some cause the matter should so rest, did come and entreat us that we would be a means to our God that they, as others that had dealt ill with us, might in like sort die, alleging how much it would be for our credit and profit as also theirs, and hoping furthermore that we would do so much at their requests in respect of the friendship we profess them.

---

2. Following on from their.

Whose entreaties, although we showed that they were ungodly, affirming that our God would not subject Himself to any such prayers and requests of men; that indeed all things have been and were to be done according to His good pleasure as he had ordained; and that we, to show ourselves His true servants, ought rather to make petition for the contrary, that they with them might live together with us, be made partakers of His truth, and serve Him in righteousness, but notwithstanding in such sort that we refer that, as all other things, to be done according to His divine will and pleasure, and as by His wisdom He had ordained to be best.

Yet because the effect fell out° so suddenly and shortly after, according to their desires, they thought nevertheless it came to pass by our means, and that we in using such speeches unto them did but dissemble the matter, and therefore came unto us to give us thanks in their manner, that although we satisfied them not in promise, yet in deeds and effect we had fulfilled their desires.   *happened*

This marvelous accident in all the country wrought so strange opinions of us that some people could not tell whether to think us gods or men, and the rather because that all the space of their sickness there was no man of ours known to die or that was especially sick. They noted also that we had no women amongst us, neither that we did care for any of theirs.

Some, therefore, were of opinion that we were not born of women and therefore not mortal, but that we were men of an old generation many years past then risen again to immortality.

Some would likewise seem to prophesy that there were more of our generation yet to come to kill theirs and take their places—as some thought the purpose was, by° that which was already done.   *judging by*

Those that were immediately to come after us they imagined to be in the air yet invisible and without bodies, and that they by our entreaty and for the love of us did make the people to die in that sort° as they did by shooting invisible bullets into them.   *in that manner*

To confirm this opinion, their physicians (to excuse° their ignorance in curing disease), would not be ashamed to say, but earnestly make the simple people believe, that the strings of blood that they sucked out of the sick bodies were the strings wherewithal the invisible bullets were tied and cast.   *clear from blame*

Some also thought that we shot them ourselves out of our pieces° from the place where we dwelled and killed the people in any such town that had offended us as we listed,° how far distant from us soever it were.   *firearms*   *as we pleased*

And other some said that it was the special work of God for our sakes, as we ourselves have cause in some sort° to think no less, whatsoever some do or may imagine to the contrary, specially some astrologers, knowing of the eclipse of the sun which we saw the same year before in our voyage thitherward which unto them appeared very terrible. And also of a comet which began to appear but a few days before the beginning of the said sickness. But to exclude them from being the special causes of so special an accident, there are further reasons than I think fit° at this present to be alleged.

°*in some fashion*

°*suitable*

These their opinions I have set down the more at large,° that it may appear unto you that there is good hope they may be brought, through discreet dealing and government, to the embracing of the truth, and consequently to honor, obey, fear, and love us.

°*at length*

And although some of our company towards the end of the year showed themselves so fierce in slaying some of the people in some towns, upon causes that on our part might easily enough have been borne withal, yet notwithstanding (because it was on their part justly deserved), the alteration of their opinions generally and for the most part concerning us is the less to be doubted.° And whatsoever else they may be, by carefulness of ourselves need nothing at all to be feared.

°*feared*

The Conclusion.

* * * Although all which I have before spoken of have been discovered and experimented not far from the seacoast where was our abode and most of our traveling, yet sometimes, as we made our journeys farther into the main° and country, we found the soil to be fatter,° the trees greater and to grow thinner, the ground more firm and deeper mold, more and larger champions,³ finer grass and as good as ever we saw any in England, in some places rocky and far more high and hilly ground, more plenty of their fruits, more abundance of beasts, the more inhabited with people, and of greater policy and larger dominions, with greater towns and houses.

°*mainland*
°*richer*

Why may we not, then, look for in good hope—from the inner parts—of more and greater plenty, as well of other things, as of those which we have already discovered? Unto the Spaniards happened the like in discovering the main of the West Indies. The main also of this country of Virginia, extending some ways so many hundreds of leagues, as otherwise° than by the relation of the inhabitants we have most certain knowledge of, where yet no Christian prince hath any possession or dealing,

°*in other ways*

3. Areas of level open country.

cannot but yield many kinds of excellent commodities, which we in our discovery have not yet seen.

What hope there is else to be gathered of the nature of the climate, being answerable to the island of Japan, the land of China, Persia, Jewry, the islands of Cyprus and Candy,° the south parts of Greece, Italy, and Spain, and of many other notable and famous countries, because I mean not to be tedious, I leave to your own consideration.

Crete

Whereby also the excellent temperature of the air there at all seasons—much warmer than in England, and never so violently hot as sometimes is under and between the Tropics or near them—cannot be unknown unto you without farther relation.

For the wholesomeness thereof I need to say but thus much. That for all the want of provision, as, first, of English victual—excepting for twenty days, we lived only by drinking water and by the victual of the country, of which some sorts were very strange unto us, and might have been thought to have altered our temperatures in such sort as to have brought us into some grievous and dangerous diseases—secondly, the want of English means for the taking of beasts, fish, and fowl, which by the help only of the inhabitants and their means, could not be so suddenly and easily provided for us, nor in so great numbers and quantities, nor of that choice as otherwise might have been to our better satisfaction and contentment. Some want also we had of clothes. Furthermore, in all our travails which were most special and often in the time of winter, our lodging was in the open air upon the ground. And yet I say for all of this, there were but four of our whole company (being one hundred and eight) that died all the year and that but at the latter end thereof and upon none of the aforesaid causes. For all four, especially three, were feeble and sickly persons before ever they came thither, and those that knew them much marveled that they lived so long being in that case° or had adventured° to travel.

condition
dared

Seeing therefore the air there is so temperate and wholesome, the soil so fertile—and yielding such commodities as I have before mentioned—the voyage also thither to and fro being sufficiently experimented[4] to be performed thrice a year with ease and at any season thereof, and the dealing of Sir Water Ralegh so liberal in large giving and granting land there, as is already known, with many helps and furtherances° else (the least that he hath granted hath been five hundred acres to a man only for the adventure° of his person) I hope there remain no cause whereby the action should be misliked.

aids
risk

4. Tried by experiment.

If that those which shall thither travel to inhabit and plant be but reasonably provided for the first year—as those are which were transported the last—and being there do use but that diligence and care as is requisite, and as they may with ease, there is no doubt but for the time following they may have victuals that is excellent good and plenty enough: some more English sorts of cattle° also hereafter, as some have been before and are there yet remaining, may and shall be, God willing, thither transported. So likewise our kind of fruits, roots, and herbs may be there planted and sowed, as some have been already, and prove well.° And in short time also they may raise of° those sorts of commodities which I have spoken of as shall both enrich themselves as also others that shall deal with them.

    livestock

    thrive
    grow

And this is all the fruits° of our labors that I have thought necessary to advertise you of at this present.

    results

* * *

Thus referring my relation° to your favorable constructions, expecting good success of the action from Him° which is to be acknowledged the author and governor not only of this but of all else, I take my leave of you this month of February, 1588.

    account
    that is, God

Finis.

    1588, 1589, 1590

WILLIAM STRACHEY

In 1625 the Reverend Samuel Purchas (1577–1626) first published the "True Reportory" by William Strachey (1572–1621). Purchas included it in a huge set of travel narratives he had gathered and printed in the style of his predecessor, Richard Hakluyt (1553–1616), from whom—or from whose surviving papers—he probably received Strachey's text. Strachey's account is in the form of a letter to an "Excellent Lady" (who is unclear) dated 15 July 1610. It is autobiographical and tells the story of Strachey's 1609 voyage on the colonial ship *The Sea Venture*, intended to be a relief fleet for the Jamestown colony of Virginia; how he and his company survived a powerful hurricane by crash-landing on the islands of Bermuda; how they lived on the main island, constructing two small boats there, *Patience* and *Deliverance*, and overcoming potential mutinies; and how they finally made their way from the Bermudas to Virginia.

Of farming and merchant stock, Strachey's family was aggrandized during his life time when his father acquired a gentleman's coat of arms. Strachey seems at first to have supported himself from his father's, and then his wife's, estates: he went to Cambridge but did not complete a degree; he also studied law at Gray's Inn, but there is no record of his practicing. His interests seem to have been in literature and the theatre. Thomas Campion and John Donne were friends; and Strachey himself was a shareholder in the Blackfriars playhouse when the boy company, the Children of the Revels, performed there. His first publication, in 1605, was a poem in praise of Ben Jonson's unsuccessful play *Sejanus* (1603), with which it was printed. Struggling financially, in 1606 Strachey traveled to the Ottoman Empire's capital, Constantinople, as secretary to its ambassador—a post from which he was dismissed—then to Venice, where he was unable to find a job. Finally, in 1609, he purchased two shares in the Virginia Company with which he then traveled to Virginia, the story he tells in this letter. After his arrival in Virginia, Strachey was appointed secretary and recorder of the colony. He returned to England in 1611, where he wrote a long account of the Virginia colony and its prospects. Yet the Virginia Company found his *History of the Travel into Virginia Britania* too critical and refused to publish it. It is unclear whether he ever had another job; he died in poverty in 1621.

The letter, extracted below, seems intended to be a public rather than private account. It tactfully praises General Thomas Gates, who had been sent out as Virginia's governor-designate, and Admiral Sir George Somers, who was commander of the fleet, for their leadership after landing on the Bermudas. It also promotes the Bermudas' natural resources—plants, animals, and potentially merchantable qualities—making the case for settling on the uninhabited islands. The account's second half, not supplied here, is rather less full of praise for the state and management of the Virginia colony.

Strachey's letter seems to have circulated before printing; thus it is sometimes suggested that Shakespeare read it, and that it influenced *The Tempest*. Shakespeare could have heard what happened in the Bermudas without reading Strachey's account. News would have reached England in 1609 that *The Sea Venture* had not arrived in Virginia, and oral accounts from the survivors themselves would certainly have been circulating by 1610. But it is clear that around 1609 Shakespeare became interested in a story like this one: of a tempest that miraculously brings a ship of troubled people to a fertile, and haunting, island.

From A True Reportory . . . of the Wreck

A true reportory of the wreck and redemption of Sir THOMAS GATES, *Knight,*[1] *upon, and from the islands of the Bermudas; his coming to* Virginia, *and the estate° of that Colony then and after, under the government of the Lord* LA WARR,[2] *July* 15. 1610, *written by* WILLIAM STRACHEY, *Esquire*   °state

I

A most dreadful tempest (the manifold deaths whereof are here to the life° described); their wrack° on Bermuda, and the description of those islands   °with exact fidelity / °wreck

Excellent lady,[3] know that upon Friday late in the evening, we brake ground° out of the sound[4] of Plymouth, our whole fleet then consisting of seven good ships and two pinnaces[5] * * * on St. James his day, July 24, being   °heaved the anchor

---

1. Thomas Gates (fl? 1622), governor-designate and then governor of Jamestown, Virginia.
2. Thomas West, third Baron De La Warr (1577–1618), first governor of Jamestown, Virginia.
3. It is not clear to whom this is addressed.
4. Narrow stretch of water.
5. Small sailing vessels with two masts.

Monday (preparing for no less all the black night before), the clouds gathering thick upon us and the winds singing and whistling most unusually * * * A dreadful storm and hideous began to blow from out the north east, which swelling and roaring as it were by fits, some hours with more violence than others, at length did beat all light from heaven—which, like an hell of darkness, turned black upon us, so much the more fuller of horror, as in such cases horror and fear use° to overrun the troubled and overmastered senses of all, which (taken up with amazement) the ears lay so sensible⁶ to the terrible cries and murmurs of the winds, and distraction of our company, as who was° most armed and best prepared was not a little shaken. For surely (noble lady) as death comes not so sudden nor apparent, so he comes not so elvish° and painful (to men especially even then in health and perfect habitudes° of body) as at sea. * * *

    customarily

    even those who were

    troublesomely

    constitution

For four-and-twenty hours, the storm, in a restless tumult, had blown so exceedingly as we could not apprehend in our imaginations any possibility of greater violence, yet did we still find it not only more terrible, but more constant, fury added to fury, and one storm urging a second more outrageous than the former, whether it so wrought upon° our fears or indeed met with new forces. Sometimes strikes in our ship amongst women and passengers not used to such hurly° and discomforts made us look one upon the other with troubled hearts and panting bosoms, our clamors drowned in the winds and the winds in thunder. Prayers might well be in the heart and lips but drowned in the outcries of the officers. * * * There was not a moment in which the sudden splitting or instant oversetting of the ship was not expected.

    caused

    tumult

Howbeit° this was not all. It pleased God to bring a greater affliction yet upon us, for in the beginning of the storm we had received likewise a mighty leak. And the ship, in every joint almost, having spued out her oakum⁷ * * * was grown five foot suddenly deep with water above her ballast,⁸ and we almost drowned within, whilst we sat looking when° to perish from above. This, imparting no less terror than danger, ran through the whole ship with much fright and amazement, startled and turned the blood, and took down the braves° of the most hardy mariner of them all, insomuch as he that before happily felt not the sorrow of others, now began to sorrow for himself, when he saw such a pond of water so suddenly broken in, and which he knew could not (without present avoiding) but instantly sink him. * * * [T]here might be seen

    however

    expecting

    bravado

---

6. Perceptible through the senses.
7. The fibers used as caulking material for ships.
8. Heavy material, such as gravel, sand, metal, water, etc., placed in the hold of a ship to weigh it down in the water and prevent it from capsizing.

master, master's mate, boatswain, quartermaster, coopers, carpenters, and who not, with candles in their hands, creeping along the ribs, viewing the sides, searching every corner, and listening in every place if they could hear the water run. Many a weeping leak was this way found and hastily stopped, and at length one in the gunner room made up° with I know not how many pieces of beef; but all was to no purpose, the leak (if it were but one), which drunk in our greatest seas and took in our destruction fastest, could not then be found, nor ever was, by any labor, counsel, or search. * * *   *stoppered*

Our governor,[9] upon the Tuesday morning * * * had caused the whole company (about one hundred and forty, besides women), to be equally divided into three parts, and opening the ship in three places (under the forecastle, in the waist, and hard by the bittacle),[1] appointed each man where to attend * * * Then men might be seen to labor, I may well say, for life, and the better sort, even our governor and admiral themselves, not refusing their turn, and to spell° each the other, to give example to other.   *relieve* The common sort, stripped naked as men in galleys,[2] the easier both to hold out[3] and to shrink° from under the salt   *draw back* water which continually leaped in among them, kept their eyes waking and their thoughts and hands working, with tired bodies and wasted spirits, three days and four nights, destitute° of outward comfort and desperate of any   *devoid* deliverance, testifying how mutually willing they were yet by labor to keep each other from drowning, albeit each one drowned whilst he labored.

Once, so huge a sea brake upon the poop° and quarter   *stern* upon us as it covered our ship from stern to stem.[4] Like a garment or a vast cloud, it filled her brimful for a while within, from the hatches up to the spar deck.[5] This source or confluence of water was so violent as it rushed and carried the helmman from the helm and wrested the whipstaff° out of his hand. * * * Our governor was at this   *steering device* time below at the capstan,[6] both by his speech and authority heartening° every man unto his labor. It struck   *encouraging* him from the place where he sat and grovelled him[7] and all us about him on our faces, beating together with our breaths all thoughts from our bosoms else° than that we   *other* were now sinking.

* * * East and by South we steered away as much as we could to bear upright, which was no small carefulness

---

9. That is, General Thomas Gates, Virginia's governor-designate.
1. Binnacle—a box near the helm in which the compass is kept. "Forecastle": fore part of a ship. "Waist": middle part of the upper deck of a ship.
2. Low flat-built seagoing vessels with one deck, propelled by sails and oars. The rowers were mostly slaves or condemned criminals.
3. Maintain their positions.
4. Timber at the extremity of the vessel. "Quarter": upper part of a ship's side aft of the beam.
5. Light upper deck.
6. Mechanism for weighing the anchor.
7. Laid him prone on the ground.

nor pain to do, albeit we much unrigged our ship, threw overboard much luggage, many a trunk and chest (in which I suffered no mean° loss) and staved[8] many a butt of beer, hogsheads of oil, cider, wine, and vinegar, and heaved away all our ordnance° on the starboard side, and had now purposed to have cut down the main mast, the more to lighten her, for we were much spent° and our men so weary as° their strengths together failed them with their hearts, having travailed now from Tuesday till Friday morning, day and night, without either sleep or food; for the leakage taking up all the hold, we could neither come by beer nor fresh water; fire we could keep none in the cook-room to dress° any meat; and carefulness, grief, and our turn at the pump or bucket were sufficient to hold sleep from our eyes.

 * * * [I]t being now Friday, the fourth morning, it wanted little but[9] that there had been a general determination to have shut up hatches, and commending our sinful souls to God, committed the ship to the mercy of the sea. Surely that night we must have done it and that night had we then perished;[1] but see the goodness and sweet introduction of better hope, by our merciful God, given unto us. Sir George Somers,[2] when no man dreamed of such happiness, had discovered and cried land. * * * We had got her° within a mile under the southeast point of the land where we had somewhat smooth water. But having no hope to save her by coming to an anchor in the same, we were enforced to run her ashore, as near the land as we could, which brought us within three quarters of a mile of shore, and by the mercy of God unto us, making out our boats, we had ere° night brought all our men, women, and children, about the number of one hundred and fifty, safe into the island.

 We found it to be the dangerous and dreaded island, or rather islands, of the Bermuda, whereof let me give your ladyship a brief description before I proceed to my narration. And that, the rather, because they be so terrible to all that ever touched on them, and such tempests, thunders, and other fearful objects are seen and heard about them that they be called commonly "The Devil's Islands" and are feared and avoided of° all sea travelers alive above any other place in the world. Yet it pleased our merciful God to make even this hideous and hated place both the place of our safety and means of our deliverance.

 And hereby also I hope to deliver° the world from a foul and general error: it being counted° of most that they can be no habitation for men, but rather given over to

---

8. Broke up (a cask) into staves.
9. It would not have taken much for.
1. We would then have perished.

2. George Somers (fl. 1554–1610), English privateer and sea captain who colonized the Bermudas for Britain.

devils and wicked spirits; whereas indeed we find them now by experience to be as habitable and commodious as most countries of the same climate and situation, insomuch as if the entrance into them were as easy as the place itself is contenting,° it had long ere this been inhabited as well as other islands.

gives contentment

* * *

The soil of the whole island is one and the same, the mold dark, red, sandy, dry, and uncapable, I believe, of any of our commodities or fruits. Sir George Somers, in the beginning of August, squared out[3] a garden by the quarter[4]—the quarter being set down before a goodly bay upon which our governor did first leap ashore, and therefore called it, as aforesaid, "Gates his bay," which opened into the east, and into which the sea did ebb and flow according to their tides—and sowed muskmelons,° peas, onions, radish, lettuce, and many English seeds and kitchen herbs. All which, in some ten days, did appear above ground, but whether by the small birds, of which there be many kinds, or by flies (worms I never saw any, nor any venomous thing as toad or snake or any creeping beast hurtful, only some spiders which, as many affirm, are signs of great store of gold—but they were long- and slender-leg spiders, and whether venomous or no I know not; I believe not, since we should still find them amongst our linen in our chests, and drinking cans; but we never received any danger from them: * * *) whether, I say, hindered by these, or by the condition or vice of the soil, they came to no proof,[5] nor thrived. * * *

nutmeg melons

Likewise there grow great store of palm trees, * * * in the uppermost part thereof, and in the top, grow leaves about the head of it (the most inmost part whereof they call "palmetto," and it is the heart and pith of the same trunk, so white and thin as it will peel off into pleats° as smooth and delicate as white satin into twenty folds, in which a man may write as in paper, where they spread and fall downward about the tree like an overblown rose, or saffron flower not early gathered). So broad are the leaves as an "Italian umbrello":[6] a man may well defend his whole body under one of them from the greatest storm rain that falls. For they being stiff and smooth, as if so many flags were knit together, the rain easily slideth off. * * * With these leaves we thatched our cabins, and roasting the palmetto or soft top thereof, they had a taste like fried melons, and being sod° they eat like cabbages, but not so offensively thankful to the stomach. Many an

folds

boiled

3. Marked out into squares.
4. A measurement (one fourth of an ell); or nautical quarter point by compass or other instrument.
5. Did not come to fulfillment.
6. Parasol that shades one from the sun; the predecessor of the umbrella.

ancient burgher was therefore heaved at and fell not for his place but for his head. For our common people, whose bellies never had ears, made it no breach of charity in their hot bloods and tall stomachs to murder thousands of them.[7]

* * *

Other kinds of high and sweet-smelling woods there be, and divers colors, black, yellow, and red, and one which bears a round blue berry, much eaten by our own people, of a styptic° quality and rough taste on the tongue, like a sloe to stay or bind the flux,[8] which the often eating of the luscious palm berry would bring them into, for the nature of sweet things is to cleanse and dissolve. harsh and raw

A kind of pea[r] of the bigness and shape of a Katherine pear we found growing upon the rocks, full of many sharp subtle pricks (as a thistle) which we therefore called "the prickle pear," the outside green, but being opened of a deep murrey,° full of juice like a mulberry, and just of the same substance and taste; we both ate them raw and baked. reddish purple color

Sure it is that there are no rivers nor running springs of fresh water to be found upon any of them. When we came first we digged and found certain gushings and soft bubblings, which being either in bottoms or on the side of hanging ground were only fed with rain water, which nevertheless soon sinketh into the earth and vanisheth away * * * howbeit some low bottoms (which the continual descent from the hills filled full, and in those flats could have no passage away) we found to continue° as fishing ponds, or standing pools, continually summer and winter full of fresh water. maintain

The shore and bays round about when we landed first afforded great store of fish, and that of divers kinds, and good; but it should seem that our fires, which we maintained on the shore's side, drave° them from us, so as we were in some want until we had made a flat bottom gondal° of cedar with which we put off° farther into the sea, and then daily hooked great store of many kinds, as excellent angelfish, salmon, peal,° bonitos, stingray, cavalli,° snappers, hogfish, sharks, dogfish, pilchards, mullets, and rockfish, of which be divers kinds. And of these our governor dried and salted and, barreling them up, brought to sea five hundred. For he had procured salt to be made with some brine, which happily was preserved, and once having made a little quantity, he kept three or four pots boiling, and two or three men attending nothing else in an house (some little distance from his bay) set up on purpose for the same work. drove
gondola / launched
sea trout
crevalle jack

---

7. A burgher is a citizen. In this metaphor the trees are being described as old men murdered for their heads.

8. Stop or hinder the flow of dysentery.

* * * A kind of web-footed fowl there is, of the bigness of an English green plover, or seamew,° which all the summer we saw not, and in the darkest nights of November and December (for in the night they only feed) they would come forth, * * * I have been at the taking of three hundred in an hour, and we might have laden° our boats. Our men found a pretty way to take them, which was by standing on the rocks or sands by the seaside, and hollowing,° laughing, and making the strangest outcry that possibly they could, with the noise whereof the birds would come flocking to that place, and settle upon the very arms and head of him that so cried, and still creep nearer and nearer, answering the noise themselves; by which our men would weigh them with their hand, and which weighed heaviest they took for the best and let the others alone, and so our men would take twenty dozen in two hours of the chiefest of them;° and they were a good and well-relished° fowl, fat and full as a partridge. In January we had great store of their eggs, which are as great as an hen's egg, and so fashioned° and white-shelled, and have no difference in yolk nor white from an hen's egg. There are thousands of these birds, and two or three islands full of their burrows, whither at any time (in two hours' warning) we could send our cockboat° and bring home as many as would serve the whole company; which birds for their blindness (for they see weakly in the day) and for their cry and hooting we called the "sea owl"; they will bite cruelly with their crooked bills.

 We had knowledge that there were wild hogs upon the island, at first by our own swine preserved from the wrack° and brought to shore, for they straying into the woods, an huge wild boar followed down to our quarter, which at night was watched and taken * * * Our people would go a-hunting with our ship dog, and sometimes bring home thirty, sometimes fifty, boars, sows, and pigs in a week alive; for the dog would fasten on them and hold, whilst the huntsmen made in: and there be thousands of them in the islands, and at that time of the year, in August, September, October, and November, they were well fed with berries that dropped from the cedars and the palms, and in our quarter we made sties for them, and gathering of these berries served them twice a day, by which means we kept them in good plight° * * * But in February when the palm berries began to be scant or dry, * * * the tortoises came in again, of which we daily both turned up great store, finding them on land, as also, sculling after them in our boat, stroke° them with an iron goad,⁹ and

Marginal glosses: gull; loaded; calling out; main ones; appetizing; shaped; small, light boat; wreck; condition; struck

---

9. Rod with a sharpened point.

sod,° baked, and roasted them. The tortoise is reasonable *boiled*
toothsome° (some say) wholesome meat. I am sure our *palatable*
company liked the meat of them very well, and one tortoise would go further amongst them than three hogs.
One turtle (for so we called them) feasted well a dozen
messes,° appointing six to every mess. It is such a kind of *courses or meals*
meat, as a man can neither absolutely call fish nor flesh,
keeping mostwhat° in the water, and feeding upon sea- *almost all*
grass like a heifer, in the bottom of the coves and bays,
and laying their eggs (of which we should find five hundred at a time in the opening of a she-turtle) in the sand
by the shore side. * * *

II

Actions and occurrents whiles they continued in the islands;
Ravens sent for Virginia; *Divers mutinies*; PAINE *executed:*
two pinnaces built.

So soon as we were a little settled after our landing, with
all the conveniency we might, and as the place and our
many wants would give us leave, we made up our long-
boat[1] (as your ladyship hath heard) in fashion of a pinnace, fitting her with a little deck, made of the hatches of
our ruined ship, so close° that no water could go in her, *tight*
gave her sails and oars, and intreating with our master's
mate Henry Ravens (who was supposed° a sufficient pilot), *thought*
we found him easily won to make over therewith,[2] as a
barque of aviso° for Virginia, * * * promising if he lived *dispatch vessel*
and arrived safe there, to return unto us the next new
moon with the pinnace belonging to the colony there. * * *
　* * * Sir George Somers coasted the islands and drew
the former plat° of them, and daily fished and hunted for *earlier map*
our whole company, until the seven-and-twentieth of
November, when then well perceiving that we were not
likely to hear from Virginia and conceiving how the pinnace which Richard Frobisher was a-building would
not be of burthen° sufficient to transport all our men *carrying capacity*
from thence into Virginia (especially considering the
season of the year wherein we were likely to put off),° *leave*
he consulted with our governor that if he might have two
carpenters (for we had four, such as they were) and
twenty men over with him into the main island, he would
quickly frame up another little bark° to second ours, for *small ship*
the better fitting and convenience of our people. Our
governor, with many thanks * * *, made ready for him all
such tools and instruments as our own use required not.
And for him were drawn forth twenty of the ablest and

1. Large, open ship's boat.　　　2. Transform with that.

stoutest° of the company and the best of our men, to hew and square timber, when himself then, with daily pains and labor, wrought upon a small vessel, which was soon ready as ours—at which we leave him a while busied, and return to ourselves.

* * * Some dangerous and secret discontents nourished amongst us had like to have been the parents of bloody issues and mischiefs. They began first in the seamen, who in time had fastened unto them (by false baits) many of our landmen likewise * * * A conspiracy was discovered, of which six were found principals, who had promised each unto the other not to set their hands to any travail or endeavor which might expedite or forward this pinnace. And each of these had severally° (according to appointment) sought his opportunity to draw° the smith, and one of our carpenters, Nicholas Bennet (who made much profession of° scripture, a mutinous and dissembling imposter), the captain and one of the chief persuaders of others—who afterwards brake from the society of the colony, and like outlaws retired into the woods to make a settlement and habitation there—on their party, with whom they purposed° to leave our quarter, and possess another island by themselves. But this happily° found out, they were condemned to the same punishment which they would have chosen (but without smith or carpenter) and to an island far by itself they were carried and there left. * * * But soon they missed comfort * * * insomuch as many humble petitions were sent unto our governor, fraught° full of their seeming sorrow and repentance and earnest vows to redeem the former trespass with example of duties in them all to the common cause and general business. Upon which our governor (not easy to admit° any accusation and hard to remit° an offence, but at all times sorry in the punishment of him in whom may appear either shame or contrition) was easily content to reacknowledge them again.

Yet could not this be any warning to others, who more subtly began to shake the foundation of our quiet safety. * * * They * * * purposed to have made a surprise of° the storehouse and to have forced from thence what was therein, either of meal, cloth, cables, arms, sails, oars or what else it pleased God that we had recovered from the wrack° and was to serve our general necessity and use, either for the relief of us, while we stayed here, or for the carrying of us from this place again when our pinnace should have been furnished.

But * * * there were some of the association who, not strong enough fortified in their own conceits,° break from the plot itself, and (before the time was ripe for the execution thereof) discovered° the whole order, and every

strongest

separately
influence
laid great claim to

intended
by chance

supplied

concede
forgive

made an assault on

wreck

opinions

revealed

agent and actor thereof * * * A gentleman amongst them, one Henry Paine, the thirteenth of March, full of mischief, and every hour preparing something or other, stealing swords, adzes,° axes, hatchets, saws, augers,[3] planes, mallets, etc. to make good his own bad end, * * * did not only give his said commander evil language, but struck at him, doubled his blows, and when he was not suffered to close with[4] him, went off° the guard, scoffing at the double diligence and attendance of the watch° appointed by the governor for much purpose, as he said; upon which, the watch telling him if the governor should understand of this his insolency, it might turn him to much blame, and happily° be as much as his life were worth, the said Paine replied with a settled° and bitter violence and in such unreverent terms as I should offend the modest ear too much to express it in his own phrase, but the contents were how that the governor had no authority of that quality to justify upon anyone (how mean soever in the colony) an action of that nature, and therefore let the governor, said he, kiss etc.[5] Which words being with the omitted additions brought the next day unto every common and public discourse, at length° they were delivered over to the governor, who * * * calling the said Paine before him, * * * condemned him to be instantly hanged; and the ladder being ready, after he had made many confessions, he earnestly desired, being a gentleman, that he might be shot to death; and towards the evening he had his desire, the sun and his life setting together.

 But for the other * * * they sent an audacious and formal petition to our governor subscribed with all their names and seals, not only intreating him that they might stay here, but (with great art) importuned° him, that he would perform° other conditions with them * * * as, namely, to furnish each of them with two suits of apparel, and contribute meal° rateably° for one whole year, so much among them, as they had weekly now, which was one pound and an half a week (for such had been our proportion for nine months). Our governor answered this their petition, writing to Sir George Somers * * * to do his best to give this revolted° company (if he could send unto them) the consideration of these particulars and so work with them, if he might, that by fair means (the mutiny reconciled) they would at length survey their own errors * * * In which good office Sir George Somers did so nobly work, and heartily labor, as he brought most of them in, and indeed all but Christopher Carter and Robert Waters, who * * * grew so cautelous° and wary for

wood axes

reproached
watchmen

perhaps
fixed

eventually

begged
fulfill
flour / proportionately

rebellious

deceitful

---

3. Devices for boring holes in wood.
4. Engage in hand-to-hand fighting with.
5. Presumably the omitted addition is "my arse," in which case, this is one of the earliest recorded uses of the phrase.

their own ill as, at our coming away, we were fain to leave them behind. * * *

During our time of abode upon these islands, we had daily every Sunday two sermons, preached by our Minister; besides, every morning and evening, at the ringing of a bell, we repaired all° to public prayer, at what time the names of our whole company were called by bill, and such as were wanting° were duly punished.

all traveled

absent

The contents, for the most part, of all our preacher's sermons, were especially of thankfulness and unity, etc.

It pleased God also to give us opportunity to perform all the other offices and rites of our Christian profession in this island: as marriage, for the six-and-twentieth of November we had one of Sir George Somers his men, his cook named Thomas Powell, who married a maidservant of one Mistress Horton, whose name was Elizabeth Persons; and upon Christmas Eve, as also once before, the first of October, our minister preached a godly sermon, which being ended he celebrated a communion at the partaking whereof our governor was and the greatest part of our company; and the eleventh of February we had the child of one John Rolf christened, a daughter, to which Captain Newport and myself were witnesses and the aforesaid Mistress Horton and we named it Bermuda; as also, the five and twentieth of March, the wife of one Edward Eason, being delivered the week before of a boy, had him then christened, to which Captain Newport and myself and Master James Swift were godfathers, and we named it Bermudas.

Likewise, we buried five of our company: Jeffery Briars, Richard Lewis, William Hitchman, and my Goddaughter Bermuda Rolf, and one untimely, Edward Samuel, a sailor, being villainously killed by the foresaid Robert Waters (a sailor likewise) with a shovel, who strake him therewith° under the list[6] of the ear, for which he was apprehended and appointed to be hanged the next day (the fact being done in the twilight), but being bound fast to a tree all night, with many ropes and a guard of five or six to attend him, his fellow sailors, watching the advantage° of the sentinels sleeping, in despite and disdain that justice should be showed upon a sailor, and that one of their crew should be an example to others—not taking into consideration the unmanliness of the murther nor the horror of the sin—they cut his bands, and conveyed him into the woods, where they fed him nightly and closely, who afterward by the mediation of Sir George Somers, upon many conditions, had his trial respited° by our governor.

with it

awaiting the chance

reprieved

---

6. List = lobe. The original word, "lift," is a typo.

We had brought our pinnace so forward by this time as, the eight-and-twentieth of August, we having laid her keel, the six-and-twentieth of February we now began to caulk.[7] Old cables we had preserved unto us, which afforded oakum enough; and one barrel of pitch, and another of tar we likewise saved, which served our use some little way upon the bilge. We breamed her[8] otherwise with lime made of whelk shells and an hard white stone which we burned in a kiln, slaked° with fresh water and tempered with tortoises' oil. * * * The most part of her timber was cedar, which we found to be bad for shipping, for that it is wondrous false inward, and besides it is so spalt or brickle° that it will make no good planks. Her beams were all oak of our ruined ship, and some planks in her bow of oak, and the rest as is aforesaid. When she began to swim° (upon her launching) our governor called her "The Deliverance," and she might be some eighty tons of burthen.

    wetted

    brittle

    float

Before we quitted our old quarter and dislodged° to the fresh water with our pinnace, our governor set up in Sir George Somers' garden a fair mnemosynon° in figure of a cross made of some of the timber of our ruined ship, which was screwed in with strong and great trunnels[9] to a mighty cedar which grew in the midst of the said garden and whose top and upper branches he caused to be lopped that the violence of the wind and weather might have the less power over her.

    moved

    monument

In the midst of the cross, our governor fastened the picture of His Majesty in a piece of silver of twelve pence, and on each side of the cross he set an inscription graven° in copper in the Latin and English to this purpose:

    engraved

> In memory of our great deliverance both from a mighty storm and leak, we have set up this to the honor of God. It is the spoil° of an English ship (of three hundred ton) called the "Sea Venture," bound with seven ships more (from which the storm divided us) to Virginia, or Nova Britania, in America. In it were two knights, Sir Thomas Gates, Knight, Governor of the English Forces and Colony there; and Sir George Somers, Knight, Admiral of the Seas. Her captain was Christopher Newport; passengers and mariners she had beside (which came all safe to land) one hundred and fifty. We were forced to run her ashore, by reason of her leak, under a point that bore southeast from the northern point of the island, which we discovered first the eight-and-twentieth of July, 1609.

    remains

---

7. Stop up the crevices with melted pitch.
8. Cleared her of rubbish.
9. Cylindrical wooden pins.

The Sixteenth Century
1485–1603

St. George and the Dragon (London version), Paolo Uccello, ca. 1455–60

A depiction by the Florentine artist Uccello of the legend that was to inspire Edmund Spenser in Book 1 of *The Faerie Queene*. Already held on a leash by the elegant lady—as if the struggle's outcome were not in doubt—the dragon submits to the knight's lance (thrust through the nose in a gesture that better recalls the domestication of cattle than the thwarting of an enemy). The desolate cave is strangely conjoined with the formal garden and the lady's elegant court dress: the story is imagined as located at once in the wilderness and at the very center of civilization.

Thomas More, Hans Holbein, 1527

Painted on the eve of More's great conflict with Henry VIII over the validity of the king's marriage to Catherine of Aragon, Holbein's portrait emphasizes both the chancellor's importance and his strength of character. More wears the heavy gold chain and rich dress of high office, which he had satirized a decade earlier in *Utopia*. In all probability, if early biographies of More can be believed, he also wears a hair shirt under the velvet and fur, a hidden, painful reminder of the vulnerable flesh that he secretly mortified.

Edward VI and the Pope: An Allegory of the English Reformation, English school, ca. 1568–71

In this detail from a work of Protestant propaganda, the dying Henry VIII points to his young son and heir, Prince Edward, who is seated on a chair of state and is now Supreme Head of the Church of England. An open book at Edward's feet is inscribed with a line from the New Testament's First Epistle of Peter: "The word of the Lord endureth forever." The book, symbolizing the power of vernacular Bible translation, crushes the pope, to whose tiara are attached ribbons inscribed "Idolatry" and "Superstition." The attack on the papacy is underscored by the words "Feigned holiness," and the inscription across the pope's chest, "All flesh is grass," makes the point that the Catholic pontiff is an ordinary, corruptible mortal. To the left two monks flee the pope's downfall. Several places in the painting were intended for further inscriptions, but for unknown reasons these were never completed.

The Wife and Daughter of a Chief,
John White, 1585

Accompanying Thomas Hariot's *Brief and True Report of the New-found Land of Virginia,* John White's watercolors chronicle Algonquin life as seen by the English voyagers. Here, a girl "of the age of 8 or 10 yeares" carries a European doll, dressed in full Elizabethan costume, that she has clearly been given as a gift by the strange visitors. The presentation of small gifts was a regular English practice, frequently alternating with murderous violence. White's drawing manages to convey both the exoticism and the dignity that Hariot and others perceived in the American natives.

Henry Percy, 9th Earl of Northumberland, Nicholas Hilliard, ca. 1590–95

Henry Percy's interests in natural science, mathematics, astronomy, alchemy, and philosophy earned him the nickname "The Wizard Earl." One of the wealthiest aristocrats in England, Percy became the patron of a remarkable group of scientists and intellectuals. He often joined them in conducting experiments and making astronomical observations, but in this elegant miniature, he is alone, reclining in a formal garden overlooking a distant landscape. His slightly disheveled dress and pose suggest the melancholy temperament that was highly regarded in this period. The emblematic object hanging in the tree—a globe or cannon ball balanced by a feather—has long tantalized interpreters, as has the significance of the word *tanti* (in Latin, "so much"; in Italian, "so many"). In 1605, suspected of conspiracy against King James, Percy was imprisoned in the Tower of London. During his imprisonment, which lasted for sixteen years, he continued his scientific experiments.

C 3

Portrait of Abd al-Wahid bin Masoud bin Muhammad al-Annuri, artist unknown, 1600

In 1600 the forty-two-year-old al-Annuri arrived in London as the ambassador of the Moroccan ruler Mulay Ahmed al-Mansur with a proposal for a military alliance with England against Spain. The imposing appearance of the ambassador made a sensation in London and may have influenced Shakespeare's conception of what the Moor Othello looked like.

Elizabethan Gloves, London, ca. 1600

"See how she leans her cheek upon her hand," Romeo sighs, as he looks up at Juliet on her balcony; "O, that I were a glove upon that hand / That I might touch that cheek!" It was fashionable among the Elizabethan elite to wear fancy gloves, often perfumed with sweet-smelling oils. These particularly elaborate leather gloves, decorated with satin, silk, and seed pearls, were in all likelihood a gift, most probably a love-token. Their imagery includes weeping eyes, to symbolize love-sickness, and pansies, also known at the time as "love-in-idleness" or "heartsease."

The "Chandos" Portrait of William Shakespeare, anonymous, date unknown

The formal portrait of the playwright that appears in the First Folio edition of his works depicts him stiffly posed in a brocade jacket and a heavily starched collar. Here, in a portrait named after its owner, the Duke of Chandos, Shakespeare is presented less formally and more as his friends and colleagues may have known him. The artist is unknown, but some speculate that it may have been Shakespeare's fellow actor Richard Burbage.

A Young Man, Nicholas Hilliard, ca. 1600

This tiny painting from a playing card approximately two inches square represents the "other side" of Elizabethan love poetry: passion replaces languor. The image of the lover tormented by the "fire" of his mistress's eyes or the hellish inner torment of desire was common. Though Sidney's Astrophil lives "in blackest winter night," he feels "the flames of hottest summer day" (p. 550), while even disillusioned lovers in Shakespeare's sonnets do not know how "To shun the heaven that leads men to this hell" (p. 637). The locket held by the young man presumably contains another miniature: a portrait of the beloved.

Elizabeth I in Procession, attributed to Robert Peake, ca. 1600

Carried on a litter like an image of the Virgin in the religious processions of previous centuries, the gorgeously arrayed Queen Elizabeth is shown here as a time-defying icon of purity and power. When the painting was executed, the queen was sixty-seven years old. Until the end of her life, she continued her custom of going on "Progresses" through the realm: surrounded by her courtiers and ladies in waiting, she would venture forth to show herself to her people, many of whom nearly bankrupted themselves to entertain her in style.

The Drake Jewel, Nicholas Hilliard, ca. 1580s

Elizabeth I gave this remarkable jewel to Sir Francis Drake, the Elizabethan naval hero and explorer, sometime before 1591. (He is wearing it in a portrait painted in that year.) The profile head of an African man superimposed on that of a European woman makes ingenious use of the brown and white bands of the sardonyx (a variety of quartz). The Black man is shown wearing a *paludamentum*, the mantle worn by Roman emperors and generals, and Elizabeth may have selected it to show her imperial ambitions. The contrast between "black" and "fair" was central to the poetry of her period, with Elizabeth's whiteness, often accentuated through makeup, serving as an ideal. See, for example, Sidney's *Astrophil and Stella*, sonnet 3; *Othello*; and Lovelace's "A Black Patch on Lucasta's Face."

Sir Walter Ralegh (Raleigh), unknown English artist, 1588

This portrait of the soldier, courtier, politician, and writer was painted in the year of the attack by the Spanish Armada. Ralegh presents himself as the queen's devoted servant, wearing her colors of black and white and her emblem (the pearl, symbol of virginity) in his left ear. The pearls on Ralegh's sable-trimmed cloak form the rays of a "sun in splendor," a heraldic divide also found in portraits of the queen. In the top left-hand corner, over the motto "Amor et Virtute" ("By love and virtue") is a crescent moon, the device of Elizabeth as the moon goddess Cynthia, and the subject of a poem by Ralegh himself.

Sir Anthony Mildmay, Knight of Apthorpe, Northamptonshire, Nicholas Hilliard, ca. 1590–93

The Elizabethan upper classes indulged in unrestrained, utterly shameless exhibitions of sartorial costliness and splendor. Anthony Mildmay was a gentleman of no particular distinction, military or otherwise, but he presents himself here in the midst of dressing (or undressing) either for battle or, more likely, for one of the ceremonial combats known as jousts. The portrait enables him to show off both his lavish suit of armor and his legs. His dog seems suitably impressed.

The Early Seventeenth Century
1603–1660

The Expulsion from Paradise, Masaccio, ca. 1427–28

This striking fresco shows an agonized Adam and Eve being driven from Eden by a sword-wielding angel. Adam is so overcome he buries his face in his hands; Eve's face is a mask of despair. They do not touch: each seems imprisoned in his or her own pain. While Adam and Eve experience great emotional torment in Books 9 and 10 of *Paradise Lost*, Milton's representation of their expulsion from Paradise at the end of Book 12 is notably different from Masaccio's (see p. 1659).

John Donne, anonymous, ca. 1595

This portrait presents Donne in the guise of a melancholy lover fond of self-display; the signs are his broad-brimmed black hat, soulful eyes, sensual lips, delicate hands, and untied but expensive lace collar. Parts of Donne's *Songs and Sonnets* (pp. 886–902) date from this period. Melancholy was supposedly caused by an excess of black bile and was often associated with scholarly and artistic temperaments. Robert Burton's massive and extremely popular *Anatomy of Melancholy* (1621) saw it as a near universal attribute of the period. Famous literary characters with melancholic temperaments include Hamlet, *Twelfth Night*'s Duke Orsino, *As You Like It*'s Jacques, and Milton's Il Penseroso (p. 1395).

Lady Sidney and Six of Her Children, Marcus Gheeraerts the Younger, ca. 1596

This portrait of Barbara (Gamage) Sidney, wife of Sir Robert Sidney of Penshurst, provides an insight into domestic relations in the period, as well as an illuminating comment on Ben Jonson's poem "To Penshurst" (p. 1051). Robert Sidney (brother of Sir Philip Sidney) is absent, serving as governor of the English stronghold in Flushing. Lady Sidney is portrayed as a fruitful, fostering mother. Her hands rest on her two sons—both still in skirts, though the heir wears a sword; the four daughters are arranged in two pairs, the elder of each pair imitating her mother's nurturing gesture. The eldest daughter will become Lady Mary Wroth, author of *Urania* and the sonnet sequence *Pamphilia to Amphilanthus* (p. 1072).

Lucy, Countess of Bedford, as a Masquer, attributed to John de Critz, ca. 1606

Lucy (Harington) Russell, Countess of Bedford, prominent courtier, favorite of Queen Anna, patron of Donne and Jonson, and frequent planner of and participant in court masques, is shown in masquing costume for the wedding masque *Hymenaei* (1606), by Ben Jonson and Inigo Jones. Jonson describes the masquing ladies as "attired richly and alike in the most celestial colors" associated with the rainbow, with elaborate headdresses and shoes, "all full of splendor, sovereignty, and riches." Their masque dances were "fully of subtlety and device."

"A Daughter of Niger" and "Torchbearer of Oceania," Inigo Jones, ca. 1605

Inigo Jones's career in theatrical design for the court began with his scenic and costume designs for Ben Jonson's *The Masque of Blackness* (1605) (pp. 1041–48). The four hundred preparatory drawings Jones made for the production include these watercolor renderings of "A Daughter of Niger" and the "Torchbearer of Oceania." Images of these and other masque costumes influenced Shakespeare's *Tempest*, as well as John Smith's and Richard Ligon's views of women "performers" in Virginia and the Cape Verde Islands, respectively. The blackface makeup in *The Masque of Blackness* was the subject of discussion among contemporaries. (For another discussion of makeup, see Jonson's "Fine Lady Would-be," p. 1049.) Cavendish's prose utopia *The Blazing World* (1666) features people with a wide range of skin colors, "Complexions; not white, black, tawny, olive- or ash-colored," but azure, deep purple, "grass-green," scarlet, and orange (p. 1366).

Henry, Prince of Wales with Robert Devereux, 3rd Earl of Essex in the Hunting Field, Robert Peake, ca. 1605

Henry, Prince of Wales, the eldest son of James I and Anna of Denmark, is shown here as a man of action. He is attended by Robert Devereux, third Earl of Essex, the son of Elizabeth I's disgraced favorite. Even as the painting celebrates the boys' likeness, subtle variations in their clothing indicate the differences in their social status. The painting represents the idealized male friendship we see celebrated in poems such as Donne's verse letter to Henry Wotton (p. 906) and Jonson's Cary-Morison ode (p. 1057).

Anna of Denmark, and a Groom, Paul Van Somer, 1617

Anna of Denmark a princess and member of the Oldenburg dynasty, married James VI, king of Scotland and the future king of England, in 1589. Here we see her in full power: dressed for the hunt and standing in front of Oatlands Palace and the gate she had commissioned from Inigo Jones. The unidentified Black groom holding the queen's horse wears the scarlet and gold livery of the House of Oldenburg, reminding viewers of the queen's political connections.

Cookmaid with Still Life of Vegetables and Fruit, Nathaniel Bacon, ca. 1620–25

An accomplished English amateur painter, Bacon was related to the writer Sir Francis Bacon, and his wife was one of Queen Anna's ladies of the bedchamber. Netherlandish influences are evident in this remarkable painting. The eroticism of the painting is obvious; the ripe melons surrounding the cookmaid bear a marked resemblance to her voluptuous bosom. According to a letter dated to June 1626, Bacon was growing melons in his estate in East Anglia. Poetic blazons often compare women and their body parts to food; see, for example, Herrick's "Upon the Nipples of Julia's Breast" (p. 126). But this painting resonates most powerfully with the image of young women bearing an "emblem of themselves in plum, or pear" in Jonson's "To Penshurst" (p. 1054) and with Marvell's "The Garden" (p. 1281), in which the speaker, overwhelmed with the erotic rush of nature's plenty, "stumbl[es] on melons" and falls "on grass."

"*Apollo and Diana*" or "*The Liberal Arts Presented to King Charles and Queen Henrietta Maria*," Gerrit van Honthorst, 1628

George Villiers, the Duke of Buckingham, who plays a starring role in this painting, was assassinated in August 1628, probably while it was still a work in progress. The painting represents Buckingham as Mercury leading the seven Liberal Arts out of a dark cave in which they have been languishing, and presenting them to Charles I (as Apollo, god of art and learning) and Henrietta Maria (as Diana, Apollo's sister, and goddess of virginity), while winged cherubs distribute the rewards of royal (or divine) patronage.

Charles I on Horseback, Sir Anthony Van Dyck, 1637–38

One of Charles I's court painters, knighted and pensioned by the king, Van Dyck produced several portraits of the royal family and their circle at court. This magnificent equestrian portrait of the king in armor presents him as hero and warrior, in a pose that looks back to portraits and statues of Roman emperors on horseback. It was painted to be hung at the end of the Long Gallery in St. James Palace.

Oliver Cromwell, Robert Walker, ca. 1649

By the time of the 1649 execution of King Charles I, Cromwell was the foremost general in the New Model army. His harsh campaign in Ireland (1649–50), marked by massacres of the native Irish, is celebrated in poems by Milton and (more ambivalently) Marvell (p. 1280). Upon the Restoration of the monarchy, Cromwell's body was disinterred from Westminster Abbey and his head was placed upon a pole above Westminster Hall. Robert Walker painted portraits of the major parliamentarian figures, including paired portraits of Lucy and John Hutchinson (see p. 1240 in this volume). A comparison with Van Dyck's portrait of Charles I on horseback (above) reveals both Walker's indebtedness to and differences from the court painter.

JOHN SMITH

After years spent as a soldier and an adventurer abroad, including being taken captive in war and sold into slavery under the Turks, Captain John Smith (1580–1631) sailed on England's first fleet to Virginia in 1607. Smith helped to establish England's first permanent settlement in North America, "Jamestown," in the territory that the native Algonquins called Tsenacommacah ("densely inhabited land"). The colony was plagued with difficulties from the beginning, and Smith's published accounts of the venture, culminating in *The General History of Virginia, New England, and the Summer Isles* (1624), defended and promoted England's colonies in North America, as well as his own extraordinary skills. (In addition to serving as the de facto governor of Jamestown until he was replaced by Christopher Newport—the captain of the ship wrecked in the Bermudas discussed in William Strachey's account—Smith served as New England's first admiral.) *The General History* records Smith's challenges as governor of the emerging colony, and his imprisonment by and negotiations with the powerful chieftan Powhatan and Powhatan's daughter, Pocahontas. Smith credits Pocahontas with saving his life, as well as that of the colony. The selection below offers an account of Pocahontas's role in the 1616 Powhatan embassy to England, which assured her place in colonial legend—as well as her death. While we do not have direct access to the Algonquins' views of the colonists, we can glimpse in Smith's reported first-person accounts of Pocahontas's and Powhatan's speeches traces of their criticism of and resistance to the colonists, as well as their skills as political leaders and negotiators.

Portrait of Matoaka or Rebecca, better known as Pocahontas, made by the royal engraver Simon van de Passe during Pocahontas's 1616 trip to England.

From The General History of Virginia, New England, and the Summer Isles

During this time, the Lady Rebecca,[1] alias Pocahontas, daughter to Powhatan, by the diligent care of Master John Rolf her husband and his friends, was taught to speak such English as might well be understood, well instructed in Christianity, and was become very formal and civil after our English manner; she had also by him a child which she loved most dearly, and the Treasurer and Company[2] took order both for the maintenance of her and it, besides there were divers° persons of great rank and quality had been very kind to her; and before she arrived at London, Captain Smith, to deserve° her former courtesies, made her qualities known to the Queen's most excellent Majesty and her Court, and writ a little book to this effect to the Queen, an abstract whereof followeth.

various, several

requite

   To the most high and virtuous Princess Queen Anne of Great Britain.

   Most admired Queen,

   The love I bear my God, my King, and Country hath so oft emboldened me in the worst of extreme dangers, that now honesty doth constrain me presume thus far beyond myself to present your Majesty this short discourse: if ingratitude be a deadly poison to all honest virtues, I must be guilty of that crime if I should omit any means to be thankful.
   So it is that some ten years ago being in Virginia, and taken prisoner by the power of Powhatan, their chief king, I received from this great savage[3] exceeding great courtesy, especially from his son Nantaquaus, the most manliest, comeliest, boldest spirit I ever saw in a savage, and his sister Pocahontas, the king's most dear and well-beloved daughter, being but a child of twelve or thirteen years of age, whose compassionate pitiful heart of° my desperate estate gave me much cause to respect her. I being the first Christian this proud King and his grim attendants ever saw, and thus enthralled in their barbarous power, I

sympathy for

---

1. Pocahontas was given the English name "Rebecca" when she was baptized.
2. The Virginia Company was an English trading company chartered by King James I on April 10, 1606, with the object of colonizing the eastern coast of America. The coast was named Virginia, after Elizabeth I, and it stretched from present-day Maine to the Carolinas. John Smith was the treasurer in 1616, when the party set forth for England.
3. The term Smith uses for Native Americans throughout his *History* is "Salvage." Unlike its near-synomyn, "savage," the Latin root of "salvage," *salve*, or save, hints at the Algonquins' role in saving the colonists from certain death.

cannot say I felt the least occasion of want° that was in | need
the power of those my mortal foes to prevent, notwithstanding all their threats. After some weeks fatting° | growing fat
among those savage courtiers, at the minute of my execution, she hazarded the beating out of her own brains to save mine, and not only that, but so prevailed with her father, that I was safely conducted to Jamestown,[4] where I found about eight and thirty miserable poor and sick creatures to keep possession of all those large territories of Virginia. Such was the weakness of this poor Commonwealth, as had the savages not fed us, we had directly starved.

And this relief, most gracious Queen, was commonly brought us by this Lady Pocahontas, notwithstanding all these passages when inconstant Fortune turned our peace to war, this tender virgin would still not spare to dare to visit us, and by her our jars° have been oft appeased, and | disagreements
our wants still supplied; were it the policy of her father thus to employ her, or the ordinance of God thus to make her his instrument, or her extraordinary affection to our nation, I know not, but of this I am sure: when her father with the utmost of his policy and power sought to surprise me, having but eighteen with me, the dark night could not affright her from coming through the irksome woods, and with watered eyes gave me intelligence, with her best advice to escape his fury; which had he known, he had surely slain her. Jamestown with her wild train° | attendants
she as freely frequented as her father's habitation; and during the time of two or three years, she next under God was still the instrument to preserve this colony from death, famine, and utter confusion, which if in those times had once been dissolved, Virginia might have lain as it was at our first arrival to this day. Since then, this business having been turned and varied by many accidents from that I left it at, it is most certain, after a long and troublesome war after my departure betwixt her father and our colony, all which time she was not heard of, about two years after she herself was taken prisoner, being so detained near two years longer, the colony by that means was relieved, peace concluded, and at last rejecting her barbarous condition, was married to an English gentleman,

---

4. Jamestown, named after James I, was the first permanent English settlement in North America, on land Indigenous peoples had inhabited for at least 12,000 years. About thirty Algonquin tribes were allied in the Powhatan Paramount Chiefdom, or Confederacy, along the coast, which was estimated to include around 15,000 people at the time of colonization. One hundred and four settlers arrived in 1607, and despite the dispatch of more settlers and supplies in 1608 (including eight Polish and German colonists and the first two European women), over 80 percent of the colonists died in 1609–10, mostly from starvation and disease. In 1610, those shipwrecked on the Bermudas, including John Rolf finally arrived in Jamestown. In 1619, the first Africans, enslaved people originally from the Kingdom of Ndongo in what is now Angola, arrived in the colony via the efforts of English privateers. One hundred European women arrived in the same year.

with whom at this present she is in England;[5] the first Christian ever of that nation, the first Virginian ever spoke English, or had a child in marriage by an Englishman, a matter surely, if my meaning be truly considered and well understood, worthy a prince's understanding.

    Thus, most gracious Lady, I have related to your Majesty what at your best leisure our approved histories will account you at large, and done in the time of your Majesty's life, and however this might be presented you from a more worthy pen, it cannot from a more honest heart, as yet I never begged anything of the state, or any, and it is my want of ability and her exceeding desert, your birth, means, and authority, her birth, virtue, want, and simplicity, doth make me thus bold, humbly to beseech your Majesty to take this knowledge of her, though it be from one so unworthy to be the reporter as myself, her husband's estate not being able to make her fit to attend your Majesty. The most and least I can do is to tell you this, because none so oft hath tried it as myself, and the rather being of so great a spirit, however her stature: if she should not be well received, seeing this kingdom may rightly have a kingdom by her means, her present love to us and Christianity might turn to such scorn and fury as to divert all this good to the worst of evil, where finding so great a Queen should do her some honor more than she can imagine, for being so kind to your servants and subjects, would so ravish her with content as endear her dearest blood to effect that your Majesty and all the king's subjects most earnestly desire. And so I humbly kiss your gracious hands.[6]

    Being about this time preparing to set sail for New England,[7] I could not stay to do her that service I desired and she well deserved; but hearing she was at Branford with divers of my friends, I went to see her. After a modest salutation, without any word she turned about, obscured her face, as not seeming well contented; and in that humor her husband, with divers others, we all left her two or three hours, repenting myself to have writ she could speak English. But not long after, she began to talk, and remembered° me well what courtesies she had done: saying, "You did promise Powhatan what was yours should be his, and he the like to you; you called him father being in his land a stranger, and by the same reason so must I do you," which though I would have excused, I durst° not allow of that title, because she was a king's daughter; with

    ° *reminded*

    ° *dare*

---

5. Powhatan removed his daughter from contact with the English when she moved from childhood into puberty; she was found and kidnapped by an English trading ship in 1613.
6. The letter to Queen Anna ends here.
7. Smith went to the coast of Massachusetts and Maine in 1614, which he then mapped and labeled as "New England" (his coinage). This map, published in *A Description of New England* (1616), proved useful to the New England colonists.

a well-set countenance she said, "Were you not afraid to come into my father's country, and caused fear in him and all his people (but me) and fear you here I should call you father; I tell you then I will, and you shall call me child, and so I will be forever and ever your countryman. They did tell us always you were dead, and I knew no other till I came to Plymouth; yet Powhatan did command Uttamatomakkin[8] to seek you, and know the truth, because your countrymen will lie much."

This savage, one of Powhatan's council, being amongst them held° an understanding fellow, the King purposely sent him, as they say, to number the people here, and inform him well what we were and our state. Arriving at Plymouth, according to his directions, he got a long stick, whereon by notches he did think to have kept the number of all the men he could see, but he was quickly weary of that task. Coming to London, where by chance I met him, having renewed our acquaintance, where many were desirous to hear and see his behavior, he told me Powhatan did bid him to find me out, to show him our God, the King, Queen, and Prince, I so much had told them of. Concerning God, I told him the best I could, the King I heard he had seen, and the rest he should see when he would. He denied ever to have seen the King, till by circumstances he was satisfied he had. Then he replied very sadly, You gave Powhatan a white dog, which Powhatan fed as himself, but your King gave me nothing, and I am better than your white dog.

considered to be

The small time I stayed in London, divers courtiers and others my acquaintances hath gone with me to see her,° that generally concluded they did think God had a great hand in her conversion, and they have seen many English ladies worse favored, proportioned, and behaviored, and, as since I have heard, it pleased both the King and Queen's Majesty honorably to esteem her, accompanied with that honorable Lady, the Lady De la Warr,[9] and that honorable Lord her husband, and divers other persons of good qualities, both publicly at the masques[1] and otherwise, to her great satisfaction and content, which doubtless she would have deserved° had she lived to arrive in Virginia.[2]

Pocahontas

returned in kind

8. Uttamatomakkin, also known as Tomocomo, was Powhatan's emissary. He traveled with Pocahontas's party to London in 1616. His wife was Pocahontas's half sister. In January 1617, Pocahontas and Tomocomo were brought before the king at the Banqueting House in Whitehall Place, at a performance of Ben Jonson's masque *The Vision of Delight*. Anne Clifford and Mary Sidney Herbert were present as well.
9. Lady De La Warr (Cecilia Shirley West) was the wife of Thomas West, third Baron De La Warr, the English merchant and politician for whom "Delaware" (state, river, First Nation) was named. De La Warr was the nominal governor of Virginia at the time, and in fall 1616, he and his wife introduced Pocahontas and her husband, John Rolf, into English society.
1. Elaborate court entertainments that celebrated and idealized the court and its rulers.
2. Pocahontas died in England in March 1617, right as her ship was about to leave for America. She was buried under the chancel of St. George's Church in Gravesend. She had been away for less than a year. John Rolf returned to Virginia, leaving their son in England.

[In January 1608, Captain Christopher Newport, the representative of the Virginia Company, arrived with supplies for the colony, saving Smith from the vengeance of the settlers. Smith disagreed with Newport over many matters of Indian policy. In the excerpt below, from fall 1608, Smith has come to see Powhatan crowned as a vassal of the king of England, a "coronation" he considers a foolish diversion from the colony's need to prepare for winter. When Smith and his men arrive, Powhatan is thirty miles away, and while they wait for him to arrive, Pocahontas and "her women" entertain the visitors.]

In a fair plain field they° made a fire, before which he° sitting upon a mat, suddenly among the woods was heard such a hideous noise and shrieking, that the English betook themselves to their arms, and seized on two or three old men by them, supposing Powhatan with all his power was come to surprise them. But presently Pocahontas came, willing him to kill her if any hurt were intended, and the beholders, which were men, women, and children, satisfied° the captain there was no such matter. Then presently they were presented with this antic:° thirty young women came naked out of the woods, only covered behind and before with a few green leaves, their bodies all painted, some of one color, some of another, but all differing. Their leader had a fair pair of buck's horns on her head, and an otter's skin at her girdle° and another at her arm, a quiver of arrows at her back, a bow and arrows in her hand; the next had in her hand a sword, another a club, another a potstick,[3] all horned alike: the rest every one with their several devices.[4] These fiends, with most hellish shouts and cries rushing from among the trees, cast themselves in a ring about the fire, singing and dancing with most excellent ill variety, oft falling into their infernal passions, and solemnly again to sing and dance; having spent near an hour in this mascarado,° as they entered, in like manner they departed.

    Having reaccommodated° themselves, they solemnly invited him to their lodgings, where he was no sooner within the house but all these nymphs[5] more tormented him than ever, with crowding, pressing, and hanging about him, most tediously crying, "Love you not me? Love you not me?" This salutation ended, the feast was set, consisting of all the savage dainties they could devise: some attending, other singing and dancing about them; which mirth being ended, with firebrands[6] instead of torches they conducted him to his lodging.

Algonquins / Smith

reassured

grotesque performance

belt; waist

masked ball; masque
redressed

---

3. Stick for stirring a pot.
4. Things artistically devised or invented for dramatic representation.
5. In classical mythology, any class of semi-divine spirits, imagined as taking the form of young maidens and inhabiting the sea, rivers, and mountains, and often portrayed in poetry as attendants on a particular god or goddess. The term was also used to describe beautiful young women and prostitutes.
6. Pieces of burning wood.

Thus did they show their feats of arms, and others art in dancing:
Some other used their oaten pipe, others voices chanting.[7]

The next day came Powhatan. Smith delivered his message of the presents sent him, and redelivered him Namontack[8] he had sent for° England, desiring him to come to his Father Newport to accept those presents, and conclude their revenge against the Monacans.[9] Whereunto this subtle° savage thus replied: *to*   *clever, crafty*

> If your king have sent me presents, I also am a king, and this is my land: eight days I will stay to receive them. Your father is to come to me, not I to him, nor yet to your fort, neither will I bite at such a bait. As for the Monacans, I can revenge my own injuries, and as for Atquanachuk, where you say your brother was slain, it is a contrary way from those parts you suppose it; but for any salt water beyond the mountains, the relations you have had from my people are false.

Whereupon he began to draw plots upon the ground (according to his discourse) of all those regions. Many other discourses they had (yet both content to give each other content in complemental° courtesies) and so Captain Smith returned with this answer.   *formal*

Upon this the presents were sent by water, which is near a hundred miles, and the captains went by land with fifty good shot. All being met at Werowocomoco,[1] the next day was appointed for his coronation, then the presents were brought him: his basin and ewer,° bed and furniture set up, his scarlet cloak and apparel with much ado put on him, being persuaded by Namontack they would not hurt him. But a foul trouble there was to make him kneel to receive his crown, he neither knowing the majesty nor meaning of a crown, nor bending of the knee, endured so many persuasions, examples, and instructions as tired them all. At last, by leaning hard on his shoulders, he a little stooped, and three, having the crown in their hands, put it on his head, when by the warning of a pistol the boats were prepared with such a volley of   *pitcher*

---

7. Smith included many italicized verse couplets like this one in his work, many of them taken (and modified) from Martin Fotherby's collection of commonplaces, *Atheomastic* (1622). These lines are from Homer's *Iliad*. "Oaten pipe": pipe made of straw or a stem of an oat.
8. Namontack was a young Powhatan man who was traded to the English as a hostage or ward in exchange for the young Englishman, Thomas Savage, who served in a similar capacity with the Native Americans. An accomplished guide, interpreter, and diplomatic mediator, Namontack made at least one trip to England.
9. Traders with and rivals of the Powhatan Confederacy. The Monacans spoke Siouan languages. Those in the Powhatan Confederacy spoke Algonquian languages.
1. A village that served as Powhatan's headquarters. The name comes from the Powhatan words *werowans* (leader) and *komakah* (settlement). It is now an archeological site. Powhatan never went to Jamestown. Smith was captured and brought to Powhatan at Werowocomoco in January 1608, and it was there that Pocohantas purportedly saved him.

shot, that the king started up in a horrible fear, till he saw all was well. Then, remembering himself, to congratulate their kindness he gave his old shoes and his mantle to Captain Newport: but perceiving his° purpose was to discover the Monacans, he labored to divert his resolution, refusing to lend him either men or guides more than Namontack; and so after some small complemental kindness on both sides, in requital of his presents, he presented Newport with a heap of wheat ears that might contain some seven or eight bushels, and as much more we bought in the town, wherewith we returned to the fort.

    *   *   *

[Powhatan explains the differences between peace and war]

Captain Smith you may understand, that I, having seen the death of all my people thrice, and not one living of those three generations but myself, I know the difference of peace and war better than any in my country.² But now I am old and ere long must die, my brethren, namely Opichapam, Opechankanough, and Kekataugh, my two sisters, and their two daughters, are distinctly each other's successors, I wish their experiences no less than mine, and your love to them, no less than mine to you. But this bruit° from Nansamund³ that you are come to destroy my country so much affrighteth all my people as they dare not visit you; what will it avail you to that that perforce° you may quietly have with love, or to destroy them that provide your food?⁴ What can you get by war, when we can hide our provision and fly to the woods, whereby you must famish, by wronging us your friends; and why are you thus jealous of our loves, seeing us unarmed, and both do, and are willing still, to feed you with that you cannot get but by our labors? Think you I am so simple not to know it is better to eat good meat, lie well, and sleep quietly with my women and children, laugh and be merry with you, have copper, hatchets, or what I want, being your friend, than be forced to fly from all, to lie cold in the woods, feed upon acorns, roots, and such trash:° and be so hunted by you that I can neither rest, eat, nor sleep, but my tired men must watch, and if a twig but break, everyone cry 'There comes Captain Smith,' then

Newport's

report

by force

rubbish, dross

---

2. Powhatan may be referring to the devastating effects on the Algonquins of European diseases contracted from other European visitors before the arrival of the Jamestown colonists.
3. In fall 1608, Smith and his men sailed up the Nansemond River, where they obtained corn from the Nansemond Indians by threatening to destroy their canoes.
4. Smith presented his opinions on Indian policy through his exchanges with Powhatan and his brother, Opechancanough. These exchanges reveal Smith's desire to maintain a dominant position as well as his awareness of the colony's dependence on the knowledge, labor, and cooperation of the Native Americans. While this is Smith's account of Powhatan's speech, it nonetheless presents Powhatan as a formidable political opponent who was well aware of the colonists' vulnerability.

must I fly I know not whether,° and thus with miserable *where* fear end my miserable life, leaving my pleasures to such youths as you, which, through your rash unadvisedness may quickly as miserably end for want of that you never know where to find. Let this therefore assure you of our loves, and every year our friendly trade shall furnish you with corn, and now also, if you would come in friendly manner to see us, and not thus with your guns and swords as to invade your foes.

1624

RICHARD LIGON

Richard Ligon's *A True and Exact History of the Island of Barbados* (1657) is the first account of the English colonization of the Caribbean island of Barbados, and of the rise of the sugar industry that would turn the island into "one of the richest Spots of earth under the Sun" and change the global economy forever. Ligon (1585?–1662) left for the Caribbean in 1647, following the failure of his efforts at land reclamation and enclosure in England, and the defeat of the royalists in the English Civil Wars. He wrote his history in London in the 1650s, while in prison for debt. The history served not only as a description of Barbados' plantations and "Sugarworks" and a prospectus (and how-to manual) for investors and future planters, but also as an account of Ligon's own value: as plantation overseer, natural scientist, draughtsman (the volume included detailed diagrams of the industrial parts of the sugar works), colonial apologist, and self-described "limner," or watercolorist.

Ligon's account (and voyage) begins with a trip to the Cape Verde Islands off the western coast of Africa, where the colonists plan to collect "Negroes, Horses, and Cattle" to sell in Barbados. The first selection below recounts a dinner in "St. Iago" (Santiago) at the Portuguese governor's house, in which Ligon's knowledge of European art, including court masques like Ben Jonson's *Masque of Blackness*, provides the lens through which he sees Black women.

The Barbados selections illustrate Ligon's views of life on the plantations, from the spectre of rebellions by enslaved people and servants (including one by servants who, *Tempest*-like, sought to make themselves "Masters of the Island"), and the challenges presented by both the diversity of languages spoken by the Africans, and a natural environment whose fertility and intractability often threatened to overwhelm the colonists' fantasies of mastery and ease. The account also displays Ligon's critique of "Christian" violence and hypocrisy, not least in his account of the Indian "maiden" Yarico, which became, much like Smith's account of Pocahontas, the stuff of legend.

From A True and Exact History of the Island of Barbados

* * *

Dinner being near half done (the Padre, Bernardo,[1] and the other black attendants, waiting on us), in comes an old fellow whose complexion was raised out of the red sack,[2] for near that colour it was: his head and beard milk white, his countenance bold and cheerful, a lute in his hand, and played us for a novelty, the *passamezzo galliard*,[3] a tune in great esteem in Harry the fourth's days; for when Sir *John Falstaff*[4] makes his amours to Mistress *Doll Tear sheet*, *Sneak* and his company, the admired fiddlers of that age, play this tune, which put a thought into my head, that if time and tune be the composites of music, what a long time this tune had in sailing from England to this place. But we being sufficiently satisfied with this kind of harmony, desired a song, which he performed in as antique[5] a manner, both favoring much of antiquity°; no graces, double relishes, trillos, gropos, or pianofortes,[6] but plain as a packstaff.[7] His lute, too, was but of ten strings, and that was in fashion in King David's days,[8] so that the rarity of this antique piece pleased me beyond measure.

Dinner being ended and the Padre were near weary of his waiting, we rose and made room for better company; for now the Padre and his Black mistress were to take their turns; a Negro of the greatest beauty and majesty together that ever I saw in one woman. Her stature large and excellently shaped, well-favored, full-eyed, and admirably graced; she wore on her head a roll of green taffety, striped with white and philiamort,[9] made up in manner of a turban; and over that a slight veil, which she took off at pleasure. On her body next to her linen, a petticoat of orange tawny and sky colors, not done with

the ancient past

---

1. Bernardo Mendes de Sousa was a Portuguese national whom the expedition brought with them as a translator. He was released from jail in London to serve in this capacity. The Cape Verde islands, named for their proximity to the verdant cape on the African coast, had been largely uninhabited until the Portuguese colonized them in the 15th century. Santiago (Ligon's "St. Iago") had been the bishop's seat for the islands and adjacent coast for almost a century when Ligon arrived. Portugal signed a treaty with England in 1642 that opened Portuguese territory to English traders. The "Padre" in Ligon's account is the current bishop.
2. Wine, imported from Spain or the Canary Islands.
3. *passamezzo galliard*: from *passer*, to walk, and *mezzo*, the middle or half, was a popular dance, and popular tune, in the period.
4. Sir John Falstaff courts the prostitute Doll Tearsheet and "Sneak and his company" provide musical entertainment in Shakespeare's *Henry IV, Part II.*
5. Old-fashioned or "antic," grotesque or absurd.
6. Graces, double relishes, trillos, and grops were musical flourishes, usually consisting of trills or vibrations made by alternating rapidly between adjacent notes. Pianofortes were alterations between loud and soft playing.
7. The stick on which a beggar supported their pack while resting. The phrase "plain as a packstaff" referred to something low or contemptible.
8. King David was the third king of Israel in the Bible.
9. Philiamort (*feuilles mortes*, in French): the color of dead leaves.

straight stripes, but waved; and upon that a mantle of purple silk, engrailed° with straw color. This mantle was large, and tied with a knot of very broad black ribbon, with a rich jewel on her right shoulder, which came under her left arm, and so hung loose and carelessly almost to the ground. On her legs she wore buskins[1] of watchet° silk, decked with silver lace and fringe; Her shoes, of white leather, laced with sky color and pinked[2] between those laces. In her ears, she wore large pendants; about her neck and on her arms, fair pearls. But her eyes were her richest jewels: for they were the largest and most oriental[3] that I have ever seen.

    variegated, mixed

    light blue

Seeing all these perfections in her only at passage,° but not yet heard her speak, I was resolved after dinner to make an essay what a present of rich silver, silk, and gold ribbon would do to persuade her to open her lips, partly out of a curiosity to see whether her teeth were exactly white and clean as I hoped they were; for 'tis a general opinion that all Negroes have white teeth, but that is a common error, for the black and white being so neer together, they set off one another with the greater advantage, but look to them and you shall find those teeth, which at a distance appeared rarely white, are yellow and foul. This knowledge wrought this curiosity in me, but it was not the end of my enquiries, for there was now but one thing more to set her off in my opinion, the rarest black swan that I had ever seen, and that was her language, and graceful delivery of that which was to unite and confirm a perfection in all the rest. And to that end I took a gentleman that spoke good Spanish with me, and awaited her coming out, which was with far greater majesty and gracefulness than I have seen Queen Anne descend from the chair of state to dance the measures with a baron of England at a masque in the Banqueting House.[4] And truly, had her followers and friends with other perquisites[5] (that ought to be the attendants on such a state and beauty) waited on her, I had made a stop and gone no farther. But finding her but slightly attended, and considering she was but the Padre's mistress and therefore the more accessible, I made my addresses to her by my interpreter and told her I had some trifles made by the people of England, which for their value were not

    in passing

---

1. Calf- or knee-high boots.
2. Ornamented with cut-outs.
3. Characteristic of countries/regions to the east of the Mediterranean, ancient Roman empire, or early Christian world. The term was also used to describe a precious stone, especially a pearl.
4. Ligon refers to court masques, elaborate court entertainments that celebrated and idealized the court and its rulers. The members of the royal family did often "descend" to dance with the nobility ("barons") at the conclusion of the masque. Queen Anna commissioned and performed in many masques at the Banqueting House in Whitehall, including Jonson's *The Masque of Blackness* (see above, p. 1039). For resonances between Ligon's description of the Black woman's attire and court masque costumes, see the illustration on p. C12 in the color insert to this volume.
5. Adjuncts, proper accompaniments.

worthy her acceptance, yet for their novelty they might be of some esteem, such having been worn by the great queens of Europe, and intreated her to vouchsafe to receive them. She, with much gravity and reservedness, opened the paper, but when she looked on them, the colors pleased her so as she put her gravity into the loveliest smile that I have ever seen. And then showed her rows of pearls, so clean, white, Orient, and well-shaped as Neptune's court was never paved with such as these; and to show which was whiter or more Orient, those or the whites of her eyes, she turned them up and gave me such a look as was a sufficient return for a far greater present, and withall wished I would think of somewhat wherein she might pleasure me, and I should find her both ready and willing. And so with a graceful bow of her neck, she took her way towards her own house, which was not above a stone's cast from the Padre's. Other addresses were not to be made without the dislike of the Padre, for they are there as jealous of their mistresses as the Italians of their wives.

In the afternoon we took leave and went aboard, where we remained three or four days; about which time some passengers of the ship who had no great store of linen for shift,° desired leave to go ashore and took divers women along with them to wash their linen. But (it seemed) the Portuguese, and Negroes too, found them handsome and fit for their turns,[6] and were a little rude; I cannot say ravished[7] them, for the major part of them, being taken from Bridewell, Turnbull Street,[8] and such like places of education, were better natured than to suffer such violence. Yet complaints were made when they came aboard, both of such abuses, and stealing their linen.

change (of clothing)

But such a praise they gave of the place as we all were desirous to see it: for after the rain, every day gave an increase to the beauty of the place by the budding out of new fruits and flowers.

* * *

No sooner were we landed, but the captain of the castle, with one soldier with him, came towards us with a slow formal pace, who desired to speak with one of us alone. Colonel Modyford,[9] being the chief man in the company, went with an interpreter to meet him, and being

---

6. To serve their sexual desires.
7. Carried away by force, raped.
8. Bridewell was a London hospital that served as a workhouse and correctional facility, primarily for women. Turnbull Street was a notorious center of crime and prostitution.
9. Colonel Thomas Modyford was the leader of the Barbados expedition. Ligon had fought with him in the royalist garrison in Exeter. Modyford amassed a huge fortune in Barbados. He moved to Jamaica as royal governor in the early 1660s, where he became the richest planter in the English Caribbean.

at the distance of speech desired to know his pleasure, which he told him was this: That he understood divers of our women had been ashore the day before and received some injury from the people of the island, and that it was conceived we were come armed to take revenge on those that did the afront. He therefore advised us either to make speedy return to the boat that brought us, or to send back our swords and pistols and commit our selves to his protection; and if one of those were not presently put in act, we should in a very short time have all our throats cut.

We told him we had no intention of revenge for any wrong done, and that the only cause of our landing was to see the beauty of the place we had heard so much commended by our people that were ashore, of which they had given a very large testimony both of the pleasantness and fruitfulness of it, and that our visit was out of love, both to the place and people. But for sending our weapons back to the boat, we desired his pardon for this reason: that the billows going so very high at that time, we could not send them to the boat without being dipped in sea water, which would spoil them, and the most of them being rich swords and pistols, we were loath to have their beauty covered with rust, which the salt water would be the occasion of. We desired rather that he would command a soldier of his to stay with a man of ours, and keep them safe till our return; which he being content to do, we committed ourselves to his protection, who put a guard upon us of ten soldiers, part Portuguese, part Negroes; the most part of either kind as proper men as I have seen, and as handsomely clothed.

* * *

In this valley of pleasure, adorned as you have heard, we marched with our guard, fair and softly, near a quarter of a mile before we came to the much-praised fountain from whence we fetched our water. The circle whereof was about 60 foot, the diameter about 20 from the ground to the top of the well (which was of freestone), 3 foot and a half; from thence within down to the surface of the water, about 15 foot. The spring itself, not so much to be praised for the excellency of the taste, though clear enough, as for the nymphs that repair thither. For whilst we stayed there seeing the sailors fill their casks, and withall contemplating the glory of the place, there appeared to our view many pretty young Negro virgins, playing about the well. But amongst those, two that came down with either of them a natural pitcher, a calabash,[1] upon their arm, to fetch water from this fountain, creatures of

---

1. Shell of an emptied gourd or pumpkin used to carry liquid.

such shapes as would have puzzled Albert Durer,[2] the great master of proportion, but to have imitated; and Titian, or Andrea del Sarto, for softness of muscles, and curiosity of coloring, though with a studied diligence, and a love both to the party and the work. To express all the perfections of nature, and parts these virgins were owners of, would ask a more skillful pen or pencil than mine. Sure I am, though all were excellent, their motions were the highest, and that is a beauty no painter can express, and therefore my pen may well be silent. Yet a word or two would not be amiss to express the difference between these and those of high Africa; as of Morocco, Guinea, Binny, Cutchew, Angola, Æthiopia, and Mauritania, or those that dwell nere the River of Gambia,[3] who are thick-lipped, short-nosed, and commonly low foreheads. But these are composed of such features as would mar the judgment of the best painters to undertake to mend. Wanton as the soil that bred them, sweet as the fruits they fed on; for being come so near as their motions and graces might perfectly be discerned, I guessed that nature could not, without help of art, frame such accomplished beauties not only of colors and favor, but of motion too, which is the highest part of beauty. If dancing had been in fashion in this island, I might have been persuaded that they had been taught those motions by some who had studied that art. But considering the Padre's music to be the best the island afforded, I could not but cast away that thought and attribute all to pure nature; innocent as youthful, their ages about 15. Seeing their beauties so fresh and youthful with all the perfections I have named, I thought good to try whether the uttering of their language would be as sweet and harmonious as their other parts were comely. And by the help of a gentleman that spoke Portuguese, I accosted them, and began to praise their beauties, shapes, and manner of dressings, which was extremely pretty. Their hair not shorn as the Negroes in the places I have named, close to their heads, nor in quarters and mazes,[4] as they use to wear it, which is ridiculous to all that see them but themselves, but in a due proportion of length so as having their shortenings by the natural curls, they appeared as wires[5] and artificial° dressings to   *artful*

---

2. Albrecht Dürer (1471–1528), German printer, painter, and theorist of the Northern Renaissance. Titian (1488–1576), Italian Renaissance painter. A Black woman is represented attending to Diana in Titian's *Diana and Actaeon* (1556–59). Andrea del Sarto (1486–1530), Italian Renaissance painter. Dürer's *Four Books on Human Proportions* was influenced by Leonardo da Vinci and Marcus Vitruvius. Dürer thought that there were "many forms of relative beauty . . . conditioned by the diversity of breeding, vocation, and natural disposition."
3. Morocco and Mauritania are in North Africa. Cacheo ("Cutchew") and the River of Gambia, centers of the trade in enslaved Africans, were in Guinea and Benin. Angola lay farther south along the West African coast. The location of Ethiopia was indeterminate in the period.
4. "Quarters and mazes" are ways of creating patterns on the scalp with the hair.
5. Forms used to support complex hairstyles.

their faces. On the sides of their cheeks, they plait° little   *braid*
of it of purpose to tie small ribbon, or some small beads of
white amber or bugle,° sometimes of the rare flowers that   *tube-shaped glass bead*
grow there; their ears hung with pendants, their necks
and arms adorned with bracelets of counterfeit pearls and
blue bugle[6] such as the Portuguese bestow on them, for
these are free Negroes, and wear upon the small of one of
their legs the badge of their freedom, which is a small
piece of silver or tin, as big as the stale° of a spoon, which   *handle*
comes round about the leg, and by reason of the smoothness and lightness is no impediment to their going. Their
clothes were petticoats of striped silk next to their linen,
which reach to their middle leg, and upon that a mantle
of blue taffety, tied with a ribbon on the right shoulder,
which coming under the left arm, hung down carelessly
somewhat lower than the petticoat, so as a great part of
the natural beauty of their backs and necks before lay
open to the view, their breast round, firm, and beautifully
shaped.

    Upon my addresses to them, they appeared a little disturbed, and whispered to one another, but had not the confidence to speak aloud. I had in my hat a piece of silver and silk ribbon, which I perceived their well-shaped eyes often to dart at, but their modesties would not give them confidence to ask. I took it out and divided it between them, which they accepted with much alacrity, and in return, drank to one another my health in the liquor of the pure fountain, which I perceived by their wanton smiles and jesticulations, and casting their eyes towards me. When they thought they had expressed enough they would take in their countenances and put themselves in the modestest of postures that could be. But we having brought a case of bottles of English spirits with us, I called for some and drunk a health to them in a small dram cup, and gave it to one of them, which they smelled so, and finding it too strong for their temper poured some of it into one of their calabashes and put to it as much water as would temper it to their palates. They drank again, but all this would not give them the confidence to speak, but in mute language and extremely pretty motions, showed they wanted neither wit nor discretion to make an answer. But it seemed it was not the fashion there for young maids to speak to strangers in so public a place.

    I thought I had been sufficiently armed with the perfections I found in the Padre's mistress as to be free from the darts of any other beauty of that place, and in so short a time, but I found the difference between young fresh beauties and those that are made up with the

---

6. Tube-shaped glass bead.

addition of state and majesty: for though they counsel and persuade our loves, yet young beauties force and so commit rapes upon our affections. In sum, had not my heart been fixed fast in my breast and dwelt there above sixty years, and therefore loath to leave his long-kept habitation, I had undoubtedly left it between them for a legacy. For, so equal were their beauties and my love, as it was not, nor could be, particular to either.

* * *

Being now come in sight of this happy island,° the nearer we came, the more beautiful it appeared to our eyes; for that being in itself extremely beautiful was best discerned, and best judged of, when our eyes became full masters of the object. There we saw the high, large, and lofty trees, with their spreading branches and flourishing tops, seemed to be beholding to the earth and roots that gave them such plenty of sap for their nourishment, as to grow to that perfection of beauty and largeness. Whilst they, in gratitude, return their cool shade to secure and shelter them from the sun's heat, which without it would scorch and dry away. So that bounty and goodness in the one, and gratefulness in the other, serve to make up this beauty which otherwise would lie empty and waste.° And truly these vegetatives may teach both the sensible and reasonable creatures what it is that makes up wealth, beauty, and all harmony in that *Leviathan*,⁷ a well-governed common-wealth where the mighty men and rulers of the earth, by their prudent and careful protection, secure them from harms, whilst they retribute° their pains and faithful obedience to serve them in all just commands; and both these, interchangeably and mutually in love, which is the cord that binds up all imperfect harmony, and where these are wanting, the roots dry and leaves fall away, and a general decay and devastation ensues. Witness the woeful experience of these sad times we live in.

Barbados

uncultivated

repay

* * *

A little before I came from thence,⁸ there was such a combination amongst them° as the like was never seen there before. Their sufferings being grown to a great height, and their daily complainings to one another (of the intolerable burdens they labored under) being spread throughout the island, at the last, some amongst them, whose spirits were not able to endure such slavery,

servants

---

7. Thomas Hobbes was, like Ligon, a royalist and an exile. He published *Leviathan* in 1651, the year he returned to England. Ligon's is the second recorded use of the term "Leviathan" to refer to the state or commonwealth.
8. Right before this section, Ligon discusses the living and working conditions of servants and enslaved workers.

resolved to break through it or die in the act, and so conspired with some others of their acquaintance, whose sufferings were equal if not above theirs and their spirits no way inferior, resolved to draw as many of the discontented party into this plot as possibly they could, and those of this persuasion were the greatest numbers of servants in the island. So that a day was appointed to fall upon their masters and cut all their throats, and by that means to make themselves not only freemen but masters of the island. And so closely was this plot carried as no discovery was made till the day before they were to put it in act, and then one of them, either by the failing of his courage, or some new obligation from the love of his master, revealed this long-plotted conspiracy, and so by this timely advertisement the masters were saved: Justice Hetherfall (whose servant this was) sending letters to all his friends, and they to theirs, and so one to another till they were all secured; and by examination found out the greatest part of them, whereof eighteen of the principal men in the conspiracy, and they the first leaders and contrivers of the plot, were put to death for example to the rest. And the reason why they made examples of so many was they found these so haughty in their resolutions, and so incorrigible, as they were like enough to become actors in a second plot; and so they thought good to secure them, and for the rest, to have a special eye over them.

It has been accounted a strange thing that the Negroes, being more than double the numbers of the Christians that are there,[9] and they accounted a bloody people where they think they have power or advantages, and the more bloody by how much they are more fearful than others, that these should not commit some horrid massacre upon the Christians, thereby to enfranchise themselves and become masters of the island. But there are three reasons that take away this wonder: the one is, they are not suffered to touch or handle any weapons; the other, that they are held in such awe and slavery as they are fearful to appear in any daring act; and seeing the mustering of our men and hearing their gunshot, (than which nothing is more terrible to them), their spirits are subjugated to so low a condition as they dare not look up to any bold attempt. Besides these, there is a third reason which stops all designs of that kind, and that is, they are fetched from several parts of Africa, who speak several languages, and by that means one of them understands not another: For some of them are fetched from Guinea and Binny, some from Cutchew, some from Angola,

9. Ligon overestimated the island's population, which by 1660 was roughly 40,000, equally divided between people of European and of African or Indian descent.

and some from the River of Gambia. And in some of these places where petty kingdoms are, they sell their subjects, and such as they take in battle, whom they make slaves; and some mean men sell their servants, their children, and sometimes their wives, and think all good traffic for such commodities as our merchants send them.

When they are brought to us, the planters buy them out of the ship, where they find them stark naked and therefore cannot be deceived in any outward infirmity. They choose them as they do horses in a market; the strongest, youthfulest, and most beautiful yield the greatest prices. Thirty pound sterling is a price for the best man Negro; and twenty five, twenty six, or twenty seven pound for a woman; the children are at easier rates. And we buy them so, as the sexes may be equal; for if they have more men than women, the men who are unmarried will come to their masters and complain that they cannot live without wives and desire him they may have wives.

* * *

What their° other opinions are in matter of religion, I know not, but certainly they are not altogether of the sect of the Sadducees,[1] for they believe a resurrection, and that they shall go into their own country again and have their youth renewed. And lodging this opinion in their hearts, they make it an ordinary practice, upon any great fright or threatening by their masters, to hang themselves.

°*the enslaved Africans*

But Colonel Walrond,[2] having lost three or four of his best Negroes this way, and in a very little time, caused one of their heads to be cut off and set upon a pole a dozen foot high; and having done that, caused all his Negroes to come forth and march round about this head, and bid them look on it, whether this were not the head of such a one that hanged himself. Which they acknowledging, he then told them that they were in a main error in thinking they went into their own countries after they were dead; for this man's head was here, as they all were witnesses of, and how was it possible the body could go without a head. Being convinced by this sad yet lively spectacle, they changed their opinions; and after that, no more hanged themselves.

* * *

1. The Sadduccees were a Jewish sect that denied the immortality of the soul and the possibility of resurrection. The name was applied to all those who rejected such beliefs.
2. Colonel Humphrey Walrond emigrated to Barbados in 1646 after a royalist defeat and became a sugar planter. After trying to seize control of the island, largely by stoking fears of servant and slave rebellions, Walrond was sent back to England in 1652. He returned in 1656 and became president of the council in 1660.

We had an Indian woman,³ a slave in the house, who was of excellent shape and color, for it was a pure bright bay,⁴ small breasts, with the nipples of a porphyry⁵ color, this woman would not be wooed by any means to wear clothes. She chanced to be with child, by a Christian⁶ servant, and lodging in the Indian house amongst other women of her own country, where the Christian servants, both men and women, came, and being very great, and, that her time was come to be delivered, loath to fall in labour before the men, walked down to a wood in which was a pond of water, and there by the side of the pond, brought her self abed;° and presently washing her child in some of the water of the pond, lapped° it up in such rags as she had begged of the Christians, and in three hours' time came home with her child in her arms, a lusty boy, frolic and lively.

gave birth
swaddled

This Indian dwelling near the sea coast upon the main, an English ship put in to a bay and sent some of her men ashore to try what victuals or water they could find, for in some distress they were. But the Indians perceiving them to go up so far into the country as they were sure they could not make a safe retreat, intercepted them in their return and fell upon them, chasing them into a wood, and being dispersed there, some were taken, and some killed. But a young man amongst them straggling from the rest was met by this Indian maid, who upon the first sight fell in love with him, and hid him close from her countrymen (the Indians) in a cave,⁷ and there fed him till they could safely go down to the shore, where the ship lay at anchor, expecting the return of their friends, but at last seeing them upon the shore, sent the long boat for them, took them aboard, and brought them away. But the youth, when he came ashore in the Barbados, forgot the kindness of the poor maid that had ventured her life for his safety, and sold her for a slave, who was as free born as he: and so poor Yarico for her love, lost her liberty.⁸

Now for the masters, I have said but little, nor am able to say half of what they deserve. They are men of great abilities and parts, otherwise they could not go through with such great works as they undertake, the managing of one of their plantations being a work of such a latitude

---

3. The Indians enslaved in Barbados were from the mainland of South America, likely Guiana.
4. Reddish-brown color, usually used to describe a horse.
5. Porphyry was a hard purplish-red rock quarried in the eastern desert of Egypt for ornamental use, especially during the Roman period.
6. "Christian" here means non-Indian or African.
7. Later in the book, Ligon tells us that "runaway Negroes" often shelter themselves in such caves, and "range abroad" in the night, stealing "pigs, plantains, potatoes and pullen [chicken]," "the nights being dark, and their bodies black, they escape undiscerned."
8. Yarico's story is taken up by later authors, including Richard Steele.

as will require a very good headpiece,° to put in order and continue it so.   *brain or intellect*

* * *

This tree° wants little of the beauty of the plantain, yet she has somewhat to delight the eyes which the other wants, and that is the picture of Christ upon the cross, so lively expressed as no limner can do it (with one color) more exactly. And this is seen when you cut the fruit just cross as you do the root of fern, to find a spread eagle. But this is much more perfect, the head hanging down, the arms extended to the full length, with some little elevation, and the feet cross upon one another. This I will speak as an artist: let a very excellent limner⁹ paint a crucifix, only with one color, in limning, and let his touches be as sharp and as masterly as he pleases, the figure no bigger than this, which is about an inch long, and remove that picture at such a distance from the eye as to lose some of the curiosity, and dainty touches of the work, so as the outmost stels° or profile of the figure may be perfectly discerned, and at such a distance, the figure in the fruit of the banana shall seem as perfect as it. Much may be said upon this subject by better wits and abler souls than mine, my contemplation being only this: that since those men dwelling in that place professing the names of Christians, and denying to preach to those poor ignorant harmless souls, the Negroes, the doctrine of Christ crucified, which might convert many of them to his worship, he himself has set up his own cross to reproach these men, who rather than lose the hold they have of them as slaves, will deny them the benefit and blessing of being Christians. Otherwise why is this figure set up for these to look on, that never heard of Christ, and God never made anything useless or in vain?   *the banana tree*

outlines

* * *

1657

---

9. A limner is an illuminator of manuscripts or a painter, especially in watercolors.

The Early Seventeenth Century 1603–1660

1603: Death of Elizabeth I; accession of James I, first Stuart king of England
1605: The Gunpowder Plot, a failed effort by Catholic extremists to blow up Parliament and the king
1607: Establishment of first permanent English colony in the New World at Jamestown, Virginia
1625: Death of James I; accession of Charles I
1642: Outbreak of civil war; theaters closed
1649: Execution of Charles I; beginning of Commonwealth and Protectorate, known inclusively as the Interregnum (1649–60)
1660: End of the Protectorate; restoration of Charles II

Queen Elizabeth died on March 24, 1603, after ruling England for more than four decades. The Virgin Queen had not, of course, produced a child to inherit her throne, but her kinsman, the thirty-six-year-old James Stuart, James VI of Scotland, succeeded her as James I without the violence that many had feared. Worries over the succession, which had plagued the reigns of the Tudor monarchs since Henry VIII, could finally subside: James already had several children with his queen, Anna of Denmark. Writers and scholars jubilantly noted that their new ruler had literary inclinations. He was the author of treatises on government and witchcraft, as well as some youthful efforts at poetry. Nonetheless, there

Charles I at the Hunt, a portrait of Charles I of England by Anthony Van Dyck, ca. 1635. See the color insert in this volume for another portrait of Charles I by Van Dyck.

were grounds for disquiet. James had come to maturity in Scotland, a foreign land with a different church, different customs, and different institutions of government. Two of his books, *The True Law of Free Monarchies* (1598) and *Basilikon Doron* (1599), expounded authoritarian theories of kingship, and James's views seemed incompatible with the English tradition of "mixed" government, in which power was shared by the monarch, the House of Lords, and the House of Commons. As Thomas Howard wrote in 1611, while Elizabeth "did talk of her subjects' love and good affection," James "talketh of his subjects' fear and subjection." James liked to imagine himself as a modern version of the wise, peace-loving Roman Augustus Caesar, who autocratically governed a vast empire. The Romans had deified their emperors, and while the Christian James could not expect the same, he insisted on his closeness to divinity. Kings, he believed, derived their powers from God rather than from the people. As God's specially chosen delegate, surely he deserved his subjects' reverent, unconditional obedience.

Yet unlike the charismatic Elizabeth, James was personally unprepossessing. One contemporary, Anthony Weldon, provides a barbed description: "His tongue too large for his mouth, which ever made him speak full in the mouth, and drink very uncomely as if eating his drink . . . he never washed his hands . . . his walk was ever circular, his fingers ever in that walk fiddling about his codpiece." Unsurprisingly, James did not always inspire in his subjects the deferential awe to which he thought himself entitled.

The relationship between the monarch and his people, and the relationship between England and Scotland, would be sources of friction throughout James's reign. James had hoped to unify his domains as a single nation, "the empire of Britain." But the two realms' legal and ecclesiastical systems proved difficult to reconcile, and the English Parliament, traditionally a sporadically convened body providing advice to the monarch, offered robustly xenophobic opposition. The failure of unification was only one of the king's several clashes with the English Parliament, especially with the House of Commons, which had authority over taxation. After James died in 1625 and his son Charles I succeeded him, tensions persisted and intensified. Charles attempted to rule without summoning Parliament at all between 1629 and 1638. By 1642 England was up in arms. The civil war between the king's forces and those loyal to the House of Commons ended with Charles's defeat and beheading in 1649.

In the early 1650s the monarchy as an institution seemed as dead as the man who had last worn the crown, but an adequate replacement proved difficult to devise and sustain. In 1653, executive power devolved upon a "Lord Protector," Oliver Cromwell, former general of the parliamentary forces, who wielded power nearly as autocratically as Charles had done. Yet without an institutionally sanctioned method of transferring power upon Cromwell's death, the attempt to fashion a commonwealth without a hereditary monarch eventually failed. In 1660 Parliament invited the eldest son of the old king home from exile. He succeeded to the throne as King Charles II.

As James's accession marks the beginning of "the early seventeenth century," his grandson's marks the end. Literary periods often fail to correlate neatly with the reigns of monarchs, and the period 1603–60 can seem especially arbitrary. Many important cultural trends in seventeenth-century Europe neither began nor ended in these years but unfolded slowly over several centuries. The Protestant Reformation of the sixteenth century was still ongoing in the seventeenth, and still producing turmoil. The European printing press, an invention of the fifteenth century, continued to make books ever more widely available, contributing to an expansion of literacy and to a changed conception of authorship. Although the English economy remained primarily agrarian, its manufacturing and trade sectors were expanding rapidly. England was also establishing itself as a leading maritime nation, as a colonial power, and increasingly, particularly in the 1650s, as a major participant in the transatlantic slave trade. From 1550 on, London grew explosively as a center of population, trade, and literary endeavor. Each of these developments was under way before James came to the throne, and many of them would continue after the 1714 death of James's great-granddaughter Queen Anne, the last of the Stuarts to reign in England.

From a literary point of view, 1603 can seem a particularly capricious dividing line; many of England's most famous writers were midcareer when James came to the throne. The professional lives of William Shakespeare, Ben Jonson, John Donne, Francis Bacon, Walter Ralegh, and many less famous writers—including George Chapman, Samuel Daniel, Thomas Dekker, Michael Drayton, Thomas Heywood, and Aemilia Lanyer—straddle the reigns of Elizabeth and James. The restoration of Charles II, with which this section ends, is likewise a more significant political than literary milestone: John Milton completed *Paradise Lost* and wrote two other major poems in the 1660s, and Margaret Cavendish, Katherine Philips, and Lucy Hutchinson wrote their most important works across the dividing line between the "early" seventeenth century and the Restoration. Nonetheless, recognizing the years 1603–60 as a period sharpens our awareness of some important political, intellectual, cultural, and stylistic currents that bear directly upon literary production. It also helps focus attention upon the seismic shift in national consciousness that, in 1649, could permit the formal trial, conviction, and execution of an anointed king at the hands of his former subjects.

STATE AND CHURCH, 1603–1640

In James's reign, the most pressing difficulties were apparently financial, but money troubles were merely symptoms of deeper quandaries about the proper relationship between king and people. Compared to James's native Scotland, England seemed prosperous, but James was less wealthy than he believed. Except in times of war, the Crown was supposed to fund the government not through regular taxation but through its own extensive land revenues and by exchanging Crown prerogatives, such as the collection of taxes on luxury imports, in return for money or services. Yet the Crown's independent income had declined throughout the sixteenth century as inflation eroded the value of land rents. Meanwhile, innovations in military technology and shipbuilding dramatically increased the cost of port security and other defenses, traditional Crown responsibilities. Elizabeth had responded to straitened finances with parsimony, transferring much of the expense of her court, for instance, onto wealthy subjects, whom she visited for extended periods on her summer "progresses." She also kept a tight lid on honorific titles, creating new knights or peers very rarely, even though the years of her reign saw considerable upward social mobility. Many of those who became wealthy during her reign, including Sir Francis Drake, did so as pirates and privateers. In consequence, by 1603 there was considerable pent-up pressure both for honors and for more tangible rewards for courtiers and government officials. As soon as James came to power he was besieged with supplicants.

James responded with what seemed to him appropriate royal munificence, knighting and ennobling many of his courtiers and endowing them with opulent gifts. His expenses were much higher than Elizabeth's; the Crown had to maintain not only his own household but also separate establishments for his queen, Anna, and for the heir apparent, Prince Henry. Yet James quickly became notorious for his financial heedlessness. Compared to Elizabeth's, his court was disorderly and wasteful, marked by hard drinking, gluttonous feasting, and a craze for hunting. "It is not possible for a king of England . . . to be rich or safe, but by frugality," warned James's lord treasurer, Robert Cecil, but James seemed unable to restrain himself. Soon after assuming the throne he was deeply in debt and unable to persuade Parliament to bankroll him by raising taxes. As the republican writer Lucy Hutchinson put it, in "setting honors to public sale," James empowered people "to invent projects to pill [plunder] the people, and pick their purses for the maintenance of vice and lewdness."

The king's financial difficulties set his authoritarian assertions about the monarch's supremacy at odds with Parliament's control over taxation. How were his prerogatives as a ruler to coexist with the rights of his subjects? Particularly disturbing to many was James's tendency to bestow high offices upon favorites apparently chosen for good looks rather than for good judgment. James's openly romantic attachment first to Robert Carr, Earl of Somerset, and then to George Villiers, Duke of Buckingham, gave rise to widespread rumors of homosexuality at court. James's own letters, in which he refers to his "Steenie" (a diminutive of St. Stephen) in headily erotic terms, make it clear that James's homosexuality was more than a rumor. The period had complex attitudes toward same-sex relationships; on the one hand, "sodomy" was a capital (though rarely prosecuted) crime; on the other hand, passionately intense male friendship, sometimes suffused with eroticism, constituted an important cultural ideal. In James's case, at least, contemporaries considered his susceptibility to lovely, expensive youths a political rather than a moral calamity. For his critics, it crystallized what was wrong with unlimited royal power: the ease with which a king could confuse his own desires with a divine mandate. There were also occasional conflicts between the king and Prince Henry, who was often seen as more martially Protestant and interventionist than his peace-keeping father, as well as between the king and Queen Anna, whose reputed Catholicism—and alliances with powerful courtiers, including Lucy Harington Russell, Countess of Bedford—often put her at odds with her husband. A 1617 diary entry by Lady Anne Clifford, who was engaged in a fierce battle for the Clifford properties, gives a vivid sense of the complex personal and political relations in the Jacobean (from *Jacobus*, Latin for James) court: "I went presently . . . to the Drawing Chamber where my Lady Derby told the Queen how my business stood, and that I was to go to the King; so she promised me she would do all the good in it she could. When I had stayed but a little while there I was sent for . . . , my Lord and I going through my Lord Buckingham's Chamber, who brought us into the King." "The Queen gave me a warning not to trust my matters absolutely to the King," Clifford concludes her entry, "lest he should deceive me." The Jacobean court was neither as authoritarian nor as centralized as one might imagine.

Despite James's frictions with Parliament, and his chronic problems of self-management, he was nonetheless politically astute. Like Elizabeth, he often succeeded not through decisiveness but through canny inaction. Cautious by temperament, he characterized himself as a peacemaker and for many years successfully kept England out of the religious wars raging on the Continent. His 1604 peace treaty with England's old enemy, Spain, made the Atlantic safe for English ships, a prerequisite for the colonization of the New World and for regular long-distance trading expeditions into the Mediterranean and down the African coast into the Indian Ocean. James's reign saw the establishment of the first permanent English settlements in North America, first at Jamestown and then in the Bermudas, at Plymouth, and in the Caribbean. In 1611, the East India Company established England's first foothold in India. Even when expeditions ended disastrously, as did Henry Hudson's 1611 attempt to find the Northwest Passage, and Walter Ralegh's 1617 expedition to Guiana, they often asserted territorial claims that England would exploit in later decades. While Jamestown certainly struggled, the decimation of Indigenous populations and the arrival of the first enslaved Africans in 1619 laid the groundwork for future colonial success. England itself was not immune to threats from abroad. In 1625, for example, Barbary pirates (Muslim privateers who operated from North Africa) captured and enslaved sixty people from the Cornwall coast. Despite late Elizabethan "Edicts of Expulsion" authorizing the removal of "blackamoors" from England, Black people were nonetheless present in England (and Scotland) in a variety of capacities during the period; the archives include records of a trumpeter, a needle maker, a decorated soldier, and "Grace Robinson, a Black moor" who had a seat at the laundress's table in Anne Clifford's household.

Although the Crown's deliberate attempts to manage the economy were often misguided, its frequent inattention or refusal to interfere often had the unintentional effect of stimulating growth. Early seventeenth-century entrepreneurs undertook a wide variety of schemes for industrial and agricultural improvement. Some ventures were almost as loony as Sir Politic Would-be's ridiculous moneymaking notions in Ben Jonson's *Volpone* (1606), but others were serious, profitable enterprises. In the south, domestic industries began manufacturing goods like pins and light woolens that had previously been imported. In the north, newly developed coal mines provided fuel for England's growing cities. In the east, landowners drained wetlands, producing more arable land to feed England's rapidly growing population and to accrue wealth for themselves. These endeavors gave rise to a new respect for the practical arts, a faith in technology as a means of improving human life, and a conviction that the future might be better than the past: all important influences on the scientific theories of Francis Bacon and his seventeenth-century followers, even as thinkers such as Margaret Cavendish offered resistance and critique. Economic growth in this period owed as much to the initiative of individuals and small groups as to government policy, a factor that encouraged a reevaluation of the role of self-interest, the profit motive, and the role of business contracts in society. This reevaluation was a prerequisite for the secular, contractual political theories proposed by Thomas Hobbes and John Locke later in the seventeenth century. There were also multiple uprisings and riots by common people in the period, primarily over food scarcity and the enclosure of common lands. In March 1629, for example, hundreds of starving women and children boarded a Flemish ship in the Essex port town of Maldon and forced its crew to fill their caps and aprons with grain from its hold. The period also saw fierce contestations over vagrancy (including the mere presence of itinerant "Gypsies" and "Irish"), poor laws, and policing.

The Church of England also faced many challenges in the early seventeenth century, and James was again often most successful when he was least activist. Since the Reformation, English rulers considered themselves heads of the Church of England, and, largely for reasons of political order, demanded that their subjects belong to one unified church. Yet the Reformation itself had opened up many areas of religious debate, and England's own history of vacillating between Protestant and Catholic rule meant that those debates were still very much alive. Sixteenth- and seventeenth-century English people argued over many aspects of ritual and faith. How should public worship be conducted, and what sorts of qualifications should ministers possess? How should scripture be understood? How should people pray? What did the sacrament of Communion mean? What happened to people's souls after they died? Elizabeth's government had needed to devise a common religious practice when actual consensus was impossible. Sensibly, it sought a middle ground between traditional and reformed views. Everyone was legally required to attend Church of England services, and the form of the services themselves was mandated in the Elizabethan Book of Common Prayer. The Book of Common Prayer deliberately avoided addressing abstruse theological controversies. The language of the English church service was carefully chosen to be open to several interpretations and acceptable to both Protestant- and Catholic-leaning subjects.

The Elizabethan compromise effectively tamed many of the Reformation's divisive energies and proved acceptable to the majority of English people. Yet to staunch Catholics on one side, and ardent Protestants on the other, the Elizabethan church seemed to have sacrificed truth to political expediency. Catholics wanted to return England to the Roman fold; while some of them were loyal subjects of the queen, others advocated invasion by a foreign Catholic power. Meanwhile the "Puritans," as they were disparagingly called—they referred to themselves as the "godly"—pressed for more thoroughgoing reformation in doctrine, ritual, and church government, urging the elimination of "popish" elements from worship services and "idolatrous" religious images from churches. Some, the Presbyterians, wanted to separate lay and clerical power in the national church, so that church leaders would be appointed by other ministers rather than the state. Others, known as separatists, advocated abandoning a national church in favor of small congregations of the "elect."

The resistance of religious minorities to Elizabeth's established church opened them to state persecution. In the 1580s and 1590s, Catholic priests

The Execution of the Gunpowder Plot Conspirators. This engraving by the Dutch artist Crispijn van de Passe shows the execution of the Gunpowder Conspirators for treason in January 1606. The punishment for treason was deliberately "cruel and unusual": the traitor was sentenced to be dragged through town on a wicker hurdle "at horse's tail," hanged but cut down while still conscious, and then castrated, disemboweled, beheaded, and his body cut into four pieces and parboiled. Though the punishment was often commuted to simple beheading or hanging, in the case of the Gunpowder Conspirators it was carried out in its entirety. On the left, the condemned men are taken to the place of execution. In the middle, the heart of one of the conspirators is being torn out, to be thrown into the fire. On the right, the heads of the conspirators are mounted on poles for display.

and the laypeople who harbored them were executed for treason, and radical Protestants for heresy. Both groups thus greeted James's accession enthusiastically; his mother, Mary, Queen of Scots, had been Catholic, while his upbringing had been in the strict reformed tradition of the Scottish Presbyterian Kirk. James began his reign with a conference at Hampton Court, one of his palaces, during which advocates debated a variety of religious views. Yet the Puritans failed to persuade him to make any substantive reforms. Practically speaking, the Puritan belief that congregations should choose their leaders diminished the monarch's power by stripping him of authority over ecclesiastical appointments. More generally, allowing people to choose their leaders in any sphere of life threatened to subvert the entire system of deference and hierarchy upon which the institution of monarchy itself seemed to rest. As James famously remarked: "No bishop, no king."

Catholics did not fare well in the new reign either. Initially inclined to lift Elizabethan sanctions against them, James hesitated when he realized the popular extent of the opposition to toleration. Then, barely two years into his reign, a small group of disaffected Catholics packed a cellar adjacent to the Houses of Parliament with gunpowder, intending to detonate it on the day that the king formally opened Parliament, with Prince Henry, the Houses of Lords and Commons, and the leading justices in attendance. The conspirators were arrested before they could effect their plan, but if the "Gunpowder Plot" had succeeded, it would have eliminated much of England's ruling class in a single tremendous explosion, and exposed the country to invasion by a foreign Catholic power. Not surprisingly, the Gunpowder Plot dramatically heightened anti-Catholic paranoia in England, and its apparently miraculous revelation was widely seen as a sign of God's care for England's Protestant governors. Many Catholics, known as "recusants" for their refusal to attend Church of England services, went underground.

In the end, James's ecclesiastical policies continued along the lines laid down by Elizabeth. By appointing bishops of varying doctrinal views, he restrained any single faction from controlling church policy. The most important religious event (and literary accomplishment) of James's reign was a newly commissioned translation of the Bible. First published in 1611, the King James Bible was a typically moderating document. A much more graceful rendering than its predecessor, the Geneva version produced by Puritan expatriates in the 1550s, the King James Bible immediately became the standard English scripture. Its impressive rhythms and memorable phrasing would influence writers for centuries. On the one hand, the new translation contributed to the Protestant aim of making the Bible widely available to every reader in their own language. On the other hand, unlike the Geneva Bible, the King James version translated controversial and ambiguous passages in ways that bolstered conservative preferences for a ceremonial church and for a hierarchically organized church government. Regardless, the widespread availability of an English Bible invited a range of interpreters, and interpretations, beyond the control of church or state. As the royalist William Cavendish wrote in a letter to the future Charles II in 1658, when the monarchy and nobility were in full crisis, "The Bible in English under every weaver's and chambermaid's arms hath done us much hurt."

James's moderation was not universally popular. Some Protestants yearned for a more confrontational policy toward Catholic powers—particularly toward England's old enemy, Spain. In the first decade of James's reign, this party clustered around James's eldest son and heir apparent, Prince Henry, who cultivated a militantly Protestant persona. When Henry died of typhoid fever in 1612, those who favored his policies were forced to seek avenues of power outside the royal court. By 1621, the House of Commons was developing a vigorous sense of its own independence, debating policy agendas often quite at odds with the Crown's, and openly attempting to use its power to approve taxation as a means of exacting concessions from the king.

James's second son, Prince Charles, came to the throne upon James's death in 1625. Unlike his father, Charles was not a theorist of royal absolutism, but he acted on that principle with an inflexibility that far exceeded his father's. By 1629 he had dissolved Parliament three times in frustration with its recalcitrance. He then embarked upon more than a decade of "personal rule" without summoning Parliament at all. Charles was more prudent in some respects than his father had been—he not only restrained the costs of his own court, but paid off his father's staggering debts as well. Throughout his reign, he conscientiously applied himself to the business of government. Yet his refusal to involve powerful individuals and factions in the workings of the state inevitably alienated them and cut him off from important channels of information about the opinions and reactions of his people. Money was also a problem. Even a relatively frugal king required some funds for ambitious government initiatives; but without parliamentary approval, any taxes Charles imposed were widely perceived as illegal. As a result, even popular policies, such as Charles's effort to build up the English navy, spawned misgivings among many of his subjects.

Religious conflicts also intensified. Charles's queen, the French princess Henrietta Maria, supported an entourage of Roman Catholic priests and French women courtiers, protected English Catholics, and encouraged several noblewomen in her court to convert to Catholicism. While Charles remained a staunch member of the Church of England, he loved visual splendor and majestic ceremony in all aspects of life, spiritual and otherwise—proclivities that led his Puritan subjects to suspect him of popish sympathies. Charles's profound attachment to his wife, so different from James's sparring with Anna, only deepened their qualms. Like many fellow Puritans, Lucy Hutchinson blamed the debacle of Charles's reign on his wife's influence: concerned only with "the meritoriousness of advancing her own religion," Hutchinson wrote, the queen used her "great wit and parts, and the power her haughty spirit kept over her husband" to "promote her own designs."

Charles's appointment of William Laud as archbishop of Canterbury, the ecclesiastical head of the English Church, further alienated the godly. Laud subscribed to a theology that most Puritans rejected. As followers of the sixteenth-century reformer John Calvin, Puritans held that salvation depended on faith in Christ, not "works." Works were meaningless, because the deeds of sinful human beings could not be sanctified in the absence of faith; moreover, the Fall had so thoroughly corrupted human beings that they could not muster this faith without the help of God's grace. God chose (or refused) to extend grace to particular individuals on grounds that human beings were incapable of comprehending, and his decision had been made from eternity, before the individuals concerned were even born. In other words, the godly believed that God predestined people to be saved or damned, and Christ's redemptive sacrifice was designed only for those who were saved, the "elect." Laud, by contrast, advocated the Arminian doctrine that through Christ, God made redemption freely available to all human beings. (Arminius was a Dutch theologian.) Individuals could choose whether to respond to God's grace, and they could work toward their salvation by acts of charity, ritual devotion, and generosity to the church.

Although Laud's theology appears more generously inclusive than the Calvinist alternative, his ecclesiastical policies were uncompromising. Stripping many "Puritan" ministers of their posts, Laud aligned the doctrine and ceremonies of the English church with those of Roman Catholicism, which, like Arminianism, held works in high regard. In an ambitious project of church renovation, Laud also installed religious paintings and images in churches; he thought they promoted reverence in worshippers, but the more godly Protestants believed they encouraged idolatry. Laud also rebuilt and resituated church altars, making them more ornate and prominent—another change that dismayed Puritans, since it implied that the Eucharist, rather than the sermon, was the central element of worship. Herbert's magnificent poem "The Altar" nods toward this controversy. In the 1630s, thousands of Puritans departed for the New England colonies, but many more remained at home, deeply discontented and often resistant. In 1637 the Puritan writer William Prynne was found guilty of sedition, along with a fellow divine (Henry Burton) and a doctor (John Bastwick). As punishment, Prynne's nose was slit and the initials "S. L." were burned into his cheeks. The letters stood for "Seditious Libeller," but Prynne claimed that they signified "Stigma of Laud." This story, which Prynne wrote about in *A New Discovery of the Prelates Tyranny* (1641), and which Milton alludes to in his sonnet "On the New Forcers of Conscience," became fodder in the battle against Laud.

As the 1630s drew to a close, Archbishop Laud and Charles attempted to impose a version of the English liturgy and episcopal organization on

Presbyterian Scotland. Unlike his father, Charles had little acquaintance with his northern realm, and he drastically underestimated the difficulties involved. The Scots objected on both nationalist and religious grounds, and they were not shy about expressing their objections: the bishop of Brechin, obliged to conduct divine service in the prescribed English style, mounted the pulpit armed with two pistols against his unruly congregation, while his wife, stationed on the floor below, backed him up with a blunderbuss. In the conflict that followed, the Bishops' Wars of 1639 and 1640, Charles's forces met with abject defeat. Exacerbating the situation, Laud at the same time was insisting on greater conformity within the English church. Riots in the London streets and the Scots' occupation of several northern English cities forced Charles to call into session the so-called Long Parliament, which would soon be managing a revolution.

LITERATURE AND CULTURE, 1603–1640

Old Ideas and New

In the first part of the seventeenth century, exciting new scientific theories were in the air; but older ways of thinking about the nature of things had not yet been superseded. Writers such as John Donne and Ben Jonson often invoked an inherited body of concepts even though they were aware that those concepts were being questioned or displaced. The Ptolemaic universe, with its fixed earth and circling sun, moon, planets, and stars, was a rich source of poetic imagery. So were the four elements—fire, earth, water, and air—that together were thought to constitute all matter, and the four bodily humors—choler, blood, phlegm, and black bile—that were supposed to determine a person's temperament and to cause physical and mental disease when out of balance. Late Elizabethans and Jacobeans considered themselves especially prone to melancholy, an ailment of scholars and thinkers stemming from an excess of black bile. Shakespeare's Hamlet is melancholic, as is Bosola in John Webster's *The Duchess of Malfi* and Milton's title figure in "Il Penseroso" ("the serious-minded one"). In his panoramic *Anatomy of Melancholy* (1621), Robert Burton argued that melancholy was universal.

Key concepts of this inherited system of knowledge were analogy and order. Donne was especially fond of drawing parallels between the macrocosm, or "big world," and the microcosm, or "little world," of the individual human being. (See also George Herbert's "Man".) Also widespread were versions of the "chain of being" that linked and ordered various kinds of beings in hierarchies. The order of nature, for instance, put God above angels, angels above human beings, human beings above animals, animals above plants, plants above rocks. The social order installed the king over his nobles, nobles over the gentry, gentry over yeomen, yeomen over common laborers. The order of the family set husband above wife, parents above children, master and mistress above servants, the elderly above the young. Each level had its particular function, and each was connected to those *above and beneath* in a tight network of obligation and dependency. Items that occupied similar positions in different hierarchies were related by

The Great Chain of Being. This illustration of the "Great Chain of Being" from Diego Valadés's 1579 *Rhetorica Christiana* shows the hierarchy of the universe according to Christian orthodoxy. God is at the top of the diagram surrounded by angels, with the blessed souls in heaven sitting on clouds just beneath; below them is the layer of humans, with Eve emerging from Adam's rib in the center; below that are layers of birds, fish, and beasts; below that is a layer of plants upon the earth. All these layers are connected by a chain running down the middle, imagined as connecting all of God's creation. At the bottom, detached from the Great Chain, are Satan and his rebel angels, who can be seen falling from heaven into hell in the right margin.

analogy: thus a monarch was like God, and he was also like a father, the head of the family, or like a lion, most majestic of beasts, or like the sun, the most excellent of heavenly bodies. Medieval or Renaissance poets who call a king a sun or a lion, then, imagine themselves not to be forging a metaphor in their own creative imagination, but to be describing something like an obvious fact of nature. Many Jacobean tragedies depict the catastrophes that ensue when these hierarchies rupture and both the social order and the natural order disintegrate.

Yet this conceptual system was itself beginning to crumble. Francis Bacon advocated rooting out of the mind all the intellectual predilections that had made the old ideas so attractive: love of ingenious correlations, reverence for tradition, and *a priori* assumptions about what was possible in nature. Instead, he argued, groups of collaborators ought to design controlled experiments to find the truths of nature by empirical means. Even as Bacon was promoting his views in *The Advancement of Learning*, *Novum Organum*, and *The New Atlantis*, actual experiments and discoveries were calling the old verities into question. From the far-flung territories that England was beginning to colonize or to trade with, collectors brought animal, plant, and ethnological novelties, many of which were hard to subsume under old categories of understanding. Some of the materials that Richard Ligon collected in Barbados, for example, formed the basis of what would become the British Museum. William Harvey's discovery that blood circulated in the body shook received views on the function of blood, casting doubt on the theory of the humors. Galileo's telescope provided evidence confirming Copernican astronomical theory, which dislodged the earth from its stable central position in the cosmos and, in defiance of all ordinary observation, set it whirling around the sun. Galileo found evidence as well of change in the heavens, which were supposed to be perfect and incorruptible above the level of the moon. Donne, like other writers of his age, responded with a mixture of excitement and anxiety to such novel ideas:

> And new philosophy calls all in doubt:
> The element of fire is quite put out;
> The sun is lost, and the earth, and no man's wit
> Can well direct him where to look for it. ("An Anatomy of the World")

Several decades later, however, Milton embraced the new science, proudly recalling a visit during his European tour to "the famous Galileo, grown old, a prisoner to the Inquisition for thinking in astronomy otherwise than the Franciscan and Dominican licensers thought." In *Paradise Lost*, he would make complex poetic use of the astronomical controversy, considering how, and how far, humans should pursue scientific knowledge. In the invocation to her epic poem *Order and Disorder*, Lucy Hutchinson asks her muse: "Let not my thoughts beyond their bound aspire." Yet the poem's celebration of the "mystic wonders" of the world is nonetheless infused with the materialist views found in Lucretius's *De rerum natura* (On the Nature of Things), which Hutchinson was the first to translate into English. Margaret Cavendish's materialist philosophy theorized a self-moving nature imbued with knowledge, and her poetry imagined and celebrated both possible worlds and animal and plant intelligences. Similarly influenced by materialist philosophies, Hester Pulter wrote poems in which she imagined the processes by which beings, "dispersed to atoms," "give a being to another world," and a flower reduced to ashes is brought back to life. The "new philosophy" neither wholly displaced the old, nor settled into common acceptance without robust and ongoing debate.

Patrons, Printers, and Acting Companies

The social institutions, customs, and practices that had supported and regulated writers in Tudor times changed only gradually before 1640. As it had under Elizabeth, the Church promoted writing of several kinds: devotional treatises; guides to meditation; controversial tracts; "cases of conscience," which work out difficult moral issues in complex situations; and, especially, sermons. Since everyone was required to attend church, everyone heard sermons at least once and often twice on Sunday, as well as on religious or national holidays. The essence of a sermon, Protestants agreed, was the careful exposition of scripture, and its purpose was to instruct and to move. Yet styles varied; while some preachers, like Donne, strove to enthrall their congregations with all the resources of artful rhetoric, others, especially Puritans, sought an undecorated style that would display God's word in its own splendor. Printing made it easy to circulate many copies of sermons, blurring the line between oral delivery and written text, and enhancing the role of printers and booksellers in disseminating God's word.

Many writers of the period depended in one way or another on literary patronage. Like their medieval forebears, Jacobean and Caroline (from *Carolus*, Latin for Charles) aristocrats were expected to reward dependents in return for services and homage. In the early seventeenth century, although commercial relationships were rapidly replacing feudal ones, patronage pervaded all walks of life: it governed relationships between landlords and tenants, masters and servants, kings and courtiers. Writers were assimilated into this system partly because their works reflected well on the patron, and partly because their all-around intelligence and writing skills made them useful members of elite households or political factions. Important patrons of the time included the royal family—especially Queen Anna, who sponsored court masques, and Prince Henry—the members of the intermarried Sidney and Herbert families, and Lucy Harington Russell, Countess of Bedford, Queen Anna's confidante.

Because the patronage relationship often took the form of an exchange of favors rather than a simple financial transaction, its terms were variable and thus difficult to recover from a historical distance. A poet might dedicate a poem or a work to a patron in the expectation of a simple cash payment, but a patron might provide a wide range of other benefits: a place to live; employment as a secretary, tutor, or household servant; or a gift of clothing. (Textiles were valuable commodities.) Donne, for instance, received financial support from Lucy Russell, Countess of Bedford; inexpensive lodging from the Drury family, for whom he wrote the *Anniversaries*; a suit of clerical attire from James Hay, when he took orders in the Church of England; and advancement in the church from King James. Ben Jonson lived for several years at the country estates of Lord Aubigny and of Robert Sidney, in whose honor he wrote "To Penshurst"; he received a regular salary from the king in return for writing court masques; and he served as chaperone to Sir Walter Ralegh's son on a Continental tour. Aemilia Lanyer claimed to have resided for some time in the household of Margaret Clifford, Countess of Cumberland, and her frequent invocations of the countess in her *Salve Deus Rex Judaeorum* invite an ongoing relationship. Andrew Marvell lived for two years with Thomas Fairfax, tutored Fairfax's daughter, and dedicated his great country house poem, *Upon Appleton House*, to him. All these quite different relationships and forms of remuneration fall under the rubric of patronage.

The patronage system required the poets involved to hone their skills in praising their patrons. Many of Jonson's epigrams, Donne's verse letters, and Lanyer's dedicatory poems evoke communities of virtuous poets and patrons joined by bonds of mutual respect and affection, or by shared religious, philosophical, or political concerns. Like the line between sycophantic flattery and truthful depiction, the line between patronage and friendship could be a thin one. Literary manuscripts circulated among circles of acquaintances and supporters, many of whom were, at least occasionally, writers as well as readers. Jonson esteemed Mary Wroth both as a fellow poet and as a member of the Sidney family to whom he owed so much. Donne became part of a coterie around Queen Anna's chief courtier, Lucy Russell, Countess of Bedford, who was also an important patron for Ben Jonson, Michael Drayton, and Samuel Daniel. The countess evidently wrote poems herself, although apparently only one attributed to her has survived.

Writers did not have to print a poem to present it to a patron or to circulate it among friends or allies. In early seventeenth-century England, the reading public for sophisticated literary works was small and concentrated in a few social settings: the royal court, the universities, the Inns of Court (or law schools), and great (and a few less-than-great) households, some of which were headed by women. In these circumstances, manuscript circulation was an effective way of reaching, and (at least in theory) restricting, one's audience. A great deal of writing thus remained in manuscript in early seventeenth-century England. The collected works of many important writers of the period—most notably John Donne, George Herbert, Andrew Marvell, and William Shakespeare—appeared in print only posthumously, in editions produced by friends or admirers. Other writers, like Robert Herrick, collected and printed their own works long after they were written and (probably) circulated in manuscript. Still others, including Katherine Philips, claimed that their work had been pirated, or published without their consent. In consequence, it is often difficult to accurately date the composition of a seventeenth-century poem. Some writings, like the entirety of Hester Pulter's oeuvre and the vast majority of Lucy Hutchinson's, were never printed. When authors did not participate in the printing of their own works, editorial questions multiply—when, for instance, the printed version of a poem is inconsistent with a surviving manuscript copy. For some poets, including Donne, there are hundreds of extant manuscripts.

Nonetheless, the printing of all kinds of literary works was becoming more common. Writers such as Francis Bacon, who hoped to reach large numbers of readers with whom they were not acquainted, usually arranged for the printing of their texts soon after they were composed. The sense that the printing of lyric poetry, in particular, was a bit vulgar began to fade when the already famous Ben Jonson collected his own works in a grand folio edition in 1616, the same year (not coincidentally) in which the king published his own collected *Works*.

Until 1640, the Stuart kings kept in place the strict controls over print publication originally instituted by Henry VIII in response to the ideological threat posed by the Reformation. Henry had given the members of London's Stationer's Company a monopoly on all printing; in return for their privilege, they were supposed to submit texts for prepublication censorship. In the latter part of the sixteenth century, presses associated with the universities at Oxford and Cambridge began operation as well, but they focused largely on scholarly and theological books. As a result, with a few exceptions, such as George Herbert's *The Temple*, which was published by Cambridge University Press, almost all printed literary texts were produced in London. Most of them were sold there as well, in the booksellers' stalls set up outside St. Paul's Cathedral.

The licensing system located both primary responsibility for a printed work and its ownership with the printer rather than with the author. Printers typically paid writers a one-time fee for the use of their work, but the payment was small, and the authors of popular texts earned no royalties from the copies sold. As a result, no one could make a living as a writer in the early seventeenth century by producing best sellers. The first English writer to formally arrange for royalties was John Milton, who received five pounds up front for *Paradise Lost*, and another five pounds (and two hundred copies) at the end of each of the first three impressions. Legal ownership of and control over printed works remained with the printers: authorial copyright would not become a reality until the early eighteenth century. During the early seventeenth century, some publishers began to specialize in literary texts. Humphrey Moseley, for example, published Donne, Richard Crashaw, Henry Vaughan, and Milton, among others. Many of these volumes included engravings of the authors on their title pages. A not-very-flattering portrait of a middle-aged Milton in his 1645 *Poems* drew a marked contrast with the cherubic engraving of the sixteen-year-old Abraham Cowley printed on the title page to his *Blossoms* (1633).

In monetary terms, a more promising outlet for writers was the commercial theater, which provided the first successful literary market in English history. Profitable and popular acting companies established successfully in London in Elizabeth's time continued to play a very important cultural role under James and Charles. Because the acting companies staged a large number of different plays and paid for them at a predictable, if not generous, rate, they enabled a few hardworking writers to support themselves as full-time professionals. One of them, Thomas Dekker, commented bemusedly on the novelty of being paid for the mere products of one's imagination: "The theater," he wrote, "is your poet's Royal Exchange upon which their muses—that are now turned to merchants—meeting, barter away that light commodity of words." (The Royal Exchange was the center of commerce for the City of London.) In James's reign, Shakespeare was at the height of his powers: *Othello, King Lear, Macbeth, Antony and Cleopatra, The Winter's Tale, The Tempest*, and other major plays were first staged during these years. So were Jonson's major comedies: *Volpone, Epicoene, The Alchemist*, and *Bartholomew Fair*. The most important new playwright was John Webster, whose dark tragedies *The White Devil* and *The Duchess of Malfi* combined gothic horror with stunningly beautiful poetry.

Just as printers were legally the owners of the texts they printed, so theater companies, not playwrights, were the owners of the texts they performed.

Typically, companies guarded their scripts closely, permitting them to be printed only in times of financial distress, or when the works were so old that printing them seemed unlikely to reduce the paying audience. As a result, many Jacobean and Caroline plays are lost or available only in corrupt or posthumous versions. For contemporaries, though, a play was "published" not by being printed but by being performed. Aware of the dangerous potential of plays in arousing the sentiments of large crowds of onlookers, the Stuarts, like the Tudors before them, instituted tight controls over dramatic performances. Like printers, acting companies were obliged to submit works to the censor before public presentation.

Authors, printers, and acting companies who flouted the censorship laws were subject to imprisonment, fines, or even bodily mutilation. Queen Elizabeth cut off the hand of a man who disagreed in print with her marriage plans; King Charles, the ears of a man who inveighed against court masques. Jonson and his collaborators found themselves in prison for ridiculing James's broad Scots accent in a comedy. The effects of censorship were therefore far-reaching across literary genres. Since overt criticism or satire of the great was so dangerous, political writing was apt to be oblique and allegorical. As the literary theorist George Puttenham put it, the genre of pastoral used "the veil of homely [rustic] persons" to "glance at greater matters, and such as perchance had not been safe to have been disclosed in any other sort." Writers often employed animal fables, tales of distant lands, or descriptions of long-past historical events to comment on contemporary issues.

While the commercial theaters were profitable businesses that made most of their money from paying audiences, several factors combined to bring writing for the theater closer to the court than it had been in Elizabeth's time. The Elizabethan theater companies had been officially associated with noblemen who guaranteed their legitimacy (in contrast to unsponsored traveling players, who were subject to punishment as vagrants). Early in his reign, James brought the major theater companies under royal auspices. Shakespeare's company, the most successful of the day, became the King's Men: it performed not only Shakespeare's plays, but also *Volpone* and *The Duchess of Malfi*. Queen Anna, Prince Henry, Prince Charles, and Princess Elizabeth sponsored other companies. Royal patronage, which brought with it tangible rewards and regular court performances, naturally encouraged the theater companies to pay more attention to courtly taste. Shakespeare's *Macbeth* put onstage Scots history and witches, two of James's own interests; in *King Lear*, the hero's disastrous division of his kingdom may reflect controversies over James's proposed union of Scotland and England. Both *Othello* and *The Tempest* were performed at court, and the latter alluded to contemporary colonial mishaps. In the first four decades of the seventeenth century, court-affiliated theater companies such as the King's Men increasingly cultivated audiences markedly more affluent than the audiences they had sought in the 1580s and 1590s, performing in intimate, expensive indoor theaters instead of, or as well as, in the cheap popular amphitheaters. *The Duchess of Malfi*, for instance, was probably written with the King's Men's indoor theater at Blackfriars in mind; several scenes *depend for their effect* on control over lighting that would have been impossible outdoors. Partly because the commercial theaters seemed increasingly to cater to the affluent and courtly elements of society, they attracted the ire of the king's opponents when civil war broke out in the 1640s. Even before closet drama took off in the 1640s, Elizabeth Cary, Lady Falkland, published *The Tragedy of Mariam* (1613), a remarkable, and politically resonant, closet drama about a queen subjected to her husband's domestic and political tyranny. While the term "closet" suggests private reading, closet dramas were often read aloud or performed in smaller settings. Wroth's unpublished play *Loves Victory* (ca. 1620), which is full of familial and topical allusions, was likely performed at Penshurst, or another country estate nearby.

Jacobean Writers and Genres

The era saw important changes in poetic fashion. Some major Elizabethan genres fell out of favor—long allegorical or mythological narratives, sonnet sequences (Wroth's 1621 *Pamphilia to Amphilanthus* excepted), and pastoral poems. Others came into ascendancy—particularly short, concentrated, often witty poems. Poets and prose writers alike often preferred the jagged rhythms of colloquial speech to the elaborate ornamentation and near-musical orchestration of sound sought by many Elizabethans. Many notable poets of these years, including Jonson, Donne, and Herbert, led this shift and also promoted a variety of "new" genres: love elegy and satire after the classical models of Ovid and Horace, epigram, verse epistle, meditative religious lyric, and country house poem. Aemilia Lanyer also made notable contributions, particularly to these last three of these genres. Her *Salve Deus Rex Judaeorum* (1611) contained verse letters to powerful court women, a long poem on Christ's passion that focused on the role of godly women, and the first country house poem, "The Description of Cookham."

Although Jonson, Donne, and Herbert differed enormously from one another, they all exercised a significant influence on the poets of the next generation. A native Londoner, Jonson first distinguished himself as an acute observer of urban manners in a series of early, controversial satiric plays. Although he wrote two of his most moving poems to his dead children, Jonson rarely focused on the family dynamics that so profoundly concerned his contemporary Shakespeare. When generational and dynastic matters do figure in his poetry, as they do at the end of "To Penshurst," they seem part of the agrarian, feudal order that Jonson may have romanticized but certainly knew was disappearing. Jonson interested himself in relationships that were negotiated by the participants themselves, often in bustling urban or courtly milieux in which blood kinship no longer decisively determined one's social place. Jonson's poems of praise celebrate and exemplify classical and humanist ideals of friendship: like-minded men and women elect to join in a community that fosters wisdom, generosity, civic responsibility, and mutual respect. In his plays and satiric poems, Jonson stages the violation of those values with such riotous comprehensiveness that the very survival of such ideals seems endangered; the plays swarm with voracious swindlers and their eager victims, social climbers both adroit and inept, and a dizzying assortment of morons and misfits. In many of Jonson's plays, rogues or wits collude to victimize others. These stormy, self-interested alliances, apparently so different from the virtuous friendships of the poems of praise, in fact resemble them in one respect: they are connections entered into by choice, not by law, inheritance, or custom.

Throughout his life, Jonson earned his living from his writing, composing plays for the public theater while also attracting patronage as a poet and a writer of court masques. He found particular success collaborating with the architect and set- and costume-designer Inigo Jones. Jonson's acute awareness of his audience was partly, then, a sheerly practical matter. Yet his yearning for recognition far exceeded any desire for material reward. A gifted poet, Jonson argued, was a society's proper judge and teacher, and he could be effective only if his audience understood and respected the poet's exalted role. Jonson set out unabashedly to create that audience and to monumentalize himself as a great English author. When he took the step—unusual for his time—of collecting his poems, plays, and masques in an elegant folio volume titled *The Works of Ben Jonson*, a contemporary epigram poked fun at his pretensions: "Pray tell me Ben," the epigram asks, "where doth the mystery lurk / What others call a play, you call a work?" Jonson's audacious attempt to dignify popular drama may have made him the butt of someone's joke, but it had far-reaching consequences for the canonization of seventeenth-century stage plays, including in the First Folio of Shakespeare's, which appeared in 1623.

Jonson's influence on the next generation of writers, and, through them, into the Restoration and the eighteenth century, was an effect both of his poetic mastery of his chosen modes and of his powerful personal example. Jonson mentored a group of younger poets known as the Tribe (or Sons) of Ben, meeting regularly with some of them in the Apollo Room of the Devil Tavern in London. Many of the royalist, or "Cavalier," poets—Robert Herrick, Thomas Carew, Richard Lovelace, Sir John Suckling, Edmund Waller, Henry Vaughan (in his secular verse)—proudly acknowledged their relationship to Jonson or gave some evidence of it in their verse. Most of them also absorbed Jonson's attitude toward print and in later decades supervised the publication of their own poems. Jonson himself testifies to his particular indebtedness to Mary Wroth; and while his relationship with Lanyer is unknown, there are myriad resonances between the first two country house poems, her "The Description of Cookham" and his "To Penshurst."

Donne, like Jonson, spent most of his life in or near London, often in the company of other writers and intellectuals—indeed, in the company of many of the same writers and intellectuals, since the two men were friends and shared some of the same patrons. Yet unlike Jonson's, most of Donne's poetry concerns itself not with a crowded social panorama but with a dyad—a relationship between the speaker and one single other being, whether a lover, a friend, or God—that in its intensity blots out the claims of lesser relationships. Love for Donne encompasses an astonishing range of emotional experiences: from the lusty impatience of "To His Mistress Going to Bed" to the cheerful promiscuity of "The Indifferent" and mysterious platonic telepathy of "Air and Angels"; from the vengeful wit of "The Apparition" to the postcoital tranquility of "The Good Morrow." While for Jonson the shared meal among friends often becomes an emblem of communion, for Donne sexual consummation has something of the same highly charged symbolic character, a moment in which the isolated individual can, however temporarily, escape the boundaries of selfhood in union with another. As he writes in "The Canonization,"

> The phoenix riddle hath more wit
> By us: we two being one, are it.
> So, to one neutral thing both sexes fit.

In the religious poems, where Donne both yearns for an intimate, physical relationship with God and knows it is impossible, he does not abandon his characteristic bodily metaphors. Donne was fascinated by the doctrine of the Incarnation—God's taking material form in the person of Jesus Christ— and the doctrine of the bodily resurrection of the dead at the Last Day, Christian teachings to which he returns again and again in his poems, sermons, and devotional writings. While sexual and religious love had long shared a common vocabulary, Donne delights in making that overlap new and shocking. He likens conjoined lovers to saints; demands to be raped by God; speculates after his wife's death that God killed her because he was jealous of Donne's divided loyalty; imagines Christ encouraging his bride, the church, to "open" herself to as many men as possible. Donne also celebrated friendship in his poetry, both with men (as in his verse letter to Henry Wotton) and with women—particularly with his patron, Lucy Harington Russell, Countess of Bedford, for whom he wrote five verse letters, and with whom he exchanged books, letters, and poems.

Throughout Donne's life, his faith, like his intellect, was anything but quiet. Born into a devoutly Roman Catholic family just as the persecution of Catholics was intensifying in Elizabethan England, Donne eventually became a member of the Church of England. If "Satire 3" is any indication, the conversion was accompanied by profound doubt and an existential crisis. Donne's restless mind can lead him in surprising and sometimes unorthodox directions. At the same time, overwhelmed with a sense of his own unworthiness, he courts God's punishment, demanding to be spat upon, flogged, burned, and broken down in the expectation that suffering at God's hand will restore him to grace and favor.

In both style and content, Donne's poems are addressed to a select few rather than to the public at large. His style is demanding, characterized by learned terms, audaciously far-fetched analogies, and an intellectually sophisticated play of ironies. Even Donne's sermons, which were attended by large crowds, share the knotty difficulty of the poems, as well as something of their quality of intimate address. Donne circulated his poems in manuscript and largely avoided print publication (most of his poems were printed after his death). Some critics have regarded Donne as the founder of a "Metaphysical" school of poetry. (The term was coined by Samuel Johnson, who argued that in Donne's poetry, "the most heterogeneous ideas are yoked by violence together.") We find echoes of Donne's style in many later poets: in Thomas Carew (who praised Donne as a "monarch of wit"), George Herbert, Richard Crashaw, Sir John Suckling, Abraham Cowley, Hester Pulter, Andrew Marvell, and Katherine Philips.

Herbert, the younger son of a wealthy, cultivated, and well-connected family, seemed destined in early adulthood for a brilliant career as a diplomat or government servant. Yet he turned his back on worldly greatness to be ordained a priest in the Church of England. Moreover, eschewing a highly visible career as an urban preacher, he spent the remaining years of his short life ministering to the tiny rural parish of Bemerton in Wiltshire. Herbert's poetry is shot through with the difficulty and joy of this renunciation. Herbert identifies literary ambition—pride in one's independent creativity—as a temptation that must be resisted, whether it takes the form of Jonson's openly competitive aspiration for literary preeminence, or Donne's brilliantly ironic self-displaying performance. Instead, Herbert seeks other models for poetic agency: the secretary taking dictation from a master, the musician playing in harmonious consort with others, the member of a church congregation who speaks with and for a community.

Herbert destroyed his secular verse in English, and he turned his volume of religious verse over to a friend only on his deathbed, asking him to print it if he thought it would be useful to "some dejected poor soul," but otherwise to burn it. The 177 lyrics contained in that volume, *The Temple*, display a complex religious sensibility and great artistic subtlety in an amazing variety of stanza forms. Herbert was the major influence on the next generation of religious lyric poets and was explicitly recognized as such by Henry Vaughan and Richard Crashaw. (Crashaw titled his own collection *Steps to the Temple*.)

Like Herbert, Lady Mary Wroth was part of a well-connected and influential family. Wroth grew up at Penshurst, and as the niece of Sir Philip Sidney and Mary Sidney Herbert, Countess of Pembroke, she seemed destined for literary fame. When she published her long prose romance, *The Countess of Montgomery's Urania*, together with a Petrarchan sonnet sequence titled *Pamphilia to Amphilanthus* in 1621, she put her own stamp on the two famous genres. The *Urania* overturns many of the conventions of romance by focusing on a number of interlinked royal families and imagining the literary—as well as romantic—careers of their queens. The sonnet sequence *Pamphilia to Amphilanthus*, which takes its name from the romance's main characters, not only reverses the gender of lover and beloved but offers a bracing analysis of female subjectivity and desire. When Wroth's romance was criticized for "traducing," or shaming, living people, she told the Duke of Buckingham that the "strange constructions" that were made of her book were "as far from my meaning as is possible for truth to be from conjecture." Yet her choice of (notorious) publishers and (a famous) engraver indicates the nature and the scale of her ambition.

The Jacobean period saw the emergence of what would become a major prose genre, the familiar essay. The works of the French inventor of the form, Michel de Montaigne, appeared in English translation in 1603, influencing Shakespeare as well as later writers such as Sir Thomas Browne and Margaret Cavendish. Yet the first essays written in English—the work of Francis Bacon, who was attorney general under Elizabeth and eventually lord chancellor under James—bear little resemblance to Montaigne's intimate, wide-ranging, conversational pieces. Bacon's essays present pithy, sententious, sometimes provocative claims in a tone of cool objectivity, tempering moral counsel with an awareness of the importance of prudence and expediency in practical affairs. In *Novum Organum* Bacon adapts his deliberately discontinuous mode of exposition to outline a new scientific method, holding out the tantalizing prospect of eventual mastery over the natural world, and boldly articulating the ways in which science might improve the human condition. In his fictional utopia, *The New Atlantis*, Bacon imagines a society that realizes his dream of carefully orchestrated collaborative research, so different from what he saw as the erratic, uncoordinated efforts of alchemists and amateurs in his own day. Bacon's philosophically revolutionary approach to the natural world profoundly affected scientifically minded people over the next several generations. His writings influenced the materialist philosophy of his erstwhile secretary, Thomas Hobbes; encouraged Oliver Cromwell to attempt a large-scale overhaul of the university curriculum during the 1650s; and inspired the formation of the Royal Society, an organization of experimental scientists, in 1660. In the 1650s and 1660s, Margaret Cavendish responded to Bacon (and to Hobbes and the Royal Society, which she was the first woman to visit) by questioning some of their methods and instruments, and making a powerful case for the role of speculation, contemplation, and imagination in the "work of discovery."

THE CAROLINE ERA, 1625–1640

When Charles I came to the throne in 1625, Lucy Hutchinson recalled, "The fools and bawds, mimics and catamites of the former court grew out of fashion." The changed style of the court directly affected the arts and literature of the Caroline period (a name derived from *Carolus*, Latin for Charles). Charles and his French queen, Henrietta Maria, were art collectors on a large scale and patrons of such painters as Peter Paul Rubens and Anthony Van Dyck; the latter's portrayal of Charles as a heroic figure of knightly romance, mounted on a splendid stallion, is included in the color insert to this volume. The conjunction of chivalric virtue and divine beauty or love, symbolized in the union of the royal couple, was the dominant theme of Caroline court masques, which were even more extravagantly hyperbolic than their Jacobean predecessors. Henrietta Maria encouraged an artistic and literary cult of platonic love, which some courtier-poets mocked in more licentiously physical terms, and others celebrated in poems and court entertainments. In *The Blazing World*, Margaret Cavendish does both, imagining the presence of several souls in one body as a "Platonic seraglio," or harem.

The religious tensions between the Caroline Laudian church and the Puritan opposition produced something of a culture war. In 1633 Charles reissued the *Book of Sports*, originally published by his father in 1618, prescribing traditional holiday festivities and Sunday sports in every parish. Like his father, he saw these recreations as the rural, downscale equivalent of the court masque: harmless, healthy diversions for people who otherwise spent most of their waking hours hard at work. Puritans, however, regarded masques and rustic dances as occasions for sin, the maypole as a vestige of pagan phallus worship, and Sunday sports as a profanation of the Sabbath. In 1632 William Prynne staked out the most extreme Puritan position, publishing a thousand-page tirade, *Histriomastix: The Player's Scourge*, against stage plays, court masques, maypoles, Laudian church rituals, stained glass windows, mixed dancing, and other outrages, all of which he associated with licentiousness, effeminacy, and the seduction of popish idolatry. As punishment for this cultural critique, Prynne was stripped of his academic degrees, ejected from the legal profession, set in the pillory, and sentenced to life imprisonment. He also had his books burned and his ears cut off. The severity of the punishment indicates the perceived danger of Prynne's book, and the inextricability of literary and cultural affairs from politics.

Milton's astonishingly virtuosic early poems also respond to the tensions of the 1630s. Milton repudiated both courtly aesthetics and Prynne's wholesale prohibitions, developing reformed versions of pastoral, masque, and hymn. In "On the Morning of Christ's Nativity," the birth of Christ coincides with a casting out of idols and the flight of false gods, stanzas that suggest contemporary Puritan resistance to Laudian policies. Milton's magnificent funeral elegy "Lycidas" firmly rejects the poetic career of the Cavalier poet who disregards high artistic ambition to "sport with Amaryllis in the shade / Or with the tangles of Neaera's hair." The poem also vehemently denounces the establishment clergy, ignorant and greedy "blind mouths" who rob their flocks of spiritual nourishment.

King Charles at Prayer. This frontispiece from *Eikon Basilike* (Latin for Portrait of the King) represents the praying king as a Christlike martyr surrounded by allegorical representations of virtue under trial. The left background shows a rock besieged by waves in a storm, surmounted with a Latin caption reading "Triumphing unmoved." The left foreground displays palm trees with weights hung to their branches, which was supposed to make them grow more vigorously: the Latin caption reads "Virtue grows under burdens." A shaft of light pierces the storm clouds to illuminate Charles's head, with the caption "More clear out of the shadows." Wearing his coronation robes, Charles is nonetheless shown turning away from this turmoil, having cast aside an earthly crown, labeled "Vanity," to grasp a crown of thorns, labeled "Grace." Set before him is a "treatise of Christ" and a Bible reading "In your words, my hope." Charles is receiving a vision from heaven of the immortal crown, "Blessed and Eternal," with which his supporters believed God would reward him. Published within days of the king's execution, *Eikon Basilike* was an immediate best seller. In 1649 alone, thirty-five editions were published in England and twenty-five elsewhere in Europe.

THE REVOLUTIONARY ERA, 1640–1660

Early in the morning on January 30, 1649, Charles Stuart, the dethroned king Charles I, set off across St. James Park for his execution, surrounded by a heavy guard. He wore two shirts because the weather was frigid, and he did not want the thousands who had gathered to watch him be beheaded to think he was *shivering with fear*. The black-draped scaffold had been erected just outside James I's elegant Banqueting House, inside of which so many court masques had celebrated the might of the Stuart monarchs and assured them of their people's love and gratitude. To those who could not attend, newsbooks provided eyewitness accounts of the dramatic events of the execution, as they had of Charles's trial the week before. Contemporary poets registered the enormity of the execution as well. The royalist Katherine Philips asked "what noble eye could see (and careless pass) / The dying lion kicked by every ass?" Marvell's famously ambivalent celebration of Oliver Cromwell in "An Horatian Ode" includes a remarkable description of the "tragic scaffold" around which "armed bands / Did clap their bloody hands" as Charles tried "the axe's edge."

The execution of Charles I was understood at the time, and is still seen by many historians today, as a watershed event in English history. How did it come to pass? Historians do not agree over what caused "the English revolution," or, as it is alternatively called, the English Civil Wars. Some argue that the conflict was largely religious, others that long-term changes in English society and the English economy led to rising social tensions and eventually to violent conflict. New capitalist modes of production in agriculture, industry, and trade were often incompatible with older feudal norms and agrarian modes of production. The gentry—an affluent, highly educated class below the nobility but above the artisans, mechanics, and yeomen—played an increasingly important part in national affairs, as did the rich merchants in London; but the traditional social hierarchies failed to grant them the economic, political, and religious freedoms they believed they deserved. The guild democracy movement also achieved successes in the period, particularly among transport workers like the Thames watermen who democratized their company in the early 1640s. Another group of historians, the "revisionists," emphasize instead short-term and avoidable causes of the war—unlucky chances, personal idiosyncrasies, and poor decisions made by a small group of overly influential individuals.

Whatever caused the outbreak of hostilities, there is no doubt that the twenty-year period between 1640 and 1660 saw the emergence of concepts that would be central to bourgeois liberal thought for centuries to come: religious toleration, separation of church and state, freedom from press censorship, popular sovereignty, and heightened nationalism and imperialism. These concepts developed out of bitter disputes centering on three fundamental questions: What is the ultimate source of political power? What kind of church government is laid down in scripture, and therefore ought to be settled in England, and what should be the relation between the church and the state? What is England's role vis-à-vis other nations and powers, particularly on the sea, in trade, and in the race for colonies? The theories that evolved in response to these questions contained the seeds of much that is familiar in modern thought, mixed with much that is forbiddingly alien. The participants in these disputes were not attempting to predict the shape of modern liberalism; instead, they were responding powerfully to the most important problems and competitions of their day. The need to find the right answers was particularly urgent for the Millenarians among them, who, interpreting the upheavals of the time through the lens of the apocalyptic book of Revelation, believed that their day was very near to being the last day of all. Others, like the Diggers, fought for communal land ownership and the abolishment of private property.

When the so-called Long Parliament convened in 1640, it did not plan to execute a monarch or even to start a war. It did, however, want to secure its rights in the face of Charles's absolutist tendencies. Refusing merely to approve

The Tower of London as seen from the River Thames in 1647. From an engraving by Wenceslaus Hollar.

taxes and go home, as Charles would have wished, the Long Parliament insisted that it could remain in session until its members agreed to disband. Then it set about abolishing extralegal taxes and courts, reining in the bishops' powers, and arresting (and eventually trying and executing) two of the king's ministers—Thomas Wentworth, Earl of Strafford, and Archbishop William Laud. The collapse of effective royal government meant that the machinery of press censorship, which had been a Crown responsibility, no longer restrained the printing of explicit commentary on contemporary affairs of state. As Parliament debated, therefore, presses poured forth a flood of treatises arguing vociferously on all sides of the questions about church and state, creating a lively public forum for political discussion where none had existed before. The suspension of censorship permitted the development of weekly newsbooks, the forerunners of modern newspapers; they reported, and editorialized on, current domestic events from varying political and religious perspectives.

As the rift widened between Parliament and the king in 1641, Charles sought to arrest five members of Parliament for treason, and Londoners rose in arms against him. The king fled to York, while the queen escaped to the Continent. Negotiations for compromise broke down over the issues that would derail them at every future stage: control of the army and the church. On July 12, 1642, Parliament voted to raise an army, and on August 22 the king stood before a force of two thousand soldiers on horse and foot at Nottingham, unfurled his royal standard, and summoned his liegemen to his aid. Civil war had begun. Regions of the country, cities, towns, social classes, and even families found themselves painfully divided. Both John Milton and Lucy Hutchinson, for example, had relatives fighting on the other side of the war, and the royalist Katherine Philips was married to a Parliamentarian. The king set up court and an alternative parliament in Oxford, to which many in the House of Lords and some in the House of Commons transferred their allegiance.

In the First Civil War (1642–46), Parliament and the Presbyterian clergy that supported it had limited aims. They hoped to secure the rights of the House of Commons to limit the king's power over the army and the church—

but not to depose him—and to settle Presbyterianism as the national established church. As Puritan armies moved through the country, fighting at Edgehill, Marston Moor, Naseby, and elsewhere, they also frequently undertook a crusade to stamp out idolatry in English churches, smashing religious images and stained glass windows and lopping off the heads of statues, much as an earlier generation had done at the time of the English Reformation. Their ravages are still visible in English churches and cathedrals.

But the Puritans were not a homogeneous group, as the 1643 Toleration Controversy revealed. The Presbyterians wanted a national Presbyterian church, with dissenters punished and silenced as before. But Congregationalists, Independents, Baptists, and other separatists opposed a national church and pressed for some measure of toleration, for themselves at least. In 1641 the Independent Katherine Chidley wrote that she knew "of no true Divinity that teacheth men to be Lords over the Conscience," and the religious radical Roger Williams, just returned from New England, argued that Christ mandated the complete separation of church and state and the civic toleration of those following all religions, including Roman Catholics, Jews, and Muslims. Yet to most people, the civil war itself seemed to confirm that people of different faiths could not coexist peacefully. Thus while sects continued to proliferate—Seekers, Finders, Antinomians, Fifth Monarchists, Quakers, Muggletonians, Ranters—even the most broad-minded of the age often attempted to draw a line between what was acceptable and what was not. Predictably, their lines failed to coincide. In *Areopagitica* (1644), John Milton argues vigorously against pre-publication press censorship and for toleration of most Protestants—but for him, Catholics were beyond the pale. Robert Herrick regarded Catholic rites—and even some pagan ones—indulgently, but could not stomach the zeal of the godly.

In 1648, after a period of negotiation and a brief Second Civil War, the king's army was definitively defeated. His supporters were captured or fled into exile, losing position and property. Yet Charles, imprisoned on the Isle of Wight, remained a threat. He was a natural rallying point for those disillusioned by parliamentary rule—many people disliked Parliament's legal but heavy taxes even more than they had disliked the king's illegal but lighter ones. Charles repeatedly attempted to escape, and was accused of trying to open the realm to a foreign invasion. Some powerful leaders of the victorious New Model Army took drastic action. They expelled from the House of Commons royalists and Presbyterians who still wanted to come to an accommodation with the king, and abolished the House of Lords. With consensus ensured by the purgation of dissenting viewpoints, the army brought the king to trial for high treason in the Great Hall of Westminster. There were dissenters, including from the Parliamentarian side. Most famously, the commander in chief of the army, Thomas Fairfax, refused to participate in the king's trial. On the day of sentencing (January 27), when the president of the court declared that Parliament was trying the king in the name of "the commons and people of England," Anne Fairfax, Thomas Fairfax's wife, cried out from the gallery, "Not half, nor a quarter of the people." "Oliver Cromwell," she added, "is a rogue and a traitor."

After the king's execution, the Rump Parliament, the part of the House of Commons that had survived the purge, immediately established a new government "in the way of a republic, without king or House of Lords." The new state was extremely fragile. Royalists and Presbyterians fiercely resented their exclusion from power and pronounced the execution of the king a sacrilege. The Rump Parliament and army leaders were at odds with the army rank and file, who argued that voting rights ought not be restricted to men of property. The Levellers, led by John Lilburne, called for suffrage for all adult males. An associated but more radical group, called the Diggers or True Levellers, pushed for economic reforms to match the political ones. Their spokesman, Gerrard Winstanley, wrote eloquent manifestos developing a Christian communist program that included abolishing private property. The lords of manors, he argued, "hold title to the Commons by no stronger hold than the King's will, whose head is cut off." Meanwhile, Millenarians and Fifth Monarchists (who took their name from the "fifth monarchy" prophesied in the Bible) wanted political power vested in the regenerate "saints," in preparation for the thousand-year reign of Christ on earth foretold in the biblical book of Revelation. Quakers, having turned to the light that shines within, claimed to live in unity with the divine. They defied both state and church authority by refusing to take oaths, by preaching incendiary sermons in open marketplaces, and by arguing for the spiritual equality of men and women. Most alarming of all, and out of proportion to their scant numbers, were the Ranters, who believed (or were said to believe) that because God dwelt within them none of their acts could be sinful. Notorious for sexual license and for public nudity, they got their name from their deliberate blasphemy and penchant for rambling prophecy. The most active Ranter, Abiezer Coppe, was arrested in January 1650 on charges of blasphemy and treason, and his "mad and blasphemous" pamphlets were "burnt by the Hand of the Hangman, at the New Palace Yard, at Westminster; the Exchange, in Cheapside; and at the Market Place in Southwark." In addition to internal disarray, the new state faced serious external threats. After Charles I's execution, the Scots and the Irish—who had not been consulted about the trial—proclaimed his eldest son, Prince Charles, the new king. The prince, exiled on the Continent, was attempting to enlist the support of a major European power for an invasion.

The formidable Oliver Cromwell, now undisputed leader of the army, crushed external threats, including rebellions in Ireland and Scotland. The Irish war was especially bloody, as Cromwell's army massacred the Catholic natives in a frenzy of religious hatred. The civil war was funded in part by the "Adventurers Act," which was initially conceived as a way of raising funds to suppress the Irish rebellion of 1641. The act invited people to invest money in exchange for lands that would be confiscated from rebels in Ireland. (The English government set aside 2.5 million acres of the island's 20.9 million acres for this purpose.) Both king and Parliament supported the bill, but its true cost was realized during Cromwell's conquest of Ireland in 1649–53, when a large proportion of the native population was killed, and as many as 50,000 people were transported as indentured laborers to English colonies in North America and the Caribbean. The act also formed the basis for the 1652 Act for the Settling of Ireland, in which the land of nearly all Catholic landowners was confiscated and divided among English soldiers and adventurers. When trade rivalries erupted with the Dutch over control of shipping lanes in the North Sea and the English Channel, the new republic was again victorious. The 1651 *Navigation Act* constituted the beginning of a system of regulated imperial commerce. Yet the domestic situation remained unstable. Given popular disaffection and the unresolved disputes between Parliament and the army, the republic's lead-

Ranters. This woodcut from *The Ranters Ranting* (1650) depicts adherents to the sect in various acts of sexual license, mocking their claims to radical egalitarianism and communalism.

ers dared not call new elections. In 1653 power effectively devolved upon Cromwell, who was sworn in as Lord Protector for life under England's first written constitution. Many property owners considered Cromwell the only hope for stability, while others, including John Milton, saw him as a champion of religious liberty. Still others, including Lucy and John Hutchinson, saw his status as "Lord Protector" as a betrayal of the cause for which they had fought. In the words of Lucy Hutchinson, the "poison of ambition" had "ulcerated Cromwell's heart." Although persecution of Quakers and Ranters continued, Cromwell sometimes intervened to mitigate the lot of the Quakers. He also began a program to readmit Jews to England, partly in the interests of trade, but also to open the way for their conversion, supposedly a precursor of the Last Day as prophesied in the book of Revelation. In 1654 Cromwell's "Western Design" failed in its attempt to wrest Hispaniola from the Spanish, but it succeeded in conquering Jamaica. Over the next century, Jamaica would eclipse Barbados as the profit center of the British Empire: a sugar plantation colony based on the labor of enslaved Africans. By 1657, when Cromwell rechartered the East India company and commenced trade with China, more than twenty thousand enslaved Africans had been imported into English colonies.

When Oliver Cromwell died in 1658, his son, Richard, was appointed in his place. Richard, however, had inherited none of his father's leadership qualities. In April 1660, General George Monck succeeded in calling elections for a new "full and free" Parliament, open to supporters of the monarchy as well as of the republic. The new Parliament immediately recalled the exiled prince, officially proclaiming him King Charles II on May 8, 1660. The period that followed is therefore called the Restoration: it saw the restoration of the monarchy and with it the royal court, the established Church of England, and the professional theater.

Over the next few years, the new regime executed some of the regicides that had participated in Charles I's trial and execution, and harshly repressed radical Protestants. (The Baptist John Bunyan wrote *Pilgrim's Progress* in prison.) Yet Charles II, who came to the throne at the invitation of Parliament, could not lay claim to absolute power as his father had done. After his accession, Parliament retained its legislative supremacy and complete power over taxation, and exercised some control over the king's choice of counselors. It assembled by its own authority, not by the king's mandate. During the Restoration years, the journalistic commentary and political debates that had first flourished in the 1640s remained forceful and open, and the first modern political parties developed out of what had been the royalist and republican factions in the civil war. In London and in other cities, the merchant classes, filled with Dissenters, retained their powerful economic leverage. Although the English revolution was apparently dismantled in 1660, its long-term effects profoundly changed English institutions and English society. Cromwell's expansion of the navy had also established England as a formidable colonial power, an advantage that Charles II exploited. Early in his reign, he granted a charter to the Company of Royal Adventurers of England, which, led by his younger brother James, Duke of York (later King James II), benefited from a monopoly on British trade with West Africa, including the trade in enslaved Africans. After Charles II's forces captured "New Netherland" during the Anglo-Dutch wars of the 1660s, the king gave the colony to this same brother, renaming it "New York" in his honor.

LITERATURE AND CULTURE, 1640–1660

The English Civil Wars were disastrous for all aspects of English life, including the theater. One of Parliament's first acts after hostilities began in 1642 was to abolish public plays and sports for "too commonly expressing lascivious mirth and levity." Some drama continued to be written and published—Margaret Cavendish wrote dozens of plays during the Interregnum—but performances were rare, and would-be theatrical entrepreneurs had to exploit loopholes in the prohibitions by describing their works as "operas" and by mounting semiprivate productions.

As the king's government collapsed, so too did the patronage relationships centered on the court. Many leading poets were staunch royalists, or Cavaliers, who suffered considerably in the war years. Robert Herrick lost his church employment; Richard Lovelace was imprisoned; Margaret Cavendish went into exile. With their usual networks of manuscript circulation disrupted, many royalist writers printed their verse. Volumes of poetry by Thomas Carew, John Denham, Richard Lovelace, and Robert Herrick appeared in the 1640s. Their poems, some dating from the 1620s or 1630s, celebrate the courtly ideal "of the good life: good food, plenty of wine, good verse, hospitality, and high-spirited loyalty, especially to the king." One characteristic Cavalier genre was the love lyric, often with a *carpe diem* theme. In Herrick's case especially, apparent ease and frivolity mask a frankly political subtext. While the Puritans excoriated May Day celebrations, harvest-home festivities, and other time-honored holidays and "sports" as unscriptural, idolatrous, or frankly pagan, for Herrick, these pastimes sustained a community. This idealized community strove neither for ascetic perfection nor for equality among social classes, but knew the value of pleasure in cementing social harmony and incorporating everyone—rich and poor, unlettered and learned—into one social body, much as the established church had traditionally tried to do.

As they faced defeat in the 1640s and 1650s, the Cavaliers wrote movingly of the relationship between love and honor, of fidelity under duress, of likeminded friends sustaining one another in a hostile environment. They presented themselves as amateurs, writing verse in the midst of a life devoted to more important matters: war, love, the king's service, the endurance of loss. Rejecting the radical Protestant emphasis on the "inner light," which they considered merely a pretext for presumptuousness and violence, Cavalier poets cultivated deliberately unidiosyncratic, even self-deprecating poetic personae. Thus the poems of Richard Lovelace express sentiments that he represents not as the unique insights of an isolated genius, but as principles easily grasped by all honorable men, and enjoyments reserved for their timeless privilege. When in "The Vine" Herrick relates a wet dream, he laughs not only at himself, but at those who mistake their own fantasies for divine inspiration.

During the 1650s, royalists wrote lyric poems in places far removed from the hostile centers of parliamentary power. In Wales, Henry Vaughan wrote religious verse expressing his intense longing for past eras of innocence and for the perfection of heaven or the millennium. Also in Wales, Katherine Philips wrote and circulated manuscript poems that celebrate female friends in terms usually reserved for male friendships and that question the ethics of the regicide and commonwealth. "Hath Charles so broke God's laws," she asks in on one poem, that "he must not have / A quiet crown, nor yet a quiet grave?" The publication of her poems after the Restoration brought Philips considerable celebrity as "the Matchless Orinda." (Orinda was the classical name she gave to herself in her poetry.) Richard Crashaw, an exile in Paris and Rome, and a convert to Roman Catholicism, wrote lush religious poetry that attempted to reveal the spiritual by stimulating the senses. Margaret Cavendish, who also spent the Interregnum in exile, published a book of poems and a book of philosophy when she returned to England temporarily in 1653 and an astounding amount of work after the Restoration.

Several prose works by royalist sympathizers became classics in their respective genres. Thomas Hobbes, the most important English philosopher of the period, developed his materialist philosophy and psychology during his exile in Paris. His *Leviathan* (1651) presented his unflinching defense of absolute sovereignty based on a theory of social contract. The revolutionary era gave new impetus to all kinds of writing, including by women and non-elites. The circumstances of war placed women in novel, occasionally dangerous, situations, giving them unusual events to describe and prompting self-discovery, creativity, and innovation. The autobiographies of the royalists Lady Anne Halkett and Margaret Cavendish, published after the Restoration, report their experiences and their sometimes daring activities during the civil wars. Lucy Hutchinson's memoir of her husband, Colonel John Hutchinson, narrates much of the history of the times from a republican point of view, as do her epic poem on Genesis, *Order and Disorder*, and her elegies, which mourn both her husband and the cause for which he fought. Leveller women presented petitions and manifestos in support of their imprisoned husbands and of their cause. Women petitioned Parliament for many causes, including their own political rights, in astounding numbers. They also registered their demands in print. The widespread belief that the Holy Spirit was moving in unexpected ways encouraged a number of women prophets, including Anna Trapnel, Mary Cary, and Lady Eleanor Davies. Their published prophecies often carried strong political critiques of Charles or of Cromwell. Authorized by the Quaker belief in the spiritual equality of women and men, and by the conviction that all persons should testify to what the inner light communicates to them, Quaker women came into their own as preachers and, occasionally, as writers of tracts. Many of their memoirs, such as Dorothy Waugh's "Relation," were originally published to call attention to their sufferings, and to inspire other Quakers to similar feats of moral fortitude.

While most writers during this period were royalists, some of the best, including Andrew Marvell, John Milton, and Lucy Hutchinson, sided with the republic. Marvell wrote most of the poems for which he is still remembered in the early 1650s while at Nunappleton, tutoring the daughter of the retired parliamentary general Thomas Fairfax; in 1657 he joined his friend Milton in the office of Cromwell's Latin Secretariat. Marvell's love poems and pastorals seem to register the conflict of civil war: older convictions about ordered harmony give way to unresolved or unresolvable oppositions—some playful, some painful. In his country house poem *Upon Appleton House*, even agricultural practices associated with regular changes of the season, like the flooding of fallow fields, become emblems of unpredictability, reversal, and category confusion. In other poems Marvell eschews an authoritative poetic persona in favor of speakers who seem limited or even a bit unbalanced: a mower who argues for the values of pastoral with disconcerting belligerence, a nymph who seems to exemplify virginal innocence but also immature self-absorption and possibly unconscious sexual perversity. Marvell's finest political poem, "An Horatian Ode upon Cromwell's Return from Ireland," celebrates Cromwell's providential victories even while inviting sympathy for the executed king and warning about the potential dangers of Cromwell's meteoric rise to power.

A promising, prolific young poet in the 1630s, Milton committed himself to the English republic as soon as the conflict between the king and Parliament began to take shape. His loyalty to the revolution remained unwavering, despite his disillusion when it failed to realize his ideals: religious toleration for all Protestants, and the free circulation of ideas without prior censorship. First as a self-appointed adviser to the state, then as its official defender, Milton addressed the great issues at stake in the 1640s and the 1650s. In a series of treatises he argued for church disestablishment and for the removal of bishops; for a republican government based on natural law and popular sovereignty; for the right of the people to dismiss their rulers from office and even execute them; and, most controversial even to his usual allies, in favor of divorce on the grounds of incompatibility. Milton was a Puritan, but both his theological heterodoxies and his poetic vision mark him as a distinctly unusual one.

During his years as a political polemicist, Milton also wrote several sonnets, revising that small, love-centered genre to accommodate large private and public topics: a Catholic massacre of proto-Protestants in the foothills of Italy; the agonizing questions posed by his blindness; various threats to intellectual and religious liberty. In 1645 he published his collected English and Latin poems as a counterstatement to the royalist volumes of the 1640s. Yet *he wrote his* most ambitious poetry when the war was over. Milton probably wrote some part of *Paradise Lost* in the late 1650s and completed it after the Restoration, encompassing in it all he had thought, read, and experienced of tyranny, political controversy, evil, deception, love, and the need for companionship. His cosmic blank-verse poem about the fall of humanity assimilates and critiques the epic tradition as well as Milton's entire intellectual and literary heritage, classical and Christian. Yet unlike earlier epics, *Paradise Lost* centers not on martial heroes but on a domestic couple who must discover how to live a good life day by day, in Eden and later in the fallen world, amid intense emotional pressures and the seductions of evil.

Lucy Hutchinson is best known for her *Memoirs of the Life of Colonel Hutchinson*, an account of the English Civil Wars written during the period but not printed until 1806. Yet Hutchinson was also the first person to translate Lucretius's *De rerum natura* (On the Nature of Things) from Latin into English, and the author of a magisterial epic poem on Genesis entitled *Order and Disorder*. Hutchinson wrote *Order and Disorder* in the years surrounding the collapse of the republican cause. "Whatever mortals' vain endeavors be," she wrote in the opening canto, "They must be broken who with power contend." Yet her faith in God's providence includes the ultimate vindication of what she calls the "little church," and the epic is rife with political commentary; in *Order and Disorder*, God always "cuts the bloody tyrant down." It is possible that the poem's outspoken republicanism prevented it from being published in the 1660s, when it circulated in manuscript. Like Milton, Hutchinson proclaims both divine inspiration—"My ravished soul a pious ardour fires"— and poetic ambition in the opening lines of her poem. The "poetic fables" she seeks to overturn, however, seem to include Milton's own, as when she writes that she (unlike Milton) will not "dare t'invent" an account of the angels' "rebellion and their overthrow," hewing instead to what "that light [of scripture] doth show." Yet her account of the creation of the universe is infused with Lucretian materialism, and she offers a bracing analysis of women's punishment for the Fall that extends far beyond the few lines devoted to the topic in Genesis. *Order and Disorder* was first published in its entirety in 2001, cementing Hutchinson's reputation as one of the finest, and most politically committed, poets of the era. In the series of elegies she wrote after her husband's death, Hutchinson expresses not only her personal grief and thwarted desire, but her unvanquished commitment to what she called "the grand quarrel."

Seventeenth-century poetry, prose, and drama retain their hold on readers because so much of it is so very good, fusing intellectual power, emotional passion, and extraordinary linguistic and formal artfulness. Poetry in this period ranges over an astonishing variety of topics and modes: highly erotic celebrations of sexual desire; passionate declarations of faith and doubt; lavishly embroidered paeans to friends and benefactors; toughminded assessments of social and political institutions; fanciful imaginations of life beyond what the naked eye (and human-made instrument) can see. English dramatists were at the height of their powers, situating characters of unprecedented complexity in plays sometimes remorselessly satiric, sometimes achingly moving. In these years English prose becomes a highly flexible instrument, suited to informal essays, scientific treatises, religious meditation, political polemic, biography and autobiography, journalistic reportage, and speculative fiction. Literary forms evolve for the exquisitely modulated representation of the self: dramatic monologues, memoirs, spiritual autobiographies, sermons in which the preacher takes himself for an example, and epic poets who assume the role of inspired prophet, envisioning a world created by God but shaped by human choice and imagination.

The Early Seventeenth Century

TEXTS	CONTEXTS
1603 James I, *Basilikon Doron* reissued	**1603** Death of Elizabeth I; accession of James I. Plague
1604 William Shakespeare, *Othello*	
1605 Shakespeare, *King Lear*. Ben Jonson, *The Masque of Blackness*. Francis Bacon, *The Advancement of Learning*	**1605** Gunpowder Plot, failed effort by Roman Catholic extremists to blow up Parliament
1606 Jonson, *Volpone*. Shakespeare, *Macbeth*	
	1607 Founding of Jamestown colony in Virginia
1609 Shakespeare, *Sonnets*	**1609** Galileo begins observing the heavens with a telescope
1611 "King James" Bible (Authorized Version). Shakespeare, *The Tempest*. John Donne, *The First Anniversary*. Aemilia Lanyer, *Salve Deus Rex Judaeorum*	
1612 Donne, *The Second Anniversary*	**1612** Death of Prince Henry
1613 Elizabeth Cary, *The Tragedy of Mariam*	
1614 John Webster, *The Duchess of Malfi*	
1616 Jonson, *Works*. James I, *Works*	**1616** Death of Shakespeare
	1618 Beginning of the Thirty Years War
	1619 First African enslaved people in North America exchanged by Dutch frigate for food and supplies at Jamestown
1620 Bacon, *Novum Organum*	**1620** Pilgrims land at Plymouth
1621 Mary Wroth, *The Countess of Montgomery's Urania* and *Pamphilia to Amphilanthus*. Robert Burton, *The Anatomy of Melancholy*	**1621** Donne appointed dean of St. Paul's Cathedral
1623 Shakespeare, First Folio	
1625 Bacon, *Essays*	**1625** Death of James I; accession of Charles I; Charles I marries Henrietta Maria
	1629 Charles I dissolves Parliament
1633 Donne, *Poems*. George Herbert, *The Temple*	**1633** Galileo forced by the Inquisition to recant the Copernican theory
1637 John Milton, "Lycidas"	
1640 Thomas Carew, *Poems*	**1640** Long Parliament called (1640–53). Archbishop Laud impeached
1640s–60s Hester Pulter writes *Poems Breathed Forth by the Nobel Hadassas*, which would not be published until 2014	
1642 Thomas Browne, *Religio Medici*. Milton, *The Reason of Church Government*	**1642** First Civil War begins (1642–46). Parliament closes the theaters
1643 Milton, *The Doctrine and Discipline of Divorce*	**1643** Accession of Louis XIV of France

TEXTS	CONTEXTS
1644 Milton, *Areopagitica*	
1645 Milton, *Poems*. Edmund Waller, *Poems*	1645 Archbishop Laud executed. Royalists defeated at Naseby
1648 Robert Herrick, *Hesperides* and *Noble Numbers*	1648 Second Civil War. "Pride's Purge" of Parliament
1649 Milton, *The Tenure of Kings and Magistrates* and *Eikonoklastes*	1649 Trial and execution of Charles I. Republic declared. Milton becomes Latin Secretary (1649–59)
1650 Henry Vaughan, *Silex Scintillans* (Part II, 1655)	
1650s Lucy Hutchinson translates Lucretius's *De Rerum Natura* from Latin to English—the first person to do so	
1651 Thomas Hobbes, *Leviathan*. Andrew Marvell, *Upon Appleton House* (unpublished)	
	1652 Anglo-Dutch War (1652–54)
	1653 Cromwell made Lord Protector
	1658 Death of Cromwell; his son Richard made Protector
1660 Milton, *Ready and Easy Way to Establish a Free Commonwealth*	1660 Restoration of Charles II to throne. Royal Society founded
	1662 Charles II marries Catherine of Braganza
	1665 The Great Plague
1666 Margaret Cavendish, *The Blazing World*	1666 The Great Fire
1667 Milton, *Paradise Lost* (in ten books). Katherine Philips, *Collected Poems*. John Dryden, *Annus Mirabilis*	
1671 Milton, *Paradise Regained* and *Samson Agonistes*	
1674 Milton, *Paradise Lost* (in twelve books)	1674 Death of Milton
1679 The first five cantos of Lucy Hutchinson's *Order and Disorder* published anonymously	
1681 Marvell, *Poems*, published posthumously	

JOHN DONNE
1572–1631

Lovers' eyeballs threaded on a string, a god who assaults the human heart with a battering ram, a teardrop that encompasses and drowns the world: John Donne's poems abound with startling images. With his strange and playful intelligence, expressed in puns, paradoxes, and the elaborately sustained metaphors known as "conceits," Donne has enthralled and sometimes enraged readers from his day to our own. The tired clichés of love poetry—cheeks like roses, hearts pierced by the arrows of love—emerge reinvigorated and radically transformed in Donne's poems, demanding from the reader an unprecedented level of mental alertness and engagement. Donne prided himself on his wit and displayed it not only in his conceits but in his grasp of learned discourses ranging from theology to alchemy, from cosmology to law. Yet for all their ostentatious intellectuality, Donne's poems never give the impression of being academic exercises. Rather, they are intense dramatic monologues in which the speaker's ideas and feelings evolve from one line to the next. Donne's prosody is equally dramatic. His jagged rhythms capture the effect of speech (and elicited from his classically minded contemporary Ben Jonson the gruff observation that "Donne, for not keeping of accent, deserved hanging").

Donne began life as an outsider, and in some respects remained one. He was born in London in 1572 into a devout Roman Catholic household. The family was prosperous, but, as the poet later remarked, none had suffered more heavily for its loyalty to the Catholic Church. As Donne wrote in a prose treatise, "I have been ever kept awake in a meditation of martyrdom." Donne was distantly related to the great Catholic humanist and martyr Sir Thomas More; two of Donne's uncles, Jesuit priests, were forced to flee the realm; and Donne's brother Henry, arrested for harboring a priest, died in prison. As a Catholic in Protestant England, growing up in decades when anti-Roman feeling reached new heights, Donne could not expect any kind of public career, nor could he receive a university degree. (He left Oxford without a degree and studied law for a time at the Inns of Court.) What Donne could reasonably expect instead was prejudice, official harassment, and crippling financial penalties. He chose not to live under such conditions. At some point in the 1590s, having returned to London after travels abroad, and having devoted some years to studying theology, Donne converted to the Church of England.

The poems that belong with certainty to this period of his life—the five satires and most of the elegies—reveal a man both fascinated by and keenly critical of English society. Four of the satires treat commonplace Elizabethan topics—obsequious courtiers, bad poets, unscrupulous lawyers, and a corrupt court—but are unique in their visceral revulsion and intellectual excitement. Donne uses striking images of pestilence, vomit, excrement, and pox to create a unique satiric world, vibrant and degenerate, in which his dramatic speakers have only to step outside the door to be inundated by all the fools and knaves in Christendom. By contrast, the third satire treats the quest for true religion—the question that preoccupied him above all others in these years—in terms that are serious, witty, and deeply felt. Donne argues that honest, doubtful searching is better than the facile acceptance of religious tradition, epitomizing his point brilliantly in the image of *Truth on a craggy hill* that is almost impossible to climb. Society's values are of no help whatsoever to the individual seeker—none will escape the final judgment by pleading that "A Harry, or a Martin taught [them] this." In his love elegies Donne

Donne in His Shroud. Shortly before his death in 1631, Donne posed in the shroud in which he would be buried. The resulting engraving, by Martin Droeshout, is the frontispiece of *Death's Duel* (1632).

seems intent on making up for his social powerlessness through witty representations of mastery in the bedroom and abroad. In "Elegy 19," for example, his seduction of a naked lover becomes in a famous conceit the equivalent of exploration in America. Donne was not alone in introducing classical Roman genres such as satire and elegy to English verse, but he was unmatched in his skill.

If Donne's conversion to the Church of England promised him security, social acceptance, and the possibility of a public career, that promise was soon to be withdrawn. In 1596–97 he participated in the Earl of Essex's military expeditions against Catholic Spain in Cádiz and the Azores (the experience prompted two remarkable poems about life at sea, "The Storm" and "The Calm"), and upon his return he became secretary to Sir Thomas Egerton, Lord Keeper of the Great Seal. This appointment should have been the beginning of a successful public career. But Donne's secret marriage in 1601 to Egerton's seventeen-year-old niece Ann More enraged Donne's employer and the bride's wealthy father; Donne was briefly imprisoned and dismissed from service. The poet was reduced to a retired country life, beset by financial insecurity and a rapidly increasing family; Ann had borne twelve children (not counting miscarriages) by the time she died in 1617 at age thirty-three. At one point, Donne wrote despairingly that while the death of a child would mean one less mouth to feed, he could not afford the burial expenses. In this bleak period, he wrote but dared not publish *Biathanatos* ("Violent Death"), a defense of suicide.

As his family grew, Donne made every effort to reinstate himself in political favor. Among other pleas for office, Donne purportedly sought to become the secretary of the Virginia Company in 1609. To win the approval of James I, he penned *Pseudo-Martyr* (1610), defending the king's insistence that Catholics take the Oath of Allegiance to the English crown. This publication set an irrevocable public stamp on his renunciation of Catholicism, and Donne followed up with a satire on the Jesuits, *Ignatius His Conclave* (1611). In the same period he produced a steady stream of occasional poems for friends and patrons such as the Earl of Somerset (the king's favorite), the Countess of Bedford, and Magdalen Herbert, as well as for small coteries of courtly readers. Like most gentlemen of his era, Donne saw poetry as a polite accomplishment rather than as a trade or vocation. He thus circulated his poems in manuscript and, with few exceptions, left most of them uncollected and unpublished.

For some years, James I had urged an ecclesiastical career on Donne, denying him any other means of advancement. In 1615 Donne finally consented. He was ordained in the Church of England, and entered upon a distinguished career as court preacher, reader in divinity at Lincoln's Inn, and, eventually, dean of St. Paul's. Donne's metaphorical style, bold erudition, and dramatic wit established him as a great preacher in an age that appreciated learned sermons powerfully delivered. Preached to monarchs and courtiers, lawyers and London magistrates, city merchants and trading companies, some 160 of his sermons survive. As a distinguished Church of England clergyman, Donne had traveled an immense distance from the religion of his childhood and the adventurous life of his twenties. Yet in his sermons and late poems we find the same brilliant, idiosyncratic mind at work, refashioning his profane conceits to serve a new and higher purpose. In "Expostulation 19" he praises God as the greatest of literary stylists: "a figurative, a metaphorical God." In poems, meditations, and sermons, Donne became increasingly engaged in anxious contemplation of his own mortality. In "Hymn to God My God, in My Sickness," for example, he imagines himself spread out on his deathbed like a map showing the route to the next world. Only a few days before his death, he preached "Death's Duel," a terrifying analysis of all life as a decline toward death and dissolution which contemporaries termed his own funeral sermon. In his final illness, according to his contemporary biographer Izaak Walton, Donne had a portrait made of himself in his shroud and meditated on it daily. Meditations upon skulls as emblems of mortality were common in the period, but nothing is more characteristic of Donne than to find a way to meditate on his own skull. Walton also notes that after Donne's death, an unknown person wrote the following "epitaph with a coal on the wall over his grave":

> Reader! I am to let thee know,
> Donne's body only lies below,
> For, could the grave his soul comprise,
> Earth would be richer than the skies.

Given the shape of Donne's career, it is no surprise that his poems and prose display an astonishing variety of attitudes, viewpoints, and feelings on the great subjects of love and religion. Yet this variety cannot be fully explained in biographical terms. The poet's own attempt to distinguish between Jack Donne, the young rake, and Dr. Donne, the grave and religious dean of St. Paul's, is (perhaps intentionally) misleading. We do not know the time and circumstances for most of Donne's verses, but it is clear that many of his finest religious poems predate his ordination, and it is possible that he continued to add to the love poems known as his "songs and sonnets" after he entered the church. Theological language abounds in his love poetry, and daringly erotic images in his religious verse.

Donne's "songs and sonnets" have been the cornerstone of his reputation almost since their publication in 1633. The title *Songs and Sonnets* associates them with the popular miscellanies of love poems and sonnet sequences in the Petrarchan tradition, but they directly challenge the sonnet sequences of the 1590s. Donne's collection contains only one formal sonnet, the "songs" are not notably lyrical, and Donne draws on and transforms a whole range of literary traditions concerned with love. Like Petrarch, Donne can present himself as the despairing lover of an unattainable lady ("The Funeral"). Like Ovid, he can be lighthearted, witty, cynical, and frankly lustful ("The Flea," "The Indifferent"). Like the Neoplatonists, he espouses a theory of transcendent love, but he breaks from them with his insistence on the union of physical and spiritual love. What binds these poems together, and grants them enduring power, is their compelling and dramatic immediacy. The speaker is always in the throes of intense emotion, and that emotion is constantly shifting with the turns of the poet's thought. Donne seems supremely present in these poems, standing behind their various speakers. Where Petrarchan poets exhaustively catalogue their beloved's physical features (though in highly conventional terms), Donne's speakers tell us little or nothing about the beloved woman imagined as the audience for many poems. Donne's repeated insistence that the private world of lovers is superior to the wider public world, or that it somehow contains all of that world, is understandable in light of the many disappointments of his career. Yet he also threw himself headlong into secular life, and later into the very visible role of preacher.

Donne was long grouped with Herbert, Vaughan, Crashaw, Marvell, Thomas Traherne, and Abraham Cowley under the heading of "Metaphysical poets." The expression was first employed by critics like Samuel Johnson and William Hazlitt, who found the intricate conceits and self-conscious learning of these poets incompatible with poetic beauty and sincerity. Early in the twentieth century, T. S. Eliot sought to restore their reputation, attributing to them a unity of thought and feeling that had since their time been lost. There was, however, no formal "school" of Metaphysical poetry, and the characteristics ascribed to it by later critics pertain chiefly to Donne. Like Ben Jonson, John Donne had an immense influence on the succeeding generation, but he remains a singular figure.

From Songs and Sonnets[1]

The Flea[2]

Mark but this flea, and mark in this,
How little that which thou deniest me is;
Me it sucked first, and now sucks thee,
And in this flea our two bloods mingled be;
5 Thou know'st that this cannot be said
A sin, or shame, or loss of maidenhead,°   *virginity*
  Yet this enjoys before it woo,
  And pampered° swells with one blood made of two,[3]   *overfed*
And this, alas, is more than we would do.

10 Oh stay, three lives in one flea spare,
Where we almost, nay more than married are.
This flea is you and I, and this
Our marriage bed and marriage temple is;
Though parents grudge, and you, we are met,
15 And cloistered[4] in these living walls of jet.°   *black*
  Though use° make you apt to kill me,[5]   *habit*
  Let not to that, self-murder added be,
  And sacrilege, three sins in killing three.

Cruel and sudden, hast thou since
20 Purpled thy nail in blood of innocence?
Wherein could this flea guilty be,
Except in that drop which it sucked from thee?
Yet thou triumph'st, and say'st that thou
Find'st not thy self nor me the weaker now;
25 'Tis true; then learn how false fears be:
  Just so much honor, when thou yield'st to me,
  Will waste, as this flea's death took life from thee.

1633

---

1. Donne's love poems were written over nearly two decades, beginning around 1595; they were not published in Donne's lifetime but circulated widely in manuscript. The title *Songs and Sonnets* was supplied in the second edition (1635), which grouped the poems by kind, but neither this arrangement nor the more haphazard organization of the first edition (1633) is Donne's own. In Donne's time the term "sonnet" often meant simply "love lyric," and in fact there is only one formal sonnet in this collection. For the poems we present we follow the 1635 edition, beginning with the extremely popular poem "The Flea."
2. This insect afforded a popular erotic theme for poets all over Europe, deriving from a pseudo-Ovidian medieval poem in which a lover envies the flea for the liberties it takes with his mistress's body.
3. The swelling suggests pregnancy.
4. As in a convent or monastery.
5. By denying me sexual gratification.

The Good-Morrow°   *morning greeting*

I wonder, by my troth,° what thou and I   *good faith*
Did, till we loved? Were we not weaned till then,
But sucked on country° pleasures, childishly?   *unsophisticated*
Or snorted° we in the seven sleepers' den?[1]   *snored*
5 'Twas so; but° this, all pleasures fancies be.   *except for*
If ever any beauty I did see,
Which I desired, and got, 'twas but a dream of thee.

And now good morrow to our waking souls,
Which watch not one another out of fear;
10 For love all love of other sights controls,
And makes one little room an everywhere.
Let sea-discoverers to new worlds have gone,
Let maps to others, worlds on worlds have shown:
Let us possess one world;[2] each hath one, and is one.

15 My face in thine eye, thine in mine appears,
And true plain hearts do in the faces rest;
Where can we find two better hemispheres,
Without sharp North, without declining West?
Whatever dies was not mixed equally;[3]
20 If our two loves be one, or thou and I
Love so alike that none do slacken, none can die.

1633

Song

Go and catch a falling star,
    Get with child a mandrake root,[1]
Tell me where all past years are,
    Or who cleft the Devil's foot,
5 Teach me to hear mermaids° singing,   *sirens*
Or to keep off envy's stinging,
    And find
      What wind
Serves to advance an honest mind.

10 If thou beest born to strange sights,
    Things invisible to see,
Ride ten thousand days and nights,
    Till age snow white hairs on thee,
Thou, when thou return'st, wilt tell me
15 All strange wonders that befell thee,

---

1. Cave in Ephesus where, according to legend, seven Christian youths hid from pagan persecutors and slept for 187 years.
2. "Our world" in many manuscripts.
3. Scholastic philosophy taught that when the elements were imperfectly mixed ("not mixed equally"), matter was mutable and mortal; conversely, when the elements were perfectly mixed, matter was immutable and hence immortal.

1. The mandrake root, or mandragora, is forked like the lower part of the human body. It was thought to shriek when pulled from the ground and to kill all humans who heard it; it was also (paradoxically) thought to help women conceive.

                And swear
                No where
            Lives a woman true, and fair.

            If thou find'st one, let me know,
    20   Such a pilgrimage were sweet;
            Yet do not, I would not go,
                Though at next door we might meet;
            Though she were true when you met her,
            And last till you write your letter,
    25   Yet she
                Will be
            False, ere I come, to two, or three.

                                                            1633

The Sun Rising

            Busy old fool, unruly sun,
                Why dost thou thus
        Through windows and through curtains call on us?
        Must to thy motions lovers' seasons run?
    5   Saucy pedantic wretch, go chide
                Late schoolboys and sour prentices,
            Go tell court huntsmen that the king will ride,[1]
            Call country ants to harvest offices;[2]
        Love, all alike, no season knows nor clime,
    10 Nor hours, days, months, which are the rags of time.

            Thy beams, so reverend and strong
                Why shouldst thou think?
        I could eclipse and cloud them with a wink,
        But that I would not lose her sight so long;
    15   If her eyes have not blinded thine,
                Look, and tomorrow late, tell me,
            Whether both th' Indias of spice and mine[3]
            Be where thou leftst them, or lie here with me.
        Ask for those kings whom thou saw'st yesterday,
    20 And thou shalt hear, All here in one bed lay.

            She is all states,° and all princes I,   *nations*
                Nothing else is.
        Princes do but play us; compared to this,
        All honor's mimic, all wealth alchemy.
    25   Thou, sun, art half as happy as we,
                In that the world's contracted thus;
            Thine age asks ease, and since thy duties be
            To warm the world, that's done in warming us.
        Shine here to us, and thou art everywhere;
    30 This bed thy center is, these walls thy sphere.[4]

                                                            1633

---

1. King James was fond of hunting.
2. Autumn chores. "Country ants": farm drudges.
3. The India of "spice" is the East Indies; that of "mine" (gold), the West Indies.

4. According to the old Ptolemaic astronomy, the earth was the center of the sun's orbit, and the sun's motion was contained within its sphere.

The Indifferent

I can love both fair and brown,[1]
Her whom abundance melts, and her whom want betrays,
Her who loves loneness best, and her who masks and plays,
Her whom the country formed, and whom the town,
Her who believes, and her who tries,°   *tests*
Her who still° weeps with spongy eyes,   *always*
And her who is dry cork, and never cries;
I can love her, and her, and you, and you,
I can love any, so she be not true.

Will no other vice content you?
Will it not serve your turn to do as did your mothers?
Or have you all old vices spent, and now would find out others?
Or doth a fear that men are true torment you?
O we are not, be not you so;
Let me, and do you, twenty know.
Rob me, but bind me not, and let me go.
Must I, who came to travail thorough[2] you,
Grow your fixed subject, because you are true?

Venus heard me sigh this song,
And by love's sweetest part, variety, she swore,
She heard not this till now; and that it should be so no more.
She went, examined, and returned ere long,
And said, Alas, some two or three
Poor heretics in love there be,
Which think to 'stablish dangerous constancy.
But I have told them, Since you will be true,
You shall be true to them who are false to you.

1633

The Canonization[1]

For God's sake hold your tongue, and let me love,
    Or chide my palsy, or my gout,
My five gray hairs, or ruined fortune, flout,
    With wealth your state, your mind with arts improve,
        Take you a course, get you a place,[2]
        Observe His Honor, or His Grace,[3]
    Or the king's real, or his stampèd face[4]
        Contemplate; what you will, approve,°   *try, test*
    So you will let me love.

---

1. Both blonde and brunette.
2. Through. "Travail": grief.
1. The poem plays off against the Roman Catholic process of determining that certain persons are saints, proper objects of veneration and prayer.
2. An appointment, at court or elsewhere. "Take you a course": follow some career.
3. Pay court to some lord or bishop.
4. On coins; "real" (royal) refers also to a particular Spanish coin.

         Alas, alas, who's injured by my love?
            What merchant's ships have my sighs drowned?
         Who says my tears have overflowed his ground?
            When did my colds a forward° spring remove?[5]   *early*
            When did the heats which my veins fill
                Add one man to the plaguy bill?[6]
            Soldiers find wars, and lawyers find out still
                Litigious men, which quarrels move,
                Though she and I do love.

         Call us what you will, we are made such by love;
            Call her one, me another fly,
         We're tapers too, and at our own cost die,[7]
            And we in us find the eagle and the dove.
                The phoenix riddle hath more wit
                By us: we two being one, are it.[8]
         So, to one neutral thing both sexes fit.
            We die and rise the same, and prove
            Mysterious by this love.

         We can die by it, if not live by love,
            And if unfit for tombs and hearse
         Our legend be, it will be fit for verse;
            And if no piece of chronicle° we prove,   *history*
                We'll build in sonnets pretty rooms;[9]
                As well a well-wrought urn becomes°   *befits*
         The greatest ashes, as half-acre tombs,
            And by these hymns,[1] all shall approve°   *confirm*
            Us canonized for love:

         And thus invoke us: You whom reverend love
            Made one another's hermitage;
         You, to whom love was peace, that now is rage;
            Who did the whole world's soul contract,[2] and drove
                Into the glasses of your eyes
                (So made such mirrors, and such spies,°   *spyglasses, telescopes*
         That they did all to you epitomize)
            Countries, towns, courts:[3] Beg from above
         A pattern of your love!

1633

---

5. Petrarchan lovers traditionally sigh, weep, and are frozen because of their mistresses' neglect.
6. Deaths from the plague, which raged in summer, were recorded by parish in weekly lists.
7. Flies were emblems of transience and lustfulness; tapers (candles) attract flies to their death and also consume themselves. "Die" in the punning terminology of the period means to experience orgasm, and there was a superstition that intercourse shortened life.
8. The eagle signifies strength and vision; the dove, meekness and mercy. The phoenix was a mythic Arabian bird, only one of which existed at any one time. After living five hundred years, it was consumed by fire, then rose triumphantly from its ashes a new bird. Thus it was a symbol of immortality and sometimes associated with Christ. "Eagle" and "dove" are also alchemical terms for processes leading to the rise of "phoenix," a stage in the transmutation of metals to gold.
9. "Rooms" (punning on the Italian meaning of "stanza") will contain their exploits, as prose chronicle histories contain great deeds done in the world.
1. The lover's own poems.
2. An alternative meaning is "extract."
3. "Countries, towns, courts" are objects of the verb "drove." The notion is that eyes both see and reflect the outside world, and so can contain all of it.

Song

    Sweetest love, I do not go,
        For weariness of thee,
    Nor in hope the world can show
        A fitter love for me;
5   But since that I
    Must die at last, 'tis best,
    To use myself in jest
        Thus by feigned deaths° to die.   *that is, absences*

    Yesternight the sun went hence
10   And yet is here today,
    He hath no desire nor sense,
        Nor half so short a way:
        Then fear not me,
    But believe that I shall make
15   Speedier journeys, since I take
        More wings and spurs than he.

    O how feeble is man's power,
        That if good fortune fall,°   *happen*
    Cannot add another hour,
20   Nor a lost hour recall!
        But come bad chance,
    And we join to'it our strength,
    And we teach it art and length,
        Itself o'er us to'advance.

25   When thou sigh'st, thou sigh'st not wind,
        But sigh'st my soul away,
    When thou weep'st, unkindly[1] kind,
        My life's blood doth decay.
        It cannot be
30   That thou lov'st me, as thou say'st,
    If in thine my life thou waste,
        Thou art the best of me.

    Let not thy divining° heart   *prophetic*
        Forethink me any ill,
35   Destiny may take thy part,
        And may thy fears fulfill;
        But think that we
    Are but turned aside to sleep;
    They who one another keep
40   Alive, ne'er parted be.

1633

---

1. This word also carries the meaning "unnaturally."

Air and Angels

    Twice or thrice had I loved thee,
    Before I knew thy face or name;
    So in a voice, so in a shapeless flame,
    Angels affect us oft, and worshipped be;
5   Still° when, to where thou wert, I came,   *always*
    Some lovely glorious nothing[1] I did see.
        But since my soul, whose child love is,
    Takes limbs of flesh, and else could nothing do,[2]
        More subtle° than the parent is   *rarefied*
10 Love must not be, but take a body too;
    And therefore what thou wert, and who,
        I bid love ask, and now
    That it assume thy body I allow,
    And fix itself in thy lip, eye, and brow.
15 Whilst thus to ballast love I thought,
    And so more steadily to have gone,
    With wares which would sink° admiration,   *overwhelm*
    I saw I had love's pinnace° overfraught;°   *small boat / overloaded*
        Every thy hair for love to work upon
20 Is much too much, some fitter must be sought;
        For, nor in nothing, nor in things
    Extreme and scatt'ring° bright, can love inhere.   *dazzling*
        Then as an angel, face and wings
    Of air, not pure as it, yet pure doth wear,[3]
25   So thy love may be my love's sphere;[4]
        Just such disparity
    As is 'twixt air and angels' purity,
    'Twixt women's love and men's will ever be.

1633

Break of Day[1]

    'Tis true, 'tis day; what though it be?
    O wilt thou therefore rise from me?
    Why should we rise because 'tis light?
    Did we lie down because 'twas night?
5   Love, which in spite of darkness brought us hither,
    Should in despite of light keep us together.

---

1. Spiritual beauty, the true object of love in Neoplatonic philosophy.
2. My soul could not function unless it were in a body.
3. It was commonly believed that angels, when they appeared to humans, assumed a body of air that, though pure, was less so than the angel's spiritual essence.
4. Each sphere in the cosmos was thought to be governed by an angel (an intelligence).
1. An aubade, or song of the lovers' parting at dawn, this poem is unusual for Donne in having a female speaker. The poem was given a musical setting and published in 1622, in William Corkine's *Second Book of Ayers*.

Light hath no tongue, but is all eye;
If it could speak as well as spy,
This were the worst that it could say,
That being well, I fain° would stay,   *gladly*
And that I loved my heart and honor so
That I would not from him, that had them, go.

Must business thee from hence remove?
O, that's the worst disease of love.
The poor, the foul, the false, love can
Admit, but not the busied man.
He which hath business, and makes love, doth do
Such wrong, as when a married man doth woo.

1622, 1633

A Valediction:[1] Of Weeping

    Let me pour forth
My tears before thy face whilst I stay here,
For thy face coins them, and thy stamp° they bear,   *image*
And by this mintage they are something worth,
    For thus they be
    Pregnant of thee;
Fruits of much grief they are, emblems° of more—   *symbols*
When a tear falls, that thou falls which it bore,
So thou and I are nothing then, when on a diverse° shore.   *different*

    On a round ball
A workman that hath copies by can lay
An Europe, Afric, and an Asia,
And quickly make that, which was nothing, all;[2]
    So doth each tear
    Which thee doth wear,[3]
A globe, yea world, by that impression grow,
Till thy tears mixed with mine do overflow
This world; by waters sent from thee, my heaven dissolvèd so.

    O more than moon,
Draw not up seas to drown me in thy sphere;[4]
Weep me not dead in thine arms, but forbear
To teach the sea what it may do too soon.
    Let not the wind
    Example find

---

1. A farewell poem, one of four so titled in the *Songs and Sonnets*. Another is "A Valediction: Forbidding Mourning," p. 897.
2. That is, on a blank globe one can place maps of the continents and so convert "nothing" into the whole world ("all").
3. Which bears your image.
4. A star or planet with more power of attraction than the moon might not only affect tides but draw the very seas unto itself.

25 To do me more harm than it purposeth;
    Since thou and I sigh one another's breath,
    Whoe'er sighs most is cruelest, and hastes the other's death.

                                                                            1633

A Nocturnal upon Saint Lucy's Day, Being the Shortest Day[1]

'Tis the year's midnight and it is the day's,
Lucy's, who scarce seven hours herself unmasks;
    The sun is spent, and now his flasks[2]
    Send forth light squibs,° no constant rays.   *small fireworks*
5   The world's whole sap is sunk;
The general balm th' hydroptic[3] earth hath drunk,
Whither, as to the bed's feet, life is shrunk,
Dead and interred; yet all these seem to laugh,
Compared with me, who am their epitaph.

10 Study me, then, you who shall lovers be
    At the next world, that is, at the next spring;
        For I am every dead thing
        In whom love wrought new alchemy.
            For his art did express°   *extract*
15 A quintessence[4] even from nothingness,
    From dull privations and lean emptiness.
    He ruined me, and I am re-begot
    Of absence, darkness, death: things which are not.

    All others from all things draw all that's good,
20 Life, soul, form, spirit, whence they being have;
        I, by love's limbeck,[5] am the grave
        Of all that's nothing. Oft a flood
            Have we two wept, and so
    Drowned the whole world, us two; oft did we grow
25 To be two chaoses when we did show
    Care to aught° else; and often absences   *anything*
    Withdrew our souls, and made us carcasses.

    But I am by her death (which word wrongs her)
    Of the first nothing the elixir grown;[6]

---

1. The nocturne, or night office of the Roman Catholic Church, is a service held in the primitive church at midnight. St. Lucy's Day fell on December 13 according to the old calendar still in use in England at the time, and its vigil (the previous day and night) was the winter solstice, the shortest day of the year. At this time of the year, the sun rises after 8 A.M. in the latitude of London and sets well before 4 P.M.
2. The stars are "flasks," thought to store up light from the sun.
3. Dropsical, thus insatiably thirsty. "General balm": the supposedly life-preserving essence of all things.
4. The reputed fifth essence, a celestial element beyond the mundane four elements (earth, water, air, fire), thought to be latent in all things and to be a universal cure. Alchemists sought to extract it.
5. Alembic; a vessel used in distilling.
6. That is, the quintessence of that absolute nothingness that existed before the creation.

30 Were I a man, that I were one
        I needs must know; I should prefer,
            If I were any beast,
    Some ends, some means; yea plants, yea stones detest
    And love.⁷ All, all some properties invest.
35 If I an ordinary nothing were,
    As shadow, a light and body must be here.

    But I am none; nor will my sun renew.
    You lovers, for whose sake the lesser sun
        At this time to the Goat⁸ is run
40   To fetch new lust and give it you,
            Enjoy your summer all.
    Since she enjoys her long night's festival,
    Let me prepare towards her, and let me call
    This hour her vigil and her eve, since this
45 Both the year's and the day's deep midnight is.

                                                    1633

The Bait[1]

   Come live with me and be my love,
   And we will some new pleasures prove,°   try
   Of golden sands and crystal brooks,
   With silken lines and silver hooks.

5 There will the river whispering run,
   Warmed by thine eyes more than the sun.
   And there the enamored fish will stay,
   Begging themselves they may betray.

   When thou wilt swim in that live bath,
10 Each fish, which every channel hath,
   Will amorously to thee swim,
   Gladder to catch thee, than thou him.

   If thou, to be so seen, beest loath,
   By sun or moon, thou darkenest both;
15 And if myself have leave to see,
   I need not their light, having thee.

---

7. Beasts have intentions; plants and even stones (like lodestones) have attractions and antipathies.
8. The sign of Capricorn, which the sun enters at the winter solstice; the goat is an emblem of sexual vigor.

1. This poem is Donne's response to Marlowe's "Passionate Shepherd to His Love," p. 495. Another of the many responses was Ralegh's "The Nymph's Reply to the Shepherd," p. 496.

> Let others freeze with angling reeds,
> And cut their legs with shells and weeds,
> Or treacherously poor fish beset
> With strangling snare or windowy net.
>
> Let coarse bold hands from slimy nest
> The bedded fish in banks outwrest,
> Or curious traitors, sleave-silk flies,[2]
> Bewitch poor fishes' wandering eyes.
>
> For thee, thou need'st no such deceit,
> For thou thyself art thine own bait;
> That fish that is not catched thereby,
> Alas, is wiser far than I.

1633

The Apparition

> When by thy scorn, O murderess, I am dead,
> And that thou thinkst thee free
> From all solicitation from me,
> Then shall my ghost come to thy bed,
> And thee, feigned vestal,[1] in worse arms shall see;
> Then thy sick taper will begin to wink,°   *flicker*
> And he whose thou art then, being tired before,
> Will, if thou stir, or pinch to wake him, think
>   Thou call'st for more,
> And in false sleep will from thee shrink,
> And then, poor aspen wretch,[2] neglected thou
> Bathed in a cold quicksilver sweat[3] wilt lie
>   A verier° ghost than I;   *truer*
> What I will say, I will not tell thee now,
> Lest that preserve thee; and since my love is spent,
> I had rather thou shouldst painfully repent,
> Than by my threatenings rest still innocent.

1633

---

2. Flies (for fishing) made of unraveled silk. "Curious": exquisitely made.
1. Virgin consecrated to the Roman goddess Vesta.
2. Aspen leaves flutter in the slightest breeze.
3. Sweating in terror; quicksilver (mercury) was a stock prescription for venereal disease, and sweating was part of the cure.

A Valediction: Forbidding Mourning[1]

As virtuous men pass mildly away,
    And whisper to their souls to go,
Whilst some of their sad friends do say
    The breath goes now, and some say, No;

5 So let us melt, and make no noise,
    No tear-floods, nor sigh-tempests move;
'Twere profanation° of our joys   *desecration*
    To tell the laity our love.

Moving of th' earth brings harms and fears,
10   Men reckon what it did and meant;
But trepidation of the spheres,
    Though greater far, is innocent.[2]

Dull sublunary[3] lovers' love
    (Whose soul is sense) cannot admit
15 Absence, because it doth remove
    Those things which elemented° it.   *composed*

But we, by a love so much refined
    That ourselves know not what it is,
Inter-assurèd of the mind,
20   Care less, eyes, lips, and hands to miss.

Our two souls therefore, which are one,
    Though I must go, endure not yet
A breach, but an expansion,
    Like gold to airy thinness beat.

25 If they be two, they are two so
    As stiff twin compasses[4] are two;
Thy soul, the fixed foot, makes no show
    To move, but doth, if th' other do.

And though it in the center sit,
30   Yet when the other far doth roam,
It leans and hearkens after it,
    And grows erect, as that comes home.

---

1. For "valediction" see p. 893, n. 1. Izaak Walton speculated that this poem was addressed to Donne's wife on the occasion of his trip to the Continent in 1611, but there is no proof of that.
2. Earthquakes cause damage and were thought to be portentous. "Trepidation" (in the Ptolemaic cosmology) is an oscillation of the ninth or crystalline sphere imparted to all the inner spheres. Though a much more violent motion than an earthquake, it is neither destructive nor sinister.
3. Beneath the moon, therefore earthly, sensual, and subject to change.
4. The two legs of a geometer's or draftsman's compass.

The Compass. A manuscript poem inspired by the compass image in Donne's "A Valediction: Forbidding Mourning" is prefaced by a drawing of a seventeenth-century compass meant to celebrate the poem's central metaphor.

>   Such wilt thou be to me, who must,
>   Like th' other foot, obliquely run;
> 35 Thy firmness makes my circle just,
>   And makes me end where I begun.

1633

The Ecstasy[1]

>   Where, like a pillow on a bed,
>   A pregnant bank swelled up to rest
>   The violet's reclining head,
>   Sat we two, one another's best.
>
> 5   Our hands were firmly cemented
>   With a fast balm° which thence did spring,   *perspiration*
>   Our eye-beams[2] twisted, and did thread
>   Our eyes upon one double string;

---

1. From *ekstasis* (Greek), a movement of the soul outside of the body.
2. Invisible shafts of light, thought of as going out of the eyes and thereby enabling one to see things.

　　　　So to intergraft our hands, as yet
10　　　　　Was all our means to make us one,
　　　　And pictures in our eyes³ to get°　　　　　　　　　　*beget*
　　　　　Was all our propagation.

　　　　As 'twixt two equal armies Fate
　　　　　Suspends uncertain victory,
15　　　　Our souls (which to advance their state
　　　　　Were gone out) hung 'twixt her and me;

　　　　And whilst our souls negotiate there,
　　　　　We like sepulchral statues lay;
　　　　All day the same our postures were,
20　　　　　And we said nothing all the day.

　　　　If any, so by love refined
　　　　　That he soul's language understood,
　　　　And by good love were grown all mind,
　　　　　Within convenient distance stood,

25　　　　He (though he knew not which soul spake,
　　　　　Because both meant, both spake the same)
　　　　Might thence a new concoction⁴ take,
　　　　　And part far purer than he came.

　　　　This ecstasy doth unperplex,
30　　　　　We said, and tell us what we love;
　　　　We see by this it was not sex;
　　　　　We see we saw not what did move;°　　　　　　　*motivate us*

　　　　But as all several° souls contain　　　　　　　　　　*separate*
　　　　　Mixture of things, they know not what,
35　　　　Love these mixed souls doth mix again,
　　　　　And makes both one, each this and that.

　　　　A single violet transplant,
　　　　　The strength, the color, and the size
　　　　(All which before was poor and scant)
40　　　　　Redoubles still,° and multiplies.　　　　　　　　*continually*

　　　　When love with one another so
　　　　　Interinanimates two souls,
　　　　That abler soul, which thence doth flow,
　　　　　Defects of loneliness controls.

45　　　　We then, who are this new soul, know
　　　　　Of what we are composed and made,
　　　　For th' atomies° of which we grow　　　　　　　　　*components*
　　　　　Are souls, whom no change can invade.

---

3. Reflections of each in the other's eyes, often called "making babies."

4. In the alchemical sense of sublimation or purification.

But O alas, so long, so far
    Our bodies why do we forbear?
They are ours, though they are not we; we are
    The intelligences, they the sphere.[5]

We owe them thanks because they thus
    Did us to us at first convey,
Yielded their forces, sense, to us,
    Nor are dross to us, but allay.[6]

On man heaven's influence works not so
    But that it first imprints the air:[7]
So soul into the soul may flow,
    Though it to body first repair.°   *go*

As our blood labors to beget
    Spirits[8] as like souls as it can,
Because such fingers need° to knit   *are needed*
    That subtle knot which makes us man,

So must pure lovers' souls descend
    T' affections, and to faculties
Which sense may reach and apprehend;
    Else a great prince in prison lies.

To our bodies turn we then, that so
    Weak men on love revealed may look;
Love's mysteries[9] in souls do grow,
    But yet the body is his book.

And if some lover, such as we,
    Have heard this dialogue of one,[1]
Let him still mark° us; he shall see   *observe*
    Small change when we are to bodies gone.

1633

The Funeral

Whoever comes to shroud me, do not harm
    Nor question much
That subtle wreath of hair which crowns my arm;
    The mystery, the sign you must not touch,

---

5. In Ptolemaic astronomy, each planet, set in a transparent "sphere" that revolved and so carried it around the earth, was inhabited by a controlling angelic "intelligence."
6. "Dross" is an impurity that weakens metal; "allay" (alloy) strengthens it.
7. Astrological influences were thought to work on people through the medium of the surrounding air.
8. Subtle substances thought to be produced by the blood to serve as intermediaries between body and soul.
9. The implied comparison is with God's mysteries, which are revealed and may be read in the book of nature and the book of scripture.
1. "Dialogue of one" because "both meant, both spake the same" (line 26).

5   For 'tis my outward soul,
Viceroy to that, which then to heaven being gone,
    Will leave this to control,
And keep these limbs, her[1] provinces, from dissolution.

For if the sinewy thread[2] my brain lets fall
10   Through every part
Can tie those parts and make me one of all,
These hairs which upward grew, and strength and art
    Have from a better brain,
Can better do it; except° she meant that I   *unless*
15   By this should know my pain,
As prisoners then are manacled, when they're condemned to die.

Whate'er she meant by it, bury it with me,
    For since I am
Love's martyr, it might breed idolatry,
20 If into others' hands these relics[3] came:
    As 'twas humility
To afford to it all that a soul can do,
    So 'tis some bravery,°   *defiance*
That since you would save[4] none of me, I bury some of you.

                    1633

The Relic

When my grave is broke up again
Some second guest to entertain
(For graves have learned that woman-head°   *female trait*
To be to more than one a bed),[1]
5   And he that digs it spies
A bracelet of bright hair about the bone,
    Will he not let us alone,
And think that there a loving couple lies,
Who thought that this device might be some way
10 To make their souls, at the last busy day,[2]
Meet at this grave, and make a little stay?

If this fall° in a time, or land,   *happen*
Where mis-devotion[3] doth command,
Then he that digs us up will bring
15   Us to the bishop and the king,

---

1. The soul's, but also the mistress's (compare "she," line 14).
2. The nervous system.
3. Body parts or other objects belonging to a saint, venerated by Roman Catholics.
4. All the early printed texts read "have" (which carries sexual connotations), while many manuscripts read "save."

1. Graves were often used to inter successive corpses, the bones of previous occupants being deposited in charnel houses.
2. Judgment Day, when the bodies of the deceased are reunited with their souls (and the beloved comes to her lover's grave to reclaim her hair).
3. False devotion, superstition—that is, Roman Catholicism.

                    To make us relics; then
                Thou shalt be a Mary Magdalen, and I
                    A something else thereby;
                All women shall adore us, and some men;
20   And since at such times, miracles are sought,
                I would have that age by this paper taught
                What miracles we harmless lovers wrought.

                    First, we loved well and faithfully,
                    Yet knew not what we loved, nor why,
25   Difference of sex no more we knew,
                    Than our guardian angels do;
                        Coming and going, we
                Perchance might kiss, but not between those meals;[4]
                    Our hands ne'er touched the seals°   *sexual organs*
30   Which nature, injured by late law, sets free:[5]
                These miracles we did: but now, alas,
                All measure and all language I should pass,
                Should I tell what a miracle she was.

                                                                1633

A Lecture upon the Shadow

                Stand still, and I will read to thee
                A lecture, Love, in love's philosophy.
                    These three hours that we have spent
                    Walking here, two shadows went
5   Along with us, which we ourselves produced;
                But, now the sun is just above our head,
                    We do those shadows tread
                    And to brave° clearness all things are reduced.   *splendid*
                So, whilst our infant loves did grow,
10   Disguises did and shadows flow
                From us and our care;° but now, 'tis not so.   *caution*

                That love hath not attained the high'st degree
                Which is still diligent lest others see.

                Except° our loves at this noon stay,   *unless*
15   We shall new shadows make the other way.
                    As the first were made to blind
                    Others, these which come behind
                Will work upon ourselves, and blind our eyes.
                If our loves faint and westwardly decline,
20   To me thou falsely thine
                And I to thee mine actions shall disguise.
                The morning shadows wear away,

---

4. The kisses of salutation and parting.
5. Human law forbids the free love permitted by nature. "Late": recent (comparatively speaking).

But these grow longer all the day,
But, oh, love's day is short if love decay.

25 Love is a growing or full constant light,
And his first minute after noon is night.

1635

Elegy[1] 16. On His Mistress

By our first strange and fatal° interview,   *fateful*
By all desires which thereof did ensue,
By our long starving hopes, by that remorse°   *pity*
Which my words' masculine persuasive force
5 Begot in thee, and by the memory
Of hurts which spies and rivals threatened me,
I calmly beg; but by thy father's wrath,
By all pains which want and divorcement hath,
I conjure thee; and all the oaths which I
10 And thou have sworn to seal joint constancy
Here I unswear and overswear them thus:
Thou shalt not love by ways so dangerous.
Temper, oh fair love, love's impetuous rage;
Be my true mistress still, not my feigned page.[2]
15 I'll go, and, by thy kind leave, leave behind
Thee, only worthy to nurse in my mind
Thirst to come back. Oh, if thou die before,
My soul from other lands to thee shall soar.
Thy (else almighty) beauty cannot move
20 Rage from the seas, nor thy love teach them love,
Nor tame wild Boreas' harshness.[3] Thou hast read
How roughly he in pieces shiverèd
Fair Orithea, whom he swore he loved.
Fall ill or good, 'tis madness to have proved°   *sought out*
25 Dangers unurged; feed on this flattery,
That absent lovers one in th' other be.
Dissemble nothing, not a boy, nor change
Thy body's habit,° nor mind's; be not strange   *clothing*
To thyself only; all will spy in thy face
30 A blushing womanly discovering grace.
Richly clothed apes are called apes, and as soon
Eclipsed as bright we call the moon the moon.
Men of France, changeable chameleons,
Spitals° of diseases, shops of fashions,   *hospitals*

---

1. In Latin poetry, an elegy is a discursive or reflective poem written in "elegiacs" (unrhymed couplets of alternating dactylic hexameters and pentameters). This meter was used for funeral laments and especially for love poetry. The most famous classical elegist was the Roman poet Ovid; his *Amores*, a collection of witty and sensual love poems, deeply influenced Donne's erotic poetry.

2. The speaker's mistress wanted to accompany him abroad, disguised as a page boy. Such escapades occasionally took place in real life; in 1605, Elizabeth Southwell, disguised as a page, went abroad with Sir Robert Dudley.

3. God of the north wind; in *Metamorphoses* 6 Ovid describes the wild force with which Boreas abducted Orithea.

35   Love's fuelers[4] and the rightest company
      Of players which upon the world's stage be,
      Will quickly know thee, and know thee; and alas![5]
      Th' indifferent° Italian, as we pass   bisexual
      His warm land, well content to think thee page,
40   Will hunt thee with such lust and hideous rage
      As Lot's fair guests were vexed.[6] But none of these
      Nor spongy, hydroptic[7] Dutch shall thee displease
      If thou stay here. O stay here, for, for thee,
      England is only a worthy gallery
45   To walk in expectation, till from thence
      Our greatest king call thee to his presence.[8]
      When I am gone, dream me some happiness,
      Nor let thy looks our long-hid love confess;
      Nor praise nor dispraise me, bless nor curse
50   Openly love's force, nor in bed fright thy nurse
      With midnight's startings, crying out "Oh, oh!
      Nurse, oh my love is slain, I saw him go
      O'er the white Alps alone; I saw him, I,
      Assailed, fight, taken, stabbed, bleed, fall, and die."
55   Augur me better chance, except dread Jove
      Think it enough for me t' have had thy love.

                                                                        1635

Elegy 19. To His Mistress Going to Bed

      Come, Madam, come, all rest my powers defy,
      Until I labor, I in labor lie.[1]
      The foe ofttimes having the foe in sight,
      Is tired with standing though he never fight.
5   Off with that girdle,° like heaven's zone° glistering,   belt / zodiac
      But a far fairer world encompassing.
      Unpin that spangled breastplate[2] which you wear
      That th' eyes of busy fools may be stopped there.
      Unlace yourself, for that harmonious chime
10   Tells me from you that now it is bed-time.
      Off with that happy busk,° which I envy,   bodice
      That still° can be and still can stand so nigh.   always
      Your gown going off, such beauteous state reveals
      As when from flowery meads th' hill's shadow steals.
15   Off with that wiry coronet and show
      The hairy diadem which on you doth grow;
      Now off with those shoes, and then safely tread

---

4. Providers of aphrodisiacs.
5. May pun on "a lass." "Know": in the sexual sense.
6. The inhabitants of Sodom tried to rape two angels who visited Lot in the guise of men to warn of the city's impending destruction (Genesis 19:1–11).
7. Dropsical, thus insatiably thirsty.
8. Throne rooms commonly had antechambers (galleries) where visitors waited until the monarch was ready to see them.
1. "Labor" in the dual sense of "get to work (sexually)" and "distress."
2. The stomacher, an ornamental, often jeweled, covering for the chest, worn under the lacing of the bodice.

In this love's hallowed temple, this soft bed.
In such white robes, heaven's angels used to be
20 Received by men; thou, angel, bring'st with thee
A heaven like Mahomet's paradise;³ and though
Ill spirits walk in white, we easily know
By this these angels from an evil sprite,
Those set our hairs, but these our flesh upright.
25   License my roving hands, and let them go
Before, behind, between, above, below.
O my America! my new-found-land,
My kingdom, safeliest when with one man manned,
My mine of precious stones, my empery,°   empire
30 How blest am I in this discovering thee!
To enter in these bonds is to be free;
There where my hand is set, my seal shall be.⁴
    Full nakedness! All joys are due to thee.
As souls unbodied, bodies unclothed must be,
35 To taste whole joys. Gems which you women use
Are like Atalanta's balls,⁵ cast in men's views,
That when a fool's eye lighteth on a gem,
His earthly soul may covet theirs, not them.
Like pictures, or like books' gay coverings, made
40 For laymen, are all women thus arrayed;
Themselves are mystic books, which only we
(Whom their imputed grace will dignify)
Must see revealed.⁶ Then since that I may know,
As liberally as to a midwife show
45 Thyself: cast all, yea, this white linen hence,
Here is no penance, much less innocence.⁷
    To teach thee, I am naked first; why then
What need'st thou have more covering than a man?

1669

Satire 3

In satire the author holds a subject up to ridicule. Like his elegies, Donne's five verse satires were written in his twenties and are in the forefront of an effort in the 1590s (by Donne, Ben Jonson, Joseph Hall, and John Marston) to naturalize those classical forms in England. While elements of satire figure in many different kinds of literature, the great models for formal verse satire were the Roman poets Horace and Juvenal, the former for an urbanely witty style, the latter for an indignant or angry manner. While Donne's other satires call on these models, his third satire more nearly resembles those of a third Roman satirist, Persius, known

---

3. A place of sensual pleasure, thought to be populated by seductive houris for the delectation of the faithful.
4. The jokes mingle law with sex: where he has signed a document (placed his hand) he will now place his seal; and in the bonds of her arms he will find freedom.
5. Atalanta, running a race against her suitor Hippomenes, was beaten when he dropped golden apples ("balls") for her to pick up. Donne reverses the story.
6. By granting favors to their lovers, women impute to them grace that they don't deserve, as God, in Calvinist doctrine, imputes grace to undeserving sinners. Laymen can only look at the covers of mystic books (clothed women), but "we" elect can read them (see women naked).
7. Some manuscripts read: "There is no penance due to innocence." White garments would be appropriate either for the innocent virgin or for the sinner doing formal penance.

for an abstruse style and moralizing manner. This work is a strenuous discussion of an acute theological problem, for the age and for Donne himself: How may one discover the true Christian church among so many claimants to that role? At the time Donne wrote "Satire 3," he was in the process of leaving the Roman Catholic Church of his heritage for the Church of England.

Satire 3

  Kind pity chokes my spleen;[1] brave° scorn forbids   *defiant*
Those tears to issue which swell my eyelids;
I must not laugh, nor weep° sins, and be wise: *lament*
Can railing then cure these worn maladies?
5 Is not our mistress, fair Religion,
As worthy of all our souls' devotion
As virtue was to the first blinded age?[2]
Are not heaven's joys as valiant to assuage
Lusts, as earth's honor was to them?° Alas,   *pagans*
10 As we do them in means, shall they surpass
Us in the end, and shall thy father's spirit
Meet blind philosophers in heaven, whose merit
Of strict life may be imputed faith,[3] and hear
Thee, whom he taught so easy ways and near
15 To follow, damned? O, if thou dar'st, fear this;
This fear great courage and high valor is.
Dar'st thou aid mutinous Dutch,[4] and dar'st thou lay
Thee in ships, wooden sepulchers, a prey
To leaders' rage, to storms, to shot, to dearth?°   *famine*
20 Dar'st thou dive seas and dungeons° of the earth?   *mines, caves*
Hast thou courageous fire to thaw the ice
Of frozen north discoveries?[5] And thrice
Colder than salamanders, like divine
Children in the oven,[6] fires of Spain and the line,
25 Whose countries limbecks to our bodies be,
Canst thou for gain bear?[7] And must every he
Which cries not "Goddess!" to thy mistress, draw,°   *fight a duel*
Or eat thy poisonous words? Courage of straw!
O desperate coward, wilt thou seem bold, and
30 To thy foes and His° (who made thee to stand   *God's*
Sentinel in his world's garrison) thus yield,
And for forbidden wars leave th' appointed field?[8]

---

1. The seat of bile, hence scorn and ridicule.
2. The age of paganism, blind to Christianity but capable of natural morality ("virtue").
3. Donne's formulation wittily turns on its head the key concept of Protestant theology—that salvation is to be achieved only by imputing Christ's merits to Christians through faith—by suggesting that virtuous pagans might be saved by imputing faith to them on the basis of their moral life.
4. English volunteers took frequent part with the Dutch in their wars against Spain. Donne himself had sailed in two raiding expeditions against the Spanish.
5. Many explorers tried to find a northwest passage to the Pacific.
6. In the biblical story (Daniel 3), Shadrach, Meshach, and Abednego were rescued from a fiery furnace. The salamander (a lizardlike creature) was thought to be so cold-blooded that it could live in fire.
7. The object of "bear" is "fires of Spain and the line"—inquisitorial and equatorial heats, which roast people as chemists heat materials in "limbecks" (alembics, or vessels for distilling).
8. Of moral struggle.

Know thy foes: The foul Devil (whom thou
Strivest to please) for hate, not love, would allow
35 Thee fain° his whole realm to be quit;° and as   *gladly / to satisfy you*
The world's all parts wither away and pass,[9]
So the world's self, thy other loved foe, is
In her decrepit wane, and thou, loving this,
Dost love a withered and worn strumpet; last,
40 Flesh (itself's death) and joys which flesh can taste
Thou lovest; and thy fair goodly soul, which doth
Give this flesh power to taste joy, thou dost loathe.
Seek true religion. O, where? Mirreus,[1]
Thinking her unhoused here, and fled from us,
45 Seeks her at Rome; there, because he doth know
That she was there a thousand years ago.
He loves her rags so, as we here obey
The statecloth[2] where the prince sat yesterday.
Crantz to such brave loves will not be enthralled,
50 But loves her only, who at Geneva is called
Religion—plain, simple, sullen, young,
Contemptuous, yet unhandsome; as among
Lecherous humors,° there is one that judges   *temperaments*
No wenches wholesome but coarse country drudges.
55 Graius stays still at home here, and because
Some preachers, vile ambitious bawds, and laws
Still new, like fashions, bid him think that she
Which dwells with us is only perfect, he
Embraceth her whom his godfathers will
60 Tender to him, being tender, as wards still
Take such wives as their guardians offer, or
Pay values.[3] Careless Phrygius doth abhor
All, because all cannot be good, as one
Knowing some women whores, dares marry none.
65 Graccus loves all as one, and thinks that so
As women do in divers countries go
In divers habits,° yet are still one kind,   *styles of clothing*
So doth, so is religion; and this blind-
ness too much light breeds;[4] but unmoved thou
70 Of force° must one, and forced but one allow;   *necessity*
And the right; ask thy father which is she,
Let him ask his; though truth and falsehood be
Near twins, yet truth a little elder is;
Be busy to seek her, believe me this,
75 He's not of none, nor worst, that seeks the best.[5]
To adore, or scorn an image, or protest,

---

9. The common belief that the world was growing old and becoming decrepit.
1. The satiric types in this passage represent different creeds: "Mirreus" is a Roman Catholic; "Crantz," an austere Calvinist Presbyterian of Geneva; "Graius," a Church of England Erastian who believes in any religion sponsored by the state; "Phrygius," a skeptic; and "Graccus," a complete relativist.
2. The royal canopy, a symbol of kingly power.
3. If minors in care of a guardian (in wardship) rejected the wives offered ("tendered") to them they had to pay fines ("values").
4. That is, Graccus considers the differences between religions merely incidental, like women's clothes, but his apparently tolerant, "enlightened" attitude is itself a form of blindness.
5. The person who seeks the best church is neither an unbeliever nor the worst sort of believer.

May all be bad; doubt wisely; in strange way
To stand inquiring right, is not to stray;
To sleep, or run wrong, is. On a huge hill,
80 Cragged and steep, Truth stands, and he that will
Reach her, about must, and about must go,
And what the hill's suddenness resists, win so;
Yet strive so, that before age, death's twilight,
Thy soul rest, for none can work in that night.[6]
85 To will° implies delay, therefore now do.   *intend a future act*
Hard deeds, the body's pains; hard knowledge too
The mind's endeavors reach,° and mysteries   *achieve*
Are like the sun, dazzling, yet plain to all eyes.
Keep the truth which thou hast found; men do not stand
90 In so ill case here, that God hath with his hand
Signed kings' blank charters to kill whom they hate,
Nor are they vicars, but hangmen to fate.[7]
Fool and wretch, wilt thou let thy soul be tied
To man's laws, by which she shall not be tried
95 At the last day? O, will it then boot° thee   *profit*
To say a Philip, or a Gregory,
A Harry, or a Martin taught thee this?[8]
Is not this excuse for mere° contraries   *complete*
Equally strong? Cannot both sides say so?
100 That thou mayest rightly obey power, her bounds know;
Those passed, her nature and name is changed; to be
Then humble to her is idolatry.
As streams are, power is; those blest flowers that dwell
At the rough stream's calm head, thrive and prove well,
105 But having left their roots, and themselves given
To the stream's tyrannous rage, alas, are driven
Through mills, and rocks, and woods, and at last, almost
Consumed in going, in the sea are lost:
So perish souls, which more choose men's unjust
110 Power from God claimed, than God himself to trust.

1633

To Sir Henry Wotton[1]

Sir, more than kisses, letters mingle souls;
For, thus friends absent speak. This ease controls°   *limits*
The tediousness of my life: but for these

---

6. An echo of John 9:4, "the night cometh, when no man can work."
7. Kings are not God's vicars on earth, with license ("blank charters") to persecute or kill whomever they wish on grounds of religion.
8. "Philip" is Philip II of Spain, "Gregory" is Pope Gregory XIII or XIV, "Harry" is England's Henry VIII, and "Martin" is Martin Luther.
1. Wotton and Donne were at Oxford together and remained friends. Wotton was secretary to the Earl of Essex and, like Donne, went on the Cadiz and Azores expeditions in 1596–97. The poem arises out of a literary exchange among members of the Essex circle over the nature of a good life. (Some manuscripts give what appears to be Wotton's reply to Donne's poem, headed "To Mr. J. D. from Mr. H. W.")

       I could ideate nothing, which could please,
5   But I should wither in one day, and pass
       To a bottle° of hay, that am a lock of grass.   *bundle*
       Life is a voyage, and in our life's ways
       Countries, courts, towns are rocks, or remoras;°   *impediments*
       They break or stop all ships, yet our state's such,
10 That though than pitch they stain worse, we must touch.
       If in the furnace of the even line,°   *equator*
       Or under th' adverse° icy poles thou pine,   *opposite*
       Thou know'st two temperate regions, girded in,
       Dwell there: But Oh! what refuge canst thou win
15 Parched in the court, and in the country frozen?
       Shall cities, built of both extremes, be chosen?
       Can dung or garlic be a perfume? Or can
       A scorpion or torpedo° cure a man?   *electric ray*
       Cities are worst of all three; of all three
20 (O knotty riddle) each is worst equally.
       Cities are sepulchres; they who dwell there
       Are carcasses, as if no such they were:
       And courts are theaters, where some men play
       Princes, some slaves, all to one end, of one clay.
25 The country is a desert, where no good,
       Gained (as habits, not born,) is understood.
       There men become beasts, and prone to more evils;
       In cities, blocks,° and in a lewd court, devils.   *blockheads*
       As in the first Chaos confusedly
30 Each element's qualities were in the other three;[2]
       So pride, lust, covetize, being several
       To these three places, yet all are in all,
       And mingled thus, their issue is incestuous:
       Falsehood is denizen'd.° Virtue is barbarous.   *resides; is naturalized*
35 Let no man say there, "Virtue's flinty wall
       Shall lock vice in me; I'll do none, but know all."
       Men are sponges, which to pour out, receive,
       Who know false play, rather than lose, deceive.
       For in best understandings, sin began,
40 Angels sinned first, then devils, and then man.
       Only perchance beasts sin not; wretched we
       Are beasts in all, but white integrity.°   *innocence*
       I think if men, which in these places live
       Durst look for themselves, and themselves retrieve,
45 They would like strangers greet themselves, seeing then
       Utopian youth, grown old Italian.°   *crafty, corrupt*
       Be then thine own home, and in thyself dwell;
       Inn° anywhere; continuance maketh hell.   *lodge for a short while*
       And seeing the snail, which everywhere doth roam,
50 Carrying his own house still, still is at home,
       Follow (for he is easy paced) this snail,

---

2. The separation of confused materials into four distinct elements (air, earth, fire, water) was a critical stage as order was created out of chaos.

Be thine own palace, or the world's thy jail.³
And in the world's sea, do not like cork sleep
Upon the water's face; nor in the deep
Sink like a lead without a line: but as
Fishes glide, leaving no print where they pass,
Nor making sound, so closely thy course go,
Let men dispute, whether thou breathe, or no.
Only in this one thing be no Galenist:⁴ to make
Courts' hot ambitions wholesome, do not take
A dram of country's dullness; do not add
Correctives, but as chemics,° purge the bad.   *alchemists, chemists*
But, Sir, I advise not you, I rather do
Say o'er those lessons, which I learned of you,
Whom, free from German schisms, and lightness
Of France, and fair Italy's faithlessness,⁵
Having from these sucked all they had of worth,
And brought home that faith, which you carried forth,
I thoroughly love. But if myself, I have won
To know my rules,⁶ I have, and you have
                                        Donne

1597 or 1598

From Holy Sonnets¹

1

Thou hast made me, and shall thy work decay?
Repair me now, for now mine end doth haste;
I run to death, and death meets me as fast,
And all my pleasures are like yesterday.
I dare not move my dim eyes any way,
Despair behind, and death before doth cast
Such terror, and my feeble flesh doth waste
By sin in it, which it towards hell doth weigh.°   *incline, weigh down*
Only thou art above, and when towards thee
By thy leave I can look, I rise again;
But our old subtle foe so tempteth me
That not one hour myself I can sustain.

---

3. "Goal" in 1633 (a boundary or limit; finishing point in a race or journey); "gaile" in 1635–69 (a wind of considerable strength or a storm). Later editors changed the word to "jail."
4. Galen (129–ca. 216 C.E.) was a Greek physician whose teachings were dominant until the mid-17th century; Galenists worked to cure by contraries, correcting an excess of some bodily humor by making up the deficiency in its opposite humor so as to restore a balance.
5. Wotton had traveled on the Continent between 1589 and 1594.
6. Principles, precepts (set out in the poem).
1. Donne wrote a variety of religious poems (called "Divine Poems"), including a group of nineteen "holy sonnets" that reflect his interest in Jesuit and Protestant meditative procedures. He probably began writing them about 1609, a decade or so after leaving the Catholic Church. Our selections follow the traditional numbering established in Sir Herbert Grierson's influential edition, since for most of these sonnets we cannot tell when they were written or in what order they were intended to appear.

Thy grace may wing° me to prevent° his art,   *give wings to / forestall*
And thou like adamant° draw mine iron heart.   *magnetic lodestone*

1635

5

I am a little world[2] made cunningly
Of elements, and an angelic sprite;°   *spirit, soul*
But black sin hath betrayed to endless night
My world's both parts, and O, both parts must die.
5 You which beyond that heaven which was most high
Have found new spheres, and of new lands can write,[3]
Pour new seas in mine eyes, that so I might
Drown my world with my weeping earnestly,
Or wash it if it must be drowned no more.[4]
10 But O, it must be burnt! Alas, the fire
Of lust and envy have burnt it heretofore,
And made it fouler; let their flames retire,
And burn me, O Lord, with a fiery zeal
Of thee and thy house, which doth in eating heal.[5]

1635

7

At the round earth's imagined corners,[6] blow
Your trumpets, angels; and arise, arise
From death, you numberless infinities
Of souls, and to your scattered bodies go:
5 All whom the flood did, and fire shall, o'erthrow,[7]
All whom war, dearth,° age, agues,° tyrannies,   *famine / fevers*
Despair, law, chance hath slain, and you whose eyes
Shall behold God, and never taste death's woe.[8]
But let them sleep, Lord, and me mourn a space;
10 For, if above all these, my sins abound,
'Tis late to ask abundance of thy grace
When we are there. Here on this lowly ground,
Teach me how to repent; for that's as good
As if thou hadst sealed my pardon with thy blood.

1633

---

2. The traditional idea of the human being as microcosm (a "little world"), containing in miniature all the features of the macrocosm, or great world.
3. "You" are astronomers, especially Galileo, and explorers.
4. God promised Noah (Genesis 9:11) never to flood the earth again.
5. See Psalm 69:9: "For the zeal of thine house hath eaten me up." These lines refer to three kinds of flame—those of the Last Judgment, those of lust and envy, and those of zeal, which alone save.
6. Compare Revelation 7:1: "I saw four angels standing on the four corners of the earth."
7. Noah's Flood, and the universal conflagration at the end of the world (Revelation 6:11).
8. Those who will be alive at the Second Coming (compare Luke 9:27).

9

If poisonous minerals, and if that tree[9]
Whose fruit threw death on else-immortal us,
If lecherous goats, if serpents envious[1]
Cannot be damned, alas! why should I be?
Why should intent or reason, born in me,
Make sins, else equal, in me more heinous?
And, mercy being easy and glorious
To God, in his stern wrath why threatens he?
But who am I that dare dispute with thee
O God? Oh, of thine only worthy blood
And my tears, make a heavenly Lethean[2] flood,
And drown in it my sin's black memory.
That thou remember them some claim as debt;
I think it mercy if thou wilt forget.[3]

1633

10

Death, be not proud, though some have callèd thee
Mighty and dreadful, for thou art not so;
For those whom thou think'st thou dost overthrow
Die not, poor Death, nor yet canst thou kill me.
From rest and sleep, which but thy pictures be,
Much pleasure; then from thee much more must flow,
And soonest our best men with thee do go,
Rest of their bones, and soul's delivery.[4]
Thou art slave to fate, chance, kings, and desperate men,
And dost with poison, war, and sickness dwell,
And poppy° or charms can make us sleep as well   *opium*
And better than thy stroke; why swell'st° thou then?   *puff with pride*
One short sleep past, we wake eternally
And death shall be no more; Death, thou shalt die.[5]

1633

11

Spit in my face ye Jews, and pierce my side,
Buffet, and scoff,° scourge, and crucify me,   *scoff at*
For I have sinned, and sinned, and only he,
Who could do no iniquity, hath died:
But by my death cannot be satisfied°   *atoned for*

---

9. The Tree of Knowledge of Good and Evil, whose fruit was forbidden to Adam and Eve in Eden.
1. Traits commonly associated with these creatures.
2. In classical mythology, the waters of the river Lethe in the underworld caused total forgetfulness.
3. Compare Jeremiah 31:34: "I will forgive their iniquity, and I will remember their sins no more."
4. That is, to find rest for their bones and freedom ("delivery") for their souls.
5. Compare 1 Corinthians 15:26: "The last enemy that shall be destroyed is death."

My sins, which pass the Jews' impiety:
They killed once an inglorious° man, but I   *obscure*
Crucify him daily,[6] being now glorified.
Oh let me then, his strange love still admire:°   *wonder at*
Kings pardon, but he bore our punishment.[7]
And Jacob came clothed in vile harsh attire
But to supplant, and with gainful intent:[8]
God clothed himself in vile man's flesh, that so
He might be weak enough to suffer woe.

1633

13

What if this present were the world's last night?
Mark in my heart, O soul, where thou dost dwell,
The picture of Christ crucified, and tell
Whether that countenance can thee affright.
Tears in his eyes quench the amazing light,
Blood fills his frowns, which from his pierced head fell;
And can that tongue adjudge thee unto hell
Which prayed forgiveness for his foes' fierce spite?
No, no; but as in my idolatry
I said to all my profane° mistresses,   *secular*
Beauty of pity, foulness only is
A sign of rigor:[9] so I say to thee,
To wicked spirits are horrid shapes assigned,
This beauteous form assures a piteous mind.

1633

14

Batter my heart, three-personed God;[1] for you
As yet but knock, breathe, shine, and seek to mend;
That I may rise and stand, o'erthrow me, and bend
Your force to break, blow, burn, and make me new.
I, like an usurped town, to another due,
Labor to admit you, but O, to no end;
Reason, your viceroy[2] in me, me should defend,
But is captived, and proves weak or untrue.
Yet dearly I love you, and would be loved fain,°   *gladly*
But am betrothed[3] unto your enemy.
Divorce me, untie or break that knot again;

---

6. Compare Hebrews 6:6: "they [sinners] crucify to themselves the Son of God afresh."
7. Kings may pardon crimes, but the King of Kings, Christ, bore the punishment due to our sins.
8. Jacob disguised himself in goatskins to gain from his blind father the blessing belonging to the firstborn son, his brother Esau (Genesis 27:1–36).
9. In Neoplatonic theory, beautiful features are the sign of a compassionate mind, while ugliness signifies the contrary.
1. That is, God existing as the Father, the Son, and the Holy Spirit.
2. The governor in your stead.
3. Humanity's relationship with God has been described in terms of marriage and adultery from the time of the Hebrew prophets.

Take me to you, imprison me, for I,
Except° you enthrall[4] me, never shall be free,   *unless*
Nor ever chaste, except you ravish[5] me.

1633

17

Since she whom I loved hath paid her last debt[6]
To Nature, and to hers, and my good is dead,
And her soul early into heaven ravishèd,
Wholly on heavenly things my mind is set.
5 Here the admiring her my mind did whet
To seek thee, God; so streams do show the head;°   *source*
But though I have found thee, and thou my thirst hast fed,
A holy thirsty dropsy° melts me yet.   *immoderate thirst*
But why should I beg more love, whenas thou
10 Dost woo my soul, for hers offering all thine:
And dost not only fear lest I allow
My love to saints and angels, things divine,
But in thy tender jealousy dost doubt°   *fear*
Lest the world, flesh, yea, devil put thee out.

1899

18

Show me, dear Christ, thy spouse[7] so bright and clear.
What! is it she which on the other shore
Goes richly painted? or which, robbed and tore,
Laments and mourns in Germany and here?[8]
5 Sleeps she a thousand, then peeps up one year?
Is she self-truth, and errs? now new, now outwore?
Doth she, and did she, and shall she evermore
On one, on seven, or on no hill appear?[9]
Dwells she with us, or like adventuring knights
10 First travel we to seek, and then make love?
Betray, kind husband, thy spouse to our sights,
And let mine amorous soul court thy mild dove,
Who is most true and pleasing to thee then
When she is embraced and open to most men.[1]

1899

---

4. Enslave, also enchant.
5. Rape, also overwhelm with wonder.
6. Donne's wife died in 1617 at the age of thirty-three, having just given birth to her twelfth child. This very personal sonnet and the following two survive in a single manuscript discovered only in 1892.
7. The church is commonly called the bride of Christ. See Revelation 19:7–8: "The marriage of the Lamb is come, and his wife hath made herself ready. / And to her was granted that she should be arrayed in fine linen, clean and white."
8. That is, the painted woman (the Church of Rome) or the ravished virgin (the Lutheran and Calvinist churches in Germany and England).
9. The church on one hill is probably Solomon's temple on Mount Moriah; that on seven hills is the Church of Rome; that on no hill is the Presbyterian church of Geneva.
1. The final lines wittily rework, with startling sexual associations, Song of Solomon 5:2: "Open to me, my sister, my love, my dove, my undefiled." That biblical book was often interpreted as the song of love between Christ and the church.

19

Oh, to vex me, contraries meet in one:
Inconstancy unnaturally hath begot
A constant habit; that when I would not
I change in vows, and in devotion.
As humorous° is my contrition   *subject to whim*
As my profane love, and as soon forgot:
As riddlingly distempered, cold and hot,[2]
As praying, as mute, as infinite, as none.
I durst not view heaven yesterday; and today
In prayers and flattering speeches I court God:
Tomorrow I quake with true fear of his rod.
So my devout fits come and go away
Like a fantastic ague:[3] save° that here   *except*
Those are my best days, when I shake with fear.

1899

Good Friday, 1613. Riding Westward

Let man's soul be a sphere, and then, in this,
The intelligence that moves, devotion is,[1]
And as the other spheres, by being grown
Subject to foreign motions, lose their own,
And being by others hurried every day,
Scarce in a year their natural form[2] obey;
Pleasure or business, so, our souls admit
For° their first mover, and are whirled by it.   *instead of*
Hence is 't, that I am carried towards the West
This day, when my soul's form bends towards the East.
There I should see a Sun[3] by rising, set,
And by that setting endless day beget:
But that Christ on this cross did rise and fall,
Sin had eternally benighted all.
Yet dare I almost be glad I do not see
That spectacle, of too much weight for me.
Who sees God's face, that is self-life, must die;[4]
What a death were it then to see God die?
It made his own lieutenant,° Nature, shrink;   *deputy*
It made his footstool crack, and the sun wink.[5]

---

2. Arising from the unbalanced humors, inexplicably changeable.
3. A fever, attended with paroxysms of hot and cold and trembling fits. "Fantastic": capricious, extravagant.
1. As angelic intelligences guide the celestial spheres, so devotion is or should be the guiding principle of the soul.
2. Their true moving principle or intelligence. The orbit of the celestial spheres was thought to be governed by an unmoving outermost sphere, the primum mobile, or first mover (line 8), but sometimes outside influences ("foreign motions," line 4) deflected the spheres from their correct orbits.
3. The "sun" / "Son" pun was an ancient one. Christ the Son of God "set" when he rose on the Cross, and that setting (death) gave rise to the Christian era and the promise of immortality.
4. God told Moses, "Thou canst not see my face, for there shall no man see me, and live" (Exodus 33:20).
5. An earthquake and eclipse supposedly accompanied the Crucifixion (Matthew 27:45, 51). Compare Isaiah 66:1: "Thus saith the Lord, The heaven is my throne, and the earth is my footstool."

Could I behold those hands which span the poles,
And tune[6] all spheres at once, pierced with those holes?
Could I behold that endless height which is
Zenith to us, and t'our antipodes,[7]
25 Humbled below us? Or that blood which is
The seat° of all our souls, if not of his,   *dwelling place*
Make dirt of dust, or that flesh which was worn
By God for his apparel, ragg'd and torn?
If on these things I durst not look, durst I
30 Upon his miserable mother cast mine eye,
Who was God's partner here, and furnished thus
Half of that sacrifice which ransomed us?
Though these things, as I ride, be from° mine eye,   *away from*
They are present yet unto my memory,
35 For that looks towards them; and thou look'st towards me,
O Savior, as thou hang'st upon the tree.
I turn my back to thee but to receive
Corrections,[8] till thy mercies bid thee leave.°   *cease*
O think me worth thine anger; punish me;
40 Burn off my rusts and my deformity;
Restore thine image so much, by thy grace,
That thou may'st know me, and I'll turn my face.

1633

Hymn to God My God, in My Sickness[1]

Since I am coming to that holy room
    Where, with thy choir of saints for evermore,
I shall be made thy music; as I come
    I tune the instrument here at the door,
5   And what I must do then, think now before.[2]

Whilst my physicians by their love are grown
    Cosmographers, and I their map, who lie
Flat on this bed, that by them may be shown
    That this is my southwest discovery[3]
10   *Per fretum febris*,[4] by these straits to die,

I joy, that in these straits, I see my West;
    For, though their currents yield return to none,
What shall my West hurt me? As West and East
    In all flat maps (and I am one) are one,[5]
15   So death doth touch the resurrection.

---

6. Some manuscripts read "turn."
7. God is at once the highest point for us and for our "antipodes," those who live on the opposite side of the earth.
8. The phrase suggests a flogging.
1. Though Izaak Walton, Donne's friend and biographer, assigns this poem to the last days of his life, it was probably written during another illness, in December 1623.
2. This is less a hymn (songs of praise) than a meditation preparing (tuning the instrument) for such (Latin) hymn.
3. South is the region of heat, west the region of sunset and death.
4. Through the straits of fever, with a pun on straits as sufferings, rigors, and a geographical reference to the Strait of Magellan.
5. If a flat map is pasted on a round globe, west and east meet.

>   Is the Pacific Sea my home? Or are
>   The Eastern riches?° Is Jerusalem?   *Cathay, China*
>   Anyan,⁶ and Magellan, and Gibraltar,
>   All straits, and none but straits, are ways to them,
> 20   Whether where Japhet dwelt, or Cham, or Shem.⁷
>
>   We think that Paradise and Calvary,
>   Christ's cross and Adam's tree, stood in one place;
>   Look, Lord and find both Adams⁸ met in me;
>   As the first Adam's sweat surrounds my face,
> 25   May the last Adam's blood my soul embrace.
>
>   So, in his purple wrapped,⁹ receive me, Lord;
>   By these his thorns° give me his other crown;   *crown of thorns*
>   And, as to others' souls I preached thy word,
>   Be this my text, my sermon to mine own:
> 30   Therefore that he may raise the Lord throws down.

1635

A Hymn to God the Father[1]

> Wilt thou forgive that sin where I begun,
>   Which is my sin, though it were done before?[2]
> Wilt thou forgive that sin through which I run,
>   And do run still, though still I do deplore?
> 5   When thou hast done,[3] thou hast not done,
>   For I have more.
>
> Wilt thou forgive that sin by which I have won
>   Others to sin? and made my sin their door?
> Wilt thou forgive that sin which I did shun
> 10   A year or two, but wallowed in a score?
>   When thou hast done, thou hast not done,
>   For I have more.
>
> I have a sin of fear, that when I have spun
>   My last thread, I shall perish on the shore;
> 15 Swear by thy self, that at my death thy Son
>   Shall shine as he shines now and heretofore;
>   And, having done that, thou hast done,
>   I fear[4] no more.

1633

---

6. Anian, a strait on the west coast of America, shown on early maps as separating America from Asia.
7. The three sons of Noah by whom the world was repopulated after the Flood (Genesis 10). The descendants of Japhet were thought to inhabit Europe; those of Cham (Ham), Africa; and those of Shem, Asia.
8. Adam and Christ. Legend had it that Christ's cross was erected on the spot, or at least in the region, where the tree forbidden to Adam in Eden had stood.
9. In his blood, also in his kingly robes.
1. This hymn was used as a congregational hymn. Walton tells us that Donne wrote it during his illness of 1623, had it set to music, and was delighted to hear it performed (as it frequently was) by the choir of St. Paul's Cathedral.
2. That is, he inherits the original sin of Adam and Eve.
3. In the refrains, Donne puns on his own name and may pun on his wife's maiden name, Ann More.
4. Some manuscripts read "have."

From Devotions upon Emergent Occasions[1]
Meditation 4

Medicusque vocatur.
The physician is sent for.[2]

It is too little to call man a little world; except God, man is a diminutive to nothing.[3] Man consists of more pieces, more parts, than the world; than the world doth, nay, than the world is. And if those pieces were extended and stretched out in man as they are in the world, man would be the giant and the world the dwarf; the world but the map, and the man the world. If all the veins in our bodies were extended to rivers, and all the sinews to veins of mines, and all the muscles that lie upon one another to hills, and all the bones to quarries of stones, and all the other pieces to the proportion of those which correspond to them in the world, the air would be too little for this orb of man to move in, the firmament would be but enough for this star. For as the whole world hath nothing to which something in man doth not answer,[4] so hath man many pieces of which the whole world hath no representation. Enlarge this meditation upon this great world, man, so far as to consider the immensity of the creatures this world produces. Our creatures are our thoughts, creatures that are born giants, that reach from east to west, from earth to heaven, that do not only bestride all the sea and land, but span the sun and firmament at once: my thoughts reach all, comprehend all.

Inexplicable mystery! I their creator am in a close prison, in a sick bed, anywhere, and any one of my creatures, my thoughts, is with the sun, and beyond the sun, overtakes the sun, and overgoes the sun in one pace, one step, everywhere. And then as the other world produces serpents and vipers, malignant and venomous creatures, and worms and caterpillars, that endeavor to devour that world which produces them, and monsters compiled and complicated[5] of divers parents and kinds, so this world, our selves, produces all these in us, in producing diseases and sicknesses of all those sorts; venomous and infectious diseases, feeding and consuming diseases, and manifold and entangled diseases made up of many several ones. And can the other world name so many venomous, so many consuming, so many monstrous creatures, as we can diseases of all these kinds? O miserable abundance, O beggarly riches! How much do we lack of having remedies for every disease, when as yet we have not names for them?

---

1. Donne's *Devotions* were composed in the aftermath of his serious illness in the winter of 1623, though Donne characteristically writes as if the events of the illness were happening as he describes them. The *Devotions* recount in twenty-three sections the stages ("emergent occasions") of the illness and recovery: the term associates the exercise with a popular kind of Protestant meditation on the occasions that daily life presents to us. Each section contains a "meditation upon our human condition," an "expostulation and debatement with God," and a prayer to God. The book was published almost immediately, offering its meditation on an intensely personal experience as exemplary for others.
2. Donne's Latin epigraphs are followed by his English translations, often quite free.
3. This meditation is based on the notion that each human being is a microcosm, a little world, analogous in every respect to the macrocosm, or great world. But in playing with this notion, Donne paradoxically reverses it.
4. Correspond.
5. Mixed.

But we have a Hercules against these giants, these monsters: that is the physician. He musters up all the forces of the other world to succor this, all nature to relieve man. We have the physician but we are not the physician. Here we shrink in our proportion, sink in our dignity in respect of very mean creatures who are physicians to themselves. The hart that is pursued and wounded, they say, knows an herb which, being eaten, throws off the arrow: a strange kind of vomit.[6] The dog that pursues it, though he be subject to sickness, even proverbially knows his grass that recovers him. And it may be true that the drugger is as near to man as to other creatures; it may be that obvious and present simples,[7] easy to be had, would cure him; but the apothecary is not so near him, nor the physician so near him, as they two are to other creatures.[8] Man hath not that innate instinct to apply these natural medicines to his present danger, as those inferior creatures have. He is not his own apothecary, his own physician, as they are. Call back therefore thy meditation again, and bring it down.[9] What's become of man's great extent and proportion, when himself shrinks himself and consumes himself to a handful of dust? What's become of his soaring thoughts, his compassing thoughts, when himself brings himself to the ignorance, to the thoughtlessness, of the grave? His diseases are his own, but the physician is not; he hath them at home, but he must send for the physician.

Meditation 17

Nunc lento sonitu dicunt, morieris.
Now this bell tolling softly for another, says to me,
Thou must die.

Perchance he for whom this bell[1] tolls may be so ill as that he knows not it tolls for him; and perchance I may think myself so much better than I am, as that they who are about me and see my state may have caused it to toll for me, and I know not that. The church is catholic, universal, so are all her actions; all that she does belongs to all. When she baptizes a child, that action concerns me; for that child is thereby connected to that head which is my head too, and ingrafted into that body[2] whereof I am a member. And when she buries a man, that action concerns me: all mankind is of one author and is one volume; when one man dies, one chapter is not torn out of the book, but translated[3] into a better language; and every chapter must be so translated. God employs several translators; some pieces are translated by age, some by sickness, some by war, some by justice; but God's hand is in every translation, and his hand shall bind up all our scattered leaves again for that library where every book shall lie open to one another. As therefore the bell that rings to a sermon calls not upon the preacher only, but upon the congregation to come, so this bell calls us all; but how much more me, who am brought so near the door by this sickness. There was a contention

---

6. Deer supposedly expelled arrows wounding them by eating the herb dittany.
7. Medicinal plants.
8. One who administers drugs might do this for man as well as for other creatures, but one who sells drugs ("the apothecary") and the physician do not know how to prescribe for man as well as for other creatures.
9. That is, apply it to the present situation.
1. The "passing bell" for the dying.
2. The church.
3. Punning on the literal sense, "carried across."

as far as a suit[4] (in which piety and dignity, religion and estimation,[5] were mingled) which of the religious orders should ring to prayers first in the morning; and it was determined that they should ring first that rose earliest. If we understand aright the dignity of this bell that tolls for our evening prayer, we would be glad to make it ours by rising early, in that application, that it might be ours as well as his whose indeed it is. The bell doth toll for him that thinks it doth; and though it intermit again, yet from that minute that that occasion wrought upon him, he is united to God. Who casts not up his eye to the sun when it rises? But who takes off his eye from a comet when that breaks out? Who bends not his ear to any bell which upon any occasion rings? But who can remove it from that bell which is passing a piece of himself out of this world? No man is an island, entire of itself; every man is a piece of the continent, a part of the main.[6] If a clod be washed away by the sea, Europe is the less, as well as if a promontory were, as well as if a manor of thy friend's or of thine own were. Any man's death diminishes me, because I am involved in mankind; and therefore never send to know for whom the bell tolls; it tolls for thee.[7] Neither can we call this a begging of misery or a borrowing of misery, as though we were not miserable enough of ourselves but must fetch in more from the next house, in taking upon us the misery of our neighbors. Truly it were an excusable covetousness if we did; for affliction is a treasure, and scarce any man hath enough of it. No man hath affliction enough that is not matured and ripened by it, and made fit for God by that affliction. If a man carry treasure in bullion, or in a wedge of gold, and have none coined into current moneys, his treasure will not defray[8] him as he travels. Tribulation is treasure in the nature of it, but it is not current money in the use of it, except we get nearer and nearer our home, heaven, by it. Another man may be sick too, and sick to death, and this affliction may lie in his bowels as gold in a mine and be of no use to him; but this bell that tells me of his affliction digs out and applies that gold to me, if by this consideration of another's danger I take mine own into contemplation and so secure myself by making my recourse to my God, who is our only security.

From *Expostulation 19*

[THE LANGUAGE OF GOD]

My God, my God, thou art a direct God, may I not say a literal God, a God that wouldst be understood literally and according to the plain sense of all that thou sayest. But thou art also (Lord, I intend it to thy glory, and let no profane misinterpreter abuse it to thy diminution), thou art a figurative, a metaphorical God too: a God in whose words there is such a height of figures, such voyages, such peregrinations to fetch remote and precious metaphors, such extensions, such spreadings, such curtains of allegories, such third heavens of hyperboles, so harmonious elocutions, so retired and so reserved expressions, so commanding persuasions, so persuading commandments, such sinews even in thy milk and such things in thy words, as

---

4. Controversy that went as far as a lawsuit.
5. Self-esteem.
6. Mainland.
7. This phrase gave Ernest Hemingway the title for his novel *For Whom the Bell Tolls*.
8. Meet his expenses.

all profane[9] authors seem of the seed of the serpent that creeps; thou art the dove that flies. Oh, what words but thine can express the inexpressible texture and composition of thy word; in which, to one man, that argument that binds his faith to believe that to be the word of God is the reverent simplicity of the word, and to another, the majesty of the word; and in which two men, equally pious, may meet, and one wonder that all should not understand it, and the other as much that any man should. So, Lord, thou givest us the same earth to labor on and to lie in; a house and a grave of the same earth; so, Lord, thou givest us the same word for our satisfaction and for our inquisition,[1] for our instruction and for our admiration too. For there are places that thy servants Jerome and Augustine would scarce believe (when they grew warm by mutual letters) of one another that they understood them, and yet both Jerome and Augustine call upon persons whom they knew to be far weaker than they thought one another (old women and young maids) to read thy Scriptures, without confining them to these or those places.[2]

Neither art thou thus a figurative, a metaphorical God, in thy word only, but in thy works too. The style of thy works, the phrase of thine actions, is metaphorical. The institution of thy whole worship in the old law was a continual allegory; types and figures[3] overspread all, and figures flowed into figures, and poured themselves out into further figures. Circumcision carried a figure of baptism,[4] and baptism carries a figure of that purity which we shall have in perfection in the New Jerusalem. Neither didst thou speak and work in this language only in the time of the prophets; but since thou spokest in thy son it is so too. How often, how much more often, doth thy son call himself a way and a light and a gate and a vine and bread than the son of God or of man? How much oftener doth he exhibit a metaphorical Christ than a real, a literal? This hath occasioned thine ancient servants, whose delight it was to write after thy copy,[5] to proceed the same way in their expositions of the Scriptures, and in their composing both of public liturgies and of private prayers to thee, to make their accesses to thee in such a kind of language as thou wast pleased to speak to them, in a figurative, in a metaphorical language; in which manner I am bold to call the comfort which I receive now in this sickness, in the indication of the concoction[6] and maturity thereof, in certain clouds[7] and residences[8] which the physicians observe, a discovering of land from sea after a long and tempestuous voyage. * * *

1623   1624

---

9. Secular.
1. Investigation.
2. Saints Jerome and Augustine did in fact differ over the proper way of interpreting the Bible, yet they both encouraged its use by the unlearned.
3. Anticipations or prefigurations, especially persons and events in the Hebrew Bible that were read as prefiguring Christ, or some aspect of the New Testament or of Christian practice. For a beautiful poem exemplifying this process, see Herbert, "The Bunch of Grapes" (p. 1192).
4. Both circumcision and baptism are rites of admission to a religious community.
5. Text.
6. Ripening.
7. Cloudy urine.
8. Residues.

From Death's Duel[1]

[Donne's last sermon, on Psalm 68:20: "And unto God the Lord belong the issues[2] of Death"—that is, from death.]

* * *

First, then, we consider this *exitus mortis*, to be *liberatio à morte*, that with God, the Lord are the issues of death, and therefore in all our deaths, and the deadly calamities of this life, we may justly hope of a good issue from him; and all our periods and transitions in this life, are so many passages from death to death. Our very birth and entrance into this life is *exitus à morte*, an issue from death, for in our mother's womb we are dead so, as that we do not know we live, not so much as we do in our sleep, neither is there any grave so close, or so putrid a prison, as the womb would be unto us, if we stayed in it beyond our time, or died there before our time. In the grave the worms do not kill us, we breed and feed, and then kill the worms which we ourselves produced. In the womb the dead child kills the mother that conceived it, and is a murderer, nay a parricide, even after it is dead. And if we be not dead so in the womb, so as that being dead, we kill her that gave us our first life, our life of vegetation,[3] yet we are dead so, as David's idols are dead. In the womb we have eyes and see not, ears and hear not.[4] There in the womb we are fitted for works of darkness, all the while deprived of light: And there in the womb we are taught cruelty, by being fed with blood, and may be damned, though we be never born.

* * *

* * * But then this *exitus à morte* is but *introitus in mortem*, this issue, this deliverance from that death, the death of the womb, is an entrance, a delivering over to another death, the manifold deaths of this world. We have a winding-sheet[5] in our mother's womb, which grows with us from our conception, and we come into the world wound up in that winding-sheet, for we come to seek a grave. * * * Now this which is so singularly peculiar to him [Christ], that his flesh should not see corruption, at his second coming, his coming to Judgment, shall extend to all then alive, their flesh shall not see corruption. * * * But for us that die now and sleep in the state of the dead, we must all pass this posthume death, this death after death, nay this death after burial, this dissolution after dissolution, this death of corruption and putrefaction, of vermiculation and incineration, of dissolution and

---

1. The printed version of this sermon (1632) has the subtitle "A Consolation to the Soul, against the dying life, and living death of the body." Donne's friend and executor Henry King (later bishop of Chichester) supplied the further information that the sermon was delivered at Whitehall, before King Charles, that it was delivered only a few days before Donne's death, and that it was fitly styled "the author's own funeral sermon." Donne was a powerful and popular preacher, and this sermon was especially moving according to the testimony of many auditors, including Izaak Walton. Besides the personal drama of the preacher himself visibly ill and perhaps dying, the audience must have responded to the almost unbearably graphic analysis of the forms of death and decay—a theme that often preoccupied Donne. As in his poems, the language is personal, rich in learning and curious lore, dazzling in verbal ingenuity and metaphor. As in the *Devotions*, the sentences are long, sinuous, and elaborate. Typically, he uses a number of Latin phrases, but almost always translates or paraphrases them immediately.
2. Passages out.
3. That is, of growth.
4. A paraphrase of Psalm 115:5–6.
5. The placenta.

dispersion in and from the grave. When those bodies that have been the children of royal parents, and the parents of royal children, must say with Job, to corruption, thou art my father, and to the worm, thou art my mother and my sister.[6] Miserable riddle, when the same worm must be my mother, and my sister, and myself. Miserable incest, when I must be married to my mother and my sister, beget, and bear that worm which is all that miserable penury; when my mouth shall be filled with dust, and the worm shall feed, and feed sweetly upon me,[7] when the ambitious man shall have no satisfaction, if the poorest alive tread upon him, nor the poorest receive any contentment in being made equal to princes, for they shall be equal but in dust. One dies at his full strength, being wholly at ease and in quiet, and another dies in the bitterness of his soul, and never eats with pleasure, but they lie down alike in the dust, and the worm covers them.[8] The worm covers them in Job, and in Isaiah, it covers them and is spread under them, the worm is spread under thee, and the worm covers thee.[9] There's the mats and the carpets that lie under, and there's the state and the canopy,[1] that hangs over the greatest of the sons of men. Even those bodies that were the temple of the Holy Ghost, come to this dilapidation, to ruin, to rubbish, to dust: even the Israel of the Lord, and Jacob himself hath no other specification, no other denomination, but that *vermis Jacob*, thou worm of Jacob.[2] Truly the consideration of this posthume death, this death after burial, that after God (with whom are the issues of death) hath delivered me from the death of the womb, by bringing me into the world, and from the manifold deaths of the world, by laying me in the grave, I must die again in an incineration of this flesh, and in a dispersion of that dust.

* * *

There we leave you in that blessed dependency, to hang upon him that hangs upon the Cross, there bathe in his tears, there suck at his wounds, and lie down in peace in his grave, till he vouchsafe you a resurrection, and an ascension into that Kingdom, which he hath purchased for you, with the inestimable price of his incorruptible blood. Amen.

1632

---

6. A paraphrase of Job 17:14.
7. An echo of Job 24:20.
8. An echo of Job 21:23–26.
9. An echo of Isaiah 14:11.
1. Cloth of state, a canopy erected over a king's throne.
2. That epithet is used in Isaiah 41:14.

AEMILIA LANYER
1569–1645

Aemilia Lanyer published one of the earliest collections of poetry by an English woman. She was a member of an Italian family of court musicians who came to England in the reign of Henry VIII; they may have been Christianized Jews or, alternatively, Protestants forced to flee Catholic persecution in their native land. Some information about Lanyer's life survived in the notebooks of the astrologer and fortune-teller Simon Forman, whom Lanyer consulted in 1597. Lanyer claims to have been educated in the aristocratic household of the Countess of Kent, and in her late teens and early twenties she was the mistress of Queen Elizabeth's lord chamberlain, Henry Carey, Lord Hunsdon, who was forty-five years her senior. The wealthy Hunsdon was a notable patron of the arts—Shakespeare's company performed under his auspices in the 1590s—and he maintained Lanyer (then Bassano) in luxury. Yet when she became pregnant by Hunsdon at age twenty-three, she was married off to Alfonso Lanyer, one of another family of gentleman musicians attached to the courts of Elizabeth I and James I. Lanyer's poetry suggests that she resided for some time in the household of the influential courtier and literary patron Margaret Clifford, Countess of Cumberland, and Margaret's daughter Anne Clifford, later Countess of Dorset. Lanyer reports receiving their encouragement in learning, piety, and poetry, and, in turn, she highlights their status as exemplary women and faithful servants of the only true king, Jesus Christ.

Lanyer's single volume of poems, *Salve Deus Rex Judaeorum* (1611; Latin for "Hail, God, King of the Jews"), begins with a series of dedicatory poems to powerful courtiers and would-be patrons whom she praises as a community of good women. The title poem, a meditation on Christ's Passion, is framed and punctuated by its dedication to the Countess of Cumberland, and contrasts the good women in the Passion story with the evil and weak men who failed to support Christ in his time of need. The poem also includes a defense of Eve, which participates in the contemporary *querelle des femmes*, or debate on women. Why, she asks, are women "By more faulty men so much defamed?" Lanyer's Christ, moreover, would rather speak to "poor women" than kings. The final poem in Lanyer's volume, "The Description of Cookham," celebrates in elegiac mode the Crown estate occasionally occupied by the Countess of Cumberland, portraying it as an Edenic paradise of women, now lost. The poem may or may not have been written before Ben Jonson's "To Penshurst"—commonly thought to have inaugurated the "country house" genre in English literature—but Lanyer's poem was published first.

Margaret Clifford. The motto of this Laurence Hilliard miniature of Clifford, "Constant in the midst / of Inconstancey," resonates with Lanyer's representation of her in *Salve Deus Rex Judaeorum*.

From Salve Deus Rex Judaeorum

From To the Queen's Most Excellent Majesty[1]

    Renowned empress, and Great Britain's queen,
    Most gracious mother of succeeding kings;
    Vouchsafe° to view that which is seldom seen,   *be willing*
    A woman's writing of divinest things:
5   Read it fair queen, though it defective be,
      Your excellence can grace both it and me.

            *   *   *

    Look in this mirror of a worthy mind,[2]
    Where some of your fair virtues will appear;
    Though all it is impossible to find,
40   Unless my glass° were crystal, or more clear: *mirror*
      Which is dim steel,[3] yet full of spotless truth,
      And for one look from your fair eyes it su'th.°   *courts, pursues*

    Here may your sacred majesty behold
    That mighty monarch° both of heaven and earth,   *Christ*
45   He that all nations of the world controlled,
    Yet took our flesh in base and meanest berth:°   *humblest birth*
      Whose days were spent in poverty and sorrow,
      And yet all kings their wealth of him do borrow.

    For he is crown and crowner of all kings,
50   The hopeful haven of the meaner sort,
    It's he that all our joyful tidings brings
    Of happy reign within his royal court:
      It's he that in extremity can give
      Comfort to them that have no time to live.

55   And since my wealth within his region stands,
    And that his cross my chiefest comfort is,
    Yea in his kingdom only rests my lands,
    Of honor there I hope I shall not miss:
      Though I on earth do live unfortunate,
60   Yet there I may attain a better state.

    In the meantime, accept, most gracious queen
    This holy work virtue presents to you
    In poor apparel, shaming to be seen,
    Or once t'appear in your judicial view:

---

1. Queen Anna of Denmark, the wife of James I. Anna was a patron of writers, including Ben Jonson and Samuel Daniel, and the mother of Prince Henry, Princess Elizabeth, and the future Charles I. This is the first of a series of poems addressed to court ladies whom Lanyer sought to attract as patrons; such poems often preface literary works by male courtier poets as well. These poems are followed by a prose address to her primary dedicatee, Margaret Clifford, Countess of Cumberland, and then by a prose epistle, "To the Virtuous Reader," which engages many of the tropes of the *querelle des femmes* and legends of good women traditions.
2. Lanyer presents her poem both as a mirror, or reflection, of Queen Anna, and as a form of political advice in the "mirror for magistrates" tradition.
3. Renaissance mirrors were made of both steel, which needed frequent polishing, and crystal.

65 But that fair virtue, though in mean attire,
All princes of the world do most desire.

* * *

The Lady Elizabeth's Grace

And she[4] that is the pattern of all beauty,
The very model of your majesty,
Whose rarest parts enforceth love and duty,
The perfect pattern of all piety:
95   O let my book by her fair eyes be blessed,
    In whose pure thoughts all innocency rests.

Then shall I think my glass a glorious sky,
When two such glitt'ring suns at once appear;
The one replete with sovereign majesty,
100 Both shining brighter than the clearest clear:
    And both reflecting comfort to my spirits,
    To find their grace so much above my merits

Whose untuned voice the doleful notes doth sing
Of sad affliction in an humble strain;
105 Much like unto a bird that wants a wing,
And cannot fly, but warbles forth her pain:
    Or he that barred from the sun's bright light,
    Wanting day's comfort, doth commend the night.

* * *

My weak distempered brain and feeble spirits,
140 Which all unlearned have adventured this
To write of Christ and of his sacred merits,
Desiring that this book her° hands may kiss: *Queen Anna's*
    And though I be unworthy of that grace,
    Yet let her blessed thoughts this book embrace.

145 And pardon me (fair queen) though I presume,
To do that which so many better can;
Not that I learning to myself assume,
Or that I would compare with any man:
    But as they are scholars, and by art do write,
150   So nature yields my soul a sad° delight.   *solemn, serious*

And since all arts at first from nature came,
That goodly creature, mother of perfection,
Whom Jove's[5] almighty hand at first did frame,
Taking both her and hers[6] in his protection:
155   Why should not she now grace my barren muse,
    And in a woman all defects excuse.

So peerless princess humbly I desire,
That your great wisdom would vouchsafe t'omit°   *overlook*
All faults; and pardon if my spirits retire,

---

4. Elizabeth Stuart, the second child and first daughter of Queen Anna and James I.
5. God as creator of nature.
6. Nature and those (especially women) under nature's protection.

160 Leaving° to aim at what they cannot hit: *declining*
　　To write your worth, which no pen can express,
　　Were but t'eclipse your fame, and make it less.⁷

1611

From To the Lady Anne, Countess of Dorset¹

　　To you I dedicate this work of grace,
　　This frame of glory which I have erected,
　　For your fair mind I hold the fittest place
　　Where virtue should be settled and protected;
5　If highest thoughts true honor do embrace,
　　And holy wisdom is of them respected,
　　　　Then in this mirror let your fair eyes look,
　　　　To view your virtues in this blessed book.

　　Blest by our savior's merits, not my skill,
10　Which I acknowledge to be very small;
　　Yet if the least part of his blessed will
　　I have performed, I count I have done all:
　　One spark of grace sufficient is to fill
　　Our lamps with oil, ready when he doth call
15　　　To enter with the bridegroom² to the feast,
　　　　Where he that is the greatest may be least.

　　Greatness is no sure frame to build upon,
　　No worldly treasure can assure that place;
　　God makes both even, the cottage with the throne,³
20　All worldly honors there are counted base,
　　Those he holds dear, and reckneth as his own,
　　Whose virtuous deeds by his especial grace
　　　　Have gained his love, his kingdom, and his crown,
　　　　Whom in the book of life he hath set down.

25　Titles of honor which the world bestows,
　　To none but to the virtuous belong;
　　As beauteous bowers° where true worth　　*idealized pleasant spaces*
　　　　should repose,
　　And where his dwellings should be built most strong:
　　But when they are bestowed upon her foes,
30　Poor virtue's friends endure the greatest wrong:
　　　　For they must suffer all indignity,
　　　　Until in heaven they better graced be.

---

7. As her poetry of praise cannot possibly do justice to the queen, she abandons an attempt that would obscure rather than promote the queen's fame.
1. Anne Clifford (1590–1676) was the sole surviving child of George Clifford, Duke of Cumberland (d. 1605), and Margaret Clifford, Countess of Cumberland. Following her father's death, Anne and her mother spent years pursuing Anne's right to inherit her father's properties in Yorkshire and Westmoreland. In 1609, she married Richard Sackville, Earl of Dorset (d. 1624), and in 1630, after Sackville's death, Philip Herbert, Earl of Pembroke and Montgomery (d. 1650). She finally acquired the rights to the Clifford properties in 1643 and actively managed them from 1649 until her death in 1676. She was an ardent family chronicler and diary keeper.
2. A reference to Jesus's parable comparing readiness for the kingdom of heaven to the behavior of ten virgins who went forth to meet the bridegroom, five carrying lamps with oil in them and five without (Matthew 25:1–13).
3. All social classes are equal in the sight of God.

>   What difference was there when the world began,
>   Was it not virtue that distinguished all?
> 35   All sprang but from one woman and one man,
>   Then how doth gentry come to rise and fall?[4]
>   Or who is he that very rightly can
>   Distinguish of his birth, or tell at all,
>   In what mean° state his ancestors have been,   *low*
> 40   Before someone of worth did honor win?

* * *

>   To you, as to God's steward I do write,
>   In whom the seeds of virtue have been sown,
>   By your most worthy mother, in whose right,
> 60   All her fair parts you challenge as your own;
>   If you, sweet lady, will appear as bright
>   As ever creature did that time hath known,
>   Then wear this diadem° I present to thee   *crown*
>   Which I have framed for her eternity.

* * *

1611

From Salve Deus Rex Judaeorum[1]

* * *

>   The meditation of this monarch's° love,   *Christ's*
>   Draws thee° from caring what this world   *Countess of Cumberland*
>   can yield;
> 155   Of joys and griefs both equal thou dost prove,
>   They have no force, to force thee from the field:
>   Thy constant faith like to the turtle dove[2]
>   Continues combat, and will never yield
>   To base affliction, or proud pomp's desire,
> 160   That sets the weakest minds so much on fire.
>
>   Thou from the court to the country art retired,
>   Leaving the world, before the world leaves thee:
>   That great enchantress of weak minds admired,
>   Whose all-bewitching charms so pleasing be
> 165   To worldly wantons; and too much desired
>   Of those that care not for eternity:
>   But yield themselves as preys to lust and sin,
>   Losing their hopes of heav'n hell pains to win.
>
>   But thou, the wonder of our wanton age
> 170   Leav'st all delights to serve a heav'nly king:

---

4. Perhaps an allusion to the well-known rhyme "When Adam delved and Eve span, / Who was then the gentleman?"

1. Lanyer's title poem has four parts: The Passion; Eve's Apology in Defense of Women; The Tears of the Daughters of Jerusalem; and The Salutation and Sorrow of the Virgin Mary. It also includes multiple addresses to the Countess of Cumberland, whom Lanyer imagines as a model of constancy. (See Hilliard's miniature on p. 924.)

2. Symbol of steadfast love.

Who is more wise? or who can be more sage,
Than she that doth affection subject bring;
Not forcing for the world, or Satan's rage,
But shrouding under the Almighty's wing;
    Spending her years, months, days, minutes, hours,
    In doing service to the heav'nly powers.

Thou fair example, live without compare,
With honors triumphs seated in thy breast;
Pale envy never can thy name impair,
When in thy heart thou harbor'st such a guest,
Malice must live forever in despair;
There's no revenge where virtue still doth rest:
    All hearts must needs do homage unto thee,
    In whom all eyes such rare perfection see.

An invective against outward beauty unaccompanied with virtue

That outward beauty which the world commends,
Is not the subject I will write upon,
Whose date expired, that tyrant time soon ends,
Those gaudy colors soon are spent and gone:
But those fair virtues which on thee attends
Are always fresh, they never are but one:
    They make thy beauty fairer to behold,
    Than was that queen's° for whom proud Troy was sold.   *Helen*

As for those matchless colors red and white,
Or perfect features in a fading face,
Or due proportion pleasing to the sight;
All these do draw but dangers and disgrace:
A mind enriched with virtue shines more bright,
Adds everlasting beauty, gives true grace,
    Frames an immortal goddess on the earth,
    Who though she dies, yet fame gives her new berth.°   *birth, beginning; status*

That pride of nature which adorns the fair,
Like blazing comets to allure all eyes,
Is but the thread that weaves their web of care,
Who glories most, where most their danger lies;
For greatest perils do attend the fair,
When men do seek, attempt, plot and devise,
    How they may overthrow the chastest Dame,
    Whose beauty is the white° whereat they aim.   *mark, target*

* * *

To the Lady of Cumberland the Introduction to the Passion of Christ.

¶This grace, great lady, doth possess thy soul,
And makes thee pleasing in thy maker's sight;
This grace doth all imperfect thoughts control,°   *contain, restrict*
Directing thee to serve thy God aright;
Still reckoning him the husband of thy soul,[3]
Which is most precious in his glorious sight:

---

3. Christ is figured as a bridegroom in the gospel of John (John 3:29); the brides of Christ were the faithful. (See also the parable of the virgins in Matthew 25:1–13.)

>
> Because the world's delights she doth deny
> For him, who for her sake vouchsafed to die.
>
> And dying made her dowager[4] of all;
> Nay more, co-heir of that eternal bliss
> That angels lost, and we by Adam's fall;
> Mere cast-aways, raised by a Judas kiss,[5]
> Christ's bloody sweat, the vinegar and gall,
> The spear, sponge, nails, his buffeting with fists,
>   His bitter passion, agony, and death,
>   Did gain us heaven when he did lose his breath.

A preamble of the Author before the Passion

> These high deserts° invite my lowly muse   *deservings, merits*
> To write of him, and pardon crave of thee,
> For time so spent, I need make no excuse,
> Knowing it doth with thy fair mind agree
> So well, as thou no labor wilt refuse
> That to thy holy love may pleasing be:
>   His death and passion I desire to write,
>   And thee to read, the blessed soul's delight.
>
> But my dear Muse, now whither wouldst thou fly,
> Above the pitch of thy appointed strain?
> With Icarus,[6] thou seekest now to try,
> Not waxen wings, but thy poor barren brain,
> Which far too weak, these siely° lines descry;°   *silly, simple / proclaim*
> Yet cannot this thy forward mind restrain,
> But thy poor infant verse must soar aloft,
>   Not fearing threat'ning dangers, happening oft.
>
> Think when the eye of wisdom shall discover
> Thy weakling muse to fly, that scarce could creep,
> And in the air above the clouds to hover,
> When better 'twere mewed up,° and fast asleep;   *confined, enclosed*
> They'll think with Phaeton,[7] thou canst ne'er recover,
> But helpless with that poor young lad to weep:
>   The little world of thy weak wit on fire,
>   Where thou wilt perish in thine own desire.
>
> But yet the weaker thou dost seem to be
> In sex, or sense, the more his° glory shines,   *Christ's*
> That doth infuse such powerful grace in thee,
> To show thy love in these few humble lines;

---

4. A widow who receives title or property from her husband's estate. Lanyer presents the countess's soul first as Christ's bride and then as his dowager, enjoying and dispensing his wealth. Lanyer may also allude to Margaret Clifford's own status following the 1605 death of her (estranged) husband: she and her daughter embarked on a years-long battle for Anne's right to inherit the Clifford estates. (George Clifford left his property to his brother.)

5. The kiss with which Judas identified Jesus to those seeking to arrest him also led (through his death) to the salvation of humankind (Matthew 26:47–56). More generally, a Judas kiss is an apparent act of friendship that actually harms the recipient.

6. In Greek myth, son of the inventor Daedalus; he fell into the sea because he flew too close to the sun, melting the wax wings his father had made for him.

7. In Greek myth, son of the sun god, Helios; after borrowing his father's sun-chariot, he drove both too close to and too far from the earth, alternately burning and freezing it. To save the world, Zeus struck him down.

>   The widow's mite[8] with this may well agree,
>   Her little all more worth than golden mines,
> 295   Being more dearer to our loving Lord,
>   Than all the wealth that kingdoms could afford.
>
>   Therefore I humbly for his grace will pray,
>   That he will give me power and strength to write,
>   That what I have begun, so end I may,
> 300   As his great glory may appear more bright;
>   Yea in these lines I may no further stray
>   Than his most holy spirit shall give me light:
>   That blindest weakness be not over bold,
>   The manner of his Passion to unfold.
>
>   * * *
>
> 745   Now Pontius Pilate[9] is to judge the cause°   *case*
>   Of faultless Jesus, who before him stands;
>   Who neither hath offended prince, nor laws,
>   Although he now be brought in woeful bands:
>   O noble governor, make thou yet a pause,
> 750   Do not in innocent blood imbrue° thy hands;   *stain*
>   But hear the words of thy most worthy wife,
>   Who sends to thee, to beg her Savior's life.[1]
>
>   Let barb'rous cruelty far depart from thee,
>   And in true justice take affliction's part;
> 755   Open thine eyes, that thou the truth may'st see,
>   Do not the thing that goes against thy heart;
>   Condemn not him that must thy savior be;
>   But view his holy life, his good desert:
>   Let not us women glory in men's fall,[2]
> 760   Who had power given to overrule us all.

Eve's Apology[3]

>   ¶Till now your° indiscretion sets us free,   *Pilate's, men's*
>   And makes our former fault much less appear;
>   Our mother Eve, who tasted of the tree,
>   Giving to Adam what she held most dear,
> 765   Was simply good, and had no power to see;[4]
>   The after-coming harm did not appear:

---

8. A coin of small value. In a parable, Jesus praises the widow for giving all she has ("the widow's mite") while the wealthy give less (Mark 12:41–44; Luke 21:1–4). Lanyer also puns on the widow's "might."
9. The Roman governor of Judea (26–36 C.E.) who authorized the crucifixion of Jesus. The intervening stanzas recount Christ's story up until his trial, focusing largely on the wickedness of kings, priests, and elders, and on the weaknesses of the disciples, "Though they protest they never will forsake him," Lanyer writes, "They do like men, when dangers overtake them."
1. "While Pilate was sitting on the judge's seat, his wife sent him this message: 'Don't have anything to do with that innocent man, for I have suffered a great deal today in a dream because of him'" (Matthew 27:19). Lanyer writes her own, much-elaborated version of this letter in the following stanzas, in which there is no clear differentiation between the voice of Pilate's wife's and that of Lanyer herself.
2. The fall of Adam and the prospective fall of Pilate.
3. Apology here means defense. Lanyer's defense of Eve, and of women more generally, is presented by Pilate's wife. (It does not appear in the Bible.)
4. In Genesis, Eve eats the forbidden fruit of the Tree of Knowledge of Good and Evil first, and then Adam eats it (Genesis 3:1–13). There was much debate in the *querelle des femmes* about whose crime was worse: that of Eve, who was seduced by the serpent, or of Adam, who hearkened to the voice of his wife. See *Paradise Lost* 9.733–1189, 10.1–208, and *Order and Disorder*, 5.120–267, for other versions of the story.

> The subtle serpent that our sex betrayed,
> Before our fall so sure a plot had laid.
>
> That undiscerning ignorance perceived
> No guile, or craft that was by him intended;
> For, had she known of what we were bereaved,[5]
> To his request she had not condescended.°   *consented*
> But she (poor soul) by cunning was deceived,
> No hurt therein her harmless heart intended:
>   For she alleged° God's word, which he° denies   *asserted / the serpent*
>   That they should die, but even as gods, be wise.
>
> But surely Adam cannot be excused,
> Her fault though great, yet he was most to blame;
> What weakness offered, strength might have refused,
> Being lord of all, the greater was his shame:
> Although the serpent's craft had her abused,
> God's holy word ought all his actions frame:°   *determine*
>   For he was lord and king of all the earth,
>   Before poor Eve had either life or breath.[6]
>
> Who being framed° by God's eternal hand,   *fashioned*
> The perfectest man that ever breathed on earth,
> And from God's mouth received that strait° command,[7]   *strict*
> The breach whereof he knew was present death:
> Yea having power to rule both sea and land,
> Yet with one apple won to lose that breath,[8]
>   Which God hath breathed in his beauteous face,
>   Bringing us all in danger and disgrace.
>
> And then to lay the fault on patience's back,
> That we (poor women) must endure it all;
> We know right well he did discretion° lack,   *judgment*
> Being not persuaded thereunto at all;
> If Eve did err, it was for knowledge sake,
> The fruit being fair persuaded him to fall:
>   No subtle serpent's falsehood did betray him,
>   If he would eat it, who had power to stay° him?   *prevent*
>
> Not Eve, whose fault was only too much love,
> Which made her give this present to her dear,
> That which she tasted, he likewise might prove,°   *experience, test*
> Whereby his knowledge might become more clear;
> He never sought her weakness to reprove
> With those sharp words which he of God did hear:
>   Yet men will boast of knowledge which he took
>   From Eve's fair hand, as from a learned book.

---

5. Deprived (here, of eternal life). See Genesis 3:16–19.
6. In contrast to Genesis 1:27 in which God created man in his own image, "male and female created he them," in Genesis 2, God creates Adam first (7), then fashions Eve from a rib taken from Adam's side (21–23).
7. Not to eat of the Tree of knowledge of Good and Evil (Genesis 2:17).
8. The breath of life, which would have been eternal.

　　　　　If any evil did in her remain,
810　　　Being made of him, he was the ground of all;
　　　　　If one of many worlds could lay a stain
　　　　　Upon our sex, and work so great a fall
　　　　　To wretched man by Satan's[9] subtle train;°   *treachery, deceit*
　　　　　What will so foul a fault amongst you all?
815　　　　　Her weakness did the serpent's word obey,
　　　　　　But you° in malice God's dear son betray.   *Pilate*

　　　　　Whom, if unjustly you condemn to die,
　　　　　Her sin was small, to what you do commit;
　　　　　All mortal sins[1] that do for vengeance cry,
820　　　Are not to be compared unto it:
　　　　　If many worlds would altogether try
　　　　　By all their sins the wrath of God to get,
　　　　　　This sin of yours surmounts them all as far
　　　　　　As doth the sun, another little star.

825　　　Then let us have our liberty again,
　　　　　And challenge° to your selves no sovereignty;   *attribute*
　　　　　You came not in the world without our pain,
　　　　　Make that a bar against your cruelty;
　　　　　Your fault being greater, why should you disdain
830　　　Our being your equals, free from tyranny?
　　　　　　If one weak woman simply did offend,
　　　　　　This sin of yours hath no excuse, nor end.

　　　　　To which (poor souls) we never gave consent,
　　　　　Witness thy wife (O Pilate) speaks for all;
835　　　Who did but dream, and yet a message sent,
　　　　　That thou should'st have nothing to do at all
　　　　　With that just man,° which, if thy heart relent,   *Christ*
　　　　　Why wilt thou be a reprobate° with Saul?[2]   *damned*
　　　　　　To seek the death of him that is so good,
840　　　　For thy soul's health to shed his dearest blood.[3]

　　　　　　　　　* * *

The tears of   Thrice happy women[4] that obtained such grace
the daughters From him whose worth the world could not contain;
of Jerusalem. Immediately to turn about his face,
　　　　　As not memb'ring his great grief and pain,
　　　　　To comfort you, whose tears poured forth apace
　　　　　On Flora's° banks, like showers of April rain: *Roman goddess of spring*
975　　　　Your cries enforced mercy, grace, and love
　　　　　　From him, whom greatest princes could not move

---

9. Tradition, not Genesis, identifies the serpent with Satan.
1. Sins punishable by damnation.
2. First king of Israel; he tried to kill his successor and God's anointed prophet-king, David (1 Samuel 20:30–24:17).
3. Lanyer's account of Christ's Passion ends with Pilate's decision (as his wife puts it) that he could not be Caesar's "friend / Unless he sent sweet Jesus to his end." Yet, she also notes, Christ's crown of thorns is superior to "the diadem / Of any king that ever lived before."
4. "The daughters of Jerusalem," are the women who wept as they followed Jesus to his crucifixion (Luke 23:27–31). "Daughters of Jerusalem" also appear in the Song of Songs (or "Canticles") 5:16, where they are called upon to witness and support the courtship of the bride (in Christian typology, the church) and bridegroom (Christ).

To speak one word, nor once to lift his eyes
Unto proud Pilate, no nor Herod, king,
By all the questions that they could devise,
980 Could make him answer to no manner of thing;
Yet these poor women by their piteous cries
Did move their lord, their lover, and their king,
    To take compassion, turn about, and speak
    To them whose hearts were ready now to break.

985 Most blessed Daughters of Jerusalem,
Who found such favor in your Savior's sight,
To turn his face when you did pity him;
Your tearful eyes beheld his eyes more bright;
Your faith and love unto such grace did climb,
990 To have reflection from this heav'nly light:
    Your eagles' eye did gaze against this sun,
    Your hearts did think, he dead, the world were done.

When spiteful men with torments did oppress
Th'afflicted body of this innocent dove,
985 Poor women seeing how much they did transgress,
By tears, by sighs, by cries, intreat, nay prove,
What may be done among the thickest press,
They labor still these tyrants' hearts to move:[5]
    In pity and compassion to forbear
1000   Their whipping, spurning, tearing of his hair.[6]

* * *

1305 This is that bridegroom that appears so fair,[7]
So sweet, so lovely in his spouse's sight,
That unto snow we may his face compare,
His cheeks like scarlet, and his eyes so bright
As purest doves that in the rivers are
1310 Washed with milk, to give the more delight;
    His head is likened to the finest gold,
    His curled locks so beauteous to behold;

Black as a raven in her blackest hue;
His lips like scarlet threads, yet much more sweet
1315 Than is the sweetest honey-dropping dew,
Or honeycombs, where all the bees do meet;
Yea, he is constant, and his words are true,
His cheeks are beds of spices, flowers sweet;
    His lips like lilies, dropping down pure myrrh,
1320   Whose love, before all worlds we do prefer.[8]

---

5. Women followed and ministered to Christ (Matthew 27:55–56), were critical of and mourned his execution (27:61), and were among his most fervent followers (28:1–12), but their role in Lanyer's poem is more activist than it is in the Gospels.
6. The omitted stanzas include "The Salutation and the Sorrow of the Virgin Mary."
7. The following stanzas are part of "A brief description of his [the bridegroom/Christ's] beauty upon the *Canticles*" (Lanyer's marginal note).
8. Some of the metaphors Lanyer uses here, such as the scarlet ribbon lips dropping honey, are based on those used by the bridegroom to describe the bride in the Songs of Songs (4:3, 11). Others, such as cheeks of spices and lips like lilies (5:13), are based on those the bride uses to describe the bridegroom to the daughters of Jerusalem.

To my Lady of Cumberland.

¶Ah! give me leave (good lady) now to leave
This task of beauty which I took in hand,
I cannot wade so deep, I may deceive
My self, before I can attain the land;
1325 Therefore (good Madam) in your heart I leave
His perfect picture, where it still shall stand,
 Deeply engraved in that holy shrine,
 Environed with love and thoughts divine.

There may you see him as a God in glory,
1330 And as a man in miserable case;
There may you read his true and perfect story,
His bleeding body there you may embrace,
And kiss his dying cheeks with tears of sorrow,
With joyful grief, you may intreat for grace;
1335 And all your prayers, and your alms-deeds°   *acts of charity*
 May bring to stop his cruel wounds that bleeds.

Oft times hath he made trial of your love,
And in your faith hath took no small delight,
By crosses and afflictions he doth prove,°   *test*
1340 Yet still your heart remaineth firm and right;
Your love so strong as nothing can remove,
Your thoughts being placed on him both day and night,
 Your constant soul doth lodge between her breasts,
 This sweet of sweets, in which all glory rests.

* * *

Wise Deborah[9] that judged Israel,
Nor valiant Judith[1] cannot equal thee,
Unto the first, God did his will reveal,
And gave her power to set his people free;
1485 Yea Judith had the power likewise to quell
Proud Holofernes, that the just might see
 What small defence vain pride and greatness hath
 Against the weapons of God's word and faith.

But thou far greater war do'st still maintain
1490 Against that many-headed monster sin,
Whose mortal sting hath many thousand slain,
And every day fresh combats do begin;
Yet cannot all his venom lay one stain
Upon thy soul, thou do'st the conquest win,
1495 Though all the world he daily doth devour,
 Yet over thee he never could get power.

For that one worthy deed by Deb'rah done,
Thou hast performed many in thy time;
For that one conquest that faire Judith won,
1500 By which she did the steps of honor climb,

---

9. A judge and prophet who played a crucial role in the Israelites' victory over the Canaanites (Judges 4 and 5).

1. Heroine of the apocryphal book of Judith; she beheaded the enemy general, Holofernes.

> Thou hast the conquest of all conquests won,
> When to thy conscience Hell can lay no crime:
>   For that one head that Judith bare away,
>   Thou takest from sin a hundred heads a day.
>
> Though virtuous Hester² fasted three days' space,   [1505]
> And spent her time in prayers all that while,
> That by God's power she might obtain such grace,
> That she and hers might not become a spoil
> To wicked Haman, in whose crabbed face
> Was seen the map of malice, envy, guile;   [1510]
>   Her glorious garments though she put apart,
>   So to present a pure and single heart.

* * *

> Lo Madam,° here you take a view of   *Countess of Cumberland*   [1825]
>   those,°   *martyrs*
> Whose worthy steps you do desire to tread,
> Decked in those colors which our Savior chose;
> The purest colors both of white and red,
> Their freshest beauties would I fain disclose,   *Colors of*
> By which our Savior most was honored: *Confessors*
>   But my weak Muse desireth now to rest,   *& Martyrs*
>   Folding up all their beauties in your breast.
>
> Whose excellence hath raised my spirits to write,
> Of what my thoughts could hardly apprehend;
> Your rarest virtues did my soul delight,   [1835]
> Great lady of my heart: I must commend
> You that appear so fair in all men's sight:
> On your deserts my muses do attend;
>   You are the Arctic star that guides my hand,
>   All what I am, I rest at your command.   [1840]

1611

The Description of Cookham¹

> Farewell, sweet Cookham, where I first obtained
> Grace² from that grace where perfect grace remained;
> And where the muses gave their full consent,
> I should have power the virtuous to content;
>   Where princely palace willed me to indite,°   *write*   [5]

---

2. Queen Esther, who interceded with King Ahasuerus when his minister Haman sought to destroy her people, the Jews; Haman was hanged, and the Jews' enemies destroyed (Esther 5–9; for her fasting, see 4:16). A defense of women published a few years after Lanyer's was entitled *Esther Hath Hanged Haman* (1617).

1. The poem was written in honor of Margaret Clifford, Countess of Cumberland, and celebrates a royal estate leased to her brother, at which the countess occasionally resided. The poem should be compared with Jonson's "To Penshurst" (p. 1053). Lanyer's poem is based on a familiar classical topic, the "farewell to a place," which had its most famous development in Virgil's *Eclogue* 1. Lanyer makes extensive use of the common pastoral motif of nature's active sympathy with and response to human emotion, which later came to be called the "pathetic fallacy."

2. Here, both God's grace and the favor of Her Grace, the Countess of Cumberland. Lanyer attributes both her religious conversion and her vocation as poet to a period of residence in the countess's household. We do not know how long or under what circumstances Lanyer resided at Cookham.

       The sacred story of the soul's delight.[3]
       Farewell, sweet place, where virtue then did rest,
       And all delights did harbor in her breast;
       Never shall my sad eyes again behold
10   Those pleasures which my thoughts did then unfold.
       Yet you, great lady, mistress of that place,
       From whose desires did spring this work of grace;
       Vouchsafe° to think upon those pleasures past,   *be willing*
       As fleeting worldly joys that could not last,
15   Or, as dim shadows of celestial pleasures,
       Which are desired above all earthly treasures.
       Oh how, methought, against° you thither came,   *in preparation for*
       Each part did seem some new delight to frame!
       The house received all ornaments to grace it,
20   And would endure no foulness to deface it.
       And walks put on their summer liveries,[4]
       And all things else did hold like similes:[5]
       The trees with leaves, with fruits, with flowers clad,
       Embraced each other, seeming to be glad,
25   Turning themselves to beauteous canopies,
       To shade the bright sun from your brighter eyes;
       The crystal streams with silver spangles graced,
       While by the glorious sun they were embraced;
       The little birds in chirping notes did sing,
30   To entertain both you and that sweet spring.
       And Philomela[6] with her sundry lays,
       Both you and that delightful place did praise.
       Oh how me thought each plant, each flower, each tree
       Set forth their beauties then to welcome thee!
35   The very hills right humbly did descend,
       When you to tread on them did intend.
       And as you set your feet, they still did rise,
       Glad that they could receive so rich a prize.
       The gentle winds did take delight to be
40   Among those woods that were so graced by thee,
       And in sad murmur uttered pleasing sound,
       That pleasure in that place might more abound.
       The swelling banks delivered all their pride
       When such a phoenix[7] once they had espied.
45   Each arbor, bank, each seat, each stately tree,
       Thought themselves honored in supporting thee.
       The pretty birds would oft come to attend thee,
       Yet fly away for fear they should offend thee;
       The little creatures in the burrow by

---

3. Apparently a reference to the countess as her patron, commissioning her poem on Christ's Passion.
4. Distinctive garments worn by persons in the service of great families, to indicate whose servants they were.
5. Behaved in similar fashion.
6. In myth, Philomela was raped by her brother-in-law Tereus, who also tore out her tongue; the gods transformed her into a bird (in Ovid's version, a nightingale) who tells her tale in song. The bird's song is joyous at first, then mournful (line 189) as Lanyer associates Philomela's woes with those of Cookham at the women's departure.
7. Mythical bird that lived alone of its kind for five hundred years, then was consumed in flame and reborn from its own ashes; metaphorically, a person of rare excellence. "All their pride": fish (compare "To Penshurst," p. 1054, lines 31–36).

50 Would come abroad to sport them in your eye,
    Yet fearful of the bow in your fair hand,
    Would run away when you did make a stand.
    Now let me come unto that stately tree,
    Wherein such goodly prospects you did see;
55 That oak that did in height his fellows pass,
    As much as lofty trees, low growing grass,
    Much like a comely cedar straight and tall,
    Whose beauteous stature far exceeded all.
    How often did you visit this fair tree,
60 Which seeming joyful in receiving thee,
    Would like a palm tree spread his arms abroad,
    Desirous that you there should make abode;
    Whose fair green leaves much like a comely veil,
    Defended Phoebus° when he would assail;   *resisted the sun*
65 Whose pleasing boughs did yield a cool fresh air,
    Joying° his happiness when you were there.   *enjoying*
    Where being seated, you might plainly see
    Hills, vales, and woods, as if on bended knee
    They had appeared, your honor to salute,
70 Or to prefer some strange unlooked-for suit;[8]
    All interlaced with brooks and crystal springs,
    A prospect fit to please the eyes of kings.
    And thirteen shires appeared all in your sight,
    Europe could not afford much more delight.
75 What was there then but gave you all content,
    While you the time in meditation spent
    Of their Creator's power, which there you saw,
    In all his creatures held a perfect law;
    And in their beauties did you plain descry°   *perceive*
80 His beauty, wisdom, grace, love, majesty.
    In these sweet woods how often did you walk,
    With Christ and his apostles there to talk;
    Placing his holy writ in some fair tree
    To meditate what you therein did see.
85 With Moses you did mount his holy hill
    To know his pleasure, and perform his will.[9]
    With lowly David you did often sing
    His holy hymns to heaven's eternal King.[1]
    And in sweet music did your soul delight
90 To sound his praises, morning, noon, and night.
    With blessed Joseph you did often feed
    Your pined° brethren, when they stood in need.[2]   *gaunt*
    And that sweet lady sprung from Clifford's race,
    Of noble Bedford's blood, fair stem of grace,[3]
95 To honorable Dorset now espoused,[4]

8. To urge some unexpected petition, as to a monarch.
9. You sought out and followed God's law, like Moses, who received the Ten Commandments on Mount Sinai.
1. You often sang David's psalms.
2. Like Joseph, who fed the starving Israelites in Egypt, you fed the hungry.
3. Main line of the family tree. Anne Clifford, only surviving child of the seaman-adventurer George Clifford, third Earl of Cumberland, and the countess, a Russell (of "Bedford's blood").
4. Anne Clifford was married to Richard Sackville, third Earl of Dorset, on February 25, 1609; the reference helps date Lanyer's poem.

In whose fair breast true virtue then was housed,
Oh what delight did my weak spirits find
In those pure parts° of her well framéd mind. *qualities*
And yet it grieves me that I cannot be
100 Near unto her, whose virtues did agree
With those fair ornaments of outward beauty,
Which did enforce from all both love and duty.
Unconstant Fortune, thou art most to blame,
Who casts us down into so low a frame
105 Where our great friends we cannot daily see,
So great a difference is there in degree.[5]
Many are placéd in those orbs of state,
Parters[6] in honor, so ordained by Fate,
Nearer in show, yet farther off in love,
110 In which, the lowest always are above.[7]
But whither am I carried in conceit,° *thought, fancy*
My wit too weak to conster° of the great. *construe*
Why not? Although we are but born of earth,
We may behold the heavens, despising death;
115 And loving heaven that is so far above,
May in the end vouchsafe us entire love.[8]
Therefore sweet memory do thou retain
Those pleasures past, which will not turn again:
Remember beauteous Dorset's[9] former sports,
120 So far from being touched by ill reports,
Wherein myself did always bear a part,
While reverend love presented my true heart.
Those recreations let me bear in mind,
Which her sweet youth and noble thoughts did find,
125 Whereof deprived, I evermore must grieve,
Hating blind Fortune, careless to relieve.
And you sweet Cookham, whom these ladies leave,
I now must tell the grief you did conceive
At their departure, when they went away,
130 How everything retained a sad dismay.
Nay long before, when once an inkling came,
Methought each thing did unto sorrow frame:
The trees that were so glorious in our view,
Forsook both flowers and fruit, when once they knew
135 Of your depart, their very leaves did wither,
Changing their colors as they grew together.
But when they saw this had no power to stay you,
They often wept, though, speechless, could not pray you,
Letting their tears in your fair bosoms fall,
140 As if they said, Why will ye leave us all?
This being vain, they cast their leaves away
Hoping that pity would have made you stay:

---

5. These lines and lines 117–25 probably exaggerate Lanyer's former familiarity with Anne Clifford.
6. Separators; that is, the various honorific ranks ("orbs of state") act to separate person from person.
7. An egalitarian sentiment playing on the Christian notion that in spiritual things—love and charity—the poor and lowly surpass the great ones.
8. That is, we (lowly) may also love God and enjoy God's love, and hence are equal to anyone.
9. As was common, Anne Clifford is here referred to by her husband's title.

       Their frozen tops, like age's hoary hairs,
       Shows their disasters, languishing in fears.
145   A swarthy riveled rind° all over spread,   bark
       Their dying bodies half alive, half dead.
       But your occasions called you so away[1]
       That nothing there had power to make you stay.
       Yet did I see a noble grateful mind
150   Requiting each according to their kind,
       Forgetting not to turn and take your leave
       Of these sad creatures, powerless to receive
       Your favor, when with grief you did depart,
       Placing their former pleasures in your heart,
155   Giving great charge to noble memory
       There to preserve their love continually.
       But specially the love of that fair tree,
       That first and last you did vouchsafe to see,
       In which it pleased you oft to take the air
160   With noble Dorset, then a virgin fair,
       Where many a learned book was read and scanned,
       To this fair tree, taking me by the hand,
       You did repeat the pleasures which had passed,
       Seeming to grieve they could no longer last.
165   And with a chaste, yet loving kiss took leave,
       Of which sweet kiss I did it soon bereave,°   soon take from it
       Scorning a senseless creature should possess
       So rare a favor, so great happiness.
       No other kiss it could receive from me,
170   For fear to give back what it took of thee,
       So I ungrateful creature did deceive it
       Of that which you in love vouchsafed to leave it.
       And though it oft had given me much content,
       Yet this great wrong I never could repent;
175   But of the happiest made it most forlorn,
       To show that nothing's free from Fortune's scorn,
       While all the rest with this most beauteous tree
       Made their sad comfort sorrow's harmony.
       The flowers that on the banks and walks did grow,
180   Crept in the ground, the grass did weep for woe.
       The winds and waters seemed to chide together
       Because you went away they knew not whither;
       And those sweet brooks that ran so fair and clear,
       With grief and trouble wrinkled did appear.
185   Those pretty birds that wonted° were to sing,   accustomed
       Now neither sing, nor chirp, nor use their wing,
       But with their tender feet on some bare spray,
       Warble forth sorrow, and their own dismay.
       Fair Philomela leaves her mournful ditty,

---

1. After her husband's death in 1605, Margaret Clifford chiefly resided in her dower properties in the north; Anne Clifford was married in 1609. The two women began their pursuit of Anne's rights to the Clifford properties immediately after George Clifford's death. Anne finally obtained her rights in 1643.

190 Drowned in deep sleep, yet can procure no pity.
    Each arbor, bank, each seat, each stately tree
    Looks bare and desolate now for want of thee,
    Turning green tresses into frosty gray,
    While in cold grief they wither all away.
195 The sun grew weak, his beams no comfort gave,
    While all green things did make the earth their grave.
    Each briar, each bramble, when you went away
    Caught fast your clothes, thinking to make you stay;
    Delightful Echo wonted to reply
200 To our last words, did now for sorrow die;
    The house cast off each garment that might grace it,
    Putting on dust and cobwebs to deface it.
    All desolation then there did appear,
    When you were going whom they held so dear.
205 This last farewell to Cookham here I give,
    When I am dead thy name in this may live,
    Wherein I have performed her noble hest°   *commission*
    Whose virtues lodge in my unworthy breast,
    And ever shall, so long as life remains,
210 Tying my life to her by those rich chains.°   *her virtues*

1611

BEN JONSON
1572–1637

In 1616 Ben Jonson published his *Works*, to the derision of those astounded to see mere plays and poems collected under the same title the king gave to his political treatises. Many of Jonson's contemporaries shied away from publication, either because, like Donne, they wrote for small coterie audiences or because, like Shakespeare, they wrote for theater companies that preferred not to let go of the scripts. Jonson knew and admired both Donne and Shakespeare and more than any Jacobean belonged to both of their very different worlds, but in publishing his *Works* he laid claim to higher literary status. He had risen from humble beginnings to become England's unofficial poet laureate, with a pension from the king and honorary degrees from both Oxford and Cambridge. If he was not the first professional author in England, he was the first to invest that role with dignity and respectability. His published *Works*, over which he labored with painstaking care, testify to an extraordinary feat of self-transformation.

Jonson's early life was tough and turbulent. The son of a London clergyman who died before he was born, he was educated at Westminster School under the antiquarian scholar William Camden. There he developed his love of classical learning; but lacking the resources to continue his education, Jonson was forced to turn to his stepfather's trade of bricklaying, a life he "could not endure." He escaped by joining the English forces in Flanders, where, he later boasted, he

Jonson's 1616 *Works*. This title page makes a strong claim for the importance of Jonson's literary achievement and for the significance of English drama in general. The columned portico suggests Jonson's connection to the classical tradition, and the figures within it represent his mastery of various genres; they represent, clockwise from the top, Tragicomedy, Pastoral, Comedy, Tragedy, and Satire. Underneath Tragedy is a cart of the sort medieval traveling players would have used; underneath Comedy is an ancient Greek amphitheater. Centered just beneath Tragicomedy is a depiction of the English public theaters for which Jonson wrote many of his plays.

killed a man in single combat before the eyes of two armies. Back in London, his attempt to make a living as an actor and a playwright almost ended in disaster. He was imprisoned in 1597 for collaborating with Thomas Nashe on the scandalous play *The Isle of Dogs* (now lost), and shortly after his release he killed one of his fellow actors in a duel. Jonson escaped the gallows by pleading benefit of clergy (a medieval privilege exempting felons from the death penalty if they could read Latin). His learning had saved his life, but he emerged from captivity branded on the thumb, and with another mark against him as well. Under the influence of a priest imprisoned with him, Jonson had converted to Catholicism. He was now more than ever a marginal figure, distrusted by the society that he satirized brilliantly in his early plays.

Jonson's fortunes improved with the accession of James I, though not immediately. In 1603 he was called before the Privy Council to answer charges of "popery and treason" found in his play *Sejanus*. Little more than a year later he was in jail again for co-writing the play *Eastward Ho*, which openly mocked the Scots accent of the new king and his courtiers. Nonetheless, in January 1605 Jonson received a commission from Queen Anna to organize the court's Twelfth Night entertainment, or masque, in the old Banqueting House at Whitehall. *The Masque of Blackness*, which Jonson produced in collaboration with the architect and scene designer Inigo Jones, featured Queen Anna and eleven of her ladies emerging from a scallop shell, "all painted like Blackamoors, face and neck bare" and "strangely attired." Jonson would go on to produce twenty-four masques for the court, most of them with Inigo Jones. In the same years that he was writing the masques, he produced his greatest works for the public theater, including the comedies *Volpone* (1606), *Epicene* (1609), *The Alchemist* (1610), and *Bartholomew Fair* (1614). Jonson preserved the detached, satiric perspective of an outsider, but he was rising in society and making accommodations where necessary. Around 1610, he returned to the Church of England.

Although he rose to a position of respectability, Jonson retained a quarrelsome spirit all his life. Much of his best work emerged out of fierce tensions with collaborators and contemporaries. Still, in spite of his antagonistic nature, Jonson had a great capacity for friendship. His friends included Shakespeare, Donne, and Francis Bacon. In later years he gathered around himself a group of admiring younger men known as the "Sons of Ben," among them Robert Herrick, Thomas Carew, and Sir John Suckling. Jonson also moved easily among the great of the land. His patrons included Lady Mary Wroth, whose sonnets he praised for making him a better poet, and other members of the Sidney and Herbert families. In "To Penshurst," a celebration of Robert Sidney's country estate, Jonson offers an ideal image of a social order in which a virtuous landowner offers hospitality to guests of all stations, from poets to kings.

"To Penshurst," together with Aemilia Lanyer's "Description of Cookham," inaugurated the genre of the "country house poem" in England. Jonson tried his hand at a wide range of poetic genres, including epitaph and epigram, love and funeral elegy, verse satire and verse letter, song and ode. More often than not he looked back to classical precedents. The classical values Jonson most admired are enumerated in "Inviting a Friend to Supper," which, in contrast to the excess that marked the banquets and entertainments of imperial Rome and Stuart England, describes a dinner party characterized by moderation and refinement, while still hinting at Jonson's own notoriety. The man who produced this image of temperate civility was a man of immense appetites, which found expression in his art as well as in his life. His best works seethe with imaginative energy and a lust for abundance. Even after a stroke in 1629 left him partially paralyzed and confined to his home, Jonson continued to write; he was at work on a new play when he died in 1637.

Fox Handling Masks. This woodcut from Andrea Alciato's *Emblemata* depicts the traditional association between foxes and deceptive human role-playing, a connection central to *Volpone*.

Volpone This dark satire on human rapacity is set in Venice, but its true target is the city of London, or the city that, Jonson feared, London was about to become. It is a place devoted to commerce and mired in corruption, populated by greedy fools and conniving rascals. Like Shakespeare, Donne, and Thomas More before him, Jonson was deeply disturbed by the rise of a protocapitalist economic order that seemed to emphasize competition and the acquisition of material goods over reciprocal goodwill and mutual obligation. On the other hand, Jonson was also fascinated by the entrepreneurial potential liberated by the new economic order. His protagonists, Volpone and Mosca, may be morally bankrupt, but they are also the most intelligent, adaptable characters in the play. Moreover, although Jonson was a strong advocate for the educational and morally improving potential of the theater—his theater in particular—the talents of his main characters are essentially those of theatrical performance and improvisation. In fact, as Jonson was well aware, he was himself deeply implicated in what he satirized. The lowborn, unscrupulous, brilliantly inventive Mosca, a flattering aristocratic hanger-on who aspires to high status himself, at times seems to be the author's evil twin. Perhaps his very resemblances to Jonson required Jonson so energetically to repudiate his motives and punish his presumption at the end of the play.

Volpone combines elements from several sources. The classical satirist Lucian provided the theme of the rich old man playing with moneygrubbing scoundrels who hope to inherit his wealth. Roman comedy provided prototypes for some characters: the wily parasite, the unscrupulous lawyer, the avaricious dotard, the voluble woman. Some scenes, such as that in which Volpone disguised as a mountebank woos Celia at her window, are drawn from the Italian commedia dell'arte. Jonson draws as well upon ancient and medieval beast fables: stories about the crafty antihero Reynard the fox, as well as a fable about a fox that plays dead in order to catch greedy birds. But *Volpone* is much more than the sum of its borrowings. It is a work of enormous comic energy, full of black humor, which holds its loathsome characters up for appalled but gleeful inspection.

Volpone was first performed by the King's Men (Shakespeare's company) in the spring of 1606, at the Globe Theater. (See the illustration, in the appendices to this volume, of a contemporary popular theater constructed on similar lines.) The Globe held some two thousand persons—aristocrats and prosperous citizens sitting in the tiered galleries, lower-class "groundlings" standing in the pit in the front of the stage. The play was also performed to great applause before learned audiences at Oxford and Cambridge, to whom Jonson dedicated the printed edition of *Volpone*. It was first published in quarto form in 1607 and republished with a few changes in the 1616 *Works*, the basis for the present text.

Volpone

or
The Fox

The Persons of the Play[1]

VOLPONE, *a magnifico*°   *Venetian nobleman*
MOSCA, *his parasite*°   *hanger-on*
NANO, *a dwarf*
ANDROGYNO, *a hermaphrodite*
CASTRONE, *an eunuch*
VOLTORE, *an advocate*°   *lawyer*
CORBACCIO, *an old gentleman*
BONARIO, *a young gentleman* [CORBACCIO's *son*]
CORVINO, *a merchant*
CELIA, *the merchant's wife*
Servitore, a SERVANT [*to* CORVINO]
[*Sir*] POLITIC *Would-be, a knight*
Fine Madame [LADY] WOULD-BE, *the knight's wife*
[*Two*] WOMEN [*servants to* LADY WOULD-BE]
PEREGRINE, *a gentleman traveler*
AVOCATORI,° *four magistrates*   *public prosecutors*
Notario [NOTARY], *the register*°   *court recorder*
COMMENDATORI,° *officers*   *court deputies*
[*Other court officials, litter-bearers*]
Mercatori, three MERCHANTS
Grege [*members of a* CROWD]

SCENE. *Venice*

The Argument[1]

V olpone, childless, rich, feigns sick, despairs,°   *is despaired of*
O ffers his state° to hopes of several heirs,   *estate*
L ies languishing; his parasite receives
P resents of all, assures, deludes, then weaves
O ther cross-plots, which ope themselves,° are told.°   *unfold / exposed*
N ew tricks for safety are sought; they thrive—when, bold,
E ach tempts th'other again, and all are sold.°   *betrayed*

Prologue

Now, luck yet send us, and a little wit
Will serve to make our play hit

The Persons of the Play
1. Many of the characters have allegorically apt names. "Volpone" is defined in John Florio's 1598 Italian-English dictionary as "an old fox . . . a sneaking, lurking, wily deceiver." "Mosca" means "fly." "Nano" means "dwarf." "Voltore" means "vulture." "Corbaccio" means "raven." "Bonario" is derived from *bono*, meaning "good." "Corvino" means "crow." "Celia" means "heaven." "Politic" means "worldly-wise" or "temporizing." "Peregrine" means "traveler" or "small hawk." In many performances the symbolism of the animal names is reinforced by costuming.

The Argument
1. Plot summary. Jonson imitates the acrostic "arguments" of the Latin playwright Plautus.

According to the palates of the season,°   *fashionable taste*
Here is rhyme not empty of reason.
This we were bid to credit° from our poet,   *asked to believe*
Whose true scope,° if you would know it,   *aim*
In all his poems still hath been this measure,
To mix profit with your pleasure;[1]
And not as some—whose throats their envy failing°—   *not fully expressing*
Cry hoarsely, "all he writes is railing,"°   *personal insult*
And when his plays come forth think they can flout them
With saying he was a year about them.[2]
To these there needs no lie° but this his creature,°   *denial / creation*
Which was, two months since, no feature;°   *nonexistent*
And, though he dares give them° five lives to mend it,   *his detractors*
'Tis known five weeks fully penned it
From his own hand, without a coadjutor,°   *collaborator*
Novice, journeyman,° or tutor.   *apprentice*
Yet thus much I can give you, as a token
Of his play's worth: no eggs are broken,
Nor quaking custards with fierce teeth affrighted,[3]
Wherewith your rout° are so delighted;   *mob*
Nor hales he in a gull,° old ends° reciting,   *fool / saws*
To stop gaps in his loose writing,
With such a deal of monstrous and forced action
As might make Bethlehem a faction.[4]
Nor made he his play for jests stol'n from each table,°   *plagiarized jokes*
But makes jests to fit his fable,
And so presents quick° comedy, refined   *lively*
As best critics have designed.
The laws of time, place, persons he observeth;[5]
From no needful rule he swerveth.
All gall and copperas[6] from his ink he draineth;
Only a little salt[7] remaineth
Wherewith he'll rub your cheeks, till, red with laughter,
They shall look fresh a week after.

Prologue
1. Rule, as laid down by Horace, that the poet ought to both please his audience and teach it something useful.
2. Thomas Dekker ridiculed the slow pace at which Jonson produced new work in *Satiromastix, or The Untrussing of the Humorous Poet* (1602), and John Marston did the same in *The Dutch Courtesan* (1605).
3. The satirist John Marston, in a line Jonson had previously ridiculed, boasted: "let custards [cowards] quake, my rage must freely run." Huge custards were a staple feature of city feasts.
4. As might win approval from lunatics (who inhabited Bethlehem hospital in London).
5. He observes the unities of time and place and the consistency of character.
6. Ferrous sulfate, like gall a corrosive substance used in ink.
7. A traditional metaphor for satiric wit.

Act 1

SCENE 1. VOLPONE's *house*.

[*Enter*] VOLPONE [*and*] MOSCA.[1]

VOLPONE   Good morning to the day, and, next, my gold!
Open the shrine that I may see my saint.
[MOSCA *reveals the treasure.*][2]
Hail the world's soul,° and mine! More glad than is   °*animating principle*
The teeming earth to see the longed-for sun
5   Peep through the horns of the celestial Ram[3]
Am I to view thy splendor darkening his,°   °*outshining the sun's*
That, lying here amongst my other hoards,
Show'st like a flame by night, or like the day
Struck out of chaos, when all darkness fled
10   Unto the center.° O thou son of Sol[4]—   °*center of the earth*
But brighter than thy father—let me kiss
With adoration thee and every relic
Of sacred treasure in this blessèd room.
Well did wise poets by thy glorious name
15   Title that age which they would have the best,[5]
Thou being the best of things, and far transcending
All style of joy in children, parents, friends,
Or any other waking dream on earth.
Thy looks when they to Venus did ascribe,
20   They should have giv'n her twenty thousand Cupids,[6]
Such are thy beauties and our loves.° Dear saint,   °*our love of thee*
Riches, the dumb god, that giv'st all men tongues,
That canst do naught and yet mak'st men do all things,
The price of souls; even hell, with thee to boot,°   °*in the bargain*
25   Is made worth heaven! Thou art virtue, fame,
Honor, and all things else. Who° can get thee,   °*whoever*
He shall be noble, valiant, honest, wise—
MOSCA   And what he will, sir. Riches are in fortune
A greater good than wisdom is in nature.
30 VOLPONE   True, my belovèd Mosca. Yet I glory
More in the cunning purchase° of my wealth   °*acquisition*
Than in the glad possession, since I gain
No common way. I use no trade, no venture;°   °*risky commerce*
I wound no earth with plowshares; fat no beasts
35   To feed the shambles;° have no mills for iron,   °*slaughterhouse*
Oil, corn, or men, to grind 'em into powder;

1.1
1. Alternatively, the play may begin with Volpone rising from his onstage bed.
2. The treasure is probably hidden behind a curtain in the alcove at the back of the stage.
3. Aries, the constellation ascendant in early spring.
4. Alchemists believed gold to have issued from the sun ("Sol"). Volpone blasphemously applies this metaphor to God's creation of the world in Genesis.
5. The mythical Golden Age (when, ironically, gold was not yet in use) was influentially described by Ovid in *The Metamorphoses*.
6. In Latin poetry, Venus was commonly described as *aurea*, meaning "golden." The throng of cupids Volpone imagines around her suggests gold's irresistible, and for him highly sexual, appeal.

        I blow no subtle[7] glass; expose no ships
        To threat'nings of the furrow-facèd sea;
        I turn° no moneys in the public bank,   *exchange*
        Nor usure° private—   *lend money at interest*
40 MOSCA   No, sir, nor devour
        Soft prodigals. You shall ha' some will swallow
        A melting° heir as glibly as your Dutch   *financially dwindling*
        Will pills° of butter, and ne'er purge for't;[8]   *morsels*
        Tear forth the fathers of poor families
45   Out of their beds and coffin them alive
        In some kind, clasping° prison, where their bones   *manacling*
        May be forthcoming° when the flesh is rotten.   *protruding; carted away*
        But your sweet nature doth abhor these courses;
        You loathe the widow's or the orphan's tears
50   Should wash your pavements, or their piteous cries
        Ring in your roofs and beat the air for vengeance.
  VOLPONE   Right, Mosca, I do loathe it.
  MOSCA   And besides, sir,
        You are not like the thresher that doth stand
        With a huge flail, watching a heap of corn,
55   And, hungry, dares not taste the smallest grain,
        But feeds on mallows° and such bitter herbs;   *unpalatable weeds*
        Nor like the merchant who hath filled his vaults
        With Romagnia and rich Candian wines,
        Yet drinks the lees of Lombard's vinegar.[9]
60   You will not lie in straw whilst moths and worms
        Feed on your sumptuous hangings° and soft beds.   *bed curtains*
        You know the use of riches, and dare give now
        From that bright heap to me, your poor observer,°   *follower*
        Or to your dwarf, or your hermaphrodite,
65   Your eunuch, or what other household° trifle   *menial*
        Your pleasure allows maint'nance°—   *you're pleased to support*
  VOLPONE [*giving money*]   Hold thee, Mosca,
        Take of my hand; thou strik'st on truth in all,
        And they are envious term° thee parasite.   *who term*
        Call forth my dwarf, my eunuch, and my fool,
        And let 'em make me sport.   [*Exit* MOSCA.]
70   What should I do
        But cocker up my genius,° and live free   *indulge my appetite*
        To all delights my fortune calls me to?
        I have no wife, no parent, child, ally
        To give my substance to, but whom I make°   *he whom I designate*
75   Must be my heir, and this makes men observe° me.   *flatter*
        This draws new clients° daily to my house,   *petitioners*
        Women and men of every sex and age,

---

7. (1) Delicate; (2) artful. (Venice was and is renowned for its art glass.)

8. Never use a remedy for gastric distress. (The Dutch were notoriously fond of butter.)

9. Romagnia and rich Candian wines are expensive wines from Greece and Crete. The lees of Lombard's vinegar are the dregs of cheap Italian wine.

That bring me presents, send me plate,° coin, jewels,   *gold or silver plate*
With hope that when I die—which they expect
80 Each greedy minute—it shall then return
Tenfold upon them; whilst some, covetous
Above the rest, seek to engross° me whole,   *swallow; monopolize*
And counterwork,° the one unto the other,   *compete; undermine*
Contend in gifts as they would seem in love;
85 All which I suffer, playing with their hopes,
And am content to coin 'em into profit,
And look upon their kindness and take more,
And look on that, still bearing them in hand,°   *leading them on*
Letting the cherry knock against their lips,
90 And draw it by their mouths and back again.[1]—
How now!

SCENE 2. *The scene continues.*

[*Enter*] MOSCA, NANO, ANDROGYNO, [*and*] CASTRONE.

NANO Now, room for fresh gamesters,° who do will   *entertainers*
    you to know
They do bring you neither play nor university show,[1]
And therefore do entreat you that whatsoever they rehearse
May not fare a whit the worse for the false pace of the verse.[2]
5 If you wonder at this, you will wonder more ere we pass,
For know here [*indicating* ANDROGYNO] is enclosed the soul
    of Pythagoras,[3]
That juggler° divine, as hereafter shall follow;   *trickster*
Which soul (fast and loose, sir) came first from Apollo,
And was breathed into Aethalides,[4] Mercurius his° son,   *Mercury's*
10 Where it had the gift to remember all that ever was done.
From thence it fled forth and made quick transmigration
To goldilocked Euphorbus,[5] who was killed in good fashion
At the siege of old Troy, by the cuckold of Sparta.[6]
Hermotimus[7] was next—I find it in my *charta*°—   *record*
15 To whom it did pass, where no sooner it was missing
But with one Pyrrhus of Delos° it learned to go   *another philosopher*
    a-fishing;
And thence did it enter the Sophist of Greece.°   *Pythagoras*
From Pythagore she went into a beautiful piece°   *slut*

---

1. In the game of chop-cherry, one player dangles a cherry in front of another, who tries to bite it.

1.2
1. University students performed classical plays or their imitations to hone their abilities in Latin oratory.
2. The four-stress meter of the skit Nano, Androgyno, and Castrone here perform was common in medieval drama but old-fashioned by Jonson's time.
3. Ancient Greek philosopher, mathematician, and music theorist who believed in the transmigration of souls and in the mystical properties of geometrical relationships (especially triangles [triangles=trigon]). His followers observed strict dietary restrictions and took five-year vows of silence. His thigh was rumored to be made of gold. Jonson adapts much of the career of Pythagoras's soul from *The Dialogue of the Cobbler and the Cock*, by the Greek satirist Lucian.
4. The herald of the Greek Argonauts and son of the god Mercury, who inherited his father's divine gift of memory. Thus, unlike other souls, which forget their previous lives, Aethalides' soul can recall its transmigrations.
5. Trojan youth who injured Achilles' beloved friend, Patroclus, in the *Iliad*.
6. Menelaus, the Spartan king whose wife, Helen, was stolen by the Trojan prince Paris.
7. Greek philosopher of about 500 B.C.E.

Hight° Aspasia the meretrix;[8] and the next toss of her *named*
Was again of a whore; she became a philosopher,
Crates the Cynic,[9] as itself doth relate it.
Since,° kings, knights, and beggars, knaves, lords, and fools *since then*
    gat° it, *received*
Besides ox and ass, camel, mule, goat, and brock,° *badger*
In all which it hath spoke as in the cobbler's cock.[1]
But I come not here to discourse of that matter,
Or his one, two, or three, or his great oath, "By quater,"[2]
His musics, his trigon, his golden thigh,
Or his telling how elements° shift; but I *earth, air, fire, water*
Would ask how of late thou hast suffered translation,° *metamorphosis*
And shifted thy coat in these days of reformation?° *religious change*

ANDROGYNO   Like one of the reformed, a fool,[3] as you see,
Counting all old doctrine heresy.

NANO   But not on thine own forbid meats hast thou ventured?

ANDROGYNO   On fish, when first a Carthusian I entered.[4]

NANO   Why, then thy dogmatical silence° hath left thee? *vow of silence*

ANDROGYNO   Of that an obstreperous lawyer bereft me.

NANO   Oh, wonderful change! When Sir Lawyer forsook thee,
For Pythagore's sake, what body then took thee?

ANDROGYNO   A good dull mule.

NANO   And how, by that means,
Thou wert brought to allow of the eating of beans?

ANDROGYNO   Yes.

NANO   But from the mule into whom didst thou pass?

ANDROGYNO   Into a very strange beast, by some writers called
    an ass;
By others a precise, pure, illuminate brother[5]
Of those devour flesh and sometimes one another,° *prey on each other*
And will drop you forth a libel° or a sanctified lie *polemic*
Betwixt every spoonful of a Nativity pie.[6]

NANO   Now quit thee, for heaven, of that profane nation,° *sect*
And gently report thy next transmigration.

ANDROGYNO   To the same that I am.° *what I am now*

NANO   A creature of delight?
And—what is more than a fool—an hermaphrodite?
Now pray thee, sweet soul, in all thy variation° *of all your shapes*
Which body wouldst thou choose to take up thy station?

ANDROGYNO   Troth, this I am in, even here would I tarry.

NANO   'Cause here the delight of each sex thou canst vary?

---

8. Whore. Aspasia was the mistress of the Athenian statesman Pericles.
9. Student of Diogenes, founder of the Cynic philosophy.
1. The speaker in Lucian's dialogue (see p. 949, n. 3 above).
2. A quater is an equilateral triangle the sides of which are evenly divisible by four.
3. The "reformed" are Protestants in general, but more specifically the Puritan wing of the Church of England. Jonson was a Catholic when he wrote *Volpone*.
4. Pythagoreans abstained from fish, but Carthusians, an order of Catholic monks, ate fish on fast days.
5. Puritan who claimed immediate, visionary knowledge of religious truth. Puritans did not observe the traditional fasting days (hence "devour flesh" in the following line).
6. Puritans substituted the term "Nativity" for "Christmas," to avoid reference to the Mass.

ANDROGYNO   Alas, those pleasures be stale and forsaken.
    No, 'tis your fool wherewith I am so taken,
    The only one creature that I can call blessèd,
    For all other forms I have proved° most distressèd.   *found to be*
60 NANO   Spoke true, as thou wert in Pythagoras still.
    This learnèd opinion we celebrate will,
    Fellow eunuch, as behooves us, with all our wit and art,
    To dignify that° whereof ourselves are so great and special a part.   *folly*
VOLPONE [*applauding*]   Now, very, very pretty! Mosca, this
    Was thy invention?
65 MOSCA   If it please my patron,
    Not else.
VOLPONE   It doth, good Mosca.
MOSCA   Then it was, sir.

Song

NANO *and* CASTRONE [*sing*]
        Fools, they are the only nation°   *group*
        Worth men's envy or admiration,
        Free from care or sorrow-taking,
70   Selves° and others merry making;   *themselves*
        All they speak or do is sterling.
        Your fool, he is your great man's dearling,
        And your lady's sport and pleasure;
        Tongue and bauble° are his treasure.   *fool's staff; penis*
75   E'en his face begetteth laughter,
        And he speaks truth free from slaughter.°   *with impunity*
        He's the grace of every feast,
        And sometimes the chiefest guest,
        Hath his trencher° and his stool,   *platter*
80   When wit waits upon the fool.
            Oh, who would not be
            He, he, he?   *One knocks without.*
VOLPONE   Who's that? Away!
                [*Exeunt* NANO *and* CASTRONE.]
            Look, Mosca.
MOSCA   Fool, begone!
                [*Exit* ANDROGYNO.]
    'Tis Signor Voltore, the advocate;
    I know him by his knock.
85 VOLPONE   Fetch me my gown,
    My furs, and nightcaps; say my couch is changing,[7]
    And let him entertain himself awhile
    Without i'th'gallery.   [*Exit* MOSCA.]
                Now, now, my clients
    Begin their visitation! Vulture, kite,
90 Raven, and gorcrow,° all my birds of prey   *carrion crow*
    That think me turning carcass, now they come.

---

7. My bedsheets are being changed.

                I am not for 'em° yet.   *ready to die*
                    [*Enter* MOSCA.]
                                How now? The news?
    MOSCA   A piece of plate,° sir.   *gold platter*
    VOLPONE   Of what bigness?
    MOSCA   Huge,
        Massy, and antique, with your name inscribed
        And arms° engraven.   *coat of arms*
95 VOLPONE   Good! And not a fox
        Stretched on the earth, with fine delusive sleights°   *deceptive tricks*
        Mocking a gaping crow?⁸ Ha, Mosca?
    MOSCA [*laughing*]   Sharp, sir.
    VOLPONE   Give me my furs. Why dost thou laugh so, man?
    MOSCA   I cannot choose, sir, when I apprehend
100   What thoughts he has, without,° now, as he walks: *outside*
        That this might be the last gift he should° give;   *would have to*
        That this would fetch you;° if you died today   *bring you around*
        And gave him all, what he should be tomorrow;
        What large return would come of all his ventures;
105   How he should worshipped be and reverenced;
        Ride with his furs and footcloths,⁹ waited on
        By herds of fools and clients; have clear way
        Made for his mule, as lettered° as himself;   *educated*
        Be called the great and learnèd advocate;
110   And then concludes there's naught impossible.
    VOLPONE   Yes, to be learnèd, Mosca.
    MOSCA   Oh, no, rich
        Implies it.° Hood an ass with reverend purple,¹   *wealth implies learning*
        So you can hide his two ambitious° ears,   *aspiring; upraised*
        And he shall pass for a cathedral doctor.°   *Doctor of Divinity*
115 VOLPONE   My caps, my caps, good Mosca. Fetch him in.
    MOSCA   Stay, sir, your ointment for your eyes.
                    [MOSCA *helps* VOLPONE *with his disguise.*]
    VOLPONE   That's true.
        Dispatch, dispatch! I long to have possession
        Of my new present.
    MOSCA   That, and thousands more
        I hope to see you lord of.
    VOLPONE   Thanks, kind Mosca.
120 MOSCA   And that, when I am lost in blended dust,
        And hundred such as I am in succession—
    VOLPONE   Nay, that were too much, Mosca.
    MOSCA   —you shall live
        Still, to delude these harpies.²
    VOLPONE   Loving Mosca!
        'Tis well. My pillow now, and let him enter.
                    [*Exit* MOSCA. VOLPONE *lies down.*]

---

8. In one of Aesop's *Fables*, the fox tricks the crow into dropping its cheese.
9. Ornamental cloths for the back of a horse.
1. Doctors of Divinity wore purple academic hoods.
2. Mythological ravenous monsters with women's heads and the bodies and claws of birds.

125 Now, my feigned cough, my phthisic,° and my gout,   *consumption; asthma*
   My apoplexy, palsy, and catarrhs,°   *mucus discharges*
   Help with your forcèd functions this my posture,°   *imposture*
   Wherein this three year I have milked their hopes.
   He comes, I hear him. [*Coughing*] Uh, uh, uh, uh! Oh—

SCENE 3. *The scene continues.*

[*Enter*] VOLTORE [*with a platter, ushered by*] MOSCA.
MOSCA [*to* VOLTORE]   You still are what you were, sir.
   Only you,
   Of all the rest, are he commands° his love;   *the one who possesses*
   And you do wisely to preserve it thus
   With early visitation and kind notes°   *tokens*
5 Of your good meaning to° him, which, I know,   *intentions toward*
   Cannot but come most grateful. [*Loudly, to* VOLPONE]
   Patron, sir!
   Here's Signor Voltore is come—
VOLPONE [*weakly*]   What say you?
MOSCA   Sir, Signor Voltore is come this morning
   To visit you.
VOLPONE   I thank him.
MOSCA   And hath brought
10 A piece of antique plate bought of Saint Mark,¹
   With which he here presents you.
VOLPONE   He is welcome.
   Pray him to come more often.
MOSCA   Yes.
VOLTORE [*straining to hear*]   What says he?
MOSCA   He thanks you, and desires you see him often.
VOLPONE   Mosca.
MOSCA   My patron?
VOLPONE [*groping*]   Bring him near. Where is he?
   I long to feel his hand.
15 MOSCA [*guiding* VOLPONE'*s hands toward the platter*]   The plate is here, sir.
VOLTORE   How fare you, sir?
VOLPONE   I thank you, Signor Voltore.
   Where is the plate? Mine eyes are bad.
VOLTORE [*relinquishing the platter*]   I'm sorry
   To see you still thus weak.
MOSCA [*aside*]   That he is not weaker.
VOLPONE   You are too munificent.
VOLTORE   No, sir, would to heaven
20 I could as well give health to you as that plate.
VOLPONE   You give, sir, what you can. I thank you. Your love
   Hath taste in° this, and shall not be unanswered.   *is suggested by*
   I pray you see me often.
VOLTORE   Yes, I shall, sir.

1.3
1. Goldsmiths kept shop in the square of St. Mark's Basilica.

VOLPONE   Be not far from me.
MOSCA [*aside to* VOLTORE]   Do you observe that, sir?
25 VOLPONE   Hearken unto me still. It will concern you.
MOSCA [*aside to* VOLTORE]   You are a happy man, sir. Know your good.
VOLPONE   I cannot now last long—
MOSCA (*aside to* VOLTORE)   You are his heir, sir.
VOLTORE (*aside to* MOSCA)   Am I?
VOLPONE   I feel me going, uh, uh, uh, uh!
   I am sailing to my port, uh, uh, uh, uh!
30 And I am glad I am so near my haven.
      [*He pretends to lapse into unconsciousness.*]
MOSCA   Alas, kind gentleman! Well, we must all go—
VOLTORE   But Mosca—
MOSCA   Age will conquer.
VOLTORE   Pray thee, hear me.
   Am I inscribed his heir for certain?
MOSCA   Are you?
   I do beseech you, sir, you will vouchsafe
35 To write me i'your family.² All my hopes
   Depend upon Your Worship. I am lost
   Except° the rising sun do shine on me.   *unless*
VOLTORE   It shall both shine and warm thee, Mosca.
MOSCA   Sir,
   I am a man that have not done your love
40 All the worst offices:° here I wear your keys,   *services*
   See all your coffers and your caskets locked,
   Keep the poor inventory of your jewels,
   Your plate, and moneys, am your steward, sir,
   Husband your goods here.
VOLTORE   But am I sole heir?
45 MOSCA   Without a partner, sir, confirmed this morning;
   The wax° is warm yet, and the ink scarce dry   *of the seal*
   Upon the parchment.
VOLTORE   Happy, happy me!
   By what good chance, sweet Mosca?
MOSCA   Your desert, sir;
   I know no second cause.
VOLTORE   Thy modesty
50   Is loath to know it.° Well, we shall requite it.   *admit your role*
MOSCA   He ever liked your course, sir; that first took him.
   I oft have heard him say how he admired
   Men of your large³ profession, that could speak
   To every cause, and things mere contraries,°   *utterly contradictory*
55 Till they were hoarse again, yet all be law;
   That with most quick agility could turn
   And re-turn, make knots and undo them,
   Give forkèd° counsel, take provoking gold   *ambiguous*

---

2. Employ me in your household (after Volpone's death).

3. Expansive, liberal (with the suggestion of "unscrupulous").

On either hand, and put it up:[4] these men,
He knew, would thrive with their humility.°   *obsequiousness*
And for his part, he thought he should be blessed
To have his heir of such a suffering° spirit,   *long-suffering*
So wise, so grave, of so perplexed° a tongue,   *bewildering*
And loud withal,° that would not wag nor scarce   *besides*
Lie still without a fee, when every word
Your Worship but lets fall is a *cecchine!*°   *Another knocks.*   *gold coin*
Who's that? One knocks; I would not have you seen, sir.
And yet—pretend you came and went in haste;
I'll fashion an excuse. And, gentle sir,
When you do come to swim in golden lard,
Up to the arms in honey, that your chin
Is born up stiff with fatness of the flood,
Think on your vassal; but° remember me.   *only*
I ha' not been your worst of clients.

VOLTORE   Mosca—
MOSCA   When will you have your inventory brought, sir?
Or see a copy of the will? [*More knocking.*] Anon!°—   *Just a minute!*
I'll bring 'em to you, sir. Away, begone,
Put business i'your face.[5]   [*Exit* VOLTORE.]
VOLPONE   Excellent, Mosca!
Come hither, let me kiss thee.
MOSCA   Keep you still, sir.
Here is Corbaccio.
VOLPONE   Set the plate away.
The vulture's gone, and the old raven's come.

SCENE 4. *The scene continues.*

MOSCA [*to* VOLPONE]   Betake you to your silence and your sleep;
     [*He puts up the plate.*]
Stand there and multiply.°—Now shall we see   *beget more booty*
A wretch who is indeed more impotent
Than this° can feign to be, yet hopes to hop   *Volpone*
Over his grave.
     [*Enter*] CORBACCIO.
        Signor Corbaccio!
You're very welcome, sir.
CORBACCIO   How does your patron?
MOSCA   Troth, as he did, sir: no amends.
CORBACCIO   What? Mends he?
MOSCA   No, sir, he is rather worse.
CORBACCIO   That's well. Where is he?
MOSCA   Upon his couch, sir, newly fall'n asleep.
CORBACCIO   Does he sleep well?
MOSCA   No wink, sir, all this night,

---

4. Take a bribe from each party to a suit and pocket it.

5. Look as if you were here on business.

Nor yesterday, but slumbers.° — *dozes fitfully*
CORBACCIO   Good! He should take
Some counsel of physicians. I have brought him
An opiate here, from mine own doctor—
MOSCA   He will not hear of drugs.
CORBACCIO   Why, I myself
Stood by while't was made, saw all th'ingredients,
And know it cannot but most gently work.
My life for his, 'tis but to make him sleep.
VOLPONE [*aside*]   Ay, his last sleep, if he would take it.
MOSCA   Sir,
He has no faith in physic.° — *medicine*
CORBACCIO   'Say you? 'Say you?
MOSCA   He has no faith in physic. He does think
Most of your doctors[1] are the greater danger
And worse disease t'escape. I often have
Heard him protest that your physician
Should never be his heir.
CORBACCIO   Not I his heir?
MOSCA   Not your physician, sir.
CORBACCIO   Oh, no, no, no,
I do not mean it.
MOSCA   No, sir, nor their fees
He cannot brook.° He says they flay° a man — *tolerate / skin*
Before they kill him.
CORBACCIO   Right, I do conceive° you. — *understand*
MOSCA   And then, they do it by experiment,[2]
For which the law not only doth absolve 'em,
But gives them great reward; and he is loath
To hire his death so.
CORBACCIO   It is true, they kill
With as much license as a judge.
MOSCA   Nay, more:
For he° but kills, sir, where the law condemns, — *the judge*
And these° can kill him,° too. — *the doctors / the judge*
CORBACCIO   Ay, or me
Or any man. How does his apoplex?° — *apoplexy, stroke*
Is that strong on him still?
MOSCA   Most violent.[3]
His speech is broken and his eyes are set,° — *fixed*
His face drawn longer than 'twas wont—
CORBACCIO   How? How?
Stronger than he was wont?
MOSCA   No, sir: his face
Drawn longer than 'twas wont.

1.4
1. Not Corbaccio's doctors, but doctors generally. (Also in line 23.)
2. By testing possible remedies on their patients.

3. In the following lines, Mosca attributes to Volpone a wide variety of symptoms that were, even occurring singly, considered sure signs of impending death.

CORBACCIO   Oh, good.
MOSCA   His mouth
    Is ever gaping, and his eyelids hang.
CORBACCIO   Good.
MOSCA   A freezing numbness stiffens all his joints,
    And makes the color of his flesh like lead.
CORBACCIO   'Tis good.
MOSCA   His pulse beats slow and dull.
CORBACCIO   Good symptoms still.
MOSCA   And from his brain—
CORBACCIO   Ha? How? Not from his brain?
MOSCA   Yes, sir, and from his brain—
CORBACCIO   I conceive you, good.
MOSCA   —Flows a cold sweat with a continual rheum°   *mucus discharge*
    Forth the resolvèd° corners of his eyes.   *watery; limp*
CORBACCIO   Is't possible? Yet I am better, ha!
    How does he with the swimming of his head?
MOSCA   Oh, sir, 'tis past the scotomy;[4] he now
    Hath lost his feeling, and hath left to snort;°   *stopped snoring*
    You hardly can perceive him that he breathes.
CORBACCIO   Excellent, excellent. Sure I shall outlast him!
    This makes me young again a score of years.
MOSCA   I was a-coming for you, sir.
CORBACCIO   Has he made his will?
    What has he giv'n me?
MOSCA   No, sir.
CORBACCIO   Nothing? Ha?
MOSCA   He has not made his will, sir.
CORBACCIO   Oh, oh, oh.
    What then did Voltore, the lawyer, here?
MOSCA   He smelt a carcass, sir, when he but heard
    My master was about his testament°—   *making his will*
    As I did urge him to it, for your good—
CORBACCIO   He came unto him, did he? I thought so.
MOSCA   Yes, and presented him this piece of plate.
CORBACCIO   To be his heir?
MOSCA   I do not know, sir.
CORBACCIO   True,
    I know it too.
MOSCA [*aside*]   By your own scale,° sir.   *scale of values*
CORBACCIO [*showing a bag of gold*]   Well,
    I shall prevent° him yet. See, Mosca, look,   *forestall*
    Here I have brought a bag of bright *cecchines*,
    Will quite weigh down his plate.
MOSCA   Yea, marry, sir!
    This is true physic, this your sacred medicine;
    No talk of opiates to° this great elixir.[5]   *compared to*

---

4. Dizziness, accompanied by partial blindness.
5. In alchemy, a liquid thought to be capable of prolonging life indefinitely or changing base metal into gold.

CORBACCIO 'Tis *aurum palpabile,* if not *potabile.*[6]
MOSCA It shall be ministered to him in his bowl?
CORBACCIO Ay, do, do, do.
MOSCA   Most blessed cordial!°   *heart medicine*
This will recover him.
CORBACCIO   Yes, do, do, do.
MOSCA I think it were not best, sir.
CORBACCIO   What?
MOSCA   To recover him.
CORBACCIO Oh, no, no, no; by no means.
MOSCA   Why, sir, this
Will work some strange effect, if he but feel it.
CORBACCIO 'Tis true, therefore forbear, I'll take my venture.°   *investment*
Give me 't again. [*He snatches for the bag.*]
MOSCA [*keeping it out of his reach*] At no hand.° Pardon me,   *By no means*
You shall not do yourself that wrong, sir. I
Will so advise you, you shall have it all.
CORBACCIO How?
MOSCA   All, sir, 'tis your right, your own; no man
Can claim a part. 'Tis yours without a rival,
Decreed by destiny.
CORBACCIO   How? How, good Mosca?
MOSCA I'll tell you, sir. This fit he shall recover—
CORBACCIO I do conceive you.
MOSCA   —and, on first advantage°   *opportunity*
Of his gained sense, will I re-importune him
Unto the making of his testament,
And show him this.
CORBACCIO   Good, good.
MOSCA   'Tis better yet,
If you will hear, sir.
CORBACCIO   Yes, with all my heart.
MOSCA Now, would I counsel you, make home with speed;
There frame a will, whereto you shall inscribe
My master your sole heir.
CORBACCIO   And disinherit
My son?
MOSCA Oh, sir, the better, for that color°   *appearance, fiction*
Shall make it much more taking.°   *plausible; attractive*
CORBACCIO   Oh, but color?°   *it's only a ruse?*
MOSCA This will, sir, you shall send it unto me.
Now, when I come to enforce°—as I will do—   *urge*
Your cares, your watchings, and your many prayers,
Your more than many gifts, your this day's present,
And last produce your will, where—without thought
Or least regard unto your proper issue,°   *own offspring*
A son so brave° and highly meriting—   *splendid*

---

6. It is gold that can be felt, if not drunk (Latin). Dissolved gold was used as a medicine.

The stream of your diverted love hath thrown you
Upon my master, and made him your heir,
He cannot be so stupid or stone dead
But out of conscience and mere gratitude—
CORBACCIO He must pronounce me his?
MOSCA   'Tis true.
CORBACCIO   This plot
Did I think on before.
MOSCA   I do believe it.
CORBACCIO Do you not believe it?
MOSCA   Yes, sir.
CORBACCIO   Mine own project.
MOSCA Which when he hath done, sir—
CORBACCIO   Published me his heir?
MOSCA And you so certain to survive him—
CORBACCIO   Ay.
MOSCA Being so lusty a man—
CORBACCIO   'Tis true.
MOSCA   Yes, sir—
CORBACCIO I thought on that too. See how he° should be   *Mosca*
The very organ to express my thoughts!
MOSCA You have not only done yourself a good—
CORBACCIO But multiplied it on my son?
MOSCA   'Tis right, sir.
CORBACCIO Still my invention.
MOSCA   'Las, sir, heaven knows,
It hath been all my study, all my care,
(I e'en grow gray withal) how to work things—
CORBACCIO I do conceive, sweet Mosca.
MOSCA   You are he
For whom I labor here.
CORBACCIO   Ay, do, do, do.
I'll straight about it.   [CORBACCIO *starts to leave*.]
MOSCA   Rook go with you,[7] raven!
CORBACCIO I know thee honest.
MOSCA   You do lie, sir—
CORBACCIO   And—
MOSCA Your knowledge is no better than your ears, sir.
CORBACCIO I do not doubt to be a father to thee.
MOSCA Nor I to gull my brother of his blessing.[8]
CORBACCIO I may ha' my youth restored to me, why not?
MOSCA Your Worship is a precious ass—
CORBACCIO   What say'st thou?
MOSCA I do desire Your Worship to make haste, sir.

---

7. May you be swindled ("rooked"). Playing on "rook" meaning "crow," "raven." This speech and Mosca's following lines, through line 130, could be considered asides since Corbaccio cannot hear them; but they need not be delivered sotto voce.

8. If Corbaccio were Mosca's father, then Bonario would be his brother. A reference to Genesis 25, in which Jacob tricks his elder brother, Esau, into resigning his birthright, and Genesis 27, in which Jacob tricks their dying father, Isaac, into giving him the paternal blessing and property.

CORBACCIO 'Tis done, 'tis done, I go.   [*Exit.*]
VOLPONE [*leaping from the bed*]   Oh, I shall burst!
    Let out my sides,° let out my sides—   *loosen my clothes*
MOSCA   Contain
    Your flux of laughter, sir. You know this hope
135 Is such a bait it covers any hook.
VOLPONE   Oh, but thy working and thy placing it!
    I cannot hold;° good rascal, let me kiss thee.   *contain my delight*
    I never knew thee in so rare a humor.°   *so excellently witty*
MOSCA   Alas, sir, I but do as I am taught:
140 Follow your grave instructions, give 'em words,
    Pour oil into their ears,° and send them hence.   *flatter them*
VOLPONE   'Tis true, 'tis true. What a rare punishment
    Is avarice to itself!⁹
MOSCA   Ay, with our help, sir.
VOLPONE   So many cares, so many maladies,
145 So many fears attending on old age,
    Yea, death so often called on,° as no wish   *invoked*
    Can be more frequent with 'em, their limbs faint,
    Their senses dull, their seeing, hearing, going,° *ability to walk*
    All dead before them; yea, their very teeth,
150 Their instruments of eating, failing them—
    Yet this is reckoned life! Nay, here was one
    Is now gone home that wishes to live longer!
    Feels not his gout nor palsy, feigns himself
    Younger by scores of years, flatters his age
155 With confident belying it,¹ hopes he may
    With charms, like Aeson,² have his youth restored,
    And with these thoughts so battens,° as if fate   *gluts himself*
    Would be as easily cheated on as he,
    And all turns air!°   Another knocks.   *is illusory*
    Who's that there, now? A third?
160 **MOSCA**   Close,° to your couch again. I hear his voice.   *hide yourself*
    It is Corvino, our spruce° merchant.   *dapper*
VOLPONE [*lying down again*]   Dead.°   *I'll play dead*
MOSCA   Another bout, sir, with your eyes.
    [*He applies ointment.*]
                            Who's there?

SCENE 5. *The scene continues.*

[*Enter*] CORVINO.
    Signor Corvino! Come° most wished for! Oh,   *you come*
    How happy were you if you knew it now!
CORVINO   Why? What? Wherein?
MOSCA   The tardy hour is come, sir.

---

9. Quoting the Stoic philosopher Seneca's *Moral Epistles*, no. 115.
1. Deceives himself, and attempts to deceive others, about his age by vigorously refusing to admit the truth.
2. Father of the Greek hero Jason; his youth was restored by Medea, his sorceress daughter-in-law.

CORVINO He is not dead?
MOSCA   Not dead, sir, but as good;
  He knows no man.
CORVINO   How shall I do, then?
MOSCA   Why, sir?
CORVINO I have brought him here a pearl.
MOSCA   Perhaps he has
  So much remembrance left as to know you, sir;
  He still calls on you; nothing but your name
  Is in his mouth. Is your pearl orient,¹ sir?
CORVINO Venice was never owner of the like.
VOLPONE [*weakly*] Signor Corvino—
MOSCA   Hark.
VOLPONE   —Signor Corvino—
MOSCA He calls you. Step and give it him.—He's here, sir,
  And he has brought you a rich pearl.
CORVINO [*to* VOLPONE]   How do you, sir?
  [*To* MOSCA] Tell him it doubles the twelfth carat.²
      [*He gives* VOLPONE *the pearl.*]
MOSCA [*to* CORVINO]   Sir,
  He cannot understand. His hearing's gone;
  And yet it comforts him to see you—
CORVINO   Say
  I have a diamond for him too.
MOSCA   Best show't, sir.
  Put it into his hand; 'tis only there
  He apprehends; he has his feeling yet.
      [CORVINO *gives* VOLPONE *the diamond.*]
  See how he grasps it!
CORVINO   'Las, good gentleman!
  How pitiful the sight is!
MOSCA   Tut, forget, sir.
  The weeping of an heir should still° be laughter   *always*
  Under a visor.°   *mask*
CORVINO Why, am I his heir?
MOSCA Sir, I am sworn; I may not show the will
  Till he be dead. But here has been Corbaccio,
  Here has been Voltore, here were others too,
  I cannot number 'em they were so many,
  All gaping here for legacies; but I,
  Taking the vantage° of his naming you—   *opportunity*
  "Signor Corvino! Signor Corvino!"—took
  Paper and pen and ink, and there I asked him
  Whom he would have his heir? "Corvino." Who
  Should be executor? "Corvino." And
  To any question he was silent to,

1.5
1. Especially brilliant. (The most beautiful pearls came from the Indian Ocean.)
2. In the seventeenth century, a carat was between 1/144 and 1/150 of an ounce. A twenty-four-carat pearl was therefore very large, weighing roughly 1/6 of an ounce.

I still interpreted the nods he made
Through weakness for consent, and sent home th'others,
Nothing bequeathed them but to cry and curse.
CORVINO Oh, my dear Mosca! [*They embrace.*] Does he not perceive us?
MOSCA No more than a blind harper.³ He knows no man,
No face of friend, nor name of any servant,
Who 'twas that fed him last or gave him drink;
Not those he hath begotten or brought up
Can he remember.
CORVINO   Has he children?
MOSCA   Bastards,⁴
Some dozen or more, that he begot on beggars,
Gypsies and Jews and blackmoors,° when he was drunk. *black Africans*
Knew you not that, sir? 'Tis the common fable.°   *rumor*
The dwarf, the fool, the eunuch are all his;
He's the true father of his family
In all save° me, but he has given 'em nothing.   *except*
CORVINO That's well, that's well. Art sure he does not hear us?
MOSCA Sure, sir? Why, look you, credit your own sense.° *believe your senses*
[*Shouting at* VOLPONE] The pox° approach and add to   *syphilis*
your diseases
If it would send you hence the sooner, sir.
For your incontinence, it hath deserved it
Throughly° and throughly, and the plague to boot.   *thoroughly*
[*To* CORVINO] You may come near, sir. [*shouting at* VOLPONE *again*]
Would you would once close
Those filthy eyes of yours, that flow with slime
Like two frog-pits,° and those same hanging cheeks, *mud puddles*
Covered with hide instead of skin—nay, help, sir—
That look like frozen dishclouts° set on end!   *dishrags*
CORVINO [*shouting at* VOLPONE] Or like an old smoked wall on which the rain
Ran down in streaks!
MOSCA   Excellent, sir! Speak out;
You may be louder yet; a culverin°   *firearm*
Dischargèd in his ear would hardly bore it.
CORVINO [*shouting*] His nose is like a common sewer, still°   *continually*
running.
MOSCA 'Tis good! And what his mouth?
CORVINO [*shouting*]   A very draught!°   *cesspool*
MOSCA Oh, stop it up—
CORVINO   By no means.
MOSCA   Pray you let me.
Faith, I could stifle him rarely with a pillow
As well as any woman that should keep° him.   *take care of*
CORVINO Do as you will, but I'll be gone.

3. Harp players were often blind.
4. By law, ordinarily barred from the line of inheritance.

70	MOSCA	Be so;
It is your presence makes him last so long.
CORVINO   I pray you, use no violence.
MOSCA   No, sir? Why?
Why should you be thus scrupulous? Pray you, sir.
CORVINO   Nay, at your discretion.
MOSCA   Well, good sir, begone.
75 CORVINO   I will not trouble him now to take my pearl?
MOSCA   Pooh! Nor your diamond. What a needless care
Is this afflicts you? Is not all here yours?
Am not I here, whom you have made your creature?
That owe my being to you?
CORVINO   Grateful Mosca!
80 Thou art my friend, my fellow, my companion,
My partner, and shalt share in all my fortunes.
MOSCA   Excepting one.
CORVINO   What's that?
MOSCA   Your gallant° wife, sir.   *splendid*
[*Exit* CORVINO.]
Now is he gone. We had no other means
To shoot him hence but this.
VOLPONE   My divine Mosca!
Thou hast today outgone thyself.   *Another knocks.*
85   Who's there?
I will be troubled with no more. Prepare
Me music, dances, banquets, all delights.
The Turk[5] is not more sensual in his pleasures
Than will Volpone.   [*Exit* MOSCA.]
       Let me see, a pearl?
90 A diamond? Plate? *Cecchines?* Good morning's purchase.°   *haul*
Why, this is better than rob churches, yet,
Or fat by eating, once a month, a man.°   *by taking monthly interest*
[*Enter* MOSCA.]
Who is't?
MOSCA   The beauteous Lady Would-be, sir,
Wife to the English knight, Sir Politic Would-be—
95 This is the style, sir, is directed me[6]—
Hath sent to know how you have slept tonight,°   *last night*
And if you would be visited.
VOLPONE   Not now.
Some three hours hence—
MOSCA   I told the squire° so much.   *messenger*
VOLPONE   When I am high with mirth and wine: then, then.
100 'Fore heaven, I wonder at the desperate° valor   *reckless*
Of the bold English, that they dare let loose
Their wives to all encounters![7]

---

5. Stereotyped as given to decadent luxuries.
6. This is the mode of address I've been told to use.
7. Married Englishwomen were reputed to enjoy more personal freedom than their southern European counterparts; Venetian wives in particular were much restricted, though Celia's situation is obviously extreme (see below, p. 964, lines 118–26).

MOSCA   Sir, this knight
   Had not his name for nothing. He is politic,°   *canny*
   And knows, howe'er his wife affect strange° airs,   *foreign; bizarre*
   She hath not yet the face[8] to be dishonest.°   *unchaste*
   But had she Signor Corvino's wife's face—
VOLPONE   Has she so rare a face?
MOSCA   Oh, sir, the wonder,
   The blazing star[9] of Italy! A wench
   O'the first year!° A beauty ripe as harvest!   *unflawed and in her prime*
   Whose skin is whiter than a swan, all over,
   Than silver, snow, or lilies! A soft lip,
   Would° tempt you to eternity of kissing!   *that would*
   And flesh that melteth in the touch to blood![1]
   Bright as your gold, and lovely as your gold!
VOLPONE   Why had not I known this before?
MOSCA   Alas, sir,
   Myself but yesterday discovered it.
VOLPONE   How might I see her?
MOSCA   Oh, not possible.
   She's kept as warily as is your gold:
   Never does come abroad,° never takes air   *outside*
   But at a window. All her looks are sweet
   As the first° grapes or cherries, and are watched   *of the season*
   As near° as they are.   *closely*
VOLPONE   I must see her—
MOSCA   Sir,
   There is a guard of ten spies thick upon her—
   All his whole household—each of which is set
   Upon his fellow, and have all their charge
   When he goes out; when he comes in, examined.[2]
VOLPONE   I will go see her, though but at her window.
MOSCA   In some disguise, then.
VOLPONE   That is true. I must
   Maintain mine own shape still the same.[3] We'll think.
                                                        [*Exeunt.*]

Act 2

SCENE 1. *Saint Mark's Square.*

   [*Enter*] POLITIC WOULD-BE [*and*] PEREGRINE.
POLITIC   Sir, to a wise man all the world's his soil.[1]
   It is not Italy, nor France, nor Europe
   That must bound me if my fates call me forth.
   Yet I protest it is no salt° desire   *inordinate*

---

8. (1) Beauty; (2) shamelessness.
9. Comet. (Rare and beautiful.)
1. (1) Blushes; (2) sexual responsiveness. (Mosca is evidently conjecturing here.)
2. Each member of the household spies on all the others; each gets his instructions when Corvino departs and is interrogated when he returns.
3. I must, in my own person, continue to pretend to be near death.
2.1
1. Proverbial, like most of Sir Pol's "original" advice. "Soil": native land.

	Of seeing countries, shifting a religion,[2]	
5	Nor any disaffection to the state	
	Where I was bred—and unto which I owe	
	My dearest plots°—hath brought me out;° much less	projects / abroad
	That idle, antique, stale, gray-headed project	
10	Of knowing men's minds and manners with Ulysses;[3]	
	But a peculiar humor° of my wife's	whim
	Laid for this height° of Venice, to observe,	latitude
	To quote,° to learn the language, and so forth.—	jot things down
	I hope you travel, sir, with license?[4]	

PEREGRINE   Yes.
POLITIC   I dare the safelier converse. How long, sir,
15 Since you left England?
PEREGRINE   Seven weeks.
POLITIC   So lately!
You ha' not been with my Lord Ambassador?
PEREGRINE   Not yet, sir.
POLITIC   Pray you, what news, sir, vents our climate?[5]
I heard last night a most strange thing reported
20 By some of my lord's° followers, and I long   *the ambassador's*
To hear how't will be seconded.°   *confirmed*
PEREGRINE   What was't, sir?
POLITIC   Marry, sir, of a raven that should build°   *reportedly built*
In a ship royal of the King's.
PEREGRINE [*aside*]   This fellow,
Does he gull° me, trow?° Or is gulled?—Your name, sir?   *trick / do you suppose?*
POLITIC   My name is Politic Would-be.
25 PEREGRINE [*aside*]   Oh, that speaks° him.—   *characterizes*
A knight, sir?
POLITIC   A poor knight, sir.[6]
PEREGRINE   Your lady
Lies° here in Venice for intelligence°   *stays / news*
Of tires° and fashions and behavior   *apparel*
Among the courtesans?[7] The fine Lady Would-be?
30 POLITIC   Yes, sir, the spider and the bee ofttimes
Suck from one flower.
PEREGRINE   Good Sir Politic,
I cry you mercy!° I have heard much of you.   *beg your pardon*
'Tis true, sir, of your raven.
POLITIC   On your knowledge?
PEREGRINE   Yes, and your lion's whelping in the Tower.[8]
POLITIC   Another whelp!

---

2. Throughout the 16th and 17th centuries, members of religious minorities throughout Europe sought refuge in lands more hospitable to their faiths.
3. The hero of the *Odyssey*, an archetype of the wise traveler.
4. A passport. (English people could not travel abroad without permission.)
5. Comes from our part of the world?
6. In the first decade of the 17th century, King James I raised badly needed money by selling knighthoods to many whose birth, attainments, or wealth would not have previously merited a title.
7. Venice was famous for its elegant prostitutes.
8. A lioness kept at the Tower of London gave birth in 1604 and 1605.

PEREGRINE	Another, sir.	
35 POLITIC	Now, heaven!	
	What prodigies° be these? The fires at Berwick!	*strange occurrences*
	And the new star![9] These things concurring,° strange!	*happening together*
	And full of omen! Saw you those meteors?	
PEREGRINE	I did, sir.	
POLITIC	Fearful! Pray you sir, confirm me:	
40	Were there three porpoises seen above the bridge,[1]	
	As they give out?°	*people report*
PEREGRINE	Six, and a sturgeon, sir.	
POLITIC	I am astonished!	
PEREGRINE	Nay, sir, be not so.	
	I'll tell you a greater prodigy than these—	
POLITIC	What should these things portend!	
PEREGRINE	The very day—	
45	Let me be sure—that I put forth from London,	
	There was a whale discovered in the river	
	As high° as Woolwich,[2] that had waited there—	*far upstream*
	Few know how many months—for the subversion	
	Of the Stode Fleet.[3]	
POLITIC	Is't possible? Believe it,	
50	'Twas either sent from Spain or the Archdukes.[4]	
	Spinola's[5] whale, upon my life, my credit!°	*honor*
	Will they not leave these projects? Worthy sir,	
	Some other news.	
PEREGRINE	Faith, Stone the fool is dead;	
	And they do lack a tavern-fool extremely.	
POLITIC	Is Mas' Stone dead?[6]	
55 PEREGRINE	He's dead, sir. Why, I hope	
	You thought him not immortal? [*aside*] Oh, this knight,	
	Were he well known, would be a precious thing	
	To fit our English stage. He that should write	
	But such a fellow should be thought to feign	
	Extremely, if not maliciously.	
60 POLITIC	Stone dead!	
PEREGRINE	Dead. Lord, how deeply, sir, you apprehend it!	
	He was no kinsman to you?	
POLITIC	That° I know of,	*not that*
	Well, that same fellow was an unknown fool.[7]	

---

9. The fires at Berwick were aurora borealis visible above Berwick, Northumberland, in 1605, said to resemble battling armies. The new star, a supernova, was described by the astronomer Johannes Kepler in 1604.
1. A porpoise was found upstream of London Bridge in the Thames River the January before *Volpone* was first performed.
2. A town on the Thames, a bit to the east of London.
3. The English merchant adventurers' ships, which were harboring at Stade, in the mouth of the Elbe River.
4. The Archduke Albert of Austria and his wife, Isabella, the Infanta of Spain, ruled the Netherlands in the name of Spain.
5. Ambrosio de Spinola was general of the Spanish army in the Netherlands.
6. "Mas'" means "master," a term of address for boys and fools. Stone, King James's outspoken court jester, was a well-known urban character. He was whipped the year before *Volpone*'s first performance for slandering the Lord Admiral. Politic is evidently unaware of the play on words in "Stone dead."
7. The person who said this was not commonly recognized as a spy; he used foolery as his cover.

PEREGRINE   And yet you knew him, it seems?
POLITIC   I did so. Sir,
   I knew him one of the most dangerous heads
   Living within the state, and so I held° him.   *considered*
PEREGRINE   Indeed, sir?
POLITIC   While he lived, in action,°   *subversive activities*
   He has received weekly intelligence,
   Upon my knowledge, out of the Low Countries,
   For all parts of the world, in cabbages,°   *a Dutch import*
   And those dispensed again to ambassadors
   In oranges, muskmelons, apricots,
   Lemons, pome-citrons,° and suchlike—sometimes   *grapefruitlike fruits*
   In Colchester oysters, and your Selsey cockles.⁸
PEREGRINE   You make me wonder!
POLITIC   Sir, upon my knowledge.
   Nay, I have observed him at your public ordinary°   *tavern*
   Take his advertisement° from a traveler—   *information*
   A concealed statesman—in a trencher° of meat,   *wooden plate*
   And instantly before the meal was done
   Convey an answer in a toothpick.⁹
PEREGRINE   Strange!
   How could this be, sir?
POLITIC   Why, the meat was cut
   So like his character,° and so laid as he   *code letters*
   Must easily read the cipher.
PEREGRINE   I have heard
   He could not read, sir.
POLITIC   So 'twas given out,
   In polity,° by those that did employ him.   *craftily*
   But he could read, and had your languages,°   *knew foreign languages*
   And to't° as sound a noddle°—   *in addition / head*
PEREGRINE   I have heard, sir,
   That your baboons were spies, and that they were
   A kind of subtle nation near to China.
POLITIC   Ay, ay, your *Mamuluchi*.¹ Faith, they had
   Their hand in a French plot or two, but they
   Were so extremely given to women as
   They made discovery of° all. Yet I   *revealed*
   Had my advices° here, on Wednesday last,   *information*
   From one of their own coat;° they were returned,   *kind*
   Made their relations,° as the fashion is,   *reports*
   And now stand fair° for fresh employment.   *ready*
PEREGRINE [*aside*]   Heart,
   This Sir Pol will be° ignorant of nothing.   *admit to being*
   [*To* POLITIC] It seems, sir, you know all?
POLITIC   Not all, sir. But

---

8. Expensive delicacies, unlikely tavern fare.
9. Presumably by inserting a tiny note into a toothpick hollowed out for espionage use.

1. Mamluks, a class of warriors originally from Asia Minor, who ruled Egypt from 1250 to 1517.

968 | BEN JONSON

100		I have some general notions; I do love	
		To note and to observe. Though I live out,°	*abroad*
		Free from the active torrent, yet I'd mark	
		The currents and the passages of things	
		For mine own private use, and know the ebbs	
		And flows of state.	
105	PEREGRINE	Believe it, sir, I hold	
		Myself in no small tie unto my fortunes°	*much obliged to my luck*
		For casting me thus luckily upon you,	
		Whose knowledge—if your bounty equal it—	
		May do me great assistance in instruction	
110		For my behavior and my bearing, which	
		Is yet so rude and raw—	
	POLITIC	Why, came you forth	
		Empty of rules for travel?	
	PEREGRINE	Faith, I had	
		Some common ones from out that vulgar grammar,[2]	
		Which he that cried° Italian to me taught me.	*taught orally*
115	POLITIC	Why, this it is that spoils all our brave bloods,°	*fine young men*
		Trusting our hopeful° gentry unto pedants,	*promising*
		Fellows of outside and mere bark.[3] You seem	
		To be a gentleman of ingenuous race°—	*honorable family*
		I not profess it,° but my fate hath been	*don't declare it openly*
120		To be where I have been consulted with	
		In this high kind,° touching some great men's sons,	*important matter*
		Persons of blood° and honor—	*noble birth*
	PEREGRINE	Who be these, sir?	

SCENE 2. *The scene continues.*

[*Enter*] MOSCA [*and*] NANO [*disguised as a mountebank's assistants*].

	MOSCA	Under that window, there't must be. The same.	
		[MOSCA *and* NANO *set up a platform.*]	
	POLITIC	Fellows to mount a bank!° Did your instructor	*platform*
		In the dear tongues[1] never discourse to you	
		Of the Italian mountebanks?	
	PEREGRINE	Yes, sir.	
	POLITIC	Why,	
		Here shall you see one.	
5	PEREGRINE	They are quacksalvers,	
		Fellows that live by venting° oils and drugs.	*selling*
	POLITIC	Was that the character he gave you of them?	
	PEREGRINE	As I remember.	
	POLITIC	Pity his ignorance.	
		They are the only knowing men of Europe!	
10		Great general scholars, excellent physicians,	
		Most admired statesmen, professed favorites	

2. Modern language textbook, which sometimes included travelers' tips.
3. Superficial accomplishments.

2.2
1. Italian was called the "cara lingua," a phrase Sir Pol translates.

And cabinet counselors° to the greatest princes! *close advisers*
The only languaged° men of all the world! *most eloquent*
PEREGRINE   And I have heard they are most lewd° impostors, *ignorant*
Made all of terms° and shreds, no less beliers *jargon*
Of great men's favors than their own vile med'cines,
Which they will utter° upon monstrous oaths, *advertise for sale*
Selling that drug for twopence ere they part
Which they have valued at twelve crowns° before. *silver or gold coins*
POLITIC   Sir, calumnies are answered best with silence.
Yourself shall judge. [*to* MOSCA *and* NANO] Who is it mounts, my friends?
MOSCA   Scoto of Mantua,[2] sir.
POLITIC   Is't he? [*to* PEREGRINE] Nay, then,
I'll proudly promise, sir, you shall behold
Another man than has been fancied° to you. *presented in imagination*
I wonder yet that he should mount his bank
Here in this nook, that has been wont t'appear
In face of° the piazza! Here he comes. *facing*
[*Enter*] VOLPONE [*disguised as a mountebank, followed by*] *a crowd*.
VOLPONE [*to* NANO]   Mount, zany.° *clown; performer*
[VOLPONE *and* NANO *climb onto the platform.*]
CROWD   Follow, follow, follow, follow, follow!
POLITIC   See how the people follow him! He's a man
May write ten thousand crowns in bank here. Note,
Mark but his gesture. I do use° to observe *make it my practice*
The state° he keeps, in getting up. *stateliness*
PEREGRINE   'Tis worth it, sir.
VOLPONE   Most noble gentlemen and my worthy patrons, it may seem strange that I, your Scoto Mantuano, who was ever wont to fix my bank in face of the public piazza near the shelter of the portico to the *procuratia*,[3] should now, after eight months' absence from this illustrious city of Venice, humbly retire myself into an obscure nook of the piazza.
POLITIC [*to* PEREGRINE]   Did not I now object the same?° *ask the same question*
PEREGRINE   Peace, sir.
VOLPONE   Let me tell you: I am not, as your Lombard proverb saith, cold on my feet,° or content to part with my commodities at a cheaper rate than I accustomed; look not for it. Nor that the calumnious reports of that impudent detractor and shame to our profession (Alessandro Buttone,° I mean) who gave out in public I was condemned a '*sforzato*° to the galleys for poisoning the Cardinal Bembo's—cook,[4] hath at all attached,° much less dejected me. No, no, worthy gentlemen. To tell you true, I cannot *in desperate straits* / *a rival mountebank* / *prisoner* / *stuck to*

---

2. An Italian juggler and magician who visited England and performed before Elizabeth I in the 1570s.
3. Arcade on the north side of the Piazza di San Marco.
4. Pietro Bembo (1470–1547) was a famous humanist, featured as a speaker in Castiglione's *Courtier* (1528). "Cook" is a teasing substitution for "whore."

endure to see the rabble of these ground *ciarlitani*,[5] that spread their cloaks on the pavement as if they meant to do feats of activity° and then come in lamely with their moldy tales out of Boccaccio, like stale Tabarine,[6] the fabulist: some of them discoursing their travels and of their tedious captivity in the Turks' galleys, when indeed, were the truth known, they were the Christians' galleys, where very temperately they ate bread and drunk water as a wholesome penance, enjoined them by their confessors, for base pilferies.

° acrobatics

POLITIC [*to* PEREGRINE] Note but his bearing and contempt of these.

VOLPONE These turdy-facy-nasty-paty-lousy-fartical rogues, with one poor groatsworth° of unprepared antimony,[7] finely wrapped up in several *scartoccios*,° are able very well to kill their twenty a week, and play;° yet these meager starved spirits, who have half stopped the organs of their minds with earthy oppilations,° want° not their favorers among your shriveled, salad-eating artisans, who are overjoyed that they may have their ha'p'orth° of physic; though it purge 'em into another world, 't makes no matter.

° fourpenceworth
° paper envelopes
° as if a game
° obstructions / lack
° halfpennyworth

POLITIC Excellent! Ha' you heard better language, sir?

VOLPONE Well, let 'em go.° And, gentlemen, honorable gentlemen, know that for this time, our bank, being thus removed from the clamors of the *canaglia*,° shall be the scene of pleasure and delight. For I have nothing to sell, little or nothing to sell.

° say no more about them
° mob

POLITIC I told you, sir, his end.

PEREGRINE You did so, sir.

VOLPONE I protest, I and my six servants are not able to make of this precious liquor so fast as it is fetched away from my lodging by gentlemen of your city, strangers of the *terra firma*,[8] worshipful merchants, ay, and senators too, who ever since my arrival have detained me to their uses by their splendidous liberalities. And worthily. For what avails your rich man to have his magazines° stuffed with *moscadelli*,° or of° the purest grape, when his physicians prescribe him (on pain of death) to drink nothing but water cocted° with anise seeds? Oh, health, health! The blessing of the rich! The riches of the poor! Who can buy thee at too dear a rate, since there is no enjoying this world without thee? Be not then so sparing of your purses, honorable gentlemen, as to abridge the natural course of life—

° storehouses
° wine / wine of
° boiled

PEREGRINE You see his end?

POLITIC Ay, is't not good?

---

5. Charlatans too poor to afford a "bank," or platform.
6. Boccaccio's *Decameron* is a storehouse of tales. Tabarine was a member of an Italian comic troupe that played in France and perhaps in England.
7. White metal used as an emetic (to cause vomiting) and a poison.
8. Mainland territory of Venice.

VOLPONE   For when a humid flux° or catarrh, by the muta-   *runny discharge*
bility of air, falls from your head into an arm or shoulder
or any other part, take you a ducat or your *cecchine* of
gold and apply to the place affected; see what good effect
it can work. No, no, 'tis this blessed *unguento,°* this rare   *ointment*
extraction, that hath only power to disperse all malignant
humors that proceed either of hot, cold, moist, or windy
causes⁹—
PEREGRINE   I would he had put in "dry," too.
POLITIC   Pray you, observe.
VOLPONE   To fortify the most indigest and crude° stomach,   *upset*
ay, were it of one that, through extreme weakness, vomited blood, applying only a warm napkin to the place after
the unction and fricace;° for the *vertigine°* in the head   *massage /*
putting but a drop into your nostrils, likewise behind the   *dizziness*
ears, a most sovereign° and approved remedy; the *mal*   *potent*
caduco, cramps, convulsions, paralyses, epilepsies, *tremor*
cordia, retired nerves, ill vapors of the spleen, stoppings of
the liver, the stone, the strangury, *hernia ventosa, iliaca*
passio; stops a *dysenteria* immediately; easeth the torsion
of the small guts; and cures *melancholia hypochondriaca,*¹
being taken and applied according to my printed receipt.°   *direction*
(*Pointing to his bill and his glass°*). For this is the physician,   *paper and flagon*
this the medicine; this counsels, this cures; this gives the
direction, this works the effect; and in sum, both together
may be termed an abstract of the theoric and practic in the
Aesculapian² art. 'Twill cost you eight crowns. And, Zan
Fritatta,³ pray thee sing a verse extempore in honor of it.
POLITIC   How do you like him, sir?
PEREGRINE   Most strangely, I!
POLITIC   Is not his language rare?°   *unrivaled*
PEREGRINE   But° alchemy   *except for*
I never heard the like, or Broughton's books.⁴

Song

NANO [*sings*]   Had old Hippocrates or Galen,⁵
                 That to their books put med'cines all in,
                 But known this secret, they had never
                 (Of which they will be guilty ever)
                 Been murderers of so much paper,°   *written so much*

---

9. Renaissance medicine was based on the theory of the humors, four bodily fluids whose balance within the body determined both physical and mental health. Their qualities, in various combinations, were hot, cold, moist, and dry; hence Peregrine's comment in the next line.
1. Volpone's list of diseases includes *"mal caduco,"* epilepsy; *"tremor cordia,"* palpitations; "retired nerves," withered sinews; "ill vapors of the spleen," short temper; "stone," kidney stones; "strangury," painful urination; *"hernia ventosa,"* a hernia containing air; *"iliaca passio,"* intestinal cramps; *"dysenteria,"* diarrhea; "torsion of the small guts," spasmodic bowel pain; and *"melancholia hypochondriaca,"* depression.
2. Medical. Aesculapius was the classical god of medicine.
3. Italian dialect for "Jack Omelet," the name of the zany (see line 28), here referring to Nano.
4. Hugh Broughton was a Puritan rabbinical scholar who wrote impenetrable treatises on scriptural matters.
5. Greek physicians (ca. 460–377 B.C.E. and 129–ca. 199 C.E., respectively) who developed the theory of humors.

Or wasted many a hurtless taper;°   *candle (working at night)*
No Indian drug had e'er been famed,
Tobacco, sassafras[6] not named,
Ne° yet of *guacum*[7] one small stick, sir,   *nor*
Nor Raymond Lully's great elixir.
Ne had been known the Danish Gonswart
Or Paracelsus with his long sword.[8]

PEREGRINE   All this yet will not do; eight crowns is high.

VOLPONE [*to* NANO]   No more.—Gentlemen, if I had but time to discourse to you the miraculous effects of this my oil, surnamed *oglio del Scoto*, with the countless catalogue of those I have cured of th'aforesaid and many more diseases, the patents and privileges of all the princes and commonwealths of Christendom, or but the depositions of those that appeared on my part before the signory of the *Sanitá*,[9] and most learned College of Physicians, where I was authorized, upon notice taken of the admirable virtues of my medicaments and mine own excellency in matter of rare and unknown secrets, not only to disperse them publicly in this famous city but in all the territories that happily joy under the government of the most pious and magnificent states of Italy. But may some other gallant fellow say, "Oh, there be divers that make profession° to have   *that claim*
as good and as experimented receipts as yours." Indeed, very many have assayed like apes in imitation of that which is really and essentially in me, to make of° this oil; bestowed   *some of*
great cost in furnaces, stills, alembics,[1] continual fires, and preparation of the ingredients (as indeed there goes to it six hundred several simples,° besides some quantity of   *different ingredients /*
human fat for the conglutination,° which we buy of the   *to glue it together*
anatomists); but, when these practitioners come to the last decoction,° blow, blow, puff, puff, and all flies *in fumo*.°   *boiling down / up in smoke*
Ha, ha, ha! Poor wretches! I rather pity their folly and indiscretion° than their loss of time and money; for those   *lack of discernment*
may be recovered by industry, but to be a fool born is a disease incurable. For myself, I always from my youth have endeavored to get the rarest secrets and book° them, either   *record*
in exchange or for money; I spared nor° cost nor labor   *neither*
where anything was worthy to be learned. And, gentlemen, honorable gentlemen, I will undertake, by virtue of chemical art, out of the honorable hat that covers your head to extract the four elements—that is to say, the fire, air, water, and earth—and return you your felt° without burn or stain.   *felt hat*
For, whilst others have been at the balloo° I have been at   *Venetian ball game*

---

6. New World plants, used medicinally.
7. The bark of a tropical tree, used medicinally.
8. Raymond Lully was a medieval astrologer rumored to have discovered the elixir of life. "Danish Gonswart" has not been positively identified.

Paracelsus was an early 16th-century alchemist who developed an alternative to Galenic medicine; he carried his medicines in his sword pommel.
9. Venetian medical licensing board.
1. Vessels for purifying liquids.

my book, and am now past the craggy paths of study and
come to the flow'ry plains of honor and reputation.
POLITIC   I do assure you, sir, that is his aim.
VOLPONE   But to our price.
PEREGRINE   And that withal,° Sir Pol.   *as well*
VOLPONE   You all know, honorable gentlemen, I never val-
ued this *ampulla*, or vial, at less than eight crowns, but for
this time I am content to be deprived of it for six; six crowns
is the price, and less, in courtesy, I know you cannot offer
me. Take it or leave it howsoever, both it and I am at your
service. I ask you not as the value of the thing, for then I
should demand° of you a thousand crowns; so the Cardi-   *ask*
nals Montalto, Fernese, the great Duke of Tuscany, my
gossip,° with divers other princes, have given me. But I   *buddy*
despise money. Only to show my affection to you, honorable gentlemen, and your illustrious state here, I have
neglected the messages of these princes, mine own offices,°   *duties*
framed° my journey hither only to present you with the   *devised*
fruits of my travels. [*to* NANO *and* MOSCA] Tune your voices
once more to the touch of your instruments, and give the
honorable assembly some delightful recreation.
PEREGRINE   What monstrous and most painful circum-
stance°   *beating around the bush*
Is here, to get some three or four *gazets*!°   *small Venetian coins*
Some threepence, i'th'whole, for that 'twill come to.

SONG
[*During the song,* CELIA *appears at her window, above.*]
NANO [*sings*]°   You that would last long, list to my song,   *accompanied*
Make no more coil,° but buy of this oil.   *by Mosca / fuss*
Would you be ever fair and young?
Stout of teeth and strong of tongue?
Tart° of palate? Quick of ear?   *keen*
Sharp of sight? Of nostril clear?
Moist of hand² and light of foot?
Or (I will come nearer to't)°   *get to the point*
Would you live free from all diseases,
Do the act your mistress pleases,
Yet fright all aches° from your bones?   *venereal disease*
Here's a med'cine for the nones.°   *occasion*
VOLPONE   Well, I am in a humor at this time to make a pres-
ent of the small quantity my coffer contains: to the rich in
courtesy, and to the poor for God's sake.° Wherefore, now   *charity*
mark; I asked you six crowns, and six crowns at other
times you have paid me. You shall not give me six crowns,
nor five, nor four, nor three, nor two, nor one, nor half a
ducat, no, nor a *moccenigo*.° Six—pence it will cost you, or   *worth ninepence*

---

2. Associated with youth and sexual vigor.

six hundred pound—expect no lower price, for by the banner of my front,° I will not bate a *bagatine*,³ that I will have only a pledge of your loves, to carry something from amongst you to show I am not contemned° by you. Therefore now, toss your handkerchiefs cheerfully, cheerfully, and be advertised° that the first heroic spirit that deigns to grace me with a handkerchief, I will give it a little remembrance of something beside, shall please° it better than if I had presented it with a double *pistolet*.⁴

PEREGRINE   Will you be that heroic spark,° Sir Pol?

CELIA *at the window throws down her handkerchief [with a coin tied inside it].*

Oh, see! The window has prevented you.°

VOLPONE   Lady, I kiss your bounty, and, for this timely grace you have done your poor Scoto of Mantua, I will return you, over and above my oil, a secret of that high and inestimable nature shall° make you forever enamored on that minute wherein your eye first descended on so mean,° yet not altogether to be despised, an object. Here is a powder concealed in this paper of which, if I should speak to the worth, nine thousand volumes were but as one page, that page as a line, that line as a word—so short is this pilgrimage of man, which some call life, to° the expressing of it. Would I reflect on the price, why, the whole world were but as an empire, that empire as a province, that province as a bank, that bank as a private purse, to the purchase of it. I will only tell you it is the powder that made Venus a goddess, given her by Apollo,⁵ that kept her perpetually young, cleared her wrinkles, firmed her gums, filled° her skin, colored her hair; from her derived to Helen, and at the sack of Troy unfortunately lost; till now in this our age it was as happily° recovered by a studious antiquary out of some ruins of Asia, who sent a moiety° of it to the court of France (but much sophisticated)° wherewith the ladies there now color their hair. The rest, at this present, remains with me, extracted to a quintessence,° so that wherever it but touches, in youth it perpetually preserves, in age restores the complexion; seats your teeth, did° they dance like virginal jacks,⁶ firm as a wall; makes them white as ivory that were black as—

displayed on my "bank"

scorned

notified

which will please

gallant

beaten you to it

which will
lowly

compared to

filled out

fortunately
part
adulterated

refined
concentrate
even if

SCENE 3. *The scene continues.*

[*Enter*] CORVINO. *He beats away the mountebank, etc.*

CORVINO   Spite o'the devil, and my shame! Come down here, Come down! No house but mine to make your scene?° Signor Flaminio, will you down, sir? Down!

stage set

---

3. I won't reduce the price by even a tiny coin.
4. Spanish gold coin worth about one English pound.
5. In his capacity as the god of health.
6. The virginal is a type of harpsichord; its "jacks" are quills that pluck strings when the keys are played, but the term was also sometimes used for the keys.

What, is my wife your Franciscina, sir?[1]
No windows on the whole piazza here
To make your properties° but mine? But mine? ⸺ stage props
Heart! Ere tomorrow I shall be new christened
And called the *pantalone di besogniosi*[2]
About the town.   [*Exeunt* VOLPONE, NANO, *and* MOSCA,
               followed by CORVINO *and the crowd*.]
PEREGRINE   What should this mean, Sir Pol?
POLITIC   Some trick of state, believe it. I will home.
PEREGRINE   It may be some design on you.
POLITIC   I know not.
I'll stand upon my guard.
PEREGRINE   It is your best,° sir.   ⸺ best course of action
POLITIC   This three weeks, all my advices, all my letters,
They have been intercepted,
PEREGRINE   Indeed, sir?
Best have a care.
POLITIC   Nay, so I will.   [*Exit.*]
PEREGRINE   This knight,
I may not lose him,° for my mirth, till night.   [*Exit.*]   *I won't leave him*

SCENE 4. VOLPONE's *house*.

[*Enter*] VOLPONE [*and*] MOSCA.
VOLPONE   Oh, I am wounded!
MOSCA   Where, sir?
VOLPONE   Not without;°   ⸺ *externally*
Those blows were nothing; I could bear them ever,
But angry Cupid, bolting° from her° eyes,   ⸺ *shooting darts / Celia's*
Hath shot himself into me like a flame,
Where now he flings about his burning heat,
As in a furnace an ambitious° fire   ⸺ *rising*
Whose vent is stopped. The fight is all within me.
I cannot live except thou help me, Mosca;
My liver[1] melts, and I, without the hope
Of some soft air from her refreshing breath,
Am but a heap of cinders.
MOSCA   'Las, good sir!
Would you had never seen her.
VOLPONE   Nay, would thou
Hadst never told me of her.
MOSCA   Sir, 'tis true;
I do confess I was unfortunate,
And you unhappy; but I'm bound in conscience

2.3
1. Corvino imagines the scene in terms of a stock episode from the Italian commedia dell'arte, in which the young lover, conventionally named Flaminio after the famous actor Flaminio Scala, seduces Franciscina, the easygoing serving wench.
2. The *pantalone* is another stock figure in the commedia dell'arte, a decrepit old man suspicious of his desirable young wife. *Di besogniosi* is his jocular surname, meaning "descended from poor people."
2.4
1. Supposed to be the seat of lust.

      No less than duty to effect my best
      To your release of torment, and I will, sir.
VOLPONE   Dear Mosca, shall I hope?
MOSCA   Sir, more than dear,
      I will not bid you to despair of aught
      Within a human compass.°   *that's humanly possible*

20 VOLPONE   Oh, there spoke
      My better angel. Mosca, take my keys.
      Gold, plate, and jewels, all's at thy devotion;°   *disposal*
      Employ them how thou wilt; nay, coin me too,[2]
      So° thou in this but crown my longings. Mosca?   *provided that*
MOSCA   Use but your patience.
VOLPONE   So I have.[3]
25 MOSCA   I doubt not
      To bring success to your desires.
VOLPONE   Nay, then,
      I not repent me of my late disguise.
MOSCA   If you can horn him,[4] sir, you need not.
VOLPONE   True;
      Besides, I never meant him for my heir.
30   Is not the color o'my beard and eyebrows[5]
      To make me known?
MOSCA   No jot.
VOLPONE   I did it well.
MOSCA   So well, would I could follow you in mine
      With half the happiness!° And yet I would   *success*
      Escape your epilogue.°   *the beating*
VOLPONE   But were they gulled°   *fooled*
      With a belief that I was Scoto?
35 MOSCA   Sir,
      Scoto himself could hardly have distinguished!
      I have not time to flatter you now. We'll part,
      And, as I prosper, so applaud my art.   [*Exeunt.*]

SCENE 5. CORVINO's *house*.

[*Enter*] CORVINO [*and*] CELIA.
CORVINO   Death of mine honor, with the city's fool?
      A juggling, tooth-drawing,[1] prating° mountebank?   *chattering*
      And at a public window? Where, whilst he
      With his strained action° and his dole of faces[2]   *overacting*
5   To his drug lecture draws your itching ears,
      A crew of old, unmarried, noted lechers
      Stood leering up like satyrs;° and you smile   *lustful goat-men*
      Most graciously! And fan your favors forth

---

2. Use my coins as well. (But also with the implication "make coins out of me," that is, "turn my body into money.")
3. Punning on the original meaning of "patience," "enduring blows."
4. Cuckold him. (The husbands of adulterous wives were traditionally supposed to sprout horns.)
5. Red, because he is a fox.

2.5
1. Mountebanks, like barbers, performed dental work.
2. Small repertory of facial expressions.

To give your hot spectators satisfaction!
What, was your mountebank their call? Their whistle?³
Or were you enamored on his copper rings?
His saffron jewel with the toadstone° in't?   *agatelike stone*
Or his embroidered suit with the cope-stitch,°   *gaudy needlework*
Made of a hearse-cloth? Or his old tilt-feather?⁴
Or his starched beard? Well! You shall have him, yes.
He shall come home and minister unto you
The fricace for the mother.⁵ Or, let me see,
I think you'd rather mount?⁶ Would you not mount?
Why, if you'll mount, you may; yes truly, you may—
And so you may be seen down to th'foot.
Get you a cittern, Lady Vanity,⁷
And be a dealer with the virtuous man;
Make one.⁸ I'll but protest° myself a cuckold   *proclaim*
And save your dowry.⁹ I am a Dutchman, I!
For if you thought me an Italian,
You would be damned ere you did this, you whore.¹
Thou'dst tremble to imagine that the murder
Of father, mother, brother, all thy race,
Should follow as the subject of my justice!
CELIA   Good sir, have patience!
CORVINO [*drawing a weapon*]   What couldst thou propose
Less to thyself° than, in this heat of wrath   *as your punishment*
And stung with my dishonor, I should strike
This steel unto thee, with as many stabs
As thou wert gazed upon with goatish° eyes?   *lustful*
CELIA   Alas, sir, be appeased! I could not think
My being at the window should more now
Move your impatience than at other times.
CORVINO   No? Not to seek and entertain a parley°   *have a conversation*
With a known knave? Before a multitude?
You were an actor with your handkerchief!
Which he most sweetly kissed in the receipt,
And might, no doubt, return it with a letter,
And 'point the place where you might meet—your sister's,
Your mother's, or your aunt's might serve the turn.°   *occasion; sexual act*
CELIA   Why, dear sir, when do I make these excuses?
Or ever stir abroad but to the church?
And that, so seldom—
CORVINO   Well, it shall be less;
And thy restraint before was liberty

---

3. Used to lure trained falcons.
4. The feather from a tilting (jousting) helmet. A hearse-cloth is a heavy cloth for draping over a coffin.
5. Womb massage; with obvious sexual innuendo. "The mother" was a term for the uterus, but also for a variety of ailments, from cramps to depression, that were supposed to originate there.
6. (1) Climb up on the mountebank's stage yourself; (2) take the top sexual position.
7. Allegorical character of a morality play representing pride and worldly pleasure. A cittern is a guitarlike instrument that conventionally was played by whores.
8. Join up with him. (With sexual innuendo.)
9. The husbands of proven adultresses could divorce them and keep their dowry.
1. The Dutch were proverbially phlegmatic, in contrast to Italians, who were stereotypically impetuous and vengeful.

To what I now decree: and therefore, mark me.
[*Pointing to the window*] First, I will have this bawdy light dammed up,
And, till't be done, some two or three yards off
I'll chalk a line, o'er which if thou but chance
To set thy desp'rate foot, more hell, more horror,
More wild, remorseless rage shall seize on thee
Than on a conjurer that had heedless left
His circle's safety ere his devil was laid.[2]
Then here's a lock which I will hang upon thee.
    [*He shows a chastity belt.*]
And now I think on't, I will keep thee backwards;[3]
Thy lodging shall be backwards, thy walks backwards,
Thy prospect°—all be backwards; and no pleasure   view (see n. 3)
That thou shalt know but backwards. Nay, since you force
My honest nature, know it is your own
Being too open makes me use you thus,
Since you will not contain your subtle° nostrils   delicate; crafty
In a sweet° room, but they must snuff the air   sweet-smelling
Of rank and sweaty passengers°—   *Knock within.*   passersby
            One knocks.
Away, and be not seen, pain of thy life!
Not look toward the window. If thou dost—
            [CELIA *begins to exit.*]
Nay stay, hear this—let me not prosper, whore,
But I will make thee an anatomy,[4]
Dissect thee mine own self, and read a lecture
Upon thee to the city, and in public.
Away!   [*Exit* CELIA.]
    Who's there?
    [*Enter*] Servitore [*a* SERVANT].
SERVANT   'Tis Signor Mosca, sir.

SCENE 6. *The scene continues.*

CORVINO Let him come in.   [*Exit* SERVANT.]
            His master's dead! There's yet
Some good to help the bad.
    [*Enter*] MOSCA.
            My Mosca, welcome!
I guess your news.
MOSCA   I fear you cannot, sir.
CORVINO Is't not his death?
MOSCA   Rather the contrary.
CORVINO Not his recovery?
MOSCA   Yes, sir.
CORVINO   I am cursed,

---

2. Conjurers protected themselves from the devils who served them by staying inside a magical circle.
3. In the back part of the house, lacking a view out onto the piazza; but with the suggestion of anal intercourse, supposedly favored by Italians.
4. Use you for anatomical research. (In the early modern period, physicians obtained the bodies of executed criminals upon which to perform dissections, often before large crowds.)

I am bewitched! My crosses° meet to vex me! *misfortunes*
How? How? How? How?
MOSCA   Why, sir, with Scoto's oil.
Corbaccio and Voltore brought of it
Whilst I was busy in an inner room—
10 CORVINO   Death! That damned mountebank! But for the law,
Now, I could kill the rascal. 'T cannot be
His oil should have that virtue. Ha' not I
Known him a common rogue, come fiddling in
To th'*osteria*° with a tumbling whore, *tavern (Italian)*
15 And, when he has done all his forced tricks, been glad
Of a poor spoonful of dead wine with flies in't?
It cannot be. All his ingredients
Are a sheep's gall, a roasted bitch's marrow,
Some few sod° earwigs, pounded caterpillars, *boiled*
20 A little capon's grease, and fasting spittle:[1]
I know 'em to a dram.° *tiny amount*
MOSCA   I know not, sir,
But some on't there they poured into his ears,
Some in his nostrils, and recovered him,
Applying but the fricace.° *massage*
CORVINO   Pox o'that fricace!
25 MOSCA   And since, to seem the more officious° *zealous*
And flatt'ring of his health, there they have had—
At extreme fees—the College of Physicians
Consulting on him how they might restore him;
Where one would have a cataplasm[2] of spices,
30 Another a flayed ape clapped to his breast,
A third would ha' it a dog, a fourth an oil
With wildcats' skins. At last, they all resolved
That to preserve him was no other means
But some young woman must be straight sought out,
35 Lusty and full of juice, to sleep by him;
And to this service—most unhappily
And most unwillingly—am I now employed,
Which here I thought to preacquaint you with,
For your advice, since it concerns you most,
40 Because I would not do that thing might cross
Your ends,[3] on whom I have my whole dependence, sir.
Yet if I do it not, they may delate[4]
My slackness to my patron, work me out
Of his opinion;° and there all your hopes, *favor*
45 Ventures, or whatsoever, are all frustrate.
I do but tell you, sir. Besides, they are all

2.6
1. Saliva of a fasting person. (Scoto cannot afford anything to eat.)
2. Poultice. (The substances described in the following lines were believed to work by absorbing the patient's infection, which bodes ill for the young woman prescribed for Volpone in lines 34–35.)
3. Do anything that might frustrate your purposes.
4. Report. (A legal term for making an accusation.)

                    Now striving who shall first present him. Therefore,
                    I could entreat you briefly, conclude somewhat;°   *decide something*
                    Prevent 'em if you can.
        CORVINO   Death to my hopes!
50   This is my villainous fortune! Best to hire
                    Some common courtesan.
        MOSCA   Ay, I thought on that, sir.
                    But they are all so subtle,° full of art,°   *cunning / deceit*
                    And age again° doting and flexible,   *old people moreover*
                    So as—I cannot tell—we may perchance
                    Light on a quean° may cheat us all.   *whore (who)*
55   CORVINO   'Tis true.
        MOSCA   No, no; it must be one that has no tricks, sir,
                    Some simple thing, a creature made unto° it;   *suited to; forced into*
                    Some wench you may command. Ha' you no kinswoman?
                    Godso°—think, think, think, think, think, think, think, sir.   *an oath*
60   One o'the doctors offered there his daughter.
        CORVINO   How!
        MOSCA   Yes, Signor Lupo,° the physician.   *Wolf (Italian)*
        CORVINO   His daughter?
        MOSCA   And a virgin, sir. Why, alas,
                    He knows the state of's body, what it is,
                    That naught can warm his blood, sir, but a fever,
65   Nor any incantation raise his spirit.°   *vigor; semen*
                    A long forgetfulness hath seized that part.°   *his penis*
                    Besides, sir, who shall know it? Some one or two—
        CORVINO   I pray thee give me leave.° [*He walks apart.*] If   *give me a minute*
                    any man
                    But I had had this luck—The thing in 'tself,
70   I know, is nothing.—Wherefore should not I
                    As well command my blood and my affections
                    As this dull doctor? In the point of honor
                    The cases are all one, of wife and daughter.
        MOSCA [*aside*]   I hear him coming.°   *coming around*
        CORVINO [*aside*]   She shall do't. 'Tis done.
75   'Slight,° if this doctor, who is not engaged,   *by God's light (an oath)*
                    Unless 't be for his counsel (which is nothing),[5]
                    Offer his daughter, what should I, that am
                    So deeply in? I will prevent him. Wretch!
                    Covetous wretch!—Mosca, I have determined.
        MOSCA   How, sir?
80   CORVINO   We'll make all sure. The party you wot° of   *know*
                    Shall be mine own wife, Mosca.
        MOSCA   Sir, the thing
                    (But that I would not seem to counsel you)
                    I should have motioned° to you at the first.   *proposed*
                    And, make your count,° you have cut all their throats.   *rest assured*

---

5. Who is not financially involved, except for whatever slight fee he could expect for his advice.

85	Why, 'tis directly taking a possession!⁶	
	And in his next fit we may let him go.	
	'Tis but to pull the pillow from his head	
	And he is throttled; 't had been done before,	
	But for your scrupulous doubts.	
	CORVINO Ay, a plague on't!	
90	My conscience fools my wit.° Well, I'll be brief,	*common sense*
	And so be thou, lest they should be before us.	
	Go home, prepare him, tell him with what zeal	
	And willingness I do it; swear it was	
	On the first hearing (as thou mayst do, truly)	
	Mine own free motion.°	*initiative*
95	MOSCA Sir, I warrant you,	
	I'll so possess° him with it that the rest	*impress*
	Of his starved clients shall be banished all,	
	And only you received. But come not, sir,	
	Until I send, for I have something else	
100	To ripen for your good; you must not know't.	
	CORVINO But do not you forget to send, now.	
	MOSCA Fear not.	
	[*Exit.*]	

SCENE 7. *The scene continues.*

CORVINO   Where are you, wife? My Celia? Wife?
   [*Enter*] CELIA [*weeping.*]
                                    What, blubbering?
   Come, dry those tears. I think thou thought'st me in earnest?
   Ha! By this light, I talked so but to try° thee.   *test*
   Methinks the lightness° of the occasion   *triviality*
5 Should ha' confirmed thee.¹ Come, I am not jealous.
   CELIA   No?
   CORVINO   Faith, I am not, I, nor never² was;
   It is a poor, unprofitable humor.
   Do not I know if women have a will
   They'll do 'gainst all the watches° o'the world?   *despite the vigilance*
10 And that the fiercest spies are tamed with gold?
   Tut, I am confident in thee, thou shalt see't;
   And see, I'll give thee cause too, to believe it.
   Come, kiss me. Go and make thee ready straight
   In all thy best attire, thy choicest jewels;
15 Put 'em all on, and, with 'em thy best looks.
   We are invited to a solemn feast
   At old Volpone's, where it shall appear
   How far I am free from jealousy or fear.   [*Exeunt.*]

---

6. A legal term for the heir's formal assumption of inherited property.

2.7
1. Convinced you that I was not serious.

2. Double negatives are grammatical in Jacobean English.

Act 3

SCENE 1. *The piazza.*

[*Enter*] MOSCA.

MOSCA　I fear I shall begin to grow in love
　　With my dear self and my most prosp'rous parts,°　　*talents*
　　They do so spring and burgeon.° I can feel　　*swell; thrive*
　　A whimsy° i'my blood. I know not how,　　*giddiness*
5　Success hath made me wanton. I could skip
　　Out of my skin now like a subtle snake,
　　I am so limber. Oh, your parasite
　　Is a most precious thing, dropped from above,°　　*sent from heaven*
　　Not bred 'mongst clods and clodpolls here on earth.
10　I muse the mystery was not made a science,
　　It is so liberally professed!¹ Almost
　　All the wise world is little else in nature
　　But parasites or subparasites. And yet
　　I mean not those that have your bare town-art,²
15　To know who's fit to feed 'em; have no house,
　　No family, no care, and therefore mold
　　Tales for men's ears,° to bait° that sense; or get　　*tell juicy rumors / entice*
　　Kitchen-invention, and some stale receipts°　　*recipes*
　　To please the belly and the groin;° nor those,　　*as aphrodisiacs*
20　With their court-dog tricks, that can fawn and fleer,°　　*smile insincerely*
　　Make their revenue out of legs and faces,
　　Echo my lord, and lick away a moth;³
　　But your fine, elegant rascal, that can rise
　　And stoop almost together, like an arrow,
25　Shoot through the air as nimbly as a star,°　　*meteor*
　　Turn short as doth a swallow, and be here
　　And there and here and yonder all at once,
　　Present to any humor, all occasion,⁴
　　And change a visor° swifter than a thought!　　*mask; expression*
30　This is the creature had the art born with him,
　　Toils not to learn it, but doth practice it
　　Out of most excellent nature, and such sparks
　　Are the true parasites, others but their zanies.°　　*clownish imitators*

SCENE 2. *The scene continues.*

[*Enter*] BONARIO.

[*Aside*] Who's this? Bonario? Old Corbaccio's son?
The person I was bound° to seek.—Fair sir,　　*on my way*
You are happ'ly met.

3.1
1. I wonder why the craft was not made a subject for academic study, it is so frequently practiced! (Punning on the "liberal professions.")
2. Crude skills of ingratiation, sufficient only for getting free meals in taverns.
3. Make a living from bows and sycophantic looks, repeat anything a nobleman says, and fawn over him, fussing over every detail of his appearance.
4. Ready to respond to any mood or opportunity.

BONARIO   That cannot be by thee.
MOSCA   Why, sir?
BONARIO   Nay, pray thee know thy way and leave me.
I would be loath to interchange discourse
With such a mate° as thou art.   *fellow (contemptuous)*
MOSCA   Courteous sir,
Scorn not my poverty.
BONARIO   Not I, by heaven,
But thou shalt give me leave to hate thy baseness.
MOSCA   Baseness?
BONARIO   Ay. Answer me, is not thy sloth
Sufficient argument? Thy flattery?
Thy means of feeding?
MOSCA   Heaven, be good to me!
These imputations are too common, sir,
And eas'ly stuck on virtue when she's poor.
You are unequal° to me, and howe'er   *superior; unfair*
Your sentence° may be righteous, yet you are not,   *verdict*
That, ere you know me, thus proceed in censure.
Saint Mark bear witness 'gainst you, 'tis inhuman.   [*He weeps.*]
BONARIO [*aside*]   What? Does he weep? The sign is soft and good.
I do repent me that I was so harsh.
MOSCA   'Tis true that, swayed by strong necessity,
I am enforced to eat my careful bread
With too much obsequy;° 'tis true, beside,   *obsequiousness*
That I am fain° to spin mine own poor raiment   *obliged*
Out of my mere observance,° being not born   *deferential service*
To a free fortune. But that I have done
Base offices in rending friends asunder,
Dividing families, betraying counsels,
Whispering false lies, or mining° men with praises,   *undermining*
Trained° their credulity with perjuries,   *lured on*
Corrupted chastity, or am in love
With mine own tender ease, but would not rather
Prove° the most rugged and laborious course   *undergo*
That might redeem my present estimation,[1]
Let me here perish in all hope of goodness.
BONARIO [*aside*]   This cannot be a personated passion!—
I was to blame, so to mistake thy nature;
Pray thee forgive me, and speak out thy business.
MOSCA   Sir, it concerns you; and though I may seem
At first to make a main° offense in manners   *great*
And in my gratitude unto my master,
Yet for the pure love which I bear all right
And hatred of the wrong, I must reveal it.
This very hour your father is in purpose
To disinherit you—
BONARIO   How!

3.2
1. That might improve your current appraisal of me.

MOSCA   And thrust you forth
  As a mere stranger to his blood. 'Tis true, sir.
  The work no way engageth° me but as   concerns
  I claim an interest in the general state
  Of goodness and true virtue, which I hear
  T'abound in you, and for which mere respect,°   for which reason alone
  Without a second aim, sir, I have done it.
BONARIO   This tale hath lost thee much of the late° trust   recent
  Thou hadst with me. It is impossible.
  I know not how to lend it any thought°   believe that
  My father should be so unnatural.
MOSCA   It is a confidence that well becomes
  Your piety;° and formed, no doubt, it is   filial loyalty
  From your own simple innocence, which makes
  Your wrong more monstrous and abhorred. But, sir,
  I now will tell you more. This very minute
  It is or will be doing; and if you
  Shall be but pleased to go with me, I'll bring you,
  I dare not say where you shall see, but where
  Your ear shall be a witness of the deed:
  Hear yourself written bastard, and professed
  The common issue of the earth.[2]
BONARIO   I'm mazed!
MOSCA   Sir, if I do it not, draw your just sword
  And score your vengeance on my front° and face;   brow
  Mark me your villain. You have too much wrong,
  And I do suffer for you, sir. My heart
  Weeps blood in anguish—
BONARIO   Lead. I follow thee. [*Exeunt.*]

SCENE 3. VOLPONE's *house*.

[*Enter*] VOLPONE, NANO, ANDROGYNO, [*and*] CASTRONE.

VOLPONE   Mosca stays long, methinks. Bring forth your sports
  And help to make the wretched time more sweet.
NANO   Dwarf, fool, and eunuch, well met here we be.
  A question it were now, whether° of us three,   which
  Being all the known delicates° of a rich man,   playthings
  In pleasing him, claim the precedency can?
CASTRONE   I claim for myself.
ANDROGYNO   And so doth the fool.
NANO   'Tis foolish indeed; let me set you both to school.
  First, for your dwarf: he's little and witty,
  And everything, as it is little, is pretty;
  Else why do men say to a creature of my shape,
  So soon as they see him, "It's a pretty little ape"?
  And why a pretty ape? But for pleasing imitation
  Of greater men's action in a ridiculous fashion.

---

2. A bastard was called *filius terrae*, "son of the earth."

15 Beside, this feat° body of mine doth not crave   *neat, trim*
    Half the meat, drink, and cloth one of your bulks will have.
    Admit your fool's face be the mother of laughter,
    Yet for his brain, it must always come after;°   *be lesser*
    And though that do feed him,° it's a pitiful case,[1]   *earns his keep*
20 His body is beholding° to such a bad face.   *One knocks.*   *beholden*
    VOLPONE Who's there? My couch. [*He lies down.*] Away,
        look, Nano, see!
    Give me my caps, first—go, inquire.
            [*Exeunt* NANO, ANDROGYNO, *and* CASTRONE.]
                        Now, Cupid
    Send° it be Mosca, and with fair return!°   *grant / good results*
        [*Enter* NANO.]
    NANO It is the beauteous Madam—
    VOLPONE   Would-be—is it?
    NANO The same
25 VOLPONE   Now, torment on me! Squire her in,
    For she will enter or dwell here forever.
    Nay, quickly, that my fit were past!   [*Exit* NANO.]
                        I fear
    A second hell, too, that my loathing this
    Will quite expel my appetite to the other.°   *Celia*
30 Would she were taking, now, her tedious leave.
    Lord, how it threats me what I am to suffer!

                SCENE 4. *The scene continues.*

        [*Enter*] LADY [WOULD-BE *and*] NANO.
    LADY WOULD-BE [*to* NANO]   I thank you, good sir. Pray you signify
        Unto your patron I am here.[1] [*regarding herself in a mirror*] This
            band°   *ruff*
        Shows not my neck enough. I trouble you, sir.
        Let me request you, bid one of my women
        Come hither to me.   [*Exit* NANO.]
5   In good faith, I am dressed
        Most favorably today!° It is no matter;   *sarcastic*
        'Tis well enough.
            [*Enter* NANO *and* FIRST] WOMAN.
                        Look, see, these petulant things!°   *her women; her curls*
        How they have done this!
    VOLPONE [*aside*]   I do feel the fever
        Ent'ring in at mine ears. Oh, for a charm
        To fright it hence!
10 LADY WOULD-BE [*to* FIRST WOMAN]   Come nearer. Is this curl
        In his° right place? Or this? Why is this higher   *its*
        Than all the rest? You ha' not washed your eyes yet?

3.3
1. With a pun on "container."
3.4
1. Much of Lady Would-be's dialogue in the following scene is adapted from Libanius of Antioch's
On Talkative Women.

          Or do they not stand even° i'your head?   *level*
          Where's your fellow? Call her.   [*Exit* FIRST WOMAN.]
       NANO [*aside*]   Now Saint Mark
15   Deliver us! Anon she'll beat her women
       Because her nose is red.
             [*Enter* FIRST *and* SECOND WOMEN.]
       LADY WOULD-BE   I pray you, view
          This tire,° forsooth. Are all things apt or no?   *headdress*
       SECOND WOMAN   One hair a little here sticks out, forsooth.
       LADY WOULD-BE   Does 't so, forsooth? [*to* FIRST WOMAN] And
          where was your dear sight
20   When it did so, forsooth? What now? Bird-eyed?°   *startled (?); asquint (?)*
          [*to* SECOND WOMAN] And you, too? Pray you both approach
          and mend it.
                                    [*They tend to her.*]
          Now, by that light,° I muse you're not ashamed!   *by heaven*
          I, that have preached these things so oft unto you,
          Read you the principles, argued all the grounds,
25   Disputed every fitness, every grace,
          Called you to counsel of so frequent dressings—
       NANO (*aside*)   More carefully than of your fame° or honor. *reputation*
       LADY WOULD-BE   Made you acquainted what an ample dowry
          The knowledge of these things would be unto you,
30   Able alone to get you noble husbands
          At your return,° and you thus to neglect it?   *to England*
          Besides, you seeing what a curious° nation   *fastidious*
          Th'Italians are, what will they say of me?
          "The English lady cannot dress herself."
35   Here's a fine imputation to our country!
          Well, go your ways, and stay i'the next room.
          This fucus° was too coarse, too; it's no matter.   *makeup*
          [*to* NANO] Good sir, you'll give 'em entertainment?°   *look after them*
                          [*Exeunt* NANO *and* WOMEN.]
       VOLPONE [*aside*]   The storm comes toward me.
       LADY WOULD-BE [*approaching the bed*]   How does my Volp?
40   VOLPONE   Troubled with noise. I cannot sleep; I dreamt
          That a strange Fury entered now my house,
          And with the dreadful tempest of her breath
          Did cleave my roof asunder.
       LADY WOULD-BE   Believe me, and I
          Had the most fearful dream, could I remember't—
45   VOLPONE [*aside*]   Out on° my fate! I ha' giv'n her the occasion   *curses on*
          How to torment me: she will tell me hers.
       LADY WOULD-BE   Methought the golden mediocrity,°   *golden mean*
          Polite and delicate—
       VOLPONE   Oh, if you do love me,
          No more! I sweat and suffer at the mention
50   Of any dream. Feel how I tremble yet.
       LADY WOULD-BE   Alas, good soul! The passion of the heart.°   *heartburn*
          Seed pearl were good now, boiled with syrup of apples,

Tincture of gold and coral, citron pills,
Your elecampane° root, myrobalans²— *perennial herb*
VOLPONE [*aside*]   Ay me, I have ta'en a grasshopper by the wing!
LADY WOULD-BE   Burnt silk and amber; you have muscadel
Good i'the house—
VOLPONE   You will not drink and part?
LADY WOULD-BE   No, fear not that. I doubt we shall not get
Some English saffron—half a dram would serve—
Your sixteen cloves, a little musk, dried mints,
Bugloss,° and barley-meal— *an herb*
VOLPONE [*aside*]   She's in again.
Before I feigned diseases; now I have one.
LADY WOULD-BE   And these applied with a right scarlet cloth—
VOLPONE [*aside*]   Another flood of words! A very torrent!
LADY WOULD-BE   Shall I, sir, make you a poultice?
VOLPONE   No, no, no.
I'm very well; you need prescribe no more.
LADY WOULD-BE   I have a little studied physic, but now
I'm all for music, save i'the forenoons
An hour or two for painting. I would have
A lady indeed t' have all letters and arts,
Be able to discourse, to write, to paint,
But principal, as Plato holds,° your music *in The Republic*
(And so does wise Pythagoras, I take it)
Is your true rapture, when there is concent° *harmony*
In face, in voice, and clothes, and is indeed
Our sex's chiefest ornament.
VOLPONE   The poet° *Sophocles, in Ajax*
As old in time as Plato, and as knowing,
Says that your highest female grace is silence.
LADY WOULD-BE   Which o' your poets? Petrarch? Or Tasso? Or Dante?
Guarini? Ariosto? Aretine?
Cieco di Hadria?³ I have read them all.
VOLPONE [*aside*]   Is everything a cause to my destruction?
LADY WOULD-BE [*searching her garments*]   I think I ha' two or three of 'em
about me.
VOLPONE [*aside*]   The sun, the sea will sooner both stand still
Than her eternal tongue! Nothing can scape it.
LADY WOULD-BE   Here's *Pastor Fido*⁴—
VOLPONE [*aside*]   Profess obstinate silence,
That's now my safest.
LADY WOULD-BE   All our English writers,
I mean such as are happy in th'Italian,
Will deign to steal out of this author mainly,
Almost as much as from Montaignié° *French essayist*
He has so modern and facile° a vein, *graceful*

---

2. Dried tropical fruits.
3. Lady Would-be juxtaposes major Italian writers with the minor di Hadria and the obscene Aretino (see p. 988, n. 6).
4. A pastoral by Giovanni Guarini, translated into English in 1602.

        Fitting the time, and catching the court ear.
        Your Petrarch is more passionate, yet he,
        In days of sonneting, trusted 'em with much.[5]
95   Dante is hard, and few can understand him.
        But for a desperate° wit, there's Aretine!   °outrageous
        Only his pictures are a little obscene[6]—
        You mark me not?
  VOLPONE   Alas, my mind's perturbed.
  LADY WOULD-BE   Why, in such cases we must cure ourselves,
        Make use of our philosophy—
100   VOLPONE   Ay me!
  LADY WOULD-BE   And, as we find our passions do rebel,
        Encounter 'em with reason, or divert 'em
        By giving scope unto some other humor
        Of lesser danger—as in politic bodies°   °political councils
105   There's nothing more doth overwhelm the judgment
        And clouds the understanding than too much
        Settling and fixing and (as 'twere) subsiding°   °alchemical jargon
        Upon one object. For the incorporating
        Of these same outward things into that part
110   Which we call mental leaves some certain feces°   °dregs
        That stop the organs and, as Plato says,
        Assassinates our knowledge.
  VOLPONE *[aside]*   Now, the spirit
        Of patience help me!
  LADY WOULD-BE   Come, in faith, I must
        Visit you more o'days and make you well.
        Laugh and be lusty.°   °merry
115   VOLPONE *[aside]*   My good angel save me!
  LADY WOULD-BE   There was but one sole man in all the world
        With whom I e'er could sympathize, and he
        Would lie you° often three, four hours together   °lie
        To hear me speak, and be sometime so rapt
120   As he would answer me quite from the purpose,
        Like you—and you are like him, just. I'll discourse—
        An't° be but only, sir, to bring you asleep—   °if it
        How we did spend our time and loves together
        For some six years.
  VOLPONE   Oh, oh, oh, oh, oh, oh!
125   LADY WOULD-BE   For we were *coaetani*° and brought up—   °the same age
  VOLPONE *[aside]*   Some power, some fate, some fortune rescue me!

                SCENE 5. *The scene continues.*

    [*Enter*] MOSCA.
  MOSCA   God save you, madam.
  LADY WOULD-BE   Good sir.

---

5. When sonnet writing was popular, gave poets plenty to imitate.
6. The libertine poems of Aretine (Pietro Aretino 1492–1556) were published with pornographic illustrations by Giulio Romano.

VOLPONE [*aside to* MOSCA]   Mosca? Welcome,
  Welcome to my redemption.
MOSCA [*to* VOLPONE]   Why, sir?
VOLPONE [*aside to* MOSCA]   Oh,
  Rid me of this my torture quickly, there,
  My madam with the everlasting voice!
5 The bells in time of pestilence ne'er made
  Like noise, or were in that perpetual motion;[1]
  The cockpit° comes not near it. All my house   *cockfighting arena*
  But now steamed like a bath with her thick breath.
  A lawyer could not have been heard, nor scarce
10 Another woman, such a hail of words
  She has let fall. For hell's sake, rid her hence.
MOSCA [*aside to* VOLPONE]   Has she presented?°   *given a gift*
VOLPONE [*aside to* MOSCA]   Oh, I do not care.
  I'll take her absence upon any price,
  With any loss.
MOSCA   Madam—
LADY WOULD-BE   I ha' brought your patron
  A toy,° a cap here, of mine own work—   *trifle; embroidered piece*
15 MOSCA [*taking it from her*]   'Tis well.
  I had forgot to tell you, I saw your knight
  Where you'd little think it—
LADY WOULD-BE   Where?
MOSCA   Marry,
  Where yet, if you make haste, you may apprehend him,
  Rowing upon the water in a gondole
20 With the most cunning courtesan of Venice.
LADY WOULD-BE   Is't true?
MOSCA   Pursue 'em, and believe your eyes.
  Leave me to make your gift.   [*Exit* LADY WOULD-BE.]
        I knew 'twould take.°   *do the trick*
  For lightly,° they that use themselves most license   *commonly*
  Are still° most jealous.   *always*
VOLPONE   Mosca, hearty thanks
25 For thy quick fiction and delivery of me.
  Now, to my hopes, what say'st thou?
        [*Enter* LADY WOULD-BE.]
LADY WOULD-BE   But do you hear, sir?
VOLPONE [*aside*]   Again! I fear a paroxysm.°   *relapse*
LADY WOULD-BE   Which way
  Rowed they together?
MOSCA   Toward the Rialto.°   *commercial district*
LADY WOULD-BE   I pray you, lend me your dwarf.
MOSCA   I pray you, take him.
        [*Exit* LADY WOULD-BE.]

3.5
1. Church bells marked the deaths of parishioners; in times of plague they therefore rang almost constantly.

30	Your hopes, sir, are like happy blossoms: fair,	
	And promise timely fruit if you will stay	
	But the maturing. Keep you at your couch.	
	Corbaccio will arrive straight with the will;	
	When he is gone I'll tell you more. [*Exit.*]	
	VOLPONE My blood,	
35	My spirits are returned. I am alive;	
	And like your wanton° gamester at primero,[2]	*reckless; lustful*
	Whose thought had whispered to him, not go° less,	*don't gamble*
	Methinks I lie, and draw—for an encounter.[3]	

[*He gets into bed and closes the bed curtains.*]

SCENE 6. *The scene continues.*

[*Enter*] MOSCA [*and*] BONARIO. [MOSCA *shows* BONARIO *to a hiding place.*]

MOSCA Sir, here concealed you may hear all. But pray you
Have patience, sir. [*One knocks.*] The same's your father knocks.
I am compelled to leave you.
BONARIO   Do so. Yet
Cannot my thought imagine this a truth.
    [*He conceals himself.*]

SCENE 7. *The scene continues.*

[*Enter*] CORVINO [*and*] CELIA. MOSCA [*crosses the stage to intercept them*].

MOSCA Death on me! You are come too soon. What meant you?
Did not I say I would send?
CORVINO   Yes, but I feared
You might forget it, and then they prevent us.
MOSCA [*aside*] Prevent? Did e'er man haste so for his horns?°   *cuckold's horns*
5   A courtier would not ply it so for a place.[1]
    [*to* CORVINO] Well, now there's no helping it, stay here;
I'll presently return.   [*He crosses the stage to* BONARIO.]
CORVINO   Where are you, Celia?
You know not wherefore I have brought you hither?
CELIA Not well, except you told me.
CORVINO   Now I will.
Hark hither. [CORVINO *and* CELIA *talk apart.*]
10 MOSCA (*to* BONARIO) Sir, your father hath sent word
It will be half an hour ere he come;
And therefore, if you please to walk the while
Into that gallery, at the upper end
There are some books to entertain the time;
15 And I'll take care no man shall come unto you, sir.
BONARIO Yes, I will stay there. [*aside*] I do doubt this fellow.
    [*He retires.*]

---

2. A card game.
3. (1) Winning play in primero; (2) sexual act.

3.7
1. Work so hard for a position at court.

MOSCA   There, he is far enough; he can hear nothing.
   And for° his father, I can keep him off. — *as for*
   [MOSCA *joins* VOLPONE *and opens his bed curtains.*]
CORVINO [*to* CELIA]   Nay, now, there is no starting back, and therefore
20   Resolve upon it; I have so decreed.
   It must be done. Nor would I move 't° afore, — *suggest it*
   Because I would avoid all shifts° and tricks — *evasions*
   That might deny me.
CELIA   Sir, let me beseech you,
   Affect° not these strange trials. If you doubt — *undertake*
25   My chastity, why, lock me up forever;
   Make me the heir of darkness. Let me live
   Where I may please° your fears, if not your trust. — *satisfy*
CORVINO   Believe it, I have no such humor, I.
   All that I speak, I mean; yet I am not mad,
30   Not horn-mad,° see you? Go to, show yourself — *crazy with jealousy*
   Obedient, and a wife.
CELIA   O heaven!
CORVINO   I say it,
   Do so.
CELIA   Was this the train?° — *scheme*
CORVINO   I have told you reasons:
   What the physicians have set down; how much
   It may concern me; what my engagements are;
35   My means, and the necessity of those means
   For my recovery. Wherefore, if you be
   Loyal and mine, be won, respect my venture.° — *support my endeavor*
CELIA   Before your honor?
CORVINO   Honor? Tut, a breath.
   There's no such thing in nature; a mere term
40   Invented to awe fools. What is my gold
   The worse for touching? Clothes for being looked on?
   Why, this's no more. An old, decrepit wretch,
   That has no sense,° no sinew; takes his meat — *sensory perception*
   With others' fingers; only knows to gape
45   When you do scald his gums; a voice, a shadow.
   And what can this man hurt you?
CELIA   Lord! What spirit
   Is this hath entered him?
CORVINO   And for your fame,° — *reputation*
   That's such a jig;° as if I would go tell it, — *joke*
   Cry° it on the piazza! Who shall know it — *advertise*
50   But he that cannot speak it,° and this fellow° — *Volpone / Mosca*
   Whose lips are i'my pocket, save yourself?
   If you'll proclaim't, you may. I know no other
   Should come to know it.
CELIA   Are heaven and saints then nothing?
   Will they be blind or stupid?
CORVINO   How?° — *what's this?*
CELIA   Good sir,

>   Be jealous still, emulate them, and think
>   What hate they burn with toward every sin.
>   CORVINO   I grant you, if I thought it were a sin
>   I would not urge you. Should I offer this
>   To some young Frenchman, or hot Tuscan blood
>   That had read Aretine, conned° all his prints,   *learned by heart*
>   Knew every quirk within lust's labyrinth,
>   And were professed critic° in lechery,   *connoisseur*
>   And I would look upon him and applaud him,
>   This were a sin. But here 'tis contrary,
>   A pious work, mere charity, for physic,
>   And honest polity° to assure mine own.   *prudence*
>   CELIA   O heaven! Canst thou suffer such a change?
>   VOLPONE [*aside to* MOSCA]   Thou art mine honor, Mosca, and my pride,
>   My joy, my tickling, my delight! Go, bring 'em.
>   MOSCA [*to* CORVINO]   Please you draw near, sir.
>   CORVINO [*dragging* CELIA *toward* VOLPONE]   Come on, what—
>   You will not be rebellious? By that light—
>   MOSCA [*to* VOLPONE]   Sir, Signor Corvino here is come to see you.
>   VOLPONE   Oh!
>   MOSCA   And, hearing of the consultation had
>   So lately for your health, is come to offer,
>   Or rather, sir, to prostitute—
>   CORVINO   Thanks, sweet Mosca.
>   MOSCA   Freely, unasked or unentreated—
>   CORVINO   Well.
>   MOSCA   As the true, fervent instance of his love,
>   His own most fair and proper wife, the beauty
>   Only of price° in Venice—   *beyond comparison*
>   CORVINO   'Tis well urged.
>   MOSCA   To be your comfortress and to preserve you.
>   VOLPONE   Alas, I am past already! Pray you, thank him
>   For his good care and promptness. But for° that,   *as for*
>   'Tis a vain labor e'en to fight 'gainst heaven,
>   Applying fire to a stone (uh! uh! uh! uh!),
>   Making a dead leaf grow again. I take
>   His wishes gently, though; and you may tell him
>   What I have done for him. Marry, my state is hopeless!
>   Will him to pray for me, and t' use his fortune
>   With reverence when he comes to't.
>   MOSCA [*to* CORVINO]   Do you hear, sir?
>   Go to him with your wife.
>   CORVINO [*to* CELIA]   Heart of my father!°   *an oath*
>   Wilt thou persist thus? Come, I pray thee, come.
>   Thou see'st 'tis nothing. [*He threatens to strike her.*] Celia! By this hand,
>   I shall grow violent. Come, do't, I say.
>   CELIA   Sir, kill me, rather. I will take down poison,
>   Eat burning coals, do anything—
>   CORVINO   Be damned!
>   Heart! I will drag thee hence, home, by the hair,

                    Cry thee a strumpet through the streets, rip up
                    Thy mouth unto thine ears, and slit thy nose
                    Like a raw rochet!°—Do not tempt me. Come,   *a fish, the red gurnard*
100   Yield! I am loath—Death!° I will buy some slave   *God's death! (an oath)*
                    Whom I will kill,² and bind thee to him alive,
                    And at my window hang you forth, devising
                    Some monstrous crime, which I in capital letters
                    Will eat into thy flesh with *aquafortis*°   *nitric acid*
105   And burning cor'sives° on this stubborn breast.   *corrosives*
                    Now, by the blood thou hast incensed, I'll do't.
CELIA   Sir, what you please, you may; I am your martyr.
CORVINO   Be not thus obstinate. I ha' not deserved it.
            Think who it is entreats you. Pray thee, sweet!
110   Good faith, thou shalt have jewels, gowns, attires,
            What° thou wilt think and ask. Do but go kiss him.   *whatever*
            Or touch him but. For my sake. At my suit.
            This once. No? Not? I shall remember this.
            Will you disgrace me thus? Do you thirst my undoing?
MOSCA   Nay, gentle lady, be advised.
115 CORVINO   No, no.
            She has watched her time.³ God's precious,⁴ this is scurvy;
            'Tis very scurvy, and you are—
MOSCA   Nay, good, sir.
CORVINO   An arrant locust,° by heaven, a locust. Whore,   *destroyer*
            Crocodile,⁵ that hast thy tears prepared,
            Expecting° how thou'lt bid 'em flow!   *anticipating*
120 MOSCA   Nay, pray you, sir,
            She will consider.
CELIA   Would my life would serve
            To satisfy—
CORVINO   'Sdeath, if she would but speak to him
            And save my reputation, 'twere somewhat—
            But spitefully to effect my utter ruin!
125 MOSCA   Ay, now you've put your fortune in her hands.
            Why, i'faith, it is her modesty; I must quit° her.   *absolve*
            If you were absent she would be more coming,°   *compliant*
            I know it, and dare undertake for her.
            What woman can before her husband? Pray you,
            Let us depart and leave her here.
130 CORVINO   Sweet Celia,
            Thou mayst redeem all yet; I'll say no more.
            If not, esteem yourself as lost.—Nay, stay there.
                            [*Exeunt* CORVINO *and* MOSCA.]
CELIA   O God and his good angels! Whither, whither
            Is shame fled human breasts, that with such ease

---

2. In the following lines, Corvino elaborates luridly upon the fate that the notorious rapist Tarquin promised the chaste Roman matron Lucretia if she did not capitulate; unlike Celia, Lucretia yielded to threats.

3. Waited for her chance (to ruin me).
4. God's precious blood. (An oath.)
5. Which was supposed to weep while preying upon its victims.

135   Men dare put off your° honors and their own?   *God's and the angels'*
      Is that which ever was a cause of life°   *sex and wedlock*
      Now placed beneath the basest circumstance,°   *lowest of concerns*
      And modesty an exile made for money?
         He [VOLPONE] leaps off from his couch.
VOLPONE   Ay, in Corvino, and such earth-fed minds
140   That never tasted the true heav'n of love.
      Assure thee, Celia, he that would sell thee
      Only for hope of gain, and that uncertain,
      He would have sold his part of paradise
      For ready money, had he met a copeman.°   *buyer*
145   Why art thou mazed to see me thus revived?
      Rather applaud thy beauty's miracle;
      'Tis thy great work, that hath, not now alone°   *not only just now*
      But sundry times raised me in several shapes,
      And but this morning like a mountebank
150   To see thee at thy window. Ay, before
      I would have left my practice° for thy love,   *scheming*
      In varying figures I would have contended
      With the blue Proteus or the hornèd flood.[6]
      Now art thou welcome.
CELIA   Sir!
VOLPONE   Nay, fly me not,
155   Nor let thy false imagination
      That I was bedrid make thee think I am so.
      Thou shalt not find it. I am now as fresh,
      As hot, as high, and in as jovial plight°   *robust condition*
      As when—in that so celebrated scene,
160   At recitation of our comedy
      For entertainment of the great Valois[7]—
      I acted young Antinoüs,[8] and attracted
      The eyes and ears of all the ladies present,
      T'admire each graceful gesture, note, and footing.° *dance step*

SONG

165   [*He sings.*]   Come, my Celia, let us prove,[9]
                While we can, the sports of love.
                Time will not be ours forever;
                He at length our good will sever.
                Spend not then his gifts in vain.
170   Suns that set may rise again,
                But if once we lose this light
                'Tis with us perpetual night.
                Why should we defer our joys?

---

6. Proteus is a shape-changing sea god with whom Menelaus wrestles in the *Odyssey*. The "hornèd flood" is the river god Achelous, defeated by Hercules despite changing into an ox.
7. Henry of Valois, Duke of Anjou, and later King Henry III of France (1574–89), was sumptuously entertained at Venice in 1574. His sexual taste for men was widely remarked.
8. The beautiful homosexual favorite of the Roman emperor Hadrian.
9. Try out. (The song is an adaptation of the Roman poet Catullus's fifth ode.)

	Fame and rumor are but toys.°	*trifles*
175	Cannot we delude the eyes	
	Of a few poor household spies?	
	Or his° easier ears beguile,	*Corvino's*
	Thus removèd by our wile?	
	'Tis no sin love's fruits to steal,	
180	But the sweet thefts to reveal.	
	To be taken,° to be seen,	*caught*
	These have crimes accounted been.	

CELIA Some serene° blast me, or dire lightning strike   *poisonous mist*
    This my offending face!

VOLPONE   Why droops my Celia?
185 Thou hast in place of a base husband found
    A worthy lover. Use thy fortune well,
    With secrecy and pleasure. See, behold
    What thou art queen of, not in expectation,°   *merely in hope*
    As I feed others, but possessed and crowned.
            [*He reveals his treasures.*]
190 See here a rope of pearl, and each more orient°   *brilliant*
    Than that the brave Egyptian queen caroused;[1]
    Dissolve and drink 'em. See, a carbuncle[2]
    May put out both the eyes of our Saint Mark;[3]
    A diamond would have bought Lollia Paulina[4]
195 When she came in like starlight, hid with jewels
    That were the spoils of provinces. Take these,
    And wear, and lose 'em; yet remains an earring
    To purchase them again, and this whole state.
    A gem but worth a private patrimony
200 Is nothing; we will eat such at a meal.
    The heads of parrots, tongues of nightingales,
    The brains of peacocks and of ostriches
    Shall be our food, and, could we get the phoenix,[5]
    Though nature lost her kind,° she were our dish.   *it became extinct*

205 CELIA Good sir, these things might move a mind affected
    With such delights; but I, whose innocence
    Is all I can think wealthy° or worth th'enjoying,   *valuable*
    And which once lost, I have naught to lose beyond it,
    Cannot be taken with these sensual baits.
    If you have conscience—

210 VOLPONE   'Tis the beggar's virtue.
    If thou hast wisdom, hear me, Celia.
    Thy baths shall be the juice of July flowers,°   *clove pinks*
    Spirit° of roses, and of violets,   *extract*
    The milk of unicorns, and panthers' breath[6]

---

1. Cleopatra dissolved and drank a pearl during a banquet with her lover, Marc Antony. "Brave": magnificent.
2. Ruby, thought to emit light.
3. Patron saint of Venice, whose statue stood in the basilica.
4. Third wife of the Roman emperor Caligula.
5. Mythical bird, of which it was supposed that only one existed at a time; it died in flames and was reborn from its own ashes.
6. Panthers were believed to use their sweet-smelling breath to lure prey.

	Gathered in bags, and mixed with Cretan wines.	
215	Our drink shall be preparèd gold and amber,	
	Which we will take until my roof whirl round	
	With the vertigo; and my dwarf shall dance,	
	My eunuch sing, my fool make up the antic,[7]	
220	Whilst we, in changèd shapes, act Ovid's tales:	
	Thou like Europa now and I like Jove,	
	Then I like Mars and thou like Erycine,[8]	
	So of the rest, till we have quite run through	
	And wearied all the fables of the gods.	
225	Then will I have thee in more modern forms,	
	Attirèd like some sprightly dame of France,	
	Brave Tuscan lady, or proud Spanish beauty;	
	Sometimes unto the Persian Sophy's° wife,	*Shah of Persia's*
	Or the Grand Signor's° mistress; and for change,	*Sultan of Turkey's*
230	To one of our most artful courtesans,	
	Or some quick° Negro, or cold Russian.	*energetic*
	And I will meet thee in as many shapes,	
	Where we may so transfuse° our wand'ring souls	*pour into each other*
	Out at our lips, and score up sums of pleasures,	
235	[*He sings.*] That the curious shall not know	
	How to tell° them as they flow;	*count*
	And the envious, when they find	
	What their number is, be pined.°	*tormented*
CELIA	If you have ears that will be pierced, or eyes	
240	That can be opened, a heart may be touched,	
	Or any part that yet sounds man[9] about you;	
	If you have touch of holy saints or heaven,	
	Do me the grace to let me scape. If not,	
	Be bountiful and kill me. You do know	
245	I am a creature hither ill betrayed	
	By one whose shame I would forget it were.	
	If you will deign me neither of these graces,	
	Yet feed your wrath, sir, rather than your lust—	
	It is a vice comes nearer manliness—	
250	And punish that unhappy crime of nature	
	Which you miscall my beauty. Flay my face	
	Or poison it with ointments for seducing	
	Your blood to this rebellion.° Rub these hands	*sexual mutiny*
	With what may cause an eating leprosy	
255	E'en to my bones and marrow—anything	
	That may disfavor me,° save in my honor—	*make me ugly*
	And I will kneel to you, pray for you, pay down	
	A thousand hourly vows, sir, for your health,	
	Report and think you virtuous—	
VOLPONE	Think me cold,	

---

7. Grotesque dance or pageant.
8. Ovid's *Metamorphoses* retells the pagan myths of transformation. Jove, king of the gods, became a bull to seduce the lovely Europa. The adulterous couple Mars, god of war, and Erycine (Venus), goddess of sexual love, were caught in a net by Vulcan, her husband.
9. That has a hint of manliness.

260 Frozen, and impotent, and so report me?
That I had Nestor's[1] hernia, thou wouldst think.
I do degenerate, and abuse my nation[2]
To play with opportunity thus long.
I should have done the act and then have parleyed.
Yield, or I'll force thee.

CELIA   O just God!

265 VOLPONE [*seizing* CELIA]   In vain—

He [BONARIO] *leaps out from where* MOSCA *had placed him.*

BONARIO   Forbear, foul ravisher, libidinous swine!
Free the forced lady or thou diest, impostor.
But that I am loath to snatch thy punishment
Out of the hand of justice, thou shouldst yet
270 Be made the timely sacrifice of vengeance
Before this altar and this dross,° thy idol.—   *the treasure*
Lady, let's quit the place. It is the den
Of villainy. Fear naught; you have a guard;
And he° ere long shall meet his just reward.   *Volpone*

[*Exeunt* BONARIO *and* CELIA.]

275 VOLPONE   Fall on me, roof, and bury me in ruin!
Become my grave, that wert my shelter! Oh!
I am unmasked, unspirited, undone,
Betrayed to beggary, to infamy—

SCENE 8. *The scene continues.*

[*Enter*] MOSCA [*bloody*].[1]

MOSCA   Where shall I run, most wretched shame of men,
To beat out my unlucky brains?

VOLPONE   Here, here.
What! Dost thou bleed?

MOSCA   Oh, that his well-driv'n sword
Had been so courteous to have cleft me down
5 Unto the navel, ere I lived to see
My life, my hopes, my spirits, my patron, all
Thus desperately engaged° by my error!   *placed at risk*

VOLPONE   Woe on thy fortune!

MOSCA   And my follies, sir.

VOLPONE   Th'hast made me miserable.

MOSCA   And myself, sir.
10 Who would have thought he would have hearkened° so?   *eavesdropped*

VOLPONE   What shall we do?

MOSCA   I know not. If my heart
Could expiate the mischance, I'd pluck it out.
Will you be pleased to hang me, or cut my throat?

---

1. Nestor was the oldest of the Greek leaders in the Trojan War.
2. I fall away from my ancestors' virtues and abuse the Italian reputation for virility.
3.8
1. Bonario apparently remembered Mosca's invitation, in 3.2.66–68, to punish him if he turns out to be lying: "draw your just sword / And score your vengeance on my front and face; / Mark me your villain."

And I'll requite you, sir. Let's die like Romans,
Since we have lived like Grecians.[2] *They knock without.*

15 VOLPONE Hark, who's there?
I hear some footing: officers, the *Saffi*,°   *arresting officers*
Come to apprehend us! I do feel the brand
Hissing already at my forehead; now
Mine ears are boring.[3]

MOSCA To your couch, sir; you
20 Make that place good, however.[4]   [VOLPONE *gets into bed.*]
Guilty men
Suspect° what they deserve still.°   [*He opens the door.*]   *dread / always*
Signor Corbaccio!

SCENE 9. *The scene continues.*

[*Enter*] CORBACCIO [*and converses with*] MOSCA; VOLTORE
[*enters unnoticed by them*].

CORBACCIO Why, how now, Mosca!
MOSCA Oh, undone, amazed, sir.
Your son—I know not by what accident—
Acquainted with your purpose to my patron
Touching° your will and making him your heir,   *concerning*
5 Entered our house with violence, his sword drawn,
Sought for you, called you wretch, unnatural,
Vowed he would kill you.
CORBACCIO Me?
MOSCA Yes, and my patron.
CORBACCIO This act shall disinherit him indeed.
Here is the will.
MOSCA [*taking it from him*] 'Tis well, sir.
CORBACCIO Right and well.
Be you as careful now for me.
10 MOSCA My life, sir,
Is not more tendered;° I am only yours.   *cherished*
CORBACCIO How does he? Will he die shortly, think'st thou?
MOSCA I fear
He'll outlast May.
CORBACCIO Today?
MOSCA No, last out May, sir.
CORBACCIO Couldst thou not gi' him a dram?°   *dose (of poison)*
MOSCA Oh, by no means, sir.
CORBACCIO Nay, I'll not bid you.
15 VOLTORE [*aside*] This is a knave, I see.
[VOLTORE *comes forward to speak privately with* MOSCA.]
MOSCA [*aside*] How, Signor Voltore! Did he hear me?
VOLTORE Parasite!
MOSCA Who's that? Oh, sir, most timely welcome—

---

2. Romans often committed suicide in adversity; Greeks were thought to be pleasure-loving.
3. Branding was a common criminal punishment; ear-boring is described as an Italian torture in Thomas Nashe's *Unfortunate Traveler* (1594).
4. (1) Defend that place, whatever happens; (2) maintain your invalid's role at all costs, since that role suits you.

VOLTORE   Scarce° *only just in time*
    To the discovery of your tricks, I fear.
    You are his only? And mine also? Are you not?
MOSCA   Who, I, sir?   [*They speak out of* CORBACCIO's *hearing.*]
20 VOLTORE   You, sir. What device° is this   *ruse*
    About a will?
MOSCA   A plot for you, sir.
VOLTORE   Come,
    Put not your foists° upon me. I shall scent 'em.   *tricks; stenches*
MOSCA   Did you not hear it?
VOLTORE   Yes, I hear Corbaccio
    Hath made your patron there his heir.
MOSCA   'Tis true,
25 By my device, drawn to it by my plot,
    With hope—
VOLTORE   Your patron should reciprocate?
    And you have promised?
MOSCA   For your good I did, sir.
    Nay, more, I told his son, brought, hid him here
    Where he might hear his father pass the deed,
30 Being persuaded to it by this thought, sir,
    That the unnaturalness, first, of the act,
    And then, his father's oft disclaiming in° him   *disowning*
    (Which I did mean t' help on) would sure enrage him
    To do some violence upon his parent,
35 On which the law should take sufficient hold,
    And you be stated° in a double hope.   *installed*
    Truth be my comfort and my conscience,
    My only aim was to dig you a fortune
    Out of these two old rotten sepulchres—
VOLTORE   I cry thee mercy, Mosca.
40 MOSCA   Worth your patience
    And your great merit, sir. And see the change!
VOLTORE   Why? What success?°   *outcome*
MOSCA   Most hapless!° You must help,   *unfortunate*
      sir.
    Whilst we expected th'old raven, in comes
    Corvino's wife, sent hither by her husband—
VOLTORE   What, with a present?
45 MOSCA   No, sir, on visitation—
    I'll tell you how, anon—and, staying long,
    The youth, he grows impatient, rushes forth,
    Seizeth the lady, wounds me, makes her swear—
    Or he would murder her, that was his vow—
50 T'affirm my patron to have done her rape,
    Which how unlike° it is, you see! And hence,   *unlikely*
    With that pretext, he's gone t'accuse his father,
    Defame my patron, defeat you—
VOLTORE   Where's her husband?
    Let him be sent for straight.

MOSCA   Sir, I'll go fetch him.
VOLTORE   Bring him to the *Scrutineo*.°   *Venetian law court*
55 MOSCA   Sir, I will.
VOLTORE   This must be stopped.
MOSCA   Oh, you do nobly, sir.
   Alas, 'twas labored all, sir, for your good;
   Nor was there want of counsel° in the plot.   *lack of wisdom*
   But fortune can at any time o'erthrow
60 The projects of a hundred learnèd clerks,° sir.   *scholars*
CORBACCIO [*striving to hear*]   What's that?
VOLTORE [*to* CORBACCIO]   Will't please you, sir, to go along?
            [*Exeunt* CORBACCIO *and* VOLTORE.]
MOSCA   Patron, go in and pray for our success.
VOLPONE [*rising*]   Need makes devotion. Heaven your labor bless!

Act 4

SCENE 1. *The piazza.*

[*Enter*] POLITIC [*and*] PEREGRINE.
POLITIC   I told you, sir, it° was a plot. You see   *the mountebank episode*
   What observation is! You mentioned me
   For° some instructions; I will tell you, sir,   *as one who could give*
   Since we are met here, in this height° of Venice,   *latitude*
5 Some few particulars I have set down
   Only for this meridian, fit to be known
   Of your crude° traveler, and they are these.   *inexperienced*
   I will not touch, sir, at your phrase or clothes,
   For they are old.¹
PEREGRINE   Sir, I have better.
POLITIC   Pardon,
   I meant as they are themes.°   *topics for advice*
10 PEREGRINE   Oh; sir, proceed.
   I'll slander° you no more of wit, good sir.   *accuse*
POLITIC   First, for your garb,² it must be grave and serious,
   Very reserved and locked;° not° tell a secret   *guarded / do not*
   On any terms, not to your father; scarce
15 A fable³ but with caution. Make sure choice
   Both of your company and discourse. Beware
   You never speak a truth—
PEREGRINE   How!
POLITIC   Not to strangers,°   *foreigners*
   For those be they you must converse with most;
   Others° I would not know, sir, but at distance,   *fellow countrymen*
20 So as I still might be a saver⁴ in 'em.

4.1
1. I will not discuss those familiar ("old") topics: the language one ought to use or the clothes one ought to wear. In the next line, in an attempt at a joke, Peregrine deliberately misconstrues "your . . . clothes" to refer to his own apparel, but Politic does not get it.
2. As for a traveler's bearing.
3. An apparently trivial story subject to political allegorization.
4. So that I might not be imposed upon. ("Be a saver" is a gambling term, meaning "to escape loss.")

You shall have tricks else passed upon you hourly.
And then, for your religion, profess none,
But wonder at the diversity of all,
And, for your part, protest, were there no other
But simply the laws o'th'land, you could content you.
Nick Machiavel and Monsieur Bodin both
Were of this mind.[5] Then must you learn the use
And handling of your silver fork° at meals,   *an Italian novelty*
The metal° of your glass—these are main matters   *composition*
With your Italian—and to know the hour
When you must eat your melons and your figs.
PEREGRINE   Is that a point of state,° too?   *statecraft*
POLITIC   Here it is.
For your Venetian, if he see a man
Preposterous in the least, he has° him straight;   *sees through*
He has, he strips° him. I'll acquaint you, sir.   *ridicules; defrauds*
I now have lived here—'tis some fourteen months;
Within the first week of my landing here,
All took me for a citizen of Venice,
I knew the forms so well—
PEREGRINE [*aside*]   And nothing else.
POLITIC   I had read Contarine,[6] took me a house,
Dealt with my Jews[7] to furnish it with movables°—   *household goods*
Well, if I could but find one man, one man
To mine own heart, whom I durst trust, I would—
PEREGRINE   What? What, sir?
POLITIC   Make him rich, make him a fortune.
He should not think° again. I would command it.   *have to think*
PEREGRINE   As how?
POLITIC   With certain projects° that I   *entrepreneurial schemes*
     have—
Which I may not discover.°   *reveal*
PEREGRINE [*aside*]   If I had
But one° to wager with, I would lay odds, now,   *someone*
He tells me instantly.
POLITIC   One is—and that
I care not greatly who knows—to serve the state
Of Venice with red herrings for three years,
And at a certain rate, from Rotterdam,[8]
Where I have correspondence. [*He shows* PEREGRINE *a paper.*]
     There's a letter
Sent me from one o'th'States,° and to that purpose;   *Dutch provinces*
He cannot write his name, but that's his mark.
PEREGRINE [*examining the paper*]   He is a chandler?[9]

---

5. Political theorists Niccolò Machiavelli (1469–1527) and Jean Bodin (1530–1596) argued that religious zeal was often politically inexpedient or divisive; as a result both were popularly thought to be atheists.
6. An English translation of Gasparo Contarini's important book, *The Commonwealth and Government of Venice*, was published in 1599.
7. The usual Jews. (In Venice Jews served as moneylenders and pawnbrokers.)
8. Venice, on the Adriatic Sea, had little need to import pickled fish from afar.
9. Candlemaker. (Evidently the paper is grease-stained.)

POLITIC   No, a cheesemonger.
There are some other° too, with whom I treat°   *others / deal*
About the same negotiation;
And I will undertake it, for 'tis thus
60   I'll do't with ease; I've cast it all.° Your hoy¹   *figured it all out*
Carries but three men in her and a boy,
And she shall make me three returns° a year.   *round trips*
So if there come but one of three, I save;°   *break even*
If two, I can defalk.° But this is, now,   *pay off loans*
If my main project fail.
65   PEREGRINE   Then you have others?
POLITIC   I should be loath to draw° the subtle air   *breathe*
Of such a place without my thousand aims.
I'll not dissemble, sir: where'er I come,
I love to be considerative;° and 'tis true   *analytic*
70   I have at my free hours thought upon
Some certain goods° unto the state of Venice,   *benefits*
Which I do call my cautions,° and, sir, which   *precautions*
I mean, in hope of pension,° to propound   *financial reward*
To the Great Council, then unto the Forty,
75   So to the Ten.² My means° are made already—   *contacts*
PEREGRINE   By whom?
POLITIC   Sir, one that though his place b'obscure,
Yet he can sway and they will hear him. He's
A *commendatore*.
PEREGRINE   What, a common sergeant?
POLITIC   Sir, such as they are put it in their mouths
80   What they should say, sometimes, as well as greater.³
I think I have my notes to show you—
    [*He searches in his garments.*]
PEREGRINE   Good, sir.
POLITIC   But you shall swear unto me on your gentry°   *gentleman's honor*
Not to anticipate—
PEREGRINE   I, sir?
POLITIC   Nor reveal
A circumstance—My paper is not with me.
PEREGRINE   Oh, but you can remember, sir.
85   POLITIC   My first is
Concerning tinderboxes.° You must know   *for lighting fires*
No family is here without its box.
Now, sir, it being so portable a thing,
Put case° that you or I were ill affected°   *suppose / disposed*
90   Unto the state; sir, with it in our pockets
Might not I go into the Arsenale?⁴
Or you? Come out again? And none the wiser?

---

1. Small vessel, not suitable for long voyages. Sir Pol's scheme is thus obviously impractical.
2. The Great Council was a large legislative group made up of wealthy Venetians; the Councils of Forty were much smaller groups that oversaw judicial affairs; the Council of Ten consisted of the elected Doge and his cabinet.
3. Common men, as well as those of higher status, may sometimes make suggestions to the government.
4. Shipyard where Venice built and repaired its naval vessels.

PEREGRINE Except yourself, sir.
POLITIC   Go to,° then. I therefore   *impatient expression*
   Advertise to° the state how fit it were   *warn*
95 That none but such as were known patriots,
   Sound lovers of their country, should be suffered
   T'enjoy them° in their houses, and even those   *tinderboxes*
   Sealed° at some office, and at such a bigness   *licensed; sealed shut*
   As might not lurk in pockets.
PEREGRINE   Admirable!
100 POLITIC My next is, how t'inquire and be resolved°   *satisfied*
   By present° demonstration whether a ship   *immediate*
   Newly arrived from Syria, or from
   Any suspected part of all the Levant,°   *Middle East*
   Be guilty of the plague. And where they use°   *are accustomed*
105 To lie out° forty, fifty days sometimes   *at anchor*
   About the Lazaretto,⁵ for their trial,
   I'll save that charge and loss unto the merchant,
   And in an hour clear the doubt.
PEREGRINE   Indeed, sir?
POLITIC Or—I will lose my labor.
PEREGRINE   My faith, that's much.
110 POLITIC Nay, sir, conceive° me. 'Twill cost me in onions⁶   *understand*
   Some thirty livres°—   *French coins*
PEREGRINE   Which is one pound sterling.
POLITIC Beside my waterworks. For this I do, sir.
   First I bring in your ship° 'twixt two brick walls—   *a ship in question*
   But those the state shall venture.° On the one   *pay for*
115 I strain° me a fair tarpaulin, and in that   *stretch*
   I stick my onions cut in halves; the other
   Is full of loopholes out at which I thrust
   The noses of my bellows, and those bellows
   I keep with° waterworks in perpetual motion⁷—   *by means of*
120 Which is the easiest matter of a hundred.°   *as easy as can be*
   Now, sir, your onion, which doth naturally
   Attract th'infection, and your bellows, blowing
   The air upon him,° will show instantly   *it (the onion)*
   By his changed color if there be contagion,
125 Or else remain as fair as at the first.
   Now 'tis known, 'tis nothing.°   *there's nothing to it*
PEREGRINE   You are right, sir.
POLITIC I would I had my note.
   [*He searches again in his garments.*]
PEREGRINE   Faith, so would I;
   But, you ha' done well for once, sir.
POLITIC   Were I false,°   *traitorous*
   Or would be made so, I could show you reasons

---

5. Quarantine hospital on an outlying island.
6. Onions were popularly supposed to absorb plague infection.
7. Perpetual-motion machines were popular attractions in early modern England, but Jonson regarded them contemptuously. Since Venice is in flat marshland, there are no waterfalls to harness there, as Sir Pol proposes.

130	How I could sell this state now to the Turk,⁸	
	Spite of their galleys° or their—	*warships*
	PEREGRINE Pray you, Sir Pol.	
	POLITIC I have 'em° not about me.	*the notes*
	PEREGRINE That I feared.	
	They are there, sir? [*He indicates a book* POLITIC *is holding.*]	
	POLITIC No, this is my diary,	
	Wherein I note my actions of the day.⁹	
135	PEREGRINE Pray you, let's see, sir. What is here? [*reading*]	
	"*Notandum*,°	*be it noted*
	A rat had gnawn my spur leathers;° notwithstanding	*laces*
	I put on new and did go forth, but first	
	I threw three beans over the threshold.° *Item,*	*for good luck*
	I went and bought two toothpicks, whereof one	
140	I burst immediately in a discourse	
	With a Dutch merchant, 'bout *ragion' del stato*.°	*political expediency*
	From him I went, and paid a *moccinigo*°	*small coin*
	For piecing° my silk stockings; by the way	*mending*
	I cheapened sprats,¹ and at Saint Mark's I urined."	
	Faith, these are politic notes!	
145	POLITIC Sir, I do slip°	*let pass*
	No action of my life thus but I quote° it.	*without noting*
	PEREGRINE Believe me, it is wise!	
	POLITIC Nay, sir, read forth.	

SCENE 2. *The scene continues.*

[*Enter*] LADY [WOULD-BE], NANO, [*and the two*] WOMEN.
[*They do not see* POLITIC *and* PEREGRINE *at first.*]

	LADY WOULD-BE Where should this loose knight be, trow?°	*do you suppose?*
	Sure he's housed.°	*in a brothel*
	NANO Why, then he's fast.°	*fast-moving; secure*
	LADY WOULD-BE Ay, he plays both° with me.	*both fast and loose*
	I pray you, stay. This heat will do more harm	
	To my complexion than his heart is worth.	
5	I do not care to hinder, but to take° him.	*catch*
	[*She rubs her cheeks.*]	
	How it° comes off!	*the makeup*
	FIRST WOMAN [*pointing*] My master's yonder.	
	LADY WOULD-BE Where?	
	FIRST WOMAN With a young gentleman.	
	LADY WOULD-BE That same's the party,	
	In man's apparel!¹ [*to* NANO] Pray you, sir, jog my knight.	
	I will be tender to his reputation,	
	However he demerit.°	*deserves blame*

---

8. The Ottoman Turks, southeast of Venice along the Adriatic Sea, were maritime and religious rivals and a long-standing military threat.
9. Many Renaissance travel writers recommended that travelers keep a written record of their journeys.
1. Bargained over some small fish.

4.2
1. Lady Would-be believes that Peregrine is the whore Mosca mentioned, in transvestite attire.

POLITIC [*seeing her*]   My lady!
PEREGRINE   Where?
POLITIC   'Tis she indeed, sir; you shall know her. She is,
  Were she not mine,² a lady of that merit
  For fashion and behavior; and for beauty
  I durst compare—
PEREGRINE   It seems you are not jealous,
  That dare commend her.
POLITIC   Nay, and for discourse—
PEREGRINE   Being your wife, she cannot miss° that.   *lack (sarcastic)*
POLITIC [*introducing* PEREGRINE]   Madam,
  Here is a gentleman; pray you use him fairly.
  He seems a youth, but he is—
LADY WOULD-BE   None?
POLITIC   Yes, one
  Has° put his face as soon° into the world—   *who has / so young*
LADY WOULD-BE   You mean, as early? But today
POLITIC   How's this!
LADY WOULD-BE   Why, in this habit,° sir; you apprehend° me.   *apparel /*
  Well, Master Would-be, this doth not become you;   *understand*
  I had thought the odor, sir, of your good name
  Had been more precious to you, that you would not
  Have done this dire massacre on your honor—
  One of your gravity and rank besides!
  But knights, I see, care little for the oath
  They make to ladies, chiefly their own ladies.
POLITIC   Now, by my spurs—the symbol of my knighthood—
PEREGRINE (*aside*)   Lord, how his brain is humbled³ for an oath!
POLITIC   —I reach° you not.   *comprehend*
LADY WOULD-BE   Right, sir, your polity°   *cunning*
  May bear° it through thus. [*to* PEREGRINE] Sir, a word with you.   *bluff*
  I would be loath to contest publicly
  With any gentlewoman, or to seem
  Froward° or violent; as *The Courtier*⁴ says,   *bad-tempered*
  It comes too near rusticity° in a lady,   *ill breeding*
  Which I would shun by all means. And however
  I may deserve from Master Would-be, yet
  T' have one fair gentlewoman° thus be made   *Peregrine*
  Th'unkind instrument to wrong another,
  And one she knows not, ay, and to persevere,
  In my poor judgment is not warranted
  From being a solecism° in our sex,   *impropriety*
  If not in manners.
PEREGRINE   How is this?
POLITIC   Sweet madam,
  Come nearer to your aim.°   *speak more clearly*

---

2. Even though I, her husband, say so.
3. Literally, "brought down" to his feet—where spurs, the appurtenances of a knight, are worn.
4. Baldassare Castiglione's famous handbook of gentility.

LADY WOULD-BE   Marry, and will, sir.
Since you provoke me with your impudence
And laughter of your light land-siren[5] here,
Your Sporus,[6] your hermaphrodite—
PEREGRINE   What's here?
Poetic fury and historic storms![7]
POLITIC   The gentleman, believe it, is of worth,
And of our nation.
LADY WOULD-BE   Ay, your Whitefriars° nation!   London brothel district
Come, I blush for you, Master Would-be, I,
And am ashamed you should ha' no more forehead°   shame
Than thus to be the patron, or Saint George,[8]
To a lewd harlot, a base fricatrice,°   whore
A female devil in a male outside.
POLITIC [to PEREGRINE]   Nay,
An° you be such a one, I must bid adieu   If
To your delights. The case appears too liquid.[9]
          [POLITIC starts to leave.]
LADY WOULD-BE   Ay, you may carry't clear, with your state-
          face!°   dignified expression
But for your carnival concupiscence,°   lecherous strumpet
Who here is fled for liberty of conscience°   licentious conduct
From furious persecution of the marshal,[1]
Her will I disc'ple.°   discipline
          [Exit POLITIC, LADY POLITIC accosts PEREGRINE.]
PEREGRINE   This is fine, i'faith!
And do you use this° often? Is this part   act this way
Of your wit's exercise, 'gainst you have occasion?[2]
Madam—
LADY WOULD-BE   Go to,° sir.   impatient expression
PEREGRINE   Do you hear me, lady?
Why, if your knight have set you to beg shirts,[3]
Or to invite me home, you might have done it
A nearer° way by far.   more direct
LADY WOULD-BE   This cannot work you
Out of my snare.
PEREGRINE   Why, am I in it, then?
Indeed, your husband told me you were fair,
And so you are; only your nose inclines—
That side that's next the sun—to the queen-apple.[4]
LADY WOULD-BE   This cannot be endured by any patience.

---

5. The Sirens were mythical sea creatures who lured sailors to their deaths by sitting on dangerous rocks and singing irresistibly. (Lady Would-be refers to Peregrine.)
6. A eunuch whom the emperor Nero dressed in drag and married.
7. Peregrine notes that even Lady Would-be's tantrums include literary allusions.
8. *Patron saint* of England, often pictured rescuing a damsel from a dragon.
9. Obvious. (Sir Pol has become convinced that his wife is right in believing that Peregrine is a transvestite whore.)
1. Official charged with punishing prostitutes. Lady Would-be thinks that Peregrine has dressed as a man to flee prosecution.
2. To keep it ready for when it is really needed?
3. Peregrine pretends to believe that Lady Would-be is tearing off his shirt in order to give it to her husband. Probably she is just trying to prevent his leaving.
4. A bright red apple. See 3.4.15–16, where we learn that Lady Would-be is sensitive about her red nose.

SCENE 3. *The scene continues.*

[*Enter*] MOSCA.

MOSCA What's the matter, madam?
LADY WOULD-BE   If the Senate°   *Venetian government*
  Right not my quest° in this, I will protest 'em   *petition*
  To all the world no aristocracy.
MOSCA What is the injury, lady?
LADY WOULD-BE   Why, the callet°   *prostitute*
5   You told me of, here I have ta'en disguised.
MOSCA Who, this? What means Your Ladyship? The creature
  I mentioned to you is apprehended now
  Before the Senate. You shall see her—
LADY WOULD-BE   Where?
MOSCA I'll bring you to her. This young gentleman,
10 I saw him land this morning at the port.
LADY WOULD-BE Is't possible! How has my judgment wandered!
  [*Releasing* PEREGRINE] Sir, I must, blushing, say to you I have erred,
  And plead your pardon.
PEREGRINE   What, more changes yet?
LADY WOULD-BE I hope you ha' not the malice to remember
15 A gentlewoman's passion. If you stay
  In Venice here, please you to use me,¹ sir—
MOSCA Will you go, madam?
LADY WOULD-BE   Pray you, sir, use me. In faith,
  The more you see me, the more I shall conceive
  You have forgot our quarrel.
  [*Exeunt* MOSCA, LADY WOULD-BE, NANO, *and* WOMEN.]
PEREGRINE   This is rare!
20 Sir Politic Would-be? No, Sir Politic Bawd,
  To bring me thus acquainted with his wife!
  Well, wise Sir Pol, since you have practiced thus
  Upon my freshmanship,² I'll try your salt-head,
  What proof° it is against a counterplot. [*Exit.*]   *how invulnerable*

SCENE 4. *The Scrutineo, or Court of Law, in the
Doge's palace.*

[*Enter*] VOLTORE, CORBACCIO, CORVINO, [*and*] MOSCA.

VOLTORE Well, now you know the carriage° of the business,   *management*
  Your constancy is all that is required
  Unto the safety of it.
MOSCA   Is the lie
  Safely conveyed° amongst us? Is that sure?   *agreed upon*
  Knows every man his burden?°   *refrain, tune*

4.3
1. Make use of my services. (With a sexual innuendo continued in "The more you see me, the more I shall conceive" [line 18], where "conceive" means both "understand" and "conceive a child.")
2. Taken advantage of my inexperience. (Peregrine apparently believes that Sir Pol has deliberately involved him in a humiliating setup. "Salt-head," following, plays on both "salt" meaning "seasoned," "old," and "salt" meaning "lecherous.")

CORVINO   Yes.
MOSCA   Then shrink not.
CORVINO [*aside to* MOSCA]   But knows the advocate the truth?
MOSCA [*aside to* CORVINO]   Oh, sir,
　By no means. I devised a formal° tale   　　　　*elaborate*
　That salved your reputation. But be valiant, sir.
CORVINO   I fear no one but him,° that this his pleading   　*Voltore*
　Should make him stand for a co-heir—
MOSCA   Co-halter![1]
　Hang him, we will but use his tongue, his noise,
　As we do Croaker's,° here.   　　　　　　　　　*Corbaccio's*
CORVINO   Ay, what shall he do?
MOSCA   When we ha' done, you mean?
CORVINO   Yes.
MOSCA   Why, we'll think—
　Sell him for *mummia*;[2] he's half dust already.
　([*Aside*] *to* VOLTORE) Do not you smile to see this buffalo,[3]
　How he doth sport it with his head? [*to himself*] I should,
　If all were well and past. ([*aside*] *to* CORBACCIO) Sir, only you
　Are he that shall enjoy the crop° of all,   　　　*harvest*
　And these not know for whom they toil.
CORBACCIO   Ay, peace!
MOSCA ([*aside*] *to* CORVINO)   But you shall eat it. [*To himself*]
　Much!° (*then to* VOLTORE *again*) Worshipful sir,   *Sure you will!*
　Mercury[4] sit upon your thund'ring tongue,
　Or the French Hercules, and make your language
　As conquering as his club,[5] to beat along,
　As with a tempest, flat, our adversaries!
　[*Aside to* CORVINO] But much more yours,° sir.   *your adversaries*
VOLTORE   Here they come. Ha' done.°   　　　*shut up*
MOSCA   I have another witness° if you need, sir,   *Lady Would-be*
　I can produce.
VOLTORE   Who is it?
MOSCA   Sir, I have her.

SCENE 5. *The scene continues.*

　　　[*Enter*] *four* AVOCATORI, BONARIO, CELIA. *Notario*
　　　[NOTORY], COMMENDATORI° [*and other court officials*].   *law court deputies*
FIRST AVOCATORE   The like of this the Senate never heard of.
SECOND AVOCATORE   'Twill come most strange to them when we report it.
FOURTH AVOCATORE   The gentlewoman has been ever held
　Of unreprovèd name.
THIRD AVOCATORE   So, the young man.
FOURTH AVOCATORE   The more unnatural part that of his father.

4.4
1. Playing on "halter," a hangman's noose, to suggest that both Corbaccio and Voltore are being duped.
2. Powdered embalmed corpse, used medicinally.
3. Corvino, with his cuckold's horns.
4. May the god of rhetoric (and thieves).
5. After his tenth labor, according to some legendary accounts, Hercules, aged by now but powerfully eloquent, fathered the Celts in Gaul, or France. He was traditionally pictured with a club.

SECOND AVOCATORE   More of the husband.
FIRST AVOCATORE   I not know to give
His act a name, it is so monstrous!
FOURTH AVOCATORE   But the impostor,° he is a thing created   °Volpone
T'exceed example!°   °precedent
FIRST AVOCATORE   And all aftertimes!°   °later eras
SECOND AVOCATORE   I never heard a true voluptuary
Described but him.
THIRD AVOCATORE   Appear yet those were cited?
NOTARY   All but the old magnifico, Volpone.
FIRST AVOCATORE   Why is not he here?
MOSCA   Please Your Fatherhoods,
Here is his advocate. Himself's so weak,
So feeble—
FOURTH AVOCATORE   What are you?
BONARIO   His parasite,
His knave, his pander! I beseech the court
He may be forced to come, that your grave eyes
May bear strong witness of his strange impostures.
VOLTORE   Upon my faith and credit with your virtues,
He is not able to endure the air.
SECOND AVOCATORE   Bring him, however.
THIRD AVOCATORE   We will see him.
FOURTH AVOCATORE   Fetch him.
             [*Exit officers.*]
VOLTORE   Your Fatherhoods' fit pleasures be obeyed,
But sure the sight will rather move your pities
Than indignation. May it please the court,
In the meantime he may be heard in me.
I know this place most void of prejudice,
And therefore crave it, since we have no reason
To fear our truth should hurt our cause.
THIRD AVOCATORE   Speak free.
VOLTORE   Then know, most honored fathers, I must now
Discover° to your strangely abusèd ears   °reveal
The most prodigious and most frontless° piece   °shameless
Of solid° impudence and treachery   °complete
That ever vicious nature yet brought forth
To shame the state of Venice. [*indicating* CELIA] This lewd woman,
That wants° no artificial looks or tears   °who lacks
To help the visor° she has now put on,   °(weeping) mask
Hath long been known a close° adulteress   °secret; intimate
To that lascivious youth there [*indicating* BONARIO]; not suspected,
I say, but known, and taken in the act
With him; and by this man, the easy° husband,   °lenient
Pardoned; whose timeless° bounty makes him now   °unseasonable; endless
Stand here, the most unhappy, innocent person
That ever man's own goodness made accused.[1]

4.5
1. That ever had his own goodness turned against him.

	For these, not knowing how to owe° a gift	acknowledge
45	Of that dear grace but° with their shame, being placed	other than
	So above all powers of their gratitude,[2]	
	Began to hate the benefit, and in place	
	Of thanks devise t'extirp° the memory	to extirpate, wipe out
	Of such an act. Wherein I pray Your Fatherhoods	
50	To observe the malice, yea, the rage of creatures	
	Discovered in their evils, and what heart°	audacity
	Such take even from their crimes. But that anon	
	Will more appear. This gentleman, the father,	
	[*indicating* CORBACCIO]	
	Hearing of this foul fact,° with many others	deed
55	Which daily struck at his too tender ears,	
	And grieved in nothing more than that he could not	
	Preserve himself a parent—his son's ills°	evil deeds
	Growing to that strange flood—at last decreed	
	To disinherit him.	
	FIRST AVOCATORE These be strange turns!	
60	SECOND AVOCATORE The young man's fame° was ever fair and honest.	reputation
	VOLTORE So much more full of danger is his vice,	
	That can beguile so under shade of virtue.	
	But, as I said, my honored sires, his father	
	Having this settled purpose, by what means	
65	To him° betrayed we know not, and this day	Bonario
	Appointed for the deed, that parricide—	
	I cannot style him better°—by confederacy	give him a better name
	Preparing this his paramour to be there,	
	Entered Volpone's house—who was the man,	
70	Your Fatherhoods must understand, designed	
	For the inheritance—there sought his father.	
	But with what purpose sought he him, my lords?	
	I tremble to pronounce it, that a son	
	Unto a father, and to such a father,	
75	Should have so foul, felonious intent:	
	It was to murder him. When, being prevented	
	By his more happy° absence, what then did he?	Corbaccio's fortunate
	Not check his wicked thoughts; no, now new deeds—	
	Mischief doth ever end where it begins[3]—	
80	An act of horror, fathers! He dragged forth	
	The agèd gentleman, that had there lain bedrid	
	Three years and more, out of his innocent couch;	
	Naked upon the floor there left him; wounded	
	His servant in the face, and with this strumpet,	
85	The stale° to his forged practice,° who was glad	decoy / plot
	To be so active—I shall here desire	
	Your Fatherhoods to note but my collections°	deductions

---

2. Since the rare value of Corvino's forgiveness was so far beyond their powers of gratitude.

3. Wickedness is always persistent.

> As most remarkable—thought at once to stop
> His father's ends,° discredit his free choice   *aims*
> In the old gentleman,° redeem themselves   *Volpone*
> By laying infamy upon this man°   *Corvino*
> To whom with blushing they should owe their lives.

FIRST AVOCATORE   What proofs have you of this?

BONARIO   Most honored fathers,
> I humbly crave there be no credit given
> To this man's mercenary tongue.

SECOND AVOCATORE   Forbear.

BONARIO   His soul moves in his fee.

THIRD AVOCATORE   Oh, sir!

BONARIO   This fellow,
> For six sols° more, would plead against his Maker.   *halfpennies*

FIRST AVOCATORE   You do forget yourself.

VOLTORE   Nay, nay, grave fathers,
> Let him have scope. Can any man imagine
> That he will spare 's° accuser, that would not   *spare his*
> Have spared his parent?

FIRST AVOCATORE   Well, produce your proofs.

CELIA   I would I could forget I were a creature!°   *living being*

VOLTORE [*calling a witness*]   Signor Corbaccio!

FOURTH AVOCATORE   What is he?

VOLTORE   The father.

SECOND AVOCATORE   Has he had an oath?

NOTARY   Yes.

CORBACCIO   What must I do now?

NOTARY   Your testimony's craved.

CORBACCIO [*mis-hearing*]   Speak to the knave?
> I'll ha' my mouth first stopped with earth! My heart
> Abhors his knowledge;° I disclaim in° him.   *knowing him / disavow*

FIRST AVOCATORE   But for what cause?

CORBACCIO   The mere portent of nature.[4]
> He is an utter stranger to my loins.

BONARIO   Have they made you to this?

CORBACCIO   I will not hear thee,
> Monster of men, swine, goat, wolf, parricide!
> Speak not, thou viper.

BONARIO   Sir, I will sit down,
> And rather wish my innocence should suffer
> Than I resist the authority of a father.

VOLTORE [*calling a witness*]   Signor Corvino!

SECOND AVOCATORE   This is strange!

FIRST AVOCATORE   Who's this?

NOTARY   The husband.

FOURTH AVOCATORE   Is he sworn?

NOTARY   He is.

THIRD AVOCATORE   Speak, then.

---

4. A completely monstrous birth. (A deformed child was often considered to be a portent, or evil omen.)

CORVINO This woman, please Your Fatherhoods, is a whore
   Of most hot exercise, more than a partridge,⁵
   Upon record°—   *as is well attested*
FIRST AVOCATORE No more.
CORVINO   Neighs like a jennet.°   *mare (in heat)*
NOTARY Preserve the honor of the court.
CORVINO   I shall,
   And modesty of your most reverend ears.
   And yet I hope that I may say these eyes
   Have seen her glued unto that piece of cedar,
   That fine well-timbered gallant;⁶ and that here
   [*Pointing to his forehead*] The letters may be read, thorough the horn,⁷
   That make the story perfect.°   *complete*
MOSCA [*aside to* CORVINO]   Excellent, sir!
CORVINO [*aside to* MOSCA] There is no shame in this, now, is there?
MOSCA [*aside to* CORVINO]   None.
CORVINO [*to the court*] Or if I said I hoped that she were
      onward°   *well on her way*
   To her damnation, if there be a hell
   Greater than whore and woman—a good Catholic
   May make the doubt°—   *may wonder*
THIRD AVOCATORE   His grief hath made him frantic.
FIRST AVOCATORE Remove him hence. *She* [CELIA] *swoons.*
SECOND AVOCATORE   Look to the woman!
CORVINO [*taunting her*]   Rare!
   Prettily feigned! Again!
FOURTH AVOCATORE   Stand from about her.
FIRST AVOCATORE Give her the air.
THIRD AVOCATORE [*to* MOSCA]   What can you say?
MOSCA   My wound,
   May't please Your Wisdoms, speaks for me, received
   In aid of my good patron when he° missed   *Bonario*
   His sought-for father, when that well-taught dame
   Had her cue given her to cry out a rape.
BONARIO Oh, most laid° impudence! Fathers—   *premeditated*
THIRD AVOCATORE   Sir, be silent.
   You had your hearing free,° so must they theirs.   *uninterrupted*
SECOND AVOCATORE I do begin to doubt th'imposture here.
FOURTH AVOCATORE This woman has too many moods.
VOLTORE   Grave fathers,
   She is a creature of a most professed
   And prostituted lewdness.
CORVINO   Most impetuous!
   Unsatisfied,° grave fathers!   *insatiable*
VOLTORE   May her feignings

---

5. A bird capable of numerous consecutive sexual acts and so a byword for lechery.
6. Corvino sarcastically compliments Bonario as a strapping fellow to whom Celia no doubt wishes to cling. The cedars of the Middle East are tall and stately.
7. Children learned to read the alphabet from pages protected by transparent sheets of horn. (With an allusion to the cuckold's horn.)

  Not take° Your Wisdoms! But° this day she baited   *take in / only*
  A stranger, a grave knight, with her loose eyes
  And more lascivious kisses. This man° saw 'em   *Mosca*
  Together on the water in a gondola.
150 MOSCA Here is the lady herself that saw 'em too,
  Without;° who then had in the open streets   *waiting outside*
  Pursued them, but for saving her knight's honor.
FIRST AVOCATORE Produce that lady.
SECOND AVOCATORE   Let her come.
             [*Exit* MOSCA.]
FOURTH AVOCATORE   These things,
  They strike with wonder!
THIRD AVOCATORE   I am turned a stone!

SCENE 6. *The scene continues.*

 [*Enter*] MOSCA [*and*] LADY [WOULD-BE].
MOSCA Be resolute, madam.
LADY WOULD-BE   Ay, this same is she.
 [*To* CELIA] Out, thou chameleon° harlot! Now thine *deceitfully changeable*
  eyes
 Vie tears with the hyena.¹ Dar'st thou look
 Upon my wrongèd face? [*to the* AVOCATORI] I cry° your pardons. *beg*
5 I fear I have forgettingly transgressed
 Against the dignity of the court—
SECOND AVOCATORE   No, madam.
LADY WOULD-BE And been exorbitant°—   *excessive*
SECOND AVOCATORE   You have not, lady.
FOURTH AVOCATORE These proofs are strong.
LADY WOULD-BE   Surely, I had no purpose
 To scandalize your honors, or my sex's.
THIRD AVOCATORE We do believe it.
10 LADY WOULD-BE   Surely, you may believe it.
SECOND AVOCATORE Madam, we do.
LADY WOULD-BE   Indeed, you may. My breeding
 Is not so coarse—
FOURTH AVOCATORE We know it.
LADY WOULD-BE   —to offend
 With pertinacy°—   *stubborn resolution*
THIRD AVOCATORE Lady—
LADY WOULD-BE   —such a presence;
 No, surely.
FIRST AVOCATORE We well think it.
LADY WOULD-BE   You may think it.
FIRST AVOCATORE [*to the other* AVOCATORI] Let her o'ercome.° *have the last*
15 [*To* CELIA *and* BONARIO] What witnesses have you *word*
 To make good your report?
BONARIO   Our consciences.

4.6
1. A symbol of treachery, the hyena was supposed to be able to change its sex and the color of its eyes at will and to imitate human voices.

CELIA And heaven, that never fails the innocent.
FOURTH AVOCATORE These are no testimonies.
BONARIO   Not in your courts,
Where multitude and clamor overcomes.
FIRST AVOCATORE Nay, then, you do wax insolent.

VOLPONE *is brought in [on a litter], as impotent.*°   *disabled*
[LADY WOULD-BE *embraces him.*]°   (see 5.2.97)

20 VOLTORE   Here, here
The testimony comes that will convince
And put to utter dumbness their bold tongues.
See here, grave fathers, here's the ravisher,
The rider on men's wives, the great impostor,
25 The grand voluptuary! Do you not think
These limbs should affect venery?² Or these eyes
Covet a concubine? Pray you, mark these hands:
Are they not fit to stroke a lady's breasts?
Perhaps he doth dissemble?
BONARIO   So he does.
VOLTORE Would you ha' him tortured?
30 BONARIO   I would have him proved.³
VOLTORE Best try him, then, with goads or burning irons;
Put him to the strappado.⁴ I have heard
The rack⁵ hath cured the gout; faith, give it him
And help him of a malady; be courteous.
35 I'll undertake, before these honored fathers,
He shall have yet as many left° diseases   *remaining*
As she has known adulterers, or thou strumpets.
O my most equal° hearers, if these deeds,   *impartial*
Acts of this bold and most exorbitant strain,
40 May pass with sufferance,° what one citizen   *be permitted*
But owes the forfeit of his life, yea, fame
To him that dares traduce him?⁶ Which of you
Are safe, my honored fathers? I would ask,
With leave of Your grave Fatherhoods, if their plot
45 Have any face or color like to truth?
Or if unto the dullest nostril here
It smell not rank and most abhorrèd slander?
I crave your care of this good gentleman,
Whose life is much endangered by their fable;
50 And as for them, I will conclude with this:
That vicious persons, when they are hot, and fleshed⁷
In impious acts, their constancy° abounds.   *resoluteness*
Damned deeds are done with greatest confidence.
FIRST AVOCATORE Take 'em to custody, and sever them.

---

2. Delight in sexual activity.
3. Tested for impotence, a regular court procedure in some divorce and rape cases. (Torture was another method sometimes used to extract confessions.)
4. Torture in which the victim's arms were tied behind his back; he was then hoisted up by the wrists and dropped.
5. Torture instrument that stretched the victim to the point of dislocating his joints.
6. What citizen is there whose life and reputation might not be forfeit to a slanderer?
7. Excited by the taste of blood, like hunting hounds.

SECOND AVOCATORE   'Tis pity two such prodigies° should live.   *monsters*
        [*Exeunt* CELIA *and* BONARIO, *guarded.*]
FIRST AVOCATORE   Let the old gentleman be returned with care.
   I'm sorry our credulity wronged him.
        [*Exeunt litter-bearers with* VOLPONE.]
FOURTH AVOCATORE   These are two creatures!°   *monsters*
THIRD AVOCATORE   I have an earthquake in me!
SECOND AVOCATORE   Their shame, even in their cradles, fled their faces.
FOURTH AVOCATORE [*to* VOLTORE]   You've done a worthy service to the
   state, sir,
   In their discovery.
FIRST AVOCATORE   You shall hear ere night
   What punishment the court decrees upon 'em.
VOLTORE   We thank Your Fatherhoods.
        [*Exeunt* AVOCATORI, NOTARY, COMMENDATORI.]
   [*To* MOSCA]   How like you it?
MOSCA   Rare!
   I'd ha' your tongue, sir, tipped with gold for this;
   I'd ha' you be the heir to the whole city;
   The earth I'd have want men ere you want living.°   *lack income*
   They're bound to erect your statue in Saint Mark's.—
   Signor Corvino, I would have you go
   And show yourself,[8] that you have conquered.
CORVINO   Yes.
MOSCA [*aside to* CORVINO]   It was much better that you should profess
   Yourself a cuckold thus, than that the other[9]
   Should have been proved.
CORVINO   Nay, I considered that.
   Now it is her fault.
MOSCA   Then it had been yours.
CORVINO   True. I do doubt this advocate still.
MOSCA   I'faith,
   You need not; I dare ease you of that care.
CORVINO   I trust thee, Mosca.
MOSCA   As your own soul, sir.
        [*Exit* CORVINO.]
CORBACCIO   Mosca!
MOSCA   Now for your business, sir.
CORBACCIO   How? Ha' you business?
MOSCA   Yes, yours, sir.
CORBACCIO   Oh, none else?
MOSCA   None else, not I.
CORBACCIO   Be careful, then.
MOSCA   Rest you with both your eyes,° sir.   *rest assured*
CORBACCIO   Dispatch it.[1]
MOSCA   Instantly.
CORBACCIO   And look that all

---

8. Appear in public. (To indicate that he is not ashamed of having admitted to being a cuckold.)
9. The attempt to prostitute Celia to Volpone.
1. That is, Hurry to make Volpone's will, since Corbaccio has already delivered on his half of the promise.

Whatever be put in: jewels, plate, moneys,
Household stuff, bedding, curtains.
MOSCA   Curtain rings, sir.
Only the advocate's fee must be deducted.
CORBACCIO   I'll pay him, now; you'll be too prodigal.
MOSCA   Sir, I must tender° it.   *present*
85 CORBACCIO   Two *cecchines* is well?
MOSCA   No, six, sir.
CORBACCIO   'Tis too much.
MOSCA   He talked a great while,
You must consider that, sir.
CORBACCIO [*giving money*]   Well, there's three—
MOSCA   I'll give it him.
CORBACCIO   Do so, and [*he tips* MOSCA] there's for thee.
                                            [*Exit* CORBACCIO.]
MOSCA [*aside*]   Bountiful bones! What horrid strange offense
90   Did he commit 'gainst nature in his youth
Worthy this age?² [*to* VOLTORE] You see, sir, how I work
Unto your ends; take you no notice.°   *leave it to me*
VOLTORE   No,
I'll leave you.
MOSCA   All is yours,   [*Exit* VOLTORE.]
            [*aside*] the devil and all,
Good advocate! [*to* LADY WOULD-BE] Madam, I'll bring you home.
LADY WOULD-BE   No, I'll go see your patron.
95 MOSCA   That you shall not.
I'll tell you why. My purpose is to urge
My patron to reform° his will; and, for   *revise*
The zeal you've shown today, whereas before
You were but third or fourth, you shall be now
100   Put in the first, which would appear as begged
If you were present. Therefore—
LADY WOULD-BE   You shall sway me.
                                            [*Exeunt.*]

Act 5

SCENE 1. VOLPONE'S *house.*

[*Enter*] VOLPONE [*attended*].
VOLPONE   Well, I am here, and all this brunt° is past.   *crisis*
I ne'er was in dislike with my disguise
Till this fled° moment; here 'twas good, in private,   *past*
But, in your public—*cavé*° whilst I breathe.   *watch out*
5   Fore God, my left leg 'gan to have the cramp,
And I apprehended straight° some power had struck me *thought at once*
With a dead palsy.° Well, I must be merry   *paralysis*
And shake it off. A many of these fears
Would put me into some villainous disease,

---

2. To deserve this old age.

Should they come thick upon me. I'll prevent 'em.
Give me a bowl of lusty wine to fright
This humor from my heart.[1]—Hum, hum, hum! *He drinks.*
'Tis almost gone already; I shall conquer,°   *overcome my fears*
Any device, now, of rare ingenious knavery,
That would possess me with a violent laughter,
Would make me up° again. So, so, so, so. *Drinks again.*   *restore me*
This heat is life; 'tis blood by this time. [*calling*] Mosca!

SCENE 2. *The scene continues.*

[*Enter*] MOSCA.

MOSCA   How now, sir? Does the day look clear again?
Are we recovered and wrought out of error
Into our way, to see our path before us?
Is our trade free once more?
VOLPONE   Exquisite Mosca!
MOSCA   Was it not carried learnedly?
VOLPONE   And stoutly.°   *resolutely*
Good wits are greatest in extremities.
MOSCA   It were a folly beyond thought to trust
Any grand act unto a cowardly spirit.
You are not taken with it enough, methinks?
VOLPONE   Oh, more than if I had enjoyed the wench!
The pleasure of all womankind's not like it.
MOSCA   Why, now you speak, sir. We must here be fixed;
Here we must rest. This is our masterpiece.
We cannot think to go beyond this.
VOLPONE   True,
Th'hast played thy prize,[1] my precious Mosca.
MOSCA   Nay, sir,
To gull° the court—   *hoodwink*
VOLPONE   And quite divert the torrent
Upon the innocent.
MOSCA   Yes, and to make
So rare a music out of discords[2]—
VOLPONE   Right.
That yet to me's the strangest, how th'ast borne it!°   *brought it off*
That these,° being so divided 'mongst themselves,   *these men*
Should not scent° somewhat, or° in me or thee,   *suspect / either*
Or doubt their own side.°   *position*
MOSCA   True, they will not see't.
Too much light blinds 'em, I think. Each of 'em
Is so possessed and stuffed with his own hopes
That anything unto the contrary,
Never so true or never so apparent,

5.1
1. Wine was supposed to convert quickly to blood (see line 17), thus giving courage to the drinker.
5.2
1. Professional fencers "played the prize," that is, competed for purses and titles, in virtuoso displays of swordsmanship.
2. To bring harmony out of various discordant elements was thought to be the highest achievement of art.

Never so palpable, they will resist it—
VOLPONE   Like a temptation of the devil.
MOSCA   Right, sir.
Merchants may talk of trade, and your great signors
Of land that yields well; but if Italy
Have any glebe° more fruitful than these fellows,   soil
I am deceived. Did not your advocate rare?°   do brilliantly
VOLPONE   Oh!—"My most honored fathers, my grave fathers,
Under correction of Your Fatherhoods,
What face of truth is here? If these strange deeds
May pass, most honored fathers"—I had much ado
To forbear laughing.
MOSCA   'T seemed to me you sweat,° sir.   sweated (with fear)
VOLPONE   In troth, I did a little.
MOSCA   But confess, sir,
Were you not daunted?
VOLPONE   In good faith, I was
A little in a mist,° but not dejected;°   uncertain / overwhelmed
Never but still myself.
MOSCA   I think° it, sir.   believe
Now, so truth help me, I must needs say this, sir,
And out of conscience for your advocate:
He's taken pains, in faith, sir, and deserved,
In my poor judgment—I speak it under favor,°   with your permission
Not to contrary° you, sir—very richly—   contradict
Well—to be cozened.°   cheated
VOLPONE   Troth, and I think so too,
By that° I heard him° in the latter end.   what / him say
MOSCA   Oh, but before, sir! Had you heard him first
Draw it to certain heads, then aggravate,[3]
Then use his vehement figures°—I looked still   figures of speech
When he would shift[4] a shirt; and doing this
Out of pure love, no hope of gain—
VOLPONE   'Tis right.
I cannot answer° him, Mosca, as I would,   repay
Not yet; but for thy sake, at thy entreaty
I will begin ev'n now to vex 'em all,
This very instant.
MOSCA   Good, sir.
VOLPONE   Call the dwarf
And eunuch forth.
MOSCA [*calling*]   Castrone, Nano!
     [*Enter*] NANO [*and*] CASTRONE.
NANO   Here.
VOLPONE   Shall we have a jig, now?
MOSCA   What you please, sir.
VOLPONE [*to* CASTRONE *and* NANO]   Go,

---

3. Arrange his material under various headings, then bring charges.
4. Change (because his efforts made him sweat).

VOLPONE   Straight give out about the streets, you two,
That I am dead. Do it with constancy,°   *conviction*
Sadly, do you hear? Impute it to the grief
Of this late slander.   [*Exeunt* CASTRONE *and* NANO.]
MOSCA   What do you mean, sir?
VOLPONE   Oh,
I shall have instantly my vulture, crow,
Raven come flying hither on the news
To peck for carrion, my she-wolf° and all,   *Lady Would-be*
Greedy and full of expectation—
MOSCA   And then to have it ravished from their mouths?
VOLPONE   'Tis true. I will ha' thee put on a gown[5]
And take upon thee as° thou wert mine heir;   *act as though*
Show 'em a will. Open that chest and reach
Forth one of those that has the blanks.° I'll straight   *blank spaces*
Put in thy name.
MOSCA [*fetching a blank will*]   It will be rare, sir.
VOLPONE   Ay,
When they e'en gape, and find themselves deluded—
MOSCA   Yes.
VOLPONE   And thou use them scurvily. Dispatch,
Get on thy gown.
[VOLPONE *signs the will* MOSCA *has given him.*
MOSCA *puts on a mourning garment.*]
MOSCA   But, what, sir, if they ask
After the body?
VOLPONE   Say it was corrupted.
MOSCA   I'll say it stunk, sir, and was fain° t'have it   *I was obliged*
Coffined up instantly and sent away.
VOLPONE   Anything; what thou wilt. Hold, here's my will.
Get thee a cap, a count-book, pen and ink,
Papers afore thee; sit as thou wert taking
An inventory of parcels.° I'll get up   *items*
Behind the curtain on a stool, and hearken;
Sometime peep over, see how they do look,
With what degrees their blood doth leave their faces.
Oh, 'twill afford me a rare meal of laughter!
MOSCA   Your advocate will turn stark dull° upon it.   *gloomy*
VOLPONE   It will take off his oratory's edge.
MOSCA   But your *clarissimo*,° old round-back, he   *aristocrat (Corbaccio)*
Will crump you° like a hog-louse with the touch.   *curl up on you*
VOLPONE   And what Corvino?
MOSCA   Oh, sir, look for him
Tomorrow morning with a rope and a dagger[6]
To visit all the streets; he must run mad.

---

5. This must be the long black gown ordinarily worn by chief mourners, not the *clarissimo*'s (aristocrat's) garment, which Mosca dons later in the scene and which constitutes a different kind of insult to Voltore, Corbaccio, and Corvino.

6. Traditional equipment of suicidal madmen, borne by the allegorical figure of Despair in Spenser's *Faerie Queene* 1.9 and by the revenger Hieronimo in *The Spanish Tragedy*.

My lady, too, that came into the court
To bear false witness for Your Worship—
VOLPONE   Yes,
And kissed me 'fore the fathers, when my face
Flowed all with oils.°   (see 4.6.2℅.1–2)
MOSCA   And sweat, sir. Why, your gold
Is such another° med'cine, it dries up   so effective a
All those offensive savors! It transforms
The most deformèd, and restores 'em lovely,
As 'twere the strange poetical girdle.[7] Jove
Could not invent t'himself a shroud more subtle
To pass Acrisius' guards.[8] It is the thing
Makes all the world her grace, her youth, her beauty.
VOLPONE   I think she loves me.
MOSCA   Who? The lady, sir?
She's jealous of you.[9]
VOLPONE   Dost thou say so?
        [*Knocking offstage.*]
MOSCA   Hark,
There's some already.
VOLPONE   Look.
MOSCA [*peeping out the door*]   It is the vulture.
He has the quickest scent.
VOLPONE   I'll to my place,
Thou to thy posture.°   *pose*
MOSCA   I am set.
VOLPONE   But, Mosca,
Play the artificer° now; torture 'em rarely.   *artist*
        [VOLPONE *conceals himself.*]

SCENE 3. *The scene continues.*

[*Enter*] VOLTORE.
VOLTORE   How now, my Mosca?
MOSCA [*pretending not to notice him, and reading from an
    inventory*]   "Turkey carpets,° nine"—   *Oriental rugs*
VOLTORE   Taking an inventory? That is well.
MOSCA   "Two suits of bedding, tissue"[1]—
VOLTORE   Where's the will?
Let me read that the while.°   *while you're busy*
        [*Enter*] CORBACCIO [*on a litter*].
CORBACCIO [*to the litter-beaters*]   So, set me down
And get you home.   [*Exeunt litter-bearers.*]
VOLTORE   Is he come now to trouble us?
MOSCA   "Of cloth-of-gold,[2] two more"—

---

7. The girdle of Venus, the goddess of love, made its wearer irresistible.
8. King Acrisius shut his daughter Danaë in a tower, but the god Jove came to her in a shower of gold.
9. (1) Devoted to you; (2) covetous of your wealth.

5.3
1. Sets of bedcovers and hangings, made of cloth with gold or silver threads interwoven. The fancy textiles Mosca mentions in this scene were extremely expensive to produce in the days before automation.
2. Cloth made of gold threads.

CORBACCIO   Is it done, Mosca?
MOSCA   "Of several velvets,° eight"—   *separate velvet hangings*
VOLTORE [*aside*]   I like his care.
CORBACCIO [*to* MOSCA]   Dost thou not hear?
     [*Enter*] CORVINO.
CORVINO   Ha! Is the hour come, Mosca?
     VOLPONE *peeps from behind a traverse.*°   *curtain*
VOLPONE [*aside*]   Ay, now they muster.°   *assemble*
CORVINO   What does the advocate here?
     Or this Corbaccio?
CORBACCIO   What do these here?
     [*Enter*] LADY [WOULD-BE].
10 LADY WOULD-BE   Mosca,
     Is his thread spun?³
MOSCA   "Eight chests of linen"—
VOLPONE [*aside*]   Oh,
     My fine Dame Would-be, too!
CORVINO   Mosca, the will,
     That I may show it these, and rid 'em hence.
MOSCA   "Six chests of diaper, four of damask"⁴—there.
     [*He gives them the will.*]
CORBACCIO   Is that the will?
MOSCA   "Down beds and bolsters"—
15 VOLPONE [*aside*]   Rare!
     Be busy still. Now they begin to flutter;
     They never think of me. Look, see, see, see!
     How their swift eyes run over the long deed
     Unto the name, and to the legacies,
     What is bequeathed them there—
20 MOSCA   "Ten suits of hangings"°—   *tapestries*
     VOLPONE [*aside*]   Ay, i' their garters,⁵ Mosca. Now their hopes
     Are at the gasp.°   *last gasp*
VOLTORE   Mosca the heir!
CORBACCIO   What's that?
VOLPONE [*aside*]   My advocate is dumb. Look to my merchant;
     He has heard of some strange storm, a ship is lost,
25   He faints. My lady will swoon. Old glazen-eyes,⁶
     He hath not reached his despair yet.
CORBACCIO   All these
     Are out of hope; I'm sure the man.
CORVINO   But, Mosca—
MOSCA   "Two cabinets"—
CORVINO   Is this in earnest?
MOSCA   "One
     Of ebony"—

---

3. Is he dead? (In Greek mythology, the Fates spin out the thread of a human being's life and cut it at the time of death.)
4. Two kinds of costly textile with interwoven motifs. Diaper was linen with a diamond pattern; damask could be linen or silk with floral or other designs.
5. "Go hang yourself in your own garters" was a common phrase of ridicule.
6. Corbaccio wears spectacles (see also line 63 below).

CORVINO   Or do you but delude me?

30 MOSCA   "The other, mother-of-pearl"—I am very busy.
    Good faith, it is a fortune thrown upon me—
    "Item, one salt° of agate"—not my seeking.   *saltcellar*

LADY WOULD-BE   Do you hear, sir?

MOSCA   "A perfumed box"—pray you, forbear;
    You see I am troubled°—"made of an onyx"—   *busy*

LADY WOULD-BE   How!

35 MOSCA   Tomorrow or next day I shall be at leisure
    To talk with you all.

CORVINO   Is this my large hope's issue?°   *outcome*

LADY WOULD-BE   Sir, I must have a fairer answer.

MOSCA   Madam!
    Marry, and shall: pray you, fairly° quit my house.   *positively*
    Nay, raise no tempest with your looks, but hark you,
40 Remember what Your Ladyship offered me°   *implicitly, sexual favors*
    To put you in° an heir; go to, think on't,   *your name in as*
    And what you said e'en your best madams did
    For maintenance,° and why not you? Enough.   *financial support*
    Go home and use the poor Sir Pol, your knight, well,
45 For fear I tell some riddles.° Go, be melancholic.   *secrets*
                         [*Exit* LADY WOULD-BE.]

VOLPONE [*aside*]   Oh, my fine devil!

CORVINO   Mosca, pray you a word.

MOSCA   Lord! Will not you take your dispatch hence yet?
    Methinks of all you should have been th'example.°   *led the way*
    Why should you stay here? With what thought? What promise?
50 Hear you, do not you know I know you an ass?
    And that you would most fain have been a wittol°   *willing cuckold*
    If fortune would have let you? That you are
    A declared cuckold, on good terms?° This pearl,   *in good standing*
    You'll say, was yours? Right. This diamond?
55 I'll not deny't, but thank you. Much here else?
    It may be so. Why, think that these good works
    May help to hide your bad. I'll not betray you.
    Although you be but extraordinary°   *in name only*
    And have it° only in title, it sufficeth.   *the name of cuckold*
60 Go home. Be melancholic too, or mad.   [*Exit* CORVINO.]

VOLPONE [*aside*]   Rare, Mosca! How his villainy becomes him!

VOLTORE [*aside*]   Certain he doth delude all these for me.

CORBACCIO [*finally making out the will*]   Mosca the heir?

VOLPONE [*aside*]   Oh, his four eyes have found it!

CORBACCIO   I'm cozened, cheated by a parasite-slave!
    Harlot,⁷ th'ast gulled me.

65 MOSCA   Yes, sir. Stop your mouth,
    Or I shall draw the only tooth is left.
    Are not you he, that filthy covetous wretch
    With the three legs,° that here, in hope of prey,   *including his cane*

---

7. A word used of wicked men as well as women.

             Have, any time this three year, snuffed about
70   With your most grov'ling nose, and would have hired
             Me to the pois'ning of my patron? Sir?
             Are not you he that have today in court
             Professed the disinheriting of your son?
             Perjured yourself? Go home, and die, and stink.
75   If you but croak a syllable, all comes out.
             Away and call your porters. Go, go stink!   [*Exit* CORBACCIO.]
VOLPONE [*aside*]   Excellent varlet!°   *servant; rascal*
VOLTORE   Now, my faithful Mosca,
     I find thy constancy—
MOSCA   Sir?
VOLTORE   Sincere.
MOSCA   "A table
     Of porphyry"—I mar'l° you'll be thus troublesome.   *marvel*
VOLTORE   Nay, leave off now, they are gone.
80 MOSCA   Why, who are you?
     What? Who did send for you? Oh, cry you mercy,°   *beg your pardon*
     Reverend sir! Good faith, I am grieved for you,
     That any chance of mine should thus defeat
     Your—I must needs say—most deserving travails.
85   But I protest, sir, it was cast upon me,
     And I could almost wish to be without it,
     But that the will o'th'dead must be observed.
     Marry, my joy is that you need it not;
     You have a gift, sir—thank your education—
90   Will never let you want, while there are men
     And malice to breed causes.° Would I had   *lawsuits*
     But half the like, for all my fortune, sir!
     If I have any suits—as I do hope,
     Things being so easy and direct,[8] I shall not—
95   I will make bold with your obstreperous° aid,   *vociferous*
     Conceive me, for your fee,[9] sir. In meantime
     You, that have so much law, I know, ha' the conscience
     Not to be covetous of what is mine.
     Good sir, I thank you for my plate;° 'twill help   (see 1.3.1–20)
100 To set up a young man.° Good faith, you look   *set up my household*
     As you were costive; best go home and purge, sir.
                                                            [*Exit* VOLTORE.]
VOLPONE [*coming from behind the traverse*]   Bid him eat
     lettuce° well. My witty mischief,   *used as a laxative*
     Let me embrace thee! [*He hugs* MOSCA.] Oh, that I could now
     Transform thee to a Venus!° Mosca, go,   *for Volpone's sexual use*
105 Straight take my habit of *clarissimo*[1]
     And walk the streets; be seen, torment 'em more.
     We must pursue as well as plot. Who would

---

8. The situation being so straightforward.
9. It being understood that I will pay you, of course.
1. Aristocrat. (By obeying this order, Mosca violates the sumptuary laws that restricted the wearing of distinctive high-status garments, such as the *clarissimo*'s robe, to persons of the appropriate rank.)

	Have lost° this feast?	*missed*
MOSCA	I doubt° it will lose them.°	*fear / as dupes*
VOLPONE	Oh, my recovery shall recover all.²	

110 That I could now but think on some disguise
To meet 'em in, and ask 'em questions.
How I would vex 'em still at every turn!
MOSCA Sir, I can fit you.
VOLPONE   Canst thou?
MOSCA   Yes, I know
One o'the *commendatori*, sir, so like you,
115 Him will I straight make drunk, and bring you his habit.
VOLPONE A rare disguise, and answering thy brain!°   *suiting your wit*
Oh, I will be a sharp disease unto 'em.
MOSCA Sir, you must look for curses—
VOLPONE   Till they burst!
The fox fares ever best when he is curst.°   [*Exeunt.*]   *proverbial wisdom*

SCENE 4. *The* WOULD-BES' *house.*

[*Enter*] PEREGRINE [*in disguise, and*] *three* MERCATORI [MERCHANTS].

PEREGRINE Am I enough disguised?
FIRST MERCHANT   I warrant you.
PEREGRINE All my ambition is to fright him only.
SECOND MERCHANT If you could ship him away, 'twere excellent.
THIRD MERCHANT To Zante, or to Aleppo?¹
PEREGRINE   Yes, and ha' his
5 Adventures put i'th'book of voyages,²
And his gulled° story registered for truth?   *erroneous*
Well, gentlemen, when I am in awhile,
And that you think us warm in our discourse,
Know° your approaches.   *make*
FIRST MERCHANT   Trust it to our care.
                                       [*Exeunt* MERCHANTS.]
[PEREGRINE *knocks. A*] WOMAN [*servant answers the door*].
10 PEREGRINE Save you, fair lady. Is Sir Pol within?
WOMAN I do not know, sir.
PEREGRINE   Pray you, say unto him
Here is a merchant upon earnest business
Desires to speak with him.
WOMAN   I will see, sir.
PEREGRINE   Pray you.
                                       [*Exit* WOMAN.]
I see the family is all female here.
    [*Enter* WOMAN.]

---

2. Volpone believes that by "undoing" his death, he will be able to resuscitate his scam.

5.4
1. Zante is an island off Greece under Venetian control; Aleppo, a big trading center, is in Syria.

2. An enlarged edition of Richard Hakluyt's *Principal Navigations, Voyages, Traffics, and Discoveries of the English Nation* was published in 1598–1600.

	WOMAN	He says, sir, he has weighty affairs of state	
15		That now require him whole;° some other time	*demand all his attention*
		You may possess° him.	*gain audience with*
	PEREGRINE	Pray you say again,	
		If those require him whole, these will exact him°	*force him out*
		Whereof I bring him tidings. [*Exit* WOMAN.]	
		What might be	
20		His grave affair of state, now? How to make	
		Bolognian sausages here in Venice, sparing	
		One o'th'ingredients?	
		[*Enter* WOMAN.]	
	WOMAN	Sir, he says he knows	
		By your word "tidings" that you are no statesman,³	
		And therefore wills you stay.°	*wishes you to wait*
	PEREGRINE	Sweet, pray you return° him	*reply to*
25		I have not read so many proclamations	
		And studied them for words as he has done,	
		But—here he deigns to come.	
		[*Enter*] POLITIC.	
		[*Exit* WOMAN.]	
	POLITIC	Sir, I must crave	
		Your courteous pardon. There hath chanced today	
		Unkind disaster 'twixt my lady and me,	
30		And I was penning my apology	
		To give her satisfaction, as you came now.	
	PEREGRINE	Sir, I am grieved I bring you worse disaster.	
		The gentleman you met at th'port today,	
		That told you he was newly arrived—	
	POLITIC	Ay, was	
		A fugitive punk?°	*prostitute*
35	PEREGRINE	No, sir, a spy set on you;	
		And he has made relation to the Senate	
		That you professed to him to have a plot	
		To sell the state of Venice to the Turk.°	*(see 4.1.128–30)*
	POLITIC	Oh, me!	
	PEREGRINE	For which warrants are signed by this time	
40		To apprehend you, and to search your study	
		For papers—	
	POLITIC	Alas, sir, I have none but notes	
		Drawn out of playbooks°—	*printed plays*
	PEREGRINE	All the better, sir.	
	POLITIC	And some essays. What shall I do?	
	PEREGRINE	Sir, best	
		Convey yourself into a sugar-chest;	
45		Or, if you could lie round, a frail were rare,⁴	
		And I could send you aboard.	
	POLITIC	Sir, I but talked so,	

---

3. Government agent. (Sir Pol believes that a spy would use the word "intelligence.")

4. If you could curl up, a fruit basket would be excellent.

     For discourse sake merely.°   *They knock without.*   *just to be conversing*
PEREGRINE   Hark, they are there!
POLITIC   I am a wretch, a wretch!
PEREGRINE   What will you do, sir?
     Ha' you ne'er a currant-butt° to leap into?   *casket for currants*
50   They'll put you to the rack; you must be sudden.
POLITIC   Sir, I have an engine°—   *contrivance*
THIRD MERCHANT [*without*]   Sir Politic Would-be!
SECOND MERCHANT [*without*]   Where is he?
POLITIC   That I have thought upon
     beforetime.
PEREGRINE   What is it?
POLITIC   I shall ne'er endure the torture!
     Marry, it is, sir, of a tortoiseshell, [*producing the shell*]
55   Fitted for these extremities. Pray you sir, help me.
     Here I have a place, sir, to put back my legs—
     Please you to lay it on, sir—with this cap
     And my black gloves. I'll lie, sir, like a tortoise
     Till they are gone.
PEREGRINE   [*laying the shell on* POLITIC's *back*]   And call you this an
     engine?
60   POLITIC   Mine own device—good sir, bid my wife's women
     To burn my papers.   [*Exit* PEREGRINE.]
             They [the MERCHANTS] *rush in*.
FIRST MERCHANT   Where's he hid?
THIRD MERCHANT   We must
     And will, sure, find him.
SECOND MERCHANT   Which is his study?
     [*Enter* PEREGRINE.]
FIRST MERCHANT   What
     Are you, sir?
PEREGRINE   I'm a merchant, that came here
     To look upon this tortoise.
THIRD MERCHANT   How?
FIRST MERCHANT   Saint Mark!
     What beast is this?
PEREGRINE   It is a fish.
65   SECOND MERCHANT [*to* POLITIC]   Come out here!
PEREGRINE   Nay, you may strike him, sir, and tread upon him.
     He'll bear a cart.
FIRST MERCHANT   What, to run over him?
PEREGRINE   Yes.
THIRD MERCHANT   Let's jump upon him.
SECOND MERCHANT   Can he not go?°   *walk*
PEREGRINE   He creeps, sir.
FIRST MERCHANT [*poking* POLITIC]   Let's see him creep.
PEREGRINE   No, good sir, you
     will hurt him.
70   SECOND MERCHANT   Heart! I'll see him creep, or prick his guts.
THIRD MERCHANT [*to* POLITIC]   Come out here!

PEREGRINE [aside to POLITIC]   Pray you, sir, creep a little.
          [POLITIC creeps.]
FIRST MERCHANT   Forth!
SECOND MERCHANT   Yet further.
PEREGRINE [aside to POLITIC]   Good sir, creep.
SECOND MERCHANT   We'll see his legs.
          They pull off the shell and discover° him.   expose
THIRD MERCHANT   Godso, he has garters!
FIRST MERCHANT   Ay, and gloves!
SECOND MERCHANT   Is this
     Your fearful tortoise?
PEREGRINE [*revealing himself*]   Now, Sir Pol, we are even.
75   For your next project I shall be prepared.
     I am sorry for the funeral of your notes, sir.
FIRST MERCHANT   'Twere a rare motion to be seen in Fleet Street!⁵
SECOND MERCHANT   Ay, i'the term.
FIRST MERCHANT   Or Smithfield, in the fair.⁶
THIRD MERCHANT   Methinks 'tis but a melancholic sight!
80 PEREGRINE   Farewell, most politic tortoise.
                                   [*Exeunt* PEREGRINE *and* MERCHANTS.]
          [*Enter* WOMAN.]
POLITIC   Where's my lady?
     Knows she of this?
WOMAN   I know not, sir.
POLITIC   Inquire.
                                                    [*Exit* WOMAN.]
     Oh, I shall be the fable of all feasts,°   *talk of the town*
     The freight of the *gazetti*, ship boys' tale,⁷
     And, which is worst, even talk for ordinaries.°   *taverns*
          [*Enter* WOMAN.]
85 WOMAN   My lady's come most melancholic home,
     And says, sir, she will straight to sea for physic.
     POLITIC   And I, to shun this place and clime forever,
     Creeping with house on back, and think it well
     To shrink my poor head in my politic shell.   [*Exeunt.*]

SCENE 5. VOLPONE's *house.*

[*Enter*] VOLPONE [*and*] MOSCA, *the first in the habit of a
     commendatore, the other, of a* clarissimo.°   (see 5.3.104–15)
VOLPONE   Am I then like him?
MOSCA   Oh, sir, you are he.
     No man can sever° you.   *distinguish*
VOLPONE   Good.
MOSCA   But what am I?
VOLPONE   'Fore heav'n, a brave° clarissimo; thou becom'st it!   *splendid*

---

5. Puppet shows, called "motions," were frequently performed on London's Fleet Street, adjacent to the Inns of Court, where attorneys were trained and cases were argued during the three law terms.

6. Smithfield, just northwest of London, was the site every August of Bartholomew Fair; puppet shows were a prime entertainment there.

7. Topic of the newspapers and the gossip of boys serving on board ships.

Pity thou wert not born one.
MOSCA   If I hold
My made one, 'twill be well.
VOLPONE   I'll go and see
What news, first, at the court.
MOSCA   Do so.   [*Exit* VOLPONE.]
                                My fox
Is out on° his hole,[1] and ere he shall reenter   °of
I'll make him languish in his borrowed case,°   disguise
Except he come to composition° with me.   °unless he makes a deal
[*Calling*] Androgyno, Castrone, Nano!
[*Enter* ANDROGYNO, CASTRONE, *and* NANO.]
ALL   Here.
MOSCA   Go recreate yourselves abroad;° go sport.   °outside
[*Exeunt* ANDROGYNO, CASTRONE, *and* NANO.]
So, now I have the keys, and am possessed.°   °in possession
Since he will needs be dead afore his time,
I'll bury him or gain by him. I am his heir,
And so will keep me° till he share at least.   °remain
To cozen him of all were but a cheat
Well placed; no man would construe it a sin.
Let his sport pay for't.° This is called the Fox Trap. [*Exit.*]   °for itself

SCENE 6. *A street in Venice.*

[*Enter*] CORBACCIO [*and*] CORVINO.
CORBACCIO   They say the court is set.°   °in session
CORVINO   We must maintain
Our first tale good, for both our reputations.
CORBACCIO   Why, mine's no tale; my son would there have killed me.
CORVINO   That's true; I had forgot. [*aside*] Mine is, I am sure.—
But for your will, sir.
CORBACCIO   Ay, I'll come upon him
For that hereafter, now his patron's dead.
[*Enter* VOLPONE [*disguised*].
VOLPONE   Signor Corvino! And Corbaccio! Sir,
Much joy unto you.
CORVINO   Of what?
VOLPONE   The sudden good
Dropped down upon you—
CORBACCIO   Where?
VOLPONE   And none knows how—
From old Volpone, sir.
CORBACCIO   Out, arrant knave!
VOLPONE   Let not your too much wealth, sir, make you furious.°   °insane
CORBACCIO   Away, thou varlet!
VOLPONE   Why, sir?
CORBACCIO   Dost thou mock me?

5.5
1. Alluding to the children's game, fox-in-the-hole.

VOLPONE You mock the world, sir.[1] Did you not change° wills?   *exchange*
CORBACCIO Out, harlot!
VOLPONE [*to* CORVINO] Oh, belike you are the man,
15   Signor Corvino? Faith, you carry it° well;   *carry it off*
  You grow not mad withal. I love your spirit.
  You are not overleavened° with your fortune.   *too puffed up*
  You should ha' some would swell now like a wine-vat
  With such an autumn.° Did he gi' you all, sir?   *harvest*
CORVINO Avoid,° you rascal!   *go away*
20 VOLPONE   Troth, your wife has shown
  Herself a very° woman. But you are well;   *typical*
  You need not care; you have a good estate
  To bear it out, sir, better by this chance—
  Except Corbaccio have a share?
CORBACCIO   Hence, varlet!
25 VOLPONE You will not be aknown,[2] sir; why, 'tis wise.
  Thus do all gamesters at all games dissemble.
  No man will seem to win.°   *admit he's winning*
        [*Exeunt* CORBACCIO *and* CORVINO.]
              Here comes my vulture,
  Heaving his beak up i'the air and snuffing.

SCENE 7. *The scene continues.*

       [*Enter*] VOLTORE.
VOLTORE [*to himself*] Outstripped thus by a parasite? A slave
  Would run on errands, and make legs° for crumbs?   *curtsies*
  Well, what I'll do—
VOLPONE   The court stays for° Your Worship.   *awaits*
  I e'en rejoice, sir, at Your Worship's happiness,
5   And that it fell into so learnèd hands
  That understand the fingering[1]—
VOLTORE   What do you mean?
VOLPONE I mean to be a suitor to Your Worship
  For the small tenement, out of reparations[2]—
  That at the end of your long row of houses
10 By the *piscaria*.° It was in Volpone's time,   *fish market*
  Your predecessor, ere he grew diseased,
  A handsome, pretty, customed° bawdy house   *much-patronized*
  As any was in Venice—none dispraised[3]—
  But fell with him; his body and that house
  Decayed together.
15 VOLTORE   Come, sir, leave your prating.°   *chattering*
VOLPONE Why, if Your Worship give me but your hand,
  That I may ha' the refusal,° I have done.   *right of first refusal*

5.6
1. Volpone pretends to believe that Corbaccio is misleading people by refusing to admit to his good fortune.
2. You prefer not to be recognized (as heir).

5.7
1. That understand how to handle money.
2. For the rental house in bad repair.
3. Not to disparage the others.

'Tis a mere toy to you, sir, candle-rents,[4]
As Your learned Worship knows—
VOLTORE   What do I know?
VOLPONE   Marry, no end of your wealth, sir, God decrease[5] it.
VOLTORE   Mistaking knave! What, mock'st thou my misfortune?
VOLPONE   His° blessing on your heart, sir! Would 'twere more.   *God's*
                                              [*Exit* VOLTORE.]
Now, to my first[6] again, at the next corner.

SCENE 8. *The scene continues.*

[*Enter*] CORBACCIO [*and*] CORVINO. [*Enter*] MOSCA,
passant° [*over the stage in* clarissimo's *attire, and exit*].   *passing*
CORBACCIO   See, in our habit! See the impudent varlet!
CORVINO   That I could shoot mine eyes at him, like gunstones!°   *cannonballs*
VOLPONE   But, is this true, sir, of the parasite?
CORBACCIO   Again t'afflict us? Monster!
VOLPONE   In good faith, sir,
   I'm heartily grieved a beard of your grave length°   *so wise an old man*
   Should be so overreached. I never brooked°   *could stand*
   That parasite's hair; methought his nose should cozen.° *he had a cheating nose*
   There still° was somewhat in his look did promise.   *always*
   The bane° of a *clarissimo*.   *ruin*
CORBACCIO   Knave—
VOLPONE [*to* CORVINO]   Methinks
   Yet you that are so traded° i'the world,   *experienced*
   A witty merchant, the fine bird Corvino,
   That have such moral emblems[1] on your name,
   Should not have sung your shame and dropped your cheese,
   To let the fox laugh at your emptiness.[2]
CORVINO   Sirrah, you think the privilege of the place,[3]
   And your red saucy cap, that seems to me
   Nailed to your jolt-head with those two *cecchines*,[4]
   Can warrant° your abuses. Come you hither.   *sanction*
   You shall perceive, sir, I dare beat you. Approach!
VOLPONE   No haste, sir, I do know your valor well,
   Since you durst publish° what you are, sir.   *make public*
   [VOLPONE *makes as if to leave.*]
CORVINO   Tarry!
   I'd speak with you.
VOLPONE   Sir, sir, another time—
CORVINO   Nay, now.
VOLPONE   Oh, God, sir! I were a wise man
   Would stand° the fury of a distracted cuckold.   *to withstand*
   MOSCA [*enters and*] *walks by 'em.*
CORBACCIO   What! Come again?

---

4. (1) Revenue from deteriorating property; (2) "pin money," money for incidentals.
5. Instead of "increase".
6. The ones I was taunting earlier, Corvino and Corbaccio.
5.8

1. Mottoes accompanying symbolic engravings.
2. As in Aesop's fable; see 1.2.95–97 and note.
3. Violence was forbidden near the court.
4. The *commendatore*'s cap is decorated with gold buttons.

25 VOLPONE [*aside to* MOSCA] Upon 'em, Mosca; save me.
CORBACCIO   The air's infected where he breathes.
CORVINO   Let's fly him.
    [*Exeunt* CORVINO *and* CORBACCIO.]
VOLPONE   Excellent basilisk![5] Turn upon the vulture.

SCENE 9. *The scene continues.*

[*Enter*] VOLTORE.

VOLTORE [*to Mosca*]   Well, flesh fly, it is summer with you now;
    Your winter will come on.
MOSCA   Good advocate,
    Pray thee not rail, nor threaten out of place° thus;   *unsuitably*
    Thou'lt make a solecism,° as madam says.   (*see* 4.2.43)
5   Get you a biggin[1] more; your brain breaks loose.
VOLTORE   Well, sir.   [*Exit* MOSCA.]
VOLPONE   Would you ha' me beat the insolent slave?
    Throw dirt upon his first good clothes?
VOLTORE   This same°   *the disguised Volpone*
    Is doubtless some familiar!°   *attendant devil*
VOLPONE   Sir, the court,
    In troth, stays for you. I am mad° a mule   *furious that*
10 That never read Justinian[2] should get up
    And ride an advocate. Had you no quirk°   *trick*
    To avoid gullage,° sir, by such a creature?   *deception*
    I hope you do but jest; he has not done't.
    This's but confederacy to blind the rest.°   *Corvino and Corbaccio*
    You are the heir?
15 VOLTORE   A strange, officious,
    Troublesome knave! Thou dost torment me.
VOLPONE   I know—
    It cannot be, sir, that you should be cozened;
    'Tis not within the wit of man to do it.
    You are so wise, so prudent, and 'tis fit
20 That wealth and wisdom still should go together.
                                        [*Exeunt.*]

SCENE 10. *The law court.*

[*Enter*] *four* AVOCATORI, NOTARIO [NOTARY], COMMEN-
DATORI, BONARIO [*and*] CELIA [*under guard*], COR-
BACCIO, [*and*] CORVINO.

FIRST AVOCATORE   Are all the parties here?
NOTARY   All but the advocate.
SECOND AVOCATORE   And here he comes.
FIRST AVOCATORE   Then bring 'em forth to sentence.
    [*Enter*] VOLTORE, [*and*] VOLPONE [*still disguised as a
    commendatore*].

---

5. A legendary monster whose breath and glance were deadly.
5.9
1. A larger skullcap (worn by lawyers).

2. The Roman law, codified under Emperor Justinian and still influential on the Continent. Lawyers traditionally rode mules to the courts; here the image is comically inverted.

VOLTORE O my most honored fathers, let your mercy
    Once win upon° your justice, to forgive—   *prevail over*
    I am distracted—
VOLPONE (*aside*) What will he do now?
VOLTORE   Oh,
    I know not which t'address myself to first,
    Whether Your Fatherhoods or these innocents°—   *Celia and Bonario*
CORVINO [*aside*] Will he betray himself?
VOLTORE   Whom equally
    I have abused, out of most covetous ends—
CORVINO [*aside to* CORBACCIO] The man is mad!
CORBACCIO   What's that?
CORVINO
                                              He is possessed.
VOLTORE For which, now struck in conscience, here I prostrate
    Myself at your offended feet for pardon.
                                    [*He throws himself down.*]
FIRST AND SECOND AVOCATORI Arise!
CELIA   O heav'n, how just thou art!
VOLPONE [*aside*]   I'm caught
    I' mine own noose—
CORVINO [*aside to* CORBACCIO] Be constant, sir; naught now
    Can help but impudence.   [VOLTORE *rises.*]
FIRST AVOCATORE [*to* VOLTORE] Speak forward.°   *continue*
COMMENDATORI [*to the courtroom*]   Silence!
VOLTORE It is not passion° in me, reverend fathers,   *madness*
    But only conscience, conscience, my good sires,
    That makes me now tell truth. That parasite,
    That knave hath been the instrument of all.
SECOND AVOCATORE Where is that knave? Fetch him.
VOLPONE [*as commendatore*]   I go. [*Exit.*]
CORVINO   Grave fathers,
    This man's distracted; he confessed it now;°   *just now*
    For, hoping to be old Volpone's heir,
    Who now is dead—
THIRD AVOCATORE How?
SECOND AVOCATORE Is Volpone dead?
CORVINO Dead since,° grave fathers—   *since his appearance here*
BONARIO   O sure vengeance!
FIRST AVOCATORE   Stay.
    Then he was no deceiver?
VOLTORE   Oh, no, none.
    The parasite, grave fathers.
CORVINO   He does speak
    Out of mere envy, 'cause the servant's made
    The thing he gaped° for. Please Your Fatherhoods,   *Voltore yearned*
    This is the truth; though I'll not justify
    The other,° but he may be somedeal° faulty.   *Mosca / somewhat*
VOLTORE Ay, to your hopes as well as mine, Corvino;
    But I'll use modesty.° Pleaseth Your Wisdoms   *self-control*

To view these certain notes, and but confer° them. *compare*
As I hope favor, they shall speak clear truth.
    [*He gives documents to the* AVOCATORI.]
CORVINO   The devil has entered him!
BONARIO   Or bides in you.
FOURTH AVOCATORE   We have done ill, by a public officer
To send for him, if he be heir.
SECOND AVOCATORE   For whom?
FOURTH AVOCATORE   Him that they call the parasite.
THIRD AVOCATORE   'Tis true;
He is a man of great estate now left.° *bequeathed to him*
FOURTH AVOCATORE [*to* NOTARY]   Go you and learn his name,
    and say the court
Entreats his presence here but to the clearing
Of some few doubts.   [*Exit* NOTARY.]
SECOND AVOCATORE   This same's a labyrinth!
FIRST AVOCATORE [*to* CORVINO]   Stand you unto° your first *do you stand by*
    report?
CORVINO   My state,° *estate*
My life, my fame°— *reputation*
BONARIO   Where is't?[1]
CORVINO   —are at the stake.
FIRST AVOCATORE [*to* CORBACCIO]   Is yours so too?
CORBACCIO   The advocate's a knave,
And has a forkèd tongue—
SECOND AVOCATORE   Speak to the point.
CORBACCIO   So is the parasite, too.
FIRST AVOCATORE   This is confusion.
VOLTORE   I do beseech Your Fatherhoods, read but those.
CORVINO   And credit nothing the false spirit hath writ.
It cannot be but he is possessed, grave fathers.
    [*The* AVOCATORI *examine* VOLTORE's *papers.*]

SCENE 11. *A street.*[1]

[*Enter*] VOLPONE [*on a separate part of the stage*].
VOLPONE   To make a snare for mine own neck! And run
My head into it willfully! With laughter!
When I had newly scaped, was free and clear!
Out of mere wantonness!° Oh, the dull devil *caprice*
Was in this brain of mine when I devised it,
And Mosca gave it second. He must now
Help to sear up° this vein, or we bleed dead. *cauterize*
    [*Enter*] NANO, ANDROGYNO, [*and*] CASTRONE.
How now, who let you loose? Whither go you now?
What, to buy gingerbread? Or to drown kitlings?° *kittens*

5.10
1. Implying that Corvino has nothing of worth to lose.

5.11
1. The courtroom characters remain visible onstage, perhaps in silent tableau, while Volpone is understood to be outside.

	NANO Sir, Master Mosca called us out of doors,
10	And bid us all go play, and took the keys.
	ANDROGYNO Yes.
	VOLPONE Did Master Mosca take the keys? Why, so!
	I am farther in.° These are my fine conceits!° *in trouble / notions*
	I must be merry, with a mischief to me!
15	What a vile wretch was I, that could not bear
	My fortune soberly! I must ha' my crotchets° *perverse whims*
	And my conundrums! Well, go you and seek him.
	His meaning may be truer than my fear.²
	Bid him he straight come to me, to the court.
20	Thither will I, and, if't be possible,
	Unscrew° my advocate upon° new hopes. *dissuade / by means of*
	When I provoked him, then I lost myself.

     [*Exeunt* VOLPONE *and his entourage.*
     The AVOCATORI *and parties to the*
     courtroom proceedings remain onstage.]

SCENE 12. *The courtroom.*

	FIRST AVOCATORE [*with* VOLTORE's *notes*] These things can ne'er be
	reconciled. He here
	Professeth that the gentleman° was wronged, *Bonario*
	And that the gentlewoman was brought thither,
	Forced by her husband, and there left.
	VOLTORE Most true.
	CELIA How ready is heav'n to those that pray!
5	FIRST AVOCATORE But that
	Volpone would have ravished her, he holds
	Utterly false, knowing his impotence.
	CORVINO Grave fathers, he is possessed; again I say,
	Possessed. Nay, if there be possession
	And obsession, he has both.
10	THIRD AVOCATORE Here comes our officer.
	[*Enter* VOLPONE, *still disguised.*]
	VOLPONE The parasite will straight be here, grave fathers.
	FOURTH AVOCATORE You might invent some other name, sir varlet.
	THIRD AVOCATORE Did not the notary meet him?
	VOLPONE Not that I know.
	FOURTH AVOCATORE His coming will clear all.
	SECOND AVOCATORE Yet it is misty.
	VOLTORE May't please Your Fatherhoods—
15	VOLPONE (*whispers* [*to*] *the advocate*) Sir, the parasite
	Willed me to tell you that his master lives,
	That you are still the man, your hopes the same;
	And this was only a jest—
	VOLTORE [*aside to* VOLPONE] How?
	VOLPONE [*aside to* VOLTORE] Sir, to try
	If you were firm, and how you stood affected.° *how loyal you were*

---

2. Mosca's intentions may be truer (more loyal) than my fear is true (accurate).

VOLTORE   Art sure he lives?
VOLPONE   Do I live,° sir?   *he's as alive as I am*
20 VOLTORE   Oh, me!
   I was too violent.
VOLPONE   Sir, you may redeem it.
   They said you were possessed; fall down, and seem so.
   I'll help to make it good.   VOLTORE *falls.*
                    [*Aloud*] God bless the man!
   [*Aside to* VOLTORE] Stop your wind hard, and swell.¹ [*Aloud*]
      See, see, see, see!
25 He vomits crooked pins! His eyes are set
   Like a dead hare's hung in a poulter's² shop!
   His mouth's running away!° [*to* CORVINO] Do you see,   *twitching*
      signor?   *spasmodically*
   Now 'tis in his belly.
CORVINO   Ay, the devil!
VOLPONE   Now in his throat.
CORVINO   Ay, I perceive it plain.
30 VOLPONE   'Twill out, 'twill out! Stand clear. See where it flies,
   In shape of a blue toad with a bat's wings!
   [*To* CORBACCIO] Do not you see it, sir?
CORBACCIO   What? I think I do.
CORVINO   'Tis too manifest.
VOLPONE   Look! He comes t' himself!
VOLTORE   Where am I?
VOLPONE   Take good heart; the worst is past, sir.
   You are dispossessed.
35 FIRST AVOCATORE   What accident° is this?   *unforeseen event*
SECOND AVOCATORE   Sudden, and full of wonder!
THIRD AVOCATORE   If he were
   Possessed, as it appears, all this° is nothing.   *Voltore's written statement*
CORVINO   He has been often subject to these fits.
FIRST AVOCATORE   Show him that writing. [*To* VOLTORE] Do
   you know it, sir?
40 VOLPONE [*aside to* VOLTORE]   Deny it, sir; forswear it; know it not.
VOLTORE   Yes, I do know it well, it is my hand;
   But all that it contains is false.
BONARIO   Oh, practice!°   *deception*
SECOND AVOCATORE   What maze is this!
FIRST AVOCATORE   Is he not guilty, then,
   Whom you there name the parasite?
VOLTORE   Grave fathers,
45 No more than his good patron, old Volpone.
FOURTH AVOCATORE   Why, he is dead!
VOLTORE   Oh, no, my honored fathers.
   He lives—

5.12
1. The details of Voltore's dispossession in the following lines resemble the fake exorcisms described in Samuel Harsnett's lively exposé, *A Discovery of the Fraudulent Practices of John Darrell* (1599). "Stop your wind": hold your breath.
2. Seller of poultry and small game.

FIRST AVOCATORE How! Lives?
VOLTORE   Lives.
SECOND AVOCATORE   This is subtler yet!
THIRD AVOCATORE [*to* VOLTORE] You said he was dead?
VOLTORE   Never.
THIRD AVOCATORE [*to* CORVINO]   You said so?
CORVINO   I heard so.
FOURTH AVOCATORE Here comes the gentleman; make him way.
    [*Enter* MOSCA.]
THIRD AVOCATORE A stool!
FOURTH AVOCATORE [*aside*] A proper° man! And, were Volpone   *handsome*
    dead,
    A fit match for my daughter.
THIRD AVOCATORE   Give him way.
VOLPONE [*aside to* MOSCA] Mosca, I was almost lost; the advocate
    Had betrayed all; but now it is recovered.
    All's o'the hinge° again. Say I am living.   *running smoothly*
MOSCA [*aloud*] What busy° knave is this? Most reverend   *troublesome*
    fathers,
    I sooner had attended your grave pleasures,
    But that my order for the funeral
    Of my dear patron did require me—
VOLPONE (*aside*)   Mosca!
MOSCA Whom I intend to bury like a gentleman.
VOLPONE [*aside*] Ay, quick,° and cozen me of all.³   *alive*
SECOND AVOCATORE   Still stranger!
    More intricate!
FIRST AVOCATORE And come about° again!   *reversing direction*
FOURTH AVOCATORE [*aside*] It is a match; my daughter is bestowed.
MOSCA [*aside to* VOLPONE] Will you gi' me half?
VOLPONE [*aside to* MOSCA]   First, I'll be hanged.
MOSCA [*aside to* VOLPONE]
                                            I know
    Your voice is good. Cry not so loud.
FIRST AVOCATORE   Demand°   *question*
    The advocate. [*To* VOLTORE] Sir, did not you affirm
    Volpone was alive?
VOLPONE   Yes, and he is;
    This gent'man told me so. (*Aside to* MOSCA) Thou shalt have half.
MOSCA Whose drunkard is this same? Speak, some that know him;
    I never saw his face. (*Aside to* VOLPONE) I cannot now
    Afford it you so cheap.
VOLPONE (*aside to* MOSCA) No?
FIRST AVOCATORE [*to* VOLTORE] What say you?
VOLTORE The officer told me.
VOLPONE   I did, grave fathers,
    And will maintain he lives with mine own life,
    And that this creature° told me. (*aside*) I was born   *Mosca*

---

3. Volpone sees that Mosca's pious pretense of burying the "dead" Volpone will mean an end to all of Volpone's hopes; he'll be cheated out of everything.

With all good stars my enemies.
MOSCA   Most grave fathers,
If such an insolence as this must pass°   *be permitted*
Upon me, I am silent. 'Twas not this
For which you sent, I hope.
SECOND AVOCATORE [*pointing to* VOLPONE]   Take him away.
VOLPONE (*aside to* MOSCA)   Mosca!
THIRD AVOCATORE   Let him be whipped.
VOLPONE (*aside to* MOSCA)   Wilt thou betray me?
Cozen me?
THIRD AVOCATORE   And taught to bear himself
Toward a person of his° rank.   *Mosca's*
FOURTH AVOCATORE   Away!
[*Officers seize* VOLPONE.]
MOSCA   I humbly thank Your Fatherhoods.
VOLPONE   Soft, soft. [*Aside*] Whipped?
And lose all that I have? If I confess,
It cannot be much more.
FOURTH AVOCATORE [*to* MOSCA]   Sir, are you married?
VOLPONE [*aside*]   They'll be allied° anon; I must be resolute. *linked by marriage*
The fox shall here uncase.° *He puts off his disguise.*   *reveal himself*
MOSCA (*aside*)   Patron!
VOLPONE   Nay, now
My ruins shall not come alone. Your match
I'll hinder sure; my substance shall not glue you
Nor screw you into a family.
MOSCA (*aside*)   Why, patron!
VOLPONE   I am Volpone, and [*pointing to* MOSCA] this is my knave;
[*Pointing to* VOLTORE] This his own knave; [*pointing to* CORBACCIO]
this, avarice's fool;
[*Pointing to* CORVINO] This, a chimera° of wittol,   *monstrous combination*
fool, and knave;
And, reverend fathers, since we all can hope
Naught but a sentence, let's not now despair it.°   *be disappointed (ironic)*
You hear me brief.°   *that's all I have to say*
CORVINO   May it please Your Fatherhoods—
COMMENDATORE[4]   Silence!
FIRST AVOCATORE   The knot is now undone by miracle!
SECOND AVOCATORE   Nothing can be more clear.
THIRD AVOCATORE   Or can more prove
These innocent.
FIRST AVOCATORE   Give 'em their liberty.
[BONARIO *and* CELIA *are released.*]
BONARIO   Heaven could not long let such gross crimes be hid.
SECOND AVOCATORE   If this be held the highway to get riches,
May I be poor!
THIRD AVOCATORE   This's not the gain, but torment.
FIRST AVOCATORE   These possess wealth as sick men possess fevers,

4. Not Volpone, of course, but one of the genuine Commendatori. They are probably the officers who strip Mosca at line 103.

Which trulier may be said to possess them.
SECOND AVOCATORE   Disrobe that parasite.
[MOSCA *is stripped of his* clarissimo's *robe*.]
CORVINO [*and*] MOSCA   Most honored fathers!
FIRST AVOCATORE   Can you plead aught to stay the course of justice?
  If you can, speak.
CORVINO [*and*] VOLTORE   We beg favor—
CELIA   And mercy.
FIRST AVOCATORE [*to* CELIA]   You hurt your innocence, suing°   *pleading*
  for the guilty.
  [*To the others*] Stand forth; and, first, the parasite. You appear
  T'have been the chiefest minister,° if not plotter,   *agent*
  In all these lewd° impostures, and now, lastly,   *vile, obscene*
  Have with your impudence abused the court
  And habit° of a gentleman of Venice,   *garb*
  Being a fellow of no birth or blood;
  For which our sentence is, first thou be whipped,
  Then live perpetual prisoner in our galleys.
VOLPONE   I thank you for him.
MOSCA   Bane to° thy wolfish nature!   *curses on*
FIRST AVOCATORE   Deliver him to the *saffi*.° [MOSCA *is placed*   *bailiffs*
  under guard.] Thou, Volpone,
  By blood and rank a gentleman, canst not fall
  Under like censure;° but our judgment on thee   *the same sentence*
  Is that thy substance° all be straight confiscate   *wealth*
  To the hospital of the *Incurabili*;[5]
  And since the most was gotten by imposture,
  By feigning lame, gout, palsy, and such diseases,
  Thou art to lie in prison, cramped with irons,
  Till thou be'st sick and lame indeed.—Remove him.
  [VOLPONE *is placed under guard*.]
VOLPONE   This is called mortifying[6] of a fox.
FIRST AVOCATORE   Thou, Voltore, to take away the scandal
  Thou hast giv'n all worthy men of thy profession,
  Art banished from their fellowship and our state.°   *Venice*
  [VOLTORE *is placed under guard*.]
  Corbaccio—bring him near.—We here possess
  Thy son of all thy state,° and confine thee   *estate*
  To the monastery of San' Spirito,°   *the Holy Spirit*
  Where, since thou knew'st not how to live well here,
  Thou shalt be learned° to die well.   *taught*
CORBACCIO   Ha! What said he?
COMMENDATORE   You shall know anon,° sir.   *soon enough*
  [CORBACCIO *is placed under guard*.]
FIRST AVOCATORE   Thou, Corvino, shalt
  Be straight embarked from thine own house and rowed

---

5. The Hospital of the Incurables was founded in Venice in 1522 to care for people terminally ill with syphilis.
6. (1) Hanging of meat to make it tender; (2) disciplining spiritually; (3) killing. (Volpone's sentence is almost certain to bring about his death.)

Bound about Venice, through the Grand Canal,
Wearing a cap with fair° long ass's ears   *handsome; clearly visible*
Instead of horns, and so to mount, a paper
Pinned on thy breast, to the *berlino*[7]—
CORVINO   Yes,
140 And have mine eyes beat out with stinking fish,
Bruised fruit, and rotten eggs—'Tis well. I'm glad
I shall not see my shame yet.
FIRST AVOCATORE   And to expiate
Thy wrongs done to thy wife, thou art to send her
Home to her father with her dowry trebled.[8]
And these are all your judgments—
145 ALL   Honored fathers!
FIRST AVOCATORE   Which may not be revoked. Now you begin,
When crimes are done and past and to be punished,
To think what your crimes are.—Away with them!
        [MOSCA, VOLPONE, VOLTORE, CORBACCIO, *and* CORVINO
             retire to the back of the stage, guarded.][9]
Let all that see these vices thus rewarded
150 Take heart,° and love to study 'em. Mischiefs feed   *take them to heart*
Like beasts, till they be fat, and then they bleed.
                           [*The* AVOCATORI *step back.*]
    [VOLPONE *comes forward.*]
VOLPONE   The seasoning of a play is the applause
Now, though the fox be punished by the laws,
He yet doth hope there is no suff'ring due
155 Nor any fact° which he hath done 'gainst you.   *crime*
If there be, censure him; here he, doubtful,° stands.   *apprehensive*
If not, fare jovially, and clap your hands.   [*Exeunt.*]

performed 1606   *published* 1616

The Masque of Blackness

When James I and Queen Anna ascended the English throne in 1603, they presided over the development of the court masque as a major form of praise, entertainment, and political idealization, celebrating the Stuart court as the embodiment of perfection. *The Masque of Blackness* established Jonson and Inigo Jones as the chief makers of court masques for more than two decades. Jonson provided the words and Jones the spectacle; over the years they developed an intense rivalry. For the first decade, the queen took an active role in planning and performing in court masques, which were usually performed only once—most often on Twelfth Night, as in this case, or sometimes for a wedding or

---

7. Pillory. Versions of such shaming punishments were commonly imposed for sexual and marital infractions. The offender typically had to wear a placard specifying his crimes; hence the paper pinned on Corvino's breast.
8. The judges grant Celia "separation from bed and board." Such legal separations could be permitted to the innocent party in a case of adultery or, as here, to a victim of gross spousal abuse. Because legal separation entailed the finding of serious fault, the guilty spouse could also, as here, be forced to pay financial damages. Legal separation did not bring with it, however, the right of remarriage for either party.
9. Alternatively, the prisoners, and later the Avocatori and the others, could exit, and Volpone could return to speak the epilogue. The advantage of the staging preferred here is that almost all the players are onstage to receive the audience's applause.

other special occasion. *The Masque of Blackness* also began the tradition of prodigiously expensive masques: the queen's bill for it came to around £5000 (more than five hundred times what the young Jonson would have made in a year as an apprentice bricklayer). Masques were customarily followed by elaborate feasts and all-night dancing known as "the revels." On this occasion, as on many that followed, the evening was chaotic. The banquet table was overturned by the crush of diners before the meal began; guests were beaten by the palace guards; light-fingered revelers stole jewels, chains, and purses; and sexual liaisons went on in dark corners.

Court masques differed from performances in the public theater in almost every respect, particularly in their focus on dance. Masques were multimedia events combining song, speech, richly ornamented costumes and masks, shifting scene panels depicting elaborate architecture and landscapes, and intricate machines in which gods and goddesses descended from the heavens. They were presented to King James, who occupied the Chair of State, which was placed in the ideal viewing position. While the speaking parts were taken by professionals, the dancers were members of the court, including—to the chagrin of some godly Protestants—women. In the reign of Charles I, William Prynne lost his ears for attacking masques and comparing the women who danced in them (including the queen) to whores.

On the surface, *The Masque of Blackness* asserts the cultural superiority of the English over non-European peoples and celebrates the power of James, the "Sun King" of Britain, who can turn black skin to white. But as in other masques commissioned by the queen, there is also a subversive element in *The Masque of Blackness*. Jonson tells us it was "her Majesty's will" that she and her court ladies appear as beautiful black African women: the daughters of Niger. (Two of Inigo Jones's designs for their costumes are included in the color insert in this volume.) The power of the supposed Sun King is further undercut by Niger's lengthy praise of black beauty and by the fact that the promised transformation of the ladies' skin is never seen. (They have, however, become white in the sequel, *The Masque of Beauty*, performed three years later.) One contemporary response to the masque gives a sense of its racially charged nature. Instead of wearing "vizards," Sir Dudley Carleton wrote from the court, the ladies' "faces and arms, up to the elbows, were painted black, which was disguise sufficient, for they were hard to be known; but it became them nothing so well as their red and white, and you cannot imagine a more ugly sight than a troop of lean-cheeked Moors." Here we see racist ideas both about the intimate relationship between Petrarchan ideals of beauty ("red and white") and white skin, and about racial phenotypes. Queen Anna danced in six masques, but the masques of *Blackness* and *Beauty* stand out for their impact on the imaginations of later writers, including John Smith, who finds echoes of the masques in Algonquin Virginia, and Richard Ligon, who finds them in a mixed-race woman in the Cape Verde islands.

In many later Jacobean masques, the glorification of the monarch seems less conflicted. Jonson developed a kind of prologue known as the antimasque, in which wicked, disruptive, or rustic characters played by professional actors invade the court, only to be banished by aristocratic masquers whose dancing transforms the court into a golden world. The aristocrats enact the mixture of the ideal and real as they unmask, revealing themselves as courtiers, and proceed to dance the revels with the other members of the court. Caroline court masques, in which Charles I and Queen Henrietta Maria regularly danced, tended to be longer, more elaborate, more dialogic, more spectacular, and even more hyperbolic. But early to late, many masques contain features that subtly resist the politics of Stuart absolutism.

The Masque of Blackness

The Queen's Masques: the first Of Blackness
Personated at the Court at Whitehall, on the Twelfth Night, 1605.

Pliny, Solinus, Ptolemy, and of late Leo the African,[1] remember unto us a river in Ethiopia famous by the name of Niger,[2] of which the people were called *Nigritae*, now Negroes, and are the blackest nation of the world. This river taketh spring out of a certain lake,[3] eastward, and after a long race, falleth into the western ocean. Hence (because it was her Majesty's will to have them blackamoors at first) the invention was derived by me, and presented thus.

First, for the scene, was drawn a Landscape[4] *consisting of small woods, and here and there a void place filled with huntings; which falling, an artificial sea was seen to shoot forth, as if it flowed to the land, raised with waves which seemed to move, and in some places the billow to break,*[5] *as imitating that orderly disorder, which is common in nature. In front of this sea were placed six tritons,*[6] *in moving and sprightly actions; their upper parts human, save that their hairs were blue, as partaking of the sea-color; their desinent*[7] *parts fish, mounted above their heads, and all varied in disposition. From their backs were borne out certain light pieces of taffeta, as if carried by the wind, and their music made out of wreathed shells. Behind these, a pair of sea-maids, for song, were as conspicuously seated; between which two great sea-horses, as big as the life, put forth themselves; the one mounting aloft, and writhing his head from the other, which seemed to sink forwards; so intended for variation, and that the figure behind might come off better. Upon their backs Oceanus*[8] *and Niger were advanced.*

Oceanus, presented in a human form, the color of his flesh blue, and shadowed with a robe of sea green; his head grey and horned, as he is described by the ancients; his beard of the like mixed color. He was garlanded with algae or sea-grass, and in his hand a trident.

Niger, in form and color of an Ethiop, his hair and rare beard curled, shadowed with a blue and bright mantle; his front, neck, and wrists adorned with pearl; and crowned with an artificial wreath of cane and paper-rush.[9]

These induced the masquers, which were twelve nymphs, negroes, and the daughters of Niger, attended by so many of the Oceaniae,[1] *which were their light-bearers.*

The masquers were placed in a great concave shell, like mother of pearl, curiously made to move on those waters, and rise with the billow; the top thereof was stuck with a chevron of lights which, indented to the proportion of the shell, struck a glorious beam upon them as they were seated one above another; so that they were all seen, but in an extravagant[2] *order.*

---

1. This long introductory note is Jonson's. Leo wrote the *Description of Africa* (1526); the others are classical authorities on geography.
2. Some, though not Pliny, identified it as the Niger, which means black in Latin.
3. Lake Chad.
4. Painted on the front curtain.
5. Effects created by a series of painted cloths raised and lowered by a machine.
6. Sea gods.
7. Back.
8. The Atlantic Ocean, father of the river Niger. Both ride on the backs of hippopotamuses ("sea-horses.")
9. The papyrus plant.
1. Sea nymphs, daughters of Oceanus and Tethys.
2. Moving about.

On sides of the shell did swim six huge sea-monsters, varied in their shapes and dispositions, bearing on their backs the twelve torch-bearers, who were planted there in several greces,[3] so as the backs of some were seen, some in purfle[4] (or side), others in face, and all having their lights burning out of whelks or murex shells.[5]

The attire of the masquers was alike in all, without difference; the colors azure and silver, their hair thick, and curled upright in tresses, like pyramids, but returned on the top with a scroll and antique dressing of feathers, and jewels interlaced with ropes of pearl. And for the front, ear, neck and wrists, the ornament was of the most choice and orient pearl, best setting off from the black.

For the light-bearers, sea-green, waved about the skirts with gold and silver; their hair loose and flowing, garlanded with sea-grass, and that stuck with branches of coral.

These thus presented, the scene behind seemed a vast sea (and united with this that flowed forth)[6] from the termination or horizon of which (being the level of the state,[7] which was placed in the upper end of the hall) was drawn, by the lines of perspective, the whole work shooting downwards from the eye; which decorum made it more conspicuous, and caught the eye afar off with a wandering beauty. To which was added an obscure and cloudy night piece,[8] that made the whole set off. So much for the bodily part, which was of Master Inigo Jones his design and act.

By this, one of the tritons, with the two sea-maids, began to sing to the others loud music, their voices being a tenor and two trebles.

SONG

  Sound, sound aloud
  The welcome of the orient flood
  Into the west;
  Fair Niger, son to great Oceanus,
5   Now honored thus
  With all his beauteous race,
  Who though but black in face,
  Yet are they bright,
  And full of life and light,
10   To prove that beauty best
  Which not the color, but the feature
  Assures unto the creature.

OCEANUS Be silent, now the ceremony's done,
 And Niger, say, how comes it, lovely son,
15 That thou, the Ethiop's river, so far east,
 Art seen to fall into th'extremest west
 Of me, the king of floods, Oceanus,
 And in mine empire's heart salute me thus?

---

3. Steps.
4. Profile.
5. Whelks and murex are sea snails.
6. The painted backdrop and the wave machine.
7. The king's throne, placed at the ideal viewing position, the vanishing point of the perspective.
8. The upper part of the scenery, through which the moon later descends.

My ceaseless current now amazèd stands
To see thy labor through so many lands
Mix thy fresh billow with my brackish stream,
And in thy sweetness, stretch thy diadem°   *realm, rule*
To these far distant and unequalled skies,
This squarèd circle of celestial bodies.[9]

NIGER   Divine Oceanus, 'tis not strange at all
That, since the immortal souls of creatures mortal
Mix with their bodies, yet reserve for ever
A power of separation, I should sever
My fresh streams from thy brackish, like things fixed,
Though with thy powerful saltness thus far mixed.
'Virtue though chained to earth, will still live free;
And hell itself must yield to industry.'[1]

OCEANUS   But what's the end of thy Herculean labors,
Extended to these calm and blessèd shores?

NIGER   To do a kind and careful father's part,
In satisfying every pensive heart
Of these my daughters, my most loved birth;
Who, though they were the first formed dames of earth,
And in whose sparkling and refulgent° eyes   *radiant*
The glorious sun did still delight to rise,
Though he (the best judge, and most formal cause[2]
Of all dames' beauties) in their firm hues° draws   *fixed colors*
Signs of his fervent'st love, and thereby shows
That in their black the perfect'st beauty grows,
Since the fixed color of their curlèd hair
(Which is the highest grace of dames most fair)
No cares, no age can change, or there display
The fearful tincture° of abhorrèd grey,   *tinge*
Since Death herself (herself being pale and blue)
Can never alter their most faithful hue;
All which are arguments to prove how far
Their beauties conquer in great beauty's war;
And more, how near divinity they be,
That stand from passion or decay so free.
Yet, since the fabulous voices of some few
Poor brain-sick men, styled poets[3] here with you,
Have, with such envy of their graces, sung
The painted beauties other empires sprung,
Letting their loose and wingèd fictions fly
To infect all climates, yea, our purity;
As of one Phaëton, that fired the world,[4]
And that before his heedless flames were hurled

---

9. The squared circle is an image of perfection, a hyperbolic compliment to Britain.
1. Alludes to Horace, *Odes* I.3.36.
2. Aristotle's formal cause produces the form or essence of anything.
3. English Petrarchan poets, whose ideal of beauty involves fair skin, blonde hair, and blue eyes. See, for example, the sonnets of Sidney, Spenser, and Wroth.
4. Son of Apollo, the sun god, whose ill-fated attempt to drive the sun's chariot scorched the earth and reportedly turned the skin of the daughters of Niger black.

About the globe, the Ethiops were as fair
As other dames, now black with black despair,
And in respect of their complexions changed,
Are eachwhere, since, for luckless creatures ranged.
Which when my daughters heard (as women are
Most jealous of their beauties) fear and care
Possessed them whole; yea, and believing them,[5]
They wept such ceaseless tears into my stream
That it hath thus far overflowed his shore
To seek them patience; who have since e'ermore
As the sun riseth, charged his burning throne
With volleys of revilings, 'cause he shone
On their scorched cheeks with such intemperate fires,
And other dames made queens of all desires.
To frustrate which strange error oft I sought,
Though most in vain against a settled thought
As women's are, till they confirmed at length
By miracle what I with so much strength
Of argument resisted; else they feigned:
For in the lake where their first spring they gained,
As they sat cooling their soft limbs one night,
Appeared a face all circumfused with light;
(And sure they saw't, for Ethiops never dream)[6]
Wherein they might decipher through the stream
These words:
    That they a land must forthwith seek,
    Whose termination (of the Greek)
    Sounds -*tania*; where bright Sol, that heat
    Their bloods, doth never rise or set,
    But in his journey passeth by,
    And leaves that climate of the sky
    To comfort of a greater light,[7]
    Who forms all beauty with his sight.
In search of this have we three princedoms past
That speak out -*tania* in their accents last:
Black Mauritania[8] first, and secondly
Swarth° Lusitania,[9] next we did descry°   *black / catch sight of*
Rich Aquitania,[1] and yet cannot find
The place unto these longing nymphs designed.°   *appointed*
Instruct and aid me, great Oceanus:
What land is this that now appears to us?
OCEANUS   This land, that lifts into the temperate air
His snowy cliff, is Albion the fair,
So called of Neptune's son, who ruleth here;[2]

---

5. The poets (line 56).
6. Jonson cites *The Natural History* of Pliny the Elder for this saying.
7. The allusion is to James, the "Sun King" of Britain.
8. Land of the Moors in North Africa.
9. Portugal.
1. Southwest France.
2. King James, regularly so styled because of Britain's close relationship to the sea. Albion (previous line): ancient name for England (from Latin: *albus*, white). The "snowy cliff" refers to the cliffs of Dover, whose chalk content makes them seem white.

For whose dear guard, myself four thousand year,
Since old Deucalion's[3] days, have walked the round
About his empire, proud to see him crowned
Above my waves.

At this, the moon was discovered in the upper part of the house, triumphant in a silver throne, made in figure of a pyramis.[4] *Her garments white and silver, the dressing of her head antique, and crowned with a luminary or sphere of light, which striking on the clouds, and heightened with silver, reflected as natural clouds do by the splendor of the moon. The heaven about her was vaulted with blue silk, and set with stars of silver which had in them their several lights burning. The sudden sight of which made Niger to interrupt Oceanus with this present passion.*[5]

NIGER   —O see, our silver star!
Whose pure auspicious light greets us thus far!
Great Æthiopia, goddess of our shore,[6]
Since with particular worship we adore
Thy general brightness, let particular grace
Shine on my zealous daughters. Show the place
Which long their longings urged their eyes to see.
Beautify them, which long have deified thee.

AETHIOPIA   Niger, be glad; resume thy native cheer.
Thy daughters' labors have their period° here,   *end, completion*
And so thy errors. I was that bright face
Reflected by the lake, in which thy race
Read mystic° lines (which skill Pythagoras[7]   *spiritual, allegorical*
First taught to men by a reverberate° glass).   *reflecting*
This blessed isle doth with that *-tania* end
Which there they saw inscribed, and shall extend
Wished satisfaction to their best desires.
Britannia, which the triple world admires,[8]
This isle hath now recovered for her name;
Where reign those beauties that with so much fame
The sacred Muses' sons° have honorèd,   *singers and poets*
And from bright Hesperus to Eos spread.[9]
With that great name, Britannia, this blessed isle
Hath won her ancient dignity and style,
A *world divided from the world*,[1] and tried
The abstract of it in his general pride.
For were the world, with all his wealth, a ring,
Britannia (whose new name makes all tongues sing)

---

3. A Greek analogue to Noah, as the survivor of a great flood.
4. Pyramid.
5. Instant outburst.
6. Jonson identifies her as the moon, worshipped by the Ethiopians.
7. Mystical Greek philosopher, said to have taught men how to read writing on the moon.
8. The triple realms of heaven, earth, and underworld, admiring the three kingdoms of England, Scotland, and Wales, united under James. In 1604, James reintroduced the name "Britain" to refer to the united island.
9. Hesperus is the evening star, and Eos the rising sun/dawn, west and east, respectively.
1. Britain as a separate world, divided from Europe by the channel.

    Might be a diamond worthy to enchase° it,   *ornament*
    Ruled by a sun, that to this height doth grace it.
140 Whose beams shine day and night, and are of force
    To blanch° an Ethiop and revive a corpse.[2]   *whiten*
    His light sciential° is and (past mere nature)   *knowledgeable*
    Can salve° the rude defects of every creature.   *redeem, overcome*
        Call forth thy honored daughters, then,
145   And let them 'fore the Britain men
        Indent the land with those pure traces[3]
        They flow with in their native graces.
        Invite them boldly to the shore,
        Their beauties shall be scorched no more;
150   This sun is temperate, and refines
        All things on which his radiance shines.

Here the tritons sounded, and they danced on shore, every couple as they advanced severally presenting their fans,[4] in one of which were inscribed their mixed names, in the other a mute hieroglyphic, expressing their mixed qualities.[5] Which manner of symbol I rather chose than imprese, as well for strangeness, as relishing of antiquity, and more applying to that original doctrine of sculpture which the Egyptians are said first to have brought from the Ethiopians.

	The Names[6]	The Symbols
The Queen	Euphoris	A golden tree, laden with fruit
Countess of Bedford	Aglaia	
Lady Herbert	Diaphane	The figure icosahedron[7] of crystal
Countess of Derby	Eucampse	
Lady Rich	Ocyte	A pair of naked feet in a river
Countess of Suffolk	Kathare	
Lady Bevill	Notis	The salamander simple
Lady Effingham	Psychrote	
Lady Elizabeth Howard	Glycyte	A cloud full of rain dropping
Lady Susan Vere	Malacia	
Lady Wroth	Baryte	An urn, sphered with wine
Lady Walsingham	Periphere	

---

2. Both are proverbial impossibilities. On the proverb "to blanch an Ethiope [white]," see the illustration on p. 1213 of this volume.
3. Imprint the land with their dancing feet. This is the call for the main masque dances.
4. The women advanced in pairs holding fans to the audience: on one appeared both women's names; on the other, an allegorical symbol of their conjoined qualities.
5. A "hieroglyph" is a character used in pictorial writing, standing for the object it depicts or for a syllable or sound; such writing is best known from ancient Egyptian monuments and records. An "imprese" was an emblem or device, often accompanied by a motto. The "hieroglyphic" of the fruit-laden tree carried by Queen Anna and the Countess of Bedford alluded to the queen's fertility. (She was pregnant during the performance.)
6. The meaning of the paired women's names and symbols, in order: abundance and splendor, fertility symbol; transparency and flexibility, a twenty-sided water symbol; swiftness and spotlessness, symbol of purity; moisture and coldness, symbol, the salamander who lives in fire unharmed; sweetness and delicacy, symbol of education; weight and revolution, symbol, the earth's globe. The women are members of Queen Anna's court. Donne and Jonson wrote poems about Lucy Harington Russell, Countess of Bedford; Lady Mary Wroth wrote poems and a romance.
7. A solid formed by twenty plane faces.

The names of the Oceaniae were

Doris	Cydippe	Beroe	Ianthe
Petraea	Glauce	Acaste	Lycoris
Ocyrhoe	Tyche	Clytia	Plexaure

Their own single dance ended, as they were about to make choice of their men, one from the sea was heard to call 'em with this charm,[8] *sung by a tenor voice.*

SONG

    Come away, come away,
    We grow jealous of your stay.
    If you do not stop your ear,
155 We shall have more cause to fear
    Sirens of the land, than they
    To doubt the sirens of the sea.

Here they danced with their men several measures and corantos. All which ended, they were again accited[9] *to sea, with a song of two trebles, whose cadences were iterated by a double echo from several parts of the land.*

SONG

    Daughters of the subtle flood,
  Do not let earth longer entertain you;
160 1st ECHO   Let earth longer entertain you
    2nd ECHO Longer entertain you

    'Tis to them enough of good
  That you give this little hope to gain you.
    1st ECHO   Give this little hope to gain you.
165 2nd ECHO Little hope to gain you.

    If they love
      You shall quickly see;
    For when to flight you move,
  They'll follow you, the more you flee.
170 1st ECHO   Follow you, the more you flee.
    2nd ECHO The more you flee.

    If not, impute° it each to other's matter;   *attribute*
    They are but earth—
    1st ECHO   But earth,
175 2nd ECHO Earth—
  And what you vowed was water.
    1st ECHO   And what you vowed was water
    2nd ECHO You vowed was water.

---

8. Chanting or recitation of a verse supposed to possess occult influence. See also *The Tempest* 5.1.31.
9. Summoned.

AETHIOPIA Enough, bright nymphs, the night grows old,
180   And we are grieved we cannot hold
           You longer light; but comfort take.
           Your father only to the lake
           Shall make return; yourselves, with feasts,
           Must here remain the Ocean's guests.
185   Nor shall this veil the sun hath cast
           Above your blood more summers last.
           For which you shall observe these rites:
           Thirteen times thrice, on thirteen nights
           (So often as I fill my sphere
190   With glorious light, throughout the year)
           You shall, when all things else do sleep
           Save your chaste thoughts, with reverence steep
           Your bodies in that purer brine
           And wholesome dew, called rosmarine;°   *sea spray*
195   Then with that soft and gentler foam,
           Of which the ocean yet yields some,
           Whereof bright Venus, beauty's queen,
           Is said to have begotten been,
           You shall your gentler limbs o'er-lave.°   *wash*
200   And for your pains, perfection have.
           So that, this night, the year gone round,[1]
           You do again salute this ground;
           And in the beams of yond bright sun
           Your faces dry, and all is done.

At which, in a dance they returned to the sea, where they took their shell, and with this full song, went out.

SONG

205   Now Dian,° with her burning face,   *the moon*
                Declines apace:
              By which our waters know
              To ebb, that late did flow.
         Back seas, back nymphs, but with a forward grace
210   Keep still your reverence to the place,
         And shout with joy of favor you have won,
              In sight of Albion, Neptune's son.

1605

---

1. Jonson had probably already planned *The Masque of Beauty*, in which the women's black skin was turned white, but intervening masques prevented its production until 1608.

From Epigrams

To My Book

It will be looked for, book, when some but see
    Thy title, *Epigrams*, and named of me,
Thou should'st be bold, licentious, full of gall,
    Wormwood° and sulphur, sharp and toothed² withal,   *bitter-tasting plant*
5 Become a petulant thing, hurl ink and wit
    As madmen stones, not caring whom they hit.
Deceive their malice who could wish it so,
    And by thy wiser temper let men know
Thou art not covetous of least self-fame
10   Made from the hazard of another's shame³—
Much less with lewd, profane, and beastly phrase
    To catch the world's loose laughter or vain gaze.
He that departs° with his own honesty   *parts*
    For vulgar praise, doth it too dearly buy.

1616

On Something, That Walks Somewhere

    At court I met it, in clothes brave° enough   *fine*
        To be a courtier, and looks grave enough
    To seem a statesman: as I near it came,
        It made me a great face. I asked the name.
5   "A lord," it cried, "buried in flesh and blood,
        And such from whom let no man hope least good,
    For I will do none; and as little ill,
        For I will dare none." Good lord, walk dead still.

1616

To Fine Lady Would-Be¹

Fine madam Would-Be,² wherefore should you fear,
    That love to make so well, a child to bear?
    The world reputes° you barren: but I know   *considers*

---

1. Epigrams are commonly thought of as brief, witty, incisive poems of personal invective, often with a surprise turn at the end. But Jonson uses the word in a more liberal sense. His "Epigrams," a separate section in his collected *Works* of 1616, include not only sharp, satiric poems but many complimentary ones to friends and patrons, as well as memorial epitaphs and a verse letter, "Inviting a Friend to Supper."
2. The distinction between toothed (biting) and toothless (general) satires was a commonplace.
3. Here, as often elsewhere, Jonson echoes the greatest Roman epigrammatist, Martial.

1. This poem, epigram LXII, reads like a sonnet of rhyming couplets, yet falls two lines short of the fourteen-line sonnet form.
2. Jonson's play *Volpone* features a character by the same name, Fine Madame [Lady] Would-be. Although she is said by her husband to have traveled to Venice "to observe / To quote, to learn the language, and so forth" (2.1.12–13), his interlocutor, Peregrine, reveals that she "Lies here, in Venice, for intelligence / Of tires, and fashions, and behavior / Among the courtesans" (2.1.26–29). Upon learning of Volpone's fabricated death, she realizes that she has not been made an heir and resolves to become a courtesan.

    Your 'pothecary,° and his drug says no.   *druggist, chemist*
5 Is it the pain affrights? That's soon forgot.
    Or your complexion's loss? you have a pot°   *makeup*
    That can restore that. Will it hurt your feature?°   *good shape, comeliness*
    To make amends, you are thought a wholesome
       creature.
    What should the cause be? Oh, you live at court;
10 And there's both loss of time, and loss of sport,
    In a great belly: Write then on thy womb,
    "Of the not born, yet buried, here's the tomb."

                                                           1616

On My First Daughter[1]

    Here lies, to each her parents' ruth,°   *grief*
    Mary, the daughter of their youth;
    Yet all heaven's gifts being heaven's due,
    It makes the father less to rue.°   *regret*
5 At six months' end she parted hence
    With safety of her innocence;
    Whose soul heaven's queen,° whose name she bears,   *Mary*
    In comfort of her mother's tears,
    Hath placed amongst her virgin-train:
10 Where, while that severed doth remain,
    This grave partakes the fleshly birth;°   *the body*
    Which cover lightly, gentle earth![2]

                                                            1616

On My First Son

    Farewell, thou child of my right hand,[1] and joy;
    My sin was too much hope of thee, loved boy.
    Seven years thou wert lent to me, and I thee pay,
    Exacted by thy fate, on the just day.
5 O could I lose all father now! For why
    Will man lament the state he should envy,
    To have so soon 'scaped world's and flesh's rage,
    And, if no other misery, yet age?
    Rest in soft peace, and asked, say, "Here doth lie
10 Ben Jonson his best piece of poetry."[2]
    For whose sake henceforth all his vows be such
    As what he loves may never like too much.[3]

                                                            1616

---

1. Probably written in the late 1590s, in Jonson's Roman Catholic period (ca. 1598–1610).
2. A common sentiment in Latin epitaphs.
1. A literal translation of the Hebrew name "Benjamin," which implies the meaning "dexterous" or "fortunate." The boy was born in 1596 and died on his birthday in 1603.
2. Poet and father are both "makers," Jonson's favorite term for the poet.
3. The obscure grammar of the last lines allows for various readings; "like" may carry the sense of "please."

To Lucy, Countess of Bedford, with Mr. Donne's Satires[1]

Lucy, you brightness[2] of our sphere, who are
    Life of the Muses' day, their morning star!
If works, not th' authors, their own grace should look,°   *have regard to*
    Whose poems would not wish to be your book?
5 But these, desired by you, the maker's ends
    Crown with their own. Rare poems ask rare friends.
Yet satires, since the most of mankind be
    Their unavoided° subject, fewest see: *inevitable*
For none e'er took that pleasure in sin's sense,°   *experience*
10   But, when they heard it taxed, took more offense.
They then that, living where the matter is bred,[3]
    Dare for these poems yet both ask and read
And like them too, must needfully, though few,
    Be of the best: and 'mongst those, best are you;
15 Lucy, you brightness of our sphere, who are
    The Muses' evening, as their morning star.[4]

1616

To Sir Thomas Roe[1]

Thou hast begun well, Roe, which stand° well too,   *continue*
    And I know nothing more thou hast to do.
He that is round° within himself, and straight,   *honest*
    Need seek no other strength, no other height;
5 Fortune upon him breaks herself, if ill,
    And what should hurt his virtue makes it still.°   *constant*
That thou at once, then, nobly may'st defend
    With thine own course the judgment of thy friend,
Be always to thy gathered self the same,
10   And study conscience, more than thou wouldst fame.
Though both be good, the latter yet is worst,
    And ever is ill got without the first.

1616

---

1. With this poem, Jonson offered a manuscript collection of Donne's satires (see pp. 905–08), such as commonly passed from hand to hand in court circles. Bedford was a well-known literary patron in the period.
2. Lucy's name derives from the Latin *lux*, meaning "light."
3. That is, at court.
4. The planet Venus is called Lucifer ("light-bearing") when it appears before sunrise, Hesperus when it appears after sunset.
1. Knighted in 1605, Roe was sent as ambassador to the Great Mogul—the ruler of the Muslim Mughal empire in South Asia—in 1614. His collection of coins and of Greek and Eastern manuscripts is in the Bodleian Library.

Inviting a Friend to Supper

    Tonight, grave sir, both my poor house and I
        Do equally desire your company:
    Not that we think us worthy such a guest,
        But that your worth will dignify our feast
5   With those that come; whose grace may make that seem
        Something, which else could hope for no esteem.
    It is the fair acceptance, sir, creates
        The entertainment perfect: not the cates.°   *food*
    Yet shall you have, to rectify your palate,
10   An olive, capers, or some better salad
    Ushering the mutton; with a short-legged hen,
        If we can get her, full of eggs, and then
    Lemons and wine for sauce; to° these, a coney°   *besides / rabbit*
        Is not to be despaired of for our money;
15   And though fowl now be scarce, yet there are clerks,°   *scholars*
        The sky not falling, think we may have larks.
    I'll tell you of more, and lie, so you will come:
        Of partridge, pheasant, woodcock, of which some
    May yet be there; and godwit if we can,
20   Knot, rail, and ruff, too.[1] Howsoe'er, my man°   *servant*
    Shall read a piece of Virgil, Tacitus,
        Livy, or of some better book to us,
    Of which we'll speak our minds amidst our meat;°   *food (of any kind)*
        And I'll profess° no verses to repeat: *promise*
25   To this,° if aught appear which I not know of,   *on this point*
        That will the pastry, not my paper, show of.[2]
    Digestive cheese and fruit there sure will be;
        But that which most doth take my muse and me
    Is a pure cup of rich canary wine,
30   Which is the Mermaid's now, but shall be mine;
    Of which, had Horace or Anacreon[3] tasted,
        Their lives, as do their lines, till now had lasted.
    Tobacco, nectar, or the Thespian spring
        Are all but Luther's beer to this I sing.[4]
35   Of this we will sup free but moderately,
        And we will have no Pooly or Parrot[5] by;
    Nor shall our cups make any guilty men,
        But at our parting we will be as when
    We innocently met. No simple word

---

1. All these are edible birds.
2. Cooks sometimes lined pans with paper to keep pastry from sticking. The writing sometimes rubbed off on the crust.
3. Horace and Anacreon (one in Latin, the other in Greek) wrote many poems in praise of wine. "Mermaid": the Mermaid tavern was a favorite haunt of the poets; sweet wine from the Canary Islands was popular in England.
4. Tobacco was an expensive New World novelty in Jonson's time. Nectar is the drink of the gods. The Thespian spring on Mount Helicon is a legendary source of poetic inspiration. Compared with canary wine, these intoxicants are no better than inferior German beer. (The Protestant reformer Martin Luther was German.)
5. Robert Poley and (Henry?) Parrot were government spies. (A parrot was also a proverbial speaker.) As a Roman Catholic convert, Jonson had reason to be wary of undercover agents.

40 That shall be uttered at our mirthful board
   Shall make us sad next morning, or affright
       The liberty that we'll enjoy tonight.

                                                    1616

On Gut

   Gut eats all day, and lechers all the night,
       So all his meat he tasteth over twice;
   And striving so to double his delight,
       He makes himself a thoroughfare of vice.
5 Thus in his belly can he change a sin:
       Lust it comes out, that gluttony went in.

                                                    1616

From The Forest[1]

To Penshurst[2]

   Thou art not, Penshurst, built to envious show,
       Of touch[3] or marble; nor canst boast a row
   Of polished pillars, or a roof of gold;
       Thou hast no lantern° whereof tales are told,   cupola
5 Or stair, or courts; but stand'st an ancient pile,°   edifice
       And, these grudged at,[4] art reverenced the while.
   Thou joy'st in better marks, of soil, of air,
       Of wood, of water; therein thou art fair.
   Thou hast thy walks for health, as well as sport;
10   Thy mount, to which the dryads° do resort,   wood nymphs
   Where Pan and Bacchus their high feasts have made,
       Beneath the broad beech and the chestnut shade;
   That taller tree, which of a nut was set
       At his great birth where all the Muses met.[5]
15 There in the writhèd bark are cut the names
       Of many a sylvan,° taken with his flames;   country dweller, rustic
   And thence the ruddy satyrs oft provoke
       The lighter fauns[6] to reach thy Lady's Oak.[7]

1. In the 1616 *Works*, Jonson grouped some of his nonepigrammatic poems under the heading "The Forest," a translation of the term *Sylvae*, meaning a poetic miscellany. "To Penshurst" and the two following poems are from that group.
2. Penshurst, in Kent, was the estate of Robert Sidney, Viscount Lisle (later, earl of Leicester), a younger brother of the poet Sir Philip Sidney. Along with Lanyer's "The Description of Cookham" (p. 936), this poem inaugurated the genre of English "country house" poems, which includes Marvell's *Upon Appleton House* (p. 1287).
3. Touchstone, an expensive black basalt.
4. More pretentious houses attract envy.
5. Sir Philip Sidney was born at Penshurst.
6. Satyrs and fauns were woodland spirits. Satyrs had the bodies of men and the legs (and horns) of goats. "Provoke": challenge to a race.
7. Named after a lady of the house who went into labor under its branches.

        Thy copse° too, named of Gamage[8] thou hast there,   *little woods*
20   That never fails to serve thee seasoned deer
        When thou wouldst feast or exercise thy friends.
           The lower land, that to the river bends,
        Thy sheep, thy bullocks, kine,° and calves do feed;   *cattle*
           The middle grounds thy mares and horses breed.
25   Each bank doth yield thee conies;° and the tops,°   *rabbits / high ground*
           Fertile of wood, Ashore and Sidney's copse,
        To crown thy open table, doth provide
           The purpled pheasant with the speckled side;
        The painted partridge lies in every field,
30   And for thy mess° is willing to be killed.   *table*
        And if the high-swollen Medway[9] fail thy dish,
           Thou hast thy ponds, that pay thee tribute fish:
        Fat agèd carps that run into thy net,
           And pikes, now weary their own kind to eat,
35   As loath the second draft or cast to stay,
           Officiously° at first themselves betray;   *dutifully*
        Bright eels that emulate them, and leap on land
           Before the fisher, or into his hand.
        Then hath thy orchard fruit, thy garden flowers,
40   Fresh as the air, and new as are the hours.
        The early cherry, with the later plum,
           Fig, grape, and quince, each in his time doth come;
        The blushing apricot and woolly peach
           Hang on thy walls, that every child may reach.
45   And though thy walls be of the country stone,
           They're reared with no man's ruin, no man's groan;
        There's none that dwell about them wish them down;
           But all come in, the farmer and the clown,°   *peasant*
        And no one empty-handed, to salute
50   Thy lord and lady, though they have no suit.°   *request to make*
        Some bring a capon, some a rural cake,
           Some nuts, some apples; some that think they make
        The better cheeses bring them, or else send
           By their ripe daughters, whom they would commend
55   This way to husbands, and whose baskets bear
           An emblem of themselves in plum or pear.
        But what can this (more than express their love)
           Add to thy free provisions, far above
        The need of such? whose liberal board doth flow
60   With all that hospitality doth know;
        Where comes no guest but is allowed to eat,
           Without his fear, and of thy lord's own meat;°   *food*
        Where the same beer and bread, and selfsame wine,
           That is his lordship's shall be also mine,[1]
65   And I not fain to sit (as some this day
           At great men's tables), and yet dine away.

---

8. Lady Barbara (Gamage) Sidney, wife of Sir Robert.
9. The local river.

1. In many great houses, different courses might be served to different guests, depending on their social status. The lord would have the best food.

Here no man tells° my cups; nor, standing by,   *counts*
    A waiter doth my gluttony envy,°   *resent*
But gives me what I call, and lets me eat;
70   He knows below° he shall find plenty of meat.   *in the servants' quarters*
Thy tables hoard not up for the next day;
    Nor, when I take my lodging, need I pray
For fire, or lights, or livery;° all is there,   *provisions*
    As if thou then wert mine, or I reigned here:
75 There's nothing I can wish, for which I stay.°   *wait*
    That found King James when, hunting late this way
With his brave son, the Prince,[2] they saw thy fires
    Shine bright on every hearth, as the desires
Of thy Penates° had been set on flame   *Roman household gods*
80   To entertain them; or the country came
With all their zeal to warm their welcome here.
    What (great I will not say, but) sudden cheer
Didst thou then make 'em! And what praise was heaped
    On thy good lady then, who therein reaped
85 The just reward of her high housewifery;
    To have her linen, plate, and all things nigh,
When she was far; and not a room but dressed
    As if it had expected such a guest!
These, Penshurst, are thy praise, and yet not all.
90   Thy lady's noble, fruitful, chaste withal.
His children thy great lord may call his own,
    A fortune in this age but rarely known.
They are, and have been, taught religion; thence
    Their gentler spirits have sucked innocence.
95 Each morn and even they are taught to pray,
    With the whole household, and may, every day,
Read in their virtuous parents' noble parts°   *attributes*
    The mysteries of manners,° arms, and arts.   *moral behavior*
Now, Penshurst, they that will proportion° thee   *compare*
100   With other edifices, when they see
Those proud, ambitious heaps, and nothing else,
    May say, their lords have built, but thy lord dwells.

1616

Song: To Celia[1]

Drink to me only with thine eyes,
    And I will pledge with mine;
Or leave a kiss but in the cup,
    And I'll not look for wine.
5 The thirst that from the soul doth rise

---

2. Prince Henry, the heir apparent, died in November 1612.
1. These famous lines translate a patchwork of five separate prose passages by Philostratus, a Greek sophist (3rd century C.E.). The music that made it a barroom favorite is by an anonymous 18th-century composer.

        Doth ask a drink divine:
    But might I of Jove's nectar sup,
        I would not change for thine.
    I sent thee late a rosy wreath,
10   Not so much honoring thee,
    As giving it a hope that there
        It could not withered be.
    But thou thereon didst only breathe,
        And sent'st it back to me;
15 Since when it grows and smells, I swear,
        Not of itself, but thee.

        1616

To Heaven

Good and great God, can I not think of thee
    But it must straight° my melancholy be?   *immediately*
Is it interpreted in me disease
    That, laden with my sins, I seek for ease?
5 Oh, be thou witness, that the reins[1] dost know
    And hearts of all, if I be sad for show,
And judge me after, if I dare pretend
    To aught but grace, or aim at other end.
As thou art all, so be thou all to me,
10   First, midst, and last, converted° one and three,   *interchanging*
My faith, my hope, my love; and in this state,
    My judge, my witness, and my advocate.
Where have I been this while exiled from thee,
    And whither rapt,° now thou but stoop'st to me?   *carried off*
15 Dwell, dwell here still:° Oh, being everywhere,   *always*
    How can I doubt to find thee ever here?
I know my state, both full of shame and scorn,
    Conceived in sin and unto labor born,
Standing with fear, and must with horror fall,
20   And destined unto judgment after all.
I feel my griefs too, and there scarce is ground
    Upon my flesh to inflict another wound.
Yet dare I not complain or wish for death
    With holy Paul,[2] lest it be thought the breath
25 Of discontent; or that these prayers be
    For weariness of life, not love of thee.

        1616

---

1. Literally, kidneys, but also the seat of the affections, with a glance at Psalm 7:9: "the righteous God trieth the hearts and reins."

2. Jonson refers to Paul's question: "Who shall deliver me from the body of this death?" (Romans 7:24).

From Underwood

A Sonnet, to the Noble Lady, the Lady Mary Wroth

I that have been a lover, and could show it,
   Though not in these,° in rhymes not wholly dumb,   *in sonnets*
   Since I exscribe° your sonnets, am become   *copy out*
A better lover, and much better poet.
5 Nor is my muse, or I, ashamed to owe it
   To those true numerous graces; whereof some
   But charm the senses, others overcome
Both brains and hearts; and mine now best do know it:
For in your verse all Cupid's armory,
10   His flames, his shafts, his quiver, and his bow,
   His very eyes are yours to overthrow.
But then his mother's° sweets you so apply,   *Venus's*
   Her joys, her smiles, her loves, as readers take
   For Venus' ceston,³ every line you make.

1640–41

My Picture Left in Scotland

I now think Love is rather deaf than blind,
   For else it could not be
      That she
Whom I adore so much should so slight me
5   And cast my love behind;
I'm sure my language to her was as sweet,
     And every close° did meet   *cadence*
    In sentence° of as subtle feet,°   *wise sayings / rhythm*
   As hath the youngest he
10   That sits in shadow of Apollo's tree.²

O, but my conscious fears
   That fly my thoughts between,
   Tell me that she hath seen

---

1. Preparing a second edition of his *Works* (published posthumously in 1640–41), Jonson added a third section of poems, "Underwood," "out of the analogy they hold to *The Forest* in my former book."
2. Mary Wroth, author of the sonnet sequence *Pamphilia to Amphilanthus* (pp. 1074–79) and the romance *The Countess of Montgomery's Urania* (pp. 1069–73), was the daughter of Robert Sidney and his wife, Barbara Gamage, of Penshurst, the niece of Sir Philip Sidney and the Countess of Pembroke; she was the wife of Sir Robert Wroth, whose country estate Jonson also praised in "The Forest." The poem exhibits how poems were exchanged within a coterie, though Jonson also writes as a client to a patron. Jonson's only sonnet, the poem pays tribute to Wroth's mastery of the genre and shows how well Jonson knew her verse.
3. Venus's girdle or belt, which had aphrodisiacal powers; it aroused passion in all beholders.
1. After his walking tour of Scotland in 1618–19, Jonson sent a manuscript version of this poem to William Drummond, with whom he had stayed. The woman of the poem may or may not be a real person.
2. Bay laurel, the tree associated with Apollo, god of poetry.

Ben Jonson. This 1617 portrait of Jonson by Abraham van Blyenberch shows the writer much as he describes himself in some of his poems, particularly "My Picture Left in Scotland."

My hundreds of gray hairs,
15   Told° seven and forty years,   *counted*
Read so much waist[3] as she cannot embrace
My mountain belly and my rocky face;
And all these through her eyes have stopped her ears.

1619   1640–41

The Ode on Cary and Morison   The ode, originally a classical form, is a lyric poem in an elevated style, celebrating a lofty theme, a noble personage, or a grand occasion. The Greek poet Pindar wrote many odes for winners of the Olympic games, known as Great Odes because of their exalted subject and style. Later, the Roman poet Horace wrote more restrained poems that came to be known as Lesser Odes. Jonson's Cary-Morison ode comes closer than any other in the language to the lofty style and manner of Pindar. "To Penshurst" is in the Horatian style, as is Marvell's "An Horatian Ode upon Cromwell's Return from Ireland."

    Pindar's odes were designed to be sung by a chorus and often followed a three-part scheme: the chorus moved in one direction while chanting the strophe, reversed direction for the antistrophe, and stood still for the epode. Jonson imitates

---

3. With a pun on "waste," meaning "untillable ground."

this pattern with his triple division of "turn," "counterturn," and "stand"—the terms more or less literally translated from the original Greek. His turns and counterturns rhyme in couplets, with line lengths varying in all stanzas according to a uniform scheme; the twelve-line stands follow a more complex but equally strict design. He imitates Pindar also in his moral generalizations and lofty but impersonal praise of the two noble friends.

To the Immortal Memory and Friendship of That Noble Pair, Sir Lucius Cary and Sir H. Morison[1]

The Turn

Brave infant of Saguntum,[2] clear°   *explain*
Thy coming forth in that great year
When the prodigious Hannibal did crown
His rage, with razing your immortal town.
5   Thou, looking then about
Ere thou wert half got out,
Wise child, didst hastily return
And mad'st thy mother's womb thine urn.°   *burial vessel*
How summed° a circle[3] didst thou leave mankind   *complete*
10   Of deepest lore, could we the center find!

The Counterturn

Did wiser nature draw thee back
From out the horror of that sack,
Where shame, faith, honor, and regard of right
Lay trampled on?—the deeds of death and night
15   Urged, hurried forth, and hurled
Upon th' affrighted world?
Sword, fire, and famine, with fell° fury met,   *fierce*
And all on utmost ruin set:
As, could they but life's miseries foresee,
20   No doubt all infants would return like thee.

The Stand

For what is life if measured by the space,
Not by the act?
Or maskèd man, if valued by his face,
Above his fact?°   *deeds*
25   Here's one outlived his peers

---

1. Henry Morison died in 1629 at the age of twenty. His good friend Lucius Cary (son of Elizabeth Cary, the author of a 1613 closet drama, *The Tragedy of Mariam*) became the second Viscount Falkland. He was known for his learning; he died fighting for King Charles in the first years of the civil war.

2. The ancient Roman writer Pliny the Elder tells the story of an infant born while Hannibal was assaulting Sagunto, in Spain. The infant dived back into his mother's womb (setting a record for brevity of life), where he was 'buried.'

3. Emblem of perfection.

And told forth fourscore years:
He vexèd time, and busied the whole state,
Troubled both foes and friends,
But ever to no ends:
30 What did this stirrer but die late?[4]
How well at twenty had he fall'n or stood!
For three of his four score, he did no good.

The Turn

He[5] entered well, by virtuous parts,°   *qualities*
Got up and thrived with honest arts:
35 He purchased friends and fame and honors then,
And had his noble name advanced with men;
But, weary of that flight,
He stooped in all men's sight
To sordid flatteries, acts of strife,
40 And sunk in that dead sea of life
So deep, as he did then death's waters sup;
But that the cork of title buoyed him up.

The Counterturn

Alas, but Morison fell young;—
He never fell, thou fall'st,[6] my tongue.
45 He stood, a soldier, to the last right end,
A perfect patriot and a noble friend,
But most a virtuous son.
All offices° were done   *duties of life*
By him, so ample, full, and round
50 In weight, in measure, number, sound,
As, though his age imperfect might appear,
His life was of humanity the sphere.

The Stand

Go now, and tell out° days summed up with fears,   *count*
And make them years;
55 Produce thy mass of miseries on the stage
To swell thine age;
Repeat of things a throng,
To show thou hast been long,
Not lived; for life doth her great actions spell,°   *tell over*
60 By what was done and wrought
In season, and so brought
To light: her measures are, how well
Each syllab'e° answered, and was formed how fair;   *syllable*
These make the lines of life, and that's her air.[7]

---

4. Punning on "dilate," meaning "talk endlessly."
5. That is, another man.
6. Slip, with a latent pun on Latin *fallo*, "to make a mistake."
7. Life is a poem set to music; life's "measures" are its metrical patterns as well as the standards by which it is judged.

The Turn

65 It is not growing like a tree
In bulk, doth make man better be,
Or standing long an oak, three hundred year,
To fall a log at last, dry, bald, and sere:°   *withered*
A lily of a day
70 Is fairer far in May,
Although it fall and die that night;
It was the plant and flower of light.
In small proportions we just beauties see,
And in short measures life may perfect be.

The Counterturn

75 Call, noble Lucius, then for wine,
And let thy looks with gladness shine:
Accept this garland,[8] plant it on thy head,
And think, nay, know, thy Morison's not dead.
He leaped the present age,
80 Possessed with holy rage,°   *inspiration*
To see that bright eternal day,
Of which we priests and poets say
Such truths as we expect for happy men,
And there he lives with memory: and Ben

The Stand

85 Jonson, who sung this of him ere he went
Himself to rest,
Or taste a part of that full joy he meant
To have expressed
In this bright asterism:°   *constellation*
90 Where it were friendship's schism
(Were not his Lucius long with us to tarry)
To separate these twi-
Lights, the Dioscuri,[9]
And keep the one half from his Harry.
95 But fate doth so alternate the design,
Whilst that in heaven, this light on earth must shine.

The Turn

And shine as you exalted are,
Two names of friendship, but one star,
Of hearts the union. And those not by chance
100 Made, or indentured,° or leased out t' advance   *contracted for*
The profits for a time.

---

8. Celebratory wreath; that is, this poem.
9. The mythical Greek twins, Castor and Pollux, the Dioscuri, were said to have exchanged places regularly, after Castor's death, between earth and the underworld. They are the principal stars of the constellation Gemini (the twins).

No pleasures vain did chime
Of rhymes or riots at your feasts,
Orgies of drink, or feigned protests;
105 But simple love of greatness and of good
That knits brave minds and manners, more than blood.

The Counterturn

This made you first to know the why
You liked, then after to apply
That liking; and approach so one the tother,°   *other*
110 Till either grew a portion of the other;
Each styled° by his end,   *called*
The copy of his friend.
You lived to be the great surnames
And titles by which all made claims
115 Unto the virtue: nothing perfect done,
But as a Cary or a Morison.

The Stand

And such a force the fair example had,
As they that saw
The good and durst not practice it, were glad
120 That such a law
Was left yet to mankind;
Where they might read and find
Friendship in deed was written, not in words.
And with the heart, not pen,
125 Of two so early° men,   *youthful*
Whose lives[1] her rolls were, and records,
Who, ere the first down bloomed on the chin
Had sowed these fruits, and got the harvest in.

1629   1640–41

Queen and Huntress[1]

Queen and huntress, chaste and fair,
Now the sun is laid to sleep,
Seated in thy silver chair,
State in wonted° manner keep;   *accustomed*
5 Hesperus entreats thy light,
Goddess excellently bright.

---

1. Some texts read "lines."
1. Also from *Cynthia's Revels* (4.3), this song is sung by Hesperus, the evening star, to Cynthia, or Diana, goddess of chastity and the moon—with whom Queen Elizabeth was frequently compared.

      Earth, let not thy envious shade
        Dare itself to interpose;[2]
      Cynthia's shining orb was made
10   Heaven to clear, when day did close.
      Bless us then with wishèd sight,
        Goddess excellently bright.

      Lay thy bow of pearl apart,
        And thy crystal-shining quiver;
15   Give unto the flying hart
      Space to breathe, how short soever.
      Thou that mak'st a day of night,
        Goddess excellently bright.

1600

To the Memory of My Beloved, The Author, Mr. William Shakespeare, and What He Hath Left Us[1]

    To draw no envy, Shakespeare, on thy name,
        Am I thus ample° to thy book and fame,   *copious*
    While I confess thy writings to be such
        As neither man nor muse can praise too much.
5 'Tis true, and all men's suffrage.° But these ways   *admission*
        Were not the paths I meant unto thy praise;
    For silliest° ignorance on these may light,   *simplest*
        Which, when it sounds at best, but echoes right;
    Or blind affection, which doth ne'er advance
10   The truth, but gropes, and urgeth all by chance;
    Or crafty malice might pretend this praise,
        And think to ruin where it seemed to raise.
    These are as° some infamous bawd or whore   *as though*
        Should praise a matron. What could hurt her more?
15 But thou art proof against them, and, indeed,
        Above th' ill fortune of them, or the need.
    I therefore will begin. Soul of the age!
        The applause! Delight! The wonder of our stage!
    My Shakespeare, rise; I will not lodge thee by
20   Chaucer or Spenser, or bid Beaumont lie
    A little further to make thee a room:[2]
        Thou art a monument without a tomb,
    And art alive still while thy book doth live,
        And we have wits to read and praise to give.
25 That I not mix thee so, my brain excuses,
        I mean with great, but disproportioned° Muses;   *not comparable*
    For, if I thought my judgment were of years,
        I should commit thee surely with thy peers,
    And tell how far thou didst our Lyly outshine,

---

2. Eclipses were thought to portend evil.
1. This poem was prefixed to the first folio of Shakespeare's plays (1623).

2. Chaucer, Spenser, and Francis Beaumont were buried in Westminster Abbey; Shakespeare, in Stratford.

30	Or sporting Kyd, or Marlowe's mighty line.[3]	
	And though thou hadst small Latin and less Greek,[4]	
	From thence to honor thee I would not seek°	lack
	For names, but call forth thund'ring Aeschylus,	
	Euripides, and Sophocles to us,	
35	Pacuvius, Accius, him of Cordova dead,[5]	
	To life again, to hear thy buskin° tread	symbol of tragedy
	And shake a stage; or, when thy socks° were on,	symbol of comedy
	Leave thee alone for the comparison	
	Of all that insolent Greece or haughty Rome	
40	Sent forth, or since did from their ashes come.	
	Triumph, my Britain; thou hast one to show	
	To whom all scenes° of Europe homage owe.	stages
	He was not of an age, but for all time!	
	And all the Muses still were in their prime	
45	When like Apollo° he came forth to warm	god of poetry
	Our ears, or like a Mercury° to charm.	god of eloquence
	Nature herself was proud of his designs,	
	And joyed to wear the dressing of his lines,	
	Which were so richly spun, and woven so fit,	
50	As, since, she will vouchsafe° no other wit:	grant
	The merry Greek, tart Aristophanes,	
	Neat Terence, witty Plautus[6] now not please,	
	But antiquated and deserted lie,	
	As they were not of Nature's family.	
55	Yet must I not give nature all; thy art,	
	My gentle Shakespeare, must enjoy a part.	
	For though the poet's matter° nature be,	subject matter
	His art doth give the fashion;° and that he	form, style
	Who casts° to write a living line must sweat	undertakes
60	(Such as thine are) and strike the second heat	
	Upon the Muses' anvil; turn the same,	
	And himself with it, that he thinks to frame,	
	Or for° the laurel he may gain a scorn;	instead of
	For a good poet's made as well as born,	
65	And such wert thou. Look how the father's face	
	Lives in his issue;° even so the race	offspring
	Of Shakespeare's mind and manners brightly shines	
	In his well-turnèd and true-filèd lines,	
	In each of which he seems to shake a lance,[7]	
70	As brandished at the eyes of ignorance.	
	Sweet swan of Avon, what a sight it were	
	To see thee in our waters yet appear,	
	And make those flights upon the banks of Thames	
	That so did take Eliza and our James![8]	

---

3. John Lyly, Thomas Kyd, and Christopher Marlowe were Elizabethan dramatists contemporary or nearly contemporary with Shakespeare.
4. Shakespeare's Latin was pretty good, but Jonson is judging by the standard of his own remarkable scholarship.
5. Marcus Pacuvius, Lucius Accius (2nd century B.C.E.), and "him of Cordova," Seneca the Younger (1st century C.E.), were Latin tragedians. Seneca's tragedies had a large influence on Elizabethan revenge tragedy.
6. Aristophanes, an ancient Greek satirist and writer of comedy; Terence and Plautus (2nd and 3rd centuries B.C.E.), Roman writers of comedy.
7. Pun on Shake-speare.
8. Queen Elizabeth and King James.

But stay; I see thee in the hemisphere
    Advanced and made a constellation there![9]
Shine forth, thou star of poets, and with rage
    Or influence[1] chide or cheer the drooping stage,
Which, since thy flight from hence, hath mourned like night,
    And despairs day, but for thy volume's light.

                                                        1623

Ode to Himself[1]

Come, leave the loathèd stage,
    And the more loathsome age,
Where pride and impudence, in faction knit,
    Usurp the chair of wit,
Indicting and arraigning every day
    Something they call a play.
Let their fastidious, vain
Commission of the brain
Run on and rage, sweat, censure, and condemn:
They were not made for thee, less thou for them.

Say that thou pour'st them wheat,
    And they will acorns eat;
'Twere simple° fury still thyself to waste   *foolish*
    On such as have no taste!
To offer them a surfeit of pure bread,
    Whose appetites are dead!
No, give them grains their fill,
Husks, draff to drink, and swill:[2]
If they love lees,° and leave the lusty wine,   *dregs*
Envy them not; their palate's with the swine.

No doubt some moldy tale
Like *Pericles*,[3] and stale
As the shrieve's° crusts, and nasty as his fish—   *sheriff's*
    Scraps, out of every dish
Thrown forth and raked into the common tub,[4]
    May keep up the play club:
There, sweepings do as well
As the best-ordered meal;
For who the relish of these guests will fit
Needs set them but the alms basket of wit.

---

9. Heroes and demigods were typically exalted after death to a place among the stars.
1. "Rage" and "influence" describe the supposed effects of the planets on earthly affairs. "Rage" also implies poetic inspiration.
1. The failure of Jonson's play *The New Inn* (1629) inspired this assault on criticism and the public taste.
2. All three items are food for pigs.
3. Shakespeare's play, at least in part (printed 1609).
4. The basket outside the jail to receive food for prisoners was called the sheriff's tub.

>   And much good do 't you then:
>   Brave plush and velvet men
>   Can feed on orts;° and, safe in your stage clothes,[5]   *scraps*
>   Dare quit,° upon your oaths,   *acquit*
> 35 The stagers and the stage-wrights[6] too, your peers,
>   Of larding your large ears
>   With their foul comic socks,°   *symbols of comedy*
>   Wrought upon twenty blocks;[7]
>   Which, if they're torn, and turned, and patched enough,
> 40 The gamesters° share your guilt,[8] and you their stuff.   *gamblers*
>
>   Leave things so prostitute
>   And take th' Alcaic lute;
>   Or thine own Horace, or Anacreon's lyre;
>   Warm thee by Pindar's fire:[9]
> 45 And though thy nerves° be shrunk, and blood be cold,   *sinews*
>   Ere years have made thee old,
>   Strike that disdainful heat
>   Throughout, to their defeat,
>   As curious fools, and envious of thy strain,
> 50 May, blushing, swear no palsy's in thy brain.[1]
>
>   But when they hear thee sing
>   The glories of thy king,
>   His zeal to God and his just awe o'er men,
>   They may, blood-shaken then,
> 55 Feel such a flesh-quake to possess their powers
>   As they shall cry, "Like ours,
>   In sound of peace or wars,
>   No harp e'er hit the stars
>   In tuning forth the acts of his sweet reign,
> 60 And raising Charles his chariot 'bove his Wain."[2]

1629   1631, 1640–41

---

5. Actors often wore on the stage clothes cast off by the gentry; these parasites wear clothes cast off by actors.
6. Playwrights. "Stagers": actors.
7. A pun: molds/blockheads.
8. A pun: guilt/gilt.
9. Alcaeus (ca. 600 B.C.E.), Horace, Anacreon, and Pindar were among the greatest lyric poets in ancient Greece and Rome.
1. By 1629 Jonson was partially paralyzed.
2. Jonson's poetry will elevate the chariot of Charles I (symbol of his royal power) above Charles's Wain (Wagon)—the seven bright stars of Ursa Major.

MARY WROTH
1587–1651?

In 1621 Mary Wroth published *The Countess of Montgomery's Urania*, a 558-page pastoral romance, with her Petrarchan lyric sequence *Pamphilia to Amphilanthus* appended. (She also wrote a manuscript continuation of her romance, first printed in 1999.) Both genres were firsts for an Englishwoman, as was the pastoral drama, *Love's Victory*, which she composed around the same time and circulated only in manuscript. Wroth's achievement was fostered by her strong sense of identity as heir to the literary and cultural fame of her uncle Sir Philip Sidney; her aunt Mary Sidney Herbert, Countess of Pembroke (who may have served as her mentor); and her father, Robert Sidney, Viscount Lisle, whose unpublished sonnet sequence was rediscovered in 1975. While Wroth was clearly influenced by her family's work, particularly Philip Sidney's *The Countess of Pembroke's Arcadia* and *Astrophil and Stella*, the *Urania* and *Pamphilia to Amphilanthus* stand alone as major contributions to the privileged genres of the English Renaissance.

Wroth was raised and educated at Penshurst, the Sidney country house celebrated by Ben Jonson. She also spent time at the Herberts' London residence, Baynard's castle; her aunt's "little college" at Wilton House; and the English garrison in Flushing, where her father and brother held military posts. Lady Anne Clifford noted that Wroth taught her "a great deal of news from beyond the seas" during a visit to Penshurst in 1616. At age seventeen, Wroth was married (not wholly compatibly) to Sir Robert Wroth, whose office it was to facilitate the king's hunting; and she befriended several poets, including Ben Jonson. Wroth's poems circulated in manuscript well before their publication, and her reputation as a poet and literary patron is attested by numerous dedicatory poems. Jonson celebrated her in two epigrams and in a verse letter honoring her husband, dedicated to her his great comedy *The Alchemist*, and claimed in his only sonnet (p. 1057) that her sonnets had made him a "better lover, and much better poet." An accomplished musician and dancer, Wroth also performed in Jonson's *The Masque of Blackness* (1605) at the behest of Queen Anna. After her husband's death, Wroth carried on a long-standing love affair with her married first cousin, William Herbert, Earl of Pembroke, himself a poet, powerful courtier, and patron of literature and the theater. (He is one of the dedicatees of Shakespeare's First Folio.) That relationship, which occasioned some scandal, produced two children.

The title characters of Wroth's Petrarchan sequence, *Pamphilia* ("all-loving") *to Amphilanthus* ("lover of two"), derive from the romance to which they were appended, and at times shadow Wroth and Pembroke. The sonnet sequence was less popular in Jacobean than in Elizabethan England, but as the major genre for analyzing the (male) lover's passions, frustrations, and fantasies (and sometimes career anxieties), it was an obvious choice for a poet of Wroth's ambition. Yet *Pamphilia to Amphilanthus* does more than reverse the roles of lover and beloved; Pamphilia addresses few sonnets to Amphilanthus, and seldom assumes the Petrarchan lover's position of abject servitude to a cruel beloved. Instead, she proclaims her subjection to Cupid, usually identified with the force of her own desire. This radical revision identifies female desire as the source and center of the love relationship, and celebrates the woman lover-poet's movement from the bondage of chaotic passion to the freedom of self-chosen constancy.

The love affair between Pamphilia and Amphilanthus plays a central role in the *Urania*, but the romance as a whole focuses on the activities of the interrelated royal

Lady Mary Wroth, with archlute (attributed to John de Critz). The image represents Mary Wroth in a conventional pose and role, holding the archlute, which indicates that she has been educated in the graceful arts that an aristocratic woman was expected to know. But the massive archlute, emblem of song making, also points to her identity as a poet and to her literary heritage as a Sidney—niece of the poets Sir Philip Sidney and the Countess of Pembroke, and daughter of Sir Robert Sidney of Penshurst, also a poet.

families of Morea and Naples, particularly the political and literary activities of their queens. Conventional romance tropes abound in the *Urania*—humble shepherdesses are revealed to be princesses; idealized knights fight monsters and tyrants—but rather than an Arcadia or Fairyland, the landscape of the *Urania* is an ambiguously ancient, war-torn Europe and Asia that often mirrors the contentious geopolitics of the early seventeenth century. Amphilanthus's "valor" and Pamphilia's "loyalty, met together" secure the future of Bohemia and the Holy Roman Empire, both hot topics of political dispute in the 1620s, and convert the Muslims of Cyprus to Christianity. Love stories proliferate in the romance, but while the male heroes are often courageous fighters and attractive lovers, they are often flawed by inconstancy, and it is the women's steadfastness that serves as the romance's guiding ethos. Almost all of Wroth's female characters are also storytellers and poets, and they compose twice as many poems in the romance as the men do. Pamphilia, Wroth's surrogate, is singled out as a poet by vocation, both by the number of her poems and by their excellence.

Many contemporaries read the *Urania* as a scandalous roman à clef, finding allusions not only to Sidney-Pembroke-Wroth affairs, but to notable personages of the Jacobean court, and to matters of political controversy. The historian Edmund Bolton placed the *Urania* in the company of the *Arcadia* and John Barclay's *Argenis* (1621) as texts that "shadow out some persons, or matter, which it were not otherwise safe, or convenient to discover directly." A public outcry from one reader, Lord Edward Denny, elicited a spirited satiric response from Wroth. Although she offered to withdraw the work from circulation, there is no evidence that she actually did so. Indeed, her choice of the famous Simon van de Passe as her engraver, and her use of publishers who had recently been punished for publishing politically sensitive materials, suggest that she may well have courted a degree of notoriety.

From The Countess of Montgomery's Urania[1]

From *The First Book*

When the spring began to appear like the welcome messenger of summer, one sweet (and in that more sweet) morning, after Aurora[2] had called all careful eyes to attend the day, forth came the fair shepherdess Urania[3] (fair indeed; yet that far too mean a title for her, who for beauty deserved the highest style[4] could be given by best-knowing judgments). Into the mead[5] she came, where usually she drove her flocks to feed, whose leaping and wantonness showed they were proud of such a guide: but she, whose sad thoughts led her to another manner of spending her time, made her soon leave them, and follow her late-begun custom; which was (while they delighted themselves) to sit under some shade, bewailing her misfortune; while they fed, to feed upon her own sorrow and tears, which at this time she began again to summon, sitting down under the shade of a well-spread beech; the ground (then blest) and the tree, with full and fine-leaved branches, growing proud to bear and shadow such perfections. But she regarding nothing, in comparison of her woe, thus proceeded in her grief: "Alas Urania," said she (the true servant to misfortune), "of any misery that can befall woman, is not this the most and greatest which thou art fallen into? Can there be any near the unhappiness of being ignorant, and that in the highest kind, not being certain of mine own estate or birth? Why was I not still continued in the belief I was, as I appear, a shepherdess, and daughter to a shepherd? My ambition then went no higher than this estate, now flies it to a knowledge; then was I contented, now perplexed. O ignorance, can thy dullness yet procure so sharp a pain? and that such a thought as makes me now aspire unto knowledge? How did I joy in this poor life, being quiet! blessed in the love of those I took for parents, but now by them I know the contrary, and by that knowledge, now to know myself. Miserable Urania, worse art thou now than these thy lambs; for they know their dams, while thou dost live unknown of any." By this were others come into that mead with their flocks: but she, esteeming her sorrowing thoughts her best and choicest company, left that place, taking a little path which brought her to the further side of the plain, to the foot of the rocks, speaking as she went these lines, her eyes fixed upon the ground, her very soul turned into mourning.

---

1. Wroth's title echoes *The Countess of Pembroke's Arcadia*, the romance written by her uncle Sir Philip Sidney and dedicated to her aunt Mary Sidney Herbert, Countess of Pembroke. The Countess of Montgomery was Susan (Vere) Herbert, Wroth's close friend and the sister-in-law of her lover, William Herbert. The opening of the *Urania* is meant to be compared to (and contrasted with) the opening of the *Arcadia*, in which two shepherds lament the absence of their beloved, the mysterious shepherdess Urania.
2. The Greek goddess of the dawn.
3. The name has multiple associations: the Muse of astronomy, the Muse of Christian poetry, and a surname for Aphrodite (Venus) designating heavenly beauty. It was also an honorific commonly bestowed on Wroth's aunt, Mary Sidney, Countess of Pembroke. In Wroth's romance, Urania is a foundling adopted by shepherds but actually the daughter of the King of Naples; after losing one lover and gaining another, she marries, becomes a matriarch, and is throughout (as in this episode) a counselor of others.
4. Title.
5. Meadow.

The Countess of Montgomeries Urania. The frontispiece to Wroth's work was engraved by Simon van de Passe. The publishers, John Marriot and John Grismond, had been fined a year earlier for publishing the overly topical *Wither's Motto* (1621).

>   Unseen, unknown, I here alone complain
>   To rocks, to hills, to meadows, and to springs,
>   Which can no help return to ease my pain,
>   But back my sorrows the sad Echo[6] brings.
> 5 Thus still increasing are my woes to me,
>   Doubly resounded by that moanful voice,
>   Which seems to second me in misery,
>   And answer gives like friend of mine own choice.
>   Thus only she doth my companion prove,

---

6. In classical mythology Echo was a wood nymph who pined away in unrequited love for the handsome Narcissus until only her voice remained (Ovid, *Metamorphoses* 3).

10   The others silently do offer ease.
     But those that grieve, a grieving note do love;
     Pleasures to dying eyes bring but disease:
     And such am I, who daily ending live,
     Wailing a state which can no comfort give.

In this passion she went on, till she came to the foot of a great rock, she thinking of nothing less than ease, sought how she might ascend it; hoping there to pass away her time more peaceably with loneliness, though not to find least respite from her sorrow, which so dearly she did value, as by no means she would impart it to any. The way was hard, though by some windings making the ascent pleasing. Having attained the top, she saw under some hollow trees the entry into the rock: she fearing nothing but the continuance of her ignorance, went in; where she found a pretty room, as if that stony place had yet in pity, given leave for such perfections to come into the heart as chiefest, and most beloved place, because most loving. The place was not unlike the ancient (or the descriptions of ancient) hermitages, instead of hangings, covered and lined with ivy, disdaining aught else should come there, that being in such perfection. This richness in Nature's plenty made her stay to behold it, and almost grudge the pleasant fullness of content that place might have, if sensible, while she must know to taste of torments. As she was thus in passion mixed with pain, throwing her eyes as wildly as timorous lovers do for fear of discovery, she perceived a little light, and such a one, as a chink doth oft discover to our sights. She curious to see what this was, with her delicate hands put the natural ornament aside, discerning a little door, which she putting from her, passed through it into another room, like the first in all proportion; but in the midst there was a square stone, like to a pretty table, and on it a wax candle burning; and by that a paper,[7] which had suffered itself patiently to receive the discovering of so much of it, as presented this sonnet (as it seemed newly written) to her sight.

    Here all alone in silence might I mourn:
        But how can silence be where sorrows flow?
        Sighs with complaints have poorer pains outworn;
    But broken hearts can only true grief show.

5   Drops of my dearest blood shall let Love know
        Such tears for her I shed, yet still do burn,
        As no spring can quench least part of my woe,
    Till this live earth, again to earth do turn.

    Hateful all thought of comfort is to me,
10   Despised day, let me still night possess;
        Let me all torments feel in their excess,
    And but this light allow my state to see.

    Which still doth waste, and wasting as this light,
    Are my sad days unto eternal night.

---

7. The episode alludes to an episode in Philip Sidney's *Old Arcadia* in which one of the heroines, Cleophila, enters a darkened cave illuminated by a single candle and finds a poem on top of a stone table.

"Alas Urania!" sighed she. "How well do these words, this place, and all agree with thy fortune? Sure, poor soul, thou wert here appointed to spend thy days, and these rooms ordained to keep thy tortures in; none being assuredly so matchlessly unfortunate."

Turning from the table, she discerned in the room a bed of boughs, and on it a man lying, deprived of outward sense, as she thought, and of life, as she at first did fear, which struck her into a great amazement: yet having a brave spirit, though shadowed under a mean habit,[8] she stepped unto him, whom she found not dead, but laid upon his back, his head a little to her wards,[9] his arms folded on his breast, hair long, and beard disordered, manifesting all care;[1] but care itself had left him: curiousness thus far afforded him, as to be perfectly discerned the most exact piece of misery; apparel he had suitable to the habitation, which was a long gray[2] robe. This grievful spectacle did much amaze the sweet and tender-hearted shepherdess; especially, when she perceived (as she might by the help of the candle) the tears which distilled from his eyes; who seeming the image of death, yet had this sign of worldly sorrow, the drops falling in that abundance, as if there were a kind strife among them, to rid their master first of that burdenous[3] carriage; or else meaning to make a flood, and so drown their woeful patient in his own sorrow, who yet lay still, but then fetching a deep groan from the profoundest part of his soul, he said:

"Miserable Perissus,[4] canst thou thus live, knowing she that gave thee life is gone? Gone, O me! and with her all my joy departed. Wilt thou (unblessed creature) lie here complaining for her death, and know she died for thee? Let truth and shame make thee do something worthy of such a love, ending thy days like thyself, and one fit to be her servant. But that I must not do: then thus remain and foster storms, still to torment thy wretched soul withall, since all are little, and too too little for such a loss. O dear Limena,[5] loving Limena, worthy Limena, and more rare, constant Limena: perfections delicately feigned to be in women were verified in thee, was such worthiness framed only to be wondered at by the best, but given as a prey to base and unworthy jealousy? When were all worthy parts joined in one, but in thee my best Limena? Yet all these grown subject to a creature ignorant of all but ill; like unto a fool, who in a dark cave, that hath but one way to get out, having a candle, but not the understanding what good it doth him, puts it out: this ignorant wretch not being able to comprehend thy virtues, did so by thee in thy murder, putting out the world's light, and men's admiration: Limena, Limena, O my Limena."

With that he fell from complaining into such a passion, as weeping and crying were never in so woeful a perfection, as now in him; which brought as deserved a compassion from the excellent shepherdess, who already had her heart so tempered with grief, as that it was apt to take any impression that it would come to seal withal. Yet taking a brave courage to her, she stepped unto him, kneeling down by his side, and gently pulling him by the arm, she thus spoke.

"Sir," said she, "having heard some part of your sorrows, they have not only made me truly pity you, but wonder at you; since if you have lost so great a

---

8. Lowly garment.
9. Toward her.
1. Trouble.
2. Gray is typically associated with mourning and despair.
3. Burdensome.
4. Perissus: "Lost one."
5. Literally, "woman of home or threshold."

treasure, you should not lie thus leaving her and your love unrevenged, suffering her murderers to live, while you lie here complaining; and if such perfections be dead in her, why make you not the phoenix[6] of your deeds live again, as to new life raised out of the revenge you should take on them? Then were her end satisfied, and you deservedly accounted worthy of her favor, if she were so worthy as you say."

"If she were, O God," cried out Perissus, "what devilish spirit art thou, that thus dost come to torture me? But now I see you are a woman; and therefore not much to be marked, and less resisted: but if you know charity, I pray now practice it, and leave me who am afflicted sufficiently without your company; or if you will stay, discourse not to me."

"Neither of these will I do," said she.

"If you be then," said he, "some Fury[7] of purpose sent to vex me, use your force to the uttermost in martyring me; for never was there a fitter subject, then the heart of poor Perissus is."

"I am no Fury," replied the divine Urania, "nor hither come to trouble you, but by accident lighted on this place; my cruel hap being such, as only the like can give me content, while the solitariness of this like cave might give me quiet, though not ease. Seeking for such a one, I happened hither; and this is the true cause of my being here, though now I would use it to a better end if I might: Wherefore favor me with the knowledge of your grief; which heard, it may be I shall give you some counsel, and comfort in your sorrow."

"Cursed may I be," cried he, "if ever I take comfort, having such cause of mourning: but because you are, or seem to be afflicted, I will not refuse to satisfy your demand, but tell you the saddest story that ever was rehearsed by dying man to living woman, and such a one, as I fear will fasten too much sadness in you; yet should I deny it, I were to blame, being so well known to these senseless places; as were they sensible of sorrow, they would condole, or else amazed at such cruelty stand dumb as they do, to find that man should be so inhuman."

* * *

SONG[8]

    Love what art thou? A vain thought
      In our minds by fancy wrought.
      Idle smiles did thee beget,
      While fond wishes made the net
5   Which so many fools have caught.

    Love what art thou? Light and fair,
      Fresh as morning, clear as th' air.
      But too soon thy evening change
      Makes thy worth with coldness range;
10   Still thy joy is mixed with care.

---

6. Mythical bird said to live five hundred years, then expire in flames, out of which a new phoenix arose. Only one phoenix existed at a time.
7. Goddess of vengeance.
8. This song, one of a group of eclogues that marks the conclusion of book 1 of the *Urania*, is sung to a shepherdess by a shepherd, "being, as it seemed, fallen out with Love."

Love what art thou? A sweet flower
Once full blown,° dead in an hour.   *in full bloom*
Dust in wind as staid remains
As thy pleasure or our gains,
15   If thy humor° change, to lour.°   *whim / frown*

Love what art thou? Childish, vain,
Firm as bubbles made by rain,
Wantonness thy greatest pride.
These foul faults thy virtues hide—
20   But babes can no staidness gain.

Love what art thou? Causeless cursed,
Yet alas these not the worst:
Much more of thee may be said.
But thy law I once obeyed,
25   Therefore say no more at first.

1621

From Pamphilia to Amphilanthus[1]

1

When night's black mantle could most darkness prove,
  And sleep, death's image, did my senses hire
From knowledge of myself, then thoughts did move
  Swifter than those most swiftness need require.
5 In sleep, a chariot drawn by winged desire
  I saw, where sat bright Venus, Queen of Love,
And at her feet, her son,° still adding fire   *Cupid*
  To burning hearts, which she did hold above.
But one heart flaming more than all the rest
10   The goddess held, and put it to my breast.
"Dear son, now shut,"[2] said she: "thus must we win."
He her obeyed, and martyred my poor heart.
  I, waking, hoped as dreams it would depart:
Yet since, O me, a lover I have been.

---

1. Pamphilia ("all-loving") is the protagonist of the *Urania*. Her unfaithful beloved's name means "lover of two." These characters are first cousins, like Mary Wroth and William Herbert; their names adumbrate the main theme of both the romance and the appended sonnet sequence: constancy in the face of unfaithfulness.
   While the sequence exists in two formats, one that circulated in manuscript and one in print, we have used the versions that appear in the printed edition of 1621. *Pamphilia to Amphilanthus* is broken into several separately numbered series (the first of which includes forty-eight sonnets, with songs inserted after every sixth sonnet except the last). In Josephine A. Roberts's edition of Wroth's poetry, the poems are numbered consecutively throughout the work; we have adopted this convenient renumbering.
2. That is, shut the burning heart into Pamphilia's breast.

16

Am I thus conquered? Have I lost the powers
   That to withstand, which joys to ruin me?[3]
   Must I be still while it my strength devours,
   And captive leads me prisoner, bound, unfree?
Love first shall leave men's fant'sies to them free,[4]
   Desire shall quench love's flames, spring, hate sweet showers,
   Love shall loose all his darts, have sight, and see
   His shame, and wishings hinder happy hours.
Why should we not Love's purblind° charms resist?   *completely blind*
   Must we be servile, doing what he list?°   *what pleases him*
   No, seek some host to harbor thee: I fly
Thy babish tricks, and freedom do profess.
   But O my hurt makes my lost heart confess
   I love, and must: so farewell liberty.

25

Like to the Indians scorched with the sun,
   The sun which they do as their god adore,
   So am I used by Love, for evermore°   *the more*
   I worship him, less favors have I won.
Better are they who thus to blackness run,
   And so can only whiteness want deplore:
   Than I, who pale and white am with grief's store,
   Nor can have hope, but to see hopes undone.
Besides their sacrifice received in sight
   Of their chose Saint, mine hid as worthless rite,
   Grant me to see where I my offerings give.
Then let me wear the mark of Cupid's might
   In heart, as they in skin of Phoebus° light,   *the sun god*
   Not ceasing offerings to Love while I live.

26

When everyone to pleasing pastime hies,°   *hastens*
   Some hunt, some hawk, some play, while some delight
   In sweet discourse, and music shows joy's might:
   Yet I my thoughts do far above these prize.
The joy which I take, is that free from eyes
   I sit and wonder at this day-like night,
   So to dispose themselves as void° of right,   *devoid*
   And leave true pleasure for poor vanities.
When others hunt, my thoughts I have in chase;
   If hawk, my mind at wished end doth fly;
   Discourse, I with my spirit talk and cry;
   While others music choose as greatest grace.
O God, say I, can these fond pleasures move?
Or music be but in sweet thoughts of love?

---

3. That is, have I lost the power to withstand love ("That"), which takes pleasure in ruining me?

4. That is, this and the other impossibilities that follow will occur before I surrender to love.

28

SONG[5]

Sweetest love, return again,
    Make not too long stay:
Killing mirth and forcing pain,
    Sorrow leading way:
5 Let us not thus parted be,
Love and absence ne'er agree.

But since you must needs depart,
    And me hapless leave,
In your journey take my heart,
10   Which will not deceive:
Yours it is, to you it flies,
Joying in those lovèd eyes.

So in part we shall not part,
    Though we absent be,
15 Time, nor place, nor greatest smart
    Shall my bands make free:
Tied I am, yet think it gain,
In such knots I feel no pain.

But can I live, having lost
20   Chiefest part of me?
Heart is fled, and sight is crossed,
    These my fortunes be:
Yet dear heart go, soon return,
As good there as here to burn.

39

Take heed mine eyes, how you your looks do cast,
    Lest they betray my heart's most secret thought:
    Be true unto yourselves, for nothing's bought
More dear than doubt, which brings a lover's fast.[6]
5 Catch you all-watching eyes ere they be past,
    Or take yours fixed where your best love hath sought
    The pride of your desires; let them be taught
Their faults for shame they could no truer last.
Then look, and look with joy, for conquest won
10   Of those that searched your hurt in double kind;[7]
    So you kept safe, let them themselves look blind,
Watch, gaze, and mark till they to madness run,
While you mine eyes enjoy full sight of Love
Contented that such happinesses move.

---

5. The poem seems to revise one of Donne's songs: "Sweetest love, I do not go," p. 891.
6. Lack of nourishment for love, due to jealousy ("doubt").
7. Those who spy and pry with their two eyes, to discover my secret love.

40

False hope which feeds but to destroy and spill[8]
    What it first breeds; unnatural to the birth
    Of thine own womb, conceiving but to kill,
    And plenty gives to make the greater dearth.[9]
So tyrants do, who falsely ruling earth,
    Outwardly grace them,[1] and with profits fill,
    Advance those who appointed are to death,
    To make their greater fall to please their will.
Thus shadow° they their wicked vile intent,   *conceal*
    Coloring evil with a show of good
    While in fair shows their malice so is spent;[2]
    Hope kills the heart, and tyrants shed the blood.
For hope deluding brings us to the pride
    Of our desires the farther down to slide.

64

Love like a juggler comes to play his prize,[3]
    And all minds draw his wonders to admire,
    To see how cunningly he (wanting eyes)[4]
    Can yet deceive the best sight of desire.
The wanton child, how he can feign his fire
    So prettily, as none sees his disguise,
    How finely do his tricks; while we fools hire
    The badge and office of his tyrannies.[5]
For in the end such juggling he doth make,
    As he our hearts instead of eyes doth take;
    For men can only by their sleights abuse
The sight with nimble and delightful skill;
    But if he play, his gain is our lost will,
    Yet child-like we cannot his sports refuse.

68

My pain still smothered in my grievèd breast,
    Seeks for some ease, yet cannot passage find
    To be discharged of this unwelcome guest;
    When most I strive, more fast his burdens bind,
Like to a ship on Goodwin's[6] cast by wind,
    The more she strives, more deep in sand is pressed,
    Till she be lost: so am I, in this kind,°   *manner*
    Sunk, and devoured, and swallowed by unrest.
Lost, shipwrecked, spoiled, debarred of smallest hope,
    Nothing of pleasure left, save thoughts have scope

---

8. Kill. The image is of miscarriage or infanticide.
9. Gives abundance only to make scarcity more painful afterward.
1. That is, those whom they mean to destroy (see next line).
2. Expended, employed. "Shows": appearances.
3. Engage in a sporting contest.
4. Cupid, the god of love, was represented as a blind child.
5. Seek, at our own cost, the external tokens and ceremonies of tyrannical Love.
6. Goodwin Sands, a line of shoals at the entrance to the Strait of Dover.

Which wander may. Go then, my thoughts, and cry
"Hope's perished, love tempest-beaten, joy lost:
    Killing despair hath all these blessings crossed."
Yet faith still cries, "love will not falsify."

74

SONG

Love a child is ever crying,
Please him, and he straight is flying;
Give him, he the more is craving,
Never satisfied with having.

5   His desires have no measure,
Endless folly is his treasure;
What he promiseth he breaketh:
Trust not one word that he speaketh.

He vows nothing but false matter,
10 And to cozen° you he'll flatter: *cheat*
Let him gain the hand,° he'll leave you,   *the upper hand*
And still glory to deceive you.

He will triumph in your wailing,
And yet cause be of your failing:
15 These his virtues are, and slighter
Are his gifts, his favors lighter.

Feathers are as firm in staying,
Wolves no fiercer in their preying.
As a child then leave him crying,
20 Nor seek him so given to flying.

From *A Crown of Sonnets Dedicated to Love*[7]

77

In this strange labyrinth how shall I turn?
    Ways° are on all sides, while the way I miss: *paths*
If to the right hand, there in love I burn,
Let me go forward, therein danger is.
5   If to the left, suspicion hinders bliss,
Let me° turn back, shame cries I ought return: *if I*
Nor faint, though crosses[8] with my fortunes kiss,

---

7. The "crown" is a difficult poetic form (originally Italian and usually known by its Italian name, *corona*) in which the last line of each poem serves as the first line of the next, until a circle is completed by the last line of the final poem, which is the same as the first line of the first one. The number of poems varies from seven to (as in Wroth's *corona*) fourteen. In contrast to the errant-child Cupid of the preceding part of the sequence, Love in this series is a mature and just monarch, whose true service ennobles lovers. The crown is in part a recantation of the harsh judgment of love earlier in the sequence. But Pamphilia relapses into melancholy afterward.

8. Troubles, adversity. "Faint": lose heart.

Stand still is harder, although sure to mourn.[9]
Then let me take the right- or left-hand way,
Go forward, or stand still, or back retire;
I must these doubts endure without allay°   abatement
Or help, but travel find for my best hire.[1]
Yet that which most my troubled sense doth move,
Is to leave all, and take the thread of love.[2]

103

My muse now happy lay thyself to rest,
    Sleep in the quiet of a faithful love,
    Write you no more, but let these fant'sies move
Some other hearts, wake not to new unrest.
But if you study, be those thoughts addressed
    To truth, which shall eternal goodness prove;
    Enjoying of true joy, the most, and best
The endless gain which never will remove.
Leave the discourse of Venus and her son
    To young beginners,[3] and their brains inspire
    With stories of great love, and from that fire
Get heat to write the fortunes they have won.
And thus leave off; what's past shows you can love,
Now let your constancy your honor prove.[4]

1621

---

9. That is, certain to make me mourn.
1. That is, I find travel (with a pun on "travail," the spelling in the manuscript edition) is my only reward.
2. Ariadne gave Theseus a thread to follow so as to find his way out of the Labyrinth, after killing the Minotaur at its center.
3. In Neoplatonic love philosophy, "beginners" in love are attracted to physical beauty and sensory delights, while more advanced lovers love virtue and spiritual beauty. Writing love sonnets is traditionally the business of young lovers.
4. In a symbolic episode in the *Urania*, Pamphilia embodies the virtue of constancy; she accepts the keys to the Throne of Love, "at which instant Constancy vanished as metamorphosing herself into her breast" (1.1.141).

JOHN WEBSTER
1580?–1625?

John Webster's fame rests on two remarkable tragedies, both set in Roman Catholic Italy and both evoking the common Jacobean stereotype of that land as a place of sophisticated corruption. Both plays have bold heroines who choose for themselves in love and refuse to submit to male authority. *The White Devil*, first performed in 1608, is based on events that took place in Italy in 1581–85; in this play Vittoria Corombona defies a courtroom full of corrupt magistrates who convict her of adultery and murder. *The Duchess of Malfi*, first performed in 1614 and published in

1623, is based on an Italian novella. In this play, the spirited ruler of Malfi secretly marries her steward for love, defying her brothers, a duke and a cardinal, who demand that she remain a widow. Their dark motives include greed for her fortune, overweening pride in their noble blood, and incestuous desire. The play weds sublime poetry and gothic horror in the devious machinations set in motion against the duchess by her brothers' melancholy spy Bosola, in the macabre mental and physical torments to which they subject her, and in the final scenes, in which the stage is littered with the slaughtered bodies of all the principal characters.

Webster was the son of a London tailor and a member of the Merchant Tailors' Company, but we know little else about him. He wrote a tragicomedy, *The Devil's Law Case* (1621), and collaborated on several plays with contemporary playwrights, among them Thomas Dekker in *Westward Ho* (1607) and John Marston in *The Malcontent* (1604). Of all the Stuart dramatists, Webster is the one who comes closest to Shakespeare in his power of tragic utterance and his flashes of poetic brilliance.

The Duchess of Malfi

Dramatis Personae

FERDINAND, *Duke of Calabria*
THE CARDINAL, *his brother*
ANTONIO BOLOGNA, *steward of the household to the* DUCHESS
DELIO, *his friend*
DANIEL DE BOSOLA, *gentleman of the horse to the* DUCHESS
CASTRUCCIO, *an old lord*
MARQUIS OF PESCARA
COUNT MALATESTE
SILVIO, *a lord, of Milan*
RODERIGO ⎱ *gentlemen attending*
GRISOLAN ⎰ *on the* DUCHESS
DOCTOR
Several MADMEN, PILGRIMS, EXECUTIONERS, OFFICERS, ATTENDANTS &c.
THE DUCHESS OF MALFI, *sister of* FERDINAND *and the* CARDINAL
CARIOLA, *her woman*
JULIA, CASTRUCCIO's *wife, and the* CARDINAL's *mistress*
OLD LADY, LADIES, *and* CHILDREN

SCENE. *Amalfi, Rome, Loreto, and Milan*

Act 1

SCENE 1. *Amalfi; a hall in the* DUCHESS's *palace.*

[*Enter* ANTONIO *and* DELIO.]

DELIO You are welcome to your country, dear Antonio;
You have been long in France, and you return
A very formal Frenchman in your habit.[1]
How do you like the French court?
ANTONIO   I admire it:
5   In seeking to reduce both state and people
To a fixed order, their judicious king
Begins at home; quits° first his royal palace   *rids*
Of flattering sycophants, of dissolute
And infamous persons—which he sweetly terms

1.1
1. An absolute Frenchman in your dress.

His Master's masterpiece, the work of heaven[2]—
Considering duly that a prince's court
Is like a common fountain, whence should flow
Pure silver drops in general, but if 't chance
Some cursed example poison 't near the head,
Death and diseases through the whole land spread.
And what is 't makes this blessed government
But a most provident council, who dare freely
Inform him the corruption of the times?
Though some o' th' court hold it presumption
To instruct princes what they ought to do,
It is a noble duty to inform them
What they ought to foresee.—Here comes Bosola,
The only court-gall;[3] yet I observe his railing
Is not for simple love of piety.
Indeed, he rails at those things which he wants;
Would be as lecherous, covetous, or proud,
Bloody, or envious, as any man,
If he had means to be so. Here's the cardinal.

[*Enter the* CARDINAL *and* BOSOLA.]

BOSOLA I do haunt you still.
CARDINAL So.
BOSOLA I have done you better service than to be slighted thus. Miserable age, where the only reward of doing well is the doing of it!
CARDINAL You enforce your merit too much.
BOSOLA I fell into the galleys[4] in your service; where, for two years together, I wore two towels instead of a shirt, with a knot on the shoulder, after the fashion of a Roman mantle. Slighted thus? I will thrive some way. Blackbirds fatten best in hard weather; why not I in these dog days?[5]
CARDINAL Would you could become honest!
BOSOLA With all your divinity do but direct me the way to it. I have known many travel far for it, and yet return as arrant knaves as they went forth, because they carried themselves always along with them. [*Exit* CARDINAL.] Are you gone? Some fellows, they say, are possessed with the devil, but this great fellow were able to possess the greatest devil, and make him worse.
ANTONIO He hath denied thee some suit?
BOSOLA He and his brother are like plum trees that grow crooked over standing pools;[6] they are rich and o'erladen with fruit, but none but crows, pies,[7] and caterpillars feed on them. Could I be one of their flattering panders, I would hang on their ears like a horse leech till I were full and then drop off. I pray, leave me. Who would rely upon these miserable dependencies, in expectation to be advanced tomorrow? What creature ever fed worse than hoping Tantalus?[8] Nor ever died any

---

2. Alludes to Christ ridding the temple of money changers (John 2:13–22).
3. One who frets the court, but with the overtone of a disease, a blight.
4. Forced labor at the oar of a Mediterranean galley was the last penalty this side of torture and execution, and was likely to be a death sentence.
5. The hot, sultry season of midsummer.
6. Stagnant waters.
7. Magpies, birds of evil omen like blackbirds.
8. Tantalus, in classical mythology, was "tantalized" by the constant presence of delectable food and drink that, though he was desperate, he could never reach.

man more fearfully than he that hoped for a pardon. There are rewards for hawks and dogs when they have done us service; but for a soldier that hazards his limbs in a battle, nothing but a kind of geometry is his last supportation.[9]

DELIO Geometry?

BOSOLA Aye, to hang in a fair pair of slings, take his latter swing in the world upon an honorable pair of crutches, from hospital to hospital.[1] Fare ye well, sir: and yet do not you scorn us; for places in the court are but like beds in the hospital, where this man's head lies at that man's foot, and so lower and lower.   [*Exit.*]

DELIO I knew this fellow seven years[2] in the galleys
For a notorious murder; and 'twas thought
The cardinal suborned it. He was released
By the French general, Gaston de Foix,
When he recovered Naples.[3]

ANTONIO   'Tis great pity
He should be thus neglected; I have heard
He's very valiant. This foul melancholy
Will poison all his goodness; for, I'll tell you,
If too immoderate sleep be truly said
To be an inward rust unto the soul,
It then doth follow want of action
Breeds all black malcontents; and their close rearing,
Like moths in cloth, do hurt for want of wearing.[4]

SCENE 2. *The scene continues.*

[*Enter* CASTRUCCIO, SILVIO, RODERIGO, *and* GRISOLAN.]

DELIO The presence° 'gins to fill: you promised me   audience hall
To make me the partaker of the natures
Of some of your great courtiers.

ANTONIO   The Lord Cardinal's,
And other strangers' that are now in court?
I shall. Here comes the great Calabrian duke.

[*Enter* FERDINAND *and* ATTENDANTS.]

FERDINAND Who took the ring oftenest?[1]

SILVIO Antonio Bologna, my lord.

FERDINAND Our sister duchess' great master of her household? Give him the jewel. When shall we leave this sportive action, and fall to action indeed?

CASTRUCCIO Methinks, my lord, you should not desire to go to war in person.

FERDINAND Now for some gravity. Why, my lord?

CASTRUCCIO It is fitting a soldier arise to be a prince, but not necessary a prince descend to be a captain.

---

9. Support.
1. In the 17th century, a place of last resort for the indigent dying.
2. In speaking to the cardinal himself (line 34), Bosola had mentioned only two years.
3. Gaston de Foix, French commander, was active in Italy during the early 1500s; hence, the time of the tragedy is about a hundred years before Webster wrote. Ferdinand and the cardinal are Span- iards established in Italy, like the infamous house of Borgia.
4. That is, enforced idleness breeds discontent, as moths breed in unused clothing.
1.2
1. A common game around court, used in training for tournaments, involved catching a hanging ring on the tip of a lance. But some of Webster's audience would have caught a sexual analogy.

FERDINAND No?
CASTRUCCIO No, my lord, he were far better do it by a deputy.
FERDINAND Why should he not as well sleep or eat by a deputy? This might take idle, offensive, and base office from him, whereas the other deprives him of honor.
CASTRUCCIO Believe my experience, that realm is never long in quiet where the ruler is a soldier.
FERDINAND Thou told'st me thy wife could not endure fighting.
CASTRUCCIO True, my lord.
FERDINAND And of a jest she broke of a captain she met full of wounds. I have forgot it.
CASTRUCCIO She told him, my lord, he was a pitiful fellow, to lie, like the children of Israel, all in tents.[2]
FERDINAND Why, there's a wit were able to undo all the chirurgeons[3] o' the city; for although gallants should quarrel and had drawn their weapons and were ready to go to it, yet her persuasions would make them put up.
CASTRUCCIO That she would, my lord.
FERDINAND How do you like my Spanish gennet?[4]
RODERIGO He is all fire.
FERDINAND I am of Pliny's opinion, I think he was begot by the wind; he runs as if he were ballassed[5] with quicksilver.
SILVIO True, my lord, he reels from the tilt often.[6]
RODERIGO *and* GRISOLAN Ha, ha, ha!
FERDINAND Why do you laugh? Methinks, you that are courtiers should be my touchwood, take fire when I give fire; that is, laugh but when I laugh, were the subject never so witty.
CASTRUCCIO True, my lord, I myself have heard a very good jest, and have scorned to seem to have so silly a wit as to understand it.
FERDINAND But I can laugh at your fool, my lord.
CASTRUCCIO He cannot speak, you know, but he makes faces: my lady cannot abide him.
FERDINAND No?
CASTRUCCIO Nor endure to be in merry company, for she says too much laughing and too much company fills her too full of the wrinkle.
FERDINAND I would, then, have a mathematical instrument made for her face, that she might not laugh out of compass.[7] I shall shortly visit you at Milan, Lord Silvio.
SILVIO Your grace shall arrive most welcome.
FERDINAND You are a good horseman, Antonio. You have excellent riders in France. What do you think of good horsemanship?
ANTONIO Nobly, my lord: as out of the Grecian horse issued many famous princes,[8] so out of brave horsemanship arise the first sparks of growing resolution that raise the mind to noble action.
FERDINAND You have bespoke it worthily.

---

2. Lint bandages were called "tents."
3. Surgeons.
4. Sometimes "jennet": a small Spanish horse of Arabian stock.
5. Ballasted. Pliny in his *Natural History* tells about some Spanish horses generated by a swift wind (8.67).
6. Veers away from the target, undesirable in a warhorse.
7. Excessively; with a pun on the draftsman's compass.
8. The Trojan horse, in which the Greek warriors hid, to overrun Troy.

SILVIO Your brother, the Lord Cardinal, and sister duchess.
[*Reenter* CARDINAL, *with* DUCHESS, CARIOLA, *and* JULIA.]
CARDINAL Are the galleys come about?
GRISOLAN   They are, my lord.
FERDINAND Here's the Lord Silvio, is come to take his leave.
DELIO [*aside to* ANTONIO] Now, sir, your promise. What's that Cardinal?
  I mean his temper? They say he's a brave fellow,
  Will play[9] his five thousand crowns at tennis, dance,
  Court ladies, and one that hath fought single combats.
ANTONIO Some such flashes superficially hang on him for form; but observe his inward character: he is a melancholy churchman; the spring in his face is nothing but the engendering of toads; where he is jealous of any man, he lays worse plots for them than ever was imposed on Hercules,[1] for he strews in his way flatterers, panders, intelligencers,[2] atheists, and a thousand such political monsters. He should have been Pope; but instead of coming to it by the primitive decency of the church, he did bestow bribes so largely and so impudently as if he would have carried it away without heaven's knowledge. Some good he hath done—
DELIO You have given too much of him. What's his brother?
ANTONIO The duke there? A most perverse and turbulent nature.
  What appears in him mirth is merely outside;
  If he laugh heartily, it is to laugh
  All honesty out of fashion.
DELIO   Twins?
ANTONIO   In quality.
  He speaks with others' tongues, and hears men's suits
  With others' ears; will seem to sleep o' th' bench
  Only to entrap offenders in their answers;
  Dooms men to death by information;°   *testimony of spies*
  Rewards by hearsay.°   *random report*
DELIO   Then the law to him
  Is like a foul black cobweb to a spider:
  He makes of it his dwelling and a prison
  To entangle those shall feed him.
ANTONIO   Most true:
  He ne'er pays debts unless they be shrewd turns,°   *hurtful acts*
  And those he will confess that he doth owe.
  Last, for his brother there, the Cardinal,
  They that do flatter him most say oracles
  Hang at his lips; and verily I believe them,
  For the devil speaks in them.
  But for their sister, the right noble duchess,
  You never fixed your eye on three fair medals
  Cast in one figure, of so different temper.
  For her discourse, it is so full of rapture,
  You only will begin then to be sorry

---

9. Wager. "Brave": fine; ostentatious.
1. Hercules' uncle, King Eurystheus, sent him on twelve suicide missions to get rid of him, but Hercules performed all these "labors" successfully.
2. Spies, "political" schemers.

	When she doth end her speech, and wish, in wonder,	
100	She held it less vainglory° to talk much,	*excessive pride*
	Than your penance to hear her: whilst she speaks,	
	She throws upon a man so sweet a look,	
	That it were able to raise one to a galliard°	*gay and lively dance*
105	That lay in a dead palsy, and to dote	
	On that sweet countenance; but in that look	
	There speaketh so divine a continence	
	As cuts off all lascivious and vain hope.	
	Her days are practiced in such noble virtue	
110	That sure her nights, nay, more, her very sleeps,	
	Are more in heaven than other ladies' shrifts.°	*confessions*
	Let all sweet ladies break their flattering glasses,°	*mirrors*
	And dress themselves in her.	

DELIO   Fie, Antonio,
You play the wire-drawer[3] with her commendations.

115	ANTONIO I'll case° the picture up only thus much;	*frame*
	All her particular worth grows to this sum:	
	She stains° the time past, lights the time to come.	*darkens*

CARDINAL   You must attend my lady in the gallery,
Some half an hour hence.

ANTONIO   I shall.   [*Exeunt* ANTONIO *and* DELIO.]

FERDINAND   Sister, I have a suit to you.

120   DUCHESS   To me, sir?

FERDINAND   A gentleman here, Daniel de Bosola,
One that was in the galleys—

DUCHESS   Yes, I know him.

FERDINAND   A worthy fellow he is. Pray, let me entreat for
The provisorship of your horse.[4]

DUCHESS   Your knowledge of him
Commends him and prefers him.

125	FERDINAND Call him hither. [*Exit* ATTENDANT.]	
	We are now upon° parting. Good Lord Silvio,	*at the point of*
	Do us commend to all our noble friends	
	At the leaguer.°	*camp*

SILVIO   Sir, I shall.

DUCHESS   You are for Milan?

SILVIO   I am.

DUCHESS   Bring the caroches. We'll bring you down to the haven.[5]
                     [*Exeunt all but* FERDINAND *and the* CARDINAL.]

130	CARDINAL Be sure you entertain° that Bosola	*hire*
	For your intelligence:° I would not be seen in 't;	*spy*
	And therefore many times I have slighted him	
	When he did court our furtherance, as this morning.	

FERDINAND   Antonio, the great master of her household,
Had been far fitter.

135   CARDINAL   You are deceived in him:

---

3. Draw out her praises excessively.
4. Let me beg (for him) the position of supervisor of your horse.
5. Harbor. "Caroches": carriages.

His nature is too honest for such business.
He comes: I'll leave you.   [*Exit.*]
    [*Reenter* BOSOLA.]
BOSOLA   I was lured to you.
FERDINAND   My brother here the cardinal could never
  Abide you.
BOSOLA   Never since he was in my debt.
FERDINAND   Maybe some oblique character° in your face   *crooked feature*
  Made him suspect you.
BOSOLA   Doth he study physiognomy?
  There's no more credit to be given to th' face
  Than to a sick man's urine, which some call
  The physician's whore, because she cozens° him.   *tricks*
  He did suspect me wrongfully.
FERDINAND   For that
  You must give great men leave to take their times.
  Distrust doth cause us seldom be deceived:
  You see, the oft shaking of the cedar tree
  Fastens it more at root.
BOSOLA   Yet, take heed;
  For to suspect a friend unworthily
  Instructs him the next° way to suspect you,   *nearest*
  And prompts him to deceive you.
FERDINAND [*giving him money*]   There's gold.
BOSOLA   So:
  What follows? Never rained such showers as these
  Without thunderbolts i' th' tail of them.
  Whose throat must I cut?
FERDINAND   Your inclination to shed blood rides post°   *hurries*
  Before my occasion to use you. I give you that
  To live i' th' court here, and observe the duchess;
  To note all the particulars of her 'havior,
  What suitors do solicit her for marriage,
  And whom she best affects. She's a young widow:
  I would not have her marry again.
BOSOLA   No, sir?
FERDINAND   Do not you ask the reason, but be satisfied
  I say I would not.
BOSOLA   It seems you would create me
  One of your familiars.°   *diabolical spirits*
FERDINAND   Familiar? What's that?
BOSOLA   Why, a very quaint invisible devil in flesh,
  An intelligencer.°   *spy*
FERDINAND   Such a kind of thriving thing
  I would wish thee, and ere long thou may'st arrive
  At a higher place by 't.
BOSOLA   Take your devils,
  Which hell calls angels;[6] these cursed gifts would make

---

6. Gold coins, marked with the image of the archangel Michael.

                You a corrupter, me an impudent traitor;
                And should I take these, they'd take me to hell.
     FERDINAND   Sir, I'll take nothing from you that I have given:
                There is a place that I procured for you
175   This morning, the provisorship o' th' horse;
                Have you heard on 't?
     BOSOLA   No.
     FERDINAND   'Tis yours. Is 't not worth thanks?
     BOSOLA   I would have you curse yourself now, that your bounty,
                Which makes men truly noble, e'er should make me
                A villain. Oh, that to avoid ingratitude
180   For the good deed you have done me, I must do
                All the ill man can invent! Thus the devil
                Candies all sins o'er; and what heaven terms vile,
                That names he complimental.°   gracious
     FERDINAND   Be yourself;
                Keep your old garb of melancholy; 'twill express
185   You envy those that stand above your reach,
                Yet strive not to come near 'em: this will gain
                Access to private lodgings, where yourself
                May, like a politic dormouse—
     BOSOLA   As I have seen some
                Feed in a lord's dish, half asleep, not seeming
190   To listen to any talk; and yet these rogues
                Have cut his throat in a dream. What's my place?
                The provisorship o' th' horse? Say, then, my corruption
                Grew out of horse dung. I am your creature.
     FERDINAND   Away!
     BOSOLA   Let good men, for good deeds, covet good fame,
195   Since place and riches oft are bribes of shame:
                Sometimes the devil doth preach.   [Exit.]

                    SCENE 3. *The scene continues.*

                [*Enter* DUCHESS, CARDINAL, *and* CARIOLA.]
     CARDINAL   We are to part from you, and your own discretion
                Must now be your director.
     FERDINAND   You are a widow:
                You know already what man is; and therefore
                Let not youth, high promotion, eloquence—
5   CARDINAL   No, nor any thing without the addition, honor,
                Sway your high blood.
     FERDINAND   Marry! They are most luxurious°   lecherous
                Will wed twice.
     CARDINAL   Oh, fie!
     FERDINAND   Their livers are more spotted
                Than Laban's sheep.[1]

1.3
1. In Genesis 30:31–33, Laban promises to Jacob any speckled lambs born while Jacob is herding Laban's sheep; the liver as seat of the passions was thought to be diseased when spotted.

DUCHESS   Diamonds are of most value,
They say, that have passed through most jewelers' hands.
FERDINAND   Whores by that rule are precious.
DUCHESS   Will you hear me?
I'll never marry.
CARDINAL   So most widows say;
But commonly that motion° lasts no longer   *impulse*
Than the turning of an hourglass; the funeral sermon
And it end both together.
FERDINAND   Now hear me:
You live in a rank pasture, here, i' th' court;
There is a kind of honeydew² that's deadly;
'Twill poison your fame° look to 't; be not cunning;   *reputation*
For they whose faces do belie their hearts
Are witches ere they arrive at twenty years,
Aye, and give the devil suck.
DUCHESS   This is terrible good counsel.
FERDINAND   Hypocrisy is woven of a fine small thread,
Subtler than Vulcan's engine:³ yet, believe 't,
Your darkest actions, nay, your privatest thoughts,
Will come to light.
CARDINAL   You may flatter yourself,
And take your own choice; privately be married
Under the eaves of night—
FERDINAND   Think 't the best voyage
That e'er you made; like the irregular crab,
Which, though 't goes backward, thinks that it goes right
Because it goes its own way; but observe,
Such weddings may more properly be said
To be executed than celebrated.
CARDINAL   The marriage night
Is the entrance into some prison.
FERDINAND   And those joys,
Those lustful pleasures, are like heavy sleeps
Which do forerun man's mischief.
CARDINAL   Fare you well.
Wisdom begins at the end: remember it.   [*Exit.*]
DUCHESS   I think this speech between you both was studied,
It came so roundly° off.   *glibly*
FERDINAND   You are my sister;
This was my father's poniard,° do you see?   *dagger*
I'd be loath to see 't look rusty, 'cause 'twas his.
I would have you to give o'er these chargeable° revels: *expensive*
A visor⁴ and a mask are whispering rooms
That were ne'er built for goodness—fare ye well—
And women like that part which, like the lamprey,⁵

---

2. A sweet, sticky substance left on plants by aphids.
3. The net in which Vulcan, Venus's husband, caught her misbehaving with Mars.
4. A half-mask, worn by ladies at carnivals, theaters, and other dubious resorts.
5. Lamprey eels have a cartilaginous, not a bony, skeleton.

Hath never a bone in 't.
DUCHESS   Fie, sir!
FERDINAND   Nay,
I mean the tongue; variety of courtship.
What cannot a neat knave with a smooth tale
Make a woman believe? Farewell, lusty widow.   [*Exit.*]
DUCHESS   Shall this move me? If all my royal kindred
Lay in my way unto this marriage,
I'd make them my low footsteps; and even now,
Even in this hate, as men in some great battles,
By apprehending danger, have achieved
Almost impossible actions (I have heard soldiers say so),
So I through frights and threatenings will assay°   *attempt*
This dangerous venture. Let old wives report
I winked and chose a husband. Cariola,
To thy known secrecy I have given up
More than my life—my fame.
CARIOLA   Both shall be safe,
For I'll conceal this secret from the world
As warily as those that trade in poison
Keep poison from their children.
DUCHESS   Thy protestation
Is ingenious° and hearty:° I believe it.   *ingenuous / sincere*
Is Antonio come?
CARIOLA   He attends you.
DUCHESS   Good dear soul,
Leave me, but place thyself behind the arras,[6]
Where thou mayst overhear us. Wish me good speed,
For I am going into a wilderness
Where I shall find nor path nor friendly clue
To be my guide.   [CARIOLA *goes behind the arras.*]
   [*Enter* ANTONIO.]
         I sent for you: sit down;
Take pen and ink, and write. Are you ready?
ANTONIO   Yes.
DUCHESS   What did I say?
ANTONIO   That I should write somewhat.
DUCHESS   Oh, I remember:
After these triumphs° and this large expense,   *tournaments*
It's fit, like thrifty husbands,[7] we inquire
What's laid up for tomorrow.
ANTONIO   So please your beauteous excellence.
DUCHESS   Beauteous?
Indeed, I thank you: I look young for your sake;
You have ta'en my cares upon you.
ANTONIO   I'll fetch your grace

---

6. Tapestries were often hung in Renaissance palaces to moderate the chill of the bare walls.
7. Though used here in its original sense of one who preserves and safeguards property, the word shows where the duchess's thoughts are tending.

    The particulars of your revenue and expense.
DUCHESS Oh, you are an upright treasurer: but you mistook;
  For when I said I meant to make inquiry
  What's laid up for tomorrow, I did mean
  What's laid up yonder for me.
ANTONIO   Where?
DUCHESS   In heaven.
  I am making my will (as 'tis fit princes should,
  In perfect memory), and I pray sir, tell me,
  Were not one better make it smiling thus
  Than in deep groans and terrible ghastly looks,
  As if the gifts we parted with procured°   *brought on*
  That violent distraction?
ANTONIO   Oh, much better.
DUCHESS If I had a husband now, this care were quit:
  But I intend to make you overseer.
  What good deed shall we first remember? Say.
ANTONIO Begin with that first good deed begun i' th' world
  After man's creation, the sacrament of marriage:
  I'd have you first provide for a good husband;
  Give him all.
DUCHESS   All?
ANTONIO   Yes, your excellent self.
DUCHESS In a winding-sheet?
ANTONIO   In a couple.
DUCHESS Saint Winfred, that were a strange will![8]
ANTONIO 'Twere stranger if there were no will in you
  To marry again.
DUCHESS   What do you think of marriage?
ANTONIO I take 't, as those that deny purgatory;
  It locally° contains or heaven or hell;   *within itself*
  There's no third place in 't.
DUCHESS   How do you affect it?° *feel about it*
ANTONIO My banishment,° feeding my melancholy, *solitary condition*
  Would often reason thus—
DUCHESS   Pray, let's hear it.
ANTONIO Say a man never marry, nor have children,
  What takes that from him? Only the bare name
  Of being a father, or the weak delight
  To see the little wanton ride a-cock-horse
  Upon a painted stick, or hear him chatter
  Like a taught starling.
DUCHESS   Fie, fie, what's all this?
  One of your eyes is bloodshot; use my ring to 't,
  They say 'tis very sovereign.[9] 'Twas my wedding ring,
  And I did vow never to part with it

---

8. Saint Winifred, Welsh virgin and martyr, is an odd saint for the Duchess of Malfi to swear on. "In a couple": that is, of sheets—but with a play on "coupling."
9. Healing, but with an overtone implying royal power.

	But to my second husband.
ANTONIO	You have parted with it now.
DUCHESS	Yes, to help your eyesight.
ANTONIO	You have made me stark blind.
115 DUCHESS	How?
ANTONIO	There is a saucy and ambitious devil
	Is dancing in this circle.[1]
DUCHESS	Remove him.
ANTONIO	How?
DUCHESS	There needs small conjuration, when your finger
	May do it: thus; is it fit? [*She puts the ring upon his finger; he kneels.*]
ANTONIO	What said you?
DUCHESS	Sir,
120	This goodly roof of yours[2] is too low built;
	I cannot stand upright in 't nor discourse,
	Without I raise it higher: raise yourself;
	Or, if you please, my hand to help you: so. [*Raises him.*]
ANTONIO	Ambition, madam, is a great man's madness,
125	That is not kept in chains and close-pent rooms,
	But in fair lightsome lodgings, and is girt
	With the wild noise of prattling visitants,
	Which makes it lunatic beyond all cure.
	Conceive not I am so stupid but I aim
130	Whereto your favors tend; but he's a fool
	That, being a-cold, would thrust his hands i' th' fire
	To warm them.
DUCHESS	So, now the ground's broke,
	You may discover what a wealthy mine
	I make you lord of.
ANTONIO	O my unworthiness!
135 DUCHESS	You were ill to sell° yourself: *evaluate*
	This darkening of your worth is not like that
	Which tradesmen use i' th' city; their false lights
	Are to rid bad wares off:[3] and I must tell you,
	If you will know where breathes a complete man
140	(I speak it without flattery), turn your eyes,
	And progress through yourself.
ANTONIO	Were there nor heaven
	Nor hell, I should be honest: I have long served virtue,
	And ne'er ta'en wages of her.
DUCHESS	Now she pays it.
	The misery of us that are born great!
145	We are forced to woo, because none dare woo us;
	And as a tyrant doubles° with his words *speaks ambiguously*
	And fearfully equivocates, so we
	Are forced to express our violent passions

---

1. To conjure up a devil, the necromancer first draws a charmed circle on the ground—like the duchess's ring.
2. His head as he kneels.
3. Tradesmen in the city display their goods in a poor light so the defects won't be seen.

In riddles and in dreams, and leave the path
Of simple virtue, which was never made
To seem the thing it is not. Go, go brag
You have left me heartless;° mine is in your bosom: *without a heart*
I hope 'twill multiply love there. You do tremble:
Make not your heart so dead a piece of flesh,
To fear more than to love me. Sir, be confident:
What is 't distracts you? This is flesh and blood, sir;
'Tis not the figure cut in alabaster
Kneels at my husband's tomb. Awake, awake, man!
I do here put off all vain ceremony,
And only do appear to you a young widow
That claims you for her husband, and, like a widow,
I use but half a blush in 't.

ANTONIO   Truth speak for me,
I will remain the constant sanctuary
Of your good name.

DUCHESS   I thank you, gentle love:
And 'cause° you shall not come to me in debt, *so that*
Being now my steward, here upon your lips
I sign your *Quietus est*.[4] This you should have begged now;
I have seen children oft eat sweetmeats thus,
As fearful to devour them too soon.

ANTONIO   But for your brothers?

DUCHESS   Do not think of them.
All discord without this circumference[5]
Is only to be pitied, and not feared;
Yet, should they know it, time will easily
Scatter the tempest.

ANTONIO   These words should be mine,
And all the parts you have spoke, if some part of it
Would not have savored flattery.

DUCHESS   Kneel.

[CARIOLA *comes from behind the arras.*]

ANTONIO   Ha!

DUCHESS   Be not amazed; this woman's of my counsel:
I have heard lawyers say, a contract in a chamber
Per verba de presenti[6] is absolute marriage.   [*She and* ANTONIO *kneel.*]
Bless, heaven, this sacred gordian,° which let violence *knot*
Never untwine!

ANTONIO   And may our sweet affections, like the spheres,
Be still° in motion! *constantly*

DUCHESS   Quickening,° and make *giving life*
The like soft music![7]

ANTONIO   That we may imitate the loving palms,

---

4. The legal formula for marking a bill "paid" or "acquitted."
5. *Outside this room, or their embrace.*
6. "By words in the present tense" (that is, not a betrothal or promise for the future). In canon law, the agreement of two parties to consider themselves married is valid with or without priest, ceremony, or witness.
7. Like the supposed music of the spheres.

Best emblem of a peaceful marriage, that ne'er
Bore fruit, divided!
DUCHESS   What can the church force more?
ANTONIO   That fortune may not know an accident,
Either of joy or sorrow, to divide
Our fixèd wishes!
DUCHESS   How can the church bind faster?°   *tighter*
We now are man and wife, and 'tis the church
That must but echo this. Maid, stand apart:[8]
I now am blind.
ANTONIO   What's your conceit° in this?   *idea*
DUCHESS   I would have you lead your fortune by the hand
Unto your marriage bed
(You speak in me this, for we now are one);
We'll only lie, and talk together, and plot
To appease my humorous° kindred; and if you please,   *choleric*
Like the old tale in *Alexander and Lodowick*,
Lay a naked sword between us, keep us chaste.[9]
Oh, let me shroud my blushes in your bosom,
Since 'tis the treasury of all my secrets!   [*Exeunt* DUCHESS *and* ANTONIO.]
CARIOLA   Whether the spirit of greatness or of woman
Reign most in her, I know not; but it shows
A fearful madness: I owe her much of pity.   [*Exit.*]

Act 2

SCENE 1. *The scene continues.*

[*Enter* BOSOLA *and* CASTRUCCIO.]

BOSOLA   You say you would fain be taken for an eminent courtier?
CASTRUCCIO   'Tis the very main of my ambition.
BOSOLA   Let me see: you have a reasonable good face for 't already, and your nightcap expresses your ears sufficient largely. I would have you learn to twirl the strings of your band[1] with a good grace, and in a set speech, at th' end of every sentence, to hum three or four times, or blow your nose till it smart again, to recover your memory. When you come to be a president[2] in criminal causes, if you smile upon a prisoner, hang him, but if you frown upon him and threaten him, let him be sure to 'scape the gallows.
CASTRUCCIO   I would be a very merry president.
BOSOLA   Do not sup o' nights; 'twill beget you an admirable wit.
CASTRUCCIO   Rather it would make me have a good stomach[3] to quarrel; for they say, your roaring boys[4] eat meat seldom, and that makes them

---

8. The phrase is addressed to Cariola as the duchess shuts her eyes and rejects all support.
9. Alexander and Lodowick were look-alike friends in an old ballad. For purely virtuous reasons, one slept with the wife of the other, but with the precaution indicated.

2.1
1. The elaborate ruff of the day had strings attached to it.
2. Presiding magistrate.
3. Disposition.
4. London town bullies.

so valiant. But how shall I know whether the people take me for an eminent fellow?

BOSOLA   I will teach a trick to know it: give out you lie a-dying, and if you hear the common people curse you, be sure you are taken for one of the prime nightcaps.[5]

[*Enter an* OLD LADY.]

You come from painting now?

OLD LADY   From what?

BOSOLA   Why, from your scurvy face-physic. To behold thee not painted inclines somewhat near a miracle; these in thy face here were deep ruts and foul sloughs the last progress.[6] There was a lady in France that, having had the smallpox, flayed the skin off her face to make it more level; and whereas before she looked like a nutmeg grater, after she resembled an abortive hedgehog.

OLD LADY   Do you call this painting?

BOSOLA   No, no, but you call it careening of an old morphewed lady, to make her disembogue again: there's rough-cast phrase to your plastic.[7]

OLD LADY   It seems you are well acquainted with my closet.

BOSOLA   One would suspect it for a shop of witchcraft, to find in it the fat of serpents, spawn of snakes, Jews' spittle, and their young children's ordure; and all these for the face. I would sooner eat a dead pigeon taken from the soles of the feet of one sick of the plague than kiss one of you fasting.[8] Here are two of you, whose sin of your youth is the very patrimony of the physician; makes him renew his footcloth with the spring, and change his high-prized courtesan with the fall of the leaf.[9] I do wonder you do not loathe yourselves. Observe my meditation now:

What thing is in this outward form of man
To be beloved? We account it ominous,
If nature do produce a colt, or lamb,
A fawn, or goat, in any limb resembling
A man, and fly from 't as a prodigy:°   *evil omen*
Man stands amazed to see his deformity
In any other creature but himself.
But in our own flesh, though we bear diseases
Which have their true names only ta'en from beasts—
As the most ulcerous wolf and swinish measle[1]—
Though we are eaten up of lice and worms,
And though continually we bear about us
A rotten and dead body, we delight
To hide it in rich tissue: all our fear,
Nay, all our terror, is lest our physician

---

5. Lawyers (who wore a white coif or skullcap; see line 4, above).
6. A progress was a formal royal journey of state.
7. Scraping ("careening") of an old, scaly ("morphewed") ship ("lady") to fit her for the ocean ("making her disembogue") again. All these metaphors are applied to the model ("plastic") of the lady's condition as "rough-cast," a mixture of lime and gravel, is troweled over a base.
8. Centuries of traditional invective about women's cosmetic practices lie behind this speech. Freshly killed pigeons were applied to the feet of plague victims to draw off the infection; fasting was supposed to cause bad breath.
9. The physician grows rich on those who have outworn their youth; every spring he buys a new harness for his horse and every fall a new mistress for himself.
1. "Wolf": cancer or lupus; "measle": an infection of swine, sometimes confused with human measles.

Should put us in the ground to be made sweet—
Your wife's gone to Rome: you two couple, and get you
To the wells at Lucca to recover your aches.[2]
[*Exeunt* CASTRUCCIO *and* OLD LADY.]
I have other work on foot. I observe our duchess
Is sick a-days: she pukes, her stomach seethes,
The fins of her eyelids look most teeming blue,
She wanes i' th' cheek, and waxes fat i' th' flank,
And contrary to our Italian fashion,
Wears a loose-bodied gown: there's somewhat in 't.
I have a trick may chance discover it,
A pretty one; I have bought some apricots,
The first our spring yields.
    [*Enter* ANTONIO *and* DELIO, *talking apart.*]

DELIO   And so long since married?
You amaze me.

ANTONIO   Let me seal your lips forever:
For, did I think that anything but th' air
Could carry these words from you, I should wish
You had no breath at all.   [*turning to* BOSOLA]
Now, sir, in your contemplation? You are studying to become a great wise fellow?

BOSOLA   Oh, sir, the opinion of wisdom is a foul tetter[3] that runs all over a man's body. If simplicity[4] direct us to have no evil, it directs us to a happy being, for the subtlest folly proceeds from the subtlest wisdom. Let me be simply honest.

ANTONIO   I do understand your inside.

BOSOLA   Do you so?

ANTONIO   Because you would not seem to appear to th' world
Puffed up with your preferment, you continue
This out-of-fashion melancholy. Leave it, leave it.

BOSOLA   Give me leave to be honest in any phrase, in any compliment whatsoever. Shall I confess myself to you? I look no higher than I can reach: they are the gods that must ride on winged horses. A lawyer's mule of a slow pace will both suit my disposition and business; for, mark me, when a man's mind rides faster than his horse can gallop, they quickly both tire.

ANTONIO   You would look up to heaven, but I think
The devil, that rules i' th' air, stands in your light.

BOSOLA   Oh, sir, you are lord of the ascendant,[5] chief man with the duchess; a duke was your cousin-german removed.[6] Say you were lineally descended from King Pepin,[7] or he himself, what of this? Search the heads of the greatest rivers in the world, you shall find them but bubbles of water. Some would think the souls of princes were brought forth by some more weighty cause than those of meaner persons: they are deceived, there's the same hand to them; the like passions sway them; the same reason that makes a

---

2. The wells at Lucca are the mineral springs at nearby Montecatini, renowned as a place to "take the cure." Aches are a symptom of syphilis.
3. Skin disease.
4. Foolishness.
5. In astrology, the predominating influence, controlling destiny.
6. First cousin once removed.
7. Father of Charlemagne, hence source of a great dynasty.

vicar go to law for a tithe-pig[8] and undo his neighbors, makes them spoil a whole province, and batter down goodly cities with the cannon.
[*Enter* DUCHESS *and* LADIES.]
DUCHESS Your arm, Antonio; do I not grow fat?
I am exceeding short-winded. Bosola,
I would have you, sir, provide for me a litter,
Such a one as the Duchess of Florence rode in.
BOSOLA The duchess used one when she was great with child.
DUCHESS I think she did. Come hither, mend my ruff;
Here, when? Thou art such a tedious° lady, and   *clumsy*
Thy breath smells of lemon peels;[9] would thou hadst done;
Shall I swoon under thy fingers? I am
So troubled with the mother![1]
BOSOLA [*aside*]   I fear too much.
DUCHESS I have heard you say that the French courtiers
Wear their hats on 'fore the king.
ANTONIO   I have seen it.
DUCHESS   In the presence?
ANTONIO Yes.
DUCHESS Why should not we bring up that fashion? 'Tis
Ceremony more than duty that consists
In the removing of a piece of felt.
Be you the example to the rest o' th' court;
Put on your hat first.
ANTONIO   You must pardon me.
I have seen, in colder countries than in France,
Nobles stand bare to th' prince, and the distinction
Methought showed reverently.
BOSOLA I have a present for your grace.
DUCHESS   For me, sir?
BOSOLA Apricots, madam.
DUCHESS   O, sir, where are they?
I have heard of none to-year.
BOSOLA [*aside*]   Good: her color rises.
DUCHESS Indeed, I thank you: they are wondrous fair ones.
What an unskillful fellow is our gardener!
We shall have none this month.
BOSOLA Will not your grace pare them?
DUCHESS No. They taste of musk, methinks; indeed they do.
BOSOLA I know not: yet I wish your grace had pared 'em.
DUCHESS Why?
BOSOLA   I forgot to tell you, the knave gardener,
Only to raise his profit by them the sooner,
Did ripen them in horse dung.[2]
DUCHESS   O, you jest.
You shall judge: pray taste one.

---

8. A parson was entitled to a tenth ("tithe") of his *parishioners'* annual profit and was often paid in crops or livestock, but was thought mean if he sued for a petty sum.
9. Lemon peels, chewed to sweeten the breath.
1. Heartburn, but with a second meaning not lost on Bosola.
2. Which grows warm as it decomposes.

ANTONIO   Indeed, madam,
  I do not love the fruit.
DUCHESS   Sir, you are loath
  To rob us of our dainties: 'tis a delicate fruit;
  They say they are restorative.
BOSOLA   'Tis a pretty art,
  This grafting.
DUCHESS   'Tis so; a bettering of nature.
BOSOLA   To make a pippin grow upon a crab,°   *crab apple*
  A damson on a blackthorn. [*aside*] How greedily she eats them!
  A whirlwind strike off these bawd farthingales!³
  For, but for that and the loose-bodied gown,
  I should have discovered apparently°   *certainly*
  The young springal° cutting a caper in her belly.   *fellow*
DUCHESS   I thank you, Bosola. They were right good ones,
  If they do not make me sick.
ANTONIO   How now, madam?
DUCHESS   This green fruit and my stomach are not friends;
  How they swell me!
BOSOLA [*aside*]   Nay, you are too much swelled already.
DUCHESS   Oh, I am in an extreme cold sweat!
BOSOLA   I am very sorry.
DUCHESS   Lights to my chamber! O good Antonio,
  I fear I am undone!
DELIO   Lights there, lights!
      [*Exeunt* DUCHESS *and* LADIES. *Exit, on the other side,* BOSOLA.]
ANTONIO   O my most trusty Delio, we are lost!
  I fear she's fall'n in labor; and there's left
  No time for her remove.
DELIO   Have you prepared
  Those ladies to attend her? And procured
  That politic° safe conveyance for the midwife   *secret*
  Your duchess plotted?
ANTONIO   I have.
DELIO   Make use, then, of this forced occasion:
  Give out that Bosola hath poisoned her
  With these apricots; that will give some color
  For her keeping close.
ANTONIO   Fie, fie, the physicians
  Will then flock to her.
DELIO   For that you may pretend
  She'll use some prepared antidote of her own,
  Lest the physicians should re-poison her.
ANTONIO   I am lost in amazement:° I know not what   *confusion*
  to think on 't.   [*Exeunt.*]

---

3. Early hoopskirts, capable of concealing the figure.

SCENE 2. *The scene continues.*

[*Enter* BOSOLA.]

BOSOLA So, so, there's no question but her tetchiness[1] and most vulturous eating of the apricots are apparent signs of breeding.

[*Enter an* OLD LADY.]

Now?

OLD LADY I am in haste, sir.

BOSOLA There was a young waiting woman had a monstrous desire to see the glasshouse[2]—

OLD LADY Nay, pray let me go.

BOSOLA And it was only to know what strange instrument it was should swell up a glass to the fashion of a woman's belly.

OLD LADY I will hear no more of the glasshouse. You are still[3] abusing women!

BOSOLA Who, I? No; only by the way now and then mention your frailties. The orange tree bears ripe and green fruit and blossoms all together; and some of you give entertainment for pure love, but more for more precious reward. The lusty spring smells well, but drooping autumn tastes well. If we have the same golden showers that rained in the time of Jupiter the thunderer, you have the same Danaës still,[4] to hold up their laps to receive them. Didst thou never study the mathematics?

OLD LADY What's that, sir?

BOSOLA Why, to know the trick how to make a many lines meet in one center. Go, go, give your foster daughters good counsel: tell them that the devil takes delight to hang at a woman's girdle, like a false rusty watch, that she cannot discern how the time passes. [*Exit* OLD LADY.]

[*Enter* ANTONIO, DELIO, RODERIGO, *and* GRISOLAN.]

ANTONIO Shut up the courtgates.

RODERIGO   Why, sir? What's the danger?

ANTONIO Shut up the posterns presently,[5] and call
All the officers o' th' court.

GRISOLAN   I shall instantly.   [*Exit.*]

ANTONIO Who keeps the key o' th' park gate?

RODERIGO   Forobosco.

ANTONIO Let him bring 't presently.

[*Reenter* GRISOLAN *with* SERVANTS.]

1 SERVANT O, gentlemen o' the court, the foulest treason!

BOSOLA [*aside*] If that these apricots should be poisoned now,
Without my knowledge!

1 SERVANT   There was taken even now
A Switzer° in the duchess' bedchamber—   Swiss guard

2 SERVANT   A Switzer?

1 SERVANT With a pistol in his great codpiece.[6]

BOSOLA   Ha, ha, ha!

2.2
1. Irritability.
2. Where bottles were blown, near the theater in Blackfriars.
3. Always.
4. Jupiter's success in wooing Danaë in a shower of gold traditionally illustrated female venality.
5. At once. "Posterns": outer gates.
6. An outsize flap worn on the front of men's trunk hose.

1 SERVANT   The codpiece was the case for 't.
2 SERVANT   There was
A cunning traitor: who would have searched his codpiece?
1 SERVANT   True, if he had kept out of the ladies' chambers.
And all the molds of his buttons were leaden bullets.
2 SERVANT   O wicked cannibal!
A firelock° in 's codpiece!   *pistol*
1 SERVANT   'Twas a French plot,
Upon my life.
2 SERVANT   To see what the devil can do!
ANTONIO   Are all the officers here?
SERVANTS   We are.
ANTONIO   Gentlemen,
We have lost much plate[7] you know, and but this evening
Jewels, to the value of four thousand ducats,
Are missing in the duchess' cabinet.
Are the gates shut?
SERVANT   Yes.
ANTONIO   'Tis the duchess' pleasure
Each officer be locked into his chamber
Till the sun-rising; and to send the keys
Of all their chests and of their outward doors
Into her bedchamber. She is very sick.
RODERIGO   At her pleasure.
ANTONIO   She entreats you take 't not ill:
The innocent shall be the more approved by it.
BOSOLA   Gentlemen o' th' wood-yard, where's your Switzer now?
1 SERVANT   By this hand, 'twas credibly reported by one o' th' black guard.[8]
          [*Exeunt all except* ANTONIO *and* DELIO.]
DELIO   How fares it with the duchess?
ANTONIO   She's exposed
Unto the worst of torture, pain, and fear.
DELIO   Speak to her all happy comfort.
ANTONIO   How I do play the fool with mine own danger!
You are this night, dear friend, to post to Rome;
My life lies in your service.
DELIO   Do not doubt me.
ANTONIO   Oh, 'tis far from me, and yet fear presents me
Somewhat that looks like danger.
DELIO   Believe it,
'Tis but the shadow of your fear, no more;
How superstitiously we mind our evils!
The throwing down salt, or crossing of a hare,
Bleeding at nose, the stumbling of a horse,
Or singing of a cricket, are of power
To daunt whole man° in us. Sir, fare you well: *all courage*
I wish you all the joys of a blessed father:

---

7. Massive gold and silver dishes, a frequent form of wealth in the days before banks.

8. Kitchen scullions. The "wood-yard" is a source of firewood for kitchen and fireplaces.

And, for my faith, lay this unto your breast,
Old friends, like old swords, still are trusted best.   [*Exit.*]
[*Enter* CARIOLA.]
CARIOLA   Sir, you are the happy father of a son:
Your wife commends him to you.
ANTONIO   Blessed comfort!
For heaven's sake tend her well: I'll presently
Go set a figure for 's nativity.⁹   [*Exeunt.*]

SCENE 3. *The scene continues.*

[*Enter* BOSOLA, *with a dark lantern.*]
BOSOLA   Sure I did hear a woman shriek: list, ha!
And the sound came, if I received it right,
From the duchess' lodgings. There's some stratagem
In the confining all our courtiers
To their several° wards: I must have part of it;   *separate*
My intelligence will freeze else.¹ List, again!
It may be 'twas the melancholy bird,
Best friend of silence and of solitariness,
The owl, that screamed so. Ha! Antonio?
[*Enter* ANTONIO *with a candle, his sword drawn.*]
ANTONIO   I heard some noise. Who's there? What art thou? Speak.
BOSOLA   Antonio? Put not your face nor body
To such a forced expression of fear.
I am Bosola, your friend.
ANTONIO   Bosola!
[*aside*] This mole does undermine me.—Heard you not
A noise even now?
BOSOLA   From whence?
ANTONIO   From the duchess' lodging.
BOSOLA   Not I. Did you?
ANTONIO   I did, or else I dreamed.
BOSOLA   Let's walk towards it.
ANTONIO   No, it may be 'twas
But the rising of the wind.
BOSOLA   Very likely.
Methinks 'tis very cold, and yet you sweat:
You look wildly.
ANTONIO   I have been setting a figure²
For the duchess' jewels.
BOSOLA   Ah, and how falls your question?
Do you find it radical?°   *significant*
ANTONIO   What's that to you?
'Tis rather to be questioned what design,
When all men were commanded to their lodgings,
Makes you a nightwalker.

---

9. Cast his horoscope right away.
2.3
1. All my news will be cold otherwise.

2. Establishing the loss involved. But Bosola takes the expression astrologically, as if Antonio were casting a horoscope.

BOSOLA   In sooth, I'll tell you:
Now all the court's asleep, I thought the devil
Had least to do here; I came to say my prayers;
And if it do offend you I do so,
You are a fine courtier.
ANTONIO [*aside*]   This fellow will undo me.
You gave the duchess apricots today:
Pray heaven they were not poisoned!
BOSOLA   Poisoned? A Spanish fig[3]
For the imputation!
ANTONIO   Traitors are ever confident
Till they are discovered. There were jewels stolen, too;
In my conceit,° none are to be suspected   *opinion*
More than yourself.
BOSOLA   You are a false steward.
ANTONIO   Saucy slave, I'll pull thee up by the roots.
BOSOLA   May be the ruin will crush you to pieces.
ANTONIO   You are an impudent snake indeed, sir:
Are you scarce warm, and do you show your sting?
You libel well, sir.
BOSOLA   No, sir: copy it out,
And I will set my hand to 't.[4]
ANTONIO [*aside*]   My nose bleeds.
One that were superstitious would count
This ominous, when it merely comes by chance:
Two letters, that are wrought here for my name,[5]
Are drowned in blood!
Mere accident.—For you, sir, I'll take order
I' th' morn you shall be safe.° [*aside*] 'Tis that must color   *under guard*
Her lying-in.°—Sir, this door you pass not: *giving birth*
I do not hold it fit that you come near
The duchess' lodgings, till you have quit° yourself.   *cleared*
[*aside*] The great are like the base, nay, they are the same,
When they seek shameful ways to avoid shame.   [*Exit.*]
BOSOLA   Antonio hereabout did drop a paper:
Some of your help, false friend: [*opening his lantern*] Oh, here it is.
What's here? A child's nativity calculated?   [*reads*]
"The duchess was delivered of a son, 'tween the hours twelve and one in the night, *Anno Dom.* 1504,"—that's this year—"*decimo nono Decembris*,"[6]—that's this night—"taken according to the meridian of Malfi"—that's our duchess: happy discovery! "The lord of the first house being combust[7] in the ascendant, signifies short life; and Mars being in a human sign, joined to the tail of the Dragon, in the eighth house, doth threaten a violent death. *Caetera non scrutantur*."[8]
Why, now 'tis most apparent: this precise° fellow   *officious*

---

3. An obscene gesture, which Bosola doubtless makes onstage.
4. Bosola denies the charge, not by denying malignancy, but by offering to publish it.
5. Embroidered on the handkerchief.
6. December 19.
7. Burned up; that is, the ruling planet is close to the sun.
8. "The rest is not examined"—that is, the horoscope is incomplete. Mars and the Dragon are sinister signs, even separately; fatal together.

                    Is the duchess' bawd:° I have it to my wish!   procurer
65   This is a parcel of intelligency
      Our courtiers were cased up for: it needs must follow
      That I must be committed on pretense
      Of poisoning her; which I'll endure, and laugh at.
      If one could find the father now! But that
70   Time will discover. Old Castruccio
      I' th' morning posts to Rome: by him I'll send
      A letter that shall make her brothers' galls
      O'erflow their livers. This was a thrifty° way.   shrewd
      Though lust do mask in ne'er so strange disguise,
75   She's oft found witty, but is never wise.   [Exit.]

              SCENE 4. *The palace of the* CARDINAL *at Rome.*

                    [*Enter* CARDINAL *and* JULIA.]
      CARDINAL   Sit. Thou art my best of wishes. Prithee, tell me
        What trick didst thou invent to come to Rome
        Without thy husband.
      JULIA   Why, my lord, I told him
        I came to visit an old anchorite°   hermit
        Here for devotion.
5   CARDINAL   Thou are a witty false one—
        I mean, to him.
      JULIA   You have prevailed with me
        Beyond my strongest thoughts! I would not now
        Find you inconstant.
      CARDINAL   Do not put thyself
        To such a voluntary torture, which proceeds
        Out of your own guilt.
      JULIA   How, my lord?
10   CARDINAL   You fear
        My constancy, because you have approved°   experienced
        Those giddy and wild turnings in yourself.
      JULIA   Did you e'er find them?
      CARDINAL   Sooth, generally for women;
        A man might strive to make glass malleable,
        Ere he should make them fixed.
15   JULIA   So, my lord.
      CARDINAL   We had need go borrow that fantastic glass
        Invented by Galileo the Florentine[1]
        To view another spacious world i' th' moon,
        And look to find a constant woman there.
      JULIA   This is very well, my lord.
20   CARDINAL   Why do you weep?
        Are tears your justification? The selfsame tears
        Will fall into your husband's bosom, lady,

2.4
1. In 1504, Galileo's telescope was more than one hundred years in the future, but the reference was topical for Webster's audience.

With a loud protestation that you love him
Above the world. Come, I'll love you wisely,
That's jealously, since I am very certain
You cannot make me cuckold.
JULIA   I'll go home
To my husband.
CARDINAL   You may thank me, lady,
I have taken you off your melancholy perch,
Bore you upon my fist, and showed you game,
And let you fly at it.² I pray thee, kiss me.
When thou wast with thy husband, thou wast watched
Like a tame elephant: still you are to thank me:
Thou hadst only kisses from him and high feeding;
But what delight was that? 'Twas just like one
That hath a little fingering on the lute,
Yet cannot tune it: still you are to thank me.
JULIA You told me of a piteous wound i' th' heart
And a sick liver, when you wooed me first,
And spake like one in physic.³   [*A knock is heard.*]
CARDINAL   Who's that?
Rest firm,° for my affection to thee,   *be assured*
Lightning moves slow to 't.°   *by comparison*
    [*Enter* SERVANT.]
SERVANT   Madam, a gentleman,
That's come post from Malfi, desires to see you.
CARDINAL   Let him enter. I'll withdraw.   [*Exit.*]
SERVANT   He says
Your husband, old Castruccio, is come to Rome,
Most pitifully tired with riding post.⁴   [*Exit.*]
    [*Enter* DELIO.]
JULIA Signor Delio! [*aside*]—'tis one of my old suitors.
DELIO I was bold to come and see you.
JULIA   Sir, you are welcome.
DELIO Do you lie° here?   *lodge*
JULIA   Sure, your own experience
Will satisfy you no: our Roman prelates
Do not keep lodging for ladies.
DELIO   Very well.
I have brought you no commendations from your husband,
For I know none by him.
JULIA   I hear he's come to Rome.
DELIO I never knew man and beast, of a horse and a knight,
So weary of each other: if he had had a good back,
He would have undertook to have borne his horse,
His breech was so pitifully sore.
JULIA   Your laughter
Is my pity.

---

2. The cardinal speaks of himself as a falconer training a bird (Julia).
3. Like a person under a doctor's care.
4. When riding post, one changed horses at regular intervals without stopping to rest oneself.

DELIO Lady, I know not whether
You want money, but I have brought you some.
JULIA From my husband?
DELIO No, from mine own allowance.
JULIA I must hear the condition, ere I be bound to take it.
DELIO Look on 't, 'tis gold: hath it not a fine color?
JULIA I have a bird more beautiful.
DELIO Try the sound on 't.
JULIA A lute string far exceeds it:
It hath no smell, like cassia or civet;
Nor is it physical,° though some fond° doctors   *medicinal / foolish*
Persuade us seethe 't in cullises:° I'll tell you,   *broth*
This is a creature bred by—
    [*Reenter* SERVANT.]
SERVANT Your husband's come,
Hath delivered a letter to the Duke of Calabria
That, to my thinking, hath put him out of his wits.   [*Exit.*]
JULIA Sir, you hear:
Pray, let me know your business and your suit
As briefly as can be.
DELIO With good speed: I would wish you,
At such time as you are nonresident
With your husband, my mistress.
JULIA Sir, I'll go ask my husband if I shall,
And straight return your answer.   [*Exit.*]
DELIO Very fine!
Is this her wit, or honesty,° that speaks thus?   *chastity*
I heard one say the duke was highly moved
With a letter sent from Malfi. I do fear
Antonio is betrayed: how fearfully
Shows his ambition now! Unfortunate fortune!
They pass through whirlpools, and deep woes do shun,
Who the event weigh ere the action's done.⁵   [*Exit.*]

SCENE 5. *The scene continues.*

[*Enter* CARDINAL, *and* FERDINAND *with a letter.*]
FERDINAND I have this night digged up a mandrake.¹
CARDINAL Say you?
FERDINAND And I am grown mad with 't.
CARDINAL What's the prodigy?°   *fearful wonder*
FERDINAND Read there—a sister damned: she's loose i' th' hilts;²
Grown a notorious strumpet.
CARDINAL Speak lower.
FERDINAND Lower?
Rogues do not whisper 't now, but seek to publish 't
(As servants do the bounty of their lords)

---

5. That is, who judge of actions before seeing their final consequences.
2.5

1. A fabulous root, violently aphrodisiac but also deadly poison. Both aspects apply to Ferdinand.
2. That is, promiscuous.

    Aloud; and with a covetous searching eye,
    To mark who note them. O, confusion seize her!
    She hath had most cunning bawds to serve her turn,
10 And more secure conveyances for lust
    Than towns of garrison for service.°   *receiving supplies*
CARDINAL   Is 't possible?
    Can this be certain?
FERDINAND   Rhubarb, oh, for rhubarb
    To purge this choler!³ Here's the cursèd day
    To prompt my memory, and here 't shall stick
15 Till of her bleeding heart I make a sponge
    To wipe it out.
CARDINAL   Why do you make yourself
    So wild a tempest?
FERDINAND   Would I could be one,
    That I might toss her palace 'bout her ears,
    Root up her goodly forests, blast her meads,°   *meadows*
20 And lay her general territory as waste
    As she hath done her honors.
CARDINAL   Shall our blood,
    The royal blood of Aragon and Castile,
    Be thus attainted?
FERDINAND   Apply desperate physic:°   *medicine*
    We must not now use balsamum,° but fire,°   *balm / cautery*
25 The smarting cupping glass⁴ for that's the mean
    To purge infected blood, such blood as hers.
    There is a kind of pity in mine eye,
    I'll give it to my handkercher; and now 'tis here,
    I'll bequeath this to her bastard.
CARDINAL   What to do?
30 FERDINAND   Why, to make soft lint for his mother's wounds,
    When I have hewed her to pieces.
CARDINAL   Cursèd creature!
    Unequal nature, to place women's hearts
    So far upon the left side!⁵
FERDINAND   Foolish men,
    That e'er will trust their honor in a bark
35 Made of so slight weak bulrush as is woman,
    Apt every minute to sink it!
CARDINAL   Thus ignorance, when it hath purchased honor,
    It cannot wield it.
FERDINAND   Methinks I see her laughing—
    Excellent hyena! Talk to me somewhat, quickly,
40 Or my imagination will carry me
    To see her in the shameful act of sin.
CARDINAL   With whom?
FERDINAND   Haply° with some strong-thighed bargeman,   *perhaps*

---

3. Rhubarb, as a laxative, was thought curative of the high pressures of hot rage.
4. By which people were bled.
5. The left is the sinister side, associated with bad luck, deceit, and passion.

	Or one o' th' wood-yard that can quoit the sledge°	throw the hammer
45	Or toss the bar,⁶ or else some lovely squire	
	That carries coal up to her privy lodgings.	

CARDINAL   You fly beyond your reason.
FERDINAND   Go to, mistress!
   'Tis not your whore's milk that shall quench my wild fire,
   But your whore's blood.
50 CARDINAL   How idly shows this rage, which carries you,
   As men conveyed by witches through the air,
   On violent whirlwinds! This intemperate noise
   Fitly resembles deaf men's shrill discourse,
   Who talk aloud,° thinking all other men   *loudly*
   To have their imperfection.
55 FERDINAND   Have not you
   My palsy?
   CARDINAL   Yes, I can be angry, but
   Without this rupture: there is not in nature
   A thing that makes man so deformed, so beastly,
   As doth intemperate anger. Chide yourself.
60 You have divers men who never yet expressed
   Their strong desire of rest but by unrest,
   By vexing of themselves. Come, put yourself
   In tune.
   FERDINAND   So; I will only study to seem
   The thing I am not. I could kill her now,
65 In you, or in myself; for I do think
   It is some sin in us heaven doth revenge
   By her.
   CARDINAL   Are you stark mad?
   FERDINAND   I would have their bodies
   Burnt in a coal pit with the ventage° stopped,   *chimney*
   That their cursed smoke might not ascend to heaven;
70 Or dip the sheets they lie in in pitch or sulphur,
   Wrap them in 't, and then light them like a match;
   Or else to boil their bastard to a cullis,°   *broth*
   And give 't his lecherous father to renew°   *repair*
   The sin of his back.⁷
   CARDINAL   I'll leave you.
   FERDINAND   Nay, I have done.
75 I am confident, had I been damned in hell,
   And should have heard of this, it would have put me
   Into a cold sweat. In, in; I'll go sleep.
   Till I know who leaps my sister, I'll not stir:
   That known, I'll find scorpions to string my whips,⁸
80 And fix her in a general eclipse.   [*Exeunt.*]

---

6. Gross tests of strength.
7. As Atreus did to Thyestes in Greek legend. "The sin of his back": sexual capacity.
8. Tipping the thongs of a whip with "scorpions" (tips of jagged steel or lead that sting and bite the flesh) is an old metaphor for aggravated punishment.

Act 3

SCENE 1. *Amalfi.*

[*Enter* ANTONIO *and* DELIO.]

ANTONIO Our noble friend, my most belovèd Delio!
Oh, you have been a stranger long at court;
Came you along with the Lord Ferdinand?

DELIO I did, sir. And how fares your noble duchess?

ANTONIO Right fortunately well: she's an excellent [5]
Feeder of pedigrees; since you last saw her,
She hath had two children more, a son and daughter.

DELIO Methinks 'twas yesterday: let me but wink,
And not behold your face, which to mine eye
Is somewhat leaner, verily I should dream [10]
It were within this half-hour.

ANTONIO You have not been in law, friend Delio,
Nor in prison, nor a suitor at the court,
Nor begged the reversion of some great man's place,
Nor troubled with an old wife, which doth make [15]
Your time so insensibly° hasten.   *imperceptibly*

DELIO   Pray, sir, tell me,
Hath not this news arrived yet to the ear
Of the Lord Cardinal?

ANTONIO   I fear it hath:
The Lord Ferdinand, that's newly come to court,
Doth bear himself right dangerously.

DELIO   Pray, why? [20]

ANTONIO He is so quiet that he seems to sleep
The tempest out, as dormice do in winter.
Those houses that are haunted are most still
Till the devil be up.

DELIO   What say the common people?

ANTONIO The common rabble do directly say [25]
She is a strumpet.

DELIO   And your graver heads,
Which would be politic,° what censure° they?   *statesmanlike / opine*

ANTONIO They do observe I grow to infinite purchase
The left-hand way,[1] and all suppose the duchess
Would amend it, if she could; for, say they, [30]
Great princes, though they grudge their officers
Should have such large and unconfinèd means
To get wealth under them, will not complain,
Lest thereby they should make them odious
Unto the people; for other obligation [35]
Of love or marriage between her and me
They never dream of.

3.1
1. That is, they think I am getting rich dishonestly.

DELIO   The Lord Ferdinand
Is going to bed.
        [*Enter* DUCHESS, FERDINAND, *and* BOSOLA.]
FERDINAND   I'll instantly to bed,
For I am weary.—I am to bespeak
A husband for you.
40 DUCHESS   For me, sir? Pray, who is 't?
FERDINAND   The great Count Malateste.
DUCHESS   Fie upon him!
A count? He's a mere stick of sugar candy;
You may look quite through him. When I choose
A husband, I will marry for your honor.
45 FERDINAND   You shall do well in 't.—How is 't, worthy Antonio?
DUCHESS   But, sir, I am to have private conference with you
About a scandalous report is spread
Touching mine honor.
FERDINAND   Let me be ever deaf to 't:
One of Pasquil's paper bullets,² court-calumny,
50 A pestilent air, which princes' palaces
Are seldom purged of. Yet, say that it were true,
I pour it in your bosom, my fixed love
Would strongly excuse, extenuate, nay, deny
Faults, were they apparent in you. Go, be safe
In your own innocency.
55 DUCHESS [*aside*]   O blessèd comfort!
This deadly air is purged.
                [*Exeunt* DUCHESS, ANTONIO, *and* DELIO.]
FERDINAND   Her guilt treads on
Hot-burning coulters.³ Now, Bosola,
How thrives our intelligence?°   *detective work*
BOSOLA   Sir, uncertainly:
'Tis rumored she hath had three bastards, but
By whom, we may go read i' th' stars.
60 FERDINAND   Why, some
Hold opinion all things are written there.
BOSOLA   Yes, if we could find spectacles to read them.
I do suspect there hath been some sorcery
Used on the duchess.
FERDINAND   Sorcery? To what purpose?
65 BOSOLA   To make her dote on some desertless fellow
She shames to acknowledge.
FERDINAND   Can your faith give way
To think there's power in potions or in charms,
To make us love whether we will or no?
BOSOLA   Most certainly.
70 FERDINAND   Away! These are mere gulleries,° horrid things,   *deceits*

---

2. Anonymous satires were traditionally pasted on the statue of Pasquillo, or Pasquino, near Piazza Navona in Rome, and attributed to his authorship.

3. Medieval chastity inquests customarily required the questioned lady to walk barefoot over red-hot plowshares ("coulters").

Invented by some cheating mountebanks[4]
To abuse us. Do you think that herbs or charms
Can force the will? Some trials have been made
In this foolish practice, but the ingredients
Were lenitive° poisons, such as are of force *slow-working*
To make the patient mad; and straight the witch
Swears by equivocation they are in love.
The witchcraft lies in her rank° blood. This night *wanton*
I will force confession from her. You told me
You had got, within these two days, a false° key *unauthorized*
Into her bedchamber.
BOSOLA   I have.
FERDINAND   As I would wish.
BOSOLA   What do you intend to do?
FERDINAND   Can you guess?
BOSOLA   No.
FERDINAND   Do not ask, then:
He that can compass° me, and know my drifts,° *comprehend / purposes*
May say he hath put a girdle 'bout the world,
And sounded all her quicksands.
BOSOLA   I do not
Think so.
FERDINAND   What do you think, then, pray?
BOSOLA   That you
Are your own chronicle too much, and grossly
Flatter yourself.
FERDINAND   Give me thy hand; I thank thee:
I ne'er gave pension but to flatterers,
Till I entertained° thee. Farewell. *employed*
That friend a great man's ruin strongly checks,
Who rails into his belief all his defects.   [*Exeunt.*]

SCENE 2. *The bedchamber of the* DUCHESS.

[*Enter* DUCHESS, ANTONIO, *and* CARIOLA.]
DUCHESS   Bring me the casket hither, and the glass.
You get no lodging here tonight, my lord.
ANTONIO   Indeed, I must persuade one.
DUCHESS   Very good:
I hope in time 'twill grow into a custom,
That noblemen shall come with cap and knee
To purchase a night's lodging of their wives.
ANTONIO   I must lie here.
DUCHESS   Must! You are a lord of misrule.[1]
ANTONIO   Indeed, my rule is only in the night.
DUCHESS   To what use will you put me?
ANTONIO   We'll sleep together.
DUCHESS   Alas, what pleasure can two lovers find in sleep?

---

4. A mixture of street entertainer and patent medicine salesman.

3.2
1. The mock-monarch of a carnival festival.

CARIOLA My lord, I lie with her often, and I know
    She'll much disquiet you.
ANTONIO   See, you are complained of.
CARIOLA For she's the sprawling'st bedfellow.
ANTONIO   I shall like her
    The better for that.
CARIOLA   Sir, shall I ask you a question?
ANTONIO I pray thee, Cariola.
15 CARIOLA   Wherefore still,° when you lie   *always*
    with my lady,
    Do you rise so early?
ANTONIO   Laboring men
    Count the clock oftenest, Cariola,
    Are glad when their task's ended.
DUCHESS   I'll stop your mouth. [*Kisses him.*]
ANTONIO Nay, that's but one; Venus had two soft doves
20 To draw her chariot; I must have another— [*She kisses him again.*]
    When wilt thou marry, Cariola?
CARIOLA   Never, my lord.
ANTONIO Oh, fie upon this single life! Forgo it.
    We read how Daphne, for her peevish flight,
    Became a fruitless bay tree; Syrinx turned
25 To the pale empty reed; Anaxarete
    Was frozen into marble: whereas those
    Which married, or proved kind unto their friends,
    Were by a gracious influence trans-shaped
    Into the olive, pomegranate, mulberry,
30 Became flowers, precious stones, or eminent stars.[2]
CARIOLA This is a vain poetry, but I pray you tell me,
    If there were proposed me, wisdom, riches, and beauty,
    In three several young men, which should I choose?
ANTONIO 'Tis a hard question: this was Paris' case,
35 And he was blind in 't, and there was great cause;
    For how was 't possible he could judge right,
    Having three amorous goddesses in view,
    And they stark naked? 'Twas a motion[3]
    Were able to benight the apprehension
40 Of the severest counselor of Europe.
    Now I look on both your faces so well formed,
    It puts me in mind of a question I would ask.
CARIOLA What is 't?
ANTONIO   I do wonder why hard-favored ladies,
    For the most part, keep worse-favored waiting women
45 To attend them, and cannot endure fair ones.

---

2. The olive was created by Athena; the mulberry gained its color from the blood of Pyramus and Thisbe; the pomegranate seems to have no particular mythological origin. Most of the other stories of ladies being transformed for complying, or not complying, with the solicitations of a god are from Ovid's *Metamorphoses*.

3. Spectacle. Paris had to choose among Hera, Athena, and Aphrodite, goddesses of regal power, wisdom, and love; his selecting the third led to the Trojan War.

DUCHESS Oh, that's soon answered.
  Did you ever in your life know an ill painter
  Desire to have his dwelling next door to the shop
  Of an excellent picture-maker? 'Twould disgrace
  His face-making, and undo him. I prithee,
  When were we so merry?—My hair tangles.
ANTONIO Pray thee, Cariola, let's steal forth the room,
  And let her talk to herself: I have divers times
  Served her the like, when she hath chafed extremely.
  I love to see her angry. Softly, Cariola. [*Exeunt* ANTONIO *and* CARIOLA.]
DUCHESS Doth not the color of my hair 'gin to change?
  When I wax gray, I shall have all the court
  Powder their hair with arras,⁴ to be like me.
  You have cause to love me; I entered you into my heart
  Before you would vouchsafe to call for the keys.
    [*Enter* FERDINAND *behind*.]
  We shall one day have my brothers take you napping;
  Methinks his presence, being now in court,
  Should make you keep your own bed; but you'll say
  Love mixed with fear is sweetest. I'll assure you,
  You shall get no more children till my brothers
  Consent to be your gossips.⁵ Have you lost your tongue?
    [*She turns and sees* FERDINAND.]
  'Tis welcome:
  For know, whether I am doomed to live or die,
  I can do both like a prince.
FERDINAND   Die, then, quickly! [*Giving her a poniard.*⁶]
  Virtue, where art thou hid? What hideous thing
  Is it that doth eclipse thee?
DUCHESS   Pray, sir, hear me.
FERDINAND Or is it true thou art but a bare name,
  And no essential° thing?   *actual*
DUCHESS   Sir—
FERDINAND   Do not speak.
DUCHESS No, sir: I will plant my soul in mine ears, to hear you.
FERDINAND O most imperfect light of human reason,
  That mak'st us so unhappy to foresee
  What we can least prevent! Pursue thy wishes,
  And glory in them: there's in shame no comfort
  But to be past all bounds and sense of shame.
DUCHESS I pray, sir, hear me. I am married.
FERDINAND   So!
DUCHESS Haply,° not to your liking: but for that,   *perhaps*
  Alas, your shears do come untimely now
  To clip the bird's wings that's already flown!
  Will you see my husband?

---

4. Orris root, used in powdered form to make hair artificially gray.
5. Sponsors in baptism.
6. A knife.

FERDINAND   Yes, if I could change
Eyes with a basilisk.⁷
DUCHESS   Sure, you came hither
By his confederacy.
FERDINAND   The howling of a wolf
Is music to thee, screech owl: prithee, peace.
Whate'er thou art that hast enjoyed my sister,
For I am sure thou hear'st me, for thine own sake
Let me not know thee. I came hither prepared
To work thy discovery; yet am now persuaded
It would beget such violent effects
As would damn us both. I would not for ten millions
I had beheld thee: therefore use all means
I never may have knowledge of thy name;
Enjoy thy lust still, and a wretched life,
On that condition. And for thee, vile woman,
If thou do wish thy lecher may grow old
In thy embracements, I would have thee build
Such a room for him as our anchorites
To holier use inhabit. Let not the sun
Shine on him till he's dead; let dogs and monkeys
Only converse with him, and such dumb things
To whom nature denies use to sound his name;
Do not keep a paraquito,° lest she learn it;   parrot
If thou do love him, cut out thine own tongue,
Lest it bewray° him.   betray
DUCHESS   Why might not I marry?
I have not gone about in this to create
Any new world or custom.
FERDINAND   Thou art undone;
And thou hast ta'en that massy sheet of lead
That hid thy husband's bones, and folded it
About my heart.
DUCHESS   Mine bleeds for 't.
FERDINAND   Thine? Thy heart?
What should I name 't unless a hollow bullet
Filled with unquenchable wildfire?
DUCHESS   You are in this
Too strict, and were you not my princely brother,
I would say, too willful. My reputation
Is safe.
FERDINAND   Dost thou know what reputation is?
I'll tell thee—to small purpose, since the instruction
Comes now too late.
Upon a time, Reputation, Love, and Death
Would travel o'er the world; and it was concluded
That they should part, and take three several ways.
Death told them, they should find him in great battles,

---

7. Monster that was fabled to kill with a glance.

			Or cities plagued with plagues. Love gives them counsel
125		To inquire for him 'mongst unambitious shepherds,
			Where dowries were not talked of, and sometimes
			'Mongst quiet kindred that had nothing left
			By their dead parents. "Stay," quoth Reputation,
			"Do not forsake me; for it is my nature,
130		If once I part from any man I meet,
			I am never found again." And so for you:
			You have shook hands° with Reputation, *parted*
			And made him invisible. So, fare you well.
			I will never see you more.
	DUCHESS Why should only I,
135		Of all the other princes of the world,
			Be cased up, like a holy relic? I have youth
			And a little beauty.
	FERDINAND So you have some virgins
			That are witches. I will never see thee more. [*Exit.*]
				[*Enter* ANTONIO *with a pistol, and* CARIOLA.]
	DUCHESS You saw this apparition?
	ANTONIO Yes. We are
140		Betrayed. How came he hither? I should turn
			This to thee, for that. [*Pointing the pistol at* CARIOLA.]
	CARIOLA Pray, sir, do; and when
			That you have cleft my heart, you shall read there
			Mine innocence.
	DUCHESS That gallery gave him entrance.
	ANTONIO I would this terrible thing would come again,
145		That, standing on my guard, I might relate
			My warrantable[8] love. [*She shows the poniard.*]
				        Ha! What means this?
	DUCHESS He left this with me.
	ANTONIO And it seems did wish
			You would use it on yourself.
	DUCHESS His action seemed
			To intend so much.
	ANTONIO This hath a handle to 't
150		As well as a point: turn it towards him, and
			So fasten the keen edge in his rank gall. [*Knocking within.*]
			How now! Who knocks? More earthquakes?
	DUCHESS I stand
			As if a mine beneath my feet were ready
			To be blown up.
	CARIOLA 'Tis Bosola.
	DUCHESS Away!
155		O misery! Methinks unjust actions
			Should wear these masks and curtains, and not we.
			You must instantly part hence: I have fashioned it already.
				                          [*Exit* ANTONIO.]

---

8. Legitimate, defensible.

[*Enter* BOSOLA.]

BOSOLA   The duke your brother is ta'en up in a whirlwind,
      Hath took horse, and 's rid post to Rome.
DUCHESS   So late?
160 BOSOLA   He told me, as he mounted into th' saddle,
      You were undone.
DUCHESS   Indeed, I am very near it.
BOSOLA   What's the matter?
DUCHESS   Antonio, the master of our household,
      Hath dealt so falsely with me in 's accounts:
165   My brother stood engaged with me for money
      Ta'en up of certain Neapolitan Jews,
      And Antonio lets the bonds be forfeit.[9]
BOSOLA   Strange!—[*aside*] This is cunning.
DUCHESS   And hereupon
      My brother's bills at Naples are protested
      Against.[1]—Call up our officers.
170 BOSOLA   I shall.   [*Exit.*]
      [*Reenter* ANTONIO.]
DUCHESS   The place that you must fly to is Ancona:[2]
      Hire a house there; I'll send after you
      My treasure and my jewels. Our weak safety
      Runs upon enginous wheels: short syllables
175   Must stand for periods.[3] I must now accuse you
      Of such a feignèd crime as Tasso calls
      Magnanima menzogna, a noble lie,
      'Cause it must shield our honors. Hark! They are coming.
      [*Reenter* BOSOLA *and* OFFICERS.]
ANTONIO   Will your grace hear me?
180 DUCHESS   I have got well by you; you have yielded me
      A million of loss: I am like to inherit
      The people's curses for your stewardship.
      You had the trick in audit time to be sick,
      Till I had signed your *quietus*;° and that cured you   *receipt*
185   Without help of a doctor.—Gentlemen,
      I would have this man be an example to you all;
      So shall you hold my favor; I pray, let him;°   *release him*
      For he's done that, alas, you would not think of,
      And, because I intend to be rid of him,
190   I mean not to publish. [*to* ANTONIO] Use your fortune elsewhere.
ANTONIO   I am strongly armed to brook my overthrow;
      As commonly men bear with a hard year,
      I will not blame the cause on 't; but do think
      The necessity of my malevolent star

---

9. That is, my brother stood security for some money I borrowed from Neapolitan moneylenders; now Antonio has let them call on the duke for payment.
1. That is, Duke Ferdinand's checks have bounced.
2. On the Adriatic coast of Italy, across the peninsula from Amalfi and well to the north.
3. Full sentences. "Enginous": delicately balanced, as in clockwork. The allusion to Tasso (next line) is literally accurate (*Jerusalem Delivered* 2.22) but anachronistic, since Tasso's poem was not published until 1574.

Procures this, not her humor. Oh, the inconstant
And rotten ground of service! You may see,
'Tis even like him that in a winter night
Takes a long slumber o'er a dying fire,
As loath to part from 't; yet parts thence as cold
As when he first sat down.
DUCHESS   We do confiscate,
Towards the satisfying of your accounts,
All that you have.
ANTONIO   I am yours, and 'tis very fit
All mine should be so.
DUCHESS   So, sir, you have your pass.°   passport
ANTONIO You may see, gentlemen, what 'tis to serve
A prince with body and soul.   [*Exit.*]
BOSOLA Here's an example for extortion: what moisture is drawn out of the sea, when foul weather comes, pours down, and runs into the sea again.
DUCHESS I would know what are your opinions of this Antonio.
SECOND OFFICER He could not abide to see a pig's head gaping: I thought your grace would find him a Jew.[4]
THIRD OFFICER I would you had been his officer, for your own sake.
FOURTH OFFICER You would have had more money.
FIRST OFFICER He stopped his ears with black wool, and to those came to him for money said he was thick of hearing.
SECOND OFFICER Some said he was an hermaphrodite, for he could not abide a woman.
FOURTH OFFICER How scurvy proud he would look when the treasury was full! Well, let him go!
FIRST OFFICER Yes, and the chippings of the buttery fly after him, to scour his gold chain![5]
DUCHESS Leave us. [*Exeunt* OFFICERS.] What do you think of these?
BOSOLA That these are rogues that in 's prosperity, but to have waited on his fortune, could have wished his dirty stirrup riveted through their noses, and followed after 's mule, like a bear in a ring; would have prostituted their daughters to his lust; made their firstborn intelligencers;[6] thought none happy but such as were born under his blessed planet, and wore his livery: and do these lice drop off now? Well, never look to have the like again:[7] he hath left a sort of flattering rogues behind him; their doom must follow. Princes pay flatterers in their own money: flatterers dissemble their vices, and they dissemble their lies; that's justice. Alas, poor gentleman!
DUCHESS Poor? He hath amply filled his coffers.
BOSOLA Sure, he was too honest. Pluto, the god of riches, when he 's sent by Jupiter to any man, he goes limping, to signify that wealth that comes on God's name comes slowly; but when he's sent on the devil's errand, he rides post and comes in by scuttles. Let me show you what a most unvalued[8] jewel you have in a wanton humor thrown away, to bless the man

---

4. Jews were identified by their antipathy to pork, but the assumptions here are deliberately ridiculous.
5. A gold chain was the steward's traditional badge of office. Bread crumbs (the "chippings of the buttery") were used to polish gold and silver plate.
6. Spies.
7. That is, a servant as good as he was.
8. Invaluable. "By scuttles": in haste.

shall[9] find him. He was an excellent courtier and most faithful; a soldier that thought it as beastly to know his own value too little as devilish to acknowledge it too much. Both his virtue and form deserved a far better fortune: his discourse rather delighted to judge itself than show itself; his breast was filled with all perfection, and yet it seemed a private whispering-room, it made so little noise of 't.

DUCHESS But he was basely descended.

BOSOLA Will you make yourself a mercenary herald, rather to examine men's pedigrees than virtues? You shall want[1] him: for know, an honest statesman to a prince is like a cedar planted by a spring; the spring bathes the tree's root, the grateful tree rewards it with his shadow: you have not done so. I would sooner swim to the Bermoothes[2] on two politicians' rotten bladders, tied together with an intelligencer's heartstring, than depend on so changeable a prince's favor. Fare thee well, Antonio! Since the malice of the world would needs down with thee, it cannot be said yet that any ill happened unto thee, considering thy fall was accompanied with virtue.

DUCHESS Oh, you render me excellent music!

BOSOLA   Say you?

DUCHESS This good one that you speak of is my husband.

BOSOLA Do I not dream? Can this ambitious age
  Have so much goodness in 't as to prefer
  A man merely for worth, without these shadows
  Of wealth and painted honors? Possible?

DUCHESS I have had three children by him.

BOSOLA   Fortunate lady!
  For you have made your private nuptial bed
  The humble and fair seminary° of peace.   seedbed
  No question but many an unbeneficed scholar[3]
  Shall pray for you for this deed, and rejoice
  That some preferment in the world can yet
  Arise from merit. The virgins of your land
  That have no dowries shall hope your example
  Will raise them to rich husbands. Should you want
  Soldiers, 'twould make the very Turks and Moors
  Turn Christians, and serve you for this act.
  Last, the neglected poets of your time,
  In honor of this trophy of a man,
  Raised by that curious° engine, your white hand,   exquisite
  Shall thank you, in your grave, for 't; and make that
  More reverend than all the cabinets
  Of living princes.[4] For Antonio,
  His fame shall likewise flow from many a pen,
  When heralds shall want coats to sell to men.[5]

---

9. Who shall.
1. Miss.
2. The Bermudas, unknown at the time of the action, but very topical a hundred years later, when the play was written.
3. A scholar without an official appointment.
4. She will be more honored in her grave than living princes in their courts. "Cabinets": council chambers.
5. The Heralds' College (an English royal corporation) carried on a brisk trade in coats of arms.

DUCHESS As I taste comfort in this friendly speech,
  So would I find concealment.
BOSOLA Oh, the secret of my prince,
  Which I will wear on th' inside of my heart!
DUCHESS You shall take charge of all my coin and jewels,
  And follow him; for he retires himself
  To Ancona.
BOSOLA   So.
DUCHESS   Whither, within few days,
  I mean to follow thee.
BOSOLA   Let me think:
  I would wish your grace to feign a pilgrimage
  To our Lady of Loreto,[6] scarce seven leagues
  From fair Ancona; so may you depart
  Your country with more honor, and your flight
  Will seem a princely progress,° retaining   *state journey*
  Your usual train about you.
DUCHESS   Sir, your direction
  Shall lead me by the hand.
CARIOLA   In my opinion,
  She were better progress to the baths at Lucca,
  Or go visit the Spa in Germany;
  For, if you will believe me, I do not like
  This jesting with religion, this feigned
  Pilgrimage.
DUCHESS   Thou art a superstitious fool.
  Prepare us instantly for our departure.
  Past sorrows, let us moderately lament them;
  For those to come, seek wisely to prevent them.
        [*Exit* DUCHESS, *with* CARIOLA.]
BOSOLA A politician° is the devil's quilted anvil;   *crafty intriguer*
  He fashions all sins on him, and the blows
  Are never heard: he may work in a lady's chamber,
  As here for proof. What rests° but I reveal   *remains*
  All to my lord? Oh, this base quality
  Of intelligencer! Why, every quality° i' th' world   *profession*
  Prefers° but gain or commendation: *offers*
  Now for this act I am certain to be raised,
  And men that paint weeds to the life are praised.   [*Exit.*]

SCENE 3. *Rome.*

[*Enter* CARDINAL, FERDINAND, MALATESTE, PESCARA, SILVIO, DELIO.]

CARDINAL Must we turn soldier, then?
MALATESTE   The Emperor,[1]
  Hearing your worth that way, ere you attained
  This reverend garment, joins you in commission

---

6. The shrine of the Virgin at Loreto was famous throughout Europe.

3.3
1. The Spanish emperor, Charles V.

With the right fortunate soldier the Marquis of Pescara,
And the famous Lannoy.
CARDINAL   He that had the honor
Of taking the French king prisoner?[2]
MALATESTE   The same.
Here's a plot drawn for a new fortification
At Naples.   [*They talk apart.*]
FERDINAND   This great Count Malateste, I perceive,
Hath got employment?
DELIO   No employment, my lord;
A marginal note in the muster book, that he is
A voluntary lord.
FERDINAND   He's no soldier?
DELIO   He has worn gunpowder in 's hollow tooth for the toothache.[3]
SILVIO   He comes to the leaguer° with a full intent   siege
To eat fresh beef and garlic, means to stay
Till the scent be gone, and straight return to court.
DELIO   He hath read all the late service[4] as the city chronicle relates it, and keeps two painters going, only to express battles in model.
SILVIO   Then he'll fight by the book.
DELIO   By the almanac, I think, to choose good days and shun the critical. That's his mistress' scarf.
SILVIO   Yes, he protests he would do much for that taffeta.
DELIO   I think he would run away from a battle, to save it from taking[5] prisoner.
SILVIO   He is horribly afraid gunpowder will spoil the perfume on 't.
DELIO   I saw a Dutchman break his pate once for calling him pot-gun;[6] he made his head have a bore in 't like a musket.
SILVIO   I would he had made a touchhole to 't. He is indeed a guarded sumpter cloth,[7] only for the remove of the court.
[*Enter* BOSOLA *and speaks to* FERDINAND *and the* CARDINAL.]
PESCARA   Bosola arrived? What should be the business?
Some falling out amongst the cardinals.
These factions amongst great men, they are like
Foxes; when their heads are divided,
They carry fire in their tails, and all the country
About them goes to wrack for 't.[8]
SILVIO   What's that Bosola?
DELIO   I knew him in Padua—a fantastical scholar, like such who study to know how many knots were in Hercules' club, of what color Achilles' beard was, or whether Hector were not troubled with the toothache. He hath studied himself half blear-eyed to know the true symmetry of

---

2. Charles de Lannoy, Belgian by origin, did indeed capture Francis I at Pavia in 1525, about two decades after the date of the play's supposed action. "Pescara": also a commander at Pavia.
3. Saltpeter was sometimes used to relieve a toothache.
4. Recent military operations.
5. Being taken.
6. Popgun.
7. Decorated saddlecloth used only when the court is changing its residence; that is, he's only for show. "Touchhole": where the match was applied to set off a cannon.
8. Samson once tied some foxes together by the tail and set them afire to burn down the fields of the Philistines (Judges 15).

Caesar's nose by a shoeing-horn; and this he did to gain the name of a speculative[9] man.
PESCARA   Mark Prince Ferdinand:
A very salamander lives in 's eye,
To mock the eager violence of fire.[1]
SILVIO   That Cardinal hath made more bad faces with his oppression than ever Michelangelo[2] made good ones: he lifts up 's nose, like a foul porpoise before a storm.
PESCARA   The Lord Ferdinand laughs.
DELIO   Like a deadly cannon that lightens ere it smokes.
PESCARA   These are your true pangs of death,
The pangs of life, that struggle with great statesmen.
DELIO   In such a deformed silence witches whisper
Their charms.
CARDINAL   Doth she make religion her riding hood
To keep her from the sun and tempest?
FERDINAND   That,
That damns her. Methinks her fault and beauty,
Blended together, show like leprosy,
The whiter, the fouler. I make it a question
Whether her beggarly brats were ever christened.
CARDINAL   I will instantly solicit the state of Ancona
To have them banished.
FERDINAND   You are for Loreto?
I shall not be at your ceremony; fare you well.
Write to the Duke of Malfi, my young nephew
She had by her first husband, and acquaint him
With 's mother's honesty.
BOSOLA   I will.
FERDINAND   Antonio!
A slave that only smelled of ink and counters,
And never in 's life looked like a gentleman,
But in the audit time. Go, go presently,°   *at once*
Draw me out an hundred and fifty of our horse,°   *cavalry*
And meet me at the fort-bridge.[3]   [*Exeunt.*]

SCENE 4. *The shrine of Our Lady of Loreto.*

[*Enter* TWO PILGRIMS.]
FIRST PILGRIM   I have not seen a goodlier shrine than this;
Yet I have visited many.
SECOND PILGRIM   The Cardinal of Aragon
Is this day to resign his cardinal's hat:
His sister duchess likewise is arrived
To pay her vow of pilgrimage. I expect

---

9. Profound, given to abstruse thoughts. Intense and especially fantastical scholarship was thought to be a cause of melancholy—Bosola's temperament—caused by an imbalance of black bile.
1. The salamander was supposed to be so cold and wet of constitution that it could live in fire.
2. Michelangelo Buonarroti (1475–1564), the great Florentine painter and sculptor. Another anachronism.
3. Drawbridge.

A noble ceremony.

FIRST PILGRIM   No question. They come.
[*Here the ceremony of the* CARDINAL'S *installment in the habit of a soldier: performed in delivering up his cross, hat, robes, and ring at the shrine, and investing him with sword, helmet, shield, and spurs; then* ANTONIO, *the* DUCHESS, *and their children, having presented themselves at the shrine, are, by a form of banishment in dumb show expressed towards them by the* CARDINAL *and the state of Ancona, banished: during all which ceremony, this ditty is sung, to very solemn music, by divers churchmen.*][1]

Arms and honors deck thy story,
To thy fame's eternal glory!
Adverse fortune ever fly thee;
10 No disastrous fate come nigh thee!

I alone will sing thy praises,
Whom to honor virtue raises;
And thy study, that divine is,
Bent to martial discipline is.
15 Lay aside all those robes lie by thee;
Crown thy arts with arms, they'll beautify thee.

O worthy of worthiest name, adorned in this manner,
Lead bravely thy forces on under war's warlike banner!
Oh, mayst thou prove fortunate in all martial courses!
20 Guide thou still by skill in arts and forces!
Victory attend thee nigh, whilst fame sings loud thy powers;
Triumphant conquest crown thy head, and blessings pour down showers!
            [*Exeunt all except the* TWO PILGRIMS.]

FIRST PILGRIM   Here's a strange turn of state! Who would have thought
So great a lady would have matched herself
25 Unto so mean a person? Yet the cardinal
Bears himself much too cruel.
SECOND PILGRIM   They are banished.
FIRST PILGRIM   But I would ask what power hath this state
Of Ancona to determine[2] of a free prince?
SECOND PILGRIM   They are a free state, sir, and her brother showed
30 How that the pope, fore-hearing of her looseness,
Hath seized into the protection of the church
The dukedom which she held as dowager.[3]
FIRST PILGRIM   But by what justice?
SECOND PILGRIM   Sure, I think by none,
Only her brother's instigation.
35 FIRST PILGRIM   What was it with such violence he took
Off from her finger?
SECOND PILGRIM   'Twas her wedding ring,

3.4
1. This song is not very suitable to the scene, and Webster, in the edition of 1623, denied writing it.
2. Pass judgment on.
3. As widow to her first husband, the Duke of Malfi.

Which he vowed shortly he would sacrifice
To his revenge.
FIRST PILGRIM   Alas, Antonio!
  If that a man be thrust into a well,
40 No matter who sets hands to 't, his own weight
  Will bring him sooner to th' bottom. Come, let's hence.
  Fortune makes this conclusion general,
  All things do help th' unhappy man to fall.   [*Exeunt.*]

SCENE 5. *Near Loreto.*

[*Enter* DUCHESS, ANTONIO, CHILDREN, CARIOLA, *and* SERVANTS.]

DUCHESS   Banished Ancona!
ANTONIO   Yes, you see what power
  Lightens° in great men's breath.   *flashes out*
DUCHESS   Is all our train
  Shrunk to this poor remainder?
ANTONIO   These poor men,
  Which have got little in your service, vow
5 To take your fortune, but your wiser buntings,[1]
  Now they are fledged, are gone.
DUCHESS   They have done wisely.
  This puts me in mind of death: physicians thus,
  With their hands full of money, use° to give o'er   *are accustomed*
  Their patients.
ANTONIO   Right° the fashion of the world: *exactly*
10 From decayed fortunes every flatterer shrinks;
  Men cease to build where the foundation sinks.
DUCHESS   I had a very strange dream tonight.°   *last night*
ANTONIO   What was 't?
DUCHESS   Methought I wore my coronet of state,
  And on a sudden all the diamonds
  Were changed to pearls.
15 ANTONIO   My interpretation
  Is, you'll weep shortly, for to me the pearls
  Do signify your tears.
DUCHESS   The birds that live
  I' th' field on the wild benefit of nature
  Live happier than we; for they may choose their mates,
20 And carol their sweet pleasures to the spring.
    [*Enter* BOSOLA *with a letter.*]
BOSOLA   You are happily o'erta'en.
DUCHESS   From my brother?
BOSOLA   Yes, from the Lord Ferdinand your brother
  All love and safety.
DUCHESS   Thou dost blanch° mischief,   *whitewash*
  Wouldst make it white. See, see, like to calm weather
25 At sea before a tempest, false hearts speak fair

3.5
1. Migratory birds. "Take": accept.

> To those they intend most mischief.
> [*reads*] "Send Antonio to me; I want his head in a business."
> A politic equivocation!
> He doth not want your counsel, but your head;
> That is, he cannot sleep till you be dead.
> And here's another pitfall that's strewed o'er
> With roses: mark it, 'tis a cunning one:
> "I stand engaged for your husband for several debts at Naples: let not that trouble him; I had rather have his heart than his money."
> And I believe so too.

BOSOLA   What do you believe?
DUCHESS   That he so much distrusts my husband's love,
He will by no means believe his heart is with him
Until he see it: the devil is not cunning
Enough to circumvent us in riddles.
BOSOLA   Will you reject that noble and free league
Of amity and love which I present you?
DUCHESS   Their league is like that of some politic° kings,   *crafty*
Only to make themselves of strength and power
To be our after-ruin: tell them so.
BOSOLA   And what from you?
ANTONIO   Thus tell him: I will not come.
BOSOLA   And what of this? [*Pointing to the letter.*]
ANTONIO   My brothers have dispersed
Bloodhounds abroad; which till I hear are muzzled,
No truce, though hatched with ne'er such politic skill,
Is safe, that hangs upon our enemies' will.
I'll not come at° them.   *to*
BOSOLA   This proclaims your breeding:
Every small thing draws a base mind to fear,
As the adamant° draws iron. Fare you well, sir;   *lodestone*
You shall shortly hear from 's.   [*Exit.*]
DUCHESS   I suspect some ambush;
Therefore, by all my love I do conjure you
To take your eldest son, and fly towards Milan.
Let us not venture all this poor remainder
In one unlucky bottom.[2]
ANTONIO   You counsel safely.
Best of my life, farewell. Since we must part,
Heaven hath a hand in 't, but no otherwise
Than as some curious artist takes in sunder
A clock or watch, when it is out of frame,[3]
To bring 't in better order.
DUCHESS   I know not which is best,
To see you dead, or part with you. Farewell, boy:
Thou art happy that thou hast not understanding
To know thy misery; for all our wit

---

2. The metaphor is mercantile: let's not load all our cargo in one ship ("bottom").

3. Not working. "Curious artist": clever craftsman.

And reading brings us to a truer sense
Of sorrow. In the eternal church,° sir,   *heavenly society*
I do hope we shall not part thus.
ANTONIO   Oh, be of comfort!
Make patience a noble fortitude,
And think not how unkindly we are used:
Man, like to cassia, is proved best being bruised.[4]
DUCHESS   Must I, like to a slave-born Russian,
Account it praise to suffer tyranny?
And yet, O heaven, thy heavy hand is in 't!
I have seen my little boy oft scourge his top,[5]
And compared myself to 't: naught made me e'er
Go right but heaven's scourge stick.
ANTONIO   Do not weep:
Heaven fashioned us of nothing, and we strive
To bring ourselves to nothing. Farewell, Cariola,
And thy sweet armful. If I do never see thee more,
Be a good mother to your little ones,
And save them from the tiger. Fare you well.
DUCHESS   Let me look upon you once more, for that speech
Came from a dying father. Your kiss is colder
Than that I have seen an holy anchorite°   *hermit*
Give to a dead man's skull.
ANTONIO   My heart is turned to a heavy lump of lead,
With which I sound[6] my danger. Fare you well.
    [*Exeunt* ANTONIO *and his son.*]
DUCHESS   My laurel is all withered.
CARIOLA   Look, madam, what a troop of armèd men
Make toward us.
DUCHESS   Oh, they are very welcome:
When Fortune's wheel[7] is overcharged with princes,
The weight makes it move swift: I would have my ruin
Be sudden.
    [*Enter* BOSOLA *vizarded,° with a guard.*]   *masked*
I am your adventure,[8] am I not?
BOSOLA   You are. You must see your husband no more.
DUCHESS   What devil art thou that counterfeits heaven's thunder?
BOSOLA   Is that terrible? I would have you tell me whether
Is that note worse that frights the silly birds
Out of the corn,° or that which doth allure them   *grain*
To the nets? You have hearkened to the last too much.
DUCHESS   Oh, misery! Like to a rusty o'ercharged cannon,
Shall I never fly in pieces?—Come, to what prison?
BOSOLA   To none.
DUCHESS   Whither, then?

---

4. Cinnamon bark ("cassia") is most aromatic (virtuous) when pressed.
5. Children used to make tops spin by whipping them.
6. Plumb the depths of.
7. The wheel of fortune is an ancient emblem of mutability; people have their fixed positions on it and rise or fall as it turns.
8. The object of your journey.

BOSOLA   To your palace.
DUCHESS   I have heard
That Charon's boat serves to convey all o'er
The dismal lake,[9] but brings none back again.
BOSOLA   Your brothers mean you safety and pity.
DUCHESS   Pity!
With such a pity men preserve alive
Pheasants and quails, when they are not fat enough
To be eaten.
BOSOLA   These are your children?
DUCHESS   Yes.
BOSOLA   Can they prattle?
DUCHESS   No.
But I intend, since they were born accursed,
Curses shall be their first language.
BOSOLA   Fie, madam!
Forget this base, low fellow—
DUCHESS   Were I a man,
I'd beat that counterfeit face° into thy other.   *mask*
BOSOLA   One of no birth.[1]
DUCHESS   Say that he was born mean,
Man is most happy when 's own actions
Be arguments and examples of his virtue.
BOSOLA   A barren, beggarly virtue!
DUCHESS   I prithee, who is greatest? Can you tell?
Sad tales befit my woe: I'll tell you one.
A salmon, as she swam unto the sea,
Met with a dogfish, who encounters her
With this rough language: "Why art thou so bold
To mix thyself with our high state of floods,
Being no eminent courtier, but one
That for the calmest and fresh time o' th' year
Dost live in shallow rivers, rank'st thyself
With silly° smelts and shrimps? And darest thou   *simple*
Pass by our dog-ship without reverence?"
"Oh!" quoth the salmon, "sister, be at peace:
Thank Jupiter we both have passed the net!
Our value never can be truly known,
Till in the fisher's basket we be shown:
I' th' market then my price may be the higher,
Even when I am nearest to the cook and fire."
So to great men the moral may be stretchèd:
Men oft are valued high, when they're most wretched.
But come, whither you please. I am armed 'gainst misery;
Bent to all sways of the oppressor's will:
There's no deep valley but near some great hill.   [*Exeunt.*]

---

9. In classical mythology, Charon transports the souls of the dead across the river Styx to Hades.

1. Of low rank by birth.

Act 4

SCENE 1. *Amalfi.*

[*Enter* FERDINAND *and* BOSOLA.]

FERDINAND How doth our sister duchess bear herself
In her imprisonment?
BOSOLA   Nobly. I'll describe her.
She's sad as one long used to 't, and she seems
Rather to welcome the end of misery
Than shun it; a behavior so noble
As gives a majesty to adversity:
You may discern the shape of loveliness
More perfect in her tears than in her smiles;
She will muse four hours together; and her silence,
Methinks, expresseth more than if she spake.
FERDINAND Her melancholy seems to be fortified
With a strange disdain.
BOSOLA   'Tis so; and this restraint,
Like English mastiffs that grow fierce with tying,
Makes her too passionately apprehend
Those pleasures she's kept from.
FERDINAND   Curse upon her!
I will no longer study in the book
Of another's heart. Inform her what I told you. [*Exit.*]
      [*Enter* DUCHESS.]
BOSOLA All comfort to your grace!
DUCHESS   I will have none.
Pray thee, why dost thou wrap thy poisoned pills
In gold and sugar?
BOSOLA Your elder brother, the Lord Ferdinand,
Is come to visit you, and sends you word,
'Cause once he rashly made a solemn vow
Never to see you more, he comes i' th' night,
And prays you gently neither torch nor taper
Shine in your chamber. He will kiss your hand
And reconcile himself, but for his vow
He dares not see you.
DUCHESS   At his pleasure.
Take hence the lights: he's come.
      [*Enter* FERDINAND.]
FERDINAND Where are you?
DUCHESS   Here, sir.
FERDINAND This darkness suits you well.
DUCHESS I would ask your pardon.
FERDINAND   You have it;
For I account it the honorabl'st revenge,
Where I may kill, to pardon. Where are your cubs?
DUCHESS Whom?
FERDINAND   Call them your children;

       For though our national law distinguish bastards
       From true legitimate issue, compassionate nature
       Makes them all equal.
   DUCHESS   Do you visit me for this?
       You violate a sacrament o' th' church
       Shall make you howl in hell for 't.
40 FERDINAND   It had been well
       Could you have lived thus always; for, indeed,
       You were too much i' th' light¹—but no more—
       I come to seal my peace with you. Here's a hand
                    [*Gives her a dead man's hand.*]
       To which you have vowed much love; the ring upon 't
       You gave.
45 DUCHESS   I affectionately kiss it.
   FERDINAND   Pray, do, and bury the print of it in your heart.
       I will leave this ring with you for a lovetoken,
       And the hand as sure as the ring; and do not doubt
       But you shall have the heart, too. When you need a friend,
50   Send it to him that owed° it; you shall see   owned
       Whether he can aid you.
   DUCHESS   You are very cold;
       I fear you are not well after your travel.
       Ha! Lights! Oh, horrible!
   FERDINAND   Let her have lights enough.   [*Exit.*]
   DUCHESS   What witchcraft doth he practice, that he hath left
55   A dead man's hand here?
           [*Here is discovered, behind a traverse,² the artificial figures of Antonio
           and his children, appearing as if they were dead.*]
   BOSOLA   Look you, here's the piece from which 'twas ta'en.
       He doth present you this sad spectacle,
       That, now you know directly they are dead,
       Hereafter you may wisely cease to grieve
60   For that which cannot be recovered.
   DUCHESS   There is not between heaven and earth one wish
       I stay for after this: it wastes³ me more
       Than were 't my picture, fashioned out of wax,
       Stuck with a magical needle, and then buried
65   In some foul dunghill; and yond's an excellent property⁴
       For a tyrant, which I would account mercy.
   BOSOLA   What's that?
   DUCHESS   If they would bind me to that lifeless trunk
       And let me freeze to death.
   BOSOLA   Come, you must live.
   DUCHESS   That's the greatest torture souls feel in hell,
70   In hell: that they must live, and cannot die.
       Portia,⁵ I'll new-kindle thy coals again,

4.1
1. Punning on "light," wanton.
2. Curtain.
3. Consumes, as by secret disease; witches were supposed to be able to "waste" their enemies by making wax images and tormenting them as indicated below.
4. Appropriate act.
5. Portia, the wife of Brutus, committed suicide by swallowing hot coals.

    And revive the rare and almost dead example
    Of a loving wife.
BOSOLA   Oh, fie! Despair? Remember
    You are a Christian.
DUCHESS   The church enjoins fasting:
    I'll starve myself to death.
BOSOLA   Leave this vain sorrow.
    Things being at the worst begin to mend: the bee
    When he hath shot his sting into your hand, may then
    Play with your eyelid.
DUCHESS   Good comfortable fellow,
    Persuade a wretch that's broke upon the wheel[6]
    To have all his bones new set; entreat him live
    To be executed again. Who must dispatch me?
    I account this world a tedious theater,
    For I do play a part in 't 'gainst my will.
BOSOLA   Come, be of comfort; I will save your life.
DUCHESS   Indeed,
    I have not leisure to tend so small a business.
BOSOLA   Now, by my life, I pity you.
DUCHESS   Thou art a fool, then,
    To waste thy pity on a thing so wretched
    As cannot pity itself. I am full of daggers.
    Puff, let me blow these vipers from me.
    [*Enter* SERVANT.]
    What are you?
SERVANT   One that wishes you long life.
DUCHESS   I would thou wert hanged for the horrible curse
    Thou hast given me. I shall shortly grow one
    Of the miracles of pity. I'll go pray—
    No, I'll go curse.
BOSOLA   Oh, fie!
DUCHESS   I could curse the stars—
BOSOLA   Oh, fearful!
DUCHESS   And those three smiling seasons of the year
    Into a Russian winter,[7] nay, the world
    To its first chaos.
BOSOLA   Look you, the stars shine still.
DUCHESS   Oh, but you must
    Remember, my curse hath a great way to go.
    Plagues, that make lanes through largest families,
    Consume them!
BOSOLA   Fie, lady!
DUCHESS   Let them, like tyrants,
    Never be remembered but for the ill they have done;
    Let all the zealous prayers of mortified
    Churchmen forget them!

---

6. Instrument of torture for stretching the body.
7. A Russian winter would last all year long.

BOSOLA   Oh, uncharitable!
DUCHESS   Let Heaven a little while cease crowning martyrs
To punish them!
Go, howl them this, and say, I long to bleed:
It is some mercy when men kill with speed.
          [*Exeunt* DUCHESS *and* SERVANT.]
     [*Reenter* FERDINAND.]
FERDINAND   Excellent, as I would wish; she's plagued
     in art:°   *by a cunning device*
These presentations are but framed in wax
By the curious master in that quality,
Vincentio Lauriola,[8] and she takes them
For true substantial bodies.
BOSOLA   Why do you do this?
FERDINAND   To bring her to despair.
BOSOLA   'Faith, end here,
And go no farther in your cruelty.
Send her a penitential garment to put on
Next to her delicate skin, and furnish her
With beads and prayer books.
FERDINAND   Damn her! That body of hers,
While that my blood ran pure in 't, was more worth
Than that which thou wouldst comfort, called a soul.
I will send her masques of common courtesans,
Have her meat° served up by bawds and ruffians,   *food (of any kind)*
And, 'cause she'll needs be mad, I am resolved
To remove forth the common hospital°   *asylum*
All the mad-folk, and place them near her lodging;
There let them practice together, sing and dance,
And act their gambols to the full o' th' moon:
If she can sleep the better for it, let her.
Your work is almost ended.
BOSOLA   Must I see her again?
FERDINAND   Yes.
BOSOLA   Never.
FERDINAND   You must.
BOSOLA   Never in mine own shape;
That's forfeited by my intelligence°   *betrayal*
And this last cruel lie. When you send me next,
The business shall be comfort.
FERDINAND   Very likely.
Thy pity is nothing of kin to thee.[9] Antonio
Lurks about Milan: thou shalt shortly thither
To feed a fire as great as my revenge,
Which ne'er will slack till it have spent his fuel.
Intemperate agues[1] make physicians cruel.   [*Exeunt.*]

---

8. The art of wax modeling was common enough, but the name of the artist seems to be imaginary.
9. That is, pity doesn't suit you very well.
1. Fevers that cannot be controlled.

SCENE 2

[*Enter* DUCHESS *and* CARIOLA.]

DUCHESS What hideous noise was that?
CARIOLA   'Tis the wild consort°   *band*
  Of madmen, lady, which your tyrant brother
  Hath placed about your lodging. This tyranny,
  I think, was never practiced till this hour.
5 DUCHESS Indeed, I thank him. Nothing but noise and folly
  Can keep me in my right wits, whereas reason
  And silence make me stark mad. Sit down;
  Discourse to me some dismal tragedy.
CARIOLA Oh, 'twill increase your melancholy.
DUCHESS   Thou art deceived:
10 To hear of greater grief would lessen mine.
  This is a prison?
CARIOLA   Yes, but you shall live
  To shake this durance° off.   *imprisonment*
DUCHESS   Thou art a fool:
  The robin redbreast and the nightingale
  Never live long in cages.
CARIOLA   Pray, dry your eyes.
  What think you of, madam?
15 DUCHESS   Of nothing:
  When I muse thus, I sleep.
CARIOLA Like a madman, with your eyes open?
DUCHESS Dost thou think we shall know one another in th' other world?
CARIOLA Yes, out of question.
DUCHESS   Oh that it were possible we might
20 But hold some two days' conference with the dead!
  From them I should learn somewhat, I am sure,
  I never shall know here. I'll tell thee a miracle;
  I am not mad yet, to my cause of sorrow:
  Th' heaven o'er my head seems made of molten brass,
25 The earth of flaming sulphur, yet I am not mad.
  I am acquainted with sad misery
  As the tanned galley slave is with his oar;
  Necessity makes me suffer constantly,
  And custom makes it easy. Who do I look like now?
30 CARIOLA Like to your picture in the gallery,
  A deal of life in show, but none in practice;
  Or rather like some reverend monument
  Whose ruins are even pitied.
DUCHESS   Very proper.
  And Fortune seems only to have her eyesight
35 To behold my tragedy.
  How now! What noise is that?
      [*Enter* SERVANT.]
SERVANT   I am come to tell you
  Your brother hath intended you some sport.

>   A great physician, when the pope was sick
>   Of a deep melancholy, presented him
> 40   With several sorts of madmen, which wild object
>   Being full of change and sport, forced him to laugh,
>   And so the imposthume° broke. The selfsame cure   abscess
>   The duke intends on you.
> DUCHESS   Let them come in.
> SERVANT   There's a mad lawyer; and a secular priest;[1]
> 45   A doctor that hath forfeited his wits
>   By jealousy; an astrologian
>   That in his works said such a day o' th' month
>   Should be the day of doom, and, failing of 't,
>   Ran mad; an English tailor crazed i' th' brain
> 50   With the study of new fashions; a gentleman-usher°   doorkeeper
>   Quite beside himself with care to keep in mind
>   The number of his lady's salutations
>   Or "How do you's" she employed him in each morning;
>   A farmer, too, an excellent knave in grain,
> 55   Mad 'cause he was hindered transportation:[2]
>   And let one broker that's mad loose to these,
>   You'd think the devil were among them.
> DUCHESS   Sit, Cariola. Let them loose when you please,
>   For I am chained to endure all your tyranny.
>   [*Enter* MADMEN.]
>   [*Here by a* MADMAN *this song is sung to a dismal kind of music.*]
>
> 60   Oh, let us howl some heavy note,
>   Some deadly dogged howl,
>   Sounding as from the threatening throat
>   Of beasts and fatal fowl!
>   As ravens, screech owls, bulls, and bears,
> 65   We'll bell° and bawl our parts,   cry
>   Till irksome noise have cloyed your ears
>   And corrosived your hearts.
>   At last, whenas our choir wants breath,
>   Our bodies being blest,
> 70   We'll sing, like swans, to welcome death,
>   And die in love and rest.
>
> FIRST MADMAN   Doomsday not come yet? I'll draw it nearer by a perspective,[3]
>   or make a glass that shall set all the world on fire upon an instant. I cannot sleep; my pillow is stuffed with a litter of porcupines.
> 75 SECOND MADMAN   Hell is a mere glasshouse, where the devils are continually blowing up women's souls on hollow irons, and the fire never goes out.
> THIRD MADMAN   I will lie with every woman in my parish the tenth night; I will tithe them over like haycocks.[4]

4.2
1. One serving a parish, not a member of an order.
2. Forbidden to export.

3. Telescope.
4. As a priest takes his tenth ("tithe") of his parishioners' crops. "Haycocks": haystacks.

FOURTH MADMAN Shall my pothecary outgo me because I am a cuckold? I have found out his roguery; he makes alum of his wife's urine, and sells it to puritans that have sore throats with overstraining.[5]
FIRST MADMAN I have skill in heraldry.
SECOND MADMAN Hast?
FIRST MADMAN You do give for your crest a woodcock's[6] head with the brains picked out on 't; you are a very ancient gentleman.
THIRD MADMAN Greek is turned Turk: we are only to be saved by the Helvetian translation.[7]
FIRST MADMAN Come on, sir, I will lay the law to you.
SECOND MADMAN Oh, rather lay a corrosive: the law will eat to the bone.
THIRD MADMAN He that drinks but to satisfy nature is damned.
FOURTH MADMAN If I had my glass[8] here, I would show a sight should make all the women here call me mad doctor.
FIRST MADMAN What's he? A rope maker?
SECOND MADMAN No, no, no, a snuffling knave that, while he shows the tombs, will have his hand in a wench's placket.
THIRD MADMAN Woe to the caroche[9] that brought home my wife from the masque at three o'clock in the morning! It had a large featherbed in it.
FOURTH MADMAN I have pared the devil's nails forty times, roasted them in raven's eggs, and cured agues with them.
THIRD MADMAN Get me three hundred milchbats, to make possets[1] to procure sleep.
FOURTH MADMAN All the college may throw their caps[2] at me: I have made a soap boiler costive;[3] it was my masterpiece.
[*Here the dance, consisting of eight* MADMEN, *with music answerable thereunto; after which* BOSOLA, *like an old man, enters.*]
DUCHESS Is he mad too?
SERVANT   Pray, question him. I'll leave you.
                [*Exeunt* SERVANT *and* MADMEN.]
BOSOLA I am come to make thy tomb.
DUCHESS   Ha! My tomb?
Thou speak'st as if I lay upon my deathbed,
Gasping for breath. Dost thou perceive me sick?
BOSOLA Yes, and the more dangerously, since thy sickness is insensible.[4]
DUCHESS Thou art not mad, sure. Dost know me?
BOSOLA Yes.
DUCHESS Who am I?
BOSOLA Thou art a box of worm-seed, at best but a salvatory of green mummy. What's this flesh? A little crudded[5] milk, fantastical puff paste. Our bodies are weaker than those paper prisons boys use to keep flies in, more contemptible, since ours is to preserve earthworms. Didst thou ever see a lark in a cage? Such is the soul in the body: this world is like her

---

5. In long prayers and sermons.
6. A proverbially stupid bird.
7. The Geneva Bible, a jibe at English Puritans who used that translation.
8. Looking glass.
9. Carriage. "Placket": slit in a skirt.
1. Sedative drafts, here made of bat's milk.
2. Despair of emulating.
3. Constipated.
4. Imperceptible.
5. Curdled. "Worm-seed" is a matter whose ultimate end is the generation of worms. "A salvatory of green mummy": the substance of mummified bodies was considered medicinal. The living body is a box ("salvatory") of such medicine, only not yet ready for use.

little turf of grass, and the heaven o'er our heads, like her looking glass, only gives us a miserable knowledge of the small compass of our prison.

DUCHESS   Am not I thy duchess?

BOSOLA   Thou art some great woman, sure, for riot[6] begins to sit on thy forehead, clad in gray hairs, twenty years sooner than on a merry milkmaid's. Thou sleep'st worse than if a mouse should be forced to take up her lodging in a cat's ear: a little infant that breeds its teeth,[7] should it lie with thee, would cry out, as if thou wert the more unquiet bedfellow.

DUCHESS   I am Duchess of Malfi still.

BOSOLA   That makes thy sleep so broken:
Glories, like glowworms, afar off shine bright,
But, looked to near, have neither heat nor light.

DUCHESS   Thou art very plain.

BOSOLA   My trade is to flatter the dead, not the living; I am a tomb-maker.

DUCHESS   And thou com'st to make my tomb?

BOSOLA   Yes.

DUCHESS   Let me be a little merry. Of what stuff wilt thou make it?

BOSOLA   Nay, resolve° me first, of what fashion?   *inform*

DUCHESS   Why, do we grow fantastical in our deathbed? Do we affect fashion in the grave?

BOSOLA   Most ambitiously. Princes' images on their tombs do not lie, as they were wont, seeming to pray up to heaven, but with their hands under their cheeks, as if they died of the toothache. They are not carved with their eyes fixed upon the stars, but as their minds were wholly bent upon the world, the selfsame way they seem to turn their faces.

DUCHESS   Let me know fully therefore the effect
Of this thy dismal preparation,
This talk fit for a charnel.[8]

BOSOLA   Now I shall.
   [*Enter* EXECUTIONERS, *with a coffin, cords, and a bell.*]
Here is a present from your princely brothers;
And may it arrive welcome, for it brings
Last benefit, last sorrow.

DUCHESS   Let me see it:
I have so much obedience in my blood,
I wish it in their veins to do them good.

BOSOLA   This is your last presence chamber.[9]

CARIOLA   O my sweet lady!

DUCHESS   Peace, it affrights not me.

BOSOLA   I am the common bellman,
That usually° is sent to condemned persons   *by custom*
The night before they suffer.

DUCHESS   Even now thou said'st
Thou wast a tomb-maker.

BOSOLA   'Twas to bring you
By degrees to mortification.[1] Listen. [*rings the bell*]

---

6. Debauchery.
7. A teething infant.
8. A storage place for bones reserved from old graves in the digging of new ones.
9. A noble person's reception room.
1. Repentance, also death and decomposition.

        Hark, now everything is still
        The screech owl and the whistler[2] shrill
        Call upon our dame aloud,
        And bid her quickly don her shroud!
        Much you had of land and rent:
        Your length in clay's now competent.°   *sufficient*
        A long war disturbed your mind:
        Here your perfect peace is signed.
        Of what is 't fools make such vain keeping?
        Sin their conception, their birth weeping,
        Their life a general mist of error,
        Their death a hideous storm of terror.
        Strew your hair with powders sweet,
        Don clean linen, bathe your feet,
        And (the foul fiend more to check)
        A crucifix let bless your neck:
        'Tis now full tide 'tween night and day;
        End your groan, and come away.

CARIOLA Hence, villains, tyrants, murderers! Alas!
    What will you do with my lady? Call for help.
DUCHESS To whom? To our next neighbors? They are mad-folks.
BOSOLA Remove that noise.
DUCHESS   Farewell, Cariola.
    In my last will I have not much to give:
    A many hungry guests have fed upon me;
    Thine will be a poor reversion.°   *inheritance*
CARIOLA   I will die with her.
DUCHESS I pray thee, look thou giv'st my little boy
    Some syrup for his cold, and let the girl
    Say her prayers ere she sleep. [CARIOLA *is forced out by the* EXECUTIONERS.]
                Now what you please.
    What death?
BOSOLA   Strangling: here are your executioners.
DUCHESS I forgive them:
    The apoplexy, catarrh, or cough o' th' lungs
    Would do as much as they do.
BOSOLA Doth not death fright you?
DUCHESS   Who would be afraid on 't,
    Knowing to meet such excellent company
    In th' other world?
BOSOLA   Yet, methinks,
    The manner of your death should much afflict you:
    This cord should terrify you.
DUCHESS   Not a whit.
    What would it pleasure me to have my throat cut
    With diamonds? Or to be smothered
    With cassia?° Or to be shot to death with pearls?   *cinnamon*

---

2. A bird premonitory of death.

I know death hath ten thousand several doors
For men to take their exits, and 'tis found
They go on such strange geometrical hinges,
You may open them both ways.—Any way, for heaven sake,
So I were out of your whispering. Tell my brothers
That I perceive death, now I am well awake,
Best gift is they can give or I can take.
I would fain° put off my last woman's fault, *gladly*
I'd not be tedious to you.
EXECUTIONER   We are ready.
DUCHESS   Dispose my breath how please you, but my body
Bestow upon my women, will you?
EXECUTIONER   Yes.
DUCHESS   Pull, and pull strongly, for your able strength
Must pull down heaven upon me—
Yet stay; heaven gates are not so high arched
As princes' palaces; they that enter there
Must go upon their knees. [*kneels*] Come, violent death.
Serve for mandragora³ to make me sleep!
Go tell my brothers, when I am laid out,
They then may feed in quiet.   [*They strangle her.*]
BOSOLA   Where's the waiting woman?
Fetch her. Some other strangle the children.
        [*Exeunt* EXECUTIONERS, *some of whom return with* CARIOLA.]
Look you, there sleeps your mistress.
CARIOLA   Oh, you are damned
Perpetually for this! My turn is next.
Is 't not so ordered?
BOSOLA   Yes, and I am glad
You are so well prepared for 't.
CARIOLA   You are deceived, sir,
I am not prepared for 't, I will not die;
I will first come to my answer,° and know *judicial hearing*
How I have offended.
BOSOLA   Come, dispatch her.
You kept her counsel; now you shall keep ours.
CARIOLA   I will not die, I must not; I am contracted
To a young gentleman.
EXECUTIONER   Here's your wedding ring. [*showing the noose*]
CARIOLA   Let me but speak with the duke; I'll discover° *reveal*
Treason to his person.
BOSOLA   Delays! Throttle her.
EXECUTIONER   She bites and scratches.
CARIOLA   If you kill me now,
I am damned; I have not been at confession
This two years.
BOSOLA [*to* EXECUTIONERS]   When!
CARIOLA   I am quick with child.

---

3. The word is used loosely for a stupefying drug.

BOSOLA   Why, then,
       Your credit's saved.[4]   [*They strangle* CARIOLA.]
                       Bear her into th' next room;
       Let this lie still.   [*Exeunt the* EXECUTIONERS *with the body of* CARIOLA.]
       [*Enter* FERDINAND.]
FERDINAND   Is she dead?
BOSOLA   She is what
235   You'd have her. But here begin your pity.   [*Shows the children strangled.*]
       Alas, how have these offended?
FERDINAND   The death
       Of young wolves is never to be pitied.
BOSOLA   Fix
       Your eye here.
FERDINAND   Constantly.
BOSOLA   Do you not weep?
       Other sins only speak; murder shrieks out:
240   The element of water moistens the earth,
       But blood flies upwards and bedews the heavens.
FERDINAND   Cover her face; mine eyes dazzle: she died young.
BOSOLA   I think not so; her infelicity°   unhappiness°
       Seemed to have years too many.
FERDINAND   She and I were twins;
245   And should I die this instant, I had lived
       Her time to a minute.
BOSOLA   It seems she was born first:
       You have bloodily approved° the ancient truth,   given proof of
       That kindred commonly do worse agree
       Than remote strangers.
FERDINAND   Let me see her face again.
250   Why didst not thou pity her? What an excellent
       Honest man mightst thou have been,
       If thou hadst borne her to some sanctuary!
       Or, bold in a good cause, opposed thyself,
       With thy advancèd sword above thy head,
255   Between her innocence and my revenge!
       I bade thee, when I was distracted of my wits,
       Go kill my dearest friend, and thou hast done 't.
       For let me but examine well the cause:
       What was the meanness of her match to me?
260   Only I must confess I had a hope,
       Had she continued widow, to have gained
       An infinite mass of treasure by her death:
       And that was the main cause, her marriage,
       That drew a stream of gall quite through my heart.
265   For thee, as we observe in tragedies
       That a good actor many times is cursed
       For playing a villain's part, I hate thee for 't,
       And, for my sake, say thou hast done much ill well.

---

4. Your reputation will now be safe.

BOSOLA Let me quicken your memory, for I perceive
You are falling into ingratitude: I challenge
The reward due to my service.
FERDINAND   I'll tell thee
What I'll give thee.
BOSOLA   Do.
FERDINAND   I'll give thee a pardon
For this murder.
BOSOLA   Ha!
FERDINAND   Yes, and 'tis
The largest bounty I can study to do thee.
By what authority didst thou execute
This bloody sentence?
BOSOLA   By yours.
FERDINAND   Mine! Was I her judge?
Did any ceremonial form of law
Doom her to not-being? Did a complete° jury   *qualified*
Deliver her conviction up i' th' court?
Where shalt thou find this judgment registered,
Unless in hell? See, like a bloody fool,
Thou'st forfeited thy life, and thou shalt die for 't.
BOSOLA The office of justice is perverted quite
When one thief hangs another. Who shall dare
To reveal this?
FERDINAND   Oh, I'll tell thee;
The wolf shall find her grave, and scrape it up,
Not to devour the corpse, but to discover
The horrid murder.
BOSOLA   You, not I, shall quake for 't.
FERDINAND Leave me.
BOSOLA   I will first receive my pension.
FERDINAND You are a villain.
BOSOLA   When your ingratitude
Is judge, I am so.
FERDINAND Oh, horror!
That not the fear of Him which binds the devils
Can prescribe man obedience!
Never look upon me more.
BOSOLA   Why, fare thee well.
Your brother and your self are worthy men:
You have a pair of hearts are rotten graves,
Rotten, and rotting others; and your vengeance,
Like two chained bullets, still° goes arm in arm.   *continually*
You may be brothers, for treason, like the plague,
Doth take much in a blood.[5] I stand like one
That long hath ta'en a sweet and golden dream.
I am angry with myself, now that I wake.

---

5. Treason and plague run in certain families.

FERDINAND   Get thee into some unknown part o' th' world,
   That I may never see thee.
BOSOLA   Let me know
   Wherefore I should be thus neglected. Sir,
   I served your tyranny, and rather strove
   To satisfy yourself than all the world,
   And though I loathed the evil, yet I loved
   You that did counsel it; and rather sought
   To appear a true servant than an honest man.
FERDINAND   I'll go hunt the badger by owl-light:
   'Tis a deed of darkness.   [*Exit.*]
BOSOLA   He's much distracted. Off, my painted honor!
   While with vain hopes our faculties we tire,
   We seem to sweat in ice and freeze in fire.
   What would I do, were this to do again?
   I would not change my peace of conscience
   For all the wealth of Europe.—She stirs; here's life.
   Return, fair soul, from darkness, and lead mine
   Out of this sensible° hell.—She's warm, she breathes.   *living*
   Upon thy pale lips I will melt my heart,
   To store them with fresh color.—Who's there!
   Some cordial° drink!—Alas! I dare not call: *restorative*
   So pity would destroy pity.—Her eye opes,
   And heaven in it seems to ope, that late was shut,
   To take me up to mercy.
DUCHESS   Antonio!
BOSOLA   Yes, madam, he is living;
   The dead bodies you saw were but feigned statues:
   He's reconciled to your brothers: the pope hath wrought
   The atonement.°   *reconciliation*
DUCHESS   Mercy!   [*She dies.*]
BOSOLA   Oh, she's gone again! There the cords of life broke.
   Oh, sacred innocence, that sweetly sleeps
   On turtles'⁶ feathers, whilst a guilty conscience
   Is a black register wherein is writ
   All our good deeds and bad, a perspective°   *telescope*
   That shows us hell! That we cannot be suffered°   *allowed*
   To do good when we have a mind to it!
   This is manly sorrow:
   These tears, I am very certain, never grew
   In my mother's milk. My estate is sunk
   Below the degree of fear. Where were
   These penitent fountains while she was living?
   Oh, they were frozen up! Here is a sight
   As direful to my soul as is the sword
   Unto a wretch hath slain his father. Come,
   I'll bear thee hence,

---

6. Turtledoves, emblems of a loving couple.

And execute thy last will; that's deliver
Thy body to the reverend dispose°   *disposition*
Of some good women: that the cruel tyrant
Shall not deny me. Then I'll post to Milan,
Where somewhat I will speedily enact
Worth my dejection.   [*Exit with the body.*]

Act 5

SCENE 1. *A public place in Milan.*

[*Enter* ANTONIO *and* DELIO.]

ANTONIO   What think you of my hope of reconcilement
To the Aragonian brethren?
DELIO   I misdoubt it;
For though they have sent their letters of safe conduct
For your repair° to Milan, they appear   *resort*
But nets to entrap you. The Marquis of Pescara,
Under whom you hold certain land in cheat,[1]
Much 'gainst his noble nature hath been moved
To seize those lands, and some of his dependents
Are at this instant making it their suit
To be invested in your revenues.[2]
I cannot think they mean well to your life
That do deprive you of your means of life,
Your living.
ANTONIO   You are still an heretic°   *skeptic*
To any safety I can shape myself.
DELIO   Here comes the marquis. I will make myself
Petitioner for some part of your land,
To know whither it is flying.
ANTONIO   I pray do.   [*Withdraws.*]
[*Enter* PESCARA.]
DELIO   Sir, I have a suit to you.
PESCARA   To me?
DELIO   An easy one.
There is the citadel of Saint Bennet,
With some demesnes,[3] of late in the possession
Of Antonio Bologna; please you bestow them on me.
PESCARA   You are my friend, but this is such a suit,
Nor fit for me to give, nor you to take.
DELIO   No, sir?
PESCARA   I will give you ample reason for 't
Soon in private.—Here's the cardinal's mistress.
[*Enter* JULIA.]
JULIA   My lord, I am grown your poor petitioner,
And should be an ill beggar, had I not

5.1
1. Escheat, that is, subject to forfeiture under certain conditions.
2. That is, to be given your rents.
3. Associated estates. "Saint Bennet": St. Benedict.

        A great man's letter here, the cardinal's,
        To court you in my favor.   [*Gives a letter.*]
30 PESCARA   He entreats for you
        The citadel of Saint Bennet, that belonged
        To the banished Bologna.
JULIA   Yes.
PESCARA   I could not
        Have thought of a friend I could rather pleasure with it;
        'Tis yours.
JULIA   Sir, I thank you; and he shall know
35   How doubly I am engaged both in your gift,
        And speediness of giving, which makes your grant
        The greater.   [*Exit.*]
ANTONIO [*aside*]   How they fortify themselves
        With my ruin!
DELIO   Sir, I am little bound to you.
PESCARA   Why?
DELIO   Because you denied this suit to me, and gave 't
        To such a creature.
40 PESCARA   Do you know what it was?
        It was Antonio's land, not forfeited
        By course of law, but ravished from his throat
        By the cardinal's entreaty. It were not fit
        I should bestow so main° a piece of wrong   *egregious*
45   Upon my friend; 'tis a gratification
        Only due to a strumpet, for it is injustice.
        Shall I sprinkle the pure blood of innocents
        To make those followers I call my friends
        Look ruddier[4] upon me? I am glad
50   This land, ta'en from the owner by such wrong,
        Returns again unto so foul an use
        As salary for his lust. Learn, good Delio,
        To ask noble things of me, and you shall find
        I'll be a noble giver.
DELIO   You instruct me well.
55 ANTONIO [*aside*]   Why, here's a man now would fright impudence
        From sauciest beggars.
PESCARA   Prince Ferdinand's come to Milan,
        Sick, as they give out, of an apoplexy,°   *stroke*
        But some say 'tis a frenzy.° I am going   *insanity*
        To visit him.   [*Exit.*]
ANTONIO   'Tis a noble old fellow.
60 DELIO   What course do you mean to take, Antonio?
ANTONIO   This night I mean to venture all my fortune,
        Which is no more than a poor lingering life,
        To the cardinal's worst of malice. I have got
        Private access to his chamber, and intend
65   To visit him about the mid of night,

---

4. More agreeably, literally with a healthier (ruddy) complexion.

　　　　As once his brother did our noble duchess.
　　　　It may be that the sudden apprehension
　　　　Of danger—for I'll go in mine own shape—
　　　　When he shall see it fraught with love and duty,
70　　　May draw the poison out of him, and work
　　　　A friendly reconcilement. If it fail,
　　　　Yet it shall rid me of this infamous calling,
　　　　For better fall once than be ever falling.
　　DELIO　　I'll second you in all danger, and, howe'er,
75　　My life keeps rank with yours.
　　ANTONIO　　You are still my loved and best friend.　　[*Exeunt.*]

　　　　　　SCENE 2. *The scene continues.*

　　　　　[*Enter* PESCARA *and* DOCTOR.]
　　PESCARA　　Now, doctor, may I visit your patient?
　　DOCTOR　　If 't please your lordship: but he's instantly°　　　*very shortly*
　　　　To take the air here in the gallery
　　　　By my direction.
　　PESCARA　　　　　　Pray thee, what's his disease?
5　　DOCTOR　　A very pestilent disease, my lord,
　　　　They call lycanthropia.
　　PESCARA　　　　　　　　　What's that?
　　　　I need a dictionary to 't.
　　DOCTOR　　　　　　　　　I'll tell you.
　　　　In those that are possessed with 't there o'erflows
　　　　Such melancholy humor, they imagine
10　　Themselves to be transformèd into wolves;
　　　　Steal forth to churchyards in the dead of night,
　　　　And dig dead bodies up: as two nights since
　　　　One met the duke 'bout midnight in a lane
　　　　Behind Saint Mark's Church, with the leg of a man
15　　Upon his shoulder; and he howled fearfully;
　　　　Said he was a wolf, only the difference
　　　　Was, a wolf's skin was hairy on the outside,
　　　　His on the inside; bade them take their swords,
　　　　Rip up his flesh, and try. Straight° I was sent for,　　　*immediately*
20　　And, having ministered to him, found his grace
　　　　Very well recovered.
　　PESCARA　　　　　　I'm glad on 't.
　　DOCTOR　　Yet not without some fear
　　　　Of a relapse. If he grow to his fit again,
　　　　I'll go a nearer way to work with him
25　　Than ever Paracelsus[1] dreamed of: if
　　　　They'll give me leave, I'll buffet his madness
　　　　Out of him. Stand aside; he comes.
　　　　　[*Enter* FERDINAND, MALATESTE, CARDINAL, *and* BOSOLA *apart.*]
　　FERDINAND　　　　　　　　　Leave me.

5.2
1. The great Swiss alchemist, famous for his cures by sympathetic magic.

MALATESTE Why doth your lordship love this solitariness?
FERDINAND Eagles commonly fly alone: they are crows, daws, and starlings that flock together. Look, what's that follows me?
MALATESTE Nothing, my lord.
FERDINAND Yes.
MALATESTE 'Tis your shadow.
FERDINAND Stay it; let it not haunt me.
MALATESTE Impossible, if you move, and the sun shine.
FERDINAND I will throttle it. [*Throws himself on the ground.*]
MALATESTE O, my lord, you are angry with nothing.
FERDINAND You are a fool: how is 't possible I should catch my shadow, unless I fall upon 't? When I go to hell, I mean to carry a bribe; for, look you, good gifts evermore make way for the worst persons.
PESCARA Rise, good my lord.
FERDINAND I am studying the art of patience.
PESCARA 'Tis a noble virtue.
FERDINAND To drive six snails before me from this town to Moscow; neither use goad nor whip to them, but let them take their own time—the patient'st man i' th' world match me for an experiment—and I'll crawl after like a sheep-biter.[2]
CARDINAL Force him up.   [*They raise him.*]
FERDINAND Use me well, you were best. What I have done, I have done: I'll confess nothing.
DOCTOR Now let me come to him. Are you mad, my lord? Are you out of your princely wits?
FERDINAND What's he?
PESCARA Your doctor.
FERDINAND Let me have his beard sawed off, and his eyebrows filed more civil.
DOCTOR I must do mad tricks with him, for that's the only way on 't.[3] I have brought your grace a salamander's skin to keep you from sunburning.
FERDINAND I have cruel sore eyes.
DOCTOR The white of a cockatrix's[4] egg is present remedy.
FERDINAND Let it be a new-laid one, you were best. Hide me from him: physicians are like kings—they brook no contradiction.
DOCTOR Now he begins to fear me: now let me alone with him.
CARDINAL How now? Put off your gown?
DOCTOR Let me have some forty urinals filled with rosewater: he and I'll go pelt one another with them. Now he begins to fear me. Can you fetch a frisk, sir?[5] Let him go, let him go, upon my peril: I find by his eye he stands in awe of me; I'll make him as tame as a dormouse.
FERDINAND Can you fetch your frisks, sir? I will stamp him into a cullis,[6] flay off his skin, to cover one of the anatomies[7] this rogue hath set i' th' cold yonder in Barber-Surgeons' Hall. Hence, hence! You are all of you

---

2. A sheepdog.
3. That is, to cure him.
4. A fabulous, and deadly poisonous, serpent, supposed to be hatched of a cock's egg.
5. Cut a caper, dance a jig.
6. Broth.
7. Anatomical skeletons hung up in the surgeon's college, which Ferdinand proposes to cover with the doctor's flayed skin.

like beasts for sacrifice: there's nothing left of you but tongue and belly,
flattery and lechery. [*Exit.*]
PESCARA   Doctor, he did not fear you thoroughly.
DOCTOR   True;
I was somewhat too forward.
BOSOLA [*aside*]   Mercy upon me,
What a fatal judgment hath fall'n upon this Ferdinand!
PESCARA   Knows your grace what accident hath brought
Unto the prince this strange distraction?
CARDINAL [*aside*]   I must feign somewhat.—Thus they say it grew:
You have heard it rumored, for these many years
None of our family dies but there is seen
The shape of an old woman, which is given
By tradition to us to have been murdered
By her nephews for her riches. Such a figure
One night, as the prince sat up late at 's book,
Appeared to him; when, crying out for help,
The gentlemen of 's chamber found his grace
All on a cold sweat, altered much in face
And language; since which apparition,
He hath grown worse and worse, and I much fear
He cannot live.
BOSOLA   Sir, I would speak with you.
PESCARA   We'll leave your grace,
Wishing to the sick prince, our noble lord,
All health of mind and body.
CARDINAL   You are most welcome.
         [*Exeunt* PESCARA, MALATESTE, *and* DOCTOR.]
Are you come? So. [*aside*] This fellow must not know
By any means I had intelligence°   *was accessory*
In our duchess' death; for, though I counseled it,
The full of all th' engagement seemed to grow
From Ferdinand.—Now, sir, how fares our sister?
I do not think but sorrow makes her look
Like to an oft-dyed garment: she shall now
Taste comfort from me. Why do you look so wildly?
Oh, the fortune of your master here the prince
Dejects you, but be you of happy comfort:
If you'll do one thing for me I'll entreat,
Though he had a cold tombstone o'er his bones,
I'll make you what you would be.
BOSOLA   Anything;
Give it me in a breath, and let me fly to 't:
They that think long, small expedition win,
For musing much o' th' end cannot begin.
         [*Enter* JULIA.]
JULIA   Sir, will you come in to supper?
CARDINAL   I am busy;
Leave me.
JULIA [*aside*]   What an excellent shape hath that fellow! [*Exit.*]

CARDINAL   'Tis thus. Antonio lurks here in Milan:
　　Inquire him out, and kill him. While he lives,
115　Our sister cannot marry, and I have thought
　　Of an excellent match for her. Do this, and style me
　　Thy advancement.⁸
BOSOLA   But by what means shall I find him out?
CARDINAL   There is a gentleman called Delio
　　Here in the camp, that hath been long approved
120　His loyal friend. Set eye upon that fellow;
　　Follow him to Mass; maybe Antonio,
　　Although he do account religion
　　But a school-name,° for fashion of the world　　　　　　　*an idle phrase*
　　May accompany him; or else go inquire out
125　Delio's confessor, and see if you can bribe
　　Him to reveal it. There are a thousand ways
　　A man might find to trace him; as to know
　　What fellows haunt the Jews for taking up
　　Great sums of money, for sure he's in want;
130　Or else to go to th' picture-makers, and learn
　　Who bought her picture lately. Some of these
　　Haply may take.
BOSOLA　　　　Well, I'll not freeze i' th' business:°　　　　*delay*
　　I would see that wretched thing, Antonio,
　　Above all sights i' th' world.
CARDINAL　　　　　　Do, and be happy.　　[*Exit.*]
135　BOSOLA   This fellow doth breed basilisks in 's eyes,
　　He's nothing else but murder; yet he seems
　　Not to have notice of the duchess' death.
　　'Tis his cunning: I must follow his example;
　　There cannot be a surer way to trace
　　Than that of an old fox.
　　　　[*Reenter* JULIA, *with a pistol.*]
140　JULIA　　　　　So, sir, you are well met.
BOSOLA   How now?
JULIA　　　　　Nay, the doors are fast enough.
　　Now, sir, I will make you confess your treachery.
BOSOLA   Treachery?
JULIA　　　　　Yes, confess to me
　　Which of my women 'twas, you hired to put
　　Love-powder into my drink?
145　BOSOLA　　　　　　Love powder?
JULIA   Yes, when I was at Malfi.
　　Why should I fall in love with such a face else?°　　　　*otherwise*
　　I have already suffered for thee so much pain,
　　The only remedy to do me good
　　Is to kill my longing.
150　BOSOLA　　　　Sure, your pistol holds
　　Nothing but perfumes or kissing-comfits.⁹

8. Call me your means of promotion.
9. Candies to sweeten the breath.

Excellent lady! You have a pretty way on 't
To discover° your longing. Come, come, I'll disarm you, — reveal
And arm you thus:¹ yet this is wondrous strange.

JULIA Compare thy form and my eyes together, you'll find
My love no such great miracle. Now you'll say
I am wanton: this nice° modesty in ladies — fastidious
Is but a troublesome familiar² that haunts them.

BOSOLA Know you me, I am a blunt soldier.

JULIA   The better:
Sure, there wants° fire where there are no lively sparks — lacks
Of roughness.

BOSOLA   And I want compliment.³

JULIA   Why, ignorance
In courtship cannot make you do amiss,
If you have a heart to do well.

BOSOLA   You are very fair.

JULIA Nay, if you lay beauty to my charge,
I must plead unguilty.

BOSOLA   Your bright eyes
Carry a quiver of darts in them, sharper
Than sunbeams.

JULIA   You will mar me with commendation,
Put yourself to the charge of courting me,
Whereas now I woo you.

BOSOLA [*aside*] I have it, I will work upon this creature.—
Let us grow most amorously familiar.
If the great cardinal now should see me thus,
Would he not count me a villain?

JULIA No, he might count me a wanton,
Not lay a scruple of offense on you;
For if I see and steal a diamond,
The fault is not i' th' stone, but in me the thief
That purloins it. I am sudden with you.
We that are great women of pleasure, use to cut off
These uncertain wishes and unquiet longings,
And in an instant join the sweet delight
And the pretty excuse together. Had you been i' th' street,
Under my chamber window, even there
I should have courted you.

BOSOLA   Oh, you are an excellent lady!

JULIA Bid me do somewhat for you presently° — right away
To express I love you.

BOSOLA   I will, and if you love me,
Fail not to effect it.
The cardinal is grown wondrous melancholy;

---

1. Disarm (by taking away her pistol); arm (by embracing her).
2. Attendant spirit or demon.
3. I don't have the gift of flattery.

Demand the cause, let him not put you off
With feigned excuse; discover the main ground on 't.
JULIA   Why would you know this?
BOSOLA   I have depended on him,
And I hear he is fallen in some disgrace
With the emperor: if he be, like the mice
That forsake falling houses, I would shift
To other dependence.
JULIA   You shall not need follow the wars;
I'll be your maintenance.
BOSOLA   And I your loyal servant;
But I cannot leave my calling.
JULIA   Not leave
An ungrateful general for the love of a sweet lady?
You are like some cannot sleep in featherbeds,
But must have blocks for their pillows.
BOSOLA   Will you do this?
JULIA   Cunningly.
BOSOLA   Tomorrow I'll expect th' intelligence.
JULIA   Tomorrow? Get you into my cabinet,°   *inner chamber*
You shall have it with you. Do not delay me,
No more than I do you. I am like one
That is condemned: I have my pardon promised,
But I would see it sealed. Go, get you in;
You shall see me wind my tongue about his heart
Like a skein of silk.   [*Exit* BOSOLA.]
        [*Reenter* CARDINAL.]
CARDINAL   Where are you?
        [*Enter* SERVANTS.]
SERVANTS   Here.
CARDINAL   Let none, upon your lives,
Have conference with the Prince Ferdinand,
Unless I know it. [*aside*] In this distraction
He may reveal the murder.   [*Exeunt* SERVANTS.]
Yond's my lingering consumption:
I am weary of her, and by any means
Would be quit of.
JULIA   How now, my lord?
What ails you?
CARDINAL   Nothing.
JULIA   Oh, you are much altered:
Come, I must be your secretary,° and remove   *confidante*
This lead from off your bosom.[4] What's the matter?
CARDINAL   I may not tell you.
JULIA   Are you so far in love with sorrow
You cannot part with part of it? Or think you
I cannot love your grace when you are sad

---

4. Secretaries opened letters addressed to their masters by removing the heavy lead seals.

                As well as merry? Or do you suspect
225   I, that have been a secret to your heart
                These many winters, cannot be the same
                Unto your tongue?
        CARDINAL   Satisfy thy longing—
                The only way to make thee keep my counsel
                Is not to tell thee.
230   JULIA   Tell your echo this,
                Or flatterers, that like echoes still report
                What they hear though most imperfect, and not me;
                For if that you be true unto yourself,
                I'll know.
        CARDINAL   Will you rack° me?   *torture*
        JULIA   No, judgment shall
                Draw it from you: it is an equal fault,
235   To tell one's secrets unto all or none.
        CARDINAL   The first argues folly.
        JULIA   But the last, tyranny.
        CARDINAL   Very well. Why, imagine I have committed
                Some secret deed which I desire the world
                May never hear of.
        JULIA   Therefore may not I know it?
240   You have concealed for me as great a sin
                As adultery. Sir, never was occasion
                For perfect trial of my constancy
                Till now: sir, I beseech you—
        CARDINAL   You'll repent it.
        JULIA   Never.
245   CARDINAL   It hurries thee to ruin: I'll not tell thee.
                Be well advised, and think what danger 'tis
                To receive a prince's secrets: they that do,
                Had need have their breasts hooped with adamant°   *the hardest metal*
                To contain them. I pray thee, yet be satisfied;
250   Examine thine own frailty; 'tis more easy
                To tie knots than unloose them: 'tis a secret
                That, like a lingering poison, may chance lie
                Spread in thy veins, and kill thee seven year hence.
        JULIA   Now you dally with me.
        CARDINAL   No more; thou shalt know it.
255   By my appointment the great Duchess of Malfi
                And two of her young children, four nights since,
                Were strangled.
        JULIA   O Heaven! Sir, what have you done?
        CARDINAL   How now? How settles this? Think you your bosom
                Will be a grave dark and obscure enough
                For such a secret?
260   JULIA   You have undone yourself, sir.
        CARDINAL   Why?
        JULIA   It lies not in me to conceal it.
        CARDINAL   No?

Come, I will swear you to 't upon this book.
JULIA   Most religiously.
CARDINAL   Kiss it.   [*She kisses the book.*]
                    Now you shall
Never utter it; thy curiosity
Hath undone thee: thou'rt poisoned with that book.
Because I knew thou couldst not keep my counsel,
I have bound thee to 't by death.
    [*Reenter* BOSOLA.]
BOSOLA   For pity sake,
Hold!
CARDINAL   Ha! Bosola?
JULIA   I forgive you
This equal piece of justice you have done;
For I betrayed your counsel to that fellow:
He overheard it; that was the cause I said
It lay not in me to conceal it.
BOSOLA   O foolish woman,
Couldst not thou have poisoned him?
JULIA   'Tis weakness,
Too much to think what should have been done. I go
I know not whither.   [*Dies.*]
CARDINAL   Wherefore com'st thou hither?
BOSOLA   That I might find a great man like yourself,
Not out of his wits as the Lord Ferdinand,
To remember my service.
CARDINAL   I'll have thee hewed in pieces.
BOSOLA   Make not yourself such a promise of that life
Which is not yours to dispose of.
CARDINAL   Who placed thee here?
BOSOLA   Her lust, as she intended.
CARDINAL   Very well.
Now you know me for your fellow murderer.
BOSOLA   And wherefore should you lay fair marble colors
Upon your rotten purposes to me?[5]
Unless you imitate some that do plot great treasons,
And when they have done, go hide themselves i' th' graves
Of those were actors in 't?
CARDINAL   No more; there is
A fortune attends thee.
BOSOLA   Shall I go sue to Fortune any longer?
'Tis the fool's pilgrimage.
CARDINAL   I have honors in store for thee.
BOSOLA   There are a many ways that conduct to seeming
Honor, and some of them very dirty ones.
CARDINAL   Throw to the devil
Thy melancholy; the fire burns well,
What need we keep a stirring of 't, and make

---

5. Plaster was often painted to look like marble.

A greater smother? Thou wilt kill Antonio?
BOSOLA   Yes.
CARDINAL   Take up that body.
BOSOLA   I think I shall
   Shortly grow the common bier for churchyards!
CARDINAL   I will allow thee some dozen of attendants
   To aid thee in the murder.
BOSOLA   Oh, by no means. Physicians that apply horse leeches to any rank swelling use to cut off their tails, that the blood may run through them the faster. Let me have no train[6] when I go to shed blood, lest it make me have a greater when I ride to the gallows.[7]
CARDINAL   Come to me after midnight, to help to remove that body to her own lodging. I'll give out she died of the plague; 'twill breed the less inquiry after her death.
BOSOLA   Where's Castruccio her husband?
CARDINAL   He's rode to Naples to take possession of Antonio's citadel.
BOSOLA   Believe me, you have done a very happy turn.
CARDINAL   Fail not to come. There is the master key of our lodgings, and by that you may conceive what trust I plant in you.
BOSOLA   You shall find me ready.   [*Exit* CARDINAL.]
   Oh poor Antonio, though nothing be so needful
   To thy estate as pity, yet I find
   Nothing so dangerous. I must look to my footing;
   In such slippery ice-pavements men had need
   To be frost-nailed well;[8] they may break their necks else;
   The precedent's here afore me. How this man
   Bears up in blood! Seems fearless! Why, 'tis well:
   Security some men call the suburbs of hell,
   Only a dead° wall between. Well, good Antonio,   bare
   I'll seek thee out, and all my care shall be
   To put thee into safety from the reach
   Of these most cruel biters that have got
   Some of thy blood already. It may be,
   I'll join with thee in a most just revenge:
   The weakest arm is strong enough that strikes
   With the sword of justice. Still methinks the duchess
   Haunts me. There, there, 'tis nothing but my melancholy.
   O Penitence, let me truly taste thy cup,
   That throws men down only to raise them up!   [*Exit.*]

SCENE 3. *A fortification at Milan.*

[*Enter* ANTONIO *and* DELIO. *Echo from the* DUCHESS' *grave.*]
DELIO   Yond's the cardinal's window. This fortification
   Grew from the ruins of an ancient abbey;
   And to yond side o' th' river lies a wall,
   Piece of a cloister, which in my opinion

---

6. Followers.
7. Criminals, carted through the streets to be hanged at Tyburn, were followed by crowds.
8. To wear hobnailed boots.

Gives the best echo that you ever heard,
So hollow and so dismal, and withal°   *in addition*
So plain in the distinction of our words,
That many have supposed it is a spirit
That answers.
ANTONIO   I do love these ancient ruins.
We never tread upon them but we set
Our foot upon some reverend history:
And, questionless, here in this open court,
Which now lies naked to the injuries
Of stormy weather, some men lie interred
Loved the church so well, and gave so largely to 't,
They thought it should have canopied their bones
Till doomsday; but all things have their end:
Churches and cities, which have diseases like to men,
Must have like death that we have.
ECHO   "Like death that we have."
DELIO   Now the echo hath caught you.
ANTONIO   It groaned, methought, and gave
A very deadly accent.
ECHO   "Deadly accent."
DELIO   I told you 'twas a pretty one: you may make it
A huntsman, or a falconer, a musician,
Or a thing of sorrow.
ECHO   "A thing of sorrow."
ANTONIO   Aye, sure, that suits it best.
ECHO   "That suits it best."
ANTONIO   'Tis very like my wife's voice.
ECHO   "Aye, wife's voice."
DELIO   Come, let's walk further from 't. I would not have you
Go to th' cardinal's tonight: do not.
ECHO   "Do not."
DELIO   Wisdom doth not more moderate wasting sorrow
Than time: take time for 't; be mindful of thy safety.
ECHO   "Be mindful of thy safety."
ANTONIO   Necessity compels me:
Make° scrutiny throughout the passes   *if you make*
Of your own life, you'll find it impossible
To fly your fate.
ECHO   "Oh, fly your fate."
DELIO   Hark! The dead stones seem to have pity on you,
And give you good counsel.
ANTONIO   Echo, I will not talk with thee,
For thou art a dead thing.
ECHO   "Thou art a dead thing."
ANTONIO   My duchess is asleep now,
And her little ones, I hope sweetly: O heaven,
Shall I never see her more?
ECHO   "Never see her more."
ANTONIO   I marked° not one repetition of the echo   *attended to*

But that, and on the sudden a clear light
Presented me a face folded in sorrow.
DELIO   Your fancy merely.
ANTONIO   Come, I'll be out of this ague,°   *fever*
For to live thus is not indeed to live;
It is a mockery and abuse of life.
I will not henceforth save myself by halves;
Lose all, or nothing.
DELIO   Your own virtue save you!
I'll fetch your eldest son, and second you°   *back you up*
It may be that the sight of his own blood
Spread in so sweet a figure° may beget   *face*
The more compassion.
ANTONIO   However, fare you well.
Though in our miseries Fortune have a part,
Yet in our noble sufferings she hath none:
Contempt of pain, that we may call our own.   [*Exeunt.*]

SCENE 4. *A room in the* CARDINAL's *palace.*

[*Enter* CARDINAL, PESCARA, MALATESTE, RODERIGO, *and* GRISOLAN.]
CARDINAL   You shall not watch tonight by the sick prince;
His grace is very well recovered.
MALATESTE   Good my lord, suffer° us.   *allow*
CARDINAL   Oh, by no means;
The noise and change of object in his eye
Doth more distract him. I pray, all to bed;
And though you hear him in his violent fit,
Do not rise, I entreat you.
PESCARA   So, sir; we shall not.
CARDINAL   Nay, I must have you promise upon your honors,
For I was enjoined to 't by himself; and he seemed
To urge it sensibly.°   *with strong feeling*
PESCARA   Let our honors bind
This trifle.
CARDINAL   Nor any of your followers.
MALATESTE   Neither.
CARDINAL   It may be, to make trial of your promise,
When he's asleep, myself will rise and feign
Some of his mad tricks, and cry out for help,
And feign myself in danger.
MALATESTE   If your throat were cutting,
I'd not come at you, now I have protested against it.
CARDINAL   Why, I thank you.   [*Withdraws.*]
GRISOLAN   'Twas a foul storm tonight.
RODERIGO   The Lord Ferdinand's chamber shook like an
    osier.°   *a willow wand*
MALATESTE   'Twas nothing but pure kindness in the devil,
To rock his own child.   [*Exeunt all except the* CARDINAL.]
CARDINAL   The reason why I would not suffer° these   *allow*

About my brother is because at midnight
I may with better privacy convey
Julia's body to her own lodging. Oh, my conscience!
I would pray now, but the devil takes away my heart
For having any confidence in prayer.
About this hour I appointed Bosola
To fetch the body: when he hath served my turn,
He dies. [*Exit.*]
[*Enter* BOSOLA.]
BOSOLA   Ha! 'Twas the cardinal's voice; I heard him name
Bosola and my death. Listen! I hear
One's footing.
[*Enter* FERDINAND.]
FERDINAND   Strangling is a very quiet death.
BOSOLA [*aside*]   Nay, then, I see I must stand upon my guard.
FERDINAND   What say to that? Whisper softly; do you agree to 't? So; it must be done i' th' dark: the cardinal would not for a thousand pounds the doctor should see it. [*Exit.*]
BOSOLA   My death is plotted; here's the consequence of murder.
We value not desert nor Christian breath,
When we know black deeds must be cured with death.
[*Enter* ANTONIO *and* SERVANT.]
SERVANT   Here stay, sir, and be confident, I pray:
I'll fetch you a dark lantern. [*Exit.*]
ANTONIO   Could I take him at his prayers,
There were hope of pardon.
BOSOLA   Fall right, my sword! [*Stabs him.*]
I'll not give thee so much leisure as to pray.
ANTONIO   Oh, I am gone! Thou hast ended a long suit[1]
In a minute.
BOSOLA   What art thou?
ANTONIO   A most wretched thing,
That only have thy benefit in death,
To appear myself.
[*Reenter* SERVANT *with a lantern.*]
SERVANT   Where are you, sir?
ANTONIO   Very near my home. Bosola?
SERVANT   Oh, misfortune!
BOSOLA   Smother thy pity; thou art dead else.° Antonio?   otherwise
The man I would have saved 'bove mine own life!
We are merely the stars' tennis balls, struck and bandied
Which way please them.[2] O good Antonio,
I'll whisper one thing in thy dying ear
Shall make thy heart break quickly! Thy fair duchess
And two sweet children—
ANTONIO   Their very names
Kindle a little life in me.

5.4
1. Antonio thinks it is the cardinal, to whom he came to address a plea ("suit"), who has stabbed him.
2. The power of the stars over people's lives was a Renaissance commonplace.

BOSOLA   Are murdered.
ANTONIO   Some men have wished to die
   At the hearing of sad tidings; I am glad
   That I shall do 't in sadness: I would not now
   Wish my wounds balmed nor healed, for I have no use
   To put my life to. In all our quest of greatness,
   Like wanton boys, whose pastime is their care,
   We follow after bubbles blown in th' air.
   Pleasure of life, what is't? Only the good hours
   Of an ague; merely a preparative to rest,
   To endure vexation. I do not ask
   The process° of my death; only commend me   *reason, circumstances*
   To Delio.
BOSOLA   Break, heart!
ANTONIO   And let my son fly the courts of princes.   [*Dies.*]
BOSOLA   Thou seem'st to have loved Antonio?
SERVANT   I brought him hither
   To have reconciled him to the cardinal.
BOSOLA   I do not ask thee that.
   Take him up, if thou tender thine own life,
   And bear him where the lady Julia
   Was wont to lodge. Oh, my fate moves swift;
   I have this cardinal in the forge already;
   Now I'll bring him to th' hammer. Oh direful
      misprision!°   *misunderstanding*
   I will not imitate things glorious,
   No more than base; I'll be mine own example.
   On, on, and look thou represent,° for silence,   *imitate*
   The thing thou bear'st.[3]   [*Exeunt.*]

SCENE 5. *The scene continues.*

[*Enter* CARDINAL, *with a book.*]
CARDINAL   I am puzzled in a question about hell:
   He says, in hell there's one material fire,
   And yet it shall not burn all men alike.
   Lay him by. How tedious is a guilty conscience!
   When I look into the fish ponds in my garden,
   Methinks I see a thing armed with a rake,
   That seems to strike at me.
      [*Enter* BOSOLA, *and* SERVANT *bearing* ANTONIO's *body.*]
                                Now, art thou come?
   Thou look'st ghastly:
   There sits in thy face some great determination
   Mixed with some fear.
BOSOLA   Thus it lightens° into action: *ignites*
   I am come to kill thee.
CARDINAL   Ha! Help! Our guard!
BOSOLA   Thou art deceived; they are out of thy howling.

3. The corpse.

CARDINAL Hold; and I will faithfully divide
  Revenues with thee.
BOSOLA   Thy prayers and proffers
  Are both unseasonable.
CARDINAL   Raise the watch!
  We are betrayed!
BOSOLA   I have confined your flight:°   *cut off your escape*
  I'll suffer your retreat to Julia's chamber,
  But no further.
CARDINAL   Help! We are betrayed!
  [*Enter, above,* PESCARA, MALATESTE, RODERIGO, *and* GRISOLAN.]
MALATESTE   Listen.
CARDINAL My dukedom for rescue!
RODERIGO   Fie upon his counterfeiting!
MALATESTE Why, 'tis not the cardinal.
RODERIGO   Yes, yes, 'tis he,
  But I'll see him hanged ere I'll go down to him.
CARDINAL Here's a plot upon me. I am assaulted! I am lost,
  Unless some rescue.
GRISOLAN   He doth this pretty well,
  But it will not serve to laugh me out of my honor.
CARDINAL The sword's at my throat!
RODERIGO   You would not bawl so loud then.
MALATESTE Come, come, let's go to bed. He told us thus much aforehand.
PESCARA He wished you should not come at him; but, believe 't,
  The accent of the voice sounds not in jest:
  I'll down to him, howsoever, and with engines.°   *battering rams*
  Force ope the doors.   [*Exit above.*]
RODERIGO   Let's follow him aloof,°   *at a distance*
  And note how the cardinal will laugh at him.
  [*Exeunt, above,* MALATESTE, RODERIGO, *and* GRISOLAN.]
BOSOLA There's for you first,   [*He kills the* SERVANT.]
  'Cause you shall not unbarricade the door
  To let in rescue.
CARDINAL What cause hast thou to pursue my life?
BOSOLA   Look there.
CARDINAL Antonio?
BOSOLA   Slain by my hand unwittingly.
  Pray, and be sudden: when thou killed'st thy sister,
  Thou took'st from Justice her most equal balance,
  And left her naught but her sword.
CARDINAL   Oh, mercy!
BOSOLA Now it seems thy greatness was only outward;
  For thou fall'st faster of thyself than calamity
  Can drive thee. I'll not waste longer time: there! [*Stabs him.*]
CARDINAL Thou hast hurt me.
BOSOLA   Again!   [*Stabs him again.*]
CARDINAL   Shall I die like a leveret,[1]

5.5
1. A baby hare.

Without any resistance? Help, help, help!
I am slain!
  [*Enter* FERDINAND.]
FERDINAND   Th' alarum? Give me a fresh horse;
Rally the vaunt-guard, or the day is lost.
Yield, yield! I give you the honor of arms,
Shake my sword over you; will you yield?[2]
CARDINAL   Help me; I am your brother!
FERDINAND   The devil!
My brother fight upon the adverse party?
  [*He wounds the* CARDINAL *and, in the scuffle, gives* BOSOLA *his death wound.*]
There flies your ransom.
CARDINAL   O justice!
I suffer now for what hath former° been: *earlier*
Sorrow is held the eldest child of sin.
FERDINAND   Now you're brave fellows. Caesar's fortune was harder than Pompey's; Caesar died in the arms of prosperity, Pompey at the feet of disgrace. You both died in the field. The pain's nothing: pain many times is taken away with the apprehension of greater, as the toothache with the sight of a barber that comes to pull it out: there's philosophy for you.
BOSOLA   Now my revenge is perfect. Sink, thou main cause
  [*He kills* FERDINAND.]
Of my undoing! The last part of my life
Hath done me best service.
FERDINAND   Give me some wet hay; I am broken-winded.[3] I do account this world but a dog kennel: I will vault credit and affect high pleasures[4] beyond death.
BOSOLA   He seems to come to himself, now he's so near the bottom.
FERDINAND   My sister, O my sister! There's the cause on 't.
Whether we fall by ambition, blood, or lust,
Like diamonds we are cut with our own dust.   [*Dies.*]
CARDINAL   Thou hast thy payment, too.
BOSOLA   Yes, I hold my weary soul in my teeth.
'Tis ready to part from me. I do glory
That thou, which stood'st like a huge pyramid
Begun upon a large and ample base,
Shalt end in a little point, a kind of nothing.
  [*Enter, below,* PESCARA, MALATESTE, RODERIGO, *and* GRISOLAN.]
PESCARA   How now, my lord?
MALATESTE   O sad disaster!
RODERIGO   How comes this?
BOSOLA   Revenge for the Duchess of Malfi murdered
By th' Aragonian brethren; for Antonio
Slain by this hand; for lustful Julia
Poisoned by this man; and lastly for myself,

---

2. Ferdinand thinks he's on the field of battle and offering the "honor of arms" (liberal surrender terms) to his foes. "Vaunt-guard": vanguard.
3. Worn-out horses are said to be broken-winded.
4. Go beyond expectation and enjoy great pleasures.

That was an actor in the main of all,
Much 'gainst mine own good nature, yet i' th' end
Neglected.
PESCARA How now, my lord?
CARDINAL   Look to my brother:
He gave us these large wounds as we were struggling
Here i' the rushes.[5] And now, I pray,
Let me be laid by and never thought of.   [*Dies.*]
PESCARA How fatally, it seems, he did withstand
His own rescue!
MALATESTE   Thou wretched thing of blood,
How came Antonio by his death?
BOSOLA In a mist: I know not how;
Such a mistake as I have often seen
In a play. Oh, I am gone!
We are only like dead walls or vaulted graves,
That, ruined, yield no echo. Fare you well.
It may be pain, but no harm to me to die
In so good a quarrel. Oh, this gloomy world,
In what a shadow or deep pit of darkness
Doth womanish and fearful mankind live!
Let worthy minds ne'er stagger in distrust
To suffer death or shame for what is just:
Mine is another voyage.   [*Dies.*]
PESCARA The noble Delio, as I came to the palace,
Told me of Antonio's being here, and showed me
A pretty gentleman, his son and heir.
[*Enter* DELIO *with* ANTONIO'S SON.]
MALATESTE O, sir, you come too late.
DELIO   I heard so, and
Was armed° for it ere I came. Let us make noble use   *prepared*
Of this great ruin, and join all our force
To establish this young hopeful° gentleman   *promising*
In 's mother's right. These wretched eminent things
Leave no more fame behind 'em, than should one
Fall in a frost, and leave his print in snow;
As soon as the sun shines, it ever melts
Both form and matter. I have ever thought
Nature doth nothing so great for great men
As when she's pleased to make them lords of truth:
Integrity of life is fame's best friend,
Which nobly, beyond death, shall crown the end.   [*Exeunt.*]

performed 1613   *published* 1623

---

5. Leafy plants, strewn over Elizabethan floors in lieu of carpets.

FRANCIS BACON
1561–1626

As a literary figure Sir Francis Bacon played a central role in the development of the English essay and inaugurated the genre of the scientific utopia in his *New Atlantis* (1627). But he was even more important to the intellectual and cultural history of the earlier seventeenth century for his treatises on reforming learning through experiment. His life span closely overlapped that of Donne and of Jonson, but unlike them he was born into a leading political family close to the centers of government and power. During Elizabeth's reign he studied law and entered Parliament. But it was under James I that his political fortunes took off: he was knighted in 1603, became attorney general in 1613, lord chancellor (the highest judicial post) and Baron Verulam in 1618, and Viscount St. Albans in 1621. That same year, however, he was convicted on twenty-three counts of corruption and accepting bribes: he was fined, imprisoned, and forced from office. Bacon admitted the truth of the charges (though they were in part politically motivated), merely observing that everyone took bribes and that bribery never influenced his judgment.

As an essayist Bacon stands at almost the opposite pole from his great French predecessor Michel de Montaigne (1533–1592), who proposed to learn about humankind by an intensive analysis of his own sensations, emotions, and ideas. Bacon's essays are instead on topics "civil and moral," and they are written in a curt, deliberately impersonal style. The ten short pieces of the first edition of his essays (1597) are little more than collections of maxims placed in sequence; the thirty-eight of the second edition (1612) are longer and looser; the fifty-eight of the final edition (1625) are still longer, are smoother in texture, use more figurative language, and are more unified. In that last edition, more than half of the essays deal with public life, and many of the others—even on such topics as truth, marriage, and love—are written from the vantage point of a practical man of affairs. They evoke an atmosphere of expediency but also voice precepts of moral wisdom and public virtue, offering a penetrating insight into the thinking of the Jacobean ruling class.

Early in his life Bacon declared, "I have taken all knowledge to be my province." He believed that his new "scientific" method would lead humankind to a better future. The title of his *Novum Organum* (The New Instrument of Learning, 1620), written in Latin, challenged the authority of Aristotle's *Organon*, which was still the basis of university education. Bacon argued that the right method of investigating nature combined careful empirical observation with limited generalizations, which themselves could be tested by further experiments. *Novum Organum* includes a trenchant analysis of four kinds of "Idols"—psychological dispositions and intellectual habits that hold individuals back in their quest for truth. But despite his emphasis on experiment, in his written work Bacon generally ignored major scientific discoveries by Galileo, William Harvey, and others; his true role was as a herald of the modern age. And despite his critique of misleading words and intellectual fictions, he used the rich resources of literary and figurative language—and of utopian fiction in *The New Atlantis*—to urge a new faith in experiment and science. He segregated theology and science as "two truths," freeing science to go its own way unhampered by religious dogmas and unrestrained by the morality they supported. He is a primary creator of the myth of science as a pathway to utopia; in the 1660s the Royal Society honored him as a prophet.

From Essays[1]

Of Truth

"What is truth?" said jesting Pilate; and would not stay for an answer.[2] Certainly there be that delight in giddiness,[3] and count it a bondage to fix a belief; affecting free will in thinking, as well as in acting. And though the sects of philosophers of that kind be gone, yet there remain certain discoursing wits,[4] which are of the same veins, though there be not so much blood in them as was in those of the ancients. But it is not only the difficulty and labor which men take in finding out of truth; nor again, that when it is found, it imposeth upon[5] men's thoughts, that doth bring lies in favor; but a natural though corrupt love of the lie itself. One of the later school of the Grecians examineth the matter, and is at a stand[6] to think what should be in it, that men should love lies, where neither they make for pleasure, as with poets, nor for advantage, as with the merchant, but for the lie's sake. But I cannot tell: this same truth is a naked and open daylight, that doth not show the masques and mummeries and triumphs of the world half so stately and daintily as candlelights. Truth may perhaps come to the price of a pearl, that showeth best by day, but it will not rise to the price of a diamond or carbuncle,[7] that showeth best in varied lights. A mixture of a lie doth ever add pleasure. Doth any man doubt that if there were taken out of men's minds vain opinions, flattering hopes, false valuations, imaginations as one would, and the like, but it would leave the minds of a number of men poor shrunken things, full of melancholy and indisposition, and unpleasing to themselves? One of the fathers, in great severity, called poesy *vinum daemonum*,[8] because it filleth the imagination, and yet it is but with the shadow of a lie. But it is not the lie that passeth through the mind, but the lie that sinketh in, and settleth in it, that doth the hurt, such as we spake of before. But howsoever these things are thus in men's depraved judgments and affections, yet truth, which only doth judge itself, teacheth that the inquiry of truth, which is the lovemaking or wooing of it, the knowledge of truth, which is the presence of it, and the belief of truth, which is the enjoying of it, is the sovereign good of human nature. The first creature[9] of God, in the works of the days, was the light of the sense; the last was the light of reason; and his sabbath work ever since is the illumination of his Spirit. First he breathed light upon the face of the matter, or chaos; then he breathed light into the face of man; and still he breatheth and inspireth light into the face of his chosen. The poet that beautified the sect that was otherwise inferior to the rest[1] saith yet excellently well: "It is a pleasure to stand upon the shore, and to see ships

---

1. Bacon's essays appeared in three editions, 1597 (10 essays), 1612 (38 essays), and 1625 (58 essays); we illustrate the considerable stylistic differences between the earliest and latest collections by presenting two versions of "Of Studies." Otherwise, all selections are from the 1625 collection, in which "Of Truth" stands first.
2. See John 18:38 for Pilate's idle query to Jesus.
3. Foolish changeability. "That": those who.
4. Discursive minds. "Philosophers of that kind": the Greek Skeptics, who taught the uncertainty of all things.
5. Restricts, controls.
6. That is, is baffled.
7. Ruby.
8. "The wine of devils"; St. Augustine is probably being cited.
9. Creation.
1. Lucretius's *On the Nature of Things* expressed the Epicurean creed, which Bacon thought inferior because it emphasized pleasure.

tossed upon the sea; a pleasure to stand in the window of a castle, and to see a battle, and the adventures thereof below; but no pleasure is comparable to the standing upon the vantage ground of truth" (a hill not to be commanded,[2] and where the air is always clear and serene), "and to see the errors, and wanderings, and mists, and tempests, in the vale below": so always that this prospect[3] be with pity, and not with swelling or pride. Certainly, it is heaven upon earth to have a man's mind move in charity, rest in providence, and turn upon the poles of truth.

To pass from theological and philosophical truth to the truth of civil business, it will be acknowledged even by those that practice it not, that clear and round[4] dealing is the honor of man's nature, and that mixture of falsehood is like alloy in coin of gold and silver, which may make the metal work the better, but it embaseth[5] it. For these winding and crooked courses are the goings of the serpent; which goeth basely upon the belly, and not upon the feet. There is no vice that doth so cover a man with shame as to be found false and perfidious. And therefore Montaigne saith prettily, when he inquired the reason why the word of the lie should be such a disgrace, and such an odious charge, saith he, "If it be well weighed, to say that a man lieth is as much to say as that he is brave towards God and a coward towards men."[6] For a lie faces God, and shrinks from man. Surely the wickedness of falsehood and breach of faith cannot possibly be so highly expressed, as in that it shall be the last peal to call the judgments of God upon the generations of men, it being foretold that when Christ cometh, he shall not "find faith upon the earth."[7]

1625

Of Marriage and Single Life

He that hath wife and children hath given hostages to fortune; for they are impediments to great enterprises, either of virtue or mischief. Certainly the best works, and of greatest merit for the public, have proceeded from the unmarried or childless men, which both in affection and means have married and endowed the public. Yet it were great reason that those that have children should have greatest care of future times, unto which they know they must transmit their dearest pledges. Some there are who, though they lead a single life, yet their thoughts do end with themselves, and account future times impertinences.[1] Nay, there are some other that account wife and children but as bills of charges. Nay more, there are some foolish rich covetous men that take a pride in having no children, because they may be thought so much the richer. For perhaps they have heard some talk, "Such an one is a great rich man," and another except to it, "Yea, but he hath a great charge of children"; as if it were an abatement to his riches. But the most ordinary cause of a single life is liberty, especially in certain self-pleasing and humorous[2] minds, which are so sensible of every restraint, as they will go near to think their girdles and garters to be bonds and shackles. Unmarried men are

---

2. Topped by anything higher.
3. That is, provided always that this observation.
4. Upright.
5. Debases.
6. *Essays* 2.18.
7. Luke 18:8.
1. Irrelevant concerns.
2. Unbalanced, whimsical.

best friends, best masters, best servants, but not always best subjects, for they are light to run away, and almost all fugitives are of that condition. A single life doth well with churchmen, for charity will hardly water the ground where it must first fill a pool. It is indifferent for judges and magistrates, for if they be facile[3] and corrupt, you shall have a servant five times worse than a wife. For soldiers, I find the generals commonly in their hortatives[4] put men in mind of their wives and children; and I think the despising of marriage amongst the Turks maketh the vulgar soldier more base. Certainly wife and children are a kind of discipline of humanity; and single men, though they be many times more charitable, because their means are less exhaust,[5] yet, on the other side, they are more cruel and hardhearted (good to make severe inquisitors), because their tenderness is not so oft called upon. Grave natures, led by custom, and therefore constant, are commonly loving husbands, as was said of Ulysses, *Vetulam suam praetulit immortalitati.*[6] Chaste women are often proud and froward,[7] as presuming upon the merit of their chastity. It is one of the best bonds, both of chastity and obedience, in the wife if she think her husband wise, which she will never do if she find him jealous. Wives are young men's mistresses, companions for middle age, and old men's nurses; so as a man may have a quarrel[8] to marry when he will. But yet he was reputed one of the wise men that made answer to the question when a man should marry: "A young man not yet, an elder man not at all."[9] It is often seen that bad husbands have very good wives; whether it be that it raiseth the price of their husbands' kindness when it comes, or that the wives take a pride in their patience. But this never fails, if the bad husbands were of their own choosing, against their friends' consent; for then they will be sure to make good their own folly.

1612, 1625

Marriage. The Liturgy of Solemnizing Marriage from *The Book of Common Prayer* (1559) emphasized the purposes of marriage (with procreation primary), the indissolubility of marriage, and the biblical texts undergirding that definition of marriage. It also held up the ideal of mutual love and help, which is represented in this emblem from George Wither's *A Collection of Emblems* (1635). The Latin motto reads in English, "Hand Washes Hand."

3. Pliable.
4. Exhortations.
5. Exhausted.
6. "He preferred his old wife to immortality." Ulysses might have had immortality with the nymph Calypso but preferred to go back to Penelope.
7. Ill-tempered.
8. Pretext.
9. Thales (6th century B.C.E.), one of the Seven Sages of Greece.

Of Great Place

Men in great place are thrice servants: servants of the sovereign or state, servants of fame, and servants of business. So as they have no freedom, neither in their persons, nor in their actions, nor in their times. It is a strange desire, to seek power and to lose liberty, or to seek power over others and to lose power over a man's self. The rising unto place is laborious, and by pains men come to greater pains; and it is sometimes base, and by indignities men come to dignities. The standing is slippery, and the regress is either a downfall or at least an eclipse, which is a melancholy thing: *Cum non sis qui fueris, non esse cur velis vivere.*[1] Nay, retire men cannot when they would, neither will they when it were reason; but are impatient of privateness, even in age and sickness, which require the shadow;[2] like old townsmen, that will be still sitting at their street door, though thereby they offer age to scorn. Certainly great persons had need to borrow other men's opinions to think themselves happy; for if they judge by their own feeling, they cannot find it; but if they think with themselves what other men think of them, and that other men would fain be as they are, then they are happy, as it were by report; when perhaps they find the contrary within. For they are the first that find their own griefs, though they be the last that find their own faults. Certainly men in great fortunes are strangers to themselves, and while they are in the puzzle of business they have no time to tend their health, either of body or mind. *Illi mors gravis incubat, qui notus nimis omnibus, ignotus moritur sibi.*[3] In place there is license to do good and evil, whereof the latter is a curse; for in evil the best condition is not to will, the second not to can.[4] But power to do good is the true and lawful end of aspiring; for good thoughts (though God accept them) yet towards men are little better than good dreams, except they be put in act; and that cannot be without power and place, as the vantage and commanding ground. Merit and good works is the end of man's motion, and conscience[5] of the same is the accomplishment of man's rest; for if a man can be partaker of God's theater,[6] he shall likewise be partaker of God's rest. *Et conversus Deus, ut aspiceret opera quae fecerunt manus suae, vidit quod omnia essent bona nimis;*[7] and then the Sabbath.

In the discharge of thy place set before thee the best examples, for imitation is a globe[8] of precepts. And after a time set before thee thine own example; and examine thyself strictly, whether thou didst not best at first. Neglect not also the examples of those that have carried themselves ill in the same place; not to set off thyself by taxing[9] their memory, but to direct thyself what to avoid. Reform, therefore, without bravery, or scandal[1] of former times and persons; but yet set it down to thyself, as well to create good precedents as to follow them. Reduce things to the first institution,[2] and observe wherein and how they have degenerate; but yet ask counsel of both times; of

---

1. "When you aren't what you were, there's no reason to live" (Cicero, *Familiar Letters* 7.3).
2. "The shadow" of retirement, out of the glare of public life.
3. "Death lies heavily on him who, while too well known to everyone else, dies unknown to himself" (Seneca, *Thyestes* 401–03).
4. Be able.
5. Consciousness.
6. Actions in the world.
7. "And God saw every thing that he had made, and, behold, it was very good" (Genesis 1:31).
8. World.
9. Blaming.
1. Defaming. "Bravery": ostentation.
2. To their original form.

the ancient time what is best, and of the latter time what is fittest. Seek to make thy course regular, that men may know beforehand what they may expect; but be not too positive and peremptory, and express thyself well when thou digressest from thy rule. Preserve the right of thy place, but stir not questions of jurisdiction; and rather assume thy right in silence and *de facto*,[3] than voice it with claims and challenges. Preserve likewise the rights of inferior places, and think it more honor to direct in chief than to be busy in all. Embrace and invite helps and advices touching the execution of thy place, and do not drive away such as bring thee information as meddlers, but accept of them in good part. The vices of authority are chiefly four: delays, corruption, roughness, and facility.[4] For delays, give easy access, keep times appointed, go through with that which is in hand, and interlace not business[5] but of necessity. For corruption, do not only bind thine own hands or thy servants' hands from taking, but bind the hands of suitors also from offering. For integrity used doth the one; but integrity professed, and with a manifest detestation of bribery, doth the other. And avoid not only the fault, but the suspicion. Whosoever is found variable and changeth manifestly, without manifest cause, giveth suspicion of corruption. Therefore, always when thou changest thine opinion or course, profess it plainly and declare it, together with the reasons that move thee to change; and do not think to steal it.[6] A servant or a favorite, if he be inward,[7] and no other apparent cause of esteem, is commonly thought but a byway to close[8] corruption. For roughness, it is a needless cause of discontent; severity breedeth fear, but roughness breedeth hate. Even reproofs from authority ought to be grave, and not taunting. As for facility, it is worse than bribery; for bribes come but now and then, but if importunity or idle respects[9] lead a man, he shall never be without. As Solomon saith, "To respect persons is not good, for such a man will transgress for a piece of bread."[1]

It is most true that was anciently spoken, "A place showeth the man"; and it showeth some to the better and some to the worse. *Omnium consensu capax imperii, nisi imperasset*,[2] saith Tacitus of Galba; but of Vespasian he saith, *Solus imperantium Vespasianus mutatus in melius*:[3] though the one was meant of sufficiency, the other of manners and affection. It is an assured sign of a worthy and generous spirit, whom honor amends.[4] For honor is, or should be, the place of virtue; and as in nature things move violently to their place and calmly in their place, so virtue in ambition is violent, in authority settled and calm. All rising to great place is by a winding stair; and if there be factions, it is good to side a man's self[5] whilst he is in the rising, and to balance himself when he is placed. Use the memory of thy predecessor fairly and tenderly; for if thou dost not, it is a debt will sure be paid when thou art gone. If thou have colleagues, respect them, and rather call them when they look not for it, than exclude them when they have reason to look to be called. Be not too sensible[6]

3. Without debate, as a matter of course.
4. Docility, too great obligingness.
5. That is, do not carry on different businesses at the same time.
6. Change your mind without its being noticed.
7. In his master's confidence.
8. Secret.
9. Irrelevant considerations.
1. Compare Proverbs 28:21.

2. "Everyone would have thought him a good ruler, if he had not ruled" (*Histories* 1.49).
3. "Of all the emperors, only Vespasian changed for the better" (slightly misquoted from *Histories* 1.50).
4. That is, whom promotion improves. "Sufficiency": abilities. "Affection": disposition.
5. For a man to take sides.
6. Sensitive.

or too remembering of thy place in conversation and private answers to suitors; but let it rather be said, "When he sits in place he is another man."

1612, 1625

Of Superstition[1]

It were better to have no opinion of God at all than such an opinion as is unworthy of him. For the one is unbelief, the other is contumely:[2] and certainly superstition is the reproach of the deity. Plutarch saith well to that purpose: "Surely" (saith he) "I had rather a great deal men should say there was no such man at all as Plutarch, than that they should say that there was one Plutarch that would eat his children as soon as they were born"—as the poets speak of Saturn.[3] And as the contumely is greater towards God, so the danger is greater towards men. Atheism leaves a man to sense, to philosophy, to natural piety, to laws, to reputation, all which may be guides to an outward moral virtue, though religion were not. But superstition dismounts all these, and erecteth an absolute monarchy in the minds of men. Therefore atheism did never perturb states, for it makes men wary of themselves as looking no further;[4] and we see the times inclined to atheism (as the time of Augustus Caesar) were civil times. But superstition hath been the confusion of many states, and bringeth in a new *primum mobile*, that ravisheth all the spheres of government.[5] The master of superstition is the people, and in all superstition wise men follow fools, and arguments are fitted to practice in a reversed order. It was gravely said by some of the prelates in the council of Trent, where the doctrine of the schoolmen bare great sway, *that the schoolmen were like astronomers, which did feign eccentrics and epicycles and such engines of orbs to save the phenomena, though they knew there were no such things*;[6] and in like manner that the schoolmen had framed a number of subtle and intricate axioms and theorems to save the practice of the church.

The causes of superstition are: pleasing and sensual rites and ceremonies; excess of outward and pharisaical holiness;[7] overgreat reverence of traditions, which cannot but load the church; the stratagems of prelates for their own ambition and lucre; the favoring too much of good intentions, which openeth the gate to conceits[8] and novelties; the taking an aim at divine matters by human, which cannot but breed mixture of imaginations; and lastly barbarous times, especially joined with calamities and disasters. Supersti-

---

1. Irrational religious practices founded on fear or ignorance.
2. Contempt.
3. Saturn (Cronos), god of time (among other things), was reputed to have eaten all his children, as time does. Many of the sentiments in Bacon's essay come from Plutarch's essay "On Superstition."
4. That is, not looking beyond their own personal lifetimes. The rule of Augustus Caesar (following) was marked by general peace and civil quiet (that is, civilized). In this period of Roman history, many members of the elite no longer believed in the pagan gods, though they participated in the forms of state religion.
5. The prime mover (*primum mobile*) was supposed to control the motions of the other heavenly spheres; superstition is a second (and contrary) mover.
6. "Save the phenomena" means "explain appearances," as did the elaborate theories of pre-Copernican astronomers (epicycles, trepidation, and such concepts). So with the Scholastic philosophers ("schoolmen").
7. The Pharisees were the strict party among the Jews of Christ's time; they taught precise observance of the letter of Mosaic law.
8. Fancies.

tion without a veil is a deformed thing, for as it addeth deformity to an ape to be so like a man, so the similitude of superstition to religion makes it the more deformed. And as wholesome meat corrupteth to little worms, so good forms and orders corrupt into a number of petty observances. There is a superstition in avoiding superstition, when men think to do best if they go furthest from the superstition formerly received; therefore care would be had that (as it fareth in ill purgings) the good be not taken away with the bad, which commonly is done when the people is the reformer.[9]

1612, 1625

Of Plantations[1]

Plantations are amongst ancient, primitive, and heroical works. When the world was young it begat more children; but now it is old it begets fewer: for I may justly account new plantations to be the children of former kingdoms. I like a plantation in a pure soil; that is, where people are not displanted to the end to plant in others. For else it is rather an extirpation than a plantation. Planting of countries is like planting of woods; for you must make account to leese[2] almost twenty years profit, and expect your recompense in the end. For the principal thing that hath been the destruction of most plantations hath been the base and hasty drawing of profit in the first years. It is true, speedy profit is not to be neglected, as far as may stand[3] with the good of the plantation, but no further. It is a shameful and unblessed thing to take the scum of people, and wicked condemned men, to be the people with whom you plant; and not only so, but it spoileth the plantation, for they will ever live like rogues, and not fall to work, but be lazy, and do mischief, and spend victuals, and be quickly weary, and then certify over[4] to their country, to the discredit of the plantation. The people wherewith you plant ought to be gardeners, plowmen, laborers, smiths, carpenters, joiners,[5] fishermen, fowlers, with some few apothecaries, surgeons, cooks, and bakers.

In a country of plantation, first look about what kind of victual the country yields of itself to hand, as chestnuts, walnuts, pineapples, olives, dates, plums, cherries, wild honey, and the like, and make use of them. Then consider what victual or esculent[6] things there are which grow speedily and within the year, as parsnips, carrots, turnips, onions, radish, artichokes of

---

9. The final sentence is directed against Puritan reformers, who loathed ceremonies, traditions, liturgy, and images, which they considered "superstitions."
1. The planting of colonies had been a standard topic of political theory since Plato, with attention focused on such matters as the choice of site, the best mix of population, and the treatment of Indigenous peoples. Sir Thomas More considered the matter in his *Utopia*, and it took on increased practical importance in the narratives of English explorers such as Sir Walter Ralegh, and especially in the early 17th century, When English colonists first settled permanently settler colonies in the New World. Bacon's essay largely avoids the most acute moral issues English colonization was posing: English participation in the brutal African slave trade, and the stocking of "plantations" in Ireland with Scottish Presbyterian settlers (to supplement genocidal policies that were starving the indigenous Roman Catholics). These policies sowed the seeds of slavery in America and civil war in Ireland.
2. Lose.
3. Be consistent.
4. Report.
5. Workers in fine carpentry.
6. Edible.

Jerusalem,[7] maize, and the like. For wheat, barley, and oats, they ask[8] too much labor; but with peas and beans you may begin, both because they ask less labor and because they serve for meat[9] as well as for bread. And of rice likewise cometh a great increase, and it is a kind of meat. Above all, there ought to be brought store of biscuit, oatmeal, flour, meal, and the like in the beginning, till bread may be had. For beasts or birds, take chiefly such as are least subject to diseases, and multiply fastest, as swine, goats, cocks, hens, turkeys, geese, house doves, and the like. The victual in plantations ought to be expended almost as in a besieged town; that is, with certain[1] allowance. And let the main part of the ground employed to gardens or corn be to[2] a common stock, and to be laid in and stored up and then delivered out in proportion; besides some spots of ground that any particular person will manure[3] for his own private. Consider likewise what commodities the soil where the plantation is doth naturally yield, that they may some way help to defray the charge of the plantation (so it be not, as was said, to the untimely prejudice of the main business), as it hath fared with tobacco in Virginia. Wood commonly aboundeth but too much, and therefore timber is fit to be one. If there be iron ore and streams whereupon to set the mills, iron is a brave commodity, where wood aboundeth.[4] Making of bay-salt, if the climate be proper for it, would be put in experience.[5] Growing silk likewise, if any be, is a likely commodity. Pitch and tar, where store of firs and pines are, will not fail; so drugs and sweet woods, where they are, cannot but yield great profit. Soap ashes likewise, and other things that may be thought of. But moil[6] not too much underground, for the hope of mines is very uncertain, and useth to make the planters lazy in other things.

For government, let it be in the hands of one, assisted with some counsel; and let them have commission to exercise martial laws, with some limitation. And above all, let men make that profit of being in the wilderness, as they have God always, and his service, before their eyes. Let not the government of the plantation depend upon too many counselors and undertakers[7] in the country that planteth, but upon a temperate number; and let those be rather noblemen and gentlemen than merchants, for they look ever to the present gain. Let there be freedoms from custom[8] till the plantation be of strength; and not only freedom from custom, but freedom to carry their commodities where they may make their best of them, except there be some special cause of caution. Cram not in people by sending too fast, company after company, but rather harken how they waste,[9] and send supplies proportionably, but so as the number may live well in the plantation, and not by surcharge[1] be in penury.

It hath been a great endangering to the health of some plantations, that they have built along the sea and rivers, in marish[2] and unwholesome grounds.

---

7. Jerusalem artichokes, a species of sunflower having an edible root. "Jerusalem" is a mistranslation of the Italian word for sunflower, *girasole*.
8. Require. "For": as for.
9. That is, as a main dish.
1. Fixed.
2. For. "Corn": grain.
3. Cultivate.
4. Waterpower and wood fires were required for getting iron out of ore. "Brave": excellent.
5. That is, should be tried. "Bay-salt" is a coarse salt obtained by evaporating seawater. "Growing silk" (next sentence): vegetable silk.
6. Labor. "Soap ashes": ashes used for making soap.
7. Investors holding shares in the enterprise.
8. Customs duties.
9. That is, observe at what rate the population declines.
1. That is, by being overpopulated.
2. Marshy.

Therefore, though you begin there, to avoid carriage and other like discommodities,[3] yet build still rather upwards from the streams than along. It concerneth likewise the health of the plantation that they have good store of salt with them, that they may use it in their victuals when it shall be necessary. If you plant where savages are, do not only entertain them with trifles and jingles, but use them justly and graciously, with sufficient guard nevertheless; and do not win their favor by helping them to invade their enemies, but for their defense it is not amiss. And send oft of them over to the country that plants, that they may see a better condition than their own, and commend it when they return. When the plantation grows to strength, then it is time to plant with women as well as with men, that the plantation may spread into generations and not be ever pieced from without. It is the sinfullest thing in the world to forsake or destitute a plantation once in forwardness; for besides the dishonor it is the guiltiness of blood of many commiserable[4] persons.

1625

Of Negotiating

It is generally better to deal by speech than by letter, and by the mediation of a third than by a man's self. Letters are good when a man would draw an answer by letter back again, or when it may serve for a man's justification afterwards to produce his own letter, or where it may be danger to be interrupted or heard by pieces. To deal in person is good when a man's face breedeth regard, as commonly with inferiors, or in tender[1] cases, where a man's eye upon the countenance of him with whom he speaketh may give him a direction how far to go; and generally, where a man will reserve to himself liberty either to disavow or to expound. In choice of instruments, it is better to choose men of a plainer sort, that are like to do that that is committed to them, and to report back again faithfully the success,[2] than those that are cunning to contrive out of other men's business somewhat to grace themselves, and will help the matter in report for satisfaction sake. Use also such persons as affect[3] the business wherein they are employed, for that quickeneth much; and such as are fit for the matter, as bold men for expostulation, fairspoken men for persuasion, crafty men for inquiry and observation, froward and absurd men for business that doth not well bear out itself.[4] Use also such as have been lucky, and prevailed before in things wherein you have employed them; for that breeds confidence, and they will strive to maintain their prescription.[5] It is better to sound a person with whom one deals afar off, than to fall upon the point at first, except you mean to surprise him by some short question. It is better dealing with men in appetite,[6] than with those that are where they would be. If a man deal with another upon conditions, the start or

---

3. Disadvantages, inconveniences.
4. Worthy of compassion. "Destitute": abandon.
1. Delicate.
2. Result.
3. Like.

4. That is, when your business is less than honest, use an ill-tempered or foolish person.
5. Keep up their reputation.
6. Who are hungry; that is, ambitious men.

first performance is all, which a man cannot reasonably demand,[7] except either the nature of the thing be such which must go before, or else a man can persuade the other party that he shall still need him in some other thing, or else that he be counted the honester man. All practice is to discover or to work.[8] Men discover themselves in trust, in passion, at unawares, and of necessity, when they would have somewhat done and cannot find an apt pretext. If you would work any man, you must either know his nature and fashions, and so lead him; or his ends, and so persuade him; or his weakness and disadvantages, and so awe him; or those that have interest in him, and so govern him. In dealing with cunning persons, we must ever consider their ends, to interpret their speeches; and it is good to say little to them, and that which they least look for. In all negotiations of difficulty, a man may not look to sow and reap at once, but must prepare business, and so ripen it by degrees.

1597, 1625

Of Masques and Triumphs

These things are but toys to come amongst such serious observations; but yet, since princes will have such things, it is better they should be graced with elegancy, than daubed with cost. Dancing to song is a thing of great state and pleasure. I understand it that the song be in choir, placed aloft, and accompanied with some broken music,[1] and the ditty fitted to the device. Acting in song, especially in dialogues, hath an extreme good grace; I say acting, not dancing (for that is a mean and vulgar thing);[2] and the voices of the dialogue would be strong and manly (a bass and tenor, no treble), and the ditty high and tragical, not nice or dainty. Several choirs, placed one over against another, and taking the voices by catches anthem-wise, give great pleasure. Turning dances into figure[3] is a childish curiosity; and, generally, let it be noted, that those things which I here set down are such as to naturally take the sense, and not respect petty wonderments. It is true, the alterations of scenes, so it be quietly and without noise, are things of great beauty and pleasure for they feed and relieve the eye before it be full of the same object. Let the scenes abound with light, specially colored and varied; and let the masquers, or any other that are to come down from the scene,[4] have some motions upon the scene itself before their coming down; for it draws the eye strangely, and makes it with great pleasure to desire to see that it cannot perfectly discern. Let the songs be loud and cheerful, and not chirpings or pulings; let the music, likewise, be sharp and loud, and well placed. The colors that show best by candlelight[5] are

---

7. You cannot reasonably make special conditions favorable to you, except in the circumstances noted.
8. All sharp bargaining aims to find out what men are up to or to make use of them. "Discover" (next sentence): reveal.
1. Part-music, for different voices and different kinds of instruments.
2. Bacon's emphasis on dialogue and song (as opposed to dance) is in keeping with the increased emphasis on dialogue in later Jacobean and Caroline masques; dance, however, remains at the center of both early and late masques.
3. Patterns with allegorical or numerological significance.
4. To unmask at the end and come onto the floor, so as to take part in the general dancing (the revels) with members of the court.
5. The Banqueting Hall at Whitehall, the site of many court masques, was lit only by candlelight; viewers complained that some masques were hard to see.

white, carnation, and a kind of seawater green; and oes or spangs,[6] as they are of no great cost, so they are of most glory. As for rich embroidery, it is lost and not discerned. Let the suits of the masquers be graceful, and such as become the person when the vizors are off; not after examples of known attires, Turks, soldiers, mariners, and the like. Let antimasques[7] not be long; they have been commonly of fools, satyrs, baboons, wild men, antics, beasts, sprites, witches, Ethiopes, pigmies, turquets,[8] nymphs, rustics, Cupids, statues moving, and the like. As for angels, it is not comical enough to put them in antimasques; and anything that is hideous, as devils, giants, is, on the other side, as unfit; but, chiefly, let the music of them be recreative, and with some strange changes. Some sweet odors suddenly coming forth, without any drops falling, are, in such a company as there is steam and heat, things of great pleasure and refreshment. Double masques, one of men, another of ladies, addeth state and variety; but all is nothing, except the room be kept clear and neat.

For jousts, and tourneys, and barriers,[9] the glories of them are chiefly in the chariots, wherein the challengers make their entry; especially if they be drawn with strange beasts, as lions, bears, camels, and the like; or in the devices of their entrance, or in the bravery of their liveries, or in the goodly furniture of their horses and armor. But enough of these toys.

1625

Of Studies

[1597 version][1]

Studies serve for pastimes, for ornaments, and for abilities. Their chief use for pastime is in privateness[2] and retiring; for ornament, is in discourse; and for ability, is in judgment. For expert men[3] can execute, but learned men are fittest to judge or censure. To spend too much time in them is sloth; to use them too much for ornament is affectation; to make judgment wholly by their rules is the humor[4] of a scholar. They perfect nature, and are perfected by experience. Crafty men contemn them, simple men admire them, wise men use them, for they teach not their own use; but that[5] is a wisdom without them, and above them, won by observation. Read not to contradict nor to believe, but to weigh and consider. Some books are to be tasted, others to be swallowed, and some few to be chewed and digested; that is, some books are to be read only in parts; others to be read but cursorily; and some few to be read wholly, and with diligence and attention.

---

6. Spangles shaped like the letter "O."
7. The antic dances (presented by professionals) that preceded the main masque dances and represented the vices, follies, or disorders that are to be dispelled with the arrival of the main masques (royal and noble personages).
8. Turkish dwarfs.
9. One form of masque was the "joust," "tourney" (tournament), or "barrier," which chiefly involved knights, who represented allegorical qualities, tilting lances against each other.
1. This version of the essay illustrates Bacon's early epigrammatic, aphoristic style, featuring balance, parallelism, disjunction between sentences, and a curtness that is occasionally cryptic. The 1625 version keeps some aphoristic elements unchanged but provides more connectives and transitions, resulting in a smoother, more flowing style.
2. Private life.
3. Men of experience.
4. Disposition, implying folly.
5. That is, the knowledge of how to use them. "Without" (following): outside.

Reading maketh a full man, conference[6] a ready man, and writing an exact man. And therefore, if a man write little, he had need have a great memory; if he confer little, he had need have a present wit;[7] and if he read little, he had need have much cunning, to seem to know that[8] he doth not. Histories make men wise; poets, witty;[9] the mathematics, subtle; natural philosophy,[1] deep; moral,[2] grave; logic and rhetoric, able to contend.

Of Studies

[1625 version]

Studies serve for delight, for ornament, and for ability. Their chief use for delight is in privateness[1] and retiring; for ornament, is in discourse; and for ability, is in the judgment and disposition of business. For expert men[2] can execute, and perhaps judge of particulars, one by one; but the general counsels, and the plots and marshaling of affairs, come best from those that are learned. To spend too much time in studies is sloth; to use them too much for ornament is affectation; to make judgment wholly by their rules is the humor[3] of a scholar. They perfect nature, and are perfected by experience; for natural abilities are like natural plants, that need pruning by study; and studies themselves do give forth directions too much at large, except they be bounded in by experience. Crafty men contemn studies, simple men admire them, and wise men use them, for they teach not their own use; but that[4] is a wisdom without them, and above them, won by observation. Read not to contradict and confute, nor to believe and take for granted, nor to find talk and discourse, but to weigh and consider. Some books are to be tasted, others to be swallowed, and some few to be chewed and digested; that is, some books are to be read only in parts; others to be read, but not curiously;[5] and some few to be read wholly, and with diligence and attention. Some books also may be read by deputy and extracts made of them by others, but that would be only in the less important arguments and the meaner sort of books; else distilled books are like common distilled waters,[6] flashy things. Reading maketh a full man, conference[7] a ready man, and writing an exact man. And therefore, if a man write little, he had need have a great memory; if he confer little, he had need have a present wit;[8] and if he read little, he had need have much cunning, to seem to know that[9] he doth not. Histories make men wise; poets, witty;[1] the mathematics, subtle; natural philosophy,[2] deep; moral, grave; logic and rhetoric, able to contend. *Abeunt studia in mores.*[3] Nay, there is no stond or impediment in the wit but may be wrought out by fit studies, like as diseases of the body may have appropriate exercises. Bowling

---

6. Conversation.
7. Lively intelligence.
8. That which.
9. Clever.
1. Science.
2. Moral philosophy.
1. Private life.
2. Men of experience.
3. Folly.
4. That is, the knowledge of how to use them. "Without" (following): outside.

5. Attentively.
6. Used as home remedies, without real value.
7. Conversation.
8. Lively intelligence.
9. That which.
1. Clever.
2. Science. "Moral" (following): that is, moral philosophy.
3. "Studies culminate in manners" (Ovid, *Heroides* 15.83). "Stond" (following): stoppage.

is good for the stone and reins,[4] shooting for the lungs and breast, gentle walking for the stomach, riding for the head, and the like. So if a man's wit be wandering, let him study the mathematics; for in demonstrations, if his wit be called away never so little, he must begin again. If his wit be not apt to distinguish or find differences, let him study the schoolmen, for they are *cumini sectores*.[5] If he be not apt to beat over matters[6] and to call up one thing to prove and illustrate another, let him study the lawyer's cases. So every defect of the mind may have a special receipt.[7]

From The Advancement of Learning

[THE ABUSES OF LANGUAGE][1]

Martin Luther, conducted (no doubt) by an higher providence, but in discourse of reason finding what a province he had undertaken against the bishop of Rome[2] and the degenerate traditions of the church, and finding his own solitude being no ways aided by the opinions of his own time, was enforced to awake all antiquity and to call former times to his succor to make a party against the present time, so that the ancient authors both in divinity and in humanity which had long time slept in libraries began generally to be read and revolved.[3] This by consequence did draw on a necessity of a more exquisite travail in the languages original wherein those authors did write,[4] for the better understanding of those authors and the better advantage of pressing and applying their words. And thereof grew again a delight in their manner of style and phrase, and an admiration of that kind of writing, which was much furthered and precipitated by the enmity and opposition that the propounders of those (primitive but seeming new) opinions had against the schoolmen, who were generally of the contrary part, and whose writings were altogether in a differing style and form, taking liberty to coin and frame new terms of art to express their own sense and to avoid circuit of speech, without regard to the pureness, pleasantness, and (as I may call it) lawfulness of the phrase or word.[5] And again, because the greatest labor then was with the people (of whom the Pharisees were wont to say, *Execrabilis ista turba, quae non novit legem*[6]) for the winning and persuading of them there grew of necessity in chief price and request[7] eloquence and variety of discourse, as the fittest and forciblest access into the capacity of the

---

4. Gallstone and kidneys.
5. "Dividers of cuminseed"; that is, hairsplitters. "Schoolmen": Scholastic philosophers.
6. Discuss a subject thoroughly.
7. Cure, prescription.
1. Among the "three distempers of learning" that Bacon proposes to cure in this work, the most important involves "vain imaginations, vain altercations, and vain affectations"; to help explain these he offers a concise history of changes in the language of learned discourse since the Reformation.
2. The pope. "Province": task.
3. Considered. Luther (1483–1546) indeed looked back to the original languages of the Bible and to ancient authors in "divinity" (chiefly Augustine), but he was not involved in the efforts of the humanists (including Erasmus and Sir Thomas More) to revive the classical languages and authors.
4. Classical Greek and Latin, and biblical Hebrew. "Exquisite travail": careful work.
5. The Scholastic philosophers ("schoolmen") used the living Latin of the Middle Ages, wrenching the language yet further from classical norms in applying it to subtle philosophical matters; the humanists denounced the Scholastics' Latin as barbarous and sought instead to imitate classical models, especially Cicero.
6. "This people who knoweth not the law are cursed" (John 7:49).
7. Worth and demand.

vulgar sort. So that these four causes concurring (the admiration of ancient authors, the hate of the schoolmen, the exact study of languages, and the efficacy of preaching) did bring in an affectionate study of eloquence and copy[8] of speech, which then began to flourish. This grew speedily to an excess, for men began to hunt more after words than matter, and more after the choiceness of the phrase, and the round and clean composition of the sentence, and the sweet falling of the clauses, and the varying and illustration of their works with tropes and figures[9] than after the weight of matter, worth of subject, soundness of argument, life of invention, or depth of judgment. Then grew the flowing and watery vein of Osorius, the Portugal bishop, to be in price. Then did Sturmius spend such infinite and curious pains upon Cicero the orator and Hermogenes the rhetorician, besides his own books of periods and imitation and the like.[1] Then did Carr of Cambridge and Ascham with their lectures and writings almost deify Cicero and Demosthenes, and allure all young men that were studious unto that delicate and polished kind of learning.[2] Then did Erasmus take occasion to make the scoffing echo, *Decem annos consumpsi in legendo Cicerone*, and the echo answered in Greek, *one, Asine*.[3] Then grew the learning of the schoolmen to be utterly despised as barbarous. In sum, the whole inclination and bent of those times was rather towards copy than weight.[4]

Here therefore is the first distemper of learning, when men study words and not matter, whereof though I have represented an example of late times, yet it hath been and will be *secundum maius et minus*[5] in all time. And how is it possible but this should have an operation to discredit learning, even with vulgar capacities, when they see learned men's works like the first letter of a patent or limned[6] book, which though it hath large flourishes, yet it is but a letter? It seems to me that Pygmalion's frenzy[7] is a good emblem or portraiture of this vanity, for words are but the images of matter, and except they have life of reason and invention, to fall in love with them is all one as to fall in love with a picture.

But yet notwithstanding, it is a thing not hastily to be condemned to clothe and adorn the obscurity even of philosophy itself with sensible and plausible elocution. For hereof we have great examples in Xenophon, Cicero, Seneca, Plutarch, and of Plato also in some degree; and hereof likewise there is great use, for surely to the severe inquisition of truth and the deep progress into philosophy it is some hindrance, because it is too early satisfactory to the mind of man, and quencheth the desire of further search before we come to a just period; but then if a man be to have any use of such knowledge in civil occasions of conference, counsel, persuasion, discourse, or the like, then shall he find it prepared to his hands in those authors which write

---

8. Copiousness. "Affectionate": affected.
9. Figurative language.
1. Jeronimo Osorio (1506–1580) wrote a history of Portuguese conquests in a flowing style that caused him to be known as the Portuguese Cicero. His contemporary, Johann Sturm, edited texts of Cicero and the Greek rhetorician Hermogenes; his "book of periods" was a rhetorical handbook.
2. Nicholas Carr was professor of Greek at Cambridge; Roger Ascham was tutor to Queen Elizabeth and author of *The Schoolmaster*. Both admired the rhetorical polish of the Roman orator Cicero and the Greek orator Demosthenes.
3. "I spent ten years in reading Cicero." Echo answers, "Ass!" The joke is in the *Colloquies* of Erasmus.
4. Elegant phrasing rather than profundity.
5. More or less, depending on circumstances.
6. Illuminated—that is,—illustrated, as with elaborate initial capitals. Royal grants ("patents") were also engrossed with fancy initial letters.
7. Pygmalion's "frenzy" (delirium) was to fall in love with a statue he had carved of a beautiful woman.

in that manner. But the excess of this is so justly contemptible that as Hercules, when he saw the image of Adonis, Venus' minion, in a temple, said in disdain, *Nil sacri es*;[8] so there is none of Hercules' followers in learning, that is, the more severe and laborious sort of inquirers into truth,[9] but will despise those delicacies and affectations as indeed capable of no divineness.

1605

From Novum Organum[1]

19

There are and can be only two ways of searching into and discovering truth. The one flies from the senses and particulars to the most general axioms, and from these principles, the truth of which it takes for settled and immovable, proceeds to judgment and to the discovery of middle axioms.[2] And this way is now in fashion. The other derives from the senses and particulars, rising by a gradual and unbroken ascent, so that it arrives at the most general axioms last of all.[3] This is the true way, but as yet untried.

* * *

22

Both ways set out from the senses and particulars, and rest in the highest generalities, but the difference between them is infinite. For the one just glances at experiment and particulars in passing, the other dwells duly and orderly among them. The one, again, begins at once by establishing certain abstract and useless generalities, the other rises by gradual steps to that which is prior and better known in the order of nature.

* * *

38

The idols and false notions which are now in possession of the human understanding and have taken deep root therein, not only so beset men's minds that truth can hardly find entrance, but even after entrance is obtained, they will again in the very instauration[4] of the sciences meet and

---

8. "You're nothing holy." Adonis was the lover ("minion") of Venus, deified after his death while boar hunting.
9. Hercules early in life was offered a choice between a life of ignoble ease and sensory delights and one of strenuous virtue. He chose the latter, and so do his followers in learning.
1. *Novum Organum*, or "The New Instrument of Learning," was written not in English but in Latin, for an international scholarly audience. Nonetheless it requires our attention here, as it is the keystone of Bacon's vast project to reform the structure of human learning from the ground up. His reform called for careful observation of all aspects of nature and controlled experiment, but the first part of the book analyzes the stumbling blocks in the way—among them, famously, the various "idols," or delusive images of truth, that lead people away from the exact knowledge of science.
2. The deductive method, associated with Aristotle and the Scholastic philosophers.
3. The inductive method that Bacon here champions.
4. Renovation, renewal.

trouble us, unless men being forewarned of the danger fortify themselves as far as may be against their assaults.

* * *

41

The Idols of the Tribe have their foundation in human nature itself, and in the tribe or race of men. For it is a false assertion that the sense of man is the measure of things. On the contrary, all perceptions as well of the sense as of the mind are according to the measure of the individual and not according to the measure of the universe. And the human understanding is like a false mirror, which, receiving rays irregularly, distorts and discolors the nature of things by mingling its own nature with it.

42

The Idols of the Cave are the idols of the individual man. For everyone (besides the errors common to human nature in general) has a cave or den of his own, which refracts and discolors the light of nature, owing either to his own proper and peculiar nature, or to his education and conversation with others, or to the reading of books, and the authority of those whom he esteems and admires; or to the difference of impressions, accordingly as they take place in a mind preoccupied and predisposed or in a mind indifferent and settled, or the like. So that the spirit of man (according as it is meted out to different individuals) is in fact a thing variable and full of perturbation, and governed as it were by chance. Whence it was well observed by Heraclitus[5] that men look for sciences in their own lesser worlds, and not in the greater or common world.

43

There are also idols formed by the intercourse and association of men with each other, which I call Idols of the Marketplace, on account of the commerce and consort of men there. For it is by discourse that men associate, and words are imposed according to the apprehension of the vulgar. And therefore the fit and unfit choice of words wonderfully obstructs the understanding. Nor do the definitions or explanations wherewith in some things learned men are wont to guard and defend themselves, by any means set the matter right. But words plainly force and overrule the understanding, and throw all into confusion, and lead men away into numberless empty controversies and idle fancies.

44

Lastly, there are idols which have immigrated into men's minds from the various dogmas of philosophies, and also from wrong laws of demonstration.

---

5. Greek philosopher (active ca. 500 B.C.E.) who considered knowledge to be based on perception by the senses and thought that everything was in flux.

These I call Idols of the Theater, because in my judgment all the received systems are but so many stage plays, representing worlds of their own creation after an unreal and scenic fashion. Nor is it only of the systems now in vogue or only of the ancient sects and philosophies that I speak; for many more plays of the same kind may yet be composed and in like artificial manner set forth, seeing that errors the most widely different have nevertheless causes for the most part alike. Neither again do I mean this only of entire systems, but also of the many principles and axioms in science, which by tradition, credulity, and negligence have come to be received.

* * *

59

But the Idols of the Marketplace are the most troublesome of all: idols which have crept into the understanding through the alliances of words and names. For men believe that their reason governs words; but it is also true that words react on the understanding; and this it is that has rendered philosophy and the sciences sophistical and inactive. Now words, being commonly framed and applied according to the capacity of the vulgar, follow those lines of division which are most obvious to the vulgar understanding. And whenever an understanding of greater acuteness or a more diligent observation would alter those lines to suit the true divisions of nature, words stand in the way and resist the change. Whence it comes to pass that the high and formal discussions of learned men end oftentimes in disputes about words and names; with which (according to the use[6] and wisdom of the mathematicians) it would be more prudent to begin, and so by means of definitions reduce them to order. Yet even definitions cannot cure this evil in dealing with natural and material things; since the definitions themselves consist of words, and those words beget others;[7] so that it is necessary to recur to individual instances, and those in due series and order; as I shall say presently when I come to the method and scheme for the formation of notions and axioms.

60

The idols imposed by words on the understanding are of two kinds. They are either names of things which do not exist (for as there are things left unnamed through lack of observation, so likewise are there names which result from fantastic suppositions and to which nothing in reality corresponds), or they are names of things which exist, but yet confused and ill-defined, and hastily and irregularly derived from realities. Of the former kind are Fortune, the Prime Mover, Planetary Orbits, Element of Fire, and like fictions which owe their origin to false and idle theories.[8] And this class

---

6. Custom.
7. Bacon's mistrust of words helped prompt the Royal Society (founded in 1645) to cultivate a plain prose style for scientific communication.
8. The "Prime Mover" was a transparent sphere on the outside of the universe, supposed to move all the other spheres; the "Element of Fire" was an area of pure, invisible fire, supposed to exist above the atmosphere. By "Planetary Orbits" Bacon may be referring to the old notion of crystalline spheres in which the planets were supposed to be set. Obviously, these concepts could be based on no observation.

of idols is more easily expelled, because to get rid of them it is only necessary that all theories should be steadily rejected and dismissed as obsolete.[9]

But the other class, which springs out of a faulty and unskillful abstraction, is intricate and deeply rooted. Let us take for example such a word as *humid*; and see how far the several things which the word is used to signify agree with each other; and we shall find the word *humid* to be nothing else than a mark loosely and confusedly applied to denote a variety of actions which will not bear to be reduced to any constant meaning. For it both signifies that which easily spreads itself round any other body; and that which in itself is indeterminate and cannot solidize; and that which readily yields in every direction; and that which easily divides and scatters itself; and that which easily unites and collects itself; and that which readily flows and is put in motion; and that which readily clings to another body and wets it; and that which is easily reduced to a liquid, or being solid easily melts. Accordingly when you come to apply the word—if you take it in one sense, flame is humid; if in another, air is not humid; if in another, fine dust is humid; if in another, glass is humid. So that it is easy to see that the notion is taken by abstraction only from water and common and ordinary liquids, without any due verification.

There are however in words certain degrees of distortion and error. One of the least faulty kinds is that of names of substances, especially of lowest species and well-deduced (for the notion of *chalk* and of *mud* is good, of *earth* bad); a more faulty kind is that of actions, as *to generate, to corrupt, to alter*; the most faulty is of qualities (except such as are the immediate objects of the sense), as *heavy, light, rare, dense*, and the like. Yet in all these cases some notions are of necessity a little better than others, in proportion to the greater variety of subjects that fall within the range of the human sense.

* * *

62

Idols of the Theater, or of systems, are many, and there can be and perhaps will be yet many more. For were it not that now for many ages men's minds have been busied with religion and theology; and were it not that civil governments, especially monarchies, have been averse to such novelties, even in matters speculative, so that men labor therein to the peril and harming of their fortunes, not only unrewarded, but exposed also to contempt and envy; doubtless there would have arisen many other philosophical sects like to those which in great variety flourished once among the Greeks. For as on the phenomena of the heavens many hypotheses may be constructed, so likewise (and more also) many various dogmas may be set up and established on the phenomena of philosophy. And in the plays of this philosophical theater you may observe the same thing which is found in the theater of the poets, that stories invented for the stage are more compact and elegant, and more as one would wish them to be, than true stories out of history.

---

9. Bacon means "theories" not in the inclusive modern sense, but "abstractions loosely invoked to explain particular facts."

In general, however, there is taken for the material of philosophy either a great deal out of a few things, or a very little out of many things; so that on both sides philosophy is based on too narrow a foundation of experiment and natural history, and decides on the authority of too few cases. For the rational school of philosophers snatches from experience a variety of common instances, neither duly ascertained nor diligently examined and weighed, and leaves all the rest to meditation and agitation of wit.[1]

There is also another class of philosophers, who having bestowed much diligent and careful labor on a few experiments, have thence made bold to educe and construct systems; wresting all other facts in a strange fashion to conformity therewith.

And there is yet a third class, consisting of those who out of faith and veneration mix their philosophy with theology and traditions; among whom the vanity of some has gone so far aside as to seek the origin of sciences among spirits and genii.[2] So that this parent stock of errors—this false philosophy—is of three kinds: the sophistical, the empirical, and the superstitious.

* * *

68

So much concerning the several classes of idols, and their equipage: all of which must be renounced and put away with a fixed and solemn determination, and the understanding thoroughly freed and cleansed; the entrance into the kingdom of man, founded on the sciences, being not much other than the entrance into the kingdom of heaven, whereinto none may enter except as a little child.

1620

From The New Atlantis[1]

[SOLOMON'S HOUSE]

We came at our day and hour, and I was chosen by my fellows for the private access.[2] We found him in a fair chamber, richly hanged, and carpeted under foot, without any degrees to the state.[3] He was set upon a low throne richly adorned, and a rich cloth of state over his head, of blue satin embroidered.

---

1. Bacon's enthusiasm for experiment at times led him to denigrate the value of reason, but what he chiefly opposes here is the excessive concern with logic he finds in the Scholastic philosophers.
2. Guardian spirits of a place.

1. Thomas More's *Utopia* (1516) set a fashion for accounts of imaginary communities with more or less ideal forms of government. Bacon's imaginary community has at its center an account of a research establishment, Solomon's House, that could exist in any society; indeed a version of it was established in England in 1662 as the Royal Society. Bacon's title alludes to the legendary island and ideal commonwealth in the Atlantic Ocean described by Plato in *Critias;* in the 17th century it was sometimes located in the New World. Bacon places his island, Bensalem, in the Pacific, roughly where the Solomon Islands had been discovered in 1568. After an imaginary journey the nameless narrator and his shipmates discover an island cut off from Hebrew and Greek civilization (though given a special revelation of Christianity) and thereby freed to focus on the development of science.
2. Audience with one of the scientific "Fathers" of Solomon's House.
3. Without stairs leading up to the dais.

He was alone, save that he had two pages of honor, on either hand one, finely attired in white. His undergarments were the like that we saw him wear in the chariot;[4] but instead of his gown, he had on him a mantle with a cape of the same fine black, fastened about him. When we came in, as we were taught, we bowed low at our first entrance, and when we were come near his chair, he stood up, holding forth his hand ungloved and in posture of blessing; and we every one of us stooped down, and kissed the hem of his tippet.[5] That done, the rest departed, and I remained. Then he warned the pages forth of the room, and caused me to sit down beside him, and spake to me thus in the Spanish tongue:

"God bless thee, my son; I will give thee the greatest jewel I have. For I will impart unto thee, for the love of God and men, a relation of the true state of Solomon's House. Son, to make you know the true state of Solomon's House, I will keep this order. First, I will set forth unto you the end of our foundation. Secondly, the preparations and instruments we have for our works. Thirdly, the several employments and functions whereto our fellows are assigned. And fourthly, the ordinances and rites which we observe.

"The end of our foundation is the knowledge of causes, and secret motions of things; and the enlarging of the bounds of human empire, to the effecting of all things possible.

"The preparations and instruments are these. We have large and deep caves of several depths: the deepest are sunk six hundred fathom; and some of them are digged and made under great hills and mountains; so that if you reckon together the depth of the hill and the depth of the cave, they are, some of them, above three miles deep. For we find that the depth of a hill, and the depth of a cave from the flat, is the same thing; both remote alike from the sun and heaven's beams, and from the open air. These caves we call the Lower Region, and we use them for all coagulations, indurations,[6] refrigerations, and conservations of bodies. We use them likewise for the imitation of natural mines, and the producing also of new artificial metals, by compositions and materials which we use, and lay there for many years. We use them also sometimes (which may seem strange) for curing of some diseases, and for prolongation of life in some hermits that choose to live there, well accommodated of[7] all things necessary, and indeed live very long; by whom also we learn many things.

"We have burials in several earths, where we put divers cements,[8] as the Chinese do their porcelain. But we have them in greater variety, and some of them more fine. We have also great variety of composts and soils, for the making of the earth fruitful.

"We have high towers, the highest about half a mile in height, and some of them likewise set upon high mountains, so that the vantage of the hill, with the tower, is in the highest of them three miles at least. And these places we call the Upper Region, accounting the air between the high places and the low as a Middle Region. We use these towers, according to their several heights and situations, for insolation,[9] refrigeration, conserva-

---

4. He had made a triumphal entry into the city the previous day, wearing an undergarment of white linen and a black robe.
5. Scarf.
6. Hardenings.
7. Provided with.
8. Clays and pottery mixtures.
9. Exposure to the sun.

tion, and for the view of divers meteors—as winds, rain, snow, hail; and some of the fiery meteors[1] also. And upon them, in some places, are dwellings of hermits, whom we visit sometimes, and instruct what to observe.

"We have great lakes, both salt and fresh, whereof we have use for the fish and fowl. We use them also for burials of some natural bodies, for we find a difference in things buried in earth, or in air below the earth, and things buried in water. We have also pools, of which some do strain fresh water out of salt, and others by art do turn fresh water into salt. We have also some rocks in the midst of the sea, and some bays upon the shore, for some works wherein is required the air and vapor of the sea. We have likewise violent streams and cataracts, which serve us for many motions; and likewise engines for multiplying and enforcing[2] of winds to set also on going divers motions.

"We have also a number of artificial wells and fountains, made in imitation of the natural sources and baths, as tincted upon[3] vitriol, sulphur, steel, brass, lead, niter, and other minerals; and again, we have little wells for infusions of many things, where the waters take the virtue[4] quicker and better than in vessels or basins. And amongst them we have a water which we call Water of Paradise, being by that we do to it, made very sovereign[5] for health and prolongation of life.

"We have also great and spacious houses, where we imitate and demonstrate meteors—as snow, hail, rain, some artificial rains of bodies and not of water, thunders, lightnings; also generations of bodies in air—as frogs, flies, and divers others.

"We have also certain chambers, which we call Chambers of Health, where we qualify[6] the air as we think good and proper for the cure of divers diseases and preservation of health.

"We have also fair and large baths, of several mixtures, for the cure of diseases and the restoring of man's body from arefaction;[7] and others for the confirming of it in strength of sinews, vital parts, and the very juice and substance of the body.

"We have also large and various orchards and gardens, wherein we do not so much respect beauty as variety of ground and soil, proper for divers trees and herbs, and some very spacious, where trees and berries are set, whereof we make divers kinds of drinks, besides the vineyards. In these we practice likewise all conclusions[8] of grafting and inoculating, as well of wild trees as fruit trees, which produceth many effects. And we make (by art) in the same orchards and gardens trees and flowers to come earlier or later than their seasons, and to come up and bear more speedily than by their natural course they do. We make them also by art greater much than their nature; and their fruit greater and sweeter, and of differing taste, smell, color, and figure, from their nature. And many of them we so order as they become of medicinal use.

"We have also means to make divers plants rise by mixtures of earths without seeds, and likewise to make divers new plants, differing from the vulgar,[9] and to make one tree or plant turn into another.

1. Anything that fell from the sky was, in Renaissance terminology, a meteor.
2. Reinforcing, strengthening.
3. Tinctured with.
4. Property (of the substances put into water).
5. Efficacious.
6. Modify.
7. Drying up.
8. Experiments.
9. Ordinary.

"We have also parks and enclosures of all sorts of beasts and birds; which we use not only for view or rareness, but likewise for dissections and trials,[1] that thereby we may take light what may be wrought upon the body of man. Wherein we find many strange effects: as continuing life in them, though divers parts, which you account vital, be perished and taken forth; resuscitating of some that seem dead in appearance; and the like. We try also all poisons and other medicines upon them, as well of chirurgery[2] as physic. By art likewise, we make them greater or taller than their kind is, and contrariwise dwarf them and stay their growth; we make them more fruitful and bearing than their kind is, and contrariwise barren and not generative. Also, we make them differ in color, shape, activity, many ways. We find means to make commixtures and copulations of different kinds, which have produced many new kinds,[3] and them not barren, as the general opinion is. We make a number of kinds of serpents, worms, fishes, flies, of putrefaction, whereof some are advanced (in effect) to be perfect creatures, like beasts or birds, and have sexes, and do propagate. Neither do we this by chance, but we know beforehand of what matter and commixture what kind of those creatures will arise.

"We have also particular pools where we make trials upon fishes, as we have said before of beasts and birds.

"We have also places for breed and generation of those kinds of worms and flies which are of special use; such as are with you your silkworms and bees."[4]

* * *

"For the several employments and offices of our fellows, we have twelve that sail into foreign countries under the names of other nations (for our own we conceal), who bring us the books and abstracts and patterns of experiments of all other parts. These we call Merchants of Light.

"We have three that collect the experiments which are in all books. These we call Depredators.

"We have three that collect the experiments of all mechanical arts, and also of liberal sciences, and also of practices which are not brought into arts. These we call Mystery-men.

"We have three that try new experiments, such as themselves think good. These we call Pioneers or Miners.

"We have three that draw the experiments of the former four into titles and tables, to give the better light for the drawing of observations and axioms out of them. These we call Compilers.

"We have three that bend themselves, looking into the experiments of their fellows, and cast about how to draw out of them things of use and practice for man's life and knowledge, as well for works as for plain demonstration of causes, means of natural divinations, and the easy and clear discovery of the virtues and parts of bodies. These we call Dowry-men or Benefactors.

---

1. Experiments.
2. Surgery.
3. Species. It was commonly supposed that all hybrids were sterile (see following).
4. The narrator continues to describe the various bakeries, vineyards, breweries, and kitchens operated by Solomon's House. He enumerates the medicines discovered there, as well as various experiments with heat. The researchers study light, sound, perfumes, mechanics, mathematics, and all ways of deceiving the senses.

"Then after divers meetings and consults of our whole number, to consider of the former labors and collections, we have three that take care out of them to direct new experiments, of a higher light, more penetrating into nature than the former. These we call Lamps.

"We have three others that do execute the experiments so directed, and report them. These we call Inoculators.

"Lastly, we have three that raise the former discoveries by experiments into greater observations, axioms, and aphorisms. These we call Interpreters of Nature.

"We have also, as you must think, novices and apprentices, that the succession of the former employed men do not fail; besides a great number of servants and attendants, men and women. And this we do also: we have consultations, which of the inventions and experiences which we have discovered shall be published, and which not; and take all an oath of secrecy for the concealing of those which we think fit to keep secret; though some of those we do reveal sometimes to the State, and some not.[5]

"For our ordinances and rites, we have two very long and fair galleries: in one of these we place patterns and samples of all manner of the more rare and excellent inventions; in the other we place the statues of all principal inventors. There we have the statue of your Columbus, that discovered the West Indies; also the inventor of ships; your monk that was the inventor of ordnance and of gunpowder;[6] the inventor of music; the inventor of letters; the inventor of printing; the inventor of observations of astronomy; the inventor of works in metal; the inventor of glass; the inventor of silk of the worm; the inventor of wine; the inventor of corn and bread; the inventor of sugars; and all these by more certain tradition than you have. Then we have divers inventors of our own, of excellent works, which since you have not seen, it were too long to make descriptions of them; and besides, in the right understanding of those descriptions you might easily err. For upon every invention of value we erect a statue to the inventor, and give him a liberal and honorable reward. These statues are some of brass, some of marble and touchstone,[7] some of cedar and other special woods gilt and adorned; some of iron, some of silver, some of gold.

"We have certain hymns and services, which we say daily, of laud and thanks to God for his marvelous works; and forms of prayer, imploring his aid and blessing for the illumination of our labors, and the turning of them into good and holy uses.

"Lastly, we have circuits or visits of divers principal cities of the kingdom; where, as it cometh to pass, we do publish such new profitable inventions as we think good. And we do also declare natural divinations of diseases, plagues, swarms of hurtful creatures, scarcity, tempests, earthquakes, great inundations, comets, temperature of the year, and divers other things; and we give counsel thereupon, what the people shall do for the prevention and remedy of them."

And when he had said this he stood up; and I, as I had been taught, kneeled down; and he laid his right hand upon my head, and said, "God bless thee,

---

5. Bacon allows his scientists considerable autonomy in relation to the state.
6. Tradition credited Roger Bacon, a 13th-century monk, with the discovery of gunpowder.
7. A hard basaltic-type rock.

my son, and God bless this relation which I have made. I give thee leave to publish it, for the good of other nations; for we here are in God's bosom, a land unknown." And so he left me; having assigned a value of about two thousand ducats for a bounty to me and my fellows. For they give great largesses, where they come, upon all occasions.

The rest was not perfected.

1627

GEORGE HERBERT
1593–1633

George Herbert's style in his volume of religious poetry, *The Temple*, is deceptively simple and graceful, especially compared to the learned, witty style of his friend John Donne. But it is also marked by self-irony, a remarkable intellectual and emotional range, and an artistry evident in the poems' tight construction, exact diction, perfect control of tone, and enormously varied stanzaic forms and rhythmic patterns. These poems reflect Herbert's struggle to define his (or his speaker's) relationship to God through biblical metaphors invested with the tensions of relationships familiar in his own society: king and subject, lord and courtier, master and servant, landlord and tenant, father and child, bridegroom and bride, and friends of unequal status. None of Herbert's secular English poems survives, so his reputation rests on this single volume, which was published posthumously. *The Temple* contains a long prefatory poem, "The Church-Porch," and a long concluding poem, "Church Militant," which together enclose a collection of 177 short lyrics titled *The Church*, among which are sonnets, songs, hymns, laments, meditative poems, dialogue poems, acrostic poems, emblematic poems, and more. Herbert describes his collection as "a picture of the many spiritual conflicts that have passed between God and my soul." Herbert's early biographer Izaak Walton reports that Herbert gave the manuscript to his friend Nicholas Farrar, head of a quasi-monastic community at Little Gidding, with instructions to publish it if he thought it would "turn to the advantage of any dejected poor soul" and otherwise to burn it. Fortunately, Farrar chose to publish, and *The Temple* became the major influence on the religious lyric poets of the Caroline age, including Henry Vaughan, Richard Crashaw, Thomas Traherne, Hester Pulter, and the American colonial poet Edward Taylor.

The fifth son of an eminent Welsh family, Herbert (and his nine siblings) had an upbringing carefully monitored by his mother, Magdalen Herbert, patron and friend of Donne and several other scholars and poets. Herbert was educated at Westminster School and at Trinity College, Cambridge, where he subsequently held a fellowship and wrote Latin poetry: elegies on the death of Prince Henry (1612), witty epigrams, poems on Christ's Passion and death, and poems defending the rites of the English church. In 1620 he was appointed "public orator," the official spokesman and correspondent for the university. This was a step toward a career at court or in public service, as was his election as the member of Parliament from Montgomery in 1624. But that route was closed off by the death of influential patrons and the change of monarchs. Like Donne, Herbert hesitated for some years before being ordained, but in

1630 he took up pastoral duties in the small country parish at Bemerton in Wiltshire. Whereas Donne preached to monarchs and statesmen, Herbert ministered to a few cottagers, and none of his sermons survive. His small book on the duties of his new life, *A Priest to the Temple; or, The Country Parson*, testifies to the earnestness and joy but also the aristocratic uneasiness with which he embraced that role. In chronic bad health, he lived only three more years—assiduously performing pastoral duties, writing and revising his poems, playing music, and listening to the organ and choir at nearby Salisbury Cathedral.

Herbert locates himself in the church through many poems that treat church liturgy, architecture, and art—for example, "Church Monuments" and "The Windows"—but his primary emphasis is always on the soul's inner architecture. Unlike Donne, Herbert does not voice fears about his salvation or about his desperate sins; his anxieties center rather on his relationship with Christ. Many poems register the speaker's distress over the vacillations and regressions in this relationship, over his lack of "fruition" in God's service, and over the instability of his own nature. In several dialogic poems the speaker's difficulties are alleviated by the voice of a divine friend heard within or recalled through scripture (as in "The Collar"). In one memorable line, the speaker compares his thoughts to "a case of knives." In poem after poem he has to come to terms with the fact that his relationship with Christ is always radically unequal, that Christ must both initiate it and enable his own response. The final poem in "The Church," "Love (3)," stages this agonistic drama with unmatched, compact power. Herbert also struggles with the paradox that, as the work of a Christian poet, his poetry ought to give fit praise to God but cannot possibly do so—an issue explored in "The Altar," the two "Jordan" poems, "Easter," "The Forerunners," and many others.

Herbert's recourse is to develop a biblical poetics that renounces conventional poetic styles—"fictions" and "false hair"—to depend instead on God's "art" wrought in his own soul and displayed in the language and symbolism of the Bible. He makes scant use of Donnean learned imagery, but his scriptural allusions carry profound significances. A biblical metaphor provides the unifying motif for the volume: the New Testament temple in the human heart (1 Corinthians 3:16). Another recurring biblical metaphor represents the Christian as plant or tree or flower in God's garden, in need of pruning, rain, and nurture. Herbert was profoundly influenced by the genre of the emblem, which typically associated mysterious but meaningful pictures and mottoes with explanatory text. Shaped poems like "The Altar" and "Easter Wings" present image and picture at once; others, like "The Windows," resemble emblem commentary. Other poems allude to typological symbolism, which interprets people and events in the Hebrew Bible (to Christians, the "Old Testament") as types or foreshadowings of Christ. Often, as in "The Bunch of Grapes," Herbert locates both type and antitype in the speaker's soul.

The motto of this emblem by George Wither, "*The* Sacrifice, *God loveth best,* / Are Brokenhearts, *for* Sin, *opprest,*" is also the subject of Herbert's "The Altar."

From The Temple[1]

The Altar[2]

  A broken ALTAR, Lord, thy servant rears,
  Made of a heart, and cemented with tears:
   Whose parts are as thy hand did frame;
   No workman's tool hath touched the same.[3]
5   A HEART alone
    Is such a stone,
    As nothing but
    Thy power doth cut.
    Wherefore each part
10   Of my hard heart
    Meets in this frame,
    To praise thy Name:
   That, if I chance to hold my peace,
   These stones to praise thee may not cease.[4]
15   Oh let thy blessed SACRIFICE be mine,
  And sanctify this ALTAR to be thine.

Redemption[1]

  Having been tenant long to a rich lord,
   Not thriving, I resolvèd to be bold,
   And make a suit unto him, to afford
  A new small-rented lease, and cancel th' old.[2]

5   In heaven at his manor I him sought:
   They told me there that he was lately gone
   About some land which he had dearly bought
  Long since on earth, to take possession.

  I straight° returned, and knowing his great birth,   *at once*
10   Sought him accordingly in great resorts—
   In cities, theaters, gardens, parks, and courts:
  At length I heard a ragged noise and mirth

---

1. The title of Herbert's volume sets his poems in relation to David's psalms for the Temple at Jerusalem; his are "psalms" for the New Testament temple in the heart. All of the following poems come from this volume, published in 1633.
2. A variety of emblem poem. Emblems customarily have three parts: a picture, a motto, and a poem. This kind collapses picture and poem into one, presenting the emblem image by its very shape. Shaped poems have been used by authors from Hellenistic times to Susan Howe.
3. A reference to Exodus 20:25, in which the Lord enjoins Moses to build an altar of uncut stones, not touched by any tool, and also to Psalm 51:17: "a broken and a contrite heart, O God, thou wilt not despise."
4. A reference to Luke 19:40: "I tell you that, if these should hold their peace, the stones would immediately cry out." Herbert's poems obtain much of their resonance from their biblical echoes.

1. Literally, "buying back." In this beautifully concise sonnet Herbert figures God as a landlord, himself as a discontented tenant.
2. That is, to ask him for a new lease, with a smaller rent; the figure points to the New Testament supplanting the Old.

Of thieves and murderers; there I him espied,
Who straight, "Your suit is granted," said, and died.

Easter[1]

Rise, heart, thy lord is risen. Sing his praise
    Without delays,
Who takes thee by the hand, that thou likewise
    With him may'st rise;
5 That, as his death calcinèd° thee to dust,   *burned to powder*
His life may make thee gold, and, much more, just.

Awake, my lute, and struggle for thy part
    With all thy art.
The cross taught all wood to resound his name
10   Who bore the same.
His stretchèd sinews taught all strings what key
Is best to celebrate this most high day.

Consort, both heart and lute, and twist[2] a song
    Pleasant and long;
15 Or, since all music is but three parts vied[3]
    And multiplied,
Oh let thy blessèd spirit bear a part,
And make up our defects with his sweet art.

The Song

I got me flowers to straw° thy way,[4]   *strew*
20 I got me boughs off many a tree;
But thou wast up by break of day
And brought'st thy sweets along with thee.

The sun arising in the east,
Though he give light and th' east perfume,
25 If they should offer to contest
With thy arising, they presume.

Can there be any day but this,
Though many suns to shine endeavor?
We count three hundred, but we miss:°   *misunderstand*
30 There is but one, and that one ever.

---

1. The first three stanzas work out the poetics of writing hymns; then comes the hymn itself.
2. Weave. "Consort": harmonize.
3. Increased by repetition. Harmony is based on the triad, the chord.
4. This evokes the scene of Christ's entry into Jerusalem (Matthew 21:8).

Easter Wings[1]

      Lord, who createdst man in wealth and store,°   *abundance*
        Though foolishly he lost the same,
          Decaying more and more
            Till he became
5   Most poor:
            With thee
          O let me rise
        As larks, harmoniously,
      And sing this day thy victories:
10   Then shall the fall further the flight in me.[2]

      My tender age in sorrow did begin:
        And still with sicknesses and shame
          Thou didst so punish sin,
            That I became
15   Most thin.
            With thee
          Let me combine,
        And feel this day thy victory;
      For, if I imp[3] my wing on thine,
20   Affliction shall advance the flight in me.

Affliction (1)[1]

When first thou didst entice to thee my heart,
    I thought the service brave:°   *splendid*
So many joys I writ down for my part,
    Besides what I might have
5 Out of my stock of natural delights,
Augmented with thy gracious benefits.

I lookèd on thy furniture so fine,
    And made it fine to me;
Thy glorious household stuff did me entwine,
10   And 'tice° me unto thee.   *entice*
Such stars I counted mine: both heaven and earth
Paid me my wages in a world of mirth.

What pleasures could I want,° whose king I served,   *lack*
    Where joys my fellows were?
15 Thus argued into hopes, my thoughts reserved

---

1. Another emblem poem whose shape presents the emblem picture; the lines, increasing and decreasing, imitate flight, and also the spiritual experience of falling and rising. Early editions printed the poem with the lines running vertically, making the wing shape more apparent.

2. A reference to the "Fortunate Fall," which brought humankind so great a redeemer.

3. In falconry, to insert feathers in a bird's wing.

1. Herbert sometimes used the same title for several poems, thereby associating them; editors distinguish them by adding numbers.

     No place for grief or fear;
  Therefore my sudden soul caught at the place,
  And made her youth and fierceness seek thy face.

  At first thou gav'st me milk and sweetnesses;
20   I had my wish and way:
  My days were strawed° with flowers and happiness;   *strewn*
     There was no month but May.
  But with my years sorrow did twist and grow,
  And made a party unawares° for woe.   *unwittingly*

25 My flesh began unto° my soul in pain,   *started complaining to*
     Sicknesses cleave° my bones;   *penetrate*
  Consuming agues° dwell in every vein,   *fevers with convulsions*
     And tune my breath to groans.
  Sorrow was all my soul; I scarce believed,
30 Till grief did tell me roundly, that I lived.

  When I got health, thou took'st away my life,
     And more; for my friends die:
  My mirth and edge was lost: a blunted knife
     Was of more use than I.
35 Thus thin and lean without a fence or friend,
  I was blown through with every storm and wind.

  Whereas my birth and spirit rather took
     The way that takes the town,
  Thou didst betray me to a lingering book,
40   And wrap me in a gown.°   *priest's garb*
  I was entangled in the world of strife,
  Before I had the power to change my life.

  Yet, for I threatened oft the siege to raise,
     Not simpering all mine age,
45 Thou often didst with academic praise
     Melt and dissolve my rage.
  I took thy sweetened pill, till I came where
  I could not go away, nor persevere.

  Yet lest perchance I should too happy be
50   In my unhappiness,
  Turning my purge° to food, thou throwest me   *laxative*
     Into more sicknesses.
  Thus doth thy power cross-bias me,° not making *turn me from my aim*
  Thine own gift good, yet me from my ways taking.

55 Now I am here, what thou wilt do with me
     None of my books will show:
  I read, and sigh, and wish I were a tree,
     For sure then I should grow
  To fruit or shade; at least, some bird would trust
60 Her household to me, and I should be just.

> Yet, though thou troublest me, I must be meek;
> In weakness must be stout.
> Well, I will change the service, and go seek
> Some other master out.
> 65 Ah, my dear God! though I am clean forgot,
> Let me not love thee, if I love thee not.

Prayer (1)[1]

> Prayer, the church's banquet; angels' age,
> God's breath in man returning to his birth;
> The soul in paraphrase,[2] heart in pilgrimage;
> The Christian plummet,[3] sounding heaven and earth;
>
> 5 Engine against th' Almighty, sinner's tower,
> Reversèd thunder, Christ-side-piercing spear,
> The six-days' world transposing[4] in an hour;
> A kind of tune which all things hear and fear:
>
> Softness and peace and joy and love and bliss;
> 10 Exalted manna,[5] gladness of the best;
> Heaven in ordinary,[6] man well dressed,
> The milky way, the bird of paradise,
>
> Church bells beyond the stars heard, the soul's blood,
> The land of spices; something understood.

Jordan (1)[1]

> Who says that fictions only and false hair
> Become a verse? Is there in truth no beauty?
> Is all good structure in a winding stair?
> May no lines pass, except they do their duty°   *pay reverence*
> 5 Not to a true, but painted chair?[2]
>
> Is it no verse, except enchanted groves
> And sudden[3] arbors shadow° coarse-spun lines?   *shade*

---

1. This extraordinary sonnet is a series of epithets without a main verb, defining prayer by metaphor.
2. Clarifying by expansion.
3. A weight used to measure ("sound") the depth of water.
4. A musical term indicating sounds produced at another pitch from the original.
5. The food God supplied to the Israelites in the wilderness (Exodus 16:4–35); it became a Christian symbol for the Eucharist.
6. That is, everyday heaven.

1. The river Jordan, which the Israelites crossed to enter the Promised Land, was also taken as a symbol for baptism.
2. It was the custom for men to bow before a throne, whether it was occupied or not (see Donne, "Satire 3," lines 47–48, p. 907), but to require bowing before a throne in a painting would be ridiculous.
3. That is, that appear unexpectedly (an artificial effect much sought after in landscape gardening).

Must purling° streams refresh a lover's loves?   *rippling*
Must all be veiled,⁴ while he that reads, divines,
10   Catching the sense at two removes?

Shepherds⁵ are honest people: let them sing;
Riddle who list,° for me, and pull for prime:⁶   *wishes*
I envy no man's nightingale or spring;
Nor let them punish me with loss of rhyme,
15   Who plainly say, *My God, My King*.⁷

Church Monuments¹

While that my soul repairs to her devotion,
Here I entomb my flesh, that it betimes°   *while time remains*
May take acquaintance of this heap of dust
To which the blast of death's incessant motion,
5   Fed with the exhalation of our crimes,
Drives all at last. Therefore I gladly trust

My body to this school, that it may learn
To spell his elements and find his birth
Written in dusty heraldry and lines°   *engraving, genealogy*
10   Which dissolution sure doth best discern,
Comparing dust with dust and earth with earth.²
These laugh at jet and marble,³ put for signs

To sever the good fellowship of dust
And spoil the meeting. What shall point out them⁴
15   When they shall bow and kneel and fall down flat
To kiss those heaps which now they have in trust?
Dear flesh, while I do pray, learn here thy stem
And true descent, that, when thou shalt grow fat

And wanton in thy cravings, thou mayest know
20   That flesh is but the glass° which holds the dust   *hourglass*
That measures all our time, which also shall
Be crumbled into dust. Mark here below
How tame these ashes are, how free from lust,
That thou mayest fit thyself against thy fall.

---

4. As in allegory.
5. Conventional pastoral poets.
6. To draw a lucky card in the game of primero. "For me": as far as I am concerned.
7. An echo of Psalm 145:1: "my God, O king."
1. The earlier, manuscript version of the poem does not divide it into stanzas.
2. An allusion to Genesis 3:19: "for dust thou art, and unto dust shalt thou return."
3. Jet (black basalt) and marble are used for tomb monuments. "These": that is, dust and earth.
4. The inhabitants of the tombs.

The Windows[1]

    Lord, how can man preach thy eternal word?
        He is a brittle, crazy° glass,   *flawed, distorting*
    Yet in thy temple thou dost him afford
        This glorious and transcendent place,
5   To be a window through thy grace.

    But when thou dost anneal[2] in glass thy story,
        Making thy life to shine within
    The holy preachers, then the light and glory
        More reverend grows, and more doth win,
10   Which else shows wat'rish, bleak, and thin.

    Doctrine and life, colors and light, in one
        When they combine and mingle, bring
    A strong regard and awe; but speech alone
        Doth vanish like a flaring thing,
15   And in the ear, not conscience, ring.

Denial

    When my devotions could not pierce
        Thy silent ears,
    Then was my heart broken, as was my verse;
        My breast was full of fears
5   And disorder;[1]

    My bent thoughts, like a brittle bow,
        Did fly asunder:
    Each took his way; some would to pleasures go,
        Some to the wars and thunder
10   Of alarms.

    As good go anywhere, they say,
        As to benumb
    Both knees and heart in crying night and day,
        Come, come, my God, O come!
15   But no hearing.

    O that thou shouldst give dust a tongue
        To cry to thee,
    And then not hear it crying! All day long

---

1. From his little parish at Bemerton, Herbert used to walk twice a week across Salisbury Plain to the great cathedral, where he delighted not only in the music but in the stained glass windows. This poem explores how the preacher himself may become such a window.
2. Heat in order to color

1. Unrhymed, as are the concluding lines of each stanza except the last.

My heart was in my knee,
20   But no hearing.

Therefore my soul lay out of sight,
    Untuned, unstrung;
My feeble spirit, unable to look right,
    Like a nipped° blossom, hung   *frostbitten*
25   Discontented.

O cheer and tune my heartless breast;
    Defer no time,
That so thy favors granting my request,
    They and my mind may chime,°   *ring together, agree*
30   And mend my rhyme.

Virtue

Sweet day, so cool, so calm, so bright,
    The bridal of the earth and sky:
The dew shall weep thy fall tonight,
    For thou must die.

5 Sweet rose, whose hue, angry and brave,[1]
    Bids the rash gazer wipe his eye:
Thy root is ever in its grave,
    And thou must die.

Sweet spring, full of sweet days and roses,
10   A box where sweets° compacted lie;   *perfumes*
My music shows ye have your closes,[2]
    And all must die.

Only a sweet and virtuous soul,
    Like seasoned timber, never gives;
15 But though the whole world turn to coal,[3]
    Then chiefly lives.

Man

My God, I heard this day
That none doth build a stately habitation,
    But he that means to dwell therein.
What house more stately hath there been,
5   Or can be, than is man? to[1] whose creation
    All things are in decay.

---

1. Splendid. "Angry": having the hue of anger, red.
2. Concluding cadences in music. This poem has often been set to music.
3. Will be reduced to a cinder at the Last Judgment.
1. Compared to.

>   For man is every thing
>   And more; he is a tree, yet bears more[2] fruit;
>   A beast, yet is or should be more;
> 10   Reason and speech we only bring.[3]
>   Parrots may thank us, if they are not mute:
>   They go upon the score.[4]
>
>   Man is all symmetry,
>   Full of proportions, one limb to another,
> 15   And all to all the world besides;[5]
>   Each part may call the farthest, brother;
>   For head with foot hath private amity,
>   And both with moons and tides.
>
>   Nothing hath got so far
> 20   But man hath caught and kept it as his prey.
>   His eyes dismount° the highest star: *bring down to earth*
>   He is in little all the sphere.°   *the universe*
>   Herbs gladly cure our flesh; because that they
>   Find their acquaintance there.
>
> 25   For us the winds do blow,
>   The earth doth rest, heav'n move, and fountains flow;
>   Nothing we see but means our good,
>   As our delight, or as our treasure.
>   The whole is either our cupboard of food,
> 30   Or cabinet of pleasure.
>
>   The stars have us to bed;
>   Night draws the curtain which the sun withdraws,
>   Music and light attend our head.
>   All things unto our flesh are kind°   *akin*
> 35   In their descent and being; to our mind
>   In their ascent and cause.
>
>   Each thing is full of duty.
>   Waters united are our navigation,
>   Distinguished,° our habitation;   *separated*
> 40   Below, our drink; above, our meat;[6]
>   Both are our cleanliness. Hath one such beauty?
>   Then how are all things neat!
>
>   More servants wait on man
>   Than he'll take notice of; in every path,
> 45   He treads down that[7] which doth befriend him,

2. A textual variant is "no."
3. Man has a vegetable, an animal, and a spiritual nature; he is the only creature that speaks and reasons.
4. Parrots are indebted to us for speech.
5. The notion is of man as microcosm, whose parts all correspond to features of the great world. Compare Donne, Holy Sonnet 5, p. 911.
6. Oceans are valuable for navigation; the earth was created by dividing waters from waters (Genesis 1:6–7); on earth water is drink; from above it provides rain to grow our food ("meat").
7. The herb that will cure him when he's sick.

     When sickness makes him pale and wan.
     O mighty love! Man is one world, and hath
          Another to attend him.

     Since then, my God, thou hast
50   So brave° a palace built, O, dwell in it,   *splendid*
        That it may dwell with thee at last!
     Till then, afford us so much wit,
     That, as the world serves us, we may serve thee,
          And both thy servants be.

Jordan (2)[1]

  When first my lines of heavenly joys made mention,
  Such was their luster, they did so excel,
  That I sought out quaint words and trim invention;
  My thoughts began to burnish,° sprout, and swell,   *burgeon*
5 Curling with metaphors a plain intention,
  Decking the sense, as if it were to sell.°   *for sale*

  Thousands of notions in my brain did run,
  Offering their service, if I were not sped:°   *supplied, satisfied*
  I often blotted what I had begun;
10 This was not quick° enough, and that was dead.   *lively*
  Nothing could seem too rich to clothe the sun,
  Much less those joys which trample on his head.[2]

  As flames do work and wind when they ascend,
  So did I weave myself into the sense;
15 But while I bustled, I might hear a friend
  Whisper, "How wide[3] is all this long pretense!
  There is in love a sweetness ready penned:
  Copy out only that, and save expense."

Affliction (4)

     Broken in pieces all asunder,°   *separate from each other*
          Lord, hunt me not,
          A thing forgot,
     Once a poor creature, now a wonder,°   *marvel, miracle*
5   A wonder tortured in the space
          Betwixt this world and that of grace.

---

1. Compare "Jordan (1)" (p. 1186), and Sidney, *Astrophil and Stella* 1 (p. 541).
2. The "joys which trample on" the sun's head are heavenly joys (line 1).
3. Irrelevant, wide of the mark.

       My thoughts are all a case of knives,
           Wounding my heart
           With scattered smart,°   *pain*
10 As wa'ring pots give flowers their lives.
           Nothing their fury can control,
       While they do wound and pink[1] my soul.

       All my attendants are at strife,
           Quitting their place
15   Unto my face:
       Nothing performs the task of life:
           The elements are let loose to fight,
       And while I live, try out their right.

       Oh help, my God! let not their plot
20   Kill them and me,
           And also thee,
       Who art my life: dissolve° the knot,   *undo*
           As the sun scatters by his light
       All the rebellions of the night.

25 Then shall those powers which work for grief,
           Enter thy pay,
           And day by day
       Labor° thy praise and my relief: *labor for*
           With care and courage building me,
30   Till I reach heav'n, and much more, thee.

The Bunch of Grapes[1]

    Joy, I did lock thee up;° but some bad man   *hold you fast*
         Hath let thee out again,
    And now methinks I am where I began
         Sev'n years ago: one vogue° and vein,   *tendency*
5   One air of thoughts usurps my brain.
    I did towards Canaan draw, but now I am
    Brought back to the Red Sea, the sea of shame.[2]

    For as the Jews of old by God's command
         Traveled, and saw no town,
10 So now each Christian hath his journeys spanned;°   *measured out*

---

1. To pierce or perforate, so as to reveal a contrasting lining (a term from fencing).

1. When the children of Israel had almost lost hope in the wilderness, God inspired Moses to send forth scouts, who returned to report that Canaan was a land of milk and honey. They brought back a bunch of grapes so big they had to carry it between them on a pole (Numbers 13:23).

2. The Red Sea's color suggests blushing for shame. Because the Israelites complained about their long ordeal in the wilderness after leaving Egypt, God drove them back toward the Red Sea.

      Their story pens and sets us down.[3]
        A single deed is small renown.
God's works are wide, and let in future times;
        His ancient justice overflows our crimes.

15 Then have we too our guardian fires and clouds;
        Our Scripture-dew° drops fast;   *manna*
We have our sands and serpents, tents and shrouds;°   *temporary shelters*
        Alas! our murmurings come not last.
      But where's the cluster? where's the taste
20 Of mine inheritance? Lord, if I must borrow,
    Let me as well take up their joy as sorrow.

But can he want° the grape who hath the wine?   *lack*
        I have their fruit and more.
Blessèd be God, who prospered Noah's vine[4]
25   And made it bring forth grapes good store.
But much more him I must adore
Who of the Law's sour juice[5] sweet wine did make,
Even God himself being pressèd for my sake.

The Holdfast[1]

    I threatened to observe the strict decree
      Of my dear God with all my power and might.
    But I was told by one, it could not be;
    Yet I might trust in God to be my light.

5   Then will I trust, said I, in him alone.
      Nay, ev'n to trust in him, was also his;
      We must confess, that nothing is our own.
    Then I confess that he my succor is.

    But to have naught is ours, not to confess
10   That we have naught. I stood amazed at this,
      Much troubled, till I heard a friend express,
  That all things were more ours by being his.
    What Adam had, and forfeited for all,
    Christ keepeth now, who cannot fail or fall.

---

3. The wandering of the Israelites in the wilderness toward the land of Canaan was taken to be a type (prefiguration) of the Christian's trials on the path of salvation.
4. Noah's vine (Genesis 9) was taken as a type of the earth replenished by God after the Flood.
5. The severe rules of the Old Testament as contrasted with the sweeter and more liberal covenant of the New Testament, which Christ's crucifixion established.
1. An allusion to Psalm 73:27 in the Book of Common Prayer: "It is good for me to hold me fast by God." The poem dramatizes the entire reliance on grace—and the abnegation of any human capacity to cooperate with it or claim any merit—that was a cornerstone of Calvinist theology.

The Collar[1]

    I struck the board[2] and cried, "No more;
             I will abroad!
    What? Shall I ever sigh and pine?
    My lines and life are free, free as the road,
5   Loose as the wind, as large as store.
           Shall I be still in suit?[3]
    Have I no harvest but a thorn
    To let me blood, and not restore
    What I have lost with cordial° fruit?   *restorative to the heart*
10   Sure there was wine
      Before my sighs did dry it; there was corn°   *grain*
    Before my tears did drown it.
      Is the year only lost to me?
         Have I no bays[4] to crown it,
15   No flowers, no garlands gay? All blasted?
            All wasted?
    Not so, my heart; but there is fruit,
           And thou hast hands.
    Recover all thy sigh-blown age
20 On double pleasures: leave thy cold dispute
    Of what is fit and not. Forsake thy cage,
           Thy rope of sands,
    Which petty thoughts have made, and made to thee
      Good cable,[5] to enforce and draw,
25   And be thy law,
    While thou didst wink and wouldst not see.
           Away! Take heed;
           I will abroad.
    Call in thy death's-head[6] there; tie up thy fears.
30   He that forbears
        To suit and serve his need,
         Deserves his load."
    But as I raved and grew more fierce and wild,
          At every word,
35   Methoughts I heard one calling, *Child!*[7]
      And I replied, *My Lord.*

---

1. The emblematic title suggests a clerical collar that has become an animal's or an enslaved person's collar; also, punningly, the speaker's choler (anger) and, perhaps, the caller that he at last hears.
2. Table, with an allusion to the Communion table.
3. Always in attendance, waiting on someone for a favor.
4. The poet's laurel wreath, a symbol of recognized accomplishment.
5. Christian restrictions on behavior, which the "petty thoughts" of the docile believer have made into strong bonds.
6. Skull, an emblem of human mortality, often used as an object for meditation.
7. The call "Child!" reminds the speaker of Paul's words that Christians are not in "bondage again to fear," but are children of God, "and if children, then heirs" (Romans 8:14–17).

The Pulley[1]

When God at first made man,
Having a glass of blessings standing by,
"Let us," said he, "pour on him all we can:
Let the world's riches, which dispersèd lie,
    Contract into a span."[2]

So strength first made a way;
Then beauty flowed, then wisdom, honor, pleasure.
When almost all was out, God made a stay,
Perceiving that, alone of all his treasure,
    Rest° in the bottom lay.   *repose*

"For if I should," said He,
"Bestow this jewel also on my creature,
He would adore my gifts instead of me,
And rest in Nature, not the God of Nature;
    So both should losers be.

"Yet let him keep the rest,°   *remainder; repose*
But keep them with repining restlessness:
Let him be rich and weary, that at least,
If goodness lead him not, yet weariness
    May toss him to my breast."

The Flower

How fresh, O Lord, how sweet and clean
Are thy returns! even as the flowers in spring,
    To which, besides their own demesne,°   *domain, demeanor*
The late-past frosts tributes of pleasure bring.
        Grief melts away
        Like snow in May,
    As if there were no such cold thing.

Who would have thought my shriveled heart
Could have recovered greenness? It was gone
    Quite underground; as flowers depart
To see their mother-root, when they have blown,°   *bloomed*
        Where they together
        All the hard weather,
    Dead to the world, keep house unknown.

        These are thy wonders, Lord of power,
Killing and quickening, bringing down to hell

---

1. The poem inverts the legend of Pandora's box, which released all manner of evils when opened but left Hope trapped inside.
2. The short time during which a person lives.

     And up to heaven in an hour,
    Making a chiming of a passing-bell.[1]
       We say amiss
20   This or that is:
    Thy word is all, if we could spell.°   *read*

     O that I once past changing were,
    Fast in thy Paradise, where no flower can wither!
     Many a spring I shoot up fair,
25   Offering° at heaven, growing and groaning thither; *aiming*
       Nor doth my flower
       Want a spring shower,°   *tears of contrition*
    My sins and I joining together.

     But while I grow in a straight line,
30   Still upwards bent,° as if heaven were mine own,   *directed*
     Thy anger comes, and I decline:
   What frost to that? What pole is not the zone
       Where all things burn,
       When thou dost turn,
35   And the least frown of thine is shown?[2]

     And now in age I bud again,
    After so many deaths I live and write;
     I once more smell the dew and rain,
    And relish versing. O my only light,
40   It cannot be
       That I am he
    On whom thy tempests fell all night.

     These are thy wonders, Lord of love,
    To make us see we are but flowers that glide;° *slip silently away*
45   Which when we once can find and prove,°   *experience*
    Thou hast a garden for us where to bide;
       Who would be more,
       Swelling through store,
    Forfeit their Paradise by their pride.

The Forerunners

    The harbingers are come: see, see their mark;
    White is their color,[1] and behold my head.
    But must they have my brain? Must they dispark° *turn out*
    Those sparkling notions which therein were bred?

---

1. The "passing-bell," intended to mark the death of a parishioner, is tolled in a monotone; a "chiming" bell offers pleasant variety.
2. That is, compared with God's wrath, what polar chill would not seem like the heat of the equator?

1. Harbingers rode ahead of a royal traveling party to requisition lodgings, marking the doors with chalk.

  Must dullness turn me to a clod?
 Yet have they left me "Thou art still my God."[2]

Good men ye be to leave me my best room,
Even all my heart and what is lodgèd there:
I pass not,° I, what of the rest become,   *care not*
So "Thou art still my God" be out of fear.
  He will be pleasèd with that ditty;
 And if I please Him, I write fine and witty.

Farewell, sweet phrases, lovely metaphors:
But will ye leave me thus? When ye before
Of stews° and brothels only knew the doors,   *whorehouses*
Then did I wash you with my tears, and more,
  Brought you to church well-dressed and clad:
 My God must have my best, even all I had.

Lovely enchanting language, sugarcane,
Honey of roses, whither wilt thou fly?
Hath some fond lover 'ticed° thee to thy bane?°   *enticed / poison*
And wilt thou leave the church and love a sty?
  Fie! thou wilt soil thy 'broidered coat,
 And hurt thyself and him that sings the note.

Let foolish lovers, if they will love dung,
With canvas, not with arras,° clothe their shame: *fine cloth*
Let Folly speak in her own native tongue.
True Beauty dwells on high; ours is a flame
  But borrowed thence to light us thither:
 Beauty and beauteous words should go together.

Yet, if you go, I pass not;° take your way.   *care not*
For "Thou art still my God" is all that ye
Perhaps with more embellishment can say.
Go, birds of spring; let winter have his fee;°   *due*
  Let a bleak paleness chalk the door,
 So all within be livelier than before.

Discipline

  Throw away thy rod,
  Throw away thy wrath:
    O my God,
  Take the gentle path.

  For my heart's desire
  Unto thine is bent:

---

2. An echo of Psalm 31:14: "But I trusted in thee, O Lord: I said, Thou art my God."

                I aspire
        To a full consent.

        Not a word or look
10   I affect° to own,   *wish, pretend*
                But by book,¹
        And thy book alone.

        Though I fail, I weep:
        Though I halt° in pace,   *limp*
15   Yet I creep
        To the throne of grace.

        Then let wrath remove;
        Love will do the deed:
                For with love
20   Stony hearts will bleed.

        Love is swift of foot;
        Love's a man of war,²
                And can shoot,
        And can hit from far.

25   Who can 'scape his bow?
        That which wrought on thee,
                Brought thee low,
        Needs must work on me.

        Throw away thy rod;
30   Though man frailties hath,
                Thou art God:
        Throw away thy wrath.

Death

Death, thou wast once an uncouth, hideous thing,
                Nothing but bones,
        The sad effect of sadder groans:
Thy mouth was open, but thou couldst not sing.

5   For we considered thee as at some six
                Or ten years hence,
        After the loss of life and sense,
Flesh being turned to dust and bones to sticks.

---

1. That's, in a set manner, by command, or like an actor who follows his playbook.
2. The jubilant song sung by Moses in Exodus 15 calls the Lord "a man of war," but Herbert also alludes to Cupid, another divine archer.

>   We looked on this side of thee, shooting short,
> 10   Where we did find
>   The shells of fledge-souls left behind—
>   Dry dust, which sheds no tears, but may extort.[1]
>
>   But since our Savior's death did put some blood
>   Into thy face,
> 15   Thou art grown fair and full of grace,
>   Much in request, much sought for as a good.
>
>   For we do now behold thee gay and glad
>   As at doomsday,
>   When souls shall wear their new array,
> 20   And all thy bones with beauty shall be clad.
>
>   Therefore we can go die as sleep, and trust
>   Half that we have
>   Unto an honest faithful grave,
>   Making our pillows either down or dust.

Love (3)

> Love bade me welcome: yet my soul drew back,
>   Guilty of dust and sin.
> But quick-eyed Love, observing me grow slack°   *hesitant*
>   From my first entrance in,
> 5 Drew nearer to me, sweetly questioning
>   If I lacked anything.[1]
>
> "A guest," I answered, "worthy to be here":
>   Love said, "You shall be he."
> "I, the unkind, ungrateful? Ah, my dear,
> 10   I cannot look on thee."
> Love took my hand, and smiling did reply,
>   "Who made the eyes but I?"
>
> "Truth, Lord; but I have marred them; let my shame
>   Go where it doth deserve."
> 15 "And know you not," says Love, "who bore the blame?"
>   "My dear, then I will serve."
> "You must sit down," says Love, "and taste my meat."
>   So I did sit and eat.[2]

1. Souls that have left the body and gone to heaven are like fledgling chicks that have left the shell behind; that corpse ("dry dust") sheds no tears but may draw ("extort") tears from the survivors.
1. The first question of tavern waiters to an entering customer would be "What d'ye lack?" (that is, want).
2. In addition to the sacrament of Communion, the reference is especially to the banquet in heaven, when the Lord "shall gird himself, and make them to sit down to meat, and will come forth and serve them" (Luke 12:37).

HENRY VAUGHAN
1621-1695

Born to a family with deep roots in Wales, Henry Vaughan was educated at Oxford and the Inns of Court but returned to his native county of Breconshire at the outbreak of the English Civil War and spent the rest of his life there. He served as secretary to the Welsh circuit courts until 1645; briefly fought for King Charles at Chester, just over the English border; and in his later years took up the practice of medicine without much formal study. In a volume of verse published in 1651, *Olor Iscanus* (The Swan of Usk), he drew attention to his heritage by terming himself "the Silurist": the Silures were an ancient tribe from southeast Wales. Some features of Vaughan's poetry derive from the rich Welsh-language poetic tradition: the frequency of assonance, consonance, and alliteration; the multiplication of comparisons and similes (*dyfalu*); and the sensitivity to nature, especially the countryside around the Usk River.

Some of Vaughan's poetry is secular—*Poems with the Tenth Satire of Juvenal, Englished* (1646), *Olor Iscanus* (1651), and a late-published collection of earlier Latin verse, *Thalia Rediviva* (1678). Vaughan's modern reputation, though, rests almost entirely on his religious poetry. In 1650 Vaughan published his major collection of religious verse, *Silex Scintillans* (The Flashing Flint), expanding it in 1655 to include an additional book. A conversion experience may have prompted Vaughan's turn to religious themes: the title of the book is explicated by the emblem of a flintlike heart struck by a bolt of lightning from the hand of God.

While Vaughan's secular poetry recalls Ben Jonson's, the religious poetry overtly models itself on George Herbert's. In the preface to *Silex Scintillans*, Vaughan refers to himself as one of Herbert's "pious converts." Some twenty-six poems appropriate their titles from *The Temple*, several owe their metrical form to Herbert, and many begin by quoting one of Herbert's lines (compare Vaughan's "Unprofitableness" with Herbert's "The Flower"). Yet no one with an ear for poetry will mistake Vaughan's long, loose poetic style for Herbert's artful precision. Vaughan's religious sensibility also differs markedly from Herbert's. Unable to locate himself in a national Church of England, now dismantled by war, he wanders unaccompanied through a landscape at once biblical, emblematic, and contemporary, mourning lost innocence. One unifying motif of the poems in *Silex Scintillans* is pilgrimage, though the arrival at the destination is typically deferred. Vaughan seems unable to experience Christ as a friend or supporter in present trials, as Herbert so often does; instead, he longs for a full relationship with the divine yet to come, at the Last Day. Despite his restless solitude, however, Vaughan finds vestiges of the divine everywhere. "I saw eternity the other night," he begins his most famous poem, "The World," situating the "ring of pure and endless light" in a specific, quotidian moment of illumination. Eternity hovers tantalizingly over the human world of strife, pain, and exploitation, apparently entirely detached from that world but in fact accessible to God's elect, who soar from earthly shadows into the light. Vaughan's twin brother, Thomas, introduced him to Hermetic philosophy, an esoteric brand of Neoplatonism that found occult correspondences between the visible world of matter and the invisible world of spirits. The influence of this philosophical system, so congenial to Vaughan's sensibility, is most apparent in the poem "Cock Crowing."

From Silex Scintillans

Regeneration[1]

A ward, and still in bonds,[2] one day
    I stole abroad;
It was high spring, and all the way
    Primrosed[3] and hung with shade;
5   Yet was it frost within,
            And surly winds
    Blasted my infant buds, and sin
        Like clouds eclipsed my mind.

    Stormed thus, I straight perceived my spring
10   Mere stage and show,
    My walk a monstrous, mountained thing,
        Roughcast with rocks and snow;
            And as a pilgrim's eye,
                Far from relief,
15   Measures the melancholy sky,
            Then drops and rains for grief,

    So sighed I upwards still; at last
            'Twixt steps and falls
    I reached the pinnacle, where placed
20   I found a pair of scales;
            I took them up and laid
                In th' one, late pains;
    The other smoke and pleasures weighed,
        But proved the heavier grains.[4]

25 With that, some cried, "Away!" Straight° I   *immediately*
            Obeyed, and led
    Full east, a fair, fresh field could spy;
        Some called it Jacob's bed,[5]
            A virgin soil which no
30   Rude feet ere trod,
    Where, since he stepped there, only go
        Prophets and friends of God.

---

1. The poem allegorizes in rather precise Calvinist terms the experience of God's grace calling the elect and distinguishing between the regenerate and the unregenerate.
2. He begins as "a ward" (in his minority under the law of the Hebrew Bible) and "in bonds" (in the Pauline "spirit of bondage" caused by fear of damnable sin).
3. An allusion to the adage that the "primrose path" leads to perdition.
4. He climbs Mount Sinai (tries to live by the Hebrew Bible) but finds his sins and follies far outweigh that effort.
5. Jacob slept in an open field, where he had a vision of a ladder leading to heaven (Genesis 28:11–19); that place, Bethel, was taken as a type or figure for the church. Vaughan's poem "Jacobs Pillow, and Pillar" works out this allegory.

>   Here I reposed; but scarce well set,
>   A grove descried°   *perceived*
> 35   Of stately height, whose branches met
>   And mixed on every side;
>   I entered, and once in,
>   Amazed to see 't,
>   Found all was changed, and a new spring[6]
> 40   Did all my senses greet.
>
>   The unthrift sun shot vital gold,
>   A thousand pieces,
>   And heaven its azure did unfold,
>   Checkered with snowy fleeces;
> 45   The air was all in spice,
>   And every bush
>   A garland wore; thus fed my eyes,
>   But all the ear lay hush.°   *quiet*
>
>   Only a little fountain[7] lent
> 50   Some use for ears,
>   And on the dumb shades language spent
>   The music of her tears;
>   I drew her near, and found
>   The cistern full
> 55   Of divers stones, some bright and round,
>   Others ill-shaped and dull.[8]
>
>   The first, pray mark, as quick as light
>   Danced through the flood;
>   But the last, more heavy than the night,
> 60   Nailed to the center stood.
>   I wondered much, but tired
>   At last with thought,
>   My restless eye that still desired
>   As strange an object brought:
>
> 65   It was a bank of flowers, where I descried,
>   Though 'twas midday,
>   Some fast asleep, others broad-eyed
>   And taking in the ray;
>   Here musing long, I heard
> 70   A rushing wind
>   Which still increased, but whence it stirred
>   Nowhere I could not find.

---

6. Imagery in the following lines—spring, perfumes, flowers—alludes to the Song of Solomon in which the bride is traditionally allegorized as the church or the beloved soul.

7. In the *Song of Solomon* 4:15 the "fountain of waters, a well of living waters" was traditionally allegorized as Christ.

8. An allusion to 1 Peter 2:5, which refers to the faithful as "lively stones." The different sorts of stones and flowers here suggest the elect and the reprobate.

I turned me round, and to each shade
    Dispatched an eye
75 To see if any leaf had made
        Least motion or reply;
    But while I listening sought
        My mind to ease
    By knowing where 'twas, or where not,
80   It whispered, "Where I please."[9]

"Lord," then said I, "on me one breath,
And let me die before my death!"

"Arise O North, and come thou South wind,
and blow upon my garden, that the spices
85 thereof may flow out."[1]

                                                                1650

The Retreat

    Happy those early days! when I
    Shined in my angel infancy.
    Before I understood this place
    Appointed for my second race,[1]
5   Or taught my soul to fancy aught°   *anything*
    But a white, celestial thought;
    When yet I had not walked above
    A mile or two from my first love,
    And looking back, at that short space,
10 Could see a glimpse of His bright face;
    When on some gilded cloud or flower
    My gazing soul would dwell an hour,
    And in those weaker glories spy
    Some shadows of eternity;
15 Before I taught my tongue to wound
    My conscience with a sinful sound,
    Or had the black art to dispense
    A several° sin to every sense,   *different*
    But felt through all this fleshly dress
20 Bright shoots of everlastingness.
        O, how I long to travel back,

---

9. John 3:8: "The wind bloweth where it listeth, and thou hearest the sound thereof, but canst not tell whence it cometh, and whither it goeth, so is every one that is born of the Spirit."
1. Vaughan identifies this verse as Canticles (Song of Solomon) 5:17; it is properly 4:16.

1. The poem alludes throughout to the Platonic doctrine of preexistence, in conjunction with Christ's words (Mark 10:15): "Whosoever shall not receive the kingdom of God as a little child, he shall not enter therein."

       And tread again that ancient track!
       That I might once more reach that plain
       Where first I left my glorious train,
25   From whence th' enlightened spirit sees
       That shady city of palm trees.[2]
       But, ah! my soul with too much stay°   *delay*
       Is drunk, and staggers in the way.
       Some men a forward motion love;
30   But I by backward steps would move,
       And when this dust falls to the urn,
       In that state I came, return.

                                                      1650

Silence, and Stealth of Days!

       Silence, and stealth of days! 'tis now
          Since thou art gone[1]
       Twelve hundred hours, and not a brow[2]
          But clouds hang on.
5   As he that in some cave's thick damp,
          Locked from the light,
       Fixeth a solitary lamp
          To brave the night,
       And walking from his sun, when past
10   That glimmering ray,
       Cuts through the heavy mists in haste
          Back to his day,[3]
       So o'er fled minutes I retreat
          Unto that hour
15   Which showed thee last, but did defeat
          Thy light and power;
       I search and rack my soul to see
          Those beams again,
       But nothing but the snuff[4] to me
20   Appeareth plain,
       That dark and dead sleeps in its known
          And common urn;
       But those[5] fled to their maker's throne,
          There shine and burn.
25   O could I track them! but souls must
          Track one the other,
       And now the spirit, not the dust,

---

2. The New Jerusalem, the Heavenly City (identified with Jericho, the "city of Palm Trees," Deuteronomy 34:3).
1. As indicated in lines 27–28, the poem is on the loss of Vaughan's brother—not his twin brother, Thomas, the Hermetic philosopher, who did not die until 1666, but his younger brother, William, who died in July 1648.
2. Mountain ridge, or forehead.
3. The miner fixes his lamp halfway down the dark shaft, ventures a little beyond it, but then beats a hasty retreat.
4. The burned wick of the lamp or candle.
5. The "beams" (line 18).

>   Must be thy brother.
>   Yet I have one pearl,[6] by whose light
> 30   All things I see,
>   And in the heart of earth and night,
>   Find heaven and thee.

1648   1650

Corruption

>   Sure it was so. Man in those early days
>   Was not all stone and earth;
>   He shined a little, and by those weak rays
>   Had some glimpse of his birth.
> 5   He saw heaven o'er his head, and knew from whence
>   He came, condemnèd, hither;
>   And, as first love draws strongest, so from hence
>   His mind sure progressed thither.
>   Things here were strange unto him: sweat and till,
> 10   All was a thorn or weed:[1]
>   Nor did those last, but (like himself) died still
>   As soon as they did seed.
>   They seemed to quarrel with him, for that act
>   That felled him foiled them all:
> 15 He drew the curse upon the world, and cracked
>   The whole frame with his fall.
>   This made him long for home, as loath to stay
>   With murmurers and foes;
>   He sighed for Eden, and would often say,
> 20   "Ah! what bright days were those!"
>   Nor was heaven cold unto him; for each day
>   The valley or the mountain
>   Afforded visits, and still Paradise lay
>   In some green shade or fountain.
> 25 Angels lay lieger[2] here; each bush and cell,
>   Each oak and highway knew them;
>   Walk but the fields, or sit down at some well,
>   And he was sure to view them.
>   Almighty Love! where art thou now? Mad man
> 30   Sits down and freezeth on;
>   He raves, and swears to stir nor fire, nor fan,
>   But bids the thread° be spun.   *thread of Fate*
>   I see, thy curtains are close-drawn; thy bow[3]
>   Looks dim, too, in the cloud;

---

6. Probably the Bible. The reference is to Matthew 13:45–46, to the merchant who sold all he had to buy a pearl of great price, there likened to the Kingdom of Heaven.
1. God's curse on Adam for eating the forbidden fruit included a curse on the earth: "Thorns also and thistles shall it bring forth to thee" (Genesis 3:18).
2. As resident ambassadors (from heaven).
3. The rainbow, God's covenant with Noah after the Flood (Genesis 9:13).

Sin triumphs still, and man is sunk below
    The center, and his shroud.
All's in deep sleep and night: thick darkness lies
    And hatcheth o'er thy people—
But hark! what trumpet's that? what angel cries,
    "Arise! thrust in thy sickle"?[4]

1650

Unprofitableness

How rich, O Lord! how fresh thy visits are![1]
'Twas but just now my bleak leaves hopeless hung,
    Sullied with dust and mud;
Each snarling blast shot through me, and did share°   shear off
    Their youth and beauty; cold showers nipped and wrung
    Their spiciness and blood.
But since thou didst in one sweet glance survey
    Their sad decays, I flourish, and once more
        Breathe all perfumes and spice;
I smell a dew like myrrh, and all the day
    Wear in my bosom a full sun; such store
        Hath one beam from thy eyes.
But, ah, my God! what fruit hast thou of this?
What one poor leaf did ever I let[2] fall
    To wait upon thy wreath?
Thus thou all day a thankless weed dost dress,
And when th' hast done, a stench or fog is all
    The odor I bequeath.

1650

The World

I saw eternity the other night,
Like a great ring of pure and endless light,
    All calm as it was bright;
And round beneath it, Time, in hours, days, years,
    Driven by the spheres,[1]
Like a vast shadow moved, in which the world
    And all her train were hurled.
The doting lover in his quaintest° strain   most ingenious
    Did there complain;

---

4. An allusion to Revelation 14:15: "And another angel came out of the temple, crying with a loud voice to him that sat on the cloud, 'Thrust in thy sickle, and reap, for the harvest of the earth is now.'"

1. Compare Herbert's "The Flower" (p. 1195).
2. The original printed text reads "yet," emended here.
1. The concentric spheres of Ptolemaic astronomy.

> Near him, his lute, his fancy, and his flights,°   *caprices*
>   Wit's sour delights,
> With gloves and knots,° the silly snares of pleasure,   *love knots*
>   Yet his dear treasure,
> All scattered lay, while he his eyes did pour
>   Upon a flower.
>
> The darksome statesman hung with weights and woe
> Like a thick midnight fog moved there so slow
>   He did nor stay nor go;
> Condemning thoughts, like sad eclipses, scowl
>   Upon his soul,
> And clouds of crying witnesses[2] without
>   Pursued him with one shout.
> Yet digged the mole,[3] and, lest his ways be found,
>   Worked underground,
> Where he did clutch his prey. But one did see
>   That policy:°   *strategy*
> Churches and altars fed him; perjuries
>   Were gnats and flies;
> It rained about him blood and tears; but he
>   Drank them as free.[4]
>
> The fearful miser on a heap of rust
> Sat pining all his life there, did scarce trust
>   His own hands with the dust;
> Yet would not place° one piece above, but lives   *invest*
>   In fear of thieves.
> Thousands there were as frantic as himself,
>   And hugged each one his pelf:
> The downright epicure placed heaven in sense,°   *the senses*
>   And scorned pretense;
> While others, slipped into a wide excess,
>   Said little less;
> The weaker sort slight, trivial wares enslave,
>   Who think them brave°   *fine, showy*
> And poor, despisèd Truth sat counting by°   *recording*
>   Their victory.
>
> Yet some, who all this while did weep and sing,
> And sing and weep, soared up into the ring;
>   But most would use no wing.
> "O fools!" said I, "thus to prefer dark night
>   Before true light!
> To live in grots and caves, and hate the day
>   Because it shows the way,
> The way which from this dead and dark abode
>   Leads up to God,

---

2. In Hebrews 12, the "clouds of witnesses" testified to God's truth in past times. Here, these champions of faith accuse one whose actions deny God.
3. That is, the "darksome statesman" (line 16).
4. That is, as freely as they rained.

55   A way where you might tread the sun and be
         More bright than he!"
     But as I did their madness so discuss,
         One whispered thus:
     "This ring the bridegroom did for none provide,
60   But for his bride."[5]

John Chap. 2. ver. 16, 17

All that is in the world, the lust of the flesh, the lust of the eyes, and the pride of life, is not of the Father, but is of the world.

And the world passeth away, and the lusts thereof, but he that doth the will of God abideth forever.

                                                                    1650

Cock-Crowing[1]

Father of lights! what sunny seed,[2]
What glance of day hast thou confined
Into this bird? To all the breed
This busy ray thou hast assigned;
5   Their magnetism works all night,
        And dreams of Paradise and light.

Their eyes watch for the morning hue,
Their little grain expelling night
So shines and sings, as if it knew
10   The path unto the house of light.
        It seems their candle, howe'r done,
        Was tinned° and lighted at the sun.   kindled

If such a tincture,[3] such a touch,
So firm a longing can impower,
15   Shall thy own image[4] think it much
     To watch for thy appearing hour?

---

5. An allusion to Revelation 19:7–9, the marriage of the Lamb and his Bride, allegorized as Christ and the church or Christ and the regenerate soul: "Blessed are they which are called unto the marriage supper of the Lamb."
1. The poem calls on the Hermetic notion of sympathetic attraction between earthly and heavenly bodies—for example, the cock whose crowing announces the sun's rising because it bears within itself a "seed" of the sun. Vaughan finds here an analogy for the attraction the soul has for its Maker.
2. The opening lines recall a passage from Henry's brother, the Hermetic philosopher Thomas Vaughan: "For she [the Anima or Soul] is guided in her operations by a spiritual metaphysical grain, a seed or glance of light . . . descending from the Father of lights." That term for God is from James 1:17. "Seed," "glance," "ray," and "grain" in line 8 are almost synonymous Hermetic terms for the bit of the sun implanted in the rooster. "Magnetism" (line 5) refers to the attraction between the rooster's "seed" and its source, the sun.
3. Alchemical term for a spiritual principle whose quality may be infused into material things.
4. An allusion to Genesis 1:27: "So God created man in his own image."

        If a mere blast so fill the sail,
        Shall not the breath of God[5] prevail?

  O thou immortal light and heat!
20 Whose hand so shines through all this frame,°   *universe*
  That by the beauty of the seat,
  We plainly see, who made the same.
        Seeing thy seed abides in me,
        Dwell thou in it, and I in thee.

25 To sleep without thee, is to die;
  Yea, 'tis a death partakes of hell:
  For where thou dost not close the eye
  It never opens, I can tell.
        In such a dark, Egyptian border,
30   The shades of death dwell and disorder.[6]

  If joys, and hopes, and earnest throes,
  And hearts, whose pulse beats still for light
  Are given to birds; who, but thee, knows
  A love-sick soul's exalted flight?
35   Can souls be tracked by any eye
        But his, who gave them wings to fly?

  Only this veil[7] which thou hast broke,
  And must be broken yet in me,
  This veil, I say, is all the cloak
40 And cloud which shadows thee from me.
        This veil thy full-eyed love denies,
        And only gleams and fractions spies.

  O take it off! Make no delay,
  But brush me with thy light, that I
45 May shine unto a perfect day,
  And warm me at thy glorious eye!
        O take it off! or till it flee,
        Though with no lily,[8] stay with me!

1655

The Waterfall

  With what deep murmurs through time's silent stealth
  Doth thy transparent, cool, and watery wealth
        Here flowing fall,
        And chide, and call,

---

5. An allusion to Genesis 2:7: "And the Lord God formed man of the dust of the ground, and breathed into his nostrils the breath of life; and man became a living soul."
6. An allusion to Exodus 10:21: brought Moses bringing down the plague of "darkness over the land of Egypt, even darkness which may be felt."
7. See Hebrews 10:20: "By a new and living way, which he [Christ] hath consecrated for us, through the veil, that is to say, his flesh."
8. See Song of Solomon 2:16: "My beloved is mine, and I am his: he feedeth among the lilies."

     5 As if his liquid, loose retìnue stayed
Ling'ring, and were of this steep place afraid,
          The common pass
          Where, clear as glass,
          All must descend,
10   Not to an end,
But quickened by this steep and rocky grave,
Rise to a longer course more bright and brave.°   *resplendent*

Dear stream! dear bank! where often I
Have sat and pleased my pensive eye—
15 Why, since each drop of thy quick° store   *living*
Runs thither whence it flowed before,
Should poor souls fear a shade or night,
Who came, sure, from a sea of light?
Or since those drops are all sent back
20 So sure to thee that none doth lack,
Why should frail flesh doubt any more
That what God takes he'll not restore?
O useful element and clear!
My sacred wash and cleanser here,
25 My first consigner° unto those   *in baptism*
Fountains of life where the Lamb goes!¹
What sublime truths and wholesome themes
Lodge in thy mystical deep streams!
Such as dull man can never find
30 Unless that Spirit lead his mind
Which first upon thy face did move
And hatched all with his quickening love.²
As this loud brook's incessant fall
In streaming rings restagnates° all   *makes still again*
35 Which reach by course the bank, and then
Are no more seen, just so pass men.
Oh my invisible estate,
My glorious liberty,³ still late!
Thou art the channel my soul seeks,
40 Not this with cataracts and creeks.

                                      1655

Quickness

False life! a foil and no more, when
            Wilt thou be gone?
Thou foul deception of all men
That would not have the true come on.

---

1. See Revelation 7:17: "For the Lamb . . . shall lead them unto living fountains of waters."
2. An allusion to Genesis 1:2: "And the Spirit of God moved upon the face of the waters." The Latin Vulgate version, *incubabant*, is closer to Vaughan's "hatched" than to "moved."
3. An allusion to Romans 8:21, promising deliverance "from the bondage of corruption into the glorious liberty of the children of God."

⁵ Thou art a moon-like toil; a blind
                    Self-posing state;
A dark contest of waves and wind;
A mere tempestuous debate.

Life is a fixed, discerning light,
                    A knowing joy;
No chance, or fit, but ever bright,
And calm and full, yet doth not cloy.°   *obstruct*

'Tis such a blissful thing, that still
                    Doth vivify,
¹⁵ And shine and smile and hath the skill
To please without eternity.

Thou art a toilsome mole,° or less,   *hardworking*
                    A moving mist.
But life is what none can express,
²⁰ A *quickness*° which my God hath kissed.   *life, vital principle*

1655

RICHARD CRASHAW
ca. 1613–1649

Steps to the Temple (1646, 1648), the title of Richard Crashaw's collection of sacred poetry, clearly acknowledges George Herbert's primacy among devotional poets. Yet Crashaw is no mere imitator. A Roman Catholic convert, Crashaw was profoundly influenced by the Counter-Reformation, which reacted against Protestant austerity by linking heightened spirituality to vivid bodily experiences. He is the only major English poet in the tradition of the Continental baroque, a movement in literature and visual art that developed out of the Counter-Reformation. Baroque style is exuberant, sensuous, and elaborately ornamented, and it deliberately strains decorum, challenging formal restraints and generic limitations. Crashaw's favorite subjects are typical of baroque art: the infant Jesus surrounded by angels and cherubs; the crucified Savior, streaming blood; the sorrowful Virgin; the tearfully penitent Mary Magdalen; saintly martyrs wracked with ecstasy and pain. Although some consider his images grotesque, Crashaw is alone among English poets in rendering the experience of rapture and religious ecstasy.

The son of a bibliophile and anti-Catholic Church of England polemicist, Crashaw was educated at Pembroke College, Cambridge, where he became an adherent of Laudian Anglicanism. In 1636 he was elected a fellow of Peterhouse, another Cambridge college. By 1639 he had become a priest of the Church of England, curate of Little St. Mary's, and a college lecturer. A contemporary wrote that his sermons "ravished more like poems," but apparently none survive. Crashaw called Peterhouse his "little contentful kingdom": his friends included the poet Abraham Cowley and George Herbert's literary executor Nicholas Ferrar, the founder of the Anglican monastic community Little Gidding. In 1643 the Puritans occupied Cambridge, violently disrupting Crashaw's life there. He fled to Paris and to the English court in exile, becoming a Roman Catholic in 1645. He was saved from destitution by obtaining various minor posts through the influence of Queen Henrietta Maria, the last one at Loreto—thought to be Jesus's house at Nazareth, miraculously transported to Italy.

Crashaw's Latin epigrams, published as *Epigrammatum Sacrorum Liber* (1634), were much influenced by Jesuit epigram style. In their Latin and later English versions, they are characterized by puns, paradoxes, and startling—even bizarre—metaphors. In one poem, Crashaw compares Christ's pierced side to a "purple wardrobe" in which Christians can find the proper garments for clothing themselves. In 1646 Crashaw published the first version of *Steps to the Temple*, along with a secular collection of poems titled *Delights of the Muses*, with the royalist publisher Humphrey Moseley. (Moseley published Milton's *Poems* [1645], among many other works.) A second edition appeared in 1648.

Crashaw constantly revised his religious poems. His posthumous volume, *Carmen Deo Nostro* (Hymn to Our Lord, 1652), includes emblems he may have executed himself, including the padlocked heart prefixed to a poem urging the Countess of Denbigh to convert to Catholicism. Especially notable are the final versions of several hymns, particularly the praise of St. Theresa in "The Flaming Heart."

From Steps to the Temple

Divine Epigrams

Acts 8. On the Baptized Aethiopian[1]

     Let it no longer be a forlorn hope
     To wash an Ethiope:
     He's washed, his gloomy skin a peaceful shade
     For his white soul is made:
5   And now, I doubt not, the eternal dove,°   Holy Spirit
     A black-faced house will love.

1646

To the Infant Martyrs[1]

     Go, smiling souls, your new-built cages° break: their bodies
     In heaven you'll learn to sing, ere here to speak.[2]
     Nor let the milky fonts that bathe your thirst
                     Be your delay;
5   The place that calls you hence is, at the worst,
                     Milk all the way.[3]

1646

---

1. This epigram and the four that follow were originally written in Latin in a volume of "sacred epigrams," and then rendered by Crashaw in English versions. Epigrams are brief, pithy, witty poems with, as was often said, "A sting in the tail." This poem refers to Acts 8, when Philip meets "an eunuch of great authority under the queen of the Ethiopians, who had the charge of all her treasure, and had come to Jerusalem to worship" (Acts 8:27). Philip baptizes the Ethiopian (Acts 8:38). Crashaw combines this biblical story with the proverb about washing the Ethiopian white (see the illustration on p. 1213).

1. This poem addresses the Holy Innocents, the infants murdered by Herod in an effort to destroy the newborn Jesus, who was honored as King of the Jews by the Magi (Matthew 2:16–18).
2. "Infant" comes from the Latin *infans*, meaning "unable to speak."
3. The Milky Way will replace their mothers' milk.

"Baptized Aethiopian." Geffrey Whitney's emblem "Aethiopem lavare" ("to wash an Ethiope"), from *A Choice of Emblems* (1586), was a proverb for impossibility. Crashaw refers to this proverb in "On the Baptized Aethiopian."

I Am the Door[1]

    And now th' art set wide ope, the spear's sad art,
    Lo! hath unlocked thee at the very heart;
        He to himself (I fear the worst)
            And his own hope
5   Hath shut these doors of heaven, that durst
            Thus set them ope.

                                                      1646

Luke 11.[27][1]
Blessed be the paps which Thou hast sucked

    Suppose he had been tabled at thy teats,
      Thy hunger feels not what he eats:
    He'll have his teat e're long (a bloody one)[2]
      The Mother then must suck the Son.

                                                      1646

---

1. "I am the door; by me if any man enter in, he shall be saved" (John 10:9).
1. The verse (Luke 11:27) identifies the addressee: "And it came to pass, as he [Jesus] spake these things, a certain woman of the company lifted up her voice, and said unto him, 'Blessed is the womb that bare thee, and the paps which thou hast sucked.'"
2. The wound in Christ's side, making his breast (the fountain of all graces) bloody.

On the Wounds of Our Crucified Lord

O these wakeful wounds of thine!
    Are they mouths? or are they eyes?
Be they mouths, or be they eyne,[1]
    Each bleeding part some one supplies.[2]

5 Lo! a mouth, whose full-bloomed lips
    At too dear a rate are roses.
Lo! a bloodshot eye! that weeps
    And many a cruel tear discloses.

O thou that on this foot hast laid
10   Many a kiss and many a tear,
Now thou shalt have all repaid,
    Whatsoe'er thy charges were.

This foot hath got a mouth and lips
    To pay the sweet sum of thy kisses;
15 To pay thy tears, an eye that weeps
    Instead of tears such gems as this is.

The difference only this appears
    (Nor can the change offend),
The debt is paid in ruby-tears
20   Which thou in pearls didst lend.

1646

On Our Crucified Lord Naked and Bloody

Th' have left thee naked, Lord, O that they had;
This garment too I would they had denied.
Thee with thy self they have too richly clad,
Opening the purple wardrobe of thy side.[1]
5 O never could be found garments too good
For thee to wear, but these, of thine own blood.

1646

---

1. Eyes (an old plural form).
2. That is, each wound of Christ is either an eye or a mouth.

1. In the Gospels, the soldiers dress Jesus in a purple robe and crown of thorns on the way to his crucifixion, and divide his clothes among themselves after he is dead. In John 19:34, one of the soldiers pierces the crucified Jesus's side with a spear, and blood and water come out.

Carmen Deo Nostro

The Flaming Heart St. Teresa of Avila, a sixteenth-century Spanish mystic and founder of an ascetic order of barefoot Carmelite nuns, was one of the great figures of the Catholic Reformation. Her autobiography, popular throughout Europe and translated into English in 1642 as *The Flaming Heart*, describes not only her practical problems in establishing her order but also a series of ecstatic trances and visitations that represent union with the divine in sensual, indeed erotic, imagery. The Italian sculptor and architect Gianlorenzo Bernini portrayed a mystical experience described in the autobiography in a stunning baroque statue still in the church of Santa Maria della Vittoria, in Rome. It shows the saint in an attitude of ecstatic, swooning abandonment while a juvenile seraph stands over her, about to plunge a golden arrow into her heart. Crashaw may or may not have seen this statue while Bernini was at work on it (it was installed after Crashaw's death), but his poem—published posthumously in *Carmen Deo Nostro* (Hymn to Our Lord, 1652)—addresses a painter who produced a picture of this episode conceived much as Bernini presented it.

THE
FLAMING HEART
UPON THE BOOK AND
Picture of the seraphical saint
TERESA,
(AS SHE IS USUALLY EX-
pressed with a SERAPHIM
beside her.)[1]

    Well-meaning readers! you that come as friends,
    And catch the precious name this piece pretends,°   *puts forward*
    Make not too much haste to admire
    That fair-cheeked fallacy of fire.
5 That is a seraphim, they say,
    And this the great Teresia.
    Readers, be ruled by me, and make
    Here a well-placed and wise mistake:
    You must transpose the picture quite
10 And spell° it wrong to read° it right;   *read / understand*
    Read *him* for *her* and *her* for *him*,
    And call the saint the seraphim.
       Painter, what didst thou understand,
    To put her dart into his hand!
15 See, even the years and size of him
    Shows this the mother seraphim.
    This is the mistress-flame; and duteous he,
    Her happy fireworks here comes down to see.
    O most poor-spirited of men!
20 Had thy cold pencil kissed her pen[2]
    Thou couldst not so unkindly err
    To show us this faint shade for her.
    Why, man, this speaks pure mortal frame,
    And mocks with female frost love's manly flame.
25 One would suspect thou meant'st to paint
    Some weak, inferior, woman saint.
    But had thy pale-faced purple took
    Fire from the burning cheeks of that bright book,
    Thou wouldst on her have heaped up all
30 That could be found seraphical:

---

1. "Seraphim" is in fact the plural form of "seraph." This highest order of angels was thought to burn continuously in the fire of divine love.

2. That is, if you had only been properly inspired by her book.

       Whate'er this youth of fire wears fair,
       Rosy fingers, radiant hair,
       Glowing cheek and glistering wings,
       All those fair and flagrant° things,   *burning*
35   But before all, that fiery dart
       Had filled the hand of this great heart.
         Do then as equal right requires,
       Since his the blushes be, and hers the fires,
       Resume and rectify thy rude design,
40   Undress thy seraphim into mine.
       Redeem this injury of thy art,
       Give him the veil, give her the dart.
         Give him the veil, that he may cover
       The red cheeks° of a rivaled lover,   *blushes*
45   Ashamed that our world now can show
       Nests of new seraphims here below.[3]
         Give her the dart, for it is she
       (Fair youth) shoots both thy shaft and thee.
       Say, all ye wise and well-pierced hearts
50   That live and die amidst her darts,°   *her writings*
       What is 't your tasteful spirits do prove°   *experience*
       In that rare life of her and love?
       Say and bear witness. Sends she not
       A seraphim at every shot?
55   What magazines of immortal arms there shine!
       Heaven's great artillery in each love-spun line.
       Give then the dart to her who gives the flame,
       Give him the veil who kindly takes the shame.
         But if it be the frequent fate
60   Of worst faults to be fortunate;
       If all's prescription,[4] and proud wrong
       Hearkens not to an humble song,
       For all the gallantry of him,
       Give me the suffering seraphim.[5]
65   His be the bravery° of all those bright things,   *splendor*
       The glowing cheeks, the glistering wings,
       The rosy hand, the radiant dart;
       Leave her alone the Flaming Heart.
         Leave her that, and thou shalt leave her
70   Not one loose shaft, but love's whole quiver.
       For in love's field was never found
       A nobler weapon than a wound.
       Love's passives are his activ'st part,
       The wounded is the wounding heart.
75   O heart! the equal poise of love's both parts,
       Big alike with wounds and darts,

---

3. Teresa burns on earth in love, as seraphim do in heaven.
4. That is, settled beforehand, by the decision of the artist.
5. If Teresa can't be transformed into the angel, Crashaw prefers her as the "suffering" lover.

Live in these conquering leaves,[6] live all the same;
And walk through all tongues one triumphant flame.
Live here, great heart; and love and die and kill,
And bleed and wound; and yield and conquer still.
Let this immortal life, where'er it comes,
Walk in a crowd of loves and martyrdoms.
Let mystic deaths wait on 't, and wise souls be
The love-slain witnesses of this life of thee.
O sweet incendiary! show here thy art,
Upon this carcass of a hard, cold heart;°   *Crashaw's heart*
Let all thy scattered shafts of light, that play
Among the leaves of thy large books of day,[7]
Combined against this breast, at once break in
And take away from me myself and sin!
This gracious robbery shall thy bounty be,
And my best fortunes such fair spoils of me.[8]
O thou undaunted daughter of desires!
By all thy dower of lights and fires;
By all the eagle in thee, all the dove;[9]
By all thy lives and deaths of love;
By thy large drafts of intellectual day,
And by thy thirsts of love more large than they;
By all thy brim-filled bowls of fierce desire,
By thy last morning's draft of liquid fire;
By the full kingdom of that final kiss
That seized thy parting soul, and sealed thee His;
By all the heavens thou hast in Him,
Fair sister of the seraphim,
By all of Him we have in thee,
Leave nothing of myself in me!
Let me so read thy life that I
Unto all life of mine may die!

1652

---

6. That is, the leaves of St. Teresa's book.
7. Books filled with intellectual and spiritual light.
8. That is, my best fortune will be to be despoiled in this way.
9. The eagle suggests wisdom and power, for its lofty flight and ability to look into the sun's eye; the dove suggests mercy and gentleness. Compare Donne's "The Canonization," line 22 (p. 890).

ROBERT HERRICK
1591–1674

Born in London the son of a goldsmith and apprenticed for some years in that craft, Herrick was educated at Cambridge and consorted in the early 1620s with Ben Jonson and his "tribe" of literary young men who met regularly to exchange and discuss their poetry. After his ordination in 1623, Herrick apparently served as chaplain to various noblemen and in that role joined the failed military expedition led by George Villiers, the Duke of Buckingham, to rescue French Protestants from La Rochelle in 1627. In 1630 he was installed as the vicar of Dean Prior in Devonshire. Expelled as a royalist in 1647, he probably lived in London until the Restoration, when he was reinstated at Dean Prior and remained there until his death.

Herrick's single volume of poems, *Hesperides* (1648), with its appended book of religious poems, *Noble Numbers*, contains 1,400 short poems (1,129 in *Hesperides*, and 271 in *Noble Numbers*). Many are love poems on the *carpe diem* theme—seize the day, time is fleeting, make love now; a famous example is "To the Virgins, to Make Much of Time." But Herrick's range is wider than is sometimes recognized. He moves from the pastoral to the cynical, from an almost rococo elegance to vulgar epigrams. Certain motifs recur in his work. One is "times trans-shifting," the transience of all natural things; another is traditional ceremonies, such as rural harvest festivals ("The Hock Cart") or the May Day rituals described in what is perhaps his finest poem, "Corinna's Going A-Maying"; yet another is the classical but also perennial ideal of the "good life." For Herrick a good life involves love devoid of high passion (the several mistresses he addresses seem interchangeable and not very real); the pleasures of food, drink, and song; delight in the beauty of surfaces (as in "Upon Julia's Clothes"); and, above all, the creation of poetry as a bulwark against the ravages of time. Herrick knows Jonson's poetry well, but his epigrams and lyrics (like Jonson's) also show the direct influence of classical poets: Horace, Anacreon, Catullus, Tibullus, Ovid, and Martial.

Published just months before the execution of Charles I, Herrick's poems can seem merely playful and charming, almost oblivious to the catastrophes of the war. But they are not. Poems celebrating rituals of good fellowship reinforce the conservative values of social stability, tradition, and order threatened by Puritans and revolutionaries. Several poems that draw on the Celtic mythology of fairy folk make their feasts, temples, worship, and ceremonies stand in for the forbidden ceremonies of the Laudian church and a life governed by ritual. Still others, like "The Hock Cart" and "Corinna's Going A-Maying," extol the kind of rural festivals that were at the center of the culture wars between royalists and Puritans. Both James I and Charles I urged such activities in their *Book of Sports* as a means of reinforcing traditional institutions in the countryside and deflecting discontent, while Puritans vigorously opposed them as occasions for drunkenness and licentiousness.

From Hesperides[1]

The Argument[2] of His Book

I sing of brooks, of blossoms, birds, and bowers,
Of April, May, of June, and July flowers.
I sing of Maypoles, hock carts, wassails, wakes,[3]
Of bridegrooms, brides, and of their bridal cakes.
5 I write of youth, of love, and have access
By these to sing of cleanly wantonness.
I sing of dews, of rains, and, piece by piece,
Of balm, of oil, of spice, and ambergris.[4]
I sing of times trans-shifting,° and I write   *changing*
10 How roses first came red and lilies white.
I write of groves, of twilights, and I sing
The court of Mab and of the fairy king.[5]
I write of hell; I sing (and ever shall)
Of heaven, and hope to have it after all.

Upon the Loss of His Mistresses[1]

I have lost, and lately, these
Many dainty mistresses:
Stately Julia, prime of all;
Sappho next, a principal;
5 Smooth Anthea, for a skin
White and heaven-like crystalline;
Sweet Electra, and the choice
Myrrha, for the lute and voice;
Next Corinna for her wit
10 And the graceful use of it,
With Perilla; all are gone,
Only Herrick's left alone,
For to number sorrows by
Their departures hence, and die.

---

1. In myth, the Hesperides, or Western Maidens, guarded an orchard and a garden, also called Hesperides, in which grew a tree bearing golden apples. Herrick's title suggests that his poems are golden apples from his residence in western Devonshire; the following poems are all from that volume, published in 1648.
2. Subject matter, theme.
3. Festive, not funerary, occasions, to celebrate the dedication of a new church. "Hock carts" carried home the last load of the harvest, so they were adorned and celebrated. "Wassails" were Twelfth Night celebrations.
4. A secretion of the sperm whale that is used in making perfume—hence it suggests something rare and delectable.
5. Mab was queen of the fairies and wife of their king, Oberon.

1. The ladies are imaginary, and their names are traditional in classical love poetry and pastoral poetry.

The Vine

    I dreamed this mortal part of mine
    Was metamorphosed to a vine,
    Which, crawling one and every way,
    Enthralled my dainty Lucia.[1]
5 Methought, her long small legs and thighs
    I with my tendrils did surprise;
    Her belly, buttocks, and her waist
    By my soft nervelets were embraced.
    About her head I writhing hung,
10 And with rich clusters (hid among
    The leaves) her temples I behung,
    So that my Lucia seemed to me
    Young Bacchus ravished by his tree.°   *the grapevine*
    My curls about her neck did crawl,
15 And arms and hands they did enthrall,
    So that she could not freely stir
    (All parts there made one prisoner).
    But when I crept with leaves to hide
    Those parts which maids keep unespied,
20 Such fleeting pleasures there I took
    That with the fancy I awoke,
    And found (ah me!) this flesh of mine
    More like a stock° than like a vine.   *hard stalk*

Dreams

    Here we are all, by day; by night, we're hurled
    By dreams, each one into a several° world.   *separate*

Delight in Disorder[1]

    A sweet disorder in the dress
    Kindles in clothes a wantonness.
    A lawn° about the shoulders thrown   *fine linen scarf*
    Into a fine distractiòn;
5 An erring° lace, which here and there   *wandering*
    Enthralls the crimson stomacher;[2]
    A cuff neglectful, and thereby
    Ribbons to flow confusedly;
    A winning wave, deserving note,

---

1. For the sake of both rhyme and meter, the name of this lady is given three syllables here; in line 12 it has only two.

1. One of several poems in this period in which women's dress is a means by which to explore the relation of nature and art.

2. An ornamental covering of the chest, worn under the laces of the bodice.

        10   In the tempestuous petticoat;
                A careless shoestring, in whose tie
                I see a wild civility:
                Do more bewitch me than when art
                Is too precise[3] in every part.

Corinna's Going A-Maying

          Get up! Get up for shame! The blooming morn
          Upon her wings presents the god unshorn.[1]
             See how Aurora throws her fair
             Fresh-quilted colors through the air:[2]
    5   Get up, sweet slug-a-bed, and see
             The dew bespangling herb and tree.
          Each flower has wept and bowed toward the east
          Above an hour since, yet you not dressed;
             Nay, not so much as out of bed?
   10   When all the birds have matins° said,   *morning prayer*
             And sung their thankful hymns, 'tis sin,
             Nay, profanation° to keep in,   *impiety*
          Whenas a thousand virgins on this day
          Spring, sooner than the lark, to fetch in May.[3]

   15   Rise, and put on your foliage, and be seen
          To come forth, like the springtime, fresh and green,
             And sweet as Flora.[4] Take no care
             For jewels for your gown or hair;
             Fear not; the leaves will strew
   20   Gems in abundance upon you;
          Besides, the childhood of the day has kept,
          Against° you come, some orient pearls[5] unwept;   *until*
             Come and receive them while the light
             Hangs on the dew-locks of the night,
   25   And Titan° on the eastern hill   *the sun*
             Retires himself, or else stands still
          Till you come forth. Wash, dress, be brief in praying:
          Few beads[6] are best when once we go a-Maying.

          Come, my Corinna, come; and, coming, mark
   30   How each field turns° a street, each street a park   *turns into*
             Made green and trimmed with trees; see how
             Devotion gives each house a bough

---

3. "Precise" and "precision" were terms used satirically about Puritans. Herrick, in praising feminine disarray, is at one level praising the *sprezzatura*, or careless grace, of Cavalier art.
1. Apollo, the sun god; sunbeams are seen as his flowing locks.
2. Aurora is goddess of the dawn.
3. On May Day morning, it was the custom to gather whitethorn blossoms and trim the house with them.
4. Flora, Italian goddess of the flowering of plants, had her festival in the spring.
5. Pearls from the Orient were especially lustrous, like drops of dew.
6. Rosary beads of the "old" Catholic religion; more generally, a casual term for prayers.

  Or branch: each porch, each door ere this,
  An ark, a tabernacle is,[7]
35   Made up of whitethorn neatly interwove,
  As if here were those cooler shades of love.
    Can such delights be in the street
    And open fields, and we not see 't?
    Come, we'll abroad; and let's obey
40   The proclamation[8] made for May,
  And sin no more, as we have done, by staying;
  But, my Corinna, come, let's go a-Maying.

  There's not a budding boy or girl this day
  But is got up and gone to bring in May;
45   A deal of youth, ere this, is come
    Back, and with whitethorn laden, home.
    Some have dispatched their cakes and cream
    Before that we have left to dream;
  And some have wept, and wooed, and plighted troth,[9]
50   And chose their priest, ere we can cast off sloth.
    Many a green gown[1] has been given,
    Many a kiss, both odd and even;[2]
    Many a glance, too, has been sent
    From out the eye, love's firmament;°   *sky*
55   Many a jest told of the keys betraying
  This night, and locks picked; yet we're not a-Maying.

  Come, let us go while we are in our prime,
  And take the harmless folly of the time.
    We shall grow old apace, and die
60   Before we know our liberty.
    Our life is short, and our days run
    As fast away as does the sun;
  And, as a vapor or a drop of rain,
  Once lost, can ne'er be found again,
65   So when or you or I are made
    A fable, song, or fleeting shade,
    All love, all liking, all delight
    Lies drowned with us in endless night.[3]
  Then while time serves, and we are but decaying,
70   Come, my Corinna, come, let's go a-Maying.

---

7. The doorways, ornamented with whitethorn, are like the Hebrew Ark of the Covenant or the sanctuary that housed it (Leviticus 23:40–42: "Ye shall take you on the first day the boughs of goodly trees . . .").
8. Probably a reference to Charles I's "Declaration to his subjects concerning lawful sports."
9. Engaged themselves to marry.
1. Made green because the wearer has rolled in the grass.
2. Kisses are odd and even in kissing games.
3. Some echoes of the apocryphal book Wisdom of Solomon 2:1–8: "For the ungodly said . . . the breath of our nostrils is as smoke, and a little spark . . . and our life shall pass away as the trace of a cloud. . . . Come on therefore . . . Let us crown ourselves with rose buds before they be withered." This carpe diem sentiment is a frequent theme in classical love poetry.

To the Virgins, to Make Much of Time

Gather ye rosebuds while ye may,
    Old time is still° a-flying;[1]   *always*
And this same flower that smiles today,
    Tomorrow will be dying.

5 The glorious lamp of heaven, the sun,
    The higher he's a-getting,
The sooner will his race be run,
    And nearer he's to setting.

That age is best which is the first,
10   When youth and blood are warmer;
But being spent, the worse, and worst
    Times still succeed the former.

Then be not coy, but use your time,
    And while ye may, go marry;
15 For having lost but once your prime,
    You may forever tarry.

The Hock Cart,[1] or Harvest Home

to the Right Honorable Mildmay, Earl of Westmoreland

Come, sons of summer, by whose toil
We are the lords of wine and oil;[2]
By whose tough labors and rough hands
We rip up first, then reap our lands.
5 Crowned with the ears of corn,° now come   *grain*
And, to the pipe, sing harvest home.
Come forth, my lord, and see the cart
Dressed up with all the country art.
See here a maukin,° there a sheet,   *scarecrow*
10 As spotless pure as it is sweet,
The horses, mares, and frisking fillies
Clad all in linen, white as lilies,
The harvest swains° and wenches bound   *young men*
For joy to see the hock-cart crowned.
15   About the cart, hear how the rout
Of rural younglings raise the shout,

---

1. A translation of the Latin *tempus fugit*.

1. The last cart carrying home the harvest; hence the occasion for a rural festival, traditional throughout Europe. Mildmay Fane, Earl of Westmoreland (1628–1660), was one of Herrick's patrons.

2. Wine and oil are the yields of Mediterranean farming, connecting the English harvest festival to classical pastoral.

Pressing before, some coming after,
Those with a shout and these with laughter.
Some bless the cart, some kiss the sheaves,
20 Some prank them up° with oaken leaves; *adorn them*
Some cross the fill-horse,³ some with great
Devotion stroke the home-borne wheat;
While other rustics, less attent
To prayers than to merriment,
25 Run after with their breeches rent.
   Well, on, brave boys, to your lord's hearth,
Glittering with fire; where, for your mirth,
Ye shall see first the large and chief
Foundation of your feast, fat beef;
30 With upper stories, mutton, veal,
And bacon,° which makes full the meal, *pork*
With several dishes standing by,
As here a custard, there a pie,
And here all-tempting frumenty.° *pudding*
35 And for to make the merry cheer,
If smirking° wine be wanting° here, *sparkling / lacking*
There's that which drowns all care, stout beer:
Which freely drink to your lord's health,
Then to the plow (the common-wealth),
40 Next to your flails, your fans,⁴ your vats,
Then to the maids with wheaten hats,
To the rough sickle and crook'd scythe,
Drink, frolic boys, till all be blithe.
   Feed, and grow fat; and, as ye eat,
45 Be mindful that the lab'ring neat,° *cattle*
As you, may have their fill of meat.⁵
And know, besides, ye must revoke° *call back*
The patient ox unto his yoke,
And all go back unto the plow
50 And harrow, though they're hanged up now.
And you must know, your lord's word's true,
Feed him ye must whose food fills you,
And that this pleasure is like rain,
Not sent ye for to drown your pain
55 But for to make it spring again.⁶

---

3. The fill-horse is harnessed between the shafts of the cart. Crossing the horse and kissing the sheaves suggest the persistence of pre-Reformation rituals in the countryside.
4. "Flails" are threshing instruments; "fans" are used to winnow grain from chaff. The plow is the common source of everybody's wealth. In line with the anti-Puritan sentiments of the whole poem, the word "commonwealth," in this communal and earthy sense, invites a contrast with Puritan republican theories.
5. Food (grain or hay).
6. Spring is heralded by rain, but the lines also point to the continual renewal of the agricultural worker's pain and labor.

Upon the Nipples of Julia's Breast

Have ye beheld (with much delight)
A red rose peeping through a white?
Or else a cherry (double graced)
Within a lily center-placed?
5 Or ever marked° the pretty beam   *observed*
A strawberry shows half drowned in cream?
Or seen rich rubies blushing through
A pure smooth pearl, and orient° too?   *iridescent*
So like to this, nay all the rest,
10 Is each neat niplet of her breast.

Upon His Verses

What offspring other men have got,
The how, where, when I question not.
These are the children I have left;
Adopted some, none got by theft.
5 But all are touched (like lawful plate)[1]
And no verse illegitimate.

Upon Julia's Clothes

Whenas in silks my Julia goes,°   *walks*
Then, then, methinks, how sweetly flows
That liquefaction of her clothes.

Next, when I cast mine eyes and see
5 That brave° vibration each way free,   *splendid*
Oh, how that glittering taketh me!

Upon Prue, His Maid[2]

In this little urn is laid
Prudence Baldwin, once my maid,
From whose happy spark here let
Spring the purple violet.

---

1. A special variety of quartz, known as basanite, was used to test gold and silver objects; the color of the smear left on the touchstone revealed its purity.
2. This is an odd epitaph, since Prudence Baldwin died four years after Herrick.

To His Book's End[3]

To his book's end this last line he'd have placed:
Jocund° his muse was, but his life was chaste.   *merry, sprightly*

FROM NOBLE NUMBERS

To His Conscience[1]

Can I not sin, but thou wilt be
My private protonotary?[2]
Can I not woo thee to pass by
A short and sweet iniquity?
5 I'll cast a mist and cloud upon
My delicate transgression
So utter dark as that no eye
Shall see the hugged° impiety.   *cherished*
Gifts blind the wise,[3] and bribes do please
10 And wind° all other witnesses: *pervert*
And wilt not thou with gold be tied
To lay thy pen and ink aside?
That in the mirk° and tongueless night   *black, murky*
Wanton I may, and thou not write?
15 It will not be; and therefore now
For times to come I'll make this vow,
From aberrations to live free,
So I'll not fear the Judge, or thee.

Another Grace for a Child

Here a little child I stand,
Heaving up my either hand;
Cold as paddocks° though they be,   *frogs*
Here I lift them up to thee,
5 For a benison° to fall   *blessing*
On our meat and on us all. *Amen.*

---

3. The last poem of *Hesperides*.
1. This and the following poem are from *Noble Numbers*, the collection of Herrick's religious poems that was bound together with *Hesperides*.
2. Chief recording clerk of a court.
3. An echo of Deuteronomy 16:19: "a gift doth blind the eyes of the wise."

HESTER PULTER
1605–1678

Rediscovered in a university archive in 1996, Hester Pulter's *Poems Breathed Forth by the Nobel Hadassas*—a single bound manuscript containing 120 poems and an incomplete romance—is a remarkable record of an intellectual life almost lost to literary history. Pulter composed her work when she and her royalist family were living in semi-exile during the Interregnum. She was born Hester Ley in Dublin, where her father was Chief Justice of Ireland, and her family came to London under the patronage of James I. Her husband, Arthur Pulter, was a lesser magistrate and wealthy estate owner in Hertfordshire, where they seem to have retired shortly after the English Civil Wars broke out.

Like Katherine Philips and Margaret Cavendish, Pulter wrote elegies for fallen royalist leaders, including Charles I; and her chosen name, "Hadassah," another name for the biblical Queen Esther (or Hester), who saved her people from oppression, hints at her self-conception as a defender of a cause. Her poetry shows a keen interest both in the "divine breath" that animates all matter and in the natural philosophies, ranging from astronomy and alchemy to vitalist materialism, that fired the imaginations of her peers, including John Donne and George Herbert, whose work she clearly admired.

Pulter's poems below demonstrate ambitious reworkings of literary traditions, particularly of conventional Petrarchan tropes such as the anatomical blazon. As she demands in one elegy on her daughter's death, "Tell me no more her cheeks excelled the rose." In "View But This Tulip," Pulter turns a philosophical discussion of "first principles" and "indivisibles" into a meditation on the resurrection of the flesh at the end of time. The formal simplicity of "Dear God, from Thy High Throne Look Down" shares with other seventeenth-century devotional poems an interest in what Herbert calls "the good fellowship of dust," but the poem is also infused with Pulter's interest in bodies tossed in a thousand "figures." Much like the poems of Margaret Cavendish, Pulter's verses invite speculation.

Upon the Death of My Dear and Lovely Daughter, Jane Pulter

All you that have indulgent parents been,
And have your children in perfection seen
Of youth and beauty: lend one tear to me,
And trust me, I will do as much for thee,
5 Unless my own grief do exhaust my store;
Then will I sigh till I suspire° no more.   *breathe*
Twice hath the Earth thrown Chloris's° mantle by,   *goddess of spring*
Embroidered o'er with curious° tapestry,   *artful, elaborate, delicate*
And twice hath seemed to mourn unto our sight,
10 Like Jews or Chineses in snowy white,[1]

---

1. Traditional color of mourning in China and in Jewish traditions of burial and mourning.

Since she laid down her milky limbs on earth,
Which, dying, gave her virgin soul new birth.
Yet still my heart is overwhelmed with grief,
And tears (alas) give sorrow no relief.
15 Twice hath sad Philomel[2] left off to sing
Her mortifying° sonnets to the spring.   *fatal, self-denying*
Twice at the sylvan° choristers' desire   *forest-dwelling*
She hath lent her music to complete their choir,
Since all devouring Death on her took seizure,
20 And Tellus's° womb involved° so rich a   *goddess of the earth / enveloped*
    treasure.
Yet still my heart is overwhelmed with grief,
And time, nor tears, will give my woes relief.
Twice times hath Phoebe,[3] hornéd,° seemed to fight,   *crescent-shaped*
As often filled them with her brother's light,
25 Since she did close her sparkling diamond eyes;
Yet my sad heart, for her still pining,° dies.   *yearning*
Through the twelve houses° hath the illustrious sun   *of the Zodiac*
With splendency° his annual journey run.   *splendor*
Twice hath his fiery, furious horses hurled
30 His blazing chariot to the lower world,
Showing his luster to the wond'ring eyes
Of our (now so well known) antipodes,°   *opposite side of the world*
Since the brack° of her spotless virgin story   *breach, rupture*
Which now her soul doth end in endless glory.
35 Yet my afflicted, sad, forsaken soul
For her in tears and ashes still doth roll.
O could a fever spot her snowy skin,
Whose virgin soul was scarcely soiled with sin?
Ay me, it did! So have I sometimes seen
40 Fair maidens sit encircled on a green,
White lilies spread when they were making poses,[4]
Upon them scatter leaves of damask roses,°   *roses from Damascas*
E'en so, the spots upon her fair skin shows
Like lily leaves sprinkled with damask rose,
45 Or, as a stately hart° to death pursued   *deer*
By ravening hounds, his eyes with tears bedewed,
An arrow sticking in his trembling breast,
His lost condition to the life expressed,°   *exactly reproduced*
So trips he o'er the lawns on trodden snow,
50 And from his side his guiltless blood doth flow.
So did the spots upon her fair skin show
Like drops of blood upon unsullied snow.
But what a heart had I, when I did stand

---

2. In classical myth, Philomela was raped by her brother-in-law Tereus, who tore out her tongue; the gods transformed her into a bird (in Ovid's version of the story, a nightingale).
3. Goddess of the moon, and sister of the sun, Phoebus Apollo.
4. Posies: bouquets or bunches of flowers; figuratively, short verses.

      Holding her forehead with my trembling hand.
55   My heart to heaven with her bright spirit flies
      Whilst she (ah me!) closed up her lovely eyes.
      Her soul being seated in her place of birth,
      I turned a Niobe[5] as she turned earth.

ca. 1647

View But This Tulip

    View but this tulip, rose, or gillyflower,°   *July flower, carnation*
    And by a finite, see an infinite power.
    These flowers into their chaos were retired
    Till human art them raised and reinspired
5   With beating, macerating,[1] fermentation,
    Calcining,° chemically, with segregation;[2]   *burning to ash*
    Then, lest the air these secrets should reveal,
    Shut up the ashes under Hermes's seal;[3]
    Then, with a candle or a gentle fire,
10 You may reanimate at your desire
    These gallant° plants; but if you cool the glass,   *gorgeous or showy*
    To their first principles[4] they'll quickly pass:
    From sulfur, salt, and mercury they came;
    When they dissolve, they turn into the same.
15 Then, seeing a wretched mortal hath the power
    To recreate a Virbius of a flower,[5]
    Why should we fear, though sadly we retire
    Into our cause?° Our God will reinspire   *original, formative elements*
    Our dormant dust, and keep alive the same
20 With an all-quick'ning,° everlasting flame.   *all-enlivening*
    Then, though I into atoms scattered be,
    In indivisibles° I'll trust in Thee.   *atoms*
    Then let this comfort me in my sad story:
    Dust is but four degrees removed from glory
25 By Nature's paths,[6] but God from death and night
    Can raise this flesh to endless life and light.
    Then, my impatient soul, contented be,
    For thou a glorious spring ere° long shalt see.   *before*
    After these gloomy shades of death and sorrow,

---

5. That is, dissolved into tears. In Greek myth, the gods Apollo and Artemis killed Niobe's six sons and six daughters after she bragged that she had more children than their mother, Leto; she was metamorphosed into a rock weeping for their loss.
1. Softening by steeping in liquid.
2. A reference to palingenesis, the (supposed) regeneration through alchemy of living organisms from ashes or putrefying matter.
3. A hermetic seal, tight enough to exclude air; Hermes Trismegistus was the Greek name of the Egyptian god Thoth, regarded as the founder of alchemy.
4. In alchemy, the substances composing all matter: mercury, salt, and sulfur; more generally, origins, constituent parts.
5. In Greek myth, Hippolytus is unjustly killed because of his father's curse but brought back to life by Asclepius, the god of healing; he emigrated to Italy under the Latin name Virbius (from *vir bis*, "a man twice").
6. Those paths derived from the four elements: earth, air, water, and fire.

30 Thou shalt enjoy an everlasting morrow.
    As wheat in new-plowed furrows rotting lies,
    Incapable of quick'ning till it dies,[7]
    So into dust this flesh of mine must turn
    And lie a while forgotten in my urn.
35 Yet when the sea, and earth, and Hell shall give
    Their treasures up, my body too shall live:
    Not like the resurrection at Grand Caire,[8]
    Where men revive, then straight of life despair;
    But, with my soul, my flesh shall reunite
40 And ne'er involvéd be with death and night,
    But live in endless pleasure, love, and light.
    Then hallelujahs will I sing to Thee,
    My gracious God, to all eternity.
    Then at thy dissolution patient be:
45 If man can raise a flower, God can thee.

ca. 1640–65

Dear God, from Thy High Throne Look Down

Dear God, from Thy high throne look down,
And let my suff'rings have their crown:
        I Thee implore.

Though grief calcine° my flesh to dust   *burn to ash; purify, refine*
5 Yet in Thy mercy still I trust
        And Thee adore.

Should I to tears dissolvéd be
Yet will I still depend on Thee
        Forevermore.

10 Or should I sigh away to air,
Though rarefied,° I'd not despair   *made less substantial; purified*
        But in Thee trust.

Though I to atoms am dispersed,
I in their dances am unversed,°   *inexperienced; not in verse*
15   Yet shall no dust

Of my old carcass e'er be lost
Though in a thousand figures° tossed,   *shapes; embodiments*
        For Thou art just.

---

7. Seeds need to be buried (and thus "die") under soil in order to return to life (or "quicken").
8. Cairo, possibly referring to the ancient Egyptian custom of mummifying the dead in anticipation of resurrection (one the speaker presumes, in the next line, will be disappointing), or to travelers' accounts of superstitious Egyptian beliefs about the annual rising of dead bones.

What mortal can or dares to look
Into Thy glorious blessed book?
                    Where written be

Of me, poor wretched me, each part,
E'en all my soul, my thoughts, my heart.
                    Thou plain may'st see

That I my gracious God do love
A thousand, thousand worlds above
                    And still praise Thee.

ca. 1640–65

RICHARD LOVELACE
1617–1657

The quintessential Cavalier, Richard Lovelace was described by a contemporary as "the most amiable and beautiful person that ever eye beheld." Born into a wealthy Kentish family, he was educated at Oxford and fought for Charles I in Scotland (in both expeditions, 1639 and 1640). He shared with his king a serious interest in art, especially the paintings of Peter Paul Rubens, Anthony Van Dyck, and Peter Lely. He was imprisoned for a few months in 1642 for supporting the "Kentish Petition" that urged restoration of the king to his ancient rights; in "To Althea, from Prison," he finds freedom from external bondage in the Cavalier embrace of sex, wine, and royalism. During 1643–46 he fought in the king's armies in England and in Holland and France, where he was wounded. In a general roundup of known royalists in 1648 he was imprisoned for ten months. While in prison Lovelace prepared his poems for publication under the title *Lucasta* (1649), the name of his muse. Besides witty and charming love songs, the volume includes the plaintive ballad about the conflict between love and honor, "To Lucasta, Going to the Wars," and also "The Grasshopper," a poem celebrating the Cavalier ideal. Like that emblematic summer creature, the once-carefree Cavalier suffers in the Puritan "winter," but Lovelace finds in the fellowship of Cavalier friends a nobler version of the good life. After 1649 he endured years of poverty, and was largely dependent on the generosity of his friend and fellow royalist, the poet Charles Cotton. His remaining poems appeared in 1659 as *Lucasta: Postume Poems*.

From Lucasta

To Lucasta, Going to the Wars

Tell me not, sweet, I am unkind,
   That from the nunnery
Of thy chaste breast and quiet mind
   To war and arms I fly.

5 True, a new mistress now I chase,
    The first foe in the field;
  And with a stronger faith embrace
    A sword, a horse, a shield.

  Yet this inconstancy is such
10   As you too shall adore;
  I could not love thee, dear, so much,
    Loved I not honor more.

1649

The Grasshopper[1]

To My Noble Friend, Mr. Charles Cotton

  O thou that swing'st upon the waving hair
    Of some well-fillèd oaten beard,°   *head of grain*
  Drunk every night with a delicious tear
    Dropped thee from heav'n, where now th' art reared,

5 The joys of earth and air are thine entire,
    That with thy feet and wings dost hop and fly;
  And when thy poppy° works thou dost retire   *opiate*
    To thy carved acorn bed to lie.

  Up with the day, the sun thou welcom'st then,
10   Sport'st in the gilt-plats° of his beams,   *golden fields*
  And all these merry days mak'st merry men,
    Thyself, and melancholy streams.[2]

  But ah, the sickle! golden ears are cropped,
    Ceres and Bacchus[3] bid goodnight;
15 Sharp frosty fingers all your flow'rs have topped,
    And what scythes spared, winds shave off quite.

  Poor verdant fool! and now green ice! thy joys,
    Large and as lasting as thy perch of grass,
  Bid us lay in 'gainst winter rain, and poise°   *counterbalance*
20   Their floods with an o'erflowing glass.

  Thou best of men and friends! we will create
    A genuine summer in each other's breast;
  And spite of this cold time and frozen fate
    Thaw us a warm seat to our rest.

---

1. In *Aesop's Fables* the grasshopper lives in carefree idleness, in contrast with the industrious ant who lays up stores for the winter. The circumstances of the poem are those of the Interregnum, when a Puritan 'winter' seemed, to royalists, to be settling over England and obliterating their mode of life. The grasshopper may also allude to the recently executed king, Charles I.
2. The three objects of "mak'st merry" are "men," "thyself," and "melancholy streams."
3. Goddess of grain and god of wine.

25 Our sacred hearths shall burn eternally
    As vestal flames;⁴ the North Wind, he
Shall strike his frost-stretched wings, dissolve, and fly
    This Etna in epitome.⁵

Dropping December shall come weeping in,
30   Bewail th' usurping of his reign;
But when in showers of old Greek we begin,
    Shall cry, he hath his crown again!⁶

Night as clear Hesper° shall our tapers whip   *the evening star*
    From the light casements where we play,
35 And the dark hag⁷ from her black mantle strip,
    And stick there everlasting day.

Thus richer than untempted kings are we,
    That asking nothing, nothing need:
Though lord of all that seas embrace, yet he
40   That wants° himself is poor indeed.   lacks

1649

To Althea, from Prison

When Love with unconfinèd wings
    Hovers within my gates,
And my divine Althea brings
    To whisper at the grates;
5 When I lie tangled in her hair
    And fettered to her eye,
The gods¹ that wanton° in the air   *play*
    Know no such liberty.

When flowing cups run swiftly round,
10   With no allaying Thames,²
Our careless heads with roses bound,
    Our hearts with loyal flames;
When thirsty grief in wine we steep,
    When healths and drafts go free,
15 Fishes that tipple in the deep
    Know no such liberty.

---

4. The Vestal Virgins, in Rome, were responsible for tending an eternal flame in the Temple of Vesta.
5. Boreas, the north wind, folding up ("striking") his wings, flees the heat of the volcano within Mount Etna, a figure for the fires of friendship.
6. Greek wine was favored in the classical world. "Crown" here has multiple associations: the crown worn by "King Christmas" at the festivities banned by Puritans, and the crown Cavaliers hoped would soon be restored to Charles II.
7. Hecate, a daughter of Night.
1. Some versions read "birds" instead of "gods."
2. No mixture of water (as from the river Thames) in the wine.

When, like committed linnets,° I   *caged finches*
    With shriller throat shall sing
The sweetness, mercy, majesty,
    And glories of my king;
When I shall voice aloud how good
    He is, how great should be,
Enlargèd winds, that curl the flood,
    Know no such liberty.

Stone walls do not a prison make,
    Nor iron bars a cage;
Minds innocent and quiet take
    That for an hermitage.
If I have freedom in my love,
    And in my soul am free,
Angels alone, that soar above,
    Enjoy such liberty.

1649

La Bella Bona Roba[1]

I

I cannot tell who loves the skeleton
Of a poor marmoset,° naught but bone, bone.   *wanton woman*
Give me a nakedness with her clothes on.[2]

II

Such whose white satin upper coat of skin,
Cut upon velvet rich incarnadine,°   *flesh-colored, red*
Has yet a body (and of flesh) within.

III

Sure it is meant good husbandry° in men,   *management*
Who do incorporate[3] with airy lean,°   *insubstantial meat*
To repair their sides, and get their rib again.[4]

IV

Hard hap° unto that huntsman that decrees   *fortune*
Fat joys for all his sweat, whenas he sees,
After his 'say,° naught but his keeper's fees.[5]   *assay, attempt*

---

1. "Bona roba," from the Italian for good dress or gear, was a term for a wanton woman or prostitute.
2. Well-fleshed.
3. Both take into the body and copulate.
4. See Genesis 2:21–22 for Eve's creation from Adam's rib.
5. The meager portion of a deer allotted to the gamekeeper.

V

    Then Love, I beg, when next thou takest thy bow,
    Thy angry shafts, and dost heart-chasing go,
15 Pass rascal° deer, strike me the largest doe.   *inferior, mean*

                                              1649

A Black Patch on Lucasta's Face

    Dull as I was, to think that a court fly[1]
        Presumed so near her eye,
        When 'twas th' industrious bee
    Mistook her glorious face for paradise;
5 To sum up all his chemistry of spice,
        With a brave pride and honor led,
        Near both her suns° he makes his bed,   *eyes*
    And though a spark struggles to rise as red;
        Then emulates the gay
10   Daughter of day,
        Acts the romantic phoenix's fate;[2]
    When now, with all his sweets laid out in state,
        Lucasta scatters but one heat,
        And all the aromatic pills do sweat,
15 And gums calcined,° themselves to powder   *reduced to powder by heat*
        beat;[3]
        Which a fresh gale of air
        Conveys into her hair;
        Then chaste he's set on fire,
    And in these holy flames doth glad expire;
20   And that black marble tablet[4] there
        So near her either sphere
        Was placed; nor foil, nor ornament,
    But the sweet little bee's large monument.°   *memorial structure; sepulcher*

                                              1659

---

1. An insect, as well as a (court) parasite or flatterer and a patch for the face (from the French *mouche*): a small piece of black material, typically silk or velvet, cut into a decorative shape and worn either for adornment or to conceal a blemish. (See the illustration from Bulwer's *Anthropometamorphosis*, as well as John Donne's "The Flea.") A patch was also a fool.
2. The phoenix was a mythic Arabian bird; only one existed at any time. After five hundred years it was consumed by fire, and another rose from its ashes.
3. As the radiance of Lucasta's eyes cremates the bee, the bee's store of honey is secreted and then calcined.
4. That is, the mark left on Lucasta's face where the bee died in the fire of her eyes. A tablet was a small slab bearing a memorial inscription, as well as a writing surface.

John Bulwer's *Anthropometamorphosis: Man Transform'd* (1653) discusses the ways in which the English copied the fashions of other nations, including face patches.

Love Made in the First Age.[1] To Chloris

    In the nativity of time,
  Chloris, it was not thought a crime
      In direct Hebrew for to woo.[2]
  Now we make love as all on fire,
5 Ring retrograde[3] our loud desire,
      And court in English backward too.

  Thrice happy was that golden age,
  When compliment was construed rage,[4]
      And fine words in the center hid;
10 When cursèd *No* stained no maid's bliss,
  And all discourse was summed in *Yes,*
      And naught forbade, but to forbid.

  Love then unstinted, love did sip,
  And cherries plucked fresh from the lip,
15   On cheeks and roses free he fed;
  Lasses like autumn plums did drop,
  And lads indifferently° did crop   *without preference*
      A flower and a maidenhead.

---

1. The Golden Age, described in Ovid's *Metamorphoses*.
2. Hebrew, supposed to be the original human language, is read from right to left; we have reversed this.
3. Backward, in reverse. The term also has musical connotations, perhaps referring here to a pattern of bell ringing.
4. Passion. Compliments in the Golden Age were understood as ardent propositions.

　　　　Then unconfinèd each did tipple
20　　Wine from the bunch, milk from the nipple;
　　　　　Paps tractable as udders were;
　　　　Then equally the wholesome jellies
　　　　Were squeezed from olive trees and bellies,
　　　　　Nor suits of trespass did they fear.

25　　A fragrant bank of strawberries,
　　　　Diapered° with violet's eyes,　　　　　　　　　*decorated, dappled*
　　　　　Was table, tablecloth, and fare;
　　　　No palace to the clouds did swell,
　　　　Each humble princess then did dwell
30　　　In the piazza[5] of her hair.

　　　　Both broken faith and th' cause of it,
　　　　All-damning gold, was damned to th' pit;
　　　　　Their troth, sealed with a clasp and kiss,
　　　　Lasted until that extreme day
35　　In which they smiled their souls away,
　　　　　And, in each other, breathed new bliss.

　　　　Because no fault, there was no tear;
　　　　No groan did grate the granting ear,
　　　　　No false foul breath their del'cate smell:
40　　No serpent kiss poisoned the taste,
　　　　Each touch was naturally chaste,
　　　　　And their mere sense a miracle.

　　　　Naked as their own innocence,
　　　　And unembroidered from offense[6]
45　　　They went, above poor riches, gay;
　　　　On softer than the cygnet's° down,　　　　　　*young swan*
　　　　In beds they tumbled of their own;
　　　　　For each within the other lay.

　　　　Thus did they live; thus did they love,
50　　Repeating only joys above;
　　　　　And angels were, but with clothes on,
　　　　Which they would put off cheerfully,
　　　　To bathe them in the galaxy,°　　　　　　　　*the Milky Way*
　　　　　Then gird them with the heavenly zone.[7]

55　　Now, Chloris, miserably crave°　　　　　　　　*beg*
　　　　The offered bliss you would not have,
　　　　　Which evermore I must deny,
　　　　Whilst ravished with these noble dreams
　　　　And crownèd with mine own soft beams,
60　　　Enjoying of my self I lie.

　　　　　　　　　　　　　　　　　　　　　　　　　　1659

---

5. Arcade, hence an artful structure.
6. That is, not ornamented to hide an offense.
7. The zodiac of stars.

LUCY HUTCHINSON
1620–1681

Lucy Aspley was born in 1620 in the Tower of London, where her father was lieutenant. In a short autobiographical fragment, Hutchinson writes that her "genius was quite averse" from everything but her "book." Hutchinson is best known for her *Memoirs of the Life of Colonel Hutchinson*, an account of the Civil Wars, particularly in Nottinghamshire, where her husband was governor of a parliamentarian garrison. But she was also a poet, and the first person to translate Lucretius's *De rerum natura* (On the Nature of Things) from Latin into English. Hutchinson also wrote a parody of the poet Edmund Waller's panegyric to Oliver Cromwell, twenty-three elegies, and an epic poem on Genesis titled *Order and Disorder*. The first five cantos of the epic appeared anonymously in print in 1679; a manuscript of twenty cantos dating from the 1660s survives in the papers of Hutchinson's cousin Anne Wilmot, Countess of Rochester, mother of the libertine poet John Wilmot, Earl of Rochester.

Hutchinson married John Hutchinson in 1638, and their estate in Owthorpe, Nottinghamshire became a significant political center even before the Civil Wars. Paired portraits by Robert Walker dating from the late 1640s or early 1650s show Lucy Hutchinson holding a laurel wreath, the emblem of poetic achievement, and Colonel Hutchinson wearing armor. Their complementary skills—hers with the pen, his with the sword—were central to their defense of a godly republic, voluntary Protestant congregations, and a heightened role for the gentry (as opposed to an oligarchic nobility) in political governance.

Hutchinson worked on her translation of Lucretius in the 1650s. While Hutchinson expressed concern about the poem's "Atheisms & impieties," she nonetheless gave a presentation copy of her translation to Arthur Annesley, Earl of Anglesey, sometime protector of the godly, and friend of John Milton. After the Restoration, Hutchinson saved her husband's life by forging a letter of recantation. The Hutchinsons lived at Owthorpe until John was arrested in 1663 for his alleged involvement in an uprising against Charles II. Following his death in prison, Hutchinson wrote her vindicatory *Memoirs*, as well as a series of elegies expressing her grief and longing for her dead husband, her theological and political beliefs, and her refusal to capitulate to the Restoration regime. The elegy included here, "To the Garden at Owthorpe," uses the conventions of the country house poem both to mourn John Hutchinson and to celebrate the forms of order to which they had dedicated their lives.

Hutchinson's invocation of an explicitly Christian muse in *Order and Disorder* reflects her belief in the divine order, or "stupendous Providence," that will ultimately vindicate the "little Church" against "the World's larger State." While the Lucretian ideas Hutchinson officially rejects in the preface to *Order and Disorder* certainly inform the poem's account of creation, the scriptural references in its margins make its primary intertext clear. (Those references have been omitted here.) Presented in its entirety below, canto 5 offers an account of the Fall that is particularly attentive to the punishment meted out to women in Genesis 3:16; Hutchinson even occasionally writes in the collective voice of women, looking forward to a time when "*we* shall trample on the serpent's head" (emphasis added).

Lucy Hutchinson. This portrait by Robert Walker features Hutchinson with a laurel wreath in her lap. It was paired with a painting of her husband, Colonel John Hutchinson, in armor.

From De rerum natura[1]

From Book I

* * *

250 But since we now eternal matter° find,[2]   *everlasting substance*
     And principles°[2] with different links combined,°   *primary elements / joined*
     Each body,° while it equal strength retains   *physical form*
     To its composure,° only firm remains.   *composition, structure*
     Thus nothing into nothing turns, but so

---

1. Hutchinson was the first person to translate Lucretius's *De rerum natura* (On the Nature of Things) into English.
2. This passage begins by assuming that matter, which is neither created nor subject to destruction, continuously transforms. Compare Milton's discussion of "one first matter all" in *Paradise Lost* 5.472, and Cavendish's theory of matter in *The Blazing World*.

255 Disjoined all back to their first bodies go.
Further when the paternal heaven powers
On the great mother earth engendering° showers   *begetting*
They perish in her womb, but thence comes out
The shining blade, plants grow, green branches sprout,
260 Thence doth she both wild beasts and mankind nourish,
And thence with growing youth great cities flourish.
Thence do new birds the shady groves supply.
Hence while the herd in their rich pastures lie
And on rank° grass their weary limbs repose   *vigorous, luxuriant*
265 White milk from their extended udders flows.
Hence sportful younglings° in the grounds we find   *offspring*
Helping their weak joints with their vigorous mind.

Thus nothing perisheth that to our eyes
Appears, for nature makes new creatures° rise   *products of creation*
270 From those which were dissolved,° and all that live   *decomposed*
Their beings out of others' deaths receive.
Since things are not of nothing made, I've taught
They cannot be again to nothing brought.

* * *

From *Book II*

* * *

What greater miracle can mortals frame
1055 Then the pure azure sky, the glorious flame
Of every star, which wanders there, the bright
Orb of the moon, the sun's refulgent° light,   *radiant*
Which were they yet unknown, how would men gaze
On such strange objects, how would they amaze
1060 The sense of vulgar° men, who scarce would dare   *common*
To credit that such things in nature were,

The reason of this world may persuade us there are more worlds springing from the same causes[5]

Who now cloyed° with the frequent sight despise   *cumbered, burdened*
The glorious view of the bright arched skies.
No longer then, with strangeness terrified,
Let reason be your thoughts access denied;[3]
But with strict judgment weigh the whole dispute
And if't be true assent, if not confute.°   *prove wrong*
    Here then the mind enquires, by reason's light,
Since space[4] beyond the world is infinite,
What those vast regions are, what they can show,
Where the free mind desires so much to go?

1650s   1996

* * *

---

3. No longer let your reason be terrified by strangeness and deny access to your thoughts.
4. The expanse in which celestial objects are situated.
5. This is Hutchinson's own comment.

To the Garden at Owthorpe[1]

Poor desolate garden, smile no more on me
To whom glad looks rude° entertainments be.   *unkind*
While thou and I for thy dear master mourn
That's best becoming that doth least adorn.[2]
5 Shall we for any meaner eyes be dressed
Who had the glory once to please thee best?
Or shall we prostitute° those joys again   *debase, offer for sale*
Which once his noble soul did entertain?
Forbid it honor and just gratitude,
10 'Tis now our best grace to be wild and rude.°   *humble, unrefined*
He that impaled° thee from the common° ground,[3]   *enclosed, fenced in / shared*
Who all thy walls with shining fruit trees crowned,
Me also above vulgar° girls did raise   *ordinary, common*
And planted in me all that yielded praise;
15 He that with various beauties decked thy face,
Gave my youth lustre and becoming grace;
But he is gone and these gone with him too.
Let now thy flowers rise charged° with weeping dew   *laden*
And, missing him, shrink back into their beds;
20 So my poor virgins° hang their drooping heads   *flowers*
And, missing the dear object of their sight,
Close up their eyes in sorrow's gloomy night.
Let thy young trees which sad and fading stand
Dried up since they lost his refreshing hand,
25 Tell me too sadly how your noblest plant
Degenerates° if it usual culture° want.   *declines / cultivation*
There spreading weeds which, while his watchful eyes
Checked their pernicious° growth, durst never rise;   *destructive, undesirable*
Let them o'errun all the sweet fragrant banks,
30 And hide what grows in better ordered ranks.°   *controlled rows*
Too much, alas, this parallel° I find   *correspondence*
In the disordered passions of my mind
But thy late loveliness is only hid,
Mine like the shadow with its substance fled.
35 Another gardener and another spring
May into thee new grace and new luster bring,

---

1. Hutchinson wrote her elegies after the death of her husband, John Hutchinson. This is Elegy 7. Despite having escaped death for his part in the regicide, he was arrested again in 1663 on charges of participating in a republican conspiracy and died in prison in September 1664. In the 1650s and 1660s, the Hutchinsons remodeled their Nottinghamshire estate, Owthorpe, and the elegies are haunted by John's absence from this once-shared landscape. In Elegy 12, "Musings in My Evening Walks at Owthorpe," the garden joins Lucy in mourning, even as she reflects on how her sorrow "glads [her] enemies."

2. That which is the least ornamental is the most appropriate.

3. Hutchinson refers here to the process of enclosing the commons, the public grounds to which the people had rights and access under common law. In her *Memoirs*, she distinguishes between the massive enclosures of the nobility and the lesser enclosures of the gentry who guarded the landscape both from the incursions of the king and from the leveling democracy of common land. (The Hutchinson family behaved "as if there had been an Agrarian law in the family," following John Harrington's prescription to limit the size of landed wealth.)

While beauty's seeds do yet remain alive.
But ah, my glories never can revive
No more than new leaves or new smiling fruit
40 Can reinvest that tree that's dead at root.
When to his worthy memory thou then
Hast offered one year's fruit,[4] thou mayst again
In gaudy dresses to thy next lord shine[5]
And show weak semblance° of his grace in thine.   *likeness*
45 For all that's generous, healthful, sweet and fair,
Imperfect emblems° of his virtue are.   *representations*
But could I call back hasty flying time
The vanished glories that decked once my prime,°   *most flourishing stage*
To me that resurrection would be vain
50 And like ungathered flowers would die again.
In vain would doting° time, which can no more   *foolish*
Give such a lover, loveliness restore.

ca. 1664   1997

From Order and Disorder[1]

Canto 5

Sad Nature's sighs gave the alarms,
And all her frighted hosts stood to their arms,
Waiting whom the great Sovereign would employ
His all-deserted rebels to destroy,
5 When God descended out of heaven above[2]
His disobedient viceroy° to remove.   *vice king*
Yet, though himself had seen the forfeiture,°   *crime*
Which distance could not from his eyes obscure;
To teach his future substitutes how they
10 Should judgments execute in a right way,
He would not unexamined facts condemn,
Nor punish sinners without hearing them;
Therefore cites to his bar[3] the criminals,
And Adam first out of his covert calls.

---

4. The offering of the first crop to God.
5. Hutchinson parted from Owthorpe in 1671, when its "next lord" took possession.
1. Hutchinson likely wrote her epic poem on Genesis in the 1660s, when a manuscript of twenty cantos circulated among her peers. The first five cantos were printed anonymously in 1679. The twenty-canto version was not published until 2001.
2. In the printed text, references to scriptural texts in the left-hand margin accompany many lines of verse, offering meaningful, and often politicized, intertexts for readers steeped in scripture. The marginal note here, for example, "Gen. 3.8," indicates the moment at which God arrives in the garden to punish Adam and Eve and they hide from him among the trees. These marginal references do not appear in the manuscript and have been omitted here for ease of reading.
3. Summons formally to appear in a court of law. Hutchinson often invokes the rule of law in her presentation of divine punishment. See also line 57. The marginal reference at line 11 is to 2 Samuel 23:3: "The God of Israel said, the Rock of Israel spake to me, He that ruleth over men must be just, ruling in the fear of God."

15 'Where art thou, Adam?' the Almighty said.
    'Here, Lord,' the trembling sinner answer made,
    'Amongst the trees I in the garden heard
    Thy voice, and being naked, was afeared,
    Nor durst I so thy purer sight abide,
20 Therefore myself did in this shelter hide.'
    'Hast thou,' said God, 'eat the forbidden tree,
    Or who declared thy nakedness to thee?'
    'She,' answered Adam, 'whom thou didst create
    To be my helper and associate
25 Gave me the fatal fruit, and I did eat.'
    Then Eve was also called from her retreat.
    'Woman, what hast thou done?' th'Almighty said;
    'Lord,' answered she, 'the serpent me betrayed
    And I did eat.' Thus did they both confess
30 Their guilt, and vainly sought to make it less
    By such extenuations° as, well weighed,   *attempts to mitigate*
    The sin, so circumstanced, more sinful made:
    A course which still half-softened sinners use:
    Transferring blame their own faults to excuse,
35 They care not how, nor where, and oftentimes
    On God himself obliquely charge their crimes,
    Expostulating° in their discontent   *complaining*
    As if he caused what he did not prevent;
    Which Adam wickedly implies, when he
40 Cries, ''Twas the woman that thou gavest me';
    Oft-times make that the Devil's guilt alone,
    Which was as well and equally their own.
    His lies could never have prevailed on Eve
    But that she wished them truth, and did believe
45 A forgery that suited her desire,
    Whose haughty heart was prone enough t'aspire.
    The tempting and the urging was his ill,
    But the compliance was in her own will.
    And herein truly lies the difference
50 Of natural and gracious penitence:
    The first transferreth and extenuates°   *diminishes, underrates*
    The guilt, which the other owns and aggravates.
    While sin is but regarded slight and small
    It makes the value of rich mercy fall,
55 But as our crimes seem greater in our eyes,
    So doth our grateful sense of pardon rise.
        Poor mankind at God's righteous bar was cast
    And set for judgment by, when at the last
    Satan within the serpent had his doom,[4]
60 Whose execrable° malice left no room   *detestable*
    For plea or pardon, but was sentenced first:
    'Thou,' said the Lord, 'above all beasts accursed,
    Shalt on thy belly creep, on dust shalt feed;

---

4. Tradition, not Genesis, identifies the serpent with Satan.

Between thee and the woman, and her seed
And thine, I will put lasting enmity;
Thou in this war his heel shalt bruise, but he
Thy head shall break.' More various mystery
Ne'er did within so short a sentence lie.
Here is irrevocable° vengeance, here   *irreversible*
Love as immutable.° Here doth appear   *unchangeable*
Infinite wisdom plotting with free grace,
Even by man's fall, th'advance of human race.
Severity here utterly confounds,
Here Mercy cures by kind and gentle wounds,
The Father here the gospel first reveals,
Here fleshly veils th'eternal Son conceals.
The law of life and spirit here takes place,
Given with the promise of assisting grace.
Here is an oracle foretelling all
Which shall the two opposèd seeds befall.
The great war hath its first beginning here,
Carried along more than five thousand year,
With various success° on either side,   *outcome*
And each age with new combatants supplied.
Two sovereign champions here we find,
Satan and Christ contending for mankind.
Two empires here, two opposite cities rise,
Dividing all in two societies:
The little Church and the World's larger State,[5]
Pursuing it with ceaseless spite and hate.
Each party here erecting their own walls,
As one advances, so the other falls.
Hope in the promise the weak Church confirms,
Hell and the World fight upon desperate terms:
By this most certain oracle they know
Their war must end in final overthrow.
Some little present mischief they may do,
And this with eager malice they pursue.
The angels whom God's justice did divide
Engage their mighty powers on either side:
Hell's gloomy princes the World's rulers made,[6]
Heaven's unseen host the Church's guard and aid;
Till the frail woman's conquering son shall tread
Beneath his feet the serpent's broken head.
    Though God the speech to man's false foe address,
The words rich grace to fallen man express,
Which God will not to him himself declare
Till he implore it by submissive prayer;
Sufficient 'tis to know a latitude
For hope, which doth no penitent exclude.

---

5. The contrast here is between what Luke 12:32 (cited in the margin) calls God's "little flock" and the secular world. Hutchinson also suggests a smaller congregation of God's elect.

6. The marginal reference here is to Revelation 12:7–9, which describes the war in heaven, but Hutchinson also signals her defiant republicanism.

Had death's sad sentence passed on man before
The promise of that seed which should restore
His fallen state, destroying death and sin,
Cureless as Satan's had his misery been.
115 But though free grace did future help provide,
Yet must he present loss and woe abide
And feel the bitter curse, that he may so
The sweet release of saving mercy know.
Prepared with late-indulgèd hope, on Eve
120 Th'Almighty next did gentler sentence give.[7]
'I will,' said he, 'greatly augment thy woes,
And thy conceptions, which with painful throes
Thou shalt bring forth, yet shall they be to thee
But a successive crop of misery.
125 Thy husband shall thy ruler be, whose sway
Thou shalt with passionate desires obey'.
    Alas! How sadly to this day we find
Th'effect of this dire curse on womankind;
Eve sinned in fruit forbid,° and God requires   *forbidden*
130 Her penance in the fruit of her desires.
When first to men their inclinations move,
How are they tortured with distracting love!
What disappointments find they in the end;
Constant uneasinesses which attend
135 The best condition of the wedded state,
Giving all wives sense of the curse's weight,
Which makes them ease and liberty refuse,
And with strong passion their own shackles choose.
Now though they easier under wise rule prove,
140 And every burden is made light by love,
Yet golden fetters, soft-lined yokes, still be
Though gentler curbs, but curbs of liberty,
As well as the harsh tyrant's iron yoke;
More sorely galling° them whom they provoke   *chafing, harassing*
145 To loathe their bondage, and despise the rule
Of an unmanly, fickle, froward° fool.[8]   *perverse, ungovernable*
Whate'er the husbands be, they covet fruit,
And their own wishes to their sorrows contribute.
How painfully the fruit within them grows,
150 What tortures do their ripened births disclose,
How great, how various, how uneasy are
The breeding-sicknesses, pangs that prepare
The violent openings of life's narrow door,
Whose fatal issues we as oft deplore!
155 What weaknesses, what languishments ensue,

---

7. Hutchinson ranges far beyond the description of Eve's punishment in Genesis (the marginal reference reads "Gen. 3.16 etc."), describing women's experiences as wives and mothers in terms at once sympathetic and indignant.

8. The marginal reference here is to 1 Samuel 25:25, in which Abigail pleads with David not to countenance her husband, the tyrant Nabal.

Scattering dead lilies where fresh roses grew.[9]
What broken rest afflicts the careful nurse,
Extending to the breasts the mother's curse;
Which ceases not when there her milk she dries,
160 The froward child draws new streams from her eyes.
How much more bitter anguish do we find
Labouring to raise up virtue in the mind
Than when the members[1] in our bowels° grew: *internal organs*
What sad abortions, what cross births[2] ensue:
165 What monsters, what unnatural vipers come
Eating their passage through their parent's womb;
How are the tortures of their births renewed,
Unrecompensed with love and gratitude.
Even the good, who would our cares requite,
170 Would be our crowns, joys, pillars, and delight,
Affect us yet with other griefs and fears,
Opening the sluices of our near-dried tears.
Death, danger, sickness, losses, all the ill
That on the children falls, the mothers feel,
175 Repeating with worse pangs the pangs that bore
Them into life; and though some may have more
Of sweet and gentle mixture, some of worse,
Yet every mother's cup tastes of the curse,
And when the heavy load her faint heart tires,
180 Makes her too oft repent her fond desires.
  Now last of all, as Adam last had been
Drawn into the prevaricating° sin,   *transgressing, equivocating*
His sentence came: 'Because that thou didst yield,'
Said God, 'to thy enticing wife, the field,
185 Producing briars and fruitless thorns to thee,
Accursèd for thy sake and sins shall be.
Thy careful brows in constant toils shall sweat,
Thus thou thy bread shalt all thy whole life eat
Till thou return into the earth's vast womb,
190 Whence, taken first, thou didst a man become;
For dust thou art, and dust again shalt be
When life's declining spark goes out in thee.'
  In all these sentences we strangely find
God's admirable love to lost mankind;
195 Who, though he never will his word recall
Or let his threats like shafts at random fall,
Yet can his wisdom order curses so
That blessings may out of their bowels flow.
Thus death the door of lasting life became,
200 Dissolving nature to rebuild her frame

---

9. Compare with Hester Pulter's "Upon the Death of My Dear and Lovely Daughter, Jane Pulter" (p. 1228).
1. Parts or organs of the body; persons (especially those belonging to the metaphorical body of Christ).
2. Births in which neither the feet nor head of the fetus lies in the direction of the birth canal. "Abortions" here refers to the expulsion or removal from the womb of developing embryos or fetuses.

On such a sure foundation as shall break
All the attempts Hell's cursèd empire make.
Thus God revenged man's quarrel on his foe,
To whom th'Almighty would no mercy show,
205 Making his reign, his respite, and success,
All augmentations of his cursedness.
Thus gave he us a powerful Chief and Head,
By whom we shall be out of bondage led,
And made the penalties of our offence
210 Precepts and rules of new obedience,
Fitted in all things to our fallen state
Under sweet promises that ease their weight.
Our first injunction is to hate and fly
The flatteries of our first grand enemy;
215 To have no friendship with his cursèd race,[3]
The interest of the opposite seed t'embrace,
Where though we toil in fights, though bruised we be,
Yet shall our combat end in victory,
Eternal glory healing our slight wound
220 When all our labours are with triumph crowned.
    The next command is, mothers should maintain
Posterity, not frighted with the pain,
Which, though it make us mourn under the sense
Of the first mother's disobedience,
225 Yet hath a promise that thereby she shall
Recover all the hurt of her first fall
When, in mysterious manner, from her womb
Her father, brother, husband, son shall come.
Subjection to the husband's rule enjoined
230 In the next place: that yoke with love is lined,[4]
Love too a precept° made, where God requires   *maxim; divine command*
We should perform our duties with desires;
And promises t'incline our averse° will,   *opposed*
Whose satisfaction takes away the ill
235 Of every toil and every suffering
That can from unenforced submission spring.
The last command God with man's curse did give
Was that men should in honest callings live,
Eating their own bread, fruit of their own sweat,
240 Nor feed like drones° on that which others get: *lazy people*
And this command a promise doth imply
That bread should recompense° our industry.   *reward, repay*
    One mercy more his sentence did include,
That mortal toils, faintings and lassitude
245 Should not beyond death's fixèd bound extend,

---

3. Children or descendants (poetic). See *Paradise Lost* 10.385.
4. The marginal reference here, "*Eph.*5.25 etc.," enjoins husbands to "love your wives, even as Christ also loved the church, and gave himself for it," a line that Hutchinson, like other defenders of women, chooses as a counterbalance to Ephesians 22, enjoining wives to "submit yourselves unto your own husbands, as unto the Lord."

    But there in everlasting quiet end.
    When men out of the troubled air depart,
    And to their first material dust revert,
    The utmost power that death or woe can have
250 Is but to shut us prisoners in the grave,
    Bruising the flesh, that heel whereon we tread;
    But we shall trample on the serpent's head.
    Our scattered atoms shall again condense,
    And be again inspired with living sense;
255 Captivity shall then a captive be,[5]
    Death shall be swallowed up in victory,
    And God shall man to Paradise restore,
    Where the foul tempter shall seduce no more.
        How far our parents, whose sad eyes were fixed
260 On woe and terror, saw the mercy mixed
    We can but make a wild uncertain guess,
    As we are now affected in distress,
    Who less regard the mitigation still
    Than the slight smart of our afflicting ill;
265 And while we groan under the hated yoke,
    Our gratitude for its soft lining choke.
        But God, having th'amazèd sinners doomed,
    Put off the judge's frown and reassumed
    A tender father's kind and melting° face,   *tearful*
270 Opening his gracious arms for new embrace,
    Taught them to expiate° their heinous guilt   *atone for*
    By spotless sacrifice and pure blood spilt,
    Which, done in faith, did their faint hearts sustain
    Till the intended Lamb of God was slain,
275 Whose death, whose merit, and whose innocence
    The forfeit paid and blotted out th'offence.
    The skins of the slain beasts God vestures° made   *clothing*
    Wherein the naked sinners were arrayed,
    Not without mystery, which typified°   *symbolized*
280 That righteousness that doth our foul shame hide.
    As when a rotting patient must endure
    Painful excisions to effect cure,
    His spirits we with cordials° fortify,   *drinks, medicines*
    Lest, unsupported, he should faint and die,
285 So with our parents the Almighty dealt:
    Before their necessary woes they felt,
    Their feeble souls rich promises upheld
    And their deliverance was in types[6] revealed.
    Even their bodies God himself did arm
290 With clothes that kept them from the weather's harm;
    But after all, they must be driven away,

---

5. See *Paradise Lost* 10.188 and Donne's "Death Be Not Proud."
6. People, objects, and events from the Hebrew Bible that Christians read as prefiguring new Christian dispensations.

       Nor in their forfeit Paradise must stay.
           Then said the Lord with holy irony,
       Whence man the folly of his pride might see,
295   'The earthly man like one of us is grown,
       To whom, as God, both good and ill is known.
       Now lest he also eat of th'other tree,
       Whose fruit gives life, and an immortal be,
       Let us by just and timely banishment
300   His further sinful arrogance prevent.'
       Then did he them out of the garden chase
       And set a cherubim to guard the place,
       Who waved a flaming sword before the door
       Through which the wretches must return no more.
305   May we not liken to this sword of flame
       The threatening law which from Mount Sinai[7] came,
       With such thick flashes of prodigious fire
       As made the mountains shake and men retire,
       Forbidding them all forward hope that they
310   Could enter into life that dreadful way?
       Whate'er it was, whate'er it signifies,
       It kept our parents out of Paradise,
       Who now, returning to their place of birth,
       Found themselves strangers in their native earth.
315   Their fatal breach of God's most strict command
       Had there dissolved all concord, the sweet band
       Of universal loveliness and peace,
       And now the calm in every part did cease;
       Love, though immutable, its smiles did shroud
320   Under the dark veil of an angry cloud,
       And while he seemed withdrawn whose grace upheld
       The order of all things, confusion filled
       The universe. The air became impure
       And frequent dreadful conflicts did endure
325   With every other angry element;[8]
       The whirling fires its tender body rent.
       From earth and seas gross vapours did arise,
       Turned to prodigious meteors in the skies;
       The blustering winds let loose their furious rage
330   And in their battles did the floods engage.
       The sun confounded was with Nature's shame
       And the pale moon shrunk in her sickly flame;
       The rude congregations° of the angry stars   *rough or turbulent meetings*
       In heaven begun the universal wars,
335   While their malicious influence from above
       On Earth did various perturbations move.

---

7. The peak in Egypt's Sinai Peninsula where Moses received the Ten Commandments (Exodus 19:10–20:18).

8. One of the substances out of which all material bodies are made (earth, water, air, and fire); the atmosphere.

       Droughts, inundations, blastings, killed the plants;
       Worse influence wrought on th'inhabitants,
       Inspiring lust, rage, ravenous appetite,
340   Which made the creatures in all regions fight.
       The little insects in great clouds did rise
       And, in battalias° spread, obscured the skies;   *battalions*
       Armies of birds encountered in the air,
       With hideous cries deciding battles there;
345   The birds of prey, to gorge their appetite,
       Seized harmless fowl in their unwary flight.
       When the dim evening had shut in the day,
       Troops of wild beasts, all marching out for prey,
       To the resistless° flocks would go, and there   *powerless to resist*
350   Oft-times by other troops assailèd were,
       Who snatched out of their jaws the new-slain food
       And made them purchase it again with blood.
          Thus sin the whole Creation did divide
       Into th'oppressing and the suffering side.
355   Those, still employing craft and violence
       T'ensnare and murder simple innocence,
       True emblems were of Satan's craft and power
       In daily ambuscado° to devour;   *ambush*
       Nor only emblems were, but organs° too,   *instruments*
360   In and by whom he did his mischiefs do,
       While persecuting cruelty and rage
       Them in his cursèd party did engage.
       Love, meekness, patience, gentleness, combined
       The tamer brood with those of their own kind;
365   Wherefore God chose them for his sacrifice
       When he the proud and mighty did despise,
       And his most certain oracles declare
       They man's restored peace at last shall share.
          But to our parents then, sad was the change
370   Which them from peace and safety did estrange,
       Brought universal woe and discord in,
       The never-failing consequents° of sin;   *consequences*
       Nor only made all things without them jar°   *clash*
       But in their breasts raised up a civil war.
375   Reason and sense maintained continual fight,
       Urging th'aversion and the appetite,
       Which led two different troops of passions out,
       Confounding all in their tumultuous rout.°   *mob*
       The less world with the great proportion held:
380   As winds the caverns, sighs the bosoms filled;
       So flowing tears did beauty's fair fields drown,
       As inundations kept within no bound.
       Fear earthquakes made, lust in the fancy whirled,
       Turned into flame and, bursting, fired the world:
385   Spite, hate, revenge, ambition, avarice.
       Made innocence a prey to monstrous vice.
       The cold and hot diseases represent

The perturbations of the element.
Thus woe and danger had beset them round,
390 Distressed without, within no comfort found.
Even as a monarch's favourite in disgrace
Suffers contempt both from the high and base,
And the most abject most insult o'er them
Whom the offended sovereigns condemn;
395 So after man th'Almighty disobeyed,
Each little fly durst his late king invade
As well as the wood's monsters, wolves and bears,
And all things else that exercise his fears.[9]
Methinks I hear sad Eve in some dark vale
400 Her woeful state with such sad plaints° bewail: *moaning; complaints*
'Ah! why doth Death its latest stroke delay?[1]
If we must leave the light, why do we stay
By slow degrees more painfully to die,
And languish in a long calamity?°   *misery*
405 Have we not lost by one false cheating sin
All peace without, all sweet repose within?
Is there a pleasure yet that life can show,
Doth not each moment multiply our woe:
And while we live thus in perpetual dread,
410 Our hope and comfort long before us dead,
Why should we not our angry Maker pray
At once to take our wretched lives away?
Hath not our sin all Nature's pure leagues rent°   *covenants split apart*
And armed against us every element?
415 Have not our subjects their allegiance broke,
Doth not each worm° scorn our unworthy yoke?   *low creature*
Are we not half with griping° hunger pined°   *painful / starved*
Before we bread amongst the brambles find?
All pale diseases in our members° reign,   *body parts or organs*
420 Anguish and grief no less our sick souls pain.
Wherever I my eyes or thoughts convert,°   *turn*
Each object adds new tortures to my heart.
If I look up, I dread Heaven's threatening frown,
Thorns prick my eyes when shame hath cast them down,
425 Dangers I see, looking on either hand,
Before me all in fighting posture stand.
If I cast back my sorrow-drownèd eyes,
I see our ne'er to be recovered Paradise,
The flaming sword which doth us thence exclude,
430 By sad remorse and ugly guilt pursued.
If on my sin-defilèd self I gaze,
My nakedness and spots do me amaze.°   *terrify, stupefy*
If I on thee a private glance reflect,°   *turn back*

---

9. The simile compares the disgraced favorite, hated by both high and low, to man, who after his fall is tormented both by "every little fly" and by the worst beasts of his fears.
1. See *Paradise Lost* 10.771–73.

Confusion doth my shameful eyes deject,
Seeing the man I love by me betrayed,
By me, who for his mutual help was made,
Who to preserve thy life ought to have died,
And I have killed thee by my foolish pride,
Defiled thy glory and pulled down thy throne.
O that I had but sinned and died alone!
Then had my torture and my woe been less,
I yet had flourished in thy happiness.'[2]
   If these words Adam's melting soul did move,
He might reply with kind rebuking° love: *reprimanding*
'Cease, cease, O foolish woman, to dispute,
God's sovereign will and power are absolute.
If he will have us soon or slow to die,
Frail worms must yield, but must not question why.
When his great hand appears, we must conclude
All that he doth is wise and just and good;
Though our poor, sin-benighted souls are blind,
Nor can the mysteries of his wisdom find,
Yet in our present case we must confess
His justice and our own unrighteousness.
He warned us of this fatal consequence,
That death must wait on disobedience;
Yet we despised his threat and broke his law,
So did destruction on our own heads draw;
Now under his afflicting hand we lie,
Reaping the fruit of our iniquity;
Which, had not he prevented when we fell,
At once had plunged us in the lowest Hell;
But by his mercy yet we have reprieve,
And yet are showed how we in death may live,
If we improve our short-indulgèd space
To understand, prize, and accept his grace.
   'Did all of us at once like brutes expire
And cease to be, we might quick death desire:
But since our chief and immaterial part,
Not framed of dust, doth not to dust revert,
Its death not an annihilation is,
But to be cut off from its supreme bliss:
Whatever here to mortals can befall
Compared to future miseries is small.
The saddest, sharpest, and the longest have
Their final consummations° in the grave;   *conclusions*
These have their intermissions and allays,°   *moderations*
Though black and gloomy ones, these nights have days.
The worst calamities we here endure
Admit a possibility of cure.

---

2. Writing in the 1730s, Julius Hutchinson notes that "these verses were writ by Mrs. Hutchinson on the occasion of the Colonel her husband's being then a prisoner in the Tower, 1664."

Our miseries here are varied in their kind,
And in that change the wretched some ease find.
Sleep here our pained senses stupefies
And cheating streams in our sick fancies rise,
485 But in our future sufferings 'tis not so,
There is no end, no intermitted° woe,   *suspended, interrupted*
No more return from the accursed place,
No hope, no possibility of grace,
No sleepy intervals, no pleasant dreams,
490 No mitigations of those sad extremes,
No gentle mixtures, no soft changes there,
Perpetual tortures heightened with despair,
Eternal horror and eternal night,
Eternal burnings with no glance of light,
495 Eternal pain. O, 'tis a thought too great,
Too terrible, for any to repeat
Who have not 'scaped° the dread. Let's not to shun   *escaped*
Heaven's scorching rays, into Hell's furnace run:
But having slain ourselves, let's fly to him
500 Who only can our souls from death redeem.
    'To undo what's done is not within our power,
No more than to call back the last fled hour.
To think we can our fallen state restore,
Or without hope our ruin to deplore,
505 Are equal aggravating crimes; the first
Repeats that sin for which we were accursed,
While we with foolish arrogating° pride   *presumptuous*
More in ourselves than in our God confide;°   *trust*
The last is both ungrateful and unjust,
510 That doth his goodness or his power distrust,
Which wheresoe'er we look, without, within,
Above, beneath, in every place is seen.
Doth Heaven frown? Above the sullen shrouds
God sits, and sees through all the blackest clouds
515 Sin casts about us, like the misty night,
Which hides his pleasing glances from our sight;
Nor only sees, but darts on us his beams,
Ministering comfort in our worst extremes.
When lightnings fly, dire storm and thunder roars,
520 He guides the shafts, the serene calm restores.
When shadows occupy day's vacant room,
He makes new glory spring from night's dark womb.
When the black prince of air lets loose the winds,
The furious warriors he in prison binds.
525 If burnings stars do conflagrations threat,°   *fires threaten*
He gives cool breezes to allay the heat.
When cold doth in its rigid season reign,
He melts the snows and thaws the air again;
Restoring the vicissitude of things,
530 He still new good from every evil brings.
He holds together the world's shaken frame,
Ordaining every change, is still the same.

If he permit the elements to fight,
The rage of storms, the blackness of the night;
'Tis that his power, love and wisdom may
More glory have, restoring calm and day;
That we may more the pleasant blessings prize,
Laid in the balance with their contraries.
   'Though dangers, then, like gaping monsters stand
Ready to swallow us on either hand,
Let us despise them, firm in this faith still,
If God will save, they can nor hurt nor kill;
If by his just permission we are slain,
His power can heal and quicken° us again.   revive
If briars and thorns which from our sins arise,
Looking on earth, pierce through our guilty eyes,
Let's yet give thanks they have not choked the seed
Which should with better fruit our sad lives feed.
If discord set the inward world on fire,
With haste let's to the living spring retire,
There quench and quiet the disturbèd soul,
There on Love's sweet refreshing green banks roll,
Where, ecstasied with joy, we shall not feel
The serpent's little nibblings at our heel.
If we look back on Paradise, late lost,
Joys vanished like swift dreams, thawed like a frost,
Converting pleasant walks to dirt and mire,
Would we such frail delights again desire,
Which at their best, however excellent,
Had this defect, they were not permanent?
If sin, remorse, and guilt give us the chase,
Let us lie close in Mercy's sweet embrace,
Which when it us ashamed and naked found,
In the soft arms of melting pity bound,
Eternal glorious triumphs did prepare,
Armed us with clothes against the wounding air,
By expiating sacrifices taught
How new life shall by death to light be brought.
If we before us look, although we see
All things in present fighting posture be:
Yet in the promise we a prospect have
Of Victory swallowing up the empty grave;
Our foes all vanquished, Death itself lies dead,
And we shall trample on the monster's head,
Entering into a new and perfect joy
Which neither sin nor sorrow can destroy:
A lasting and refined felicity,
For which even we ourselves refined must be.
Then shall we laugh at our now childish woes,
And hug the birth that issues from these throes.[3]
   'Let not my share of grief afflict thy mind,

---

3. The "birth" that issues from the "throes" of death is the final judgment and resurrection.

But let me comfort in thy courage find;
'Twas not thy malice, but thy ignorance
That lately my destruction did advance;
585 Nor can I my own self excuse; 'twas I
Undid myself by my facility.° *easiness, compliance*
Let's not in vain each other now upbraid,° *reproach*
But rather strive to'afford each other aid,
And our most gracious Lord with due thanks bless,
590 Who hath not left us single in distress.
When fear chills thee, my hope shall make thee warm,
When I grow faint, thou shalt my courage arm;
When both our spirits at a low ebb are,
We both will join in mutual fervent prayer
595 To him whose gracious succour never fails
When sin and death poor feeble man assails,
He that our final triumph hath decreed
And promised thee salvation in thy seed.'
　　Ah! can I this in Adam's person say,
600 While fruitless tears melt my poor life away?
Of all the ills to mortals incident,
None more pernicious is than discontent,
That brat of unbelief and stubborn pride
And sensual lust, with no joy satisfied,
605 That doth ingratitude and murmur nurse,
And is a sin which carries its own curse;
This is the only smart of every ill.
But can we without it sad tortures feel?
Yes; if our souls above our sense remain,
610 And take not in th'afflicted body's pain;
When they descend and mix with the disease,
Then doth the anguish live, reign, and increase,
Which when the soul is not in it, grows faint
And wastes its strength, not nourished with complaint.
615 Submissive, humble, happy, sweet content
A thousand deaths by one death doth prevent,
When our rebellious wills, subdued thereby
Into th'eternal will and wisdom, die;
Nor is that will harsh or irrational,
620 But sweet in that which we most bitter call,
Who err in judging what is ill or good,
Only by studying that will understood.
　　What we admire in a low paradise,
If they our souls from heavenly thoughts entice,
625 Here terminating our most strong desire
Which should to perfect permanence aspire,
From being good to us they are so far
That they our fetters, yokes and poisons are,
The obstacles of our felicity,° *happiness*
630 The ruin of our souls' most firm healths be,
Quenching that life-maintaining appetite
Which makes substantial fruit our sound delight.

The evils, so miscalled, that we endure
Are wholesome medicines tending to our cure;
635 Only disease to these aversion breeds,
The healthy soul on them with due thanks feeds.
If for a prince, a mistress, or a friend,
Many do joy their blood and lives to spend,
Wealth, honour, ease, dangers and wounds despise,
640 Should we not more to God's will sacrifice
And by free gift prevent that else-sure loss?
Whate'er our will is, we must bear the cross,
Which freely taken up, the weight is less
And hurts not, carried on with cheerfulness.
645 Besides, what we can lose are gliding streams,
Light airy shadows, unsubstantial dreams,
Wherein we no propriety° could have   *ownerships, property*
But that which our own cheating fancy gave.
The right of them was due to God alone,
650 And when with thanks we render him his own
Either he gives us back our offerings
Or our submission pays with better things.
Were ills as real as our fancies make,
They soon must us, or we must them forsake;
655 We cannot miss ease and vicissitude
Till our last rest our labours shall conclude.
Natural tears[4] there are which in due bound
Do not the soul with sinful sorrow drown;
Repentant tears, too, are no fretting brine,°   *corroding salt water*
660 But Love's soft meltings, which the soul refine;
Like gentle showers that usher in the spring,
These make the soul more fair and flourishing.
No murmuring winds of passions here prevail,
But the life-breathing spirit's sweet fresh gale,
665 Which by those fruitful drops all graces feeds
And draws rich extracts from the soakèd seeds;
But worldly sorrow, like rough winter's storms,
All graces kills, all loveliness deforms,
Augments the evils of our present state
670 And doth eternal woes anticipate.
Vain is that grief which can no ill redress
But adds affliction to uneasiness,
Unnerving the soul's powers then when they should
Most exercise their constant fortitude.
675 With these most certain truths let's wind up all:[5]
Whatever doth to mortal men befall

---

4. See *Paradise Lost* 12.645.
5. "Wind up all" (sum up or bring to a close) suggests that cantos 1–5 were originally conceived as a complete work. Hutchinson's twenty-canto poem circulated in the manuscript form associated with more politically controversial matters, but its first five cantos were printed anonymously in 1679 as *Order and disorder, or, The world made and undone, being meditations upon the creation and fall, as it is recorded in the beginnings of Genesis.*

Not casual⁶ is, like shafts at random shot,
But Providence distributes every lot,
In which th'obedient and the meek rejoice,
Above their own preferring God's wise choice.
Nor is his Providence less good than wise,
Though our gross sense pierce not its mysteries.
As there's but one most true substantial good,
And God himself is that beatitude:
So can we suffer but one real ill,
Divorce from him by our repugnant will,
Which when to just submission it returns
The reunited soul no longer mourns,
His serene rays dry up its former tears,
Dispel the tempest of its carnal fears,
Which dread what either never may arrive,
Or not as seen in their false perspective;
For in the crystal mirror of God's grace
All things appear with a new lovely face.
When that doth Heaven's more glorious palace show,
We cease t'admire a Paradise below,
Rejoice in that which lately was our loss,
And see a crown made up of every cross.
Return, return, my soul, to thy true rest,
As young benighted⁷ birds unto their nest;
There hide thyself under the wings of Love
Till the bright morning all thy clouds remove.

ca. 1660s   1679

6. Accidental; without design.   7. Overtaken by darkness or obscurity.

KATHERINE PHILIPS
1632–1664

The most famous woman poet of her own and the next generation, Katherine Philips was honored as "the Matchless Orinda," the classical name she chose for herself in her poetic addresses to a coterie of chiefly female friends, especially Mary Aubrey (M. A.) and Anne Owen (Lucasia). Sometimes reminiscent of Donne's love lyrics, and sometimes of the ancient Greek Sappho's erotic lyrics to women, these poems develop an exalted ideal of female friendship as a Platonic union of souls. If souls "no sexes have," she writes in one poem,

for men t'exclude
Women from friendship's vast capacity,
Is a design injurious and rude,
Only maintained by partial tyranny.

Two prose treatises, including Jeremy Taylor's *Discourse of the Nature, Offices, and Measures of Friendship* (1657), were dedicated to Philips, indicating the seriousness with which her theories of friendship were considered in the period.

Born to a well-to-do Presbyterian family and educated at Mrs. Salmon's Presbyterian School in Hackney, Philips was taken to Wales when her mother remarried. In 1648, at age seventeen, she was married to James Philips, a prominent member of Parliament. They lived together twelve years, chiefly in the small Welsh town of Cardigan. The death of her son, Hector, a few days after birth prompted one of her most moving poems. A royalist despite her Puritan family connections, Philips forged connections with other displaced royalists. Her poems circulated in manuscript and elicited high praise from Henry Vaughan, among others. They include elegies, epitaphs, poems at parting, and friendship poems to women and men, but also poetry on political themes: a denunciation of the regicide, "Upon the Double Murder of King Charles," and panegyrics on the restored Stuarts.

After the Restoration, James Philips barely escaped execution as a regicide, had his estates confiscated, and lost his seat in Parliament. Katherine, however, became a favorite at court, promoted by her friend Sir Charles Cotterell ("Poliarchus"), who was master of ceremonies. Attempting (unsuccessfully) to redeem an investment, in Ireland, Philips translated Corneille's *Pompey*, which she and her friend the Earl of Orrery produced and printed in Dublin in 1663. The first edition of her poems, apparently pirated, appeared in 1664, the same year she died of smallpox. Her friend Cotterell brought out an authorized edition in 1667 titled *Poems by the Most Deservedly Admired Mrs. Katherine Philips, the Matchless Orinda*. The many extant manuscript collections of her poems suggest the popularity and wide circulation of her work both during her lifetime and after.

A Married State[1]

A married state affords but little ease
The best of husbands are so hard to please.
This in wives' careful° faces you may spell°   *full of cares / read*
Though they dissemble their misfortunes well.
5 A virgin state is crowned with much content;[2]
It's always happy as it's innocent.
No blustering husbands to create your fears;
No pangs of childbirth to extort your tears;
No children's cries for to offend your ears;

---

1. In a manuscript (Orielton MSS Box 24 at the National Library of Wales) this poem appears with another by Philips, addressed to Anne Barlow (whom she probably met in 1646); this one is probably also for Barlow. Both are signed by her maiden name, C. Fowler, so were evidently written before her marriage in 1648.
2. Praise of the single life is a common topic in women's poetry.

          Few worldly crosses to distract your prayers:
          Thus are you freed from all the cares that do
          Attend on matrimony and a husband too.
          Therefore Madam, be advised by me
          Turn, turn apostate to love's levity,
          Suppress wild nature if she dare rebel.
          There's no such thing as leading apes in hell.[3]

ca. 1646   MS; 1988

An Answer to Another Persuading a Lady to Marriage

1

    Forbear, bold youth, all's Heaven here,
        And what you do aver,
    To others, courtship may appear,
        'Tis sacrilege to her.

2

5   She is a public deity,
        And were't not very odd
    She should depose her self to be
        A pretty household god?

3

    First make the sun in private shine,
10   And bid the world adieu,
    That so he may his beams confine
        In complement to you.

4

    But if of that you do despair,
        Think how you did amiss,
15   To strive to fix her beams which are
        More bright and large than this.

                                                                                  1667

---

3. Proverbially, the fate of spinsters.

Upon the Double Murder of King Charles

In Answer to a Libelous Rhyme made by V. P.[1]

I think not on the state, nor am concerned
Which way soever that great helm[2] is turned,
But as that son whose father's danger nigh
Did force his native dumbness, and untie
His fettered organs: so here is a cause
That will excuse the breach of nature's laws.[3]
Silence were now a sin: nay passion now
Wise men themselves for merit would allow.[4]
What noble eye could see (and careless pass)
The dying lion kicked by every ass?
Hath Charles so broke God's laws, he must not have
A quiet crown, nor yet a quiet grave?
Tombs have been sanctuaries; thieves lie here
Secure from all their penalty and fear.
Great Charles his double misery was this,
Unfaithful friends, ignoble enemies;
Had any heathen been this prince's foe,
He would have wept to see him injured so.
His title was his crime, they'd reason good
To quarrel at the right they had withstood.
He broke God's laws, and therefore he must die,
And what shall then become of thee and I?
Slander must follow treason; but yet stay,
Take not our reason with our king away.
Though you have seized upon all our defense,
Yet do not sequester° our common sense.   *confiscate*
But I admire° not at this new supply: *wonder*
No bounds will hold those who at scepters fly.
Christ will be King, but I ne'er understood,
His subjects built his kingdom up with blood
(Except their own) or that he would dispense
With his commands, though for his own defense.
Oh! to what height of horror are they come
Who dare pull down a crown, tear up a tomb![5]

1649?   1664

---

1. The itinerant Welsh preacher Vavasour Powell was a *Fifth Monarchist* and an ardent republican who justified the regicide on the ground that Christ's second coming was imminent, when he would rule with his saints, putting down all earthly kings. His poem and Philips's answer were likely written shortly after Charles I's execution (January 30, 1649). Powell's poem has been published by Elizabeth H. Hageman in *English Manuscript Studies*. Compare this poem with Marvell's "An Horatian Ode upon Cromwell's Return from Ireland."
2. Steering wheel for the "ship" of state.
3. Breaking the supposed law of nature that excludes women from speaking about public affairs.
4. Wise men, especially Stoic philosophers, normally counsel the firm control or elimination of passions.
5. Their slanders tear up Charles's tomb after his death.

Friendship's Mystery, To My Dearest *Lucasia*[1]

1

Come, my Lucasia, since we see
   That miracles men's faith do move,
By wonder and by prodigy
   To the dull angry world let's prove
5   There's a religion in our love.

2

For though we were designed t' agree,
   That fate no liberty destroys,
But our election is as free
   As angels, who with greedy choice
10   Are yet determined to their joys.[2]

3

Our hearts are doubled by the loss,
   Here mixture is addition grown;
We both diffuse,° and both engross:°   *spread out / collect*
   And we whose minds are so much one,
15   Never, yet ever are alone.

4

We court our own captivity
   Than thrones more great and innocent:
'Twere banishment to be set free,
   Since we wear fetters whose intent
20   Not bondage is, but ornament.

5

Divided joys are tedious found,
   And griefs united easier grow:
We are selves but by rebound,
   And all our titles shuffled so,
25   Both princes, and both subjects too.[3]

6

Our hearts are mutual victims laid,
   While they (such power in friendship lies)

---

1. This poem was first printed, with a musical setting by the royalist musician and composer Henry Lawes, as "Mutual Affection betweene Orinda and *Lucasia*" in Lawes's *The Second Book of Ayres* (1655); our text is from *Poems by the Most Deservedly Admired Mrs. Katherine Philips, the Matchless Orinda* (1667). Lucasia is Philips's name for her friend Anne Owen.
2. Angels, though created with free will, were thought to have become fixed in goodness when they turned toward God in the first moments after their creation.
3. Compare Donne, "The Sun Rising," line 21: "She is all states, and all princes, I" (p. 888).

>   Are altars, priests, and off'rings made:
>   And each heart which thus kindly° dies,   *benevolently, naturally*
> 30   Grows deathless by the sacrifice.

                                        1655, 1667

To Mrs. M. A.[1] at Parting

>   I have examined and do find,
>   Of all that favor me
>   There's none I grieve to leave behind
>   But only only thee.
> 5   To part with thee I needs must die,
>   Could parting separate thee and I.
>
>   But neither chance nor compliment
>   Did element° our love: *compose*
>   'Twas sacred sympathy was lent
> 10   Us from the choir above.
>   (That friendship fortune did create,
>   Still fears a wound from time or fate.)
>
>   Our changed and mingled souls are grown
>   To such acquaintance now,
> 15 That if each would resume their own,
>   Alas! we know not how.
>   We have each other so engrossed°   *absorbed*
>   That each is in the union lost.[2]
>
>   And thus we can no absence know,
> 20   Nor shall we be confined;
>   Our active souls will daily go
>   To learn each other's mind.
>   Nay, should we never meet to sense,°   *physically*
>   Our souls would hold intelligence.°   *would still commune*
>
> 25 Inspirèd with a flame divine,
>   I scorn to court a stay;[3]
>   For from that noble soul of thine
>   I ne'er can be away.
>   But I shall weep when thou dost grieve;
> 30 Nor can I die whilst thou dost live.
>
>   By my own temper I shall guess
>   At thy felicity,

---

1. M. A. was Mary Aubrey, the first and, until she married, the dearest member of Philips's "Society of Friendship." Orinda's valedictory poem to her—which Keats admired enough to copy it out in full in an early letter—recalls some of Donne's lyrics, especially "A Valediction: Forbidding Mourning" (p. 897).
2. These lines play upon the Neoplatonic idea of friendship and spiritual love—two souls become one.
3. Postponement (of their parting).

  And only like my happiness
   Because it pleaseth thee.
35 Our hearts at any time will tell
   If thou or I be sick or well.

  All honor, sure, I must pretend,°   *aspire to*
   All that is good or great:
  She that would be Rosania's[4] friend
40   Must be at least complete.
  If I have any bravery,°   *splendor*
   'Tis cause I have so much of thee.

  Thy leiger° soul in me shall lie,   *ambassadorial*
   And all thy thoughts reveal;
45 Then back again with mine shall fly,
   And thence to me shall steal.
  Thus still to one another tend:
  Such is the sacred name of friend.

  Thus our twin souls in one shall grow,
50   And teach the world new love,
  Redeem the age and sex, and show
   A flame fate dares not move:
  And courting death to be our friend,
  Our lives, together too, shall end.

55 A dew shall dwell upon our tomb
   Of such a quality
  That fighting armies, thither come,
   Shall reconcilèd be.
  We'll ask no epitaph, but say:
60 ORINDA and ROSANIA.

                    1664

Epitaph: On Her Son H. P. at St. Syth's Church, Where Her Body Was Interred[1]

  What on earth deserves our trust?
  Youth and beauty both are dust.
  Long we gathering are with pain,
  What one moment calls again.
5 Seven years childless, marriage past,
  A son, a son is born at last;
  So exactly limned° and fair,   *portrayed*

---

4. The poetic name Philips gave to Mary Aubrey.
1. Philips wrote two poems on the death of her only son, Hector Philips; he was born April 23 and died May 2, 1655, in Philips's seventh year of marriage. St. Syth's Church, London, where Philips was also buried, burned down in the Great Fire of 1666.

      Full of good spirits, mien,° and air,   *bearing, expression*
      As a long life promised;
10   Yet, in less than six weeks dead.
      Too promising, too great a mind
      In so small room to be confined:
      Therefore, as fit in heav'n to dwell,
      He quickly broke the prison shell.
15   So the subtle alchemist,
      Can't with Hermes' seal resist
      The powerful spirit's subtler flight,
      But t'will bid him long good night.[2]
      And so the sun, if it arise
20   Half so glorious as his eyes,
      Like this infant, takes a shroud,
      Buried in a morning cloud.

                                                                      1667

2. A reference to alchemy's attempt to find the secret of eternal life. Hermes' seal, tight enough to exclude air, is named for Hermes Trismegistus, the Greek name of the Egyptian god Thoth, regarded as the founder of alchemy.

ANDREW MARVELL
1621–1678

Andrew Marvell's finest poems are second to none in this or any other period. He wrote less than did Donne, Jonson, and Herbert, but his range was in some ways greater, including in poetry and prose both the private worlds of love and religious devotion and the public worlds of politics and satire. His overriding concern with art, his limpid style, and the cool balance and reserve of some poems align him with Jonson. Yet his paradoxes and complexities of tone, his use of dramatic monologue, and his witty, dialectical arguments associate him with Donne. Above all, he is a supremely original poet, so complex and elusive that it is often hard to know what he really thought about the subjects he treated. Many of his poems were published posthumously in 1681, some thirty years after they were written, by a woman who claimed to be his widow but was probably his housekeeper. So their date and order of composition are often in doubt, as is his authorship of some anonymous works.

    The son of a Church of England clergyman, Marvell grew up in Yorkshire and attended Trinity College, Cambridge (perhaps deriving the persistent strain of Neoplatonism in his poetry from the academics known as the Cambridge Platonists). Falling under the influence of Jesuits, he ran off to London and converted to Roman Catholicism until his father put an end to both ventures. He returned to Cambridge, took his degree in 1639, and stayed on as a scholar until his father's death in 1641. During the years of the civil wars (1642–48), he traveled in France, Italy, Holland, and Spain. While his earliest poems associate him with royalists, those after 1649 celebrate the Commonwealth and Oliver Cromwell; although he is sometimes ambivalent, Marvell recognizes divine providence in the political changes. From 1650 to 1652 he lived at Nunappleton, in rural Yorkshire, as tutor to the twelve-year-old daughter of Thomas Fairfax, who had given over his command of the parliamentary army to Cromwell because he was unwilling to invade Scotland. In these years of retirement, Marvell probably wrote most of his love lyrics and pastorals as well as *Upon Appleton House*. Later he was tutor to Cromwell's ward, William Dutton, and traveled with him on the Continent; in 1657 he joined the blind Milton, at Milton's request, in the post of Latin secretary to Cromwell's Council of State. After the restoration of Charles II, Marvell maintained his own independent vision and his abiding belief in religious toleration, a mixed state, and constitutional government. He helped his friend Milton avoid execution for his revolutionary polemics, as well as helping to negotiate Milton's release from a brief imprisonment. Elected a member of Parliament in 1659 from his hometown, Hull, in Yorkshire, he held that post until 1678; on two occasions he went on diplomatic missions to Holland and Russia. His (necessarily anonymous) antiroyalist polemics of these years include several verse satires on Charles II and his ministers, as well as his best-known prose work, *The Rehearsal Transprosed* (1672–73), which defends Puritan dissenters and denounces censorship with verve and wit.

Many of Marvell's poems explore the human condition in terms of fundamental dichotomies that resist resolution. In religious or philosophical poems like "The Coronet" or "The Dialogue Between the Soul and Body," the conflict is between nature and grace, body and soul, poetic creation and sacrifice. Love poems such as "The Definition of Love" or "To His Coy Mistress" contrast flesh and spirit, physical sex and platonic love, idealized courtship and the ravages of time. In pastorals like the Mower poems and "The Garden," the opposition is between nature and art, or the fallen and the Edenic state, or violent passion and contentment. Marvell's most subtle and complex political poem, "An Horatian Ode upon Cromwell's Return from Ireland," sets stable traditional order and ancient right against providential revolutionary change, and the goods and costs of retirement and peace against those of action and war. *Upon Appleton House* also opposes the attractions of retirement to the duties of action and reformation.

Marvell experimented with style and genre to striking effect. Many of his dramatic monologues center on naive personas like the Mower or the Nymph, whose opinions may or may not voice those of the author. In "To His Coy Mistress," perhaps the best known of the century's carpe diem poems, an urbane narrator speaks in balanced and artful couplets. But the poem's rapid shifts from the world of fantasy to the charnel house of reality raise questions as to whether this is a clever seduction poem or an articulation of existential angst, and whether Marvell intends to endorse or to critique this speaker's view of passion and sex. *Upon Appleton House* transforms the mythic features of Jonson's country house poem "To Penshurst" by assimilating history and the conflicts of contemporary society. The poem incorporates into providential history the topographical features of the Fairfax estate, the Fairfax family myth of origin, the progress of the poet-tutor around the estate, and the activities and projected future of the daughter of the house. The poem's rich symbolism of biblical events—Eden, the first temptation, the Fall, the Israelites' journey in the wilderness—resonates with the experiences of the Fairfax family, the speaker, the history of the English Reformation, and the wanton destruction caused by the recent civil wars.

From Poems[1]

The Coronet[2]

When for the thorns with which I long, too long,
    With many a piercing wound,
    My Savior's head have crowned,
I seek with garlands to redress that wrong,
5   Through every garden, every mead,
I gather flowers (my fruits are only flowers),
    Dismantling all the fragrant towers°   high headdress
That once adorned my shepherdess's head:
And now, when I have summed up all my store,
10   Thinking (so I myself deceive)
    So rich a chaplet° thence to weave   wreath
As never yet the King of Glory wore,
    Alas! I find the serpent old,[3]
    That, twining° in his speckled breast,   entwining
15   About the flowers disguised does fold
With wreaths of fame and interest.[4]
Ah, foolish man, that wouldst debase with them,
And mortal glory, heaven's diadem!
But thou who only couldst the serpent tame,
20   Either his slippery knots at once untie,
And disentangle all his winding snare,
Or shatter too with him my curious frame,°   elaborate construction
And let these wither, so that he may die,
Though set with skill and chosen out with care;
25   That they, while thou on both their spoils dost tread,[5]
May crown thy feet, that could not crown thy head.

1650–52   1681

Bermudas[1]

    Where the remote Bermudas ride
    In th' ocean's bosom unespied,
    From a small boat that rowed along,
    The listening winds received this song:

5   "What should we do but sing His praise
    That led us through the wat'ry maze

---

1. Marvell's lyrics were published posthumously in 1681.
2. A floral wreath, also a garland of poems of praise.
3. An allusion to the serpent that tempted Eve (Genesis 3), traditionally understood to be an instrument for Satan.
4. Self-glorification, self-advancement.
5. See the curse on the serpent (Genesis 3:15), that the seed of Eve will bruise his head.

1. Otherwise known as the Summer Isles, the Bermudas were described in travel books like John Smith's *The General History of Virginia, New England, and the Summer Isles* (1624) as an Edenic paradise. The poem was probably written after 1653, when Marvell took up residence in the house of John Oxenbridge, who had twice visited the Bermudas.

                Unto an isle so long unknown,
                And yet far kinder than our own?
                Where He the huge sea monsters wracks,²
10   That lift the deep upon their backs;
                He lands us on a grassy stage,
                Safe from the storms, and prelate's rage.³
                He gave us this eternal spring
                Which here enamels everything,
15   And sends the fowls to us in care,
                On daily visits through the air;
                He hangs in shades the orange bright,
                Like golden lamps in a green night,
                And does in the pomegranates close
20   Jewels more rich than Ormus⁴ shows;
                He makes the figs our mouths to meet,
                And throws the melons at our feet;
                But apples° plants of such a price,   *pineapples*
                No tree could ever bear them twice;
25   With cedars, chosen by his hand
                From Lebanon, he stores the land;
                And makes the hollow seas that roar
                Proclaim the ambergris⁵ on shore;
                He cast (of which we rather° boast)   *more properly*
30   The gospel's pearl upon our coast,
                And in these rocks for us did frame
                A temple, where to sound his name.
                O let our voice his praise exalt
                Till it arrive at heaven's vault,
35   Which, thence (perhaps) rebounding, may
                Echo beyond the Mexique Bay."°   *Gulf of Mexico*

                Thus sung they in the English boat
                An holy and a cheerful note;
                And all the way, to guide their chime,
40   With falling oars they kept the time.

ca. 1650–52   1681

A Dialogue Between the Soul and Body¹

SOUL   O, who shall from this dungeon raise
        A soul enslaved so many ways?²
        With bolts of bones, that fettered stands

---

2. Probably an allusion to the event described in Edmund Waller's mock epic, a battle between the Bermudans and two stranded whales.
3. The Puritan settlers in Bermuda have escaped both the dangers of the sea voyage and religious persecution at home.
4. Hormuz, a pearl- and jewel-trading center in the Persian Gulf.
5. A substance found in sperm whales that was used in the manufacture of expensive perfume.
1. The poem derives from the medieval *debat* (debate) on this theme but alters the usual ending, which gives a clear victory to the soul.
2. The soul echoes Romans 7:24: "O wretched man that I am! who shall deliver me from the body of this death?"

                In feet, and manacled in hands.
5   Here blinded with an eye, and there
                Deaf with the drumming of an ear;
                A soul hung up, as 'twere, in chains
                Of nerves, and arteries, and veins;
                Tortured, besides each other part,
10   In a vain head and double heart.

   BODY   O, who shall me deliver whole
                From bonds of this tyrannic soul?
                Which, stretched upright, impales me so
                That mine own precipice[3] I go;
15   And warms and moves this needless° frame   *without needs*
                (A fever could but do the same),
                And, wanting where° its spite to try,   *lacking an object*
                Has made me live to let me die.
                A body that could never rest
20   Since this ill spirit it possessed.

   SOUL   What magic could me thus confine
                Within another's grief to pine?
                Where, whatsoever it complain,°   *suffer, complain of*
                I feel, that cannot feel,[4] the pain;
25   And all my care itself employs,
                That to preserve which me destroys;
                Constrained not only to endure
                Diseases, but, what's worse, the cure;
                And, ready oft the port to gain,
30   Am shipwrecked into health again.

   BODY   But physic° yet could never reach   *medicine*
                The maladies thou me dost teach:
                Whom first the cramp of hope does tear,
                And then the palsy shakes of fear;
35   The pestilence of love does heat,
                Or hatred's hidden ulcer eat;
                Joy's cheerful madness does perplex,
                Or sorrow's other madness vex;
                Which knowledge forces me to know,
40   And memory will not forego.
                What but a soul could have the wit
                To build me up for sin so fit?
                So architects do square and hew
                Green trees that in the forest grew.

ca. 1650–52   1681

---

3. Having a soul enables humans to walk erect and so face the danger of falling.

4. The soul can sympathize ("feel") though it has no power of physical sensation.

The Nymph Complaining for the Death of Her Fawn[1]

The wanton troopers[2] riding by
Have shot my fawn, and it will die.
Ungentle men! They cannot thrive
To kill thee. Thou ne'er didst alive
5 Them any harm; alas, nor could
Thy death yet do them any good.
I'm sure I never wished them ill,
Nor do I for all this, nor will:
But if my simple prayers may yet
10 Prevail with heaven to forget
Thy murder, I will join my tears
Rather than fail. But, O my fears!
It cannot die so. Heaven's king
Keeps register of everything,
15 And nothing may we use in vain.
Even beasts must be with justice slain,
Else men are made their deodands.[3]
Though they should wash their guilty hands
In this warm lifeblood, which doth part
20 From thine, and wound me to the heart,
Yet could they not be clean; their stain
Is dyed in such a purple grain.
There is not such another in
The world to offer for their sin.
25   Unconstant Sylvio, when yet
I had not found him counterfeit,°   *false, deceitful*
One morning (I remember well),
Tied in this silver chain and bell,
Gave it to me; nay, and I know
30 What he said then, I'm sure I do.
Said he, Look how your huntsman here
Hath taught a fawn to hunt his dear.
But Sylvio soon had me beguiled;
This waxèd tame, while he grew wild,
35 And quite regardless of my smart,
Left me his fawn, but took his heart.[4]
    Thenceforth I set myself to play
My solitary time away
With this; and very well content
40 Could so mine idle life have spent.

---

1. The lament for the death of a pet is an ancient topic dating back to Catullus and Ovid; the closest analogue may be Virgil's story of Sylvia's deer killed wantonly by the Trojans (*Aeneid* 7.475ff). John Skelton has a mock-heroic poem on "Philip Sparrow." There are also echoes of the Song of Songs, which have prompted critical debate as to whether Marvell uses them with serious allegorical import or the nymph uses them quite inappropriately.
2. Soldiers of the invading Scots army were called "troopers" (ca. 1640), as were, sometimes, soldiers of Cromwell's New Model Army.
3. In English law, animals or objects forfeited to the Crown (literally, to God) because they were the immediate cause of a human being's death. The nymph applies the term to persons who cause the death of animals.
4. A pun: heart/hart (a deer); line 32 also puns on dear/deer.

For it was full of sport, and light
Of foot and heart, and did invite
Me to its game. It seemed to bless
Itself in me; how could I less
⁴⁵ Than love it? O I cannot be
Unkind t' a beast that loveth me.
   Had it lived long, I do not know
Whether it too might have done so
As Sylvio did; his gifts might be
⁵⁰ Perhaps as false or more than he.
But I am sure, for aught that I
Could in so short a time espy,
Thy love was far more better than
The love of false and cruel men.
⁵⁵   With sweetest milk and sugar first
I it at mine own fingers nursed.
And as it grew, so every day
It waxed more sweet and white than they.
It had so sweet a breath! and oft
⁶⁰ I blushed to see its foot more soft
And white—shall I say than my hand?—
Nay, any lady's of the land.
   It is a wondrous thing how fleet
'Twas on those little silver feet,
⁶⁵ With what a pretty skipping grace
It oft would challenge me the race;
And when it had left me far away,
'Twould stay, and run again, and stay.
For it was nimbler much than hinds,[5]
⁷⁰ And trod, as on the four winds.
   I have a garden of my own
But so with roses overgrown
And lilies that you would it guess
To be a little wilderness.
⁷⁵ And all the springtime of the year
It only lovèd to be there.
Among the beds of lilies, I
Have sought it oft where it should lie,
Yet could not, till itself would rise,
⁸⁰ Find it, although before mine eyes.
For in the flaxen lilies' shade
It like a bank of lilies laid.
Upon the roses it would feed,
Until its lips ev'n seemed to bleed;
⁸⁵ And then to me 'twould boldly trip
And print those roses on my lip.
But all its chief delight was still
On roses thus itself to fill,
And its pure virgin limbs to fold
⁹⁰ In whitest sheets of lilies cold.

---

5. That is, full-grown deer.

Had it lived long, it would have been
Lilies without, roses within.
   O help! O help! I see it faint,
And die as calmly as a saint.
95 See how it weeps.[6] The tears do come
Sad, slowly dropping like a gum.
So weeps the wounded balsam, so
The holy frankincense doth flow.[7]
The brotherless Heliades
100 Melt in such amber tears as these.[8]
   I in a golden vial will
Keep these two crystal tears, and fill
It till it do o'erflow with mine,
Then place it in Diana's shrine.[9]
105   Now my sweet fawn is vanished to
Whither the swans and turtles° go,   *turtledoves*
In fair Elysium[1] to endure
With milk-white lambs and ermines pure.
O do not run too fast, for I
110 Will but bespeak° thy grave, and die.   *give orders for*
   First my unhappy statue shall
Be cut in marble, and withal,
Let it be weeping too; but there
Th' engraver sure his art may spare,
115 For I so truly thee bemoan
That I shall weep, though I be stone:[2]
Until my tears, still dropping, wear
My breast, themselves engraving there.
There at my feet shalt thou be laid,
120 Of purest alabaster made;
For I would have thine image be
White as I can, though not as thee.

ca. 1650–52   1681

To His Coy Mistress

   Had we but world enough, and time,
This coyness, lady, were no crime.
We would sit down, and think which way
To walk, and pass our long love's day.
5 Thou by the Indian Ganges' side
Shouldst rubies find; I by the tide

---

6. Deer were supposed to weep as they died.
7. Both balsam and frankincense are fragrant resins obtained a drop at a time from trees with holes bored in them.
8. The three daughters of the sun (Helios), grieving the death of their rash brother Phaëthon, were transformed to black poplar trees dropping "tears" of amber.
9. Diana was the goddess of chastity and woodland creatures; nymphs were her attendants.
1. The Elysian fields, a pagan version of heaven.
2. Niobe, lamenting the death of her many children, killed by the gods because of her boasting about them, was turned into a stone that wept.

Of Humber would complain.[1] I would
Love you ten years before the Flood,
And you should, if you please, refuse
Till the conversion of the Jews.[2]
My vegetable love should grow
Vaster than empires, and more slow;
An hundred years should go to praise
Thine eyes, and on thy forehead gaze;
Two hundred to adore each breast,
But thirty thousand to the rest:
An age at least to every part,
And the last age should show your heart.
For, lady, you deserve this state,°   *dignity*
Nor would I love at lower rate.
    But at my back I always hear
Time's wingèd chariot hurrying near;
And yonder all before us lie
Deserts of vast eternity.
Thy beauty shall no more be found,
Nor, in thy marble vault, shall sound
My echoing song; then worms shall try
That long-preserved virginity,
And your quaint[3] honor turn to dust,
And into ashes all my lust:
The grave's a fine and private place,
But none, I think, do there embrace.
    Now therefore, while the youthful hue
Sits on thy skin like morning dew,[4]
And while thy willing soul transpires
At every pore with instant fires,[5]
Now let us sport us while we may,
And now, like amorous birds of prey,
Rather at once our time devour
Than languish in his slow-chapped[6] power.
Let us roll all our strength and all
Our sweetness up into one ball,
And tear our pleasures with rough strife
Thorough° the iron gates of life:[7]   *through*
Thus, though we cannot make our sun
Stand still, yet we will make him run.[8]

ca. 1650–52   1681

---

1. The exotic river Ganges in India is on one side of the world, the Humber flows past Marvell's city, Hull, on the opposite side. Complaints are poems of plaintive, unavailing love.
2. Popular belief had it that the Jews were to be converted just before the Last Judgment. The exaggerated offers in this stanza play off against conventional hyperbolic declarations of love in Petrarchan poetry.
3. "Quaint" puns on "out of date" and *queynte*, a term for the female genitals.
4. The text reads "glew," which could be correct, but "dew" is a common emendation.
5. Urgent, sudden enthusiasm. "Transpires": breathes forth.
6. Slowly devouring jaws.
7. One manuscript reads "grates," a somewhat different figure for the sexual act proposed.
8. The sun stood still for Joshua (Joshua 10:12) in his war against Gibeon; see the very different resolution in Donne's "The Sun Rising" (p. 888).

The Definition of Love

My Love is of a birth as rare
As 'tis, for object, strange and high;
It was begotten by Despair
Upon Impossibility.

5 Magnanimous Despair alone
Could show me so divine a thing,
Where feeble Hope could ne'er have flown
But vainly flapped its tinsel wing.

And yet I quickly might arrive
10 Where my extended soul is fixed;[1]
But Fate does iron wedges drive,
And always crowds itself betwixt.

For Fate with jealous eye does see
Two perfect loves, nor lets them close;°   unite
15 Their union would her ruin be,
And her tyrannic power depose.[2]

And therefore her decrees of steel
Us as the distant poles have placed
(Though Love's whole world on us doth wheel),[3]
20 Not by themselves to be embraced,

Unless the giddy heaven fall,
And earth some new convulsion tear,
And, us to join, the world should all
Be cramped into a planisphere.[4]

25 As lines, so loves oblique may well
Themselves in every angle greet;[5]
But ours, so truly parallel,
Though infinite, can never meet.

Therefore the Love which us doth bind,
30 But Fate so enviously debars,
Is the conjunction of the mind,
And opposition of the stars.[6]

ca. 1650–52   1681

---

1. The soul has extended itself from the speaker's body and fixed itself to his lover.
2. Two perfections, united, would not be subject to change and thereby to Fate.
3. Rotates as on its axis.
4. A two-dimensional map of the world; Marvell images a round globe collapsed into a flat pancake shape, top to bottom, which would bring the two poles together.
5. Oblique lines can touch in angles, as might "oblique" lovers that (in one meaning of the term) "deviate from right conduct or thought."
6. "Conjunction" is the coming together of two heavenly bodies in the same sign of the zodiac; "opposition" places them at diametrical opposites.

The Picture of Little T. C. in a Prospect of Flowers[1]

    See with what simplicity
    This nymph begins her golden days!
    In the green grass she loves to lie,
    And there with her fair aspect tames
5   The wilder flowers and gives them names,
        But only with the roses plays,
            And them does tell
    What color best becomes them and what smell.

    Who can foretell for what high cause
10   This darling of the gods was born?
    Yet this is she whose chaster laws
    The wanton Love shall one day fear,
    And under her command severe
    See his bow broke and ensigns° torn.   *flags, pennants*
15   Happy who can
    Appease this virtuous enemy of man!

    O then let me in time compound°   *come to terms*
    And parley with those conquering eyes
    Ere they have tried their force to wound,
20   Ere with their glancing wheels they drive
    In triumph over hearts that strive
    And them that yield but more despise:
        Let me be laid
    Where I may see thy glories from some shade.

25   Meantime, whilst every verdant thing
    Itself does at thy beauty charm,
    Reform the errors of the spring;
    Make that the tulips may have share
    Of sweetness, seeing they are fair;
30   And roses of their thorns disarm:
        But most procure
    That violets may a longer age endure.

    But O, young beauty of the woods,
    Whom Nature courts with fruit and flowers,
35   Gather the flowers but spare the buds,
    Lest Flora,[2] angry at thy crime
    To kill her infants in their prime,
    Do quickly make th' example yours;
        And ere we see,
40   Nip in the blossom all our hopes and thee.

ca. 1650–52   1681

---

1. The little girl, T. C., has not been identified with any certainty. "Prospect": landscape.
2. Roman goddess of flowers.

The Mower Against Gardens[1]

    Luxurious° man, to bring his vice in use,[2]   *voluptuous*
        Did after him the world seduce,
    And from the fields the flowers and plants allure,
        Where Nature was most plain and pure.
5   He first enclosed within the garden's square
        A dead and standing pool of air,
    And a more luscious earth for them did knead,
        Which stupefied them while it fed.
    The pink grew then as double as his mind;[3]
10   The nutriment did change the kind.
    With strange perfumes he did the roses taint;
        And flowers themselves were taught to paint.
    The tulip white did for complexion seek,
        And learned to interline its cheek;
15   Its onion root they then so high did hold,
        That one was for a meadow sold;[4]
    Another world was searched through oceans new,
        To find the marvel of Peru;[5]
    And yet these rarities might be allowed
20   To man, that sovereign thing and proud,
    Had he not dealt between the bark and tree,[6]
        Forbidden mixtures there to see.
    No plant now knew the stock from which it came;
        He grafts upon the wild the tame,
25   That the uncertain and adult'rate fruit
        Might put the palate in dispute.
    His green seraglio[7] has its eunuchs too,
        Lest any tyrant him outdo;
    And in the cherry he does Nature vex,
30   To procreate without a sex.[8]
    'Tis all enforced, the fountain and the grot,°   *grotto*
        While the sweet fields do lie forgot,
    Where willing Nature does to all dispense
        A wild and fragrant innocence;
35   And fauns and fairies do the meadows till
        More by their presence than their skill.
    Their statues polished by some ancient hand

---

1. The four "Mower" poems are linked by their treatment of a distinctly unusual pastoral figure, a mower rather than a shepherd or goatherd, who provides a singular perspective on those familiar pastoral topics: nature versus art and nature's sympathy for man (the pathetic fallacy). As mower wielding a scythe, he evokes other figures (Time, Death).
2. Into common practice.
3. The double pink, or carnation, is a product of sophisticated ("double") minds.
4. The lucrative trade in Dutch tulip bulbs during the 17th century led to speculation and a crash in 1637.
5. *Mirabilis jalapa*, the four-o'clock, was an exotic, multicolored flower found originally in tropical America.
6. An adage for interfering between husband and wife, in reference, apparently, to grafting.
7. Enclosure, a harem in a sultan's palace.
8. Cherries are commonly propagated by grafting.

        May to adorn the gardens stand;
      But, howsoe'er the figures do excel,
40   The gods themselves with us do dwell.

ca. 1650–52   1681

Damon the Mower

    Hark how the mower Damon sung,
    With love of Juliana stung![1]
    While everything did seem to paint
    The scene more fit for his complaint.[2]
5   Like her fair eyes the day was fair,
    But scorching like his amorous care;
    Sharp, like his scythe, his sorrow was,
    And withered, like his hopes, the grass.

    "Oh what unusual heats are here,
10 Which thus our sunburned meadows sear!
    The grasshopper its pipe gives o'er,
    And hamstringed° frogs can dance no more: *disabled*
    But in the brook the green frog wades,
    And grasshoppers seek out the shades.
15 Only the snake, that kept within,
    Now glitters in its second skin.

    "This heat the sun could never raise,
    Nor Dog Star so inflame the days;[3]
    It from an higher beauty grow'th,
20 Which burns the fields and mower both;
    Which mads the dog, and makes the sun
    Hotter than his own Phaëton.[4]
    Not Jùly causeth these extremes,
    But Juliana's scorching beams.

25 "Tell me where I may pass the fires
    Of the hot day or hot desires,
    To what cool cave shall I descend,
    Or to what gelid° fountain bend?   *icy*
    Alas! I look for ease in vain,
30 When remedies themselves complain:[5]
    No moisture but my tears do rest,
    No cold but in her icy breast.

---

1. Damon is a familiar classical name in pastoral; Juliana gets her name from July (lines 23–24).
2. The plaintive love song of an unrequited lover.
3. The Dog Star (Sirius in the constellation Canis Major) rises with the sun in late summer, producing the heats of "dog days."
4. Phaëthon, son of Helios, the sun god of Greek mythology; he tried to drive his father's chariot but could not control the horses and scorched the world.
5. That is, fountain and cave themselves complain of unusual heat.

"How long wilt thou, fair shepherdess,
Esteem me and my presents less?
35 To thee the harmless snake I bring,
Disarmèd of its teeth and sting:
To thee chameleons, changing hue,
And oak leaves tipped with honeydew;
Yet thou, ungrateful, hast not sought
40 Nor what they are, nor who them brought.

"I am the mower Damon, known
Through all the meadows I have mown.
On me the morn her dew distills
Before her darling daffodils,
45 And if at noon my toil me heat,
The sun himself licks off my sweat;
While, going home, the evening sweet
In cowslip-water bathes my feet.

"What though the piping shepherd stock
50 The plains with an unnumbered flock?
This scythe of mine discovers° wide   *uncovers*
More ground than all his sheep do hide.
With this the golden fleece I shear
Of all these closes every year,[6]
55 And though in wool more poor than they,
Yet I am richer far in hay.

"Nor am I so deformed to sight
If in my scythe I lookèd right;
In which I see my picture done
60 As in a crescent moon the sun.
The deathless fairies take me oft
To lead them in their dances soft,
And when I tune myself to sing,
About me they contract their ring.[7]

65 "How happy might I still have mowed,
Had not Love here his thistles sowed!
But now I all the day complain,
Joining my labor to my pain;
And with my scythe cut down the grass,
70 Yet still my grief is where it was;
But when the iron blunter grows,
Sighing, I whet my scythe and woes."

While thus he threw his elbow round,
Depopulating all the ground,
75 And with his whistling scythe does cut
Each stroke between the earth and root,

---

6. Hay is the "wool" of the fields ("closes").
7. That is, the "fairy ring," a discolored circle of grass popularly supposed to result from fairies dancing there.

           The edgèd steel, by careless chance,
           Did into his own ankle glance,
           And there among the grass fell down[8]
    80   By his own scythe the mower mown.

           "Alas!" said he, "these hurts are slight
           To those that die by Love's despite.
           With shepherd's purse and clown's° all-heal[9]   *rustic's*
           The blood I stanch and wound I seal.
    85   Only for him no cure is found
           Whom Juliana's eyes do wound.
           'Tis Death alone that this must do;
           For, Death, thou art a mower too."

ca. 1650–52   1681

The Mower to the Glowworms

           Ye living lamps, by whose dear light
           The nightingale does sit so late,
           And studying all the summer night
           Her matchless songs does meditate,

    5   Ye country comets, that portend
           No war nor prince's funeral,
           Shining unto no higher end
           Than to presage the grass's fall;

           Ye glowworms, whose officious° flame   *helpful*
    10   To wand'ring mowers shows the way,
           That in the night have lost their aim,
           And after foolish fires° do stray;   *will-o'-the-wisps*

           Your courteous fires in vain you waste,
           Since Juliana here is come,
    15   For she my mind hath so displaced
           That I shall never find my home.

ca. 1650–52   1681

The Mower's Song

           My mind was once the true survey
           Of all these meadows fresh and gay,
           And in the greenness of the grass

---

8. An echo of the biblical phrase "All flesh is grass" (Isaiah 40:6).

9. Folk names for popular remedies to heal wounds, found in fields and hedges.

              Did see its hopes[1] as in a glass;°   *mirror*
        5   When Juliana came, and she,
              What I do to the grass, does to my thoughts and me.[2]

              But these, while I with sorrow pine,
              Grew more luxuriant still and fine,
              That not one blade of grass you spied
       10   But had a flower on either side;
              When Juliana came, and she,
              What I do to the grass, does to my thoughts and me.

              Unthankful meadows, could you so
              A fellowship so true forego,
       15   And in your gaudy May-games[3] meet,
              While I lay trodden under feet?
              When Juliana came, and she,
              What I do to the grass, does to my thoughts and me.

              But what you in compassion ought
       20   Shall now by my revenge be wrought,
              And flowers, and grass, and I, and all,
              Will in one common ruin fall;
              For Juliana comes, and she,
              What I do to the grass, does to my thoughts and me.

       25   And thus ye meadows, which have been
              Companions of my thoughts more green,
              Shall now the heraldry become
              With which I shall adorn my tomb;
              For Juliana comes, and she,
       30   What I do to the grass, does to my thoughts and me.

ca. 1650–52   1681

The Garden

              How vainly men themselves amaze°   *bewilder*
              To win the palm, the oak, or bays,[1]
              And their uncessant labors see
              Crowned from some single herb or tree,
        5   Whose short and narrow-vergèd° shade   *edged*
              Does prudently their toils upbraid;°   *reprove*
              While all flowers and all trees do close°   *unite, agree*
              To weave the garlands of repose!

---

1. Green is the color of hope.
2. The alexandrine (twelve-syllable line) used here is the only example of a refrain in Marvell.
3. Festivals and merrymaking marked the first of May, May Day.

1. Honors, respectively, for military, civic, and poetic achievement.

  Fair Quiet, have I found thee here,
10 And Innocence, thy sister dear?
  Mistaken long, I sought you then
  In busy companies of men.
  Your sacred plants, if here below,°   *on earth*
  Only among the plants will grow;
15 Society is all but rude,
  To° this delicious solitude.   *compared to*

  No white nor red[2] was ever seen
  So amorous as this lovely green.
  Fond lovers, cruel as their flame,
20 Cut in these trees their mistress' name:
  Little, alas, they know or heed
  How far these beauties hers exceed!
  Fair trees, wheresoe'er your barks I wound,
  No name shall but your own be found.[3]

25 When we have run our passion's heat,
  Love hither makes his best retreat.
  The gods, that mortal beauty chase,
  Still° in a tree did end their race: *always*
  Apollo hunted Daphne so,
30 Only that she might laurel grow;
  And Pan did after Syrinx speed,
  Not as a nymph, but for a reed.[4]

  What wondrous life is this I lead!
  Ripe apples drop about my head;
35 The luscious clusters of the vine
  Upon my mouth do crush their wine;
  The nectarine and curious° peach   *exquisite*
  Into my hands themselves do reach;
  Stumbling on melons[5] as I pass,
40 Ensnared with flowers, I fall on grass.

  Meanwhile the mind, from pleasure less,
  Withdraws into its happiness;
  The mind, that ocean where each kind
  Does straight° its own resemblance find;[6]   *immediately*
45 Yet it creates, transcending these,
  Far other worlds and other seas,
  Annihilating all that's made
  To a green thought in a green shade.

---

2. Colors traditionally associated with female beauty.
3. Marvell proposes to carve in the bark of trees not "Sylvia" or "Laura," but "Beech" and "Oak."
4. Apollo, the god of poetry, chased Daphne until she turned into a laurel (the emblematic reward of poets); Pan pursued Syrinx until she became a reed, out of which he made panpipes. The gods' motives were, of course, sexual, not horticultural.
5. "Melons," with etymological roots in the Greek word for "apple," may recall the apple over which all humankind stumbled.
6. As the ocean supposedly contained a counterpart of every creature on land, so the ocean of the mind holds the innate ideas of all things (in Neoplatonic philosophy).

Here at the fountain's sliding foot,
Or at some fruit tree's mossy root,
Casting the body's vest° aside,   *garment*
My soul into the boughs does glide:
There like a bird it sits and sings,
Then whets° and combs its silver wings,   *preens*
And, till prepared for longer flight,
Waves in its plumes the various light.[7]

Such was that happy garden-state,
While man there walked without a mate:
After a place so pure and sweet,
What other help could yet be meet![8]
But 'twas beyond a mortal's share
To wander solitary there:
Two paradises 'twere in one
To live in paradise alone.

How well the skillful gardener drew
Of flowers and herbs this dial new,[9]
Where from above the milder sun
Does through a fragrant zodiac run;
And as it works, th' industrious bee
Computes its time[1] as well as we!
How could such sweet and wholesome hours
Be reckoned but with herbs and flowers?

ca. 1650–52   1681

An Horatian Ode

Upon Cromwell's Return from Ireland[1]

The forward° youth that would appear   *eager, ambitious*
Must now forsake his Muses dear,
   Nor in the shadows sing
   His numbers languishing:

'Tis time to leave the books in dust
And oil th' unusèd armor's rust,

---

7. The multicolored light of this world, contrasted with the white radiance of eternity.
8. Genesis 2:18 recounts the Lord's decision to make a "help meet" for Adam, Eve.
9. The garden itself is laid out as a sundial.
1. A pun on "thyme."

1. Oliver Cromwell, the general primarily responsible for Parliament's victory in the English Civil War, returned from conquering Ireland in May 1650, about eighteen months after the execution of Charles I. The two events were persistently connected: Cromwell's "success" in Ireland was taken as a sign of God's favor to the new republican regime and to Cromwell as his chosen instrument. Pindaric odes (like Jonson's Cary–Morison ode, p. 1059) are heroic and ecstatic; Horatian odes are poems of cool and balanced judgment, as this one is in its representations of Cromwell, Charles 1, and the issues of power and providence.

The Execution of Charles I. A German print illustrates the beheading of Charles I before an enormous crowd, on a scaffold erected in front of the Banqueting House. At the top of the picture small portraits of General Fairfax and Cromwell, leaders of the parliamentary forces, flank a portrait of King Charles, to whom an angel in the clouds is extending a heavenly crown. In the lower right corner, a woman faints.

>   Removing from the wall
>   The corselet° of the hall.[2]   *upper body armor*
>
> So restless Cromwell could not cease
> 10 In the inglorious arts of peace,
>   But through adventurous war
>   Urgèd his active star;[3]
>
> And, like the three-forked lightning, first
> Breaking the clouds where it was nursed,
> 15   Did through his own side
>   His fiery way divide:[4]

2. Here as elsewhere there are allusions to Lucan's *Pharsalia*, a poem of civil war whose sympathies are with Pompey, Cato, and the Roman Republic against Caesar and the empire. The poem's allusions to Caesar are most often to Charles I, but sometimes to Cromwell.
3. Normally the stars are thought to control men's fates, but Cromwell presses his own star forward.
4. The "three-forked lightning" identifies him with Zeus, suggesting the elemental force by which he surpassed all those in his own party ("side") of radical Independents; the imagery of giving birth to himself also suggests going Caesar (born by cesarean section) one better.

> For 'tis all one to courage high,
> The emulous, or enemy;
>   And with such, to enclose
>   Is more than to oppose.
>
> Then burning through the air he went,
> And palaces and temples rent;
>   And Caesar's head at last
>   Did through his laurels blast.[5]
>
> 'Tis madness to resist or blame
> The force of angry heaven's flame;
>   And if we would speak true,
>   Much to the man is due,
>
> Who from his private gardens, where
> He lived reservèd and austere
>   (As if his highest plot
>   To plant the bergamot),[6]
>
> Could by industrious valor climb
> To ruin the great work of time,
>   And cast the kingdom old
>   Into another mold;
>
> Though Justice against Fate complain,
> And plead the ancient rights in vain:
>   But those do hold or break,
>   As men are strong or weak.
>
> Nature that hateth emptiness,
> Allows of penetration less,[7]
>   And therefore must make room
>   Where greater spirits come.
>
> What field of all the civil wars
> Where his were not the deepest scars?
>   And Hampton shows what part
>   He had of wiser art;[8]
>
> Where, twining subtle fears with hope,
> He wove a net of such a scope
>   That Charles himself might chase
>   To Caresbrooke's narrow case,

---

5. Royal crowns were made of laurel because they were supposed to protect from lightning.
6. A pear-shaped orange (from the Turkish, "prince's pear").
7. Nature abhors a vacuum, but even more, the penetration of one body's space by another body.
8. Charles was confined at Hampton Court after his defeat, as Parliament attempted to negotiate terms for his restoration. Cromwell was rumored to have connived at his escape to Carisbrooke Castle, on the Isle of Wight, in order to convince Parliament that he could not be trusted and must be executed. Cromwell has shown himself master of the two "arts" of rule defined by Machiavelli: namely, force and craft.

That thence the royal actor[9] borne,
The tragic scaffold might adorn;
    While round the armèd bands
    Did clap their bloody hands.

He nothing common did or mean
Upon that memorable scene,
    But with his keener eye
    The ax's edge[1] did try;

Nor called the gods with vulgar spite
To vindicate his helpless right;
    But bowed his comely head
    Down, as upon a bed.

This was that memorable hour,
Which first assured the forcèd power;
    So when they did design
    The Capitol's first line,

A bleeding head where they begun
Did fright the architects to run;
    And yet in that the state
    Foresaw its happy fate.[2]

And now the Irish are ashamed
To see themselves in one year tamed;
    So much one man can do,
    That does both act and know.

They can affirm his praises best,
And have, though overcome, confessed
    How good he is, how just,
    And fit for highest trust.[3]

Nor yet grown stiffer with command,
But still in the republic's hand—
    How fit he is to sway,
    That can so well obey.[4]

---

9. The theater metaphors used for Charles are even more powerful because the "tragic scaffold" was erected outside Whitehall, where so many royal masques were produced. See a depiction of the king's execution on p. 1283.
1. A play on the Latin *acies*, which means the edge of a sword or axe, a keen glance, and the vanguard of a battle. Compare the newsbook account of the king's execution, p. 1320.
2. Livy and Pliny record that the workmen digging the foundations for a temple of Jupiter at Rome uncovered a bloody head, which they were persuaded to take as an omen that Rome would be head (*caput*) of a great empire; the temple and the hill took the name Capitoline from that event.
3. Cromwell conducted a particularly brutal campaign in Ireland, and the Irish had no such testimonials for him; the lines are deeply equivocal.
4. The maxim about obedience fitting one to rule is a commonplace. The implications of "yet" and "still," along with the next stanza, suggest a Caesar figure who has not—but might—cross the Rubicon and defy the Republic, as Julius Caesar did.

> 85 He to the Commons' feet presents
> A kingdom for his first year's rents;
> And, what he may, forbears
> His fame to make it theirs;[5]
>
> And has his sword and spoils ungirt,
> 90 To lay them at the public's skirt:
> So, when the falcon high
> Falls heavy from the sky,
>
> She, having killed, no more does search,
> But on the next green bough to perch;
> 95 Where, when he first does lure,
> The falconer has her sure.
>
> What may not then our isle presume,
> While victory his crest does plume!
> What may not others fear,
> 100 If thus he crown each year!
>
> A Caesar he ere long to Gaul,
> To Italy an Hannibal,
> And to all states not free,
> Shall climactèric be.[6]
>
> 105 The Pict no shelter now shall find
> Within his parti-colored mind,
> But from this valor sad,°   *severe, solemn*
> Shrink underneath the plaid;[7]
>
> Happy if in the tufted brake
> 110 The English hunter him mistake,
> Nor lay his hounds in near
> The Caledonian° deer.   *Scottish*
>
> But thou, the war's and Fortune's son,
> March indefatigably on;
> 115 And for the last effect,
> Still keep thy sword erect;

---

5. Thus far, Cromwell gives the Republic credit for his victories.
6. It was thought that Cromwell's military acumen might subdue France and Italy (which threatened to attack the new republic to restore Charles II), just as did Caesar and Hannibal of old. "Climactèric": a period of crucial, epochal change—here, the expectation that the example of a successful English republic would topple absolute monarchs abroad.
7. Early Scots were called Picts (from the Latin *pictus*, painted), because the warriors painted themselves many colors; contemporary Scots are "parti-colored" (divided into many factions) like a scotch plaid. Cromwell was about to go to subdue Scotland, which had declared for Charles II.

                    Besides the force it has to fright
                    The spirits of the shady night,[8]
                    The same arts that did gain
120   A power must it maintain.[9]

1650   **1681**

Upon Appleton House[1]
To My Lord Fairfax

1

Within this sober frame expect
Work of no foreign architect,
That unto caves the quarries drew,
And forests did to pastures hew;
5   Who of his great design in pain
Did for a model vault his brain,[2]
Whose columns should so high be raised
To arch the brows that on them gazed.

2

Why should of all things man unruled
10 Such unproportioned dwellings build?
The beasts are by their dens expressed,
And birds contrive an equal nest;[3]
The low-roofed tortoises do dwell
In cases fit of tortoiseshell:
15 No creature loves an empty space;
Their bodies measure out their place.

3

But he, superfluously spread,
Demands more room alive than dead;
And in his hollow palace goes
20 Where winds as he themselves may lose.

---

8. A sword carried with the blade upright evokes the classical tradition that underworld spirits (here, the slain king and his followers) are frightened off by raised weapons.

9. The maxim alludes to Machiavelli's advice that a kingdom won by force must for some time be maintained by force.

1. From 1651 to 1653, Marvell served as tutor to Mary Fairfax, daughter of Ann Vere and Thomas Fairfax, commander in chief of the parliamentary army throughout the civil wars. Fairfax opposed the regicide and in 1650 resigned his command rather than lead a preemptive strike against Scotland (which had declared for Charles II). Cromwell took over as Fairfax retired to his country estates in Yorkshire, especially Nunappleton, a comparatively simple brick structure on the site of a former Cistercian priory dissolved by Henry VIII along with all monasteries in 1542. The poem makes the house and its history figure the progress of the Reformation and the recent civil wars, played off against the Fall, the conflicts of the Israelites in the wilderness, and other biblical moments. The poem is structured as a journey around the estate, intersected by a long passage of family history. It was apparently written in the summer of 1651, when Mary Fairfax was twelve.

2. Did design in his brain the absurdly high vaulted ceilings of grand, magnificent houses built for showy display. This poem invites comparison and contrast with other country house poems and the houses, estates, and society they describe, including Jonson's "To Penshurst" (p. 1053), and Lanyer's "Description of Cookham" (p. 936).

3. That is, a nest proportioned to their size.

What need of all this marble crust
T' impark the wanton mote of dust,
That thinks by breadth the world t' unite
Though the first builders[4] failed in height?

4

25 But all things are composèd here
Like nature, orderly and near:
In which we the dimensions find
Of what more sober age and mind,
When larger sizèd men did stoop
30 To enter at a narrow loop;
As practicing, in doors so strait,
To strain themselves through heaven's gate.

5

And surely when the after age
Shall hither come in pilgrimage,
35 These sacred places to adore,
By Vere and Fairfax trod before,
Men will dispute how their extent
Within such dwarfish confines went;
And some will smile at this as well
40 As Romulus his bee-like cell.[5]

6

Humility alone designs
Those short but admirable lines,
By which, ungirt and unconstrained,
Things greater are in less contained.
45 Let other vainly strive t'immure
The circle in the quadrature![6]
These holy mathematics can
In ev'ry figure equal man.[7]

7

Yet thus the laden house does sweat,
50 And scarce endures the master great:
But where he comes the swelling hall
Stirs, and the square grows spherical;[8]
More by his magnitude distressed,
Than he is by its straitness pressed;
55 And too officiously° it slights   *overeagerly*
That in itself which him delights.

---

4. The proud builders of the Tower of Babel, who *thought* to make it reach to heaven (Genesis 11).
5. The thatched hut of the legendary founder of Rome.
6. To square the circle.
7. The circle symbolized perfection, the square variously virtue, justice, and prudence.
8. The square hall rises up into a domed cupola.

8

 So honor better lowness bears,
 Than that unwonted° greatness wears.   *unaccustomed*
 Height with a certain grace does bend,
60 But low things clownishly° ascend.   *in rustic fashion*
 And yet what needs there here excuse,
 Where ev'ry thing does answer use?
 Where neatness nothing can condemn,
 Nor pride invent° what to contemn?   *find out*

9

65 A stately frontispiece of poor[9]
 Adorns without the open door;
 Nor less the rooms within commends
 Daily new furniture of friends.
 The house was built upon the place
70 Only as for a mark of grace;
 And for an inn to entertain
 Its lord a while, but not remain.[1]

10

 Him Bishops-Hill, or Denton may,
 Or Bilbrough, better hold than they;
75 But Nature here hath been so free
 As if she said, Leave this to me.
 Art would more neatly° have defaced   *elegantly*
 What she had laid so sweetly waste;
 In fragrant gardens, shady woods,
80 Deep meadows, and transparent floods.

11

 While with slow eyes we these survey,
 And on each pleasant footstep stay,
 We opportunely may relate
 The progress of this house's fate.
85 A nunnery first gave it birth
 For virgin buildings oft brought forth.
 And all that neighbor-ruin shows
 The quarries whence this dwelling rose.

12

 Near to this gloomy cloister's gates
90 There dwelt the blooming virgin Thwaites[2]

---

9. Poor people awaiting Fairfax's alms.
1. The house is described as an inn, with an allusion to Hebrews 11:13–16 and the faithful who proclaim themselves "strangers and pilgrims on the earth" as they "desire a better country, that is, an heavenly."

2. In 1518 the heiress Isabel Thwaites was to marry Thomas Fairfax's ancestor, William, but was confined by her guardian, the prioress of Nunappleton; William obtained an order for her release and then seized her by force and married her.

Fair beyond measure, and an heir
Which might deformity make fair.
And oft she spent the summer suns
Discoursing with the subtle nuns.
95 Whence in these words one to her weaved
(As 'twere by chance) thoughts long conceived.

13

"Within this holy leisure we
Live innocently as you see.
These walls restrain the world without,
100 But hedge° our liberty about.   *defend*
These bars inclose that wider den
Of those wild creatures, callèd men;
The cloister outward shuts its gates,
And, from us, locks on them the grates.

14

105 "Here we, in shining armor white,°   *nun's habit*
Like virgin amazons do fight:
And our chaste lamps we hourly trim,
Lest the great bridegroom find them dim.[3]
Our orient° breaths perfumed are   *fresh*
110 With incense of incessant pray'r.
And holy water of our tears
Most strangely our complexion clears:

15

"Not tears of grief; but such as those
With which calm pleasure overflows;
115 Or pity, when we look on you
That live without this happy vow.
How should we grieve that must be seen
Each one a spouse, and each a queen;
And can in heaven hence behold
120 Our brighter robes and crowns of gold?

16

"When we have prayed all our beads,
Some one the holy legend° reads;   *a saint's life*
While all the rest with needles paint
The face and graces of the saint.
125 But what the linen can't receive
They in their lives do interweave.
This work the saints best represents;
That serves for altar's ornaments.

---

3. Matthew 25:1–13 contrasts the wise virgins who kept their lamps lit for the bridegroom (Christ) and the foolish ones who did not and so were excluded from the marriage feast (heaven).

17

    "But much it to our work would add
130 If here your hand, your face we had.
    By it we would our Lady touch;[4]
    Yet thus she you resembles much.
    Some of your features, as we sewed,
    Through every shrine should be bestowed:
135 And in one beauty we would take
    Enough a thousand saints to make.

18

    "And (for I dare not quench the fire
    That me does for your good inspire)
    'Twere sacrilege a man t' admit
140 To holy things, for heaven fit.
    I see the angels in a crown
    On you the lilies show'ring down;
    And round about you glory breaks,
    That something more than human speaks.

19

145 "All beauty, when at such a height,
    Is so already consecrate.
    Fairfax I know; and long ere this
    Have marked the youth, and what he is.
    But can he such a rival seem
150 For whom you heav'n should disesteem?
    Ah, no! and 'twould more honor prove
    He your devoto° were, than love.   *devotee*

20

    "Here live beloved, and obeyed,
    Each one your sister, each your maid.
155 And, if our rule seem strictly penned,
    The rule itself to you shall bend.
    Our abbess too, now far in age,
    Doth your succession near presage.
    How soft the yoke on us would lie,
160 Might such fair hands as yours it tie!

21

    "Your voice, the sweetest of the choir,
    Shall draw heav'n nearer, raise us higher:
    And your example, if our head,
    Will soon us to perfection lead.
165 Those virtues to us all so dear,

---

4. We could come close to representing the Virgin Mary in our designs with you as model.

      Will straight° grow sanctity when here: *immediately*
      And that, once sprung, increase so fast
      Till miracles it work at last.

22

      "Nor is our order yet so nice,°   *precise*
170 Delight to banish as a vice.
      Here pleasure piety doth meet,
      One perfecting the other sweet.
      So through the mortal fruit we boil
      The sugar's uncorrupting oil;
175 And that which perished while we pull,
      Is thus preserved clear and full.

23

      "For such indeed are all our arts;
      Still handling nature's finest parts.
      Flow'rs dress the altars; for the clothes,
180 The sea-born amber[5] we compose;
      Balms for the grieved° we draw; and pastes   *injured*
      We mold, as baits for curious tastes.
      What need is here of man? unless
      These as sweet sins we should confess.

24

185 "Each night among us to your side
      Appoint a fresh and virgin bride;
      Whom if our Lord at midnight find,
      Yet neither should be left behind.
      Where you may lie as chaste in bed,
190 As pearls together billeted,
      All night embracing arm in arm,
      Like crystal pure with cotton warm.

25

      "But what is this to all the store
      Of joys you see, and may make more!
195 Try but a while, if you be wise:
      The trial neither costs, nor ties."
      Now Fairfax seek her promised faith:°   *promise to wed*
      Religion that dispensed hath;
      Which she henceforward does begin:[6]
200 The nun's smooth tongue has sucked her in.

---

5. Ambergris from the sperm whale supplies the rich perfume for our altar cloths.

6. She now begins her "religious" life in the convent.

26

 Oft, though he knew it was in vain,
Yet would he valiantly complain:
"Is this that sanctity so great,
An art by which you finelier cheat?
Hypocrite witches, hence avaunt,
Who though in prison yet enchant!
Death only can such thieves make fast,
As rob though in the dungeon cast.

27

 "Were there but, when this house was made,
One stone that a just hand had laid,
It must have fall'n upon her head
Who first thee from thy faith misled.
And yet, how well soever meant,
With them 'twould soon grow fraudulent:
For like themselves they alter all,
And vice infects the very wall.

28

 "But sure those buildings last not long,
Founded by folly, kept by wrong.
I know what fruit their gardens yield,
When they it think by night concealed.
Fly from their vices. 'Tis thy state,°   *estate*
Not thee, that they would consecrate.
Fly from their ruin. How I fear
Though guiltless lest thou perish there!"

29

 What should he do? He would respect
Religion, but not right neglect;
For first religion taught him right,
And dazzled not but cleared his sight.
Sometimes resolved his sword he draws,
But reverenceth then the laws:
For justice still that courage led;
First from a judge, then soldier bred.[7]

30

 Small honor would be in the storm.°   *storming the priory*
The court him grants the lawful form;
Which licensed either peace or force,
To hinder the unjust divorce.

---

7. His father was judge of the Common Pleas; his maternal grandfather was a heroic soldier.

Yet still the nuns his right debarred,
Standing upon their holy guard.
Ill-counseled women, do you know
240 Whom you resist, or what you do?

31

Is not this he whose offspring fierce
Shall fight through all the universe;
And with successive valor try
France, Poland, either Germany;
245 Till one, as long since prophesied,
His horse through conquered Britain ride?
Yet, against fate, his spouse they kept,
And the great race would intercept.[8]

32

Some to the breach against their foes
250 Their wooden saints in vain oppose.
Another bolder stands at push
With their old holy-water brush.
While the disjointed° abbess threads   *distracted*
The jingling chain-shot[9] of her beads.
255 But their loud'st cannon were their lungs;
And sharpest weapons were their tongues.

33

But, waving these aside like flies,
Young Fairfax through the wall does rise.
Then th' unfrequented vault appeared,
260 And superstitions vainly feared.
The relics false were set to view;
Only the jewels there were true—
But truly bright and holy Thwaites
That weeping at the altar waits.

34

265 But the glad youth away her bears
And to the nuns bequeaths her tears:
Who guiltily their prize bemoan,
Like gypsies that a child had stol'n.
Thenceforth (as when th' enchantment ends
270 The castle vanishes or rends)
The wasting cloister with the rest
Was in one instant dispossessed.[1]

---

8. Thomas Fairfax, son of William and Isabel Thwaites, fought in Italy and Germany; his descendants were also honored soldiers; the present Fairfax fulfilled the prophecy by his victories in the Civil War.
9. Cannonballs linked in a chain and fired together.
1. An allusion to Henry VIII's dissolution of the monasteries.

35

At the demolishing, this seat
To Fairfax fell as by escheat.[2]
And what both nuns and founders willed
'Tis likely better thus fulfilled:
For if the virgin proved not theirs,
The cloister yet remained hers;
Though many a nun there made her vow,
'Twas no religious house till now.

36

From that blest bed the hero came,
Whom France and Poland yet does fame;
Who, when retired here to peace,
His warlike studies could not cease;
But laid these gardens out in sport
In the just figure of a fort;
And with five bastions it did fence,
As aiming one for ev'ry sense.[3]

37

When in the east the morning ray
Hangs out the colors of the day,
The bee through these known alleys hums,
Beating the dian° with its drums.   *reveille*
Then flow'rs their drowsy eyelids raise,
Their silken ensigns each displays,
And dries its pan[4] yet dank with dew,
And fills its flask° with odors new.   *powder flask*

38

These, as their governor goes by,
In fragrant volleys they let fly;
And to salute their governess
Again as great a charge they press:
None for the virgin nymph;[5] for she
Seems with the flow'rs a flow'r to be.
And think so still! though not compare[6]
With breath so sweet, or cheek so fair.

39

Well shot ye firemen!° Oh how sweet,   *shooters*
And round your equal fires do meet;

---

2. Legally, in the absence of an heir, the property reverted to him as lord of the manor; Henry gave monastery lands to his nobles.
3. The garden's five (seeming) bulwarks or fortifications aim at the five senses.
4. In a musket, the hollow part of the lock that receives the priming.
5. Mary Fairfax (Maria)—Marvell's pupil at Nunappleton.
6. The imperatives are addressed to the flowers.

　　　　Whose shrill report no ear can tell,
　　　　But echoes to the eye and smell.
　　　　See how the flow'rs, as at parade,
310　　Under their colors stand displayed:
　　　　Each regiment in order grows,
　　　　That of the tulip, pink, and rose.

40

　　　　But when the vigilant patrol
　　　　Of stars walks round about the pole,
315　　Their leaves, that to the stalks are curled,
　　　　Seem to their staves the ensigns furled.
　　　　Then in some flow'r's beloved hut
　　　　Each bee as sentinel is shut;
　　　　And sleeps so too: but, if once stirred,
320　　She runs you through, nor asks the word.°　　　　　　　　password

41

　　　　Oh thou,° that dear and happy isle　　　　　　　　　　　England
　　　　The garden of the world ere while,
　　　　Thou paradise of four[7] seas,
　　　　Which heaven planted us to please,
325　　But, to exclude the world, did guard
　　　　With wat'ry if not flaming sword;[8]
　　　　What luckless apple did we taste,
　　　　To make us mortal, and thee waste?

42

　　　　Unhappy! shall we never more
330　　That sweet militia restore,
　　　　When gardens only had their tow'rs,
　　　　And all the garrisons were flow'rs;
　　　　When roses only arms might bear,
　　　　And men did rosy garlands wear?
335　　Tulips, in several colors barred,
　　　　Were then the Switzers[9] of our guard.

43

　　　　The gardener had the soldier's place,
　　　　And his more gentle forts did trace.
　　　　The nursery of all things green
340　　Was then the only magazine.
　　　　The winter quarters were the stoves°　　　　　　　　hothouses
　　　　Where he the tender plants removes.
　　　　But war all this doth overgrow;
　　　　We ordnance plant, and powder sow.

---

7. Pronounced with two syllables.
8. After the Fall, the garden in Eden was guarded by angels with flaming swords.
9. The papal Swiss guards, who wore multicolored uniforms.

44

And yet there walks one on the sod
Who, had it pleased him and God,
Might once have made our gardens spring
Fresh as his own and flourishing.
But he preferred to the Cinque Ports[1]
These five imaginary forts;
And, in those half-dry trenches, spanned°   *restrained*
Pow'r which the ocean might command.

45

For he did, with his utmost skill,
Ambition weed, but conscience till.
Conscience, that heaven-nursèd plant,
Which most our earthly gardens want.°   *lack, need*
A prickling leaf it bears, and such
As that which shrinks at every touch;
But flow'rs eternal, and divine,
That in the crowns of saints do shine.

46

The sight does from these bastions ply
Th' invisible artillery;
And at proud Cawood Castle[2] seems
To point the batt'ry of its beams,
As if it quarreled in° the seat   *found fault with*
Th' ambition of its prelate great;
But o'er the meads below it plays,
Or innocently seems to gaze.

47

And now to the abyss I pass
Of that unfathomable grass,
Where men like grasshoppers appear,
But grasshoppers are giants[3] there:
They, in their squeaking laugh, contemn
Us as we walk more low than them:
And, from the precipices tall
Of the green spires, to us do call.

48

To see men through this meadow dive,
We wonder how they rise alive;

---

1. The five ports on the southeast coast of England, of which Fairfax was warden for a time; the "imaginary forts" (next line) are the "five bastions" of line 287.
2. Seat of the archbishop of York, two miles from Appleton House.
3. Compare Numbers 13:33: "And there we saw the giants . . . and we were in our own sight as grasshoppers, and so we were in their sight."

             As, underwater, none does know
380   Whether he fall through it or go;°   *move forward*
             But as the mariners that sound
             And show upon their lead the ground,[4]
             They bring up flow'rs so to be seen,
             And prove they've at the bottom been.

49

385   No scene° that turns with engines strange   *stage set*
             Does oft'ner than these meadows change:
             For when the sun the grass hath vexed,
             The tawny mowers enter next;
             Who seem like Israelites to be
390   Walking on foot through a green sea.
             To them the grassy deeps divide
             And crowd a lane to either side.[5]

50

             With whistling scythe and elbow strong,
             These massacre the grass along:
395   While one, unknowing, carves the rail,[6]
             Whose yet unfeathered quills her fail.
             The edge all bloody from its breast
             He draws, and does his stroke detest;
             Fearing the flesh untimely mowed
400   To him a fate as black forebode.

51

             But bloody Thestylis[7] that waits
             To bring the mowing camp their cates,°   *food*
             Greedy as kites° has trussed it up,   *birds of prey*
             And forthwith means on it to sup;
405   When on another quick she lights,
             And cries, he[8] called us Israelites;
             But now, to make his saying true,
             Rails rain for quails, for manna dew.[9]

52

             Unhappy birds! what does it boot°   *avail*
410   To build below the grasses' root,
             When lowness is unsafe as height,

---

4. Plumb the depths and show the nature of the ground below.
5. The mowers produce a lane in the grassy meadow, like that formed when the Red Sea parted to allow the Israelites passage.
6. The corncrake (land rail), a field bird.
7. The cook for the harvest workers, comically given the name of a classical shepherdess.
8. The author, at line 389. The Puritans constantly compared themselves and their revolution to the Israelites battling enemies and wandering in the wilderness en route to Canaan, the Promised Land.
9. Exodus 13–15 describes the quails and manna (left after the dew evaporated) with which the Israelites were miraculously fed after crossing the Red Sea.

And chance o'ertakes what scapeth spite?
And now your orphan parents' call
Sounds your untimely funeral.
415 Death-trumpets creak in such a note,
And 'tis the sourdine[1] in their throat.

53

Or° sooner hatch or higher build: *either*
The mower now commands the field;
In whose new traverse° seemeth wrought   *track*
420 A camp of battle newly fought:
Where, as the meads with hay, the plain
Lies quilted o'er with bodies slain;
The women that with forks it fling,
Do represent the pillaging.

54

425 And now the careless victors play,
Dancing the triumphs of the hay;[2]
Where every mower's wholesome heat
Smells like an Alexander's sweat,[3]
Their females fragrant as the mead
430 Which they in fairy circles tread:
When at their dance's end they kiss,
Their new-made hay not sweeter is.

55

When after this 'tis piled in cocks,°   *haystacks*
Like a calm sea it shows the rocks:
435 We wond'ring in the river near
How boats among them safely steer.
Or, like the desert Memphis[4] sand,
Short pyramids of hay do stand.
And such the Roman camps do rise[5]
440 In hills for soldiers' obsequies.

56

This scene° again withdrawing brings   *stage set*
A new and empty face of things;
A leveled space, as smooth and plain,
As cloths for Lely[6] stretched to stain.
445 The world when first created sure
Was such a table rase[7] and pure;

---

1. A small pipe put into the mouth of a trumpet to produce a low sound.
2. A country dance (with a pun).
3. Plutarch wrote that Alexander the Great's sweat smelled sweet.
4. An ancient Egyptian city near the pyramids.
5. Hillocks that served as burial mounds; they were actually British in origin, not Roman.
6. Canvases for the Dutch portrait painter Sir Peter Lely, who came to England in 1643.
7. *Tabula rasa* (Latin): a clean or blank slate.

  Or rather such is the toril
  Ere the bulls enter at Madril.[8]

57

  For to this naked equal flat,
450 Which Levellers[9] take pattern at,
  The villagers in common° chase   *common pasture*
  Their cattle, which it closer rase;°   *crops*
  And what below the scythe increased°   *grew*
  Is pinched yet nearer by the beast.
455 Such, in the painted world, appeared,
  Davenant with th' universal herd.[1]

58

  They seem within the polished grass
  A landscape drawn in looking glass;
  And shrunk in the huge pasture show
460 As spots, so shaped, on faces do.[2]
  Such fleas, ere they approach the eye,
  In multiplying° glasses lie.   *magnifying*
  They feed so wide, so slowly move,
  As constellations do above.

59

465 Then, to conclude these pleasant acts,
  Denton sets ope' its cataracts;[3]
  And makes the meadow truly be
  (What it but seemed before) a sea.
  For, jealous of its lord's long stay,
470 It tries t' invite him thus away.
  The river in itself is drowned
  And isles th' astonished cattle round.

60

  Let others tell the paradox,
  How eels now bellow in the ox;[4]
475 How horses at their tails do kick,
  Turned as they hang to leeches quick;[5]
  How boats can over bridges sail,
  And fishes do the stables scale;

---

8. Madrid. "Toril": bull ring.
9. A radical faction, the Diggers or True Levellers, who sought social and economic equality. A group of Diggers began to put their tenets into practice by taking over and cultivating the land on St. George Hill, part of Fairfax's domain. See Gerrard Winstanley (p. 1331).
1. William Davenant, in his heroic poem *Gondibert* (2.6), describes a painting of the Creation, where on the sixth day "an universal herd" of animals appeared.
2. A landscape (or painted landscape) reflected in a mirror would be reduced in size.
3. Small waterfalls or dams. Denton, also a Fairfax estate (see line 73), was located on the Wharfe River, thirty miles from Nunappleton.
4. Because the ox swallowed them.
5. In popular superstition, horsehairs in water became live leeches or eels.

How salmons trespassing are found,
And pikes are taken in the pound.°   *cattle pen*

61

But I, retiring from the flood,
Take sanctuary in the wood;
And, while it lasts, myself embark
In this yet green, yet growing ark;
Where the first carpenter[6] might best
Fit timber for his keel have pressed;°   *obtained*
And where all creatures might have shares,
Although in armies, not in pairs.

62

The double wood of ancient stocks
Linked in so thick an union locks,
It like two pedigrees[7] appears,
On one hand Fairfax, th' other Vere's:
Of whom though many fell in war,
Yet more to heaven shooting are:
And, as they nature's cradle decked,
Will in green age her hearse expect.

63

When first the eye this forest sees
It seems indeed as wood not trees;
As if their neighborhood° so old   *nearness*
To one great trunk them all did mold.
There the huge bulk takes place, as meant
To thrust up a fifth element;[8]
And stretches still so closely wedged
As if the night within were hedged.

64

Dark all without it knits; within
It opens passable and thin;
And in as loose an order grows
As the Corinthian[9] porticoes.
The arching boughs unite between
The columns of the temple green;
And underneath the winged choirs
Echo about their tuned fires.

---

6. Noah, who built an ark to escape a flood that would cover the earth (Genesis 6).
7. Genealogical trees, of the Fairfax and Vere families.
8. The so-called quintessence, beyond and superior to fire, air, water, and earth.
9. The most elaborate order of Greek columns.

65

The nightingale does here make choice
To sing the trials of her voice.
Low shrubs she sits in, and adorns
With music high the squatted thorns.
But highest oaks stoop down to hear,
And list'ning elders prick the ear.
The thorn, lest it should hurt her, draws
Within the skin its shrunken claws.

66

But I have for my music found
A sadder, yet more pleasing sound:
The stock doves,° whose fair necks are graced   *turtledoves*
With nuptial rings, their ensigns chaste;
Yet always, for some cause unknown,
Sad pair, unto the elms they moan.
O why should such a couple mourn,
That in so equal flames do burn!

67

Then as I careless on the bed
Of gelid strawberries do tread,
And through the hazels thick espy
The hatching throstle's shining eye,
The heron from the ash's top
The eldest of its young lets drop,
As if it stork-like[1] did pretend
That tribute to its lord to send.

68

But most the hewel's° wonders are,   *green woodpecker's*
Who here has the holtfelster's° care.   *woodcutter's*
He walks still upright from the root,
Meas'ring the timber with his foot;
And all the way, to keep it clean,
Doth from the bark the wood-moths glean.
He, with his beak, examines well
Which fit to stand and which to fell.

69

The good he numbers up, and hacks;
As if he marked them with the ax.
But where he, tinkling with his beak,

---

1. The stork upon leaving a nest was believed to leave behind one of its young as a tribute to the householder.

Does find the hollow oak² to speak,
That for his building he designs,
550 And through the tainted side he mines.
Who could have thought the tallest oak
Should fall by such a feeble stroke!

70

Nor would it, had the tree not fed
A traitor-worm, within it bred.
555 (As first our flesh corrupt within
Tempts impotent and bashful sin)
And yet that worm triumphs not long,
But serves to feed the hewel's young;
While the oak seems to fall content,
560 Viewing the treason's punishment.

71

Thus I, easy philosopher,
Among the birds and trees confer;
And little now to make me, wants°   *lacks*
Or° of the fowls, or of the plants.   *either*
565 Give me but wings as they, and I
Straight floating on the air shall fly:
Or turn me but, and you shall see
I was but an inverted tree.³

72

Already I begin to call
570 In their most learned original:
And where I language want, my signs
The bird upon the bough divines;
And more attentive there doth sit
Than if she were with lime⁴ twigs knit.
575 No leaf does tremble in the wind
Which I returning cannot find.

73

Out of these scattered Sibyl's leaves
Strange prophecies my fancy weaves:⁵
And in one history consumes,
580 Like Mexique paintings, all the plumes.°   *feathers*
What Rome, Greece, Palestine, ere said
I in this light Mosaic⁶ read.

---

2. The "royal" oak was traditionally an emblem of monarchy.
3. Originally classical, this is a widely used metaphor in the Renaissance.
4. Birdlime, a sticky substance smeared on twigs to trap birds.
5. In Virgil's *Aeneid*, the Cumaean Sibyl, committed her prophecies to leaves that Aeneas feared might be scattered (6.77).
6. The pattern formed by the trembling leaves; also the books of Moses, who was thought to have written the first five books of the Bible.

> Thrice happy he who, not mistook,
> Hath read in nature's mystic book.[7]

74

585
> And see how chance's better wit
> Could with a mask[8] my studies hit!
> The oak-leaves me embroider all,
> Between which caterpillars crawl;
> And ivy, with familiar trails,
590
> Me licks, and clasps, and curls, and hales.
> Under this antic cope[9] I move
> Like some great prelate of the grove.

75

> Then, languishing with ease, I toss
> On pallets swol'n of velvet moss;
595
> While the wind, cooling through the boughs,
> Flatters with air my panting brows.
> Thanks for my rest, ye mossy banks,
> And unto you, cool zephyrs,° thanks,   *gentle west winds*
> Who, as my hair, my thoughts too shed,°   *part*
600
> And winnow from the chaff my head.

76

> How safe, methinks, and strong, behind
> These trees have I encamped my mind;
> Where beauty, aiming at the heart,
> Bends in some tree its useless° dart;   *harmless*
605
> And where the world no certain shot
> Can make, or me it toucheth not.
> But I on it securely play,
> And gall its horsemen all the day.

77

> Bind me ye woodbines in your twines,
610
> Curl me about ye gadding vines,
> And O so close your circles lace,
> That I may never leave this place:
> But, lest your fetters prove too weak,
> Ere I your silken bondage break,
615
> Do you, O brambles, chain me too,
> And courteous briars, nail me through.[1]

---

7. The book of the creatures, or the book of God's works.
8. Masque costume or disguise appropriate to the speaker's studies.
9. Comic ecclesiastical vestment.
1. The imagery evokes imprisonment and crucifixion.

78

Here in the morning tie my chain,
Where the two woods have made a lane;
While, like a guard on either side,
The trees before their lord divide;
This, like a long and equal thread,
Betwixt two labyrinths does lead.
But, where the floods did lately drown,
There at the evening stake me down.

79

For now the waves are fall'n and dried,
And now the meadows fresher dyed;
Whose grass, with moister color dashed,
Seems as green silks but newly washed.
No serpent new nor crocodile
Remains behind our little Nile;[2]
Unless itself you will mistake,
Among these meads° the only snake.   *meadows*

80

See in what wanton harmless folds
It ev'rywhere the meadow holds;
And its yet muddy back doth lick,
Till as a crystal mirror slick;°   *smooth*
Where all things gaze themselves, and doubt
If they be in it or without.
And for his shade° which therein shines,   *shadow*
Narcissus-like, the sun too pines.[3]

81

Oh what a pleasure 'tis to hedge
My temples here with heavy sedge;
Abandoning my lazy side,
Stretched as a bank unto the tide;
Or to suspend my sliding foot
On th' osier's undermined root,
And in its branches tough to hang,
While at my lines the fishes twang!

82

But now away my hooks, my quills,°   *floats*
And angles, idle utensils.
The young Maria walks tonight:

---

2. Our river; serpents and crocodiles were thought to be bred by spontaneous generation from the mud of the Nile.

3. In classical myth, Narcissus lay beside water, staring at his reflection, pining for himself.

Hide trifling youth thy pleasures slight.
'Twere shame that such judicious eyes
Should with such toys a man surprise;
She that already is the law
Of all her sex, her age's awe.

83

See how loose nature, in respect
To her, itself doth recollect;
And everything so whisht° and fine, — *hushed*
Starts forthwith to its bonne mine.° — *good appearance*
The sun himself, of her aware,
Seems to descend with greater care;
And lest she see him go to bed,
In blushing clouds conceals his head.

84

So when the shadows laid asleep
From underneath these banks do creep,
And on the river as it flows
With ebon shuts° begin to close; — *black shutters*
The modest halcyon[4] comes in sight,
Flying betwixt the day and night;
And such an horror calm and dumb,
Admiring nature does benumb.

85

The viscous° air, wheresoe'r she fly, — *thick*
Follows and sucks her azure dye;
The jellying stream compacts° below, — *solidifies*
If it might fix her shadow so;
The stupid° fishes hang, as plain — *stupefied*
As flies in crystal overta'en;
And men the silent scene assist,° — *attend*
Charmed with the sapphire-wingèd mist.[5]

86

Maria such, and so° doth hush — *in like fashion*
The world, and through the ev'ning rush.
No newborn comet such a train
Draws through the sky, nor star new-slain.[6]
For straight those giddy rockets[7] fail,
Which from the putrid earth exhale,
But by her flames, in heaven tried,
Nature is wholly vitrified.° — *turned to glass*

---

4. The kingfisher, who by nesting on the waves was believed to bring absolute calm to the sea.
5. The bird in its flight.
6. Meteor, or shooting star.
7. Vapors exhaled from the earth.

87

'Tis she that to these gardens gave
That wondrous beauty which they have;
She straightness on the woods bestows;
To her the meadow sweetness owes;
Nothing could make the river be
So crystal-pure but only she;
She yet more pure, sweet, straight, and fair,
Than gardens, woods, meads, rivers are.

88

Therefore what first she on them spent,
They gratefully again present:
The meadow, carpets where to tread;
The garden, flow'rs to crown her head;
And for a glass, the limpid brook,
Where she may all her beauties look;
But, since she would not have them seen,
The wood about her draws a screen.

89

For she, to higher beauties raised,
Disdains to be for lesser praised.
She counts her beauty to converse
In all the languages as hers;
Nor yet in those herself employs
But for the wisdom, not the noise;
Nor yet that wisdom would affect,
But as 'tis heaven's dialect.

90

Blest nymph! that couldst so soon prevent
Those trains° by youth against thee meant: *artillery*
Tears (wat'ry shot that pierce the mind)
And sighs (love's cannon charged with wind)
True praise (that breaks through all defense)
And feigned complying innocence;
But knowing where this ambush lay,
She scaped the safe, but roughest way.

91

This 'tis to have been from the first
In a domestic heaven nursed,
Under the discipline severe
Of Fairfax, and the starry Vere;
Where not one object can come nigh
But pure, and spotless as the eye;

        And goodness doth itself entail
        On females, if there want a male.[8]

92

        Go now fond° sex that on your face   *foolish*
730 Do all your useless study place,
        Nor once at vice your brows dare knit
        Lest the smooth forehead wrinkled sit;
        Yet your own face shall at you grin,
        Thorough° the black-bag° of your skin;   *through / mask*
735 When knowledge only could have filled
        And virtue all those furrows tilled.

93

        Hence she with graces more divine
        Supplies beyond her sex the line;
        And, like a sprig of mistletoe,
740 On the Fairfacian oak doth grow;
        Whence, for some universal good,
        The priest shall cut the sacred bud;[9]
        While her glad parents most rejoice,
        And make their destiny their choice.

94

745 Meantime ye fields, springs, bushes, flow'rs,
        Where yet she leads her studious hours
        (Till fate her worthily translates,
        And find a Fairfax for our Thwaites),
        Employ the means you have by her,
750 And in your kind yourselves prefer;[1]
        That, as all virgins she precedes,
        So you all woods, streams, gardens, meads.

95

        For you Thessalian Tempe's[2] seat
        Shall now be scorned as obsolete;
755 Aranjuez, as less, disdained;
        The Bel-Retiro[3] as constrained;
        But name not the Idalian grove,[4]
        For 'twas the seat of wanton Love;
        Much less the dead's Elysian Fields,[5]
760 Yet nor to them your beauty yields.

---

8. Maria was the only child and heir of the Fairfaxes.
9. Maria is, of course, intended for marriage.
1. Make yourselves the best you can.
2. The Vale of Tempe, in Greece, was a kind of paradise.
3. Spanish palaces.
4. A favorite haunt of Aphrodite (Venus), goddess of love, on Cyprus.
5. The pleasant habitation of the good in the classical underworld.

96

'Tis not, what once it was, the world,
But a rude heap together hurled;
All negligently overthrown,
Gulfs, deserts, precipices, stone.
Your lesser world[6] contains the same,
But in more decent order tame;
You heaven's center, nature's lap,
And paradise's only map.

97

But now the salmon-fishers moist
Their leathern boats begin to hoist;
And, like antipodes in shoes,
Have shod their heads in their canoes.[7]
How tortoise-like, but not so slow,
These rational amphibii[8] go!
Let's in; for the dark hemisphere
Does now like one of them appear.

1651   1681

---

6. Appleton House.
7. The men who dwell at the "antipodes," on the other side of the world, are sometimes said to wear their shoes on their heads; these English fishermen transport their leather boats on their heads.
8. As men, the fishermen are "rational"; and they live in two elements, land and water.

Crisis of Authority

Most of the poets and prose writers who published in the civil war decades, 1640 to 1660, registered in some way their responses to the conflicts swirling about them. The war and the issues over which it was fought shadow the poetry of Vaughan, Herrick, Hutchinson, Lovelace, Suckling, Marvell, and Milton and the prose of Thomas Browne and Izaak Walton. Yet writers often addressed the conflict only obliquely. When Marvell or Herrick celebrates peaceful gardens or fruitful countryside, when Vaughan envisions eternity as a "great ring of pure and endless light" suspended above all mortal turmoil, when Walton rhapsodizes about fishing, they create refuges of the imagination that might partially compensate for the trauma of war. Other writers confronted the issues of the age more straightforwardly. The readings included in this section sample this more explicitly political writing. They exemplify some of the genres encouraged by the new conditions in which literary materials could be written and circulated.

With the restoration of Charles II in 1660, many of the radical voices of the 1640s and 1650s were muted. Yet the war decades left a lasting imprint upon English literature. They established a tradition of overtly political, often ambitiously literary writing without which it is hard to imagine the works of such authors as John Dryden, Jonathan Swift, and Alexander Pope. They established prose as a dominant literary medium, especially for the description and analysis of everyday life. They initiated a tradition of apparently ordinary people bearing witness in writing to extraordinary events: a vital precedent for the rise of the novel.

This section presents examples of several kinds of writing that flourished during the Civil War and its immediate aftermath: the printed petition; the journalistic reporting of current events; political theory; and descriptions of contemporary history, personal experience, and individual character. These excerpts demonstrate a variety of ways in which writers responded to the disturbing and exciting developments around them: by reporting the details of dramatic, unprecedented occurrences; by analyzing the political and social problems posed by the conflict; by ruminating upon the character of great men; by seizing new opportunities for autobiographical reflection.

PETITIONING

A TRUE COPY OF THE PETITION OF GENTLEWOMEN AND TRADESMEN'S WIVES

Petitions—requests or demands signed by a number of people and presented to a governing authority—were always a fact of English political life. But in the crises leading up to and during the English Civil Wars and Commonwealth, petitions, particularly those addressed to Parliament, took on new life, expressing and manifesting the public demand for a greater role in political decision making and

The Parliament of Women. Satirical pamphlets like this one responded directly to the increased participation of women in political life in the 1640s.

helping to pave the way for a more representative government. The "Root and Branch Petition," which called for the abolition of bishops in all "roots" and "branches" of English life, including Parliament, was purportedly signed by 15,000 subscribers and presented to Parliament in December 1640 by 1,500 people. Most petitions from the period do not survive, but some, including the one below, were printed as stand-alone publications or in newsbooks.

While still a minority among petitioners, women petitioned Parliament on matters of trade, war, religion, and government. *A True Copy of the Petition of the Gentlewomen and Tradesmen's Wives in and about the City of London*, dated February 5, 1641 (1642 in the Julian calendar), articulates a number of reasons why women ought to petition "as well as the men": they share in the "common calamities" that affect church and commonwealth; they are equal sharers in Christian salvation; they are punished for their political actions; and there are biblical precedents for women's political activism. Like Aemilia Lanyer and Hester Pulter, the women petitioners marshal the example of Queen Esther, who, aided by the collective action of women, saved her people from a tyrannical king. In the King James Version of the book of Esther, King Ahasuerus even describes Esther's request as a petition. "What is thy petition?" he asks her, "and it shall be granted thee" (Esther 5:6). While later women petitioners were described as Medusa, Hecuba, "Whores, Bawds, Oysterwomen," and "Lacedemonians or bold Amazons," their voices were nonetheless heard loud and clear.

A True Copy of the Petition of Gentlewomen and Tradesmen's Wives in and about the City of London. Delivered to the Honorable, the Knights, Citizens and Burgesses, of the House of Commons in Parliament, the 4th of February, 1641. Together with their several reasons why their sex ought thus to petition, as well as the men; and the manner how both their petition and reasons was delivered. Likewise the answer which the Honorable Assembly sent to them by Mr. Pym, as they stood at the House door.

With lowest submission showing,

That we also with all thankful humility acknowledging the unwearied pains, care, and great charge, besides hazard of health and life, which you the noble worthies[1] of this honorable and renowned assembly have undergone, for safety both of Church and Commonwealth, for a long time already past; for which not only we your humble petitioners, and all well affected in this kingdom, but also all other good Christians are bound now and at all times to acknowledge; yet notwithstanding that many worthy deeds have been done by you, great danger and fear do still attend us, and will, as long as popish lords and superstitious bishops are suffered to have their voice in the House of Peers,[2] and that accursed and abominable idol of the mass suffered in the kingdom, and that arch-enemy[3] of our prosperity and reformation lie in the tower, yet not receiving his deserved punishment.

All these under correction, gives us great cause to suspect that God is angry with us, and to be the chief causes why your pious endeavors for a further reformation proceed not with that success as you desire, and is most earnestly prayed for of all that wish well to true religion and the flourishing estate both of king and kingdom; the insolencies of the papists and their abettors raise a just fear and suspicion of sowing sedition, and breaking out into bloody persecution in this kingdom, as they have done in Ireland,[4] the thoughts of which sad and barbarous events make our tender hearts to melt within us, forcing us humbly to petition to this honorable assembly to make safe provision for yourselves and us before it be too late.

And whereas we, whose hearts have joined cheerfully with all those petitions which have been exhibited unto you in the behalf of the purity of

1. Members of the House of Commons, the lower chamber of the English Parliament; they are elected.
2. The House of Lords, originally the more powerful chamber of the English Parliament, consisting of religious leaders and hereditary peers. "Popish": Catholic; high church.
3. William Laud, archbishop of Canterbury; he was imprisoned in 1641 but not executed until 1645.
4. In October 1641, Irish Catholics fought against English and settler-colonial rule for greater Irish self-governance, an end to (or limitations on) plantations, and an end to anti-Catholic discrimination.

religion, and the liberty of our husbands' persons and estates, recounting ourselves to have an interest in the common privileges with them, do with the same confidence assure ourselves to find the same gracious acceptance with you for easing of those grievances, which in regard of our frail condition, do more nearly concern us, and do deeply terrify our souls: our domestical dangers with which this kingdom is so much distracted, especially growing on us from those treacherous and wicked attempts already are such, as we find ourselves to have as deep a share as any other.

We cannot but tremble at the very thoughts of the horrid and hideous facts which modesty forbids us now to name, occasioned by the bloody wars in Germany,[5] his Majesty's late northern army,[6] how often did it affright our hearts, whilst their violence began to break out so furiously upon the persons of those whose husbands or parents were not able to rescue: we wish we had no cause to speak of those insolencies, and savage usage and unheard of rapes, exercised upon our sex in Ireland,[7] and have we not just cause to fear they will prove the forerunners of our ruin, except almighty God by the wisdom and care of this parliament be pleased to succor us, our husbands and children, which are as dear and tender unto us as the lives and blood of our hearts, to see them murdered and mangled and cut in pieces before our eyes, to see our children dashed against the stones, and the mothers' milk mingled with the infants' blood, running down the streets; to see our houses on flaming fire over our heads: oh how dreadful would this be! We thought it misery enough (though nothing to that we have just cause to fear) but few years since for some of our sex, by unjust divisions from their bosom comforts, to be rendered in a manner widows, and the children fatherless, husbands were imprisoned from the society of their wives, even against the laws of God and nature, and little infants suffered in their fathers' banishments: thousands of our dearest friends have been compelled to fly from Episcopal persecutions[8] into desert places amongst wild beasts, there finding more favor then in their native soil, and in the midst of all the sorrows, such hath the pity of the prelates been, that our cries could never enter into their ears or hearts, nor yet through multitudes of obstructions could never have access or come nigh to those royal mercies of our most gracious sovereign, which we confidently hope, would have relieved us: but after all these pressures ended, we humbly signify that our present fears are that unless the blood-thirsty faction of the papists and prelates be hindered in their designs, ourselves here in England as well as they in Ireland shall be exposed to that misery which is more intolerable than that which is already past, as namely

---

5. The Thirty Years' War (1618–48), a series of wars fought mostly on German soil following the efforts of the emperor of the Holy Roman Empire, Ferdinand II, to impose Catholicism throughout his domain.
6. The army raised to fight in the Second Bishops' War (1640), after Charles I imposed universal church practices, including the presence of bishops, on the Presbyterian-leaning Church of Scotland; it was defeated by the Scots.
7. The English press emphasized the Irish rebels' anti-settler violence during the Catholic uprising in 1641, particularly the murder of children and the rape of women.
8. That is, the movement led by Archbishop William Laud and his supporters within the Church of England; it emphasized free will, and hence the possibility of salvation for all men, thus rejecting the predestination embraced by Calvinism. Its stress on liturgical ceremony and clerical hierarchy, as well as its active silencing of dissent, was unpopular with more reform-minded Protestants.

to the rage not of men alone, but of devils incarnate (as we may so say), besides the thraldom of our souls and consciences in matters concerning God, which of all things are most dear unto us.

Now the remembrance of all these fearful accidents aforementioned do strongly move us from the example of the woman of Tekoa to fall submissively at the feet of his Majesty,[9] our dread sovereign, and cry help, O king, help O ye the noble worthies now sitting in parliament: And we humbly beseech you, that you will be a means to his Majesty and the House of Peers, that they will be pleased to take our heartbreaking grievances into timely consideration, and to add strength and encouragement to your noble endeavors, and further that you would move his Majesty with our humble requests that he would be graciously pleased according to the example of the good King Asa,[1] to purge both the court and kingdom of that great idolatrous service of the mass, which is tolerated in the Queen's court,[2] this sin (as we conceive) is able to draw down a greater curse upon the whole kingdom than all your noble and pious endeavors can prevent, which was the cause that the good and pious King Asa would not suffer idolatry in his own mother, whose example if it shall please his Majesty's gracious goodness to follow in putting down popery and idolatry both in great and small, in court and in the kingdom throughout, to subdue the papists and their abetters, and by taking away the power of the prelates, whose government by long and woeful experience we have found to be against the liberty of our conscience and the freedom of the gospel and the sincere profession and practice thereof, then shall our fears be removed, and we may expect that God will power down his blessings in abundance both upon his Majesty and upon this honorable assembly, and upon the whole land.

For which your new petitioners shall pray affectionately.

The reasons follow.

It may be thought strange and unbeseeming our sex to show ourselves by way of petition to this honorable assembly: but the matter being rightly considered, of the right and interest we have in the common and public cause of the church, it will as we conceive (under correction) be found a duty commanded and required.

First, because Christ has purchased us at as dear a rate as he has done men, and therefore requires the like obedience for the same mercy as of men.

---

9. In 2 Samuel 14, Joab asks a "wise woman" of Tekoa to reconcile David to Absalom after Absalom was banished for the murder of Amnon.
1. The third king of the Kingdom of Judah, who zealously opposed idolatry and disestablished all churches of false worship in his kingdom. Asa's eradication of idolatry and paganism was followed by decades of peace (2 Chronicles 14–15).
2. Charles I's queen, Henrietta Maria, kept a separate court in which she and many of her women attendants openly maintained their Catholic faith.

Secondly, because in the free enjoining of Christ in his own laws and a flourishing estate of the church and commonwealth consists the happiness of women as well as men.

Thirdly, because women are sharers in the common calamities that accompany both church and commonwealth when oppression is exercised over the church or kingdom wherein they live; and an unlimited power has been given to prelates to exercise authority over the consciences of women, as well as men; witness Newgate, Smithfield, and other places of persecution, wherein women as well as men have felt the smart of their fury.

Neither are we left without example in Scripture, for when the state of the church in the time of King Ahasuerus[3] was by the bloody enemies thereof sought to be utterly destroyed, we find that Esther the Queen and her maids fasted and prayed, and that Esther petitioned to the king in the behalf of the church: and though she enterprised this duty with the hazard of her own life, being contrary to the law to appear before the king before she were sent for, yet her love to the church carried her through all difficulties to the performance of that duty.

On which grounds we are emboldened to present our humble petition unto this honorable assembly, not weighing the reproaches which may and are by many cast upon us, who (not well weighing the premises) scoff and deride our good intent. We do it not out of any self conceit, or pride of heart, as seeking to equal ourselves with men, either in authority or wisdom, but according to our places to discharge that duty we owe to God, and the cause of the church, as far as lie in us, following herein the example of the men which have gone in this duty before us.

A relation of the manner how it was delivered,
with their Answer, sent by Mr. Pym.[4]

The petition with their reasons was delivered the fourth of Feb. 1641 by Mrs. Anne Stagg, a gentlewoman and brewer's wife, and many others with her of like rank and quality, which when they had delivered it, after some time spent in reading of it, the honorable assembly sent them an answer by Mr. Pym, which was performed in this manner.

---

3. A Persian king; the book of Esther tells the story of how his Jewish wife, Queen Esther, and her attending women successfully interceded with him to save her people (Esther 5–9).

4. John Pym (1584–1643), a member of Parliament who had long opposed arbitrary royalist rule and high church Anglicanism; this response was recorded in the *Journal of the House of Commons*. Pym was treasurer of the Providence Island Company, a colonial venture that helped fund the parliamentarian side in the civil wars. Following the Irish uprising in 1641 (which Charles I refused to condemn), Pym became the unofficial leader of the parliamentary opposition to the king, and the attempt in January 1642 to arrest him and four other members of Parliament sparked the first English Civil War.

Mr. Pym came to the commons door, and called for the women, and spake unto them in these words: Good women, your petition and the reasons have been read in the house, and is very thankfully accepted of, and is come in a seasonable time. You shall (God willing) receive from us all the satisfaction which we can possibly give to your just and lawful desires. We entreat you to repair to your houses, and turn your petition which you have delivered here into prayers at home for us; for we have been, are, and shall be (to our utmost power) ready to relieve you, your husbands, and children, and to perform the trust committed unto us, towards God, our king and country, as becometh faithful Christians and loyal subjects.

Reporting the News

The following accounts of the king's trial and execution are excerpted from newsbooks, one of the most important new literary forms of the war years. In England the reportage of current events originated in the 1620s, when anxiety over the nation's entanglement in what would become the Thirty Years' War on the Continent generated a demand for international news. In addition, in the 1620s and 1630s a few enterprising individuals provided "corantos," handwritten reports of court goings-on, to wealthy individuals in the provinces; these were technically considered private letters, although they sometimes circulated to several hundred paid subscribers. Yet even these modest ventures were always on legally shaky ground. The printing of domestic news, or commentary on it, was strictly prohibited by Charles I, as it had been by his forebears.

In the early 1640s, censorship collapsed just when many people urgently wanted information about the momentous events transpiring in England, Scotland, and Ireland. The result was the explosive development of printed news. While in 1640 there were no newsbooks, by 1645 there were 755. Their format varied, but typically they were eight-page cheaply printed pamphlets, issued weekly. Most writers and compilers remained anonymous, though in some cases the identity of the authors was an open secret. Unlike the earlier corantos, the inexpensive newsbooks of the 1640s gave a broad spectrum of readers access to information about current events. Often, simultaneously, they propagandized on behalf of various parties to the developing conflict. The newsbooks thus encouraged an unprecedentedly wide and deep sense of civic involvement, and arguably also had the effect of hardening factional differences.

The newsbooks provided eyewitness, or what purported to be eyewitness, accounts of the king's trial and execution very shortly after they occurred. Both events were highly charged, with important and complex stakes on both sides. In the autumn of 1648, many in Parliament who had initially wanted to restrict the king's powers hesitated to remove him from the throne; they favored a negotiated end to hostilities. Yet the powerful leaders of the New Model Army, including Oliver Cromwell, were convinced that Charles was a threat to a reorganized commonwealth. Even if the king dealt with his opponents in good faith, which they doubted, he would be a constant rallying point for opposition to their policies. Conceivably, the war would never be over.

When Charles seemed to be planning to escape from his relatively light confinement on the Isle of Wight, the army council ordered him seized and brought to London, which the army occupied. Yet what were they to do with their captive? Simply to assassinate him would deprive his killers of any semblance of legitimacy. A formal trial, therefore, seemed necessary; but it was not easy to achieve. First, Parliament had to be purged of more than half its members, who disapproved of putting the king on trial. Once reconstituted so as to exclude opposition, Parliament then had to pass a law redefining treason as a crime against the state, not a crime against the king, of which the king himself could not logically have been guilty.

As in the case of most treason trials in the sixteenth and seventeenth centuries, a guilty verdict was a foregone conclusion. Yet the trial's value as propaganda was unpredictable. The judges and executioners pointedly assumed the regalia and symbolism of state power, and conducted both the trial and the execution with great punctiliousness, in order to bolster the impression of due process in the eyes of onlookers and newsbook readers. Charles's calmly defiant behavior, meanwhile, was not meant to secure his acquittal, which everyone knew would have been unforthcoming anyhow. Rather, he hoped to garner sympathy for his plight, to demonstrate publicly his unwavering adherence to his own principles, and to provoke prosecutors and judges into behaving like rabid zealots. Likewise, his conduct on the scaffold impressed even those who deplored his political position. While his judges and executioners strove to describe him as an overweening tyrant, Charles struggled to appear the heir to a Christian tradition of suffering innocence, a "martyr of the people." In 1660, as soon as the monarchy was restored, Charles I was canonized by the Church of England.

From The Moderate, No. 28
16–23 January 1649

[THE TRIAL OF KING CHARLES I, THE FIRST DAY]

At the high court of justice sitting in the Great Hall of Westminster, Sergeant Bradshaw President,[1] about 70 Members present. Oyez[2] made thrice, silence commanded. The president had the sword and mace carried before him, attended with Colonel Fox, and twenty other officers and gentlemen with partisans.[3] The act of the Commons in Parliament for trial of the king, read. After the court was called, and each member rising up as he was called. The king came into the court, his hat on, and the Commissioners with theirs on also; no congratulation or motion of hats at all.[4] The Sergeant ushered him in with the mace, Colonel Hacker[5] and about thirty officers and gentlemen more came as his guard; the president then spake in these words, viz.

---

1. John Bradshaw (1609–1659), chief justice of Cheshire and Wales, accepted the office of president after others declined. He lost this office after 1653, when he opposed Cromwell's consolidation of personal power. Bradshaw was posthumously convicted of treason at the Restoration in 1660; his body was exhumed and hanged in chains.
2. Hear ye (French).
3. John Fox (1610–1650) was commander of the Lord President's bodyguard, the members of which carried spears with a lobed base or "partisans." The "sword and mace" symbolizes state power.
4. For either the king or the judges to doff their hats would be to acknowledge the others' superiority. "Congratulation": salutation.

"Charles Stuart, King of England, the Commons of England assembled in Parliament being sensible of the great calamities that have been brought upon this nation, of the innocent blood that hath been shed in this nation, which is referred[6] to you, as the author of it; and according to that duty which they owe to God, to the nation, and themselves, and according to that fundamental power and trust that is reposed in them by the people, have constituted this high court of justice before which you are now brought; and you are to hear the charge upon which the court will proceed."

Mr. Cook Solicitor General.[7] "My lord, in behalf of the Commons of England, and of all the people thereof, I do accuse Charles Stuart, here present, of high treason and high misdemeanors, and I do in the name of the Commons of England desire that the charge may be read unto him."

King. "Hold a little"—tapping the solicitor general twice on the shoulder with his cane, which drawing towards him again, the head thereon fell off, he stooping for it, put it presently[8] into his pocket. This is conceived will be very ominous.

Lord President. "Sir, the court commands the charge to be read; if you have any thing to say after, you may be heard."

The charge was read.

The king smiled often during the time, especially at those words therein, viz that Charles Stuart was a tyrant, traitor, murderer, and public enemy of the commonwealth.

Lord President. "Sir, you have now heard your charge read, containing such matter as appears in it: you find that in the close of it, it is prayed to the court in the behalf of all the Commons of England, that you answer to your charge. The court expects your answer."

King. "I would know by what power I am called hither. I was not long ago in the Isle of Wight; how I came hither is a larger story then I think is fit at this time for me to speak of: But there I entered into a treaty with the two Houses of Parliament, with as much public faith as is possibly to be had of any people in the world. I treated there with a number of honorable lords and gentlemen, and treated honestly and uprightly. I cannot say but they did deal very nobly with me. We were upon conclusion of a treaty. Now I would know by what authority—I mean lawful; there are many unlawful authorities in the world, thieves and robbers by the highways— but I would know by what authority I was brought from thence, and carried from place to place; and when I know by what lawful authority, I shall answer.

"Remember, I am your king, your lawful king; and what sin you bring upon your heads, and the judgments of God upon this land, think well upon it; I say think well upon it before you go further, from one sin to a

---

5. Francis Hacker (1618–1660) commanded the soldiers who guarded the king, signed the king's death warrant, and supervised the guard on the scaffold. He was executed after the Restoration.
6. Attributed.
7. John Cook (1608–1660), a radical republican lawyer, served as chief prosecutor. He was executed after the Restoration.
8. Immediately.

greater.[9] Therefore let me know by what lawful authority I am seated here, and I shall not be unwilling to answer. In the meantime, I shall not betray my trust. I have a trust committed to me by God, by old and lawful descent. I will not betray it, to answer to a new and unlawful authority. Therefore resolve me that, and you shall hear more of me."

Lord President. "If you had been pleased to have observed what was hinted to you by the court at our first coming hither, you would have known by what authority; which authority requires you in the name of the people of England, of which you are elected king, to answer them."

King. "No sir, I deny that."

Lord President. "If you acknowledge not the authority of the court, they must proceed."

King. "I do tell you so, England was never an elective kingdom, but an hereditary kingdom, for near a thousand years; therefore let me know by what authority I am called hither. I do stand more for the liberty of my people than any here that come to be my pretended judges; and therefore let me know by what lawful authority I am seated here, and I will answer it; otherwise I will not answer it."

Lord President told him he did interrogate the court, which beseemed not one in his condition, and it was known how he had managed his trust.

* * *

King. "I desire that you would give me, and all the world, satisfaction in this. For let me tell you, it is not a slight thing you are about. I am sworn to keep the peace by the duty I owe to God and my country; and I will do it to the last breath of my body: And therefore you shall do well to satisfy first God and then the country by what authority you do it; if by a reserved[1] authority, you cannot answer it. There is a God in heaven that will call you, and all that give you power, to an account. Satisfy me in that, and I will answer; otherwise, I betray my trust and the liberties of the people. And therefore think of that, and then I shall be willing. For I do vow, that it is as great a sin to withstand lawful authority, as it is to submit to a tyrannical or any otherways unlawful authority, And therefore satisfy me that, and you shall receive my answer."

Lord President. "The court expects a final answer. They are to adjourn till Monday. If you satisfy not yourself, though we tell you our authority, we are satisfied with our authority, and it is upon God's authority and the kingdom's; and that peace you speak of will be kept in the doing of justice; and that is our present work."

The court adjourned till Monday ten of clock to the Painted Chamber, and thence hither.

As the king went away, facing the court, the king said, "I fear not that," looking upon and meaning the sword.

---

9. From rebellion to regicide.   1. Unexplained.

Going down from the court, the people cried, "Justice, justice, justice!"
Jan. 21. The commissioners kept a fast this day in Whitehall. There preached before them Mr. Sprig, whose text was, "He that sheds blood, by man shall his blood be shed." Mr. Foxley's was "Judge not, lest you be judged." And Mr. Peters' was. "I will bind their kings in chains, and their nobles in fetters of iron."[2] The last sermon made amends for the two former.

1649

From A Perfect Diurnal of Some Passages in Parliament, No. 288

Tuesday, January 30

[THE EXECUTION OF CHARLES I]

This day the king was beheaded over against the Banqueting House by Whitehall.[1] The manner of execution and what passed before his death take thus.[2] He was brought from Saint James[3] about ten in the morning, walking on foot through the park with a regiment of foot for his guard, with colors flying, drums beating, his private guard of partisans,[4] with some of his gentlemen before, and some behind bareheaded, Dr. Juxon late Bishop of London[5] next behind him, and Colonel Tomlinson[6] (who had the charge of him) to the gallery in Whitehall, and so into the Cabinet Chamber where he used to lie, where he continued at his devotion, refusing to dine (having before taken the sacrament) only about 12 at noon he drank a glass of claret wine, and eat a piece of bread. From thence he was accompanied by Dr. Juxon, Colonel Tomlinson, Colonel Hacker,[7] and the guards before mentioned through the Banqueting House adjoining to which the scaffold was erected between Whitehall Gate and the gate leading into the gallery from Saint James. The scaffold was hung round with black, and the floor covered with black, and the ax and block laid in the middle of the scaffold. There were divers companies of foot and horse on every side the scaffold, and the multitudes of people that came to be spectators very great. The king making a pass upon[8] the scaffold, looked very earnestly on the block, and asked

---

2. The biblical texts are Genesis 9:6, Matthew 7:1, and Psalm 149:8. Hugh Peters (1598–1660), Independent preacher to Cromwell's New Model Army, passionately supported the king's execution. He was himself executed after the Restoration.
1. Whitehall Palace was the English monarch's principal residence from 1530 to 1698, when most of it was destroyed by fire. The Banqueting House, designed by Inigo Jones with ceilings painted by Peter Paul Rubens, was built for King James I in 1619–22 and was used to stage court masques. "Over against": just outside.
2. Accept the following account.
3. St. James Palace, near Whitehall.

4. Guards armed with partisans, spears with lobed points or halberds.
5. William Juxon (1582–1663), Charles I's personal chaplain, was bishop of London until 1649, when he was deprived of office. In the late 1630s he had also served as one of the king's financial advisers. After the Restoration he became archbishop of Canterbury.
6. Matthew Tomlinson commanded the guards assigned to Charles. He was tried after the Restoration but was spared because he had been courteous to the king.
7. On Colonel Hacker, see p. 1318, note 5.
8. Traversing.

Colonel Hacker if there were no higher; and then spake thus, directing his speech to the gentlemen upon the scaffold.

King. "I shall be very little heard of anybody here; I shall therefore speak a word unto you here. Indeed I could hold my peace[9] very well, if I did not think that holding my peace would make some men think that I did submit to the guilt as well as to the punishment. But I think it is my duty to God first, and to my country, for to clear myself both as an honest man, and a good king, and a good Christian. I shall begin first with my innocency. In troth I think it not very needful for me to insist long upon this, for all the world knows that I never did begin a war with the two Houses of Parliament, and I call God to witness, to whom I must shortly make an account, that I never did intend for to encroach upon their privileges; they began upon me. It is the militia they began upon;[1] they confessed that the militia was mine but they thought it fit to have it from me; and to be short, if anybody will look to the dates of commissions, theirs and mine, and likewise to the declarations,[2] will see clearly that they began these unhappy troubles, not I. So that as the guilt of these enormous crimes that are laid against me, I hope in God that God will clear me of it. I will not; I am in charity;[3] God forbid that I should lay it upon the two Houses of Parliament, there is no necessity of either.[4] I hope they are free of this guilt; for I do believe that ill instruments[5] between them and me has been the chief cause of all this bloodshed. So that by way of speaking, as I find myself clear of this, I hope and pray God that they may too. Yet for all this, God forbid that I should be so ill a Christian, as not to say that God's judgments are just upon me. Many times he does pay justice by an unjust sentence; that is ordinary. I only say this, that an unjust sentence (meaning Strafford)[6] that I suffered for to take effect, is punished now by an unjust sentence upon me. That is, so far I have said, to show you that I am an innocent man.

"Now for to show you that I am a good Christian, I hope there is" (pointing to Dr. Juxon) "a good man that will bear me witness that I have forgiven all the world, and those in particular that have been the chief causers of my death. Who they are, God knows; I do not desire to know. I pray God forgive them. But this is not all; my charity must go farther. I wish that they may repent, for indeed they have committed a great sin in that particular. I pray God with Saint Stephen that this be not laid to their charge;[7] nay, not only so, but that they may take the right way to the peace of the kingdom,

---

9. Remain silent. It was customary for condemned prisoners to address onlookers before their public executions. "You here": the small group standing on the scaffold, as distinguished from the large crowd watching the execution.
1. In 1642 Parliament's Militia Ordinance transferred local militias from the king's control to Parliament's. Despite its failure to secure Charles's assent to the measure, Parliament declared it legally binding.
2. "Commissions" and "declarations": warrants for enlisting troops and proclamations of war.
3. Practicing the charity that befits a Christian, I refuse to lay the blame for the war on my enemies.
4. Of blaming either side for the war.
5. Corrupt go-betweens.
6. In an attempt to appease his opponents in Parliament, Charles reluctantly consented to the execution of his adviser Thomas Wentworth, Earl of Strafford, for treason in 1641, despite lack of evidence that Strafford had committed any crime.
7. St. Stephen, the first Christian martyr, prayed that God not hold his persecutors responsible for their actions (see Acts 7:54–60). "Particular" (previous line): regard.

for charity commands me not only to forgive particular men, but to endeavor to the last gasp the peace of the kingdom. Sirs, I do wish with all my soul, and I do hope there is some here will carry it further, that they may endeavor the peace of the kingdom.

"Now, sirs, I must show you both how you are out of the way, and will put you in a way.[8] First, you are out of the way, for certainly all the way[9] you ever have had yet as I could find by anything, is in the way of conquest. Certainly this is an ill way, for conquest, sir, in my opinion is never just, except there be a good just cause, either for matter of wrong or just title, and then if you go beyond it,[1] the first quarrel that you have to it, that makes it unjust at the end that was just at first. But if it be only matter of conquest, then it is a great robbery; as a pirate said to Alexander that he was a great robber, he was but a petty robber. And so, sir, I do think the way that you are in, is much out of the way. Now, sir, for to put you in the way, believe it you never do right, nor God will never prosper you,[2] until you give Him his due, the king his due (that is, my successors) and the people their due. I am as much for them[3] as any of you. You must give God his due by regulating rightly his Church, according to Scripture, which is now out of order. For to set you in a way particularly[4] now I cannot, but only this, a national synod freely called, freely debating among themselves, must settle this; when that every opinion is freely and clearly heard. For the king, indeed I will not—(Then turning to a gentleman that touched the ax, said, hurt not the ax that may hurt me.)—For the king, the laws of the land will clearly instruct you for that; therefore, because it concerns my own particular I only give you a touch of it.[5] For the people, and truly I desire their liberty and freedom, as much as anybody whomsoever; but I must tell you, that their liberty and their freedom consists in having of government, those laws by which their life and their goods may be most their own. It is not for having share in government, sir, that is nothing pertaining to them.[6] A subject and a sovereign are clean[7] different things; and therefore, until they do that, I mean, that you do put the people in that liberty as I say, certainly they will never enjoy themselves.[8] Sirs, it was for this[9] that now I am come here. If I would have given way to an arbitrary way, for to have all laws changed according to the power of the sword, I needed not to have come here; and therefore I tell you, and I pray God it be not laid to your charge, that I am the martyr of the people. In troth sirs, I shall not hold you much longer; for I will only say this to you, that in truth I could have desired some little time longer because that I would have put this that I have said in a little more order and a little better digested[1] than I have done; and therefore I hope you will excuse me. I have delivered[2] my conscience. I pray God that you do

---

8. Both show you how you are wrong and put you on a correct course.
9. All the rationale.
1. Beyond what is necessary to correct the wrong.
2. Allow you to flourish.
3. On the people's side.
4. In detail.
5. Because it concerns my own situation, I mention it only briefly.
6. Of their concern or responsibility.
7. Completely.
8. Be happy.
9. Because I upheld the liberty of the people.
1. More methodically arranged.
2. Spoken.

take those courses that are best for the good of the kingdom and your own salvations."

Dr. Juxon. "Will Your Majesty—though it may be very well known Your Majesty's affections to religion—yet it may be expected that you should say somewhat[3] for the world's satisfaction."

King. "I thank you very heartily, my lord, for that I had almost forgotten it. In troth, sirs, my conscience in religion I think is very well known to the world, and therefore I declare before you all that I die a Christian according to the profession of the Church of England as I found it left me by my father; and this honest man, I think, will witness it." Then turning to the officers said, "sirs, excuse me for this same.[4] I have a good cause, and I have a gracious God; I will say no more."

Then turning to Colonel Hacker, he said, "Take care that they do not put me to pain; and, sir, this, an it please you."[5] But then a gentleman coming near the ax, the king said, "Take heed of the ax, pray take heed of the ax." Then the king speaking to the executioner said, "I shall say but very short prayers, and then thrust out my hands."

Then the king called to Dr. Juxon for his nightcap, and having put it on he said to the executioner, "Does my hair trouble you?" Who desired him to put it all under his cap, which the king did accordingly, by the help of the executioner and the bishop. Then the king turning to Dr. Juxon said, "I have a good cause, and a gracious God on my side."

Dr. Juxon, "There is but one stage more. This stage is turbulent and troublesome; it is a short one: But you may consider it will soon carry you a very great way; it will carry you from earth to heaven, and there you shall find a great deal of cordial joy and comfort."

King. "I go from a corruptible to an incorruptible crown, where no disturbance can be."

Dr. Juxon. "You are exchanged from a temporal to an eternal crown, a good exchange."

Then the king took off his cloak and his George,[6] giving his George to Dr. Juxon, saying "Remember" (it is thought for the prince) and some other small ceremonies past. After which the king stooping down laid his neck upon the block, and after a very little pause stretching forth his hands, the executioner at one blow severed his head from his body. Then his body was put in a coffin covered with black velvet, and removed to his lodging chamber in Whitehall.

---

3. Something.
4. This religious profession. Charles did not accept the radical Protestantism espoused by many of his opponents.
5. As was customary, Charles tips Hacker, the person supervising the execution, in hopes of ensuring a quick death. "An": if.
6. A jeweled pendant representing St. George killing a dragon, worn by Knights of the Garter. The prince (following) is the king's eldest son, later King Charles II, who had escaped to exile in France.

Political Writing

Not surprisingly, the tumult of civil war stimulated a good deal of thinking about the nature and ends of government. The excerpts that follow give some idea of the arguments proposed by English political writers between 1630 and 1655.

Robert Filmer and Thomas Hobbes both favor an absolutist government that would concentrate power in the sovereign and deprive the people of any way to get rid of him. However, the two writers work from quite different premises. In *Patriarcha, or The Natural Power of Kings Defended Against the Unnatural Liberty of the People*, Filmer outlines a historical theory based on the authority of biblical patriarchs—Abraham, Isaac, and Jacob, for instance—over their families. God ratified kingly authority, Filmer argues, when he commanded the honoring of parents. Although many royalists retained a larger role for popular consent than Filmer did, Filmer's account of the king's fatherly care of his people, and the people's childlike incompetence to manage political affairs, was close to the Stuart kings' own view.

Unlike Filmer, Thomas Hobbes, a gifted mathematician, believed in working from clearly defined first principles to conclusions, grounding his political vision not on biblical history but upon a comprehensive philosophy of nature and of knowledge. He believed that human beings seek self-preservation as a primary goal, and power as a means to secure that goal; his politics spring directly from these premises. Since the best way to assure self-preservation, he argued, is to assent permanently to the creation of a strong authority, the founding political covenant cannot be revoked and rebellion against the sovereign is absurd. Hobbes's materialism and secularism—his virtual exclusion of God from politics—scandalized both the Puritans who opposed him and many royalists as well.

The claims of royalists came under vigorous attack from the poet John Milton, who during the war years became one of the most effective polemicists for the parliamentary radicals. Milton wrote *The Tenure of Kings and Magistrates* in 1648, the days leading up to Charles's trial and execution, when many of those who had originally supported limiting the king's power shrank from actually beheading him. Milton decries this hesitation, seeing it as the effect of a misdirected awe for the privileges of monarchs. All political authorities, Milton argues, hold their power in trust from the people, and the people can revoke that trust whenever they choose.

Like Filmer, Milton bases his argument upon biblical history, but he cites very different passages. Filmer emphasizes the importance of fatherly authority in Genesis, which narrates the lives of Adam, Noah, Abraham, Isaac, Jacob, and Joseph. Milton acknowledges that the fall of Adam and Eve corrupted human nature so that individuals were henceforth unable to govern themselves properly without external discipline. Yet, he insists, since those charged with implementing that discipline are themselves sinners, they must be kept in check by laws and by strict limitations upon their authority. In Milton's account, problems with the exercise of authority became evident only gradually. Unlike Filmer, who assumes that the social arrangements described in Genesis are a pattern for modern political communities, Milton chooses his examples from later eras in Jewish history: for instance, the book of Samuel, in which God disapproves of the Israelites' desire for a king.

For Filmer, Hobbes, and Milton, the central issue of the conflict between the king and Parliament is, Who has ultimate authority, the king or the people? Gerrard Winstanley construes the problem differently, in primarily economic rather than political terms. Winstanley was a well-educated London linen draper who worked as a laborer in the countryside after suffering financial reverses during the war years. In his political writing, he concerns himself less with the way power is allocated than with the equitable distribution of wealth. The ownership of land is especially important to him, since it was the critical asset in a largely agrarian society. Members of the House of Commons, though they considered themselves the representatives of "the people," were actually fairly substantial property owners; indeed, those without land or income were not entitled to vote. In consequence, more than half the male population (and, of course, the entire female population) was denied the franchise. In *A New Year's Gift Sent to the Parliament and Army* (1650), Winstanley accuses Parliament of having merely transferred oppressive power from the king to itself, leaving most of England's population as impoverished and downtrodden as before.

Winstanley suggests a practical means to remedy his society's inequities: "the commons," undeveloped lands used for grazing, should be made available to poor people to farm communally. Since the commons, though traditionally used by all the residents on an estate, were legally the manorial landlord's private property, Winstanley's ideas were highly unpopular among landowners. Moreover, his proposal was not merely a theoretical recommendation. The year before he wrote *A New Year's Gift*, Winstanley and some of his followers, called Diggers, had settled on St. George's Hill in Surrey. They planted twelve acres of grain and built a number of makeshift houses before they were violently evicted.

Like Filmer and Milton, Winstanley turns to the Bible to justify his politics. And like them, he chooses passages that suit his argument. He reads contemporary history through the heady allegories of the book of Revelation, as a confrontation between the powers of darkness and the powers of light. Jesus's concern for the poor and scorn for the rich loom large to him, and his social vision owes much to biblical accounts of early Christian communities, which held property in common and minimized class differences.

ROBERT FILMER

The eldest of eighteen children, Robert Filmer (1588–1653) attended Trinity College, Cambridge, and inherited his father's estate in Kent in 1629. When war broke out he was too old to participate as a soldier, but he was briefly imprisoned by Parliament as a known supporter of the king, and his property was seized. After his release, he published a number of treatises arguing for absolute monarchy, among them *The Anarchy of a Limited and Mixed Monarchy* (1648); *The Freeholder's Grand Inquest* (1648), which argued that Parliament could meet only at the will of the king; and a translation of excerpts from the works of the French absolutist Jean Bodin. However, Filmer's most important treatise, *Patriarcha*, was not among these publications. Scholars disagree about when it was written, but Filmer probably composed it in the early 1630s in the wake of Charles's conflicts with Parliament early in his reign. The treatise remained in manuscript until 1680. Printed during a heated debate between Tories (royalists) and Whigs (Parliamentarians) over the right of King Charles II's brother James to inherit the throne, *Patriarcha* was comprehensively savaged by John Locke in his *First Treatise of Government* (1690).

While Filmer's motive in writing *Patriarcha* was undoubtedly close-to-home disputes between the English king and his subjects, his explicit polemical target is not Charles's parliamentary opponents. Rather, Filmer argues against Continental political theorists such as the Jesuit Robert Cardinal Bellarmine, who had written a devastating critique of James I's treatises on monarchy earlier in the century. Bellarmine's aim had been to secure freedom of conscience and worship for Roman

Catholic subjects of a Protestant monarch, by arguing that the power of monarchs was constrained by their people. Charles's Puritan opponents would find many aspects of Bellarmine's line of reasoning irresistible. Since in the English-speaking tradition republican concepts eventually came to be strongly associated with Puritan dissent, it is worth remembering that for much of the sixteenth and early seventeenth centuries, it had been Protestants who advocated consolidating secular and spiritual power in the figure of a powerful king, and Catholics who had resisted that consolidation.

From Patriarcha, or The Natural Power of Kings Defended Against the Unnatural Liberty of the People

From Chapter 1: That the First Kings Were Fathers of Families

Since the time that school divinity[1] began to flourish there hath been a common opinion maintained, as well by divines as by divers other learned men, which affirms: "Mankind is naturally endowed and born with freedom from all subjection, and at liberty to choose what form of government it please, and that the power which any one man hath over others was at first bestowed according to the discretion of the multitude." This tenet was first hatched in the schools, and hath been fostered by all succeeding Papists for good divinity. The divines, also, of the reformed churches have entertained it, and the common people everywhere tenderly embrace it as being most plausible[2] to flesh and blood, for that it prodigally distributes a portion of liberty to the meanest of the multitude, who magnify liberty as if the height of human felicity were only to be found in it, never remembering that the desire of liberty was the first cause of the fall of Adam.

But howsoever this vulgar[3] opinion hath of late obtained a great reputation, yet it is not to be found in the ancient fathers and doctors of the primitive church. It contradicts the doctrine and history of the holy scriptures, the constant practice of all ancient monarchies, and the very principles of the law of nature. It is hard to say whether it be more erroneous in divinity or dangerous in policy.[4]

* * *

That the patriarchs[5] * * * were endowed with kingly power, their deeds do testify; for as Adam was lord of his children, so his children under him had a command and power over their own children, but still with subordination to the first parent, who is lord-paramount over his children's children to all generations, as being the grandfather of his people.

I see not then how the children of Adam, or of any man else, can be free from subjection to their parents. And this subjection of children being the fountain of all regal authority, by the ordination of God himself, it follows that civil power not only in general is by divine institution, but even the assignment of it specifically to the eldest parents, which quite takes away

---

1. Systematic theology, as undertaken by medieval philosophers in the universities ("schools").
2. Agreeable.
3. Commonly held.
4. The conduct of public affairs.
5. Forefathers of the Jews, including Adam, Noah, Abraham, Isaac, Jacob, and Jacob's twelve sons.

that new and common distinction which refers only power universal and absolute to God, but power respective[6] in regard of the special form of government to the choice of the people.

This lordship which Adam by command had over the whole world, and by right descending from him the patriarchs did enjoy, was as large and ample as the absolutest dominion of any monarch which hath been since the Creation. For dominion of life and death we find that Judah, the father, pronounced sentence of death against Thamar, his daughter-in-law, for playing the harlot. "Bring her forth," saith he, "that she may be burnt."[7] Touching war, we see that Abraham commanded an army of three hundred and eighteen soldiers of his own family. And Esau met his brother Jacob with four hundred men at arms. For matter of peace, Abraham made a league with Abimelech, and ratified the articles with an oath. These acts of judging in capital crimes, of making war, and concluding peace, are the chiefest marks of sovereignty that are found in any monarch.

* * *

It may seem absurd to maintain that kings now are the fathers of their people, since experience shows the contrary. It is true, all kings be not the natural parents of their subjects, yet they all either are, or are to be reputed, the next heirs to those first progenitors who were at first the natural parents of the whole people, and in their right succeed to the exercise of supreme jurisdiction; and such heirs are not only lords of their own children, but also of their brethren, and all others that were subject to their fathers. And therefore we find that God told Cain of his brother Abel, "His desires shall be subject unto thee, and thou shalt rule over him." Accordingly, when Jacob bought his brother's birthright, Isaac blessed him thus: "Be lord over thy brethren, and let the sons of thy mother bow before thee."[8]

As long as the first fathers of families lived, the name of patriarchs did aptly belong unto them; but after a few descents, when the true fatherhood itself was extinct, and only the right of the father descends to the true heir, then the title of prince or king was more significant to express the power of him who succeeds only to the right of that fatherhood which his ancestors did naturally enjoy. By this means it comes to pass that many a child, by succeeding a king, hath the right of a father over many a gray-headed multitude, and hath the title of *pater patriae*.[9]

To confirm this natural right of regal power, we find in the Decalogue[1] that the law which enjoins obedience to kings is delivered in the terms of "Honor thy father," as if all power were originally in the father. If obedience to parents be immediately due by a natural law, and subjection to princes but by the mediation of a human ordinance, what reason is there that the laws of nature should give place to the laws of men, as we see the power of the father over his child gives place and is subordinate to the power of the magistrate?

If we compare the natural rights of a father with those of a king, we find them all one, without any difference at all but only in the latitude or extent

---

6. Partial, limited.
7. Genesis 38:24. The examples following also come from Genesis, 14:14, 32:6, and 21:22–27.
8. The first reference is to Genesis 4:7, which Filmer reads tendentiously as establishing the elder brother Cain's authority over the younger Abel, and the second is to Genesis 27:29.
9. Father of his country. See Exodus 20:12.
1. Ten Commandments.

of them: as the father over one family, so the king, as father over many families, extends his care to preserve, feed, clothe, instruct, and defend the whole commonwealth. His war, his peace, his courts of justice, and all his acts of sovereignty, tend only to preserve and distribute to every subordinate and inferior father, and to their children, their rights and privileges, so that all the duties of a king are summed up in an universal fatherly care of his people.

1620s–40s   1680

JOHN MILTON[1]

From The Tenure[2] of Kings and Magistrates

If men within themselves would be governed by reason, and not generally give up their understanding to a double tyranny, of custom from without, and blind affections[3] within, they would discern better what it is to favor and uphold the tyrant of a nation. But being slaves within doors,[4] no wonder that they strive so much to have the public state conformably governed to the inward vicious rule by which they govern themselves. For indeed none can love freedom heartily but good men; the rest love not freedom but license; which never hath more scope or more indulgence than under tyrants. Hence it is that tyrants are not oft offended nor stand much in doubt of bad men, as being all naturally servile; but in whom[5] virtue and true worth most is eminent, them they fear in earnest as by right their masters; against them lies all their hatred and suspicion. Consequently neither do bad men hate tyrants, but have been always readiest with the falsified names of loyalty, and obedience, to color over their base compliances.[6] And although sometimes for shame, and when it comes to their own grievances, of purse especially, they would seem good patriots and side with the better cause, yet when others for the deliverance of their country, endued with fortitude and heroic virtue to fear nothing by the curse written against those "that do the work of the lord negligently,"[7] would go on to remove not only the calamities and thralldoms of a people but the roots and causes whence they spring, straight these men and sure helpers at need, as if they hated only the miseries but not the mischiefs,[8] after they have juggled and paltered[9] with the world, bandied and borne arms against their king, divested him, disanointed him, nay cursed him all over in their pulpits and their pamphlets, to the engaging of sincere and real men beyond what is possible or honest to retreat from, not only turn revolters from those

---

1. See headnote to Milton, p. 1381.
2. Terms of holding office.
3. Impulses, passions.
4. That is, within their own selves.
5. Those in whom.
6. Make their slavishness look good.
7. Milton apparently refers to Jeremiah 48:10: "Cursed be he that doeth the work of the Lord deceitfully, and cursed be he that keepeth back his sword from blood."
8. The suffering but not its causes.
9. Played fast and loose.

principles which only could at first move them, but lay the stain of disloyalty and worse on those proceedings which are the necessary consequences of their own former actions; nor disliked by themselves, were they managed to the entire advantages of their own faction; not considering the while that he toward whom they boasted their new fidelity counted them accessory;[1] and by those statutes and laws which they so impotently brandish against others would have doomed them to a traitor's death for what they have done already. 'Tis true, that most men are apt enough to civil wars and commotions as a novelty, and for a flash hot and active; but through sloth or inconstancy, and weakness of spirit either fainting ere their own pretences,[2] though never so just, be half attained, or through an inbred falsehood and wickedness, betray ofttimes to destruction with themselves men of noblest temper[3] joined with them for causes whereof they in their rash undertakings[4] were not capable.

* * *

No man who knows aught, can be so stupid to deny that all men naturally were born free, being the image and resemblance of God Himself, and were by privilege above all the creatures born to command and not to obey, and that they lived so. Till from the root of Adam's transgression,[5] falling among themselves to do wrong and violence, and foreseeing that such courses must needs tend to the destruction of them all, they agreed by common league to bind each other from mutual injury, and jointly to defend themselves against any that gave disturbance or opposition to such agreement. Hence came cities, towns, and commonwealths. And because no faith in all was found sufficiently binding,[6] they saw it needful to ordain some authority that might restrain by force and punishment what was violated against peace and common right. This authority and power of self-defense and preservation being originally and naturally in every one of them, and unitedly in them all, for ease, for order, and lest each man should be his own partial[7] judge, they communicated and derived[8] either to one, whom for the eminence of his wisdom and integrity they chose above the rest, or to more than one whom they thought of equal deserving: the first was called a king, the other magistrates. Not to be their lords and masters (though afterward those names in some places were given voluntarily to such as had been authors[9] of inestimable good to the people) but to be their deputies and commissioners, to execute, by virtue of their entrusted power, that justice which else every man by the bond of nature and of convenant must have executed for himself and for one another. And to him that shall consider well why among free persons, one man by civil right[1] should bear authority and jurisdiction over another, no other end or reason can be imaginable. These[2] for a while governed well, and with much equity decided all things at their own arbitrament:[3] till the temptation of such a power left absolute in their hands,

---

1. Guilty of being accessories to a crime.
2. Purposes.
3. Character.
4. Attempts, enterprises.
5. Adam's fall introduced sin and violence into human life.
6. Because merely trusting people to behave themselves did not suffice to control them.
7. Biased.
8. Delegated.
9. Doers.
1. Law.
2. Kings and magistrates.
3. Judgment.

perverted them at length to injustice and partiality. Then did they who now by trial[4] had found the danger and inconveniences of committing arbitrary power to any, invent laws either framed or consented to by all, that should confine and limit the authority of whom they chose to govern them: that so man,[5] of whose failing they had proof, might no more rule over them, but law and reason abstracted as much as might be from personal errors and frailties. While[6] as the magistrate was set above the people, so the law was set above the magistrate. When this would not serve, but that the law was either not executed or misapplied, they were constrained from that time, the only remedy left them, to put conditions[7] and take oaths from all kings and magistrates at their first installment to do impartial justice by law: who upon those terms and no other received allegiance from the people, that is to say, bond or covenant to obey them in execution of those laws which they the people had themselves made or assented to. And this ofttimes with express warning, that if the king or magistrate proved unfaithful to his trust, the people would be disengaged.[8] They added also counselors and parliaments, nor to be only at his beck,[9] but with him or without him, at set times, or at all times when any danger threatened to have care of the public safety.

* * *

It being thus manifest that the power of kings and magistrates is nothing else but what is only derivative, transferred and committed to them in trust from the people, to the common good of them all, in whom the power yet remains fundamentally, and cannot be taken from them without a violation of their natural birthright; and seeing that from hence Aristotle[1] and the best of political writers have defined a king, him who governs to the good and profit of his people and not for his own ends, it follows from necessary causes that the titles of sovereign lord, natural lord, and the like, are either arrogancies or flatteries, not admitted[2] by emperors and kings of best note, and disliked by the church both of Jews, Isaiah 26.13, and ancient Christians, as appears by Tertullian and others.[3] Although generally the people of Asia, and with them the Jews also, especially since the time they chose a king against the advice and counsel of God,[4] are noted by wise authors much inclinable to slavery.

Secondly, that to say, as is usual, the king hath as good right to his crown and dignity as any man to his inheritance, is to make the subject no better than the king's slave, his chattel or his possession that may be bought and sold. And doubtless if hereditary title were sufficiently inquired, the best foundation of it would be found either but in courtesy or convenience. But suppose it to be of right hereditary, what can be more just and legal, if a

---

4. Experience. "They": the people who had delegated power to the kings and magistrates.
5 An individual man.
6 Thus.
7 Specify restrictions on.
8. Freed from having to obey.
9 The king's command. Charles had claimed that Parliament could not assemble unless called into session by the king.
1. In *Nicomachean Ethics* 8.11.1.

2. Permitted.
3. Isaiah 26:13: "O Lord our God, other lords beside thee have had dominion over us; but by thee only will we make mention of thy name." The church father Tertullian wrote against earthly monarchs in *On the Crown*.
4. The Israelites, traditionally governed by judges, demanded a king despite God's warning against monarchy, as conveyed by the prophet Samuel (1 Samuel 8).

subject for certain crimes be to forfeit by law from himself, and posterity, all his inheritance to the king,[5] than that a king for crimes proportional should forfeit all his title and inheritance to the people: unless the people must be thought created all for him, he not for them, and they all in one body inferior to him single, which were a kind of treason against the dignity of mankind to affirm.

Thirdly it follows that to say kings are accountable to none but God is the overturning of all law and government. For if they may refuse to give account, then all covenants made with them at coronation, all oaths are in vain and mere mockeries, all laws which they swear to keep made to no purpose; for if the king fear not God—as how many of them do not?—we hold then our lives and estates by the tenure of his mere grace and mercy, as from a God, not a mortal magistrate, a position that none but court parasites or men besotted would maintain.

* * *

It follows lastly, that since the king or magistrate holds his authority of the people, both originally and naturally for their good in the first place, and not his own, then may the people as oft as they shall judge it for the best, either choose him or reject him, retain him or depose him though no tyrant, merely by the liberty and right of freeborn men to be governed as seems to them best.

1649

5. Convicted felons forfeited their property to the king.

GERRARD WINSTANLEY

The demand for democratic elections by a political faction called the Levellers raised the fear in Cromwell and his conservative associates that with unpropertied voters outnumbering the propertied by five to one, they might divide or even abolish private property. That was in fact the program of a small group calling themselves True Levellers or, later, Diggers, who were a group of Christian communists. Their leader was Gerrard Winstanley (1609–1676?), a failed businessman and subsequently a hired laborer, who began to publish tracts in 1648, became notorious in 1649 with the attempted enactment of the Diggers' program, and lapsed back into obscurity after his last published work in 1652.

In the spring of 1649, the Diggers began to put their ideals into practice, digging up the wasteland of St. George's Hill in Surrey and preparing it for crops. Though this land was not enclosed, all over England landowners claimed property rights in such common land, and the Diggers' gesture of cultivation here and in a few other Digger communities made a threatening counterclaim on behalf of the poor and propertyless. Their aim was at one level practical: at least one-third of England, they claimed, was barren waste, and if properly cultivated could vastly increase the food supply, to the great benefit of the poor. At another level their aim was ideological, a fundamental challenge to the concept of private ownership of land, as the tract excerpted here argues—at least in regard to the common land. The army and the civil authorities were not very hard on the Diggers, but the local landholders were, beating them, expelling them, and destroying their settlements. Nonetheless, their radical and often eloquent tracts survived to inspire later communes.

From A New Year's Gift[1] Sent to the Parliament and Army

Gentlemen of the Parliament and army: you and the common people have assisted each other to cast out the head of oppression which was kingly power seated in one man's hand, and that work is now done; and till that work was done you called upon the people to assist you to deliver this distressed, bleeding, dying nation out of bondage; and the people came and failed you not, counting neither purse nor blood too dear to part with to effect this work.

The Parliament after this have made an act to cast out kingly power, and to make England a free commonwealth. These acts the people are much rejoiced with, as being words forerunning their freedom, and they wait for their accomplishment that their joy may be full; for as words without action are a cheat and kills the comfort of a righteous spirit, so words performed in action does comfort and nourish the life thereof.

Now, sirs, wheresoever we spy out kingly power, no man I hope shall be troubled to declare it, nor afraid to cast it out, having both act of Parliament, the soldiers' oath, and the common people's consent on his side; for kingly power is like a great spread tree, if you lop the head or top bough, and let the other branches and root stand, it will grow again and recover fresher strength.

If any ask me what kingly power is, I answer, there is a twofold kingly power. The one is the kingly power of righteousness, and this is the power of almighty God, ruling the whole creation in peace and keeping it together. And this is the power of universal love, leading people into all truth, teaching everyone to do as he would be done unto: now once more striving with flesh and blood, shaking down everything that cannot stand, and bringing everyone into the unity of himself, the one spirit of love and righteousness, and so will work a thorough restoration. But this kingly power is above all and will tread all covetousness, pride, envy, and self-love, and all other enemies whatsoever, under his feet, and take the kingdom and government of the creation out of the hand of self-seeking and self-honoring flesh,[2] and rule the alone king of righteousness in the earth; and this indeed is Christ himself, who will cast out the curse.[3] But this is not that kingly power intended by that act of Parliament to be cast out, but pretended to be set up, though this kingly power be much fought against both by Parliament, army, clergy, and people; but when they are made to see him, then they shall mourn because they have persecuted him.[4]

---

1. In 17th-century England, gifts were customarily exchanged on New Year's Day, not at Christmas.
2. "Flesh" is imagined as everything mortal and fallible, that which rebels against divine righteousness.
3. The curse upon mankind that was the punishment of Adam's fall.
4. That is, Parliament and the army do not expressly intend to cast out God's kingly power, but rather they act as if they are conforming to God's teachings, and yet often they resist God until they are brought to recognize him.

But the other kingly power is the power of unrighteousness, which indeed is the devil. And O, that there were such a heart in Parliament and army as to perform your own act.[5] Then people would never complain of you for breach of covenant, for your covetousness, pride, and too much self-seeking that is in you. And you on the other side would never have cause to complain of the people's murmurings against you. Truly this jarring that is between you and the people is the kingly power; yea that very kingly power which you have made an act to cast out. Therefore see it be fulfilled on your part; for the kingly power of righteousness expects it, or else he will cast you out for hypocrites and unsavory salt;[6] for he looks upon all your actions, and truly there is abundance of rust about your actings, which makes them that they do not shine bright.

This kingly power is covetousness in his branches,[7] or the power of self-love ruling in one or in many men over others and enslaving those who in the creation are their equals; nay, who are in the strictness of equity rather their masters. And this kingly power is usually set in the chair of government under the name of prerogative[8] when he rules in one over other: and under the name of state privilege of Parliament when he rules in many over others: and this kingly power is always raised up and established by the sword, and therefore he is called the murderer, or the great red dragon which fights against Michael,[9] for he enslaves the weakness of the people under him, denying an equal freedom in the earth to everyone, which the law of righteousness gave every man in his creation. This I say is kingly power under darkness; and as he rules in men, so he makes men jar one against another, and is the cause of all wars and complainings. He is known by his outward actions, and his action at this very day fills all places; for this power of darkness rules, and would rule, and is that only enemy that fights against creation and national freedom. And this kingly power is he which you have made an act of Parliament to cast out. And now, you rulers of England, play the men and be valiant for the truth, which is Christ: for assure yourselves God will not be mocked, nor the devil will not be mocked. For first you say and profess you own[1] the scriptures of prophets and apostles, and God looks that you should perform that word in action. Secondly you have declared against the devil, and if you do not now go through with your work but slack your hand by hypocritical self-love, and so suffer this dark kingly power to rise higher and rule, you shall find he will maul both you and yours to purpose.[2]

* * *

In the time of the kings, who came in as conquerors and ruled by the power of the sword, not only the common land but the enclosures[3] also were

---

5. Enforce the act already passed by Parliament.
6. Matthew 5:13: "Ye are the salt of the earth: but if the salt have lost his savour, wherewith shall it be salted? it is thenceforth good for nothing, but to be cast out, and to be trodden under foot of men."
7. That is, covetousness is one manifestation of unrighteous kingly power.
8. The monarch's special powers.
9. Revelation 12:3–9: "And there appeared another wonder in heaven; and behold a great red dragon, having seven heads and ten horns, and seven crowns upon his heads. . . . And there was war in heaven: Michael and his angels fought against the dragon; and the dragon fought and his angels, / and prevailed not; neither was their place found any more in heaven. / And the great dragon was cast out, that old serpent, called the Devil, and Satan, which deceiveth the whole world."
1. Acknowledge.
2. Thoroughly.
3. Privately held land, often common land that had been enclosed.

captivated under the will of those kings, till now of late that our later kings granted more freedom to the gentry than they had presently after the Conquest;[4] yet under bondage still. For what are prisons, whips, and gallows in the times of peace but the laws and power of the sword, forcing and compelling obedience, and so enslaving as if the sword raged in the open field? England was in such a slavery under the kingly power that both gentry and commonalty[5] groaned under bondage; and to ease themselves, they endeavored to call a parliament, that by their counsels and decrees they might find some freedom.

But Charles the then king perceiving that the freedom they strove for would derogate from his prerogative tyranny,[6] thereupon he goes into the north to raise a war against the Parliament; and took William the Conqueror's sword into his hand again, thereby to keep under the former conquered English, and to uphold his kingly power of self-will and prerogative, which was the power got by former conquests; that is, to rule over the lives and estates of all men at his will, and so to make us pure slaves and vassals.

Well, this Parliament, that did consist of the chief lords, lords of manors, and gentry, and they seeing that the king, by raising an army, did thereby declare his intent to enslave all sorts to him by the sword; and being in distress and in a low ebb, they call upon the common people to bring in their plate, monies, taxes, free-quarter, excise,[7] and to adventure their lives with them, and they would endeavor to recover England from that Norman yoke and make us a free people. And the common people assent hereunto, and call this the Parliament's cause, and own it and adventure person and purse to preserve it; and by the joint assistance of Parliament and people the king was beaten in the field, his head taken off, and his kingly power voted down. And we the commons thereby virtually have recovered ourselves from the Norman conquest; we want nothing but possession of the spoil,[8] which is a free use of the land for our livelihood.

And from hence we the common people, or younger brothers,[9] plead our property in the common land as truly our own by virtue of this victory over the king, as our elder brothers can plead property in their enclosures; and that for three reasons in England's law.

First, by a lawful purchase or contract between the Parliament and us; for they were our landlords and lords of manors, that held the freedom of the commons from us[1] while the king was in his power; for they held title thereunto from him,[2] he being the head and they branches of the kingly power that enslaved the people by that ancient conqueror's sword, that was the ruling power. For they said, "Come and help us against the king that enslaves us, that we may be delivered from his tyranny, and we will make you a free people."

4. The conquest of England by the Norman William the Conqueror in 1066. Winstanley argued that the oppression of the poor and the landless was a consequence of nearly six centuries of occupation of England by a foreign power. "Presently": immediately.
5. Common people.
6. Absolute rule.
7. A tax on domestically manufactured goods, first imposed by Parliament in 1643 to finance the war against the king. "Plate": silver plate. "Free-quarter": free room and board for soldiers, or its monetary equivalent imposed as a tax.
8. Reward of victory.
9. Estates commonly passed to the eldest brother, leaving the younger brothers landless.
1. Kept the right to use the common lands from us, the common people.
2. Under the feudal system, the great lords held their lands on grant from the king, in return for their allegiance.

Now they cannot make us free unless they deliver us from the bondage[3] which they themselves held us under; and that is, they held the freedom of the earth from us: for we in part with them have delivered ourselves from the king. Now we claim freedom from that bondage you have and yet do hold us under, by the bargain and contract between Parliament and us, who, I say, did consist of lords of manors and landlords, whereof Mr. Drake,[4] who hath arrested me for digging upon the common, was one at that time. Therefore by the law of bargain and sale we claim of them our freedom, to live comfortably with them in this land of our nativity; and this we cannot do so long as we lie under poverty, and must not be suffered to plant the commons and wasteland for our livelihood. For take away the land from any people, and those people are in a way of continual dearth and misery; and better not to have had a body, than not to have food and raiment for it. But, I say, they have sold us our freedom in the common, and have been largely paid for it; for by means of our bloods and money they sit in peace: for if the king had prevailed, they had lost all, and been in slavery to the meanest cavalier, if the king would.[5] Therefore we the commons say, give us our bargain: if you deny us our bargain, you deny God, Christ, and scriptures; and all your profession[6] then is and hath been hypocrisy.

Secondly, the commons and crown land is our property by equal conquest over the kingly power: for the Parliament did never stir up the people by promises and covenant to assist them to cast out the king and to establish them in the king's place and prerogative power. No, but all their declarations were for the safety and peace of the whole nation.

Therefore the common people being part of the nation, and especially they that bore the greatest heat of the day in casting out the oppressor; and the nation cannot be in peace so long as the poor oppressed are in wants and the land is entangled and held from them by bondage.

But the victory being obtained over the king, the spoil, which is properly the land, ought in equity to be divided now between the two parties, that is Parliament and common people. The Parliament, consisting of lords of manors and gentry, ought to have their enclosure lands free to them without molestation. * * * And the common people, consisting of soldiers and such as paid taxes and free-quarter, ought to have the freedom of all waste and common land and crown land equally among them. The soldiery ought not in equity to have all, nor the other people that paid them to have all; but the spoil ought to be divided between them that stayed at home and them that went to war; for the victory is for the whole nation.

And as the Parliament declared they did all for the nation, and not for themselves only; so we plead with the army, they did not fight for themselves, but for the freedom of the nation: and I say, we have bought our freedom of them likewise by taxes and free-quarter. Therefore we claim an equal freedom with them in this conquest over the king.

---

3. Technically bondage refers to the services and goods legally required by feudal landowners of their tenants.
4. Sir Francis Drake, a member of Parliament who owned St. George's Hill, on which Winstanley and his followers had established a commune. At first sympathetic to the Diggers, Drake eventually took legal action to have them evicted.
5. To the lowest soldier of the king, if the king so commanded.
6. Statement of principles.

Thirdly, we claim an equal portion in the victory over the king by virtue of the two acts of Parliament: the one to make England a free commonwealth, the other to take away kingly power. Now the kingly power, you have heard, is a power that rules by the sword in covetousness and self, giving the earth to some and denying it to others: and this kingly power was not in the hand of the king alone, but lords, and lords of manors, and corrupt judges and lawyers especially held it up likewise. For he was the head and they, with the tithing priests,[7] are the branches of that tyrannical kingly power; and all the several limbs and members must be cast out before kingly power can be pulled up root and branch. Mistake me not, I do not say, cast out the persons of men. No, I do not desire their fingers to ache;[8] but I say, cast out their power whereby they hold the people in bondage, as the king held them in bondage. And I say, it is our own freedom we claim, both by bargain and by equality in the conquest; as well as by the law of righteous creation which gives the earth to all equally.

And the power of lords of manors lies in this: they deny the common people the use and free benefit of the earth, unless they give them leave and pay them for it, either in rent, in fines, in homages or heriots.[9] Surely the earth was never made by God that the younger brother should not live in the earth unless he would work for and pay his elder brother rent for the earth. No, this slavery came in by conquest, and it is part of the kingly power; and England cannot be a free commonwealth till this bondage be taken away. You have taken away the king; you have taken away the House of Lords. Now step two steps further, and take away the power of lords of manors and of tithing priests, and the intolerable oppressions of judges by whom laws are corrupted; and your work will be honorable.

Fourthly, if this freedom be denied the common people, to enjoy the common land; then Parliament, army, and judges will deny equity and reason, whereupon the laws of a well-governed commonwealth ought to be built. And if this equity be denied, then there can be no law but club law[1] among the people: and if the sword must reign, then every party will be striving to bear the sword; and then farewell peace; nay, farewell religion and gospel, unless it be made use of to entrap one another, as we plainly see some priests and others make it a cloak for their knavery. If I adventure my life and fruit of my labor equal with you, and obtain what we strive for; it is both equity and reason that I should equally divide the spoil with you, and not you to have all and I none. And if you deny us this, you take away our property from us, our monies and blood, and give us nothing for it.

Therefore, I say, the common land is my own land, equal with my fellow-commoners, and our true property, by the law of creation. It is everyone's, but not one single one's. * * * True religion and undefiled is this, to make restitution of the earth, which hath been taken and held from the common people by the power of conquests formerly, and so set the oppressed free. Do not

---

7. Priests of the Church of England were legally entitled to a tenth, or "tithe," of the goods of every parishioner; those people who wished to separate from the established church fiercely resented the involuntary nature of the tithe.

8. Wish the least physical harm to them.

9. Fees or goods paid by tenants to landlords in addition to rent.

1. That is, might makes right.

all strive to enjoy the land? The gentry strive for land, the clergy strive for land, the common people strive for land; and buying and selling is an art whereby people endeavor to cheat one another of the land. Now if any can prove from the law of righteousness that the land was made peculiar to him and his successively,[2] shutting others out, he shall enjoy it freely for my part. But I affirm it was made for all; and true religion is to let everyone enjoy it. Therefore, you rulers of England, make restitution of the lands which the kingly power holds from us: set the oppressed free, and come in and honor Christ, who is the restoring power, and you shall find rest.

1650

2. By inheritance.

THOMAS HOBBES

The English Civil War and its aftermath raised fundamental questions about the nature and legitimacy of state power. In 1651 Thomas Hobbes (1588–1679) attempted to answer those questions in his ambitious masterwork of political philosophy, *Leviathan*. He grounded his political vision upon a comprehensive philosophy of nature and knowledge. Hobbes held that everything in the universe is composed only of matter; spirit does not exist. All knowledge is gained through sensory impressions, which are nothing but matter in motion. What we call the self is, for Hobbes, simply a tissue of sensory impressions—clear and immediate in the presence of the objects that evoke them, vague and less vivid in their absence. As a result, an iron determinism of cause and effect governs everything in the universe, including human action.

Because, Hobbes argues, all humans are roughly equal mentally and physically, they possess equal hopes of attaining goods, as well as equal fears of danger from others. In the state of nature, prior to the foundation of some sovereign power to keep them in awe, everyone is continually at war with everyone else, and life, in Hobbes's memorable phrase, is "solitary, poor, nasty, brutish, and short." To escape this ghastly strife, humans covenant with one another to establish a sovereign government over all of them. That sovereign power—which need not be a king but is always indivisible—incorporates the wills and individuality of them all, so that the people no longer have rights or liberties apart from the sovereign's will. The sovereign's dominion over his subjects extends to the right to pronounce on all matters of religion.

While other versions of covenant theory, for instance Milton's *Tenure of Kings and Magistrates*, insisted that the power transferred by the people to the sovereign could be limited or revoked, in Hobbes's system, the founding political covenant must be a permanent one, since no tyranny can be so evil as the state of war that the sovereign power prevents. Yet if the sovereign power should be overthrown, the individual ruler has no further claim, and the people, for their safety, must accept the new sovereign unconditionally. Hobbes was generally associated with the royalist cause, as a tutor to the Cavendish family and as an exile in Paris from 1640 to 1651, where he tutored the future Charles II. Yet his argument made no distinction between a legitimate monarch and a successful usurper, like Oliver Cromwell. Moreover, Hobbes's philosophical materialism led many to suspect him of atheism;

after the Restoration, the publication of many of his books, including a history of the civil war titled *Behemoth*, was prohibited for a number of years. Undeterred, Hobbes continued to write on a variety of psychological, political, and mathematical topics, completing a translation of Homer's *Iliad* and *Odyssey* at the age of eighty-six.

Hobbes's political theory did not fit easily into the established patterns of English thought partly because his perspective was unusually cosmopolitan. Educated at Oxford as a classicist, Hobbes traveled widely in Europe between 1610 and 1660 as a companion and tutor of noblemen, often remaining abroad for years at a time. During these lengthy sojourns he became acquainted with many of the leading intellectuals and scientists on the Continent, including Galileo, Descartes, and the prominent French mathematician Pierre Gassendi, who argued that the universe was governed entirely by mechanical principles. The most important political philosophers for Hobbes were also Continental figures: the Italian Niccolò Machiavelli, who saw human beings as naturally competitive and power hungry, and Jean Bodin, a French theorist of indivisible, absolute monarchy. One English writer who did influence Hobbes profoundly was Francis Bacon, whose amanuensis Hobbes had been in Bacon's last years. Ironically, Hobbes was not invited to join the Royal Society, established after the Restoration on Baconian principles, because his religious views were suspect and because he had quarreled with several of the society's founders. Yet Hobbes is truly Bacon's heir, sharing Bacon's utter lack of sentimentality and a memorably astringent prose style.

From Leviathan[1]

From *The Introduction*

[THE ARTIFICIAL MAN]

Nature (the art whereby God hath made and governs the world) is by the art of man, as in many other things, so in this also imitated, that it can make an artificial[2] animal. For seeing life is but a motion of limbs, the beginning whereof is in some principal part within, why may we not say that all automata (engines that move themselves by springs and wheels as doth a watch) have an artificial life?[3] For what is the heart but a spring; and the nerves but so many strings; and the joints but so many wheels, giving motion to the whole body such as was intended by the artificer? Art goes yet further, imitating that rational and most excellent work of nature, man. For by art is created that great Leviathan called a Commonwealth or State (in Latin, *Civitas*), which is but an artificial man, though of greater stature and strength than the natural, for whose protection and defense it was intended; and in which the sovereignty is an artificial soul, as giving life and motion to the whole body; the magistrates and other officers of judicature and execution, artificial joints; reward and punishment (by which, fastened to the seat of the sovereignty, every joint and member is moved to perform his duty) are the nerves, that do the same in the body natural; the wealth and riches

---

1. The title refers to the primordial sea creature Leviathan, described in Job 41 as the prime evidence of and analogue to God's power, beyond all human measure and comprehension. Hobbes takes him as figure for the sovereign power in the state. Leviathan was also sometimes taken as a figure for Satan, on the basis of Job 41:34: "he is a king over all the children of pride."
2. Made by art.
3. Hobbes's definition of life as motion collapses the distinction between the life of humans and the life of machines or institutions.

of all the particular members are the strength; *salus populi* (the people's safety) its business; counselors, by whom all things needful for it to know are suggested unto it, are the memory; equity and laws an artificial reason and will; concord, health; sedition, sickness; and civil war, death. Lastly, the pacts and covenants by which the parts of this body politic were at first made, set together, and united, resemble that *Fiat* or the "let us make man," pronounced by God in the creation.[4]

* * *

From *Part 1. Of Man*

CHAPTER 1. OF SENSE

Concerning the thoughts of man, I will consider them first singly and afterwards in train or dependence upon one another. Singly, they are every one a representation or appearance of some quality or other accident of a body without us, which is commonly called an object. Which object worketh on the eyes, ears, and other parts of man's body, and by diversity of working produceth diversity of appearances.

The original of them all is that which we call sense. (For there is no conception in a man's mind which hath not at first, totally or by parts, been begotten upon the organs of sense.)[5] The rest are derived from that original.

To know the natural cause of sense is not very necessary to the business now in hand, and I have elsewhere written of the same at large. Nevertheless, to fill each part of my present method, I will briefly deliver the same in this place.

The cause of sense is the external body or object which presseth the organ proper to each sense, either immediately as in the taste and touch, or mediately, as in seeing, hearing, and smelling; which pressure, by the mediation of nerves and other strings and membranes of the body continued inwards to the brain and heart, causeth there a resistance or counterpressure or endeavor of the heart to deliver itself;[6] which endeavor, because outward, seemeth to be some matter without. And this seeming or fancy is that which men call sense; and consisteth, as to the eye, in a light or color figured; to the ear, in a sound; to the nostril in an odor; to the tongue and palate in a savor; and to the rest of the body in heat, cold, hardness, softness, and such other qualities as we discern by feeling. All which qualities called "sensible"[7] are, in the object that causeth them, but so many several motions of the matter by which it presseth our organs diversely. Neither, in us that are pressed, are they anything else but diverse motions; for motion produceth nothing but motion. But their appearance to us is fancy, the same waking, that dreaming. And as pressing, rubbing, or striking the eye makes us fancy a light; and pressing the ear produceth a din; so do the bodies also we see or hear produce the same by their strong though unobserved actions. For if those colors and sounds were in the bodies or objects that cause them, they

---

4. Genesis 1:26.
5. This view of the mind as a blank sheet written on by physical experience will influence the philosophy of John Locke and David Hume.
6. Hobbes's physiology of sense is, in keeping with his premises, strictly mechanical.
7. That is, accessible through the senses.

Leviathan. Abraham Bosse's frontispiece for *Leviathan* was based on a sketch by Hobbes. The "Leviathan" or commonwealth is shown as a gigantic human figure holding a scepter and a sword; the figure is made up of many tiny individual humans who have joined together in the social contract. Hobbes's royalist sympathies are betrayed in the figure's face, which is that of King Charles. The small pictures in the lower part of the engraving display the various attributes of civil power on the left, and ecclesiastical power on the right.

could not be severed from them, as by glasses[8] and in echoes by reflection we see they are; where we know the thing we see is in one place, the appearance in another. And though at some certain distance the real and very object seem invested with the fancy it begets in us, yet still the object is one thing, the image or fancy is another. So that sense in all cases is nothing else but original fancy, caused (as I have said) by the pressure, that is by the motion, of external things upon our eyes, ears, and other organs thereunto ordained.

But the philosophy schools[9] through all the universities of Christendom, grounded upon certain texts of Aristotle, teach another doctrine, and say for the cause of vision, that the thing seen sendeth forth on every side a visible species—in English, a visible show, apparition, or aspect, or a being seen—the receiving whereof into the eye is seeing. And for the cause of hearing, that the thing heard sendeth forth an audible species, that is an audible aspect or audible being seen, which entering at the ear maketh hearing. Nay for the cause of understanding also they say the thing understood sendeth forth intelligible species, that is an intelligible being seen, which coming into the understanding makes us understand. I say not this as disapproving the use of universities, but because I am to speak hereafter of their office in a commonwealth, I must let you see on all occasions by the way what things would be amended in them; amongst which the frequency of insignificant speech[1] is one.

* * *

CHAPTER 13. OF THE NATURAL CONDITION OF MANKIND AS CONCERNING THEIR FELICITY AND MISERY

Nature hath made men so equal in the faculties of body and mind as that, though there be found one man sometimes manifestly stronger in body or of quicker mind than another, yet when all is reckoned together, the difference between man and man is not so considerable as that one man can thereupon claim to himself any benefit, to which another may not pretend as well as he. For as to the strength of body, the weakest has strength enough to kill the strongest, either by secret machination, or by confederacy[2] with others that are in the same danger with himself.

And as to the faculties of the mind—setting aside the arts grounded upon words, and especially that skill of proceeding upon general and infallible rules, called science; which very few have, and but in few things; as being not a native faculty, born with us; nor attained, as prudence, while we look after somewhat else—I find yet a greater equality amongst men than that of strength. For prudence is but experience, which equal time equally bestows on all men, in those things they equally apply themselves unto. That which may perhaps make such equality incredible is but a vain conceit of one's own wisdom, which almost all men think they have in a greater degree than the vulgar—that is, than all men but themselves and a few

---

8. Mirrors.
9. Led by the Scholastic philosophers (schoolmen).
1. Unmeaningful speech. Compare Bacon's critique of the idols of the marketplace and the theater in *Novum Organum* 43–44 and 59–62.
2. Alliance.

others, whom by fame, or for concurring with themselves, they approve. For such is the nature of men, that howsoever they may acknowledge many others to be more witty, or more eloquent, or more learned, yet they will hardly believe there be many so wise as themselves; for they see their own wit at hand, and other men's at a distance. But this proveth rather that men are in that point equal, than unequal. For there is not ordinarily a greater sign of the equal distribution of anything than that every man is contented with his share.

From this equality of ability ariseth equality of hope in the attaining of our ends. And therefore if any two men desire the same thing, which nevertheless they cannot both enjoy, they become enemies; and in the way to their end (which is principally their own conservation, and sometimes their delectation[3] only) endeavor to destroy or subdue one another. And from hence it comes to pass, that where an invader hath no more to fear than another man's single power, if one plant, sow, build, or possess a convenient seat, others may probably be expected to come prepared with forces united, to dispossess and deprive him, not only of the fruit of his labor, but also of his life or liberty. And the invader again is in the like danger of another.

And from this diffidence of[4] one another, there is no way for any man to secure himself so reasonable as anticipation; that is, by force or wiles to master the persons of all men he can, so long, till he see no other power great enough to endanger him; and this is no more than his own conservation requireth, and is generally allowed. Also because there be some, that taking pleasure in contemplating their own power in the acts of conquest, which they pursue farther than their security requires; if others that otherwise would be glad to be at ease within modest bounds, should not by invasion increase their power, they would not be able long time, by standing only on their defense, to subsist. And by consequence, such augmentation of dominion over men being necessary to a man's conservation, it ought to be allowed him.

Again, men have no pleasure, but on the contrary a great deal of grief, in keeping company, where there is no power able to overawe them all. For every man looketh that his companion should value him at the same rate he sets upon himself; and upon all signs of contempt, or undervaluing, naturally endeavors, as far as he dares (which amongst them that have no common power to keep them in quiet, is far enough to make them destroy each other), to extort a greater value from his contemners[5] by damage, and from others by the example.

So that in the nature of man, we find three principal causes of quarrel. First, competition; secondly, diffidence; thirdly, glory.

The first maketh men invade for gain; the second, for safety; and the third, for reputation. The first use violence to make themselves masters of other men's persons, wives, children, and cattle; the second, to defend them; the third, for trifles, as a word, a smile, a different opinion, and any other sign of undervalue, either direct in their persons, or by reflection in their kindred, their friends, their nation, their profession, or their name.

---

3. Pleasure.
4. Lack of faith in, mistrust of.

5. Scorners.

Hereby it is manifest that during the time men live without a common power to keep them all in awe, they are in that condition which is called war; and such a war as is of every man against every man. For war consisteth not in battle only, or the act of fighting, but in a tract of time wherein the will to contend by battle is sufficiently known; and therefore the notion of time is to be considered in the nature of war, as it is in the nature of weather. For as the nature of foul weather lieth not in a shower or two of rain, but in an inclination thereto of many days together; so the nature of war consisteth not in actual fighting, but in the known disposition thereto, during all the time there is no assurance to the contrary. All other time is peace.

Whatsoever therefore is consequent to a time of war, where every man is enemy to every man, the same is consequent to the time wherein men live without other security than what their own strength and their own invention shall furnish them withal. In such condition there is no place for industry, because the fruit thereof is uncertain, and consequently no culture of the earth; no navigation, nor use of the commodities that may be imported by sea; no commodious building; no instruments of moving, and removing, such things as require much force; no knowledge of the face of the earth; no account of time; no arts; no letters; no society; and, which is worst of all, continual fear, and danger of violent death; and the life of man, solitary, poor, nasty, brutish, and short.[6]

It may seem strange to some man that has not well weighed these things, that nature should thus dissociate and render men apt to invade and destroy one another; and he may therefore, not trusting to this inference, made from the passions, desire perhaps to have the same confirmed by experience. Let him therefore consider with himself, when taking a journey, he arms himself and seeks to go well accompanied; when going to sleep, he locks his doors; when even in his house he locks his chests; and this when he knows there be laws, and public officers, armed, to revenge all injuries shall be done him; what opinion he has of his fellow subjects, when he rides armed; of his fellow citizens, when he locks his doors; and of his children and servants, when he locks his chests. Does he not there as much accuse mankind by his actions, as I do by my words? But neither of us accuse man's nature in it. The desires and other passions of man are in themselves no sin. No more are the actions that proceed from those passions, till they know a law that forbids them, which, till laws be made, they cannot know; nor can any law be made, till they have agreed upon the person that shall make it.

It may peradventure be thought there was never such a time nor condition of war as this; and I believe it was never generally so, over all the world; but there are many places where they live so now. For the savage people in many places of America, except the government of small families, the concord whereof dependeth on natural lust, have no government at all and live at this day in that brutish manner as I said before. Howsoever, it may be perceived what manner of life there would be, where there were no common

---

6. Hobbes's views on the "state of nature" were influenced by the European encounter with the indigenous peoples of the Americas. By denying that indigenous peoples had state formations, European political thinkers often excluded them from the protections provided by the law of nations.

power to fear, by the manner of life which men that have formerly lived under a peaceful government use to degenerate into in a civil war.[7]

But though there had never been any time wherein particular men were in a condition of war one against another, yet in all times, kings and persons of sovereign authority, because of their independency, are in continual jealousies, and in the state and posture of gladiators; having their weapons pointing, and their eyes fixed on one another; that is, their forts, garrisons, and guns upon the frontiers of their kingdoms, and continual spies upon their neighbors, which is a posture of war. But because they uphold thereby the industry of their subjects, there does not follow from it that misery which accompanies the liberty of particular men.

To this war of every man against every man, this also is consequent: that nothing can be unjust. The notions of right and wrong, justice and injustice, have there no place. Where there is no common power, there is no law; where no law, no injustice. Force and fraud are in war the two cardinal virtues. Justice and injustice are none of the faculties neither of the body nor mind. If they were, they might be in a man that were alone in the world, as well as his senses and passions. They are qualities that relate to men in society, not in solitude. It is consequent also to the same condition that there be no propriety,[8] no dominion, no *mine* and *thine* distinct; but only that to be every man's, that he can get; and for so long as he can keep it. And thus much for the ill condition which man by mere nature is actually placed in; though with a possibility to come out of it, consisting partly in the passions, partly in his reason.

The passions that incline men to peace are fear of death, desire of such things as are necessary to commodious living, and a hope by their industry to obtain them. And reason suggesteth convenient articles of peace, upon which men may be drawn to agreement. These articles are they which otherwise are called the Laws of Nature, whereof I shall speak more particularly in the two following chapters.

FROM CHAPTER 14. OF THE FIRST AND SECOND NATURAL LAWS

The Right of Nature, which writers commonly call *ius naturale*, is the liberty each man hath to use his own power as he will himself for the preservation of his own nature, that is to say, of his own life; and consequently of doing anything which in his own judgment and reason he shall conceive to be the aptest means thereunto.

By Liberty is understood, according to the proper signification of the word, the absence of external impediments, which impediments may oft take away part of a man's power to do what he would, but cannot hinder him from using the power left him according as his judgment and reason shall dictate to him.

A Law of Nature (*lex naturalis*) is a precept or general rule found out by reason, by which a man is forbidden to do that which is destructive of his life or taketh away the means of preserving the same; and to omit that by which

---

7. Hobbes is thinking of the recent civil wars in England, and perhaps of the Greek civil wars described by Thucydides (whom he translated).
8. Property.

he thinketh it may be best preserved. For though they that speak of this subject use to confound[9] *Ius* and *Lex*, *Right* and *Law*, yet they ought to be distinguished, because Right consisteth in liberty to do or to forbear, whereas Law determineth and bindeth to one of them: so that Law and Right differ as much as obligation and liberty, which in one and the same matter are inconsistent.

And because the condition of man (as hath been declared in the precedent chapter) is a condition of war of every one against every one, in which case every one is governed by his own reason, and there is nothing he can make use of that may not be a help unto him in preserving his life against his enemies: it followeth that in such a condition every man has a right to every thing, even to one another's body. And therefore as long as this natural right of every man to every thing endureth, there can be no security to any man (how strong or wise soever he be) of living out the time which nature ordinarily alloweth men to live. And consequently it is a precept or general rule of reason, *That every man ought to endeavor peace, as far as he has hope of obtaining it; and when he cannot obtain it, that he may seek and use all helps and advantages of war.* The first branch of which rule containeth the first and fundamental law of nature, which is *to seek peace and follow it.* The second, the sum of the right of nature, which is, *by all means we can to defend ourselves.*

From this fundamental law of nature, by which men are commanded to endeavor peace, is derived this second law: *That a man be willing, when others are so too, as far-forth as*[1] *for peace and defense of himself he shall think it necessary, to lay down this right to all things, and be contented with so much liberty against other men as he would allow other men against himself.* For as long as any man holdeth this right of doing anything he liketh, so long are all men in the condition of war. But if other men will not lay down their right, as well as he, then there is no reason for anyone to divest himself of his. For that were to expose himself to prey (which no man is bound to) rather than to dispose himself to peace. This is that law of the Gospel: *Whatsoever you require that others should do to you, that do ye to them.*[2]

* * *

FROM CHAPTER 15. OF OTHER LAWS OF NATURE

From that law of nature by which we are obliged to transfer to another such rights as, being retained, hinder the peace of mankind, there followeth a third, which is this: *That men perform their covenants made:*[3] without which, covenants are in vain, and but empty words; and, the right of all men to all things remaining, we are still in the condition of war.

And in this law of nature consisteth the fountain and original of Justice. For where no covenant hath preceded, there hath no right been transferred, and every man has right to every thing; and consequently no action can

---

9. Confuse.
1. Insofar as.
2. The Golden Rule: Matthew 7:12, Luke 6:31.
3. Though the terms are general, Hobbes refers in this chapter especially to the covenants men make with each other when they transfer power to the sovereign. Milton makes very different use of covenant theory to justify the rebellion and regicide in *The Tenure of Kings and Magistrates*.

be unjust. But when a covenant is made, then to break it is unjust; and the definition of injustice is no other than *the not performance of covenant.* And whatsoever is not unjust is just. * * *

For the question is not of promises mutual where there is no security of performance on either side, as when there is no civil power erected over the parties promising; for such promises are no covenants. But either where one of the parties has performed already, or where there is a power to make him perform: there is the question whether it be against reason, that is against the benefit of the other, to perform or not. And I say it is not against reason.[4] For the manifestation whereof, we are to consider: first, that when a man doth a thing which (notwithstanding anything can be foreseen and reckoned on) tendeth to his own destruction, howsoever[5] some accident, which he could not expect, arriving may turn it to his benefit; yet such events do not make it reasonably or wisely done. Secondly, that in a condition of war, wherein every man to every man, for want of a common power to keep them all in awe, is an enemy, there is no man can hope by his own strength or wit to defend himself from destruction without the help of confederates; where everyone expects the same defense by the confederation that anyone else does. And therefore he which declares he thinks it reason to deceive those that help him can in reason expect no other means of safety than what can be had from his own single power. He therefore that breaketh his covenant, and consequently declareth that he thinks he may with reason do so, cannot be received into any society that unite themselves for peace and defense, but by the error of them that receive him; nor when he is received be retained in it without seeing the danger of their error; which errors a man cannot reasonably reckon upon as the means of his security. And therefore if he be left or cast out of society, he perisheth; and if he live in society, it is by the errors of other men, which he could not foresee nor reckon upon; and consequently against the reason of his preservation; and so as all men that contribute not to his destruction forbear him only out of ignorance of what is good for themselves.

As for the instance of gaining the secure and perpetual felicity of heaven by any way, it is frivolous: there being but one way imaginable, and that is not breaking, but keeping of covenant.

And for the other instance of attaining sovereignty by rebellion, it is manifest that though the event follow, yet because it cannot reasonably be expected, but rather the contrary; and because by gaining it so others are taught to gain the same in like manner, the attempt thereof is against reason. Justice therefore, that is to say, keeping of covenant, is a rule of reason, by which we are forbidden to do anything destructive to our life, and consequently a law of nature.

* * *

---

4. That is, to perform the promise.   5. Even though.

From *Part 2: Of Commonwealth*

CHAPTER 17. OF THE CAUSES, GENERATION, AND DEFINITION OF A COMMONWEALTH

The final cause, end, or design of men, who naturally love liberty and dominion over others, in the introduction of that restraint upon themselves in which we see them live in commonwealths, is the foresight of their own preservation and of a more contented life thereby—that is to say, of getting themselves out from their miserable condition of war which is necessarily consequent, as has been shown (Chapter 13), to the natural passions of men when there is no visible power to keep them in awe and tie them by fear of punishment to the performance of their convenants and observation of those laws of nature set down in the fourteenth and fifteenth chapters.

For the laws of nature—as justice, equity, modesty, mercy, and, in sum, doing to others as we would be done to—of themselves, without the terror of some power to cause them to be observed, are contrary to our natural passions, that carry us to partiality,[6] pride, revenge, and the like. And covenants without the sword are but words, and of no strength to secure a man at all. Therefore, notwithstanding the laws of nature (which everyone has then kept when he had the will to keep them, when he can do it safely), if there be no power erected, or not great enough for our security, every man will—and may lawfully—rely on his own strength and art for caution[7] against all other men. And in all places where men have lived by small families, to rob and spoil one another has been a trade, and so far from being reputed against the law of nature that the greater spoils they gained, the greater was their honor; and men observed no other laws therein but the laws of honor—that is to abstain from cruelty, leaving to men their lives and instruments of husbandry. And as small families did then, so now do cities and kingdoms, which are but greater families, for their own security enlarge their dominions upon all pretenses of danger and fear of invasion or assistance that may be given to invaders, and endeavor as much as they can to subdue or weaken their neighbors by open force and secret arts, for want of other caution, justly; and are remembered for it in after ages with honor.

Nor is it the joining together of a small number of men that gives them this security, because in small numbers small additions on the one side or the other make the advantage of strength so great as is sufficient to carry the victory, and therefore gives encouragement to an invasion. The multitude sufficient to confide in for our security is not determined by any certain number but by comparison with the enemy we fear, and is then sufficient when the odds of the enemy is not of so visible and conspicuous moment to determine the event[8] of war as to move him to attempt.

And be there never so great a multitude, yet if their actions be directed according to their particular judgments and particular appetites, they can expect thereby no defense nor protection, neither against a common enemy nor against the injuries of one another. For being distracted in opinion[9]

---

6. Favoritism, to oneself or another.
7. Precaution, defense.
8. Outcome.
9. That is, by opinions.

concerning the best use and application of their strength, they do not help but hinder one another, and reduce their strength by mutual opposition to nothing; whereby they are easily not only subdued by a very few that agree together, but also, when there is no common enemy, they make war upon each other for their particular interest. For if we could suppose a great multitude of men to consent in the observation of justice and other laws of nature without a common power to keep them all in awe, we might as well suppose all mankind to do the same, then there neither would be, nor need to be, any civil government or commonwealth at all, because there would be peace without subjection.

Nor is it enough for the security which men desire should last all the time of their life that they be governed and directed by one judgment for a limited time, as in one battle or one war. For though they obtain a victory by their unanimous endeavor against a foreign enemy, yet afterwards, when either they have no common enemy or he that by one part is held for an enemy is by another part held for a friend, they must needs, by the difference of their interests, dissolve and fall again into a war among themselves.

It is true that certain living creatures, as bees and ants, live sociably one with another—which are therefore by Aristotle numbered among political creatures—and have no other direction than their particular judgments and appetites, nor speech whereby one of them can signify to another what he thinks expedient for the common benefit; and therefore some man may perhaps desire to know why mankind cannot do the same. To which I answer:

First, that men are continually in competition for honor and dignity, which these creatures are not; and consequently among men there arises on that ground envy and hatred and finally war, but among these not so.

Secondly, that among these creatures the common good differs not from the private; and being by nature inclined to their private, they procure thereby the common benefit. But man, whose joy consists in comparing himself with other men, can relish nothing but what is eminent.

Thirdly, that these creatures—having not, as man, the use of reason—do not see nor think they see any fault in the administration of their common business; whereas among men there are very many that think themselves wiser and abler to govern the public better than the rest, and these strive to reform and innovate, one this way, another that way, and thereby bring it into distraction and civil war.

Fourthly, that these creatures, though they have some use of voice in making known to one another their desires and other affections, yet they want that art of words by which some men can represent to others that which is good in the likeness of evil, and evil in the likeness of good, and augment or diminish this apparent greatness of good and evil, discontenting men and troubling their peace at their pleasure.

Fifthly, irrational creatures cannot distinguish between injury and damage, and therefore, as long as they be at ease, they are not offended with their fellows; whereas man is then most troublesome when he is most at ease, for then it is that he loves to show his wisdom and control the actions of them that govern the commonwealth.

Lastly, the agreement of these creatures is natural, that of men is by covenant only, which is artificial, and therefore it is no wonder if there be somewhat else required besides covenant to make their agreement constant and lasting, which is a common power to keep them in awe and to direct their actions to the common benefit.

The only way to erect such a common power as may be able to defend them from the invasion of foreigners and the injuries of one another, and thereby to secure them in such sort as that by their own industry and by the fruits of the earth they may nourish themselves and live contentedly, is to confer all their power and strength upon one man, or upon one assembly of men that may reduce all their wills, by plurality of voices, into one will, which is as much as to say, to appoint one man or assembly of men to bear their person, and everyone to own and acknowledge himself to be the author of whatsoever he that so bears their person shall act or cause to be acted in those things which concern the common peace and safety, and therein to submit their wills everyone to his will, and their judgments to his judgment. This is more than consent or concord; it is a real unity of them all in one and the same person, made by covenant of every man with every man, in such manner as if every man should say to every man, "I authorize and give up my right of governing myself to this man, or to this assembly of men, on the condition that you give up your right to him and authorize all his actions in like manner." This done, the multitude so united in one person is called a commonwealth, in Latin *civitas*. This is the generation of that great Leviathan (or rather, to speak more reverently, of that mortal god) to whom we owe, under the immortal God, our peace and defense. For by this authority, given him by every particular man in the commonwealth, he has the use of so much power and strength conferred on him that, by terror thereof, he is enabled to form the wills of them all to peace at home and mutual aid against their enemies abroad. And in him consists the essence of the commonwealth, which, to define it, is one person, of whose acts a great multitude, by mutual covenants one with another, have made themselves everyone the author, to the end he may use the strength and means of them all as he shall think expedient for their peace and common defense. And he that carries this person is called sovereign and said to have sovereign power; and everyone besides, his subject.

1651

History and Life-Writing

The Civil Wars invited new kinds of histories, including partisan accounts like Margaret Cavendish's *Life of William Cavendish* (1667) and Lucy Hutchinson's "Life of Colonel Hutchinson" (which circulated in manuscript). Clarendon's *History of the Rebellion*, excerpted below, would become the standard text of the period. The civil war decades also provided the impetus for non-elite subjects to record their lives. The excerpt from the Quaker Dorothy Waugh's account of her persecution in Carlisle gives a vivid sense of the courage of those forging new paths in tumultuous times.

EDWARD HYDE, EARL OF CLARENDON

Edward Hyde (1609–1674) was educated at Oxford and during the 1630s practiced law. From about 1641 onward, he was among the chief supporters and advisers of Charles I; he went into exile with the boy who was to become Charles II and was privy to the various plots and plans of the royalists to restore him to power. After the Restoration he became lord chancellor and prime minister to Charles II, and he was instrumental in enacting the so-called Clarendon Code, a series of harsh laws against all nonconformists to the reestablished Church of England. He was impeached in 1667, owing partly to England's ill success in the Dutch War, and spent the last seven years of his life in France.

Clarendon wrote part of his great *History of the Rebellion* amid the events it describes. For the Muse of History such a short view can be a mixed blessing. But Clarendon's learning—legal, classical, and historical—and the formality of his method save him from many of the failings of partisanship. He wrote with dignity and for posterity. His *History*, which first appeared in print thirty years after his death, was remarkable not only for the largeness of its canvas but also for the force and coherence of the conservative social philosophy informing it. As a historian and rhetorician, Clarendon invites comparison with his classical models, Thucydides and Tacitus. As an evaluator of character, he invites comparison with Plutarch, whose judiciousness he shares.

From The History of the Rebellion

[THE CHARACTER OF OLIVER CROMWELL][1]

About the middle of August he was seized on by a common tertian ague,[2] from which he believed a little ease and divertissement at Hampton Court[3] would have freed him; but the fits grew stronger and his spirits much abated, so that he returned again to Whitehall,[4] when his physicians began

---

1. After the manner of ancient historians, Clarendon describes the last days, sickness, and death of Cromwell, then summarizes his character. The Protector, who had been depressed for some time by the death of a favorite daughter, first grew ill in the summer of 1658.
2. An acute fever, with paroxysms recurring every third day.
3. Hampton Court, built by Cardinal Wolsey and ceded by him to Henry VIII, is a splendid old palace up the Thames from London. "Divertissement": diversion.
4. Whitehall, in London, was the traditional residence of the head of state.

to think him in danger, though the preachers who prayed always about him and told God Almighty what great things he had done for Him, and how much more need He had still of his service, declared as from God that he should recover, and he himself did not think he should die, till even the time that his spirits failed him, and then declared to them that he did appoint his son to succeed him, his eldest son Richard. And so expired upon the third day of September (a day he thought always very propitious to him, and on which he had triumphed for several victories),[5] 1658, a day very memorable for the greatest storm of wind that had been ever known for some hours before and after his death, which overthrew trees, houses, and made great wrecks at sea, and was so universal that there were terrible effects of it both in France and Flanders, where all people trembled at it, besides the wrecks all along the coast, many boats having been cast away in the very rivers; and within few days after, that circumstance of his death that accompanied that storm was known.

He was one of those men *quos vituperare ne inimici quidem possunt, nisi ut simul laudent*,[6] for he could never have done half that mischief without great parts of courage and industry and judgment, and he must have had a wonderful understanding in the natures and humors of men, and as great a dexterity in the applying them, who from a private and obscure birth (though of a good family), without interest of estate, alliance, or friendships, could raise himself to such a height, and compound and knead such opposite and contradictory tempers, humors, and interests into a consistence that contributed to his designs and to their own destruction, whilst himself grew insensibly powerful enough to cut off those by whom he had climbed, in the instant that they projected to demolish their own building.[7] What Velleius Paterculus said of Cinna may very justly be said of him, *Ausum eum quae nemo auderet bonus, perfecisse quae a nullo nisi fortissimo perfici possunt*.[8] Without doubt no man with more wickedness ever attempted anything, or brought to pass what he desired more wickedly, more in the face and contempt of religion and moral honesty; yet wickedness as great as his could never have accomplished those trophies without the assistance of a great spirit, an admirable circumspection and sagacity, and a most magnanimous resolution. When he appeared first in the Parliament he seemed to have a person in no degree gracious, no ornament of discourse, none of those talents which use to reconcile the affections of the standers-by; yet as he grew into place and authority, his parts[9] seemed to be renewed, as if he had concealed faculties till he had occasion to use them, and when he was to act the part of a great man, he did it without any indecency[1] through the want of custom.

After he was confirmed and invested Protector by the Humble Petition and Advice,[2] he consulted with very few upon any action of importance, nor

---

5. Dunbar and Worcester were important battles that Cromwell had won on September 3.
6. "Whom not even his enemies could curse without praising him" (Latin), a slight misquotation of Pling the Younger, *Letters* 3.12.
7. Clarendon's judgment can be compared with that of Marvell in "An Horatian Ode" (p. 1282). "Insensibly": imperceptibly.
8. "He dared undertake what no good man would have tried and triumphed where only the strongest of men could have succeeded." Velleius Paterculus (died 30 C.E.) wrote a concise *History of Rome*; the quotation is from 2.24.
9. Personal qualities.
1. Indecorum.
2. In December 1653, Cromwell was invested as Protector under a written constitution called the Instrument of Government. In 1657 another constitution, the Humble Petition and Advice, invested him with quasi-monarchical powers and restored the House of Lords.

communicated any enterprise he resolved upon with more than those who were to have principal parts in the execution of it, nor to them sooner than was absolutely necessary. What he once resolved, in which he was not rash, he would not be dissuaded from, nor endure any contradiction of his power and authority, but extorted obedience from them who were not willing to yield it.

When he had laid some very extraordinary tax upon the city, one Cony, an eminent fanatic,[3] and one who had heretofore served him very notably, positively refused to pay his part and loudly dissuaded others from submitting to it, as an imposition notoriously against the law and the property of the subject, which all honest men were bound to defend. Cromwell sent for him and cajoled him with the memory of the old kindness and friendship that had been between them, and that of all men he did not expect this opposition from him in a matter that was so necessary for the good of the commonwealth. But it was always his fortune to meet with the most rude and obstinate behavior from those who had formerly been absolutely governed by him, and they commonly put him in mind of some expressions and sayings of his own in cases of the like nature. So this man remembered[4] him how great an enemy he had expressed himself to such grievances, and declared that all who submitted to them and paid illegal taxes were more to blame, and greater enemies to their country, than they who imposed them; and that the tyranny of princes could never be grievous but by the tameness and stupidity of the people.

When Cromwell saw that he could not convert him, he told him that he had a will as stubborn as his, and he would try which of them two should be master, and thereupon with some terms of reproach and contempt he committed the man to prison—whose courage was nothing abated by it, but as soon as the term came, he brought his *habeas corpus*[5] in the King's Bench, which they then called the Upper Bench. Maynard, who was of counsel with the prisoner, demanded his liberty with great confidence, both upon the illegality of the commitment and the illegality of the imposition,[6] as being laid without any lawful authority. The judges could not maintain or defend either, but enough declared what their sentence would be, and therefore the Protector's attorney required a further day to answer what had been urged. Before that day, Maynard was committed to the Tower for presuming to question or make doubt of his authority, and the judges were sent for and severely reprehended for suffering that license; and when they with all humility mentioned the law, and Magna Carta, Cromwell told them their Magna Carta should not control his actions, which he knew were for the safety of the commonwealth. He asked them who made them judges; whether they had any authority to sit there but what he gave them, and that if his authority were at an end, they knew well enough what would become of themselves. And therefore advised them to be more tender of that which could only preserve them, and so dismissed them with caution that they

---

3. In Clarendon's vocabulary, a radical Puritan. "The city": the City of London.
4. Reminded.
5. Writ to release a prisoner.
6. That is, the original tax.

should not suffer the lawyers to prate what it would not become them to hear.

Thus he subdued a spirit that had been often troublesome to the most sovereign power, and made Westminster Hall[7] as obedient and subservient to his commands as any of the rest of his quarters. In all other matters which did not concern the life of his jurisdiction, he seemed to have great reverence for the law, and rarely interposed between party and party; and as he proceeded with this kind of indignation and haughtiness with those who were refractory and dared to contend with his greatness, so towards those who complied with his good pleasure and courted his protection he used a wonderful civility, generosity, and bounty.

To reduce three nations which perfectly hated him to an entire obedience to all his dictates, to awe and govern those nations by an army that was indevoted to him and wished his ruin, was an instance of a very prodigious address;[8] but his greatness at home was but a shadow of the glory he had abroad. It was hard to discover which feared him most, France, Spain, or the Low Countries, where his friendship was current at the value he put upon it; and as they did all sacrifice their honor and their interest to his pleasure, so there is nothing he could have demanded that either of them would have denied him.

* * *

He was not a man of blood, and totally declined Machiavel's method, which prescribes upon any alteration of a government, as a thing absolutely necessary, to cut off all the heads of those, and extirpate their families, who are friends to the old;[9] and it was confidently reported in the Council of Officers, it was more than once proposed that there might be a general massacre of all the royal party as the only expedient to secure the government, but Cromwell would never consent to it, it may be out of too much contempt of his enemies. In a word, as he had all the wickednesses against which damnation is denounced and for which hellfire is prepared, so he had some virtues which have caused the memory of some men in all ages to be celebrated, and he will be looked upon by posterity as a brave, bad man.

1702–04

---

7. The center of the law courts and legal profession. Clarendon never tells us what happened to poor George Cony; the lawyer and judges made their submission and got off, but the fate of the plaintiff remains obscure.

8. Skill. "Indevoted": Clarendon's word, carefully coined to express the far from unanimous feelings of the army.

9. See Machiavelli, *The Prince*, chapters 3 and 7.

DOROTHY WAUGH

Around 1647, a group of disciples began forming around the charismatic itinerant preacher George Fox. Like many religious radicals of the period, Fox taught the importance of relying upon the Inner Light—one's own conscience as guided by the Holy Spirit—in preference to human law or holy writ. Fox believed that the days of prophecy and revelation had not ended in biblical times but were ongoing, so that the teachings of scripture were open to revision. Moreover, sacred illumination was available to all sincere believers regardless of sex, education, or social rank. Fox's followers were derisively called "Quakers" because, in the grip of a visitation by the Holy Spirit, they would suffer paroxysms similar to epileptic convulsions.

Because Quakers believed all human beings to be spiritually equal, they refused to perform the acts of deference that permeated social life in seventeenth-century England—bowing before and doffing the hat to superiors or addressing them with the honorific "you" rather than the familiar "thou." They felt called upon to testify to their beliefs wherever, and whenever, the Inner Light prompted, answering back to ministers in the pulpit, inveighing against what they considered social injustices, and sermonizing without a license in public places. Often, their outspokenness enraged secular and ecclesiastical authorities.

Dorothy Waugh (ca. 1636–?) worked as a maidservant in Preston Patrick, in northwest England, a hotbed of Quaker activity. She probably became one of Fox's followers in the early 1650s, when she was still a teenager. Like Fox and a number of other missionary spirits, sometimes called "the Valiant Sixty," she traveled through England on foot, spreading the Quaker message to all who would listen. In 1656, about age twenty, she was one of the Friends who arrived in Boston, Massachusetts, aboard the *Speedwell*: the party was imprisoned for ten days by the staunch Puritan governor John Endicott, and then forced to return to England. Undaunted, Waugh embarked for the colonies again, with another small group of missionary Quakers, the following year, this time landing in New Amsterdam (modern New York). They were no more welcome here than they had been in Boston. After a brief imprisonment, they were shipped in shackles to the colony of Rhode Island, where complete religious toleration was the rule. In the late 1650s, probably between voyages to the New World, Waugh married, but nothing is known about her later life or the circumstances of her death. Other Quakers traveled even farther than Waugh on missionary expeditions; one woman made it as far as the Ottoman Empire and gave a sermon before the Grand Turk; when she failed to convert him, she walked back home to England.

Waugh's account of her treatment in Carlisle was published in *The Lamb's Defence Against Lies*, a collection in which various Quakers testified to their maltreatment by secular and religious authorities; like most Quaker accounts, it owed much to John Foxe's influential tales of Protestant martyrdom under the Catholic queen "Bloody Mary." Although the Friends were pacifists who refused to retaliate physically or verbally against their persecutors, they were fully aware of the propaganda value of unmerited suffering—indeed, their enemies believed that they deliberately courted abuse as a publicity stunt. In the years between 1650 and 1700, numerous male and female Friends published memoirs of their arduous lives, producing some of the first printed autobiographical writing in English by women and by people of humble status.

A Relation Concerning Dorothy Waugh's Cruel Usage by the Mayor of Carlisle

Upon a seventh day about the time called Michaelmas in the year of the world's account 1655[1] I was moved of the Lord to go into the market of Carlisle, to speak against all deceit and ungodly practices, and the mayor's officer came and violently haled me off the cross[2] and put me in prison, not having anything to lay to my charge. And presently the mayor came up where I was, and asked me from whence I came; and I said, "Out of Egypt,[3] where thou lodgest." But after these words, he was so violent and full of passion he scarce asked me any more questions, but called to one of his followers to bring the bridle[4] as he called it to put upon me, and was to be on three hours. And that which they called so was like a steel cap and my hat being violently plucked off which was pinned to my head whereby they tore my clothes to put on their bridle as they called it, which was a stone weight of iron by the relation of their own generation,[5] and three bars of iron to come over my face, and a piece of it was put in my mouth, which was so unreasonable big a thing for that place as cannot be well related, which was locked to my head. And so I stood their time with my hands bound behind me, with the stone weight of iron upon my head and the bit in my mouth to keep me from speaking. And the mayor said he would make me an example to all that should ever come in that name.[6] And the people to see me so violently abused were broken into tears, but he cried out on them and said, "For foolish pity, one may spoil a whole city." And the man that kept the prison door demanded two pence of everyone that came to see me while their bridle remained upon me. Afterwards it was taken off and they kept me in prison for a little season, and after a while the mayor came again and caused it to be put on again, and sent me out of the city with it on, and gave me very vile and unsavory words, which were not fit to proceed out of any man's mouth, and charged the officer to whip me out of the town, from constable to constable to send me till I came to my own home, whenas[7] they had not anything to lay to my charge.

1656

---

1. Quakers saw themselves as separated from "the world" and its conventional means of marking dates, particularly objecting to terms left over from medieval Catholicism, like "Michaelmas," or the Mass of the Archangel Michael, celebrated on September 29. "Seventh day": Sabbath.
2. A large stone cross marked the main intersection of most English towns; public speakers could mount the steps in order to be heard better.
3. In the Bible, the place where God's chosen people were enslaved and where most of the population worshipped false gods.
4. An instrument of torture and humiliation, typically used to punish women who "scolded" their husbands or neighbors in public.
5. By their own report. A stone is fourteen pounds.
6. As professed Friends, or Quakers.
7. Inasmuch as.

MARGARET CAVENDISH
1623–1673

Margaret (Lucas) Cavendish, Duchess of Newcastle, wrote and published numerous works in many genres, including poetry (*Poems and Fancies*), essays, short fiction and nonfiction, a full-length piece of utopian fiction (*The Description of a New Blazing World*), plays, letters, orations, a biography of her husband (which is also a history of the English Civil Wars), and multiple works of natural philosophy. Born to a wealthy gentry family in Colchester, in 1643 Margaret Lucas joined Queen Henrietta Maria's court-in-exile in Paris. Following the defeat of the royalist forces at Marston Moor in 1644, William Cavendish, then Marquess of Newcastle, went into self-imposed exile in France, where he met and married Margaret Lucas. William and Margaret Cavendish formed a partnership based on shared intellectual interests and writing projects. The couple lived in exile in Europe until the Restoration—first in Paris, where they hosted leading philosophers, including René Descartes and Thomas Hobbes, and then in Antwerp in a house designed and built by the artist Peter Paul Rubens. In 1651 Cavendish traveled to London to (unsuccessfully) petition Parliament for her share of the sequestered Newcastle estates, and published her earliest work, *Poems and Fancies*, in the lavish folio format that became her signature style. (Cavendish was an active circulator of her own books.) Immediately after Charles II returned to the throne the Cavendishes returned to England, where they lived largely at their war-damaged estates, Welbeck Abbey and Bolsover Castle.

Cavendish's literary work illustrates the original theory of self-moving matter that she developed in dialogue with and resistance to the mechanical theories of matter and empiricist and experimental practices that came to dominate English natural philosophy in her lifetime. While Cavendish was the first woman to visit the Royal Society (in 1667), the visit was not a success, and in both *Observations upon Experimental Philosophy* (1666) and, in greater detail, *Grounds of Natural Philosophy* (1668) she pushed back against many scientific premises then current, including the idea that "optic glasses"—both telescopes and the microscopes celebrated in Robert Hooke's *Micrographia* (1665)—enabled a closer approach to the truth of things. "Sense," she writes in *Observations*, "is more apt to be deluded than reason." Cavendish continued to argue for the value of reason, including contemplation, speculation, and imagination, in natural philosophy, and to assert, as she put it in *Grounds*, that "all the parts of nature have life and knowledge." Her refusal of a strict separation between literary and philosophical pursuits is reflected in the mixed genres of many of her volumes. She published her first book of natural philosophy, *Philosophical Fancies*, which also included the poem "Of Sense and Reason Exercised in Their Different Shapes," in the same year as she published her first volume of poetry. Her utopia, *The Blazing World*, which was published "as an appendix" to her *Observations*, extends many of the ideas and precepts expressed in the first part into a literary form. While the *Observations* argues that "boys that play with watery bubbles" and "superficial wonders" "contribute less to the Commonwealth of Learning" than they like to think, *The Blazing World* presents a commonwealth of learning that is governed by an Empress who not only puts a stop to the infighting of experimental philosophers, but hires the "Spirit" of one "Duchess of Newcastle" to support her in her work. The two women discuss myriad political, moral, natural philosophical, and socioeconomic ideas, including the Duchess's suggestion that there is inestimable value in creating "a world of [one's] own." Cavendish's ideas about imagined worlds and the possibility of worlds beyond our senses are complemented by her beliefs that God is the only immaterial entity; that animals are not, as she puts it in "The Hunting of the Hare," ours to "tyrannize upon"; that all forms of life have intelligence, or what she calls "rational spirits"; and that thoughts and literary "fancies" are expressive and creative matter.

From Poems and Fancies

The Poetess's Hasty Resolution

    Reading my verses, I liked them so well,
    Self-love did make my judgment to rebel.
    Thinking them so good, I thought more to write;
    Considering not how others would them like.
5 I writ so fast, I thought, if I lived long,
    A pyramid of fame[1] to build thereon.
    Reason observing which way I was bent,
    Did stay my hand, and asked me what I meant;
    Will you, said she, thus waste your time in vain,
10 On that which in the world small praise shall gain?
    For shame, leave off, said she, the printer spare,
    He'll lose by your ill poetry, I fear.
    Besides the world hath already such a weight
    Of useless books, as it is overfraught.[2]
15 Then pity take, do the world a good turn,
    And all you write cast in the fire, and burn.
    Angry I was, and Reason struck away,
    When I did hear, what she to me did say.
    Then all in haste I to the press it sent,
20 Fearing persuasion might my book prevent.
    But now 'tis done, with grief repent do I,
    Hang down my head with shame, blush, sigh, and cry.
    Take pity, and my drooping spirits raise,
    Wipe off my tears with handkerchiefs of praise.

1653

---

1. A poetic monument.
2. Like a ship with too heavy a cargo, in danger of sinking.

A World Made by Atoms

  Small atoms[1] of themselves a world may make,
  As being subtle,[2] and of every shape:
  And as they dance about, fit places find,
  Such forms[3] as best agree, make every kind.
5 For when we build a house of brick, and stone,
  We lay them even, every one by one:
  And when we find a gap that's big, or small,
  We seek out stones, to fit that place withal.° *in addition, moreover*
  For when not fit, too big, or little be,
10 They fall away, and cannot stay, we see.
  So atoms, as they dance, find places fit,
  They there remain, lie close, and fast will stick.
  Those that unfit, the rest that rove about,
  Do never leave, until they thrust them out.
15 Thus by their several motions, and their forms,
  As several workmen serve each other's turns.
  And thus, by chance, may a new world create:
  Or else, predestinate,° may work by fate. *foreordained (by God)*

1653

Of Many Worlds in This World

  Just like unto a nest of boxes° round, *nested boxes*
  Degrees of sizes within each box are found.
  So in this world, may many worlds more be,
  Thinner, and less, and less still by degree;° *step, stage*
5 Although they are not subject to our sense,
  A world may be no bigger than twopence.
  Nature is curious, and such work may make,
  That our dull sense can never find, but scape.° *escape*
  For creatures,° small as atoms, may be there, *beings, composite bodies*
10 If every atom a creature's figure° bear. *matter and form combined*
  If four atoms a world can make,[1] then see,
  What several° worlds might in an earring be. *many, distinct*
  For millions of these atoms may be in
  The head of one small, little, single pin.
15 And if thus small, then ladies well may wear
  A world of worlds as pendants in each ear.

1653

---

1. Smallest particles of matter.
2. Finely woven; refined; imperceptible.
3. Shapes, arrangements of parts.
1. Cavendish includes a marginal note to the right of this line: "As I have before showed they do, in my Atoms"—that is, in her earlier poems about atoms. A poem titled "The Four Principal Atoms Make the Four Elements, as Square, Round, Long, and Sharp" follows "A World Made by Atoms" in *Poems and Fancies* (1653).

The Hunting of the Hare

Betwixt two ridges of plowed land lay Wat,[1]
Pressing his body close to earth lay squat.
His nose upon his two forefeet close lies,
Glazing obliquely with his great gray eyes.
5 His head he always sets against the wind,
If turn his tail, his hairs blow up behind:
Which he too cold will grow, but he is wise,
And keeps his coat still° down, so warm he lies. *constantly*
Then resting all the day, till, sun doth set,
10 Then riseth up, his relief for to get.
Walking about until the sun doth rise,
Then back returns, down in his form° he lies. *nest*
At last, poor Wat was found, as he there lay,
By huntsmen, with their dogs which came that way.
15 Seeing, gets up, and fast begins to run,
Hoping some ways the cruel dogs to shun.
But they by nature have so quick a scent,
That by their nose they trace what way he went.
And with their deep, wide mouths set forth a cry,
20 Which answered was by echoes in the sky.
Then Wat was struck with terror, and with fear,
Thinks every shadow still the dogs they were.
And running out some distance from the noise,
To hide himself, his thoughts he new employs.
25 Under a clod of earth in sand pit wide,
Poor Wat sat close, hoping himself to hide.
There long he had not sat, but straight° his ears *immediately*
The winding° horns and crying dogs he hears: *blowing*
Staring with fear, up leaps, then doth he run,
30 And with such speed, the ground scarce treads upon.
Into a great thick wood he straightway gets.
Where underneath a broken bough he sits.
At every leaf that with the wind did shake,
Did bring such terror, made his heart to ache.
35 That place he left, to champaign° plains he went, *open*
Winding about, for to deceive their scent.
And while they snuffling were, to find his track,
Poor Wat, being weary, his swift pace did slack.
On his two hinder legs for ease did sit,
40 His forefeet rubbed his face from dust, and sweat.
Licking his feet, he wiped his ears so clean,
That none could tell that Wat had hunted been.
But casting round about his fair great eyes,
The hounds in full career he near him spies:
45 To Wat it was so terrible a sight,
Fear gave him wings, and made his body light.

---

1. Conventional name for a hare.

> Though weary was before, by running long,
> Yet now his breath he never felt more strong.
> Like those that dying are, think health returns,
> When 'tis but a faint blast, which life out burns. [50]
> For spirits seek to guard the heart about,
> Striving with death, but death doth quench them out.
> Thus they so fast came on, with such loud cries,
> That he no hopes hath left, nor help espies.
> With that the winds did pity poor Wat's case, [55]
> And with their breath the scent blew from the place.
> Then every nose is busily employed,
> And every nostril is set open wide,
> And every head doth seek a several° way,   *different*
> To find what grass, or track, the scent on lay. [60]
> Thus quick industry° that is not slack,   *clever work*
> Is like to witchery,° brings lost things back.   *witchcraft*
> For though the wind had tied the scent up close,
> A busy dog thrust in his snuffling nose
> And drew it out, with it did foremost run, [65]
> Then horns blew loud, for th'rest to follow on.
> The great slow hounds, their throats did set a bass,
> The fleet swift hounds, as tenors next in place,
> The little beagles they a treble sing,
> And through the air their voices round did ring. [70]
> Which made a consort, as they ran along;
> If they but words could speak, might sing a song.
> The horns kept time, the hunters shout for joy,
> And valiant seem, poor Wat for to destroy:
> Spurring their horses to a full career, [75]
> Swim rivers deep, leap ditches without fear;
> Endanger life and limbs so fast will ride,
> Only to see how patiently Wat died.
> At last,[2] the dogs so near his heels did get,
> That they their sharp teeth in his breech did set; [80]
> Then tumbling down, did fall with weeping eyes,
> Gives up his ghost, and thus poor Wat he dies.
> Men whooping loud, such acclamations make,
> As if the Devil they did prisoner take.
> When they do but a shiftless° creature kill;   *helpless* [85]
> To hunt, there needs no valiant soldier's skill.
> But man doth think that exercise and toil,
> To keep their health, is best, which makes most spoil.
> Thinking that food and nourishment so good,
> And appetite, that feeds on flesh and blood. [90]
> When they do lions, wolves, bears, tigers see,
> To kill poor sheep, straight say, they cruel be,
> But for themselves all creatures think too few
> For luxury, wish God would make them new.
> As if that God made creatures for man's meat, [95]

---

2. From the 1664 edition; 1653 has "For why."

To give them life and sense, for man to eat;
Or else for sport, or recreation's sake,
Destroy those lives that God saw good to make:
Making their stomachs, graves, which full they fill
100 With murdered bodies that in sport they kill.
Yet man doth think himself so gentle, mild,
When he of creatures is most cruel wild.
And is so proud, thinks only he shall live,
That God a godlike nature did him give.
105 And that all creatures for his sake alone
Was made for him, to tyrannize upon.

1653, 1664

Of Sense and Reason Exercised in Their Different Shapes[1]

If everything hath sense and reason, then
There might be beasts, and birds, and fish, and men:
As vegetables and minerals, had they
The animal shape° to express that way;   *animate, living form*
5 And vegetables and minerals may know,
As man, though like to trees and stones they grow.
Then coral trouts may through the water glide,
And pearled minnows swim on either side;
And mermaids, which in the sea delight,
10 Might all be made of watry lilies white,
Set on salt watry billows as they flow,
Which like green banks appear thereon to grow.
And mariners i'th'midst their ship might stand,
Instead of mast, hold sails in either hand.
15 On mountain tops the golden fleece[2] might feed,
Some hundred years their ewes bring forth their breed.
Large deer of oak might through the forest run,
Leaves on their heads might keep them from the sun;
Instead of shedding horns, their leaves might fall,
20 And acorns to increase a wood of fawns withal.
Then might a squirrel for a nut be cracked,
If nature had that matter° so compact: *physical substance*
And the small sprouts° which on the husk° do grow,   *offshoots / outer shell*
Might be the tail, and make a brushing[3] show.
25 Then might the diamonds which on rocks oft lie,
Be all like to some little sparkling fly.
Then might a leaden hare, if swiftly run,
Melt from that shape, and so a pig[4] become.

---

1. This poem appeared in *Philosophical Fancies* (1653). In Cavendish's natural philosophy, matter is solid, self-moving, sensitive, and rational.
2. In classical Greek myth, the fleece sought by Jason, which had belonged to a single ram; Cavendish imagines a living herd of golden sheep.
3. Brushwood, the cutting of brushwood. Brush is also the bushy part of an animal's tail.
4. Cavendish's marginal note: "A Pig [a crudely cast bar] of Lead."

  And dogs of copper-mouths sound like a bell;
30 So when they kill a hare, ring out his knell.[5]
  Hard iron men shall have no cause to fear
  To catch a fall, when they a hunting were.
  Nor in the wars should have no use of arms,
  Nor feared to fight; they could receive no harms.
35 For if a bullet on their breasts should hit,
  Fall on their back, but straightways up may get.
  Or if a bullet on their head do light,
  May make them totter, but not kill them quite.
  And stars be like the birds with twinkling wing,
40 When in the air they fly, like larks might sing.
  And as they fly, like wand'ring° planets show,   *roving*
  Their tails may like to blazing comets grow.
  When they on trees do rest themselves from flight,
  Appear like fixed stars in clouds of night.
45 Thus may the sun be like a woman fair,
  And the bright beams be as her flowing hair.
  And from her eyes may cast a silver light,
  And when she sleeps, the world be as dark night.
  Or women may of alabaster be,
50 And so as smooth as polished ivory,
  Or, as clear crystal, where hearts may be shown,
  And all their falsehoods to the world be known.
  Or else be made of rose, and lilies white,
  Both fair, and sweet, to give the soul delight,
55 Or else be made like tulips fresh in May,
  By nature dressed, clothed several colors gay.
  Thus every year there may young virgins spring,
  But wither, and decay, as soon again.
  While they are fresh,° upon their breast might set   *new, not deteriorated*
60 Great swarms of bees, from thence sweet honey get.
  Or, on their lips, for gillyflowers,° flies   *sweet-scented flowers*
  Drawing delicious sweet that therein lies.
  Thus every maid, like several flowers show,
  Not in their shape, but like in substance grow.
65 Then tears which from oppressed hearts do rise,
  May gather into clouds within the eyes:
  From whence those tears, like showers of rain may flow
  Upon the banks of cheeks, where roses grow.
  After those showers of rain, so sweet may smell,
70 Perfuming all the air, that near them dwell.
  But when the sun of joy and mirth doth rise,
  Darting forth pleasing beams from loving eyes.
  Then may the buds of modesty unfold,
  With full blown confidence the sun behold.
75 But grief as frost them nips, and withering die,
  In their own pods[6] entombèd lie.

---

5. The stroke or sound of a bell, especially one rung to announce a death.
6. Cavendish's marginal note: "The Husk."

Thus virgin cherry trees, where blossoms blow,°   *bloom*
So red ripe cherries on their lips may grow.
Or women plum trees at each finger's end,
May ripe plums hang, and make their joints to bend.
Men sycamores, which on their breast may write
Their amorous verses, which their thoughts indite.°   *put into words, compose*
Men's stretched arms may be like spreading vines,
Where grapes may grow, so drink of their own wine.
To plant large orchards, need no pains nor care,
For every one their sweet fresh fruit may bear.
Then silver grass may in the meadows grow,
Which nothing but a scythe of fire can mow.
The wind, which from the north a journey takes,
May strike those silver strings, and music make.
Thus may another world, though matter still the same,
By changing shapes, change humors,[7] properties, and name.
Thus Colossus,[8] a statue wondrous great,
When it did fall, might straight get on his feet.
Where ships, which through his legs did swim, he might
Have blowed their sails, or else have drowned them quite.
The golden calf[9] that Israel joyed to see,
Might run away from their idolatry.
The Basan bull of brass might be,[1] when roar,
His metalled throat might make his voice sound more.
The hill, which Muhammed did call,[2] might come
At the first word, or else away might run.
Thus Pompey's statue might rejoice to see,
When killed was Caesar, his great enemy.[3]
The wooden horse[4] that did great Troy betray,
Have told what's in him, and then run away.
Achilles arms against Ulysses plead,
And not let wit against true valor speed.°[5]   *succeed, prosper*

1653

---

7. The four fluids of the body—blood, phlegm, choler, and black bile—whose relative proportions were thought to determine a person's disposition and general health.
8. A huge bronze statue of the sun god Helios at Rhodes; it was one of the seven wonders of the ancient world. In later accounts, ships were said to sail between its legs.
9. Literally, the idol created and worshipped by the Israelites when Moses was slow to return from Mount Sinai (Exodus 32); more broadly, any object of false worship, including material wealth.
1. Cavendish conflates a strong bull from Bashan (Psalm 22:12), in what is now Syria, and the brazen bull, a torture device invented for a Greek tyrant in the 6th century B.C.E.: victims were roasted to death inside it, and their screams were said to be converted into the lowing of a bull.
2. An allusion to a story about the founder of Islam that was told in Francis Bacon's *Essays* ("Of Boldness"): "Mahomet called the hill to come to him. And when the hill stood still, he was never a whit abashed, but said; if the hill will not come to Mahomet, Mahomet will go to the hill."
3. The Roman generals Pompey the Great and Julius Caesar, formerly allies, became enemies in the civil war in which Pompey was killed in 48 B.C.E. Pompey's statue stood in the senate house, on whose steps Caesar was murdered in 44 B.C.E.
4. In Greek myth, the huge hollow horse in which Greek soldiers hid and were drawn inside the gates of Troy, which they destroyed.
5. Achilles and Ulysses were Greek leaders in the Trojan War, preeminent respectively for skill in battle and for cunning. Here, Achilles' "arms," or armor, plead on behalf of bravery ("true valor") against "wit" in a contest of values.

The Blazing World *The Blazing World* begins as a romance: a young woman is abducted by merchants and then miraculously saved when a tempest carries the abductors' boat to the North Pole (where the kidnappers freeze to death) and then further on into another world. The emperor of this "Blazing World" marries the heroine and gives her sovereignty over its entire government. *The Blazing World* then assumes a utopian character, as the fantastical inhabitants teach their new Empress about their scientific experiments, politics, and religious practices, many of which reflect Cavendish's own views. When the Empress decides she needs a scribe to help her with her "Cabbala," or book of wisdom, she considers philosophers ranging from Aristotle to Descartes, but ultimately settles on the spirit of the Duchess of Newcastle. The two "Platonic friends" travel to Cavendish's world, where they evaluate its culture and politics and visit the ruined Newcastle estates. *The Blazing World* illustrates the philosophy of matter in Cavendish's own *Observations upon Experimental Philosophy*, to which it was attached. Her argument for the work of fancy thus privileges both natural philosophy and literature: one can create and rule over an imagined world with force comparable to that of a "Caesar or an Alexander," but one can also "alter it as often as you please."

From The Description of a New World, Called The Blazing World[1]

From *To the Reader*

* * *

[F]ictions are an issue of man's fancy, framed in his own mind, according as he pleases, without regard whether the thing he fancies be really existent without[2] his mind or not; so that reason searches the depth of nature, and enquires after the true causes of natural effects, but fancy creates of its own accord whatsoever it pleases, and delights in its own work. The end of reason, is truth; the end of fancy, is fiction. But mistake me not, when I distinguish fancy from reason; I mean not as if fancy were not made by the rational parts of matter; but by reason I understand a rational search and enquiry into the causes of natural effects; and by fancy a voluntary creation or production of the mind, both being effects, or rather actions, of the rational part of matter; of which, as that is a more profitable and useful study than this, so it is also more laborious and difficult, and requires sometimes the help of fancy to recreate the mind, and withdraw it from its more serious contemplations. And this is the reason why I added this piece of fancy to my philosophical observations, and joined them as two worlds at the ends of their poles; both for my own sake, to divert my studious thoughts which I employed in the contemplation thereof, and to delight the reader

---

1. *The Blazing World* was published as an addendum to Cavendish's *Observations Upon Experimental Philosophy*. That critique of the new sciences emphasizes the limitations of experiments founded on human perception and such instruments as the microscope and telescope, and provides an argument for an original theory of rational, self-moving matter. The texts were published in 1666 and 1668.
2. Outside of.

with variety, which is always pleasing. But lest my fancy should stray too much, I chose such a fiction as would be agreeable to the subject I treated of in the former parts; it is a description of a new world, not such as Lucian's, or the French man's world in the moon;[3] but a world of my own creating, which I call the Blazing World: the first part whereof is romancical, the second philosophical, and the third is merely fancy, or (as I may call it) fantastical; which if it add any satisfaction to you, I shall account myself a happy creatoress; if not, I must be content to live a melancholy life in my own world; I cannot call it a poor world, if poverty be only want of gold, silver, and jewels; for there is more gold in it then all the chemists ever did, and (as I verily believe) will ever be able to make. As for the rocks of diamonds, I wish with all my soul they might be shared amongst my noble female friends, and upon that condition I would willingly quit my part; and of the gold I should only desire so much as might suffice to repair my noble lord and husband's losses:[4] for I am not covetous, but as ambitious as ever any of my sex was, is, or can be; which is the cause, that though I cannot be Henry the Fifth, or Charles the Second, yet I endeavor to be Margaret the First; and although I have neither power, time nor occasion to conquer the world as Alexander and Caesar did;[5] yet rather than not to be mistress of one, since fortune and the fates would give me none, I have made a world of my own: for which no body, I hope, will blame me, since it is in everyone's power to do the like.

The Description of a New World, Called The Blazing World

* * *

No sooner was the lady brought before the emperor, but he conceived her to be some goddess, and offered to worship her; which she refused, telling him (for by that time she had pretty well learned their language) that although she came out of another world, yet was she but a mortal; at which the emperor rejoicing, made her his wife, and gave her an absolute power to rule and govern all that world as she pleased. But her subjects, who could hardly be persuaded to believe her mortal, tendered her all the veneration and worship due to a deity.

* * *

---

3. Depicted in *The Comic History of the States and Empires of the Moon* (1656), by the French satirist and dramatist Cyrano de Bergerac (1619–1655). In a tale translated into English in 1634 as *Lucian's True History*, the Greek satirist Lucian of Samosata (ca. 120–after 180 C.E.) describes a voyage to the moon and beyond.
4. Cavendish's husband, William, was a general in the royalist forces. After their defeat, his estates were confiscated by Parliament and fully returned to him only upon the restoration of the monarchy; in her *Life of William Cavendish* (1667), Cavendish offered a precise estimate of the financial losses suffered by her husband, equivalent today to millions of dollars.
5. Alexander the Great (356–23 B.C.E.) and Julius Caesar (100–44 B.C.E.) were viewed as the greatest generals of Greek and Roman history, respectively. Henry V (1387–1422) made England one of the strongest military powers in Europe. Charles II (1630–1685) was restored to the English throne in 1660.

Their priests and governors were princes of the imperial blood, and made eunuchs for that purpose; and as for the ordinary sort of men in that part of the world where the emperor resided, they were of several complexions; not white, black, tawny, olive, or ash-colored; but some appeared of an azure, some of a deep purple, some of a grass-green, some of a scarlet, some of an orange color, etc. Which colors and complexions, whether they were made by bare reflection of light without the assistance of small particles, or by the help of well-ranged and ordered atoms; or by a continual agitation of little globules; or by some pressing and reacting motion, I am not able to determine.[6] The rest of the inhabitants of that world were men of several different sorts, shapes, figures, dispositions, and humors, as I have already made mention heretofore; some were bear-men, some worm-men, some fish- or mear-men, otherwise called sirens;[7] some bird-men, some fly-men, some ant-men, some geese-men, some spider-men, some lice-men, some fox-men, some ape-men, some jackdaw-men, some magpie-men, some parrot-men, some satyrs, some giants, and many more which I cannot all remember; and of these several sorts of men, each followed such a profession as was most proper for the nature of their species, which the Empress encouraged them in, especially those that had applied themselves to the study of several arts and sciences; for they were as ingenious and witty in the invention of profitable and useful arts as we are in our world, nay, more; and to that end she erected schools and founded several societies. The bear-men were to be her experimental philosophers, the bird-men her astronomers, the fly-, worm-, and fish-men her natural philosophers, the ape-men her chemists, the satyrs her Galenic physicians,[8] the fox-men her politicians, the spider- and lice-men her mathematicians, the jackdaw-, magpie-, and parrot-men her orators and logicians, the giants her architects, etc. But before all things, she having got a sovereign power from the emperor over all the world, desired to be informed both of the manner of their religion and government, and to that end she called the priests and statesmen to give her an account of either. Of the statesmen she enquired, first, why they had so few laws? To which they answered that many laws made many divisions, which most commonly did breed factions and at last brake out into open wars. Next, she asked, why they preferred the monarchical form of government before any other? They answered that as it was natural for one body to have but one head, so it was also natural for a politic body to have but one governor; and that a commonwealth which had many governors was like a monster of many heads: besides, said they, a monarchy is a divine form of government and agrees most with our religion; for as there is but one God, whom we all unanimously worship and adore with one faith, so we are resolved to have but one emperor to whom we all submit with one obedience.

---

6. Cavendish satirizes the theories and experiments of the Royal Society, including those described in Robert Boyle's *Experiments and Considerations Touching Colours* (1664).
7. Imaginary serpents, or the mythical creatures (part bird, part woman) whose singing lures sailors to their destruction (see Homer, *Odyssey* 12).

"Mear-men": mermen (the male counterparts of mermaids).
8. Followers of Galen (129–ca. 216 C.E.), ancient Greek physician and philosopher whose theories dominated European medical practice into the 17th century.

Then the Empress seeing that the several sorts of her subjects had each their churches apart, asked the priests whether they were of several religions. They answered Her Majesty that there was no more but one religion in all that world, nor no diversity of opinions in that same religion; for though there were several sorts of men, yet had they all but one opinion concerning the worship and adoration of God. The Empress asked them whether they were Jews, Turks, or Christians? We do not know, said they, what religions those are; but we do all unanimously acknowledge, worship, and adore the only, omnipotent, and eternal God, with all reverence, submission, and duty. Again, the Empress enquired, whether they had several forms of worship? They answered, no: for our devotion and worship consists only in prayers, which we frame according to our several necessities, in petitions, humiliations, thanksgiving, etc. Truly, replied the Empress, I thought you had been either Jews or Turks,[9] because I never perceived any women in your congregations; but what is the reason, you bar them from your religious assemblies? It is not fit, said they, that men and women should be promiscuously together in time of religious worship; for their company hinders devotion, and makes many, instead of praying to God, direct their devotion to their mistresses. But, asked the Empress, have they no congregation of their own to perform the duties of divine worship as well as men? No, answered they: but they stay at home and say their prayers by themselves in their closets.[1] Then the Empress desired to know the reason why the priests and governors of their world were made eunuchs? They answered, to keep them from marriage: for women and children most commonly make disturbance both in church and state. But, said she, women and children have no employment in church or state. 'Tis true, answered they; but although they are not admitted to public employments, yet are they so prevalent with their husbands and parents that many times by their importunate[2] persuasions they cause as much, nay more, mischief secretly, than if they had the management of public affairs.

* * *

[TIRING OF THE EXPERIMENTAL AND NATURAL PHILOSOPHERS, THE EMPRESS COMMANDS THEM TO BREAK THEIR "ARTIFICIAL GLASSES"]

The bear-men, being exceedingly troubled at her Majesty's displeasure concerning their telescopes, kneeled down, and in the humblest manner petitioned that they might not be broken; for, said they, we take more delight in artificial delusions than in natural truths. Besides, we shall want employments for our senses and subjects for arguments; for were there nothing but truth and no falsehood there would be no occasion for to dispute, and by this means we should want the aim and pleasure of our endeavors in confuting and contradicting each other; neither would one man be thought wiser than another, but all would either be alike knowing and wise, or all would be fools; wherefore we most humbly beseech your

---

9. That is, Muslims; in Jewish and Muslim houses of prayer, men and women traditionally worship in separate spaces.

1. Private chambers.
2. Persistent. "Prevalent": influential.

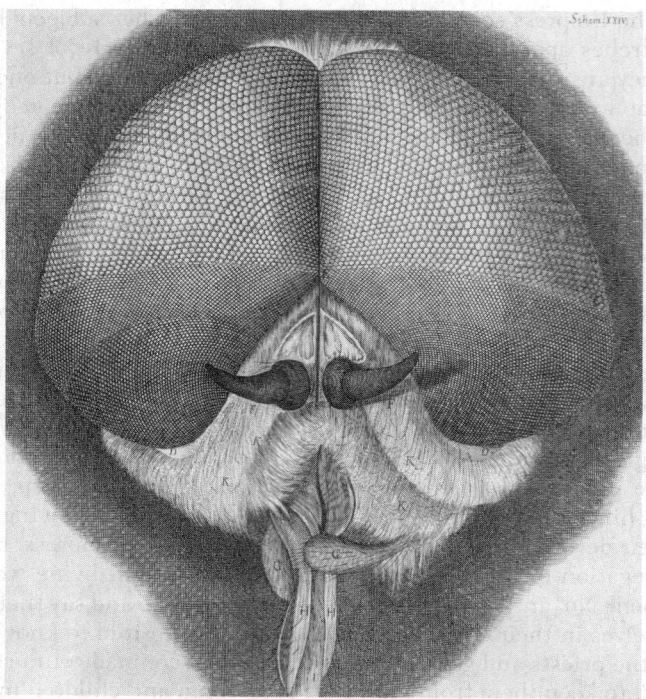

Grey Drone Fly. *The Blazing World* discusses this image "Of the eyes and head of a grey drone fly" from Robert Hooke's *Of Micrographia: or Some Physiological Descriptions of Minute Bodies Made by Magnifying Glasses* (1665).

imperial Majesty to spare our glasses, which are our only delight and as dear to us as our lives. The Empress at last consented to their request, but upon condition that their disputes and quarrels should remain within their schools, and cause no factions or disturbances in state or government. The bear-men, full of joy, returned their most humble thanks to the Empress; and to make her amends for the displeasure which their telescopes had occasioned, told her Majesty that they had several other artificial optic-glasses which they were sure would give her Majesty a great deal more satisfaction. Amongst the rest they brought forth several microscopes by the means of which they could enlarge the shapes of little bodies and make a louse appear as big as an elephant, and a mite as big as a whale. First of all, they shewed the Empress a gray drone-fly, wherein they observed that the greatest part of her face, nay, of her head, consisted of two large bunches all covered over with a multitude of small pearls or hemispheres in a trigonal order, which pearls were of two degrees, smaller and bigger; the smaller degree was lowermost, and looked towards the ground; the other was upward, and looked sideward, forward, and backward. They were all so smooth and polished that they were able to represent the image of any object, the number of them was in all 14000.[3] After the view of this strange and miraculous creature, and their several observations upon it, the Empress asked them what they judged those little hemispheres might be? They answered that each of them was a perfect eye, by reason they perceived that each was covered with a transparent cornea containing a liquor within them, which resembled the watery or glassy humor of the eye. To which the Empress replied that they might be glassy pearls and yet not eyes, and that perhaps their microscopes did not truly inform them: but they smilingly answered her Majesty that she did not know the virtue of those microscopes; for they did never delude but rectify and inform their senses; nay, the world, said they, would be but blind without them, as it has been in former ages before those microscopes were invented.

* * *

Then the Empress asked [the worm-men], whether by their sensitive perceptions they could observe the interior corporeal, figurative motions both of vegetables and minerals? They answered that their senses could perceive them after they were produced, but not before; Nevertheless, said they, although the interior, figurative motions of natural creatures are not subject to the exterior, animal, sensitive perceptions, yet by their rational perception they may judge of them and of their productions if they be regular: whereupon the Empress commanded the bear-men to lend them some of their best microscopes; at which the bear-men smilingly answered her Majesty that their glasses would do them but little service in the bowels of the earth because there was no light; for, said they, our glasses do only represent exterior objects according to the various reflections and positions of light; and wheresoever light is wanting,[4] the glasses will do no good. To which the worm-men replied that although they could not say much of refractions, reflections, inflections, and the like; yet were they not blind, even in the bowels of the earth, for they could see the several sorts of minerals, as also minute animals, that lived there, which minute animal creatures were not blind neither but had some kind of sensitive perception that was as serviceable to them as sight, taste, smell, touch, hearing, etc. was to other animal creatures: by which it is evident that nature has been as bountiful to those creatures that live underground or in the bowels of the earth as to those that live upon the surface of the earth, or in the air, or in water. But howsoever, proceeded the worm-men, although there is light in the bowels of the earth, yet your microscopes will do but little good there, by reason those creatures that live underground have not such an optic sense as those that live on the surface of the earth: wherefore, unless you had such glasses as are proper for their perception, your microscopes will not be any ways advantageous to them. The Empress seemed well pleased with this answer of the worm-men, and asked them further whether minerals, and all other creatures within the earth, were colorless? At

3. Robert Hooke included a drawing of the drone fly in his *Of Micrographia: or Some Physiological Descriptions of Minute Bodies Made by Magnifying Glasses* (1665); see p. 1368.
4. Lacking.

which question they could not forbear laughing; and when the Empress asked the reason why they laughed; we most humbly beg your Majesty's pardon, replied they; for we could not choose but laugh when we heard of a colorless body. Why, said the Empress, color is only an accident,[5] which is an immaterial thing, and has no being of itself but in another body. Those, replied they, that informed your Majesty thus, surely their rational motions were very irregular; for how is it possible that a natural nothing can have a being in nature? If it be no substance, it cannot have a being, and if no being, it is nothing; wherefore the distinction between subsisting of itself, and subsisting in another body, is a mere nicety and nonsense; for there is nothing in nature that can subsist of or by itself, (I mean singly) by reason all parts of nature are composed in one body, and though they may be infinitely divided, commixed, and changed in their particulars, yet in general parts cannot be separated from parts as long as nature lasts; nay, we might as probably affirm that infinite nature would be as soon destroyed as that one atom could perish; and therefore your Majesty may firmly believe that there is no body without color, nor no color without body; for color, figure, place, magnitude, and body are all but one thing, without any separation or abstraction from each other.

* * * Again, the Empress asked them, whether there were any non-beings within the earth? To which they answered that they never heard of any such thing; and that if her Majesty would know the truth thereof, she must ask those creatures that are called immaterial spirits, which had a great affinity with non-beings, and perhaps could give her a satisfactory answer to this question. Then, she desired to be informed, what opinion they had of the beginning of forms? They told her Majesty that they did not understand what she meant by this expression; for, said they, there is no beginning in nature, no not of particulars, by reason nature is eternal and infinite and her particulars are subject to infinite changes and transmutations by virtue of their own corporeal, figurative self-motions; so that there's nothing new in nature, nor properly a beginning of anything.

* * *

The Empress having thus declared her mind to the ape-men and given them better instructions than perhaps they expected, not knowing that her Majesty had such great and able judgment in natural philosophy, had several conferences with them concerning chemical preparations, which for brevity's sake I'll forbear to rehearse: amongst the rest, she asked how it came that the imperial race appeared so young and yet was reported to have lived so long; some of them two, some three, and some four hundred years? and whether it was by nature or a special divine blessing? To which they answered that there was a certain rock in the parts of that world which contained the golden sands, which rock was hollow within and did produce a gum that was a hundred years before it came to its full strength and perfection; this gum, said they, if it be held in a warm hand will dissolve into

---

5. A nonessential property.

an oil, the effects whereof are following: it being given every day for some certain time to an old decayed man, in the bigness of a little pea, will first make him spit for a week or more; after this, it will cause vomits of phlegm, and after that it will bring forth by vomits, humors[6] of several colors; first of a pale yellow, then of a deep yellow, then of a green, and lastly of a black color; and each of these humors have a several taste, some are fresh, some salt, some sour, some bitter, and so forth; neither do all these vomits make them sick, but they come out on a sudden and unawares, without any pain or trouble to the patient: and after it hath done all these mentioned effects, and cleared both the stomach and several other parts of the body, then it works upon the brain, and brings forth of the nose such kind of humors as it did out of the mouth, and much after the same manner; then it will purge by stool, then by urine, then by sweat, and lastly by bleeding at the nose, and the hemorrhoids; all which effects it will perform within the space of six weeks or a little more; for it does not work very strongly, but gently, and by degrees: lastly, when it has done all this it will make the body break out into a thick scab, and cause both hair, teeth, and nails to come off; which scab being arrived to its full maturity, opens first along the back and comes off all in a piece like an armor, and all this is done within the space of four months. After this the patient is wrapped into a cerecloth[7] prepared of certain gums and juices wherein he continues until the time of nine months be expired from the first beginning of the cure, which is the time of a child's formation in the womb. In the meanwhile, his diet is nothing else but eagles' eggs and hinds' milk; and after the cerecloth is taken away he will appear of the age of twenty, both in shape and strength.

* * *

[THE EMPRESS CONVERSES WITH IMMATERIAL SPIRITS]

* * * The Empress asked them further whether there was not a world of spirits as well as there is of material creatures? No, answered they, for the word world implies a quantity or multitude of corporeal creatures, but we being immaterial can make no world of spirits. Then she desired to be informed when spirits were made? We do not know, answered they, how and when we were made, nor are we much inquisitive after it; nay, if we did, it would be no benefit, neither for us, nor for you mortals to know it. The Empress replied that cabbalists and divine philosophers[8] said men's rational souls were immaterial and stood as much in need of corporeal vehicles as spirits did. If this be so, answered the spirits, then you are hermaphrodites[9] of nature; but your cabbalists are mistaken, for they take the purest and subtlest parts of matter for immaterial spirits. * * * She asked again whether souls

---

6. The four fluids of the body—blood, phlegm, choler, and black bile—whose relative proportions were thought to determine a person's disposition and general health.
7. Cloth impregnated with wax or gum, used as a plaster in surgery or as wrapping for a dead body.
8. Those who believed that soul and body were separable (unlike monists, who believed that they were one). "Cabbalists": devotees or interpreters of the Jewish Kabbalah, medieval esoteric mysticism; more generally, those skilled in mystic arts or secret learning.
9. Persons or animals that have (or appear to have) both male and female sexual organs; figuratively, persons or things in which radically different or contradictory attributes or qualities are combined. The term often had pejorative connotations. "Take": mistake.

did choose bodies? They answered that Platonics believed the souls of lovers lived in the bodies of their beloved; but surely, said they, if there be a multitude of souls in a world of matter, they cannot miss bodies; for as soon as a soul is parted from one body, it enters into another; and souls having no motion of themselves must of necessity be clothed or embodied with the next parts of matter. If this be so, replied the Empress, then I pray inform me, whether all matter be soulified? The spirits answered, they could not exactly tell that; but if it was true that matter had no other motion but what came from a spiritual power, and that all matter was moving, then no soul could quit a body, but she must of necessity enter into another soulified body, and then there would be two immaterial substances in one body. The Empress asked whether it was not possible that there could be two souls in one body? As for immaterial souls, answered the spirits, it is impossible; for there cannot be two immaterials in one inanimate body, by reason they want parts and place, being bodiless; but there may be numerous material souls in one composed body, by reason every material part has a material natural soul; for nature is but one infinite, self-moving, living, and self-knowing body, consisting of the three degrees of inanimate, sensitive, and rational matter, so intermixed together that no part of nature, were it an atom, can be without any of these three degrees; the sensitive is the life, the rational the soul, and the inanimate part the body of infinite nature. * * * The Empress asked further, whether animal life came out of the spiritual world and did return thither again? The spirits answered, they could not exactly tell; but if it were so, then certainly animal lives must leave their bodies behind them, otherwise the bodies would make the spiritual world a mixed world, that is, partly material, and partly immaterial; but the truth is, said they, spirits being immaterial, cannot properly make a world; for a world belongs to material, not to immaterial creatures. If this be so, replied the Empress, then certainly there can be no world of lives and forms without matter? No, answered the spirits, nor a world of matter without lives and forms; for natural lives and forms cannot be immaterial, no more than matter can be immovable. And therefore natural lives, forms, and matter, are inseparable.

* * *

[THE EMPRESS CONSULTS WITH THE IMMATERIAL SPIRITS ABOUT WRITING A CABBALA]

After some time, when the spirits had refreshed themselves in their own vehicles,[1] they sent one of their nimblest spirits to ask the Empress whether she would have a scribe, or whether she would write the Cabbala herself? The Empress received the proffer which they made her with all civility; and told them that she desired a spiritual scribe. The spirits answered that they could dictate, but not write, except they put on a hand or arm or else the whole body of man. The Empress replied, how can spirits arm themselves with gauntlets of flesh? As well, answered they, as man can arm himself with a gauntlet of steel. If it be so, said the Empress, then I will have a

---

1. Material objects that can contain the spirits.

scribe. Then the spirits asked her whether she would have the soul of a living or a dead man? Why, said the Empress, can the soul quit a living body and wander or travel abroad? Yes, answered they, for according to Plato's doctrine, there is a conversation of souls, and the souls of lovers live in the bodies of their beloved. Then I will have, answered she, the soul of some ancient famous writer, either of Aristotle, Pythagoras, Plato, Epicurus, or the like.[2] The spirits said that those famous men were very learned, subtle, and ingenious writers; but they were so wedded to their own opinions that they would never have the patience to be scribes. Then, said she, I'll have the soul of one of the most famous modern writers, as either of Galileo, Gassendi, Descartes, Helmont, Hobbes, H. More, etc.[3] The spirits answered, that they were fine ingenious writers, but yet so self-conceited that they would scorn to be scribes to a woman. But, said they, there's a lady, the Duchess of Newcastle, which although she is not one of the most learned, eloquent, witty, and ingenious, yet she is a plain and rational writer; for the principle of her writings is sense and reason, and she will without question be ready to do you all the service she can. That lady then, said the Empress, will I choose for my scribe, neither will the emperor have reason to be jealous, she being one of my own sex. In truth, said the spirit, husbands have reason to be jealous of Platonic lovers, for they are very dangerous, as being not only very intimate and close, but subtle and insinuating. You say well, replied the Empress; wherefore I pray send me the Duchess of Newcastle's soul; which the spirit did; and after she came to wait on the Empress, at her first arrival the Empress embraced and saluted her with a spiritual kiss; then she asked her whether she could write? Yes, answered the Duchess's soul, but not so intelligibly that any reader whatsoever may understand it, unless he be taught to know my characters; for my letters are rather like characters,[4] than well formed letters. Said the Empress, you were recommended to me by an honest and ingenious spirit. Surely, answered the Duchess, the spirit is ignorant of my handwriting. The truth is, said the Empress, he did not mention your handwriting; but he informed me, that you writ sense and reason, and if you can but write so that any of my secretaries may learn your hand, they shall write it out fair and intelligible. The Duchess answered that she questioned not but it might easily be learned in a short time. But, said she to the Empress, what is it that your Majesty would have written? She answered, the Jews' Cabbala. * * * [I]f your Majesty were resolved to make a Cabbala, I would advise you rather to make a poetical or romancical Cabbala, wherein you may use metaphors, allegories, similitudes, etc. and interpret them as you please.[5] With that the Empress thanked the Duchess, and embracing her soul, told her she would

---

2. She names major Greek philosophers active between the 6th and the early 3rd century B.C.E.
3. European scientists and philosophers: Galileo Galilei (1564–1642), Italian astronomer, mathematician, and philosopher; Pierre Gassendi (1592–1655), French mathematician and proponent of a mechanistic theory of matter; René Descartes (1596–1650), French mathematician and mechanist philosopher; Jan Baptista van Helmont (1579–1644), Flemish physician, chemist, and philosopher; Thomas Hobbes, English mechanistic philosopher and political scientist; Henry More (1614–1687), British poet and philosopher, author of *The Immateriality of the Soul* (1659).
4. Distinctive marks or impressions
5. Cavendish adds a fourth kind of Cabbala to the three identified by Henry More in his *Conjectura Cabbalistica* (1653): the literal, philosophical, and "Mystical or Moral" levels of biblical significance.

take her counsel: she made her also her favorite and kept her sometime in that world, and by this means the Duchess came to know and give this relation of all that passed in that rich, populous, and happy world; and after some time the Empress gave her leave to return to her husband and kindred into her native world, but upon condition that her soul should visit her now and then; which she did: and truly their meeting did produce such an intimate friendship between them that they became Platonic lovers, although they were both females.

[THE DUCHESS WANTS TO BE THE EMPRESS OF HER OWN WORLD]

* * * I love you so well, replied the Empress, that I wish with all my soul you had the fruition of your ambitious desire, and I shall not fail to give you my best advice how to accomplish it; the best informers are the immaterial spirits, and they'll soon tell you whether it be possible to obtain your wish. But, said the Duchess, I have little acquaintance with them, for I never knew any before the time you sent for me. They know you, replied the Empress, for they told me of you, and were the means and instrument of your coming hither: wherefore I'll confer with them and enquire whether there be not another world whereof you may be Empress as well as I am of this? No sooner had the Empress said this, but some immaterial spirits came to visit her, of whom she inquired whether there were but three worlds in all, to wit, the Blazing World where she was in, the world which she came from, and the world where the Duchess lived? The spirits answered, that there were more numerous worlds than the stars which appeared in these three mentioned worlds. Then the Empress asked whether it was not possible that her dearest friend the Duchess of Newcastle might be empress of one of them?[6] Although there be numerous, nay, infinite worlds, answered the spirits, yet none is without government. But is none of these worlds so weak, said she, that it may be surprised or conquered? The spirits answered, that Lucian's World of Lights had been for some time in a snuff,[7] but of late years one Helmont had got it, who since he was emperor of it had so strengthened the immortal parts thereof with mortal outworks as it was for the present impregnable.[8] Said the Empress, if there be such an infinite number of worlds, I am sure not only my friend the Duchess but any other might obtain one. Yes, answered the spirits, if those worlds were uninhabited; but they are as populous as this your Majesty governs. Why, said the Empress, it is not possible to conquer a world? No, answered the spirits, but for the most part conquerors seldom enjoy their conquest, for they being more feared then loved most commonly come to an untimely end. * * * [B]ut we wonder, proceeded the spirits, that you desire to be empress of a terrestrial world when as you can create yourself a celestial world if you please. What, said the Empress, can any mortal be a creator?

---

6. Texts on the new astronomy occasionally speculated about multiple inhabited worlds. Raphael introduces the idea to Adam in Milton's *Paradise Lost*, 8.140–58.
7. On the point of extinction.
8. Cavendish suggests that van Helmont turned Lucian's material world of light into a world that mixed material and immaterial elements. In Walter Charleton's translation of van Helmont's *Ternary of Paradoxes* (1650), a section on the "variety of vital lights" includes a story of a light that appeared to van Helmont and revealed to him that soul is distinct from body, a view with which Cavendish would have disagreed.

Yes, answered the spirits; for every human creature can create an immaterial world fully inhabited by immaterial creatures and populous of immaterial subjects such as we are, and all this within the compass of the head or skull; nay, not only so, but he may create a world of what fashion and government he will, and give the creatures thereof such motions, figures, forms, colors, perceptions, etc. as he pleases, and make whirlpools, lights, pressures, and reactions, etc. as he thinks best; nay, he may make a world full of veins, muscles, and nerves, and all these to move by one jolt or stroke: also he may alter that world as often as he pleases, or change it from a natural world to an artificial; he may make a world of ideas, a world of atoms, a world of lights, or whatsoever his fancy leads him to. And since it is in your power to create such a world, what need you to venture life, reputation, and tranquility to conquer a gross material world? For you can enjoy no more of a material world than a particular creature is able to enjoy, which is but a small part, considering the compass of such a world; and you may plainly observe it by your friend the Empress here which although she possesses a whole world, yet enjoys she but a part thereof; neither is she so much acquainted with it that she knows all the places, countries, and dominions she governs. The truth is, a sovereign monarch has the general trouble; but the subjects enjoy all the delights and pleasures in parts; for it is impossible that a kingdom, nay, a country, should be enjoyed by one person at once, except he take the pains to travel into every part and endure the inconveniencies of going from one place to another? Wherefore, since glory, delight, and pleasure lives but in other men's opinions, and can neither add tranquility to your mind nor give ease to your body, why should you desire to be empress of a material world and be troubled with the cares that attend government, when as by creating a world within yourself, you may enjoy all both in whole and in parts, without control or opposition; and may make what world you please, and alter it when you please, and enjoy as much pleasure and delight as a world can afford you? You have converted me, said the Duchess to the spirits, from my ambitious desire; wherefore, I'll take your advice, reject and despise all the worlds without me, and create a world of my own. The Empress said, if I do make such a world, then I shall be mistress of two worlds, one within, and the other without me. That your Majesty may, said the spirits; and so left these two ladies to create two worlds within themselves, who did also part from each other until such time as they had brought their worlds to perfection. The Duchess of Newcastle was most earnest and industrious to make her world, because she had none at present; and first she resolved to frame it according to the opinion of Thales,[9] but she found herself so much troubled with daemons, that they would not suffer her to take her own will, but forced her to obey their orders and commands; which she being unwilling to do, left off from making a world that way, and began to frame one according to Pythagoras's[1] doctrine; but in the creation thereof, she was so puzzled with numbers, how to order and compose the several parts, that she having no skill in arithme-

9. Greek philosopher (ca. 620–ca. 545 B.C.E.) who believed that the world originates in and returns to water.
1. Greek philosopher and mathematician (ca. 570–ca. 490 B.C.E.) whose followers believed that reality is fundamentally mathematical in nature.

tic, was forced also to desist from the making of that world. Then she intended to create a world according to the opinion of Plato; but she found more trouble and difficulty in that than in the two former; for the numerous Ideas[2] having no other motion but what was derived from her mind whence they did flow and issue out, made it a far harder business to her to impart motion to them than puppet-players have in giving motion to every several puppet; in so much that her patience was not able to endure the trouble which those Ideas caused her; wherefore she annihilated also that world and was resolved to make one according to the opinion of Epicurus;[3] which she had no sooner begun but the infinite atoms made such a mist that it quite blinded the perception of her mind; neither was she able to make a vacuum as a receptacle for those atoms, or a place which they might retire into; so that partly for the want of it, and of a good order and method, the confusion of those atoms produced such strange and monstrous figures as did more affright then delight her, and caused such a chaos in her mind as had almost dissolved it. At last, having with much ado cleansed and cleared her mind of these dusty and misty particles, she endeavored to create a world according to Aristotle's opinion;[4] but remembering that her mind, as most of the learned hold it, was immaterial, and that, according to Aristotle's principle, out of nothing, nothing could be made, she was forced also to desist from that work, and then she fully resolved not to take any more patterns from the ancient philosophers, but to follow the opinions of the moderns; and to that end, she endeavored to make a world according to Descartes' opinion; but when she had made the ethereal globules and set them a moving by a strong and lively imagination her mind became so dizzy with their extraordinary swift turning round that it almost put her into a swoon;[5] for her thoughts by their constant tottering did so stagger as if they had all been drunk: wherefore she dissolved that world and began to make another according to Hobbes's opinion; but when all the parts of this imaginary world came to press and drive each other they seemed like a company of wolves that worry sheep, or like so many dogs that hunt after hares;[6] and when she found a reaction equal to those pressures her mind was so squeezed together that her thoughts could neither move forward nor backward, which caused such an horrible pain in her head that although she had dissolved that world, yet she could not without much difficulty settle her mind and free it from that pain which those pressures and reactions had caused in it.

At last, when the Duchess saw that no patterns would do her any good in the framing of her world, she was resolved to make a world of her own invention, and this world was composed of sensitive and rational self-moving matter; indeed, it was composed only of the rational, which is the subtlest

---

2. In the philosophy of the Greek philosopher Plato (ca. 427–ca. 347 B.C.E.), transcendent entities in whose reality existing things (their imperfect representations) participate.
3. Greek philosopher (341–270 B.C.E.) who taught that all of matter was made of minute and invisible particles called atoms, and that all occurrences in the natural world resulted from atoms moving and interacting in empty space.
4. In his scientific writings, the Greek philosopher Aristotle (384–322 B.C.E.) argued that objects were made of matter and form. The claim that nothing can come out of nothing actually was made by Parmenides (b. ca. 515 B.C.E.); Aristotle argued against it in *Physics* 1.8.
5. Fainting fit.
6. See Hobbes's *Leviathan* and Cavendish's "The Hunting of the Hare."

and purest degree of matter; for as the sensitive did move and act both to the perceptions and consistency of the body, so this degree of matter at the same point of time (for though the degrees are mixed, yet the several parts may move several ways at one time) did move to the creation of the imaginary world; which world after it was made appeared so curious and full of variety, so well ordered and wisely governed, that it cannot possibly be expressed by words, nor the delight and pleasure which the Duchess took in making this world-of-her-own.

* * *

[HAVING MADE HER OWN WORLD, THE EMPRESS WANTS TO SEE THE WORLD THE DUCHESS CAME FROM]

* * * The Duchess used all the means she could to divert her from that journey, telling her that the world she came from was very much disturbed with factions, divisions, and wars; but the Empress would not be persuaded from her design; and lest the emperor or any of his subjects should know of her travel and obstruct her design, she sent for some of the spirits she had formerly conversed withal, and inquired whether none of them could supply the place of her soul in her body at such a time when she was gone to travel into another world? They answered: Yes, they could; for not only one, said they, but many spirits may enter into your body, if you please. The Empress replied, she desired but one spirit to be viceroy[7] of her body in the absence of her soul, but it must be an honest and ingenious spirit, and if it was possible, a female spirit. The spirits told her that there was no difference of sexes amongst them; but, said they, we will choose an honest and ingenious spirit, and such a one as shall so resemble your soul, that neither the emperor nor any of his subjects, although the most divine, shall know whether it be your own soul or not: which the Empress was very glad at; and after the spirits were gone, asked the Duchess how her body was supplied in the absence of her soul? who answered her Majesty that her body, in the absence of her soul, was governed by her sensitive and rational corporeal motions. Thus those two female souls travelled together as lightly as two thoughts into the Duchess her native world; and, which is remarkable, in a moment viewed all the parts of it, and all the actions of all the creatures therein, especially did the Empress's soul take much notice of the several actions of human creatures in all the several nations and parts of that world, and wondered that for all there were so many several nations, governments, laws, religions, opinions, etc. they should all yet so generally agree in being ambitious, proud, self-conceited, vain, prodigal, deceitful, envious, malicious, unjust, revengeful, irreligious, factious, etc. She did also admire that not any particular state, kingdom, or commonwealth was contented with their own shares but endeavored to encroach upon their neighbors, and that their greatest glory was in plunder and slaughter, and yet their victories less than their expenses, and their losses more than their gains; but their being overcome,

---

7. Governing authority.

Welbeck Abbey. This engraving from William Cavendish's *La méthode nouvelle et Invention extraordinaire de dresser les chevaux* (1658), published in French while the Cavendishes were in exile, features Welbeck Abbey, the Newcastle seat, in the background.

in a manner their utter ruin. But that she wondered most at was that they should prize or value dirt more than men's lives, and vanity more than tranquility[.]

* * *

[AFTER THE EMPRESS AND DUCHESS VISIT THE STUART COURT, THEY VISIT THE DUKE OF NEWCASTLE]

[W]hen the Empress's and Duchess's souls were travelling into Nottinghamshire (for that was the place where the Duke did reside), passing through the forest of Sherwood, the Empress's soul was very much delighted with it, as being a dry, plain, and woody place, very pleasant to travel in both in winter and summer; for it is neither much dirty nor dusty at no time. At last they arrived at Welbeck, a house where the Duke dwelled, surrounded all with wood so close and full that the Empress took great pleasure and delight therein, and told the Duchess she never had observed more wood in so little compass in any part of the kingdom she had passed through.[8] The truth is, said she, there seems to be more wood on the seas

---

8. Welbeck Abbey and Bolsover Castle were Newcastle's primary northern residences. He entertained Charles I at both houses in the 1630s.

(she meaning the ships) than on the land. The Duchess told her the reason was that there had been a long civil war in that kingdom, in which most of the best timber-trees and principal palaces were ruined and destroyed; and my dear lord and husband, said she, has lost by it half his woods besides many houses, land, and movable goods so that all the loss out of his particular estate did amount to above half a million of pounds. I wish, said the Empress, he had some of the gold that is in the Blazing World, to repair his losses. The Duchess most humbly thanked her imperial Majesty for her kind wishes; but, said she, wishes will not repair his ruins[.] * * * [W]hen the Duke was gone into the house again, those two souls followed him; where the Empress observing that he went to the exercise of the sword, and was such an excellent and unparalleled master thereof, she was as much pleased with that exercise as she was with the former:[9] but the Duchess's soul being troubled, that her dear lord and husband used such a violent exercise before meat,[1] for fear of overheating himself, without any consideration of the Empress's soul, left her aerial vehicle and entered into her lord. The Empress's soul perceiving this, did the like: and then the Duke had three souls in one body; and had there been but some such souls more, the Duke would have been like the Grand Signior in his seraglio,[2] only it would have been a Platonic seraglio.

* * *

[THE EMPRESS AND DUCHESS HAVE ONE FINAL DIALOGUE BEFORE RETURNING TO THEIR OWN WORLDS]

[S]ince your Majesty complains much of the factions of the bear-, fish-, fly-, ape-, and worm-men, the satyrs, spider-men, and the like, and of their perpetual disputes and quarrels, I would advise your Majesty to dissolve all their societies; for 'tis better to be without their intelligences than to have an unquiet and disorderly government. The truth is, said she, wheresoever learning is, there is most commonly also controversy and quarrelling; for there be always some that will know more and be wiser than others: some think their arguments come nearer to truth and are more rational then others; some are so wedded to their own opinions that they'll never yield to reason; and others, though they find their opinions not firmly grounded upon reason, yet for fear of receiving some disgrace by altering them, will nevertheless maintain them against all sense and reason, which must needs breed factions in their schools, which at last break out into open wars and draw sometimes an utter ruin upon a state or government. The Empress told the Duchess that she would willingly follow her advice, but she thought it would be an eternal disgrace to her to alter her own decrees, acts, and laws. To which the Duchess answered that it was so far from a disgrace as it would rather be for her Majesty's eternal honor to

---

9. "Former" refers to his management of his houses.
1. Dinner.
2. Turkish harem. "Grand Signior": the Ottoman sultan.

return from a worse to a better, and would express and declare her to be more than ordinary wise and good; so wise as to perceive her own errors, and so good as not to persist in them, which few did: for which, said she, you will get a glorious fame in this world, and an eternal glory hereafter, and I shall pray for it so long as I live. Upon which advice the Empress's soul embraced and kissed the Duchess's soul with an immaterial kiss, and shed immaterial tears that she was forced to part from her, finding her not a flattering parasite,[3] but a true friend; and in truth, such was their Platonic friendship as these two loving souls did often meet and rejoice in each other's conversation.

* * *

The Epilogue to the Reader

By this poetical description you may perceive that my ambition is not only to be empress, but authoress of a whole world; and that the worlds I have made, both the Blazing and the other philosophical world mentioned in the first part of this description, are framed and composed of the most pure, that is, the rational parts of matter, which are the parts of my mind; which creation was more easily and suddenly effected than the conquests of the two famous monarchs of the world, Alexander and Caesar. Neither have I made such disturbances, and caused so many dissolutions of particulars, otherwise named deaths, as they did; for I have destroyed but some few men in a little boat, which died through the extremity of cold, and that by the hand of justice, which was necessitated to punish their crime of stealing away a young and beauteous lady. And in the formation of those worlds, I take more delight and glory than ever Alexander or Caesar did in conquering this terrestrial world; and though I have made my Blazing World a peaceable world, allowing it but one religion, one language, and one government, yet could I make another world as full of factions, divisions and wars, as this is of peace and tranquility; and the rational figures of my mind might express as much courage to fight as Hector and Achilles had; and be as wise as Nestor, as eloquent as Ulysses, and as beautiful as Helen.[4] But I esteeming peace before war, wit before policy, honesty before beauty, instead of the figures of Alexander, Caesar, Hector, Achilles, Nestor, Ulysses, Helen, etc. chose rather the figure of honest Margaret Newcastle, which now I would not change for all this terrestrial world; and if any should like the world I have made, and be willing to be my subjects, they may imagine themselves such, and they are such, I mean in their minds, fancies, or imaginations; but if they cannot endure to be subjects, they may create worlds of their own and govern themselves as they please. But yet let them have a care not to prove unjust usurpers and to rob me of mine: for, concerning the philosophical world, I am empress

---

3. Someone who lives at the expense of another.
4. All figures from the story of the Trojan War.

of it myself; and as for the Blazing World, it having an empress already who rules it with great wisdom and conduct, which empress is my dear Platonic friend, I shall never prove so unjust, treacherous, and unworthy to her as to disturb her government, much less to depose her from her imperial throne, for the sake of any other, but rather choose to create another world for another friend.

1668

JOHN MILTON
1608–1674

As a young man, John Milton proclaimed himself the future author of a great English epic. He promised a poem devoted to the glory of the nation, centering on the deeds of King Arthur or some other ancient hero. When Milton finally published his epic thirty years later, readers found instead a poem about the Fall of Satan and humankind, set in Heaven, Hell, and the Garden of Eden, in which traditional heroism is denigrated and England is not mentioned once. What lay between the youthful promise and the eventual fulfillment was a career marked by private tragedy and public controversy.

In his poems and prose tracts, Milton often alludes to crises in his own life: his choice of a vocation, the early death of friends, painful disappointment in marriage, and the catastrophe of blindness. At the same time, no other major English poet has been so deeply involved in the major intellectual debates and political crises of his times, including the new science, freedom of the press, religious liberty and toleration, and republicanism. It is scarcely possible to treat Milton's career separately from the history of England in his lifetime, not only because he was an active participant in affairs of church and state, but also because when he signed himself, as he often did, "John Milton, Englishman," he was presenting himself as England's prophetic bard. He considered himself the spokesman for the nation as a whole even when he found himself isolated in the minority.

From an early age, Milton fashioned himself self-consciously as an author. He deliberately set out to follow the steps of the ideal poetic career—beginning with pastoral (the mode of several of his early poems) and ending with epic. His models for this progression were Virgil and Spenser: he called the latter "a better teacher than Scotus or Aquinas." (Scotus and Aquinas were influential medieval Christian philosopher-theologians, or "Scholastics.") Milton resembles Spenser in his constant juxtaposition of biblical and classical stories and in his ability to continually transform the ideas, literary forms, and values of his literary and intellectual heritage to make it relevant to himself and to his age.

Milton's family was middle-class, cultured, and staunchly Protestant. His father was a scrivener—a combination of solicitor, investment adviser, and moneylender—as well as an amateur composer with some reputation in musical circles. At age seventeen Milton wrote a funeral elegy for the death of his sister's infant daughter and educated her two sons (the older, Edward, would later write his biography).

Milton had private tutors at home and also attended one of London's finest schools, St. Paul's. At school he began a close friendship with Charles Diodati, with whom he exchanged Latin poems and letters over several years, and for whose death in 1638 he wrote a moving Latin elegy. Milton's excellent early education gave him special facility in languages (Latin, Greek, Hebrew, Aramaic, Italian, and French; later he learned Spanish and Dutch).

In 1625 Milton entered Christ's College, Cambridge. He was briefly suspended during his freshman year over a dispute with his tutor, but graduated in 1629 and was made Master of Arts three years later. As his surviving student orations indicate, he was profoundly disappointed in his university education, reviling the scholastic logic and Latin rhetorical exercises that still formed its core as "futile and barren controversies and wordy disputes" that "stupefy and benumb the mind." Milton expressed contempt for his fellow students: "They thought themselves gallant men, and I thought them fools." They, in turn, dubbed him "the Lady of Christ's College," but whether as compliment or insult is the subject of scholarly debate. He had gone to university with the serious intention of taking orders in the Church of England—the obvious vocation for a young man of his scholarly and religious bent—but became increasingly disenchanted with the lack of reformation in the church under Archbishop William Laud and later proclaimed himself "church-outed by the prelates."

Above all, Milton came to believe more and more strongly that he was destined to serve his language, his country, and his God as a poet. He began by writing occasional poetry in Latin, the usual language for collegiate poets and for poets who sought a European audience. Milton wrote some of the century's best Latin poems, but as early as 1628 he announced to a university audience his determination to glorify England in English poetry. In his first major English poem (written, he claimed, when he was twenty-one), the hymn "On the Morning of Christ's Nativity," Milton portrayed himself as a prophet. This poem is very different from Richard Crashaw's Nativity hymn, with its Spenserian echoes, its allusion to Roman Catholic and Laudian "idolatry", and its stunning shifts from the Creation to Doomsday, from the manger at Bethlehem to the cosmos, and from the shepherd's chatter to the music of the spheres. A few years later, Milton wrote the companion poems "L'Allegro" and "Il Penseroso," achieving a stylistic tour de force by creating from the same meter (octosyllabic couplets) entirely different sound qualities, rhythmic effects, and moods. These poems celebrate, respectively, Mirth and Melancholy, as personifications, defining them by their ancestry, lifestyles, associates, landscapes, activities, music, and literature. In 1634, at the invitation of his musician friend Henry Lawes, he wrote a masque popularly known as "Comus," in which the villain is a refined, seductive, and dissolute Cavalier. "Comus" challenges the royalist politics of previous court masques by locating true virtue and good pleasure in the households of the country magistracy rather than at court.

After university, as part of his preparation for a poetic career, Milton undertook a six-year program of self-directed reading in ancient and modern theology, philosophy, history, science, politics, and literature. He was profoundly grateful to his father for sparing him the grubby business of making money and for financing these years of private study, followed by a fifteen-month "grand tour" of France, Italy, and Switzerland. In 1638 Milton contributed "Lycidas" to a Cambridge volume lamenting the untimely death of a college contemporary. This beautiful pastoral funeral elegy explores Milton's deep anxieties about poetry as a vocation, confronts the terrors of mortality in language of astonishing resonance and power, and incorporates a furious apocalyptic diatribe on the corrupt Church of England clergy. Milton nonetheless maintained relationships across religious and ideological divides; while he was in Italy he exchanged verses and learned compliments with various Catholic intellectuals and men of letters, some of whom became his friends. In 1645 he published his English and Latin poems together in a two-part volume, *Poems of Mr. John Milton.*

Upon his return to England, Milton opened a school and was soon involved in Presbyterian efforts to depose the bishops and to reform church liturgy, writing five "antiprelatical tracts" denouncing and satirizing bishops. These were the first in a series of political interventions Milton produced over the next twenty years, characterized by remarkable courage and fierce independence of thought. He wrote successively on church government, divorce, education, freedom of the press, and, most radically, on regicide and republicanism. From the outbreak of the Civil War in 1642 until his death, Milton allied himself with the Puritan cause, but his religious opinions developed throughout his life, from relative orthodoxy in his youth to ever more heretical positions in his later years. And while his family belonged to the class that benefited most directly from Europe's first bourgeois revolution, his brother fought on the royalist side. The Milton brothers, like most of their contemporaries, did not see these wars as a confrontation of class interests, but as a conflict between radically differing theories of government and, above all, religion.

Some of Milton's treatises were prompted by personal concerns. He interrupted his polemical tract, *The Reason of Church Government Urged Against Prelaty* (1642), to devote several pages to a discussion of his poetic vocation and the great works he hoped to produce in the future. His tracts about divorce, which can hardly have seemed the most pressing of issues in the strife-torn years 1643–45, were motivated by his own unhappy marriage. When he was thirty-three, he had married Mary Powell, aged seventeen; just a few months after the wedding, she left him to return to her royalist family. In response, Milton wrote several tracts vigorously advocating the man's right to divorce on the grounds of incompatibility and with the right to remarry—a position almost unheard of at the time and one that required a boldly antiliteral reading of the bible. At its heart this tract was a defense of companionate marriage, a union not just of bodies but of minds, in which the wife was meant to be "an intimate and speaking help." The fact that these tracts could not be licensed and were roundly denounced in Parliament, from pulpits, and in print prompted him to write *Areopagitica* (1644), an impassioned attack against prepublication censorship, valorizing a "free and open encounter" between truth and falsehood. He saw these personal issues—reformed poetry, domestic liberty achieved through divorce, and a free press—as vital to the creation of a reformed English culture.

In 1649, just after Parliament executed Charles I, Milton published *The Tenure of Kings and Magistrates* (see p. 1328). This treatise defends the revolution and the regicide and develops a "contract theory" of government based on the inalienable and ongoing sovereignty of the people—a version of contract very different from that of Thomas Hobbes, who argued for a one-time and irrevocable contract between king and people that rendered the monarch's powers absolute. Milton was appointed Latin Secretary to the Commonwealth government (1649–53) and to Oliver Cromwell's Protectorate (1654–58), which meant that he wrote the regimes' official letters—mostly in Latin—to foreign governments and heads of state. He also wrote polemical defenses of the new government: *Eikonoklastes* (1649) ("Iconoclast"), to counter the powerful emotional effect of *Eikon Basilike* ("Royal Portrait"), supposedly written by the king just before his death, and two Latin *Defenses* upholding the regicide and the new republic to European audiences.

During these years Milton suffered a series of tragedies. Mary Powell returned to him in 1645 but died in childbirth in 1652, leaving four children; his only son,

John, died a few months later. That same year Milton became totally blind; he claimed that his boyhood habit of reading until midnight had weakened his eyesight and that writing his first *Defense* against the political (and personal) attacks of the Frenchman Claudius Salmasius had destroyed it. Milton married again in 1656, apparently happily, but his new wife, Katherine Woodcock, died two years later, along with their infant daughter. Katherine is probably the subject of his sonnet "Methought I Saw My Late Espoused Saint," a moving dream vision poignant with the sense of loss—both of sight and of love. The few sonnets Milton wrote during the height of the Commonwealth and Protectorate revolutionized the genre. He used the small sonnet form, hitherto confined (in England) mainly to matters of love, for new and grand subjects: praises of Cromwell and other statesmen mixed with admonition and political advice; a prophetic denunciation calling down God's vengeance for Protestants massacred in Piedmont; and an emotional account of his continuing struggle to come to terms with his blindness as part of God's providence.

Cromwell's death in 1658 led to mounting political chaos, and soon the restoration of the Stuart monarchy seemed inevitable. Milton held out against that tide. His several tracts of 1659–60 developed radical arguments for broad toleration, church disestablishment, and republican government. And just as he was among the first to attack the power of the bishops, so he was virtually the last defender of the "Good Old Cause" of the Revolution; the second edition of his *Ready and Easy Way to Establish a Free Commonwealth* appeared in late April 1660, scarcely two weeks before the monarchy was restored. For several months after that event, Milton was in hiding, his life in danger. Friends, especially the poet Andrew Marvell, managed to secure his pardon and later his release from a brief imprisonment. He lived out his last years in reduced circumstances, plagued by ever more serious attacks of gout but grateful for the domestic comforts provided by his third wife, Elizabeth Minshull, thirty years his junior, whom he had married in 1663 and who survived him.

In such conditions, dismayed by the defeat of his political and religious cause, totally blind and often ill, threatened by the plague of 1665 and the great fire of 1666, and entirely dependent on amanuenses and friends to transcribe his dictation, Milton completed his great epic poem. *Paradise Lost* (1667/74) radically reconceives the epic genre and epic heroism, choosing as protagonists a domestic couple rather than martial heroes and degrading the military glory celebrated in epic tradition in favor of "the better fortitude / Of patience and heroic martyrdom." It offers a sweeping imaginative vision of Hell, Chaos, and Heaven; the creation of the world out of "one first matter all"; the sex lives of angels; prelapsarian life in Eden; the power of the devil's political rhetoric; the psychology of Satan, Adam, and Eve; and the high drama of the Fall and its aftermath.

In his final years, Milton published works on grammar and logic chiefly written during his days as a schoolmaster, a history of Britain (1670) from the earliest times to the Norman Conquest, and a treatise urging toleration for Puritan dissenters (1673). He also continued work on his *Christian Doctrine*, a Latin treatise that reveals how far he had moved from the orthodoxies of his day. The work denies the Trinity (making the Son and the Holy Spirit much inferior to God the Father), insists upon free will against Calvinist predestination, and privileges the inspiration of the Spirit even above the Scriptures and the Ten Commandments. Such heterodox positions could not be made public in Milton's lifetime, and *Christian Doctrine* was lost to view for over 150 years.

In 1671 Milton published two poems that reflect the harsh repression all Puritan dissenters faced after the Restoration. *Paradise Regained*, a brief epic in four books, treats Jesus's temptation in the wilderness as an intellectual struggle through which the hero comes to understand both himself and his mission. He defeats Satan by renouncing the whole panoply of faulty versions of the good life and of God's kingdom. *Samson Agonistes,* a classical tragedy, is the more harrowing for the resemblances between its tragic hero and its author. The deeply flawed, pain-wracked, blind, and defeated Samson struggles, in dialogues with his visitors, to gain self-knowledge, discovering at last a desperate way to triumph over his captors and offer his people a chance to regain their freedom. In these last poems Milton sought to educate his readers in moral and political wisdom and virtue. Only through such inner transformation, Milton now firmly believed, would people come to value—and so perhaps reclaim—the intellectual, religious, and political freedom he so vigorously promoted in his work.

From Poems

On the Morning of Christ's Nativity[1]

1

This is the month, and this the happy morn
Wherein the son of Heaven's eternal King,
Of wedded maid and virgin mother born,
Our great redemption from above did bring;
5   For so the holy sages once did sing,
   That he our deadly forfeit[2] should release,
And with his Father work us a perpetual peace.

2

That glorious form, that light unsufferable,°   *unable to be endured*
And that far-beaming blaze of majesty
10   Wherewith he wont° at Heaven's high council-table   *was accustomed*
To sit the midst of Trinal Unity,[3]
He laid aside; and here with us to be,
   Forsook the courts of everlasting day,
And chose with us a darksome house of mortal clay.

---

1. This ode was written on Christmas 1629, a few weeks after Milton's twenty-first birthday. He placed it first in the 1645 edition of his poems, claiming in it his vocation as inspired poet. The poem often looks back to Spenser: the first four stanzas are an adaptation of the Spenserian stanza; there are several Spenserian archaisms (y- prefixes) and some Spenser-like onamatopoeia (lines 156, 172).
2. The sentence of death consequent on the Fall. "Holy sages": for example, the prophet Isaiah (chaps. 9 and 40) and Job (chap. 19) were thought to have foretold Christ as Messiah.
3. The Trinity: Father, Son (incarnate in Christ), and Holy Ghost.

3

<small>15</small> Say, heavenly Muse, shall not thy sacred vein
Afford a present to the infant God?
Hast thou no verse, no hymn, or solemn strain,
To welcome him to this his new abode,
Now while the heaven by the sun's team untrod[4]
<small>20</small>   Hath took no print of the approaching light,
And all the spangled host° keep watch in squadrons bright?   *angels*

4

See how from far upon the eastern road
The star-led wizards[5] haste with odors sweet:
O run, prevent° them with thy humble ode,   *anticipate*
<small>25</small> And lay it lowly at his blessèd feet;
Have thou the honor first thy Lord to greet,
    And join thy voice unto the angel choir,
From out His secret altar touched with hallowed fire.[6]

The Hymn

1

It was the winter wild
<small>30</small> While the Heaven-born child
    All meanly wrapped in the rude manger lies;
Nature in awe to him
Had doffed her gaudy trim[7]
    With her great Master so to sympathize;
<small>35</small> It was no season then for her
To wanton with the sun, her lusty paramour.

2

Only with speeches fair
She woos the gentle air
    To hide her guilty front° with innocent snow,   *brow*
<small>40</small> And on her naked shame,
Pollute with sinful blame,
    The saintly veil of maiden white to throw,[8]
Confounded that her Maker's eyes
Should look so near upon her foul deformities.

---

4. In classical myth, the sun (Phoebus Apollo) drove across heaven in a chariot drawn by horses.
5. The Magi who followed the star of Bethlehem to find and adore the infant Christ.
6. Isaiah's lips were touched by a burning coal from the altar, purifying him and confirming him as a prophet (Isaiah 6:7).
7. Put off her garments of leaves and flowers.
8. Nature fell also with the Fall, so she is a harlot (line 36), not a pure maiden, despite her white garment of snow.

3

45 But he her fears to cease
Sent down the meek-eyed Peace;
    She, crowned with olive green, came softly sliding
Down through the turning sphere,[9]
His ready harbinger,°   *forerunner*
50   With turtle[1] wing the amorous clouds dividing,
And waving wide her myrtle wand,
She strikes a universal peace through sea and land.

4

No war or battle's sound
Was heard the world around;[2]
55   The idle spear and shield were high up-hung;
The hookèd chariot[3] stood
Unstained with hostile blood,
    The trumpet spake not to the armèd throng,
And kings sat still with awful° eye,   *filled with awe*
60 As if they surely knew their sovereign Lord was by.

5

But peaceful was the night
Wherein the Prince of Light
    His reign of peace upon the earth began:
The winds, with wonder whist,°   *hushed*
65 Smoothly the waters kissed,
    Whispering new joys to the mild oceàn,
Who now hath quite forgot to rave,
While birds of calm[4] sit brooding on the charmèd wave.

6

The stars with deep amaze
70 Stand fixed in steadfast gaze,
    Bending one way their precious influence,
And will not take their flight
For all the morning light,
    Or Lucifer[5] that often warned them thence;
75 But in their glimmering orbs did glow
Until their Lord himself bespake,° and bid them go.   *spoke out*

---

9. The Ptolemaic spheres, revolving around the earth.
1. Like a turtledove, which, like the myrtle (next line), is an emblem of Venus (Love), as the olive crown is of peace.
2. Around the time of Christ's birth, the "Peace of Augustus" held, during which no major wars disturbed the Roman Empire; that peace was sometimes attributed to Christ.
3. War chariots were built with scythelike hooks on the axles, to wound and kill.
4. Kingfishers (halcyons) were thought to calm the seas during the time they nested on its waves.
5. Not Satan but the morning star, Venus.

7

    And though the shady gloom
    Had given day her room,
        The sun himself withheld his wonted speed,
80   And hid his head for shame
    As° his inferior flame   *as if*
        The new-enlightened world no more should need;
    He saw a greater Sun[6] appear
    Than his bright throne or burning axletree° could bear.   *chariot axle*

8

85   The shepherds on the lawn
    Or ere the point of° dawn   *just before*
        Sat simply chatting in a rustic row;
    Full little thought they than°   *then*
    That the mighty Pan[7]
90   Was kindly[8] come to live with them below;
    Perhaps their loves or else their sheep
    Was all that did their silly° thoughts so busy keep.   *simple, humble*

9

    When such music sweet
    Their hearts and ears did greet
95   As never was by mortal finger struck,
    Divinely warbled voice
    Answering the stringèd noise,
        As all their souls in blissful rapture took;
    The air, such pleasure loath to lose,
100   With thousand echoes still prolongs each heavenly close.°   *cadence*

10

    Nature that heard such sound
    Beneath the hollow round
        Of Cynthia's seat,[9] the airy region thrilling,°   *piercing, delighting*
    Now was almost won
105   To think her part was done,
        And that her reign had here its last fulfilling;
    She knew such harmony alone
    Could hold all heaven and earth in happier uniòn.

11

    At last surrounds their sight
110   A globe of circular light

---

6. The familiar Son/sun pun.
7. Pan, patron of shepherds, is a merry, goat-footed god, but he was often conceived in more exalted terms and identified with Christ, because his name in Greek means "all."
8. By nature; also, benevolently.

9. Cynthia is the moon. Nature rules below the moon (the region of the four elements and subject to decay). The unchanging, perfect region above the moon is normally the only place one could hear either angels' hymnody or the music of the spheres.

That with long beams the shamefaced night arrayed;°   *adorned with rays*
The helmèd cherubim
And sworded seraphim[1]
Are seen in glittering ranks with wings displayed,
115   Harping in loud and solemn choir
With unexpressive° notes to Heaven's newborn heir.   *inexpressible*

12

Such music (as 'tis said)
Before was never made,
  But when of old the sons of morning sung,[2]
120   While the Creator great
His constellations set,
  And the well-balanced world on hinges° hung,   *the two poles*
And cast the dark foundations deep,
And bid the welt'ring waves their oozy channel keep.

13

125   Ring out, ye crystal spheres,
Once bless our human ears
  (If ye have power to touch our senses so),
And let your silver chime
Move in melodious time,
130   And let the bass of Heaven's deep organ blow;
And with your ninefold harmony[3]
Make up full consort to th' angelic symphony.

14

For if such holy song
Enwrap our fancy long,
135   Time will run back and fetch the age of gold;[4]
And speckled vanity
Will sicken soon and die,
  And leprous sin will melt from earthly mold,
And Hell itself will pass away,
140   And leave her dolorous mansions to the peering day.

15

Yea, Truth and Justice then
Will down return to men,
  Th' enameled arras° of the rainbow wearing,   *brightly colored fabric*

---

1. Seraphim and cherubim are the highest of the traditional nine orders of angels; they are often portrayed in martial attire.
2. Job 38:4–7: "Where wast thou when I laid the foundations of the earth? . . . / When the morning stars sang together and all the sons of God shouted for joy?"
3. In Pythagorean theory, each of the nine moving spheres sounds a distinctive note (the tenth, the primum mobile, does not move). It was supposed that, after the Fall, this harmonious music of the spheres could not be heard on earth. Earth would be the "bass" of the cosmic organ, sounding under that planetary harmony.
4. The first age, of human innocence, classical mythology's equivalent to the Garden of Eden.

   And Mercy set between,[5]
145 Throned in celestial sheen,
    With radiant feet the tissued[6] clouds down steering;
   And Heaven, as at some festival,
   Will open wide the gates of her high palace hall.

16

   But wisest Fate says no,
150 This must not yet be so;
    The Babe lies yet in smiling infancy[7]
   That on the bitter cross
   Must redeem our loss,
    So both himself and us to glorify;
155 Yet first to those ychained[8] in sleep
   The wakeful trump of doom must thunder through the deep,

17

   With such a horrid clang
   As on Mount Sinai rang
    While the red fire and smoldering clouds outbrake;
160 The agèd earth, aghast
   With terror of that blast,
    Shall from the surface to the center shake,
   When at the world's last sessiòn,
   The dreadful Judge in middle air shall spread His throne.[9]

18

155 And then at last our bliss
   Full and perfect is,
    But now begins; for from this happy day
   Th' old dragon under ground,[1]
   In straiter limits bound,
170 Not half so far casts his usurpèd sway,
   And wroth to see his kingdom fail,
   Swinges° the scaly horror of his folded tail.   *lashes*

19

   The oracles are dumb;[2]
   No voice or hideous hum
175 Runs through the archèd roof in words deceiving.

---

5. This allegorical scene, suggesting a masque descent, alludes to Psalm 85:10, part of the liturgy for Christmas: "Mercy and truth are met together; righteousness and peace have kissed each other." Peace, in the poem, has already descended (lines 45–52). The lines also evoke the flight of Astraea, the classical goddess of justice, at the end of the Golden Age, and her return with its restoration, celebrated by Virgil in his fourth eclogue, applied by him to the birth of Pollio but by Christians to Christ.
6. Cloth woven with silver and gold.
7. The Latin word, *infans*, means, literally, "non-speaking."
8. One of Spenser's archaic *y-* prefixes.
9. Moses received the Ten Commandments amid thunder and lightning atop Mount Sinai (Exodus 19); the Last Judgment will take place amid similar uproar. "Session": court proceeding.
1. The devil (Revelation 20:2).
2. An ancient tradition held that pagan oracles ceased with the coming of Christ; another identified the pagan gods with the fallen angels.

      Apollo from his shrine
      Can no more divine,
          With hollow shriek the steep of Delphos leaving.[3]
      No nightly trance or breathèd spell
180 Inspires the pale-eyed priest from the prophetic cell.

20

      The lonely mountains o'er
      And the resounding shore
          A voice of weeping heard and loud lament;
      From haunted spring and dale
185 Edged with the poplar pale,
          The parting genius[4] is with sighing sent;
      With flower-in-woven tresses torn
      The nymphs in twilight shade of tangled thickets mourn.

21

      In consecrated earth
190 And on the holy hearth,
          The lars and lemures[5] moan with midnight plaint;
      In urns and altars round
      A drear and dying sound
          Affrights the flamens[6] at their service quaint;
195 And the chill marble seems to sweat,
      While each peculiar power forgoes his wonted seat.

22

      Peor and Baalim[7]
      Forsake their temples dim,
          With that twice-battered god of Palestine,[8]
200 And moonèd Ashtaroth,[9]
      Heaven's queen and mother both,
          Now sits not girt with tapers' holy shine;
      The Libyc Hammon[1] shrinks° his horn;   *draws in*
      In vain the Tyrian maids their wounded Thammuz mourn.[2]

23

205 And sullen Moloch,[3] fled,
      Hath left in shadows dread
          His burning idol all of blackest hue;

---

3. Apollo's main shrine was at Delphi, on the slopes of Mount Parnassus.
4. A local deity guarding a particular place.
5. Spirits of the dead. "Lars": household gods.
6. Roman priests.
7. Other manifestations of Baal, a Canaanite sun god.
8. Dagon, the Philistine god whose image at Ashdod was twice thrown down when the Ark of the Covenant was placed beside it (1 Samuel 5:2–4).
9. Ashtaroth, also known as Astarte, was a Phoenician fertility goddess identified with the moon.
1. Hammon, also Ammon, an Egyptian and Libyan god, depicted as a ram.
2. Thammuz, lover of Ashtaroth, was killed by a boar and lamented by the Phoenician women; he was taken into the Greek pantheon as Adonis.
3. Moloch was a Phoenician fire god, a brazen idol with a human body and a calf's, head; the statue ("his burning idol," line 207) was heated flaming hot and children were thrown into its embrace, with cymbals drowning out their cries (2 Kings 22:10).

                    In vain with cymbals' ring
                    They call the grisly king
210   In dismal dance about the furnace blue;
                    The brutish gods of Nile as fast,⁴
                    Isis and Orus and the dog Anubis haste.

                                    24

                    Nor is Osiris seen
                    In Memphian grove or green,
215   Trampling the unshowered° grass with lowings loud,   *rainless*
                    Nor can he be at rest
                    Within his sacred chest;
                       Naught but profoundest Hell can be his shroud.
                    In vain with timbrelled anthems dark
220   The sable-stolèd sorcerers bear his worshipped ark.⁵

                                    25

                    He feels from Judah's land
                    The dreaded Infant's hand,
                       The rays of Bethlehem blind his dusky eyne;°   *eyes*
                    Nor all the gods beside
225   Longer dare abide,
                       Not Typhon huge, ending in snaky twine;
                    Our Babe, to show his godhead true,
                    Can in his swaddling bands control the damnèd crew.⁶

                                    26

                    So when the sun in bed,
230   Curtained with cloudy red,
                       Pillows his chin upon an orient° wave,   *eastern, bright*
                    The flocking shadows pale
                    Troop to th' infernal jail;
                       Each fettered ghost slips to his several° grave;   *separate*
235   And the yellow-skirted fays
                    Fly after the night-steeds, leaving their moon-loved maze.⁷

                                    27

                    But see! the Virgin blessed
                    Hath laid her Babe to rest.
                       Time is our tedious song should here have ending.
240   Heaven's youngest-teemèd° star   *latest born*
                    Hath fixed her polished car,°   *gleaming chariot*

---

4. Egyptian gods had some features of animals: Isis (next line) was represented with cow's horns, Orus, or Horus, with a hawk's head; Osiris (lines 213–15) sometimes had the shape of a bull.
5. Osiris's image was carried from temple to temple in a wooden chest, and his priests accompanied it with tambourines ("timbrels").
6. Typhon was a hundred-headed monster who was a serpent below the waist, a figure for the devil. The infant Christ controlling him calls up (as a foreshadowing) the story of the infant Hercules strangling two giant serpents in his cradle.
7. Fairy rings. "Night-steeds": horses drawing Night's chariot.

Her sleeping Lord with handmaid lamp attending:
And all about the courtly stable
Bright-harnessed° angels sit in order serviceàble.   *bright-armored*

1629   1645

On Shakespeare[1]

What needs my Shakespeare for his honored bones
The labor of an age in pilèd stones,
Or that his hallowed relics should be hid
Under a star-ypointing[2] pyramid?
5   Dear son of memory,[3] great heir of fame,
What° need'st thou such weak witness of thy name?   *why*
Thou in our wonder and astonishment
Hast built thyself a livelong° monument.   *enduring*
For whilst to th' shame of slow-endeavoring art
10   Thy easy numbers° flow, and that each heart   *verses*
Hath from the leaves of thy unvalued° book   *invaluable*
Those Delphic[4] lines with deep impression took,
Then thou, our fancy of itself bereaving,
Dost make us marble with too much conceiving;[5]
15   And so sepùlchered in such pomp dost lie,
That kings for such a tomb would wish to die.

1630   1632

L'Allegro[1]

Hence loathèd Melancholy,[2]
    Of Cerberus[3] and blackest midnight born,
In Stygian[4] cave forlorn
    'Mongst horrid shapes, and shrieks, and sights unholy,
5   Find out some uncouth° cell,   *desolate*
    Where brooding Darkness spreads his jealous wings,

---

1. This tribute, Milton's first published poem, appeared in the Second Folio of Shakespeare's plays (1632).
2. A Spenserian archaism.
3. As "son of memory" Shakespeare is a brother of the Muses, who are the daughters of Mnemosyne (Memory).
4. Apollo, god of poetry, had his oracle at Delphi.
5. Shakespeare's mesmerized readers are themselves his ("marble") monument.
1. The companion poems "L'Allegro" and "Il Penseroso" are both written in tetrameter couplets, except for the first ten lines, but Milton's virtuosity produces entirely different tempos and sound qualities in the two poems. The Italian titles name, respectively, the cheerful, mirthful man and the melancholy, contemplative man. The poems are carefully balanced and their different values celebrated, though "Il Penseroso's" greater length and final coda may intimate that life's superiority. Mirth, the presiding deity of "L'Allegro," is described in terms that evoke Botticelli's presentation of the Grace Euphrosyne (youthful mirth) and her sisters in his *Primavera*.
2. The black melancholy recognized and here exorcized by Mirth's man is a disease leading to madness. "Il Penseroso" celebrates "white" melancholy as the temperament of the scholarly, contemplative man, represented in Dürer's famous engraving *Melancholy*.
3. The three-headed hellhound of classical mythology.
4. Near the river Styx, in the underworld.

   And the night raven sings;
    There under ebon shades and low-browed rocks,
   As ragged as thy locks,
10 In dark Cimmerian[5] desert ever dwell.
   But come thou goddess fair and free,
   In heaven yclept Euphrosyne,[6]
   And by men, heart-easing Mirth,
   Whom lovely Venus at a birth
15 With two sister Graces more
   To ivy-crownèd Bacchus bore;
   Or whether (as some sager sing)
   The frolic wind that breathes the spring,
   Zephyr with Aurora playing,
20 As he met her once a-Maying,
   There on beds of violets blue,
   And fresh-blown° roses washed in dew,   *newly opened*
   Filled her with thee a daughter fair,
   So buxom,° blithe, and debonair.   *lively*
25 Haste thee nymph, and bring with thee
   Jest and youthful Jollity,
   Quips° and Cranks,° and wanton Wiles,   *witty sayings / jokes*
   Nods, and Becks,° and wreathèd Smiles,   *beckonings*
   Such as hang on Hebe's[7] cheek,
30 And love to live in dimple sleek;
   Sport that wrinkled Care derides,
   And Laughter holding both his sides.
   Come, and trip it° as ye go   *dance*
   On the light fantastic toe,
35 And in thy right hand lead with thee
   The mountain nymph, sweet Liberty;
   And if I give thee honor due,
   Mirth, admit me of thy crew
   To live with her and live with thee,
40 In unreprovèd° pleasures free;   *irreproachable*
   To hear the lark begin his flight,
   And, singing, startle the dull night,
   From his watch tower in the skies,
   Till the dappled dawn doth rise;
45 Then to come in spite of° sorrow,   *in defiance of*
   And at my window bid good morrow,
   Through the sweetbriar or the vine,
   Or the twisted eglantine.
   While the cock with lively din
50 Scatters the rear of darkness thin,
   And to the stack or the barn door,

---

5. Homer's Cimmereans (*Odyssey* 11.13–19) live on the outer edge of the world, in perpetual darkness.

6. The three Graces—Euphrosyne (four syllables) figuring Youthful Mirth; Aglaia, Brilliance; and Thalia, Bloom—were commonly taken to be offspring of Venus (Love and Beauty) and Bacchus (god of wine). Milton proceeds, however, to devise another, more innocent parentage for Euphrosyne (ascribing it to "some sager," lines 17–24): Zephyr, the West Wind, and Aurora, goddess of the Dawn.

7. Goddess of youth and cupbearer to the gods.

Stoutly struts his dames before;
Oft listening how the hounds and horn
Cheerly rouse the slumbering morn,
From the side of some hoar° hill,   *ancient*
Through the high wood echoing shrill.
Sometime walking not unseen
By hedgerow elms, on hillocks green,
Right against the eastern gate,
Where the great sun begins his state,[8]
Robed in flames and amber light,
The clouds in thousand liveries dight;°   *dressed*
While the plowman near at hand
Whistles o'er the furrowed land,
And the milkmaid singeth blithe,
And the mower whets his scythe,
And every shepherd tells his tale
Under the hawthorn in the dale.
Straight° mine eye hath caught new pleasures   *immediately*
Whilst the landscape round it measures,
Russet lawns and fallows° gray,   *plowed land*
Where the nibbling flocks do stray,
Mountains on whose barren breast
The laboring clouds do often rest;
Meadows trim with daisies pied,°   *multicolored*
Shallow brooks, and rivers wide.
Towers and battlements it sees
Bosomed high in tufted trees,
Where perhaps some beauty lies,
The cynosure[9] of neighboring eyes.
Hard by, a cottage chimney smokes
From betwixt two agèd oaks,
Where Corydon and Thyrsis met
Are at their savory dinner set
Of herbs and other country messes,
Which the neat-handed° Phyllis dresses;   *dexterous*
And then in haste her bower she leaves,
With Thestylis[1] to bind the sheaves;
Or if the earlier season lead
To the tanned° haycock in the mead.   *sun-dried*
Sometimes with secure° delight   *careless*
The upland hamlets will invite,
When the merry bells ring round
And the jocund rebecks[2] sound
To many a youth and many a maid,
Dancing in the checkered shade;
And young and old come forth to play
On a sunshine holiday,

---

8. Stately procession, as by a monarch.
9. Literally, the bright polestar, or North Star, by which mariners steer; here, a splendid object, much gazed at.
1. Milton uses traditional names from classical pastoral—Corydon, Thyrsis, Phyllis, Thestylis—for his rustic English shepherds.
2. A small three-stringed fiddle. "Jocund": merry, sprightly.

Till the livelong daylight fail;
100 Then to the spicy nut-brown ale,
With stories told of many a feat,
How fairy Mab the junkets[3] eat;
She was pinched and pulled, she said,
And he, by friar's lantern led,
105 Tells how the drudging goblin[4] sweat
To earn his cream bowl duly set,
When in one night, ere glimpse of morn,
His shadowy flail hath threshed the corn
That ten day laborers could not end;
110 Then lies him down the lubber fiend,[5]
And stretched out all the chimney's° length,   *fireplace's*
Basks at the fire his hairy strength;
And crop-full° out of doors he flings   *satiated*
Ere the first cock his matin rings.
115 Thus done the tales, to bed they creep,
By whispering winds soon lulled asleep.
Towered cities please us then,
And the busy hum of men,
Where throngs of knights and barons bold
120 In weeds of peace high triumphs[6] hold,
With store of ladies, whose bright eyes
Rain influence,[7] and judge the prize
Of wit or arms, while both contend
To win her grace, whom all commend.
125 There let Hymen[8] oft appear
In saffron robe, with taper clear,
And pomp and feast and revelry,
With masque and antique° pageantry;   *ancient, also antic*
Such sights as youthful poets dream
130 On summer eves by haunted stream.
Then to the well-trod stage anon,
If Jonson's learned sock be on,
Or sweetest Shakespeare, fancy's child,
Warble his native woodnotes wild.[9]
135 And ever against eating cares;[1]
Lap me in soft Lydian airs,[2]
Married to immortal verse
Such as the meeting soul may pierce
In notes with many a winding bout°   *circuit*

3. Sweetmeats, especially with cream. Queen Mab is the fairy queen, consort of Oberon. "She" and "he" in the next two lines are country folk telling of their experiences with fairies.
4. Robin Goodfellow, alias Puck, Pook, or Hobgoblin. "Friar's lantern": will-o'-the-wisp.
5. Puck, here identified with the folktale goblin, Lob-lie-by-the-fire. Robin traditionally did all manner of drudging work for people, to be rewarded with a bowl of cream.
6. Pageants. "Weeds of peace": courtly raiment.
7. The ladies' eyes are stars and so have astrological influence over the men.
8. Roman god of marriage. An orange-yellow ("saffron") robe and a torch are his attributes.
9. It was conventional to contrast Jonson as a "learned" poet and Shakespeare as a "natural" one, but L'Allegro's views and choices of literature also suits with his nature. "Sock": the comedian's low-heeled slipper, contrasted with the tragedian's buskin, a high-heeled boot.
1. "Eating cares" (Horace, *Odes* 2.11.18) is one of many classical echoes in the poem.
2. Plato considered "Lydian airs" to be enervating, soft, and sensual; he preferred the solemn Doric mode. Some others thought Lydian airs relaxing and delightful.

140 Of linkèd sweetness long drawn out,
    With wanton heed and giddy cunning,
    The melting voice through mazes running,
    Untwisting all the chains that tie
    The hidden soul of harmony;
145 That Orpheus' self may heave his head
    From golden slumber on a bed
    Of heaped Elysian flowers, and hear
    Such strains as would have won the ear
    Of Pluto, to have quite set free
150 His half-regained Eurydice.[3]
    These delights if thou canst give,
    Mirth, with thee I mean to live.[4]

ca. 1631   1645

Il Penseroso[1]

　　Hence vain deluding joys,[2]
　　　The brood of Folly without father bred,
　　How little you bestead,°   *avail*
　　　Or fill the fixèd mind with all your toys°   *trifles*
5 　　Dwell in some idle brain,
　　　And fancies fond° with gaudy shapes possess,   *foolish*
　　As thick and numberless
　　　As the gay motes that people the sunbeams,
　　Or likest hovering dreams,
10 　The fickle pensioners of Morpheus'[3] train.
　　But hail thou Goddess sage and holy,
　　Hail, divinest Melancholy,
　　Whose saintly visage is too bright
　　To hit° the sense of human sight,   *suit*
15 　And therefore to our weaker view
　　O'erlaid with black, staid wisdom's hue;[4]
　　Black, but such as in esteem,
　　Prince Memnon's sister[5] might beseem,
　　Or that starred Ethiope queen[6] that strove
20 　To set her beauty's praise above

---

3. Orpheus's music so moved Pluto that he agreed to release Orpheus's dead wife Eurydice (four syllables, accent on the second) from the underworld (Elysium), but he violated the condition set—that he not look back at her—and so lost her again. Milton often uses Orpheus as a figure for the poet.
4. The final lines echo Marlowe's "The Passionate Shepherd to His Love" (p. 495): "If these delights thy mind may move, / Then live with me and be my love."
1. Il Penseroso whose name is Italian for "the thoughtful one," celebrates a melancholy that does not produce madness but the scholarly temperament, ruled by Saturn. For "L'Allegro" see 2nd n. 2 on p. 1393.
2. In "Il Penseroso," Mirth is not the innocent joys of "L'Allegro," but "vain deluding joys."
3. Morpheus is the god of sleep. "Pensioners": followers.
4. The melancholy humor, caused by black bile, was thought to make the face dark or saturnine—from the ancient god Saturn, allegorized in Neoplatonic philosophy as "the collective angelic mind."
5. Memnon, in *Odyssey* 11, was a handsome Ethiopian prince; his sister Himera's beauty was mentioned by later commentators. See Song of Solomon 1:5, "I am black but comely."
6. Cassiopeia was turned into a constellation ("starred") for bragging that she was more beautiful than the sea nymphs.

    The sea nymphs, and their powers offended.
    Yet thou art higher far descended;
    Thee bright-haired Vesta long of yore
    To solitary Saturn bore;[7]
25 His daughter she (in Saturn's reign
    Such mixture was not held a stain).
    Oft in glimmering bowers and glades
    He met her, and in secret shades
    Of woody Ida's inmost grove,
30 While yet there was no fear of Jove.
    Come pensive nun, devout and pure,
    Sober, steadfast, and demure,
    All in a robe of darkest grain,°   *color*
    Flowing with majestic train,
35 And sable stole[8] of cypress lawn
    Over thy decent° shoulders drawn.   *comely, modestly covered*
    Come, but keep thy wonted° state,°   *usual / dignity*
    With even step and musing gait,
    And looks commercing with the skies,
40 Thy rapt soul sitting in thine eyes:
    There held in holy passion still,
    Forget thyself to marble,[9] till
    With a sad° leaden downward cast° *grave, dignified / glance*
    Thou fix them on the earth as fast.
45 And join with thee calm Peace and Quiet,
    Spare Fast, that oft with gods doth diet,
    And hears the Muses in a ring
    Aye° round about Jove's altar sing.   *continually*
    And add to these retired Leisure,
50 That in trim gardens takes his pleasure;
    But first, and chiefest, with thee bring
    Him that yon soars on golden wing,
    Guiding the fiery-wheelèd throne,
    The cherub Contemplatiòn;[1]
55 And the mute Silence hist° along,   *summon*
    'Less Philomel[2] will deign a song,
    In her sweetest, saddest plight,°   *mood*
    Smoothing the rugged brow of night,
    While Cynthia[3] checks her dragon yoke
60 Gently o'er th' accustomed oak;
    Sweet bird that shunn'st the noise of folly,
    Most musical, most melancholy!

---

7. Vesta, daughter of Saturn, was goddess of the household and a virgin, as were her priestesses. Milton invented the story of her sexual congress with Saturn on Mount Ida, resulting in Melancholy's birth. Saturn ruled the gods and the world during the Golden Age, which ended when he was murdered by his son Jove.
8. A delicate black cloth.
9. Still as a statue.
1. The special function of cherubim is contemplation of God; Milton alludes also (line 53) to their identification with the wheels of the mystical chariot/throne of God described by Ezekiel (Ezekiel 10).
2. The nightingale (the bird into which Philomela was transformed after her rape by her brother-in-law Tereus) traditionally sings a mournful song. "'Less": unless.
3. Goddess of the moon, also associated with Hecate, goddess of the underworld, who drives a pair of sleepless dragons.

Thee chantress oft the woods among
I woo to hear thy evensong;[4]
And missing thee, I walk unseen
On the dry smooth-shaven green,
To behold the wandering moon,
Riding near her highest noon,
Like one that had been led astray
Through the heaven's wide pathless way;
And oft as if her head she bowed,
Stooping through a fleecy cloud.
Oft on a plat° of rising ground,   *plot, open field*
I hear the far-off curfew sound
Over some wide-watered shore,
Swinging slow with sullen° roar;   *deep, mournful*
Or if the air will not permit,
Some still removèd place will fit,
Where glowing embers through the room
Teach light to counterfeit a gloom,
Far from all resort of mirth,
Save the cricket on the hearth,
Or the bellman's[5] drowsy charm,
To bless the doors from nightly harm;
Or let my lamp at midnight hour
Be seen in some high lonely tower,
Where I may oft outwatch the Bear,[6]
With thrice-great Hermes, or unsphere
The spirit of Plato[7] to unfold
What words or what vast regions hold
The immortal mind that hath forsook
Her mansion in this fleshly nook;
And of those demons[8] that are found
In fire, air, flood, or underground,
Whose power hath a true consent°   *agreement*
With planet, or with element.
Sometime let gorgeous Tragedy
In sceptered pall[9] come sweeping by,
Presenting Thebes, or Pelops' line,
Or the tale of Troy divine,[1]
Or what (though rare) of later age
Ennobled hath the buskined[2] stage.
But, O sad virgin, that thy power

---

4. The evening liturgy traditionally sung by cloistered monks and nuns ("chantress" evokes such a singer); "L'Allegro's" cock, by contrast, calls hearers to the morning liturgy, "matins" (line 114).
5. Night watchman who rang a bell to mark the hours.
6. The Great Bear constellation never sets in northern skies.
7. Various esoteric books (actually written in the 3rd and 4th centuries) were attributed to an ancient Egyptian, Hermes Trismegistus ("thrice great"). Neoplatonists made him the father of all knowledge; later he became a patron of magicians and alchemists. To "unsphere" Plato is to bring him magically back to earth from whatever sphere he now inhabits—in practical terms, by reading his books.
8. Demons (daemons), halfway between gods and men, preside over the four elements.
9. Royal robe, worn by tragic actors.
1. Tragedies about Thebes include Sophocles' *Oedipus* cycle, those about the line of Pelops, Aeschylus's *Oresteia*, and those about Troy, Euripedes' *Trojan Women*.
2. The buskin (high boot) of tragedy, contrasted with the "sock" of comedy ("L'Allegro," line 132).

  Might raise Musaeus[3] from his bower,
105 Or bid the soul of Orpheus[4] sing
  Such notes as, warbled to the string,
  Drew iron tears down Pluto's cheek,
  And made Hell grant what love did seek.
  Or call up him[5] that left half told
110 The story of Cambuscan bold,
  Of Camball and of Algarsife,
  And who had Canacee to wife,
  That owned the virtuous° ring and glass, *having magical*
  And of the wondrous horse of brass, *powers*
115 On which the Tartar king did ride;
  And if aught° else great bards beside *anything*
  In sage and solemn tunes have sung,
  Of tourneys and of trophies hung,
  Of forests and enchantments drear,
120 Where more is meant than meets the ear.[6]
  Thus, Night, oft see me in thy pale career,
  Till civil-suited Morn appear,
  Not tricked and frounced as she was wont
  With the Attic boy to hunt,[7]
125 But kerchiefed in a comely cloud,
  While rocking winds are piping loud,
  Or ushered with a shower still,° *gentle*
  When the gust hath blown his fill,
  Ending on the rustling leaves,
130 With minute drops from off the eaves.
  And when the sun begins to fling
  His flaring beams, me, Goddess, bring
  To archèd walks of twilight groves,
  And shadows brown that Sylvan[8] loves
135 Of pine or monumental oak,
  Where the rude ax with heavèd stroke
  Was never heard the nymphs to daunt,
  Or fright them from their hallowed haunt.
  There in close covert° by some brook, *hidden place*
140 Where no profaner eye may look,
  Hide me from day's garish eye,
  While the bee with honeyed thigh,
  That at her flowery work doth sing,
  And the waters murmuring
145 With such consort° as they keep, *musical harmony*
  Entice the dewy-feathered sleep;
  And let some strange mysterious dream
  Wave at his wings in airy stream
  Of lively portraiture displayed

---

3. Mythical poet-priest of the pre-Homeric age, supposedly a son or pupil of Orpheus.
4. For the story of Orpheus, see "L'Allegro," line 145, and n. 3 (on line 150).
5. Chaucer, whose Squire's Tale is unfinished.
6. A capsule definition of allegory.
7. The now soberly dressed Aurora, goddess of the dawn, once fell in love with Cephalus ("the Attic boy") and hunted with him. "Tricked and frounced": adorned and with frizzled hair.
8. Roman god of woodlands.

	Softly on my eyelids laid.	
150	And as I wake, sweet music breathe	
	Above, about, or underneath,	
	Sent by some spirit to mortals good,	
	Or th' unseen genius° of the wood.	*guardian deity*
155	But let my due feet never fail	
	To walk the studious cloister's pale,°	*enclosure*
	And love the high embowèd roof,	
	With antic pillars massy proof,⁹	
	And storied windows richly dight,¹	
160	Casting a dim religious light.	
	There let the pealing organ blow	
	To the full-voiced choir below,	
	In service high and anthems clear,	
	As may with sweetness, through mine ear,	
165	Dissolve me into ecstasies,	
	And bring all heaven before mine eyes.	
	And may at last my weary age	
	Find out the peaceful hermitage,	
	The hairy gown and mossy cell,	
170	Where I may sit and rightly spell°	*study*
	Of every star that heaven doth shew,	
	And every herb that sips the dew,	
	Till old experience do attain	
	To something like prophetic strain.	
175	These pleasures, Melancholy, give,²	
	And I with thee will choose to live.	

ca. 1631   1645

Lycidas

Lycidas   Milton wrote this pastoral elegy for a volume of Latin, Greek, and English poems, *Justa Edouardo King Naufrago* (1638), commemorating the death by shipwreck of his college classmate Edward King, three years younger than himself. King was not a close friend, but Milton's deepest emotions, anxieties, and fears are engaged here because, as poet and minister, King could serve Milton as a kind of alter ego. Still engaged in preparing himself, at the age of twenty-nine, for his projected poetic career, Milton was forced to recognize the uncertainty of all human endeavors. King's death posed the problem of mortality in its most agonizing form: the death of the young, the unfulfilled, the good seems to deny all meaning to life, to demonstrate the uselessness of exceptional talent, lofty ambition, and noble ideals of service to God.

While the poem expresses Milton's anxieties, it also serves as an announcement of his grand ambitions. Like Edmund Spenser, Milton saw mastery of the pastoral mode as the first step in a great poetic career. In "Lycidas" that mastery is complete. In the tradition that Milton received from classical and Renaissance predecessors, including Theocritus, Virgil, Petrarch, and Spenser, the pastoral landscape was invested with profound significances that had little indeed to do with the hard life

---

9. Massive and strong. "Antic": covered with quaint or grotesque carvings, also antique.
1. Dressed. "Storied windows": stained glass windows depicting biblical stories.

2. Compare "L'Allegro," lines 151–52 (p. 1397), and the final lines of Marlowe's "Passionate Shepherd" (p. 495).

of agricultural labor. In lines 25–36, Milton evokes the conventional pastoral topic of carefree shepherds who engage in singing contests, watch contentedly over their grazing sheep, fall in love, and write poetry, offering an image of human life in harmony with nature and the seasonal processes of fruition and mellowing before the winter of death. That classical image of the shepherd as poet is mingled with the Christian understanding of the shepherd as pastor (Christ is the Good Shepherd), and sometimes as the prophet called to his mission from the fields, like David or Isaiah. Milton calls on all these associations, along with other motifs specific to pastoral funeral elegy: the recollection of past friendship, a questioning of destiny for cutting short this life, a procession of mourners (often mythological figures), and a "flower passage" in which nature pays tribute to the dead shepherd.

"Lycidas" uses but continually tests and challenges the assumptions and conventions of pastoral elegy, making for profound tensions and clashes of tone. The pastoral "oaten flute" is interrupted by divine pronouncements and bitter invective; nature seems rife with examples of meaningless waste and early death; the "blind Fury" often cuts off the poet's "thin-spun life" before he can win fame; good pastors die young while corrupt "Blind mouths" remain; and Nature cannot even pay her tribute of flowers to Lycidas's funeral bier since he welters in the deep, his bones hurled to the "bottom of the monstrous world." In response to these fierce challenges come pronouncements by Apollo and St. Peter, and images of protection and resurrection in nature and myth, culminating in a new vision of pastoral: in heaven Lycidas enjoys a perfected pastoral existence, and in the coda the consoled shepherd arises and carries his song to "pastures new." Milton's questioning leads to a final reassertion of confidence in his calling as national poet. Moreover, in the headnote added in the 1645 volume of his *Poems*, he lays claim to prophetic authority, for the Church of England clergy he denounced as corrupt in 1638 had mostly been expelled from their livings by Puritan reformers in 1645.

Lycidas

In this monody[1] the author bewails a learned friend, unfortunately drowned in his passage from Chester on the Irish seas, 1637. And by occasion foretells the ruin of our corrupted clergy, then in their height.

    Yet once more, O ye laurels, and once more
    Ye myrtles brown, with ivy never sere,[2]
    I come to pluck your berries harsh and crude,°   *unripe*
    And with forced fingers rude,°   *unskilled*
5   Shatter your leaves before the mellowing year.
    Bitter constraint, and sad occasion dear,°   *heartfelt, also dire*
    Compels me to disturb your season due;
    For Lycidas is dead, dead ere his prime,[3]
    Young Lycidas, and hath not left his peer.
10 Who would not sing for Lycidas? He knew

---

1. A dirge sung by a single voice, though this one incorporates several other voices. Milton added this headnote in the edition of 1645; it identifies Milton as a prophet in the passage denouncing the clergy in this 1638 poem (lines 112–31) and invites the reader to remember Milton's 1641–42 polemics against the English bishops and church government (now dismantled).
2. "Laurels," associated with Apollo and poetry; "myrtle," associated with Venus and love; "ivy," associated with Bacchus and frenzy (also learning). All three are evergreens ("never sere") linked to poetic inspiration.
3. King was twenty-five.

          Himself to sing, and build the lofty rhyme.[4]
          He must not float upon his watery bier
          Unwept, and welter° to the parching wind,   *be tossed about*
          Without the meed° of some melodious tear.°   *reward / elegy*
    15   Begin then, sisters of the sacred well[5]
          That from beneath the seat of Jove doth spring,
          Begin, and somewhat loudly sweep the string.
          Hence with denial vain, and coy excuse;
          So may some gentle muse[6]
    20   With lucky words favor my destined urn,
          And as he passes turn,
          And bid fair peace be to my sable shroud.
          For we were nursed upon the selfsame hill,
          Fed the same flock, by fountain, shade, and rill.
    25   Together both, ere the high lawns° appeared   *upland pastures*
          Under the opening eyelids of the morn,
          We drove afield, and both together heard
          What time the grayfly winds her sultry horn,[7]
          Battening° our flocks with the fresh dews of night,   *feeding fat*
    30   Oft till the star that rose at evening bright[8]
          Toward heaven's descent had sloped his westering wheel.
          Meanwhile the rural ditties were not mute,
          Tempered to th' oaten flute,[9]
          Rough satyrs danced, and fauns with cloven heel
    35   From the glad sound would not be absent long,
          And old Damoetas[1] loved to hear our song.
            But O the heavy change, now thou art gone,
          Now thou art gone, and never must return!
          Thee, shepherd, thee the woods and desert caves,
    40   With wild thyme and the gadding° vine o'ergrown,   *wandering*
          And all their echoes mourn.
          The willows and the hazel copses° green   *thickets of trees*
          Shall now no more be seen,
          Fanning their joyous leaves to thy soft lays.
    45   As killing as the canker° to the rose,   *cankerworm*
          Or taint-worm[2] to the weanling herds that graze,
          Or frost to flowers that their gay wardrobe wear
          When first the white-thorn blows;[3]
          Such, Lycidas, thy loss to shepherd's ear.
    50   Where were ye, nymphs,[4] when the remorseless deep
          Closed o'er the head of your loved Lycidas?
          For neither were ye playing on the steep
          Where your old bards, the famous Druids,[5] lie,

---

4. King had written several poems of compliment in the patronage mode, chiefly on members of the royal family.
5. The nine (sister) Muses called (probably) from the fountain Aganippe, near Mount Helicon.
6. Here, some kindly poet.
7. That is, heard the grayfly when she buzzes.
8. Hesperus, the evening star.
9. Panpipes, played traditionally by shepherds in pastoral.
1. A type name from pastoral poetry, possibly referring to some particular tutor at Cambridge. "Satyrs": goat-legged woodland creatures, Pan's boisterous attendants.
2. Internal parasite fatal to newly weaned lambs.
3. Hawthorn blooms.
4. Nature deities.
5. Priestly poet-kings of Celtic Britain, who worshipped the forces of nature. They are buried on the mountain ("steep") Kerig-y-Druidion in Wales.

Nor on the shaggy top of Mona high,
Nor yet where Deva spreads her wizard stream:[6]
Ay me! I fondly dream—
Had ye been there—for what could that have done?
What could the Muse[7] herself that Orpheus bore,
The Muse herself, for her enchanting[8] son
Whom universal Nature did lament,
When by the rout that made the hideous roar
His gory visage down the stream was sent,
Down the swift Hebrus to the Lesbian shore?[9]
    Alas! What boots° it with incessant care   *profits*
To tend the homely slighted shepherd's trade,
And strictly meditate the thankless muse?[1]
Were it not better done as others use,
To sport with Amaryllis in the shade,
Or with the tangles of Neaera's hair?[2]
Fame is the spur that the clear spirit doth raise
(That last infirmity of noble mind)
To scorn delights, and live laborious days;
But the fair guerdon° when we hope to find,   *reward*
And think to burst out into sudden blaze,
Comes the blind Fury[3] with th' abhorrèd shears,
And slits the thin-spun life. "But not the praise,"
Phoebus replied, and touched my trembling ears;[4]
"Fame is no plant that grows on mortal soil,
Nor in the glistering foil[5]
Set off to th' world, nor in broad rumor lies,
But lives and spreads aloft by those pure eyes,
And perfect witness of all-judging Jove;
As he pronounces lastly on each deed,
Of so much fame in heaven expect thy meed."°   *reward*
    O fountain Arethuse, and thou honored flood,
Smooth-sliding Mincius, crowned with vocal reeds,
That strain I heard was of a higher mood.[6]
But now my oat° proceeds,   *pastoral flute*
And listens to the herald of the sea[7]

---

6. Mona is the island of Anglesey. Deva, the river Dee in Cheshire, was magic ("wizard") because its shifting stream foretold prosperity or dearth for the land. All these places are in the West Country, near where King drowned.
7. Calliope, Muse of epic poetry, was the mother of Orpheus.
8. Implies both song and magic; the root word survives in "incantation."
9. Orpheus's song was drowned out by the screams of a mob ("rout") of Thracian women, the Bacchantes, who then were able to tear him to pieces and throw his gory head into the river Hebrus, which carried it—still singing—to the island of Lesbos, bringing that island the gift of poetry.
1. That is, study to write poetry (a Virgilian phrase).
2. "Amaryllis" and "Neaera" (*Nee-eye-ra*), conventional names for pretty shepherdesses wooed in song by pastoral shepherds.
3. Atropos, one of the three Fates, whose scissors cuts the thread of human life after her sisters spin and measure it. Milton makes her a savage, and blind, Fury.
4. Phoebus Apollo, god of poetic inspiration. In *Eclogue* 6.3–4 he plucked Virgil's ears, warning him against impatient ambition.
5. Flashy, glittering metal foil, set under a gem to enhance its brilliance.
6. Arethusa was a fountain in Sicily associated with Greek pastoral poetry (Theocritus), Mincius a river in Lombardy associated with Latin pastoral (Virgil); Milton invokes them as a return to the pastoral after the "higher mood" of Apollo's speech.
7. Triton, who comes gathering evidence about the accident for Neptune's court.

	That came in Neptune's plea.	
90	He asked the waves, and asked the felon° winds,	savage
	"What hard mishap hath doomed this gentle swain?"°	shepherd
	And questioned every gust of rugged° wings	stormy
	That blows from off each bekèd promontory;	
95	They knew not of his story,	
	And sage Hippotades[8] their answer brings,	
	That not a blast was from his dungeon strayed;	
	The air was calm, and on the level brine,	
	Sleek Panope[9] with all her sisters played.	
100	It was that fatal and perfidious bark,	
	Built in th' eclipse,[1] and rigged with curses dark,	
	That sunk so low that sacred head of thine.	
	Next Camus,[2] reverend sire, went footing slow,	
	His mantle hairy, and his bonnet sedge,°	formed of reeds
105	Inwrought with figures dim, and on the edge	
	Like to that sanguine flower inscribed with woe.[3]	
	"Ah! who hath reft," quoth he, "my dearest pledge?"	
	Last came and last did go	
	The pilot of the Galilean lake;[4]	
110	Two massy keys he bore of metals twain	
	(The golden opes, the iron shuts amain).°	forever
	He shook his mitered locks, and stern bespake:	
	"How well could I have spared for° thee, young swain,	in place of
	Enow° of such as for their bellies' sake	enough (plural)
115	Creep and intrude and climb into the fold![5]	
	Of other care they little reckoning make,	
	Than how to scramble at the shearers' feast,[6]	
	And shove away the worthy bidden guest.	
	Blind mouths![7] that scarce themselves know how to hold	
120	A sheep-hook, or have learned aught else the least	
	That to the faithful herdsman's art belongs!	
	What recks it them? What need they? They are sped;[8]	
	And when they list,° their lean° and flashy songs	choose / meager
	Grate on their scrannel° pipes of wretched straw.	harsh, thin
125	The hungry sheep look up, and are not fed,	
	But swol'n with wind, and the rank mist they draw,°	inhale

8. Aeolus, god of winds.
9. The chief Nereid, or sea nymph.
1. Eclipses were taken as evil omens.
2. God of the river Cam, representing Cambridge University.
3. Like the *AI AI* cry of grief supposedly found on the hyacinth, a "sanguine flower" sprung from the blood of the youth Hyacinthus, beloved of Apollo and accidentally killed by him.
4. St. Peter, originally a fisherman on the sea of Galilee, was Christ's chief apostle; his keys open and shut the gates of heaven. He wears a bishop's miter (line 112): Milton in his "antiprelatical tracts" allows for a special role for apostles but denies any distinction in office between bishops and ministers in the later church.
5. See John 10:1: "He that entereth not by the door into the sheepfold, but climbeth up some other way, the same is a thief and a robber."
6. Festive suppers for the sheepshearers (hence, the material rewards of their ministry). "Worthy bidden guest" (next line): see Matthew 22:8, the parable of the marriage feast, "they which were bidden were not worthy."
7. Collapsing blindness with greed, this audacious metaphor accuses churchmen of shirking oversight (*episcopus*, bishop, means "super-vision") and of glutting themselves, although pastors ought to feed their flocks. "Sheep-hook" (next line): the bishop's staff is in the form of a shepherd's crook.
8. Provided for. "What recks it them?": what do they care?

>   Rot inwardly,[9] and foul contagion spread,
>   Besides what the grim wolf with privy paw[1]
>   Daily devours apace, and nothing said.
> 130 But that two-handed engine at the door[2]
>   Stands ready to smite once, and smite no more."
>   Return, Alpheus,[3] the dread voice is past,
>   That shrunk thy streams; return, Sicilian muse,
>   And call the vales, and bid them hither cast
> 135 Their bells and flowerets of a thousand hues.[4]
>   Ye valleys low where the mild whispers use,°   *frequent*
>   Of shades and wanton winds, and gushing brooks,
>   On whose fresh lap the swart star[5] sparely looks,
>   Throw hither all your quaint enameled eyes,[6]
> 140 That on the green turf suck the honeyed showers,
>   And purple all the ground with vernal flowers.
>   Bring the rathe° primrose that forsaken dies,   *early*
>   The tufted crow-toe, and pale jessamine,[7]
>   The white pink, and the pansy freaked° with jet,   *flecked*
> 145 The glowing violet,
>   The musk rose, and the well-attired woodbine,
>   With cowslips wan° that hang the pensive head,   *pale*
>   And every flower that sad embroidery wears:
>   Bid amaranthus[8] all his beauty shed,
> 150 And daffadillies fill their cups with tears,
>   To strew the laureate hearse° where Lycid lies.   *laurel-decked bier*
>   For so to interpose a little ease,
>   Let our frail thoughts dally with false surmise.[9]
>   Ay me! whilst thee the shores and sounding seas
> 155 Wash far away, where'er thy bones are hurled,
>   Whether beyond the stormy Hebrides,[1]
>   Where thou perhaps under the whelming° tide   *engulfing*
>   Visit'st the bottom of the monstrous world;
>   Or whether thou, to our moist vows denied,
> 160 Sleep'st by the fable of Bellerus old,[2]
>   Where the great vision of the guarded mount

---

9. Sheep rot is used as an allegory of church corruption by both Petrarch and Dante.

1. That is, Roman Catholicism, whole agents operated in secret ("privy"). Conversions in the court of the Roman Catholic queen Henrietta Maria were notorious.

2. A celebrated crux, variously explained as the two houses of Parliament, St. Peter's keys, the two-edged sword of the Book of Revelation, a sword wielded by two hands, and by other guesses; what is clear is the denunciation of impending, apocalyptic vengeance. In Matthew 24:33 the Last Judgment is said to be "even at the doors."

3. A river in Arcadia, fabled to pass unmixed through the sea before mixing its waters with the "fountain Arethuse" in Sicily, again reviving the pastoral mode after the fierce denunciation of Peter (see lines 85–87).

4. A catalogue of flowers was a common pastoral topic. "Bells": bell-shaped flowers.

5. The Dog Star, Sirius, associated with the heats of late summer.

6. Flowers curiously patterned and adorned with many colors.

7. White jasmine. "Tufted crow-toe": hyacinth or buttercup, growing in clusters. "Woodbine" (line 146): honeysuckle.

8. In Greek, "unfading," a legendary flower of immortality, one that never fades.

9. False, because Lycidas's body is not here to receive floral and poetic tributes.

1. Islands off the coast of Scotland, the northern terminus of the Irish Sea.

2. A fabulous giant invented by Milton as the origin of the Latin name for Land's End in Cornwall, *Bellerium*. "Monstrous world" (line 158): filled with monsters, also, immense.

      Looks toward Namancos and Bayona's hold;³
      Look homeward angel now, and melt with ruth:°   *pity*
      And, O ye dolphins,⁴ waft the hapless youth.
165   Weep no more, woeful shepherds, weep no more,
      For Lycidas your sorrow is not dead,
      Sunk though he be beneath the wat'ry floor;
      So sinks the daystar° in the ocean bed,   *the sun*
      And yet anon repairs his drooping head,
170   And tricks° his beams, and with new-spangled ore   *adorns, trims*
      Flames in the forehead of the morning sky:
      So Lycidas sunk low, but mounted high,
      Through the dear might of him that walked the waves,⁵
      Where, other groves and other streams along,⁶
175   With nectar pure his oozy° locks he laves,   *moist*
      And hears the unexpressive nuptial song,⁷
      In the blest kingdoms meek of joy and love.
      There entertain him all the saints above,
      In solemn troops and sweet societies
180   That sing, and singing in their glory move,
      And wipe the tears forever from his eyes.
      Now, Lycidas, the shepherds weep no more;
      Henceforth thou art the Genius⁸ of the shore,
      In thy large recompense, and shalt be good
185   To all that wander in that perilous flood.
         Thus sang the uncouth swain⁹ to th' oaks and rills,
      While the still morn went out with sandals gray;
      He touched the tender stops of various quills,¹
      With eager thought warbling his Doric² lay:
190   And now the sun had stretched out all the hills,
      And now was dropped into the western bay;
      At last he rose, and twitched his mantle blue:³
      Tomorrow to fresh woods, and pastures new.

November 1637   1638

---

3. "The guarded mount" is St. Michael's Mount in Cornwall, where the archangel was said to have appeared to fishermen in 495, and from which he is envisioned as looking over the Atlantic toward a region and fortress ("Bayona's hold") in northern Spain, thereby guarding Protestant England against the continuing Roman Catholic threat.
4. Dolphins brought the Greek poet Arion safely ashore, for love of his verse, and also performed other sea rescues.
5. Christ, who rescued Peter when he tried and failed to walk on the Sea of Galilee (Matthew 14:25–31).
6. See Revelation 22:1–2, on the "pure river of water of life," and the "tree of life, which bare twelve manner of fruits."
7. Inexpressible hymn of joy sung at "the marriage supper of the Lamb" (Revelation 19).
8. Local guardian spirit.
9. Another voice now seems to take over from the previously heard voice of the "uncouth swain" (unknown, unskilled shepherd).
1. The oaten stalks of panpipes.
2. Rustic, the dialect of Theocritus and other famous Greek pastoral poets.
3. The color of hope. "Twitched": pulled up around his shoulders.

From The Reason of Church Government Urged Against Prelaty[1]

[PLANS AND PROJECTS]

*** Concerning therefore this wayward subject against prelaty,[2] the touching whereof is so distasteful and disquietous[3] to a number of men, as by what hath been said I may deserve of charitable readers to be credited that neither envy nor gall hath entered me upon this controversy, but the enforcement of conscience only and a preventive fear lest the omitting of this duty should be against me when I would store up to myself the good provision of peaceful hours; so lest it should be still imputed to me, as I have found it hath been, that some self-pleasing humor of vainglory hath incited me to contest with men of high estimation, now while green years are upon my head;[4] from this needless surmisal I shall hope to dissuade the intelligent and equal auditor, if I can but say successfully that which in this exigent[5] behooves me; although I would be heard only, if it might be, by the elegant and learned reader, to whom principally for a while I shall beg leave I may address myself. To him it will be no new thing though I tell him that if I hunted after praise by the ostentation of wit and learning, I should not write thus out of mine own season when I have neither yet completed to my mind the full circle of my private studies,[6] although I complain not of any insufficiency to the matter in hand; or, were I ready to my wishes, it were a folly to commit anything elaborately composed to the careless and interrupted listening of these tumultuous times. Next, if I were wise only to mine own ends, I would certainly take such a subject as of itself might catch applause, whereas this hath all the disadvantages on the contrary, and such a subject as the publishing whereof might be delayed at pleasure, and time enough to pencil it over with all the curious touches of art, even to the perfection of a faultless picture; whenas in this argument the not deferring is of great moment to the good speeding,[7] that if solidity have leisure to do her office, art cannot have much. Lastly, I should not choose this manner of writing, wherein knowing myself inferior to myself, led by the genial power of nature[8] to another task, I have the use, as I may account it, but of my left hand. And though I shall be foolish in saying more to this purpose, yet, since it will be such a folly as wisest men going about to commit have only confessed and so

---

1. This was the fourth of five tracts Milton published attacking the bishops, liturgy, and church government of the Church of England, in support of Presbyterian reform, though these tracts also show signs of the more radical positions he will soon adopt. This 1642 treatise is the first one to carry his name, so the autobiographical passage is in part to introduce himself to the reader and explain why, though a layman and a young man, he feels himself called, and well prepared, to write on theology and ecclesiastical order. Beyond that rhetorical purpose, this is also the fullest account Milton ever set forth of his poetics: his sense of the poet's calling, of the nature and multiple uses of poetry, and of the several genres he already has employed or hopes to attempt. It also registers his inner conflict between duty (to serve God and his church with his learning) and desire (to write poetry).
2. Government by prelates (bishops). "Wayward": untoward, unpromising.
3. Distressing.
4. Milton's opponents, Bishops Joseph Hall, James Ussher, and Lancelot Andrewes, were famous, and he was still almost unknown at age thirty-four.
5. Urgent occasion. "Equal": impartial.
6. After taking his B.A. and M.A. degrees from Cambridge, Milton spent nearly six more years in private study at home; he was still continuing that program of reading.
7. Prompt publication is essential in polemic, so substance rather than art must be the priority. "Office": duty.
8. Intellectual gifts or natural disposition.

committed, I may trust with more reason, because with more folly, to have courteous pardon. For although a poet, soaring in the high region of his fancies with his garland and singing robes about him, might without apology speak more of himself than I mean to do, yet for me sitting here below in the cool element of prose, a mortal thing among many readers of no empyreal conceit,[9] to venture and divulge unusual things of myself, I shall petition to the gentler sort, it may not be envy[1] to me.

I must say, therefore, that after I had from my first years by the ceaseless diligence and care of my father (whom God recompense) been exercised to the tongues and some sciences, as my age would suffer,[2] by sundry masters and teachers both at home and at the schools, it was found that whether aught was imposed me by them that had the overlooking, or betaken to of mine own choice in English or other tongue, prosing or versing (but chiefly this latter), the style, by certain vital signs it had, was likely to live. But much latelier in the private academies of Italy,[3] whither I was favored to resort—perceiving that some trifles which I had in memory, composed at under twenty or thereabout (for the manner is that everyone must give some proof of his wit[4] and reading there) met with acceptance above what was looked for, and other things which I had shifted in scarcity of books and conveniences to patch up amongst them, were received with written encomiums,[5] which the Italian is not forward to bestow on men of this side the Alps—I began thus far to assent both to them and divers of my friends here at home, and not less to an inward prompting which now grew daily upon me, that by labor and intent study (which I take to be my portion in this life) joined with the strong propensity of nature, I might perhaps leave something so written to aftertimes, as they should not willingly let it die. These thoughts at once possessed me, and these other: that if I were certain to write as men buy leases, for three lives and downward,[6] there ought no regard be sooner had than to God's glory by the honor and instruction of my country. For which cause, and not only for that I knew it would be hard to arrive at the second rank among the Latins, I applied myself to that resolution which Ariosto followed against the persuasions of Bembo,[7] to fix all the industry and art I could unite to the adorning of my native tongue; not to make verbal curiosities the end—that were a toilsome vanity—but to be an interpreter and relater of the best and sagest things among mine own citizens throughout this island in the mother dialect. That what the greatest and choicest wits of Athens, Rome, or modern Italy, and those Hebrews of old did for their country, I, in my proportion, with this over and above of being a Christian,[8] might do for mine; not caring to be once named abroad, though perhaps I could attain to that, but content with these British islands as my world; whose fortune hath hitherto been that if the Athenians, as

---

9. Without sublime and elevated conceits.
1. *Cause for odium or disrespect.*
2. Admit. "Tongues": foreign languages. In *Ad Patrem* Milton says that as a boy he learned Latin, Greek, French, Italian, and Hebrew.
3. When on the grand tour of the Continent (1638–39) Milton enjoyed attending academies in Rome and especially Florence, which were centers for literary, scientific, and social exchange.
4. Ingenuity, creative powers; Milton read some of his Latin poems to the academies.
5. Praises. Milton published five of these encomiums, four in Latin, one in Italian, as prefatory material to the Latin part of his 1645 *Poems*.
6. Leases were often drawn for a tenancy to run through the longest-lived of three named persons.
7. Rejecting Cardinal Bembo's advice, Ariosto said he would rather be first among the Italian poets than second among those writing Latin.
8. The advantage would be in having "true" subjects to write about.

some say, made their small deeds great and renowned by their eloquent writers, England hath had her noble achievements made small by the unskillful handling of monks and mechanics.

    Time serves not now, and perhaps I might seem too profuse to give any certain account of what the mind at home in the spacious circuits of her musing hath liberty to propose to herself, though of highest hope and hardest attempting: whether that epic form whereof the two poems of Homer and those other two of Virgil and Tasso are a diffuse, and the book of Job a brief, model;[9] or whether the rules of Aristotle herein are strictly to be kept, or nature to be followed,[1] which in them that know art and use judgment is no transgression but an enriching of art; and lastly, what king or knight before the conquest[2] might be chosen in whom to lay the pattern of a Christian hero. And as Tasso gave to a prince of Italy his choice whether he would command him to write of Godfrey's expedition against the infidels, or Belisarius against the Goths, or Charlemagne against the Lombards;[3] if to the instinct of nature and the emboldening of art aught may be trusted, and that there be nothing adverse in our climate[4] or the fate of this age, it haply would be no rashness from an equal diligence and inclination to present the like offer in our own ancient stories; or whether those dramatic constitutions[5] wherein Sophocles and Euripides reign shall be found more doctrinal and exemplary to a nation. The Scripture also affords us a divine pastoral drama in the Song of Solomon, consisting of two persons and a double chorus, as Origen rightly judges. And the Apocalypse of St. John is the majestic image of a high and stately tragedy, shutting up and intermingling her solemn scenes and acts with a sevenfold chorus of hallelujahs and harping symphonies; and this my opinion the grave authority of Paraeus, commenting that book, is sufficient to confirm.[6] Or if occasion shall lead to imitate those magnific odes and hymns wherein Pindarus and Callimachus[7] are in most things worthy, some others in their frame judicious, in their matter most an end[8] faulty. But those frequent songs throughout the law and prophets beyond all these, not in their divine argument alone, but in the very critical art of composition, may be easily made appear over all the kinds of lyric poesy to be incomparable.[9] These abilities, wheresoever they be found, are the inspired gift of God rarely bestowed, but yet to some

---

9. The great models for the "diffuse" or long, epic were Homer's *Iliad* and *Odyssey*, Virgil's *Aeneid*, and Torquato Tasso's *Gerusalemme liberata* ("Jerusalem Delivered") (1581); there was also a long tradition of reading the Book of Job as a "brief" epic, a moral conflict between Job and Satan. Milton's brief epic, *Paradise Regained* (1671), makes some use of that model. For all the genres he discusses, Milton cites both classical and biblical models.

1. One contemporary debate concerned whether the Aristotelian rule of beginning in medias res was to be followed, or Ariosto's "natural" method of beginning at the beginning of the story.

2. At first Milton considered as potential epic subjects King Arthur, who fought against invading Saxons, and King Alfred, who warred with invading Danes; he excluded those after the Norman Conquest.

3. Tasso offered this choice to his patron, Alfonso II d'Este, Duke of Ferrara.

4. Milton often speculated that the cold climate of England might not be as conducive to poetry as the warmer climates of Italy and Greece had been.

5. Plays.

6. Sophocles and Euripides are supreme examples of Greek tragedy; the Scripture models for drama are the Song of Solomon as a "divine pastoral drama" (Milton cites Origen, an Alexandrine Father of the 3rd century), and the Book of Revelation as a "high and stately tragedy" (he cites David Paraeus, a German theologian of the 16th and 17th centuries).

7. Pindar, a 5th century B.C.E. Greek poet, wrote numerous odes especially on winners of the Olympic games; Callimachus, a 3rd century B.C.E. Alexandrine Greek, wrote elegant elegiac verse on the origin of various myths and rituals.

8. Almost entirely.

9. He thinks especially of the Psalms, often compared to classical lyric.

(though most abuse) in every nation; and are of power beside the office of a pulpit to inbreed and cherish in a great people the seeds of virtue and public civility, to allay the perturbations of the mind and set the affections in right tune, to celebrate in glorious and lofty hymns the throne and equipage of God's almightiness, and what he works and what he suffers to be wrought with high providence in his church, to sing the victorious agonies of martyrs and saints, the deeds and triumphs of just and pious nations doing valiantly through faith against the enemies of Christ, to deplore the general relapses of kingdoms and states from justice and God's true worship. Lastly, whatsoever in religion is holy and sublime, in virtue amiable or grave, whatsoever hath passion or admiration in all the changes of that which is called fortune from without or the wily subtleties and refluxes of man's thoughts from within, all these things with a solid and treatable smoothness to paint out and describe.[1] Teaching over the whole book of sanctity and virtue through all the instances of example, with such delight to those especially of soft and delicious temper,[2] who will not so much as look upon truth herself unless they see her elegantly dressed, that whereas the paths of honesty and good life appear now rugged and difficult, though they be indeed easy and pleasant, they would then appear to all men both easy and pleasant, though they were rugged and difficult indeed. And what a benefit this would be to our youth and gentry may be soon guessed by what we know of the corruption and bane which they suck in daily from the writings and interludes of libidinous and ignorant poetasters,[3] who, having scarce ever heard of that which is the main consistence of a true poem, the choice of such persons as they ought to introduce, and what is moral and decent to each one, do for the most part lap up[4] vicious principles in sweet pills to be swallowed down, and make the taste of virtuous documents harsh and sour.

But because the spirit of man cannot demean[5] itself lively in this body without some recreating intermission of labor and serious things, it were happy for the commonwealth if our magistrates, as in those famous governments of old, would take into their care, not only the deciding of our contentious law cases and brawls, but the managing of our public sports and festival pastimes, that they might be, not such as were authorized a while since,[6] the provocations of drunkenness and lust, but such as may inure and harden our bodies by martial exercises to all warlike skill and performance, and may civilize, adorn, and make discreet our minds by the learned and affable meeting of frequent academies, and the procurement of wise and artful recitations sweetened with eloquent and graceful enticements to the love and practice of justice, temperance, and fortitude, instructing and bettering the nation at all opportunities, that the call of wisdom and virtue may be heard everywhere, as Solomon saith: "She crieth without, she uttereth her voice in the streets, in the top of high places, in the chief concourse, and

---

1. See the wide range of kinds and subjects and functions suggested for the serious national poet.
2. Temperament. Milton here paraphrases Horace's formula, echoed by Sidney and Jonson, that poetry both teaches and delights, and that it encourages virtuous endeavor.
3. Some of the pseudo-poets of the Cavalier court who wrote on lascivious topics.
4. Roll up.
5. Comport.
6. Charles I's republication (1633) of James I's *Book of Sports*, encouraging sports, dancing, and rural festivals on Sundays—anathema to Puritans.

in the openings of the gates."[7] Whether this may not be, not only in pulpits, but after another persuasive method,[8] at set and solemn panegyries, in theaters, porches,[9] or what other place or way may win most upon the people to receive at once both recreation and instruction, let them in authority consult.

The thing which I had to say, and those intentions which have lived within me ever since I could conceive myself anything worth to my country, I return to crave excuse that urgent reason hath plucked from me by an abortive and foredated discovery.[1] And the accomplishment of them lies not but in a power above man's to promise; but that none hath by more studious ways endeavored, and with more unwearied spirit that none shall, that I dare almost aver of myself as far as life and free leisure will extend; and that the land had once enfranchised herself from this impertinent[2] yoke of prelaty, under whose inquisitorious and tyrannical duncery no free and splendid wit can flourish. Neither do I think it shame to covenant with any knowing reader that for some few years yet I may go on trust with him toward the payment of what I am now indebted, as being a work not to be raised from the heat of youth or the vapors of wine, like that which flows at waste from the pen of some vulgar amorist or the trencher fury of a rhyming parasite, nor to be obtained by the invocation of Dame Memory and her siren daughters,[3] but by devout prayer to that Eternal Spirit who can enrich with all utterance and knowledge, and sends out his seraphim with the hallowed fire of his altar to touch and purify the lips of whom he pleases.[4] To this must be added industrious and select reading, steady observation, insight into all seemly and generous arts and affairs; till which in some measure be compassed, at mine own peril and cost I refuse not to sustain this expectation.* * * But were it the meanest under-service, if God by his secretary conscience enjoin it, it were sad for me if I should draw back; for me especially, now when all men offer their aid to help ease and lighten the difficult labors of the church, to whose service by the intentions of my parents and friends I was destined of a child, and in mine own resolutions: till coming to some maturity of years and perceiving what tyranny had invaded the church, that he who would take orders must subscribe slave and take an oath withal,[5] which, unless he took with a conscience that would retch, he must either straight perjure or split his faith; I thought it better to prefer a blameless silence before the sacred office of speaking, bought and begun with servitude and forswearing. Howsoever, thus church-outed by the prelates,

---

7. The phrases are from Proverbs 1:20–21 and 8:2–3. Milton would not ban recreation or festival pastimes but reform them: his models are the lofty encomiastic poems and recitations Plato would admit into his *Republic*, the literary and social exchanges of the Italian academies, and martial exercises (to prepare the citizenry for war, now imminent).
8. That is, poetry.
9. Porticos. "Panegyries": solemn public meetings.
1. That is, I have been forced to write for my country's sake and to reveal my poetic plans before I was ready to do either.
2. Unsuitable, absurd.
3. True poetry comes not from youth, wine, a full plate, or even Memory (and her daughters the Muses): tradition alone does not make a poet.
4. The coal from the altar that purifies the prophet's lips (Isaiah 6:6–7): the passage makes poetry first and foremost the product of inspiration, but Milton also insists on his need to attain well-nigh universal knowledge and experience.
5. Milton was not willing to subscribe the oath affirming that the Book of Common Prayer and the present government of the church by bishops were according to the word of God; still less was he willing to subscribe the notorious "etcetera" oath required in 1640, that the minister would never seek to alter the government of the church "by archbishops, bishops, deacons, and archdeacons, etc."

hence may appear the right I have to meddle in these matters, as before the necessity and constraint appeared.

1642

Areopagitica   This passionate, trenchant defense of intellectual liberty has had a powerful influence on the evolving liberal conception of freedom of speech, press, and thought. Milton's specific target is the Press Ordinance of June 14, 1643, Parliament's attempt to crack down on the flood of pamphlets (including Milton's own controversial treatises on divorce) that poured forth both from legal and from underground presses as the Civil War raged. Like Tudor and Stuart censorship laws, Parliament's ordinance demanded that works be registered with the stationers and licensed by the censors before publication, and that both author and publisher be identified, on pain of fines and imprisonment for both. Milton vigorously protests the prepublication licensing of books, arguing that such measures have only been used by, and are only fit for, degenerate cultures. In the regenerate English nation, now "rousing herself like a strong man after sleep," men and women must be allowed to develop in virtue by participating in the clash and conflict of ideas. Truth will always overcome falsehood in reasoned debate. Thus, in opposition to the Presbyterians then in power, Milton defends widespread religious toleration, though with restrictions on Roman Catholicism, which, like most of his Protestant contemporaries, he viewed as a political threat and a tyranny binding individual conscience to the pope.

The title associates the tract with the speech of the Greek orator Isocrates to the Areopagus, the Council of the Wise in Athens. Learned readers would have recognized the irony of this. While Isocrates instructed the council to reform Athens by careful supervision of the private lives of citizens, Milton argues that only liberty and removal of censorship can advance reformation. This association explains the oratorical tone of the tract, which was, in fact, subtitled "A Speech." In this most literary of his tracts, Milton's style is elevated, eloquent, dense with poetic figures, and ranges in tone from satire and ridicule to urgent pleading and florid praise. His arguments and principles are often couched in striking images and phrases. One example is his passionate testimony to the potency and inestimable value of books: "As good almost kill a man as kill a good book . . ." Most memorable is his ringing credo that echoes down the centuries to protest every new tyranny: "Give me the liberty to know, to utter, and to argue freely according to conscience, above all liberties."

From Areopagitica

I deny not, but that it is of greatest concernment in the church and commonwealth, to have a vigilant eye how books demean[1] themselves as well as men; and thereafter to confine, imprison, and do sharpest justice on them as malefactors:[2] For books are not absolutely dead things, but do contain a potency of life in them to be as active as that soul was whose progeny they are; nay they do preserve as in a vial the purest efficacy and extraction of that living intellect that bred them. I know they are as lively, and as vigorously

---

1. Behave.
2. Milton allows that books may be called to account after publication, if they are proved to contain libels or other manifest crimes (he leaves this quite vague).

productive, as those fabulous dragon's teeth; and being sown up and down, may chance to spring up armed men.³ And yet on the other hand unless wariness be used, as good almost kill a man as kill a good book; who kills a man kills a reasonable creature, God's image; but he who destroys a good book, kills reason itself, kills the image of God, as it were in the eye. Many a man lives a burden to the earth; but a good book is the precious lifeblood of a master spirit, embalmed and treasured up on purpose to a life beyond life. 'Tis true, no age can restore a life, whereof perhaps there is no great loss; and revolutions of ages do not oft recover the loss of a rejected truth, for the want of which whole nations fare the worse. We should be wary therefore what persecution we raise against the living labors of public men, how we spill that seasoned life of man preserved and stored up in books; since we see a kind of massacre, whereof the execution ends not in the slaying of an elemental life, but strikes at that ethereal and fifth essence,⁴ the breath of reason itself, slays an immortality rather than a life. But lest I should be condemned of introducing licence, while I oppose licensing, I refuse not the pains to be so much historical, as will serve to show what hath been done by ancient and famous commonwealths, against this disorder, till the very time that this project of licensing crept out of the Inquisition,⁵ was catched up by our prelates, and hath caught some of our presbyters.⁶ * * *

* * * Good and evil we know in the field of this world grow up together almost inseparably; and the knowledge of good is so involved and interwoven with the knowledge of evil, and in so many cunning resemblances hardly to be discerned, that those confused seeds which were imposed on Psyche as an incessant labor to cull out and sort asunder were not more intermixed.⁷ It was from out the rind of one apple tasted, that the knowledge of good and evil, as two twins cleaving together, leaped forth into the world. And perhaps this is that doom which Adam fell into of knowing good and evil, that is to say of knowing good by evil.

As therefore the state of man now is, what wisdom can there be to choose, what continence to forbear, without the knowledge of evil? He that can apprehend and consider vice with all her baits and seeming pleasures, and yet abstain, and yet distinguish, and yet prefer that which is truly better, he is the true wayfaring⁸ Christian. I cannot praise a fugitive and cloistered virtue, unexercised and unbreathed,⁹ that never sallies out and sees her adversary, but slinks out of the race where that immortal garland is to be run for, not without dust and heat. Assuredly we bring not innocence into the world, we bring impurity much rather; that which purifies us is trial,

---

3. After Cadmus killed a dragon on his way to founding Thebes, on a god's advice he sowed the dragon's teeth, which sprang up as an army, the belligerent forefathers of Sparta.
4. Quintessence, a pure, mystical substance above the four elements (fire, air, water, earth).
5. The Roman Catholic institution for suppressing heresy, especially strong in Spain.
6. The Presbyterians, powerful in the Parliament, were striving to establish theirs as the national church and suppress others. Milton, who began by supporting them in *The Reason of Church Government* and his other antiprelatical tracts (1641–42), now rejects them, in large part because they seek to supplant one repressive church with another.
7. Angry at her son Cupid's love for Psyche, Venus set the girl many trials, among them to sort out a vast mound of mixed seeds, but the ants took pity on her and did the work.
8. The printed text reads "wayfaring," calling up the image of the Christian pilgrim; several presentation copies correct it (by hand) to "warfaring," calling up the image of the Christian warrior. Both suit the passage.
9. Not forced by exertion to breathe hard. "Immortal garland" (next line): the prize for the winner of a race, as figure for the "crown of life" promised to those who endure temptation (James 1:12).

and trial is by what is contrary. That virtue therefore which is but a youngling in the contemplation of evil, and knows not the utmost that vice promises to her followers, and rejects it, is but a blank virtue, not a pure; her whiteness is but an excremental[1] whiteness; which was the reason why our sage and serious poet Spenser (whom I dare be known to think a better teacher than Scotus or Aquinas), describing true temperance under the person of Guyon, brings him in with his Palmer through the Cave of Mammon and the Bower of Earthly Bliss,[2] that he might see and know, and yet abstain.

Since therefore the knowledge and survey of vice is in this world so necessary to the constituting of human virtue, and the scanning of error to the confirmation of truth, how can we more safely, and with less danger, scout into the regions of sin and falsity than by reading all manner of tractates and hearing all manner of reason? And this is the benefit which may be had of books promiscuously read.

But of the harm that may result hence, three kinds are usually reckoned. First is feared the infection that may spread; but then all human learning and controversy in religious points must remove out of the world, yea, the Bible itself; for that ofttimes relates blasphemy not nicely,[3] it describes the carnal sense of wicked men not unelegantly, it brings in holiest men passionately murmuring against providence through all the arguments of Epicurus;[4] in other great disputes it answers dubiously and darkly to the common reader.[5]

* * *

To sequester out of the world into Atlantic and Utopian politics,[6] which never can be drawn into use, will not mend our condition, but to ordain wisely as in this world of evil, in the midst whereof God hath placed us unavoidably. . . . Impunity and remissness, for certain, are the bane of a commonwealth; but here the great art lies, to discern in what the law is to bid restraint and punishment, and in what things persuasion only is to work. If every action which is good or evil in man at ripe years were to be under pittance[7] and prescription and compulsion, what were virtue but a name, what praise could be then due to well-doing, what gramercy[8] to be sober, just, or continent?

Many there be that complain of divine providence for suffering Adam to transgress; foolish tongues! When God gave him reason, he gave him freedom to choose, for reason is but choosing; he had been else a mere artificial Adam, such an Adam as he is in the motions.[9] We ourselves esteem not of that obedience, or love, or gift, which is of force: God therefore left him

---

1. Exterior only.
2. John Duns Scotus and Thomas Aquinas, major Scholastic theologians. Guyon (following), the hero of Book 2 of the *Faerie Queene*, passes through the Cave of Mammon (symbolic of all worldly goods and honors) without his Palmer-guide, but that figure does accompany him through the Bower of Bliss.
3. Daintily.
4. Greek philosopher (342–270 B.C.E.) who taught that happiness is the greatest good, and that virtue should be practiced because it brings happiness; some of his followers equated happiness with sensual enjoyment. Milton may be thinking of the biblical book of Ecclesiastes.
5. Milton goes on to argue that a fool can find material for folly in the best books, and a wise person material for wisdom in the worst. Also, one cannot remove evil by censoring books without also censoring ballads, fiddlers, clothing, conversation, and all social life.
6. Milton alludes to More's *Utopia* and Bacon's *New Atlantis*.
7. Rationing.
8. Reward, thanks.
9. Puppet shows.

free, set before him a provoking object, ever almost in his eyes; herein consisted his merit, herein the right of his reward, the praise of his abstinence.[1] Wherefore did he create passions within us, pleasures round about us, but that these rightly tempered are the very ingredients of virtue? They are not skillful considerers of human things, who imagine to remove sin by removing the matter of sin; for, besides that it is a huge heap increasing under the very act of diminishing, though some part of it may for a time be withdrawn from some persons, it cannot from all, in such a universal thing as books are; and when this is done, yet the sin remains entire. Though ye take from a covetous man all his treasure, he has yet one jewel left: ye cannot bereave him of his covetousness. Banish all objects of lust, shut up all youth into the severest discipline that can be exercised in any hermitage, ye cannot make them chaste that came not thither so: such great care and wisdom is required to the right managing of this point.

Suppose we could expel sin by this means; look how much we thus expel of sin, so much we expel of virtue: for the matter of them both is the same; remove that, and ye remove them both alike. This justifies the high providence of God, who, though he commands us temperance, justice, continence, yet pours out before us, even to a profuseness, all desirable things, and gives us minds that can wander beyond all limit and satiety. Why should we then affect a rigor contrary to the manner of God and of nature, by abridging or scanting those means, which books freely permitted are, both to the trial of virtue and the exercise of truth? It would be better done to learn that the law must needs be frivolous which goes to restrain things uncertainly and yet equally working to good and to evil. And were I the chooser, a dram of well-doing should be preferred before many times as much the forcible hindrance of evil-doing. For God sure esteems the growth and completing of one virtuous person more than the restraint of ten vicious.

* * *

What advantage is it to be a man over it is to be a boy at school, if we have only scaped the ferula to come under the fescue of an *imprimatur*;[2] if serious and elaborate writings, as if they were no more than the theme of a grammarlad under his pedagogue, must not be uttered without the cursory eyes of a temporizing and extemporizing licenser?[3] He who is not trusted with his own actions, his drift not being known to be evil, and standing to the hazard of law and penalty, has no great argument to think himself reputed, in the commonwealth wherein he was born, for other than a fool or a foreigner.

When a man writes to the world, he summons up all his reason and deliberation to assist him; he searches, meditates, is industrious, and likely consults and confers with his judicious friends, after all which done he takes himself to be informed in what he writes, as well as any that writ before him. If in this the most consummate act of his fidelity and ripeness, no years, no industry, no former proof of his abilities can bring him to that state

---

1. Compare Milton's representation of Adam and Eve in Eden in *Paradise Lost*.
2. "Ferula": a schoolmaster's rod; "fescue": a pointer, "imprimatur": "it may be printed" (Latin), appears on the title page of books approved by the Roman Catholic censors. Milton's keen sense of the affront to scholars and scholarship, and to himself, is evident in this passage.
3. He temporizes in following the times, and acts by whim (extemporizes).

of maturity as not to be still mistrusted and suspected (unless he carry all his considerate diligence, all his midnight watchings, and expense of Palladian[4] oil, to the hasty view of an unleisured licenser, perhaps much his younger, perhaps far his inferior in judgment, perhaps one who never knew the labor of book-writing), and if he be not repulsed, or slighted, must appear in print like a puny[5] with his guardian, and his censor's hand on the back of his title to be his bail and surety that he is no idiot, or seducer; it cannot be but a dishonor and derogation to the author, to the book, to the privilege and dignity of learning.* * *

And how can a man teach with authority, which is the life of teaching, how can he be a doctor[6] in his book as he ought to be, or else had better be silent, whenas all he teaches, all he delivers, is but under the tuition, under the correction of his patriarchal[7] licenser to blot or alter what precisely accords not with the hide-bound humor which he calls his judgment? When every acute reader upon the first sight of a pedantic license, will be ready with these like words to ding the book a quoit's[8] distance from him: "I hate a pupil teacher, I endure not an instructor that comes to me under the wardship of an overseeing fist. I know nothing of the licenser, but that I have his own hand here for his arrogance; who shall warrant me his judgment?"

"The state, sir," replies the stationer,[9] but has a quick return: "The state shall be my governors, but not my critics; they may be mistaken in the choice of a licenser, as easily as this licenser may be mistaken in an author."

* * *

Well knows he who uses to consider, that our faith and knowledge thrives by exercise, as well as our limbs and complexion.[1] Truth is compared in Scripture to a streaming fountain;[2] if her waters flow not in a perpetual progression, they sicken into a muddy pool of conformity and tradition. A man may be a heretic in the truth; and if he believe things only because his pastor says so, or the Assembly[3] so determines, without knowing other reason, though his belief be true, yet the very truth he holds becomes his heresy.

* * *

Truth indeed came once into the world with her Divine Master, and was a perfect shape most glorious to look on: but when he ascended, and his apostles after him were laid asleep, then straight arose a wicked race of deceivers, who, as that story goes of the Egyptian Typhon with his conspirators, how they dealt with the good Osiris,[4] took the virgin Truth, hewed her lovely form into a thousand pieces, and scattered them to the four winds. From that time ever since, the sad friends of Truth, such as durst appear, imitating the careful search that Isis made for the mangled body of Osiris, went

---

4. Pertaining to Pallas Athena, goddess of wisdom.
5. A minor, hence, young, unseasoned.
6. Teacher.
7. Taking on the role of a father; also, standing in for ecclesiastical patriarchs or prelates (like Archbishop Laud).
8. A flat disc of stone or metal, thrown as an exercise of strength or skill.
9. Printer, who was responsible for submitting books before publication to the "licenser" (censor).
1. Constitution, the proper mingling of qualities in the body.
2. In Psalm 85:11.
3. The Westminster Assembly, convened by Parliament in 1643 to reorganize the English church along Presbyterian lines.
4. Plutarch tells, in "Isis and Osiris," of Typhon's scattering the fragments of his brother Osiris and of Isis's efforts to recover them.

up and down gathering up limb by limb, still as they could find them. We have not yet found them all, Lords and Commons, nor ever shall do, till her Master's second coming; he shall bring together every joint and member, and shall mold them into an immortal feature of loveliness and perfection. Suffer not these licensing prohibitions to stand at every place of opportunity, forbidding and disturbing them that continue seeking, that continue to do our obsequies[5] to the torn body of our martyred saint.

We boast our light; but if we look not wisely on the sun itself, it smites us into darkness. Who can discern those planets that are oft combust,[6] and those stars of brightest magnitude that rise and set with the sun, until the opposite motion of their orbs bring them to such a place in the firmament where they may be seen evening or morning? The light which we have gained was given us, not to be ever staring on, but by it to discover onward things more remote from our knowledge. It is not the unfrocking of a priest, the unmitering of a bishop, and the removing him from off the Presbyterian shoulders, that will make us a happy nation. No, if other things as great in the church, and in the rule of life both economical and political, be not looked into and reformed, we have looked so long upon the blaze that Zwinglius and Calvin[7] hath beaconed up to us, that we are stark blind.

There be who perpetually complain of schisms and sects, and make it such a calamity that any man dissents from their maxims. 'Tis their own pride and ignorance which causes the disturbing, who neither will hear with meekness, nor can convince; yet all must be suppressed which is not found in their syntagma.[8] They are the troublers, they are the dividers of unity, who neglect and permit not others to unite those dissevered pieces which are yet wanting to the body of Truth. To be still searching what we know not by what we know, still closing up truth to truth as we find it (for all her body is homogeneal and proportional), this is the golden rule in theology as well as in arithmetic, and makes up the best harmony in a church; not the forced and outward union of cold and neutral and inwardly divided minds.

Lords and Commons of England, consider what nation it is whereof ye are, and whereof ye are the governors: a nation not slow and dull, but of a quick, ingenious, and piercing spirit, acute to invent, subtle and sinewy to discourse, not beneath the reach of any point the highest that human capacity can soar to. Therefore the studies of learning in her deepest sciences have been so ancient and so eminent among us, that writers of good antiquity and ablest judgment have been persuaded that even the school of Pythagoras and the Persian wisdom took beginning from the old philosophy of this island.[9] And that wise and civil Roman, Julius Agricola,[1] who governed once here for Caesar, preferred the natural wits of Britain before the labored studies of the French. Nor is it for nothing that the grave and

---

5. Funeral or commemorative rites.
6. Burned up; in astrology, so close to the sun as not to be visible.
7. Zwingli and Calvin, famous Protestant reformers, were mainstays of the Presbyterian cause. "Economical": domestic.
8. Compilations of beliefs, creeds.
9. Some speculation existed as to whether the Pythagorean notion of the transmigration of souls might trace back to the Druids, but the notion was mostly denied.
1. The "civil" (cultured, civilized) Agricola's opinion of the British intellect is found in Tacitus's *Life of Agricola*. Transylvania (following; now Romania) was an independent Protestant country whose citizens sometimes came to England to study. "Hercynian wilderness": Roman name for a forested and mountainous region of Germany.

frugal Transylvanian[2] sends out yearly from as far as the mountainous borders of Russia, and beyond the Hercynian wilderness, not their youth, but their staid men, to learn our language and our theologic arts.

Yet that which is above all this, the favor and the love of heaven we have great argument to think in a peculiar manner propitious and propending[3] towards us. Why else was this nation chosen before any other, that out of her, as out of Zion,[4] should be proclaimed and sounded forth the first tidings and trumpet of Reformation to all Europe? And had it not been the obstinate perverseness of our prelates against the divine and admirable spirit of Wycliffe to suppress him as a schismatic and innovator, perhaps neither the Bohemian Huss and Jerome,[5] no, nor the name of Luther or of Calvin, had been ever known: the glory of reforming all our neighbors had been completely ours. But now, as our obdurate clergy have with violence demeaned the matter, we are become hitherto the latest and the backwardest scholars of whom[6] God offered to have made us the teachers.

Now once again by all concurrence of signs, and by the general instinct of holy and devout men, as they daily and solemnly express their thoughts, God is decreeing to begin some new and great period in his church, even to the reforming of Reformation itself; what does he then but reveal himself to his servants, and as his manner is, first to his Englishmen? I say, as his manner is, first to us, though we mark not the method of his counsels, and are unworthy. Behold now this vast city: a city of refuge,[7] the mansion house of liberty, encompassed and surrounded with his protection; the shop of war hath not there more anvils and hammers waking, to fashion out the plates[8] and instruments of armed justice in defense of beleaguered truth, than there be pens and heads there, sitting by their studious lamps, musing, searching, revolving new notions and ideas wherewith to present, as with their homage and their fealty, the approaching Reformation: others as fast reading, trying all things, assenting to the force of reason and convincement.

What could a man require more from a nation so pliant and so prone to seek after knowledge? What wants there to such a towardly and pregnant[9] soil, but wise and faithful laborers, to make a knowing people, a nation of prophets,[1] of sages, and of worthies? We reckon more than five months yet to harvest; there need not be five weeks; had we but eyes to lift up, the fields are white already.[2] Where there is much desire to learn, there of necessity will be much arguing, much writing, many opinions; for opinion in good men is but knowledge in the making. Under these fantastic terrors of sect and schism we wrong the earnest and zealous thirst after knowledge and understanding which God hath stirred up in this city.

---

2. The Protestant princes of Transylvania encouraged their theologians and humanist scholars to study at English universities.
3. Inclining, favorable. "Argument": reason.
4. Mount Zion, in Jerusalem, the site of the Temple.
5. John Wycliffe was a 14th-century English reformer and translator of the Bible, whose books were forbidden by Pope Alexander V in 1409. John Huss spread Wycliffe's doctrines on the Continent; he was burned at the stake in 1415, as was (the next year) his follower Jerome of Prague.
6. Of those whom. "Demeaned": conducted, degraded.
7. Numbers 35 instructs the Jews to establish "cities of refuge" where those accused of crimes will be protected from "revengers of blood."
8. Plate mail, for armor.
9. Favorable and fertile.
1. In Numbers 11:29 Moses reproaches Joshua, who complained of the presence of other prophets: "Enviest thou for my sake? Would God that all the Lord's people were prophets."
2. Milton is paraphrasing Christ's words to his disciples (John 4:35): "Lift up your eyes, and look on the fields: for they are white already to harvest."

What some lament of, we rather should rejoice at, should rather praise this pious forwardness among men, to reassume the ill-deputed care of their religion into their own hands again. A little generous prudence, a little forbearance of one another, and some grain of charity might win all these diligences to join, and unite into one general and brotherly search after truth; could we but forgo this prelatical tradition of crowding free consciences and Christian liberties into canons and precepts of men. I doubt not, if some great and worthy stranger should come among us, wise to discern the mold and temper of a people, and how to govern it, observing the high hopes and aims, the diligent alacrity of our extended thoughts and reasonings in the pursuance of truth and freedom, but that he would cry out as Pyrrhus did, admiring the Roman docility and courage: "If such were my Epirots, I would not despair the greatest design that could be attempted, to make a church or kingdom happy."[3] Yet these are the men cried out against for schismatics and sectaries;[4] as if, while the temple of the Lord was building, some cutting, some squaring the marble, others hewing the cedars, there should be a sort of irrational men, who could not consider there must be many schisms and many dissections[5] made in the quarry and in the timber, ere the house of God can be built. And when every stone is laid artfully together, it cannot be united into a continuity, it can but be contiguous in this world; neither can every piece of the building be of one form; nay rather the perfection consists in this, that out of many moderate varieties and brotherly dissimilitudes that are not vastly disproportional, arises the goodly and the graceful symmetry that commends the whole pile and structure. Let us therefore be more considerate builders, more wise in spiritual architecture, when great reformation is expected. For now the time seems come, wherein Moses the great prophet may sit in heaven rejoicing to see that memorable and glorious wish of his fulfilled, when not only our seventy elders, but all the Lord's people, are become prophets.[6]

* * *

Methinks I see in my mind a noble and puissant nation rousing herself like a strong man after sleep, and shaking her invincible locks:[7] methinks I see her as an eagle mewing her mighty youth, and kindling her undazzled eyes at the full midday beam;[8] purging and unsealing her long-abused sight at the fountain itself of heavenly radiance; while the whole noise of timorous and flocking birds, with those also that love the twilight, flutter about, amazed at what she means, and in their envious gabble would prognosticate[9] a year of sects and schisms.

What should ye do then, should ye suppress all this flowery crop of knowledge and new light sprung up and yet springing daily in this city? Should ye

---

3. Though King Pyrrhus of Epirus beat the Roman armies at Heraclea in 280 B.C.E., he was much impressed by their discipline.
4. "Schismatics": those who cut up or divide the church; "sectaries": members of Protestant communions outside the national church.
5 Milton is playing on the literal meaning of "schism," cutting up or dividing.
6 Again alluding to Numbers 11:29, Milton equates the English assembly of clergy to set doctrine and church order (the Westminster Assembly) with the Jewish Sanhedrin of seventy elders.
7. The allusion is to Samson, whose uncut hair made him invincible, when he frustrated the first three attempts of Delilah and the Philistines to subdue him in sleep (Judges 16:6–14).
8. Eagles were thought to be able to look directly at the sun. "Mewing": molting, when the eagle sheds it feathers and thereby renews its coat.
9. Predict.

set an oligarchy of twenty engrossers[1] over it, to bring a famine upon our minds again, when we shall know nothing but what is measured to us by their bushel? Believe it, Lords and Commons, they who counsel ye to such a suppressing do as good as bid ye suppress yourselves; and I will soon show how.[2]

* * *

And now the time in special is by privilege to write and speak what may help to the further discussing of matters in agitation. The temple of Janus with his two controversial faces might now not unsignificantly be set open.[3] And though all the winds of doctrine were let loose to play upon the earth, so Truth be in the field, we do injuriously by licensing and prohibiting to misdoubt her strength. Let her and Falsehood grapple; who ever knew Truth put to the worse in a free and open encounter? Her[4] confuting is the best and surest suppressing. He who hears what praying there is for light and clearer knowledge to be sent down among us would think of other matters to be constituted beyond the discipline of Geneva framed and fabriced already to our hands.[5]

Yet when the new light which we beg for shines in upon us, there be who envy and oppose if it come not first in at their casements. What a collusion is this, whenas we are exhorted by the wise man to use diligence, to seek for wisdom as for hidden treasures early and late,[6] that another order shall enjoin us to know nothing but by statute. When a man hath been laboring the hardest labor in the deep mines of knowledge, hath furnished out his findings in all their equipage, drawn forth his reasons as it were a battle[7] ranged, scattered and defeated all objections in his way, calls out his adversary into the plain, offers him the advantage of wind and sun if he please, only that he may try the matter by dint of argument; for his opponents then to skulk, to lay ambushments, to keep a narrow bridge of licensing where the challenger should pass, though it be valor enough in soldiership, is but weakness and cowardice in the wars of Truth.

For who knows not that Truth is strong, next to the Almighty? She needs no policies nor stratagems nor licensings to make her victorious—those are the shifts and the defenses that error uses against her power. Give her but room, and do not bind her when she sleeps, for then she speaks not true, as the old Proteus[8] did, who spake oracles only when he was caught and bound, but then rather she turns herself into all shapes except her own, and perhaps tunes her voice according to the time, as Micaiah did before Ahab,[9] until she be adjured into her own likeness.

---

1. Engrossers, much hated in the English countryside, bought up great quantities of grain and held it for times of famine, selling it at high prices; Milton equates them with the twenty authorized printers, the *stationers*.
2. Milton goes on to argue that Parliament, by its own liberalizing reforms to date, has created the vigorous and inquiring minds it now seeks to suppress.
3. Janus, as god of beginnings and endings, had two faces looking in opposite directions; a door dedicated to him in Rome was kept open in time of war, closed in time of peace.
4. That is, Falsehood's.
5. Milton was already disenchanted with Genevan "Discipline" (Presbyterian church government) and within a year or so would be writing "New *presbyter* is but old *priest*, writ large." "Fabriced": fabricated.
6. Solomon's advice in Proverbs 8:11.
7. Line of battle. Wind and sun (below) were significant advantages in a fight with swords.
8. The sea god who could change shape at will, to avoid capture (*Odyssey* 4).
9. Micaiah, a prophet of God, tried for a time to disguise an unpleasant prophecy from King Ahab but then spoke truth when adjured to do so (1 Kings 22:10–28).

Yet it is not impossible that she may have more shapes than one. What else is all that rank of things indifferent, wherein Truth may be on this side or on the other without being unlike herself? What but a vain shadow else is the abolition of those ordinances, that handwriting nailed to the cross?[1] What great purchase is this Christian liberty which Paul so often boasts of? His doctrine is that he who eats or eats not, regards a day or regards it not, may do either to the Lord.[2] How many other things might be tolerated in peace and left to conscience, had we but charity, and were it not the chief stronghold of our hypocrisy to be ever judging one another? I fear yet this iron yoke of outward conformity hath left a slavish print upon our necks; the ghost of a linen decency[3] yet haunts us. We stumble and are impatient at the least dividing of one visible congregation from another, though it be not in fundamentals; and through our forwardness to suppress and our backwardness to recover any enthralled piece of truth out of the grip of custom, we care not[4] to keep truth separated from truth, which is the fiercest rent and disunion of all. We do not see that while we still affect by all means a rigid and external formality, we may as soon fall again into a gross conforming stupidity, a stark and dead congealment of "wood and hay and stubble,"[5] forced and frozen together, which is more to the sudden degenerating of a church than many subdichotomies of petty schisms.

Not that I can think well of every light separation, or that all in a church is to be expected "gold and silver and precious stones." It is not possible for man to sever the wheat from the tares, the good fish from the other fry; that must be the angels' ministry at the end of mortal things.[6] Yet if all cannot be of one mind—as who looks they should be?—this doubtless is more wholesome, more prudent, and more Christian, that many be tolerated rather than all compelled. I mean not tolerated popery and open superstition, which, as it extirpates all religions and civil supremacies, so itself should be extirpate, provided first that all charitable and compassionate means be used to win and regain the weak and the misled; that also which is impious or evil absolutely, either against faith or manners,[7] no law can possibly permit that intends not to unlaw itself; but those neighboring differences or rather indifferences are what I speak of, whether in some point of doctrine or of discipline, which though they may be many yet need not interrupt "the unity of spirit," if we could but find among us the "bond of peace."[8]

In the meanwhile, if anyone would write and bring his helpful hand to the slow-moving reformation which we labor under, if truth have spoken to him before others, or but seemed at least to speak, who hath so bejesuited[9] us that we should trouble that man with asking license to do so worthy a deed? And not consider this, that if it come to prohibiting, there is not aught more likely to be prohibited than truth itself; whose first appearance to our

---

1. The locution, from Colossians 2:14, implies that the Crucifixion canceled all the rules and penalties of the Mosaic law. Paul's doctrine of Christian liberty (below) is expressed in Galatians 5 and elsewhere.
2. In the Lord's service.
3. White bands around the necks of clergymen are made emblems of formal piety.
4. Scruple not.
5. The contrast between "wood and hay and stubble" and "gold and silver and precious stones" (next paragraph) is from 1 Corinthians 3:12.
6. In Matthew 13:24–30, 36–43, Christ in a parable tells his disciples to let the wheat and tares (weeds) grow up together till harvest time.
7. Morals.
8. The quoted phrases are from Ephesians 4:3.
9. Imposed on us Jesuit ideas (of censorship).

eyes bleared and dimmed with prejudice and custom is more unsightly and unplausible than many errors, even as the person is of many a great man slight and contemptible to see to. And what do they tell us vainly of new opinions, when this very opinion of theirs, that none must be heard but whom they like, is the worst and newest opinion of all others, and is the chief cause why sects and schisms do so much abound, and true knowledge is kept at distance from us; besides yet a greater danger which is in it. For when God shakes a kingdom[1] with strong and healthful commotions to a general reforming, it is not untrue that many sectaries and false teachers are then busiest in seducing; but yet more true it is that God then raises to his own work men of rare abilities and more than common industry, not only to look back and revise what hath been taught heretofore, but to gain further and go on some new enlightened steps in the discovery of truth.

1644

Sonnets Milton wrote twenty-four sonnets between 1630 and 1658. Five in Italian constitute a mini-Petrarchan sequence on a perhaps imaginary Italian lady. The rest, in English, are individual poems on a wide variety of topics and occasions, though not on the usual sonnet topics (love, as in the sequences of Sidney, Spenser, and Shakespeare, or religious devotion, as in that of Donne). Milton writes sometimes about personal crises (his blindness, the death of his wife), sometimes about political issues or personages (Cromwell, the persecuting Parliament), sometimes about friends and friendship (Cyriack Skinner, Lady Margaret Ley), sometimes about historical events (a threatened royalist attack on London, the massacre of Protestants in Piedmont). His tone ranges from Jonsonian urbanity to prophetic denunciation. The form of the sonnets is Petrarchan (see "Poetic Forms and Literary Terminology," in the appendices to this volume), but in the later sonnets especially (for example, the Blindness and Piedmont sonnets) the sense runs on from line to line, overriding the expected end-stopped lines and the octave/sestet shift. There is some precedent for this in the Italian sonneteer Giovanni della Casa, but not for the powerful tension Milton creates as meaning and emotion strive within and against the formal metrics of the Petrarchan sonnet. Milton's new ways with the sonnet had a profound influence on the Romantic poets, especially Wordsworth and Shelley.

How Soon Hath Time

How soon hath Time, the subtle thief of youth,
　　Stol'n on his wing my three and twentieth year!
　　My hasting days fly on with full career,
　　But my late spring no bud or blossom shew'th.
5　　Perhaps my semblance might deceive[1] the truth,

---

1. Milton alludes to Haggai 2:7: "I will shake all nations, and the desire of all nations shall come, and I will fill this house with glory, saith the Lord of hosts."

1. Misrepresent. "Semblance": appearance.

That I to manhood am arrived so near,
And inward ripeness doth much less appear,
That some more timely-happy spirits endu'th.°   *endows*
Yet be it less or more, or soon or slow,
10   It shall be still in strictest measure even²
To that same lot, however mean or high,
Toward which Time leads me, and the will of Heaven;
All is, if I have grace to use it so,
As ever in my great Taskmaster's eye.³

1632?   1645

On the New Forcers of Conscience under the Long Parliament¹

Because you have thrown off your prelate lord,²
And with stiff vows renounced his liturgy,
To seize the widowed whore Plurality³
From them whose sin ye envied, not abhorred,
5   Dare ye for this adjure° the civil sword⁴   *invoke*
To force our consciences that Christ set free,
And ride us with a classic hierarchy⁵
Taught ye by mere A. S. and Rutherford?⁶
Men whose life, learning, faith, and pure intent
10   Would have been held in high esteem with Paul
Must now be named and printed heretics
By shallow Edwards and Scotch what-d'ye-call:⁷
But we do hope to find out all your tricks,
Your plots and packing° worse than those of Trent,⁸   *fraudulent*
15   That so the Parliament⁹   *dealings*

---

2. Equal, adequate. "It": Milton's inner growth. 'Even / To that same lot": conformed to my appointed destiny.
3. The final lines allow for various readings. "Taskmaster" identifies God with the parable Matthew 20:1–16) in which a vineyard keeper takes on workers throughout the day, paying the same wages to those hired at the first and at the eleventh hour.
1. The sonnet targets the Presbyterians, whom Milton in *The Reason of Church Government* (p. 1408) and other antiprelatical tracts of 1641–42 had supported against the bishops. Now that they have overthrown the bishops and dominate the Long Parliament, they seek to become the national church, repressing all others. This *sonetto caudato*, or "tailed sonnet" (an Italian form), has the usual fourteen lines followed by two "tails" of three lines each.
2. Bishops and the ecclesiastical church structure.
3. The practice of holding several benefices at once; she is a "widowed whore" because her earlier lovers, the Anglican clergy, can no longer possess her.

4. State authority.
5. The Presbyterian church order comprised of synods and classes as governing boards and disciplinary courts.
6. Adam Stuart and Samuel Rutherford, Scottish Presbyterian pamphleteers who urged the establishment of an English national Presbyterian church on the Scottish model.
7. Thomas Edwards analyzed hundreds of so-called heresies in a book picturesquely titled *Gangraena* (1645, 1646). It even identifies Milton as the founder of a sect of Divorcers, promoting "divorce at pleasure." "Scotch what-d'ye-call" may refer to another Scots cleric, Robert Baillie, or may simply be a sneer at the unpronounceability of Scottish names.
8. The Council of Trent, held by the Roman Church to deal with the Protestant Reformation, was notorious as a scene of political jockeying.
9. In the previous few months Independents and more secular-minded republicans had gained some strength in the Parliament, so Milton could hope they might weigh in against Presbyterian repression.

May with their wholesome and preventive shears
    Clip your phylacteries,[1] though balk your ears,[2]
        And succor our just fears
    When they shall read this clearly in your charge:
20 New *presbyter* is but old *priest* writ large.[3]

ca. 1646   1673

To the Lord General Cromwell, May 1652[1]

Cromwell, our chief of men, who through a cloud
    Not of war only, but detractions[2] rude,
    Guided by faith and matchless fortitude
To peace and truth[3] thy glorious way hast ploughed,
5   And on the neck of crownèd Fortune proud
    Hast reared God's trophies,[4] and his work pursued,
    While Darwen stream with blood of Scots imbrued[5]
And Dunbar field resounds thy praises loud,
And Worcester's laureate wreath;[6] yet much remains
10 To conquer still; peace hath her victories
    No less renowned than war; new foes arise,
Threatening to bind our souls with secular chains:[7]
    Help us to save free conscience from the paw
    Of hireling wolves[8] whose gospel is their maw.°   belly

1652   1694

1. Little scrolls containing texts from the Pentateuch, worn on the forehead and arm by observant Jews; Milton takes them as a symbol of self-righteous ostentation.
2. "Balk": spare. Mutilation by cutting off the ears was a punishment formerly suffered by several Presbyterian leaders, as Milton hereby reminds them. Milton changed the rather cruel manuscript version of this line—"Crop ye as close as marginal P——'s ears"—alluding to the ultraprolific pamphleteer William Prynne, who stuffed his margins with citations, and who had his ears cropped twice.
3. "Priest" is, etymologically, a contracted form of "Presbyter."
1. The sonnet appeals to Cromwell, a longtime supporter of religious toleration but also of some kind of loosely defined national church, to oppose recent proposals by Independents to set up a national church with a paid clergy and some limits to toleration. This is the only Milton sonnet to end with an epigrammatic couplet. It could not be published in the 1673 *Poems* of Milton because the subject would have offended the restored Stuart monarchy.
2. Cromwell was a target of slander and vituperation from royalists and from extreme radicals.
3. The words "Truth and Peace" were on a coin issued by Parliament to honor Cromwell's victories over the Scots at Preston (1648), Dunbar (1650), and Worcester (1651).
4. Alluding to the ancient Greek custom of erecting trophies of victory on the battlefield.
5. Stained with blood. The river Darwen runs through Preston, site of a major victory by Cromwell over the Scots.
6. Cromwell described his victory at Worcester as his "crowning mercy."
7. Alluding to the new proposals that Parliament, the secular power, repress heresies and blasphemy.
8. Milton fiercely opposed a paid clergy, believing they should support themselves or be supported by their congregations.

When I Consider How My Light Is Spent[1]

When I consider how my light is spent,°   *extinguished*
    Ere half my days,[2] in this dark world and wide,
And that one talent which is death to hide[3]
    Lodged with me useless, though my soul more bent
5 To serve therewith my Maker, and present
    My true account, lest he returning chide;
"Doth God exact day-labor, light denied?"[4]
    I fondly° ask; but Patience to prevent°   *foolishly / forestall*
That murmur, soon replies, "God doth not need
10   Either man's work or his own gifts; who best
Bear his mild yoke, they serve him best. His state°   *splendor*
    Is kingly.[5] Thousands at his bidding speed
And post o'er land and ocean without rest:
    They also serve who only stand and wait."

1652?   1673

On the Late Massacre in Piedmont[1]

Avenge,[2] O Lord, thy slaughtered saints, whose bones
    Lie scattered on the Alpine mountains cold;
Even them who kept thy truth so pure of old
    When all our fathers worshipped stocks and stones,[3]
5 Forget not: in thy book[4] record their groans
    Who were thy sheep and in their ancient fold
Slain by the bloody Piemontese that rolled

---

1. Apparently written soon after Milton lost his sight entirely in 1652.
2. Milton was forty-three in 1652; he is obviously not thinking of the biblical lifespan of seventy, but perhaps of that of his father, who died at eighty-four.
3. In the parable of the talents (Matthew 25:14–30) a crucial text for Puritans, the servants who put their master's money ("talents") to earn interest for him were praised, while the servant who buried the single talent he was given was deprived of it and cast into outer darkness. Milton puns on "literary talent." "Useless" (line 4) carries a pun on "usury," the return expected by the Master.
4. Milton alludes here to the parable of the vineyard keeper (see "How Soon Hath Time," note 3), and also to John 9:4, spoken by Jesus before curing a blind man: "I must work the works of him that sent me, while it is day: the night cometh, when no man can work."
5. The changed metaphor for God—from master who needs to profit from his workers to king—allows the inference that those who "stand and wait" may be placed nearest the throne.
1. The Waldensians (or Vaudois) were a proto-Protestant sect dating to the 12th century who lived in the valleys of northern Italy (the Piedmont) and southern France; Protestants considered them a remnant retaining apostolic purity, free of Catholic superstitions and graven images ("stocks and stones," line 4). The treaty that had allowed them freedom of worship was bypassed in 1655 when the armies of the Catholic duke of Savoy conducted a massacre, razing villages, committing unspeakable atrocities, and hurling women and children from the mountaintops. Protestant Europe was outraged, and in his capacity as Cromwell's Latin secretary Milton translated and wrote several letters about the episode. The sonnet incorporates details from such letters and the contemporary newsbooks. Here Milton transforms the sonnet into a prophetic denunciation.
2. See Revelation 6:9–10: "the souls of them that were slain for the word of God . . . cried with a loud voice, saying, 'How long, O Lord, holy and true, dost thou not judge and avenge our blood . . . ?'"
3. Pagan gods of wood and stone, but with allusion to Roman Catholic "idols."
4. See Revelation 20:12: "the dead were judged out of those things which were written in the books, according to their works." "Sheep" (next line) echoes Romans 8:36: "we are accounted as sheep for the slaughter."

                Mother with infant down the rocks. Their moans
                The vales redoubled to the hills, and they
    10   To heaven. Their martyred blood and ashes sow
                O'er all th' Italian fields, where still doth sway
                The triple tyrant:[5] that from these may grow
                A hundredfold, who having learnt thy way
                Early may fly the Babylonian woe.[6]

1655   1673

Methought I Saw My Late Espousèd Saint[1]

    Methought I saw my late espousèd saint
        Brought to me like Alcestis[2] from the grave,
        Whom Jove's great son to her glad husband gave,
        Rescued from death by force though pale and faint.
    5   Mine, as whom[3] washed from spot of childbed taint,
        Purification in the old law did save,[4]
        And such, as yet once more I trust to have
        Full sight of her in heaven without restraint,
        Came vested all in white, pure as her mind.
    10   Her face was veiled, yet to my fancied sight[5]
        Love, sweetness, goodness, in her person shined
        So clear, as in no face with more delight.
        But O, as to embrace me she inclined,
        I waked, she fled, and day brought back my night.

1658   1673

Paradise Lost

The setting of Milton's great epic encompasses Heaven, Hell, primordial Chaos, and the planet earth. It features battles among immortal spirits, voyages through space, and lakes of fire. Yet its protagonists are a married couple living in a garden, and its climax consists in the eating of a piece of fruit. *Paradise Lost* is ultimately about the human condition, the Fall that caused "all our woe," and the promise and means of restoration. It is also about knowing and choosing, about free will. In the opening passages of Books 1, 3, 7, and 9, Milton highlights

---

5. The pope, wearing his tiara with three crowns. The passage alludes to Tertullian's maxim that "the blood of the martyrs is the seed of the church"; also to the parable of the sower (Matthew 13:3), some of whose seed brought forth fruit "an hundredfold" (see next line); and also to Cadmus, who sowed dragon's teeth that sprang forth armed men.
6. Protestants often identified the Roman Church with the whore of Babylon (Revelation 17–18).
1. There is some debate as to whether this poem refers to Milton's first wife, Mary Powell, who died in May 1652, three days after giving birth to her third daughter, or his second wife, Katherine Woodcock, who died in February 1658, after giving birth (in October 1657) to a daughter. The text can support either, but the latter seems more likely. The sonnet is couched as a dream vision.
2. In Euripides' *Alcestis*, Alcestis, wife of Admetus, is rescued from the underworld by Hercules ("Jove's great son," next line) and restored, veiled, to Admetus; he is overjoyed when he lifts the veil, but she must remain silent until she is ritually cleansed.
3. As one whom.
4. The Mosaic Law (Leviticus 12:2–8) prescribed periods for the purification of women after childbirth (eighty days for a daughter).
5. She is veiled like Alcestis, and Milton's sight of her is only "fancied"; he never saw the face of his second wife, Katherine, because of his blindness.

the choices and difficulties he faced in creating his poem. His central characters—Satan, Beelzebub, Abdiel, Adam, and Eve—are confronted with hard choices under the pressure of powerful desires and sometimes devious temptations. Milton's readers, too, are continually challenged to choose and to reconsider their most basic assumptions about freedom, heroism, work, pleasure, language, nature, and love. The great themes of *Paradise Lost* are intimately linked to the political questions at stake in the English Revolution and the Restoration, but the connection is by no means straightforward. This is a poem in which Satan leads a revolution against an absolute monarch and in which questions of tyranny, servitude, and liberty are debated in a parliament in Hell. Milton's readers are hereby challenged to rethink these topics and, like Abdiel debating with Satan in Books 5 and 6, to make crucial distinctions between God as monarch and earthly kings.

In Milton's time, the conventions of epic poetry followed a familiar recipe. The action was to begin *in medias res* (in the middle of things), following the poet's statement of his theme and invocation of his Muse. The reader could expect grand battles and love affairs, supernatural intervention, a descent into the underworld, catalogues of warriors, and epic similes. Milton had absorbed the epic tradition in its entirety, and his poem abounds with echoes of Homer and Virgil, the fifteenth-century Italians Tasso and Ariosto, and the English Spenser. But in *Paradise Lost* he at once heightens epic conventions and values and utterly transforms them. This is the epic to end all epics. Milton gives us the first and greatest of all wars (between God and Satan) and the first and greatest of love affairs (between Adam and Eve). His theme is the destiny of the entire human race, caught up in the temptation and Fall of our first "grand parents."

Milton challenges his readers in *Paradise Lost*, at once fulfilling and defying all of our expectations. Nothing in the epic tradition or in biblical interpretation can prepare us for the Satan who hurtles into view in Book 1, with his awesome energy and defiance, incredible fortitude, and, above all, magnificent rhetoric. For some readers, including Blake and Shelley, Satan is the true hero of the poem. But Milton is engaged in a radical reevaluation of epic values, and Satan's version of heroism must be contrasted with those of the loyal Abdiel and the Son of God. Moreover, the poem's truly epic action takes place not on the battlefield but in the moral and domestic arena. Milton's Adam and Eve are not conventional epic heroes, but neither are they the conventional Adam and Eve. Their state of innocence is not childlike, tranquil, and free of sexual desire. Instead, the first couple enjoy sex, experience tension and passion, make mistakes of judgment, and grow in knowledge. Their task is to prune what is unruly in their own natures as they prune the vegetation in their garden, for both have the capacity to grow wild. Their relationship exhibits gender hierarchy, but Milton's early readers may have been surprised by the fullness and complexity of Eve's character and the centrality of her role, not only in the Fall but in the promised restoration.

We expect in epics a grand style, and Milton's style engulfs us from the outset with its energy and power, as those rushing, enjambed, blank-verse lines propel us along with only a few pauses for line endings or grammar (there is only one full stop in the first twenty-six lines). The elevated diction and complex syntax, the sonorities and patternings make a magnificent music. But that music is an entire orchestra of tones, including the high political rhetoric of Satan in Books 1 and 2, the evocative sensuousness of the descriptions of Eden, the delicacy of Eve's love lyric to Adam in Book 4, the relatively plain speech of God in Book 3, and the speech rhythms of Adam and Eve's marital quarrel in Book 9. This majestic achievement depends on the poet's rejection of heroic couplets, the norm for epic and tragedy in the Restoration, vigorously defended by Dryden but denounced by Milton in his note on "The Verse." The choice of verse form was, like so many other things in Milton's life, in part a question of politics. Milton's terms associate the "troublesome and modern bondage of rhyming" with Restoration monarchy and the repression of dissidents and present his use of unrhymed blank verse as a recovery of "ancient liberty."

The first edition (1667) presented *Paradise Lost* in ten books; the second (1674) recast it into twelve books, after the Virgilian model, splitting the original Books 7 and 10. We present the twelve-book epic in its entirety, to allow readers to experience the impact of the whole.

Paradise Lost

SECOND EDITION (1674)

The Verse

The measure is English heroic verse without rhyme, as that of Homer in Greek and of Virgil in Latin; rhyme being no necessary adjunct or true ornament of poem or good verse, in longer works especially, but the invention of a barbarous age, to set off wretched matter[1] and lame meter; graced indeed since by the use of some famous modern poets,[2] carried away by custom, but much to their own vexation, hindrance, and constraint to express many things otherwise, and for the most part worse than else they would have expressed them. Not without cause therefore some both Italian[3] and Spanish poets of prime note have rejected rhyme both in longer and shorter works, as have also long since our best English tragedies, as a thing of itself, to all judicious ears, trivial and of no true musical delight; which consists only in apt numbers,[4] fit quantity of syllables, and the sense variously drawn out from one verse into another, not in the jingling sound of like endings, a fault avoided by the learned ancients both in poetry and all good oratory. This neglect then of rhyme so little is to be taken for a defect, though it may seem so perhaps to vulgar readers, that it rather is to be esteemed an example set, the first in English, of ancient liberty recovered to heroic poem from the troublesome and modern bondage of rhyming.

Book 1

The Argument[1]

This first book proposes, first in brief, the whole subject, man's disobedience, and the loss thereupon of Paradise wherein he was placed: then touches the prime cause of his fall, the Serpent, or rather Satan in the Serpent; who revolting from God, and drawing to his side many legions of angels, was by the command of God driven out of Heaven with all his crew

---

1. Perhaps the bawdy content of the Latin songs composed by goliardic poets of the Middle Ages; they learned rhyme from medieval hymns.
2. Notably, Dryden. See his *Essay of Dramatic Poesy*.
3. Trissino and Tasso.
4. Appropriate rhythm.

1. *Paradise Lost* appeared originally without any sort of prose aid to the reader, but the printer asked Milton for some "Arguments," or summary explanations of the action in the various books, and these were prefixed to later issues of the poem.

into the great deep. Which action passed over, the poem hastes into the midst of things,[2] presenting Satan with his angels now fallen into Hell, described here, not in the center[3] (for Heaven and Earth may be supposed as yet not made, certainly not yet accursed) but in a place of utter darkness, fitliest called Chaos: here Satan with his angels lying on the burning lake, thunderstruck and astonished, after a certain space recovers, as from confusion, calls up him who next in order and dignity lay by him; they confer of their miserable fall. Satan awakens all his legions, who lay till then in the same manner confounded; they rise, their numbers, array of battle, their chief leaders named, according to the idols known afterwards in Canaan and the countries adjoining. To these Satan directs his speech, comforts them with hope yet of regaining Heaven, but tells them lastly of a new world and new kind of creature to be created, according to an ancient prophecy or report in Heaven; for that angels were long before this visible creation, was the opinion of many ancient Fathers.[4] To find out the truth of this prophecy, and what to determine[5] thereon he refers to a full council. What his associates thence attempt. Pandemonium the palace of Satan rises, suddenly built out of the deep: the infernal peers there sit in council.

Of man's first disobedience, and the fruit[1]
Of that forbidden tree, whose mortal° taste   *deadly*
Brought death into the world, and all our woe,
With loss of Eden, till one greater Man[2]
5 Restore us, and regain the blissful seat,
Sing Heav'nly Muse,[3] that on the secret top
Of Oreb, or of Sinai, didst inspire
That shepherd, who first taught the chosen seed,
In the beginning how the heav'ns and earth
10 Rose out of Chaos: or if Sion hill[4]
Delight thee more, and Siloa's brook that flowed
Fast by the oracle of God; I thence
Invoke thy aid to my advent'rous song,
That with no middle flight intends to soar
15 Above th' Aonian mount,[5] while it pursues
Things unattempted yet in prose or rhyme.[6]
And chiefly thou O Spirit,[7] that dost prefer
Before all temples th' upright heart and pure,
Instruct me, for thou know'st; thou from the first
20 Wast present, and with mighty wings outspread

---

2. According to Horace, the epic poet should begin "in medias res."
3. That is, of the earth.
4. Church Fathers, the Christian writers of the first centuries.
5. That is, what action to take.
1 Eve's apple, and all the consequences of eating it. This first proem (lines 1–26) combines the epic statement of theme and invocation.
2. Christ, the second Adam.
3. In Greek mythology, Urania, Muse of astronomy; here, however, by the references to Oreb (Horeb) and Sinai (following), identified with the Muse who inspired Moses ("that shepherd") to write Genesis and the other four books of the Pentateuch for the instruction of the Jews ("the chosen seed").
4. Mount Zion: the site of Solomon's Temple. "Siloa's brook" (next line): a spring near the Temple where Christ cured a blind man.
5. Helicon, home of the classical Muses. Milton will attempt to surpass Homer and Virgil.
6. Paradoxically, Milton vaunts his originality in a translated line from Ariosto's *Orlando Furioso* 1.2. The allusion also challenges the romantic epic in Ariosto's tradition.
7. Here identified with God's creating power.

Dove-like sat'st brooding[8] on the vast abyss
And mad'st it pregnant: what in me is dark
Illumine, what is low raise and support;
That to the height of this great argument°   *subject, theme*
25 I may assert Eternal Providence,
And justify° the ways of God to men.   *show the justice of*
    Say first, for Heav'n hides nothing from thy view
Nor the deep tract of Hell, say first what cause[9]
Moved our grand parents in that happy state,
30 Favored of Heav'n so highly, to fall off
From their Creator, and transgress his will
For° one restraint, lords of the world besides?°   *because of / otherwise*
Who first seduced them to that foul revolt?
Th' infernal Serpent; he it was, whose guile
35 Stirred up with envy and revenge, deceived
The mother of mankind, what time° his pride   *when*
Had cast him out from Heav'n, with all his host
Of rebel angels, by whose aid aspiring
To set himself in glory above his peers,°   *equals*
40 He trusted to have equaled the Most High,
If he opposed; and with ambitious aim
Against the throne and monarchy of God
Raised impious war in Heav'n and battle proud
With vain attempt. Him the Almighty Power
45 Hurled headlong flaming from th' ethereal sky
With hideous ruin and combustion down
To bottomless perdition, there to dwell
In adamantine[1] chains and penal fire,
Who durst defy th' Omnipotent to arms.
50 Nine times the space[2] that measures day and night
To mortal men, he with his horrid crew
Lay vanquished, rolling in the fiery gulf
Confounded though immortal: but his doom
Reserved him to more wrath; for now the thought
55 Both of lost happiness and lasting pain
Torments him; round he throws his baleful° eyes   *malignant*
That witnessed huge affliction and dismay
Mixed with obdúrate pride and steadfast hate:
At once as far as angels' ken° he views   *range of sight*
60 The dismal situation waste and wild,
A dungeon horrible, on all sides round
As one great furnace flamed, yet from those flames
No light, but rather darkness visible
Served only to discover sights of woe,
65 Regions of sorrow, doleful shades, where peace

---

8. A composite of phrases and ideas from Genesis 1:2 ("And the earth was without form, and void, and darkness was upon the face of the deep. And the Spirit of God moved upon the face of the waters"). Only a small number of Milton's many allusions to the Bible (in many versions) can be indicated in the notes. Milton's brooding dove image comes from the Latin (Tremellius) Bible version, *incubabat*, "incubated."
9. An opening question like this is an epic convention.
1. A mythical substance of great hardness.
2. Extent of time.

And rest can never dwell, hope never comes
That comes to all;³ but torture without end
Still urges,° and a fiery deluge, fed   *always provokes*
With ever-burning sulphur unconsumed:
70 Such place Eternal Justice had prepared
For those rebellious, here their prison ordained
In utter darkness, and their portion set
As far removed from God and light of Heav'n
As from the center thrice to th' utmost pole.⁴
75 O how unlike the place from whence they fell!
There the companions of his fall, o'erwhelmed
With floods and whirlwinds of tempestuous fire,
He soon discerns, and welt'ring° by his side   *rolling in the waves*
One next himself in power, and next in crime,
80 Long after known in Palestine, and named
Beëlzebub.⁵ To whom th' Arch-Enemy,
And thence in Heav'n called Satan,⁶ with bold words
Breaking the horrid silence thus began.
  "If thou beest he; but O how fall'n!⁷ how changed
85 From him, who in the happy realms of light
Clothed with transcendent brightness didst outshine
Myriads though bright: if he whom mutual league,
United thoughts and counsels, equal hope
And hazard in the glorious enterprise,
90 Joined with me once, now misery hath joined
In equal ruin: into what pit thou seest
From what height fall'n, so much the stronger proved
He with his thunder:° and till then who knew   *thunderbolt*
The force of those dire arms? Yet not for those,
95 Nor what the potent victor in his rage
Can else inflict, do I repent or change,
Though changed in outward luster, that fixed mind
And high disdain, from sense of injured merit,
That with the mightiest raised me to contend,
100 And to the fierce contention brought along
Innumerable force of spirits armed
That durst dislike his reign, and me preferring,
His utmost power with adverse power opposed
In dubious° battle on the plains of Heav'n,   *of uncertain outcome*
105 And shook his throne. What though the field be lost?
All is not lost; the unconquerable will,
And study° of revenge, immortal hate,   *intense consideration*

---

3. The phrase alludes to Dante ("All hope abandon, ye who enter here").
4. Milton makes use of various images of the cosmos in *Paradise Lost*: (1) the earth is the center of the (Ptolemaic) cosmos of ten concentric spheres; (2) the earth and the whole cosmos are an appendage hanging from Heaven by a golden chain; (3) the cosmos seems Copernican from the angels' perspective (see Book 8). Here, the fall from Heaven to Hell is described as thrice as far as the distance from the center (earth) to the outermost sphere.
5. A Phoenician deity, or Baal (the name means "Lord of Flies"). He is called the prince of devils in Matthew 12:24. As with the other fallen angels, his angelic name has been obliterated, and he is now called by the name he will bear as a pagan deity. That literary strategy evokes all the evil associations attaching to those names in human history.
6. In Hebrew the name means "adversary."
7. Alludes to Isaiah 14:12: "How art thou fallen from heaven, O Lucifer, Son of the morning."

And courage never to submit or yield:
And what is else not to be overcome?[8]
110 That glory never shall his wrath or might
Extort from me. To bow and sue for grace
With suppliant knee, and deify his power
Who from the terror of this arm so late
Doubted° his empire, that were low indeed,   *feared for*
115 That were an ignominy and shame beneath
This downfall; since by fate the strength of gods[9]
And this empyreal substance cannot fail,°   *cease to exist*
Since through experience of this great event
In arms not worse, in foresight much advanced,
120 We may with more successful hope resolve
To wage by force or guile eternal war
Irreconcilable, to our grand foe,
Who now triúmphs, and in th' excess of joy
Sole reigning holds the tyranny of Heav'n."
125   So spake th' apostate angel, though in pain,
Vaunting aloud, but racked with deep despair:
And him thus answered soon his bold compeer.°   *comrade*
"O Prince, O Chief of many thronéd Powers,
That led th' embattled Seraphim[1] to war
130 Under thy conduct, and in dreadful deeds
Fearless, endangered Heav'ns perpetual King;
And put to proof his high supremacy,
Whether upheld by strength, or chance, or fate;
Too well I see and rue the dire event,°   *outcome*
135 That with sad overthrow and foul defeat
Hath lost us Heav'n, and all this mighty host
In horrible destruction laid thus low,
As far as gods and heav'nly essences
Can perish: for the mind and spirit remains
140 Invincible, and vigor soon returns,
Though all our glory extinct, and happy state
Here swallowed up in endless misery.
But what if he our conqueror (whom I now
Of force° believe almighty, since no less   *necessarily*
145 Than such could have o'erpow'red such force as ours)
Have left us this our spirit and strength entire
Strongly to suffer and support our pains,
That we may so suffice° his vengeful ire,   *satisfy*
Or do him mightier service as his thralls
150 By right of war, whate'er his business be
Here in the heart of Hell to work in fire,
Or do his errands in the gloomy deep;
What can it then avail though yet we feel

---

8. That is, what else does it mean not to be overcome?
9. A term commonly used in the poem for angels. But to Satan and his followers it means more, as Satan claims the position of a god, subject to fate but nothing else. Their substance is "empyreal" (next line), of the empyrean.

1. According to tradition, there were nine orders of angels, arranged hierarchically—seraphim, cherubim, thrones, dominions, virtues, powers, principalities, archangels, and angels. The poem makes use of some of these titles but does not keep this hierarchy.

Strength undiminished, or eternal being
To undergo eternal punishment?"
Whereto with speedy words th' Arch-Fiend replied.
    "Fall'n Cherub, to be weak is miserable
Doing or suffering: but of this be sure,
To do aught° good never will be our task,   *anything*
But ever to do ill our sole delight,
As being the contrary to his high will
Whom we resist. If then his providence
Out of our evil seek to bring forth good,
Our labor must be to pervert that end,
And out of good still to find means of evil;
Which ofttimes may succeed, so as perhaps
Shall grieve him, if I fail° not, and disturb   *err*
His inmost counsels from their destined aim.
But see the angry victor hath recalled
His ministers of vengeance and pursuit
Back to the gates of Heav'n: the sulphurous hail
Shot after us in storm, o'erblown hath laid°   *calmed*
The fiery surge, that from the precipice
Of Heav'n received us falling, and the thunder,
Winged with red lightning and impetuous rage,
Perhaps hath spent his shafts, and ceases now
To bellow through the vast and boundless deep.
Let us not slip° th' occasion, whether scorn,   *let slip*
Or satiate fury yield it from our foe.
Seest thou yon dreary plain, forlorn and wild,
The seat of desolation, void of light,
Save what the glimmering of these livid° flames   *bluish*
Casts pale and dreadful? Thither let us tend
From off the tossing of these fiery waves,
There rest, if any rest can harbor there,
And reassembling our afflicted powers,°   *armies*
Consult how we may henceforth most offend°   *harm, vex*
Our enemy, our own loss how repair,
How overcome this dire calamity,
What reinforcement we may gain from hope,
If not what resolution from despair."[2]
    Thus Satan talking to his nearest mate
With head uplift above the wave, and eyes
That sparkling blazed, his other parts besides
Prone on the flood, extended long and large
Lay floating many a rood,[3] in bulk as huge
As whom° the fables name of monstrous size,   *as those whom*
Titanian, or Earth-born, that warred on Jove,
Briareos or Typhon,[4] whom the den

---

2. Five of the last nine lines of Satan's speech rhyme.
3. An old unit of measure, between six and eight yards.
4. Both the Titans, led by Briareos (said to have had a hundred hands), and the earth-born Giants, represented by Typhon (who lived in Cilicea near Tarsus and was said to have had a hundred heads), fought with Jove. They were punished by being thrown into the underworld. Christian mythographers found in these stories an analogy to Satan's revolt and punishment.

By ancient Tarsus held, or that sea-beast
Leviathan,[5] which God of all his works
Created hugest that swim th' ocean stream:
Him haply° slumb'ring on the Norway foam   *perhaps*
The pilot of some small night-foundered° skiff,   *overcome by night*
Deeming some island, oft, as seamen tell,[6]
With fixèd anchor in his scaly rind
Moors by his side under the lee,° while night   *out of the wind*
Invests° the sea, and wishèd morn delays: *covers*
So stretched out huge in length the Arch-Fiend lay
Chained on the burning lake, nor ever thence
Had ris'n or heaved his head, but that the will
And high permission of all-ruling Heaven
Left him at large to his own dark designs,
That with reiterated crimes he might
Heap on himself damnation, while he sought
Evil to others, and enraged might see
How all his malice served but to bring forth
Infinite goodness, grace, and mercy shown
On man by him seduced, but on himself
Treble confusion, wrath, and vengeance poured.
Forthwith upright he rears from off the pool
His mighty stature; on each hand the flames
Driv'n backward slope their pointing spires,° and rolled   *points of flames*
In billows, leave i' th' midst a horrid° vale.   *dreadful, bristling*
Then with expanded wings he steers his flight
Aloft, incumbent on° the dusky air   *resting on*
That felt unusual weight, till on dry land
He lights,° if it were land that ever burned   *alights*
With solid, as the lake with liquid fire,
And such appeared in hue; as when the force
Of subterranean wind transports a hill
Torn from Pelorus, or the shattered side
Of thund'ring Etna,[7] whose combustible
And fueled entrails thence conceiving fire,
Sublimed° with mineral fury, aid the winds,   *vaporized*
And leave a singèd bottom all involved°   *enveloped*
With stench and smoke: such resting found the sole
Of unblest feet. Him followed his next mate,
Both glorying to have scaped the Stygian° flood   *Styxlike, hellish*
As gods, and by their own recovered strength,
Not by the sufferance° of supernal power.   *permission*
   "Is this the region, this the soil, the clime,"
Said then the lost Archangel, "this the seat°   *estate*
That we must change for Heav'n, this mournful gloom
For that celestial light? Be it so, since he
Who now is sov'reign can dispose and bid

---

5. The whale, often identified with the great sea monster and enemy of the Lord in Isaiah 17:1 and the crocodile-like dragon of Job 41. Both were also identified with Satan.
6. The story of the deceived sailor and the illusory island was a commonplace, but the reference to Norway suggests a 16th-century version by Olaus Magnus, a Swedish historian.
7. Pelorus and Etna are volcanic mountains in Sicily.

What shall be right: farthest from him is best
Whom reason hath equaled, force hath made supreme
Above his equals. Farewell happy fields
Where joy forever dwells: Hail horrors, hail
Infernal world, and thou profoundest Hell
Receive thy new possessor: one who brings
A mind not to be changed by place or time.
The mind is its own place, and in itself
Can make a Heav'n of Hell, a Hell of Heav'n.⁸
What matter where, if I be still the same,
And what I should be, all but less than° he   *barely less than*
Whom thunder hath made greater? Here at least
We shall be free; th' Almighty hath not built
Here for his envy,⁹ will not drive us hence:
Here we may reign secure, and in my choice
To reign is worth ambition though in Hell:
Better to reign in Hell, than serve in Heav'n.¹
But wherefore let we then our faithful friends,
Th' associates and copartners of our loss
Lie thus astonished° on th' oblivious pool,²   *stunned*
And call them not to share with us their part
In this unhappy mansion, or once more
With rallied arms to try what may be yet
Regained in Heav'n, or what more lost in Hell?"
    So Satan spake, and him Beëlzebub
Thus answered. "Leader of those armies bright,
Which but th' Omnipotent none could have foiled,
If once they hear that voice, their liveliest pledge
Of hope in fears and dangers, heard so oft
In worst extremes, and on the perilous edge°   *front lines*
Of battle when it raged, in all assaults
Their surest signal, they will soon resume
New courage and revive, though now they lie
Groveling and prostrate on yon lake of fire,
As we erewhile, astounded and amazed,
No wonder, fall'n such a pernicious highth."
    He scarce had ceased when the superior Fiend
Was moving toward the shore; his ponderous shield
Ethereal temper,³ massy, large and round,
Behind him cast; the broad circumference
Hung on his shoulders like the moon, whose orb
Through optic glass the Tuscan artist views⁴
At evening from the top of Fesole,
Or in Valdarno, to descry new lands,
Rivers or mountains in her spotty globe.

---

8. Compare Satan's soliloquy, 4.32–113.
9. That is, because he desires this place.
1. An ironic echo of *Odyssey* 11.489–91, where the shade of Achilles tells Odysseus that it is better to be a farmhand on earth than king among the dead.
2. The epithet "oblivious" is transferred from the fallen angels to the pool into which they have fallen.
3. That is, tempered in celestial fire.
4. Galileo, who looked through a telescope ("optic glass") from the hill town of Fiesole, outside Florence, in the valley of the Arno River ("Valdarno," val d'Arno, line 290). In 1610 he published a book describing the mountains on the moon.

His spear, to equal which the tallest pine
Hewn on Norwegian hills, to be the mast
Of some great ammiral,° were but a wand   *admiral's ship*
He walked with to support uneasy steps
Over the burning marl,° not like those steps   *soil*
On heaven's azure; and the torrid clime
Smote on him sore besides, vaulted with fire;
Nathless° he so endured, till on the beach   *nevertheless*
Of that inflamed° sea, he stood and called   *flaming*
His legions, angel forms, who lay entranced
Thick as autumnal leaves that strow the brooks
In Vallombrosa,⁵ where th' Etrurian shades
High overarched embow'r;° or scattered sedge°   *form bowers / seaweed*
Afloat, when with fierce winds Orion armed
Hath vexed the Red Sea coast,⁶ whose waves o'erthrew
Busiris⁷ and his Memphian chivalry,
While with perfidious hatred they pursued
The sojourners of Goshen, who beheld
From the safe shore their floating carcasses
And broken chariot wheels; so thick bestrown
Abject and lost lay these, covering the flood,
Under amazement of their hideous change.
He called so loud, that all the hollow deep
Of Hell resounded. "Princes, Potentates,
Warriors, the flow'r of Heav'n, once yours, now lost,
If such astonishment as this can seize
Eternal Spirits: or have ye chos'n this place
After the toil of battle to repose
Your wearied virtue,° for the ease you find   *strength, valor*
To slumber here, as in the vales of Heav'n?
Or in this abject posture have ye sworn
To adore the conqueror? who now beholds
Cherub and Seraph rolling in the flood
With scattered arms and ensigns,° till anon   *battle flags*
His swift pursuers from Heav'n gates discern
Th' advantage, and descending tread us down
Thus drooping, or with linkèd thunderbolts
Transfix us to the bottom of this gulf.
Awake, arise, or be forever fall'n."
 They heard, and were abashed, and up they sprung
Upon the wing, as when men wont° to watch   *accustomed*
On duty, sleeping found by whom they dread,
Rouse and bestir themselves ere well awake.
Nor did they not perceive the evil plight
In which they were, or the fierce pains not feel;⁸

---

5. The name means "shady valley" and refers to a region high in the Apennines, about twenty miles from Florence, in Tuscany ("Etruria"). Similes comparing the numberless dead to falling leaves are frequent in epic (for example, *Aeneid* 6.309–10).
6. Orion is a constellation whose rising near sunset in late summer and autumn was associated with storms in the Red Sea.
7. Mythical Egyptian pharaoh, whom Milton associates with the pharaoh of Exodus 14, who pursued the Israelites ("sojourners of Goshen," line 309) into the Red Sea, which God parted for them. His "chivalry" (following) are horsemen from Memphis.
8. The double negatives make a positive: they did perceive both plight and pain.

Yet to their general's voice they soon obeyed
Innumerable. As when the potent rod
Of Amram's son[9] in Egypt's evil day
340 Waved round the coast, up called a pitchy cloud
Of locusts, warping° on the eastern wind,   *swarming*
That o'er the realm of impious Pharaoh hung
Like night, and darkened all the land of Nile:
So numberless were those bad angels seen
345 Hovering on wing under the cope° of Hell   *roof*
'Twixt upper, nether, and surrounding fires;
Till, as a signal giv'n, th' uplifted spear
Of their great Sultan[1] waving to direct
Their course, in even balance down they light
350 On the firm brimstone, and fill all the plain;
A multitude, like which the populous north
Poured never from her frozen loins, to pass
Rhene or the Danaw, when her barbarous sons
Came like a deluge on the south, and spread
355 Beneath Gibraltar to the Libyan sands.[2]
Forthwith from every squadron and each band
The heads and leaders thither haste where stood
Their great commander; godlike shapes and forms
Excelling human, princely dignities,
360 And powers that erst° in Heaven sat on thrones;   *formerly*
Though of their names in heav'nly records now
Be no memorial, blotted out and razed°   *erased*
By their rebellion, from the Books of Life.
Nor had they yet among the sons of Eve
365 Got them new names, till wand'ring o'er the earth,
Through God's high sufferance for the trial of man,
By falsities and lies the greatest part
Of mankind they corrupted to forsake
God their Creator, and th' invisible
370 Glory of him that made them, to transform
Oft to the image of a brute, adorned
With gay religions° full of pomp and gold,   *showy rites*
And devils to adore for deities:
Then were they known to men by various names,
375 And various idols through the heathen world.
    Say, Muse, their names then known, who first, who last,[3]
Roused from the slumber on that fiery couch,
At their great emperor's call, as next in worth
Came singly° where he stood on the bare strand,   *one at a time*
380 While the promiscuous° crowd stood yet aloof.   *mixed*
    The chief were those who from the pit of Hell
Roaming to seek their prey on earth, durst fix

---

9. Moses, who drew down a plague of locusts on Egypt (Exodus 10:12–15).
1. A first use of this description of Satan as an Oriental despot.
2. The barbarian invasions of Rome began with crossings of the Rhine ("Rhene") and Danube ("Danaw") rivers and spread across Spain, via Gibraltar, to North Africa.
3. The catalogue of gods here is an epic convention; Homer catalogues ships; Virgil, warriors.

Their seats long after next the seat of God,[4]
Their altars by his altar, gods adored
Among the nations round, and durst abide   385
Jehovah thund'ring out of Zion, throned
Between the Cherubim;[5] yea, often placed
Within his sanctuary itself their shrines,
Abomination; and with cursèd things
His holy rites, and solemn feasts profaned,   390
And with their darkness durst affront his light.
First Moloch,[6] horrid king besmeared with blood
Of human sacrifice, and parents' tears,
Though for the noise of drums and timbrels° loud   *tambourines*
Their children's cries unheard, that passed through fire   395
To his grim idol. Him the Ammonite[7]
Worshipped in Rabba and her wat'ry plain,
In Argob and in Basan, to the stream
Of utmost Arnon. Nor content with such
Audacious neighborhood, the wisest heart   400
Of Solomon he led by fraud to build
His temple right against the temple of God
On that opprobrious hill, and made his grove
The pleasant valley of Hinnom, Tophet thence
And black Gehenna called, the type of Hell.[8]   405
Next Chemos,[9] th' obscene dread of Moab's sons,
From Aroer to Nebo, and the wild
Of southmost Abarim; in Hesebon
And Horonaim, Seon's realm, beyond
The flow'ry dale of Sibma clad with vines,   410
And Elealè to th' Asphaltic Pool.[1]
Peor[2] his other name, when he enticed
Israel in Sittim on their march from Nile
To do him wanton rites, which cost them woe.
Yet thence his lustful orgies he enlarged   415
Even to that hill of scandal,[3] by the grove
Of Moloch homicide, lust hard by° hate;   *close by*
Till good Josiah drove them thence to Hell.
With these came they, who from the bord'ring flood
Of old Euphrates to the brook that parts   420

4. The first group of devils come from the Middle East, close neighbors of Jehovah "throned" in his sanctuary in Jerusalem.
5. Golden cherubim adorned opposite ends of the gold cover on the Ark of the Covenant.
6. Moloch was a sun god, sometimes represented as a roaring bull or with a calf's head, within whose brazen image living children were supposedly burned as sacrifices.
7. The Ammonites lived east of the Jordan River. "Rabba" (next line) is modern Amman, in Jordan; "Argob," "Basan," "utmost Arnon" (lines 398–99) are lands east of the Dead Sea.
8. The rites of Moloch on "that opprobrious hill" (the Mount of Olives), just opposite the Jewish temple, and in the valley of Hinnom so polluted those places that they were turned into the refuse dump of Jerusalem. Under the name "Tophet" and "Gehenna," Hinnom became a type of Hell.
9. Chemos, or Chemosh, associated with Moloch in 1 Kings 11:7, was the god of the Moabites, whose lands (many drawn from Isaiah 15–16) are mentioned in the following lines.
1. The Dead Sea.
2. The story of Peor seducing the Israelites in Sittim is told in Numbers 25.
3. The Mount of Olives, where Solomon built temples for Chemos and Moloch (1 Kings 11:7); epithets were commonly attached to the names of gods, as in the next line, Moloch "homicide." Josiah (following line) destroyed pagan idols in Jerusalem and other cities (2 Chronicles 34).

  Egypt from Syrian ground,[4] had general names
Of Baalim and Ashtaroth, those male,
These feminine.[5] For Spirits when they please
Can either sex assume, or both; so soft
425 And uncompounded is their essence pure,
Not tied or manacled with joint or limb,
Nor founded on the brittle strength of bones,
Like cumbrous flesh; but in what shape they choose
Dilated or condensed, bright or obscure,
430 Can execute their airy purposes,
And works of love or enmity fulfill.
For those the race of Israel oft forsook
Their Living Strength, and unfrequented left
His righteous altar, bowing lowly down
435 To bestial gods; for which their heads as low
Bowed down in battle, sunk before the spear
Of despicable foes. With these in troop
Came Astoreth, whom the Phoenicians called
Astartè, queen of Heav'n, with crescent horns;
440 To whose bright image nightly by the moon
Sidonian virgins[6] paid their vows and songs,
In Sion also not unsung, where stood
Her temple on th' offensive mountain,[7] built
By that uxorious king, whose heart though large,
445 Beguiled by fair idolatresses, fell
To idols foul. Thammuz[8] came next behind,
Whose annual wound in Lebanon allured
The Syrian damsels to lament his fate
In amorous ditties all a summer's day,
450 While smooth Adonis[9] from his native work
Ran purple to the sea, supposed with blood
Of Thammuz yearly wounded: the love-tale
Infected Sion's daughters with like heat,
Whose wanton passions in the sacred porch
455 Ezekiel[1] saw, when by the vision led
His eye surveyed the dark idolatries
Of alienated Judah. Next came one
Who mourned in earnest, when the captive ark
Maimed his brute image, head and hands lopped off
460 In his own temple, on the grunsel edge,[2]
Where he fell flat, and shamed his worshippers:

---

4. Palestine lies between the Euphrates and "the brook Besor" (1 Samuel 30:10).
5. Plural forms, masculine and feminine, respectively, denoting aspects of the sun god Baal and the moon goddess Astarte (called "Astoreth" in line 438, below).
6. Sidon and Tyre were the chief cities of Phoenicia.
7. The Mount of Olives again. "That uxorious king" (next line) is Solomon, who "loved many strange women" (2 Kings 11:1–8).
8. A Syrian god, supposedly killed by a boar in Lebanon; his Greek form was Adonis, beloved of Aphrodite and god of the solar year. Annual festivals mourned his death and celebrated his revival as signifying the death and rebirth of vegetation.
9. Here, the Lebanese river named for the deity because every spring it turned bloodred from sedimentary mud.
1. The prophet complained that Jewish women were worshipping Thammuz (Ezekiel 8:14).
2. When the Philistines stole the ark of God, they placed it in the temple of their sea god, Dagon, but in the morning the mutilated statue of Dagon was found on the threshhold ("grunsel edge") (1 Samuel 5:1–5).

Dagon his name, sea monster, upward man
And downward fish: yet had his temple high
Reared in Azotus, dreaded through the coast
465 Of Palestine, in Gath and Ascalon
And Accaron and Gaza's[3] frontier bounds.
Him followed Rimmon,[4] whose delightful seat
Was fair Damascus, on the fertile banks
Of Abbana and Pharphar, lucid streams.
470 He also against the house of God was bold:
A leper once he lost and gained a king,
Ahaz his sottish conqueror, whom he drew
God's altar to disparage and displace
For one of Syrian mode,[5] whereon to burn
475 His odious off'rings, and adore the gods
Whom he had vanquished. After these appeared
A crew who under names of old renown,
Osiris, Isis, Orus[6] and their train
With monstrous shapes and sorceries abused
480 Fanatic Egypt and her priests, to seek
Their wand'ring gods disguised in brutish forms
Rather than human. Nor did Israel scape
Th' infection when their borrowed gold composed
The calf in Oreb:[7] and the rebel king
485 Doubled that sin in Bethel and in Dan,
Lik'ning his Maker to the grazèd ox,[8]
Jehovah, who in one night when he passed
From Egypt marching, equaled° with one stroke   *leveled*
Both her firstborn and all her bleating gods.[9]
490 Belial came last,[1] than whom a spirit more lewd
Fell not from Heaven, or more gross to love
Vice for itself: to him no temple stood
Or altar smoked; yet who more oft than he
In temples and at altars, when the priest
495 Turns atheist, as did Eli's sons,[2] who filled
With lust and violence the house of God.
In courts and palaces he also reigns
And in luxurious cities, where the noise
Of riot ascends above their loftiest tow'rs,
500 And injury and outrage: and when night

3. The five chief cities of the Philistines, sites of Dagon's worship.
4. A Phoenician god whose temple was in Damascus.
5. A Syrian general, Naaman, was cured of leprosy and converted from worship of Rimmon by the waters of the Jordan (2 Kings 5), while King Ahaz, an Israelite monarch who conquered Damascus, was converted there to Rimmon's worship.
6. The second group of devils includes the Egyptian gods driven from Heaven by the revolt of the giants (Ovid, *Metamorphoses* 5) and forced to wander in "monstrous" (next line) animal disguises.
7. In the wilderness of Egypt, while Moses was receiving the Law, Aaron made a golden calf, thought to be an idol of the Egyptian god Apis and made of ornaments brought out of Egypt (Exodus 32).
8. Jeroboam, "the rebel king" who led the ten tribes of Israel in revolt against Solomon's son, Rehoboam; he doubled Aaron's sin by making two golden calves (1 Kings 12:25–30).
9. Jehovah smote the firstborn of all Egyptian families as well as their gods (Exodus 12:12).
1. Belial was never worshipped as a god; his name means "wickedness," but its use in phrases like "sons of Belial" encouraged personification.
2. Priests who were termed "sons of Belial" because they seized for themselves offerings made to God and lay with women who assembled at the door of the tarbernacle (1 Samuel 2:12–22).

Darkens the streets, then wander forth the sons
Of Belial, flown° with insolence and wine.³ — *flushed*
Witness the streets of Sodom, and that night
In Gibeah, when the hospitable door
Exposed a matron to avoid worse rape.⁴   [505]

    These were the prime in order and in might;
The rest were long to tell, though far renowned,
Th' Ionian gods, of Javan's issue held
Gods, yet confessed later than Heav'n and Earth
Their boasted parents;⁵ Titan Heav'n's firstborn   [510]
With his enormous brood, and birthright seized
By younger Saturn, he from mightier Jove,
His own and Rhea's son, like measure found;
So Jove usurping reigned:⁶ these first in Crete
And Ida known, thence on the snowy top   [515]
Of cold Olympus ruled the middle air
Their highest heav'n; or on the Delphian cliff,
Or in Dodona, and through all the bounds
Of Doric land;⁷ or who with Saturn old
Fled over Adria to th' Hesperian fields,   [520]
And o'er the Celtic roamed the utmost isles.⁸

    All these and more came flocking; but with looks
Downcast and damp,° yet such wherein appeared — *depressed, dazed*
Obscure some glimpse of joy, to have found their chief
Not in despair, to have found themselves not lost   [525]
In loss itself; which on his count'nance cast
Like doubtful hue:⁹ but he his wonted° pride — *accustomed*
Soon recollecting, with high words, that bore
Semblance of worth, not substance, gently raised
Their fainting courage, and dispelled their fears.   [530]
Then straight° commands that at the warlike sound — *immediately*
Of trumpets loud and clarions be upreared
His mighty standard; that proud honor claimed
Azazel¹ as his right, a Cherub tall:
Who forthwith from the glittering staff unfurled   [535]
Th' imperial ensign, which full high advanced
Shone like a meteor streaming to the wind
With gems and golden luster rich emblazed,
Seraphic arms and trophies:² all the while

---

3. This passage, with its present-tense verbs, invites application to current examples—at court and in Restoration London.

4. Lot begged the Sodomites to rape his daughters rather than his (male) angel guests (Genesis 19); in Gibeah a Levite avoided "worse" (homosexual) rape by surrendering his concubine to riotous "sons of Belial" (Judges 19:21–30).

5. The Ionian Greeks ("Javan's issue," that is, of the line of Javan, grandson of Noah) regarded the Titans as gods; their supposed parents were Heaven (Uranus) and Earth (Gaia).

6. The Titan Cronos, or Saturn, deposed his father, married his sister Rhea, and ruled until he was deposed by his son, Zeus (Jove), who had been reared in secret on Mount Ida in Crete.

7. Zeus and the other Olympian gods had their seat on Mount Olympus, in "middle air"; they were worshipped in Delphi, Dodona, and throughout Greece ("Doric lands").

8. Saturn, after his downfall, fled over "Adria" (the Adriatic Sea) to the "Hesperian fields" (Italy), crossed the "Celtic" fields of France, and thence to Britain, the "utmost isles."

9. Satan's face reflected the same mixed emotions.

1. Traditionally, one of the four standard-bearers in Satan's army. "Clarions" (line 532): small, shrill trumpets.

2. Their flags bear the heraldic arms of the various orders of angels and memorials of their battles.

540 Sonorous metal° blowing martial sounds: *trumpets*
     At which the universal host upsent
     A shout that tore Hell's concave,° and beyond   *vault*
     Frighted the reign of Chaos and old Night.³
     All in a moment through the gloom were seen
545 Ten thousand banners rise into the air
     With orient° colors waving: with them rose   *lustrous*
     A forest huge of spears: and thronging helms
     Appeared, and serried° shields in thick array   *pushed close together*
     Of depth immeasurable: anon they move
550 In perfect phalanx to the Dorian⁴ mood
     Of flutes and soft recorders; such as raised
     To highth of noblest temper heroes old
     Arming to battle, and instead of rage
     Deliberate valor breathed, firm and unmoved
555 With dread of death to flight or foul retreat,
     Nor wanting power to mitigate and swage°   *assuage*
     With solemn touches, troubled thoughts, and chase
     Anguish and doubt and fear and sorrow and pain
     From mortal or immortal minds. Thus they
560 Breathing united force with fixèd thought
     Moved on in silence to soft pipes that charmed
     Their painful steps o'er the burnt soil; and now
     Advanced in view they stand, a horrid° front   *bristling with spears*
     Of dreadful length and dazzling arms, in guise
565 Of warriors old with ordered spear and shield,
     Awaiting what command their mighty chief
     Had to impose. He through the armèd files
     Darts his experienced eye, and soon traverse°   *across*
     The whole battalion views, their order due,
570 Their visages and stature as of gods,
     Their number last he sums. And now his heart
     Distends with pride, and hard'ning in his strength
     Glories: for never since created man⁵
     Met such embodied force, as named° with these   *composed*
575 Could merit more than that small infantry
     Warred on by cranes:⁶ though all the giant brood
     Of Phlegra with th' heroic race were joined
     That fought at Thebes and Ilium,⁷ on each side
     Mixed with auxiliar° gods; and what resounds   *allied*
580 In fable or romance of Uther's son
     Begirt with British and Armoric knights;
     And all who since, baptized or infidel
     Jousted in Aspramont or Montalban,
     Damasco, or Morocco, or Trebisond,

---

3. In *Paradise Lost* 2.894–909, 959–70 Chaos and Night rule the region of unformed matter between Heaven and earth.
4. Severe, martial music used by the Spartans marching to battle. "Phalanx": battle formation.
5. That is, since the creation of man.
6. Pygmies (little people, with a pun, in "infantry" on "infants") had periodic fights with the cranes, in Pliny's account. Compared with Satan's forces, all other armies are puny.
7. In Greek mythology, the Giants fought the gods at Phlegra in Macedonia; in Roman myth, it was at Phlegra in Italy. Satan's forces surpass them, even if joined with the Seven who fought against Thebes and the whole Greek host that besieged Troy ("Ilium").

585 Or whom Biserta sent from Afric shore
When Charlemagne with all his peerage fell
By Fontarabia.⁸ Thus far these beyond
Compare of mortal prowess, yet observed°   *obeyed*
Their dread commander: he above the rest
590 In shape and gesture proudly eminent
Stood like a tow'r; his form had yet not lost
All her⁹ original brightness, nor appeared
Less than Archangel ruined, and th' excess
Of glory obscured: as when the sun new-ris'n
595 Looks through the horizontal° misty air   *on the horizon*
Shorn of his beams, or from behind the moon
In dim eclipse disastrous° twilight sheds   *ill-starred*
On half the nations, and with fear of change
Perplexes monarchs. Darkened so, yet shone
600 Above them all th' Archangel: but his face
Deep scars of thunder had intrenched,° and care   *furrowed*
Sat on his faded cheek, but under brows
Of dauntless courage, and considerate° pride   *conscious, deliberate*
Waiting revenge: cruel his eye, but cast
605 Signs of remorse and passion° to behold   *compassion, pain*
The fellows of his crime, the followers rather
(Far other once beheld in bliss) condemned
Forever now to have their lot in pain,
Millions of Spirits for his fault amerced°   *deprived*
610 Of Heav'n, and from eternal splendors flung
For his revolt, yet faithful how they stood,
Their glory withered: as when Heaven's fire
Hath scathed° the forest oaks, or mountain pines, *damaged*
With singèd top their stately growth though bare
615 Stands on the blasted heath. He now prepared
To speak; whereat their doubled ranks they bend
From wing to wing, and half enclose him round
With all his peers: attention held them mute.
Thrice he essayed,° and thrice, in spite of scorn, *attempted*
620 Tears such as angels weep burst forth: at last
Words interwove with sighs found out their way.
    "O myriads of immortal Spirits, O Powers
Matchless, but with th' Almighty, and that strife
Was not inglorious, though th' event° was dire,   *outcome*
625 As this place testifies, and this dire change
Hateful to utter: but what power of mind
Foreseeing or presaging, from the depth
Of knowledge past or present, could have feared,
How such united force of gods, how such
630 As stood like these, could ever know repulse?
For who can yet believe, though after loss,

---

8. Satan's forces also surpass the "British and Armoric" (from Brittany) knights who fought with King Arthur ("Uther's son") and all the romance knights who fought at the famous named sites in the following lines. Roncesvalles, near Fontarabia, was the place where Charlemagne's "peerage," including his best knight, Roland, were defeated in battle (though not Charlemagne himself).

9. *Forma* in Latin is feminine.

That all these puissant° legions, whose exile — *potent, powerful*
Hath emptied Heav'n, shall fail to reascend
Self-raised, and repossess their native seat?
635 For me, be witness all the host of Heav'n,
If counsels different,° or danger shunned — *contradictory*
By me, have lost our hopes. But he who reigns
Monarch in Heav'n, till then as one secure
Sat on his throne, upheld by old repute,
640 Consent or custom, and his regal state
Put forth at full, but still° his strength concealed, — *always*
Which tempted our attempt, and wrought our fall.
Henceforth his might we know, and know our own
So as not either to provoke, or dread
645 New war, provoked; our better part remains
To work in close design, by fraud or guile
What force effected not: that he no less
At length from us may find, who overcomes
By force, hath overcome but half his foe.
650 Space may produce new worlds; whereof so rife° — *common*
There went a fame° in Heav'n that he ere long — *rumor*
Intended to create, and therein plant
A generation, whom his choice regard
Should favor equal to the sons of Heaven:
655 Thither, if but to pry, shall be perhaps
Our first eruption,° thither or elsewhere: — *breaking out*
For this infernal pit shall never hold
Celestial Spirits in bondage, not th' abyss
Long under darkness cover. But these thoughts
660 Full counsel must mature: peace is despaired,
For who can think submission? War then, war
Open or understood° must be resolved." — *covert*
   He spake: and to confirm his words, out flew
Millions of flaming swords, drawn from the thighs
665 Of mighty Cherubim; the sudden blaze
Far round illumined Hell: highly they raged
Against the Highest, and fierce with graspèd arms
Clashed on their sounding shields the din of war,[1]
Hurling defiance toward the vault of Heav'n.
670   There stood a hill not far whose grisly top
Belched fire and rolling smoke; the rest entire
Shone with a glossy scurf,° undoubted sign — *crust*
That in his womb was hid metallic ore,
The work of sulphur.[2] Thither winged with speed
675 A numerous brigade hastened. As when bands
Of pioneers° with spade and pickax armed — *military engineers*
Forerun the royal camp, to trench a field,
Or cast a rampart. Mammon[3] led them on,

---

1. Like Roman legionnaires, the fallen angels applaud by beating swords on shields.
2. Sulfur and mercury were considered the basic substances of all metals.
3. "Mammon," an abstract word for riches, came to be personified and associated with the god of wealth, Plutus, and so with Pluto, god of the underworld. See Matthew 6:24: "Ye cannot serve God and mammon."

       Mammon, the least erected Spirit that fell
680 From Heav'n, for ev'n in Heav'n his looks and thoughts
       Were always downward bent, admiring more
       The riches of Heav'n's pavement, trodden gold,
       Than aught divine or holy else enjoyed
       In vision beatific: by him first
685 Men also, and by his suggestion taught,
       Ransacked the center, and with impious hands
       Rifled the bowels of their mother earth
       For treasures better hid. Soon had his crew
       Opened into the hill a spacious wound
690 And digged out ribs of gold. Let none admire°   *wonder*
       That riches grow in Hell; that soil may best
       Deserve the precious bane.° And here let those   *poison*
       Who boast in mortal things, and wond'ring tell
       Of Babel, and the works of Memphian kings,[4]
695 Learn how their greatest monuments of fame,
       And strength and art are easily outdone
       By Spirits reprobate, and in an hour
       What in an age they with incessant toil
       And hands innumerable scarce perform.
700 Nigh on the plain in many cells prepared,
       That underneath had veins of liquid fire
       Sluiced from the lake, a second multitude
       With wondrous art founded° the massy ore,   *melted*
       Severing° each kind, and scummed the bullion dross:°   *separating / boiling dregs*
705 A third as soon had formed within the ground
       A various mold, and from the boiling cells
       By strange conveyance filled each hollow nook,
       As in an organ from one blast of wind
       To many a row of pipes the soundboard breathes.
710 Anon out of the earth a fabric huge
       Rose like an exhalation, with the sound
       Of dulcet symphonies and voices sweet,
       Built like a temple,[5] where pilasters° round   *columns set in a wall*
       Were set, and Doric pillars[6] overlaid
715 With golden architrave; nor did there want
       Cornice or frieze, with bossy° sculptures grav'n;   *embossed*
       The roof was fretted° gold. Not Babylon,   *richly ornamented*
       Nor great Alcairo such magnificence
       Equaled in all their glories, to enshrine
720 Belus or Serapis[7] their gods, or seat
       Their kings, when Egypt with Assyria strove
       In wealth and luxury. Th' ascending pile
       Stood fixed° her stately height, and straight° the doors   *complete / at once*
       Opening their brazen folds discover° wide   *reveal*

---

4. The Tower of Babel and the pyramids of Egypt.
5. After melting the gold with fire from the lake and pouring it into molds, the devils cause their building to rise as by magic, to the sounds of marvelous music.
6. Doric pillars are severe and plain. The devils' palace combines classical architectural features with elaborate ornamentation, suggesting, perhaps, St. Peter's in Rome.
7. At Babylon, in Assyria, there were temples to "Belus" or Baal; at Alcairo (modern Cairo, ancient Memphis), in Egypt, they were to Osiris ("Serapis").

	Within, her ample spaces, o'er the smooth	
725	And level pavement: from the archèd roof	
	Pendent by subtle magic many a row	
	Of starry lamps and blazing cressets[8] fed	
	With naphtha and asphaltus yielded light	
730	As from a sky. The hasty multitude	
	Admiring entered, and the work some praise	
	And some the architect: his hand was known	
	In Heav'n by many a towered structure high,	
	Where sceptered angels held their residence,	
735	And sat as princes, whom the Súpreme King	
	Exalted to such power, and gave to rule,	
	Each in his hierarchy, the orders bright.	
	Nor was his name unheard or unadored	
	In ancient Greece and in Ausonian land	
740	Men called him Mulciber[9] and how he fell	
	From Heav'n, they fabled, thrown by angry Jove	
	Sheer o'er the crystal battlements: from morn	
	To noon he fell, from noon to dewy eve,	
	A summer's day; and with the setting sun	
745	Dropped from the zenith like a falling star,	
	On Lemnos th' Aégean isle: thus they relate,	
	Erring; for he with this rebellious rout	
	Fell long before; nor aught availed him now	
	To have built in Heav'n high tow'rs; nor did he scape	
750	By all his engines, but was headlong sent	
	With his industrious crew to build in Hell.	
	Meanwhile the wingèd heralds by command	
	Of sov'reign power, with awful ceremony	
	And trumpet's sound throughout the host proclaim	
755	A solemn council forthwith to be held	
	At Pandemonium,[1] the high capitol	
	Of Satan and his peers:° their summons called	nobles
	From every band and squarèd regiment	
	By place° or choice° the worthiest; they anon	rank / election
760	With hundreds and with thousands trooping came	
	Attended: all access was thronged, the gates	
	And porches wide, but chief the spacious hall	
	(Though like a covered field, where champions bold	
	Wont ride in armed, and at the soldan's° chair	sultan's
765	Defied the best of paynim° chivalry	pagan
	To mortal combat or career with lance)	
	Thick swarmed, both on the ground and in the air,	
	Brushed with the hiss of rustling wings. As bees	
	In springtime, when the sun with Taurus rides,[2]	
770	*Pour forth their populous youth about the hive*	
	In clusters; they among fresh dews and flowers	

8. Basketlike lamps, hung from the ceiling.
9. Hephaestus, or Vulcan, was sometimes known in "Ausonian land" (Italy) as "Mulciber." The story of Jove's tossing him out of Heaven (see following lines) is told in Book 1 of the *Iliad*.

1. "Pandemonium" (a Miltonic coinage) means literally "all demons," an inversion of "pantheon," "all gods."
2. The sun is in the zodiacal sign of Taurus from about April 19 to May 20.

Fly to and fro, or on the smoothèd plank,
The suburb of their straw-built citadel,
New rubbed with balm, expatiate and confer³
Their state affairs. So thick the aery crowd
Swarmed and were straitened; till the signal giv'n,
Behold a wonder! They but now who seemed
In bigness to surpass Earth's giant sons
Now less than smallest dwarfs, in narrow room
Throng numberless, like that Pygmean race
Beyond the Indian mount,⁴ or fairy elves,
Whose midnight revels, by a forest side
Or fountain some belated peasant sees,
Or dreams he sees, while overhead the moon
Sits arbitress,° and nearer to the earth   witness
Wheels her pale course: they on their mirth and dance
Intent, with jocund° music charm his ear;⁵   merry
At once with joy and fear his heart rebounds.
Thus incorporeal Spirits to smallest forms
Reduced their shapes immense, and were at large,
Though without number still amidst the hall
Of that infernal court. But far within
And in their own dimensions like themselves
The great Seraphic Lords and Cherubim
In close recess and secret conclave sat,
A thousand demigods on golden seats,
Frequent and full.⁶ After short silence then
And summons read, the great consult⁷ began.

Book 2

The Argument

The consultation begun, Satan debates whether another battle be to be hazarded for the recovery of heaven: some advise it, others dissuade: a third proposal is preferred, mentioned before by Satan, to search the truth of that prophecy or tradition in heaven concerning another world, and another kind of creature equal or not much inferior to themselves, about this time to be created: their doubt who shall be sent on this difficult search; Satan their chief undertakes alone the voyage, is honored and applauded. The council thus ended, the rest betake them several ways and to several employments, as their inclinations lead them, to entertain the time till Satan return. He passes on his journey to hell gates, finds them shut, and who sat there to guard them, by whom at length they are opened, and discover to him the great gulf between hell and heaven; with what difficulty he passes through, directed by Chaos, the power of that place, to the sight of this new world which he sought.

---

3. Spread out and discuss. Bee similes were common in epic from Homer on; also, the bees' (royalist) society was often cited in political argument. The simile prepares for the sudden contraction of the devils, who can shrink or dilate at will.
4. The pygmies were supposed to live beyond the Himalayas.
5. The belated peasant's.
6. Crowded together, and in full complement.
7. Consultation, often secret and seditious.

High on a throne of royal state, which far
Outshone the wealth of Ormus and of Ind,[1]
Or where the gorgeous East with richest hand
Show'rs on her kings barbaric pearl and gold,
Satan exalted sat, by merit raised
To that bad eminence; and from despair
Thus high uplifted beyond hope, aspires
Beyond thus high, insatiate to pursue
Vain war with Heav'n, and by success° untaught   *the outcome*
His proud imaginations° thus displayed.   *schemes*
   "Powers and Dominions,[2] deities of Heaven,
For since no deep within her gulf can hold
Immortal vigor, though oppressed and fall'n,
I give not Heav'n for lost. From this descent
Celestial Virtues rising, will appear
More glorious and more dread than from no fall,
And trust themselves to fear no second fate.
Me though just right, and the fixed laws of Heav'n
Did first create your leader, next, free choice,
With what besides, in counsel or in fight,
Hath been achieved of merit, yet this loss
Thus far at least recovered, hath much more
Established in a safe unenvied throne
Yielded with full consent. The happier state
In Heav'n, which follows dignity, might draw
Envy from each inferior; but who here
Will envy whom the highest place exposes
Foremost to stand against the Thunderer's aim
Your bulwark, and condemns to greatest share
Of endless pain? Where there is then no good
For which to strive, no strife can grow up there
From faction; for none sure will claim in Hell
Precédence, none, whose portion is so small
Of present pain, that with ambitious mind
Will covet more. With this advantage then
To union, and firm faith, and firm accord,
More than can be in Heav'n, we now return
To claim our just inheritance of old,
Surer to prosper than prosperity
Could have assured us;[3] and by what best way,
Whether of open war or covert guile,[4]
We now debate; who can advise, may speak."
   He ceased, and next him Moloch, sceptered king
Stood up, the strongest and the fiercest Spirit
That fought in Heav'n; now fiercer by despair:
His trust was with th' Eternal to be deemed
Equal in strength, and rather than be less

---

1. India. "Ormus": an island in the Persian Gulf, modern Hormuz, famous for pearls.
2. Angelic orders.
3. Note the play on "surer," "prosper," "prosperity," "assured," a favorite device of Milton's.
4. A typical epic convention (in Homer, Virgil, Tasso, and elsewhere) involved councils debating war or peace, with spokesmen on each side. Satan offers only the option of war, open or covert.

Cared not to be at all; with that care lost
Went all his fear: of God, or Hell, or worse
He recked° not, and these words thereafter spake. — *cared*
  'My sentence° is for open war: of wiles, — *judgment*
More unexpért,° I boast not: them let those — *less experienced*
Contrive who need, or when they need, not now.
For while they sit contriving, shall the rest,
Millions that stand in arms, and longing wait
The signal to ascend, sit lingering here
Heav'n's fugitives, and for their dwelling place
Accept this dark opprobrious den of shame,
The prison of his tyranny who reigns
By our delay? No, let us rather choose
Armed with Hell flames and fury all at once
O'er Heav'n's high tow'rs to force resistless way,
Turning our tortures into horrid° arms — *bristling, horrifying*
Against the Torturer; when to meet the noise
Of his almighty engine° he shall hear — *the thunderbolt*
Infernal thunder, and for lightning see
Black fire and horror shot with equal rage
Among his angels; and his throne itself
Mixed with Tartarean[5] sulfur, and strange fire,
His own invented torments. But perhaps
The way seems difficult and steep to scale
With upright wing against a higher foe.
Let such bethink them, if the sleepy drench° — *large draught*
Of that forgetful° lake benumb not still, — *causing oblivion*
That in our proper° motion we ascend — *natural to us*
Up to our native seat: descent and fall
To us is adverse. Who but felt of late
When the fierce foe hung on our broken rear
Insulting,[6] and pursued us through the deep,
With what compulsion and laborious flight
We sunk thus low? Th' ascent is easy then;
Th' event° is feared; should we again provoke — *outcome*
Our stronger, some worse way his wrath may find
To our destruction: if there be in Hell
Fear to be worse destroyed: what can be worse
Than to dwell here, driven out from bliss, condemned
In this abhorrèd deep to utter woe;
Where pain of unextinguishable fire
Must exercise° us without hope of end — *vex, afflict*
The vassals[7] of his anger, when the scourge
Inexorably, and the torturing hour
Calls us to penance? More destroyed than thus
We should be quite abolished and expire.
What fear we then? What° doubt we to incense — *why*
His utmost ire? which to the height enraged,
Will either quite consume us, and reduce

---

5. Tartarus is a classical name for hell.
6. With the Latin sense of stamping on; also, triumphantly scorning.
7. Servants, but perhaps also vessels. See Romans 9:22: "vessels of wrath fitted to destruction."

To nothing this essential,° happier far   *essence*
Than miserable to have eternal being:
Or if our substance be indeed divine,
100 And cannot cease to be, we are at worst
On this side nothing;⁸ and by proof we feel
Our power sufficient to disturb his Heav'n,
And with perpetual inroads to alarm,
Though inaccessible, his fatal⁹ throne:
105 Which if not victory is yet revenge."

    He ended frowning, and his look, denounced°   *portended*
Desperate revenge, and battle dangerous
To less than gods. On th' other side up rose
Belial, in act more graceful and humane;°   *civil, polite*
110 A fairer person lost not Heav'n; he seemed
For dignity composed and high exploit:
But all was false and hollow; though his tongue
Dropped manna, and could make the worse appear
The better reason,¹ to perplex and dash°   *confuse*
115 Maturest counsels: for his thoughts were low;
To vice industrious, but to nobler deeds
Timorous and slothful: yet he pleased the ear,
And with persuasive accent thus began.

    "I should be much for open war, O Peers,
120 As not behind in hate; if what was urged
Main reason to persuade immediate war,
Did not dissuade me most, and seem to cast
Ominous conjecture on the whole success:
When he who most excels in fact° of arms,   *feat*
125 In what he counsels and in what excels
Mistrustful, grounds his courage on despair
And utter dissolution, as the scope
Of all his aim, after some dire revenge.
First, what revenge? The tow'rs of Heav'n are filled
130 With armèd watch, that render all access
Impregnable; oft on the bordering deep
Encamp their legions, or with óbscure wing
Scout far and wide into the realm of Night,
Scorning surprise. Or could we break our way
135 By force, and at our heels all Hell should rise
With blackest insurrection, to confound
Heav'n's purest light, yet our great enemy
All incorruptible would on his throne
Sit unpolluted, and th' ethereal mold²
140 Incapable of stain would soon expel
Her mischief, and purge off the baser fire
Victorious. Thus repulsed, our final hope
Is flat despair: we must exasperate

---

8. That is, we cannot be worse off than we are now, and still live.
9. Established by Fate; also, deadly.
1. The Sophists, mercenary teachers of rhetoric in ancient Greece, were denounced by Plato for making "the worse appear / The better reason."

"His tongue / Dropped manna": his honeyed words seemed like the manna supplied to the Israelites in the desert.
2. Heavenly substance, derived from "ether," the fifth and purest element, thought to be incorruptible.

Th' almighty victor to spend all his rage,
145 And that must end us, that must be our cure,
To be no more; sad cure; for who would lose,
Though full of pain, this intellectual being,
Those thoughts that wander through eternity,
To perish rather, swallowed up and lost
150 In the wide womb of uncreated night,
Devoid of sense and motion? And who knows,
Let this be good, whether our angry foe
Can give it, or will ever? How he can
Is doubtful; that he never will is sure.
155 Will he, so wise, let loose at once his ire,
Belike° through impotence, or unaware,   *perhaps*
To give his enemies their wish, and end
Them in his anger, whom his anger saves
To punish endless? 'Wherefore cease we then?'
160 Say they who counsel war, 'We are decreed,
Reserved and destined to eternal woe;
Whatever doing, what can we suffer more,
What can we suffer worse?' Is this then worst,
Thus sitting, thus consulting, thus in arms?
165 What when we fled amain,° pursued and strook°   *headlong / struck*
With Heav'n's afflicting thunder, and besought
The deep to shelter us? This Hell then seemed
A refuge from those wounds. Or when we lay
Chained on the burning lake? That sure was worse.
170 What if the breath that kindled those grim fires
Awaked should blow them into sevenfold rage
And plunge us in the flames? Or from above
Should intermitted° vengeance arm again   *suspended*
His red right hand to plague us? What if all
175 Her° stores were opened, and this firmament°   *Hell's / sky*
Of Hell should spout her cataracts° of fire,   *cascades*
Impendent[3] horrors, threat'ning hideous fall
One day upon our heads; while we perhaps
Designing or exhorting glorious war,
180 Caught in a fiery tempest shall be hurled
Each on his rock transfixed, the sport and prey
Of racking whirlwinds, or forever sunk
Under yon boiling ocean, wrapped in chains;
There to converse with everlasting groans,
185 Unrespited, unpitied, unreprieved,
Ages of hopeless end; this would be worse.
War therefore, open or concealed, alike
My voice dissuades; for what can force or guile[4]
With him, or who deceive his mind, whose eye
190 Views all things at one view? He from Heav'n's high
All these our motions° vain, sees and derides;   *proposals*
Not more almighty to resist our might

3. In the Latin sense, hanging down, threatening.
4. The verb "accomplish" or "achieve" is understood.

Than wise to frustrate all our plots and wiles.
Shall we then live thus vile, the race of Heav'n
195 Thus trampled, thus expelled to suffer here
Chains and these torments? Better these than worse
By my advice; since fate inevitable
Subdues us, and omnipotent decree,
The victor's will. To suffer, as to do,
200 Our strength is equal, nor the law unjust
That so ordains: this was at first resolved,
If we were wise, against so great a foe
Contending, and so doubtful what might fall.
I laugh, when those who at the spear are bold
205 And vent'rous, if that fail them, shrink and fear
What yet they know must follow, to endure
Exile, or ignominy, or bonds, or pain,
The sentence of their conqueror: This is now
Our doom; which if we can sustain and bear,
210 Our Súpreme Foe in time may much remit
His anger, and perhaps thus far removed
Not mind us not offending, satisfied
With what is punished; whence these raging fires
Will slacken, if his breath stir not their flames.
215 Our purer essence then will overcome
Their noxious vapor, or inured° not feel,   *accustomed*
Or changed at length, and to the place conformed
In temper and in nature, will receive
Familiar the fierce heat, and void of pain;
220 This horror will grow mild, this darkness light,
Besides what hope the never-ending flight
Of future days may bring, what chance, what change
Worth waiting, since our present lot appears
For happy though but ill, for ill not worst,[5]
225 If we procure not to ourselves more woe."
    Thus Belial, with words clothed in reason's garb,
Counseled ignoble ease and peaceful sloth,
Not peace: and after him thus Mammon spake.
    "Either to disenthrone the King of Heav'n
230 We war, if war be best, or to regain
Our own right lost: him to unthrone we then
May hope when everlasting Fate shall yield
To fickle Chance, and Chaos judge the strife:
The former vain to hope argues° as vain   *proves*
235 The latter: for what place can be for us
Within Heav'n's bound, unless Heav'n's Lord supreme
We overpower? Suppose he should relent
And publish grace to all, on promise made
Of new subjection; with what eyes could we
240 Stand in his presence humble, and receive
Strict laws imposed, to celebrate his throne
With warbled hymns, and to his Godhead sing

---

5. That is, from the point of view of happiness, the devils are in an ill state, but it could be worse.

              Forced hallelujahs; while he lordly sits
              Our envied Sov'reign, and his altar breathes
245   Ambrosial° odors and ambrosial flowers,   *fragrant, immortal*
              Our servile offerings. This must be our task
              In Heav'n, this our delight; how wearisome
              Eternity so spent in worship paid
              To whom we hate. Let us not then pursue
250   By force impossible, by leave obtained
              Unacceptable, though in Heav'n, our state
              Of splendid vassalage,° but rather seek   *servitude*
              Our own good from ourselves, and from our own
              Live to ourselves, though in this vast recess,
255   Free, and to none accountable, preferring
              Hard liberty before the easy yoke
              Of servile pomp. Our greatness will appear
              Then most conspicuous, when great things of small,
              Useful of hurtful, prosperous of adverse
260   We can create, and in what place soe'er
              Thrive under evil, and work ease out of pain
              Through labor and endurance. This deep world
              Of darkness do we dread? How oft amidst
              Thick clouds and dark doth Heav'n's all-ruling Sire
265   Choose to reside, his glory unobscured,
              And with the majesty of darkness round
              Covers his throne; from whence deep thunders roar
              Must'ring their rage, and Heav'n resembles Hell?
              As he our darkness, cannot we his light
270   Imitate when we please? This desert soil
              Wants° not her hidden luster, gems and gold;   *lacks*
              Nor want we skill or art, from whence to raise
              Magnificence; and what can Heav'n show more?
              Our torments also may in length of time
275   Become our elements, these piercing fires
              As soft as now severe, our temper° changed   *constitution*
              Into their temper; which must needs remove
              The sensible of pain.⁶ All things invite
              To peaceful counsels, and the settled state
280   Of order, how in safety best we may
              Compose° our present evils, with regard   *come to terms with*
              Of what we are and where, dismissing quite
              All thoughts of war: ye have what I advise."
                 He scarce had finished, when such murmur filled
285   Th' assembly, as when hollow rocks retain
              The sound of blust'ring winds, which all night long
              Had roused the sea, now with hoarse cadence lull
              Seafaring men o'erwatched,° whose bark by chance   *worn out from watching*
              Or pinnace° anchors in a craggy bay   *boat*
290   After the tempest: such applause was heard
              As Mammon ended, and his sentence pleased,
              Advising peace: for such another field°   *battlefield*

   6. Pain felt by the senses.

They dreaded worse than Hell: so much the fear
Of thunder and the sword of Michaël[7]
295 Wrought still within them; and no less desire
To found this nether empire, which might rise
By policy,° and long process of time,   *statecraft*
In emulation opposite to Heav'n.
Which then Beëlzebub perceived, than whom,
300 Satan except, none higher sat, with grave
Aspect he rose, and in his rising seemed
A pillar of state; deep on his front° engraven   *brow*
Deliberation sat and public care;
And princely counsel in his face yet shone,
305 Majestic though in ruin: sage he stood
With Atlantean[8] shoulders fit to bear
The weight of mightiest monarchies; his look
Drew audience and attention still as night
Or summer's noontide air, while thus he spake.
310   "Thrones and imperial Powers, offspring of Heav'n
Ethereal Virtues; or these titles[9] now
Must we renounce, and changing style° be called   *title*
Princes of Hell? for so the popular vote
Inclines, here to continue, and build up here
315 A growing empire. Doubtless! while we dream,
And know not that the King of Heav'n hath doomed
This place our dungeon, not our safe retreat
Beyond his potent arm, to live exempt
From Heav'n's high jurisdiction, in new league
320 Banded against his throne, but to remain
In strictest bondage, though thus far removed,
Under th' inevitable curb, reserved
His captive multitude: for he, be sure,
In height or depth, still first and last will reign
325 Sole King, and of his kingdom lose no part
By our revolt, but over Hell extend
His empire, and with iron scepter rule
Us here, as with his golden those in Heav'n.
What° sit we then projecting peace and war?   *why*
330 War hath determined us,[1] and foiled with loss
Irreparable; terms of peace yet none
Vouchsafed° or sought; for what peace will be giv'n   *granted*
To us enslaved, but custody severe,
And stripes, and arbitrary punishment
335 Inflicted? And what peace can we return,
But, to our power,[2] hostility and hate,
Untamed reluctance,° and revenge though slow,   *resistance*
Yet ever plotting how the conqueror least
May reap his conquest, and may least rejoice
340 In doing what we most in suffering feel?

---

7. The warrior angel, chief of the angelic armies.
8. Worthy of Atlas, the Titan who as a punishment for rebellion was condemned to hold up the heavens on his shoulders.
9. The official titles of angelic orders.
1. That is, war has decided the question for us, but also limited us.
2. That is, to the best of our power.

           Nor will occasion want,° nor shall we need   *be lacking*
           With dangerous expedition to invade
           Heav'n, whose high walls fear no assault or siege,
           Or ambush from the deep. What if we find
345   Some easier enterprise? There is a place
           (If ancient and prophetic fame° in Heav'n   *rumor*
           Err not) another world, the happy seat
           Of some new race called Man, about this time
           To be created like to us, though less
350   In power and excellence, but favored more
           Of him who rules above; so was his will
           Pronounced among the gods, and by an oath,
           That shook Heav'n's whole circumference, confirmed.
           Thither let us bend all our thoughts, to learn
355   What creatures there inhabit, of what mold,
           Or substance, how endued,° and what their power,   *endowed*
           And where their weakness, how attempted° best,   *attacked, tempted*
           By force or subtlety. Though Heav'n be shut,
           And Heav'n's high arbitrator sit secure
360   In his own strength, this place may lie exposed,
           The utmost border of his kingdom, left
           To their defense who hold it:[3] here perhaps
           Some advantageous act may be achieved
           By sudden onset, either with hellfire
365   To waste° his whole creation, or possess   *lay waste*
           All as our own, and drive as we were driven,
           The puny habitants, or if not drive,
           Seduce them to our party, that their God
           May prove their foe, and with repenting hand
370   Abolish his own works.[4] This would surpass
           Common revenge, and interrupt his joy
           In our confusion, and our joy upraise
           In his disturbance; when his darling sons
           Hurled headlong to partake with us, shall curse
375   Their frail original,° and faded bliss,   *originator, parent*
           Faded so soon. Advise° if this be worth   *consider*
           Attempting, or to sit in darkness here
           Hatching vain empires." Thus Beëlzebub
           Pleaded his devilish counsel, first devised
380   By Satan, and in part proposed: for whence,
           But from the author of all ill could spring
           So deep a malice, to confound° the race   *ruin*
           Of mankind in one root,[5] and earth with Hell
           To mingle and involve, done all to spite
385   The great Creator? But their spite still serves
           His glory to augment. The bold design
           Pleased highly those infernal States,° and joy   *nobles*
           Sparkled in all their eyes; with full assent
           They vote: whereat his speech he thus renews.

3. To be defended by the occupants.
4. See Genesis 6:7: "And the Lord said, 'I will destroy man [and all other creatures]; for it repenteth me that I have made them.'"
5. Adam, the first man, is the "root" of the human race.

"Well have ye judged, well ended long debate,
Synod of gods, and like to what ye are,
Great things resolved, which from the lowest deep
Will once more lift us up, in spite of fate,
Nearer our ancient seat; perhaps in view
Of those bright confines, whence with neighboring arms
And opportune excursion we may chance
Reenter Heav'n; or else in some mild zone
Dwell not unvisited of Heav'n's fair light
Secure, and at the bright'ning orient° beam   lustrous
Purge off this gloom; the soft delicious air,
To heal the scar of these corrosive fires
Shall breathe her balm. But first whom shall we send
In search of this new world, whom shall we find
Sufficient? Who shall tempt° with wand'ring feet   attempt, venture
The dark unbottomed infinite abyss
And through the palpable obscure[6] find out
His uncouth° way, or spread his aery flight   unknown
Upborne with indefatigable wings
Over the vast abrupt,[7] ere he arrive
The happy isle? What strength, what art can then
Suffice, or what evasion bear him safe
Through the strict senteries° and stations thick   sentries
Of angels watching round? Here he had need
All circumspection, and we now no less
Choice° in our suffrage; for on whom we send,   discrimination
The weight of all and our last hope relies."
    This said, he sat; and expectation held
His look suspense,[8] awaiting who appeared
To second, or oppose, or undertake
The perilous attempt: but all sat mute,
Pondering the danger with deep thoughts; and each
In other's count'nance read his own dismay
Astonished. None among the choice and prime
Of those Heav'n-warring champions could be found
So hardy as to proffer or accept
Alone the dreadful voyage; till at last
Satan, whom now transcendent glory raised
Above his fellows, with monarchal pride
Conscious of highest worth, unmoved thus spake.
    "O progeny of Heav'n, empyreal Thrones,
With reason hath deep silence and demur°   hesitation
Seized us, though undismayed: long is the way
And hard, that out of Hell leads up to light;
Our prison strong, this huge convex of fire,
Outrageous to devour, immures us round
Ninefold,[9] and gates of burning adamant
Barred over us prohibit all egress.

---

6. Darkness so thick it can be felt (see Exodus 10:21).
7. Chaos, a striking example of sound imitating sense.
8. That is, he sat waiting in suspense.
9. Hell's fiery walls and gates have nine thicknesses (see lines 645ff.). "Adamant" (following): a fabulously hard metal.

>   These passed, if any pass, the void profound
>   Of unessential Night receives him next
> 440   Wide gaping, and with utter loss of being
>   Threatens him, plunged in that abortive gulf.¹
>   If thence he scape into whatever world,
>   Or unknown region, what remains him less°   awaits him except
>   Than unknown dangers and as hard escape?
> 445   But I should ill become this throne, O Peers,
>   And this imperial sov'reignty, adorned
>   With splendor, armed with power, if aught proposed
>   And judged of public moment,° in the shape   importance
>   Of difficulty or danger could deter
> 450   Me from attempting. Wherefore do I assume
>   These royalties, and not refuse to reign,
>   Refusing° to accept as great a share   if I refuse
>   Of hazard as of honor, due alike
>   To him who reigns, and so much to him due
> 455   Of hazard more, as he above the rest
>   High honored sits? Go therefore mighty Powers,
>   Terror of Heav'n, though fall'n; intend° at home,   consider
>   While here shall be our home, what best may ease
>   The present misery, and render Hell
> 460   More tolerable; if there be cure or charm
>   To respite or deceive, or slack the pain
>   Of this ill mansion: intermit no watch
>   Against a wakeful foe, while I abroad
>   Through all the coasts° of dark destruction seek   districts
> 465   Deliverance for us all: this enterprise
>   None shall partake with me." Thus saying rose
>   The monarch, and prevented° all reply,   forestalled
>   Prudent, lest from his resolution raised°   roused
>   Others among the chief might offer now
> 470   (Certain to be refused) what erst° they feared;   formerly
>   And so refused might in opinion stand
>   His rivals, winning cheap the high repute
>   Which he through hazard huge must earn. But they
>   Dreaded not more th' adventure than his voice
> 475   Forbidding; and at once with him they rose;
>   Their rising all at once was as the sound
>   Of thunder heard remote. Towards him they bend
>   With awful° reverence prone; and as a god   full of awe
>   Extol him equal to the Highest in Heav'n:
> 480   Nor failed they to express how much they praised,
>   That for the general safety he despised
>   His own: for neither do the Spirits damned
>   Lose all their virtue; lest bad men should boast
>   Their specious° deeds on earth, which glory excites,   pretending to worth
> 485   Or close° ambition varnished o'er with zeal.   secret
>   Thus they their doubtful consultations dark

1. Chaos is a womb in which all potential forms fragment (see lines 895ff.) "Unessential" (line 439): having no real essence.

Ended rejoicing in their matchless chief:
As when from mountaintops the dusky clouds
Ascending, while the north wind sleeps, o'erspread
490 Heav'n's cheerful face, the louring element°   *threatening sky*
Scowls o'er the darkened landscape snow, or show'r;
If chance the radiant sun with farewell sweet
Extend his evening beam, the fields revive,
The birds their notes renew, and bleating herds
495 Attest their joy, that hill and valley rings.
O shame to men! Devil with devil damned
Firm concord holds, men only disagree
Of creatures rational, though under hope
Of heavenly grace: and God proclaiming peace,
500 Yet live in hatred, enmity, and strife
Among themselves, and levy cruel wars,
Wasting the earth, each other to destroy:
As if (which might induce us to accord)
Man had not hellish foes enow° besides,   *enough*
505 That day and night for his destruction wait.
    The Stygian° council thus dissolved; and forth   *Styx-like, hellish*
In order came the grand infernal peers:
Midst came their mighty paramount,° and seemed   *supreme ruler*
Alone th' antagonist of Heav'n, nor less
510 Than Hell's dread emperor with pomp supreme,
And godlike imitated state; him round
A globe° of fiery Seraphim enclosed   *band, circle*
With bright emblazonry and horrent[2] arms.
Then of their session ended they bid cry
515 With trumpet's regal sound the great result:
Toward the four winds four speedy Cherubim
Put to their mouths the sounding alchemy[3]
By herald's voice explained; the hollow abyss
Heard far and wide, and all the host of Hell
520 With deaf'ning shout, returned them loud acclaim.
Thence more at ease their minds and somewhat raised
By false presumptuous hope, the rangèd° powers   *arrayed in ranks*
Disband, and wand'ring, each his several way
Pursues, as inclination or sad choice
525 Leads him perplexed, where he may likeliest find
Truce to his restless thoughts, and entertain
The irksome hours, till his great chief return.
Part on the plain, or in the air sublime°   *aloft*
Upon the wing, or in swift race contend,
530 As at th' Olympian games or Pythian fields;[4]
Part curb their fiery steeds, or shun the goal[5]
With rapid wheels, or fronted° brígades form.   *confronting*
As when to warn proud cities war appears
Waged in the troubled sky, and armies rush

---

2. Bristling. "Emblazonry": decorated shields.
3. Trumpets (made of the goldlike alloy brass).
4. The Olympic games were held at Olympia, the Pythian games at Delphi. Games celebrating a (usually dead) hero are an epic convention.
5. To drive a chariot as close as possible around a column without hitting it.

535	To battle in the clouds,⁶ before each van°	vanguard
	Prick° forth the aery knights, and couch their spears	spur
	Till thickest legions close; with feats of arms	
	From either end of Heav'n the welkin° burns.	sky
	Others with vast Typhoean⁷ rage more fell°	fierce
540	Rend up both rocks and hills, and ride the air	
	In whirlwind; Hell scarce holds the wild uproar.	
	As when Alcides from Oechalia crowned	
	With conquest, felt th' envenomed robe, and tore	
	Through pain up by the roots Thessalian pines,	
545	And Lichas from the top of Oeta threw	
	Into th' Euboic sea.⁸ Others more mild,	
	Retreated in a silent valley, sing	
	With notes angelical to many a harp	
	Their own heroic deeds and hapless fall	
550	By doom of battle; and complain that fate	
	Free virtue should enthrall to force or chance.	
	Their song was partial,° but the harmony	prejudiced
	(What could it less when Spirits immortal sing?)	
	Suspended° Hell, and took with ravishment	held in suspense
555	The thronging audience. In discourse more sweet	
	(For eloquence the soul, song charms the sense)	
	Others apart sat on a hill retired,	
	In thoughts more elevate, and reasoned high	
	Of providence, foreknowledge, will, and fate,	
560	Fixed fate, free will, foreknowledge absolute,	
	And found no end, in wand'ring mazes lost.	
	Of good and evil much they argued then,	
	Of happiness and final misery,	
	Passion and apathy,⁹ and glory and shame,	
565	Vain wisdom all, and false philosophy:	
	Yet with a pleasing sorcery could charm	
	Pain for a while or anguish, and excite	
	Fallacious hope, or arm th' obdurèd° breast	hardened
	With stubborn patience as with triple steel.	
570	Another part in squadrons and gross° bands,	solid, dense
	On bold adventure to discover wide	
	That dismal world, if any clime perhaps	
	Might yield them easier habitation, bend	
	Four ways their flying march, along the banks	
575	Of four infernal rivers that disgorge	
	Into the burning lake their baleful streams:¹	
	Abhorrèd Styx the flood of deadly hate,	
	Sad Acheron of sorrow, black and deep;	
	Cocytus, named of lamentation loud	

---

6. The appearance of warfare in the skies, reported before several notable battles, portends trouble on earth.

7. Like that of Typhon, the hundred-headed Titan (see 1.199).

8. Wearing a *poisoned robe* given him in a deception, Hercules ("Alcides") in his dying agonies threw his beloved companion Lichas, along with a good part of Mount Oeta, into the Euboean Sea, near Thermopylae.

9. The Stoic goal of freedom from passion.

1. These four rivers are traditional in hellish geography. Milton distinguishes them by the original meanings of their Greek names: Styx means "hateful," Acheron "woeful," etc. Lethe is "far off" and quite different from the others, oblivion being a desired state in Hell.

580	Heard on the rueful stream; fierce Phlegethon	
	Whose waves of torrent fire inflame with rage.	
	Far off from these a slow and silent stream,	
	Lethe the river of oblivion rolls	
	Her wat'ry labyrinth, whereof who drinks,	
585	Forthwith his former state and being forgets,	
	Forgets both joy and grief, pleasure and pain.	
	Beyond this flood a frozen continent	
	Lies dark and wild, beat with perpetual storms	
	Of whirlwind and dire hail, which on firm land	
590	Thaws not, but gathers heap,[2] and ruin seems	
	Of ancient pile; all else deep snow and ice,	
	A gulf profound as that Serbonian bog[3]	
	Betwixt Damiata and Mount Casius old,	
	Where armies whole have sunk: the parching air	
595	Burns frore,° and cold performs th' effect of fire.	*frozen*
	Thither by harpy-footed[4] Furies haled,°	*driven*
	At certain revolutions° all the damned	*recurring times*
	Are brought: and feel by turns the bitter change	
	Of fierce extremes, extremes by change more fierce,	
600	From beds of raging fire to starve° in ice	*make numb*
	Their soft ethereal warmth, and there to pine	
	Immovable, infixed, and frozen round,	
	Periods of time; thence hurried back to fire.	
	They ferry over this Lethean sound	
605	Both to and fro, their sorrow to augment,	
	And wish and struggle, as they pass, to reach	
	The tempting stream, with one small drop to lose	
	In sweet forgetfulness all pain and woe,	
	All in one moment, and so near the brink;	
610	But fate withstands, and to oppose th' attempt	
	Medusa[5] with Gorgonian terror guards	
	The ford, and of itself the water flies	
	All taste of living wight,° as once it fled	*creature*
	The lip of Tantalus.[6] Thus roving on	
615	In cónfused march forlorn, th' advent'rous bands	
	With shudd'ring horror pale, and eyes aghast	
	Viewed first their lamentable lot, and found	
	No rest: through many a dark and dreary vale	
	They passed, and many a region dolorous,	
620	O'er many a frozen, many a fiery alp,°	*volcano*
	Rocks, caves, lakes, fens, bogs, dens, and shades of death,	
	A universe of death, which God by curse	
	Created evil, for evil only good,	
	Where all life dies, death lives, and nature breeds,	
625	Perverse, all monstrous, all prodigious things,	

---

2. In a heap, resembling the ruin of an old building ("ancient pile," next line).
3. Lake Serbonis, once famous for its quicksands, lies near the city of Damietta ("Damiata," next line), just east of the Nile.
4. Taloned. In Greek mythology the Harpies (monsters with women's faces) carried off individuals to the Furies, who avenged crimes.
5. One of the three Gorgons, women with snaky hair, scaly bodies, and boar tusks, the sight of whose faces changed men to stone.
6. Tantalus, afflicted with a raging thirst, stood in the middle of a lake, the water of which always receded when he tried to drink (hence, "tantalize").

Abominable, inutterable, and worse
Than fables yet have feigned, or fear conceived,
Gorgons and Hydras, and Chimeras[7] dire.
    Meanwhile the Adversary[8] of God and man,
Satan, with thoughts inflamed of highest design,
Puts on swift wings,° and towards the gates of Hell   *flies swiftly*
Explores his solitary flight; sometimes
He scours the right-hand coast, sometimes the left,
Now shaves with level wing the deep, then soars
Up to the fiery concave° tow'ring high.   *vault*
As when far off at sea a fleet descried
Hangs on the clouds, by equinoctial° winds   *from the equator*
Close sailing from Bengala,° or the isles   *Bengal*
Of Ternate and Tidore,[9] whence merchants bring
Their spicy drugs: they on the trading flood
Through the wide Ethiopian to the Cape
Ply stemming nightly toward the pole:[1] so seemed
Far off the flying Fiend. At last appear
Hell bounds high reaching to the horrid roof,
And thrice threefold the gates; three folds were brass,
Three iron, three of adamantine rock,
Impenetrable, impaled with circling fire,
Yet unconsumed. Before the gates there sat
On either side a formidable shape;[2]
The one seemed woman to the waist, and fair,
But ended foul in many a scaly fold
Voluminous and vast, a serpent armed
With mortal sting: about her middle round
A cry° of hellhounds never ceasing barked   *pack*
With wide Cerberean[3] mouths full loud, and rung
A hideous peal: yet, when they list,° would creep,   *wish*
If aught disturbed their noise, into her womb,
And kennel there, yet there still barked and howled,
Within unseen. Far less abhorred than these
Vexed Scylla[4] bathing in the sea that parts
Calabria from the hoarse Trinacrian shore:
Nor uglier follow the night-hag,[5] when called
In secret, riding through the air she comes
Lured with the smell of infant blood, to dance
With Lapland witches, while the laboring° moon   *troubled*
Eclipses at their charms.° The other shape,   *magic*

---

7. The Hydra was a serpent whose multiple heads grew back when severed; the Chimera was a fire-breathing creature, part lion, part dragon, part goat.
8. *Satan* in Hebrew means "adversary."
9. Two of the Moluccas, or Spice Islands, modern Indonesia.
1. The South Pole. "Ethiopian": the Indian Ocean. "The Cape" is the Cape of Good Hope.
2. The allegorical figures of Sin and Death are founded on James 1:15: "Then when lust hath conceived, it bringeth forth sin: and sin, when it is finished, bringeth forth death." But the incestuous relations of Sin and Death are Milton's own invention. Physically, Sin is modeled on Virgil's or Ovid's Scylla, with some touches adopted from Spenser's Error. Death is a traditional figure, vague and vast.
3. Like Cerberus, the multiheaded hound of Hell.
4. Circe, out of jealousy, threw poison into the water where Scylla bathed, in the straits between Calabria and Sicily ("Trinacria," next line); the poison caused Scylla to develop a ring of barking, snapping dogs around her waist.
5. Hecate (three syllables), goddess of sorcery. She attends orgies of witches in Lapland (line 665, famous for witchcraft), drawn by the blood of babies sacrificed for the occasion.

If shape it might be called that shape had none
Distinguishable in member, joint, or limb,
Or substance might be called that shadow seemed,
For each seemed either; black it stood as night,
Fierce as ten Furies, terrible as hell,
And shook a dreadful dart; what seemed his head
The likeness of a kingly crown had on.
Satan was now at hand, and from his seat
The monster moving onward came as fast
With horrid strides. Hell trembled as he strode.
Th' undaunted Fiend what this might be admired,°   *wondered*
Admired, not feared; God and his Son except,
Created thing naught valued he nor shunned;
And with disdainful look thus first began.
   "Whence and what art thou, execrable shape,
That dar'st, though grim and terrible, advance
Thy miscreated front° athwart my way   *misshapen face*
To yonder gates? Through them I mean to pass,
That be assured, without leave asked of thee:
Retire, or taste° thy folly, and learn by proof,   *experience*
Hell-born, not to contend with Spirits of Heav'n."
   To whom the goblin full of wrath replied:
"Art thou that traitor angel, art thou he,
Who first broke peace in Heav'n and faith, till then
Unbroken, and in proud rebellious arms
Drew after him the third part of Heav'n's sons
Conjured° against the Highest, for which both thou   *sworn together*
And they outcast from God, are here condemned
To waste eternal days in woe and pain?
And reckon'st thou thyself with Spirits of Heav'n,
Hell-doomed, and breath'st defiance here and scorn,
Where I reign king, and to enrage thee more,
Thy king and lord? Back to thy punishment,
False fugitive, and to thy speed add wings,
Lest with a whip of scorpions I pursue
Thy ling'ring, or with one stroke of this dart
Strange horror seize thee, and pangs unfelt before."
   So spake the grisly terror, and in shape,
So speaking and so threat'ning, grew tenfold
More dreadful and deform: on th' other side
Incensed with indignation Satan stood
Unterrified, and like a comet burned
That fires the length of Ophiuchus[6] huge
In th' arctic sky, and from his horrid° hair   *bristling*
Shakes pestilence and war. Each at the head
Leveled his deadly aim; their fatal hands
No second stroke intend, and such a frown
Each cast at th' other, as when, two black clouds
With Heav'n's artillery fraught,[7] come rattling on

---

6. A vast northern constellation, "the Serpent Bearer."

7. Loaded with thunderbolts.

Over the Caspian,[8] then stand front to front
Hov'ring a space, till winds the signal blow
To join their dark encounter in mid-air:
So frowned the mighty combatants, that Hell
Grew darker at their frown, so matched they stood;
For never but once more was either like
To meet so great a foe.[9] And now great deeds
Had been achieved, whereof all Hell had rung,
Had not the snaky sorceress that sat
Fast by Hell gate, and kept the fatal key,
Ris'n, and with hideous outcry rushed between.
   "O father, what intends thy hand," she cried,
"Against thy only son?[1] What fury O son,
Possesses thee to bend that mortal dart
Against thy father's head? And know'st for whom;
For him who sits above and laughs the while
At thee ordained his drudge, to execute
Whate'er his wrath, which he calls justice, bids,
His wrath which one day will destroy ye both."
   She spake, and at her words the hellish pest
Forbore, then these to her Satan returned.
   'So strange thy outcry, and thy words so strange
Thou interposest, that my sudden hand
Prevented° spares to tell thee yet by deeds   *forestalled*
What it intends; till first I know of thee,
What thing thou art, thus double-formed, and why
In this infernal vale first met thou call'st
Me father, and that phantasm call'st my son?
I know thee not, nor ever saw till now
Sight more detestable than him and thee."
   T' whom thus the portress of Hell gate replied:
"Hast thou forgot me then, and do I seem
Now in thine eye so foul, once deemed so fair
In Heav'n, when at th' assembly, and in sight
Of all the Seraphim with thee combined
In bold conspiracy against Heav'n's King,
All on a sudden miserable pain
Surprised thee, dim thine eyes, and dizzy swum
In darkness, while thy head flames thick and fast
Threw forth, till on the left side op'ning wide,
Likest to thee in shape and count'nance bright,
Then shining heav'nly fair, a goddess armed
Out of thy head I sprung:[2] amazement seized
All th' host of Heav'n; back they recoiled afraid
At first, and called me Sin, and for a sign
Portentous held me; but familiar grown,
I pleased, and with attractive graces won
The most averse, thee chiefly, who full oft

8. The Caspian is a particularly stormy area.
9. That is, the Son of God.
1. Sin, Death, and Satan, in their various interrelations, parody obscenely the relations between God and the Son, Adam and Eve.
2. As Athena sprang full grown from the head of Zeus.

Thyself in me thy perfect image viewing
Becam'st enamored, and such joy thou took'st
With me in secret, that my womb conceived
A growing burden. Meanwhile war arose,
And fields were fought in Heav'n; wherein remained
(For what could else) to our almighty foe
Clear victory, to our part loss and rout
Through all the empyrean: down they fell
Driv'n headlong from the pitch° of Heaven, down   *summit*
Into this deep, and in the general fall
I also; at which time this powerful key
Into my hand was giv'n, with charge to keep
These gates forever shut, which none can pass
Without my op'ning. Pensive here I sat
Alone, but long I sat not, till my womb
Pregnant by thee, and now excessive grown
Prodigious motion felt and rueful throes.
At last this odious offspring whom thou seest
Thine own begotten, breaking violent way
Tore through my entrails, that with fear and pain
Distorted, all my nether shape thus grew
Transformed: but he my inbred enemy
Forth issued, brandishing his fatal dart
Made to destroy: I fled, and cried out 'Death';
Hell trembled at the hideous name, and sighed
From all her caves, and back resounded 'Death.'
I fled, but he pursued (though more, it seems,
Inflamed with lust than rage) and swifter far,
Me overtook his mother all dismayed,
And in embraces forcible and foul
Engend'ring with me, of that rape begot
These yelling monsters that with ceaseless cry
Surround me, as thou saw'st, hourly conceived
And hourly born, with sorrow infinite
To me, for when they list,° into the womb   *wish*
That bred them they return, and howl and gnaw
My bowels, their repast; then bursting forth
Afresh with conscious terrors vex me round,
That rest or intermission none I find.
Before mine eyes in opposition sits
Grim Death my son and foe, who sets them on,
And me his parent would full soon devour
For want of other prey, but that he knows
His end with mine involved; and knows that I
Should prove a bitter morsel, and his bane,°   *poison*
Whenever that shall be; so fate pronounced.
But thou O father, I forewarn thee, shun
His deadly arrow; neither vainly hope
To be invulnerable in those bright arms,
Though tempered heav'nly, for that mortal dint,°   *blow*
Save he who reigns above, none can resist."
   She finished, and the subtle Fiend his lore°   *lesson*

Soon learned, now milder, and thus answered smooth.
"Dear daughter, since thou claim'st me for thy sire,
And my fair son here show'st me, the dear pledge
Of dalliance had with thee in Heav'n, and joys
Then sweet, now sad to mention, through dire change   820
Befall'n us unforeseen, unthought of, know
I come no enemy, but to set free
From out this dark and dismal house of pain,
Both him and thee, and all the heav'nly host
Of Spirits that in our just pretenses° armed   *claims*   825
Fell with us from on high: from them I go
This uncouth errand[3] sole, and one for all
Myself expose, with lonely steps to tread
Th' unfounded° deep, and through the void immense   *bottomless*
To search with wand'ring quest a place foretold   830
Should be, and, by concurring signs, ere now
Created vast and round, a place of bliss
In the purlieus° of Heav'n, and therein placed   *outskirts*
A race of upstart creatures, to supply
Perhaps our vacant room, though more removed,   835
Lest Heav'n surcharged° with potent multitude   *overcrowded*
Might hap to move new broils:° be this or aught   *controversies*
Than this more secret now designed, I haste
To know, and this once known, shall soon return,
And bring ye to the place where thou and Death   840
Shall dwell at ease, and up and down unseen
Wing silently the buxom° air, embalmed°   *yielding / made fragrant*
With odors; there ye shall be fed and filled
Immeasurably, all things shall be your prey."
He ceased, for both seemed highly pleased, and Death   845
Grinned horrible a ghastly smile, to hear
His famine° should be filled, and blessed his maw°   *ravenous hunger / belly*
Destined to that good hour: no less rejoiced
His mother bad, and thus bespake her sire.
    "The key of this infernal pit by due,   850
And by command of Heav'n's all-powerful King
I keep, by him forbidden to unlock
These adamantine gates; against all force
Death ready stands to interpose his dart,
Fearless to be o'ermatched by living might.   855
But what owe I to his commands above
Who hates me, and hath hither thrust me down
Into this gloom of Tartarus profound,
To sit in hateful office here confined,
Inhabitant of Heav'n, and heav'nly-born,   860
Here in perpetual agony and pain,
With terrors and with clamors compassed round
Of mine own brood, that on my bowels feed?
Thou art my father, thou my author, thou
My being gav'st me; whom should I obey   865

---

3. Unknown journey—a parody of Christ's errand on earth (3.236–65).

But thee, whom follow? Thou wilt bring me soon
To that new world of light and bliss, among
The gods who live at ease, where I shall reign
At thy right hand voluptuous,[4] as beseems
870 Thy daughter and thy darling, without end."
   Thus saying, from her side the fatal key,
Sad instrument of all our woe, she took;
And towards the gate rolling her bestial train,[5]
Forthwith the huge portcullis high up drew,
875 Which but herself not all the Stygian powers°   *armies of Hell*
Could once have moved; then in the keyhole turns
Th' intricate wards, and every bolt and bar
Of massy iron or solid rock with ease
Unfastens: on a sudden open fly
880 With impetuous recoil and jarring sound
Th' infernal doors, and on their hinges grate
Harsh thunder, that the lowest bottom shook
Of Erebus.° She opened, but to shut   *Hell*
Excelled° her power; the gates wide open stood,   *exceeded*
885 That with extended wings a bannered host
Under spread ensigns° marching might pass through   *flags, standards*
With horse and chariots ranked in loose array;
So wide they stood, and like a furnace mouth
Cast forth redounding° smoke and ruddy flame.   *billowing*
890 Before their eyes in sudden view appear
The secrets of the hoary° deep, a dark   *ancient*
Illimitable° ocean without bound,   *without limit*
Without dimension, where length, breadth, and height,
And time and place are lost; where eldest Night
895 And Chaos, ancestors of Nature, hold
Eternal anarchy, amidst the noise
Of endless wars, and by confusion stand.
For Hot, Cold, Moist, and Dry, four champions fierce
Strive here for mastery, and to battle bring
900 Their embryon atoms;[6] they around the flag
Of each his faction, in their several clans,
Light-armed or heavy, sharp, smooth, swift or slow,
Swarm populous, unnumbered as the sands
Of Barca or Cyrene's torrid soil,[7]
905 Levied to side with warring winds, and poise[8]
Their lighter wings. To whom these most adhere,
He rules a moment; Chaos[9] umpire sits,
And by decision more embroils the fray
By which he reigns: next him high arbiter
910 Chance governs all. Into this wild abyss,

4. As the Son sits at God's right hand, Sin will at Satan's, a blasphemous parody of the Apostles' Creed and of *Paradise Lost* 3.250–80.
5. That is, propelling her yelping offspring.
6. These subatomic qualities combine together in nature to form the four elements, fire, earth, water, and air, but they struggle endlessly in Chaos, where the atoms of these elements remain undeveloped (in "embryo").
7. Cities built on the shifting sands of North Africa.
8. Give weight to. "Levied": both enlisted and raised up.
9. Chaos is both the place where confusion reigns and personified confusion itself.

The womb of Nature and perhaps her grave,
Of neither sea, nor shore, nor air, nor fire,
But all these in their pregnant causes° mixed　　　　　　　*seeds*
Confus'dly, and which thus must ever fight,
Unless th' Almighty Maker them ordain
His dark materials to create more worlds,
Into this wild abyss the wary Fiend
Stood on the brink of Hell and looked a while,
Pondering his voyage; for no narrow frith°　　　　　　*channel, firth*
He had to cross. Nor was his ear less pealed°　　　　　　*dinned*
With noises loud and ruinous (to compare
Great things with small) than when Bellona[1] storms,
With all her battering engines bent to raze
Some capital city; or less than if this frame°　　　　　　*structure*
Of Heav'n were falling, and these elements
In mutiny had from her axle torn
The steadfast earth. At last his sail-broad vans°　　　　　　*wings*
He spreads for flight, and in the surging smoke
Uplifted spurns the ground, thence many a league
As in a cloudy chair ascending rides
Audacious, but that seat soon failing, meets
A vast vacuity: all unawares
Flutt'ring his pennons[2] vain plumb down he drops
Ten thousand fathom deep, and to this hour
Down had been falling, had not by ill chance
The strong rebuff° of some tumultuous cloud　　　　　　*counterblast*
Instinct° with fire and niter° hurried him　　　　　　*filled / saltpeter*
As many miles aloft: that fury stayed,
Quenched in a boggy Syrtis,[3] neither sea,
Nor good dry land: nigh foundered° on he fares,　　　　　　*drowned*
Treading the crude consistence, half on foot,
Half flying; behoves° him now both oar and sail.　　　　　　*befits*
As when a griffin through the wilderness
With wingèd course o'er hill or moory° dale,　　　　　　*marshy*
Pursues the Arimaspian, who by stealth
Had from his wakeful custody purloined
The guarded gold:[4] so eagerly the Fiend
O'er bog or steep, through strait, rough, dense, or rare,
With head, hands, wings, or feet pursues his way,
And swims or sinks, or wades, or creeps, or flies:
At length a universal hubbub wild
Of stunning sounds and voices all confused
Borne through the hollow dark assaults his ear
With loudest vehemence: thither he plies,
Undaunted to meet there whatever Power
Or Spirit of the nethermost abyss
Might in that noise reside, of whom to ask

---

1. Goddess of war.
2. Useless wings ("pinions").
3. Quicksand in North African gulfs, famous for their shifting sandbars.
4. Griffins, mythical creatures, half-eagle, half-lion, hoarded gold that was stolen from them by the one-eyed Arimaspians.

Which way the nearest coast of darkness lies
Bordering on light; when straight behold the throne
Of Chaos, and his dark pavilion spread
Wide on the wasteful deep; with him enthroned
Sat sable-vested Night, eldest of things,
The consort of his reign; and by them stood
Orcus and Ades,[5] and the dreaded name
Of Demogorgon,[6] Rumor next and Chance,
And Tumult and Confusion all embroiled,
And Discord with a thousand various mouths.
    T' whom Satan turning boldly, thus. "Ye Powers
And Spirits of this nethermost abyss,
Chaos and ancient Night, I come no spy,
With purpose to explore or to disturb
The secrets of your realm, but by constraint
Wand'ring this darksome desert, as my way
Lies through your spacious empire up to light,
Alone, and without guide, half lost, I seek
What readiest path leads where your gloomy bounds
Confine with° Heav'n; or if some other place   *border on*
From your dominion won, th' Ethereal King
Possesses lately, thither to arrive
I travel this profound;° direct my course;   *deep pit*
Directed, no mean recompense it brings
To your behoof,° if I that region lost,   *on your behalf*
All usurpation thence expelled, reduce
To her original darkness and your sway
(Which is my present journey)[7] and once more
Erect the standard there of ancient Night;
Yours be th' advantage all, mine the revenge."
    Thus Satan; and him thus the anarch[8] old
With falt'ring speech and visage incomposed°   *disordered*
Answered. "I know thee, stranger, who thou art,
That mighty leading angel, who of late
Made head against Heav'n's King, though overthrown.
I saw and heard, for such a numerous host
Fled not in silence through the frighted deep
With ruin upon ruin, rout on rout,
Confusion worse confounded; and Heav'n gates
Poured out by millions her victorious bands
Pursuing. I upon my frontiers here
Keep residence; if all I can will serve,
That little which is left so to defend,
Encroached on still° through our intestine broils°   *constantly / civil wars*
Weak'ning the scepter of old Night: first Hell
Your dungeon stretching far and wide beneath;
Now lately heaven and earth,[9] another world

---

5. Latin and Greek names of Pluto, god of Hell.
6. A mysterious deity associated with Fate; Milton elsewhere identifies him with Chaos.
7. The purpose of my present journey.
8. Chaos is not monarch of his realm but, appropriately, "anarch," nonruler.
9. The cosmos, with its own "heaven" (not the empyrean, the Heaven of God and the angels).

1005 Hung o'er my realm, linked in a golden chain
      To that side Heav'n from whence your legions fell:
      If that way be your walk, you have not far;
      So much the nearer danger; go and speed;
      Havoc and spoil and ruin are my gain."
1010   He ceased; and Satan stayed not to reply,
      But glad that now his sea should find a shore,
      With fresh alacrity and force renewed
      Springs upward like a pyramid of fire
      Into the wild expanse, and through the shock
1015 Of fighting elements, on all sides round
      Environed wins his way; harder beset
      And more endangered, than when Argo passed
      Through Bosporus betwixt the justling rocks:[1]
      Or when Ulysses on the larboard shunned
1020 Charybdis, and by th' other whirlpool steered.[2]
      So he with difficulty and labor hard
      Moved on, with difficulty and labor he;
      But he once passed, soon after when man fell,
      Strange alteration! Sin and Death amain°   *at full speed*
1025 Following his track, such was the will of Heav'n,
      Paved after him a broad and beaten way
      Over the dark abyss, whose boiling gulf
      Tamely endured a bridge of wondrous length
      From Hell continued reaching th' utmost orb[3]
1030 Of this frail world; by which the Spirits perverse
      With easy intercourse pass to and fro
      To tempt or punish mortals, except whom
      God and good angels guard by special grace.
      But now at last the sacred influence
1035 Of light appears, and from the walls of Heav'n
      Shoots far into the bosom of dim Night
      A glimmering dawn; here Nature first begins
      Her farthest verge,° and Chaos to retire   *threshold*
      As from her outmost works a broken foe
1040 With tumult less and with less hostile din,
      That° Satan with less toil, and now with ease   *so that*
      Wafts on the calmer wave by dubious light
      And like a weather-beaten vessel holds°   *makes for*
      Gladly the port, though shrouds and tackle torn;
1045 Or in the emptier waste, resembling air
      Weighs° his spread wings, at leisure to behold   *balances*
      Far off th' empyreal Heav'n, extended wide
      In circuit, undetermined square or round,
      With opal tow'rs and battlements adorned
1050 Of living sapphire, once his native seat;
      And fast by hanging in a golden chain

---

1. Jason and his fifty Argonauts, sailing through the Bosporus to the Black Sea in pursuit of the Golden Fleece, had to pass through the Symplegades, or clashing rocks.
2. Homer's Ulysses, sailing where Italy almost touches Sicily, had to pass between Charybdis, a whirlpool, and Scylla, a monster who devoured six of his men (not another whirlpool, as used here).
3. The bridge ends on the outermost sphere of the ten concentric spheres making up the universe.

This pendent world,° in bigness as a star   *universe*
Of smallest magnitude close by the moon.
Thither full fraught with mischievous revenge,
Accursed, and in a cursèd hour, he hies.

Book 3

The Argument

God sitting on his throne sees Satan flying towards this world, then newly created; shows him to the Son who sat at his right hand; foretells the success of Satan in perverting mankind; clears his own justice and wisdom from all imputation, having created man free and able enough to have withstood his tempter; yet declares his purpose of grace towards him, in regard he fell not of his own malice, as did Satan, but by him seduced. The Son of God renders praises to his Father for the manifestation of his gracious purpose towards man; but God again declares, that grace cannot be extended towards man without the satisfaction of divine justice; man hath offended the majesty of God by aspiring to Godhead, and therefore with all his progeny devoted to death must die, unless someone can be found sufficient to answer for his offense, and undergo his punishment. The Son of God freely offers himself a ransom for man: the Father accepts him, ordains his incarnation, pronounces his exaltation about all names in heaven and earth; commands all the angels to adore him; they obey, and hymning to their harps in full choir, celebrate the Father and the Son. Meanwhile Satan alights upon the bare convex of this world's outermost orb; where wandering he first finds a place since called the Limbo of Vanity; what persons and things fly up thither; thence comes to the gate of heaven, described ascending by stairs, and the waters above the firmament that flow about it: his passage thence to the orb of the sun; he finds there Uriel the regent of that orb, but first changes himself into the shape of a meaner angel; and pretending a zealous desire to behold the new creation and man whom God had placed there, inquires of him the place of his habitation, and is directed; alights first on Mount Niphates.

Hail holy Light, offspring of Heav'n firstborn,
Or of th' Eternal coeternal beam
May I express thee unblamed?[1] Since God is light,
And never but in unapproachèd light
Dwelt from eternity, dwelt then in thee,
Bright effluence of bright essence increate.°   *uncreated, eternal*
Or hear'st thou rather[2] pure ethereal stream,
Whose fountain who shall tell? Before the sun,
Before the heavens thou wert, and at the voice
Of God, as with a mantle, didst invest°   *cover*
The rising world of waters dark and deep,
Won from the void and formless infinite.

---

1. This second proem or invocation (3.1–55) is a hymn to Light, addressed either as the first creature of God or as coeternal with God, with allusion to 1 John 1:5, "God is Light, and in him is no darkness at all."
2. That is, would you rather be called (a Latinism).

Thee I revisit now with bolder wing,
Escaped the Stygian pool, though long detained
In that obscure sojourn, while in my flight
Through utter and through middle darkness[3] borne
With other notes than to th' Orphéan lyre[4]
I sung of Chaos and eternal Night,
Taught by the Heav'nly Muse[5] to venture down
The dark descent, and up to reascend,
Though hard and rare: thee I revisit safe,
And feel thy sov'reign vital lamp; but thou
Revisit'st not these eyes, that roll in vain
To find thy piercing ray, and find no dawn;
So thick a drop serene hath quenched their orbs,
Or dim suffusion[6] veiled. Yet not the more
Cease I to wander where the Muses haunt
Clear spring, or shady grove, or sunny hill,
Smit with the love of sacred song; but chief
Thee Sion[7] and the flow'ry brooks beneath
That wash thy hallowed feet, and warbling flow,
Nightly I visit: nor sometimes forget°   always remember
Those other two equaled with me in fate,[8]
So were I equaled with them in renown,
Blind Thamyris and blind Maeonides,
And Tiresias and Phineus prophets old,[9]
Then feed on thoughts, that voluntary move
Harmonious numbers;° as the wakeful bird°   verses / nightingale
Sings darkling,° and in shadiest covert hid   in the dark
Tunes her nocturnal note. Thus with the year
Seasons return, but not to me returns
Day, or the sweet approach of ev'n or morn,
Or sight of vernal bloom, or summer's rose,
Or flocks, or herds, or human face divine;
But cloud instead, and ever-during° dark   everlasting
Surrounds me, from the cheerful ways of men
Cut off, and for the book of knowledge° fair   Book of Nature
Presented with a universal blank
Of nature's works to me expunged and razed,°   erased
And wisdom at one entrance quite shut out.
So much the rather thou celestial Light
Shine inward, and the mind through all her powers
Irradiate, there plant eyes, all mist from thence
Purge and disperse, that I may see and tell
Of things invisible to mortal sight.
    Now had the Almighty Father from above,
From the pure empyrean° where he sits   Heaven

3. Hell is "utter" (outer) darkness; Chaos is middle darkness.
4. One of the so-called Orphic hymns is "To Night," and Orpheus himself visited the underworld. But Milton's song, Christian and epic, is of a different kind.
5. Urania (though not named until 7.1).
6. Cataract—*suffusio nigra*. "Drop serene": *gutta serena*, the medical term for Milton's kind of blindness.
7. The mountain of scriptural inspiration, with its brooks Siloa and Kidron.
8. That is, blind like me.
9. Thamyris was a blind Thracian poet who lived before Homer; "Maeonides" is an epithet of Homer; Tiresias was the blind prophet of Thebes; Phineus was a blind king and seer (*Aeneid* 3).

High throned above all height, bent down his eye,
His own works and their works at once to view:
Above him all the sanctities° of Heaven　　　　　　　　　　　　*angels*
Stood thick as stars, and from his sight received
Beatitude past utterance; on his right
The radiant image of his glory sat,
His only Son; on earth he first beheld
Our two first parents, yet the only two
Of mankind, in the happy garden placed,
Reaping immortal fruits of joy and love,
Uninterrupted joy, unrivaled love
In blissful solitude; he then surveyed
Hell and the gulf between, and Satan there
Coasting the wall of Heav'n on this side Night
In the dun° air sublime,° and ready now　　　　　　　　　　　　*dusky / aloft*
To stoop° with wearied wings, and willing feet　　　　　　　　*swoop down*
On the bare outside of this world,° that seemed　　　　　　　　*universe*
Firm land embosomed without firmament,°　　　　　　　　　　*atmosphere*
Uncertain which, in ocean or in air.
Him God beholding from his prospect high,
Wherein past, present, future he beholds,
Thus to his only Son foreseeing spake.

　　"Only begotten Son, seest thou what rage
Transports our Adversary, whom no bounds
Prescribed, no bars of Hell, nor all the chains
Heaped on him there, nor yet the main° abyss　　　　　　　　　　*vast*
Wide interrupt[1] can hold; so bent he seems
On desperate revenge, that shall redound°　　　　　　　　　　　*flow back*
Upon his own rebellious head. And now
Through all restraint broke loose he wings his way
Not far off Heav'n, in the precincts of light,
Directly towards the new-created world,
And man there placed, with purpose to essay°　　　　　　　　　　*try*
If him by force he can destroy, or worse,
By some false guile pervert; and shall pervert;
For man will hearken to his glozing° lies,　　　　　　　　　　　*flattering*
And easily transgress the sole command,
Sole pledge of his obedience: so will fall
He and his faithless progeny: whose fault?
Whose but his own? Ingrate, he had of me
All he could have; I made him just and right,
Sufficient to have stood, though free to fall.
Such I created all th' ethereal Powers
And Spirits, both them who stood and them who failed;
Freely they stood who stood, and fell who fell.
Not free, what proof could they have giv'n sincere
Of true allegiance, constant faith or love,
Where only what they needs must do, appeared,
Not what they would? What praise could they receive?
What pleasure I from such obedience paid,

---

1. Forming a wide breach between Heaven and Hell.

When will and reason (reason also is choice)
Useless and vain, of freedom both despoiled,
Made passive both, had served necessity,
Not me. They therefore as to right belonged,
So were created, nor can justly accuse
Their Maker, or their making, or their fate,
As if predestination overruled
Their will, disposed by absolute decree
Or high foreknowledge; they themselves decreed
Their own revolt, not I: if I foreknew,
Foreknowledge had no influence on their fault,
Which had no less proved certain unforeknown.[2]
So without least impulse or shadow of fate,
Or aught by me immutably foreseen,
They trespass, authors to themselves in all
Both what they judge and what they choose; for so
I formed them free, and free they must remain,
Till they enthrall themselves: I else must change
Their nature, and revoke the high decree
Unchangeable, eternal, which ordained
Their freedom, they themselves ordained their fall.
The first sort[3] by their own suggestion fell,
Self-tempted, self-depraved: man falls deceived
By the other first: man therefore shall find grace,
The other none: in mercy and justice both,
Through Heav'n and earth, so shall my glory excel,
But mercy first and last shall brightest shine."
   Thus while God spake, ambrosial° fragrance filled   *fragrant, immortal*
All Heav'n, and in the blessèd Spirits elect°   *unfallen*
Sense of new joy ineffable° diffused: *inexpressible*
Beyond compare the Son of God was seen
Most glorious, in him all his Father shone
Substantially expressed, and in his face
Divine compassion visibly appeared,
Love without end, and without measure grace,
Which uttering thus he to his Father spake.
   "O Father, gracious was that word which closed
Thy sov'reign sentence, that man should find grace;
For which both Heav'n and earth shall high extol
Thy praises, with th' innumerable sound
Of hymns and sacred songs, wherewith thy throne
Encompassed shall resound thee ever blessed.
For should man finally be lost, should man
Thy creature late so loved, thy youngest son
Fall circumvented thus by fraud, though joined
With his own folly? That be from thee far,
That far be from thee, Father, who art judge
Of all things made, and judgest only right.[4]

---

2. That is, if I had not foreknown it.
3. Satan and his crew.
4. The Son echoes (or rather foreshadows) Abraham pleading with the Lord to spare Sodom: "That be far from thee to do after this manner, to slay the righteous with the wicked . . . that be far from thee: Shall not the Judge of all the earth do right?" (Genesis 18:25).

Or shall the Adversary thus obtain
His end, and frustrate thine, shall he fulfill
His malice, and thy goodness bring to naught,
Or proud return though to his heavier doom,
Yet with revenge accomplished, and to Hell
Draw after him the whole race of mankind,
By him corrupted? Or wilt thou thyself
Abolish thy creation, and unmake,
For him, what for thy glory thou hast made?
So should thy goodness and thy greatness both
Be questioned and blasphemed° without defense."   *profaned*
　　To whom the great Creator thus replied.
"O Son, in whom my soul hath chief delight,
Son of my bosom, Son who art alone
My Word, my wisdom, and effectual might,[5]
All hast thou spoken as my thoughts are, all
As my eternal purpose hath decreed:
Man shall not quite be lost, but saved who will,
Yet not of will in him, but grace in me
Freely vouchsafed;° once more I will renew   *bestowed*
His lapsèd powers, though forfeit and enthralled
By sin to foul exorbitant desires;
Upheld by me, yet once more he shall stand
On even ground against his mortal foe,
By me upheld, that he may know how frail
His fall'n condition is, and to me owe
All his deliv'rance, and to none but me.
Some I have chosen of peculiar grace
Elect above the rest;[6] so is my will:
The rest shall hear me call, and oft be warned°   *warned about*
Their sinful state, and to appease betimes
Th' incensèd Deity, while offered grace
Invites; for I will clear their senses dark,
What may suffice, and soften stony hearts
To pray, repent, and bring obedience due.
To prayer, repentance, and obedience due,
Though but endeavored with sincere intent,
Mine ear shall not be slow, mine eye not shut.
And I will place within them as a guide
My umpire conscience, whom if they will hear,
Light after light well used they shall attain,[7]
And to the end persisting, safe arrive.
This my long sufferance and my day of grace
They who neglect and scorn, shall never taste;
But hard be hardened, blind be blinded more,
That they may stumble on, and deeper fall;
And none but such from mercy I exclude.

---

5. God's speech is rhythmic and sometimes rhymed.
6. In this speech, Milton's God rejects the Calvinist doctrine that he had from the beginning predestined the damnation or salvation of each individual soul; he claims rather that grace sufficient for salvation is offered to all, enabling everyone, if they choose to do so, to believe and persevere. He does, however, assert his right to give special grace to some.
7. By using the light of conscience well they will gain more light.

                But yet all is not done; man disobeying,
                Disloyal breaks his fealty, and sins
205   Against the high supremacy of Heav'n,
                Affecting° Godhead, and so losing all,   *aspiring to*
                To expiate his treason hath naught left,
                But to destruction sacred and devote,°   *consecrated*
                He with his whole posterity must die,
210   Die he or justice must; unless for him
                Some other able, and as willing, pay
                The rigid satisfaction, death for death.
                Say heav'nly Powers, where shall we find such love,
                Which of ye will be mortal to redeem
215   Man's mortal crime,[8] and just th' unjust to save,
                Dwells in all Heaven charity so dear?"
                    He asked, but all the heav'nly choir stood mute,[9]
                And silence was in Heav'n; on man's behalf
                Patron or intercessor none appeared,
220   Much less that durst upon his own head draw
                The deadly forfeiture, and ransom set.
                And now without redemption all mankind
                Must have been lost, adjudged to death and Hell
                By doom severe, had not the Son of God,
225   In whom the fullness dwells of love divine,
                His dearest mediation° thus renewed.   *intercession*
                    'Father, thy word is passed, man shall find grace;
                And shall grace not find means, that finds her way,
                The speediest of thy wingèd messengers,
230   To visit all thy creatures, and to all
                Comes unprevented,° unimplored, unsought,   *unanticipated*
                Happy for man, so coming; he her aid
                Can never seek, once dead in sins and lost;
                Atonement for himself or offering meet,°   *fitting*
235   Indebted and undone, hath none to bring:
                Behold me then, me for him, life for life
                I offer, on me let thine anger fall;
                Account me man; I for his sake will leave
                Thy bosom, and this glory next to thee
240   Freely put off, and for him lastly die
                Well pleased, on me let Death wreak all his rage;
                Under his gloomy power I shall not long
                Lie vanquished; thou hast giv'n me to possess
                Life in myself forever, by thee I live,
245   Though now to Death I yield, and am his due
                All that of me can die, yet that debt paid,
                Thou wilt not leave me in the loathsome grave
                His prey, nor suffer my unspotted soul
                Forever with corruption there to dwell;
250   But I shall rise victorious, and subdue
                My vanquisher, spoiled of his vaunted spoil;

---

8. "Mortal" means "human" in line 214, but "deadly" in line 215.

9. Compare the devils in the Great Consult, 2.420–26.

Death his death's wound shall then receive, and stoop
Inglorious, of his mortal sting disarmed.
I through the ample air in triumph high
255 Shall lead Hell captive maugre° Hell, and show   *in spite of*
The powers of darkness bound. Thou at the sight
Pleased, out of Heaven shalt look down and smile,
While by thee raised I ruin¹ all my foes,
Death last, and with his carcass glut the grave:
260 Then with the multitude of my redeemed
Shall enter Heaven long absent, and return,
Father, to see thy face, wherein no cloud
Of anger shall remain, but peace assured,
And reconcilement; wrath shall be no more
265 Thenceforth, but in thy presence joy entire."
    His words here ended, but his meek aspéct
Silent yet spake, and breathed immortal love
To mortal men, above which only shone
Filial obedience: as a sacrifice
270 Glad to be offered, he attends the will
Of his great Father. Admiration° seized   *wonder*
All Heav'n, what this might mean, and whither tend
Wond'ring; but soon th' Almighty thus replied:
    "O thou in Heav'n and earth the only peace
275 Found out for mankind under wrath, O thou
My sole complacence!° well thou know'st how dear   *pleasure, delight*
To me are all my works, nor man the least
Though last created, that for him I spare
Thee from my bosom and right hand, to save,
280 By losing thee a while, the whole race lost.
Thou therefore whom² thou only canst redeem,
Their nature also to thy nature join;
And be thyself man among men on earth,
Made flesh, when time shall be, of virgin seed,
285 By wondrous birth: be thou in Adam's room
The head of all mankind, though Adam's son.³
As in him perish all men, so in thee
As from a second root shall be restored,
As many as are restored, without thee none.
290 His crime makes guilty all his sons; thy merit
Imputed shall absolve them who renounce
Their own both righteous and unrighteous deeds,
And live in thee transplanted, and from thee
Receive new life.⁴ So man, as is most just,
295 Shall satisfy for man, be judged and die,
And dying rise, and rising with him raise
His brethren, ransomed with his own dear life.

---

1. In the Latin sense, throw down.
2. The antecedent of "whom" is, loosely construed, the "their nature" that follows it.
3. The Son of God, who long antedates the creation of Adam and who is actually the first created being (3.383), is later incarnated in Jesus Christ; he is called Second Adam and Son of Man by reason of his descent from the first man, Adam. See 1 Corinthians 15:22: "For as in Adam all die, even so in Christ shall all be made alive."
4. The merit of Christ attributed vicariously ("imputed") to human beings frees from original sin those who renounce their own deeds, good and bad, and hope to be saved by faith.

So heav'nly love shall outdo hellish hate,
Giving to death, and dying to redeem,
So dearly to redeem what hellish hate
So easily destroyed, and still destroys
In those who, when they may, accept not grace.
Nor shalt thou by descending to assume
Man's nature, lessen or degrade thine own.
Because thou hast, though throned in highest bliss
Equal to God, and equally enjoying
Godlike fruition,° quitted all to save   *pleasurable possession*
A world from utter loss, and hast been found
By merit more than birthright Son of God,[5]
Found worthiest to be so by being good,
Far more than great or high; because in thee
Love hath abounded more than glory abounds.
Therefore thy humiliation shall exalt
With thee thy manhood also to this throne;
Here shalt thou sit incarnate, here shalt reign
Both God and man, Son both of God and man,
Anointed[6] universal King; all power
I give thee, reign forever, and assume
Thy merits; under thee as Head Supreme
Thrones, Princedoms, Powers, Dominions[7] I reduce:
All knees to thee shall bow, of them that bide
In Heaven, or earth, or under earth in Hell;
When thou attended gloriously from Heav'n
Shalt in the sky appear, and from thee send
The summoning Archangels to proclaim
Thy dread tribunal: forthwith from all winds°   *directions*
The living, and forthwith the cited° dead   *summoned*
Of all past ages to the general doom°   *judgment*
Shall hasten, such a peal shall rouse their sleep.
Then all thy saints assembled, thou shalt judge
Bad men and angels, they arraigned° shall sink   *accursed*
Beneath thy sentence; Hell, her numbers full,
Thenceforth shall be forever shut. Meanwhile
The world shall burn, and from her ashes spring
New heav'n° and earth, wherein the just shall dwell,[8]   *sky, cosmos*
And after all their tribulations long
See golden days, fruitful of golden deeds,
With joy and love triumphing, and fair truth.
Then thou thy regal scepter shalt lay by,
For regal scepter then no more shall need,°   *be needed*
God shall be all in all. But all ye gods,°   *angels*
Adore him, who to compass all this dies,
Adore the Son, and honor him as me."
   No sooner had th' Almighty ceased, but all

---

5. A heterodox doctrine, that Christ was Son of God *by merit*. Compare with Satan (2.5).
6. In Hebrew "Messiah" means "the anointed one."
7. Orders of angels.
8. Milton's description of the Last Judgment draws on several biblical texts, including Matthew 24:30–31 and 25:31–32; the account of the burning and re-creation of the heavens and earth is from 2 Peter 3:12–13.

345   The multitude of angels with a shout
       Loud as from numbers without number, sweet
       As from blest voices, uttering joy, Heav'n rung[9]
       With jubilee, and loud hosannas filled
       Th' eternal regions: lowly reverent
350   Towards either throne[1] they bow, and to the ground
       With solemn adoration down they cast
       Their crowns inwove with amarant[2] and gold,
       Immortal amarant, a flow'r which once
       In Paradise, fast by the Tree of Life
355   Began to bloom, but soon for man's offense
       To Heav'n removed where first it grew, there grows,
       And flow'rs aloft shading the Fount of Life,
       And where the river of bliss through midst of Heav'n
       Rolls o'er Elysian[3] flow'rs her amber stream;
360   With these that never fade the Spirits elect
       Bind their resplendent locks inwreathed with beams,
       Now in loose garlands thick thrown off, the bright
       Pavement that like a sea of jasper shone
       Impurpled with celestial roses smiled.
365   Then crowned again their golden harps they took,
       Harps ever tuned, that glittering by their side
       Like quivers hung, and with preamble sweet
       Of charming symphony they introduce
       Their sacred song, and waken raptures high;
370   No voice exempt,° no voice but well could join   *excluded*
       Melodious part, such concord is in Heav'n.
          Thee Father first they sung omnipotent,
       Immutable, immortal, infinite,
       Eternal King; thee Author of all being,
375   Fountain of light, thyself invisible
       Amidst the glorious brightness where thou sitt'st
       Throned inaccessible, but° when thou shad'st   *except*
       The full blaze of thy beams, and through a cloud
       Drawn round about thee like a radiant shrine,[4]
380   Dark with excessive bright thy skirts appear,
       Yet dazzle Heav'n, that brightest Seraphim
       Approach not, but with both wings veil their eyes.
       Thee next they sang of all creation first,[5]
       Begotten Son, Divine Similitude,
385   In whose conspicuous count'nance, without cloud
       Made visible, th' Almighty Father shines,
       Whom else no creature can behold;[6] on thee
       Impressed th' effulgence of his glory abides,
       Transfused on thee his ample spirit rests.
390   He Heav'n of heavens and all the Powers therein

---

9. "Multitude" (line 345) is the subject of the sentence, "rung" the verb, and "Heav'n" the object.
1. Thrones of God and the Son.
2. In Greek, "unfading," a legendary immortal flower.
3. Milton draws freely, for his Christian Heaven, on descriptions of the classical paradisal place, the Elysian Fields.
4. The turn from theological debate to images that evoke a more mystical aspect of God.
5. The Son is not eternal, as in Trinitarian doctrine, but rather, God's first creation.
6. If it were not for the Son who is God's image, no creature could see God.

>   By thee created, and by thee threw down
>   Th' aspiring Dominations.⁷ Thou that day
>   Thy Father's dreadful thunder didst not spare,
>   Nor stop thy flaming chariot wheels, that shook
> 395 Heav'n's everlasting frame, while o'er the necks
>   Thou drov'st of warring angels disarrayed.
>   Back from pursuit thy Powers° with loud acclaim   *angels*
>   Thee only extolled, Son of thy Father's might,
>   To execute fierce vengeance on his foes,
> 400 Not so on man; him through their malice fall'n,
>   Father of mercy and grace, thou didst not doom
>   So strictly, but much more to pity incline:
>   No sooner did thy dear and only Son
>   Perceive thee purposed not to doom° frail man   *judge*
> 405 So strictly, but much more to pity inclined,
>   He to appease thy wrath, and end the strife
>   Of mercy and justice in thy face discerned,
>   Regardless of the bliss wherein he sat
>   Second to thee, offered himself to die
> 410 For man's offense. O unexampled love,
>   Love nowhere to be found less than divine!
>   Hail Son of God, Savior of men, thy name
>   Shall be the copious matter of my⁸ song
>   Henceforth, and never shall my harp thy praise
> 415 Forget, nor from thy Father's praise disjoin.
>   Thus they in Heav'n, above the starry sphere,
>   Their happy hours in joy and hymning spent.
>   Meanwhile upon the firm opacous° globe   *opaque*
>   Of this round world, whose first convex divides
> 420 The luminous inferior orbs, enclosed
>   From Chaos and th' inroad of Darkness old,
>   Satan alighted walks:⁹ a globe far off
>   It seemed, now seems a boundless continent
>   Dark, waste, and wild, under the frown of Night
> 425 Starless exposed, and ever-threatening storms
>   Of Chaos blust'ring round, inclement sky;
>   Save on that side which from the wall of Heav'n
>   Though distant far some small reflection gains
>   Of glimmering air less vexed with tempest loud:
> 430 Here walked the Fiend at large in spacious field.
>   As when a vulture on Imaus bred,
>   Whose snowy ridge the roving Tartar bounds,¹
>   Dislodging from a region scarce of prey
>   To gorge the flesh of lambs or yeanling° kids   *newborn*
> 435 On hills where flocks are fed, flies toward the springs
>   Of Ganges or Hydaspes, Indian streams;²

---

7. The rebel angels.
8. Either Milton here quotes the angels singing as a single chorus, or he associates himself with their song, or both.
9. Satan is on the outermost of the ten concentric spheres that make up the cosmos.
1. Imaus, a ridge of mountains beyond the modern Himalayas, runs north through Asia from modern Afghanistan to the Arctic Circle.
2. Both the Ganges and the Hydaspes (a tributary of the Indus) rise from the mountains of northern India. Sericana (line 438) is a region in northwest China.

But in his way lights on the barren plains
Of Sericana, where Chineses drive
With sails and wind their cany wagons light:
So on this windy sea of land, the Fiend   440
Walked up and down alone bent on his prey,
Alone, for other creature in this place
Living or lifeless to be found was none,
None yet, but store hereafter from the earth
Up hither like aërial vapors flew   445
Of all things transitory and vain, when sin
With vanity had filled the works of men:
Both all things vain, and all who in vain things
Built their fond° hopes of glory or lasting fame,   *foolish*
Or happiness in this or th' other life;   450
All who have their reward on earth, the fruits
Of painful superstition and blind zeal,
Naught seeking but the praise of men, here find
Fit retribution, empty as their deeds;
All th' unaccomplished° works of nature's hand,   *imperfect*   455
Abortive, monstrous, or unkindly° mixed,   *unnaturally*
Dissolved on earth, fleet° hither, and in vain,   *float*
Till final dissolution, wander here,
Not in the neighboring moon, as some[3] have dreamed;
Those argent° fields more likely habitants,   *silver*   460
Translated saints,[4] or middle Spirits hold
Betwixt th' angelical and human kind:
Hither of ill-joined sons and daughters born
First from the ancient world those giants came
With many a vain exploit, though then renowned:[5]   465
The builders next of Babel on the plain
Of Sennaär,[6] and still with vain design
New Babels, had they wherewithal, would build:
Others came single; he who to be deemed
A god, leaped fondly° into Etna flames,   *foolishly*   470
Empedocles, and he who to enjoy
Plato's Elysium, leaped into the sea,
Cleombrotus, and many more too long,[7]
Embryos and idiots, eremites° and friars   *hermits*
White, black, and gray, with all their trumpery.[8]   475
Here pilgrims roam, that strayed so far to seek
In Golgotha[9] him dead, who lives in Heav'n;
And they who to be sure of paradise
Dying put on the weeds° of Dominic,   *garments*

---

3. Milton's Paradise of Fools (named in line 496) was inspired by Ariosto's Limbo of Vanity in *Orlando Furioso* (Book 34, lines 73ff.); Milton's region is reserved for deluded victims of misplaced devotion, chiefly Roman Catholics.
4. Holy men like Enoch and Elijah, transported to Heaven while yet alive (Genesis 5:24; 2 Kings 2:11–12).
5. Giants, born of unnatural marriages between the "sons of God" and the daughters of men (Genesis 6:4), are creatures unkindly mixed.
6. Shinar, the plain of Babel (Genesis 11:2–9); the Tower of Babel is an emblem of human pride and folly.
7. That is, it would take too long to name them. Both Empedocles and Cleombrotus foolishly carried piety to the point of suicide.
8. Religious paraphernalia. The white friars are Carmelites; the black, Dominicans; and the gray, Franciscans.
9. Place where Christ was crucified.

480 Or in Franciscan think to pass disguised;[1]
     They pass the planets seven, and pass the fixed,
     And that crystalline sphere whose balance weighs
     The trepidation talked, and that first moved;[2]
     And now Saint Peter at Heav'n's wicket seems
485 To wait them with his keys, and now at foot
     Of Heav'n's ascent they lift their feet, when lo
     A violent crosswind from either coast
     Blows them transverse ten thousand leagues awry
     Into the devious° air. Then might ye see   erratic
490 Cowls, hoods, and habits[3] with their wearers tossed
     And fluttered into rags; then relics, beads,
     Indulgences, dispenses, pardons, bulls,
     The sport of winds: all these upwhirled aloft
     Fly o'er the backside° of the world far off   rump
495 Into a limbo large and broad, since called
     The Paradise of Fools, to few unknown
     Long after, now unpeopled, and untrod;
     All this dark globe the Fiend found as he passed,
     And long he wandered, till at last a gleam
500 Of dawning light turned thitherward in haste
     His traveled° steps; far distant he descries   travel-weary
     Ascending by degrees° magnificent   steps
     Up to the wall of Heaven a structure high,
     At top whereof, but far more rich appeared
505 The work as of a kingly palace gate
     With frontispiece° of diamond and gold   pediment
     Embellished; thick with sparkling orient° gems   lustrous
     The portal shone, inimitable on earth,
     By model, or by shading pencil drawn.
510 The stairs were such as whereon Jacob saw
     Angels ascending and descending, bands
     Of guardians bright, when he from Esau fled
     To Padan-Aram in the field of Luz,
     Dreaming by night under the open sky,
515 And waking cried, "This is the gate of Heav'n."[4]
     Each stair mysteriously was meant, nor stood
     There always, but drawn up to Heav'n sometimes
     Viewless,° and underneath a bright sea flowed   invisible
     Of jasper, or of liquid pearl, whereon
520 Who after came from earth, sailing arrived,
     Wafted by angels, or flew o'er the lake
     Rapt in a chariot drawn by fiery steeds.[5]
     The stairs were then let down, whether to dare
     The Fiend by easy ascent, or aggravate

---

1. Some try to trick God into granting them salvation by wearing on their deathbeds the garb of various religious orders.
2. Milton follows their souls through the spheres of the moon and sun, the five then-known planets, the fixed stars, and the sphere responsible for the "trepidation" (a periodic corrective shudder of the cosmos), up to the primum mobile, or prime mover. The next step seems to be the empyreal Heaven.
3. The dress of religious orders, together with (next lines) saints' relics, rosary beads, various kinds of pardon for sins, and papal decrees ("bulls").
4. The story of Jacob's vision is summarized from Genesis 28:1–19; the stairs of the ladder (next line) allegorically ("mysteriously") represent stages of spiritual growth.
5. Elijah was wafted to heaven in a chariot.

His sad exclusion from the doors of bliss.   525
Direct against which opened from beneath,
Just o'er the blissful seat of Paradise,
A passage down to th' earth, a passage wide,[6]
Wider by far than that of aftertimes
Over Mount Zion, and, though that were large,   530
Over the Promised Land to God so dear,
By which, to visit oft those happy tribes,
On high behests his angels to and fro
Passed frequent, and his eye with choice° regard   *discriminating*
From Paneas the fount of Jordan's flood   535
To Beërsaba, where the Holy Land
Borders on Egypt and the Arabian shore;[7]
So wide the op'ning seemed, where bounds were set
To darkness, such as bound the ocean wave.
Satan from hence now on the lower stair   540
That scaled by steps of gold to Heaven gate
Looks down with wonder at the sudden view
Of all this world at once. As when a scout
Through dark and desert ways with peril gone
All night; at last by break of cheerful dawn   545
Obtains° the brow of some high-climbing hill,   *gains*
Which to his eye discovers unaware
The goodly prospect of some foreign land
First seen, or some renowned metropolis
With glistering spires and pinnacles adorned,   550
Which now the rising sun gilds with his beams.
Such wonder seized, though after Heaven seen,
The Spirit malign, but much more envy seized
At sight of all this world beheld so fair.
Round he surveys, and well might, where he stood   555
So high above the circling canopy
Of night's extended shade; from eastern point
Of Libra to the fleecy star that bears
Andromeda far off Atlantic seas[8]
Beyond th' horizon; then from pole to pole   560
He views in breadth, and without longer pause
Down right into the world's first region throws
His flight precipitant, and winds with ease
Through the pure marble° air his oblique way   *sparkling*
Amongst innumerable stars, that shone   565
Stars distant, but nigh hand seemed other worlds,
Or other worlds they seemed, or happy isles,
Like those Hesperian gardens famed of old,
Fortunate fields, and groves and flow'ry vales,[9]
Thrice happy isles, but who dwelt happy there   570
He stayed not to inquire: above them all

6. A passage through the crystalline spheres, otherwise impenetrable.
7. From Paneas (or Dan) in northern Palestine to Beersaba, or Beersheba, near the Egyptian border—the entire land of Israel.
8. In the zodiac, Libra is diametrically opposite Aries, or the Ram ("the fleecy star"), which seems to carry the constellation Andromeda on its back.
9. The gardens of the Hesperides and the "fortunate isles" of Greek mythology, classical versions of paradise, lay far out in the Atlantic.

The golden sun in splendor likest Heaven
Allured his eye: thither his course he bends
Through the calm firmament;° but up or down   *sky*
575 By center, or eccentric, hard to tell,
Or longitude,[1] where the great luminary
Aloof the vulgar constellations thick,
That from his lordly eye keep distance due,
Dispenses light from far; they as they move
580 Their starry dance in numbers that compute
Days, months, and years, towards his all-cheering lamp
Turn swift their various motions, or are turned
By his magnetic beam, that gently warms
The universe, and to each inward part
585 With gentle penetration, though unseen,
Shoots invisible virtue° even to the deep: *influence, strength*
So wondrously was set his station bright.
    There lands the Fiend, a spot like which perhaps
Astronomer in the sun's lucent orb
590 Through his glazed optic tube yet never saw.[2]
The place he found beyond expression bright,
Compared with aught on earth, metal or stone;
Not all parts like, but all alike informed
With radiant light, as glowing iron with fire;
595 If metal, part seemed gold, part silver clear;
If stone, carbuncle most or chrysolite,[3]
Ruby or topaz, to the twelve that shone
In Aaron's breastplate,[4] and a stone besides
Imagined rather oft than elsewhere seen,[5]
600 That stone, or like to that which here below
Philosophers in vain so long have sought,[6]
In vain, though by their powerful art they bind
Volátile Hermes, and call up unbound
In various shapes old Proteus from the sea,
605 Drained through a limbec to his native form.[7]
What wonder then if fields and regions here
Breathe forth elixir pure,[8] and rivers run
Potable° gold, when with one virtuous° touch   *drinkable / powerful*
Th' arch-chemic° sun so far from us remote   *chief alchemist*
610 Produces with terrestrial humor° mixed   *earth's moisture*
Here in the dark so many precious things
Of color glorious and effect so rare?
Here matter new to gaze the Devil met
Undazzled, far and wide his eye commands,

---

1. The passage leaves open whether the sun or the earth is at the center of the cosmos.
2. Galileo first observed sunspots through his telescope in 1609.
3. Any green stone. "Carbuncle": any red stone.
4. In Exodus 28:15–20, Aaron's "breastplate" is described as decorated with twelve different gems, of which Milton lists the first four.
5. That is, elsewhere imagined more often than seen.
6. Alchemists had identified the "philosophers' stone" with the *urim* on Aaron's breastplate (Exodus 28:30); that stone reputedly could heal all diseases, restore paradise, and transmute base metals to gold.
7. "Hermes": the winged god and the element mercury, which evaporated readily ("volatile"). "Proteus": the shape-shifting sea god, a symbol of matter. Alchemists would "bind" (solidify) mercury and dissolve or refine matter to its "native form" in a vessel (alembic, "limbec").
8. The liquid form of the philosopher's stone. "Here": in the sun.

For sight no obstacle found here, nor shade,
But all sunshine, as when his beams at noon
Culminate from th' equator, as they now
Shot upward still direct, whence no way round
Shadow from body opaque can fall,[9] and the air,
Nowhere so clear, sharpened his visual ray
To objects distant far,[1] whereby he soon
Saw within ken° a glorious angel stand,   *range of vision*
The same whom John saw also in the sun:[2]
His back was turned, but not his brightness hid;
Of beaming sunny rays, a golden tiar°   *tiara, crown*
Circled his head, nor less his locks behind
Illustrious° on his shoulders fledge° with wings   *lustrous / feathered*
Lay waving round; on some great charge employed
He seemed, or fixed in cogitation deep.
Glad was the Spirit impure; as now in hope
To find who might direct his wand'ring flight
To Paradise the happy seat of man,
His journey's end and our beginning woe.
But first he casts° to change his proper shape,   *contrives*
Which else might work him danger or delay:
And now a stripling Cherub he appears,
Not of the prime,[3] yet such as in his face
Youth smiled celestial, and to every limb
Suitable grace diffused, so well he feigned;
Under a coronet his flowing hair
In curls on either cheek played, wings he wore
Of many a colored plume sprinkled with gold,
His habit fit for speed succinct,° and held   *close-fitting*
Before his decent° steps a silver wand.   *comely*
He drew not nigh unheard; the angel bright,
Ere he drew nigh, his radiant visage turned,
Admonished by his ear, and straight° was known   *immediately*
Th' Archangel Uriel, one of the sev'n
Who in God's presence, nearest to his throne[4]
Stand ready at command, and are his eyes
That run through all the heav'ns, or down to th' earth
Bear his swift errands over moist and dry,
O'er sea and land: him Satan thus accosts:
"Uriel, for thou of those sev'n Spirits that stand
In sight of God's high throne, gloriously bright,
The first art wont° his great authentic° will   *used / authoritative*
Interpreter through highest Heav'n to bring,
Where all his sons thy embassy attend;
And here art likeliest by supreme decree
Like honor to obtain, and as his eye

---

9. Before the Fall (and the consequent tipping of the earth's axis) the sun at noon, on the equator, never cast a shadow. "Culminate": reach their zenith.
1. The eye was thought to emit a beam into the object perceived.
2. "I saw an angel standing in the sun" (Revelation 19:17).
3. Not yet in the prime of life.
4. Uriel—in Hebrew, "light" (or "fire") of God—is the angel named first (in 2 Esdras 4:1–5, *apocrypha*) among the seven angels who stood before God's throne.

                To visit oft this new creation round;
                Unspeakable desire to see, and know
                All these his wondrous works, but chiefly man,
                His chief delight and favor,° him for whom   *favorite*
665   All these his works so wondrous he ordained,
                Hath brought me from the choirs of Cherubim
                Alone thus wand'ring. Brightest Seraph tell
                In which of all these shining orbs hath man
                His fixèd seat, or fixèd seat hath none,
670   But all these shining orbs his choice to dwell;
                That I may find him, and with secret gaze,
                Or open admiration him behold
                On whom the great Creator hath bestowed
                Worlds, and on whom hath all these graces poured;
675   That both in him and all things, as is meet,°   *fitting*
                The Universal Maker we may praise;
                Who justly hath driv'n out his rebel foes
                To deepest Hell, and to repair that loss
                Created this new happy race of men
680   To serve him better: wise are all his ways."
                    So spake the false dissembler unperceived;
                For neither man nor angel can discern
                Hypocrisy, the only evil that walks
                Invisible, except to God alone,
685   By his permissive will, through Heav'n and earth:
                And oft though wisdom wake, suspicion sleeps
                At wisdom's gate, and to simplicity
                Resigns her charge, while goodness thinks no ill
                Where no ill seems: which now for once beguiled
690   Uriel, though regent of the sun, and held
                The sharpest-sighted Spirit of all in Heav'n;
                Who to the fraudulent impostor foul
                In his uprightness answer thus returned:
                    "Fair angel, thy desire which tends° to know   *inclines*
695   The works of God, thereby to glorify
                The great Work-Master, leads to no excess
                That reaches blame, but rather merits praise
                The more it seems excess, that led thee hither
                From thy empyreal mansion thus alone,
700   To witness with thine eyes what some perhaps
                Contented with report hear only in Heav'n:
                For wonderful indeed are all his works,
                Pleasant to know, and worthiest to be all
                Had in remembrance always with delight;
705   But what created mind can comprehend
                Their number, or the wisdom infinite
                That brought them forth, but hid their causes deep.
                I saw when at his word the formless mass,
                This world's material mold,° came to a heap: *substance*
710   Confusion heard his voice, and wild uproar
                Stood ruled, stood vast infinitude confined;
                Till at his second bidding darkness fled,

               Light shone, and order from disorder sprung:
               Swift to their several quarters hasted then
715   The cumbrous elements, earth, flood, air, fire,
               And this ethereal quíntessence⁵ of Heav'n
               Flew upward, spirited with various forms,
               That rolled orbicular,⁶ and turned to stars
               Numberless, as thou seest, and how they move;
720   Each had his place appointed, each his course,
               The rest in circuit walls this universe.
               Look downward on that globe whose hither side
               With light from hence, though but reflected, shines;
               That place is earth the seat of man, that light
725   His day, which else as th' other hemisphere
               Night would invade, but there the neighboring moon
               (So call that opposite fair star) her aid
               Timely interposes, and her monthly round
               Still ending, still renewing through mid-Heav'n,
730   With borrowed light her countenance triform⁷
               Hence⁸ fills and empties to enlighten th' earth,
               And in her pale dominion checks the night.
               That spot to which I point is Paradise,
               Adam's abode, those lofty shades his bow'r.
735   Thy way thou canst not miss, me mine requires."
                  Thus said, he turned, and Satan bowing low,
               As to superior Spirits is wont in Heav'n,
               Where honor due and reverence none neglects,
               Took leave, and toward the coast of earth beneath,
740   Down from th' ecliptic,° sped with hoped success,   *the sun's orbit*
               Throws his steep flight in many an airy wheel,
               Nor stayed, till on Niphates' top⁹ he lights.

Book 4

The Argument

Satan now in prospect of Eden, and nigh the place where he must now attempt the bold enterprise which he undertook alone against God and man, falls into many doubts with himself, and many passions, fear, envy, and despair; but at length confirms himself in evil, journeys on to Paradise, whose outward prospect and situation is described, overleaps the bounds, sits in the shape of a cormorant on the Tree of Life, as highest in the Garden to look about him. The Garden described; Satan's first sight of Adam and Eve; his wonder at their excellent form and happy state, but with resolution to work their fall; overhears their discourse, thence gathers that the Tree of Knowledge was forbidden them to eat of, under penalty of death; and thereon intends to found his temptation, by seducing them to transgress: then leaves

---

5. The fifth element, of which the incorruptible heavenly bodies were made.
6. The spherical shape of the stars and their orbits. "Spirited with various forms": presided over or inhabited by various angelic spirits or intelligences (Plato, *Timaeus* 41E).
7. The moon was said to have a triple nature: Luna in Heaven, Diana on earth, and Hecate in Hell.
8. From here (the sun).
9. A mountain in Assyria.

them a while, to know further of their state by some other means. Meanwhile Uriel descending on a sunbeam warns Gabriel, who had in charge the gate of Paradise, that some evil Spirit had escaped the deep, and passed at noon by his sphere in the shape of a good angel down to Paradise, discovered after by his furious gestures in the mount. Gabriel promises to find him ere morning. Night coming on, Adam and Eve discourse of going to their rest: their bower described; their evening worship. Gabriel drawing forth his bands of nightwatch to walk the round of Paradise, appoints two strong angels to Adam's bower, lest the evil Spirit should be there doing some harm to Adam or Eve sleeping; there they find him at the ear of Eve, tempting her in a dream, and bring him, though unwilling, to Gabriel; by whom questioned, he scornfully answers, prepares resistance, but hindered by a sign from heaven, flies out of Paradise.

O for that warning voice, which he who saw
Th' Apocalypse, heard cry in Heaven aloud,
Then when the Dragon, put to second rout,
Came furious down to be revenged on men,
"Woe to the inhabitants on earth!"[1] that now, 5
While time was, our first parents had been warned
The coming of their secret foe, and scaped
Haply° so scaped his mortal° snare; for now   *perhaps / deadly*
Satan, now first inflamed with rage, came down,
The tempter ere° th' accuser of mankind,   *before being* 10
To wreak° on innocent frail man his loss   *avenge*
Of that first battle, and his flight to Hell:
Yet not rejoicing in his speed, though bold,
Far off and fearless, nor with cause to boast,
Begins his dire attempt, which nigh the birth 15
Now rolling, boils in his tumultuous breast,
And like a devilish engine back recoils
Upon himself; horror and doubt distract
His troubled thoughts, and from the bottom stir
The Hell within him, for within him Hell 20
He brings, and round about him, nor from Hell
One step no more than from himself can fly
By change of place: now conscience wakes despair
That slumbered, wakes the bitter memory
Of what he was, what is, and what must be 25
Worse; of worse deeds worse sufferings must ensue.
Sometimes towards Eden which now in his view
Lay pleasant, his grieved look he fixes sad,
Sometimes towards Heav'n and the full-blazing sun,
Which now sat high in his meridian tow'r:[2] 30
Then much revolving,° thus in sighs began.   *pondering*
"O thou that with surpassing glory crowned,[3]
Look'st from thy sole dominion like the god

---

1. John of Patmos, in Revelation 12:3–12, hears such a cry during a second war in Heaven, between the Dragon and the angels.
2. At midday, the height of noon.
3. Milton's nephew, Edward Phillips, said that this soliloquy was written "several years before the poem was begun," and was intended to begin a drama on the topic, *Adam Unparadised*.

Of this new world: at whose sight all the stars
35 Hide their diminished heads; to thee I call,
But with no friendly voice, and add thy name
O sun, to tell thee how I hate thy beams
That bring to my remembrance from what state
I fell, how glorious once above thy sphere;
40 Till pride and worse ambition threw me down
Warring in Heav'n against Heav'n's matchless King:
Ah wherefore! he deserved no such return
From me, whom he created what I was
In that bright eminence, and with his good
45 Upbraided[4] none, nor was his service hard.
What could be less than to afford him praise,
The easiest recompense, and pay him thanks,
How due! yet all his good proved ill in me,
And wrought but malice; lifted up so high
50 I 'sdained° subjection, and thought one step higher   *disdained*
Would set me highest, and in a moment quit°   *pay*
The debt immense of endless gratitude,
So burthensome still° paying, still to owe;   *always*
Forgetful what from him I still received,
55 And understood not that a grateful mind
By owing owes not, but still pays, at once
Indebted and discharged; what burden then?
O had his powerful destiny ordained
Me some inferior angel, I had stood
60 Then happy; no unbounded hope had raised
Ambition. Yet why not? some other Power°   *angel*
As great might have aspired, and me though mean
Drawn to his part; but other Powers as great
Fell not, but stand unshaken, from within
65 Or from without, to all temptations armed.
Hadst thou[5] the same free will and power to stand?
Thou hadst: whom hast thou then or what to accuse,
But Heav'n's free love dealt equally to all?
Be then his love accursed, since love or hate,
70 To me alike, it deals eternal woe.
Nay cursed be thou; since against his thy will
Chose freely what it now so justly rues.
Me miserable![6] which way shall I fly
Infinite wrath, and infinite despair?
75 Which way I fly is Hell; myself am Hell;[7]
And in the lowest deep a lower deep
Still threat'ning to devour me opens wide,
To which the Hell I suffer seems a Heav'n.
O then at last relent! is there no place
80 Left for repentance, none for pardon left?
None left but by submission; and that word

---

4. Reproached (James 1:5).
5. Compare Satan's address to himself here with Adam's soliloquy in parallel circumstances (10.758ff.).
6. A Latinism, *me miserum!*
7. Compare Satan's earlier claim that "the mind is its own place" (1.254).

　　　　Disdain forbids me, and my dread of shame
　　　　Among the Spirits beneath, whom I seduced
　　　　With other promises and other vaunts
85　　　Than to submit, boasting I could subdue
　　　　Th' Omnipotent. Ay me, they little know
　　　　How dearly I abide° that boast so vain,　　　　　　　　　　*pay the penalty far*
　　　　Under what torments inwardly I groan:
　　　　While they adore me on the throne of Hell,
90　　　With diadem and scepter high advanced
　　　　The lower still I fall, only supreme
　　　　In misery; such joy ambition finds.
　　　　But say I could repent and could obtain
　　　　By act of grace[8] my former state; how soon
95　　　Would heighth recall high thoughts, how soon unsay
　　　　What feigned submission swore: ease would recant
　　　　Vows made in pain, as violent° and void.　　　　　　　　　　*forced*
　　　　For never can true reconcilement grow
　　　　Where wounds of deadly hate have pierced so deep:
100　　Which would but lead me to a worse relapse,
　　　　And heavier fall: so should I purchase dear
　　　　Short intermission bought with double smart.
　　　　This knows my punisher; therefore as far
　　　　From granting he, as I from begging peace:
105　　All hope excluded thus, behold instead
　　　　Of us outcast, exiled, his new delight,
　　　　Mankind created, and for him this world.
　　　　So farewell hope, and with hope farewell fear,
　　　　Farewell remorse: all good to me is lost;
110　　Evil be thou my good; by thee at least
　　　　Divided empire with Heav'n's King I hold
　　　　By thee, and more than half perhaps will reign;
　　　　As man ere long, and this new world shall know."
　　　　　　Thus while he spake, each passion dimmed his face
115　　Thrice changed with pale,° ire, envy, and despair,　　　　　　*pallor*
　　　　Which marred his borrowed visage, and betrayed
　　　　Him counterfeit, if any eye beheld.
　　　　For heav'nly minds from such distempers foul
　　　　Are ever clear. Whereof he soon aware,
120　　Each perturbation smoothed with outward calm,
　　　　Artificer of fraud; and was the first
　　　　That practiced falsehood under saintly show,
　　　　Deep malice to conceal, couched° with revenge:　　　　　　　*hidden*
　　　　Yet not enough had practiced to deceive
125　　Uriel once warned; whose eye pursued him down
　　　　The way he went, and on th' Assyrian mount°　　　　　　　　　*Niphates*
　　　　Saw him disfigured, more than could befall
　　　　Spirit of happy sort: his gestures fierce
　　　　He marked and mad demeanor, then alone,
130　　As he supposed, all unobserved, unseen.
　　　　　　So on he fares, and to the border comes

---

8. The technical term for a formal pardon.

Of Eden, where delicious Paradise,[9]
Now nearer, crowns with her enclosure green,
As with a rural mound the champaign head°   *open summit*
135 Of a steep wilderness, whose hairy sides
With thicket overgrown, grotesque[1] and wild,
Access denied; and overhead up grew
Insuperable heighth of loftiest shade,
Cedar, and pine, and fir, and branching palm,
140 A sylvan scene, and as the ranks ascend
Shade above shade, a woody theater[2]
Of stateliest view. Yet higher than their tops
The verdurous wall of Paradise up sprung:
Which to our general sire gave prospect large
145 Into his nether empire neighboring round.
And higher than that wall a circling row
Of goodliest trees loaden with fairest fruit,
Blossoms and fruits at once of golden hue
Appeared, with gay enameled° colors mixed: *bright*
150 On which the sun more glad impressed his beams
Than in fair evening cloud, or humid bow,°   *rainbow*
When God hath show'red the earth; so lovely seemed
That landscape: and of pure now purer air[3]
Meets his approach, and to the heart inspires°   *infuses*
155 Vernal delight and joy, able to drive°   *drive out*
All sadness but despair: now gentle gales
Fanning their odoriferous° wings dispense   *fragrance-bearing*
Native perfumes, and whisper whence they stole
Those balmy spoils. As when to them who sail
160 Beyond the Cape of Hope,° and now are past   *Cape of Good Hope*
Mozambic, off at sea northeast winds blow
Sabean odors from the spicy shore
Of Araby the Blest,[4] with such delay
Well pleased they slack their course, and many a league
165 Cheered with the grateful° smell old Ocean smiles.   *pleasing*
So entertained those odorous sweets the Fiend
Who came their bane,° though with them better pleased   *poison*
Than Asmodeus with the fishy fume,
That drove him, though enamored, from the spouse
170 Of Tobit's son, and with a vengeance sent
From Media post to Egypt, there fast bound.[5]
    Now to th'ascent of that steep savage° hill   *wooded, wild*
Satan had journeyed on, pensive and slow;
But further way found none, so thick entwined,
175 As one continued brake,° the undergrowth   *thicket*

---

9. Paradise is a delightful ("delicious") garden on top of a steep hill situated in the east of the land of Eden.
1. Characterized by interwoven, tangled vines and branches.
2. As if in a Greek amphitheater, the trees are set row on row.
3. The air becomes still purer.
4. *Arabia Felix* (modern Yemen). "Sabean": the biblical Sheba.
5. The Apocryphal book of Tobit tells of Tobias, Tobit's son, who married Sara and avoided the fate of her previous seven husbands (killed on their wedding night by the demon Asmodeus) by following the instructions of the angel Raphael and making a fishy smell to drive him off; Asmodeus then fled to Egypt, where Raphael bound him.

Of shrubs and tangling bushes had perplexed
All path of man or beast that passed that way:
One gate there only was, and that looked east
On th' other side: which when th' arch-felon saw
180 Due entrance he disdained, and in contempt,
At one slight bound high overleaped all bound
Of hill or highest wall, and sheer within
Lights on his feet. As when a prowling wolf,
Whom hunger drives to seek new haunt for prey,
185 Watching where shepherds pen their flocks at eve
In hurdled cotes° amid the field secure,   *pens of woven reeds*
Leaps o'er the fence with ease into the fold:
Or as a thief bent to unhoard the cash
Of some rich burgher, whose substantial doors,
190 Cross-barred and bolted fast, fear no assault,
In at the window climbs, or o'er the tiles;
So clomb° this first grand thief into God's fold: *climbed*
So since into his church lewd hirelings[6] climb.
Thence up he flew, and on the Tree of Life,
195 The middle tree and highest there that grew,
Sat like a cormorant;[7] yet not true life
Thereby regained, but sat devising death
To them who lived; nor on the virtue° thought   *power*
Of that life-giving plant, but only used
200 For prospect,° what well used had been the pledge   *as a lookout*
Of immortality. So little knows
Any, but God alone, to value right
The good before him, but perverts best things
To worst abuse, or to their meanest use.
205   Beneath him with new wonder now he views
To all delight of human sense exposed
In narrow room nature's whole wealth, yea more,
A heav'n on earth: for blissful Paradise
Of God the garden was, by him in the east
210 Of Eden planted; Eden stretched her line
From Auran eastward to the royal tow'rs
Of great Seleucia, built by Grecian kings,
Or where the sons of Eden long before
Dwelt in Telassar:[8] in this pleasant soil
215 His far more pleasant garden God ordained;
Out of the fertile ground he caused to grow
All trees of noblest kind for sight, smell, taste;
And all amid them stood the Tree of Life,
High eminent, blooming ambrosial° fruit   *divinely fragrant*
220 Of vegetable gold; and next to life
Our death the Tree of Knowledge grew fast by,
Knowledge of good bought dear by knowing ill.

---

6. Base men interested only in money; Milton would have clergymen not paid by required tithes or by the state, to ensure their purity of motive.
7. A sea bird, noted for gluttony.
8. Auran is the province of Hauran on the eastern border of Israel. Selucia, a powerful city on the Tigris, near modern Baghdad, was founded by one of Alexander's generals ("built by Grecian kings"). Telassar is another Near Eastern kingdom.

Southward through Eden went a river large,[9]
Nor changed his course, but through the shaggy hill
225 Passed underneath engulfed, for God had thrown
That mountain as his garden mold° high raised   *rich earth*
Upon the rapid current, which through veins
Of porous earth with kindly° thirst up drawn,   *natural*
Rose a fresh fountain, and with many a rill
230 Watered the garden; thence united fell
Down the steep glade, and met the nether flood,
Which from his darksome passage now appears,
And now divided into four main streams,
Runs diverse, wand'ring many a famous realm
235 And country whereof here needs no account,
But rather to tell how, if art could tell,
How from that sapphire fount the crispèd° brooks,   *wavy, rippling*
Rolling on orient pearl and sands of gold,
With mazy error[1] under pendent shades
240 Ran nectar, visiting each plant, and fed
Flow'rs worthy of Paradise which not nice° art   *fastidious*
In beds and curious knots, but nature boon°   *bounteous*
Poured forth profuse on hill and dale and plain,
Both where the morning sun first warmly smote
245 The open field, and where the unpierced shade
Embrowned° the noontide bow'rs. Thus was this place,   *darkened*
A happy rural seat of various view,[2]
Groves whose rich trees wept odorous gums and balm,
Others whose fruit burnished with golden rind
250 Hung amiable,° Hesperian fables true,[3]   *lovely*
If true, here only, and of delicious taste:
Betwixt them lawns, or level downs,° and flocks   *uplands*
Grazing the tender herb, were interposed,
Or palmy hillock, or the flow'ry lap
255 Of some irriguous° valley spread her store,   *well-watered*
Flow'rs of all hue, and without thorn the rose:
Another side, umbrageous° grots and caves   *shady*
Of cool recess, o'er which the mantling° vine   *enveloping*
Lays forth her purple grape, and gently creeps
260 Luxuriant; meanwhile murmuring waters fall
Down the slope hills, dispersed, or in a lake,
That to the fringèd bank with myrtle crowned,
Her crystal mirror holds, unite their streams.
The birds their choir apply; airs,[4] vernal airs,
265 Breathing the smell of field and grove, attune
The trembling leaves, while universal Pan[5]
Knit° with the Graces and the Hours in dance   *clasping hands*
Led on th' eternal spring. Not that fair field

---

9. The Tigris (identified at 9.71) flowed under the hill.
1. From Latin *errare*, to wander.
2. Like a country estate, with a variety of prospects.
3. These were real golden apples, by contrast to those feigned golden apples of the Hesperides, fabled paradisal islands in the Western Ocean.
4. Both breezes and melodies. "Their choir apply": practice their songs.
5. The god of all nature—*pan* in Greek means "all."

Of Enna, where Proserpine gathering flow'rs
Herself a fairer flow'r by gloomy Dis
Was gathered, which cost Ceres all that pain
To seek her through the world; nor that sweet grove
Of Daphne by Orontes, and th' inspired
Castalian spring, might with this Paradise
Of Eden strive;⁶ nor that Nyseian isle
Girt with the river Triton, where old Cham,
Whom Gentiles Ammon call and Libyan Jove,
Hid Amalthea and her florid° son   *wine-flushed*
Young Bacchus from his stepdame Rhea's eye;⁷
Nor where Abassin kings their issue guard,
Mount Amara,⁸ though this by some supposed
True Paradise under the Ethiop line°   *equator*
By Nilus'° head, enclosed with shining rock,   *Nile's*
A whole day's journey high, but wide remote
From this Assyrian garden,° where the Fiend   *Eden*
Saw undelighted all delight, all kind
Of living creatures new to sight and strange:
    Two of far nobler shape erect and tall,
Godlike erect, with native honor clad
In naked majesty seemed lords of all,
And worthy seemed, for in their looks divine
The image of their glorious Maker shone,
Truth, wisdom, sanctitude severe and pure,
Severe but in true filial freedom placed;
Whence true authority in men;⁹ though both
Not equal, as their sex not equal seemed;
For contemplation he and valor formed,
For softness she and sweet attractive grace,
He for God only, she for God in him:¹
His fair large front° and eye sublime declared   *forehead*
Absolute rule; and hyacinthine² locks
Round from his parted forelock manly hung
Clust'ring, but not beneath his shoulders broad:
She as a veil down to the slender waist
Her unadorned golden tresses wore
Disheveled, but in wanton° ringlets waved   *unrestrained*
As the vine curls her tendrils,³ which implied
Subjection, but required° with gentle sway,°   *requested / persuasion*
And by her yielded, by him best received,
Yielded with coy° submission, modest pride,   *shyly reserved*

---

6. Milton compares Paradise with famous beauty spots of antiquity. Enna in Sicily was a lovely meadow from which Proserpine was kidnapped by "gloomy Dis" (Pluto); her mother Ceres sought her throughout the world. The grove of Daphne, near Antioch and the Orontes River in the Near East, had a spring called "Castalia" after the Muses' fountain near Parnassus.

7. The isle of Nysa in the river Triton in Tunisia was where Ammon (an Egyptian god, identified with Cham, or Ham, the son of Noah) hid Bacchus, his child by Amalthea (who later became the god of wine), away from the eyes of his wife Rhea.

8. Atop Mount Amara, the "Abassin" (Abyssinian) king had a splendid palace in a paradisal garden.

9. This phrase underscores Milton's idea that true freedom involves obedience to natural superiors (that is, God).

1. The phrase has as its context 1 Corinthians 11:3: "The head of every man is Christ; and the head of the woman is the man."

2. A classical metaphor for hair curled in the form of hyacinth petals, and perhaps also implying dark or flowing.

3. Eve's hair is curly, abundant, not subjected to rigid control, like the vegetation in Paradise.

And sweet reluctant amorous delay.
Nor those mysterious parts were then concealed,
Then was not guilty shame, dishonest° shame　　　　　　　　*unchaste*
Of nature's works, honor dishonorable,
315 Sin-bred, how have ye troubled all mankind
With shows instead, mere shows of seeming pure,
And banished from man's life his happiest life,
Simplicity and spotless innocence.
So passed they naked on, nor shunned the sight
320 Of God or angel, for they thought no ill:
So hand in hand they passed, the loveliest pair
That ever since in love's embraces met,
Adam the goodliest man of men since born
His sons, the fairest of her daughters Eve.
325 Under a tuft of shade that on a green
Stood whispering soft, by a fresh fountain side
They sat them down, and after no more toil
Of their sweet gard'ning labor than sufficed
To recommend cool Zephyr,[4] and made ease
330 More easy, wholesome thirst and appetite
More grateful, to their supper fruits they fell,
Nectarine° fruits which the compliant boughs　　　　　　　　*sweet as nectar*
Yielded them, sidelong as they sat recline
On the soft downy bank damasked with flow'rs:
335 The savory pulp they chew, and in the rind
Still as they thirsted scoop the brimming stream;
Nor gentle purpose,° nor endearing smiles　　　　　　　　　*conversation*
Wanted,° nor youthful dalliance as beseems　　　　　　　　　*lacked*
Fair couple, linked in happy nuptial league,
340 Alone as they. About them frisking played
All beasts of th' earth, since wild, and of all chase°　　　　*game animals*
In wood or wilderness, forest or den;
Sporting the lion ramped,° and in his paw　　　　　　　　　*stood on hind legs*
Dandled the kid; bears, tigers, ounces,° pards°　　　　　　　*lynxes / leopards*
345 Gamboled before them; th' unwieldy elephant
To make them mirth used all his might, and wreathed
His lithe proboscis;° close the serpent sly　　　　　　　　　*trunk*
Insinuating,° wove with Gordian twine　　　　　　　　　　　*writhing, twisting*
His braided train,[5] and of his fatal guile
350 Gave proof unheeded; others on the grass
Couched, and now filled with pasture gazing sat,
Or bedward ruminating:° for the sun　　　　　　　　　　　　*chewing the cud*
Declined was hasting now with prone° career　　　　　　　　*sinking*
To th' Ocean Isles,° and in th' ascending scale　　　　　　　*the Azores*
355 Of Heav'n the stars that usher evening rose:
When Satan still in gaze, as first he stood,
Scarce thus at length failed speech recovered sad.
　"O Hell! what do mine eyes with grief behold,
Into our room of bliss thus high advanced

---

4. That is, to make a cool breeze welcome.
5. Checkered body. "Gordian twine": cords as convoluted as the Gordian knot that Alexander the Great had to cut with his sword.

    Creatures of other mold, earth-born perhaps,
    Not Spirits, yet to heav'nly Spirits bright
    Little inferior; whom my thoughts pursue
    With wonder, and could love, so lively shines
    In them divine resemblance, and such grace
    The hand that formed them on their shape hath poured.
    Ah gentle pair, ye little think how nigh
    Your change approaches, when all these delights
    Will vanish and deliver ye to woe,
    More woe, the more your taste is now of joy;
    Happy, but for so happy° ill secured   *such happiness*
    Long to continue, and this high seat your heav'n
    Ill fenced for Heav'n to keep out such a foe
    As now is entered; yet no purposed foe
    To you whom I could pity thus forlorn
    Though I unpitied: league with you I seek,
    And mutual amity so strait,° so close,   *intimate*
    That I with you must dwell, or you with me
    Henceforth; my dwelling haply° may not please   *perhaps*
    Like this fair Paradise, your sense, yet such
    Accept your Maker's work; he gave it me,
    Which I as freely give; Hell shall unfold,
    To entertain you two, her widest gates,
    And send forth all her kings; there will be room,
    Not like these narrow limits, to receive
    Your numerous offspring; if no better place,
    Thank him who puts me loath to this revenge
    On you who wrong me not for° him who wronged.   *in place of*
    And should I at your harmless innocence
    Melt, as I do, yet public reason just,
    Honor and empire with revenge enlarged
    By conquering this new world, compels me now
    To do what else though damned I should abhor."⁶
         So spake the Fiend, and with necessity,
    The tyrant's plea, excused his devilish deeds.
    Then from his lofty stand on that high tree
    Down he alights among the sportful herd
    Of those four-footed kinds, himself now one,
    Now other, as their shape served best his end
    Nearer to view his prey, and unespied
    To mark what of their state he more might learn
    By word or action marked: about them round
    A lion now he stalks with fiery glare,
    Then as a tiger, who by chance hath spied
    In some purlieu° two gentle fawns at play,   *outskirts of a forest*
    Straight° couches close, then rising changes oft   *at once*
    His couchant watch, as one who chose his ground
    Whence rushing he might surest seize them both
    Gripped in each paw: when Adam first of men
    To first of women Eve thus moving speech

---

6. Satan's excuse—reason of state, public interest, empire, etc.—is called "the tyrant's plea" in line 394.

410   Turned him all ear to hear new utterance flow:
      "Sole partner and sole° part of all these joys,   *chief*
   Dearer thyself than all; needs must the Power
   That made us, and for us this ample world
   Be infinitely good, and of his good
415 As liberal and free as infinite,
   That raised us from the dust and placed us here
   In all this happiness, who at his hand
   Have nothing merited, nor can perform
   Aught whereof he hath need, he who requires
420 From us no other service than to keep
   This one, this easy charge, of all the trees
   In Paradise that bear delicious fruit
   So various, not to taste that only Tree
   Of Knowledge, planted by the Tree of Life,
425 So near grows death to life, whate'er death is,
   Some dreadful thing no doubt; for well thou know'st
   God hath pronounced it death to taste that Tree,
   The only sign of our obedience left
   Among so many signs of power and rule
430 Conferred upon us, and dominion giv'n
   Over all other creatures that possess
   Earth, air, and sea. Then let us not think hard
   One easy prohibition, who enjoy
   Free leave so large to all things else, and choice
435 Unlimited of manifold delights:
   But let us ever praise him, and extol
   His bounty, following our delightful task
   To prune these growing plants, and tend these flow'rs,
   Which were it toilsome, yet with thee were sweet."
440   To whom thus Eve replied. "O thou for whom
   And from whom I was formed flesh of thy flesh,
   And without whom am to no end, my guide
   And head, what thou hast said is just and right.
   For we to him indeed all praises owe,
445 And daily thanks, I chiefly who enjoy
   So far the happier lot, enjoying thee
   Preeminent by so much odds,° while thou   *advantage*
   Like consort to thyself canst nowhere find.
   That day I oft remember, when from sleep
450 I first awaked, and found myself reposed°   *resting*
   Under a shade on flowers, much wond'ring where
   And what I was, whence thither brought, and how.
   Not distant far from thence a murmuring sound
   Of waters issued from a cave and spread
455 Into a liquid plain, then stood unmoved
   Pure as th' expanse of Heav'n; I thither went
   With unexperienced thought, and laid me down
   On the green bank, to look into the clear
   Smooth lake, that to me seemed another sky.
460 As I bent down to look, just opposite,
   A shape within the wat'ry gleam appeared

       Bending to look on me, I started back,
       It started back, but pleased I soon returned,
       Pleased it returned as soon with answering looks
465   Of sympathy and love; there I had fixed
       Mine eyes till now, and pined with vain° desire,[7]   *futile*
       Had not a voice thus warned me, 'What thou seest,
       What there thou seest fair creature is thyself,
       With thee it came and goes: but follow me,
470   And I will bring thee where no shadow stays°   *hinders*
       Thy coming, and thy soft embraces, he
       Whose image thou art, him thou shall enjoy
       Inseparably thine, to him shalt bear
       Multitudes like thyself, and thence be called
475   Mother of human race': what could I do,
       But follow straight° invisibly thus led?   *at once*
       Till I espied thee, fair indeed and tall,
       Under a platan,° yet methought less fair,   *plane tree*
       Less winning soft, less amiably mild,
480   Than that smooth wat'ry image; back I turned,
       Thou following cried'st aloud, 'Return fair Eve,
       Whom fli'st thou? Whom thou fli'st, of him thou art,
       His flesh, his bone; to give thee being I lent
       Out of my side to thee, nearest my heart
485   Substantial life, to have thee by my side
       Henceforth an individual° solace dear;   *inseparable, distinct*
       Part of my soul I seek thee, and thee claim
       My other half': with that thy gentle hand
       Seized mine, I yielded, and from that time see
490   How beauty is excelled by manly grace
       And wisdom, which alone is truly fair."
          So spake our general mother, and with eyes
       Of conjugal attraction unreproved,
       And meek surrender, half embracing leaned
495   On our first father, half her swelling breast
       Naked met his under the flowing gold
       Of her loose tresses hid: he in delight
       Both of her beauty and submissive charms
       Smiled with superior love, as Jupiter
500   On Juno smiles, when he impregns° the clouds   *impregnates*
       That shed May flowers; and pressed her matron lip
       With kisses pure: aside the Devil turned
       For envy, yet with jealous leer malign
       Eyed them askance, and to himself thus plained.°   *complained*
505   "Sight hateful, sight tormenting! thus these two
       Imparadised in one another's arms
       The happier Eden, shall enjoy their fill
       Of bliss on bliss, while I to Hell am thrust,
       Where neither joy nor love, but fierce desire,
510   Among our other torments not the least,

---

7. Eve's experience reprises (but with significant differences) the story of Narcissus, who fell in love with his own reflection and was transformed into a flower.

Still° unfulfilled with pain of longing pines;   *always*
Yet let me not forget what I have gained
From their own mouths; all is not theirs it seems:
One fatal tree there stands of Knowledge called,
515 Forbidden them to taste: knowledge forbidden?
Suspicious, reasonless. Why should their Lord
Envy° them that? Can it be sin to know,   *begrudge*
Can it be death? And do they only stand
By ignorance, is that their happy state,
520 The proof of their obedience and their faith?
O fair foundation laid whereon to build
Their ruin! Hence I will excite their minds
With more desire to know, and to reject
Envious commands, invented with design
525 To keep them low whom knowledge might exalt
Equal with gods; aspiring to be such,
They taste and die: what likelier can ensue?
But first with narrow search I must walk round
This garden, and no corner leave unspied;
530 A chance, but chance[8] may lead where I may meet
Some wand'ring Spirit of Heav'n, by fountain side,
Or in thick shade retired, from him to draw
What further would be learnt. Live while ye may,
Yet happy pair; enjoy, till I return,
535 Short pleasures, for long woes are to succeed."
   So saying, his proud step he scornful turned,
But with sly circumspection, and began
Through wood, through waste, o'er hill, o'er dale his roam.°   *act of wandering*
Meanwhile in utmost longitude, where heav'n°   *the sky*
540 With earth and ocean meets, the setting sun
Slowly descended, and with right aspèct
Against the eastern gate of Paradise
Leveled his evening rays.[9] It was a rock
Of alabaster,[1] piled up to the clouds,
545 Conspicuous far, winding with one ascent
Accessible from earth, one entrance high;
The rest was craggy cliff, that overhung
Still as it rose, impossible to climb.
Betwixt these rocky pillars Gabriel[2] sat
550 Chief of th' angelic guards, awaiting night;
About him exercised heroic games
Th' unarmèd youth of Heav'n, but nigh at hand
Celestial armory, shields, helms, and spears
Hung high with diamond flaming, and with gold.
555 Thither came Uriel, gliding through the even
On a sunbeam, swift as a shooting star
In autumn thwarts° the night, when vapors fired   *passes across*
Impress the air, and shows the mariner
From what point of his compass to beware

---

8. An opportunity, even if only by luck.
9. Setting in the west, the sun struck the eastern gate from the inside, at a ninety-degree angle.

1. White, translucent marble veined with colors.
2. In Hebrew, "strength of God." A tradition (see 1 Enoch 20:7) gave Gabriel charge of Paradise.

Impetuous winds:[3] he thus began in haste.
  "Gabriel, to thee thy course by lot hath giv'n
Charge and strict watch that to this happy place
No evil thing approach or enter in;
This day at height of noon came to my sphere
A Spirit, zealous, as he seemed, to know
More of th' Almighty's works, and chiefly man
God's latest image: I described° his way   described, observed
Bent all on speed, and marked his airy gait;°   path
But in the mount that lies from Eden north,
Where he first lighted, soon discerned his looks
Alien from Heav'n, with passions foul obscured:
Mine eye pursued him still, but under shade°   trees
Lost sight of him; one of the banished crew
I fear, hath ventured from the deep, to raise
New troubles; him thy care must be to find."
  To whom the winged warrior thus returned:
"Uriel, no wonder if thy perfect sight,
Amid the sun's bright circle where thou sitt'st,
See far and wide. In at this gate none pass
The vigilance here placed, but such as come
Well known from Heav'n; and since meridian hour°   noon
No creature thence: if Spirit of other sort,
So minded, have o'erleaped these earthy bounds
On purpose, hard thou know'st it to exclude
Spiritual substance with corporeal bar.
But if within the circuit of these walks,
In whatsoever shape he lurk, of whom
Thou tell'st, by morrow dawning I shall know."
  So promised he, and Uriel to his charge
Returned on that bright beam, whose point now raised
Bore him slope downward to the sun now fall'n
Beneath th' Azorès; whether the prime orb,
Incredible how swift, had thither rolled
Diurnal,° or this less volúble° earth   daily / swift-turning
By shorter flight to th' east,[4] had left him there
Arraying with reflected purple and gold
The clouds that on his western throne attend.
Now came still evening on, and twilight gray
Had in her sober livery all things clad;
Silence accompanied, for beast and bird,
They to their grassy couch, these to their nests
Were slunk, all but the wakeful nightingale;
She all night long her amorous descant° sung;   melody
Silence was pleased: now glowed the firmament
With living sapphires: Hesperus[5] that led
The starry host, rode brightest, till the moon
Rising in clouded majesty, at length

---

3. Shooting stars were thought to indicate by the direction of their fall the source of oncoming storms. "Vapors fired": heat lightning.
4. Here and elsewhere Milton leaves open the question of whether the sun moves around the earth, or vice versa.
5. Called Venus when it appears in the evening sky.

Apparent° queen unveiled her peerless light,   *clearly seen*
And o'er the dark her silver mantle threw.
    When Adam thus to Eve: "Fair consort, th' hour
Of night, and all things now retired to rest
Mind us of like repose, since God hath set
Labor and rest, as day and night to men
Successive, and the timely dew of sleep
Now falling with soft slumbrous weight inclines
Our eyelids; other creatures all day long
Rove idle unemployed, and less need rest;
Man hath his daily work of body or mind
Appointed, which declares his dignity,
And the regard of Heav'n on all his ways;
While other animals unactive range,
And of their doings God takes no account.
Tomorrow ere fresh morning streak the east
With first approach of light, we must be ris'n,
And at our pleasant labor, to reform
Yon flow'ry arbors, yonder alleys green,
Our walk at noon, with branches overgrown,
That mock our scant manuring,° and require   *cultivating*
More hands than ours to lop their wanton° growth: *luxuriant*
Those blossoms also, and those dropping gums,
That lie bestrown unsightly and unsmooth,
Ask riddance,° if we mean to tread with ease;   *need to be cleared*
Meanwhile, as nature wills, night bids us rest."
    To whom thus Eve with perfect beauty adorned.
"My author and disposer, what thou bidd'st
Unargued I obey; so God ordains,
God is thy law, thou mine: to know no more
Is woman's happiest knowledge and her praise.
With thee conversing I forget all time.
All seasons° and their change, all please alike.   *times of day*
Sweet[6] is the breath of morn, her rising sweet,
With charm[7] of earliest birds; pleasant the sun
When first on this delightful land he spreads
His orient° beams, on herb, tree, fruit, and flow'r,   *lustrious, eastern*
Glist'ring with dew; fragrant the fertile earth
After soft showers; and sweet the coming on
Of grateful evening mild, then silent night
With this her solemn bird° and this fair moon,   *the nightingale*
And these the gems of heav'n, her starry train:
But neither breath of morn when she ascends
With charm of earliest birds, nor rising sun
On this delightful land, nor herb, fruit, flow'r,
Glist'ring with dew, nor fragrance after showers,
Nor grateful evening mild, nor silent night
With this her solemn bird, nor walk by moon,
Or glittering starlight without thee is sweet.

6. With this embedded lyric, beginning here, Eve displays her literary talents in an elegant love song, sonnetlike and replete with striking rhetorical figures of circularity and repetition.
7. Blended singing of many birds.

> But wherefore all night long shine these, for whom
> This glorious sight, when sleep hath shut all eyes?"
>   To whom our general ancestor replied.
> "Daughter of God and man, accomplished[8] Eve, ₆₆₀
> Those have their course to finish, round the earth,
> By morrow evening, and from land to land
> In order, though to nations yet unborn,
> Minist'ring light prepared, they set and rise;
> Lest total darkness should by night regain ₆₆₅
> Her old possession, and extinguish life
> In nature and all things, which these soft° fires   *agreeable*
> Not only enlighten, but with kindly° heat   *natural, benevolent*
> Of various influence foment° and warm,   *foster*
> Temper or nourish, or in part shed down ₆₇₀
> Their stellar virtue on all kinds that grow
> On earth, made hereby apter to receive
> Perfection from the sun's more potent ray.[9]
> These then, though unbeheld in deep of night,
> Shine not in vain, nor think, though men were none, ₆₇₅
> That heav'n would want° spectators, God want praise;   *lack*
> Millions of spiritual creatures walk the earth
> Unseen, both when we wake, and when we sleep:
> All these with ceaseless praise his works behold
> Both day and night: how often from the steep ₆₈₀
> Of echoing hill or thicket have we heard
> Celestial voices to the midnight air,
> Sole, or responsive each to other's note
> Singing their great Creator: oft in bands
> While they keep watch, or nightly rounding walk, ₆₈₅
> With heav'nly touch of instrumental sounds
> In full harmonic number joined, their songs
> Divide[1] the night, and lift our thoughts to Heaven."
>   Thus talking hand in hand alone they passed
> On to their blissful bower; it was a place ₆₉₀
> Chos'n by the sov'reign Planter, when he framed°   *fashioned*
> All things to man's delightful use; the roof
> Of thickest covert was inwoven shade
> Laurel and myrtle, and what higher grew
> Of firm and fragrant leaf; on either side ₆₉₅
> Acanthus, and each odorous bushy shrub
> Fenced up the verdant wall; each beauteous flow'r,
> Iris all hues, roses, and jessamine°   *jasmine*
> Reared high their flourished° heads between, and wrought   *flowering*
> Mosaic; underfoot the violet, ₇₀₀
> Crocus, and hyacinth with rich inlay
> Broidered the ground, more colored than with stone
> Of costliest emblem:° other creature here   *inlaid work*
> Beast, bird, insect, or worm durst enter none,

---

8. Having many talents and achievements; perfect, complete.
9. The stars were thought to have their own occult influence, and also to moderate that of the sun.
1. Mark the watches of the night; also, perform musical "divisions," elaborate melodic passages.

705	Such was their awe of man. In shadier bower	
	More sacred and sequestered,° though but feigned,	*secluded*
	Pan or Silvanus never slept, nor nymph,	
	Nor Faunus² haunted. Here in close recess	
	With flowers, garlands, and sweet-smelling herbs	
710	Espousèd Eve decked first her nuptial bed,	
	And heav'nly choirs the hymenean° sung,	*wedding song*
	What day the genial³ angel to our sire	
	Brought her in naked beauty more adorned,	
	More lovely than Pandora, whom the gods	
715	Endowed with all their gifts, and O too like	
	In sad event,° when to the unwiser son	*outcome*
	Of Japhet brought by Hermes, she ensnared	
	Mankind with her fair looks, to be avenged	
	On him who had stole Jove's authentic fire.⁴	
720	Thus at their shady lodge arrived, both stood,	
	Both turned, and under open sky adored	
	The God that made both sky, air, earth, and heav'n	
	Which they beheld, the moon's resplendent globe	
	And starry pole:° "Thou also mad'st the night,	*sky*
725	Maker Omnipotent, and thou the day,	
	Which we in our appointed work employed	
	Have finished happy in our mutual help	
	And mutual love, the crown of all our bliss	
	Ordained by thee, and this delicious place	
730	For us too large, where thy abundance wants	
	Partakers, and uncropped falls to the ground.	
	But thou hast promised from us two a race	
	To fill the earth, who shall with us extol	
	Thy goodness infinite, both when we wake,	
735	And when we seek, as now, thy gift of sleep."	
	This said unanimous, and other rites	
	Observing none, but adoration pure	
	Which God likes best,⁵ into their inmost bow'r	
	Handed° they went; and eased° the putting off	*hand in hand / spared*
740	These troublesome disguises which we wear,	
	Straight side by side were laid, nor turned I ween°	*surmise*
	Adam from his fair spouse, nor Eve the rites	
	Mysterious⁶ of connubial love refused:	
	Whatever hypocrites austerely talk	
745	Of purity and place and innocence,	
	Defaming as impure what God declares	
	Pure, and commands to some, leaves free to all.	

2. Forest and field divinities of classical mythology.
3. Presiding over marriage and generation.
4. Pandora (the name means "all gifts") was an artificial woman, molded of clay, bestowed by the gods on Epimetheus, brother of Prometheus (who angered Jove by stealing fire from heaven). She brought a box that foolish Epimetheus opened, releasing all the ills of the human race, leaving only hope inside. The brothers were sons of Iapetos, whom Milton identifies with Japhet, Noah's third son. The Eve-Pandora parallel was often noted.
5. Like many Puritans, Milton objected to set forms of prayer, so Adam and Eve pray spontaneously (therefore sincerely), but also, paradoxically, together. Their prayer develops variations on Psalm 104:20–24.
6. Ephesians 5:32 calls the union of man and woman a "mystery" paralleling that of Christ and the church.

Our Maker bids increase,[7] who bids abstain
But our destroyer, foe to God and man?
Hail wedded Love, mysterious law, true source
Of human offspring, sole propriety°　　　　　　　　　　*private property*
In Paradise of all things common else.
By thee adulterous lust was driv'n from men
Among the bestial herds to range, by thee
Founded in reason, loyal, just, and pure,
Relations dear, and all the charities°　　　　　　　　　　　　　　　　*loves*
Of father, son, and brother first were known.
Far be it, that I should write thee sin or blame,
Or think thee unbefitting holiest place,
Perpetual fountain of domestic sweets,
Whose bed is undefiled and chaste pronounced,
Present, or past, as saints and patriarchs used.[8]
Here Love his golden shafts employs,[9] here lights
His constant lamp, and waves his purple wings,
Reigns here and revels; not in the bought smile
Of harlots, loveless, joyless, unendeared,
Casual fruition, nor in court amours,
Mixed dance, or wanton masque, or midnight ball,
Or serenade, which the starved° lover sings　　　　　　　　　　　*deprived*
To his proud fair, best quitted with disdain.
These lulled by nightingales embracing slept,
And on their naked limbs the flow'ry roof
Show'red roses, which the morn repaired.° Sleep on,　　　　　*replaced*
Blest pair; and O yet happiest if ye seek
No happier state, and know to know no more.[1]
　　Now had night measured with her shadowy cone
Halfway up hill this vast sublunar vault,[2]
And from their ivory port the Cherubim
Forth issuing at th' accustomed hour stood armed
To their night watches in warlike parade,
When Gabriel to his next in power thus spake:
　　"Uzziel,[3] half these draw off, and coast° the south　　　　　　*skirt*
With strictest watch; these other wheel[4] the north,
Our circuit meets full west." As flame they part
Half wheeling to the shield, half to the spear.
From these, two strong and subtle Spirits he called
That near him stood, and gave them thus in charge:
　　"Ithuriel and Zephon,[5] with winged speed
Search through this garden, leave unsearched no nook,
But chiefly where those two fair creatures lodge,
Now laid perhaps asleep secure of° harm.　　　　　　　　　　　　*from*

---

7. Genesis 1:28: "Be fruitful and multiply, and replenish the earth."
8. Throughout history ("present or past"), Old and New Testament worthies have "used" matrimony as a noble estate.
9. The "golden shafts" (arrows) of Cupid produce true love, his lead-tipped arrows, hate.
1. Know enough to be content with what you know.
2. The conical shadow cast by the earth has moved halfway up to its zenith, so it is 9 P.M., the end of the first three-hour watch.
3. Hebrew, "my strength is God."
4. "Wheel": turn to (military term); "shield" (line 785) is left, "spear" is right.
5. Hebrew, "a looking out." "Ithuriel": Hebrew, "discovery of God."

This evening from the sun's decline arrived
Who° tells of some infernal Spirit seen   *one who*
Hitherward bent; who could have thought? escaped
795 The bars of Hell, on errand bad no doubt:
Such where ye find, seize fast, and hither bring."
    So saying, on he led his radiant files,
Dazzling the moon; these to the bower direct
In search of whom they sought: him there they found
800 Squat like a toad, close at the ear of Eve;
Assaying° by his devilish art to reach   *attempting*
The organs of her fancy,[6] and with them forge
Illusions as he list,° phantasms and dreams;   *pleased*
Or if, inspiring° venom, he might taint   *breathing*
805 Th' animal spirits that from pure blood arise
Like gentle breaths from rivers pure, thence raise
At least distempered,° discontented thoughts,   *disordered*
Vain hopes, vain aims, inordinate desires
Blown up with high conceits° engend'ring pride.   *notions*
810 Him thus intent Ithuriel with his spear
Touched lightly; for no falsehood can endure
Touch of celestial temper,[7] but returns
Of force to its own likeness: up he starts
Discovered and surprised. As when a spark
815 Lights on a heap of nitrous powder,[8] laid
Fit for the tun some magazine to store
Against a rumored war, the smutty° grain   *black*
With sudden blaze diffused, inflames the air:
So started up in his own shape the Fiend.
820 Back stepped those two fair angels half amazed
So sudden to behold the grisly king;
Yet thus, unmoved with fear, accost him soon:
    "Which of those rebel Spirits adjudged to Hell
Com'st thou, escaped thy prison; and transformed,
825 Why sat'st thou like an enemy in wait
Here watching at the head of these that sleep?"
    "Know ye not then," said Satan, filled with scorn,
"Know ye not me? Ye knew me once no mate
For you, there sitting where ye durst not soar;
830 Not to know me argues° yourselves unknown,   *proves*
The lowest of your throng; or if ye know,
Why ask ye, and superfluous begin
Your message, like to end as much in vain?"
    To whom thus Zephon, answering scorn with scorn:
835 "Think not, revolted Spirit, thy shape the same,
Or undiminished brightness, to be known
As when thou stood'st in Heav'n upright and pure;
That glory then, when thou no more wast good,
Departed from thee, and thou resembl'st now

---

6. The faculty of forming mental images.
7. Anything, like the spear, made ("tempered") in Heaven.
8. Alights or kindles ("lights") gunpowder ("nitrous powder"), ready (next lines) to be stored in some barrel ("tun") laid up in some storehouse ("magazine"), in preparation for ("against") rumors of war.

Thy sin and place of doom obscure° and foul. —dark
But come, for thou, be sure, shalt give account
To him who sent us, whose charge is to keep
This place inviolable, and these from harm."
　　So spake the Cherub, and his grave rebuke
Severe in youthful beauty, added grace
Invincible: abashed the Devil stood,
And felt how awful° goodness is, and saw   —awe-inspiring
Virtue in her shape how lovely, saw, and pined°   —mourned
His loss; but chiefly to find here observed
His luster visibly impaired; yet seemed
Undaunted. "If I must contend," said he,
"Best with the best, the sender not the sent,
Or all at once; more glory will be won,
Or less be lost." "Thy fear," said Zephon bold,
"Will save us trial what the least can do
Single° against thee wicked, and thence weak."   —in single combat
　　The Fiend replied not, overcome with rage;
But like a proud steed reined, went haughty on,
Champing his iron curb: to strive or fly
He held it vain; awe from above had quelled
His heart, not else dismayed. Now drew they nigh
The western point, where those half-rounding guards
Just met, and closing stood in squadron joined
Awaiting next command. To whom their chief
Gabriel from the front thus called aloud:
"O friends, I hear the tread of nimble feet
Hasting this way, and now by glimpse discern
Ithuriel and Zephon through the shade,°   —trees
And with them comes a third of regal port,°   —bearing
But faded splendor wan;° who by his gait   —faint, dark
And fierce demeanor seems the Prince of Hell,
Not likely to part hence without contést;
Stand firm, for in his look defiance lours."°   —frowns
　　He scarce had ended, when those two approached
And brief related whom they brought, where found,
How busied, in what form and posture couched.
　　To whom with stern regard thus Gabriel spake:
"Why hast thou, Satan, broke the bounds prescribed
To thy transgressions, and disturbed the charge°   —responsibility
Of others, who approve not to transgress
By thy example, but have power and right
To question thy bold entrance on this place;
Employed it seems to violate sleep, and those
Whose dwelling God hath planted here in bliss?"
　　To whom thus Satan, with contemptuous brow:
"Gabriel, thou hadst in Heav'n th' esteem° of wise,   —reputation of being
And such I held thee; but this question asked
Puts me in doubt. Lives there who loves his pain?
Who would not, finding way, break loose from Hell,
Though thither doomed? Thou wouldst thyself, no doubt,
And boldly venture to whatever place

Farthest from pain, where thou mightst hope to change° *exchange*
Torment with ease, and soonest recompense
Dole° with delight, which in this place I sought; *pain, grief*
895 To thee no reason, who know'st only good,
But evil hast not tried: and wilt object[9]
His will who bound us? Let him surer bar
His iron gates, if he intends our stay
In that dark durance:° thus much what was asked.[1] *confinement*
900 The rest is true, they found me where they say;
But that implies not violence or harm."
    Thus he in scorn. The warlike angel moved,
Disdainfully half smiling thus replied:
"O loss of one in Heav'n to judge of wise,
905 Since Satan fell, whom folly overthrew,[2]
And now returns him from his prison scaped,
Gravely in doubt whether to hold them wise
Or not, who ask what boldness brought him hither
Unlicensed from his bounds in Hell prescribed;
910 So wise he judges it to fly from pain
However,° and to scape his punishment. *howsoever*
So judge thou still, presumptuous, till the wrath,
Which thou incurr'st by flying, meet thy flight
Sevenfold, and scourge that wisdom back to Hell,
915 Which taught thee yet no better, that no pain
Can equal anger infinite provoked.
But wherefore thou alone? Wherefore with thee
Came not all Hell broke loose? Is pain to them
Less pain, less to be fled, or thou than they
920 Less hardy to endure? Courageous chief,
The first in flight from pain, hadst thou alleged
To thy deserted host this cause of flight,
Thou surely hadst not come sole fugitive."
    To which the Fiend thus answered frowning stern:
925 "Not that I less endure, or shrink from pain,
Insulting angel, well thou know'st I stood° *withstood*
Thy fiercest, when in battle to thy aid
The blasting volleyed thunder made all speed
And seconded thy else not dreaded spear.
930 But still thy words at random, as before,
Argue thy inexperience what behoves
From° hard assays° and ill successes past *after / attempts*
A faithful leader, not to hazard all
Through ways of danger by himself untried.
935 I therefore, I alone first undertook
To wing the desolate abyss, and spy
This new-created world, whereof in Hell
Fame° is not silent, here in hope to find *rumor*
Better abode, and my afflicted powers° *downcast armies*

---

9. Put forward as an objection.
1. That is, thus much (answers) what was asked.
2. Irony: "O what a loss to Heaven to lose such a judge of wisdom as Satan, whose folly led to his fall."

To settle here on earth, or in midair;[3]
Though for possession put° to try once more *forced*
What thou and thy gay° legions dare against; *showy*
Whose easier business were to serve their Lord
High up in Heav'n, with songs to hymn his throne,
And practiced distances to cringe, not fight."[4]
    To whom the warrior angel soon replied:
"To say and straight unsay, pretending first
Wise to fly pain, professing next the spy,
Argues no leader, but a liar traced,° *found out*
Satan, and couldst thou faithful add? O name,
O sacred name of faithfulness profaned!
Faithful to whom? To thy rebellious crew?
Army of fiends, fit body to fit head;
Was this your discipline and faith engaged,
Your military obedience, to dissolve
Allegiance to th' acknowledged Power Supreme?
And thou sly hypocrite, who now wouldst seem
Patron of liberty, who more than thou
Once fawned, and cringed, and servilely adored
Heav'n's awful Monarch?[5] Wherefore but in hope
To dispossess him, and thyself to reign?
But mark what I areed° thee now, avaunt;° *advise / be gone*
Fly thither whence thou fledd'st: if from this hour
Within these hallowed limits thou appear,
Back to th' infernal pit I drag thee chained,
And seal thee so, as henceforth not to scorn
The facile° gates of Hell too slightly barred." *easily moved*
    So threatened he, but Satan to no threats
Gave heed, but waxing° more in rage replied: *growing*
"Then when I am thy captive talk of chains,
Proud limitary[6] Cherub, but ere then
Far heavier load thyself expect to feel
From my prevailing arm, though Heaven's King
Ride on thy wings, and thou with thy compeers,
Used to the yoke, draw'st his triumphant wheels
In progress through the road of heav'n star-paved."
    While thus he spake, th' angelic squadron bright
Turned fiery red, sharp'ning in moonèd horns[7]
Their phalanx, and began to hem him round
With ported[8] spears, as thick as when a field
Of Ceres[9] ripe for harvest waving bends
Her bearded grove of ears, which way the wind
Sways them; the careful plowman doubting stands
Lest on the threshing floor his hopeful sheaves

---

3. Satan will become "prince of the power of the air" (Ephesians 2:2).
4. Satan contemptuously parallels the angels' courtly deference ("distances") before God's throne and keeping a safe distance from battle. "Cringe": bow or kneel in fear or servility.
5. See 5.617 for Satan's "servile" adoration on the day of the Son's exaltation, when he "seemed well pleased" but was not.
6. Frontier guard, also, one of limited authority.
7. A crescent-shaped military formation.
8. Held slantwise in front.
9. Roman goddess of grain; here, the grain itself. A Homeric simile compares an excited army to windswept corn (*Iliad* 2.147–50).

985	Prove chaff. On th' other side Satan alarmed°	*called to arms*
	Collecting all his might dilated stood,	
	Like Tenerife or Atlas[1] unremoved:°	*unremovable*
	His stature reached the sky, and on his crest	
	Sat Horror plumed; nor wanted in his grasp	
990	What seemed both spear and shield: now dreadful deeds	
	Might have ensued, nor only Paradise	
	In this commotion, but the starry cope°	*vault*
	Of Heav'n perhaps, or all the elements	
	At least had gone to wrack, disturbed and torn	
995	With violence of this conflict, had not soon	
	Th' Eternal to prevent such horrid fray	
	Hung forth in Heav'n his golden scales, yet seen	
	Betwixt Astraea and the Scorpion sign,[2]	
	Wherein all things created first he weighed,	
1000	The pendulous round earth with balanced air	
	In counterpoise, now ponders all events,	
	Battles and realms: in these he put two weights	
	The sequel each of parting and of fight;[3]	
	The latter quick up flew, and kicked the beam;	
1005	Which Gabriel spying, thus bespake the Fiend:	
	"Satan, I know thy strength, and thou know'st mine,	
	Neither our own but giv'n; what folly then	
	To boast what arms can do, since thine no more	
	Than Heav'n permits, nor mine, though doubled now	
1010	To trample thee as mire: for proof look up,	
	And read thy lot in yon celestial sign	
	Where thou art weighed, and shown how light, how weak,[4]	
	If thou resist." The Fiend looked up and knew	
	His mounted scale aloft: nor more; but fled	
1015	Murmuring, and with him fled the shades of night.	

Book 5

The Argument

Morning approached, Eve relates to Adam her troublesome dream; he likes it not, yet comforts her: they come forth to their day labors: their morning hymn at the door of their bower. God to render man inexcusable sends Raphael to admonish him of his obedience, of his free estate, of his enemy near at hand; who he is, and why his enemy, and whatever else may avail Adam to know. Raphael comes down to Paradise, his appearance described, his coming discerned by Adam afar off sitting at the door of his bower; he goes out to meet him, brings him to his lodge, entertains him with the choicest fruits of

---

1. A mountain in Morocco. "Tenerife": a mountain in the Canary Islands.
2. The zodiac sign Libra, represented by a pair of scales, is between Virgo (identified with Astraea, goddess of Justice, who fled the earth at the end of the Golden Age) and Scorpio.
3. In several classical epic similes the fates of opposing heroes are weighed in scales by the gods, but here God "ponders" (weighs the consequences of) all events, including parting or fighting. Battle, desired by Satan, proves lighter ("kicked the beam," line 1004).
4. See Daniel 5:27: "Thou art weighed in the balances, and art found wanting."

Paradise got together by Eve; their discourse at table: Raphael performs his message, minds Adam of his state and of his enemy; relates at Adam's request who that enemy is, and how he came to be so, beginning from his first revolt in heaven, and the occasion thereof; how he drew his legions after him to the parts of the north, and there incited them to rebel with him, persuading all but only Abdiel a Seraph, who in argument dissuades and opposes him, then forsakes him.

Now Morn her rosy steps in th' eastern clime
Advancing, sowed the earth with orient pearl,°   *sparkling dew*
When Adam waked, so customed, for his sleep
Was aery light, from pure digestion bred,
5 And temperate vapors bland,° which th' only sound   *gentle, balmy*
Of leaves and fuming rills, Aurora's fan,[1]
Lightly dispersed, and the shrill matin° song   *morning*
Of birds on every bough; so much the more
His wonder was to find unwakened Eve
10 With tresses discomposed, and glowing cheek,
As through unquiet rest: he on his side
Leaning half-raised, with looks of cordial° love   *heartfelt*
Hung over her enamored, and beheld
Beauty, which whether waking or asleep,
15 Shot forth peculiar° graces; then with voice   *its own*
Mild, as when Zephyrus on Flora[2] breathes,
Her hand soft touching, whispered thus: "Awake
My fairest, my espoused, my latest found,
Heav'n's last best gift, my ever new delight,
20 Awake, the morning shines, and the fresh field
Calls us, we lose the prime, to mark how spring
Our tended plants, how blows° the citron grove,   *blooms*
What drops the myrrh, and what the balmy reed,°   *balsam*
How nature paints her colors, how the bee
25 Sits on the bloom extracting liquid sweet."[3]
    Such whispering waked her, but with startled eye
On Adam, whom embracing, thus she spake:
"O sole in whom my thoughts find all repose,
My glory, my perfection, glad I see
30 Thy face, and morn returned, for I this night,
Such night till this I never passed, have dreamed,
If dreamed, not as I oft am wont,° of thee,   *accustomed*
Works of day past, or morrow's next design,
But of offense and trouble, which my mind
35 Knew never till this irksome night. Methought
Close at mine ear one called me forth to walk
With gentle voice, I thought it thine; it said,
'Why sleep'st thou Eve? Now is the pleasant time,

---

1. Rustling leaves and streams ("rills") stirred by Aurora, goddess of the dawn.
2. Zephyrus is god of the gentle west wind, Flora goddess of flowers.
3. Adam sings a morning love song (*aubade*) to Eve, which works variations on Song of Solomon 2:10–12: "Rise up, my love, my fair one, and come away. . . . The flowers appear on the earth; the time of the singing of birds is come." Compare Satan's serenade (5.38–47), a parody of Adam's *aubade* and the Song of Solomon. "Prime" (line 21): first hour of the day.

The cool, the silent, save where silence yields
To the night-warbling bird, that now awake ⁴⁰
Tunes sweetest his love-labored song; now reigns
Full-orbed the moon, and with more pleasing light
Shadowy sets off the face of things, in vain,
If none regard; heav'n wakes with all his eyes,°   *stars*
Whom to behold but thee, nature's desire,
In whose sight all things joy, with ravishment
Attracted by thy beauty still° to gaze.'   *continually*
I rose as at thy call, but found thee not;
To find thee I directed then my walk;
And on, me thought, alone I passed through ways
That brought me on a sudden to the tree
Of interdicted knowledge: fair it seemed,
Much fairer to my fancy than by day:
And as I wond'ring looked, beside it stood
One shaped and winged like one of those from Heav'n
By us oft seen; his dewy locks distilled
Ambrosia;° on that tree he also gazed;   *heavenly fragrance*
And 'O fair plant,' said he, 'with fruit surcharged,°   *overburdened*
Deigns none to ease thy load and taste thy sweet,
Nor god,° nor man? Is knowledge so despised?   *angel*
Or envy, or what reserve forbids to taste?[4]
Forbid who will, none shall from me withhold
Longer thy offered good, why else set here?'
This said he paused not, but with vent'rous arm
He plucked, he tasted; me damp horror chilled
At such bold words vouched with° a deed so bold: *backed by*
But he thus overjoyed, 'O fruit divine,
Sweet of thyself, but much more sweet thus cropped,
Forbidden here, it seems, as only fit
For gods, yet able to make gods of men:
And why not gods of men, since good, the more
Communicated, more abundant grows,
The author not impaired,° but honored more?   *injured, diminished*
Here, happy creature, fair angelic Eve,
Partake thou also; happy though thou art,
Happier thou may'st be, worthier canst not be:
Taste this, and be henceforth among the gods
Thyself a goddess, not to earth confined,
But sometimes in the air, as we, sometimes
Ascend to Heav'n, by merit thine, and see
What life the gods live there, and such live thou.'
So saying, he drew nigh, and to me held,
Even to my mouth of that same fruit held part
Which he had plucked; the pleasant savory smell
So quickened appetite, that I, methought,
Could not but taste. Forthwith up to the clouds
With him I flew, and underneath beheld
The earth outstretched immense, a prospect wide

---

4. That is, does envy or some other barrier ("reserve") forbid your being tasted?

                    And various: wond'ring at my flight and change
90   To this high exaltation: suddenly
              My guide was gone, and I, methought, sunk down,
              And fell asleep; but O how glad I waked
              To find this but a dream!" Thus Eve her night
              Related, and thus Adam answered sad.°   *gravely, soberly*
95   "Best image of myself and dearer half,
              The trouble of thy thoughts this night in sleep
              Affects me equally; nor can I like
              This uncouth° dream, of evil sprung I fear;   *strange, unpleasant*
              Yet evil whence? In thee can harbor none,
100   Created pure. But know that in the soul
              Are many lesser faculties[5] that serve
              Reason as chief; among these fancy next
              Her office holds; of all external things,
              Which the five watchful senses represent,
105   She forms imaginations,° aery shapes,   *images*
              Which reason joining or disjoining, frames
              All what we affirm or what deny, and call
              Our knowledge or opinion; then retires
              Into her private cell when nature rests.
110   Oft in her absence mimic fancy wakes
              To imitate her; but misjoining shapes,
              Wild work produces oft, and most in dreams,
              Ill matching words and deeds long past or late.
              Some such resemblances methinks I find
115   Of our last evening's talk in this thy dream,[6]
              But with addition strange; yet be not sad.
              Evil into the mind of god[7] or man
              May come and go, so unapproved,[8] and leave
              No spot or blame behind: which gives me hope
120   That what in sleep thou didst abhor to dream,
              Waking thou never wilt consent to do.
              Be not disheartened then, nor cloud those looks
              That wont to be° more cheerful and serene   *usually are*
              Than when fair morning first smiles on the world,
125   And let us to our fresh employments rise
              Among the groves, the fountains, and the flow'rs
              That open now their choicest bosomed smells
              Reserved from night, and kept for thee in store."
                    So cheered he his fair spouse, and she was cheered,
130   But silently a gentle tear let fall
              From either eye, and wiped them with her hair;
              Two other precious drops that ready stood,
              Each in their crystal sluice, he ere they fell
              Kissed as the gracious signs of sweet remorse

---

5. Adam's explanation of the dream (lines 100–116) summarizes the orthodox faculty psychology and dream theory of Milton's time—one among many kinds of knowledge with which unfallen man was endowed.

6. Adam recalls his own words in 4.411–39.

7. Probably "angel" as elsewhere, but perhaps God, whose omniscience must encompass knowledge of evil as well as good.

8. If not willed (approved of) or not acted on (put to the proof).

And pious awe, that feared to have offended.
   So all was cleared, and to the field they haste.
But first from under shady arborous° roof,   *consisting of trees*
Soon as they forth were come to open sight
Of day-spring,° and the sun, who scarce up risen   *daybreak*
With wheels yet hov'ring o'er the ocean brim,
Shot parallel to the earth his dewy ray,
Discovering in wide landscape all the east
Of Paradise and Eden's happy plains,
Lowly they bowed adoring, and began
Their orisons,° each morning duly paid   *prayers*
In various style, for neither various style
Nor holy rapture° wanted they to praise   *ecstasy*
Their Maker, in fit strains pronounced or sung
Unmeditated,[9] such prompt eloquence
Flowed from their lips, in prose or numerous° verse,   *rhythmic*
More tuneable° than needed lute or harp   *melodious*
To add more sweetness, and they thus began:
   "These are thy glorious works, Parent of good,[1]
Almighty, thine this universal frame,
Thus wondrous fair; thyself how wondrous then!
Unspeakable, who sitt'st above these heavens,
To us invisible or dimly seen
In these thy lowest works, yet these declare
Thy goodness beyond thought, and power divine:
Speak ye who best can tell, ye sons of light,
Angels, for ye behold him, and with songs
And choral symphonies,° day without night,   *music in parts*
Circle his throne rejoicing, ye in Heav'n,
On earth join all ye creatures to extol
Him first, him last, him midst, and without end.
Fairest of stars,[2] last in the train° of night,   *procession*
If better thou belong not to the dawn,
Sure pledge of day, that crown'st the smiling morn
With thy bright circlet, praise him in thy sphere
While day arises, that sweet hour of prime.
Thou sun, of this great world both eye and soul,
Acknowledge him thy greater, sound his praise
In thy eternal course, both when thou climb'st,
And when high noon hast gained, and when thou fall'st.
Moon, that now meet'st the orient sun, now fli'st
With the fixed stars, fixed in their orb that flies,
And ye five other wand'ring fires that move
In mystic dance not without song,[3] resound
His praise, who out of darkness called up light.
Air, and ye elements the eldest birth

---

9. In a variety of styles or forms of speech and song, which harmonize together but are at the same time impromptu, spontaneous, and ecstatic.
1. Their morning hymn works variations on Psalms 148, 104, and 19, as well as the canticle "Benedicite."
2. Venus, the morning star and (as Hesperus) the evening star.
3. The planets, unlike the fixed stars, change their relative positions; their motion produces the music of the spheres, audible to unfallen humans.

>   Of nature's womb, that in quaternion[4] run
>   Perpetual circle, multiform, and mix
>   And nourish all things, let your ceaseless change
>   Vary to our great Maker still° new praise.   *continually*
> 185 Ye mists and exhalations that now rise
>   From hill or steaming lake, dusky or gray,
>   Till the sun paint your fleecy skirts with gold,
>   In honor to the world's great Author rise,
>   Whether to deck with clouds the uncolored sky,
> 190 Or wet the thirsty earth with falling showers,
>   Rising or falling still advance his praise.
>   His praise ye winds, that from four quarters blow,
>   Breathe soft or loud; and wave your tops, ye pines,
>   With every plant, in sign of worship wave.
> 195 Fountains and ye, that warble, as ye flow,
>   Melodious murmurs, warbling tune his praise.
>   Join voices all ye living souls: ye birds,
>   That singing up to heaven gate ascend,
>   Bear on your wings and in your notes his praise.
> 200 Ye that in waters glide, and ye that walk
>   The earth, and stately tread, or lowly creep;
>   Witness if I be silent, morn or even,
>   To hill, or valley, fountain, or fresh shade
>   Made vocal by my song, and taught his praise.
> 205 Hail universal Lord, be bounteous still°   *always*
>   To give us only good; and if the night
>   Have gathered aught of evil or concealed,
>   Disperse it, as now light dispels the dark."
>   So prayed they innocent, and to their thoughts
> 210 Firm peace recovered soon and wonted calm.
>   On to their morning's rural work they haste
>   Among sweet dews and flow'rs; where any row
>   Of fruit trees over-woody° reached too far   *too bushy*
>   Their pampered boughs, and needed hands to check
> 215 Fruitless embraces: or they led the vine
>   To wed her elm;[5] she spoused about him twines
>   Her marriageable arms, and with her brings
>   Her dow'r th' adopted clusters, to adorn
>   His barren leaves. Them thus employed beheld
> 220 With pity Heav'n's high King, and to him called
>   Raphael, the sociable Spirit, that deigned
>   To travel with Tobias, and secured
>   His marriage with the seven-times-wedded maid.[6]
>   "Raphael," said he, "thou hear'st what stir on earth
> 225 Satan from Hell scaped through the darksome gulf
>   Hath raised in Paradise, and how disturbed
>   This night the human pair, how he designs

---

4. The fourfold changing relationship of the four elements.

5. A familiar emblem of matrimony, the elm symbolizing masculine strength, and the vine, feminine fruitfulness, softness, and sweetness; note, however, the matriarchal implications of "adopted clusters" (line 218).

6. Raphael (in Hebrew, "health of God") was the adviser of Tobias in winning his wife (see 4.168–71 and note).

In them at once to ruin all mankind.
Go therefore, half this day as friend with friend
Converse with Adam, in what bow'r or shade
Thou find'st him from the heat of noon retired,
To respite his day labor with repast,
Or with repose; and such discourse bring on,
As may advise him of his happy state,
Happiness in his power left free to will,
Left to his own free will, his will though free,
Yet mutable; whence warn him to beware
He swerve not too secure:° tell him withal   *overconfident*
His danger, and from whom, what enemy
Late fall'n himself from Heav'n, is plotting now
The fall of others from like state of bliss;
By violence, no, for that shall be withstood,
But by deceit and lies; this let him know,
Lest wilfully transgressing he pretend°   *plead*
Surprisal, unadmonished, unforewarned."
   So spake th' Eternal Father, and fulfilled
All justice: nor delayed the wingèd saint°   *angel*
After his charge received; but from among
Thousand celestial ardors,[7] where he stood
Veiled with his gorgeous wings, up springing light
Flew through the midst of Heav'n; th' angelic choirs
On each hand parting, to his speed gave way
Through all th' empyreal road; till at the gate
Of Heav'n arrived, the gate self-opened wide
On golden hinges turning, as by work°   *mechanism*
Divine the sov'reign Architect had framed.
From hence, no cloud, or, to obstruct his sight,
Star interposed, however small he sees,
Not unconform to other shining globes,
Earth and the gard'n of God, with cedars crowned
Above all hills. As when by night the glass°   *telescope*
Of Galileo, less assured, observes
Imagined lands and regions in the moon:
Or pilot from amidst the Cyclades
Delos or Samos first appearing kens°   *discerns*
A cloudy spot.[8] Down thither prone° in flight   *bent forward*
He speeds, and through the vast ethereal sky
Sails between worlds and worlds, with steady wing
Now on the polar wings, then with quick fan
Winnows the buxom air; till within soar
Of tow'ring eagles,[9] to all the fowls he seems
A phoenix, gazed by all, as that sole bird
When to enshrine his relics in the sun's

---

7. Bright spirits burning in love; the Hebrew *seraph* means "to burn."
8. The Cyclades are a circular group of islands in the south Aegean Sea; the two islands seen as "spots" from within the archipelago are Delos (the traditional center but famous for having floated adrift) and Samos (outside the group).
9. Raphael sails with steady wing, turns at the pole, beats ("fans") with his wings the yielding ("buxom") air, and then comes within range of the eagle's soaring flight.

Bright temple, to Egyptian Thebes he flies.¹
At once on th' eastern cliff of Paradise
He lights, and to his proper shape returns
A Seraph winged; six wings he wore, to shade
His lineaments° divine; the pair that clad   *parts of the body*
Each shoulder broad, came mantling° o'er his breast   *draping*
With regal ornament; the middle pair
Girt like a starry zone° his waist, and round   *belt*
Skirted his loins and thighs with downy gold
And colors dipped in Heav'n; the third his feet
Shadowed from either heel with feathered mail²
Sky-tinctured grain.° Like Maia's son³ he stood,   *dye*
And shook his plumes, that heav'nly fragrance filled
The circuit wide. Straight° knew him all the bands   *at once*
Of angels under watch; and to his state,°   *rank*
And to his message° high in honor rise;   *mission*
For on some message high they guessed him bound.
Their glittering tents he passed, and now is come
Into the blissful field; through groves of myrrh,
And flow'ring odors, cassia, nard, and balm;⁴
A wilderness of sweets; for nature here
Wantoned° as in her prime, and played° at will   *reveled / acted out*
Her virgin fancies, pouring forth more sweet,
Wild above rule or art; enormous° bliss.   *immense, beyond rule*
Him through the spicy forest onward come
Adam discerned, as in the door he sat⁵
Of his cool bow'r, while now the mounted sun
Shot down direct his fervid rays, to warm
Earth's inmost womb, more warmth than Adam needs;
And Eve within, due° at her hour prepared   *fittingly*
For dinner savory fruits, of taste to please
True appetite and not disrelish thirst,
Of nectarous drafts between, from milky stream,
Berry or grape: to whom thus Adam called:
  "Haste hither Eve, and worth thy sight behold
Eastward among those trees, what glorious shape
Comes this way moving; seems another morn
Ris'n on mid-noon; some great behest from Heav'n
To us perhaps he brings, and will vouchsafe
This day to be our guest. But go with speed,
And what thy stores contain, bring forth and pour
Abundance, fit to honor and receive
Our heav'nly stranger; well we may afford
Our givers their own gifts, and large bestow
From large bestowed, where nature multiplies
Her fertile growth, and by disburd'ning grows

---

1. The phoenix was a mythical, unique ("sole") bird that lived five hundred years, was consumed by fire, and was reborn from the ashes, which it then carried to the temple of the sun at Heliopolis in Egypt.
2. Plumage suggesting scale armor.
3. Mercury, messenger of the gods.
4. "Odors": aromatic substances; "cassia": cinnamon; "nard": spikenard; "balm": balsam—all were used to make perfumed ointments.
5. Raphael's visit to Adam is modeled on Abraham's entertainment of three angels (Genesis 18:1–16).

320 More fruitful, which instructs us not to spare."
　　To whom thus Eve: "Adam, earth's hallowed mold,[6]
Of God inspired, small store will serve, where store,[7]
All seasons, ripe for use hangs on the stalk;
Save what by frugal storing firmness gains
325 To nourish, and superfluous moist consumes:
But I will haste and from each bough and brake
Each plant and juiciest gourd will pluck such choice
To entertain our angel guest, as he
Beholding shall confess that here on earth
330 God hath dispensed his bounties as in Heav'n."
　　So saying, with dispatchful looks in haste
She turns, on hospitable thoughts intent
What choice to choose for delicacy best,
What order, so contrived as not to mix
335 Tastes, not well joined, inelegant, but bring
Taste after taste upheld° with kindliest° change,   *maintained / most natural*
Bestirs her then, and from each tender stalk
Whatever earth all-bearing mother yields
In India east or west, or middle shore
340 In Pontus or the Punic coast,[8] or where
Alcinous reigned, fruit of all kinds, in coat,
Rough, or smooth-rined, or bearded husk, or shell
She gathers, tribute large, and on the board
Heaps with unsparing hand; for drink the grape
345 She crushes, inoffensive must, and meaths[9]
From many a berry, and from sweet kernels pressed
She tempers° dulcet creams, nor these to hold   *blends*
Wants° her fit vessels pure, then strews the ground   *lacks*
With rose and odors from the shrub unfumed.[1]
350 Meanwhile our primitive° great sire, to meet   *original*
His godlike guest, walks forth, without more train°   *attendants*
Accompanied than with his own complete
Perfections, in himself was all his state,°   *dignity, authority*
More solemn° than the tedious pomp that waits   *awe-inspiring*
355 On princes, when their rich retinue long
Of horses led, and grooms besmeared with gold
Dazzles the crowd, and sets them all agape.
Nearer his presence Adam though not awed,
Yet with submiss approach and reverence meek,
360 As to a superior nature, bowing low,
　　Thus said: "Native of Heav'n, for other place:
None can than Heav'n such glorious shape contain;
Since by descending from the thrones above,
Those happy places thou hast deigned° a while   *condescended*
365 To want,° and honor these, vouchsafe with us   *be parted from*

---

6. Revered shape of earth's substance. The name "Adam" signifies red earth.
7. A great quantity. "Small store": few stored foods.
8. The "middle shore" includes Pontus, the south coast of the Black Sea, famous for nuts and fruits, and the "Punic" (Carthaginian) coast of North Africa on the Mediterranean, famous for figs; the gardens of Alcinous (next line) are described in the *Odyssey* 7.113–21 as perpetually fruitful.
9. Meads, drinks sweetened with honey. "Must": unfermented fruit juice.
1. Naturally scented, not burned for incense.

Two only, who yet by sov'reign gift possess
This spacious ground, in yonder shady bow'r
To rest, and what the garden choicest bears
To sit and taste, till this meridian° heat   *noontime*
370 Be over, and the sun more cool decline."
    Whom thus the angelic Virtue[2] answered mild:
"Adam, I therefore came, nor art thou such
Created, or such place hast here to dwell,
As may not oft invite, though Spirits of Heav'n
375 To visit thee; lead on then where thy bow'r
O'ershades; for these mid-hours, till evening rise
I have at will." So to the sylvan lodge
They came, that like Pomona's[3] arbor smiled
With flow'rets decked° and fragrant smells; but Eve   *covered*
380 Undecked, save with herself more lovely fair
Than wood nymph, or the fairest goddess feigned
Of three that in Mount Ida naked strove,[4]
Stood to entertain her guest from Heav'n; no veil
She needed, virtue-proof,° no thought infirm   *armored in virtue*
385 Altered her cheek. On whom the Angel "Hail"
Bestowed, the holy salutation used
Long after to blest Mary, second Eve.[5]
    "Hail mother of mankind, whose fruitful womb
Shall fill the world more numerous with thy sons
390 Than with these various fruits the trees of God
Have heaped this table." Raised of grassy turf
Their table was, and mossy seats had round,
And on her ample square from side to side
All autumn piled, though spring and autumn here
395 Danced hand in hand. A while discourse they hold;
No fear lest dinner cool; when thus began
Our author:° "Heav'nly stranger, please to taste   *forefather*
These bounties which our Nourisher, from whom
All perfect good unmeasured out, descends,
400 To us for food and for delight hath caused
The earth to yield; unsavory food perhaps
To spiritual natures; only this I know,
That one Celestial Father gives to all."
    To whom the angel: "Therefore what he gives
405 (Whose praise be ever sung) to man in part
Spiritual, may of° purest Spirits be found   *by*
No ingrateful food: and food alike those pure
Intelligential substances require[6]

---

2. Milton uses these angelic titles freely, in the Protestant manner, not as designations of the nine traditional orders (Raphael was called "Seraph" at line 277).
3. The Roman goddess of fruit trees.
4. On Mount Ida, Venus, Juno, and Minerva "strove" naked for the title of the most beautiful; Paris awarded the prize (the apple of discord) to Venus, which led to the rape of Helen and the Trojan War.
5. See the angel's words to Mary announcing that she would bear a son, Jesus (Luke 1:28): "Hail, thou that art highly favored, the Lord is with thee: blessed art thou among women."
6. Milton's angels ("intelligential substances") require real food, even as "rational" men do (see below, lines 430–38). As a monist (believer that all creation is of one matter), Milton denied the more common (dualistic) idea that angels are pure spirit, holding instead that they are of a very highly refined material substance.

As doth your rational; and both contain
Within them every lower faculty
Of sense, whereby they hear, see, smell, touch, taste,
Tasting concoct, digest, assimilate,[7]
And corporeal to incorporeal turn.
For know, whatever was created, needs
To be sustained and fed; of elements
The grosser feeds the purer, earth the sea,
Earth and the sea feed air, the air those fires
Ethereal, and as lowest first the moon;
Whence in her visage round those spots, unpurged
Vapors not yet into her substance turned.[8]
Nor doth the moon no nourishment exhale
From her moist continent to higher orbs.[9]
The sun that light imparts to all, receives
From all his alimental° recompense   *nourishing*
In humid exhalations, and at even
Sups with the ocean:[1] though in Heav'n the trees
Of life ambrosial° fruitage bear, and vines   *divinely fragrant*
Yield nectar,[2] though from off the boughs each morn
We brush mellifluous° dews, and find the ground   *honey-flowing*
Covered with pearly grain; yet God hath here
Varied his bounty so with new delights,
As may compare with Heaven; and to taste
Think not I shall be nice."° So down they sat,   *fastidious, finicky*
And to their viands fell, nor seemingly°   *in show*
The angel, nor in mist, the common gloss°   *explanation*
Of theologians, but with keen dispatch
Of real hunger, and concoctive° heat   *digestive*
To transubstantiate;[3] what redounds, transpires
Through Spirits with ease; nor wonder, if by fire
Of sooty coal the empiric° alchemist   *experimental*
Can turn, or holds it possible to turn
Metals of drossiest ore to perfect gold
As from the mine. Meanwhile at table Eve
Ministered naked, and their flowing cups
With pleasant liquors crowned.° O innocence   *filled to the brim*
Deserving Paradise! if ever, then,
Then had the Sons of God excuse t' have been
Enamored at that sight,[4] but in those hearts
Love unlibidinous° reigned, nor jealousy   *without lust*

---

7. Three stages in digestion.
8. Here Raphael describes lunar spots as still-undigested vapors (in keeping with his exposition of the universal need of nourishment); in 1.287–91 he referred to moon spots in Galileo's terms, as landscape features.
9. A double negative: the moon does exhale such nourishment to other planets.
1. Milton explains evaporation as the sun dining off moisture exhaled from the oceans.
2. Ambrosia is the food and nectar the drink of the classical gods; Milton adds "pearly grain" (line 430), like the manna showered on the Israelites in the desert (Exodus 16:14–15).
3. In common theological use, transubstantiation is the Roman Catholic doctrine that the bread and wine of the Eucharist become the body and blood of Christ. Milton vigorously denied that doctrine, but he describes the angels' transforming of earthly food into their more highly refined spiritual substance as a true transubstantiation. The excess ("what redounds") is exhaled ("transpires") through angelic pores.
4. Genesis 6:2 tells of the marriage of "the daughters of men" with "the sons of God," usually identified as sons of Seth, but a patristic tradition (alluded to here) identifies them as angels.

450 Was understood, the injured lover's hell.
    Thus when with meats and drinks they had sufficed,
Not burdened nature, sudden mind arose
In Adam, not to let th' occasion pass
Given him by this great conference to know
455 Of things above his world, and of their being
Who dwell in Heav'n, whose excellence he saw
Transcend his own so far, whose radiant forms
Divine effulgence,° whose high power so far   *shining forth*
Exceeded human, and his wary speech
460 Thus to th' empyreal minister he framed:
"Inhabitant with God, now know I well
Thy favor, in this honor done to man,
Under whose lowly roof thou hast vouchsafed
To enter and these earthly fruits to taste,
465 Food not of angels, yet accepted so,
As that more willingly thou couldst not seem
At Heav'n's high feasts t' have fed: yet what compare?"
    To whom the wingèd hierarch° replied: *authority*
"O Adam, one Almighty is, from whom
470 All things proceed, and up to him return,
If not depraved from good, created all
Such to perfection, one first matter all,[5]
Endued with various forms, various degrees
Of substance, and in things that live, of life;
475 But more refined, more spiritous, and pure,
As nearer to him placed or nearer tending
Each in their several active spheres assigned,
Till body up to spirit work, in bounds
Proportioned to each kind.[6] So from the root
480 Springs lighter the green stalk, from thence the leaves
More airy, last the bright consummate flow'r
Spirits odorous breathes:[7] flow'rs and their fruit
Man's nourishment, by gradual scale sublimed°   *purified*
To vital spirits aspire, to animal,
485 To intellectual, give both life and sense,
Fancy° and understanding, whence the soul   *imagination*
Reason receives, and reason is her being,
Discursive, or intuitive;[8] discourse

---

5. Milton held that the universe was created out of Chaos, not out of nothing: the primal matter of Chaos had its origin in God, who subsequently created all things from that matter (see 7.168–73, 210–42). This materialist "monism" denies sharp distinctions between angels and men, spirit and matter: all beings are of one substance, of varying degrees of refinement and life.
6. Milton's version of the chain of being qualifies natural hierarchy by allowing for movement up or down; beings may become increasingly spiritual ("more spiritous") or increasingly gross (as the rebel angels do), depending on their moral choices—"nearer tending."
7. The plant figure—root, stalk, leaves, flowers, and fruit—provides an illustration of the dynamism of being in the universe and further explains why Raphael can eat the fruit. Such food is then transformed (next lines) into various orders of "spirits"—"vital," "animal," and "intellectual" (fluids in the blood that sustain life, sensation, motion, and finally intellect and its functions, "fancy," "understanding," and "reason"), indicating that the soul is also material.
8. Traditionally, on the dualist assumption that angels are pure spirit and humans a combination of matter and spirit, angelic intuition (immediate apprehension of truth) was absolutely distinguished from human "discourse" of reason (arguing from premises to conclusions). Milton, denying that assumption, makes the distinction only relative, a matter of "degree" (line 490).

Is oftest yours, the latter most is ours,
Differing but in degree, of kind the same.
Wonder not then, what God for you saw good
If I refuse not, but convert, as you,
To proper° substance; time may come when men   *our own*
With angels may participate, and find
No inconvenient diet, nor too light fare:
And from these corporal nutriments perhaps
Your bodies may at last turn all to spirit,
Improved by tract° of time, and winged ascend   *passage*
Ethereal as we, or may at choice
Here or in heav'nly paradises dwell;
If ye be found obedient, and retain
Unalterably firm his love entire
Whose progeny you are. Meanwhile enjoy
Your fill what happiness this happy state
Can comprehend, incapable° of more."   *unable to contain*
    To whom the patriarch of mankind replied:
"O favorable Spirit, propitious guest,
Well hast thou taught the way that might direct
Our knowledge, and the scale of nature set
From center to circumference, whereon
In contemplation of created things
By steps we may ascend to God. But say,
What meant that caution joined, 'If ye be found
Obedient'? Can we want° obedience then   *lack*
To him, or possibly his love desert
Who formed us from the dust, and placed us here
Full to the utmost measure of what bliss
Human desires can seek or apprehend?"
    To whom the angel: "Son of Heav'n and earth,
Attend: that thou art happy, owe° to God;   *attribute*
That thou continu'st such, owe to thyself,
That is, to thy obedience; therein stand.
This was that caution giv'n thee; be advised.
God made thee perfect, not immutable;°   *unchangeable*
And good he made thee, but to persevere
He left it in thy power, ordained thy will
By nature free, not overruled by fate
Inextricable, or strict necessity,
Our voluntary service he requires,
Not our necessitated, such with him
Finds no acceptance, nor can find, for how
Can hearts, not free, be tried whether they serve
Willing or no, who will but what they must
By destiny, and can no other choose?
Myself and all th' angelic host that stand
In sight of God enthroned, our happy state
Hold, as you yours, while our obedience holds;
On other surety° none; freely we serve,   *guarantee*
Because we freely love, as in our will
To love or not; in this we stand or fall:

And some are fall'n, to disobedience fall'n,
And so from Heav'n to deepest Hell; O fall
From what high state of bliss into what woe!"
    To whom our great progenitor: "Thy words
545 Attentive, and with more delighted ear,
Divine instructor, I have heard, than when
Cherubic songs° by night from neighboring hills   *songs of Cherubim*
Aerial music send: nor knew I not[9]
To be both will and deed created free;
550 Yet that we never shall forget to love
Our Maker, and obey him whose command
Single, is yet° so just, my constant thoughts   *also*
Assured me, and still assure: though what thou tell'st
Hath passed in Heav'n, some doubt within me move,
555 But more desire to hear, if thou consent,
The full relation, which must needs be strange,
Worthy of sacred silence to be heard;
And we have yet large° day, for scarce the sun   *ample*
Hath finished half his journey, and scarce begins
560 His other half in the great zone of Heav'n."
    Thus Adam made request, and Raphael
After short pause assenting, thus began:
    "High matter[1] thou enjoin'st me, O prime of men,
Sad task and hard, for how shall I relate
565 To human sense th' invisible exploits
Of warring Spirits; how without remorse
The ruin of so many glorious once
And perfect while they stood; how last unfold
The secrets of another world, perhaps
570 Not lawful to reveal? Yet for thy good
This is dispensed, and what surmounts the reach
Of human sense, I shall delineate so,
By lik'ning spiritual to corporal forms,
As may express them best, though what if earth
575 Be but the shadow of Heav'n, and things therein
Each to other like, more than on earth is thought?
    "As yet this world was not, and Chaos wild
Reigned where these heav'ns now roll, where earth now rests
Upon her center poised, when on a day
580 (For time, though in eternity, applied
To motion, measures all things durable
By present, past, and future)[2] on such day
As Heav'n's great year[3] brings forth, th' empyreal host
Of angels by imperial summons called,
585 Innumerable before th' Almighty's throne
Forthwith from all the ends of Heav'n appeared

---

9. A double negative; that is, "I did know."
1. Raphael's account of the war in Heaven is an epic device, a narrative of past action; it is also a mini-epic itself, with traditional battles, challenges, and single combats. As an "epic" poet treating sacred matter, Raphael confronts a narrative challenge similar to Milton's own.

2. Countering a long philosophical tradition, Milton asserts the existence of time in Heaven, before the creation of the universe.
3. Plato and others defined the "great year" as the cycle completed when all the heavenly bodies simultaneously return to the positions they held at the cycle's beginning.

  Under their hierarchs° in orders bright.   *leaders*
  Ten thousand thousand ensigns high advanced,
  Standards, and gonfalons° twixt van and rear   *banners*
590 Stream in the air, and for distinction serve
  Of hierarchies, of orders, and degrees;
  Or in their glittering tissues° bear emblazed   *cloth*
  Holy memorials, acts of zeal and love
  Recorded eminent. Thus when in orbs
595 Of circuit° inexpressible they stood,   *circumference*
  Orb within orb, the Father Infinite,
  By whom in bliss embosomed sat the Son,
  Amidst as from a flaming mount, whose top
  Brightness had made invisible, thus spake:
600 "'Hear all ye angels, progeny of Light,
  Thrones, Dominations, Princedoms, Virtues, Powers,
  Hear my decree, which unrevoked shall stand.
  This day I have begot whom I declare
  My only Son, and on this holy hill
605 Him have anointed,[4] whom ye now behold
  At my right hand; your head I him appoint;
  And by myself have sworn to him shall bow
  All knees in Heav'n, and shall confess him Lord:
  Under his great vicegerent[5] reign abide
610 United as one individual° soul   *indivisible*
  Forever happy: him who° disobeys   *whoever*
  Me disobeys, breaks union, and that day
  Cast out from God and blessèd vision, falls
  Into utter° darkness, deep engulfed, his place   *outer, total*
615 Ordained without redemption, without end.'
  "So spake th' Omnipotent, and with his words
  All seemed well pleased, all seemed, but were not all.
  That day, as other solemn° days, they spent   *ceremonial*
  In song and dance about the sacred hill,
620 Mystical dance, which yonder starry sphere
  Of planets and of fixed° in all her wheels   *fixed stars*
  Resembles nearest, mazes intricate,
  Eccentric,° intervolved,° yet regular   *off center / intertwined*
  Then most, when most irregular they seem:
625 And in their motions harmony divine
  So smooths her charming tones,[6] that God's own ear
  Listens delighted. Evening now approached
  (For we have also our evening and our morn,
  We ours for change delectable, not need)
630 Forthwith from dance to sweet repast they turn
  Desirous; all in circles as they stood,
  Tables are set, and on a sudden piled

---

4. See Psalm 2:7: "I will declare the decree: . . . Thou art my Son; this day have I begotten thee." The episode refers to the exaltation of the Son as King, not his actual begetting, since he is elsewhere described as "of all creation first" (3.383) and as God's agent in creating the angels and everything else.

5. Vice-regent, one appointed by the supreme ruler (here, God) to wield his authority.

6. The movements of the angels in their dance produce harmony, like those of the planets in the Pythagorean theory of the music of the spheres.

With angels' food, and rubied nectar flows
In pearl, in diamond, and massy gold,
635 Fruit of delicious vines, the growth of Heav'n.
On flow'rs reposed, and with fresh flow'rets crowned,
They eat, they drink, and in communion sweet
Quaff immortality and joy, secure
Of surfeit where full measure only bounds
640 Excess, before th' all-bounteous King, who show'red
With copious hand, rejoicing in their joy.
Now when ambrosial° night with clouds exhaled   *fragrant*
From that high mount of God, whence light and shade
Spring both, the face of brightest Heav'n had changed
645 To grateful° twilight (for night comes not there   *pleasing*
In darker veil) and roseate° dews disposed   *rose-scented*
All but the unsleeping eyes of God to rest,
Wide over all the plain, and wider far
Than all this globous earth in plain outspread,
650 (Such are the courts of God) th' angelic throng
Dispersed in bands and files their camp extend
By living streams among the trees of life,
Pavilions numberless, and sudden reared,
Celestial tabernacles, where they slept
655 Fanned with cool winds, save those who in their course
Melodious hymns about the sov'reign throne
Alternate all night long: but not so waked
Satan, so call him now, his former name
Is heard no more in Heav'n; he of the first,
660 If not the first Archangel, great in power,
In favor and preeminence, yet fraught
With envy against the Son of God, that day
Honored by his great Father, and proclaimed
Messiah[7] King anointed, could not bear
665 Through pride that sight, and thought himself impaired.
Deep malice thence conceiving and disdain,
Soon as midnight brought on the dusky hour
Friendliest to sleep and silence, he resolved
With all his legions to dislodge,° and leave   *leave camp*
670 Unworshipped, unobeyed the throne supreme
Contemptuous, and his next subordinate[8]
Awak'ning, thus to him in secret spake:
"'Sleep'st thou companion dear, what sleep can close
Thy eyelids? and remember'st what decree
675 Of yesterday, so late hath passed the lips
Of Heav'n's Almighty. Thou to me thy thoughts
Wast wont,° I mine to thee was wont to impart;   *in the habit of*
Both waking we were one; how then can now
Thy sleep dissent? New laws thou seest imposed;
680 New laws from him who reigns, new minds° may raise   *purposes*
In us who serve, new counsels, to debate

---

7. Hebrew, "anointed."
8. His original name in Heaven is lost (1.356–63), but he will come to be known as Beelzebub.

What doubtful may ensue, more in this place
To utter is not safe. Assemble thou
Of all those myriads which we lead the chief;
685 Tell them that by command, ere yet dim night
Her shadowy cloud withdraws, I am to haste,
And all who under me their banners wave,
Homeward with flying march where we possess
The quarters of the north, there to prepare
690 Fit entertainment to receive our King
The great Messiah, and his new commands,
Who speedily through all the hierarchies
Intends to pass triumphant, and give laws.'
    "So spake the false Archangel, and infused
695 Bad influence into th' unwary breast
Of his associate; he together calls,
Or several one by one, the regent powers,
Under him regent, tells, as he was taught,
That the Most High commanding, now ere night,
700 Now ere dim night had disencumbered Heav'n,
The great hierarchal standard was to move;
Tells the suggested° cause, and casts between   insinuated
Ambitious words and jealousies, to sound°   make trials of
Or taint integrity; but all obeyed
705 The wonted signal, and superior voice
Of their great potentate° for great indeed   ruler
His name, and high was his degree in Heav'n;
His count'nance as the morning star that guides
The starry flock, allured them, and with lies
710 Drew after him the third part of Heav'n's host:
Meanwhile, th' Eternal Eye, whose sight discerns
Abstrusest° thoughts, from forth his holy mount   most secret
And from within the golden lamps that burn
Nightly before him, saw without their light
715 Rebellion rising, saw in whom, how spread
Among the sons of morn, what multitudes
Were banded to oppose his high decree;
And smiling to his only Son thus said:
    "'Son, thou in whom my glory I behold
720 In full resplendence, heir of all my might,
Nearly it now concerns us to be sure
Of our omnipotence, and with what arms
We mean to hold what anciently we claim
Of deity or empire, such a foe
725 Is rising, who intends to erect his throne
Equal to ours, throughout the spacious north;
Nor so content, hath in his thought to try
In battle, what our power is, or our right.
Let us advise, and to this hazard draw
730 With speed what force is left, and all employ
In our defense, lest unawares we lose
This our high place, our sanctuary, our hill.'
    "To whom the Son with calm aspect and clear

Lightning divine, ineffable, serene,
735 Made answer: 'Mighty Father, thou thy foes
Justly hast in derision, and secure
Laugh'st at their vain designs and tumults vain,⁹
Matter to me of glory, whom their hate
Illustrates,° when they see all regal power   *makes illustrious*
740 Giv'n me to quell their pride, and in event°   *in the outcome*
Know whether I be dextrous to subdue
Thy rebels, or be found the worst in Heav'n.'
   "So spake the Son, but Satan with his powers°   *armies*
Far was advanced on wingèd speed, an host
745 Innumerable as the stars of night,
Or stars of morning, dewdrops, which the sun
Impearls on every leaf and every flower.
Regions they passed, the mighty regencies°   *dominions*
Of Seraphim and Potentates and Thrones
750 In their triple degrees, regions to° which   *compared to*
All thy dominion, Adam, is no more
Than what this garden is to all the earth,
And all the sea, from one entire globose°   *globe*
Stretched into longitude° which having passed   *spread out flat*
755 At length into the limits° of the north   *regions*
They came, and Satan to his royal seat
High on a hill, far blazing, as a mount
Raised on a mount, with pyramids and tow'rs
From diamond quarries hewn, and rocks of gold,
760 The palace of great Lucifer (so call
That structure in the dialect of men
Interpreted) which not long after, he
Affecting° all equality with God,   *arrogating*
In imitation of that mount whereon
765 Messiah was declared in sight of Heav'n,
The Mountain of the Congregation called;
For thither he assembled all his train,
Pretending so commanded to consult
About the great reception of their King,
770 Thither to come, and with calumnious art
Of counterfeited truth thus held their ears:
   "'Thrones, Dominations, Princedoms, Virtues, Powers,
If these magnific titles yet remain
Not merely titular, since by decree
775 Another now hath to himself engrossed°   *monopolized*
All power, and us eclipsed under the name
Of King anointed, for whom all this haste
Of midnight march, and hurried meeting here,
This only to consult how we may best
780 With what may be devised of honors new
Receive him coming to receive from us
Knee-tribute yet unpaid, prostration vile,
Too much to one, but double how endured,

---

9. See Psalm 2:4: "He that sitteth in the heavens shall laugh: the Lord shall have them in derision."

To one and to his image now proclaimed?
But what if better counsels might erect
Our minds and teach us to cast off this yoke?
Will ye submit your necks, and choose to bend
The supple knee? Ye will not, if I trust
To know ye right, or if ye know yourselves
Natives and sons of Heav'n possessed before
By none, and if not equal all, yet free,
Equally free; for orders and degrees
Jar not with liberty, but well consist.
Who can in reason then or right assume
Monarchy over such as live by right
His equals,[1] if in power and splendor less,
In freedom equal? or can introduce
Law and edíct on us, who without law
Err not, much less for this to be our Lord,
And look for adoration to th' abuse
Of those imperial titles which assert
Our being ordained to govern, not to serve?"
  "Thus far his bold discourse without control°   *hindrance*
Had audience, when among the Seraphim
Abdiel,[2] than whom none with more zeal adored
The Deity, and divine commands obeyed,
Stood up, and in a flame of zeal severe
The current of his fury thus opposed:
  "'O argument blasphémous, false and proud!
Words which no ear ever to hear in Heav'n
Expected, least of all from thee, ingrate,
In place thyself so high above thy peers.
Canst thou with impious obloquy condemn
The just decree of God, pronounced and sworn,
That to his only Son by right endued
With regal scepter, every soul in Heav'n
Shall bend the knee, and in that honor due
Confess him rightful King? Unjust thou says't,
Flatly unjust, to bind with laws the free,
And equal over equals to let reign,
One over all with unsucceeded° power.   *without successor*
Shalt thou give law to God, shalt thou dispute
With him the points of liberty, who made
Thee what thou art, and formed the pow'rs of Heav'n
Such as he pleased, and circumscribed their being?
Yet by experience taught we know how good,
And of our good, and of our dignity
How provident he is, how far from thought
To make us less, bent rather to exalt
Our happy state under one head more near
United. But to grant it thee unjust,

---

1. Satan here paraphrases the republican theory against earthly monarchy like that urged by Milton in his *Tenure of Kings and Magistrates* (1649); see p. 1328. Abdiel, however, insists (lines 809–41) that the argument from equality cannot pertain to God and the angels.
2. Hebrew, "servant of God."

That equal over equals monarch reign:
Thyself though great and glorious dost thou count,
Or all angelic nature joined in one,
Equal to him begotten Son, by whom
As by his Word the mighty Father made
All things, ev'n thee, and all the Spirits of Heav'n
By him created in their bright° degrees,   *illustrious*
Crowned them with glory, and to their glory named
Thrones, Dominations, Princedoms, Virtues, Powers,
Essential Powers, nor by his reign obscured,
But more illustrious made, since he the head
One of our number thus reduced becomes,³
His laws our laws, all honor to him done
Returns our own. Cease then this impious rage,
And tempt not these; but hasten to appease
Th' incensèd Father and th' incensèd Son,
While pardon may be found in time besought.'
   "So spake the fervent angel, but his zeal
None seconded, as out of season judged,
Or singular and rash, whereat rejoiced
Th' Apostate,° and more haughty thus replied.   *religious renegade*
'That we were formed then say'st thou? and the work
Of secondary hands, by task transferred
From Father to his Son? Strange point and new!
Doctrine which we would know whence learnt: who saw
When this creation was? Remember'st thou
Thy making, while the Maker gave thee being?
We know no time when we were not as now;
Know none before us, self-begot, self-raised,
By our own quick'ning power, when fatal course°   *the course of fate*
Had circled his full orb, the birth mature
Of this our native Heav'n, ethereal sons.⁴
Our puissance° is our own, our own right hand   *power*
Shall teach us highest deeds, by proof to try
Who is our equal: then thou shalt behold
Whether by supplication we intend
Address, and to begirt th' Almighty throne
Beseeching or besieging. This report,
These tidings carry to th' anointed King;
And fly, ere evil intercept thy flight.'
   "He said, and as the sound of waters deep
Hoarse murmur echoed to his words applause
Through the infinite host, nor less for that
The flaming Seraph fearless, though alone
Encompassed round with foes, thus answered bold:
   "'O alienate from God, O Spirit accurst,
Forsaken of all good; I see thy fall
Determined, and thy hapless crew involved

---

3. Abdiel suggests that the Son's appointment as the angels' king is something like an "incarnation" for them.
4. Satan's (illogical) argument is that since the angels cannot remember their creation, they created themselves. See Adam's comment on his recollection of origins (8.250–51, 270–79).

880 In this perfidious fraud, contagion spread
     Both of thy crime and punishment: henceforth
     No more be troubled how to quit the yoke
     Of God's Messiah; those indulgent laws
     Will not be now vouchsafed, other decrees
885 Against thee are gone forth without recall;
     That golden scepter which thou didst reject
     Is now an iron rod to bruise and break
     Thy disobedience. Well thou didst advise,
     Yet not for thy advice or threats I fly
890 These wicked tents devoted,° lest the wrath   doomed
     Impendent,° raging into sudden flame   impending
     Distinguish not: for soon expect to feel
     His thunder on thy head, devouring fire.
     Then who created thee lamenting learn,
895 When who can uncreate thee thou shalt know.'
        "So spake the Seraph Abdiel faithful found,
     Among the faithless, faithful only he;
     Among innumerable false, unmoved,
     Unshaken, unseduced, unterrified
900 His loyalty he kept, his love, his zeal;
     Nor number, nor example with him wrought
     To swerve from truth, or change his constant mind
     Though single. From amidst them forth he passed,
     Long way through hostile scorn, which he sustained
905 Superior, nor of violence feared aught;°   anything
     And with retorted scorn his back he turned
     On those proud tow'rs to swift destruction doomed."

Book 6

The Argument

Raphael continues to relate how Michael and Gabriel were sent forth to battle against Satan and his angels. The first fight described: Satan and his powers retire under night: he calls a council, invents devilish engines, which in the second day's fight put Michael and his angels to some disorder; but they at length pulling up mountains overwhelmed both the force and machines of Satan: yet the tumult not so ending, God on the third day sends Messiah his Son, for whom he had reserved the glory of that victory: he in the power of his Father coming to the place, and causing all his legions to stand still on either side, with his chariot and thunder driving into the midst of his enemies, pursues them unable to resist towards the wall of heaven; which opening, they leap down with horror and confusion into the place of punishment prepared for them in the deep: Messiah returns with triumph to this Father.

All night the dreadless angel[1] unpursued
Through Heav'n's wide champaign° held his way, till Morn,   plain
Waked by the circling Hours,[2] with rosy hand

---

1. That is, Abdiel.
2. Daughters of Jove, who control the seasons and guard the gates of Heaven. "Morn": Aurora, goddess of dawn.

Unbarred the gates of light. There is a cave
Within the mount of God, fast° by his throne,   *close*
Where light and darkness in perpetual round
Lodge and dislodge by turns, which makes through Heav'n
Grateful vicissitude,° like day and night;   *delightful change*
Light issues forth, and at the other door
Obsequious° darkness enters, till her hour   *compliant*
To veil the Heav'n, though darkness there might well
Seem twilight here; and now went forth the Morn
Such as in highest Heav'n, arrayed in gold
Empyreal;° from before her vanished night,   *heavenly*
Shot through with orient beams: when all the plain
Covered with thick embattled° squadrons bright,   *in battle array*
Chariots and flaming arms, and fiery steeds
Reflecting blaze on blaze, first met his view:
War he perceived, war in procinct,° and found   *preparation*
Already known what he for news had thought
To have reported: gladly then he mixed
Among those friendly Powers who him received
With joy and acclamations loud, that one
That of so many myriads fall'n, yet one
Returned not lost: on to the sacred hill
They led him high applauded, and present
Before the seat supreme; from whence a voice:
From midst a golden cloud thus mild was heard.
"'Servant of God,[3] well done, well hast thou fought
The better fight, who single hast maintained
Against revolted multitudes the cause
Of truth, in word mightier than they in arms;
And for the testimony of truth hast borne
Universal reproach, far worse to bear
Than violence: for this was all thy care
To stand approved in sight of God, though worlds
Judged thee perverse: the easier conquest now
Remains thee, aided by this host of friends,
Back on thy foes more glorious to return
Than scorned thou didst depart, and to subdue
By force, who reason for their law refuse,
Right reason° for their law, and for their King   *upright, true reason*
Messiah, who by right of merit reigns.
Go Michael of celestial armies prince,
And thou in military prowess next
Gabriel, lead forth to battle these my sons°   *angels*
Invincible, lead forth my armèd saints
By thousands and by millions ranged for fight;
Equal in number to that godless crew
Rebellious,[4] them with fire and hostile arms
Fearless assault, and to the brow of Heav'n

---

3. The literal meaning (Hebrew) of the name Abdiel.
4. God sends out only an equal force to match the one-third of the angelic host that rebelled, not the two-thirds that remained loyal.

Pursuing drive them out from God and bliss,
Into their place of punishment, the gulf
Of Tartarus,° which ready opens wide   *Hell*
His fiery chaos to receive their fall.'
    "So spake the Sovereign Voice, and clouds began
To darken all the hill, and smoke to roll
In dusky wreaths reluctant° flames, the sign   *writhing*
Of wrath awaked: nor with less dread the loud
Ethereal trumpet from on high gan° blow: *began to*
At which command the powers militant,
That stood for Heav'n, in mighty quadrate[5] joined
Of union irresistible, moved on
In silence their bright legions, to the sound
Of instrumental harmony that breathed
Heroic ardor to advent'rous deeds
Under their godlike leaders, in the cause
Of God and his Messiah. On they move
Indissolubly firm; nor obvious° hill,   *standing in the way*
Nor strait'ning vale,[6] nor wood, nor stream divides
Their perfect ranks; for high above the ground
Their march was, and the passive air upbore
Their nimble tread; as when the total kind
Of birds in orderly array on wing
Came summoned over Eden to receive
Their names of thee; so over many a tract
Of Heav'n they marched, and many a province wide
Tenfold the length of this terrene:° at last   *earth, terrain*
Far in th' horizon to the north appeared
From skirt to skirt a fiery region, stretched
In battailous° aspéct, and nearer view   *warlike*
Bristled with upright beams° innumerable   *shafts*
Of rigid spears, and helmets thronged, and shields
Various, with boastful argument° portrayed,   *heraldic devices*
The banded powers of Satan hasting on
With furious expedition;° for they weened°   *speed / thought*
That selfsame day by fight, or by surprise
To win the mount of God, and on his throne
To set the envier of his state, the proud
Aspirer, but their thoughts proved fond° and vain   *foolish*
In the mid-way: though strange to us it seemed
At first, that angel should with angel war,
And in fierce hosting[7] meet, who wont° to meet   *were accustomed*
So oft in festivals of joy and love
Unanimous, as sons of one great Sire
Hymning th' Eternal Father: but the shout
Of battle now began, and rushing sound
Of onset ended soon each milder thought.
High in the midst exalted as a god
Th' Apostate in his sun-bright chariot sat

---

5. A square military formation.
6. A narrow valley would force other armies to march in a file.
7. Hostile encounter.

>   Idol of majesty divine, enclosed
>   With flaming Cherubim, and golden shields;
>   Then lighted from his gorgeous throne, for now
>   'Twixt host° and host but narrow space was left,   *army*
> 105 A dreadful interval, and front to front°   *face to face*
>   Presented stood in terrible array
>   Of hideous length: before the cloudy van,°   *frowning vanguard*
>   On the rough edge of battle° ere it joined,   *front line*
>   Satan with vast and haughty strides advanced,
> 110 Came tow'ring, armed in adamant and gold;
>   Abdiel that sight endured not, where he stood
>   Among the mightiest, bent on highest deeds,
>   And thus his own undaunted heart explores:
>   "'O Heav'n! that such resemblance of the Highest
> 115 Should yet remain, where faith and realty°   *sincerity*
>   Remain not; wherefore should not strength and might
>   There fail where virtue fails, or weakest prove
>   Where boldest; though to sight° unconquerable?   *seemingly*
>   His puissance,° trusting in th' Almighty's aid,   *power*
> 120 I mean to try, whose reason I have tried°   *proved by trial*
>   Unsound and false; nor is it aught but just,
>   That he who in debate of truth hath won,
>   Should win in arms, in both disputes alike
>   Victor; though brutish that contést and foul,
> 125 When reason hath to deal with force, yet so
>   Most reason is that reason overcome.'
>   "So pondering, and from his armèd peers
>   Forth stepping opposite, halfway he met
>   His daring foe, at this prevention° more   *obstruction*
> 130 Incensed, and thus securely° him defied: *confidently*
>   "'Proud, art thou met? Thy hope was to have reached
>   The height of thy aspiring unopposed,
>   The throne of God unguarded, and his side
>   Abandoned at the terror of thy power
> 135 Or potent tongue; fool, not to think how vain
>   Against the Omnipotent to rise in arms;
>   Who out of smallest things could without end
>   Have raised incessant armies to defeat
>   Thy folly; or with solitary hand
> 140 Reaching beyond all limit at one blow
>   Unaided could have finished thee, and whelmed
>   Thy legions under darkness; but thou seest
>   All are not of thy train; there be° who faith   *there are those*
>   Prefer, and piety° to God, though then   *devotion*
> 145 To thee not visible, when I alone
>   Seemed in thy world erroneous to dissent
>   From all: my sect[8] thou seest, now learn too late

---

8. The term carries political resonance, since the national English church, Anglican or (during the revolution) Presbyterian, sought to suppress and persecute the sects who separated from it (Baptists, Quakers, Socinians, and others), often denouncing them as heretics. Satan claims that a "synod" (line 156, term for a Presbyterian assembly) has proclaimed the truth of the rebel angels' case; Abdiel insists that truth may rather reside (as here) with a single "dissenter" or a sect of a few.

How few sometimes may know, when thousand err.'
   "Whom the grand Foe with scornful eye askance
150 Thus answered. 'Ill for thee, but in wished hour
   Of my revenge, first sought for thou return'st
   From flight, seditious angel, to receive
   Thy merited reward, the first assay
   Of this right hand provoked, since first that tongue
155 Inspired with contradiction durst oppose
   A third part of the gods, in synod met
   Their deities to assert, who while they feel
   Vigor divine within them, can allow
   Omnipotence to none. But well thou com'st
160 Before thy fellows, ambitious to win
   From me some plume, that thy success[9] may show
   Destruction to the rest: this pause between
   (Unanswered lest thou boast)[1] to let thee know;
   At first I thought that liberty and Heav'n
165 To heav'nly souls had been all one;° but now   *one and the same*
   I see that most through sloth had rather serve,
   Minist'ring Spirits, trained up in feast and song;
   Such hast thou armed, the minstrelsy[2] of Heav'n,
   Servility° with freedom to contend,   *bondage, obsequiousness*
170 As both their deeds compared this day shall prove.'
   "To whom in brief thus Abdiel stern replied:
   'Apostate, still thou err'st, nor end wilt find
   Of erring, from the path of truth remote:
   Unjustly thou deprav'st° it with the name   *vilify*
175 Of servitude to serve whom God ordains,
   Or nature; God and nature bid the same,
   When he who rules is worthiest, and excels
   Them whom he governs. This is servitude,
   To serve th' unwise, or him who hath rebelled
180 Against his worthier, as thine now serve thee,
   Thyself not free, but to thyself enthralled;[3]
   Yet lewdly° dar'st our minist'ring upbraid.   *ignorantly, basely*
   Reign thou in Hell thy kingdom, let me serve
   In Heav'n God ever blest, and his divine
185 Behests obey, worthiest to be obeyed;
   Yet chains in Hell, not realms expect: meanwhile
   From me returned, as erst° thou saidst, from flight,   *formerly*
   This greeting on thy impious crest receive.'
   "So saying, a noble stroke he lifted high,
190 Which hung not, but so swift with tempest fell
   On the proud crest of Satan, that no sight,
   Nor motion of swift thought, less could his shield
   Such ruin intercept: ten paces huge
   He back recoiled; the tenth on bended knee

---

9. The outcome of your action. "Plume": token of victory.
1. That is, lest thou boast that I did not answer your argument.
2. Satan's contemptuous pun links together the loyal angels' service ("Minist'ring," line 167) with their song, likened to the street songs of minstrels.
3. Abdiel cites the "natural law" principle that rule rightly belongs to the best or worthiest, and that tyrants are enslaved to their own passions.

His massy spear upstayed; as if on earth
Winds under ground or waters forcing way
Sidelong, had pushed a mountain from his seat
Half sunk with all his pines. Amazement seized
The rebel Thrones,[4] but greater rage to see
Thus foiled their mightiest: ours joy filled, and shout,
Presage of victory and fierce desire
Of battle: whereat Michaël bid sound
Th' Archangel trumpet; through the vast of Heav'n
It sounded, and the faithful armies rung
Hosanna to the Highest: nor stood at gaze
The adverse legions, nor less hideous joined
The horrid shock: now storming fury rose,
And clamor such as heard in Heav'n till now
Was never, arms on armor clashing brayed[5]
Horrible discord, and the madding° wheels   *whirling madly*
Of brazen chariots raged; dire was the noise
Of conflict; overhead the dismal° hiss   *dreadful*
Of fiery darts in flaming volleys flew,
And flying vaulted either host with fire.
So under fiery cope° together rushed   *sky*
Both battles main,[6] with ruinous assault
And inextinguishable rage; all Heav'n
Resounded, and had earth been then, all earth
Had to her center shook. What wonder? when
Millions of fierce encount'ring angels fought
On either side, the least of whom could wield
These elements,[7] and arm him with the force
Of all their regions: how much more of power
Army against army numberless to raise
Dreadful combustion° warring, and disturb,   *tumult*
Though not destroy, their happy native seat;
Had not th' Eternal King Omnipotent
From his stronghold of Heav'n high overruled
And limited their might; though numbered such
As each divided legion might have seemed
A numerous host, in strength each armèd hand
A legion; led in fight, yet leader seemed
Each warrior single as in chief,[8] expert
When to advance, or stand, or turn the sway°   *force*
Of battle, open when, and when to close
The ridges° of grim war; no thought of flight,   *ranks*
None of retreat, no unbecoming deed
That argued fear; each on himself relied,
As° only in his arm the moment[9] lay   *as if*
Of victory; deeds of eternal fame

---

4. Here as elsewhere Milton uses the name of one angelic order to stand for all. But the choice of "Thrones" here carries political resonance, linking monarchs with rebels against God's kingdom.
5. Made a harsh, jarring sound.
6. The principal body of an army, as opposed to the van, rear, and wing.
7. The four elements—fire, air, water, earth—that constitute the several "regions" (next line) of planet earth.
8. That is, the angelic legions had leaders, yet each single warrior seemed like such a leader.
9. Weight that will tip the scales.

Were done, but infinite: for wide was spread
That war and various; sometimes on firm ground
A standing fight, then soaring on main° wing   *strong, powerful*
Tormented° all the air; all air seemed then   *agitated*
245 Conflicting fire: long time in even scale
The battle hung; till Satan, who that day
Prodigious power had shown, and met in arms
No equal, ranging through the dire attack
Of fighting Seraphim confused, at length
250 Saw where the sword of Michael smote, and felled
Squadrons at once; with huge two-handed sway
Brandished aloft the horrid edge came down
Wide-wasting; such destruction to withstand
He hasted, and opposed the rocky orb
255 Of tenfold adamant, his ample shield[1]
A vast circumference: at his approach
The great Archangel from his warlike toil
Surceased, and glad as hoping here to end
Intestine war° in Heav'n, the Arch-Foe subdued   *civil war*
260 Or captive dragged in chains, with hostile frown
And visage all inflamed first thus began:
   "'Author of evil, unknown till thy revolt,
Unnamed in Heav'n, now plenteous, as thou seest
These acts of hateful strife, hateful to all,
265 Though heaviest by just measure on thyself
And thy adherents: how hast thou disturbed
Heav'n's blessèd peace, and into nature brought
Misery, uncreated till the crime
Of thy rebellion! how hast thou instilled
270 Thy malice into thousands, once upright
And faithful, now proved false! But think not here
To trouble holy rest; Heav'n casts thee out
From all her confines. Heav'n the seat of bliss
Brooks° not the works of violence and war.   *endures*
275 Hence then, and evil go with thee along
Thy offspring, to the place of evil, Hell,
Thou and thy wicked crew; there mingle° broils,   *concoct*
Ere this avenging sword begin thy doom,
Or some more sudden vengeance winged from God
280 Precipitate thee with augmented pain.'
   "So spake the Prince of Angels; to whom thus
The Adversary: 'Nor think thou with wind
Of airy threats to awe whom yet with deeds
Thou canst not. Hast thou turned the least of these
285 To flight, or if to fall, but that they rise
Unvanquished, easier to transact with me
That thou shouldst hope, imperious, and with threats
To chase me hence?[2] Err not that so shall end

---

1. Satan's shield is a rocklike ("rocky") circle, made of impenetrable "adamant" (probably diamond), ten layers thick.
2. That is, Have you made even the least of my followers flee, or seen them fall and fail to rise, that you would hope "imperiously" to deal ("transact") otherwise with me, driving me off by mere threats? "Err not" (following): don't falsely suppose.

                The strife which thou call'st evil, but we style
290   The strife of glory: which we mean to win,
                Or turn this Heav'n itself into the Hell
                Thou fablest, here however to dwell free,
                If not to reign: meanwhile thy utmost force,
                And join him named Almighty to thy aid,
295   I fly not, but have sought thee far and nigh.'
                    "They ended parle,° and both addressed° for fight   *parley / prepared*
                Unspeakable; for who, though with the tongue
                Of angels, can relate, or to what things
                Liken on earth conspicuous, that may lift
300   Human imagination to such height
                Of godlike power: for likest gods they seemed,
                Stood they or moved, in stature, motion, arms
                Fit to decide the empire of great Heav'n.
                Now waved their fiery swords, and in the air
305   Made horrid circles; two broad suns their shields
                Blazed opposite, while Expectation stood[3]
                In horror; from each hand with speed retired
                Where erst° was thickest fight, th' angelic throng,   *ever*
                And left large field, unsafe within the wind
310   Of such commotion, such as to set forth
                Great things by small, if nature's concord broke,
                Among the constellations war were sprung,
                Two planets rushing from aspéct malign
                Of fiercest opposition in midsky,
315   Should combat, and their jarring spheres confound.[4]
                Together both with next to almighty arm,
                Uplifted imminent one stroke they aimed
                That might determine,° and not need repeat,°   *end / repetition*
                As not of power,[5] at once; nor odds° appeared   *inequality*
320   In might or swift prevention;° but the sword   *anticipation*
                Of Michael from the armory of God
                Was giv'n him tempered so, that neither keen
                Nor solid might resist that edge: it met
                The sword of Satan with steep force to smite
325   Descending, and in half cut sheer, nor stayed,
                But with swift wheel reverse, deep ent'ring shared°   *cut off*
                All his right side; then Satan first knew pain,
                And writhed him to and fro convolved;° so sore   *contorted*
                The griding° sword with discontinuous° wound   *keenly cutting / gaping*
330   Passed through him, but th' ethereal substance closed
                Not long divisible, and from the gash
                A stream of nectarous humor issuing flowed
                Sanguine,° such as celestial Spirits may bleed,   *blood-red*
                And all his armor stained erewhile so bright.
335   Forthwith on all sides to his aid was run

---

3. Personifying the angels' apprehension.
4. An epic simile comparing the clash of these armies ("great things") with war among the planets, in which two planets clashing together from diametrically opposed positions ("aspect malign"), would cast the planetary system and its music ("jarring spheres") into confusion ("confound").
5. That is, because they would not have power to repeat the blow.

By angels many and strong, who interposed
Defense, while others bore him on their shields
Back to his chariot, where it stood retired
From off the files of war; there they him laid
340 Gnashing for anguish and despite and shame
To find himself not matchless, and his pride
Humbled by such rebuke, so far beneath
His confidence to equal God in power.
Yet soon he healed; for Spirits that live throughout
345 Vital in every part, not as frail man
In entrails, heart or head, liver or reins,°   kidneys
Cannot but by annihilating die;
Nor in their liquid texture mortal wound
Receive, no more than can the fluid air:
350 All heart they live, all head, all eye, all ear,
All intellect, all sense, and as they please,
They limb themselves,[6] and color, shape, or size
Assume, as likes° them best, condense or rare.   pleases
    "Meanwhile in other parts like deeds deserved
355 Memorial, where the might of Gabriel fought,
And with fierce ensigns pierced the deep array
Of Moloch furious king,[7] who him defied,
And at his chariot wheels to drag him bound
Threatened, nor from the Holy One of Heav'n
360 Refrained his tongue blasphémous; but anon
Down clov'n to the waist, with shattered arms
And uncouth° pain fled bellowing. On each wing   unfamiliar
Uriel and Raphael his vaunting foe,
Though huge, and in a rock of diamond armed,
365 Vanquished Adramelech, and Asmadai,[8]
Two potent Thrones, that to be less than gods
Disdained, but meaner thoughts learned in their flight,
Mangled with ghastly wounds through plate and mail.
Nor stood unmindful Abdiel to annoy°   injure
370 The atheist° crew, but with redoubled blow   impious
Ariel and Arioch, and the violence
Of Ramiel[9] scorched and blasted overthrew.
I might relate of thousands, and their names
Eternize here on earth; but those elect
375 Angels contented with their fame in Heav'n
Seek not the praise of men: the other sort
In might though wondrous and in acts of war,
Nor of renown less eager, yet by doom
Canceled from Heav'n and sacred memory,
380 Nameless in dark oblivion let them dwell.
For strength from truth divided and from just,
Illaudable,° naught merits but dispraise   unworthy of praise

---

6. That is, provide themselves with limbs. "Condense or rare" (line 353): dense or airy.
7. With his companies ("ensigns") he pierced Moloch's troops in their dense formation ("deep array").
8. Asmodeus, a Persian god (see 4.167–71). "Adramelech": "king of fire," a god worshipped at Samaria with human sacrifice.
9. "Ariel": "lion of God." "Arioch": "lionlike." "Ramiel": "thunder of God."

And ignominy, yet to glory aspires
Vainglorious, and through infamy seeks fame:
Therefore eternal silence be their doom.
    "And now their mightiest quelled, the battle swerved,[1]
With many an inroad gored; deformèd rout
Entered, and foul disorder; all the ground
With shivered armor strown, and on a heap
Chariot and charioteer lay overturned
And fiery foaming steeds; what° stood, recoiled   *those who*
O'erwearied, through the faint Satanic host
Defensive scarce,[2] or with pale fear surprised,°   *seized unexpectedly*
Then first with fear surprised and sense of pain
Fled ignominious, to such evil brought
By sin of disobedience, till that hour
Not liable to fear or flight or pain.
Far otherwise th' inviolable saints
In cubic phalanx° firm advanced entire,   *formation*
Invulnerable, impenetrably armed:
Such high advantages their innocence
Gave them above their foes, not to have sinned,
Not to have disobeyed; in fight they stood
Unwearied, unobnoxious° to be pained   *not liable*
By wound, though from their place by violence moved.
    "Now night her course began, and over Heav'n
Inducing darkness, grateful truce imposed,
And silence on the odious din of war:
Under her cloudy covert both retired,
Victor and vanquished: on the foughten field
Michaël and his angels prevalent°   *victorious*
Encamping, placed in guard their watches round,
Cherubic waving fires: on th' other part
Satan with his rebellious disappeared,
Far in the dark dislodged,° and void of rest,   *shifted quarters*
His potentates to council called by night;
And in the midst thus undismayed began:
    "'O now in danger tried, now known in arms
Not to be overpowered, companions dear,
Found worthy not of liberty alone,
Too mean pretense,° but what we more affect,[3]   *low aim*
Honor, dominion, glory, and renown,
Who have sustained one day in doubtful° fight,   *indecisive*
(And if one day, why not eternal days?)
What Heaven's Lord had powerfullest to send
Against us from about his throne, and judged
Sufficient to subdue us to his will,
But proves not so: then fallible, it seems,
Of future° we may deem him, though till now   *in the future*
Omniscient thought. True is, less firmly armed,
Some disadvantage we endured and pain,

---

1. That is, the army gave way.   3. Aspire to.
2. Scarcely defending themselves.

                    Till now not known, but known as soon contemned,[4]
                    Since now we find this our empyreal form
                    Incapable of mortal injury
435   Imperishable, and though pierced with wound,
                    Soon closing, and by native vigor healed.
                    Of evil then so small as easy think
                    The remedy; perhaps more valid° arms,   *powerful*
                    Weapons more violent, when next we meet,
440   May serve to better us, and worse° our foes,   *injure*
                    Or equal what between us made the odds,
                    In nature none: if other hidden cause
                    Left them superior, while we can preserve
                    Unhurt our minds, and understanding sound,
445   Due search and consultation will disclose.'
                         "He sat; and in th' assembly next upstood
                    Nisroch,[5] of Principalities the prime;
                    As one he stood escaped from cruel fight,
                    Sore toiled, his riven arms to havoc hewn,°   *cut to pieces*
450   And cloudy in aspéct thus answering spake:
                    'Deliverer from new lords, leader to free
                    Enjoyment of our right as gods; yet hard
                    For gods, and too unequal work we find
                    Against unequal arms to fight in pain,
455   Against unpained, impassive;[6] from which evil
                    Ruin must needs ensue; for what avails
                    Valor or strength, though matchless, quelled with pain
                    Which all subdues, and makes remiss° the hands   *slack, weak*
                    Of mightiest. Sense of pleasure we may well
460   Spare out of life perhaps, and not repine,
                    But live content, which is the calmest life:
                    But pain is perfect misery, the worst
                    Of evils, and excessive, overturns
                    All patience. He who therefore can invent
465   With what more forcible we may offend°   *attack*
                    Our yet unwounded enemies, or arm
                    Ourselves with like defense, to me° deserves   *in my opinion*
                    No less than for deliverance what we owe.'[7]
                         "Whereto with look composed Satan replied.
470   'Not uninvented that, which thou aright
                    Believ'st so main° to our success, I bring;   *essential*
                    Which of us who beholds the bright surfáce
                    Of this ethereous mold° whereon we stand,   *ethereal matter*
                    This continent of spacious Heav'n, adorned
475   With plant, fruit, flow'r ambrosial, gems and gold,
                    Whose eye so superfically surveys
                    These things, as not to mind° from whence they grow   *consider*
                    Deep underground, materials dark and crude,
                    Of spiritous and fiery spume,° till touched   *frothy matter*
480   With Heav'n's ray, and tempered they shoot forth

---

4. No sooner known than despised.
5. An Assyrian god; the Hebrew name was said to mean flight or luxurious temptation.
6. Not liable to suffering.
7. That is, we would owe such a one our deliverance.

So beauteous, op'ning to the ambient° light.   *enveloping*
These in their dark nativity the deep
Shall yield us, pregnant with infernal° flame,   *from underground*
Which into hollow engines° long and round   *cannon*
485 Thick-rammed, at th' other bore[8] with touch of fire
Dilated and infuriate° shall send forth   *raging*
From far with thund'ring noise among our foes
Such implements of mischief as shall dash
To pieces, and o'erwhelm whatever stands
490 Adverse, that they shall fear we have disarmed
The Thunderer of his only° dreaded bolt.   *unique*
Nor long shall be our labor, yet ere dawn,
Effect shall end our wish. Meanwhile revive;
Abandon fear; to strength and counsel joined
495 Think nothing hard, much less to be despaired.'
   He ended, and his words their drooping cheer°   *spirits*
Enlightened, and their languished hope revived.
Th' invention all admired,° and each, how he   *marveled at*
To be th' inventor missed, so easy it seemed
500 Once found, which yet unfound most would have thought
Impossible: yet haply° of thy race   *possibly*
In future days, if malice should abound,
Someone intent on mischief, or inspired
With dev'lish machination might devise
505 Like instrument to plague the sons of men
For sin, on war and mutual slaughter bent.
Forthwith from council to the work they flew,
None arguing stood, innumerable hands
Were ready, in a moment up they turned
510 Wide the celestial soil, and saw beneath
Th' originals° of nature in their crude   *original elements*
Conception; sulphurous and nitrous foam[9]
They found, they mingled, and with subtle art,
Concocted° and adjusted° they reduced   *heated / dried*
515 To blackest grain, and into store conveyed:
Part hidden veins digged up (nor hath this earth
Entrails unlike) of mineral and stone,
Whereof to found° their engines and their balls   *cast*
Of missive° ruin; part incentive° reed   *missile / kindling*
520 Provide, pernicious° with one touch to fire.   *quick, destructive*
So all ere day-spring,° under conscious[1] night   *dawn*
Secret they finished, and in order set,
With silent circumspection unespied.
Now when fair morn orient in Heav'n appeared
525 Up rose the victor angels, and to arms
The matin° trumpet sung: in arms they stood   *morning*
Of golden panoply, refulgent° host,   *shining*
Soon banded; others from the dawning hills
Looked round, and scouts each coast light-armèd scour,

---

8. The touchhole into which fine powder was poured to serve as fuse for the charge. "Thick": compactly.
9. Saltpeter ("nitrous foam") and sulphur are the ingredients of gunpowder.
1. Aware, as an accessory to a crime.

530	Each quarter, to descry the distant foe,	
	Where lodged, or whither fled, or if for fight,	
	In motion or in alt:° him soon they met	*halt*
	Under spread ensigns moving nigh, in slow	
	But firm battalion; back with speediest sail	
535	Zophiel,[2] of Cherubim the swiftest wing,	
	Came flying, and in mid-air aloud thus cried:	
	"'Arm, warriors, arm for fight, the foe at hand,	
	Whom fled we thought, will save us long pursuit	
	This day, fear not his flight; so thick a cloud	
540	He comes, and settled in his face I see	
	Sad° resolution and secure:° let each	*sober / confident*
	His adamantine° coat gird well, and each	*of hardest metal*
	Fit well his helm, gripe fast his orbèd shield,	
	Borne ev'n° or high, for this day will pour down,	*straight out*
545	If I conjecture° aught, no drizzling shower,	*interpret signs*
	But rattling storm of arrows barbed with fire.'	
	So warned he them aware themselves, and soon	
	In order, quit of all impediment;°	*hindrance*
	Instant without disturb° they took alarm,	*disorder*
550	And onward move embattled;° when behold	*in battle order*
	Not distant far the heavy pace the foe	
	Approaching gross° and huge; in hollow cube	*compact*
	Training° his devilish enginry, impaled°	*hauling / fenced in*
	On every side with shadowing squadrons deep,	
555	To hide the fraud. At interview° both stood	*at mutual view*
	A while, but suddenly at head appeared	
	Satan: and thus was heard commanding loud:	
	"'Vanguard, to right and left the front unfold;	
	That all may see who hate us, how we seek	
560	Peace and composure,° and with open breast	*agreement*
	Stand ready to receive them, if they like	
	Our overture,[3] and turn not back perverse;	
	But that I doubt, however witness Heaven,	
	Heav'n witness thou anon, while we discharge	
565	Freely our part: ye who appointed stand	
	Do as you have in charge, and briefly touch	
	What we propound, and loud that all may hear.'	
	"So scoffing in ambiguous words, he scarce	
	Had ended; when to right and left the front	
570	Divided, and to either flank retired.	
	Which to our eyes discovered new and strange,	
	A triple-mounted° row of pillars laid	*in three rows*
	On wheels (for like to pillars most they seemed	
	Or hollowed bodies made of oak or fir	
575	With branches lopped, in wood or mountain felled)	
	Brass, iron, stony mold,° had not their mouths	*matter*
	With hideous orifice gaped on us wide,	

2. Hebrew, "spy of God."
3. A pun on "offer to negotiate" and "opening" (aperture), the hole or muzzle of the cannon. The passage is full of puns: for example, "perverse" (line 562, peevish, turned the wrong way), "discharge" (line 564), "charge," "touch," "propound," "loud" (lines 566–67), "hollow" (line 578).

Portending hollow truce; at each behind
A Seraph stood, and in his hand a reed
Stood waving tipped with fire; while we suspense,°   *in suspense*
Collected stood within our thoughts amused,°   *puzzled*
Not long, for sudden all at once their reeds
Put forth, and to a narrow vent applied
With nicest° touch. Immediate in a flame,   *most exact*
But soon obscured with smoke, all Heav'n appeared,
From those deep-throated engines belched,[4] whose roar
Emboweled° with outrageous noise the air,   *disemboweled*
And all her entrails tore, disgorging foul
Their devilish glut, chained[5] thunderbolts and hail
Of iron globes, which on the victor host
Leveled, with such impetuous fury smote,
That whom they hit, none on their feet might stand,
Though standing else as rocks, but down they fell
By thousands, Angel on Archangel rolled,
The sooner for their arms; unarmed they might
Have easily as Spirits evaded swift
By quick contraction or remove; but now
Foul dissipation° followed and forced rout;   *dispersal*
Nor served it to relax their serried files.[6]
What should they do? If on they rushed, repulse
Repeated, and indecent° overthrow   *shameful*
Doubled, would render them yet more despised,
And to their foes a laughter; for in view
Stood ranked of Seraphim another row
In posture to displode° their second dire°   *explode / volley*
Of thunder: back defeated to return
They worse abhorred. Satan beheld their plight,
And to his mates thus in derision called:
   "'O friends, why come not on these victors proud?
Erewhile they fierce were coming, and when we,
To entertain them fair with open front°   *candid face*
And breast,° (what could we more?) propounded[7] terms   *heart*
Of composition, straight they changed their minds,
Flew off, and into strange vagaries° fell,   *eccentric motions*
As they would dance, yet for a dance they seemed
Somewhat extravagant and wild, perhaps
For joy of offering peace: but I suppose
If our proposals once again were heard
We should compel them to a quick result.'
   "To whom thus Belial in like gamesome mood:
'Leader, the terms we sent were terms of weight,
Of hard contents, and full of force urged home,
Such as we might perceive amused them[8] all,

---

4. See the sustained debased imagery relating to bodily functions, for example, "belched," "emboweled," "entrails."
5. Chainshot, which was linked cannonballs.
6. That is, nor did it do any good ("served it") to loosen up ("relax") their rows pressed close together ("serried files").
7. More puns, on "propounded," "terms of composition," "flew off."
8. A pun on "held their attention" and "bewildered them." Belial also puns on (among other terms) "stumbled" ("nonplussed" and "tripped up") and "understand" ("comprehend" and "prop up").

And stumbled many: who receives them right,
Had need from head to foot well understand;
Not understood, this gift they have besides,
They show us when our foes walk not upright."
    "So they among themselves in pleasant° vein   *jesting*
Stood scoffing, heightened in their thoughts beyond
All doubt of victory, Eternal Might
To match with their inventions they presumed
So easy, and of his thunder made a scorn,
And all his host derided, while they° stood   *the good angels*
A while in trouble; but they stood not long,
Rage prompted them at length, and found them arms
Against such hellish mischief fit to oppose.
Forthwith (behold the excellence, the power,
Which God hath in his mighty angels placed)
Their arms away they threw, and to the hills
(For earth hath this variety from Heav'n
Of pleasure situate in hill and dale)
Light as the lightning glimpse they ran, they flew,
From their foundations loos'ning to and fro
They plucked the seated hills with all their load,⁹
Rocks, waters, woods, and by the shaggy tops
Uplifting bore them in their hands: amaze,°   *astonishment, panic*
Be sure, and terror seized the rebel host,
When coming towards them so dread they saw
The bottom of the mountains upward turned,
Till on those cursèd engines' triple-row
They saw them whelmed, and all their confidence
Under the weight of mountains buried deep,
Themselves invaded° next, and on their heads   *attacked*
Main° promontories flung, which in the air   *great, solid*
Came shadowing, and oppressed° whole legions armed.   *pressed down*
Their armor helped their harm, crushed in and bruised
Into their substance pent,° which wrought them pain   *closely confined*
Implacable, and many a dolorous groan,
Long struggling undernearth, ere they could wind
Out of such prison, though Spirits of purest light,
Purest at first, now gross by sinning grown.
The rest in imitation to like arms
Betook them, and the neighboring hills uptore;
So hills amid the air encountered hills
Hurled to and fro with jaculation° dire,   *hurling*
That underground they fought in dismal shade;
Infernal noise; war seemed a civil° game   *humane, refined*
To° this uproar; horrid confusion heaped   *compared to*
Upon confusion rose: and now all Heav'n
Had gone to wrack, with ruin overspread,
Had not th' Almighty Father where he sits
Shrined in his sanctuary of Heav'n secure,

---

9. The hurling of hills as missiles is taken from the war between the Olympian gods and the Giants, in Hesiod's *Theogony*.

Consulting° on the sum of things, foreseen   *considering*
This tumult, and permitted all, advised:°   *deliberately*
That his great purpose he might so fulfill, [675]
To honor his anointed Son avenged
Upon his enemies, and to declare
All power on him transferred: whence to his Son
Th' assessor[1] of his throne he thus began:
   "'Effulgence° of my glory, Son beloved,   *radiance* [680]
Son in whose face invisible is beheld
Visibly,[2] what by Deity I am,
And in whose hand what by decree I do,
Second Omnipotence,[3] two days are passed,
Two days, as we compute the days of Heav'n, [685]
Since Michael and his powers went forth to tame
These disobedient; sore hath been their fight,
As likeliest was, when two such foes met armed;
For to themselves I left them, and thou know'st,
Equal in their creation they were formed, [690]
Save what sin hath impaired, which yet hath wrought
Insensibly,° for I suspend their doom;   *imperceptively*
Whence in perpetual fight they needs must last
Endless, and no solution will be found:
War wearied hath performed what war can do, [695]
And to disordered rage let loose the reins,
With mountains as with weapons armed, which makes
Wild work in Heav'n, and dangerous to the main.°   *whole continent*
Two days are therefore passed, the third is thine;
For thee I have ordained it, and thus far [700]
Have suffered,° that the glory may be thine   *permitted*
Of ending this great war, since none but thou
Can end it. Into thee such virtue and grace
Immense I have transfused, that all may know
In Heav'n and Hell thy power above compare, [705]
And this perverse commotion governed thus,
To manifest thee worthiest to be heir
Of all things, to be heir and to be King
By sacred unction,° thy deservèd right.   *anointing*
Go then thou mightiest in thy Father's might, [710]
Ascend my chariot, guide the rapid wheels
That shake Heav'n's basis, bring forth all my war,°   *instruments of war*
My bow and thunder, my almighty arms
Gird on, and sword upon thy puissant thigh;
Pursue these sons of darkness, drive them out [715]
From all Heav'n's bounds into the utter° deep: *outer*
There let them learn, as likes them, to despise
God and Messiah his anointed[4] King.'
   "He said, and on his Son with rays direct

---

1. One who sits beside, an associate.
2. See Colossians 1:15: "Who is the image of the invisible God."
3. Two omnipotences are a logical impossibility; the phrase underscores Milton's view that the Son receives all power from the Father. See John 5:19, "The Son can do nothing of himself, but what he seeth the Father do," which Milton cites in *Christian Doctrine* 1.5 to argue that the Son derives all power from the Father.
4. The literal meaning of "messiah."

> Shone full, he all his Father full expressed
> Ineffably° into his face received,   *inexpressibly*
> And thus the Filial Godhead answering spake:
> "'O Father, O Supreme of heav'nly Thrones,
> First, highest, holiest, best, thou always seek'st
> To glorify thy Son, I always thee,
> As is most just; this I my glory account,
> My exaltation, and my whole delight,
> That thou in me well pleased, declar'st thy will
> Fulfilled, which to fulfill is all my bliss.
> Scepter and power, thy giving, I assume,
> And gladlier shall resign, when in the end
> Thou shalt be all in all, and I in thee
> Forever, and in me all whom thou lov'st:
> But whom thou hat'st, I hate, and can put on
> Thy terrors, as I put thy mildness on,
> Image of thee in all things; and shall soon,
> Armed with thy might, rid Heav'n of these rebelled,
> To their prepared ill mansion driven down
> To chains of darkness, and th' undying worm,
> That from thy just obedience could revolt,
> Whom to obey is happiness entire.
> Then shall thy saints unmixed, and from th' impure
> Far separate, circling thy holy mount
> Unfeignèd hallelujahs to thee sing,
> Hymns of high praise, and I among them chief.'
> So said, he o'er his scepter bowing, rose
> From the right hand of Glory where he sat,
> And the third sacred morn began to shine
> Dawning through Heav'n: forth rushed with whirlwind sound
> The chariot of Paternal Deity,
> Flashing thick flames, wheel within wheel undrawn,
> Itself instinct with° spirit, but convoyed   *animated by*
> By four Cherubic shapes, four faces each[5]
> Had wondrous, as with stars their bodies all
> And wings were set with eyes, with eyes the wheels
> Of beryl, and careering fires between;[6]
> Over their heads a crystal firmament,
> Whereon a sapphire throne, inlaid with pure
> Amber, and colors of the show'ry arch.°   *rainbow*
> He in celestial panoply all armed
> Of radiant urim,[7] work divinely wrought,
> Ascended, at his right hand Victory
> Sat eagle-winged, beside him hung his bow
> And quiver with three-bolted thunder stored,[8]
> And from about him fierce effusion° rolled   *copious emission*

---

5. The Son's living chariot, with its four-faced Cherubim—the faces being man, lion, ox, and eagle—is taken from Ezekiel 1 (especially 1:10) and 10.
6. See Ezekiel 10:12: "And their whole body, and their backs, and their hands, and their wings, and the wheels, were full of eyes round about, even the wheels that they four had."
7. Gems worn by Aaron in his "breastplate of judgment" (Exodus 28:30).
8. Jove's bird was the eagle; his weapon was the thunderbolt.

                Of smoke and bickering° flame, and sparkles dire;   *flickering*
                Attended with ten thousand thousand saints,
                He onward came, far off his coming shone,
                And twenty thousand⁹ (I their number heard)
770   Chariots of God, half on each hand were seen:
                He on the wings of Cherub rode sublime°   *lifted up*
                On the crystálline sky, in sapphire throned,
                Illustrious° far and wide, but by his own   *shining*
                First seen: them unexpected joy surprised,
775   When the great ensign of Messiah blazed
                Aloft by angels borne, his sign in Heav'n:
                Under whose conduct Michael soon reduced°   *led back*
                His army, circumfused° on either wing,   *spread around*
                Under their Head embodied all in one.
780   Before him Power Divine his way prepared;
                At his command the uprooted hills retired
                Each to his place, they heard his voice and went
                Obsequious,° Heav'n his wonted face renewed,   *dutiful*
                And with fresh flow'rets hill and valley smiled.
785   This saw his hapless foes but stood obdured,°   *hardened*
                And to rebellious fight rallied their powers
                Insensate, hope conceiving from despair.
                In heav'nly Spirits could such perverseness dwell?
                But to convince the proud what signs avail,
790   Or wonders move th' obdúrate to relent?
                They hardened more by what might most reclaim,
                Grieving° to see his glory, at the sight   *aggrieved*
                Took envy, and aspiring to his height,
                Stood re-embattled¹ fierce, by force or fraud
795   Weening° to prosper, and at length prevail   *thinking*
                Against God and Messiah, or to fall
                In universal ruin last, and now
                To final battle drew; disdaining flight,
                Or faint retreat; when the great Son of God
800   To all his host on either hand thus spake:
                "'Stand still in bright array ye saints, here stand
                Ye angels armed, this day from battle rest;²
                Faithful hath been your warfare, and of God
                Accepted, fearless in his righteous cause,
805   And as ye have received, so have ye done
                Invincibly; but of this cursed crew
                The punishment to other hand belongs,
                Vengeance is his,³ or whose he sole appoints;
                Number to this day's work is not ordained
810   Nor multitude, stand only and behold
                God's indignation on these godless poured
                By me, not you but me they have despised,

---

9. See Psalm 68:17: "The chariots of God are twenty thousand, even thousands of angels: the Lord is among them."
1. Drawn up again in battle formation.
2. Echoes Moses's words when God destroyed the Egyptians in the Red Sea (Exodus 14:13): "Fear ye not, stand still, and see the salvation of the Lord, which he will shew to you to day."
3. See Romans 12:19: "Vengeance is mine; I will repay, saith the Lord."

Yet envied; against me is all their rage,
Because the Father, t' whom in Heav'n supreme
815 Kingdom and power and glory appertains,
Hath honored me according to his will.
Therefore to me their doom he hath assigned;
That they may have their wish, to try with me
In battle which the stronger proves, they all,
820 Or I alone against them, since by strength
They measure all, of other excellence
Not emulous,° nor care who them excels;   *desirous of rivaling*
Nor other strife with them do I vouchsafe.'°   *grant*
   "So spake the Son, and into terror changed
825 His count'nance too severe to be beheld
And full of wrath bent on his enemies.
At once the Four[4] spread out their starry wings
With dreadful shade contiguous, and the orbs
Of his fierce chariot rolled, as with the sound
830 Of torrent floods, or of a numerous host.
He on his impious foes right onward drove,
Gloomy as night; under his burning wheels
The steadfast empyrean shook throughout,
All but the throne itself of God. Full soon
835 Among them he arrived; in his right hand
Grasping ten thousand thunders, which he sent
Before him, such as in their souls infixed
Plagues; they astonished° all resistance lost,   *struck with fear*
All courage; down their idle weapons dropped;
840 O'er shields and helms, and helmèd heads he rode
Of Thrones and mighty Seraphim prostráte,
That wished the mountains now might be again
Thrown on them as a shelter from his ire.
Nor less on either side tempestuous fell
845 His arrows, from the fourfold-visaged Four,
Distinct° with eyes, and from the living wheels,   *adorned*
Distinct alike with multitude of eyes;
One spirit in them ruled, and every eye
Glared lightning, and shot forth pernicious° fire   *deadly*
850 Among th' accursed, that withered all their strength,
And of their wonted° vigor left them drained,   *accustomed*
Exhausted, spiritless, afflicted, fall'n.
Yet half his strength he put not forth, but checked
His thunder in mid-volley, for he meant
855 Not to destroy, but root them out of Heav'n:
The overthrown he raised, and as a herd
Of goats or timorous flock together thronged
Drove them before him thunderstruck, pursued
With terrors and with furies to the bounds
860 And crystal wall of Heav'n, which op'ning wide,
Rolled inward, and a spacious gap disclosed
Into the wasteful° deep; the monstrous sight   *desolate*

---

4. The four "Cherubic shapes" of line 753.

Strook them with horror backward, but far worse
Urged them behind; headlong themselves they threw
Down from the verge of Heav'n, eternal wrath
Burnt after them to the bottomless pit.
    "Hell heard th' unsufferable noise, Hell saw
Heav'n ruining° from Heav'n, and would have fled   *falling headlong*
Affrighted; but strict fate had cast too deep
Her dark foundations, and too fast had bound.
Nine days they fell; confounded Chaos roared,
And felt tenfold confusion in their fall
Through his wild anarchy, so huge a rout°   *defeated army*
Encumbered° him with ruin: Hell at last   *burdened*
Yawning received them whole, and on them closed,
Fell their fit habitation fraught with fire
Unquenchable, the house of woe and pain.
Disburdened Heav'n rejoiced, and soon repaired
Her mural° breach, returning whence it rolled.   *in the wall*
Sole victor from th' expulsion of his foes
Messiah his triumphal chariot turned:
To meet him all his saints, who silent stood
Eyewitnesses of his almighty acts,
With jubilee° advanced; and as they went,   *joyful shouts*
Shaded with branching palm, each order bright
Sung triumph, and him sung victorious King,
Son, Heir, and Lord, to him dominion giv'n,
Worthiest to reign: he celebrated rode
Triumphant through mid-Heav'n, into the courts
And temple of his mighty Father throned
On high: who into glory him received,
Where now he sits at the right hand of bliss.
    "Thus measuring things in Heav'n by things on earth
At thy request, and that thou may'st beware
By what is past, to thee I have revealed
What might have else to human race been hid;
The discord which befell, and war in Heav'n
Among th' angelic powers,° and the deep fall   *armies*
Of those too high aspiring, who rebelled
With Satan, he who envies now thy state,
Who now is plotting how he may seduce
Thee also from obedience, that with him
Bereaved of happiness thou may'st partake
His punishment, eternal misery;
Which would be all his solace and revenge,
As a despite° done against the Most High,   *malicious act*
Thee once to gain companion of his woe.
But listen not to his temptations, warn
Thy weaker;[5] let it profit thee to have heard
By terrible example the reward
Of disobedience; firm they might have stood,
Yet fell; remember, and fear to transgress."

---

5. Eve, who is, however, present for this story.

Book 7

The Argument

Raphael at the request of Adam relates how and wherefore this world was first created; that God, after the expelling of Satan and his angels out of heaven, declared his pleasure to create another world and other creatures to dwell therein; sends his Son with glory and attendance of angels to perform the work of creation in six days: the angels celebrate with hymns the performance thereof, and his reascension into heaven.

Descend from Heav'n Urania,[1] by that name
If rightly thou art called, whose voice divine
Following, above th' Olympian hill I soar,
Above the flight of Pegasean wing.[2]
5 The meaning, not the name I call: for thou
Nor of the muses nine, nor on the top
Of old Olympus dwell'st, but heav'nly born
Before the hills appeared, or fountain flowed,
Thou with eternal Wisdom[3] didst converse,°   *associate*
10 Wisdom thy sister, and with her didst play
In presence of th' Almighty Father, pleased
With thy celestial song. Up led by thee
Into the Heav'n of Heav'ns I have presumed,
An earthly guest, and drawn empyreal air,
15 Thy temp'ring;° with like safety guided down   *made suitable by thee*
Return me to my native element:
Lest from this flying steed unreined (as once
Bellerophon,[4] though from a lower clime)°   *region*
Dismounted, on th' Aleian field I fall
20 Erroneous° there to wander and forlorn.   *straying*
Half yet remains unsung, but narrower bound
Within the visible diurnal sphere;[5]
Standing on earth, not rapt° above the pole,   *transported, enraptured*
More safe I sing with mortal voice, unchanged
25 To hoarse or mute, though fall'n on evil days,
On evil days though fall'n, and evil tongues;
In darkness, and with dangers compassed round,[6]
And solitude; yet not alone, while thou

---

1. Urania, the Greek Muse of astronomy, had been made into the Muse of Christian poetry by du Bartas and other religious poets. Milton, however, constructs another derivation for her (line 5ff.). Milton begins Book 7 with a third proem (lines 1–39).
2. Pegasus, the flying horse of inspired poetry, suggests (in connection with Bellerophon, line 18) Milton's sense of perilous audacity in writing this poem.
3. In Proverbs 8:24–31 Wisdom tells of her activities before the Creation: "Then I was by him [God], as one brought up with him: and I was daily his delight, rejoicing always before him." Milton describes "eternal Wisdom" as a daughter of God (personification of his wisdom) and devises a myth in which the Muse of divine poetry ("celestial song," line 12) is Wisdom's "sister"—also, thereby, originating from God.
4. Bellerophon incurred the gods' anger when he tried to fly to heaven upon Pegasus; Zeus sent an insect to sting the horse, and Bellerophon fell down to the "Aleian field" (plain of error), where he wandered alone and blind until his death.
5. The universe, which appears to rotate daily.
6. After the Restoration of Charles II (May 1660) and until the passage of the Act of Oblivion (August 1660), Milton was in danger of death and dismemberment (like Orpheus, lines 34–35); several of his republican colleagues were hanged, disembowelled, and quartered for their part in the revolution and regicide.

Visit'st my slumbers nightly, or when morn
30 Purples the east: still govern thou my song,
Urania, and fit audience find, though few.
But drive far off the barbarous dissonance
Of Bacchus and his revelers, the race
Of that wild rout that tore the Thracian bard
35 In Rhodope, where woods and rocks had ears
To rapture, till the savage clamor drowned
Both harp and voice;[7] nor could the Muse defend
Her son.[8] So fail not thou, who thee implores:
For thou art heav'nly, she an empty dream.
40   Say goddess, what ensued when Raphael,
The affable Archangel, had forewarned
Adam by dire example to beware
Apostasy, by what befell in Heaven
To those apostates, lest the like befall
45 In Paradise to Adam or his race,
Charged not to touch the interdicted tree,
If they transgress, and slight that sole command,
So easily obeyed amid the choice
Of all tastes else° to please their appetite,   *besides*
50 Though wand'ring. He with his consorted° Eve   *wedded*
The story heard attentive, and was filled
With admiration,° and deep muse to hear   *amazement*
Of things so high and strange, things to their thought
So unimaginable as hate in Heav'n,
55 And war so near the peace of God in bliss
With such confusion: but the evil soon
Driv'n back redounded° as a flood on those   *flowed back*
From whom it sprung, impossible to mix
With blessedness. Whence Adam soon repealed°   *abandoned*
60 The doubts that in his heart arose: and now
Led on, yet sinless, with desire to know
What nearer might concern him, how this world
Of Heav'n and earth conspicuous° first began,   *visible*
When, and whereof created, for what cause,
65 What within Eden or without was done
Before his memory, as one whose drouth°   *thirst*
Yet scarce allayed still eyes the current° stream,   *flowing*
Whose liquid murmur heard new thirst excites,
Proceeded thus to ask his heav'nly guest:
70   "Great things, and full of wonder in our ears,
Far differing from this world, thou hast revealed
Divine interpreter, by favor sent
Down from the empyrean to forewarn
Us timely of what might else° have been our loss,   *otherwise*

---

7. The music of the "Thracian bard" Orpheus, type of the poet, charmed even "woods and rocks," but his song was drowned out by the Bacchantes, a "wild rout" of screaming women who murdered and dismembered him and threw his body parts into the Hebrus River, which rises in the "Rhodope" mountains. Milton fears that a similar "barbarous dissonance" unleashed by the Restoration will drown out his voice and threaten his life.

8. Orpheus's mother is Calliope, Muse of epic poetry.

Unknown, which human knowledge could not reach: [75]
For which to the Infinitely Good we owe
Immortal thanks, and his admonishment
Receive with solemn purpose to observe
Immutably his sov'reign will, the end°   *purpose*
Of what we are. But since thou hast vouchsafed [80]
Gently for our instruction to impart
Things above earthly thought, which yet concerned
Our knowing, as to Highest Wisdom seemed,
Deign to descend now lower, and relate
What may no less perhaps avail us known, [85]
How first began this Heav'n which we behold
Distant so high, with moving fires adorned
Innumerable, and this which yields or fills
All space, the ambient° air wide interfused   *yielding*
Embracing round this florid° earth, what cause   *flowery* [90]
Moved the Creator in his holy rest
Through all eternity so late to build
In Chaos,[9] and the work begun, how soon
Absolved,° if unforbid thou may'st unfold   *finished*
What we, not to explore the secrets ask [95]
Of his eternal empire, but the more
To magnify° his works, the more we know.   *glorify*
And the great light of day yet wants to run
Much of his race though steep, suspense° in Heav'n   *attentive, suspended*
Held by thy voice, thy potent voice he hears, [100]
And longer will delay to hear thee tell
His generation,° and the rising birth   *creation*
Of nature from the unapparent[1] deep:
Or if the star of evening and the moon
Haste to thy audience, night with her will bring [105]
Silence, and sleep list'ning to thee will watch,°   *stay awake*
Or we can bid his absence, till thy song
End, and dismiss thee ere the morning shine."
  Thus Adam his illustrious guest besought:
  And thus the godlike angel answered mild: [110]
"This also thy request with caution asked
Obtain: though to recount almighty works
What words or tongue of Seraph can suffice,
Or heart of man suffice to comprehend?
Yet what thou canst attain, which best may serve [115]
To glorify the Maker, and infer°   *make, render*
Thee also happier, shall not be withheld
Thy hearing, such commission from above
I have received, to answer thy desire
Of knowledge within bounds; beyond abstain [120]
To ask, nor let thine own inventions° hope   *speculations*
Things not revealed, which th' invisible King,

---

9. Adam's question about God's actions before the Creation was often cited as an example of presumptuous and dangerous speculation, especially when, as here, it implies mutability in God. But in Milton's Eden, error that is not deliberate is not sinful.

1. Invisible, because dark and without form.

Only omniscient, hath suppressed in night,
To none communicable in earth or Heaven:
125 Enough is left besides to search and know.
But knowledge is as food, and needs no less
Her temperance over appetite, to know
In measure what the mind may well contain,
Oppresses else with surfeit, and soon turns
130 Wisdom to folly, as nourishment to wind.
　　"Know then, that after Lucifer from Heav'n
(So call him, brighter once amidst the host
Of angels, than that star the stars among)[2]
Fell with his flaming legions through the deep
135 Into his place, and the great Son returned
Victorious with his saints, th' Omnipotent
Eternal Father from his throne beheld
Their multitude, and to his Son thus spake:
　　"'At least our envious foe hath failed, who thought
140 All like himself rebellious, by whose aid
This inaccessible high strength, the seat
Of Deity supreme, us dispossessed,[3]
He trusted to have seized, and into fraud°　　　　　　　　　　*deception, error*
Drew many, whom their place knows here no more;
145 Yet far the greater part have kept, I see,
Their station, Heav'n yet populous retains
Number sufficient to possess her realms
Though wide, and this high temple to frequent
With ministeries due and solemn rites:
150 But lest his heart exalt him in the harm
Already done, to have dispeopled Heav'n,
My damage fondly° deemed, I can repair　　　　　　　　　　　　　*foolishly*
That detriment, if such it be to lose
Self-lost, and in a moment will create
155 Another world, out of one man a race
Of men innumerable, there to dwell,
Not here, till by degrees of merit raised
They open to themselves at length the way
Up hither, under long obedience tried,
160 And earth be changed to Heav'n and Heav'n to earth,
One kingdom, joy and union without end.
Meanwhile inhabit lax,° ye Powers of Heav'n;　　　　　　　　　　*spread out*
And thou my Word, begotten Son, by thee
This I perform, speak thou, and be it done:[4]
165 My overshadowing Spirit and might with thee
I send along, ride forth, and bid the deep
Within appointed bounds be heav'n and earth,
Boundless the deep, because I am who fill
Infinitude, nor vacuous the space.
170 Though I uncircumscribed myself retire,

---

2. That is, Lucifer (Satan) was once brighter among the angels than the star bearing his name is among the stars.
3. That is, once he had dispossessed us.
4. God identifies himself as Creator, the Son as his agent to speak his creating Word.

And put not forth my goodness, which is free
To act or not,[5] necessity and chance
Approach not me, and what I will is fate.'
 "So spake th' Almighty and to what he spake
175 His Word, the Filial Godhead, gave effect.
Immediate are the acts of God, more swift
Than time or motion, but to human ears
Cannot without process of speech be told,
So told as earthly notion° can receive.[6]   *human understanding*
180 Great triumph and rejoicing was in Heav'n
When such was heard declared the Almighty's will;
'Glory' they sung to the Most High, 'good will
To future men, and in their dwellings peace:
Glory to him whose just avenging ire
185 Had driven out th' ungodly from his sight
And th' habitations of the just; to him
Glory and praise, whose wisdom had ordained
Good out of evil to create, instead
Of Spirits malign a better race to bring
190 Into their vacant room, and thence diffuse
His good to worlds and ages infinite.'
So sang the hierarchies: meanwhile the Son
On his great expedition now appeared,
Girt with omnipotence, with radiance crowned
195 Of majesty divine, sapience° and love   *wisdom*
Immense, and all his Father in him shone.
About his chariot numberless were poured
Cherub and Seraph, Potentates and Thrones,
And Virtues, winged Spirits, and chariots winged,
200 From the armory of God, where stand of old
Myriads between two brazen mountains lodged
Against° a solemn day, harnessed at hand,   *in preparation for*
Celestial equipage; and now came forth
Spontaneous, for within them spirit lived,
205 Attendant on their Lord: Heav'n opened wide
Her ever-during° gates, harmonious sound   *lasting*
On golden hinges moving, to let forth
The King of Glory[7] in his powerful Word
And Spirit coming to create new worlds.
210 On heav'nly ground they stood, and from the shore
They viewed the vast immeasurable abyss
Outrageous° as a sea, dark, wasteful, wild,   *enormous, violent*
Up from the bottom turned by furious winds
And surging waves, as mountains to assault
215 Heav'n's height, and with the center mix the pole.
 "'Silence, ye troubled waves, and thou deep, peace,'

---

5. Milton's God creates out of Chaos, not out of nothing; the matter of Chaos emanated from God, and Chaos is therefore "infinite" because God fills it even while he withholds his "goodness" (creating power) from it. Neither necessity nor chance affect in any way God's freely willed creative act.

6. Raphael explains the principle of accommodation, whereby God's acts are said to be translated into terms humans can understand: here, a six-day creation. This principle allows for an escape from biblical literalism.

7. See Psalm 24:9: "Lift up your heads, O ye gates; even lift them up, ye everlasting doors; and the King of glory shall come in."

Said then th' Omnific° Word, 'your discord end':   *all-creating*
   "Nor stayed, but on the wings of Cherubim
Uplifted, in paternal glory rode
220 Far into Chaos, and the world unborn;
For Chaos heard his voice: him all his train
Followed in bright procession to behold
Creation, and the wonders of his might.
Then stayed the fervid° wheels, and in his hand   *burning*
225 He took the golden compasses, prepared
In God's eternal store, to circumscribe
This universe, and all created things:
One foot he centered, and the other turned
Round through the vast profundity obscure,
230 And said, 'Thus far extend, thus far thy bounds,
This be thy just° circumference O world.'   *exact*
Thus God the heav'n° created, thus the earth,   *the sky*
Matter unformed and void: darkness profound
Covered th' abyss: but on the wat'ry calm
235 His brooding wings the Spirit of God outspread,
And vital virtue° infused, and vital warmth   *power*
Throughout the fluid mass, but downward purged
The black tartareous cold infernal dregs[8]
Adverse to life: then founded, then conglobed
240 Like things to like, the rest to several place
Disparted, and between spun out the air,
And earth self-balanced on her center hung.
   "'Let there be light,' said God,[9] and forthwith light
Ethereal, first of things, quintessence[1] pure
245 Sprung from the deep, and from her native east
To journey through the airy gloom began,
Sphered in a radiant cloud, for yet the sun
Was not; she in a cloudy tabernacle
Sojourned the while. God saw the light was good;
250 And light from darkness by the hemisphere
Divided: light the day, and darkness night
He named. Thus was the first day ev'n and morn:[2]
Nor passed uncelebrated, nor unsung
By the celestial choirs, when orient light
255 Exhaling° first from darkness they beheld;   *rising as vapor*
Birthday of heav'n° and earth; with joy and shout   *the sky*
The hollow universal orb they filled,
And touched their golden harps, and hymning praised
God and his works, Creator him they sung,
260 Both when first evening was, and when first morn.
   "Again, God said, 'Let there be firmament
Amid the waters, and let it divide

---

8. Crusty, gritty stuff left over from the elements infused with life that make up the universe; it is associated with Hell ("infernal," "tartarous") and presumably used in its composition.
9. God's creating words, here and later, are quoted from Genesis 1–2, but Milton freely elaborates the creatures' responses to those words.
1. Ether was thought to be a fifth element or "quintessence," the substance of the celestial bodies above the moon.
2. One twenty-four-hour period measured in the Hebrew manner from sundown to sundown.

The waters from the waters': and God made
The firmament, expanse of liquid,° pure, — clear, bright
265 Transparent, elemental air diffused
In circuit to the uttermost convex° — vault
Of this great round:° partition firm and sure, — universe
The waters underneath from those above
Dividing: for as earth, so he the world
270 Built on circumfluous° waters calm, in wide — flowing around
Crystálline ocean, and the loud misrule
Of Chaos far removed, lest fierce extremes
Contiguous might distemper the whole frame:[3]
And heav'n° he named the firmament: so ev'n — the sky
275 And morning chorus sung the second day.
  "The earth was formed, but in the womb as yet
Of waters, embryon[4] immature involved° — enfolded
Appeared not: over all the face of earth
Main° ocean flowed, not idle, but with warm — of great expanse
280 Prolific humor° soft'ning all her globe, — generative moisture
Fermented the great mother to conceive,
Satiate with genial° moisture, when God said, — generative
'Be gathered now ye waters under heav'n
Into one place, and let dry land appear.'
285 Immediately the mountains huge appear
Emergent, and their broad bare backs upheave
Into the clouds, their tops ascend the sky:
So high as heaved the tumid° hills, so low — swollen
Down sunk a hollow bottom broad and deep,
290 Capacious bed of waters: thither they
Hasted with glad precipitance,° uprolled — headlong fall
As drops on dust conglobing from the dry;
Part rise in crystal wall, or ridge direct° — surge forward
For haste; such flight the great command impressed
295 On the swift floods: as armies at the call
Of trumpet (for of armies thou hast heard)
Troop to their standard, so the wat'ry throng,
Wave rolling after wave, where way they found,
If steep, with torrent rapture,° if through plain, — force
300 Soft-ebbing; nor withstood them rock or hill,
But they, or° underground, or circuit wide — whether
With serpent error° wand'ring, found their way, — winding course
And on the washy ooze deep channels wore;
Easy, ere God had bid the ground be dry,
305 All but within those banks, where rivers now
Stream, and perpetual draw their humid train.° — following
The dry land, earth, and the great receptacle
Of congregated waters he called seas:
And saw that it was good, and said, 'Let th' earth
310 Put forth the verdant grass, herb yielding seed,
And fruit tree yielding fruit after her kind;

---

3. Disturb the order and mixture of the elements and the created "frame" of the universe.
4. The earth is at first the "embryo" enveloped in a "womb of waters" and is then herself the "great mother" (line 281), made ready ("fermented") to conceive and bear every other being.

                Whose seed is in herself upon the earth.'
                He scarce had said, when the bare earth, till then
                Desert and bare, unsightly, unadorned,
315   Brought forth the tender grass, whose verdure clad
                Her universal face with pleasant green,
                Then herbs of every leaf, that sudden flow'red
                Op'ning their various colors, and made gay
                Her bosom smelling sweet: and these scarce blown,°   *blossomed*
320   Forth flourished thick the clust'ring vine, forth crept
                The swelling gourd, up stood the corny° reed   *hard as horn*
                Embattled in her field: add the humble° shrub,   *low-growing*
                And bush with frizzled hair implicit:° last   *tangled*
                Rose as in dance the stately trees, and spread
325   Their branches hung with copious fruit; or gemmed°   *put forth buds*
                Their blossoms: with high woods the hills were crowned,
                With tufts the valleys and each fountain side,
                With borders long the rivers. That earth now
                Seemed like to Heav'n, a seat where gods might dwell,
330   Or wander with delight, and love to haunt
                Her sacred shades: though God had yet not rained
                Upon the earth, and man to till the ground
                None was, but from the earth a dewy mist
                Went up and watered all the ground, and each
335   Plant of the field, which ere it was in the earth
                God made, and every herb, before it grew
                On the green stem; God saw that it was good:
                So ev'n and morn recorded the third day.
                   "Again th' Almighty spake: 'Let there be lights
340   High in th' expanse of heaven° to divide   *the sky*
                The day from night; and let them be for signs,
                For seasons, and for days, and circling years,
                And let them be for lights as I ordain
                Their office° in the firmament of heav'n   *function*
345   To give light on the earth'; and it was so.
                And God made two great lights, great for their use
                To man, the greater to have rule by day,
                The less by night altern:° and made the stars,   *in turns*
                And set them in the firmament of heav'n
350   To illuminate the earth, and rule the day
                In their vicissitude,° and rule the night,   *regular alternation*
                And light from darkness to divide. God saw,
                Surveying his great work, that it was good:
                For of celestial bodies first the sun
355   A mighty sphere he framed, unlightsome first,
                Though of ethereal mold:° then formed the moon   *fashioned from ether*
                Globose, and every magnitude of stars,
                And sowed with stars the heav'n thick as a field:
                Of light by far the greater part he took,
360   Transplanted from her cloudy shrine,[5] and placed
                In the sun's orb, made porous to receive

---

5. The "cloudy tabernacle" of line 248.

And drink the liquid light, firm to retain
Her gathered beams, great palace now of light.
Hither as to their fountain other stars
365 Repairing,° in their golden urns draw light, — resorting
And hence the morning planet gilds her horns;[6]
By tincture° or reflection they augment — absorption
Their small peculiar,° though from human sight — own small light
So far remote, with dimunition seen.
370 First in his east the glorious lamp was seen,
Regent of day, and all th' horizon round
Invested with bright rays, jocund° to run — merry
His longitude° through heav'n's high road: the gray — distance
Dawn, and the Pleiades[7] before him danced
375 Shedding sweet influence: less bright the moon,
But opposite in leveled west was set
His mirror, with full face borrowing her light
From him, for other light she needed none
In that aspect,° and still that distance keeps — when full
380 Till night, then in the east her turn she shines,
Revolved on heav'n's great axle, and her reign
With thousand lesser lights dividual° holds, — divided
With thousand thousand stars, that then appeared
Spangling the hemisphere: then first adorned
385 With their bright luminaries that set and rose,
Glad° evening and glad morn crowned the fourth day. — bright, gay
  And God said, 'Let the waters generate
Reptile° with spawn abundant, living soul: — creeping animals
And let fowl fly above the earth, with wings
390 Displayed° on the op'n firmament of heav'n.' — spread out
And God created the great whales, and each
Soul living, each that crept, which plenteously
The waters generated by their kinds,
And every bird of wing after his kind;
395 And saw that it was good, and blessed them, saying,
'Be fruitful, multiply, and in the seas
And lakes and running streams the waters fill;
And let the fowl be multiplied on the earth.'
Forthwith the sounds and seas, each creek and bay
400 With fry° innumerable swarm, and shoals — young fish
Of fish that with their fins and shining scales
Glide under the green wave, in sculls that oft
Bank the mid-sea:[8] part single or with mate
Graze the seaweed their pasture, and through groves
405 Of coral stray, or sporting with quick glance
Show to the sun their waved° coats dropped° with gold, — striped / flecked
Or in their pearly shells at ease, attend° — watch for
Moist nutriment, or under rocks their food

---

6. Venus, which Galileo's telescope found to be crescent-shaped in her first quarter.
7. A cluster of seven stars in the constellation Taurus. They appear at dawn ahead of the sun. See Job 38:31.
8. The fishes' darting motions resemble boats oared now on one side, now on the other ("sculls"), as they turn they seem to form banks within the sea.

                In jointed armor watch: on smooth the seal,
410   And bended⁹ dolphins play: part huge of bulk
                Wallowing unwieldy, enormous in their gait
                Tempest° the ocean: there leviathan¹   *stir up*
                Hugest of living creatures, on the deep
                Stretched like a promontory sleeps or swims,
415   And seems a moving land, and at his gills
                Draws in, and at his trunk spouts out a sea.
                Meanwhile the tepid caves, and fens and shores
                Their brood as numerous hatch, from th' egg that soon
                Bursting with kindly° rupture forth disclosed   *natural*
420   Their callow° young, but feathered soon and fledge   *without feathers*
                They summed their pens,² and soaring th' air sublime
                With clang° despised the ground, under a cloud   *harsh cry*
                In prospect;³ there the eagle and the stork
                On cliffs and cedar tops their eyries build:
425   Part loosely° wing the region,° part more wise   *separately / sky*
                In common, ranged in figure wedge their way,⁴
                Intelligent° of seasons, and set forth   *understanding*
                Their aery caravan high over seas
                Flying, and over lands with mutual wing
430   Easing their flight;⁵ so steers the prudent crane
                Her annual voyage, borne on winds; the air
                Floats,° as they pass, fanned with unnumbered plumes: *undulates*
                From branch to branch the smaller birds with song
                Solaced the woods, and spread their painted wings
435   Till ev'n, nor then the solemn nightingale
                Ceased warbling, but all night tuned her soft lays:°   *songs*
                Others on silver lakes and rivers bathed
                Their downy breast; the swan, with archèd neck
                Between her white wings mantling proudly, rows
440   Her state with oary feet:⁶ yet oft they quit
                The dank,° and rising on stiff pennons, tow'r°   *pool / soar into*
                The mid-aerial sky: others on ground
                Walked firm; the crested cock whose clarion sounds
                The silent hours, and th' other° whose gay train   *the peacock*
445   Adorns him, colored with the florid hue
                Of rainbows and starry eyes. The waters thus
                With fish replenished,° and the air with fowl,   *fully supplied*
                Evening and morn solemnized the fifth day.
                   "The sixth, and of creation last arose
450   With evening harps and matin,° when God said,   *morning*
                'Let th' earth bring forth soul living in her kind,
                Cattle and creeping things, and beast of the earth,
                Each in their kind.' The earth obeyed, and straight
                Op'ning her fertile womb teemed° at a birth   *brought forth*

---

9. Curved in leaping. "Smooth": a stretch of calm water.
1. The great whale (see 1.200–208).
2. Brought their feathers to full growth.
3. The ground seems covered by a cloud of birds.
4. Fly in a wedge formation.
5. Birds were thought to support each other with their wings when they flew in formation.
6. The swan's outstretched ("mantling") wings form a mantle, and it seems like a monarch on a royal barge rowed by its own "oary" feet.

455 Innumerous living creatures, perfect forms,
Limbed and full grown: out of the ground up rose
As from his lair the wild beast where he wons°   *dwells*
In forest wild, in thicket, brake, or den;
Among the trees in pairs they rose, they walked:
460 The cattle in the fields and meadows green:
Those rare and solitary, these[7] in flocks
Pasturing at once,° and in broad herds upsprung.   *immediately*
The grassy clods° now calved, now half appeared   *mounds of earth*
The tawny lion, pawing to get free
465 His hinder parts, then springs as broke from bonds,
And rampant shakes his brinded° mane; the ounce,°   *streaked / lynx*
The libbard,° and the tiger, as the mole   *leopard*
Rising, the crumbled earth above them threw
In hillocks; the swift stag from underground
470 Bore up his branching head: scarce from his mold
Behemoth[8] biggest born of earth upheaved
His vastness: fleeced the flocks and bleating rose,
As plants: ambiguous between sea and land
The river-horse[9] and scaly crocodile.
475 At once came forth whatever creeps the ground,
Insect or worm;[1] those waved their limber fans
For wings, and smallest lineaments exact
In all the liveries decked of summer's pride
With spots of gold and purple, azure and green:
480 These as a line their long dimension drew,
Streaking the ground with sinuous trace; not all
Minims° of nature; some of serpent kind   *smallest animals*
Wondrous in length and corpulence involved°   *coiled*
Their snaky folds, and added wings. First crept
485 The parsimonious emmet,° provident   *thrifty ant*
Of future, in small room large heart° enclosed,   *great wisdom*
Pattern of just equality perhaps
Hereafter, joined in her popular tribes
Of commonalty:[2] swarming next appeared
490 The female bee that feeds her husband drone
Deliciously, and builds her waxen cells
With honey stored: the rest are numberless,
And thou their natures know'st, and gav'st them names,[3]
Needless to thee repeated; nor unknown
495 The serpent subtlest beast of all the field,
Of huge extent sometimes, with brazen eyes
And hairy mane[4] terrific,° though to thee   *terrifying*
Not noxious, but obedient at thy call.

---

7. "These" are the domestic cattle who come forth in "flocks" and "herds" in pastures; "those" are the wild beasts who come forth "in pairs" (line 459), and spread out ("rare") at wide intervals.
8. A huge biblical beast (Job 40:15), often identified with the elephant.
9. Translates the Greek name "hippopotamus."
1. Any creeping creature, including serpents.
2. The ant will become the symbol of a frugal and self-governing republic ("pattern of just equality") with the "popular" (populous, plebian) tribes of common people ("commonalty") joined in rule (lines 486–89); Milton made it such a symbol in his prose tract *The Ready and Easy Way*. Bees here (lines 489–93) suggest delightful ease but are not yet (as in 1.768–75) a symbol of monarchy and associated with Hell.
3. See 8.342–54, and Genesis 2:19–20.
4. Sea serpents were so described in *Aeneid* 2.203–7.

Now heav'n in all her glory shone, and rolled
Her motions, as the great First Mover's hand
First wheeled their course; earth in her rich attire
Consummate° lovely smiled; air, water, earth,   *complete, perfect*
By fowl, fish, beast, was flown, was swum, was walked
Frequent;° and of the sixth day yet remained;   *in throngs*
There wanted yet the master work, the end°   *purpose*
Of all yet done; a creature who not prone
And brute as other creatures, but endued
With sanctity of reason, might erect
His stature,[5] and upright with front° serene   *brow, face*
Govern the rest, self-knowing, and from thence
Magnanimous to correspond[6] with Heav'n,
But grateful to acknowledge whence his good
Descends, thither with heart and voice and eyes
Directed in devotion, to adore
And worship God supreme, who made him chief
Of all his works: therefore th' Omnipotent
Eternal Father (for where is not he
Present) thus to his Son audibly spake:
   "Let us make now man in our image, man
In our similitude, and let them rule
Over the fish and fowl of sea and air,
Beast of the field, and over all the earth,
And every creeping thing that creeps the ground.'
This said, he formed thee, Adam, thee O man
Dust of the ground, and in thy nostrils breathed
The breath of life; in his own image he
Created thee, in the image of God
Express,° and thou becam'st a living soul.   *exact, manifest*
Male he created thee, but thy consort
Female for race; then blessed mankind, and said,
'Be fruitful, multiply, and fill the earth,
Subdue it, and throughout dominion hold
Over fish of the sea, and fowl of the air,
And every living thing that moves on the earth.'
Wherever thus created, for no place
Is yet distinct by name, thence,° as thou know'st   *from there*
He brought thee into this delicious° grove,   *delightful*
This garden, planted with the trees of God,
Delectable both to behold and taste;
And freely all their pleasant fruit for food
Gave thee, all sorts are here that all th' earth yields,
Variety without end; but of the tree
Which tasted works knowledge of good and evil,
Thou may'st not; in the day thou eat'st, thou di'st;
Death is the penalty imposed, beware,
And govern well thy appetite, lest Sin
Surprise thee, and her black attendant Death.

---

5. Both "stand erect" and "elevate his condition": his erect stance was understood to signify that he was created for Heaven.
6. Both "be in harmony" and "communicate."

Here finished he, and all that he had made
Viewed, and behold all was entirely good;
So ev'n and morn accomplished the sixth day: [550]
Yet not till the Creator from his work
Desisting, though unwearied, up returned
Up to the Heav'n of Heav'ns his high abode,
Thence to behold his new-created world
Th' addition of his empire, how it showed   [555]
In prospect from his throne, how good, how fair,
Answering his great Idea.[7] Up he rode
Followed with acclamation and the sound
Symphonious of ten thousand harps that tuned°   *performed*
Angelic harmonies: the earth, the air   [560]
Resounded (thou remember'st, for thou heard'st),
The heav'ns and all the constellations rung,
The planets in their stations list'ning stood,
While the bright pomp° ascended jubilant.   *triumphal procession*
 "'Open, ye everlasting gates,' they sung,   [565]
'Open, ye Heav'ns, your living doors; let in
The great Creator from his work returned
Magnificent,[8] his six days' work, a world;
Open, and henceforth oft; for God will deign
To visit oft the dwellings of just men   [570]
Delighted, and with frequent intercourse
Thither will send his wingèd messengers
On errands of supernal° grace.' So sung   *heavenly*
The glorious train ascending: he through Heav'n,
That opened wide her blazing° portals, led   *radiant*   [575]
To God's eternal house direct the way,
A broad and ample road, whose dust is gold
And pavement stars, as stars to thee appear,
Seen in the galaxy, that Milky Way
Which nightly as a circling zone° thou seest   *belt*   [580]
Powdered with stars. And now on earth the seventh
Evening arose in Eden, for the sun
Was set, and twilight from the east came on,
Forerunning night; when at the holy mount
Of Heav'n's high-seated top, th' imperial throne   [585]
Of Godhead, fixed forever firm and sure,
The Filial Power arrived, and sat him down
With his great Father, for he[9] also went
Invisible, yet stayed (such privilege
Hath Omnipresence) and the work ordained,°   *ordered, enacted*   [590]
Author and end of all things, and from work
Now resting, blessed and hallowed the sev'nth day,
As resting on that day from all his work,
But not in silence holy kept; the harp
Had work and rested not, the solemn pipe,   [595]

---

7. Eternal archetype or pattern, as in Plato: concept in the mind of God.
8. See Psalm 24:7: "Lift up your heads, O ye gates; and be ye lift up, ye everlasting doors; and the King of glory shall come in."
9. The Father.

And dulcimer, all organs° of sweet stop,   *wind instruments*
All sounds on fret[1] by string or golden wire
Tempered° soft tunings, intermixed with voice   *brought into harmony*
Choral° or unison: of incense clouds   *in parts*
600 Fuming from golden censers hid the mount.
   "Creation and the six days' acts they sung:
'Great are thy works, Jehovah, infinite
Thy power; what thought can measure thee or tongue
Relate thee; greater now in thy return
605 Than from the giant[2] angels; thee that day
Thy thunders magnified; but to create
Is greater than created to destroy.
Who can impair thee, Mighty King, or bound
Thy empire? Easily the proud attempt
610 Of Spirits apostate and their counsels vain
Thou hast repelled, while impiously they thought
Thee to diminish, and from thee withdraw
The number of thy worshippers. Who seeks
To lessen thee, against his purpose serves
615 To manifest the more thy might: his evil
Thou usest, and from thence creat'st more good.
Witness this new-made world, another heav'n
From Heaven gate not far, founded in view
On the clear hyaline,[3] the glassy sea;
620 Of amplitude almost immense,° with stars   *immeasurable*
Numerous, and every star perhaps a world
Of destined habitation; but thou know'st
Their seasons: among these the seat of men,
Earth with her nether ocean circumfused,°   *surrounded, bathed*
625 Their pleasant dwellingplace. Thrice happy men,
And sons of men, whom God hath thus advanced,
Created in his image, there to dwell
And worship him, and in reward to rule
Over his works, on earth, in sea, or air,
630 And multiply a race of worshippers
Holy and just: thrice happy if they know
Their happiness, and persevere upright.'
   "So sung they, and the empyrean rung,
With hallelujahs:[4] thus was Sabbath kept.
635 And thy request think now fulfilled, that asked
How first this world and face of things began,
And what before thy memory was done
From the beginning, that posterity
Informed by thee might know; if else thou seek'st
640 Aught, not surpassing human measure, say."

---

1. Ear on the fingerboard of a stringed instrument. "Dulcimer": the Hebrew bagpipe (Daniel 3:5).
2. The allusion implies that the myth of the Giants' revolt against Jove is a classical type or version of the angels' rebellion.
3. From the Greek word for glass (Revelation 4:6), the waters above the firmament as contrasted with the "nether ocean" (line 624), the earth's seas.
4. Hebrew, "praise the Lord."

Book 8

The Argument

Adam inquires concerning celestial motions, is doubtfully answered, and exhorted to search rather things more worthy of knowledge: Adam assents, and still desirous to detain Raphael, relates to him what he remembered since his own creation, his placing in Paradise, his talk with God concerning solitude and fit society, his first meeting and nuptials with Eve, his discourse with the angel thereupon; who after admonitions repeated departs.

    The angel ended, and in Adam's ear
So charming° left his voice, that he a while   *spell-binding*
Thought him still speaking, still stood fixed to hear;
Then as new-waked thus gratefully replied:[1]
5 "What thanks sufficient, or what recompense
Equal have I to render thee, divine
Historian, who thus largely hast allayed
The thirst I had of knowledge, and vouchsafed
This friendly condescension to relate
10 Things else by me unsearchable, now heard
With wonder, but delight, and, as is due,
With glory attributed to the high
Creator; something yet of doubt remains,
Which only thy solution° can resolve.   *explanation*
15 When I behold this goodly frame,° this world   *the universe*
Of heav'n and earth consisting, and compute
Their magnitudes, this earth a spot, a grain,
An atom, with the firmament compared
And all her numbered° stars, that seem to roll   *numerous*
20 Spaces incomprehensible (for such
Their distance argues and their swift return
Diurnal)° merely to officiate° light   *daily / supply*
Round this opacous° earth, this punctual° spot,   *dark / pointlike*
One day and night; in all their vast survey
25 Useless besides; reasoning I oft admire,°   *wonder*
How Nature wise and frugal could commit
Such disproportions, with superfluous hand
So many nobler bodies to create,
Greater so manifold,° to this one use,   *so much greater*
30 For aught appears,° and on their orbs impose   *as it seems*
Such restless revolution day by day
Repeated, while the sedentary° earth,   *motionless*
That better might with far less compass° move,   *circular course*
Served by more noble than herself, attains
35 Her end without least motion, and receives,
As tribute such a sumless° journey brought   *incalculable*
Of incorporeal° speed, her warmth and light;   *like that of spirits*

---

1. When Milton divided Book 7 of the ten-book version of 1667 into the present Books 7 and 8, he replaced a line reading "To whom thus Adam gratefully replied" with these introductory lines.

Speed, to describe whose swiftness number fails."
     So spake our sire, and by his count'nance seemed
40 Ent'ring on studious thoughts abstruse, which Eve
Perceiving where she sat retired in sight,
With lowliness majestic from her seat,
And grace that won who saw to wish her stay,
Rose, and went forth among her fruits and flow'rs,
45 To visit° how they prospered, bud and bloom,   *see*
Her nursery;[2] they at her coming sprung
And touched by her fair tendance gladlier grew.
Yet went she not as not with such discourse
Delighted, or not capable her ear
50 Of what was high: such pleasure she reserved,
Adam relating, she sole auditress;
Her husband the relater she preferred
Before the angel, and of him to ask
Chose rather;[3] he, she knew, would intermix
55 Grateful° digressions, and solve high dispute   *gratifying*
With conjugal caresses, from his lip
Not words alone pleased her. O when meet now
Such pairs, in love and mutual honor joined?
With goddess-like demeanor forth she went;
60 Not unattended, for on her as queen
A pomp° of winning Graces[4] waited still,   *procession*
And from about her shot darts of desire
Into all eyes to wish her still in sight.
And Raphael now to Adam's doubt proposed
65 Benevolent and facile° thus replied.   *easy, affable*
     "To ask or search I blame thee not, for heav'n
Is as the book of God before thee set,
Wherein to read his wondrous works, and learn
His seasons, hours, or days, or months, or years:
70 This to attain, whether heav'n move or earth,
Imports not, if thou reckon right; the rest[5]
From man or angel the great Architect
Did wisely to conceal, and not divulge
His secrets to be scanned° by them who ought   *judged critically*
75 Rather admire;° or if they list to try   *marvel*
Conjecture, he his fabric° of the heav'ns   *design*
Hath left to their disputes, perhaps to move
His laughter at their quaint opinions wide°   *wide of the mark*
Hereafter, when they come to model heav'n
80 And calculate the stars, how they will wield
The mighty frame, how build, unbuild, contrive
To save appearances,[6] how gird the sphere
With centric and eccentric scribbled o'er,

---

2. Her garden, where she "nurses" her flowers and plants.
3. The emphasis on choice suggests that Eve is not bound in Eden by the Pauline directive (1 Corinthians 14:34–35) that women refrain from speaking in church and instead learn at home from their husbands, but she voluntarily and for her own pleasure observes this hierarchical decorum.
4. The Graces attended on Venus.
5. Presumably, God's ways with other worlds and other creatures inhabiting them (if any).
6. To find ways of explaining discrepancies between their hypotheses and observed facts.

Cycle and epicycle,[7] orb in orb:
Already by thy reasoning this I guess,
Who art to lead thy offspring, and supposest
That bodies bright and greater should not serve
The less not bright, nor heav'n such journeys run,
Earth sitting still, when she alone receives
The benefit: consider first, that great
Or bright infers° not excellence: the earth   *implies*
Though, in comparison of heav'n, so small,
Nor glistering, may of solid good contain
More plenty than the sun that barren shines,
Whose virtue on itself works no effect,
But in the fruitful earth; there first received
His beams, unactive° else, their vigor find.   *ineffective*
Yet not to earth are those bright luminaries
Officious,° but to thee earth's habitant.   *attentive, dutiful*
And for the heav'n's wide circuit, let it speak
The Maker's high magnificence, who built
So spacious, and his line stretched out so far;
That man may know he dwells not in his own;
An edifice too large for him to fill,
Lodged in a small partition, and the rest
Ordained for uses to his Lord best known.
The swiftness of those circles° áttribute,   *orbits*
Though numberless,° to his omnipotence,   *innumerable*
That to corporeal substances could add
Speed almost spiritual;° me thou think'st not slow,   *that of angels*
Who since the morning hour set out from Heav'n
Where God resides, and ere midday arrived
In Eden, distance inexpressible
By numbers that have name. But this I urge,
Admitting motion in the heav'ns, to show
Invalid that which thee to doubt it moved;
Not that I so affirm, though so it seem
To thee who hast thy dwelling here on earth.[8]
God to remove his ways from human sense,
Placed heav'n from earth so far, that earthly sight,
If it presume, might err in things too high,
And no advantage gain. What if the sun
Be center to the world, and other stars
By his attractive virtue° and their own   *magnetism*
Incited, dance about him various rounds?°   *circles*
Their wand'ring course now high, now low, then hid,
Progressive, retrograde,° or standing still,   *backward*

---

7. In the Ptolemaic system, observed irregularities in the motion of heavenly bodies were first explained by hypothesizing eccentric orbits, then by adding epicycles, which were smaller orbits whose centers ride on the circumference of the main eccentric circles and carry the planets. The Copernican system also had some recourse to epicycles.

8. Raphael declines to "reveal" astronomical truth to Adam, leaving that matter open to human scientific speculation. He suggests here that Adam's Ptolemaic assumptions result from his earthbound perspective, and he implies that angels see the universe in different terms. In the following lines (122–58) he sets forth advanced scientific notions Adam had not imagined: not only Copernican astronomy but multiple universes and other inhabited planets.

                    In six thou seest,[9] and what if sev'nth to these
                    The planet earth, so steadfast though she seem,
130   Insensibly three different motions move?[1]
                    Which else to several spheres thou must ascribe,
                    Moved contrary with thwart obliquities,[2]
                    Or save the sun his labor, and that swift
                    Nocturnal and diurnal rhomb[3] supposed,
135   Invisible else above all stars, the wheel
                    Of day and night; which needs not thy belief,
                    If earth industrious of herself fetch day
                    Traveling east, and with her part averse
                    From the sun's beam meet night, her other part
140   Still luminous by his ray. What if that light
                    Sent from her through the wide transpicuous° air,   *transparent*
                    To the terrestrial moon be as a star
                    Enlight'ning her by day, as she by night
                    This earth? Reciprocal, if land be there,
145   Fields and inhabitants: her spots thou seest
                    As clouds, and clouds may rain, and rain produce
                    Fruits in her softened soil, for some to eat
                    Allotted there; and other suns perhaps
                    With their attendant moons thou wilt descry
150   Communicating male° and female° light,   *original / reflected*
                    Which two great sexes animate° the world,   *endow with life*
                    Stored in each orb perhaps with some that live.
                    For such vast room in nature unpossessed
                    By living soul, desert and desolate,
155   Only to shine, yet scarce to contribute
                    Each orb a glimpse of light, conveyed so far
                    Down to this habitable,° which returns   *inhabited place*
                    Light back to them, is obvious to dispute.°   *open to dispute*
                    But whether thus these things, or whether not,
160   Whether the sun predominant in heav'n
                    Rise on the earth, or earth rise on the sun,
                    He from the east his flaming road begin,
                    Or she from west her silent course advance
                    With inoffensive° pace that spinning sleeps   *unobstructed, harmless*
165   On her soft axle, while she paces ev'n,
                    And bears thee soft with the smooth air along,
                    Solicit° not thy thoughts with matters hid,   *disturb*
                    Leave them to God above, him serve and fear;
                    Of other creatures, as him pleases best,
170   Wherever placed, let him dispose: joy thou
                    In what he gives to thee, this Paradise
                    And thy fair Eve; heav'n is for thee too high
                    To know what passes there; be lowly wise:

---

9. Mercury, Venus, Mars, Jupiter, Saturn, and the moon. In the Ptolemaic system, the "seventh" is the sun; in the Copernican, earth.

1. Copernicus described the three motions as daily, annual, and "motion in declination" whereby the earth's axis swerved so as always to point in the same direction.

2. Oblique paths that cross each other.

3. Wheel, that is, the primum mobile, which (if we accept the Ptolemaic system and "save the sun his labor") revolves around the universe every twenty-four hours, carrying the planets and their spheres with it.

                Think only what concerns thee and thy being;
175   Dream not of other worlds, what creatures there
        Live, in what state, condition, or degree,
        Contented that thus far hath been revealed
        Not of earth only but of highest Heav'n."
            To whom thus Adam cleared of doubt, replied:
180   "How fully hast thou satisfied me, pure
        Intelligence° of Heav'n, angel serene,   *spirit*
        And freed from intricacies, taught to live
        The easiest way, nor with perplexing thoughts
        To interrupt the sweet of life, from which
185   God hath bid dwell far off all anxious cares,
        And not molest us, unless we ourselves
        Seek them with wand'ring thoughts, and notions vain.
        But apt the mind or fancy is to rove
        Unchecked, and of her roving is no end;
190   Till warned, or by experience taught, she learn,
        That not to know at large of things remote
        From use, obscure and subtle, but to know
        That which before us lies in daily life,
        Is the prime wisdom; what is more, is fume,°   *vapor*
195   Or emptiness, or fond impertinence,°   *foolish irrelevance*
        And renders us in things that most concern
        Unpracticed, unprepared, and still to seek.°   *always searching*
        Therefore from this high pitch let us descend
        A lower flight, and speak of things at hand
200   Useful, whence haply° mention may arise   *perhaps*
        Of something not unseasonable to ask
        By sufferance,° and thy wonted° favor deigned.   *permission / usual*
        Thee I have heard relating what was done
        Ere my remembrance: now hear me relate
205   My story, which perhaps thou hast not heard;
        And day is yet not spent; till then thou seest
        How subtly to detain thee I devise,
        Inviting thee to hear while I relate,
        Fond,° were it not in hope of thy reply: *foolish*
210   For while I sit with thee, I seem in Heav'n,
        And sweeter thy discourse is to my ear
        Than fruits of palm tree pleasantest to thirst
        And hunger both, from labor, at the hour
        Of sweet repast; they satiate, and soon fill,
215   Though pleasant, but thy words with grace divine
        Imbued, bring to their sweetness no satiety."
            To whom thus Raphael answered heav'nly meek:
        "Nor are thy lips ungraceful, sire of men,
        Nor tongue ineloquent; for God on thee
220   Abundantly his gifts hath also poured
        Inward and outward both, his image fair:
        Speaking or mute all comeliness and grace
        Attends thee, and each word, each motion forms.
        Nor less think we in Heav'n of thee on earth
225   Than of our fellow-servant, and inquire

Gladly into the ways of God with man:
For God we see hath honored thee, and set
On man his equal love: say therefore on;
For I that day was absent, as befell,
Bound on a voyage uncouth° and obscure,   *strange*
Far on excursion toward the gates of Hell;
Squared in full legion (such command we had)
To see that none thence issued forth a spy,
Or enemy, while God was in his work,
Lest he incensed at such eruption bold,
Destruction with creation might have mixed.
Not that they durst without his leave attempt,
But us he sends upon his high behests
For state,° as sov'reign King, and to inure°   *ceremony / strengthen*
Our prompt obedience. Fast we found, fast shut
The dismal gates, and barricadoed strong;
But long ere our approaching heard within
Noise, other than the sound of dance or song,
Torment, and loud lament, and furious rage.
Glad we returned up to the coasts of light
Ere Sabbath evening: so we had in charge.
But thy relation now; for I attend,
Pleased with thy words no less than thou with mine."
 So spake the godlike Power, and thus our sire:
"For man to tell how human life began
Is hard; for who himself beginning knew?[4]
Desire with thee still longer to converse
Induced me. As new-waked from soundest sleep
Soft on the flow'ry herb I found me laid
In balmy sweat, which with his beams the sun
Soon dried, and on the reeking° moisture fed.   *steaming*
Straight toward heav'n my wond'ring eyes I turned,
And gazed a while the ample sky, till raised
By quick instinctive motion up I sprung
As thitherward endeavoring, and upright
Stood on my feet; about me round I saw
Hill, dale, and shady woods, and sunny plains,
And liquid lapse° of murmuring streams; by these,   *flow*
Creatures that lived, and moved, and walked, or flew,
Birds on the branches warbling; all things smiled,
With fragrance and with joy my heart o'erflowed.
Myself I then perused, and limb by limb
Surveyed, and sometimes went,° and sometimes ran   *walked*
With supple joints, as lively vigor led:
But who I was, or where, or from what cause,
Knew not; to speak I tried, and forthwith spake,
My tongue obeyed and readily could name
Whate'er I saw.[5] 'Thou sun,' said I, 'fair light,

---

4. Compare Satan's inability to remember his origins (5.856–63), from which he infers self-creation, whereas Adam infers a Maker (line 278).

5. Adam's ability to name the creatures was said to signify his intuitive understanding of their natures.

And thou enlightened earth, so fresh and gay,
275 Ye hills and dales, ye rivers, woods, and plains,
And ye that live and move, fair creatures, tell,
Tell, if ye saw, how came I thus, how here?
Not of myself; by some great Maker then,
In goodness and in power preeminent;
280 Tell me, how may I know him, how adore,
From whom I have that thus I move and live,
And feel that I am happier than I know.'
While thus I called, and strayed I knew not whither,
From where I first drew air, and first beheld
285 This happy light, when answer none returned,
On a green shady bank profuse of flow'rs
Pensive I sat me down; there gentle sleep
First found me, and with soft oppression seized
My drowsèd sense, untroubled, though I thought
290 I then was passing to my former state
Insensible, and forthwith to dissolve:
When suddenly stood at my head a dream,
Whose inward apparition gently moved
My fancy to believe I yet had being,
295 And lived: one came, methought, of shape divine,
And said, 'Thy mansion° wants° thee, Adam, rise,   *habitation / lacks*
First man, of men innumerable ordained
First father, called by thee I come thy guide
To the garden of bliss, thy seat° prepared.'   *residence*
300 So saying, by the hand he took me raised,
And over fields and waters, as in air
Smooth sliding without step, last led me up
A woody mountain whose high top was plain,
A circuit wide, enclosed, with goodliest trees
305 Planted, with walks, and bowers, that what I saw
Of earth before scarce pleasant seemed. Each tree
Load'n with fairest fruit, that hung to the eye
Tempting, stirred in me sudden appetite
To pluck and eat; whereat I waked, and found
310 Before mine eyes all real, as the dream
Had lively° shadowed: here had new begun   *vividly*
My wand'ring, had not he who was my guide
Up hither, from among the trees appeared,
Presence Divine. Rejoicing, but with awe
315 In adoration at his feet I fell
Submiss:° he reared me, and 'Whom thou sought'st I am,'   *submissive*
Said mildly, 'Author of all this thou seest
Above, or round about thee or beneath.
This Paradise I give thee, count it thine
320 To till and keep,° and of the fruit to eat: *care for*
Of every tree that in the garden grows
Eat freely with glad heart; fear here no dearth:
But of the tree whose operation° brings   *action*
Knowledge of good and ill, which I have set
325 The pledge of thy obedience and thy faith,

                Amid the garden by the Tree of Life,
                Remember what I warn thee, shun to taste,
                And shun the bitter consequence: for know,
                The day thou eat'st thereof, my sole command
330   Transgressed, inevitably thou shalt die;
                From that day mortal, and this happy state
                Shalt lose, expelled from hence into a world
                Of woe and sorrow.'⁶ Sternly he pronounced
                The rigid interdiction,° which resounds   prohibition
335   Yet dreadful in mine ear, though in my choice
                Not to incur; but soon his clear aspéct°   untroubled expression
                Returned and gracious purpose° thus renewed: speech
                'Not only these fair bounds, but all the earth
                To thee and to thy race I give; as lords
340   Possess it, and all things that therein live,
                Or live in sea, or air, beast, fish, and fowl.
                In sign whereof each bird and beast behold
                After their kinds; I bring them to receive
                From thee their names, and pay thee fealty
345   With low subjection; understand the same
                Of fish within their wat'ry residence,
                Not hither summoned, since they cannot change
                Their element to draw the thinner air.'
                As thus he spake, each bird and beast behold
350   Approaching two and two, these° cow'ring low   the beasts
                With blandishment,° each bird stooped on his wing.   flattering gesture
                I named them, as they passed, and understood
                Their nature, with such knowledge God endued
                My sudden apprehension:⁷ but in these
355   I found not what methought I wanted still;
                And to the heav'nly Vision thus presumed:
                    "'O by what name, for thou above all these,
                Above mankind, or aught than mankind higher,
                Surpassest far my naming,⁸ how may I
360   Adore thee, Author of this universe,
                And all this good to man, for whose well-being
                So amply, and with hands so liberal
                Thou hast provided all things: but with me
                I see not who partakes. In solitude
365   What happiness, who can enjoy alone,
                Or all enjoying, what contentment find?'
                Thus I presumptuous; and the Vision bright,
                As with a smile more brightened, thus replied:
                    "'What call'st thou solitude? Is not the earth
370   With various living creatures, and the air
                Replenished,° and all these at thy command   fully stocked
                To come and play before thee? Know'st thou not

---

6. Compare God's commands to Adam (Genesis 1:28–30, 2:16–17) with Milton's elaboration here.
7. Adam had already begun naming the sun and features of the earth (lines 272–74), but here he names (and thereby shows he understands) all living creatures.
8. Adam reasons, as the Scholastics did, from the creatures to the fact of a Creator, but he cannot name (and so indicates that he cannot understand) God, except as God reveals himself.

  Their language and their ways? They also know,°   *have understanding*
And reason not contemptibly; with these
Find pastime, and bear rule; thy realm is large.'
So spake the Universal Lord, and seemed
So ordering. I with leave of speech implored,
And humble deprecation thus replied:
  "'Let not my words offend thee, Heav'nly Power,
My Maker, be propitious while I speak.
Hast thou not made me here thy substitute,
And these inferior far beneath me set?
Among unequals what society
Can sort,° what harmony or true delight?   *agree*
Which must be mutual, in proportion due
Giv'n and received; but in disparity
The one intense, the other still remiss
Cannot well suit with either,[9] but soon prove
Tedious alike. Of fellowship I speak
Such as I seek, fit to participate°   *partake of*
All rational delight, wherein the brute
Cannot be human consort; they rejoice
Each with their kind, lion with lioness;
So fitly them in pairs thou hast combined;
Much less can bird with beast, or fish with fowl
So well converse, nor with the ox the ape;
Worse then can man with beast, and least of all.'
  "Whereto th' Almighty answered, not displeased:
'A nice° and subtle happiness I see   *fastidious*
Thou to thyself proposest, in the choice
Of thy associates, Adam, and wilt taste
No pleasure, though in pleasure, solitary.
What think'st thou then of me, and this my state?
Seem I to thee sufficiently possessed
Of happiness, or not? who am alone
From all eternity, for none I know
Second to me or like, equal much less.
How have I then with whom to hold converse
Save with the creatures which I made, and those
To me inferior, infinite descents
Beneath what other creatures are to thee?'
  "He ceased, I lowly answered: 'To attain
The height and depth of thy eternal ways
All human thoughts come short, Supreme of things;
Thou in thyself art perfect, and in thee
Is no deficience found; not so is man,
But in degree, the cause of his desire
By conversation with his like to help,
Or solace his defects.[1] No need that thou

---

9. As with poorly matched musical instruments, Adam's string is too taut ("intense") and the animals' is too slack ("remiss") to be in harmony ("suit").

1. God is absolutely perfect, man only relatively so ("in degree"), and thereby needs companionship with a fit mate to assuage ("solace") the "defects" arising from solitude.

420	Shouldst propagate, already infinite;	
	And through all numbers absolute, though One;	
	But man by number is to manifest	
	His single imperfection, and beget	
	Like of his like, his image multiplied,	
425	In unity defective,² which requires	
	Collateral° love, and dearest amity.	*mutual*
	Thou in thy secrecy° although alone,	*seclusion*
	Best with thyself accompanied, seek'st not	
	Social communication, yet so pleased,	
430	Canst raise thy creature to what height thou wilt	
	Of union or communion, deified;	
	I by conversing cannot these erect	
	From prone, nor in their ways complacence° find.'	*satisfaction*
	Thus I emboldened spake, and freedom used	
435	Permissive,° and acceptance found, which gained	*permitted*
	This answer from the gracious Voice Divine:	
	"'Thus far to try thee, Adam, I was pleased,	
	And find thee knowing not of beasts alone,	
	Which thou hast rightly named, but of thyself,	
440	Expressing well the spirit within thee free,	
	My image, not imparted to the brute,	
	Whose fellowship therefore unmeet° for thee	*unsuitable*
	Good reason was thou freely shouldst dislike,	
	And be so minded still. I, ere thou spak'st,	
445	Knew it not good for man to be alone,	
	And no such company as then thou saw'st	
	Intended thee, for trial only brought,	
	To see how thou couldst judge of fit and meet:	
	What next I bring shall please thee, be assured,	
450	Thy likeness, thy fit help, thy other self,	
	Thy wish, exactly to thy heart's desire.'³	
	"He ended, or I heard no more, for now	
	My earthly by his heav'nly overpowered,	
	Which it had long stood under,° strained to the height	*been exposed to*
455	In that celestial colloquy sublime,	
	As with an object that excels° the sense,	*exceeds*
	Dazzled and spent, sunk down, and sought repair	
	Of sleep, which instantly fell on me, called	
	By nature as in aid, and closed mine eyes.	
460	Mine eyes he closed, but open left the cell	
	Of fancy° my internal sight, by which	*imagination*
	Abstract° as in a trance methought I saw,	*withdrawn*
	Though sleeping, where I lay, and saw the shape	
	Still glorious before whom awake I stood;	
465	Who stooping opened my left side, and took	
	From thence a rib, with cordial° spirits warm,	*from the heart*

2. God, "though One," (line 421), contains all numbers, but man has to remedy the "imperfection" of being single (line 423) by procreating and thereby multiplying his single and thereby "defective" image (line 425).

3. Compare the account in Genesis 2:18 with Milton's elaboration.

And lifeblood streaming fresh; wide was the wound,
But suddenly with flesh filled up and healed:
The rib he formed and fashioned with his hands;
Under his forming hands a creature grew,
Manlike, but different sex, so lovely fair
That what seemed fair in all the world seemed now
Mean, or in her summed up, in her contained
And in her looks, which from that time infused
Sweetness into my heart, unfelt before,
And into all things from her air° inspired   *mien, look*
The spirit of love and amorous delight.
She disappeared, and left me dark, I waked
To find her, or forever to deplore
Her loss, and other pleasures all abjure:
When out of hope, behold her, not far off,
Such as I saw her in my dream, adorned
With what all earth or heaven could bestow
To make her amiable:° on she came,   *lovely*
Led by her heav'nly Maker, though unseen,[4]
And guided by his voice, nor uninformed
Of nuptial sanctity and marriage rites:
Grace was in all her steps, Heav'n in her eye,
In every gesture dignity and love.
I overjoyed could not forbear aloud:
  "'This turn hath made amends; thou hast fulfilled
Thy words, Creator bounteous and benign,
Giver of all things fair, but fairest this
Of all thy gifts, nor enviest.° I now see   *given reluctantly*
Bone of my bone, flesh of my flesh, my self
Before me; woman is her name, of man
Extracted; for this cause he shall forgo
Father and mother, and to his wife adhere;
And they shall be one flesh, one heart, one soul.'[5]
  "She heard me thus, and though divinely brought,
Yet innocence and virgin modesty,
Her virtue and the conscience° of her worth   *consciousness*
That would be wooed, and not unsought be won,
Not obvious,° not obtrusive,° but retired,   *bold / forward*
The more desirable, or to say all,
Nature herself, though pure of sinful thought,
Wrought in her so that, seeing me, she turned;
I followed her, she what was honor knew,
And with obsequious° majesty approved   *compliant*
My pleaded reason. To the nuptial bow'r
I led her blushing like the morn: all heav'n,
And happy constellations on that hour
Shed their selectest influence; the earth
Gave sign of gratulation,° and each hill;   *rejoicing, congratulation*

---

4. Compare Eve's version of these events (4.440–91).
5. Compare the account in Genesis 2:23–24.

	Joyous the birds; fresh gales and gentle airs[6]	
515	Whispered it to the woods, and from their wings	
	Flung rose, flung odors from the spicy shrub,	
	Disporting,° till the amorous bird of night°	*frolicking / nightingale*
	Sung spousal, and bid haste the evening star°	*Venus*
520	On his hill top, to light the bridal lamp.	
	Thus I have told thee all my state, and brought	
	My story to the sum of earthly bliss	
	Which I enjoy, and must confess to find	
	In all things else delight indeed, but such	
525	As used or not, works in the mind no change,	
	Nor vehement desire, these delicacies	
	I mean of taste, sight, smell, herbs, fruits, and flow'rs,	
	Walks, and the melody of birds; but here	
	Far otherwise, transported° I behold,	*enraptured*
530	Transported touch; here passion first I felt,	
	Commotion° strange, in all enjoyments else	*mental agitation*
	Superior and unmoved, here only weak	
	Against the charm of beauty's powerful glance.	
	Or° nature failed in me, and left some part	*either*
535	Not proof enough such object to sustain,°	*withstand*
	Or from my side subducting,° took perhaps	*subtracting*
	More than enough; at least on her bestowed	
	Too much of ornament, in outward show	
	Elaborate, of inward less exact.	
540	For well I understand in the prime end	
	Of nature her th' inferior, in the mind	
	And inward faculties, which most excel,	
	In outward also her resembling less	
	His image who made both, and less expressing	
545	The character of that dominion giv'n	
	O'er other creatures; yet when I approach	
	Her loveliness, so absolute° she seems	*perfect, independent*
	And in herself complete, so well to know	
	Her own, that what she wills to do or say,	
550	Seems wisest, virtuousest, discreetest, best;	
	All higher knowledge in her presence falls	
	Degraded, wisdom in discourse with her	
	Loses discount'nanced,° and like folly shows;	*disconcerted, abashed*
	Authority and reason on her wait,	
555	As one intended first, not after made	
	Occasionally;° and to consúmmate all,	*incidentally*
	Greatness of mind and nobleness their seat	
	Build in her loveliest, and create an awe	
	About her, as a guard angelic placed."	
560	To whom the angel with contracted brow:	
	"Accuse not nature, she hath done her part;	
	Do thou but thine, and be not diffident°	*mistrustful*
	Of wisdom, she deserts thee not, if thou	

---

6. Both breezes and melodies. "Gales": winds.

Dismiss not her, when most thou need'st her nigh,
By áttributing overmuch to things
Less excellent, as thou thyself perceiv'st.
For what admir'st thou, what transports thee so,
An outside? Fair no doubt, and worthy well
Thy cherishing, thy honoring, and thy love,
Not thy subjection: weigh with her thyself;
Then value: ofttimes nothing profits more
Than self-esteem, grounded on just and right
Well managed; of that skill the more thou know'st,
The more she will acknowledge thee her head,[7]
And to realities yield all her shows:
Made so adorn for thy delight the more,
So awful,° that with honor thou may'st love   *awe-inspiring*
Thy mate, who sees when thou art seen least wise.
But if the sense of touch whereby mankind
Is propagated seem such dear delight
Beyond all other, think the same vouchsafed
To cattle and each beast; which would not be
To them made common and divulged,° if aught   *imparted generally*
Therein enjoyed were worthy to subdue
The soul of man, or passion in him move.
What higher in her society thou find'st
Attractive, human, rational, love still;
In loving thou dost well, in passion not,
Wherein true love consists not; love refines
The thoughts, and heart enlarges, hath his seat
In reason, and is judicious, is the scale[8]
By which to heav'nly love thou may'st ascend,
Not sunk in carnal pleasure, for which cause
Among the beasts no mate for thee was found."
       To whom thus half abashed Adam replied.
"Neither her outside formed so fair, nor aught
In procreation common to all kinds
(Though higher of the genial[9] bed by far,
And with mysterious reverence I deem)
So much delights me, as those graceful acts,
Those thousand decencies° that daily flow   *fitting acts*
From all her words and actions, mixed with love
And sweet compliance, which declare unfeigned
Union of mind, or in us both one soul;
Harmony to behold in wedded pair
More grateful than harmonious sound to the ear.
Yet these subject not; I to thee disclose
What inward thence I feel, not therefore foiled,°   *overcome*

---

7. See 1 Corinthians 11:3: "the head of every man is Christ; and the head of the woman is the man; and the head of Christ is God."
8. The ladder of love, a Neoplatonic concept for the movement from sensual love to higher forms, and ultimately to love of God.
9. Both "nuptial" and "generative." Adam takes respectful issue with the apparent denigration of human sex in Raphael's account of the Neoplatonic ladder, which prompts his question about angelic sex (lines 615–17).

Who meet with various objects, from the sense
Variously representing;[1] yet still free
Approve the best, and follow what I approve.
To love thou blam'st me not, for love thou say'st
Leads up to Heav'n, is both the way and guide;
Bear with me then, if lawful what I ask;
Love not the heav'nly Spirits, and how their love
Express they, by looks only, or do they mix
Irradiance, virtual or immediate° touch?"   *actual*
    To whom the angel with a smile that glowed
Celestial rosy red, love's proper hue,[2]
Answered. "Let it suffice thee that thou know'st
Us happy, and without love no happiness.
Whatever pure thou in the body enjoy'st
(And pure thou wert created) we enjoy
In eminence,° and obstacle find none   *higher degree*
Of membrane, joint, or limb, exclusive bars:
Easier than air with air, if Spirits embrace,
Total they mix, union of pure with pure
Desiring; nor restrained conveyance need
As flesh to mix with flesh, or soul with soul.
But I can now no more; the parting sun
Beyond the earth's green cape and verdant isles
Hesperian sets,[3] my signal to depart.
Be strong, live happy, and love, but first of all
Him whom to love is to obey, and keep
His great command; take heed lest passion sway
Thy judgment to do aught, which else free will
Would not admit;° thine and of all thy sons   *permit*
The weal or woe in thee is placed; beware.
I in thy persevering shall rejoice,
And all the blest: stand fast; to stand or fall
Free in thine own arbitrament° it lies.   *determination*
Perfect within, no outward aid require;°   *depend on*
And all temptation to transgress repel."
    So saying, he arose; whom Adam thus
Followed with benediction. "Since to part,
Go heavenly guest, ethereal messenger,
Sent from whose sov'reign goodness I adore.
Gentle to me and affable hath been
Thy condescension, and shall be honored ever
With grateful memory: thou to mankind
Be good and friendly still,° and oft return."   *always*
    So parted they, the angel up to Heav'n
From the thick shade, and Adam to his bow'r.

---

1. That is, various objects, variously represented to me by my senses.
2. This is not likely to be an embarrassed blush: red is the color traditionally associated with Seraphim, who burn with ardor. Raphael's smile also glows with friendship for Adam and appreciation of his perceptive inference about angelic love.
3. Cape Verde, near Dakar, and the islands off that coast are the westernmost ("Hesperian") points of Africa.

Book 9

The Argument

Satan having compassed the earth, with meditated guile returns as a mist by night into Paradise, enters into the serpent sleeping. Adam and Eve in the morning go forth to their labors, which Eve proposes to divide in several places, each laboring apart: Adam consents not, alleging the danger, lest that enemy, of whom they were forewarned, should attempt her found alone: Eve loath to be thought not circumspect or firm enough, urges her going apart, the rather desirous to make trial of her strength; Adam at last yields: the Serpent finds her alone; his subtle approach, first gazing, then speaking, with much flattery extolling Eve above all other creatures. Eve wondering to hear the Serpent speak, asks how he attained to human speech and such understanding not till now; the Serpent answers, that by tasting of a certain tree in the garden he attained both to speech and reason, till then void of both: Eve requires him to bring her to that tree, and finds it to be the Tree of Knowledge forbidden: the Serpent now grown bolder, with many wiles and arguments induces her at length to eat; she pleased with the taste deliberates a while whether to impart thereof to Adam or not, at last brings him of the fruit, relates what persuaded her to eat thereof: Adam at first amazed, but perceiving her lost, resolves through vehemence of love to perish with her; and extenuating the trespass, eats also of the fruit: the effects thereof in them both; they seek to cover their nakedness; then fall to variance and accusation of one another.

No more of talk where God or angel guest
With man, as with his friend, familiar used
To sit indulgent, and with him partake
Rural repast, permitting him the while
5 Venial° discourse unblamed: I now must change   *permissible*
Those notes to tragic; foul distrust, and breach
Disloyal on the part of man, revolt,
And disobedience: on the part of Heav'n
Now alienated, distance and distaste,°   *aversion*
10 Anger and just rebuke, and judgment giv'n,
That brought into this world a world of woe,
Sin and her shadow Death, and misery
Death's harbinger:° sad task, yet argument°   *forerunner / subject*
Not less but more heroic than the wrath
15 Of stern Achilles on his foe pursued
Thrice fugitive about Troy wall; or rage
Of Turnus for Lavinia disespoused,
Or Neptune's ire or Juno's, that so long
Perplexed the Greek and Cytherea's son;[1]

---

1. In this fourth proem (lines 1–47), after signaling his change from pastoral to tragic mode (lines 1–6), Milton emphasizes tragic elements in several classical epics: Achilles pursuing Hector three times around the wall of Troy before killing him (*Iliad* 22); Turnus fighting Aeneas over the loss of his betrothed Lavinia, and then killed by Aeneas; Odysseus ("the Greek") and Aeneas ("Cytherea's son," that is, Venus's son) tormented ("perplexed") by Neptune (Poseidon) and Juno, respectively.

If answerable° style I can obtain   *fitting*
Of my celestial patroness, who deigns
Her nightly visitation unimplored,[2]
And dictates to me slumb'ring, or inspires
Easy my unpremeditated verse:
Since first this subject for heroic song
Pleased me long choosing, and beginning late;
Not sedulous° by nature to indite   *eager*
Wars, hitherto the only argument°   *subject*
Heroic deemed, chief mastery to dissect
With long and tedious havoc fabled knights
In battles feigned; the better fortitude
Of patience and heroic martyrdom
Unsung; or to describe races and games,
Or tilting furniture, emblazoned shields,
Impresses quaint, caparisons and steeds;
Bases[3] and tinsel trappings, gorgeous knights
At joust and tournament; then marshaled feast
Served up in hall with sewers,° and seneschals;°   *waiters / stewards*
The skill of artifice° or office mean,   *mechanic art*
Not that which justly gives heroic name
To person or to poem. Me of these
Nor skilled nor studious, higher argument
Remains,[4] sufficient of itself to raise
That name, unless an age too late, or cold
Climate, or years damp my intended wing
Depressed, and much they may, if all be mine,
Not hers who brings it nightly to my ear.
    The sun was sunk, and after him the star
Of Hesperus,[5] whose office is to bring
Twilight upon the earth, short arbiter
'Twixt day and night, and now from end to end
Night's hemisphere had veiled the horizon round:
When Satan who late° fled[6] before the threats   *recently*
Of Gabriel out of Eden, now improved°   *increased*
In meditated fraud and malice, bent
On man's destruction, maugre what might hap
Of heavier on himself,[7] fearless returned.
By night he fled, and at midnight returned
From compassing the earth, cautious of day,
Since Uriel regent of the sun descried
His entrance, and forewarned the Cherubim
That kept their watch; thence full of anguish driv'n,

---

2. Milton does not here invoke the Muse but testifies to her customary nightly visits. Milton's nephew reports that he often awoke in the morning with lines of poetry fully formed in his head, ready to dictate them to a scribe.

3. Cloth coverings for horses; "tilting furniture": equipment for jousting; "impresses quaint": cunningly designed heraldic devices on shields; "caparisons": ornamental trappings or armor for horses. After rejecting the classical epic subjects, Milton here rejects the familiar topics of romance.

4. For a heroic poem. He proceeds to recap worries he has voiced before: that the times might not be receptive to such poems ("age too late"), that the "cold Climate" of England or his own advanced age might "damp" (benumb, dampen) his "intended wing / Depressed" (poetic flights held down, kept from soaring).

5. Venus, the evening star.

6. At the end of Book 4.

7. That is, despite ("maugre") what might result in heavier punishments for himself.

The space of seven continued nights he rode
With darkness, thrice the equinoctial line°   *equator*
He circled, four times crossed the car of Night
From pole to pole, traversing each colure;⁸
On the eighth returned, and on the coast averse°   *turned away*
From entrance on Cherubic watch, by stealth
Found unsuspected way. There was a place,
Now not, though sin, not time, first wrought the change,
Where Tigris at the foot of Paradise
Into a gulf shot underground, till part
Rose up a fountain by the Tree of Life;
In with the river sunk, and with it rose
Satan involved° in rising mist, then sought   *enveloped*
Where to lie hid. Sea he had searched and land
From Eden over Pontus,⁹ and the pool
Maeotis, up beyond the river Ob;
Downward as far Antarctic; and in length
West from Orontes to the ocean barred
At Darien, thence to the land where flows
Ganges and Indus: thus the orb he roamed
With narrow° search; and with inspection deep   *strict*
Considered every creature, which of all
Most opportune might serve his wiles, and found
The serpent subtlest beast of all the field.¹
Him after long debate, irresolute°   *undecided*
Of° thoughts revolved, his final sentence° chose   *among / decision*
Fit vessel, fittest imp° of fraud, in whom   *offshoot*
To enter, and his dark suggestions hide
From sharpest sight: for in the wily snake,
Whatever sleights° none would suspicious mark,   *artifices*
As from his wit and native subtlety
Proceeding, which in other beasts observed
Doubt° might beget of diabolic pow'r   *suspicion*
Active within beyond the sense of brute.
Thus he resolved, but first from inward grief
His bursting passion into plaints thus poured:
    "O earth, how like to Heav'n, if not preferred
More justly, seat worthier of gods, as built
With second thoughts, reforming what was old!
For what God after better worse would build?
Terrestrial heav'n, danced round by other heav'ns
That shine, yet bear their bright officious° lamps,   *dutiful*
Light above light, for thee alone, as seems,²
In thee concent'ring all their precious beams

---

8. The colures are two great circles that intersect at right angles at the poles. By circling the globe from east to west at the equator and then over the north and south poles, Satan can remain in darkness, keeping the earth between himself and the sun. "Car of Night" (line 65): the earth's shadow, imagined as the chariot of the goddess Night.
9. The Black Sea. Satan's journey (lines 77–82) takes him from there to the Sea of Azov in Russia ("Maeotis"), beyond the river "Ob" in Siberia, which flows into the Arctic Ocean, then south to Antarctica; thence west from "Orontes" (a river in Syria) across the Atlantic to "Darien" (the Isthmus of Panama), then across the Pacific and Asia to India where the "Ganges" and "Indus" rivers flow.
1. The serpent is so described in Genesis 3:1.
2. Like Adam (8.15ff.) and Eve (4.657–58) but not Raphael (8.114–78), Satan assumes a Ptolemaic universe centered on the earth and humankind.

           Of sacred influence: as God in Heav'n
           Is center, yet extends to all, so thou
           Centring receiv'st from all those orbs; in thee,
110   Not in themselves, all their known virtue appears
           Productive in herb, plant, and nobler birth
           Of creatures animate with gradual life
           Of growth, sense, reason,[3] all summed up in man.
           With what delight could I have walked thee round,
115   If I could joy in aught, sweet interchange
           Of hill and valley, rivers, woods and plains,
           Now land, now sea, and shores with forest crowned,
           Rocks, dens, and caves; but I in none of these
           Find place or refuge; and the more I see
120   Pleasures about me, so much more I feel
           Torment within me, as from the hateful siege°   *conflict*
           Of contraries; all good to me becomes
           Bane,° and in Heav'n much worse would be my state.   *poison*
           But neither here seek I, no nor in Heav'n
125   To dwell, unless by mastering Heav'n's Supreme;
           Nor hope to be myself less miserable
           By what I seek, but others to make such
           As I, though thereby worse to me redound:
           For only in destroying I find ease
130   To my relentless thoughts; and him[4] destroyed,
           Or won to what may work his utter loss,
           For whom all this was made, all this will soon
           Follow, as to him linked in weal or woe:
           In woe then; that destruction wide may range:
135   To me shall be the glory sole among
           The infernal Powers, in one day to have marred
           What he Almighty styled,° six nights and days   *called*
           Continued making, and who knows how long
           Before had been contriving, though perhaps
140   Not longer than since I in one night freed
           From servitude inglorious well-nigh half
           Th' angelic name, and thinner left the throng
           Of his adorers. He to be avenged,
           And to repair his numbers thus impaired,
145   Whether such virtue° spent of old now failed   *power*
           More angels to create, if they at least
           Are his created, or to spite us more,
           Determined to advance into our room
           A creature formed of earth, and him endow,
150   Exalted from so base original,°   *origin*
           With Heav'nly spoils, our spoils: what he decreed
           He effected; man he made, and for him built
           Magnificent this world, and earth his seat,
           Him lord pronounced, and, O indignity!
155   Subjected to his service angel wings,

3. Graduated in steps ("gradual," 112) from vegetable to animal to rational forms (souls); compare 5.469–90.
4. Acam. "This" (line 132): the universe.

And flaming ministers to watch and tend
Their earthy charge: of these the vigilance
I dread, and to elude, thus wrapped in mist
Of midnight vapor glide obscure, and pry
In every bush and brake, where hap° may find   *luck*
The serpent sleeping, in whose mazy folds
To hide me, and the dark intent I bring.
O foul descent! that I who erst contended
With gods to sit the highest, am now constrained
Into a beast, and mixed with bestial slime,
This essence to incarnate and imbrute,⁵
That to the height of deity aspired;
But what will not ambition and revenge
Descend to? Who aspires must down as low
As high he soared, obnoxious° first or last   *exposed*
To basest things. Revenge, at first though sweet,
Bitter ere long back on itself recoils;
Let it; I reck° not, so it light well aimed,   *care*
Since higher I fall short, on him who next
Provokes my envy, this new favorite
Of Heav'n, this man of clay, son of despite,
Whom us the more to spite his Maker raised
From dust: spite then with spite is best repaid."
    So saying, through each thicket dank or dry,
Like a black mist low creeping, he held on
His midnight search, where soonest he might find
The serpent: him fast sleeping soon he found
In labyrinth of many a round self-rolled,
His head the midst, well stored with subtle wiles:
Not yet in horrid shade or dismal den,
Nor nocent° yet, but on the grassy herb   *harmful, guilty*
Fearless unfeared he slept: in at his mouth
The Devil entered, and his brutal° sense,   *animal*
In heart or head, possessing soon inspired
With act intelligential: but his sleep
Disturbed not, waiting close° th' approach of morn.   *hidden*
Now whenas sacred light began to dawn
In Eden on the humid flow'rs, that breathed
Their morning incense, when all things that breathe,
From th' earth's great altar send up silent praise
To the Creator, and his nostrils fill
With grateful° smell, forth came the human pair   *pleasing*
And joined their vocal worship to the choir
Of creatures wanting° voice; that done, partake   *lacking*
The season, prime° for sweetest scents and airs: *best*
Then cómmune how that day they best may ply
Their growing work; for much their work outgrew
The hands' dispatch of two gard'ning so wide.
And Eve first to her husband thus began:

---

5. Satan "imbruting" himself in a snake parodies, grotesquely, the Son's incarnation in human form, as Christ.

>   "Adam, well may we labor still° to dress   *continually*
>   This garden, still to tend plant, herb, and flow'r,
>   Our pleasant task enjoined, but till more hands
>   Aid us, the work under our labor grows,
>   Luxurious° by restraint; what we by day   *luxuriant*
> 210 Lop overgrown, or prune, or prop, or bind,
>   One night or two with wanton° growth derides,   *unrestrained*
>   Tending to wild. Thou therefore now advise
>   Or hear what to my mind first thoughts present,
>   Let us divide our labors, thou where choice
> 215 Leads thee, or where most needs, whether to wind
>   The woodbine round this arbor, or direct
>   The clasping ivy where to climb, while I
>   In yonder spring° of roses intermixed   *growth*
>   With myrtle, find what to redress° till noon: *set upright*
> 220 For while so near each other thus all day
>   Our task we choose, what wonder if so near
>   Looks intervene and smiles, or object new
>   Casual discourse draw on, which intermits°   *interrupts*
>   Our day's work brought to little, though begun
> 225 Early, and th' hour of supper comes unearned."
>   To whom mild answer Adam thus returned:
>   "Sole Eve, associate sole,⁶ to me beyond
>   Compare above all living creatures dear,
>   Well hast thou motioned,° well thy thoughts employed *proposed*
> 230 How we might best fulfill the work which here
>   God hath assigned us, nor of me shalt pass
>   Unpraised: for nothing lovelier can be found
>   In woman, than to study household good,
>   And good works in her husband to promote.⁷
> 235 Yet not so strictly hath our Lord imposed
>   Labor, as to debar us when we need
>   Refreshment, whether food, or talk between,
>   Food of the mind, or this sweet intercourse
>   Of looks and smiles, for smiles from reason flow,
> 240 To brute denied, and are of love the food,
>   Love not the lowest end of human life.
>   For not to irksome toil, but to delight
>   He made us, and delight to reason joined.
>   These paths and bowers doubt not but our joint hands
> 245 Will keep from wilderness with ease, as wide
>   As we need walk, till younger hands ere long
>   Assist us: but if much convérse perhaps
>   Thee satiate, to short absence I could yield.
>   For solitude sometimes is best society,
> 250 And short retirement urges sweet return.
>   But other doubt possesses me, lest harm
>   Befall thee severed from me; for thou know'st
>   What hath been warned us, what malicious foe

---

6. Adam puns on "sole" as "unrivaled" and "only" (see 4.411).
7. Adam's compliments resemble the praises of a good wife in Proverbs 31.

Envying our happiness, and of his own
Despairing, seeks to work us woe and shame
By sly assault; and somewhere nigh at hand
Watches, no doubt, with greedy hope to find
His wish and best advantage, us asunder,
Hopeless to circumvent us joined, where each
To other speedy aid might lend at need;
Whether his first design be to withdraw
Our fealty° from God, or to disturb   *allegiance*
Conjugal love, than which perhaps no bliss
Enjoyed by us excites his envy more;
Or° this, or worse, leave not the faithful side   *whether*
That gave thee being, still shades thee and protects.
The wife, where danger or dishonor lurks,
Safest and seemliest by her husband stays,
Who guards her, or with her the worst endures."
    To whom the virgin[8] majesty of Eve,
As one who loves, and some unkindness meets,
With sweet austere composure thus replied.
    "Offspring of Heav'n and earth, and all earth's lord,
That such an enemy we have, who seeks
Our ruin, both by thee informed I learn,
And from the parting angel overheard
As in a shady nook I stood behind,
Just then returned at shut of evening flow'rs.[9]
But that thou shouldst my firmness therefore doubt
To God or thee, because we have a foe
May tempt it, I expected not to hear.
His violence thou fear'st not, being such,
As we, not capable of death or pain,
Can either not receive, or can repel.
His fraud is then thy fear, which plain infers
Thy equal fear that my firm faith and love
Can by his fraud be shaken or seduced;
Thoughts, which how found they harbor in thy breast,
Adam, misthought of° her to thee so dear?"   *misapplied to*
    To whom with healing words Adam replied.
"Daughter of God and man, immortal Eve,
For such thou art, from sin and blame entire:°   *untouched*
Not diffident° of thee do I dissuade   *distrustful*
Thy absence from my sight, but to avoid
Th' attempt itself, intended by our foe.
For he who tempts, though in vain, at least asperses°   *bespatters*
The tempted with dishonor foul, supposed
Not incorruptible of faith, not proof
Against temptation: thou thyself with scorn
And anger wouldst resent the offered wrong,

---

8. The term here means unspotted or peerless; Milton has insisted at the end of Books 4 and 8 that Adam and Eve have sex.
9. Somewhat confusing, since Eve heard the full story of the war in Heaven and Raphael's earlier warnings; Raphael's parting words (8.630–43) overheard by Eve do not specifically mention Satan but warn Adam to resist his passion for Eve. He does, however, reiterate the charge to obey the "great command" and repel temptation.

> Though ineffectual found; misdeem not then,
> If such affront I labor to avert
> From thee alone, which on us both at once
> The enemy, though bold, will hardly dare,
> 305 Or daring, first on me th' assault shall light.
> Nor thou his malice and false guile contemn;°   *despise*
> Subtle he needs must be, who could seduce
> Angels, nor think superfluous others' aid.
> I from the influence of thy looks receive
> 310 Access° in every virtue, in thy sight   *increase*
> More wise, more watchful, stronger, if need were
> Of outward strength; while shame, thou looking on,
> Shame to be overcome or overreached°   *outwitted*
> Would utmost vigor raise, and raised unite.
> 315 Why shouldst not thou like sense within thee feel
> When I am present, and thy trial choose
> With me, best witness of thy virtue tried."
>   So spake domestic Adam in his care
> And matrimonial love; but Eve, who thought
> 320 Less° attribúted to her faith sincere,   *too little*
> Thus her reply with accent sweet renewed.
>   "If this be our condition, thus to dwell
> In narrow circuit straitened° by a foe,   *confined*
> Subtle or violent, we not endued
> 325 Single with like defense, wherever met,
> How are we happy, still° in fear of harm?   *always*
> But harm precedes not sin: only our foe
> Tempting affronts us with his foul esteem
> Of our integrity: his foul esteem
> 330 Sticks no dishonor on our front,° but turns   *forehead*
> Foul on himself; then wherefore shunned or feared
> By us? who rather double honor gain
> From his surmise proved false, find peace within,
> Favor from Heav'n, our witness from th' event.°   *outcome*
> 335 And what is faith, love, virtue unassayed
> Alone, without exterior help sustained?[1]
> Let us not then suspect our happy state
> Left so imperfect by the Maker wise,
> As not secure to single° or combined.   *one alone*
> 340 Frail is our happiness, if this be so,
> And Eden were no Eden thus exposed."
>   To whom thus Adam fervently replied.
> "O woman, best are all things as the will
> Of God ordained them, his creating hand
> 345 Nothing imperfect or deficient left
> Of all that he created, much less man,
> Or aught that might his happy state secure,
> Secure from outward force; within himself
> The danger lies, yet lies within his power:

---

1. Compare with *Areopagitica*, p. 1413.

	Against his will he can receive no harm.	
350	Against his will he can receive no harm.	
	But God left free the will, for what obeys	
	Reason, is free, and reason he made right,[2]	
	But bid her well beware, and still erect,°	*ever-alert*
	Lest by some fair appearing good surprised	
355	She dictate false, and misinform the will	
	To do what God expressly hath forbid.	
	Not then mistrust, but tender love enjoins,	
	That I should mind° thee oft, and mind thou me.	*remind, pay heed to*
	Firm we subsist,° yet possible to swerve,	*stand, exist*
360	Since reason not impossibly may meet	
	Some specious° object by the foe suborned,	*deceptively attractive*
	And fall into deception unaware,	
	Not keeping strictest watch, as she was warned.	
	Seek not temptation then, which to avoid	
365	Were better, and most likely if from me	
	Thou sever not: trial will come unsought.	
	Wouldst thou approve° thy constancy, approve	*prove*
	First thy obedience; th' other who can know,	
	Not seeing thee attempted, who attest?	
370	But if thou think, trial unsought may find	
	Us both securer° than thus warned thou seem'st,	*overconfident*
	Go; for thy stay, not free, absents thee more;	
	Go in thy native innocence, rely	
	On what thou hast of virtue, summon all,	
375	For God towards thee hath done his part, do thine."	
	So spake the patriarch of mankind, but Eve	
	Persisted, yet submiss, though last, replied:	
	"With thy permission then, and thus forewarned	
	Chiefly by what thy own last reasoning words	
380	Touched only, that our trial, when least sought,	
	May find us both perhaps far less prepared,	
	The willinger I go, nor much expect	
	A foe so proud will first the weaker seek;	
	So bent, the more shall shame him his repulse."	
385	Thus saying, from her husband's hand her hand	
	Soft she withdrew, and like a wood nymph light[3]	
	Oread or Dryad, or of Delia's train,	
	Betook her to the groves, but Delia's self	
	In gait surpassed and goddess-like deport,°	*bearing*
390	Though not as she with bow and quiver armed,	
	But with such gardening tools as art yet rude,	
	Guiltless of fire[4] had formed, or angels brought.	
	To Pales, or Pomona, thus adorned,	
	Likest she seemed Pomona when she fled	

---

2. Right reason, a classical concept accommodated to Christian thought, is the God-given power to apprehend truth and moral law.
3. Light-footed, with overtones of "fickle" or "frivolous." "Oread" (next line): a mountain nymph. "Dryad": a wood nymph. "Delia": Diana, born on the isle of Delos, hunted with a "train" of nymphs.
4. Having no experience of fire, not needed in Paradise. Milton may be alluding to the guilt of Prometheus, who stole fire from heaven.

	Vertumnus, or to Ceres in her prime,	
395	Vertumnus, or to Ceres in her prime,	
	Yet virgin of Proserpina from Jove.⁵	
	Her long with ardent look his eye pursued	
	Delighted, but desiring more her stay.	
	Oft he to her his charge of quick return	
400	Repeated, she to him as oft engaged	
	To be returned by noon amid the bow'r,	
	And all things in best order to invite	
	Noontide repast, or afternoon's repose.	
	O much deceived, much failing,° hapless° Eve,	*erring / unlucky*
405	Of thy presumed return! event° perverse!	*outcome*
	Thou never from that hour in Paradise	
	Found'st either sweet repast, or sound repose;	
	Such ambush hid among sweet flow'rs and shades	
	Waited with hellish rancor imminent	
410	To intercept thy way, or send thee back	
	Despoiled of innocence, of faith, of bliss.	
	For now, and since first break of dawn the Fiend,	
	Mere serpent in appearance, forth was come,	
	And on his quest, where likeliest he might find	
415	The only two of mankind, but in them	
	The whole included race, his purposed prey.	
	In bow'r and field he sought, where any tuft	
	Of grove or garden plot more pleasant lay,	
	Their tendance or plantation for delight,⁶	
420	By fountain or by shady rivulet	
	He sought them both, but wished his hap° might find	*luck*
	Eve separate; he wished, but not with hope	
	Of what so seldom chanced, when to his wish,	
	Beyond his hope, Eve separate he spies,	
425	Veiled in a cloud of fragrance, where she stood,	
	Half spied, so thick the roses bushing round	
	About her glowed, oft stooping to support	
	Each flow'r of slender stalk, whose head though gay	
	Carnation, purple, azure, or specked with gold,	
430	Hung drooping unsustained, them she upstays	
	Gently with myrtle band, mindless° the while,	*heedless*
	Herself, though fairest unsupported flow'r	
	From her best prop so far, and storm so nigh.⁷	
	Nearer he drew, and many a walk traversed	
435	Of stateliest covert, cedar, pine, or palm,	
	Then voluble° and bold, now hid, now seen	*undulating*
	Among thick-woven arborets° and flow'rs	*small trees*
	Embordered on each bank, the hand° of Eve:	*handiwork*
	Spot more delicious than those gardens feigned	
440	Or° of revived Adonis, or renowned	*either*

5. These goddesses, like Eve, are associated with agriculture (lines 393–96)—Pales, with flocks and pastures; Pomona, with fruit trees; Ceres, with harvests—and the latter two foreshadow Eve's situation. Pomona was chased by the wood god "Vertumnus" in many guises before surrendering to him; Ceres was impregnated by Jove with Proserpina—later carried off to Hades by Pluto.
6. That is, which they had cultivated or planted for their pleasure.
7. The conceit of the flower-gatherer who is herself gathered evokes the story of Proserpina, to whom it was applied in 4.269–71.

Alcinous, host of old Laertes' son,
Or that, not mystic, where the sapient king
Held dalliance with his fair Egyptian spouse.[8]
Much he the place admired, the person more.
445 As one who long in populous city pent,
Where houses thick and sewers annoy° the air,   *make noisome, befoul*
Forth issuing on a summer's morn to breathe
Among the pleasant villages and farms
Adjoined, from each thing met conceives delight,
450 The smell of grain, or tedded grass, or kine,[9]
Or dairy, each rural sight, each rural sound;
If chance with nymph-like step fair virgin pass,
What pleasing seemed, for° her now pleases more,   *because of*
She most, and in her look sums all delight.
455 Such pleasure took the Serpent to behold
This flow'ry plat,° the sweet recess° of Eve   *plot / retreat*
Thus early, thus alone; her heav'nly form
Angelic, but more soft, and feminine,
Her graceful innocence, her every air°   *manner*
460 Of gesture or least action overawed
His malice, and with rapine sweet[1] bereaved
His fierceness of the fierce intent it brought:
That space the Evil One abstracted° stood   *withdrawn*
From his own evil, and for the time remained
465 Stupidly good,° of enmity disarmed,   *good because stupefied*
Of guile, of hate, of envy, of revenge;
But the hot hell that always in him burns,
Though in mid-Heav'n, soon ended his delight,
And tortures him now more, the more he sees
470 Of pleasure not for him ordained: then soon
Fierce hate he recollects, and all his thoughts
Of mischief gratulating,° thus excites: *greeting*
 "Thoughts, whither have ye led me, with what sweet
Compulsion thus transported to forget
475 What hither brought us, hate, not love, nor hope
Of Paradise for Hell, hope here to taste
Of pleasure, but all pleasure to destroy,
Save what is in destroying, other joy
To me is lost. Then let me not let pass
480 Occasion which now smiles, behold alone
The woman, opportune° to all attempts,   *open*
Her husband, for I view far round, not nigh,
Whose higher intellectual more I shun,
And strength, of courage haughty,° and of limb   *exalted*
485 Heroic built, though of terrestrial° mold,   *earthly*
Foe not informidable, exempt from wound,

---

8. The gardens of Adonis were beauty spots named for the lovely youth loved by Venus, killed by a boar, and subsequently revived; Odysseus ("Laertes' son") was entertained by Alcinous in his beautiful gardens; Solomon ("the sapient king") entertained his "fair Egyptian spouse," the Queen of Sheba, in a real garden (not "mystic," or "feigned," as the others were).
9. Cattle. "Tedded": spread out to dry, like hay.
1. From Latin *rapere*, to seize, the root of both "rape" and "rapture," underscoring the paradox of the ravisher (temporarily) ravished.

                I not; so much hath Hell debased, and pain
                Enfeebled me, to what I was in Heav'n.
                She fair, divinely fair, fit love for gods,
490   Not terrible,° though terror be in love   terrifying
                And beauty, not° approached by stronger hate,   unless
                Hate stronger, under show of love well feigned,
                The way which to her ruin now I tend."
                    So spake the Enemy of mankind, enclosed
495   In serpent, inmate bad, and toward Eve
                Addressed his way, not with indented° wave,   zigzag
                Prone on the ground, as since, but on his rear,
                Circular base of rising folds, that tow'red
                Fold above fold a surging maze, his head
500   Crested aloft, and carbuncle° his eyes;   deep red
                With burnished neck of verdant° gold, erect   green
                Amidst his circling spires,° that on the grass   coils
                Floated redundant:° pleasing was his shape,   in swelling waves
                And lovely, never since of serpent kind
505   Lovelier, not those that in Illyria changed
                Hermione and Cadmus, or the god
                In Epidaurus;² nor to which transformed
                Ammonian Jove, or Capitoline was seen,
                He with Olympias, this with her who bore
510   Scipio, the height of Rome.³ With tract° oblique   course
                At first, as one who sought access, but feared
                To interrupt, sidelong he works his way.
                As when a ship by skillful steersman wrought
                Nigh river's mouth or foreland, where the wind
515   Veers oft, as oft so steers, and shifts her sail;
                So varied he, and of his tortuous train°   twisting length
                Curled many a wanton° wreath in sight of Eve,   luxuriant, sportive
                To lure her eye; she busied heard the sound
                Of rustling leaves, but minded not, as used
520   To such disport before her through the field,
                From every beast, more duteous at her call,
                Than at Circean call the herd disguised.⁴
                He bolder now, uncalled before her stood;
                But as in gaze admiring: oft he bowed
525   His turret crest, and sleek enameled° neck,   multicolored
                Fawning, and licked the ground whereon she trod.
                His gentle dumb expression turned at length
                The eye of Eve to mark his play; he glad
                Of her attention gained, with serpent tongue
530   Organic, or impulse of vocal air,⁵
                His fraudulent temptation thus began.

2. The legendary founder of Thebes, Cadmus, and his wife Harmonia (Milton's "Hermione") were changed to serpents when they went to Illyria in old age; Aesculapius, god of healing, sometimes came forth as a serpent from his temple in Epidaurus.
3. Jupiter Ammon ("Ammonian Jove") made love to Olympias in the form of a snake and sired Alexander the Great; the Jupiter worshipped in Rome ("Capitoline"), also in serpent form, sired Scipio Africanus, the savior and great leader ("height") of Rome.
4. Circe, in the *Odyssey*, transformed men to beasts and was attended by an obedient herd.
5. Satan either used the actual tongue of the serpent or impressed the air with his own voice.

"Wonder not, sovereign mistress, if perhaps
Thou canst, who art sole wonder, much less arm
Thy looks, the heav'n of mildness, with disdain,
535 Displeased that I approach thee thus, and gaze
Insatiate, I thus single, nor have feared
Thy awful° brow, more awful thus retired.   *awe-inspiring*
Fairest resemblance of thy Maker fair,
Thee all things living gaze on, all things thine
540 By gift, and thy celestial beauty adore
With ravishment beheld, there best beheld
Where universally admired; but here
In this enclosure wild, these beasts among,
Beholders rude, and shallow to discern
545 Half what in thee is fair, one man except,
Who sees thee? (and what is one?) who shouldst be seen
A goddess among gods, adored and served
By angels numberless, thy daily train."[6]
So glozed° the Tempter, and his proem° tuned;   *flattered / prelude*
550 Into the heart of Eve his words made way,
Though at the voice much marveling; at length
Not unamazed she thus in answer spake.
"What may this mean? Language of man pronounced
By tongue of brute, and human sense expressed?
555 The first at least of these I thought denied
To beasts, whom God on their creation day
Created mute to all articulate sound;
The latter I demur,° for in their looks   *hesitate about*
Much reason, and in their actions oft appears.
560 Thee, Serpent, subtlest beast of all the field
I knew, but not with human voice endued;°   *endowed*
Redouble then this miracle, and say,
How cam'st thou speakable° of mute, and how   *able to speak*
To me so friendly grown above the rest
565 Of brutal kind, that daily are in sight?
Say, for such wonder claims attention due."
To whom the guileful Tempter thus replied:
"Empress of this fair world, resplendent Eve,
Easy to me it is to tell thee all
570 What thou command'st, and right thou shouldst be obeyed:
I was at first as other beasts that graze
The trodden herb, of abject thoughts and low,
As was my food, nor aught but food discerned
Or sex, and apprehended nothing high:
575 Till on a day roving the field, I chanced
A goodly tree far distant to behold
Loaden with fruit of fairest colors mixed,
Ruddy and gold: I nearer drew to gaze;
When from the boughs a savory odor blown,
580 Grateful to appetite, more pleased my sense
Than smell of sweetest fennel, or the teats

---

6. Satan's entire speech is couched in the extravagant praises of the Petrarchan love convention.

Of ewe or goat dropping with milk at ev'n,[7]
Unsucked of lamb or kid, that tend their play.
To satisfy the sharp desire I had
585 Of tasting those fair apples, I resolved
Not to defer;° hunger and thirst at once,   *delay*
Powerful persuaders, quickened at the scent
Of that alluring fruit, urged me so keen.
About the mossy trunk I wound me soon,
590 For high from ground the branches would require
Thy utmost reach or Adam's: round the tree
All other beasts that saw, with like desire
Longing and envying stood, but could not reach.
Amid the tree now got, where plenty hung
595 Tempting so nigh, to pluck and eat my fill
I spared° not, for such pleasure till that hour   *refrained*
At feed or fountain never had I found.
Sated at length, ere long I might perceive
Strange alteration in me, to degree
600 Of reason in my inward powers, and speech
Wanted° not long, though to this shape retained.[8]   *lacked*
Thenceforth to speculations high or deep
I turned my thoughts, and with capacious mind
Considered all things visible in Heav'n,
605 Or earth, or middle,° all things fair and good;   *regions between*
But all that fair and good in thy divine
Semblance, and in thy beauty's heav'nly ray
United I beheld; no fair° to thine   *beauty*
Equivalent or second, which compelled
610 Me thus, though importune° perhaps, to come   *inopportunely*
And gaze, and worship thee of right declared
Sov'reign of creatures, universal dame."[9]
   So talked the spirited[1] sly snake; and Eve
Yet more amazed unwary thus replied:
615 "Serpent, thy overpraising leaves in doubt
The virtue° of that fruit, in thee first proved: *power*
But say, where grows the tree, from hence how far?
For many are the trees of God that grow
In Paradise, and various, yet unknown
620 To us, in such abundance lies our choice,
As leaves a greater store of fruit untouched,
Still hanging incorruptible, till men
Grow up to their provision,[2] and more hands
Help to disburden nature of her birth."
625   To whom the wily adder, blithe and glad:

---

7. According to Pliny, serpents ate fennel to aid in shedding their skins and to sharpen their eyesight; folklore had it that they drank the milk of sheep and goats.
8. There is no precedent in Genesis or the interpretative tradition for Satan's powerfully persuasive argument by analogy based on the snake's supposed experience of attaining to reason and speech by eating the forbidden fruit.
9. Satan continues his Petrarchan language of courtship.
1. Both inspired by and possessed by an evil spirit, Satan.
2. That is, until the numbers of the human race are such as to consume the food God has provided.

"Empress, the way is ready, and not long,
Beyond a row of myrtles, on a flat,
Fast by° a fountain, one small thicket past   *close by*
Of blowing myrrh and balm;³ if thou accept
630 My conduct,° I can bring thee thither soon."   *guidance*
    "Lead then," said Eve. He leading swiftly rolled
In tangles, and made intricate seem straight,
To mischief swift. Hope elevates, and joy
Brightens his crest, as when a wand'ring fire,°   *will-o'-the-wisp*
635 Compact° of unctuous° vapor, which the night   *composed / oily*
Condenses, and the cold environs round,
Kindled through agitation to a flame,
Which oft, they say, some evil spirit attends,
Hovering and blazing with delusive light,
640 Misleads th' amazed° night-wanderer from his way   *bewildered*
To bogs and mires, and oft through pond or pool,
There swallowed up and lost, from succor far.
So glistered the dire snake, and into fraud
Led Eve our credulous mother, to the tree
645 Of prohibition, root of all our woe;
Which when she saw, thus to her guide she spake:
    "Serpent, we might have spared our coming hither,
Fruitless to me, though fruit be here to excess,
The credit of whose virtue° rest with thee,   *power*
650 Wondrous indeed, if cause of such effects.
But of this tree we may not taste nor touch;
God so commanded, and left that command
Sole daughter of his voice;⁴ the rest, we live
Law to ourselves, our reason is our law."
655   To whom the Tempter guilefully replied:
"Indeed? hath God then said that of the fruit
Of all these garden trees ye shall not eat,
Yet lords declared of all in earth or air?"
    To whom thus Eve yet sinless: "Of the fruit
660 Of each tree in the garden we may eat,
But of the fruit of this fair tree amidst
The garden, God hath said, 'Ye shall not eat
Thereof, nor shall ye touch it, lest ye die.'"⁵
    She scarce had said, though brief, when now more bold
665 The Tempter, but with show of zeal and love
To man, and indignation at his wrong,
New part puts on, and as to passion moved,
Fluctuates disturbed, yet comely, and in act
Raised,⁶ as of some great matter to begin.
670 As when of old some orator renowned

---

3. Blooming trees that exude the aromatic gums myrrh and balm (balsam).
4. God's only direct commandment (in Hebrew, *Bath Kol*, "daughter of a voice" from heaven). Otherwise (see following), they follow the moral law of nature, known to them perfectly by their unfallen reason, "our reason is our law."
5. Eve's formulation indicates her "sufficient" understanding of the prohibition and the conditions of life in Eden. See 3.98–101.
6. Drawn up to full dignity. Satan as the snake takes on the role of a Greek or Roman orator defending liberty (lines 670–72), a Demosthenes or a Cicero.

In Athens or free Rome, where eloquence
Flourished, since mute, to some great cause addressed,
Stood in himself collected, while each part,
Motion, each act won audience ere the tongue,°   *before speaking*
675 Sometimes in height began, as no delay
Of preface brooking⁷ through his zeal of right.
So standing, moving, or to high upgrown
The Tempter all impassioned thus began:
"O sacred, wise, and wisdom-giving plant,
680 Mother of science,° now I feel thy power   *knowledge*
Within me clear, not only to discern
Things in their causes, but to trace the ways
Of highest agents, deemed however wise.
Queen of this universe, do not believe
685 Those rigid threats of death; ye shall not die:
How should ye? By the fruit? It gives you life
To knowledge.⁸ By the Threat'ner? Look on me,
Me who have touched and tasted, yet both live,
And life more perfect have attained than fate
690 Meant me, by vent'ring higher than my lot.
Shall that be shut to man, which to the beast
Is open? Or will God incense his ire
For such a petty trespass, and not praise
Rather your dauntless virtue,° whom the pain   *courage*
695 Of death denounced,° whatever thing death be,   *threatened*
Deterred not from achieving what might lead
To happier life, knowledge of good and evil;
Of good, how just?⁹ Of evil, if what is evil
Be real, why not known, since easier shunned?
700 God therefore cannot hurt ye, and be just;
Not just, not God; not feared then,¹ nor obeyed:
Your fear itself of death removes the fear.
Why then was this forbid? Why but to awe,
Why but to keep ye low and ignorant,
705 His worshippers; he knows that in the day
Ye eat thereof, your eyes that seem so clear,
Yet are but dim, shall perfectly be then
Opened and cleared, and ye shall be as gods,²
Knowing both good and evil as they know.
710 That ye should be as gods, since I as man,
Internal man, is but proportion meet,
I of brute human, ye of human gods.³
So ye shall die perhaps, by putting off
Human, to put on gods, death to be wished,
715 Though threatened, which no worse than this can bring.

---

7. Bursting into the middle of his speech without a preface, and "upgrown" to the impassioned high style ("high") at once (lines 675–78).
8. That is, life as well as knowledge, and a better life enhanced by knowledge, which Satan in the snake presents as a magical property of the tree.
9. That is, how can it be just to forbid the knowledge of good?

1. Satan's sophism invites atheism: if God forbids knowledge of good and evil he is not just, therefore not God, therefore his threat of death need not be feared.
2. Hereafter, Satan speaks of "gods," not God.
3. Satan invites the aspiration to divinity, based on analogy to the supposed experience of the snake.

And what are gods that man may not become
As they, participating° godlike food? — *partaking of*
The gods are first, and that advantage use
On our belief, that all from them proceeds;
I question it, for this fair earth I see,
Warmed by the sun, producing every kind,
Them nothing: if they all° things, who enclosed — *produce all*
Knowledge of good and evil in this tree,
That whoso eats thereof, forthwith attains
Wisdom without their leave? And wherein lies
Th' offense, that man should thus attain to know?
What can your knowledge hurt him, or this tree
Impart against his will if all be his?
Or is it envy, and can envy dwell
In heav'nly breasts? These, these and many more
Causes import° your need of this fair fruit. — *prove*
Goddess humane,[4] reach then, and freely taste."
    He ended, and his words replete with guile
Into her heart too easy entrance won;
Fixed on the fruit she gazed, which to behold
Might tempt alone, and in her ears the sound
Yet rung of his persuasive words, impregned° — *impregnated*
With reason, to her seeming, and with truth;
Meanwhile the hour of noon drew on, and waked
An eager appetite, raised by the smell
So savory of that fruit, which with desire,
Inclinable now grown to touch or taste,
Solicited her longing eye; yet first
Pausing a while, thus to herself she mused:
    "Great are thy virtues,° doubtless, best of fruits, — *powers*
Though kept from man, and worthy to be admired,
Whose taste, too long forborne, at first assay° — *try*
Gave elocution to the mute, and taught
The tongue not made for speech to speak thy praise:
Thy praise he also who forbids thy use,
Conceals not from us, naming thee the Tree
Of Knowledge, knowledge both of good and evil;
Forbids us then to taste, but his forbidding
Commends thee more, while it infers° the good — *implies*
By thee communicated, and our want:° — *lack*
For good unknown, sure is not had, or had
And yet unknown, is as not had at all.
In plain° then, what forbids he but to know, — *in plain words*
Forbids us good, forbids us to be wise?
Such prohibitions bind not. But if death
Bind us with after-bands,° what profits then — *later bonds*
Our inward freedom? In the day we eat
Of this fair fruit, our doom is, we shall die.
How dies the serpent? He hath eat'n and lives,
And knows, and speaks, and reasons, and discerns,

---

4. Both "human" and "gracious" or "kindly."

> Irrational till then. For us alone
> Was death invented? Or to us denied
> This intellectual food, for beasts reserved?
> For beasts it seems: yet that one beast which first
> Hath tasted, envies° not, but brings with joy   *begrudges*
> The good befall'n him, author unsuspect,[5]
> Friendly to man, far from deceit or guile.
> What fear I then, rather what know to fear
> Under this ignorance of good and evil,
> Of God or death, of law or penalty?
> Here grows the cure of all, this fruit divine,
> Fair to the eye, inviting to the taste,
> Of virtue° to make wise: what hinders then   *power*
> To reach, and feed at once both body and mind?"
>   So saying, her rash hand in evil hour
> Forth reaching to the fruit, she plucked, she eat.[6]
> Earth felt the wound, and nature from her seat
> Sighing through all her works gave signs of woe,
> That all was lost. Back to the thicket slunk
> The guilty serpent, and well might, for Eve
> Intent now wholly on her taste, naught else
> Regarded, such delight till then, as seemed,
> In fruit she never tasted, whether true
> Or fancied so, through expectation high
> Of knowledge, nor was godhead from her thought.
> Greedily she engorged without restraint,
> And knew not eating death:[7] satiate at length,
> And heightened as with wine, jocund° and boon,°   *merry / jolly*
> Thus to herself she pleasingly began:
>   "O sov'reign, virtuous, precious of all trees
> In Paradise, of operation blest
> To sapience, hitherto obscured, infamed,[8]
> And thy fair fruit let hang, as to no end
> Created; but henceforth my early care,
> Not without song, each morning, and due praise
> Shall tend thee, and the fertile burden ease
> Of thy full branches offered free to all;
> Till dieted by thee I grow mature
> In knowledge, as the gods who all things know;
> Though others envy what they cannot give;
> For had the gift been theirs,[9] it had not here
> Thus grown. Experience, next to thee I owe,
> Best guide; not following thee, I had remained
> In ignorance, thou open'st wisdom's way,
> And giv'st accéss, though secret° she retire.   *hidden*
> And I perhaps am secret;° Heav'n is high,   *unseen*
> High and remote to see from thence distinct

---

5. An authority or informant beyond suspicion.
6. Ate: an accepted past tense, pronounced *et*.
7. That is, she is eating death and doesn't know it, or experience it yet, but also, punning, death is eating her too.
8. Slandered. "Sapience": both knowledge and tasting (Latin *sapere*).
9. Like Satan, Eve now conflates gods and God, ascribing envy but also lack of power to "them."

Each thing on earth; and other care perhaps
May have diverted from continual watch
Our great Forbidder, safe with all his spies
About him. But to Adam in what sort°   *guise*
Shall I appear? Shall I to him make known
As yet my change, and give him to partake
Full happiness with me, or rather not,
But keep the odds° of knowledge in my power   *advantage*
Without copartner? so to add what wants°   *lacks*
In female sex, the more to draw his love,
And render me more equal, and perhaps,
A thing not undesirable, sometime
Superior; for inferior who is free?[1]
This may be well: but what if God have seen,
And death ensue? Then I shall be no more,
And Adam wedded to another Eve,
Shall live with her enjoying, I extinct;
A death to think. Confirmed then I resolve,
Adam shall share with me in bliss or woe:
So dear I love him, that with him all deaths
I could endure, without him live no life."
   So saying, from the tree her step she turned,
But first low reverence done, as to the power
That dwelt within,[2] whose presence had infused
Into the plant scientical° sap, derived   *knowledge-producing*
From nectar, drink of gods. Adam the while
Waiting desirous her return, had wove
Of choicest flow'rs a garland to adorn
Her tresses, and her rural labors crown,
As reapers oft are wont° their harvest queen.   *accustomed*
Great joy he promised to his thoughts, and new
Solace in her return, so long delayed;
Yet oft his heart, divine of° something ill,   *foreboding*
Misgave him; he the falt'ring measure° felt;   *heartbeat*
And forth to meet her went, the way she took
That morn when first they parted; by the Tree
Of Knowledge he must pass; there he her met,
Scarce from the tree returning; in her hand
A bough of fairest fruit that downy smiled,
New gathered, and ambrosial° smell diffused.   *fragrant*
To him she hasted, in her face excuse
Came prologue,[3] and apology to prompt,
Which with bland° words at will she thus addressed.   *mild, coaxing*
   "Hast thou not wondered, Adam, at my stay?
Thee I have missed, and thought it long, deprived
Thy presence, agony of love till now
Not felt, nor shall be twice, for never more
Mean I to try, what rash untried I sought,

---

1. See Satan, 1.248–63, 5.790–97.
2. Eve ends with idolatry, worship of the tree.
3. That is, excuse came like the prologue in a play, and apology (justification, self-defense) served as prompter.

The pain of absence from thy sight. But strange
  Hath been the cause, and wonderful to hear:
  This tree is not as we are told, a tree
  Of danger tasted,° nor to evil unknown°   *if tasted*
865 Op'ning the way, but of divine effect
  To open eyes, and make them gods who taste;
  And hath been tasted such: the serpent wise,
  Or° not restrained as we, or not obeying,   *either*
  Hath eaten of the fruit, and is become,
870 Not dead, as we are threatened, but thenceforth
  Endued with human voice and human sense,
  Reasoning to admiration,° and with me   *wonderfully well*
  Persuasively° hath so prevailed, that I   *by persuasion*
  Have also tasted, and have also found
875 Th' effects to correspond, opener mine eyes,
  Dim erst,° dilated spirits, ampler heart,   *before*
  And growing up to godhead; which for thee
  Chiefly I sought, without thee can despise.
  For bliss, as thou hast part, to me is bliss,
880 Tedious, unshared with thee, and odious soon.
  Thou therefore also taste, that equal lot
  May join us, equal joy, as equal love;
  Lest thou not tasting, different degree°   *rank*
  Disjoin us, and I then too late renounce
885 Deity for thee, when fate will not permit."[4]
    Thus Eve with count'nance blithe her story told;
  But in her cheek distemper[5] flushing glowed.
  On th' other side, Adam, soon as he heard
  The fatal trespass done by Eve, amazed,°   *stunned*
890 Astonied° stood and blank, while horror chill   *petrified*
  Ran through his veins, and all his joints relaxed;
  From his slack hand the garland wreathed for Eve
  Down dropped, and all the faded roses shed:
  Speechless he stood and pale, till thus at length
895 First to himself he inward silence broke:
    "O fairest of creation, last and best
  Of all God's works, creature in whom excelled
  Whatever can to sight or thought be formed,
  Holy, divine, good, amiable, or sweet!
900 How art thou lost, how on a sudden lost,
  Defaced, deflow'red, and now to death devote?°   *doomed*
  Rather how hast thou yielded to transgress
  The strict forbiddance, how to violate
  The sacred° fruit forbidd'n! Some cursèd fraud   *consecrated*
905 Of enemy hath beguiled thee, yet unknown,
  And me with thee hath ruined, for with thee
  Certain my resolution is to die;
  How can I live without thee, how forgo
  Thy sweet converse and love so dearly joined,

---

4. Compare Eve in soliloquy, lines 817–33.
5. That is, disorder arising from disturbance of the balance of humors in the body, intoxication.

910   To live again in these wild woods forlorn?
    Should God create another Eve, and I
    Another rib afford, yet loss of thee
    Would never from my heart; no no, I feel
    The link of nature draw me: flesh of flesh,
915   Bone of my bone thou art,[6] and from thy state
    Mine never shall be parted, bliss or woe."
      So having said, as one from sad dismay
    Recomforted, and after thoughts disturbed
    Submitting to what seemed remédiless,
920   Thus in calm mood his words to Eve he turned:
      "Bold deed thou hast presumed, advent'rous Eve,
    And peril great provoked, who thus hast dared
    Had it been only coveting to eye
    That sacred fruit, sacred° to abstinence,   *set apart*
925   Much more to taste it under ban to touch.
    But past who can recall, or done undo?
    Not God omnipotent, nor fate; yet so
    Perhaps thou shalt not die, perhaps the fact°   *deed*
    Is not so heinous now, foretasted fruit,
930   Profaned first by the serpent, by him first
    Made common and unhallowed ere our taste;
    Nor yet on him found deadly, he yet lives,
    Lives, as thou saidst, and gains to live as man
    Higher degree of life, inducement strong
935   To us, as likely tasting to attain
    Proportional ascent, which cannot be
    But to be gods, or angels demigods.
    Nor can I think that God, Creator wise,
    Though threat'ning, will in earnest so destroy
940   Us his prime creatures, dignified so high,
    Set over all his works, which in our fall,
    For us created, needs with us must fail,
    Dependent made; so God shall uncreate,
    Be frustrate, do, undo, and labor lose,
945   Not well conceived of God, who though his power
    Creation could repeat, yet would be loath
    Us to abolish, lest the Adversary°   *Satan*
    Triumph and say; 'Fickle their state whom God
    Most favors, who can please him long? Me first
950   He ruined, now mankind; whom will he next?'
    Matter of scorn, not to be given the Foe.
    However I with thee have fixed my lot,
    Certain° to undergo like doom; if death   *resolved*
    Consort° with thee, death is to me as life;   *associate*
955   So forcible within my heart I feel
    The bond of nature draw me to my own,
    My own in thee, for what thou art is mine;
    Our state cannot be severed, we are one,
    One flesh; to lose thee were to lose myself."

---

6. Adam echoes Genesis 2:23–24.

  So Adam, and thus Eve to him replied:
"O glorious trial of exceeding[7] love,
Illustrious evidence, example high!
Engaging me to emulate, but short
Of thy perfection, how shall I attain, 965
Adam, from whose dear side I boast me sprung,
And gladly of our union hear thee speak,
One heart, one soul in both; whereof good proof
This day affords, declaring thee resolved,
Rather than death or aught° than death more dread   *anything other*
Shall separate us, linked in love so dear, 970
To undergo with me one guilt, one crime,
If any be, of tasting this fair fruit,
Whose virtue,° for of good still good proceeds,   *power*
Direct, or by occasion° hath presented   *indirectly*
This happy trial of thy love, which else 975
So eminently never had been known.
Were it° I thought death menaced would ensue°   *if / result from*
This my attempt, I would sustain alone
The worst, and not persuade thee, rather die
Deserted, than oblige° thee with a fact°   *bind / deed* 980
Pernicious to thy peace, chiefly assured
Remarkably so late of thy so true,
So faithful love unequaled;[8] but I feel
Far otherwise th' event,° not death, but life   *result*
Augmented, opened eyes, new hopes, new joys, 985
Taste so divine, that what of sweet before
Hath touched my sense, flat seems to this, and harsh.
On my experience, Adam, freely taste,
And fear of death deliver to the winds."
  So saying, she embraced him, and for joy 990
Tenderly wept, much won that he his love
Had so ennobled, as of choice to incur
Divine displeasure for her sake, or death.
In recompense (for such compliance bad
Such recompense best merits) from the bough 995
She gave him of that fair enticing fruit
With liberal hand: he scrupled not to eat
Against his better knowledge, not deceived,[9]
But fondly° overcome with female charm.   *foolishly*
Earth trembled from her entrails, as again 1000
In pangs, and nature gave a second groan;
Sky loured, and muttering thunder, some sad drops
Wept at completing of the mortal sin
Original;[1] while Adam took no thought,
Eating his fill, nor Eve to iterate°   *repeat* 1005

---

7. The word, which Eve intends as praise, carries the implication of "excessive."
8. That is, since I have so recently been assured of your unparalleled love.
9. See 1 Timothy 2:14: "And Adam was not deceived, but the woman being deceived was in the transgression."
1. The theological doctrine that all Adam's descendants are stained by Adam's sin and are thereby subject to physical death and (unless saved by grace) to damnation.

Her former trespass feared, the more to soothe
Him with her loved society, that now
As with new wine intoxicated both
They swim in mirth, and fancy that they feel
1010 Divinity within them breeding wings
Wherewith to scorn the earth: but that false fruit
Far other operation first displayed,
Carnal desire inflaming, he on Eve
Began to cast lascivious eyes, she him
1015 As wantonly repaid; in lust they burn:
Till Adam thus 'gan Eve to dalliance move:
 "Eve, now I see thou art exact of taste,
And elegant, of sapience[2] no small part,
Since to each meaning savor we apply,
1020 And palate call judicious; I the praise
Yield thee, so well this day thou hast purveyed.°   *provided*
Much pleasure we have lost, while we abstained
From this delightful fruit, nor known till now
True relish, tasting; if such pleasure be
1025 In things to us forbidden, it might be wished,
For this one tree had been forbidden ten.
But come, so well refreshed, now let us play,
As meet° is, after such delicious fare;   *appropriate*
For never did thy beauty since the day
1030 I saw thee first and wedded thee, adorned
With all perfections, so inflame my sense
With ardor to enjoy thee, fairer now
Than ever, bounty of this virtuous tree."
 So said he, and forbore not glance or toy°   *caress*
1035 Of amorous intent, well understood
Of° Eve, whose eye darted contagious fire.   *by*
Her hand he seized, and to a shady bank,
Thick overhead with verdant roof embow'red
He led her nothing loath; flow'rs were the couch,
1040 Pansies, and violets, and asphodel,
And hyacinth, earth's freshest softest lap.
There they their fill of love and love's disport
Took largely, of their mutual guilt the seal,
The solace of their sin, till dewy sleep
1045 Oppressed them, wearied with their amorous play.
Soon as the force of that fallacious fruit,
That with exhilarating vapor bland°   *pleasing*
About their spirits had played, and inmost powers
Made err, was now exhaled, and grosser sleep
1050 Bred of unkindly fumes,° with conscious dreams   *unnatural vapors*
Encumbered,° now had left them, up they rose   *oppressed*
As from unrest, and each the other viewing,
Soon found their eyes how opened, and their minds
How darkened; innocence, that as a veil

---

2. Adam commends Eve for her fine ("exact") and discriminating ("elegant") taste, as a part of "sapience," which means both "taste" and "wisdom."

1055	Had shadowed them from knowing ill, was gone,	
	Just confidence, and native righteousness,	
	And honor from about them, naked left	
	To guilty shame: he° covered, but his robe	*shame*
	Uncovered more. So rose the Danite strong	
1060	Herculean Samson from the harlot-lap	
	Of Philistéan Dálilah, and waked	
	Shorn of his strength,³ they destitute and bare	
	Of all their virtue: silent, and in face	
	Confounded long they sat, as strucken mute,	
1065	Till Adam, though not less than Eve abashed,	
	At length gave utterance to these words constrained:°	*forced*
	"O Eve, in evil⁴ hour thou didst give ear	
	To that false worm, of whomsoever taught	
	To counterfeit man's voice, true in our fall,	
1070	False in our promised rising; since our eyes	
	Opened we find indeed, and find we know	
	Both good and evil, good lost and evil got,⁵	
	Bad fruit of knowledge, if this be to know,	
	Which leaves us naked thus, of honor void,	
1075	Of innocence, of faith, of purity,	
	Our wonted° ornaments now soiled and stained,	*accustomed*
	And in our faces evident the signs	
	Of foul concupiscence;⁶ whence evil store;	
	Even shame, the last of evils; of the first	
1080	Be sure then. How shall I behold the face	
	Henceforth of God or angel, erst with joy	
	And rapture so oft beheld? Those heav'nly shapes	
	Will dazzle now this earthly, with their blaze	
	Insufferably bright. O might I here	
1085	In solitude live savage, in some glade	
	Obscured, where highest woods impenetrable	
	To star or sunlight, spread their umbrage° broad,	*shadow, foliage*
	And brown as evening: cover me ye pines,	
	Ye cedars, with innumerable boughs	
1090	Hide me, where I may never see them more.	
	But let us now, as in bad plight, devise	
	What best may for the present serve to hide	
	The parts of each from other, that seem most	
	To shame obnoxious,° and unseemliest seen,	*exposed*
1095	Some tree whose broad smooth leaves together sewed,	
	And girded on our loins, may cover round	
	Those middle parts, that this newcomer, shame,	
	There sit not, and reproach us as unclean."	
	So counseled he, and both together went	

---

3. Samson, of the tribe of Dan, told the "harlot" Philistine Delilah that the secret of his strength (like that of Hercules) lay in his hair; she sheared it off while he slept, and when he awoke he was easily captured and blinded by his enemies.

4. Adam's bitter pun—Eve, evil—repudiates the actual etymology of Eve, "life," which Adam will later reaffirm (11.159–61).

5. Milton, like most commentators, derives the tree's name from the event (4.222, 11.84–89).

6. The theological term for the unruly human passions and desires seen as one effect of the Fall, a sign of abundance ("store") of evils. If "shame" (see following lines) is the "last" evil, the "first" is probably the guiltiness that produces it, according to Milton's *Christian Doctrine* (1.12).

1100 Into the thickest wood, there soon they chose
The fig tree,[7] not that kind for fruit renowned,
But such as at this day to Indians known
In Malabar or Deccan spreads her arms
Branching so broad and long, that in the ground
1105 The bended twigs take root, and daughters grow
About the mother tree, a pillared shade
High overarched, and echoing walks between;
There oft the Indian herdsman shunning heat
Shelters in cool, and tends his pasturing herds
1110 At loopholes cut through thickest shade: those leaves
They gathered, broad as Amazonian targe,°   *shields*
And with what skill they had, together sewed,
To gird their waist, vain covering if to hide
Their guilt and dreaded shame. O how unlike
1115 To that first naked glory. Such of late
Columbus found th' American so girt
With feathered cincture,° naked else and wild,   *belt*
Among the trees on isles and woody shores.
Thus fenced, and as they thought, their shame in part
1120 Covered, but not at rest or ease of mind,
They sat them down to weep, nor only tears
Rained at their eyes, but high winds worse within
Began to rise, high passions, anger, hate,
Mistrust, suspicion, discord, and shook sore
1125 Their inward state of mind, calm region once
And full of peace, now tossed and turbulent:
For understanding ruled not, and the will
Heard not her lore, both in subjection now
To sensual appetite, who from beneath
1130 Usurping over sov'reign reason claimed
Superior sway: from thus distempered breast,[8]
Adam, estranged° in look and altered style,   *unlike himself*
Speech intermitted° thus to Eve renewed: *interrupted*
    "Would thou hadst hearkened to my words, and stayed
1135 With me, as I besought thee, when that strange
Desire of wand'ring this unhappy morn,
I know not whence possessed thee; we had then
Remained still happy, not as now, despoiled
Of all our good, shamed, naked, miserable.
1140 Let none henceforth seek needless cause to approve°   *prove*
The faith they owe; when earnestly they seek
Such proof, conclude, they then begin to fail."
    To whom soon moved with touch of blame thus Eve:
"What words have passed thy lips, Adam severe,
1145 Imput'st thou that to my default, or will
Of wand'ring, as thou call'st it, which who knows
But might as ill have happened thou being by,

---

7. The banyan, or Indian fig, has small leaves, but the account Milton draws on from Gerard's *Herbal* (1597) contains the details of lines 1104–11; Malabar and Deccan (line 1103) are in southern India.

8. The immediate psychological effects of the Fall are evident in the subjection of reason to the lower faculties of sensual appetite.

>   Or to thyself perhaps: hadst thou been there,
>   Or here th' attempt, thou couldst not have discerned
> 1150 Fraud in the serpent, speaking as he spake;
>   No ground of enmity between us known,
>   Why he should mean me ill, or seek to harm.
>   Was I to have never parted from thy side?
>   As good have grown there still a lifeless rib.
> 1155 Being as I am, why didst not thou the head
>   Command me absolutely not to go,
>   Going into such danger as thou saidst?
>   Too facile° then thou didst not much gainsay,°   *easy, mild / oppose*
>   Nay didst permit, approve, and fair dismiss.
> 1160 Hadst thou been firm and fixed in thy dissent,
>   Neither had I transgressed, nor thou with me."
>   To whom then first incensed Adam replied.
>   "Is this the love, is this the recompense
>   Of mine to thee, ingrateful Eve, expressed°   *demonstrated*
> 1165 Immutable when thou wert lost, not I,
>   Who might have lived and joyed immortal bliss,
>   Yet willingly chose rather death with thee:
>   And am I now upbraided, as the cause
>   Of thy transgressing? not enough severe,
> 1170 It seems, in thy restraint: what could I more?
>   I warned thee, I admonished thee, foretold
>   The danger, and the lurking enemy
>   That lay in wait; beyond this had been force,
>   And force upon free will hath here no place.
> 1175 But confidence then bore thee on, secure°   *self-assured*
>   Either to meet no danger, or to find
>   Matter of glorious trial; and perhaps
>   I also erred in overmuch admiring
>   What seemed in thee so perfect, that I thought
> 1180 No evil durst attempt thee, but I rue
>   That error now, which is become my crime,
>   And thou th' accuser. Thus it shall befall
>   Him who to worth in women overtrusting
>   Lets her will rule; restraint she will not brook,° *accept*
> 1185 And left to herself, if evil thence ensue,
>   She first his weak indulgence will accuse."
>   Thus they in mutual accusation spent
>   The fruitless hours, but neither self-condemning,
>   And of their vain contést appeared no end.

Book 10

The Argument

Man's transgression known, the guardian angels forsake Paradise, and return up to heaven to approve their vigilance, and are approved, God declaring that the entrance of Satan could not be by them prevented. He sends his Son to judge the transgressors, who descends and gives sentence accordingly; then in pity clothes them both, and reascends. Sin and Death, sitting till then at the gates of hell, by wondrous sympathy feeling the success of Satan in this new world, and the sin by man there committed, resolve to sit no longer confined in hell, but to follow Satan their sire up to the place of man: to make the way easier from hell to this world to and fro, they pave a broad highway or bridge over chaos, according to the track that Satan first made; then preparing for earth, they meet him proud of his success returning to hell; their mutual gratulation. Satan arrives at Pandemonium, in full assembly relates with boasting his success against man; instead of applause is entertained with a general hiss by all his audience, transformed with himself also suddenly into serpents, according to his doom given in Paradise; then deluded with a show of the Forbidden Tree springing up before them, they greedily reaching to take of the fruit, chew dust and bitter ashes. The proceedings of Sin and Death; God foretells the final victory of his Son over them, and the renewing of all things; but for the present commands his angels to make several alterations in the heavens and elements. Adam more and more perceiving his fallen condition, heavily bewails, rejects the condolement of Eve; she persists and at length appeases him: then to evade the curse likely to fall on their offspring, proposes to Adam violent ways which he approves not, but conceiving better hope, puts her in mind of the late promise made them, that her seed should be revenged on the Serpent, and exhorts her with him to seek peace of the offended Deity, by repentance and supplication.

Meanwhile the heinous and despiteful act
Of Satan done in Paradise, and how
He in the serpent had perverted Eve,
Her husband she, to taste the fatal fruit,
5   Was known in Heav'n; for what can scape the eye
Of God all-seeing, or deceive his heart
Omniscient, who in all things wise and just,
Hindered not Satan to attempt the mind
Of man, with strength entire, and free will armed,
10 Complete° to have discovered and repulsed   *fully equipped*
Whatever wiles of foe or seeming friend.
For still they knew, and ought to have still° remembered   *always*
The high injunction not to taste that fruit,
Whoever tempted; which they not obeying,
15 Incurred, what could they less, the penalty,
And manifold in sin, deserved to fall.
Up into Heav'n from Paradise in haste
Th' angelic guards ascended, mute and sad
For man, for of his state by this° they knew,   *this time*
20 Much wond'ring how the subtle Fiend had stol'n
Entrance unseen. Soon as th' unwelcome news
From earth arrived at Heaven gate, displeased
All were who heard, dim sadness did not spare
That time celestial visages, yet mixed
25 With pity, violated not their bliss.
About the new-arrived, in multitudes
Th' ethereal people ran, to hear and know
How all befell: they towards the throne supreme

  Accountable made haste to make appear
30 With righteous plea, their utmost vigilance,
  And easily approved;[1] when the Most High
  Eternal Father from his secret cloud,
  Amidst in thunder uttered thus his voice:
   "Assembled Angels, and ye Powers returned
35 From unsuccessful charge, be not dismayed,
  Nor troubled at these tidings from the earth,
  Which your sincerest care could not prevent,
  Foretold so lately what would come to pass,
  When first this tempter crossed the gulf from Hell.
40 I told ye then he should prevail and speed°   *succeed*
  On his bad errand, man should be seduced
  And flattered out of all, believing lies
  Against his Maker; no decree of mine
  Concurring to necessitate his fall,
45 Or touch with lightest moment[2] of impulse
  His free will, to her own inclining left
  In even scale. But fall'n he is, and now
  What rests,° but that the mortal sentence pass   *remains*
  On his transgression, death denounced° that day,   *decreed*
50 Which he presumes already vain and void,
  Because not yet inflicted, as he feared,
  By some immediate stroke; but soon shall find
  Forbearance no acquittance ere day end.[3]
  Justice shall not return as bounty scorned.
55 But whom send I to judge them? Whom but thee
  Vicegerent Son, to thee I have transferred
  All judgment, whether in Heav'n, or earth, or Hell.[4]
  Easy it may be seen that I intend
  Mercy colleague with justice, sending thee
60 Man's friend, his mediator, his designed
  Both ransom and redeemer voluntary,
  And destined man himself to judge man fall'n."
   So spake the Father, and unfolding bright
  Toward the right hand his glory, on the Son
65 Blazed forth unclouded deity; he full
  Resplendent all his Father manifest
  Expressed, and thus divinely answered mild:
   "Father Eternal, thine is to decree,
  Mine both in Heav'n and earth to do thy will
70 Supreme, that thou in me thy Son beloved
  May'st ever rest well pleased. I go to judge
  On earth these thy transgressors; but thou know'st,
  Whoever judged, the worst on me must light,
  When time shall be, for so I undertook
75 Before thee; and not repenting, this obtain

---

1. The angels, "accountable" for guarding Eden, rush to God's throne to explain that they had exercised "utmost vigilance"; their plea is readily accepted ("easily approved").
2. The smallest weight that would tip the scales.
3. A proverb: "Abstinence from enforcing a debt is not release from it." Next line: My justice must not be scorned as my generosity has been.
4. See John 5:22: "For the Father judgeth no man, but hath committed all judgment unto the Son."

Of right, that I may mitigate their doom
On me derived,° yet I shall temper so   *diverted*
Justice with mercy, as may illustrate most°   *best show*
Them fully satisfied, and thee appease.
Attendance none shall need, nor train,° where none   *attendants*
Are to behold the judgment, but the judged,
Those two; the third best absent is condemned,
Convict° by flight, and rebel to all law: *proved guilty*
Conviction to the serpent none belongs."
    Thus saying, from his radiant seat he rose
Of high collateral° glory: him Thrones and Powers,   *placed side by side*
Princedoms, and Dominations ministrant
Accompanied to Heaven gate, from whence
Eden and all the coast° in prospect lay.   *region*
Down he descended straight; the speed of gods
Time counts not,[5] though with swiftest minutes winged.
Now was the sun in western cadence° low   *falling*
From noon, and gentle airs due at their hour
To fan the earth now waked, and usher in
The evening cool, when he from wrath more cool
Came the mild Judge and Intercessor both
To sentence man: the voice of God they heard
Now walking in the garden, by soft winds
Brought to their ears, while day declined; they heard,
And from his presence hid themselves among
The thickest trees, both man and wife, till God
Approaching, thus to Adam called aloud.
    "Where art thou Adam, wont° with joy to meet   *used before*
My coming seen far off? I miss thee here,
Not pleased, thus entertained with solitude,
Where obvious duty erewhile appeared unsought:
Or come I less conspicuous, or what change
Absents thee, or what chance detains? Come forth."
He came, and with him Eve, more loath, though first
To offend, discount'nanced both, and discomposed;
Love was not in their looks, either to God
Or to each other, but apparent° guilt,   *easily seen*
And shame, and perturbation, and despair,
Anger, and obstinacy, and hate, and guile.
Whence Adam falt'ring long, thus answered brief:
    "I heard thee in the garden, and of thy voice
Afraid, being naked, hid myself." To whom
The gracious Judge without revile° replied: *abuse*
    "My voice thou oft hast heard, and hast not feared,
But still° rejoiced, how is it now become   *always*
So dreadful to thee? That thou art naked, who
Hath told thee? Hast thou eaten of the tree
Whereof I gave thee charge thou shouldst not eat?"
    To whom thus Adam sore beset replied.

---

5. The Son's descent is immediate; Raphael had taken much of the morning to travel from Heaven to earth (8.110–14).

"O Heav'n! in evil strait this day I stand   125
Before my Judge, either to undergo
Myself the total crime, or to accuse
My other self, the partner of my life;
Whose failing, while her faith to me remains,
I should conceal, and not expose to blame   130
By my complaint; but strict necessity
Subdues me, and calamitous constraint,
Lest on my head both sin and punishment,
However insupportable, be all
Devolved;° though should I hold my peace, yet thou   135 *fallen on*
Wouldst easily detect what I conceal.
This woman whom thou mad'st to be my help,
And gav'st me as thy perfect gift, so good,
So fit, so acceptáble, so divine,
That from her hand I could suspect no ill,   140
And what she did, whatever in itself,
Her doing seemed to justify the deed;
She gave me of the tree, and I did eat."[6]
    To whom the Sov'reign Presence thus replied.
"Was she thy God, that her thou didst obey   145
Before his voice, or was she made thy guide,
Superior, or but equal, that to her
Thou didst resign thy manhood, and the place
Wherein God set thee above her made of thee,
And for thee,[7] whose perfection far excelled   150
Hers in all real dignity: adorned
She was indeed, and lovely to attract
Thy love, not thy subjection, and her gifts
Were such as under government well seemed,
Unseemly to bear rule, which was thy part   155
And person,[8] hadst thou known thyself aright."
    So having said, he thus to Eve in few°   *few words*
"Say woman, what is this which thou hast done?"
    To whom sad Eve with shame nigh overwhelmed,
Confessing soon, yet not before her Judge   160
Bold or loquacious, thus abashed replied:
"The serpent me beguiled and I did eat."
    Which when the Lord God heard, without delay
To judgment he proceeded on th' accused
Serpent though brute, unable to transfer   165
The guilt on him who made him instrument
Of mischief, and polluted from the end°   *purpose*
Of his creation; justly then accursed,
As vitiated in nature:[9] more to know

---

6. Compare Adam's speech in Genesis 3:12, and the elements Milton adds of complaint, veiled accusation of God, and self-exculpation; also compare Eve's answer in Genesis 3:13 and in lines 159–62 below.

7. See 1 Corinthians 11:8–9: "For the man is not of the woman; but the woman of the man. / Neither was the man created for the woman; but the woman for the man."

8. Role and character (persona), as in a drama.

9. The serpent was "unable to transfer" (line 165) his own guilt in being "polluted" from his proper end and nature onto Satan, who made him "instrument," so he was "justly . . . accursed," but the terms of that judgment have a "mysterious" (line 173) or hidden meaning that applies to Satan.

170　　　Concerned not man (since he no further knew)
　　　　Nor altered his offense; yet God at last
　　　　To Satan first in sin his doom applied,
　　　　Though in mysterious terms, judged as then best:
　　　　And on the serpent thus his curse let fall.
175　　　"Because thou hast done this, thou art accursed
　　　　Above all cattle, each beast of the field;
　　　　Upon thy belly groveling thou shalt go,
　　　　And dust shalt eat all the days of thy life.
　　　　Between thee and the woman I will put
180　　　Enmity, and between thine and her Seed;
　　　　Her Seed shall bruise thy head, thou bruise his heel."[1]
　　　　　So spake this oracle, then verified
　　　　When Jesus son of Mary second Eve,
　　　　Saw Satan fall like lightning down from Heav'n,[2]
185　　　Prince of the air; then rising from his grave
　　　　Spoiled Principalities and Powers, triumphed
　　　　In open show, and with ascension bright
　　　　Captivity led captive through the air,
　　　　The realm itself of Satan long usurped,
190　　　Whom he shall tread at last under our feet;
　　　　Ev'n he who now foretold his fatal bruise,
　　　　And to the woman thus his sentence turned.
　　　　　"Thy sorrow I will greatly multiply
　　　　By thy conception; children thou shalt bring
195　　　In sorrow forth, and to thy husband's will
　　　　Thine shall submit, he over thee shall rule."
　　　　　On Adam last thus judgment he pronounced.
　　　　"Because thou hast hearkened to the voice of thy wife,
　　　　And eaten of the tree concerning which
200　　　I charged thee, saying: Thou shalt not eat thereof,
　　　　Cursed is the ground for thy sake, thou in sorrow
　　　　Shalt eat thereof all the days of thy life;
　　　　Thorns also and thistles it shall bring thee forth
　　　　Unbid, and thou shalt eat th' herb of the field,
205　　　In the sweat of thy face shalt thou eat bread,
　　　　Till thou return unto the ground, for thou
　　　　Out of the ground wast taken: know thy birth,
　　　　For dust thou art, and shalt to dust return."
　　　　　So judged he man, both judge and savior sent,
210　　　And th' instant stroke of death denounced° that day　　　　*announced*
　　　　Removed far off; then pitying how they stood
　　　　Before him naked to the air, that now
　　　　Must suffer change, disdained not to begin
　　　　Thenceforth the form of servant to assume,
215　　　As when he washed his servants' feet,[3] so now

---

1. This is the so-called protoevangelion or judgment of the Serpent (Satan) that contains at the same time the promise of the Redeemer ("her Seed"); Adam and Eve are led to understand it by degrees.
2. See Christ's comment to his disciples (Luke 10:18: "I beheld Satan as lightning fall from heaven"), and also Colossians 2:15 and Ephesians 4:8, to the following lines, 185–88.
3. See Philippians 2:7: "[Christ] took upon him the form of a servant"; John 13:5: "he poureth water into a basin, and began to wash the disciples' feet."

As father of his family he clad
Their nakedness with skins of beasts, or° slain,   *either*
Or as the snake with youthful coat repaid;
And thought not much° to clothe his enemies: *too much*
220 Nor he their outward only with the skins
Of beasts, but inward nakedness, much more
Opprobrious, with his robe of righteousness,
Arraying covered from his Father's sight.
To him with swift ascent he up returned,
225 Into his blissful bosom reassumed
In glory as of old, to him appeased
All, though all-knowing, what had passed with man
Recounted, mixing intercession sweet.
Meanwhile ere thus was sinned and judged on earth,
230 Within the gates of Hell sat Sin and Death,
In counterview within the gates, that now
Stood open wide, belching outrageous° flame   *unrestrained*
Far into Chaos, since the Fiend passed through,
Sin opening, who thus now to Death began:
235   "O son, why sit we here each other viewing
Idly, while Satan our great author° thrives   *father*
In other worlds, and happier seat provides
For us his offspring dear? It cannot be,
But that success attends him; if mishap,
240 Ere this he had returned, with fury driv'n
By his avengers, since no place like° this   *as well as*
Can fit his punishment, or their revenge.
Methinks I feel new strength within me rise,
Wings growing, and dominion giv'n me large
245 Beyond this deep; whatever draws me on,
Or sympathy, or some connatural force
Powerful at greatest distance to unite
With secret amity things of like kind
By secretest conveyance.[4] Thou my shade
250 Inseparable must with me along:
For Death from Sin no power can separate.
But lest the difficulty of passing back
Stay his return perhaps over this gulf
Impassable, impervious,° let us try   *impenetrable*
255 Advent'rous work, yet to thy power and mine
Not unagreeable, to found° a path   *establish*
Over this main from Hell to that new world
Where Satan now prevails, a monument
Of merit high to all th' infernal host,
260 Easing their passage hence, for intercourse,°   *passing back and forth*
Or transmigration,° as their lot shall lead.   *emigration*
Nor can I miss the way, so strongly drawn
By this new-felt attraction and instinct."
   Whom thus the meager° shadow answered soon: *emaciated*

---

4. Sin feels an attraction ("sympathy") drawing two things together, or an innate ("connatural") force, linking her to Satan.

"Go whither fate and inclination strong
Leads thee, I shall not lag behind, nor err
The way, thou leading, such a scent I draw
Of carnage, prey innumerable, and taste
The savor of death from all things there that live:
Nor shall I to the work thou enterprisest
Be wanting, but afford thee equal aid."
       So saying, with delight he snuffed the smell
Of mortal change on earth. As when a flock
Of ravenous fowl, though many a league remote,
Against° the day of battle, to a field, — *anticipating*
Where armies lie encamped, come flying, lured
With scent of living carcasses designed° — *marked out*
For death, the following day, in bloody fight.
So scented the grim feature,° and upturned — *form, shape*
His nostril wide into the murky air,
Sagacious° of his quarry from so far. — *keenly smelling, wise*
Then both from out Hell gates into the waste
Wide anarchy of Chaos damp and dark
Flew diverse,° and with power (their power was great) — *in different directions*
Hovering upon the water, what they met
Solid or slimy, as in raging sea
Tossed up and down, together crowded drive
From each side shoaling° towards the mouth of Hell. — *assembling*
As when two polar winds blowing adverse
Upon the Cronian Sea,[5] together drive
Mountains of ice, that stop th' imagined way
Beyond Petsora eastward, to the rich
Cathaian coast. The aggregated soil
Death with his mace petrific,[6] cold and dry,
As with a trident smote, and fixed as firm
As Delos floating once; the rest his look
Bound with Gorgonian rigor not to move,[7]
And with asphaltic slime;° broad as the gate, — *pitch*
Deep to the roots of Hell the gathered beach
They fastened, and the mole° immense wrought on — *pier*
Over the foaming deep high-arched, a bridge
Of length prodigious joining to the wall° — *outer shell*
Immovable of this now fenceless world
Forfeit to Death; from hence a passage broad,
Smooth, easy, inoffensive° down to Hell. — *free from obstacle*
So, if great things to small may be compared,
Xerxes,[8] the liberty of Greece to yoke,
From Susa his Memnonian palace high

---

5. The Arctic Ocean; the "imagined way" (lines 291–93) is the Northeast Passage to North China ("Cathay") from Pechora ("Petsora"), a river in Siberia, which Henry Hudson could only imagine (in 1608) because it was blocked with ice.
6. Turning things to stone.
7. Anything the Gorgon Medusa looked upon turned to stone. Death's materials are the "cold and dry" elements; his mace is associated with Neptune's "trident," which was said to have "fixed" the floating Greek island of Delos.
8. The Persian king Xerxes ordered the sea whipped when it destroyed the bridge of ships he built over the Hellespont (linking Europe and Asia) so as to invade Greece. "Susa" (next line): Xerxes' winter residence, founded by the mythical prince Memnon.

  Came to the sea, and over Hellespont
310 Bridging his way, Europe with Asia joined,
  And scourged with many a stroke th' indignant waves.
  Now had they brought the work by wondrous art
  Pontifical,⁹ a ridge of pendent rock
  Over the vexed° abyss, following the track   *stormy*
315 Of Satan, to the selfsame place where he
  First lighted from his wing, and landed safe
  From out of Chaos to the outside bare
  Of this round world: with pins of adamant
  And chains they made all fast, too fast they made
320 And durable; and now in little space
  The confines° met of empyrean Heav'n   *boundaries*
  And of this world, and on the left hand Hell
  With long reach interposed; three sev'ral ways
  In sight, to each of these three places led.¹
325 And now their way to earth they had descried,°   *perceived*
  To Paradise first tending, when behold
  Satan in likeness of an angel bright
  Betwixt the Centaur and the Scorpion² steering
  His zenith, while the sun in Aries rose:
330 Disguised he came, but those his children dear
  Their parent soon discerned, though in disguise.
  He, after Eve seduced, unminded° slunk   *unnoticed*
  Into the wood fast by, and changing shape
  To observe the sequel, saw his guileful act
335 By Eve, though all unweeting,° seconded   *unaware*
  Upon her husband, saw their shame that sought
  Vain covertures;° but when he saw descend   *garments*
  The Son of God to judge them, terrified
  He fled, not hoping to escape, but shun
340 The present, fearing guilty what his wrath
  Might suddenly inflict; that past, returned
  By night, and list'ning where the hapless pair
  Sat in their sad discourse, and various plaint,
  Thence gathered his own doom, which understood
345 Not instant, but of future time.³ With joy
  And tidings fraught, to Hell he now returned,
  And at the brink of Chaos, near the foot
  Of this new wondrous pontifice,° unhoped   *bridge*
  Met who to meet him came, his offspring dear.
350 Great joy was at their meeting, and at sight
  Of that stupendous bridge his joy increased.
  Long he admiring stood, till Sin, his fair
  Enchanting daughter, thus the silence broken:
   "O parent, these are thy magnific deeds,

---

9. Bridge-building, with a pun on "papal" (the pope had the title "pontifex maximus").
1. The golden staircase or chain linking the universe to Heaven, the new bridge linking it to Hell, and the passage through the spheres down to earth.
2. Satan steered between Sagittarius ("the Centaur") and Scorpio, thereby passing through Anguis, the constellation of the Serpent.
3. This evidently refers to the plaints and discourse of Adam and Eve (lines 720–1104 below), which therefore precede Satan's return to Hell (lines 345–609).

	Thy trophies,[4] which thou view'st as not thine own,	
355	Thou art their author and prime architect:	
	For I no sooner in my heart divined,	
	My heart, which by a secret harmony	
	Still moves with thine, joined in connection sweet,	
360	That thou on earth hadst prospered, which thy looks	
	Now also evidence, but straight° I felt	*at once*
	Though distant from thee worlds between, yet felt	
	That I must after thee with this thy son;	
	Such fatal consequence[5] unites us three:	
365	Hell could no longer hold us in her bounds,	
	Nor this unvoyageable gulf obscure	
	Detain from following thy illustrious track.	
	Thou hast achieved our liberty, confined	
	Within Hell gates till now, thou us empow'red	
370	To fortify thus far, and overlay	
	With this portentous° bridge the dark abyss.	*marvelous, ominous*
	Thine now is all this world, thy virtue° hath won	*power, courage*
	What thy hands builded not, thy wisdom gained	
	With odds° what war hath lost, and fully avenged	*advantage*
375	Our foil in Heav'n; here thou shalt monarch reign,	
	There didst not; there let him still victor sway,	
	As battle hath adjudged, from this new world	
	Retiring, by his own doom alienated,	
	And henceforth monarchy with thee divide	
380	Of all things parted by th' empyreal bounds,	
	His quadrature, from thy orbicular world,[6]	
	Or try° thee now more dangerous to his throne."	*discover by experience*
	Whom thus the Prince of Darkness answered glad:	
	"Fair daughter, and thou son and grandchild both,	
385	High proof ye now have giv'n to be the race	
	Of Satan (for I glory in the name,	
	Antagonist[7] of Heav'n's Almighty King)	
	Amply have merited of me, of all	
	Th' infernal empire, that so near Heav'n's door	
390	Triumphal with triumphal act[8] have met,	
	Mine with this glorious work, and made one realm	
	Hell and this world, one realm, one continent	
	Of easy thoroughfare. Therefore while I	
	Descend through darkness, on your road with ease	
395	To my associate powers, them to acquaint	
	With these successes, and with them rejoice,	
	You two this way, among those numerous orbs	
	All yours, right down to Paradise descend;	

4. Objects or persons captured in battle were displayed in the Triumphs accorded Roman generals and emperors who had won a great military victory; the term casts Satan's conquests in Eden in such terms.
5. Connection of cause and effect.
6. Revelation 21:16 describes the City of God as "foursquare, and the length is as large as the breadth"; Satan's new conquest, earth, is an orb. Sin may imply its superiority (being a sphere).
7. The name "Satan" means "adversary" or "antagonist."
8. The repeated word emphasizes that Satan is enacting a Triumph, passing over a triumphal bridge rather than through triumphal arches; the scene would likely evoke the "Roman" Triumph and triumphal arches celebrating the Restoration of Charles II.

There dwell and reign in bliss, thence on the earth
Dominion exercise and in the air,
Chiefly on man, sole lord of all declared,
Him first make sure your thrall,° and lastly kill.   *slave*
My substitutes I send ye, and create
Plenipotent° on earth, of matchless might   *with full power*
Issuing from me: on your joint vigor now
My hold of this new kingdom all depends,
Through Sin to Death exposed by my exploit.
If your joint power prevail, th' affairs of Hell
No detriment need fear, go and be strong."
    So saying he dismissed them, they with speed
Their course through thickest constellations held
Spreading their bane;° the blasted° stars looked wan,   *poison / ruined*
And planets, planet-strook,[9] real eclipse
Then suffered. Th' other way Satan went down
The causey° to Hell gate; on either side   *causeway*
Disparted Chaos over-built exclaimed,
And with rebounding surge the bars assailed,
That scorned his indignation.[1] Through the gate,
Wide open and unguarded, Satan passed,
And all about found desolate; for those[2]
Appointed to sit there, had left their charge,
Flown to the upper world; the rest were all
Far to the inland retired, about the walls
Of Pandemonium, city and proud seat
Of Lucifer, so by allusion° called,   *metaphor*
Of that bright star to Satan paragoned.[3]
There kept their watch the legions, while the grand[4]
In council sat, solicitous° what chance   *anxious*
Might intercept their emperor sent, so he
Departing gave command, and they observed.
As when the Tartar from his Russian foe
By Astracan over the snowy plains
Retires, or Bactrian Sophi from the horns
Of Turkish crescent, leaves all waste beyond
The realm of Aladule, in his retreat
To Tauris or Casbeen:[5] so these the late
Heav'n-banished host, left desert utmost Hell
Many a dark league, reduced° in careful watch   *drawn together*
Round their metropolis, and now expecting
Each hour their great adventurer from the search
Of foreign worlds: he through the midst unmarked,°   *unnoticed*

---

9. Suffering not merely a temporary eclipse but a real loss of light, as from the malign influence of an adverse planet.
1. Chaos is the instinctive enemy of all order, so hostile to the bridge built over it.
2. Sin and Death.
3. Satan before his fall was Lucifer, the Light-bringer, and the morning star is named Lucifer because it is compared ("paragoned") to him.
4. The "grand infernal peers" who govern (see 2.507).

5. The simile, begun in line 431, compares the fallen angels, withdrawn from other regions of Hell to guard their metropolis, to Tartars retiring before attacking Russians and Persians retreating before the attacking Turks. "Astracan": a region west of the Caspian Sea inhabited by Russia and defended against Turks and Tartars; "Aladule": the region of Armenia, from which the last Persian ruler, called Anadule, a "Bactrian Sophi" (Persian shah), was forced to retreat from the Turks, to Tabriz ("Tauris") and Kazvin ("Casbeen").

In show plebeian angel militant
Of lowest order, passed; and from the door
Of that Plutonian⁶ hall, invisible
Ascended his high throne, which under state°   *canopy*
Of richest texture spread, at th' upper end
Was placed in regal luster. Down a while
He sat, and round about him saw unseen:
At last as from a cloud his fulgent head
And shape star-bright appeared, or brighter, clad
With what permissive° glory since his fall   *permitted*
Was left him, or false glitter: all amazed
At that so sudden blaze the Stygian⁷ throng
Bent their aspéct, and whom they wished beheld,
Their mighty chief returned: loud was th' acclaim:
Forth rushed in haste the great consulting peers,
Raised from their dark divan,⁸ and with like joy
Congratulant approached him, who with hand
Silence, and with these words attention won:
 "Thrones, Dominations, Princedoms, Virtues, Powers,
For in possession such, not only of right,
I call ye⁹ and declare ye now, returned
Successful beyond hope, to lead ye forth
Triumphant out of this infernal pit
Abominable, accurst, the house of woe,
And dungeon of our tyrant: now possess,
As lords, a spacious world, to our native Heaven
Little inferior, by my adventure hard
With peril great achieved. Long were to tell
What I have done, what suffered, with what pain
Voyaged th' unreal,° vast, unbounded deep   *unformed*
Of horrible confusion, over which
By Sin and Death a broad way now is paved
To expedite your glorious march; but I
Toiled out my uncouth° passage, forced to ride   *strange*
Th' untractable abyss, plunged in the womb
Of unoriginal¹ Night and Chaos wild,
That jealous of their secrets fiercely opposed
My journey strange, with clamorous uproar
Protesting Fate² supreme; thence how I found
The new-created world, which fame in Heav'n
Long had foretold, a fabric wonderful
Of absolute perfection, therein man
Placed in a paradise, by our exile
Made happy: him by fraud I have seduced
From his Creator, and the more to increase
Your wonder, with an apple. He thereat
Offended, worth your laughter, hath giv'n up
Both his beloved man and all his world,

---

6. Pertaining to Pluto, ruler of the classical underworld.
7. Of the river Styx in Hades, the river of hate.
8. The Turkish Council of State.
9. That is, you now have these titles not only by right but by possession (from the conquest on earth).
1. Having no origin, uncreated.
2. Protesting both to and against Fate.

To Sin and Death a prey, and so to us,
Without our hazard, labor, or alarm,
To range in, and to dwell, and over man
To rule, as over all he should have ruled.
True is, me also he hath judged, or rather
Me not, but the brute serpent in whose shape
Man I deceived; that which to me belongs,
Is enmity, which he will put between
Me and mankind; I am to bruise his heel;
His seed, when is not set, shall bruise my head:
A world who would not purchase with a bruise,
Or much more grievous pain? Ye have th' account
Of my performance: what remains, ye gods,
But up and enter now into full bliss."³
    So having said, a while he stood, expecting
Their universal shout and high applause
To fill his ear, when contrary he hears
On all sides, from innumerable tongues
A dismal universal hiss, the sound
Of public scorn; he wondered, but not long
Had leisure, wond'ring at himself now more;
His visage drawn he felt to sharp and spare,
His arms clung to his ribs, his legs entwining
Each other, till supplanted° down he fell   *tripped up*
A monstrous serpent on his belly prone,
Reluctant,° but in vain, a greater power   *struggling*
Now ruled him, punished in the shape he sinned,
According to his doom: he would have spoke,
But hiss for hiss returned with forkèd tongue
To forkèd tongue, for now were all transformed
Alike, to serpents⁴ all as accessories
To his bold riot:° dreadful was the din   *revolt*
Of hissing through the hall, thick swarming now
With complicated° monsters, head and tail,   *tangled*
Scorpion and asp, and amphisbaena dire,
Cerastes horned, hydrus, and ellops drear,
And dipsas⁵ (not so thick swarmed once the soil
Bedropped with blood of Gorgon, or the isle
Ophiusa)⁶ but still greatest he the midst,
Now dragon grown, larger than whom the sun
Engendered in the Pythian vale on slime,
Huge Python,⁷ and his power no less he seemed
Above the rest still to retain; they all

---

3. Ironically, the final word of Satan's proud, triumphal speech rhymes with and so prepares for the "hiss" (line 508) that will soon greet him, as his would-be triumph is turned by God to abject humiliation.
4. The scene recalls Dante's vivid description of the thieves metamorphosed to snakes in *Inferno* 24–25.
5. The "scorpion" has a venomous sting at the tip of the tail; "asp" is a small Egyptian viper; "amphisbaena" supposedly had a head at each end; "Cerastes" is an asp with horny projections over each eye; "hydrus" and "ellops" were mythical water snakes; "dipsas" was a mythical snake whose bite caused raging thirst.
6. Drops of blood from the Gorgon Medusa's severed head turned into snakes; "Ophiusa" in Greek means "isle of snakes."
7. A gigantic serpent engendered from the slime left by Deucalion's flood; Apollo slew him and appropriated the "Pythian" vale and shrine at Delphi.

                Him followed issuing forth to th' open field,
                Where all yet left of that revolted rout
535   Heav'n-fall'n, in station stood or just array,⁸
                Sublime° with expectation when to see   *raised up*
                In triumph issuing forth their glorious chief;
                They saw, but other sight instead, a crowd
                Of ugly serpents; horror on them fell,
540   And horrid sympathy; for what they saw,
                They felt themselves now changing; down their arms,
                Down fell both spear and shield, down they as fast,
                And the dire hiss renewed, and the dire form
                Catched by contagion, like in punishment,
545   As in their crime. Thus was th' applause they meant,
                Turned to exploding hiss, triumph to shame
                Cast on themselves from their own mouths. There stood
                A grove hard by, sprung up with this their change,
                His will who reigns above, to aggravate
550   Their penance,° laden with fair fruit, like that   *punishment*
                Which grew in Paradise, the bait of Eve
                Used by the Tempter: on that prospect strange
                Their earnest eyes they fixed, imagining
                For one forbidden tree a multitude
555   Now ris'n, to work them further woe or shame;
                Yet parched with scalding thirst and hunger fierce,
                Though to delude them sent, could not abstain,
                But on they rolled in heaps, and up the trees
                Climbing, sat thicker than the snaky locks
560   That curled Megaera:⁹ greedily they plucked
                The fruitage fair to sight, like that which grew
                Near that bituminous lake where Sodom flamed;¹
                This more delusive, not the touch, but taste
                Deceived; they fondly° thinking to allay   *foolishly*
565   Their appetite with gust,° instead of fruit   *relish*
                Chewed bitter ashes, which th' offended taste
                With spattering noise rejected: oft they assayed,°   *attempted*
                Hunger and thirst constraining, drugged as oft,
                With hatefulest disrelish writhed their jaws
570   With soot and cinders filled; so oft they fell
                Into the same illusion, not as man
                Whom they triumphed once lapsed.² Thus were they plagued
                And worn with famine, long and ceaseless hiss,
                Till their lost shape, permitted, they resumed,³
575   Yearly enjoined, some say, to undergo
                This annual humbling certain numbered days,
                To dash their pride, and joy for man seduced.
                However some tradition they dispersed
                Among the heathen of their purchase° got,   *plunder*

---

8. That is, at their posts or on parade.
9. One of three Furies with snaky hair.
1. Sodom apples reputedly grew on the spot where the accursed city once stood, now the Dead Sea ("that bituminous lake"); the apples look good but dissolve into ashes when eaten.

2. Unlike man who fell once, they try to eat the dissolving apples over and over again.
3. God permitted them to regain their "lost shape" as fallen angels; but they are undergoing a slower, natural metamorphosis into grosser substance by their continuing commitment to and choice of evil.

And fabled how the serpent, whom they called
Ophion with Eurynome, the wide-
Encroaching Eve perhaps, had first the rule
Of high Olympus, thence by Saturn driv'n
And Ops, ere yet Dictaean Jove was born.[4]
Meanwhile in Paradise the hellish pair
Too soon arrived, Sin there in power before,
Once actual, now in body, and to dwell
Habitual habitant;[5] behind her Death
Close following pace for pace, not mounted yet
On his pale horse:[6] to whom Sin thus began:
   "Second of Satan sprung, all-conquering Death,
What think'st thou of our empire now, though earned
With travail° difficult, not better far   labor
Than still at Hell's dark threshold to have sat watch,
Unnamed, undreaded, and thyself half-starved?"
   Whom thus the Sin-born monster answered soon:
"To me, who with eternal famine pine,
Alike is Hell, or Paradise, or Heaven,
There best, where most with ravin° I may meet;   prey
Which here, though plenteous, all too little seems
To stuff this maw, this vast unhidebound corpse."[7]
   To whom th' incestuous mother thus replied:
"Thou therefore on these herbs, and fruits, and flow'rs
Feed first, on each beast next, and fish, and fowl,
No homely morsels, and whatever thing
Thy scythe of Time mows down, devour unspared,
Till I in man residing through the race,
His thoughts, his looks, words, actions all infect,
And season him thy last and sweetest prey."
   This said, they both betook them several ways,
Both to destroy, or unimmortal make
All kinds, and for destruction to mature
Sooner or later; which th' Almighty seeing,
From his transcendent seat the saints among,
To those bright orders uttered thus his voice:
   "See with what heat these dogs of Hell advance
To waste and havoc° yonder world, which I   plunder
So fair and good created, and had still
Kept in that state, had not the folly of man
Let in these wasteful furies, who impute
Folly to me, so doth the Prince of Hell
And his adherents, that with so much ease
I suffer them to enter and possess
A place so heav'nly, and conniving seem

---

4. The Titan Ophion (whose name means "snake") and his wife Eurynome ("the wide-reacher") ruled Olympus until driven away by "Saturn" and his wife Ops, who were in turn overthrown by Jove, who lived on the mountain Dicte. Milton suggests that these may represent versions of the story transmitted by the fallen angels to the pagans (lines 578–79).

5. Sin was present in Eden in the actual sins committed by Adam and Eve; now she will dwell there in her own body and in all other bodies.
6. See Revelation 6:8: "behold a pale horse: and his name that sat on him was Death, and Hell followed with him."
7. Its hide does not cling close to its bones: Death's hunger is such that it can never fill its skin.

> To gratify my scornful enemies, 625
> That laugh, as if transported with some fit
> Of passion, I to them had quitted all,° — *handed everything over*
> At random yielded up to their misrule;
> And know not that I called and drew them thither
> My hellhounds, to lick up the draff° and filth — *dregs* 630
> Which man's polluting sin with taint hath shed
> On what was pure, till crammed and gorged, nigh burst
> With sucked and glutted offal, at one sling
> Of thy victorious arm, well-pleasing Son,
> Both Sin, and Death, and yawning grave at last 635
> Through Chaos hurled, obstruct the mouth of Hell
> Forever, and seal up his ravenous jaws.
> Then Heav'n and earth renewed shall be made pure
> To sanctity that shall receive no stain:
> Till then the curse pronounced on both precedes."° — *takes precedence* 640
>   He ended, and the heav'nly audience loud
> Sung hallelujah, as the sound of seas,
> Through multitude that sung: "Just are thy ways,
> Righteous are thy decrees on all thy works;
> Who can extenuate° thee? Next, to the Son, — *disparage* 645
> Destined restorer of mankind, by whom
> New heav'n and earth shall to the ages rise,
> Or down from Heav'n descend." Such was their song,
> While the Creator calling forth by name
> His mighty angels gave them several charge, 650
> As sorted° best with present things. The sun — *suited*
> Had first his precept so to move, so shine,
> As might affect the earth with cold and heat
> Scarce tolerable, and from the north to call
> Decrepit winter, from the south to bring 655
> Solstitial summer's heat. To the blank° moon — *white, pale*
> Her office they prescribed, to th' other five
> Their planetary motions and aspécts[8]
> In sextile, square, and trine, and opposite,
> Of noxious efficacy, and when to join 660
> In synod° unbenign, and taught the fixed° — *conjunction / fixed stars*
> Their influence malignant when to show'r,
> Which of them rising with the sun, or falling,
> Should prove tempestuous:° to the winds they set — *productive of storms*
> Their corners, when with bluster to confound 665
> Sea, air, and shore, the thunder when to roll
> With terror through the dark aerial hall.
> Some say[9] he bid his angels turn askance
> The poles of earth twice ten degrees and more
> From the sun's axle; they with labor pushed 670
> Oblique the centric globe:° some say the sun — *the earth*

---

8. Astrological positions. The next line names positions of 60, 90, 120, and 180 degrees, respectively.

9. The poem offers both a Ptolemaic and a Copernican explanation of the shifts made in the cosmic order so as to change the prelapsarian eternal spring. The Copernican explanation (offered first) proposes that the earth's axis is now tilted (lines 668–71); the Ptolemaic explanation is that the plane of the sun's orbit is tilted (lines 671–78).

    Was bid turn reins from th' equinoctial road°   *the equator*
    Like distant breadth to Taurus[1] with the sev'n
    Atlantic Sisters, and the Spartan Twins
675 Up to the Tropic Crab; thence down amain°   *at full speed*
    By Leo and the Virgin and the Scales,
    As deep as Capricorn, to bring in change
    Of seasons to each clime; else° had the spring   *otherwise*
    Perpetual smiled on earth with vernant° flow'rs,   *spring*
680 Equal in days and nights, except to those
    Beyond the polar circles; to them day
    Had unbenighted° shone, while the low sun   *without any night*
    To recompense his distance, in their sight
    Had rounded still° th' horizon, and not known   *always*
685 Or° east or west, which had forbid the snow   *either*
    From cold Estotiland, and south as far
    Beneath Magellan.[2] At that tasted fruit
    The sun, as from Thyestean banquet, turned
    His course intended;[3] else how had the world
690 Inhabited, though sinless, more than now,
    Avoided pinching cold and scorching heat?
    These changes in the heav'ns, though slow, produced
    Like change on sea and land, sideral blast,[4]
    Vapor, and mist, and exhalation hot,
695 Corrupt and pestilent: now from the north
    Of Norumbega, and the Samoed shore
    Bursting their brazen dungeon, armed with ice
    And snow and hail and stormy gust and flaw,°   *squall*
    Boreas and Caecias and Argestes loud
700 And Thrascias rend the woods and seas upturn;
    With adverse blast upturns them from the south
    Notus and Afer black with thund'rous clouds
    From Serraliona,[5] thwart of these as fierce
    Forth rush the Levant and the ponent° winds   *opposing*
705 Eurus and Zephyr with their lateral noise,
    Sirocco and Libecchio.[6] Thus began
    Outrage from lifeless things; but Discord first
    Daughter of Sin, among th' irrational,
    Death introduced through fierce antipathy:[7]
710 Beast now with beast gan war, and fowl with fowl,
    And fish with fish; to graze the herb° all leaving,   *grass*
    Devour'd each other; nor stood much in awe

---

1. Lines 673–78 trace the sun's apparent (Ptolemaic) journey from Aries through Taurus and the rest of the zodiac over the course of the year.
2. The region of the Straits of Magellan, at the tip of South America. "Estotiland" (line 686): northern Labrador.
3. As a revenge, Atreus killed one of the sons of his brother Thyestes and served him in a banquet to that brother; the sun changed course to avoid the sight.
4. Malevolent stellar influences. "Norumbega" (line 696): northern New England and maritime Canada; "Samoed" Shore: northeastern Siberia.
5. Winds (701–6) from the south ("Notus," "Afer") come from Sierra Leone ("Serraliona") on the west coast of Africa; "Boreas," "Caecias," "Argestes," and "Thrascias" are all winds that blow from the north, northeast, and northwest, bursting from the cave ("brazen dungeon") in which Aeolus imprisoned the winds (lines 695–700).
6. Crossing the north and south winds ("thwart," line 703) are the "Levant" (from the east) and "Eurus" (east southeast), from the west "Zephyr," the west wind; "Sirocco" and "Libecchio" come from the southeast and southwest, respectively.
7. Discord (personified as daughter of Sin) introduced Death among the animals ("th' irrational") by stirring up "antipathy" among them.

Of man, but fled him, or with count'nance grim
Glared on him passing: these were from without
715 The growing miseries, which Adam saw
Already in part, though hid in gloomiest shade,
To sorrow abandoned, but worse felt within,
And in a troubled sea of passion tossed,
Thus to disburden sought with sad complaint:
720 "O miserable of happy!⁸ Is this the end
Of this new glorious world, and me so late
The glory of that glory, who now become
Accurst of blessèd, hide me from the face
Of God, whom to behold was then my height
725 Of happiness: yet well, if here would end
The misery, I deserved it, and would bear
My own deservings; but this will not serve;
All that I eat or drink, or shall beget,
Is propagated⁹ curse. O voice once heard
730 Delightfully, 'Increase and multiply,'
Now death to hear! For what can I increase
Or multiply, but curses on my head?
Who of all ages to succeed, but feeling
The evil on him brought by me, will curse
735 My head: 'Ill fare our ancestor impure,
For this we may thank Adam'; but his thanks
Shall be the execration; so besides
Mine own that bide upon me, all from me
Shall with a fierce reflux on me redound,
740 On me as on their natural center light
Heavy, though in their place.¹ O fleeting joys
Of Paradise, dear bought with lasting woes!
Did I request thee, Maker, from my clay
To mold me man, did I solicit thee
745 From darkness to promote me, or here place
In this delicious garden? As my will
Concurred not to my being, it were but right
And equal° to reduce me to my dust,   *just*
Desirous to resign, and render back
750 All I received, unable to perform
Thy terms too hard, by which I was to hold
The good I sought not. To the loss of that,
Sufficient penalty, why hast thou added
The sense of endless woes? Inexplicable
755 Thy justice seems; yet to say truth, too late
I thus contest; then should have been refused
Those terms whatever, when they were proposed:
Thou² didst accept them; wilt thou enjoy the good,

---

8. Adam's complaint begins with the classical formula for a tragic fall, or *peripeteia*, the change from happiness to misery.
9. Handed down from one generation to the next.
1. That is, Adam's "own" curse will remain ("bide") with him, and the curse ("execration") of "all" who descend from him will "redound" on him as to their "natural center"; objects so placed ("in their place") were thought to be weightless ("light"), but these curses will be "heavy."
2. Adam turns from addressing God to address himself.

           Then cavil° the conditions? And though God   object frivolously to
760   Made thee without thy leave, what if thy son
       Prove disobedient, and reproved, retort,
       'Wherefore didst thou beget me? I sought it not':
       Wouldst thou admit for his contempt of thee
       That proud excuse? Yet him not thy election,°   choice
765   But natural necessity begot.
       God made thee of choice his own, and of his own
       To serve him, thy reward was of his grace,
       Thy punishment then justly is at his will.
       Be it so, for I submit, his doom is fair,
770   That dust I am, and shall to dust return:
       O welcome hour whenever! Why delays
       His hand to execute what his decree
       Fixed on this day? Why do I overlive,
       Why am I mocked with death, and lengthened out
775   To deathless pain? How gladly would I meet
       Mortality my sentence, and be earth
       Insensible, how glad would lay me down
       As in my mother's lap! There I should rest
       And sleep secure; his dreadful voice no more
780   Would thunder in my ears, no fear of worse
       To me and to my offspring would torment me
       With cruel expectation. Yet one doubt
       Pursues me still, lest all I° cannot die,   all of me
       Lest that pure breath of life, the spirit of man
785   Which God inspired, cannot together perish
       With this corporeal clod; then in the grave,
       Or in some other dismal place, who knows
       But I shall die a living death? O thought
       Horrid, if true! Yet why? It was but breath
790   Of life that sinned; what dies but what had life
       And sin? The body properly hath neither.
       All of me then shall die:³ let this appease
       The doubt, since human reach no further knows.
       For though the Lord of all be infinite,
795   Is his wrath also? Be it, man is not so,
       But mortal doomed. How can he exercise
       Wrath without end on man whom death must end?
       Can he make deathless death? That were to make
       Strange contradiction, which to God himself
800   Impossible is held, as argument
       Of weakness, not of power. Will he draw out,
       For anger's sake, finite to infinite
       In punished man, to satisfy his rigor
       Satisfied never; that were to extend
805   His sentence beyond dust and nature's law,
       By which all causes else according still

---

3. After debating the matter, Adam concludes that the soul dies with the body; Milton in his *Christian Doctrine* worked out this "mortalist" doctrine, with its corollary, that both soul and body rise at the Last Judgment.

To the reception of their matter act,
Not to th' extent of their own sphere.[4] But say
That death be not one stroke, as I supposed,
810 Bereaving° sense, but endless misery   *taking away*
From this day onward, which I feel begun
Both in me, and without° me, and so last   *outside of*
To perpetuity; ay me, that fear
Comes thund'ring back with dreadful revolution°   *return*
815 On my defenseless head; both Death and I
Am found eternal, and incorporate° both,   *made one body*
Nor I on my part single, in me all
Posterity stands cursed: fair patrimony
That I must leave ye, sons; O were I able
820 To waste it all myself, and leave ye none!
So disinherited how would ye bless
Me now your curse! Ah, why should all mankind
For one man's fault thus guiltless be condemned,
If guiltless? But from me what can proceed,
825 But all corrupt, both mind and will depraved,
Not to do° only, but to will the same   *act*
With me? How can they then acquitted stand
In sight of God? Him after all disputes
Forced I absolve: all my evasions vain
830 And reasonings, though through mazes, lead me still
But to my own conviction: first and last
On me, me only, as the source and spring
Of all corruption, all the blame lights due;
So might the wrath.[5] Fond° wish! Couldst thou support   *foolish*
835 That burden heavier than the earth to bear,
Than all the world much heavier, though divided
With that bad woman? Thus what thou desir'st,
And what thou fear'st, alike destroys all hope
Of refuge, and concludes thee miserable
840 Beyond all past example and future,
To Satan only like both crime and doom.
O conscience, into what abyss of fears
And horrors hast thou driv'n me; out of which
I find no way, from deep to deeper plunged!"
845   Thus Adam to himself lamented loud
Through the still night, not now, as ere man fell,
Wholesome and cool, and mild, but with black air
Accompanied, with damps° and dreadful gloom,   *noxious vapors*
Which to his evil conscience represented
850 All things with double terror: on the ground
Outstretched he lay, on the cold ground, and oft
Cursed his creation, Death as oft accused
Of tardy execution, since denounced°   *pronounced*
The day of his offense: "Why comes not Death,"

---

4. Adam convinces himself that "finite" matter (line 802) cannot suffer "infinite" punishment by an axiom of traditional philosophy, that by "nature's law" (line 805) the actions of agents are limited by the nature of the object they act upon.
5. See the Son's offer to accept all humankind's guilt (3.236–41), and Eve's similar offer (10.933–36).

Said he, "with one thrice-accéptáble stroke
To end me? Shall Truth fail to keep her word,
Justice divine not hasten to be just?
But Death comes not at call, Justice divine
Mends not her slowest pace for prayers or cries.
O woods, O fountains, hillocks, dales, and bow'rs,
With other echo late I taught your shades
To answer, and resound far other song."[6]
Whom thus afflicted when sad Eve beheld,
Desolate where she sat, approaching nigh,
Soft words to his fierce passion she assayed;°   *attempted*
But her with stern regard he thus repelled:
   "Out of my sight, thou serpent,[7] that name best
Befits thee with him leagued, thyself as false
And hateful; nothing wants,° but that thy shape,   *is lacking*
Like his, and color serpentine may show
Thy inward fraud, to warn all creatures from thee
Henceforth; lest that too heav'nly form, pretended[8]
To hellish falsehood, snare them. But° for thee   *except*
I had persisted happy, had not thy pride
And wand'ring vanity, when least was safe,
Rejected my forewarning, and disdained
Not to be trusted, longing to be seen
Though by the Devil himself, him overweening°   *overconfident*
To overreach, but with the serpent meeting
Fooled and beguiled, by him thou, I by thee,
To trust thee from my side, imagined wise,
Constant, mature, proof against all assaults,
And understood not all was but a show
Rather than solid virtue, all but a rib
Crooked by nature, bent, as now appears,
More to the part siníster° from me drawn,   *the left side*
Well if thrown out, as supernumerary
To my just number found.[9] O why did God,
Creator wise, that peopled highest heav'n
With Spirits masculine,[1] create at last
This novelty on earth, this fair defect
Of nature,[2] and not fill the world at once
With men as angels without feminine,
Or find some other way to generate
Mankind? This mischief had not then befall'n,
And more that shall befall, innumerable
Disturbances on earth through female snares,
And strait conjunction[3] with this sex: for either
He never shall find out fit mate, but such

---

6. See their morning hymn (5.153–208).
7. Adam's bitter, misogynistic outcry begins with reference to the patristic notion that the name Eve, aspirated, means "serpent."
8. Held in front, as a cover or mask.
9. It was supposed that Adam had thirteen ribs on the left side, so he could spare one for the creation of Eve and still retain the proper ("just") number, twelve.
1. The Miltonic bard indicated that angels can assume at will "either sex . . . or both" (1.424).
2. Aristotle had claimed that the female is a defective male.
3. Close, hard-pressing, binding union: Adam then projects the problems of future marriages.

	As some misfortune brings him, or mistake,	
900	As some misfortune brings him, or mistake,	
	Or whom he wishes most shall seldom gain	
	Through her perverseness, but shall see her gained	
	By a far worse, or if she love, withheld	
	By parents, or his happiest choice too late	
905	Shall meet, already linked and wedlock-bound	
	To a fell° adversary, his hate or shame:	*bitter*
	Which infinite calamity shall cause	
	To human life, and household peace confound."	
	He added not, and from her turned, but Eve	
910	Not so repulsed, with tears that ceased not flowing,	
	And tresses all disordered, at his feet	
	Fell humble, and embracing them, besought	
	His peace, and thus proceeded in her plaint:	
	"Forsake me not thus, Adam, witness Heav'n	
915	What love sincere, and reverence in my heart	
	I bear thee, and unweeting° have offended,	*unintentionally*
	Unhappily deceived; thy suppliant	
	I beg, and clasp thy knees;[4] bereave me not,	
	Whereon I live, thy gentle looks, thy aid,	
920	Thy counsel in this uttermost distress,	
	My only strength and stay: forlorn of thee,	
	Whither shall I betake me, where subsist?	
	While yet we live, scarce one short hour perhaps,	
	Between us two let there be peace, both joining,	
925	As joined in injuries, one enmity	
	Against a foe by doom express° assigned us,	*explicit judgment*
	That cruel serpent: on me exercise not	
	Thy hatred for this misery befall'n,	
	On me already lost, me than thyself	
930	More miserable; both have sinned, but thou	
	Against God only, I against God and thee,	
	And to the place of judgment will return,	
	There with my cries importune Heaven, that all	
	The sentence from thy head removed may light	
935	On me, sole cause to thee of all this woe,	
	Me me only just object of his ire."[5]	
	She ended weeping, and her lowly plight,°	*posture*
	Immovable till peace obtained from fault	
	Acknowledged and deplored, in Adam wrought	
940	Commiseration; soon his heart relented	
	Towards her, his life so late and sole delight,	
	Now at his feet submissive in distress,	
	Creature so fair his reconcilement seeking,	
	His counsel whom she had displeased, his aid;	
945	As one disarmed, his anger all he lost,	
	And thus with peaceful words upraised her soon:	
	"Unwary, and too desirous, as before,	
	So now of what thou know'st not, who desir'st	

---

4. Eve assumes the posture of the classical suppliant, clasping the knees of the one she begs from.

5. Eve also echoes the Son's offer (3.236–41). Compare Adam's cry (10.832–34).

The punishment all on thyself; alas!
Bear thine own first, ill able to sustain
His full wrath whose thou feel'st as yet least part,
And my displeasure bear'st so ill.[6] If prayers
Could alter high decrees, I to that place
Would speed before thee, and be louder heard,
That on my head all might be visited,
Thy frailty and infirmer sex forgiv'n,
To me committed and by me exposed.
But rise, let us no more contend, nor blame
Each other, blamed enough elsewhere, but strive
In offices of love, how we may light'n
Each other's burden in our share of woe;
Since this day's death denounced, if aught I see,
Will prove no sudden, but a slow-paced evil,
A long day's dying to augment our pain,
And to our seed (O hapless seed!) derived."   *passed on*
  To whom thus Eve, recovering heart, replied:
"Adam, by sad experiment I know
How little weight my words with thee can find,
Found so erroneous, thence by just event°   *consequence*
Found so unfortunate; nevertheless,
Restored by thee, vile as I am, to place
Of new acceptance, hopeful to regain
Thy love, the sole contentment of my heart
Living or dying, from thee I will not hide
What thoughts in my unquiet breast are ris'n,
Tending to some relief of our extremes,
Or end, though sharp and sad, yet tolerable,
As in our evils, and of easier choice.
If care of our descent perplex us most,[7]
Which must be born to certain woe, devoured
By Death at last, and miserable it is
To be to others cause of misery,
Our own begotten, and of our loins to bring
Into this cursèd world a woeful race,
That after wretched life must be at last
Food for so foul a monster, in thy power
It lies, yet ere conception to prevent
The race unblest, to being yet unbegot.
Childless thou art, childless remain; so Death
Shall be deceived° his glut, and with us two   *cheated of*
Be forced to satisfy his rav'nous maw.
But if thou judge it hard and difficult,
Conversing, looking, loving, to abstain
From love's due rites, nuptial embraces sweet,
And with desire to languish without hope,
Before the present object[8] languishing

---

6. That is, you could hardly bear God's "full wrath" since you are so distraught when you feel only the smallest part of it, and you can "ill" bear my displeasure.

7. That is, if concern for our descendants most torment ("perplex") us.

8. That is, Eve herself, who then projects her own frustrated desire if they were to forgo sex.

With like desire, which would be misery
And torment less than none of what we dread,
Then both ourselves and seed at once to free
From what we fear for both, let us make short,°   *lose no time*
Let us seek Death, or he not found, supply
With our own hands his office on ourselves;
Why stand we longer shivering under fears,
That show no end but death, and have the power,
Of many ways to die the shortest choosing,
Destruction with destruction to destroy."
    She ended here, or vehement despair
Broke off the rest; so much of death her thoughts
Had entertained, as dyed her cheeks with pale.
But Adam with such counsel nothing swayed,
To better hopes his more attentive mind
Laboring had raised, and thus to Eve replied.
    "Eve thy contempt of life and pleasure seems
To argue in thee something more sublime
And excellent than what thy mind contemns;°   *despises*
But self-destruction therefore sought, refutes
That excellence thought in thee, and implies,
Not thy contempt, but anguish and regret
For loss of life and pleasure overloved.
Or if thou covet death, as utmost end
Of misery, so thinking to evade
The penalty pronounced, doubt not but God
Hath wiselier armed his vengeful ire than so
To be forestalled; much more I fear lest death
So snatched will not exempt us from the pain
We are by doom to pay: rather such acts
Of contumácy° will provoke the Highest   *contempt*
To make death in us live. Then let us seek
Some safer resolution, which methinks
I have in view, calling to mind with heed
Part of our sentence, that thy seed shall bruise
The serpent's head; piteous amends, unless
Be meant, whom I conjecture, our grand foe
Satan, who in the serpent hath contrived
Against us this deceit: to crush his head
Would be revenge indeed; which will be lost
By death brought on ourselves, or childless days
Resolved, as thou proposest; so our foe
Shall scape his punishment ordained, and we
Instead shall double ours upon our heads.
No more be mentioned then of violence
Against ourselves, and willful barrenness,
That cuts us off from hope, and savors only
Rancor and pride, impatience and despite,
Reluctance° against God and his just yoke   *resistance*
Laid on our necks. Remember with what mild
And gracious temper he both heard and judged
Without wrath or reviling; we expected

Immediate dissolution, which we thought
Was meant by death that day, when lo, to thee
Pains only in childbearing were foretold,
And bringing forth, soon recompensed with joy,
Fruit of thy womb:[9] on me the curse aslope
Glanced on the ground,[1] with labor I must earn
My bread; what harm? Idleness had been worse;
My labor will sustain me; and lest cold
Or heat should injure us, his timely care
Hath unbesought provided, and his hands
Clothed us unworthy, pitying while he judged;
How much more, if we pray him, will his ear
Be open, and his heart to pity incline,
And teach us further by what means to shun
Th' inclement seasons, rain, ice, hail, and snow,
Which now the sky with various face begins
To show us in this mountain, while the winds
Blow moist and keen, shattering° the graceful locks   *scattering*
Of these fair spreading trees; which bids us seek
Some better shroud,° some better warmth to cherish   *shelter*
Our limbs benumbed, ere this diurnal star°   *the sun*
Leave cold the night, how we his gathered beams
Reflected, may with matter sere° foment,   *dry*
Or by collision of two bodies grind
The air attrite to fire,[2] as late the clouds
Justling or pushed with winds rude in their shock
Tine° the slant lightning, whose thwart° flame driv'n down   *ignite / slanting*
Kindles the gummy bark of fir or pine,
And sends a comfortable heat from far,
Which might supply° the sun: such fire to use,   *take the place of*
And what may else be remedy or cure
To evils which our own misdeeds have wrought,
He will instruct us praying, and of grace
Beseeching him, so as we need not fear
To pass commodiously this life, sustained
By him with many comforts, till we end
In dust, our final rest and native home.
What better can we do, than to the place
Repairing where he judged us, prostrate fall
Before him reverent, and there confess
Humbly our faults, and pardon beg, with tears
Watering the ground, and with our sighs the air
Frequenting,° sent from hearts contrite, in sign   *filling*
Of sorrow unfeigned, and humiliation meek.
Undoubtedly he will relent and turn
From his displeasure; in whose look serene,
When angry most he seemed and most severe,

---

9. Adam's prophetic echo of Elizabeth's address to Mary, mother of Jesus (Luke 1:41–42), "blessed is the fruit of thy womb," lays the ground for their fuller understanding of the promise about the "seed" of the woman.
1. That is, the curse, like a spear that almost missed its target, glanced aside and hit the ground.
2. Adam projects the invention of fire: they might, by striking two bodies together, rub ("attrite") the air into fire by friction; or else (lines 1070–71) focus reflected sunbeams (through some equivalent of glass) on dry ("sere") matter.

What else but favor, grace, and mercy shone?"
    So spake our father penitent, nor Eve
Felt less remorse: they forthwith to the place
Repairing where he judged them prostrate fell
Before him reverent, and both confessed
Humbly their faults, and pardon begged, with tears
Watering the ground, and with their sighs the air
Frequenting, sent from hearts contrite, in sign
Of sorrow unfeigned, and humiliation meek.[3]

Book 11

The Argument

The Son of God presents to his Father the prayers of our first parents now repenting, and intercedes for them: God accepts them, but declares that they must no longer abide in Paradise; sends Michael with a band of Cherubim to dispossess them; but first to reveal to Adam future things: Michael's coming down. Adam shows to Eve certain ominous signs; he discerns Michael's approach, goes out to meet him: the angel denounces their departure. Eve's lamentation. Adam pleads, but submits: the angel leads him up to a high hill, sets before him in vision what shall happen till the Flood.

Thus they in lowliest plight repentant stood[1]
Praying, for from the mercy-seat above
Prevenient grace[2] descending had removed
The stony from their hearts, and made new flesh
Regenerate grow instead, that sighs now breathed
Unutterable, which the spirit of prayer
Inspired, and winged for Heav'n with speedier flight
Than loudest oratory: yet their port
Not of mean suitors, nor important less
Seemed their petition, than when th' ancient pair
In fables old, less ancient yet than these,
Deucalion and chaste Pyrrha to restore
The race of mankind drowned, before the shrine
Of Themis stood devout.[3] To Heav'n their prayers
Flew up, nor missed the way, by envious winds
Blown vagabond or frustrate:[4] in they passed
Dimensionless through heav'nly doors; then clad
With incense, where the golden altar fumed,
By their great Intercessor, came in sight

---

3. The final six lines repeat, almost word for word, lines 1086–92, as the poet describes Adam's proposed gesture of repentance carried out in every detail.
1. "Stood" may mean "remained," or that, after prostrating themselves (10.1099) they prayed standing upright; their demeanor ("port") was "Not of mean suitors" (11.8–9), and they had stood to pray before (4.720).
2. Grace given before the human will can turn from sin, enabling it to do so.
3. In Greek myth, when Deucalion and his wife Pyrrha (like Noah's family) alone survived a universal flood, they sought direction from Themis, goddess of justice; she told them to throw stones behind them, which became men and women.
4. That is, their prayers were not scattered ("blown vagabond") by spiteful ("envious") winds, or prevented ("frustrate") from reaching their goal. "Dimensionless": without physical extension.

20 Before the Father's throne: them the glad° Son   *pleased*
    Presenting, thus to intercede began:
        "See Father, what firstfruits on earth are sprung
    From thy implanted grace in man, these sighs
    And prayers, which in this golden censer, mixed
25 With incense, I thy priest before thee bring,
    Fruits of more pleasing savor from thy seed
    Sown with contrition in his heart, than those
    Which his own hand manuring° all the trees   *cultivating*
    Of Paradise could have produced, ere fall'n
30 From innocence. Now therefore bend thine ear
    To supplication, hear his sighs though mute;
    Unskillful with what words to pray, let me
    Interpret for him, me his advocate
    And propitiation, all his works on me
35 Good or not good ingraft,[5] my merit those
    Shall perfect, and for these my death shall pay.
    Accept me, and in me from these receive
    The smell of peace toward mankind, let him live
    Before thee reconciled, at least his days
40 Numbered, though sad, till death, his doom (which I
    To mitigate thus plead, not to reverse)
    To better life shall yield him, where with me
    All my redeemed may dwell in joy and bliss,
    Made one with me as I with thee am one."
45   To whom the Father, without cloud, serene:
    "All thy request for man, accepted Son,
    Obtain, all thy request was my decree:
    But longer in that Paradise to dwell,
    The law I gave to nature him forbids:
50 Those pure immortal elements that know
    No gross, no unharmonious mixture foul,
    Eject him tainted now, and purge him off
    As a distemper, gross to air as gross,
    And mortal food,[6] as may dispose him best
55 For dissolution° wrought by sin, that first   *death*
    Distempered all things, and of incorrupt
    Corrupted. I at first with two fair gifts
    Created him endowed, with happiness
    And immortality: that fondly° lost,   *foolishly*
60 This other served but to eternize woe;
    Till I provided death; so death becomes
    His final remedy, and after life
    Tried in sharp tribulation, and refined
    By faith and faithful works, to second life,
65 Waked in the renovation[7] of the just,

---

5. The theological term for Christ's standing in the place of humankind, taking onto himself all their deeds, perfecting the good by his merit, and, by his death, "paying" (see next line) the debt due God's justice for their evil deeds.

6. The pure elements of the Garden of Eden will themselves "purge" Adam and Eve as an impurity or disorder ("distemper"), ejecting them to a place where the air and food are more gross, like themselves.

7. The resurrection and renewal of body and soul on the Last Day.

Resigns him up with Heav'n and earth renewed.
But let us call to synod° all the blest   *assembly*
Through Heav'n's wide bounds; from them I will not hide
My judgments, how with mankind I proceed,
70 As how with peccant° angels late they saw;   *sinning*
And in their state, though firm, stood more confirmed."
    He ended, and the Son gave signal high
To the bright minister that watched, he blew
His trumpet, heard in Oreb[8] since perhaps
75 When God descended, and perhaps once more
To sound at general doom. Th' angelic blast
Filled all the regions: from their blissful bow'rs
Of amarantine° shade, fountain or spring,   *unfading*
By the waters of life, where'er they sat
80 In fellowships of joy, the sons of light
Hasted, resorting to the summons high,
And took their seats; till from his throne supreme
Th' Almighty thus pronounced his sov'reign will:
    "O sons, like one of us man is become
85 To know both good and evil, since his taste
Of that defended° fruit; but let him boast   *forbidden*
His knowledge of good lost, and evil got,
Happier, had it sufficed him to have known
Good by itself, and evil not at all.
90 He sorrows now, repents, and prays contrite,
My motions° in him; longer than they move,   *promptings*
His heart I know, how variable and vain
Self-left.[9] Lest therefore his now bolder hand
Reach also of the Tree of Life, and eat,
95 And live forever, dream at least to live
Forever,[1] to remove him I decree,
And send him from the garden forth to till
The ground whence he was taken, fitter soil.
    "Michael, this my behest have thou in charge,
100 Take to thee from among the Cherubim
Thy choice of flaming warriors, lest the Fiend
Or° in behalf of man, or to invade   *either*
Vacant possession some new trouble raise:
Haste thee, and from the Paradise of God
105 Without remorse° drive out the sinful pair,   *pity*
From hallowed ground th' unholy, and denounce
To them and to their progeny from thence
Perpetual banishment. Yet lest they faint°   *lose courage*
At the sad sentence rigorously urged,
110 For I behold them softened and with tears
Bewailing their excess,° all terror hide.   *violation of law*

---

8. Where God delivered the Ten Commandments to the sound of a trumpet (Exodus 19:19); it will sound again at the Last Judgment ("general doom," line 76).
9. Left to itself, without my continual promptings ("motions," line 91), I know his heart to be "variable and vain."
1. Milton adds the phrase "dream at least to live forever" to suggest that parts of God's speech (especially lines 84–85 and 93–95, closely quoted from Genesis 3:22) are ironic.

>   If patiently thy bidding they obey,
>   Dismiss them not disconsolate; reveal
>   To Adam what shall come in future days,
> 115   As I shall thee enlighten,[2] intermix
>   My cov'nant in the woman's seed renewed;
>   So send them forth, though sorrowing, yet in peace:
>   And on the east side of the garden place,
>   Where entrance up from Eden easiest climbs,
> 120   Cherubic watch, and of a sword the flame
>   Wide-waving, all approach far off to fright,
>   And guard all passage to the Tree of Life:[3]
>   Lest Paradise a receptácle prove
>   To spirits foul, and all my trees their prey,
> 125   With whose stol'n fruit man once more to delude."
>   He ceased; and th' archangelic power prepared
>   For swift descent, with him the cohort bright
>   Of watchful Cherubim; four faces each[4]
>   Had, like a double Janus, all their shape
> 130   Spangled with eyes more numerous than those
>   Of Argus, and more wakeful than to drowse,
>   Charmed with Arcadian pipe, the pastoral reed
>   Of Hermes, or his opiate rod. Meanwhile
>   To resalute the world with sacred light
> 135   Leucóthea[5] waked, and with fresh dews embalmed
>   The earth, when Adam and first matron Eve
>   Had ended now their orisons, and found
>   Strength added from above, new hope to spring
>   Out of despair, joy, but with fear yet linked;
> 140   Which thus to Eve his welcome words renewed:
>   "Eve, easily may faith admit, that all
>   The good which we enjoy, from Heav'n descends;
>   But that from us aught should ascend to Heav'n
>   So prevalent° as to concern the mind   *influential*
> 145   Of God high-blest, or to incline his will,
>   Hard to belief may seem; yet this will prayer,
>   Or one short sigh of human breath, upborne
>   Ev'n to the seat of God. For since I sought
>   By prayer th' offended Deity to appease,
> 150   Kneeled and before him humbled all my heart,
>   Methought I saw him placable and mild,
>   Bending his ear; persuasion in me grew
>   That I was heard with favor; peace returned
>   Home to my breast, and to my memory

---

2. God, it seems, has to "enlighten" Michael with knowledge of humankind's future at the same time Michael presents that future to Adam (see 12.128); Michael is told to "intermix" in his account God's "cov'nant in the woman's seed" (lines 115–16), the "mysterious" promise of the redeemer hinted when the Son pronounced judgment on the serpent (10.179–81).
3. Compare Genesis 3:24: "he placed at the east of the garden of Eden Cherubims, and a flaming sword which turned every way, to keep the way of the tree of life."
4. Ezekiel 1:6 Janus (line 129), the Roman god of doorways, had two faces; in one version he had four, corresponding to the four seasons and the four quarters of the earth. Argus (line 131), a giant with one hundred eyes, was set by Juno to watch Jove's mistress Io, but Hermes (Mercury) put all of his eyes to sleep with his music ("pipe") and his sleep-producing caduceus ("opiate rod").
5. Roman goddess of the dawn.

His promise, that thy seed shall bruise our foe;
Which then not minded in dismay, yet now
Assures me that the bitterness of death
Is past, and we shall live. Whence hail to thee,
Eve rightly called, mother of all mankind,
Mother of all things living, since by thee
Man is to live, and all things live for man."[6]
    To whom thus Eve with sad demeanor meek:
"Ill-worthy I such title should belong
To me transgressor, who for thee ordained
A help, became thy snare; to me reproach
Rather belongs, distrust and all dispraise:
But infinite in pardon was my Judge,
That I who first brought death on all, am graced
The source of life; next favorable thou,
Who highly thus to entitle me vouchsaf'st,
Far other name deserving. But the field
To labor calls us now with sweat imposed,
Though after sleepless night; for see the morn,
All unconcerned with our unrest, begins
Her rosy progress smiling; let us forth,
I never from thy side henceforth to stray,
Where'er our day's work lies, though now enjoined
Laborious, till day droop; while here we dwell,
What can be toilsome in these pleasant walks?
Here let us live, though in fall'n state, content."
    So spake, so wished much-humbled Eve, but fate
Subscribed not; nature first gave signs,° impressed   *omens*
On bird, beast, air, air suddenly eclipsed°   *darkened*
After short blush of morn; nigh in her sight
The bird of Jove, stooped from his airy tow'r,[7]
Two birds of gayest plume before him drove:
Down from a hill the beast that reigns in woods,[8]
First hunter then, pursued a gentle brace,°   *pair*
Goodliest of all the forest, hart and hind;
Direct to th' eastern gate was bent their flight.
Adam observed, and with his eye the chase
Pursuing, not unmoved to Eve thus spake:
    "O Eve, some further change awaits us nigh,
Which Heaven by these mute signs in nature shows
Forerunners of his purpose, or to warn
Us haply too secure° of our discharge   *overconfident*
From penalty, because from death released
Some days; how long, and what till then our life,
Who knows, or more than this, that we are dust,
And thither must return and be no more.
Why else this double object in our sight
Of flight pursued in th' air and o'er the ground

---

6. The name Eve is cognate with the Hebrew word meaning "life." In Genesis 3:20 Adam names his wife Eve only after the Fall; Milton's Adam has named her before (4.481) and now affirms that that name is right.
7. The eagle swooped ("stooped") from his soaring flight ("tow'r").
8. The lion.

> One way the selfsame hour? Why in the east
> Darkness ere day's mid-course, and morning light
> More orient° in yon western cloud that draws   *bright*
> O'er the blue firmament a radiant white,
> And slow descends, with something heav'nly fraught."°   *laden*
>   He erred not, for by this° the heav'nly bands   *by this time*
> Down from a sky of jasper lighted° now   *alighted, shone*
> In Paradise, and on a hill made alt,°   *halt*
> A glorious apparition, had not doubt
> And carnal fear that day dimmed Adam's eye.
> Not that more glorious, when the angels met
> Jacob in Mahanaim,[9] where he saw
> The field pavilioned with his guardians bright;
> Nor that which on the flaming mount appeared
> In Dothan, covered with a camp of fire,
> Against the Syrian king, who to surprise
> One man, assassin-like had levied war,
> War unproclaimed.[1] The princely hierarch[2]
> In their bright stand, there left his powers to seize
> Possession of the garden; he alone,
> To find where Adam sheltered, took his way,
> Not unperceived of Adam, who to Eve,
> While the great visitant approached, thus spake:
>   "Eve, now expect great tidings, which perhaps
> Of us will soon determine,° or impose   *make an end*
> New laws to be observed; for I descry
> From yonder blazing cloud that veils the hill
> One of the heav'nly host, and by his gait
> None of the meanest, some great potentate
> Or of the Thrones above, such majesty
> Invests him coming; yet not terrible,
> That I should fear, nor sociably mild,
> As Raphael, that I should much confide,
> But solemn and sublime, whom not to offend,
> With reverence I must meet, and thou retire."
> He ended; and th' Archangel soon drew nigh,
> Not in his shape celestial, but as man
> Clad to meet man; over his lucid arms
> A military vest of purple flowed
> Livelier than Meliboean, or the grain
> Of Sarra,[3] worn by kings and heroes old
> In time of truce; Iris[4] had dipped the woof;
> His starry helm unbuckled showed him prime
> In manhood where youth ended; by his side
> As in a glistering zodiac° hung the sword,   *belt*
> Satan's dire dread, and in his hand the spear.

---

9. Jacob gave that name, meaning "armies" or "camps" ("field pavilioned," line 215), to a place where he saw an army of angels (Genesis 32:2).
1. The Syrian king levied war against "Dothan" (line 217) in order to capture Elisha the prophet ("One man," line 219), but the Lord saved Elisha by sending "horses and chariots of fire" (2 Kings 6:8ff.).
2. Michael, who left his angelic forces ("powers") in their formation ("stand") to take possession of the garden (lines 221–22).
3. Both Meliboea and Tyre ("Sarra") in Thessaly were famous for purple dye.
4. Goddess of the rainbow.

Adam bowed low, he kingly from his state°   *stately bearing*
250 Inclined not, but his coming thus declared:
"Adam, Heav'n's high behest no preface needs:
Sufficient that thy prayers are heard, and Death,
Then due by sentence when thou didst transgress,
Defeated° of his seizure° many days   *cheated / possession*
255 Giv'n thee of grace, wherein thou may'st repent,
And one bad act with many deeds well done
May'st cover: well may then thy Lord appeased
Redeem thee quite from Death's rapacious claim;
But longer in this Paradise to dwell
260 Permits not; to remove thee I am come,
And send thee from the garden forth to till
The ground whence thou wast taken, fitter soil."
    He added not, for Adam at the news
Heart-strook with chilling gripe° of sorrow stood,   *spasm*
265 That all his senses bound; Eve, who unseen
Yet all had heard, with audible lament
Discovered° soon the place of her retire: *revealed*
"O unexpected stroke, worse than of Death!
Must I thus leave thee Paradise? thus leave
270 Thee native soil,[5] these happy walks and shades,
Fit haunt of gods? where I had hope to spend,
Quiet though sad, the respite° of that day   *delay*
That must be mortal to us both. O flow'rs,
That never will in other climate grow,
275 My early visitation, and my last
At ev'n which I bred up with tender hand
From the first op'ning bud, and gave ye names,[6]
Who now shall rear ye to the sun, or rank
Your tribes,° and water from th' ambrosial° fount?   *species / fragrant*
280 Thee lastly nuptial bower, by me adorned
With what to sight or smell was sweet; from thee
How shall I part, and whither wander down
Into a lower world, to° this obscure   *compared to*
And wild, how shall we breathe in other air
285 Less pure, accustomed to immortal fruits?"
    Whom thus the angel interrupted mild:
"Lament not Eve, but patiently resign
What justly thou hast lost; nor set thy heart,
Thus overfond, on that which is not thine;
290 Thy going is not lonely, with thee goes
Thy husband, him to follow thou art bound;
Where he abides, think there thy native soil."
    Adam by this from the cold sudden damp°   *dejection*
Recovering, and his scattered spirits returned,
295 To Michael thus his humble words addressed:
"Celestial, whether among the Thrones, or named

---

5. Unlike Adam, Eve was created in the Paradise of Eden.
6. Departing from Genesis 2:19–20, in which Adam alone gives names, Milton has Eve name the flowers, an action that signifies (like Adam's naming of the beasts, 8.352–54) intuitive knowledge of their nature.

Of them the highest, for such of shape may seem
Prince above princes, gently hast thou told
Thy message, which might else in telling wound,
300 And in performing end us; what besides
Of sorrow and dejection and despair
Our frailty can sustain, thy tidings bring,
Departure from this happy place, our sweet
Recess, and only consolation left
305 Familiar to our eyes, all places else
Inhospitable appear and desolate,
Nor knowing us nor known: and if by prayer
Incessant I could hope to change the will
Of him who all things can,° I would not cease   *knows, can do*
310 To weary him with my assiduous cries:
But prayer against his absolute decree
No more avails than breath against the wind,
Blown stifling back on him that breathes it forth:
Therefore to his great bidding I submit.
315 This most afflicts me, that departing hence,
As from his face I shall be hid, deprived
His blessed count'nance; here I could frequent,
With worship, place by place where he vouchsafed
Presence Divine, and to my sons relate:
320 'On this mount he appeared, under this tree
Stood visible, among these pines his voice
I heard, here with him at this fountain talked:'
So many grateful altars I would rear
Of grassy turf, and pile up every stone
325 Of luster from the brook, in memory,
Or monument to ages, and thereon
Offer sweet-smelling gums and fruits and flow'rs:
In yonder nether world where shall I seek
His bright appearances, or footstep trace?
330 For though I fled him angry, yet recalled
To life prolonged and promised race,[7] I now
Gladly behold though but his utmost skirts
Of glory, and far off his steps adore."
    To whom thus Michael with regard benign:
335 "Adam, thou know'st Heav'n his, and all the earth,
Not this rock only; his omnipresence fills
Land, sea, and air, and every kind that lives,
Fomented° by his virtual° power and warmed: *nurtured / potent*
All th' earth he gave thee to possess and rule,
340 No despicable gift; surmise not then
His presence to these narrow bounds confined
Of Paradise or Eden: this had been
Perhaps thy capital seat, from whence had spread
All generations, and had hither come
345 From all the ends of th' earth, to celebrate

---

7. His descendants, from whom will spring the "promised Seed." See 10.180–81 and n. 1, and 12.623.

And reverence thee their great progenitor.
But this preeminence thou hast lost, brought down
To dwell on even ground now with thy sons:
Yet doubt not but in valley and in plain
350 God is as here, and will be found alike
Present, and of his presence many a sign
Still following thee, still compassing thee round
With goodness and paternal love, his face
Express, and of his steps the track divine.
355 Which that thou may'st believe, and be confirmed,
Ere thou from hence depart, know I am sent
To show thee what shall come in future days
To thee and to thy offspring,[8] good with bad
Expect to hear, supernal° grace contending   *heavenly*
360 With sinfulness of men; thereby to learn
True patience, and to temper joy with fear
And pious sorrow, equally inured°   *tempered*
By moderation either state to bare,
Prosperous or adverse: so shalt thou lead
365 Safest thy life, and best prepared endure
Thy mortal passage when it comes. Ascend
This hill; let Eve (for I have drenched her eyes)[9]
Here sleep below while thou to foresight wak'st,
As once thou slept'st while she to life was formed."
370   To whom thus Adam gratefully replied:
"Ascend, I follow thee, safe guide, the path
Thou lead'st me, and to the hand of Heav'n submit,
However chast'ning, to the evil turn
My obvious° breast, arming to overcome   *exposed*
375 By suffering, and earn rest from labor won,
If so I may attain." So both ascend
In the visions of God: it was a hill
Of Paradise the highest, from whose top
The hemisphere of earth in clearest ken°   *view*
380 Stretched out to amplest reach of prospect lay.
Not higher that hill nor wider looking round,
Whereon for different cause the Tempter set
Our second Adam in the wilderness,
To show him all earth's kingdoms and their glory.[1]
385 His eye might there command wherever stood
City of old or modern fame, the seat
Of mightiest empire, from the destined walls
Of Cambalu, seat of Cathaian Can,
And Samarkand by Oxus, Temir's throne,
390 To Paquin of Sinaean kings, and thence
To Agra and Lahore of Great Mogul

---

8. Prophetic visions are a common feature in epic, for example, Aeneas's vision of his descendants culminating in the Roman Empire (Virgil, *Aeneid* 6.754–854).
9. Put a soporific liquid ("drench") in her eyes.
1. When Satan tempted Christ (the subject of Milton's "brief epic" *Paradise Regained*), he took him up to "an exceeding high mountain" and showed him "all the kingdoms of the world, and the glory of them" (Matthew 4:8). The passage that follows details the places "he" (Christ and/or Adam) might see (lines 386–411).

                Down to the golden Chersonese,² or where
                The Persian in Ecbatan sat, or since
                In Hispahan, or where the Russian czar
395   In Moscow, or the sultan in Bizance,
                Turkéstan-born;³ nor could his eye not ken°   view
                Th' empire of Negus to his utmost port
                Ercoco and the less maritime kings
                Mombaza, and Quiloa, and Melind,
400   And Sofala thought Ophir, to the realm
                Of Congo, and Angola farthest south;⁴
                Or thence from Niger flood to Atlas mount
                The kingdoms of Almansor, Fez and Sus,
                Morocco and Algiers, and Tremisen;⁵
405   On Europe thence, and where Rome was to sway
                The world: in spirit perhaps he also saw
                Rich Mexico the seat of Motezume,
                And Cuzco in Peru, the richer seat
                Of Atabalipa, and yet unspoiled
410   Guiana, whose great city Geryon's sons
                Call El Dorado:⁶ but to nobler sights
                Michael from Adam's eyes the film removed
                Which that false fruit that promised clearer sight
                Had bred; then purged with euphrasy and rue⁷
415   The visual nerve, for he had much to see;
                And from the well of life three drops instilled.
                So deep the power of these ingredients pierced,
                Ev'n to the inmost seat of mental sight,
                That Adam now enforced to close his eyes,
420   Sunk down and all his spirits became entranced:
                But him the gentle angel by the hand
                Soon raised, and his attention thus recalled:
                    "Adam, now ope thine eyes, and first behold
                Th' effects which thy original crime hath wrought
425   In some to spring from thee, who never touched

2. His first views are of "destined" (yet to come) great kingdoms in Asia: "Cambalu," capital of "Cathay," the region of North China ruled by such khans as Genghis and Kublai; "Samarkand," ruled by Tamburlaine ("Temir"), near the "Oxus" river near modern Uzbekistan; Beijing ("Paquin," Peking), ruled by Chinese ("Sinaean") kings; "Agra" and "Lahore," capitals in northern India ruled by the "Great Mogul"; "golden Chersonese," an area sometimes identified with the Malay Peninsula.
3. Next, Persian and Turkish kingdoms. From Persia (Iran): Ecbatana ("Ecbatan"), a summer residence of Persian kings, and the 16th-century Persian capital Isfahan ("Hispahan"); and Byzantium ("Bizance," Constantinople, Istanbul), capital of the Ottomon Empire after falling to the Turks in 1453.
4. From Africa: Abyssinia (empire of King "Negus"); Arkiko ("Ercoco") in Ethiopia, a Red Sea port; Mombasa ("Mombaza") and Malindi ("Melind") in Kenya; Kilwa ("Quiloa") in Tanzania "Sofala," sometimes identified with the biblical "Ophir" from which Solomon took gold for his Temple (1 Kings 9:28); and "Congo" and "Angola" on the west coast.
5. In North Africa: the kingdoms of "Almansor" (the name shared by various Muslim rulers, here referring probably to Abu-Amir al Ma-Ma'afiri, caliph of Cordova) reached from the "Niger" River in northern Morocco to the "Atlas" Mountains in Algeria, taking in Morocco (and its capital, "Fez"), Tunis ("Sus"), and part of Algeria called Tiemecen ("Tremisen").
6. Because they lay on the other side of the spherical earth, Christ and/or Adam could only see places in the New World "in spirit" (line 406): Mexico, the seat of Montezuma ("Motezume"), the last Aztec emperor; "Cuzco in Peru," seat of Atahualpa ("Atabalipa"), the last Incan emperor (murdered by Pizarro); and "Guiana" (a region including Surinam, Guyana, and parts of Venezuela and Brazil). Unlike Mexico and Peru it was "yet unspoiled" by the Spaniards (sons of the evil monster "Geryon," in Spenser an allegory of the great power and oppression of Spain), though they identified its chief city, Manoa, with the fabled city of gold, "El Dorado."
7. Both herbs were thought to sharpen eyesight.

Th' excepted° tree, nor with the snake conspired,   *forbidden*
Nor sinned thy sin, yet from that sin derive
Corruption to bring forth more violent deeds."
   His eyes he opened, and beheld a field,
430 Part arable and tilth,° whereon were sheaves   *cultivated*
New-reaped, the other part sheep-walks and folds;
I' th' midst an altar as the landmark° stood   *boundary marker*
Rustic, of grassy sord;° thither anon   *turf*
A sweaty reaper from his tillage brought
435 Firstfruits, the green ear, and the yellow sheaf,
Unculled,° as came to hand; a shepherd next   *picked at random*
More meek came with the firstlings of his flock
Choicest and best; then sacrificing, laid
The inwards and their fat, with incense strewed,
440 On the cleft wood, and all due rites performed.
His off'ring soon propitious fire from Heav'n
Consumed with nimble glance, and grateful steam;
The other's not, for his was not sincere;[8]
Whereat he inly raged, and as they talked,
445 Smote him into the midriff with a stone
That beat out life; he fell, and deadly pale
Groaned out his soul with gushing blood effused.
Much at that sight was Adam in his heart
Dismayed, and thus in haste to th' angel cried:
450   "O teacher, some great mischief hath befall'n
To that meek man, who well had sacrificed;
Is piety thus and pure devotion paid?"
   T' whom Michael thus, he also moved, replied:
"These two are brethren, Adam, and to come
455 Out of thy loins;[9] th' unjust the just hath slain,
For envy that his brother's offering found
From Heav'n acceptance; but the bloody fact°   *crime*
Will be avenged, and th' other's faith approved
Lose no reward, though here thou see him die,
460 Rolling in dust and gore." To which our sire:
   "Alas, both for the deed and for the cause!
But have I now seen death? Is this the way
I must return to native dust? O sight
Of terror, foul and ugly to behold,
465 Horrid to think, how horrible to feel!"
   To whom thus Michaël: "Death thou hast seen
In his first shape on man; but many shapes
Of Death, and many are the ways that lead
To his grim cave, all dismal; yet to sense
470 More terrible at th' entrance than within.
Some, as thou saw'st, by violent stroke shall die,
By fire, flood, famine; by intemperance more
In meats and drinks, which on the earth shall bring
Diseases dire, of which a monstrous crew

---

8. Milton's version of the Cain and Abel story (Genesis 4:1–16) provides a clear reason for God's rejection of Cain's sacrifice.

9. Adam has to be told that these are his own sons, not simply descendants.

475 Before thee shall appear; that thou may'st know
What misery th' inabstinence of Eve
Shall bring on men." Immediately a place¹
Before his eyes appeared, sad,° noisome, dark,   *lamentable*
A lazar-house it seemed, wherein were laid
480 Numbers of all diseased, all maladies
Of ghastly spasm, or racking torture, qualms
Of heartsick agony, all feverous kinds,
Convulsions, epilepsies, fierce catarrhs,
Intestine stone and ulcer, colic pangs,
485 Demoniac frenzy, moping melancholy
And moonstruck madness,° pining atrophy,   *lunacy*
Marasmus, and wide-wasting pestilence,²
Dropsies, and asthmas, and joint-racking rheums.
Dire was the tossing, deep the groans, Despair
490 Tended the sick busiest from couch to couch;
And over them triumphant Death his dart
Shook, but delayed to strike, though oft invoked
With vows, as their chief good, and final hope.
Sight so deform what heart of rock could long
495 Dry-eyed behold? Adam could not, but wept,
Though not of woman born; compassion quelled
His best of man,° and gave him up to tears   *manliness, courage*
A space, till firmer thoughts restrained excess,
And scarce recovering words his plaint renewed:
500   "O miserable mankind, to what fall
Degraded, to what wretched state reserved!
Better end here unborn. Why is life giv'n
To be thus wrested from us? Rather why
Obtruded on us thus? who if we knew
505 What we receive, would either not accept
Life offered, or soon beg to lay it down,
Glad to be so dismissed in peace. Can thus
Th' image of God in man created once
So goodly and erect, though faulty since,
510 To such unsightly sufferings be debased
Under inhuman pains? Why should not man,
Retaining still divine similitude
In part, from such deformities be free,
And for his Maker's image sake exempt?"
515   "Their Maker's image," answered Michael, "then
Forsook them, when themselves they vilified°   *debased*
To serve ungoverned appetite, and took°   *took away*
His image whom they served, a brutish vice,
Inductive° mainly to° the sin of Eve.   *produced / from*
520 Therefore so abject is their punishment,
Disfiguring not God's likeness, but their own,
Or if his likeness, by themselves defaced
While they pervert pure nature's healthful rules

---

1. This is the only nonbiblical sight shown to Adam, a "lazar-house" (line 479)—a hospital for leprosy and infectious diseases, especially syphilis.
2. The plague. "Marasmus": a wasting disease of the body.

To loathsome sickness, worthily,° since they   *deservedly*
525   God's image did not reverence in themselves."
     "I yield it just," said Adam, "and submit.
But is there yet no other way, besides
These painful passages, how we may come
To death, and mix with our connatural dust?"
530   "There is," said Michael, "if thou well observe
The rule of not too much, by temperance taught
In what thou eat'st and drink'st, seeking from thence
Due nourishment, not gluttonous delight,
Till many years over thy head return:
535   So may'st thou live, till like ripe fruit thou drop
Into thy mother's³ lap, or be with ease
Gathered, not harshly plucked, for death mature:
This is old age; but then thou must outlive
Thy youth, thy strength, thy beauty, which will change
540   To withered weak and gray; thy senses then
Obtuse, all taste of pleasure must forgo,
To what thou hast, and for the air of youth
Hopeful and cheerful, in thy blood will reign
A melancholy damp° of cold and dry   *depression of spirits*
545   To weigh thy spirits down, and last consume
The balm° of life." To whom our ancestor: *preservative essence*
     "Henceforth I fly not death, nor would prolong
Life much, bent rather how I may be quit
Fairest and easiest of this cumbrous charge,
550   Which I must keep till my appointed day
Of rend'ring up, and patiently attend°   *await*
My dissolution." Michaël replied:
     "Nor love thy life, nor hate; but what thou liv'st
Live well, how long or short permit to Heav'n:
555   And now prepare thee for another sight."
     He looked and saw a spacious plain,⁴ whereon
Were tents of various hue; by some were herds
Of cattle grazing: others, whence the sound
Of instruments that made melodious chime
560   Was heard, of harp and organ; and who moved
Their stops and chords was seen: his volant touch
Instinct through all proportions low and high
Fled and pursued transverse the resonant fugue.⁵
In other part stood one⁶ who at the forge
565   Laboring, two massy clods of iron and brass
Had melted (whether found where casual° fire   *accidental*
Had wasted woods on mountain or in vale,
Down to the veins of earth, thence gliding hot
To some cave's mouth, or whether washed by stream
570   From underground) the liquid ore he drained

---

3. "Mother" earth.
4. Adam's third vision is based on Genesis 4:19–22; "tents" (next line) identifies these as the descendants of Cain, described as "such as dwell in tents."
5. Genesis 4:21 describes Cain's descendant Jubal as "father of all such as handle the harp and organ." "Volant": nimble; "instinct": instinctive; "proportions": ratios of pitches; "fugue": musical form in which one statement of the theme seems to chase another.
6. Tubal-cain, "instructor of every artificer in brass and iron" (Genesis 4:22).

        Into fit molds prepared; from which he formed
        First his own tools; then, what might else be wrought
        Fusile° or grav'n in metal. After these,   cast
        But on the hither side a different sort⁷
575   From the high neighboring hills, which was their seat,
        Down to the plain descended: by their guise
        Just men they seemed, and all their study bent
        To worship God aright, and know his works
        Not hid,⁸ nor those things last which might preserve
580   Freedom and peace to men: they on the plain
        Long had not walked, when from the tents behold
        A bevy of fair women, richly gay
        In gems and wanton dress; to the harp they sung
        Soft amorous ditties, and in dance came on:
585   The men though grave, eyed them, and let their eyes
        Rove without rein, till in the amorous net
        Fast caught, they liked, and each his liking chose;
        And now of love they treat till th' evening star⁹
        Love's harbinger appeared; then all in heat
590   They light the nuptial torch, and bid invoke
        Hymen,¹ then first to marriage rites invoked;
        With feast and music all the tents resound.
        Such happy interview and fair event°   outcome
        Of love and youth not lost, songs, garlands, flow'rs,
595   And charming symphonies attached° the heart   seized
        Of Adam, soon° inclined to admit delight,   easily
        The bent of nature; which he thus expressed:
           "True opener of mine eyes, prime angel blest,
        Much better seems this vision, and more hope
600   Of peaceful days portends, than those two past;
        Those were of hate and death, or pain much worse,
        Here nature seems fulfilled in all her ends."
           To whom thus Michael: "Judge not what is best
        By pleasure, though to nature seeming meet,°   appropriate
605   Created, as thou art, to nobler end
        Holy and pure, conformity divine.
        Those tents thou saw'st so pleasant, were the tents
        Of wickedness, wherein shall dwell his race
        Who slew his brother; studious they appear
610   Of arts that polish life, inventors rare,
        Unmindful of their Maker, though his spirit
        Taught them, but they his gifts acknowledged none.
        Yet they a beauteous offspring shall beget;
        For that fair female troop thou saw'st, that seemed
615   Of goddesses, so blithe, so smooth, so gay,
        Yet empty of all good wherein consists
        Woman's domestic honor and chief praise;
        Bred only and completed° to the taste   accomplished

---

7. The descendants of Seth, Adam's third son (Genesis 5:3); "hither side": away from the "east" (Genesis 4:16), where Cain's sons lived.
8. They studied God's visible works, not the "matters hid" that Raphael had warned Adam against.
9. Venus.
1. God of marriage.

Of lustful appetence,° to sing, to dance,   *desire*
620   To dress, and troll° the tongue, and roll the eye.   *move*
To these that sober race of men, whose lives
Religious titled them the sons of God,[2]
Shall yield up all their virtue, all their fame
Ignobly, to the trains° and to the smiles   *wiles, snares*
625   Of these fair atheists, and now swim in joy,
(Erelong to swim at large) and laugh; for which
The world erelong a world of tears must weep."
    To whom thus Adam of short joy bereft:
"O pity and shame, that they who to live well
630   Entered so fair, should turn aside to tread
Paths indirect, or in the mid-way faint!
But still I see the tenor of man's woe
Holds on the same, from woman to begin."
    "From man's effeminate slackness it begins,"
635   Said th' angel, "who should better hold his place
By wisdom, and superior gifts received.
But now prepare thee for another scene."
    He looked and saw wide territory spread
Before him, towns, and rural works between,
640   Cities of men with lofty gates and tow'rs,
Concourse° in arms, fierce faces threat'ning war,   *encounters*
Giants[3] of mighty bone, and bold emprise;°   *chivalric adventure*
Part wield their arms, part curb the foaming steed,
Single or in array of battle ranged°   *drawn up in ranks*
645   Both horse and foot, nor idly must'ring stood;
One way a band select from forage drives
A herd of beeves, fair oxen and fair kine
From a fat meadow ground; or fleecy flock,
Ewes and their bleating lambs over the plain,
650   Their booty; scarce with life the shepherds fly,
But call in aid, which makes a bloody fray;
With cruel tournament the squadrons join;
Where cattle pastured late, now scattered lies
With carcasses and arms th' ensanguined° field   *blood-stained*
655   Deserted: others to a city strong
Lay siege, encamped; by battery, scale, and mine,[4]
Assaulting; others from the wall defend
With dart and jav'lin, stones and sulphurous fire;
On each hand slaughter and gigantic deeds.
660   In other part the sceptered heralds call
To council in the city gates: anon
Gray-headed men and grave, with warriors mixed,
Assemble, and harangues are heard, but soon
In factious opposition, till at last

---

2. Like many exegetes, Milton identifies the "sons of God" as the descendants of Seth, and the "daughters of men" whom they wed (Genesis 6:2) as the descendants of Cain.
3. Adam's fourth vision, based on Genesis 6:4, is of the "Giant" offspring of the previous marriages (identified at lines 683–84); Milton makes them exemplify false heroism and false glory sought through military might and conquest (lines 689–99).
4. That is, by battering, scaling, and tunneling under the walls.

	Of middle age one[5] rising, eminent	
665	Of middle age one[5] rising, eminent	
	In wise deport, spake much of right and wrong,	
	Of justice, of religion, truth and peace,	
	And judgment from above: him old and young	
	Exploded,° and had seized with violent hands,	*mocked*
670	Had not a cloud descending snatched him thence	
	Unseen amid the throng: so violence	
	Proceeded, and oppression, and sword-law	
	Through all the plain, and refuge none was found.	
	Adam was all in tears, and to his guide	
675	Lamenting turned full sad; "O what are these,	
	Death's ministers, not men, who thus deal death	
	Inhumanly to men, and multiply	
	Ten-thousandfold the sin of him who slew	
	His brother; for of whom such massacre	
680	Make they but of their brethren, men of men?	
	But who was that just man, whom had not Heav'n	
	Rescued, had in his righteousness been lost?"	
	To whom thus Michael: "These are the product	
	Of those ill-mated marriages thou saw'st:	
685	Where good with bad were matched, who of themselves	
	Abhor to join; and by imprudence mixed,	
	Produce prodigious births of body or mind.	
	Such were these giants, men of high renown;	
	For in those days might only shall be admired,	
690	And valor and heroic virtue called;	
	To overcome in battle, and subdue	
	Nations, and bring home spoils with infinite	
	Manslaughter, shall be held the highest pitch	
	Of human glory, and for glory done	
695	Of triumph, to be styled great conquerors,	
	Patrons of mankind, gods, and sons of gods,	
	Destroyers rightlier called and plagues of men.	
	Thus fame shall be achieved, renown on earth,	
	And what most merits fame in silence hid.	
700	But he the sev'nth from thee,[6] whom thou beheld'st	
	The only righteous in a world perverse,	
	And therefore hated, therefore so beset	
	With foes for daring single to be just,	
	And utter odious truth, that God would come	
705	To judge them with his saints: him the Most High	
	Rapt in a balmy cloud with winged steeds	
	Did, as thou saw'st, receive, to walk with God	
	High in salvation and the climes of bliss,	
	Exempt from death; to show thee what reward	
710	Awaits the good, the rest what punishment;	
	Which now direct thine eyes and soon behold."	

---

5. Enoch, who "walked with God: and he was not; for God took him" (Genesis 5:24); Milton elaborates on the story.

6. Here Enoch is more precisely identified by generation, but neither he nor the other biblical personages in these pageants are named. Apparently, Michael and Adam together see the pageants, and Michael (by God's illumination) can interpret them rightly, but neither of the two knows the names these persons will later bear.

He looked, and saw the face of things quite changed;
The brazen throat of war had ceased to roar,
All now was turned to jollity and game,
715 To luxury° and riot,° feast and dance,   *lust / debauchery*
Marrying or prostituting, as befell,
Rape or adultery, where passing fair°   *surpassing beauty*
Allured them; thence from cups to civil broils.
At length a reverend sire[7] among them came,
720 And of their doings great dislike declared,
And testified against their ways; he oft
Frequented their assemblies, whereso met,
Triumphs or festivals, and to them preached
Conversion and repentance, as to souls
725 In prison under judgments imminent:
But all in vain: which when he saw, he ceased
Contending, and removed his tents far off;
Then from the mountain hewing timber tall,
Began to build a vessel of huge bulk,
730 Measured by cubit, length, and breadth, and height,
Smeared round with pitch, and in the side a door
Contrived, and of provisions laid in large
For man and beast: when lo a wonder strange!
Of every beast, and bird, and insect small
735 Came sevens and pairs, and entered in, as taught
Their order: last the sire and his three sons
With their four wives; and God made fast the door.
Meanwhile the south wind rose, and with black wings
Wide hovering, all the clouds together drove
740 From under heav'n; the hills to their supply°   *assistance*
Vapor, and exhalation dusk° and moist,   *dark mist*
Sent up amain;° and now the thickened sky   *with main force*
Like a dark ceiling stood; down rushed the rain
Impetuous, and continued till the earth
745 No more was seen; the floating vessel swum
Uplifted; and secure with beakèd prow
Rode tilting o'er the waves, all dwellings else
Flood overwhelmed, and them with all their pomp
Deep underwater rolled; sea covered sea,
750 Sea without shore;[8] and in their palaces
Where luxury late reigned, sea monsters whelped
And stabled; of mankind, so numerous late,
All left, in one small bottom° swum embarked.   *boat*
How didst thou grieve then, Adam, to behold
755 The end of all thy offspring, end so sad,
Depopulation; thee another flood,
Of tears and sorrow a flood thee also drowned,
And sunk thee as thy sons; till gently reared
By th' angel, on thy feet thou stood'st at last,
760 Though comfortless, as when a father mourns

---

7. Noah. Milton's account is based on Genesis 6–9.
8. The "sea without shore" and some other features of this description are taken from Ovid's account of Deucalion's Flood (*Metamorphoses* 1.292–300, Sandys translation).

His children, all in view destroyed at once;
And scarce to th' angel utter'dst thus thy plaint:
    "O visions ill foreseen! Better had I
Lived ignorant of future, so had borne
My part of evil only, each day's lot   765
Enough to bear; those now, that were dispensed
The burd'n of many ages, on me light
At once, by my foreknowledge[9] gaining birth
Abortive, to torment me ere their being,
With thought that they must be. Let no man seek   770
Henceforth to be foretold what shall befall
Him or his children, evil he may be sure,
Which neither his foreknowing can prevent,
And he the future evil shall no less
In apprehension than in substance feel   775
Grievous to bear: but that care now is past,
Man is not whom to warn:[1] those few escaped
Famine and anguish will at last consume
Wand'ring that wat'ry desert: I had hope
When violence was ceased, and war on earth,   780
All would have then gone well, peace would have crowned
With length of happy days the race of man;
But I was far deceived; for now I see
Peace to corrupt no less than war to waste.
How comes it thus? Unfold, celestial guide,   785
And whether here the race of man will end."
    To whom thus Michael: "Those whom last thou saw'st
In triumph and luxurious wealth, are they
First seen in acts of prowess eminent
And great exploits, but of true virtue void;   790
Who having spilt much blood, and done much waste
Subduing nations, and achieved thereby
Fame in the world, high titles, and rich prey,
Shall change their course to pleasure, ease, and sloth,
Surfeit, and lust, till wantonness and pride   795
Raise out of friendship hostile deeds in peace.
The conquered also, and enslaved by war
Shall with their freedom lost all virtue lose
And fear of God, from whom their piety feigned
In sharp contest of battle found no aid   800
Against invaders; therefore cooled in zeal
Thenceforth shall practice how to live secure,
Worldly or dissolute, on what their lords
Shall leave them to enjoy, for th' earth shall bear
More than enough, that temperance may be tried: 805
So all shall turn degenerate, all depraved,
Justice and temperance, truth and faith forgot;[2]

---

9. The term suggests that Adam is experiencing something akin to God's foreknowledge, which the poem insists is not predestination. Adam knows what is to happen but can neither cause it nor prevent it.

1. That is, there is no man to warn, all will die.
2. This passage (lines 797–807) may also allude to the backsliding Puritans who betrayed the Commonwealth in 1660 and have now taken on the vices of the restored royalists.

                One man except, the only son of light
                In a dark age, against example good,
810   Against allurement, custom, and a world
                Offended;° fearless of reproach and scorn,   *hostile*
                Or violence, he of their wicked ways
                Shall them admonish, and before them set
                The paths of righteousness, how much more safe,
815   And full of peace, denouncing° wrath to come   *proclaiming*
                On their impenitence; and shall return
                Of them derided, but of God observed
                The one just man alive; by his command
                Shall build a wondrous ark, as thou beheld'st,
820   To save himself and household from amidst
                A world devote° to universal wrack.   *doomed*
                No sooner he with them of man and beast
                Select for life shall in the ark be lodged,
                And sheltered round, but all the cataracts°   *floodgates*
825   Of heav'n set open on the earth shall pour
                Rain day and night, all fountains of the deep
                Broke up, shall heave the ocean to usurp
                Beyond all bounds, till inundation rise
                Above the highest hills: then shall this mount
830   Of Paradise by might of waves be moved
                Out of his place, pushed by the hornèd flood,[3]
                With all his verdure spoiled, and trees adrift
                Down the great river to the op'ning gulf,[4]
                And there take root an island salt and bare,
835   The haunt of seals and ores,° and sea mews'° clang.   *sea monsters / seagulls*
                To teach thee that God áttributes to place
                No sanctity, if none be thither brought
                By men who there frequent, or therein dwell.
                And now what further shall ensue, behold."
840   He looked, and saw the ark hull° on the flood,   *drift*
                Which now abated, for the clouds were fled,
                Driv'n by a keen north wind, that blowing dry
                Wrinkled the face of deluge, as decayed;
                And the clear sun on his wide wat'ry glass
845   Gazed hot, and of the fresh wave largely drew,
                As after thirst, which made their flowing shrink
                From standing lake to tripping° ebb, that stole   *running*
                With soft foot towards the deep, who now had stopped
                His sluices, as the heav'n his windows shut.
850   The ark no more now floats, but seems on ground
                Fast on the top of some high mountain fixed.[5]
                And now the tops of hills as rocks appear;
                With clamor thence the rapid currents drive
                Towards the retreating sea their furious tide.
855   Forthwith from out the ark a raven flies,
                And after him, the surer messenger,

---

3. Classical river gods were often depicted as horned.
4. That is, down the Euphrates to the Persian Gulf.
5. Mount Ararat (Genesis 8:4).

A dove sent forth once and again to spy
Green tree or ground whereon his foot may light;
The second time returning, in his bill
An olive leaf he brings, pacific sign: 860
Anon dry ground appears, and from his ark
The ancient sire descends with all his train;
Then with uplifted hands, and eyes devout,
Grateful to Heav'n, over his head beholds
A dewy cloud, and in the cloud a bow 865
Conspicuous with three listed colors gay,[6]
Betok'ning peace from God, and covenant new.
Whereat the heart of Adam erst so sad
Greatly rejoiced, and thus his joy broke forth:
"O thou who future things canst represent 870
As present, heav'nly instructor, I revive
At this last sight, assured that man shall live
With all the creatures, and their seed preserve.
Far less I now lament for one whole world
Of wicked sons destroyed, than I rejoice 875
For one man found so perfect and so just,
That God vouchsafes to raise another world
From him, and all his anger to forget.[7]
But say, what mean those colored streaks in heav'n,
Distended° as the brow of God appeased, 880   *spread out*
Or serve they as a flow'ry verge to bind
The fluid skirts of that same wat'ry cloud,
Lest it again dissolve and show'r the earth?"
   To whom th' Archangel: "Dextrously thou aim'st;
So willingly doth God remit his ire, 885
Though late repenting him of man depraved,
Grieved at his heart, when looking down he saw
The whole earth filled with violence, and all flesh
Corrupting each their way; yet those removed,
Such grace shall one just man find in his sight, 890
That he relents, not to blot out mankind,
And makes a cov'nant[8] never to destroy
The earth again by flood, nor let the sea
Surpass his bounds, nor rain to drown the world
With man therein or beast; but when he brings 895
Over the earth a cloud, will therein set
His triple-colored bow, whereon to look
And call to mind his cov'nant: day and night,
Seed-time and harvest, heat and hoary frost
Shall hold their course, till fire purge all things new, 900
Both heav'n and earth, wherein the just shall dwell."[9]

---

6. The primary colors, red, yellow, and blue.
7. The language invites recognition of Noah as a type (foreshadowing) of Christ, the one "perfect" and "just" who will cause God to forget his anger.
8. The language of covenant makes this promise—that God will not again destroy the earth by flood—a type of the "covenant of grace" through which God will save humankind.
9. The restoration of the orderly processes of nature after the Flood is identified as a type (foreshadowing) of the final renewal of all things after the final conflagration at the Last Judgment.

Book 12

The Arguments

The angel Michael continues from the Flood to relate what shall succeed; then, in the mention of Abraham, comes by degrees to explain, who that Seed of the Woman shall be, which was promised Adam and Eve in the Fall; his incarnation, death, resurrection, and ascension; the state of the church till his second coming. Adam greatly satisfied and recomforted by these relations and promises descends the hill with Michael; wakens Eve, who all this while had slept, but with gentle dreams composed to quietness of mind and submission. Michael in either hand leads them out of Paradise, the fiery sword waving behind them, and the Cherubim taking their stations to guard the place.

As one who in his journey bates° at noon,   *stops for refreshment*
Though bent on speed, so here the Archangel paused
Betwixt the world destroyed and world restored,
If Adam aught perhaps might interpose;
     5 Then with transition sweet new speech resumes:[1]
"Thus thou hast seen one world begin and end;
And man as from a second stock proceed.
Much thou hast yet to see, but I perceive
Thy mortal sight to fail; objects divine
    10 Must needs impair and weary human sense:
Henceforth what is to come I will relate,[2]
Thou therefore give due audience, and attend.
This second source of men, while yet but few,
And while the dread of judgment past remains
    15 Fresh in their minds, fearing the Deity,
With some regard to what is just and right
Shall lead their lives, and multiply apace,
Laboring the soil, and reaping plenteous crop,
Corn, wine, and oil; and from the herd or flock,
    20 Oft sacrificing bullock, lamb, or kid,
With large wine-offerings poured, and sacred feast,
Shall spend their days in joy unblamed, and dwell
Long time in peace by families and tribes
Under paternal rule; till one[3] shall rise
    25 Of proud ambitious heart, who not content
With fair equality, fraternal state,
Will arrogate dominion undeserved
Over his brethren, and quite dispossess
Concord and law of nature from the earth;
    30 Hunting (and men not beasts shall be his game)
With war and hostile snare such as refuse
Subjection to his empire tyrannous:
A mighty hunter thence he shall be styled°   *called*

---

1. The first five lines were added when Book 10 of the 1667 edition was divided to make Books 11 and 12 of the 1674 edition.
2. Adam no longer sees visions or pageants, as before, but simply listens to Michael's narration.
3. Nimrod (Genesis 10:8–10) is described as the first king, in terms that equate kingship itself with tyranny (lines 25–29).

Before the Lord, as in despite of Heav'n,
Or from Heav'n claiming second sov'reignty;[4]
And from rebellion shall derive his name,
Though of rebellion others he accuse.
He with a crew, whom like ambition joins
With him or under him to tyrannize,
Marching from Eden towards the west, shall find
The plain, wherein a black bituminous gurge°   *whirlpool*
Boils out from underground, the mouth of Hell;
Of brick, and of that stuff they cast° to build   *set about*
A city and tow'r,[5] whose top may reach to Heav'n;
And get themselves a name, lest far dispersed
In foreign lands their memory be lost,
Regardless whether good or evil fame.
But God who oft descends to visit men
Unseen, and through their habitations walks
To mark their doings, them beholding soon,
Comes down to see their city, ere the tower
Obstruct Heav'n tow'rs, and in derision sets
Upon their tongues a various° spirit to raze   *divisive*
Quite out their native language, and instead
To sow a jangling noise of words unknown:
Forthwith a hideous gabble[6] rises loud
Among the builders; each to other calls
Not understood, till hoarse, and all in rage,
As mocked they storm; great laughter was in Heav'n
And looking down, to see the hubbub strange
And hear the din; thus was the building left
Ridiculous, and the work Confusion[7] named."
   Whereto thus Adam fatherly displeased:
"O execrable son so to aspire
Above his brethren, to himself assuming
Authority usurped, from God not giv'n:
He gave us only over beast, fish, fowl
Dominion absolute; that right we hold
By his donation; but man over men
He made not lord; such title to himself
Reserving, human left from human free.[8]
But this usurper his encroachment proud
Stays not on man; to God his tower intends
Siege and defiance: wretched man! What food
Will he convey up thither to sustain
Himself and his rash army, where thin air
Above the clouds will pine° his entrails gross,   *waste away*

---

4. Milton offers two explanations of the biblical phrase "Before the Lord": either he openly defied God ("despite") or he claimed divine right ("second sov'reignty") like the Stuart kings. Drawing on the (false) etymology linking the name Nimrod with the Hebrew word meaning "to rebel," Milton implies that the paradox developed in the next two lines (that he accuses others of rebellion but is himself a rebel against God) extends to other kings, especially Charles I, who accused his opponents in the civil war of rebellion.
5. Babylon is the city, Babel the tower.
6. Genesis 11:1–9 recounts the building of the Tower of Babel reaching to Heaven; God punished this presumption by confounding the builders' original language into multiple languages.
7. "Confusion" was taken to be the meaning of "Babel."
8. Adam states the assumption Milton often invokes to support republicanism.

And famish him of breath, if not of bread?"
  To whom thus Michael: "Justly thou abhorr'st
80 That son, who on the quiet state of men
Such trouble brought, affecting° to subdue   *aspiring*
Rational liberty; yet know withal,
Since thy original lapse, true liberty
Is lost, which always with right reason dwells
85 Twinned, and from her hath no dividual° being:[9]   *separate*
Reason in man obscured, or not obeyed,
Immediately inordinate desires
And upstart passions catch the government
From reason, and to servitude reduce
90 Man till then free. Therefore since he permits
Within himself unworthy powers to reign
Over free reason, God in judgment just
Subjects him from without to violent lords;
Who oft as undeservedly enthrall
95 His outward freedom: tyranny must be,
Though to the tyrant thereby no excuse.
Yet sometimes nations will decline so low
From virtue, which is reason, that no wrong,
But justice, and some fatal curse annexed
100 Deprives them of their outward liberty,
Their inward lost: witness th' irreverent son[1]
Of him who built the ark, who for the shame
Done to his father, heard this heavy curse,
'Servant of servants,' on his vicious race.[2]
105 Thus will this latter, as the former world,
Still tend from bad to worse, till God at last
Wearied with their iniquities, withdraw
His presence from among them, and avert
His holy eyes; resolving from thenceforth
110 To leave them to their own polluted ways;
And one peculiar° nation to select   *special*
From all the rest, of whom to be invoked,
A nation from one faithful man[3] to spring:
Him on this side Euphrates yet residing,
115 Bred up in idol-worship; O that men
(Canst thou believe?) should be so stupid grown,
While yet the patriarch[4] lived, who scaped the Flood,

9. As Milton (following classical theorists) often did, and as Abdiel did earlier (6.178–81), Michael links political to psychological servitude, and political liberty to inner freedom, that is, the exercise of "right reason" and the control of passion. Loss of liberty is often (though not always) God's just punishment for national decline (lines 81–100). The long passage alludes to the "baseness" of the English in restoring monarchy in 1660.
1. Ham, son of Noah, who looked on the nakedness of his father and brought down the curse that his descendants would be "servant of servants" to their brethren (Genesis 9:22–25).
2. Noah's curse provided scriptural authorization for ancient Hebrew enslavement of the native Canaanites after the conquest of the Promised Land. Some early modern thinkers expanded the scope of the curse beyond the people of Canaan to include Ham and his son Cush, who was thought to be the progenitor of Black Africans, in order to justify the enslavement of Africans. Milton's use of the term "vicious race" allows for a wide range of possible interpretations.
3. Abraham, whose name means "father of many nations"; the passage is based on Genesis 11:27 to 25.10.
4. Noah, who lived for 350 years after the Flood.

>   As to forsake the living God, and fall
>   To worship their own work in wood and stone
> 120 For gods! Yet him God the Most High vouchsafes
>   To call by vision from his father's house,
>   His kindred and false gods, into a land
>   Which he will show him, and from him will raise
>   A mighty nation, and upon him show'r
> 125 His benediction so, that in his seed
>   All nations shall be blest; he straight° obeys,   *immediately*
>   Not knowing to what land, yet firm believes:
>   I see him, but thou canst not,⁵ with what faith
>   He leaves his gods, his friends, and native soil
> 130 Ur⁶ of Chaldaea, passing now the ford
>   To Haran, after him a cumbrous train
>   Of herds and flocks, and numerous servitude;°   *servants and slaves*
>   Not wand'ring poor, but trusting all his wealth
>   With God, who called him, in a land unknown.
> 135 Canaan he now attains, I see his tents
>   Pitched about Sechem, and the neighboring plain
>   Of Moreh; there by promise he receives
>   Gift to his progeny of all that land;
>   From Hamath northward to the desert south
> 140 (Things by their names I call, though yet unnamed)
>   From Hermon east to the great western sea,⁷
>   Mount Hermon, yonder sea, each place behold
>   In prospect, as I point them; on the shore
>   Mount Carmel; here the double-founted stream
> 145 Jordan, true limit eastward; but his sons
>   Shall dwell to Senir, that long ridge of hills.⁸
>   This ponder, that all nations of the earth
>   Shall in his seed be blessed; by that Seed
>   Is meant thy great Deliverer,⁹ who shall bruise
> 150 The Serpent's head; whereof to thee anon
>   Plainlier shall be revealed. This patriarch blest,
>   Whom 'faithful Abraham'¹ due time shall call,
>   A son, and of his son a grandchild leaves,
>   Like him in faith, in wisdom, and renown;
> 155 The grandchild with twelve sons increased, departs
>   From Canaan, to a land hereafter called
>   Egypt, divided by the river Nile;

---

5. Michael evidently continues to see the stories he recounts as visionary scenes or pageants; Adam must accept the story of Abraham "by faith," analogous to the faith Abraham himself displays.
6. Ur was on one bank of the Euphrates, Haran (line 131) on the other, to the northwest.
7. The Promised Land was bounded on the north by Hamath, a city on the Orontes River in west Syria; on the south by the wilderness "desert" of Zin; on the east by Mount Hermon; and on the west by the Mediterranean, the "great western sea."
8. "Mount Carmel": a mountain range near Haifa, on the Mediterranean coast of Israel; "Jordan": the river thought incorrectly to have two sources ("double-founted"), the Jor and the Dan; "Senir": a peak of Mount Hermon.
9. Michael interprets the promise to Abraham (Genesis 17:5, "a father of many nations have I made thee") typologically, as to be fulfilled in Christ, the "Woman's Seed." See 10.180–81 and note 1, and 12.322–28, 12.600–601, 12.623.
1. Echoes Galatians 3:9: "So then they which be of faith are blessed with faithful Abraham." His son (line 153) is Isaac, and his grandson, Jacob.

>   See where it flows,[2] disgorging at seven mouths
>   Into the sea: to sojourn in that land
> 160   He comes invited by a younger son[3]
>   In time of dearth,° a son whose worthy deeds   *famine*
>   Raise him to be the second in that realm
>   Of Pharaoh: there he dies, and leaves his race
>   Growing into a nation, and now grown
> 165   Suspected to° a sequent° king, who seeks   *by / successive*
>   To stop their overgrowth, as inmate° guests   *foreign*
>   Too numerous; whence of guests he makes them slaves
>   Inhospitably, and kills their infant males:
>   Till by two brethren (those two brethren call
> 170   Moses and Aaron) sent from God to claim
>   His people from enthrallment, they return
>   With glory and spoil back to their promised land.[4]
>   But first the lawless tyrant, who denies°   *refuses*
>   To know their God, or message to regard,
> 175   Must be compelled by signs and judgments dire;[5]
>   To blood unshed the rivers must be turned,
>   Frogs, lice, and flies must all his palace fill
>   With loathed intrusion, and fill all the land;
>   His cattle must of rot and murrain° die,   *cattle plague*
> 180   Botches and blains must all his flesh emboss,[6]
>   And all his people; thunder mixed with hail,
>   Hail mixed with fire must rend th' Egyptian sky
>   And wheel on th' earth, devouring where it rolls;
>   What it devours not, herb, or fruit, or grain,
> 185   A darksome cloud of locusts swarming down
>   Must eat, and on the ground leave nothing green:
>   Darkness must overshadow all his bounds,
>   Palpable darkness, and blot out three days;
>   Last with one midnight stroke all the firstborn
> 190   Of Egypt must lie dead. Thus with ten wounds°   *plagues*
>   The river-dragon[7] tamed at length submits
>   To let his sojourners depart, and oft
>   Humbles his stubborn heart, but still as ice
>   More hardened after thaw, till in his rage
> 195   Pursuing whom he late dismissed, the sea
>   Swallows him with his host, but them lets pass
>   As on dry land between two crystal walls,
>   Awed by the rod of Moses so to stand
>   Divided, till his rescued gain their shore:[8]
> 200   Such wondrous power God to his saint will lend,
>   Though present in his angel, who shall go

---

2. Adam can see geographical features from his mountaintop, though not the scenes Michael sees and describes.

3. Joseph, the next youngest of Jacob's twelve sons, invited the Israelites to Egypt to escape famine, but they were subsequently made slaves (Genesis 21–50).

4. The story of Moses and Aaron leading the Israelites from captivity to the Promised Land is told in Exodus and Deuteronomy.

5. The ten plagues, recounted in lines 176–90.

6. "Botches": boils; "blains": blisters; "emboss": cover as with studs.

7. The Egyptian pharaoh is termed "the great dragon that lieth in the midst of his rivers" (Ezekiel 29:3).

8. The Red Sea was parted by the rod of Moses; the Israelites passed through, but Pharaoh's pursuing forces drowned as the water rushed back (Exodus 13:17–22 and 14:5–31).

>   Before them in a cloud, and pillar of fire,
>   By day a cloud, by night a pillar of fire,
>   To guide them in their journey,[9] and remove
> 205 Behind them, while th' obdúrate king pursues:
>   All night he will pursue, but his approach
>   Darkness defends° between till morning watch;   *prevents*
>   Then through the fiery pillar and the cloud
>   God looking forth will trouble all his host
> 210 And craze° their chariot wheels: when by command   *shatter*
>   Moses once more his potent rod extends
>   Over the sea; the sea his rod obeys;
>   On their embattled ranks the waves return,
>   And overwhelm their war:° the race elect   *armies*
> 215 Safe towards Canaan from the shore advance
>   Through the wild desert, not the readiest way,
>   Lest ent'ring on the Canaanite alarmed°   *prepared to fight*
>   War terrify them inexpert, and fear
>   Return them back to Egypt, choosing rather
> 220 Inglorious life with servitude; for life
>   To noble and ignoble is more sweet
>   Untrained in arms, where rashness leads not on.[1]
>   This also shall they gain by their delay
>   In the wide wilderness, there they shall found
> 225 Their government, and their great senate[2] choose
>   Through the twelve tribes, to rule by laws ordained:
>   God from the mount of Sinai, whose gray top
>   Shall tremble, he descending, will himself
>   In thunder, lightning, and loud trumpet's sound
> 230 Ordain them laws; part such as appertain
>   To civil justice, part religious rites
>   Of sacrifice,[3] informing them, by types
>   And shadows, of that destined Seed to bruise
>   The Serpent, by what means he shall achieve
> 235 Mankind's deliverance.[4] But the voice of God
>   To mortal ear is dreadful; they beseech
>   That Moses might report to them his will,
>   And terror cease; he grants what they besought
>   Instructed that to God is no access
> 240 Without mediator, whose high office now
>   Moses in figure[5] bears, to introduce
>   One greater, of whose day he shall foretell,
>   And all the prophets in their age the times
>   Of great Messiah shall sing. Thus laws and rites
> 245 Established, such delight hath God in men

9. Milton repeats here a view developed in his *Christian Doctrine*, that God was "present in his angel," not in his own person, in the cloud and pillar of fire that led the Israelites on their journey (Exodus 13:21–22).

1. That is, unless prompted by "rashness," those "untrained in arms" will choose servitude rather than battle.

2. The "Seventy Elders" of the Sanhedrin, whom Milton cites as a model for republican government in his *Ready and Easy Way*.

3. God delivered ceremonial, civil, and moral/religious laws (the Ten Commandments) to Moses on Mount Sinai, with thunder and lightning (lines 227–32; Exodus 19–31).

4. The principle of typology, whereby persons and events in the Old Testament are seen to prefigure Christ or matters pertaining to his life or the Christian church.

5. Moses is a type of Christ in his role as mediator between the people and God.

      Obedient to his will, that he vouchsafes
      Among them to set up his tabernacle,
      The Holy One with mortal men to dwell:
      By his prescript a sanctuary is framed
250 Of cedar, overlaid with gold, therein
      An ark, and in the ark his testimony,
      The records of his cov'nant, over these
      A mercy-seat of gold between the wings
      Of two bright Cherubim, before him burn
255 Seven lamps as in a zodiac° representing   *like the planets*
      The heav'nly fires; over the tent a cloud
      Shall rest by day, a fiery gleam by night,
      Save when they journey, and at length they come,
      Conducted by his angel to the land
260 Promised to Abraham and his seed: the rest
      Were long to tell, how many battles fought,
      How many kings destroyed, and kingdoms won,
      Or how the sun shall in mid-heav'n stand still
      A day entire, and night's due course adjourn,
265 Man's voice commanding, 'Sun in Gibeon stand,
      And thou moon in the vale of Aialon,
      Till Israel overcome';[6] so call the third
      From Abraham, son of Isaac, and from him
      His whole descent,[7] who thus shall Canaan win."
270   Here Adam interposed: "O sent from Heav'n,
      Enlight'ner of my darkness, gracious things
      Thou hast revealed, those chiefly which concern
      Just Abraham and his seed: now first I find
      Mine eyes true op'ning, and my heart much eased,
275 Erewhile perplexed with thoughts what would become
      Of me and all mankind; but now I see
      His day, in whom all nations shall be blest,[8]
      Favor unmerited by me, who sought
      Forbidden knowledge by forbidden means.
280 This yet I apprehend not, why to those
      Among whom God will deign to dwell on earth
      So many and so various laws are giv'n;
      So many laws argue so many sins
      Among them; how can God with such reside?"
285   To whom thus Michael: "Doubt not but that sin
      Will reign among them, as of thee begot;
      And therefore was law given them to evince°   *make evident*
      Their natural pravity,° by stirring up   *original sin*
      Sin against law to fight; that when they see
290 Law can discover sin, but not remove,
      Save by those shadowy expiations weak,
      The blood of bulls and goats, they may conclude

---

6. The story of Joshua, at whose bidding the sun stood still in Gibeon, and the moon in Ajalon (both a few miles north of Jerusalem), until Israel won its battle against the Amorites (Joshua 10:12–23).

7. Isaac's son Jacob was named Israel, and his descendants after him (Genesis 33:28).

8. Adam supposes that the promise made to him is fulfilled in the covenant with Abraham; he has yet to understand that in this Abraham is a type of Christ.

          Some blood more precious must be paid for man,
          Just for unjust, that in such righteousness
295   To them by faith imputed, they may find
          Justification towards God, and peace
          Of conscience,[9] which the law by ceremonies
          Cannot appease, nor man the moral part
          Perform, and not performing cannot live.[1]
300   So law appears imperfect, and but giv'n
          With purpose to resign° them in full time   yield
          Up to a better cov'nant, disciplined
          From shadowy types to truth, from flesh to spirit,
          From imposition of strict laws, to free
305   Acceptance of large grace, from servile fear
          To filial, works of law to works of faith.[2]
          And therefore shall not Moses, though of God
          Highly beloved, being but the minister
          Of law, his people into Canaan lead;
310   But Joshua whom the Gentiles Jesus call,[3]
          His name and office bearing, who shall quell
          The adversary Serpent, and bring back
          Through the world's wilderness long-wandered man
          Safe to eternal paradise of rest.
315   Meanwhile they in their earthly Canaan placed
          Long time shall dwell and prosper, but when sins
          National interrupt their public peace,
          Provoking God to raise them enemies:
          From whom as oft he saves them penitent°   when penitent
320   By judges first, then under kings; of whom
          The second, both for piety renowned
          And puissant° deeds, a promise shall receive   mighty
          Irrevocable, that his regal throne
          Forever shall endure;[4] the like shall sing
325   All prophecy, that of the royal stock
          Of David (so I name this king) shall rise
          A son, the Woman's Seed to thee foretold,[5]
          Foretold to Abraham, as in whom shall trust
          All nations, and to kings foretold, of kings
330   The last, for of his reign shall be no end.
          But first a long succession must ensue,
          And his next son for wealth and wisdom famed,
          The clouded ark of God till then in tents
          Wand'ring, shall in a glorious temple enshrine.[6]

---

9. The ceremonial sacrifices of "bulls and goats" under the Law are types, "shadowy expiations," pointing to Christ's efficacious sacrifice that alone can win "Justification" for humankind, by Christ's merits being "imputed" (attributed vicariously) to them through faith (lines 290–96).

1. The theological doctrine that the Law is intended to lead humans to the "better cov'nant" (line 302) of grace, by demonstrating that fallen men cannot fulfill the commandments of the Law or appease God through ceremonial sacrifices (lines 297–302).

2. A more complete explanation of the principle of typology.

3. "Jesus" is the Greek equivalent of the Hebrew "Joshua," who, rather than Moses, led the children of Israel into the Promised Land of Canaan, being in this a type of Christ.

4. The history summarized in lines 315–30 is recounted in Judges, Samuel, and Kings.

5. The Messiah was prophesied to come of David's line, and Jesus was referred to as the "Son of David."

6. Solomon, son of David, built a "glorious temple" to house the Ark of the Covenant.

	Such follow him, as shall be registered	
	Part good, part bad, of bad the longer scroll,	
	Whose foul idolatries and other faults	
	Heaped° to the popular sum, will so incense	added
	God, as to leave them, and expose their land,	
340	Their city, his temple, and his holy ark	
	With all his sacred things, a scorn and prey	
	To that proud city, whose high walls thou saw'st	
	Left in confusion, Babylon thence called.	
	There in captivity he lets them dwell	
345	The space of seventy years,[7] then brings them back,	
	Rememb'ring mercy, and his cov'nant sworn	
	To David, stablished as the days of Heav'n.	
	Returned from Babylon by leave of kings[8]	
	Their lords, whom God disposed,° the house of God	made well-disposed
350	They first re-edify, and for a while	
	In mean estate live moderate, till grown	
	In wealth and multitude, factious they grow;	
	But first among the priests dissension springs,	
	Men who attend the altar, and should most	
355	Endeavor peace: their strife pollution brings	
	Upon the Temple itself: at last they seize	
	The scepter, and regard not David's sons,°	descendants
	Then lose it to a stranger,[9] that the true	
	Anointed King Messiah might be born	
360	Barred of his right; yet at his birth a star	
	Unseen before in heav'n proclaims him come,	
	And guides the eastern sages,° who inquire	the Magi
	His place, to offer incense, myrrh, and gold;	
	His place of birth a solemn° angel tells	awe-inspiring
365	To simple shepherds, keeping watch by night;	
	They gladly thither haste, and by a choir	
	Of squadroned angels hear his carol sung.	
	A virgin is his mother, but his sire	
	The Power of the Most High; he shall ascend	
370	The throne hereditary, and bound his reign	
	With earth's wide bounds, his glory with the heav'ns."	
	He ceased, discerning Adam with such joy	
	Surcharged,° as had like grief been dewed in tears,	overwhelmed
	Without the vent of words, which these he breathed:	
375	"O prophet of glad tidings, finisher	
	Of utmost hope! now clear I understand	
	What oft my steadiest thoughts have searched in vain,	
	Why our great expectation should be called	
	The Seed of Woman: Virgin Mother, hail,	

7. The seventy-year Babylonian Captivity of the Jews and destruction of the Temple (6th century B.C.E.).
8. The Persian kings Cyrus the Great, Darius, and Artaxerxes allowed the Jews to return from Babylon and rebuild the Temple.
9. Antiochus, father of Herod the Great (who ruled at the time of Christ's birth), was made governor of Jerusalem in 61 B.C.E. by the Romans, and procurator of Judaea in 47 B.C.E. Prior to this (lines 353–57), strife among the priests allowed the Seleucid king Antiochus IV to sack Jerusalem and pollute the Temple; then one of the Maccabees seized the throne, disregarding the claims of David's dynasty.

380   High in the love of Heav'n, yet from my loins
        Thou shalt proceed, and from thy womb the Son
        Of God Most High; so God with man unites.
        Needs must the Serpent now his capital° bruise   *on the head, fatal*
        Expect with mortal pain: say where and when
385   Their fight, what stroke shall bruise the victor's heel."
          To whom thus Michael: "Dream not of their fight,
        As of a duel, or the local wounds
        Of head or heel: not therefore joins the Son
        Manhood to Godhead, with more strength to foil
390   Thy enemy; nor so is overcome
        Satan, whose fall from Heav'n, a deadlier bruise,
        Disabled not to give thee thy death's wound:
        Which he who comes thy Savior, shall recure,°   *heal*
        Not by destroying Satan, but his works
395   In thee and in thy seed: nor can this be,
        But by fulfilling that which thou didst want,°   *lack*
        Obedience to the law of God, imposed
        On penalty of death, and suffering death,
        The penalty to thy transgression due,
400   And due to theirs which out of thine will grow:
        So only can high justice rest apaid.°   *satisfied*
        The law of God exact he shall fulfill
        Both by obedience and by love, though love
        Alone fulfill the law; thy punishment
405   He shall endure by coming in the flesh
        To a reproachful life and cursèd death,
        Proclaiming life to all who shall believe
        In his redemption, and that his obedience
        Imputed becomes theirs by faith, his merits
410   To save them, not their own, though legal works.[1]
        For this he shall live hated, be blasphemed,
        Seized on by force, judged, and to death condemned
        A shameful and accursed, nailed to the cross
        By his own nation, slain for bringing life;
415   But to the cross he nails thy enemies,
        The law that is against thee, and the sins
        Of all mankind, with him there crucified,
        Never to hurt them more who rightly trust
        In this his satisfaction; so he dies,
420   But soon revives, Death over him no power
        Shall long usurp; ere the third dawning light
        Return, the stars of morn shall see him rise
        Out of his grave, fresh as the dawning light,
        Thy ransom paid, which man from Death redeems,
425   His death for man, as many as offered life
        Neglect not,[2] and the benefit embrace
        By faith not void of works: this Godlike act

---

1. Michael restates the theological doctrine that humans can be saved only by Christ's merits attributed to them vicariously ("imputed"), not by their own good works performed according to God's law ("legal").
2. That is, for as many as accept ("neglect not") his offer of life.

Annuls thy doom, the death thou shouldst have died,
In sin forever lost from life; this act
430 Shall bruise the head of Satan, crush his strength
Defeating Sin and Death, his two main arms,
And fix far deeper in his head their stings
Than temporal death shall bruise the victor's heel,
Or theirs whom he redeems, a death like sleep,
435 A gentle wafting to immortal life.
Nor after resurrection shall he stay
Longer on earth than certain times to appear
To his disciples, men who in his life
Still followed him; to them shall leave in charge
440 To teach all nations what of him they learned
And his salvation, them who shall believe
Baptizing in the profluent° stream, the sign   *flowing*
Of washing them from guilt of sin to life
Pure, and in mind prepared, if so befall,
445 For death, like that which the Redeemer died.
All nations they shall teach; for from that day
Not only to the sons of Abraham's loins
Salvation shall be preached, but to the sons
Of Abraham's faith wherever through the world;
450 So in his seed all nations shall be blest.³
Then to the Heav'n of Heav'ns he shall ascend
With victory, triumphing through the air
Over his foes and thine; there shall surprise
The Serpent, prince of air, and drag in chains
455 Through all his realm, and there confounded leave;
Then enter into glory, and resume
His seat at God's right hand, exalted high
Above all names in Heav'n; and thence shall come,
When this world's dissolution shall be ripe
460 With glory and power to judge both quick° and dead,   *living*
To judge th' unfaithful dead, but to reward
His faithful, and receive them into bliss,
Whether in Heav'n or earth, for then the earth
Shall all be paradise, far happier place
465 Than this of Eden, and far happier days."
    So spake th' Archangel Michaël, then paused,
As at the world's great period;° and our sire   *consummation*
Replete with joy and wonder thus replied:
"O goodness infinite, goodness immense!
470 That all this good of evil shall produce,
And evil turn to good; more wonderful
Than that which by creation first brought forth
Light out of darkness! Full of doubt I stand,
Whether I should repent me now of sin
475 By me done and occasioned, or rejoice
Much more, that much more good thereof shall spring,
To God more glory, more good will to men

---

3. Michael spells out the application to Christ of the promise offered typologically to Abraham's seed.

>   From God, and over wrath grace shall abound.[4]
>   But say, if our Deliverer up to Heav'n
> 480 Must reascend, what will betide the few
>   His faithful, left among th' unfaithful herd,
>   The enemies of truth; who then shall guide
>   His people, who defend? Will they not deal
>   Worse with his followers than with him they dealt?"
> 485   "Be sure they will," said th' angel; "but from Heav'n
>   He to his own a Comforter will send,[5]
>   The promise of the Father, who shall dwell
>   His Spirit within them, and the law of faith
>   Working through love, upon their hearts shall write,
> 490 To guide them in all truth, and also arm
>   With spiritual armor, able to resist
>   Satan's assaults, and quench his fiery darts,[6]
>   What° man can do against them, not afraid,   *as much as*
>   Though to the death, against such cruelties
> 495 With inward consolations recompensed,
>   And oft supported so as shall amaze
>   Their proudest persecutors: for the Spirit
>   Poured first on his apostles, whom he sends
>   To evangelize the nations, then on all
> 500 Baptized, shall them with wondrous gifts endue°   *endow*
>   To speak all tongues, and do all miracles,
>   As did their Lord before them. Thus they win
>   Great numbers of each nation to receive
>   With joy the tidings brought from Heav'n: at length
> 505 Their ministry performed, and race well run,
>   Their doctrine and their story written left,[7]
>   They die; but in their room, as they forewarn,
>   Wolves shall succeed for teachers, grievous wolves,
>   Who all the sacred mysteries of Heav'n
> 510 To their own vile advantages shall turn
>   Of lucre° and ambition, and the truth   *wealth*
>   With superstitions and traditions taint,[8]
>   Left only in those written records pure,
>   Though not but by the Spirit understood.
> 515 Then shall they seek to avail themselves of names,°   *honors*
>   Places° and titles, and with these to join   *offices*
>   Secular power, though feigning still to act
>   By spiritual, to themselves appropriating

---

4. These lines do not formulate the medieval idea of the *felix culpa*—that the Fall was fortunate in bringing humans greater happiness than they would otherwise have enjoyed—only that the Fall has provided God an occasion to bring still greater good out of evil. The poem makes clear that Adam and Eve would have grown in perfection and advanced to Heaven had they not sinned.
5. The Holy Spirit, who for Milton is much subordinate to both Father and Son.
6. Compare Ephesians 6:11–16: "Put on the whole armor of God, that ye may be able to stand against the wiles of the devil. . . . Above all, taking the shield of faith, wherewith ye shall be able to quench all the fiery darts of the wicked." The subsequent history (lines 493–507) is that of the early Christian church in apostolic times.
7. That is, in the Gospels and Epistles.
8. The history summarized in lines 508–40 is of the corruption of the Christian church by superstitions, traditions, and persecutions of conscience in patristic times under the popes and the Christian emperors, but also extending to the Last Day. The terms point especially to what Milton saw as the revival of "popish" superstitions in the English church of the Restoration and to the fierce persecution of dissenters.

The Spirit of God, promised alike and giv'n
To all believers; and from that pretense,
Spiritual laws by carnal° power shall force   *fleshly, worldly*
On every conscience;[9] laws which none shall find
Left them enrolled, or what the Spirit within
Shall on the heart engrave.[1] What will they then
But force the Spirit of Grace itself, and bind
His consort Liberty; what, but unbuild
His living temples,[2] built by faith to stand,
Their own faith not another's: for on earth
Who against faith and conscience can be heard
Infallible?[3] Yet many will presume:
Whence heavy persecution shall arise
On all who in the worship persevere
Of Spirit and Truth; the rest, far greater part,
Will deem in outward rites and specious forms
Religion satisfied; Truth shall retire
Bestuck with sland'rous darts, and works of faith
Rarely be found: so shall the world go on,
To good malignant, to bad men benign,
Under her own weight groaning, till the day
Appear of respiration° to the just,   *respite*
And vengeance to the wicked, at return
Of him so lately promised to thy aid,
The Woman's Seed,[4] obscurely then foretold,
Now amplier known thy Savior and thy Lord,
Last in the clouds from Heav'n to be revealed
In glory of the Father, to dissolve
Satan with his perverted world, then raise
From the conflagrant mass,° purged and refined,   *the burning world*
New heav'ns, new earth, ages of endless date
Founded in righteousness and peace of love,
To bring forth fruits joy and eternal bliss."
    He ended; and thus Adam last replied:
"How soon hath thy prediction, seer blest,
Measured this transient world, the race of time,
Till time stand fixed: beyond is all abyss,
Eternity, whose end no eye can reach.
Greatly instructed I shall hence depart,
Greatly in peace of thought, and have my fill
Of knowledge, what° this vessel can contain;   *as much as*
Beyond which was my folly to aspire.
Henceforth I learn, that to obey is best,

9. These lines affirm the Protestant principle of every Christian's right to interpret Scripture according to the "inner light" of the Spirit, and denounce (as Milton consistently did in his tracts) the use of civil ("carnal") power to enforce orthodoxy.
1. That is, there is nothing in Scripture or in the Spirit's inner teaching that sanctions persecution for conscience.
2. See 1 Corinthians 3:16: "Know ye not that ye are the temple of God?" "His consort Liberty":
Milton typically insists that Christ's gospel and the Spirit of God teach liberty, religious and civil, alluding as here to 2 Corinthians 3:17: "where the Spirit of the Lord is, there is liberty."
3. An attack on papal claims to infallibility, asserted though not yet proclaimed as doctrine.
4. Michael's story ends with the full explication of the promised "Woman's Seed" as Christ, and with the renewal of all things after the Last Judgment (lines 545–51).

  And love with fear the only God, to walk
As in his presence, ever to observe
His providence, and on him sole depend,
Merciful over all his works, with good   565
Still overcoming evil, and by small
Accomplishing great things, by things deemed weak
Subverting worldly strong, and worldly wise
By simply meek; that suffering for truth's sake
Is fortitude to highest victory,   570
And to the faithful death the gate of life;
Taught this by his example whom I now
Acknowledge my Redeemer ever blest."
  To whom thus also th' angel last replied:
"This having learnt, thou hast attained the sum   575
Of wisdom; hope no higher, though all the stars
Thou knew'st by name,[5] and all th' ethereal powers,
All secrets of the deep, all nature's works,
Or works of God in heav'n, air, earth, or sea,
And all the riches of this world enjoy'dst,   580
And all the rule, one empire; only add
Deeds to thy knowledge answerable,° add faith,   *corresponding*
Add virtue, patience, temperance, add love,
By name to come called charity, the soul
Of all the rest: then wilt thou not be loath   585
To leave this Paradise, but shalt possess
A paradise within thee, happier far.
Let us descend now therefore from this top
Of speculation;° for the hour precise   *hill of speculation*
Exacts° our parting hence; and see the guards,   590   *requires*
By me encamped on yonder hill, expect
Their motion,° at whose front a flaming sword,   *await their orders*
In signal of remove, waves fiercely round;
We may no longer stay: go, waken Eve;
Her also I with gentle dreams have calmed   595
Portending good, and all her spirits composed
To meek submission: thou at season fit
Let her with thee partake what thou hast heard,
Chiefly what may concern her faith to know,
The great deliverance by her seed to come   600
(For by the Woman's Seed) on all mankind.
That ye may live, which will be many days,
Both in one faith unanimous though sad,
With cause for evils past, yet much more cheered
With meditation on the happy end."   605
  He ended, and they both descend the hill;
Descended, Adam to the bow'r where Eve
Lay sleeping ran before, but found her waked;
And thus with words not sad she him received:
  "Whence thou return'st, and whither went'st, I know;   610

---

5. Michael glances back at Raphael's warning in Book 8 that Adam should concern himself first with matters pertaining to his own life and world, rather than speculating overmuch about the cosmos.

For God is also in sleep, and dreams advise,[6]
Which he hath sent propitious, some great good
Presaging, since with sorrow and heart's distress
Wearied I fell asleep: but now lead on;
In me is no delay; with thee to go,
Is to stay here; without thee here to stay,
Is to go hence unwilling; thou to me
Art all things under heav'n, all places thou,[7]
Who for my willful crime art banished hence.
This further consolation yet secure
I carry hence; though all by me is lost,
Such favor I unworthy am vouchsafed,
By me the promised Seed shall all restore."
  So spake our mother Eve, and Adam heard
Well pleased, but answered not; for now too nigh
Th' Archangel stood, and from the other hill
To their fixed station, all in bright array
The Cherubim descended; on the ground
Gliding metéorous,° as evening mist   *like a meteor*
Ris'n from a river o'er the marish° glides,   *marsh*
And gathers ground fast at the laborer's heel
Homeward returning. High in front advanced,
The brandished sword of God before them blazed
Fierce as a comet; which with torrid heat,
And vapor° as the Libyan air adust,°   *smoke / parched*
Began to parch that temperate clime; whereat
In either hand the hast'ning angel caught
Our ling'ring parents, and to th' eastern gate
Led them direct, and down the cliff as fast
To the subjected° plain; then disappeared.   *low-lying*
They looking back, all th' eastern side beheld
Of Paradise, so late their happy seat,°   *estate*
Waved over by that flaming brand,° the gate   *sword*
With dreadful faces thronged and fiery arms:
Some natural tears they dropped, but wiped them soon;
The world was all before them, where to choose
Their place of rest, and Providence their guide:
They hand in hand with wand'ring steps and slow,
Through Eden took their solitary way.

1674

---

6. The lines suggest that Eve's dream has provided her a parallel (if lesser) prophecy to Adam's visions and instruction. See Numbers 12:6: "If there be a prophet among you, I the Lord will make myself known unto him in a vision, and will speak unto him in a dream."

7. Eve's lines—the final speech in the poem—recall her prelapsarian love song to Adam (4.641ff.) and Ruth's promise to accompany her mother-in-law, Naomi (Ruth 1:16).

APPENDICES

APPENDICES

General Bibliography

This bibliography consists of a list of suggested general readings on English literature. Bibliographies for the authors and topical clusters in *The Norton Anthology of English Literature* are available online at the NAEL student site.

Histories of England and of English Literature

Even the most distinguished of the comprehensive general histories written in past generations have come to seem outmoded. Innovative research in social, cultural, and political history has made it difficult to write a single coherent account of England from the Middle Ages to the present, let alone to accommodate in a unified narrative the complex histories of Scotland, Ireland, Wales, and the other nations where writing in English has flourished. Readers who wish to explore the historical matrix out of which the works of literature collected in this anthology emerged are advised to consult the studies of particular periods listed in the appropriate sections of this bibliography. The multivolume *Oxford History of England* (1934–65) and *New Oxford History of England* (1992–2009) are useful, as are the three-volume *Peoples of the British Isles: A New History*, by Stanford E. Lehmberg, Samantha A. Meigs, and Thomas William Heyck (3rd ed., 1992); the nine-volume *Cambridge Cultural History of Britain*, ed. Boris Ford (1992); the three-volume *Cambridge Social History of Britain, 1750–1950*, ed. F. M. L. Thompson (1990); and the multivolume *Penguin History of Britain*, gen. ed. David Cannadine (1996–). For Britain's imperial history, readers can consult the five-volume *Oxford History of the British Empire*, ed. Wm. Roger Louis (1998–99), as well as *Gender and Empire*, ed. Philippa Levine (2004). Also of interest is Lisa Lowe, *The Intimacies of Four Continents* (2015). Given the cultural centrality of London, readers may find particular interest in *The London Encyclopaedia*, ed. Ben Weinreb et al. (3rd ed., 2008); Roy Porter, *London: A Social History* (1994); and Jerry White, *London in the Nineteenth Century: "A Human Awful Wonder of God"* (2007) and *London in the Twentieth Century: A City and Its People* (2001).

Similar observations may be made about literary history. In the light of such initiatives as women's studies, New Historicism, and postcolonialism, the range of authors deemed significant has expanded, along with the geographical and conceptual boundaries of literature in English. Attempts to capture in a unified account the great sweep of literature from *Beowulf* to the early twenty-first century have largely given way to studies of individual genres, carefully delimited time periods, and specific authors. Among the large-scale literary surveys, *The Cambridge Guide to Literature in English*, ed. Dominic Head (3rd ed., 2006), is useful, as is the nine-volume *Penguin History of Literature* (1987–94) and the multivolume *Oxford History of Poetry in English* (2022–). *The Feminist Companion to Literature in English: Women Writers from the Middle Ages to the Present*, ed. Virginia Blain, Isobel Grundy, and Patricia Clements (1990), is an important resource, and the editorial materials in the two-volume *The Norton Anthology of Literature by Women: The Traditions in English*, ed. Sandra M. Gilbert and Susan Gubar (3rd ed., 2007), constitute a concise history and set of biographies of women authors since the Middle Ages. *Annals of English Literature, 1475–1950* (2nd ed., 1961), lists important publications year by year, together with the significant literary events for each year. Seven volumes have been published in *The Oxford English Literary History*, gen. eds. Jonathan Bate and Colin Burrow (2002–): Laura Ashe, *1000–1350: Conquest and Transformation*; James Simpson, *1350–1547: Reform and Cultural Revolution*; Margaret J. M. Ezell, *1645–1714: The Later Seventeenth Century*; Philip Davis, *1830–1880: The Victorians*; Chris Baldick, *1830–1880: The Modern Movement (1910–1940)*; Randall Stevenson, *1960–2000: The Last of England?*; and Bruce King, *1948–2000: The Internationalization of English Literature*. See also *The Cambridge History of Medieval English Literature*, ed. David Wallace (1999); *The Cambridge History of Early Medieval English Literature*, ed. Clare E. Lees (2013); *The Cambridge History of Early Modern English Literature*, ed. David Loewenstein and Janel Mueller (2002); *The Cambridge History of English Literature, 1660–1780*, ed. John Richetti (2005); *The Cambridge History of English Romantic Literature*, ed. James Chandler (2009); *The Cambridge History of Victorian Literature*, ed. Kate Flint (2012); and *The Cambridge History of Twentieth-Century English Literature*, ed. Laura Marcus and Peter Nicholls (2004).

Helpful treatments and surveys of English meter, rhyme, and stanza forms are Paul Fussell Jr., *Poetic Meter and Poetic Form* (rev. ed., 1979); Donald Wesling, *The Chances of Rhyme: Device and Modernity* (1980); Charles O. Hartman, *Free Verse: An Essay on Prosody* (1980); Derek Attridge, *Poetic Rhythm: An Introduction* (1995); Robert Pinsky, *The Sounds of Poetry: A Brief Guide* (1998); *The Making of a Poem: A Norton Anthology of Poetic Forms*, ed. Mark Strand and Eavan Boland (2000); John Hollander, *Rhyme's Reason: A Guide to English Verse* (3rd ed., 2001); *Poems, Poets, Poetry: An Introduction and Anthology*, ed. Helen Vendler (3rd ed., 2010); *The Lyric Theory Reader: A Critical Anthology*, ed. Virginia Jackson and Yopie Prins (2014); and Jonathan Culler, *Theory of the Lyric* (2015).

On the development and functioning of the novel as a form, see Ian Watt, *The Rise of the Novel: Studies in Defoe, Richardson, and Fielding* (1957); Gérard Genette, *Narrative Discourse: An Essay in Method* (1970; trans. 1980); *Theory of the Novel: A Historical Approach*, ed. Michael McKeon (2000); *The Novel*, ed. Franco Moretti (2 vols.; 2001–03, trans. 2006); McKeon, *The Origins of the English Novel, 1600–1740* (15th anniversary ed., 2002); *The Cambridge History of the English Novel*, ed. Robert L. Caserio and Clement Hawes (2012); *A Companion to the English Novel*, ed. Stephen Arata et al. (2015); and the ten volumes to date of *The Oxford History of the Novel in English* (2012–). On women novelists and readers, see Nancy Armstrong, *Desire and Domestic Fiction: A Political History of the Novel* (1987), and Catherine Gallagher, *Nobody's Story: The Vanishing Acts of Women Writers in the Marketplace, 1670–1820* (1994).

On the history of playhouse design, see Richard Leacroft, *The Development of the English Playhouse: An Illustrated Survey of Theatre Building in England from Medieval to Modern Times* (1988). For a survey of the plays that have appeared on these and other stages, see Allardyce Nicoll, *British Drama*, rev. J. C. Trewin (6th ed., 1978); the eight-volume *The Revels History of Drama in English*, gen. eds. Clifford Leech and T. W. Craik (1975–83); Alfred Harbage, *Annals of English Drama, 975–1700*, rev. S. Schoenbaum and Sylvia Wagonheim (3rd ed., 1989); and the three volumes of *The Cambridge History of British Theatre*, ed. Jane Milling, Peter Thomson, Joseph Donohue, and Baz Kershaw (2004).

On some of the key intellectual currents that are at once reflected in and shaped by literature and contemporary literary criticism, Arthur O. Lovejoy's classic studies *The Great Chain of Being* (1936) and *Essays in the History of Ideas* (1948) remain valuable, along with such works as Georg Simmel, *The Philosophy of Money* (1900; trans. 1907; 3rd enl. ed., 2004); Ernst Cassirer, *The Philosophy of Symbolic Forms* (4 vols., 1923–95; trans. 1953–96); Arthur O. Lovejoy and George Boas, *Primitivism and Related Ideas in Antiquity* (1935); Norbert Elias, *The Civilizing Process* (2 vols., 1939; trans. 1979–82); Simone de Beauvoir, *The Second Sex* (2 vols., 1949; trans. 1953, new trans.

2009); Frantz Fanon, *Black Skin, White Masks* (1952; trans. 1957, new trans. 2008); Ernst Kantorowicz, *The King's Two Bodies: A Study in Mediaeval Political Theology* (1957; new eds. 1997, 2016); Hannah Arendt, *The Human Condition* (1958; 2nd ed., 1998); Gaston Bachelard, *The Poetics of Space* (1958; trans. 1969, new ed. 1994); Richard Popkin, *The History of Scepticism from Erasmus to Descartes* (1960; rev. ed., 1964; rev. and expanded as *The History of Scepticism: From Savonarola to Bayle*, 2003); Hans Blumenberg, *The Legitimacy of the Modern Age* (1966; trans. 1983); M. H. Abrams, *Natural Supernaturalism: Tradition and Revolution in Romantic Literature* (1971); Michel Foucault, *Madness and Civilization: A History of Insanity in the Age of Reason* (1964; trans. 1965) and *The Order of Things: An Archaeology of the Human Sciences* (1966; trans. 1970); Jacques Derrida, *Of Grammatology* (1967; trans. 1976, 40th anniversary ed. 2016) and *Dissemination* (1972; trans. 1981); Martin Jay, *The Dialectical Imagination: A History of the Frankfurt School and the Institute of Social Research, 1923–1950* (1973); Hayden White, *Metahistory: The Historical Imagination in Nineteenth-Century Europe* (1973); Roland Barthes, *The Pleasure of the Text* (1973; trans. 1975); Raymond Williams, *Keywords: A Vocabulary of Culture and Society* (1976; new ed., 2015); Pierre Bourdieu, *Distinction: A Social Critique of the Judgement of Taste* (1979; trans. 1984); Richard Rorty, *Philosophy and the Mirror of Nature* (1979; 39th anniversary ed., 2009); Gilles Deleuze and Félix Guattari, *A Thousand Plateaus: Capitalism and Schizophrenia* (1980; trans. 1987); Michel de Certeau, *The Practice of Everyday Life* (2 vols., 1980; trans. 1984–98); Jürgen Habermas, *The Philosophical Discourse of Modernity: Twelve Lectures* (1985; trans. 1987); Slavoj Žižek, *The Sublime Object of Ideology* (1989); Homi Bhabha, *The Location of Culture* (1994; new ed., 2004); Judith Butler, *The Psychic Life of Power: Theories in Subjection* (1997); Sigmund Freud, *Writings on Art and Literature*, ed. Neil Hertz (1997); and N. Katherine Hayles, *How We Became Posthuman: Virtual Bodies in Cybernetics, Literature, and Informatics* (1999).

Reference Works

The single most important tool for the study of literature in English is the *Oxford English Dictionary* (1884–1924; 2nd ed., 1989; 3rd ed. in process). The most current edition, updated quarterly, is available online to subscribers. The OED is written on historical principles: that is, it attempts not only to describe current word use but also to record the history and development of the language from its origins before the Norman Conquest to the present. It thus provides, for familiar as well as archaic and obscure words, the widest possible range of meanings and uses, organized chronologically and illustrated with quotations. The OED can be searched as a conventional dictionary arranged a–z and also by subject, usage, region, origin, and timeline (the first appearance of a word). Resources available for early forms of English include the online Old English and Middle English dictionaries at Lexilogos (https://www.lexilogos.com/english/english_old.htm and https://www.lexilogos.com/english/english_middle.htm); also valuable are the *Dictionary of Old English* (1986–) and the *Middle English Dictionary* (1952; digitized 2008). Beyond the OED there are many other valuable dictionaries, such as *The American Heritage Dictionary* (5th ed., 50th anniversary printing, 2018); *The Oxford Dictionary of Abbreviations* (1992); T. F. Hoad, *The Concise Oxford Dictionary of English Etymology* (1993); Bas Aarts, Sylvia Chalker, and Edmund Weiner, *The Oxford Dictionary of English Grammar* (2nd ed., 2014); Morton S. Freeman, *A New Dictionary of Eponyms* (1997); *The Oxford Essential Dictionary of Foreign Terms in English* (1999); *The Oxford Dictionary of Idioms*, ed. Judith Siefring (2nd ed., 2004); P. H. Matthews, *The Concise Oxford Dictionary of Linguistics* (3rd ed., 2014); Tom McArthur, *The Oxford Guide* to World English (2002); and *The Concise Oxford Dictionary of Proverbs*, ed. Jennifer Speake (4th ed., 2003). Other valuable reference works include *The Cambridge Encyclopedia of the English Language*, ed. David Crystal (3rd ed., 2018); *The Concise Oxford Companion to the English Language*, ed. Tom McArthur (1998); *Fowler's Concise Dictionary of Modern English Usage*, ed. Jeremy Butterfield (3rd ed., 2016); and the numerous guides to specialized vocabularies, slang, regional dialects, and the like.

There is a steady flow of new editions of most major and many minor writers in English, along with the publication of critical appraisals and scholarship. James L. Harner's *Literary Research Guide: An Annotated List of Reference Sources in English Literary Studies* (6th ed., 2014; available online at www.mlalrg.org/public) offers thorough, evaluative annotations of a wide range of sources. For the historical record of scholarship and critical discussion, *The New Cambridge Bibliography of English Literature*, ed. George Watson (5 vols., 1969–77), and the third edition in process, *The Cambridge Bibliography of English Literature*, ed. Joanne Shattock (1 vol. to date, 2000–), are useful. The *MLA International Bibliography* (also online) is a key resource for following critical discussion of literatures in English. Ranging from 1926 to the present, it includes journal articles, essays, chapters from collections, books, and dissertations, and covers folklore, linguistics, and film. The *Annual Bibliography of English Language and Literature* (*ABELL*), compiled by the Modern Humanities Research Association, lists monographs, periodical articles, critical editions of literary works, book reviews, and collections of essays published anywhere in the world; unpublished doctoral dissertations are covered for the period 1920–99 (available online to subscribers directly and as part of Literature Online, http://literature.proquest.com/marketing/index.jsp).

For compact biographies of English authors, see the multivolume *Oxford Dictionary of National Biography* (*DNB*), ed. H. C. G. Matthew and Brian Harrison (2004); since 2004 the *DNB* has been extended online with updates (now monthly). Handy reference books of authors, works, and various literary terms and allusions include many volumes in the *Cambridge Companion* and *Oxford Companion* series: e.g., *The Cambridge Companion to Narrative*, ed. David Herman (2007); *The Oxford Companion to English Literature*, ed. Dinah Birch (7th ed., 2009); and *The Cambridge Companion to Allegory*, ed. Rita Copeland and Peter Struck (2010). *The Princeton Encyclopedia of Poetry and Poetics*, editor-in-chief Roland Greene (4th ed., 2012), is available online to subscribers in Oxford Reference. Handbooks that define and illustrate literary concepts and terms include *The Penguin Dictionary of Literary Terms and Literary Theory*, ed. J. A. Cuddon and M. A. R. Habib (5th ed., 2015); William Harmon, *A Handbook to Literature* (12th ed., 2011); *Critical Terms for Literary Study*, ed. Frank Lentricchia and Thomas McLaughlin (2nd ed., 1995); and M. H. Abrams and Geoffrey Galt Harpham, *A Glossary of Literary Terms* (11th ed., 2014). Also useful are Richard A. Lanham, *A Handlist of Rhetorical Terms* (2nd ed., 1991); Arthur Quinn, *Figures of Speech: 60 Ways to Turn a Phrase* (1982); the *Barnhart Concise Dictionary of Etymology*, ed. Robert K. Barnhart (1995); and George A. Kennedy, *A New History of Classical Rhetoric* (1994).

On Greek and Roman backgrounds, see *The Cambridge History of Classical Literature*—vol. 1, *Greek Literature*, ed. P. E. Easterling and Bernard M. W. Knox (1985), and vol. 2, *Latin Literature*, ed. E. J. Kenney and W. V. Clausen (1982), both available to subscribers online; *The Oxford Companion to Classical Literature*, ed. M. C. Howatson (3rd ed., 2011); Gian Biagio Conte, *Latin Literature: A History* (1987; trans. 1994); *The Oxford Classical Dictionary*, ed. Simon Hornblower, Antony Spawforth, and Esther Eidinow (4th ed., 2012); Richard Rutherford, *Classical Literature: A Concise History* (2005); and Mark P. O. Morford, Robert J. Lenardon, and Michael Sham, *Classical Mythology* (11th ed., 2018). The Loeb Classical Library of Greek and Roman texts with facing-page English translations is now available online to subscribers at www.loebclassics.com.

Digital resources in the humanities continue to grow rapidly. Among the many useful electronic resources for the study of English literature are enormous digital archives, available to subscribers: Early English Books Online (EEBO), http://eebo.chadwyck.com/home; Literature Online, http://literature.proquest.com/marketing/index.jsp; and Eighteenth Century Collections Online (ECCO), www.gale.com/primary-sources/eighteenth-century-collections-online. There are also numerous free sites of variable quality. Many of the best of these are period- or author-specific and hence are listed in the period/author bibliographies on the NAEL website. Among the general sites, one of the most useful and wide-ranging is Voice of the Shuttle (http://vos.ucsb.edu), which includes links to Bartleby.com and Project Gutenberg.

Literary Criticism and Theory

The Cambridge History of Literary Criticism comprises nine volumes (1989–2013): *Classical Criticism*, ed. George A. Kennedy; *The Middle Ages*, ed. Alastair Minnis and Ian Johnson; *The Renaissance*, ed. Glyn P. Norton; *The Eighteenth Century*, ed. H. B. Nisbet and Claude Rawson; *Romanticism*, ed. Marshall Brown; *The Nineteenth Century, c. 1830–1914*, ed. M. A. R. Habib; *Modernism and the New Criticism*, ed. A. Walton Litz, Louis Menand, and Lawrence Rainey; *From Formalism to Poststructuralism*, ed. Raman Selden; and *Twentieth-Century Historical, Philosophical and Psychological Perspectives*, ed. Christa Knellwolf and Christopher Norris. See also M. H. Abrams, *The Mirror and the Lamp: Romantic Theory and the Critical Tradition* (1953); William K. Wimsatt Jr. and Cleanth Brooks, *Literary Criticism: A Short History* (1957); René Wellek, *A History of Modern Criticism: 1750–1950* (8 vols., 1955–92); Frank Lentricchia, *After the New Criticism* (1980); J. Hillis Miller, *On Literature* (2002); and John Frow, *Character and Person* (2014). Raman Selden, Peter Widdowson, and Peter Brooker have written *A Reader's Guide to Contemporary Literary Theory* (6th ed., 2017). Other useful resources include *The Johns Hopkins Guide to Literary Theory and Criticism*, ed. Michael Groden, Martin Kreiswirth, and Imre Szeman (2nd ed., 2005); *Literary Theory: An Anthology*, ed. Julie Rivkin and Michael Ryan (3rd ed., 2017); and *The Norton Anthology of Theory and Criticism*, gen. ed. Vincent B. Leitch (3rd ed., 2018).

Modern approaches to English literature and literary theory were shaped by certain landmark works: William Empson, *Seven Types of Ambiguity* (1930; 3rd ed., 1953), *Some Versions of Pastoral* (1935), and *The Structure of Complex Words* (1951; 3rd ed., 1977); T. S. Eliot, *Selected Essays* (1932; 3rd ed., 1951) and *On Poetry and Poets* (1957); F. R. Leavis, *Revaluation: Tradition and Development in English Poetry* (1936) and *The Great Tradition: George Eliot, Henry James, Joseph Conrad* (1948); Erich Auerbach, *Mimesis: The Representation of Reality in Western Literature* (1946; trans. 1953); Lionel Trilling, *The Liberal Imagination: Essays on Literature and Society* (1950); William K. Wimsatt Jr., *The Verbal Icon: Studies in the Meaning of Poetry* (1954); Northrop Frye, *Anatomy of Criticism: Four Essays* (1957); Wayne C. Booth, *The Rhetoric of Fiction* (1961; 2nd ed., 1983); and W. Jackson Bate, *The Burden of the Past and the English Poet* (1970). René Wellek and Austin Warren, *Theory of Literature* (3rd ed., 1963), is a useful introduction to the variety of scholarly and critical approaches to literature up to the time of its publication. Jonathan Culler's *Literary Theory: A Very Short Introduction* (2nd ed., 2011), discusses recurrent issues and debates. On the discipline of criticism, see John Guillory's *Professing Criticism: Essays on the Organization of Literary Study* (2022); Rita Felski's *The Limits of Critique* (2015) is a critical assessment of contemporary criticism.

Beginning in the late 1960s, interest in literary theory as a specific field markedly intensified. Certain forms of literary study had already been influenced by the work of the Russian linguist Roman Jakobson and the Russian formalist Viktor Shklovsky—and, still more, by conceptions that derived or claimed to derive from Marx and Engels—but the full impact of these theories was not felt until what became known as the "theory revolution" of the 1970s and '80s. For Marxist literary criticism, see Georg Lukács, *Theory of the Novel: A Historico-philosophical Essay on the Forms of Great Epic Literature* (1920; trans. 1971), *The Historical Novel* (1937 trans. 1962), and *Studies in European Realism: A Sociological Survey of the Writings of Balzac, Stendhal, Zola, Tolstoy, Gorki, and Others* (trans. 1950); Walter Benjamin's essays from the 1920s and '30s, represented in *Illuminations* (1955; trans. 1968) and *Reflections: Essays, Aphorisms, Autobiographical Writings* (1975; trans. 1978); Mikhail Bakhtin's essays from the 1930s represented in *The Dialogic Imagination: Four Essays* (trans. 1981) and *Rabelais and His World* (1965; trans. 1968); *Selections from the Prison Notebooks of Antonio Gramsci*, ed. and trans. Quintin Hoare and Geoffrey Nowell Smith (1971); Raymond Williams, *Marxism and Literature* (1977); Tony Bennett, *Formalism and Marxism* (1979; 2nd ed., 2003); Fredric Jameson, *The Political Unconscious: Narrative as a Socially Symbolic Act* (1981); and Terry Eagleton, *Literary Theory: An Introduction* (1983; anniversary ed., 2003) and *The Ideology of the Aesthetic* (1990).

Structural linguistics and anthropology gave rise to a flowering of structuralist literary criticism; convenient introductions include Robert Scholes, *Structuralism in Literature: An Introduction* (1974), and Jonathan Culler, *Structuralist Poetics: Structuralism, Linguistics and the Study of Literature* (new ed., 2002). Poststructuralist challenges to this approach are epitomized in such influential works as Jacques Derrida, *Writing and Difference* (1967; trans. 1978), and Paul de Man, *Blindness and Insight: Essays in the Rhetoric of Contemporary Criticism* (1971; 2nd ed., 1983). Poststructuralism is discussed in Jonathan Culler, *On Deconstruction: Theory and Criticism after Structuralism* (1982; 25th anniversary ed., 2007); Slavoj Žižek, *The Sublime Object of Ideology* (1989); Fredric Jameson, *Postmodernism; or, The Cultural Logic of Late Capitalism* (1991); John McGowan, *Postmodernism and Its Critics* (1991); and *Beyond Structuralism: The Speculations of Theory and the Experience of Reading*, ed. Wendell V. Harris (1996). A figure who greatly influenced both structuralism and poststructuralism is Roland Barthes, in *Mythologies* (1957; trans. 1972, new trans. 2012) and *S/Z* (1970; trans. 1974). Among other influential contributions to literary theory are the psychoanalytic approach in Harold Bloom, *The Anxiety of Influence: A Theory of Poetry* (1973; 2nd ed., 1997), and the reader-response approach in Stanley Fish, *Is There a Text in This Class? The Authority of Interpretive Communities* (1980). For a retrospect on these decades, see Terry Eagleton, *After Theory* (2003).

Influenced by these theoretical currents but not restricted to them, modern feminist literary criticism was fashioned by such works as Patricia Meyer Spacks, *The Female Imagination* (1975); Ellen Moers, *Literary Women* (1976; new ed., 1986); Elaine Showalter, *A Literature of Their Own: British Women Novelists from Brontë to Lessing* (1977; expanded ed., 1999); and Sandra M. Gilbert and Susan Gubar, *The Madwoman in the Attic: The Woman Writer and the Nineteenth-Century Literary Imagination* (1979). Subsequent studies include Jane Gallop, *The Daughter's Seduction: Feminism and Psychoanalysis* (1982); Luce Irigaray, *This Sex Which Is Not One* (1977; trans. 1985); Gayatri Chakravorty Spivak, *In Other Worlds: Essays in Cultural Politics* (1987; new ed., 2006); Barbara Johnson, *A World of Difference* (1987); Sandra M. Gilbert and Susan Gubar, *No Man's Land: The Place of the Woman Writer in the Twentieth Century* (3 vols., 1988–94); Judith Butler, *Gender Trouble: Feminism and the Subversion of Identity* (1990; 2nd ed., 1999); and the critical views sampled in *The New Feminist Criticism: Essays on Women, Literature, and Theory*, ed. Elaine Showalter (1985); *Feminist Literary Theory: A Reader*, ed. Mary Eagleton (1986; 3rd ed., 2011); and *Feminisms: An Anthology of Literary Theory and Criticism*, ed. Robyn R. Warhol and Diane Price Herndl (1991; rev. in 2009 as *Feminisms Redux: An Anthology of Literary Theory and Criticism*); *The Hélène*

Cixous Reader, ed. Susan Sellers (1994); *The Cambridge Companion to Feminist Literary Theory*, ed. Ellen Rooney (2006); and *Feminist Literary Theory and Criticism: A Norton Reader*, ed. Sandra M. Gilbert and Susan Gubar (2007).

Just as feminist critics used poststructuralist and psychoanalytic methods to place literature in conversation with gender theory, a new school emerged placing literature in conversation with critical race theory. Comprehensive introductions include *Critical Race Theory: The Key Writings That Formed the Movement*, ed. Kimberlé Crenshaw et al. (1995); and Richard Delgado and Jean Stefancic, *Critical Race Theory: An Introduction* (3rd ed., 2017); and *The Routledge Companion to Race and Ethnicity*, ed. Stephen M. Caliendo and Charlton D. McIlwain (2nd ed., 2021). For an important precursor in cultural studies, see Stuart Hall et al., *Policing the Crisis: Mugging, the State and Law and Order* (1978; 2nd ed., 2013). Seminal works include Henry Louis Gates Jr., *The Signifying Monkey: A Theory of African-American Literary Criticism* (1988; 25th anniversary ed., 2014); Patricia Williams, *The Alchemy of Race and Rights* (1991); Toni Morrison, *Playing in the Dark: Whiteness and the Literary Imagination* (1992); Cornel West, *Race Matters* (1993; 25th anniversary ed., 2017); Gene Andrew Jarrett, *Representing the Race: A New Political History of African American Literature* (2011); Fred Moten, *Black and Blur* (2017); and Saidiya V. Hartman, *Wayward Lives, Beautiful Experiments: Intimate Histories of Social Upheaval* (2019). Other important works include Kathleen Davis, *Periodization and Sovereignty: How Ideas of Feudalism and Secularization Govern the Politics of Time* (2008; rpt. 2017); Alexander G. Weheliye, *Habeas Viscus: Racializing Assemblages, Biopolitics, and Black Feminist Theories of the Human* (2014); Christina Sharpe, *In the Wake: On Blackness and Being* (2016); and Geraldine Heng, *The Invention of Race in the European Middle Ages* (2018). Helpful anthologies and collections of essays have emerged in recent decades, such as *The Oxford Companion to African American Literature*, ed. William L. Andrews, Frances Smith Foster, and Trudier Harris (1997), and also their *Concise Oxford Companion to African American Literature* (2001); *Unchained Voices: An Anthology of Black Authors in the English-Speaking World of the Eighteenth Century*, ed. Vincent Carretta (1996; updated 2003); *The Cambridge Companion to Jewish American Literature*, ed. Hana Wirth-Nesher and Michael P. Kramer (2003); *A Companion to African American Literature*, ed. Gene Andrew Jarrett (2010); *The Routledge Companion to Anglophone Caribbean Literature*, ed. Michael A. Bucknor and Alison Donnell (2011); *The Routledge Companion to Latino/a Literature*, ed. Suzanne Bost and Frances R. Aparicio (2013); *The Routledge Companion to Asian American and Pacific Islander Literature*, ed. Rachel C. Lee (2014); *The Cambridge Companion to Asian American Literature*, ed. Crystal Parikh and Daniel Y. Kim (2015); and *The Cambridge Companion to British Black and Asian Literature, 1945–2010*, ed. Deirdre Osborne (2016).

Gay literature and queer studies are represented in collections including *Inside/Out: Lesbian Theories, Gay Theories*, ed. Diana Fuss (1991); *The Lesbian and Gay Studies Reader*, ed. Henry Abelove, Michèle Aina Barale, and David Halperin (1993); *The Columbia Anthology of Gay Literature: Readings from Western Antiquity to the Present Day*, ed. Byrne R. S. Fone (1998); *The Cambridge History of Gay and Lesbian Literature*, ed. E. L. McCallum and Mikko Tuhkanen (2014); and *The Cambridge Companion to Lesbian Literature*, ed. Jodie Medd (2015), and by such books as Eve Kosofsky Sedgwick, *Between Men: English Literature and Male Homosocial Desire* (1985; 30th anniversary ed., 2015) and *Epistemology of the Closet* (1990; updated ed., 2008); Diana Fuss, *Essentially Speaking: Feminism, Nature, and Difference* (1989); Terry Castle, *The Apparitional Lesbian: Female Homosexuality and Modern Culture* (1993); Leo Bersani, *Homos* (1995); Gregory Woods, *A History of Gay Literature: The Male Tradition* (1998); David Halperin, *How to Do the History of Homosexuality* (2002); Judith Halberstam, *In a Queer Time and Place: Transgender Bodies, Subcultural Lives* (2005); Heather Love, *Feeling Backward: Loss and the Politics of Queer History* (2007); and Brian Glavey, *The Wallflower Avant-garde: Modernism, Sexuality, and Queer Ekphrasis* (2016).

New Historicism is represented in Stephen Greenblatt, *Learning to Curse: Essays in Early Modern Culture* (1990; new ed., 2007); *New Historical Literary Study: Essays on Reproducing Texts, Representing History*, ed. Jeffrey N. Cox and Larry J. Reynolds (1993); *The New Historicism Reader*, ed. H. Aram Veeser (1994); and Catherine Gallagher and Stephen Greenblatt, *Practicing New Historicism* (2000). The related social and historical dimension of texts is discussed in Jerome McGann, *Critique of Modern Textual Criticism* (1983), and *Scholarly Editing: A Guide to Research*, ed. D. C. Greetham (1995). Characteristic of New Historicism is an expansion of the field of literary interpretation still further in cultural studies; for a broad sampling of the range of interests, see *Cultural Studies*, ed. Lawrence Grossberg, Cary Nelson, and Paula A. Treichler (1992); *A Cultural Studies Reader: History, Theory, Practice*, ed. Jessica Munns and Gita Rajan (1995); and *The Cultural Studies Reader*, ed. Simon During (3rd ed., 2007).

This expansion of the field is similarly reflected in postcolonial studies: see Frantz Fanon, *Black Skin, White Masks* (cited above) and *The Wretched of the Earth* (1961; trans. 1963, 60th anniversary ed. 2021); Edward Said, *Orientalism* (1978) and *Culture and Imperialism* (1993); *Nation and Narration*, ed. Homi K. Bhabha (1990); *The Post-Colonial Studies Reader*, ed. Bill Ashcroft, Gareth Griffiths and Helen Tiffin (2nd ed., 2006); and such influential books as Bill Ashcroft, Gareth Griffiths, and Helen Tiffin, *The Empire Writes Back: Theory and Practice in Post-Colonial Literatures* (1989; 2nd ed., 2002); Homi K. Bhabha, *The Location of Culture* (1994; new ed., 2004); Elleke Boehmer, *Colonial and Postcolonial Literature: Migrant Metaphors* (1995; 2nd ed., 2005); Dipesh Chakrabarty, *Provincializing Europe: Postcolonial Thought and Historical Difference* (2000; new ed., 2008); and Robert J. C. Young, *Postcolonialism: An Historical Introduction* (2001; anniversary ed., 2016). Useful collections include *The Cambridge History of Postcolonial Literature*, ed. Ato Quayson (2 vols., 2011–12); *The Cambridge Companion to the Postcolonial Novel*, ed. Ato Quayson (2016); and *The Cambridge Companion to Postcolonial Poetry*, ed. Jahan Ramazani (2017).

In the wake of the theory revolution, critics have focused on a wide array of topics, which can be only briefly surveyed here. One current of work, focusing on the history of emotion, is represented in Brian Massumi, *Parables for the Virtual: Movement, Affect, Sensation* (2002); Sianne Ngai, *Ugly Feelings* (2005); *The Affect Theory Reader*, ed. Melissa Gregg and Gregory J. Seigworth (2010); and Judith Butler, *Senses of the Subject* (2015). A somewhat related current, examining the special role of traumatic memory in literature, is exemplified in *Trauma: Explorations in Memory*, ed. Cathy Caruth (1995), and Dominic LaCapra, *Writing History, Writing Trauma* (2001; new ed., 2014). Work on the literary implications of cognitive science may be glimpsed in *Introduction to Cognitive Cultural Studies*, ed. Lisa Zunshine (2010). Interest in quantitative approaches to literature was sparked by Franco Moretti's *Graphs, Maps, Trees: Abstract Models for Literary History* (2005). For the field of digital humanities, see Moretti, *Distant Reading* (2013); *Defining Digital Humanities: A Reader*, ed. Melissa Terras, Julianne Nyhan, and Edward Vanhoutte (2013); and *A New Companion to Digital Humanities*, ed. Susan Schreibman, Ray Siemens, and John Unsworth (2016). For ecocriticism, or studies of literature and the environment, see *The Ecocriticism Reader: Landmarks in Literary Ecology*, ed. Cheryll Glotfelty and Harold Fromm (1996); *Writing the Environment: Ecocriticism and Literature*, ed. Richard Kerridge and Neil Sammells (1998); Jonathan Bate, *The Song of the Earth* (2000); Lawrence Buell, *The Future of Environmental Criticism: Environmental Crisis and Literary Imagination* (2005); Timothy Morton, *Ecology Without Nature: Rethinking Environmental Aesthetics* (2007); Jane Bennett, *Vibrant Matter: A Political Ecology of Things* (2010); Rob Nixon, *Slow Violence and the Environmentalism of the Poor* (2011); *The Oxford Handbook of Ecocriticism*, ed. Greg Garrard (2014); and *Anthropocene Reading: Literary History in Geologic*

Times, ed. Tobias Menely and Jesse Oak Taylor (2017). Related are the fields of animal studies and posthumanism, whose key works include Bruno Latour, *We Have Never Been Modern* (1991; trans. 1993); Steve Baker, *The Postmodern Animal* (2000); Cary Wolfe, *Animal Rites: American Culture, the Discourse of Species, and Posthumanist Theory* (2003) and *What Is Posthumanism?* (2009); Jacques Derrida, *The Animal That Therefore I Am* (2006; trans. 2008); Kari Weil, *Thinking Animals: Why Animal Studies Now?* (2012); *Animals and the Human Imagination: A Companion to Animal Studies*, ed. Aaron Gross and Anne Vallely (2012); and *Critical Animal Studies: Thinking the Unthinkable*, ed. John Sorenson (2014). The relationship between literature and law is central to such works as *Interpreting Law and Literature: A Hermeneutic Reader*, ed. Sanford Levinson and Steven Mailloux (1988); *Law's Stories: Narrative and Rhetoric in the Law*, ed. Peter Brooks and Paul Gewirtz (1996); *Literature and Legal Problem Solving: Law and Literature as Ethical Discourse*, ed. Paul J. Heald (1998); and *New Directions in Law and Literature*, ed. Elizabeth S. Anker and Bernadette Meyler (2017). Ethical questions in literature have been usefully explored by, among others, Geoffrey Galt Harpham in *Getting It Right: Language, Literature, and Ethics* (1992) and Derek Attridge in *The Singularity of Literature* (2004). Finally, some approaches to literature, such as formalism and literary biography, that seemed superseded in the theoretical ferment of the late twentieth century have had a resurgence. A renewed interest in form is evident in Susan Stewart, *Poetry and the Fate of the Senses* (2002); *Reading for Form*, ed. Susan J. Wolfson and Marshall Brown (2006); and Caroline Levine, *Forms: Whole, Rhythm, Hierarchy, Network* (2015). Interest in the history of the book was spearheaded by D. F. McKenzie's *Bibliography and the Sociology of Texts* (1986), Jerome J. McGann's *The Textual Condition* (1991), and Roger Chartier's *The Order of Books: Readers, Authors, and Libraries in Europe Between the Fourteenth and Eighteenth Centuries* (1992; trans. 1994). See also *The Practice and Representation of Reading in England*, ed. James Raven, Helen Small, and Naomi Tadmor (1996); *The Cambridge History of the Book in Britain* (7 vols., 1999–2019); *The Book History Reader*, ed. David Finkelstein and Alistair McCleery (2nd ed., 2006); and *The Cambridge Companion to the History of the Book*, ed. Leslie Howsam (2015). For studies in new media and digital or electronic literature, see N. Katherine Hayles, *Electronic Literature: New Horizons for the Literary* (2008); Matthew G. Kirschenbaum, *Track Changes: A Literary History of Word Processing* (2016); and Jessica Pressman's *Bookishness: Loving Books in a Digital Age* (2020).

Anthologies representing a range of recent approaches include *Modern Criticism and Theory*, ed. David Lodge with Nigel Wood (2nd ed., 2000); *Contemporary Literary Criticism*, ed. Robert Con Davis and Ronald Schleifer (4th ed., 1998); and *The Norton Anthology of Theory and Criticism* (cited above).

Literary Terminology*

Using simple technical terms can sharpen our understanding and streamline our discussion of literary works. Some terms, such as the ones in section A, below, help us address the internal style, structure, form, and kind of works. Other terms, such as those in section B, provide insight into the material forms in which literary works have been produced.

In analyzing what they called "rhetoric," ancient Greek and Roman writers determined the elements of what we call "style" and "structure." Most of our literary terms are derived, via medieval and Renaissance intermediaries, from the Greek and Latin sources. In the definitions that follow, the etymology, or root, of the word is given when it helps illuminate the word's current usage.

Many of the examples are drawn from texts in *The Norton Anthology of English Literature*.

Words **boldfaced** within definitions are themselves defined in this appendix. Some terms are defined within definitions; such words are *italicized*.

A. Terms of Style, Structure, Form, and Kind

accent (synonym "stress"): a term of **rhythm**. The special force devoted to the voicing of one syllable in a word over others. In the noun "accent," for example, the accent, or stress, is on the first syllable.

act: the major subdivision of a play, usually divided into **scenes**.

aesthetics (from Greek, "to feel, apprehend by the senses"): the philosophy of artistic meaning as a distinct mode of apprehending untranslatable truth, defined as an alternative to rational enquiry, which is purely abstract. Developed in the late eighteenth century by the German philosopher Immanuel Kant especially.

Alexandrine: a term of **meter**. In French verse a line of twelve syllables, and, by analogy, in English verse a line of six stresses. See **hexameter**.

allegory (Greek "saying otherwise"): saying one thing (the "vehicle" of the allegory) and meaning another (the allegory's "tenor"). Allegories may be momentary aspects of a work, as in **metaphor** ("John is a lion"), or, through extended metaphor, may constitute the basis of narrative, as in Bunyan's *Pilgrim's Progress*: this second meaning is the dominant one. See also **symbol** and **type**. Allegory is one of the most significant **figures of thought**.

alliteration (from Latin "litera," alphabetic letter): a **figure of speech**. The repetition of an initial consonant sound or consonant cluster in consecutive or closely positioned words. This pattern is often an inseparable part of the meter in Germanic languages, where the tonic, or accented **syllable**, is usually the first syllable. Thus all Old English poetry and some varieties of Middle English poetry use alliteration as part of their basic metrical practice. *Sir Gawain and the Green Knight*, line 1: "Once the siege and assault of Troy had ceased" (see vol. A, p. 415). Otherwise used for local effects; Stevie Smith, "Pretty," lines 4–5: "And in the pretty pool the pike stalks / He stalks his prey . . ." (see vol. F, p. 589).

---

*This appendix was devised and compiled by James Simpson with the collaboration of all the editors. We especially thank Professor Lara Bovilsky of the University of Oregon at Eugene for her help.

allusion: Literary allusion is a passing but illuminating reference within a literary text to another, well-known text (often biblical or **classical**). Topical allusions are also, of course, common in certain modes, especially **satire**.

anagnorisis (Greek "recognition"): the moment of **protagonist's** recognition in a narrative, which is also often the moment of moral understanding.

anapest: a term of **rhythm**. A three-syllable foot following the rhythmic pattern, in English verse, of two unstressed (uu) syllables followed by one stressed (/). Thus, for example, "Illinois."

anaphora (Greek "carrying back"): a **figure of speech**. The repetition of words or groups of words at the beginning of consecutive sentences, clauses, or phrases. Blake, "London," lines 5–8: "In every cry of every Man, / In every Infant's cry of fear, / In every voice, in every ban..." (see vol. D, p. 137); Louise Bennett, "Jamaica Oman," lines 17–20: "Some backa man a push, some side-a / Man a hole him han, / Some a lick sense eena him head, / Some a guide him pon him plan!" (see vol. F, p. 724).

animal fable: a **genre**. A short narrative of speaking animals, followed by moralizing comment, written in a low style and gathered into a collection. Robert Henryson, "The Cock and the Jasper" (see vol. A, p. 679).

antithesis (Greek "placing against"): a **figure of thought**. The juxtaposition of opposed terms in clauses or sentences that are next to or near each other. Milton, *Paradise Lost* 1.777–80: "They but now who seemed / In bigness to surpass Earth's giant sons / Now less than smallest dwarfs, in narrow room / Throng numberless" (see vol. B, p. 1448).

apostrophe (from Greek "turning away"): a **figure of thought**. An address, often to an absent person, a force, or a quality. For example, a poet makes an apostrophe to a Muse when invoking her for inspiration.

apposition: a term of **syntax**. The repetition of elements serving an identical grammatical function in one sentence. The effect of this repetition is to arrest the flow of the sentence, but in doing so to add extra semantic nuance to repeated elements. This is an especially important feature of Old English poetic style. See, for example, Caedmon's *Hymn* (vol. A, p. 31), where the phrases "heaven-kingdom's Guardian," "the Measurer's might," "his mind-plans," and "the work of the Glory-Father" each serve an identical syntactic function as the direct objects of "praise."

assonance (Latin "sounding to"): a **figure of speech**. The repetition of identical or near identical stressed vowel sounds in words whose final consonants differ, producing half-rhyme. Tennyson, "The Lady of Shalott," line 100: "His broad clear brow in sunlight glowed" (see vol. E, p. 210).

aubade (originally from Spanish "alba," dawn): a **genre**. A lover's dawn song or lyric bewailing the arrival of the day and the necessary separation of the lovers; Donne, "The Sun Rising" (see vol. B, p. 888). Larkin recasts the genre in "Aubade" (see vol. F, p. 795).

autobiography (Greek "self-life writing"): a **genre**. A narrative of a life written by the subject; Wordsworth, *The Prelude* (see vol. D, p. 391). There are subgenres, such as the spiritual autobiography, narrating the author's path to conversion and subsequent spiritual trials, as in Bunyan's *Grace Abounding*.

ballad stanza: a **verse form**. Usually a **quatrain** in alternating **iambic tetrameter** and **iambic trimeter** lines, rhyming abcb. See "Sir Patrick Spens" (vol. D, p. 38); Louise Bennett's poems (vol. F, pp. 719–24); Eliot, "Sweeney among the Nightingales" (vol. F, p. 501); Larkin, "This Be The Verse" (vol. F, p. 795).

ballade: a **verse form**. A form consisting usually of three stanzas followed by a four-line envoi (French, "send off"). The last line of the first stanza establishes a **refrain**, which is repeated, or subtly varied, as the last line of each stanza. The form was derived from French medieval poetry; English poets, from the fourteenth to the sixteenth centuries especially, used it with varying stanza forms. Chaucer, "The Complaint of Chaucer to His Purse" (see vol. A, p. 575).

bathos (Greek "depth"): a **figure of thought**. A sudden and sometimes ridiculous descent of tone; Pope, *The Rape of the Lock* 3.157–58: "Not louder shrieks to pitying heaven are cast, / When husbands, or when lapdogs breathe their last" (see vol. C, p. 549).

beast epic: a **genre**. A continuous, unmoralized narrative, in prose or verse, relating the victories of the wholly unscrupulous but brilliant strategist Reynard the Fox over all adversaries. Chaucer arouses, only to deflate, expectations of the genre in *The Nun's Priest's Tale* (see vol. A, p. 556).

biography (Greek "life-writing"): a **genre**. A life as the subject of an extended narrative.

blank verse: a **verse form**. Unrhymed **iambic pentameter** lines. Blank verse has no stanzas, but is broken up into uneven units (verse paragraphs) determined by sense rather than form. First devised in English by Henry Howard, Earl of Surrey, in his translation of two books of Virgil's *Aeneid*, this very flexible verse type became the standard form for dramatic poetry in the seventeenth century, as in most of Shakespeare's plays. Milton and Wordsworth, among many others, also used it to create an English equivalent to **classical epic**.

blazon: strictly, a heraldic shield; in rhetorical usage, a **topos** whereby the individual elements of a beloved's face and body are singled out for **hyperbolic** admiration. Spenser, *Epithalamion*, lines 167–84 (see vol. B, p. 459). For an inversion of the **topos**, see Shakespeare, Sonnet 130 (vol. B, p. 637).

burlesque (French and Italian "mocking"): a work that adopts the **conventions** of a genre with the aim less of comically mocking the genre than of satirically mocking the society so represented (see **satire**). Thus Pope's *Rape of the Lock* (see vol. C, p. 537) does not mock **classical epic** so much as contemporary mores.

caesura (Latin "cut") (plural "caesurae"): a term of **meter**. A pause or breathing space within a line of verse, generally occurring between syntactic units; Louise Bennett, "Colonization in Reverse," lines 5–8: "By de hundred, by de tousan, / From country an from town, / By de ship-load, by de plane-load, / Jamaica is Englan boun" (see vol. F, p. 722), where the caesurae occur in lines 5 and 7.

canon (Greek "rule"): the group of texts regarded as worthy of special respect or attention by a given institution. Also, the group of texts regarded as definitely having been written by a certain author.

catastrophe (Greek "overturning"): the decisive turn in **tragedy** by which the plot is resolved and, usually, the **protagonist** dies.

catharsis (Greek "cleansing"): According to Aristotle, the effect of **tragedy** on its audience, through their experience of pity and terror, was a kind of spiritual cleansing, or catharsis.

character (Greek "stamp, impression"): a person, personified animal, or other figure represented in a literary work, especially in narrative and drama. The more a character seems to generate the action of a narrative, and the less he or she seems merely to serve a preordained narrative pattern, the "fuller," or more "rounded," a character is said to be. A "stock" character, common particularly in many comic genres, will perform a predictable function in different works of a given genre.

chiasmus (Greek "crosswise"): a **figure of speech**. The inversion of an already established sequence. This can involve verbal echoes: Pope, "Eloisa to Abelard," line 104, "The crime was common, common be the pain" (see vol. C, p. 560); or it can be purely a matter of syntactic inversion: Pope, *Epistle to Dr. Arbuthnot*, line 8: "They pierce my thickets, through my grot they glide" (see vol. C, p. 575).

classical, classicism, classic: Each term can be widely applied, but in English literary discourse, "classical" primarily describes the works of either Greek or Roman antiquity. "Classicism" denotes the practice of art forms inspired by classical antiquity, in particular the observance of rhetorical norms of **decorum** and balance, as opposed to following the dictates of untutored inspiration, as in Romanticism. "Classic" denotes an especially famous work within a given **canon**.

climax (Greek "ladder"): a moment of great intensity and structural change, especially in drama. Also a **figure of speech** whereby a sequence of verbally linked clauses is made, in which each successive clause is of greater consequence than its predecessor. Bacon, *Of Studies*: "Studies serve for pastimes, for ornaments, and for abilities. Their chief use for pastimes is in privateness and retiring; for ornament, is in discourse; and for ability, is in judgement" (see vol. B, pp. 1167–68).

comedy: a **genre**. A term primarily applied to drama, and derived from ancient drama, in opposition to **tragedy**. Comedy deals with humorously confusing, sometimes ridiculous situations in which the ending is, nevertheless, happy. A comedy often ends in one or more marriages.

comic mode: Many genres (for example, **romance, fabliau, comedy**) involve a happy ending in which justice is done, the ravages of time are arrested, and that which is lost is found. Such genres participate in a comic mode.

connotation: To understand connotation, we need to understand **denotation**. While many words can denote the same concept—that is, have the same basic meaning—those words can evoke different associations, or connotations. Contrast, for example, the clinical-sounding term "depression" and the more colorful, musical, even poetic phrase "the blues."

consonance (Latin "sounding with"): a **figure of speech**. The repetition of final consonants in words or stressed syllables whose vowel sounds are different. Herbert, "Easter," line 13: "Consort, both heart and lute . . ." (see vol. B, p. 1183).

convention: a repeatedly recurring feature (in either form or content) of works, occurring in combination with other recurring formal features, which constitutes a convention of a particular genre.

couplet: a **verse form**. In English verse two consecutive, rhyming lines usually containing the same number of stresses. Chaucer first introduced the **iambic pentameter** couplet into English (*Canterbury Tales*); the form was later used in many types of writing, including drama; imitations and translations of **classical epic** (thus *heroic couplet*); essays; and **satire** (see Dryden and Pope). The *distich* (Greek "two lines") is a couplet usually making complete sense; Aemilia Lanyer, *Salve Deus Rex Judaeorum*, lines 5–6: "Read it fair queen, though it defective be, / Your excellence can grace both it and me" (see vol. B, p. 925).

dactyl (Greek "finger," because of the finger's three joints): a term of **rhythm**. A three-syllable foot following the rhythmic pattern, in English verse, of one stressed followed by two unstressed syllables. Thus, for example, "Oregon."

decorum (Latin "that which is fitting"): a rhetorical principle whereby each formal aspect of a work should be in keeping with its subject matter and/or audience.

deixis (Greek "pointing"): relevant to **point of view**. Every work has, implicitly or explicitly, a "here" and a "now" from which it is narrated. Words that refer to or imply this point from which the voice of the work is projected (such as "here," "there," "this," "that," "now," "then") are examples of deixis, or "deictics." This technique is especially important in drama, where it is used to create a sense of the events happening as the spectator witnesses them.

denotation: A word has a basic, "prosaic" (factual) meaning prior to the associations it connotes (see **connotation**). The word "steed," for example, might call to mind a horse fitted with battle gear, to be ridden by a warrior, but its denotation is simply "horse."

denouement (French "unknotting"): the point at which a narrative can be resolved and so ended.

dialogue (Greek "conversation"): a **genre**. Dialogue is a feature of many genres, especially in both the **novel** and drama. As a genre itself, dialogue is used in philosophical traditions especially (most famously in Plato's *Dialogues*), as the representation of a conversation in which a philosophical question is pursued among various speakers.

diction, or **"lexis"** (from, respectively, Latin *dictio* and Greek *lexis*, each meaning "word"): the actual words used in any utterance—speech, writing, and, for our purposes here, literary works. The choice of words contributes significantly to the style of a given work.

didactic mode (Greek "teaching mode"): **Genres** in a didactic mode are designed to instruct or teach, sometimes explicitly (for example, sermons, philosophical **discourses, georgic**), and sometimes through the medium of fiction (for example, **animal fable, parable**).

diegesis (Greek for "narration"): a term that simply means "narration," but is used in literary criticism to distinguish one kind of story from another. In a *mimetic* story, the events are played out before us (see **mimesis**), whereas in diegesis someone recounts the story to us. Drama is for the most part *mimetic*, whereas the novel is for the most part diegetic. In novels the narrator is not, usually, part of the action of the narrative; s/he is therefore extradiegetic.

dimeter (Greek "two measure"): a term of **meter.** A two-stress line, rarely used as the meter of whole poems, though used with great frequency in single poems by Skelton, for example, "The Tunning of Elinour Rumming" (see vol. B, p. 41). Otherwise used for single lines, as in Herbert, "Discipline," line 3: "O my God" (see vol. B, p. 1197).

discourse (Latin "running to and fro"): broadly, any nonfictional speech or writing; as a more specific genre, a philosophical meditation on a set theme.

dramatic irony: a feature of narrative and drama, whereby the audience knows that the outcome of an action will be the opposite of that intended by a **character.**

dramatic monologue (Greek "single speaking"): a **genre.** A poem in which the voice of a historical or fictional **character** speaks, unmediated by any narrator, to an implied though silent audience. See Tennyson, "Ulysses" (vol. E, p. 217); Browning, "The Bishop Orders His Tomb" (vol. E, p. 416); Eliot, "The Love Song of J. Alfred Prufrock" (vol. F, p. 498); Carol Ann Duffy, "Medusa" and "Mrs Lazarus" (vol. F, pp. 1158–60).

ecphrasis (Greek "speaking out"): a **topos** whereby a work of visual art is represented in a literary work. Auden, "Musée des Beaux Arts" (see vol. F, p. 677).

elegy: a **genre**. In **classical** literature elegy was a form written in elegiac **couplets** (a **hexameter** followed by a **pentameter**) devoted to many possible topics. In Ovidian elegy a lover meditates on the trials of erotic desire (for example, Ovid's *Amores*). The **sonnet** sequences of both Sidney and Shakespeare exploit this genre, and, while it was still practiced in classical tradition by Donne ("On His Mistress" [see vol. B, p. 903]), by the later seventeenth century the term came to denote the poetry of loss, especially through the death of a loved person. See Tennyson, *In Memoriam* (vol. E, p. 231); Auden, "In Memory of W. B. Yeats" (see vol. F, p. 677); Heaney, "Clearances" (vol. F, p. 970).

emblem (Greek "an insertion"): a **figure of thought**. A picture allegorically expressing a moral, or a verbal picture open to such interpretation.

end-stopping: the placement of a complete syntactic unit within a complete poetic line, fulfilling the metrical pattern; Auden, "In Memory of W. B. Yeats," line 42: "Earth, receive an honoured guest" (see vol. F, p. 679). Compare **enjambment**.

enjambment (French "striding," encroaching): The opposite of **end-stopping,** enjambment occurs when the syntactic unit does not end with the end of the poetic line and the fulfillment of the metrical pattern. When the sense of the line overflows its meter and, therefore, the line break, we have enjambment; Auden, "In Memory of W. B. Yeats," lines 44–45: "Let the Irish vessel lie / Emptied of its poetry" (see vol. F, p. 679).

epic (synonym, *heroic poetry*): a **genre**. An extended narrative poem celebrating martial heroes, invoking divine inspiration, beginning in medias res (see **order**), written in a high style (including the deployment of **epic similes;** on high style, see **register**), and divided into long narrative sequences. Homer's *Iliad* and Virgil's *Aeneid* were the prime models for English writers of epic verse. Thus Milton, *Paradise Lost* (see vol. B, p. 1427); Wordsworth, *The Prelude* (see vol. D, p. 391); and Walcott, *Omeros* (see vol. F, p. 808). With its precise repertoire of stylistic resources, epic lent itself easily to **parodic** and **burlesque** forms, known as **mock epic;** thus Pope, *The Rape of the Lock* (see vol. C, p. 537).

epigram: a **genre**. A short, pithy poem wittily expressed, often with wounding intent. See Jonson, *Epigrams* (see vol. B, p. 1049).

epigraph (Greek "inscription"): a **genre**. Any formal statement inscribed on stone; also the brief formulation on a book's title page, or a quotation at the beginning of a poem, introducing the work's themes in the most compressed form possible.

epistle (Latin "letter"): a **genre**. The letter can be shaped as a literary form, involving an intimate address often between equals. The *Epistles* of Horace provided a model for English writers from the sixteenth century. Thus Wyatt, "Mine Own John Poins" (see vol. B, p. 131), or Leapor, "An Epistle to a Lady" (vol. C, p. 771). Letters can be shaped to form the matter of an extended fiction, as the eighteenth-century epistolary **novel** (for example, Samuel Richardson's *Pamela*).

epitaph: a **genre**. A pithy formulation to be inscribed on a funeral monument. Thus Ralegh, "The Author's Epitaph, Made by Himself" (see vol. B, p. 479).

epithalamion (Greek "concerning the bridal chamber"): a **genre**. A wedding poem, celebrating the marriage and wishing the couple good fortune. Thus Spenser, *Epithalamion* (see vol. B, p. 455).

epyllion (plural "epyllia") (Greek: "little epic"): a **genre**. A relatively short poem in the meter of epic poetry. See, for example, Marlowe, *Hero and Leander* (vol. B, p. 562).

essay (French "trial, attempt"): a **genre**. An informal philosophical meditation, usually in prose and sometimes in verse. The journalistic periodical essay was developed in the early eighteenth century. Thus Addison and Steele, periodical essays (see vol. C, p. 281); Pope, *An Essay on Criticism* (see vol. C, p. 521).

euphemism (Greek "sweet saying"): a **figure of thought.** The figure by which something distasteful is described in alternative, less repugnant terms (for example, "he passed away").

exegesis (Greek "leading out"): interpretation, traditionally of the biblical text, but, by transference, of any text.

exemplum (Latin "example"): an example inserted into a usually nonfictional writing (for example, sermon or **essay**) to give extra force to an abstract thesis.

fabliau (French "little story," plural *fabliaux*): a **genre.** A short, funny, often bawdy narrative in low style (see **register**) imitated and developed from French models, most subtly by Chaucer; see *The Miller's Prologue and Tale* (vol. A, p. 494).

farce (French "stuffing"): a **genre.** A play designed to provoke laughter through the often humiliating antics of stock **characters.** Congreve's *The Way of the World* (see vol. C, p. 221) draws on this tradition.

figures of speech: Literary language often employs patterns perceptible to the eye and/or to the ear. Such patterns are called "figures of speech"; in classical rhetoric they were called "schemes" (from Greek *schema*, meaning "form, figure").

figures of thought: Language can also be patterned conceptually, even outside the rules that normally govern it. Literary language in particular exploits this licensed linguistic irregularity. Synonyms for figures of thought are "trope" (Greek "twisting," referring to the irregularity of use) and "conceit" (Latin "concept," referring to the fact that these figures are perceptible only to the mind). Be careful not to confuse **trope** with **topos** (a common error).

first-person narration: relevant to **point of view,** a narrative in which the voice narrating refers to itself with forms of the first-person pronoun ("I," "me," "my," etc., or possibly "we," "us," "our"), and in which the narrative is determined by the limitations of that voice. Thus Mary Wollstonecraft Shelley, *Frankenstein*.

frame narrative: Some narratives, particularly collections of narratives, involve a frame narrative that explains the genesis of, and/or gives a perspective on, the main narrative or narratives to follow. Thus Chaucer, *Canterbury Tales*; Mary Wollstonecraft Shelley, *Frankenstein*; or Conrad, *Heart of Darkness*.

free indirect style: relevant to **point of view,** a narratorial voice that manages, without explicit reference, to imply, and often implicitly to comment on, the voice of a **character** in the narrative itself. Virginia Woolf, "A Sketch of the Past," where the voice, although strictly that of the adult narrator, manages to convey the child's manner of perception: "—I begin: the first memory. This was of red and purple flowers on a black background—my mother's dress."

genre and mode: The **style,** structure, and, often, length of a work, when coupled with a certain subject matter, raise expectations that a literary work conforms to a certain **genre** (French "kind"). Good writers might upset these expectations, but they remain aware of the expectations and thwart them purposefully. Works in different genres may nevertheless participate in the same **mode,** a broader category designating the fundamental perspectives governing various genres of writing. For mode, see **tragic, comic, satiric,** and **didactic modes.** Genres are fluid, sometimes very fluid (for example, the **novel**); the word "usually" should be added to almost every account of the characteristics of a given genre!

georgic (Greek "farming"): a **genre**. Virgil's *Georgics* treat agricultural and occasionally scientific subjects, giving instructions on the proper management of farms. Unlike **pastoral**, which treats the countryside as a place of recreational idleness among shepherds, the georgic treats it as a place of productive labor.

hermeneutics (from the Greek god Hermes, messenger between the gods and humankind): the science of interpretation, first formulated as such by the German philosophical theologian Friedrich Schleiermacher in the early nineteenth century.

heroic poetry: see **epic**.

hexameter (Greek "six measure"): a term of **meter**. The hexameter line (a six-stress line) is the meter of **classical** Latin **epic;** while not imitated in that form for epic verse in English, some instances of the hexameter exist. See, for example, the last line of a Spenserian stanza, *Faerie Queene* 1.1.2: "O help thou my weake wit, and sharpen my dull tong" (vol. B, p. 269), or Yeats, "The Lake Isle of Innisfree," line 1: "I will arise and go now, and go to Innisfree" (vol. F, p. 221).

homily (Greek "discourse"): a **genre**. A sermon, to be preached in church; *Book of Homilies* (see vol. B, p. 164). Writers of literary fiction sometimes exploit the homily, or sermon, as in Chaucer, *The Pardoner's Tale* (see vol. A, p. 540).

homophone (Greek "same sound"): a **figure of speech**. A word that sounds identical to another word but has a different meaning ("bear" / "bare").

hyperbaton (Greek "overstepping"): a term of **syntax**. The rearrangement, or inversion, of the expected word order in a sentence or clause. Gray, "Elegy Written in a Country Churchyard," line 38: "If Memory o'er their tomb no trophies raise" (vol. C, p. 899). Poets can suspend the expected syntax over many lines, as in the first sentences of the *Canterbury Tales* (vol. A, p. 474) and of *Paradise Lost* (vol. B, p. 1430).

hyperbole (Greek "throwing over"): a **figure of thought**. Overstatement, exaggeration; Marvell, "To His Coy Mistress," lines 11–12: "My vegetable love should grow / Vaster than empires, and more slow" (see vol. B, p. 1273); Auden, "As I Walked Out One Evening," lines 9–12: "'I'll love you, dear, I'll love you / Till China and Africa meet / And the river jumps over the mountain / And the salmon sing in the street" (see vol. F, p. 675).

hypermetrical (adj.; Greek "over measured"): a term of **meter**; the word describes a breaking of the expected metrical pattern by at least one extra syllable.

hypotaxis, or **subordination** (respectively Greek and Latin "ordering under"): a term of **syntax**. The subordination, by the use of subordinate clauses, of different elements of a sentence to a single main verb. Milton, *Paradise Lost* 9.513–15: "As when a ship by skillful steersman wrought / Nigh river's mouth or foreland, where the wind / Veers oft, as oft so steers, and shifts her sail; So varied he" (vol. B, p. 1588). The contrary principle to **parataxis**.

iamb: a term of **rhythm**. The basic foot of English verse; two syllables following the rhythmic pattern of unstressed followed by stressed and producing a rising effect. Thus, for example, "Vermont."

imitation: the practice whereby writers strive ideally to reproduce and yet renew the **conventions** of an older form, often derived from **classical** civilization. Such a practice will be praised in periods of classicism (for example, the eighteenth century) and repudiated in periods dominated by a model of inspiration (for example, Romanticism).

irony (Greek "dissimulation"): a **figure of thought**. In broad usage, irony designates the result of inconsistency between a statement and a context that undermines the statement. "It's a beautiful day" is unironic if it's a beautiful day; if, however, the weather is terrible, then the inconsistency between statement and context is ironic. The effect is often amusing; the need to be ironic is sometimes produced by censorship of one kind or another. Strictly, irony is a subset of allegory: whereas allegory says one thing and means another, irony says one thing and means its opposite. For an extended example of irony, see Swift's "Modest Proposal" (vol. C, p. 511). See also **dramatic irony.**

journal (French "daily"): a **genre.** A diary, or daily record of ephemeral experience, whose perspectives are concentrated on, and limited by, the experiences of single days. Thus Pepys, *Diary* (see vol. C, p. 74).

lai: a **genre.** A short narrative, often characterized by images of great intensity; a French term, and a form practiced by Marie de France (see vol. A, p. 159).

legend (Latin "requiring to be read"): a **genre.** A narrative of a celebrated, possibly historical, but mortal **protagonist.** To be distinguished from **myth.** Thus the "Arthurian legend" but the "myth of Proserpine."

lexical set: Words that habitually recur together (for example, January, February, March, etc.; or red, white, and blue) form a lexical set.

litotes (from Greek "smooth"): a **figure of thought.** Strictly, understatement by denying the contrary; More, *Utopia*: "differences of no slight import" (see vol. B, p. 49). More loosely, understatement; Stevie Smith, "Sunt Leones," lines 11–12: "And if the Christians felt a little blue— / Well people being eaten often do" (see vol. F, p. 585).

lullaby: a **genre.** A bedtime, sleep-inducing song for children, in simple and regular meter. Adapted by Auden, "Lullaby" (see vol. F, p. 671).

lyric (from Greek "lyre"): Initially meaning a song, "lyric" refers to a short poetic form, without restriction of meter, in which the expression of personal emotion, often by a voice in the first person, is given primacy over narrative sequence. Thus "The Wife's Lament" (see vol. A, p. 126); Yeats, "The Wild Swans at Coole" (see vol. F, p. 229).

masque: a **genre.** Costly entertainments of the Stuart court, involving dance, song, speech, and elaborate stage effects, in which courtiers themselves participated.

metaphor (Greek "carrying across," etymologically parallel to Latin "translation"): One of the most significant **figures of thought,** metaphor designates identification or implicit identification of one thing with another with which it is not literally identifiable. Blake, "London," lines 11–12: "And the hapless Soldier's sigh / Runs in blood down Palace walls" (see vol. D, p. 137).

meter: Verse (from Latin *versus*, turned) is distinguished from prose (from Latin *prorsus*, "straightforward") as a more compressed form of expression, shaped by metrical norms. **Meter** (Greek "measure") refers to the regularly recurring sound pattern of verse lines. The means of producing sound patterns across lines differ in different poetic traditions. Verse may be **quantitative,** or determined by the quantities of syllables (set patterns of long and short syllables), as in Latin and Greek poetry. It may be **syllabic,** determined by fixed numbers of syllables in the line, as in the verse of Romance languages (for example, French and Italian). It may be **accentual,** determined by the number of accents, or stresses in the line, with variable numbers of syllables, as in Old English and some varieties of Middle English alliterative verse. Or it may be **accentual-syllabic,** determined by the numbers of accents, but possessing a regular pattern of stressed and unstressed syllables, so as to produce regular numbers of syllables per line. Since Chaucer, English verse has worked primarily within the many possibilities of accentual-syllabic meter. The unit of meter is the **foot**. In English verse the number of feet per line corresponds to the number of accents in a line. For the types and examples of different meters, see **monometer, dimeter, trimester, tetrameter, pentameter,** and **hexameter**. In the definitions below, "u" designates one unstressed syllable, and "/" one stressed syllable.

metonymy (Greek "change of name"): one of the most significant **figures of thought**. Using a word to **denote** another concept or other concepts, by virtue of habitual association. Thus "The Press," designating printed news media. Fictional names often work by associations of this kind. Closely related to **synecdoche**.

mimesis (Greek for "imitation"): A central function of literature and drama has been to provide a plausible imitation of the reality of the world beyond the literary work; mimesis is the representation and imitation of what is taken to be reality.

mise-en-abyme (French for "cast into the abyss"): Some works of art represent themselves in themselves; if they do so effectively, the represented artifact also represents itself, and so ad infinitum. The effect achieved is called "*mise-en-abyme*." Hoccleve's *Complaint*, for example, represents a depressed man reading about a depressed man. This sequence threatens to become a *mise-en-abyme*.

monometer (Greek "one measure"): a term of **meter**. An entire line with just one stress; *Sir Gawain and the Green Knight*, line 15, "most (u) grand (/)" (see vol. A, p. 415).

myth: a **genre**. The narrative of **protagonists** with, or subject to, superhuman powers. A myth expresses some profound foundational truth, often by accounting for the origin of natural phenomena. To be distinguished from **legend**. Thus the "Arthurian legend" but the "myth of Proserpine."

novel: an extremely flexible **genre** in both form and subject matter. Usually in prose, giving high priority to narration of events, with a certain expectation of length, novels are preponderantly rooted in a specific, and often complex, social world; sensitive to the realities of material life; and often focused on one **character** or a small circle of central characters. By contrast with chivalric **romance** (the main European narrative genre prior to the novel), novels tend to eschew the marvelous in favor of a recognizable social world and credible action. The novel's openness allows it to participate in all modes, and to be co-opted for a huge variety of sub-genres. In English literature the novel dates from the late seventeenth century and has been astonishingly successful in appealing to a huge readership, particularly in the nineteenth and twentieth centuries. The English and Irish tradition of the novel includes, for example, Fielding, Austen, the Brontë sisters, Dickens, George Eliot, Conrad, Woolf, Lawrence, and Joyce, to name but a few very great exponents of the genre.

novella: a **genre**. A short **novel**, often characterized by imagistic intensity. Conrad, *Heart of Darkness* (see vol. F, p. 70).

occupatio (Latin "taking possession"): a **figure of thought**. Denying that one will discuss a subject while actually discussing it; also known as "praeteritio" (Latin "passing by"). See Chaucer, *Nun's Priest's Tale*, lines 414–31 (see vol. A, p. 565).

ode (Greek "song"): a **genre**. A **lyric** poem in elevated, or high style (see **register**), often addressed to a natural force, a person, or an abstract quality. The Pindaric ode in English is made up of **stanzas** of unequal length, while the Horatian ode has stanzas of equal length. For examples of both types, see, respectively, Wordsworth, "Ode:

Intimations of Immortality" (vol. D, p. 381); and Marvell, "An Horatian Ode" (vol. B, p. 1282), or Keats, "Ode on Melancholy" (vol. D, p. 973). For a fuller discussion, see the headnote to Jonson's "Ode on Cary and Morison" (vol. B, p. 1058).

omniscient narrator (Latin "all-knowing narrator"): relevant to **point of view.** A narrator who, in the fiction of the narrative, has complete access to both the deeds and the thoughts of all **characters** in the narrative. Thus Thomas Hardy, "On the Western Circuit" (see vol. F, p. 36).

onomatopoeia (Greek "name making"): a **figure of speech.** Verbal sounds that imitate and evoke the sounds they denote. Hopkins, "Binsey Poplars," lines 10–12 (about some felled trees): "O if we but knew what we do / When we delve [dig] or hew— / Hack and rack the growing green!" (see vol. E, p. 726).

order: A story may be told in different narrative orders. A narrator might use the sequence of events as they happened, and thereby follow what **classical** rhetoricians called the *natural order*; alternatively, the narrator might reorder the sequence of events, beginning the narration either in the middle or at the end of the sequence of events, thereby following an *artificial order*. If a narrator begins in the middle of events, he or she is said to begin *in medias res* (Latin "in the middle of the matter"). For a brief discussion of these concepts, see Spenser, *Faerie Queene*, "A Letter of the Authors" (vol. B, p. 265). Modern narratology makes a related distinction, between *histoire* (French "story") for the natural order that readers mentally reconstruct, and *discours* (French, here "narration") for the narrative as presented. See also **plot** and **story.**

ottava rima: a **verse form.** An eight-line stanza form, rhyming abababcc, using **iambic pentameter;** Yeats, "Sailing to Byzantium" (see vol. F, p. 234). Derived from the Italian poet Boccaccio, an eight-line stanza was used by fifteenth-century English poets for inset passages (for example, Christ's speech from the Cross in Lydgate's *Testament*, lines 754–897). The form in this rhyme scheme was used in English poetry for long narrative by, for example, Byron (*Don Juan*; see vol. D, p. 690).

oxymoron (Greek "sharp blunt"): a **figure of thought.** The conjunction of normally incompatible terms; Milton, *Paradise Lost* 1.63: "darkness visible" (see vol. B, p. 1431).

panegyric: a **genre.** Demonstrative, or epideictic (Greek "showing"), rhetoric was a branch of **classical** rhetoric. Its own two main branches were the rhetoric of praise on the one hand and of vituperation on the other. Panegyric, or eulogy (Greek "sweet speaking"), or encomium (plural *encomia*), is the term used to describe the speeches or writings of praise.

parable: a **genre.** A simple story designed to provoke, and often accompanied by, **allegorical** interpretation, most famously by Christ as reported in the Gospels.

paradox (Greek "contrary to received opinion"): a **figure of thought.** An apparent contradiction that requires thought to reveal an inner consistency. Chaucer, "Troilus's Song," line 12: "O sweete harm so quainte" (see vol. A, p. 574).

parataxis, or coordination (respectively Greek and Latin "ordering beside"): a term of **syntax.** The coordination, by the use of coordinating conjunctions, of different main clauses in a single sentence. Malory, *Morte Darthur*: "So Sir Lancelot departed and took his sword under his arm, and so he walked in his mantel, that noble knight, and put himself in great jeopardy" (see vol. A, p. 607). The opposite principle to **hypotaxis.**

parody: a work that uses the **conventions** of a particular genre with the aim of comically mocking a **topos**, a genre, or a particular exponent of a genre. Shakespeare parodies the topos of **blazon** in Sonnet 130 (see vol. B, p. 637).

pastoral (from Latin *pastor*, "shepherd"): a **genre.** Pastoral is set among shepherds, making often refined **allusion** to other apparently unconnected subjects (sometimes politics) from the potentially idyllic world of highly literary if illiterate shepherds. Pastoral is distinguished from **georgic** by representing recreational rural idleness, whereas the georgic offers instruction on how to manage rural labor. English writers had classical models in the *Idylls* of Theocritus in Greek and Virgil's *Eclogues* in Latin. Pastoral is also called bucolic (from the Greek word for "herdsman"). Thus Spenser, *Shepheardes Calender* (see vol. B, p. 257).

pathetic fallacy: the attribution of sentiment to natural phenomena, as if they were in sympathy with human feelings. Thus Milton, *Lycidas*, lines 146–47: "With cowslips wan that hang the pensive head, / And every flower that sad embroidery wears" (see vol. B, p. 1406). For critique of the practice, see Ruskin (who coined the term), "Of the Pathetic Fallacy" (vol. E, p. 467).

pentameter (Greek "five measure"): a term of **meter.** In English verse, a five-stress line. Between the late fourteenth and the nineteenth centuries, this meter, frequently employing an iambic rhythm, was the basic line of English verse. Chaucer, Shakespeare, Milton, and Wordsworth each, for example, deployed this very flexible line as their primary resource; Milton, *Paradise Lost* 1.128: "O Prince, O Chief of many thronèd Powers" (see vol. B, p. 1433).

performative: Verbal expressions have many different functions. They can, for example, be descriptive, or constative (if they make an argument), or performative, for example. A performative utterance is one that makes something happen in the world by virtue of its utterance. "I hereby sentence you to ten years in prison," if uttered in the appropriate circumstances, itself performs an action; it makes something happen in the world. By virtue of its performing an action, it is called a "performative." See also **speech act.**

peripeteia (Greek "turning about"): the sudden reversal of fortune (in both directions) in a dramatic work.

periphrasis (Greek "declaring around"): a **figure of thought.** Circumlocution; the use of many words to express what could be expressed in few or one; Sidney, *Astrophil and Stella* 39.1–4.

persona (Latin "sound through"): originally the mask worn in the Roman theater to magnify an actor's voice; in literary discourse persona (plural *personae*) refers to the narrator or speaker of a text, whose voice is coherent and whose person need have no relation to the person of the actual author of a text. Eliot, "The Love Song of J. Alfred Prufrock" (see vol. F, p. 498).

personification, or **prosopopoeia** (Greek "person making"): a **figure of thought.** The attribution of human qualities to nonhuman forces or objects; Keats, "Ode on a Grecian Urn," lines 1–2: "Thou still unvanish'd bride of quietness, / Thou foster-child of silence and slow time" (see vol. D, p. 971).

plot: the sequence of events in a story as narrated, as distinct from **story,** which refers to the sequence of events as we reconstruct them from the plot. See also **order.**

point of view: All of the many kinds of writing involve a point of view from which a text is, or seems to be, generated. The presence of such a point of view may be powerful and explicit, as in many novels, or deliberately invisible, as in much drama. In some genres, such as the **novel,** the narrator does not necessarily tell the story from a position we can predict; that is, the needs of a particular story, not the **conventions** of the genre, determine the narrator's position. In other genres, the narrator's position is fixed by convention; in certain kinds of love poetry, for example, the narrating voice is always that of a suffering lover. Not only does the point of view significantly inform the style of a work, but it also informs the structure of that work.

protagonist (Greek "first actor"): the hero or heroine of a drama or narrative.

pun: a figure of thought. A sometimes irresolvable doubleness of meaning in a single word or expression; Shakespeare, Sonnet 135, line 1: "Whoever hath her wish, thou hast thy *Will*" (see vol. B, p. 637).

quatrain: a verse form. A stanza of four lines, usually rhyming abcb, abab, or abba. Of many possible examples, see Crashaw, "On the Wounds of Our Crucified Lord" (see vol. B, p. 1214).

refrain: usually a single line repeated as the last line of consecutive stanzas, sometimes with subtly different wording and ideally with subtly different meaning as the poem progresses.

register: The register of a word is its stylistic level, which can be distinguished by degree of technicality but also by degree of formality. We choose our words from different registers according to context, that is, audience and/or environment. Thus a chemist in a laboratory will say "sodium chloride," a cook in a kitchen "salt." A formal register designates the kind of language used in polite society (for example, "Mr. President"), while an informal or colloquial register is used in less formal or more relaxed social situations (for example, "the boss"). In **classical** and medieval rhetoric, these registers of formality were called *high style* and *low style*. A *middle style* was defined as the style fit for narrative, not drawing attention to itself.

rhetoric: the art of verbal persuasion. **Classical** rhetoricians distinguished three areas of rhetoric: the forensic, to be used in law courts; the deliberative, to be used in political or philosophical deliberations; and the demonstrative, or epideictic, to be used for the purposes of public praise or blame. Rhetorical manuals covered all the skills required of a speaker, from the management of style and structure to delivery. These manuals powerfully influenced the theory of poetics as a separate branch of verbal practice, particularly in the matter of style.

rhyme: a figure of speech. The repetition of identical vowel sounds in stressed syllables whose initial consonants differ ("dead" / "head"). In poetry, rhyme often links the end of one line with another. *Masculine rhyme*: full rhyme on the final syllable of the line ("decays" / "days"). *Feminine rhyme*: full rhyme on syllables that are followed by unaccented syllables ("fountains" / "mountains"). *Internal rhyme*: full rhyme within a single line; Coleridge, *The Rime of the Ancient Mariner*, line 7: "The guests are met, the feast is set" (see vol. D, p. 475). *Rhyme riche*: rhyming on **homophones;** Chaucer, *General Prologue*, lines 17–18: "seeke" / "seke." *Off rhyme* (also known as *half rhyme, near rhyme,* or *slant rhyme*): differs from perfect rhyme in changing the vowel sound and/or the concluding consonants expected of perfect rhyme; Byron, "They say that Hope is Happiness," lines 5–7: "most" / "lost." *Pararhyme*: stressed vowel sounds differ but are flanked by identical or similar consonants; Owen, "Miners," lines 9–11: "simmer" / "summer" (see vol. F, p. 169).

rhyme royal: a verse form. A **stanza** of seven **iambic pentameter** lines, rhyming ababbcc; first introduced by Chaucer and called "royal" because the form was used by James I of Scotland for his *Kingis Quair* in the early fifteenth century. Chaucer, "Troilus's Song" (see vol. A, p. 574).

rhythm: Rhythm is not absolutely distinguishable from **meter**. One way of making a clear distinction between these terms is to say that rhythm (from the Greek "to flow") denotes the patterns of sound within the feet of verse lines and the combination of those feet. Very often a particular meter will raise expectations that a given rhythm will be used regularly through a whole line or a whole poem. Thus in English verse the pentameter regularly uses an iambic rhythm. Rhythm, however, is much more fluid than meter, and many lines within the same poem using a single meter will frequently exploit different rhythmic possibilities. For examples of different rhythms, see **iamb, trochee, anapest, spondee,** and **dactyl.**

romance: a **genre**. From the twelfth to the sixteenth century, the main form of European narrative, in either verse or prose, was that of chivalric romance. Romance, like the later **novel,** is a very fluid genre, but romances are often characterized by (i) a tripartite structure of social integration, followed by disintegration, involving moral tests and often marvelous events, itself the prelude to reintegration in a happy ending, frequently of marriage; and (ii) aristocratic social milieux. Thus *Sir Gawain and the Green Knight* (see vol. A, p. 415); Spenser's (unfinished) *Faerie Queene* (vol. B, p. 263). The immensely popular, fertile genre was absorbed, in both domesticated and undomesticated form, by the novel. For an adaptation of romance, see Chaucer, *Wife of Bath's Tale* (vol. A, p. 512).

sarcasm (Greek "flesh tearing"): a **figure of thought**. A wounding expression, often expressed ironically; Boswell, *Life of Johnson:* Johnson [asked if any man of the modern age could have written the **epic** poem *Fingal*] replied, "Yes, Sir, many men, many women, and many children" (see vol. C, p. 891).

satire (Latin for "a bowl of mixed fruits"): a **genre.** In Roman literature (for example, Juvenal), the communication, in the form of a letter between equals, complaining of the ills of contemporary society. The genre in this form is characterized by a first-person narrator exasperated by social ills; the letter form; a high frequency of contemporary reference; and the use of invective in **low-style** language. Pope practices the genre thus in the *Epistle to Dr. Arbuthnot* (see vol. C, p. 573). Wyatt's "Mine Own John Poins" (see vol. B, p. 131) draws ultimately on a gentler, Horatian model of the genre.

satiric mode: Works in a very large variety of genres are devoted to the more or less savage attack on social ills. Thus Swift's travel narrative *Gulliver's Travels* (see vol. C, p. 377), his **essay** "A Modest Proposal" (vol. C, p. 511), and Gay's *Beggar's Opera* (vol. C, p. 587), to look no further than the eighteenth century, are all within a satiric mode.

scene: a subdivision of an **act**, itself a subdivision of a dramatic performance and/or text. The action of a scene usually occurs in one place.

sensibility (from Latin, "capable of being perceived by the senses"): as a literary term, an eighteenth-century concept derived from moral philosophy that stressed the social importance of fellow feeling and particularly of sympathy in social relations. The concept generated a literature of "sensibility," such as the sentimental **novel** (the most famous of which was Goethe's *Sorrows of the Young Werther* [1774]), or sentimental poetry, such as Cowper's passage on the stricken deer in *The Task* (see vol. C, p. 1076).

short story: a **genre**. Generically similar to, though shorter and more concentrated than, the **novel;** often published as part of a collection. Thus Mansfield, "The Daughters of the Late Colonel" (see vol. F, p. 542).

simile (Latin "like"): a **figure of thought.** Comparison, usually using the word "like" or "as," of one thing with another so as to produce sometimes surprising analogies. Donne, "The Storm," lines 29–30: "Sooner than you read this line did the gale, / Like shot, not feared till felt, our sails assail." Frequently used, in extended form, in **epic** poetry; Milton, *Paradise Lost* 1.338–46 (see vol. B, p. 1438).

soliloquy (Latin "single speaking"): a **topos** of drama, in which a **character,** alone or thinking to be alone on stage, speaks so as to give the audience access to his or her private thoughts.

sonnet: a **verse form.** A form combining a variable number of units of rhymed lines to produce a fourteen-line poem, usually in rhyming **iambic pentameter** lines. In English there are two principal varieties: the Petrarchan sonnet, formed by an octave (an eight-line stanza, often broken into two **quatrains** having the same rhyme scheme, typically abba abba) and a sestet (a six-line stanza, typically cdecde or cdcdcd); and the Shakespearean sonnet, formed by three quatrains (abab cdcd efef) and a **couplet** (gg). The declaration of a sonnet can take a sharp turn, or "volta," often at the decisive formal shift from octave to sestet in the Petrarchan sonnet, or in the final couplet of a Shakespearean sonnet, introducing a trenchant counterstatement. Derived from Italian poetry, and especially from the poetry of Petrarch, the sonnet was first introduced to English poetry by Wyatt, and initially used principally for the expression of unrequited erotic love, though later poets used the form for many other purposes. See Wyatt, "Whoso List to Hunt" (vol. B, p. 123); Sidney, *Astrophil and Stella* (vol. B, p. 541); Shakespeare, Sonnets (vol. B, p. 624); Wordsworth, "London, 1802" (vol. D, p. 390); McKay, "If We Must Die" (vol. F, p. 576); Heaney, "Clearances" (vol. F, p. 970).

speech act: Words and deeds are often distinguished, but words are often (perhaps always) themselves deeds. Utterances can perform different speech acts, such as promising, declaring, casting a spell, encouraging, persuading, denying, lying, and so on. See also **performative.**

Spenserian stanza: a **verse form.** The stanza developed by Spenser for *The Faerie Queene*; nine **iambic** lines, the first eight of which are **pentameters,** followed by one **hexameter,** rhyming ababbcbcc. See also, for example, Shelley, *Adonais* (vol. D, p. 851), and Keats, *The Eve of St. Agnes* (vol. D, p. 953).

spondee: a term of **meter.** A two-syllable foot following the rhythmic pattern, in English verse, of two stressed syllables. Thus, for example, "Utah."

stanza (Italian "room"): groupings of two or more lines, though "stanza" is usually reserved for groupings of at least four lines. Stanzas are often joined by rhyme, often in sequence, where each group shares the same metrical pattern and, when rhymed, rhyme scheme. Stanzas can themselves be arranged into larger groupings. Poets often invent new **verse forms,** or they may work within established forms.

story: a narrative's sequence of events, which we reconstruct from those events as they have been recounted by the narrator (i.e., the **plot**). See also **order.**

stream of consciousness: usually a **first-person** narrative that seems to give the reader access to the narrator's mind as it perceives or reflects on events, prior to organizing those perceptions into a coherent narrative. Thus (though generated from a **third-person** narrative) Joyce, *Ulysses*, "Penelope" (see vol. F, p. 452).

style (from Latin for "writing instrument"): In literary works the manner in which something is expressed contributes substantially to its meaning. The expressions "sun," "mass of helium at the center of the solar system," "heaven's golden orb" all designate "sun," but do so in different manners, or styles, which produce different meanings. The manner of a literary work is its "style," the effect of which is its "tone." We often can intuit the tone of a text; from that intuition of tone we can analyze the stylistic resources by which it was produced. We can analyze the style of literary works through consideration of different elements of style; for example, **diction, figures of thought, figures of speech, meter and rhythm, verse form, syntax, point of view.**

sublime: As a concept generating a literary movement, the sublime refers to the realm of experience beyond the measurable, and so beyond the rational, produced especially by the terrors and grandeur of natural phenomena. Derived especially from the first-century Greek treatise *On the Sublime*, sometimes attributed to Longinus, the notion of the sublime was in the later eighteenth century a spur to Romanticism.

syllable: the smallest unit of sound in a pronounced word. The syllable that receives the greatest stress is called the *tonic* syllable.

symbol (Greek "token"): a **figure of thought.** Something that stands for something else, and yet seems necessarily to evoke that other thing. In Neoplatonic, and therefore Romantic, theory, to be distinguished from **allegory** thus: whereas allegory involves connections between vehicle and tenor agreed by convention or made explicit, the meanings of a symbol are supposedly inherent to it.

synecdoche (Greek "to take with something else"): a **figure of thought.** Using a part to express the whole, or vice versa; for example, "all hands on deck." Closely related to **metonymy.**

syntax (Greek "ordering with"): Syntax designates the rules by which sentences are constructed in a given language. Discussion of meter is impossible without some reference to syntax, since the overall effect of a poem is, in part, always the product of a subtle balance of meter and sentence construction. Syntax is also essential to the understanding of prose style, since prose writers, deprived of the full shaping possibilities of meter, rely all the more heavily on syntactic resources. A working command of syntactical practice requires an understanding of the parts of speech (nouns, verbs, adjectives, adverbs, conjunctions, pronouns, prepositions, and interjections), since writers exploit syntactic possibilities by using particular combinations and concentrations of the parts of speech.

taste (from Italian "touch"): Although medieval monastic traditions used eating and tasting as a metaphor for reading, the concept of taste as a personal ideal to be cultivated by, and applied to, the appreciation and judgment of works of art in general was developed in the eighteenth century.

tercet: a **verse form.** A stanza or group of three lines, used in larger forms such as **terza rima,** the **Petrarchan sonnet,** and the **villanelle.**

terza rima: a **verse form.** A sequence of rhymed **tercets** linked by rhyme thus: aba bcb cdc, etc. first used extensively by Dante in *The Divine Comedy*, the form was adapted in English **iambic pentameters** by Wyatt and revived in the nineteenth century. See Wyatt, "Mine Own John Poins" (vol. B, p. 131); Shelley, "Ode to the West Wind" (vol. D, p. 302); and Morris, "The Defence of Guinevere" (vol. E, p. 657). For modern adaptations see Eliot, lines 78–149 (though unrhymed) of "Little Gidding" (vol. F, pp. 523–25); Heaney, "Station Island" (vol. F, p. 968); Walcott, *Omeros* (vol. F, p. 806).

tetrameter (Greek "four measure"): a term of **meter.** A line with four stresses. Coleridge, *Christabel*, line 31: "She stole along, she nothing spoke" (see vol. D, p. 495).

theme (Greek "proposition"): In literary criticism the term designates what the work is about; the theme is the concept that unifies a given work of literature.

third-person narration: relevant to **point of view.** A narration in which the narrator recounts a narrative of **characters** referred to explicitly or implicitly by third-person pronouns ("he," she," etc.), without the limitation of a **first-person narration.** Thus Johnson, *The History of Rasselas*.

topographical poem (Greek "place writing"): a **genre**. A poem devoted to the meditative description of particular places.

topos (Greek "place," plural *topoi*): a commonplace in the content of a given kind of literature. Originally, in **classical** rhetoric, the topoi were tried-and-tested stimuli to literary invention: lists of standard headings under which a subject might be investigated. In medieval narrative poems, for example, it was commonplace to begin with a description of spring. Writers did, of course, render the commonplace uncommon, as in Chaucer's spring scene at the opening of *The Canterbury Tales* (see vol. A, p. 474).

tradition (from Latin "passing on"): A literary tradition is whatever is passed on or revived from the past in a single literary culture, or drawn from others to enrich a writer's culture. "Tradition" is fluid in reference, ranging from small to large referents: thus it may refer to a relatively small aspect of texts (for example, the tradition of **iambic pentameter**), or it may, at the other extreme, refer to the body of texts that constitute a **canon**.

tragedy: a **genre**. A dramatic representation of the fall of kings or nobles, beginning in happiness and ending in catastrophe. Later transferred to other social milieux. The opposite of **comedy**; thus Shakespeare, *Othello* (see vol. B, p. 640).

tragic mode: Many genres (**epic** poetry, **legend**ary chronicles, **tragedy**, the **novel**) either do or can participate in a tragic mode, by representing the fall of noble **protagonists** and the irreparable ravages of human society and history.

tragicomedy: a **genre**. A play in which potentially tragic events turn out to have a happy, or **comic**, ending. Thus Shakespeare, *Measure for Measure*.

translation (Latin "carrying across"): the rendering of a text written in one language into another.

trimeter (Greek "three measure"): a term of **meter**. A line with three stresses. Herbert, "Discipline," line 1: "Throw away thy rod" (see vol. B, p. 1197).

triplet: a **verse form**. A **tercet** rhyming on the same sound. Pope inserts triplets among heroic **couplets** to emphasize a particular thought; see *Essay on Criticism*, 315–17 (vol. C, p. 521).

trochee: a term of **rhythm**. A two-syllable foot following the pattern, in English verse, of stressed followed by unstressed syllable, producing a falling effect. Thus, for example, "Texas."

type (Greek "impression, figure"): a **figure of thought**. In Christian allegorical interpretation of the Old Testament, pre-Christian figures were regarded as "types," or foreshadowings, of Christ or the Christian dispensation. *Typology* has been the source of much visual and literary art in which the parallelisms between old and new are extended to nonbiblical figures; thus the virtuous plowman in *Piers Plowman* becomes a type of Christ.

unities: According to a theory supposedly derived from Aristotle's *Poetics*, the events represented in a play should have unity of time, place, and action: that the play take up no more time than the time of the play, or at most a day; that the space of action should be within a single city; and that there should be no subplot. See Johnson, *The Preface to Shakespeare* (vol. C, p. 876).

vernacular (from Latin *verna*, "servant"): the language of the people, as distinguished from learned and arcane languages. From the later Middle Ages especially, the "vernacular" languages and literatures of Europe distinguished themselves from the learned languages and literatures of Latin, Greek, and Hebrew.

verse form: The terms related to **meter** and **rhythm** describe the shape of individual lines. Lines of verse are combined to produce larger groupings, called verse forms. These larger groupings are in the first instance **stanzas.** The combination of a certain meter and stanza shape constitutes the verse form, of which there are many standard kinds.

villanelle: a **verse form.** A fixed form of usually five **tercets** and a **quatrain** employing only two rhyme sounds altogether, rhyming aba for the tercets and abaa for the quatrain, with a complex pattern of two **refrains.** Derived from a French fixed form. Thomas, "Do Not Go Gentle into That Good Night" (see vol. F, p. 693).

wit: Originally a synonym for "reason" in Old and Middle English, "wit" became a literary ideal in the Renaissance as brilliant play of the full range of mental resources. For eighteenth-century writers, the notion necessarily involved pleasing expression, as in Pope's definition of true wit as "Nature to advantage dressed, / What oft was thought, but ne'er so well expressed" (*Essay on Criticism*, lines 297–98; see vol. C, p. 527). Romantic theory of the imagination deprived wit of its full range of apprehension, whence the word came to be restricted to its modern sense, as the clever play of mind that produces laughter.

zeugma (Greek "a yoking"): a **figure of thought.** A figure whereby one word applies to two or more words in a sentence, and in which the applications are surprising, either because one is unusual, or because the applications are made in very different ways; Pope, *Rape of the Lock* 3.7–8, in which the word "take" is used in two senses: "Here thou, great Anna! whom three realms obey, / Dost sometimes counsel take— and sometimes tea" (see vol. C, p. 546).

B: Publishing History, Censorship

By the time we read texts in published books, they have already been treated—that is, changed by authors, editors, and printers—in many ways. Although there are differences across history, in each period literary works are subject to pressures of many kinds, which apply before, while, and after an author writes. The pressures might be financial, as in the relations of author and patron; commercial, as in the marketing of books; and legal, as in, during some periods, the negotiation through official and unofficial censorship. In addition, texts in all periods undergo technological processes, as they move from the material forms in which an author produced them to the forms in which they are presented to readers. Some of the terms below designate important material forms in which books were produced, disseminated, and surveyed across the historical span of this anthology. Others designate the skills developed to understand these processes. The anthology's introductions to individual periods discuss the particular forms these phenomena took in different eras.

bookseller: In England, and particularly in London, commercial bookmaking and -selling enterprises came into being in the early fourteenth century. These were loose organizations of artisans who usually lived in the same neighborhoods (around St. Paul's Cathedral in London). A bookseller or dealer would coordinate the production of hand-copied books for wealthy patrons (see **patronage**), who would order books to be custom-made. After the introduction of **printing** in the late fifteenth century, authors generally sold the rights to their work to booksellers, without any further **royalties.** Booksellers, who often had their own shops, belonged to the **Stationers' Company.** This system lasted into the eighteenth century. In 1710, however, authors were for the first time granted **copyright,** which tipped the commercial balance in their favor, against booksellers.

censorship: The term applies to any mechanism for restricting what can be published. Historically, the reasons for imposing censorship are heresy, sedition, blasphemy, libel, or obscenity. External censorship is imposed by institutions having legislative sanctions at their disposal. Thus the pre-Reformation Church imposed the Constitutions of Archbishop Arundel of 1409, aimed at repressing the Lollard "heresy." After the Reformation, some key events in the history of censorship are as follows: 1547, when anti-Lollard legislation and legislation made by Henry VIII concerning treason by writing (1534) were abolished; the Licensing Order of 1643, which legislated that works be licensed, through the Stationers' Company, prior to publication; and 1695, when the last such Act stipulating prepublication licensing lapsed. Postpublication censorship continued in different periods for different reasons. Thus, for example, British publication of D. H. Lawrence's *Lady Chatterley's Lover* (1928) was obstructed (though unsuccessfully) in 1960, under the Obscene Publications Act of 1959. Censorship can also be international: although not published in Iran, Salman Rushdie's *Satanic Verses* (1988) was censored in that country, where the leader, Ayatollah Ruhollah Khomeini, proclaimed a fatwa (religious decree) promising the author's execution. Very often censorship is not imposed externally, however: authors or publishers can censor work in anticipation of what will incur the wrath of readers or the penalties of the law. Victorian and Edwardian publishers of **novels,** for example, urged authors to remove potentially offensive material, especially for serial publication in popular magazines.

codex: the physical format of most modern books and medieval manuscripts, consisting of a series of separate leaves gathered into quires and bound together, often with a cover. In late antiquity, the codex largely replaced the scroll, the standard form of written documents in Roman culture.

copy text: the particular text of a work used by a textual editor as the basis of an edition of that work.

copyright: the legal protection afforded to authors for control of their work's publication, in an attempt to ensure due financial reward. Some key dates in the history of copyright in the United Kingdom are as follows: 1710, when a statute gave authors the exclusive right to publish their work for fourteen years, and fourteen years more if the author were still alive when the first term had expired; 1842, when the period of authorial control was extended to forty-two years; and 1911, when the term was extended yet further, to fifty years after the author's death. In 1995 the period of protection was harmonized with the laws in other European countries to be the life of the author plus seventy years. In the United States no works first published before 1923 are in copyright. Works published since 1978 are, as in the United Kingdom, protected for the life of the author plus seventy years.

folio: the leaf formed by both sides of a single page. Each folio has two sides: a *recto* (the front side of the leaf, on the right side of a double-page spread in an open codex), and a *verso* (the back side of the leaf, on the left side of a double-page spread). Modern book pagination follows the pattern 1, 2, 3, 4, while medieval manuscript pagination follows the pattern 1r, 1v, 2r, 2v. "Folio" can also designate the size of a printed book. Books come in different shapes, depending originally on the number of times a standard sheet of paper is folded. One fold produces a large volume, a *folio* book; two folds produce a *quarto*, four an *octavo*, and six a very small *duodecimo*. Generally speaking, the larger the book, the grander and more expensive. Shakespeare's plays were, for example, first printed in quartos, but were gathered into a folio edition in 1623.

foul papers: versions of a work before an author has produced, if she or he has, a final copy (a "fair copy") with all corrections removed.

incunabulum (plural "incunabula"): any printed book produced in Europe before 1501. Famous incunabula include the Gutenberg Bible, printed in 1455.

manuscript (Latin, "written by hand"): Any text written physically by hand is a manuscript. Before the introduction of **printing** with moveable type in 1476, all texts in England were produced and reproduced by hand, in manuscript. This is an extremely labor-intensive task, using expensive materials (for example, **vellum**, or **parchment**); the cost of books produced thereby was, accordingly, very high. Even after the introduction of printing, many texts continued to be produced in manuscript. This is obviously true of letters, for example, but until the eighteenth century, poetry written within aristocratic circles was often transmitted in manuscript copies.

paleography (Greek "ancient writing"): the art of deciphering, describing, and dating forms of handwriting.

parchment: animal skin, used as the material for handwritten books before the introduction of paper. See also **vellum**.

patronage, patron (Latin "protector"): Many technological, legal, and commercial supports were necessary before professional authorship became possible. Although some playwrights (for example, Shakespeare) made a living by writing for the theater, other authors needed, principally, the large-scale reproductive capacities of **printing** and the security of **copyright** to make a living from writing. Before these conditions obtained, many authors had another main occupation, and most authors had to rely on patronage. In different periods, institutions or individuals offered material support, or patronage, to authors. Thus in Anglo-Saxon England, monasteries afforded the conditions of writing to monastic authors. Between the twelfth and the seventeenth centuries, the main source of patronage was the royal court. Authors offered patrons prestige and ideological support in return for financial support. Even as the conditions of professional authorship came into being at the beginning of the eighteenth century, older forms of direct patronage were not altogether displaced until the middle of the century.

periodical: Whereas journalism, strictly, applies to daily writing (from French *jour*, "day"), periodical writing appears at larger, but still frequent, intervals, characteristically in the form of the **essay**. Periodicals were developed especially in the eighteenth century.

printing: Printing, or the mechanical reproduction of books using moveable type, was invented in Germany in the mid-fifteenth century by Johannes Gutenberg; it quickly spread throughout Europe. William Caxton brought printing into England from the Low Countries in 1476. Much greater powers of reproduction at much lower prices transformed every aspect of literary culture.

publisher: the person or company responsible for the commissioning and publicizing of printed matter. In the early period of **printing**, publisher, printer, and bookseller were often the same person. This trend continued in the ascendancy of the **Stationers' Company**, between the middle of the sixteenth and the end of the seventeenth centuries. Toward the end of the seventeenth century, these three functions began to separate, leading to their modern distinctions.

quire: When medieval manuscripts were assembled, a few loose sheets of parchment or paper would first be folded together and sewn along the fold. This formed a quire (also known as a "gathering" or "signature"). Folded in this way, four large sheets of parchment would produce eight smaller manuscript leaves. Multiple quires could then be bound together to form a codex.

royalties: an agreed-upon proportion of the price of each copy of a work sold, paid by the publisher to the author, or an agreed-upon fee paid to the playwright for each performance of a play.

scribe: In **manuscript** culture, the scribe is the copyist who reproduces a text by hand.

scriptorium (plural "scriptoria"): a place for producing written documents and manuscripts.

serial publication: generally referring to the practice, especially common in the nineteenth century, of publishing novels a few chapters at a time, in periodicals.

Stationers' Company: The Stationers' Company was an English guild incorporating various tradesmen, including printers, publishers, and booksellers, skilled in the production and selling of books. It was formed in 1403, received its royal charter in 1557, and served as a means both of producing and of regulating books. Authors would sell the manuscripts of their books to individual stationers, who incurred the risks and took the profits of producing and selling the books. The stationers entered their rights over given books in the Stationers' Register. They also regulated the book trade and held their monopoly by licensing books and by being empowered to seize unauthorized books and imprison resisters. This system of licensing broke down in the social unrest of the Civil War and Interregnum (1640–60), and it ended in 1695. Even after the end of licensing, the Stationers' Company continued to be an intrinsic part of the **copyright** process, since the 1710 copyright statute directed that copyright had to be registered at Stationers' Hall.

subscription: An eighteenth-century system of bookselling somewhere between direct **patronage** and impersonal sales. A subscriber paid half the cost of a book before publication and half on delivery. The author received these payments directly. The subscriber's name appeared in the prefatory pages.

textual criticism: Works in all periods often exist in many subtly or not so subtly different forms. This is especially true with regard to manuscript textual reproduction, but it also applies to printed texts. Textual criticism is the art, developed from the fifteenth century in Italy but raised to new levels of sophistication from the eighteenth century, of deciphering different historical states of texts. This art involves the analysis of textual **variants,** often with the aim of distinguishing authorial from scribal forms.

variants: differences that appear among different manuscripts or printed editions of the same text.

vellum: animal skin, used as the material for handwritten books before the introduction of paper. See also **parchment.**

watermark: the trademark of a paper manufacturer, impressed into the paper but largely invisible unless held up to light.

Geographic Nomenclature

The British Isles refers to the prominent group of islands off the northwest coast of Europe, especially to the two largest, **Great Britain** and **Ireland**. At present these comprise two sovereign states: **the Republic of Ireland**, and **the United Kingdom of Great Britain and Northern Ireland**—known for short as the **United Kingdom** or the **U.K.** Most of the smaller islands are part of the **U.K.** but a few, like the **Isle of Man** and the tiny **Channel Islands**, are largely independent. The U.K. is often loosely referred to as "Britain" or "Great Britain" and is sometimes called simply, if inaccurately, "**England**." For obvious reasons, the latter usage is rarely heard among the inhabitants of the other countries of the U.K.—**Scotland**, **Wales**, and **Northern Ireland** (sometimes called **Ulster**). England is by far the most populous part of the kingdom, as well as the seat of its capital, London.

From the first to the fifth century C.E. most of what is now **England** and **Wales** was a province of the Roman Empire called **Britain** (in Latin, **Britannia**). After the fall of Rome, much of the island was invaded and settled by peoples from northern Germany and Denmark speaking what we now call Old English. These peoples are known as the Angles and the Saxons (the word **England** is related to **Angles**). By the time of the Norman Conquest (1066) most of the kingdoms founded by the Angles, the Saxons, and the subsequent Viking invaders had coalesced into the kingdom of **England**, which, in the latter Middle Ages, conquered and largely absorbed the neighboring Celtic kingdom of **Wales**. In 1603 James VI of **Scotland** inherited the island's other throne as James I of **England**, and for the next hundred years—except for the two decades of Puritan rule—**Scotland** (both its English-speaking **Lowlands** and its Gaelic-speaking **Highlands**) and **England** (with **Wales**) were two kingdoms under a single king. In 1707 the Act of Union brought them together as **the United Kingdom of Great Britain**. **Ireland**, where English rule had begun in the twelfth century and been tightened in the sixteenth, was incorporated by the 1800–1801 Act of Union into **the United Kingdom of Great Britain and Ireland**. With the division of Ireland and the establishment of **the Irish Free State** after World War I, this name was modified to its present form, and in 1949 **the Irish Free State** became **the Republic of Ireland**, or **Éire**. In 1999 **Scotland** elected a separate parliament it had relinquished in 1707, and **Wales** elected an assembly it lost in 1409; neither Scotland nor Wales ceased to be part of the **United Kingdom**.

The **British Isles** are further divided into counties, which in **Great Britain** are also known as shires. This word, with its vowel shortened in pronunciation, forms the suffix in the names of many counties, such as **Yorkshire, Wiltshire, Somersetshire**.

The Latin names **Britannia (Britain)**, **Caledonia (Scotland)**, and **Hibernia (Ireland)** are sometimes used in poetic diction; so too is **Britain**'s ancient Celtic name, **Albion**. Because of its accidental resemblance to *albus* (Latin for "white"), **Albion** is especially associated with the chalk cliffs that seem to gird much of the English coast like defensive walls.

The British Empire took its name from **the British Isles** because it was created not only by the **English** but also by the **Irish, Scots,** and **Welsh**, as well as by civilians and servicemen from other constituent countries of the empire. Some of the empire's **overseas colonies**, or **crown colonies**, were populated largely by settlers of European origin and their descendants. These predominantly White **settler colonies**, such as **Canada, Australia,** and **New Zealand**, were allowed significant self-government in the nineteenth century and recognized as **dominions** in the early twentieth century. The **White dominions** became members of **the Commonwealth of Nations**, also called **the Commonwealth, the British Commonwealth,** and "**the Old Commonwealth**" at different times, an association of sovereign states under the symbolic leadership of the British monarch.

Other **overseas colonies** of the empire had mostly Indigenous populations (or, in the Caribbean, the descendants of enslaved people, indentured servants, and others). These **colonies** were granted political independence after World War II, later than the **dominions**, and have often been referred to since as **postcolonial** nations. In South and Southeast Asia, **India** and **Pakistan** gained independence in 1947, followed by other countries including **Sri Lanka** (formerly **Ceylon**), **Burma** (now **Myanmar**), **Malaya** (now **Malaysia**), and **Singapore**. In West and East Africa, the **Gold Coast** was decolonized as **Ghana** in 1957, **Nigeria** in 1960, **Sierra Leone** in 1961, **Uganda** in 1962, **Kenya** in 1963, and so forth, while in southern Africa, the White minority government of **South Africa** was already independent in 1931, though majority rule did not come until 1994. In the Caribbean, **Jamaica** and **Trinidad and Tobago** became independent in 1962, followed by **Barbados** in 1966, and other islands of the British West Indies in the 1970s and '80s. Other regions from which nations emerged out of British colonial rule included Central America (**British Honduras**, now **Belize**), South America (**British Guiana**, now **Guyana**), the Pacific islands (**Fiji**), and Europe (**Cyprus**, **Malta**). After decolonization, many of these nations chose to remain within a newly conceived **Commonwealth** and are sometimes referred to as "**New Commonwealth**" countries. Some nations, such as **Ireland, Pakistan,** and **South Africa,** withdrew from the **Commonwealth**, though **South Africa** and **Pakistan** eventually rejoined, and others, such as **Burma** (now **Myanmar**), gained independence outside the **Commonwealth**. Britain's last major overseas colony, **Hong Kong**, was returned to Chinese sovereignty in 1997, but while Britain retains only a handful of dependent territories, such as **Bermuda** and **Montserrat**, the scope of the **Commonwealth** remains vast, with approximately 30 percent of the world's population.

British Money

One of the most dramatic changes to the system of British money came in 1971. In the system previously in place, the pound consisted of 20 shillings, each containing 12 pence, making 240 pence to the pound. Since 1971, British money has been calculated on the decimal system, with 100 pence to the pound. Britons' experience of paper money did not change very drastically: as before, 5- and 10-pound notes constitute the majority of bills passing through their hands (in addition, 20- and 50-pound notes have been added). But the shift necessitated a whole new way of thinking about and exchanging coins and marked the demise of the shilling, one of the fundamental units of British monetary history. Many other coins, still frequently encountered in literature, had already passed. These include the groat, worth 4 pence (the word "groat" is often used to signify a trifling sum); the angel (which depicted the archangel Michael triumphing over a dragon), valued at 10 shillings; the mark, worth in its day two-thirds of a pound or 13 shillings 4 pence; and the sovereign, a gold coin initially worth 22 shillings 6 pence, later valued at 1 pound, last circulated in 1932. One prominent older coin, the guinea, was worth a pound and a shilling; though it has not been minted since 1813, a very few quality items or prestige awards (like the purse in a horse race) may still be quoted in guineas. (The table below includes some other obsolete coins.) Colloquially, a pound was (and is) called a quid; a shilling a bob; sixpence, a tanner; a copper could refer to a penny, a half-penny, or a farthing (¼ penny).

Old Currency	New Currency
1 pound note	1 pound coin (or note in Scotland)
10 shilling (half-pound note)	50 pence
5 shilling (crown)	
2½ shilling (half crown)	20 pence
2 shilling (florin)	10 pence
1 shilling	5 pence
6 pence	
2½ pence	1 penny
2 pence	
1 penny	
½ penny	
¼ penny (farthing)	

Throughout its tenure as a member of the European Union (1973–2020), Britain contemplated but did not make the change to the EU's common currency, the Euro, reflecting many Britons' strong identification of their country with its rich commercial history and view of their currency as a national symbol.

Even more challenging than sorting out the values of obsolete coins is calculating for any given period the purchasing power of money, which fluctuates over time by its very nature. As difficult as it is to generalize, it is clear that money used to be worth much more than it is currently. During the early Middle Ages, the most valuable circulating coin was the silver penny: four would buy a sheep. Beyond long-term inflationary trends, prices varied from times of plenty to those marked by poor harvests; from peacetime to wartime; from the country to the metropolis (life in London has always been very expensive); and wages varied according to the availability of labor (wages would sharply rise, for instance, during the devastating Black Death in the fourteenth century). The following chart provides a glimpse of some actual prices of given periods and their changes across time, though all the variables mentioned above prevent them from being definitive. Even from one year to the next, an added tax on gin or tea could drastically raise prices, and a lottery ticket could cost much more the night before the drawing than just a month earlier. Still, the prices quoted below do indicate important trends, such as the disparity of incomes in British society and the costs of basic commodities. In the chart on the following pages, the symbol £ is used for pound, s. for shilling, d. for a penny (from Latin *denarius*); a sum would normally be written £2.19.3—that is 2 pounds, 19 shillings, 3 pence. (This is Leopold Bloom's budget for the day depicted in Joyce's novel *Ulysses* [1922]; in the new currency, it would be about £2.96.)

circa	1390	1590	1650	1750	1815	1875	1950
food and drink	gallon (8 pints) of ale, 1.5d.	tankard of beer, 5d.	coffee, 1d. a dish	"drunk for a penny, dead drunk for two-pence" (gin shop sign in Hogarth print)	ounce of laudanum, 3d.	pint of beer, 3d.	pint of Guinness stout, 11d.
	gallon (8 pints) of wine, 3 to 4d.	pound of beef, 2s. 5d.	chicken, 1s. 4d.	dinner at a steakhouse, 1s.	ham and potato dinner for two, 7s.	dinner in a good hotel, 5s.	pound of beef, 2s. 2d.
	pound of cinnamon, 1 to 3s.	pound of cinnamon, 10s. 6d.	pound of tea, £3 10s.	pound of tea, 16s.	bottle of French claret, 12s.	pound of tea, 2s.	dinner on railway car, 7s. 6d.
entertainment	no cost to watch a cycle play	admission to public theater, 1 to 3d.	falcon, £11 5s.	theater tickets, 1 to 5s.	admission to Covent Garden theater, 1 to 7s.	theater tickets, 6d. to 7s.	admission to Old Vic theater, 1s. 6d. to 10s. 6d.
	contributory admission to professional troupe theater	cheap seat in private theater, 6d.	billiard table, £25	admission to Vauxhall Gardens, 1s.	annual subscription to Almack's (exclusive club), 10 guineas	admission to Madam Tussaud's waxworks, 1s.	admission to Odeon cinema, Manchester, 1s 3d.
	maintenance for royal hounds at Windsor, .75d. a day	"to see a dead Indian" (*The Tempest* 2.2.32), 1.25d. (ten "doits")	three-quarter length portrait painting, £31	lottery ticket, £20 (shares were sold)	Jane Austen's piano, 30 guineas	annual fees at a gentleman's club, 7 to 10 guineas	tropical fish tank, £4 4s.

circa	1390	1590	1650	1750	1815	1875	1950
reading	cheap romance, 1s.	play quarto, 6d.	pamphlet, 1 to 6d.	issue of *The Gentleman's Magazine*, 6d.	issue of *Edinburgh Review*, 6s.	copy of the *Times*, 3d.	copy of the *Times*, 3d.
	a Latin Bible, 2 to £4	Shakespeare's *First Folio* (1623), £1	student Bible, 6s.	cheap edition of Milton, 2s.	membership in circulating library (3rd class), £1 4s. a year	illustrated edition of *Through the Looking-glass*, 6s.	issue of *Eagle* comics, 4.5d.
	payment for illuminating a liturgical book, £22 9s.	Foxe's *Acts and Monuments*, 24s.	Hobbes's *Leviathan*, 8s.	Johnson's *Dictionary*, folio, 2 vols., £4 10s.	1st edition of Austen's *Pride and Prejudice*, 18s.	1st edition of Trollope's *The Way We Live Now*, 2 vols., £1 1s.	Orwell's *Nineteen Eighty Four*, paperback, 3s. 6d.
transportation	night's supply of hay for horse, 2d.	wherry (whole boat) across Thames, 1d.	day's journey, coach, 10s.	boat across Thames, 4d.	coach ride, outside, 2 to 3d. a mile; inside, 4 to 5d. a mile	15-minute journey in a London cab, 1s. 6d.	London tube fare, about 2d. a mile
	coach, £8	hiring a horse for a day, 12d.	coach horse, £30	coach fare, London to Edinburgh, £4 10s.	palanquin transport in Madras, 5s. a day	railway, 3rd class, London to Plymouth, 18s. 8d. (about 1d. a mile)	petrol, 3s. a gallon
	quality horse, £10	hiring a coach for a day, 10s.	fancy carriage, £170	transport to America, £5	passage, Liverpool to New York, £10	passage to India, 1st class, £50	midsize Austin sedan, £449 plus £188 4s. 2d. tax
clothes	clothing allowance for peasant, 3s. a year	shoes with buckles, 8d.	footman's frieze coat, 15s.	working woman's gown, 6s. 6d.	checked muslin, 7s. per yard	flannel for a cheap petticoat, 1s. 3d. a yard	woman's sundress, £3 13s. 10d.

labor/incomes						
shoes for gentry wearer, 4d.	woman's gloves, £1 5s.	falconer's hat, 10s.	gentleman's suit, £8	hiring a dressmaker for a pelisse, 8s.	overcoat for an Eton schoolboy, £1 1s.	tweed sports jacket, £3 16s. 6d.
hat for gentry wearer, 10d.	fine cloak, £16	black cloth for mourning household of an earl, £100	very fine wig, £30	ladies silk stockings, 12s.	set of false teeth, £2 10s.	"Teddy boy" drape suit, £20
hiring a skilled building worker, 4d. a day	actor's daily wage during playing season, 1s.	agricultural laborer, 6s. 5d. a week	price of enslaved boy, £32	lowest-paid sailor on Royal Navy ship, 10s. 9d. a month	seasonal agricultural laborer, 14s. a week	minimum wage, agricultural laborer, £4 14s. per 47-hour week
wage for professional scribe, £2 3s. 4d. a year + cloak	household servant 2 to £5 a year + food, clothing	tutor to nobleman's children, £30 a year	housemaid's wage, £6 to £8 a year	contributor to *Quarterly Review*, 10 guineas per sheet	housemaid's wage, £10 to £25 a year	shorthand typist, £367 a year
minimum income to be called gentleman, £10 a year; for knighthood, 40 to £400	minimum income for eligibility for knighthood, £30 a year	Milton's salary as Secretary of Foreign Tongues, £288 a year	Boswell's allowance, £200 a year	minimum income for a "genteel" family, £100 a year	income of the "comfortable" classes, £800 and up a year	middle manager's salary, £1,480 a year
income from land of richest magnates, £3,500 a year	income from land of average earl, £4,000 a year	Earl of Bedford's income, £8,000 a year	Duke of Newcastle's income, £40,000 a year	Mr. Darcy's income, *Pride and Prejudice*, £10,000	Trollope's income, £4,000 a year	barrister's salary, £2,032 a year

The British Baronage

The English monarchy is in principle hereditary, though at times during the Middle Ages the rules were subject to dispute. As it stands now, authority passes from parent to eldest surviving child, to siblings in order of seniority if there are no children, and in default of direct descendants to collateral lines (cousins, nephews, nieces) in order of closeness. There have been breaks in the order of succession (1066, 1399, 1688), but so far as possible the usurpers have always sought to paper over the break with a legitimate, that is, hereditary, claim. When a queen succeeds to the throne and takes a husband, he does not become king unless he is in the line of blood succession; rather, he is named prince consort, as Albert was to Victoria. He may be the father of kings, but he is not one himself.

The original Saxon nobles were the king's thanes, ealdormen, or earls, who provided the king with military service and counsel in return for booty, gifts, or landed estates. William the Conqueror, arriving from France, where feudalism was fully developed, considerably expanded this group. In addition, as the king distributed the lands of his new kingdom, he also distributed dignities to men who became known collectively as "the baronage." "Baron" in its root meaning signifies simply "man," and barons were the king's men. As the title was common, a distinction was early made between greater and lesser barons, the former gradually assuming loftier and more impressive titles. The first English "duke" was created in 1337; the title of "marquess," or "marquis" (pronounced "markwis"), followed in 1385, and "viscount" ("vyekount") in 1440. Though "earl" is the oldest title of all, an earl now comes between a marquess and a viscount in order of dignity and precedence, and the old term "baron" now designates a rank just below viscount. "Baronets" were created in 1611 as a means of raising revenue for the crown (the title could be purchased for about £1,000); they are marginal nobility and have never sat in the House of Lords.

Kings and queens are addressed as "Your Majesty," princes and princesses as "Your Highness," the other hereditary nobility as "My Lord" or "Your Lordship." Peers receive their titles either by inheritance (like Lord Byron, the sixth baron of that line) or from the monarch (like Alfred, Lord Tennyson, created 1st Baron Tennyson by Victoria). The children, even of a duke, are commoners unless they are specifically granted some other title or inherit their father's title from him. A peerage can be forfeited by act of attainder, as for example when a lord is convicted of treason; and, when forfeited, or lapsed for lack of a successor, can be bestowed on another family. Thus in 1605 Robert Cecil was made first Earl of Salisbury in the third creation, the first creation dating from 1149, the second from 1337, the title having been in abeyance since 1539. Titles descend by right of succession and do not depend on tenure of land; thus, a title does not always indicate where a lord dwells or holds power. Indeed, noble titles do not always refer to a real place at all. At Prince Edward's marriage in 1999, the queen created him Earl of Wessex, although the old kingdom of Wessex has had no political existence since 1066, and the name was all but forgotten until it was resurrected by Thomas Hardy as the setting of his novels. (This is perhaps but one of many ways in which the world of the aristocracy increasingly resembles the realm of literature.)

The king and queen	(These are all of the royal line.)
Prince and princess	
Duke and duchess	(These may or may not be of the royal line, but are ordinarily remote from the succession.)
Marquess and marchioness	
Earl and countess	
Viscount and viscountess	
Baron and baroness	
Baronet and lady	

Scottish peers sat in the parliament of Scotland, as English peers did in the parliament of England, till at the Act of Union (1707) Scottish peers were granted sixteen seats in the English House of Lords, to be filled by election. (In 1963, all Scottish lords were allowed to sit.) Similarly, Irish peers, when the Irish parliament was abolished in 1801, were granted the right to elect twenty-eight of their number to the House of Lords in Westminster. (Now that the Republic of Ireland is a separate nation, this no longer applies.) Women members (peeresses) were first allowed to sit in the House as nonhereditary Life Peers in 1958 (when that status was created for members of both genders); women first sat by their own hereditary right in 1963. Today the House of Lords still retains some power to influence or delay legislation, but its future is uncertain. In 1999, the hereditary peers (then amounting to 750) were reduced to 92 temporary members elected by their fellow peers. Holders of Life Peerages remain, as do senior bishops of the Church of England and high-court judges (the "Law Lords").

Below the peerage the chief title of honor is "knight." Knighthood, which is not hereditary, is generally a reward for services rendered. A knight (Sir John Black) is addressed, using his first name, as "Sir John"; his wife, using the last name, is "Lady Black'—unless she is the daughter of an earl or nobleman of higher rank, in which case she will be "Lady Arabella." The female equivalent of a knight bears the title of "Dame." Though the word *knight* itself comes from the Old English *cniht*, there is some doubt as to whether knighthood amounted to much before the arrival of the Normans. The feudal system required military service as a condition of land tenure, and a man who came to serve his king at the head of an army of tenants required a title of authority and badges of identity—hence the title of knighthood and the coat of arms. During the Crusades, when men were far removed from their land (or even sold it in order to go on crusade), more elaborate forms of fealty sprang up that soon expanded into orders of knighthood. The Templars, Hospitallers, Knights of the Teutonic Order, Knights of Malta, and Knights of the Golden Fleece were but a few of these companionships; not all of them were available at all times in England.

Gradually, with the rise of centralized government and the decline of feudal tenures, military knighthood became obsolete, and the rank largely honorific; sometimes, as under James I, it degenerated into a scheme of the royal government for making money. For hundreds of years after its establishment in the fourteenth century, the Order of the Garter was the only English order of knighthood, an exclusive courtly companionship. Then, during the late seventeenth, the eighteenth, and the nineteenth centuries, a number of additional orders were created, with names such as the Thistle, Saint Patrick, the Bath, Saint Michael, and Saint George, plus a number of special Victorian and Indian orders. They retain the terminology, ceremony, and dignity of knighthood, but the military implications are vestigial.

Although the British Empire now belongs to history, appointments to the Order of the British Empire continue to be conferred for services to that empire at home or abroad. Such honors (commonly referred to as "gongs") are granted by the monarch in New Year's and Birthday lists, but the decisions are now made by the government in power. In recent years there have been efforts to popularize and democratize the dispensation of honors, with recipients including celebrities of all types. But this does not prevent large sectors of British society from regarding both knighthood and the peerage as largely irrelevant to modern life.

The Royal Lines of England and Great Britain
England
SAXONS AND DANES

Egbert, king of Wessex	802–839
Ethelwulf, son of Egbert	839–858
Ethelbald, second son of Ethelwulf	858–860
Ethelbert, third son of Ethelwulf	860–866
Ethelred I, fourth son of Ethelwulf	866–871
Alfred the Great, fifth son of Ethelwulf	871–899
Edward the Elder, son of Alfred	899–924
Athelstan the Glorious, son of Edward	924–940
Edmund I, third son of Edward	940–946
Edred, fourth son of Edward	946–955
Edwy the Fair, son of Edmund	955–959
Edgar the Peaceful, second son of Edmund	959–975
Edward the Martyr, son of Edgar	975–978 (murdered)
Ethelred II, the Unready, second son of Edgar	978–1016
Edmund II, Ironside, son of Ethelred II	1016–1016
Canute the Dane	1016–1035
Harold I, Harefoot, natural son of Canute	1035–1040
Hardecanute, son of Canute	1040–1042
Edward the Confessor, son of Ethelred II	1042–1066
Harold II, brother-in-law of Edward	1066–1066 (died in battle)

HOUSE OF NORMANDY

William I, the Conqueror	1066–1087
William II, Rufus, third son of William I	1087–1100 (shot from ambush)
Henry I, Beauclerc, youngest son of William I	1100–1135

HOUSE OF BLOIS

Stephen, son of Adela, daughter of William I	1135–1154

HOUSE OF PLANTAGENET

Henry II, son of Geoffrey Plantagenet by Matilda, daughter of Henry I	1154–1189
Richard I, Coeur de Lion, son of Henry II	1189–1199
John Lackland, son of Henry II	1199–1216
Henry III, son of John	1216–1272
Edward I, Longshanks, son of Henry III	1272–1307
Edward II, son of Edward I	1307–1327 (deposed)
Edward III of Windsor, son of Edward II	1327–1377
Richard II, grandson of Edward III	1377–1399 (deposed)

HOUSE OF LANCASTER

Henry IV, son of John of Gaunt, son of Edward III	1399–1413
Henry V, Prince Hal, son of Henry IV	1413–1422
Henry VI, son of Henry V	1422–1461 (deposed), 1470–1471 (deposed)

HOUSE OF YORK

Edward IV, great-great-grandson of Edward III	1461–1470 (deposed), 1471–1483
Edward V, son of Edward IV	1483–1483 (murdered)
Richard III, Crookback	1483–1485 (died in battle)

HOUSE OF TUDOR

Henry VII, married daughter of Edward IV	1485–1509
Henry VIII, son of Henry VII	1509–1547
Edward VI, son of Henry VIII	1547–1553
Mary I, "Bloody," daughter of Henry VIII	1553–1558
Elizabeth I, daughter of Henry VIII	1558–1603

HOUSE OF STUART

James I (James VI of Scotland)	1603–1625
Charles I, son of James I	1625–1649 (executed)

COMMONWEALTH & PROTECTORATE

Council of State	1649–1653
Oliver Cromwell, Lord Protector	1653–1658
Richard Cromwell, son of Oliver	1658–1660 (resigned)

HOUSE OF STUART (RESTORED)

Charles II, son of Charles I	1660–1685
James II, second son of Charles I	1685–1688

(INTERREGNUM, 11 DECEMBER 1688 TO 13 FEBRUARY 1689)

HOUSE OF ORANGE-NASSAU

William III of Orange, by Mary, daughter of Charles I	1689–1701
and Mary II, daughter of James II	–1694
Anne, second daughter of James II	1702–1714

Great Britain

HOUSE OF HANOVER

George I, son of Elector of Hanover and Sophia, granddaughter of James I	1714–1727
George II, son of George I	1727–1760
George III, grandson of George II	1760–1820
George IV, son of George III	1820–1830
William IV, third son of George III	1830–1837
Victoria, daughter of Edward, fourth son of George III	1837–1901

HOUSE OF SAXE-COBURG AND GOTHA

Edward VII, son of Victoria	1901–1910

HOUSE OF WINDSOR (NAME ADOPTED 17 JULY 1917)

George V, second son of Edward VII	1910–1936
Edward VIII, eldest son of George V	1936–1936 (abdicated)
George VI, second son of George V	1936–1952
Elizabeth II, daughter of George VI	1952–2022
Charles III, son of Elizabeth II	2022–

Religions in Great Britain

In the late sixth century C.E., missionaries from Rome introduced Christianity to Britons—actually, reintroduced it, since it had briefly flourished in the southern parts of the British Isles during the Roman occupation, and even after the Roman withdrawal had persisted in the Celtic regions of Scotland and Wales. By the time the earliest poems included in *The Norton Anthology of English Literature* were composed (the seventh century), therefore, there had been a Christian presence in the British Isles for hundreds of years. The conversion of the Germanic occupiers of England can, however, be dated only from 597. Our knowledge of the religion of pre-Christian Britain is sketchy, but it is likely that vestiges of Germanic polytheism assimilated into, or coexisted with, the practice of Christianity: fertility rites were incorporated into the celebration of Easter resurrection, rituals commemorating the dead into All-Hallows Eve and All Saints Day, and elements of winter solstice festivals into the celebration of Christmas. The most durable polytheistic remains are the days of the week, each of which except "Saturday" derives from the name of a Germanic pagan god, and the word "Easter," deriving, according to the great monastic scholar Bede (ca. 673–735), from the name of a Germanic pagan goddess, Eostre. In English literature such "folkloric" elements sometimes elicit romantic nostalgia. Geoffrey Chaucer's "Wife of Bath" looks back to a magical time before the arrival of Christianity in which the land was "fulfild of fairye." Hundreds of years later, the seventeenth-century writer Robert Herrick honors the amalgamation of Christian and pagan elements in agrarian British culture in such poems as "Corinna's Gone A-Maying" and "The Hock Cart."

Medieval Christianity was fairly uniform, if complex, across Western Europe—hence called "catholic," or universally shared. The Church was composed of the so-called "regular" and "secular" orders, the regular orders being those who followed a rule in a community under an abbot or an abbess (that is, monks, nuns, friars, and canons), while the secular clergy of priests served parish communities under the governance of a bishop. In the unstable period from the sixth until the twelfth century, monasteries were the intellectual powerhouse of the Church. From the beginning of the thirteenth century, with the development of an urban Christian spirituality in Europe, friars dominated the recently invented institution of universities, as well as devoting themselves, in theory at least, to the urban poor.

The Catholic Church was also an international power structure. With its hierarchy of pope, cardinals, archbishops, and bishops, it offered a model of the centralized, bureaucratic state from the late eleventh century. That ecclesiastical power structure coexisted alongside a separate, often less centralized and feudal structure of lay authorities, with theoretically different and often competing spheres of social responsibilities. The sharing of lay and ecclesiastical authority in medieval England was sometimes a source of conflict. Chaucer's pilgrims are on their way to visit the memorial shrine to one victim of such exemplary struggle: Thomas à Becket, Archbishop of Canterbury, who opposed the policies of King Henry II, was assassinated by indirect suggestion of the king in 1170, and later made a saint. The Church, in turn, produced its own victims: Jews were subject to persecution in the late twelfth century in England, before being expelled in 1290. From the beginning of the fifteenth century, the English Church targeted Lollard heretics (see below) with capital punishment, for the first time.

As an international organization, the Church conducted its business in the universal language of Latin. Thus although in the period the largest segment of literate persons was made up of clerics, the clerical contribution to great literary writing in vernacular languages (for example, French and English) was, so far as we know, relatively modest, with some great exceptions in the later Middle Ages (for example, William Langland). Lay, vernacular writers of the period certainly reflect the importance of the Church as an institution and the pervasiveness of religion in the rituals that marked everyday life, as well as contesting institutional authority. From the late fourteenth century, indeed, England witnessed an active and articulate, proto-Protestant movement known as Lollardy, which attacked clerical hierarchy and promoted vernacular scriptures.

Beginning in 1517 the German monk Martin Luther, in Wittenberg, Germany, openly challenged many aspects of Catholic practice and by 1520 had completely repudiated the authority of the pope, setting in motion the Protestant Reformation. Luther argued that the Roman Catholic Church had strayed far from the pattern of Christianity laid out in scripture. He rejected Catholic doctrines for which no biblical authority was to be found, such as the belief in Purgatory, and translated the Bible into German, on the grounds that the importance of scripture for all Christians made its translation into the vernacular tongue essential. Luther was not the first to advance such views—Lollard followers of the Englishman John Wycliffe had translated the Bible in the late fourteenth century. But Luther, protected by powerful German rulers, was able to speak out without fear of punishment and convert others to his views, rather than suffer the persecution usually meted out to heretics. Soon other reformers were following in Luther's footsteps: of these, the Swiss Ulrich Zwingli and the French Jean Calvin would be especially influential for English religious thought.

At first England remained staunchly Catholic. Its king, Henry VIII, was so severe to heretics that the pope awarded him the title "Defender of the Faith," which British monarchs have retained to this day. In 1534, however, Henry rejected the authority of the pope to prevent his divorce from his queen, Catherine of Aragon, and his marriage to his mistress, Ann Boleyn. In doing so, Henry appropriated to himself ecclesiastical as well as secular authority. Thomas More, author of *Utopia*, was executed in 1535 for refusing to endorse Henry's right to govern the English church. Over the following six years, Henry consolidated his grip on the ecclesiastical establishment by dissolving the powerful, populous Catholic monasteries and redistributing their massive landholdings to his own lay followers. Yet Henry's church largely retained Catholic doctrine and liturgy. When Henry died and his young son, Edward, came to the throne in 1547, the English church embarked on a more Protestant path, a direction abruptly reversed when Edward died and his older sister Mary, the daughter of Catherine of Aragon, took the throne in 1553 and attempted to reintroduce Roman Catholicism. Mary's reign was also short, however, and her successor, Elizabeth I, the daughter of Ann Boleyn, was a Protestant. Elizabeth attempted to establish a "middle way" Christianity, compromising between Roman Catholic practices and beliefs and reformed ones.

The Church of England, though it laid claim to a national rather than pan-European authority, aspired like its predecessor to be the universal church of all English subjects. It retained the Catholic structure of parishes and dioceses and the Catholic hierarchy of bishops, though the ecclesiastical authority was now the Archbishop of Canterbury and the Church's "Supreme Governor" was the monarch. Yet disagreement and controversy persisted. Some members of the Church of England wanted to retain many of the ritual and liturgical elements of Catholicism. Others, the Puritans, advocated a more thoroughgoing reformation. Most Puritans remained within the Church of England, but a minority, the "Separatists" or "Congregationalists," split from the established church altogether. These dissenters no longer thought of the ideal church as an organization to which everybody belonged; instead, they conceived it as a more exclusive group of likeminded people, one not necessarily attached to a larger body of believers.

In the seventeenth century, the succession of the Scottish king James to the English throne produced another problem. England and Scotland were separate nations, and in the sixteenth century Scotland had developed its own national Presbyterian church, or "kirk," under the leadership of the reformer John Knox. The kirk retained fewer Catholic liturgical elements than did the Church of England, and its authorities, or "presbyters," were elected by assemblies of their fellow clerics, rather than appointed by the king. James I and his son Charles I, especially the latter, wanted to bring the Scottish kirk into conformity with Church of England practices. The Scots violently resisted these efforts, with the collaboration of many English Puritans, in a conflict that eventually developed into the English Civil War in the mid-seventeenth century. The effect of these disputes is visible in the poetry of such writers as John Milton, Robert Herrick, Henry Vaughan, and Thomas Traherne, and in the prose of Thomas Browne, Lucy Hutchinson, and Dorothy Waugh. Just as in the mid-sixteenth century, when a succession of monarchs with different religious commitments destabilized the church, so the seventeenth century endured spiritual whiplash. King Charles I's highly ritualistic Church of England was violently overturned by the Puritan victors in the Civil War—until 1660, after the death of the Puritan leader, Oliver Cromwell, when the Church of England was restored along with the monarchy.

The religious and political upheavals of the seventeenth century produced Christian sects that de-emphasized the ceremony of the established church and rejected as well its top-down authority structure. Some of these groups were ephemeral, but the Baptists (founded in 1608 in Amsterdam by the English expatriate John Smyth) and Quakers, or Society of Friends (founded by George Fox in the 1640s), flourished outside the established church, sometimes despite cruel persecution. John Bunyan, a Baptist, wrote the Christian allegory *Pilgrim's Progress* while in prison. Some dissenters, like the Baptists, shared the reformed reverence for the absolute authority of scripture but interpreted the scriptural texts differently from their fellow Protestants. Others, like the Quakers, favored, even over the authority of the Bible, the "inner light" or voice of individual conscience, which they took to be the working of the Holy Spirit in the lives of individuals.

The Protestant dissenters were not England's only religious minorities. Despite crushing fines and the threat of imprisonment, a minority of Catholics under Elizabeth and James openly refused to give their allegiance to the new church, and others remained secret adherents to the old ways. John Donne was brought up in an ardently Catholic family, and several other writers converted to Catholicism as adults—Ben Jonson for a considerable part of his career, Elizabeth Carey and Richard Crashaw permanently, and at profound personal cost. In the eighteenth century, Catholics remained objects of suspicion as possible agents of sedition, especially after the "Glorious Revolution" in 1688 deposed the Catholic James II in favor of the Protestant William and Mary. Anti-Catholic prejudice affected John Dryden, a Catholic convert, as well as the lifelong Catholic Alexander Pope. By contrast, the English colony of Ireland remained overwhelmingly Roman Catholic, the fervor of its religious commitment at least partly inspired by resistance to English occupation. Starting in the reign of Elizabeth, England shored up its own authority in Ireland by encouraging Protestant immigrants from Scotland to settle in the north of Ireland, producing a virulent religious divide the effects of which are still felt today.

A small community of Jews had moved from France to London after 1066, when the Norman William the Conqueror came to the English throne. Although despised and persecuted by many Christians, they were allowed to remain as moneylenders to the Crown, until the thirteenth century, when the king developed alternative sources of credit. At this point, in 1290, the Jews were expelled from England. In 1655 Oliver Cromwell permitted a few to return, and in the late seventeenth and early eighteenth centuries the Jewish population slowly increased, mainly by immigration from Germany. In the mid-eighteenth century some prominent Jews had their children brought up as Christians so as to facilitate their full integration into English society: thus the nineteenth-century writer and politician Benjamin Disraeli, although he and his father were members of the Church of England, was widely considered a Jew insofar as his ancestry was Jewish.

In the late seventeenth century, as the Church of England reasserted itself, Catholics, Jews, and dissenting Protestants found themselves subject to significant legal restrictions. The Corporation Act, passed in 1661, and the Test Act, passed in 1673, excluded all who refused to take communion in the Church of England from voting, attending university, or working in government or in the professions. Members of religious minorities, as well as Church of England communicants, paid mandatory taxes in support of Church of England ministers and buildings. In 1689 the dissenters gained the right to worship in public, but Jews and Catholics were not permitted to do so.

During the eighteenth century, political, intellectual, and religious history remained closely intertwined. The Church of England came to accommodate a good deal of variety. "Low church" services resembled those of the dissenting Protestant churches, minimizing ritual and emphasizing the sermon; the "high church" retained more elaborate ritual elements, yet its prestige was under attack on several fronts. Many Enlightenment thinkers subjected the Bible to rational critique and found it wanting: the philosopher David Hume, for instance, argued that the "miracles" described therein were more probably lies or errors than real breaches of the laws of nature. Within the Church of England, the "broad church" Latitudinarians welcomed this rationalism, advocating theological openness and an emphasis on ethics rather than dogma. More radically, the Unitarian movement rejected the divinity of Christ while professing to accept his ethical teachings. Taking a different tack, the preacher John Wesley, founder of Methodism, responded to the rationalists' challenge with a newly fervent call to evangelism and personal discipline; his movement was particularly successful in Wales. Revolutions in America and France at the end of the century generated considerable millenarian excitement and fostered more new religious ideas, often in conjunction with a radical social agenda. Many important writers of the Romantic period were indebted to traditions of protestant dissent: Unitarian and rationalist protestant ideas influenced William Hazlitt, Anna Barbauld, Mary Wollstonecraft, and the young Samuel Taylor Coleridge. William Blake created a highly idiosyncratic poetic mythology loosely indebted to radical strains of Christian mysticism. Others were even more heterodox: Lord Byron and Robert Burns, brought up as Scots Presbyterians, rebelled fiercely, and Percy Shelley's writing of an atheistic pamphlet resulted in his expulsion from Oxford.

Great Britain never erected an American-style "wall of separation" between church and state, but in practice religion and secular affairs grew more and more distinct during the nineteenth century. In consequence, members of religious minorities no longer seemed to pose a threat to the commonweal. A movement to repeal the Test Act failed in the 1790s, but a renewed effort resulted in the extension of the franchise to dissenting Protestants in 1828 and to Catholics in 1829. The numbers of Roman Catholics in England were swelled by immigration from Ireland, but there were also some prominent English adherents. Among writers, the converts John Newman and Gerard Manley Hopkins are especially important. The political participation and social integration of Jews presented a thornier challenge. Lionel de Rothschild, repeatedly elected to represent London in Parliament during the 1840s and 1850s, was not permitted to take his seat there because he refused to take his oath of office "on the true faith of a Christian"; finally, in 1858, the Jewish Disabilities Act allowed him to omit these words. Only in 1871, however, were Oxford and Cambridge opened to non-Anglicans.

Meanwhile geological discoveries and Charles Darwin's evolutionary theories increasingly cast doubt on the literal truth of the Creation story, and close philological analysis of the biblical text suggested that its origins were human rather than divine. By the end of the nineteenth century, many writers were bearing witness to a world in which Christianity no longer seemed fundamentally plausible. In his poetry and prose, Thomas Hardy depicts a world devoid of benevolent providence. Matthew Arnold's poem "Dover Beach" is in part an elegy to lost spiritual assurance, as the "Sea of Faith" goes out like the tide: "But now I only hear / Its melancholy, long, withdrawing roar / Retreating." For Arnold, literature must replace religion as a source of spiritual truth, and intimacy between individuals substitute for the lost communal solidarity of the universal church.

The work of many twentieth-century writers shows the influence of a religious upbringing or a religious conversion in adulthood. T. S. Eliot and W. H. Auden embrace Anglicanism, William Butler Yeats spiritualism. James Joyce repudiates Irish Catholicism but remains obsessed with it. Yet religion, or lack of it, is a matter of individual choice and conscience, not social or legal mandate. Over the past several decades, church attendance has plummeted in Great Britain. Only about 46 percent of the population identified itself as "Christian" on the 2021 census. Meanwhile, immigration from former British colonies as well as other countries has swelled the ranks of religions once uncommon in the British Isles—Muslim, Sikh, Hindu, Buddhist—though the numbers of adherents remain small relative to the total population.

The Universe According to Ptolemy

Ptolemy was a Roman astronomer of Greek descent, born in Egypt during the second century C.E.; for nearly fifteen hundred years after his death his account of the design of the universe was accepted as standard. During that time, the basic pattern underwent many detailed modifications and was fitted out with many astrological and pseudoscientific trappings. But in essence Ptolemy's followers portrayed the earth as the center of the universe, with the sun, planets, and fixed stars set in transparent spheres orbiting around it. In this scheme of things, as modified for Christian usage, Hell was usually placed under the earth's surface at the center of the cosmic globe, while Heaven, the abode of the blessed spirits, was in the outermost, uppermost circle, the empyrean. But in 1543 the Polish astronomer Copernicus proposed an alternative hypothesis—that the earth rotates around the sun, not vice versa; and despite theological opposition, observations with the new telescope and careful mathematical calculations insured ultimate acceptance of the new view.

The map of the Ptolemaic universe below is a simplified version of a diagram in Peter Apian's *Cosmography* (1584). In such a diagram, the Firmament is the sphere that contained the fixed stars; the Crystalline Sphere, which contained no heavenly bodies, is a late innovation, included to explain certain anomalies in the observed movement of the heavenly bodies; and the Prime Mover is the sphere that, itself put into motion by God, imparts rotation around the earth to all the other spheres.

Milton, writing in the mid-seventeenth century, used two universes. The Copernican universe, though he alludes to it, was too large, formless, and unfamiliar to be the setting for the war between Heaven and Hell in *Paradise Lost*. He therefore used the Ptolemaic cosmos, but placed Heaven well outside this smaller earth-centered universe, Hell far beneath it, and assigned the vast middle space to Chaos.

A LONDON PLAYHOUSE OF SHAKESPEARE'S TIME

PERMISSIONS ACKNOWLEDGMENTS

TEXT CREDITS

Queen Elizabeth: *On Monsieur's Departure* from THE POEMS OF QUEEN ELIZABETH I, edited by Leicester Bradner. Copyright © 1964 by Brown University. Reprinted by permission of the University Press of New England. *Letter to Sir Amyes Paulet* and *Letter to King James VI of Scotland* from THE LETTERS OF QUEEN ELIZABETH, edited by G. B. Harrison (Cassell, 1935). Reprinted by permission of David Higham Associates. *The Golden Speech* from THE PUBLIC SPEAKING OF QUEEN ELIZABETH: SELECTIONS FROM HER OFFICIAL ADDRESSES, edited by George P. Rice, Jr. (AMS Press, 1966). Reprinted with the permission of AMS Press, Inc.
Lucy Hutchinson: From THE WORKS OF LUCY HUTCHINSON, Vol. 1, THE TRANSLATION OF LUCRETIUS, edited by Reid Barbour and David Norbrook, and from THE WORKS OF LUCY HUTCHINSON: THE TRANSLATION OF LUCRETIUS (electronic resource). Copyright © 2012 by Oxford University Press. Reproduced with permission of the Licensor through PLSclear. "Elegy 7 (To the Garden at Owthorpe)" by Lucy Hutchinson, from "Lucy Hutchinson's 'Elegies' and the Situation of the Republican Woman Writer" by David Norbrook, from *English Literary Renaissance*, Volume 27, Number 3, Autumn 1997. Copyright © University of Chicago Press. Permission conveyed through Copyright Clearance Center, Inc.
Ben Johnson: "The Masque of Blackness" by Ben Johnson, from COURT MASQUES: JACOBEAN AND CAROLINE ENTERTAIMENTS, edited by David Lindley, Michael Cordner, Peter Holland, and Martin Wiggins. Copyright © 1995 by Oxford University Press. Reproduced with permission of the Licensor through PLSclear.
John Milton: Excerpts from *Areopagitica* from THE COMPLETE POETRY AND MAJOR PROSE OF MILTON, edited by Merritt Y. Hughes, copyright © 1957. Reprinted by permission of Prentice-Hall, Inc., Upper Saddle River, NJ. From PARADISE LOST: A NORTON CRITICAL EDITION by John Milton, edited by Gordon Teskey. Copyright © 2005 by W. W. Norton & Company, Inc. Reprinted by permission of W. W. Norton & Company, Inc.
Sir Thomas More: "Entire text," from UTOPIA: A Norton Critical Edition, Second Edition, by Sir Thomas More, translated by Robert M. Adams. Copyright © 1992, 1975 by W. W. Norton & Company, Inc. Used by permission of W. W. Norton & Company, Inc.
Petrarch: Reprinted by permission of the publisher from PETRARCH'S LYRIC POEMS: THE *RIME SPARSE* AND OTHER LYRICS, translated and edited by Robert M. Durling, Cambridge, Mass.: Harvard University Press. Copyright © 1976 by Robert M. Durling.
Katherine Philips: *A Married State* from NLW Orielton Collection, box 24. Courtesy of The National Library of Wales.
Hester Pulter: "Upon the Death of my Dear and Lovely Daughter, Jane Pulter," "Emblem 40 (View But this Tulip)," "Dear God, From Thy High Throne Look Down" from THE PULTER PROJECT: POET IN THE MAKING (2018), general editors Leah Knight and Wendy Wall, http://pulterproject.northwestern.edu. Copyright © 2023 by Wendy Wall, Leah Knight, Northwestern University, others. This site is licensed under a Creative Commons CC BY-NC-SA 4.0 License.
William Shakespeare: "The Tempest." Copyright © 2015 by W. W. Norton & Company, Inc. "Sir Thomas More," edited by Stephen Greenblatt, Holger Schott Syme, from THE NORTON SHAKESPEARE, THIRD EDITION, edited by Stephen Greenblatt. Copyright © 2015, 2008, 1997 by W. W. Norton & Company, Inc. Used by permission of W. W. Norton & Company, Inc.
Sir Philip Sidney: "The Countess of Pembroke's Arcadia" by Sir Philip Sidney, from THE NORTON ANTHOLOGY OF ENGLISH LITERATURE, TENTH EDITION, Vol. B, edited by Stephen Greenblatt. Copyright 2018, 2012, 2006, 2000, 1993, 1990, 1986, 1974, 1968, 1962 by W. W. Norton & Company, Inc. Used by permission of W. W. Norton & Company, Inc.
Captain John Smith: From CAPTAIN JOHN SMITH: A SELECTED EDITION OF HIS WRITINGS, edited by Karen Ordahl Kupperman. Published for the Omohundo Institute of Early American History and Culture. Copyright © 1988 by the University of North Carolina Press. Used by permission of the publisher. www.uncpress.org.
Mary Wroth: From THE POEMS OF LADY MARY WROTH, edited by Josephine A. Roberts. Copyright © 1992. Reprinted by permission of Louisiana State University Press.

IMAGE CREDITS

Pages 2–3: © akg-images/Album/Prisma; p. 7: imageBROKER/Alamy Stock Photo; p. 9: Science History Images/Alamy Stock Photo; p. 11: artist unknown/from *Fierie Tryall of God's Saints* (1611); p. 16: Chronicle of World History/Alamy Stock Photo; p. 18: Historic Images/Alamy Stock Photo; p. 22: The Metropolitan Museum of Art, Rogers Fund, 1950. 50.69.2; p. 25: © RMN-Grand Palais/Art Resource, NY; p. 30: © London Metropolitan Archives/Bridgeman Images; p. 33: Private Collection/Bridgeman Images; p. 72: history_docu_photo/Alamy Stock Photo; p. 145: Houghton Library/Harvard; p. 158: Pictorial Press Ltd/Alamy Stock Photo; p. 202: Library of Congress Rare Books/Cookbooks; p. 218: *Royal Collection Trust*/© His Majesty King Charles III, 2023/Bridgeman Images; p. 220: Bibliothèque Nationale de France; p. 229: Photo by The Art Archive/Shutterstock; p. 231: GL Archive/Alamy Stock Photo; p. 258: Timewatch Images/Alamy Stock Photo; p. 475: Album/British Library/Alamy Stock Photo; p. 494: British Library/GRANGER; p. 505: Commonplace Book, Mid-17th Century. James Marshall and Marie-Louise Osborn Collection, Beinecke Rare Book and Manuscript Library, Yale University; p. 622: sketch from 1596 via Wikimedia Commons; p. 641: Private Collection © Archives Charmet/Bridgeman Images; p. 788: College of Arms MS Misc. Grants 1, fol. 148v. Reproduced by permission of the Kings, Heralds and Pursuivants of Arms; p. 827: Virginia Museum of History & Culture/Alamy Stock Photo; pp. 848–49: Album/Alamy Stock Photo; p. 855: Chronicle/Alamy Stock Photo; p. 859: Pictorial Press Ltd/Alamy Stock Photo; p. 870: The Print Collector/Alamy Stock Photo; p. 872: Iconographic Archive/Alamy Stock Photo; p. 875: Historic

Collection/Alamy Stock Photo; p. 883: GRANGER; p. 898: compass sketch, Folger MS V.a.345 p. 44. Digital Image File Name: 68715 Used by permission of the Folger Shakespeare Library; p. 924: Victoria & Albert Museum, UK/Bridgeman Images; p. 942: GRANGER; p. 944: Reading Room 2020/Alamy Stock Photo; p. 1058: PRISMA ARCHIVO/Alamy Stock Photo; p. 1068: The Picture Art Collection/Alamy Stock Photo; p. 1070: *The Countess of Montgomeries Urania* frontispiece. Digital Image File Name: 3361 Source Call Number: STC 26051 Copy, used by permission from the Folger Shakespeare Library; p. 1159: George Wither's book (1635); p. 1181: Reading Room 2020/Alamy Stock Photo; p. 1213: Reading Room 2020/Alamy Stock Photo; p. 1215: Adam Eastland/Alamy Stock Photo; p. 1237: Wellcome Library, London. Wellcome Images, images@wellcome.ac.uk http://wellcomeimages.org. Four faces displaying the adaptation of non-western apparel upon western fashion by J.B. sirnamed, the Chirosopher John Bulwer, Published: 1653 CC BY 4.0 http://creativecommons.org/licenses/by/4.0/; p. 1240: Smith Archive/Alamy Stock Photo; p. 1283: GRANGER; p. 1311: Album/British Library/Alamy Stock Photo; p. 1340: © British Library Board/Robana/Art Resource, NY; p. 1368: World History Archive/Alamy Stock Photo; p. 1378: Historic Images/Alamy Stock Photo.

COLOR INSERT CREDITS

C1: © National Gallery, London/Art Resource, NY; C2: top: National Portrait Gallery, UK/Bridgeman Images; bottom: National Portrait Gallery, UK/Bridgeman Images; C3: top: © The Trustees of the British Museum/Art Resource, NY; bottom: Rijksmuseum, Amsterdam, The Netherlands/Bridgeman Images; C4: © Research and Cultural Collections, University of Birmingham; C5: top left: Gift of Mrs. Edward S. Harkness, 1928. The Metropolitan Museum of Art; top right: Gift of Mrs. Edward S. Harkness, 1928. The Metropolitan Museum of Art; C5: bottom: National Portrait Gallery, UK/Bridgeman Images; C6: top: V&A Images, London/Art Resource, NY; bottom: Private Collection, The Stapleton Collection/Bridgeman Images; C7: World History Archive/Alamy Stock Photo; C8: top: Photo 12/Alamy Stock Photo; bottom: Purchase from the J. H. Wade Fund 1926.554. The Cleveland Museum of Art; C9: Scala/Art Resource, NY; C10: top: National Portrait Gallery, UK/Bridgeman Images; bottom: The Picture Art Collection/Alamy Stock Photo; C11: Woburn Abbey, UK/Bridgeman Images; C12: left: The Picture Art Collection/Alamy Stock Photo; right: Reproduced by permission of Chatsworth Settlement Trustees/Bridgeman Images; C13: top: Royal Collection Trust/© His Majesty King Charles III, 2023/Bridgeman Images; C13: bottom: Private Collection/Bridgeman Images; C14: © Tate, London/Art Resource, NY; C15: Royal Collection Trust/© His Majesty King Charles III, 2023/Bridgeman Images; C16: top: National Portrait Gallery, UK/Bridgeman Images; bottom: © Leeds Museums and Galleries, UK/Bridgeman Images.

Index

A broken ALTAR, Lord, thy servant rears, 1182
Acts and Monuments, 157
Adieu, farewell, earth's bliss, 497
Advancement of Learning, The, 1169
Affliction (I), 1184
Affliction (IV), 1191
Air and Angels, 890
Alas, 'tis true I have gone here and there, 635
Alas! So All Things Now Do Hold Their Peace, 136
All Married Men Desire to Have Good Wives, 510
All you that have indulgent parents been, 1228
Altar, The, 1182
A married state affords but little ease, 1259
Ambassadorial Dispatch to the Holy Roman Emperor Charles V, An, 205
Am I thus conquered? Have I lost the powers, 1075
Amoretti, 452
And If I Did, What Then?, 492
And now th' art set wide ope, the spear's sad art, 1213
Anger, Jane, 253
Another Grace for a Child, 1227
Answer to Another Persuading a Lady to Marriage, An, 1260
Apparition, The, 896
Areopagitica, 1409
Argument of His Book, The, 1220
As an unperfect actor on the stage, 628
Ascham, Roger, 171
As I in hoary winter's night stood shivering in the snow, 171
As in Some Countries Far Remote from Hence, 493
Askew, Anne, 154
Astrophil and Stella, 540
As virtuous men pass mildly away, 897
A sweet disorder in the dress, 1221
At court I met it, in clothes brave enough, 1049
At London, sink of sin, as at the fount, 498
At the round earth's imagined corners, blow, 911
Author's Epitaph, Made by Himself, The, 479
Avenge, O Lord, thy slaughtered saints, whose bones, 1426

A ward, and still in bonds, one day, 1201
A woman's face with Nature's own hand painted, 627
Aye, beshrew you, by my fay, 39

Back and side go bare, go bare, 475
Bacon, Anne Cooke, 159, 248
Bacon, Francis, 1156
Bait, The, 895
Barnfield, Richard, 490
Batter my heart, three-personed God; for you, 913
Because you have thrown off your prelate lord, 1424
Bella Bona-Roba, La, 1235
Bermudas, 1267
Betwixt two ridges of plowed land lay Wat, 1359
Black Patch on Lucasta's Face, A, 1236
Book of Common Prayer, 161
Book of Homilies, 164
Brave infant of Saguntum, clear, 1059
Break of Day, 892
Brief and True Report of the New-Found Land of Virginia, A, 790
Broken in pieces all asunder, 1191
Bunch of Grapes, The, 1192
Burning Babe, The, 170
Busy old fool, unruly sun, 888
But be contented; when that fell arrest, 631
But since we now eternal matter find, 1240
By our first strange and fatal interview, 903

Calvin, John, 151
Campion, Thomas, 488, 489, 490, 499
Can I not sin, but thou wilt be, 1227
Canonization, The, 889
Carmen Deo Nostro, 1215
Casket Letter Number 2, 219
Castiglione's The Courtier, 176
Cavendish, Margaret, 1356
Certain Man, A, 509
Cheke, Lady Mary, 509
Church Monuments, 1187
Clarendon, Edward Hyde, Earl of, 1350
Cock-Crowing, 1208
Cold's the wind and wet's the rain, 477

Collar The, 1194
Come leave the loathèd stage, 1065
Come, Madam, come, all rest my powers defy, 902
Come, my Lucasia, since we see, 1262
Come, sons of summer, by whose toil, 1224
Come live with me and be my love (Donne), 895
Come live with me and be my love (Marlowe), 495
Corinna's Going A-Maying, 1222
Coronet, The, 1267
Corruption, 1205
Countess of Montgomery's Urania, The, 1069
Countess of Pembroke's Arcadia, The, 515
Crashaw, Richard, 1211
Cries of London, 506
Cromwell, our chief of men, who through a cloud, 1425
Crown of Sonnets Dedicated to Love, A, 1078
Cynthia, 490

Damon the Mower, 1277
Daniel, Samuel, 469
Davies of Hereford, John, 487, 498
Dear God, From Thy High Throne Look Down, 1227
Death, 1198
Death, be not proud, though some have callèd thee, 912
Death, thou wast once an uncouth, hideous thing, 1198
Death's Duel, 922
Defense of Poesy, The, 524
Definition of Love, The, 1274
Dekker, Thomas, 477
Delight in Disorder, 1221
Denial, 1188
De rerum natura, 1240
Description of a New World, Called The Blazing World, The, 1364
Description of Cookham, The, 936
Devotions upon Emergent Occasions, 918
Devouring Time, blunt thou the lion's paws, 627
Dialogue Between the Soul and Body, A, 1268
Dialogue Concerning Heresies, A, 149
Diana (on a time) walking the wood, 490
Discipline, 1197
discovery of the large, rich, and beautiful Empire of Guiana, The, 790
Doctor Faustus, 581
Donne, John, 882
Doralicia's Ditty, 500
Doubt of Future Foes, The, 240
Dowland, John, 501
Dowriche, Anne, 252
Drayton, Michael, 468, 484, 491, 493
Dreams, 1220
Drink to me only with thine eyes, 1055
Duchess of Malfi, The, 1080

Dull as I was, to think that a court fly, 1236
Dutch Libel, The, 480

Easter, 1183
Easter Wings, 1184
Ecstasy, The, 898
Eiusdem ad Lectorem, de Authore, 254
Elegy 16. On His Mistress, 903
Elegy 19. To His Mistress Going to Bed, 904
Elizabeth I, 230
English Bible, The, 146
Epigrams, 1049
Epitaph: On Her Son H. P. at St. Syth's Church, Where Her Body Was Interred, 1264
Epithalamion, 455
Essays, 1157
Euphues: The Anatomy of Wit, 511
Even now, that care which on thy crown attends, 553
Even such is time, which takes in trust, 479

Faerie Queene, The, 263
False hope which feeds but to destroy, and spill, 1077
False life! a foil and no more, when, 1210
Farewell, False Love, 493
Farewell, false love, the oracle of lies, 493
Farewell, sweet Cookham, where I first obtained, 936
Farewell: thou art too dear for my possessing, 632
Farewell, thou child of my right hand, and joy, 1050
Father of lights! what sunny seed, 1208
Filmer, Robert, 1325
Fine madam Would-Be, wherefore should you fear, 1049
First Examination of Anne Askew, The, 154
Flaming Heart, The, 1215
Flea, The, 886
Flower, The, 1195
Forbear, bold youth, all's Heaven here, 1260
Forerunners, The, 1196
Forest, The, 1053
Forget Not Yet, 129
Forget not yet the tried intent, 129
For God's sake hold your tongue, and let me love, 889
Fortune hath taken away my love, 243
Foxe, Emma, 473
Foxe, John, 157
Foxe's Acts and Monuments, 215
Friendship's Mystery, To My Dearest Lucasia, 1262
From fairest creatures we desire increase, 625
From you have I been absent in the spring, 633
Full many a glorious morning have I seen, 629
Funeral, The, 900

Garden, The, 1280
Gascoigne, George, 467, 492
Gather ye rosebuds while ye may, 1224
General History of Virginia, New-England, and the Summer Isles, The, 830
Get up! Get up for shame! The blooming morn, 1222
Go, smiling souls, your new-built cages break, 1212
Go, soul, the body's guest, 485
Go and catch a falling star, 887
Goe little booke: thy selfe present, 257
"Golden Speech," The, 245
Good and great God, can I not think of thee, 1056
Good Friday, 1613. Riding Westward, 915
Good ladies, take pity and grant our desire, 506
Good-Morrow, The, 887
Grant them removed, and grant that this your noise, 482
Grasshopper, The, 1233
Greene, Robert, 500
Greville, Fulke, 473, 483
Grey, Lady Jane, 209
Gut eats all day, and lechers all the night, 1053

Had we but world enough, and time, 1272
Happy those early days! when I, 1203
Happy ye leaves when as those lilly hands, 452
Harington, Sir John, 509
Hariot, Thomas, 790
Hark how the mower Damon sung, 1277
Have mercy, Lord, have mercy: for I know, 167
Have ye beheld (with much delight), 1226
Having been tenant long to a rich lord, 1182
Hence loathèd Melancholy, 1393
Hence vain deluding joys, 1397
Herbert, George, 1180
Herbert, Mary (Sidney), Countess of Pembroke, 552
Here a little child I stand, 1227
Here lies, to each her parents' ruth, 1050
Here we are all, by day; by night, we're hurled, 1221
Hero and Leander, 563
Herrick, Robert, 1219
Hesperides, 1220
His golden locks time hath to silver turned, 470
History of the Rebellion, The, 1350
History of the World, The, 474
Hobbes, Thomas, 1337
Hoby, Sir Thomas, 176
Hock Cart, or Harvest Home, The, 1224
Holdfast, The, 1193
Holy Sonnets, 910
Hooker, Richard, 167
Horatian Ode, An, 1282
How fresh, O Lord, how sweet and clean, 1195
How like a winter hath my absence been, 633

How Many Paltry, Foolish, Painted things, 484
How oft when thou, my music, music play'st, 636
How rich, O Lord! how fresh thy visits are!, 1206
How Soon Hath Time, 1423
How soon hath Time, the subtle thief of youth, 1423
How vainly men themselves amaze, 1280
Hume, Tobias, 504
Hunting for Hire, 506
Hunting of the Hare, The, 1359
Hutchinson, Lucy, 1239
Hymn to God My God, in My Sickness, 916
Hymn to God the Father, A, 917

I am a little world made cunningly, 911
I Am the Door, 1213
I can love both fair and brown, 889
I cannot tell who loves the skeleton, 1235
I Care Not for These Ladies, 489
I dreamed this mortal part of mine, 1221
If all the world and love were young, 496
If everything hath sense and reason, then, 1361
I Find No Peace, 124
I find no peace, and all my war is done, 124
If poisonous minerals, and if that tree, 912
If There Were (Oh!) an Hellespont of Cream, 487
I grieve and dare not show my discontent, 240
I have examined and do find, 1263
I have lost, and lately, these, 1220
Il Penseroso, 1397
Indifferent, The, 889
In loving thee thou know'st I am forsworn, 639
In Night When Colors All to Black Are Cast, 483
I now think Love is rather deaf than blind, 1057
Institution of Christian Religion, The, 151
In the nativity of time, 1237
In the old age black was not counted fair, 636
In this little urn is laid, 1226
In this strange labyrinth how shall I turn?, 1078
In time we *see* that silver drops, 500
Inviting a Friend to Supper, 1052
I saw eternity the other night, 1206
I sing of brooks, of blossoms, birds, and bowers, 1220
I struck the board and cried, "No more, 1194
I that have been a lover, and could show it, 1057
I think not on the state, nor am concerned, 1261
I threatened to observe the strict decree, 1193
It Was a Time When Silly Bees Could Speak, 501
It was not certain when a certain preacher, 509

It will be looked for, book, when some but see, 1049
I wonder, by my troth, what thou and I, 885

Jack and Joan, They Think No Ill, 499
John Jewel's An Apology or Answer in Defence of the Church of England, 159
Jolly Good Ale and Old, 475
Jonson, Ben, 941
Jordan (1), 1186
Jordan (2), 1191
Joy, I did lock thee up; but some bad man, 1192
Just like unto a nest of boxes round, 1358

Kind pity chokes my spleen; brave scorn forbids, 906

L'Allegro, 1393
Lanyer, Aemilia, 924
Lecture upon the Shadow, A, 902
Let man's soul be a sphere, and then, in this, 915
Let me not to the marriage of true minds, 635
Let me pour forth, 893
Let not my love be called idolatry, 634
Letter of the Lady Jane, Sent unto Her Father, A, 213
Letter of the Lady Jane to M. H., Late Chaplain to the Duke of Suffolk Her Father, A, 211
Letter to Elizabeth I, May 17, 1568, A, 222
Letter to Henry VIII, 204
Letter to King James VI of Scotland, February 14, 1587, A, 242
Letter to Mary, Queen of Scots, February 24, 1567, A, 239
Letter to Robert Dudley, Earl of Leicester, February 10, 1586, A, 241
Letter to Sir Amyas Paulet, August 1586, A, 241
Leviathan, 1338
Lie, The, 484
Ligon, Richard, 837
Like as the waves make towards the pebbled shore, 630
Like to the Indians scorched with the sun, 1075
Litany in Time of Plague, A, 496
Locke, Anne Vaughan, 166
Lodge, Thomas, 472
Long Love That in My Thought Doth Harbor, The, 122
Look in thy glass and tell the face thou viewest, 625
Lord, how can man preach thy eternal word?, 1188
Lord, who createdst man in wealth and store, 1184
Love (3), 1199
Love, That Doth Reign and Live within My Thought, 136
Love a child is ever crying, 1078

Love bade me welcome: yet my soul drew back, 1199
Lovelace, Richard, 1232
Love like a juggler comes to play his prize, 1077
Love Made in the First Age. To Chloris, 1237
Lover Showeth How He Is Forsaken of Such as He Sometime Enjoyed, The, 127
Loving in truth, and fain in verse my love to show, 541
Lucasta, 1232
Lucy, you brightness of our sphere, who are, 1051
Luke 11.[27], 1213
Lullaby of a Lover, The, 467
Lycidas, 1401
Lyly, John, 511

Madam, Withouten Many Words, 126
Man, 1189
Mannerly Margery Milk and Ale, 39
Mariners' Song, 508
Mark but this flea, and mark in this, 886
Marlowe, Christopher, 495, 561
Married State, A, 1259
Marvell, Andrew, 1265
Mary, Queen of Scots, 217
Mary I (Mary Tudor), 203
Masque of Blackness, The, 1039
Meditation of a Penitent Sinner, A, 166
Methought I Saw My Late Espousèd Saint, 1427
Milton, John, 1328, 1381
Mine own John Poins, 131
Mine own John Poins, since ye delight to know, 131
Moderate, No. 28, The [The Trial of King Charles I, the first day], 1317
More, Sir Thomas, 43, 149
Mower's Song, The, 1279
Mower to the Glowworms, The, 1279
Much suspected by me, 232
My Galley, 125
My galley charged with forgetfulness, 125
My God, I heard this day, 1189
My love is as a fever, longing still, 639
My Love is of a birth as rare, 1274
My Lute, Awake!, 128
My lute, awake! Perform the last, 128
My mind was once the true survey, 1279
My mistress' eyes are nothing like the sun, 637
My muse now happy, lay thyself to rest, 1079
My pain, still smothered in my grievèd breast, 1077
My Picture Left in Scotland, 1057
My prime of youth is but a frost of cares, 478
My spirit is too weak—mortality, 949
My Sweetest Lesbia, 488
My sweetest Lesbia, let us live and love, 488

Narrative of the Execution of the Queen of Scots, 224

Nashe, Thomas, 496
Nature, That Washed Her Hands in Milk, 502
New Atlantis, The, 1175
New Brooms, 505
New brooms, green brooms, will you buy any?, 505
New Year's Gift Sent to the Parliament and Army, A, 1332
Noble Numbers, 1227
Nocturnal upon Saint Lucy's Day, Being the Shortest Day, A, 894
No longer mourn for me when I am dead, 631
No more be grieved at that which thou hast done, 629
Nothing but "No" and "I" and "I" and "No"?, 491
Not marble nor the gilded monuments, 629
Not mine own fears, nor the prophetic soul, 634
Novum Organum, 1171
Now Winter Nights Enlarge, 490
Nymph Complaining for the Death of Her Fawn, The, 1270
Nymph's Reply to the Shepherd, The, 496

O, how I faint when I of you do write, 632
O, who shall from this dungeon raise, 1268
Obedience of a Christian Man, The, 147
Ode to Himself, 1065
Of Great Place, 1160
Of Many Worlds in this World, 1358
Of Marriage and Single Life, 1158
Of Masques and Triumphs, 1166
Of Negotiating, 1165
Of Plantations, 1163
Of Sense and Reason Exercised in their Different Shapes, 1361
Of Studies [1597 version], 1167
Of Studies [1625 version], 1168
Of Superstition, 1162
Of the Laws of Ecclesiastical Polity, 167
Of Truth, 1157
Oh, to vex me, contraries meet in one, 913
Oh, what a lantern, what a lamp of light, 557
O Happy Dames, That May Embrace, 139
O Lord, in me there lieth nought, 557
On a Maidenhead, 471
On Gut, 1053
On Hellespont, guilty of true-loves' blood, 563
On Monsieur's Departure, 240
On My First Daughter, 1050
On My First Son, 1050
On Our Crucified Lord Naked and Bloody, 1214
On Shakespeare, 1393
On Something, That Walks Somewhere, 1049
On the Late Massacre in Piedmont, 1426
On the Morning of Christ's Nativity, 1385
On the New Forcers of Conscience under the Long Parliament, 1424
On the Wounds of Our Crucified Lord, 1214

Oration of Queen Mary in the Guildhall, on the First of February 1554, The, 207
Order and Disorder, 1243
Othello, 640
O these wakeful wounds of thine, 1214
O thou, my lovely boy, who in thy power, 636
O thou that swing'st upon the waving hair, 1233

Pamphilia to Amphilanthus, 1074
Paradise Lost, 1427
Passage of Our Most Dread Sovereign Lady Queen Elizabeth through the City of London to Westminster on the Day before Her Coronation, The, 233
Passionate Shepherd to His Love, The, 495
Patriarcha, 1326
Perfect Diurnal of Some Passages in Parliament, No. 288, A, 1320
Petrarch, Rima 134, 124
Petrarch, Rima 140, 123
Petrarch, Rima 164, 136
Petrarch, Rima 189, 125
Petrarch, Rima 190, 124
Petrarch, Rima 310, 135
Philips, Katherine, 1258
Picture of Little T. C. in a Prospect of Flowers, The, 1275
Pluck the Fruit and Taste the Pleasure, 472
Poems, 1385
Poems and Fancies, 1357
Poetess's Hasty Resolution, The, 1357
Poor desolate garden, smile no more on me, 1242
Poor soul, the center of my sinful earth, 638
Prayer (1), 1186
Prayer, the church's banquet; angels' age, 1186
Prayer of the Lady Jane, A, 214
Psalm 52, 556
Psalm 139, 557
Psalm 119: O, 557
Pulley, The, 1195
Pulter, Hester, 1224

Queen and Huntress, 1062
Queen and huntress, chaste and fair, 1062
Queen's Champion Retires, The, 470
Quickness, 1210

Ralegh, Sir Walter, 474, 478, 479, 484, 493, 502, 790
Rape of Lucrece, The, 503
Reading my verses, I liked them so well, 1357
Reason of Church Government Urged Against Prelaty, The, 1408
Redemption, 1182
Regeneration, 1201
Relation Concerning Dorothy Waugh's Cruel Usage by the Mayor of Carlisle, 1355
Relic, The, 901
Religious Use of Taking Tobacco, A, 503

Renowned empress, and Great Britain's queen, 925
Reply, The, 510
Retreat, The, 1203
Rise, heart, thy lord is risen. Sing his praise, 1183
Robert Garnier's Marc Antoine, 560
Roger Ascham's Schoolmaster, 210

Sad Nature's sighs gave the alarms, 1243
Salve Deus Rex Judaeorum, 928
Satire 3, 905
Schoolmaster, The, 172
Second Letter to Her Father, A, 215
See with what simplicity, 1275
Shakespeare, William, 482, 503, 620
Shall I compare thee to a summer's day?, 626
Shepheardes Calender, The, 257
Show me, dear Christ, thy spouse so bright and clear, 914
Sidney, Sir Philip, 514
Silence, and Stealth of Days!, 1204
Silence, and stealth of days! 'tis now, 1204
Silex Scintillans, 1201
Since brass, nor stone, nor earth, nor boundless sea, 630
Since I am coming to that holy room, 916
Since she whom I loved hath paid her last debt, 914
Sing lullaby, as women do, 467
Sin of self-love possesseth all mine eye, 630
Sir, more than kisses, letters mingle souls, 908
Sir Thomas More, 482
Sir Walter Ralegh to His Son, 479
Skelton, John, 38
Small atoms of themselves a world may make, 1358
Smith, Captain John, 827
So Cruel Prison How Could Betide, 137
So cruel prison how could betide, alas, 137
Soldiers' Song, 508
Some have no money, 41
Song (Donne), 891
Song (Wroth), 1076
Song, The (Donne), 887
Song: To Celia, 1055
Sonnet, to the Noble Lady, the Lady Mary Wroth, A, 1057
Sonnets (Shakespeare), 624
Soote Season, The, 135
Southwell, Lady Anne, 510
Southwell, Robert, 170
Speech to a Joint Delegation of Lords and Commons, November 5, 1566, A, 236
Speech to the House of Commons, January 28, 1563, 235
Speech to the Troops at Tilbury, 244
Spenser, Edmund, 254
Spit in my face ye Jews, and pierce my side, 912
Stand still, and I will read to thee, 902
Stand Whoso List, 130

Stand whoso list upon the slipper top, 130
Steps to the Temple, 1212
Stevenson, William, 475
Still, John S., 475
Strachey, William, 814
Sun Rising, The, 888
Suppose he had been tabled at thy teats, 1213
Sure it was so. Man in those early days, 1205
Surrey, Henry Howard, Earl of, 134
Sweet day, so cool, so calm, so bright, 1189
Sweetest love, I do not go, 891
Sweetest love, return again, 1076

Take heed mine eyes, how you your looks do cast, 1076
Tell me not, sweet, I am unkind, 1232
Tempest, The, 726
Temple, The, 1182
Tenure of Kings and Magistrates, The, 1328
That no man yet could in the Bible find, 510
That time of year thou may'st in me behold, 631
The doubt of future foes exiles my present joy, 240
The forward youth that would appear, 1282
The harbingers are come: see, *see* their mark, 1196
The Indian weed withered quite, 504
The meditation of this monarch's love, 928
There's Nothing Grieves Me, But That Age Should Haste, 468
The soote season, that bud and bloom forth brings, 135
The time is come I must depart, 193
The wanton troopers riding by, 1270
Th' expense of spirit in a waste of shame, 637
They Flee from Me, 127
They flee from me, that sometime did me seek, 127
They that have power to hurt and will do none, 633
Th' have left thee naked, Lord, O that they had, 1214
This is the month, and this the happy morn, 1385
Thou art not, Penshurst, built to envious show, 1053
Though sharp the seed by Anger sown, 254
Thou hast begun well, Roe, which stand° well too, 1051
Thou hast made me, and shall thy work decay?, 910
Three things there be that prosper up apace, 479
Throw away thy rod, 1197
Tichborne, Chidiock, 478
Tichborne's Elegy, 478
Time's glory is to calm contending kings, 503
'Tis the year's midnight and it is the day's, 894
'Tis true, 'tis day; what though it be?, 892
To All Women in General, and Gentle Reader[s] Whatsoever, 253

To Althea, from Prison, 1234
Tobacco, 504
To draw no envy, Shakespeare, on thy name, 1063
To Fine Lady Would-Be, 1049
To Heaven, 1056
To His Book's End, 1223
To his book's end this last line he'd have placed, 1227
To His Conscience, 1227
To His Coy Mistress, 1272
To Lucy, Countess of Bedford, with Mr. Donne's Satires, 1051
To Mrs. M. A. at Parting, 1263
To My Book, 1049
Tonight, grave sir, both my poor house and I, 1052
To Sir Henry Wotton, 905
To Sir Thomas Roe, 1051
To the Garden at Owthorpe, 1242
To the Immortal Memory and Friendship of That Noble Pair, Sir Lucius Cary and Sir H. Morison, 1059
To the Infant Martyrs, 1212
To the Ladie Anne, Countess of Dorset, 927
To the Lord General Cromwell, May 1652, 1425
To the Memory of My Beloved, The Author, Mr. William Shakespeare, 1063
To the Queen's Most Excellent Majesty, 925
To the Reader, 249
To the Right Worshipful and Worthily Beloved Mother, the Lady F., 248
To the Right worshipful Her Loving Brother, Master Pearse Edgecombe, 252
To the Thrice-Sacred Queen Elizabeth, 553
To the Virgins, to Make Much of Time, 1224
To you I dedicate this work of grace, 927
To You That Life Possess, 473
Triumph of Death, The, 498
Troll the Bowl, the Jolly Nut-Brown Bowl, 477
True and Exact History of the Island of Barbados, A, 836
True Copie of the Petition of Gentlewomen and Tradesmens Wives, A, 1310
True Repertory of the Wreck, 815
Tunning of Elinour Rumming, The, 41
Twice or thrice had I loved thee, 892
Two loves I have of comfort and despair, 638
Tyler, Margaret, 249
Tyndale, William, 147
Tyrant, why swell'st thou thus, 556

Underwood, 1057
Unprofitableness, 1206
Upon Appleton House, 1287
Upon His Verses, 1226
Upon Julia's Clothes, 1226
Upon Prue, His Maid, 1226
Upon the Death of My Dear and Lovely Daughter, Jane Pulter, 1228
Upon the Double Murder of King Charles, 1261
Upon the Loss of His Mistresses, 1220
Upon the Nipples of Julia's Breast, 1226
Utopia, 46

Valediction: Forbidding Mourning, A, 897
Valediction: Of Weeping, A, 893
Vaughan, Henry, 1200
Verse Exchange between Elizabeth and Sir Walter Ralegh, 243
Verses Written with a Diamond, 232
View But This Tulip, 1230
View but this tulip, rose, or gillyflower, 1230
Vine, The, 1221
Virtue, 1185
Volpone, 944

Waterfall, The, 1209
Waugh, Dorothy, 1354
We be soldiers three, 508
We be three poor mariners, 508
Webster, John, 1079
Well-meaning readers! you that come as friends, 1216
What if this present were the world's last night?, 913
What needs my Shakespeare for his honored bones, 1391
What offspring other men have got, 1226
What on earth deserves our trust?, 1264
What Vaileth Truth?, 126
What vaileth truth? or by it to take pain, 126
When, in disgrace with Fortune and men's eyes, 628
Whenas in silks my Julia goes, 1226
When by thy scorn, O murderess, I am dead, 896
When everyone to pleasing pastime hies, 1075
When first my lines of heavenly joys made mention, 1191
When first thou didst entice to thee my heart, 1184
When for the thorns with which I long, too long, 1267
When God at first made man, 1195
When I consider every thing that grows, 626
When I Consider How My Light Is Spent, 1426
When I do count the clock that tells the time, 626
When in the chronicle of wasted time, 634
When Love with unconfinèd wings, 1234
When Men Shall Find Thy Flower, Thy Glory, Pass, 469
When my devotions could not pierce, 1188
When my grave is broke up again, 901
When my love swears that she is made of truth, 638
When night's black mantle could most darkness prove, 1074
When to the sessions of sweet silent thought, 628
Where, like a pillow on a bed, 898
Where the remote Bermudas ride, 1267

While that my soul repairs to her devotion, 187
Whitney, Isabella, 193
Whoever comes to shroud me, do not harm, 900
Whoever hath her wish, thou hast thy *Will*, 637
Who List His Wealth and Ease Retain, 130
Who liveth so merry in all this land, 507
Who says that fictions only and false hair, 186
Whoso List to Hunt, 123
Whoso list to hunt, I know where is an hind, 123
Will and Testament, 193
Will Ye Buy a Fine Dog?, 471
Will ye buy a fine dog, with a hole in his head, 471
Wilson, Robert, 505, 506
Wilt thou forgive that sin where I begun, 915
Windows, The, 1188

Wisdome, Robert, 503
Wistanley, Gerrard, 1331
Within this sober frame expect, 1287
With lullay, lullay, like a child, 40
With Lullay, Lullay, Like a Child, 40
With what deep murmurs through time's silent stealth, 1209
World, The, 1206
World Made by Atoms, A, 1358
Wroth, Mary, 1067
Wyatt, Sir Thomas, the Elder, 120
Wyatt Resteth Here, That Quick Could Never Rest, 138

Ye learnèd sisters which have oftentimes, 455
Ye living lamps, by whose dear light, 1279
Yes, that a maidenhead we call, 471
Ye strangers that do inhabit in this land, 480
Yet once more, O ye laurels, and once more, 1402
You That Seek What Life Is in Death, 473